Roger Ebert's
Movie Yearbook
2007

Other Books by Roger Ebert

An Illini Century

A Kiss Is Still a Kiss

Two Weeks in the Midday Sun:
A Cannes Notebook

Behind the Phantom's Mask

Roger Ebert's Little Movie Glossary

Roger Ebert's Movie Home Companion
annually 1986–1993

Roger Ebert's Video Companion
annually 1994–1998

Roger Ebert's Movie Yearbook
annually 1999–

Questions for the Movie Answer Man

Roger Ebert's Book of Film: An Anthology

Ebert's Bigger Little Movie Glossary

I Hated, Hated, Hated This Movie

The Great Movies

The Great Movies II

With Daniel Curley
The Perfect London Walk

With Gene Siskel
The Future of the Movies: Interviews with
Martin Scorsese, Steven Spielberg, and
George Lucas

DVD Commentary Tracks
Beyond the Valley of the Dolls
Citizen Kane
Dark City
Casablanca
Floating Weeds

Roger Ebert's Movie Yearbook 2007

**Andrews McMeel
Publishing, LLC**
Kansas City

1736 98 77 1

Roger Ebert's Movie Yearbook 2006
copyright © 1999, 2000, 2001, 2002, 2003,
2004, 2005, 2006, 2007
by Roger Ebert
For information write
Andrews McMeel Publishing,
an Andrews McMeel Universal company,
4520 Main Street,
Kansas City, Missouri 64111.

06 07 08 09 10 BBG 10 9 8 7 6 5 4 3 2 1

ISBN-13: 978-0-7407-6157-7
ISBN-10: 0-7407-6157-9

www.andrewsmcmeel.com

All the reviews in this book originally appeared
in the *Chicago Sun-Times.*

This book is dedicated
to my Aunt Martha, who
took me to the movies.

Contents

Introduction

In six decades there have been three revolutions in the way movies are distributed. The first was in 1948, when the Supreme Court found the big studios in violation of antitrust laws and ordered them to sell their theater chains. Until then, the majors owned theaters and booked their own movies into them; afterward, the playing field was more level for independent producers.

The second came when "platforming" was replaced by mass national bookings of major new films. For decades, a new film would open in a few big markets, typically New York and Los Angeles, and then trickle through to the rest of the country. This provided a way for audience word-of-mouth to spread and was a godsend for smaller films that needed time to win a reputation. Three films that especially benefited from platforming were *Bonnie and Clyde*, *My Dinner with Andre*, and *Chariots of Fire*.

That model changed when studios started using national TV ad campaigns for their movies. At about the same time, more movie stars became willing to appear on television; for years, many of them had refused. Now the pieces were in place for the modern system in which a big movie will open in thousands of theaters on the same day, backed by an advertising and publicity blitz.

A drawback of this model is that it is best suited to blockbuster films. The opening-night audience for a mass-market action picture is made up mostly of teenagers, who have free time; adults need more warning to gear up for a visit to the movies, and often the movie closes before they can get to it. This has created a loop in which more and more Hollywood movies are aimed at young action and comedy audiences. To some degree, the pattern has been offset by the rise of independent films and the theaters that show them, including the Landmark chain.

The third revolution is happening right now. It involves a fundamental shift in the medium chosen by moviegoers. The studios get more of their revenue from DVDs than from ticket sales, and if you consider that much of that revenue comes from rentals, it's apparent that most people see more movies on DVD than in theaters. Sure, these movies would look better in a theater, but if they are getting to audiences that want to see them, that's a good thing. There are precedents. When Allen Lane introduced Penguin paperbacks, he was told he would destroy the book publishing industry. When the first Betamax home video machines came onto the market, the studios sued to block home videos, which would eventually earn them billions. If I were a director, I would prefer for my work to be seen in a theater but would be happy for it to find an audience anywhere. And the extras on DVDs now mean moviegoers can learn more about the making of a film than any one filmmaking professional used to know.

Movies also have a big presence on television, and the studios are correctly experimenting with technology that will allow viewers to rent "movies on demand" via cable, satellite, or the Internet. The danger of such digital distribution, from the studios' point of view, is that movies in digital form are easier to pirate than those on 35 mm film.

That's one reason that digital projection, which was supposed to replace film in theaters, seems stalled (another is that no one wants to foot the $100,000 per booth price tag).

I believe that the best way to see a movie is in a theater with an audience, and that light-through-celluloid is still better than any digital projection system I have seen. But this is not the way most people now see movies, and there is a bright side to the digital revolution. Home video itself meant that for the first time viewers could program their own viewing; they were no longer at the mercy of theaters and TV stations. There has been a big jump in the quality of home entertainment systems (and a rapid fall in their prices), and it is no longer unusual for a consumer to have a big flat-screen or front-projection screen and a surround sound system. Movies shown on these systems look impressive when seen on high-quality DVDs and will look even better when HD-DVD comes in, although that switch has been stalled by a war between two formats.

Last year Steven Soderbergh, who makes both big commercial movies (*Ocean's Eleven*) and small indie films (*Sex, Lies, and Videotape*) did some lateral thinking about the problem of distribution, especially for smaller films. It costs a fortune to open any first-run movie in New York City and, in a sense, if it hasn't made it there, it can't make it anywhere. But what's the point of producing a $100,000 movie when it costs more than that for an ad campaign in the *New York Times*?

What Soderbergh tried with his film *Bubble* was revolutionary: He would release it more or less simultaneously in theaters, on DVD, and on pay cable. This strategy was not welcomed by theater owners, needless to say, but it had the advantage of concentrating all of the publicity and advertising efforts at one time. The heat generated in each medium would in theory help the film in the others.

At Cannes 2006 I ran into Jonathan Sehring, the inventive and risk-taking producer of nearly fifty independent pictures, many of them for IFC Films and its digital spin-off, InDiGent. He said the Soderbergh model seemed to hold hope for his kind of film, and he cited one title whose box office take went up 15 percent in New York in its second week, apparently because of word-of-mouth inspired by cable.

My guess is that theaters are wrong to oppose this form of distribution, which will apply mostly to smaller films. Although the window between theater and DVD has been growing smaller for all releases, it is probably true that for many more years big Hollywood movies like *Superman Returns* will open exclusively in theaters. But smaller indie films like *Me and You and Everyone We Know*, *The Proposition*, *L'Enfant*, and *Water* could benefit from cross-platform openings.

Moviegoers know that all movies will eventually be on DVD; they choose to go to theaters because they like that experience, but they can't see every film that way. Imagine a scenario in which Landmark, say, sells DVDs in its lobby. A hypothetical customer buys a ticket to *Lonesome Jim*, and on the way out runs into friends who have just liked *The Notorious Bettie Page*. On an impulse, he might buy the *Bettie Page* DVD. If theaters limited themselves to movies currently in release, it wouldn't involve a lot of inventory and sales space; it would be more like the CDs displayed at Starbucks.

Another major distribution channel is Netflix and its clones, which have a large customer base seriously interested in a *lot* of movies. How do I know this? Because Netflix has a stock of about 60,000 films, and two-thirds of them are rented on a given day (if only by one person). That contradicts the Blockbuster model, in which new releases are piled in big displays but the backlist is limited. This is called the phenomenon of the Long Tail, and it benefits Web sites like Amazon, which does more business selling a few copies of countless books than a lot of copies of a few.

There may be only one person in a city who wants to see a film or read a review, but because of Netflix and the Internet, that person can do it. We observe that pattern at www.rogerebert.com, where there are more than ten thousand reviews and our Web traffic statistics show that even the most popular film represents less than 1 percent of our business. As of June 15, 2006, *The Da Vinci Code* and *Brokeback Mountain* were tied at 0.8 percent of our page views; the next most requested reviews in 2006 have been for *V for Vendetta* (0.7), *X-Men: The Last Stand* (0.6), and *An Inconvenient Truth* (0.5). The lesson: People are curious about a lot of different movies. (Of course, all of these titles will pick up hits as the year advances; in 2005, the most-requested review was *Wolf Creek*, followed by *Munich* and *Brokeback*.)

Twenty years ago when we reviewed a new art, indie, foreign, or documentary film on the TV show, we would hear from viewers complaining, "That movie will never open in my state." Now they thank us: "I've put it in my Netflix queue." Some analysts think that the Netflix model will eventually be replaced by video-on-demand, but I don't think that will happen until you can demand just about any movie you've ever heard of. The current pay-for-view titles on cable and satellite are sadly limited to recent wide commercial releases. Look at those Netflix "shared lists" and you see people renting the damnedest and most obscure titles.

Eventually HDTV and HD-DVD will become so affordable and so good that its quality will rival theatrical projection. If the theaters have switched to digital projection, consumers will rightly notice that they get the same quality at home that they get in a theater. That's why American theater chains desperately need to upgrade the quality of their projection, not settle for a questionable sideways move.

For years and years I have stubbornly been writing about MaxiVision 48, a system that provides a 400 percent improvement in picture quality over current 35 mm projection and involves a per-booth cost of only about $12,000 (only the front end of the projector changes; the housing remains the same). MV48 shoots at forty-eight frames a second but doesn't require twice as much film; because of the way it uses the real estate on a frame of film, it needs only 50 percent more, and it has an economy mode that slows to the standard 24 fps. It can switch seamlessly between frame rates, because it doesn't use sprockets to pull the film through but a nonvibrating electric motor and compressed air (that means no scratches). In March 2006 I visited Eastman House in Rochester, New York, and had a talk with their best film people. They all knew about MaxiVision, they all knew Kodak could sell more film if it were introduced, and not a single person in the room thought they had seen digital projection comparable even to ordinary 35 mm. But they said Kodak was being "repositioned" as a digital company and would not be investing in new film projection systems. That may work in the short run and be suicidal in the long run.

In the past, theaters have responded to competition from other media by upgrading their projection. Radio brought the talkies. TV brought wide screen. Stereo brought surround sound. All of these revolutions required visionaries in Hollywood boardrooms. The time is here for someone to step up to the plate with MV48. The obvious candidate is the IMAX chain, which could use MV48 to project a picture at much higher quality than current IMAX offerings and at smaller cost, because the big 70 mm IMAX format is costlier and more cumbersome than MaxiVision. That there is an eager market for high-quality sound and picture is shown by the success IMAX has had with ordinary 35 mm films like *Batman Begins* and *King Kong*, not to mention the enormous success of its 3-D version of *Polar Express*. If *Polar Express* could be released in 3-D and flat versions, why not in MV48 and standard versions? The IMAX box office alone makes it plausible.

What I foresee happening in American exhibition is the more or less simultaneous release of smaller films in theaters, on video, on cable/satellite, and on the Internet. I see big films continuing to showcase in standard theaters, but only if the theaters offer a clear improvement over home video standards.

*   *   *

This is the twenty-first annual edition of this Yearbook and its predecessors. My thoughts go back to the original *Movie Home Companion* and to Donna Martin, the editor who conceived it and later persuaded me to switch to the *Yearbook* format. My sincere thanks to her, and to Dorothy O'Brien, who has been the book's valued editor at Andrews McMeel Publishing in recent years. Also to Sue Roush, my editor at Universal Press Syndicate, and to Laura Emerick, Miriam Dinunzio, Teresa Budasi, Thomas Conner, and all the other heroes at the *Chicago Sun-Times*, and Jim Emerson and Cathy Williams at www.rogerebert.com. Many others are thanked in the acknowledgments.

In autumn 2006, the University of Chicago Press published *Awake in the Dark*, a survey of my forty years of writing about the movies. As for the Great Movies books, as I write this I've written the first fifty-seven of one hundred reviews for *The Great Movies III*, which should be published in 2008.

ROGER EBERT

Acknowledgments

My editor is Dorothy O'Brien, tireless, cheerful, all-noticing. She is assisted by the equally invaluable Julie Roberts. My friend and longtime editor Donna Martin suggested this new approach to the annual volume. The design is by Cameron Poulter, the typographical genius of Hyde Park. My thanks to production editor Christi Clemons-Hoffman, who renders Cameron's design into reality. I have been blessed with the expert and discriminating editing of John Barron, Laura Emerick, Miriam DiNunzio, Jeff Wisser, Darel Jevins, Avis Weathersbee, Jeff Johnson, and Teresa Budasi at the *Chicago Sun-Times;* Sue Roush at Universal Press Syndicate; and Michelle Daniel at Andrews McMeel Publishing. Many thanks are also due to the production staff at *Ebert & Roeper,* and to Marsha Jordan at WLS-TV. My gratitude goes to Carol Iwata, my expert personal assistant, and to Marlene Gelfond, at the *Sun-Times.* And special thanks and love to my wife, Chaz, for whom I can only say: If more film critics had a spouse just like her, the level of cheer in the field would rise dramatically.

ROGER EBERT

Key to Symbols

★★★★	A great film
★★★	A good film
★★	Fair
★	Poor

G, PG, PG-13, R, NC-17:
Ratings of the Motion Picture
Association of America

G   Indicates that the movie is
suitable for general audiences

PG   Suitable for general audiences
but parental guidance is
suggested

PG-13   Recommended for viewers
13 years or above; may contain
material inappropriate for
younger children

R   Recommended for viewers
17 or older

NC-17   Intended for adults only

141 m.   Running time

2006   Year of theatrical release

☞   Refers to "Questions for the
Movie Answer Man"

Reviews

A

Adam & Steve ★ ★

NO MPAA RATING, 100 m., 2006

Craig Chester (Adam), Malcolm Gets (Steve), Parker Posey (Rhonda), Chris Kattan (Michael), Noah Segan (Twink), Sally Kirkland (Mary), Julie Hagerty (Sheila). Directed by Craig Chester and produced by Kirkland Tibbels and George Bendele. Screenplay by Chester.

Adam & Steve exerts a strange fascination with its balancing act between scenes that work and others so clunky that, I dunno, is it possible to be this awkward by accident? There is an underlying story here, and some comic ideas, that in the hands of a better director (or more ruthless editor) could have become an entertaining romantic comedy. But the couple in love is forced to enact so many directorial conceits that the movie trips over itself. The director, Craig Chester, is also the costar; as an actor, he has the wrong director.

Chester stars as Adam Bernstein, first seen in the 1980s with best pal Rhonda (Parker Posey), dressed as Goths and entering a gay disco on Glitter Night, the wrong night for them. Adam makes eye contact with a dancer named Steve (Malcolm Gets), and it's love at first sight, but, "We don't dance," they explain. "We're Goths. We're dead." Not too dead for Steve to give Adam his first hit of cocaine, which makes him instantly addicted. The coke is laced with baby laxative, leading to a scene in which so many bodily wastes and fluids are ejected or vomited that a serious plot miscalculation is involved, evoking such a strong "ewww!" reflex that it takes the audience five minutes and a "17 Years Later" subtitle to get back on track.

Adam and Steve meet again in their late thirties, neither one remembering their first meeting (or perhaps much else of the late 1980s). Adam is clean and sober now, a pet lover who accidentally stabs his dog while slicing sausage and takes him to a human emergency room, where Steve, a psychiatrist who "trained as a veterinarian" (does that make him a pet psychiatrist?), treats the wound. For the two men, it's love at second sight.

Their romance develops despite the usual plot convenience (fear of commitment), but there's a crisis when Steve realizes who Adam is and flees rather than confess he made the deposit on Adam's rug seventeen years ago. Will they reconcile? Can Rhonda and Steve's straight roommate, Michael (Chris Kattan), be the go-betweens? Before we can learn the answer to that question, we get a scene both bizarre and weirdly funny.

Remember those old musicals such as *Seven Brides for Seven Brothers*, where lumberjacks would stage dance duels for the favor of the girl? Steve and Adam face off in a disco where western line dancing and two-steps in cowboy boots are the dance style, and both men instantly acquire backup dancers for a meticulously choreographed confrontation that's as well-staged as it is dramatically inexplicable. That scene, and one where Steve serenades Adam by singing to him at brunch, show how the movie uses any genre that can be plundered for effect, and does it with humor and sometimes charm.

I liked, for example, the visit to Adam's parents, who are the nicest people in the world although they suffer from the "Bernstein curse" (mother in neck brace, father in wheelchair, sister bites tongue). I liked the deadpan way Posey plays the formerly fat Goth who has become a slender stand-up comic who still tells fat jokes. The scene where Adam, leading a bird-watching tour in Central Park, meets Steve again after a tragic duck shooting. And Sally Kirkland as an AA group leader shouting "no cross-talking!" during a verbal fight.

But what can we make of other scenes that destroy any dramatic effect and all but shout, "This cumbersome scene is being committed to film by ham-handed amateurs"? I'm thinking of a conversation that is observed by a man in the center background who stares at the camera, reacts to the conversation, and closes the scene with an unintelligible comment. Who was that man? Friend of the director? Investor? In another scene a drunken girl, trying to pick up Michael in a bar, is so self-consciously awful in her awkward overacting that you can see

Kattan, a pro, wishing himself elsewhere. Or a scene where Adam and Rhonda have a talk on a bench in a gay sculpture park, and in the last shot they awkwardly "happen" to take the same pose as the sculptures they're seated next to. What does a shot like that mean? Where does it go? How do we react?—Wow! They're in the same pose as the sculpture!

There is a gay-bashing montage in which Adam and Steve try to pursue their courtship while offscreen homophobes throw beer bottles at them. Far from funny, and it isn't saved by a pan up to the street sign: "Gay Street." And a scene where Steve gets fed up with a homophobic neighbor who screams insults at them and drags him, beaten and bloody, into a bar so that the gay-basher can get his arm twisted while he speaks for Steve in proposing marriage to Adam. This is an agonizingly bad idea.

The movie is one hundred minutes long. My guess is that by taking out maybe fifteen judicious minutes, it could be cut into a measurably better film—funnier, more romantic, more professional. The sad thing is to watch it finding a rhythm and beginning to work as a comedy, then running into a brick wall of miscalculation or incompetence. Any professional film editor watching this movie is going to suffer through one moment after another that begs to be ripped from the film and cut up into ukulele picks. Never mind the film editor: A lot of audiences, with all the best will in the world, are going to feel the same way.

The Adventures of Sharkboy and Lavagirl in 3-D ★ ★
PG, 94 m., 2005

Cayden Boyd (Max), David Arquette (Dad), Kristin Davis (Mom), Taylor Dooley (Lavagirl), Taylor Lautner (Sharkboy), George Lopez (Mr. Electricidad), Sasha Pieterse (Ice Princess), Jacob Davich (Minus). Directed by Robert Rodriguez and produced by Elizabeth Avellan and Robert Rodriguez. Screenplay by Racer Rodriguez and Robert Rodriguez.

The Adventures of Sharkboy and Lavagirl in 3-D is an innocent and delightful children's tale that is spoiled by a disastrous decision to film most of it in lousy 3-D. Fully three-quarters of the movie is in "3"-D, which looks more like 1-D to me, removing the brightness and life of the movie's colors and replacing them with a drab, listless palette that is about as exciting as looking at a 3-D bowl of oatmeal. The 3-D process subtracts instead of adding. Ordinary 2-D movies look perfectly real enough for audiences and have for years; if it's not broke, don't fix it. Paradoxically, since it allegedly resembles our real-world vision, 3-D is less real than standard flat movies; 3-D acts as a distraction from character and story, giving us something to think about that during a good movie we should not be thinking about.

To be sure, there is a new 3-D process that is pretty good. That would be the IMAX process that uses oversized glasses and creates a convincing 3-D effect, as in James Cameron's *Aliens of the Deep*. That is not the process used in *Sharkboy and Lavagirl*, which settles for those crummy old cardboard glasses where the left lens is such a dark red that the whole movie seems seen through a glass, darkly.

What a shame. I assume the unaltered original color footage of the movie exists, and no doubt will be used for the DVD. My suggestion to Robert Rodriguez, who directed the movie from a screenplay by one of his sons and uses three of them as actors, would be to make a non–3-D version available theatrically as soon as possible. This is a movie aimed at younger kids, who may be willing to sit through almost anything, but they're going to know something is wrong and they're not going to like it.

The origin of the film makes a good story. Rodriguez's son Racer, then seven, told him a story about a boy who grew gills and a fin and became half-shark, and a girl who incorporated fiery volcanic elements. He encouraged his son to keep working on the story, in which the young hero, Max (Cayden Boyd), is a daydreamer. Max is mocked by Linus, the school bully, because of his Dream Journal, where he documents the adventures of Sharkboy and Lavagirl. Then a tornado appears out of a clear sky, bringing with it Sharkboy (Taylor Lautner) and Lavagirl (Taylor Dooley), who explain they have been created by Max's dreams and now need his help; the world he created for them, Planet Drool, will be destroyed by darkness in forty-five minutes. I may not have followed these details with perfect fidelity, but you get the drift.

Max, SB, and LG go on a journey that takes them on the Stream of Consciousness to the Sea of Confusion; they ride a Train of Thought, and eventually arrive at a Dream Lair. There they find the nasty Minus, played by the same actor (Jacob Davich) who was the bully in Max's classroom. Many adventures result, some of them involving an Ice Princess and a robot named Tobor, as well as an all-knowing character named Mr. Electric, who looks exactly like Max's teacher Mr. Electricidad (George Lopez).

Mr. Electric appears as a big, round smiling face in a frame outfitted with spindly arms and legs. He reminded me of someone, which was odd, since he looked like nobody I've ever seen. Nobody, I realized, except the Man in the Moon in Georges Melies's *A Trip to the Moon* (1902). Mr. Electric floats about like a busybody commentator, offering advice, issuing warnings, and making a general nuisance of himself; one of his peculiarities is that he won't allow the kids on the planet to stop playing—ever. One group is trapped on a roller coaster that never stops.

Sharkboy and Lavagirl has the same upbeat charm as Rodriguez's *Spy Kids* movies, and it must be said that the screenplay by Racer Rodriguez involves the kind of free-wheeling invention that kids enjoy; this is a movie where dream logic prevails. Their movie also resembles *Spy Kids* in having roles for parents, including Max's dad and mom (David Arquette and Kristin Davis).

Because the real-world scenes are in 2-D and the dream and fantasy scenes are in 3-D, we get an idea of what the movie would have looked like without the unnecessary dimension. Signs flash on the screen to tell us when to put on and take off our polarizing glasses, and I felt regret every time I had to shut out those colorful images and return to the dim and dreary 3-D world. On DVD, this is going to be a great-looking movie.

After the Sunset ★ ★
PG-13, 100 m., 2004

Pierce Brosnan (Max Burdett), Salma Hayek (Lola Cirillo), Woody Harrelson (Stan Lloyd), Don Cheadle (Kingpin), Kate Walsh (Sheila), Naomie Harris (Sophie), Rachael Harris (June), Jeff Garlin (Ron). Directed by Brett Ratner and produced by Beau Flynn and Jay Stern. Screenplay by Paul Zbyszewski and Craig Rosenberg.

I am bemused by what a movie expects us to accept on faith. Consider the opening sequence of *After the Sunset*, a diamond heist movie. Woody Harrelson plays Stan, an FBI agent who is a passenger in an SUV; he holds a briefcase that contains a precious jewel. After the driver gets out of the SUV, the thief Max (Pierce Brosnan) uses a PDA to assume control of the vehicle, backs it up at high speed, and speeds away from the FBI security escort. On a side street, it halts in front of a garage door, and a semitruck pushes it sideways through the door, which slams shut behind it. Stan is relieved of the jewel and foiled again by his longtime arch-enemy.

Very good. But now think some more. Max's partner in the heist was Lola (Salma Hayek), who disguised herself as a bearded squeegee guy at a stoplight, using her squeegee to read the bar code on the SUV window so Max could key in the vehicle on his PDA. Very good. But why did he need to know the vehicle identification number when he manifestly had already customized the vehicle? After all, it contains the remote controls he is manipulating. Even the best-equipped SUVs don't come loaded with equipment allowing them to be driven automatically by PDAs. We're distracted from this logic by the obligatory scene in which Lola rips off her whiskers and wig, looking of course perfectly made up underneath.

All very well. But hold on: Did I say Max was on a rooftop? Yes, because that's how he can look down and see the SUV that he takes control of. Excellent. Except, what happens after the SUV turns the corner and races down the street and turns another corner? How can Max still see it? How does he know where to steer it? How come it doesn't run through a crosswalk containing a baby carriage, two nuns with six orphans, and a couple of guys carrying a sheet of plate glass? And how could they be sure the SUV would stop exactly in front of the open garage door, especially since Brosnan can't see what's happening? Maybe it was remote-controlled too.

The movies are never more mysterious

than when they show us something that is completely preposterous, and get away with it. Not 1 viewer in 100 will ask the questions I've just asked, because in movies like this we go along with the flow. And this whole movie is flow.

After the Sunset is skillfully made, but it's not necessary. I can think of no compelling reason to see it during a time when your choices also include *Sideways, Ray, The Polar Express, The Incredibles, Primer, Vera Drake,* and *Undertow.* On the other hand, should you see it, the time will pass pleasantly.

The actors are good company. Pierce Brosnan and Salma Hayek hurl themselves into their roles—but gently, so nothing gets broken. She's in full plunging-neckline-in-the-sunset mode. Woody Harrelson has the necessary ambiguity to play the FBI agent's love-hate relationship with Max. Don Cheadle has fun as the American-born Bahamian gangster who wants to become Brosnan's partner in stealing a precious diamond from a cruise ship. Naomie Harris is intriguing as a local cop. The locations are sun-drenched, and there are enough plugs for the Atlantis resort hotel so that we know the cast enjoyed their stay on the island.

But what, really, is *After the Sunset* other than behavior-circling clichés? The heist itself, with its entrance through the ceiling, etc., is recycled from other films. However, the method by which Max establishes his alibi is clever. I can't describe it without giving away too much, but should you watch the film, ask yourself (1) if there's really enough time to do what he does, and (2) how likely it is that a nondiving FBI agent would agree to come along with a couple of thieves on a midnight scuba expedition to an old wreck?

The subplot is the old standby about the crooks who pull off one last job and plan to retire. Of course the woman is in favor of this, but the man grows restless and misses his old life. The same thing that happens to Max happened to Mr. Incredible. The female lead always gets the thankless task of trying to talk the hero out of doing what he obviously must do, or there would be no movie. "Now the challenge is to find joy in simple things," Lola tells Max. *After the Sunset* is a simple thing, so we could start there.

Against the Ropes ★ ★ ★
PG-13, 111 m., 2004

Meg Ryan (Jackie Kallen), Omar Epps (Luther Shaw), Charles S. Dutton (Felix Reynolds), Tony Shalhoub (Sam Larocca), Timothy Daly (Gavin Reese), Joseph Cortese (Irving Abel), Kerry Washington (Renee), Skye McCole Bartusiak (Young Jackie Kallen). Directed by Charles S. Dutton and produced by Robert W. Cort and David Madden. Screenplay by Cheryl Edwards.

You know the slow clap scene, where the key character walks into the room and it falls silent? And everybody is alert and tense and waiting to see what will happen? And then one person slowly starts to clap, and then two, three, four, and then suddenly the tension breaks and everyone is clapping, even the sourpuss holdouts? Can we agree that this scene is an ancient cliché? We can. And yet occasionally I am amazed when it works, all the same.

It works near the end of *Against the Ropes*, a biopic about Jackie Kallen, who was (and is) the first female fight promoter in the all-male world of professional boxing. It works, and another cliché works, too: the big fight scene, right out of *Rocky* and every other boxing movie, in which the hero gets pounded silly but then somehow, after becoming inspired between rounds, comes back and is filled with skill and fury.

Against the Ropes meanders until it gets to the final third of its running time, and then it catches fire. Its setup story is flat and lacks authenticity. Meg Ryan is barely adequate as Jackie Kallen, and Omar Epps, as her boxer, Luther Shaw, is convincing but underwritten. The film plays like a quick, shallow, made-for-TV biopic, but then it relies on those ancient conventions, and they pull it through.

When we meet Kallen, she is the assistant to Cleveland's top boxing promoter. She grew up in boxing; her dad ran a gym and when she was a little girl he sometimes had to chase her out of the ring. Now she knows as much about boxing as anyone, but of course as a woman isn't allowed to use that knowledge. Then, observing a fight in a ghetto drug apartment, she sees a (nondrug-related) guy waltz in and cream everyone, and she intuits that he could be a great fighter.

This is Luther Shaw, played by Epps as a man with psychic wounds from childhood that sometimes unleash a terrible fury. Kallen persuades him he can be a fighter, signs him, hires a trainer to prepare him, edges around the Cleveland boycott against her by convincing a Buffalo promoter it's time for him to return the favors he got from her dad. Many of the scenes in this stretch are routine, although the performance by Charles Dutton as a veteran trainer has a persuasive authenticity; he also directs.

Meg Ryan works hard at Jackie Kallen, but this is not a role she was born to play. Ryan is a gifted actress, best at comedy but with lots of *noir* in her; she's good in thrillers, too. But she's not naturally a brassy exhibitionist, and that's what this role calls for. Kallen, who seems to buy her wardrobe from Trashy Lingerie and Victoria's Secret, and who talks like a girl who grew up in a gym, might have better been cast with someone with rougher notes—Gina Gershon. Ryan seems to be pushing it.

There's also a problem with Renee (Kerry Washington), Kallen's best friend, who becomes Luther's girlfriend, I think. I say "I think" because the role is so seriously underwritten that the movie would have been better off just not including it. Although Luther and Kallen are never romantically attracted, theirs is the movie's central relationship. Dutton (working from a screenplay by Cheryl Edwards) doesn't seem much interested in Luther's private emotional life, and so we get inexplicable scenes in which Luther and Renee seem to be best friends, or are hanging out together, or—what? The two of them have hardly any dialogue with each other, and although Renee is cheering during the big fight, there's no scene resolving her feelings for her man; the spotlight is on Kallen, which is all right, but it leaves a loose end.

Epps is always convincing, however, and by the last act of the movie we make our accommodation with Ryan because the character has grown more interesting. Intoxicated by the spotlight of publicity, she starts to think it's about her, not her boxer, and eventually she turns into a media caricature and finds herself forced outside the world she helped to create. Then comes the big fight, and the slow clap, and I'm damned if I wasn't really moved by the payoff.

Agent Cody Banks 2: Destination London ★ ★ ½
PG, 93 m., 2004

Frankie Muniz (Cody Banks), Anthony Anderson (Derek), Hannah Spearritt (Emily), Daniel Roebuck (Mr. Banks), Keith Allen (Diaz), Keith David (CIA Director), Cynthia Stevenson (Mrs. Banks), Connor Widdows (Alex Banks). Directed by Kevin Allen and produced by David Glasser, Andreas Klein, David Nicksay, Guy Oseary, and Dylan Sellers. Screenplay Don Rhymer.

I've been trying to mind-control myself into the head of a kid the right age to enjoy *Agent Cody Banks 2: Destination London*, but either I was never that age, or I haven't reached it yet. I'm capable of enjoying the *Spy Kids* movies, so I know I'm not totally lacking in range, but the movie seems preassembled, like those kits where it takes more time to open the box than build the airplane.

The movie opens at a secret summer camp where the CIA trains teenagers to become junior James Bonds. The opening scene, in fact, is uncanny in the way it resembles the prologue of David Mamet's *Spartan*. In both movies, characters in combat uniforms with lots of camouflage paint on their faces creep through trees and try to cream one another. For Mamet, that is not the high point of his movie.

Cody Banks (Frankie Muniz) is a smart, resourceful kid who thinks there may be something fishy at the camp, which is run by Diaz (Keith Allen), love child of Patton and Rambo. After a secret plot is revealed, Cody finds himself on assignment in London, where his handler is Derek (Anthony Anderson) and his mission is to prevent the CIA's bad apples from gaining possession of a mind-control device that fits inside a tooth and turns its wearer into a zombie.

It's a pretty nifty device: At one point, its mad inventor fits it to a dog which then sits upright at a piano and plays a little tune, reminding me inevitably of Dr. Johnson's observation that when a dog walks on its hind legs, "it is not done well, but one is surprised to find it done at all." The dog is impressive but no pianist, and Derek, watching the demonstration on a spycam with Cody, decides he won't buy the CD.

The agency, as in the previous film, supplies Cody with various secret weapons, including a pack of Mentos that explode when moistened. Turns out the evil master plan is to subvert a conference of world leaders at Buckingham Palace; to infiltrate the palace, Cody must join a world-class youth orchestra—not easy, since he doesn't play an instrument, but easier than you might think, since his agency-supplied clarinet plays itself. It seems to know only "Flight of the Bumble Bee," unfortunately.

Hilary Duff, who played Cody's sidekick in the previous movie, is MIA this time, and her place is taken, sort of, by Emily (Hannah Spearritt), a British agent who looks in a certain light as if she might be a teenager, and in another as if she might be, oh, exactly twenty-three. You will recall from the previous film that Cody is too busy being an agent to date much, and his little brother sees more action. (That produced a good exchange: Cody says most of the brother's dating doesn't count because it's limited to a tree house, and the brother replies, "It does if you're playing Doctor.")

The big climax at Buckingham Palace features look-alikes for Tony Blair and the queen, and a scene that is supposed to be funny because the youth orchestra stalls for time by improvising a song with a funky rhythm and the queen boogies with the heads of state. Since I am enough of a realist to believe that a large part of the target audience for this movie doesn't know who the queen is or what she looks like, it's a good thing the action starts up again real soon.

There is a mind-controlled food fight that begins promisingly but is awkwardly handled, and a chase through London that is (sigh) just one more chase through London, and apart from funny supporting work by the inventor of the mind control and the guy in the "Q" role, the movie is pretty routine. I wanted to be able to tell you the names of the actors in those two entertaining roles, but half an hour's research has not discovered them, although the movie's Website has signed me up for junior agent training.

The Agronomist ★ ★ ★ ½

NO MPAA RATING, 90 m., 2004

A documentary directed by Jonathan Demme and produced by Demme, Bevin McNamara, and Peter Saraf.

Jean Dominique was a brave man in a danger-ous country, and Jonathan Demme's *The Agronomist* shows him telling the truth as he sees it, day after day, on the radio in Haiti. It is obvious that sooner or later he will be assassinated. Dissent cannot be tolerated in a nation that depends on secrecy to protect its powerful. What is remarkable is how long he survived, and how courageously he owned and operated Radio Haiti-Inter; it became the voice of the powerless in great part because it broadcast in Creole, the language they spoke, instead of in the French of their masters.

Jonathan Demme, who made the documentary, is a man who seems to lead parallel lives. In one, he is the successful director of such films as *The Silence of the Lambs, Philadelphia, Married to the Mob,* and *Melvin and Howard.* In the other, he has made documentaries about Haiti, has visited there countless times, has helped promote Haitian art and music, and has a heart that aches as he sees the country victimized by powerful interests both within and without.

In Jean Dominique and his wife, Michele Montas, Demme finds subjects who reflect the agony of Haiti's struggle. His documentary draws on hundreds of hours of filming and conversations from 1991 until Dominique's death in 2000. It begins at the moment when President Jean-Claude Aristide was overthrown in 1991, follows the Dominiques into exile in New York, watches as they return to Haiti and Aristide is restored to power, and observes how Dominique, originally a supporter of Aristide, became one of his critics.

Dominique is a man who seems to have come to heroism because it was the only choice for a man of his nature. His college education was in agriculture (which explains the movie's title), and he first came up against the ruling clique through his efforts for land reform. He was interested in the arts, started a cinema club in Port-au-Prince, and was shut down by the dictator "Papa Doc" Duvalier after showing Alain Resnais's *Night and Fog.* That was a film about the evil of Nazism; why Papa Doc found it unacceptable is easy to imagine.

At first it seemed that the rebel priest Aristide might force a change in his nation's destiny, but soon he, too, was employing the tactics of those he replaced. There is a sequence in the film where Dominique interviews Aristide and challenges him with pointed questions. The president responds with measured sound bites that repeat the same inanities again and again, as if he is incapable of understanding the actual meaning of the questions he has been asked.

Dominique and Montas are persons of great cheer and energy, leaping into each day with such zeal that they sometimes seem to forget the risks they are taking. Their problem in Haiti is that by honestly speaking to the ordinary people in their own language, they offend not only their obvious enemies but even those they do not know they have made. A nation built on lies cannot tolerate truth even when it agrees with it.

Radio Haiti-Inter comes under siege more than once, and Demme's camera does not overlook the bullet holes in the exterior walls. The station seems to be run informally, as a mixture of music, gossip, local news, and political opinion; at times of crisis, Dominique stays on the air as long as he can, until power outages or the government shut him down.

This is a couple who could have led the good life in Haiti. With the light complexions of the French-speaking Haitian establishment, with education and some wealth, they could have gone along with the ruling elite and earned a nice little fortune with their radio station or other enterprises. What fascinates us is Dominique's inability to do that. He is well enough connected to know what is going wrong, and too principled to ignore it.

Did he know he would be killed? Who can say? His country was in tumult, and the inconsistent policies of the United States did little to help. The country seemed almost to force its rulers into fearful and repressive policies. The wise course for Dominique would have been to return in exile to New York and use a dissenting magazine or Web site to spread his beliefs.

But no. When he could go back, he went back. Demme often followed him. We watch Dominique use humor and cynicism as well as anger, and we understand he is not a zealot but simply a reasonable man saying reasonable things in an unreasonable country. After his murder, Michele Montas goes on the air to insist that Jean Dominique is still alive, because his spirit lives on. But in this film Haiti seems to be a country that can kill the spirit, too.

Aileen: The Life and Death of a Serial Killer ★ ★ ★ ½
NO MPAA RATING, 89 m., 2004

A documentary directed by Nick Broomfield and Joan Churchill and produced by Jo Human.

Aileen Wuornos was trashed by life. That she committed seven murders is beyond dispute and unforgivable, but what can we expect from a child who was beaten by her grandfather, molested by a pedophile, abandoned by her mother, and raped by her brother and other neighborhood boys and men? A child who was selling sex for cigarettes at the age of nine, who had a baby at thirteen and was thrown out of the house, who lived for two years in the woods at the end of the street or, in cold weather, in the backseat of a car, wrapped in a single blanket? Society made Aileen into a weapon and turned her loose.

Aileen: The Life and Death of a Serial Killer is a documentary by Nick Broomfield, the guerrilla filmmaker who works with a crew of one (cinematographer and codirector Joan Churchill) and structures his films into the stories of how he made them. He met Aileen, invariably described as "America's first female serial killer," soon after her original arrest, and made the 1992 documentary *Aileen Wuornos: The Selling of a Serial Killer* about the media zoo and bidding war that surrounded her sudden notoriety. Florida police officers were fired after it was disclosed they were negotiating for a Hollywood deal, and Aileen, meanwhile, was represented by "Dr. Legal," a bearded, pot-smoking ex-hippie who was incompetent and clueless. She saw his ad on late-night TV. She couldn't pay him, but he figured he could cash in, too.

As Wuornos's often-delayed execution date inexorably closed in, Broomfield returned to the story for this film, made in 2002. He had become friendly, if that is the word, with Aileen, and indeed she gave him her last interview. He also interviewed many people instrumental in her life, including childhood friends, former sexual partners, and even her long-lost mother. The portrait he builds of her life is one of cruel suffering and mistreatment. This was a young woman who hitchhiked to Florida when she was thirteen because she was tired of sleeping in the rough, and who became a roadside pros-

7

titute because, really, what else was open to her? Social services? Invisible in her case.

Wuornos herself is onscreen for much of the film. Charlize Theron has earned almost unanimous praise for her portrayal of Aileen in the film *Monster,* and her performance stands up to direct comparison with the real woman. There were times, indeed, when I perceived no significant difference between the woman in the documentary and the one in the feature film. Theron has internalized and empathized with Wuornos so successfully that to experience the real woman is only to understand more completely how remarkable her performance is.

Wuornos talks and talks and talks to Broomfield. She confesses and recants. She says at one point that her original defense (she was raped and attacked by her victims, and shot them in self-defense) was a lie—that she was in the "stealing biz" and killed them to cover her tracks. On another day she is likely to return to her original story. We hear her describing a man who tortured her with acid in a Visine bottle, and her vivid details make us feel we were there. Then she tells Broomfield she made it all up. What can we believe? Broomfield's theory is that after more than a decade on Death Row, Wuornos was insane, and that she used her last remaining shreds of reason to hasten the day of her execution. She said whatever she thought would speed her date with death.

Oh, yes, it's clear she was crazy on the day she died. She talks to Broomfield about secret signals and radio waves being beamed into her cell, about how the police knew she was the killer but let her keep on killing because it would make a better story for them to sell, about how she would be beamed up "like on *Star Trek*" to a spaceship waiting for her in Earth orbit.

Remarkably, three psychiatrists "examined" her right before her death and found her sane. No person who sees this film would agree with them. Florida Governor Jeb Bush was scarcely less enthusiastic about the death penalty than his brother George, who supported the notorious execution assembly line in Texas. Aileen died in October of an election year, just in time to send a law-and-order message to the voters. Should she have died? That depends on whether you support the death penalty. She was certainly guilty. The film makes it clear her imprisonment would simply have continued a lifelong sentence that began when she was born. No one should have to endure the life that Aileen Wuornos led, and we leave the movie believing that if someone, somehow, had been able to help that little girl, her seven victims would never have died.

Akeelah and the Bee ★ ★ ★ ★
PG-13, 112 m., 2006

Angela Bassett (Tanya Anderson), Keke Palmer (Akeelah Anderson), Laurence Fishburne (Dr. Joshua Larabee), Curtis Armstrong (Mr. Welch), J. R. Villarreal (Javier), Sahara Garey (Georgia), Sean Michael Afable (Dylan), Erica Hubbard (Kiana Anderson). Directed by Doug Atchison and produced by Laurence Fishburne, Sidney Ganis, Nancy Hult Ganis, Daniel Llewelyn, and Michael Romersa. Screenplay by Atchison.

Akeelah Anderson can spell. She can spell better than anyone in her school in south central Los Angeles, and she might have a chance at the nationals. Who can say? She sees the national spelling bee on ESPN and is intrigued. But she is also wary, because in her school there is danger in being labeled a "brainiac," and it's wiser to keep your smarts to yourself. This is a tragedy in some predominantly black schools: Excellence is punished by the other students, possibly as an expression of their own low self-esteem.

The thing with Akeelah (Keke Palmer) is that she *can* spell, whether she wants to or not. Beating time with her hand against her thigh as sort of a metronome, she cranks out the letters and arrives triumphantly at the words. No, she doesn't have a photographic memory, nor is she channeling the occult, as the heroine of *Bee Season* does. She's just a good speller.

The story of Akeelah's ascent to the finals of the National Spelling Bee makes an uncommonly good movie, entertaining and actually inspirational, and with a few tears along the way. Her real chance at national success comes after a reluctant English professor agrees to act as her coach. This is Dr. Joshua Larabee (Laurence Fishburne), on a leave of absence after the death of his daughter. Coaching her is a way out of his own shell. And for Fishburne, it's a reminder of his work in *Searching for Bobby Fischer* (1993), another movie where he coached a prodigy.

Akeelah is not mocked only at school. Her own mother is against her. Tanya Anderson (Angela Bassett) has issues after the death of her husband, and she values Akeelah's homework above all else, including silly after-school activities such as spelling bees. Akeelah practices in secret, and after she wins a few bees, even the tough kids in the neighborhood start cheering for her.

Keke Palmer, a young Chicago actress whose first role was as Queen Latifah's niece in *Barber Shop 2*, becomes an important young star with this movie. It puts her in Dakota Fanning and Flora Cross territory, and there's something about her poise and self-possession that hints she will grow up to be a considerable actress. The movie depends on her, and she deserves its trust.

So far I imagine *Akeelah and The Bee* sounds like a nice but fairly conventional movie. What makes it transcend the material is the way she relates to the professor and to two fellow contestants: a Mexican-American named Javier (J. R. Villarreal) and an Asian-American named Dylan (Sean Michael Afable). Javier, who lives with his family in the upscale Woodland Hills neighborhood, invites Akeelah to his birthday party (unaware of what a long bus trip it involves). Dylan, driven by an obsessive father, treats the spelling bee like life and death, and takes no hostages. Hearing Dylan's father berate him, Akeelah feels an instinctive sympathy. And as for Javier's feelings for Akeelah, at his party he impulsively kisses her.

"Why'd you do that?" she asks him.

"I had an impulse. Are you gonna sue me for sexual harassment?"

The sessions between Akeelah and the professor are crucial to the film, because he is teaching her not only strategy but also how to be willing to win. No, he doesn't use self-help clichés. He is demanding and uncompromising, and he tells her again and again, "Our deepest fear is that we are powerful beyond measure." This quote, often attributed to Nelson Mandela, is actually from Marianne Williamson but is no less true for Akeelah (the movie does not attribute it).

Now I am going to start dancing around the plot. Something happens during the finals of the national bee that you are not going to see coming, and it may move you as deeply as it did me. I've often said it's not sadness that touches me the most in a movie, but goodness. Under enormous pressure, at a crucial moment, Akeelah does something good. Its results I will leave for you to discover. What is ingenious about the plot construction of writer-director Doug Atchison is that he creates this moment so that we understand what's happening, but there's no way to say for sure. Even the judges sense or suspect something. But Akeelah, improvising in the moment and out of her heart, makes it airtight. There is only one person who absolutely must understand what she is doing, and why—and he does.

This ending answers one of my problems with spelling bees and spelling-bee movies. It removes winning as the only objective. Vince Lombardi was dead wrong when he said, "Winning isn't everything. It's the only thing" (a quote, by the way, first said not by Lombardi but in the 1930s by UCLA coach Henry "Red" Sanders—but since everybody thinks Lombardi said it, he won, I guess). The saying is mistaken because to win for the wrong reason or in the wrong way is to lose. Something called sportsmanship is involved.

In our winning-obsessed culture, it is inspiring to see a young woman like Akeelah Anderson instinctively understand, with empathy and generosity, that doing the right thing involves more than winning. That's what makes the film particularly valuable for young audiences. I don't care if they leave the theater wanting to spell better, but if they have learned from Akeelah, they will want to live better.

The Alamo ★ ★ ★ ½
PG-13, 137 m., 2004

Dennis Quaid (Sam Houston), Billy Bob Thornton (Davy Crockett), Jason Patric (James Bowie), Patrick Wilson (William Barrett Travis), Emilio Echevarria (Santa Anna), Jordi Molla (Juan Seguin), Laura Clifton (Susanna Dickinson), Leon Rippy (Sergeant William Ward). Directed by John Lee Hancock and produced by Brian Grazer, Ron Howard, and Mark Johnson. Screenplay by Leslie Bohem, Stephen Gaghan, and Hancock.

The advance buzz on *The Alamo* was negative,

and now I know why: This is a good movie. Conventional wisdom in Hollywood is that any movie named *The Alamo* must be simplistic and rousing, despite the fact that we already know all the defenders got killed. (If we don't know it, we find out in the first scene.) Here is a movie that captures the loneliness and dread of men waiting for two weeks for what they expect to be certain death, and it somehow succeeds in taking those pop culture brand names like Davy Crockett and James Bowie and giving them human form.

The arc of the Alamo story is a daunting one for any filmmaker: long days and nights of waiting, followed by a massacre. Even though the eventual defeat of Santa Anna by Sam Houston provides an upbeat coda, it's of little consolation to the dead defenders. This movie deals frankly with the long wait and the deadly conclusion by focusing on the characters of the leaders; it's about what they're made of, and how they face a bleak situation.

Davy Crockett, the man in the coonskin hat, surprisingly becomes the most three-dimensional of the Alamo heroes, in one of Billy Bob Thornton's best performances. We see him first in a theater box, attending a play inspired by his exploits. We learn of his legend; even Santa Anna's men whisper that he can leap rivers in a single bound and wrestle grizzly bears to death. And then we watch Crockett with a rueful smile as he patiently explains that he did not do and cannot do any of those things, and that his reputation has a life apart from his reality.

Crockett, who was a U.S. congressman before fate led him to the Alamo, has two scenes in particular that are extraordinary, and Thornton brings a poignant dignity to them. One is his memory of a U.S. Army massacre of Indians. The other occurs when the Mexicans, who have brought along a band, have their drummers put on a show. Crockett knows just what the percussion needs, climbs one of the battlements, takes out his violin and serenades both sides. It is one of those moments, like the Christmas Eve truce in World War I, when fighting men on both sides are reminded of the innocence they have lost. Crockett also has a line that somehow reminded me of the need, in *Jaws*, for a bigger boat: "We're going to need more men."

Leadership of the Alamo is contested between Colonel James Bowie (Jason Patric) and Lieutenant Colonel William Barrett Travis (Patrick Wilson). It involves a show of hands, a contest of wills, a truce, and then the inexorable weakening of Bowie, who is dying of tuberculosis and, it is murmured, other diseases. Travis is a humorless patriot who would rather, he tells us, have moments of glory than a lifetime of drudgery, and he strikes the men as over the top. But he is true to his principles, and at one point, although he has to be informed that the time has come to talk to his men, he delivers a speech filled with fire and resolve, reminding me of Henry V on the night before Agincourt.

Bowie faces the fact that he is a dying man, and it is agonizing to watch him attempt to button up his vest and climb from his deathbed to join in the battle. A revolver is placed in each of his hands, and when the Mexicans burst in, he takes two lives before they claim the few hours of life left in him. Both Travis and Bowie could have been caricatures; Wilson and Patric find their humanity.

The director and cowriter, John Lee Hancock, occupies more than an hour with scenes leading up to the final battle, as the Alamo defenders make their plans and wait for reinforcements that never arrive. As his troops surround them, General Santa Anna (Emilio Echevarria) struts and poses in front of his officers, who are appalled by his ignorance but intimidated by his temper. Ordering the final charge, he's told a twelve-pound cannon will arrive tomorrow that would breach the Alamo's walls without sacrifice of countless Mexican lives, but he disdains to wait, and dismisses the lives with a wave of his hand. (His own life was much more precious to him; he traded it for Texas.)

There are two scenes involving surrender that make an ironic contrast. Surrounded by dead bodies, himself gravely wounded, Davy Crockett is offered surrender terms by Santa Anna and replies by defiantly offering to accept Santa Anna's surrender. This is matched by the scene at the end where Houston (Dennis Quaid) has Santa Anna on his knees, and the general will agree to anything.

Much of the picture takes place at night, illuminated by campfires and candlelight, and Hancock's cinematographer, the gifted Dean Semler, finds color and texture in the shadows that evoke those hours between midnight and dawn that Fitzgerald called the dark night of the soul. Oddly enough, as Santa Anna's troops march up to within one hundred yards of the Alamo, there seem to be no watchmen to see them, and when they attack it is a surprise.

The battle scenes, when they come, are brutal and unforgiving; we reflect that the first Mexicans up the scaling ladders must have known they would certainly die, and yet they climbed them heedlessly. This intimate, hand-to-hand conflict is balanced by awesome long shots, combining the largest sets ever built by modern Hollywood with some special effects shots that are generally convincing.

Although the battle for the Alamo has taken its place as a sacred chapter in American history, the movie deals with the fact that it all came down to one thing: Mexico owned Texas, and ambitious Americans and Texans (or "Texians") wanted it. Many of the fighters had been promised 760 acres of land as a bonus for enlisting. For Bowie, Crockett, and Travis, the challenge was to rehabilitate reputations that had gone astray—to redeem themselves. For Sam Houston, who never sent reinforcements, it was an opportunity to apply Wellington's strategy in leading Napoleon on a chase until Napoleon's army was splintered and weakened. Houston was too wise to commit his army to the Alamo; that took foolishness, bravery, and a certain poetry of the soul.

Alexander ★ ★
R, 175 m., 2004

Colin Farrell (Alexander), Angelina Jolie (Olympias), Val Kilmer (Philip), Rosario Dawson (Roxane), Jared Leto (Hephaistion), Anthony Hopkins (Ptolemy), Christopher Plummer (Aristotle). Directed by Oliver Stone and produced by Moritz Borman, Jon Kilik, Thomas Schuhly, Iain Smith, and Stone. Screenplay by Stone, Christopher Kyle, and Laeta Kalogridis.

When the mighty fall, it is from a greater height. So it was with Alexander the Great, and so it is with Oliver Stone's *Alexander*. Here is an ambitious and sincere film that fails to find a focus for its elusive subject. Stone is fascinated by two aspects of Alexander: his pannationalism, and his pansexualism. He shows him trying to unite many peoples under one throne while remaining equally inclusive with his choices of lovers.

But it remains unclear if Alexander has united those peoples or simply conquered them, and his sexuality is made murky by the film's shyness about gay sex and its ambiguity about Alexander's relationships with his "barbarian" bride and his tigress mother. We welcome the movie's scenes of battle, pomp, and circumstance because at least for a time we are free of sociopolitical concepts and the endless narration of Ptolemy the historian, who functions here like the Bill Kurtis of antiquity ("No tyrant ever gave back so much . . .").

The facts are quickly summarized. Alexander (Colin Farrell) is the son of Philip of Macedonia (Val Kilmer) and Queen Olympias (Angelina Jolie). As a boy, he sees his drunken father all but rape his mother, who for her part insists Alexander's actual father is Zeus, but doesn't give details. Young Alexander impresses his father by taming an intractable horse, but both mother and son are banished from the kingdom, Olympias advising her son to seize the throne before Philip has him murdered. In the event, Philip is murdered, and Alexander rules Macedonia.

Still a very young man, he sets out to conquer the known world. Told by Aristotle (Christopher Plummer) where the world ends, he finds it keeps on going, and so he keeps on conquering, defeating the other Greek city states, the Persians, and all the other peoples he confronts until he is finally defeated not so much by the rulers of India as by India itself. He dies at 32.

He is, in Stone's version, remarkably open-minded for a tyrant. There are many scenes in which he debates strategy and goals with the members of his army, something we cannot easily imagine Philip (or Patton) doing. He takes the Asian bride Roxane (Rosario Dawson) instead of choosing a nice Greek girl as his advisers recommend. He spends eight years in battle, taking with him his army, their wives and lovers, their servants and households, in a sort of movable empire. And always smoldering in the shadows is Hephaistion (Jared Leto), his closest friend since childhood.

In ancient times, we are told, powerful men often took men or boys as their lovers, reserving women for childbearing and suchlike.

Alexander seems to be following that tradition to the extent that Stone (and perhaps the MPAA production code) will permit it. Hephaistion doesn't even go through the motions of taking a wife; he is always there for Alexander—but for what? They have what looks like the beginning of a love scene before it fades out, and the rest of the time, they hug a lot.

As for Alexander's sex life with Roxane, it is not surprising but nevertheless worthy of notice that we see a great deal more of her body than Hephaistion's, and observe them during a sex scene that begins with her fighting him off and ends with them engaged in the kind of unbridled passion where you hope nobody gets hurt. All right, so they have great sex—once. Then we learn that three years pass and she provides no male heir, although for all we see of them together, the fault may be Zeus's.

It's clear enough that Alexander loves Hephaistion and has married Roxane as a political gesture. In that case it is a miscalculation by Stone to make Hephaistion into a pouting sideline figure who specializes in significant glances, the significance of which the movie does not explore, while making Roxane into such an exciting hellion that we're disappointed Alexander doesn't let us spend more time with her, even if he doesn't want to. Dawson's Roxane is truly sexy, but Jared Leto's Hephaistion is not allowed to be seen as a male beauty; he looks like a drag queen, with more eye-liner than Elizabeth Taylor as Cleopatra. If Stone is not willing to make Hephaistion at least potentially as erotic a character as Roxane, he is not really engaging the logic of the story.

The ambiguities are not assisted by Colin Farrell's less-than-wholehearted embrace of his bisexuality. He goes after Roxane at first with the gusto of a rugby player, but approaches Hephaistion with a solemnity that borders on the doleful. Nor is he convincing as a conqueror. Farrell is a fine actor, but on a human scale; he's not cut out for philosopher-king. One needs to sense a certain madness in a colossus; George C. Scott brought it to Patton, Peter O'Toole brought it to Lawrence, Klaus Kinski to Fitzcarraldo, Mel Gibson had it as William Wallace, Willem Dafoe had it in Stone's *Platoon*, but Farrell seems too reasonable, too much of ordinary scale to drive men to the ends of the world with his unbending

will. Of other actors Stone has worked with, perhaps Woody Harrelson has the strange light in his eyes that the role requires.

The running narration by Ptolemy (Anthony Hopkins) is a road map through three decades of history, but there are so many names, places, and dates that finally we want to ask, please, sir, will this be on the final? Perhaps the narration is supposed to bridge gaps in the disjointed narrative. Even so, at one late point the movie comes to a jarring halt with the title "Macedonia—Eight Years Earlier," and we get a flashback to scenes involving Philip that don't feel like a flashback at all, but more like material plucked from its place in the chronology and inserted later to clarify what the filmmakers fear we will not otherwise understand.

Alexander and Ptolemy both talk a lot about incorporating conquered peoples into the expanding empire. Their clothes, languages, foods, and customs are embraced, we hear, but the movie spends more energy telling us this than showing us. Even though the movie's battle scenes are impressive and sometimes brilliant, Alexander's opponents have the human dimension of video-game figures. They attack, are vanquished, are replaced by new foes. The battles in India are masterful, with Alexander's men and horses terrified by war elephants, and an earlier battle against the Persians at Gaugamela has scope and grandeur. It looks as if there might be real men on the ground, instead of the digital ants in *Troy*. But we don't get a sense of the humans on the other side.

To mention Wolfgang Petersen's *Troy*, the 2004 epic about Grecian myth, is to make a comparison necessary. *Alexander* far outreaches *Troy* in ambition, its action scenes seem at least conceivably plausible, and it is based on ideas, not formulas. Yet *Troy* tells a story that has some structure and clarity, and those are precisely the qualities that *Alexander* lacks. The parts don't fit together in *Alexander*. Transitions and segues are missing, and we seem to be looking at disconnected parts from a much larger whole—two wholes, perhaps, one involving Alexander's military and political careers, and the other his confused emotional life.

While we can at least process the problems in his marriage with Roxane (he lost interest), we are left baffled by his tangled relationship with his mother. Angelina Jolie seems so young and sexy as Olympias, especially in scenes involving Alexander, that we wonder if she will start raiding cradles instead of tombs. She hates Philip, and no wonder, for he is a drunken lout, but are her hopes for Alexander entirely geopolitical? She regards him in a way Roxane never does, and one of the reasons for the "Eight Years Earlier" flashback is to get her back into the film after a too-lengthy absence.

I have always admired Oliver Stone's courage in taking on big, challenging films, and his gift for marrying action and ideas. *Alexander* is not a success, but it is ambitious and risky, and incapable of the inanities of *Troy*. Fascinated by his subject, he has things he urgently wants to say about Alexander, but his urgency outraces his narrative; he gives us provocative notes and sketches but not a final draft. The film doesn't feel at ease with itself. It says too much, and yet leaves too much unsaid.

Alfie ★ ★ ★
R, 106 m., 2004

Jude Law (Alfie), Marisa Tomei (Julie), Omar Epps (Marlon), Nia Long (Lonette), Jane Krakowski (Dorie), Sienna Miller (Nikki), Susan Sarandon (Liz). Directed by Charles Shyer and produced by Shyer and Elaine Pope. Screenplay by Bill Naughton, Pope, and Shyer, based on the play by Naughton.

Strange, that *Alfie* (1966) is halfway remembered as a comedy, when it was actually about a man who attempted to live life as comedy despite the lowering gloom that he thoroughly deserved. Alfie, in 1966 and again in the 2004 version, desperately wants to keep smiling, have a great time, and be lover to a parade of women who are willing and friendly, and never complain, and make no demands, and understand his need to be unfaithful. Such a woman, if she exists, would not be worth having, but tell that to Alfie.

Michael Caine made *Alfie* and *The Ipcress File* (1965) back-to-back, and they made him a star. He had a brash Cockney self-confidence that suggested a hardness beneath the kidding around. Jude Law is already a movie star, currently one of the busiest, and in *Alfie* he is less a predator than Caine, more a needy hedonist

who is wounded and even surprised when women won't put up with him.

Of course, he meets a different kind of woman in 2004 than Caine met in 1966; the feminist revolution, the rise and fall of the one-night stand, and the specter of AIDS all happened between those two dates, and today a compulsively promiscuous man is more of a danger to himself and his partners than he was then. In 1966 the worst thing Alfie brings about is an abortion; in the 2004 version, his greatest crime is essentially to throw away the love of the only woman he really cares for.

That would be Julie (Marisa Tomei), who is honest and grounded and has a young son to care for, and absolutely will not share Alfie with other women. Of course, for a time she doesn't know about the other women. Alfie confesses, in one of his rueful speeches directly to the camera, that the tricky thing about dating a woman with a kid is that you get to really like the kid. It's also tricky, as Alfie discovers, when you get to like the woman.

Alfie is still British in this version, but more upmarket, and now living in Manhattan, where his job as a limo driver gives him access to a lot of women, and they to him. We meet them as he does: Dorie (Jane Krakowski), the lonely married woman; Liz (Susan Sarandon), a successful businesswoman with a no-nonsense approach to obtaining sex; and Nikki (Sienna Miller), a beautiful model who wanders into his life and seems to be the undemanding woman of his dreams. Then there's Lonette (Nia Long), the girlfriend of his best friend, Marlon (Omar Epps). She should be forbidden territory, but to Alfie borders are made to be crossed.

The first film, directed by Lewis Gilbert, closely followed the era of the British Angry Young Men movies, and contained echoes of the proletarian anger of characters played by such as Albert Finney and Tom Courtenay. The new film comes out of a lad-mag era, in which Alfie is better dressed, smoother, and smoldering not with anger but with a spoiled boy's desire to be indulged. Both 1966 and 2004 are probably getting the characters they deserve; narcissism has evolved in thirty-eight years from a character flaw to a male fashion attribute.

The women have evolved, too. Marisa

Tomei's Julie might have felt helpless in 1966—felt she had to put up with Alfie because she had no choice. Now she has choices. The sexy businesswoman (Sarandon) is no longer seen as aging and needy (as Shelley Winters was in the original) but as desirable and independent; when Alfie finds her with another man, he asks, "What's he got better than me?" and her answer feels a little sorry for him: "He's younger than you." And when Lonette gets pregnant, abortion doesn't seem inevitable, even though the mixed race of her child will betray its father to her boyfriend. In 2004 it is possible for a woman to have a child outside the traditional rules; in 1966, that was not common.

But we don't go to see *Alfie* in order to make a sociological comparison of the two films; indeed, most of the audience members on opening night may not even know it's a remake. On its own terms, it's funny at times and finally sad and sweet. Alfie learns that to lie to women is to lie to himself about them. Jude Law's best scenes are when he doggedly tries to keep smiling as his lifestyle grows grim and depressing. He's sold himself on life as a ladies' man, and is beginning to realize he is his only customer.

Aliens of the Deep ★ ★ ★
G, 45 m., 2005

With James Cameron, Pamela Conrad, Djanna Figueroa, Kevin Hand, Loretta Hidalgo, and Maya Tolstoy. A documentary directed by James Cameron and Steven Quayle and produced by Cameron and Andrew Wight.

The timing of *Aliens of the Deep* couldn't be better. Days after a space probe landed successfully on Saturn's moon Titan and sent back spectacular photographs of its surface, here is a movie that explores the depths of the seas of Earth and then uses animation to imagine a probe that would fly to Jupiter's moon Europa and drill through its ice layer to the liquid water thought to be below. By finding living creatures on Earth that live under extreme conditions—no sunlight, no photosynthesis, incredible pressure, extremes of hot and cold—James Cameron convincingly argues that life could exist in the seas of Europa, or, for that matter, in any number of harrowing environments.

For Cameron, the film continues an obses-sion. When he wrote and directed *The Abyss* in 1989, his story involved scientists venturing into the deepest parts of the ocean. The movie was a box-office disappointment, not least because the director's cut reveals that the studio chopped crucial and amazing footage—and also, reportedly, because many potential ticket buyers did not know what an "abyss" is. For Cameron, it was an epiphany.

He returned to the sea bed for *Titanic* (1997), still the highest-grossing movie of all time, and essentially never came up for air. In 2002 his *Expedition: Bismarck*, made for the Discovery Channel, used deep-water submersibles to visit the grave of the doomed battleship, and in 2003 he made the 3-D IMAX movie *Ghosts of the Abyss*, which visited the wreck of the *Titanic* itself.

That was a movie with fascinating content, but I found the 3-D format unsatisfactory, and thought it might have been better to forget the gimmick and just give us the images. Now comes Cameron's *Aliens of the Deep*, also in IMAX 3-D, also fascinating, and with much-improved 3-D. After tinkering with the format for years, the IMAX technicians have devised oversized glasses that fit easily over existing eyeglasses and cover the entire field of vision. I saw the first 3-D movie, *Bwana Devil*, in 1952, and have been tired of the format ever since, but IMAX finally seems to be getting it right.

The movie is about expeditions to the deepest seas on Earth, where life is found to flourish under incredible conditions. We've read reports of some of these discoveries before—the worms that live around the sulphurous vents of hot water on the cold sea bottom, for example—but now we see them, photographed in lonely and splendid isolation, and the sights are magnificent.

What are these creatures? A good question, and one you might well still be asking after the movie, since it is high on amazement but low on information. His aquanauts, all real scientists or students, keep saying their discoveries are magnificent, beautiful, unbelievable, incredible, etc., and so they are, but only rudimentary facts are supplied about these life forms.

That didn't bother me as much as it might have, because *Aliens of the Deep* is not a scientific documentary so much as a journey to an alien world, and basically what we want to do is peer out the portholes along with the explorers. We see a vast, drifting, transparent creature, looking like nothing so much as a linen scarf, with a fragile network of vessels holding itself together. How does it feed? What does it know?

The tube worms are fascinating because they exist in symbiosis with bacteria that live inside of them. They have no digestive facility, and the bacteria have no food-gathering ability, but working together they both make a living. Astonishingly, we see shrimp, millions of them, darting endlessly through superheated vents of escaping lava-heated water, which is hundreds of degrees warmer than the icy water around it. How do these creatures move through such extremes of hot and cold so quickly, when either by itself would kill them?

Aliens of the Deep is a convincing demonstration of Darwin's theory of evolution because it shows creatures not only adapted perfectly to their environment but obviously generated by that environment. It drives me crazy when people say evolution is "only a theory," because that reveals they don't know what a scientific theory is. As *National Geographic* pointed out, a theory is a scientific hypothesis that is consistent with observed and experimental data, and the observations and experiments must be able to be repeated. Darwin passes that test. His rival, creationism, is not a theory, but a belief. There is a big difference.

Evolution aside, there are some wonderful images in *Aliens of the Deep,* even if the crew members say how much they love their jobs about six times too often. In a late segment of the film, Cameron uses special effects to imagine a visit to Europa, where a nuclear-heated probe would melt and drill its way down to the liquid seas thought to be three to fourteen miles below ice, and find there—well, life, perhaps. He even envisions an underwater city that belongs on the cover of *Amazing Stories,* circa 1940. It's not a million miles different from the one in the director's cut of *The Abyss.* That his city was astonishingly cut from the theatrical version of *The Abyss* to make more room for the love story is no doubt one of the several reasons Cameron has recently worked in documentary instead of fiction. It's tempting to say that Cameron should have stayed with the wonders of Earth and not created

imaginary civilizations on Europa, but I was enthralled by those fictional sequences, unlikely as they are. I would suggest that if an advanced civilization has evolved on Europa, however, it is unlikely to have cities, since interior rooms and corridors would not occur naturally to swimming creatures. More likely, like dolphins, the Europans will fully exploit their given habitat. Or maybe they will all look like pond scum, which as discoveries go would also be quite amazing enough.

Almost Peaceful ★ ★ ★
NO MPAA RATING, 94 m., 2004

Simon Abkarian (Albert), Zabou Breitman (Lea), Denis Podalydes (Charles), Vincent Elbaz (Leon), Lubna Azabal (Jacqueline), Stanislas Merhar (Maurice), Clotilde Courau (Simone), Julie Gaynet (Mme. Andree), Malik Zidi (Joseph). Directed by Michel Deville and produced by Rosalinde Deville. Screenplay by Michel Deville and Rosalinde Deville, based on a novel by Robert Bober.

In a sunny upstairs room in Paris, eight or nine people gather daily to tailor clothes. The room is in a flat belonging to Albert and Lea, who run the business and have hired these people quite recently, for it is 1946 and all but one of them is Jewish and they have returned to their trade after the horror of the war. The atmosphere in the room is cozy and chatty, relaxed almost to a fault, as if these people have been holding their breath for years and are grateful for a day that passes without event.

Michel Deville's *Almost Peaceful* is unlike any other film I have seen about the Holocaust. Indeed, the abstract concept of a holocaust has not yet been formed as these people reassemble their ordinary lives. They speak about what happened, about "the camps" where their loved ones disappeared, about the war, but they do not go into detail because they lived through it firsthand and do not need to be reminded—none of them except the one gentile woman, who is puzzled when a new employee introduces himself and the others burst into laughter. What's so funny? What's funny, or at least what's able to be laughed about, is that he can say his Jewish name loudly and freely in Paris once again.

Albert (Simon Abkarian) and Lea (Zabou Breitman) own the business. Their children are away in the south of France, at summer camp, sending back letters and drawings that are eagerly awaited. Of the others, there is a man who returned to the neighborhood hoping any of his surviving relatives would find their way there, and an unemployed actor with a pregnant wife, and a new employee fit only to cut and trim, and a young man named Maurice (Stanislas Merhar), who visits the prostitutes at a nearby hotel. The gentile woman goes out to lunch one day with Albert to ask if he can find a job for her sister, who had a child by a German soldier and after the war had her head shaved and was made to run naked through the town. She tells it as a sad story. But Albert cannot help her. A lot of people had sad experiences in the war, he says, quietly.

The new employee, Joseph (Malik Zidi), goes around to the police station to have his papers put in order, and recognizes the cop behind the desk. He has seen this man before, through the crack in a wardrobe where his parents concealed him before the cop took them away, never to return. The cop is insolent. Joseph walks out, pauses on the pavement, goes back in and tells the man he knows who he is and what he did, and he wants to inform him that he, Joseph, is here and will remain here and has a right to be here. Then Joseph walks out again and goes to a café and collapses at a table with a release of tension and a certain sad joy.

There are little plots involving the people, their children, their friends, their romantic intrigues (Maurice finds himself always returning to the same prostitute, Simone, who likes him well enough and prostitution not so much). Customers come and go. Albert must approve any garment that leaves the shop. He and Lea are happy beyond happiness. There is a woman who comes around twice a week with things to sell. Today she is selling scented soaps. She is also a matchmaker, and in her valise has letters and photographs of single people looking for a spouse. "Your marriageable people smell of soap," one of the tailors' kids her. "Was it better," she asks, "when soap smelled of marriageable people?"

In a line like that, which passes quickly and is not commented upon, an abyss of evil is glimpsed. These people live gently and embrace routine and love their jobs because they are still walking on ice, still aware of how fragile a life can be, how deceptive security can seem. The film ends with a picnic, and the sound of children playing. There is a new generation. There is the feeling that marriageable people should be married and having children. Maurice and Simone seem to be arriving at that conclusion. Life goes on, and that is what the movie is about, and all it is about, except for the unspeakable horrors it is not about.

Along Came Polly ★ ★
PG-13, 90 m., 2004

Ben Stiller (Reuben Feffer), Jennifer Aniston (Polly Prince), Philip Seymour Hoffman (Sandy Lyle), Debra Messing (Lisa Kramer), Alec Baldwin (Stan Indursky), Hank Azaria (Claude), Bryan Brown (Leland Van Lew), Jsu Garcia (Javier). Directed by John Hamburg and produced by Danny DeVito, Michael Shamberg, and Stacey Sher. Screenplay by Hamburg.

I will never eat free nuts from the bowl on the bar again, having seen *Along Came Polly*. Not after hearing the expert risk-assessor Reuben Feffer (Ben Stiller) explain who has already handled them, what adventures they have had, and, for all we know, where they might have been. It's his job to know the risks of every situation, which is why his marriage seems like such a sure thing: His new bride, Lisa (Debra Messing), is like a computer printout of an ideal mate for life.

But it doesn't work out that way in *Along Came Polly*, a movie where a lot of things don't work out, including, alas, the movie itself. On the second day of their honeymoon in Saint Bart's, Lisa cheats on Reuben with a muscular scuba instructor (Hank Azaria), and he returns to New York crushed and betrayed. When he meets Polly (Jennifer Aniston), an old school chum, he doubts they can be happy together (assessing the risks, he sees the two of them as totally incompatible), but to his amazement they are soon involved in a neurotic but not boring relationship.

The problem is that their relationship, and indeed Reuben's entire array of friendships and business associations, are implausible not in a funny way but in a distracting way: We keep doubting that this person would be acting this way in this situation. What kind of a risk assessor is Reuben if he *knows* he has irritable bowel syndrome, and nevertheless goes on a first date with Polly to dinner at a North African spice palace? Yes, his dinner gives the movie the opportunity to launch one of those extended sequences involving spectacular digestive, eliminatory, and regurgitative adventures, but we're aware it's a setup. As Stiller himself classically demonstrated in *There's Something About Mary*, embarrassment is comic when it is thrust upon you by accident or bad luck, not when you go looking for it yourself.

Of the Polly character, it can be said that the risk of her ever falling in love with a man like Reuben is a very long shot. What attracts her? His constipated personality? Low self-esteem? Workaholism? Neurotic inability to engage spontaneously with fun? She's a free spirit who lives in one of those apartments that look like they were inspired by an old Sandy Dennis movie. Her favorite occupation is salsa dancing, which for her approaches virtual sex, especially with her favorite partner, Javier (Jsu Garcia). Reuben, uncoordinated and inhibited, is jealous of Javier until he signs up for salsa lessons, which could have been funny, but are not.

There isn't a lot in the movie that is funny. I did like Philip Seymour Hoffman as Sandy, Reuben's best man; he's a former child star, now reduced to having strangers tell him how amazed they are that he's still alive. How he responds to this in one early scene is a small masterpiece of facial melodrama, but how many times does he have to slip and fall on slick floors before we get tired of it? I grant him this: He knows exactly how a fat man looks in a red cummerbund from a tuxedo rental agency.

Alec Baldwin does a lot of good supporting work (notably in *The Cooler*), and he's Reuben's boss, the head of the agency, a slickster whose toast at the wedding skates artfully at the edge of crudeness and then pirouettes out of danger. He assigns Reuben to somehow make a case for insuring the high-risk Leland Van Lew (Bryan Brown), leading to still more fish-out-of-water material. Reuben's fish is so consistently out of water in this movie, indeed, that after a while we begin to wish it was smoked.

American Dreamz ★ ★ ★
PG-13, 107 m., 2006

Hugh Grant (Martin Tweed), Dennis Quaid (President Staton), Mandy Moore (Sally Kendoo), Marcia Gay Harden (First Lady Staton), Chris Klein (William Williams), Jennifer Coolidge (Martha Kendoo), Sam Golzari (Omer), Adam Busch (Sholem), Seth Meyers (Chet Krogl). Directed by Paul Weitz and produced by Rodney M. Liber, Andrew Miano, and Weitz. Screenplay by Weitz.

American Dreamz is a comedy, not a satire. We have that on the authority of its writer-director, Paul Weitz, who told *Variety*: "Satire is what closes on Saturday night. So it's a comedy." Actually, it's a satire. Its comedy is only fairly funny, but its satire is mean, tending toward vicious. The movie is more slapdash than smooth, more impulsive than calculating, and it takes cheap shots. I responded to its savage, sloppy zeal.

The movie has two targets, *American Idol* and President George W. Bush, not in that order. As it opens, a TV producer and star named Martin Tweed (Hugh Grant) is planning the new season of his hit show. On camera, he's Simon Cowell. Off camera, he's Machiavelli, scheming for contestants who get the highest ratings. The season will end in a three-way contest between a Hasidic Jew rapper (Adam Busch), a corn-fed Ohio blonde (Mandy Moore), and a theater buff from Iraq (Sam Golzari) who is secretly a terrorist.

Meanwhile, in the White House, President Staton (Dennis Quaid) awakens after his reelection victory and has an impulse: "I'm gonna read the newspaper!" He asks for the *New York Times*. "We can get one," an aide assures him uncertainly. He finds the paper instructive. "Did you know there are three kinds of Iraqistans?" he asks his chief of staff (Willem Dafoe), who looks uncannily like Dick Cheney. Surrounding himself with books and even the left-wing *Guardian* from England, the president isn't seen in public for weeks. "There is a lot of interesting things in the paper!" he marvels.

The plot chugs forward on two fronts. On the TV program, we see Sally Kendoo (Moore) playing the role of a screamingly delirious young contestant, pushed by her mother (Jennifer Coolidge) and superagent (Seth Meyers), and dumping her boyfriend (Chris Klein) because he's going nowhere and she's going up-up-up. As the godlike *American Dreamz* producer and judge, Grant does what he's curiously good at, playing an enormously likable SOB.

When the president is finally blasted out of his bedroom in the White House, he resumes public life with an earpiece so his chief of staff can dictate, word for word, his response in every situation. That many Americans believe Bush has used such earpieces, and that he rarely if ever reads a newspaper, brings a certain poignancy to these scenes. The first lady (Marcia Gay Harden) labors behind the scenes to counsel and advise him, and to explain stuff to him. Badgered by publicity about his "reclusive" chief executive, the chief of staff decides to book the president on the season finale of *American Dreamz* to show what a great guy he is. The terrorist, who seems headed for the final round, is ordered by his handlers to wear a bomb into the studio.

This is dark comedy in the spirit of *Dr. Strangelove*, a movie that thought the unthinkable. *American Dreamz* isn't nearly as good as *Strangelove*, perhaps because it lacks its merciless ironic detachment. But I was surprised at the movie's daring, at its frank depiction of the Bush-like president as the clueless puppet of his staff. His mom wanted him to run for president, he says, "to show my dad any idiot could do it." Quaid looks and sounds a little like Bush, and Dafoe looks a little and sounds a lot like Cheney. Grant, for that matter, could stand in for Simon Cowell.

Weitz was only thirty-three when he directed *American Pie*. It looked like a teenage sex comedy, played like a teenage sex comedy, and was a teenage sex comedy—and a lot more. He proved with *About a Boy* (2002) that he was a director of considerable gifts; working with his brother Chris, he adapted a Nick Hornby novel into the perfect setting for Grant's merger of selfishness and charm. *In Good Company* (2004), which he wrote and directed, starred Quaid as an aging executive bossed by a young hotshot who is also dating his daughter. Now Quaid, Grant, and Weitz are together on a project that lacks the polish and assurance of those earlier films but has a

kind of reckless nerve. *American Dreamz* looks like a sitcom, plays like a sitcom, and is a sitcom—and is the riskiest political satire since *Wag the Dog*.

At a time when I am already receiving messages of alarm about Oliver Stone's forthcoming *World Trade Center*, does *American Dreamz* go too far? Is it in bad taste? That would depend on what you think satire is supposed to do. Satire by definition goes beyond the norm, exaggerates, is partisan, is unfair. It offends those who believe others (not themselves) are too stupid to know it's satire. And it alarms those who think some things are not laughing matters. To them I recommend Lord Byron: "And if I laugh at any mortal thing, 'tis that I may not weep."

The buried message of the film, perhaps, is that our political system resembles *American Idol*. Contestants are chosen on the basis of superficial marketability, and they go through a series of primaries and debates while the pollsters keep score. The winner is not necessarily the deserving contestant from an objective point of view but the one with the best poll numbers. A candidate from either party will be defeated if he is not entertaining. His intelligence and matters of right or wrong don't have much to do with it. In this scenario, satire plays the role in politics that Simon Cowell plays on TV.

Americanese ★ ★ ★ ½
NO MPAA RATING, 108 m., 2006

Chris Tashima (Raymond Ding), Allison Sie (Aurora Crane), Joan Chen (Betty Nguyen), Kelly Hu (Brenda Nishitani), Ben Shenkman (Steve), Sab Shimono (Wood Ding), Michael Paul Chan (Jimmy Chan). Directed by Eric Byler and produced by Lisa Onodera. Screenplay by Byler, based on a novel by Shawn Wong.

Americanese is the second feature I've seen by Eric Byler, who has a quiet confidence not only about film but about life. Byler deals with characters who have lived their years, have learned from them, and try to apply their values to their lives. Their romances are not heedless but wary and involve a lot of negotiation. Listen to Betty calmly tell Raymond, after their first date, "We can be friends, or we can be something more." The choice is theirs. But they must make it, and with their eyes wide open. And they have to start out knowing that.

There's none of the silliness of an Adult Teenager Movie where romance is a montage of candlelight and sailboats, and the characters never have a conversation of any substance. Don't these people know that you have to be able to *talk* with the other person for hours, days, and years, or the relationship is doomed? Watching *Americanese* after movies like *Failure to Launch*, I felt like I'd wandered into the grown-up cinema.

Raymond Ding (Chris Tashima) meets Betty Nguyen (Joan Chen) on a double rebound. He's a university professor in San Francisco whose first marriage ended in divorce. For three years he lived with Aurora Crane (Allison Sie), but they've broken up, in a strange, sad, subdued process that's not quite finished. They're still "friends." She kept their apartment. During the day, when he knows she's not at home, he enters it and pokes around, as if looking for clues to what went wrong. She knows he does this.

Raymond is Chinese-American. Aurora is half-Asian; her dad is white. Betty is from Vietnam. Before Raymond and Betty make love for the first time, she tells him he will find scars on her legs. Later, they talk about that. "Did you . . . get them all at once?" he asks her. "Yes, all the same time," she says quietly. And later: "It's not your job to heal me." In her sleep, she says the name "Amy." Amy is her daughter by her first marriage, to a long-haul trucker in Houston. She lost custody because she made mistakes. In a few words, Byler creates a character who was wounded in Vietnam, came to America, made a bad marriage, walked out on it, went to the University of Texas to start her life over again, is now in San Francisco, and is, as they say, strongest at the broken places.

But Betty is not even the central character in the movie. Byler establishes his characters with a few words or quick strokes, like a short-story writer. Nothing is hammered home. These lives are still being lived. One of the reasons Raymond and Aurora broke up, we learn, is that he never believed she accepted her Asian identity. There is a scene where Aurora goes home for a weekend with her white father, her Asian mother, and her sister. The sister is engaged to a black man, whom we meet and like. A good man. Her father doesn't want this man coming to his retirement party; he wants to save "possible embarrassment." He explains to Aurora: "I'm not a racist; otherwise, I wouldn't have married your mom." That's when Aurora realizes he's a racist.

Raymond tells Aurora, not making a big deal of it, that her father thinks of her as white. That in her father's mind, there is a difference between him marrying an Asian woman and a black man marrying his daughter. "When you let something slide," he tells her, "you're essentially passing as white." Until Aurora can accept both sides of herself, Raymond cannot feel accepted. It is perhaps no surprise that Aurora's new boyfriend is white. "When am I gonna meet your new guy?" Raymond asks her. "You've met, actually," she says. Those three words do the work of a scene in someone else's movie.

The film centers on the performance of Tashima, handsome but not thinking about it, playing an inward man whose view of race is not confrontational but observational. He wants to be a good man, and the breakup with Aurora hurts. He senses in the Vietnamese woman Betty another kind of gulf: She accepts her Asian identity, all right, but when she looks at him she sees not an Asian but an Asian-American, more American than Asian. This is true. "I don't read Chinese," Raymond casually reminds his father, Wood (Sab Shimono). He's startled when his dad, a widower, announces plans to go to China and find a wife. Just like that? Why not? To Raymond, marriage is a minefield of emotional and intellectual challenges. To his dad, it's a necessity: "It's not good to live without a wife."

I've been writing in such a way you'd think *Americanese* is a movie entirely about the theory and practice of race in America. Not at all, based on a novel by Shawn Wong, it is above all about people seeking love and happiness in their lives. I've spoken with Byler several times since seeing his *Charlotte Sometimes* (2002) for the first time, and I know that when he grew up in Hawaii he sometimes felt like an outsider because he, like Aurora, is half-Asian. Standing on the divide, he opens his arms and his artistic imagination to those who let it separate them. That they are Asian in one way or another is a reality of their search, but not a condition of it. It's a strange thing about characters in movies: The more "universal" they are, the more provincial. The more specific they are, the more they are exactly themselves, the more we can identify with them.

American Gun ★ ★ ★

R, 95 m., 2006

Donald Sutherland (Carl), Forest Whitaker (Carter), Marcia Gay Harden (Janet), Linda Cardellini (Mary Anne), Tony Goldwyn (Frank), Chris Marquette (David), Arlen Escarpeta (Jay), Garcelle Beauvais-Nilon (Sara), Nikki Reed (Tally). Directed by Aric Avelino and produced by Ted Kroeber. Screenplay by Steven Bagatourian and Avelino.

American Gun tells three stories that are small, even quiet. The stories are not strident but sad, and one of them is open-ended. They are about people who find that guns in the hands of others have made their own lives almost impossible to live.

The first story involves a mother named Janet, played by Marcia Gay Harden, whose son shot and killed other students at his Oregon high school three years ago and then was shot dead. She carries on with her remaining son, David (Chris Marquette), who attends a private school. She needs money. She agrees to a paid interview with a local television station, during which she seems inarticulate about her older son's rampage. Well, what can she say? Like other parents, she lost a child in the shooting. Perhaps it is harder to be the parent of a killer than the parent of a victim. Then David has to leave the private school and enroll in the very same school where his brother did the shooting.

Also interviewed is a cop (Tony Goldwyn) who some people feel should have been able to save lives that day. He knows he followed department procedures but feels blamed for the deaths. Both the mother and the cop are at a loss for words when TV reporters ask them questions beginning with "How does it make you feel?" They're not glib and don't fall easily into the clichés of remorse and redemption.

The second story stars Forest Whitaker as Carter, the principal of an inner-city high school in Chicago. He moved to the big city from Ohio, thinking he could make a difference, but now his wife (Garcelle Beauvais-Nilon) feels she is losing him to his job. He is discouraged, weary beyond belief, despairing. One of his honor students, Jay (Arlen Escarpeta), is found with a gun near the school and faces expulsion. We follow Jay to his job inside a padlocked cashier's station at an all-night gas station where any customer might confront him with a gun. He needs to carry a gun, he feels, for protection, even though it isn't loaded.

The third story, the open-ended one, involves a gentle old man named Carl (Donald Sutherland) who runs a gun shop in Charlottesville, Virginia. His granddaughter Mary Anne (Linda Cardellini) enrolls at the university and works part time in the store. Carl is not a gun nut. He might as well be selling fishing tackle. Mary Anne feels uneasy working in the store, however, and then one of her friends is assaulted.

All three stories ask the same question: How do you lead a reasonable life in a world where a lot of your fellow citizens can and do walk around armed? Two answers seem to be possible: They should be disarmed, or you should be armed. A third answer, implied by some gun owners, is that they should be armed but many other categories of people should not be. They never include themselves in those categories. I am reminded of my friend McHugh, who was shown a gun by a guy in a bar. "Why do you carry that?" McHugh asked him. "I live in a dangerous neighborhood," the guy said. "It would be safer," McHugh told him, "if you moved."

At one point in the movie, the neighbors of Janet, the mother, observe the third anniversary of the high school massacre by planting flags on their lawns, including a black flag on hers. They are vindictive and revengeful. Did it occur to them to plant signs asking for a ban on handguns? No. Guns don't kill people. Janet's son does.

American Gun is a first feature by Aric Avelino, who cowrote it with Steven Bagatourian. He shows an almost tender restraint in his storytelling, not pounding us with a message but simply looking steadily at how guns have made these lives difficult. The mother's real answer to the TV interviewer could have been: "My son killed his school-mates because he had a gun and he could." The Columbine shooters without weapons still would have been antisocial psychopaths, but they would not have been killers.

As for the Chicago school principal, his despair is easy to understand. During the same week I saw *American Gun*, two children were shot dead in Chicago just as a byproduct of guns. They were not targets, but accidental victims. The cost of guns is multiplied day after day, year after year, body after body, in our society. The rest of the world looks on in wonder. The right to bear arms is being defended by the sacrifice of the lives of their victims. That doesn't mean gun owners are all bad people. Sutherland's gun dealer seems like one of the nicest people you would ever want to meet. On the door of his store there is a sign: WE BUY USED GUNS. Just a sign. No big deal. It's the final image in the movie.

America's Heart & Soul ★ ★
PG, 84 m., 2004

A documentary directed and produced by Louis Schwartzberg.

America's Heart & Soul may be the first feature-length documentary filmed entirely in the style of a television commercial. It tells the stories of about twenty Americans who are colorful, eccentric, courageous, goofy, or musically talented—sometimes all five—and it uses the shorthand of TV spots, in which the point is that these people are wonderful and so, gosh darn it, are the good folks at (insert name of corporation). In this case, the sponsor is America, a nation where, in this film, poverty is an opportunity, racism doesn't exist, and (most miraculous of all) everyone is self-employed doing a job they love. Nobody grinds away for the minimum wage in this America.

Even though the method of the filmmaker, Louis Schwartzberg, is slick, superficial, and relentlessly upbeat, the people he finds are genuine treasures. I wanted to see a whole film about most of them, which means this film is a series of frustrations. Still, it underlines a point I like to make when students ask me about employment prospects: Figure out what you love and find a way to do it, no matter how badly it

pays, because you will enjoy yourself and probably end up happy. Midcareer test: If retirement seems better than the job you're doing, you're doing the wrong job.

The first character we meet in *America's Heart & Soul* is Thomas "Roudy" Roudebush, a cowboy in Telluride, Colorado, whose life has much improved since he got sober, but who still rides his horse into a bar for a drink (water, straight up). Then we meet Marc and Ann Savoy, Cajun musicians, and watch them making gumbo, and visit a black gospel singer named Mosie Burks, and a weaver named Minnie Yancey ("If I've woven ten feet into the rug and it still doesn't say 'yes,' I'll cut it right off and start again"). As she weaves, she looks out the window at her husband, plowing a field on one of the few surviving family farms.

In Vermont, George Woodard, a dairy farmer, milks his cows, plays in a string band, and stars as Dracula in a local production. We say hello to Ben Cohen, of Ben & Jerry's, as he invents a new flavor. We meet a hat maker. A chair maker. A wine maker. Men who fight oil well fires. A New Orleans jazz band. Patty Wagstaff of Florida, who is a champion acrobatic pilot.

Also, people who dance on cliffs at the ends of ropes. A blind mountain climber. Rick Hoyt, a marathon runner with cerebral palsy whose father, Dick, pushes his wheelchair. Paul Stone of Creede, Colorado, who spends his winters blowing up stuff real good (one of his cannon shells is made of ham and cheese). And David Krakauer, a klezmer musician influenced by Jimi Hendrix.

An opera singer. Salsa dancers. Michael Bennett of Chicago, an armed robber who started boxing in the pen, became captain of the U.S. Olympic boxing team, and works to keep kids off the streets. Cecil Williams, the pastor of the progressive Glide Church in San Francisco, which supplies a million meals for the homeless every year. People who decorate their cars as works of art. A Manhattan bike messenger who loves racing through traffic. Dan Klennert, who makes art out of junk. The Indian elder Charles Jimmie Sr., who releases a healed eagle back into the skies.

All of these people are happy, productive, creative, and unconventional, and if there were more of them in our society the news would be a lot more cheerful. They live in a parallel universe where everyone is oddball and fascinating and has a story that can be neatly wrapped up in a few minutes. Surely there is more to all of these people, a lot more, but *America's Heart & Soul* has miles to go before it sleeps.

In the middle of a montage I saw one shot, a few seconds long, that was unmistakably of Howard Armstrong, the legendary African-American string musician who died in August 2003 at the age of ninety-three. At my Overlooked Film Festival, I showed two documentaries made fifteen years apart about this miraculous man, whose art was as distinctive as his music, and whose life was a work in progress. Because I know how much there was to say about him, I can guess how much there is to say about the others in *America's Heart & Soul*. But this movie doesn't pause to find out; it's in such a hurry, it uses "&" because "and" would take too long. Working within the limitations of the star rating system, I give four stars to the subjects of this movie, and two stars to the way they have been boiled down into cute pictures and sound bites.

Anacondas: The Hunt for the Blood Orchid ★ ★

PG-13, 93 m., 2004

Johnny Messner (Bill Johnson), KaDee Strickland (Samantha Rogers), Matthew Marsden (Dr. Jack Byron), Morris Chestnut (Gordon Mitchell), Karl Yune (Tran), Salli Richardson-Whitfield (Gail Stern), Eugene Byrd (Cole Burris), Nicholas Gonzalez (Ben Douglas). Directed by Dwight H. Little and produced by Verna Harrah. Screenplay by John Claflin, Daniel Zelman, Michael Miner, and Edward Neumeier.

Deep in the jungles of Borneo lurks the blood orchid, which blooms only once in seven years, and whose red flowers contain a mysterious ingredient that extends the ability of living cells to reproduce themselves. A pill based on this substance would allow you to live forever, or at least long enough to feel like you had. "This is bigger than Viagra!" observes a drug company executive. Yes, and creates a whole new market for it. The notion of using Viagra when you're 150 is a little daunting, but at least, unlike George Burns, you could find plenty of girls your age.

Alas, there's a catch. The only existing samples of the blood orchid were "destroyed in testing," so it's necessary to return to Borneo for more blooms—and the blooming season ends in two weeks. There's barely time for an emergency expedition, and besides, it's the rainy season. We read a lot about how their profits allow drug companies to spend billions on research, but in the quest for eternal life this company is able to lease only the *Bloody Mary*, a river boat that looks hammered together out of spare parts from the tree house in *Benji: Off the Leash.*

The boat is commanded by Bill Johnson (Johnny Messner), who proves that even with the face of a Calvin Klein model he can earn a living piloting a leaky gutbucket into the jaws of hell. The scientific team includes four serious men, Dr. Jack Byron (Matthew Marsden), Gordon Mitchell (Morris Chestnut), Ben Douglas (Nicholas Gonzalez), and Tran (Karl Yune); two serious women, Gail Stern (Salli Richardson) and Samantha Rogers (KaDee Strickland); and a comic relief guy named Cole Burris (Eugene Byrd), who is always scared of everything. There is also a pet monkey that gets way, way too many reaction shots as it plays essentially the same role that Fred Willard filled in *Best in Show.*

It is dangerous to travel the rivers of Borneo even in the best of times, and treacherous in the rainy season, when the rivers overflow their banks, navigation is uncertain, alligators are hungry, submerged logs can rip the bottom out of your boat, and if you miss a turn you could go over a waterfall. Bill Johnson demands 50 grand to make the journey and later collects another 50 grand; looking at the *Bloody Mary,* we realize he's not so much charging for the trip as getting a good price on a used boat.

Ah, but there's a catch. The jungle where the blood orchid blooms is inhabited by giant anacondas. In fact, although they are solitary creatures, the snakes congregate in this very place during the rainy season, to form (or attend, perhaps) a "mating ball," so that the river and the jungle seem to be teeming with them. We have heard about salmon swimming upstream to mate and birds flying thousands of miles to their summer nesting homes, and perhaps that explains why the anaconda, which is a native of the South American rain forests and is unknown in Borneo, makes the arduous journey across the Pacific and up the river to the precise location of this movie.

No matter how they get there, they hang around a long while. That's because, of course, they eat the blood orchid and therefore do not die, but simply grow bigger and bigger. Perhaps they are immune to the bite of a local spider, which causes paralysis for forty-eight hours, although the cast of the movie certainly is not. You know when a spider paralyzes you and then you see an anaconda starting to eat you? I hate it when that happens.

There comes a point when we realize that *Anacondas: The Hunt for the Blood Orchid* is hunting not so much for orchids as for trouble. The cast is so large because one must be eaten every so often, and the attrition rate grows after they fall into a cave. Bill Johnson keeps their spirits up: "There's a way in—there's a way out." True, but what if it's the way in?

Faithful readers will recall that I immensely enjoyed the original *Anaconda* (1997). It was a superb example of exactly what it was, and Jon Voight's final scene in the movie retains a sublime perfection. But I've seen *Anaconda* and, senator, *Anacondas* is no *Anaconda*. The director, Dwight H. Little, has done a lot of TV and retains the annoying TV practice of the reaction-shot whip-round, in which A says something witty, B hears it and grins and looks at C, who smiles and shrugs, while D looks on, amused. With the monkey playing the E position, this can get monotonous.

The movie, however, is competent at a basic level, doing a good job of using its locations and a hardworking, fearless cast. The beautiful Salli Richardson-Whitfield continues the great tradition of the late Fay Wray as she struggles to escape the clutches of danger, and Matthew Marsden, obsessed with the millions to be made from the new drug, is suitably treacherous. The movie is competent formula entertainment, but doesn't make that leap into pure barminess that inspired *Anaconda*.

Anatomy of Hell ★
NO MPAA RATING, 77 m., 2004

Amira Casar (The Woman), Rocco Siffredi (The Man). Directed by Catherine Breillat and produced by Jean-Francois Lepetit. Screenplay by Breillat, based on her novel *Pornocratie*.

She is the only woman in a gay nightclub. She goes into the toilet and cuts her wrist. He follows her in, sees what she has done, and takes her to a drug store, where the wound is bandaged. If you cut your wrist and there's time to go to the drugstore, maybe you weren't really trying. He asks her why she did it. "Because I'm a woman," she says, although she might more accurately have replied, "Because I'm a woman in a Catherine Breillat movie."

Breillat is the bold French director whose specialty is female sexuality. Sometimes she is wise about it, as in *36 Fillette* (1989), the story of a troubled teenager who begins a series of risky flirtations with older men. Or in *Fat Girl* (2001), about the seething resentment of a pudgy twenty-year-old toward her sexpot older sister. Sometimes she is provocative about it, as in *Romance* (1999), which is about a frustrated woman's dogged search for orgasm. But sometimes she is just plain goofy, as in *Anatomy of Hell*, which plays like porn dubbed by bitter deconstructionist theoreticians.

The Woman makes an offer to The Man. She will pay him good money to watch her, simply watch her, for four nights. He keeps his end of the bargain, but there were times when I would have paid good money to not watch them, simply not watch them. I remember when hard-core first became commonplace, and there were discussions about what it would be like if a serious director ever made a porn movie. The answer, judging by *Anatomy of Hell*, is that the audience would decide they did not require such a serious director after all.

The Woman believes men hate women, and that gay men hate them even more than straight men, who, however, hate them quite enough. Men fear women, fear their menstrual secrets, fear their gynecological mysteries, fear that during sex they might disappear entirely within the woman and be imprisoned again by the womb. To demonstrate her beliefs, The Woman disrobes completely and displays herself on a bed, while The Man sits in a chair and watches her, occasionally rousing himself for a shot of Jack on the rocks.

They talk. They speak as only the French can speak, as if it is not enough for a concept to be difficult, it must be impenetrable. No two real people in the history of mankind have ever spoken like this, save perhaps for some of Catherine Breillat's friends that even she gets bored by. "Your words are inept reproaches," they say, and "I bless the day I was made immune to you and all your kind." After a few days of epigrams, they suddenly and sullenly have sex, and make a mess of the sheets.

Some events in this movie cannot be hinted at in a family newspaper. Objects emerge to the light of day that would distinguish target-practice in a Bangkok sex show. There are moments when you wish they'd lighten up a little by bringing in the guy who bites off chicken heads.

Of course we are expected to respond on a visceral level to the movie's dirge about the crimes of men against women, which, it must be said, are hard to keep in mind given the crimes of The Woman against The Man, and the transgressions committed by The Director against Us. The poor guy is just as much a prop here as men usually are in porn films. He is played by Rocco Siffredi, an Italian porn star. The Woman is played by Amira Casar, who is completely nude most of the time, although the opening titles inform us that a body double will be playing her close-ups in the more action-packed scenes. "It's not her body," the titles explain, "it's an extension of a fictional character." Tell that to the double.

No doubt the truth can be unpleasant, but I am not sure that unpleasantness is the same as the truth. There are scenes here where Breillat deliberately disgusts us, not because we are disgusted by the natural life functions of women, as she implies, but simply because The Woman does things that would make any reasonable Man, or Woman, for that matter, throw up.

Anchorman ★ ★ ★
PG-13, 94 m., 2004

Will Ferrell (Ron Burgundy), Christina Applegate (Veronica Corningstone), David Koechner (Champ Kind), Steven Carell (Brick Tamland), Paul Rudd (Brian Fantana), Fred Willard (Ed Harken), Chris Parnell (Garth Holliday). Directed by Adam McKay and produced by Judd Apatow. Screenplay by Will Ferrell and McKay.

Sometimes the key to satire is to stay fairly close to the source. *Anchorman*, like *This Is Spinal Tap*, works best when it's only a degree or two removed from the excesses of the real thing. When the news director goes ape over stories about cute animals at the zoo, when the promos make the news "team" look like a happy family, the movie is right on target. But when rival local news teams engage in what looks like a free-for-all from a Roman arena, it doesn't work. Most of the time, though, *Anchorman* works, and a lot of the time it's very funny.

The movie centers on Ron Burgundy (Will Ferrell), the legendary top local anchor in San Diego in the early 1970s. Ron has bought into his legend, believes his promos, and informs a blond at a pool party: "I have many very important leather-bound books, and my apartment smells of rich mahogany." His weakness is that he will read anything that is typed into his prompter. Anything. The words pass from his eyes into his mouth without passing through his brain.

There are viewers in every city who will think they know who this character is based on. Certainly anyone who was around Chicago TV news in the 1970s will instantly think of one name. I will not reveal the name here, but I will tell a story. A friend of mine was an assignment editor on this nameless anchor's station. One day he gave a juicy assignment to the man's coanchor and rival. The next day the nameless one leaned casually against my friend's door:

"Say, John, that was a great story you had for Maury yesterday. What do you have for me today?"

"Contempt."

True story. *Anchorman* also shows promotional spots in which Burgundy and his news teammates smile at each other lots and lots. Richard Roeper and I reviewed promos at PROMAX, the annual convention of TV promotion people. One spot showed the members of a news team doing magic tricks, performing with a hula hoop, playing a ukulele, etc. Yes, it was intended to be funny. And it was funny, especially if that's how you want to think of the people you trust for your news.

As *Anchorman* opens, Ron Burgundy faces a crisis. Ed Harken, the station's news director, played by the invaluable Fred Willard, wants to add "diversity" to the newsroom by hiring a woman—no, a *woman!*—as Burgundy's coanchor. This cannot be. It is not right. It is against nature. Burgundy is appalled. The new coanchor will be the efficiently named Veronica Corningstone (Christina Applegate), and, yes, reader, she was the blond Burgundy tried to pick up with the leather-and-mahogany line.

The other news team members include the wonderfully named Champ Kind (David Koechner), Brick Tamland (Steven Carell), and Brian Fantana (Paul Rudd). And yes, sometimes when they're together, they actually do sing "Afternoon Delight." They are united in their fear of adding a woman to the team. "I read somewhere," one of them ominously warns, "that their periods attract bears." Odors play an important role in the movie. Hoping to attract Corningstone, Brian Fantana splashes on a high-octane cologne that smells, the newsroom agrees, "like the time the raccoon got in the copier."

If the movie simply focused on making Ron and his team look ridiculous, it might grow tedious, because that would be such an easy thing to do. But it has a kind of sweetness to it. Despite his weaknesses, Ron is sort of a nice guy, darn it all, and Veronica Corningstone, despite her desire to project a serious image, kinda likes the guy—especially when he reveals an unsuspected musical talent in a lounge one night, after he's asked to "sit in on jazz flute."

The movie contains a lot of cameo appearances by other stars of the current comedy movie tour. Their names I will not reveal. Well, a character's name I will reveal: an anchorman named Wes Mantooth is Burgundy's archenemy. When the news teams clash in a free-for-all, it's over the top. But a lot of the quieter moments of rivalry are on target.

I have known and worked with a lot of anchorpersons, even female anchorpersons, over the years, and I can tell you that almost all of them are good people—smart professionals who don't take themselves too seriously. But every once in a while you get a Ron Burgundy, and you kind of treasure him, because you can dine out on the stories for years.

Annapolis ★ ½
PG-13, 108 m., 2006

James Franco (Jake Huard), Tyrese Gibson (Lieutenant Cole), Jordana Brewster (Ali), Donnie Wahlberg (Lieutenant Commander Burton), Chi McBride (McNally), Vicellous Shannon (Twins), Roger Fan (Loo), McCaleb Burnett (Whitaker), Wilmer Calderon (Estrada), Brian Goodman (Bill Huard). Directed by Justin Lin and produced by Mark Vahradian and Damien Saccani. Screenplay by David Collard.

Here I am at Sundance 2006. Four years ago I sat in the Park City Library and saw a film named *Better Luck Tomorrow* by a young man named Justin Lin, and I joined in the cheers. This was a risky, original film by a brilliant new director who told the story of a group of Asian kids from affluent families in Orange County, who backed into a life of crime with their eyes wide open.

Now it is Sundance again, but I must pause to review *Annapolis*, which is opening in the nation's multiplexes. Let the young directors at Sundance 2006 set aside their glowing reviews and gaze with sad eyes upon this movie, for it is a cautionary lesson. It is the anti-Sundance film, an exhausted wheeze of bankrupt clichés and cardboard characters, the kind of film that has no visible reason for existing, except that everybody got paid.

The movie stars James Franco as Jake Huard, a working-class kid who works as a riveter in a Chesapeake Bay shipyard and gazes in yearning across the waters to the U.S. Naval Academy, which his dead mother always wanted him to attend. His father, Bill (Brian Goodman), opposes the idea: He thinks his kid is too hotheaded to stick it out. But Jake is accepted for an unlikely last-minute opening, and the movie is the story of his plebe year.

That year is the present time, I guess, since Jake is referred to as a member of the class that will graduate in 2008. That means that the Navy is presumably fighting a war somewhere or other in this old world of ours, although there is not a single word about it in the movie. The plebes seem mostly engaged in memorizing the longitude and latitude of Annapolis to avoid doing push-ups.

There is a subplot involving Jake's fat African-American roommate, nicknamed Twins (Vicellous Shannon). There is much suspense over whether Twins can complete the obstacle course in less than five minutes by the end of the year. If I had a year to train under a brutal Marine drill sergeant with his boot up my butt, I could complete the goddamn obstacle course in under five minutes, and so could Queen Latifah.

The drill sergeant is Lieutenant Cole (Tyrese Gibson), who is a combat-veteran Marine on loan to the academy. Where he saw combat is never mentioned, even when he returns to it at the end of the movie. I've got my money on Iraq. But this movie is not about war. It is about boxing.

Yes, *Annapolis* takes the subject of a young man training to be a Navy officer in a time of war and focuses its entire plot on whether he can win the Brigades, which is the academy-wide boxing championship held every spring. It switches from one set of clichés to another in the middle of the film, without missing a single misstep. Because Jake has an attitude and because Cole doubts his ability to lead men, they become enemies, and everything points toward the big match where Jake and Cole will be able to hammer each other in the ring.

I forgot to mention that Jake was an amateur fighter before he entered the academy. His father thought he was a loser at that, too. He tells the old man he's boxing in the finals, but of course the old man doesn't attend. Or could it possibly be that the father, let's say, does attend, but arrives late and sees the fight, and then his eyes meet the eyes of his son, who is able to spot him immediately in that vast crowd? And does the father give him that curt little nod that means, "I was wrong, son, and you have the right stuff"? Surely a movie made in 2006 would not recycle the Parent Arriving Late and Giving Little Nod of Recognition Scene? Surely a director who made *Better Luck Tomorrow* would have nothing to do with such an ancient wheeze, which is not only off the shelf, but off the shelf at the resale store?

Yes, the Navy is at war, and it all comes down to a boxing match. Oh, and a big romance with another of Jake's superiors, the cute Ali (Jordana Brewster), who is twenty-five in real life and looks about nineteen in the movie. I have not been to Annapolis, but I think plebes and officers are not supposed to fraternize, kiss, and/or dance and do who knows what else with each other, in spite of the fact that they Meet Cute after he thinks she is a hooker (ho, ho). Ali and the academy's boxing coach (Chi McBride) help train Jake for his big bout.

Here is a movie with dialogue such as: "You just don't get it, do you, Huard?" "I don't need advice from you." Or . . . "You aren't good enough." "I've heard that all my life."

Is there a little store in Westwood that sells dialogue like this on rubber stamps? There is only one character in the movie who comes alive and whose dialogue is worth being heard. That is the fat kid, Twins. His story is infinitely more touching than Jake's; he comes from a small Southern town that gave him a parade before he went off to the academy, and if he flunks out, he can't face the folks at home. When Jake's other roommates move out because they don't want to bunk with a loser, Twins stays. Why? His reason may not make audiences in Arkansas and Mississippi very happy, but at least it has the quality of sounding as if a human being might say it out loud.   ☞

Après Vous ★ ★

R, 110 m., 2005

Daniel Auteuil (Antoine), José Garcia (Louis), Sandrine Kiberlain (Blanche), Marilyne Canto (Christine), Michèle Moretti (Martine), Garence Clavel (Karine), Fabio Zenoni (André). Directed by Pierre Salvadori and produced by Philippe Martin. Screenplay by Benoît Graffin, David Léotard, and Salvadori

Daniel Auteuil, who seems to be the busiest actor in France, has that look about him of a man worried about whether he is doing the right thing. In *Après Vous* he does the right thing and it results in nothing but trouble for him. He rescues a man in the act of committing suicide, and then, in an irony that is probably covered by several ancient proverbs, he feels responsible for the man's life.

Auteuil plays Antoine, the maître d' at a Paris brasserie that, if the customers typically endure as much incompetence as they experience during this movie, must have great food. Taking a shortcut through a park late one night, Antoine comes upon Louis (the sad-eyed, hangdog José Garcia) just as he kicks the suitcase out from under his feet to hang himself from a tree. Antoine saves him, brings him home, introduces him to his uneasy girlfriend, Christine (Marilyne Canto), and cares more about Louis than Louis does.

Louis, in fact, wishes he had committed suicide. He is heartbroken over the end of his romance with Blanche (Sandrine Kiberlain), and suddenly remembers he has written a letter bidding farewell from life and mailed it to the grandmother who raised him. Antoine promptly drives through the night with him to intercept the letter, and finds himself living Louis's life for him.

Après Vous is intended as a farce, but lacks farcical insanity and settles for being a sitcom, not a very good one. One problem is that neither Louis nor his dilemma is amusing. Another is that Antoine is too sincere and single-minded to suggest a man being driven buggy by the situation; he seems more earnest than beleaguered.

Farces often involve cases of mistaken or misunderstood identities, and that's what happens this time as Antoine seeks out Blanche, finds her in a florist shop, and falls in love with her. That would be a simple enough matter, since after all, she has already broken up with Louis, but Antoine is conscientious to a fault, and feels it is somehow his responsibility to deny himself romantic happiness and try to reconcile Louis and Blanche. Since there is nothing in the movie to suggest they would bring each other anything but misery, this compulsion seems more masochistic than generous.

Much of the action centers on the brasserie, Chez Jean, where I would like to eat the next time I am in Paris, always assuming Louis and Antoine no longer work there. Antoine gets Louis the wine steward's job, despite Louis's complete lack of knowledge about wine; he develops a neat trick of describing a wine by its results rather than its qualities, recommending expensive labels because they will make the customer feel cheery. This at least has the advantage of making him less boring than most wine stewards.

Blanche meanwhile doesn't realize the two men know each other, and that leads of course to a scene in which she finds that out and feels betrayed, as women always do in such situations, instead of being grateful that two men have gone to such pains to make her the center of their deceptions. There are also scenes

that I guess are inevitable in romantic comedies of a certain sort, in which one character and then another scales a vine-covered trellis to Blanche's balcony, risking their lives in order to spy on her. I don't know about you, but when I see a guy climbing to a balcony and his name's not Romeo, I wish I'd brought along my iPod.

There is a kind of mental efficiency meter that ticks away during comedies, in which we keep an informal accounting: Is the movie providing enough laughter to justify its running time? If the movie falls below its recommended laughter saturation level, I begin to make use of the Indiglo feature on my Timex. Antoine and Louis and Blanche make two or three or even four too many trips around the maypole of comic misunderstandings, giving us time to realize that we don't really care how they end up anyway.

Aquamarine ★ ★
PG, 109 m., 2006

Emma Roberts (Claire), JoJo (Hailey), Sara Paxton (Aquamarine), Jake McDorman (Raymond), Arielle Kebbel (Cecilia), Bruce Spence (Leonard). Directed by Elizabeth Allen and produced by Susan Cartsonis. Screenplay by John Quaintance and Jessica Bendinger, based on the novel by Alice Hoffman.

Aquamarine is another movie where an event of earthshaking astonishment takes place and is safely contained within a sitcom plot. In this case, a mermaid comes ashore at a Florida beach resort, makes friends with two thirteen-year-old girls, and dates a cute lifeguard. Oh, and of course there's a bitchy blonde with her posse to make life miserable for everybody.

And yet—well, the movie is awfully sweet. The young actresses playing eighth-graders look their age, for once, and have an unstudied charm. I know there's an audience for this movie just as surely as I know I am not that audience. It's clever in the way the two heroines get a crush on the lifeguard and then use the mermaid as their designated hitter; they coach her on how to win a boy's attention, and watch fascinated as she dazzles the boy they can only dream about.

The girls are Claire and Hailey, played by

Emma Roberts and JoJo (aka Joanna Levesque). They're best friends, but when the summer ends in a few days, Hailey has to move to Australia with her mom. Meanwhile, they fantasize about Raymond (Jake McDorman), who is blond and muscular and awfully nice. They study his body language: how he shakes his hair and stretches his arms to flex his biceps.

One night there's a big storm, and the next day Claire, who is afraid of the water, falls into a swimming pool and glimpses a mermaid who washed up during the night. Soon the girls are best friends with Aquamarine (Sara Paxton), who despite having swum several times around the world and having a father who can create tsunamis, behaves like a Nickelodeon star. She explains her rules: Merpeople can speak all human languages and can grow legs on dry land, but the legs turn back into a tail after dark, or when they get wet. "We are not fictional," Aquamarine tells the girls. "We're discreet." She has nail polish that changes colors to reflect her moods.

Her mission on land is to prove that love exists. This is because her father has arranged a marriage for her. She doesn't love the proposed husband and has been given three days to prove to her dad that there is such a thing as love. Hailey and Claire coach her in the art of getting a boy's attention. Step One: Call him and hang up. Step Two: Walk past and don't seem to notice him. Soon Aquamarine and Raymond are holding hands and stuff like that, which enrages the scheming Cecilia (Arielle Kebbel). She snoops around trying to discover Aquamarine's secret, and what with one thing and another the mermaid is trapped overnight inside the big water tank outside town.

So you get the idea. Suspense builds as Cecilia and Aquamarine compete to be Raymond's date for the Final Splash, a big block party on the last day of summer. Meanwhile, Hailey learns that mermaids can grant a wish and wonders if she can use hers to make her mother stay in Florida and forget about Australia. And gee, that's about it.

A movie like this does not engage the mind, but it engages the eyes. It shows pleasant and cheerful young people on screen looking as if it's still fun for them to be making movies. It stays so far away from specific sexual content

that the PG rating, "for mild language and sensuality," seems severe. The plot is predictable, the emotions are obvious, and the mermaid reminds me of my friend McHugh explaining why lobsters make ideal pets: They don't bark, and they know the secrets of the deep.

Oh, I almost forgot Leonard (Bruce Spence), the beach handyman, who looks so ominous that one girl whispers to another, "He knows what you did last summer." I learn from IMDb.com that he stands 6 feet 7 inches tall, and his role as the Mouth of Sauron in *The Lord of the Rings: The Return of the King* was cut from the movie but has been restored in the extended edition. I tell you these things because when Leonard comes on the screen you will want to know more about him. He plays the only character of which that can be said.

Are We There Yet? ★ ★
PG, 91 m., 2005

Ice Cube (Nick Persons), Nia Long (Suzanne Kingston), Aleisha Allen (Lindsey Kingston), Philip Bolden (Kevin Kingston), Jay Mohr (Marty). Directed by Brian Levant and produced by Matt Alvarez, Ice Cube, and Dan Kolsrud. Screenplay by Steven Gary Banks, Claudia Grazioso, J. David Stem, and David N. Weiss.

Ice Cube is an effortlessly likable actor, which presents two problems for *Are We There Yet?* Problem No. 1 is that he has to play a bachelor who hates kids, and No. 2 is that two kids make his life miserable in ways that are supposed to be funny but are mean and painful.

Mr. Cube plays Nick, owner of a sports memorabilia store, who one day is struck by the lightning bolt of love when he gazes upon Suzanne (Nia Long), who runs an event-management service across the street. There is a problem. She is the divorced mom of two kids. Nick hates kids. But one Dark and Stormy Night he passes Suzanne next to her stalled car and offers her a lift. There is chemistry, and it seems likely to lead to physics, but then she sadly observes that they can only be "good friends" because he doesn't really care for kids.

But . . . but . . . Nick cares so much for her that he's willing to learn. Suzanne is needed in Vancouver to coordinate a New Year's Eve party, her ex-husband breaks a promise to baby-sit the kids, and Nick agrees to bring the kids to Vancouver. That's when the trouble starts.

We've already seen what these kids are capable of. One of their mom's dates arrives on the front sidewalk, hits a trip wire, and is pelted with buckets of glue before losing his footing on dozens of marbles and falling hard to the ground. Hilarious, right?

Now it's Nick's turn. He attempts to take the kids north by plane and train before settling on automobile—in his case, a brand-new Lincoln Navigator, curiously enough the same vehicle that was used in *Johnson Family Vacation*. It's the SUV of choice for destruction in bizarre ways through family adventures.

Young Lindsey (Aleisha Allen) and younger Kevin (Philip Bolden) retain the delusion that their father will come back home someday, and have dedicated themselves to discouraging their mother's would-be boyfriends. This leads to such stunts as writing "Help us!" on a card and holding it to the car window so a trucker will think they're the captives of a child abuser. It also leads to several potentially fatal traffic adventures, a boxing match with a deer that stands on its hind legs and seems to think it's a kangaroo, and the complete destruction of the Navigator.

Nick displays the patience of a saint. Far from being the child-hater he thinks he is, he's gentle, understanding, forgiving, and empathetic. The kids are little monsters. What they do to him is so far over the top that it's sadistic, not funny, and it doesn't help when they finally get to Vancouver and Suzanne cruelly misreads the situation.

I would have loved to see a genuine love story involving Ice Cube, Nia Long, and the challenge of a lifelong bachelor dating a woman with children. Sad that a story like that couldn't get made, but this shrill "comedy" could. Maybe it's the filmmakers who don't like children. They certainly don't seem to know very much about them.

The Aristocrats ★ ★ ½
NO MPAA RATING, 92 m., 2005

Featuring Jason Alexander, Shelley Berman, Lewis Black, David Brenner, Drew Carey, George Carlin, Tim Conway, Andy Dick, Phyllis Diller, Joe Franklin, Judy Gold, Whoopi Goldberg, Gilbert Gottfried, Eric Idle, Eddie Izzard, Richard Lewis, Bill Maher, Howie Mandel, Merrill Markoe, Jackie "The Joke Man" Martling, Michael McKean, Larry Miller, Martin Mull, Kevin Nealon, the *Onion* editorial staff, Penn & Teller, Emo Philips, Kevin Pollak, Andy Richter, Don Rickles, Chris Rock, Bob Saget, Harry Shearer, the Smothers Brothers, David Steinberg, Jon Stewart, Larry Storch, Rip Taylor, Dave Thomas, Peter Tilden, Bruce Vilanch, Fred Willard, Robin Williams, Steven Wright. Directed by Paul Provenza and produced by Penn Jillette and Peter Adam Golden.

Two extremes in joke-telling:

Style No. 1. As tight as a haiku. Not one wasted word. Told with aggressive brutality. Ends with a punch line that ends with the punch word. The last word delivers the joke. Then, bang, it's over.

Style No. 2. The joke-teller's purpose is to sadistically control the time and attention of the other person by an elaborate and unnecessary recital of the setup. He lovingly adds irrelevant details. Uses one or more accents. Chuckles during the telling to prompt you that he's funny. Inverts the punch line, so the payoff comes at the start, not the end, of the final sentence, which then meanders in anticlimax. Then provides a helpful explanation of the joke. ("See, the bartender was talking to the duck, not the woman.") In the worst of all possible worlds, he finds his joke so funny that he actually repeats it, to be sure you properly appreciated it. Anyone who tells a joke this way should not be trusted in positions of authority.

The perfect joke in Style No. 1, as told by Henny Youngman, Rodney Dangerfield, Lou Jacobi:

Guy goes to a psychiatrist.

Psychiatrist says, "You're crazy!"

"I want a second opinion!"

"All right, you're ugly!"

Now for a joke in Style No. 2, which can easily go five minutes. I will mercifully condense it. A carpenter dies and goes to heaven, and he tells St. Peter he is looking for his son. His description of the son matches Jesus. The son appears. "Father?" says the son. "Pinocchio!" says the father.

I am constantly amazed that the people

who tell this joke don't realize that *every single person in the English-speaking world has already heard this joke five hundred times.* The joke-teller relentlessly spins it out for minute after minute, while his captives stand there with glazed eyes and a rictus that he mistakes for a grin.

I will now describe two versions of another joke.

Style No. 1:

Guy goes into a talent agency to pitch his act. "What do you do?" asks the agent.

"We come out and crap on the stage."

"What do you call yourselves?"

"The Aristocrats."

Style No. 2 now has an entire movie devoted to it. It is famous among professional comedians, we're told, as the dirtiest joke of all time. Here's how you tell it. After the talent agent asks, "What do you do?" the other guy describes a long series of the most depraved and disgusting words, images, and actions that he can string together. Absolutely nothing is off-limits. The act can involve incest, bestiality, matricide, bodily waste, vomiting and other sudden voidings, necrophilia, bondage, whatever. It is described in racist, sexist, and obscene terms. After the litany is complete, the agent asks, What do you call yourselves? and the guy replies, etc.

No less than one hundred comedians appear in *The Aristocrats,* according to someone who kept score. I think the editorial board of the *Onion* is counted as one. It's observed by several of them that professional comedians don't tell "jokes" onstage; they do an act, often involving their cosmic struggle with life. The dirtiest joke is reserved for when they hang out with each other. There's a competition: Who can make it longer and dirtier? Michael O'Donoghue once told a version that lasted ninety minutes.

I am an expert on joke-telling and often hold audiences spellbound with my mastery of the topic. I contend that this joke cannot be funny one-on-one or in a small group. It must be performed before a larger group, preferably in a situation where it is transgressive and dangerous. That's because it is not a funny joke, but it can potentially create a funny situation, or an interesting one. That explains why, with all the firepower in this movie (George Carlin, Andy Dick, Richard Lewis, Chris Rock, and

ninety-six more), the funniest version ever told, everyone agrees, was by Gilbert Gottfried at a 2001 Friar's Club roast of Hugh Hefner.

Gottfried had a lot of things going for him. 1) Every comic in the room knew the joke and couldn't believe he was telling it. 2) Hefner was seated in a wingback chair next to the podium and seemed uncertain if he should laugh at its extreme political incorrectness. 3) The roast was held not long after 9/11, and from the audience there were shouts of "Too soon!" to warn that New York, in mourning, was not ready for it. 4) He tells it with breakneck, manic intensity, so that the point is not the joke, but the reckless, heedless performance. All the conditions are in place for Gottfried to have a big success, because at last the joke has found a setting in which it can actually offend.

In *The Aristocrats,* which was directed by Paul Provenza and coproduced by Penn Jillette, we hear the joke in many versions and styles. Sometimes we cut between takes of the same guy telling it two or three times. It is theorized about. It is marveled at. What's remarkable is that no one, except Dick Smothers and Phyllis Diller, thinks that it isn't funny. Everything depends on the risk involved in telling it; without risk, no joke.

The Aristocrats might have made a nice short subject. At ninety-two minutes, it's like the boozy salesman who corners you with the Pinocchio torture. I am left with three observations. 1) If Buddy Hackett were still alive, he could have told it better than Gilbert Gottfried. 2) Whatever happened to Andrew Dice Clay? 3) The punch line stinks. These are better:

"The Brothers Two."

"The Mellow Tones."

"Penn and Teller." ☞

Around the Bend ★ ★ ½
R, 85 m., 2004

Michael Caine (Henry Lair), Christopher Walken (Turner Lair), Josh Lucas (Jason Lair), Jonah Bobo (Zach), Glenne Headly (Katrina). Directed by Jordan Roberts and produced by Elliott Lewitt and Julie Kirkham. Screenplay by Roberts.

Christopher Walken has become so expert at finely tuned walk-ons that he rarely stays around for a whole movie. His cameos are like the prize in a Cracker Jack box: You don't buy the ticket to see Walken, but you keep looking for him. In *Around the Bend* he has a role big enough to move around inside, and he reminds us what a very good actor he is. The movie, unfortunately, doesn't really work; it's one of those films where the characters always seem to be Behaving, as if ordinary life has to be jacked up into eccentricity.

The film opens with Michael Caine as old Henry, bedridden and being cared for by his adult grandson, Jason (Josh Lucas), his great-grandson, Zach (Jonah Bobo), and Katrina (Glenne Headly), the Danish live-in. He has one of those unspecified illnesses that permit grand gestures before the final exit. There is a generation missing from this picture, but the portrait is filled out when Turner (Christopher Walken) amazingly returns home for the first time in thirty years.

Jason doesn't much like his father, who abandoned him. Young Zach is impressed: You're not dead anymore! Turner says he must leave again the following day, but won't give his reasons (which turn out, in fact, to be excellent). Henry rouses himself for one last journey into the world with Zach, and the old man and the boy settle into a booth at the nearby Kentucky Fried Chicken restaurant, where Henry scribbles instructions on Post-it notes and stuffs them into KFC bags, one inside another, outlining a sort of scavenger hunt. Then he dies.

The opening of the KFC bags, which takes on the solemnity of the reading of a will, reveals Henry's plan. He wants to be cremated along with his dog, and he wants his son, grandson, and great-grandson to make a journey from Los Angeles to New Mexico, scattering ashes along the way. One specification: Every bag must be opened in a KFC restaurant, and the ashes scattered nearby.

Turner, the Walken character, decides he will go along with this plan. Of course, there are poignant reasons why he should not, even apart from the fact that he walked away from a prison, but one grand gesture deserves another.

The three men pilot a very old VW van down the desert highways from one chicken outlet to the next, faithfully consuming fried chicken at every meal, as if this were the sequel to *Super Size Me.* Why, we may ask, did Henry insist on KFC? Does it have anything to do with product placement? Is KFC trying to drum up postinterment business? I doubt it. I think they go to KFC because Jordan Roberts, the writer-director, wanted to make them into Characters and thought KFC would be quirky or funny or something.

But this is not exactly a comedy. It is, alas, a voyage of discovery, during which old secrets are revealed, new ones are shared, and the generations find peace with one another. These passages are well acted by Walken, Lucas, and young Bobo, but I always felt as if they were inhabiting a story, not their lives. Walken has some nice moments, though, and I love the way he releases dialogue as if first giving every word a friendly pat. There's a good scene where his son accuses him of stealing a spoon, and the explanation reveals important things about the way he lives now.

Around the Bend has the best will in the world, and its heart is in the right place. Walken is a pleasure to watch in a role he can stretch in, and there may be some audience members who get involved in these men trying to figure out how to talk to one another. But I dunno. It all seemed like a setup job to me. I know movie characters usually follow a script, but I don't like it when it feels like they are.

Around the World in 80 Days ★ ★ ★
PG, 120 m., 2004

Jackie Chan (Passepartout), Steve Coogan (Phileas Fogg), Cecile De France (Monique La Roche), Jim Broadbent (Lord Kelvin), Kathy Bates (Queen Victoria), Arnold Schwarzenegger (Prince Hapi), John Cleese (Grizzled Sergeant), Owen Wilson (Wilbur Wright), Luke Wilson (Orville Wright), Karen Mok (General Fang). Directed by Frank Coraci and produced by Bill Badalato and Hal Lieberman. Screenplay by David N. Titcher, David Benullo, and David Goldstein, based on the novel by Jules Verne.

Here against all probability is a jolly comedy made from that wheezy high concept, *Around the World in 80 Days*. I grew up with Phileas Fogg and his picaresque journey, plundered the Classics Illustrated comic, read the Jules

Verne novel, and attended Michael Todd's 1956 film, but I never thought the story was much of a cliff-hanger. Even in its time, eighty days seemed doable. Verne's *20,000 Leagues Under the Sea* and *From the Earth to the Moon* were more like it.

But here's a film version that does some lateral thinking, that moves Fogg off dead center and makes Jackie Chan's Passepartout the real hero, and lingers for comic effect instead of always looking at its watch. The Todd production was famous for its wall-to-wall cameos ("Look! That piano player! Why, it's Frank Sinatra!"). And here we have Kathy Bates as Queen Victoria, Owen and Luke Wilson as the Wright brothers, John Cleese as a British sergeant, and, funniest of all, Arnold Schwarzenegger as a Turkish prince.

The setup is familiar. Phileas Fogg is much resented by the members of the fogbound Explorers' Club because of his crackpot inventions and fevered schemes. Lord Kelvin (Jim Broadbent), president of the club, is a mainstream scientist who no doubt gave his name to the scientific term "kelvin," which measures how many degrees of separation there are between you and Sir Kelvin Bacon, the inventor of gravity.

Fogg claims the world can be circled in eighty days. Kelvin is outraged by his presumption, and makes him dare: Either (a) Fogg circles the globe by the deadline and Kelvin resigns from the club, or (b) Fogg resigns and discontinues his confounded experiments. Fogg (Steve Coogan) accepts the bet, and as he's preparing for his journey he hires a new valet, Passepartout (Jackie Chan).

This valet we have already met, making a sudden exit from the Bank of England after having stolen the priceless Jade Buddha, a relic much treasured by his native village in China, but nabbed by the Black Scorpions, hirelings of the evil warlord Fang. Passepartout's hidden motive for joining the journey is to elude the police, sneak out of England, and return the Buddha to China.

So off we go, by horse, train, ship, hot air balloon, and so on. There is a brief stop at an art fair in France, where the beautiful Monique (Cecile De France) insists on joining their expedition and cannot be dissuaded; we think at first she has a nefarious motive, but no, she's probably taken a class in screenplay construction and

knows that the film requires a sexy female lead. This is not the first case in cinematic history of a character voluntarily entering a movie because of the objective fact that she is required.

Fogg is the straight man to Passepartout for much of the journey, allowing Chan to steal scenes with shameless mugging, astonished double-takes, and his remarkable physical agility. But all goes more or less as expected until the three arrive in Turkey and are made guests of Prince Hapi (Arnold Schwarzenegger), whose hospitality is hard to distinguish from captivity. Smitten by the fragrant Monique, he invites all three to join him in the Turkish equivalent of a hot tub, observing ruefully, "I'm always embarrassing myself in front of visiting dignitaries." It may not be worth the price of admission, but it almost is, to hear Schwarzenegger proudly boast, "Guess who else was in this pool? U.S. president Rutherford B. Hayes!"

The director, Frank Coraci, takes advantage of Verne's structure to avoid the need for any real continuity. When one location runs out of gags, the three move on to the next, including an extended stay in Passepartout's native China, where Fang and the Black Scorpions do all they can to win back the Jade Buddha from the grateful village where it has exerted its benign charm for centuries.

Then across the Pacific and into the American desert, where the travelers encounter a couple of traveling bicycle salesmen, Wilbur and Orville Wright (Owen and Luke Wilson). They generously share their ideas for an airplane, and that comes in handy in the mid-Atlantic, when Fogg's chartered steamer runs out of fuel and the intrepid circumnavigators invent an airplane and fly to London. Oh, and before that there's an extended martial arts scene in the New York warehouse where the head of the Statue of Liberty provides a gigantic prop.

None of this amounts to anything more than goofy fun, but that's what the ads promise, and the movie delivers. It's light as a fly, but springs some genuinely funny moments, especially by Schwarzenegger, the Wilsons, and the irrepressible Chan.

The California governor's scenes were shot before he took office, and arguably represent his last appearance in a fiction film; if so, he leaves the movies as he entered, a man who shares our amusement at his improbability, and has a canny sense of his own image and possibilities. I met him when the documentary *Pumping Iron* was being released, and Mr. Universe was the first of the offices he would hold. I liked him then, I like him now, and I remember that when I introduced the film at the USA Film Festival in Dallas, he greeted the audience and then slipped off to the green room to study his business textbooks. He refused to be dismissed as muscles with an accent, but he got the joke.

Art School Confidential ★ ★ ★
R, 102 m., 2006

Max Minghella (Jerome), Sophia Myles (Audrey), John Malkovich (Professor Sandiford), Anjelica Huston (Sophie), Jim Broadbent (Jimmy), Ethan Suplee (Vince), Matt Keeslar (Jonah), Joel David Moore (Bardo), Steve Buscemi (Broadway Bob). Directed by Terry Zwigoff and produced by Lianne Halfon, John Malkovich, and Russell Smith. Screenplay by Daniel Clowes.

I believe you can go to school to learn to be an accountant, a doctor, a physicist, an engineer, an astronaut. I am not sure you can learn to be an artist. Artists are born, not made, and the real reason to study the arts is to have fun, learn technical skills, network with other creative types, fall in love with people who are not boring, and do the work you probably would have done anyway. That said, I highly recommend college. I majored in English and journalism, and I wanted to be a graduate student forever.

I am writing this the morning after my wife and I attended the Head to Toe Gala, at which students of the School of the Art Institute of Chicago presented their spring fashion show. We saw about half of the work presented a week earlier at the school's 2006 Fashion Show at Marshall Field's, which sounds ever so much more upscale than the 2007 Fashion Show at Macy's. I was astonished. The creativity and wit in their designs would have made Fellini envious. These were not items of clothing; these were visual arts. I could imagine the same models, wearing the same designs, walking up the red carpet at the Cannes Film Festival and sending the designers of Paris weeping and gnashing into the shadows.

Then we learned that the first third of the show, featuring white clothing, was all by freshmen. They didn't learn to create those fashions between September and May. Therefore, apparently, they always could design. I am not suggesting the school's faculty serves no purpose; indeed, as a teacher of film appreciation, I believe faculties in the arts are sainted. They must guide, advise, moderate, encourage, teach methods, provide a context, share secrets, and declare an informed opinion on the worth of the work. They create a world within which such work is possible and valued. What they cannot do, I suspect, is teach a student how to be original and creative.

Art School Confidential, the new comedy by Terry Zwigoff, seems to share these sentiments. It was written, like his *Ghost World*, by the artist Daniel Clowes and is based on one of Clowes's graphic novels. Zwigoff also made the great documentary *Crumb*, about another artist who is entirely his own creation. *Art School*'s hero is Jerome (Max Minghella), already an extraordinary draftsman when he enters the school; his drawings glow from the page with conviction and love. "I want to be the next Picasso," he claims, which indicates his vision is indeed inward and personal, since he does not know enough about Picasso to see that his work does not have a single line in common with that master. Perhaps he simply means he wants to be famous, make lots of money, and grow old while making love to beautiful women. Honorable goals.

There is a moment in the film when the students are asked to create a self-portrait. Jerome's work bears comparison with the pre-Raphaelites. The student whose self-portrait is most highly praised has created an assemblage of lines and squiggles that "looks like a Cy Twombly," someone says—in praise. I'm not saying a nineteenth-century representational style is superior to Twombly, but I do believe that in a freshman class the purpose of a self-portrait assignment is to draw something that looks like it might be you. Students have to learn to walk before they can crawl.

Jerome's teacher is Professor Sandiford (John Malkovich), who paces the classroom talking on his cell phone, trying to get a gallery to give him a show. Sandiford draws triangles. "I was one of the first," he says, to paint triangles—in his mind, perhaps second only to Euclid. Malkovich's character issues dire warnings about the future awaiting any would-be artist, conceals rage about his own neglect, and in general provides the kind of forbidding detachment that drives students crazy trying to please him.

Jerome falls in love with the artists' model Audrey (Sophia Myles). She likes the drawing he does of her, as who would not, and is kind to him, and as a nerd in high school he is thrilled that his talent at last has brought him the affection of a beautiful girl. Jerome's roommates are Vince (Ethan Suplee) and Bardo (Joel David Moore), who, like all roommates (in the words of John D. McDonald), deprive him of solitude without providing him with companionship. The Vince character is a wonderful creation, an unkempt underground filmmaker, making a work of enthusiasm and incoherence; much of his time is spent rearranging 3-by-5 cards describing hypothetical scenes. Bardo is helpful on practical stuff, explaining the politics of the Strathmore school of art and briefing him on his fellow students.

There is a wise and understanding teacher on the faculty, played by Anjelica Huston. Defending the work of Dead White Males, she sensibly observes that when they did their best work "they weren't dead yet." Even more wisdom and certainly more weariness come when Jerome visits the squalid apartment of the drunken old artist Jimmy (Jim Broadbent), who might once have been young and might once have had hopes but now festers in cynicism, anger, despair, and the need for a drink. There is something in the Zwigoffian universe that values such characters; having abandoned all illusions, they offer the possibility of truth. I also much enjoyed Broadway Bob (Steve Buscemi); his café is a hangout for the students, who hope he will hang their work on his walls. Bob at this point is more important to them than the art critic of the New York Times.

Now I regret to tell you that the plot also involves a serial killer who is stalking the campus and has claimed several victims. The police investigate, the students become paranoid, and some of the characters fall under suspicion. There is nothing particularly wrong with this subplot except that it is completely unnecessary and imposes a generic story structure on a film that might better have just grown from scene to scene like an experience. I wasn't interested in the killer and would have rather seen more of Jerome interacting with his professors, with Broadway Bob and old Jimmy, and with the beautiful Audrey, who will surely see that her future lies with the next Picasso, since she was born too late to lie with the previous one.

Ask the Dust ★ ★ ★
R, 117 m., 2006

Colin Farrell (Arturo Bandini), Salma Hayek (Camilla Lopez), Donald Sutherland (Hellfrick), Eileen Atkins (Mrs. Hargraves), Justin Kirk (Sammy), Idina Menzel (Vera Rivkin). Directed by Robert Towne, and produced by Tom Cruise, Paula Wagner, Don Granger, and Jonas McCord. Screenplay by Towne, based on the novel by John Fante.

Who is harder to portray in a movie than a writer? The standard portrait is familiar: the shabby room, the typewriter, the bottle, the cigarettes, the crazy neighbors, the nickel cup of coffee, the smoldering sexuality of the woman who comes into his life. Robert Towne's Ask the Dust is not the first film to evoke this vision of a writer's life, and not the first to find that typing is not a cinematic activity. Just the week before, Winter Passing starred Ed Harris in a version of the same kind of character at the other end of his career.

Still, in its wider focus, Ask the Dust finds a kind of poetry because although we may not find it noble and romantic to sit alone in a room, broke and hungover and dreaming of glory, a writer can, and must. The film stars Colin Farrell as Arturo Bandini, who lives in a Los Angeles rooming house during the Depression. He has sold one story to the American Mercury, edited by H. L. Mencken, the god of American letters, and now he tries to write more: "The greatest man in America—do you want to let him down?"

Arturo has one nickel, with which he buys a cup of coffee in a diner where Camilla (Salma Hayek) is the waitress. Something happens between them, but it is expressed curiously. One day she gives him a free beer, which he pours into a spittoon. She takes the magazine with his story, tears it up, and throws it into the same spittoon. Why this hostility, which is meant to mask lust but seems gratuitous?

The answer may be in the source of the material. *Ask the Dust* is a novel by John Fante, a writer of the generation just before Charles Bukowski, who saw to it that the book was reissued by his publisher, the Black Sparrow Press. It shares Bukowski's view of women who are attracted to a courtship consisting largely of hostility. In *Ask the Dust,* there is the additional element of racism; Camilla is wounded, as she should be, by prejudice against Mexicans in the city, and Bandini is uneasy about his Italian heritage. When they go to the movies together, Anglos pointedly move away from them, but the movie evokes racism without really engaging it, and the crucial scenes in their romance take place in a cottage on a deserted Laguna Beach, where they create a world of their own. There is also the mysterious Jewish woman, Vera (Idina Menzel), who comes into his life, makes a sudden and deep impression, reveals to him her scarred body, and then departs from the plot in a particularly Los Angeles sort of way.

What the movie is about, above all, is the bittersweet solitude of the would-be great writer. Whether Arturo will become the next Hemingway (or Fante or Bukowski) is uncertain, but Farrell shows him as a young man capable of playing the role should he win it. He could also possibly live a long and happy life with Camilla, but stories like this exist in the short run and are about problems, not solutions.

I did not feel a strong chemistry between Farrell and Hayek, but I have started to write the word "chemistry" with growing doubts. What is it, anyway? William Hurt and Kathleen Turner had it in *Body Heat,* and Nicolas Cage and Cher in *Moonstruck,* but *Ask the Dust* does not provide a setting for great, dramatic, towering lust and love: It is about poverty, fatigue, lives that are young but already old in discouragement. Perhaps what we are meant to feel between Arturo and Camilla is not chemistry but geometry: They could fit well together and provide each other's missing angles.

I enjoyed and admired the film without being grabbed or shaken by it. Where can such a story lead? I have been lucky enough to know a great writer in his shabby apartment, with his typewriter, his bottle, and his cigarettes, and I know he had a famous romance, and that later he hated the woman, and having achieved all possible success was perhaps not as happy as when it was still before him.

What immediately impressed me about *Ask the Dust* was its evocation of time and place. The cinematographer, Caleb Deschanel, creates Depression-era Los Angeles with the same love the 2005 *King Kong* lavished on New York at the same period, and although one is a smaller film about a writer and the other is an epic about an ape, the cityscapes are so evocative they take on a character of their own. In the case of *King Kong,* much of the city was special effects; in *Ask the Dust* there are some effects, but Deschanel in large part is working with reality.

Towne filmed on location in Cape Town, a city I lived in for a year, and I agree with him that it can double for prewar Los Angeles. Just keep Table Mountain out of the shot and you have storefront cafés, rooming houses built on hillsides with the front door on the top floor, palm trees, and a feeling in some neighborhoods of strangers who don't know what brought them together or why they wait. Such a person is Hellfrick (Donald Sutherland), Arturo's wise, weary neighbor, who shuffles onstage to provide the ghost of Arturo's possible future.

Ask the Dust requires an audience with a special love for film noir, with a feeling for the loneliness and misery of the writer, and with an understanding that any woman he meets will be beautiful. Such stories are never about understanding landladies. I am not sure the film achieves great things, but it achieves its smaller things perfectly. ☞

The Assassination of Richard Nixon ★ ★ ★ ½
R, 95 m., 2005

Sean Penn (Samuel Bicke), Naomi Watts (Marie Bicke), Don Cheadle (Bonny Simmons), Jack Thompson (Jack Jones), Mykelti Williamson (Harold Mann), Michael Wincott (Julius Bicke). Directed by Niels Mueller and produced by Alfonso Cuaron and Jorge Vergara. Screenplay by Kevin Kennedy and Mueller.

Baltimore, 1974. Sam Bicke explains and explains and explains. He has it all worked out, why he is right and the world is wrong, and he has a fierce obsession with injustice. "My name is Sam Bicke," he says at the beginning of one of the tapes he mails to Leonard Bernstein, "and I consider myself a grain of sand." He sells office supplies, very badly. His marriage is at an end. The Small Business Administration is not acting on his loan application. Nixon is still in the White House. The Black Panthers are being persecuted. It is all part of the same rage coiling within him.

Sean Penn plays Bicke as a man who has always been socially inept and now, as his life comes apart, descends into madness. His own frustration and the evils in the world are all the same, all somehow someone else's fault, and in the opening scene of *The Assassination of Richard Nixon,* we see him in an airport parking garage, concealing a pistol in a leg brace. He mails one last tape to Leonard Bernstein. He plans to hijack a plane and fly it into the White House.

There was a real Sam Bicke (spelled Byck), whose plan of course failed. Niels Mueller's movie is based on his botched assassination scheme, but many of the other details, including some scenes of mordant humor, are the invention of Mueller and his cowriter, Kevin Kennedy. This is a character study of a marginal man who goes off the rails, and Penn is brilliant at evoking how daily life itself is filled, for Bicke, with countless challenges to his rigid sense of right and wrong.

Consider his job as an office supply salesman. He is selling chairs covered in Naugahyde. The client asks if they are leather. He says they are not. His boss, Jack Jones (Jack Thompson), steps in and smoothly explains they are "Naugahyde-covered leather." Uh-huh. When Sam offers a client a discount to close a sale, Jack calls him into his office and screams at him for selling the desk at a loss. The client overhears. Later Sam finds out the joke was on him. Jack wants to help him, and recommends reading *The Power of Positive Thinking* and *How to Win Friends and Influence People.*

His sense of honesty offended by his job, Sam becomes obsessed with Nixon: "He made us a promise—he didn't deliver. Then he sold us on the exact same promise and he got elected again." He visits the local Black Panther office to make a donation and, as a Panther official (Mykelti Williamson) listens

incredulously, shares his ideas about renaming the Panthers the Zebras and admitting white members—like Sam Bicke, for example.

Sam is separated from his wife, Marie (Naomi Watts), and two daughters. He dreams of saving his marriage. She can't make him understand it's over. He is served with divorce papers and protests, "We're supposed to be working this out!" In one of the movie's most painful moments, he talks to the family dog: "You love me, don't you?" The dog seems indifferent.

Sam dreams of starting a limousine company with his closest friend, Bonny Simmons (Don Cheadle). This depends on a small business loan. Sam and Bonny are a poor risk, the bank drags out the paperwork, and Sam explains and explains and explains how important the loan is, and how urgent it is that it comes quickly.

Sean Penn conveys anger through small, contained details. He is one of our great actors, able to invest insignificant characters with importance because their lives are so urgent to themselves. Was it Penn or the filmmakers who thought of the touch where Sam puts on a false mustache in the airport parking lot. What for? Nobody knows who he is or what he looks like, and if his plan succeeds there will be no Sam Bicke left, mustache or not.

Penn shows him always on the outside. Kept out of his house. Turned away by the bank. Ineligible for the Black Panthers. The outsider at the office, listening to his boss and a coworker snickering about him. The only person he can confide in is Leonard Bernstein, whose music he admires. (The real Bernstein, who received tapes from the real Byck, was mystified to be attached however distantly to a hijacking plot.)

The Assassination of Richard Nixon is about a man on a collision course; given the stark terms in which he arranges right and wrong, he will sooner or later crack up. He hasn't a clue about appropriate behavior, about how others perceive him, about what may be right but is nevertheless impossible. The movie's title has one effect before we see it, and another afterward, when we can see the grandiosity and self-deceit that it implies. What really happens is that Sam Bicke assassinates himself.

Does the film have a message? I don't think it wants one. It is about the journey of a man going mad. A film can simply be a character study, as this one is. That is sufficient. A message might seem trundled in and gratuitous. Certainly our opinions of Nixon, Vietnam, and the Black Panthers are irrelevant; they enter the movie only as objects of Bicke's obsessions. We cannot help but sense a connection with another would-be assassin from the 1970s, another obsessed loner, Travis Bickle. Travis pours out his thoughts in journals; Sam uses tapes. They feel the need to justify themselves, and lack even a listener.

Assault on Precinct 13 ★ ★ ★

R, 109 m., 2005

Ethan Hawke (Jake Roenick), Laurence Fishburne (Marion Bishop), Drea de Matteo (Iris Ferry), Brian Dennehy (Jasper O'Shea), John Leguizamo (Beck), Jeffrey "Ja Rule" Atkins (Smiley), Maria Bello (Alex Sabian), Gabriel Byrne (Marcus Duvall). Directed by Jean-Francois Richet and produced by Pascal Caucheteux, Stephane Sperry, and Jeffrey Silver. Screenplay by James DeMonaco, based on the film by John Carpenter.

Assault on Precinct 13 is not so much a remake as a riff on an old familiar plot: The fort is surrounded, and the defenders have to fight off the attackers and deal with possible traitors in their midst. Howard Hawks did versions of this so often that after John Wayne starred for him in *Rio Bravo* (1959) and *El Dorado* (1966), he told Wayne he was sending over a script for *Rio Lobo,* and Wayne told him, "I'll make it, but I don't need to read it. We've already made it twice."

John Carpenter's 1976 film, made just before his famous *Halloween,* added some touches from George Romero's *Night of the Living Dead* and moved the action from a threatened sheriff's office in the Old West to a threatened police station in the inner city. Now French director Jean-Francois Richet takes essentially the same material and makes it work with strong performances and a couple of new twists.

Precinct 13, in this version, is scheduled to close forever at midnight. Burnt-out desk sergeant Jake Roenick (Ethan Hawke), still traumatized by the death of two partners, is on the graveyard shift with old-timer Jasper O'Shea (Brian Dennehy), who in a revelation fraught with omens announces he will soon retire. Also in the station is the buxom secretary Iris (Drea de Matteo).

There's basically nothing for them to do except for Jake to pop some more painkillers and chase them with booze from the office bottle. Then everything changes. An ubercriminal named Bishop (Laurence Fishburne) has been arrested, and is being transported by police bus with some other detainees, including the motormouth Beck (John Leguizamo), a crew-cut girl crook (Aisha Hinds), and a counterfeiter named Smiley (Jeffrey Atkins, a.k.a Ja Rule). It's New Year's Eve, a Dark and Stormy Night, the highway is blocked by an accident, the officers on the bus decide to dump the prisoners at Precinct 13, and then things get dicey when it appears that Bishop's men are determined to break him free. It's up to Jake to pull himself together and command the defense of the surrounded station; he can't call for help because the phones, cell phones, and radios are all conveniently inoperable—all because of the Dark and Stormy, etc., I think.

Turns out the forces surrounding the station are not quite who they seem, ratcheting up the level of interest and danger, and providing Gabriel Byrne with one of his thankless roles in which he is hard, taciturn, and one-dimensional enough to qualify for Flatland. Never mind; an interesting dynamic develops inside the station, especially after Jake's psychiatrist, Alex Sabian (Maria Bello), comes to visit, leaves for home, has to return to the station because of the Dark, etc., and ends up as part of the defense team. Also recruited are the prisoners, who must fight for their own lives alongside the cops who have imprisoned them.

All classic and airtight, and handled by Richet with economy and a sturdy clarity of action; he doesn't go overboard with manic action scenes. There are, however, a few plot points that confused me. One is the way a forest seems to materialize near the station, which seemed in an overhead shot to be in an urban wasteland. My other problem is with a character who, in order to be who he is and what he is, would have to have known that Bishop would end up at Precinct 13, even though Bishop clearly ends up there by accident. Oh, and a tunnel turns up at a convenient moment, as tunnels so often do.

Problems like these amuse me with the nerve shown in trying to ignore them. Everybody is in a forest in the middle of downtown Detroit? Okay, then everybody can hide behind trees. They're running down a long-forgotten sewage tunnel? Okay, but not so forgotten that it doesn't have electric lights. There's no way for that particular character to have prior knowledge of where Bishop would be, and no way for him to communicate plans that are essential to the outcome? Okay, then just ignore those technicalities, and concentrate on such delightful synchronicities as that John Wayne played characters named both Ethan and Hawk.

Asylum ★ ★

R, 90 m., 2005

Natasha Richardson (Stella Raphael), Ian McKellen (Peter Cleave), Marton Csokas (Edgar Stark), Hugh Bonneville (Max Raphael), Sean Harris (Nick), Gus Lewis (Charlie Raphael), Joss Ackland (Straffen), Robert Willox (Archer). Directed by David Mackenzie and produced by David E. Allen, Laurie Borg, and Mace Neufeld. Screenplay by Patrick Marber and Chrysanthy Balis, based on the novel by Patrick McGrath.

Asylum is well titled, since everyone in it is more or less crazy, mostly more. It's an overwrought Gothic melodrama that has a nice first act before it descends into shameless absurdity. To care about the story you would have to believe it, which you cannot, so there you are. Yet the movie is well made, and the actors courageously try to bring life into the preposterous story. Perhaps the original novel by Patrick McGrath held up better, or perhaps imagined images have a plausibility that gets lost when a movie makes them literal.

The story is set circa 1960 in a vast old asylum built in the Victorian era—one of those buildings looking like an architectural shriek. Max Raphael (Hugh Bonneville) has arrived to become the new superintendent; he brings his wife, Stella (Natasha Richardson), and their son, Charlie (Gus Lewis). All is not well in this family, but, then, nothing is right in the asylum, where the long-serving Peter Cleave (Ian McKellen) resents being passed over for Max's job. He's expected to serve as Max's sec-

ond-in-command, leading to acid one-liners that McKellen delivers like dagger thrusts:

Max: "May I remind you that I am your superior?"

Peter: "In what sense?"

Max and Stella seem separated by a vast emotional gulf. Charlie is not much loved by his parents. He finds a friend in one of the patients, Edgar (Marton Csokas), who becomes his buddy and sort of a father figure, which would be heartening if Edgar had not been declared insane after murdering his wife, decapitating her, and so on and so forth.

Edgar undertakes to rebuild a gardener's shed that Stella wants to make use of. Soon she is making use of it with Edgar. There is this to be said for Richardson: Required to play an asylum-keeper's wife who has sudden, frequent, and heedless sex with an inmate, she doesn't leave a heed standing.

Edgar's diagnosis is "severe personality disorder with features of morbid jealousy." With admirable economy, the movie eventually applies this diagnosis to just about everyone in it except little Charlie, who is way too trusting, and not just of Edgar. There are lots of scenes involving British twits who are well dressed but with subtly disturbing details about their haberdashery and styles of smoking. They sit or stand across desks from one another and exchange technical jargon that translates as, "I hate you and your kind." Meanwhile, the cinematographer, Giles Nuttgens, makes the asylum into a place so large, gloomy, and foreboding that we suspect maybe *Eyes with No Face* is being filmed elsewhere on the premises.

If I'm spinning my wheels, it's because we've arrived (already) at a point in the plot where major developments start to tumble over one another in their eagerness to bewilder us. In my notes I find many entries beginning with such words as:

"Yes, but . . ."

"Why would . . ."

"Surely they . . ."

"Yet he . . ."

"How could . . ."

And then several one-word entries followed by too many exclamation points, such as:

"Drowns!!!"

But I do not want to spoil these developments and so will not reveal who drowns, except to say it's not every movie that reminds you of *Leave Her to Heaven*. There is also a question, some distance into the film, of the plausibility of certain living arrangements. Also of their wisdom, of course, but wisdom at this point has been left so far behind, it's churlish to double back for it.

The director, David Mackenzie, made *Young Adam*, also the story of a married woman attracted to a young and possibly dangerous man. The screenplay is cowritten by Patrick Marber, who wrote *Closer*, a movie about four-way sexual infidelity involving characters who deserved one another. Certainly the characters in *Asylum* richly earn their fates, and by the end we are forced to reflect that although they are indeed mad, at least the villain is acting reasonably under the circumstances.

ATL ★ ★ ★
PG-13, 105 m., 2006

Tip Harris (Rashad), Evan Ross (Anton "Ant"), Mykelti Williamson (Uncle George), Lauren London (New-New), Keith David (John Garnett), Jackie Long (Esquire), Jason Weaver (Teddy), Albert Daniels (Brooklyn), Antwan Andre Patton (Marcus). Directed by Chris Robinson and produced by Dallas Austin, Jody Gerson, James Lassiter, and Will Smith. Screenplay by Tina Gordon Chism, based on a story by Antwone Fisher.

Since their parents died in a car crash, Rashad and Anton have been living with their Uncle George, or maybe he's been living with them, since it was their parents' house. Rashad is seventeen, a high school senior, working part time to save money for his kid brother "to make it out of here"—out of their poor black neighborhood in Atlanta. Anton, known as "Ant," sees a faster route, standing on a corner selling drugs for a local dealer.

But no, *ATL* isn't a drug movie, and it doesn't send its characters on a harrowing journey into danger. It's a film about growing up and working, about falling in love, about planning for your future, and about the importance of friends. For Rashad (Tip Harris),

the best day of the week is Sunday because that's when he and three friends head for the Cascade, a roller rink where they show off with intricately choreographed moves on the floor.

Rashad's friends are Esquire (Jackie Long), Teddy (Jason Weaver), and Brooklyn (Albert Daniels). They're solid and will last for a lifetime. Esquire, who has top grades, is a waiter at a country club, where he meets the black millionaire John Garnett (Keith David). He needs a letter of recommendation to go with his Ivy League scholarship application. Garnett is happy to give him one and to invite the smart, polite kid to his mansion on the other side of town. And that's when . . .

But let's back up to New-New (Lauren London). Rashad meets her at the Cascade, they like each other, they start spending time together, and it looks like love. But there is something she doesn't tell him—although she almost does, before he interrupts her. I'm not going to reveal her secret, except to say that it threatens to sink their romance and their trust in each other. And for a while it looks like it may destroy Rashad's friendship with Esquire.

What this plot outline doesn't describe is the warmth and heart of *ATL*, which is about good kids more or less raising themselves. Uncle George is not a bad man, and at forty-one he has been a janitor long enough to plead with his nephews to get themselves an education. But when he finds out Ant (Evan Ross) is selling drugs, his immediate reaction is pragmatic: "We can always use some money in this house." Rashad is a lot more disturbed and takes action.

But even before that, the movie offers an unusual portrait of the fourteen-year-old as drug dealer. Yes, he works for a guy with a big, expensive car (the rumbles of the sound system are an advance warning system). But Ant's own job is to stand on a corner, hour after hour, lonely, cold, hungry, scared, not making much money and then getting that stolen. The movie is lacking the false sense of empowerment that sometimes seems to surround drugs in the movies.

Apart from its other qualities, which are real, the movie has a lot of music. The director, Chris Robinson, has made many music videos, and two of his actors are rap artists: Tip Harris records as T.I. (and did a lot of the sound track) and Antwon Andre Patton records as Big Boi. Their music, plus the mix at the Cascade, creates a sound track that drives the movie, especially in the roller-skating scenes, which are choreographed to make the rink look like a magical place. And yes, there is a Cascade in Atlanta and it's just as popular as it seems in the movie. I know this because my wife is visiting relatives there and they took her to the Cascade, and she called me half an hour ago and was having a great time. Small world.

The screenplay, by Tina Gordon Chism, is based on a story by Antwone Fisher, and do I have to say, yes, *that* Antwone Fisher? I doubt *ATL* is as autobiographical as his 2002 film, but it reflects lives of focus and determination; Rashad and his friends *are* young and sometimes foolish and like to party, but they're also smart and determined to survive and prevail. That's why Rashad can't understand it when ... well, you'll find out if you see the film.

What I liked most was its unforced, genuine affection for its characters. Rashad likes his friends, and so do we. He realizes Uncle George is not a paragon, but Mykelti Williamson has a strong scene where he defends his life from his point of view. He's forty-one, no wife, pushing a broom, trying to hold a home together for two nephews he didn't ask for, and he's doing his best. I sense that somewhere in the film, if we know where to look, maybe in the support of Uncle George, the friendships involving Rashad, Esquire, and New-New, we can find clues about how Antwone Fisher evolved from a kid with a shaky future into a screenwriter with a big one.

The Aviator ★ ★ ★ ★
PG-13, 166 m., 2004

Leonardo DiCaprio (Howard Hughes), Cate Blanchett (Katharine Hepburn), Kate Beckinsale (Ava Gardner), Alec Baldwin (Juan Trippe), John C. Reilly (Noah Dietrich), Alan Alda (Senator Brewster), Gwen Stefani (Jean Harlow), Kelli Garner (Faith Domergue), Adam Scott (Johnny Meyer), Ian Holm (Professor Fitz), Danny Huston (Jack Frye), Jude Law (Errol Flynn), Matt Ross (Glenn Odekirk), Edward Herrmann (Joseph Breen). Directed by Martin Scorsese and produced by Michael Mann, Sandy Climan, Graham King, and Charles Evans Jr. Screenplay by John Logan.

Howard Hughes in his last two decades sealed himself away from the world. At first he haunted a penthouse in Las Vegas, and then he moved to a bungalow behind the Beverly Hills Hotel. He was the world's richest man, and with his billions bought himself a room he never left.

In a sense, his life was a journey to that lonely room. But he took the long way around: As a rich young man from Texas, the heir to his father's fortune, he made movies, bought airlines, was a playboy who dated Hollywood's famous beauties. If he had died in one of the airplane crashes he survived, he would have been remembered as a golden boy. Martin Scorsese's *The Aviator* wisely focuses on the glory years, although we can see the shadows falling, and so can Hughes. Some of the film's most harrowing moments show him fighting his demons; he knows what is normal and sometimes it seems almost within reach.

The Aviator celebrates Scorsese's zest for finding excitement in a period setting, re-creating the kind of glamour he heard about when he was growing up. It is possible to imagine him wanting to be Howard Hughes. Their lives, in fact, are even a little similar: heedless ambition and talent when young, great early success, tempestuous romances, and a dark period, although with Hughes it got darker and darker, while Scorsese has emerged into the full flower of his gifts.

The movie achieves the difficult feat of following two intersecting story arcs, one in which everything goes right for Hughes, and the other in which everything goes wrong. Scorsese chronicled similar life patterns in *GoodFellas, Raging Bull, The King of Comedy, Casino,* actually even *The Last Temptation of Christ.* Leonardo DiCaprio is convincing in his transitions between these emotional weathers; playing madness is a notorious invitation to overact, but he shows Hughes contained, even trapped, within his secrets, able to put on a public act even when his private moments are desperate.

His Howard Hughes arrives in Los Angeles as a good-looking young man with a lot of money, who plunges right in, directing a World War I aviation adventure named *Hell's*

Angels, which was the most expensive movie ever made. The industry laughed at him, but he finished the movie and it made money, and so did most of his other films. As his attention drifted from movies to the airplanes in his films, he began designing and building aircraft, and eventually bought his own airline.

Women were his for the asking, but he didn't go for the easy kill. Jean Harlow was no pushover, Ava Gardner wouldn't take gifts of jewelry ("I am not for sale!"), and during his relationship with Katharine Hepburn, they both wore the pants in the family. Hepburn liked his sense of adventure, she was thrilled when he let her pilot his planes, she worried about him, she noted the growing signs of his eccentricity, and then she met Spencer Tracy and that was that. Hughes found Jane Russell and invented a pneumatic bra to make her bosom heave in *The Outlaw*, and by the end he had starlets on retainer in case he ever called them, but he never did.

DiCaprio is nobody's idea of what Hughes looked like (that would be a young Sam Shepard), but he vibrates with the reckless spirit of the man. John C. Reilly plays the hapless Noah Dietrich, his right-hand man and flunky, routinely ordered to mortgage everything for one of Hughes's sudden inspirations; Hughes apparently became the world's richest man by going bankrupt at higher and higher levels.

Scorsese shows a sure sense for the Hollywood of that time, as in a scene where Hughes, new in town, approaches the mogul L. B. Mayer at the Coconut Grove and asks to borrow two cameras for a big *Hell's Angels* scene. He already had twenty-four, but that was not enough. Mayer regards him as a child psychiatrist might have regarded the young Jim Carrey. Scorsese adds subtle continuity: Every time we see Mayer, he seems to be surrounded by the same flunkies.

The women in the film are wonderfully well cast. Cate Blanchett has the task of playing Katharine Hepburn, who was herself so close to caricature that to play her accurately involves some risk. Blanchett succeeds in a performance that is delightful and yet touching; mannered and tomboyish, delighting in saying exactly what she means, she shrewdly sizes up

Hughes and is quick to be concerned about his eccentricities. Kate Beckinsale is Ava Gardner, aware of her power and self-protective; Gwen Stefani is Jean Harlow, whose stardom overshadows the unknown Texas rich boy; and Kelli Garner is Faith Domergue, "the next Jane Russell" at a time when Hughes became obsessed with bosoms. Jane Russell doesn't appear in the movie as a character, but her cleavage does, in a hilarious scene before the Breen office, which ran the Hollywood censorship system. Hughes brings his tame meteorology professor (Ian Holm) to the censorship hearing, introduces him as a systems analyst, and has him prove with calipers and mathematics that Russell displays no more cleavage than a control group of five other actresses.

Special effects can distract from a film or enhance it. Scorsese knows how to use them. There is a sensational sequence when Hughes crash-lands in Beverly Hills, his plane's wingtip slicing through living room walls seen from the inside. Much is made of the *Spruce Goose*, the largest airplane ever built, which inspires Senator Owen Brewster (Alan Alda) to charge in congressional hearings that Hughes was a war profiteer. Hughes, already in the spiral to madness, rises to the occasion, defeats Brewster on his own territory, and vows that the plane will fly—as indeed it does, in a CGI sequence that is convincing and kind of awesome.

By the end, darkness is gathering around Hughes. He gets stuck on words, and keeps repeating them. He walks into a men's room and then is too phobic about germs to touch the doorknob in order to leave; with all his power and wealth, he has to lurk next to the door until someone else walks in and he can sneak through without touching anything. His aides, especially the long-suffering Dietrich, try to protect him, but eventually he disappears into seclusion. What a sad man. What brief glory. What an enthralling film—166 minutes, and it races past. There's a match here between Scorsese and his subject, perhaps because the director's own life journey allows him to see Howard Hughes with insight, sympathy—and, up to a point, with admiration. This is one of the year's best films.

B

Baadasssss! ★ ★ ★ ★
R, 108 m., 2004

Mario Van Peebles (Melvin Van Peebles), Joy Bryant (Priscilla), T. K. Carter (Bill Cosby), Terry Crews (Big T), Khleo Thomas (Mario Van Peebles), Ossie Davis (Grandad), David Alan Grier (Clyde Houston), Nia Long (Sandra), Paul Rodriguez (Jose Garcia), Saul Rubinek (Howie), Len Lesser (Manny/Mort Goldberg). Directed by Mario Van Peebles and produced by Bruce Wayne Gillies, Dennis Haggerty, G. Marq Roswell, and Van Peebles. Screenplay by Van Peebles and Haggerty, based on the book by Van Peebles.

I want to show all the faces that Norman Rockwell never painted.
—Melvin Van Peebles

It would be nice if movies were always made the way they are in Truffaut's *Day for Night*, with idealism and romance, or Minnelli's *The Bad and the Beautiful*, with glamour and intrigue. But sometimes they are made the way they are in Mario Van Peebles's *Baadasssss!*, with desperation, deception, and cunning. Here is one of the best movies I've seen about the making of a movie—a fictionalized eyewitness account by Mario of how and why his father, Melvin Van Peebles, made *Sweet Sweetback's Baadasssss Song*, a landmark in the birth of African-American cinema.

The original 1971 movie was scruffy and raw, the story of a man born in a brothel and initiated to sex at the age of twelve, who grows up as an urban survivor, attacks two racist cops, and eludes capture. That Sweetback got away with it electrified the movie's first audiences, who were intrigued by ad lines like "Rated X by an All-White Jury." Although it was not an exploitation film, it was credited by *Variety* with creating "blaxploitation," a genre that gave us Pam Grier, Shaft, Superfly, and a generation of black filmmakers who moved into the mainstream.

That a big-budget action film is unthinkable today without a black costar is a direct consequence of Melvin Van Peebles's $150,000 fly-by-night movie. *Sweet Sweetback* did astonishing business, proving that a viable market existed for movies made by, for, and about blacks. When the movie opened at the Oriental Theater in Chicago, the marquee proclaimed: "The Oriental Is Yo-riental Now!"

Mario Van Peebles was thirteen when the movie was being made, and was pressed into service by his father to play Sweetback as a boy. That involved a scene with a hooker in the brothel that still, today, Mario must feel resentment about, since in *Baadasssss!* he makes a point of showing that some of the crew members and his father's girlfriend, Sandra (Nia Long), objected to it. But Melvin was a force of nature, a cigar-chewing Renaissance man who got his own way. Only sheer willpower forced the production ahead despite cash and personnel emergencies, and *Sweet Sweetback* is like a textbook on guerrilla filmmaking.

Aware that he could not possibly afford to pay union wages (there were days when he could pay no wages at all), Melvin disguises the production as a porn film to elude union rules. The day the union reps visit the set is the day he shoots a sex scene—a little more explicit, of course, than the one he would use in the movie. Determined to have a crew that included at least 50 percent minorities (in an industry where most crews were all white), he trained some of them on the job. At the end of *Baadasssss!*, a white sound man has hired his assistant, a tough black street guy who doubles as security, to be his partner; that detail, like most of the film, is based on fact. Surveying the set, he observes, "No crew has ever looked like this."

Mario plays his own father in the movie, and Khleo Thomas plays Mario. It's clear that (the real) Mario admires his father while at the same time harbors some resentment against his old man's strong-willed, single-minded treatment of people. We see Melvin bouncing checks, telling lies, roughing up a crew member who wants to quit, and even getting a free shot courtesy of the Los Angeles Fire Department when their trucks respond to an alarm for a car fire. The car was blown up for a scene in the movie, and Melvin kept the cameras rolling to get the firemen for free.

As a director, Mario keeps the large cast alive, from Melvin's alluring, exasperated assistant, Priscilla (Joy Bryant), to his long-suffering agent, Howie (Saul Rubinek), his hard-pressed producer, Clyde Houston (David Alan Grier), and Bill Cosby (T. K. Carter), whose $50,000 check bailed out Melvin at a crisis point. There is a double role for Len Lesser as Manny and Mort Goldberg, the dubious Detroit exhibitors who premiere *Sweetback* and are ready to close it after one screening, until they see the lines in front of the theater.

Mario could make another movie about the rest of his father's life, which has included being an officer in the U.S. Air Force, making art films in Paris, working as a trader on Wall Street, composing, painting, winning eleven Tony nominations for Broadway plays, and winning the French Legion of Honor. The last shot in the film is a wink and a cloud of cigar smoke from this living legend, now seventy-one.

What's fascinating is the way Mario, working from his father's autobiography and his own memories, has somehow used his firsthand experience without being cornered by it. He keeps a certain objectivity in considering the character of Melvin, seeing him as brave and gifted and determined, but also as a hustler who gets his movie made, in the words of Malcolm X, "by any means necessary." He steps on toes, hurts feelings, expects sacrifices, doesn't hesitate to use his own son in a scene that no professional child actor would have been allowed to touch.

To one degree or another, all low-budget films are like this one, with cast and crew members bludgeoned into hard work at low pay in the service of the director's ego. Mario Van Peebles captures the elusive sense of family that forms on a movie set, the moments of despair, the times when it seems impossible to continue, the sexual intrigue and (always) the bitching over the food. *Sweet Sweetback's Baadasssss Song* was historically a film of great importance, but in another sense it was just another low-rent, fly-by-night production. *Baadasssss!* manages to get both of those aspects just about right.

Note: This film's original title was How to Get the Man's Foot Outta Your Ass.

Bad Education ★ ★ ★ ½
NC-17, 104 m., 2004

Fele Martinez (Enrique Goded), Gael Garcia Bernal (Ignacio/Zahara), Daniel Gimenez Cacho (Father Manolo), Lluis Homar (Mr. Berenguer), Javier Camara (Paquito), Nacho Perez (Young Ignacio), Raul Garcia Forneiro (Young Enrique). Directed by Pedro Almodóvar and produced by Agustin Almodóvar and Pedro Almodóvar. Screenplay by Pedro Almodóvar.

I've just thrown out the first 500 words of my review and am starting again with a sense of joy and release. I was attempting to describe the plot of *Bad Education*. It was quicksand and I was sinking fast. You and I have less than 1,000 words to spend together discussing this fascinating film, and not only would the plot take up half of that, but if I were by some miracle to succeed in making it clear, that would only diminish your pleasure. This is a movie we are *intended* to wander around in. It begins in the present with a story about the past, presents that story as a film within the film, and then, if I am not mistaken, there is a paradoxical moment when the two categories leak into each other. It's like *Citizen Kane*, where the memories of one character curiously contain the memories of another.

So there's 152 words right there, and my guess is, you're thinking the hell with it, just tell us what it's about and if it's any good. Your instincts are sound. Pedro Almodóvar's new movie is like an ingenious toy that is a joy to behold, until you take it apart to see what makes it work, and then it never works again. While you're watching it you don't realize how confused you are, because it either makes sense from moment to moment or, when it doesn't, you're distracted by the sex. Life is like that.

The story, which I will not describe, involves a young movie director named Enrique (Fele Martinez) who is visited one day by Ignacio (Gael Garcia Bernal). Ignacio has written a story he wants Enrique to read. Enrique would ordinarily not be interested, but he learns that his visitor is *the* Ignacio—the boy who was his first adolescent love, back in school, and that the story is set in their school days and involves Ignacio being sexually abused by a priest at the school. Indeed, he permitted the abuse in order to get Enrique out of some trouble: "I sold myself for the first time that night in the sacristy."

That is all of the story you will hear from me, although to fan your interest I will note that Gael Garcia Bernal, an actor who is turning out to be as versatile as Johnny Depp, portrays a drag queen in the movie, and does it so well that if he had played Hephaistion, Alexander would have stayed at home in Macedonia and they could have opened an antique shop, antiquities being dirt cheap at the time.

Almodóvar loves melodrama. So do I. "Lurid" for me is usually a word of praise. The film within the film allows Almodóvar to show transgressive sexual behavior at a time during Franco's fascist regime in Spain, when it was illegal and so twice as exciting. There is enough sex in the movie to earn it an NC-17 rating, although not enough to make it even distantly pornographic. You see hands and heads moving and it's up to you to figure out why.

Sex is a given in an Almodóvar movie, anyway. It's what his characters do. His movies are never about sex but about consequences and emotions. In *Bad Education*, he uses straight and gay (and for that matter, transvestite and transsexual) as categories that the "real" characters and the "fictional" characters use as roles, disguises, strategies, deceptions, or simply as a way to make a living. There's no doubt in my mind that Almodóvar screened Hitchcock's *Vertigo* before making the movie, and was fascinated by the idea of a man asking a woman to pretend to be the woman he loves, without knowing she actually *is* the woman he loves. When she's not playing that woman she's giving a performance—in his life, although it works the other way around in hers.

In Almodóvar's story, the Hitckcockian identity puzzle is even more labyrinthine, because the past depicted in Ignacio's screenplay is not quite the past either Ignacio or Enrique remembers, and, for that matter, although Enrique loved Ignacio only fifteen years ago, he doesn't think Ignacio looks much like Ignacio anymore. "Zahara," the drag queen, begins to take on a separate identity of his or her own, and then the guilty priest turns up with his own version of events.

Almodóvar wants to intrigue and entertain us, and he certainly does, proving along the way that Gael Garcia Bernal has the same kind of screen presence that Antonio Banderas brought to Almodóvar's earlier movies. For that matter, as Zahara, he also has the kind of presence that Carmen Maura brought. Whether Almodóvar has a message, I am not

quite sure. The movie is not an attack on sexually abusive priests, nor does it have a statement to make about homosexuality, which for Almodóvar is no more of a topic than heterosexuality is for Clint Eastwood. I think it's really more about erotic role-playing: about the roles we play, the roles other people play, and the roles we imagine them playing and they imagine us playing. If Almodóvar is right, some of our most exciting sexual experiences take place entirely within the minds of other people.

Bad News Bears ★ ★ ★
PG-13, 111 m., 2005

Billy Bob Thornton (Morris Buttermaker), Greg Kinnear (Roy Bullock), Marcia Gay Harden (Liz Whitewood), Sammi Kane Kraft (Amanda Whurlitzer), Jeffrey Davies (Kelly Leak), Carter Jenkins (Joey Bullock). Directed by Richard Linklater and produced by J. Geyer Kosinski and Linklater. Screenplay by John Requa and Glenn Ficarra, based on a screenplay by Bill Lancaster.

Billy Bob Thornton stages a head-on collision between two previous roles in *Bad News Bears*, a movie in which he plays, and I quote, "a drunk who makes a living killing rats to live in a trailer." The movie is like a merger of his ugly drunk in *Bad Santa* and his football coach in *Friday Night Lights*, yet he doesn't recycle from either movie; he modulates the manic anger of the Santa and the intensity of the coach and produces a morose loser whom we like better than he likes himself.

The movie, directed by Richard Linklater, is a fairly faithful remake of the 1976 film starring Walter Matthau, which inspired sequels starring William Devane and Tony Curtis. They had strengths of their own, but following Matthau's boozy vulgarian was not one of them. Thornton's performance is obviously fond of the Matthau approach but finds a weary sadness in Coach Morris Buttermaker, who made it out of the minor leagues long enough to play in one major league game.

His team, the Bears, exists only because of a lawsuit filed by attorney Liz Whitewood (Marcia Gay Harden), who believes the Little League discriminates; she files a class-action suit demanding that the league accept all players. The Bears end up with bad players in several categories: a black kid, two Spanish speakers, an Indian, a kid almost too little to hold the bat, and another one in a motorized wheelchair. What they have in common is not their minority status, but their inability to play the game.

They revived my own childhood memories of Little League, which I hated; it was a meritocracy in which good players were heroes and I was pointed toward right field with the hope that I would just keep on walking. Well, of course it was a meritocracy. Sports involves winning, and winning involves skills. What I could never figure out was how some kids had always been good at sports and others would never be any good, no matter how hard they tried: Kids like me, so nearsighted that the approach of a ball had to be described to me by teammates.

If Matthau was a grumpy old drunk, Thornton descends still further into self-loathing; he's coaching only for the money, keeps his "nonalcoholic" beer can filled with bourbon, and recruits some of the kids to crawl under houses and spray dangerous chemicals. When Liz Whitewood thinks she smells booze on his breath, he uses the "nonalcoholic" line and points out he is driving. "That's right! Never drink and drive," she tells her son, Toby. Coach Buttermaker adds helpful details: "Stay away from crack, too. You'll wake up in prison married to some guy named Big Bear."

The progress of the story is predictable, as it is in all movies about underdogs. They are bad and will get better. In the case of the Bad News Bears, this process is aided when Buttermaker recruits his daughter, Amanda (Sammi Kane Kraft), from a failed marriage. She's a gifted pitcher. He also recruits a strong hitter named Kelly Leak (Jeffrey Davies), advises one kid to deliberately get hit by a ball in order to get on base, and another one to lie to his parents. Buttermaker is not a role model, and his private life is untidy; required to find a sponsor willing to pay for the Bears' uniforms, he recruits—well, it gets a big laugh.

The movie works on two levels. On the top level it's a dark but traditional PG-13 version of a kids' sports movie, with everything but the f-word in the dialogue. The plot leads inexorably up to the last inning of the final game; we know the routine.

On a more insidious level, the movie suggests that America has embraced a new approach to winning. Where sportsmanship and fair play once counted for something, success now often includes lying, cheating, and stealing, as demonstrated in criminal trials sending millionaire executives off to prison in chains.

Whether Coach Buttermaker develops better values by the end of the film, I will leave for you to discover. Thornton, in the opening and middle innings, displays a nice touch for cynical vulgarity. His archenemy in the league is Coach Bullock (Greg Kinnear), whose Yankees, like the real ones, usually win. Bullock, however, is not a paragon compared to Buttermaker, but vile in his own right, and really tough on his own kid. He's actually more in the tradition of Vince Lombardi ("Winning isn't everything; it's the only thing") than Buttermaker ("Baseball. Once you love it, it doesn't always love you back. It's like dating a German chick"). When he does finally edge toward a change of heart, it involves replacing false phony team spirit with real phony team spirit.

That the movie lacks the evil genius of *Bad Santa* is perhaps inevitable; you couldn't put a character as misogynistic and vulgar as Billy Bob's Santa in a movie where he's surrounded by kids. There's a limit. But Buttermaker does his best to be politically incorrect ("You guys are acting like Helen Keller at a piñata party"), and when it comes time for him to utter his big inspirational speech, it is grounded in dour reality.

What I liked most about the movie, I think, is that it undermines the self-congratulatory myths we cultivate about sports in America. It writes the obituary of good sportsmanship. Grantland Rice wrote, "It's not whether you win or lose; it's how you play the game," to which, according to the *Baseball Almanac,* celebrated baseball team owner Gene Autry replied: "Grantland Rice can go to hell as far as I'm concerned."

Note: The language in the movie pushes the limits of the PG-13 rating.

The Ballad of Jack and Rose ★ ★ ★
R, 111 m., 2005

Daniel Day-Lewis (Jack), Camilla Belle (Rose), Catherine Keener (Kathleen), Paul Dano (Thaddius), Ryan McDonald (Rodney), Jena Malone (Red Berry), Beau Bridges (Marty

Rance). Directed by Rebecca Miller and produced by Lemore Syvan. Screenplay by Miller.

The Ballad of Jack and Rose is the last sad song of 1960s flower power. On an island off the East Coast, a craggy middle-aged hippie and his teenage daughter live alone in the remains of a commune. A generator is powered by wind. There is no television. Seaweed fertilizes the garden. They read. He homeschools her. They divide up the tasks. When Rose looks at Jack, her eyes glow with worship, and there is something wrong about that. When they lie side by side on the turf roof of their cottage, finding cloud patterns in the sky, they could be lovers. She is at an age when her hormones vibrate around men, and there is only one in her life.

Rebecca Miller's film is not about incest, but it is about incestuous feelings, and about the father's efforts, almost too late, to veer away from danger. Jack (Daniel Day-Lewis) is a fierce idealist who occasionally visits the other side of the island to fire shotgun blasts over the heads of workers building a housing development. Rose (Camilla Belle) admires him as her hero. "If you die, then I'm going to die," she tells him. "If you die," he says, "there will have been no point to my living."

This is not an academic discussion. He's had a heart attack, and he may die. She regularly takes away his home-rolled cigarettes, but out of her sight he's a chain-smoker, painfully thin, his idealistic serenity sometimes revealing a fierce anger just below the surface. He hates the developer (Beau Bridges) who is building the new homes on what Jack believes are wetlands: "That's not a house. It's a thing to keep the TV dry," he says, and, "They all want to live in places with people exactly like themselves, and have private police forces to keep their greedy little children safe."

Jack is being forced to think about the future. His daughter, he finally realizes, is too fixated on him. He visits the mainland, where for six months he has been dating Kathleen (Catherine Keener). He asks her to move with her two teenage boys out to the island and live with them: "It will be an experiment." Because he has a trust fund, he can write her a handsome check to make the move more practical. Kathleen, who lives at home with her mother,

needs the money and is realistic about that, while at the same time genuinely liking Jack. But how much does she know about him? She has never been to the island.

The film's best scenes involve the introduction of these three outsiders into the solitude of Jack and Rose. The sons, by different fathers, are different creatures. Rodney (Ryan McDonald) is an endomorphic sweetheart; Thaddius (Paul Dano) is a skinny pothead. "I'm studying to be a woman's hair dresser," Rodney tells Rose. "I wanted to be a barber, but men don't get enough pleasure out of their hair."

Having possibly fantasized herself as her father's lover, Rose reacts with anger to the newcomers and determines in revenge to lose her virginity as soon as possible. She asks Rodney to sleep with her, but he demurs ("I am sure my brother will be happy to oblige") and suggests a haircut instead. The short-haired Rose seems to have grown up overnight, and in reaction to her father's "experiment" offers him evidence of an experiment of her own.

The fundamental flaws in their idyllic island hideaway become obvious. As long as Jack and Rose lived in isolation, a certain continuity could be maintained. But the introduction of Kathleen as her father's lover, and the news that she is to start attending a school in town, cause Rose to rage against the loss of—what? Her innocence, or her ideas about her father's innocence?

Rebecca Miller, the writer and director, had a strong father of her own, the playwright Arthur Miller. She had a strong mother, too, the photographer Inge Morath. That she is now essentially the photographer (although the cinematography is by the visual poet Ellen Kuras) and her subject is a father and daughter may be less of a case of acting out her own childhood, as some writers have suggested, as identifying with her mother. It would be reckless and probably wrong to find literal parallels between Rebecca and Rose, but perhaps the film's emotional conflicts have an autobiographical engine.

Toward the end of the film, events pile up a little too quickly; there are poisonous snakes and sudden injuries, confrontations with the builder and medical concerns, and Jack resembles a lot of dying characters in the movies: His health closely mirrors the requirements of the story. By the end I had too much of a sense of story strands that had strayed too far to be neatly concluded, and there is an epilogue that could have been done without.

Despite these complaints, *The Ballad of Jack and Rose* is an absorbing experience. Consider the care with which Miller handles a confrontation between Jack and the homebuilder. Countless clichés are sidestepped when Jack finally sees their conflict for what it is, not right against wrong, but "a matter of taste." Is it idealistic to want a whole island to yourself, and venal to believe that other people might enjoy having homes there? The movie has a sly scene where Jack and Rose visit one of the model homes, which to Jack is an abomination and to Rose a dream.

Balzac and the Little Chinese Seamstress ★ ★ ½
NO MPAA RATING, 111 m., 2005

Xun Zhou (Little Seamstress), Kun Chen (Luo), Ye Liu (Ma), Shuangbao Wang (Village Chief), Zhijun Cong (Old Tailor), Hong Wei Wang (Four Eyes), Xiong Xiao (Mother of Four Eyes). Directed by Sijie Dai and produced by Lise Fayolle. Screenplay by Sijie Dai and Nadine Perront, based on the novel by Dai.

Balzac and the Little Chinese Seamstress is artfully designed to appeal to lovers of romance and books, but by the end of the film I was not convinced it knew much about either. The romance is sincere but lacking in passion, and the books have the strange result of sending the heroine away from both men who love her, and toward an unknown future in the big city.

The story takes place in 1971, when two city boys are sent to a remote mountain area to be "reeducated" under the Cultural Revolution. Luo (Kun Chen) confesses to the village chief that his father is a "reactionary dentist" who committed the sin of once treating Chiang Kai-shek. Ma (Ye Liu) is the child of intellectuals. Enough said. In the rural vastness, surrounded by breathtaking scenery, they stagger up a mountainside with barrels of waste and work in a copper mine.

The chief (Shuangbao Wang) takes a hard line at first. He goes through the young men's possessions, throwing a cookbook into the fire because in the village they will eat not bourgeois chicken but proletarian cabbage and corn. Ma has a violin, which the chief thinks is a toy until Ma begins to play Mozart. Everyone in the village is enchanted by the music, which the chief allows after being informed the composition is in honor of Chairman Mao. Nearby lives the little seamstress (Xun Zhou), with her ancient grandfather, the tailor (Zhijun Cong). The boys are attracted to her beauty and grace, and Luo courts her while Ma feels the same way.

The movie has been cowritten and directed by Sijie Dai, based on his own best seller in which the young men find a cache of forbidden Western books and read them aloud to the seamstress. They also teach her to read and write. The novels are by Balzac, Dumas, and Flaubert, whose *Madame Bovary* perhaps inspires the seamstress to one day leave the village and set out alone to walk to the city. The boys protest, passively, and let her go. To be sure, by this time she's been through harrowing experiences and is no longer the innocent we first met, but still: Is this a success story about literacy, or a failure to communicate?

Some of my favorite episodes from the novel are well visualized in the movie, including the way Luo and Ma travel to a nearby town, watch Korean films, and return to describe them to the villagers with great drama (making up most of the details). There's also the drama of Luo's sudden departure for the city, and an emergency that Ma helps the seamstress survive. But somehow the principal characters seem oddly remote from their own lives. We're not sure what literature means to them (aside from the sentimental assumption that it is redemptive). And we're not sure how deep the love between Luo and the seamstress can possibly be, considering the way they eventually part.

When the movie violently yanks us twenty years into the future for the epilogue, it is an unsatisfactory one in which one character shows his video footage of how the mountain district was flooded after a new dam was built, but the two men are never really clear about their feelings for the seamstress, or each other. There should have been more urgency at the time, more powerful memories afterward, and less complacency about the way the seamstress disappears from the story.

I do believe that books are redemptive. I believe that no child who can read and has access to books and the time to read them is without hope. That alone can change a life. But in *Balzac and the Little Chinese Seamstress*, the city boys go through the motions of transforming the seamstress through books, without the how and why. What does she think—do any of them think—about the strange foreign worlds described by Balzac and the others?

I am reminded of the scene in Truffaut's *The 400 Blows* where the young hero has a shrine to Balzac; *Seamstress* has a sort of shrine, too, a hidden grotto, but without Truffaut's perception about how his character changes. And after some initial hardships, the lives of the boys seem to become easier and filled with free time; there's no sense that the village chief represents a real danger to them, and a scene where Luo treats his tooth is badly acted and seems awkward. The elements in the story push all the right buttons, but the buttons don't seem to be wired to anything.

Barbershop 2: Back in Business ★ ★ ½
PG-13, 118 m., 2004

Ice Cube (Calvin Palmer), Cedric the Entertainer (Eddie), Sean Patrick Thomas (Jimmy James), Eve (Terri Jones), Troy Garity (Isaac Rosenberg), Michael Ealy (Ricky Nash), Leonard Earl Howze (Dinka), Harry Lennix (Quentin Leroux), Kenan Thompson (Kenard), Queen Latifah (Gina). Directed by Kevin Rodney Sullivan and produced by Alex Gartner, Robert Teitel, and George Tillman Jr. Screenplay by Don D. Scott.

Calvin's Barbershop is still in business as *Barbershop 2* opens, and the same barbers are at the same chairs, dealing with the usual customers discussing the day's events, and providing free advice on each other's lives. Just like the first movie, the shop is a talk show where everybody is the host. The talk could go on forever, coiling from current events to current romances, but then danger strikes: Nappy Cutz, a slick franchise haircut emporium, is opening across the street, and it may put the little neighborhood shop out of business.

This would be a disaster for Calvin (Ice Cube), whose operation is not single-mindedly devoted to profit. If it were, why would he give a prized chair to Eddie (Cedric the Entertainer), who hardly ever seems to cut any hair?

We learn the answer to that mystery in the course of this movie, along with a little of Eddie's background: We see him in a flashback, protecting the shop from rioters and winning the lifelong gratitude of Calvin's father.

Even back then, Eddie was on the conservative side, and again in this movie he delivers his trademark riffs against African-American icons. Although others in the shop cringed when they learned the D.C. sniper was black, for Eddie the contrarian that's something to be proud of: "He's the Jackie Robinson of crime." Alas, Eddie's I-Can't-Believe-He-Said-That act, which worked so well in the original *Barbershop*, seems a little perfunctory and obligatory this time, and it's often hard to understand what Cedric the E is saying; a little work in postproduction could have clarified his dialogue and allowed the zingers to land with more impact.

The plot, just like last time, involves a threat to the beloved neighborhood institution. An entrepreneur named Quentin Leroux (Harry Lennix) has purchased the property across the street and is erecting a huge Nappy Cutz emporium which, it is rumored, will even feature a basketball court. Calvin's could be doomed. And there's a larger issue, because the Chicago City Council, in the pockets of developers, seems bent on tearing down all the little neighborhood stores and moving in giant franchisers.

This could have headed in an interesting direction if the movie wanted to be political, but it doesn't (the talkative crowd in Calvin's never mentions a name like, oh, say, "Daley"). There is an arm's-length recognition of city hall in the character of Jimmy (Sean Patrick Thomas), who used to work in the shop but now has the inside track to a powerful alderman.

Calvin struggles with the idea of new competition, and meanwhile Terri (Eve), the only female barber, tries to decide if there's any future with Ricky (Michael Ealy), and Eddie himself is flummoxed by the arrival of a flame from his torrid past. The only white barber, Isaac (Troy Garity), remains convinced he is the blackest man in the shop, and the African-born barber Dinka (Leonard Earl Howze) has a futile crush on Eve. Jimmy's empty chair is taken over by Calvin's cousin Kenard (Kenan Thompson), who doesn't seem to understand the fundamental purpose of a barbershop, which is to provide a refuge, affirmation, confirmation, entertainment, and occasionally haircuts.

Next door in a beauty salon, stylist Gina (Queen Latifah) stands by for several almost self-contained supporting scenes, including an insult contest with Eddie in which it sounds like Eddie has won, and we would be sure if we could understand him. The Queen has a high-energy presence in the film, and just as well, because she'll star in *Beauty Shop*.

Did I like the film? Yeah, kinda, but not enough to recommend. The first film arrived with freshness and an unexpected zing, but this one seems too content to follow in its footsteps. Maybe *Beauty Shop* is the one to wait for, if they can find half a dozen high-powered foils for the Queen. Prediction: Terri (Eve) will get tired of everyone stealing her apple juice and move next door.

Basic Instinct 2 ★ ½
R, 113 m., 2006

Sharon Stone (Catherine Tramell), David Morrissey (Dr. Michael Glass), Charlotte Rampling (Milena Gardosh), David Thewlis (Roy Washburn), Hugh Dancy (Adam Towers), Indira Varma (Denise Glass), Heathcote Williams (Jakob Gerst). Directed by Michael Caton-Jones and produced by Moritz Borman, Joel B. Michaels, Mario Kassar, and Andrew G. Vajna. Screenplay by Leora Barish and Henry Bean.

Basic Instinct 2 resembles its heroine: It gets off by living dangerously. Here is a movie so outrageous and preposterous it is either a) suicidal or b) throbbing with a horrible fascination. I lean toward b). It's a lot of things, but boring is not one of them. I cannot recommend the movie, but . . . why the hell can't I? Just because it's godawful? What kind of reason is that for staying away from a movie? Godawful and boring, *that* would be a reason.

I have here an e-mail from Adam Burke, a reader who says: "I'm tired of reading your reviews where you give a movie three stars but make sure we know it isn't a great movie. You always seem to want to cover your ass, making sure we know you're smarter than the movie." He has a point. Of course, I am smarter than most movies, but so are you. That doesn't always prevent us from enjoying them. What

Burke doesn't mention is my other maddening tendency, which is to give a movie 1½ stars and then hint that it's really better than that.

Which brings us full circle to *Basic Instinct 2*. It has an audacious plot, which depends on a) a psychopathic serial killer being able to manipulate everyone in her life, or b) a woman who uncannily seems to be a psychopathic serial killer, while there is c) an alternative explanation for everything. True, a), b), or c) are equally impossible, but they're the only possibilities, I think. That leaves us feeling screwed at the end, which is how everyone in the film feels, so we cross the finish line together.

So much for the plot. Now for Sharon Stone. She may get some of the worst reviews in years, but she delivers the goods. Playing Catherine Tramell, a trashy novelist who toys with life, death, and sex while doing "research" for her next best seller, Stone brings a hypnotic fascination to her performance. You don't believe it, but you can't tear your eyes away. She talks dirty better than anyone in the movies. She can spend hours working her way through "every position in Masters and Johnson," she sighs wistfully, and forget all about it in a week, "but I'd remember it if a man died while having sex with me."

She says this, and lots of other things, to a shrink named Dr. Michael Glass (David Morrissey). He's appointed by the courts to evaluate her sanity after the car she is driving goes off a bridge at 110 mph and her passenger, a soccer star, drowns. In court we learn she has a "risk addiction" so severe that "the only limit for her would be her own death." They say that with any addiction you have to hit bottom. Death may be taking it too far.

Back on the street after unlikely legal technicalities, she comes salivating after Dr. Glass, who insanely accepts her as a client. Also involved in the tangled web are his ex-wife (Indira Varma); a gossip writer (Hugh Dancy) the ex-wife is currently bonking; a Freudian in a fright wig (Heathcote Williams); a fellow shrink (Charlotte Rampling) who warns Glass he is playing with fire; and a cop (David Thewlis) who sniffs around the case like a dog convinced that if liverwurst is not in the room at this moment, it was here not very long ago.

Some of these people die unpleasantly during the course of the film, possibly giving Tramell something to remember. Some of them are suspected of the murders. The details are not very important. What matters are the long scenes of dialogue in which Tramell mind-whacks Dr. Glass with speculations so detailed they rival the limerick about who did what, and with which, and to whom.

The Catherine Tramell role cannot be played well, but Sharon Stone can play it badly better than any other actress alive. The director, Michael Caton-Jones, alternates smoldering close-ups with towering dominatrix poses, and there's an extended Jacuzzi sequence in which we get the much-advertised full frontal nudity—which does not, somehow, manage to be full, frontal, and nude all at the same time. First a little nude, then a little full, then a little frontal, driving us crazy trying to load her simultaneously onto our hard drive.

Dr. Glass is played by Morrissey as a subdued, repressed basket case who listens to Tramell with a stony expression on his face. This is because he is either a) suppressing his desire to ravage her in lustful abandon, or b) suppressing delirious laughter. I'll bet there are outtakes of Stone and Morrissey cracking up. How else to respond to dialogue such as, "Don't take it so hard—even Oedipus didn't see his mother coming."

Basic Instinct 2 is not good in any rational or defensible way, but not bad in irrational and indefensible ways. I savored the icy abstraction of the modern architecture, which made the people look like they came with the building. I grinned at that absurd phallic skyscraper that really does exist in London. I liked the recklessness of the sex-and-speed sequence that opens the movie (and, curiously, looks to have been shot in Chicago). I could appreciate the plot once I accepted that it was simply jerking my chain. You can wallow in it.

Speaking of wallowing in the plot, I am reminded of another of today's e-mails, from Coralyn Sheridan, who tells me that in Parma they say, "The music of Verdi is like a pig: Nothing goes to waste." Those Parmesans.

Of Sharon Stone, what can I say except that there is within most men a private place that responds to an aggressive sexual challenge, especially when it's delivered like a lurid torch song, and Stone plays those notes like she worked out her own fingering.

Note No. 1: The last shot in the film is wrong. It should show only the eyes.

Note No. 2: My 1¹/₂-star rating is like a cold shower, designed to take my mind away from giving it four stars. I expect to hear from Adam Burke about this. ☞

Batman Begins ★ ★ ★ ★
PG-13, 140 m., 2005

Christian Bale (Bruce Wayne/Batman), Michael Caine (Alfred Pennyworth), Liam Neeson (Henri Ducard), Katie Holmes (Rachel Dawes), Morgan Freeman (Lucius Fox), Gary Oldman (Lieutenant James Gordon), Cillian Murphy (Dr. Jonathan Crane), Tom Wilkinson (Carmine Falcone), Rutger Hauer (Richard Earle), Ken Watanabe (Ra's Al Ghul). Directed by Christopher Nolan and produced by Larry J. Franco, Charles Roven, and Emma Thomas. Screenplay by David S. Goyer and Nolan.

Batman Begins at last penetrates to the dark and troubled depths of the Batman legend, creating a superhero who, if not plausible, is at least persuasive as a man driven to dress like a bat and become a vigilante. The movie doesn't simply supply Batman's beginnings in the tradition of a comic book origin story, but explores the tortured path that led Bruce Wayne from a parentless childhood to a friendless adult existence. The movie is not realistic, because how could it be, but it acts as if it is.

Opening in a prison camp in an unnamed nation, *Batman Begins* shows Bruce Wayne (Christian Bale) enduring brutal treatment as a prisoner as part of his research into the nature of evil. He is rescued by the mysterious Henri Ducard (Liam Neeson), who appoints himself Wayne's mentor, teaches him sword-fighting and mind control, and tries to enlist him in his amoral League of Shadows ("We burned London to the ground"). When Wayne refuses to kill someone as a membership requirement, Ducard becomes his enemy; the reclusive millionaire returns to Gotham determined to fight evil, without realizing quite how much trouble he is in.

The story of why he identifies with bats (childhood trauma) and hates evildoers (he saw his parents killed by a mugger) has been referred to many times in the various incarnations of the Batman legend, including four previous films. This time it is given weight and depth.

Wayne discovers in Gotham that the family Wayne Corp. is run by a venal corporate monster (Rutger Hauer), but that in its depths labors the almost-forgotten scientific genius Lucius Fox (Morgan Freeman), who understands that Wayne wants to fight crime and offers him the weaponry. Lucius happens to have on hand a prototype Batmobile, which unlike the streamlined models in the earlier movies is a big, unlovely juggernaut that looks like a Humvee's wet dream. He also devises a Bat Cape with surprising properties.

These preparations, Gotham crime details, and the counsel of the faithful family servant Alfred (Michael Caine) delay the actual appearance of a Batman until the second act of the movie. We don't mind. Unlike the earlier films, which delighted in extravagant special-effects action, Batman Begins is shrouded in shadow; instead of high-detail, sharp-edged special effects, we get obscure developments in fog and smoke, their effect reinforced by a superb sound effects design. And Wayne himself is a slow learner, clumsy at times, taking foolish chances, inventing Batman as he goes along ("People need dramatic examples to shake them out of fear and apathy, and I can't do that as a human being").

This is at last the Batman movie I've been waiting for. The character resonates more deeply with me than the other comic superheroes, perhaps because when I discovered him as a child he seemed darker and more grown-up than the cheerful Superman. He has secrets. As Alfred muses: "Strange injuries and a nonexistent social life. These things beg the question, what does Bruce Wayne do with his time?"

What he does is create a high profile as a millionaire playboy who gets drunk and causes scenes. This disappoints his friend since childhood, Rachel Dawes (Katie Holmes), who is now an assistant D.A. She and Lieutenant James Gordon (Gary Oldman), apparently Gotham's only honest cop, are faced with a local crime syndicate led by Carmine Falcone (Tom Wilkinson). But Falcone's gang is child's play compared to the deep scheme being hatched by the corrupt psychiatrist Dr. Jonathan Crane (Cillian Murphy), who in the tradition of Victorian alienists likes to declare his enemies insane and lock them up.

Crane's secret identity as the Scarecrow fits into a scheme to lace the Gotham water supply with a psychedelic drug. Then a superweapon will be used to vaporize the water, citizens will inhale the drug, and it will drive them crazy, for reasons the Scarecrow and his confederates explain with more detail than clarity. Meanwhile, flashbacks establish Wayne's deepest traumas, including his special relationship with bats and his guilt because he thinks he is responsible for his parents' mugging.

I admire, among other things, the way the movie doesn't have the gloss of the earlier films. The Batman costume is an early design. The Bat Cave is an actual cave beneath Wayne Manor. The Batmobile enters and leaves it by leaping across a chasm and through a waterfall. The early Bat Signal is crude and out of focus. The movie was shot on location in Chicago, making good use of the murky depths of Lower Wacker Drive (you may remember it from Henry: Portrait of a Serial Killer) and the Board of Trade building (now the Wayne Corp.). Special effects add a spectacular monorail straight down LaSalle Street, which derails in the best scene along those lines since The Fugitive.

Christian Bale is just right for this emerging version of Batman. It's strange to see him muscular and toned, after his cadaverous appearance in The Machinist, but he suggests an inward quality that suits the character. His old friend Rachel is at first fooled by his facade of playboy irresponsibility, but Lieutenant Gordon (destined to become in the fullness of time Commissioner Gordon) figures out fairly quickly what Batman is doing, and why. Instead of one villain as the headliner, Batman Begins has a whole population, including Falcone, the Scarecrow, the Asian League of Shadows leader Ra's Al Ghul (Ken Watanabe), and a surprise bonus pick.

The movie has been directed by Christopher Nolan, still only thirty-five, whose Memento (2000) took Sundance by storm and was followed by Insomnia (2002), a police procedural starring Al Pacino. What Warner Bros. saw in those pictures that inspired it to think of Nolan for Batman is hard to say, but the studio guessed correctly, and after an eight-year hiatus the Batman franchise has finally found its way.

I said this is the Batman movie I've been

waiting for; more correctly, this is the movie I did not realize I was waiting for, because I didn't realize that more emphasis on story and character and less emphasis on high-tech action was just what was needed. The movie works dramatically in addition to being an entertainment. There's something to it. ☞

The Baxter ★ ★
PG-13, 91 m., 2005

Michael Showalter (Elliot Sherman), Elizabeth Banks (Caroline Swann), Justin Theroux (Bradley Lake), Michelle Williams (Cecil Mills), Michael Ian Black (Ed), Peter Dinklage (Benson Hedges), Paul Rudd (Dan Abbott). Directed by Michael Showalter and produced by Daniela Taplin Lundberg, Galt Niederhoffer, Celine Rattray, and Reagan Silber. Screenplay by Showalter.

We are informed early in *The Baxter* that "the baxter" is a term for the guy in a movie who never gets the girl. This came as news to me, and I expect it will come as a shock to my friend Billy "Silver Dollar" Baxter, who always gets more or less what he wants, especially when he wants a good seat in a restaurant, which is usually harder to get than the girl.

The movie stars Michael Showalter as Elliot Sherman, who is the baxter, and has been told about baxters by his grandmother, which means baxters are entering their third generation of nobody ever having heard about them. Given the definition of a baxter, I guess that makes sense. The opening scene shows Elliot at the altar, about to marry a girl, when the man she truly loves bursts into the church and sweeps her away. That's the baxter: the guy left at the altar. I'm trying to think of the name of the baxter in *The Graduate*.

Elliot, it must be said, richly deserves to be a baxter. He is a certified public accountant who is engaged to a smart, hot, successful young woman named Caroline (Elizabeth Banks), who is playing well below her league. Maybe she wants to marry Elliot so she won't always be bothered by having a husband. But when her high-school honey, Bradley (Justin Theroux), turns up, she forgets all her reasons for wanting to marry Elliot, if there are any.

Actually, there aren't any. It is Showalter's misfortune to be releasing a movie about a boring and unlikable nerd only two weeks after the opening of *The 40-Year-Old Virgin*, which stars Steve Carell as a fascinating and lovable nerd. The thing you have to remember about movie nerds is that they're *movie* nerds; they're nerds for the convenience of the plot, but secretly fascinating. To be a good nerd in a movie, a nerd should resemble a baked potato, as I have so often heard them described by Billy "Silver Dollar" Baxter: "I've been tubbed, I've been scrubbed, I've been rubbed! I'm lovable, huggable, and eatable!"

There is, luckily, a baked potato in *The Baxter*. She is played by Michelle Williams, as Cecil Mills, the cute temp who is right there in Elliot's outer office and adores him and is perfect for him and is cuter than a button and almost as cute as two buttons. She glows in the movie. She glows so much, indeed, that I was waiting for her to dump Elliot, too. She's too good for a baxter.

There's also a hilarious supporting performance by Peter Dinklage as a wedding planner named Benson Hedges. His name reminds me of the year Edy Williams introduced me to her date on Oscar night: "I'd like you to meet Dean Witter." Dinklage, whom you may remember from *The Station Agent* (and if you don't, that is the next movie you should rent), plays a gay dwarf who not only steals every scene he's in but pawns it and buys more scenes and walks off with them, too. He has a little routine with cute guys on a city sidewalk that is like a meditation on hope and lust. Benson may be a Hedges, but he will never be a baxter.

The problem with *The Baxter* is right there at the center of the movie, and maybe it is unavoidable: Showalter makes too good a baxter. He deserves to be dumped. At some point everyone in the movie should have jilted him and gone off and started a movie of their own. If Elliot ever gets to the altar with Cecil, Benson Hedges the wedding planner should march in and sweep her away. Yes, he's gay, but maybe they could work out something. He could plan her into another wedding.

The Beat That My Heart Skipped ★ ★ ★
NO MPAA RATING, 107 m., 2005

Romain Duris (Thomas), Niels Arestrup (Robert), Linh-Dan Pham (Miao-Lin), Aure Atika

(Aline), Emmanuelle Devos (Chris), Jonathan Zaccaï (Fabrice), Gilles Cohen (Sami), Anton Yakovlev (Minskov). Directed by Jacques Audiard and produced by Pascal Caucheteux. Screenplay by Audiard and Tonino Benacquista, based on the film *Fingers* by James Toback.

The first time we see Thomas, he's carrying a sack squirming with movement. It contains rats he will set loose in a building he wants to buy cheaply; he has to persuade the current tenants to leave. Later, with two sidekicks, he smashes windows and intimidates squatters in another desirable property. This is how the real estate business operates at his level in Paris. He learned it from his father, Robert, a seedy soak with a big gut, who has been an insidious influence in his son's life.

A more beneficent influence, his mother, is dead. She was a concert pianist, and as a young man Thomas studied the piano seriously. One day he meets the impresario who booked his mother's concerts, and the man remembers his talent and invites him to audition. Thomas is stirred, and torn. He is working at a job he loathes, doing things that make him despise himself, but is reluctant to defy his father. He loves classical music but doubts his ability to regain whatever talent he once had.

This story, told in Jacques Audiard's *The Beat That My Heart Skipped*, will sound familiar to anyone who has seen *Fingers* (1978), the first film directed by James Toback, who himself has always been torn between his good and bad angels. The Toback film, filled with fierce energy and desire, starred Harvey Keitel, torn between Bach and brutality, as the son of a mafioso (Michael V. Gazzo).

The French movie is not a remake so much as a riff on the same material, seen in a more realistic, less emotionally extreme way. Thomas, played by Romain Duris with self-contempt that translates into coiled energy, is fully capable of violence. His anger may be fueled by frustration at the piano keyboard.

He hires a coach. This is Miao-Lin (Linh-Dan Pham), a Chinese pianist, newly arrived in Paris and without a word of French. They communicate through the music. In her own way she is as demanding and unforgiving as his father, forcing him to repeat passages again and again. Thomas's whole life comes down to

the inability to satisfy authority figures. After a long but unspecified period of practice, he is ready for his audition, but the impresario represents yet one more test he fears he will fail.

In a different kind of movie, Thomas and Miao-Lin would fall in love. There is certainly feeling between them, but unrealized; they are an intriguing mystery to each other. Thomas has an affair with the wife of one of his shady partners, but regards in puzzlement his father's new "fiancée," Chris (Emmanuelle Devos), who is deluded if she thinks she has a future with Robert. Yes, Robert (Niels Arestrup) exhibits her with pride, as proof that he is still the man he has always played for his son, but clearly he is a heart attack on hold, an overweight, florid-cheeked shambles with a yellow sport coat and tangled hair. He no doubt thinks his hair, probably dyed, preserves the dash he had in the 1960s, but it's a discouraged mop of worn-out bravado.

What hold does Robert have over his son? Why will Thomas do his dirty work? The times have bypassed Robert, as Thomas tries to explain when his dad has a deal that goes bad with a Russian mobster named Minskov (Anton Yakovlev). He tries to tell his father to stay clear of Minskov, to forget the bad deal and write off the loss; Minskov is dangerous and out of their league. But the father sits implacably in a series of shabby cafés, smoking and drinking and setting tests for his son.

The 1978 Toback film was crazier and edgier than this one; the young Keitel brought it a desperate energy, and Gazzo had a charisma that helped you understand why the son loved his father so. *The Beat That My Heart Skipped* is a darker and more downbeat enterprise, with a hero who is as conflicted, but not as mad, as the Toback original. There is nothing in this movie to match Toback's famous shot of Keitel crouched naked behind a piano, but there is a noir grunginess that is always convincing. The film seems to argue that a man who conducts his life like Thomas cannot successfully play classical music because he cannot feel its exaltation.

Audiard is a considerable filmmaker. His *Read My Lips* (2001), like this one cowritten with Tonino Benacquista, was a superb psycho-thriller involving a hearing-impaired office worker (again, Devos) who gets involved with an ex-con (Vincent Cassel) in a situation where lip-reading takes on a startling urgency. Both of these films occupy the meeting point between crime and middle-class respectability, and have central characters who are not prepared to live in both of those worlds, but cannot choose. *The Beat That My Heart Skipped* doesn't replace *Fingers*, but joins it as the portrait of a man reaching out desperately toward his dying ideals.

Beauty Shop ★ ★ ★
PG-13, 105 m., 2005

Queen Latifah (Gina Norris), Alicia Silverstone (Lynn), Andie MacDowell (Terri Green), Alfre Woodard (Miss Josephine), Mena Suvari (Joanne Marcus), Djimon Hounsou (Joe), Kevin Bacon (Jorge Christophe), Keshia Knight Pulliam (Darnelle), Paige Hurd (Vanessa), Bryce Wilson (James). Directed by Bille Woodruff and produced by Robert Teitel, George Tillman Jr., Queen Latifah, David Hoberman, Shakim Compere, and Elizabeth Cantillon. Screenplay by Kate Lanier and Norman Vance Jr.

Early in *Beauty Shop*, Queen Latifah asks her daughter if her pants make her butt look big. When the answer is "yes," she slaps it and says, "Good!" And means it. Latifah is profoundly comfortable with herself, and *Beauty Shop* is comfortable with itself. It isn't simply trying to turn up the heat under a *Barber Shop* clone, but to be more plausible (not a lot, but a little) in the story of a woman starting her own business. It's more of a human comedy than stand-up or slapstick.

Queen Latifah stars as Gina, recently arrived in Atlanta from Chicago (where she appeared briefly in *Barber Shop 2*). She's already the top stylist in an upscale salon run by the improbable Jorge Christophe, a streaked blond self-promoter who keeps Latifah from being the only queen in the movie. Jorge is over the top in every possible way, and you have to blink a couple of times before you realize he's being played by—Kevin Bacon?

It's very funny work, and sets up Gina for a big showdown where she walks out on Jorge and starts her own beauty shop. There's nothing terrifically original in the way she finds an old salon, remodels and repaints it, and staffs

it with a shampoo girl from Jorge's (Alicia Silverstone) and an array of expert and verbal hairdressers, most notably Miss Josephine (Alfre Woodard) and Darnelle (Keshia Knight Pulliam, from *Cosby*). But consider the scene where she applies for a bank loan, and gets it after she shows the loan officer what she should be doing with her hair.

It is a convention of these movies that the shop is under threat from a landlord, a developer, or another ominous menace. This time it is the jealous Jorge, bribing a corrupt city inspector to put Gina out of business, and later taking more drastic measures. The movie wisely doesn't treat the threats as the whole plot, and it's refreshing how most of the movie is essentially about the characters, their stories, their lives.

Gina, for example, is a widow raising her daughter, Vanessa (Paige Hurd), a promising pianist. The man who lives upstairs over the beauty shop is Joe (Djimon Hounsou), an African who is both an electrician and a pianist. That sets up a sweet romance that isn't the usual bawdiness, but kind of touching, especially since Hounsou has so much warmth as an actor.

Just as *Barber Shop* had one white barber (Troy Garrity), *Beauty Shop* has one white beautician (Silverstone, promoted from shampoo). Andie MacDowell plays a customer from Jorge's shop who makes a crucial trip across town to follow Gina, her favorite hairdresser, and Mena Suvari is another customer from the old shop, not so nice. Some of the other employees, including the outspoken Miss Josephine, came with the old shop; others walk in through the door, including Bryce Wilson as James, an ex-con truck driver who knows so much about braids that Gina hires him on the spot, setting off intense speculation in the shop about his sexuality.

The beauty of the *Beauty* movies is that they provide a stage for lively characters. Countless plays have been set in bars for the same reason. The format almost works like a variety show, allowing each character to get a solo, as when Woodard's Miss Josephine takes the floor for a passionate recital of Maya Angelou's "Still I Rise."

Presiding like a den mother and emcee, Queen Latifah exudes a quiet confidence that sort of hugs the movie, making it feel warmer than the *Barber Shop* films. *Beauty Shop* doesn't shout at us, not even when catastrophe strikes; it's more about choosing a goal, being confident you can get there, and having some fun along the way.

Because of Winn-Dixie ★ ★

PG, 105 m., 2005

AnnaSophia Robb (Opal), Jeff Daniels (Preacher), Cicely Tyson (Gloria Dump), Dave Matthews (Otis), Eva Marie Saint (Miss Franny). Directed by Wayne Wang and produced by Trevor Albert and Joan Singleton. Screenplay by Singleton, based on the novel by Kate DiCamillo.

Because of Winn-Dixie tells the story of a lonely girl with a distant father, who is adopted by a dog. The dog changes her life, helps her make friends, and gives her someone to confide in for the first time. All without doubt sweet and warmhearted, but there is another film with a similar story that is boundlessly better, and that is *My Dog Skip* (2000). Also with the lonely kid. Also with the dog who makes friends. Also with the dad who thinks the dog should go back to the pound.

The difference between the two films is that *My Dog Skip* is made with a complexity that appeals to adults as much as children, while *Because of Winn-Dixie* seems pretty firmly aimed at middle school and below. Its portrait of the adult world comes from storybooks, not life, and its small town is populated entirely by (1) eccentric characters, and (2) anonymous people seen from a distance.

The little girl is named Opal (AnnaSophia Robb). She is ten, and lives in a house trailer supplied rent-free to her dad, who preaches in a church that uses the corner convenience store. When Opal was three, her mother ran away from the family for reasons unknown. Preacher (apparently his only name) has been depressed ever since, and spends long hours gazing out the window and "working on a sermon."

He sends Opal to the Winn-Dixie supermarket, and while she's there a dog runs up and down the aisles and is chased by countless clerks, who skid into piles of cans and knock over pyramids of boxes; destruction during a supermarket chase is the indoor shopping equivalent of the Fruit Cart Scene. Opal rescues the dog, claims it is hers, and names it Winn-Dixie.

Although both her dad and Mr. Alfred, the mean old man who runs the trailer park, want the dog to go to the pound, Opal stubbornly bonds with Winn-Dixie, and together they meet (1) Otis, played by Dave Matthews, who is the temporary clerk at the local pet store; (2) Gloria Dump, played by Cicely Tyson, who is blind and very wise; (3) Miss Franny, played by Eva Marie Saint, who is a fading southern belle with genteel airs; and (4) various local kids.

Otis takes out his guitar and sings her his story one day, in a nice scene. But is he really the clerk in the pet shop? What happened to the owner? And why, for that matter, does this pet shop stock ducks, chickens, pigs, and pigeons in addition to cats and dogs and hamsters? Is this a pet store, or an ark? Another local business, now defunct, once made Luttmuss Lozenges; when you put one in your mouth, you think it tastes like emotions. No surprise to me; I've always thought M&Ms tasted like uncertainty, Peppermint Patties like sarcasm, and Tootsie Rolls like sweet revenge.

Although the movie has heartfelt conversations about the absence of Opal's mother, and scenes in which dog ownership is viewed as a great philosophical consolation, the picture mainly meanders until a big party scene at Miss Gloria's, to which all of the characters are invited—even Preacher, who, true to the ancient tradition of movie fathers, arrives late but then recognizes that his daughter has done a good thing.

It is one of those parties you see only in the movies, where the people may be poor, but they have an unlimited budget for candles. Hundreds of them. Thousands, maybe, all over the yard outside Miss Gloria's house. Covered dishes are uncovered, and meanwhile the stage has been set for drama.

"We have to be sure Winn-Dixie doesn't get out during a thunderstorm," Opal says. "He might run away." This makes it absolutely certain there will be a thunderstorm, right in the middle of the party, and that Winn-Dixie will run away, and have to be searched for all over town, with Opal's little voice piping, "Winn-Dixie! Winn-Dixie!" until . . . well, until the thunderstorm clears as quickly as it sprang up, and the party resumes, and so on.

Because of Winn-Dixie doesn't have a mean bone in its body, but it's dead in the water. It was directed by Wayne Wang, who usually (how can I put this?) makes films for grown-ups *(The Joy Luck Club, Smoke, The Center of the World, Maid in Manhattan)*. Why did he choose this project? Why did he feel it had to be made? Did he screen *My Dog Skip* and realize he'd been dealt a weak hand? I don't know, and maybe I don't want to know.

Be Cool ★ ½
PG-13, 112 m., 2005

John Travolta (Chili Palmer), Uma Thurman (Edie Athens), Vince Vaughn (Raji), Cedric the Entertainer (Sin LaSalle), Andre 3000 (Dabu), Steven Tyler (Himself), Christina Milian (Linda Moon), Harvey Keitel (Nicki Carr), Danny DeVito (Martin Weir), The Rock (Elliot Wilhelm). Directed by F. Gary Gray and produced by Danny DeVito, David Nicksay, Michael Shamberg, and Stacey Sher. Screenplay by Peter Steinfeld, based on the novel by Elmore Leonard.

John Travolta became a movie star by playing a Brooklyn kid who wins a dance contest in *Saturday Night Fever* (1977). He revived his career by dancing with Uma Thurman in *Pulp Fiction* (1994). In *Be Cool*, Uma Thurman asks if he dances. "I'm from Brooklyn," he says, and then they dance. So we get it: "Brooklyn" connects with *Fever*, Thurman connects with *Pulp*. That's the easy part. The hard part is, what do we do with it?

Be Cool is a movie that knows it is a movie. It knows it is a sequel, and contains disparaging references to sequels. All very cute at the screenplay stage, where everybody can sit around at story conferences and assume that a scene will work because the scene it refers to worked. But that's the case only when the new scene is also good as itself, apart from what it refers to.

Quentin Tarantino's *Pulp Fiction* knew that Travolta won the disco contest in *Saturday Night Fever*. But Tarantino's scene didn't depend on that; it built from it. Travolta was graceful beyond compare in *Fever*, but in *Pulp Fiction* he's dancing with a gangster's girlfriend on orders from the gangster, and part of the point of the scene is that both Travolta and

Thurman look like they're dancing not out of joy, but out of duty. So we remember *Fever* and then we forget it, because the new scene is working on its own.

Now look at the dance scene in *Be Cool*. Travolta and Thurman dance in a perfectly competent way that is neither good nor bad. Emotionally they are neither happy nor sad. The scene is not necessary to the story. The filmmakers have put them on the dance floor without a safety net. And so we watch them dancing and we think, yeah, *Saturday Night Fever* and *Pulp Fiction*, and when that thought has been exhausted, they're still dancing.

The whole movie has the same problem. It is a sequel to *Get Shorty* (1995), which was based on a novel by Elmore Leonard just as this is based on a sequel to that novel. Travolta once again plays Chili Palmer, onetime Miami loan shark, who in the first novel traveled to Los Angeles to collect a debt from a movie producer, and ended up pitching him on a movie based on the story of why he was in the producer's living room in the middle of the night threatening his life.

This time Chili has moved into the music business, which is less convincing because, while Chili was plausibly a fan of the producer's sleazy movies, he cannot be expected, ten years down the road, to know or care much about music. Funnier if he had advanced to the front ranks of movie producers and was making a movie with A-list stars when his past catches up with him.

Instead, he tries to take over the contract of a singer named Linda Moon (Christina Milian), whose agent (Vince Vaughn) acts as if he is black. He is not black, and that's the joke, I guess. But where do you go with it? Maybe by sinking him so deeply into dialect that he cannot make himself understood, and has to write notes. Chili also ventures into the hip-hop culture; he runs up against a Suge Knight type named Sin LaSalle (Cedric the Entertainer), who has a bodyguard named Elliot Wilhelm, played by The Rock.

I pause here long enough to note that Elliot Wilhelm is the name of a friend of mine who runs the Detroit Film Theater, and that Elmore Leonard undoubtedly knows this because he also lives in Detroit. It's the kind of in-joke that doesn't hurt a movie unless you happen to know Elliot Wilhelm, in which case you can think of nothing else every second The Rock is on the screen.

The deal with The Rock's character is that he is manifestly gay, although he doesn't seem to realize it. He makes dire threats against Chili Palmer, who disarms him with flattery, telling him in the middle of a confrontation that he has all the right elements to be a movie star. Just as the sleazy producer in *Get Shorty* saved his own life by listening to Chili's pitch, now Chili saves his life by pitching The Rock.

There are other casting decisions that are intended to be hilarious. Sin LaSalle has a chief of staff played by Andre 3000, who is a famous music type, although I did not know that and neither, in my opinion, would Chili. There is also a gag involving Steven Tyler turning up as himself.

Be Cool becomes a classic species of bore: a self-referential movie with no self to refer to. One character after another, one scene after another, one cute line of dialogue after another, refers to another movie, a similar character, a contrasting image, or whatever. The movie is like a bureaucrat who keeps sending you to another office.

It doesn't take the in-joke satire to an additional level that might skew it funny. To have The Rock play a gay narcissist is not funny because all we can think about is that The Rock is not a gay narcissist. But if they had cast someone who was *also* not The Rock, but someone removed from The Rock at right angles, like Steve Buscemi or John Malkovich, then that might have worked, and The Rock could have played another character at right angles to himself—for example, the character played here by Harvey Keitel as your basic Harvey Keitel character. Think what The Rock could do with a Harvey Keitel character.

In other words: (1) Come up with an actual story, and (2) if you must have satire and self-reference, rotate it 90 degrees off the horizontal instead of making it ground-level. Also (3) go easy on the material that requires a familiarity with the earlier movie, as in the scenes with Danny DeVito, who can be the funniest man in a movie, but not when it has to be a movie other than the one he is appearing in.

Bee Season ★ ★ ★ ★
PG-13, 104 m., 2005

Richard Gere (Saul Naumann), Juliette Binoche (Miriam Naumann), Flora Cross (Eliza Naumann), Max Minghella (Aaron Naumann), Kate Bosworth (Chali), Justin Alioto (Kevin). Directed by Scott McGehee and David Siegel and produced by Albert Berger and Ron Yerxa. Screenplay by Naomi Foner Gyllenhaal, based on the novel by Myla Goldberg.

Bee Season involves one of those crazy families that cluster around universities: an intellectual husband who is clueless about human emotions, a wife who married him because she was afraid to be loved and he didn't know how to, a son who rebels by being more like his father than his father is, and a daughter who retreats into secret survival strategies. There are many movies about families sharing problems; in this one the members are isolated by them. They meet mostly at meals, which the father cooks and serves with a frightening intensity.

Like many families without centers, this one finds obsessions to focus on. Saul Naumann (Richard Gere) is a professor at Berkeley, specializing in Jewish theology and the Kabbalah. His wife, Miriam (Juliette Binoche), emotionally wounded by the early loss of her own parents, slips into the homes of strangers to steal small glittering things. Their teenage son, Aaron (Max Minghella), watches his father intimidate students with icy theological superiority and does the one thing best calculated to enrage him; he joins the Hare Krishnas. Their daughter, Eliza (Flora Cross), who is about twelve, seems to be trying to pass as unobserved and ordinary, but her inner life has a fierce complexity.

The father teaches Judaism and follows its forms, but his spiritual life is academic, not mystical. What no one in the family perceives is that Eliza is a genuine mystic, for whom the Kabbalah is not a theory but a reality. One of the things that Kabbalah believes is that words not only reflect reality but in a sense create it. God and the name of God are in this way the same thing.

How could this association enter into the life of a twelve-year-old in a practical way? Eliza finds out when she enters a spelling bee. Because she exists in the same world with words, because words create her world, she doesn't need to "know" how to spell a word. It needs merely to be evoked, and it materializes in a kind of vision: "I see the words." Although this gift gets her into the national finals, *Bee Season* is not a movie about spelling bees. It is a movie about a spiritual choice that calls everyone's bluff; it involves the sort of refusal and rebellion seen in that half-forgotten masterpiece *The Loneliness of the Long-Distance Runner* (1962).

Eliza is at the center of the film, and Cross carries its weight in a performance of quiet, compelling wisdom; the foreground character in the early scenes is Saul, the father. The members of his family swim in and out of focus. He is proud that Miriam is a scientist, in the sense that "my wife is a scientist," but does he know what enormous secrets she keeps from him? He is proud that his son is a gifted musician, and joins him in violin and cello duets. But Eliza is essentially invisible to Saul, because she has no particular accomplishments. Only when she wins a spelling bee does he start to focus on her, "helping" her train, pushing her to the next level, sitting proudly in the audience. He is proud not so much of her as of himself, for fathering such a prodigy.

The performance by Cross is haunting in its seriousness. She doesn't act out; she acts in. She suggests that Eliza has grown up in this family as a wise, often-overlooked observer, who keeps her own counsel and has her own values, the most important being her autonomy. In her father's manic kitchen behavior as he prepares and serves unwanted meals, she sees people-pleasing that exists apart from people who are pleased. In her fellow contestants in the spelling bees, she sees the same thing: Young people who are devoting their lives to mastering useless information for the glory of themselves and their parents. Yes, it is necessary to be able to spell in an ordinary sort of way, but to be able to spell every word is to aim for perfection, and perfection will drive you crazy, because our software isn't designed for it.

The movie, directed by Scott McGehee and David Siegel, is based on a novel by Myla Goldberg, unread by me. They made *Suture* (1993), a film about "identical" brothers played by actors of different races; you can deal with this apparent inconsistency by saying it doesn't matter—but in that case, why doesn't it? And their powerful *Deep End* (2001) starred Tilda Swinton as a mother scarcely less secretive than the Binoche character here.

Neither prepares us for *Bee Season*, which represents Eliza's decision to insist on herself as a being apart from the requirements of theology and authority, a person who insists on exercising her free will. This is a stick in the eye of her father. When people say they are "doing God's will," I am struck by the egotism of such a statement. What Eliza is doing at the end of *Bee Season* is Eliza's will. Does that make her God? No. It makes her Eliza.

Before Sunset ★ ★ ★ ½
R, 80 m., 2004

Ethan Hawke (Jesse), Julie Delpy (Celine). Directed by Richard Linklater and produced by Linklater and Anne Walker-McBay. Screenplay by Linklater, Julie Delpy, and Ethan Hawke.

Nine years have passed since Jesse and Celine met in Vienna and walked all over the city, talking as if there would be no tomorrow, and then promising to meet again in six months. "Were you there in Vienna, in December?" she asks him. Nine years have passed and they have met again in Paris. Jesse wrote a novel about their long night together, and at a book signing he looks up, and there she is. They begin to talk again, in a rush, before he must leave to catch his flight back to America.

Before Sunset continues the conversation that began in *Before Sunrise* (1995), but at a riskier level. Jesse (Ethan Hawke) and Celine (Julie Delpy) are over thirty now, have made commitments in life, no longer feel as they did in 1995 that everything was possible. One thing they have learned, although they are slow to reveal it, is how rare it is to meet someone you feel an instinctive connection with. They walk out of the bookstore and around the corner and walk, and talk, and director Richard Linklater films them in long, uninterrupted takes, so that the film feels like it exists in real time.

Before Sunset is a remarkable achievement in several ways, most obviously in its technical skill. It is not easy to shoot a take that is six or seven minutes long, not easy for actors to walk through a real city while dealing with dialogue that has been scripted but must sound natural and spontaneous. Yet we accept, almost at once, that this conversation is really happening. There's no sense of contrivance or technical difficulty.

Hawke and Delpy wrote the screenplay themselves, beginning from the characters and dialogue created the first time around by Linklater and Kim Krizan. They lead up to personal details very delicately; at the beginning they talk politely and in abstractions, edging around the topics we (and they) want answers to: Is either one married? Are they happy? Do they still feel that deep attraction? Were they intended to spend their lives together?

There is the feeling, as they discuss how their adult lives are unfolding, that sometimes the actors may be skirting autobiography. Certainly there is an unmistakable truth when Jesse, trying to describe what marriage is like, says, "I feel like I'm running a small nursery with someone I used to date." But the movie is not a confessional, and the characters don't rush into revelations. There is a patience at work, even a reticence, that reflects who they have become. They have responsibilities. They no longer have a quick instinctive trust. They are wary of revealing too much. They are grown-ups, although at least for this afternoon in Paris they are in touch with the open, spontaneous, hopeful kids they were nine years before.

Before Sunrise was a remarkable celebration of the fascination of good dialogue. But *Before Sunset* is better, perhaps because the characters are older and wiser, perhaps because they have more to lose (or win), and perhaps because Hawke and Delpy wrote the dialogue themselves. The film has the materials for a lifetime project; like the *7-Up* series, this is a conversation that could be returned to every ten years or so, as Celine and Jesse grow older.

Delpy worked often with Krzysztof Kieslowski, the Polish master of coincidence and synchronicity, and perhaps it's from that experience that *Before Sunset* draws its fascination with intersecting time lines. When Celine and Jesse parted, they didn't know each other's last names or addresses; they staked everything on that promise to meet again in six months. We find out what happened in Vienna in December, but we also find out that

Celine studied for several years at New York University (just as Delpy did) while Jesse was living there (just as Hawke was). "In the months leading up to my wedding, I was thinking of you," he tells her. He even thought he saw her once, in the deli at 17th and Broadway. She knows the deli. Maybe he did.

What they are really discussing, as they trade these kinds of details, is the possibility that they missed a lifetime they were intended to spend together. Jesse eventually confesses that he wrote his book and came to Paris for a book signing because that was the only way he could think of to find her again. A little later, in a subtle moment of body language, she reaches out to touch him and then pulls back her hand before he sees it.

All this time they are walking and talking. Down streets, through gardens, past shops, into a café, out of the café, toward the courtyard where she has the flat she has lived in for four years. And it is getting later, and the time for his flight is approaching, just as he had to catch the train in Vienna. But what is free will for, if not to defy our plans? "Baby, you are gonna miss that plane," she says.

Being Julia ★ ★ ½
R, 105 m., 2004

Annette Bening (Julia Lambert), Jeremy Irons (Michael Gosselyn), Michael Gambon (Jimmie Langton), Shaun Evans (Tom Fennel), Bruce Greenwood (Lord Charles), Juliet Stevenson (Evie), Rosemary Harris (Mrs. Lambert), Miriam Margolyes (Dolly de Vries), Lucy Punch (Avice Crichton), Thomas Sturridge (Roger Gosselyn). Directed by Istvan Szabo and produced by Robert Lantos. Screenplay by Ronald Harwood, based on the novel by W. Somerset Maugham.

Old Jimmie Langdon, the impresario who taught the young Julia Langdon much of what she knows about the world, refers at one point to "what civilians call the real world." Theater people know better. All the world's a stage, and Julia is but a player on it. At one point, when she's asked for a loan, she replies with the same speech she used earlier in a play. Her marriage is "in name only." Even her extramarital affair is a performance; her lover, Lord Charles, finally confesses, "I play for the other side." Her son, Roger, says: "You have a performance for everybody. I don't think you really exist."

In *Being Julia*, she departs from the playwright's lines and improvises a new closing act right there on the stage, and it's appropriate that her professional and personal problems should be resolved in front of an audience. Like Margo Channing, the Bette Davis character in *All About Eve*, Julia draws little distinction between her public and private selves. She lives to be on the stage, and when, at forty-five, she perceives that her star is dimming, she fights back with theatrical strategies.

Annette Bening plays Julia in a performance that has great verve and energy, and just as well, because the basic material is wheezy melodrama. *All About Eve* breathed new life into it all those years ago, but now it's gasping again. The film is based on *Theater*, a 1937 novel by W. Somerset Maugham that was not one of his few great works, and has been adapted by a director and a writer who have separately created much more important fictions about the theater. Istvan Szabo directed *Mephisto*, with its brilliant performance by Klaus Maria Brandauer as an actor who sells out to the Nazis to protect his career, and Ronald Harwood wrote *The Dresser*, one of the most knowledgeable of backstage plays.

Here they all seem to have followed Maugham into a soap opera. Bening is fresh and alive (is there another actress who smiles and laughs so generously and naturally?), but she's surrounded by stock characters. Jeremy Irons plays her husband and producer, Michael, who turns a blind eye to her lover, Lord Charles (Bruce Greenwood), and why should he not, since Charles actually decides to break up with her because of all the gossip—and isn't gossip surely the best reason to have an affair with an actress?

They are all in the middle of an enormously successful play, but Julia has tired of it, complaining that the world is too much for her, she is weary and bored, she thinks she may retire. Circling her like moons, reflecting her light, are not only Michael and Charles but her loyal dresser Evie (Juliet Stevenson), her hopeful lesbian admirer Dolly (Miriam Margolyes), and the ghost of old Jimmie (Michael Gambon), who advises for practical reasons that she sleep with her young leading man: "If

that doesn't improve your performance, then nothing will."

What happens instead is that she meets the callow young American theatrical accountant Tom Fennel (Shaun Evans), a man as exciting as the seed after which he is named. He's seen all of her plays—some of them three times!—and Julia is flattered, not so much by his praise as by sex with a man half her age. In a world with few secrets, Lord Charles frets: "I trust she doesn't tell the boy she loves him—that's always fatal."

She sort of does and it sort of is, especially after the arrival of the young ingenue Avice Crichton (Lucy Punch), in the Eve Harrington role. Not only does Avice feel warmly toward Tom, but she also sparks interest in old Michael, Julia's husband, whose genitals may be able to revive for a farewell tour.

All of this is fitfully entertaining, but it seems to be happening for the first time to only the Bening character. The others seem trapped in loops, as if they've traveled these clichés before. All comes to a head during rehearsals for a new play in which Avice seems to have better lines and staging than Julia. ("I'm going to give my all in this part!" she gushes to Julia, who replies, "Mustn't be a little spendthrift.") It's by departing from the staging and the lines, and improvising in an entirely different direction that Julia delivers Avice's comeuppance.

But it doesn't happen that way in the theater. An actor may improvise a line or two, or a bit of business, or communicate in an occult way with the audience, or if he's Groucho Marx or Alfie even address us directly, but is it possible to improvise an entire act with the other actors on stage, and somehow incorporate them in such a way that they're not left standing there and gawking at you? I don't think so. I think the movie leads up to a denouement that would work only if the improvisation (as it is here) were carefully scripted and rehearsed. There's never the feeling that poor Avice is really out to sea, because even her discomfiture seems carefully blocked.

I liked the movie in its own way, while it was cheerfully chugging along, but the ending let me down; the materials are past their sell-by date, and were when Maugham first retailed them. The pleasures are in the actual presence of the actors, Bening most of all, and the droll Irons, and Juliet Stevenson as the practical aide-de-camp, and Thomas Sturridge, so good as Julia's son that I wonder why he wasn't given the role of her young lover.

Benji: Off the Leash! ★ ★ ★
PG, 100 m., 2004

Benji (Puppy), Shaggy (Lizard Tongue), Nick Whitaker (Colby), Nate Bynum (Sheriff Ozzie), Chris Kendrick (Hatchett), Randall Newsome (Livingston), Duane Stephens (Sheldon), Christy Summerhays (Claire). Directed by Joe Camp and produced by Margaret Loesch and Camp. Screenplay by Camp.

Benji: Off the Leash! isn't one of the great dog movies, but it's a good one, abandoning wall-to-wall cuteness for a drama about a homeless puppy. And it sends a valuable message: Mongrels are just as lovable as pure breeds, or maybe in the case of Benji and Shaggy, the stars of this film, more so.

The movie resembles *Shiloh* in its story about a young boy who loves a dog and tries to protect it from the cruelty of an adult. Nick Whitaker stars as Colby, a fourteen-year-old whose stepfather, Hatchett (Chris Kendrick), breeds dogs in crowded kennels in the backyard. When one of his prize breeders gives birth to a white mongrel, he finds the dog useless and plans to put it to death. Colby steals it, names it Puppy, and successfully protects it for months, hiding it in a playhouse so interestingly designed he will no doubt grow up to become an architect. The playhouse is shared by a parrot named Merlin, who proves the point that parrots are not nearly as funny as they think they are.

The plot is not entirely about Colby and his mean stepfather, however. Its real costars are Benji and a dog named Shaggy, who was discovered in a Chicago animal shelter. Shaggy plays Lizard Tongue, a dog of the streets, who knows the ropes and provides invaluable help to Puppy in a world populated not only by cruel breeders but, inevitably, by dogcatchers.

The movie's PG-rated bad guys are carefully modulated to be evil but not too evil. The animal control wardens, named Livingston and Sheldon (Randall Newsome and Duane Stephens), are comic relief: bumbling flatfoots

who actually kinda like dogs. Like all goofy characters in movies like this, they exhibit a genius for finding and falling facedown in mud puddles.

As for Hatchett, he is stern, heartless, and hateful, but never physically abuses Colby; his mom, Claire, played by Christy Summerhays, makes sure of that. There's a scene between Colby and his mother where she tries to explain to her son why she has stayed in her marriage; it's heartfelt and sincere, and could be useful to kids in the audience who are going through similar experiences in their families.

Joe Camp, who has directed a series of Benjis in six movies and a TV series, is a master at getting his animals to seem as smart as Lassie (who, as Dave Barry has pointed out, was smarter and possibly more articulate than any of the humans in her family). He has a winning character actor in Shaggy, a playful roughhouse type, and the latest Benji, of course, is cuteness squared.

The movie opens and closes with quasi-documentary footage about Camp's search for a new dog to play Benji. You might be tempted to wonder if being cast as Benji is something Puppy would prefer to life with Shaggy and Colby, but a paradox is involved, since the new Benji has already been discovered and is playing Puppy in this movie.

The drama continues. There have been recent medical bulletins about Benji's need for eye surgery; the movie's Web site says Benji underwent retinal reattachment. Dr. Sam Vainisi of Wheeling, Illinois, described as "the top veterinary ophthalmologist in the country," said the surgery was complicated because of inflammation from an earlier cataract operation, and an allergic reaction to an antibiotic. One wishes Benji a complete and speedy recovery, and prays that Shaggy doesn't have to go into training as Benji's Seeing Eye dog.

The Best of Youth ★ ★ ★ ★
R, 366 m., 2005

Luigi Lo Cascio (Nicola Carati), Alessio Boni (Matteo Carati), Adriana Asti (Adriana Carati), Sonia Bergamasco (Giulia Monfalco), Fabrizio Gifuni (Carlo Tommasi), Maya Sansa (Mirella Utano), Valentina Carnelutti (Francesca Carati), Jasmine Trinca (Giorgia), Andrea Tidona (Angelo Carati), Lidia Vitale (Giovanna Carati).

Directed by Marco Tullio Giordana and produced by Angelo Barbagallo. Screenplay by Sandro Petraglia and Stefano Rulli.

Every review of *The Best of Youth* begins with the information that it is six hours long. No good movie is too long, just as no bad movie is short enough. I dropped outside of time and was carried along by the narrative flow; when the film was over, I had no particular desire to leave the theater, and would happily have stayed another three hours. The two-hour limit on most films makes them essentially short stories. *The Best of Youth* is a novel.

The film is ambitious. It wants no less than to follow two brothers and the people in their lives from 1963 to 2000, following them from Rome to Norway to Turin to Florence to Palermo and back to Rome again. The lives intersect with the politics and history of Italy during the period: the hippies, the ruinous flood in Florence, the Red Brigades, kidnappings, hard times and layoffs at Fiat, and finally a certain peace for some of the characters, and for their nation.

The brothers are Nicola and Matteo Carati (Luigi Lo Cascio and Alessio Boni). We meet their parents, Angelo (Andrea Tidona) and Adriana (Adriana Asti), their older sister, Giovanna (Lidia Vitale), and their kid sister, Francesca (Valentina Carnelutti). And we meet their friends, their lovers, and others who drift through, including a mental patient whose life seems to follow in parallel.

As the film opens, Nicola has qualified as a doctor and Matteo is still taking literature classes. Matteo, looking for a job, has been hired as a "logotherapist"—literally, a person who takes mental patients for walks. One of the women he walks with is Giorgia (Jasmine Trinca), who is beautiful, deeply wounded by electroshock therapy, and afraid of the world. On the spur of the moment, Matteo decides to spring her from the institution and take her along when he and Nicola take a summer trip to the "end of the world," the tip of Norway.

Giorgia is found by the police, but has the presence of mind to protect the brothers. Nicola continues on his journey and gets a job as a lumberjack, and Matteo returns to Rome and, impulsively, joins the army. They are to meet again in Florence, where catastrophic floods have drowned the city. Nicola is a volunteer, Matteo is a soldier assigned to the emergency effort, and in the middle of the mud and ruins Nicola hears a young woman playing a piano that has been left in the middle of the street.

This is Giulia (Sonia Bergamasco). Their eyes meet and lock, and so do their destinies. They live together without marrying, and have a daughter, Sara. Giulia is drawn into a secret Red Brigade cell. She draws apart from her family. One night she packs to leave the house. He tries to block her way, then lets her go. She disappears into the terrorist underground.

Matteo meanwhile joins the police, takes an assignment in Sicily because no one else wants to go there, and meets a photographer in a café. This is Mirella (Maya Sansa). She wants to be a librarian, and he advises her to work at a beautiful library in Rome. Years later, he walks into the library and sees her for the second time in his life. They become lovers, but there is a great unexplained rage within Matteo, maybe also self-hatred, and he will not allow anyone very close.

Enough about the plot. These people, all of them, will meet again—even Giorgia, who is found by Nicola in the most extraordinary circumstances, and who will cause a meeting that no one in the movie could have anticipated, because neither person involved knows the other exists. Because of the length of the film, the director, Marco Tullio Giordana, has time and space to work with, and we get a tangible sense of the characters growing older, learning about themselves, dealing with hardship. The journey of Giulia, the radical, is the most difficult and in some ways the most touching. The way Nicola finally finds happiness is particularly satisfying because it takes him so long to realize that it is right there before him for the taking.

The film must have deep resonances for Italians, where it was made for national television; because of its politics, sexuality, and grown-up characters, it would be impossible on American networks. It is not easy on Italy. As he is graduating from medical school, Nicola is advised by his professor: "Do you have any ambition? Then leave Italy. Go to London, Paris, America if you can. Italy is a beautiful country. But it is a place to die, run by dinosaurs." Nicola asks the professor why he stays. "I'm one of the dinosaurs."

Nicola stays. Another who stays is his brother-in-law, who is marked for kidnapping and assassination but won't leave, "because then they will have won." There is a scene where he stands in front of windows late at night and we feel real dread for him. With the politics and the personal drama there is also the sense of a nation that beneath the turbulent surface is deeply supportive of its citizens. Some of that is sensed through the lives of the parents of the Carati family: The father busies himself with optimistic schemes; the mother meets a grandchild who brings joy into her old age.

The film is being shown in two parts, three hours each, with separate admissions. You don't have to see both parts on the same day, but you may want to. It is a luxury to be enveloped in a good film, and to know there's a lot more of it—that it is not moving inexorably toward an ending you can anticipate, but moving indefinitely into a future that is free to be shaped in surprising ways. When you hear that it is six hours long, reflect that it is therefore also six hours deep.

Bewitched ★ ★ ½
PG-13, 100 m., 2005

Nicole Kidman (Isabel Bigelow), Will Ferrell (Jack Wyatt), Shirley MacLaine (Iris Smythson), Michael Caine (Nigel Bigelow), Jason Schwartzman (Richie), Kristin Chenoweth (Maria Kelly), Heather Burns (Nina), Steve Carell (Uncle Arthur), Stephen Colbert (Stu Robison). Directed by Nora Ephron and produced by Nora Ephron, Penny Marshall, Douglas Wick, and Lucy Fisher. Screenplay by Nora Ephron and Delia Ephron.

One of the many areas in which I am spectacularly ill-informed is prime-time television. You would be amazed at the numbers of sitcoms I have never seen, not even once. When you see 500 movies a year, you don't have a lot of leftover yearning for watching television. In the evenings, you involve yourself in more human pursuits. On TV you watch the news, talk shows, or old movies. You don't watch sports unless your team is in the finals. You can sense I am edging up to the admission that I have never seen a single episode of *Bewitched*. I knew it existed, however, because of my reading.

That makes me well prepared to review the movie *Bewitched*, since I have nothing to compare it with and have to take it on its own terms. It is tolerably entertaining. Many of its parts work, although not together. Will Ferrell and Nicole Kidman are funny and likable, but they're in a plot that doesn't allow them to aim for the same ending with the same reason. It's one of those movies where you smile and laugh and are reasonably entertained, but you get no sense of a mighty enterprise sweeping you along with its comedic force. There is not a movie here. Just scenes in search of one.

The joke is this: Will Ferrell plays Jack Wyatt, a movie star whose career has hit bottom. Sales of his last DVD: zero. In desperation he turns to television and finds himself considered for a starring role in a revival of *Bewitched*. He will play the Darrin role. At least that's what everyone says. I assume Darrin was a character on the original show. I know (from my reading) that the show's interest centered on Samantha, who was played by Elizabeth Montgomery. I know from the movie that Samantha had a way of twitching her nose that was very special, and that they can't find an actress with twitchability until Jack spots Isabel Bigelow (Nicole Kidman) in Book Soup on Sunset.

He insists on using her in the role because (a) he wants a complete unknown, so he'll get all the attention, (b) the twitch, and (c) already he is falling in love with her. What he doesn't realize, oh, delicious irony, is that Isabel is in fact a real witch. She has, however, just decided to move to the Valley, get a house with a VW bug in the garage, live a normal life, and find a guy who loves her for herself and not because she put a hex on him. Her father (Michael Caine) warns her that this dream is not possible, and indeed she has a lot of trouble giving up witchcraft. It's so tempting to charge your purchases on a Tarot card.

The movie has been directed by Nora Ephron (*Sleepless in Seattle, You've Got Mail*), and written by her with her sister Delia. They have a lot of cute scenes. I like the way they make Jack Wyatt an egotistical monster who wants three trailers, star billing, and cake every Wednesday. He's hysterically in love with himself. His ego is, of course, no match for Samantha, who can make him act in Spanish if she wants to. Occasionally when things go wrong she rewinds the arrow of time, although even after a rewind, it's a funny thing: Something magical happens anyway.

The movie has fun with Ferrell on the star trip, and fun with Kidman's love-hate relationship with magic. It has a lot of good supporting work, including Jason Schwartzman as Jack's desperate agent, and Shirley MacLaine as Samantha's mother (her theory on actors: "Sometimes, deep down, there is no deep down"). If you watch *The Daily Show* you'll enjoy cameos by Stephen Colbert and Steve Carell. It might have been a good idea to bring in Samantha Bee, too, and have her interview Jack Wyatt ("You're staring at my boobs!").

Will Ferrell has become a major star in almost no time at all. One moment he was a *Saturday Night Live* veteran who had played backup in a lot of movies, and the next moment he had made *Old School* and *Elf* and *Anchorman* and *Melinda and Melinda* and had *The Producers* on the way, and he was bigtime. One reason for that is, you like the guy. He has a brawny, take-no-prisoners style of comedy that suggests he's having a lot of fun.

Nicole Kidman, on the other hand, is an actor with more notes in her repertoire (maybe Ferrell could have played a role in *The Hours*, but that remains to be seen). Here, she is fetching and somehow more relaxed than usual as Samantha, and makes witchcraft seem like a bad habit rather than a cosmic force.

But what are they doing in the same movie? You have two immovable objects or two irresistible forces. Both characters are complete, right off the shelf. There's no room for them to move. Yes, Jack becomes a nicer guy after he falls in love, and yes, Samantha realizes that magic is sometimes just not fair. But they are separate at the beginning and essentially still self-contained at the end, and the movie never works them both into the same narrative logic. Still, that's a great moment when Jack shouts: "Guys! Make me 200 cappuccinos! Bring me the best one!"   ☞

Beyond the Sea ★ ★ ★
PG-13, 121 m., 2004

Kevin Spacey (Bobby Darin), Kate Bosworth (Sandra Dee), John Goodman (Steve Blauner), Bob Hoskins (Charlie Maffia), Brenda Blethyn (Polly Cassotto), Greta Scacchi (Mary Duvan), Caroline Aaron (Nina Cassotto Maffia), Peter Cincotti (Dick Behrke), William Ullrich (Young Bobby). Directed by Kevin Spacey and produced by Jan Fantl, Arthur Friedman, Andy Paterson, and Spacey. Screenplay by Spacey and Lewis Colick.

Kevin Spacey believes he was born to play Bobby Darin. I believe he was born to play more interesting characters, and has, and will, but I can see his point. He looks a little like Darin and sounds a lot like him, and apparently when he was growing up he formed one of those emotional connections with a performer where admiration is mixed with pity.

Darin's own emotional connection was apparently with Frank Sinatra, a pop singer he hoped to displace. That wasn't going to happen; there is a point beyond which talent cannot be extended into genius. He died young, at thirty-seven, having lived most of his life on borrowed time. After rheumatic fever at seven, he wasn't expected to live past fifteen. That he found twenty-two more years, had great success, and made recordings that are still popular today is an achievement, but not one that makes a biopic necessary, unless the filmmaker is moved by a personal obsession.

Kevin Spacey was, and *Beyond the Sea* is at least as much about Spacey playing Darin as about Darin himself. Is Spacey too old to be convincing as a singer in his teens, twenties, and thirties? Yes, but not too old to play an actor in his forties who feels driven to play such a role. Perhaps there are parallels. Spacey has struggled, been misunderstood, had triumphs and disasters, has recently been the target of malicious coverage in the British press (his sin was to presume to contribute to the London stage even though he is a Movie Star). In his own best work, Spacey has achieved genius; he is better as an actor than Darin ever was as a singer, but there must have been a time when Spacey identified strongly with Darin's disappointments and defeats, and *Beyond the Sea* is about those feelings.

It is also probably relevant that Spacey, in preparing the project, knew something we could not guess: He is a superb pop singer. In a rash ad lib on *Ebert and Roeper*, I said I thought he was probably even a better singer than

Darin. A statement like that has an apples-and-oranges foolishness; Darin was himself and nobody else ever will be, and it's enough to observe that although many actors think they are wonderful singers, Spacey is correct.

He constructs the picture as a film within a film, to provide an explanation for the spectacle of an older man playing a much younger one. The film begins with Darin onstage at the Copacabana night club, and then pulls back to reveal that we're on a sound stage; the adult Darin is confronted by himself as a young boy, arguing that he's gotten it all wrong, and in a weird way the whole movie will be an argument among the various ages of Bobby Darin. There is a parallel with *De-Lovely*, in which the ancient Cole Porter reviews a musical about his life; in both cases, the POV is essentially posthumous.

Darin as a boy is the darling of his mother (Brenda Blethyn) and sister, Nina (Caroline Aaron), although his relationship with them is not quite what he believes. Nina's husband, Charlie (Bob Hoskins), helps start his career, a manager (John Goodman) signs aboard, and with big teeny-bopper hits like "Splish Splash," he becomes a star.

Darin hungers to grow, and moves into the mainstream of popular music with hits like "Mack the Knife" and "Beyond the Sea." On a movie set, he falls in love with Sandra Dee (Kate Bosworth) and marries her, at a time when their careers were both soaring. The marriage goes wrong for reasons that seem to have more to do with biopic conventions than real life; their careers keep them apart, etc., although there is a moment with the hard truth of *A Star Is Born* when Darin is nominated for an Oscar, loses, goes ballistic, and screams: "Warren Beatty is there with Leslie Caron and I'm there with Gidget!"

Darin's career collapse led at one point to exile in a house trailer, and then to a comeback in which he tried to cross over into politically conscious acoustic folk singing, which was not a good fit for his talent. He was born to play Vegas, but not as an aging hippie. His Vegas debut flops, but he returns in triumph after restaging his show to include a black gospel choir, which brings a lot of energy onto the stage. He is advised of audiences, "remember—they hear what they see," and he nods at

this wise insight, although I am not sure exactly what it means.

Bobby Darin's life provides a less-than-perfect template for a biopic, because he achieved success up to a certain point, then failed, then did not really have much of a comeback, then died young. Not precisely the inspirational ascent of a biographical Everest. But the movie possesses genuine feeling because Spacey is there with Darin during all the steps of this journey, up and down, all the way into death. Not all stories have happy endings. Not all lives have third acts. This was a life, too, and although it was a disappointment, it also contained more success and maybe even more happiness than Darin could have reasonably expected at age fifteen, his presumed cut-off date. What I sensed above all in *Beyond the Sea* was Spacey's sympathy with and for Bobby Darin. There have been biopics inspired by less worthy motivations.

The Big Animal ★ ★ ★
NO MPAA RATING, 72 m., 2004

Jerzy Stuhr (Zygmunt Sawicki), Anna Dymna (Marysia Sawicki), Dominika Bednarczyk (Bank Clerk), Blazej Wojcik (Bank Clerk), Andrzej Franczyk (Bank Manager), Feliks Szajnert (Drunkard), Rublo from Zalewski Circus (Camel). Directed by Jerzy Stuhr and produced by Janusz Morgenstern and Slawomir Rogowski. Screenplay by Krzysztof Kieslowski, based on a novel by Kazimierz Orlos.

One day a camel appears in a Polish village. It must have been left behind by a circus. Bereft and abandoned, it seeks out the garden of the Sawicki family, Zygmunt and Marysia, and they are happy to give it a home. Not everyone has a camel, and Marysia feels as if there's another guest for dinner when the beast peers through their dining room window during meals.

So begins *The Big Animal*, a fable written by Krzysztof Kieslowski, the Polish poet of serendipity and coincidence, who died in 1996, leaving behind such masterpieces as *The Double Life of Veronique* and the Three Colors Trilogy *(Blue, White,* and *Red)*. He wrote this screenplay in 1973, adapted from a novel, six years before *Camera Buff* brought him his first wide attention. Now it has been filmed by his best friend, Jerzy Stuhr, who stars as Zygmunt and appeared in many Kieslowski films, including *White*.

This is not a major Kieslowski work, nor was it intended to be. Kieslowski sometimes liked to work in a minor key, and some of the ten-hour-long films in his masterful *Decalogue* (1988) occupy similar territory: They are small parables about trying to make moral choices in an indifferent universe. He finds unexpected connections between characters, and unexpected meetings, and unintended consequences. Surely, to acquire an orphaned camel is such an event.

At first the village is happy to have a camel in its midst. That may be because the villagers have never seen a camel molting in the spring, when for several weeks it resembles a sofa abandoned to the rain. The camel (played by Rublo the camel) is a docile creature who often seems to be trying to recapture a lost train of thought. Zygmunt takes it for strolls around the village, schoolchildren are delighted by it, and Marysia knits it a shawl that leaves holes for its two humps.

All is well until stirrings of discontent are heard. Even in the most hospitable of communities, there are always malcontents who don't want a camel hanging around. The camel smells, and is unlovely, and it relieves itself in the street. And the Sawickis begin to stand out from the crowd: They are the People Who Have the Camel. In 1973 when Kieslowski wrote his screenplay, perhaps he saw it as a parable about life under the sameness and regimentation of communism. But even in a democracy human nature is intolerant of those who are different, and to own a camel is to be different.

In a capitalist society, this film might not be made because the story is not commercial. In 1973, there were state sources in Poland for production funds, but I have no idea if *The Big Animal* was turned down by the authorities. It is the kind of story that could be seen as a satirical attack on the government, or on the other hand it might simply be the tale of a camel. You never know. It is whimsical, bittersweet, wise in a minor key.

I am reminded of a story Dusan Makavejev told me. When there was a Yugoslavia, it had a censor whose job was to approve film scripts. The censor was a friend of Makavejev's; they had gone to school together. Makavejev submitted a script, and the censor called him into his office. "Dusan, Dusan, Dusan," he said sorrowfully, "you know what this story is about, and I know what this story is about. Now go home and rewrite it so only the audience knows what it is about."

The Big Bounce ★ ★

PG-13, 89 m., 2004

Owen Wilson (Jack Ryan), Charlie Sheen (Bob Rogers Jr.), Vinnie Jones (Lou Harris), Sara Foster (Nancy Hayes), Morgan Freeman (Walter Crewes), Gary Sinise (Ray Ritchie), Willie Nelson (Joe Lurie), Harry Dean Stanton (Bob Rogers Sr.), Butch Helemano (Hawaiian Priest). Directed by George Armitage and produced by Jorge Saralegui and Steve Bing. Screenplay by Sebastian Gutierrez, based on a novel by Elmore Leonard.

Elmore Leonard is a writer you read with your fingers crossed, amazed at his high-wire act, reading dialogue that always sounds like Leonard even though the characters never quite sound the same. You love the jargon as they explain their criminal specialties. You savor the way he pulls oddballs and misfits out of the shrubbery and sets them to work at strange day jobs and illegal night jobs, and shows them wise to the heartbreaks of the world but vulnerable to them. Just today I bought Leonard's new novel, because I never miss one. Most of the time they're clear sailing right to the end, and you close the covers with a grin.

Such a distinctive voice translates only rarely to the movies. Although Leonard's plots are ingenious and delightful, they're not the reason we read the books; Agatha Christie, poor soul, has delightful and ingenious plots. It's not the what but the how with Leonard, and the movies (his work has generated thirty of them) are mostly distant echoes of the genius. Of those I've seen, the ones that seem to channel him more or less successfully are John Frankenheimer's *52 Pick-Up*, Barry Sonnenfeld's *Get Shorty*, Quentin Tarantino's *Jackie Brown*, and Steven Soderbergh's *Out of Sight*, although all four cross the Leonard voice with the distinctive voices of their directors.

Now here is *The Big Bounce*, the second screen version of this Leonard novel, which was first filmed in California in 1969 with Ryan

O'Neal and Leigh Taylor-Young and has now been transferred to Hawaii. There's a dream cast: Owen Wilson, Charlie Sheen, Vinnie Jones, Sara Foster, Morgan Freeman, Gary Sinise and, I am not kidding you, Willie Nelson and Harry Dean Stanton. And the location is well visualized: not the commercialized Hawaii of so many movies, but a more secluded area with colorful local characters, not least at the resort bungalows managed by Freeman (also the local lawman), where Wilson gets a job halfway between janitor and gigolo.

The area's bad guy is Ray Ritchie (Gary Sinise), a developer who wants to put up high-rise hotels and spoil the flavor of paradise. His foreman, Lou Harris (Vinnie Jones), gets into a televised fight with Jack Ryan (Wilson), a beach bum and sometime athlete. That brings in Ritchie's enforcer, Bob Jr. (Charlie Sheen). And then there's the lithesome Nancy Hayes (Sara Foster), who is Ritchie's mistress but has a jones for criminals and gets really turned on when Jack demonstrates his skills as a burglar.

The destinies of all of these characters intersect in a way it would be unfair to describe, except to say that Leonard has a gift for surprising us with the hidden motives of some of his characters, and their allegiances can shift in an instant. What they want and what they do are not the point, really; that's the excuse for providing them with a stage. The pleasure in the film comes from watching them and listening to them, and Owen Wilson is especially good with his dialogue, which masks hostility with sweet reason.

The movie doesn't work. It meanders and drifts and riffs. There is a part of me that enjoyed its leisurely celebration of its characters. I wanted more focus, and so will you, but on TV late some night you may stumble across it and find yourself bemused for a time by the way they live their lives as if there's nothing more fun than being an Elmore Leonard character. Maybe they're right.

Birth ★ ★ ★ ½
R, 100 m., 2004

Nicole Kidman (Anna), Cameron Bright (Sean), Danny Huston (Joseph), Lauren Bacall (Eleanor), Alison Elliott (Laura), Arliss Howard (Bob), Anne Heche (Clara), Peter Stormare (Clifford). Directed by Jonathan Glazer and produced by Jean-Louis Piel, Nick Morris, and Lizie Gower. Screenplay by Jean-Claude Carriere, Milo Addica, and Glazer.

Nobody sees the little boy come into the apartment, but suddenly there he is, a stranger in the room at a family birthday party. "I am Sean," he says. Sean is the name of Anna's husband, who died ten years ago. The boy's name is Sean, but that's not what he means. What he means is that he *is* Sean—in that when Sean died while jogging in Central Park, he was reborn and now here he stands, aged ten.

Since the first two scenes of *Birth* show the death and the birth, we're prepared for the reincarnation. What I wasn't expecting was a film that treats it as intelligent, skeptical adults might. They don't believe in reincarnation. Neither did the original Sean; the movie opens with a black screen and we hear him giving a speech: "As a man of science, I just don't believe that mumbo jumbo."

Birth is an effective thriller precisely because it is true to the way sophisticated people might behave in this situation. Its characters are not movie creatures, gullible, emotional, and quickly moved to tears. They're realists, rich, a little jaded. At first they simply laugh at the boy (Cameron Bright). Even when he seems to know things that only her husband would know, Anna (Nicole Kidman) is slow to allow herself to be convinced. She loved Sean and mourned him a long time, but after ten years it is time to resume her life, and she has just announced her engagement to Joseph (Danny Huston).

Anna lives with her mother, Eleanor (Lauren Bacall), in a luxurious Manhattan duplex. The family includes her sister Laura (Alison Elliott), her brother-in-law Bob (Arliss Howard), and her close friends Clara (Anne Heche) and Clifford (Peter Stormare). Since they're all present when Sean first appears, they're all involved in the dilemma of what to do about him. Sean's parents order him not to annoy Anna anymore, but he turns up anyway, an unsettling combination of a kid and a solemn, unblinking presence.

When Anna tells him she simply doesn't believe him, he says, "What if Bob comes to my house and asks me some questions?" "How do you know Bob?" "He was my brother-in-law."

Bob comes and asks some questions, and as the family gathers to listen to a tape recording of Sean's answers, it's clear something exceedingly strange is going on.

Anna becomes convinced, reluctantly, but then firmly, that Sean really is her reincarnated husband. She arrives at this decision, I think, during an extraordinary shot: a close-up of her face for a full three minutes, during an opera performance. And then the film ventures into the delicate area of exactly how a woman in her thirties goes about relating to a ten-year-old boy who is or was or will again be her husband. In one mordantly funny scene, they eat ice cream while she asks him how they will live, and he says, "I'll get a job." And, "Have you ever made love to a girl?" Well, yes and no. Yes, as Sean One, and no, as Sean Two; one of the film's mysteries is that Sean seems to be simultaneously the dead husband and an actual little boy.

Much has been said about a scene where Sean boldly gets into the bathtub with her, but the movie handles it with such care and tact that it sidesteps controversy. Anna's mother, for her part, thinks the whole situation is dangerous nonsense, and could develop into a crime. As played by Bacall, Eleanor is tart and decisive. When it appears Anna is considering living with Sean, her mother says: "I will call his mother, and his mother will call the police." Anna's fiancé, Joseph, is the wild card, reacting first with disbelief and then with restraint, before . . .

Of course there's a lot I haven't described, including the role of Clara (Heche), Anna's best friend. The movie goes deep, and then it takes a turn and leaves us asking fundamental questions. There seem to be two possible explanations for what finally happens; neither one is consistent with all of the facts. At a point when the characters seem satisfied they have arrived at the truth, I believed them, but it wasn't truth enough for me.

Birth is a dark, brooding film, with lots of kettledrums and ominous violins on Alexandre Desplat's sound track. Harris Savides's cinematography avoids surprises and gimmicks and uses the same kind of level gaze that Sean employs. Echoes of *Rosemary's Baby* are inevitable, given the similarity of the apartment locations and Nicole Kidman's haircut, so similar to Mia Farrow's. But *Birth* is less sensational and more ominous, and also more intriguing, because instead of going for quick thrills it explores what might really happen if a ten-year-old turned up and said what Sean says. Because it is about adults who act like adults, who are skeptical and wary, it's all the creepier, especially since Cameron Bright is so effective as the uninflected and noncute Sean. Like M. Night Shyamalan's best work, *Birth* works less with action than with implication.

Blade: Trinity ★ ½

R, 105 m., 2004

Wesley Snipes (Blade), Kris Kristofferson (Whistler), Jessica Biel (Abigail Whistler), Ryan Reynolds (Hannibal King), Parker Posey (Danica Talos), Dominic Purcell (Dracula/Drake). Directed by David Goyer and produced by Goyer, Peter Frankfurt, and Lynn Harris. Screenplay by Goyer.

I liked the first two *Blade* movies, although my description of *Blade II* as "a really rather brilliant vomitorium of viscera" might have sounded like faint praise. The second film was directed by Guillermo del Toro, a gifted horror director with a sure feel for the quease-inducing, and was even better, I thought, than the first. Now comes *Blade: Trinity*, which is a mess. It lacks the sharp narrative line and crisp comic-book clarity of the earlier films, and descends too easily into shapeless fight scenes that are chopped into so many cuts that they lack all form or rhythm.

The setup is a continuation of the earlier films. Vampires are waging a war to infect humanity, and the most potent fighter against them is the half-human, half-vampire Blade (Wesley Snipes). He has been raised from childhood by Whistler (Kris Kristofferson), who recognized his unique ability to move between two worlds, and is a fearsome warrior, but, despite some teammates, is seriously outnumbered.

As *Trinity* opens, the Vampire Nation and its leader, Danica (played by Parker Posey—yes, Parker Posey), convince the FBI that Blade is responsible for, if I heard correctly, 1,182 murders. "They're waging a goddamned publicity campaign," Whistler grumbles, in that great Kris Kristofferson seen-it-all voice.

Agents surround Blade headquarters, which is your basic action movie space combining the ambience of a warehouse with lots of catwalks and high places to fall from and stuff that blows up good. Whistler goes down fighting (although a shotgun seems retro given the sci-fi weapons elsewhere in the movie), and Blade is recruited by the Night Stalkers, who reach him through Whistler's daughter, Abigail (Jessica Biel). It would have been too much, I suppose, to hope for Whistler's mother.

The Night Stalkers have information that the Vampire Nation is seeking the original Dracula because, to spread the vampire virus, "they need better DNA; they need Dracula's blood." Dracula's superior DNA means he can operate by day, unlike his descendants, who must operate by night. The notion that DNA degrades or is somehow diluted over the centuries flies in the face of what we know about the double helix, but who needs science when you know what's right? "They found Dracula in Iraq about six months ago," we learn, and if that's not a straight line, I'm not Jon Stewart.

Dracula is some kinduva guy. Played by Dominic Purcell, he isn't your usual vampire in evening dress with overdeveloped canines, but a creature whose DNA seems to have been infected with the virus of Hollywood monster effects. His mouth and lower face unfold into a series of ever more horrifying fangs and suchlike, until he looks like a mug shot of the original *Alien*. He doesn't suck blood; he vacuums it.

Parker Posey is an actress I have always had affection for, and now it is mixed with increased admiration for the way she soldiers through an impossible role, sneering like the good sport she is. Jessica Biel becomes the first heroine of a vampire movie to listen to her iPod during slayings. That's an excuse to get the sound track by Ramin Djawadi and RZA into the movie, I guess, although I hope she downloaded it from the iTunes Store and isn't a pirate on top of being a vampire.

Vampires in this movie look about as easy to kill as the ghouls in *Dawn of the Dead*. They have a way of suddenly fizzing up into electric sparks, and then collapsing in a pile of ash. One of the weapons used against them by the Night Stalkers is a light-saber device that is,

and I'm sure I have this right, "half as hot as the sun." Switch on one of those babies and you'd zap not only the vampires but British Columbia and large parts of Alberta and Washington State.

Jessica Biel is the resident babe, wearing fetishistic costumes to match Blade's, and teaming up with Hannibal King (Ryan Reynolds), no relation to Hannibal Lecter, a former vampire who has come over to the good side. The vampire killers and their fellow Night Stalkers engage in an increasingly murky series of battles with the vampires, leading you to ask this simple strategic question: Why, since the whole world is theirs for the taking, do the vampires have to turn up and fight the Night Stalkers in the first place? Why not just figure out that since the Stalkers are in Vancouver, the vampires should concentrate on, say, Montreal?

Bobby Jones: Stroke of Genius ★ ★ ★
PG, 120 m., 2004

James Caviezel (Bobby Jones), Claire Forlani (Mary Jones), Jeremy Northam (Walter Hagen), Malcolm McDowell (O. B. Keeler), Connie Ray (Clara Jones), Brett Rice ("Big Bob" Jones), Aidan Quinn (Harry Vardon), Larry Thompson (John Malone). Directed by Rowdy Herrington and produced by Kim Dawson, Kim Moore, and John Shepherd. Screenplay by Herrington and Bill Pryor.

Bobby Jones (1902–1971) was perhaps the greatest golfer who ever lived. Not even Tiger Woods has equaled Jones's triumph in 1930, when he became the only player to win the U.S. Open, the British Open, the U.S. Amateur, and the British Amateur in the same year. Then he retired from competition—still only twenty-eight. Odds are good no golfer will ever equal that record—if only because no golfer good enough to do it will be an amateur. Jones also won seven U.S. titles in a row, an achievement that may be unmatchable.

Jones was not only an amateur, but an amateur who had to earn a living, so that he couldn't play golf every day and mostly played only in championship-level tournaments. This makes him sound like a man who played simply for love of the game, but *Bobby Jones: Stroke of Genius* shows us a man who seems driven to play, a man obsessed; there seems less joy than compulsion in his career, and the movie contrasts him with the era's top professional, Walter Hagen (Jeremy Northam), who seems to enjoy himself a lot more.

Jim Caviezel *(The Passion of the Christ)* plays Jones as an adult, after childhood scenes showing a young boy who becomes fascinated by the game and watches great players while hiding in the rough. He comes from a family dominated by a strict, puritanical grandfather, but Jones's father, "Big Bob" (Brett Rice), is supportive. Not so Jones's wife, Mary (Claire Forlani), who plays a role that has become standard in the biographies of great men—the woman who wishes her man would give up his dream and spend more time at home with her and the children.

Of course, Mary sees a side of Bobby that's invisible to the world. The man is tortured. He feels he must enter tournaments and win them to prove something he can never quite articulate, to show "them" without being sure who they are. And he is often in physical pain. After a sickly childhood, he grows up into a reed-thin man with a tense face, and doctors have only to look at him to prescribe rest. His stomach starts to hurt at about the same time he begins to drink and smoke, and although the movie does not portray him as an alcoholic, we hold that as a hypothesis until we find the pain is caused by syringomyelia, a spinal disease that would cripple him later in life.

Bobby Jones: Stroke of Genius tells this story in a straightforward, calm way that works ideally as the chronicle of a man's life but perhaps less ideally as drama. No doubt we should be grateful that Jones's story isn't churned up into soap opera and hyped with false crises and climaxes; it is the story of a golfer, and it contains a lot of golf. Much of the golf is photographed at the treacherous Old Course in St Andrews, Scotland, where the game began, and where we learn why there are eighteen holes: "A bottle of Scotch has eighteen shots," an old-timer explains, "and they reckoned that when it was empty, the game was over."

A major player in Jones' life is O. B. Keeler (Malcolm McDowell), his friend and "official biographer," and if Jones was an amateur golfer, Keeler seems to be an amateur biographer, with all day free, every day, to follow Jones around,

carry his stomach medicine (and his whisky), and chronicle his exploits, sometimes typing while leaning against a stone wall on a course. Little wonder that although Jones retired in 1930, Keeler did not publish his "authorized biography" until 1953.

The director, Rowdy Herrington, has made more excited movies, including *Road House* (1989), legendary for its over-the-top performances by Patrick Swayze, Kelly Lynch, and Ben Gazzara. *Bobby Jones* is more solemn, more the kind of movie you're not surprised was financed by the Bobby Jones Film Co., and authorized by the Jones trustees, who also oversee lines of clothing and the like. It is also not astonishing, I suppose, that although the film mentions that Jones founded the Augusta National Golf Club and started the Masters tournament there, and although a photo over the end credits shows Jones with the course's favorite golfer, Dwight D. Eisenhower, there is no mention of the club's exclusion of blacks and women.

To be fair, the movie isn't really about Jones's entire life; it focuses on his youth and his championship golf. I am not a golfer, although I took the sport in P.E. class in college and have played a few rounds. There are too many movies to see, books to read, cities to explore, and conversations to hold for me to spend great parts of the day following that little ball around and around and around. I do concede that everyone I know who plays golf loves the game, and that most of them seem to derive more cheer from it than Bobby Jones does in this movie.

That Jones should obtain more pleasure than he does is all the more certain because the movie mostly shows him making impossible shots, at one point chipping the ball into the hole from close to the wall of a sand trap higher than his head. Walter Hagen spends a lot of the movie raising his eyebrows and grimacing in reaction shots, after Jones sinks another miracle.

Bon Voyage ★ ★ ★ ½
PG-13, 114 m., 2004

Isabelle Adjani (Viviane Denvers), Gerard Depardieu (Jean-Etienne Beaufort), Virginie Ledoyen (Camille), Yvan Attal (Raoul), Gregori Derangere (Frederic), Peter Coyote (Alex Winckler), Jean-Marc Stehle (Professeur

Kopolski). Directed by Jean-Paul Rappeneau and produced by Laurent Petin and Michele Petin. Screenplay by Patrick Modiano, Gilles Marhand, Jean-Paul Rappeneau, Julien Rappeneau, and Jerome Tonnerre.

The Nazi occupation of France may seem like a strange backdrop for an adventure comedy, but consider how *Casablanca* found humor, irony, and courage in a related situation. Not that *Bon Voyage* is *Casablanca*, but it proceeds from the same cynicism, and unites the worlds of politics, science, and the movies. It also provides Isabelle Adjani with one of the best roles of her career, as a movie star who will do anything, say anything, and sleep with anybody, first to further her career and then to save her life.

The movie is a lavish, expensive period production by Jean-Paul Rappeneau, who also made Gérard Depardieu's rabble-rousing *Cyrano de Bergerac* in 1990 and the exhilarating *The Horseman on the Roof* (1995). Depardieu returns in *Bon Voyage*, and he is an unmade bed no longer; he is astonishingly slimmed down, his hair trimmed and slicked back, wearing the tailored suits of a cabinet minister.

The movie opens in Paris, as the Nazis are moving into the city and many prudent citizens with the means or clout are moving to Bordeaux, which they think might be Nazi-free, at least for a while. Adjani plays Viviane Denvers, a great movie star and apparently an even greater lover. To say that she looks much younger than her forty-eight years is not flattery but the simple truth; Adjani was able to play a convincing teenager in *Camille Claudel* (1990). Here her character functions instinctively as a woman who is attracted to men who offer her money and safety. Her fatal flaw is that she is also attracted to men she loves. These tastes become thoroughly confused during the film, as she seeks money, safety, and love simultaneously, which means that no one man is going to be able to fill the bill.

Jean-Etienne Beaufort (Depardieu) is the harassed cabinet minister she's attached to as the movie opens. As some ministers urge collaboration with the Nazis, he commands a car and Viviane joins him on the exodus. But then she is astonished to see a childhood friend named Frederic (Gregori Derangere) on the streets— astonished because she thought he was in jail charged with murder. Such is her power over

men that, some days earlier, after she murdered a blackmailer in her apartment, she called him up and because he had always been in love with her, he allowed the police to arrest him. He's free because his jailers helpfully released their prisoners ahead of the Nazi advance.

So now there is a man to care for her, and a man for her to care for. And not to forget Alex Winckler (Peter Coyote), a journalist who seems to have a lot of influence and is mesmerized by her. Can he be trusted? He speaks with an accent, and movie fans will know he has the same last name as one of the Nazi creeps in *The Third Man*. Viviane's strategy is to accept protection from the man of the moment, convince him she loves only him, and jump ship when necessary. How does Adjani create the character? Not by vamping, not by flaunting sexuality, but by creating a kind of vacuum of need that draws men so close they cannot resist the lure of her large, liquid eyes—pools to drown in.

The film introduces a tributary that will eventually join with the mainstream, although at first we can't see how. This involves an emigré Jewish professor named Kopolski (Jean-Marc Stehle), an intellectual temperamentally unsuited to survive in an evil world. He is in possession of several very large bottles of heavy water, needed for nuclear experiments, and he wants to keep them away from the Nazis and somehow get them to England. (The heavy water bottles here, like the wine bottles filled with heavy earth in Hitchcock's *Notorious*, function essentially as a MacGuffin.) Professor Kopolski's only hope is a young assistant named Camille (Virginie Ledoyen), who rises to the occasion, saving both the professor and the heavy water from Nazi capture; she transports the bottles in the back of a station wagon, where we constantly expect them to break.

There are other characters, a lot of them, including a set of rich aristocrats and tourists who keep turning up in all of the hotels, demanding what cannot be had. But the underlying structure of the movie is farce crossed with action and oiled by romance, and Rappeneau and his four cowriters are virtuosos at keeping all of their balls in the air. The lives and fates of the characters crisscross, their motives are subject to sudden adjustments, and Viviane is like Eliza on the ice floes, leaping from one man to another.

The movie is funny, not in a ho-ho way, but

in the way it surprises us with delights and blindsides us with hazards. There's a lot of contrivance involved—it is, after all, improbable that these characters would not only constantly cross paths, but always at moments of crisis. But once we accept the movie's method, it implicates us; the sudden separations and reunions are devices for testing Viviane's powers of romantic invention and Camille's desperate improvisations. There is also the amusement that men, especially powerful men, are powerless in the hands of a woman like Viviane. Their mistake is to love someone who loves only herself; their excuse is that she loves herself so much she loves them, too, or is able to make them believe she does, which comes to the same thing.

I haven't even mentioned the costumes, the sets, the ambience. If Rappeneau's *The Horseman on the Roof* was the most expensive French film to date, *Bon Voyage* must be in the same league. He uses the money not to manufacture a big, clunky entertainment, but to facilitate a world that seems real even into the farthest corners of Paris, Bordeaux, hotels, cabinet meetings, boudoirs, dark roads, and desperate rendezvous. This is a grand, confident entertainment, sure of the power of Adjani, Depardieu, and the others, and sure of itself.

Born into Brothels: Calcutta's Red Light Kids ★ ★ ★ ½
R, 85 m., 2005

A documentary directed and produced by Zana Briski and Ross Kauffman.

In a movie named *The Five Obstructions*, the Danish director Lars von Trier creates an ordeal for his mentor, Jorgen Leth. The older director will have to remake a short film in five different ways, involving five obstructions that von Trier will devise. One of the five involves making a film in "the most miserable place on Earth," which they decide is the red light district of Mumbai. The director is unable to deal with this assignment.

Now here is a documentary made in a place that is by definition as miserable: the red light district of Calcutta. I thought of the Danish film as I was watching this one, because the makers of *Born into Brothels: Calcutta's Red Light Kids* also find it almost impossible to

make. They are shooting in an area where no one wants to be photographed, where lives are hidden behind doors or curtains, where with their Western features and cameras they are as obvious as the police, and indeed suspected of working for them.

Zana Briski, an American photographer, and Ross Kauffman, her collaborator, went to Calcutta to film prostitution and found that it melted out of sight as they appeared. It was all around them, it put them in danger, but it was invisible to their camera. What they did see were the children, because the kids of the district followed the visitors, fascinated. Briski hit upon the idea of giving cameras to these children of prostitutes, and asking them to take photos of the world in which they lived.

It is a productive idea, and has a precedent of sorts in a 1993 project by National Public Radio in Chicago; two teenagers, LeAlan Jones and Lloyd Newman, were given tape recorders and asked to make an audio documentary of the Ida B. Wells public housing project, where they lived and where a young child had been thrown from a high window in a fight over candy. Their work won a Peabody Award.

The kids in *Born into Brothels* (which won the 2005 Oscar) take photos with zest and imagination, squint at the contact sheets to choose their favorite shots, and mark them with crayons. Their pictures capture life, and a kind of beauty and squalor that depend on each other. One child, Avijit, is so gifted he wins a week's trip to Amsterdam for an exhibition of photography by children.

Over a couple of years, Briski teaches photo classes and meets some of the parents of the children—made difficult because she must work through interpreters. Prostitution in this district is not a choice but a settled way of life. We meet a grandmother, mother, and daughter, the adults engaged in prostitution, and the granddaughter seems destined to join them. Curiously, the movie does not suggest that the boys will also be used as prostitutes, although it seems inevitable. The age of entry into prostitution seems to be puberty. There are no scenes that could be described as sexually explicit, partly because of the filmmakers' tact in not wanting to exploit their subjects, partly no doubt because the prostitutes refused to be filmed except in innocuous settings.

Briski becomes determined to get several of the children out of the district and into a boarding school, where they will have a chance at different lives. She encounters opposition from their parents and roadblocks from the Indian bureaucracy, which seems to create jobs by requiring the same piece of paper to be meaninglessly stamped, marked, read, or filed in countless different offices. She goes almost mad trying to get a passport for Avijit, the winner of the Amsterdam trip; of course with his background he lacks the "required" papers.

The film is narrated mostly by Briski, who is a good teacher and brings out the innate intelligence of the children as they use their cameras to see their world in a different way. The faces of the children are heartbreaking, because we reflect that in the time since the film was finished, most of them have lost childhood forever, some their lives. Far away offscreen is the prosperous India with middle-class enclaves, an executive class, and a booming economy. These wretched poor exist in a separate and parallel universe, without an exit.

The movie is a record by well-meaning people who try to make a difference for the better, and succeed to a small degree while all around them the horror continues unaffected. Yes, a few children stay in boarding schools. Others are taken out by their parents, drop out, or are asked to leave. The red light district has existed for centuries and will exist for centuries more. I was reminded of a scene in Buñuel's *Viridiana*. A man is disturbed by the sight of a dog tied to a wagon and being dragged along faster than it can run. The man buys the dog to free it, but does not notice, in the background, another cart pulling another dog.

The Bourne Supremacy ★ ★ ★
PG-13, 109 m., 2004

Matt Damon (Jason Bourne), Joan Allen (Agent Pamela Landy), Brian Cox (Ward Abbott), Karl Urban (Kirill), Franka Potente (Marie Helena Kreutz), Julia Stiles (Nicky). Directed by Paul Greengrass and produced by Patrick Crowley, Frank Marshall, and Paul Sandberg. Screenplay by Tony Gilroy, based on the novel by Robert Ludlum.

Jason Bourne obtained an identity in *The Bourne Identity* (2002), and the title of *The Bourne Supremacy* hints that he is not going to die—not with *The Bourne Ultimatum* still to go. He may not die even then, but live on like James Bond, caught in a time loop, repeating the same archetypal pattern again and again as his persona is inhabited by generations of actors.

Bourne may live forever, but the bad news is, people will always want to kill him; that is the defining reality of his life. The plot of *Supremacy*, like *Identity*, involves Bourne trying to survive the shadowy forces against him by using his awesome skills in spycraft, the martial arts, and running real fast. The movie works because he does these things well, and because Matt Damon embodies Bourne without adding any flashy heroism. A show-off would be deadly in this role.

The movie skillfully delivers a series of fights, stalkings, plottings, and chases, punctuated by a little brooding. The best word for Bourne is "dogged." After a brief illusion of happiness, he puts his head down and marches relentlessly ahead into the lairs of his enemies, not even bothering with disguises, because he's using himself as bait. He always wears the same black shirt, pants, and jacket, in scenes taking him from India to Italy to Germany to Russia (no one complains).

Bourne awakened from amnesia, we recall from the first movie, possessed of skills he did not even know he had, and with a cache of passports and other aids to survival, a cache left to him by—well, you remember. As *Supremacy* opens, he has gone as far away as he can go, dropping out with Marie (Franka Potente), the woman he met in the first adventure. They're living on the beach in Goa, in southern India, happy as clams until Bourne spots a stranger who is wearing the wrong clothes, driving the wrong car, and turning up in all the wrong places.

They're still after him, or someone is. What is it about Bourne that makes his enemies prepared to spend millions to wipe him out? Sometimes he seems tantalizingly close to remembering. He suffers from Manchurian Candidate's syndrome, a malady that fills your nightmares with disconnected flashes of something dreadful that may or may not have happened to you. I saw *The Bourne Supremacy* on the very same day I saw the new remake of

73

The Manchurian Candidate, and I was able to compare the symptoms, which involve quick cuts of fragmentary images.

The movie is assembled from standard thriller ingredients, and hurtles from one action sequence to another in India and Europe, with cuts to parallel action in Washington and New York. What distinguishes it is Bourne's inventiveness. There's a scene where he takes about four seconds to disable an armed agent and steal his cell phone contact list, and you're thinking, this is a guy who knows what he's doing. And how about the innovative use he finds for a toaster? It's neat to see him read a situation and instantaneously improvise a response, often by using lateral thinking.

What Bourne doesn't know about his pursuers, we find out as the movie intercuts with a plot involving a CIA agent named Pamela Landy (Joan Allen) and her boss, Ward Abbott (Brian Cox). Julia Stiles plays a younger agent under Landy's direction. They've found Bourne's fingerprints at the scene of a murder in Berlin involving a CIA agent and his high-level criminal contact. But Bourne was in Goa at the time, so who's framing him?

We have a pretty good idea, long before anyone else does, because the movie observes the Law of Economy of Character Development, which teaches us that when an important actor is used in an apparently subordinate role, he's the villain. But the movie doesn't depend on its big revelations for its impact; the mystery is not why Bourne is targeted, but whether he will die. He survives one lethal trap or ambush after another, leaping off bridges, crashing cars, killing assailants, and finally limping a little after a chase that should have killed him.

I have the weakness of bringing logic to movies where it is not required. There's a chase scene where he commandeers a taxicab and leads a posse of squad cars through an urban version of a demo derby. Although the film does not linger over the victims, we assume dozens of cars were destroyed and dozens of people killed or maimed in this crash, and we have to ask ourselves: Is this cost in innocent victims justified in the cause of saving Jason Bourne's life? At the end of the film there is a heartfelt scene where he delivers an apology. If he ever goes back to Berlin,

he'll have to apologize to hundreds if not thousands of people, assuming a lynch mob doesn't get to him first.

But I digress. Thrillers don't exist in a plausible universe. They consist of preposterous situations survived by skill, courage, craft, and luck. That Matt Damon is able to bring some poignancy to Jason Bourne makes the process more interesting, because we care more about the character. That the director, Paul Greengrass, treats the material with gravity and uses good actors in well-written supporting roles elevates the movie above its genre, but not quite out of it.

The Boys of Baraka ★ ★ ★
NO MPAA RATING, 84 m., 2006

Featuring Devon Brown, Darius Chambers, Richard Keyser, Justin Mackall, Montrey Moore, and Romesh Vance. A documentary produced and directed by Heidi Ewing and Rachel Grady.

Here is a movie that makes you want to do something. Cry, or write a check, or howl with rage. It tells the story of twenty "high-risk" inner-city black boys, twelve and thirteen years old, who are lifted out of the Baltimore school system and given scholarships to the Baraka School. Where is Baraka? In Kenya, in an area poorer than the ghettos of Baltimore. There's not even full-time electricity. Here they are told, "Fail one class and you go home."

Two boys who fight are taken on a hike to "base camp," given a two-man tent, and told to spend the night. How do you assemble the tent? They have to figure it out together. One boy refuses to do it. Fine, says the teacher. Sleep outdoors. We see a process at work. The tent gets assembled. The fights stop.

The movie, by Heidi Ewing and Rachel Grady, begins in Baltimore, where 76 percent of African-American boys do not graduate from high school. A recruiter for Baraka speaks at an assembly, telling potential students they have three choices: jail, death, or high school graduation. Despairing parents and grandparents embrace the idea of this strange school in Africa because nothing could be worse than the children's present reality. Two brothers apply. The school asks their mother what would happen if only one was selected. "Don't make one a king and the other a killer," she says. Both are given scholarships.

All the teachers we see at Baraka School are white; it is not an African school but one run by American volunteers who chose Kenya, among other reasons, because it is cheap, and because "boys can live the lives of boys"—running around, swimming in streams, seeing wild animals, climbing Mount Kenya. In Baltimore it can be dangerous for them to go outside, and they stare at television. The boys thrive at Baraka. Their behavior is transformed, their grades improve, and they think differently of themselves.

Then everything changes. Because of terrorist attacks and the closure of the American embassy in Nairobi, Baraka has to shut down at the end of the first of the boys' two years. In Baltimore that summer, they're told they won't be going back. One review actually complains that the movie is "unsatisfactory" because unforeseen events prevented the filmmakers from "completing" their story. Oh, it's complete, all right. "All our lives gonna be bad now," one tearful boy says. One parent on the terrorist threat: "They're more likely to be killed right here in Baltimore." Another parent: "If you send them to Baltimore, you're sending them to jail."

Some of the boys seem to return to the same aimless lives they were leading before. But a boy named Devon is elected president of his ninth-grade class, and we see him already beginning his life's work, as a preacher. Montrey, the boy with the worst attitude and behavior problems, is so changed by one year at Baraka that at the end of the next year he gets the top score in all of Maryland on a math test and is admitted to the most competitive high school in Baltimore. He speaks at the close of the film: "People think we ain't got a future. I'm gonna make a difference. I'm gonna be on the map."

In a simple, direct way, without a lot of filmmaking sophistication, *The Boys of Baraka* makes this argument: Many of our schools are failing, and many of our neighborhoods are poisonous. Individual parents and children make an effort, but the system is against them, and hope is hard to find. One of the mothers in the film goes back to drugs and is jailed during the Baraka year. Grandparents realistically look at the city and see a death sentence for their grandchildren. The recruiter for Baraka says, "Nothing's out there for them other than a new jail they just built." These children are born into a version of genocide.

If I were in charge of everything, and I certainly should be, I would divert billions of dollars into an emergency fund for our schools. I would reduce classroom size to fifteen or twenty. I would double teachers' salaries. I would fund boarding schools to remove the most endangered children from environments that are killing them. I would be generous and vigilant about school lunch programs and medical care for kids. I would install monitors on the television sets in the homes of these children and pay a cash bonus for every hour they are not turned on during homework time. I would open a storefront library on every other block. And although there are two sides to the question, I would consider legalizing drugs; illegal drugs are destroying countless lives, and legalizing them would destroy the profit motive for promoting and selling them.

All of this would cost a fraction of—well, of the cost of the government undertaking of your choice. It would pay dividends in one generation. There is something wrong when, as our own officials say, we depend on immigration to supply us with scientists. A kid like Montrey, who goes from a standing start to the top state score in math in one year, can supply us with an invaluable resource, but he has to be given a chance. We look at TV and see stories of drugs and gang bangers and despair, and we assume the victims bring it on themselves. If we had been born and raised as they were, in areas abandoned by hope and opportunity, the odds are good we would be dead, or watching TV in prison.

Breakfast on Pluto ★ ★ ★ ½
R, 135 m., 2005

Cillian Murphy (Patrick "Kitten" Braden), Liam Neeson (Father Bernard), Stephen Rea (Bertie), Ruth Negga (Charlie), Laurence Kinlan (Irwin), Gavin Friday (Billy Hatchet), Bryan Ferry (Mr. Silky String), Brendan Gleeson (John-Joe). Directed by Neil Jordan and produced by Stephen Woolley, Alan Moloney, and Jordan.

Screenplay by Jordan and Patrick McCabe, based on the novel by McCabe.

We'll fly to the stars . . .
Journey to Mars . . .
And find our breakfast on Pluto.

I heard this song performed in London by a blind man in a pub on Portobello Road in the early 1970s, and remembered it during Neil Jordan's new film. His hero, Patrick Braden, known as Kitten, would have heard it at about the same time, and needed to, because he needed all the cheering-up he could get, and usually breakfast, too. *Breakfast on Pluto* tells the story of an Irish orphan, left on the steps of a priest's rectory and raised by a strict foster mother. Patrick discovers his identity at an early age. One day the woman finds him trying on her dresses and shoes.

"I'll walk you up and down the streets before the whole town in disgrace!" she screams.

"Promise?" says Patrick.

He is then about ten. Too young to have such feelings and smart answers? Not if you have seen Jonathan Caouette's documentary *Tarnation,* which contains a home movie of Jonathan in drag at about the same age, with something of the same personality. Patrick decides that his name is Kitten, insists on being called by it, and is not a boy trapped in a girl's body but a boy trapped in a transvestite's body—or, more accurately, a boy trapped in a world he desperately wants to escape, using his imagination to reinvent himself and escape it. He is, as they say, not like the other boys.

The enchanting and hopeful *Breakfast on Pluto,* adapted by Jordan from a novel by Patrick McCabe, has a hero who is a little mad and a little saintly. Many saints insist on living in their own way regardless of what the world thinks. Some climb trees or pray in caves. Some work among the poor. Some, like Kitten, insist on optimism in the face of absolutely everything. In his case, it could be sainthood, could be denial, could be insanity. Whatever it is, Kitten so stubbornly insists on it that motorcycle gangs, London cops, and IRA killers all realize they can kill him but they can't change him.

The movie is like a Dickens novel in which the hero moves through the underskirts of so-ciety, encountering one colorful character after another. Kitten believes his birth mother may have moved to London. His only clue is that she looked like Mitzi Gaynor. Of course Kitten would know who that was. In the course of his journey to find her, he sings with a rock band, becomes a magician's assistant, is a suspected IRA bomber, and is reduced to street prostitution, although he handles it with a kind of dreamy denial. The movie becomes a series of seductions, with the goal not sex but acceptance.

Consider that Kitten is unluckily in a London pub when it's bombed by the IRA. The cops suspect him as a cross-dressing bomber and interrogate him for a week, not gently. At the end of that time they give up and accept him for who and what he says he is. A little later, one of the same cops who beat him sees him working the streets, knows Kitten is no match for the life, drives him to Soho, drops him outside a peep show, and says, with real concern, "Get a job here. It's safe and it's legal."

Kitten depends on the kindness of strangers. Played by Cillian Murphy with a bemused and hopeful voice, he meets such characters as Billy (Gavin Friday), leader of the scruffy rock band Billy Hatchet and the Mohawks, and soon Kitten is onstage as a squaw, helping out during the performance of *Running Bear.* Billy falls in love with him, but eventually "the band thinks the squaw is not working out," and Kitten finds a job being sawed in two by a magician named Bertie (Stephen Rea). In Jordan's *The Crying Game,* Rea fell in love with a cross-dressing hairdresser. But no one is deceived by Kitten, who doesn't care if you think he's male or female, as long as you think he's Kitten.

That's the part of the story Dickens would have agreed with. His heroes, from Pip to Oliver Twist to Nicholas Nickleby to David Copperfield, travel bleak landscapes of gruesome betrayal and disappointment and meet villains of every description but never lose their innocence. Dickens also would have enjoyed the story's use of melodrama and improbable coincidence, and the way the hero befriends and is befriended just when it's needed the most.

Consider Father Bernard (Liam Neeson), whose rectory steps are Kitten's first home. The priest is one of those good souls bumbling through, doing what good he can. And John-Joe (Brendan Gleeson), a streetwise hobo who shares what he has. And Charlie (Ruth Negga), a black girl who becomes Kitten's closest friend. And consider the story of how Kitten does, or does not, find his mother, or Mitzi Gaynor, or whoever, and what he finds out then.

Breakfast on Pluto is being included in earnest analytical articles about this being the season of homosexuals *(Brokeback Mountain)*, transsexuals *(Transamerica)*, transvestites (this movie), or all three *(Rent)*. As a "trend," this means absolutely nothing, although as a coincidence it is worth notice, however slight. What these titles have in common with many other good current films are characters who are given the challenge to be true to their own natures and either rise to the occasion or descend into misery.

Kitten has less to do with sexual unorthodoxy than knowing what you must be and do, and being and doing it: characters like those played by Terrence Howard in *Hustle and Flow,* Anthony Hopkins in *The World's Fastest Indian,* Amy Adams in *Junebug,* Naomi Watts in *Ellie Parker,* Miranda July in *Me and You and Everyone We Know,* Tommy Lee Jones in *The Three Burials of Melquiades Estrada,* Charlize Theron in *North Country,* and King Kong. This drive toward individualism is an encouraging counterforce to the relentless team spirit that seems to drive so much unhappiness in our society. Although it is true that in some times and places Kitten would be murdered (the fear that haunts Ennis in *Brokeback Mountain*), it is also true that Kitten might be given a pass by dangerous characters who either recognize a kindred independence, or envy it.

Breakin' All the Rules ★ ★ ★
PG-13, 85 m., 2004

Jamie Foxx (Quincy Watson), Gabrielle Union (Nicky Callas), Morris Chestnut (Evan Fields), Peter MacNicol (Philip Gascon), Jennifer Esposito (Rita Monroe), Bianca Lawson (Helen Sharp). Directed by Daniel Taplitz and produced by Lisa Tornell. Screenplay by Taplitz.

Breakin' All the Rules combines a romantic comedy, a little mistaken identity, and some satire about office politics into one of those genial movies where you know everything is going to turn out all right in the end. The movie depends for its success on the likability of Jamie Foxx, Morris Chestnut, and Gabrielle Union, and because they're funny and pleasant we enjoy the ride even though the destination is preordained.

Foxx plays Quincy Watson, a writer for *Spoils* magazine, one of those men's lifestyle books edited for readers who believe they can become rich, successful, and well groomed by studying a magazine. The magazine has fallen upon hard times, and the editor summons Quincy and gives him a list of people to fire. Quincy recoils; he hates the idea of firing anybody. So does Philip the editor (Peter MacNicol), who explains that one of the spoils of being the boss is that you can get other people to do your dirty work.

Rather than fire anyone, Quincy quits. He's depressed anyway; his fiancée, Helen Sharp (Bianca Lawson), has just broken up with him. He starts writing versions of a wounded, angry letter to her, and somehow the correspondence grows into a book titled *Break Up Handbook,* about how to break up with a girl before she can break up with you (danger signal: she says she "wants to have a talk").

Enter Quincy's cousin, Evan (Morris Chestnut), a moving target who prides himself on breaking up with girls as a preemptive strategy. His girl, Nicky (Gabrielle Union), says she wants to have a talk, and to deny her the opportunity of breaking up with him, Evan sends Quincy to a bar to meet her and tell her the relationship is over. Alas, Nicky has cut her hair and doesn't fit Evan's description; Quincy starts talking with her, and soon they're flirting with love. If the hair trick sounds contrived, recall that Shakespeare was not above mistaken identities even more absurd. Not that I hold it against him.

Gabrielle Union is one of those actresses whose smile is so warm you hope the other characters will say something just to make her happy. As a counterbalance, the movie supplies Rita (Jennifer Esposito), a mercenary mantrap who wants to get her hooks into Philip the editor. Quincy is called in as a consultant on this case, too, but Rita is too crafty to be easily fooled by tricks learned from a book.

There will, of course, be a scene of wounded betrayal, when Evan discovers that Quincy is dating Nicky and decides he loves her after all.

And a titanic battle of the wills between Rita and Philip. And jokes about being the author of a best-seller; Quincy's book seems to hit the charts within days after he finishes it, having apparently been printed by magic.

Breakin' All the Rules is not a comic masterpiece, but it's entertaining and efficient and provides a showcase for its stars. It's on the level of a good sitcom. It's unusual in this way: Writer-director Daniel Taplitz has come up with a magazine title that would probably work on the newsstands, and a book idea that would probably sell. Most magazines in movies are completely implausible (in *13 Going on 30*, the heroine redesigned the magazine as a school yearbook). And most best-sellers in the movies sound way too good to ever sell many copies.

The Break-Up ★ ★

PG-13, 106 m., 2006

Vince Vaughn (Gary Grobowski), Jennifer Aniston (Brooke Meyers), Joey Lauren Adams (Addie), John Michael Higgins (Richard Meyers), Jon Favreau (Johnny O), Vincent D'Onofrio (Dennis Grobowski), Justin Long (Christopher), Cole Hauser (Lupus Grobowski), Judy Davis (Marilyn Dean), Ann-Margret (Wendy Meyers), Jason Bateman (Riggleman). Directed by Peyton Reed and produced by Vince Vaughn and Scott Stuber. Screenplay by Jeremy Garelick and Jay Lavender.

The Break-Up hints that the broken-up couple will get back together, but that doesn't make us eager for a sequel. The movie stars Vince Vaughn and Jennifer Aniston as Gary and Brooke, a steady couple who have many reasons to break up but none to get together, except that they fall in love. Since the scenes where they're together are so much less convincing than the ones where they fall apart, watching the movie is like being on a double date from hell.

Gary is obsessed with the Chicago Cubs and video games, and thinks if they moved the dining table into the living room, that would make space for a pool table. He and his brothers run a Chicago tour bus company, and he is the tour guide. Brooke works in a high-powered Chicago art gallery. They break up because she says he never listens to her, or appreciates all the work she does around the house or how she cooks his meals and picks up his laundry. All true, but these are not merely faults; they are his essential nature, and he will never, ever be interested in her world. Not when he thinks Michelangelo painted the ceiling of the "Sixteenth Chapel."

True, their arguments are funny, at least while they're still getting along. They have a fight right at the beginning that had me nodding my head and recognizing my own shortcomings. At the thirty-minute mark, I thought the movie had a chance, but it grew dreary and sad, especially when they both receive spectacularly bad advice from their best friends (Joey Lauren Adams and Jon Favreau). There's a stretch when Gary's sleeping on the sofa surrounded by dirty underwear, and she's trying to make him jealous by being picked up at home by a series of handsome studs. Would any woman really do this? The way to make a guy jealous is by seeming to really like someone else, not acting like first prize on Match.com.

Gary, on the other hand, tries to make Brooke jealous by hiring hookers to join his buddies in a strip poker game. Believe it or not, this doesn't work, either. By the time they have a heart-to-heart, it's way too late because both hearts are broken, and it isn't a pretty sight. What the movie lacks is warmth, optimism, and insight into human nature. I point you to *Fever Pitch* (2005), with Jimmy Fallon as a schoolteacher and Red Sox fan, and Drew Barrymore as a business executive. It begins by showing them really and truly falling in love, and then baseball season starts, and she realizes that he is two guys: the guy she fell in love with, and the Red Sox fan. If she can accept both of these personalities and he can accept her needs, they can repair their problems.

The problem with Gary is that he has only the one personality, and even if he starts listening to her and thanking her for picking up his dirty socks, they still will be profoundly incompatible. For the movie to work, we would have to like the couple and want them to succeed. Despite some sincere eleventh-hour soul-searching by Vaughn, we're sorry, but we don't want them back together. We want them to end their misery.

The supporting cast adds variety, to be sure, but of a strange kind. Occasionally, supporting actors will be so effective you want the movie to be about them. *The Break-Up* is filled with actors who seem to be auditioning for that role. John Michael Higgins, as Brooke's brother, is the leader of a men's choir and tries to turn a family dinner party into a sing-along; this scene might be funny in theory, but in practice, it's ungainly. Favreau and Adams, as the best friends, get whiplash from a plot that requires them to give one kind of advice at the beginning and another kind toward the end, as if they hadn't been listening to themselves. And Judy Davis, as the art gallery owner, behaves as if she should be carrying a whip. The best supporting performance is by Vincent D'Onofrio, as Gary's older brother: He does exactly what is required, finds the right notes, and is so convincing we hardly notice he is cleaning his ears with separate handkerchiefs.

That Aniston and Vaughn are such likable actors compounds the problem. They're not convincing as sadistic meanies, and when the movie makes them act that way, we feel sorrier for them than for their characters. Their problems start in the first scene, at Wrigley Field, where Gary is a jerk who forces Brooke to accept a hot dog she doesn't want and then insults her date. Why would a girl end up with a guy who acts like that the first time she meets him? We never find out. The next time we see them, they're living together. Must have been some courtship.   ☞

Brick ★ ★ ★
R, 110 m., 2006

Joseph Gordon-Levitt (Brendan Frye), Nora Zehetner (Laura Dannon), Lukas Haas (The Pin), Noah Fleiss (Tugger), Matt O'Leary (The Brain), Emilie de Ravin (Emily Kostach), Noah Segan (Dode), Richard Roundtree (Mr. Trueman), Meagan Good (Kara), Brian White (Brad Bramish). Directed by Rian Johnson and produced by Ram Bergman and Mark G. Mathis. Screenplay by Johnson.

You have preserved in your own lifetime, sir, a way of life that was dead before you were born.
—the butler in Elaine May's
A New Leaf (1971)

You will forgive me for reaching back thirty-five years for a quotation to open this review of *Brick,* since the movie itself is inspired by hard-boiled crime novels written by Dashiell Hammett between 1929 and 1934. What is unexpected, and daring, is that *Brick* transposes the attitudes and dialogue of classic detective fiction to a modern Southern California high school. These are contemporary characters who say things like, "I got all five senses and I slept last night. That puts me six up on the lot of you." Or, "Act smarter than you look, and drop it."

What is the audience for this movie? It is carrying on in its own lifetime a style of film that was dead before it was born. Are teenage moviegoers familiar with movies like *The Maltese Falcon?* Do they know who Humphrey Bogart was? Maybe it doesn't matter. They're generally familiar with black-and-white classics on cable and will understand the strategy: The students inhabit personal styles from an earlier time.

This mixing of styles and ages has been done before. Alan Parker's *Bugsy Malone* (1976) was a 1930s gangster movie cast with preteen kids (including Jodie Foster). Once you accepted the idea, it worked, and so does *Brick.* The crucial decision by writer-director Rian Johnson is to play it straight; this isn't a put-on, and the characters don't act as if they think their behavior is funny.

The movie opens in James Ellroy territory, with the hero, Brendan (Joseph Gordon-Levitt), finding the dead body of his onetime girlfriend in a drainage ditch. From the mouth of a tunnel comes the sound, perhaps, of her murderer escaping. The victim is Emily (Emilie de Ravin), who called him earlier for help; from a lonely phone booth (itself a relic of pre-cellular movies) he sees her being taken past in a car, possibly a captive.

Brendan turns into a classic 1930s gumshoe, tracing Emily's movements back through a high school drug ring and ignoring threats from a high school principal who tries to pull him off the case (this is the role police captains filled in old private-eye movies). True to the genre that inspired it, the movie has tough and dippy dames, an eccentric crime kingpin, some would-be toughs who can be slapped around like Elisha Cook Jr. in *The Maltese Falcon,* and an enigmatic know-it-all. This last character was, in the old days, an informer, bookie, or newspaper reporter often found in the shadows of a bar; in *Brick*, he apparently exists permanently sitting against a back wall of the high school, from which vantage point he sees and knows, or guesses, everything.

Does the movie work on its own terms as a crime story? Yes, in the sense that the classic Hollywood noirs worked: The story is never clear while it unfolds, but it provides a rich source of dialogue, behavior, and incidents. Then, at the end, if it doesn't all hold water, who cares as long as all the characters think it does? *The Big Sleep* is famous for the loophole of a killer who is already dead when he commits his crime. At the Madison Film Festival this year, I saw *Laura* again and was reminded that it is entirely a movie about atmosphere, dialogue, and acting styles, in which the very realities of murder are arbitrary. It makes no difference who committed the central killing; what's important is that everyone acts as if it does.

Brick is a movie reportedly made with great determination and not much money by Johnson, who did the editing on his Macintosh (less impressive than it sounds, since desktop machines are now often used even on big-budget movies). What is impressive is his absolute commitment to his idea of the movie's style. He relates to the classic crime novels and movies, he notes the way their mannered dialogue and behavior elevate the characters into archetypes, and he uses the strategy to make his teenagers into hard-boiled guys and dolls. The actors enter into the spirit; we never catch them winking.

The movie has one inevitable point of vulnerability: Because we can't believe in the characters, we can't care about their fates. They have lifestyles, not lives. The same can be said of many (not all) noir films, and it is because of style that we treasure them. This movie leaves me looking forward to the director's next film; we can say of Johnson, as somebody once said about a dame named Brigid O'Shaughnessy, "You're good. You're very good."

Bride and Prejudice ★ ★ ★
PG-13, 110 m., 2005

Aishwarya Rai (Lalita Bakshi), Martin Henderson (Will Darcy), Naveen Andrews (Balraj), Indira Varma (Kiran Bingley), Nitin Chandra Ganatra (Mr. Kholi), Daniel Gillies (Johnny Wickham), Anupam Kher (Mr. Bakshi), Nadira Babbar (Mrs. Bakshi), Namrata Shirodkar (Jaya Bakshi), Meghna Kothari (Maya Bakshi), Peeya Rai Chowdhary (Lucky Bakshi), Marsha Mason (Will's Mother). Directed by Gurinder Chadha and produced by Deepak Nayar and Chadha. Screenplay by Paul Mayeda Berges and Chadha, inspired by Jane Austen's *Pride and Prejudice.*

Bollywood musicals are the Swiss Army knives of the cinema, with a tool for every job: comedy, drama, song and dance, farce, pathos, adventure, great scenery, improbably handsome heroes, teeth-gnashing villains, marriage-obsessed mothers and their tragically unmarried daughters, who are invariably ethereal beauties. "You get everything in one film," my friend Uma da Cuhna told me, as she took me to see *Taal* in Hyderabad. "No need to run around here and there, looking for a musical or an action picture." The movie lasted more than three hours, including an intermission, which Uma employed by correctly predicting everything that would happen during the rest of the film.

Bollywood, is, of course, Bombay—or Mumbai, as it is now called, although there has been no movement to rename the genre Mumblywood. Although Western exhibitors aren't crazy about a movie they can show only twice a night, instead of three times, Bollywood has developed a healthy audience in London, where the Bollywood Oscars were held a year ago. Now comes *Bride and Prejudice*, which adds the BritLit genre to the mix.

Directed by Gurinder Chadha, whose *What's Cooking?* (2000) and *Bend It Like Beckham* (2002) make you smile just thinking about them, this is a free-spirited adaptation of the Jane Austen novel, in which Mr. Darcy and the unmarried sisters and their family are plugged into a modern plot that spans London, New York, Bombay, and Goa. Darcy is an American played by Martin Henderson, and Lizzie Bennett becomes Lalita Bakshi, second of four daughters in Amritsar, India—true to Austen, a country town.

Lalita is played by Aishwarya Rai, Miss World of 1994, recently described by at least one film critic (me) as not only the first but also the second most beautiful woman in the world.

According to the Internet Movie Database, "The Queen of Bollywood" is so popular she was actually able to get away with appearing in ads for both Coke and Pepsi. I also learn she carried the Olympic Torch in 2004, has a puppy named Sunshine, and was listed by *Time* as one of the 100 most influential people in the world. If this review is not accompanied by a photograph of her, you have grounds for a lawsuit.

Aishwarya (ash-waar-e-ah) Rai exudes not the frightening seriousness of a woman who thinks she is being sexy, but the grace and ease of a woman who knows she is fun to look at and be around. What a smile. What eyes. Rai is not remotely overweight, but neither is she alarmingly skinny; having deliberately gained twenty pounds for this role, she is the flower of splendid nutrition.

Sorry, I got a little distracted there. Gurinder Chadha, who was born in Kenya, raised in London, and is married to a Japanese-American, seems attracted to ethnic multitasking. Her *What's Cooking?* is set in Los Angeles and tells parallel stories about families with Vietnamese, African-American, Mexican, and Jewish roots. *Bend it Like Beckham* was about a London girl from a Kenyan family with Punjabi roots, who wants to play soccer.

In *Bride and Prejudice* Chadha once again transcends boundaries. This is not a Bollywood movie, but a Hollywood musical comedy incorporating Bollywood elements. Her characters burst into song and dance at the slightest provocation, backed up by a dance corps that materializes with the second verse and disappears at the end of the scene. That's Bollywood. So is the emphasis on the mother and father; the lovers in most American romantic comedies seem to be orphans. And she employs the Bollywood strategy for using color, which comes down to: If it's a color, use it.

Will Darcy (Henderson) is a rich young New York hotel man, visiting India because his old friend from London, Balraj (Naveen Andrews), is the best man at a wedding. The Bakshi family is friendly with the family of the bride, and Mrs. Bakshi (Nadira Babbar) hopes her four daughters can meet eligible husbands at the event. That strategy works immediately for Balraj and Jaya Bakshi (Namrata Shirodkar), Lalita's older sister. For them, it's love at first sight. For Darcy and Lalita, it's not.

Darcy makes tactless remarks, disagrees with the custom of arranged marriages, seems stuck-up, is distracted by business, and creates the possibility that Lalita may have to follow her mother's instructions and marry the creepy Hollywood mogul Mr. Kholi (Nitin Chandra Ganatra). Things could be worse; Harvey Weinstein is also visiting India. We know Lalita won't really marry Mr. Kholi, since he is never provided with a first name, but in stories of this sort it's necessary for Darcy and Lalita to rub each other the wrong way, so that later they can rub each other the right way.

This plot, recycled from Austen, is the clothesline for a series of dance numbers that, like Hong Kong action sequences, are set in unlikely locations and use props found there; how else to explain the sequence set in, yes, a Mexican restaurant? Even the most strenuous dances are intercut with perfectly composed close-ups of Aishwarya Rai, never sweaty, never short of breath. What a smile. Did I say that?

Bridget Jones: The Edge of Reason ★ ★ ★
R, 108 m., 2004

Renee Zellweger (Bridget Jones), Hugh Grant (Daniel Cleaver), Colin Firth (Mark Darcy), Gemma Jones (Mum), Jim Broadbent (Dad), Jacinda Barrett (Rebecca), Sally Phillips (Shazzer), James Callis (Tom), Shirley Henderson (Jude). Directed by Beeban Kidron and produced by Tim Bevan, Jonathan Cavendish, and Eric Fellner. Screenplay by Andrew Davies, Helen Fielding, Richard Curtis, and Adam Brooks, based on the novel by Fielding.

You ever have the kind of friend where for a long time you shake your head in admiration, and then gradually realize you're shaking your head in despair? Bridget Jones would be a friend like that. She's hopelessly lovable, and she's always going to be your friend no matter what, but really, who but Bridget, with her guilt-ridden diary entries for alcohol and nicotine units per day, would manage to get jailed in Thailand on drug-smuggling charges?

Bridget, of course, is not a drug smuggler, but being Bridget she did the one thing no tourist should *ever* do, and that is to carry in her luggage a souvenir given to her girlfriend by a guy. But Bridget has pluck. In no time at all, she's traded her pink bra for cigarettes, organized her prison inmates into a Madonna class, and they're rehearsing "Like a Virgin."

Bridget Jones: The Edge of Reason is a jolly movie, and I smiled pretty much all the way through, but it doesn't shift into high with a solid thunk, the way *Bridget Jones' Diary* (2001) did. In the first movie, things happened to Bridget. In the sequel, Bridget happens to things.

As the story opens, Bridget is happily involved with Mark Darcy (Colin Firth), who to her astonishment became her boyfriend in the earlier film. Plump Bridget, in love with a hunk! She's still working as an on-air personality for a TV show which seems to be running its private version of *Fear Factor* just for Bridget; surely this girl is not ready to sky dive? Or ski? Or manage a romance without getting unreasonably jealous of the quality time Mark seems to be spending with his colleague Rebecca (Jacinda Barrett). But she loves the guy. Who else could keep him standing outside her door while she finishes leaving a message for him on his answering machine? Especially when the message is, essentially, that he is standing outside even as she speaks?

Bridget depends as before on the wisdom of three friends whose advice is infallibly dangerous. They are Shazzer (Sally Phillips), Tom (James Callis), and Jude (Shirley Henderson), and they support her when she and Mark have a completely unreasonable fight. Bridget flies off to Thailand on assignment, and discovers that her former boyfriend Daniel (Hugh Grant) is already there. This is a man she should never, ever, have anything to do with, but because she is mad at Mark she allows herself to be maneuvered into a position where Daniel can cry with glee: "Please! Please be wearing the giant panties!"

Renée Zellweger is lovable to begin with, and combining her with Bridget Jones creates a critical mass of cuteness: You don't want to just watch her, you want to tickle her ears and scratch under her chin. She has that desperately hopeful smile, and the endearing optimism of a woman in a dress two sizes too small. When she embarrasses herself, it's bigtime, as when she single-handedly causes

Mark's table to lose the annual quiz at the Law Society dinner.

The scenes in Thailand, it must be said, venture beyond contrivance. Bridget is the kind of woman who is more at home dealing with the sorts of things that could happen to anybody, like dropping a rock Cornish game hen down the front of her dress. She isn't made for cocaine busts. And it's a little mystifying why Daniel and Mark, two relatively important and successful men no longer in their first youth, have *another* brawl over her. Their motivation, I think, is that the fight in the first movie was so funny. Hugh Grant is so good at losing his dignity that we forget what skillful acting it requires to assure us he has any. Colin Firth plays the basically good guy, never a plum role; rascals always have more fun in comedies.

Standing back from *Bridget Jones: The Edge of Reason*, I can see that the perfection of the first film has been replaced here by a series of comic episodes that could as easily be about anything else. The movie doesn't have the dire necessity of Bridget One's quest for true love. If we didn't know better, we'd suspect that Bridget Two subtly engineers her way into pickles because she knows how cute she looks when she gets in trouble. Still, at the end of the day, I left hoping there will be a Bridget Three. Long may she squint and bravely smile and keep tugging her neckline up and believe in love.

Bright Leaves ★ ★ ★
NO MPAA RATING, 107 m., 2004

A documentary, directed and produced by Ross McElwee. Screenplay by McElwee.

Two scenes from *Bright Leaves*. In the first, Ross McElwee visits the fifty-two-room Duke mansion in Charlotte, North Carolina. In the second, he sits on the only bench in a threadbare little park in Charlotte—McElwee Park, named after his great-grandfather. If things had worked out differently, he would be living in the mansion and the Dukes would be sitting on the bench.

McElwee is a great-grandson of John McElwee, who patented the famous line of Bull Durham tobacco. John McElwee and Washington Duke, founder of the Duke dynasty, were rivals at the birth of the modern tobacco industry, and Duke essentially destroyed McElwee (whose warehouse was burned down three times by suspicious fires). The Dukes went on to found Duke University. Three generations of John McElwee's descendants became doctors, and Ross became a documentarian who films introspective essays about his life.

Bright Leaves is not a documentary about anything in particular. That is its charm. It's a meandering visit by a curious man with a quiet sense of humor, who pokes here and there in his family history and the history of tobacco. The title refers to the particular beauty of tobacco leaves, both in the fields and after they have been cured, and perhaps also to the leaves of his family's history.

McElwee's odyssey begins with a second cousin, a fanatic film buff who is convinced that *Bright Leaf,* a 1950 movie starring Gary Cooper and Patricia Neal, was inspired by the rivalry of Washington Duke and John McElwee. There do seem to be a lot of parallels in its story of the triumph of one family over another. McElwee interviews Patricia Neal, who knows nothing about the origins of the story, but does helpfully volunteer that Cooper was "the love of my life." Then he tracks down Marian Fitz-Simons, the widow of the writer, who assures him her husband did not have real people in mind.

Well, maybe not, but the parallels are uncanny. Unwilling to entirely let go of his notion, McElwee wanders about the area where he grew up, remembering that his childhood home, while large and comfortable, was known as the "Dukes' outhouse." He ruminates on the addiction of smoking, which he has given up while still understanding its appeal. He chats with five beauty-school students as they puff away on the sidewalk outside their classes, and with a couple who give him their deadlines for stopping smoking: When they get married, after the millennium, whenever. He also visits people who are dying of cigarette-related illnesses, but he doesn't preach about the evils of tobacco; it's more that he regrets that such a beautiful plant, which produces so much pleasure, should be lethal. Think how happy it would make so many people if smoking were good for you.

McElwee's lifework is his life. He has been making autobiographical films since 1976,

taking as his subjects his father, his southern heritage, his favorite teacher, his marriage, his son, his prospects. His most famous work is *Sherman's March* (1986), which traces the footsteps of the Civil War general while musing about southernness and whatever else occurs along the way.

In all of his films, McElwee runs into people by chance, and pauses to film them. In *Bright Leaves,* one of his discoveries is Vlada Petric, a film historian he consults for information about the Gary Cooper film. Almost immediately, the subject becomes not Gary Cooper, but Vlada Petric, who refuses to be interviewed in one of those boring shots where the camera looks at a guy sitting in a chair. Instead, Petric orders McElwee to sit in a wheelchair with his hand-held camera, while Petric looms over him, pushing the chair backward while being interviewed. Petric is right and the shot is interesting, but not as interesting as the shots of Petric insisting on it.

Others we meet along the way include Charleen Swansea, the inspirational teacher who has been in several of McElwee's films, and now talks about her dying sister, a smoker made ill by cigarettes. He talks with a civic booster about Charlotte's Tobacco Festival and its annual parade, only to discover that, starting next year, it will be renamed Farmer's Day. He finds that local residents have "mixed feelings" about tobacco, which has been so good to them financially and yet killed so many along the way.

McElwee's films are always, in a way, about why he makes them. He looks at faded home movies of his father, trying to recapture his memories of the man, and then he films his son and wonders how the son will feel, someday, seeing this film. Always at his back he hears time's winged chariot, hurrying near, and is fascinated by the way film seems to freeze time, or at least preserve it. He doesn't really much care that his family lost an incalculable fortune to the Dukes; he is content to be who he is, doing what he does, and his motivation for making the film is not to complain, but simply to meditate on how events in the past reverberate in our own lives. He goes back to the park, and sits on the bench again. McElwee Park. It's not much, but it's something.

Bright Young Things ★ ★ ★ ½
R, 106 m., 2004

Stephen Campbell Moore (Adam Symes), Emily Mortimer (Nina), Fenella Woolgar (Agatha Runcible), James McAvoy (Simon Balcairn), Dan Aykroyd (Lord Monomark), Peter O'Toole (Colonel Blount), David Tennant (Ginger Littlejohn), Jim Broadbent (Drunken Major), Stockard Channing (Mrs. Melrose Ape). Directed by Stephen Fry and produced by Gina Carter and Miranda Davis. Screenplay by Fry, based on the novel *Vile Bodies* by Evelyn Waugh.

If *Bright Young Things* were set today in Manhattan, it would be about Paris and Nicky Hilton and their circle, Rupert Murdoch, the gossip writers of Page Six, and bloggers for sites like defamer.com. That might make a good movie. Certainly it would if it were done in the spirit of Stephen Fry's new film, based on Evelyn Waugh's *Vile Bodies* (1930), which has been called the funniest English novel of the century. Five or six books by Wodehouse may outrank it, but never mind; what's striking about the Fry version is how clearly he sees the underlying sadness. Until a few years ago he was a Bright Young Thing himself, and there may be elements of autobiography lurking here somewhere. "What a lot of parties!" one of the exhausted young things sighs late one night.

The story takes place in London and English country houses between the two wars, and, like Anthony Powell's *A Dance to the Music of Time*, occupies the intersection of the aristocratic, the rich, the ambitious, the decadent, the fraudulent, and the bohemian. The most important requirement for BYT membership is never to be boring, although one can often be bored. Alcoholism is the recommended lifestyle.

The hero, as so often in comic novels, is an earnest young man who wants to get married but lacks the money. Adam Symes (Stephen Campbell Moore) has great hopes for his new novel, having already spent his publisher's advance, and when his only manuscript is seized as pornography at customs, he is in despair. How can he marry the fragrant Nina (Emily Mortimer) without the money to support her in the style to which she wants to become accustomed? Nina loves him, truly she does, but she hates poverty more.

Adam moves in circles that spin more quickly after midnight, and is a friend of the titled but impoverished Lord Simon Balcairn (James McAvoy), who attends all the best parties and then, as Mr. Chatterbox, writes anonymous scandal about them for a popular newspaper. His publisher is Lord Monomark (Dan Aykroyd), a Canadian press baron who seems to combine the worst (and, it must be said, the best) qualities of Murdoch and Conrad Black, although Monomark is of course the original. Simon has a crisis when his friends discover his double-dealing, and he is uninvited to a crucial party; he implores his friend Adam to cover for him, Adam produces a sensational (if libelous) scoop, and Lord Monomark (who likes to print tonight and call the lawyers in the morning) gives him the Chatterbox column.

This provides Adam with the money to marry Nina, but of course he will lose and regain his stake several times during the film; Waugh's novel, like so much of Wodehouse, is about characters who are realistic about romance but idealistic about money. Adam's rival for the hand of Nina is Ginger Littlejohn (David Tennant), who has money but is boring. Too bad, but to be poor like Adam is boring, too, and if she has to choose, Nina would rather be bored in comfort.

These friends are like sparrows in the springtime, all landing on a branch, chattering deliriously, and then at an invisible signal fluttering off together to perch on another tree. They move from restaurants to clubs to private parties, from town to the country, often awakening hungover to discover that their genitals have misbehaved during a spell of drunken inattention. The most desperate in their circle is the movie's manic party animal, Agatha Runcible (Fenella Woolgar). In a scene that transcends invention and moves into inspired lunacy, Agatha is invited back to spend the night at the house of a tipsy new girlfriend, blunders into the breakfast room in the morning, and as those around the table regard her with horror, reads in the morning paper about where she spent (and is still spending) the night.

Like *The Great Gatsby*, the works of Dawn Powell, Jay McInerney, and all the other novels about heedless romance and debauchery, *Bright Young Things* is about people who think they can live forever, and discover that to live forever in the way they are living is not only impossible but would become exhausting and discouraging. Agatha is the poster girl for this discovery. Adam and Nina are luckier, redeemed by pluck and optimism and, it must be admitted, their real love for each other (this despite Adam's offer at one point to sell his share in her to Ginger for £100; later in the movie, after another setback, she asks bravely, "Oh, dear, have I been sold again?").

Fry, who as a younger actor was the obvious choice to play Bertie Wooster's butler Jeeves (and did), is also the obvious choice to direct this material. He has a feel for it; to spend a little time talking with him is to hear inherited echoes from characters just like those in the story. He supplies a roll call of supporting actors who turn up just long enough to convince us entire movies could be made about their characters. Among these are Peter O'Toole (who here, and in *Troy*, steals his scenes almost kindly from his fellow actors); he plays Nina's decaying old pater, Lord Blount, who has a gift for saying what he thinks while not seeming to know what he's saying. Jim Broadbent pops up regularly as a perpetually drunken army officer who makes extravagant promises to Adam, gives him tips on race horses ("Indian Runner at 37-to-1"), promises him money, disappears for months at a time, seems likely to be a fraud, and always remembers what he said when he was loaded, even though that may be of no help to Adam. The only character who doesn't really fit in is Mrs. Ape (Stockard Channing), a religious zealot whose appeal to bright young things is questionable, especially while she sings "Ain't No Flies on the Lamb of God."

As pure comedy, *Bright Young Things* would be funny up to a point, and then repetitive. Waugh's novel and Fry's movie wisely see that their characters live by spending their comic capital and ending up emotionally overdrawn. They begin by being awake when everyone else is asleep, and end by being asleep while everyone else is awake. The funniest person in a bar is rarely the happiest. The movie has a sweetness and tenderness for these characters, poor lambs, blissfully unaware that they're about to be flattened by World War II.

Brokeback Mountain ★ ★ ★ ★
R, 134 m., 2005

Heath Ledger (Ennis Del Mar), Jake Gyllenhaal (Jack Twist), Michelle Williams (Alma Del Mar), Anne Hathaway (Lureen Twist), Randy Quaid (Joe Aguirre), Linda Cardellini (Cassie Cartwright), Anna Faris (LaShawn Malone). Directed by Ang Lee and produced by Diana Ossana and James Schamus. Screenplay by Larry McMurtry and Ossana, based on the short story by E. Annie Proulx.

Ennis tells Jack about something he saw as a boy. "There were two old guys shacked up together. They were the joke of the town, even though they were pretty tough old birds." One day they were found beaten to death. Ennis says: "My dad, he made sure me and my brother saw it. For all I know, he did it."

This childhood memory is always there, the ghost in the room, in Ang Lee's *Brokeback Mountain*. When he was taught by his father to hate homosexuals, Ennis was taught to hate his own feelings. Years after he first makes love with Jack on a Wyoming mountainside, after his marriage has failed, after his world has compressed to a mobile home, the Laundromat, the TV, he still feels the same pain: "Why don't you let me be? It's because of you, Jack, that I'm like this—nothing, and nobody."

But it's not because of Jack. It's because Ennis and Jack love each other and can find no way to deal with that. *Brokeback Mountain* has been described as "a gay cowboy movie," which is a cruel simplification. It is the story of a time and place where two men are forced to deny the only great passion either one will ever feel. Their tragedy is universal. It could be about two women, or lovers from different religious or ethnic groups—any "forbidden" love.

The movie wisely never steps back to look at the larger picture, or deliver the "message." It is specifically the story of these men, this love. It stays in close-up. That's how Jack and Ennis see it. "You know I ain't queer," Ennis tells Jack after their first night together. "Me neither," says Jack.

Their story begins in Wyoming in 1963, when Ennis (Heath Ledger) and Jack (Jake Gyllenhaal) are about nineteen years old and get jobs tending sheep on a mountainside.

Ennis is a boy of so few words he can barely open his mouth to release them; he learned to be guarded and fearful long before he knew what he feared. Jack, who has done some rodeo riding, is a little more outgoing. After some days have passed on the mountain and some whiskey has been drunk, they suddenly and almost violently have sex.

"This is a one-shot thing we got going on here," Ennis says the next day. Jack agrees. But it's not. When the summer is over, they part laconically: "I guess I'll see ya around, huh?" Their boss (Randy Quaid) tells Jack he doesn't want him back next summer: "You guys sure found a way to make the time pass up there. You weren't getting paid to let the dogs guard the sheep while you stemmed the rose."

Some years pass. Both men get married. Then Jack goes to visit Ennis and the undiminished urgency of their passion stuns them. Their lives settle down into a routine, punctuated less often than Jack would like by "fishing trips." Ennis's wife, who has seen them kissing, says nothing about it for a long time. But she notices there are never any fish.

The movie is based on a short story by E. Annie Proulx. The screenplay is by Larry McMurtry and Diana Ossana. Last summer I read McMurtry's *Lonesome Dove* books, and as I saw the movie I was reminded of Gus and Woodrow, the two cowboys who spend a lifetime together. They aren't gay; one of them is a womanizer, and the other spends his whole life regretting the loss of the one woman he loved. They're straight but just as crippled by a society that tells them how a man must behave and what he must feel.

Brokeback Mountain could tell its story and not necessarily be a great movie. It could be a melodrama. It *could* be a "gay cowboy movie." But the filmmakers have focused so intently and with such feeling on Jack and Ennis that the movie is as observant as work by Bergman. Strange but true: The more specific a film is, the more universal, because the more it understands individual characters, the more it applies to everyone. I can imagine someone weeping at this film, identifying with it because he always wanted to stay in the Marines, or be an artist or a cabinetmaker.

Jack is able to accept a little more willingly that he is inescapably gay. In frustration and need he goes to Mexico one night and finds a male prostitute. Prostitution is a calling with hazards, sadness, and tragedy, but it accepts human nature. It knows what some people need, and perhaps that is why every society has found a way to accommodate it.

Jack thinks he and Ennis might someday buy themselves a ranch and settle down. Ennis, who remembers what he saw as a boy: "This thing gets hold of us at the wrong time and wrong place and we're dead." Well, wasn't Matthew Shepard murdered in Wyoming in 1998? And Brandon Teena in Nebraska in 1993? Haven't brothers killed their sisters in the Muslim world to defend "family honor"?

There are gentle and nuanced portraits of Ennis's wife, Alma (Michelle Williams), and Jack's wife, Lureen (Anne Hathaway), who are important characters, seen as victims, too. Williams has a powerful scene where she finally calls Ennis on his "fishing trips," but she takes a long time to do that, because nothing in her background prepares her for what she has found out about her husband. In their own way, programs like *Jerry Springer* provide a service by focusing on people, however pathetic, who are prepared to defend what they feel. In 1963 there was nothing like that on TV. And in 2005, the situation has not entirely changed. One of the ads for *Brokeback Mountain*'s Oscar campaign shows Ledger and Williams together, although the movie's posters are certainly honest.

Ang Lee is a director whose films are set in many nations and many times. What they have in common is an instinctive sympathy for the characters. Born Chinese, he makes movies about Americans, British, Chinese, straights, gays; his sci-fi movie *Hulk* was about a misunderstood outsider. Here he respects the entire arc of his story, right down to the lonely conclusion.

A closing scene involving a visit by Ennis to Jack's parents is heartbreaking in what is said, and not said, about their world. A look around Jack's childhood bedroom suggests what he overcame to make room for his feelings. What we cannot be sure is this: In the flashback, are we witnessing what really happened to Jack, or how Ennis sees it in his imagination? Ennis, whose father "made sure me and my brother saw it." ☞

Broken Flowers ★ ★ ★ ★
R, 105 m., 2005

Bill Murray (Don Johnston), Jeffrey Wright (Winston), Sharon Stone (Laura), Frances Conroy (Dora), Jessica Lange (Carmen), Tilda Swinton (Penny), Julie Delpy (Sherry), Alexis Dziena (Lolita), Chloë Sevigny (Carmen's Assistant), Chris Bauer (Dan). Directed by Jim Jarmusch and produced by Jon Kilik and Stacey Smith. Screenplay by Jarmusch.

Broken Flowers stars Bill Murray as Don Johnston, a man who made his money in computers and now doesn't even own one. To sit at the keyboard would mean moving from his sofa, where he seems to be stuck. As the film opens, his latest girlfriend (Julie Delpy) is moving out. She doesn't want to spend any more time with "an over-the-hill Don Juan." After she leaves, he remains on the sofa, listening to music. He reaches out for a glass of wine, changes his mind, lets the hand drop.

This is a man whose life is set on idle. His neighbor Winston (Jeffrey Wright), on the other hand, is a go-getter from Ethiopia who supports a wife and five kids with three jobs and still has time to surf the Net as an amateur detective. One day, Don receives a letter suggesting that twenty years ago he fathered a son and that a nineteen-year-old boy may be searching for him at this very moment. Don is unmoved by this intelligence, but Winston is energized; he extracts from Don the names of all the women who could possibly be the mother, and he supplies Don with plane tickets and an itinerary so that he can visit the candidates and figure out which one might have sent the letter.

"The letter is on pink stationery," Winston says. "Give them pink flowers and watch their reaction." Don nods, barely, and embarks on his journey—not to discover if he has a child so much as to discover if he wants a child. At one point, he phones Winston from the road, complaining that he has been supplied with conventional rental cars. Why couldn't he have a Porsche? "I'm a stalker in a Taurus."

No actor is better than Murray at doing nothing at all and being fascinating while not doing it. Buster Keaton had the same gift for contemplating astonishing developments with absolute calm. Keaton surrounded himself with slapstick, and in *Broken Flowers*, Jim Jarmusch surrounds Murray with a parade of formidable women.

First stop, Laura (Sharon Stone). Her husband was a NASCAR champion but "died in a wall of flame." Her daughter (Alexis Dziena), who is named Lolita, offers Don her Popsicle and, unmistakably, herself. Neither daughter nor mother seems to know that the name Lolita has literary associations. Don does in fact spend the night with the mother, but we do not see precisely what goes on, and just as well: The sight of this passive and withdrawn man making love might be sad beyond calculation.

Second woman: Dora (Frances Conroy), who with her husband, Dan (Chris Bauer), is a Realtor, specializing in selling "quality prefabs" and currently living in a "wonderful example." Don's dinner with Dora and Dan grows unspeakably depressing after he asks the wrong question.

Third woman: Carmen (Jessica Lange), protected by her ambiguous assistant (Chloë Sevigny). Carmen is an "animal communicator," who talks to people's pets on their behalf. The movie doesn't take cheap shots at this occupation but suggests Carmen may be the real thing. "Is he saying something?" Don asks, as Carmen converses with her cat. Carmen: "He says you have a hidden agenda."

The fourth woman, Penny (Tilda Swinton), has a front yard full of motorcycles and lives in an atmosphere that makes Don feel threatened, not without reason. There was a fifth possible candidate, who has been eliminated from Don's list because, well, she's dead.

Were any of these women the mother of his child? I will leave that for you, and Don, to discover. After the film's premiere at Cannes, I observed: "Some actors give the kinds of performances where we want to get out of the room, stand on the lawn, and watch them through a window. Murray has the uncanny ability to invite us into his performance, into his stillness and sadness. I don't know how he does it. A Bill Murray imitation would be a pitiful sight: Passive immobility, small gestures of the eyes, enigmatic comments, yes, those would be easy, but how does he suggest the low tones of crashing chaotic uncertainty?"

Jarmusch first came into focus in 1983 with *Stranger than Paradise*, about a slick New Yorker who gets an unexpected visit from his Hungarian cousin, who is sexy and naive and soon leaves to visit her aunt in Cleveland. Then followed a series of films of various degrees of wonderfulness; I have admired them all except for *Dead Man* (1995); the critic Jonathan Rosenbaum regards me sadly every time this title is mentioned. Jarmusch makes films about outsiders, but they're not loners; they're soloists. Murray's character here is the ultimate Jarmusch soloist, in that he lacks even an instrument. His act is to walk onto the stage and not play.

How did Don fascinate these women in the first place? Why are most of them (relatively) happy to see him again? Perhaps they were simply curious. Perhaps they embodied nature, and he embodied a vacuum. At the end, there is an enigmatic scene that explains little or nothing. Still, it opens up the possibility that if Don ever did discover he had a son, he would try to do the right thing. That would mean he was doing something, and that would be a start. ☞

Broken Lizard's Club Dread ★ ★ ½
R, 103 m., 2004

Jay Chandrasekhar (Putman), Steve Lemme (Juan), Paul Soter (Dave), Britanny Daniel (Jenny), Erik Stolhanske (Sam), Kevin Heffernan (Lars), M. C. Gainey (Hank), Greg Cipes (Trevor), Bill Paxton (Coconut Pete). Directed by Jay Chandrasekhar and produced by Richard Perello. Screenplay by Broken Lizard.

Broken Lizard's Club Dread is a definitive demonstration, if one is needed, that *The Real Cancun* was way too real. Filmed in Mexico but allegedly set on Coconut Pete's Pleasure Island off the coast of Costa Rica, it's a head-on smashup between spring break weekend and a machete-swinging slasher. Whether it works or not is a little hard to say; like *Super Troopers* (2001), the previous film by the Broken Lizard comedy troupe, it has lovable performances, very big laughs, and then some downtime while everybody (in the cast as well as the audience) waits to see what will happen next.

The leader of the troupe and director of both films is Jay Chandrasekhar, whose character in *Super Troopers* delighted in spreading confusing hints about his ethnic origin. Here he's the dreadlocked Indian (or perhaps British or Caribbean) tennis instructor, whose serve is so powerful that at one point he actually tries to kill the slasher by hitting balls at him.

Pleasure Island is run by Coconut Pete (Bill Paxton), who very briefly, a long time ago, had a record that was a hit for five minutes. It was called "Pina Colada-berg," and who knows what heights it might have reached on the charts had it not been for the treachery of "Margaritaville." Pete presides over an endless boozy sex-'n'-sand party that looks recycled out of every other movie ever made about beach blanket bingo, and if there is a babe (the film's preferred word) who ever wears anything other than a bikini, my memory fails me.

Alas, this island idyll is marred by the presence of a mad slasher, who stalks about garbed as if he (or she) once saw *I Know What You Did Last Summer* but either forgot how the fisherman dressed, or the costume supply store ran out of Groton's outfits. How a killer can roam a small tropical island dressed like Death in *The Seventh Seal* and never be noticed is one of the many questions this movie answers by keeping the bar open twenty-four hours a day.

The cast includes a cop in charge of enforcing fun, a six-foot-one Swedish masseuse who turns out, to intense disappointment, to be a six-foot-two Swedish masseur, and an aerobics instructor whose best exercises are horizontal. Characters are periodically killed, and at one point a severed head turns up on the deejay's turntable, but the fun goes on because these characters, while admittedly brighter and more articulate than the real people in *The Real Cancun*, realize that the slightest insight would solve the mystery and terminate the movie right then and there, and if we paid for feature length, that's what we deserve.

Do I recommend this movie or not? I am at a loss to say. It is what it is. Criticism is irrelevant. Why are you even reading a review of *Club Dread*? You've seen the TV ads and you already know (a) you won't miss it or (b) not in a million years. There will be better movies playing in the same theater, even if it is a duplex, but on the other hand there is something to be said for goofiness without apology by broken lizards who just wanna have fun. I think I'll give it two and a half stars plus a nudge and a wink, as a signal to those who liked *Super Troopers* and know what they're in for. I gave *Super Troopers* two and a half stars, too, but I'd rather see it again than certain distinguished movies I could mention.

Brooklyn Lobster ★ ★ ★
NO MPAA RATING, 90 m., 2006

Danny Aiello (Frank Giorgio), Jane Curtin (Maureen Giorgio), Daniel Sauli (Michael Giorgio), Marisa Ryan (Lauren Giorgio-Wallace), Ian Kahn (Justin Wallace), Heather Burns (Kerry Miller). Directed by Kevin Jordan and produced by Darren Jordan, Kevin Jordan, and Chris Valentino. Screenplay by Kevin Jordan.

Danny Aiello is an actor to depend on when you want a tough guy with a tender side, a sweet guy who can turn hard, and *Brooklyn Lobster* is a movie founded on his ability to show those two sides without seeming to shift gears. It's as if his nature is at war with itself. He loves his family with a genuine passion, and he runs a lobster house in Brooklyn that is his life's blood, and he's one of those guys, we all know a few, who thinks he expresses his love by the way he works so hard. It's a surprise to him, and it hurts, when his wife of many years tells him, "I've been alone throughout this entire marriage."

If you merge your family and your work, they are likely to go down together. It is Christmastime at Giorgio's Lobster Bar in Brooklyn, as you can tell by the large inflated Santa lobster balloon that floats above the restaurant. But inside not all is well, even before the lobsters die. Frank Giorgio (Aiello) is in trouble: "My bank forecloses, and the FDIC puts a gun to my head." His wife, Maureen (Jane Curtin), has moved out. His daughter, Lauren (Marisa Ryan), continues to run the bookkeeping side of the business, and knows better than anyone how desperate the situation is. Giorgio's has been in the family since 1938, but opening a restaurant on top of the basic lobster business was a mistake.

Frank's son, Michael (Daniel Sauli), might have been expected to take over as the third

generation, but he got as far away as he could (Seattle) and is back now for the holidays with his fiancée, Kerry (Heather Burns). Her family has some money, and there's the possibility that they might want to invest, and the excellent possibility that it would be a mistake for everybody.

Meanwhile, Frank, facing a bank auction and forced by law to advertise it, puts a tiny ad in the Pets section of the classified ads. He figures lobsters are pets. As faithful readers will know from my review of *Aquamarine*, he is right. Lobsters make perfect pets. As the French poet Nerval observed, lobsters are "peaceful, serious creatures, who know the secrets of the sea, and don't bark." Amazing, isn't it, how that has come up twice in two recent reviews.

The movie, written and directed by Kevin Jordan, has a spontaneous, confident realism about it, and no wonder: It was inspired by his family's business, Jordan's Lobster Dock, in Brooklyn. I looked it up on the Web. It gets good reviews from CitySearch: prompt seating, good for groups, good for kids, but "Romantic? No." And, warning: "Stay away from the corn in the platters." Overcooked. The *Village Voice* says the whole steamed lobsters are "excellent, served with drawn butter" but says the illusion of a Maine lobster pound "is marred somewhat by the garish franchise restaurant next door."

The *Voice* will be happy to learn that in *Brooklyn Lobster*, the Aiello character is given the opportunity to sell out to a garish franchise restaurant, and responds with garish language of his own. Meanwhile, his son moves into the cramped quarters above the restaurant and bunks with his dad, the fiancée camps out in a motel, Frank's wife stays with her daughter, and there is every prospect that Christmas will be unhappy and New Year's miserable. But watch the quiet way Jordan and his actors pull redemption out of the gloom. There is a subtle way that the father and son begin to share unspoken conclusions. There is the feeling that a restaurant that has been in the family since 1938 is more than a restaurant, and its absence will leave less than a family.

I first encountered Jordan's work in 1999, when his *Goat on Fire and Smiling Fish* played at Toronto, charming audiences with its story of two brothers and their romantic and professional lives. It was picked up by distributors who insisted on renaming it. The new name: *Smiling Fish and Goat on Fire.*

Both *Fish* and *Lobster* have a strong feeling for family, and a way of allowing the action to grow out of the characters instead of being required by the script. People do goofy things in real life, including building a tent over their desk in the office or, in this film, taking out that ad in the Pets section. Watch Aiello try to remain self-righteous as he defends the placement of that ad. *Brooklyn Lobster* is a sweet and touching film, worth a visit. So, by the sound of it, is Jordan's Lobster Dock, which is at 3165 Harkness Ave. in Brooklyn, telephone (718) 934–6300.

Brothers ★ ★ ★ ½
R, 110 m., 2005

Connie Nielsen (Sarah), Ulrich Thomsen (Michael), Nikolaj Lie Kaas (Jannik), Bent Mejding (Henning), Solbjorg Hojfeldt (Else). Directed by Susanne Bier and produced by Sisse Graum Olsen. Screenplay by Anders Thomas Jensen, based on the story by Bier.

Jannik has always been the embarrassment of the family, an aimless younger brother who, as *Brothers* opens, is being released from prison after committing a crime hardly worth his time and effort. Was he breaking the law simply to play his usual role in the family drama?

Michael is the good brother, a loving husband, a responsible father, a man who does his duty. When his Danish military unit is sent to Afghanistan, he goes without complaint, because he sees it as the right thing to do. Within a shockingly short time, his helicopter is shot down, and his wife, Sarah, is told he was killed.

Jannik, with no better choice, tries to do what he sees as his duty: to be kind to Sarah, to be a good uncle to the children, to help around the house. In subtle ways that are never underlined, he starts acting from a different script in his life; with Michael gone, a vacancy has been created in the family, and Jannik steps into it. Now he is the person you can trust.

It is not a spoiler to reveal that Michael was not killed in the helicopter crash, but captured by Afghan enemies. This is made clear very early; the movie is not about mysteries and suspense, but about behavior. As a prisoner he is treated badly, but his real punishment comes when his captors force an impossible choice upon him. If he wants to save his own life, he will have to take the life of a fellow prisoner, a man he likes, who is counting on him.

Strangely enough, this parallels Paul Schrader's *Dominion*, in which a priest is told that if he doesn't choose some villagers to be killed, the whole village will die. Michael's choice is more direct: Either he will die, or the other prisoner will. In theory, Michael should choose death. Not so clear is what the priest should have done; theology certainly teaches him to do no evil, but does theology account for a world where good has been eliminated as a choice?

Michael saves his own life; let the first stones be cast by those who would choose to die. Eventually he is freed and returns home to find things somehow different. He is no longer able to subtly condescend to his screwed-up little brother because Jannik has changed. And Michael has changed too. Sarah senses it immediately. There is a torment in him that we know is an expression of guilt.

It shows itself in strange ways: in his anger, for example, about the new kitchen cabinets that Jannik installed in his absence, and at the love the children have for their uncle. And in Michael's own relentlessly growing jealousy. "It's all right if you did," he tells his brother, "since you both thought I was dead. But I have to know: Did you make love?"

The answer to the question is simple (and perhaps not the one you expect). The meaning of the answer is very tricky, because Michael is a time bomb, waiting to explode. He has lost his view of himself in Afghanistan, and back at home in Denmark he cannot find it again, perhaps because the way is blocked by Jannik.

The movie was directed by Susanne Bier, who wrote a story that was turned into a screenplay by Anders Thomas Jensen. They worked together once before, on *Open Hearts* (2003), the story of a couple engaged to be married when the young man is paralyzed from the neck down in a senseless accident.

Will she still love him? Will she stay with him? How does he feel about that? Bier and Jensen are drawn to situations in which every answer leads to a question.

The central performance in *Brothers* is by Connie Nielsen, as Sarah, who is strong, deep, and true. You may remember her from *The Devil's Advocate* and *Gladiator*. What is she doing in a Danish movie? She is Danish, although this is her first Danish film.

The brothers are Ulrich Thomsen as Michael and Nikolaj Lie Kaas as Jannik. Both have to undergo fundamental transformations, and both must be grateful to Bier and Jensen for not getting all psychological on them. *Brothers* treats the situation as a real-life dilemma in which the characters behave according to how they are made and what they are capable of doing.

Like *Open Hearts*, this is the kind of movie that doesn't solve everything at the end—that observes some situations are capable not of solution but only of accommodation. That's more true to life than the countless movies with neat endings—happy endings, and even sad ones. In the world, sometimes the problem comes and stays forever, and the question with the hardest answer is, well, okay, how are you going to live with it?

The Brothers Grimm ★ ★
PG-13, 118 m., 2005

Matt Damon (Wilhelm Grimm), Heath Ledger (Jacob Grimm), Peter Stormare (Cavaldi), Lena Headey (Angelika), Jonathan Pryce (General Delatombe), Monica Bellucci (Mirror Queen). Directed by Terry Gilliam and produced by Daniel Bobker and Charles Roven. Screenplay by Ehren Kruger.

Terry Gilliam's *The Brothers Grimm* is a work of limitless invention, but it is invention without pattern, chasing itself around the screen without finding a plot. Watching it is a little exhausting. If the images in the movie had been put to the service of a story we could care about, he might have had something. But the movie seems like a style in search of a purpose.

He begins with the Brothers Grimm, whose fairy tales enchant those lucky children whose parents still read to them. There is an eerie quality to the Grimm stories that's lacking in their Hollywood versions; no modern version of *Little Red Riding Hood* approaches the scariness of the original story, where the Big Bad Wolf was generated not by computers but by my quaking imagination.

Gilliam's intention is not to tell the fairy tales, however, although some of them have walk-ons in his movie; he makes the Brothers Grimm into con artists, circa 1796, who travel from village to village in Germany, staging phony magic and claiming it is real. Wilhelm Grimm (Matt Damon) is the hustler of the outfit, a mercenary cynic. His brother, Jacob (Heath Ledger), sort of believes in magic. It has been thus since "Jake" and "Will" were children, and Jacob sold the family cow for a handful of magic beans.

The con artists are unmasked by Delatombe (Jonathan Pryce), Napoleon's man in Germany. But instead of punishing them, he dispatches the lads to the village of Marbaden, where children are missing and it appears that in the haunted forest "the trees themselves set upon them." Delatombe's bizarre torturer, Cavaldi (Peter Stormare), is sent along to be sure the Grimms deliver the goods; they are apparently supposed to be eighteenth-century ghostbusters, or maybe the equivalents of the Amazing Randi, unmasking fraud.

The problem is, the forest really is enchanted. A local huntswoman named Angelika (Lena Headey) knows it is and tries to convince the boys, who become convinced only that they love her. There is another romantic complication when the evil five-hundred-year-old Mirror Queen (Monica Bellucci) casts a spell over events; when the Grimms attempt to enter her castle and break the spell, they're up against the real thing: A kiss from her can kill. Jacob is tempted. Considering that she is five-hundred years old, I am reminded of Mark Twain's first words after being shown an ancient Egyptian mummy: "Is he, ah . . . is he dead?"

A great deal more happens in *The Brothers Grimm*, and none of it is as easy to follow as I have made it sound. The film is constructed of elements that probably seemed like a great idea in themselves but have not been assembled into a narrative we can follow and care about. There is also the problem of who exactly Gilliam thinks the Brothers Grimm are. At times they seem like romantic heroes, at times like clowns, at times like fake magicians, at times like real ones. Their own fairy tales had the virtue of being tightly focused and implacable in their sense of justice: Misbehavior was cruelly punished as often as virtue was rewarded. Their strict code is lacking in the movie, which is based on shifting moral sands. At times the Grimms are liars and charlatans, at times brave and true. Those times seem chosen at the convenience of the movie.

Gilliam has always been a director who fills the screen with rich visual spectacle. In *Brazil* and *12 Monkeys* and *The Adventures of Baron Munchausen*, in the past and in the future, his world is always hallucinatory in its richness of detail. Here the haunted forest is really very impressive, but to what end? In a movie like Tim Burton's *The Legend of Sleepy Hollow*, the night and shadows hold real menace. Here the trees seem more like an idea than a danger. And the movie, for all of its fantastic striving, stays on the screen and fails to engage our imagination.

The Brown Bunny ★ ★ ★
NO MPAA RATING, 92 m., 2004

Vincent Gallo (Bud Clay), Chloe Sevigny (Daisy), Cheryl Tiegs (Lilly), Elizabeth Blake (Rose), Anna Vareschi (Violet), Mary Morasky (Mrs. Lemon). Directed and produced by Vincent Gallo. Screenplay by Gallo.

In May 2003, I walked out of the press screening of Vincent Gallo's *The Brown Bunny* at the Cannes Film Festival and was asked by a camera crew what I thought of the film. I said I thought it was the worst film in the history of the festival. That was hyperbole—I hadn't seen every film in the history of the festival—but I was still vibrating from one of the most disastrous screenings I had ever attended.

The audience was loud and scornful in its dislike for the movie; hundreds walked out, and many of those who remained stayed only because they wanted to boo. Imagine, I wrote, a film so unendurably boring that when the hero changes into a clean shirt, there is applause. The panel of critics convened by *Screen International*, the British trade paper,

gave the movie the lowest rating in the history of their annual voting.

But then a funny thing happened. Gallo went back into the editing room and cut 26 minutes of his 118-minute film, or almost a fourth of the running time. And in the process he transformed it. The film's form and purpose now emerge from the miasma of the original cut, and are quietly, sadly effective. It is said that editing is the soul of the cinema; in the case of *The Brown Bunny*, it is its salvation.

Critics who saw the film last autumn at the Venice and Toronto festivals walked in expecting the disaster they'd read about from Cannes. Here is Bill Chambers of Film Freak Central, writing from Toronto: "Ebert catalogued his mainstream biases (unbroken takes: bad; nonclassical structure: bad; name actresses being aggressively sexual: bad) . . . and then had a bigger delusion of grandeur than *The Brown Bunny*'s Gallo-centric credit assignations: 'I will one day be thin, but Vincent Gallo will always be the director of *The Brown Bunny*.'"

Faithful readers will know that I admire long takes, especially by Ozu, that I hunger for nonclassical structure, and that I have absolutely nothing against sex in the cinema. In quoting my line about one day being thin, Chambers might in fairness have explained that I was responding to Gallo calling me a "fat pig"—and, for that matter, since I made that statement I have lost eighty-six pounds and Gallo is indeed still the director of *The Brown Bunny*.

But he is not the director of the same *Brown Bunny* I saw at Cannes, and the film now plays so differently that I suggest the original Cannes cut be included as part of the eventual DVD, so that viewers can see for themselves how twenty-six minutes of aggressively pointless and empty footage can sink a potentially successful film. To cite but one cut: From Cannes, I wrote: "Imagine a long shot on the Bonneville Salt Flats where he races his motorcycle until it disappears as a speck in the distance, followed by another long shot in which a speck in the distance becomes his motorcycle." In the new version we see the motorcycle disappear, but the second half of the shot has been completely cut. That helps in two ways: (1) It saves the scene from an unintended laugh, and (2) it provides an emotional purpose, since to disappear into the distance is a much different thing than to ride away and then ride back again.

The movie stars Gallo as Bud Clay, a professional motorcycle racer who loses a race on the East Coast and then drives his van cross-country. (The race in the original film lasted 270 seconds longer than in the current version, and was all in one shot, of cycles going around and around a track.) Bud is a lonely, inward, needy man, who thinks much about a former lover whose name in American literature has come to embody idealized, inaccessible love: Daisy.

Gallo allows himself to be defenseless and unprotected in front of the camera, and that is a strength. Consider an early scene where he asks a girl behind the counter at a convenience store to join him on the trip to California. When she declines, he says "please" in a pleading tone of voice not one actor in a hundred would have the nerve to imitate. There's another scene not long after that has a sorrowful poetry. In a town somewhere in the middle of America, at a table in a park, a woman (Cheryl Tiegs) sits by herself. Bud Clay parks his van, walks over to her, senses her despair, asks her some questions, and wordlessly hugs and kisses her. She never says a word. After a time he leaves again. There is a kind of communication going on here that is complete and heartbreaking, and needs not one word of explanation, and gets none.

In the original version, there was an endless, pointless sequence of Bud driving through Western states and collecting bug splats on his windshield; the eight and a half minutes Gallo has taken out of that sequence were as exciting as watching paint after it has already dried. Now he arrives sooner in California, and there is the now-famous scene in a motel room involving Daisy (Chloe Sevigny). Yes, it is explicit, and no, it is not gratuitous.

But to reveal how it works on a level more complex than the physical would be to undermine the way the scene pays off. The scene, and its dialogue, and a flashback to the Daisy character at a party, work together to illuminate complex things about Bud's sexuality, his guilt, and his feelings about women. Even at Cannes, even after unendurably superfluous footage, that scene worked, and I wrote: "It must be said that [Sevigny] brings a truth and vulnerability to her scene that exists on a level far above the movie it is in." Gallo takes the materials of pornography and repurposes them into a scene about control and need, fantasy, and perhaps even madness. That scene is many things, but erotic is not one of them. (A female friend of mine observed that Bud Clay, like many men, has a way of asking a woman questions just when she is least prepared to answer them.)

When movies were cut on Movieolas, there was a saying that they could be "saved on the green machine." Make no mistake: The Cannes version was a bad film, but now Gallo's editing has set free the good film inside. *The Brown Bunny* is still not a complete success—it is odd and off-putting when it doesn't want to be—but as a study of loneliness and need, it evokes a tender sadness. I will always be grateful I saw the movie at Cannes; you can't understand where Gallo has arrived unless you know where he started.

Bubble ★ ★ ★ ★
R, 73 m., 2006

Debbie Doebereiner (Martha), Dustin James Ashley (Kyle), Misty Dawn Wilkins (Rose), Omar Cowan (Martha's Dad), Laurie Lee (Kyle's Mother), David Hubbard (Pastor), Kyle Smith (Jake), Decker Moody (Detective Don). Directed by Steven Soderbergh and produced by Gregory Jacobs. Screenplay by Coleman Hough.

Steven Soderbergh's *Bubble* approaches with awe and caution the rhythms of ordinary life itself. He tells the stories of three Ohio factory workers who have been cornered by life. They work two low-paying jobs, they dream of getting a few bucks ahead, they eat fast food without noticing it, two of them live with their parents, one of them has a car. Their speech is such a monotone of commonplaces that we have to guess about how they really feel, and sometimes, we suspect, so do they.

I haven't made the movie sound enthralling. But it is. The characters are so closely observed and played with such exacting accuracy and conviction that *Bubble* becomes quietly, inexorably hypnotic. Soderbergh never underlines, never points, never uses music to suggest emotion, never shows the characters thinking ahead, watches appalled as small shifts in orderly lives lead to a murder.

Everything about the film—its casting, its filming, its release—is daring and innovative. Soderbergh, the poster boy of the Sundance generation (for *sex, lies . . . and videotape* sixteen years ago), has moved confidently ever since between commercial projects *(Ocean's Eleven)* and cutting-edge experiments like *Bubble*. The movie was cast with local people who were not actors. They participated in the creation of their dialogue. Their own homes were used as sets. The film was shot quickly in high-definition video.

And when it opens in theaters, it will simultaneously play on HDNet cable and four days later be released on DVD. Here is an experiment to see if there is a way to bring a small art film to a larger audience; most films like this would play in a handful of big-city art houses, and you'd read this review and maybe reflect that it sounded interesting and then lose track of it. In a time when audiences are pounded into theaters with multimillion-dollar ad campaigns, here's a small film with a big idea behind it.

As the film opens, Martha (Debbie Doebereiner) awakens, brings breakfast to her elderly father, picks up Kyle (Dustin James Ashley) at his mobile home, stops at a bakery, and arrives at the doll factory where they both work. He operates machinery to create plastic body parts. She paints the faces and adds the eyelashes and hair. During their lunch hour in a room of Formica and fluorescence, they talk about nothing much. He doesn't have time to date. He'd like to get the money together to buy a car. He'd like a ride after work to his other job. Martha, who is fat and ten or fifteen years older than Kyle, watches him carefully, looking for clues in his shy and inward speech.

Rose (Misty Dawn Wilkins) begins work at the factory. She is introduced to the workforce and provides Kyle with a smile so small he may not even see it, but Martha does. How should we read this? In a conventional movie, Kyle would be attracted to Rose, and Martha would be jealous. But *Bubble* is more cautiously modulated. Martha, I believe, has never allowed herself to think Kyle would be

attracted to her. What she wants from him is what she already has: a form of possession in the way he depends on her for rides and chats with her at lunch. Nor does Kyle seem prepared to go after Rose. He is shy, quiet, and withdrawn, smokes pot at home, keeps a low profile at work.

Rose at least represents change. She takes Martha along to a suburban house that she cleans, and Martha is shocked to find her taking a bubble bath. Rose explains that her apartment, which she shares with her two-year-old daughter, has only a shower. "I'm not too sure about her," Martha tells Kyle. "She scares me a little."

Rose asks Kyle out. In a bar, they share their reasons for dropping out of high school. Their date goes nowhere—not even when Rose gets herself asked into his bedroom—because Kyle is too passive to make a move, or maybe even to respond to one. He's too beaten down by life. "I'm very ready to get out of this area," says Rose, who observes that everybody is poor and there are no opportunities.

I am describing the events but not the fascination they create. The uncanny effect comes in large part from the actors. I learn that Debbie Doebereiner is the manager of a KFC. That Misty Dawn Wilkins is a hairdresser, and her own daughter plays her daughter in the movie. They are not playing themselves, but they are playing people they know from the inside out, and although Soderbergh must have worked closely with them, his most important work was in the casting: Not everybody could carry a feature film made of everyday life and make it work, but these three do. The movie feels so real a hush falls upon the audience, and we are made aware of how much artifice there is in conventional acting. You wouldn't want to spend the rest of your life watching movies like this, because artifice has its uses, but in this film, with these actors, something mysterious happens.

I said there was a murder. That's all I'll say about it. The local police inspector (Decker Moody) handles the case. He is played by an actual local police inspector. We have seen a hundred or a thousand movies where a cop visits the crime scene and later cross-examines people. There has never been one like this. In the flat, experienced, businesslike way he does his job, and in the way his instincts guide him past misleading evidence, the inspector depends not on crime-movie suspense but on implacable logic. *Bubble* ends not with the solution to a crime but with the revelation of the depths of a lonely heart.

Some theater owners are boycotting *Bubble* because they hate the idea of a simultaneous release on cable and DVD. I think it's the only hope for a movie like this. Let's face it. Even though I call the film a masterpiece (and I do), my plot description has not set you afire with desire to see the film. Unless you admire Soderbergh or can guess what I'm saying about the performances, you'll be there in line for *Annapolis* or *Nanny McPhee*. But maybe you're curious enough to check it out on cable, or rent it on DVD, or put it in your Netflix queue. That's how movies like this can have a chance. And how you can have a chance to see them. ☞

Bukowski: Born Into This ★ ★ ★ ½
NO MPAA RATING, 130 m., 2004

A documentary directed and produced by John Dullaghan.

Charles Bukowski was blessed, as if to compensate for everything else, with the most beautiful smile. It was, as more than one woman probably told him, his best feature. When he was not smiling he was craggy at best; when he was angry he was unlovely. His early years, punctuated by regular beatings from his father, were scarred by acne so disfiguring it left him with a face pitted like the surface of the moon. He told a friend about standing outside his school prom—he didn't dare to ask a girl to be his date—with his pimply face wrapped in toilet paper, holes cut for the eyes, blood seeping through.

He was twenty-four when he had sex for the first time. She was a 300-pound prostitute. He remembers her name. As he tells the story, he does an extraordinary thing. He blushes. Here was a man who made a living and became a legend by being hard-boiled, and he blushes, and in that moment we glimpse the lonely, wounded little boy inside.

John Dullaghan's *Bukowski: Born Into This* is a documentary about the poet and novelist who died in 1994. It draws from many interviews, from footage of poetry readings and from the testimony of his friends, who include Sean Penn, Harry Dean Stanton, Bono, and the publisher John Martin, who started Black Sparrow Press specifically to publish Bukowski's work. There are also the memories of his wife, Linda Lee Bukowski, who loved him and cared for him, despite scenes like one in the film where he kicks her and curses at her.

That was the booze talking, you could say, except when precisely was Bukowski sober? He drank with dedication and abandon for most of his adult years, slowed only by illness toward the end. And he chain-smoked little cigarettes named Mangalore Ganesh Beedies. "You can get them in any Indian or Pakistani store," he told me in 1987. "They're what the poor, poor people smoke in India. I like them because they contain no chemicals and no nicotine, and they go very well with red wine."

Linda Lee Bukowski, it must be said, possessed extraordinary patience to put up with him, but then she understood him, and his life was often as simple as that: a plea for understanding. I sense from his work and from a long day spent with him that even when he was drunk and angry, obscene and hurtful, he was not the aggressor; he was fighting back.

The movie opens with Bukowski on a stage for a reading, very drunk, threatening to come down into the audience and kick some ass. There is another reading where, backstage, he asks the organizer, "You got a little pot on the stage I can vomit in?" He drank most every day, red wine his preference, and his routine usually included a visit to the track, a return home, and long hours at his typewriter with classical music on the radio. For all of his boozing, he was, like the prodigious Thomas Wolfe, amazingly productive.

He wrote poems as if the words were bricks to be laid. He cut through the labyrinthine, indulgent difficulty of much modern verse, and wrote poems anyone could understand. Yet they *were* poems, real poems, and the film director Taylor Hackford remembers the first time he heard Bukowski reading; he was presented by Lawrence Ferlinghetti, one of the founding Beats, at Ferlinghetti's City Lights Bookstore in San Francisco—where to this day you can find a shelf of Bukowski, most of it with the bold Black Sparrow lettering on the spine.

John Martin, the publisher, says he offered Bukowski a monthly stipend to live on, with the condition that he quit his job at the post office. One of his first novels was *Post Office*, a snarl at the daily torture of hard work under stupid bureaucrats. It snarled, yes, but it also sang, and was romantic and funny. It came directly from Bukowski's life, as did such autobiographical novels as *Women* and *Hollywood*.

The Hollywood book was inspired by his experiences when his *Barfly* was adapted into a movie starring Mickey Rourke and Faye Dunaway. He didn't like the movie much—he thought Rourke was a "showoff." I thought it was a good movie, and wondered if part of his dislike was because he was played by a handsome man who had never suffered the agonies of being Charles Bukowski. It is probably also true that in his barfly days he was rarely fortunate enough to be the lover of a woman who looked like Faye Dunaway.

On the set one day, Dunaway turned up to question him, doing research on the character she would play.

"This woman," she asked him, "what would she put under her pillow?"

"A rosary."

"What sort of perfume did she wear?"

He looked at her incredulously.

"Perfume?"

I can testify to the way his life became his fiction because the day I spent on the set of the movie became part of *Hollywood*, and the movie critic in the book is a fair enough portrait of me. Central to his fiction and poetry was his lifelong love-hate relationship with women; by the time his fame began to attract groupies, he complains, "it was too late."

The movie is valuable because it provides a face and a voice to go with the work. Ten years have passed since Bukowski's death, and he seems likely to last, if not forever, then longer than many of his contemporaries. He outsells Kerouac and Kesey, and his poems, it almost goes without saying, outsell any other modern poet on the shelf.

How much was legend, how much was pose, how much was real? I think it was all real, and the documentary suggests as much. There were no shields separating the real Bukowski, the public Bukowski, and the autobiographical hero of his work. They were all the same man. Maybe that's why his work remains so immediate and affecting: The wounded man is the man who writes, and the wounds he writes about are his own.

The Butterfly Effect ★ ★ ½
R, 113 m., 2004

Ashton Kutcher (Evan Treborn), Amy Smart (Kayleigh Miller), William Lee Scott (Tommy Miller), Elden Henson (Lenny), Eric Stoltz (George Miller), Kevin Schmidt (Lenny at Thirteen), Melora Walters (Andrea Treborn), John Patrick Amedori (Evan at Thirteen), Cameron Bright (Tommy at Eight). Directed by Eric Bress and J. Mackye Gruber and produced by Chris Bender, A. J. Dix, Anthony Rhulen, Lisa Richardson, and J. C. Spink. Screenplay by Bress and Gruber.

Chaos theory teaches us that small events can have enormous consequences. An opening title informs us that a butterfly flapping its wings in Asia could result in a hurricane halfway around the world. Yes, although given the number of butterflies and the determination with which they flap their little wings, isn't it extraordinary how rarely that happens? *The Butterfly Effect* applies this theory to the lives of four children whose early lives are marred by tragedy. When one of them finds he can go back in time and make changes, he tries to improve the present by altering the past.

The characters as young adults are played by Ashton Kutcher, as Evan, a college psych major; Amy Smart and William Lee Scott as Kayleigh and Tommy, a brother and sister with a pedophile father; and Elden Henson as Lenny, their friend. The story opens in childhood, with little Evan seriously weird. His drawings in kindergarten are sick and twisted (and also, although nobody ever mentions it, improbably good for a child). He has blackouts, grabs kitchen knives, frightens his mother (Melora Walters), becomes a suitable case for treatment.

A shrink suggests that he keep a daily journal. This he does, although apparently neither the shrink nor the mother ever read it, or their attention might have been snagged by entries about how Mr. Miller (Eric Stoltz), father of

Kayleigh and Tommy, forced them all to act in kiddie porn movies. Evan hangs onto the journals, and one day while reading an old one at school he's jerked back into the past and experiences a previously buried memory.

One thing he'd always done, after moving from the old neighborhood, was to promise Kayleigh "I'll come back for you." (This promise is made with handwriting as precocious as his drawing skills.) The flashbacks give him a chance to do that, and eventually he figures out that by reading a journal entry, he can return to that page in his life and relive it. The only problem is, he then returns to a present that is different than the one he departed from—because his actions have changed everything that happened since.

This is a premise not unknown to science fiction, where one famous story by Ray Bradbury has a time traveler stepping on a butterfly millions of years ago and wiping out humanity. The remarkable thing about the changes in *The Butterfly Effect* is that they're so precisely aimed: They apparently affect only the characters in the movie. From one reality to the next, Kayleigh goes from sorority girl to hooker, Evan zaps from intellectual to frat boy to prisoner, and poor Lenny spends some time as Kayleigh's boyfriend and more time as a hopeless mental patient.

Do their lives have no effect on the wider world? Apparently not. External reality remains the same, apart from minute adjustments to college and prison enrollment statistics. But it's unfair to bring such logic to bear on the story, which doesn't want to *really* study the butterfly effect, but simply to exploit a device to jerk the characters through a series of startling life changes. Strange, that Evan can remember everything that happened in the alternate lifetimes, even though by the theory of the movie, once he changes something, they didn't happen.

Ashton Kutcher has become a target lately; the gossip press can't forgive him for dating Demi Moore, although that is a thing many sensible young men dream of doing. He was allegedly fired from a recent film after the director told him he needed acting lessons. Can he act? He can certainly do everything that's required in *The Butterfly Effect*. He plays a convincing kid in his early twenties, treating each new reality with a straightforward realism when most actors would be tempted to hyperventilate under the circumstances.

The plot provides a showcase for acting talent, since the actors have to play characters who go through wild swings (even Evan's mom has a wild ride between good health and death's door). And there's a certain grim humor in the way the movie illustrates the truth that you can make plans, but you can't make results. Some of the futures Evan returns to are so seriously wrong from his point of view that he's lucky he doesn't just disappear from the picture, having been killed at fifteen, say, because of his meddling.

I enjoyed *The Butterfly Effect*, up to a point. That point was reached too long before the end of the movie. There's so much flashing forward and backward, so many spins of fate, so many chapters in the journals, that after a while I felt that I, as well as time, was being jerked around. Eric Bress and J. Mackye Gruber, the cowriters and directors, also collaborated on *Final Destination 2* (2003), another film in which fate works in mysterious ways, its ironies to reveal. I gave that one half a star, so *The Butterfly Effect* is five times better. And outside, the wind is rising . . .

C

Caché ★ ★ ★ ★
R, 121 m., 2006

Daniel Auteuil (Georges Laurent), Juliette Binoche (Anne Laurent), Maurice Benichou (Majid), Annie Girardot (Georges' Mom), Bernard Le Coq (Georges' Editor), Daniel Duval (Pierre), Lester Makedonsky (Pierrot Laurent), Walid Afkir (Majid's Son). Directed by Michael Haneke and produced by Veit Heiduschka. Screenplay by Haneke.

The opening shot of Michael Haneke's *Caché* shows the facade of a townhouse on a side street in Paris. As the credits roll, ordinary events take place on the street. Then we discover that this footage is a video and that it is being watched by Anne and Georges Laurent (Juliette Binoche and Daniel Auteuil). It is their house. They have absolutely no idea who took the video, or why it was sent to them.

So opens a perplexing and disturbing film of great effect, showing how comfortable lives are disrupted by the simple fact that someone is watching. Georges is the host of a TV program about books; yes, in France they have shows where intellectuals argue about books and an audience that actually watches them. Georges and Anne live in their book-lined house with their son, Pierrot Laurent (Lester Makedonsky), a teenager who is sulky and distracted in the way that teenagers can be when they have little to complain about except their discontent.

Another video arrives, showing the farmhouse where Georges and his family lived when he was a child. All the videos they receive will have the same style: a camera at some distance, simply looking. Many of the shots in the film itself are set up and filmed in the same way, so that *Caché* could be watching itself just as the videos watch the Laurents. No comment is made in the videos through camera position, movement, editing—or perhaps there is the same comment all the time: Someone wants them to know that they are being watched.

Another video arrives, showing a journey down a suburban street and into a building. Georges is able to freeze a frame and make out a street name; going off alone, he follows the path of the video and finds himself in front of a door in an apartment building. The person inside is someone he knows, but this person (whom I will not describe) is unlikely to be the author of the alarming videos.

Georges conceals the results of his trip from his wife. Then another video arrives, showing him speaking with the occupant of the apartment. Now there is a fierce argument between Georges and Anne: She cannot trust him, she feels. He must tell her who the person is. He will not. In a way, he cannot. She feels threatened by the videos, and now threatened because her husband may be withholding information she needs to know. Binoche trembles with fury as the wife who feels betrayed by her husband; Auteuil, a master of detachment, folds into himself as a man who simply cannot talk about his deepest feelings.

Meanwhile, their lives continue. Georges does the TV show. Their son goes to school. There is a dinner party, at which a story about a dog will give you something to recycle with great effect at your own next dinner party. Georges goes to visit his mother. He asks about events that happened in 1961, when he was a boy. His mother asks him if something is wrong. He denies it. She simply regards him. She knows her son, and she knows something is wrong.

I have deliberately left out a great deal of information, because the experience of *Caché* builds as we experience the film. There are parallels, for example, between the TV news that is often on in the background, and some of the events in Georges' past. We expect that the mystery of the videos will be solved, explained, and make sense. But perhaps not. Here is a curious thing: In some of the videos, the camera seems to be in a position where anyone could see it, but no one ever does.

When *Caché* played at Cannes 2005 (where it won the prize for best direction), it had an English title, *Hidden*. That may be a better title than *Caché*, which can also be an English word, but more obscure. In the film, the camera is hidden. So are events in Georges' life. Some of what he knows is hidden from his wife. The son keeps secrets from his parents, and so on. The film seems to argue that life would have gone on well enough for the Laurents had it not been for the unsettling knowledge that they had become visible, that someone knew something about them, that someone was watching.

The last shot of the film, like many others, is taken from a camera that does not move. It regards events on the outside staircase of a building. There are a lot of people moving around. Closer to us than most of them is a figure with her back turned, placed just to the right of center; given basic rules of composition, this is where our eye will fall if all else in the shot is equal. Many viewers will not notice another element in the shot. Stop reading now if you plan to see the film, and save the review . . .

. . . and now observe that two people meet and talk on the upper left-hand side of the screen. They are two characters we recognize, and who should not know each other or have any way of meeting. Why do they know each other? What does it explain, that they do? Does it explain anything? Are there not still questions without answers? *Caché* is a film of bottomless intrigue. "The unexamined life is not worth living," said Socrates. An examined life may bring its own form of disquiet.

When *Caché* played at Cannes, some critics deplored its lack of a resolution. I think it works precisely because it leaves us hanging. It proposes not to solve the mystery of the videos but to portray the paranoia and distrust that they create. If the film merely revealed in its closing scenes who was sending the videos and why, it would belittle itself. We are left feeling as the characters feel, uneasy, violated, spied upon, surrounded by faceless observers. The nonexplanation supplied by the enigmatic last scene opens a new area of speculation that also lacks any solution or closure. And the secrets of Georges' past reach out their guilty tendrils to the next generation.   ☞

Callas Forever ★ ★ ½
NO MPAA RATING, 108 m., 2004

Fanny Ardant (Maria Callas), Jeremy Irons (Larry Kelly), Joan Plowright (Sarah Keller), Jay Rodan (Michael), Gabriel Garko (Marco), Manuel de Blas (Esteban Gomez), Justino Diaz (Scarpia), Jean Dalric (Gerard). Directed by Franco Zeffirelli and produced by Riccardo Tozzi and Giovannella Zannoni. Screenplay by Zeffirelli and Martin Sherman.

In 1977, when she is fifty-three and near the end of her life, the great diva Maria Callas is approached by a man who directed some of her greatest performances. He wants to film her in *Carmen*. Impossible! she says, playing him a tape of her final concert, in Tokyo, where the great voice was in ruins. His idea: Use the Callas of today and the voice of Callas in her prime. "But—it's dishonest!" she says. Still, since almost all European movies until recent years were lip-synched anyway, it is not such a transgression as it seems, and it would at least make possible the great opera film that Callas never made.

This fictional story, told in *Callas Forever*, has parallels with real life. Franco Zeffirelli, who directed and cowrote the film, directed Callas on stage in *Norma, La Traviata,* and *Tosca.* In 1964, he directed her TV special "Maria Callas at Covent Garden," and he remained a friend of the singer until the end. In addition to his famous feature work like *Romeo and Juliet* (1967), he directed several films of operas, notably *La Traviata* (1982) and *Pagliacci* (1982) with Placido Domingo and Teresa Stratas, and *Cavalleria Rusticana* (1982) and *Otello* (1986) with Domingo. He must have dreamed of one grand final film for Callas, and might even have spoken with her about it.

What else in the movie is based on fact, we cannot know. Terrence McNally's play *Master Class*, which shows Callas teaching opera students, shows her at a similar time in her life, but the story structure of *Callas Forever* is original, and pointed in another direction. It is perhaps Zeffirelli's consolation for the film he was never able to make. (It is small consolation, however, for Faye Dunaway, who starred powerfully in *Master Class* for a year and dreamed of making a film version of the play.)

Callas is played in *Callas Forever* by Fanny Ardant, that tall, grave French actress with the facial structure of a Greek heroine (one thinks of Irene Papas in *Electra*). Ardant (who starred in Paris in *Master Class*) cannot sing, but then neither could Callas at the time. What she does have is the fiery passion needed for *Carmen*, and Zeffirelli stages several scenes from the opera in the style, we can only assume, that he would have used had he made the actual film. These show Callas in her impetuous, imperious, man-scorning pride, physically dominating the production. And the voice is . . . Callas.

The visual style is all Zeffirelli, and it is interesting that the opera-within-the-film is not skimped on, as is usually the case in films containing scenes from other productions. Indeed, most of the budget seems to have gone to the moments of *Carmen* that we see; they look sumptuous and robust, and the surrounding film looks, well, like a low-budget art movie.

Callas shares the story with Larry Kelly (Jeremy Irons), probably meant to be Zeffirelli, a hardworking professional director, gay, whose infatuation with a young man named Michael (Jay Rodan) seems like a slight embarrassment, and seems meant to be; he drags Callas over to the youth's studio to look at his paintings, and Callas praises him because she knows that at some level Larry has to deliver her as part of his romantic bargain with Michael. These scenes are a distraction, and slow down the main line of the movie.

Ardant excels at playing a temperamental diva, whose entrances transform a room, who is instantly the center of attention, who gives orders and expects to be obeyed. This is all true to life. Callas was famous in a way no other twentieth-century opera singer was famous, and she deserved her fame, not only for the toll she paid through her celebrated liaison with Aristotle Onassis, but also because her voice was called the voice of the century, and that may have been true.

Her problems with *Carmen* involve more than the dubbed sound track. She is concerned about how she looks. Half-persuaded she should let her fans remember her as she was. Uncertain about a flirtation with a young man on the set. And, for that matter, just generally flighty on principle, as a diva has a right to be.

The Larry Kelly character is patient, flattering, persuasive, insidious. To his credit, he seems to want to make the film not so much for himself as to collaborate with Callas on a film she should have made and never did. But there is a crucial moment when he visits her apartment late at night and sees her singing along with her recordings and then sobbing, and he realizes that anyone who sang as Callas did must always live with the pain of having lost her gift.

Callas Forever reminded me a little of two documentaries by Maximilian Schell, *Marlene* (1984) and *My Sister Maria* (2002). Both were about great beauties, now reclusive. His friend

Marlene Dietrich refused to be seen on camera. His sister Maria did not. Dietrich made the wiser decision, and in *Callas Forever* we are asked to decide if Callas does too.

Note: It is amusing, in a movie where dubbing is one of the subjects, that the opening airport scene is so poorly dubbed.

Cape of Good Hope ★ ★ ★
PG-13, 107 m., 2006

Debbie Brown (Kate), Eriq Ebouaney (Jean Claude), Nthati Moshesh (Lindiwe), Morne Visser (Morne), Quanita Adams (Sharifa), David Isaacs (Habib), Kamo Masilo (Thabo), Nick Boraine (Stephen van Heern). Directed by Mark Bamford and produced by Suzanne Kay Bamford and Genevieve Hofmeyr. Screenplay by Mark and Suzanne Kay Bamford.

In Cape Town, one of the most beautiful cities on Earth, we meet people who move uncertainly into their own futures. The iron curtain separating the races has lifted, and they are all (except one) citizens on equal footing, but Mark Bamford's *Cape of Good Hope* is a postapartheid film in which the characters are less concerned with politics than with matters of the heart. Of course, political and economic concerns drift in (they do regardless of whether we admit it), but the title is a good one, standing not only for that point at the bottom of Africa where the Indian and Atlantic oceans meet, but also for good hope itself, about love, choices, and the future.

The movie belongs to a genre that has been named "hyperlink cinema" by the critic Alissa Quart in Film Comment. She suggests the structure was invented by Robert Altman, and Altman certainly brought it into modern times and made it particularly useful for showing interlocking stories in a world where lives seem to crash into each other heedlessly. *Crash*, indeed, is an example of the genre, as are Altman's *The Player* and *Short Cuts*, and such films as *Traffic*, *Syriana*, *City of God*, *Amores Perros*, and *Nine Lives*.

Cape of Good Hope transports the hyperlink movie to South Africa, to show how lives previously divided by race and class now connect more unpredictably. Two women (one white, one Indian) work at an animal shelter with a refugee from the Congo. We meet an African maid and her mother and son, a white veterinarian, an older woman trying to fool herself into romance with a younger man, and others whose lives are more connected than they realize. Most of the hidden connections eventually have positive results; this is a movie with characters we care about, living ordinary lives with reasonable goals.

Kate (Debbie Brown) is the white woman who runs the animal shelter. She has never married, is having an affair with a married man. Her best friend is Sharifa (Quanita Adams), a Muslim woman who works with her at the shelter; Sharifa is married to Habib (David Isaacs), and they are a childless couple who argue over their inability to conceive a child. One day Kate meets young Thabo (Kamo Masilo), a boy who lives in a nearby African township. He has a clever dog named Tupac (when will the hyperlinks end?), and Kate hires him and his dog to entertain at the shelter's open house. Through Thabo we meet his mother, Lindiwe (Nthati Moshesh), the maid, and his grandmother, who is conspiring to marry Lindiwe to an elderly but affluent local minister. Oh, and Kate has dealings with a veterinarian named Morne (Morne Visser), who likes her, although she seems to prefer the detachment of an affair.

These characters are introduced briskly in their everyday lives against the backdrop of the Cape Town suburb of Hout Bay, one of those communities that are strung along the lower slopes of Table Mountain, which so benevolently looks down on rich and poor, happy and miserable.

For me, the most interesting character it overlooks is Jean Claude (Eriq Ebouaney, who played the title role in *Lumumba* and had a key role in Brian de Palma's *Femme Fatale*). He is a French-speaking refugee from the violence of the Congo who works at the animal shelter cleaning the cages. On Sundays, he volunteers at the Cape Town Observatory. As a volunteer, his official job is to sweep and clean, although he often engages young students in stories of the universe that leave them goggle-eyed. Jean Claude in fact has a Ph.D. in astronomy, but like the Beirut surgeon in *Yes* who works in London as a waiter, he cannot as a refugee find the employment he was trained for. There is a colossal irony when Jean Claude

is fired by the head of the observatory because government policy dictates that such jobs should go to locals. "But I am not paid!" he points out. Nevertheless, he has to go.

Jean Claude meets Lindiwe and her son, Thabo, falls in love with her, is idolized by the boy, is an alternative to the loathed elderly minister. But if his application for Canadian citizenship comes through, will he have to leave her behind? Meanwhile, Kate continues to befriend Thabo, which leads her to an after-dark visit to a nearby African township where, as any city-smart person should know, she might not be entirely safe wandering the streets by herself. These stories are intercut, or hyperlinked, to reveal more and unexpected connections. Will Kate dump the married man and find room in her life for the veterinarian? Will Sharifa and her husband be able to conceive? Do Jean Claude and Lindiwe have a future? And what about the dog at the shelter who was trained to attack blacks? Will it learn to get along with all races in the new South Africa?

While we are absorbed in these stories, while some of the characters appeal enormously to us, we are at the same time being drawn subtly into the emerging South African multiracialism. What *Cape of Good Hope* argues, I think, is that we live in sad times if political issues define our lives. When politics do not create walls (as apartheid did), most people are primarily interested in their families, their romances, and their jobs. They hope to improve all three. The movie is about their hope.

The movie was directed by Mark Bamford; his wife, Suzanne Kay Bamford, cowrote and coproduced. At the Toronto festival, they told me they were Americans who were unable to interest Hollywood in the stories they wanted to tell. They moved to Cape Town "for one year" and are still there after four. Ironically, their screenplay for *Cape of Good Hope* attracted the interest of Hollywood, but the studios wanted to use an American cast to play the South Africans. That would have lost the particular local flavor that is one of the film's assets.

Capote ★ ★ ★ ★
R, 114 m., 2005

Philip Seymour Hoffman (Truman Capote), Catherine Keener (Nelle Harper Lee), Clifton

Collins Jr. (Perry Smith), Chris Cooper (Alvin Dewey), Bruce Greenwood (Jack Dunphy), Bob Balaban (William Shawn), Amy Ryan (Marie Dewey), Mark Pellegrino (Dick Hickock). Directed by Bennett Miller and produced by Caroline Baron, William Vince, and Michael Ohoven. Screenplay by Dan Futterman, based on the book *Capote* by Gerald Clarke.

On November 15, 1959, Truman Capote noticed a news item about four members of a Kansas farm family who were shotgunned to death. He telephoned William Shawn, editor of the *New Yorker*, wondering if Shawn would be interested in an article about the murders. Later in his life Capote said that if he had known what would happen as a result of this impulse, he would not have stopped in Holcomb, Kansas, but would have kept right on going "like a bat out of hell."

At first Capote thought the story would be about how a rural community was dealing with the tragedy. "I don't care one way or the other if you catch who did this," he tells an agent from the Kansas Bureau of Investigation. Then two drifters, Perry Smith and Richard Hickock, are arrested and charged with the crime. As Capote gets to know them, he's consumed by a story that would make him rich and famous, and destroy him. His "nonfiction novel," *In Cold Blood*, became a best seller and inspired a movie, but Capote was emotionally devastated by the experience and it hastened his death.

Bennett Miller's *Capote* is about that crucial period of fewer than six years in Capote's life. As he talks to the killers, to law officers, and to the neighbors of the murdered Clutter family, Capote's project takes on depth and shape as the story of conflicting fates. But at the heart of his reporting is an irredeemable conflict: He wins the trust of the two convicted killers and essentially falls in love with Perry Smith, while needing them to die to supply an ending for his book. "If they win this appeal," he tells his friend Harper Lee, "I may have a complete nervous breakdown." After they are hanged on April 14, 1965, he tells Harper, "There wasn't anything I could have done to save them." She says: "Maybe, but the fact is you didn't want to."

Capote is a film of uncommon strength and insight, about a man whose great achievement requires the surrender of his self-respect. Philip

Seymour Hoffman's precise, uncanny performance as Capote doesn't imitate the author so much as channel him, as a man whose peculiarities mask great intelligence and deep wounds.

As the story opens, Capote is a well-known writer (of *Breakfast at Tiffany's*, among others), a popular guest on talk shows, a man whose small stature, large ego, and affectations of speech and appearance make him an outsider wherever he goes. Trying to win the confidence of a young girl in Kansas, he tells her: "Ever since I was a child, folks have thought they had me pegged because of the way I am, the way I talk." But he was able to enter a world far removed from Manhattan and write a great book about ordinary Midwesterners and two pathetic, heartless killers. Could anyone be less like Truman Capote than Perry Smith? Yet they were both mistreated and passed around as children, had issues with distant and remote mothers, had secret fantasies. "It's like Perry and I grew up in the same house, and one day he went out the back door and I went out the front," he tells Harper Lee.

The film, written by Dan Futterman and based on the book *Capote* by Gerald Clarke, focuses on the way a writer works on a story and the story works on him. Capote wins the wary acceptance of Alvin Dewey (Chris Cooper), the agent assigned to the case. Over dinner in Alvin and Marie Dewey's kitchen, he entertains them with stories of John Huston and Humphrey Bogart. As he talks, he studies their house like an anthropologist. He convinces the local funeral director to let him view the mutilated bodies of the Clutters. Later, Perry Smith will tell him he liked the father, Herb Clutter: "I thought he was a very nice, gentle man. I thought so right up until I slit his throat."

On his trips to Kansas, Capote takes along a Southern friend from childhood, Harper Lee (Catherine Keener). So long does it take him to finish his book that Lee in the meantime has time to publish her famous novel, *To Kill a Mockingbird*, sell it to the movies, and attend the world premiere with Gregory Peck. Harper Lee is a practical, grounded woman who clearly sees that Truman cares for Smith and yet will exploit him for his book. "Do you hold him in esteem, Truman?" she asks, and he is defensive: "Well, he's a gold mine."

Perry Smith and Dick Hickock are played

by Clifton Collins Jr. and Mark Pellegrino. Hickock is not developed as deeply as in Richard Brooks's film *In Cold Blood* (1967), where he was played by Scott Wilson; the emphasis this time is on Smith, played in 1967 by Robert Blake and here by Collins as a haunted, repressed man in constant pain who chews aspirin by the handful and yet shelters a certain poetry; his drawings and journal move Capote, who sees him as a man who was born a victim and deserves not forgiveness but pity.

The other key characters are Capote's lover, Jack Dunphy (Bruce Greenwood), and his editor at the *New Yorker*, William Shawn (Bob Balaban). "Jack thinks I'm using Perry," Truman tells Harper. "He also thinks I fell in love with him in Kansas." Shawn thinks *In Cold Blood*, when it is finally written, is "going to change how people write." He prints the entire book in his magazine.

The movie *In Cold Blood* had no speaking role for Capote, who in a sense stood behind the camera with the director. If *Capote* had simply flipped the coin and told the story of the Clutter murders from Capote's point of view, it might have been a good movie, but what makes it so powerful is that it looks with merciless perception at Capote's moral disintegration.

"If I leave here without understanding you," Capote tells Perry Smith during one of many visits to his cell, "the world will see you as a monster. I don't want that." He is able to convince Smith and Hickock to tell him what happened on the night of the murders. He learns heartbreaking details, such as that they "put a different pillow under the boy's head just to shoot him." Capote tells them he will support their appeals and help them find another lawyer. He betrays them. Smith eventually understands that and accepts his fate. "Two weeks, and finito," he tells Capote as his execution draws near. Another good line for the book.

Carandiru ★ ★ ★
R, 148 m., 2004

Luiz Carlos Vasconcelos (Doctor), Milton Goncalves (Chico), Ivan de Almeida (Ebony), Ailton Graca (Majestade), Maria Luisa Mendonca (Dalva), Aide Leiner (Rosirene), Rodrigo Santoro (Lady Di), Gero Camilo (No Way). Directed by Hector Babenco and produced by Babenco and Oscar Kramer. Screenplay by Babenco, Fernando Bonassi, and Victor Navas, based on the book *Estacao Carandiru* by Dr. Drauzio Varella.

In the Brazilian documentary *Bus 174*, there is a scene that could have been shot in hell. Using the night-vision capability of a digital camera, the film ventures into an unlit Brazilian prison to show desperate souls reaching through the bars. Jammed so closely they have to sit down in shifts, with temperatures above 100 degrees Fahrenheit, with rotten food and dirty water, many jailed without any charges being filed, they cry out for rescue.

Hector Babenco's *Carandiru* is a drama that adds a human dimension to that Dantean vision. Shot on location inside a notorious prison in São Paolo, it shows 8,000 men jammed into space meant for 4,000, and enforcing their own laws in a place their society has abandoned. The film, based on life, climaxes with a 1992 police attack on the prison during which 111 inmates were killed.

How this film came to be made is also a story. Babenco is the gifted director of *Pixote, Kiss of the Spider Woman*, and *At Play in the Fields of the Lord*. An illness put him out of action for several years, and he credits his doctor, Drauzio Varella, with saving his life. As it happens, Varella was for years the physician on duty inside the prison, and his memoir *Carandiru Station* inspired Babenco to make this film, with Varella as his guide.

What we see at first looks like lawless anarchy. But as characters develop and social rules become clear, we see that the prisoners have imposed their own order in the absence of outside authority. The prison is run more or less by the prisoners, with the warden and guards looking on helplessly; stronger or more powerful prisoners decorate their cells like private rooms, while the weak are crammed in head to toe. Respected prisoners act as judges when crimes are committed. A code permits homosexuality but forbids rape. And the prison has such a liberal policy involving conjugal visits that a prisoner with two wives has to deal with both of them on the same day. Some prisoners continue to function as the heads of their families, advising their children, counseling their wives, approving marriages, managing the finances.

Dr. Varella, played in the film by Luiz Carlos Vasconcelos, originally went to Carandiru when AIDS was still a new disease; he lectures on the use of condoms, advises against sharing needles, but is in a society where one of his self-taught assistants sews up wounds without anesthetic or sanitation. The prisoners come to trust the doctor and confide in him, and as some of them tell their stories, the movie flashes back to show what they did to earn their sentences.

In a prison filled with vivid, Dickensian characters, several stand out. There is, for example, the unlikely couple of Lady Di (Rodrigo Santoro), tall and muscular, and No Way (Gero Camilo), a stunted little man. They are the great loves of each other's lives. Their marriage scene is an occasion for celebration in the prison, and later, when the police murder squads arrive, it is No Way, the husband, who fearlessly uses his little body to protect the great hulk of his frightened bride. Their story and several others are memorably told, although the film is a little too episodic and meandering.

Although there are weapons everywhere in the prison, the doctor walks unarmed and without fear, because he is known and valued. The warden is not so trusted, and with good reason. After a prison soccer match ends in a fight that escalates into a protest, he stands in the courtyard, begs for a truce, and asks the inmates to throw down their weapons. In an astonishing scene, hundreds or even thousands of knives rain down from the cell windows. And then, when the prisoners are unarmed, the police attack.

The movie observes laconically that the police were "defending themselves," even though 111 prisoners and no police were killed. The prison was finally closed in 2002, and the film's last shot shows it being leveled by dynamite. Strange, how by then we have grown to respect some of the inmates and at least understand others. *Bus 174* is a reminder that although Carandiru has disappeared, prison conditions in Brazil continue to be inhuman.

Cars ★ ★ ★
G, 118 m., 2006

Voices of: Owen Wilson (Lightning McQueen), Paul Newman (Doc Hudson), Bonnie Hunt (Sally Carrera), Larry the Cable Guy (Mater), George Carlin (Fillmore), Paul Dooley (Sarge), Cheech Marin (Ramone), Jenifer Lewis (Flo), Tony Shalhoub (Luigi), Michael Wallis (The Sheriff), Richard Petty (The King), Michael Keaton (Chick Hicks), John Ratzenberger (Mack). Directed by John Lasseter and produced by Darla K. Anderson. Screenplay by Dan Fogelman, Lasseter, Kiel Murray, and Phil Lorin.

I wouldn't have thought that even in animation a 1951 Hudson Hornet could look simultaneously like itself and like Paul Newman, but you will witness that feat, and others, in *Cars*. This is the new animated feature by John Lasseter (*Toy Story, A Bug's Life*); it tells a bright and cheery story and then has a little something profound lurking around the edges. In this case, it's a sense of loss.

What have we lost? The movie's hero, a racing car named Lightning McQueen (voice by Owen Wilson), has just lost a big race, and then one day on the highway he goes astray and rolls into the forgotten hamlet of Radiator Springs, in Carburetor County. This was a happenin' town back when Route 66 was the way to get from Chicago to L.A., passing through Flagstaff, Arizona, and don't forget Winona. But now the interstates and time itself have passed it by, and the town slumbers on, a memory of an earlier America.

Lightning's dream is to win the Piston Cup, the grand prix of American racing. He's on his way to the race when he gets lost and then, more humiliating, impounded. Once released, he meets the population of Radiator Springs, led by Doc Hudson (Paul Newman), who may be an old-timer but probably knows something about Hudsons that Lightning doesn't: Because of their "step-down design," they had a lower center of gravity than the Big 3 models of their time and won stock car races by making tighter turns.

Other citizens include Mater (rhymes with *tow-mater*) the Tow Truck (Larry the Cable Guy), Sally the sexy Porsche (Bonnie Hunt), Fillmore the hippie VW bus (George Carlin), and Sarge the veteran Jeep (Paul Dooley). Tractors serve as the cows of Radiator Springs and even chew their cud, although what that cud consists of I'm not sure. Fan belts, maybe.

The message in *Cars* is simplicity itself: Life was better in the old days, when it revolved around small towns where everybody knew each other, and around small highways such as Route 66, where you made new friends, sometimes even between Flagstaff and Winona. This older America long has been much beloved by Hollywood, and apparently it survives in Radiator Springs as sort of a time capsule. Doc Hudson, it turns out, was a famous race car in his day. That leads up to a race in which the vet and the kid face off, although how that race ends I would not dream of revealing. What I will reveal, with regret, is that the movie lacks a single Studebaker. The 1950s Studebakers are much beloved by all period movies, because they so clearly signal their period, from the classic Raymond Loewy–designed models to the Golden Hawk, which left Corvettes and T-Birds eating its dust. Maybe there's no Hawk in Radiator Springs because then Doc Hudson would lose his bragging rights.

The movie is great to look at and a lot of fun but somehow lacks the extra push of the other Pixar films. Maybe that's because there's less at stake here, and no child-surrogate to identify with. I wonder if the movie's primary audience, which skews young, will care much about the 1950s and its cars. Maybe they will. Of all decades, the 1950s seems to have the most staying power; like Archie and Jughead, the decade stays forever young, perhaps because that's when modern teenagers were invented.

Casanova ★ ★
R, 108 m., 2005

Heath Ledger (Casanova), Sienna Miller (Francesca Bruni), Oliver Platt (Paprizzio), Jeremy Irons (Bishop Pucci), Lena Olin (Andrea Bruni), Charlie Cox (Giovanni), Natalie Dormer (Victoria). Directed by Lasse Hallstrom and produced by Betsy Beers, Mark Gordon, and Leslie Holleran. Screenplay by Jeffrey Hatcher and Kimberly Simi.

I have just been idly paging through volume three of Casanova's Memoirs, which covers the circa 1753 time frame of Lasse Hallstrom's new film. Casanova was a busy man. He found himself in Parma ("perplexities concerning my female traveling companion"), Bologna ("Henriette resumes the dress of her sex"), Geneva ("unpleasant adventure with an actress"), Venice ("adventure with the Marchetti girl"), Paris ("I

practice cabalism for the duchess of Chartres"), Padua ("her father refuses and puts her in a convent"), and Vicenza ("my tragicomic scene at the inn"). That he also found the will and the way to undertake the adventures in this film is explained only because it is fictional.

Its most imaginary aspect might appear to be his love affair with a swashbuckling cross-dressing feminist named Francesca Bruni, but, as we have seen, he had already met a cross-dresser in 1753 and, for that matter, had been one. As for feminism as it existed at that time, all its beliefs seem to have included the implicit footnote "except for Casanova." What is accurate about the movie is that he was the quarry of the Inquisition and doomed to be locked up in the infamous dungeon reached from the Ducal Palace by the Bridge of Sighs, which even then had tourists lined up three deep on the nearby Ponte della Paglia, awaiting the invention of the Instamatic.

Casanova was such a genuinely fascinating person, so tireless, seductive, brilliant, revolutionary, and daring, that Hallstrom's Casanova hardly does him justice. He was a magician, an author, a lawyer, the secretary to a cardinal, a politician, and a violinist; invented the national lottery; was a spy and a diplomat; and has been played by Bela Lugosi, Donald Sutherland, Peter O'Toole, and now by Heath Ledger, whose other current film, Brokeback Mountain, has him playing a gay cowboy, a role that eluded Casanova only because cowboys hadn't been invented yet.

The film is no more implausible than Casanova's actual adventures. It shows him returning in Venice (he did), running across the rooftops (he did) while being chased by the Inquisition (he was) and protected by the ruler of Venice, the doge (also true). The doge orders him to get married. He selects the virginal Victoria (Natalie Dormer), only to find she is already affianced to Giovanni (Charlie Cox), whose sister Francesca (Sienna Miller) is a feminist who dons male garb and impersonates Giovanni after her brother (Giovanni, that is) challenges Casanova to a sword fight. She is the more skilled swordsperson, and Casanova, keen student of swordsmanship, transfers his lust to her, only to learn that she is engaged to Paprizzio (Oliver Platt), who is, according to my notes, "the lard king of Genoa."

It must be a wondrous thing to be the lard king of Genoa, and I would have wished Casanova time to quiz Paprizzio about his lofty estate, but the Inquisition is fed up with Casanova's flaunting of morality and appoints Pucci (Jeremy Irons) to apprehend and imprison him. By this time Casanova has grown somewhat weary, although when he resumes his real-life *Autobiography* it still has eight more volumes of tireless lubricity to go. As I watched the film, I kept having flash-forwards, or were they flash-sidewayses, to the forthcoming film *The Libertine*, in which Johnny Depp plays a Casanova wannabe who spends so much time sticking his nose into other people's business that it eventually falls off and has to be replaced by a silver one.

I also had flashbacks to *Dangerous Beauty* (1998), a film about romance and Venice that is so much better than *Casanova* that you might as well just go ahead and rent it. Catherine McCormick stars as a woman who is forced by circumstances to become a courtesan and so convincingly entertains King Henry of France that he saves Venice from the Turkish fleet. I quote from my review:

"'What do you yearn for, King Henry?' asks Veronica. 'Your tears,' he says, pressing a knife to her throat. 'I don't think so,' she says, and a shadow of doubt crosses his face. 'Then what do I yearn for?' he asks. She graces him with a cold smile: 'Why don't we find out?' Cut to the next morning, as the doge and other nobles nervously await the king's reappearance. He emerges, settles himself somewhat painfully on a cushion, and says, 'You'll get your ships.'"

That the new *Casanova* lacks such wit is fatal. Ledger is a good actor, but Hallstrom's film is busy and unfocused, giving us the view of Casanova's ceaseless activity but not the excitement. It's a sitcom when what is wanted is comic opera.

The fictional character of Francesca Bruni is, oddly enough, not making her first appearance in a film about Casanova. In the 1954 comedy *Casanova's Big Night,* she is courted by Pippo Popolino (Bob Hope), a Casanova impersonator who puts on a mask and tries to seduce her.

"Take your mask off!" Francesca (Joan Fontaine) tells him.

"I couldn't do that," he says. "I haven't got anything on underneath it."

Catch That Kid ★ ★ ★
PG, 92 m., 2004

Kristen Stewart (Maddy Phillips), Corbin Bleu (Austin), Max Thieriot (Gus), Jennifer Beals (Molly), Sam Robards (Tom), Michael Des Barres (Brisbane). Directed by Bart Freundlich and produced by Andrew Lazar and Uwe Schott. Screenplay by Nicolai Arcel, Hans Fabian Wullenweber, Erlend Loe, Michael Brandt, and Derek Haas.

Now here's something you don't see every day: a heist movie involving twelve-year-old kids. *Catch That Kid* respects all of the requirements of the genre, and the heist itself is worthy of *Ocean's Eleven* (either one; take your pick). Kristen Stewart's plucky heroine will win the hearts of the same young audiences who liked *Bend It Like Beckham* and *Whale Rider*.

This is not, to be sure, a movie as good as those two wonderful titles. But it's plenty good, and it has the same buried theme: Anything a guy can do, a girl can do too. It stars Stewart as Maddy Phillips, an athletic young girl whose father, Tom (Sam Robards), once climbed Mount Everest. He had a nasty fall on the way down, which is why he discourages Maddy from climbing, while her mother, Molly (Jennifer Beals), forbids it. But as the movie opens, she's scaling the local water tower.

Maddy has two best friends. Austin (Corbin Bleu) is a computer geek. Gus (Max Thieriot) is a mechanic at the go-kart track operated by her father. They both have crushes on her, although at one point, when she's hanging in danger high in the air during the heist, Gus complains that he never even got a chance to kiss her once.

A crisis comes into her life with all the melodrama of a silent movie. One night while her dad and mom are dancing in the living room, he falls to the floor and says, "I can't feel my legs!" It's paralysis—whether from the neck or waist down, we don't learn, but in any event the condition is incurable, except for an experimental procedure offered in Europe; it costs $250,000 the family doesn't have.

Common sense at this point steps in and suggests that if such an operation really existed,

Christopher Reeve would already be on site with a charity to help the Toms of the world, but no: Molly the mother is turned down for a loan at the bank where she has installed the security system. The bank president, named Brisbane (Michael Des Barres), is a teeth-gnashing, scenery-chewing villain whose origins go back even before silent films—back to Horatio Alger, if anybody remembers who that was. Been a while since we've had a banker this evil in the movies.

So the kids take things into their own hands. With Maddy's climbing skills, Austin to hack into the bank's security system, and Gus to devise mechanical devices and the getaway, they'll break into the bank vault and steal the $250,000. This is not so easy, since the vault is suspended in midair, surrounded by motion detectors, protected by savage rottweilers, etc.

The movie is a remake of a Danish film, unseen by me, named *Klatretøsen*, which was hailed at the Berlin Film Festival. This version, directed by Bart Freundlich and sporting five writing credits, is well made, straightforward, and entertaining. It doesn't bog down in a lot of cute kid stuff, but gets on with telling the story, and has some unexpected touches. For example, the getaway scene with the kids in go-karts. Yes, and the police chase them, shouting on loudspeakers: "You kids in the go-karts! Pull over! You're leaving the scene of a crime." Sure, because any cop seeing kids on a city street in go-karts is instinctively going to link them to a bank robbery.

Kristen Stewart is at the center of the movie, stalwart and sure. You may remember her as Jodie Foster's daughter in a more harrowing thriller, *Panic Room* (2002). Corbin Bleu and Max Thieriot, as her two pals, are just plain likable, and the attraction between Bleu and Stewart may be the screen's first example of interracial puppy love. For that matter, Jennifer Beals is cast as a possibly mixed-race mother, and I would not bother to make this point except to observe that all of a sudden racial categories are evaporating in mainstream movies, and for the first time in history actors are being cast because they're right for a role, not because they passed an identity check.

Catch That Kid doesn't have the flash of *Spy Kids*, but it's solid entertainment—better than *Agent Cody Banks*. Faithful readers know that my definition of a good family film is one the parents can enjoy, and you know

what? In the middle of the heist scene, we're just about as involved as if the movie starred George Clooney and Julia Roberts. A heist is a heist, and a good one works no matter what.

Catwoman ★
PG-13, 91m., 2004

Halle Berry (Patience Philips), Benjamin Bratt (Detective Tom Lone), Lambert Wilson (George Hedare), Frances Conroy (Ophelia Powers), Sharon Stone (Laurel Hedare). Directed by Pitof and produced by Denise Di Novi and Edward McDonnell. Screenplay by John Rogers, John Brancato, and Michael Ferris.

Catwoman is a movie about Halle Berry's beauty, sex appeal, figure, eyes, lips, and costume design. It gets those right. Everything else is secondary, except for the plot, which is tertiary. What a letdown. The filmmakers have given great thought to photographing Berry, who looks fabulous, and little thought to providing her with a strong character, story, supporting characters, or action sequences. When *Spider-Man 2* represents the state of the art, *Catwoman* is tired and dated.

Although the movie's faults are many, the crucial one is that we never get any sense of what it feels like to turn into a catwoman. The strength of *Spider-Man 2* is in the ambivalence that Peter Parker has about being part nerdy student, part superhero. In *Catwoman,* where are the scenes where a woman comes to grips with the fact that her entire nature and even her species seems to have changed?

Berry plays Patience Philips, a designer for an ad agency, who dies and is reborn after Midnight, a cat with ties to ancient Egypt, breathes new life into her. She becomes Catwoman, but what is a catwoman? She can leap like a cat, strut around on top of her furniture, survive great falls, and hiss. Halle Berry looks great doing these things, and spends a lot of time on all fours, inspiring our almost unseemly gratitude for her cleavage.

She gobbles down tuna and sushi. Her eyes have vertical pupils instead of horizontal ones. She sleeps on a shelf. The movie doesn't get into the litter box situation. What does she *think* about all of this? Why isn't she more astonished that it has happened to her? How

107

does it affect her relationship with that cute cop, Tom Lone (Benjamin Bratt)?

The movie makes it clear that they make love at least once, but we don't see that happening because *Catwoman*, a film that was born to be rated R, has been squeezed into the PG-13 category to rake in every last teenage dollar. From what we know about Catwoman, her style in bed has probably changed along with everything else, and sure enough the next day Tom notices a claw mark on his shoulder. Given the MPAA's preference for violence over sex, this might have been one sex scene that could have sneaked in under the PG-13.

Catwoman dresses like a dominatrix, with the high heels and the leather skirt, brassiere, mask, and whip. But why? Because the costume sketches looked great, is my opinion. The film gives her a plot that could have been phoned in from the 1960s: She works for a corporation that's introducing a new beauty product that gives women eternal youth, unless they stop taking it, in which case they look like burn victims. When Patience stumbles over this unfortunate side effect, she is attacked by security guards, flushed out of a waste pipe, and is dead when Midnight finds her.

Soon she has a dual identity: Patience by day, Catwoman by night. She already knows Tom Lone. They met when she crawled out of her window and balanced on an air conditioner to rescue Midnight, and Tom thought she was committing suicide and saved her after she slipped. Uh, huh. That meeting begins a romance between Patience and Tom that is remarkable for its complete lack of energy, passion, and chemistry. If the movie had been ten minutes longer it would have needed a scene where they sigh and sadly agree their relationship is just not working out. One of those things. Not meant to be.

The villains are Laurel and George Hedare (Sharon Stone and Lambert Wilson). He runs the cosmetics company and fires his wife as its model when she turns forty. She is not to be trifled with, especially not in a movie where the big fight scene is a real catfight, so to speak, between the two women. Stone's character is laughably one-dimensional, but then that's a good fit for this movie, in which none of the characters suggest any human dimensions and seem to be posing more than relat-

ing. Take George, for example, whose obnoxious mannerisms are so grotesque he's like the *Saturday Night Live* version of Vincent Price.

Among many silly scenes, the silliest has to be the Ferris wheel sequence, which isn't even as thrilling as the one in *The Notebook*. Wouldn't you just know that after the wheel stalls, the operator would recklessly strip the gears, and the little boy riding alone would be in a chair where the guard rail falls off, and then the seat comes loose, and then the wheel tries to shake him loose and no doubt would try to electrocute him if it could.

The score by Klaus Badelt is particularly annoying; it faithfully mirrors every action with what occasionally sounds like a karaoke rhythm section. The director, whose name is given as Pitof, was probably issued with two names at birth, and would be wise to use the other one on his next project.

Cellular ★ ★ ★ ½
PG-13, 94 m., 2004

Kim Basinger (Jessica Martin), Chris Evans (Ryan), Eric Christian Olsen (Chad), William H. Macy (Mooney), Jason Statham (Greer), Adam Taylor Gordon (Ricky Martin), Rick Hoffman (Porsche Owner), Richard Burgi (Craig Martin). Directed by David R. Ellis and produced by Dean Devlin and Lauren Lloyd. Screenplay by Larry Cohen and Chris Morgan.

Cellular stands *Phone Booth* on its head. The 2003 thriller was about a psychopath who threatens Colin Farrell with death if he leaves a Manhattan phone booth. The new one has Chris Evans racing desperately all over Los Angeles as he tries to stay on his cell phone with a woman who says she's been kidnapped. The same writer, Larry Cohen, collaborated on both projects and is no doubt currently involved in a thriller about chat rooms.

The plot of *Cellular* sounds like a gimmick, and no wonder: It *is* a gimmick. What's surprising is how convincing it is, under the circumstances, and how willingly we accept the premise and get involved in it. The movie is skillfully plotted, halfway plausible, and well acted; the craftsmanship is in the details, including the astonishing number of different ways in which a cell phone can be made to function—both as a telephone and as a plot device.

Kim Basinger stars as Jessica, a high school science teacher who is kidnapped by violent home invaders and held prisoner in an attic. The men who have taken her want something from her husband—something she knows nothing about. They know where her young son, Ricky (Adam Taylor Gordon), attends school and plan to kidnap him too. The kidnappers are hard men, especially their cold, intense leader, Greer, played by Jason Statham. Because they've allowed Jessica to see them, she assumes they will eventually kill her.

The attic has a wall phone, which a kidnapper smashes to bits. But Jessica the science teacher is able to fit some of the parts back together and click on the wires to make a call—at random. She reaches Ryan (Chris Evans), a twenty-something kid who at first doesn't believe her when she says she has been kidnapped. At one point, he even puts her on hold; that's part of the movie's strategy of building our frustration by creating one believable obstacle after another. Jessica pleads with him not to hang up: to trust her enough to hand his cell phone to a cop. Something in her voice convinces him. He walks into a police station and hands the phone to a desk cop named Mooney (William H. Macy), who gets sidetracked and advises him to go to homicide, up on the fourth floor. Uh-huh. But Mooney, too, hears something in her voice, and later in the day it still resonates. He's not your typical hot-dog movie cop, but a quiet, thoughtful professional with unexpected resources.

The movie's surprises, when they come, mostly seem to make sense. When we find out who the kidnappers are and what it is they want from Jessica's husband, it doesn't seem like too much of a reach. But the real fun of the movie comes from the hoops Ryan has to jump through in order to somehow stay on the line with Jessica, convince people he's not crazy, and get personally involved in the deadly climax. Yes, the action scenes are over the top, and yes, the chase scenes involve unthinkable carnage on the freeways, but, yes, we go along because the motivations and strategies of the characters are strong and clear.

About the crime and the criminals I will say no more. What's ingenious about the movie is the way it uses telephones—and the people who use them. At one point Ryan gets a "low battery" warning and desperately needs a charger, so of course he finds himself in a cell phone store where he is instructed with maddening condescension to take a number and wait his place in line. At another point he comes into the life of a spectacularly obnoxious lawyer (Rick Hoffman), and steals his Porsche not once but twice.

And then there are the ways phones can be used for things other than making calls. Ways they can preserve evidence, maintain callback records, function as an emergency alarm system, convey unintended information, or even betray themselves. Larry Cohen and his cowriter, Chris Morgan, must have spent days with their yellow pads, jotting down every use they could think of for a cell phone.

The director, David R. Ellis, does have the usual chases and shoot-outs, but he doesn't depend on them to make his movie work. He's attentive to how and why the characters behave, he makes it clear what they're thinking, and he has a good feel for situations in which everything depends on human nature. Kim Basinger, who for such a healthy-looking woman has always been so good at seeming vulnerable, is ideally cast here, and young Chris Evans (from *Not Another Teen Movie*) has a star-making role. But the real juice comes from the old pros William H. Macy, as a dogged cop who might surprise you in a tight spot, and Jason Statham as the leader of the kidnappers. By occupying their roles believably, by acting as we think their characters probably would, they save the movie from feeling like basic Hollywood action (even when it probably is). This is one of the year's best thrillers. Better than *Phone Booth*, for my money, and I liked that too.

Chaos no stars
NO MPAA RATING, 78 m., 2005

Kevin Gage (Chaos), Stephen Wozniak (Frankie), Kelly K. C. Quann (Sadie), Sage Stallone (Swan), Chantal Degroat (Emily), Maya Barovich (Angelica), Ken Medlock (Sheriff). Directed by David DeFalco and produced by Steven Jay Bernheim. Screenplay by DeFalco.

Chaos is ugly, nihilistic and cruel—a film I regret having seen. I urge you to avoid it.

Don't make the mistake of thinking it's "only" a horror film, or a slasher film. It is an exercise in heartless cruelty and it ends with careless brutality. The movie denies not only the value of life but also the possibility of hope.

The movie premiered in late July at Flashback Weekend, a Chicago convention devoted to horror and exploitation films. As I write, it remains unreviewed in *Variety,* unlisted on Rotten Tomatoes. As an unabashed retread of *The Last House on the Left* (itself inspired by Ingmar Bergman's *The Virgin Spring*), it may develop a certain notoriety, but you don't judge a book by its cover or a remake by its inspiration. A few Web writers have seen it and try to deal with their feelings:

"What is inflicted upon these women is degrading, humiliating, and terrible on every level."
—Capone, Ain't It Cool News

"Disgusting, shocking, and laced with humiliation, nudity, profanity, and limit-shoving tastelessness."
—John Gray, Pitofhorror.com

"What's the point of this s—t anyway?"
—Ed Gonzalez, slantmagazine.com

But Capone finds the film "highly effective" if "painful and difficult to watch." And Gray looks on the bright side: David DeFalco "manages to shock and disturb as well as give fans a glimpse of hope that some people are still trying to make good, sleazy exploitation films." Gonzalez finds no redeeming features, adding, "DeFalco directs the whole thing with all the finesse of someone who has been hit on the head one too many times (is this a good time to say he was a wrestler?)."

I quote these reviews because I'm fascinated by their strategies for dealing with a film that transcends all barriers of decency. There are two scenes so gruesome I cannot describe them in a newspaper, no matter what words I use. Having seen it, I cannot ignore it, nor can I deny that it affected me strongly: I recoiled during some of the most cruel moments, and when the film was over I was filled with sadness and disquiet.

The plot: Angelica and Emily (Chantal Degroat and Maya Barovich) are UCLA students, visiting the country cabin of Emily's parents, an interracial couple. They hear about a rave in the woods, drive off to party, meet a lout named Swan (Sage Stallone), and ask him where they can find some Ecstasy. He leads them to a cabin occupied by Chaos (Kevin Gage), already wanted for serial killing, Frankie (Stephen Wozniak), and Sadie (Kelly K. C. Quann). They're a Manson family in microcosm. By the end of the film, they will have raped and murdered the girls, not always in that order. Nor does the bloodshed stop there. The violence is sadistic, graphic, savage, and heartless. Much of the action involves the girls weeping and pleading for their lives. When the film pauses for dialogue, it is often racist.

So that's it. DeFalco directs with a crude, efficient gusto, as a man with an ax makes short work of firewood. Gage makes Chaos repulsive and cruel, Quann is effective as a pathetic, dim-witted sex slave, and the young victims are played with relentless sincerity; to the degree that we are repelled by the killers and feel pity for the victims, the movie "works." It works, all right, but I'm with Gonzalez: Why do we need this s—t? ☞

Charlie and the Chocolate Factory ★ ★ ★
PG, 115 m., 2005

Johnny Depp (Willy Wonka), Freddie Highmore (Charlie Bucket), David Kelly (Grandpa Joe), Helena Bonham Carter (Mrs. Bucket), Noah Taylor (Mr. Bucket), Missi Pyle (Mrs. Beauregarde), James Fox (Mr. Salt), Deep Roy (Oompa Loompa), Christopher Lee (Dr. Wonka), Julia Winter (Veruca Salt), AnnaSophia Robb (Violet Beauregarde), Jordan Fry (Mike Teavee), Philip Wiegratz (Augustus Gloop). Directed by Tim Burton and produced by Brad Grey and Richard D. Zanuck. Screenplay by John August, based on the book by Roald Dahl.

Now this is strange. *Charlie and the Chocolate Factory* succeeds in spite of Johnny Depp's performance, which should have been the high point of the movie. Depp, an actor of considerable gifts, has never been afraid to take a chance, but this time he takes the wrong one. His Willy Wonka is an enigma in an otherwise mostly delightful movie from Tim Burton, where the visual invention is a wonderment.

The movie is correctly titled. Unlike *Willy Wonka and the Chocolate Factory* (1971), which depends on Gene Wilder's twinkling air of mystery, *Charlie and the Chocolate Factory* is mostly about—Charlie. Young Charlie Bucket (Freddie Highmore) is so plucky and likable, and comes from such an eccentric and marvelous household, that the wonders inside the chocolate factory are no more amusing than everyday life at the Bucket residence.

The Buckets live in a house that leans crazily in all directions and seems to have been designed by Dr. Caligari along the lines of his cabinet. The family is very poor. Charlie sleeps in a garret that is open to the weather, and his four grandparents all sleep (and live, apparently) in the same bed, two at one end, two at the other. His mother (Helena Bonham Carter) maintains the serenity of the home, while his father (Noah Taylor) seeks employment. Grandpa Joe (David Kelly) remembers the happy decades when he and everyone else in the neighborhood worked in the chocolate factory.

Alas, fifteen years before the story begins, Willy Wonka dismissed his employees and locked his factory gates. Yet the world still enjoys Wonka products; how does Willy produce them? One day, astonishingly, Wonka announces a contest: For the five lucky children who find golden tickets in their Wonka Bars, the long-locked factory gates will open, and Willy will personally escort them through the factory. A special surprise is promised for one of them. Of course Charlie wins one of the tickets, not without suspense.

This stretch of the film has a charm not unlike *Babe* or the undervalued *Babe: Pig in the City*. A metropolis is remade to the requirements of fantasy. Tim Burton is cheerfully inventive in imagining the city and the factory, and the film's production design, by Alex McDowell, is a wonder. David Kelly, as Grandpa Joe, is a lovable geezer who agrees to accompany Charlie to the factory; you may remember him racing off naked on a motorcycle in *Waking Ned Devine* (1998). And young Freddie Highmore, who was so good opposite Depp in *Finding Neverland*, is hopeful and brave and always convincing as Charlie.

The problem is that this time, he finds Neverland. Depp may deny that he had Michael Jackson in mind when he created the look and feel of Willy Wonka, but moviegoers trust their eyes, and when they see Willy opening the doors of the factory to welcome the five little winners, they will be relieved that the kids brought along adult guardians. Depp's Wonka—his dandy's clothes, his unnaturally pale face, his makeup and lipstick, his hat, his manner—reminds me inescapably of Jackson (and, oddly, in a certain use of the teeth, chin, and bobbed hairstyle, of Carol Burnett).

The problem is not simply that Willy Wonka looks like Michael Jackson; it's that in a creepy way we're not sure of his motives. The story of Willy and his factory has had disturbing undertones ever since it first appeared in Roald Dahl's 1964 novel (also named after Charlie, not Willy). Nasty and frightening things happen to the children inside the factory in the book and both movies; perhaps Willy is using the tour to punish the behavior of little brats, while rewarding the good, poor, and decent Charlie. (How does it happen that each of the other four winners illustrates a naughty childhood trait? Just Willy's good luck, I guess.)

We see the wondrous workings of the factory in the opening titles, a CGI assembly-line sequence that swoops like a roller coaster. When the five kids and their adult guardians finally get inside, their first sight is a marvel of imagination: a sugary landscape of chocolate rivers, gumdrop trees, and (no doubt) rock candy mountains. Behind his locked doors, Willy has created this fantastical playground for—himself, apparently. As the tour continues, we learn the secret of his workforce: He uses Oompa Loompas, earnest and dedicated workers all looking exactly the same and all played, through a digital miracle, by the vaguely ominous Deep Roy. We're reminded of Santa's identical helpers in *Polar Express*.

It is essential to the story that the bad children be punished. Their sins are various: Veruca Salt (Julia Winter) is a spoiled brat; Violet Beauregarde (Annasophia Robb) is a competitive perfectionist; Mike Teavee (Jordan Fry) approaches the world with the skills and tastes he has learned through video games; and Augustus Gloop (Philip Wiegratz) likes to make a little pig out of himself.

All of these children meet fates appropriate to their misdemeanors. I might be tempted to wonder if smaller children will find the movie too scary, but I know from long experience with the first film that kids, for some reason, instinctively know this is a cautionary tale, and that even when a character is suctioned up by a chocolate conduit, all is not lost.

Charlie and his grandfather join wide-eyed in the tour, and there are subplots, especially involving Violet Beauregarde, before the happy ending. What is especially delightful are the musical numbers involving the Oompa Loompas, who seem to have spent a lot of time studying Hollywood musicals. The kids, their adventures and the song-and-dance numbers are so entertaining that Depp's strange Willy Wonka is not fatal to the movie, although it's at right angles to it.

What was he thinking of? In *Pirates of the Caribbean*, Depp was famously channeling Keith Richards, which may have primed us to look for possible inspirations for this performance. But leaving *Pirates* aside, can anyone look at Willy Wonka and not think of Michael Jackson? Consider the reclusive lifestyle, the fetishes of wardrobe and accessories, the elaborate playground built by an adult for the child inside. What's going on here?

But here is the important thing: Depp's miscalculated performance seems to exist almost outside the movie. It's fun despite his character. *Charlie and the Chocolate Factory* has its own life and energy, generated by Charlie and Grandpa Joe and their wacky household, by the other kids, by the special effects, and by the Oompa Loompas. While Willy pursues his mysterious concerns, the adventures go on without him. ☞

Chasing Liberty ★ ★
PG-13, 111 m., 2004

Mandy Moore (Anna Foster), Matthew Goode (Ben Calder), Jeremy Piven (Alan Weiss), Annabella Sciorra (Cynthia Morales), Mark Harmon (James Foster), Caroline Goodall (Michelle Foster). Directed by Andy Cadiff and produced by Broderick Johnson, Andrew A. Kosove, and David Parfitt. Screenplay by Derek Guiley and David Schneiderman.

Chasing Liberty is surprisingly good in areas where it doesn't need to be good at all, and pretty awful in areas where it has to succeed. It centers on a couple of engaging performances in impossible roles, and involves a madcap romp through a Europe where 9/11 never happened and *Roman Holiday* was never made. The movie is ideal for audiences who kinda know that we have a president, and he could have a teenage daughter, and she might be protected by the Secret Service, but don't know a whole lot else.

The movie has a view of reality, danger, romance, foreigners, sex, and impulsive behavior that would have made ideal honeymoon viewing for Britney and Jason, had their marriage not tragically ended before the movie could open. It reflects precisely the prudence and forethought of two people who could get married at 5:30 A.M. in a Vegas chapel after seeing *The Texas Chainsaw Massacre* and then file for an annulment after belatedly realizing they hadn't discussed having children, where they want to live, community property, religious affiliation, and whether the toilet paper should roll out or in.

You may protest that I'm hauling Britney and Jason into a review of a movie they have nothing to do with, but you would be wrong. There are going to be people who say that no one could possibly be as glamorous and yet as stupid as the characters in this film, and I give you Jason and Britney, case closed.

The movie stars Mandy Moore, a singer-actress of precisely Britney's generation, who has undeniable screen presence and inspires instant affection. Britney used to inspire instant affection herself, but now inspires instant alarm and concern. Mandy Moore is just plain likable, a Slurpee blended from scoops of Mary Tyler Moore, Sally Field, and Doris Day.

In *Chasing Liberty* she plays Anna Foster, code-named Liberty, who is the only daughter of U.S. president James Foster (Mark Harmon) and his first lady (Caroline Goodall). Her dating life is impossible. A hapless kid from her class arrives at the White House to take her out on a date, and the Secret Service strips the petals from the sweet little bouquet he brought her, seeking tiny and fragrant weapons of mass destruction.

The president is planning a state visit to Prague, and she wants to go along. What's more, she wants to hook up (in the old-fashioned sense, let us pray) with the daughter of the French ambassador, so they can skip over to Berlin for the annual Love Parade. And she demands freedom from the omnipresent Secret Service.

Her father nixes the Love Parade, promises to assign only two Secret Service agents, and is alarmed when Anna pulls a fast one, slips out of a nightclub, and is able to escape her agents by hitching a ride on the back of a motorcycle driven by Ben Calder (Matthew Goode). Ben is a saturnine Brit of about thirty, very dry and mysterious, and she knows absolutely nothing about him as she entrusts her life to him by embarking on a tour of Berlin, Venice, London, and other popular tourist destinations. Life on the road is easier when, by pure charm, for example, you can find a gondolier in Venice who not only waives his fee but invites you home so his mother can cook dinner for you and you can spend the night. Why does this gondolier remind me of the joke about the housewife who invites the mailman in for breakfast?

Anna doesn't know who Ben is, but she knows who she is, and it's fairly inconsiderate of her to run away and inspire a vast Euro hunt involving the Secret Service, Interpol, countless black helicopters, and millions of the taxpayers' dollars; this is one child who could have been left behind. Ben, however, does know who he is and so do we—he's working for the Secret Service, and has been assigned by the president to keep an eye on Anna while letting her think she's getting away with something.

Mandy Moore and Matthew Goode have a quirky and appealing chemistry, based on her confusion over whether she wants to have sex or not, or maybe over whether she's had sex or not, and his confusion when his private emotions begin to interfere with his job. There's a scene where Anna goes bungee-jumping and you want to explain to Ben that his job is to *prevent* her from bungee-jumping, not to tie himself to her bungee so they can die together. That would be a job for the Last Samurai.

I liked Goode's dry way of sardonically holding his distance, and Moore's unforced charm. It was a useful contrast to the movie's parallel romance between two agents named Weiss and Morales (Jeremy Piven and Annabella Sciorra), who grumble their way into love in dialogue that seems recycled from a shelved sitcom. Harmon is singularly unconvincing as the president, not only because he recklessly endangers his daughter's life and his country's fortune, but also because he reads the newspaper, and there's no telling where that could lead.

Cheaper by the Dozen 2 ★ ★ ★
PG, 94 m., 2005

Steve Martin (Tom "Dad" Baker), Bonnie Hunt (Kate "Mom" Baker), Eugene Levy (Jimmy Murtaugh), Piper Perabo (Nora Baker), Hilary Duff (Lorraine Baker), Alyson Stoner (Sarah Baker), Taylor Lautner (Eliot Murtaugh), Tom Welling (Charlie Baker), Jacob Smith (Jake Baker), Kevin Schmidt (Henry Baker), Carmen Electra (Sarina Murtaugh). Directed by Adam Shankman and produced by Shawn Levy and Ben Myron. Screenplay by Sam Harper, based on the novel by Frank B. Gilbreth Jr. and Ernestine Gilbreth Carey.

Cheaper by the Dozen 2 is the kind of title, like *The Other Side of the Mountain 2*, that starts you wondering why they didn't call it *This Side of the Mountain*. Or, more to the point, *Even Cheaper by Two Dozen*. All sequel titles tell you is that if you liked the doughnuts, why not buy another box. At which your mother would tell you to save some room for dinner, and I would suggest a new movie.

Still, as I watched this sequel, a certain good feeling began to make itself known. Yes, the movie is unnecessary. On the other hand, it is unnecessary at a higher level of warmth and humor than the recent remake *Yours, Mine and Ours*. And it has more plausible parents, even though neither one, so far as I know, is played by actors who have any children.

Steve Martin, whose adamant loner in *Shopgirl* is possibly autobiographical (he wrote the original novel), uses his status as a non-accumulator of kids as a basis for Dad Baker here, who is affectionate but not soppy. And Bonnie Hunt, as Mom, is the kind of mother who understands she essentially has a job in management. I am not even a little surprised that Hunt has three brothers and three sisters and used to work as a nurse in the oncology ward at Northwestern Memorial Hospital in Chicago.

What I liked the most about the second *Dozen*, however, was another performance, the one by Alyson Stoner as their daughter Sarah. As a girl poised on the first scary steps of adolescence, she finds the kind of vulnerability and shy hope that Reese Witherspoon projected in *The Man in the Moon* (1991), which contains a first kiss so sweet you remember it fifteen years later.

113

In Sarah's case, romance finds her after her parents assemble the Fabulous Baker Boys and Girls for one last summer at a rented lake cottage. Kids are growing up fast. The daughters played by Hilary Duff and Piper Perabo have already flown the coop, college is looming for others, and the parents want to assemble the whole brood.

Since their earlier summer at the ramshackle beach rental on Lake Winnetka, Dad Baker's high school rival, Jimmy Murtaugh (Eugene Levy), has erected his own gargantuan family home, the Boulders, directly across the waters. He's made a lot more money than Tom Baker, whose job as a college football coach evaporates in some vague dialogue. The two fathers resume their lifelong rivalry, and Murtaugh shows off at a fancy Fourth of July clambake at the lake club, where the fireworks go off prematurely and destroy everything in sight. It is a rule of the cinema that all fireworks always go off prematurely except those used in sex scenes, and sometimes then, too.

Countering these predictabilities is the wonderful little subplot. For Sarah Baker and Eliot Murtaugh (Taylor Lautner), it's first love at first sight. This leads Sarah to experiment with makeup, because like all girls her age she is convinced she is an ugly duckling. God, thirteen can be horrible. I remember as a high school freshman, standing around at the Tigers' Den teenage hangout in Urbana, Illinois, cupping my hand to my mouth and checking to see if I had bad breath. At any given moment there would be half a dozen other kids also sniffing in dread and suspicion, all of us chewing Doublemint like crazy. If some girl had told us she didn't dance with boys who chewed gum, we would have gone home and wept ourselves to sleep.

Anyway, *Dozen 2* remembers that kind of suffering, and the way kids are supersensitive. Any teasing, however slight, however kind, however well-meaning, comes as a crushing blow. Mom Baker (Hunt) sees what's happening, calls Sarah "sweetheart," and sympathizes, but what's especially touching is when Sarah's older sister Lorraine (Hilary Duff) takes her upstairs and expertly applies the right style of makeup for a girl that age—which means, in effect, that when Sarah tremulously exposes herself to the family view, she looks absolutely lovely and you really

can't notice much makeup at all. I personally couldn't see any, but then I hardly notice makeup unless we're talking Tommy Lee Jones as Two-Face in *Batman Forever*.

Speaking of makeup, Jimmy Murtaugh's new wife of six months' standing is Sarina, played by Carmen Electra, and the movie surprises us by making her nice. She's sexy, yes, but she really cares for her eight new stepkids, intervenes with her husband's monstrous ego, and passes the acid test, which is that Bonnie Hunt's character accepts her as (provisionally) human.

The movie is otherwise about what you'd expect. As family movies go, it skews younger than the better *Rumor Has It* and *The Family Stone*. It's a lot better than *Yours, Mine and Ours*, which has inexplicably grossed more than forty-five million dollars, all of which could have been more usefully dropped into Santa's little red bucket outside the theater.

Chicken Little ★ ★ ½
G, 82 m., 2005

With the voices of: Zach Braff (Chicken Little), Joan Cusack (Abby Mallard), Steve Zahn (Runt of the Litter), Amy Sedaris (Foxy Loxy), Mark Walton (Goosey Loosey), Garry Marshall (Buck Cluck), Don Knotts (Mayor Turkey Lurkey), Patrick Stewart (Mr. Woolensworth), Wallace Shawn (Principal Fetchit), Fred Willard (Melvin [Alien Dad]), Catherine O'Hara (Tina [Alien Mom]). Directed by Mark Dindal and produced by Randy Fullmer. Screenplay by Steve Bencich and Ron J. Friedman.

As the hero of a story, Chicken Little is the poultry equivalent of the Boy Who Cried Wolf. Once you understand their mistakes, their stories are over and attention passes to the results of their errors. In Chicken Little's case, the sky was not falling. In the case of the Boy Who Cried Wolf, I cannot remember if he was eaten by one, but he was asking for it.

There is one way for Chicken Little to redeem himself, and that would be for the sky to actually fall. *Chicken Little*, a new animated cartoon from Disney, wisely takes this approach and even provides an explanation: Earth is being attacked from outer space. When Chicken Little claims he was hit on the head by a chunk of blue sky and the townspeople think it was only an acorn, the chicken is telling the truth.

The movie takes place in an all-purpose small town named Oakey Oaks, where chameleons change color while functioning as traffic signals. In a salute to the original British children's story, the film has a Turkey Lurkey (he's the mayor) and a Foxy Loxy (she's foxy, all right, but not very nice) and even a Goosey Loosey (Mark Walton, who will be cautious in adding this credit to his résumé). Chicken Little is voiced by Zach Braff; his father, Buck Cluck (Garry Marshall), obviously moved here from Brooklyn.

The plot: Chicken Little thinks the sky is falling, and he seems to be mistaken. He is ambushed and hounded by the press. There are no skies of mass destruction. He is shamed and humiliated. His friends loyally stand by him; they would be the goths, nerds, geeks, and outsiders in a human town: Abby (the Ugly Duckling) Mallard, voiced by Joan Cusack; Fish Out of Water, who wears a diver's helmet filled not with air but water and is not voiced because he doesn't talk, and you couldn't hear him anyway; and Runt of the Litter (Steve Zahn), who is so fat he can hardly see his stomach, let alone his feet.

Will Chicken Little ever be able to hold his head up again? In an attempt to redeem himself, he joins the town baseball team, but even though he plays in the big game, this sequence feels, frankly, as if the plot is killing time. That's because it is.

Then the heavy-duty plotting arrives, as the town is attacked by animated versions of the alien creatures, who remind us of Spielberg's *War of the Worlds* crossed with other alien-invasion pictures. Does Chicken Little save the day? Let's put it this way: Here is a movie where you don't have to wonder what a bear does in the woods.

The problem, I think, lies with the story. As a general rule, if a movie is not about baseball or aliens from outer space and you have to use them anyway, you should have started with a better premise. The best animated films are based on sturdy fables that deserve retelling (*Beauty and the Beast*), new stories involving archetypal emotions (*Finding Nemo*) or satire (*The Incredibles*). *Chicken Little* seems uncomfortably close to the Three Little Pigs and other not-ready-for-prime-time players. Yes, it's funny

how they involve animal traits in the daily affairs of the town, and yes, the voice talent (especially Marshall and such verbal originals as Wallace Shawn, Fred Willard, and Don Knotts) is sometimes funny just because of the performers.

The movie did make me smile. It didn't make me laugh, and it didn't involve my emotions, or the higher regions of my intellect, for that matter. It's a perfectly acceptable feature cartoon for kids up to a certain age, but it doesn't have the universal appeal of some of the best recent animation.   ☞

The Chorus ★ ★ ½
PG-13, 95 m., 2005

Gerard Jugnot (Clement Mathieu), Jean-Baptiste Maunier (Pierre Morhange [young]), Jacques Perrin (Pierre Morhange [adult]), Francois Berleand (Rachin), Kad Merad (Chabert), Marie Bunel (Violette Morhange). Directed by Christophe Barratier and produced by Arthur Cohn, Nicolas Mauvernay, and Jacques Perrin. Screenplay by Barratier and Philippe Lopes-Curval.

This time the teacher is named Clement Mathieu. In earlier films it was Mr. Chips, Miss Jean Brodie, Mr. Holland, Mr. Crocker-Harris (in *The Browning Version*), John Keating (in *Dead Poets Society*), Joe Clark (in *Lean on Me*), Katherine Ann Watson (in *Mona Lisa Smile*), Jaime A. Escalante (in *Stand and Deliver*), and Roberta Guaspari (in *Music of the Heart*). In theaters right now, his name is Coach Carter. The actors have included Morgan Freeman, Meryl Streep, Edward James Olmos, Albert Finney, Robin Williams, Samuel L. Jackson, Julia Roberts, Maggie Smith, Richard Dreyfuss, and even, in one version of *Chips*, Peter O'Toole. They all have two things in common: Their influence will forever change the lives of their students, and we can see that coming from the opening frame.

I have nothing against the formula. Done well, it can be moving, as it was in *Mr. Holland's Opus*. But *The Chorus*, the film France selected as its Oscar candidate this year, does it by the numbers, so efficiently this feels more like a Hollywood wannabe than a French film. Where's the quirkiness, the nuance, the deeper levels?

The movie begins with a middle-aged man named Pierre (Jacques Perrin) being awakened from his slumber by the news of a death. That night he conducts an orchestra, and we learn that he is the world's greatest conductor. I would have been better pleased if he had merely been a really good conductor. Then Pierre makes a journey to the country to attend the funeral of the teacher who found him as a juvenile delinquent and instilled a love of music and learning in him.

All of this is quickly known, and more details are easy to come by because in the town, he meets his old classmate Pepinot, who produces the diary kept fifty years ago by Mr. Mathieu. It is the kind of helpful journal that seems to have been written as the treatment for a film.

But perhaps I am too cynical about a perfectly sincere sentimental exercise. We flash back to 1949 and the Fond de d'Etang boarding school; the name means (not its official title, I believe) something like the bottom of the pond. Here the students are considered pond scum, too impossible to reach in ordinary schools, and the headmaster maintains an iron discipline. Young Pierre (now played by young Jean-Baptiste Maunier) is a handful, sent to the school by a single mom who despairs for him.

Also new to the school this term is Clement Mathieu (Gerard Jugnot), a pudgy and somewhat unfocused middle-aged man who is hired as a teacher's assistant. He loves music, and one day when he hears the boys singing, a light glows in his eye and he decides to begin a boys' choir in the school. This, of course, is frowned upon by the headmaster, who disapproves of anything even remotely educational, as such headmasters always do, and hates even more the idea of students having fun. But Mr. Mathieu holds rehearsals anyway, secretly, in sort of a boarding school parallel of the Resistance.

We know without having to see the movie that there will be vignettes establishing how troubled the kids are, and scenes in which Mr. Mathieu loses all hope, and a scene where the kids surprise him, and a scene of triumph, and a glorious performance at the end. All done competently. What is disconcerting, however, is how well these boys sing. After a few months of secret lessons, they sing as well as—well, as well as Les Petits Chanteurs de Saint-Marc Choir, the professional boys' choir that does the actual singing. Every time those little rascals open their mouths, somebody seems to have slipped a CD into the stereo.

Wouldn't it work better for the movie if they were simply a really good choir? The choice of a real choir makes for a better sound track album, no doubt, but causes a disconnect in the film's reality. I guess we have to accept this, along with the cruel fate that inevitably awaits any teacher who dares to break the mold, defy the establishment, and challenge his students with the wonders of the world.

The Great Teacher Who Forever Changes Lives is not as rare as these movies would suggest.

As it happens, I have had several such teachers, none more lovably eccentric than Mrs. Seward of Urbana High School, who taught senior rhetoric by gazing out the window and rhapsodizing about the worms on her farm, who came up after heavy rains and glistened in their wormy perfection. She also taught us to write. I had been working for two years as a sportswriter on the local daily, but she disabused me of the notion that a sentence equaled a paragraph, and gently suggested that the day would come when I would no longer find Thomas Wolfe readable.

The Chorus is only a fair example of its genre. I would rank it below Mr. Holland's Opus and Music of the Heart. Am I wearied because I have seen too many movies telling similar stories? No, it is just that since I know the story and so does everybody else in the theater, it should have added something new and unexpected, and by that I do not mean hiring Les Petits Chanteurs de Saint-Marc.

Christmas in the Clouds ★ ★ ★
PG, 97 m., 2005

Tim Vahle (Ray Clouds on Fire), MariAna Tosca (Tina Pisati Little Hawk), Sam Vlahos (Joe Clouds on Fire), M. Emmet Walsh (Stu O'Malley), Graham Greene (Earl), Sheila Tousey (Mary), Rosalind Ayres (Mabel Winright), Jonathan Joss (Phil). Directed by Kate Montgomery and produced by Montgomery and Sarah Wasserman. Screenplay by Montgomery.

Christmas in the Clouds is part romantic comedy, part screwball comedy, and part historic breakthrough. The history is made because the movie is about affluent Native American yuppies. So many movies about American Indians deal in negative stereotypes that it's nice to find one that takes place at an upscale Indian-owned ski resort. The only alcoholic in the cast is a white undercover investigator for a guidebook. The romance begins through a misunderstanding. Through an online dating service, Joe Clouds on Fire (Sam Vlahos) is paired off with Tina Pisati (MariAna Tosca). She's a chic New York professional woman whose name sounds Italian but whose family name is Little Hawk. He's a likable codger whose son, Ray Clouds on Fire (Tim Vahle), manages the resort. Joe has not been entirely honest about his age and is about thirty years older than Tina. Meanwhile, the resort is expecting a surprise visit from the critic of luxury hotels, and Mary the reservations manager (Sheila Tousey) keeps an eagle eye for anyone checking in who looks like he can spell Zagat.

This is the setup for an Idiot Plot, in which all misunderstandings could be cleared up with one or two lines of dialogue. Yes, but some Idiot Plots are charming, while most are merely dumb. This one I enjoyed, mostly because the actors have so much quiet fun with it. Of course Mary the manager thinks Tina Pisati is the critic. Of course Tina thinks that handsome young Ray is her pen pal, not crusty old Joe. And of course when Stu O'Malley checks in, no one fingers him as the critic, because he is grumpy, unkempt, and half loaded; it's M. Emmet Walsh, playing his usual role.

Tina is upgraded to a luxury corner suite. O'Malley gets shunted to a budget room, where he suffers from what passes for flu and may involve a large percentage of hangover. Tina has her eye on Ray. Ray thinks Tina is beautiful and sexy but refuses to cater to her because he is too ethical to kowtow to a critic. Old Joe knows the score but maintains a studious silence about his pen-pal correspondence, which no one at the resort knows about.

And then there is the matter of Earl (Graham Greene), the resort's chef, who has become a devout vegetarian and tries to discourage the customers from eating meat. He has a disconcerting way of referring to the animals on the menu by their first names and grows sorrowful when someone orders the turkey, which is a beloved pet.

Old Joe dreams of winning a Jeep Cherokee in an approaching bingo tournament. Grumpy old O'Malley hauls out of bed to play bingo. Eventually the two old-timers both end up in the Cherokee, stranded in a blizzard, while misunderstandings pile up back at the resort.

There is nothing here of earthshaking originality, but Kate Montgomery, the writer-director, has such affection for these characters that we can feel it through the screen. They're not simply pawns in the plot, we sense; they represent something she wants to say about the Native Americans she knows. And the actors, all with successful careers behind them, must be fed up with playing losers in social problem dramas; Greene, a natural comedian, expands magnificently as the vegetarian chef with an effortless line of patter about soy products, analog foods, and healthy nutrition. There may be a sitcom job for him lingering somewhere near this role.

As for Ray and Tina, well, in all versions of basic romantic comedy, we want them to kiss, they want to kiss, and the plot perversely frustrates all of us. But at the end of *Christmas in the Clouds,* after everything has worked out more or less as we hoped it would, I felt a surprising affection and warmth. There will be holiday pictures that are more high-tech than this one, more sensational, with bigger stars and higher budgets and indeed greater artistry. But there may not be many with such good cheer.

Christmas with the Kranks ★

PG, 98 m., 2004

Tim Allen (Luther Krank), Jamie Lee Curtis (Nora Krank), Dan Aykroyd (Vic Frohmeyer), Erik Per Sullivan (Spike Frohmeyer), Cheech Marin (Officer Salino), Jake Busey (Officer Treen), M. Emmet Walsh (Walt Scheel), Julie Gonzalo (Blair Krank). Directed by Joe Roth and produced by Michael Barnathan, Chris Columbus, and Mark Radcliffe. Screenplay by Columbus, based on a novel by John Grisham.

Christmas with the Kranks doesn't have anything wrong with it that couldn't be fixed by adding Ebenezer Scrooge and Bad Santa to the cast. It's a holiday movie of stunning awfulness that gets even worse when it turns gooey at the end. And what is it finally so happy about? Why, that the Kranks's neighbors succeed in enforcing their lockstep conformity upon them. They form a herd mentality, without the mentality.

The movie is not funny, ever, in any way, beginning to end. It's a colossal miscalculation. Tim Allen and Jamie Lee Curtis star, as Luther and Nora Krank, who live in a Chicago suburb with their daughter, Blair (Julie Gonzalo). Julie is going to Peru in the Peace Corps, so this will be their first Christmas without her, and Luther suggests that instead of spending $6,000 on Christmas, he and Nora spend $3,000 on a Caribbean cruise.

Sounds reasonable to me. But perhaps you're wondering how a couple with one child and no other apparent relatives on either side of the family spends $6,000 on Christmas. The answer is, they decorate. Their street coordinates a Christmas display every year in which neighbors compete to hang the most lights from their eaves and clutter the lawn with secular symbolism. Everyone has Frosty on their rooftop.

When the word gets around that the Kranks are taking a year off, the neighborhood posse gets alarmed. Their leader is Vic Frohmeyer (Dan Aykroyd), who leads a delegation to berate them. Before long, pickets are on the front lawn, chanting "Free Frosty!" and the local paper writes a story about "The only house on the block that's keeping Frosty in the basement."

As a satire against neighborhood conformity, *Christmas with the Kranks* might have found a way to be entertaining. But no. The reasonable Kranks are pounded down by the neighbors, and then their daughter decides, after having been away only about two weeks, to fly home for Christmas with her new Peruvian fiancé. So the Kranks of course must have their traditional Christmas Eve party after all, and the third act consists of all the neighbors pitching in to decorate the house, prepare the food and decorations, etc., in a display of self-righteous cooperation that is supposed to be merry but frankly is a little scary. Here's an idea: Why don't the Kranks meet Blair and her fiance in Miami and go on the cruise together?

The movie's complete lack of a sense of humor is proven by its inability to see that the Kranks are reasonable people and their neighbors are monstrous. What it affirms is not the Christmas spirit but the Kranks caving in. What is the movie really about? I think it may play as a veiled threat against non-conformists

who don't want to go along with the majority opinion in their community. What used to be known as American individualism is now interpreted as ominous. We're supposed to think there's something wrong with the Kranks. The buried message is: Go along, and follow the lead of the most obnoxious loudmouth on the block.

Christmas, some of my older readers may recall, was once a religious holiday. Not in this movie. Not a single crucifix, not a single creche, not a single mention of the J-name. It's not that I want *Christmas with the Kranks* to get all religious, but that I think it's secular as a cop-out, to avoid any implication of religious intolerance. No matter what your beliefs or lack of them, you can celebrate Christmas in this neighborhood, because it's not about beliefs; it's about a shopping season.

So distant are the spiritual origins of the holiday, indeed, that on Christmas Eve one of the guests at the Kranks's big party is the local priest (Tom Poston), who hangs around gratefully with a benevolent smile. You don't have to be raised Catholic to know that priests do not have time off on Christmas Eve. Why isn't he preparing for Midnight Mass? Apparently because no one in the Kranks's neighborhood is going to attend—they're too busy falling off ladders while stringing decorations on rooftops.

There is, however, one supernatural creature in the movie, and I hope I'm not giving away any secrets by revealing that it is Santa Claus. The beauty of this approach is that Santa is a nonsectarian saint, a supernatural being who exists free of theology. Frosty, on the other hand, is apparently only a snowman.

The Chronicles of Narnia: The Lion, the Witch and the Wardrobe ★ ★ ★
PG, 139 m., 2005

Tilda Swinton (White Witch), Georgie Henley (Lucy Pevensie), Skandar Keynes (Edmund Pevensie), William Moseley (Peter Pevensie), Anna Popplewell (Susan Pevensie), James McAvoy (Mr. Tumnus), Jim Broadbent (Professor Kirke); and the voices of: Liam Neeson (Aslan), Ray Winstone (Mr. Beaver), Dawn French (Mrs. Beaver), Rupert Everett (Fox). Directed by Andrew Adamson and produced by Mark Johnson and Philip Steuer.

Screenplay by Ann Peacock, Adamson, Christopher Markus, and Stephen McFeely, based on the novel by C. S. Lewis.

C. S. Lewis, who wrote the Narnia books, and J. R. R. Tolkien, who wrote the Ring trilogy, were friends who taught at Oxford at the same time, were pipe-smokers, drank in the same pub, and took Christianity seriously, but although Lewis loved Tolkien's universe, the affection was not returned. Well, no wonder. When you've created your own universe, how do you feel when, in the words of a poem by e. e. cummings: "Listen: there's a hell / of a good universe next door; let's go."

Tolkien's universe was in unspecified Middle Earth, but Lewis's really was next door. In the opening scenes of *The Chronicles of Narnia: The Lion, the Witch and the Wardrobe,* two brothers and two sisters from the Pevensie family are evacuated from London and sent to live in a vast country house where they will be safe from the nightly Nazi air raids. Playing hide-and-seek, Lucy, the youngest, ventures into a wardrobe that opens directly onto a snowy landscape where before long Mr. Tumnus is explaining to her that he is a faun.

Fauns, like leprechauns, are creatures in the public domain, unlike Hobbits, who are under copyright. There are mythological creatures in Narnia, but most of the speaking roles go to humans such as the White Witch (if indeed she is human) and animals who would be right at home in the zoo (if indeed they are animals). The kids are from a tradition that requires that British children be polite and well-spoken, no doubt because Lewis preferred them that way. What is remarkable is that this bookish bachelor who did not marry until he was nearly sixty would create four children so filled with life and pluck.

That's the charm of the Narnia stories: They contain magic and myth, but their mysteries are resolved not by the kinds of rabbits Tolkien pulls out of his hat but by the determination and resolve of the Pevensie kids— who have a good deal of help, to be sure, from Aslan the Lion. For those who read the Lewis books as a Christian parable, Aslan fills the role of Christ because he is resurrected from the dead. I don't know if that makes the White Witch into Satan, but Tilda Swinton plays the role as if she has not ruled out the possibility.

The adventures that Lucy has in Narnia, at first by herself, then with her brother Edmund, and finally with the older Peter and Susan, are the sorts of things that might happen in any British forest, always assuming fauns, lions, and witches can be found there, as I am sure they can. Only toward the end of this film do the special effects ramp up into spectacular extravaganzas that might have caused Lewis to snap his pipe stem.

It is the witch who has kept Narnia in frigid cold for a century, no doubt because she is descended from Aberdeen landladies. Under the rules, Tumnus (James McAvoy) is supposed to deliver Lucy (Georgie Henley) to the witch forthwith, but fauns are not heavy hitters, and he takes mercy. Lucy returns to the country house and pops out of the wardrobe, where no time at all has passed and no one will believe her story. It is only after Edmund (Skandar Keynes) follows her into the wardrobe that evening that her breathless reports are taken seriously.

Edmund is gob-smacked by the White Witch, who proposes to make him a prince. Peter (William Moseley) and Susan (Anna Popplewell) believe Lucy and Edmund, and soon all four children are back in Narnia. They meet the first of the movie's CGI characters, Mr. and Mrs. Beaver (voices by Ray Winstone and Dawn French), who invite them into their home, which is delightfully cozy for being made of largish sticks. The Beavers explain the Narnian situation to them, just before an attack by computerized wolves whose dripping fangs reach hungrily through the twigs.

Edmund by now has gone off on his own and gotten himself taken hostage, and the Beavers hold out hope that perhaps the legendary Aslan (voice by Liam Neeson) can save him. This involves Aslan dying for Edmund's sins, much as Christ died for ours. Aslan's eventual resurrection leads into an apocalyptic climax that may be inspired by Revelations. Since there are six more books in the Narnia chronicles, however, we reach the end of the movie while still far from the Last Days.

These events, fantastical as they sound, take place on a more human, or at least more earthly, scale than those in *The Lord of the Rings.* The personalities and character traits of the children have something to do with the outcome, which is not being decided by wizards on another level of reality but will be duked out right there in Narnia. That the battle owes something to Lewis's thoughts about the first two world wars is likely, although nothing in Narnia is as horrible as the trench warfare of the first or the Nazis of the second.

The film has been directed by Andrew Adamson, who directed both of the *Shrek* movies and supervised the special effects on both of Joel Schumacher's *Batman* movies. He knows his way around both comedy and action, and here combines them in a way that makes Narnia a charming place with fearsome interludes. We suspect that the Beavers are living on temporary reprieve and that wolves have dined on their relatives, but this is not the kind of movie where you bring up things like that.

Lewis famously said he never wanted the Narnia books to be filmed because he feared the animals would "turn into buffoonery or nightmare." But he said that in 1959, when he might have been thinking of a man wearing a lion suit, or puppets. The effects in this movie are so skillful that the animals look about as real as any of the other characters, and the critic Emanuel Levy explains the secret: "Aslan speaks in a natural, organic manner (which meant mapping the movement of his speech unto the whole musculature of the animal, not just his mouth)." Aslan is neither as frankly animated as the Lion King nor as real as the cheetah in *Duma*, but halfway in between, as if an animal were inhabited by an archbishop.

This is a film situated precisely on the dividing line between traditional family entertainment and the newer action-oriented family films. It is charming and scary in about equal measure, and confident for the first two acts that it can be wonderful without having to hammer us into enjoying it, or else. Then it starts hammering. Some of the scenes toward the end push the edge of the PG envelope, and like the Harry Potter series, the Narnia stories may eventually tilt over into R. But it's remarkable, isn't it, that the Brits have produced Narnia, the Ring, Hogwarts, Gormenghast, James Bond, Alice, and Pooh, and what have we produced for them in return? I was going to say the cuckoo clock, but for that you would require a three-way Google of Italy, Switzerland, and Harry Lime. ☞

The Chronicles of Riddick ★ ★
PG-13, 118 m., 2004

Vin Diesel (Richard B. Riddick), Colm Feore (Lord Marshal), Alexa Davalos (Kyra), Karl Urban (Vaako), Thandie Newton (Dame Vaako), Judi Dench (Aereon), Keith David (Abu "Imam" al-Walid), Alexis Llewellyn (Ziza). Directed by David Twohy and produced by Vin Diesel and Scott Kroopf. Screenplay by Twohy.

"In normal times, evil should be fought by good, but in times like this, well, it should be fought by another kind of evil."

So says a character named Aereon in the opening moments of *The Chronicles of Riddick,* a futuristic battle between a fascist misfit and a fascist master race. The opening shot shows a gargantuan steel face that looks like Mussolini after a face-lift, and when the evil Necromongers rally to hail their Lord Marshal, it looks like they've been studying *The Triumph of the Will.*

Against this intergalactic tribe stands a man, a man with the somewhat anticlimactic name of Richard B. Riddick. He is one of the few surviving Furions, fierce warriors who have, alas, mostly been captured and turned into Necromongers. Such is his prowess that with merely his flesh and blood he can defeat and capture a Necromonger fighter ship. What a guy. Riddick, played by Vin Diesel, is a character we first encountered in *Pitch Black,* the 2000 film by the same director, David Twohy. Although a few other characters repeat from that film, notably Abu "Imam" al-Walid (Keith David), there's no real connection between them, apart from Riddick's knack of finding himself on absurdly inhospitable planets. Here he fights for life on Crematoria, a planet whose blazing sun rockets over the horizon every fifteeen minutes or so and bakes everything beneath it. That you can shield yourself from it behind rocks is helpful, although it begs the question of why, since the atmosphere is breathable, the air is not superheated.

But never mind. The Necromongers want everybody to be a Necromonger, and they line up behind the Lord Marshal (Colm Feore), who alone among his race has visited the Underverse. Aereon tells us he returned "half alive and half . . . something else." This Aereon, she's awfully well informed, and has a way of materializing out of thin air. She's a member of the race of Elementals, a fact I share with you since I have no idea what an Elemental is, or was, or wants to be.

Her character is one of several who are introduced with great fanfare and then misplaced. There's also a big-eyed, beautiful little girl named Ziza (Alexis Llewellyn), who keeps asking Riddick if he will fight the monsters, and Riddick keeps looking like he may have a heart of stone but this little girl melts it, and we're all set up for a big scene of monster-bashing and little-girl-saving that somehow never comes. (In this movie, a setup is as good as a payoff, since the last shot clearly establishes that there will be a sequel, and we can find out about all the missing stuff then.)

The Chronicles of Riddick is above all an exercise in computer-generated effects, and indeed the project represents the direction action movies are taking, as its human actors (or their digital clones) are inserted into manifestly artificial scenes that look like frames from the darkest of superhero comic books. The jolly reds, yellows, and blues of the classic Superman and Spiderman have been replaced in these grim days with black and gunmetal gray. *Chronicles* doesn't pause for much character development, and is in such a hurry that even the fight scenes are abbreviated chop-chop sessions. There are a lot of violent fights (the movie is made of them, which explains the PG-13 rating), but never do we get a clear idea of the spatial locations of the characters or their complete physical movements. Twohy breaks the fights down into disconnected flashes of extreme action in close-up, just as a comic book would, and maybe this is a style. It's certainly no more boring than most conventional CGI fight scenes.

I think the Lord Marshal wants to conquer all planets colonized by humans and make them Necromongers, but I was never sure that Richard B. Riddick didn't approve of that. Riddick seems more angered that there is a bounty on his head, and when he wreaks vengeance against the Necromongers, it's personal. His travails are intercut with the story of Vaako and Dame Vaako (Karl Urban and Thandie Newton), who want to overthrow the Lord Marshal, although whether they constitute a movement or just a coterie, I cannot say.

Vin Diesel was born to play a character like Riddick, and he growls and scowls impressively. I like Diesel as an actor and trust he was born to play other, better characters, in movies that make sense. None of the other actors do anything we couldn't do if we looked like them. Films like *The Chronicles of Riddick* gather about them cadres of fans who obsess about every smallest detail, but somehow I don't think *Riddick* will make as many converts as *The Matrix*. In fact, I owe an apology to fans of *The Lord of the Rings* trilogy.

When Richard Roeper reviewed the current two-disc DVD of *The Lord of the Rings: The Return of the King* on TV, I noted that a four-disc set of the movie was coming out later. He observed that the complete trilogy will come out on "an accordion-size set that will take up the next six years of your life." I observed that *LOTR* fans should "get a life." I meant this as an affectionate, ironic throwaway, but have received dozens of wounded e-mails from *Ring* devotees who believe *LOTR* has, indeed, given them a life, and after seeing *The Chronicles of Riddick*, I agree. They have a life. The prospect of becoming an expert on *Riddick*, in contrast, is too depressing to contemplate.

Cinderella Man ★ ★ ★ ½
PG-13, 144 m., 2005

Russell Crowe (Jim Braddock), Renée Zellweger (Mae Braddock), Paul Giamatti (Joe Gould), Craig Bierko (Max Baer), Bruce McGill (Jimmy Johnston), Paddy Considine (Mike Wilson), Ron Canada (Joe Jeanette), Connor Price (Jay Braddock). Directed by Ron Howard and produced by Brian Grazer, Howard, and Penny Marshall. Screenplay by Cliff Hollingsworth and Akiva Goldsman.

There is a moment early in *Cinderella Man* when we see Russell Crowe in the boxing ring, filled with cocky self-confidence, and I thought I knew what direction the story would take. I could not have been more mistaken. I walked in knowing nothing about Jim Braddock, "The Bulldog of Bergen," whose riches-to-rags-to-riches career inspired the movie. My friend Bill Nack of *Sports Illustrated*, who just won the A.J. Liebling Award, the highest honor a boxing writer can attain, could have told me all about Braddock, but I am just as happy to have gone in cold, so that I could be astonished by Crowe's performance.

I think of Crowe as a tough customer, known to get in the occasional brawl. Yes, he plays men who are inward and complex, as in *The Insider* and *A Beautiful Mind*, or men who are tempered and wise, as in *Master and Commander*. But neither he nor anyone else in a long time has played such a *nice* man as the boxer Jim Braddock. You'd have to go back to actors like James Stewart and Spencer Tracy to find such goodness and gentleness. Tom Hanks could handle the assignment, but do you see any one of them as a prize-fighter? Tracy, maybe.

As the film opens, Braddock is riding high with a series of victories that buy a comfortable, but not opulent, lifestyle for his wife, Mae (Renée Zellweger), and their children, Jay, Rosemarie, and Howard. Also doing okay is Braddock's loyal manager, Joe Gould (Paul Giamatti, in a third home run after *American Splendor* and *Sideways*). Then Braddock breaks his right hand, loses some matches so badly his license is taken away, and descends with his family to grim poverty in the early days of the Great Depression.

What is remarkable during both the highs and the lows is that Jim Braddock, as Crowe plays him, remains level-headed, sweet-tempered, and concerned about his family above all. Perhaps it takes a tough guy like Crowe to make Braddock's goodness believable. Mae is just the wife he deserves, filled with love and loyalty, and so terrified he will be hurt that she refuses to attend his fights and won't even listen on the radio.

Their poverty takes them from a nice family house to a cramped little apartment where there is no heat and hardly anything to eat. Braddock gets a job on the docks in Hoboken, slinging sacks of grain and coal, using his left arm because of his injured right hand, and although that job is a low point, it is also the secret to the left hook that will eventually get him named "Cinderella Man" by Damon Runyon.

The movie teams Crowe once again with director Ron Howard; they made *A Beautiful Mind* together, and the screenwriter of that film, Akiva Goldsman, cowrote this one with Cliff Hollingsworth. They find human ways to mirror the descent into despair; the Braddock family's poverty, for example, seems to weigh most heavily on the oldest son, Jay (Connor Price), who fears above all being sent away to live with "rich" relatives—rich here meaning those with something to eat. He steals a sausage from a butcher shop, is caught, and then, in a scene typical of Braddock's gentle wisdom, is not punished by his father, but talked to, softly and earnestly, because his father instinctively knows why his son stole the sausage, and that the kid's daring was almost noble.

Up to this point, there would not be a comeback, and no occasion for Damon Runyon nicknames. Jim Braddock gets one more chance at a fight, as Gould edges him past the doubts of promoter Jimmy Johnston (Bruce McGill). Without much time to train, he takes on a leading contender and to everyone's amazement wins the fight. One victory leads to another, and finally Gould is able to broker a title fight with the heavyweight champion Max Baer (Craig Bierko), who has killed two of his opponents and seems likely to kill the outweighed and outclassed Braddock.

What happens in the fight you will see. Ron Howard, Russell Crowe, Craig Bierko, the cinematographer Salvatore Totino, and the editors Daniel P. Hanley and Mike Hill step into a ring already populated by the ghosts of countless movie fights, most memorably those in *Raging Bull*, *Million Dollar Baby*, and the *Rocky* movies. They don't try to outfight those movies, but to outmaneuver them emotionally. The closest connection is with *Million Dollar Baby*, also a film about a fighter whose deepest motivation is the fear of poverty (at a press conference, Braddock says he fights in order to be able to buy milk for his family). The visual strategy of the big fight is direct and brutal, but depends not so much on the technical depiction of boxing as on the development of the emotional duel going on in the ring. When an underdog fights from "heart" after his strength and skill are not enough, the result is almost always unconvincing—but not always.

Cinderella Man is a terrific boxing picture, but there's no great need for another one. The need it fills is for a full-length portrait of a good man. Most serious movies live in a world of cynicism and irony, and most good-hearted movie characters live in bad movies. Here is a movie where a good man prevails in a world where every day is an invitation to despair, where resentment would seem fully justified, where doing the right thing seems almost gratuitous, because nobody is looking and nobody cares. Jim Braddock is almost transparent in the simple goodness of his character; that must have made him almost impossible to play. Russell Crowe makes him fascinating, and it takes a moment or two of thought to appreciate how difficult that must have been.   ☞

A Cinderella Story ★
PG, 96 m., 2004

Hilary Duff (Sam), Jennifer Coolidge (Fiona), Chad Michael Murray (Austin), Dan Byrd (Carter), Regina King (Rhonda), Julie Gonzalo (Shelby), Lin Shaye (Mrs. Wells), Madeline Zima (Brianna), Andrea Avery (Gabriella). Directed by Mark Rosman and produced by Ilyssa Goodman, Casey La Scala, Hunt Lowry, Dylan Sellers, and Clifford Werber. Screenplay by Leigh Dunlap.

Ernest Madison says he swore off movie critics when they panned Dragonslayer, *one of the favorites of his childhood. "I stopped paying attention to critics because they kept giving bad reviews to good movies," says Madison, now thirty-five.*

Fourteen-year-old Byron Turner feels the same way. He turns to the Web for movie information and trailers, then shares what he's discovered with his friends, his sister, Jasmine, even his mother, Toni.

"I used to watch Roger Ebert, but now I get most of my information from Byron," Toni Turner says. "I don't really pay attention to critics anymore."

—story by Bob Curtright
in the *Wichita Eagle*

Dear Byron,

I know what your mother means because when I was fourteen I was also pummeling my parents with information about new movies and singing stars. I didn't have the Internet, but I grabbed information anywhere I could—mostly from other kids, Hollywood newspaper columnists, and what disk jockeys said. Of course, that was a more innocent time, when movies slowly crept around the

country and there was time to get advance warning of a turkey.

Your task is harder than mine was because the typical multiplex movie is heralded by an ad campaign costing anywhere from $20 million to $50 million. Fast-food restaurants now have tie-ins with everyone from Shrek to Spider-Man; when I was a kid we were lucky to get ketchup with the fries. Enormous pressure is put on the target audience to turn out on opening weekends. And Hollywood's most valued target audience, Byron, is teenage males. In other words, you.

So I am writing you in the hope of saving your friends, your sister, Jasmine, and your mother, Toni, from going to see a truly dismal new movie. It is called *A Cinderella Story*, and they may think they'll like it because it stars Hilary Duff. I liked her in *Cheaper by the Dozen*, and said she was "beautiful and skilled" in *The Lizzie McGuire Movie*, but wrote:

"As a role model, Lizzie functions essentially as a spokeswoman for the teen retail fashion industry, and the most-quoted line in the movie is likely to be when the catty Kate accuses her of being an 'outfit repeater.' Since many of the kids in the audience will not be millionaires and do indeed wear the same outfit more than once, this is a little cruel, but there you go." That's probably something your mother might agree with.

In *A Cinderella Story*, Hilary plays Sam, a Valley Girl whose happy adolescence ends when her dad is killed in an earthquake. That puts her in the clutches of an evil stepmother (Jennifer Coolidge, whom you may remember fondly as Stifler's mom in the *American Pie* movies, although since they were rated R, of course you haven't seen them). Sam also naturally has two evil stepsisters. Half the girls in school have a crush on Austin (Chad Michael Murray), a handsome football star, but Sam never guesses that Austin is secretly kind of poetic—and is, in fact, her best chat-room buddy. She agrees to meet him at the big Halloween dance, wearing a mask to preserve her anonymity; as a disguise, the mask makes her look uncannily like Hilary Duff wearing a mask.

Anyway, this is a lame, stupid movie, but Warner Bros. is spending a fortune, Byron, to convince you to see it and recommend it to your mom and Jasmine. So you must be strong and wise, and do your research. Even though your mother no longer watches my TV show, you use the Internet as a resource and no doubt know about movie review sources like rottentomatoes.com, metacritic.com, and even (pardon me while I wipe away a tear) rogerebert.com. Even when a critic dislikes a movie, if it's a good review, it has enough information so you can figure out whether you'd like it anyway.

For example, this review is a splendid review because it lets you know you'd hate *A Cinderella Story*, and I am pretty much 100 percent sure that you would. So I offer the following advice. Urgently counsel your mom and sister to forget about going out to the movies this week, and instead rent *Ella Enchanted*. This is a movie that sank without a trace, despite the fact that it was magical, funny, intelligent, romantic, and charming. It stars the beautiful Anne Hathaway (from *The Princess Diaries*) as a young girl whose fairy godmother (Vivica A. Fox) puts a spell on her that makes her life extremely complicated. She has the usual evil stepmother and two jealous stepsisters. Will she win the love of Prince Charmont (Hugh Dancy)? *A Cinderella Story* is a terrible movie, sappy and dead in the water, but *Ella Enchanted* is a wonderful movie, and if Jasmine and your mom insist on *Cinderella* you can casually point out what "Ella" is short for.

As for that guy Ernest Madison, he was about eleven when *Dragonslayer* came out. He must have been a child prodigy, to swear off movie critics at an age when most kids don't even know they exist. If he still feels the same way, I hope he goes to see *A Cinderella Story*. That'll teach him.

Your fellow critic,
Roger

Classe Tous Risques ★ ★ ★

NO MPAA RATING, 110 m., 1960 (rereleased 2006)

Lino Ventura (Abel Davos), Jean-Paul Belmondo (Eric Stark), Sandra Milo (Liliane), Marcel Dalio (Arthur Gibelin), Michel Ardan (Riton Vintran), Stan Krol (Raymond Naldi), Claude Cerval (Raoul Fargier), Simone France (Therese Davos), Michele Meritz (Sophie Fargier). Directed by Claude Sautet and produced by Jean Darvey. Screenplay by Sautet, Jose Giovanni, and Pascal Jardin, based on the novel by Jose Giovanni.

Abel is a convicted killer on the lam from the French who has lived in Italy long enough to acquire a wife and two sons. He loves his family more than crime. He thinks it is time to return to France. One last job should do it. If he went to more movies, he'd know that calling it your "last job" seems to put the jinx in.

Abel is played by Lino Ventura, with a sad, lived-in face. At the train station in Milan, he meets his wife, Therese (Simone France), their sons, and his partner, Raymond (Stan Krol). The details of the plan have been carefully prepared: They'll put the wife and kids on the train to a town just the other side of the French border, then stick up a bank messenger, make a getaway, switch cars, meet up again, and cross into France. Abel has pals in Paris he's sure will be happy to see him again. He did them a lot of favors.

The snatch-and-grab on a Milan street takes place, but the getaway is not as planned, and Abel and Raymond end up hiring a boat to get them to Nice. Here I will cloud certain details, moving ahead to a call Abel makes to Paris. He needs his old pals to drive down to Nice and meet him. This they are not eager to do. We see them hemming and hawing and explaining to each other how one needs to check in with his probation officer and another—anyway, what happens is, they recruit a kid none of them knows very well and hire him to drive down and look for the old man.

This kid is Eric Stark, played by Jean-Paul Belmondo at the dawn of his stardom. He makes the kind of entrance you notice, wearing a loud tweed overcoat that would be perfect for a stickup because witnesses would remember the coat instead of the guy inside. His entrance is an important moment in movie history. The French New Wave descended more or less directly from mainstream French crime films made in the 1950s, and if there is a missing link in that evolution, it might be this one. Claude Sautet's *Classe Tous Risques* was made in 1960, the same year Jean-Luc Godard's *Breathless* came out, and both starred Belmondo, who was the flavor of the year; he had appeared in ten other recent films and would have six more starring roles in 1960, usually playing a plug-ugly who was after the girl.

Breathless got all the publicity, and *Classe Tous Risques* hardly opened in America, although Sautet later would make many international successes *(Un Coeur en Hiver, Vincent, Francois, Paul . . . and the Others)*. It arrives now in a restored print with rewritten subtitles, a crisp, smart, cynical film about dishonor among thieves.

Sautet's film grows out of work like Jacques Becker's *Touchez Pas au Grisbi* (1954) and Jean-Pierre Melville's *Bob le Flambeur* (1955) and shares their affection for a middle-aged thief who would like to retire but finds that his old life reaches out and nails him. Jean Gabin gave one of his best performances in the Becker, and Melville's star, Roger Duchesne, made Bob the High Roller so likable that the movie inspired three *Ocean's Eleven* remakes. Ventura lacks Gabin's star power and Duchesne's silky, regretful heroism, but he has an implacable, lived-in face, and like them he embodies a code his world has abandoned.

By sending a kid for him, Abel's pals in Paris have insulted his ideas of loyalty and friendship. And who is this kid, anyway? Why did he take the job? Can he be trusted? Why is he fooling around with an actress (Sandra Milo) he just met, who is down on her luck when there isn't enough luck to go around? After the quick-moving opening episodes, the movie comes down to the relationship between the old guy and the kid—who has no reason at all to risk his life for Abel, except that he knows class when he sees it, understands the code the Parisians have forgotten, and wants to live by it.

The film doesn't make it a big point, but consider the meetings in Paris where Abel's pals recruit and hire Eric Stark. As moviegoers we are focusing on a) Belmondo, so young, his career ahead of him, and b) the evasions by which the pals hire a kid to do the job they are morally bound to do themselves. But in Sautet's mind, the scenes might equally have been c) about the kid listening to them betraying a man who is counting on them. It's possible that before Eric ever sees Abel, he has already decided that Abel is the real thing, the kind of guy Eric could respect and trust.

Abel asks Eric more than once why he took the job. He doesn't get much of an answer, but then, men in such trades aren't big on discussing their philosophies. There is also the way Milo plays Liliane, the new girlfriend. She's in the tradition of women in gangster movies who sign on with a guy they like because he treats them right and isn't a rat. They're usually running away from a guy who treated them wrong and was a rat. Hard to believe this is the same actress who played Mastroianni's pouty, flamboyant mistress in Federico Fellini's *8½* (1963). Here she seems dialed down, wearier, just as she should.

Classe Tous Risques isn't a film in the same league with the titles by Becker, Melville, and Godard, but how many films are? It's more like one of those Humphrey Bogart films that isn't *The Big Sleep*, but you're glad you saw it anyway. Studying the Hollywood crime films of the 1930s and 1940s, the French gave them their name, "film noir," and embraced them with a particular Gallic offhandedness. Their French gangsters crossed hardness with cool and style. In *Touchez Pas au Grisbi, Bob le Flambeur*, and *Classe Tous Risques*, the heroes have not only loyalty but also a certain tenderness, a friendship that survives even when their friends act stupidly and get them all in trouble. In *Breathless*, the Belmondo hero acts stupidly himself and gets himself in trouble, and the modern age of crime films begins.

Ebert's essays on Breathless, Touchez Pas au Grisbi, *and* Bob le Flambeur *are in the Great Movies series at www.rogerebert.com.*

Clean ★ ★ ★ ½
R, 110 m., 2006

Maggie Cheung (Emily Wang), Nick Nolte (Albrecht Hauser), James Dennis (Jay), Beatrice Dalle (Elena), Jeanne Balibar (Irene Paolini), Don McKellar (Vernon), Martha Henry (Rosemary Hauser), James Johnston (Lee Hauser). Directed by Olivier Assayas and produced by Niv Fichman, Xavier Giannoli, Xavier Marchand, and Edouard Weil. Screenplay by Assayas.

Emily is always in motion, driven by disquiet, unhappy with herself and the decisions that got her here. Her mind seems elsewhere, focusing on what would bring her peace: heroin. She and her partner, Lee, are rock stars whose moment of fame has passed and stranded

125

them in a Canadian motel. They fight, she drives off into the night, scores drugs, shoots up, and sleeps in the car. When she returns to the motel, Lee is dead of an overdose. She should quietly back away and leave town. Instead, she gets herself arrested and sentenced to six months for possession.

Maggie Cheung plays Emily with such intense desperation that she won the best actress award at Cannes 2004. Only a few actresses in the world could have handled this role from a technical point of view: Born in Hong Kong, a citizen of the movie world, she acts here mostly in English, with some French and Cantonese, and moves confidently through Vancouver, Paris, and London. She always looks as if she knows the rules, even when she has broken them; despite being broke and strung out, she retains enough personal authority to call in favors and ask old friends for jobs.

She and Lee (James Johnston) had a child named Jay (James Dennis), who is about six. She loves him, and maybe she tells herself she isn't raising him because it's better that way for Jay. The boy is living with Lee's parents, Albrecht and Rosemary Hauser (Nick Nolte and Martha Henry). When Emily goes to jail, of course she loses custody. She loses more than that, and observe how low her voice is, and how downcast her eyes, as she answers questions at an interrogation. She is defeated; she knows precisely how she destroyed her life and lost her boy.

Clean, written and directed by Cheung's former husband, Olivier Assayas, does a brisk, understated job of implying Emily's past by observing her present. In the eyes of her old friends, we understand what she used to be, and what they see now. She lives in the moment. Consider the steps in Paris by which she begins by asking for a job and ends up with a free room.

Cheung is on screen for most of *Clean,* but Nolte's smaller role is equally important. His wife is dying of cancer. They were in London when she fell ill, and now he and the boy live in a hotel and visit her in the hospital. His wife is bitter about Emily, but Albrecht is realistic: "Someday we won't be here. And she is the boy's mother." He talks with her soberly and with searching eyes, and she responds to his seriousness. She is a damaged person but not a bad one, wants her boy back again, and

knows it will be some time before she can meet that responsibility.

Cheung is a considerable actress, famous in Asia for Hong Kong action pictures, respected in the West at film festivals. Incredibly, she has made about eighty movies; raised from the age of eight in England, she returned to Hong Kong as a model and got into movies at a time when the industry churned them out. I haven't seen most of her action films but have admired her in Wong Kar-Wai's *In the Mood for Love* (2000) and Wayne Wang's *Chinese Box* (1997), and was part of an audience at the Hawaii Film Festival that was fascinated by *The Soong Sisters* (1997), where she, Vivian Wu, and Michelle Yeoh played sisters who married three of the most powerful men of their time.

Those roles all, in one way or another, required her to be a great and grave beauty. It is astonishing how different the character in *Clean* is, with her restless style of smoking, walking, imploring, protesting. When her character grows anxious or angry, Cheung doesn't make the mistake of overacting; Emily is always closer to her bottoms than her tops. Watch her when her little boy tells her, "You killed my father." Her instincts as she handles that moment suggest she may make a good mother, after all.

I wonder what audiences will make of the last shot of the movie. Is it too inconclusive, or too upbeat? You can read it either way, but I believe it is appropriate because what it says is, tomorrow we start again. Every tomorrow.

The Clearing ★ ★ ★
R, 91 m., 2004

Robert Redford (Wayne Hayes), Helen Mirren (Eileen Hayes), Willem Dafoe (Arnold Mack), Alessandro Nivola (Tim Hayes), Matt Craven (Agent Ray Fuller), Melissa Sagemiller (Jill Hayes), Wendy Crewson (Louise Miller). Directed by Pieter Jan Brugge and produced by Brugge, Jonah Smith, and Palmer West. Screenplay by Justin Haythe and Brugge.

A movie that begins with a pleasant morning in an ordinary marriage is never about mornings or marriages. As *The Clearing* opens, we meet Wayne and Eileen Hayes, long and apparently happily married, in their elegant stone-walled mansion in a woodsy suburb. Wayne (Robert

Redford) gets in his car, at the end of his driveway stops for a man who seems to know him, and finds himself kidnapped at gunpoint. Eileen (Helen Mirren) has a cup of coffee at the side of their pool.

We've already met the kidnapper, a man named Arnold Mack (Willem Dafoe). He lives with his perpetually disappointed wife and her father in a row house in a nearby city. We see him paste on a mustache in the mirror, which seems odd, and we follow him as he travels to his work (kidnapping) on a commuter train. Arnold approaches Wayne with such easy familiarity, waving a manila envelope as if it contained important papers, that Wayne automatically stops and puts down the car window for him. Perhaps he even sort of remembers him, or feels that good manners require him to say that he does.

The movie intercuts between two story lines: Wayne, his hands tied, led by Arnold on a long trek at gunpoint through a wooded area; and Eileen, concerned when he doesn't return home and eventually calling in the FBI. These time lines are not parallel, a fact that eventually occurs to us, along with its implications.

We learn a lot about Wayne as he and Arnold talk. Arnold has studied up on him, knows he's a self-made millionaire who bought and sold a car rental company at the right time. Wayne is rich, lives surrounded by luxury, and is expensively dressed, but he has the tough instincts of a negotiator, and tries to talk Arnold out of the kidnapping. Arnold says the men who hired him are waiting in a cottage at the end of their walk, and Wayne asks him why those men should honor their deal with him. Arnold, who is not a professional criminal, listens politely and perhaps agrees with some of what Wayne says.

In the mansion, Eileen deals with an FBI agent (Matt Craven) who is all business, too much business. Her children, Tim and Jill (Alessandro Nivola and Melissa Sagemiller), join the vigil with their mother, and privately share an interesting insight: At first, their mother was afraid Wayne might simply have run away from the marriage. The FBI man finds out about an affair Wayne had, and discusses it in front of the children. That angers Eileen, who knew about it but didn't want them to know. And it sets up one of the most extraordinary scenes in the movie, a meeting between

Eileen and Louise Miller (Wendy Crewson), who was her husband's mistress. This scene is written so precisely and acted so well that it sidesteps all the hazards of jealousy and sensation, and becomes simply a discussion of emotional realities.

What happens, of course, I cannot reveal, nor will it be what you expect. Indeed, the events in a late scene are so unexpected and yet so logical that we are nodding with agreement as we react with surprise. And there is another scene, after that, indirectly dealing with psychological truth, with why people do the things they do, although I must say no more.

The Clearing is the first film directed by the successful producer Pieter Jan Brugge *(The Insider, The Pelican Brief, Heat)*. The screenplay is by Brugge and Justin Haythe, a British novelist. They know how to make a conventional thriller, but are not interested in making one. Instead, they use the crime here as the engine to drive their parallel psychological portraits. While Eileen has the reality of her marriage made uncomfortably clear, Wayne and Arnold engage in a little subtle class warfare. Wayne acts as if he was born to lead, and Arnold thinks of himself as a born loser with one last chance to hit a jackpot. Certainly, kidnapping offers enormous penalties and uncertain rewards, and Wayne thinks maybe Arnold doesn't really have the stomach for it.

What finally happens, and how, has a certain inevitable rightness to it, but you can't say you see it coming, especially since *The Clearing* doesn't feel bound by the usual formulas of crime movies. What eventually happens will emerge from the personalities of the characters, not from the requirements of Hollywood endings. Sensing that, we grow absorbed in the story, knowing that what happens along the way will decide what happens at the end.

Click ★ ★
PG-13, 98 m., 2006

Adam Sandler (Michael Newman), Kate Beckinsale (Donna Newman), Christopher Walken (Morty), Henry Winkler (Ted Newman), David Hasselhoff (Mr. Ammer), Julie Kavner (Trudy Newman), Sean Astin (Bill Rando). Directed by Frank Coraci and produced by Steve Koren, Mark O'Keefe, Adam Sandler,

Jack Giarraputo, and Neal H. Moritz. Screenplay by Koren and O'Keefe.

Scrooge was granted visions of Christmas Past and Christmas Future, and reformed his life. What happens to Adam Sandler in *Click* is like what happened to Scrooge, except with a lot more Christmases. He needs more than one lesson, and he gets more than one lesson. Way more.

In *Being There*, the hero, Chance, has spent all his life watching television. When he wanders out to freedom and is threatened on the street, he clicks a TV remote control to get another channel. In *Click*, Adam Sandler plays Michael, an architect who is given a universal remote that's truly universal. With it, he can take control of his life: freeze a scene, fast-forward, reverse, mute the sound, select the chapters of his choice, and even witness his parents at the moment of his conception (that's, of course, in the "Making of" documentary).

The movie is being sold as a comedy, but you know what? This isn't funny. Yes, there are some laughs, as when he finds he can turn the dog's barking up and down, or play around with the settings for hue and contrast, or when he discovers the picture-in-picture feature, which allows him to watch the ball game no matter what else is going on around him. But the movie essentially involves a workaholic who uses the universal remote to skip over all the bad stuff in his life and discovers in the process that he is missing life itself. Take away the gimmick of the universal remote and this is what a lot of us do, and it's sad.

It's not just sad, it's brutal. There's an undercurrent of cold, detached cruelty in the way Michael uses the magical device. He turns off the volume during an argument with his wife. He fast-forwards through a boring family dinner and, later, through foreplay. He skips ahead to avoid a bad cold. He jumps to the chapter where he gets a promotion. Eventually he realizes the family dog has died and been replaced by another, his kids have grown up, his wife is married to someone else, and he weighs four hundred pounds. It happened while he wasn't paying attention.

Like many another Sandler movie, this one lingers studiously over bodily functions. After losing enormous amounts of weight, for ex-

ample, Michael plays with a big flap of loose skin around his stomach, plopping it up and down long after any possible audience curiosity has been satisfied. During an argument with his boss (David Hasselhoff), he freeze-frames the boss, jumps on his desk, and farts. When he puts his boss back on "play," the boss inexplicably decides his secretary has put feces in his salad. Anyone who can't tell poop from lettuce doesn't deserve to be a senior partner. They teach you that in business school.

Michael is surrounded by patient and saintly people. His wife, Donna (Kate Beckinsale), loves him but despairs of reaching him. She has that standard wifely role of complaining when he has to work late and can't be at the swimming meet/Fourth of July party, etc. Michael's parents (Henry Winkler and Julie Kavner) are sweet and loving but kvetch too much and talk too slowly, so Michael zaps right through the time he has remaining with them.

I am not sure if this story device could possibly have been made funny. It could have been elevated into a metaphysical adventure, as in *Eternal Sunshine of the Spotless Mind*, or made to generate a series of paradoxes, as in *Being John Malkovich*, but *Click* stays resolutely at level one—the tiresome explication of the basic premise. Once we get the idea, there are no more surprises, only variations on the first one.

The movie does have some wit about its product placement. The plot is set in motion when Michael goes out late at night to buy a universal remote, and only one store is open: Bed, Bath & Beyond. As a retail store name, this has always reminded me of the final subtitle in Kubrick's *2001*, which was "Jupiter and Beyond the Infinite." *Beyond* the infinite. That's a fair piece. In the store Michael enters, Bed and Bath are easy to find, but Beyond is behind a mysterious door at the end of a very long corridor, where a man named Morty (Christopher Walken) makes him a gift of the universal remote. If they make *Click 2*, I want it to be about Morty.

Closer ★ ★ ★ ★
R, 101 m., 2004

Julia Roberts (Anna), Jude Law (Dan), Natalie Portman (Alice), Clive Owen (Larry). Directed by Mike Nichols and produced by Cary Brokaw,

John Calley, and Nichols. Screenplay by Patrick Marber, based on his play.

Mike Nichols's *Closer* is a movie about four people who richly deserve one another. Fascinated by the game of love, seduced by seduction itself, they play at sincere, truthful relationships that are lies in almost every respect except their desire to sleep with each other. All four are smart and ferociously articulate, adept at seeming forthright and sincere even in their most shameless deceptions.

"The truth," one says. "Without it, we're animals." Actually, truth causes them more trouble than it saves, because they seem compelled to be most truthful about the ways in which they have been untruthful. There is a difference between confessing you've cheated because you feel guilt and seek forgiveness, and confessing merely to cause pain.

The movie stars, in order of appearance, Jude Law, Natalie Portman, Julia Roberts, and Clive Owen. Law plays Dan, who writes obituaries for his London newspaper; Portman is Alice, an American who says she was a stripper and fled New York to end a relationship; Roberts is Anna, an American photographer; and Owen is Larry, a dermatologist. The characters connect in a series of Meet Cutes that are perhaps no more contrived than in real life.

In the opening sequence, the eyes of Alice and Dan (Portman and Law) meet as they approach each other on a London street. Eye contact leads to an amused flirtation, and then Alice, distracted, steps into the path of a taxicab. Knocked on her back, she opens her eyes, sees Dan, and says "Hello, stranger." Time passes. Dan writes a novel based on his relationship with Alice, and has his book jacket photo taken by Anna, whom he immediately desires. More time passes. Dan, who has been with Anna, impersonates a woman named "Anna" on a chat line, and sets up a date with Larry, a stranger. When Larry turns up as planned at the Aquarium, Anna is there, but when he describes "their" chat, she disillusions him: "I think you were talking with Daniel Wolf."

Eventually both men will have sex with both women, occasionally as a round trip back to the woman they started with. There is no constancy in this crowd: When they're not with the one they love, they love the one they're with. It is a good question, actually, whether any of them are ever in love at all, although they do a good job of saying they are.

They are all so very articulate, which is refreshing in a time when literate and evocative speech has been devalued in the movies. Their words are by Patrick Marber, based on his award-winning play. Consider Dan as he explains to Alice his job writing obituaries. There is a kind of shorthand, he tells her: "If you say someone was 'convivial,' that means he was an alcoholic. 'He was a private person' means he was gay. 'Enjoyed his privacy' means he was a raging queen."

Forced to rank the four characters in order of their nastiness, I would place Dr. Larry at the top of the list. He seems to derive genuine enjoyment from the verbal lacerations he administers, pointing out the hypocrisies and evasions of the others. Dan is an innocent by comparison; he wants to be bad, but isn't good at it. Anna, the photographer, is accurately sniffed out by Alice as a possible lover of Dan. "I'm not a thief, Alice," she says, but she is. Alice seems the most innocent and blameless of the four until the very end of the movie, when we are forced to ask if everything she did was a form of stripping, in which much is revealed, but little is surrendered. "Lying is the most fun a girl can have without taking her clothes off," she tells Dr. Larry, "but it's more fun if you do."

There's a creepy fascination in the way these four characters stage their affairs while occupying impeccable lifestyles. They dress and present themselves handsomely. They fit right in at the opening of Anna's photography exhibition. (One of the photos shows Alice with tears on her face as she discerns that Dan was unfaithful with Anna; that's the stuff that art is made of, isn't it?) They move in that London tourists never quite see, the London of trendy restaurants on dodgy streets, and flats that are a compromise between affluence and the exorbitant price of housing. There is the sense that their trusts and betrayals are not fundamentally important to them; "You've ruined my life," one says, and is told, "You'll get over it."

Yes, unless, fatally, true love does strike at just that point when all the lies have made it impossible. Is there anything more pathetic than a lover who realizes he (or she) really is in love, after all the trust has been lost, all the bridges burnt, and all the reconciliations used up?

Mike Nichols has been through the gender wars before, in films like *Carnal Knowledge* and *Who's Afraid of Virginia Woolf?* Those films, especially *Woolf,* were about people who knew and understood each other with a fearsome intimacy, and knew all the right buttons to push. What is unique about *Closer,* making it seem right for these insincere times, is that the characters do not understand each other, or themselves. They know how to go through the motions of pushing the right buttons, and how to pretend their buttons have been pushed, but do they truly experience anything at all except their own pleasure?

Coach Carter ★ ★ ★
PG-13, 140 m., 2005

Samuel L. Jackson (Coach Ken Carter), Robert Ri'chard (Damien Carter), Rob Brown (Kenyon Stone), Debbi Morgan (Tonya Carter), Ashanti (Kyra), Rick Gonzalez (Timo Cruz). Directed by Thomas Carter and produced by David Gale, Brian Robbins, and Michael Tollin. Screenplay by Mark Schwahn and John Gatins.

Samuel L. Jackson made news by refusing to costar with 50 Cent in a movie based on the rapper's life. He not only refused, but did it publicly, even though the film is to be directed by six-time Oscar nominee Jim Sheridan *(In America).* A clue to Jackson's thinking may be found in his film, *Coach Carter,* based on the true story of a California high school basketball coach who placed grades ahead of sports. Like Bill Cosby, Jackson is arguing against the antiintellectual message that success for young black males is better sought in the worlds of rap and sports than in the classroom.

There is, however, another aspect to Jackson's refusal: He said he thought Sheridan wanted him to "lend legitimacy" to 50 Cent's acting debut. He might have something there. Jackson has an authority on the screen; he occupies a character with compelling force, commanding attention, and can bring class to a movie. He might, he said, be interested in working with 50 Cent after the rapper makes another five movies or so, and earns his chops. This reasoning may not be fair. Consider the

work that Ice Cube did in *Boyz N the Hood* (1991), his first movie and the beginning of a successful acting career. Or look at the promise that Tupac Shakur showed, especially in his last feature, *Gridlock'd* (1997), holding his own with the veteran Tim Roth. Maybe 50 Cent has the stuff to be an actor. Maybe not. Jackson's decision may have more to do with the underlying values of the rapper's life; he may not consider 50 Cent's career, so often involving violent episodes, to be much of a role model.

Role models are what *Coach Carter,* Jackson's film, is all about. He plays Ken Carter, who began as a sports star at Richmond (California) High School, setting records that still stand, and then had success in the military and as a small businessman. He's asked to take over as basketball coach, an unpaid volunteer position; the former coach tells him, "I can't get them to show up for school." Ken Carter thinks he can fix that.

The movie was directed by Thomas Carter *(Save the Last Dance),* no relation to the coach. It follows long-established genre patterns; it's not only a sports movie with the usual big games and important shots, but also a coach movie, with inspiring locker-room speeches and difficult moral decisions. There are certain parallels with *Friday Night Lights,* although there it's the movie itself, and not the coach, that underlines the futility of high school stars planning on pro sports as a career.

Certainly both movies give full weight to public opinion in the communities where they're set—places where the public's interest in secondary education seems entirely focused on sports, where coaches are more important than teachers, where scores are more important than grades.

Coach Carter wants to change all that. He walks into a gymnasium ruled by loud, arrogant, disrespectful student jocks, and commands attention with the fierceness of his attitude. He makes rules. He requires the students to sign a contract, promising to maintain a decent grade-point average as the price of being on the team. He deals with the usual personnel problems; a star player named Kenyon Stone (Ron Brown) has a pregnant girlfriend named Kyra (Ashanti, in her, a-hem, first role), and she sees a threat to her future in Carter's determination to get his players into college.

Ken Carter's most dramatic decision, which got news coverage in 1999, was to lock the gymnasium, forfeit games, and endanger the team's title chances after some of his players refused to live up to the terms of the contract. The community, of course, is outraged that a coach would put grades above winning games; for them, the future for the student athletes lies in the NBA, not education. Given the odds against making it in the NBA (dramatically demonstrated in the great documentary *Hoop Dreams*), this reasoning is like considering the lottery a better bet than working for a living.

Jackson has the usual big speeches assigned to all coaches in all sports movies, and delivers on them, big time. His passion makes familiar scenes feel new. "I see a system that's designed for you to fail," he tells his players, pointing out that young black men are 80 percent more likely to go to prison than to go to college. The movie's closing credits indicate that six of the team members did go on to college, five with scholarships. Lives, not games, were won.

Code 46 ★ ★ ½
R, 92 m., 2004

Tim Robbins (William), Samantha Morton (Maria), Om Puri (Backland), Jeanne Balibar (Sylvie). Directed by Michael Winterbottom and produced by Andrew Eaton. Screenplay by Frank Cottrell Boyce.

Michael Winterbottom's *Code 46* reminds me of a William Gibson novel; the values and mood of *film noir* are linked with modern alienation and futuristic newspeak. The film takes place in cities named Seattle and Shanghai, although they may not be the cities of today, and the hero ventures from one to the other to track down traffickers in stolen or forged "papelles"—papers necessary to travel from one zone of this world to another.

The papelles function not like passports but like genetic ID codes. In this future, couples are forbidden to reproduce unless their DNA is a good match: no more first cousins or recessive negative traits in the bedroom. This positive breeding strategy is not racist but a form of quality control, and indeed, races and cultures seem mingled in Winterbottom's new world, and words from many languages are mixed into everyday speech. Samantha Morton, who plays the heroine, looks as British as the queen but is named Maria Gonzalez, perhaps suggesting ethnic distinctions have been lost in generations of government-supervised DNA matchups.

The hero, played by Tim Robbins, has a name well suited to this context: William Geld. He's on assignment to Shanghai to investigate Maria, a suspect in the papelle operation, but is thunderstruck by love the moment he sets eyes on her. This may be because romance in science fiction is more often a plot convenience than an emotional process. Or it may be because William has been injected with an "empathy virus" that allows him powerful intuitive powers. He investigates in the Dr. Phil style, by feeling your pain. He sees into souls. And in the case of Maria, to know, know, know her is to love, love, love her.

The viruses are an ingenious idea, one of many enriching the screenplay by Frank Cottrell Boyce, who undoubtedly contracted the empathy virus himself before writing *Hilary and Jackie*, and whose intelligence and imagination are well suited for collaboration with the restless, eclectic, never predictable Winterbottom. If you're familiar with the titles *Butterfly Kiss, Welcome to Sarajevo, The Claim*, and *24 Hour Party People*, ask yourself how these films and *Code 46* could possibly have been created by the same two people. Their luncheon conversations must resemble a season of Charlie Rose.

Viruses, of course, carry information. That's what they do, and zoologist Richard Dawkins points out that from their point of view, they are the life form and we are simply the carriers to get them from one generation to the next. Boyce indirectly but amusingly suggests how they work when Maria mentions she once tried a virus that allowed her to speak Mandarin: "Chinese people could understand what I was saying, but I couldn't." Why does that line make me think of Groucho Marx?

Maria and William engage in a daring, forbidden romance and exchange information that's subversive under the new laws. Her crime was to help a friend get papelles in order to travel to India to study a rare breed of bats. India, apparently, is not part of the DNA-protected zone, and indeed there are "freeports" throughout the world where the rules don't apply. That raises the question of why anybody would go to the trouble of living under these rules: It's like moving all the way to Singapore just in case you're ever seized with the need to chew gum or spit on the sidewalk. The love scenes between Maria and William are enlivened by his empathy virus, as you might imagine; I assume it makes him a rare male who knows *and* cares how his partner is feeling. Such science fiction aids to romance have been insufficiently explored. If Lois Lane gets Clark Kent into the sack, I hope she shares with us about the Man of Steel.

But I digress. The problem with *Code 46* is that the movie, filled with ideas and imagination, is murky in its rules and intentions. I cannot say I understand the hows and whys of this future world, nor do I much care, since it's mostly a clever backdrop to a love affair that would easily teleport to many other genres: Investigator falls in love with mystery woman, helps her commit crime, risks being left hanging out to dry. *Double Indemnity.*

William knows she's guilty, frames someone else, leaves after their affair to go home to his wife and family, then returns to Maria because his wife offers less to empathize with, or perhaps because neither one of them understands when he speaks Mandarin. But back in Shanghai, he finds that Maria's memory of him has been erased, indicating that the future didn't learn its lesson from *Eternal Sunshine of the Spotless Mind.* And then the freeport business at the end isn't so much like lovers leaving paradise to live in hell, as like suburbanites moving to San Francisco.

Code 46 is filled with ideas. Robbins and Morton in their scenes together suggest the same kind of lonely sharing of needs I responded to in *Lost in Translation* (a movie about people trying to catch the empathy virus but ending up with its antibody, jet lag). There's nice control of moods in the intimate dialogue scenes, but the movie is more successful at introducing the slang and science of the future than incorporating it into a story.

Coffee and Cigarettes ★ ★ ★
R, 96 m., 2004

With Roberto Benigni, Steven Wright, Joie Lee, Cinque Lee, Steve Buscemi, Iggy Pop, Tom Waits, Joe Rigano, Vinny Vella, Vinny Vella Jr., Renee French, E. J. Rodriguez, Alex Descas, Isaach De Bankole, Cate Blanchett, Meg White, Jack White, Alfred Molina, Steve Coogan, GZA, RZA, Bill Murray, Bill Rice, and Taylor Mead. Directed by Jim Jarmusch and produced by Joana Vicente and Jason Kliot. Screenplay by Jarmusch.

Jim Jarmusch has been working on *Coffee and Cigarettes* for so long that when he started the project, you could still smoke in a coffee shop. The idea was to gather unexpected combinations of actors and, well, let them talk over coffee and cigarettes. He began with the short film *Coffee and Cigarettes I,* filmed in 1986, before we knew who Roberto Benigni was (unless we'd seen Jarmusch's *Down by Law*). Benigni the verbal hurricane strikes the withdrawn Steven Wright, and is so eager to do him a favor that he eventually goes to the dentist for him.

There's no more to it than that, but how much more do you need? A few minutes, and the skit is over. None of these eleven vignettes overstays its welcome, although a few seem to lose their way. And although Jarmusch has the writing credit, we have the feeling at various moments (as when Bill Murray walks in on a conversation between RZA and GZA of Wu-Tang Clan and exchanges herbal remedies with them) that improvisation plays a part.

My favorite among the segments is one of the longest, starring the actors Alfred Molina and Steve Coogan. Molina has asked for the meeting. Coogan is not sure why, and grows more condescending as Molina, all politeness and charm, explains that his genealogical researchers have discovered that the two men are related through a common Italian ancestor centuries ago. Molina hopes perhaps this connection might lead to them becoming friends and "doing things together." Coogan is distinctly unenthusiastic, until Molina says something that impresses him, and then he becomes ingratiating. In its compact way, this segment contains a lot of human nature.

The structure—smoking and drinking—provides all the explanation we need for the meetings, although sometimes the actors seem to smoke a little too self-consciously, and Murray drinks his coffee straight from the pot. The prize for virtuosity goes to Cate Blanchett, who plays a dual role: herself and her cousin. As herself, she is the movie star Cate Blanchett. As her cousin, she is quietly jealous of Cate's success, and feels patronized when Cate gives her some perfume—a bottle, she correctly guesses, that the star just received as a freebie.

The third of the segments to be filmed, "Somewhere in California," won the award for best short at Cannes and is a little masterpiece of observation about two musicians acutely aware of who they are and who the other one is, while trying to appear unimpressed. Tom Waits and Iggy Pop star, in a subtle bout of one-upmanship. Agreeing that they have given up smoking, they smoke—which is okay, they agree, as long as they've given it up. They're sitting next to a jukebox, which leads to a little understated competition over who does, or doesn't, have songs on the machine.

Sometimes a segment depends largely on the screen persona of an actor. That's the case with a conversation between Cinque and Joie Lee and Steve Buscemi, who confides incredible facts to them in an all-knowing style, so confident they are powerless to penetrate it. Elvis was replaced by his twin brother, Buscemi explains, but it's not the theory that's amusing so much as his determination to force it upon two listeners manifestly not eager to hear it.

Sometimes movies tire us by trying too relentlessly to pound us with their brilliance and energy. Here is a movie pitched at about the energy level of a coffee break. That the people are oddly assorted and sometimes very strange is not so very unusual, considering some of the conversations you overhear in Starbucks.

Collateral ★ ★ ★ ½
R, 119 m., 2004

Tom Cruise (Vincent), Jamie Foxx (Max), Jada Pinkett Smith (Annie), Mark Ruffalo (Fanning), Peter Berg (Weidner), Bruce McGill (Pedrosea), Barry Shabaka Henley (Daniel), Irma P. Hall (Ida). Directed by Michael Mann and produced by Mann and Julie Richardson. Screenplay by Stuart Beattie.

Collateral opens with Tom Cruise exchanging briefcases with a stranger in an airport. Then, intriguingly, it seems to turn into another movie. We meet a cab driver named Max (Jamie Foxx), who picks up a ride named Annie (Jada Pinkett Smith). She's all business. She rattles off the streets he should take to get her to downtown Los Angeles. He says he knows a faster route. They end up making a bet: The ride will be free if he doesn't get them downtown faster.

The scene continues. It's not about flirtation. Sometimes you need to have only a few words with a person to know you would like to have many more. They open up. She's a federal prosecutor who confesses she's so nervous the night before a big case that she cries. He says he plans to own his own limousine service. They like each other. He lets her get out of the cab and knows he should have asked for her number. Then she taps on the window and gives him her card.

This is a long scene to come at the beginning of a thriller, but a good one, establishing two important characters. It is also good on its own terms, like a self-contained short film. It allows us to learn things about Max we could not possibly learn in the scenes to follow, and adds a subtext after the next customer into his cab is Tom Cruise.

Cruise plays a man named Vincent, who seems certain, centered, and nice. He needs a driver to spend all night with him, driving to five destinations, and offers Max six crisp $100 bills as persuasion. First stop, an apartment building. No parking in front. Vincent tells Max to wait for him in the alley. If you know nothing about the film, save this review until after.

A body lands on top of the cab. "You threw him out of the window and killed him?" Max asks incredulously. No, says Vincent, the bullets killed him, *then* he went out the window. So now we know more about Vincent. The movie is structured to make his occupation a surprise, but how much of a surprise can it be when the movie's Web site cheerfully blurts out: "Vincent is a contract killer." Never mind. The surprise about Vincent's occupation is the least of the movie's pleasures.

Collateral is essentially a long conversation between a killer and a man who fears for his life. Director Michael Mann punctuates the conversation with what happens at each of the five stops, where he uses detailed character roles and convincing dialogue by writer Stuart Beattie to create, essentially, more short films that could be freestanding. Look at the heart-

133

breaking scene where Vincent takes Max along with him into a nightclub, where they have a late-night talk with Daniel (Barry Shabaka Henley), the owner. Daniel remembers a night Miles Davis came into the club, recalling it with such warmth and wonder, such regret for his own missed opportunities as a musician, that we're looking into the window of his life.

Mann is working in a genre with *Collateral*, as he was in *Heat* (1995), but he deepens the genre through the kind of specific detail that would grace a straight drama. Consider a scene where Vincent asks (or orders) Max to take him to the hospital where Max's mother is a patient. The mother is played by Irma P. Hall (the old lady in the Coens' *The Lady-killers*), and she makes an instant impression, as a woman who looks at this man with her son, intuits that everything might not be right, and keeps that to herself.

These scenes are so much more interesting than the standard approach of the shifty club owner or the comic-relief Big Mama. Mann allows dialogue into the kind of movie that many directors now approach as wall-to-wall action. Action gains a lot when it happens to convincing individuals, instead of to off-the-shelf action figures.

What's particularly interesting is the way he, and Cruise, modulate the development of Vincent as a character. Vincent is not what he seems, but his secret is not that he's a killer; that's merely his occupation. His secret is his hidden psychological life going back to childhood, and in the way he thinks all the time about what life means, even as he takes it. When Max tells him the taxi job is "temporary" and talks about his business plans, Vincent finds out how long he's been driving a cab (twelve years) and quotes John Lennon: "Life is what happens while you're making other plans." Max tells Vincent something, too: "You lack standard parts that are supposed to be there in most people."

I would have preferred for the movie to end in something other than a chase scene, particularly one involving a subway train, but Mann directs it well. And he sets it up with a cat-and-mouse situation in a darkened office, which is very effective; it opens with a touch of *Rear Window* as Max watches what's happening on different floors of an office building.

Cruise and the filmmakers bring a great deal more to his character than we expect in a thriller. What he reveals about Vincent, deliberately and unintentionally, leads up to a final line that is worthy of one of those nihilistic French crime movies from the 1950s. Jamie Foxx's work is a revelation. I've thought of him in terms of comedy *(Booty Call, Breakin' All the Rules)*, but here he steps into a dramatic lead and is always convincing and involving. Now I'm looking forward to him playing Ray Charles; before, I wasn't so sure. And observe the way Jada Pinkett Smith sidesteps the conventions of the Meet Cute and brings everyday plausibility to every moment of Annie's first meeting with Max. This is a rare thriller that's as much character study as sound and fury.

Colossal Sensation! ★ ★ ★
NO MPAA RATING, 97 m., 2005

Róbert Koltai (Naftalin), Sándor Gáspár (Dodo), Orsolya Tóth (Pipitér). Directed by Róbert Koltai and produced by Gábor P. Koltai. Screenplay by Péter Horváth and Róbert Koltai.

Colossal Sensation! sees the history of Hungary in the twentieth century through the eyes of twin circus clowns. For them, as for all Hungarians, it is a story of feast and famine, nostalgia and regret, suffering and triumph, although not all Hungarians had the misfortune (or was it the opportunity?) to destroy a wristwatch given to the Hungarian party leader by Stalin himself.

The year, 1903. Nonidentical twin boys are born into a circus family. One afternoon, they are jumping over an alligator, as circus kids will do, when the beast snaps at little Naftalin, leaving him with a lifelong limp. Dodo is taller, better-looking, and straighter-walking, and he becomes their leader. When he gets engaged, his fiancée is alarmed to find that Naftalin (Róbert Koltai) may come along on the honeymoon. Dodo (Sándor Gáspár) doesn't have the heart to leave him behind.

The movie begins in monochrome, switches to color in 1949, and fills the screen with brilliant reds for events in 1953, when the twins are employed by the Budapest Grand Circus. They do that trick where they pretend to smash a watch borrowed from the audience and then return it unharmed. Naftalin, alas, borrows the party leader's watch, and let us say the party leader is not amused by the results.

Dodo, who has spent his life looking out for his slightly smaller and younger brother, takes the rap and goes to prison. In 1956, during the Hungarian uprising, Naftalin and Dodo's girl, Pipitér (Orsolya Tóth), make friends with the clueless crew of a wandering Russian tank, leading to a series of events surreal enough for *Catch-22.*

The movie follows the grim reality of the Soviet occupation but is not itself grim; director Koltai, who wrote it with Péter Horváth, at one point has a character say, "We are very small dots in this, comrade." And indeed, instead of making his heroes the center of the world, he shows them making a living on the fringes; showbiz provides them with a home, but only limited success, and what little we see of their clown act seems routine and perfunctory. What they are good at is improvising a response to the emergencies of life.

Colossal Sensation! had its American premiere at the Wilmette Theater in suburban Chicago, where two years ago the Hungarian film *Gloomy Sunday* also played for the first time in the United States. The big art distributors won't risk their limited funds on sweet little comedies from Hungary (or on gloomy big tragedies). *Gloomy Sunday* was accomplished and ambitious in a way *Colossal Sensation!* doesn't really intend to be. But in its own modest way, the movie is a whimsical charmer.

Connie and Carla ★ ½

PG-13, 98 m., 2004

Nia Vardalos (Connie), Toni Collette (Carla), David Duchovny (Jeff), Stephen Spinella (Robert/Peaches), Alec Mapa (Lee/N'Cream), Chris Logan (Brian/Brianna), Robert Kaiser (Paul), Debbie Reynolds (Herself). Directed by Michael Lembeck and produced by Gary Barber, Roger Birnbaum, Jonathan Glickman, Tom Hanks, and Rita Wilson. Screenplay by Nia Vardalos.

Connie and Carla plays like a genial amateur theatrical, the kind of production where you'd like it more if you were friends with the cast. The plot is creaky, the jokes are laborious, and total implausibility is not considered the slightest problem. Written by and starring Nia Vardalos, it's a disappointment after her hilarious *My Big Fat Greek Wedding.*

This time, in a retread of *Some Like It Hot,* Vardalos and Toni Collette play Connie and Carla, two friends who have been a singing duo since schooldays. Now they're in their thirties, stardom has definitely passed them by, and they perform a medley of musical comedy hits in an airport lounge that resembles no airport lounge in history, but does look a lot like somebody's rec room with some tables and chairs and a cheesy stage.

The guys they date beg them to face facts: They'll never really be any good. But they still dream the dream, and then, in a direct lift from *Some Like It Hot,* they witness a mob murder and have to go on the lam. The way this scene is handled is typical of the film's ham-handed approach: They're hiding in a parking garage when their boss is rubbed out, so what do they do? Stay hidden? Nope, they both stand up, scream, and wave their hands. They have to: Otherwise, there wouldn't be any movie.

Connie and Carla hit the road, head for Los Angeles, happen into a drag bar, and inspiration strikes: They can pretend to be female impersonators! That way no one will find them, or even know where to look. One of the running gags in *Some Like It Hot* was that Jack Lemmon and Tony Curtis did not make very plausible women, but the movie handled that by surrounding them with dim bulbs like the characters played by Marilyn Monroe and Joe E. Brown. *Connie and Carla* is set in today's Los Angeles gay community, where the other characters are supposed to be real, I guess, and where never in a million years could they pass as boys passing as girls.

Their danger from the mob is put on hold as the movie switches to another reliable formula, the showbiz rags-to-riches epic. Their act, of course, is an immediate hit, they make lots of buddies among the other drag queens, and there are many close calls as they're almost discovered out of drag, or would that be not out of drag? The time scheme of the movie is sufficiently forgiving for them to suggest that their little club remodel itself and double in size; and there is actually a scene where the show goes on while plastic sheeting separates the old club from the new addition. Next scene, the construction work is finished. Forget the drag queens, get the names of those contractors.

Nia Vardalos was of course wonderful in *My Big Fat Greek Wedding,* and Toni Collette has proven she can do about anything—but she can't do this. The movie masks desperation with frenzied slapstick and forced laughs. And when Connie meets a straight guy she likes (David Duchovny), we groan as the plot manufactures Meet Cutes by having them repeatedly run into each other and knock each other down. Uh-huh. I think maybe the point in *Some Like It Hot* was that Joe E. Brown fell in love with Jack Lemmon, not Marilyn Monroe. I'm not saying *Connie and Carla* would have been better if Connie had attracted a gay guy, or maybe a lesbian who saw through the drag, but at least that would have supplied a comic problem, not a romantic one.

My Big Fat Greek Wedding was such a huge success that it gave Vardalos a free ticket for her next movie. Someone should have advised her this wasn't the right screenplay to cash in the pass. Nor does director Michael Lembeck save the day. He's done a lot of TV sitcoms, including many episodes of *Friends,* and his only other feature film, *The Santa Clause 2,* was funny enough, but here he took on an unfilmable premise and goes down with it. By the end, as the gangsters, the midwestern boyfriends, Duchovny, various drag queens, and Debbie Reynolds (herself) all descend on the finale, we're not watching a comedy, we're watching a traffic jam.

The Constant Gardener ★ ★ ★ ★
R, 129 m., 2005

Ralph Fiennes (Justin Quayle), Rachel Weisz (Tessa Quayle), Danny Huston (Sandy Woodrow), Hubert Kounde (Arnold Bluhm), Bill Nighy (Sir Bernard Pellegrin), Pete Postlethwaite (Marcus Lorbeer). Directed by Fernando Meirelles and produced by Simon Channing-Williams. Screenplay by Jeffrey Caine, based on the novel by John le Carre.

They meet as strangers who plunge at once into sudden sex. They catch their breath, marry, and begin to learn about each other. Justin is an official in the British government. Tessa is an activist. She goes to Africa with Justin, her mo-

tives unclear in his mind, and witnesses what she thinks is murder in an African hospital. Then she is murdered at a crossroads, along with her African driver. And a doctor named Arnold, whom she works with, is found dead, too. But why, Justin needs to know, did Tessa receive an e-mail asking her, "What were you and Arnold doing in the Nairobi Hilton Friday night? Does Justin know?"

The murder of Tessa takes place right at the start of *The Constant Gardener,* so it is not revealing too much to mention it. The movie is a progress back into her life, and a journey of discovery for Justin, who learns about a woman he never really knew. The flashback structure, told in remembered moments, passages of dialogue, scenes that are interrupted and completed later, is typical of John le Carre, whose novels resemble chess problems in which one solution is elegant and all of the others take too many moves. It is a style suited to the gifts of the Brazilian director Fernando Meirelles, whose great *City of God* (2003) told a story that was composed of countless tributaries that all flowed together into a mighty narrative stream.

The fragmented style is the best way to tell this story, for both the novel and the movie. *The Constant Gardener* is not a logical exercise beginning with mystery and ending at truth, but a circling around an elusive conspiracy. Understand who the players are and how they are willing to compromise themselves, and you can glimpse cruel outlines beneath the public relations facade. As the drug companies pour AIDS drugs into Africa, are they using their programs to mask the test of other drugs? "No drug company does something for nothing," le Carre has a character observe.

The Constant Gardener may be the angriest story le Carre has ever told. Certainly his elegant prose and the oblique shorthand of the dialogue show the writer forcing himself to turn fury into style. His novel involves drug companies that test their products on the poor of the Third World, and are willing to accept the deaths that may occur because, after all, those people don't count. Why not? Because no one is there to count them.

Do drug companies really do this? Facts are the bones beneath the skin of a le Carre novel. Either he knows what he's talking about, or he is uncommonly persuasive in seeming to. *The*

Constant Gardener at times plays like a movie that will result in indictments. What makes it extraordinary is that it also plays as a love story, and as an examination of the mysteries of the heart.

The performances need to be very good to carry us through sequences in which nobody, good or evil, seems very sure of the total picture. Ralph Fiennes plays Justin as a bureaucrat who seems detached from issues; he's the opposite of Tessa. As he tries to get to the bottom of her death, he sifts through his discoveries like an accountant unwilling to go home for the day until the books are balanced.

One way of looking at Tessa's death is that she was a hothead who had an affair with a handsome African man, went where she shouldn't have been, and got caught in one of those African border killings where toll-collecting soldiers with AK-47s enforce whatever they think is the law. Another way to look at it is to give her the benefit of the doubt. To wonder what was behind the embarrassing questions she asked at a press conference. To ask why statistics seem to be missing, if a drug study is designed to generate them.

As he probes through the wreckage of his wife's life, Justin encounters an array of characters who could have been airlifted in from Graham Greene—or from other le Carre novels, of course. Hubert Kounde plays Arnold Bluhm, the African who is not, in fact, Tessa's driver, but a doctor who is her colleague. Danny Huston, tall and courtly like his father, John, and like John often smiling at a private joke, plays Sandy Woodrow, the British high commissioner on the scene. Bill Nighy, that actor who often seems to be frowning through a migraine, is Sir Bernard Pellegrin, head of the Foreign Office and thus Justin and Sandy's boss. And Pete Postlethwaite, looking as if he has been left out too long in the weather, is Lorbeer, a drug company man who works in the field—at what, it is dangerous to say.

The Constant Gardener begins with a strong, angry story and peoples it with actors who let it happen to them, instead of rushing ahead to check off the surprises. It seems solidly grounded in its Kenyan locations; like *City of God*, it feels organically rooted. Like many le Carre stories, it begins with grief and proceeds with sadness toward horror. Its closing scenes are as cynical about international politics and commerce as I can imagine. I would like to believe they are an exaggeration, but I fear they are not. This is one of the year's best films.

Constantine ★ ½
R, 120 m., 2005

Keanu Reeves (John Constantine), Rachel Weisz (Angela and Isabel Dodson), Shia LeBeouf (Chas), Djimon Hounsou (Midnite), Max Baker (Beeman), Pruitt Taylor Vince (Father Hennessy), Gavin Rossdale (Balthazar), Tilda Swinton (Gabriel), Peter Stormare (Satan). Directed by Francis Lawrence and produced by Lauren Shuler Donner, Benjamin Melniker, Michael E. Uslan, Erwin Stoff, Lorenzo di Bonaventura, and Akiva Goldsman. Screenplay by Kevin Brodbin and Frank Cappello, based on the comic book *Hellblazer* by Jamie Delano and Garth Ennis.

No, *Constantine* is not part of a trilogy including *Troy* and *Alexander*. It's not about the emperor at all, but about a man who can see the world behind the world, and is waging war against the scavengers of the damned. There was a nice documentary about emperor penguins, however, at Sundance. The males sit on the eggs all winter long in, like, 60 degrees below zero.

Keanu Reeves plays Constantine as a chain-smoking, depressed demon-hunter who lives above a bowling alley in Los Angeles. Since he was a child, he has been able to see that not all who walk among us are human. Some are penguins. Sorry about that. Some are half-angels and half-devils. Constantine knows he is doomed to hell because he once tried to kill himself, and is trying to rack up enough frames against the demons to earn his way into heaven.

There is a scene early in the movie where Constantine and his doctor look at his X-rays, never a good sign in a superhero movie. He has lung cancer. The angel Gabriel (Tilda Swinton) tells him, "You are going to die young because you've smoked thirty cigarettes a day since you were thirteen." Gabriel has made more interesting announcements. Constantine has already spent some time in hell, which looks like a postnuclear Los Angeles created by animators with a hangover. No doubt it is filled with carcinogens.

137

The half-angels and half-devils are earthly proxies in the war between God and Satan. You would think that God would be the New England Patriots of this contest, but apparently there is a chance that Satan could win. Constantine's lonely mission is to track down half-demons and cast them back to the fires below. Like Blade, the vampire-killer, he is surprisingly optimistic, considering he is one guy in one city dealing on a case-by-case basis, and the enemy is global.

Constantine has a technical adviser named Beeman (Max Baker), who lives in the ceiling of the bowling alley among the pin-spotting machines, and functions like Q in the James Bond movies. Here he is loading Constantine with the latest weaponry: "Bullet shavings from the assassination attempt on the pope, holy water from the river of Jordan, and, you'll love this, screech beetles." The screech beetles come in a little matchbox. "To the fallen," Beeman explains, "the sound is like nails on a blackboard." Later there is a scene where Constantine is inundated by the creatures of hell, and desperately tries to reach the matchbox and *get* those beetles to *screeching*.

Rachel Weisz plays Angela Dodson, an L.A. police detective whose twin sister, Isabel, has apparently committed suicide. Isabel reported seeing demons, so Angela consults Constantine, who nods wisely and wonders if Isabel jumped, or was metaphysically pushed. Later in the film, to show Angela that she also has the gift of seeing the world behind the world, Constantine holds her underwater in a bathtub until she passes out and sees the torments of hell. No bright white corridors and old friends and Yanni for her. You wonder what kind of an L.A. cop would allow herself to be experimentally drowned in a bathtub by a guy who lives over a bowling alley.

Together, they prowl the nighttime streets. At one point, Constantine needs to consult Midnite (Djimon Hounsou), a former witch doctor who runs a private nightclub where half-angels and half-demons can get half-loaded and talk shop. There is a doorman. To gain admittance, you have to read his mind and tell him what's on the other side of the card he's holding up. "Two frogs on a bench," Constantine says. Could have been a lucky guess.

There is a priest in the film, the alcoholic Father Hennessy (Pruitt Taylor Vince), whose name, I guess, is product placement. Strange that there is a priest, since that opens the door to Catholicism and therefore to the news that Constantine is not doomed unless he wages a lifelong war against demons, but needs merely go to confession; three Our Fathers, three Hail Marys, and he's outta there. Strange that movies about Satan always require Catholics. You never see your Presbyterians or Episcopalians hurling down demons.

The forces of hell manifest themselves in many ways. One victim is eaten by flies. A young girl is possessed by a devil, and Constantine shouts, "I need a mirror! Now! At least three feet high!" He can capture the demon in the mirror and throw it out the window, see, although you wonder why supernatural beings would have such low-tech security holes.

Keanu Reeves has a deliberately morose energy level in the movie, as befits one who has seen hell, walks among half-demons, and is dying. He keeps on smoking. Eventually he confronts Satan (Peter Stormare), who wears a white suit. (Satan to tailor: "I want a suit just like God's.") Oh, and the plot also involves the Spear of Destiny, which is the spear that killed Christ, and which has been missing since World War II, which seems to open a window to the possibility of Nazi villains, but no.

Control Room ★ ★ ★
NO MPAA RATING, 84 m., 2004

With Sameer Khader, Lieutenant Josh Rushing, Tom Mintier, Hassan Ibrahim, David Shuster, and Deema Khatib. A documentary directed by Jehane Noujaim and produced by Hani Salama and Rosadel Varela. Screenplay by Noujaim.

The final film I saw at Cannes 2004 came from Egypt and contained a surprise. It was *Alexandrie . . . New York,* by the veteran director Youssef Chahine, and it told the autobiographical story of an Egyptian who comes to America in 1950 to study at the Pasadena Playhouse, and returns again in 1975 and 2000. There is a lot more to it than that, but what struck me was when the student joined his classmates in singing "God Bless America" at the graduation. I hadn't heard that in an American film since *The Deer Hunter* in 1978. The character in 1950, and apparently the seventy-eight-year-old Egyptian who told his story, loved America.

I thought of them as I watched *Control Room*, an enlightening documentary about how the U.S. networks and the Arab satellite news channel Al Jazeera covered the early days of the war in Iraq. If Americans are familiar with Al Jazeera at all, it is because, as Donald Rumsfeld charges in the film, it is a source of anti-American propaganda, "willing to lie to the world to make their case." Yet there is an extraordinary moment in the film when Sameer Khadar, an engaging and articulate producer for Al Jazeera, confides that if he were offered a job with Fox News, he would take it. He wants his children to seek their futures in the United States, he says, and I carefully wrote down his next words: "to exchange the Arab nightmare for the American dream." These are the words of a man Rumsfeld calls a liar. That many American news organizations, including the *New York Times*, have had to apologize for errors in their coverage of Iraq may indicate that Rumsfeld and his teammates may also have supplied them with . . . inaccuracies.

Khadar is seen in action, interviewing an American "analyst" named Jeffrey Steinberg who attacks U.S. policy. Afterward, Khadar is angry that his network arranged the interview: "He's just a crazy activist. He wasn't an analyst. He was just against America." We also see correspondents from CNN, Fox, and the networks attempting to stay objective, although they collectively lose it when a military spokesman holds up the famous deck of cards with the faces of Iraq's "most wanted" on it, announces the decks will be distributed by the thousands throughout the country, and then refuses to let the journalists see the cards.

The documentary is low-key for the most part, just watching and listening. Many of its scenes take place in and around CentCom, the temporary media center in Qatar where the world's journalists gathered during the run-up to the invasion of Iraq. Here Americans have long conversations with their counterparts at Al Jazeera, which is privately owned and heavily watched in Arab countries because viewers trust it more than their own government channels.

I have not seen Al Jazeera and am in no position to comment on its accuracy. I have seen this film, however, which contains enlightening moments. Remember the TV scene when joyous Iraqis toppled the statue of Saddam Hussein after the capture of Baghdad? TV pictures on the monitors at CentCom clearly see something American audiences were not shown: The square was not filled with cheering citizens, but was completely empty except for the small band of young men who toppled the statue. Al Jazeera producers watch the footage with their U.S. counterparts and observe that those who are interviewed "do not have Baghdad accents." They wonder why one "happened to have the old Iraqi flag in his pocket." The implication: This was a staged event, initiated by the U.S. occupation and bought into by the U.S. media.

The movie listens in on many philosophical bull sessions between a U.S. marine press spokesman, Lieutenant Josh Rushing, and an Al Jazeera producer named Hassan Ibrahim, who once worked for the BBC. Rushing defends the American line, but is willing to listen to Ibrahim, who deconstructs some of the American claims (his version: "Democratize or we'll shoot you"). Some of Rushing's statements ring a little hollow, as when he says, "The American POWs expect to be treated humanely, just like we are treating our prisoners humanely."

The correspondents are saddened when three journalists are killed in Baghdad by U.S. strikes. We see one of them, working for Al Jazeera, sitting sadly behind sandbags on the roof of a building, looking like a man who has had his last meal. The network carefully informed American authorities of the location of their bureau, it's noted, and American rockets struck that location not long after Rumsfeld and others complained about Al Jazeera's coverage. An accident of war.

Control Room was directed by Jehane Noujaim, an Arab-American documentarian who made *Startup.com*, the absorbing 2001 doc about an ambitious Web site that got caught in the collapse of the Internet bubble. In this film, she seems content to watch and listen as journalists do their jobs and talk about them. She doesn't take sides, but in insisting that there is something to be said for both sides she offends those who want to hear only one side.

What is clear is that the Al Jazeera journalists feel more disappointment than hatred for America. During one of those bull sessions, there's a rhetorical question: "Who's going to stop the United States?" And an Arab replies: "The United States is going to stop the United States. I have absolute confidence in the U.S. Constitution and the U.S. people." The film's buried message is that there is a reservoir of admiration and affection for America, at least among the educated classes in the Arab world, and they do not equate the current administration with America.

Note: Salon.com reported June 6 that Lieutenant Josh Rushing was ordered by the Pentagon not to comment on this film, "and as a result, the fourteen-year career military man, recently promoted to captain, plans to leave the Marines."

The Corporation ★ ★ ★
NO MPAA RATING, 145 m., 2004

A documentary directed by Jennifer Abbott and Mark Achbar and produced by Achbar and Bart Simpson. Screenplay by Joel Bakan and Harold Crooks.

Muley: *Who's the Shawnee Land and Cattle Co.?*
Land agent: *It ain't anybody. It's a company.*
—*The Grapes of Wrath*

I was at a health ranch last week, where the idea is to clear your mind for serene thoughts. At dinner one night, a woman at the table referred to Arizona as a "right to work state." Unwisely, I replied: "Yeah—the right to work cheap." She said, "I think you'll find the nonunion workers are quite well paid." Exercising a supreme effort of will to avoid pronouncing the syllables "Wal-Mart," I replied: "If so, that's because unions have helped raise salaries for everybody." She replied: "The unions steal their members' dues." I replied, "How much money would you guess the unions have stolen compared to corporations like Enron?" At this point our exchange was punctuated by a kick under the table from my wife, and we went back to positive thinking.

The Corporation is not a film my dinner companion would enjoy. It begins with the unsettling information that, under the law, a corporation is not a thing but a person. The U.S. Supreme Court so ruled, in a decision based, bizarrely, on the 14th Amendment to the Constitution. That was the one that guar-

anteed former slaves equal rights. The court ruling meant corporations were given the rights of individuals in our society. They are free at last.

If Monsanto and WorldCom and Enron are indeed people, what kind of people are they? The movie asks Robert Hare, a consultant who helps the FBI profile its suspects. His diagnosis: Corporations by definition have a personality disorder and can be categorized as psychopathic. That is because they singlemindedly pursue their own wills and desires without any consideration for other people (or corporations) and without reference to conventional morality. They don't act that way to be evil; it's just, as the scorpion explained to the frog, that it's in their nature.

Having more or less avoided the corporate world by living in my little movie critic corner, I've been struck by the way classmates and friends identify with their corporations. They are loyal to an entity that exists only to perpetuate itself. Any job that requires you to wear a corporate lapel pin is taking more precious things from you than display space. Although I was greatly cheered to see Ken Lay in handcuffs, I can believe he thinks he's innocent. In corporate terms, he is: He was only doing his job in reflecting Enron's psychopathic nature.

The movie assembles a laundry list of corporate sins: bovine growth hormone, Agent Orange, marketing research on how to inspire children to nag their parents to buy products. It is in the interest of corporations to sell products, and therefore in their interest to have those products certified as safe, desirable, and good for us. No one who knows anything about the assembly-line production of chickens would eat a nonorganic chicken. Cows, which are vegetarians, have been fed processed animal protein, leading to the charming possibility that they can pass along mad cow disease. Farm-raised salmon contains mercury. And so on.

If corporations are maximizing profits by feeding Strangelovian chemicals to unsuspecting animals, what are we to make of the U.S. Supreme Court decision that living organisms can be patented? Yes, strains of laboratory mice, cultures of bacteria, even bits of DNA, can now be privately owned.

Fascinated as I am by the labyrinthine reasoning by which stem-cell research somehow violates the right to life, I have been waiting for opponents of stem cell to attack the private ownership and patenting of actual living organisms, but I wait in vain. If there is one thing more sacred than the right to life, it is the corporation's right to patent, market, and exploit life.

If I seem to have strayed from the abstract idea of a corporation, *The Corporation* does some straying itself. It produces saintly figures like Ray Anderson, chairman of Interface, the largest rug manufacturer in the world, who tells his fellow executives they are all "plundering" the globe, and tries to move his corporation toward sustainable production. All living organisms on Earth are in decline, the documentary argues, mostly because corporations are stealing from the future to enrich themselves in the present.

The Corporation is an impassioned polemic, filled with information sure to break up any dinner-table conversation. Its fault is that of the dinner guest who tells you something fascinating, and then tells you again, and then a third time. At 145 minutes, it overstays its welcome. The wise documentarian should treat film stock as a nonrenewable commodity.

Crash ★ ★ ★ ★

R, 100 m., 2005

Sandra Bullock (Jean), Don Cheadle (Graham), Matt Dillon (Officer Ryan), Jennifer Esposito (Ria), William Fichtner (Flanagan), Brendan Fraser (Rick), Terrence Dashon Howard (Cameron), Ludacris (Anthony), Thandie Newton (Christine), Ryan Phillippe (Officer Hansen), Larenz Tate (Peter), Shaun Toub (Farhad), Michael Pena (Daniel). Directed by Paul Haggis and produced by Haggis, Mark R. Harris, Robert Moresco, Cathy Schulman, and Tom Nunan. Screenplay by Haggis and Moresco.

Crash tells interlocking stories of whites, blacks, Latinos, Koreans, Iranians, cops and criminals, the rich and the poor, the powerful and powerless, all defined in one way or another by racism. All are victims of it, and all are guilty of it. Sometimes, yes, they rise above it, although it is never that simple. Their negative impulses may be instinctive, their posi-

tive impulses may be dangerous, and who knows what the other person is thinking?

The result is a movie of intense fascination; we understand quickly enough who the characters are and what their lives are like, but we have no idea how they will behave because so much depends on accident. Most movies enact rituals; we know the form and watch for variations. *Crash* is a movie with free will, and anything can happen. Because we care about the characters, the movie is uncanny in its ability to rope us in and get us involved.

Crash was directed by Paul Haggis, whose screenplay for *Million Dollar Baby* led to Academy Awards. It connects stories based on coincidence, serendipity, and luck, as the lives of the characters crash against each other like pinballs. The movie presumes that most people feel prejudice and resentment against members of other groups, and observes the consequences of those feelings.

One thing that happens, again and again, is that peoples' assumptions prevent them from seeing the actual person standing before them. An Iranian (Shaun Toub) is thought to be an Arab, although Iranians are Persian. Both the Iranian and the white wife of the district attorney (Sandra Bullock) believe a Mexican-American locksmith (Michael Pena) is a gang member and a crook, but he is a family man.

A black cop (Don Cheadle) is having an affair with his Latino partner (Jennifer Esposito), but never gets it straight which country she's from. A cop (Matt Dillon) thinks a light-skinned black woman (Thandie Newton) is white. When a white producer tells a black TV director (Terrence Dashon Howard) that a black character "doesn't sound black enough," it never occurs to him that the director doesn't "sound black," either. For that matter, neither do two young black men (Larenz Tate and Ludacris), who dress and act like college students, but have a surprise for us.

You see how it goes. Along the way, these people say exactly what they are thinking, without the filters of political correctness. The district attorney's wife is so frightened by a street encounter that she has the locks changed, then assumes the locksmith will be back with his "homies" to attack them. The white cop can't get medical care for his dying father, and accuses a black woman at his HMO of taking advantage of preferential racial treatment. The Iranian can't understand what the locksmith is trying to tell him, freaks out, and buys a gun to protect himself. The gun dealer and the Iranian get into a shouting match.

I make this sound almost like episodic TV, but Haggis writes with such directness and such a good ear for everyday speech that the characters seem real and plausible after only a few words. His cast is uniformly strong; the actors sidestep clichés and make their characters particular.

For me, the strongest performance is by Matt Dillon, as the racist cop in anguish over his father. He makes an unnecessary traffic stop when he thinks he sees the black TV director and his light-skinned wife doing something they really shouldn't be doing at the same time they're driving. True enough, but he wouldn't have stopped a black couple or a white couple. He humiliates the woman with an invasive body search, while her husband is forced to stand by powerless, because the cops have the guns—Dillon, and also a unseasoned rookie (Ryan Phillippe), who hates what he's seeing but has to back up his partner.

That traffic stop shows Dillon's cop as vile and hateful. But later we see him trying to care for his sick father, and we understand why he explodes at the HMO worker (whose race is only an excuse for his anger). He victimizes others by exercising his power, and is impotent when it comes to helping his father.

Then the plot turns ironically on itself, and both of the cops find themselves, in very different ways, saving the lives of the very same TV director and his wife. Is this just manipulative storytelling? It didn't feel that way to me because it serves a deeper purpose than mere irony: Haggis is telling parables, in which the characters learn the lessons they have earned by their behavior.

Other cross-cutting Los Angeles stories come to mind, especially Lawrence Kasdan's more optimistic *Grand Canyon* and Robert Altman's more humanistic *Short Cuts*. But *Crash* finds a way of its own. It shows the way we all leap to conclusions based on race—yes, all of us, of all races, and however fair-minded we may try to be—and we pay a price for that. If there is hope in the story, it comes because as the characters crash into one another, they

learn things, mostly about themselves. Almost all of them are still alive at the end, and are better people because of what has happened to them. Not happier, not calmer, not even wiser, but better. Then there are those few who kill or get killed; racism has tragedy built in.

Not many films have the possibility of making their audiences better people. I don't expect *Crash* to work any miracles, but I believe anyone seeing it is likely to be moved to have a little more sympathy for people not like themselves. The movie contains hurt, coldness, and cruelty, but is it without hope? Not at all.

Stand back and consider. All of these people, superficially so different, share the city and learn that they share similar fears and hopes. Until several hundred years ago, most people everywhere on Earth never saw anybody who didn't look like them. They were not racist because, as far as they knew, there was only one race. You may have to look hard to see it, but *Crash* is a film about progress. ☞

Criminal ★ ★ ½
R, 87 m., 2004

John C. Reilly (Richard Gaddis), Diego Luna (Rodrigo), Maggie Gyllenhaal (Valerie Gaddis), Jonathan Tucker (Michael Gaddis), Peter Mullan (William Hannigan), Zitto Kazann (Ochoa). Directed by Gregory Jacobs and produced by George Clooney, Steven Soderbergh, and Jacobs. Screenplay by Jacobs and Soderbergh, based on the screenplay by Fabian Bielinsky.

It comes down to this: *Criminal* is an English-language remake of *Nine Queens*, an Argentinean film I saw in 2002 and remember well. *Criminal* follows the original fairly closely, and because I already knew the plot secrets, it couldn't work on me in its intended way. As the recycled characters, dialogue, and events turned up, there seemed to be an echo in the room.

The film may work for you. *Nine Queens* worked for me and I gave it three stars. Much depends on whether you enjoy films that deliberately set out to mislead you. This one is a con about a con, and occupies the territory staked out so perfectly by such as David Mamet's *House of Games* and Ridley Scott's *Matchstick Men*. Odds are you'll have an inkling of what's going on under the surface, but the ending is likely to surprise you—not in what it reveals, but in how it forces you to think again about parts you thought were on the level.

John C. Reilly and Diego Luna costar, as Richard and Rodrigo, who meet in a casino when Richard, a veteran con man, observes Rodrigo clumsily trying to trick waitresses into giving him his change twice. Richard steps in, tells casino security he's a cop, and leads Rodrigo away in handcuffs he conveniently carries in his pocket. Then he explains that he went to all this trouble because he needs a partner for a few days, and Rodrigo looks promising.

They warm up slowly, conning waiters and little old ladies, and then a larger quarry swims into view. Richard's sister Valerie (Maggie Gyllenhaal), who works in a hotel, calls him to say an old forger pal of his (Zitto Kazann) is sick in the men's room, and needs help. That leads to Richard and Rodrigo's involvement in the forger's scheme to sell a counterfeit bank note to a wealthy collector named Hannigan (Peter Mullan), who is staying in the hotel.

The plot as it uncoils is indeed ingenious. Like many such plots, it depends on outrageous coincidence, lucky timing, and the ability to think through the con and come out on the other side. I'm convinced there's a logical flaw in the story structure, having to do with why Richard thinks he needs Rodrigo before he finds out what makes Rodrigo of interest to him. And no, that's not giving anything away, as you will discover when you see the film.

The actors do a good job of giving edge and momentum to the material: John C. Reilly is always in character (as his character, if you see what I mean), and Diego Luna, from *Y Tu Mama Tambien,* walks a fine line between being a novice con man and being a very quick study. It's all done well. The director is Gregory Jacobs, who has worked as an assistant director for Stephen Soderbergh (the film's producer) and no doubt learned a thing or two about cons on *Ocean's 11* and *Out of Sight.* His decision to remake this recent film is defensible, since the plot of *Nine Queens* was what distinguished it, and plots translate better than intangibles like, oh, say, artistry.

Because I had an excellent idea of what was really happening and why, however, the film

couldn't work on me in its intended way. Some con-game films have such great dialogue *(House of Games)* or such intense acting *(Matchstick Men)* that they work entirely apart from the con. But *Criminal* needs the element of puzzlement and surprise. Since you have probably not seen *Nine Queens* (which grossed less than $2 million at the North American box office), *Criminal* will be new to you, and I predict you'll like the remake about as much as I liked the original—three stars' worth. If, however, you've seen *Nine Queens,* you may agree that some journeys, however entertaining, need only be taken once.

Crimson Gold ★ ★ ★

NO MPAA RATING, 97 m., 2004

Hussein Emadeddin (Hussein), Kamyar Sheissi (Ali), Azita Rayeji (Bride), Shahram Vaziri (Jeweler), Ehsan Amani (Man in the Tea House), Pourang Nakhayi (Rich Man), Kavey Najmabadi (Seller), Saber Safael (Soldier). Directed by Jafar Panahi and produced by Panahi. Screenplay by Abbas Kiarostami.

The success of *Crimson Gold* depends to an intriguing degree on the performance of its leading actor, a large, phlegmatic man who embodies the rule that an object at rest will stay at rest until some other force sets it into motion. The character, named Hussein and played by Hussein Emadeddin, is a pizza deliveryman in Tehran, heavy-set, tall, undemonstrative. He sits where he sits as if planted there, and when he rides his scooter around the city streets he doesn't lean and dart like most scooter drivers, but seems at one with his machine in implacable motion. When he smokes, he is like an automaton programmed to move the cigarette toward and away from his lips.

He has a friend named Ali (Kamyar Sheissi). We meet Ali for the first time in a teahouse, where he produces a purse he has just found. Its contents are disappointing—a broken gold ring. Another man overhears their conversation, assumes they stole the purse, and delivers a little lecture on the morality of theft. He believes the rewards should suit the crime; you should not put your targets through a great deal of suffering just to relieve them of pocket change.

Hussein, who is engaged to Ali's sister, seems

an unlikely candidate for marriage. We learn indirectly that he was wounded in the Iraq-Iran War, and Ali refers to his "medication." Perhaps that accounts for his sphinxlike detachment; he acts as little as it is possible to act and yet, paradoxically, we can't take our eyes off of him.

The film uses Hussein and his life as a lens to look at Tehran today. The director, Jafar Panahi, also made *The Circle* (2000), a film showing the impossibility of being a single woman in modern Iran without having a man to explain your status. *Crimson Gold* was written by Abbas Kiarostami, the best-known Iranian director, and includes his trademark: long, unbroken shots of a character driving somewhere. In this case, it is Hussein on his scooter, sometimes with Ali as a passenger.

Hussein lives a solitary existence in an untidy little flat, venturing out at night to deliver pizzas. One night he delivers a stack of pizzas to the penthouse of an apartment building in a wealthy neighborhood. He is greeted at the door by the occupant (Pourang Nakhayi), who complains that "the women have gone" and he doesn't need the pizza. But he invites Hussein in, asks him to eat the pizza, and talks obsessively about himself: How his parents only lived in the apartment for a month before moving overseas, how he has just returned to Iran and finds it not organized to his liking, how women are crazy and unpredictable.

Hussein eats steadily and regards him. Later, as the man is on the telephone, he walks around the apartment (he has never been so high up in his life), looks at the skyline, visits a bathroom more luxurious than any he could imagine, dives fully clothed into the swimming pool, and is seen later wrapped in towels.

When he leaves the apartment he goes directly to a jewelry store that he and Ali had visited twice before. The first time, they wanted to get a price on the gold ring, and were treated rudely and with suspicion by the store owner and guard. Returning, wearing ties and with Ali's sister along, they said they were shopping for a wedding ring—but were treated rudely again; it is a high-end store and they look like low-end people.

After he leaves the high-rise apartment, Hussein returns to the store. We already know much of what will happen now, because *Crim-* son *Gold* opens with a version of the same scene it closes with. But I will not discuss the opening (and closing) because they proceed with a kind of implacable logic. What seems impulsive and reckless at the beginning of the film takes on a certain logic after we have spent some time in Hussein's company. In his case, still waters run deep and cold. He has been still and implacable for the entire film, but now we understand he was not frozen, but waiting.

Note: In real life, Hussein Emadeddin, a non-actor, is a paranoid schizophrenic. Having learned this information, I felt obliged to share it with you, but the film does not refer to the disease; perhaps Jafar Panahi found that Emadeddin's demeanor, whatever its source, provided the kind of detachment he needed for his character. Hussein (the character) is doubly effective because he does not seem to be an active participant in the story, but an observer carried along by the currents of chance.

Cronicas ★ ★ ★
R, 98 m., 2005

John Leguizamo (Manolo Bonilla), Leonor Watling (Marisa Iturralde), Damián Alcázar (Vinicio Cepeda), Jóse María Yazpik (Iván Suárez), Alfred Molina (Victor Hugo Puente), Camilo Luzuriaga (Bolivar Rojas). Directed by Sebastian Cordero and produced by Alfonso Cuaron, Berta Navarro, Guillermo del Toro, Jorge Vergara, and Isabel Davalos. Screenplay by Cordero.

I don't know if John Leguizamo was thinking of Geraldo Rivera when he made *Cronicas*, but I was. Leguizamo plays the same kind of swashbuckling TV reporter who likes to be in the middle of breaking news stories, standing on camera in front of amazing events. Nothing wrong with that, unless you start thinking of yourself as the foreground and the story as the setting.

In *Cronicas*, Leguizamo plays Manolo Bonilla, a Miami-based star reporter for a Spanish-language network that blankets Latin America. He's in Ecuador covering the story of the Monster of Babahoyo, a serial killer who has murdered at least 150 young children. During a funeral for the latest victims, a man in a pickup truck grows confused and runs over a small boy. The funeral mob turns ugly, drags the man from his truck, beats him, dowses him with gasoline, and is prepared to set him afire.

Bonilla and his crew film the mob scene right up to the point the match is thrown. Then they're involved, along with Bolivar Rojas, a local policeman (Camilo Luzuriaga), in saving the man's life. But a lynching still seems likely, and the man, named Vinicio (Damian Alcazar) bargains with the reporter, telling him he has inside knowledge of the Monster and his methods.

At this point I am prepared to believe that Leguizamo can play just about anyone, and do it well. A list of his roles would take us from a drag queen *(To Wong Foo)* to Toulouse-Lautrec *(Moulin Rouge!)* to a dog whisperer *(The Honeymooners)* to a Shakespeare character *(Romeo + Juliet)* to a zombie hunter *(Land of the Dead)*. Here he convincingly plays an experienced TV reporter, in a performance that knows the type and knows the job, and strikes a nice balance between how he covers the story and gets publicity for himself, two tasks he is equally suited for.

What's remarkable is that he plays the character while mostly speaking in Spanish. Yes, Leguizamo was born in Colombia, but his family soon moved to America, and he is not fluent in Spanish; the performance required him to learn the language and use a dialogue coach for line-by-line readings. That he could do that and stay in character as the persuasive, fast-talking media star Bonilla is remarkable.

Bonilla's conversations with Vinicio arouse in him, and in the audience, the suspicion that this man, who says he is a traveling Bible salesman, might actually be the Monster. He claims he gave the real Monster a lift one day, "and he needed someone to talk to." He claims that he can lead Bonilla to a grave that contains a body not discovered by the authorities —and Bonilla, hot for a scoop, deliberately keeps this secret from the cops and digs up the evidence himself.

He does his job with a two-person crew. Marisa Iturralde (Leonor Watling, from *Bad Education*) is his producer, and Ivan Suarez (Jose Maria Yazpik) is his cameraman; the movie knows, as not every movie does, that the cameraman is as instrumental in covering a story as the reporter, sometimes more. The dynamic is complicated because Marisa's hus-band, back in Miami, is Victor Hugo Puente (Alfred Molina), anchor of their sensationalistic newscast and a flamboyant ham with his own hunger for publicity.

The movie too quickly leads us to suspect Vinicio as the real Monster, I think, although the Law of Economy of Characters would probably lead us to suspect him no matter what. The question becomes: What will Bonilla do with the information he's gathering, how can he get the scoop without damaging the investigation, how can he keep Victor Hugo in Miami and away from the action, and how, for that matter, can the movie generate much suspense? Bonilla's private sleuthing is complicated, he complains to Marisa, because "we're stuck with the only honest cop in Latin America."

It goes without saying that Bonilla and Marisa are attracted to each other, but whether they do or don't betray Victor Hugo really has nothing to do with anything; it's just the obligatory romantic interlude. More interesting is whether Marisa betrays herself, since she has a journalistic conscience, and Bonilla seems to have mislaid his. Although I understand the strategy of keeping Victor Hugo in Miami, so that he's seen only on a TV monitor, Alfred Molina is such a gifted actor that I imagine his physical presence in Ecuador would have generated more dramatic interest than his absence.

As it is, the movie loses tension the moment we guess the essential truth behind the story, and the rest is all details. Mostly accurate details, however, in a rare movie that knows TV journalism inside-out; the director, Sebastian Cordero, an Ecuador-born UCLA graduate, gets the right feel for his news crew at work in the field, and Leguizamo and Watling bring a fascination to their characters that the story doesn't always deserve. There are also nice small moments, as when a great deal depends on knowing the Spanish word for *twin*. *Cronicas* is the kind of movie that grabs you while you're watching, even if later you wish it had grabbed a little harder.

Curious George ★ ★ ★
G, 86 m., 2006

With the voices of: Drew Barrymore (Maggie), Will Ferrell (Man in the Yellow Hat),

Eugene Levy (Clovis), Joan Plowright (Miss Plushbottom), David Cross (Bloomsberry Jr.), Dick Van Dyke (Mr. Bloomsberry), Frank Welker (George). Directed by Matthew O'Callaghan and produced by Brian Grazer, Ron Howard, David Kirschner, Bonne Radford, and Jon Shapiro. Screenplay by Ken Kaufman, based on the books by Margret and H. A. Rey.

Definition of a good family movie: one that appeals to all members of the family. *Curious George* is not a family movie. It is a children's movie. There is nothing wrong with that, and a great deal that is admirable. For once, the younger children can watch a movie where they have a good chance of understanding everything that happens and everything that's said. The new generation of mainstream animation has so many in-jokes that even the editors of *People* magazine miss some of them. How many of the preschoolers watching *Shark Tale* realized that Sykes was named after a Charles Dickens character and looked like Martin Scorsese?

On the *Ebert & Roeper* TV show, Roeper and I technically disagreed about *Curious George,* even though our opinions of the movie were approximately the same. He voted thumbs down because it was aimed at children. I voted thumbs up because it was aimed at children. We agreed it was not going to be an ecstatic viewing experience for parents.

In theory, I should have voted against it. The critic must recommend what he or she enjoys, not what some hypothetical audience will enjoy. Critics who say, "This is sure to be enjoyed by teenagers," when they are not teenagers are dummies, and the audience is the ventriloquist. Some of my colleagues say their editors require them to recommend movies on the basis of the tastes of the readers. An editor who does that is instructing the critic in falsehood and incompetence.

Having said that, and since I am not a child, how can I ethically recommend *Curious George* as a movie for children? I will quote Walt Whitman: "Do I contradict myself? Very well, then I contradict myself. I am large, I contain multitudes." I have no idea what teenagers think, but I know what four-year-olds think because I was one, an expert one, and I believe that up to a certain age all children enjoy more or less the same things: bright colors, vivid drawings, encouraging music, a plot that is exciting but not too scary, and a character they can identify with. This character should have an older friend who guides him through neat adventures and keeps things from getting too scary. If that doesn't describe what you liked when you were three or four, then I blame your parents, Mr. and Mrs. Chainsaw.

George the monkey is easy for any kid to identify with. They have so much in common. George cannot make himself understood, he is driven here and there in mechanical vehicles without his consent, adults talk about things he does not understand, and sometimes it's just not fair how he's treated. Then he meets the Man in the Yellow Hat (the movie reveals that the man's name is Ted). Ted (voice by Will Ferrell) makes friends with him, and because he is alone in the world, George stows away on Ted's ship and ends up in New York, where Ted is trying to save a museum. This undertaking requires Ted and George to fly above the city while holding on to a big bunch of balloons. Meanwhile, Ted has a girlfriend named Maggie (Drew Barrymore), but that's fine with George, because it means he gets another friend.

I am not sure Ted saves the museum in any meaningful way (it becomes a gallery of virtual-reality experiences), but George has a lot of fun and gets to paint lots of surfaces with bright primary colors, which passes the time pleasantly. There are songs sung by Jack Johnson, which are pleasant if kind of innocuous. The movie is faithful to the spirit and innocence of the books, and director Matthew O'Callaghan and his team create a visual look that is uncluttered, charming, and not so realistic that it undermines the fantasies on the screen.

Is this a movie for the whole family to attend? No, it is a movie for small children and their parents or adult guardians, who will take them because they love them very much. Even if they love them very much, they will have to be very, very patient, so maybe waiting for the DVD is a good idea, except then, of course, you will have to experience it over and over and over and over and over again.

D

Danny Deckchair ★ ★
PG-13, 100 m., 2004

Rhys Ifans (Danny Morgan), Miranda Otto (Glenda Lake), Justine Clarke (Trudy Dunphy), Rhys Muldoon (Sandy Upman). Directed by Jeff Balsmeyer and produced by Andrew Mason. Screenplay by Balsmeyer.

You don't have to be a bigwig to be a somebody.
— Danny

There really was a Danny Deckchair. His name was Larry Walters, and the Web site snopes.com reports that on July 2, 1982, he "filled 45 weather balloons with helium and tethered them in four tiers to an aluminum lawn chair he purchased at Sears for $110, loading his makeshift aircraft with a large bottle of soda, milk jugs full of water for ballast, a pellet gun, a portable CB radio, an altimeter and a camera." The pellet gun was to shoot at balloons when he wanted to come down. That worked fine until he dropped the gun.

His flight was all too successful, the site says; he was seen by commercial airline pilots at 16,000 feet above Long Beach, California, was a guest of the Carson and Letterman shows, received an award from the Bonehead Club of Dallas, and was fined by the FAA for, among other transgressions, "operating a civil aircraft for which there is not currently in effect an air-worthiness certificate."

Danny Deckchair is a splendid movie while its hero is preparing for his flight and actually experiencing it, but it's not nearly as interesting once he descends to Earth. The hero is Danny Morgan, played by Rhys Ifans, that guy you see in a lot of movies and you always think, "I've seen that guy in a lot of movies." Ifans is a splendid actor in both serious and comic roles, but once he lands after his flight, the movie provides him with a role neither serious nor comic but, I fear, uplifting.

Danny is unhappily married to a Realtor named Trudy (Justine Clarke), who doesn't understand him, as indeed who could. He makes his escape from his backyard, lands in a small town, and more or less falls in love with Glenda, the town cop (Miranda Otto). Although his flight and disappearance have received national publicity, no one in the small town watches TV or reads the papers, I guess, and so they buy his story that he's Glenda's former teacher. Soon he's been promoted to the town's wise guru, this being one of those movie towns where the citizens have nothing better to do than congregate for speeches at which Danny informs them of truths like the one that prefaces this review.

Every single shred of the movie's plot after Danny ends his flight is unnecessary, contrived, unlikely, or simply not interesting. Even when a man has done an amazing thing, that doesn't make him an authority on anything except his amazing thing, if that. Here is a man who knows more than anyone alive about manned flight using a lawn chair and helium balloons, and that is the one thing he never gets to talk about.

The movie is sweet enough in its barmy way, partly because of the charm of Ifans and Otto, partly because the writer-director, Jeff Balsmeyer, must have a certain hopefulness about things. To have made this movie at all probably shows he has a good heart; it is not the work of a cynic. But if only the people in that small town had known Danny Deckchair's real identity, the movie might have been rescued from smarminess. It is human nature to believe whatever an expert tells you if the expert has descended from the clouds, but it is prudent to determine whether you're dealing with a "deus ex machina" or only a "doofus ex deckchair."

Dark Water ★ ★ ★
PG-13, 120 m., 2005

Jennifer Connelly (Dahlia Williams), Ariel Gade (Cecilia Williams), Dougray Scott (Kyle), Pete Postlethwaite (Veeck), Tim Roth (Jeff Platzer), John C. Reilly (Mr. Murray), Perla Haney-Jardine (Natasha), Camryn Manheim (Mrs. Finkle). Directed by Walter Salles and produced by Doug Davison, Roy Lee, and Bill Mechanic. Screenplay by Rafael Yglesias, based on the film by Hideo Nakata.

Art Buchwald said the plot of *Last Tango in Paris* could be understood as the story of what people were willing to do to get an apartment in Paris. *Dark Water,* a new horror film starring Jennifer Connelly, suggests that in New York, people not only are willing to kill for an affordable apartment but may have to die, too. The movie is a remake of a 2002 thriller by the Japanese horror specialist Hideo Nakata, whose work also inspired the *Ring* pictures.

As *Dark Water* opens, Dahlia Williams (Connelly) is splitting up with her husband, Kyle (Dougray Scott), and needs to find a new home for herself and her daughter, Ceci (Ariel Gade). Her search takes her to Roosevelt Island, where a real estate agent named Murray (John C. Reilly) cheerfully shows them a flat that could be the New York pied-à-terre of the Amityville Horror.

The entrance hall is dark and dank. The superintendent (Pete Postlethwaite) lurks in his cubicle like a poisonous toad. The elevator seems programmed to devour little girls or their mothers. The rooms are dark and dank. Murray talks optimistically about a new coat of paint, and when he fails to find the second bedroom, he instantly redefines the living room as "dual-use." Little Ceci, who thinks the building is "yucky," is right on the money.

Still, the rent is right, and Dahlia is desperate. She takes the apartment, violating the ancient tradition that movie characters always live in apartments they could never afford in real life. She can afford this one. It's just that, well, that stain in the ceiling seems sort of malevolent and alive, as if it were eating up the apartment and will eat them, too. And a trip upstairs reveals unspeakable horrors.

What went on in this building? Who is the imaginary friend Ceci seems to have made? Her mother has fears of abandonment from her own childhood, and we wonder if she will allow her child to be endangered. Here is a world with few friendly faces: Reilly as the real estate agent would praise a death chamber for its square footage, Postlethwaite as the super seems to be harboring alien parasites in his eyebrows, and Dahlia's lawyer is played by Tim Roth, which is all you need to know.

Dark Water is the first film in English by Walter Salles (*Central Station, The Motorcycle Diaries*), and he has a dark visual style that matches the building's pulsing gloominess. Like other recent horror directors, he is intrigued by the challenges of bathtubs and shower stalls, and the ways in which people can be trapped in them and drown, and the tendency of tap water to turn the color of blood, or Pennzoil. He is also aware of the possibilities in scenes where heedless children defy instructions and wander off on their own.

I have been criticized recently for giving a pass to films of moderate achievement because they accomplish what the audience expects, while penalizing more ambitious films for falling short of greater expectations. There may be some truth in such observations, but on the other hand, nobody in the real world goes to every movie with the same kind of anticipation. If I see a film by Ingmar Bergman, as I recently did, I expect it to be a masterpiece, and if it is not, Bergman has disappointed me. If I attend a horror film in which Connelly and her daughter are trapped in the evil web of a malevolent apartment building, I do not expect Bergman; if the movie does what it can do as well as it can be done, then it has achieved perfection within its own terms.

The Bergman film (*Saraband*) was a masterpiece. *Dark Water* achieves some, but not all, of what we might hope for. It is not *Rosemary's Baby.* The acting is effective, the supporting roles are performed with relish by the skilled technicians Postlethwaite, Reilly, and Roth, and the cinematographer, Affonso Beato, succeeds in making the stain on the ceiling look like an evil vastation and not just a leaky sink. The climax is certainly over the top, and we're never quite sure how all the parts of the mystery fit together, but, then, the movie is about the horror of the mystery, not about its solution. Most important, I cared about the Jennifer Connelly character; she is not a horror heroine, but an actress playing a mother faced with horror. There is a difference, and because of that difference, *Dark Water* works.

Dave Chappelle's Block Party ★ ★ ★

R, 100 m., 2006

Featuring Dave Chappelle, Mos Def, Erykah Badu, Lauryn Hill, Kanye West, Talib Kweli, Dead Prez, Jill Scott, the Roots, the Fugees, and Bilal. Directed by Michel Gondry and produced by Bob Yari, Dave Chappelle, and Gondry. Screenplay by Chappelle.

Dave Chappelle's Block Party is a fairly disorganized film about a fairly disorganized concert, redeemed by the good feeling that Chappelle sheds like a sunbeam on every scene. I came away from the movie with three observations: 1) I find a lot of rap nihilistic and negative, but the musicians featured here seemed accessible and positive. 2) Nevertheless, I was pathetically grateful when Lauryn Hill and the Fugees sang "Killing Me Softly with His Song" and when many of the others sang what used to be called songs. Thank God for melody. 3) Chappelle appears to be a nice man, in addition to being a funny one, and the buried message in this movie may be: "Can I sign a $50 million contract and still remain the person I am happy to be?"

The movie is a documentary about Chappelle's sudden inspiration to hold a rap and comedy concert at a free block party in Brooklyn. The location would be kept secret to avoid a mob scene, and the audience would include people from the block and others who were bused in. And by bused in, I mean from Dayton, Ohio, which is about twenty miles from Yellow Springs, where Chappelle lives. The film opens with him handing out tickets good for a bus ride, a hotel room, food, and admission to the concert. He offers them to the nice lady who runs the shop where he buys his cigarettes, and to a couple of young men on the street, and to a man who says he is too deaf to hear the music, and then, in an expansive mood, he invites the entire Central State College marching band. (The two young men from Ohio stand on a rooftop and say now they really feel they're in New York, because in the movies everybody is always standing on rooftops.)

That some of the lucky ticket winners are white and even middle-aged is part of the point: He wants them to come to a rap concert in Brooklyn, and he wants it to be a rap concert where everybody will feel at home. In this connection the musicians do not reflect a gangsta image, they use lyrics that are not particularly hostile or angry, and they employ the n-word, the f-word, and the mf-word only about every twenty words, instead of every fifth word.

On the stage is an all-star cast, including Mos Def, Erykah Badu, Kanye West, Talib Kweli, Dead Prez, Jill Scott, the Roots, Bilal, and Lauryn Hill with the reunited Fugees. If I told you I knew who all of them were, I'd be lying. The women (Badu, Scott, Hill) seem to please the crowd more than the men, maybe because their material leans more toward jazz and R&B. Mos Def is a surprise because a day earlier I'd seen him costarring with Bruce Willis in *16 Blocks*, a movie where his character talks incessantly in a high-pitched screech; on stage with Dave, he's got an entirely different personality, a different voice even, and seems cool, authoritative, likable. Kanye West you know about, and he wears his superstardom lightly.

There is an audience for rap and, let's face it, I am not a member of that audience. That's why I was surprised to enjoy so many of the performances in the film. Not that I am likely to become a convert. As I write this, I'm listening to the Dianne Reeves sound track album from *Good Night, and Good Luck,* and it is wonderful. Not that you are likely to become a convert. Maybe we can meet in the middle.

The concert doesn't exactly proceed like clockwork, and it doesn't help (or hurt much) that it rains. Chappelle is onstage most of the time, does a lot of spontaneous comedy, makes the crowd feel good. There is a lot of backstage footage of Chappelle talking about how the concert will go, how it is going, and how it went. He has a theory about musicians and comedians: All comedians wish they were musicians, and all musicians think they are funny. "I'm mediocre at both," he says, "but have managed to talk my way into a fortune."

It's that fortune that seems to be the problem. The concert was held on Sept. 18, 2004. It was on Aug. 3, 2004, that Chappelle signed his infamous $50 million contract with Comedy Central. In this movie, long before his "disappearance" and his confessional with Oprah, you can see those millions nagging at him. His block party seems like an apology or an amends for the $50 million, an effort to reach out to people, to protect his ability to walk down the street like an ordinary man.

Having watched Chappelle on his show, on Oprah, and now in this movie, filmed at the dawn of his life as the $50 Million Man, I get a sense of how he feels. There is something about a $50 million contract that feels wrong to him, that threatens to build a wall between his personality and the way he likes to use it. His Comedy Central show is (was?) so funny because he worked without a net. He was willing to try anything. He didn't obsess about whether it worked. Here he makes some ominous comments about executives and you intuit he's saying that the *Dave Chappelle Show* will never work if anyone other than Dave Chappelle has a license to provide input.

As for the movie, I've seen better comedy films and better concert films. It noodles around too much and gets distracted from the music. Michel Gondry, who directed, makes good fiction films (*Eternal Sunshine of the Spotless Mind*) but is not an instinctive documentarian and forgets that even a fly on the wall should occasionally find some peanut butter. As the record of a state of mind, however, the film is uncanny.

The Da Vinci Code ★ ★ ★
PG-13, 148 m., 2006

Tom Hanks (Robert Langdon), Audrey Tautou (Sophie Neveu), Ian McKellen (Sir Leigh Teabing), Alfred Molina (Manuel Aringarosa), Jean Reno (Bezu Fache), Paul Bettany (Silas), Jurgen Prochnow (Andre Vernet), Jean-Pierre Marielle (Jacques Sauniere). Directed by Ron Howard and produced by John Calley and Brian Grazer. Screenplay by Akiva Goldsman, based on the novel by Dan Brown.

They say *The Da Vinci Code* has sold more copies than any book since the Bible. Good thing it has a different ending. Dan Brown's novel is utterly preposterous; Ron Howard's movie is preposterously entertaining. Both contain accusations against the Catholic Church and its order of Opus Dei that would be scandalous, if anyone of sound mind could possibly entertain them. I know there are people who believe Brown's fantasies about the Holy Grail, the descendants of Jesus, the Knights Templar, Opus Dei, and the true story of Mary Magdalene. This has the advantage of distracting them from the theory that the Pentagon was not hit by an airplane.

Let us begin, then, by agreeing that *The Da Vinci Code* is a work of fiction. And that since everyone has read the novel, I need only give away one secret—that the movie follows the book religiously. Although the book is a potboiler written with little grace or style, it does supply an intriguing plot. Luckily Ron Howard is a better filmmaker than Dan Brown is a novelist, and he follows Brown's formula (exotic location, startling revelation, desperate chase scene, repeat as needed) and elevates it into a superior entertainment, with Tom Hanks as a theo-intellectual Indiana Jones.

Hanks stars as Robert Langdon, a Harvard semiotician in Paris for a lecture when Inspector Fache (Jean Reno) informs him of the murder of the museum curator Jacques Sauniere (Jean-Pierre Marielle). This poor man has been shot and killed late at night inside the Louvre; his wounds, although mortal, fortunately leave him time enough to conceal a safe-deposit key, strip himself, cover his body with symbols written in his own blood, arrange his body in a pose and within a design by Da Vinci, and write out, also in blood, an encrypted message, a scrambled numerical sequence, and a footnote to Sophie Neveu (Audrey Tautou), the pretty French policewoman he raised after the death of her parents. Most people are content with a dying word or two; Jacques leaves us with a film treatment.

Having read the novel, we know what happens then. Sophie warns Robert he is in danger from Fache, and they elude capture in the Louvre and set off on a quest that leads them to the vault of a private bank, to the French villa of Sir Leigh Teabing (Ian McKellen), to the Temple Church in London, to an isolated Templar church in the British countryside, to a hidden crypt, and then back to the Louvre again. The police, both French and British, are one step behind them all this time, but Sophie and Robert are facile, inventive, and daring. Also, perhaps, they have God on their side.

This series of chases, discoveries, and escapes is intercut with another story, involving an albino named Silas (Paul Bettany), who works under the command of The Teacher, a mysterious figure at the center of a conspiracy to conceal the location of the Holy Grail, and what it really is, and what that implies. The conspiracy involves members of Opus Dei, a society of Catholics who in real life (I learn from a recent issue of the *Spectator*) are rather conventionally devout and prayerful. Although the movie describes their practices as "maso-chastity," not all of them are chaste and hardly any practice self-flagellation. In the months ahead, I would advise Opus Dei to carefully scrutinize membership applications.

Opus Dei works within but not with the church, which also harbors a secret cell of cardinals who are in on the conspiracy (the pope and most other Catholics apparently don't have backstage passes). These men keep a secret that, if known, could destroy the church. That's why they keep it. If I were their adviser, I would point out that by preserving the secret they preserve the threat to the church, and the wisest strategy would have been to destroy the secret, say, 1,000 years ago.

But one of the fascinations of the Catholic Church is that it is the oldest continuously surviving organization in the world, and that's why movies such as *The Da Vinci Code* are more fascinating than thrillers about religions founded, for example, by a science-fiction author in the 1950s. All the places in *The Da Vinci Code* really exist, although the last time I visited the Temple Church I was disappointed to find it closed for "repairs." A likely story.

Hanks, Tautou, and Reno do a good job of not overplaying their roles, and McKellen overplays his in just the right way, making Sir Leigh into a fanatic whose study just happens to contain all the materials for an audiovisual presentation that briefs his visitors on the secrets of Leonardo's *The Last Supper* and other matters. Apparently he keeps in close touch with other initiates. On the one hand, we have a conspiracy that lasts 2,000 years and threatens the very foundations of Christianity, and on the other hand a network of rich dilettantes who resemble a theological branch of the Baker Street Irregulars.

Yes, the plot is absurd, but then most movie plots are absurd. That's what we pay to see. What Howard brings to the material is tone and style, and an aura of mystery that is undeniable. He begins right at the top; the Columbia Pictures logo falls into shadow as Hans Zimmer's music sounds simultaneously liturgical and ominous. The murder scene in the Louvre is creepy in a ritualistic way, and it's clever the way Robert Langdon is able to look at letters, numbers, and symbols and mentally rearrange them to yield their secrets. He's like the Flora Cross character in *Bee Season*, who used Kabbalistic magic to visualize spelling words floating before her in the air.

The movie works; it's involving, is intriguing, and constantly seems on the edge of star-

tling revelations. After it's over and we're back on the street, we wonder why this crucial secret needed to be protected by the equivalent of a brain-twister puzzle crossed with a scavenger hunt. The trail that Robert and Sophie follow is so difficult and convoluted that it seems impossible that anyone, including them, could ever follow it. The secret needs to be protected up to a point; beyond that it is absolutely lost, and the whole point of protecting it is beside the point. Here's another question: Considering where the trail begins, isn't it sort of curious where it leads? Still, as T. S. Eliot wrote, "In my beginning is my end." Maybe he was onto something. ☞

Dawn of the Dead ★ ★ ★
R, 100 m., 2004

Sarah Polley (Ana), Ving Rhames (Kenneth), Jake Weber (Michael), Mekhi Phifer (Andre), Inna Korobkina (Luda), Michael Kelly (CJ). Directed by Zack Snyder and produced by Marc Abraham, Eric Newman, and Richard P. Rubinstein. Screenplay by James Gunn, based on the original by George A. Romero.

The contrast between this new version of *Dawn of the Dead* and the 1979 George Romero original is instructive in the ways that Hollywood has grown more skillful and less daring over the years. From a technical point of view, the new *Dawn* is slicker and more polished, and the acting is better, too. But it lacks the mordant humor of the Romero version, and although both films are mostly set inside a shopping mall, only Romero uses that as an occasion for satirical jabs at a consumer society. The 1979 film dug deeper in another way, by showing two groups of healthy humans fighting each other; the new version draws a line between the healthy and the zombies and maintains it. Since the zombies cannot be blamed for their behavior, there is no real conflict between good and evil in Zack Snyder's new version; just humans fighting ghouls. The conflict between the two healthy groups in the Romero film does have a pale shadow in the new one; a hard-nosed security guard (Michael Kelly) likes to wave his gun and order people around, and is set up as the bad guy, but his character undergoes an inexplicable change just for the convenience of the plot.

All of which is not to say that the new *Dawn of the Dead* doesn't do an efficient job of delivering the goods. The screenplay, credited to James Gunn (based on Romero's original screenplay), has been coproduced by Richard P. Rubinstein, who produced the original. They use the same premise: An unexplained disease or virus, spread by human bites, kills its victims and then resurrects them as zombies. The creatures then run berserk, attacking healthy humans, infecting them, and so on. The only way to kill them is to shoot them in the head. True to the general speed-up in modern Hollywood, these new-issue zombies run fast, unlike the earlier ones, who lurched along. They also seem smarter and make decisions faster, unlike the 1979 models, who were likely to lurch up the down escalator.

The story begins with Ana (Sarah Polley) greeting a young girl who lives in the neighborhood. As the girl skates away on her in-lines, the shot is held just a little longer than seems natural, informing us that Something Bad Will Happen to Her. And does, as the next morning she attacks Ana's boyfriend, and Ana barely escapes with her life. After zombies roam the streets, newscasters fight hysteria, and neighborhoods burn, Ana eventually finds herself part of a small group in the local shopping mall.

Well, not such a small group. Unlike the tight little group of survivors in *28 Days Later,* this one expands to the point where we don't much care about some of the characters (the blond with the red lipstick, for example). But we do care about Kenneth (Ving Rhames), a gravel-voiced cop with hard-edged authority. We care about Michael (Jake Weber), a decent guy who tries to make the right decisions. And we care about Andre (Mekhi Phifer), whose wife, Luda (Inna Korobkina), is great with child and will give birth at any moment; the way that plot plays out is touching and horrifying. We even work up some feeling for the guy marooned on the roof of the gun shop across the street, who communicates with Kenneth by holding up signs.

For the rest, the movie consists mostly of dialogue and character scenes, alternating with violent attacks by zombies. The movie wisely doesn't give us too many of those scenes where one guy wanders off by himself when we're mentally screaming, "Stick together!" And although there is a cute dog, at least it's made useful in the plot. Of course, the movie makes full

use of the shock shot where a zombie suddenly appears in the foreground from out of nowhere.

Of gore and blood there is a sufficiency. When the survivors devise a risky way to escape from the mall (which I will not reveal), a chain saw plays a key role. The survivors take chances that are probably unwise; maybe they should stay in a safe place, since the zombies will presumably sooner or later run out of gas. But taking chances makes for good action scenes, and exploding propane is always useful.

So, yes, *Dawn of the Dead* works, and it delivers just about what you expect when you buy your ticket. My only complaint is that its plot flat-lines compared to the 1979 version, which was trickier, wittier, and smarter. Romero was not above finding parallels between zombies and mall shoppers; in the new version, the mall is just a useful location, although at least there are still a few jokes about the Muzak.

The Day After Tomorrow ★ ★ ★
PG-13, 124 m., 2004

Dennis Quaid (Jack Hall), Jake Gyllenhaal (Sam Hall), Ian Holm (Terry Rapson), Emmy Rossum (Laura Chapman), Sela Ward (Dr. Lucy Hall), Dash Mihok (Jason Evans), Kenneth Welsh (Vice President Becker), Jay O. Sanders (Frank Harris), Austin Nichols (J.D.), Perry King (President), Arjay Smith (Brian Parks). Directed by Roland Emmerich and produced by Emmerich and Mark Gordon. Screenplay by Emmerich and Jeffrey Nachmanoff.

It is such a relief to hear the music swell up at the end of a Roland Emmerich movie, its restorative power giving us new hope. Billions of people may have died, but at least the major characters have survived. Los Angeles was wiped out by flying saucers in Emmerich's *Independence Day,* New York was assaulted in his *Godzilla,* and now, in *The Day After Tomorrow,* Emmerich outdoes himself: Los Angeles is leveled by multiple tornadoes, New York is buried under ice and snow, the United Kingdom is flash-frozen, and lots of the Northern Hemisphere is wiped out for good measure. Thank God that Jack, Sam, Laura, Jason, and Dr. Lucy Hall survive, along with Dr. Hall's little cancer patient.

So, yes, the movie is profoundly silly. What surprised me is that it's also very scary. The special effects are on such an awesome scale that the movie works in spite of its cornball plotting. When tornadoes rip apart Los Angeles (not sparing the Hollywood sign), when a wall of water roars into New York, when a Russian tanker floats down a Manhattan street, when snow buries skyscrapers, when the crew of a space station can see nothing but violent storm systems—well, you pay attention.

No doubt some readers are already angry with me for revealing that Jack, Sam, Laura, Jason, Dr. Lucy Hall, and the little cancer patient survive. Have I given away the plot? This plot gives itself away. When cataclysmic events shred uncounted lives but the movie zeroes in on only a few people, of *course* they survive, although some supporting characters may have to be sacrificed. What's amusing in movies like *The Day After Tomorrow* is the way the screenplay veers from the annihilation of subcontinents to whether Sam should tell Laura he loves her.

The movie stars Dennis Quaid as the paleoclimatologist Jack Hall, whose computer models predict that global warming will lead to a new ice age. He issues a warning at a New Delhi conference, but is sarcastically dismissed by the American vice president (Kenneth Welsh), whom the movie doesn't even try to pretend doesn't look just like Dick Cheney. "Our economy is every bit as fragile as the environment," the vice president says, dismissing Jack's "sensational claims."

Before long, however, it is snowing in India, and hailstones the size of softballs are ripping into Tokyo. Birds, which are always wise in matters of global disaster, fly south double-time. Turbulence tears airplanes from the sky. The president (Perry King) learns the FAA wants to ground all flights, and asks the vice president, "What do you think we should do?"

Meanwhile, young Sam Hall (Jake Gyllenhaal) goes to New York with an academic decathlon team, which includes Laura (Emmy Rossum of *Mystic River*) and Brian (Arjay Smith). They're stranded there. Ominous portents abound and Jack finally gets his message through to the administration ("This time," says a friend within the White House, "it will be different. You've got to brief the president directly.")

Jack draws a slash across a map of the United States and writes off everybody north of it. He issues a warning that supercooled air will kill anybody exposed to it, advises those in its path to stay inside, and then ... well, then he sets off to walk from Washington to New York to get to his son. Two of his buddies, also veterans of Arctic treks, come along.

We are wondering (a) why walk to New York when his expertise is desperately needed to save millions, (b) won't his son be either dead or alive whether or not he makes the trek? And (c) how quickly *can* you walk from Washington to New York over ice sheets and through a howling blizzard? As nearly as I can calculate, this movie believes it can be done in two nights and most of three days. Oh, I forgot; they drive part of the way, on highways that are gridlocked and buried in snow, except for where they're driving. How they get gas is not discussed in any detail.

As for the answer to (a), anyone familiar with the formula will know it is because he Feels Guilty About Neglecting His Son by spending all that time being a paleoclimatologist. It took him a lot of that time just to spell it. So okay, the human subplots are nonsense—all except for the quiet scenes anchored by Ian Holm, as a sad, wise Scottish meteorologist. Just like Peter O'Toole in *Troy*, Holm proves that a British-trained actor can walk into almost any scene and make it seem like it means something.

Quaid and Gyllenhaal and the small band of New York survivors do what can be done with impossible dialogue in an unlikely situation. And Dr. Lucy Hall (Sela Ward), Jack's wife and Sam's mother, struggles nobly in her subplot, which involves the little cancer patient named Peter. She stays by his side after the hospital is evacuated, calling for an ambulance, which we think is a tad optimistic, since Manhattan has been flooded up to about the eighth floor, the water has frozen, and it's snowing. But does the ambulance arrive? Here's another one for you: Remember those wolves that escaped from the zoo? Think we'll see them again?

Of the science in this movie I have no opinion. I am sure global warming is real, and I regret that the Bush administration rejected the Kyoto treaty, but I doubt that the cataclysm, if it comes, will come like this. It makes for a fun movie, though. Especially the parts where Americans become illegal immigrants in Mexico, and the vice president addresses the world via the Weather Channel. *The Day After Tomorrow* is ridiculous, yes, but sublimely ridiculous—and the special effects are stupendous.

Deadline ★ ★ ★

NO MPAA RATING, 93 m., 2004

A documentary directed by Katy Chevigny and Kirsten Johnson and produced by Dallas Brennan and Chevigny.

If there were one hundred condemned prisoners on death row and one of them was innocent, would it be defensible to kill all one hundred on the grounds that the other ninety-nine deserved to die? Most reasonable people would answer that it would be wrong. Yet evidence has been gathering for years that far more than 1 percent of the inhabitants of death row are innocent. In the Illinois penal system, for example, a study following twenty-five condemned men ended after twelve of them had been executed, and the other thirteen had been exonerated of their crimes after new evidence was produced.

Deadline is a sober, even low-key documentary about how the American death penalty system is broken and probably can't be fixed. It climaxes with the extraordinary January 2003 press conference at which Republican Governor George Ryan commuted the death sentences of all 167 prisoners awaiting execution in Illinois. His action followed a long, anguished, public process scrutinizing the death penalty in Illinois—a penalty here, as throughout the United States, administered overwhelmingly upon defendants who are poor and/or belong to minority groups.

The film opens with Ryan speaking to students at Northwestern University, where students in an investigative journalism class had been successful in proving the innocence of three men on death row. That was a tribute not only to their skills as student journalists but also to the ease with which the evidence against the prisoners could be disproved. Many thoughtful observations in the doc come from Scott Turow, the Chicago lawyer and crime novelist who was appointed by Ryan to a commission to consider clemency for Illinois's condemned. He is not against the death penalty itself, he says, and was completely comfortable with the execution of John Wayne Gacy, killer of thirty-three young men. "But can we construct a system that *only* executes the John Wayne Gacys, without executing the innocent?" Turow doubts it.

Murder cases have high profiles, and the police are under pressure for arrests and charges. They don't precisely frame innocent people, the movie argues, but when they find someone who looks like a plausible perpetrator they tend to zero in with high-pressure tactics, willing their prisoner to be guilty. Confessions were tortured out of some of the Illinois prisoners in *Deadline*, including one who was dangled out of a high window by his handcuffs, and another who signed a confession in English even though he could not speak it.

The death penalty was briefly outlawed by the U.S. Supreme Court in 1972, and then reinstated in 1976 after the justices were persuaded the system's flaws had been repaired. It was during that time, the movie says, that Richard M. Nixon "discovered crime as a national issue." Before then, it had been thought of as a local problem and did not enter into presidential campaigns. After Nixon's law-and-order rhetoric, politicians of both parties followed his lead. "All politicians want to be seen as tough on crime," observes Illinois GOP house leader Tom Cross.

Since 1976 there has been a startling rise in executions in America, one of the few Western countries that still allow the death penalty. The movie cites statistics for American prisoners put to death:

1976–1980: 3 executions.
1981–1990: 140 executions.
1991–2000: 540 executions.

That latest figure was enhanced by just one governor, George W. Bush of Texas; 152 prisoners were executed under his watch between 1995 and 2000, as Texas in five years outstripped the entire nation in the previous decade. In a speech, Bush says he is absolutely certain they were all guilty. For that matter, Bill Clinton must have known one of his Arkansas prisoners was so brain-damaged he asked the warden after his last meal, "Save my dessert so I can have it after the execution." But Clinton was running for president and dared not pardon this man, lest he be seen as soft on crime.

Some of the movie's most dramatic moments take place during hearings before Ryan's clemency commission, which reheard all 167 pending cases. The relatives of many victims say they will not be able to rest until the guilty have been put to death. But then we hear testimony from a group called Murder Victims' Families Against the Death Penalty. Among their witnesses are the father of a woman killed in the Oklahoma City terror attack, and the mother of the Chicago youth Emmett Till, murdered by southern racists fifty years ago. They say they do not want revenge and are opposed to the death penalty.

Deadline is all the more effective because it is calm, factual and unsensational. There are times when we are confused by its chronology and by how its story threads fit together, but it makes an irrefutable argument: Our criminal justice system is so flawed, especially when it deals with the poor and the nonwhite, that we cannot be sure of the guilt of many of those we put to death. George Ryan, not running for reelection, faced that truth and commuted those sentences, and said he could live with his decision. George Bush was absolutely confident he was right to allow 152 prisoners to die. He could live with his decision too.

The Deal ★ ★ ½
R, 107 m., 2005

Christian Slater (Tom Hanson), Selma Blair (Abbey Gallagher), Robert Loggia (Jared Tolson), John Heard (Professor Roseman), Colm Feore (Hank Weiss), Angie Harmon (Anna), Kevin Tighe (John Cortland), Françoise Yip (Janice Long). Directed by Harvey Kahn and produced by Chris Dorr, Ruth Epstein, Kahn, and Robert Lee. Screenplay by Epstein.

The Deal is a thriller about Wall Street insiders, set during an oil crisis a few years in the future. The United States is at war with the "Confederation of Arab States," gas is $6 a gallon and getting more expensive, and there's enormous pressure to find new sources for oil.

More than most thrillers, this one seems to be based on expert insights; its author, Ruth Epstein, wrote the screenplay against a background of Wall Street experience, and its view of boardroom politics has a convincing level of detail. It's not in every thriller that you hear someone say, "Oil is a fungible commodity." Christian Slater stars as Tom Hanson, an associate with an old-line Wall Street investment firm that has kept its reputation during

a period of corporate scandals. That's why the firm is attractive to the giant Condor Corp. and its sleek president, Jared Tolson (Robert Loggia, never scarier than when he smiles).

Condor wants to merge with Black Star, a privately held Russian oil company that controls massive oil reserves. We know from the start that the deal is fishy because at the top of the film a lawyer tells Tolson he can't continue to work on the deal; a few hours later the lawyer is shot dead. Hanson, the Slater character, is brought in as his replacement. His assignment: Perform due diligence to be sure Black Star is sound and the merger is in the best interests of Condor's shareholders.

The movie surrounds this main story line with several other intersecting strands, of which the most interesting involves young Abbey Gallagher (Selma Blair), a graduate student and "tree hugger" from Harvard who is recruited by Hanson to join his firm on the grounds that she can get a better hearing for her environmental concerns from inside the establishment.

Blair does specific things with her character that are interesting; she makes Abbey not one of those Harvard superhumans but a sincere, sometimes naive young woman who could use some social polish. Soon she is working with Hanson, and although they are indeed attracted to each other, romance is not the focus of this movie.

The Deal appreciates how big institutions like Slater's have factions and infighting; when he lands the Condor account, there's jealousy from Hank Weiss (a leaner, meaner Colm Feore), who is supposed to be the firm's oil expert.

There is also a middle-aged woman in research who knows all sorts of things that nobody ever asks her about: for example, that there is no oil in the "oil fields" controlled by Black Star. What's going on? "Oil may have been shipped from there," Hanson is told by a cryptic insider, "but I can't tell you where it came out of the ground."

The movie is a little too laden with details for its own good, and it has more characters than it needs, but sometimes that complexity works; like the hero, we're feeling our way through a maze of motives and possibilities, and although it's fairly clear who cannot be trusted, it's not always clear who can be. "He's my only friend at the firm," Hanson says of one associate, "and he'd stab me in the back in a second."

The pressure to close the deal is enormous; Hanson's firm alone expects to bank $25 million in commissions. But would it be worth it if Black Star were phony and Condor's shareholders were buying a worthless company? More to the point, what if Black Star is the front for an oil-laundering scheme?

Plots like this once seemed paranoid, but no one who has seen the documentary *Enron: The Smartest Guys in the Room* will find the lies and deceit in this film surprising. It expresses a system of moral values that keeps running into the discovery that "in the real world," as they say, "things don't work that way." The last scenes of the movie are deeply cynical and yet, we have a sinking feeling, not a million miles from the way Wall Street and the federal government actually do business.

There is of course always the Ethics Task Force, set up by the SEC and the FBI to guard against Wall Street fraud. One of the movie's continuing puzzles involves the possibility that several characters may be working undercover for the task force or Black Star. Secret information has a way of getting around, and the seriousness of the people behind the deal is made fairly clear when Hanson finds a bleeding heart in his refrigerator. "Not a human heart," the cops quickly reassure him.

I admire the film's anger and intelligence, and the generally persuasive level of the performances; Robert Loggia really seems like a CEO, and Selma Blair really seems like an idealistic college graduate. Françoise Yip, for that matter, seems like the sort of best corporate friend who always seems to know more than she should, and to be trying to tell you more than she can say.

But the problem is, *The Deal*, like a lot of real-life Wall Street deals, is a labyrinth into which the plot tends to disappear. The ideas in the film are challenging, the level of expertise is high, the performances are convincing, and it's only at the level of story construction and dramatic clarity that the film doesn't succeed. One more rewrite might have been a good idea. I can't quite recommend it purely as a film, but as a double feature with *Enron: The Smartest Guys in the Room*, it's a slam dunk.

Dear Frankie ★ ★ ★ ½
PG-13, 102 m., 2005

Emily Mortimer (Lizzie Morrison), Gerard Butler (The Stranger), Sharon Small (Marie), Jack McElhone (Frankie Morrison), Mary Riggans (Nell Morrison). Directed by Shona Auerbach and produced by Caroline Wood. Screenplay by Andrea Gibb.

There is a shot toward the end of *Dear Frankie* when a man and a woman stand on either side of a doorway and look at each other, just simply look at each other. During this time they say nothing, and yet everything they need to say is communicated: their doubts, cautions, hopes. The woman is named Lizzie (Emily Mortimer), and the man, known in the movie only as "The Stranger," is played by Gerard Butler. Here is how they meet.

Lizzie has fled from her abusive husband, and is raising her deaf son, Frankie (Jack McElhone) with the help of her mother (Mary Riggans). Instead of telling Frankie the truth about his father, Lizzie creates the fiction that he is away at sea—a crew member on a freighter named the *Accra*. Frankie writes to his dad, and his mother intercepts the letters and answers them herself. Frankie's letters are important to her "because it's the only way I can hear his voice."

The deception works until, one day, a ship named the *Accra* actually docks in Glasgow. Frankie assumes his father is on board, but a schoolmate bets his dad doesn't care enough to come and see him. After all, Frankie is nine and his father has never visited once.

Lizzie decides to find a man who will pretend, for one day, to be Frankie's father. Her friend Marie (Sharon Small), who runs the fish and chips shop downstairs, says she can supply a man, and introduces The Stranger, who Lizzie pays to pretend to be Frankie's dad for one day.

This sounds, I know, like the plot of a melodramatic tearjerker, but the filmmakers work close to the bone, finding emotional truth in hard, lonely lives. The missing father was brutal; Lizzie reveals to The Stranger, "Frankie wasn't born deaf. It was a gift from his dad." But Frankie has been shielded from this reality in his life and is a sunny, smart boy, who helps people deal with his deafness by acting in a gently funny way. When the kid at the next desk in school writes "Def Boy" on Frankie's desk, Frankie grins and corrects his spelling.

"Call me Davey," The Stranger says, since that is the name of Frankie's dad. So we will call him Davey, too. He is a man who reveals nothing about himself, who holds himself behind a wall of reserve, who makes the arrangement strictly business. We follow Frankie and his "dad" through a day that includes a soccer game, and the inevitable visit to an ice-cream shop. At the end of the day, Davey tells Lizzie and Frankie that his ship isn't sailing tomorrow after all—he'll be able to spend another day with his son. This wasn't part of the deal. But then Davey didn't guess how much he would grow to care about the boy, and his mother.

A movie like this is all in the details. The director, Shona Auerbach, and her writer, Andrea Gibb, see Lizzie, Frankie, and his grandmother not as archetypes in a formula, but as very particular, cautious, wounded people, living just a step above poverty, precariously shielding themselves from a violent past. The grandmother gives every sign of having grown up on the wrong side of town, a chain-smoker who moved in with her daughter "to make sure" she didn't go back to the husband.

Davey, or whatever his name is, comes into the picture as a man who wants to have his exit strategy nailed down. He insists money is his only motive. It is quietly impressive how the young actor Jack McElhone as Frankie understands the task of his character, which is to encourage this man to release his better nature. There is also the matter of how much Frankie knows, or intuits, about his father's long absence.

What eventually happens, while not entirely unpredictable, benefits from close observation, understated emotions, unspoken feelings, and the movie's tact; it doesn't require its characters to speak about their feelings simply so that we can hear them. That tact is embodied in the shot I started out by describing: Lizzie and The Stranger looking at each other.

"We shot several takes," Emily Mortimer told me after the film's premiere. "Shona knew it had to be long, but she didn't know how long, and she had to go into the edit and find out which length worked. She is a very brave director in that way, allowing space around the action."

Every once in a long while, a director and actors will discover, or rediscover, the dramatic power of silence and time. They are moving pictures, but that doesn't mean they always have to be moving. In Miranda July's *You and Me and Everyone We Know,* there is a scene where a man and a woman who don't really know each other walk down a sidewalk and engage in a kind of casual word play that leads to a defining moment in their lives. The scene is infinitely more effective than all the countless conventional ways of obtaining the same result. In the same way, the bold long shot near the end of *Dear Frankie* allows the film to move straight as an arrow toward its emotional truth, without a single word or plot manipulation to distract us. While they are looking at each other, we are looking at them, and for a breathless, true moment, we are all looking at exactly the same fact.

Dear Wendy ★ ½
NO MPAA RATING, 105 m., 2005

Jamie Bell (Dick), Bill Pullman (Krugsby), Mark Webber (Stevie), Alison Pill (Susan), Chris Owen (Huey), Michael Angarano (Freddie), Danso Gordon (Sebastian), Novella Nelson (Clarabelle). Directed by Thomas Vinterberg and produced by Sisse Graum Olsen. Screenplay by Lars von Trier.

Thomas Vinterberg's *Dear Wendy* is a tedious exercise in style, intended as a meditation on guns and violence in America but more of a meditation on itself, the kind of meditation that invites the mind to stray. Mine strayed to the fact that the screenplay is by Vinterberg's Danish mentor, Lars von Trier, and the movie, although filmed on three-dimensional sets, feels as artificial and staged as his *Dogville* (2003). Once again a small group of people inhabits a small space, can all see each other out the window, and lives in each other's pockets.

The movie is set in Electric Park, a set in which two rows of buildings face each other and a third row supplies the end of the street. Towering overhead is the elevator for the mine shaft; the locals were mostly miners, but the mines are nearly played out. Dick (Jamie Bell), the orphaned son of a miner, lives with his protective black housekeeper, Clarabelle

(Novella Nelson), and his life lacks purpose until he goes into a store to buy a toy gun. The weapon, as it happens, is real. Dick is a pacifist but falls in love with the gun, which he names Wendy. Much of the movie consists of a letter he writes to Wendy, about how he loved her and lost her, and how everything went wrong. He descends into an abandoned mine for target practice, finds he has a psychic bond with Wendy (he can hit a bull's-eye blindfolded), and soon enlists other people his age into a secret society named the Dandies.

They meet in the mine, which they redecorate as the "Temple," and begin to dress in oddments of haberdashery, like fools or clowns. They have the obligatory unlimited supply of candles. They take a vow of nonviolence. Then Clarabelle's grandson Sebastian (Danso Gordon) appears on the scene, fresh from jail. The local sheriff (Bill Pullman) suggests that Dick "could be like Sebastian's friend, and keep an eye on him."

Sebastian is black because he is Clarabelle's grandson, of course, but also because as the only young black man in the film he is made into the catalyst for violence. This is the Vinterberg/von Trier version of insight into America, roughly as profound as the scene in *Dirty Love* where Carmen Electra holds a gun to a man's head simply because she likes to act black and thinks that will help. To call such reasoning racist is tempting, and yet I suspect in both movies the real reasons for it are stupidity and cluelessness.

Right away there is trouble. A romantic triangle forms, as Sebastian holds Wendy tenderly and Dick gets jealous. Sebastian helpfully supplies all of the Dandies with guns, and then a challenge emerges: Clarabelle visits her granddaughter at the end of the street every year and has become afraid to leave the house. The Dandies devise an ingenious scheme to protect her from danger during her one-block walk, despite the fact that the town seems to contain no danger. I am reminded of a guy I knew who said he carried a gun because he lived in a dangerous neighborhood, and another guy told him, "It would be a lot safer if you moved."

What happens during Clarabelle's progress down the street I will leave for you to experience if you are unwise enough to see the film. As the Dandies plan their operation, Dick draws a diagram of the town that looks uncan-

nily like an aerial view of the chalk outlines on a soundstage floor that von Trier used to create Dogville. Odd, that the Dogma movement from Denmark, which originally seemed to call for the use of actual locations exactly as they were, has become more stylized and artificial than German Expressionism.

It is true that America has problems and that many of them are caused by a culture of guns and violence. It is also true that a movie like David Cronenberg's *A History of Violence* (or I could name countless others) is wiser and more useful on the subject than the dim conceit of *Dear Wendy*.

Apart from what the movie says, which is shallow and questionable, there is the problem of how it says it. The style is so labored and obvious that with all the goodwill in the world you cannot care what happens next. It is all just going through the motions, silly and pointless motions, with no depth, humor, edge, or timing. Vinterberg has made wonderful films, such as *The Celebration* (1998), filled with life and emotion. Here he seems drained of energy, plodding listlessly on the treadmill of style, racking up minutes on the clock but not getting anywhere.

The Death of Mr. Lazarescu ★ ★ ★ ★
R, 154 m., 2006

Ion Fiscuteanu (Mr. Lazarescu), Luminita Gheorghiu (Mioara Avram), Gabriel Spahiu (Leo), Doru Ana (Sandu Sterian), Dana Dogaru (Miki Sterian), Florin Zamfirescu (Dr. Ardelean), Mimi Branescu (Dr. Mirica). Directed by Cristi Puiu and produced by Alexandru Munteanu. Screenplay by Puiu and Razvan Radulescu.

It must be like this with many people, and not just in Romania. A smelly old drunk calls for an ambulance after having a headache for four days. The ambulance service asks him so many questions, he doubts they believe him, and he asks his neighbors for help. They stretch him out on a sofa, ask him how he feels, and complain about the stink of his cats. They call the ambulance again.

The Death of Mr. Lazarescu will follow this dying man for most of the night, as he gradually slips away from the world and the world little notices. The movie is not heartless, but it is matter-of-fact and makes no attempt to heighten the drama. In its relentless gaze at exactly what happens, it reminds me of the Dardenne brothers (*The Son, The Child*), whose films see everything but do not intervene.

Mr. Lazarescu (Ion Fiscuteanu) has long lived in his cluttered Bucharest apartment. He has a sister in a nearby town and a child in Canada, neither much concerned with him. He gives such information to his neighbors, while slowly drifting out of contact with reality. Then the ambulance arrives, with the attendant Mioara (Luminita Gheorghiu) and the driver Leo (Gabriel Spahiu). In the course of this night, they will take him to four hospitals. It is a long night and a long film, but not a slow one because we are drawn so deeply into it.

At hospitals, the obviously incompetent Mr. Lazarescu is asked to fill out forms, sign consents, and answer questions he does not understand. Each hospital suggests sending him to another one. He is nevertheless given a scan that reveals a blood clot on his brain, and a problem with his liver that "nobody," a doctor observes, "is going to be able to do anything about." One of the CT scan technicians almost rejoices: "These neoplasms are Discovery Channel stuff."

The film's focus is never on Mr. Lazarescu, who becomes disoriented and finally almost speechless, and who was probably not good company on his best days. It does not help that he wets himself during a CT scan, then soils his pants. We focus on the ambulance attendant, who is given one opportunity after another to dump her patient but stubbornly wants to be sure someone actually pays him attention. Her job is to take sick people to hospitals. If they are not admitted, her life is meaningless.

She is not portrayed as a heroine and indeed is passive in the face of sarcasm by a smart-ass resident who mocks her description of Mr. Lazarescu's problems. She knows that what he needs immediately is brain surgery to relieve the clot. One doctor who agrees with this diagnosis nevertheless insists on a signature of consent: "If I operate without his signature, I could go to jail." The doctor's solution is a perfect catch-22: "Drive him for a while until he's comatose and then bring him back."

At the fourth hospital, Mioara finds a doctor who is just ending her shift but wearily agrees to take the patient. And only then can Mioara

leave—and disappear from the film because we follow the dying body of Mr. Lazarescu through the hands of all these strangers who have only an immediate role in his final day. Even in the first three hospitals, he has continued to wear his ratty stocking cap and threadbare knit sweater. Now at last he is undressed and bathed, the nurses sponging him and shaving his head with quiet professionalism.

The film, directed and cowritten by Cristi Puiu, has been described as a criticism of the health services in Romania. At least in Romania he is not asked for his insurance company, and he has a theoretical right to free medical care. On Cinematical.com, a doctor posted this message: "As a Romanian physician, I would say it's worse than shown. The misery of Romanian hospitals is not shown at all. By the way, this is based on a true story of a man turned down at five Bucharest hospitals in 1997 and eventually left in the street by the paramedics and found dead next morning (the paramedic got fired)."

There is no need to fire Mioara and her driver, although in the film's final shot we wonder whether Mr. Lazarescu is still alive. I have undergone various medical adventures in recent years and have been moved by the unfailing competence and care of the doctors and nurses I have come into contact with; I admire them even more because I sense this movie is accurate about many hospitals everywhere, in which everyone is overworked, there are more problems than solutions, and the smelly, incoherent Mr. Lazarescu seems doomed no matter what is done. He is not a candidate for triage.

I keep thinking about Mioara. She is insulted by young residents whose experience is far less than hers. She carries Mr. Lazarescu's X-rays around with her from one set of uncaring eyes to another. She could get angry, but she has been on the job too long for that. They all have. Here are no *E.R.*-style interns calling for transfusions or racing down corridors with gurneys. In *The Death of Mr. Lazarescu,* the patient is another detail in an endless series of impossible situations and exhausting overnight shifts. If you start thinking of Lazarescu, of all the Lazarescus, as people who deserve your full concern and attention, you could go mad. Yes, the doctors and nurses chat about getting an espresso or using each other's cell phones. Life goes on.

There is a rule about the movies: Never take an expert to a movie about his or her specialty. *The Death of Mr. Lazarescu* is an exception. I suspect medical professionals would see much they recognize in this movie. The credits include a long list of technical advisers, but it doesn't take an adviser to convince you the movie is authentic. Like *United 93* and the work of the Dardenne brothers, it lives entirely in the moment, seeing what happens as it happens, drawing no conclusions, making no speeches, creating no artificial dramatic conflicts, just showing people living one moment after another, as they must.

Note: The man's full name is Dante Remus Lazarescu. Dante wrote of the circles of hell. Remus was a cofounder of ancient Rome, killed by his twin. "Lazarescu" reminds us of Lazarus, who was lucky enough to find someone who could raise him from the dead.

D.E.B.S. ★ ½
PG-13, 91 m., 2005

Sara Foster (Amy), Meagan Good (Max), Jill Ritchie (Janet), Devon Aoki (Dominique), Jordana Brewster (Lucy), Jessica Cauffiel (Ninotchka), Michael Clarke Duncan (Academy President), Holland Taylor (Mrs. Peatree). Directed by Angela Robinson and produced by Jasmine Kosovic and Andrea Sperling. Screenplay by Robinson.

At some point during the pitch meetings for *D.E.B.S.* someone must certainly have used the words "Charlie's Lesbians." The formula is perfectly obvious: Four sexy young women work for a secret agency as a team that is gifted at lying, cheating, stealing, and killing. How do we know they have these gifts? Because of the movie's funniest moment, during the opening narration, when we learn that trick questions on SAT exams allow an agency to select high school graduates who can and will lie, cheat, steal, kill.

Amy (Sara Foster), the leader of the group, is a latent lesbian. Lucy Diamond (Jordana Brewster), a thief and master criminal, goes on a blind date with a semi-retired Russian assassin named Ninotchka (Jessica Cauffiel). When the D.E.B.S. monitor the date on a surveillance assignment, Amy is attracted to the smiling, seductive Lucy, which causes security complications. Pause for a moment to ask with me, would this movie be as interesting if the blind date had been with a guy? I submit it would not, because the lesbian material is all that separates *D.E.B.S.* from the standard teenage Insta-Flick.

The character traits of the "D.E.B.S." are only slightly more useful than the color-coded uniforms of the Teenage Mutant Ninja Turtles. In such movies, taxonomy is personality; once you've got the label straight, you know all you're ever going to know about the character. In addition to Amy, who is a lesbian, we meet Max (Meagan Good), who is black, Janet (Jill Ritchie), who is white, and Dominique (Devon Aoki), who corners the market on character attributes by being an Asian with a French accent who smokes all the time. I would not identify the characters by race, but the movie leaves us with no other way to differentiate them.

Dominique's smoking fascinates me. She never lights a cigarette, extinguishes one, or taps an ash. She simply exists with a freshly lit filter tip in her mouth, occasionally removing it to emit a perky little puff of uninhaled smoke. I wish I had stayed through the credits to see if there was a cigarette wrangler. Dominique's very presence on the screen inspires me to imagine an excited pitch meeting during which the writer-director, Angela Robinson, said with enthusiasm: "And Dominique, the Asian chick, smokes all the time!" At which the studio executives no doubt thanked the gods for blessing them with such richness and originality in character formation.

I have mentioned the pitch more than once because this movie is all pitch. It began as a popular short subject at Sundance, where audiences were reportedly amused by a send-up of the *Charlie's Angels* formula in which the angels were teenagers and one was a lesbian. The problem is, a short subject need only delight while a feature must deliver.

At one point in *D.E.B.S.* a team member uses the term "supervillain," not ironically but descriptively, leading to a new rule for *Ebert's Little Movie Glossary*: "Movies that refer to supervillains not ironically but descriptively reveal an insufficient disconnect between the pitch and the story." The rule has countless subsets, such as characters referring to themselves or others as heroes. Best friends who say, "I'm only comic relief" are given a provisional pass.

The Charlie figure in the movie is the president of the D.E.B.S. Academy, played by Michael Clarke Duncan, who looks spiffy in a tailored suit and rimless glasses. He gives them their orders, while never asking himself, I guess, how goes the homeland security when bimbos are minding the front lines. For that matter, Lucy Diamond, whose middle name I hope is Intheskywith, would rather make love than war, which leads to some PG-13 smooching.

Mrs. Peatree (Holland Taylor), headmistress of the D.E.B.S. Academy, asks Amy to turn the situation to her advantage by using herself as bait ("like Jodie did in that movie—you know the one, what was its name?"). I confess at this point I was less interested in Jodie's filmography than in the news that the D.E.B.S. Academy has a headmistress. I found myself wanting to know more about the academy's school song, lunchroom menu, student council, and parents' day. ("Janet has perfect scores in lying and cheating, but needs work on her stealing, and is flunking murder.") The uniform is cute little plaid skirts and white blouses, with matching plaid ties.

Other notes: I think I heard correctly, but may not have, that one character's "Freudian analysis" is that she suffers from a "dangerous Jungian symbiosis." Now there's a Freudian analysis you don't hear every day. I know I heard correctly when two of the girls share their dream: "Let's pretend we're in Barcelona, and you're at art school and I'm renting boats to tourists." The young people today, send them on junior year abroad, they go nuts. I note in passing that the movie quotes accurately from the famous shot in *Citizen Kane* where the camera moves straight up past the catwalks, drops, ropes, and pulleys above a stage. For me, that shot was like the toy in a box of Cracker-Jacks: not worth much, but you're glad they put it in there.

De-Lovely ★ ★ ★ ½

PG-13, 125 m., 2004

Kevin Kline (Cole Porter), Ashley Judd (Linda Lee Porter), Jonathan Pryce (Gabe), Kevin MacNally (Gerald Murphy), Sandra Nelson (Sara Murphy), Allan Corduner (Monty Woolley), Peter Polycarpou (Louis B. Mayer), Keith Allen (Irving Berlin). Directed by Irwin Winkler and produced by Rob Cowan, Charles Winkler, and Irwin Winkler. Screenplay by Jay Cocks.

I wanted every kind of love that was available, but I could never find them in the same person, or the same sex.

—Cole Porter

Porter floated effortlessly for a time between worlds: gay and straight, Europe and America, Broadway and Hollywood, showbiz and high society. He had a lifelong love affair with his wife, and lifelong love affairs without his wife. He thrived, it seemed, on a lifestyle that would have destroyed other men (and was, in fact, illegal in most of the places that he lived), and all the time he wrote those magical songs. Then a horse fell down and crushed his legs, and he spent twenty-seven years in pain. And *still* he wrote those magical songs.

De-Lovely is a musical and a biography, and brings to both of those genres a worldly sophistication that is rare in the movies. (If you seek to find how rare, compare this film with *Night and Day*, the 1946 biopic that stars Cary Grant as a resolutely straight Porter, even sending him off to World War I). *De-Lovely* not only accepts Porter's complications, but bases the movie on them; his lyrics take on a tantalizing ambiguity once you understand that they are not necessarily written about love with a woman:

It's the wrong game, with the wrong chips
Though your lips are tempting, they're
    the wrong lips
They're not her lips, but they're such
    tempting lips
That, if some night, you're free
Then it's all right, yes, it's all right with me.

It would appear from *De-Lovely* that on many nights Porter was free, and yet Linda Lee Porter was the love and solace of his life, and she accepted him as he was. One night in Paris they put their cards on the table.

"You know then, that I have other interests," he says.

"Like men."

"Yes, men."

"You like them more than I do. Nothing is cruel if it fulfills your promise."

Dialogue like this requires a certain wistful detachment, and Kevin Kline is ideally cast as

Cole Porter: elegant, witty, always onstage, brave in the face of society and his own pain. Kline plays the piano, too, which allows the character to spend a lot of convincing time at the keyboard, writing the sound track of his life. But who might have known Ashley Judd would be so nuanced as Linda Lee? In those early scenes she lets Porter know she wants him and yet allows him his freedom, and she speaks with such tact that she is perfectly understood without really having said anything at all. Yet their relationship was by definition painful for her, because it was really all on his terms. Many of his lyrics are fair enough to reflect that from her point of view:

Every time we say goodbye, I die a little,
Every time we say goodbye, I wonder why
a little,
Why the gods above me, who must be in
the know.
Think so little of me, they allow you to go.

Cole and Linda met in Paris at that time in the twenties when expatriate Americans were creating a new kind of lifestyle. Scott and Zelda were there, too, and Hemingway, and the movie supplies as the Porters' best friends the famous American exile couple Sara and Gerald Murphy (the originals for Fitzgerald's *Tender Is the Night*). Porter was born with money, made piles more, and spent it fabulously, on parties in Venice and traveling in high style. Linda's sense of style suited his own: They always looked freshly pressed, always seemed at home, always had the last word, even if beneath the surface there was too much drinking and too many compromises. The chain smoking that eventually killed Linda was at first an expression of freedom, at the end perhaps a kind of defense.

The movie, directed by Irwin Winkler (*Life as a House*) and written by Jay Cocks (*The Age of Innocence*), is told as a series of flashbacks from a ghostly rehearsal for a stage musical based on Porter's life. Porter and a producer (Jonathan Pryce) sit in the theater, watching scenes run past, but the actors cannot see or hear Porter, and the producer may in a sense be a recording angel.

This structure allows the old, tired, widowed, wounded Porter to revisit the days of his joy, and at the same time explains the presence of many musical stars who appear, both on stage and in dramatic flashbacks, to perform Porter's songs. Porter has famously been interpreted by every modern pop singer of significance, most memorably by Ella Fitzgerald in *The Cole Porter Songbook*, but here we get a new generation trying on his lyrics: Elvis Costello, Alanis Morissette, Sheryl Crow, Natalie Cole, Robbie Williams, Diana Krall.

The movie contains more music than most musicals, yet is not a concert film because the songs seem to rise so naturally out of the material and illuminate it. We're reminded how exhilarating the classic American songbook is, and how inarticulate so much modern music sounds by contrast. Kevin Kline plays Porter as a man apparently able to write a perfect song more or less on demand, which would be preposterous if it were not more or less true. One of Porter's friends was Irving Berlin, who labored to bring forth his songs and must have given long thought to how easy it seemed for Porter.

If the film has a weakness, it is that neither Cole nor Linda ever found full, complete, passionate, satisfying romance. They couldn't find it with each other, almost by the terms of their arrangement, but there is no evidence that Porter found it in serial promiscuity, and although Linda Lee did have affairs, they are not made a significant part of this story. They were a good fit not because they were a great love story, but because they were able to provide each other consolation in its absence.

Strange, dear, but true, dear, he began a
song that confessed:
Even without you,
My arms fold about you,
You know, darling why,
So in love with you am I.

Derailed ★ ★ ½
R, 100 m., 2005

Clive Owen (Charles Schine), Jennifer Aniston (Lucinda Harris), Melissa George (Deanna Schine), Vincent Cassel (Philippe LaRouche), RZA (Winston Boyko), Xzibit (Dexter). Directed by Mikael Hafstrom and produced by Lorenzo di Bonaventura. Screenplay by Stuart Beattie, based on the novel by James Siegel.

Derailed cannot be about what it seems to be about, not with a title like *Derailed,* but the story works if you're willing to meet it halfway. Critics of thrillers are hard on the new ones, applying logic with a merciless zeal, but they cave in when the thriller is from the 1940s. Imagine this movie with Barbara Stanwyck and Fred MacMurray, and it would work for you. Better still, just rent *Double Indemnity* and the hell with it.

The movie stars Clive Owen as Charles, a man with a lot of problems on his mind. His beloved daughter has diabetes, and her third kidney transplant has just failed. He has been fired from his big account at work. When we meet him, he realizes his wife borrowed money from his billfold and he can't pay the fare on his commuter train. Luckily, the movie is set in Chicago, which means that a smart and sexy brunette with sheer stockings and high heels offers to pay for his ticket. That is so typically Chicago.

Certain spoilers follow. Others do not. The brunette is Lucinda (Jennifer Aniston). He senses an attraction between them. He wants to meet her again, allegedly to repay the train fare, more likely to tempt himself with her appeal. She smiles back. They exchange business cards. They meet for lunch. Lunch becomes dinner. Dinner becomes a hotel. Sex becomes a necessity, and then a brutal man with a French accent (Vincent Cassel) breaks into the room, knocks Charles almost unconscious, and rapes Lucinda.

Charles tells his wife, Deanna (Melissa George), that he worked late at the office and then was mugged. Deanna buys this story, I guess. She is one of the more trusting wives in movie history. But the nightmare is not over. The mugger, named Philippe, has Charles's name and phone number. He guesses, correctly, that Charles and Lucinda did not call the police (she's married, too). He has blackmail in mind.

Charles luckily has an African-American friend at the ad agency where he works. This is Winston Boyko, played (and played well) by the rap artist RZA. As all white executives know (as, indeed, all executives of every race know), when you are in trouble and need to step outside the borders of the law, there's always a black guy in the mail room whom you can count on. This guy is always smarter and more experienced in the ways of the real world than any mere executive could ever hope to be. Winston knows how Philippe's mind works. He becomes Charles's adviser and dirty-work expert, charging only 10 percent of Philippe's extortion demand, which is

kind of a finder's fee in reverse, for making sure Philippe gets lost.

More than that I will not reveal. Let me say that I was intrigued by the performances. Owen was my candidate for James Bond and can play hard and heartless rotters (see *Closer*), but here he is quiet and sad, with a sort of passivity. He lets his face relax into acceptance of his own bad fortune. Aniston does that interesting thing of not being a stereotyped sexpot but being irresistibly intriguing. That works with a man like Charles. Happily married, in debt, worried about his daughter and his job, he would be impervious to a sexy slut.

What gets him is that Lucinda has problems, too, and a sense of humor, and seems as reluctant as he is to have an affair. It's just that, well, they talk so easily together. She listens, she cares. How desperately this man needs someone to confide in, outside the world of his problems. By the time it gets around to sex, it isn't exactly sex anymore, it's more like a physical expression of the sympathy they have for each other. These are difficult notes to play, but Aniston and Owen form a little emotional duet that doesn't even need sheet music. Maybe you will approve of how the plot unfolds, or maybe not. Remember with *Unfaithful*, how you didn't know if you felt bad when Diane Lane cheated on Richard Gere, or were happy for her? Of course a lot depended on Gere not finding out.

I think probably in the last analysis, *Derailed* doesn't hold up. At the end we want more, or less, or different. But you didn't have a lousy vacation just because it rained for the last two days.

Derailed has a great setup, a good middle passage, and some convincing performances. Then it runs off the tracks. If you're an unforgiving logician, you'll be offended. If you like movies even when you know where they're going and you've been there before, *Derailed* may work for you. It depends on how willing you are to go along with it.

Deuce Bigalow: European Gigolo
no stars
R, 75 m., 2005

Rob Schneider (Deuce Bigalow), Eddie Griffin (T.J. Hicks), Til Schweiger (Heinz Hummer),

Jeroen Krabbe (Gaspar Voorsboch), Hanna Verboom (Eva Voorsboch). Directed by Mike Bigelow and produced by Jack Giarraputo, Adam Sandler, and John Schneider. Screenplay by Rob Schneider, David Garrett, and Jason Ward.

Deuce Bigalow: European Gigolo makes a living cleaning fish tanks and occasionally prostituting himself. How much he charges, I'm not sure, but the price is worth it if it keeps him off the streets and out of another movie. *Deuce Bigalow* is aggressively bad, as if it wants to cause suffering to the audience. The best thing about it is that it runs for only seventy-five minutes.

Rob Schneider is back, playing a male prostitute (or, as the movie reminds us dozens of times, a "man-whore"). He is not a gay hustler but specializes in pleasuring women, although the movie's closest thing to a sex scene is when he wears diapers on orders from a giantess. Oh, and he goes to dinner with a woman with a laryngectomy who sprays wine on him through her neck vent.

The plot: Deuce visits his friend T.J. Hicks (Eddie Griffin) in Amsterdam, where T.J. is a pimp specializing in man-whores. Business is bad because a serial killer is murdering male prostitutes, and so Deuce acts as a decoy to entrap the killer. In his investigation, he encounters a woman with a penis for a nose. You don't want to know what happens when she sneezes.

Does this sound like a movie you want to see? It sounds to me like a movie that Columbia Pictures and the film's producers (Jack Giarraputo, Adam Sandler, and John Schneider) should be discussing in long, sad conversations with their inner child.

The movie created a spot of controversy last February. According to a story by Larry Carroll of MTV News, Rob Schneider took offense when Patrick Goldstein of the *Los Angeles Times* listed this year's Best Picture nominees and wrote that they were "ignored, unloved, and turned down flat by most of the same studios that . . . bankroll hundreds of sequels, including a follow-up to *Deuce Bigalow: Male Gigolo,* a film that was sadly overlooked at Oscar time because apparently nobody had the foresight to invent a category for Best Running Penis Joke Delivered by a Third-Rate Comic."

Schneider retaliated by attacking Goldstein in full-page ads in *Daily Variety* and the *Hollywood Reporter.* In an open letter to Goldstein, Schneider wrote: "Well, Mr. Goldstein, I decided to do some research to find out what awards you have won. I went online and found that you have won nothing. Absolutely nothing. No journalistic awards of any kind. . . . Maybe you didn't win a Pulitzer Prize because they haven't invented a category for Best Third-Rate, Unfunny Pompous Reporter Who's Never Been Acknowledged by His Peers."

Reading this, I was about to observe that Schneider can dish it out, but he can't take it. Then I found he's not so good at dishing it out, either. I went online and found that Goldstein has won a National Headliner Award, a Los Angeles Press Club Award, a RockCritics.com award, and the Publicists' Guild award for lifetime achievement.

Schneider was nominated for a 2000 Razzie Award for Worst Supporting Actor but lost to Jar-Jar Binks. But Schneider is correct, and Goldstein has not yet won a Pulitzer Prize. Therefore, Goldstein is not qualified to complain that Columbia financed *Deuce Bigalow: European Gigolo* while passing on the opportunity to participate in *Million Dollar Baby, Ray, The Aviator, Sideways,* and *Finding Neverland.* As chance would have it, I *have* won the Pulitzer Prize, and so I am qualified. Speaking in my official capacity as a Pulitzer Prize winner, Mr. Schneider, your movie sucks. ☞

The Devil and Daniel Johnston ★ ★ ★
PG-13, 110 m., 2006

Featuring Daniel Johnston, Louis Black, Bill Johnston, Mabel Johnston, Jeff Tartakov, Kathy McCarty, Gibby Haynes, and Jad Fair. A documentary written and directed by Jeff Feuerzeig and produced by Henry S. Rosenthal.

The Devil and Daniel Johnston opens with Johnston being introduced at a folk club in Austin, Texas, as "the greatest singer-songwriter alive today." This sort of statement is either true or really needs to be heard by the person being described. Daniel Johnston needs all the support he can find. He is a singer-songwriter and an artist whose underground tapes and gallery shows sell out, and he is a manic-depressive with other mental problems that have had him in and out of hospitals for years.

This documentary charts his life's journey through an apparently inexhaustible archive of video- and audiotapes. Jeff Feuerzeig, who won the best director award at Sundance 2005 for this film, has started with a subject who has filmed himself and been filmed by others for more than twenty years.

That allows us to see Daniel Johnston as a bright young kid who "lost all his confidence" in junior high school, who has had a romantic obsession with a classmate all his life, who was briefly a star on MTV, whose songs have been covered by Beck and Pearl Jam, whom Kurt Cobain called the "greatest living songwriter," whose friends included members of Sonic Youth and Half Japanese, and who still lives at home with his parents, who worry about what will happen to him when they are gone. His tapes are sold on the Web by an ex-manager, still a fan of his music, whom he fired and attacked with a pipe.

Despite the loyalty it inspires, Daniel Johnston's music does not seem to deserve quite the level of praise he has received. He made a crucial early decision to move away from the piano, which he could play, to the guitar, which he has not mastered. When the *Austin Chronicle* named him Austin's Folk Artist of the Year, its editor recalls, that created some unhappiness "in a town where a lot of people *can* play the guitar."

Johnston's life has often been highly medicated, and when he goes off meds for a week or two before a concert, he sometimes gets into trouble. After a happy trip to New York, he was returning home when he got off the bus in West Virginia and was involved in an incident that led to an elderly lady breaking her ankles jumping out a window. During a trip in his dad's private airplane, he caused a crash that could have killed them both. His artwork first got publicity when Cobain wore one of his T-shirts for weeks on end (whether it was always the same shirt, the movie neglects to say), and his drawings of devils, crucifixes, and eyeballs, especially eyeballs, have become famous in some circles.

Watching the movie, I was reminded of the documentary *Crumb* and its portrait of R. Crumb's brother, Charles, who almost never left his bedroom in his mother's home, and whose drawings and notebooks, Robert Crumb says, inspired him. There is a line that sometimes runs between genius and madness, sometimes encircles them. *The Devil and Daniel Johnston* shows us a life of accomplishment and achievement, ringed with sadness, dampened by drugs both prescribed and not (bad acid trips didn't help), and supported by parents whom the film characterizes as "fundamentalist," as if that led to Daniel's troubles. It looks to me more as if Johnston's parents are the luckiest thing that has ever happened to him, as they care for him on his good days and his impossible ones.

The Devil's Rejects ★ ★ ★
R, 101 m., 2005

Sid Haig (Captain Spaulding), Bill Moseley (Otis Firefly), Sheri Moon Zombie (Baby), William Forsythe (Sheriff Wydell), Ken Foree (Charlie Altamont), Matthew McGrory (Tiny), Leslie Easterbrook (Mother Firefly). Directed by Rob Zombie and produced by Mike Elliott, Andy Gould, Michael Ohoven, and Zombie. Screenplay by Zombie.

Here is a gaudy vomitorium of a movie, violent, nauseating, and really a pretty good example of its genre. If you are a hardened horror movie fan capable of appreciating skill and wit in the service of the deliberately disgusting, *The Devil's Rejects* may exercise a certain strange charm. If, on the other hand, you close your eyes if a scene gets icky, here is a movie to see with blinders on, because it starts at icky and descends relentlessly through depraved and nauseating to the embrace of roadkill.

How can I possibly give *The Devil's Rejects* a favorable review? A kind of heedless zeal transforms its horrors. The movie is not merely disgusting but also has an attitude and a subversive sense of humor. Its actors venture into camp satire but never seem to know it's funny; their sincerity gives the jokes a kind of solemn gallows cackle. Consider the fact that it's about a depraved family of mass murderers who name themselves after Groucho Marx characters (Otis P. Driftwood, Rufus Firefly, Captain Spaulding) and that the sheriff calls in a film critic to give him insights into their pathology. The critic is such a Groucho fan that he knows Groucho played God in Otto Preminger's *Skidoo* (1968), something I also knew, but I bet you didn't. The sheriff wants to bring in Groucho for questioning, but the critic knows he died in 1977. "Elvis died three days earlier and stole all the headlines," he moans, risking death at the hands of the sheriff's department's Elvis fans.

The Devil's Rejects movie has been written and directed by Rob Zombie (aka Robert Cummings and Robert Wolfgang Zombie), a composer and music video producer whose *House of 1,000 Corpses* (2003) was a *Texas Chainsaw Massacre* wannabe. Pause for a moment to meditate on the phrase "a *Texas Chainsaw Massacre* wannabe," and you will begin to form some idea of Zombie's artistic vision. Now give him credit, in this movie, not for transcending *Chainsaw Massacre* but for sidestepping its temptations and opening up a mordantly funny approach to the material. There is actually some good writing and acting going on here, if you can step back from the material enough to see it.

The film opens with a 1978 police assault on an isolated farmhouse where, we learn, seventy-five murders have taken place. Inside the house, the Firefly family armors itself with steel masks and vests, and shoots it out with the sheriff (William Forsythe). He is a hard-bitten, vengeful man who cheerfully informs a deputy to be cautious or he'll be "cold-slabbed, toe-tagged, and mailed to your mom in a plastic bag."

Mother Firefly (Leslie Easterbrook) is captured in the raid, but Otis Firefly (Bill Moseley) and his sister, Baby (Sheri Moon Zombie), escape through a storm sewer (odd, in the Texas desert) and meet up with their father, Captain Spaulding (Sid Haig). He is a man whose teeth are so bad they're more frightening than his clown makeup. He plays such a thoroughly disgusting person, indeed, that I was driven to www.sidhaig.com to discover that in real life Haig looks, well, presentable, and even played a judge in Tarantino's *Jackie Brown*. This was a relief to me, because anyone who really looked like Captain Spaulding would send shoppers screaming from the Wal-Mart.

The sheriff pursues the fugitive Fireflys, who kidnap innocent bystanders in the kind of motel no reasonable person would ever occupy, leading to the roadkill scene, which is, of its kind, one of the best I have seen. There is also a scene in which a staple gun is used to post the photos of murder victims in a particularly gruesome manner, and one where characters are nailed to chairs in a burning building and then rescued by a character who deals with the nails in a surprisingly forthright way.

I suppose you're getting the idea. There's a sense in which a movie like this can be endured only if you distance yourself from the material and appreciate its manipulation of the genre. It can be seen as dark (very dark) satire. Or you can just throw up. At the end, when we get mellow flashbacks to the characters sharing a laugh in happier days, we are reminded of all those movies that attempt to follow a sad ending with a happy one, and we have to admire the brutality with which Zombie skewers that particular cliché.

Okay now, listen up, people. I don't want to get any e-mail messages from readers complaining that I gave the movie three stars, and so they went to it expecting to have a good time, and it was the sickest and most disgusting movie they've ever seen. My review has accurately described the movie and explained why some of you might appreciate it and most of you will not, and if you decide to go, please don't claim you were uninformed. ☞

The Devil Wears Prada ★ ½
PG-13, 106 m., 2006

Meryl Streep (Miranda Priestly), Anne Hathaway (Andy Sachs), Stanley Tucci (Nigel), Simon Baker (Christian), Emily Blunt (Emily), Adrian Grenier (Nate). Directed by David Frankel and produced by Wendy Finerman. Screenplay by Aline Brosh McKenna, based on the novel by Lauren Weisberger.

When I was young there was a series of books about boys and girls dreaming of the careers they'd have as grown-ups. I can't remember what the titles were, but let's say one was *Don Brown, Boy Announcer*. Don dreams of being a radio announcer, and one day, when an announcer falls ill at the scene of a big story, he grabs the mike and gets his chance: *The engineer nodded urgently to me and I began to de-*

scribe the fire, remembering to speak clearly. I was nervous at first, but soon the words flowed smoothly.

There were books about future coaches, nurses, doctors, pilots, senators, inventors, and so on. I also read the *Childhood of Famous Americans* series, but the "boy announcer" books were far superior, because they were about the childhood of me. *I took a deep breath and began. This was the chance I had been waiting for!*

The Devil Wears Prada is being positioned as a movie for grown-ups and others who know what, or who, or when, or where, Prada is. But while watching it I had the uncanny notion that, at last, one of those books from my childhood had been filmed. Call it *Andy Sachs, Girl Editor*. Anne Hathaway stars as a fresh-faced Midwesterner who comes to New York seeking her first job. "I just graduated from Northwestern," she explains. "I was editor of the *Daily Northwestern!*" Yes! *It had been a thrill to edit the student newspaper, but now, as I walked down Madison Avenue, I realized I was headed for the big time!*

Andy still dresses like an undergraduate, which offends Miranda Priestly (Meryl Streep), the powerful editor of *Runway,* the famous fashion magazine. Miranda, who is a cross between Anna Wintour, Graydon Carter, and a dominatrix, stands astride the world of fashion in very expensive boots. She throws things (her coat, her purse) at her assistants, rattles off tasks to be done immediately, and demands "the new Harry Potter" in "three hours." No, not the new book in the stores. The unpublished manuscript of the next book. Her twins want to read it. So get two copies.

Young Andy Sachs gets a job as the assistant to Miranda's assistant. That's Emily (Emily Blunt), who is terrified of Miranda. She is blunt to Andy: She'll need to get rid of that wardrobe, devote twenty-four hours a day to the job, and hope to God she remembers all of Miranda's commands. *I was impressed when I first saw the famous Miranda Priestly. She had the poise of Meryl Streep, the authority of Condoleezza Rice, and was better-dressed than anyone I'd ever met, except the Northwestern dean of women. And now she was calling my name! Gulp!*

Young Andy has a live-in boyfriend, which wasn't allowed in those old books. He is Nate (Adrian Grenier), who has a permanent three-day beard and loves her but wonders what has happened to "the old Andy I used to know." *I was heartbroken when I had to work late on Nate's birthday, but Miranda swamped me with last-minute demands.* Emily, the first assistant, lives for the day when she will travel to Paris with Miranda for Spring Fashion Week. But then Emily gets a cold or, as Miranda puts it, becomes "an incubus of viral plague." By this time Young Andy has impressed Miranda by getting the Harry Potter manuscript, and she's dressing better, too. *Nigel took me into the storage rooms, where I found myself surrounded by the latest and most luxurious fashion samples!* So Andy replaces Emily on the Paris trip.

"You are the one who has to tell Emily," Miranda kindly explains. *Ohmigod! I was dreaming! Paris, France! And as Miranda Priestly's assistant! But how would I break the news to Emily, who had dreamed of this day? And how could I tell Nate, whose own plans would have to be changed?* Actually, by this time Young Andy has a lot of things to discuss with Nate, including her friendship with Christian (Simon Baker), a famous writer for *New York* magazine. *Ohmigod! Simon Baker said he would read my clippings!*

The Devil Wears Prada is based on the bestselling novel by Lauren Weisberger, which oddly enough captures the exact tone, language, and sophistication of the books of my childhood: *There was nowhere to wipe my sweaty palms except for the suede Gucci pants that hugged my thighs and hips so tightly they'd both begun to tingle within minutes of my securing the final button.* This novel was on the *New York Times* best seller list for six months and has been published in twenty-seven countries. I hope some of the translators left the word "both" out of that sentence.

Streep is indeed poised and imperious as Miranda, and Hathaway is a great beauty (*Ella Enchanted, Brokeback Mountain*) who makes a convincing career girl. I liked Stanley Tucci, too, as Nigel, the magazine's fashion director, who is kind and observant despite being a careerist slave. But I thought the movie should have reversed the roles played by Grenier and Baker. Grenier comes across not like the old boyfriend but like the slick New York writer, and Baker seems the embodiment of Midwestern sincerity, which makes sense, because he is from Australia, the Midwest of the Southern Hemisphere.

Diary of a Mad Black Woman ★
PG-13, 116 m., 2005

Kimberly Elise (Helen McCarter), Shemar Moore (Orlando), Cicely Tyson (Myrtle), Steve Harris (Charles McCarter), Tyler Perry (Grandma Madea), Lisa Marcos (Brenda), Tamara Taylor (Debrah). Directed by Darren Grant and produced by Reuben Cannon and Tyler Perry. Screenplay by Perry, based on his play.

Diary of a Mad Black Woman begins as the drama of a wife of eighteen years, dumped by her cruel husband and forced to begin a new life. Then this touching story is invaded by the Grandma from Hell, who takes a chainsaw to the plot, the mood, everything. A real chainsaw, not a metaphorical one. The Grandma is not merely wrong for the movie, but fatal to it—a writing and casting disaster. And since the screenplay is by the man who plays Grandma in drag, all blame returns to Tyler Perry. What was he *thinking*?

There's a good movie buried beneath the bad one. Kimberly Elise stars as Helen, wife of Atlanta's attorney of the year. She lives with her husband, Charles (Steve Harris), in a house big enough to be the suburban headquarters of an insurance company. Their marriage seems ideal, but he cheats on her and assaults her with verbal brutality. When Helen comes home the next day, her clothes are being loaded into a U-Haul. That's how she finds out Charles is dumping her and moving in his mistress, Brenda (Lisa Marcos). Oh, and he has two children by Brenda.

Luckily for Helen, the U-Haul is driven by Orlando (Shemar Moore, from *The Young and the Restless*), who is handsome and kind and everything Charles is not. Helen weepingly flees to the house of her grandmother, and that's when everything goes spectacularly wrong.

Grandma Madea, who is built along the lines of a linebacker, is a tall, lantern-jawed, smooth-skinned, balloon-breasted gargoyle with a bad wig, who likes to wave a loaded gun and shoot test rounds into the ceiling. This person is not remotely plausible; her dialogue

is so offensively vulgar that it's impossible to believe that the intelligent, sweet, soft-spoken Helen doesn't seem to notice. Madea at one point invades Charles's mansion, tells his mistress she is a ho (which is correct), and destroys all the furniture in his living room with a chainsaw she is able to find and employ within seconds. What's with this bizarre grandmother? She's like Moms Mabley at a church social. Did nobody realize that Grandma Madea comes from Planet X, would seem loud at the Johnson Family Picnic, is playing by different rules than anyone else in the cast, and fatally sabotages Kimberly Elise's valiant attempt to create a character we can care about?

The director is Darren Grant. Did he approve as Grandma took a chainsaw to his movie? Did he see Kimberly Elise in *Beloved* and *Woman, Thou Art Loosed* and realize what she was capable of in a Grandma-free movie? I can imagine this movie working perfectly well with Grandma played as a sympathetic human being, perhaps by Irma P. Hall.

For that matter, Helen has an aunt as well as a grandmother, and her aunt, Myrtle, is played with taste and sympathy by Cicely Tyson. It is impossible that Grandma the harridan could have given life to such gentle and civilized women as Myrtle and Helen. The math doesn't work, either. We learn that Myrtle was thirty-nine when Helen was born, and that makes Grandma about eighty-five, which is too old to operate a chainsaw.

Without the interruptions by Grandma Madea, the movie would be about Helen as a shattered woman who (1) tells the judge Charles can keep all his assets, because she doesn't want a penny; (2) goes to work as a waitress; and (3) is courted by the handsome Orlando, who is kind, understanding, sincere, and knows how to listen to women. No. 1 is impossible, because no judge is going to let a wife abandoned by an adulterer after eighteen years walk away without a penny, but never mind. Does Helen find happiness with Orlando?

Not so fast. The movie has a Christian agenda, which is fine with me, if only it had been applied in a believable way. After melodramatic events occur in the life of the evil Charles, Helen gets the opportunity to practice the virtues of forgiveness and redemption, at the apparent cost of her own happiness. We hate Charles so much that it's impossible to feel sorry for him, or believe in his miraculous recovery in body or reformation of character. It just doesn't play—especially while Helen keeps poor Orlando in the dark about her true feelings, for no better reason than to generate phony romantic suspense.

At the end of the film, Orlando makes a comeback that demonstrates he has carefully studied *An Officer and Gentleman*, but before then we have had one emotionally implausible scene after another involving Charles and Helen, interrupted by periodic raids by the Grandma Madea action figure, who brings the movie to a halt every time she appears. She seems like an invasion from another movie. A very bad another movie. I've been reviewing movies for a long time, and I can't think of one that more dramatically shoots itself in the foot.

Dirty Dancing: Havana Nights ★ ★
PG-13, 87 m., 2004

Diego Luna (Javier Suarez), Romola Garai (Katey Miller), Sela Ward (Jeannie Miller), John Slattery (Bert Miller), Jonathan Jackson (James Phelps), January Jones (Eve), Rene Lavan (Carlos Suarez), Mika Boorem (Susie Miller), Mya Harrison (Lola Martinez). Directed by Guy Ferland and produced by Lawrence Bender and Sarah Green. Screenplay by Boaz Yakin and Victoria Arch.

I was not a fan of *Dirty Dancing*, although $150 million in 1987 box-office dollars attempted, unsuccessfully, to convince me I was wrong. I thought Patrick Swayze and Jennifer Grey were terrific dancers, and I thought the plot was a clunker assembled from surplus parts at the Broken Plots Store. The actions of the characters (especially her parents) were so foreordained they played like closing night of a run that had gone on way too long.

Now here is *Dirty Dancing: Havana Nights*. Same characters, new names, same plot, new location. The wealthy Miller family from St. Louis arrives in 1958 Havana with their teenage daughter, Katey (Romola Garai). She is courted by young James Phelps (Jonathan Jackson), son of a wealthier family. Has anybody in the movies named Phelps ever been poor? She meets Javier Suarez (Diego Luna), a nice Cuban

waiter about her age, and by her clumsiness gets him fired. But ...

Well, of course she finds Phelps a bore and Javier a nice and considerate friend, not nearly as sexually vibrant, by the way, as Swayze. Except when he's dancing. She has to choose between the godawful official balls and the excitement at La Rosa Negra, the club where Javier and his friends hang out—a club not a million miles distant in function from the disco in *Saturday Night Fever*.

Can this white-bread American princess learn rhythm? Of course she can, with Javier wading with her into the ocean and teaching her to feel the motion of the waves and allow her body to sway with them, and to listen to the music as if it is the waves, and meanwhile perfecting choreography so complex and demanding that it would have had Rita Moreno, in her heyday, pleading for the Sloan's Liniment.

Is it not clear to all of us that sooner or later Katey and Javier will have to defy social convention and enter the dance contest, and that Mr. and Mrs. Miller will find themselves at the big contest but astonished to discover their own daughter out there on the floor? Of course they will be shocked, but then they will be proud, and Mrs. Miller (Sela Ward), who was a heck of a dancer in her day, will realize that the fruit has not fallen far from the tree, and that Katey must follow her dream, realize her talent, go with the flow, sway with the waves, and bring home the bacon.

Meanwhile, in the hills, Fidel Castro readies his assault on the corrupt Batista regime. All very well, and his revolution could have supplied some good scenes, as we know from *Havana* and the *Godfather* saga. But is Fidel really needed in a retread of *Dirty Dancing*? And do the inevitable scenes of upheaval, people separated from each other, confusion in the streets, etc., create tension, or only tedium? How can we get excited about action that the movie isn't even about? Couldn't Castro at least have crashed the dance contest in disguise, like Douglas Fairbanks would have done?

Why, then, do I give this movie two stars and the original only one? Because I have grown mellow and forgiving? Perhaps, but perhaps too because we go to the movies to look at the pretty pictures on the screen, like infants who like bright toys dangled before us. And *Dirty*

Dancing: Havana Nights is a great movie to look at, with its period Havana (actually San Juan, Puerto Rico, with lots of 1950s cars). The dancing is well done, the music will sell a lot of sound tracks, and . . .

Romola Garai and Diego Luna. He you remember from *Y Tu Mama Tambien,* and here again he has that quirky, winning charm. She is a beauty and a gifted comedienne, who played Kate in *Nicholas Nickleby* and was the younger sister, Cassandra, in the wonderful 2003 film *I Capture the Castle.* They must be given credit for their presence and charisma in *Dirty Dancing: Havana Nights,* and together with the film's general ambience they do a lot to make amends for the lockstep plot. But here's an idea. Rent *Y Tu Mama También, Nicholas Nickleby,* and *I Capture the Castle,* and eliminate the middleman.

Dirty Love no stars

R, 95 m., 2005

Jenny McCarthy (Rebecca), Carmen Electra (Michelle), Kam Heskin (Carrie), Eddie Kaye Thomas (John), Victor Webster (Richard). Directed by John Mallory Asher and produced by Trent Walford, Jenny McCarthy, Asher, Rod Hamilton, Kimberley Kates, B. J. Davis, and Michael Manasseri. Screenplay by McCarthy.

Dirty Love wasn't written and directed; it was committed. Here is a film so pitiful it doesn't rise to the level of badness. It is hopelessly incompetent. It stars and was scripted by Jenny McCarthy, the cheerfully sexy model who, judging by this film, is fearless, plucky, and completely lacking in common sense or any instinct for self-preservation.

Yes, it takes nerve to star in a scene where you plop down in a supermarket aisle surrounded by a lake of your own menstrual blood. But to expect an audience to find that funny verges on dementia. McCarthy follows it with a scene where the cops strip-search her and she's wearing a maxi pad that would be adequate for an elephant. She doesn't need to do this. It's painful to see a pretty girl who seems nice enough humiliating herself on the screen. I feel sorry for her.

The film basically consists of McCarthy and her half-dressed friends Carmen Electra and Kam Heskin grouped awkwardly on the screen like high school girls in that last heedless showoff stage before a designated driver straps them in and takes them home. At times they literally seem to be letting the camera roll while they try to think up something goofy to do. There is also a lot of crude four-letter dialogue, pronounced as if they know the words but not the music.

The plot: McCarthy plays Rebecca, who seems well dressed and with great wheels for someone with no apparent income. She is cheated on by her boyfriend, Richard (Victor Webster), aka Dick, who looks like the model on the cover of a drugstore romance novel about a girl who doesn't know that guys who look like that spend all of their time looking like that. When she discovers his treachery, Rebecca has a grotesque emotional spasm. She weeps, wails, staggers about Hollywood Boulevard flailing her arms and screaming, crawls on the pavement, and waves her butt at strangers while begging them to ravage her because she simultaneously is worthless and wants to teach Dick a lesson. Then, to teach Dick a lesson, she dates scummy losers.

These events are directed by McCarthy's former partner John Mallory Asher and photographed by Eric Wycoff so incompetently that Todd McCarthy, the esteemed film critic of *Variety,* should have won the Jean Hersholt Humanitarian Award for generosity after writing the "whole package has a cheesy look." This movie is an affront to cheese. Also to breasts. Jenny McCarthy has a technologically splendid bosom that should, in my opinion, be put to a better use than being vomited upon.

The Electra character, meanwhile, struts around like a ho in a bad music video, speaking black street talk as if she learned it phonetically, and pulling out a gun and holding it to a man's head because she thinks, obviously, that pulling guns on guys is expected of any authentic black woman. A scene like that would be insulting in any other movie; here it possibly distracts her from doing something even more debasing.

I would like to say more, but—no, I wouldn't. I would not like to say more. I would like to say less. On the basis of *Dirty Love,* I am not certain that anyone involved has ever seen a movie, or knows what one is. I would like to invite poor Jenny McCarthy up here to the Toronto Film Festival, where I am writing this review while wonderful films are playing all over town, and get her a pass, and require her to go to four movies a day until she gets the idea.

A Dirty Shame ★
NC-17, 89 m., 2004

Tracey Ullman (Sylvia Stickles), Johnny Knoxville (Ray-Ray Perkins), Chris Isaak (Vaughn Stickles), Selma Blair (Caprice Stickles), Suzanne Shepherd (Big Ethel), Mink Stole (Marge the Neuter), Patricia Hearst (Paige). Directed by John Waters and produced by Ted Hope and Christine Vachon. Screenplay by Waters.

There is in showbiz something known as "a bad laugh." That's the laugh you don't want to get, because it indicates not amusement but incredulity, nervousness, or disapproval. John Waters's *A Dirty Shame* is the only comedy I can think of that gets more bad laughs than good ones.

Waters is the poet of bad taste, and labors mightily here to be in the worst taste he can manage. That's not the problem—no, not even when Tracey Ullman picks up a water bottle using a method usually employed only in Bangkok sex shows. We go to a Waters film expecting bad taste, but we also expect to laugh, and *A Dirty Shame* is monotonous, repetitive, and sometimes wildly wrong in what it hopes is funny.

The movie takes place in Baltimore, as most Waters films do. Stockholm got Bergman, Rome got Fellini, and Baltimore—well, it also has Barry Levinson. Ullman plays Sylvia Stickles, the owner of a 7-Eleven–type store. Chris Isaak plays Vaughn, her husband. Locked in an upstairs room is their daughter, Caprice (Selma Blair), who was a legend at the local go-go bar until her parents grounded and padlocked her. She worked under the name of Ursula Udders, a name inspired by breasts so large they are obviously produced by technology, not surgery.

Sylvia has no interest in sex until a strange thing happens. She suffers a concussion in a car crash, and it turns her into a sex maniac. Not only can't she get enough of it, she

doesn't even pause to inquire what it is before she tries to get it. This attracts the attention of a local auto mechanic named Ray-Ray Perkins, played by Johnny Knoxville, who no longer has to consider *Jackass* his worst movie. Ray-Ray has a following of sex addicts who joyfully proclaim their special tastes and gourmet leanings.

A digression. In 1996, David Cronenberg made a movie named *Crash*, about a group of people who had a sexual fetish for car crashes, wounds, broken bones, crutches, and so on. It was a good movie, but as I wrote at the time, it's about "a sexual fetish that, in fact, no one has." I didn't get a lot of letters disagreeing with me.

John Waters also goes fetish-shopping in *A Dirty Shame*, treating us to such specialties as infantilism (a cop who likes to wear diapers), bear lovers (those who lust after fat, hairy men), and Mr. Pay Day, whose fetish does not involve the candy bar of the same name. We also learn about such curious pastimes as shelf-humping, mallet whacking, and tickling. As the movie introduced one sex addiction after another, I sensed a curious current running through the screening room. How can I describe it? Not disgust, not horror, not shock, but more of a sincere wish that Waters had found a way to make his movie without being quite so encyclopedic.

The plot, such as it is, centers on Sylvia and other characters zapping in and out of sex addiction every time they hit their heads, which they do with a frequency approaching the kill rate in *Crash*. This is not really very funny the first time, and grows steadily less funny until it becomes a form of monomania.

I think the problem is fundamental: Waters hopes to get laughs because of what the characters are, not because of what they do. He works at the level of preadolescent fart jokes, hoping, as the French say, to *"epater les bourgeois."* The problem may be that Waters has grown more bourgeois than his audience, which is so epatered that he actually thinks he is being shocking.

To truly deal with a strange sexual fetish can indeed be shocking, as *Kissed* (1996) demonstrated with its quiet, observant portrait of Molly Parker playing a necrophiliac. It can also be funny, as James Spader and Maggie Gyllenhaal demonstrated in *Secretary*

(2002). Tracey Ullman is a great comic actress, but for her to make this movie funny would have required not just a performance but a rewrite and a miracle.

Fetishes are neither funny nor shocking simply because they exist. You have to do more with them than have characters gleefully celebrate them on the screen. Waters's weakness is to expect laughs because the *idea* of a moment is funny. But the idea of a moment exists only for the pitch; the movie has to develop it into a reality, a process, a payoff. An illustration of this is his persisting conviction that it is funny by definition to have Patty Hearst in his movies. It is only funny when he gives Ms. Hearst, who is a good sport, something amusing to do. She won't find it in this movie.

Distant ★ ★ ★

NO MPAA RATING, 110 m., 2004

Muzaffer Ozdemir (Mahmut), Mehmet Emin Toprak (Yusuf), Zuhal Gencer Erkaya (Nazan), Nazan Kirilmis (Lover), Feridun Koc (Janitor), Fatma Ceylan (Mother), Ebru Ceylan (Young Girl). Directed by Nuri Bilge Ceylan and produced by Ceylan. Screenplay by Ceylan.

How is it that the same movie can seem tedious on first viewing and absorbing on the second? Why doesn't it grow even more tedious? In the case of *Distant*, which I first saw at Cannes in 2003, perhaps it helped that I knew what the story offered and what it did not offer, and was able to see it again without expecting what would not come.

The film takes place in Turkey, but its dynamic could be transplanted anywhere—maybe to our own families. It is about a cousin from the country who comes to the big city searching for work, and asks to stay "for a few days" with his relative, who is a divorced photographer with walls filled with books and an apartment filled with sad memories.

Mahmut (Muzaffer Ozdemir) is the photographer, whose wife has divorced him and is marrying another man; the couple will move to Canada. What went wrong is not hard to guess: Mahmut is a man of habit, silent, introspective, exhausted by life. Yusuf (Mehmet Emin Toprak) comes from a small town where the factory has

failed and there are no jobs; he foolishly thinks he can get hired on one of the ships in the port, but there are no jobs, and an old sailor informs him that the wages are so bad he'll never have anything left over to send home.

It is the dead of winter. Yusuf tramps through the snow with no gloves and inadequate shoes, and his job search starts unpromisingly when the first ship he finds is listing and sinking. He haunts the coffee bars of the sailors, who smoke and wait. Mahmut, meanwhile, says good-bye to his wife and then secretly and sadly watches her leaving from the airport. He has a shabby affair with a woman who lives nearby, and who will not make eye contact in a restaurant. He watches art videos (Tarkovsky, I think) to drive Yusuf from the room, and then switches to porno.

For both men, smoking is a consolation, and they spend a lot of time standing alone, doing nothing, maybe thinking nothing, smoking as if it is a task that provides them with purpose. Mahmut has rules (smoking only in the kitchen or on the balcony), but Yusuf sits in his favorite chair and smokes and drinks beer when Mahmut is away, and Mahmut grows gradually furious at the disorder that has come into his life. "Close the door," he says, as Yusuf goes to the guest bedroom, because he wants to shut him away from his privacy.

A photographic expedition to the countryside, with Yusuf hired as his assistant, turns out badly for Mahmut; sharing rented rooms, they invade each other's space. Finally Mahmut has had enough and asks Yusuf, "What are your plans?" But Yusuf has none. He does not even have an opening for plans. He is trapped in unemployment, has no money, no skills, no choices.

The film, directed by Nuri Bilge Ceylan, is shot with a frequently motionless camera that regards the men as they, frequently, regard nothing in particular. It permits silences to grow. Perhaps in the hurry of Cannes, with four or five films a day, I could not slow down to occupy those silences, but seeing the film a second time I understood they were crucial: There is little these men have to say to each other and—more to the point—no one else for them to talk with. Women are a problem for them both. Yusuf shadows attractive women, but is too shy to approach them before they inevitably meet a man and walk off arm-in-arm. A man without funds is in a double bind: He has no way to attract good women, or to hire bad ones. The one sex scene we witness with Mahmut, which is out of focus at the far end of a room, is so joyless that solitude seems preferable.

A movie like this touches everyday life in a way that we can recognize as if Turkey were Peoria. I can imagine a similar film being made in America, although Americans might talk more. What do you say to a relative who is out of work and seems unlikely to ever work again? He is family, and so there is a sense of responsibility embedded in childhood, but there are no jobs and he has no skills, and your own comfort, which seems enviable to him, is little consolation to you. To have joyless work means you have employment but not an occupation. At the end, one of the men is sitting on a bench on a gray, cold day, staring at nothing, and if we could see the other man we could probably see another bench. *Distant* is a good title for this movie.

Note: At Cannes, the movie won the Jury Grand Prize, and Muzaffer Ozdemir and Mehmet Emin Toprak shared the prize as best actors. The previous December, Toprak died in a traffic accident. He was twenty-eight.

Dodgeball: A True Underdog Story ★ ★ ★
PG-13, 97 m., 2004

Vince Vaughn (Peter La Fleur), Ben Stiller (White Goodman), Christine Taylor (Kate Veatch), Rip Torn (Patches O'Houlihan), Justin Long (Justin), Stephen Root (Gordon), Joel Moore (Owen), Chris Williams (Dwight), Alan Tudyk (Steve the Pirate). Directed by Rawson Marshall Thurber and produced by Stuart Cornfeld and Ben Stiller. Screenplay by Thurber.

Dodgeball: A True Underdog Story is a title that rewards close study. It does not say it is a true story. It says it is about a true underdog. That is true. This is a movie about a spectacularly incompetent health club owner (Vince Vaughn) who tries to save his club from foreclosure by entering a team in the $50,000 world series of dodgeball in Las Vegas. Proof that the team is an underdog: One of the team members believes he is a pirate, and another team member hasn't noticed that.

Vaughn's club, Average Joe's Gym, is run-down and shabby, but has a loyal if nutty clientele. Across the street is a multimillion-dollar muscle emporium known as Globa Gym (there is no "l" in the title because it fell off). Globa is owned by Ben Stiller, overacting to the point of apoplexy as White Goodman; his manic performance is consistently funny, especially when he protects against Small Man Complex by surrounding himself with enormous bodybuilders and building an inflatable crotch into his training pants.

Vaughn, playing the absentminded Peter La Fleur, acts as a steadying influence; he plays it more or less straight, which is wise, since someone has to keep the plot on track. He's visited by the lithesome Kate Veatch (Christine Taylor), who works for the bank and explains that Average Joe's needs $50,000 in thirty days or the bank will foreclose. Standing by to turn Joe's into a parking lot: White Goodman. Among other questionable business practices, La Fleur has neglected to collect membership dues for several months.

Kate hates Globa's White Goodman, not least because at their last meeting he rudely drew attention to his extremely well-inflated crotch. One of the Average Joe staff members comes up with the idea of the dodgeball tournament, and for reasons unnecessary to explain, Kate becomes a member of the team, along with the pirate and four others.

None of them know anything about dodgeball. This may not be a handicap. My own experiences with dodgeball have led me to conclude that it is basically a game of luck; the only skill you need is to pick bigger kids for your side. But I learn that Extreme Dodgeball is actually a real sport, with its own cable TV show.

Dodgeball explains the sport by pausing for a grade-school educational documentary from 1938. It is a very short documentary, because all you need to know about the game are the Five Ds, of which both D No. 1 and D No. 5 are "Dodge!" The film is hosted by dodgeball legend Patches O'Houlihan, who must therefore be in his eighties when he appears at Average Joe's in his motorized wheelchair, and announces that he will coach them to victory. Patches is played by Rip Torn, whose training methods get enormous laughs.

173

The Las Vegas tournament itself follows the time-honored formulas of all sports movies, but is considerably enhanced by the weird teams in the finals. Weirdest is Globa Gym, captained by White Goodman and including four gigantic musclemen and a very hairy woman from an obscure former Soviet republic. The finals are telecast on ESPN8 ("If it's almost a sport, we have it here!").

I dare not say much more without giving away jokes; in a miraculous gift to the audience, 20th Century Fox does *not* reveal all of the best gags in its trailer. Therefore, let me just gently say that late in the movie a famous man approaches Peter La Fleur at the airport and gets laughs almost as big as the Patches O'Houlihan training technique.

Dogville ★ ★
R, 177 m., 2004

Nicole Kidman (Grace), Paul Bettany (Tom Edison), James Caan (The Big Man), Patricia Clarkson (Vera), Jeremy Davies (Bill Henson), Ben Gazzara (Jack McKay), Philip Baker Hall (Tom Edison Sr.), John Hurt (Narrator), Chloe Sevigny (Liz Henson), Stellan Skarsgård (Chuck), Lauren Bacall (Ma Ginger), Blair Brown (Mrs. Henson), Bill Raymond (Mr. Henson). Directed by Lars von Trier and produced by Vibeke Windelov. Screenplay by von Trier.

Lars von Trier exhibits the imagination of an artist and the pedantry of a crank in *Dogville*, a film that works as a demonstration of how a good idea can go wrong. There is potential in the concept of the film, but the execution had me tapping my wristwatch to see if it had stopped. Few people will enjoy seeing it once and, take it from one who knows, even fewer will want to see it a second time.

The underlying vision of the production has the audacity we expect from von Trier, a daring and inventive filmmaker. He sets his story in a small Rocky Mountain town during the Great Depression, but doesn't provide a real town (or a real mountain). The first shot looks straight down on the floor of a large sound stage, where the houses of the residents are marked out with chalk outlines, and there are only a few props—some doors, desks, chairs, beds. We will never leave this set and never see be-

yond it; on all sides in the background there is only blankness.

The idea reminds us of *Our Town,* but von Trier's version could be titled *Our Hell.* In his town, which I fear works as a parable of America, the citizens are xenophobic, vindictive, jealous, suspicious, and capable of rape and murder. His dislike of the United States (which he has never visited, since he is afraid of airplanes) is so palpable that it flies beyond criticism into the realm of derangement. When the film premiered at Cannes 2003, he was accused of not portraying America accurately, but how many movies do? Anything by David Spade come to mind? Von Trier could justifiably make a fantasy about America, even an anti-American fantasy, and produce a good film, but here he approaches the ideological subtlety of a raving prophet on a street corner.

The movie stars Nicole Kidman in a rather brave performance: Like all the actors, she has to act within a narrow range of tone, in an allegory that has no reference to realism. She plays a young woman named Grace who arrives in Dogville being pursued by gangsters (who here, as in Brecht, I fear, represent native American fascism). She is greeted by Tom Edison (Paul Bettany), an earnest young man, who persuades his neighbors to give her a two-week trial run before deciding whether to allow her to stay in town.

Grace meets the townspeople, played by such a large cast of stars that we suspect the original running time must have been even longer than 177 minutes. Tom's dad is the town doctor (Philip Baker Hall); Stellan Skarsgård grows apples and, crucially, owns a truck; Patricia Clarkson is his wife; Ben Gazzara is the all-seeing blind man; Lauren Bacall runs the general store; Bill Raymond and Blair Brown are the parents of Jeremy Davies and Chloe Sevigny. There are assorted other citizens and various children, and James Caan turns up at the end in a long black limousine. He's the gangster.

What von Trier is determined to show is that Americans are not friendly, we are suspicious of outsiders, we cave in to authority, we are inherently violent, etc. All of these things are true, and all of these things are untrue. It's a big country, and it has a lot of different kinds of people. Without stepping too far out on a limb, however, I doubt that we have any villages where the helpless visitor would eventually be chained to a bed and raped by every man in town. The actors (or maybe it's the characters) seem to be in a kind of trance much of the time. They talk in monotones, they seem to be reciting truisms rather than speaking spontaneously, they seem to sense the film's inevitable end. To say that the film ends in violence is not to give away the ending so much as to wonder how else it could have ended. In the apocalyptic mind-set of von Trier, no less than general destruction could conclude his fable; life in Dogville clearly cannot continue for a number of reasons, one of them perhaps that the Dogvillians would go mad.

Lars von Trier has made some of the best films of recent years (*Europa, Breaking the Waves, Dancer in the Dark*). He was a guiding force behind the Dogma movement, which has generated much heat and some light. He takes chances, and that's rare in a world where most films seem to have been banged together out of other films. But at some point his fierce determination has to confront the reality that a film does not exist without an audience. *Dogville* can be defended and even praised on pure ideological grounds, but most moviegoers, even those who are sophisticated and have open minds, are going to find it a very dry and unsatisfactory slog through conceits masquerading as ideas.

Note No. 1: Although Lars von Trier has never been to the United States, he does have one thing right: In a small town, the smashing of a collection of Hummel figurines would count as an atrocity.

Note No. 2: I learn from Variety *that* Dogville Confessions, *a making-of documentary, was filmed using a soundproof "confession box" near the soundstage where actors could unburden themselves. In it, Stellan Skarsgård describes von Trier, whom he has worked with many times, as "a hyperintelligent child who is slightly disturbed, playing with dolls in a dollhouse, cutting their heads off with nail clippers." Von Trier himself testifies that the cast is conspiring against him.* Variety *thinks this doc would make a great bell and/or whistle on the eventual DVD.*

Note No. 3: We should not be too quick to condemn von Trier, a Dane, for not filming in the United States when The Prince and Me, *a new Hollywood film about a Wisconsin farm girl who falls in love with the prince of Denmark, was filmed in Toronto and Prague.*

Dolls ★ ★ ★
NO MPAA RATING, 113 m., 2005

Miho Kanno (Sawako), Hidetoshi Nishijima (Matsumoto), Tatsuya Mihashi (Hiro, the Boss), Chieko Matsubara (Woman in the Park), Kyoko Fukada (Haruna, the Pop Star), Tsutomu Takeshige (Nukui, the Fan). Directed by Takeshi Kitano and produced by Masayuki Mori and Takio Yoshida. Screenplay by Kitano.

Takeshi Kitano is known for directing pictures in which flashes of violence are punctuated by periods of waiting, reflection, and loneliness. Using the name of Beat Takeshi, he stars in them. He is a distinctive, original director; his *The Blind Swordsman: Zatoichi* (2004) took a durable Japanese series character and transformed him into a philosophical wanderer. In his film, *Dolls*, he makes his longest journey from his action-film roots, into a land of three tragic relationships.

The title is taken from the Japanese tradition of Bunraku, or puppet plays. Elaborate dolls are moved about the stage, each one with two or three artists to manipulate their eyes, heads, arms. One artist is visible, the others hooded in black. A reader recites all of the dialogue, and there is music.

Kitano's film opens with a Bunraku performance, and then segues into the first of three live-action stories in which the characters seem moved about the stages of their own lives without wills of their own. We are reminded of Gloucester's line in *King Lear*: "As flies to wanton boys, are we to the gods; they kill us for their sport."

The first story involves Matsumoto (Hidetoshi Nishijima), who is engaged to Sawako (Miho Kanno). His parents insist he break off the engagement and marry his boss's daughter. Sawako attempts suicide, is brain-damaged, and is spirited out of a nursing home by Matsumoto, who devotes his life to being with her. They live in a hotel room, in a car, and finally in the wild; because she wanders away, he joins them with a length of rope, and as they walk through the countryside they become known as the Bound Beggars.

The second story involves a gangster boss named Hiro (Tatsuya Mihashi). As a young man he is in love with a woman (Chieko Matsubara), who meets him on a park bench every Saturday with two box lunches. One Saturday he breaks up with her; a woman would be a complication now that he has decided to become a yakuza. She says she will come every Saturday no matter what. Years later, old and disillusioned, he returns to the park to look for her.

The third story is about a pop idol named Haruna (Kyoko Fukada). A fan named Nukui (Tsutomu Takeshige) is obsessed with her. His job is to wave a warning light at a highway construction zone; Haruna is disfigured in a traffic accident that may have been caused (the movie is a little vague) by Nukui being distracted from his job by thoughts of her. After her injury she refuses to be seen by any of her fans; Nukui's determination to meet her leads to a gruesome decision.

Dolls moves with a deliberate pace. I have seen Bunraku performances in Japan, and found them long, slow, and stylized; the same can be said of the film. Kitano is not content to simply tell his stories, but wants to leave us time to contemplate them, to experience the passage of time for these characters and the way their choices will define them for the rest of their lives. The three active lovers in the film—Matsumoto, the woman, and the fan—willingly sacrifice their freedom and happiness in acts of romantic abnegation. Such gestures seem odd in the modern world, but not in classical tragedy, not in Bunraku, and not in the Japanese tradition of dramatic personal gestures.

The film has moments of great loveliness. Some of the landscapes, filled with autumn leaves of astonishing shades of red, are beautiful and lonely. The film is about three people who have unhappiness forced upon them, and three others who choose it. *Dolls* isn't a film for everybody, especially the impatient, but Kitano does succeed, I think, in drawing us into his tempo and his world, and slowing us down into the sadness of his characters.

Dominion: Prequel to the Exorcist ★ ★ ★

R, 111 m., 2005

Stellan Skarsgard (Father Merrin), Gabriel Mann (Father Francis), Clara Bellar (Rachel), Billy Crawford (Cheche), Antonie Kamerling (Lieutenant Kessel), Ralph Brown (Sergeant-Major), Julian Wadham (Major Granville), Eddie Osei (Emekwi). Directed by Paul Schrader and produced by James G. Robinson. Screenplay by Caleb Carr and William Wisher Jr.

Paul Schrader's *Dominion: Prequel to the Exorcist* does something risky and daring in this time of jaded horror movies: It takes evil seriously. There really are dark Satanic forces in the Schrader version, which takes a priest forever scarred by the Holocaust and asks if he can ever again believe in the grace of God. The movie is drenched in atmosphere and dread, as we'd expect from Schrader, but it also has spiritual weight and texture, boldly confronting the possibility that Satan may be active in the world. Instead of cheap thrills, Schrader gives us a frightening vision of a good priest who fears goodness may not be enough.

The film's hero, Merrin (Stellan Skarsgard), considers himself an ex-priest; during World War II he was forced by Nazis to choose some villagers for death in order that a whole village not be killed. This is seen by a Nazi officer as an efficient way to undermine Merrin's belief in his own goodness, and indeed forces the priest to commit evil to avoid greater evil. This is not theologically sound; the idea is to do no evil and leave it to God to sort out the consequences.

His trauma from this experience hurls Merrin out of the priesthood and into an archeological dig in Africa, where he is helping to excavate a remarkably well-preserved church buried in the sand. Why this church, in this place? It doesn't fit in architectural, historical, or religious terms, and seems intended not so much to celebrate God as to trap something unspeakably evil that lies beneath it.

Schrader is famously a director of moral values crossed with dangerous choices; his own movies (*Hardcore, Light Sleeper, The Comfort of Strangers*) and those he has written for Martin Scorsese (*Taxi Driver, Raging Bull*) deal with men obsessed with guilt and sin. His *Dominion* is not content to simply raise the curtain on William Friedkin's classic *The Exorcist* (1974), but is more ambitious: It wants to observe the ways Satan seduces man.

The film's battle between good and evil involves everyone on the dig, notably the young priest Father Francis (Gabriel Mann), who has been assigned by Rome to keep an eye on

Merrin. Then there is the doctor Rachel (Clara Bellar), whose special concern is a deformed young man named Cheche (Billy Crawford). Curiously, Cheche seems to improve beyond all expectations of medicine, as if something supernatural were going on. Also on the site, in "British East Africa," is the Sergeant-Major (Ralph Brown), a racist who assigns the devil's doings to the local Africans.

In a lesser movie, there would be humid goings-on at the camp, and a spectacular showdown between the humans and special effects. Not in the Schrader version, which trusts evil to be intrinsically fascinating and not in need of f/x enhancement. His vision, however, was not the one the powers at Morgan Creek were looking for (although Schrader was filming a script by Caleb Carr and William Wisher Jr. that the producers presumably approved). After Schrader delivered his version, a scenario developed that is, I think, unprecedented in modern movie history. The studio, having spent millions on the Schrader version, hired the director Renny Harlin to spend more millions remaking it in a presumably more commercial fashion.

Harlin kept some of the actors, including Skarsgard, and substituted others (Gabriel Mann was replaced by James D'Arcy, Clara Bellar by Izabella Scorupco). The same cinematographer, the great Vittorio Storaro, filmed for both directors. After Harlin's version, *Exorcist: The Beginning*, did a break-even $82 million at the box office but drew negative reviews, Schrader succeeded in getting his version screened at a film festival in Brussels, where the positive reception inspired this theatrical release, a resurrection fully in keeping with the film's theme.

I've seen both versions and much prefer Schrader's, and yet it must be said that Harlin did not prostitute himself in his version. Indeed, oddly, it opens with more talk and less excitement than the Schrader version (Harlin dissipates the power of the Nazi sequence by fragmenting it into flashbacks).

What is fascinating from a movie buff's point of view is that the movie has been filmed twice in different ways by different directors. Maybe this is what Gus Van Sant was getting at when he inexplicably did his (almost) shot-by-shot remake of Hitchcock's *Psycho*. Film students are often given a series of shots and assigned to edit them to tell a story. They can fit together in countless ways, to greater or less effect. Here we have the experiment conducted with $80 million.

It's eerie, to see the same locations occupied by different actors speaking similar dialogue. Odd to see the young priest and the doctor occupying the same rooms but played by different people. Strange to see Skarsgard in both versions, some shots and dialogue exactly the same, others not. Curious how the subplot about the British shrinks in the Harlin version, while the horror is ramped up. I prefer the Schrader version, certainly, but you know what? Now that two versions exist and are available, each one makes the other more interesting.

Domino ★ ★ ★
R, 128 m., 2005

Keira Knightley (Domino Harvey), Mickey Rourke (Ed Mosbey), Edgar Ramirez (Choco), Rizwan Abbasi (Alf), Ian Ziering (Himself), Brian Austin Green (Himself), Christopher Walken (Mark Heiss), Mena Suvari (Kimmie), Jacqueline Bisset (Sophie Wynn), Lucy Liu (Taryn Miles), Delroy Lindo (Claremont Williams), Mo'Nique (Lateesha Rodriguez), Macy Gray (Lashandra Davis), Shondrella Avery (Lashindra Davis), Tom Waits (The Drifter). Directed by Tony Scott and produced by Samuel Hadida and Scott. Screenplay by Richard Kelly and Steve Barancik.

A character in Tony Scott's *Domino* is described as having "the attention span of a ferret on crystal meth," and that pretty much describes the movie. Not many movies have two narrations, one written, one spoken, and not many require them. But the damned thing has its qualities, and one of them is a headlong, twisting energy, a vitality that finds comedy in carnage. Here we have a man whose arm is shot off because it has a combination tattooed on it, and thieves disguised as four recent first ladies.

The movie was inspired by Domino Harvey, a friend of Scott's who was named Bounty Hunter of the Year in 2003 and died in June 2005, perhaps of an overdose, only thirty-five years old. Her life was not merely stranger than fiction but almost beyond invention: The daughter of the movie star Laurence Harvey and the fashion model Paulene Stone, she was sent, as they say, to all the best schools. She worked at day jobs before becoming a bounty hunter—a professional paid to track down and deliver dangerous prey. "My agenda is to kick ass," she famously said, and she must have been good at it to win that honor, although the awards ceremony is a paltry affair of folding chairs in a bare room.

The movie is inspired by her story but not based on it, and although famous people filled her life, the names are all changed here, and just as well, because there are times when Scott and his writers, Richard Kelly and Steve Barancik, spin free of reality and enter a parallel universe of pulp fiction. Consider again that man whose arm is shot off and tossed around like a Frisbee. Surely it would be easier to simply look at his arm and note the combination in a PDA, instant messaging being so much more efficient than the transfer of body parts.

The plot exists at the intersection of crime and show business, which has long needed traffic signals. Domino (Keira Knightley, who won an Oscar nomination for *Pride and Prejudice*) sees an ad for a bounty-hunting course run by a bail bondsman named Claremont Williams (Delroy Lindo) and his top hunters, Ed Mosbey (Mickey Rourke) and Choco (Edgar Ramirez). They just want to collect the tuition, but she insists on being taken seriously.

Mosbey might be expected to resist working with an unseasoned sexpot, but no: "Take a look at her," he tells Choco. "Come on, man, she ain't ugly. We walk down the street and people call us losers. We add her to the equation and people are going to think we're two of the coolest mothers who have ever lived." Domino, as it turns out, is the coolest mother of all. In a situation where a bad guy seems inclined to start shooting, she distracts him with a lap dance. The things a sweet young British actress has to do when she moves from Jane Austen to Hollywood.

Oh, it gets stranger. Mosbey's team also includes Alf (Rizwan Abbasi), an Afghan who knows a lot about blowing things up and whose existence on the streets of Los Angeles is a rebuke to the dream of homeland security. Choco is a tough guy from El Salvador who is offended

that anyone would speak English in L.A. Rourke, who with this film and *Sin City* has rehabilitated his iconic status, is so hardened at times he seems to be channeling Warren Oates.

The movie has so many supporting characters it's a good thing it's edited at MTV velocity, or just introducing them would be feature-length. The funniest and most possibly true to life is Mark Heiss (Christopher Walken), a TV producer and ferret. He hires the bounty-hunting team for a reality TV show and then mixes in the (real) stars Ian Ziering and Brian Austin Green of *Beverly Hills 90210*, setting up a scene where they introduce themselves to some killers: "We're the celebrity hostages." There's also Claremont's lover, Lateesha (Mo'Nique), whose job at the Department of Motor Vehicles gives her access to a database of basically everybody. Her twin cousins, Lashandra (Macy Gray) and Lashindra (Shondrella Avery), exist in part, I suspect, so that they can be called Lashandra and Lashindra by Lateesha, although the movie gives them plenty else to do. Worth the price of admission is the Jerry Springer show where Lateesha produces a chart to explain her theory of new American racial groups, including Blacktinos and Hispanese.

All of this happens outside of any reasonable chronology. The story leaps around in time and logic, subtitles explain who characters are and then later have to correct themselves, and Domino's own narration is intercut with her cross-examination by an FBI agent (Lucy Liu). Domino is not entirely certain what she can testify about, in part because she is evasive, in part because of that time in the desert when her coffee was spiked with mescaline and a prophet (Tom Waits) appeared, or seemed to appear, or something.

Did I admire *Domino*? In a sneaky way, yes. It's fractured and maddening, but it's alive. It begins with the materials of a perfectly conventional thriller. It heeds Godard's rule that "all you need for a movie is a girl and a gun." It gives us Knightley in a role all the more astonishing because I've just seen her in *Pride and Prejudice*. It not only stars Rourke and Walken but also uses them instead of just gawking at them. It blows up a Las Vegas casino, and it's a real one, not a fictional one. And it contains the line "I'll never tell you what it all meant," as if anyone could. Seeking guidance in understanding the movie's manic narrative, I poked around online and discovered in one review the explanation that the movie "totally challenges the bourgeois notion of the nuclear family." Oh. ☞

Donkey Skin ★ ★ ★

NO MPAA RATING, 100 m., 1970 (rereleased 2005)

Catherine Deneuve (Queen/Daughter), Jean Marais (King), Jacques Perrin (Prince), Micheline Presle (Red Queen), Delphine Seyrig (Fairy Godmother), Fernand Ledoux (Red King), Henri Cremieux (Doctor), Sacha Pitoeff (Minister), Pierre Repp (Thibaud), Jean Servais (Narrator). Directed by Jacques Demy, and produced by Mag Bodard. Screenplay by Demy, based on a story by Charles Perrault.

Donkey Skin is told with the simplicity and beauty of a child's fairy tale, but with emotional undertones and a surrealistic style that adults are more likely to appreciate. A child and a parent seeing this movie would experience two different films. It was directed by the French New Wave legend Jacques Demy in 1970 and is based on a seventeenth-century tale by Charles Perrault; it's one of his original Mother Goose stories, which also include *Cinderella* and *Sleeping Beauty.*

In adapting it into a musical, Demy was probably thinking of Jean Cocteau's surrealistic masterpiece *The Beauty and the Beast* (1946), and Demy's own famous musicals, *The Umbrellas of Cherbourg* (1964) and *The Young Girls of Rochefort* (1967). His *Donkey Skin* makes the connection by costarring Jean Marais, who played three roles in *The Beauty and the Beast,* and Catherine Deneuve, who had the lead in both of the earlier Demy films.

The story involves two neighboring kingdoms. In the land ruled by Marais, the palace servants and even the horses are bright blue, like a medieval tryout for the Blue Man Group. In the land next door, ruled by Fernand Ledoux, everyone is red. Their maps must look like the Bush-Kerry election.

Sorrow in the blue kingdom. The queen (Deneuve) is dying. On her deathbed she orders the king, "Promise me you'll marry only when you find a wife more beautiful than me." This is not easily done. A search begins for

such a woman, but as the king examines the portraits of the candidates, each is more ugly than the one before. Finally his advisers decide only one woman qualifies: the king's own daughter, who is played by Catherine Deneuve and, therefore, bears a striking resemblance to her mother.

The king decrees he will marry his daughter. You are beginning to understand why Disney filmed *Sleeping Beauty* and *Cinderella* but not this one. There is also the remarkable detail that the kingdom's riches depend upon a donkey who, instead of manure, produces coins and jewels.

"Is my love a sin?" asks the blue king. "All little girls, asked who they want to marry when they grow up, say, 'I want to marry Daddy.'" Not this little girl, who escapes by boat and consults her fairy godmother (Delphine Seyrig), who suggests she make a series of impossible demands, such as a dress the color of weather. What color is weather? We find out when Deneuve appears in one of several remarkable gowns that are elegant and showy beyond any normal dimension, all but burying the princess inside.

After the king orders additional dresses the color of the moon and the sun, his daughter runs out of demands and escapes into the forest cloaked in a donkey skin. There she is seen by the prince of the red kingdom (Jacques Perrin), who falls in love and demands that his servants determine the identity of the unknown girl, etc.

To this story Demy brings a particular sense of style. A great deal of the dialogue is sung by the actors, with music by Michel Legrand, although the film doesn't approach his wall-to-wall score for *The Umbrellas of Cherbourg.* There are also incongruous elements I doubt were found in the seventeenth-century original, including a helicopter, a woman who spits toads, doorways so low everyone must stoop to get through them, and a royal throne that looks like Hello, Kitty! At times, characters fade in and out of transparency.

Despite these visual marvels, the film somehow lacks variety. It is all more or less the same; the same tone, similar songs, a level emotional field, nothing too exciting or too depressing. It requires, I hate to say it, an arc. Lacking that, it nevertheless provides a visual feast and fanciful imaginations, and Deneuve was then, as she was before and since, a great beauty with the confidence such beauty requires.

Note: This is a review of a restored print with new digital sound. Ebert's review of the Cocteau version of The Beauty and the Beast *is a Great Movie at rogerebert.com.*

Donnie Darko: The Director's Cut ★ ★ ★
R, 142 m., 2004

Jake Gyllenhaal (Donnie Darko), Mary McDonnell (Rose Darko), Holmes Osborne (Eddie Darko), Jena Malone (Gretchen Ross), Drew Barrymore (Ms. Pomeroy), Daveigh Chase (Samantha Darko), Patrick Swayze (Jim Cunningham), Katharine Ross (Dr. Thurman), Noah Wyle (Dr. Monnitoff). Directed by Richard Kelly and produced by Adam Fields and Sean McKittrick. Screenplay by Kelly.

"Pay close attention," warns the Web site for *Donnie Darko: The Director's Cut,* because "you could miss something." Damn, I missed it. I'm no closer to being able to explain the film's events than I was after seeing the 2001 version, which was about twenty minutes shorter. The difference is, that doesn't bother me so much. The movie remains impenetrable to logical analysis, but now I ask myself: What logical analysis would explain the presence of a six-foot-tall rabbit with what looks like the head of a science-fiction insect?

The director's cut adds footage that enriches and extends the material, but doesn't alter its tone. It adds footnotes that count down to a deadline, but without explaining the nature of the deadline or the usefulness of the countdown (I think it comes from an omniscient narrator who, despite his omniscience, sure does keep a lot to himself). What we have, in both versions, is a film of paradox that seems to involve either time travel or parallel universes. Having seen in *The Butterfly Effect* (2004) how a film might try to explain literally the effects of temporal travel, I am more content to accept this version of the Darko backward and abysm of time.

Let it be said that writer-director Richard Kelly's first film engages us so intriguingly

that we *desire* an explanation. It opens with Donnie Darko (Jake Gyllenhaal) sprawled at dawn in the middle of a remote road next to his bicycle. Just sleeping, he explains. He's out of his house a lot at night, apparently on the advice of the rabbit, which is named Frank. It's good advice, since Donnie returns home to find that the engine of a jet airliner has fallen from the skies into his bedroom. The strange thing is, the government has no record of a plane losing its engine.

Given the eerie national mood after 9/11, this detail did not much recommend the film to audiences when it opened on October 26, 2001. The film, a success at Sundance 2001, opened and closed in a wink, grossing only about $500,000 and inspiring some negative reviews ("Insufferable, lumpy and dolorous . . . infatuated with an aura of hand-me-down gloom."—Elvis Mitchell, *New York Times*). But it gathered a band of admirers, became a hit on DVD and at midnight shows, and is returning to theaters.

More than one critic said the movie was set in "John Hughes country," that 1980s suburban land of teenage angst and awkward love. Certainly, Jake Gyllenhaal is convincing in his convoluted relationship with Gretchen (Jena Malone), the new girl in town—who walks into the English class of Ms. Pomeroy (Drew Barrymore), asks where she should sit, and is told as only Drew Barrymore could tell her, "Sit next to the boy you think is the cutest." When she chooses Donnie, we can see why Gyllenhaal was once considered to play Spider-Man; he's got the look of a guy whose inner demons wall him off from girlfriends.

Donnie's suburb is green and leafy, and his home life happy. His mother (Mary McDonnell) is filled with warmth and love, and his father (Holmes Osborne) is not the standard monster of dad-hating Hollywood formulas. At school, Ms. Pomeroy is a good enough teacher to get herself fired. And the parent-teacher conference involving Donnie's run-in with the gym teacher is one of those scenes where parents try to look properly appalled at their son's behavior while it's all they can do to keep from laughing.

Then there's Frank, who is definitely not from Hughesland. He shows Donnie how to look into the future, and even gives him the power to visualize other people as they follow their time lines (a time line resembles a rope of coiling water, like the effect in *The Abyss*). And there is the case of the wizened old lady known as Grandma Death, who lives down the street and once wrote a book titled *The Philosophy of Time Travel*, which hinted or warned or predicted or intuited something ominous, I think, although I have no idea what it might have been.

The details of daily life are exactly right. We believe Donnie as a teenager who did not ask to be haunted by doubts and demons and is bearing up as best he can. He lives in a real world; apart, to be sure, from the rabbit and the time lines. Richard Kelly shows that he could make a straightforward movie about these characters, but *Donnie Darko* has no desire to be straightforward. I wrote in my original review: "The movie builds twists on top of turns until the plot wheel revolves one time too many and we're left scratching our heads. We don't demand answers at the end, but we want some kind of closure; Keyser Soze may not explain everything in *The Usual Suspects*, but it *feels* like he does."

In that 2001 review, I found a lot to admire and enjoy in *Donnie Darko*, including the director's control of tone and the freshness of the characters. My objection was that you couldn't understand the movie, which seemed to have parts on order. With the director's cut, I knew going in that I wouldn't understand it, so perhaps I was able to accept it in a different way. I ignored logic and responded to tone, and liked it more. There may have been another factor at work: As I grow weary of films like *The Princess Diaries II*, which follow their formulas with relentless fidelity to cliché and stereotype, I feel gratitude to directors who make something new.

Donnie Darko: The Director's Cut is alive, original, and intriguing. It's about a character who has no explanation for what is happening in his life, and is set in a world that cannot account for prescient rabbits named Frank. I think, after all, I am happier that the movie *doesn't* have closure. What kind of closure could there be? Frank takes off the insect head and reveals Drew Barrymore, who in a classroom flashback explains the plot and brings in Grandma Death as a resource person?

Don't Come Knocking ★ ★ ½
R, 122 m., 2006

Sam Shepard (Howard Spence), Jessica Lange (Doreen), Tim Roth (Sutter), Gabriel Mann (Earl), Sarah Polley (Sky), Fairuza Balk (Amber), Eva Marie Saint (Howard's Mother). Directed by Wim Wenders and produced by Peter Schwartzkopff. Screenplay by Sam Shepard.

Does every moment of a movie have to work for you? Or can you enjoy an imperfect one if it fills in places around the edges of your imagination? *Don't Come Knocking* is a curious film about a movie cowboy who walks off the set, goes seeking his past, and finds something that looks a lot more like a movie than the one he was making. There are scenes that don't even pretend to work. And others have a sweetness and visual beauty that stop time and simply invite you to share.

The opening shot is the key. On a black screen, we see two openings into the sky. From how they're placed, they could be the eyeholes in a ragged mask, maybe the Lone Ranger's. Then the shot reveals itself as a rock formation in Monument Valley; millions of years of evolution have left behind these two holes, joined by arches to the walls of a long-ago river canyon.

We are looking into the past, and at icons of the movie western; such rock formations were a backdrop in the classic films of John Ford. But the movie being filmed is far from *Stagecoach*. The mobile homes of the filmmakers are arranged in a circle, like wagons, but instead of a horse the assistant director rides a Segway. The western being made is so bad in a retro Johnny Mack Brown way that maybe it's a satire.

But, no. It's supposed to be a real western, starring Howard Spence (Sam Shepard), a once-great western star, now disappearing into cocaine and booze after a lifetime of scandal. *Don't Come Knocking* was written by Shepard and directed by Wim Wenders; they wrote and directed the great *Paris, Texas* (1984). What they should know is that once-great stars do not disappear into bargain-basement versions of their earlier work but move laterally into independent films that use their presence as an icon. That's what's hap-

181

pening here: Shepard may be playing a pathetic has-been, but what he really brings is an actor and playwright who embodies western myth in modern dress. I suppose I have seen all of Shepard's work on the screen and have never caught him being less than authentic.

That's true here, even at times when his Howard Spence is like a little boy who never grew up. Now he simply walks away from the set. He calls the mother he hasn't seen in thirty years (Eva Marie Saint) and goes to see her in Elko, Nevada. He arrives not as if decades have passed, but as if he's late coming home after school. As mothers will, she pages through the scrapbook she's kept of her famous son, and we see stories about drugs, divorces, brawls, and box-office disasters.

She tells him of a son he has in Butte, Montana. He goes to Butte in search of this unknown child and finds the boy's mother working as a waitress. She is Doreen (Jessica Lange), still attractive, amused that this joke should have walked back into her life. He follows her into a bar. "If you're looking for your son," she says, "that's him, right there in front of you."

The son is Earl (Gabriel Mann), very good as an uncertain and mannered young would-be folk singer with a lot of resentment toward his father. His girlfriend, Amber (Fairuza Balk), like a lot of young women who affect a ferocious Goth look, is timid and affectionate underneath. Howard realizes he is being followed by another young woman. This is Sky (Sarah Polley), his daughter by yet another woman, whose ashes she is carrying in an urn.

These people move in intersecting orbits through Butte, a city that seems to have essentially no traffic, and no residents not in the movie except for a few tavern extras and restaurant customers. Consider a scene where the enraged Earl throws all of his possessions out the window of his second-story apartment and into the street. His stuff remains there, undisturbed, for days. No complaints from the neighbors. No cops. Howard Spence spends a night on the sofa, sleeping, thinking, and smoking. It's a lovely scene. After Howard's meditative night, he comes to a peace of sorts with his son and daughter, and they with each other. As this process takes place, they all seem outlined against their own

mental horizons, as archetypes who represent something: a cowboy's last hurrah, a rebellious son's acceptance of his father, a lost daughter's opportunity to fabricate a funeral for her mother by going in search of the mourners.

The characters stand for so much, it's all they can do to bear the weight. Tim Roth is more realistic, as a tracer for the insurance company that holds a bond on the movie. His job is to track down Howard Spence and bring him back alive. This he does with such dispatch that he hardly seems aware he is interrupting a family drama.

The cinematography by Franz Lustig looks wonderful from beginning to end, but no shot equals one where we see Howard Spence sitting in a lonely hotel room window overlooking a desolate city street. Surely when they framed this shot, Wenders, Lustig, and Shepard were thinking of Edward Hopper crossed with "Main Line on Main Street," the famous photograph by O. Winston Link. The cinematography evokes a romantic and elegiac mood, within which the peculiarities of the characters may seem sillier than was intended.

Don't Come Knocking finally doesn't work for me because instead of embodying its themes, it seems to be regarding them from outside, with awe, as if it is the high school production of itself. The supporting characters are all genuine enough, but the central role of Howard Spence is a problem. He needs to be more heroic or more pathetic—I'm not sure which. His life seems to be lived outside his experience, as if someone else made all those headlines in his mother's scrapbook. "Nothing that happened back then happened," he says, summing up his life with one line that puts its finger directly on the character's biggest problem.

Doom ★
R, 104 m., 2005

Karl Urban (John Grimm [Reaper]), Rosamund Pike (Samantha Grimm), Raz Adoti (Duke), The Rock (Sarge), Deobia Oparei (Destroyer), Ben Daniels (Goat), Richard Brake (Portman), Al Weaver (The Kid), Yao Chin (Mac), Robert Russell (Dr. Carmack). Directed by Andrzej Bartkowiak and produced by John Wells and

Lorenzo di Bonaventura. Screenplay by David Callaham and Wesley Strick.

Doom has one great shot. It comes right at the beginning. It's the Universal logo. Instead of a spinning Earth with the letters U-N-I-V-E-R-S-A-L rising in the east and centering themselves over Lebanon, Kansas, we see the red planet, Mars. Then we fly closer to Mars until we see surface details and finally the Olduvai Research Station, helpfully described on the movie's Web site as "a remote scientific facility on Mars"—where, if you give it but a moment's thought, all of the scientific facilities are remote.

Anyway, that's the last we see of the surface of Mars. A lot of readers thought I was crazy for liking *Ghosts of Mars* (2001) and *Red Planet* (2000) and *Total Recall* (1990), but blast it all, at least in those movies *you get to see Mars*. I'm a science fiction fan from way back. I go to Mars, I expect to see it. Watching *Doom* is like visiting Vegas and never leaving your hotel room.

The movie has been "inspired by" the famous video game. No, I haven't played it, and I never will, but I know how it feels *not* to play it, because I've seen the movie. *Doom* is like some kid came over and is using your computer and won't let you play.

The movie involves a group of Marines named the Rapid Response Tactical Squad, which if they would take only the slightest trouble could be renamed the Rapid Action Tactical Squad, which would acronym into RATS. The year is 2046. In the middle of an American desert has been discovered a portal to an ancient city on Mars. The Olduvai facility has been established to study it, and now there is a "breech of level 5 security," and the RRTS is sent to Mars through the portal to take care of business. The leader is Sarge (The Rock), and their members include Reaper (Karl Urban), Destroyer (Deobia Oparei), Mac (Yao Chin), Goat (Ben Daniels), Duke (Raz Adoti), Portman (Richard Brake), and The Kid (Al Weaver). Now you know everything you need to know about them.

On Mars, we see terrified humans running from an unseen threat. Dr. Carmack (Robert Russell) closes an automatic steel door on a young woman whose arm is onscreen longer than she is, if you get my drift, and then he spends a lot of time huddled in the corner vibrating and whimpering. We meet Samantha Grimm (Rosamund Pike), sister of Reaper (aka John Grimm). She is an anthropologist at the station and has reconstructed a complete skeleton of a humanoid Martian woman huddled protectively over her child. If you know your anthropology, you gotta say those are bones that have survived a lot of geological activity.

The original Martians were not merely humanoid, Dr. Grimm speculates, but superhuman: They bioengineered a twenty-fourth chromosome. We have twenty-three. The extra chromosome made them super smart, super strong, super fast, and super quick to heal. But it turned some of them into monsters, which presumably is why the others built the portal to Earth, where—what? They became us but left the twenty-fourth chromosome behind? Is that the kind of intelligent design we want our kids studying?

Despite all of her chromosome counting, Dr. Grimm says at another point: "Ten percent of the human genome has not yet been mapped. Some say it's the soul." Whoa! The Human Genome Project was completed in 2003, something you would think a scientist like Dr. Grimm should know. I am reminded of the astronauts in *Stealth* reminding each other what a prime number is.

The monsters are still there on Mars. They are big mothers and must have awesome daily caloric requirements. How they survive, how they breathe Earth atmosphere in the station, and what, as carnivores, they eat and drink—I think we can all agree these are questions deserving serious scientific study. Meanwhile, their pastime is chasing humans, grabbing them, smashing them, eviscerating and disemboweling them, pulling them through grates, and in general doing anything that can take place obscurely in shadows and not require a lot of special effects.

Toward the end of the movie, there is a lengthy point-of-view shot looking forward over the barrel of a large weapon as it tracks the corridors of the research station. Monsters jump out from behind things and are blasted to death, in a sequence that abandons all attempts at character and dialogue and uncannily resembles a video game. Later, when the names of the actors appear on the screen, they are also blasted into little pieces. I forget whether the director, Andrzej Bartkowiak, had his name shot to smithereens, but for the DVD I recommend that a monster grab it and eat it.

The Door in the Floor ★ ★ ★
R, 111 m., 2004

Jeff Bridges (Ted Cole), Kim Basinger (Marion Cole), Jon Foster (Eddie O'Hare), Mimi Rogers (Eleanor Vaughn), Bijou Phillips (Alice), Elle Fanning (Ruth). Directed by Tod Williams and produced by Anne Carey, Michael Corrente, and Ted Hope. Screenplay by Williams, and based on the novel *A Widow for One Year* by John Irving.

What is it about Jeff Bridges, the way he can say something nice in a way that doesn't sound so nice? How does he find that balance between the sunny optimism and the buried agenda? Early in *The Door in the Floor*, playing an author named Ted Cole, he suggests to his wife, Marion (Kim Basinger), that they add a swimming pool to the lawn of their home in the East Hamptons. How do we know his proposal is like turning a knife in his wife's ribs?

I saw the movie after rewatching Bridges' first performance, in *The Last Picture Show* (1971). More than thirty years later, he still has the same open face, the same placid smile, the same level voice that never seems to try very hard for emotion, and the same ability to suggest the depths and secrets of his character. In this story of a wounded marriage, Kim Basinger is well chosen as his target in an emotional duel. There can be something hurt and vulnerable about her, a fear around the eyes, a hopeful sweetness that doesn't seem to expect much. Here she transgresses moral boundaries by deliberately seducing a sixteen-year-old boy, and yet still seems to be the victim.

The movie is about a marriage between two smart people who are too afraid, or perhaps too cruel, to fight out in the open. They play a deep game of psychological chicken, all the more hurtful because they know so well what buttons to push. We learn eventually that their two sons were killed in a car crash, that Marion in some ways blames Cole, that in middle life they've had a daughter, Ruth (Elle Fan-

ning), to try to heal the loss, and that the loss was not healed. Now Cole proposes to hire a young student as their assistant for the summer. This is Eddie (Jon Foster). Because we have already visited the upstairs corridor lined with photographs of their two dead boys, we notice immediately that Eddie looks a lot like the older boy. Marion notices too, as she is intended to.

The movie is based on an early section of John Irving's 1998 novel *A Widow for One Year*, which is mostly about Ruth growing up and developing problems of her own. This story focuses on the relationship of her parents. Ted Cole is a womanizer, a failed serious novelist who has found success with children's books that he illustrates himself; his illustrations require female models, whom he recruits from the neighborhood, and who only gradually discover that they are to be nude and to have sex with Cole. Marion, meanwhile, is stuck in a sad blankness, unable to stir herself back into life.

The boy Eddie is smart, serious, ambitious, headed for a good school, and very impressed to be working for a famous writer. Cole has little for him to do, except to drive him to and from liaisons with Mrs. Vaughn (Mimi Rogers), one of his current mistresses. Cole can't drive himself because his license is suspended.

During the course of the summer Cole says he has been "thinking," which in a marriage usually means trouble, and he suggests a "trial separation," which usually means the trial will be successful. He times this suggestion for soon after Eddie comes to work for them, and Eddie finds himself dividing his time between the beach house and the house in town. That this is part of Cole's plan to passively urge his wife into adultery is obvious to Marion if not to Eddie, who becomes sexually obsessed with the older woman. She catches him one day masturbating with the inspiration of her bra and panties.

I don't know what I think—or what I'm supposed to think—about the sex they eventually have. Certainly Basinger is perfectly modulated in the way she talks with Eddie, soothes his guilt over the masturbation scene, asks him to dinner and eventually to bed. Young men have daydreams about older women like this, just as older women have nightmares about the young men. But the director, Tod Williams, pays unseemly attention to their sex itself. The film should be about their transgression, not their technique. The relationship between Marion and Eddie is the least satisfactory in the movie, because the movie isn't really about it—it's about how Cole and Marion use it.

Cole is a thoroughgoing SOB. Marion may be evil too, but she's nicer about it. The way Cole treats the Mimi Rogers character ventures beyond cruelty into sadism, and Williams makes a mistake by allowing its tension to be released in a quasi-slapstick scene where she tries to run him over in her SUV. That's letting him off too easy. But Williams handles the main line of the story, the war between Cole and Marion, clearly and strongly; you may not always hurt the one you love, but you certainly know how to.

Bridges plays his role with an untidy beard, wild hair, and a wardrobe that ranges from ratty bathrobes to casual nudity in front of strangers. He's doing something with his lower jaw, as if he's talking with a mouthful of water, and it makes him seem more like a predator. Basinger has to internalize more. Jon Foster, the young actor, is given a good character but the screenplay denies him either an objective or a release; all he can do is escape. Ruth, the little girl, meanwhile, watches disturbing sights with big eyes, screams at the top of her lungs, and will grow up to be the heroine of a John Irving novel, not something you would wish lightly upon a child.

Dot the I ★ ★ ★
R, 92 m., 2005

Gael Garcia Bernal (Kit), Natalia Verbeke (Carmen), James D'Arcy (Barnaby), Tom Hardy (Tom), Charlie Cox (Theo). Directed by Matthew Parkhill and produced by George Duffield and Meg Thomson. Screenplay by Parkhill.

There is an ancient French tradition that on the night before her marriage, the bride-to-be can choose a handsome stranger and share with him one last kiss. If you have never heard of this tradition, neither have I, because it,

along with a great deal else, was invented for this movie. *Dot the I* is like one of those nests of Chinese boxes within boxes. The outer box is a love story. There are times when we despair of ever reaching the innermost box.

An opening scene is set in a French restaurant in London, where Carmen (Natalia Verbeke), a Spanish dancer, is having a dinner with her girlfriends on the eve of her wedding. The maitre d' explains the ancient tradition, Carmen believes him, looks around the restaurant, and her eyes settle on Kit (Gael Garcia Bernal). She kisses him. This is interesting: The kiss continues longer than we would expect. They seem to want it to go on forever. They have so much chemistry it threatens to trespass upon biology.

Kit is from Brazil, an out-of-work actor. Since Bernal is in fact from Mexico, he could perfectly well speak Spanish, which is why he is made Brazilian and would speak Portuguese, so that he and his Spanish friend will have to talk for our convenience in English. Sometimes it is jolly, this neocolonialism. As for the title, we are told that "a kiss dots the 'I' on the word 'love,'" but not in English, obviously, or Spanish or Portuguese, either (they both use "amor"). Maybe in German ("liebe"). Or maybe, we eventually realize, not in this movie.

Although Carmen and Kit are obviously made for each other, Carmen persists in her plan to marry the rich but odious Barnaby (James D'Arcy). As *Dot the I* moves along, it becomes clear that there is very little, however, that this Barnaby would not do.

The opening hour of the movie is a wonderfully complicated love story, during which Carmen goes ahead with her plans to marry Barnaby, and Kit fails in his attempt to emulate Benjamin in *The Graduate* and interrupt the ceremony with a wild goat cry of love. But Kit is not easily discouraged. He finds out Carmen's name from her friends in the restaurant, and contacts her to ask if they can meet: "Just once! Just one glass of water! In a brightly lit public place! We don't even have to speak!" She has mercy on him.

What happens next it would be unfair to reveal, and perhaps impossible. The movie not only scatters undotted I's and uncrossed T's in its wake, but unsquared circles, unfactored primes, unrisen soufflés, and unconsummated consummations. Matthew Parkhill, who wrote and directed it, is not a man to deny us the fruits of his boundless, some would say excessive, invention.

Watching the movie, I went through several stages. I liked the first half perfectly well as a love story involving sympathetic people. I hoped they would find happiness out from under the cloud of the snarfy Barnaby. Then—well, there was a surprise, and I rather liked the surprise, too, because it put things in a new light and made everyone just that much more interesting. And then another surprise, and another, until . . .

The last ten or fifteen minutes are going to require a great deal of patience with the filmmakers, as they riffle through the plot like a riverboat gambler with aces up his wazoo. I suppose that in a logical way it all makes sense—except that there is no logical way that it would happen in the first place. Having been tricked into accepting the characters as people we can trust in and care for, we now discover their world is but a stage, and they but players on it. Psychological realism and emotional continuity be damned!

Am I unhappy because the concluding scenes in the movie rob me of my feelings about the characters, or because the earlier scenes created those feelings? Certainly the film would not be better if the first hour had been given over to game-playing. The ingenuity of the film is admirable, I suppose, although we walk out of the theater with perplexing questions about motives, means, access, and techniques.

So let us observe that good work is performed here by all three of the leading actors—Bernal, who is so likable he had better play a villain soon just to add some Tabasco; Verbeke, who is so touchingly torn between love and loyalty, and then between loyalty and love; and D'Arcy, who creates a truly scary two-faced personality. To keep their emotional bearings in this plot is no small achievement. And let us concede that Matthew Parkhill has at least not taken the easy way out. Yes, we'd prefer a straightforward love triangle without the bells and whistles, but that might turn out boring, while *Dot the I* keeps our attention even while stomping on it.

Downfall ★ ★ ★ ★
R, 155 m., 2005

Bruno Ganz (Adolf Hitler), Alexandra Maria Lara (Traudl Junge), Juliane Kohler (Eva Braun), Corinna Harfouch (Magda Goebbels), Thomas Kretschmann (Hermann Fegelein), Ulrich Matthes (Joseph Goebbels), Heino Ferch (Albert Speer), Christian Berkel (Dr. Schenck), Ulrich Noethen (Heinrich Himmler). Directed by Oliver Hirschbiegel and produced by Bernd Eichinger. Screenplay by Eichinger, based on the book *Inside Hitler's Bunker* by Joachim Fest and the book *Bis zur letzten Stunde* by Traudl Junge and Melissa Muller.

Downfall takes place almost entirely inside the bunker beneath Berlin where Adolf Hitler and his inner circle spent their final days, and died. It ventures outside only to show the collapse of the Nazi defense of Berlin, the misery of the civilian population, and the burning of the bodies of Hitler, Eva Braun, and Joseph and Magda Goebbels. For the rest, it occupies a labyrinth of concrete corridors, harshly lighted, with a constant passage back and forth of aides, servants, guards, family members, and Hitler's dog, Blondi. I was reminded, oddly, of the claustrophobic sets built for *Das Boot,* which took place mostly inside a Nazi submarine.

Our entry to this sealed world is Traudl Junge (Alexandra Maria Lara), hired by Hitler as a secretary in 1942 and eyewitness to Hitler's decay in body and mind. She wrote a memoir about her experiences, which is one of the sources of this film, and *Blind Spot* (2002) was a documentary about her memories. In a clip at the end of *Downfall,* filmed shortly before her death, she says she now feels she should have known more than she did about the crimes of the Nazis. But like many secretaries the world over, she was awed by the power of her employer and not included in the information loop. Yet she could see, as anyone could see, that Hitler was a lunatic. Sometimes kind, sometimes considerate, sometimes screaming in fits of rage, but certainly cut loose from reality.

Against the overarching facts of his personal magnetism and the blind loyalty of his lieutenants, the movie observes the workings of the world within the bunker. All power flowed from Hitler. He was evil, mad, ill, but long after Hitler's war was lost he continued to wage it in fantasy. Pounding on maps, screaming ultimatums, he moved troops that no longer existed, issued orders to commanders who were dead, counted on rescue from imaginary armies.

That he was unhinged did not much affect the decisions of acolytes like Joseph and Magda Goebbels, who decided to stay with him and commit suicide as he would. "I do not want to live in a world without National Socialism," says Frau Goebbels, and she doesn't want her six children to live in one, either. In a sad, sickening scene, she gives them all a sleeping potion and then, one by one, inserts a cyanide capsule in their mouths and forces their jaws closed with a soft but audible crunch. Her oldest daughter, Helga, senses there is something wrong; senses, possibly, she is being murdered. Then Magda sits down to a game of solitaire before she and Joseph kill themselves. (By contrast, Heinrich Himmler wonders aloud, "When I meet Eisenhower, should I give the Nazi salute, or shake his hand?")

Hitler is played by Bruno Ganz, the gentle soul of *Wings of Desire*, the sad-eyed romantic or weary idealist of many roles over thirty years. Here we do not recognize him at first, hunched over, shrunken, his injured left hand fluttering behind his back like a trapped bird. If it were not for the 1942 scenes in which he hires Frau Junge as a secretary, we would not be able to picture him standing upright. He uses his hands as claws that crawl over battlefield maps, as he assures his generals that this or that impossible event will save them. And if not, well: "If the war is lost, it is immaterial if the German people survive. I will shed not one tear for them." It was his war, and they had let him down, he screams: betrayed him, lied to him, turned traitor.

Frau Junge and two other secretaries bunk in a small concrete room, and sneak away to smoke cigarettes, which Hitler cannot abide. Acting as a hostess to the death watch, his mistress, Eva Braun (Juliane Kohler), presides over meals set with fine china and crystal. She hardly seems to engage Hitler except as a social companion. Although we have heard his rants and ravings about the Jews, the Russians, his own treacherous generals, and his paranoid delusions, Braun is actually able to confide to Junge, toward the end: "He only talks about dogs and vegetarian meals. He doesn't want anyone to see deep inside of him." Seeing inside of him is no trick at all: He is flayed bare by his own rage.

Downfall was one of 2005's Oscar nominees for Best Foreign Film. It has inspired much debate about the nature of the Hitler it presents. Is it a mistake to see him, after all, not as a monster standing outside the human race, but as just another human being?

David Denby, *The New Yorker*: "Considered as biography, the achievement (if that's the right word) of *Downfall* is to insist that the monster was not invariably monstrous—that he was kind to his cook and his young female secretaries, loved his German shepherd, Blondi, and was surrounded by loyal subordinates. We get the point: Hitler was not a supernatural being; he was common clay raised to power by the desire of his followers. But is this observation a sufficient response to what Hitler actually did?"

Stanley Kauffman, *The New Republic*: "Ever since World War II, it has been clear that a fiction film could deal with the finish of Hitler and his group in one of two ways: either as ravening beasts finally getting the fate they deserved or as consecrated idealists who believed in what they had done and were willing to pay with their lives for their actions. The historical evidence of the behavior in the bunker supports the latter view .... *Downfall*, apparently faithful to the facts, evokes—torments us with—a discomfiting species of sympathy or admiration."

Admiration I did not feel. Sympathy I felt in the sense that I would feel it for a rabid dog, while accepting that it must be destroyed. I do not feel the film provides "a sufficient response to what Hitler actually did," because I feel no film can, and no response would be sufficient. All we can learn from a film like this is that millions of people can be led, and millions more killed, by madness leashed to racism and the barbaric instincts of tribalism.

What I also felt, however, was the reality of the Nazi sickness, which has been distanced and diluted by so many movies with so many

Nazi villains that it has become more like a plot device than a reality. As we regard this broken and pathetic Hitler, we realize that he did not alone create the Third Reich, but was the focus for a spontaneous uprising by many of the German people, fueled by racism, xenophobia, grandiosity, and fear. He was skilled in the ways he exploited that feeling, and surrounded himself with gifted strategists and propagandists, but he was not a great man, simply one armed by fate to unleash unimaginable evil. It is useful to reflect that racism, xenophobia, grandiosity, and fear are still with us, and the defeat of one of their manifestations does not inoculate us against others.

Down in the Valley ★ ★ ½
R, 125 m., 2006

Edward Norton (Harlan), Evan Rachel Wood (Tobe), David Morse (Wade), Bruce Dern (Charlie), Rory Culkin (Lonnie). Directed by David Jacobson and produced by Holly Wiersma, Edward Norton, and Adam Rosenfelt. Screenplay by Jacobson.

A carload of teenage girls on their way to the beach stop at a gas station, and one of them likes the look of the attendant, an older guy with bad-boy charm. She invites him along. He quits his job and jumps in the car. He says he's from South Dakota and has never seen the ocean. We don't know whether to believe that, or much of anything else he says, but she believes him, and so will her younger brother.

That's the setup for *Down in the Valley*, a movie that the actors and director take as far as they can until the story bogs down in questions too big to forgive. The first half is pitch-perfect, as Tobe (Evan Rachel Wood), who is eighteen, falls under the spell of Harlan (Edward Norton), who is thirtysomething but not quite grown up, or all there. He thinks of himself as a cowboy, loves that ten-gallon hat, takes her horseback riding, and gets into a dispute over whether the horse was stolen or only borrowed. He has a lot of misunderstandings like that.

Tobe lives in an ordinary house in the San Fernando Valley with her dad, Wade (David Morse), and thirteen-year-old brother, Lonnie (Rory Culkin). Wade works as a correc-

tions officer but doesn't bring his work home with him: He is a careless parent who makes a big show of supervising his children but seems unaware that Harlan enters his daughter's bedroom at will. When Harlan meets him for the first time, he delivers one of those sincere, forthright speeches about wanting to treat the daughter with respect and earn the trust of the father, etc. Norton is such a nuanced actor that he simultaneously makes this speech sound like the absolute truth and a bald-faced lie.

Tobe is fascinated by Harlan, by his cowboy act, by his posturing, by his (or somebody's) horse, and by the sex. But she isn't dumb, and she grows disturbed about some of the things she senses. Her kid brother, Lonnie, on the other hand, is angry with his father and ready to fall for Harlan's line, and that leads to some closing scenes that plain don't work. Wade, having been absent or inattentive at crucial moments, becomes obsessed with hunting down Harlan after the "cowboy" gets into the big trouble that we've been expecting since the first scene. The chase actually leads to the movie set of a Western town, which is not merely symbolism, or even Symbolism, but SYMBOLISM!

The ending is a mess, but the film has qualities that make me happy to have seen it. I like the peculiar loneliness of Harlan's life; he lives in the Valley as if it were the old West, he haunts hillsides and wooded areas, he hides under culverts, he conceals from Tobe the fact that, apart from her, he has no resources at all. At the end, even if he's crazy, he's consistent.

And the performances can't be faulted. Norton finds that line dividing madness from plausibility and reminds me a little of how Treat Williams talks to Laura Dern in *Smooth Talk* (1985), permanently destroying her illusions. Wood, who starred in *Thirteen*, a similar story about teenagers out of control, is fascinating in the way she wills herself to believe what cannot be true. There's a little of *Kwik Stop* (2001) in Tobe's desire to escape from her life. And Culkin is convincing when he chooses the cowboy over his strict father, but the screenplay maintains his decision long after he should abandon it. Morse finds a difficult note, as a father who wants to love and protect his children but whose mind seems elsewhere and whose common sense is lacking.

All of these qualities are worthy. But when a movie begins to present one implausible or unwise decision after another, when its world plays too easily into the hands of its story, when the taste for symbolism creates impossible scenes, we grow restless. The movie has stopped being about its characters and has started being about its concept, stranding them in ideas instead of lives.

Dreamer ★ ★ ★
PG, 98 m., 2005

Kurt Russell (Ben Crane), Dakota Fanning (Cale Crane), Kris Kristofferson (Pop Crane), Elisabeth Shue (Lily Crane), Luis Guzman (Balon), Freddy Rodriguez (Manolin), David Morse (Palmer), Oded Fehr (Prince Sadir). Directed by John Gatins and produced by Hunt Lowry, Mike Tollin, and Brian Robbins. Screenplay by Gatins.

One of the most important stories in *Sports Illustrated*'s history was written by William Nack, the great writer about horses and boxing. Nack grew up around racetracks and served in Vietnam, and when he returned noticed something new: A lot of horses were breaking down. In earlier years, it was rare for a horse to break a leg during a race. His investigation met a wall of silence, until one vet talked to him off the record, confirming his suspicions: Owners were using cortisone to deaden the pain of horses that should not be racing, and the broken bones were the result.

When a racehorse breaks a leg on the track, the horse is invariably put down. Nack's story "Breakdowns" told of the death of one such filly. I heard Nack read it once, at a signing for his book *My Turf,* and people in the audience were crying. The movie *Dreamer* is based on a true story of the unthinkable: a horse that broke a bone and came back to race again. She was Mariah's Storm, winner of the 1995 Turfway Breeder's Cup.

The movie is a well-made use of familiar materials, including the loyalty between a child and a horse that goes back to *National Velvet* (1944) and *The Black Stallion* (1979). It's aimed at an audience of teenagers that may never have heard of those films, and for them,

Dreamer will be an exciting experience. It has a first-rate cast: Dakota Fanning as young Cale Crane, Kurt Russell as her father, Ben, and Kris Kristofferson as her grandfather, Pop.

Ben is a trainer for the rich and supercilious Palmer (David Morse). He likes the prospects of a filly named Sonador, which is Spanish for "dreamy"—close enough to Dreamer, especially since the title refers to Cale. She's at the track one day when her dad tells Palmer he doesn't think Sonador should run: "She doesn't want to race today." Palmer overrules him, the horse runs, and she breaks a leg.

Ben later admits, "If Cale hadn't have been with me that night, I'd have left that horse on the track." But Cale is there, and looking at her big sad eyes, her father has the leg splinted and wrapped, and brings the horse back to the stable. This inspires an argument with Palmer, who is forced to regard the results of his own bad judgment. Ben resigns, taking a payout— and the horse.

This is not something he can afford to do. Their farm, which is already "the only horse farm in Lexington, Kentucky, without any horses," is facing foreclosure. But Sonador mends, and Ben and Pop think maybe she can be bred. That's before Cale gives Sonador her head one day, and the two men watch Cale and the horse flying across the turf.

"We could see if she perks up in a real race," Ben says, almost to himself.

"Could be easy money," says Pop.

This is a long conversation for them, since they weren't on speaking terms, Pop living on his own in a cabin on the property. The saga of Sonador has broken the ice, and now they're talking together and daring to dream. As for Cale, she knows the horse can run and win. And Pop is right: There would be long odds on a horse making a comeback after an injury.

What happens next I will leave for you to discover, including the subplot involving the two Arab brothers who are rival horse owners. What is central is young Fanning's performance, as a mite of a girl who stands up to be counted. Fanning, it is said, appears in every third movie nowadays; she's busy, all right, but that's because she's good, and here she plays Cale as a girl who has watched horses and trainers and has grown up around the track, and who tempers her sentiment for

Sonador with an instinct that the horse has more race left in her.

They say girls discover horses right before they discover boys. Whether that represents progress is a question every parent of a teenager must sometimes ponder, but certainly any girl in the target age group is going to make *Dreamer* one of her favorite films. For adults, the movie offers the appeal of solid, understated performances by Russell, Kristofferson, and Morse, whose villain doesn't gnash but simply calculates heartlessly. And then of course there is the horse racing. If your horse might win but might break the same leg again, you have so much riding on the race that the odds don't really come into it. 		☞

The Dreamers ★ ★ ★ ★
NC-17, 115 m., 2004

Michael Pitt (Matthew), Eva Green (Isabelle), Louis Garrel (Theo), Robin Renucci (Father), Anna Chancellor (Mother). Directed by Bernardo Bertolucci. and produced by Jeremy Thomas. Screenplay by Gilbert Adair, based on his novel.

In the spring of 1968, three planets—Sex, Politics, and the Cinema—came into alignment and exerted a gravitational pull on the status quo. In Paris, what began as a protest over the ouster of Henri Langlois, the legendary founder of the Cinématheque Français, grew into a popular revolt that threatened to topple the government. There were barricades in the streets, firebombs, clashes with the police, a crisis of confidence. In a way that seems inexplicable today, the director Jean-Luc Godard and his films were at the center of the maelstrom. Other New Wave directors and the cinema in general seemed to act as the agitprop arm of the revolution.

Here are two memories from that time. In the spring of 1968, I was on vacation in Paris. Demonstrators had barricaded one end of the street where my cheap Left Bank hotel was located. Police were massed at the other end. I was in the middle, standing outside my hotel, taking it all in. The police charged, I was pushed out in front of them, and rubber truncheons pounded on my legs. "Tourist!" I shouted, trying to make myself into a neutral.

Later I realized they might have thought I was saying "tourista!" which is slang for diarrhea. Unwise.

The second memory is more pleasant. In April 1969, driving past the Three Penny Cinema on Lincoln Avenue in Chicago, I saw a crowd lined up under umbrellas on the sidewalk, waiting in the rain to get into the next screening of Godard's *Weekend*. Today you couldn't pay most Chicago moviegoers to see a film by Godard, but at that moment, the year after the Battle of Grant Park, at the height of opposition to the Vietnam War, it was all part of the same alignment.

Oh, and sex. By the summer of 1969, I was in Hollywood, writing the screenplay for Russ Meyer's *Beyond the Valley of the Dolls*. It would be an X-rated movie from 20th Century-Fox, and although it seems tame today (R-rated, probably), it was part of a moment when sex had entered the mainstream and was part of a whole sense of society in flux.

I indulge in this autobiography because I have just seen Bernardo Bertolucci's *The Dreamers* and am filled with poignant and powerful nostalgia. To be sixteen in 1968 is to be fifty today, and so most younger moviegoers will find this film as historical as *Cold Mountain*. For me, it is yesterday; above all, it evokes a time when the movies—good movies, both classic and newborn—were at the center of youth culture. "The Movie Generation," *Time* magazine called us in a cover story. I got my job at the *Sun-Times* because of it; they looked around the feature department and appointed the longhaired new kid who had written a story about the underground films on Monday nights at Second City.

Bertolucci is two years older than I am, an Italian who made his first important film, *Before the Revolution*, when he was only twenty-four. He would, in 1972, make *Last Tango in Paris*, a film starring Marlon Brando and the unknown Maria Schneider in a tragedy about loss, grief, and sudden sex between two strangers who find it a form of urgent communication. Pauline Kael said, "Bertolucci and Brando have altered the face of an art form." Well, in those days we talked about movies that way.

It is important to have this background in mind when you go to see *The Dreamers* because Bertolucci certainly does. His film, like

Last Tango, takes place largely in a vast Parisian apartment. It is about transgressive sex. Outside the windows, there are riots in the streets, and indeed, in a moment of obvious symbolism, a stone thrown through a window saves the lives of the characters, the revolution interrupting their introverted triangle.

The three characters are Matthew (Michael Pitt), a young American from San Diego who is in Paris to study for a year, but actually spends all of his time at the Cinématheque, and the twins Isabelle (Eva Green) and Theo (Louis Garrel), children of a famous French poet and his British wife. They also spend all of their time at the movies. Almost the first thing Isabelle tells Matthew is, "You're awfully clean for someone who goes to the cinema so much." He's clean in more ways than one; he's a naive, idealistic American, and the movie treats him to these strange Europeans in the same way Henry James sacrifices his Yankee innocents on the altar of continental decadence.

These are the children of the cinema. Isabelle tells Matthew, "I entered this world on the Champs Élysées in 1959, and my very first words were *New York Herald Tribune!*" Bertolucci cuts to the opening scene in Godard's *Breathless* (1959), one of the founding moments of the New Wave, as Jean Seberg shouts out those words on the boulevard. In other words, the New Wave, not her parents, gave birth to Isabelle. There are many moments when the characters quiz each other about the movies, or reenact scenes they remember; a particularly lovely scene has Isabelle moving around a room, touching surfaces, in a perfect imitation of Garbo in *Queen Christina.* And there's a bitter argument between Matthew and Theo about who is greater—Keaton or Chaplin? Matthew, the American, of course, knows that the answer is Keaton. Only a Frenchman could think it was Chaplin.

But *The Dreamers* is not Bertolucci's version of Trivial Pursuit. Within the apartment, sex becomes the proving ground and then the battleground for the revolutionary ideas in the air. Matthew meets the twins at the Cinématheque during a demonstration in favor of Langlois (Bertolucci intercuts newsreel footage of Jean-Pierre Leaud in 1968 with new footage of Leaud today, and we also get glimpses of Truffaut, Godard, and Nicholas Ray). They invite him back to their parents' apartment. The parents are going to the seaside for a month, and the twins invite him to stay.

At first it is delightful. "I have at last met some real Parisians!" Matthew writes his parents. Enclosed in the claustrophobic world of the apartment, he finds himself absorbed in the sexual obsessions of the twins. He glimpses one night that they sleep together, naked. Isabelle defeats Theo in a movie quiz and orders him to masturbate (on his knees, in front of a photo of Garbo). Theo wins a quiz and orders Matthew to make love to his sister. Matthew is sometimes a little drunk, sometimes high, sometimes driven by lust, but at the bottom he knows this is wrong, and his more conventional values set up the ending of the film, in which sex and the cinema are engines, but politics is the train.

The film is extraordinarily beautiful. Bertolucci is one of the great painters of the screen. He has a voluptuous way here of bathing his characters in scenes from great movies, and referring to others. Sometimes his movie references are subtle, and you should look for a lovely one. Matthew looks out a window as rain falls on the glass, and the light through the window makes it seem that the drops are running down his face. This is a quote from a famous shot by Conrad L. Hall in Richard Brooks's *In Cold Blood* (1967). And although Michael Pitt usually looks a little like Leonardo DiCaprio, in this shot, at that angle, with that lighting, he embodies for a moment the young Marlon Brando. Another quotation: As the three young people run down an outdoor staircase, they are pursued by their own giant shadows, in a nod to *The Third Man.*

The movie is rated NC-17, for adults only, because of the themes and because of some frontal nudity. So discredited is the NC-17 rating that Fox Searchlight at first thought to edit the film for an R, but why bother to distribute a Bertolucci film except in the form he made it? The sexual content evokes that time and place. The movie is like a classic argument for an A rating, between the R and NC-17, which would identify movies intended for adults but not actually pornographic. What has happened in our society to make us embrace violence and shy away from sexuality?

Bertolucci titles his film *The Dreamers*, I think, because his characters are dreaming, until the brick through the window shatters their cocoon and the real world of tear gas and Molotov cocktails enters their lives. It is clear now that Godard and sexual liberation were never going to change the world. It only seemed that way for a time. The people who really run things do not go much to the movies, or perhaps think much about sex. They are driven by money and power. Matthew finds he cannot follow the twins into whatever fantasy the times have inspired in them. He turns away and disappears into the crowd of rioters, walking in the opposite direction. Walking into a future in which, perhaps, he will become the director of this movie.

Duane Hopwood ★ ★ ★ ½
R, 83 m., 2005

David Schwimmer (Duane Hopwood), Janeane Garofalo (Linda), Judah Friedlander (Anthony), Susan Lynch (Gina), Dick Cavett (Fred), Steve Schirripa (Steve), Jerry Grayson (Carl), Bill Buell (Wally), John Krasinski (Bob Flynn). Directed by Matt Mulhern and produced by Melissa Marr, Lemore Syvan, and Marc Turtletaub. Screenplay by Mulhern.

Duane Hopwood is the portrait of a man who loves his wife, loves his children, knows how to be a good father, and is losing everything because of alcoholism. The movie is a wise and realistic portrait of the disease, showing the drunk not as a colorful or tragic character but simply as a sad man whose days occasionally contain moments of joy and hope. He is not without friends. People care for him. His wife is not heartless, but after he drives drunk with one of their daughters in the backseat, she goes into divorce court. She has given up hope about his drinking; she needs to protect her kids and cut her losses.

Duane is played by David Schwimmer in one of those performances that transform the way we think about an actor. *Friends* was a beloved show, but like all popular shows it fixes its actors in our minds; their TV characters are like ghosts standing beside every other role they play. No one stands beside Duane Hopwood, who is all by himself on those lonely winter mornings in Atlantic City, riding his bicycle home from his job as a pit boss in the casinos—a bicycle, because his license has been revoked.

The movie has so many things right. It understands that alcoholics reach a point where their friends are mostly other people on the same drinking schedule. They date out of bars because that is where they meet people. On Thanksgiving they cannot go home because they no longer have one but are invited to dinner at the homes of friends, where they feel even more spectacularly alone.

It knows this, too: that alcoholics don't think they're alcoholics. "I'm not a drunk," they say. Sure, they *get* drunk, but that's what they do, not what they are. What's a drunk, anyway? Some bum under a bridge with a pint in a brown paper bag? Duane has endangered a daughter he loves, lost a family he cherishes, been through traffic and divorce court, and yet cannot stop himself from going to a bar after work. Sometimes he drinks way too much. Sometimes he drinks too much. Sometimes he drinks almost too much. Sometimes he doesn't drink enough. Those are the only four "sometimes" for an alcoholic.

Duane Hopwood is not, however, a movie about drinking, and it lacks spectacular scenes of colorful alcoholism. It is more about waking up at the wrong time of day, working through a hangover, having times when your good essential nature shines through, and hating it that the woman who loves you now loves someone else because she must.

As Linda, his wife, Janeane Garofalo is precise and kind, caring for the man she married, not wanting to hurt him, but too wise to share his disease. There could be spectacular scenes of overacting and souped-up drama in their relationship, but unless the drunk is also violent, those rarely happen; it is more sadness and loss, with an occasional moment of acting out, as in the baseball bat scene, where the drunk is playing a confused role generated by his murky grief.

Duane has a few close friends. One is Carl (Jerry Grayson), his boss at the casino, who likes him and wants to help him. But Duane makes a stupid mistake on the job, and Carl has to deal with that. How he does this is more human (and probably more accurate) than what we expect from casino bosses in the movies. Another friend is Anthony (Judah Friedlander), a security guard who dreams of becoming a stand-up comic. He wants to become Duane's roommate because they can share rent and he will be closer to the casino and won't have to live with his mother anymore. One of the danger signals of alcoholism that Ann Landers never listed in her columns is when you get a roommate because he needs to save on rent and move out from his mother's house, and you are both over forty.

Then there are Fred and Wally (Dick Cavett and Bill Buell), the neighbors who invite Duane over for Thanksgiving. They are good souls, gay, I suppose, who in a quiet way see Duane in need and are kind to him. And there is Gina (Susan Lynch), the bartender Duane is dating. Like many alcoholics, even his dating is about himself, and he cannot help telling her, "I still love Linda." He doesn't want a lover; he wants a confessor.

Yes, he goes to one AA meeting, which is filled with people who look at him and know exactly who he is and what he's going through. He's there, he says, because "the judge thought it might be a good idea," even though "I don't really have a problem." Uh-huh. "In our experience," a guy tells him, "most of the people who come through that door have a problem."

Duane Hopwood, written and directed by Matt Mulhern, is a wise and touching film with a lot of love in it. I may have given the wrong impression: It's not entirely about drinking, but it's entirely about a drinker. He does other things. Shares joyful little moments with his girls. Wears a turkey suit when he is actually sober. Has a dead-on conversation with "Jogger Bob" (John Krasinski), his ex-wife's new boyfriend, who lectures the youngest daughter on how she is fat. Duane may be screwed up, but he knows that for Mommy's new boyfriend to tell a little girl she is fat is not a smart thing.

The quality of this movie is in its observation. The filmmaker Mulhern and Schwimmer, Garofalo, and the other actors have real lives and experiences in mind. *Duane Hopwood* shows ordinary days in ordinary lives. Its hero is a man who grieves for the loss of his happiness and does not know he should grieve for the loss of himself. Nobody has left

him. He has gone away, into that place between himself and the next drink. That's where he lives. Everywhere else, he's only visiting. But he doesn't have a problem.

Duck Season ★ ★ ★
R, 85 m., 2006

Diego Catano (Moko), Daniel Miranda (Flama), Danny Perea (Rita), Enrique Arreola (Ulises). Directed by Fernando Eimbcke and produced by Christian Valdelievre. Screenplay by Eimbcke.

Not very much really happens in *Duck Season,* but in its rich details, it remembers how absorbing and endless every single day can seem when you're fourteen. It takes place mostly inside an apartment in a Mexican urban highrise, where best friends Moko and Flama (Diego Catano and Daniel Miranda) are left alone one Sunday with a big bottle of Coke and a video game. The Coke they share with great care, and the game (Bush vs. bin Laden) they employ for counterfeit excitement. They're kids killing time.

Then the next act in their lives opens. Rita (Danny Perea) knocks on the door. She says she's sixteen but looks older. She wants to use their oven to cook herself a birthday cake. She claims her own stove doesn't work. Maybe, or maybe she wants company. She moves into the kitchen and then into their conversations. The younger teens imply more than they're ready to say, and the older one less than she means. In such a way does emotional information float across the river of time.

To describe the actions in the film would be a mistake, both because they should happen to you in your own time, and because the movie isn't about what happens but about how it happens and why, and you shouldn't look for really deep hows and whys. One of the things I enjoyed was the way no phony melodrama is cooked up; it's the meandering quality of the material that makes it feel real. The movie invests in these lives enough that when characters are simply sitting on the sofa and staring into space, we're not staring at them but with them.

Episodes. There's a little speculative flirtation. They order a pizza. There is an argument about whether it should be free because Ulises (Enrique Arreola), the delivery boy, misses the advertised deadline. You can make whatever you want from the symbolism of his name—not too much, I hope. Now there are four people in the apartment, and several dogs, which are present in spirit.

The two boys are best friends. The two older characters are both among strangers. None of these characters has any place better to go or anything better to do, and when magic ingredients appear in the brownies, it's no big deal; it simply enhances the ennui, making it Ennui!

I was reminded of another and better film, Hirokazu Kore-Eda's *Nobody Knows* (2004), the Japanese film about four siblings who are abandoned by their mother and shift for themselves in an apartment for several months. Both movies have perfect pitch when it comes to watching kids pass time: They don't kill it so much as toy with it. *Duck Season* is shot in black and white, which is a good choice, because color might enhance an experience that is intended to seem no more than it is.

Yes, some of the dialogue is funny. One or two developments are a surprise. But not real funny, and not a big surprise. When the dispute with the pizza man comes up, it's not so much about the money, more about their gratitude for something to argue about. The title of the movie comes from a painting hanging on the wall of the apartment, the kind of painting that nobody ever buys, but that walls seem to acquire. It shows ducks in flight. Perhaps the migration of the ducks foretells the lives of these four young people who are about to take flight. "Whither, midst falling dew,/While glow the heavens with the last steps of day,/Far, through their rosy depths, dost thou pursue/Thy solitary way?" Sister Rosanne promised us if we memorized a poem we would use it someday. It looks like she was right.

The Dukes of Hazzard ★

PG-13, 105 m., 2005

Seann William Scott (Bo Duke), Johnny Knoxville (Luke Duke), Jessica Simpson (Daisy Duke), Burt Reynolds (Boss Hogg), Willie Nelson (Uncle Jesse), M. C. Gainey (Sheriff Coltrane), Lynda Carter (Pauline). Directed by Jay Chandrasekhar and produced by Bill Gerber. Screenplay by John O'Brien.

The Dukes of Hazzard is a comedy about two cousins who are closer'n brothers, and their car, which is smarter'n they are. It's a retread of a sitcom that ran from about 1979 to 1985, years during which I was able to find better ways to pass my time. Yes, it is still another TV program I have never, ever seen. As this list grows, it provides more and more clues about why I am so smart and cheerful.

The movie stars Johnny Knoxville, from *Jackass*, Seann William Scott, from *American Wedding*, and Jessica Simpson, from Mars. Judging by her recent conversation on TV with Dean Richards, Simpson is so remarkably uninformed that she should sue the public schools of Abilene, Texas, or maybe they should sue her. On the day he won his seventh Tour de France, not many people could say, as she did, that they had no idea who Lance Armstrong was.

Of course, you don't have to be smart to get into *The Dukes of Hazzard*. But people like Willie Nelson and Burt Reynolds should have been smart enough to stay out of it. Here is a lamebrained, outdated wheeze about a couple of good ol' boys who roar around the back roads of the South in the General Lee, their beloved 1969 Dodge Charger. As it happens, I also drove a 1969 Dodge Charger. You could have told them apart because mine did not have a Confederate flag painted on the roof.

Scott and Knoxville play Bo Duke and Luke Duke; the absence of a Puke Duke is a sadly missed opportunity. They deliver moonshine manufactured by their Uncle Jesse (Willie Nelson) and depend on the General to outrun the forces of Sheriff Roscoe P. Coltrane (M. C. Gainey). The movie even has one of those obligatory scenes where the car is racing along when there's a quick cut to a gigantic Mack truck, its horn blasting as it bears down on them. They steer out of the way at the last possible moment. That giant Mack truck keeps busy in the movies, turning up again and again during chase scenes and always just barely missing the car containing the heroes, but this is the first time I have seen it making 60 mph down a single-lane dirt track.

Jessica Simpson plays Daisy Duke, whose short shorts became so famous on TV that they were known as "Daisy Dukes." She models them to a certain effect in a few brief scenes but is missing from most of the movie. Maybe she isn't even smart enough to wear shorts. I learn from the Internet that Simpson has a dog named Daisy, but I have been unable to learn if she named it before or after being signed for the role, and whether the dog is named after the character, the shorts, the flower, or perhaps (a long shot) Daisy Duck.

The local ruler is Boss Jefferson Davis Hogg (Burt Reynolds), "the meanest man in Hazzard County," who issues orders to the sheriff and everybody else and who has a secret plan to strip-mine the county and turn it into a wasteland. I wonder if there were moments when Reynolds reflected that, karmawise, this movie was the second half of what *Smokey and the Bandit* was the first half of.

There are a lot of scenes in the movie where the General is racing down back roads at high speeds and becomes airborne, leaping across ditches, rivers, and suchlike, miraculously without breaking the moonshine bottles. Surely if you have seen, say, twelve scenes of a car flying through the air, you are not consumed by a need to see twelve more.

There is a NASCAR race in the film and some amusing dialogue about car sponsorship. You know the film is set in modern times because along with Castrol and Coke, one of the car sponsors is Yahoo! I noted one immortal passage of dialogue, about a charity that is raising money for "one of the bifidas." I was also amused by mention of *The Al Unser Jr. Story*, an "audiobook narrated by Laurence Fishburne."

The movie has one offensive scene, alas, that doesn't belong in a contemporary comedy. Bo and Luke are involved in a mishap that causes their faces to be blackened with soot, and then, wouldn't you know, they drive into an African-American neighborhood, where their car is surrounded by ominous young men who are not amused by blackface, or by the Confederate flag painted on the car. I was hoping maybe the boyz n the hood would carjack the General, which would provide a fresh twist to the story, but no, the scene sinks into the mire of its own despond. ☞

Duma ★ ★ ★ ½
PG, 100 m., 2005

Alex Michaeletos (Xan), Eamonn Walker (Ripkuna), Campbell Scott (Peter), Hope Davis (Kristin). Directed by Carroll Ballard and produced by Stacy Cohen, E. K. Gaylord II, Kristin Harms, Hunt Lowry, and John Wells. Screenplay by Karen Janszen and Mark St. Germain, based on the book *How It Was with Dooms* by Carol Cawthra Hopcraft and Xan Hopcraft.

The twelve-year-old boy helped raise the cheetah after he and his father found it as a cub. The boy, named Xan, lives on a farm in South Africa, where he and Duma form a strong bond, but their friendship cannot last forever. An emergency forces the family to move to the city, and Xan realizes that Duma, now fully grown, should be returned to the wild.

There might be reasonable ways of doing that. Perhaps Xan (Alex Michaeletos) could call the animal welfare people. Instead, without telling his mother (Hope Davis), he decides to personally return Duma to the wilderness. There is a scene of the cheetah riding in the sidecar of an old motorcycle, which Xan drives into the desert. It could be a cute scene, maybe funny, in a different kind of movie, but *Duma* takes itself seriously and is not a cute children's story but a grand tale of adventure.

Xan has courage but not a lot of common sense. He is headed into the Kalahari Desert, where to get lost is, usually, to die. Of course the motorcycle runs out of gas. Then he meets another wanderer in the desert, named Ripkuna (Eamonn Walker), who once worked in the mines of Johannesburg but now prefers to work alone, perhaps for reasons we would rather not know. He warns Xan of the dangers ahead ("That is a place of many teeth, my friend; that is a place to die"). He has the knowledge to save the boy and the cheetah. But what is his agenda?

Duma is an astonishing film by Carroll Ballard, the director who is fascinated by the relationship between humans, animals, and the wilderness. He works infrequently, but unforgettably. Perhaps you have seen his *The Black Stallion* (1979), about a boy and a horse who are shipwrecked and begin a friendship that leads to a crucial horse race. Or his *Never Cry Wolf* (1983), based on the Farley Mowat book about a man who goes to live in the wild with wolves. Or the wonderful *Fly Away Home* (1996), about a thirteen-year-old girl who solos in an ultralight aircraft, leading a flock of pet geese south from Canada.

The wolf and geese stories were, incredibly, based on fact. So, perhaps even more incredibly, is *Duma*. There really was a boy and a cheetah, written about in the book *How It Was with Dooms* by Xan Hopcraft and his mother, Carol Cawthra Hopcraft. Even more to the point: This movie shows a real boy and a real cheetah (actually, four cheetahs were used). There are no special effects. The cheetah is not digitized. What we see on the screen is what is happening, and that lends the film an eerie intensity. Animals are fascinating when they are free to be themselves; when they are manipulated by CGI into cute little actors who behave on cue, what's the point?

How is this film possible? There are shots showing a desert empty to the horizon, except for the boy and the cheetah. No doubt handlers are right there out of camera range, ready to act in an emergency, but it is clear the filmmakers and the boy trust the animals they are working with.

True, cheetahs are a special kind of big cat; Wikipedia informs us, "Because cheetahs are far less aggressive than other big cats, cubs are sometimes sold as pets." Yes, but a pet that can, as Xan tells his dad (Campbell Scott), "outrun your Porsche." A pet that is a carnivore. It would seem that Duma can be trusted, but as W. G. Sebald once observed, "Men and animals regard each other across a gulf of mutual incomprehension."

And if Duma can be trusted, can the African man, Ripkuna? Where is he leading them? He must know that a reward has been posted for the missing boy and that a tame cheetah can be sold for a good amount of money. While these questions circle uneasily in our minds, *Duma* creates scenes of wonderful adventure. The stalled motorcycle is turned into a wind-driven land yacht. A raft

trip on a river involves rapids and crocodiles. The cheetah itself plays a role in their survival. And the movie takes on an additional depth because Xan is not a cute one-dimensional "family movie" child, and Ripkuna is freed from the usual clichés about noble and helpful wanderers. These are characters free to hold surprises in the real world.

Watching this movie, absorbed by its storytelling, touched by its beauty, fascinated by the bond between the boy and the animal, I was also astonished by something else: The studio does not know if it is commercial! The most dismal stupidities can be inflicted on young audiences, but let a family movie come along that is ambitious and visionary, and distributors lose confidence. It's as if they fear some movies are better than the audience can handle.

Duma is an extraordinary film, and intelligent younger viewers in particular may be enthralled by it. ☞

Dust to Glory ★ ★ ★
PG, 97 m., 2005

With appearances by Mario Andretti, Sal Fish, James Garner, Ricky Johnson, Chad McQueen, Steve McQueen, Jimmy N. Roberts, and Malcolm Smith. A documentary directed by Dana Brown and produced by Mike "Mouse" McCoy and Scott Waugh.

Let's be sure we have this right. The Baja 1000 is the world's longest nonstop point-to-point race. It has more than a dozen categories of vehicles, from $2 million racing cars to motorcycles to unmodified pre-1972 VW Beetles. The course changes every year. You can leave the course and take a shortcut, but that way you might miss one of the secret checkpoints. The race includes both dirt back roads and Mexican highways. The highways are not blocked to civilian traffic during the event, and the racers have to weave in and out of ordinary traffic. Oh, and they could get stopped by the highway police.

Dust to Glory tells the story of the 2003 running of this legendary race, which offers glory but not much money; they can't even sell tickets, since the fans essentially just walk over to the edge of the road and watch the cars go by. And yet the Baja 1000 attracts stars like Mario Andretti and Parnelli Jones, and in years past, celebrities like James Garner and Steve McQueen.

The documentary was directed by Dana Brown, son of Bruce (*The Endless Summer*) Brown, who uses some fifty cameras, including lightweight digital cameras mounted on cars and motorcycles. That's helpful because there is no one place to stand in order to get a good idea of the entire race, especially since each category of vehicle is dispatched separately—the fastest cars, trucks, and motorcycles first, the Beetles last. There is a ham radio operator who keeps in touch with the checkpoints, provides weather reports, reports accidents, and communicates with the drivers' support teams, but he looks less like Command Central than like a guy in a hut on a hill with some stuff from Radio Shack.

The record time for the race is sixteen hours. There is a winner in every category. You have to finish in thirty-two hours, and in this race, to finish at all is a victory. Most of the teams have two or three drivers, but the movie's star (maybe because he is also the co-producer) is Mike "Mouse" McCoy, a motorcycle racing legend who plans to drive solo, nonstop, for all 1,000 miles.

Since the race runs through the night and passes areas where fine silt makes a dust cloud that limits visibility, this is a dangerous thing to do, but then the Baja 1000 is dangerous anyway: not least for the spectators, who seem to stand awfully close to hairpin turns where vehicles can spin out. Miraculously, only one person was killed in 2003—a spectator hit by a motorcycle belonging not to a racer, but to another spectator, who was driving the wrong way on the course.

There is a kind of madness involved in a race like this, and that's apparently its appeal. Car companies like Porsche invest big money in their teams, despite the lack of a purse or even much TV coverage (how could ESPN spot cameras along all 1,000 miles, and how would it make sense of the countless categories?). The race is more like a private poker game held upstairs in somebody's suite during the World Series of Poker.

Does Mouse make it? I would not dream of telling you. I will, however, tell you that he has

a camera on his motorcycle that records with a sickening thud an accident he has sixty miles from the finish line, during which he injures or breaks (he isn't sure) some ribs, a shoulder, and a finger.

The Dying Gaul ★ ★ ½
R, 105 m., 2005

Peter Sarsgaard (Robert), Campbell Scott (Jeffrey), Patricia Clarkson (Elaine), Robin Bartlett (Bella), Linda Emond (Dr. Foss), Ryan Miller (Max). Directed by Craig Lucas and produced by David Newman, Campbell Scott, George VanBuskirk, and Lisa Zimble. Screenplay by Lucas, based on a play by Lucas.

Woe to him who seeks to please rather than to appall.

Those words appear onscreen in the first shot of *The Dying Gaul*. Here is another quotation, from later in the film: "No one goes to the movies to have a bad time. Or to learn anything." The first quotation is from Herman Melville's *Moby Dick*. The second is by a Hollywood studio executive, about a screenplay he likes but thinks is not commercial. The screenplay is about a homosexual love affair. Make the lovers heterosexual, the executive tells the writer, and I'll cut you a check for one million dollars, here and now.

The executive is Jeffrey, played by Campbell Scott, who is becoming a master of characters with controlled but alarming emotions. The screenwriter is Robert, played by Peter Sarsgaard in a sincere and inward role a little unusual for him. His screenplay is about his former lover, who was also his agent.

"Americans hate gays," Jeffrey tells him flatly. Then he dangles temptation before Robert, who is broke and has child support to pay.

"Who do you think should direct this?"

"Gus Van Sant," says Robert, "since Truffaut is dead."

"Would you like me to show it to him?"

"Yes."

"That's good, because I already have."

This dialogue, by the writer-director Craig Lucas, depends on us to realize that Jeffrey has not shown the screenplay to Gus Van Sant and probably never will. The opening stages in a movie negotiation are like a romance, with the screenwriter as the blushing bride and the producer as the prince who strews riches at his feet. Just compromise this one time, Jeffrey tells Robert, and soon, like Spike Lee, you'll be making your own films in your own way.

The Dying Gaul grabs us immediately with this seduction by negotiation. It follows with scenes establishing another Hollywood convention: If you're doing business with someone, you are immediately "family." Robert is invited to Jeffrey's home and introduced to his wife, Elaine (Patricia Clarkson), and their children. Elaine likes his mind. On the other hand, Jeffrey likes Robert's body. "Let's hug," he tells Jeffrey at one point in their negotiations. Everybody hugs in Hollywood. It is a good way to look someone in the eye while stabbing them in the back. "You are very handsome," Jeffrey says in mid-hug. "And I'm getting a little turned on. Are you?"

Robert caves in and makes his story about heterosexuals at about the same time he and Jeffrey start having sex. It takes Robert less than ten seconds on the computer to find "Maurice" and replace it with "Maggie." Neither one of them observes that "Maurice" is the name of a novel about a gay man that E. M. Forster did not allow to be published until after his death. No doubt other rewriting will take out AIDS and substitute cancer. "It's going to be a beautiful movie," Jeffrey promises him.

At this point in *The Dying Gaul* I could see no way the movie could step wrong, but it does. The movie is based on Lucas's play and represents his directorial debut. His previous screenplays include *Longtime Companion* (1990), with its Oscar-nominated performance by Bruce Davison as the companion of a dying AIDS victim, and *The Secret Lives of Dentists* (2002), which also starred Campbell Scott and was about secrets and possessiveness in a marriage.

The Dying Gaul considers some of this same material but adds a dimension that is at first intriguing and then, I think, fatal. The troublesome device is an Internet chat room. Elaine, a former screenwriter who now has time and loneliness on her hands, likes Robert immediately. They gossip. He confesses that with his lover dead his sex life is conducted mostly online. Robert says the chat rooms are like "life after death," with disembodied voices floating in the ether. Elaine asks, "What's your favorite really dirty chat room?"

Before he answers, I should issue a spoiler warning. I will not reveal crucial details, but I will describe a few things you may prefer not to know. The movie proceeds with parallel affairs, one real, one virtual. Jeffrey and Robert become lovers, while Elaine creates a fictional identity in Robert's chat room and is soon one of Robert's regular correspondents. What she writes and what he thinks and what the result is, I will leave for you to discover. It is all done well enough. I object for two more fundamental reasons: 1) There is no reason to believe Robert particularly believes in the supernatural, and 2) Would it not occur to Robert that he had, after all, told Elaine about his favorite chat room? He has a bulb that needs to be changed, the one right above his head.

So there are implausibilities in the plot devices that lead the movie to its ultimate conclusion. And then the final developments themselves, I think, are wrong in both theory and practice. There is some ambiguity about why a final event takes place, and that's all right, but the way in which the movie reveals it is, I think, singularly ineffective. It leads to one of those endings where you sit there wishing they'd tried a little harder to think up something better.

It's all the more depressing because the performances are effective, especially the way Clarkson obliquely approaches the crisis in her marriage. And I liked the way Scott's character insists on being both gay and straight. There's a Hollywood producer for you: greedy. ☞

E

Eight Below ★ ★ ★
PG, 120 m., 2006

Paul Walker (Jerry Shepard), Bruce Greenwood (Dr. Davis McLaren), Moon Bloodgood (Katie), Jason Biggs (Cooper), Gerard Plunkett (Dr. Andy Harrison), August Schellenberg (Mindo), Wendy Crewson (Eve McLaren), Belinda Metz (Rosemary), Panou Mowling (Howard). Directed by Frank Marshall and produced by Patrick Crowley, Doug Davison, and David Hoberman. Screenplay by David DiGilio, suggested by the film *Nankyoku Monogatari*.

You think penguins have it bad? At least they're adapted to survive in Antarctica. *Eight Below* tells the harrowing story of a dogsled team left chained outside a research station when the humans pull out in a hurry. The guide who used and loved them wants to return to rescue them but is voted down: Winter has set in, and all flights are canceled until spring. Will the dogs survive? Or will the film end in the spring, with the guide uttering a prayer over their eight dead bodies?

Remarkable how in a film where we *know* with an absolute certainty that all or most of the dogs must survive, *Eight Below* succeeds as an effective story. It works by focusing on the dogs. To be sure, the guide, Jerry (Paul Walker), never stops thinking about them, but there's not much he can do. He visits Dr. Davis McLaren (Bruce Greenwood), the scientist whose research financed the dogsled expedition, and he hangs out at his mobile home on a scenic Oregon coast, and he pursues a reawakening love affair with Katie (Moon Bloodgood), the pilot who ferried them to and from the station.

To give him credit, he's depressed, really depressed, by the thought of those dogs chained up in the frigid night, but what can he do?

Meanwhile, the subtitles keep count of how long the dogs have been on their own: 50 days . . . 133 days . . . 155 days . . .

If there is a slight logical problem with their fight for survival, it's that they have plenty of daylight to work with. Isn't there almost eternal night during the Antarctic winter, just as there's almost eternal day during the summer? I suppose we have to accept the unlikely daylight because otherwise the most dramatic scenes would take place in darkness.

The dog sequences reminded me of Jack London's dog novels, especially *White Fang* and *The Call of the Wild*. Do not make the mistake of thinking London's books are for children. They can be read by kids in grade school, yes, but they were written by an adult with serious things to say about the nature of dogs and the reality of arctic existence. There's a reason they're in the Library of America.

In *Eight Below*, as in Jack London, the dogs are not turned into cute cartoon pets but are respected for their basic animal natures.

To be sure, the sled dogs here do some mighty advanced thinking, as when one dog seems to explain a fairly complex plan to the other dogs by telepathy. I was also impressed by the selfless behavior of the dogs, as they bring birds to feed a member of the pack who has been crippled. I was under the impression that if a dog died in such circumstances, the others would eat it to avoid starvation, but apparently not. (You can't assume the idea didn't occur to Frank Marshall, the director, since he made *Alive*, the story of the Andes survivors.)

Could the dogs (six huskies and two malamutes) really have survived unsheltered for five months, scavenging for themselves through an Antarctic winter? I learn from *Variety* that *Eight Below* is inspired by a Japanese film, itself based on real events, but in the 1958 "true story," seven of nine dogs died. Still, the film doesn't claim to be a documentary, and the story, believable or not, is strong and involving. It's the stuff about the humans that gets thin: The film lacks a human villain, because the decision not to return for the dogs is wise and prudent, and not made by a mean man who hates dogs.

You might think, however, that when Jerry appeals to Dr. McLaren, the scientist would exert himself a little more to save the dogs, since they saved his life. (How he gets into trouble and what the dogs do to save him I will leave for you to experience; it provides the film's most compelling moments.)

Movies about animals always live with the temptation to give the animals human characteristics. Lassie, for example, could do everything but dial the telephone and drive the car. The brilliance of the English-language *March of the Penguins* involved dropping a French sound track in which the penguins expressed themselves in voice-over dialogue, and simply trusting to the reality of their situation. *Eight Below* is restrained, for the most part, in how it presents its dogs. When there are close-ups of a dog's face, absorbed in thought, anxiety, or yearning, we aren't asked to believe anything we don't already believe about dogs: They *do* think, worry, and yearn, and they love, too. Or if they don't, I don't want to know about it.   ☞

El Crimen Perfecto ★ ★
NO MPAA RATING, 105 m., 2005

Guillermo Toledo (Rafael), Monica Cervera (Lourdes), Luis Varela (Don Antonio), Fernando Tejero (Alonso), Enrique Villen (Inspector Campoy), Javier Gutierrez (Jaime), Kira Miro (Roxanne). Directed by Alex de la Iglesia and produced by Roberto Di Girolamo, Gustavo Ferrada, and de la Iglesia. Screenplay by Jorge Guerricaechevarria and de la Iglesia.

Rafael lives for two reasons: to make love to women, and to sell them clothes. He feels blessed by his job as the department manager of ladies' wear in YeYo's, the big Madrid department store where he claims to have been born and certainly seems to live. After hours, he treats salesgirls to champagne and caviar, a race down the aisles in a shopping cart, and a passionate denouement in a dressing room. *El Crimen Perfecto* records Rafael's sudden and devastating loss of three things: his job, his happiness, and, worst of all, his bachelorhood. Alex de la Iglesia's comedy, which in many ways Jerry Lewis might have made, shows Rafael (Guillermo Toledo) as madcap and manic, a man who feels immune to ordinary laws: Witness his daily theft of a paper from a newsstand, and the way he steals kisses while walking down the street. When a security guard catches him having sex in a dressing room, Rafael bribes him and is warned he must stop—in three hours.

As the film opens, Rafael and his archenemy, Don Antonio (Luis Varela), manager of men's wear, are in a sales contest to determine who will become floor manager. Rafael seems to win, but then victory is snatched from his grasp, and in a ferocious struggle in a dressing room, Don Antonio is killed. In desperation Rafael tries to jam him into a basement incinerator that's too small for the body. Hints of Hitchcock begin to surface around here.

Rafael has been careful to hire only beautiful women as his employees, but one plain woman is on the staff. This is Lourdes (Monica Cervera), who desperately loves Rafael and is not above blackmailing him after she helps dispose of the body. Rafael would rather die than marry her, but what is he to do when he steps off the elevator one morning and is bushwhacked by a reality show on live TV? "Will you marry Lourdes?" the emcee screams. "Millions are waiting for your answer!"

El Crimen Perfecto has energy, color, spirit, and lively performances, but what it does not have are very many laughs. In a month that has seen *The 40-Year-Old Virgin*, a wonderful comedy about romance in retail, this one seems oddly old-fashioned; it has a 1950s feel. The humor is strong on sitcom complications and short on human nature, and Rafael is too likable to be as hateful as he ought to be, if he were really going to be funny.

I did like Cervera, as Lourdes, who comes on like a force of nature. Rafael is fond of lecturing to his troops that you can get anything you really set your heart on, but Lourdes is the only one who listens, believes, and puts his theories into practice. One of the movie's problems is that she's supposed to be unsympathetic, but we can't help admiring her; when the movie is cruel to her, which is often, it puts a damper on things. Better the good-hearted notes in *The 40-Year-Old Virgin*, which likes everybody in its cast, after their fashion.

The movie's third act moves beyond Jerry Lewis into desperation. Don Antonio's ghost turns up with a hatchet in his head and his hair still smoldering, to contribute cheerful suggestions; his presence is desperately not funny. A scene set on a Ferris wheel doesn't work in any of several possible ways, and a scene involving a fire sprinkler system suggests that the screenwriters' desperation was as great as the character who sounds the alarm. Watching a scene where bargain hunters storm the salesclerks seconds after the store opens, I was reminded of Harold Lloyd's

Safety Last, which has an uncannily similar scene. Maybe de la Iglesia was paying homage. In that case, maybe the Ferris wheel scene was homage to the scene where Lloyd hangs from the hands of a clock. Or maybe not.

Elektra ★ ½
PG-13, 97 m., 2005

Jennifer Garner (Elektra), Goran Visnjic (Mark Miller), Will Yun Lee (Kirigi), Cary-Hiroyuki Tagawa (Roshi), Terence Stamp (Stick), Kirsten Prout (Abby Miller). Directed by Rob Bowman and produced by Arnon Milchan, Avi Arad, and Gary Foster. Screenplay by Zak Penn, Stuart Zicherman, and Raven Metzner.

Elektra plays like a collision between leftover bits and pieces of Marvel superhero stories. It can't decide what tone to strike. It goes for satire by giving its heroine an agent who suggests mutual funds for her murder-for-hire fees, and sends her a fruit basket before her next killing. And then it goes for melancholy, by making Elektra a lonely, unfulfilled overachiever who was bullied as a child and suffers from obsessive-compulsive disorder. It goes for cheap sentiment by having her bond with a thirteen-year-old girl, and then . . . but see for yourself. The movie's a muddle in search of a rationale.

Elektra, you may recall, first appeared on screen in *Daredevil* (2003), the Marvel saga starring Ben Affleck as a blind superhero. Jennifer Garner, she of the wonderful lips, returns in the role as a killer for hire, which seems kind of sad, considering that in the earlier movie she figured in the beautiful scene where he imagines her face by listening to raindrops falling on it.

Now someone has offered her $2 million for her next assassination, requiring only that she turn up two days early for the job—on Christmas Eve, as it works out. She arrives in a luxurious lakeside vacation home and soon meets the young girl named Abby (Kirsten Prout), who lives next door. Abby's father is played by Goran Visnjic with a three-day beard, which tells you all you need to know: Powerful sexual attraction will compel them to share two PG-13-rated kisses.

The back story, which makes absolutely no mention of Daredevil, involves Elektra's training under the stern blind martial arts master Stick (Terence Stamp), who can restore people to life and apparently materialize at will, yet is reduced to martial arts when he does battle. Her enemies are assassins hired by the Order of the Hand, which is a secret Japanese society that seeks the Treasure, and the Treasure is . . . well, see for yourself.

As for the troops of the Hand, they have contracted Movie Zombie's Syndrome, which means that they are fearsome and deadly until killed, at which point they dissolve into a cloud of yellow powder. I don't have a clue whether they're real or imaginary. Neither do they, I'll bet. Eagles and wolves and snakes can materialize out of their tattoos and attack people, but they, too, disappear in clouds. Maybe this is simply to save Elektra the inconvenience of stepping over her victims in the middle of a fight.

The Order of the Hand is not very well defined. Its office is a pagoda on top of a Tokyo skyscraper, which is promising, but inside all we get is the standard scene of a bunch of suits sitting around a conference table giving orders to paid killers. Their instructions: Kill Elektra, grab the Treasure, etc. Who are they and what is their master plan? Maybe you have to study up on the comic books.

As for Elektra, she's a case study. Flashbacks show her tortured youth, in which her father made her tread water in the family's luxury indoor pool until she was afraid she'd drown. (Her mother, on balcony overlooking pool: "She's only a girl!" Her father, at poolside: "Only using your legs! Not your hands!" Elektra: "Glub.")

Whether this caused her OCD or not, I cannot say. It manifests itself not as an extreme case, like poor Howard Hughes, but fairly mildly: She counts her steps in groups of five. This has absolutely nothing to do with anything else. A superheroine with a bad case of OCD could be interesting, perhaps; maybe she would be compelled to leap tall buildings with bound after bound after bound.

The movie's fight scenes suffer from another condition, attention deficit disorder. None of their shots are more than a few seconds long, saving the actors from doing much in the way of stunts and the director from having to worry overmuch about choreography. There's one showdown between Elektra and the head killer of the Hand that involves a lot of white sheets, but all they do is flap around; we're expecting maybe an elegant Zhang Yimou sequence, and it's more like they're fighting with the laundry.

Jennifer Garner is understandably unable to make a lot of sense out of this. We get a lot of close-ups in which we would identify with what she was thinking, if we had any clue what that might be. Does she wonder why she became a paid killer instead of a virtuous superheroine? Does she wonder why her agent is a bozo? Does she clearly understand that the Order of the Hand is the group trying to kill her? At the end of the movie, having reduced her enemies to yellow poofs, she tells Goran Visnjic to "take good care" of his daughter. Does she even know those guys in suits are still up there in the pagoda, sitting around the table?

Elevator to the Gallows ★ ★ ★ ½
NO MPAA RATING, 88 m., 1958 (rereleased 2005)

Jeanne Moreau (Florence Carala), Maurice Ronet (Julien Tavernier), Georges Poujouly (Louis), Yori Bertin (Veronique), Jean Wall (Simon Carala). Directed by Louis Malle and produced by Jean Thuillier. Screenplay by Noel Calef, Malle, and Roger Nimier.

She loves him. "Je t'aime, je t'aime," she repeats into the telephone, in the desperate close-up that opens Louis Malle's *Elevator to the Gallows* (1958). He needs to know this because he is going to commit a murder for them. The woman is Jeanne Moreau, in her first feature film role, looking bruised by the pain of love. She plays Florence, wife of the millionaire arms dealer Simon Carala (Jean Wall). Her lover, Julien Tavernier (Maurice Ronet), is a paratrooper who served in Indochina and Algeria, in wars that made Carala rich. Now he works for Carala and is going to kill him and take his wife.

Because Julien has access and a motive, he must make this a perfect crime. Malle, who apprenticed with the painstaking genius Robert Bresson, devotes loving care to the details of the murder. After office hours, Julien uses a rope and a hook to climb up one floor and enter a window of Simon's office. He shoots him, makes it look like a suicide, bolts the office from inside, leaves by the window. An elegant

little locked-room mystery. Then he climbs back down and leaves to meet his mistress.

Stupidly, he has left behind evidence. It is growing dark. Perhaps no one has noticed. He hurries back to the office and gets into an elevator, but then the power is shut off in the building for the night, and he is trapped between floors. Florence, meanwhile, waits and waits in the café where they planned their rendezvous. And then, in a series of shots that became famous, she walks the streets, visiting all their usual haunts, looking for the lover she is convinced has deserted her.

Moreau plays these scenes not with frantic anxiety but with a kind of masochistic despair, not really expecting to find Julien. It rains, and she wanders drenched in the night. Malle shot her scenes using a camera in a baby carriage pushed along beside her by the cinematographer Henri Decae, who worked with Jean-Pierre Melville on another great noir of the period, *Bob le Flambeur* (1955). Her face is often illuminated only by the lights of the cafés and shops that she passes; at a time when actresses were lit and photographed with care, these scenes had a shock value and influenced many films to come. We see that Florence is a little mad. An improvised jazz score by Miles Davis seems to belong to the night as much as she does.

Meanwhile, Julien struggles to free himself from the elevator. There is a parallel story. His parked car is stolen by a teenage couple—the braggart Louis (Georges Poujouly) and his girlfriend, Veronique (Yori Bertin). They get into a fender bender with a German tourist and his wife, and the tourists rather improbably invite them to party with them at a motel. This leads to murder, and the police of course suspect Julien because his car is found at the scene.

The more I see the great French crime films of the 1950s, the earlier seems the dawning of the New Wave. The work of Melville, Jacques Becker, and their contemporaries uses the same low-budget, unsprung, jumpy style that was adapted by Truffaut in *Jules and Jim* and Godard in *Breathless* (which owes a lot to the teenage couple in *Elevator*). Malle became a card-carrying New Waver, and *Elevator to the Gallows* could be called the first New Wave title, except then what was *Bob le Flambeur*? These 1950s French noirs abandon the formality of traditional crime films, the almost ritualistic obedience to formula, and show crazy stuff happening to people who seem to be making up their lives as they go along. There is an irony that Julien, trapped in the elevator, has a perfect alibi for the murders he is suspected of but seems inescapably implicated in the one he might have gotten away with. And observe the way Moreau, wandering the streets, handles her arrest for prostitution. She is so depressed it hardly matters, and yet, is this the way the wife of a powerful man should be treated? Even one she hopes is dead?

Note: The movie played around the country in a beautifully restored 35 mm print that works as a reminder: Black and white doesn't subtract something from a film, but adds it.

Elizabethtown ★ ★ ★
PG-13, 120 m., 2005

Orlando Bloom (Drew Baylor), Kirsten Dunst (Claire Colburn), Susan Sarandon (Hollie Baylor), Alec Baldwin (Phil DeVoss), Bruce McGill (Bill Banyon), Judy Greer (Heather Baylor), Jessica Biel (Ellen Kishmore), Paul Schneider (Jessie Baylor). Directed by Cameron Crowe and produced by Crowe, Tom Cruise, and Paula Wagner. Screenplay by Crowe.

I've seen Cameron Crowe's *Elizabethtown* twice, and remarkable is the difference between the two versions. Critics were warned before seeing the Toronto film festival version that it was not the final cut, and was it ever not. The new version is eighteen minutes shorter, and more than 18 percent better, and wisely eliminates the question of why anyone would want to wear a pair of shoes that whistled.

The final version centers the story where it belongs, on the most unrelenting Meet Cute in movie history. Orlando Bloom plays Drew Baylor, a shoe designer on a red-eye flight to Kentucky, where his father has died during a family visit. Kirsten Dunst plays Claire Colburn, who is the only flight attendant on the plane, just as Drew is the only passenger. He just wants to be left alone. She insists he move up to first class, coddles him, makes bright and perky chat, and more or less insists on Meeting him, Cute or not.

Drew was contemplating suicide when the call came about his father's death. He's the designer of the Spasmodica shoe, a world-famous

but flawed new product that his boss (Alec Baldwin) informs him will lose $972 million and is "a failure of mythic proportions, a folk tale that makes other people feel better because it didn't happen to them." Drew's suicide is put on hold for the visit to Elizabethtown, where his father was related to half the population and the best friend of the other half, and where Drew's mother, Hollie (Susan Sarandon), is still hated as the woman who kidnapped this beloved man and took him away to live in California. "But we live in Oregon," Drew, his mother, and his sister, Heather (Judy Greer), keep explaining, but no one is listening.

The movie crosses two familiar kinds of material: the city slicker who encounters the salt-of-the-earth small-town types, and the romance that blossoms even while the two participants keep agreeing it is over. Both of these areas are handled gently and with affection, as when Drew offers condolences to everybody about the death of his father, and a relative gently informs him that "condolences" is "an incoming phrase."

Claire the flight attendant seems destined to save Drew's life by drawing his thoughts away from suicide, placing his failure in perspective, and insisting that he fall in love with her. For someone with a full-time job, she seems to have a lot of time on her hands and materializes where needed (and where not needed). Their in-flight relationship continues with an all-night phone call that ends with them meeting at dawn and looking out over the sunrise and deciding, after the conversation runs out, that maybe they were better on the phone. So that's the end, right? No: "You are always trying to break up with me," she tells him, "and we're not even together." And later, in exasperation: "Just tell me you love me and get it over with."

Meanwhile, Drew makes discoveries about his father and his family that are mostly positive. His mother, Hollie, and sister, Heather, fly in, the mother in the middle of manic plans for the rest of her life: "I want to learn to cook. I want to learn to laugh. I want to learn to tap dance." There is much discussion over the desire of the "Californians" to have the father cremated, this despite the family plot waiting to embrace his remains.

This being a Cameron Crowe movie, there is a great deal of music in it, some supplied by a cousin named Jessie (Paul Schneider), who was once a drummer in a band that once actually played (very, very far down) on the same bill as his idols, Lynyrd Skynyrd. How his band has a reunion at the memorial service, and how this leads to the flight of a flaming bird I will leave for you to discover.

It must be said that although Drew and Claire do seem to be falling in love, life with Claire might be maddening. She's the kind of person who would alphabetize alphabet soup. The climax of the movie is a cross-country road journey undertaken by Drew with copious maps, instructions, and CDs supplied by Claire, who instructs Drew on exactly where to go and what to see and who to meet and what to feel. All that redeems this exercise in compulsion is the fact that she is right.

This journey is charming, up to a point. In the first cut of the film, there was a great deal more of the journey, followed by a pointless epilogue in which the Spasmodica shoe turns out to be a hit after all, because with every step you take, it whistles. (Since much of the journey and all of the epilogue have been cut from the movie, this is not a spoiler unless the ban on spoilers has been extended to include deleted scenes on the DVD.)

The difference between the two versions is dramatic, even though they share most of the same footage. The longer version seemed to end, and end, and end. It was one of those situations where people in the audience were pulling on their sweaters, fishing under the seat for their empty popcorn boxes, and leaning forward ready to stand up, and *still* the movie wasn't over. The Spasmodica epilogue played like some kind of demented reluctance on Crowe's part to ever end the movie at all.

In its trimmed version, *Elizabethtown* is nowhere near one of Crowe's great films (like *Almost Famous*), but it is sweet and good-hearted and has some real laughs, and we can just about accept Claire's obsessive romantic behavior because if someone is going to insist that you have to fall in love, there are many possibilities more alarming than Claire.

Ella Enchanted ★ ★ ★ ½
PG, 95 m., 2004

Anne Hathaway (Ella), Hugh Dancy (Prince Charmont), Cary Elwes (Prince Regent Edgar), Minnie Driver (Mandy), Vivica A. Fox (Fairy Lucinda), Joanna Lumley (Dame Olga), Patrick Bergin (Sir Peter), Jimi Mistry (Benny the Book), Aiden McArdle (Slannen the Elf), Lucy Punch (Hattie), Jennifer Higham (Olive), Eric Idle (Narrator), Parminder K. Nagra (Areida). Directed by Tommy O'Haver and produced by Jane Startz. Screenplay by Laurie Craig, Karen McCullah Lutz, and Kirsten Smith, based on the novel by Gail Carson Levine.

Ella Enchanted is enchanted, all right. Based on the beloved novel by Gail Carson Levine, it's a high-spirited charmer, a fantasy that sparkles with delights. A lot of the fun is generated because it takes place in a world that is one part *Cinderella*, one part *Shrek*, and one part *The Princess Bride*. It even stars the hero from *The Princess Bride*, Cary Elwes, who has grown up to become evil Prince Regent Edgar, who killed his brother the king and now has his sights on the king's son, who will inherit the throne. So make that one part *Hamlet* crossed with one part *Macbeth*.

Anne Hathaway, that improbably beautiful young woman from *The Princess Diaries*, stars as Ella, who at her birth is burdened with a spell from her fairy godmother, Lucinda (Vivica A. Fox). In this kingdom, everyone gets a fairy spell, but Ella's is a real inconvenience: She is given the spell of obedience, which means she has to do whatever she's told. As she grows older this becomes a real problem, especially after her widowed father, Sir Peter (Patrick Bergin), provides her with an evil stepmother named Dame Olga (Joanna Lumley) and two jealous stepsisters, Hattie and Olive (Lucy Punch and Jennifer Higham).

So we get the Cinderella story, but with a twist, because Ella is sort of a medieval civil rights crusader and thinks it's wrong that Prince Edgar has condemned all the nonhumans in the kingdom to leave the city and live in the forest. That would include the giants, the ogres, and the elves. Ella is in the forest one day when she is captured by ogres, who suspend her above a boiling cauldron and prepare to boil her for lunch. An ogre asks her, "How do you like to be eaten? Baked? Boiled?" I like her answer: "Free range." Ella explains she's on their side, and as she sets out to end discrimination, she takes along a talking book named Benny; the front cover is a hologram showing Benny (Jimi Mistry), whose body was unfortunately lost in a wayward spell. Open the book and he can show you anyone you want to see, although Benny's powers are limited and he can't tell you where to find these people.

She has a Meet Cute (three, actually) with Prince Charmont (Hugh Dancy), and it's love at first, second, and third sight, plunging Ella into the middle of palace intrigue. Edgar plans to murder his nephew and assume the throne, and although Ella discovers this danger, her stepsisters know the secret of the curse and use it to alienate her from Charmont.

The look of the movie is delightful. Special effects create a picture-book kingdom in which the medieval mixes with the suburban (there is a mall). I like the casual way that computer-animated graphics are used with real foregrounds; sure, it doesn't look as convincing as it did (sometimes) in *The Lord of the Rings*, but a certain artifice adds to the style. The cast is appropriately goofy, including the household fairy, Mandy (Minnie Driver), who is not good for much in the spell department; Slannen the Elf (Aiden McArdle), Ella's plucky sidekick; a narrator played by Eric Idle, who sings a few songs; and a slithering snake named Heston, who is Edgar's chief adviser. The role of Ella's best friend, played by Parminder K. Nagra of *Bend It Like Beckham*, seems to have been much abbreviated, alas; we lose track of her for an hour, until she turns up waving happily at the end.

One of the charms of the movie is its goofiness, which extends to the songs, which verge on sing-along chestnuts; what else would the elves sing, after all, but "Let Us Entertain You"?

And Anne Hathaway is, well, kind of luminous. She has that big smile and open face, and here she's working with a witty and wicked plot, instead of with the wheezy contrivances of *The Princess Diaries*. She looks like she's having fun. So does everyone, even the snake. This is the best family film so far this year.

Ellie Parker ★ ★ ★

NO MPAA RATING, 95 m., 2005

Naomi Watts (Ellie Parker), Rebecca Riggs (Sam), Scott Coffey (Chris), Mark Pellegrino (Justin), Blair Mastbaum (Smash), Chevy Chase (Dennis). Directed by Scott Coffey and produced by Coffey, Naomi Watts, Matt Chesse, and Blair Mastbaum. Screenplay by Coffey.

To be a movie star *and* a good actor *and* a happy person is so difficult that Meryl Streep may be the only living person who has achieved it. Maybe Paul Newman, later in life. Okay, Tilda Swinton, Catherine Keener, and Morgan Freeman. Maybe Frances McDormand.

I know such speculation is goofy, but it's how I feel after seeing *Ellie Parker*, a daring and truthful film by Scott Coffey, starring Naomi Watts as an actress who is trying to get a start in Los Angeles. It is one of the ironies of this film about a failing actress that it got made only because a successful actress (the star of *King Kong*, no less) agreed to appear in it. You'd think they could have given the job to someone who needed the job, but then they couldn't have lined up the financing, modest as it is.

This is the movie they should show in college acting classes instead of tapes of *Inside the Actors' Studio*. It is about auditioning for an idiotic Southern Gothic soap opera and then changing your makeup and accent in the car on your way to audition as a hooker in a softcore sex film. About trying to impress a group of "producers" who are so stoned they don't have a sober brain cell to pass from hand to hand around the room. About suspecting that the only thing worse than not getting the job would be to get it. About being broke. About depending on your friends, who are your friends because they depend on you. About lying to the folks back home. About going to clubs to be "seen" and getting so wasted you hope no one saw you, and about suspecting that while you were in a blackout your genitals may have been leading a life of their own. And it is about having to be smart, talented, beautiful, determined, and, yes, lucky, just to get to *this* point in your career.

Ellie Parker follows its heroine through about twenty-four hours of her life. Maybe more. I'm not sure and neither is she. The character is played by Naomi Watts with courage, fearless observation, and a gift for timing that is so uncanny it can make points all by itself. Watts, as Parker, is so familiar with her look, her face, her hair, her style, her makeup that she can transform herself from a belle to a slut in the rearview mirror while driving from one audition to another, and convince us that she really could do that, and has.

She deceives herself that she might meet a nice guy who would—what? Does she have *time* for a relationship if she's really serious about her career? Would a guy that nice settle for the life she has to lead? If he shared it, wouldn't that mean he was as desperate as she was? There's a scene here where a guy has sex with her and then confesses he fantasized that she was Johnny Depp. He should have told her this before they started so that she could have fantasized that she was Johnny Depp, too, and then both people in bed could have felt successful.

In between these harrowing adventures, she engages in acting exercises where she dredges up sense memories that are worn out from overuse, and goes to see her therapist, whose occupation, she realizes, can also be spelled "the rapist." She doesn't know where to go with this, and neither does her therapist. We understand why Hollywood is such a hotbed of self-improvement beliefs, disciplines, formulas, and cults. I walked into the Bodhi Tree psychic bookstore one day and saw a big star rummaging through the shelves. What was she looking for? Didn't she know those books were written to help people get to the point she was already at? Maybe the star was trying to reverse the process. Maybe self-help bookstores should have a section named "Uninstall."

Ellie Parker is a very good movie, fearless and true, observant and merciless. Watts was brave to make it and gifted to make it so well. Coffey shot it off and on, as he was able to raise funds. The truth in this movie has been earned and paid for. Young people considering acting as a career should study it carefully. If Ellie Parker's ordeal looks like it might be fun, you may have the right stuff.

Enduring Love ★ ★ ★
R, 97 m., 2004

Daniel Craig (Joe Rose), Rhys Ifans (Jed), Samantha Morton (Claire), Bill Nighy (Robin), Andrew Lincoln (TV Producer), Helen McCrory(Mrs. Logan), Susan Lynch (Rachel). Directed by Roger Michell and produced by Kevin Loader. Screenplay by Joe Penhall, based on the novel by Ian McEwan.

In a grassy, sunlit field, the lovers Joe and Claire spread out their picnic lunch and open a bottle of champagne. Just then a hot-air balloon appears in the sky. It drifts down and lands, and a man jumps out, leaving a small boy inside. A gust of wind catches the balloon. The man tries to hold it down with a rope, but it is away. Joe runs to grab at another rope. Other men appear and grab ropes, but the balloon inexorably rises. One by one, the men let go and fall safely to Earth. One hangs on too long, past the point of no return. As the others stare silently at the long, quiet ascent of the balloon, this man hangs on as long as he can, and then he falls to Earth and is shattered.

This opening scene in *Enduring Love* is implacable in its simplicity. It literally shows death appearing from out of a clear blue sky. The others run through fields to the body of the dead man, and then one of the other survivors kneels down and asks Joe (Daniel Craig) to join him in prayer. This is Jed (Rhys Ifans), stringy-haired, skin and bones, with an intensity that is off-putting. Joe explains that he does not much believe in prayer. Jed implores him.

We follow Joe home, where he is a university lecturer and his girlfriend, Claire (Samantha Morton), is a sculptor. He is haunted by what happened in the field. The man who held on too long, he learns, was a doctor who happened on the scene entirely by fate. The balloon landed safely; the small boy was safe. The doctor died unnecessarily. Joe becomes obsessed by which of the men was first to let go of a rope. Was he the one? When one let go, all had to let go; if all had held on, he believes, the balloon would have returned to Earth and the doctor would not have died. "We let him down," Joe tells Claire.

Joe teaches a university class on love and ethics, and asks his students if love is real and ethics have meaning. His experience in the field undermines all he thinks he knows about such matters, and his classroom manner grows odd and tortured. There is another problem. Jed starts to stalk him. He stands in the park across from Joe's home. He is there when Joe visits the Tate Modern. He feels it is urgent that they know each other better. "You know what passed between us," he tells Joe. "Love—God's love. It was a sign." Jed is clearly mad. He exists at the intersection of religious hysteria and erotomania, and confuses God's love with his own sudden love for Joe. But what can Joe do? He warns him away, he tries to elude him, he changes his daily patterns. And meanwhile the specter of Jed's and Joe's haunting doubts about the death of the doctor create a tortured space between Joe and Claire.

The movie, directed by Roger Michell, has been adapted by Joe Penhall from a novel by Ian McEwan; it begins with ethical issues and then gradually descends into thriller material. The character of Jed is nicely modulated by Rhys Ifans; in the early scenes, he's the kind of man you instinctively know you want to get away from, but you nod and are polite and agree in a perfunctory way to whatever he's saying, while edging away and hoping never to see him again. Such people take such small talk literally, and convince themselves you have made promises or, worse, sent them a coded message.

The movie's questions about love take a turn when Joe goes to visit Mrs. Logan (Helen McCrory), widow of the dead doctor. She doesn't seem as grief-stricken as she should. "He was bound to die saving someone," she says. Then she asks questions about that day that must not be revealed here, but that cast the doctor's participation in a different light.

Most movies remain at the top level of action: They are about what happens. A few consider the meaning of what happened, and even fewer deal with the fact that we have a choice, some of the time, about what happens and what we do about it. It's impossible not to imagine ourselves in that field, seeing the father struggling with the rope as his son cries in the gondola. Would we run and grab a rope? Probably. Would we hang on too long? Not me. Rapid situational calculations dictate our decisions: The boy will not necessarily die if the balloon drifts away, but I will die if I lose my grip at a great height.

Joe is obsessed with the question of who let go first, but from another point of view, the doctor held on for too long. Now why did he do that? Is his widow correct in the way she

imagines the scenario? Certainly the doctor did nothing to save the boy, and everything to bring Joe and Jed together. Joe thinks of ethical questions in an objective, logical way. Jed responds emotionally to his own demons. No one thinks to blame the boy's father for getting out of the balloon too soon.

Enron: The Smartest Guys in the Room ★ ★ ★ ½
NO MPAA RATING, 110 m., 2005

Narrated by Peter Coyote. Featuring Kenneth Lay, Jeff Skilling, Lou Pai, Mike Muckleroy, Sherron Watkins, Reverend James Nutter, Bethany McLean, Peter Elkind, and others. A documentary directed by Alex Gibney and produced by Gibney, Jason Kliot, and Susan Motamed, based on the book *The Smartest Guys in the Room: The Amazing Rise and Scandalous Fall of Enron* by Bethany McLean and Peter Elkind.

This is not a political documentary. It is a crime story. No matter what your politics, *Enron: The Smartest Guys in the Room* will make you mad. It tells the story of how Enron rose to become the seventh-largest corporation in America with what was essentially a Ponzi scheme, and in its last days looted the retirement funds of its employees to buy a little more time.

There is a general impression that Enron was a good corporation that went bad. The movie argues that it was a con game almost from the start. It was "the best energy company in the world," according to its top executives, Kenneth Lay and Jeffrey Skilling. At the time they made that claim, they must have known that the company was bankrupt, had been worthless for years, had inflated its profits and concealed its losses through bookkeeping practices so corrupt that the venerable Arthur Andersen accounting firm was destroyed in the aftermath.

The film shows how it happened. To keep its stock price climbing, Enron created good quarterly returns out of thin air. One accounting tactic was called "mark to market," which meant if Enron began a venture that might make $50 million ten years from now, it could claim the $50 million as current income. In an astonishing in-house video made for employees, Skilling stars in a skit that satirizes "HFV" accounting, which he explains stands for "Hypothetical Future Value."

Little did employees suspect that was more or less what the company was counting on.

Skilling and Lay were less than circumspect at times. When a New York market analyst questions Enron's profit-and-loss statements during a conference call, Skilling can't answer and calls him an "asshole"; that causes bad buzz on the street. During a Q&A session with employees, Lay actually reads this question from the floor: "Are you on crack? If you are, that might explain a lot of things. If you aren't, maybe you should be."

One Enron tactic was to create phony offshore corporate shells and move their losses to those companies, which were off the books. We're shown a schematic diagram tracing the movement of debt to such Enron entities. Two of the companies are named "M. Smart" and "M. Yass." These "companies" were named with a reckless hubris: One stood for "Maxwell Smart" and the other one . . . well, take out the period and put a space between "y" and "a."

What did Enron buy and sell, actually? Electricity? Natural gas? It was hard to say. The corporation basically created a market in energy, gambled in it, and manipulated it. It moved on into other futures markets, even seriously considering "trading weather." At one point, we learn, its gambling traders lost the entire company in bad trades, and covered their losses by hiding the news and producing phony profit reports that drove the share price even higher. In hindsight, Enron was a corporation devoted to maintaining a high share price at any cost. That was its real product.

The documentary is based on the best-selling book of the same title, cowritten by *Fortune* magazine's Bethany McLean and Peter Elkind. It is assembled out of a wealth of documentary and video footage, narrated by Peter Coyote, from testimony at congressional hearings, and from interviews with such figures as disillusioned Enron exec Mike Muckleroy and whistle-blower Sherron Watkins. It is best when it sticks to fact, shakier when it goes for visual effects and heavy irony.

It was McLean who started the house of cards tumbling down with an innocent question about Enron's quarterly statements, which did not ever seem to add up. The movie uses in-house video made by Enron itself to show Lay and Skilling optimistically addressing employees and shareholders at a time when Skilling in particular was coming apart at the seams. Toward the end, he sells $200 million in his own Enron stock while encouraging Enron employees to invest their 401(k) retirement plans in the company. Then he suddenly resigns, but not quickly enough to escape Enron's collapse not long after. Televised taking the perp walk in handcuffs, both he and Lay face criminal trials in Texas.

The most shocking material in the film involves the fact that Enron cynically and knowingly created the phony California energy crisis. There was never a shortage of power in California. Using tape recordings of Enron traders on the phone with California power plants, the film chillingly overhears them asking plant managers to "get a little creative" in shutting down plants for "repairs." Between 30 percent and 50 percent of California's energy industry was shut down by Enron a great deal of the time, and up to 76 percent at one point, as the company drove the price of electricity higher by nine times.

We hear Enron traders laughing about "Grandma Millie," a hypothetical victim of the rolling blackouts, and boasting about the millions they made for Enron. As the company goes belly-up, 20,000 employees are fired. Their pensions are gone, their stock worthless. The usual widows and orphans are victimized. A power company lineman in Portland, who worked for the same utility all his life, observes that his retirement fund was worth $248,000 before Enron bought the utility and looted it, investing its retirement funds in Enron stock. Now, he says, his retirement fund is worth about $1,200.

Strange that there has not been more anger over the Enron scandals. The cost was incalculable, not only in lives lost during the power crisis, but in treasure: The state of California is suing for $6 billion in refunds for energy overcharges collected during the phony crisis. If the crisis had been created by al-Qaida, if terrorists had shut down half of California's power plants, consider how we would regard these same events. Yet the crisis, made possible because of legislation engineered by Enron's lobbyists, is still being blamed on "too much regulation." If there was ever a corporation that needed more regulation, that corporation was Enron.

Early in the film, there's a striking image. We see a vast, empty room, with rows of what look like abandoned lunchroom tables. Then we see the room when it was Enron's main trading floor, with countless computer monitors on the tables and hundreds of traders on the phones. Two vast staircases sweep up from either side of the trading floor to the aeries of Lay and Skilling, whose palatial offices overlook the traders. They look like the stairway to heaven in that old David Niven movie, but at the end they only led down, down, down.

Envy ★ ★

PG-13, 99 m., 2004

Ben Stiller (Tim Dingman), Jack Black (Nick Vanderpark), Rachel Weisz (Debbie Dingman), Amy Poehler (Natalie Vanderpark), Christopher Walken (J-Man), Ariel Gade (Lula Dingman), Lily Jackson (Nellie Vanderpark). Directed by Barry Levinson and produced by Levinson and Paula Weinstein. Screenplay by Steve Adams.

Jack Black becomes a zillionaire named Nick Vanderpark in *Envy*, who gets rich by inventing a product named Vapoorize. Yes, with a double O. It makes doggy-do into doggy-didn't. Spray some on your dog's morning gift and it disappears. His best friend, Tim Dingman, played by Ben Stiller, lives across the street. They share the commute every day to the sandpaper factory. When Vanderpark comes up with the idea for Vapoorize, he offers Dingman a 50 percent share, but Dingman turns it down. He can't figure out how it could possibly work. Soon, of course, he is being eaten alive by envy. My memory for some reason dredged up an ancient science fiction story in which a child's toy would zap little metal objects like paper clips into the fourth dimension. Great, until they started leaking back into our three. When you walk through a speck of paper clip, you can do serious damage. I wondered if maybe the same phenomenon would happen in *Envy*, causing, say, five years of dog poop to reappear all at once. Not a pretty picture.

The plot idea resembles that classic British comedy *The Man in the White Suit*, with Alec Guinness, who invented a fabric that never gets dirty. Of course, Guinness underplayed the comedy, a concept alien to Black and Stiller. Not that we want them to dial down; they're gifted comedians, and it's fun to watch Dingman gnashing while Vanderpark celebrates his untold riches. Vanderpark doesn't lord it over his neighbor; he builds an enormous mansion, yes, but right across the street from his best buddy because he doesn't want to leave the neighborhood. So that every time Dingman looks out the window, he has to witness Vanderpark's latest acquisition: ancient statuary, a proud white stallion, a merry-go-round, whatever.

Because Stiller and Black are in the movie, it contains laughs, and because Christopher Walken is in the movie, it contains more laughs. Walken is becoming Hollywood's version of a relief pitcher who comes on in the seventh and saves the game. You can sense the audience smiling when he appears onscreen.

Here he plays a stumblebum who calls himself J-Man, perhaps in homage to that immortal movie character Z-Man, perhaps not. After Dingman's life melts down, he turns to a saloon for consolation, and finds J-Man standing at the bar ready to provide advice and inspiration. J-Man's dialogue is Walkenized; he says strange things in strange, oracular ways.

So the movie is funny, yes, but not really funny enough. The screenplay, by Steve Adams, reportedly with uncredited input by Larry David, is best at showing a friendship being destroyed by envy, but weak at exploiting the comic potential of the invention itself. It gets sidetracked into the story of how Dingman hits Vanderpark's white horse with a bow and arrow, and we are reminded of the dog set on fire in *There's Something About Mary*. Dingman also hits J-Man with an arrow, although J-Man reacts to this development almost indifferently.

Dingman is married to Debbie (Rachel Weisz) and Vanderpark to Natalie (Amy Poehler), and there is a certain tension when the two families, plus kids, gather for dinner at Vanderpark's palatial mansion. There is also the matter of the fountain that Vanderpark gives to Dingman; it's a nice thought, but it does look a little out of scale with his little suburban home. Meanwhile, there is a certain tension between Dingman and his wife, since Stiller was, after all, *offered* 50 percent of the invention and *refused* it. (That's not the end of it, but I dare not spoil a plot point.)

Toward the end of the film, but not before the final revelations, Dingman has a speech that Stiller delivers with manic comic zeal. Allowing all of his pent-up feelings to explode, he tells Vanderpark what he really thinks about horses and offices and houses and dog poop and having flan for dessert, and his entire being quakes with Stillerian angst. Well done.

But the film, directed by Barry Levinson, doesn't generate heedless glee. Jack Black somehow feels reined in; shaved and barbered, he's lost his anarchic passion and is merely playing a comic role instead of transforming it into a personal mission. Walken, good as he is, isn't used enough by the plot, and Stiller's envy is replaced by plot logistics involving the dead horse, the merry-go-round, and so on, until the characters get mired in the requirements of the screenplay, which lumbers on its way, telling a story that increasingly strays from what was funny to begin with.

Eros
R, 104 m., 2005

The Hand ★ ★ ★ ★

Gong Li (Miss Hua), Chang Chen (Zhang). Directed by Wong Kar Wai and produced by Jacky Pang Yee Wah.

Equilibrium ★ ★ ★

Robert Downey Jr. (Nick Penrose), Alan Arkin (Dr. Pearl). Directed by Steven Soderbergh and produced by Jacques Bar, Raphael Berdugo, Gregory Jacobs, and Stephane Tchal Gadjieff.

The Dangerous Thread of Things ★

Christopher Buchholz (Christopher), Regina Nemni (Cloe), Luisa Ranieri (La Ragazza). Directed by Michelangelo Antonioni and produced by Marcantonio Borghese and Domenico Procacci. Screenplay by Antonioni and Tonino Guerra.

Are the three films in *Eros* intended to be (a) erotic, (b) about eroticism, or (c) both? The directors respond in three different ways.

Wong Kar Wai chooses (c), Steven Soderbergh chooses (b), and Michelangelo Antonioni, alas, arrives at None of the Above.

Wong Kar Wai's film, named *The Hand,* stars Gong Li as Miss Hua, a prostitute who is at the top of her game the first time the shy tailor Zhang (Chang Chen) meets her. He has been sent by his boss to design her clothes, and as he waits in her living room he clearly hears the sounds of sex on the other side of the wall. Her client leaves, she summons him, and curtly interrogates him. He passes muster. To be sure he will think about her while designing her clothes, she says, she will supply him with an aid to his memory. This she does; the film's title is a clue.

Steven Soderbergh's film, *Equilibrium,* is a sketch starring Robert Downey Jr. as the neurotic client of Dr. Pearl (Alan Arkin), his psychiatrist. Downey goes through verbal riffs as only Downey can do, moping about a recurring dream. Because the doctor is not in his line of sight, he is unaware that Dr. Pearl, between cursory responses, has seen someone through the window and is eagerly trying to mime the suggestion that they meet later.

Michelangelo Antonioni's film, *The Dangerous Thread of Things,* takes place near a resort on a lake, out of season. A man named Christopher (Christopher Buchholz) and his wife, Cloe (Regina Nemni), stroll and talk and discuss their problems, and then he sees a sexy young woman (Luisa Ranieri), and his wife tells him where she lives.

He goes to visit her, in improbable quarters inside a crumbling medieval tower, and they have sex. She laughs a lot. After he leaves, she does the kind of dance on the beach that hippies used to perform at dawn in Chicago's Lincoln Park back when the world was young and dance standards were more relaxed.

The Wong Kar Wai film is erotic. At least I found it so, and in matters of eroticism one is always the only judge who matters. It has no nudity, no explicit sex, no lingering shots of Gong Li's beauty. It is about situation and personality. She sees him, understands him, creates his obsession with her almost casually. Later, when the tailor comes to measure her again, he uses his hands instead of a tape measure. She allows him. There is an extraordinary scene in his tailor shop where his hands and arms venture inside her dress as if she were wearing it. Time passes. There is a sad and poetic closure.

The Soderbergh film makes the point that few things are more boring than what arouses someone else—unless it also arouses you, of course, in which case you can forget the other person and just get on with it. Downey's dream is all he can think of, but the psychiatrist cannot force himself to listen, and neither can we; it's much more exciting to speculate on the (unseen) object of his hoped-for tryst.

The Antonioni film is an embarrassment. Regina Nemni acts all of her scenes wearing a perfectly transparent blouse for no other reason, I am afraid, than so we can see her breasts. Luisa Ranieri acts mostly in the nude. The result is soft-core porn of the most banal variety, and when the second woman begins to gambol on the beach one yearns for Russ Meyer to come to the rescue. When a woman gambols in the nude in a Meyer film, you stay gamboled with.

I return to Wong Kar Wai's *The Hand*. It stays with me. The characters expand in my memory and imagination. I feel empathy for both of them: Miss Hua, sadly accepting the fading of her beauty, the disappearance of her clients, the loss of her health, and Mr. Zhang, who will always be in her thrall. "I became a tailor because of you," he says. It is the greatest compliment it is within his power to give, and she knows it. Knows it, and is touched by it as none of the countless words of her countless clients have ever, could ever, touch her.

Eternal Sunshine
of the Spotless Mind ★ ★ ★ ½
R, 106 m., 2004

Jim Carrey (Joel Barish), Kate Winslet (Clementine Kruczynski), Kirsten Dunst (Mary), Mark Ruffalo (Stan), Elijah Wood (Patrick), Tom Wilkinson (Dr. Howard Mierzwiak). Directed by Michel Gondry and produced by Anthony Bregman and Steve Golin. Screenplay by Charlie Kaufman.

How happy is the blameless vestal's lot! The world forgetting, by the world forgot. Eternal sunshine of the spotless mind! Each pray'r accepted, and each wish resign'd.
—Alexander Pope, "Eloisa to Abelard"

It's one thing to wash that man right outta your hair, and another to erase him from your mind. *Eternal Sunshine of the Spotless Mind* imagines a scientific procedure that can obliterate whole fields of memory—so that, for example, Clementine can forget that she ever met Joel, let alone fell in love with him. "Is there any danger of brain damage?" the inventor of the process is asked. "Well," he allows, in his most kindly voice, "technically speaking, the procedure *is* brain damage."

The movie is a labyrinth created by the screenwriter Charlie Kaufman, whose *Being John Malkovich* and *Adaptation* were neorealism compared to this. Jim Carrey and Kate Winslet play Joel and Clementine, in a movie that sometimes feels like an endless series of aborted Meet Cutes. That they lose their minds while all about them are keeping theirs is a tribute to their skill; they center their characters so that we can actually care about them even when they're constantly losing track of their own lives. ("My journal . . . ," Joel observes oddly, "is . . . just blank.")

The movie is a radical example of maze cinema, that style in which the story coils back upon itself, redefining everything and then throwing it up in the air and redefining it again. To reconstruct it in chronological order would be cheating, but I will cheat: At some point before the technical beginning of the movie, Joel and Clementine were in love, and their affair ended badly, and Clementine went to Dr. Howard Mierzwiak (Tom Wilkinson) at Lacuna Inc., to have Joel erased from her mind.

Discovering this, Joel in revenge applies to have *his* memories of her erased. But the funny thing about love is, it can survive the circumstances of its ending; we remember good times better than bad ones, and Joel decides in midprocess that maybe he would like to remember Clementine after all. He tries to squirrel away some of his memories in hidden corners of his mind, but the process is implacable.

If you think this makes the movie sound penetrable, you have no idea. As the movie opens, Joel is seized with an inexplicable compulsion to ditch work and take the train to Montauk, and on the train he meets Clementine. For all they know they have never seen each other before, but somehow there's a connection, a distant shadow of déjà vu. During the course of the film, which moves freely, dizzyingly, forward and backward in time, they will each experience fragmentary versions of relationships they had, might have had, or might be having.

Meanwhile, back at the Lacuna head office, there are more complications. Lacuna (www. lacunainc.com) seems to be a prosperous and growing firm (it advertises a Valentine's Day special), but in reality it consists only of the avuncular Dr. Mierzwiak and his team of assistants: Stan (Mark Ruffalo), Patrick (Elijah Wood), and Mary (Kirsten Dunst). There are innumerable complications involving them, which I will not describe because it would not only be unfair to reveal the plot but probably impossible.

Eternal Sunshine has been directed by Michel Gondry, a music video veteran whose first feature, *Human Nature* (2002), also written by Kaufman, had a lunacy that approached genius and then veered away. Tim Robbins starred as an overtrained child who devotes his adult life to teaching table manners to white mice. The scene where the male mouse politely pulls out the chair for the female to sit down is without doubt in a category of its own.

Despite jumping through the deliberately disorienting hoops of its story, *Eternal Sunshine* has an emotional center, and that's what makes it work. Although Joel and Clementine ping-pong through various stages of romance and reality, what remains constant is the human need for love and companionship, and the human compulsion to keep seeking it despite all odds. It may also be true that Joel and Clementine, who seem to be such opposites (he is shy and compulsive; she is extroverted and even wild), might be a good match for each other, and so if they keep on meeting they will keep on falling in love, and Lacuna Inc. may have to be replaced with the Witness Protection Program.

For Jim Carrey, this is another successful attempt, like *The Truman Show* and the underrated *The Majestic*, to extend himself beyond screwball comedy. He has an everyman appeal, and here he dials down his natural energy to give us a man who is so lonely and needy that a fragment of memory is better than none at all. Kate Winslet is the right foil for him, exasperated by Joel's peculiarities while paradoxically fond of them. The shenanigans back at

Lacuna belong on a different level of reality, but even there, secrets are revealed that are oddly touching.

Charlie Kaufman's mission seems to be the penetration of the human mind. His characters journeyed into the skull of John Malkovich, and there is a good possibility that two of them were inhabiting the same body in *Adaptation.* But both of those movies were about characters trying to achieve something outside themselves. The insight of *Eternal Sunshine* is that, at the end of the day, our memories are all we really have, and when they're gone, we're gone.

Everybody Says I'm Fine ★ ★
NO MPAA RATING, 103 m., 2004

Rehaan Engineer (Xen), Koel Purie (Nikita), Rahul Bose (Rage), Pooja Bhatt (Tanya), Anahita Oberoi (Misha), Boman Irani (Mr. Mittal), Sharokh Bharucha (Bobby), Juneli Aguiar (Tina). Directed by Rahul Bose and produced by Viveck Vaswani. Screenplay by Bose.

The English-language Indian film *Everybody Says I'm Fine* is too cluttered and busy, but as a glimpse into the affluent culture of a country with economic extremes, it's intriguing. Occasionally, it's funny and moving, too. The movie was shot in English not for the export market, but for India's domestic English speakers, who tend to be toward the top of the economic scale and are beginning to tire of endless Bollywood megaproductions. This film, at 103 minutes, almost qualifies in its market as a short subject, although true to Bollywood tradition it does include one completely arbitrary and inexplicable song-and-dance sequence.

Rehaan Engineer stars as Xen, a hairdresser whose parents died tragically when the sound board short-circuited in their recording studio. The trauma has left him with a psychic gift: When he cuts a person's hair, he can read the person's thoughts. He learns of adulteries, deceptions, and hypocrisies, and keeps them all to himself, going upstairs after work to his lonely room, where the shades are never opened and the TV sound is muted.

One day a pretty woman named Nikita (Koel Purie) arrives in his chair, and he picks up nothing. No thoughts. Is her mind a blank? He has acted as a matchmaker for some of his other customers whom he learns are attracted to one another, but now here is a challenge for him.

If the story had stayed more or less focused on Xen and his adventures, it might have been more involving, but it strays outside the salon to tell other stories, including one about a beautiful wife who has been left abandoned and penniless by her faithless husband, and a snoopy friend who has secrets of her own. There is also a flamboyant actor named Rage, played by director Rahul Bose, whose desperate attempts to find work are reflected by his bizarre hairstyles.

Movies like this are intrinsically interesting for the way they regard the culture they are immersed in, one where a Domino's pizza across the street coexists with crowds of desperate beggars. I enjoyed watching it just for the information and attitudes it contained, but as a story, it's too disorganized to really involve us.

Everything Is Illuminated ★ ★ ★ ½
PG-13, 104 m., 2005

Elijah Wood (Jonathan), Eugene Hutz (Alex), Boris Leskin (Grandfather), Laryssa Lauret (Lista). Directed by Liev Schreiber and produced by Peter Saraf and Marc Turtletaub. Screenplay by Schreiber, based on the novel by Jonathan Safran Foer.

Liev Schreiber's *Everything Is Illuminated* begins in goofiness and ends in silence and memory. How it gets from one to the other is the subject of the film, a journey undertaken by three men and a dog into the secrets of the past. The movie is narrated by Alex (Eugene Hutz), a Ukrainian whose family specializes in "tours of dead Jews." Alex and his grandfather (also named Alex) drive American Jews in search of their roots to the places where many of their ancestors died.

The trip through a bewildering but beautiful Ukrainian countryside involves a Soviet-era car that may not exactly have air bags. The grandfather is the driver, although he claims to be blind and insists on going everywhere with his "seeing-eye bitch," whose name is Sammy Davis Junior Junior. Alex's English seems learned from a thesaurus that was one

word off. He tortures words to force them into sentences from which they try to escape, and he keeps a journal with chapters like "Overture to the Commencement of a Very Rigid Search."

The movie's hero is Jonathan (Elijah Wood), a solemn, goggle-eyed American known as "The Collector" because he accumulates bits and pieces of his life and stores them in Ziploc bags, carefully labeled. He has come to Ukraine to find the woman who saved his grandfather's life. To this woman is due much gratitude, because Jonathan's grandmother passed along the belief that Ukraine treated Jews so badly that if the Nazis invaded, it might be an improvement.

The opening hour or so is a weirdly hilarious comedy, based on the intractable nature of the grandfather (Boris Leskin), his fierce love for Sammy Davis Junior Junior, and his truce with his grandson, who idolizes American popular culture, especially Michael Jackson. When Jonathan tells him Sammy Davis Jr. was Jewish, he is astonished: "What about Michael Jackson?" No, says Jonathan, definitely not Michael Jackson.

There is much perplexion (the kind of word the younger Alex savors) that Jonathan is a vegetarian, and in a hotel dining room he is told potatoes do not, cannot, have never come without meat. He is finally served one boiled potato, in a scene that develops as if Chaplin had been involved. Then he goes to his room, a narrow single bed in the midst of vast emptiness. Alex advises him to lock his door: "There are many dangerous people who would try to steal things from Americans and also kidnap them."

The journey continues. Sammy Davis Junior Junior begins to love Jonathan. Grandfather speaks like a crusty anti-Semite, Alex covers for him in his translation, and nobody seems to have heard of the hamlet of Trachimbrod, which they seek. Then abruptly the grandfather steers off the highway and into the middle of nowhere, and they find a beautiful white-haired old woman (Laryssa Lauret) living in a house in the middle of a field who simply says, "You are here. I am it."

The movie is based on a novel by Jonathan Safran Foer that reportedly includes many more scenes from the distant past, including some of magic realism in the eighteenth-century Ukrainian Jewish community. *Everything Is Illuminated* lives in the present, except for memories and enigmatic flashbacks to the Second World War. The gift that Schreiber brings to the material is his ability to move us from the broad satire of the early scenes to the solemnity of the final ones. The first third of the film could be inspired by Fellini's *Amarcord*, the last third by Bergman's darkest hours.

I described Jonathan as the hero of the film, but perhaps he is too passive to be a hero. He regards. He collects. Alex is the active character, cheerfully inventing English as he goes along, making the best of the journey's hardships, humoring his grandfather, telling the rich American what he wants to hear. Eugene Hutz, a singer in a punk gypsy band, brings notes of early John Turturro to the performance. Elijah Wood's performance is deliberately narrow and muted—pitch-perfect, although there is a distraction caused by his oversized eyeglasses, so thick they make his eyes huge. He visits, he witnesses, he puts things in Ziploc bags.

Then again, perhaps the real hero of the film is the grandfather, unless by default it is the old lady, who is a collector, too. For Grandfather, this is as much a journey of discovery as it is for Jonathan, and the changes that take place within him are all the more profound for never once being referred to in his dialogue. He never discusses his feelings or his memories, but in a way he is the purpose of the whole trip. The conclusion he draws from it is illustrated in an image that, in context, speaks more eloquently than words.

Everything Is Illuminated is a film that grows in reflection. The first time I saw it, I was hurtling down the tracks of a goofy ethnic comedy when suddenly we entered dark and dangerous territory. I admired the film but did not sufficiently appreciate its arc. I went to see it again at the Toronto Film Festival, feeling that I had missed some notes, had been distracted by Jonathan's eyeglasses and other relative irrelevancements (as Alex might say). The second time, I was more aware of the journey Schreiber was taking us on, and why it is necessary to begin where he begins to get where he's going.

The Exorcism of Emily Rose ★ ★ ★
PG-13, 114 m., 2005

Laura Linney (Erin Bruner), Tom Wilkinson (Father Moore), Campbell Scott (Ethan Thomas), Shohreh Aghdashloo (Doctor), Jennifer Carpenter (Emily Rose), Colm Feore (Karl Gunderson), Mary Beth Hurt (Judge Brewster). Directed by Scott Derrickson and produced by Paul Harris Boardman, Beau Flynn, Gary Lucchesi, Tom Rosenberg, and Tripp Vinson. Screenplay by Boardman and Derrickson.

"Demons exist whether you believe in them or not," says the priest at the center of *The Exorcism of Emily Rose*. Yes, and you could also say that demons do not exist whether you believe in them or not, because belief by definition stands outside of proof. If you can prove it, you don't need to believe it.

Such truths are at the center of this intriguing and perplexing movie, which is based on the true story of a priest who was accused of murder after a teenage girl died during an exorcism. If the priest is correct and the girl was possessed by a demon, he is innocent. If the authorities called by the prosecution are correct, she died of psychotic epileptic disorder, and the priest created complications leading to her death. If, on the other hand, the exorcism theory is correct, drugs given to the girl to treat her "disorder" made her immune to exorcism and led to her death.

The movie is told through flashbacks from a courtroom, where Father Moore (Tom Wilkinson) is on trial. He has been offered a deal (plead guilty to reckless endangerment and do six months of a twelve-month sentence), but he refuses it: "I don't care about my reputation, and I'm not afraid of jail. All I care about is telling Emily Rose's story." His lawyer, Erin Bruner (Laura Linney), despairs and yet admires him for his conviction. She herself does not believe in demons. The prosecutor, Ethan Thomas (Campbell Scott), is a churchgoer and presumably does believe, but lawyers sometimes argue against what they believe to be true. That's their job.

And who is Emily Rose? As played by Jennifer Carpenter in a grueling performance, she is a college student who sees the faces of friends and strangers turn into demonic snarls. Her nightmares are haunting. She speaks in foreign languages. She loses an alarming amount of weight. She calls home for help, in tears. Her boyfriend can't reach her. The parish priest, Father Moore, is called in and determines that an exorcism is indicated.

He has authorization from the archdiocese, but after he is charged with murder, the church authorities order him to accept plea bargaining and create as little scandal for the church as possible. The church is curiously ambivalent about exorcism. It believes that the devil and his agents can be active in the world, it has a rite of exorcism, and it has exorcists. On the other hand, it is reluctant to certify possessions and authorize exorcisms, and it avoids publicity on the issue. It's like those supporters of intelligent design who privately believe in a literal interpretation of Genesis but publicly distance themselves from it because that would undermine their plausibility in the wider world.

What is fascinating about *The Exorcism of Emily Rose* is that it asks a secular institution, the court, to decide a question that hinges on matters the court cannot have an opinion on. Either Emily was possessed by a demon and Father Moore did his best to save her, or she had a psychotic condition and he unwittingly did his best to kill her. The defense and the prosecution mount strong arguments and call persuasive witnesses, but in the end it all comes down to the personal beliefs of the jury. A juror who does not believe in demons must find Father Moore guilty, if perhaps sincere. A juror who does believe in demons must decide if Emily Rose was possessed or misdiagnosed. In a case like this, during the jury selection, are you qualified or disqualified by believing one way or the other?

The movie takes place in a small town surrounded by a Grant Wood landscape; houses and remote farms crouch in winter fields under a harsh sky. The key relationship is between the priest and his defense attorney. Erin

Bruner does not believe in devils, but she believes in Father Moore, and she believes he believes in them. "There are dark forces surrounding this trial," he warns her, suggesting that she herself might be a target of demons. In this and other scenes the movie is studiously neutral on the subject of the priest: He would look, speak, and behave exactly the same if he were sane and sincere, or deluded and sincere.

Erin works for a powerful law firm that has been retained by the archdiocese. She wants to be named a partner, but she won't be if she agrees with Father Moore's wish to appear on the witness stand; the archdiocese wants to make a deal leading to a quick settlement, with no testimony from the priest, and the archdiocese, not the priest, is the client who is paying. Which way does Erin turn? The film is fascinating in the way it makes legal and ethical issues seem as suspenseful as possession and exorcism.

The movie was directed by Scott Derrickson and written by Paul Harris Boardman and Derrickson. The screenplay is intelligent and open to occasional refreshing wit, as when prosecutor Ethan Thomas makes an objection to one witness's speculations about demonology. "On what grounds?" asks the judge (Mary Beth Hurt). "Oh . . . silliness," he says.

Somehow the movie really never takes off into the riveting fascination we expect in the opening scenes. Maybe it cannot; maybe it is too faithful to the issues it raises to exploit them. A movie like *The Exorcist* is a better film because it's a more limited one that accepts demons and exorcists lock, stock, and barrel, as its starting point. Certainly they're good showbiz. A film that keeps an open mind must necessarily lack a slam-dunk conclusion. In the end, Emily Rose's story does get told, although no one can agree about what it means. You didn't ask, but in my opinion she had psychotic epileptic disorder, but it could have been successfully treated by the psychosomatic effect of exorcism if those drugs hadn't blocked the process. ☞

F

Fahrenheit 9/11 ★ ★ ★ ½
R, 110 m., 2004

A documentary directed and produced by
Michael Moore.

Michael Moore's *Fahrenheit 9/11* is less an exposé of George W. Bush than a dramatization
of what Moore sees as a failed and dangerous
presidency. The charges in the film will not
come as news to those who pay attention to
politics, but Moore illustrates them with dramatic images and a relentless commentary
track that essentially concludes Bush is incompetent, dishonest, failing in the war on terrorism, and has bad taste in friends.

Although Moore's narration ranges from
outrage to sarcasm, the most devastating passage in the film speaks for itself. That's when
Bush, who was reading *My Pet Goat* to a classroom of Florida children, is notified of the second attack on the World Trade Center, and yet
lingers with the kids for almost seven minutes
before finally leaving the room. His inexplicable paralysis wasn't underlined in news reports
at the time, and only Moore thought to contact
the teacher in that schoolroom—who, as it
turned out, had made her own video of the
visit. The expression on Bush's face as he sits
there is odd indeed.

Bush, here and elsewhere in the film, is characterized as a man who owes a lot to his friends,
including those who helped bail him out of
business ventures. Moore places particular emphasis on what he sees as a long-term friendship between the Bush family (including both
presidents) and powerful Saudi Arabians. More
than $1.4 billion in Saudi money has flowed
into the coffers of Bush family enterprises, he
says, and after 9/11 the White House helped ex-
pedite flights out of the country carrying,
among others, members of the Bin Laden family (which disowns its most famous member).

Moore examines the military records released by Bush to explain his disappearance
from the Texas Air National Guard, and finds
that the name of another pilot has been blacked
out. This pilot, he learns, was Bush's close
friend James R. Bath, who became Texas money
manager for the billionaire Bin Ladens. An-

other indication of the closeness of the Bushes
and the Saudis: The law firm of James Baker, the
secretary of state for Bush's father, was hired by
the Saudis to defend them against a suit by a
group of 9/11 victims and survivors, who
charged that the Saudis had financed al-Qaida.

To Moore, this is more evidence that Bush
has an unhealthy relationship with the Saudis,
and that it may have influenced his decision to
go to war against Iraq at least partially on their
behalf. The war itself Moore considers un-
justified (no WMDs, no Hussein–Bin Laden
link), and he talks with American soldiers, including amputees, who complain bitterly about
Bush's proposed cuts of military salaries at the
same time he was sending them into a war that
they (at least, the ones Moore spoke to) hated.
Moore also shows American military personnel
who are apparently enjoying the war; he has
footage of soldiers who use torture techniques
not in a prison but in the field, where they hood
an Iraqi prisoner, call him "Ali Baba," and pose
for videos while touching his genitals.

Moore brings a fresh impact to familiar material by the way he marshals his images. We are
all familiar with the controversy over the 2000
election, which was settled by the U.S. Supreme
Court. What I hadn't seen before was footage of
the ratification of Bush's election by the U.S.
Congress. An election can be debated at the request of one senator and one representative;
ten representatives rise to challenge it, but not a
single senator. As Moore shows the challengers,
one after another, we cannot help noting that
they are eight black women, one Asian woman,
and one black man. They are all gaveled into silence by the chairman of the joint congressional session—Vice President Al Gore. The
urgency and futility of the scene reawaken old
feelings for those who believe Bush is an illegitimate president.

Fahrenheit 9/11 opens on a note not unlike
Moore's earlier films, such as *Roger & Me* and
Bowling for Columbine. Moore, as narrator,
brings humor and sarcasm to his comments,
and occasionally appears onscreen in a gadfly
role. It's vintage Moore, for example, when he
brings along a marine who refused to return to
Iraq; together, they confront congressmen, urging them to have their children enlist in the

service. And he makes good use of candid footage, including eerie video showing Bush practicing facial expressions before going live with his address to the nation about 9/11.

Apparently Bush and other members of his administration don't know what every TV reporter knows—that a satellite image can be live before they get the cue to start talking. That accounts for the quease-inducing footage of Deputy Defense Secretary Paul Wolfowitz wetting his pocket comb in his mouth before slicking back his hair. When that doesn't do it, he spits in his hand and wipes it down. If his mother is alive, I hope for his sake she doesn't see this film.

Such scenes are typical of vintage Moore, catching his subjects off-guard. But his film grows steadily darker, and Moore largely disappears from it, as he focuses on people such as Lila Lipscomb, from Moore's hometown of Flint, Michigan; she reads a letter from her son, written days before he was killed in Iraq. It urges his family to work for Bush's defeat.

Fahrenheit 9/11 is unashamedly partisan: Moore dislikes and distrusts Bush, and wants to motivate his viewers to vote against him. Whether his film will make a big difference is debatable, since it's likely most of the audience members will be in agreement with Moore. We tend to choose films that support our decisions, not those that challenge them. Moore's complaints are familiar to those who share his opinion of Bush; they seem to have had little effect on Bush's supporters. If the film does have an effect on the election, as Moore fervently hopes, it will be because it energizes and motivates those who already plan to vote against the president.

Fahrenheit 9/11 is a compelling and persuasive film, at odds with the White House effort to present Bush as a strong leader. He comes across as a shallow, inarticulate man, simplistic in speech and inauthentic in manner. If the film is not quite as electrifying as Moore's *Bowling for Columbine,* that may be because Moore has toned down his usual exuberance and was sobered by attacks on the factual accuracy of elements of *Columbine;* playing with larger stakes, he is more cautious here, and we get an op-ed piece, not a stand-up routine. But he remains one of the most valuable figures on the political landscape, a populist rabble-rouser,

humorous and effective; the outrage and incredulity in his film are exhilarating responses to Bush's determined repetition of the same stubborn sound bites.

Failure to Launch ★
PG-13, 97 m., 2006

Matthew McConaughey (Tripp), Sarah Jessica Parker (Paula), Zooey Deschanel (Kit), Justin Bartha (Ace), Bradley Cooper (Demo), Kathy Bates (Sue), Terry Bradshaw (Al). Directed by Tom Dey and produced by Scott Rudin and Scott Aversano. Screenplay by Tom J. Astle and Matt Ember.

During the course of *Failure to Launch,* characters are bitten by a chipmunk, a dolphin, a lizard, and a mockingbird. I am thinking my hardest why this is considered funny, and I confess defeat. Would the movie be twice as funny if the characters had also been bitten by a Chihuahua, a naked mole rat, and a donkey?

I was bitten by a donkey once. It was during a visit to Stanley Kubrick's farm outside London. I was the guest of the gracious Christiane Kubrick, who took me on a stroll and showed me the field where she cares for playground donkeys after their retirement. I rested my hand on the fence, and a donkey bit me. "Stop that!" I said, and the donkey did. If I had lost a finger, it would have been a great consolation to explain that it had been bitten off by one of Mrs. Stanley Kubrick's retired donkeys.

But I digress. *Failure to Launch* is about a thirty-five-year-old man named Tripp (Matthew McConaughey) who still lives at home with his parents. They dream of being empty nesters and hire a woman named Paula (Sarah Jessica Parker), who is a specialist at getting grown men to move out of their parents' homes. Her method is simple: You look nice, you find out what they like, and you pretend to like it, too. You encourage them to share a sad experience with you. And you ask them to teach you something. In this case, he likes paintball, her dog has to be put to sleep, and he teaches her to sail. Actually, it's not her dog and it's not really put to sleep, but never mind.

Sue and Al (Kathy Bates and Terry Bradshaw) are Tripp's parents. "I never sleep with my clients," Paula tells them. What she does is take hardened bachelors, force them to fall in love with her, and use that leverage to get them to move out of the parental home, after which she breaks up with them and they're fine. If this sounds to you like a cross between pathological cruelty and actionable fraud, I could not agree more. On the other hand, Tripp is no more benign. His strategy is to date a girl until she begins to like him and then take her home to bed, not telling her it is his parents' home. "The only reason he brings girls to dinner is because he's breaking up with them!" Sue warns Paula.

Oh, what stupid people these are. Stupid to do what they do, say what they say, think what they think, and get bitten by a chipmunk, a dolphin, a lizard, and a mockingbird. Actually, it's Tripp's friend Ace (Justin Bartha) who is bitten by the mockingbird. He is dating Paula's surly roommate, Kit (Zooey Deschanel). She hates the mockingbird because it keeps her awake at night. They hunt it with a BB gun, intending only to wound it, but alas the bird is peppered with BBs and seems to be dead, and . . . no, I'm not even going to go there. "You can't kill a mockingbird!" a gun salesman tells Kit. "Why not?" she asks. "You know!" he says. "That book, To Kill a Mockingbird!" No, she doesn't know. "I can't believe you don't know that," the guy says. Not know what? It's not titled To Kill a Mockingbird Would Be Wrong.

Ace gives the bird the kiss of life and they pump its furry little chest, and it recovers and bites Ace. Kit meanwhile has fallen in love with Ace. Which is my cue to tell you that Zooey Deschanel on this same weekend is opening in two movies; in this one she plays an airhead who saves the life of a mockingbird, and in the other one, Winter Passing, she plays an alcoholic actress who drowns her cat, which is dying from leukemia. It's an impressive stretch, like simultaneously playing Lady Macbeth and judging American Idol. Deschanel is actually very good in Winter Passing and fairly good in Failure to Launch. You know the joke about how polite Canadians are. If a movie is great they say it's "very good," and if a movie is terrible, they say it's "fairly good."

I cannot bring myself to describe how Tripp's friend Ace kidnaps him, locks him in a closet, and tricks Paula into being locked in the room with him so that they will be forced to confess their love to each other while Tripp remains tied to a chair and Ace uses hidden iSight cameras to telecast this event, live and with sound, for the entertainment of complete strangers in a restaurant, who watch it on a wall-sized video screen.

Now to get technical. The editing of the film is strangely fragmented. I first noticed this during a backyard conversation between the parents. There's unusually jerky cutting on lines of dialogue, back and forth, as if the film is unwilling to hold the characters in the same shot while they talk to one another. This turbulence continues throughout the film. Back and forth we go, as if the camera's watching a tennis match. I would question the editor, Steven Rosenblum, but he's the same man who edited Braveheart, Glory, and The Last Samurai, so I know this isn't his style. Did the director, Tom Dey, favor quick cutting for some reason? Perhaps because he couldn't stand to look at any one shot for very long? That's the way I felt.

The Family Stone ★ ★ ★
PG-13, 102 m., 2005

Claire Danes (Julie Morton), Diane Keaton (Sybil Stone), Rachel McAdams (Amy Stone), Dermot Mulroney (Everett Stone), Craig T. Nelson (Kelly Stone), Sarah Jessica Parker (Meredith Morton), Luke Wilson (Ben Stone), Tyrone Giordano (Thad Stone), Brian White (Patrick Thomas). Directed by Thomas Bezucha and produced by Michael London. Screenplay by Bezucha.

I was poised to attack The Family Stone because its story of a family of misfits is no match for the brilliance of Junebug. I was all worked up to bemoan the way a holiday release with stars such as Claire Danes, Diane Keaton, Dermot Mulroney, and Luke Wilson gets a big advertising send-off, while a brilliant film like Junebug, ambitious and truthful, is shuffled off into "art film" purgatory. Then sanity returned: Junebug intends to be a great film, and is, and The Family Stone intends to be a screwball comedy, and is, and all they have in common is an outsider coming into a family circle. To punish The Family

Stone because of Junebug would be like discovering that The Producers is not The Sweet Smell of Success.

So let's see what it is. As the movie opens, the Stones are preparing to celebrate Christmas. The oldest son, Everett (Dermot Mulroney), is bringing home his fiancée, Meredith (Sarah Jessica Parker), to meet the family. Meredith is not going to be an easy fit. She's aggressive, uptight, and hypersensitive, and dresses like someone who has never been undressed.

Waiting in the hometown are Everett's family: his mom, Sybil (Diane Keaton), his dad, Kelly (Craig T. Nelson), his brother Ben (Luke Wilson), his gay and deaf brother, Thad (Ty Giordano), and his kid sister, Amy (Rachel McAdams). We will also meet Thad's African-American partner, Patrick (Brian White), and their adopted son.

So, okay, if the Stones are okay with Patrick, they're strong on empathy and acceptance. Therefore, if they don't like Meredith, it is because she is not to be liked. And that does seem to be the case because 1) it is instantly obvious to the mother, Sybil, that this is the wrong woman for her son Everett, and 2) poor Meredith is one of those perfectionists who, in their rigid compulsion to do the right thing, always succeed in doing the wrong one.

Sir Michael Tippett, who wrote operas, said, "There is only one comic plot: the unexpected hindrances to an eventual marriage." While this definition does not encompass A Night at the Opera or Babe: Pig in the City, there is much truth in it. In Meredith's case, she is her own greatest hindrance to marriage, and the more she realizes that, the deeper the hole she digs.

The screenplay by director Thomas Bezucha establishes subplots around this central fact. We learn that Everett is drawn to Meredith partly because he believes that to be successful in business, he should be more like her and less like he really is. We learn that Ben, the Luke Wilson character, thinks of himself as a wild and crazy guy. We meet Meredith's sister Julie (Claire Danes), who flies in to rescue her sister and turns into a second fly in the same ointment. Julie is as relaxed and natural as Meredith is emotionally constipated. And then, in ways I will not reveal, it turns out there is another truth Sir Michael might have observed: Opposites attract.

The Family Stone is silly at times, leaning toward the screwball tradition of everyone racing around the house at the same time in a panic fueled by serial misunderstandings. There is also a thoughtful side, involving the long and loving marriage of Sybil and Kelly. Keaton and Nelson create touching characters in the middle of comic chaos. They have a scene together as true and intimate in its way as a scene involving a long-married couple can be. It doesn't involve a lot of dialogue, and doesn't need to, because it obviously draws on a lot of history.

There is an emerging genre of movies about family reunions at holiday time. It seems to be a truth universally acknowledged that most reunions at Christmas end happily, while most reunions at Thanksgiving end sadly. That's odd, because the way things shake out in the world of fragmented families, we tend to spend Thanksgiving with those we choose, and Christmas with those we must. If those two lists are identical in your life, your holidays must all be joyous, or all not.

What is always true is that the holiday itself imposes Aristotle's unities of time and place upon the plot. Most of the action takes place in the house or on the way to and from it, and whatever happens will have to happen before everybody heads back to the airport. That creates an artificial deadline that makes everything seem more urgent and requires that the truth be told or love declared right here and now, or not at all.

The Family Stone sorts out its characters admirably, depends on typecasting to help establish its characters more quickly, and finds a winding path between happy and sad secrets to that moment when we realize that the Family Stone will always think of this fateful Christmas with a smile, and a tear. What else do you want? If it's a lot, just rent Junebug.

Fantastic Four ★
PG-13, 123 m., 2005

Ioan Gruffudd (Reed Richards/Mr. Fantastic), Jessica Alba (Susan Storm/Invisible Woman), Michael Chiklis (Ben Grimm/Thing), Chris Evans (Johnny Storm/Human Torch), Kerry Washington (Alicia Masters), Julian McMahon (Victor Von Doom/Doctor Doom). Directed by

Tim Story and produced by Avi Arad, Chris Columbus, Bernd Eichinger, and Ralph Winter. Screenplay by Michael France and Mark Frost, based on the comic book and characters by Jack Kirby and Stan Lee.

So you get in a spaceship and you venture into orbit to research a mysterious star storm hurtling toward Earth. There's a theory it may involve properties of use to man. The ship is equipped with a shield to protect its passengers from harmful effects, but the storm arrives ahead of schedule and saturates everybody on board with unexplained but powerful energy that creates radical molecular changes in their bodies.

They return safely to Earth, only to discover that Reed Richards (Ioan Gruffudd), the leader of the group, has a body that can take any form or stretch to unimaginable lengths. Call him Mr. Fantastic. Ben Grimm (Michael Chiklis) develops superhuman powers in a vast and bulky body that seems made of stone. Call him Thing. Susan Storm (Jessica Alba) can become invisible at will and generate force fields that can contain propane explosions, in case you have a propane explosion that needs containing but want the option of being invisible. Call her Invisible Woman. And her brother, Johnny Storm (Chris Evans), has a body that can burn at supernova temperatures. Call him the Human Torch. I almost forgot the villain, Victor Von Doom (Julian McMahon), who becomes Doctor Doom and wants to use the properties of the star storm and the powers of the Fantastic Four for his own purposes. He eventually becomes metallic.

By this point in the review, are you growing a little restless? What am I gonna do, list names and actors and superpowers and nicknames forever? That's how the movie feels. It's all setup and demonstration and naming and discussing and demonstrating, and it never digests the complications of the Fantastic Four and gets on to telling a compelling story. Sure, there's a nice sequence where Thing keeps a fire truck from falling off a bridge, but you see one fire truck saved from falling off a bridge, you've seen them all.

The Fantastic Four are, in short, underwhelming. The edges kind of blur between them and other superhero teams. That's un-

derstandable. How many people could pass a test right now on who the X-Men are and what *their* powers are? Or would want to? I was watching *Fantastic Four* not to study it but to be entertained by it, but how could I be amazed by a movie that makes its own characters so indifferent about themselves? The Human Torch, to repeat, *can burn at supernova temperatures!* He can become so hot, indeed, that he could *threaten the very existence of the earth itself!* This is absolutely, stupendously amazing, wouldn't you agree? If you could burn at supernova temperatures, would you be able to stop talking about it? I know people who won't shut up about winning fifty bucks in the lottery.

But after Johnny Storm finds out he has become the Human Torch, he takes it pretty much in stride, showing off a little by setting his thumb on fire. Later he saves the earth, while Invisible Woman simultaneously contains his supernova so he doesn't destroy it. That means Invisible Woman could maybe create a force field to contain the sun, which would be a big deal, but she's too distracted to explore the possibilities: She gets uptight because she will have to be naked to be invisible, because otherwise people could see her empty clothes; it is no consolation to her that invisible nudity is more of a metaphysical concept than a condition.

Are these people complete idiots? The entire nature of their existence has radically changed, and they're about as excited as if they got a makeover on *Oprah*. The exception is Ben Grimm, as Thing, who gets depressed when he looks in the mirror. Unlike the others, who look normal except when actually exhibiting superpowers, he looks like—well, he looks like his suits would fit the Hulk, just as the Human Torch looks like the Flash, and the Invisible Woman reminds me of Storm in *X-Men*. Is this the road company? Thing clomps around on his size 18 boulders and feels like an outcast until he meets a blind woman named Alicia (Kerry Washington) who loves him, in part because she can't see him. But Thing looks like Don Rickles crossed with Mount Rushmore; he has a body that feels like a driveway and a face with crevices you could hide a toothbrush in. Alicia tenderly feels his face with her fingers, like blind people often do while falling in love in the movies, and I guess she likes what she feels. Maybe she's extrapolating.

The story involves Dr. Doom's plot to . . . but perhaps we need not concern ourselves with the plot of the movie, since it is undermined at every moment by the unwieldy need to involve a screenful of characters who, despite the most astonishing powers, have not been made exciting, or even interesting. The X-Men are major league compared to them. And the really good superhero movies, such as *Superman, Spider-Man 2,* and *Batman Begins,* leave *Fantastic Four* so far behind that the movie should almost be ashamed to show itself in some of the same theaters. ☞

The Fast and the Furious: Tokyo Drift ★ ★ ★
PG-13, 105 m., 2006

Lucas Black (Sean Boswell), Bow Wow (Twinkie), Nathalie Kelley (Neela), Brian Tee (D.K.), Sung Kang (Han), Leonardo Nam (Morimoto), Brian Goodman (Mr. Boswell), Sonny Chiba (Uncle Kamata). Directed by Justin Lin and produced by Neal H. Moritz. Screenplay by Chris Morgan.

After Sean wrecks a construction site during a car race, the judge offers him a choice: Juvenile Hall or go live with his father in Japan. So here he is in Tokyo, wearing his cute school uniform and replacing his shoes with slippers before entering a classroom where he does not read, write, or understand one word of Japanese. They say you can learn through total immersion. When he sees the beautiful Neela sitting in the front row, it's clear what he'll be immersed in.

The Fast and the Furious: Tokyo Drift is the third of the F&F movies; it delivers all the races and crashes you could possibly desire, and a little more. After only one day in school, Sean (Lucas Black) is offered a customized street speedster and is racing down the ramps of a parking garage against the malevolent D.K. (Brian Tee), who turns out to be Neela's boyfriend.

The racing strategy is called "drifting." It involves sliding sideways while braking and accelerating, and the races involve a lot of hairpin turns. The movie ends with a warning that professional stunt drivers were used and we shouldn't try this ourselves. Like the stunt in *Jackass* where the guy crawls on a rope over an alligator pit with a dead chicken hanging from his underwear, it is not the sort of thing likely to tempt me.

The movie observes two ancient Hollywood conventions. First, the actors play below their ages. Although the "students" are all said to be seventeen, Lucas Black is twenty-four, and his contemporaries in the movie range between nineteen and thirty-four. Maybe that's why the girls in the movie take their pom-poms home: They need to remind us how young they are.

They also are rich. After Sean wrecks the red racer that Han (Sung Kang) has loaned him, he has access to a steady supply of expensive customized machines, maybe because Han likes him, although the movie isn't heavy on dialogue. "I have money," Han tells Sean after the first crash. "It's trust I don't have." He lets Sean work off the cost of the car by walking into a bathhouse and trying to collect a debt from a sumo wrestler. Meanwhile, in the tiny but authentic Tokyo house occupied by his father (Brian Goodman), a U.S. military officer, Sean has to listen to a movie speech so familiar it should come on rubber stamps: "This isn't a game. If you're gonna live under my roof, you gotta live under my rules. Understood?"

Yeah, sure, Dad. Sean is scorned in Tokyo as a *gaijin,* or foreigner, and that gives him something in common with Neela (Nathalie Kelley), whose Australian mother was a "hostess" in a bar and whose father presumably was Japanese, making her half-gaijin. "Why can't you find a nice Japanese girl like all the other white guys?" Han asks him. Luckily, Neela speaks perfect English, as do Han and Twinkie (Bow Wow), another new friend, who can get you Air Jordans even before Nike puts them on the market.

The racing scenes in the movie are fast, and they are furious, and there's a scene where Sean and D.K. are going to race down a twisting mountain road, and Neela stands between the two cars and starts the race, and we wonder if anyone associated with this film possibly saw *Rebel Without a Cause.*

221

What's interesting is the way the director, Justin Lin, surrounds his gaijin with details of Japanese life, instead of simply using Tokyo as an exotic location. We meet the sumo wrestler, who will be an eye-opener for teenagers self-conscious about their weight. We see pachinko parlors, we see those little "motel rooms" the size of a large dog carrier, and we learn a little about the *yakuza* (the Japanese mafia) because D.K.'s uncle is the yakuza boss Kamata (Sonny Chiba). One nice touch happens during the race on the mountain road, which the kids are able to follow because of instant streaming video on their cell phones.

Lin, still only thirty-three, made an immediate impression with his 2002 Sundance hit, *Better Luck Tomorrow,* a satiric and coldly intelligent movie about rich Asian-American kids growing up in Orange County, California, and winning Ivy League scholarships while becoming successful criminals. That movie suggested Lin had the resources to be a great director, but since then he's chosen mainstream commercial projects. Maybe he wants to establish himself before returning to more personal work. His *Annapolis* (2006) was a sometimes incomprehensible series of off-the-shelf situations (why, during the war in Iraq, make a military academy movie about boxing?).

But in *The Fast and the Furious: Tokyo Drift* he takes an established franchise and makes it surprisingly fresh and intriguing. The movie is not exactly *Shogun* when it comes to the subject of an American in Japan (nor, on the other hand, is it *Lost in Translation*). But it's more observant than we expect and uses its Japanese locations to make the story about something more than fast cars. Lin is a skillful director, able to keep the story moving, although he needs one piece of advice. It was Chekhov, I believe, who said when you bring a gun onstage in the first act, it has to be fired in the third. Chekhov also might have agreed that when you bring Nathalie Kelley onstage in the first act, by the third act the hero at least should have been able to kiss her.

Fat Albert ★ ★
PG, 93 m., 2004

Kenan Thompson (Fat Albert), Kyla Pratt (Doris Roberts), Dania Ramirez (Lauri), Shedrack Anderson III (Rudy), Jermaine Williams (Mushmouth), Keith Robinson (Bill), Alphonso McAuley (Bucky), Aaron Frazier (Old Weird Harold), Marques Houston (Dumb Donald). Directed by Joel Zwick and produced by John Davis. Screenplay by Bill Cosby and Charles Kipps.

Now here is a movie for which the words "good-hearted" come straight into mind. It takes the characters of Bill Cosby's *Fat Albert* TV cartoon show from the 1970s, and sends them popping magically out of the TV screen and into the life of a teenage girl—where, hey-hey-hey, they give her advice that has always worked for them in Toonland.

It's ingenious in the way it shows the cartoon characters amazed by the real world (hey-hey-hey, they learn from a poster in a video store that they're on a "de-ved," or however you say "DVD"). But in a season where the standards have been set for animated entertainment by *The Polar Express* and *The Incredibles,* I don't think *Fat Albert* is up to speed; in its meandering, low-key way, it seems destined more for a future on de-ved, returning to the video world where the characters say they feel more at home.

Kyla Pratt plays Doris, a high school student who is pretty and smart but lacks self-confidence and feels left out of things. There's a big party tonight (a rich kid's father is blocking off the street), but she's not invited. Oh, she was kinda included in an invitation to her popular foster sister, Lauri (Dania Ramirez), but that's not the same thing.

Doris comes home, turns on the TV, and sheds a single tear, which falls onto the TV screen and creates a portal in space, time, and reality. On the *Fat Albert* TV show, in a Philadelphia junk yard, the characters see this glistening sphere floating in midair, take a reckless chance by jumping through it, and find themselves in Doris's living room.

Many movies have inserted cartoon characters into the real world, but usually while still representing them as cartoons, as in *Roger Rabbit, Space Jam,* and *Garfield.* In *Fat Albert,* the toons become real humans, played by actors who look amazingly like their TV counterparts, including Kenan Thompson of *Saturday Night Live,* who wears a padded costume that makes him look not like an actual fat kid, but like a cartoon fat kid who is round in all the right places and has a belt around the equator that looks drawn on. (In a poignant sequence at the very end of the film, we discover that the toons also look like Bill Cosby's real-life childhood friends, who inspired *Fat Albert and the Cosby Kids*.)

Doris, who is worried about her popularity, isn't thrilled to be joined by cartoonish caricatures like Fat Albert, Mushmouth (Jermaine Williams), Bucky (Alphonso McAuley), Old Weird Harold (Aaron Frazier), Dumb Donald (Marques Houston), and Rudy (Shedrack Anderson III). Nor are they exactly thrilled to be in the real world, where things work different than in a cartoon. They try to jump back into the screen, but the *Fat Albert* show is over, and they deduce that the magic portal opens only while they're on the air; that means they have to stick around for twenty-four hours. Alas, the bright colors of their costumes seem to be slowly fading away, as if they're losing their unreality.

There's an awkward little subplot in which Fat Albert gets a crush on Lauri, a strange moment when Dumb Donald reveals that he wears a hood "because I haven't got a face," and lots of scenes in which Doris's low self-esteem is boosted by the Cosby Kids' hey-hey-hey style of positive thinking.

The movie is sweet and gentle, but not very compelling. All but its younger viewers will be expecting a little more excitement along with Fat Albert's genial encouragement of Doris. And I was wondering, as I always do with plot devices like this, why the human characters deal so calmly with the appearance of toons. Yes, Doris is surprised when the Fat Albert gang pops through her TV set, but isn't that event more than just . . . surprising? Isn't it *incredibly amazing?* When the laws of the physical universe as we know them are fundamentally violated, shouldn't it be for more earth-shaking purposes than to cheer up Doris?

Fear and Trembling ★ ★ ★
NO MPAA RATING, 107 m., 2005

Sylvie Testud (Amelie), Kaori Tsuji (Fubuki), Taro Suwa (Monsieur Saito), Bison Katayama (Monsieur Omochi), Yasunari Kondo (Monsieur Tenshi), Sokyu Fujita (Monsieur Haneda), Gen Shimaoka (Monsieur Unaji). Directed by Alain Corneau and produced by Alain Sarde and based on the novel by Amelie Nothomb.

The opening shot of *Fear and Trembling* shows the heroine at the age of five, sitting at the edge of the ancient rock garden at the Ryoanji Zen temple in Kyoto. This is an elegant arrangement of rocks on a surface of smooth pebbles. They are so placed that no matter where you sit, you can't see all of them at the same time. Some see the garden as a metaphor for Japanese society, intricately arranged so that it looks harmonious from every viewpoint, but is never all visible at once.

The heroine, whose name is Amelie, returns with her parents to her native Belgium. But she has fallen in love with Japan, and at the age of twenty, she returns to take a job with a vast corporation and "become a real Japanese." Now played by Sylvie Testud as a college graduate who speaks perfect Japanese, she is hired as a translator and assigned to work under the beautiful Fubuki (Kaori Tsuji). She idolizes this woman, so beautiful, so flawless, so tall—too tall, probably, to ever marry, Amelie reflects.

The story of her year at the Yumimoto Corp., based on a semiautobiographical novel by Amelie Nothomb, is the story of a Westerner who speaks flawless Japanese but in another sense does not understand Japanese at all. In one way after another she commits social errors, misreads signals, violates taboos, and has her fellow workers wondering, she is told, "how the nice white geisha became a rude Yankee." That she is Belgian makes her no less a Yankee from the Japanese point of view; what is important is that she is not Japanese.

Consider her first blunder. She is ordered to serve coffee to visiting executives in a conference room. As she passes around the cups, she quietly says, "Enjoy your coffee." Soon after she leaves the room, the visitors walk out in anger, and Omochi (Bison Katayama), the boss of the boss of her boss, screams, "Who is this girl? Why does she speak Japanese?" But, she says, she was *hired* because she speaks Japanese. "How could they discuss secret matters in front of a foreigner who speaks Japanese?" the boss of her boss screams. "You no longer speak Japanese!"

She argues that it is impossible for her to forget how to speak Japanese, but this is taken as an example of her inability to understand Japan. She learns quickly that the corporate hierarchy is unbending: "You may only address your immediate superior, me," says Fubuki. Eager to find a role, Amelie begins to distribute the mail, only to find she is taking the job of the mailman. She assigns herself to updating every calendar in the office, but is told to stop because it is a distraction. That's a shame, because she finds she enjoys her simple tasks. "How silly I was to get a college degree," she says in the narration, "when my mind was satisfied by mindless repetition. How nice it was to live without pride or brains!" Eventually she is assigned to clean the toilets.

This is indeed a woman who is lost in translation. But how accurate is this portrait of Japanese corporate life? I searched for a review from Japan, but wasn't able to find one. My guess is that an actual Japanese corporation has been transformed here through a satirical filter into an exaggeration of basic truths: There is a hierarchy, there is suspicion of foreigners, no one who is not Japanese can ever possibly understand the Japanese, etc. Donald Richie has lived in Japan for most of the last fifty-six years and written invaluable books about its society and films; he was able to relax and adjust, he writes in his recently published journals, only when he realized that he would always be an invisible outsider, exempt from social laws because he was not expected to be able to understand them.

Fear and Trembling, directed by Alain Corneau, may be a sardonic view of Japanese corporate culture, but that's not all it is. The movie is also subtly sexual and erotic, despite the fact that almost every scene takes place in the office and there is not a single overt sexual act or word or gesture or reference. Sexuality in the movie's terms is transferred into the power of one person over another; Amelie begins by adoring Fubuki, but eventually realizes that the other woman hates her and is jealous of her as a competitor. Fubuki finds her one demeaning task after another, and Amelie responds simply by—doing them. By submitting.

This response has a quietly stimulating result for Fubuki, who is aroused by the other woman's submission. The brilliance of the movie is to suppress all expression of this arousal; we have to sense it in small moments of body language, in almost imperceptible pauses or reactions, in the rhythm set up between command and obedience. Understanding Fubuki better than she understands herself, Amelie is eventually able to win the game by becoming so submissive, so much in fear of the taller, more powerful woman, that a kind of erotic release takes place. She exaggerates the "fear and trembling" that, it is said, one should exhibit when addressing the emperor.

The movie that comes to mind is *Secretary*, the 2002 film with James Spader as a lawyer whose new secretary, played by Maggie Gyllenhaal, gradually enters with him in an S&M relationship that she, as the submissive one, finds a source of power (and amusement). Much the same thing happens in *Fear and Trembling*; that it happens below the level of what is said and done and acknowledged makes it doubly erotic because it cannot be admitted or acknowledged. The film ends again in the Kyoto rock garden, whose message is perhaps: If you could see all the rocks at once, what would be the point of the garden?

Fever Pitch ★ ★ ★ ½
PG-13, 98 m., 2005

Drew Barrymore (Lindsey Meeks), Jimmy Fallon (Ben Wrightman). Directed by Bobby Farrelly and Peter Farrelly and produced by Drew Barrymore, Alan Greenspan, Nancy Juvonen, Gil Netter, Amanda Posey, and Bradley Thomas. Screenplay by Lowell Ganz and Babaloo Mandel, based on the book by Nick Hornby.

It must be Nick Hornby who understands men so well, and how they think about women, and how women think about them. His books have been the starting point for three wonderful movies about the truce of the sexes: *High Fidelity* (2000), *About a Boy* (2002), and now *Fever Pitch*. Their humor all begins in the same place, with truth and close observation. We know these people. We dated these people. We are these people.

Because *Fever Pitch* involves a Boston Red Sox fan and takes place during the miraculous 2004 season, do not make the mistake of thinking it is a baseball movie. It is a movie about how men and women, filled with love and motivated by the best will in the world, simply do not speak the same emotional language. She cannot understand why he would rather go to spring training camp in Florida than meet her parents. He cannot understand why this is even an issue.

Drew Barrymore and Jimmy Fallon star, as Lindsey and Ben, both around thirty. She thinks it may be time to get married. He already seems married, to the Red Sox. His love for the team, he confesses to her, "has been a problem with me . . . and women." She is a high-paid business executive. He is a high school teacher.

Should she date below her income level? She has a strategy meeting with her girlfriends. When men have these meetings, they talk about how a woman really understands them. Women talk about how a man doesn't really understand them. Men talk about how a woman looks. Women ask questions like: "Where has he been?" Ben is thirty and single. Lindsey at least *knows* why she's still single: She works all the time.

Their first date begins unpromisingly, with food poisoning and Lindsey hurling into a garbage can. But Ben is a nice guy and cleans up, puts her to bed, sleeps on the couch. In no time at all, they're in love. What she doesn't understand is, she's in love with Winter Guy.

Summer Guy is a Red Sox fan. She is from Venus; he is from Fenway Park. He has season tickets. The people in the nearby seats are his "summer family." When they talk Red Sox lore, it sounds like they know what they're talking about. When he considers selling his season tickets, they observe that "technically" he's supposed to return them to the team. His apartment looks like a sports memorabilia store. Even the telephone is made out of a baseball mitt. She looks at the T-shirts and warm-up jackets in his closet, and says, "This is not a man's closet."

Jimmy Fallon is perfectly cast in the role. *Saturday Night Live* veterans tend to disappear into the fourth dimension of "SNL comedies" that are usually pretty bad. Only occasionally does someone like Bill Murray find a wider range of roles. Fallon was recently in the awful *Taxi*, but here it must be said (as it could be said about John Cusack in *High Fidelity* and Hugh Grant in *About a Boy*)

that you cannot imagine anyone else in the role. He achieves a kind of perfection in his high spirits, his boyish enthusiasm, his dependence on the Sox for a purpose in his life, and his bafflement about romance. He doesn't know that Freud's dying words were allegedly, "Women! What do they want?" But he would have understood them.

Drew Barrymore is also perfectly cast, in part because in real life, as in the movie, she's not only adorable but also a high-powered businesswoman (she is listed first among the film's producers). Her Lindsey likes Ben because he is a good and nice man, funny, considerate, and sexy. That's the Winter Guy. The Summer Guy is also all of those things, when his busy schedule as a Red Sox fan permits him. "All those things you feel for that team," she tells him in despair, "I feel them too, for you."

Well, come on. Think how the guy feels. The Sox are down 0-3 to the Yankees in the AL playoffs and behind in the fourth and apparently final game. He's at a party she wanted him to attend. He has a great time at the party, until he finds out *the Red Sox tied it up and won 6–4 in the 12th inning!* That will be a moment that he will always, always regret missing. Is he a fool? I would like to say that he is, but if I hadn't seen the final four minutes of the Illinois game against Arizona, *when they came from 15 behind to tie it up and win in overtime!* I would have been . . . discontented.

Yes, it's only a game. There's a bright little boy in the movie who says to Ben: "Let me just leave you with this thought. You love the Sox, but have they ever loved you back?" Lindsey loves him back. But one transgression follows another. Consider her thoughts as she watches the TV news, which shows her being hit by a foul ball and knocked out, while next to her Ben jumps up and down in excitement and hasn't noticed his girl is unconscious. Women remember things like that.

The movie has been directed by the Farrelly brothers, Peter and Bobby, who tend to make a different kind of movie (*Dumb and Dumber, Kingpin, There's Something About Mary, Stuck on You*). Here, they're sensitive and warmhearted, never push too hard, empathize with the characters, allow Lindsey and Ben to become people we care about. What's going on? first Danny (*Trainspotting*) Boyle makes *Mil-*

lions, and now this. Maybe the Farrellys were helped by the script by Lowell Ganz and Babaloo Mandel, who have nine children between them, and whose writing collaborations include *Parenthood, Forget Paris,* and *A League of Their Own*, which knew a lot about baseball.

What's really touching is the way Lindsey works and works to try to understand Ben. When he tries to tell her why he loves the Red Sox even though they always, always let him down, she says: "You have a lyrical soul. You can live under the best and worst conditions." What she doesn't understand is that the girlfriend of a Red Sox fan must also endure the best and the worst, and have a soul not only lyrical but forgiving. How does it feel when his Sox tickets are *always* more important than *anything* she suggests? "Here's a tip, Ben," she says. "When your girlfriend says let's go to Paris for the weekend—you go."

50 First Dates ★ ★ ★
PG-13, 96 m., 2004

Adam Sandler (Henry Roth), Drew Barrymore (Lucy Whitmore), Rob Schneider (Ula), Lusia Strus (Assistant Alexa), Blake Clark (Marlin Whitmore), Sean Astin (Doug Whitmore), Dan Aykroyd (Dr. Keats). Directed by Peter Segal and produced by Jack Giarraputo, Steve Golin, Nancy Juvonen, Larry Kennar, and Adam Sandler. Screenplay by George Wing.

50 First Dates is a spin on the *Groundhog Day* notion of a day that keeps repeating itself. This time, though, the recycling takes place entirely inside the mind of Lucy Whitmore (Drew Barrymore), who was in an accident that caused short-term memory loss. Every night while she sleeps, the slate of her memory is wiped clean, and when she wakes up in the morning she remembers everything that happened up to the moment of the accident, but nothing that happened afterward.

Is this possible? I'd like to bring in Oliver Sacks for a second opinion. Seems to me that short-term memory loss doesn't work on a daily timetable, but is more like the affliction of Ten-Second Tom, a character in the movie who reboots every ten seconds. Still, this isn't a psychiatric docudrama but a lighthearted romantic comedy, and the premise works to provide

Adam Sandler and Barrymore with a sweet story. They work well together, as they showed in *The Wedding Singer*. They have the same tone of smiling, coy sincerity.

The movie is sort of an experiment for Sandler. He reveals the warm side of his personality, and leaves behind the hostility, anger, and gross-out humor. To be sure, there's projectile vomiting on a vast scale in an opening scene of the movie, but it's performed by a sea lion, not one of the human characters, and the sea lion feels a lot better afterward. This is a kinder and gentler Adam Sandler.

He plays Henry Roth, a marine biologist at a Hawaiian sea world, healing walruses, sea lions, and dolphins, and moonlighting as an expert in one-night stands. He romances babes who are in Hawaii on vacation, and then forgets them when they go home, so imagine his amazement when he meets Lucy and finds that she forgets him every night. Lucy is surrounded by a lot of support (her loving dad and the staff at the local diner), and they're dubious about the motives of this guy who says he's so much in love he's willing to start over with this girl every morning.

You'd think it would be hard to construct an arc for a story that starts fresh every day, but George Wing's screenplay ingeniously uses videotape to solve that problem—so that Lucy gets a briefing every morning on what she has missed, and makes daily notes in a journal about her strange romance with Henry. Eventually this leads her to conclude that it's unfair to Henry to have to endure her daily memory losses, and she says she wants to break up. Of course, the formula requires this, but how the movie solves it is kind of charming.

The movie doesn't have the complexity and depth of *Groundhog Day* (which I recently saw described as "the most spiritual film of our time"), but as entertainment it's ingratiating and lovable. And it suggests that Adam Sandler, whose movies are so often based on hostility, has another speed, another tone, that plays very nicely.

The Final Cut ★ ★ ★
PG-13, 105 m., 2004

Robin Williams (Alan Hackman), Mira Sorvino (Delila), James Caviezel (Fletcher), Thom

Bishops (Hasan), Mimi Kuzyk (Thelma), Stephanie Romanov (Jennifer Bannister). Directed by Omar Naim and produced by Nick Wechsler. Screenplay by Naim.

There is another Robin Williams, a lonely recluse hiding inside the extrovert. Williams is able to channel this furtive, secretive persona for roles that are far removed from Mork, Mrs. Doubtfire, and *Aladdin*'s Genie. As early as *Seize the Day* (1986), a little-seen adaptation of Saul Bellow's novel about a man who loses everything of importance, Williams was accepting roles in which he would be inward, withdrawn, obsessive, peculiar. Consider his work in *The Secret Agent* (1996), as a man who prowls Edwardian London with explosives strapped to his body; *One Hour Photo* (2002), where he plays a loner who lives vicariously through the photographs he develops; and *Insomnia* (2002), where he plays a killer who forgives himself because, well, these things happen.

Williams brings this oddball outsider to a kind of perfection in Omar Naim's *The Final Cut*, a moody science fiction drama. He plays a cutter, a man who edits memories. In an unspecified time that looks like the present, it is possible to acquire "Zoe implants"—chips in the brain that record everything you see, hear, and say. After your death, a cutter can edit highlights of your memories into a two-hour video called a "rememory" for your friends and family to watch.

Of course, a cutter sees *everything*. He knows every secret, witnesses every sin, observes every lie. But a good cutter, like a good mortician, puts the best possible face on things. Alan Hackman, Williams's character, is the best: "The dead mean nothing to me," he says. "I took this job out of respect for the living." A rival cutter puts it more clearly: "If you can't bear to look at it, he will." And another says: "He's first on the list for cutting scumbags and lowlifes." He is, they say behind his back, a sin eater.

He lives alone, spending most of his time in a room with his cutting machines. A woman friend despairs of tearing him away from his work, and says, "You're like a magician—or a priest—or a taxidermist." He is especially like a taxidermist, removing the rotting parts hidden inside his subjects while preserving the external covering in its ideal form. What does he think about the horrors he witnesses, the terrible things he edits from his rememories? We don't know. We don't even know if he enjoys his voyeurism.

He looks sad and weary much of the time, like the angels in *Wings of Desire*, who also see and know all. They pity and envy their humans—pity them for the frailties, and envy them because they live in time, not eternity. It is impossible to say how Alan feels. Certainly he has no life of his own, apart from his job, which consists of rememories of other lives. I was reminded of the documentary *Cinemania*, about five or six people who plan their days in order to spend every waking moment watching a movie. Their entire lives, and Alan's, are vicarious.

There is a thriller plot of sorts, which doesn't add much to the movie, since Alan's peculiar relationship to his job is at the heart of everything. A rich, evil man, probably a child abuser, has died, and his wealthy widow (Stephanie Romanov) hires Hackman to create a rememory of her husband. She knows, or suspects, Zoe may have recorded images of their daughter being molested. She knows Hackman (what a precise name) can be trusted.

Jim Caviezel plays the leader of a group opposed to rememories. Their slogan: "Remember for yourself!" Characters argue against the Zoe implant because of its inhibiting influence on human lives: If you know everything you do is being recorded, or if you suspect you are with a person with a Zoe implant, can you behave naturally? In Catholic school we learned that God was always watching us, but God forgave, and didn't maintain digital files.

The movie is bookended with the story of a childhood tragedy that may have twisted Alan into the cutter he is today. The tragedy is well handled, but its aftermath in his adult life seems unfinished and unsatisfying. Indeed, the movie never really finds its way out of the dilemmas it has created. But Robin Williams stands apart from the problems of *The Final Cut*, just as he stands apart from the other characters. It's been said that inside every comedian is a sad man refusing to weep. Williams has extraordinary success in channeling this other person. How strange that the same actor can play some of the most uninhibited of all characters, and some of the most morose.

Final Destination 3 ★ ★
R, 92 m., 2006

Mary Elizabeth Winstead (Wendy Christensen), Ryan Merriman (Kevin Fischer), Texas Battle (Lewis Romero), Alexz Johnson (Erin), Sam Easton (Frankie), Kris Lemche (Ian McKinley), Gina Holden (Carrie Dreyer). Directed by James Wong and produced by Glen Morgan, Craig Perry, Wong, and Warren Zide. Screenplay by Morgan and Wong.

Final Destination 3 is in the relentless tradition of the original Dead Teenager Movies, which existed to kill all the teenagers in the movie except one, who was left alive to star in the sequel, explaining to fresh victims what happened at Camp Crystal Lake, or how we know what you did last summer. In *FD3*, the kids learn about their possible fates because one of them heard about the *FD1* case on the news. If the movie were self-aware, like the *Scream* pictures, he would have said, "This is just like that movie *Final Destination*."

The *FD1* opening formula is repeated. Some viewers may feel cheated by the It's Only a Dream Scene, but fans of the series will understand as a character has a premonition of disaster and watches in horror as her vision comes true. Wendy (Mary Elizabeth Winstead) is with a group of friends at a carnival and refuses to get on the roller coaster because she's convinced it will crash. It does, with many detailed scenes in which teenagers cling desperately to upside-down coaster cars, are beheaded, etc.

Wendy and her friend Kevin (Ryan Merriman) learn that the kids who didn't get on the doomed airplane in *FD1* died anyway, in the same order they were intended to board the plane. Is the same fate in store for the kids who didn't get on the roller coaster? Wendy, who was taking digital photos at the carnival, loads them into her computer and uses them to figure out what the likely order of victims will be; she and Kevin seem doomed along with the others, which is a reason right there not to spend the $79 to upgrade to iPhoto 6.

Do they all die? The point in these movies is not if they die, but how they die, and Fate must stay up nights devising ingenious executions. There is a crushing experience in the takeout lane at Fatburger, a crispy afternoon

at a tanning salon, a beheading, a gruesome death by nail gun, an unfortunate fireworks accident, and at the end, everyone gets on a train when they should be checking into an emergency room just as a precaution.

Why are teenagers attracted to movies in which teenagers die? Maybe it's related to the basic appeal of all horror films: We sit in the audience and think, there but for the grace of God go we. There is also the reassurance that the movie will not contain a lot of long speeches or deep thought, and there will be few adults in the audience to tell you to get the hell off your cell phone because they paid for their tickets, etc.

There must be dozens of films in this genre. At Sundance 2006 there was at least a positive development in *Wristcutters*, when the characters discover that after you kill yourself, the world is pretty much the same as it was before, except grungy, poverty-stricken, and depressing. In *Wristcutters 2*, they should have a Third World suicide victim who finds the afterlife an improvement and thinks he is in heaven.

The problem with *FD3* is that since it is clear to everyone who must die and in what order, the drama is reduced to a formula in which ominous events accumulate while the teenagers remain oblivious. We see oil dripping, trucks rolling out of control, and hinges working loose, and we realize: The movie is obviously filmed from the POV of Fate itself. We see a nail gun, and we start calculating which character is next to be nailed.

Final Destination 3 is good looking and made with technical skill. The director is James Wong, who made *FD1* and was once a writer on *The X-Files* and *21 Jump Street*. He and the cinematographer, Robert McLachlan, do an especially good job of evoking a creepy sense of menace on a carnival midway. Has there ever been a carnival midway in a movie that *didn't* look like a sadomasochistic nightmare? The rides look fatal, the sideshows look like portals to hell, and you know that game where you slam down a big hammer to make the weight fly up and hit the bell? One kid pounds so hard the weight crashes through the bell and flies off into the air. I expected it to land on somebody's head, or maybe on the roller coaster tracks, and maybe it did and I missed it because there was a lot going on. But as nearly as I can figure, the weight is still up there somewhere.

Note: Ebert's review was cut short when a weight from a carnival game crashed through the window and wiped out his computer. Dann Gire, president of the Chicago Film Critics Association, has sent out warnings to the next six reviewers scheduled to write about the film.

Finding Home ★
PG-13, 124 m., 2005

Lisa Brenner (Amanda), Genevieve Bujold (Katie), Louise Fletcher (Esther), Jeannetta Arnette (Grace), Misha Collins (Dave), Sherri Saum (Candace), Justin Henry (Prescott), Johnny Messner (Nick), Jason Miller (Lester), Andrew Lukich (C.J.). Directed by Lawrence D. Foldes and produced by Victoria Paige Meyerink. Screenplay by Foldes and Grafton S. Harper.

The end credits for *Finding Home* thank no fewer than six experts on false memory. If only they had consulted even one expert on flashbacks involving false memories, or memories of any kind, or flashbacks of any kind. Here is a movie in which the present functions mostly as a launching pad for the past, which is a hotbed of half-remembered out-of-focus screams, knives, secrets, blood, and piano lessons.

As the story opens, Amanda (Lisa Brenner) is planning her first visit to her grandmother, Esther (Louise Fletcher), when she gets a message that Esther has died. Esther's death doesn't deprive Fletcher of screen time, however, since she's present in so many flashbacks that the time line could have just been flipped, with the story taking place in the past with flash-forwards. To be sure, the flashbacks are confused and fragmented, but the present-day scenes don't make any more sense, even though we can see and hear them, which you might think would be an advantage.

Amanda's grandmother owned and operated an inn on a Maine island. The inn is one of those New England clapboard jobs with a dock and cozy public rooms and two or three floors of guest rooms. Hold that thought. We'll need it. Because of whatever happened more than ten years ago, Amanda has been

forbidden to ever mention the grandmother or the inn to her mother, Grace (Jeannetta Arnette). When Amanda is ferried to the island in a boat piloted by Dave (Misha Collins), she focuses on his knife with such intensity we're reminded of the zoom-lens eye belonging to Alastor "Mad-Eye" Moody in the latest Harry Potter picture. Admittedly, a character who toys with a knife all the time in a movie makes you think.

Dave is a nice young man, ostensibly, although he spends an alarming amount of time in his work shed, carving large blocks of wood into measurably smaller ones. "Who is that going to be?" Amanda asks him of one block that already looks so much like Amanda it might as well be wearing a name tag. "I don't know who is inside it yet," he says, a dead giveaway that he has read *The Agony and the Ecstasy* and knows that with Amanda he can safely steal anything Michelangelo ever said.

"You and Dave were inseparable," Amanda is told by Katie (Genevieve Bujold), her grandmother's best friend, who has managed the inn for years. Then what happened to make Amanda fear him so, and dislike him so, and stare so at his knife? I personally think Katie knows the whole story: "Something happened between your mother and grandmother that summer," she also tells Amanda. And, "Can you really believe what she tells you about that summer?"

Before we can answer these questions, Amanda's mother, Grace, herself arrives on the island, along with, let's see, thumbing through my notes here, the family lawyer (Jason Miller); Amanda's boss and boyfriend, Nick (Johnny Messner); Amanda's best friend, Candace (Sherri Saum), and *her* boyfriend, C. J. (Andrew Lukich); and the accountant Prescott (Justin Henry), who after all the trouble that nice Dustin Hoffman went to on his behalf in *Kramer vs. Kramer* has grown up to be a bad accountant. There is room for all these visitors because not a single guest is ever seen at the inn.

But hold on, how do I know Prescott is incompetent? Have you kept the inn fixed in your memory as I requested? The dock, the cozy public rooms, the clapboard siding, several acres of forested grounds? The hardwood floors, the pewter, the quilts, the Arts and Crafts furniture, the canned preserves? The smell of apple pies in the oven? Well, Amanda

229

discovers that she has inherited the inn from her grandmother, who cut off Grace with a lousy brooch. Prescott the accountant then estimates that the inn could sell for, oh, about $400,000. It is unspeakably rude for a movie critic to talk aloud during a screening, but at the screening I attended, someone cried out, "I'll buy it!" Reader, that person was me.

Are Dave and Katie the caretaker depressed that Amanda might sell her grandmother's inn? Not as much as you might think. Does this have anything to do with the flashbacks, the screams, the blood, the knife, and the piano lessons? Not as much as you might think. Did Dave sexually assault Amanda ten years ago? Not as much as you might think. Why does another character choose this moment to announce she is pregnant? Who could the father be? Given the Law of Economy of Characters, it has to be someone on the island. Or maybe it was someone in one of the flashbacks who flash-forwarded in a savage act of phallic time travel and then slunk back to the past, the beast.

The solution to the mysteries, when it comes, is not so much anticlimactic as not climactic at all. I think it is wrong to bring a false memory on board only to discover that it is really false. After what this movie puts us through, the false memory at least should have a real false memory concealed beneath it. What were all those experts for?

Finding Neverland ★ ★ ★ ½
PG, 101 m., 2004

Johnny Depp (J. M. Barrie), Kate Winslet (Sylvia Llewelyn Davies), Julie Christie (Mrs. Emma du Maurier), Dustin Hoffman (Charles Frohman), Radha Mitchell (Mary Ansell Barrie), Freddie Highmore (Peter Llewelyn Davies), Nick Roud (George Llewelyn Davies), Joe Prospero (Jack Llewelyn Davies), Luke Spill (Michael Llewelyn Davies). Directed by Marc Forster and produced by Nellie Bellflower and Richard N. Gladstein. Screenplay by David Magee, based on a play by Allan Knee.

Finding Neverland is the story of a man who doesn't want to grow up, and writes the story of a boy who never does. The boy is Peter Pan, and the man is Sir J. M. Barrie, who wrote his famous play after falling under the spell of a widow and her four young boys. That Barrie was married at the time, that he all but ignored his wife, that he all but moved into the widow's home, that his interest in the boys raised little suspicion, would make this story play very differently today. Johnny Depp's performance makes Barrie not only believable, but acceptable. And he does it without evading the implications of his behavior: The movie doesn't inoculate Barrie as a "family friend," but shows him truly and deeply in love with the widow and her boys, although in an asexual way; we wonder, indeed, if this man has ever had sex, or ever wants to.

The movie opens in 1903 in a London theater where Barrie, a Scottish playwright, has seen his latest play turn into a disaster. He needs something new, and quickly, because his impresario (Dustin Hoffman) has a lease on the house and needs to keep it filled. In Kensington Gardens, Barrie happens upon the Davies family: the mother, Sylvia (Kate Winslet), and her boys Peter, George, Jack, and Michael. As he watches them at play, a kind of spiritual hunger begins to glow in his eyes. They represent an innocence and purity that strikes him so powerfully he's unable to think of anything else.

He becomes friendly with the family. Sylvia has recently become widowed and is not interested in a new romance, but then, curiously, nothing about Barrie's behavior suggests he's attracted to her in that way. He idealizes her, he obsesses about her boys, and when he talks about his own unhappy childhood we get a glimpse of his motivation; when his older brother died, his parents started calling him by the brother's name, and perhaps he felt he lived his brother's childhood and never had his own.

He plays games with the boys. He wrestles with a big stuffed bear. He leads them in games involving pirates and cowboys and Indians. He dresses in funny costumes. The children like him, and Sylvia is grateful for his attention, especially since she has developed an alarming cough and he helps take care of the boys. The only holdout is Peter, the oldest, played by Freddie Highmore in a remarkable performance; if Barrie never grew up, Peter was perhaps never a child. He is wise and solemn, feels the loss of his father more sharply than his younger brothers, and boldly tells Barrie: "You're not my father." Nor does Barrie want to be; he wants to be his brother. Sylvia's condition worsens, and when Barrie stages a play in the family garden, it's cut short by her coughing. The boys are reassured that nothing serious is wrong, but Peter is sure they're lying to him about her illness: "I won't be made a fool!"

Two other women regard this situation with alarm. Barrie's wife, Mary (Radha Mitchell), rarely sees him at home and is understandably disturbed about his relationship with the Davies family, although she is not as angry as she might be; there is the implication that she has long since given up on expecting rational behavior from her husband. He lives in a dream world, and to some degree she understands that. Not as sympathetic is Emma du Maurier (Julie Christie), Sylvia's mother, who as the widow of the famous George du Maurier moved in sophisticated circles and is not amused by a forty-three-year-old man who wants to become the best playmate of her grandchildren.

It is Barrie's innocence, or naïveté, or perhaps even a kind of rapture, impervious to common sense, that steers him past all obstacles as he begins to form the idea of Peter Pan in his mind. The boys are his muses. He tries to explain his new play to his impresario, who has just closed one flop, doesn't want to open another, and is less than thrilled about a play involving fairies, pirates, and children who can fly. Depp in his scenes shows Barrie in the grip of a holy zeal, his mind operating on a private, almost trancelike level, as the play comes into focus for him. He knows, if nobody else does, that he is creating a myth that will powerfully involve children. His masterstroke is to invite twenty-five orphans to the play's opening night and scatter them through the audience, where their laugher and delight stirs the adults to see the magic in the play.

For Johnny Depp, Finding Neverland is the latest in an extraordinary series of performances. After his Oscar nomination for Pirates of the Caribbean (2003), here is another role that seems destined for nomination. And then think of his work in Secret Window (2004), the Stephen King story about the author caught in a nightmare, and his demented

CIA agent in Once Upon a Time in Mexico (2003), and The Libertine, as the depraved and shameless Earl of Rochester. That the flamboyance of his pirate and the debauchery of the earl could exist in the same actor as the soft-spoken, gentle, inward J. M. Barrie is remarkable. It is commonplace for actors to play widely differing roles, but Depp never makes it feel like a reach; all of these notes seem well within his range.

Finding Neverland is, finally, surprisingly moving. The screenplay by David Magee and the direction of Marc Forster (Monster's Ball) manipulate the facts to get their effect; Sylvia's husband was still alive in the original story, for example, and her illness had not taken hold. But by compressing events, the movie creates for the Barrie character an opportunity for unconditional love. What he feels for the Davies family is disinterested and pure, despite all the appearances. What he feels for his wife remains a mystery, not least to her.

Find Me Guilty ★ ★ ★
R, 125 m., 2006

Vin Diesel (Jackie DiNorscio), Peter Dinklage (Ben Klandis), Ron Silver (Judge Finestein), Linus Roache (Sean Kierney), Annabella Sciorra (Bella DiNorscio), Alex Rocco (Nick Calabrese). Directed by Sidney Lumet and produced by Bob Yari, Robert Greenhut, Bob DeBrino, T. J. Mancini, and George Vitetzakis. Screenplay by Mancini and Robert McCrea.

"When they f— with me," Jackie DiNorscio says, "they wake a sleeping giant." Actually, it's more like they bring his inner stand-up comedian to his feet. DiNorscio is the wild card in the longest trial in American history, a twenty-one-month extravaganza aimed at the Lucchese crime family of New Jersey. There are twenty defendants, and they all have defense attorneys except Jackie, who represents himself. His participation makes the trial curiously similar to Mystery Science Theater 3000, with dopey characters marching through with profundities while Jackie cracks jokes.

Jackie is played by Vin Diesel, something I didn't know going in. It took awhile to see through the makeup to Diesel, playing a paunchy goombah who is already serving a thirty-year sentence when the trial begins. He's offered a deal: testify against his fellow villains, and get a reduction in his sentence. "I don't rat on my friends," he says. That's for sure. He even forgives a cousin who pumps four bullets into him. "I love him," he says. "Live and let live." When the cops ask him to name the shooter, he intones, "My eyes were shut the whole time." Diesel is a good choice for this role, bringing it sincerity without nobility.

The movie was directed by a man who knows all about courtroom drama. Sidney Lumet directed 12 Angry Men, which takes place almost entirely within a jury room, and there are vivid scenes of testimony in his Serpico and The Verdict. What's different this time is that the battle between good and evil is murky. Yes, the defendants are killers, thieves, extortionists, drug dealers, pimps, and otherwise ill-behaved. No one doubts they are guilty. But against their predations the movie sets Jackie DiNorscio, who says he is "not a gangster but a gagster," and pisses off the prosecution, the defense, the judge, and his fellow defendants. Only the jury likes him. "They say a laughing jury is not a hanging jury," says Ben Klandis (Peter Dinklage), the brains of the defense team. He sits next to Jackie in court and occasionally whispers advice.

Jackie didn't graduate grade school. He is loyal to mobsters who ordered him to be whacked. He spends less time defending himself than offering a running commentary on the judicial system. He cuts through the fog of testimony. "How did you *know* they were Italians?" he asks an FBI witness, who says he saw defendants paying homage to crime boss Nick Calabrese (Alex Rocco). The witness babbles about how they waved their hands and had black hair and sounded like they were talking Italian. Jackie cuts him to shreds, exposing at the same time the tendency of lawmen to describe what they saw as if they were objective observers without preconceptions. The FBI agent should have replied: "I knew they were Italians because I've been on this case for years and I knew every one of them by name."

Jackie's moral position is hard to define. He seems to value friendship and loyalty above all, and to disregard imperfections such as murder. He is loyal to Calabrese even after the mobster tells him, "If you mention my name

in this courtroom one more time, I will cut your heart out." He loves the guy. Live and let live. The movie's title comes from his closing statement, in which he tells the jury he's already serving thirty years and has nothing to lose: "Find me guilty," he says, but let off his friends.

Are we cheering for him? Not precisely. But he is the underdog in a system that offends common sense with its ponderous slog through legal quicksand. A defense attorney who needs five days to summarize his argument doesn't have one. Subtitles remind us how many days the trial has lasted; they climb above five-hundred. A defendant has a heart attack, is brought into court on a bed, falls out of the bed. A mother dies. The chief prosecutor, Sean Kierney (Linus Roache), doesn't like to be laughed at and retaliates by taking away the prized Barcalounger in Jackie's jail cell. The judge (Ron Silver) would cut Jackie loose from the case, except that might lead to a mistrial.

If the movie lacks a battle between good and evil, it also lacks drama. The outcome of the trial seems to be a foregone conclusion. *Find Me Guilty* exists in its moments. There is an electric conversation between Jackie and his former wife, Bella (Annabella Sciorra), that makes it perfectly clear why they drove each other crazy, and why they got married in the first place. The defense attorneys are presented in montages of gaseous idiocies, except for Klandis, the Dinklage character, who stands apart as a man concise, articulate, and professional. He is a dwarf. A court officer wheels forward a podium on a staircase, which he climbs to face the jury. Without one word being spoken, Klandis transforms this podium from a compensation for his height into an acknowledgment of his stature. He stands above the others with or without the stairs.

This movie by its nature is not thrilling, but it is genuinely interesting, and that is rare. It's not even really about a particular trial, but about a Kafkaesque system that can only work if there are no Jackies to point out its absurdities. We in the audience are left without cheering rights. Since the defendants (except for the cousin) are not actually seen doing anything evil, we don't yearn for their conviction. But surely they cannot be found innocent. The trial comes down to: Can Jackie get away with his act? And if he does, so what? He's still facing thirty years. Good and evil seem stuck on the same treadmill, and we are invited to focus on a contest between drones and a wise guy. You'd be surprised how entertaining that can be.

Firecracker ★ ★ ★ ½
NO MPAA RATING, 112 m., 2005

Karen Black (Eleanor/Sandra), Mike Patton (David/Frank), Susan Traylor (Ed), Kathleen Wilhoite (Jessica), Jak Kendall (Jimmy), Brooke Balderson (Pearl), Paul Sizemore (Officer Harry). Directed by Steve Balderson and produced by Clark Balderson. Screenplay by Steve Balderson.

Firecracker is a movie that was made outside the factory, beyond the rules, in a far place named Wamego, Kansas. We accustom ourselves to the weekly multiplex extrusions, and then something like this slips in, fresh from the wild. It's a black-and-white crime drama and a lurid color fantasy, a slice of life crossed with grotesque sideshow performers; it contains cruel family secrets, deadpan humor, horrifying mutilations, and possibly a visit from the Virgin Mary.

The movie is profoundly odd, which qualified it to open the Chicago Underground Film Festival. Imagine *In Cold Blood* crossed with *Freaks*, with the look of Alejandro Jodorowsky's *Santa Sangre*. It was written, directed, and filmed by Steve Balderson in his hometown of Wamego, inspired by a murder that happened there fifty years ago. The movie is so rooted in this small town that one of the locations is the house where the murder took place. So rooted that Balderson got permission to shoot in the house because his father's plumber lives there now.

The movie has one of the most immediately gripping opening scenes I can remember. In everyday black-and-white, the sleepy town is alarmed as two people, and then more, desperately run across lawns and down alleys. Mothers snatch their children out of the way. The runners converge on a backyard where digging is going on inside a tool shed. A female sheriff looks on. Another woman glances inside the shed and retches.

The rest of the movie is prelude. We meet a sad, wounded family: The mother, Eleanor (Karen Black), prays the rosary and tries to keep peace between her brutal older son, David (Mike Patton), and her sensitive younger son, Jimmy (Jak Kendall). There is a father, so withdrawn he is hardly visible. David calls the shots, struts like a torturer, torments Jimmy for playing the piano: "Learn how to make a living, not sissy-boy piano recitals!"

It is the Fourth of July and the carnival is in town. Traveling carnivals often serve in horror movies as repositories of the bizarre in the wilderness of small-town boredom. Jimmy wants to go. David taunts him: "You want to see the girly show." Well, of course he does. In the world before *Playboy*, the carnival girly show was an erotic magnet; furtive men eyed the parade of strippers and followed them into the tent's smutty embrace. There was the same rumor every summer: "After the show, they do it with guys in the field behind the tent." Maybe it was true. Nobody I knew ever had the nerve to see.

The town is mostly in black and white, and the carnival is in saturated color: bold, dripping reds and yellows and dark brown shadows. The focus of attention is the "French singer" Sandra (also played by Karen Black). She is the captive, perhaps the slave, of the carnival owner, Frank (also played by Mike Patton, the rock singer). She hides herself in furs, feathers, hoods, scarves, and dresses that look shabby not because they have been worn so much but because they have been removed so often.

Jimmy wants to play for her. Maybe join the carnival and tour as her pianist. She remembers him from other summers, looking hungrily from the audience. She also remembers his brother, David, who got her pregnant last summer. The cruel Frank ended her pregnancy, but it is David she tells, "I'm not gonna let you hurt me again."

These characters and their sexual needs and fears are seen against an ominous background of sideshow people, played (as in *Freaks*) by themselves. The most striking is the Enigma, his skin entirely covered by an intricate jigsaw of blue tattoos that is beautiful or ugly, erotic or not, depending on your taste. There is also a giant, a lobster girl, and so on.

What happens between these people, I will

leave for you to discover. The plot burrows more deeply, until the line between the black-and-white town and the color carnival seems to blur, and everything seems caught up in the same nightmare. The idea of having Karen Black and Mike Patton play dual roles is not a stunt but part of the strategy; no, the mother and the whore, the brother and the owner are not "the same person" but are connected at a deeper level, perhaps in Jimmy's mind, where they perform similar functions in opposite worlds. Black is uncanny in the way she creates two characters who are so opposite and convincing.

The film is visually jarring. Some shots by cinematographer Jonah Torreano look like lab experiments with the psychology of color. A shot, for example, of a woman in a red cape fleeing across a green field, the red so red, the green so green, that the impact is aggressive. There are inexplicable images, like bright blue bottles hanging from the stark branches of a tree next to a woman gowned in white, that work because they shift the whole movie away from reality into hallucination.

Then there are strange everyday details. There's a little girl put on a leash in the back yard by her mother. She sets off firecrackers. There is a sequence where a body is carried from a house to a shed while being concealed behind a big white sheet on a clothes line; the line is on rollers, so the sheet can be pulled along as a moving screen. There is the Hitchcockian scene where the mother asks at the cleaners for an "astringent" to remove the "shoe polish" on her carpet. A good enough story, but she has foolishly ripped up some of the carpet and brought it along, and anyone can see it's soaked with blood. And a scene where the color fades from the frame as life fades from a body.

Movie critics are criticized for preferring novelty because we are jaded by the ordinary. If only that were true of everybody; how much wasted time we could recapture. I praise *Firecracker* because it is original and peculiar, but also because it is haunted; there is an uneasy spirit living within this film that stirs uneasily and regards us with cold, unblinking eyes. The calm of small-town Kansas inspires the yearnings in those who do not fit there, who are drawn to the carnival, which doesn't fit anywhere.

First Daughter ★ ★
PG, 104 m., 2004

Katie Holmes (Samantha Mackenzie), Marc Blucas (James Lansome), Amerie Rogers (Mia Thompson), Michael Keaton (President Mackenzie), Margaret Colin (Melanie Mackenzie), Lela Rochon (Liz Pappas). Directed by Forest Whitaker and produced by John Davis, Wyck Godfrey, Mike Karz, and Arnon Milcan. Screenplay by Jessica Bendinger and Kate Kondell.

First Daughter is all heart and has the best intentions in the world, but what a bore. It's a beat slower than it should be, it makes its points laboriously, and the plot surprise would be obvious even if I hadn't seen the same device used in exactly the same way in *Chasing Liberty*. Even the ending isn't as happy as it thinks it is.

Katie Holmes, so fetching in *Wonder Boys* and *Pieces of April*, stars as Samantha Mackenzie, daughter of a U.S. president whose party is carefully not mentioned even though when we learn the United Auto Workers support him, the secret is out. She has spent her entire life as a good, sweet, dutiful daughter, smiling loyally at the side of her parents (Michael Keaton and Margaret Colin) as they campaign for office. Now it is time for her to go to college, and she yearns to be treated as a normal kid. Her definition of this is that she would get to drive herself there in her little Volkswagen, with a cooler in the front seat that has a can of beer hidden under the bologna sandwiches. What is wrong with this picture? (1) As we find out at the end of the movie, it's a classic VW bug, not one of the new models, and the kids who dreamed of driving off to college in one of those are now closer in age to, oh, say, the filmmakers. (2) Today's progressive modern parents, spotting the beer and the bologna, would gasp in horror, "Bologna?" Samantha enrolls at the University of Redmond, where to her horror the school band plays "Hail to the Chief" while she walks into her dorm with the chief and first lady. Her new roomie Mia (Amerie Rogers) is a cutey-pie who's used to getting all the attention herself, and doesn't want to play second banana to the F.D. Samantha wears clothes that inspire Joan Rivers monologues on TV, she sits in a roped-off section of lecture classes, flanked by Secret Service agents, and she is thoroughly miserable.

So she stages a revolt that is painfully awkward in its conception and execution, pretending to be a bad girl, so the president will hear her cry for help. Her first transgression is to slide down a hill on a wet tarp at a frat party, which gets her on the front page of the *New York Post*, a paper more easily shocked in this movie than in life. Her slide seems to me like a plus (first daughter is real kid, has harmless fun), but no: She gets a scolding, and then she gets a *severe* scolding when Mia talks her into attending another party dressed, so help me, like a go-go dancer in the days when the words "go-go" were being used (high white lace-up boots, denim miniskirt, pink fur pimp hat, the works). Realizing Samantha is serious about wanting more privacy, or maybe fearing that she will in desperation pose for *Playboy* if he doesn't relent, the president agrees to pull back her Secret Service detail. Half of her agents disappear. Joyous with her new freedom, she has a Meet Cute with James Lansome (Marc Blucas), the handsome resident adviser who just happens to be the resident on her floor of the dorm. Soon true love blooms between them. No, really.

The stages by which the movie arrives at this point and travels onward are so deliberate the movie seems reluctant to proceed. It keeps pausing and looking back to make sure we're keeping up. Katie Holmes plays Samantha with wide-eyed wonder, underlining every point. Her normal kid is a strange anachronism, like the 1940s music that plays at all of the dances; she'd be right at home as a freshman in, say, *The Glenn Miller Story*. No first daughter in recent memory has been this square. She doesn't even seem to have met Paris and Nicky Hilton.

The surprise, when it comes, is sadly unsurprising. It leads to a formula in which Samantha must first be depressed, then be resolute, then be joyous again. All fine, except that the movie makes her be depressed again and resolute again, and ends with muted joy, and then with more resolution. Girls have renounced thrones and entered convents with less trouble. Even worse, everyone in the movie, but surely no one in the audience, believes it arrives at the correct ending. Having tortured us

with clichés for more than 100 minutes, the movie denies us the final upbeat cliché that we have paid our dues for. Who wants a movie about a first daughter who finds, loses, refinds, reloses, sort of refinds, and probably loses perfect love, only to end up alone and responsible?

First Descent ★ ½
PG-13, 110 m., 2005

Shawn Farmer (Himself), Terje Haakonsen (Himself), Nick Perata (Himself), Hannah Teter (Herself), Shaun White (Himself). Directed by Kemp Curly and Kevin Harrison, and produced by Curly and Harrison. Screenplay by Harrison.

First Descent is boring, repetitive, and maddening about a subject you'd think would be fairly interesting: snowboarding down a mountain. And not just any mountain. This isn't about snowboarders at Aspen or Park City. It's about experts who are helicoptered to the tops of virgin peaks in Alaska, and snowboard down what look like almost vertical slopes.

I know nothing about snowboarding. A question occurs to me. If it occurs to me, it will occur to other viewers. The question is this: How do the snowboarders know where they are going? In shot after shot, they hurtle off snow ledges into thin air and then land dozens or hundreds of feet lower on another slope. Here's my question: As they approach the edge of the ledge, how can they know for sure what awaits them over the edge? Wouldn't they eventually be surprised, not to say dismayed, to learn that they were about to drop half a mile? Or land on rocks? Or fall into a chasm? Shouldn't the mountains of Alaska be littered with the broken bodies of extreme snowboarders?

I search the Internet and find that indeed snowboarders die not infrequently. "All I heard was Gore-Tex on ice," one survivor recalls after two of his companions disappeared. The movie vaguely talks about scouting a mountain from the air and picking out likely descent paths, but does the mountain look the same when you're descending it at 45 degrees and high speed? Can rocks be hidden just beneath the surface? Can crevasses be hidden from the eye?

The film features five famous names in the sport: veterans Shawn Farmer, Terje Haakonsen, and Nick Perata, and teenage superstars

Hannah Teter and Shaun White. For at least twenty minutes at the top of the movie, they talk and talk about the "old days," the "new techniques," the "gradual acceptance" of snowboarding, the way ski resorts first banned snowboarders but now welcome them. "As the decade progressed, so did snowboarding," we learn at one point, leading me to reflect that as the decade progressed, so did time itself.

There are a lot of shots of snowboarders in the movie, mostly doing the same things again and again, often with the camera at such an angle that we cannot get a clear idea of the relationship between where they start and where they land. To be sure, if it's hard to ski down a virgin mountainside, it must be even harder to film someone doing it. (When I saw the IMAX documentary about climbing Everest, it occurred to me that a more interesting doc would have been about the people who carried the camera.) In this case, the action footage is repetitive and underwhelming, no match for the best docs about surfing, for example. The powerful surfing film *Riding Giants* (2004), directed by Stacy Perata, does everything right that *First Descent* does wrong.

The movie's fundamental problem, I think, is journalistic. It doesn't cover its real subject. The movie endlessly repeats how exciting, or thrilling, or awesome it is to snowboard down a mountain. I would have preferred more detail about how dangerous it is, and how one prepares to do it, and what precautions are taken, and how you can anticipate avalanches on virgin snow above where anybody has ever snowboarded before.

The kicker on the trailer says: "Unless you're fully prepared to be in a situation of life and death, you shouldn't be up here." So, okay, how can you possibly be fully prepared in a situation no one has been in before and that by definition can contain fatal surprises? Since the five stars of the movie are all still alive as I write this review, they must have answers for those questions. Maybe interesting ones. Maybe more interesting than what a thrill it is. ☞

The Five Obstructions ★ ★ ★
NO MPAA RATING, 90 m., 2004

As themselves: Jorgen Leth, Lars von Trier, Daniel Hernandez Rodriguez, Patrick Bauchau, Jacqueline Arenal, and Bob Sabiston. A documentary directed by Jorgen Leth and Lars von Trier and produced by Carsten Holst. Screenplay by Sophie Destin, Asger Leth, Leth, and von Trier, inspired by *The Perfect Human* by Leth.

The Five Obstructions is a perverse game of one-upmanship between the Danish director Lars von Trier and his mentor, Jorgen Leth. In 1967, we learn, Leth made a twelve-minute film named *The Perfect Human*. Von Trier admired it so much he saw it twenty times in a single year. Now he summons the sixty-seven-year-old Leth from retirement in Haiti and commands him to remake the film in five different ways, despite obstructions that von Trier will supply.

The first obstruction seems almost insurmountable: Von Trier commands Leth to go to Cuba (and bring back some cigars while he's at it) and remake the film in shots no more than twelve frames, or half a second, in length. "That will be totally destructive!" Leth complains. "It will be a spastic film." But when he returns after facing the first obstruction, he is all smiles, and tells von Trier: "The twelve frames were like a gift."

Von Trier accepts this news while lounging behind his desk like a headmaster. The joke seems to be that Leth, nineteen years his senior and once von Trier's teacher, is to be ordered around like an unruly schoolboy. There is an additional element in play: Leth's style is clean, spare, and classical, while von Trier is the architect of the Dogma movement, which is essentially a series of obstructions (use natural light and sound, no music except that found at the source, etc.). "I want to banalize you," von Trier cheerfully informs him.

Von Trier sends Leth out again, this time to "the most miserable place on Earth." They settle on the Falkland Road red-light district in Mumbai. Leth journeys there and films himself eating an elegant meal. "This is not the film I asked for!" growls von Trier, and offers him a choice: (1) go back to India and do it again, or (2) make a completely freestyle film, which would be against all of Leth's stylistic instincts.

Leth, who in his cool and amused way seems impervious to von Trier's challenges, emerges intact from this third obstruction with a film shot in his native Brussels. For obstruction No. 4, von Trier has a real zinger in mind. "I hate animation," he observes. "So do I," says Leth. "Make an animated film," von Trier says. Leth protests: "I can't be bothered to invent the technology, or to learn it. No stupid drawing board!" His solution is as brilliant as it is elegant. I will not reveal it, except to say the result will speak loudly to anyone who has seen Richard Linklater's *Waking Life.*

At this point Leth seems ahead 4-0, but von Trier has one more twist up his sleeve. See for yourself. A film like this has a limited audience, I suppose, but for that audience it offers a rare fascination. Von Trier has deliberately set up a contest between two generations and styles of filmmaking, and in the pose of honoring *The Perfect Human* he tries to force Leth to demolish and reinvent it. Leth is more than his equal, and the entire enterprise is infected with a spirit of mischievous play. *The Five Obstructions* clearly calls for a sequel, in which Leth requires von Trier to remake *Dogville* despite Obstructions Six through Ten.

Flight of the Phoenix ★ ★
PG-13, 112 m., 2004

Dennis Quaid (Frank Towns), Giovanni Ribisi (Elliott), Tyrese Gibson (A.J.), Mirando Otto (Kelly), Hugh Laurie (Ian). Directed by John Moore and produced by William Aldrich, Alex Blum, John Davis, and Wyck Godfrey. Screenplay by Scott Frank and Edward Burns, based on the screenplay by Lukas Heller.

Flight of the Phoenix is a fairly faithful remake of the 1965 adventure classic, with no big surprises. But it uses special effects to create scenes unavailable to the earlier film, including sensational sandstorms, a detailed crash sequence, and a convincing takeoff. If effects had been available in 1965, a life would have been saved; the older movie used a real plane, flown by legendary stunt pilot Paul Mantz, who crashed and was killed. The knowledge of that real event shadowed the 1965 film, giving it an eerie reality.

The remake follows the same story pattern: An oil company crew in the middle of a desert is picked up by a hotshot pilot. The return

flight runs into a violent sandstorm and crashes. The survivors are without a radio, and grimly add up their water and food supplies while a last-minute passenger stands aside, thinking deep thoughts to himself. He eventually announces that a new plane can be made from the wreckage of the old, and they can fly themselves to safety.

The pilot this time is Dennis Quaid, who shares with the 1965 pilot, James Stewart, the ability to be abrupt at the beginning and mellow toward the end. A woman is added to the cast: Kelly, an oil engineer played by Miranda Otto. The key role of the would-be aircraft designer is taken by Giovanni Ribisi, who has a fierce but defensive pride that is explained when more details emerge about his background.

My memory of the 1965 film, somewhat obscured by the sands of time, is that there was less sand. Yes, they crashed in the desert, but the 2004 version can whip up unlimited sandstorms on a moment's notice, and more than once the plane is completely buried except for part of its tail. This leads to a moment when the characters determine to dig it out one last time, and then a shot of the plane ready to take off, without so much as a single shot of a shovel or a bucket. Why bother to bury it if you're not going to show it being dug out? So Quaid can give his inspirational speech, I think.

When it comes to movies about people trying to return alive after catastrophic accidents, nothing else for a long time is going to be more riveting than *Touching the Void,* the film about a man climbing down from a mountain with a shattered leg. *Flight of the Phoenix* is more in the old-fashioned mold of heroes who fight among themselves but eventually decide to cooperate, depending on pluck and luck. There is also a half-realized subplot about local "nomads" or "bandits"—nobody seems quite sure—who seem to survive quite comfortably in large numbers in the desert, and whose comings and goings bear an uncanny relationship to exactly when they are required by the plot.

Because I had, in a sense, already seen this movie, it didn't have surprises or suspense for me, and the actors on their own aren't enough to save it. I'm not recommending it for those who know the original, but it might work nicely enough for those who have not.

Flightplan ★ ★ ★ ½
PG-13, 97 m., 2005

Jodie Foster (Kyle Pratt), Peter Sarsgaard (Gene Carson), Sean Bean (Captain Rich), Erika Christensen (Fiona), Kate Beahan (Stephanie), Marlene Lawston (Julia Pratt). Directed by Robert Schwentke and produced by Brian Grazer. Screenplay by Peter A. Dowling and Billy Ray.

How can a little girl simply disappear from an airplane at 37,000 feet? By asking this question and not cheating on the answer, *Flightplan* delivers a frightening thriller with an airtight plot. It's like a classic Locked Room Murder, in which the killer could not possibly enter or leave, but the victim nevertheless is dead. Such mysteries always have solutions, and so does *Flightplan,* but not one you will easily anticipate. After the movie is over and you are on your way home, some questions may occur to you, but the film proceeds with implacable logic after establishing that the little girl does not seem to be on board.

The movie stars Jodie Foster in a story that bears similarities to her *Panic Room* (2002). In both films, a woman uses courage and intelligence to defend her child against enemies who hold all the cards. The problem she faces in *Flightplan* is more baffling: Who are her enemies? Why would they kidnap her daughter? How is it possible on an airplane?

For that matter, has it really happened? Foster plays Kyle Pratt, a jet propulsion engineer who has been employed in Germany on the design of the very airplane she is now using to cross the Atlantic. She is on a sad mission. Her husband, David, has died after falling—she insists he fell and did not jump—from a rooftop. The coffin is in the hold, and she is traveling with Julia (Marlene Lawston). She falls asleep, she wakes up, and Julia is gone.

Kyle methodically looks around the airplane, calm at first, then on the edge of panic. She tries to seem more rational than she feels so the crew won't dismiss her as a madwoman. Certainly they're tempted, because the passenger list lacks Julia's name, the departure gate at Munich says she did not get on the plane, and her boarding pass and backpack are nowhere to be found. The captain is Sean

Bean, very effective as a man who knows what his job is and how to do it. Peter Sarsgaard plays the in-flight air marshal, under the captain's orders. They receive a message from Munich informing them that Julia was killed along with her father. Obviously, the traumatized mother is fantasizing.

And that's all you'll find out from me. There is no one else I want to mention, no other developments I want to discuss, no other questions I want to raise. If someone tries to tell you anything else about *Flightplan,* walk away.

The movie's excellence comes from Foster's performance as a resourceful and brave woman; from Bean, Sarsgaard, and the members of the cabin crew, all with varying degrees of doubt; from the screenplay by Peter A. Dowling and Billy Ray; and from the direction by Robert Schwentke, a German whose first two films were not much seen in North America. This one will be.

I want to get back to the notion of the airtight plot. Often in thrillers we think of obvious questions that the characters should ask, but do not, because then the problems would be solved and the movie would be over. In *Flightplan,* Jodie Foster's character asks all the right questions and plays the situation subtly and with cunning: She knows that once she crosses a line, she will no longer be able to help her daughter. There are times when she's ahead of the audience in her thinking, anticipating the next development, factoring it in.

As the situation develops, her response is flexible. Her tactics are improvised moment by moment, not out of some kind of frantic acting-out. Because she does what we would do, because she makes no obvious mistakes, because of the logic of everything the crew knows, she seems trapped. A passenger cannot disappear from an airplane, and Julia has disappeared, so either her mother is hallucinating, or something has happened that is apparently impossible.

Schwentke is limited, but not constrained, by the fact that most of his movie takes place on an airplane in midair. He uses every inch of the aircraft, and the plot depends on the mother's knowledge of its operation and construction. If she didn't know the plane better, really, than its pilots, her case would be hopeless. Even with her knowledge, she comes up against one bafflement after another. Should she doubt her sanity? Should we? We have, after all, seen Julia on the airplane. But for that matter, in two early scenes, we saw, and she saw, her husband, David, after he was dead. They spoke to each other. Didn't they? ☞

The Fog of War ★ ★ ★ ★
PG-13, 106 m., 2004

A documentary directed by Errol Morris and produced by Morris, Michael Williams, and Julie Ahlberg. Screenplay by Morris.

How strange the fate that brought together Robert McNamara and Errol Morris to make *The Fog of War*. McNamara, considered the architect of the Vietnam War, an Establishment figure who came to Washington after heading the Ford Motor Company and left to become the president of the World Bank. And Morris, the brilliant and eccentric documentarian who has chronicled pet cemeteries, Death Row, lion tamers, robots, naked mole rats, a designer of electric chairs, people who cut off their legs for the insurance money, and Stephen Hawking's *A Brief History of Time*.

McNamara agreed to talk with Morris for an hour or so, supposedly for a TV special. He eventually spent twenty hours peering into Morris's "Interrotron," a video device that allows Morris and his subjects to look into each other's eyes while also looking directly into the camera lens. Whether this invention results in better interviews is impossible to say, but it does have the uncanny result that the person on the screen never breaks eye contact with the audience.

McNamara was eighty-five when the interviews were conducted—a fit and alert eighty-five, still skiing the slopes at Aspen. Guided sometimes by Morris, sometimes taking the lead, he talks introspectively about his life, his thoughts about Vietnam, and, taking Morris where he would never have thought to go, his role in planning the firebombing of Japan, including a raid on Tokyo that claimed 100,000 lives. He speaks concisely and forcibly, rarely searching for a word, and he is not reciting boilerplate and old sound bites; there is the uncanny sensation that he is thinking as he speaks.

His thoughts are organized as *Eleven Lessons from the Life of Robert S. McNamara*, as extrap-olated by Morris, and one wonders how the planners of the war in Iraq would respond to lesson Nos. 1 and 2 ("Empathize with your enemy" and "Rationality will not save us"), or for that matter, No. 6 ("Get the data"), No. 7 ("Belief and seeing are both often wrong"), and No. 8 ("Be prepared to reexamine your reasoning"). I cannot imagine the circumstances under which Donald Rumsfeld, the current secretary of defense, would not want to see this film about his predecessor, having recycled and even improved upon McNamara's mistakes.

McNamara recalls the days of the Cuban missile crisis, when the world came to the brink of nuclear war (he holds up two fingers, almost touching, to show how close—"this close"). He recalls a meeting, years later, with Fidel Castro, who told him he was prepared to accept the destruction of Cuba if that's what the war would mean. He recalls two telegrams to Kennedy from Khrushchev, one more conciliatory, one perhaps dictated by Kremlin hard-liners, and says that JFK decided to answer the first and ignore the second. (Not quite true, as Fred Kaplan documents in an article at Slate.com.) The movie makes it clear that no one was thinking very clearly, and that the world avoided war as much by luck as by wisdom.

And then he remembers the years of the Vietnam War, inherited from JFK and greatly expanded by Lyndon Johnson. He began to realize the war could never be won, he says, and wrote a memo to the president to that effect. The result was that he resigned as secretary. (He had dinner with Kay Graham, publisher of the *Washington Post*, and told her, "Kay, I don't know if I resigned or was fired." "Oh, Bob," she told him, "of course you were fired.") He didn't resign as a matter of principle, as a British cabinet minister might; it is worth remembering that a few months later Johnson, saying he would not stand for reelection, did effectively resign.

McNamara begins by remembering how, at the age of two, he witnessed a victory parade after World War I, and engages in painful soul-searching about his role in World War II. He was a key aide to General Curtis LeMay, the hard-nosed warrior whose strategy for war was simplicity itself: kill them until they give up. Together, they planned the bombing raids before the atomic bomb ended the war, and Morris supplies a chart showing the American cities

239

equivalent in size to the ones they targeted. After the war, McNamara says, in one of the film's most astonishing moments, LeMay observed to him that if America had lost, they would have been tried as war criminals. Thinking of the 100,000 burned alive in Tokyo, McNamara finds lesson No. 5: "Proportionality should be a guideline in war." In other words, I suppose, kill enough of the enemy but don't go overboard. Lesson No. 9: "In order to do good, you may have to engage in evil."

McNamara is both forthright and elusive. He talks about a Quaker who burned himself to death below the windows of his office in the Pentagon, and finds his sacrifice somehow in the same spirit as his own thinking—but it is true he could have done more to try to end the war and did not, and will not say why he did not, although now he clearly wishes he had. He will also not say he is sorry, even though Morris prompts him; maybe he's too proud, but I get the feeling it's more a case of not wanting to make a useless gesture that could seem hypocritical. His final words in the film make it clear there are some places he is simply not prepared to go.

Although McNamara is photographed through the Interrotron, the movie is far from offering only a talking head. Morris is uncanny in his ability to bring life to the abstract, and here he uses graphics, charts, moving titles, and visual effects in counterpoint to what McNamara is saying. There's also a lot of historical footage, including some shots of Curtis LeMay with his cigar clenched between his teeth—images that describe whatever McNamara neglected to say about him. There are tape recordings of Oval Office discussions involving McNamara, Kennedy, and Johnson. And archival footage of McNamara's years at Ford (he is proud of introducing seat belts). Underneath all of them, uneasily urging the movie along, is the Philip Glass score, which sounds—what? Mournful, urgent, melancholy, driven?

The effect of *The Fog of War* is to impress upon us the frailty and uncertainty of our leaders. They are sometimes so certain of actions that do not deserve such certitude. The farce of the missing weapons of mass destruction is no less complete than the confusion in the Kennedy White House over whether there were really nuclear warheads in Cuba. Some commentators on the film, notably Kaplan in his in-

formative Slate essay, question McNamara's facts. What cannot be questioned is his ability to question them himself. At eighty-five, he knows what he knows, and what he does not know, and what cannot be known. Lesson No. 11: "You can't change human nature."

A Foreign Affair ★ ★ ★
PG-13, 94 m., 2004

David Arquette (Josh), Tim Blake Nelson (Jake), Emily Mortimer (Angela), Larry Pine (Tour Guide), Lois Smith (Ma), Megan Follows (Lena), Redmond Gleeson (Funeral Director), Allyce Beasley (Librarian). Directed by Helmut Schleppi and produced by David-Jan Bijker, Esli Bijker, Geert Heetebrij, and Schleppi. Screenplay by Heetebrij.

When their mother dies, Josh and Jake are saddened, yes, but they are also frightened, because Ma took care of everything. She cooked, she washed, she darned, she remembered where things were. Now there is no one to perform those tasks, and the boys are helpless. A farm they can manage, but a house is beyond them. *A Foreign Affair* shows them taking matters into their own hands. With the help of the friendly town librarian, they find a Web site that features young women from Russia who want to marry Americans and are apparently packed and ready to go. They sign up for the package tour, and find themselves in St. Petersburg, where they never expected to be, and considered very desirable, which they have never been before.

Their task is simpler because they are seeking only one wife. That isn't because they plan to practice reverse polygamy, or because one of them is gay, but because they do not think of this as a true marriage. Jake (Tim Blake Nelson), the serious one, is up-front with the women he interviews: no sex, but you keep house for us for a few years, and you get your citizenship.

His brother, Josh (David Arquette), agreed to this plan back on the farm, but now, attending the nightly parties arranged by the tour group, he finds delightful women throwing themselves at him, and this is a new experience he begins to enjoy. He falls in love more or less nightly, using an ancient formula: When he's not with the one he loves, he loves the one he's with.

The movie, directed by Helmut Schleppi and written by Geert Heetebrij, could have gone several ways. I can imagine it as a sex comedy, as a romance, as a bittersweet exploration of lonely people. Schleppi has a little of all three elements at work here, but it's Tim Blake Nelson's character who keeps the plot from spinning out of control, because he has a natural and unforced respect for these women that yanks his brother's chain and keeps their mission on course.

Watching Josh and Jake as they negotiate this process, Emily Mortimer plays a British documentary-maker named Angela. She's been assigned to make a film about the whole phenomenon of Internet brides, but becomes fascinated by Jake because he is not really looking for a bride in the traditional sense, and is up-front about it. As she shoots his interviews with prospective partners, we see her footage, and we sense that we are close to the line between fiction and reality. Maybe closer than we think: I was talking about the movie with Mortimer at Cannes, and she said the filmmakers and the two actors actually took the real tour to do their research.

Mortimer's character provides a subtle subtext. As she watches Jake, listens to him and films him, she begins to be moved by his honesty and his good heart. He is a simple, forthright man, unlike most of those she meets, and we begin to sense he may find a bride in the last place he's looking. Or maybe that's too easy; maybe there's no way their worlds can meet, and yet she has a way of looking at him . . .

Do marriages like this work? Many Americans find mail-order brides or arranged marriages bizarre, but think how bizarre it is to seek your spouse in a singles bar or on a blind date. There are countless possible partners out there somewhere, but we never meet most of them, and most of those we meet are impossible. Maybe it helps to use a system. If you're interested, the actual Web site is at www.aforeignaffair.com.

The Forgotten ★ ★
PG-13, 89 m., 2004

Julianne Moore (Telly Paretta), Dominic West (Ash Correll), Gary Sinise (Dr. Munce), Alfre Woodard (Detective Ann Pope), Linus Roache (Friendly Man), Anthony Edwards (Jim Paretta). Directed by Joseph Ruben and produced by Bruce Cohen, Dan Jinks, and Joe Roth. Screenplay by Gerald DiPego.

Warning: This review contains spoilers. If it didn't, I can think of no way to review it at all, short of summarizing the first three minutes and then telling you some very strange stuff happens. My advice: If you plan to see the film (which I do not recommend), hold the review until afterward.

Whenever I hear about aliens who abduct human subjects and carry them off in spaceships and conduct weird experiments on them and shove scientific probes where the sun don't shine, I ask myself this question: Why do these alien visitations always seem to be aimed at just those kinds of people who are most likely to believe in them? Why do the aliens always pick people who summer at Roswell, New Mexico, instead of choosing someone like Stephen Hawking, Howard Stern, or Dick Cheney?

The Forgotten is not a good movie, but at least it supplies a credible victim. Julianne Moore plays Telly Paretta, a mother who for fourteen months has mourned her nine-year-old son, Sam. He died in a plane crash along with nine other kids. Her psychiatrist (Gary Sinise) wonders if perhaps she is . . . enhancing . . . her memories of Sam. She tries to limit her daily visits to photo albums and home videos, and then, one horrifying day, she finds that all her photos and videos of Sam have vanished!

She blames her husband (Anthony Edwards), but then she gets the bad news: She never had a son. She had a miscarriage. All of her memories of Sam have been fabricated in some kind of posttraumatic-syndrome scenario. The shrink and her husband agree: no Sam. In desperation she turns to a neighbor (Dominic West) whose daughter also died in the same crash. He tells her he never had a daughter.

How can this be? She remembers Sam so clearly. So do we, because the director, Joseph Ruben, supplies repeated reruns of her memories, or home movies, I'm not sure which, and there's Sam, smiling at the camera and playing in the park and looking defiantly pretraumatic.

But how, and why, would her husband, and her shrink, and her neighbor, and her *other* neighbor, and even the *New York Times*, completely forget about Sam and the crash and all those little kids? The most likely hypothesis is that Telly is crazy and everybody else is right. But who would make a movie about a mother discovering her beloved child was imaginary? That would be too sad, too tragic, and, for that matter, too thought-provoking and artistically challenging, and might even make a good movie.

So we determine that Telly is not crazy. Therefore, she had a son, and she is the only person whose memory of Sam has not been erased. The whole world is arrayed against her. Even the federal government is her enemy. She's trailed by agents for the National Security Agency, who are sinister but astonishingly incompetent. A local cop (Alfre Woodard) wonders why the feds are involved: "They don't chase missing children." Being a woman, she of course intuitively believes Telly while all of the logical males diagnose her as a hysteric. She is a great help to Telly until she is suddenly pulled off the case, so to speak.

I will not spoil details of the last act, except to say that it is preposterous, and undoes a good deal of sympathy that Moore's performance has built up in the earlier scenes. There comes a point at which even the most patient moviegoer wearies of chases in which frantic female book editors outrun trained male agents. In which there is a large empty warehouse/hangar space for a dramatic confrontation. In which the Talking Killer Syndrome, by which the villain explains his misdeeds, is not a flaw but is desperately necessary if the plot is ever to be explained at all.

I will content myself with the very final scenes. You know, the ones in the playground. How are they possible? What repairs were necessary to the fabric of the physical world and remembered events? Who keeps track of this stuff? How come such stupid experiments are carried out by beings so superbly intelligent as to be able to conduct them?

The movie begins with a premise: A mother remembers her lost son, and everyone she trusts tells her she only imagines she had a son. That's a great story idea. But it's all downhill from there. *The Forgotten* is best left.

Forty Shades of Blue ★ ★ ★
NO MPAA RATING, 108 m., 2005

Rip Torn (Alan James), Dina Korzun (Laura), Darren Burrows (Michael), Paprika Steen (Lonni), Red West (Duigan). Directed by Ira Sachs and produced by Margot Bridger, Jawal Nga, and Donald Rosenfeld. Screenplay by Michael Rohatyn and Sachs.

Drunks can be such a royal pain in the ass. The falling-down ones tend to be comic or tragic or both, which keeps them from being boring. But how do you live with a maintenance drinker who has become laboriously convinced of his own great importance and who views the other people in his life as through a glass, darkly?

Consider Alan James (Rip Torn), the subject of Ira Sachs's *Forty Shades of Blue*. He is a legend in Memphis, where at a time remembered by him more vividly than by anyone else, he was instrumental in the interracial union of country, R&B, and the blues. This produced music less interesting than the pure forms of each but that could be sold to consumers who didn't know much about any. As the film opens, Alan is being honored at a banquet at which everyone except him seems to be attending as a duty. Extraordinary, how little interaction he has with any of the other guests, except for a tarty tramp he sneaks away with.

He came to the banquet with his girlfriend. This is Laura (Dina Korzun), whom he met when she was a translator for his group of English-speaking businessmen in Moscow. She has moved with him to Memphis, where they live in what she (and maybe he) thinks of as a luxury home, although it is furnished like a show home, circa 1970.

After the banquet is over, Laura lingers for a while, waiting in the bar, but Alan has disappeared. She has been left behind—not abandoned, which would be bad enough, but forgotten. She makes her way home. It is not the first time something like this has happened.

Laura has seen terrible things in her lifetime. We sense that. She puts up with almost anything from Alan because she has spent years putting up with worse. But how does Alan put up with himself? And how happy is he when Michael (Darren Burrows), his son from a previous marriage, turns up in town? We don't have to be told that Michael has seen his father at his worst, probably saw his own mother treated as Laura is now being treated, and, therefore, has none of the standard dislike for the new girlfriend. She's a victim, and they float around the house like victims of an emotional shipwreck.

There is a scene of some mastery, involving a party Alan throws in his own backyard—a big barbecue, with lots of booze and live music. His guests represent a cross section of the Memphis music communities, black and white, young and old, and they all have one thing in common: a vast indifference to Alan. Watch him move through this gathering like a ghost at a banquet. Listen to his speech, at which with a grandiose gesture he tries to make things up with Laura; he is so ignorant of healthy human emotion that he has no idea he is only insulting her again, publicly.

There is poignancy to his character, yes. He and Laura have a small son named Sam. He feels love for the boy, but it is generic love, marked down and not made of the finest ingredients. His heart is incapable of the manufacture of brand-name emotions. Every day for him is essentially a balancing act between his enormous regard for himself, his need to be drunk enough but not too drunk, and the sullen enjoyment of his possessions. His human relationships maintain his cover; he would prefer to devote his days to being pleasantly sloshed and acknowledging applause.

The story then essentially becomes Laura's, because she is the one who can feel and change. The question for her is, at what emotional cost is a comfortable life in Memphis overpriced? To be sure, Alan sometimes stirs himself to express warm sentiments and touch her gently, but she has grown beyond the point where these gestures work; he can touch, but she can't be touched, so they are working in different dimensions.

Forty Shades of Blue won the Grand Jury Prize at Sundance 2005. It might also have deserved acting awards for Torn and Korzun. I despised the character of Alan James so sincerely that I had to haul back at one point to remind myself that, hey, I've met Rip Torn and he's a nice guy and he's only acting. He's acting so well, he not only creates this character but makes him into an object lesson. Sometimes the worst drunks aren't the ones who pass out or go down in flames but the ones who just go on and on, relentlessly, staggering under the weight of their emptiness.

The 40-Year-Old Virgin ★ ★ ★ ½
R, 116 m., 2005

Steve Carell (Andy Stitzer), Catherine Keener (Trish), Paul Rudd (David), Romany Malco (Jay), Seth Rogen (Cal), Elizabeth Banks (Beth), Leslie Mann (Nicky), Jane Lynch (Paula). Directed by Judd Apatow and produced by Apatow, Shauna Robertson, and Clayton Townsend. Screenplay by Apatow and Steve Carell.

Here's a movie that could have had the same title and been a crude sex comedy with contempt for its characters. Instead, *The 40-Year-Old Virgin* is surprisingly insightful, as buddy comedies go, and it has a good heart and a lovable hero. It's not merely that Andy Stitzer rides his bike to work, it's that he signals his turns.

Andy (Steve Carell) is indeed forty and a virgin, after early defeats in the gender wars turned him into a noncombatant. His strategy for dealing with life is to surround himself with obsessions, including action figures, video games, high-tech equipment, and "collectibles," a word that, like "drinkable," never sounds like a glowing endorsement.

Andy is one of those guys whose life is a work-around. What he doesn't understand, he avoids, finesses, or fakes. On the job at the electronics superstore where he works, his fellow employees spend a lot of time talking about women, and he nods as if he speaks the language. Then they rope him into a poker game, the conversation turns to sex, and they look at him strangely when he observes enthusiastically how women's breasts feel like bags of sand.

The buddies are wonderfully cast. David (Paul Rudd) is still hopelessly in love with a woman who has long since outgrown any possible interest in him; Jay (Romany Malco) is a ladies' man who considers himself an irresistible seducer; and Cal (Seth Rogen) is the guy with practical guidance, such as "date drunks" and "never actually say anything to a woman; just ask questions." All these guys have problems of their own and seem prepared to pass them on to Andy as advice; listen with particular care to the definition of "outercourse." Also at work is Paula (Jane Lynch), Andy's boss, a tall, striking woman who is definitely not a forty-year-old virgin;

243

after asking him if he's ever heard of just being sex buddies, she promises him, "I'm discreet, and I'll haunt your dreams."

Andy would just as soon stay home and play with his action figures. But his friends consider it a sacred mission to end his forty-year drought. In a singles bar, under their coaching, he separates a tipsy babe from the crowd; his alarm should have gone off when she asks him to blow into the Breathalyzer so she can start her car. In a bookstore, he asks a cute salesclerk one question after another, which works charmingly until she finds out he has no answers. He goes to one of those dating round-robins where a buzzer goes off and you switch tables, giving the movie an opportunity to assemble a little anthology of pickup clichés.

And then there's Trish (Catherine Keener). She runs a store across the mall, where you can take in your stuff and she'll sell it on eBay. Andy knows right away that he really likes her, but he's paralyzed by shyness and fear, and the way she coaxes him into asking her out is written so well, it could be in a more serious movie. Or maybe it is; there's an insight and understanding under the surface of *The 40-Year-Old Virgin* that is subtle but sincere.

On the surface, the movie assembles a collection of ethnic types as varied as *Crash*. It has fun with them, but it likes them, and it's gentle fun that looks for humanity, not cheap laughs. Consider the character who unexpectedly performs a Guatemalan love song, or Andy's neighbors, who like to watch *Survivor* with him, although he has to bring the set. The movie approaches the subject of homosexuality without the usual gay-bashing, in a scene where the guys trade one-liners beginning "You're gay because . . ." and their reasons show more insight than prejudice.

But the best reason the movie works is that Carell and Keener have a rare kind of chemistry that is maybe better described as mutual sympathy. Keener is an actress at the top of her form, and to see her in *Lovely and Amazing* and *The Ballad of Jack and Rose* and then in *Virgin* is to watch an actress who starts every role with a complete understanding of the woman inside. Her task in the plot is to end Andy's virginity, but her challenge is to create a relationship we care about. We do. The character Trish is intuitively understanding, but

more important, she actually likes this guy. Keener's inspiration is to have Trish see Andy not as a challenge but as an opportunity.

The movie was directed by Judd Apatow, who produced *Anchorman*, and written by Apatow and Carell, the *Daily Show* veteran who first developed the idea of a closeted virgin in a Second City skit. The screenplay is filled with small but perfect one-liners (as when Andy is advised to emulate David Caruso in *Jade*). At the end, for no good reason except that it strikes exactly the perfect (if completely unexpected) note, the cast performs a Bollywood version of *The Age of Aquarius*. By then, they could have done almost anything and I would have been smiling. 🖙

Four Brothers ★ ★ ★
R, 102 m., 2005

Mark Wahlberg (Bobby Mercer), Tyrese Gibson (Angel Mercer), Andre Benjamin (Jeremiah Mercer), Garrett Hedlund (Jack Mercer), Terrence Howard (Lieutenant Green), Josh Charles (Detective Fowler), Sofia Vergara (Sofi), Taraji P. Henson (Camille), Chiwetel Ejiofor (Victor Sweet), Fionnula Flanagan (Evelyn Mercer). Directed by John Singleton and produced by Lorenzo di Bonaventura. Screenplay by David Elliot and Paul Lovett.

John Singleton's *Four Brothers* is an urban Western, or maybe it's an urban movie inspired by a Western; either way, it's intended to be more mythic than realistic. It connects with underlying moral currents in the way Westerns used to, back before greed, fear, anger, and "society" provided action movies with all the motivation they needed.

The movie opens with a sweet white-haired grandmother type who arrives at a Detroit convenience store late at night. Wrong store, wrong neighborhood, we're thinking. But Evelyn Mercer (Fionnula Flanagan) has a reason to be there: A frightened young kid has been caught shoplifting some candy, and she settles things with the store owner and puts the fear of God into the kid. Then two stickup guys walk into the store, and she is shot dead.

At the funeral, we meet her four adopted sons, two black, two white. She was a foster mother all of her life, and these were the only four she couldn't find homes for: Bobby (Mark Wahlberg), Angel (Tyrese Gibson), Jeremiah (Andre Benjamin), and Jack (Garrett Hedlund). Bobby is the oldest, the natural leader, the one with a temper. Angel is the player with a hot babe (Sofia Vergara). Jeremiah is a success; he's married (to Taraji P. Henson), has a family, is involved in real estate deals. Jack is a rock-and-roller.

They all have the name Mercer, and they all consider Evelyn their mom, but they grew up on mean streets and have not spent a lot of time getting all sentimental about being "brothers." That begins to change at the funeral, when they wordlessly agree that their mother's death requires some kind of action. Jeremiah, the businessman, observes: "The people who did this are from the same streets we're from. Mom would have been the first to forgive them." True of Mom, not true of them.

This story is inspired by Henry Hathaway's *The Sons of Katie Elder* (1965), unseen by me but cited by my fellow critic Emanuel Levy. (I am awed by the number of films I have seen, and awed by the number I have not seen.) At first it looks like an open-and-shut case: Witnesses saw two gangbangers walk in and blast the store owner. Mom was a bystander, shot in cold blood. But as the brothers look at the tape from the security camera, they're struck by how ruthlessly she was murdered; they turn up evidence suggesting maybe there was something more to this killing. As long as we're talking about the influence of old movies, a crucial clue in *Four Brothers* involves when the lights are turned off on a basketball court; I was reminded of the almanac in John Ford's *Young Mr. Lincoln* (1939) that provides the phases of the moon.

I won't describe the rest of the plot, which unfolds like a police procedural, but I will note a nice touch involving the way Jeremiah looks guilty for a moment simply because he is successful and generous. And I'll mention the key supporting characters. Terrence Howard and Josh Charles play the two cops on the case, and Chiwetel Ejiofor *(Dirty Pretty Things)*, who is one of the nicest men alive, plays one of the meanest men in Detroit. He's a crime boss whose methods for humbling his underlings pass beyond mere cruelty into demented ingenuity.

For Singleton, the movie is a return to inner-city subjects after some fairly wide excursions *(Shaft, 2 Fast 2 Furious)*. In between those two he made the provocative *Baby Boy* (2001), which attacks some young black men who feel licensed to live at home with their mothers, thoughtlessly father children, avoid work, and perpetuate the cycle. That had the kind of critical insight into the kinds of realities that distinguish his first, and greatest, film, *Boyz n the Hood* (1991). (Singleton is also the producer of the current drama *Hustle and Flow*, a more ambitious and insightful urban film that also uses the talents of Howard and Henson.) *Four Brothers* basically wants to be an entertainment, although it deliberately makes the point that in an increasingly diverse society, people of different races may belong to the same family.

Four Brothers works as an urban thriller, if not precisely as a model of logic. There is, for example, a bloody and extended gun battle involving hundreds of rounds of machine-gun bullets and a stack of dead bodies, and afterward a cop observes, "It looks like self-defense." Yes, but since that cop cannot make the point after the smoke clears, why is there no investigation to tidy up the carnage? I guess I shouldn't ask questions like that in a Western, urban or otherwise; bad guys exist to get shot and good guys exist to shoot them, with a few key exceptions to keep things interesting. If you want to know how it all turned out, you need to get a transfer to the courtroom genre.

Freedomland ★ ★
R, 113 m., 2006

Samuel L. Jackson (Lorenzo Council), Julianne Moore (Brenda Martin), Edie Falco (Karen Collucci), Ron Eldard (Danny Martin), William Forsythe (Boyle), Aunjanue Ellis (Felicia), Anthony Mackie (Billy Williams). Directed by Joe Roth and produced by Scott Rudin. Screenplay by Richard Price, based on his novel.

Freedomland assembles the elements for a superior thriller, but were the instructions lost when the box was opened? It begins with a compelling story about a woman whose car is hijacked with her four-year-old son inside. It adds racial tension and the bulldog detective work of a veteran police detective. And then it flies to pieces with unmotivated scenes, inexplicable dialogue, and sudden conclusions that may be correct but arrive from nowhere. The film seems edited none too wisely from a longer version that made more sense.

Julianne Moore appears in the opening scene, sobbing, her hands bleeding, staggering into a hospital with a story of her car being hijacked in a wooded area near a low-income housing development.

Samuel L. Jackson plays Lorenzo, the detective assigned to the case. He can't understand why her character, named Brenda, was driving through the isolated area at the time. She explains: She's a volunteer at a community children's center and took the wrong shortcut home. Lorenzo thinks she's hiding something, and she is: Her son was in the backseat of the car when it was taken.

When this story becomes public, it creates a furor. Cops from a nearby white district blanket the area, a black preacher complains that blacks are killed all the time in the district without this kind of police attention, and the woman's brother Danny (Ron Eldard) is a white cop who seems angry all the time—at his sister, at the black community, at Lorenzo.

Racial demonstrations are on the simmer, but the movie turns them on and off at will. Brenda, after all, is well-known and beloved in the area because of her volunteer work. Yet at one point a black woman tells her, "You stay away from my child!" Why would she say that? And why, for that matter, does Lorenzo announce a sudden about-face on the case when we haven't seen the evidence to support his conclusion? Why, for that matter, are untold resources used to search for the missing boy on the grounds and buildings of Freedomland, an abandoned orphanage, when there is every reason to believe he is not there?

And why, oh why, is Brenda apparently left in the personal custody of Lorenzo, who removes her from the hospital without formalities, drives her around, leaves her alone, has heart-to-heart talks with her, and ignores all police procedures for dealing with victims and/or witnesses? And what about that passionate discussion between Lorenzo and Brenda in which their body language and the close framing of the shots lead us to anticipate a development that never comes?

The scene ends weirdly with the two of them staring fiercely at each other, as if they were told to freeze while the writers came up with more dialogue.

This movie is filled with behavior that seems to exist only to provide things for the actors to do. There's an asthma attack early in the film that should pay off somehow but doesn't. Danny, the brother who is a cop, seems constantly poised to do something radical but never quite does. And why does his concern for his sister express itself in his decision essentially to ignore her and operate elsewhere in the plot? And does the angry preacher in the black neighborhood have a legitimate grievance, or is he just venting on command, to provide filler for the plot?

One scene works. It's a conversation between Brenda and Karen (Edie Falco), who is the leader of a group of mothers whose children have been kidnapped, molested, or killed. She gets Brenda alone for a fraught and crucial conversation (which is against all standard procedures, but never mind), and for the length of that conversation the movie is about something, and it works.

Freedomland is based on a novel by Richard Price, whose *Clockers* made a better film. He adapts his story for director Joe Roth as if they know a lot of places in the neighborhood but don't remember how to get from one place to another. Individual scenes feel authentic, but the story tries to build bridges between loose ends.

Friday Night Lights ★ ★ ★ ½
PG-13, 115 m., 2004

Billy Bob Thornton (Coach Gary Gaines), Tim McGraw (Charles Billingsley), Derek Luke (Boobie Miles), Jay Hernandez (Brian Chavez), Lucas Black (Mike Winchell), Garrett Hedlund (Don Billingsley), Lee Thompson Young (Chris Comer), Lee Jackson (Ivory Christian), Grover Coulson (L. V. Miles). Directed by Peter Berg and produced by Brian Grazer. Screenplay by David Aaron Cohen and Berg, based on the book *Friday Night Lights* by H. G. Bissinger.

You have the responsibility of protecting this team and this school and this town.
—Coach Gary Gaines

Protecting them against what? We're not talking about war here, we're talking about high school football. And yet as *Friday Night Lights* unfolds, we begin to understand: The role of the team is to protect against the idea that the town is inconsequential and its citizens insignificant. If Gaines can lead the Odessa-Permian team to a state championship, that will prove that Odessa is a place of consequence, a center of power and glory. Well, won't it?

Certainly there are countless citizens in Odessa who lead happy and productive lives, and are fulfilled without depending on high school football. We just don't meet any of them in the movie, which focuses on the team, the coach, and the local boosters—adults who define themselves in terms of their relationship to the team.

These people are obsessed beyond all reason with winning and losing, and the pressure they put on the kids and their coach is relentless. "Take us to State, coach," one booster tells Gaines in a supermarket parking lot. "Or what?" asks Gaines. Or else. "Are we going to be moving again?" the coach's young daughter asks after a defeat. "No, honey," says her mother, but Gaines answers: "Possibly."

Gaines is played by Billy Bob Thornton in another great performance: He played the drunken title character in *Bad Santa*, and Davy Crockett in *The Alamo*. The man has range, and he has a command of tone, too. Santa was over the top, but his Coach Gaines is a private man, inward, who finds it wise to keep his thoughts to himself. Consider the scene where he's told that his star player's injury won't prevent him from playing. Look at his eyes. He has reason to believe he is being lied to. He has reason to hope he is not.

The player is Boobie Miles (Derek Luke), a motormouth with a giant talent that comes wrapped in ego. When one of his teammates accused him of not working out in the weight room, he explains that his gift is "God-given." But in the first game of the season he injures his knee. He pretends it's nothing. Eventually the uncle who is raising him (Grover Coulson) takes him to Midland for an MRI, which reveals a badly torn ligament. Boobie dismisses the doctor as a Midland fan "jealous of Odessa," and he and his uncle tell the coach he's ready to play. He isn't. Because he depended on sports for his future, because he doesn't read very well, there is a moment when he sits on the porch and watches some garbage men at work, and contemplates his future.

The movie is based on real life, described in the best-seller *Friday Night Lights: A Town, a Team, and a Dream*, by H. G. Bissinger. It depicts Odessa as a town consumed by high school football; its stadium is larger than those at many colleges. Local talk radio keeps up a steady drumbeat of criticism against Gaines. "They're doing too much learning in the schools," one caller complains.

The movie has been directed by Peter Berg not as character studies, but as emotional snapshots. We catch on who the key characters are. Others are never identified. Gaines has enormous focus, and can deliver a powerful message at halftime, but he understands better than anyone else that football is only a game. Unfortunately, his job is not only a game, and so he must take football very seriously; his job is not to protect the town and the school, but to protect his family. At dinner parties, in restaurants, everywhere he goes, he undergoes an endless stream of comments, criticism, suggestions, threats masked as praise. The way Thornton plays him, Gaines reminds me of Hemingway's definition of courage: grace under pressure.

There is something pathetic about a grown man still living his life in terms of high school, and that's the case with Charles Billingsley (played with great power by the country singer Tim McGraw). He still wears his ring from Odessa's championship team of twenty years earlier, and bullies his son, Don (Garrett Hedlund), who is a receiver on the team. When Don fumbles early in the season, his dad actually walks onto the field to chew him out. He slaps his son around, trash-talks him, gets drunk, and directs a withering stream of sarcasm at the kid—and has a revealing moment when he tells Don that high school football will be the high point of his life.

I started in journalism at fifteen, as a sportswriter covering high school football. I thought it was the most important thing on Earth. But it was more innocent in those days. At what point in American history did the phrase "It's not whether you win or lose, but how you play the game" get replaced by "Winning is the only thing"? Today's teams are like surrogate nations for their fans. When your team wins, it enhances you.

Oddly enough, despite all these undertones, *Friday Night Lights* does also work like a traditional sports movie, and there's enormous tension and excitement at the end, when everything comes down to the last play in the State finals. The movie demonstrates the power of sports to involve us; we don't live in Odessa and are watching a game played sixteen years ago, and we get all wound up.

Friday Night Lights reminded me of another movie filmed in Texas: *The Last Picture Show,* set fifty years ago. In that one, after the local team loses another game, the players catch flak everywhere they go. It's gotten worse. I'll bet if you phoned talk radio in Odessa and argued that high school football is only a game, you'd make a lot of people mad at you. The poor kids who play it are under cruel pressure. One of the team members tells a friend, midway through the season: "I just don't feel like I'm seventeen."

Friends with Money ★ ★
R, 88 m., 2006

Jennifer Aniston (Olivia), Joan Cusack (Franny), Catherine Keener (Christine), Frances McDormand (Jane), Simon McBurney (Aaron), Jason Isaacs (David), Greg Germann (Matt), Scott Caan (Mike), Bob Stephenson (Marty). Directed by Nicole Holofcener and produced by Anthony Bregman. Screenplay by Holofcener.

Friends with Money resembles *Crash,* except that all the characters are white and the reason they keep running into one another is that the women have been friends since the dawn of time. Three of them are rich and married. The fourth is, and I quote, "single, a pothead, and a maid." That's Olivia (Jennifer Aniston), who used to teach at a fancy school in Santa Monica "but quit when the kids started giving her quarters."

The other friends are Jane (Frances McDormand), who screams at people who try to cut in line ahead of her; Christine (Catherine Keener), who writes screenplays with her husband; and Franny (Joan Cusack), whose biggest concern is that her husband spends too much money on their child's shoes. Jane's husband is Aaron (Simon McBurney). "He's so gay," says Olivia. Christine's husband is David (Jason Isaacs). They fight over what the characters should say in the screenplay they're writing, and then they simply fight: She tells him his breath stinks, and he tells her she's getting a lard butt. Not a demonstration of mutual support. Franny's husband is Matt (Greg Germann), whose problem, as far as this film is concerned, is that he has no problems.

The characters meet in various combinations and gossip about those not present, and all three couples spend a lot of time on the topic of Olivia, who they agree needs a husband, although their own marriages don't argue persuasively for wedded bliss. Olivia finally gets fixed up with a physical trainer named Mike (Scott Caan), who in some ways is the most intriguing character in the movie, and certainly the biggest louse. Consider how he asks to go along with her when she cleans houses, and what he asks her afterward, and the present he gives her, and the "friend from junior high school" he sees in a restaurant.

Meanwhile, the marriage of Jane and Aaron is melting down because of her anger. She's a famous dress designer who has decided not to wash her hair, which becomes so greasy her husband turns away from her in bed, although maybe he really is gay. Or probably not, and neither is his new friend, also named Aaron, although they do enjoy trying on sweaters together. Meanwhile, Christine and David are putting a second story on their house, which will give them a view, and we all know that if you're fighting, the best thing to do is remodel.

Friends with Money was written and directed by Nicole Holofcener, whose two previous features were wonderful studies of women and their relationships: *Walking and Talking* (1996) and *Lovely and Amazing* (2001). Both of them also starred Catherine Keener, who is expert at creating the kind of Holofcener character who speaks the truth with wit, especially when it is not required. Cusack can do that too, although she is underused here.

The movie lacks the warmth and edge of the two previous features. It seems to be more of an idea than a story. Yes, it's about how Olivia's friends all have money, and at one point Jane suggests they simply give her some to bring her up to their level. As it happens, characters do exactly that in novels I've read recently by Stendhal and Trollope, but in modern Los Angeles, it is unheard of. If you have millions and your friend is a maid, obviously what you do is tell her how much you envy her. Working for a living is a charming concept when kept at a reasonable distance.

The parts of the movie that really live are the ones involving Olivia and the two men in her life: first Mike, the fitness instructor, and then Marty (Bob Stephenson), a slob who lives alone, is very shy, and hires her to clean his house. When the rich friends go to a $1,000-a-plate benefit, they invite Olivia along and she brings Marty, and when she goes to pick him up, she suggests that maybe he should think about wearing a tie. This he is happy to do. At the dinner, he smooths down the tie with pride and satisfaction. Watch the way Aniston regards him while he does this. She is so happy for him. At last she is the friend with money. Not cash money, it's true, but a good line of credit in the bank of love.

Fun with Dick and Jane ★ ★ ½
PG-13, 90 m., 2005

Jim Carrey (Dick Harper), Téa Leoni (Jane Harper), Alec Baldwin (Jack McCallister), Richard Jenkins (Frank Bascome), Angie Harmon (Veronica), Jeff Garlin (Peter Scott). Directed by Dean Parisot and produced by Brian Grazer and Jim Carrey. Screenplay by Judd Apatow and Nicholas Stoller.

Fun with Dick and Jane recycles the 1977 comedy starring Jane Fonda and George Segal, right down to repeating the same mistakes. Those who do not learn from history are doomed to remake it. The movie stars Jim Carrey as Dick, an executive of a megacorp much like Enron who is promoted to vice president in charge of communications just in time to be its spokesman on live cable news as the corporation's stock melts down to pennies a share.

Téa Leoni plays his wife, Jane, who is a travel agent but has quit her job that very morning because of Dick's big promotion. They were looking forward to glorious affluence and now find they are broke, and the gardeners have come around to roll up the turf on their lawn and truck it away. They lose their retirement savings, their furniture, their light, their heat, and (the cruelest blow of all for their son) their flat-panel hi-def TV.

Dick goes out on job interviews, only to find that the jobs a) do not exist, b) have already been taken, or c) are in the control of chortling sadists who know by heart the tape of his meltdown on TV. Soon Dick and Jane are reduced to theft, at first small-time and then on a larger scale, and that's when this film goes kablooie, just like the 1977 movie did.

There is a large but unexploited comic premise here: One of the largest corporations in America turned out to be worth less than zero and was built from a tissue of lies. Alec Baldwin and Richard Jenkins do a merciless job of playing characters that we may, for convenience, assume are inspired by Enron's fallen giants Kenneth Lay and Jeffrey Skilling.

We have seen the Enron documentaries and know what possibilities there are for ruthless dark comedy, as in the scenes where Enron executives deliberately and cold-bloodedly mastermind the California energy crisis, chuckling that a few grandmothers may have died of heat exhaustion but Enron has made millions. The California energy "shortage" fits any definition of terrorism except that it was engineered by Americans wearing lapel pins instead of Arabs wearing beards.

But the movie avoids the rich opportunities to plop Carrey and Leoni into the middle of a political lampoon and turns to tired slapstick, wigs, false beards, "funny" bank holdups, and so on. There is a late attempt at a comeback as the Baldwin character tries to get his loot out of the country, but by then it's all too neat and too late.

If you want to taste the opportunities that *Fun with Dick and Jane* bypassed, you might want to rent Michael Tolkin's *The New Age* (1994), which stars Peter Weller and Judy Davis in the story of an affluent Los Angeles couple who lose their jobs and descend gradually, in disbelief, from luxury to destitution. Dealing with financial demolition is more than a matter of waving a water pistol in a bank lobby, as a lot of people in Houston would be happy to assure us, if their phones were working.

G

G ★ ★

R, 96 m., 2005

Richard T. Jones (Summer G), Blair Underwood (Chip Hightower), Chenoa Maxwell (Sky Hightower), Andre Royo (Tre), Jillian Lindsey (Daizy Duke), Laz Alonzo (Craig Lewis), Sonja Sohn (Shelley James), Nicoye Banks (B. Mo Smoov), Lalanya Masters (Nicole Marshall). Directed by Christopher Scott Cherot and produced by Andrew Lauren and Judd Landon. Screenplay by Cherot and Charles E. Drew Jr., loosely based on a novel by F. Scott Fitzgerald.

G enters a world not much seen in the movies, the world of affluent African-Americans whose summer places are in the Hamptons. I wish it had approached this material with a clean slate and given us a story made from scratch. That it's fitfully based on F. Scott Fitzgerald's *The Great Gatsby* is only a distraction; noting how it followed the novel and how it didn't, I wondered why the clarity of Fitzgerald's story line was replaced by such a jumble of a plot.

The film is a fictional recycling of details from its immediate inspiration, Sean Combs, aka Diddy, although still called P Diddy when the movie was filmed in 2002. *G* is based not on his life but on his lifestyle: the Hamptons place, the elegant summer parties where everyone wears white, the crowds of stars and would-be stars. The movie is being described as a "hip-hop *Gatsby*," but there's not much more hip-hop in it than there is *Gatsby*.

Richard T. Jones stars as Summer G, a famous performer and producer who presides over his newly purchased Hamptons mansion and its population of constantly changing guests. This world is seen through the eyes of Tre (Andre Royo), a journalist sent to cover the world of black affluence. He stays with his cousin Sky (Chenoa Maxwell) and her husband, Chip (Blair Underwood), who is a rich stockbroker with a mean streak. If we're keeping count, we now have the equivalents of Jay Gatsby, Nick Carraway, and Daisy and Tom Buchanan.

G and Sky were in love once, long ago. Their lives separated. She married the rich guy. G became the even richer guy. At one of G's parties, he sees Sky and the earth moves. His heart still circles around her. Like Gatsby, he overcame obscurity and poverty, built an empire, and then bought his summer palace to attract her: "I built this world for you."

G is circled by hungry and ambitious performers and producers who know he holds the keys to their success. One hopeful couple is Craig (Laz Alonzo) and the girlfriend he is jealously possessive about, Nicole (Lalanya Masters). These characters do not work as an improvement on the Fitzgerald structure and contribute to an ending that entirely misses the point.

I know, I know, I'm always saying that a movie has to work as a movie and not be "faithful" to the book that inspired it. Filmmaking is not marriage, and adaptation is not adultery. But here we begin with a novel of legendary importance, where the ending is perfectly calculated to end the summer of parties on a note of futility, irony, and loss. G rearranges plot elements to make them into a soap opera, in which Summer G suffers the wrong loss in the wrong way for the wrong reasons.

No more about that. The movie is intrinsically interesting when it touches on class differences in the African-American community. Chip Hightower, for example, comes from old money and cringes when he regards hip-hop millionaires moving to the Hamptons. There goes the neighborhood. His opinion of Sky's friendship with Summer G: "I don't want my wife socializing with gangsters." At one point he actually conspires against G with the white head of the local homeowners' association.

Interesting, how much more of the discrimination in G is inspired by class and income than by race. Consider the conversation between a Humvee-load of rap stars and a car occupied by upper-middle-class Hamptons residents, both black and white. The Humvee people, heavy with bling, ask for directions. Notice how the tone changes when the car driver's white girlfriend realizes they're talking to celebrities. This movie, like *Crash* in its very different way, realizes that the old forms of prejudice in society are giving way to new ones.

The problem with *G* is not merely that the ending doesn't work and feels hopelessly contrived. It's also that the plot adds too many unnecessary characters and subplots, so that the

250

main line gets misplaced. The question recycled through the movie (and its advertising) is, "Does hip-hop have heart?" Summer G certainly has one, and so does Sky, although she's not sure what it's telling her. In the classic form of the story, the narrator watches as the hero tries to regain the heart of his lost love, while her brutal husband mistreats her and his mistress. In *G* those functions are spread more widely among additional characters, so that A has a way of leading to C while B loses a place in line. The ending of *Gatsby* is inevitable. The ending of *G* is arbitrary and melodramatic.

If you haven't read *The Great Gatsby*, you may enjoy the movie more. On the other hand, maybe not; maybe it's too crowded and overloaded with subplots to really grab you. Either way, you can look forward to reading a great novel. The closing paragraphs contain some of the best prose ever written.

The Game of Their Lives ★ ½
PG, 95 m., 2005

Gerard Butler (Frank Borghi), Wes Bentley (Walter Bahr), Gavin Rossdale (Stanley Mortensen), Jay Rodan (Pee Wee), Zachery Bryan (Harry Keough), Jimmy Jean-Louis (Joe Gatjaens), Richard Jenik (Joe Maca), Craig Hawksley (Walter Giesler), John Rhys-Davis (Coach Bill Jeffrey). Directed by David Anspaugh and produced by Howard Baldwin, Karen Elise Baldwin, Peter Newman, and Ginger T. Perkins. Screenplay by Angelo Pizzo, based on the book by Geoffrey Douglas.

The Game of Their Lives tells the story of an astonishing soccer match in 1950, when an unsung team of Americans went to Brazil to compete in the World Cup, and defeated England, the best team in the world. So extraordinary was the upset, I learn on the Internet Movie Database, that "London bookmakers offered odds of 500-1 against such an preposterous event," and "The *New York Times* refused to run the score when it was first reported, deeming it a hoax."

So it was a hell of an upset. Pity about the movie. Obviously made with all of the best will in the world, its heart in the right place, this is a sluggish and dutiful film that plays more like a eulogy than an adventure. Strange, how it follows the form of a sports movie, but has the feeling of an educational film. And all the stranger because the director, David Anspaugh, has made two exhilarating movies about underdogs in sports, *Hoosiers* (1986) and *Rudy* (1993).

In those films he knew how to crank up the suspense and dramatize the supporting characters. Here it feels more like a group of Calvin Klein models have gathered to pose as soccer players from St. Louis. Shouldn't there be at least one player not favored by nature with improbably good looks? And at least a couple who look like they're around twenty, instead of thirty-five? And a goalie who doesn't look exactly like Gerard Butler, who played *The Phantom of the Opera*? True, Frank Borghi, the goalie, is played by Gerard Butler, but that's no excuse: In *Dear Frankie*, Butler played a perfectly believable character who didn't look like he was posing for publicity photos.

The one personal subplot involves a player who thinks he can't go to Brazil because it conflicts with his wedding day. Instead of milking this for personal conflict, Anspaugh solves it all in one perfunctory scene: The coach talks to the future father-in-law, the father-in-law talks to his daughter, she agrees to move up the wedding, and so no problem-o.

This team is so lackluster, when they go out to get drunk, they don't get drunk. It's 1950, but there's only one cigarette and three cigars in the whole movie. The sound track could have used big band hits from the period, but William Ross's score is so inspirational it belongs on a commercial.

As the movie opens, we see a St. Louis soccer club from a mostly Italian-American neighborhood, and hear a narration that sounds uncannily like an audiobook. Word comes that soccer players from New York will travel to Missouri, an American team will be chosen, and they'll travel to Brazil. The players get this information from their coach, Bill Jeffrey (John Rhys-Davis), who is so uncoachlike that at no point during the entire movie does he give them one single word of advice about the game of soccer. Both Rhys-Davis and the general manager, Walter Giesler (Craig Hawksley), are perfectly convincing in their roles, but the screenplay gives them no dialogue to suggest their characters know much about soccer.

As for the big game itself, the game was allegedly shot on location in Brazil, but never do we get a sense that the fans in the long shots are actually watching the match. The tempo of the game is monotonous, coming down to one would-be British goal after another, all of them blocked by Borghi. This was obviously an amazing athletic feat, but you don't get that sense in the movie. You don't get the sense of soccer much at all; *Bend It Like Beckham* had better soccer—*lots* better soccer, and you could follow it and get involved.

At the end of the film, before a big modern soccer match, the surviving members of that 1950 team are called out onto the field and introduced. That should provide us with a big emotional boost, as we see the real men next to insets of their characters in the movie. But it doesn't, because we never got to know the characters in the movie. *The Game of Their Lives* covers its story like an assignment, not like a mission.

Game 6 ★ ★ ★ ½
R, 83 m., 2006

Michael Keaton (Nicky Rogan), Griffin Dunne (Elliot Litvak), Shalom Harlow (Paisley Porter), Bebe Neuwirth (Joanna Bourne), Catherine O'Hara (Lillian Rogan), Robert Downey Jr. (Steven Schwimmer), Ari Graynor (Laurel Rogan), Harris Yulin (Peter Redmond). Directed by Michael Hoffman and produced by Amy Robinson, Griffin Dunne, Leslie Urdang, and Christina Weiss Lurie. Screenplay by Don DeLillo.

Michael Keaton is a talker. His strength as an actor is in roles that position him on the scale between literate and glib; even in the wonderful lost film *Touch and Go* (1986), where he played a pro hockey player, he spoke like one who had a novel in him. In *Game 6*, he plays a playwright and talks like one, taking pleasure in choosing specific words to evoke exactly what he means. He is also a Boston Red Sox fan, and when the opening night of his new play coincides with the sixth game in the 1986 World Series, he has a lot to talk about: "I've been carrying this franchise on my back since I was six years old."

The original screenplay is by the novelist Don DeLillo, and it involves subjects (or obsessions?) he used in his novels *Underworld* (1997) and *Cosmopolis* (2003). From the first comes expertise on baseball, pitched somewhere between torch songs and Greek tragedy. From the second

comes the Manhattan gridlock and the undercurrent of danger and violence in the streets. The playwright, named Nicky Rogan, abandons a cab after an exploding steam pipe sprays asbestos into the air, and retreats into a bar where he finds an old friend and fellow playwright, Elliot Litvak (Griffin Dunne). Because it is Nicky's opening night, they talk about a critic they both hate; Elliot believes this man destroyed his life and indeed seems to be entering madness.

This is DeLillo's first produced screenplay, but he has written for the stage, and perhaps his portrait of Steven Schwimmer (Robert Downey Jr.), the detested critic, is drawn from life. I can think of a candidate. Schwimmer has written such lethal reviews of plays that he lives in hiding, is forced to attend opening nights in disguise, and goes to the theater fully armed. Elliot speaks of him in wonder: "I opened a one-act play at 4 A.M. in the Fulton Fish Market. In the rain. For an audience of fish-handlers. Schwimmer was there."

In addition to his fears about opening night and his premonition that the Red Sox will once again destroy his dreams, Nicky is facing personal problems. While one of his cabs was stuck in traffic, he saw his daughter, Laurel (Ari Graynor), in another one; visits between cars stuck in traffic are also an *Underworld* theme. She informs him her mother is divorcing him: "She says Daddy's demons are so intense, he doesn't even know when he's lying." There is consolation in an affair he's having with an investor in his play (Bebe Neuwirth), but not much.

Writers find strange connections in their days and lives; they generate wormholes that connect people. How else to explain that one of the taxi drivers "used to be head of neurosurgery in the USSR," and the star of his new play (Harris Yulin) can't remember his dialogue because he has, the director says, "a parasite living in his brain." Yulin has a painful rehearsal where he fails again and again to remember the line that has just been repeated to him.

This material could be pitched at various levels. You can imagine it being incorporated into a sequel to *The Producers*, or being transformed into quasi-O'Neill. Keaton, DeLillo, and director Michael Hoffman make it into a celebration of spoken language; we're reminded that Hoffman directed *Restoration*

(1995) and the 1999 *A Midsummer Night's Dream*. After the Sundance opening of *Game 6*, I wrote, "DeLillo's dialogue allows for a complexity and richness of speech that is refreshing compared to the subject-verb-object recitation in many movies." Such dialogue requires an actor who sounds like he understands what he is saying, and Keaton goes one better and convinces us he is generating it. Life for him is a play, he is the actor, his speech is the dialogue, and he deepens and dramatizes his experience by the way he talks about it. Certainly what he says about the Red Sox has a weary grandeur.

Downey Jr., whose troubles of a few years ago were well documented, has come back with a vengeance; his career is ascendent, and since *Game 6* was finished in 2005, he has made ten other movies, ranging from *Good Night, and Good Luck* to *The Shaggy Dog*, and that's some range. Here he makes the critic Schwimmer into a study in affectation, a little Buddhist, a little loony, a little paranoid, a little fearless. Dunne, who also produced the movie with his filmmaking partner, Amy Robinson, plays the disintegrating playwright Elliot as a man halfway between barroom philosopher and Dumpster-diver. And for Nicky, everything comes down to which is more important: success for his play, or the Red Sox winning Game 6. Talk about backing yourself into a lose-lose situation.

Games People Play: New York ★ ★
NO MPAA RATING, 100 m., 2004

As themselves, more or less: Joshua Coleman, Sarah Smith, Scott Ryan, Dani Marco, David Maynard, Elisha Imani Wilson, Dr. Gilda Carle, and Jim Caruso. Directed by James Ronald Whitney and produced by Whitney and Neil Stephens. Screenplay by Whitney.

Games People Play: New York plays most of its games with the audience. It pretends to be a documentary about the filming of a pilot for a TV reality program, but it contains so much full frontal nudity, semi-explicit sex, and general raunchiness that it's impossible to imagine it anywhere on TV except pay-for-view adult cable. As viewers, we intuit that it is more, or less, than it seems: That in some sense the whole project is a scam. Yes, but a scam that involves real actors doing real things while they're really in front of the camera.

The premise: Auditions are held to select six finalists for a game-show pilot. The winner of the contest will be paid $10,000. The actors are asked to be attractive and "completely uninhibited," and so they are. They're awarded points for their success at such events as: (1) asking complete strangers for a urine sample; (2) the men: enacting casting-couch seductions with would-be actresses not in on the gag; (3) the women: seducing delivery men by dropping a towel and standing there naked; (4) persuading strangers to join a man and woman in a "naked trio" in a nearby hotel room, and (5) persuading a stranger in the next toilet stall to join them in the reading of a scene they're rehearsing.

Amazingly (or maybe not, given the times we live in), the movie not only finds actors willing to play these roles, but men and women off the street who volunteer (in the case of the urine and naked trio gags) or are at least good sports (as in the dropped towel routine). After having been tricked into appearing in the film, they actually sign releases allowing their footage to be used.

These episodes are intercut with sessions where a psychologist named Dr. Gilda Carle and a publicist named Jim Caruso interview the finalists. I have no idea if these people are real, but their cross-examinations elicit harrowing confessions: One woman was raped at four and then beaten by her father, another saw her father murdered, a third is bulimic, a man is a male prostitute, and so on. The uncanny thing about the revelations at the end of the movie is that we cannot be absolutely sure if this is all fiction, or only some of it.

The film was made by James Ronald Whitney, whose *Just, Melvin* is one of the most powerful documentaries I've seen, about a man who abused and molested many members of Whitney's extended family and is finally confronted on screen. What's odd about *Games People Play* is that Whitney seems to have set up the film and offered the $10,000 prize in order to manipulate his actors and their victims into abusing themselves.

Although acting is a noble profession, there is little nobility in being an out-of-work actor, and the ambience at a lot of auditions resembles the desperation of a soup line. *Games People Play* proves, if nothing else, that there are actors who will do almost anything to get in a movie. The actors here (Joshua Coleman, Sarah Smith, Scott Ryan, Dani Marco, David Maynard, Elisha Imani Wilson) are all effective in their scenes, sometimes moving, sometimes more convincing than they have a right to be. But we cringe at how the movie uses them.

How do you rate a movie like this? Star ratings seem irrelevant. It is either a brilliant example of an experiment in psychological manipulation (four stars) or a reprehensible exploitation of the ambitions and vulnerabilities of actors and others who did the director no harm (zero stars). Because it evokes a strange and horrible fascination, I suppose the stars must fall in the middle (two), but your reaction will swing all the way to one side or the other. I felt creepy afterward.

Garden State ★ ★ ★
R, 109 m., 2004

Zach Braff (Andrew Largeman), Natalie Portman (Sam), Peter Sarsgaard (Mark), Ian Holm (Gideon Largeman), Method Man (Diego), Jean Smart (Carol). Directed by Zach Braff and produced by Pamela Abdy, Gary Gilbert, Dan Halsted, and Richard Klubeck. Screenplay by Braff.

Andrew Largeman, the hero of *Garden State,* is almost catatonic when first we see him. He's flat on his back under an unwrinkled white sheet on a white bed in a white room with no other furnishings except for an answering machine, which is recording a message from his father informing him that his mother has drowned in the bathtub. Andrew gets up and looks into his medicine cabinet, where every shelf is filled with neatly arranged rows of prescription drugs.

We learn in the following scenes that Andrew is a would-be actor (he played a retarded quarterback on a made-for-cable movie), works in a Vietnamese restaurant, has not been home to New Jersey in nine years, and is overmedicated. When he leaves all the pills behind before flying home for the funeral, his life begins to budge again.

Garden State was written and directed by Zach Braff, who stars as Andrew. He has one of those faces, like David Schwimmer's, that seem congenitally dubious. He returns home to his father, Gideon (Ian Holm), who is very dry and

distant, masking anger: Gideon is a psychiatrist who believes Andrew will never be well "until you forgive yourself for what you did to your mother." What Andrew did, in Gideon's mind, was to make the woman into a paraplegic by pushing her so that she fell over the door of a dishwasher. What Andrew believes is that he was a very small boy, the dishwasher had a broken latch, and his father is full of it.

Andrew's new life begins when he recognizes the gravediggers at his mother's funeral. These are high school buddies he left behind. Soon he's high on Ecstasy and playing spin-the-bottle at a party, and not long after that he's unexpectedly in love. She is Sam (Natalie Portman), a local girl who is one of those creatures you sometimes find in the movies, a girl who is completely available, absolutely desirable, and really likes you. Portman's success in creating this character is all the more impressive because we learn almost nothing about her except that she's great to look at and has those positive attributes.

The movie joins Andrew, Sam, and his high school buddy Mark (Peter Sarsgaard) on an odyssey through the wilds of New Jersey, which contains stranger denizens than Oz. Mark is a stoner with a wide range of interesting friends, including a couple who live in a boat at the bottom of a stone quarry, and a high school classmate who's made millions with the invention of silent Velcro ("it doesn't make that noise when you pull it apart").

Andrew is awakening gradually from a long, sedated nothingness. He tries to communicate with his father, he tries to reconnect with his feelings, and mostly he tries to deal with the enormous puzzle that Sam represents. What is he to do about her? His romantic instincts have been on hold for so long he's like a kid with his first girlfriend.

Garden State inspires obvious comparisons with *The Graduate,* not least in the similarity of the two heroes; both Benjamin and Andrew are passive, puzzled, and quizzical in the face of incoming exhortations. The presence of Simon and Garfunkel on the sound track must not be entirely coincidental. But *The Graduate* is a critique of the world Benjamin finds himself in, and *Garden State* is the world's critique of Andrew. All of the people he meets are urging him, in one way or another, to wake up and smell the coffee. All except for his father, whose anger is so deep he prefers his son medicated into a kind of walking sleep. Ian Holm plays the role with perfect pitch, making small emotional adjustments instead of big dramatic moves.

This is not a perfect movie; it meanders and ambles and makes puzzling detours. But it's smart and unconventional, with a good eye for the perfect detail, as when Andrew arrives at work in Los Angeles and notices that the spigot from a gas pump, ripped from its hose when he drove away from a gas station, is still stuck in his gas tank. Something like that tells you a lot about a person's state of mind.

Garfield: A Tail of Two Kitties ★ ★ ★
PG, 80 m., 2006

Bill Murray (Garfield [voice]), Breckin Meyer (Jon Arbuckle), Jennifer Love Hewitt (Liz Wilson), Billy Connolly (Lord Dargis), Ian Abercrombie (Smithee), Roger Rees (Mr. Hobbs), Lucy Davis (Abby Westminster), Tim Curry (Prince [voice]), Greg Ellis (Nigel [voice]), Bob Hoskins (Winston [voice]), Richard E. Grant (Preston [voice]), Jane Horrocks (Meenie [voice]), Rhys Ifans (McBunny [voice]). Directed by Tim Hill and produced by John Davis. Screenplay by Joel Cohen and Alec Sokolow, based on the comic strip by Jim Davis.

I don't watch a lot of television, because if you spend all your time on the couch you could become the cat equivalent of a couch potato which would be one of those pillows with the crocheted message "If you can't say anything good about someone, sit right here with me." I have kneaded and nuzzled such pillows so many times I even know the author of the quotation: Alice Roosevelt Longworth, who on the basis of this pillow certainly must have been a cat lover.

But I confess I watched Ebert and Roeper on TV when they reviewed my first movie, Garfield (2004). I was eager to get my first review. Having spent years within the cramped panels of a newspaper comic strip, I gloried in the freedom of the cinema. It allowed me to show off my body language: My languorous stretches, my graceful pirouettes, my daring leaps and bounds, my shameless affection for my owner, Jon (Breckin Meyer).

There will be malcontents who will claim I am not the real author of this review, because how could a cat know that after you mention a character in a movie, you include the name of the actor in parentheses? Do these people believe a cat lives in a vacuum? I read all the movie reviews, especially those of Ebert, a graceful and witty prose stylist with profound erudition, whose reviews are worth reading just for themselves, whether or not I have any intention of viewing the movie. I need to read movie reviews because Jon watches DVDs all the time and likes to have me within petting distance, and I need advance warning about movies I will want to avoid, so I can slink off for a snooze under the sofa. Last night, for example, he watched Cat People—which, judging by the sound track, had no cats in it.

But I digress. Ebert, the smart and handsome one, gave thumbs up to my first movie, but Roeper, the other one, gave thumbs down and was particularly unkind. He went on forever, attacking Ebert for liking Garfield. This from a man with enough taste to praise Duma. How very disappointing. One of Roeper's complaints was that I was animated and all the other characters in the movie were "real." Do you have any idea how a statement like that hurts an actor who has worked all his life as a media cat? Yes, Richard Roeper, I was animated. Read my lips: I am a character in a comic strip. What Roeper should have done for perfect consistency is complain that Dennis was not animated in Dennis the Menace.

But forget his review of Garfield. No use mewling over spilled milk. This week my new movie comes out, inspired (I am happy to report) by the gratifying box office success of the previous one. Garfield: A Tail of Two Kitties is my most ambitious work to date, starring me in a dual role as (ahem) Garfield and as a British cat named Prince. As in the first movie, I do Bill Murray's voice while playing myself. In my role as Prince, I do the voice of Tim Curry, an actor I have admired ever since Jon took me to a drive-in to see Rocky Horror Picture Show while he smoked human catnip.

I physically perform both roles, which, as any cat knows, is easier for a cat than a human, because we are always playing multiple roles, such as looking gratefully toward humans while shooting daggers at dogs. I love the scene where they use visual effects to show both cats at the same time, in a kind of mirror scene inspired by the Marx Brothers.

Garfield: A Tail of Two Kitties, is actually funnier and more charming than the first film. The plot contrives to get me to England in the suitcase of my master, who has flown over to propose to his girlfriend, Liz (Jennifer Love Hewitt), who is attending a conference on animals at Castle Carlyle, which Prince has just inherited from Lady Eleanor, a cat lover. With intelligent estate planning, I'm sure we'd see a gratifying rise in the numbers of homeowning cats.

Anyway, Prince is dumped in the river by the unspeakably vile Lord Dargis (Billy Connolly), Lady Eleanor's nephew, who will inherit the castle when Prince dies. Prince is washed through the sewer systems into London, where he gets his first taste of pub life; meanwhile, I arrive at Castle Carlyle and am mistaken for Prince by the barnyard animals. These are all real animals, and good actors, too; they do the voices of such actors as Bob Hoskins, Richard E. Grant, Jane Horrocks, and Rhys Ifans.

That all of these animals can talk goes without saying. No doubt some carpers in the chat rooms will observe that Jon's other pet, a dog, does not speak but only barks. I could give you the name of Jon's dog, but (yawn) frankly I can't be bothered. In this movie, Jon's dog may not be able to speak, but he apparently can read, which was as much of a surprise to me as to everyone else. Dogs, in my experience, have hyperactivity disorders that prevent them from concentrating on reading, because they are compelled to leap up in a frenzy and bark at every moving object. Some dogs do this to frighten, but most do it as a pathetic attempt to draw attention to themselves.

In any event, my career as a movie star now seems to be the real thing, and I am speaking with my agents about a third Garfield movie, in which I would like my character to be based on Casanova or Neil Armstrong, with a score by Josie and the Pussycats. Whether I get a thumbs up from Richard Roeper is a matter of profound indifference to me. Profound. (Yawn) Really, seriously, pro . . .

Garfield: The Movie ★ ★ ★
PG, 85 m., 2004

Voice of Bill Murray (Garfield), Breckin Meyer (Jon Arbuckle), Jennifer Love Hewitt (Dr. Liz Wilson), Stephen Tobolowsky (Happy Chapman), Eve Brent (Mrs. Baker), Voice of Debra Messing (Arlene), Voice of David Eigenberg (Nermal), Voice of Brad Garrett (Luca), Voice of Alan Cumming (Persnikitty), Voice of Jimmy Kimmel (Spanky). Directed by Peter Hewitt and produced by John Davis. Screenplay by Joel Cohen and Alec Sokolow, based on the comic strip by Jim Davis.

Yep, this is Garfield, all right. *Garfield: The Movie* captures the elusive charm of the most egotistical character on the funny pages, and drops him into a story that allows him to bask in his character flaws. That Garfield is revealed to be brave and conscientious after all will not surprise anyone, although it might embarrass him.

I don't know who had the idea that Bill Murray would be the right actor to do Garfield's voice, but the casting is inspired. Murray's voice-over work finds the right balance for Garfield—between smugness and uncertainty, between affection and detachment, between jealousy and a grudging ability to see the other point of view.

In this case, the other POV belongs to Odie, a dog that is given to Jon (Breckin Meyer), Garfield's owner, by his sexy veterinarian, Dr. Liz (Jennifer Love Hewitt). Garfield is shocked and astonished to have to share pillow space with a dog, not to mention quality time with Jon ("You're not just my owner—you're my primary caregiver"). Being Garfield, he expresses his displeasure not with a humiliating public display, but by subtle subterfuge. He steers the dog outdoors, and, dogs being dogs, Odie chases a car and then another one, and gets lost, and is picked up by a little old lady who advertises him.

There's a parallel plot involving the talentless Happy Chapman (Stephen Tobolowsky), who hosts a TV show with a pet cat. He thinks maybe using a dog might bring him national exposure, tells the little old lady he is Odie's owner, and as a training strategy gives him electrical shocks from a cruel collar. Whether Garfield is able to break into and out of the pound, save Odie, expose Chapman, and reunite Jon with both the dog and Garfield's own noble presence, I will leave for you to discover.

The movie, based on the comic strip by Jim

Davis, has been directed by Peter Hewitt and written by Joel Cohen and Alec Sokolow. The filmmakers obviously understand and love Garfield, and their movie lacks that sense of smarmy slumming you sometimes get when Hollywood brings comic strips to the screen. Although Garfield claims "I don't do chases," the movie does have a big chase scene and other standard plot ingredients, but it understands that Garfield's personality, his behavior, his glorious self-absorption, are what we're really interested in. The Davis strip is not about a story but about an attitude.

If they hadn't gotten Garfield right, nothing else would have mattered. But they did. And they've also solved the perplexing problem of how to integrate a cartoon cat into a world of real humans and animals. Garfield talks all through the movie (this is one of Murray's most talkative roles), but only we can hear him; that's the equivalent of his thought bubbles in the strip. Garfield is animated, the other animals and the humans are real, and the movie does a convincing job of combining the two levels. Garfield looks like neither a cartoon nor a real cat, but like something in between—plump, squinty, and satisfied. Uncanny how when he talks his mouth looks like Murray's.

In a film mostly involved with plot, there are two scenes that are irrelevant but charming. In one of them, Garfield and Odie perform in sort of a music video, and in the other, at the end, Garfield has a solo, singing "I Feel Good" and dancing along. Oh, and Jon and Dr. Liz fall in love, although Garfield is no doubt confident he will remain the center of their attention.

George A. Romero's
Land of the Dead ★ ★ ★
R, 93 m., 2005

Simon Baker (Riley), John Leguizamo (Cholo), Asia Argento (Slack), Robert Joy (Charlie), Dennis Hopper (Kaufman), Eugene Clark (Big Daddy). Directed by George Romero and produced by Romero, Mark Canton, Bernie Goldmann, and Peter Grunwald. Screenplay by Romero.

In a world where the dead are returning to life, the word trouble has lost its meaning.
—Dennis Hopper in *Land of the Dead*

Now this is interesting. In the future world of *George A. Romero's Land of the Dead*, both zombies and their victims have started to evolve. The zombies don't simply shuffle around mindlessly, eating people. And the healthy humans don't simply shoot them. The zombies have learned to communicate on a rudimentary level, to make plans, however murky, and to learn from their tormenters. When the zombie named Big Daddy picks up a machine gun in this movie, that is an ominous sign.

The healthy humans, on the other hand, have evolved a class system. Those with money and clout live in Fiddler's Green, a luxury high-rise where all their needs are catered to under one roof—and just as well, because they are not eager to go outside. Other survivors cluster in the city at the foot of the tower, in a city barricaded against the zombie hordes outside. Mercenaries stage raids outside the safe zone in Dead Reckoning, a gigantic armored truck, and bring back canned food, gasoline, and booze.

The most intriguing single shot in *Land of the Dead* is a commercial for Fiddler's Green, showing tanned and smiling residents, dressed in elegant leisure wear, living the good life. They look like the white-haired eternally youthful golfers in ads for retirement paradises. The shot is intriguing for two reasons: (1) Why does Fiddler's Green need to advertise, when it is full and people are literally dying to get in? And (2) What is going through the minds of its residents as they relax in luxury, sip drinks, shop in designer stores, and live the good life? Don't they know the world outside is one of unremitting conflict and misery?

Well, yes, they probably do, and one of the reasons George A. Romero's zombie movies have remained fresh is that he suggests such questions. The residents of Fiddler's Green and the zombies have much the same relationship as citizens of rich nations have with starving orphans and refugees. The lesson is clear: It's good to live in Fiddler's Green.

That's why Cholo (John Leguizamo) wants to move in. He's one of the best mercenaries in the hire of Kaufman (Dennis Hopper), who is the Donald Trump of Fiddler's Green. Kaufman sits in his penthouse, smokes good cigars, sips brandy, and gets rich, although the movie never explains how money works in this economy, where possessions are acquired by looting and retained by force. How, for that matter, do the residents of Fiddler's Green earn a living? Do they spend all day in their casual wear, flashing those white teeth as they perch on the arms of each other's lounge chairs? The thing that bothers me about ads for retirement communities is that the residents seem condemned to leisure.

Cholo works under Riley (Simon Baker), the leader of Kaufman's hired force and the movie's hero. Riley is responsible, calm, and sane. Cholo is not, and Leguizamo plays another one of his off-the-wall loose cannons. He has added an unreasonable amount of interest to any number of recent movies. Also important to the plot is Slack (Asia Argento), a sometime hooker who is beautiful and heroic and intended for better things, and is thrown into a pit of zombies to fend for herself. For that matter, zombies themselves are occasionally hung by the heels with bull's-eyes painted on them for target practice. And Romero finds still new and entertaining ways for unspeakably disgusting things to happen to the zombies and their victims.

The balance of power in this ordered little world is upset when Kaufman refuses Cholo's request to move into Fiddler's Green. There is a long waiting list, etc. Cholo steals Dead Reckoning, he is pursued, the zombies get (somewhat) organized, and Big Daddy (Eugene Clark) begins to develop a gleam of intelligence in his dead blue eyes.

The puzzle in all the zombie movies is why any zombies are still—I was about to write "alive," but I guess the word is "moving." Shooting them in the head or decapitating them seems simple enough, and dozens are mowed down with machine guns by the troops in Dead Reckoning. Guards at the city barriers kill countless more. Since they are obviously zombies and no diagnosis is necessary before execution on sight, why do they seem to be winning?

This and other questions may await Romero's next movie. It's good to see him back in the genre he invented with *Night of the Living Dead*, and still using zombies not simply for target practice but as a device for social satire. It's probably not practical from a box office point of view, but I would love to see a movie set entirely inside a thriving Fiddler's Green. There would be zombies outside but we'd never see them or deal with them. We would simply regard the Good Life as it is lived by those who have walled the zombies out. Do they relax? Have they peace of mind? Do the miseries of others weigh upon them? The parallels with the real world are tantalizing.

Get Rich or Die Tryin' ★ ★ ★
R, 134 m., 2005

Curtis "50 Cent" Jackson (Marcus), Terrence Howard (Bama), Joy Bryant (Charlene), Bill Duke (Levar), Adewale Akinnuoye-Agbaje (Majestic), Omar Benson Miller (Keryl), Tory Kittles (Justice), Ashley Walters (Antwan), Viola Davis (Grandma). Directed by Jim Sheridan and produced by Dr. Dre, Jimmy Iovine, Chris Lighty, Paul Rosenberg, and Sheridan. Screenplay by Terence Winter.

Get Rich or Die Tryin' offers a limited range of choices, but we'll probably never see a film titled *Get By and Don't Die*. The film is inspired by the haunting life story of Curtis "50 Cent" Jackson, who never knew his father, whose mother was a drug dealer killed when he was young, who sold drugs on the streets of New York City, and survived gunshot wounds to become one of the best-selling recording artists of modern times. It has been an amazing life, and he is only thirty.

Of course, the odds against a young drug dealer eventually selling 4 million copies of an album are so high that by comparison, getting into the NBA is a sure thing. A more accurate title might have been, *I Got Rich but Just About Everybody Else Died Tryin', and So Did I, Almost*. Given the harrowing conditions of his early life, Jackson's movie dwells on it with a strange affection; the movie is closer in tone to *Scarface* than to *Hustle and Flow*, the year's other rags-to-riches rap story.

Billboards for the movie have been protested by citizens' groups—not do-gooders or killjoys but people who have seen the bodies on the streets and attended the funerals and seen drugs taking a deadly tax on young manhood. *Hustle and Flow* is about a man (Terrence Howard) who wants to escape the drug world and become a musical artist. *Get Rich* is about a man who hangs on in the drug world as long as possible and becomes a musician because he is talented and very lucky. There is a difference between these two life strategies.

Still, I must review the movie, not offer counseling to Curtis Jackson. *Get Rich* is a film with a rich and convincing texture, a drama with power and anger. It shows its young hero taken in by grandparents who love him (Viola Davis and Sullivan Walker) after the death of his mother, and then being lured by the streets because, quite simply, he wants money for athletic shoes and, eventually, a car. There seem to be few other avenues of employment open to him, certainly none that he seeks, and although his mother tried to shield him from her business, he saw what happened and how it worked and he knows who the players are.

Early scenes in his career involve turf wars. The question of who stands on what corner to sell drugs is sometimes settled by death. Meanwhile, the customers, a great many of them whites from the suburbs, roll up in their cars and subsidize these deaths, one purchase at a time. Although the movies have accustomed us to associate drug dealers with briefcases filled with cash, the movie provides a more realistic job description: "All you get out there is long lonely nights." And "If you would add up all the time spent standing around, it was minimum wage. If you added prison time, it was below minimum wage." The lie in the movie's title is that you get rich. Someone gets rich, yes, but then someone wins the lottery every week.

The best thing that happens to Jackson is that he is sent to prison. This probably saves his life, and it's there that he's approached by Bama (Terrence Howard again), a guy he already knows from the neighborhood, who tells him, "You need a manager." This before he has a career. Jackson has always sung along with rap recordings, has started writing his own lyrics, and observes in the narration, "After Tupac, everybody wanted to be a gangster rapper." He has the timing a little off, though. It wasn't "after Tupac," but "after Tupac's death." I remember Tupac Shakur in *Gridlock'd* (1997), where opposite Tim Roth he showed that he was a gifted actor. Now he is dead. *Tupac Resurrection* (2003), the quasi-documentary based on his life and narrated by his own words, makes an instructive parallel to this film.

Jackson is a good actor, at least in this film, playing himself. The same can be said of Eminem after *8 Mile*. Whether he makes a career

of acting is his choice. Joy Bryant is crucial in the film as Charlene, whom he has known since they were young, who loves him, who despairs of the danger he is in. There are smaller but significant roles for actors such as Bill Duke, playing a drug wholesaler who tries to run an orderly business but has too much turnover in the deadly front lines.

In an opening scene of the film, Jackson is shot and left to die. This scene might as well come early, since everyone in the audience will know this happened to the real 50 Cent. "I was about to die," he says in the narration. "I don't know why I was expecting my father to rescue me, been looking for him all my life." This theme, the search for the father, may have been one reason Jim Sheridan, an Irishman in his fifties, seemed like a good director for this assignment. He knows about fathers and prisons (see his *In the Name of the Father*) and he knows about poverty in New York (see his *In America*). Many of his visuals are brilliant; look at the way the bass on an automobile's sound system makes images in the rear-view mirrors vibrate. Sheridan has made a well-crafted film, but it contains more drugs and less music than many people will expect. I guess people don't attend movies about gangster rap looking for career guidance and inspiration, but *Hustle and Flow* has a lot more of each, and more music, too.

Gilles' Wife ★ ★ ★
NO MPAA RATING, 103 m., 2005

Emmanuelle Devos (Elisa), Clovis Cornillac (Gilles), Laura Smet (Victorine), Alice and Chloe Verlinden (Twins), Colette Emmanuelle (Elisa's Mother), Gil Lagay (Elisa's Father). Directed by Frederic Fonteyne and produced by Patrick Quinet and Claude Waringo. Screenplay by Philippe Blasband and Fonteyne, based on the novel by Madeleine Bourdouxhe.

Let us assume you are a wife deeply contented with your husband, your children, your home, and your marriage. You discover that your husband is having an affair. You know the woman well enough to feel betrayed by her as well as by him. Also well enough to know this affair cannot endure. Do you explode with fury, throw out your husband, and end the marriage? Or do you wait out the affair? Do you offer emotional support to your husband, who you know is torn to pieces by what has happened to him?

You require more detail. I will provide it. This story takes place in a small French town in the 1930s. Your husband works in the factory, marches home every evening down the hill, helps tend your kitchen garden. You are pregnant with your third child. You are beautiful in the way that makes a man want to nuzzle you and be comforted, but not with a beauty that attracts attention. The other woman is glamorous, at least by the provincial standards of the village. Certainly the most glamorous woman who ever looked seriously at him. She is your sister.

Now what do you do? You do not have a job, except the unending one of being a wife and mother. You wash, iron, teach, scold, cook, serve, clean up, mend, tend, treat, cure, bake, garden, repair, and turn warmly to your man in bed at night. You know him well enough to understand how the stupid goof would be powerless against a woman like *that* woman. You wish he were stronger, wiser, and more discerning, but he is not. He barely understands that his "lover" uses him only to supply sex and sneak away because she would not be able to stand him underfoot all day, and he would have nothing to talk to her about. He barely has anything to talk to you about. He barely has speech. John Prine wrote a song that could describe him:

"How the hell can a man
"Go off in the morning,
"Come back in the evening,
"And have nothing to say?"

Now you know what you need to know about *Gilles' Wife*, the movie by Frederic Fonteyne, based on the novel by Madeleine Bourdouxhe— all except that I have not provided you with the subject of the film, which is the face of the actress Emmanuelle Devos. Of the face of her husband (Clovis Cornillac) and her sister, Victorine (Laura Smet), I need say little. He has the face of a man waiting in line for something more interesting men do not desire. She has the face of the trophy girl of a man who cannot afford a better trophy.

The film unfolds with little dialogue. On one level it could be a Bresson film of suffering and renunciation. A slightly different angle and it could be a story by Simenon, in which people have locked themselves into intolerable

situations, thrown away the key, and now spend their days looking through their prison bars at the key, still there but just out of reach. It is a story not of passion (its passion is pathetic) but of patience.

Or perhaps it is the story of a woman who in another life would have been a social scientist but in this life is limited to one experiment, in which she tests her theory on her husband. Her theory is that no man can stand Victorine for long. Why should she lose husband, home, family, security, respectability, even the warmth they truly share, just because he wants to dart out at night and fool himself that he is a daring lover? From what we see of his sex life, he is like a motorcyclist who roars up a tricky ramp in order to leap a tiny chasm.

I do not approve of the way the movie ends, and I think Fonteyne's elaborate camera move right before the end is just showing off and is not a word in the visual language he was using. It would have taken more courage and thought for the movie to have ended as it began. But I was fascinated by the face of Devos, and her face is specifically why I recommend the movie. There are some people who keep their thoughts to themselves because they don't have a one to spare. Others who are filled with thoughts but keep them as companions. Devos, as Gilles' wife, is in the second category. She is too clever by half. What such people don't realize is that being too clever by half is only being too clever by half enough.

The Girl Next Door ½ ★

R, 110 m., 2004

Emile Hirsch (Matthew Kidman), Elisha Cuthbert (Danielle), Timothy Olyphant (Kelly), James Remar (Hugo Posh), Chris Marquette (Eli), Paul Dano (Klitz). Directed by Luke Greenfield and produced by Harry Gittes, Charles Gordon, and Marc Sternberg. Screenplay by Stuart Blumberg, David Wagner, and Brent Goldberg.

The studio should be ashamed of itself for advertising *The Girl Next Door* as a teenage comedy. It's a nasty piece of business, involving a romance between a teenage porn actress and a high school senior. A good movie could presumably be made from this premise—a good movie can be made from anything, in the right hands and way—but this is a dishonest, quease-inducing "comedy" that had me feeling uneasy and then unclean. Who in the world read this script and thought it was acceptable?

The film stars Emile Hirsch as Matthew Kidman. (Please tell me the "Kidman" is not an oblique reference to Nicole Kidman and therefore to Tom Cruise and therefore to *Risky Business,* the film this one so desperately wants to resemble.) One day he sees a sexy girl moving in next door, and soon he's watching through his bedroom window as she undresses as girls undress only in his dreams. Then she sees him, snaps off the light, and a few minutes later rings the doorbell.

Has she come to complain? No, she says nothing about the incident and introduces herself to Matthew's parents: Her aunt is on vacation, and she is house-sitting. Soon they're in her car together and Danielle is coming on to Matthew: "Did you like what you saw?" He did. She says now it's her turn to see him naked, and makes him strip and stand in the middle of the road while she shines the headlights on him. Then she scoops up his underpants and drives away, leaving him to walk home naked, ho, ho. (It is not easy to reach out of a car and scoop up underpants from the pavement while continuing to drive. Try it sometime.)

Danielle (Elisha Cuthbert) has two personalities: In one, she's a sweet, misunderstood kid who has never been loved, and in the other she's a twisted emotional sadist who amuses herself by toying with the feelings of the naive Matthew. The movie alternates between these personalities at its convenience, making her quite the most unpleasant character I have seen in some time.

They have a romance going before one of Matthew's buddies identifies her, correctly, as a porn star. The movie seems to think, along with Matthew's friends, that this information is in her favor. Matthew goes through the standard formula: first he's angry with her, then she gets through his defenses, then he believes she really loves him and that she wants to leave the life she's been leading. Problem is, her producer is angry because he wants her to keep working. This character, named Kelly, is played by Timothy Olyphant with a skill that would have distinguished a better movie, but it doesn't work here,

because the movie never levels with us. When a guy his age (thirty-six, according to IMDB) "used to be the boyfriend" of a girl her age (nineteen, according to the plot description) and she is already, at nineteen, a famous porn star, there is a good chance the creep corrupted her at an early age; think Traci Lords. That he is now her "producer" under an "exclusive contract" is an elevated form of pimping. To act in porn as a teenager is not a decision freely taken by many teenage girls, and not a life to envy.

There's worse. The movie produces a basically nice guy, named Hugo Posh (James Remar), also a porn king, who is Kelly's rival. That a porn king saves the day gives you an idea of the movie's limited moral horizons. Oh, and not to forget Matthew's best friends, named Eli and Klitz (Chris Marquette and Paul Dano). Klitz? "Spelled with a *K,*" he explains.

Kelly steals the money that Matthew has raised to bring a foreign exchange student from Cambodia, and to replace the funds, the resourceful Danielle flies in two porn star friends (played by Amanda Swisten and Sung Hi Lee), so that Matthew, Eli, and Klitz can produce a sex film during the senior prom. The nature of their film is yet another bait-and-switch, in a movie that wants to seem dirtier than it is. Like a strip show at a carnival, it lures you in with promises of sleaze, and after you have committed yourself for the filthy-minded punter you are, it professes innocence.

Risky Business (1983), you will recall, starred Tom Cruise as a young man left home alone by his parents, who wrecks the family Porsche and ends up enlisting a call girl (Rebecca De Mornay) to run a brothel out of his house to raise money to replace the car. The movie is the obvious model for *The Girl Next Door,* but it completely misses the tone and wit of the earlier film, which proved you can get away with that plot, but you have to know what you're doing and how to do it, two pieces of knowledge conspicuously absent here.

One necessary element is to distance the heroine from the seamier side of her life. *The Girl Next Door* does the opposite, actually taking Danielle and her "producer" Kelly to an adult film convention in Las Vegas, and even into a dimly lit room where adult stars apparently pleasure the clients. (There is another scene where Kelly, pretending to be Matthew's friend, takes him to a lap dance emporium and treats him.) We can deal with porn stars, lap dances, and whatever else in a movie that declares itself and plays fair, but to insert this material into something with the look and feel of a teen comedy makes it unsettling. The TV ads will attract audiences expecting something like *American Pie*; they'll be shocked by the squalid content of this film.

Glory Road ★ ★ ★
PG, 106 m., 2006

Josh Lucas (Coach Don Haskins), Derek Luke (Bobby Joe Hill), Damaine Radcliff (Willie "Scoops" Cager), Jon Voight (Coach Adolph Rupp). Directed by James Gartner and produced by Jerry Bruckheimer. Screenplay by Christopher Cleveland, Bettina Gilois, and Gregory Allen Howard.

Glory Road is like other sports movies, and different from all of them. It is the same in the way it shows a rookie coach with an underdog team; he finds resistance from his players at first, he imposes his system and is a merciless taskmaster, and do I have to ask you if they win the big game? This has been the formula for countless films, and *Glory Road* will not be the last.

But the movie is not really about underdogs and winning the big game. It's about racism in American sports and how Coach Don Haskins and his players on the 1965–66 basketball team from Texas Western University made a breakthrough comparable to that moment when Jackie Robinson was hired by the Brooklyn Dodgers. In Texas at that time, we learn, college basketball teams had been integrated, but there was an "informal rule" that you never played more than one black player at home, two on the road, or three if you were behind.

After Texas Western won the 1966 NCAA championship with an all-black team, defeating an all-white Kentucky team coached by the legendary Adolph Rupp, the rules were rewritten, and modern college and professional basketball began. Haskins and his team wrote the "emancipation proclamation of 1966," says Coach Pat Riley in an interview during the end credits. He starred on the defeated Kentucky team.

Glory Road tells its story not through personalities but in terms of the issues involved. It uses the basketball season as a backdrop to the story of how Haskins (Josh Lucas) inherited a weak, losing team at Texas Western and set out to recruit gifted black players from the schools and playgrounds of the North. The school's administration and some of the rich boosters were not very happy with him, until the team started to win. Strange how that works, isn't it?

An opening scene is brief but poignant: After Haskins coaches a girls' basketball team to victory, his players try to lift him up on their shoulders, but they aren't strong enough. Haskins is offered the head coaching position at Texas Western and jumps at it: This is his chance to coach a Division I team, no matter how weak. Haskins knows he has no chance of recruiting the best white players to come to Texas Western, so he and his assistant coach head north and find African-Americans who are happy to have scholarships and a chance to play. Chief among them are Bobby Joe Hill (Derek Luke) and Willie "Scoops" Cager (Damaine Radcliff).

They play a hotshot, Globetrotters-style basketball; Haskins thinks it is undisciplined and risky, and he drills them with his own man-on-man system. There are the predictable clashes between coach and players, but the movie doesn't linger on them. Instead, it shows Texas Western going on the road with a mostly black team in a South where the teams were mostly white. One player is beaten in a restroom. The team's motel rooms are trashed in east Texas. The white players begin to bond with their teammates who are the targets of such attacks. And then, when everything depends on the Big Game, Haskins announces that he plans to play only black athletes. He wants to make a point. By this time, the white players understand the point and agree with it.

Jon Voight plays Kentucky's Rupp, one of the most successful coaches in college history. Voight doesn't have a lot of screen time, but he uses it to create a character, not a stereotype. On the sidelines, we watch his face as he begins to realize what's happening. "This is a special team," he warns his players during a time-out. He is trying to tell them that ordinary sideline talks are irrelevant; if they cannot rise to this historic moment, they will lose.

Director James Gartner tells his story forcefully and makes a wise decision during the end titles to show black-and-white footage of many of the real people whose lives are depicted in the film. One of his decisions about the sound track is strange but perhaps effective: The play-by-play announcers somehow simultaneously seem to be the game announcers, so that loudspeakers in the gyms carry their commentary and opinions. That works for us, but how would it work with players and fans in real life?

Glory Road is an effective sports movie, yes, but as the portrait of a coach and team and the realities of administrations and booster clubs in a state obsessed with sports, it's a shadow of *Friday Night Lights* (2004). Where it succeeds is as the story of a chapter in history, the story of how one coach at one school arrived at an obvious conclusion and acted on it, and helped open up college sports in the South to generations of African-Americans. As the end credits tell us what happened in later life to the members of that 1966 Texas Western team, we realize that Haskins not only won an NCAA title but also made a contribution to the future that is still being realized.　　　　　☞

Goal! The Dream Begins ★ ★ ★
PG, 117 m., 2006

Kuno Becker (Santiago Munez), Stephen Dillane (Glen Foy), Alessandro Nivola (Gavin Harris), Anna Friel (Roz Harmison), Tony Plana (Herman Munez), Sean Pertwee (Barry Rankin), Kiernan O'Brien (Hughie Magowen), Cassandra Bell (Christina), Marcel Iures (Erik Dornhelm), Miriam Colon (Mercedes). Directed by Danny Cannon and produced by Mark Huffam, Matt Barrelle, and Mike Jefferies. Screenplay by Dick Clement and Ian La Frenais.

Goal! The Dream Begins is a rags-to-riches sports saga containing all the usual elements, arranged in the usual ways, and yet it's surprisingly effective. We have the kid from Mexico who dreams of soccer stardom, his impoverished life in Los Angeles as an undocumented immigrant, his dad who scorns soccer, his grandmother who believes in him, the scout who gets him a tryout with a top British team, the superstar who befriends him, and even a pretty nurse. There is also a great deal of soccer, some of it looking real, some of it not.

The movie works because it is, above all, sin-cere. It's not sports by the numbers. The starring performance by Kuno Becker is convincing and dimensional, and we begin to care for him. He plays Santiago Munez, a busboy in an L.A. Chinese restaurant, who plays in an after-work soccer league so deprived that he wears cardboard shin protectors. Then he's spotted by a former soccer pro (Stephen Dillane), who tells him he has potential and arranges for him to get a tryout with Newcastle United.

That would, however, involve an air ticket to England. Santiago has some money saved, but his dad (Tony Plana) nicks it to buy a pickup truck and start his own landscaping business. This is cruel, but perhaps more practical than betting the money on a future in soccer. Santiago's grandmother (Miriam Colon) says she hasn't worked for a lifetime without having some savings, and pays for him to fly to London out of Mexico City—a wise precaution, since he has no American passport or identity.

In Newcastle, Santiago undergoes a rough initiation at the hands of the hardened soccer pros, gets his first experience of soccer in the mud, and almost loses his place on the team because of his asthma. What saves him is an accidental friendship with the team's superstar, Gavin Harris (Alessandro Nivola), a party animal. How the season turns out and how Santiago fares I will leave for you to discover, not only in this movie, but in *Goal! 2: Living the Dream*, which comes out in late 2006, and in *Goal! 3*, scheduled for 2007. The fact that *Goal! 4* is not in preproduction soon will, I am sure, be remedied.

Before *Goal!* began, I moaned to a colleague that I was dreading the screening. Any movie named *Goal!* that needs an exclamation mark seems to be protesting too much, and the words *The Dream Begins* suggest that the snores will follow shortly. I see an average of one sports movie a month in which an underdog (or underhorse or undergymnast) overcomes the odds to earn an exclamation mark. I know all about the grizzled coaches, the mean teammates, the dad who doesn't understand, and the girl who does.

I was surprised, then, to find myself enjoying the movie almost from the beginning. It had some of the human reality of Gregory Nava's work in movies such as *Mi Familia* and the PBS series *American Family*. Not the depth or beauty, to be sure, but the feeling for a culture and family ties. And Becker, a Mexican star of films and

TV and three English-language films little released in America, has not only star quality but also something more rare: likability. He makes us want his character to succeed.

Where possible, director Danny Cannon sidesteps some (not all) of the clichés. We suspect Santiago's father may be proud of his son after all but are unprepared for the way that plays out, and how Santiago's toughness is both the right and wrong choice. We know all about the understanding Irish nurse Roz (Anna Friel), except that she will have insight and understanding. We are relieved, in a way, to be spared an obligatory sex scene. And it is interesting that the boss of the Newcastle United team is not made into your standard Bob Hoskins or Colm Meany role but is written as a German and cast with a Romanian, Marcel Iures.

Goal! The Dream Begins is not a great sports film, and I can easily contain my impatience for *Goal! 2* and *Goal! 3* (which should, but will not, be titled *Goal! 3: The Dreamer Awakes*). But it is good and caring work, with more human detail than we expect. Specifically, it is more about Santiago's life as a young man than it is about who wins the big match. There's a subtext about immigrants in America that is timely right now, and a certain sadness in his father's conviction that some people are intended to be rich and others poor, and that the Munez family should be content and grateful to be poor. Santiago is not content, but he is driven not so much by ambition as by pure and absolute love of soccer, and that gives the movie a purity that shines through.

Godsend ★ ★
PG-13, 102 m., 2004

Greg Kinnear (Paul Duncan), Rebecca Romijn-Stamos (Jessie Duncan), Robert De Niro (Dr. Richard Wells), Cameron Bright (Adam Duncan). Directed by Nick Hamm and produced by Marc Butan, Sean O'Keefe, and Cathy Schulman. Screenplay by Mark Bomback.

Godsend tells the story of parents whose only son is killed in an accident, and who are offered the opportunity to clone him. If all goes well, the grieving mother will bear a child genetically identical to the dead boy. I would find that unspeakably sad, but the movie isn't interested in really considering the implications; it's a thriller, a bad thriller, completely lacking in psychological or emotional truth.

Greg Kinnear and Rebecca Romijn-Stamos star, as Paul and Jessie Duncan; he's an inner-city high school teacher, and she's a photographer. Immediately after their son, Adam, is killed, they're approached by Dr. Richard Wells (Robert De Niro), who offers them an illegal opportunity to retrieve one of Adam's cells and implant it in Jessie's womb so that she can bear another Adam. At first they resist, but then they agree, and soon they have another son named Adam. Both boys are played by Cameron Bright.

Dr. Wells, who made millions earlier in his career, operates out of a vast medical laboratory in Vermont, and persuades the Duncans to move up there; they must cut all ties with former friends and family, he explains, because of course the Adam clone will raise difficult questions. To help them settle in, he provides a waterfront house that will have every real-estate agent in the audience thinking in the millions. Adam Two is born (in a particularly unconvincing live childbirth scene) and quickly reaches the same birthday that Adam One celebrated just before he was killed. Until then he has been an ideal child, but now he begins to get weird. "Dad," he tells his father, "I've been thinking. I don't think I like you so much any more." As Kinnear recoils in pain, the kid grins and says he was only kidding. Ho, ho. "There was always the possibility," Dr. Wells intones, "that things could change once he passed the age when he died."

I dare not reveal the secret around which the plot revolves, but I can say that Adam Two has visions and night terrors, and in them sees a little boy whose experiences seem to intersect with his own. At school, Adam Two is not popular, perhaps because he spits on playmates and a teacher, perhaps because he is just plain weird; the movie *Omenizes* him with big close-ups, his face pinched and ominous. At home, he has a habit of hanging around in the woodshed with sharp instruments or invading his mother's darkroom, where a lot of photos of Adam One are kept in a box that really should have been locked.

The movie's premise is fascinating, and has

stirred up a lot of interest. Some opponents of cloning reportedly confused its Web site (godsendinstitute.org) for the real thing, although that "confusion" has the aroma of a publicity stunt. No matter; *Godsend* isn't about cloning so much as about shock, horror, evil, deception, and the peculiar appeal that demonic children seem to possess for movie audiences.

The performances are ineffective. I would say they are bad, but I suppose they're as good as the material permits. Kinnear and Romijn-Stamos are required to play a couple whose entire relationship is formed and defined by plot gimmicks, and as for De Niro, there are times when he seems positively embarrassed to be seen as that character, saying those things. His final conversation with Kinnear must be the most absurd scene he has ever been asked to play seriously. The movie is so impossible that even the child actor is left stranded. He seems lovable as Adam One, but as Adam Two he seems to have been programmed, not by genetics, but by sub-"Omen" potboilers.

For a brief time, however, I thought director Nick Hamm was using at least one original strategy. During certain tense scenes, I heard a low, ominous, scraping noise, and I thought it was some kind of audible flash-forward to terrors still to come. Then I realized I was hearing carpenters at work on the floor below the screening room. I recommend they be added to an optional sound track on the DVD.

Note: That's going to be one crowded DVD. My fellow critic Joe Leydon points me to a story at sci-fifx.com reporting that director Hamm shot at least seven alternate endings to the movie, including those in which two different characters are killed two different ways, and little Adam kills everybody. Nothing like covering your bases.

Godzilla ★ ½

NO MPAA RATING, 98 m., 2004

Takashi Shimura (Dr. Kyohei Yamane), Momoko Kochi (Emiko Yamane), Akira Takarada (Hideto Ogata), Akihiko Hirata (Dr. Serizawa), Sachio Sakai (Reporter Hagiwara), Fuyuki Murakami (Dr. Tabata), Toranosuke Ogawa (CEO of Shipping Company), Ren Yamamoto (Masaji). The fiftieth-anniversary release of a film directed by Ishiro Honda and produced by Tomoyuki Tanaka. Screenplay by Takeo Murata and Honda, based on the original story by Shigeru Kayama.

Regaled for fifty years by the stupendous idiocy of the American version of *Godzilla*, audiences can now see the original 1954 Japanese version, which is equally idiotic, but, properly decoded, was the *Fahrenheit 9/11* of its time. Both films come after fearsome attacks on their nations, embody urgent warnings, and even incorporate similar dialogue, such as, "The report is of such dire importance it must not be made public." Is that from 1954 Tokyo or 2004 Washington?

The first *Godzilla* set box-office records in Japan and inspired countless sequels, remakes, and rip-offs. It was made shortly after an American H-bomb test in the Pacific contaminated a large area of ocean and gave radiation sickness to a boatload of Japanese fishermen. It refers repeatedly to Nagasaki, H-bombs, and civilian casualties, and obviously embodies Japanese fears about American nuclear tests.

But that is not the movie you have seen. For one thing, it doesn't star Raymond Burr as Steve Martin, intrepid American journalist, who helpfully explains, "I was headed for an assignment in Cairo when I dropped off for a social call in Tokyo." The American producer Joseph E. Levine bought the Japanese film, cut it by forty minutes, removed all of the political content, and awkwardly inserted Burr into scenes where he clearly did not fit. The hapless actor gives us reaction shots where he's looking in the wrong direction, listens to Japanese actors dubbed into the American idiom (they always call him "Steve Martin" or even "the famous Steve Martin"), and provides a reassuring conclusion in which Godzilla is seen as some kind of public health problem, or maybe just a malcontent.

The Japanese version, now in general U.S. release to mark the film's fiftieth anniversary, is a bad film, but with an undeniable urgency. I learn from helpful notes by Mike Flores of the Psychotronic Film Society that the opening scenes, showing fishing boats disappearing as the sea boils up, would have been read by Japanese audiences as a coded version of U.S. underwater H-bomb tests. Much is made of a scientist named Dr. Serizawa (Akihiko Hirata), who could destroy Godzilla with his secret weapon, the Oxygen Destroyer, but hesitates because he is afraid the weapon might fall into the wrong hands, just as H-bombs might, and have. The film's ending warns that atomic tests may lead to more Godzillas. All cut from the U.S. version.

In these days of flawless special effects, Godzilla and the city he destroys are equally crude. Godzilla at times looks uncannily like a man in a lizard suit, stomping on cardboard sets, as indeed he was, and did. Other scenes show him as a stiff, awkward animatronic model. This was not state-of-the-art even at the time; *King Kong* (1933) was much more convincing.

When Dr. Serizawa demonstrates the Oxygen Destroyer to the fiancée of his son, the super-weapon is somewhat anticlimactic. He drops a pill into a tank of tropical fish, the tank lights up, he shouts "Stand back!" The fiancée screams, and the fish go belly-up. Yeah, that'll stop Godzilla in his tracks.

Reporters covering Godzilla's advance are rarely seen in the same shot with the monster. Instead, they look offscreen with horror; a TV reporter, broadcasting for some reason from his station's tower, sees Godzilla looming nearby and signs off, "Sayonara, everyone!" Meanwhile, searchlights sweep the sky, in case Godzilla learns to fly.

The movie's original Japanese dialogue, subtitled, is as harebrained as Burr's dubbed lines. When the Japanese Parliament meets (in what looks like a high school home room), the dialogue is portentous but circular:

"The professor raises an interesting question! We need scientific research!"

"Yes, but at what cost?"

"Yes, that's the question!"

Is there a reason to see the original *Godzilla*? Not because of its artistic stature, but perhaps because of the feeling we can sense in its parable about the monstrous threats unleashed by the atomic age. There are shots of Godzilla's victims in hospitals, and they reminded me of documentaries of Japanese A-bomb victims. The incompetence of scientists, politicians, and the military will ring a bell. This is a bad movie, but it has earned its place in history, and the enduring popularity of Godzilla and other monsters shows that it struck a chord. Can it be a coincidence, in these years of trauma after 9/11, that in a 2005 remake, King Kong will march once again on New York?

Going Upriver: The Long War of John Kerry ★ ★ ★
PG-13, 89 m., 2004

Directed by George Butler and produced by Butler and Mark Hopkins. Screenplay by Joseph Dorman, based on the book *Tour of Duty* by Douglas Brinkley.

Of all the dirty tricks in the unhappy 2004 presidential campaign, the most outrageous was the ad campaign by the Swift Boat Veterans for Truth, attempting to discredit John Kerry's service in Vietnam. Supporters of the malingering Bush shamelessly challenged the war record of a wounded and decorated veteran. Their campaign illustrated the tactic of the Big Lie, as defined by Hitler and perfected by Goebbels: Although a little lie is laughed at, a Big Lie somehow takes on a reality of its own through its sheer effrontery.

Going Upriver: The Long War of John Kerry is a matter-of-fact documentary that describes Kerry's war service and his later role as a leader of the Vietnam Veterans Against the War. It's not an in-your-face Michael Moore–style doc, but an attempt to rationally respond to the damaging TV ads. The most remarkable connection it makes is that John O'Neill, mastermind of the Swift Boat Veterans for Truth and coauthor of the current book *Unfit for Command,* was originally recruited by the dirty tricksters in the Nixon White House to play precisely the same role!

The movie documents this with tapes of Oval Office conversations showing Richard Nixon discussing John Kerry with his aides H. R. Haldeman and Charles Colson. Kerry had made a strong impression as a spokesman for Vietnam vets who now felt the war was immoral and ill-advised. Senator J. William Fulbright, head of the Senate Foreign Relations Committee, visited the veterans' bivouac on the Mall and asked Kerry to testify before the committee. Kerry's testimony, sampled in the film, is forceful and yet not radical; essentially he was early with what has become the consensus about that war.

In the Oval Office, it is noted that Kerry made a good impression, especially on the network news programs. "He's a Kennedy-type guy. He looks like a Kennedy and sounds like a Kennedy," says Haldeman. "We have to destroy the young demagogue before he becomes another Nader," Colson tells the president. Asked to get some dirt on Kerry, Colson reports, "We couldn't find anything on him." Then he comes up with the idea of recruiting Vietnam vets who would be coached to smear Kerry. Colson enlists O'Neill, who thirty years later has revived his old role.

The film argues that Kerry has truthfully described his role in the war. This is testified to by those in the boat with him, those on the same river at the time, and a man whose life he saved. What's interesting is to learn more about the Swift Boats themselves. Since the Viet Cong blended with the civilian population, anybody could be the enemy, and the Swift Boats were sent upriver in the hopes they would be fired on by Cong troops who would therefore reveal their positions.

Patrols like those led by Kerry had casualty rates above 75 percent; no wonder he was wounded. Yet some of his opponents have questioned if Kerry actually shed blood in Vietnam. Since Kerry carries shrapnel in his leg, it must have been a neat trick to get it in there without puncturing the skin. A case for the Amazing Randi.

Going Upriver has been directed by George Butler, a longtime Kerry friend who is a veteran documentarian (he made *Pumping Iron* about young Arnold Schwarzenegger, and *Endurance,* the documentary about Ernest Shackleton's expedition to the Antarctic). His film is pro-Kerry, yes, but the focus is on history, not polemics, and provides a record of the crucial role of the Vietnam Veterans Against the War, who because of their credentials could not be dismissed as peaceniks. Kerry comes across even then not as a hotheaded young radical, but as a centered, thoughtful man whose appearance before the Foreign Relations Committee draws respectful reviews even from its Republican members.

The Nixon instinct to smear him finds an echo today in the "Veterans for Truth" ads. It is Kerry's great misfortune that Dan Rather and CBS News deflected attention from Bush's inexplicable (or at least unexplained) absence from guard duty. If the polls can be believed, many American voters are inattentive, credulous, and unable to think critically about political claims. The Swift Boat ads reportedly lost votes for Kerry, but the Rather debacle gained votes for Bush; some voters apparently believed that if Rather was wrong, then somehow Bush's military irregularities have been vindicated.

Did this film change any votes? Doubtful, since most members of the audience were Kerry supporters. It is sad but true that a thirty-second commercial, which any literate person should instinctively question, can shift votes, but the truth cannot. Not that the Swift Boat Veterans for Truth know much about truth.

Good Bye, Lenin! ★ ★ ★

R, 121 m., 2004

Katrin Sass (Christiane Kerner), Daniel Bruhl (Alex Kerner), Maria Simon (Ariane Kerner), Chulpan Khamatova (Lara), Florian Lukas (Denis). Directed by Wolfgang Becker and produced by Stefan Arndt. Screenplay by Bernd Lichtenberg, Becker, Hendrik Handloegten, and Achim von Borries.

East Berlin, 1989. In the final days before the fall of the Berlin Wall, there are riots against the regime. A loyal Communist named Christiane (Katrin Sass) sees her son Alex (Daniel Bruhl) beaten by the police on television, suffers an attack of some sort, and lapses into a coma. During the months she is unconscious, the Wall falls, Germany is reunified, and the world as she knew it disappears. When she miraculously regains consciousness, the doctors advise, as doctors always do in the movies, "the slightest shock could kill her."

What to do? After her husband abandoned her (for another woman, she told her children), the German Democratic Republic became her life. To learn that it has failed ignominiously would surely kill her, and so Alex decides to create a fictional world for her, in which Erich Honecker is still in office, consumer shortages are still the rule, and the state television still sings the praises of the regime.

Good Bye, Lenin! is a movie that must have resonated loudly in Germany when it was released; it is no doubt filled with references and in-jokes we do not quite understand. But the central idea travels well: Imagine an American Rip Van Winkle who is told that President Gore has led a United Nations coalition in liberating Afghanistan, while cutting taxes for working people, attacking polluters, and forcing the drug companies to cut their bloated profits. Sorry, something came over me for a second.

Change, when it comes to East Germany, arrives in a torrent. Alex is reduced to plundering Dumpsters for discarded cans and boxes that contained GDR consumer products, which were swept away by the arrival of competition. In his day job, he sells satellite systems with his friend Denis (Florian Lukas), and together the two of them produce phony news broadcasts to show his mom—even enlisting a former East German astronaut for plausibility.

This works fine until one day Christiane ventures outside, finds the streets awash with Westerners, and is confused by all the ads for Coke. Improvising desperately, Alex and Denis produce newscasts reporting that the West is in collapse, Westerners are fleeing to the East, and the rights to Coke reverted to the Communist nation after it was revealed that its famous formula was devised, not in Atlanta, but in East Germany.

Good Bye, Lenin! is a comedy, but a peculiar one. Peculiar, because it never quite addresses the self-deception that causes Christiane to support the Communist regime in the first place. Many people backed it through fear, ambition, or prudence, but did anyone actually love it and believe in it? The scenes of joyous East Berliners pouring across the fallen Wall are still fresh in our minds. Toward the end of the movie we get a surprise plot point that suggests Christiane may have replaced her husband with the party in an act of emotional compensation, but that seems to be a stretch.

We all feel nostalgia for the environs of our past, of course, which is why someone like me once treasured a 1957 Studebaker Golden Hawk even though new cars are incomparably better made (they aren't as sexy, though). There are fan clubs in Germany for the Trabant, the singularly ugly and poorly made official auto of the GDR, and great is Christiane's delight when Alex tells her the family now owns one. Our pasts may be flawed, but they are ours, and we are attached to them. What *Good Bye, Lenin!* never quite deals with is the wrongheadedness of its heroine. Imagine a film named *Good Bye, Hitler!* in which a loving son tries to protect his cherished mother from news of the fall of the Third Reich.

Well, maybe that's too harsh. *Good Bye, Lenin!* is not a defense of the GDR, which Alex

and his sister Ariane are happy to see gone (she's proud of her new job at Burger King). The underlying poignancy in this comedy is perhaps psychological more than political: How many of us lie to our parents, pretending a world still exists that they believe in but we have long since moved away from? And are those lies based on love or cowardice? Sometimes, despite doctors' warnings, parents have to take their chances with the truth.

Good Night, and Good Luck ★ ★ ★ ★
PG, 93 m., 2005

David Strathairn (Edward R. Murrow), Patricia Clarkson (Shirley Wershba), George Clooney (Fred Friendly), Jeff Daniels (Sig Mickelson), Robert Downey Jr. (Joe Wershba), Frank Langella (William Paley), Ray Wise (Don Hollenbeck), Dianne Reeves (Jazz Singer). Directed by George Clooney and produced by Grant Heslov. Screenplay by Clooney and Heslov.

Good Night, and Good Luck is a movie about a group of professional newsmen who with surgical precision remove a cancer from the body politic. They believe in the fundamental American freedoms, and in Senator Joseph McCarthy they see a man who would destroy those freedoms in the name of defending them. Because McCarthy is a liar and a bully, surrounded by yes-men, recklessly calling his opponents traitors, he commands great power for a time. He destroys others with lies and then himself is destroyed by the truth.

The instrument of his destruction is Edward R. Murrow, a television journalist above reproach, whose radio broadcasts from London led to a peacetime career as the most famous newsman in the new medium of television. Murrow is offended by McCarthy. He makes bold to say so, and why. He is backed by his producers and reporters and is supported by the leadership of his network, CBS, even though it loses sponsors, and even though McCarthy claims Murrow himself is a member of a subversive organization.

There are times when it is argued within CBS that Murrow has lost his objectivity, that he is not telling "both sides." He argues that he is reporting the facts, and if the facts are contrary to

McCarthy's fantasies, they are nevertheless objective. In recent years, few reporters have dared take such a stand, but at the height of Hurricane Katrina, we saw many reporters in the field who knew by their own witness that the official line on hurricane relief was a fiction, and said so.

Murrow is played in *Good Night, and Good Luck* by David Strathairn, that actor of precise inward silence. He has mastered the Murrow mannerisms, the sidelong glance from beneath lowered eyebrows, the way of sitting perfectly still and listening and watching others, the ironic underplayed wit, the unbending will. He doesn't look much like Murrow, any more than Philip Seymour Hoffman looks much like Truman Capote, but both actors create their characters from the inside, concealing behind famous mannerisms the deliberate actions that impose their will. In that they are actually a little alike.

George Clooney costars as Fred Friendly, Murrow's producer, who remained active into the 1990s. Clooney also directed and cowrote the movie. Because his father was a newscaster, he knows what the early TV studios looked like, and it is startling to see how small was Murrow's performance space: He sits close to the camera, his famous cigarette usually in the shot, and Friendly sits beside the camera, so close that he can tap Murrow's leg to cue him. They are also close as professionals who share the same beliefs about McCarthy and are aware that they risk character assassination from the Wisconsin senator.

The other key character is McCarthy himself, and Clooney uses a masterstroke: He employs actual news footage of McCarthy, who therefore plays himself. It is frightening to see him in full rant, and pathetic to see him near meltdown during the Army-McCarthy hearings, when the Army counsel Joseph Welch famously asked him, "Have you no decency?" His wild attack on Murrow has an element of humor; he claims the broadcaster is a member of the Industrial Workers of the World, the anarchist "Wobblies," who by then were more a subject of nostalgic folk songs than a functioning organization.

The movie is entirely, almost claustrophobically, about politics and the news business. Even its single subplot underlines the atmosphere of the times. We meet Shirley and Joe Wershba (Patricia Clarkson and Robert Downey Jr.), who work for CBS News and keep their marriage a secret because company policy forbids the employment of married couples. Their clandestine meetings and subtle communications raise our own suspicions and demonstrate in a way how McCarthyism works.

Apart from the Wershbas, the movie is entirely about the inner life of CBS News. Every substantial scene is played in the CBS building, except for a banquet, a bar, a bedroom, and the newsreel footage. Murrow and Friendly circulate in three arenas: their production offices, the television studio, and the offices of their boss, William Paley (Frank Langella), who ran the network as a fiefdom but granted Murrow independence and freedom from advertiser pressure.

The movie is not really about the abuses of McCarthy but about the process by which Murrow and his team eventually brought about his downfall (some would say his self-destruction). It is like a morality play, from which we learn how journalists should behave. It shows Murrow as fearless but not flawless. Paley observes that when McCarthy said that Alger Hiss was convicted of "treason," Murrow knew Hiss was convicted not of treason but of perjury and yet did not correct McCarthy. Was he afraid of seeming to support a communist, Paley asks, perhaps guessing the answer. He has a point. Murrow's response indicates he might have been a great poker player.

There are small moments of humor. After one broadcast fraught with potential hazards, Murrow waits until he's off the air and then there is the smallest possible movement of his mouth: Could that have been almost a smile? David Strathairn is a stealth actor, revealing Murrow's feelings almost in code. Clooney by contrast makes Friendly an open, forthright kinduva guy, a reliable partner for Murrow's enigmatic reserve.

As a director, Clooney does interesting things. One of them is to shoot in black and white, which is the right choice for this material, lending it period authenticity and a matter-of-factness. In a way, black and white is inevitable, since both Murrow's broadcasts and the McCarthy footage would have been in black and white. Clooney shoots close, showing men (and a few women) in business dress, talking in anonymous rooms. Everybody smokes all of the time. When they screen footage, there is an echo of *Citizen Kane*. Episodes are separated by a jazz singer

269

(Dianne Reeves), who is seen performing in a nearby studio; her songs don't parallel the action but evoke a time of piano lounges, martinis, and all those cigarettes.

Clooney's message is clear: Character assassination is wrong, McCarthy was a bully and a liar, and we must be vigilant when the emperor has no clothes and wraps himself in the flag. It was Dr. Johnson who said, "Patriotism is the last refuge of the scoundrel." That was more than two-hundred years ago. The movie quotes a more recent authority, Dwight Eisenhower, who is seen on TV defending the basic American right of habeas corpus. How many Americans know what "habeas corpus" means, or why people are still talking about it on TV?　☞

The Gospel ★ ★ ★
PG, 103 m., 2005

Boris Kodjoe (David Taylor), Idris Elba (Frank), Nona Gaye (Charlene), Clifton Powell (Pastor Fred Taylor), Aloma Wright (Ernestine), Donnie McClurkin (Terrance Hunter), Omar Gooding (Wesley), Tamyra Gray (Rain), Hezekiah Walker (Brother Gordon), Keshia Knight Pulliam (Maya), Dolores "Mom" Winans (Janet Perkins), Yolanda Adams (Herself), Fred Hammond (Himself), Martha Munizzi (Herself). Directed by Rob Hardy and produced by William Packer. Screenplay by Hardy.

The Gospel is the first mainstream movie I can remember that deals knowledgeably with the role of the church in African-American communities. It is not a particularly religious movie; the characters are believers, but the movie is not so much about faith and prayer as about the economic and social function of a church: how it operates as a stabilizing force, a stage for personalities, an arena for power struggles, and an enterprise that must make money or go out of business.

The counterpoint for all of this drama is gospel music, a lot of it, performed by such well-known singers as Yolanda Adams, Fred Hammond, Martha Munizzi, *American Idol* finalist Tamyra Gray, and inspired gospel choirs in full praise mode. If the plot wanders through several predictable situations, and it does, the movie never lingers too long on those developments before cutting back to the best gospel music I've seen on film since *Say Amen, Somebody.* Like an Astaire and Rogers musical, this is a movie you don't go to for the dialogue.

As the story opens, Pastor Fred Taylor (Clifton Powell) presides over a thriving church in Atlanta. His son David and David's best friend, Frank, are both in the youth ministry. Flash forward fifteen years. David, now played by Boris Kodjoe, is a rising hip-hop star with a hit on the charts: "Let Me Undress You." Frank (Idris Elba) is an associate minister. The church is having financial problems and must close in thirty days unless funds can be found. At a meeting of a board of church overseers, Pastor Fred collapses. His son flies home to be at his bedside, gets the bad news, and is soon enough at his funeral.

Before his death, the old pastor turned the pulpit over to Frank. There was some jealousy among more veteran pastors, but that's nothing compared to the way David feels when he sees the big billboard out in front of his father's church, showing Frank with the motto: "A new church, a new man, a new vision!" It doesn't help that Frank has married Charlene (Nona Gaye), David's cousin.

Will David return to his concert tour? His friend and manager, Wesley (Omar Gooding), certainly hopes so: They've struggled a long time to get on the charts, to get the limousines and the hotel suites and the big crowds and such perks as the groupie David wakes up with the morning he gets the bad news about his father's health. Yes, David is a sinner, but he's not into drugs or booze, and it becomes clear, as his brief trip to Atlanta stretches to a week and then longer, that his spiritual life is calling to him. For Ernestine (Aloma Wright), his father's church secretary for many years, Frank is an interloper and David belongs in the pulpit.

The plot plays out in terms of David and Frank's personal and professional rivalries, with the deadline for foreclosure looming always closer. None of these details, in themselves, are particularly new or interesting. What is new is the way the church is seen not in purely spiritual terms but as a social institution. Rob Hardy, who wrote and directed *The Gospel,* obviously knows a lot about black churches, their services, their music, their traditions, and the way the congregation interacts with the people at the altar.

There are times here when call-and-response shades into put-up-or-shut-up.

I am not an expert on African-American church services, but I have attended some, at Bishop Arthur Brazier's Apostolic Church of God and at Rev. Michael Pfleger's St. Sabina's, and I appreciate the way the choir acts as a sound track for the service, softly coming up under the preacher's exhortation, taking over, backing down for more preaching, its body language expressing as much joy as the music, the congregation fully involved. It is accurate that you see some white faces in the congregations in this film: To recycle an old British advertising slogan, these services refresh parts the others do not reach.

The Greatest Game Ever Played ★ ★ ★

PG, 115 m., 2005

Shia LaBeouf (Francis Ouimet), Stephen Dillane (Harry Vardon), Josh Flitter (Eddie Lowery), Peyton List (Sarah Wallis), Elias Koteas (Arthur Ouimet), Marnie McPhail (Mary Ouimet), Stephen Marcus (Ted Ray), Peter Firth (Lord Northcliffe), Michael Weaver (John McDermott). Directed by Bill Paxton and produced by David Blocker, Larry Brezner, Mark Frost, and David A. Steinberg. Screenplay by Frost.

The Greatest Game Ever Played was a game of golf, in case you thought your team might have been involved. In 1913, a working-class American amateur named Francis Ouimet defeated the great British player Harry Vardon to win the U.S. Open. Here is a movie that tells that story and exactly that story, devoting a considerable amount of its running time to the final games and playing like one superb sports telecast. Because some of the opening scenes seem borrowed from other underdog movies, I was surprised to realize, toward the end, how gripping the movie had become.

Shia LaBeouf stars as Francis Ouimet, a poor boy who lives with his family across from a golf course in Brookline, Massachusetts. From his windows and the front porch, Francis can see the golfers at play. So can his father, Arthur (Elias Koteas), an immigrant who steadfastly opposes his son's passion for golf: "A man should know his place." But Francis has a natural gift for the game and is encouraged by his mother (Marnie

McPhail) and two players at the local club. As a teenager, he actually attends a demonstration by the great Harry Vardon.

As for Vardon, we find that he, too, is a working-class boy, born across from a golf course. Or, more precisely, born directly on one, since in the first scene of the movie we see his family's home on the Isle of Jersey being surveyed by men who plan to tear it down for the construction of a course. He asks one of the men what "golf" is. "A game for gentlemen," he is told.

Harry is not a gentleman, but he is a class act, and as played by Stephen Dillane he becomes a perfect foil in the great 1913 game. It would be too easy to make him a villain, but Harry and Francis both embody the tradition of generosity and good sportsmanship later practiced by Sam Snead. To Francis, Harry is an unspeakably grand man. But Harry sees himself in young Francis, and he knows that in the British class system he may be a great golfer but he will never be in the Establishment.

The villain of the piece is Lord Northcliffe (Peter Firth), then the proprietor of the powerful *Daily Mail* and *Daily Mirror*, and the underwriter of the British team. He expects nothing less than a championship from Harry, confiding: "The prime minister has promised me a seat in his cabinet if I bring back this title." That seems a little unlikely, since to command the *Mail* and the *Mirror* was much more grand than a cabinet seat, but the fact that he would say it tells you a lot about him.

The other central character in the story is a pudgy ten-year-old caddy named Eddie Lowery (Josh Flitter), who works for Francis for free and offers him sound advice with unshakable self-confidence. Eddie, who seems to be ten going on forty, is one of those kids who always did and always will know it all; it helps that he is sweet. The movie also involves a romance with the fragrant Sarah Wallis (Peyton List), a young woman who begins a friendship with Francis that looks promising until the movie essentially sidelines it in the excitement of the Greatest Game.

This is the second film directed by the actor Bill Paxton and could not possibly be more different from his first, *Frailty* (2001). In that one, he played a father who leads his two sons in a series of murders that were commanded, he believes, by an angel. *Frailty* was dark and brilliant and filled with fearful prospects; now this sunny film, which plays almost as if it's emotional rehab for Paxton.

I am not a golf fan but found *The Greatest Game Ever Played* absorbing all the same, partly because of the human element, partly because Paxton and his technicians have used every trick in the book to dramatize the flight and destination of the golf balls. We follow balls through the air, we watch them creep toward the green or stray into the rough, we get not only an eagle's-eye view but a club's-eye view and sometimes, I am convinced, a ball's-eye view.

The technique is at the service of a game in which everything is at risk and we like both players; our affection for them makes everything trickier, and certainly as the final rounds are played, the games themselves seem to have been scripted to create as much suspense as possible. I have no idea if the movie is based, stroke for stroke, on the actual competition at the 1913 U.S. Open. I guess I could find out, but I don't want to know. I like it this way.

The Great Raid ★ ★ ★
R, 132 m., 2005

Benjamin Bratt (Lieutenant Colonel Henry Mucci), James Franco (Captain Bob Prince), Connie Nielsen (Margaret Utinsky), Joseph Fiennes (Major Gibson), Marton Csokas (Captain Redding), Cesar Montano (Captain Juan Pajota). Directed by John Dahl and produced by Lawrence Bender and Marty Katz. Screenplay by Carlo Bernard and Douglas Miro, based on the books *The Great Raid on Cabanatuan* by William B. Breuer and *Ghost Soldiers* by Hampton Sides.

Here is a war movie that understands how wars are actually fought. After *Stealth* and its high-tech look-alikes, which make warfare look like a video game, *The Great Raid* shows the hard work and courage of troops whose reality is danger and death. The difference between *Stealth* and *The Great Raid* is the difference between the fantasies of the Pentagon architects of "shock and awe" and the reality of the Marines who were killed in Iraq.

The movie is based on the true story of a famous raid by U.S. Army Rangers and Philippine guerrillas, who attacked the Japanese POW camp at Cabanatuan and rescued more than five-hundred Americans, with the loss of only two American and twenty-one Filipino lives. Nearly eight-hundred Japanese died in the surprise attack. These numbers are so dramatic that the movie uses end credits to inform us they are factual.

The Great Raid has the look and feel of a good war movie you might see on cable late one night, perhaps starring Robert Mitchum, Robert Ryan, or Lee Marvin. It has been made with the confidence that the story itself is the point, not the flashy graphics. The raid is outlined for the troops (and for the audience) so that, knowing what the rescuers want to do, we understand how they're trying to do it. Like soldiers on a march, it puts one step in front of another, instead of flying apart into a blizzard of quick cuts and special effects. Like the jazzier but equally realistic *Black Hawk Down*, it shows a situation that has moved beyond policy and strategy, and amounts to soldiers in the field, hoping to hell they get home alive.

"You are the best-trained troops in the U.S. Army," their commander (Benjamin Bratt) tells the 6th Army Ranger Battalion. Perhaps that is close to the truth, but they have never been tested under fire; their first assignment involves penetrating Japanese-controlled territory, creeping in daylight across an open field toward the POW camp, hiding in a ditch until night, and then depending on surprise to rescue the prisoners, most of them starving, many of them sick, all of them survivors of the Bataan Death March.

Historical narration and footage provide the context: As the Japanese retreated, they killed their prisoners, and Americans in one camp were burned alive. In both this raid and a larger, more famous one at the nearby Los Banos camp, the challenge was to rescue the POWs before the Japanese believed the enemy was close enough to trigger the deaths of their prisoners.

Commanding the Rangers are the real-life war heroes Lieutenant Colonel Henry Mucci (Bratt) and Captain Bob Prince (James Franco), who plans the raid. In parallel stories, we meet the fictional Major Gibson (Joseph Fiennes), leader of the POWs, and a brave American nurse, also from real life, named Margaret Utinsky (Connie Nielsen). She works in the Manila underground, obtaining drugs on the black market that are smuggled into the camp. She and Gibson were once lovers (in what must be a fictional invention) but have not seen each other for years. Still, it is the idea of Margaret that sustains Gibson, whose strength is being drained by malaria.

The film is unique in giving full credit to the Filipino fighters who joined the Rangers and made the local logistics possible by enlisting the secret help of local farmers and villagers (their oxcarts were employed to carry prisoners too weak to walk). The Filipinos are led by Capt. Juan Pajota (Cesar Montano), a forcible local actor who steps into the Hollywood cast and adds to its authenticity and sense of mission.

A brilliant strategic idea is to have a single American plane make several passes over the camp, lifting the eyes of the Japanese to the skies as rescuers were creeping toward them. The raid itself, when it comes, is at night, and would be hard for us to follow except that it follows so precisely the plans that were outlined earlier. One effective moment comes when an officer delays action to be absolutely sure that all is ready; with radio silence, he has to send a scout, and we grow almost as impatient as the waiting men.

The movie was directed by John Dahl, based on a screenplay by Carlo Bernard and Douglas Miro, and the books *The Great Raid on Cabanatuan* by William B. Breuer and *Ghost Soldiers* by Hampton Sides. Dahl is best known for two of the trickiest modern films noir, *Red Rock West* and *The Last Seduction*. Those films would seem to have nothing in common with a war movie, but in a way they do, because they avoid special effects and stay close to their characters while negotiating a risky and complicated plot.

The history of the movie is interesting. It was green-lighted by Harvey Weinstein of Miramax just a few days after 9/11; perhaps a story of a famous American victory seemed needed. It was completed by 2002 but, like a lot of Miramax inventory, sat on the shelf (Miramax won a "shelf award" at the Indie Spirits one year for the quality of its unreleased pictures). Now that Disney and Miramax are going separate ways, Miramax is releasing a lot of those films in the final months of its original management.

The Great Raid is perhaps more timely now than it would have been a few years ago, when "smart bombs" and a couple of weeks of warfare were supposed to solve the Iraq situation. Now that we are involved in a lengthy and

bloody ground war there, it is good to have a film that is not about entertainment for action fans but about how wars are won with great difficulty, risk, and cost.

Green Street Hooligans ★ ★ ★ ½
R, 106 m., 2005

Elijah Wood (Matt Buckner), Charlie Hunnam (Pete Dunham), Claire Forlani (Shannon Dunham), Marc Warren (Steve Dunham), Leo Gregory (Bovver), Geoff Bell (Tommy Hatcher), Kieran Bew (Ike), Henry Goodman (Carl Buckner). Directed by Lexi Alexander and produced by Gigi Pritzker, Deborah Del Prete, and Donald Zuckerman. Screenplay by Alexander, Dougie Brimson, and Josh Shelov.

"West Ham is mediocre. But their firm is first-rate." So a young American is told soon after arriving in London. West Ham is a London football team. "Firms" are the names for organized gangs of supporters who plan and provoke fights with the firms of opposing teams. The firms are quasi-military, the level of violence is brutal, and then the gang members return to their everyday lives as office workers, retail clerks, drivers, government servants, husbands, and fathers.

I first saw this world in Alan Clarke's *The Firm* (1988), one of Gary Oldman's early performances, which showed in disturbing detail how his character was drawn into what the press calls "football hooliganism." The fights can be crippling or deadly. They're all the more brutal because the gangs don't for the most part carry firearms, preferring to beat on one another with fists, bricks, iron bars, and whatever else they can pick up. Members of a firm have such fierce loyalty that they disregard risk. Unlike American street gangs, which are motivated by drug profits, British football firms are motivated by an addiction to violence.

Green Street Hooligans chooses an unexpected entry point into this world. Its hero is Matt Buckner (Elijah Wood), a bright Harvard student kicked out of school two months before graduating after his roommate forces him to take the fall for some cocaine found in their room. The Harvard business is not convincing but motivates Matt to visit his sister Shannon (Claire Forlani) in London. Her husband,

Steve (Marc Warren), more or less forces his brother Pete (Charlie Hunnam) to take Matt to a football game.

Elijah Wood, who can seem harmless enough to be cast as Frodo in *The Lord of the Rings*, might appear to be the last person who'd be interested in the violent world of a firm. But the movie is about the way men who run in packs need to belong, and to prove themselves. In a series of gradual stages that are convincing because we see his early resistance wearing down, Matt tries to become accepted by the Green Street Elite. This involves fighting at their side, which he does with more recklessness than skill. When he is finally covered with blood, he belongs.

There's a lot of plot surrounding this progression. The GSE lives with memories of its glory days, when it was led by a legendary fighter known as the General. Its rivalry with Mill Hill is so vicious that matches between the two teams have not been scheduled since the General led a particularly nasty fight several years ago. Shannon, Matt's sister, is horrified that Matt has gotten involved with the GSE, and her husband tries to warn Matt.

But he has become addicted. He was a journalist at Harvard, an editor of the *Crimson*, and now he keeps a journal: "I'd never lived closer to danger—never felt more confident." Life in the firm makes his previous life seem insubstantial and unreal; what is real is bonding with other men and beating the crap out of opposing firms.

This seems to me insane. What pleasure can be found voluntarily seeking injury every weekend? Of course, the fuel of the firm is alcohol, its meeting place is a pub, and its war song is a boozy, defiant version of the last song you would think of: "I'm Forever Blowing Bubbles." There's an intriguing montage showing GSE members at home and at their daytime jobs; the 1988 Clarke film made clear that firm members are not outcasts but jobholders and family men who have violence as a hobby.

At first I thought the character of Matt was unnecessary. Why not simply dramatize the world of firms? Do we need a Hollywood star as an entry point for non-British audiences? If you must have one, Wood seems so *very* unlikely as a street fighter that I began a list of more plausible actors for the role. Then I real-

ized that the movie's point is that someone like this nerdy Harvard boy might be transformed in a fairly short time into a bloodthirsty gang fighter. The message is that violence is hardwired into men, if only the connection is made. As someone who has never thrown a punch in his life, I find that alien to my own feelings, but I remember years ago, late on nights of drinking, when anger would come from somewhere and fill me. Certainly alcoholism is essential for firm membership: It is inconceivable that anyone would go into action sober.

The movie was directed by Lexi Alexander, a German woman who is herself a former kickboxing champion. It uses cinematography by Alexander Buono to capture the everyday reality of London streets and the kinetic energy unleashed in the fights. It also unfolds a tragic back story, as old secrets are revealed, leading up to the ultimate possibility of death. No, don't assume you know who will die. It isn't who you might think. Of the dead man, we are told: "His life taught me there's a time to stand your ground. His death taught me there's a time to walk away." I guess the time to walk away is before you get killed standing your ground, unless you have a very good reason for standing it. The most frightening thing about the members of the Green Street Elite is that they think they have such a reason, and it is loyalty to the mob.

Grizzly Man ★ ★ ★
R, 103 m., 2005

As themselves: Timothy Treadwell, Amie Huguenard, Medical Examiner Franc G. Fallico, Jewel Palovak, Willy Fulton, Sam Egli. Directed by Werner Herzog and produced by Erik Nelson. Screenplay by Herzog.

"If I show weakness, I'm dead. They will take me out, they will decapitate me, they will chop me up into bits and pieces—I'm dead. So far, I persevere. I persevere."

So speaks Timothy Treadwell, balanced somewhere between the grandiose and the manic in Werner Herzog's *Grizzly Man*. He is talking about the wild bears he came to know and love during thirteen summers spent living among them in Alaska's Katmai National Park and Preserve. In the early autumn of 2003, one of the bears took him out, decapitated him, chopped him up into bits and pieces, and he was dead. The bear also killed his girlfriend.

In happier times, we see Treadwell as a guest on the David Letterman show. "Is it going to happen," Letterman asks him, "that we read a news item one day that you have been eaten by one of these bears?" Audience laughter. Later in the film, we listen to the helicopter pilot who retrieved Treadwell's bones a few days after he died: "He was treating them like people in bear costumes. He got what he deserved. The tragedy of it is, he took the girl with him."

Grizzly Man is unlike any nature documentary I've seen; it doesn't approve of Treadwell, and it isn't sentimental about animals. It was assembled by Herzog, the great German director, from some ninety hours of video that Treadwell shot in the wild, and from interviews with those who worked with him, including Jewel Palovak of Grizzly People, the organization Treadwell founded. She knew him as well as anybody.

Treadwell was a tanned, good-looking man in his thirties with a Prince Valiant haircut who could charm people and, for thirteen years, could charm bears. He was more complex than he seemed. In rambling, confessional speeches recorded while he was alone in the wilderness, he talks of being a recovering alcoholic, of his love for the bears and his fierce determination to "protect" them—although others point out that they were safe enough in a national park, and he was doing them no favor by making them familiar with humans. He had other peculiarities, including a fake Australian accent to go with his story that he was from down under and not from New York.

"I have seen this madness on a movie set before," says Herzog, who narrates his film. "I have seen human ecstasies and darkest human turmoil." Indeed, madness has been the subject of many of his films, fact and fiction, and watching Treadwell I was reminded of the ski-jumper Steiner in another Herzog doc, the man who could fly so far that he threatened to overshoot the landing area and crash in the parking lot. Or the hero of *Fitzcarraldo*, obsessed with hauling a ship across land from one river to another.

"My life is on the precipice of death," Treadwell tells the camera. Yet he sentimentalizes the bears and is moved to ecstasy by a large steaming pile of "Wendy's poop," which is still warm, he exults, and was "inside of her" just minutes ear-lier. He names all the bears and provides a play-by-play commentary as two of the big males fight for the right to court "Satin."

During his last two or three years in the wilderness, Treadwell was joined by his new girlfriend, Amie Huguenard. Herzog is able to find only one photograph of her, and when she appears in Treadwell's footage (rarely), her face is hard to see. Treadwell liked to give the impression that he was alone with his bears, but Herzog shows one shot that is obviously handheld—by Huguenard, presumably.

Ironically, Treadwell and Huguenard had left for home in the September when they died. Treadwell got into an argument with an Air Alaska employee, canceled his plans to fly home, returned to the "Grizzly Maze" area where most of the bears he knew were already hibernating, and was killed and eaten by an unfamiliar bear that, it appears, he photographed a few hours before his death.

The cap was on his video camera during the attack, but audio was recorded. Herzog listens to the tape in the presence of Palovak and then tells her: "You must never listen to this. You should not keep it. You should destroy it because it will be like the elephant in your room all your life." His decision not to play the audio in his film is a wise one, not only out of respect to the survivors of the victims, but because to watch him listening to it is, oddly, more effective than actually hearing it. We would hear, he tells us, Treadwell screaming for Huguenard to run for her life, and we would hear the sounds of her trying to fight off the bear by banging it with a frying pan.

The documentary is an uncommon meeting between Treadwell's loony idealism and Herzog's bleak worldview. Treadwell's footage is sometimes miraculous, as when we see his close bond with a fox that has been like his pet dog for ten years. Or when he grows angry with God because a drought has dried up the salmon run and his bears are starving. He *demands* that God make it rain and, what do you know, it does.

Against this is Herzog, on the sound track: "I believe the common character of the universe is not harmony, but hostility, chaos, and murder." And over footage of one of Treadwell's beloved bears: "This blank stare" shows not the wisdom Treadwell read into it but "only the half-bored interest in food."

"I will protect these bears with my last

breath," Treadwell says. After he and Huguenard become the first and only people to be killed by bears in the park, the bear that is guilty is shot dead. His watch, still ticking, is found on his severed arm. I have a certain admiration for his courage, recklessness, idealism, whatever you want to call it, but here is a man who managed to get himself and his girlfriend eaten, and you know what? He deserves Werner Herzog. ☞

The Grudge ★
PG-13, 96 m., 2004

Sarah Michelle Gellar (Karen), Jason Behr (Doug), Clea DuVall (Jennifer Williams), William Mapother (Matthew Williams), KaDee Strickland (Susan Williams), Bill Pullman (Peter), Rosa Blasi (Maria), Grace Zabriskie (Emma). Directed by Takashi Shimizu and produced by Doug Davison, Roy Lee, and Robert G. Tapert. Screenplay by Shimizu and Stephen Susco.

The Grudge has a great opening scene, I'll grant you that. Bill Pullman wakes up next to his wife, greets the day from the balcony of their bedroom, and then—well, I, for one, was gobsmacked. I'm not sure how this scene fits into the rest of the movie, but then I'm not sure how most of the scenes fit into the movie. I do, however, understand the underlying premise: There is a haunted house, and everybody who enters it will have unspeakable things happen to them.

These are not just any old unspeakable things. They rigidly follow the age-old formula of horror movies, in which characters who hear alarming sounds go to investigate, unwisely sticking their heads/hands/body parts into places where they quickly become forensic evidence. Something attacks them in a shot so brief and murky it could be a fearsome beast, a savage ghost—or, of course, Only A Cat.

The movie, set in Japan but starring mostly American actors, has been remade by Takashi Shimizu from his original Japanese version. It loses intriguing opportunities to contrast American and Japanese cultures, alas, by allowing everyone to speak English; I was hoping it would exploit its locations and become *Lost, Eviscerated and Devoured in Translation.*

An opening title informs us that when an event causes violent rage, a curse is born that inhabits that place and is visited on others who

come there. We are eventually given a murky, black-and-white, tilt-shot flashback glimpse of the original violent rage, during which we can indistinctly spot some of the presences who haunt the house, including a small child with a big mouth and a catlike scream.

The house shelters at various times the mother of one of the characters, who spends most of her time in bed or staring vacantly into space, and a young couple who move in, and a real estate agent who sees that the bathtub is filled up and sticks his hand into the water to pull the plug, and is attacked by a woman with long hair who leaps out of the water. This woman's hair, which sometimes looks like seaweed, appears in many scenes, hanging down into the frame as if it dreams of becoming a boom mike.

Various cops and social workers enter the house, some never to emerge, but the news of its malevolence doesn't get around. You'd think that after a house has been associated with gruesome calamities on a daily basis, the neighbors could at least post an old-timer outside to opine that some mighty strange things have been a-happening in there.

I eventually lost all patience. The movie may have some subterranean level on which the story strands connect and make sense, but it eluded me. The fragmented time structure is a nuisance, not a style. The house is not particularly creepy from an architectural point of view, and if it didn't have a crawl space under the eaves, the ghosts would have to jump out from behind sofas.

Sarah Michelle Gellar, the nominal star, has been in her share of horror movies, and all by herself could have written and directed a better one than this. As for Bill Pullman, the more I think about his opening scene, the more I think it represents his state of mind after he signed up for the movie, flew all the way to Japan, and read the screenplay.

Guess Who? ★ ★ ★
PG-13, 105 m., 2005

Bernie Mac (Percy Jones), Ashton Kutcher (Simon Green), Zoe Saldana (Theresa Jones), Judith Scott (Marilyn Jones), Kellee Stewart (Keisha Jones). Directed by Kevin Rodney Sullivan and produced by Jason Goldberg,

Erwin Stoff, and Jenno Topping. Screenplay by David Ronn, Jay Scherick, and Peter Tolan.

Thirty-eight years after Katharine Houghton brought Sidney Poitier home to meet her parents in *Guess Who's Coming to Dinner,* it's time for an African-American woman to bring her white fiancé home in *Guess Who.* Not much has changed over the years, or in the parents, who go through various forms of discomfort and disapproval before finally caving in when they realize the fiancé is, after all, a heck of a nice guy with a great future ahead of him.

Although racially mixed marriages are more frequent than they were in 1967, it is still probably true that no parents of any race have ever said to a child: "You're marrying someone of another race, and that's it!" When a child chooses a spouse from another group, it is usually because they have more things in common than the bits of DNA that separate them. Most parents—not all—eventually conclude that the happiness of their child is the most important factor of all.

Parents did not come quite so willingly to that conclusion in 1967, which is why Stanley Kramer's film, now often dismissed as liberal piety, took some courage to make. No doubt it worked better because the African-American who came to dinner was played by Sidney Poitier as a famous doctor who lived in Switzerland. And it was crucial that the parents were played not merely by white actors, but by the icons Spencer Tracy and Katharine Hepburn, whose screen presence carried great authority.

In *Guess Who,* the white fiancé is not quite the world-class catch that Poitier was. Named Simon and played by Ashton Kutcher, who must have had an interesting evening when he came home for dinner with Demi Moore, he is a Wall Street trader with a bright future, who has suddenly quit his job. He's in love with Theresa (Zoe Saldana), an artist. Her parents are Percy (Bernie Mac), a bank loan officer, and Marilyn (Judith Scott). Like Tracy and Hepburn, they live in an expensive home in an upscale suburb.

"You didn't tell me your parents were black!" Simon says when he meets them, in a lame attempt at humor. The fact is, Theresa didn't tell them he was white. Simon discovers this during the cab ride to the suburbs. "Ididn't tell them because it doesn't matter," she says. The black cab driver (Mike Epps) looks in the rearview mirror and says, "It's gonna matter."

It does, and the movie is a little uneasy about how to deal with that fact. Percy has already run a credit check on Simon and discovered (a) that he has an impressive net worth, but (b) is newly unemployed. When he finds out Simon hasn't told Theresa about his joblessness, Percy decides that the young man is not to be trusted. He is also not to be trusted with Theresa's body, at least not under Percy's roof; her father insists that Simon sleep on the sofa-bed in the basement, and to be sure he stays there, Percy sleeps in the same bed with him. This leads to several scenes that are intended to be funny, but sit there uncomfortably on the screen because the humor comes from a different place than the real center of the film.

Simon and Theresa are indeed in love, indeed seem compatible, indeed have us hoping things will work out for them. But Percy is smart and suspicious, with a way of setting traps for the unsuspecting younger man. One of the film's best scenes, because it reflects fundamental truths, comes at dinner, when Simon says he doesn't approve of the "ethnic jokes" that "some people" tell at work. Percy asks him to provide a sample. Simon refuses, but then he decides, in a fatal spasm of political correctness, that it "empowers" the joke if he *doesn't* tell it.

So he does. ("How do we know Adam and Eve weren't black? Ever try to get a rib away from a black man?") Not everyone around the table may think this is funny, but they all laugh—except Theresa, who senses the danger. Percy asks for another joke, and Simon obliges. And a third. Encouraged by Percy, Simon inevitably tells one joke too many—one that isn't funny, but racist. A terrible silence falls. Percy leaves the table. Simon is aghast. "I should never have told that joke," he says to Theresa. "You should never have started," she says. His mistake was to tell the first one. But she forgives him his mistake: "He dared you."

He did. And if the movie had spent more time walking that tightrope between the acceptable and the offensive, between what we have in common and what divides us, it would have been more daring. Instead, it uses sitcom and soap opera formulas that allow the characters easy ways out. (The scene where Percy finds Simon wearing Theresa's negligee is painfully awkward.) No one in the audience of any race is going to feel uncomfortable about much of anything on the screen.

That said, *Guess Who?* works efficiently on its chosen level. Bernie Mac, who often cheerfully goes over the top in his roles, here provides a focused and effective performance as a father who would subject a boyfriend of any race to merciless scrutiny. He has a moment of sudden intuition about Simon that is perfectly realized and timed. Ashton Kutcher is not the actor Sidney Poitier was, but the movie doesn't require him to be; his assignment is to be acceptable and sympathetic in a situation where he is coached through the hazards by his girlfriend.

The movie focuses primarily on the two men. If we heard a lot about strong black women after *Diary of a Mad Black Woman*, here we have a movie about a strong black man and about male bonding that has more to do with corporate than racial politics. Zoe Saldana, a true beauty, is lovable and charming as Theresa, but in her home she's upstaged by her father. As her mother, Marilyn, Judith Scott has a much smaller role than Katharine Hepburn had in the earlier movie, and although we meet Theresa's feisty sister, Keisha (Kellee Stewart), not much is done with the character.

Interracial relationships may be an area where the daily experience of many people is better-informed and more comfortable than the movies are ready to admit. Certainly after the first few dates any relationship is based more on love, respect, and mutual care than it is on appearances. I think the couple in *Guess Who?* has figured that out, but if they haven't, I predict they'll have a wonderful starter marriage.

Gunner Palace ★ ★ ★ ½
PG-13, 85 m., 2005

A documentary directed by Michael Tucker and Petra Epperlein and produced by Epperlein.

Gunner Palace is a ground-level documentary, messy and immediate, about the daily life of a combat soldier in Iraq. It is not prowar or antiwar. It is about American soldiers, mostly young, who are strangers in a strange land, trying to do their jobs and stay alive.

It has become dangerous to be a news correspondent in Iraq. As I write this, the front-page story is about an Italian journalist who was freed from her kidnappers, only to be wounded by friendly fire while trying to cross to safety at an American checkpoint. The man who negotiated her freedom was killed. In recent months many news organizations have pulled out their reporters; even the supposedly safe Green Zone inside Baghdad has become dangerous.

That's why this film is so valuable. Not because it argues a position about the war and occupation, but because it simply goes and observes as soldiers work and play, talk and write letters home and, on a daily basis, risk their lives in sudden bursts of violence. Sometimes they translate their experiences into songs. The African-American soldiers, in particular, use hip-hop as an outlet, and their lyrics are sometimes angry, more often lonely and poetic; all wars seem to create poets, and so has this one.

The movie was directed, produced, written, and edited by Michael Tucker and Petra Epperlein, a married American couple who live in Germany and visited Iraq twice, in late 2003 and 2004. They followed the 2/3 Field Artillery Division (the "gunners") of the army's 1st Armored Division. As it happens, a platoon from that division was also being followed by *Time* magazine, which picked "The American Soldier" as its 2003 Person of the Year. The woman on the cover, SPC Billie Grimes, is the only woman seen in the film. SPC Stuart Wilf, much seen in the film, "is the centerfold" in *Time*, according to an online journal kept by Tucker, who notes that two *Time* reporters were wounded while reporting the article.

The cover story takes a large view: "About 40 percent of the troops are Southern, 60 percent are white, 22 percent are black, and a disproportionate number come from empty states like Montana and Wyoming. When they arrive at the recruiter's door, Defense Secretary Donald Rumsfeld told *Time*, 'They have purple hair and an earring, and they've never walked with another person in step in their life. And suddenly they get this training, in a matter of weeks, and they become part of a unit, a team.'"

Gunner Palace plays like the deleted scenes from the *Time* cover story. The self-proclaimed gunners of the title live in the half-destroyed ruins of a palace once occupied by

Saddam's son Uday. What's left of the furnishings make it look like a cross between a bordello and a casino, and some rooms end abruptly with bomb craters, but there is still a functioning swimming pool, and the soldiers' own rock band blasts Smokey Robinson's *My Girl* from loudspeakers during their party time. We're reminded that songs by The Doors provided a sound track for *Apocalypse Now*, with the difference that the soldiers in that film were often stoned, and these young men (and one woman) seem more sober and serious.

Their job is impossible to define, which is one of their frustrations. At some times they are peacekeepers, at other times targets; they may be overseeing a community meeting, acting like paramedics as they handle a stoned street kid, breaking down doors during raids, engaging in firefights in the midnight streets. Eight of them were killed during this period of time; one of them, known as "Super Cop," was an Iraqi attached to their unit who was famous for capturing wanted fugitives. Another trusted Iraqi, an interpreter, was charged with passing intelligence to insurgents. "If it is true," Tucker writes in his journal, "he is responsible for at least four deaths."

The filmmakers go along with the gunners on their nighttime patrols, and the camera follows them into houses harboring suspected terrorists. Gunfire breaks out at unexpected moments. You don't see this on TV. Tucker, who photographed his own movie, was willing to take risks, and the gunners were willing to have him come along with them; you can sense by the way they relax in front of the camera and confide their thoughts that they were comfortable with him, accustomed to him. What's working here is the technique Frederick Wiseman uses in his documentaries: He hangs around for so long that he disappears into the scene, and his subjects forget that they're on camera.

That doesn't mean Tucker catches them off guard, or finds them cynical or disloyal. It's a truism of war that a combat soldier of any nation is motivated in action not by his flag, his country, his cause, or his leaders, but by his buddies. He has trained with them, fought with them, seen some of them die and others take risks for him, and he doesn't want to let them down. That's what we feel here, along with the constant awareness that death can come suddenly in the middle of a routine action. We hear about "IEDs," which are Improvised Explosive Devices, easy to place, hard to spot, likely to be almost anywhere. A sequence involves the investigation of a carrier bag on a city street, a bag that turns out to contain—nothing.

It's clear the soldiers don't think their logistical support amounts to much. Long before Rumsfeld was asked the famous question about the lack of armor for military vehicles, we see these men improvising homemade armor for their trucks and joking about it. There is a serious side: The flimsy junkyard shields they add are as likely to create deadly shrapnel as to protect them.

I wondered during the movie whether a sound track album exists. Apparently not. There should be one, or perhaps the original lyrics could be covered by established artists. The lyrics composed by the soldiers provide a view of the war that is simply missing in the middle of all the political rhetoric and gaseous briefings.

On May 23, 2004, after he had finished his principal photography, director Tucker made a last entry in his online journal: "I've asked soldiers what they think about the war and their answers are surprisingly simple. After a year, the war isn't about WMDs, democracy, Donald Rumsfeld, or oil. It's about them. Simple. They just want to finish the job they were sent to do so they can go home."

H

Happily Ever After ★ ★
NO MPAA RATING, 100 m., 2005

Charlotte Gainsbourg (Gabrielle), Yvan Attal (Vincent), Alain Chabat (Georges), Emmanuelle Seigner (Nathalie), Alain Cohen (Fred), Angie David (The Mistress), Anouk Aimée (Vincent's Mother), Claude Berri (Vincent's Father), Aurore Clément (Mistress's Mother). Directed by Yvan Attal and produced by Claude Berri. Screenplay by Attal.

Happily Ever After is among other things a dirge for the death of the French style of adultery. These Parisian philanderers seem no more chic than your average cheating American. Recall the elegance of the adultery in a film such as Renoir's *The Rules of the Game*, and then regard a couple in this film having a food fight. Of course, in Renoir the elegance was all upstairs among the aristocrats, while the gamekeeper and the footman chased each other around the kitchen, fighting over the gamekeeper's wife. Has everyone in France moved into the kitchen?

The movie opens with a man making a crass pickup attempt at a bar. The woman who is his target efficiently dismisses and humiliates him, turns her attention to another man, and picks him up.

In no time at all they are plundering their netherlands in a parked car, and it is only when they get inside an apartment that we realize they are man and wife. It's a game to bring a little spice into their marriage.

That couple is Vincent, played by Yvan Attal, who also wrote and directed the movie, and Gabrielle (Charlotte Gainsbourg, his real-life wife). Another couple in the story are the miserable Georges (Alain Chabat) and his feminist wife, Nathalie (Emmanuelle Seigner), who finds fault with everything he does, including buying gender-appropriate toys for their children. What does a little boy need? A toy vacuum cleaner, obviously.

These two men join in an occasional poker game with Fred (Alain Cohen), a bachelor and obsessive ladies' man, and an Indian man who enjoys frequent and satisfying sex with his wife after twenty years. The plot, which is generous with its characters, also provides Vincent with a mistress (Angie David), who at one point is actually talking to him on her cell phone while sitting in a restaurant at the next table from Vincent's wife. We also meet Vincent's parents (Anouk Aimee and Claude Berri) and the mistress's mother (Aurore Clement), looking uncannily like a mistress herself.

If I spent a lot of time performing a census of the cast, it is because the movie seems to rotate among its characters as if taking inventory. Nothing happens in *Happily Ever After* that I cared much about.

There is a scene where Gabrielle is at a Virgin megastore, listening to an album on headphones, and Johnny Depp joins her at the same kiosk and listens to the same song. They smile enigmatically, about the album, I guess, and he walks away. Later, Gabrielle, who is a Realtor, discovers she is showing an apartment to a man who is—why, it's Johnny Depp. They get on the elevator and find themselves kissing, and the elevator goes up, and up, and up, no doubt being circled by the stairway to heaven.

Scenes like this cause me to become unreasonably restless.

Does Gabrielle know this man is Johnny Depp? Does the movie? Does Depp? Is the movie so cool everybody knows he's Johnny Depp but just doesn't say so? Is his appearance intended as an endorsement? Or is he not supposed to be Johnny Depp, in which case why was he cast?

If the movie had given Gabrielle and the man something to actually say or do, none of these questions would be anywhere near the surface of my mind. Depp would be playing a role, instead of making a cameo. The cuteness of his appearance is an emblem of the film's self-absorbed satisfaction with itself: It need not extend itself to involve or amuse us, because its characters are so content to circulate among each other's genitals.

There's nothing much wrong with the film; my complaint is that there's nothing much right about it. Why do I need to see it? What do I learn? Why should I smile? Does the movie approve of the feminist wife, disapprove, or consider her merely a collection of character traits? Why is so little made of the Indians, who after all have mastered the happiness the others seek?

What does it say about a couple when a food fight escalates into an action scene? I don't know, and I don't care, and if they are all really going to live happily ever after it will not be in this movie or even, at their rate of growth, in its sequel.

Happy Endings ★ ★ ½
R, 128 m., 2005

Maggie Gyllenhaal (Jude), Tom Arnold (Frank), Jason Ritter (Otis), Laura Dern (Pam), Lisa Kudrow (Mamie), David Sutcliffe (Gil), Bobby Cannavale (Javier), Jesse Bradford (Nicky), Steve Coogan (Charley), Sarah Clarke (Diane). Directed by Don Roos and produced by Holly Wiersma and Michael Paseornek. Screenplay by Roos.

Maggie Gyllenhaal steals the show in *Happy Endings*, as a seductive gold digger who realizes that the fastest way to a rich dad is through his gay son. Her character, Jude, is a bold tease who first convinces Otis (Jason Ritter) that he's straight, then lets his dad, Frank (Tom Arnold), know that she prefers an older man. Her cynicism is part of her allure; her journey through their family leaves them in confusion and disarray, if momentarily happier.

Elsewhere in Don Roos's *Happy Endings* are characters not so engaging. The movie itself seems discouraged by its depressed characters and tries to cheer us up with written subtitles. After the opening scene, in which a woman running in the street is struck by a car, the first title slides onto the screen: "She's not dead."

We meet Mamie at seventeen; her mother, explains a subtitle, has just married a guy who owns a chain of restaurants. She has gained a sixteen-year-old stepbrother, Charley, "who will be a virgin for ten more minutes." Her seduction technique is concise: "You know, we're not really brother and sister." She becomes pregnant and goes to Phoenix to get an abortion.

The film leaps forward to the present. Charley, now played by Steve Coogan, has inherited his father's restaurants, and runs the one that is still open. He's gay; his partner is Gil (David Sutcliffe). They're friends with a lesbian couple, Pam and Diane (Laura Dern and Sarah Clarke). Gil at one point donated sperm to help them have a baby, and indeed they have a baby, which is allegedly, however, not Gil's. Charley has deep suspicions; the kid looks a lot like Gil,

and he thinks they're lying so they don't have to share the kid.

We meet Mamie again, now played by Lisa Kudrow as a counselor in an abortion clinic. She has a paid lover named Javier (Bobby Cannavale, from *The Station Agent*), who specializes in massages with "happy endings." *Spoiler Warning:* She is visited one day by an alarming young man named Nicky (Jesse Bradford), who says he knows she didn't have an abortion in Phoenix and can provide the name and address of her son. There is a catch: Nicky wants to film their reunion for a documentary he thinks will win him a scholarship to the American Film Institute.

So, that's the setup and indeed at least half of the movie. All of these characters are connected in one way or another, even Jude and Mamie, when Jude needs counseling and Mamie seems singularly unhelpful. The film's problem is that we don't much like most of the characters, or care about them. Jude, who strictly speaking is the worst of the lot, at least has spirit and energy and tries to find happiness on her own terms.

The lesbian couple is singularly dour. The counselor needs counseling. Otis, the confused son, will be fine in a few years, but not now. The gay men, Gil and Charley, get involved in an intrigue about the baby that leads to a permanent break with Pam and Diane. Apart from the calculating Mamie, the only other sunshine in the movie comes from Arnold, as a true-blue dad who loves his son, Otis, whether he's gay or straight, and lusts for Mamie whether she's sincere or not. He probably knows she wants him for his money but is willing to overlook that because a) he thinks he can handle himself, and b) the one thing rich men believe more easily than poor men is that they are irresistible to sexy women half their age.

Happy Endings maintains a certain level of intrigue, and occasionally bursts into life, especially when Gyllenhaal or Arnold are involved. I also like the way Mamie, the Kudrow character, becomes obsessed with Nicky's documentary; Final Cut Pro becomes as addictive for her as a video game. The movie's construction is clever and the dialogue well-heard, but the movie lacks the wicked magic of Roos's *The Opposite of Sex* (1998) and *Bounce* (2000). Both of those movies also had central roles for gay characters but saw them as warmer and more dimensional. In *Happy Endings* no one, gay or

281

straight, seems much entertained by sex except when using it to manipulate, or be manipulated. For the father, and seductress and the masseur, cash seems to be crucial to sexual success; for the others, it seems to be a gloomy murkiness.

Hard Candy ★ ★ ★ ½
R, 103 m., 2006

Patrick Wilson (Jeff Kohver), Ellen Page (Hayley Stark), Sandra Oh (Judy Tokuda), Odessa Rae (Janelle Rogers), Gilbert John (Nighthawks Clerk). Directed by David Slade and produced by Michael Caldwell, David Higgins, Richard Hutton, and Jody Patton. Screenplay by Brian Nelson.

David Slade's *Hard Candy* is against pedophilia, but what does it think about sadomasochism? On one level it's a revenge picture about a fourteen-year-old girl who entraps a thirty-two-year-old pedophile on the Internet, gets herself invited to his home, and quickly has him strapped down and helpless. On another level, it plays into the classic porno scenario in which a dominating female torments her victim. That the female is a child makes it all the more disturbing. That the film is so well-made and effectively acted makes it even more challenging.

Let me put my questions to one side for a moment and simply consider the story. Jeff (Patrick Wilson) is a photographer who hangs out in Internet teen chat rooms and strikes up a predatory friendship with Hayley (Ellen Page). She agrees to meet him on neutral territory, a coffee shop, but soon suggests they go to his home. He offers her a drink. She laughs: "I know better than to accept a drink mixed by a strange man." So she mixes the drinks. And he passes out and wakes up securely tied to a table.

Now commences an extraordinary acting performance by both actors, especially Page. Although she plays fourteen, I understand she was seventeen when she made it; to involve a fourteen-year-old in this material would be wrong. As an actress, she makes Hayley into a calm, methodical, intelligent girl who announces she is going to castrate Jeff. She has medical textbooks, instructions from the Web, scalpels, and antiseptic, and he should look on

the bright side: He'll have to go through this only once.

Before she carries out her threat, however, she plays mind games with him. She has followed him into other chat rooms, she says. She suspects he may have been implicated in the death of a young person. She explores his home and finds his stash of porno. He begs for mercy. She lets him beg.

How it all turns out, you will have to discover for yourself. There are a few other characters involved, including Sandra Oh as a curious neighbor, and some suspense of a conventional thriller type. But most of the movie simply involves Hayley and Jeff talking, and we're placed in the middle: We disapprove of what she's doing to him, but in a sense he was asking for it, because her evidence against him is persuasive, and he admits to a good deal of it.

If that were that, I would give the film an admiring review with special mention to the actors. But it isn't that simple. Isn't there a sense in which this film takes away with one hand and gives with the other? While it tells its horrifying parable about pedophilia, isn't it also dealing with sexually charged images that some audience members will find appealing? True, as far as I know, there is no tradition of pornography about men being tortured by young girls; usually the dominant female is adult, as she must be to feed into her victim's fantasies about authority figures. Still, what precisely is going on here, and is it anywhere near as clear as it seems? Is Hayley perhaps getting some pleasure of her own out of the situation she has created for Jeff? Are there two perverts in the room?

The film succeeds in telling its story with no nudity; the R rating comes "for disturbing violent and aberrant sexual content involving a teen, and for language." The young girl is not objectified but has free will throughout, lives in the moment, and improvises. There is undeniable fascination in the situation as it unfolds. It is an effective film. Although I may be concerned about how some audience members may react to it, I cannot penalize it on the basis of my speculations about their private feelings. Seen as a film, seen as acting and direction, seen as just exactly how it unfolds on the screen, *Hard Candy* is impressive and effective. As for what else it may be, each audience member will have to decide.

Harlan County, USA ★ ★ ★ ★

NO MPAA RATING, 103 m., 1976 (rereleased 2006)

A documentary directed and produced by Barbara Kopple.

At Sundance 2005, I went to a tribute screening for Barbara Kopple's great documentary *Harlan County, USA*, which won the Academy Award in 1976.

The film retains all of its power, in the story of a miners' strike in Kentucky where the company employed armed goons to escort scabs into the mines, and the most effective picketers were the miners' wives—articulate, indominable, courageous. It contains a famous scene where guns are fired at the strikers in the darkness before dawn, and Kopple and her cameraman are knocked down and beaten.

"I found out later that they planned to kill us that day," Kopple said later, in a discussion I chaired at the Filmmakers' Lodge. "They wanted to knock us out because they didn't want a record of what was happening." But her cinematographer, Hart Perry, got an unforgettable shot of an armed company employee driving past in his pickup, and a warrant was issued for his arrest.

Kopple brought some friends along to the festival. Foremost among them was Hazel Dickens, a miner's wife and sister, now sixtynine, who wrote songs for the movie and led the room in singing "Which Side Are You On?" Kopple also shared the stage with Utah miners who were on strike; although the national average pay for coal miners is fifteen to sixteen dollars an hour, these workers—who were striking for a union contract—are paid seven dollars for the backbreaking and dangerous work.

Using a translator, the Spanish-speaking miners told their story. One detail struck me with curious strength. A miner complained that his foreman demanded he give him a bottle of Gatorade every day as sort of a job tax. It is the small scale of the bribe that hit me, demonstrating how desperately poor these workers are. Work it out, and the Gatorade represents 10 percent of a daily wage.

Kopple and Perry spent eighteen months in Harlan County, filming what happened as it happened. Her editor, Nancy Baker, who was also onstage, took hundreds of hours of footage

and brought it together with power and clarity. I asked Kopple what she thought about other styles of documentaries, such as Michael Moore's first-person adventures, or the Oscarnominated *Story of the Weeping Camel*, which is scripted and has people who portray themselves but is not a direct record of their daily lives.

"I accept any and all kinds of documentaries," she said. "*Harlan County* came out of the tradition of Albert Maysles and Leacock and Pennebaker, documentarians who went somewhere and stayed there and watched and listened and made a record of what happened. That is one approach. There are others, just as valid. All that matters is making a good film."

Note: The conversation at Sundance between Kopple and Ebert is on the DVD.

Harold and Kumar Go to White Castle ★ ★ ★

R, 96 m., 2004

John Cho (Harold), Kal Penn (Kumar), Paula Garces (Maria), Neil Patrick Harris (Himself), Eddie Kaye Thomas (Rosenberg), Christopher Meloni (Freakshow), Fred Willard (Dr. Woodruff), Sandy Jobin-Bevans (Officer Palumbo). Directed by Danny Leiner and produced by Nathan Kahane and Greg Shapiro. Screenplay by Jon Hurwitz and Hayden Schlossberg.

One secret of fiction is the creation of unique characters who are precisely defined. The secret of comedy is the same, with the difference that the characters must be obsessed with unwholesome but understandable human desires. Many comedies have the same starting place: a hero who *must* obtain his dream, which should if possible be difficult, impractical, eccentric, or immoral. As he marches toward his goal, scattering conventional citizens behind him, we laugh because of his selfishness, and because secretly that's how we'd like to behave, if we thought we could get away with it.

I realize this is a lofty beginning for a review about a stoner road comedy, but there you are. The summer has been filled with comedies that failed because they provided formula characters, mostly nice teenagers who wanted to be loved and popular. *Harold and Kumar Go to White Castle*, on the other hand, is about two very specific

283

roommates who want to smoke pot, meet chicks, and eat sliders in the middle of the night. Because this column is read in Turkey, Botswana, Japan, and California, I should explain that "sliders" are what fans of the White Castle chain call their hamburgers, which are small and cheap and slide right down. We buy 'em by the bag.

Is a slider worth the trouble of leaving home and journeying through two states? If you're stoned and have the munchies, as Harold and Kumar are, and if you're in the grip of a White Castle obsession, the answer is clearly yes. The only hamburger worth that much trouble when you're clean and sober is at Steak 'n Shake. Californians believe the burgers at In 'n Out are better, but that is because they do not appreciate the secret of Steak 'n Shake, expressed in its profound credo, "In Sight, It Must Be Right." (Many people believe the names of In 'n Out and Steak 'n Shake perfectly describe the contrast in bedroom techniques between the coast and the heartland.)

Harold Lee (John Cho) is a serious, bookish, shy Korean-American accountant. Kumar Patel (Kal Penn), an Indian American, is a party animal whose parents think he's about to enroll in med school. That the dean is played by the benevolent but obscurely disturbed Fred Willard lets you know this process will not be without setbacks. Harold and Kumar are getting stoned one night when a White Castle commercial plays on TV and fixates them with a slider fixation.

Kumar seems to remember that there is a White Castle near where they live in New Jersey. There is not. If there were, it's questionable whether they could find it, as they careen through the night on a journey that makes the travels of Cheech and Chong look like outings in the popemobile.

It is an item of faith in comedies that if you leave the main road, you will instantly be in a land inhabited by people who did not learn all they know about chain-saw massacres from the movies. Consider Freakshow (Christopher Meloni), an auto mechanic who comes to their rescue after they run off the road while wearing what John Prine calls illegal smiles. Freakshow has a complexion so bad it upstages sausage pizza. Alarming fluids erupt from its protuberances; volcanic activity on the Jovian moon Io comes to mind.

Harold and Kumar eventually find themselves, inexplicably as far as they are concerned, on the campus at Princeton, where the students may be Ivy Leaguers but, like students everywhere, occasionally unwind with ear-shattering demonstrations of flatulence. This is the kind of movie where they pick up a hitchhiker and ask him, "Are you Neil Patrick Harris?" and find out that he is. Later he steals Harold's car. Harold is incredulous: "Did Doogie Howser just steal my car?" Yes, but he did it for a good reason. He did it so that when they finally get to a White Castle and find him there ahead of them, Harold can ask, "Dude, where's my car?"

Danny Leiner, who directed this film, began his career with *Dude, Where's My Car?* I inexplicably missed that movie, but I laughed often enough during the screening of *Harold and Kumar* that afterward I told Dann Gire, distinguished president of the Chicago film Critics' Association, that I thought maybe I should rent *Dude* and check it out. Dann cautioned me that he did not think it was all that urgent. Still another reason our leader's photograph should be displayed in every government office and classroom.

Harry Potter and the Goblet of Fire ★ ★ ★ ½
PG-13, 157 m., 2005

Daniel Radcliffe (Harry Potter), Emma Watson (Hermione Granger), Rupert Grint (Ron Weasley), Brendan Gleeson (Alastor "Mad-Eye" Moody), Robert Pattinson (Cedric Diggory), Clemence Poesy (Fleur Delacour), Stanislav Ianevski (Viktor Krum), Ralph Fiennes (Lord Voldemort), Robbie Coltrane (Rubeus Hagrid), Katie Leung (Cho Chang), Frances de la Tour (Madame Maxime), Miranda Richardson (Rita Skeeter). Directed by Mike Newell and produced by David Heyman. Screenplay by Steven Kloves, based on the novel by J. K. Rowling.

Well into *Harry Potter and the Goblet of Fire*, Albus Dumbledore intones as only he can: "Dark and difficult times lie ahead." What does he think lay behind? In this adventure, Harry will do battle with the giant lizards, face the attack of the Death Eaters, and in perhaps the most difficult task of all for a fourteen-year-old, ask a girl to be his date at the Yule Ball. That Harry survives these challenges goes without saying, since in the world of print his next adventures have already been published, but *Goblet of Fire* provides trials that stretch his powers to the breaking point.

Harry (Daniel Radcliffe) was just turning thirteen in the previous movie, *Harry Potter and the Prisoner of Azkaban* (2004), and the Potter series turns PG-13 with this one. There is still at least a mail owl, and what looks like a mail raven (it may represent FedEx), but many of the twee touches of the earlier films have gone missing to make room for a brawnier, scarier plot. Is it fair to wonder if the series will continue to grow up with Harry, earning the R rating as he turns seventeen?

Certainly Lord Voldemort seems capable of limitless villainy. Although we glimpsed his face in *Sorcerer's Stone*, we see him full on the screen for the first time in *Goblet of Fire*, and he does not disappoint: Hairless, with the complexion of a slug, his nostrils snaky slits in his face, he's played by Ralph Fiennes as a vile creature who at last has been rejoined by his Death Eaters, who were disabled by Harry's magic earlier in the series. Hogwarts School and indeed the entire structure of Harry's world are threatened by Voldemort's return to something approaching his potential powers, and the film becomes a struggle between the civilized traditions of the school and the dark void of voldemortism.

The film is more violent, less cute than the others, but the action is not the mindless destruction of a video game; it has purpose, shape, and style, as in the Triwizard Tournament. Three finalists are chosen by the Goblet of Fire, and then the Goblet spits out an unprecedented fourth name: Harry Potter's. This is against the rules, since you have to be sixteen to compete in Triwizardry, and Harry is only fourteen, but Dumbledore's hands are tied: What the Goblet wants, the Goblet gets. The question is, who entered Harry's name, since Harry says he didn't?

The Triwizard Tournament begins near the start of the film, but after the Quidditch World Cup, which takes place within a stadium so vast it makes the Senate Chamber in *Star Wars* look like a dinner theater. The cup finals are interrupted by ominous portents; the Death Eaters attack, serving notice that Voldemort is back and

means business. But the early skirmishers are repelled and the students return to Hogwarts, joined by exchange students from two overseas magic academies: From France come the Beauxbaton girls, who march on parade like Bemelman's maids all in a row, and from Durmstrang in central Europe come clean-cut Nordic lads who look like extras from *Triumph of the Will*.

Besides Harry, Cedric Diggory is the Triwizard contestant from Hogwarts, and the other finalists are Viktor Krum, a Quidditch master from Durmstrang who looks ready to go pro, and the lithe Fleur Delacour, a Beauxbaton siren. Together they face three challenges: They must conquer fire-breathing dragons, rescue captives in a dark lagoon, and enter a maze that, seen from the air, seems limitless. The maze contains a threat for Harry that I am not sure is anticipated by the Triwizard rules; within it waits Voldemort himself, who has been lurking offstage in the first three films and now emerges in malevolent fury.

Against these trials, which are enough to put you off your homework, Harry must also negotiate his fourth year at Hogwarts. As usual, there is a bizarre new teacher on the faculty. Alastor "Mad-Eye" Moody (Brendan Gleeson) is the new professor of Defense Against the Dark Arts and seems made of spare parts; he has an artificial limb, and a glass eye that incorporates a zoom lens and can swivel independently of his real eye.

There is also, finally, full-blown adolescence to contend with. I'd always thought Harry would end up in love with Hermione Granger (Emma Watson), even though their inseparable friend Ron Weasley (Rupert Grint) clearly has the same ambition. But for the Yule Ball, Harry works up the courage to ask Cho Chang (Katie Leung), who likes him a lot. Ron asks Hermione, but she already has a date, with the student most calculated to inspire Ron's jealousy. These scenes seem almost in the spirit of John Hughes's high school movies.

Most of the Potter series regulars are back, if only for brief scenes, and it is good to see the gamekeeper Hagrid (Robbie Coltrane) find love at last with Madame Maxime (Frances de la Tour), headmistress of Beauxbaton. Hagrid, you will recall, is a hairy giant. Frances is an even taller, but mercifully less hairy, giantess. One new character is the snoopy Rita Skeeter

(Miranda Richardson), gossip columnist of the *Daily Prophet*, a paper that, like the portraits in earlier films, has pictures that talk.

With this fourth film, the Harry Potter saga demonstrates more than ever the resiliency of J. K. Rowling's original invention. Her novels have created a world that can be expanded indefinitely and produce new characters without limit. That there are schools like Hogwarts in other countries comes as news and offers many possibilities; the only barrier to the series lasting forever is Harry's inexorably advancing age. The thought of him returning to Hogwarts for old boy's day is too depressing to contemplate.

Harry Potter and the Goblet of Fire was directed by Mike Newell, the first British director in the series (he turned down the first Potter movie). Newell's credits range from the romantic *Four Weddings and a Funeral* to the devastating *Donnie Brasco* to the gentle *Enchanted April*. Such various notes serve him well in *Goblet of Fire*, which explores such a wide emotional range. Here he finds a delicate balance between whimsy and the ominous, on the uncertain middle ground where Harry lives, poised between fun at school, teenage romance, and the dark abyss.

Harry Potter and the Prisoner of Azkaban ★ ★ ★ ½
PG, 136 m., 2004

Daniel Radcliffe (Harry Potter), Rupert Grint (Ron Weasley), Emma Watson (Hermione Granger), Gary Oldman (Sirius Black), David Thewlis (Professor Lupin), Michael Gambon (Albus Dumbledore), Alan Rickman (Professor Severus Snape), Maggie Smith (Professor Minerva McGonagall), Robbie Coltrane (Rubeus Hagrid), Tom Felton (Draco Malfoy), Emma Thompson (Professor Sybil Trelawney), Julie Walters (Mrs. Weasley), Timothy Spall (Peter Pettigrew), Julie Christie (Madame Rosmerta), Richard Griffiths (Uncle Vernon), Pam Ferris (Aunt Marge). Directed by Alfonso Cuaron and produced by Chris Columbus, David Heyman, and Mark Radcliffe. Screenplay by Steven Kloves, based on the novel by J. K. Rowling.

I've just returned from London, where Daniel Radcliffe created a stir by speculating that his famous character, Harry Potter, might have to

die at the end of the series. Certainly that seems like more of a possibility in *Harry Potter and the Prisoner of Azkaban*, the third Potter film, than it did in the first two. It's not that Harry, Ron, and Hermione are faced with any really gruesome dangers (there's nothing here on the order of the spider that wrapped up Frodo for his dinner in the *Ring* trilogy), but that Harry's world has grown a little darker and more menacing.

The film centers on the escape of the sinister Sirius Black (Gary Oldman) from Azkaban Prison; Sirius was convicted in Voldemort's plot to murder Harry's parents, and now it's suspected he must finish the job by killing Harry. As Harry returns for his third year at Hogwarts, grim wraiths named Dementors are stationed at every entrance to the school to ward off Sirius, but the Dementors are hardly reassuring, with their trick of sucking away the soul essence of their victims.

Harry, too, has developed an edge. We first met him as the poor adopted relative of a suburban family who mistreated him mercilessly; this time, Harry is no longer the long-suffering victim but zaps an unpleasant dinner guest with a magical revenge that would be truly cruel if it were not, well, truly funny. Harry is no longer someone you can mess with.

Harry and his friends Ron and Hermione (Radcliffe, Rupert Grint, and Emma Watson) return to a Hogwarts that boasts, as it does every school year, peculiar new faculty members (this school policy promises years of employment for British character actors). New this year are Professor Lupin (David Thewlis), who tutors Harry in a tricky incantation said to provide protection against the dark magic of the Dementors; and Professor Sybil Trelawney (Emma Thompson), whose tea readings don't pull punches—not when she gazes into the bottom of Harry's cup and sees death in the leaves.

To distract Harry from his presumed fate, his friend the gamekeeper Hagrid (Robbie Coltrane) introduces the three friends to a wondrous new beast named Buck Beak, which is a hippogriff, half-bird, half-horse, wholly misunderstood. When a werewolf begins to prowl the grounds, a battle between the two creatures is inevitable. Who could the werewolf be by day? Does no one at Hogwarts find the Latin root of Lupus suggestive?

Among the movie's many special effects, I especially admired the gnarled tree that figures in the third act. The tree is introduced with a wink to the viewer who knows it is CGI: It shakes melting snow from its branches, and some of the snow seems to plop on the camera lens. Beneath this tree is a warren that shelters unimaginable terrors for Ron, when he is dragged into it as part of a longer climactic sequence that plays tricks with time. First the three heroes witness one version of events, and then, after reversing the flow of time, they try to alter them. The ingenuity of the time-tricks worked for me, but may puzzle some of the film's youngest viewers.

Chris Columbus, the director of the first two Potter films, remains as producer but replaces himself as director with Alfonso Cuaron, director of the wonderful *A Little Princess* (1995), as well as the brilliant *Y Tu Mama Tambien*. Cuaron continues the process, already under way in *Harry Potter and the Chamber of Secrets*, of darkening the palate. The world of the first film, with its postal owls and Quidditch matches, seems innocent now, and although there is indeed a Quidditch match in this film, it's played in a storm that seems to have blown in from *The Day After Tomorrow*. I like what Cuaron does with the look of the picture, but found the plotting a little murky; just when we should be focusing on exactly who Sirius Black is and why he killed Harry's parents, there is the sudden appearance of a more interesting, if less important character, Peter Pettigrew (Timothy Spall), a real rat who undergoes a change of purpose.

The actors playing Harry, Ron, and Hermione have outgrown their childhoods in this movie, and by the next film will have to be dealt with as teenagers, or replaced by younger actors. If they continue to grow up, I'm afraid the series may begin to tilt toward less whimsical forms of special-effects violence, but on the other hand I like Radcliffe, Grint, and Watson, and especially the way Watson's Hermione has of shouldering herself into the center of scenes and taking charge. Although the series is named for Harry, he's often an onlooker, and it's Hermione who delivers a long-delayed uppercut to the jaw of Draco Malfoy.

Unlike American movies such as *Spy Kids* where the young actors dominate most of their scenes, the Harry Potter movies weave the three

heroes into a rich tapestry of character performances. Here I savored David Thewlis as a teacher too clever by half, Emma Thompson as the embodiment of daffy enthusiasm, Alan Rickman as the meticulously snippy Snape, Robbie Coltrane as the increasingly lovable Hagrid, and Michael Gambon, stepping into the robes and beard of the late Richard Harris as Dumbledore.

Is *Harry Potter and the Prisoner of Azkaban* as good as the first two films? Not quite. It doesn't have that sense of joyously leaping through a clockwork plot, and it needs to explain more than it should. But the world of Harry Potter remains delightful, amusing, and sophisticated; the challenge in the films ahead will be to protect its fragile innocence and not descend into the world of conventional teen thrillers.

Hate Crime ★ ★ ½
No MPAA rating, 104 m., 2006

Seth Peterson (Robbie Levinson), Bruce Davison (Pastor Boyd), Chad Donella (Chris Boyd), Cindy Pickett (Barbara McCoy), Susan Blakely (Martha Boyd), Lin Shaye (Kathleen Slansky), Giancarlo Esposito (Sergeant Esposito), Farah White (Detective Fisher), Brian J. Smith (Trey McCoy), Sean Hennigan (Jim McCoy). Directed by Tommy Stovall and produced by P. Dirk Higdon and Stovall. Screenplay by Stovall.

Hate Crime is set in motion with the murder of a gay man, but the title refers to more than one kind of hate and more than one kind of crime. At the end, we're left with good and evil in a bewildering tangle. The story is sometimes overwritten, often overwrought, includes an overheard conversation on the Nancy Drew level, and yet holds our attention and contains surprises right until the end.

The story begins with Robbie and Trey (Seth Peterson and Brian J. Smith), a long-established gay couple. A new neighbor moves in next door: Chris Boyd (Chad Donella). He makes it clear he hates homosexuals: "You're going to hell." A few nights later, while Trey is walking their dog in the park, he is beaten to death with a baseball bat.

Robbie is sure he knows who did it. The new neighbor, Chris, even has a previous hate crime on his record. A detective (Farah White) is assigned to the case, considers Chris a suspect, and then is joined by a senior detective (Giancarlo Esposito) who sees the case differently and has another suspect.

Meanwhile, we see the home life of Chris Boyd. His father, Pastor Boyd (Bruce Davison), is the leader of a fundamentalist congregation much given to sermons that linger in loving detail on sinners in the hands of an angry God. His mother, Martha (Susan Blakely), is a sweet, worried woman who supports her husband primarily, it appears, because anything else might be a sin. Their family dinners are fraught with tension.

Also in the film, less crucial but well-drawn, are Cindy Pickett and Sean Hennigan as Trey's parents. Lin Shaye has a peculiar but vivid role as a neighbor who agrees with Pastor Boyd's religion in theory but considers Robbie and Trey "my family" and has reason to suspect the cops: "You can't trust anybody but yourself."

So now all the pieces are in place for a puzzle I will not reveal, since *Hate Crime* is actually more of a thriller than a social commentary. It provides a sympathetic and convincing portrait of its gay characters, but it has two weaknesses that undermine the power it might have developed.

One involves the melodramatic way the plot is resolved. The other involves Pastor Boyd, his wife, his son, and his church. Yes, plenty of fundamentalists believe homosexuals (and many others) are on the highway to hell. Yes, they are intolerant and extreme and do not do onto others as they would be done unto themselves. Yes, they talk a lot about Jesus but seem unable to practice his principles, especially those involving charity. Yes, Jesus in their theology is not a spiritual leader so much as their spokesmodel on reactionary social and political issues. To drive its point home, the movie counterpoints Pastor Boyd's hellfire and brimstone with the gentler Christianity of Robbie's church.

But there are other fundamentalists, a great many more, I believe, who are gentle and humane, positive and well-meaning, and although I may disagree with many of their beliefs, well, there are a lot of religious beliefs in the world and most people disagree with most of them. In a sense, Pastor Boyd and his team represent Islamic terrorists, and most fundamentalists are like most Muslims, religious but not extremist, valued members of the community, good citizens and neighbors.

I make this point because the portrait of the Boyds is painted by Tommy Stovall, the film's writer and director, with such broad and venomous strokes that if the gay characters had been portrayed in the same way, the film would rightly be seen as bigoted. The Boyds are such nutcases that the film is thrown out of balance; a moderated portrait of them might have made a more effective movie.

What does feel right is the tension between the two detectives, the younger woman played by White and the veteran played by Esposito. Both leap to instant conclusions about the crime, and although our sympathies are with the woman, both of their theories are inspired more by prejudice than police work.

Of the ending of the movie I will have nothing to say. I have been accused recently of "spoiling" endings by the simple act of suggesting there is something to be spoiled. Life for me was so much simpler before e-mails in which readers send bulletins: "By hinting that there is a twist, you spoiled the movie, because otherwise why would I expect a twist?" I would suggest to such readers that few movies proceed predictably on a preordained path to an obvious conclusion. If you want one that does, Lindsay Lohan's *Just My Luck* also opened the same day as *Hate Crime*. For the rest of us, the ending of *Hate Crime* raises complex moral issues that make the movie more thought-provoking than we possibly could have expected. ☞

Head in the Clouds ★ ★ ★
R, 132 m., 2004

Charlize Theron (Gilda Besse), Penelope Cruz (Mia), Stuart Townsend (Guy), Thomas Kretschmann (Major Thomas Bietrich), Steven Berkhoff (Charles Besse), David La Haye (Lucien), Karine Vanasse (Lisette). Directed by John Duigan and produced by Michael Cowan, Bertil Ohlsson, Jonathan Olsberg, Jason Piette, Andre Rouleau, and Maxime Remillard. Screenplay by Duigan.

Head in the Clouds uses World War II as the backdrop for a romantic triangle. Well, so did *Pearl Harbor*, but I liked this one more, perhaps because it isn't so serious about itself. Oh, it keeps a straight face, but the plot has been rigged so the heroine can be seen in every possible light from the noble to the sinister, occasionally at the same time. She's Gilda Besse (Charlize Theron), one of those women who is so rebellious, daring, sexy, scandalous, shocking, and brave that it's a good thing the war came around to give her a context. A woman like this in peacetime would have a terrifying volume of unreleased energy and would be driven to find a channel to vent it. Maybe that explains Martha Stewart.

The movie begins with a fortune-teller who predicts amazing things in Gilda's thirty-fourth year. This is a device to tip off the audience that it's not going to be entirely about the school days of a young woman who pops up in the rooms of an Oxford undergraduate one night. He is Guy (Stuart Townsend), and he offers Gilda refuge from the campus scouts; he knows she's having an affair with one of the dons (who at Oxford are professors, not gangsters, with occasional exceptions, especially in earlier centuries).

Gilda is already a legend. Her father, played by the alarming British actor Steven Berkhoff, is a French millionaire. Her mother is an American. Her affairs are legion, her behavior notorious. Although Guy should be beneath her radar, she kind of likes him, and he of course is smitten. One thing leads to another, and a few years later he's invited to join her in Paris, where she is now a famous photographer and lives with her model Mia (Penelope Cruz). Mia is quite a character herself: former apache dancer and stripper, probably once a hooker, also a committed political idealist who is taking nursing classes in order to volunteer against the fascists in her native Spain.

Of course Mia and Gilda are lovers, sort of; they're the kind of movie lesbians whose relationships exist primarily to accommodate the men in their lives and excite the men in their audience. Mia's reaction to Gilda's uncertain but real affection for Guy is to look pensive in quiet little shots, as if she is thinking, "I wish that was me."

Eventually, Guy gets to look pensive, too, after the war breaks out and he returns to Paris as a British spy, only to find that Gilda is now the mistress of a powerful Nazi officer. The Nazis had excellent taste in mistresses, if we can

judge by the two best recent movies on the theme, *Bon Voyage* and *Gloomy Sunday*. Their mistresses, of course, had lousy taste in men, which is why Guy can't understand what Gilda has done. Surely this great free spirit is not sleeping with a man just to get nylons, cigarettes, and champagne?

Whether she is or not, I will leave for you to determine. What is certain is that Gilda is a considerable movie character, as Gildas so often are in the movies. The function of poor Guy is to follow her from one continent to another, gaze at her in admiration, lust, shock, horror, and dismay, and then in admiration and lust again. Wonderful as Gilda is, it must be exhausting to be fascinated by her.

Charlize Theron is one of the few actresses equal to the role, bringing to it beauty, steel-edged repose, and mystery. Gilda will be compared unfavorably to her great work in *Monster*, but I find it fascinating that the two films come so close together, underlining what magic really is involved in being an actor. Penelope Cruz is given a character who seems to combine the attributes of several other people who must have been written out of the script, so that she's busy being jealous, heroic, political, seductive, and studious; she walks with a limp, except in her lesbo tango with Gilda, where we don't much miss it.

The screenplay, by director John Duigan, seems constructed to put Gilda through the paces of most of the activities that would later be described in the little green paperbacks of the Traveler's Companion series published by Olympia in postwar Paris. When Mia's date leaves her black and blue with welts from a beating, for example, Gilda calls him up, hints that she's really interested in finding out more about his techniques, and then ties him to a bed and whips him, not entirely to his disliking. What she does with her Nazi is not entirely clear, but he seems content.

All the same, what *does* she think about Guy? Does she see him as a lover, a pet, a mascot, a dupe, a friend, an enemy? That's the movie's central puzzle, and no one is more baffled than Guy. By the time he (and we) get it all figured out, the war's about over, and so is the movie. I know *Head in the Clouds* is silly and the plot is preposterous, but it labors under no delusions otherwise. It wants to be a hard-panting melodrama, with spies and sex and love and death, and there are times when a movie like this is exactly what you feel like indulging.

Head-On ★ ★ ★

NO MPAA RATING, 118 m., 2005

Birol Unel (Cahit), Sibel Kekilli (Sibel), Catrin Striebeck (Maren), Guven Kirac (Seref), Meltem Cumbul (Selma). Directed by Fatih Akin and produced by Ralph Schwingel and Stefan Schubert. Screenplay by Akin.

"Are you Turkish? Will you marry me?" This may not be the shortest marriage proposal in movie history, but it is certainly one of the most sincere. It comes early in *Head-On*, a film about two people who would deserve each other, except that no one deserves either one of them. Sibel is a Turkish woman of about twenty-two, living in Germany with her parents. Cahit, who is at least twenty years older, is also a Turk living in Germany, which is all Sibel needs to know, because what she needs is a Turkish husband (any Turkish husband will do) who can take her out of her home and the domination of her father and brother and the threat of being married off to a loathsome man of their choosing.

Not that Sibel is a prize. Her wrists are scarred after suicide attempts, and she meets Cahit in a mental institution, where he has been taken after driving his car into a wall at full speed. Not a promising couple. She explains the deal: She will cook and keep house for him, do his laundry and stay out of the way. He doesn't have to have sex with her, and she gets to have sex with anybody she wants. This sounds like a good enough deal to Cahit, who desperately needs a housecleaner (and a bath and a haircut) and is getting all the sex he needs from a buxom hairdresser who hangs out with him at the sleaziest saloon since *Barfly*.

Cahit (Birol Unel) and Sibel (Sibel Kekilli) are played with a deadpan self-destructiveness that sometimes tilts toward comedy, sometimes toward tragedy, sometimes simply toward grossing us out. Cahit picks up the empty bottles in a bar in return for free drinks, uses cocaine when he can get it, is morose about the unexplained loss of his first wife (maybe he misplaced her), and is a sight to behold when he is brought home by Sibel to meet her family. Her father, a

bearded patriarch, looks on incredulously. Her brother whispers to the old man that at least Cahit will take her off their hands. To Cahit, he says: "Your Turkish sucks. What did you do with it?" Cahit: "I threw it away."

It is not that he hates Turkish or Turkey; it is that he hates himself. He prefers to speak German because that is the language of the society he moves in, one of garish bars and sudden fights and desperate bloody hangovers. Everyone in his world is a realist with no delusions. I treasured the scene where Cahit's new brother-in-law suggests they all make a trip to a brothel and is enraged when Cahit suggests that the man return home and sleep with his wife instead.

In a conventional movie, the formula would be: They put up with each other out of necessity, she starts to care for him, he begins to like her but she draws away, he grows angry and distant, she sees that he needs her, and they end by discovering that, what do you know, they actually love each other. *Head-On* goes through these stages in five minutes, on its way to much more desperate and harrowing adventures, which you will discover for yourself.

The film won the Berlin Film Festival and a lot of European Film Awards, and was praised partly, I imagine, because it provides a portrait (however dire) of Germany's large population of Turks and other immigrants—who, like undocumented Mexicans in America, are made to feel unwelcome while at the same time being essential to the functioning of the economy. The most memorable film I've seen about immigrants in Germany was *Ali—Fear Eats the Soul* (1974), by Rainer Werner Fassbinder, a director with an uncanny resemblance to Cahit, especially in the categories of personal hygiene, barbering, and drug abuse. In *Ali*, a middle-aged cleaning woman marries a much younger Moroccan man, and when she announces this fact to her family, a son (played by Fassbinder) stares at her for a second, stands up, and kicks out the screen of her television set.

Head-On not only includes a car crash, but has the fascination of one. It is possible that no good can come to these characters, no matter what changes they make or what they can do for each other. Their marriage functions primarily to yank both parties out of their personal spirals of self-destruction and allow them to join in a double helix of personal misfortune.

From time to time, the movie cuts to a band performing on a stage of Turkish carpets on a bank of the Bosphorus strait, with Istanbul in the background. These musical interludes suggest that we may be seeing a version of a ballad or folk-legend, which has been processed through generations of urban grunge. What I can say for the film is what I could also say of *Barfly, Last Exit to Brooklyn,* and *Sid & Nancy,* which is that the characters in these movies are making their mistakes so we don't have to.

I can also observe that I watched with fascination. The movie is well and fearlessly acted, and the writer-director (Fatih Akin) is determined to follow the story to a logical and believable conclusion, rather than letting everyone off the hook with a conventional ending.

The Heart Is Deceitful Above All Things ★ ★
R, 98 m., 2006

Asia Argento (Sarah), Jimmy Bennett (Jeremiah [age seven]), Dylan and Cole Sprouse (Jeremiah [age eleven]), Peter Fonda (Grandfather), Ben Foster (Fleshy Boy), Ornella Muti (Grandmother), Kip Pardue (Luther), Michael Pitt (Buddy), Jeremy Renner (Emerson). Directed by Asia Argento and produced by Chris Hanley and Alain de la Mata. Screenplay by Argento and Alessandra Magania, based on short stories by J. T. LeRoy.

How should this movie be approached? As an exploitation of child abuse? As a fearless portrait of a childhood in hell? As an acting and filmmaking enterprise pushed to heroic extremes? *The Heart Is Deceitful Above All Things* is the unrelenting story of a little boy torn away from a loving foster home at the age of seven and subjected for years to a series of physical and psychological cruelties. There is no redemption, no surcease, and as the film ends, the barbarity continues. This film made me intensely uncomfortable, but that was its intention.

The material is drawn from short stories by J. T. LeRoy, whose work was widely considered to be autobiographical—the memories of an abused boy who grew up to become a prostitute and finally spilled out all his remembered pain in thinly disguised fiction. As it turns out, the fiction was more heavily disguised than its

admirers realized: "J. T. LeRoy" now appears to be a forty-year-old woman named Laura Albert, and when "LeRoy" appeared in public he was played by Savannah Knoop, the half-sister of Albert's lover. With wigs, hats, and dark glasses, Knoop succeeded in playing a man by presenting LeRoy as a man willing to be seen as a woman. There is probably another movie here somewhere, maybe *Transamerica Meets James Frey.*

The stories were thought to be essentially truthful when Asia Argento adapted them and made this film, in which she stars as the boy's drug-abusing, mentally deranged mother. That they are fiction makes little difference to the film, since it would have been the same film either way, and we are relieved, not disappointed, that this childhood experience did not really exist. Such childhoods do exist, however, and we read from time to time of children taken from foster parents and returned to birth parents who mistreat or kill them.

The Heart Is Deceitful Above All Things opens with young Jeremiah (Jimmy Bennett), taken at seven from the home he loves and the people he considers his parents, and returned to the custody of his mother, Sarah (Argento). She shoves a toy rabbit in his face, promises him good times, throws a paper plate of SpaghettiOs in front of him, and tells him, "If my father had let me, you would have been flushed down some toilet."

Would social workers actually turn a child over to this mother? She dresses like a hooker because she is one. Jeremiah is sometimes in the same room as she services her tricks, and is introduced to a series of temporary daddies. Sarah "marries" one of them (Jeremy Renner), and when the newlyweds head to Atlantic City on their honeymoon, they lock the child in the house with instructions not to answer the phone. "There are cheese slices in the fridge," his mother says helpfully. The man returns alone ("She run out on me") and rapes the boy.

There are beatings all through the film, and more disturbing than any of them is a scene where the little boy thinks he has been bad and solemnly offers a belt to one of the men so that he can be beaten. There is a bizarre episode when he is collected from a shelter by his grandparents (Peter Fonda and Ornella

291

Muti), who are sadistic fundamentalists. After a flash-forward, Jeremiah, now eleven and played by the twins Dylan and Cole Sprouse, is a sidewalk preacher in a little suit and tie. His mother finds him again and drags him back into her life, which for a time involves sharing the cab of a long-haul trucker. And on, and on, and on.

The cruelty of child abuse exists. It is a legitimate subject for a film. In this film, there is nothing else. The child is abused for ninety-eight minutes, and then the film is over. We know in theory that there are ways to edit around child actors so that they do not fully participate in scenes where they seem present, but what are we to make of a scene where the little boy is dressed and made up as a girl, and encouraged to approach one of Sarah's tricks? For young actors, there is not a clear distinction between performance and experience, and although I hope the child actors were not harmed in the making of the film, I feel no confidence that the experience left them untouched.

Objectively, looking at the film as an event and not as an experience, I feel admiration for Argento, who has not compromised the material or tried to force a happy ending, and is as merciless to Sarah as to Jeremiah. She is faithful to the horror in the original material. She does not exploit it in a way likely to please predators. *The Heart Is Deceitful* evokes the reality of child abuse more closely than any other film I have seen. But, oh, what a sad and painful film this is, so despairing and merciless. If "J. T. LeRoy" had been real, we would wonder how he survived to write a book—to read and write at all. Yes, the human spirit is resilient, but this is not a film about resilience; it is a film about cruelty.

Many people, even adventurous filmgoers, will find the film unwatchable. Others may have the resources to place it in a context they can find useful. To be moved by pity and outrage is a given. To demand an upbeat ending or some kind of redemption or salvation is unrealistic; most lives like this end in early and cruel death. I cannot recommend the film, or dismiss it. My two-star rating represents a compromise between admiration and horror. You have read the review. You will decide to see the film, or turn away.

The Heart of the Game ★ ★ ★ ½
PG-13, 97 m., 2006

Featuring Bill Resler, Darnellia Russell, Devon Crosby Helms, Joyce Walker, April Russell, and Maude Lepley. Narrated by Chris "Ludacris" Bridges. A documentary directed by Ward Serrill and produced by Liz Manne and Serrill. Screenplay by Serrill.

How can she finish school, get basketball taken care of, and be a mommy?
—Talk-show caller

How can she not? *The Heart of the Game* tells the story of Darnellia Russell, a young woman who leads her Seattle high school basketball team to a state championship, graduates with honors, and is a mommy—despite the Washington Interscholastic Activities Association, which sues to prevent her from playing during her senior year. It is also the story of Bill Resler, a professor of tax law who looks like Santa Claus and coaches like a saint. "Have fun!" he says after every time-out.

The Heart of the Game, like *Hoop Dreams*, is a basketball documentary that began with no idea of where its story would lead. It begins in the classroom of Resler, a professor at the University of Washington, who hears that Roosevelt High School is looking for a new girls' basketball coach and applies for the job. A man in his fifties, he has three grown daughters and always followed their teams; now he gets to coach, although he keeps the day job and we get the impression that his coaching salary is little or nothing.

Resler's coaching philosophy is simple: "A full-court press the whole game. No offensive strategy, just run like hell." He runs his first team up and down the court until they drop, but he turns Roosevelt's Roughriders around and they start winning. "You can't defend against them," an opponent complains, "because even they don't know what they're going to do next."

Resler recruits Darnellia Russell, a middle-school star across town, for Roosevelt. It's a middle-class school with a majority of white students; her closest high school, Garfield, is mostly black. Russell's mother, April, thinks her child will "do better" at Roosevelt.

At first, she doesn't. She skips practices, and

her grades are bad; the film's narrator (Ludacris) tells us she is "intimidated by how to be around so many white people." Resler works with her, encourages her studies, tells her he'll throw her off the team if she isn't at practice on time. "What I know," he says, "is that Darnellia is brilliant. The one issue she has to conquer is believing in how smart she is."

Resler names each of his Roughrider teams. We live through the seasons of the Pack of Wolves, the Tropical Storm, the Pride of Lions. He takes them to state finals during Russell's sophomore and junior years; then she gets pregnant by the boy she's been dating since ninth grade. She drops out to have the baby. Her mother and grandmother support her, and she applies to return for a senior year. That's when the WIAA steps in and sues to prevent her from playing again, threatening the Roughriders with forfeiting every game. The team votes to play anyway.

It's here that the film's politics become fascinating. The interscholastic association's bylaws allow exceptions in the cases of "hardships," but the WIAA says pregnancy is not a hardship: "She made her own choice." Callers to local talk shows argue against her; I quote one at the top of this review. But Seattle lawyer Kenyon E. Luce volunteers to represent Russell in court and wins. The WIAA appeals. His argument is that since male players are not punished when they're responsible for a pregnancy, it is discriminatory to penalize a pregnant woman.

Consider the WIAA argument: "She made her own choice." Yes, she did. She chose to have her baby. If she had chosen to have an abortion, she could have played next season, no questions asked. It is here that the values of the talk show callers get confused. They apparently believe Russell should have the baby but be penalized for having it. Yes, abstinence is also a choice, but tell that to a weeping teenage girl locked in the bathroom with a drugstore pregnancy test.

Russell's final season combines the legal court battle with a cross-town rivalry; its traditional archenemy, Garfield, is now coached by women's basketball legend Joyce Walker. Garfield has a tall team; Russell is 5-7, and Resler lists all of his starters as "guards." Director Ward Serrill, who has been following Resler since the day he took the job, is allowed into practice sessions and halftime locker rooms,

but not into the "inner circle," a meeting of the team members themselves, with no one else present—including Resler.

"Look in their eyes!" Resler screams from the sidelines, a reminder that lions are the only animal that will return man's gaze. Is he obsessed with winning? There are more important things. Since the whole team voted to risk forfeiting their season, he decides that every single team member will play in the state championship game, no matter the score.

Sports movies have a purity of form. They always end with the big game, in triumph or heartbreak. So does The Heart of the Game, although the lawsuit still hangs over the team after the final free throw. By then we have come to have real respect for Russell's determination: Her grades improve so much she's on the honor roll, her baby is getting lots of mothering, fathering, grandmothering, and great-grandmothering, and she is voted player of the year.

Only later do questions occur. Resler casually mentions getting married in Alaska. It apparently is a second marriage, but we never meet his wife, and he never talks about her. When your husband is a university professor and takes on a second job that is arguably full time, does that cause problems? And although we see Russell's boyfriend several times, we never hear from him, nor does her mother talk directly about Russell's pregnancy. There are other stories stirring below the surface.

But perhaps by focusing on basketball itself, on the game and the legal and moral issue of Darnellia's pregnancy, the movie has enough to contend with. The Heart of the Game has the potential, like Hoop Dreams, to win a large audience. And Russell, like William Gates and Arthur Agee in that film, has the potential to use basketball as a way to graduate from college and have a better life.

Heights ★ ★ ★
R, 93 m., 2005

Glenn Close (Diana), Elizabeth Banks (Isabel), James Marsden (Jonathan), Jesse Bradford (Alec), Eric Bogosian (Henry), John Light (Peter), Andrew Howard (Ian), George Segal (Rabbi Mendel). Directed by Chris Terrio and produced by Ismail Merchant and Richard Hawley.

Screenplay by Amy Fox, based on her stage play.

The most thankless task in Shakespeare may not be playing Lady Macbeth, but playing an actress who is playing Lady Macbeth. She can't even name the play she's in, referring instead to "the Scottish play," so that most people think they missed the first half of her sentence, while the rest of us reflect on what a long time has passed since we learned why she says that. In *Heights*, Glenn Close plays Diana, the actress who is playing Lady Macbeth and interrupts a rehearsal to declare, "We have forgotten passion." Yes, but in this movie they'll remember it soon enough.

The film is one of those interlocking dramas where all of the characters are involved in one another's lives, if only they knew it. We know, and one of our pleasures is waiting for the pennies to drop. Diana is the mother of Isabel (Elizabeth Banks), a photographer who is engaged to Jonathan (James Marsden). Meanwhile, Jonathan has been contacted by Peter (John Light), who is interviewing the subjects of a British photo exhibition in which a photograph of Jonathan suggests that Isabel should think twice, or three times, before marrying him.

At an audition, Diana meets Alec (Jesse Bradford), a young actor. He leaves his jacket behind. Diana discovers that Alex lives in the same building as Isabel and Jonathan, and gives the jacket to her daughter to return to the actor. The astonishing thing about this is that an unemployed actor could afford to live in the same building as two well-employed people who are sharing the rent.

Diana's husband is having an affair with a young actress, which Diana pretends to accept, while meanwhile she seems to audition young lovers everywhere she goes; she doesn't want to sleep with them so much as see if she's still famous enough that they think they have to sleep with her. Other characters include George Segal as a rabbi who is counseling the Jewish Jonathan and the Christian Isabel before their marriage; his experiment with flash cards is not successful.

That the threads of all of these lives intersect in about twenty-four hours is the movie's reality. That they are interesting is the movie's success. There is a sense in which this movie could simply play as a puzzle, but the acting is good

enough to carry the contrivance. Glenn Close, hovering over the characters like a malevolent succubus, is wonderful here; her character must have had to dial down to play Lady Macbeth.

Much in the plot depends on the discovery of a secret that is not much of a secret to us at any point during the film. Oddly enough, that's not a problem, since the drama is based not on our surprise, but on the reaction of characters in the film. Suspecting, and then knowing, what they do not suspect and do not want to know allows us a kind of superiority that is one of the pleasures of being in the audience. After everything has been revealed, we do have a question, though: Why exactly did the character with a secret make the choices that are made? What would be proven? What would be accomplished? How would happiness come that way?

Apart from the movie's mysteries and revelations, its chief pleasure comes through simple voyeurism. It is entertaining to see the lives of complex people become brutally simple all of a sudden. They build elaborate facades of belief and image, they think they know who they are and what people think of them, and suddenly they're back at the beginning. That can be a disaster, or a relief. We start with nothing, we slowly construct this person we call ourselves, and eventually we live inside that person and it is too late to bring in another architect. Idea for a movie: A character takes a year's leave of absence from his life in order to go where he is unknown, and experience the adventure of starting from scratch.

But I digress. Let me just say that another of the movie's pleasures is the way it introduces characters for brief scenes in which it's suggested that another movie could be made by following them out of this one. One of those characters is Ian (Andrew Howard), a Welsh artist whom Isabel meets, and whose life takes a sudden turn. One of the other pleasures of narrative is when elaborate fictional scenes are built up, only to be smacked down.

Heights is not a great movie, and makes no great point, unless it is "To thine own self be true." But director Chris Terrio, working from a screenplay by Amy Fox (based on her play), sees the characters clearly and watches them with accuracy as they occupy their delusions, or lose them. The movie is one of the last produced by

Ismail Merchant, who as always was attracted to stories and characters, not to genres, concepts, or marketing plans.

Hellboy ★ ★ ★ ½
PG-13, 132 m., 2004

Ron Perlman (Hellboy) John Hurt (Professor Bruttenholm), Selma Blair (Liz Sherman), Jeffrey Tambor (Tom Manning), Karel Roden (Grigori Rasputin), Rupert Evans (John Myers), Corey Johnson (Agent Clay), Doug Jones (Abe Sapien), Bridget Hodson (Ilsa), Ladislav Beran (Kroenen). Directed by Guillermo del Toro and produced by Lawrence Gordon, Lloyd Levin, and Mike Richardson. Screenplay by Guillermo del Toro, based on the comic by Mike Mignola.

Hellboy is one of those rare movies that's not only based on a comic book, but feels like a comic book. It's vibrating with energy, and you can sense the zeal and joy in its making. Of course it's constructed of nonstop special effects, bizarre makeup, and a preposterous story line, but it carries that baggage lightly; unlike some CGI movies that lumber from one set piece to another, this one skips lightheartedly through the action. And in Ron Perlman it has found an actor who is not just playing a superhero, but enjoying it; although he no doubt had to endure hours in makeup every day, he chomps his cigar, twitches his tail, and battles his demons with something approaching glee. You can see an actor in the process of making an impossible character really work.

The movie, based on comics by Mike Mignola and directed by the Mexican-born horror master Guillermo del Toro *(Cronos, Blade II),* opens with a scene involving Nazis, those most durable of comic book villains. In a desperate scheme late in World War II, they open a portal to the dark side and summon forth the Seven Gods of Chaos—or almost do, before they are thwarted by U.S. soldiers and Professor Bruttenholm (John Hurt), who is President Roosevelt's personal psychic adviser. Nothing slips through the portal but a little red baby with horns and a tail; he spits and hisses at the professor, who calms him with a Baby Ruth bar, cradles him in his arms, and raises him to become mankind's chief warrior against the forces of hell.

Meanwhile, the psychic practitioner Grigori Rasputin (Karel Roden), who is working for the Nazis, is sucked through a portal and disappears. Yes, he's *that* Rasputin. We flash-forward to the present. The professor, now in his eighties, is told he will die soon. Two of his old enemies have inexplicably not grown older, however: a Nazi named Ilsa (Bridget Hodson) and a weirdo named Kroenen (Ladislav Beran), who is addicted to surgical modifications on his body. In an icy pass in Mondavia they perform ceremonies to bring Rasputin back from the other side, and they're ready to rumble.

Cut to a secret FBI headquarters where Hellboy lives with the professor and an aquatic creature named Abe Sapien (Doug Jones)—a fishboy who got his name because he was born the day Abraham Lincoln was assassinated. The professor is showing the ropes to young FBI agent Myers (Rupert Evans) when the Nazis attack a museum and liberate a creature imprisoned inside an ancient statue. This creature, a writhing, repellant, oozing mass of tentacles and teeth, reproduces by dividing, and will soon conquer the Earth, unless Hellboy can come to the rescue.

Which he does, of course, in action sequences that seem storyboarded straight off the pages of a comic book. Hellboy gets banged up a lot, but is somehow able to pick himself up off the mat and repair himself with a little self-applied chiropractic; a crunch of his spine, a pop of his shoulders, and he's back in action. Abe the fishboy, who wears a breathing apparatus out of the water, is more of a dreamer than a fighter, with a personality that makes him a distant relative of Jar Jar Binks.

Hellboy's life is a lonely one. When you are seven feet tall and bright red, with a tail, you don't exactly fit in, even though HB tries to make himself look more normal by sawing his horns down to stumps, which he sands every morning. He is in love with another paranormal: Liz Sherman (Selma Blair), a pyrokineticist who feels guilty because she starts fires when she gets excited. There is a terrific scene where Hellboy kisses her and she bursts into flames, and we realize they were made for each other, because Hellboy, of course, is fireproof.

The FBI, which is occasionally accused of not sharing its information with other agencies, keeps Hellboy as its own deep secret; that droll actor Jeffrey Tambor plays the FBI chief, a bureaucrat who is just not cut out for battling the hounds of hell. He has some funny setup scenes, and indeed the movie is best when it's establishing all of these characters and before it descends to its apocalyptic battles.

Hellboy battles the monsters in subway tunnels and subterranean caverns, as Liz, Myers, and Abe the fishboy tag along. I know, of course, that one must accept the action in a movie like this on faith, but there was one transition I was utterly unable to follow. Liz has saved them all from the monsters by filling a cave with fire, which shrivels them and their eggs into crispy s'mores, and then—well, the movie cuts directly to another cave in which they are held captive by the evil Nazis, and Hellboy is immobilized in gigantic custom-made stocks that have an extra-large hole for his oversized left hand. How did that happen?

Never mind. Doesn't matter. Despite his sheltered upbringing, Hellboy has somehow obtained the tough-talking personality of a Brooklyn stevedore, but he has a tender side, not only for Liz but for cats and kittens. He has one scene with the FBI director that reminded me of the moment when Frankenstein enjoys a cigar with the blind man. He always lights his stogies with a lighter, and Tambor explains that cigars must always be ignited with a wooden match. Good to know when Liz isn't around.

Herbie: Fully Loaded ★ ★
G, 101 m., 2005

Lindsay Lohan (Maggie Peyton), Justin Long (Kevin), Breckin Meyer (Ray Peyton Jr.), Matt Dillon (Trip Murphy), Michael Keaton (Ray Peyton Sr.), Cheryl Hines (Sally). Directed by Angela Robinson and produced by Robert Simonds. Screenplay by Thomas Lennon, Ben Garant, Alfred Gough, and Miles Millar.

The question that haunted me during *Herbie: Fully Loaded* involved the degree of Herbie's intelligence. Is the car alive? Can it think? Does it have feelings? Can it really fall in love, or is its romance with that cute little yellow VW bug just a cynical ploy to get publicity, since it has a new movie coming out?

To the dim degree that I recall the premise of the earlier *Herbie* movies, none of which I seem to have reviewed or indeed seen, Herbie

was essentially just a car. A car with a personality, a car that feelings and emotions could be projected upon, a car that sometimes seemed to have a mind of its own, but nevertheless a car existing in the world as we know it. In *Herbie: Fully Loaded*, Herbie can blink his headlights and roll them from side to side, he can let his front bumper droop when he's depressed, and he can suddenly open his doors to cause trouble for people he doesn't like.

I see I have subconsciously stopped calling Herbie "it" and am now calling Herbie "he." Maybe I've answered my own question. If Herbie is alive, or able to seem alive, isn't this an astonishing breakthrough in the realm of Artificial Intelligence? That's if computer scientists, working secretly, programmed Herbie to act the way he does. On the other hand, if Herbie just sort of became Herbie on his own, then that would be the best argument yet for Intelligent Design.

Either way, a thinking car is a big story. It is an incredible, amazing thing. In *Herbie: Fully Loaded*, Herbie becomes the possession of a young woman named Maggie (Lindsay Lohan), who is the daughter of a famous racing family headed by her dad, Ray (Michael Keaton). The family dynasty falls on hard times after her brother Ray Jr. (Breckin Meyer) gets caught in a slump. She rescues Herbie from a junkyard, a friendly mechanic (Justin Long) rebuilds the car, and then Herbie offends the sensibilities of a hotshot racing champion (Matt Dillon). The champ challenges Herbie and Maggie, the bug is entered in a NASCAR race, and I would not dream of telling you who wins.

The movie is pretty cornball. Little kids would probably enjoy it, but their older brothers and sisters will be rolling their eyes, and their parents will be using their iPods. The story is formula from beginning to end: the plucky girl and her plucky car, both disregarded by the dominant male culture, but gritting their teeth, or radiators, for a chance to prove themselves. The ineffectual dad. The teeth-gnashing villain. The racing footage. There is a moment when Herbie narrowly escapes being crushed into scrap metal in the junkyard, and his escape is sort of ingenious, but for the most part, this movie, like Herbie, seems to have been assembled from spare parts.

But let's rewind a little. *Herbie: Fully Loaded* opens with a montage of headlines and TV coverage from Herbie's original burst of fame, as chronicled in three earlier movies. That leads me to wonder (a) why Herbie ended up in a junkyard, when such a famous car should obviously be in a classic automobile museum in Las Vegas, and (b) why, when Maggie appears with the rebuilt and customized Herbie, no one in the racing media realizes this is the same car.

Never mind. The real story is Herbie's intelligence. The car seems to be self-aware, able to make decisions on its own, and able to communicate with Maggie on an emotional level, and sometimes with pantomime or example. Why then is everyone, including Lohan, so fixated on how fast the car can go? The car could be up on blocks and be just as astonishing.

It goes to show you how we in the press so often miss the big stories that are right under our noses. There is a famous journalistic legend about the time a young reporter covered the Johnstown flood of 1889. The kid wrote: "God sat on a hillside overlooking Johnstown today and looked at the destruction He had wrought." His editor cabled back: "Forget flood. Interview God."

Her Majesty ★ ★ ½
PG, 105 m., 2005

Sally Andrews (Elizabeth Wakefield), Vicky Haughton (Hira Mata), Liddy Holloway (Virginia Hobson), Mark Clare (John Wakefield), Craig Elliott (Stuart Wakefield), Alison Routledge (Victoria Wakefield), Anna Sheridan (Annabel Leach). Directed by Mark J. Gordon and produced by Walter Coblenz. Screenplay by Gordon.

Her Majesty has all the makings of a perfectly charming family picture, and then the plot runs off the rails. At some point during the writing process, a clear-headed realist should have stepped in and restored sanity. This hypothetical person would have realized (1) that the heroine's brother is not just a nasty young boy, but a psychopath, (2) that it is not necessary for the rhododendron lady to be having an affair with the mayor in order to be reprehensible, and (3) it is not very likely that Queen Elizabeth, on a state visit to New Zealand, would go

out of her way to visit the village of Middleton and call on an old Maori lady in order to return a spear stolen from her grandfather.

I realize it is (3) where I'm asking for trouble. The notes for the movie say it is "inspired by real events." I learn that Queen Elizabeth did indeed visit New Zealand in 1953, and even the hamlet of Cambridge, which plays Middleton in the film. Now I will no doubt be informed that she also tracked down the old Maori woman on the porch of her humble shack, and gave her the spear. In that case, the scene in question will not be inaccurate, but merely unbelievable.

Her Majesty is the kind of movie where you start out smiling, and then smile more broadly, and then really smile, and then realize with a sinking heart that the filmmakers are losing it. It stars a sunny-faced twelve-year-old named Sally Andrews as Elizabeth Wakefield, who is obsessed with the young Queen Elizabeth. A panning shot across her bedroom reveals enough QEII mementoes to bring a fortune on eBay. When she learns that the queen plans to visit her subjects in New Zealand, Elizabeth (the heroine, not the II) writes her more than fifty letters, suggesting Middleton as a destination. Apparently they work.

Elizabeth the Heroine has meanwhile made fast friends with Hira Mata (Vicky Haughton), the old Maori woman whose unpainted shack is an eyesore on the road into town. Hira takes Elizabeth the Heroine to a mountaintop and shows her that all she surveys—and land, the sea, and the sky—once belonged to the Maori, but now all that is left is her little patch of land. She reveals that Elizabeth II's ancestor once gave her grandfather a brace of dueling pistols in admiration of his bravery, but that two weeks later her grandfather was murdered and the pistols and his spear were stolen.

The pistols turn up as a family heirloom of the loathsome Mrs. Hobson (Liddy Holloway), busybody and head of the Rhododendron Trust, who plans to present them to the queen during her inspection, of course, of the rhododendrons. This Hobson creature is a powdery-faced screecher whose sex life with the mayor involves unspeakable games based on bee-keeping. She is insufferable, but consider Elizabeth the H's brother, Stuart (Craig Elliott), who, if he survives his adolescence, has a good chance of developing into New Zealand's most alarming criminal case study.

Stuart throws a brick through the Maori woman's window. He steals his sister's QEII collection and burns it. He gets fired for laziness and lies about it. He sneaks out to the Maori woman's house, douses it with gasoline, and prepares to burn it down, which is not a youthful prank but a crime for which I would throw the little bastard behind bars. And he locks up Elizabeth the H on the day when Elizabeth II is coming to town.

This is going too far. Stuart's depredations break through the veneer of small-town comedy and turn into some kind of sick weirdness. Elizabeth the H keeps smiling, preserves her pluck, and dutifully rehearses with the girls' drill team, and we would like to relax and smile with her and wish her the best, but we are distracted by the vile little desperado and his band of degenerate buddies.

I agree with the Maori woman that the land was her tribe's, and was taken from them. I agree that treatment of the Maoris was a crime against humanity. I have seen *Rabbit-Proof Fence*, which is about the treatment of aboriginal orphans in Australia as recently as 1970. That a neighboring commonwealth nation engaged in such practices until 1970 argues that in 1953, Queen Elizabeth was not rummaging through the attic at Buckingham Palace looking for a Maori spear her relative might have stolen, so that she could return it to the friend of the nice young woman who has been writing her from Middleton. It's a feel-good scene for white viewers, but Maoris may view it a little more ironically.

There is a sense in which all of my logic is wasted. *Her Majesty*, directed by Mark J. Gordon, will work perfectly well for its intended audience of girls about Elizabeth the H's age, which is twelve; they will like her pluck and spirit, and won't ask themselves if her brother is a little over the top, since at that age they consider most brothers to be monsters. I do not want to discourage this audience, because entertaining family movies are hard enough to find, and maybe only a curmudgeon like me would ask the questions that distract me.

There's another movie from Down Under that is also about a small town and an important visit. That would be *The Dish* (2001), about

a little Australian town where a radio telescope has been installed that will track man's first moon landing. The U.S. ambassador and the Australian prime minister are scheduled to visit, and when things go very wrong, the way in which they are made to seem right is hilarious and inspired. I thought of *The Dish*, which found the perfect notes, and regretted that *Her Majesty*, which has all the right ingredients for its story, also has so many wrong ones.

Hero ★ ★ ★ ½
PG-13, 96 m., 2004

Jet Li (Nameless), Tony Leung (Broken Sword), Maggie Cheung (Flying Snow), Zhang Ziyi (Moon), Chen Dao Ming (King of Qin), Donnie Yen (Long Sky). Directed by Zhang Yimou and produced by Bill Kong and Yimou. Screenplay by Li Feng, Wang Bin, and Yimou.

Zhang Yimou's *Hero* is beautiful and beguiling, a martial arts extravaganza defining the styles and lives of its fighters within Chinese tradition. It is also, like *Rashomon*, a mystery told from more than one point of view; we hear several stories, which all could be true, or false. The movie opens, like many folk legends, with a storyteller before the throne of an imperious ruler, counting on his wits to protect his life.

The storyteller is Nameless (Jet Li), who comes to the imperial court of the dreaded king of Qin (Chen Dao Ming). Qin dreams of uniting all of China's warring kingdoms under his rule; his plans to end war, the opening narration observes, "were soaked in the blood of his enemies." Three assassins have vowed to kill him: Broken Sword (Tony Leung), Flying Snow (Maggie Cheung), and Long Sky (Donnie Yen). Now comes Nameless to claim he has killed all three of them. He wishes to become the king's valued retainer, and collect a reward.

These opening scenes are visually spectacular. Nameless approaches the royal residence past ranks of countless thousands of soldiers, passes through entrance rooms of great depth and richness, and is allowed to kneel within 100 paces of the king—which is closer than anyone has been allowed to approach in many years. One pace closer, he is warned, and he will be killed.

The king asks to hear his stories. Nameless explains that his martial arts skill by itself was not enough to defeat such formidable enemies. Instead, he used psychological methods to discover their weak points. The style of Broken Sword's swordplay, for example, was betrayed by the style of his calligraphy. Sword and Snow were lovers, so jealousy could be used. Perhaps Snow could discover Sword making love with the beautiful Moon (Zhang Ziyi), which would sunder their alliance. As Nameless talks, there are flashbacks to the scenes he describes.

Hero is the most expensive film in Chinese history, a frank attempt to surpass Ang Lee's *Crouching Tiger, Hidden Dragon,* and the sets, costumes, and special effects are of astonishing beauty. Consider a scene where Nameless and Long Sky fight to the death during a torrential rainstorm that pierces the ceiling of the room where they fight, while a blind musician plucks his harp in counterpoint; they pause sometimes to urge the musician to continue. At one point Nameless launches himself across the room in slow motion, through a cloud of suspended raindrops that scatter like jewels at his passage.

Consider another scene where Nameless and Broken Sword do battle while floating above the vast mirror of a lake, sometimes drawing patterns in the water with their blades; Zhang even seems to film them from below the surface of the water they're walking on. Or another scene that takes place in a rain of bright red leaves. Or another where an imperturbable master of calligraphy continues his instruction, and his students sit obediently around him, while a rain of arrows slices through the roof of their school. Never have more archers and more arrows been seen in a movie; although I knew special effects were being used, I was not particularly aware of them.

These stories are of great fascination to the king of Qin, and after each is finished he allows Nameless to approach the throne a little closer, until finally only ten paces separate them. But the king has not survived years of assassination attempts by being a fool, and after the stories, he speaks, providing his own interpretation of what must have happened. His version is also visualized by Zhang, creating the *Rashomon* effect.

We can easily imagine the king being correct in his rewriting of Nameless's stories, and we wonder if Nameless has invented them as a strategy to get closer to the throne and murder the

king himself. This idea occurs not only to us but, obviously, to the king, who may have a strategic reason in permitting Nameless to come so close. The two are playing an elaborate game of truth or consequences, in which it hardly matters what really happened to Sword, Sky, and Snow, because everything has finally come down to these two men in the throne room.

A film like *Hero* demonstrates how the martial arts genre transcends action and violence and moves into poetry, ballet, and philosophy. It is violent only incidentally. What matters is not the manner of death, but the manner of dying: In a society that takes a Zen approach to swordplay and death, one might win by losing. There is an ancient martial arts strategy in which one lures the opponent closer to throw him off balance, and yields to his thrusts in order to mislead him. This strategy works with words as well as swords. One might even defeat an opponent by dying— not in the act of killing him, but as a move in a larger game.

Every genre has its cadre of moviegoers who think they dislike it. Sometimes a movie comes along that they should see nevertheless. If you've avoided every superhero movie, for example, *Spider-Man 2* is the one to see. If you dislike martial arts even after *Crouching Tiger,* then *Hero* may be the right film. Is it better than *Crouching Tiger?* Perhaps not, because the *Rashomon* structure undermines the resonance and even the reality of the emotional relationships. But Zhang Yimou, whose *Raise the Red Lantern* was so beautiful, once again creates a visual poem of extraordinary beauty.

Hidalgo ★ ★ ★
PG-13, 135 m., 2004

Viggo Mortensen (Frank Hopkins), Omar Sharif (Sheikh Riyadh), Zuleikha Robinson (Jazira), Adam Alexi-Malle (Aziz), Louise Lombard (Lady Anne Davenport), Said Taghmaoui (Prince Bin al Reeh). Directed by Joe Johnston and produced by Casey Silver. Screenplay by John Fusco.

Hidalgo is the kind of movie Hollywood has almost become too jaundiced to make anymore. Bold, exuberant, and swashbuckling, it has the purity and simplicity of something Douglas

Fairbanks or Errol Flynn might have bounded through. Modern movies that attempt the adventure genre usually feel they have to tart it up, so in *Pirates of the Caribbean,* which once would have been played straight, we get animated cadavers and Johnny Depp channeling Keith Richards. Well, okay, *Pirates* was fun, but *Hidalgo* is a throwback to a more innocent time when heroes and their horses risked everything just because life was so damned boring in the slow lane.

The movie is a completely fictionalized version of the life of a real cowboy named Frank Hopkins; a moment's research on the Web will suggest that an accurate portrait of his life would have been much briefer and very depressing. But never mind. Let us assume, as the movie does, that Hopkins was a half-Indian cowboy who bonded with an uncommonly talented mustang pony named Hidalgo. And that after he grew drunk and morose while laboring in Buffalo Bill's Wild West Show, he risked everything to travel to the Saudi Desert and enter the Ocean of Fire, a legendary race across the sands with a $10,000 prize.

Hopkins is played by Viggo Mortensen, fresh from *The Lord of the Rings,* as a bronzed, lean loner who (if I guess right) enters the race as much for the sake of his horse as for the prize. He respects and loves Hidalgo, especially after the scornful Arab riders scoff at the notion that a mixed-breed mustang could challenge their desert stallions with their ancient lineages. Of course, Hopkins is a half-breed, too, and so we're dealing with issues here.

The race is so grueling that many men and horses die, and some are murdered by their rivals. Hopkins functions in this world like a duck in a shooting gallery. When he is discovered in the tent of the beautiful princess Jazira (Zuleikha Robinson), he is brought before her father, powerful Sheikh Riyadh (Omar Sharif), and threatened with the loss of that possession he would least like to part with, even more than his horse. But then, in the kind of development that sophisticates will deplore but true children of the movies will treasure, his manhood is spared when the sheikh discovers that Hopkins knew—actually worked with, and spoke with, and could tell stories about!—that greatest of all men, that paragon of the sheikh's favorite pulp magazines, Buffalo Bill!

Hopkins is quite a babe magnet for an ex-drunk cowpoke who bunks with his horse. Not only does the lovely Jazira hope he will rescue her from capture by her father's lustful rival, but there's a rich woman named Lady Anne Davenport (Louise Lombard), who throws herself at him in an attempt to influence the outcome of the race, or maybe just because her husband is fifty years older. Hopkins passes up so many of these opportunities that we're forced to speculate that his life might have gone on much as before if the sheikh had carried out his plans for the cowboy's netherlands.

This is a movie that has concealed pits in the sand with sharpened stakes at the bottom; exotic sprawling villas made with corridors and staircases and balconies and rooftops where countless swordsmen can leap forward to their doom; sandstorms that can be outrun by a horse like Hidalgo; tents as large and elaborately furnished as a Malcolm Forbes birthday party; blazing close-ups of the pitiless sun; poisoned oases; tantalizing mirages; parched lips; six-shooters, whips, daggers, and . . . no, I don't think there were any asps. Some will complain that Hidalgo magically arrives on the scene whenever Hopkins whistles, but Hidalgo knows that if he could whistle, Hopkins would be right there for him, too.

I have done my duty. Not a moviegoer alive will be able to attend *Hidalgo* and claim that I have not painted an accurate portrait of the film. Whether you like movies like this, only you can say. But if you do not have some secret place in your soul that still responds even a little to brave cowboys, beautiful princesses, and noble horses, then you are way too grown up and need to cut back on cable news.

Hide and Seek ★ ★
R, 100 m., 2005

Robert De Niro (Dr. David Callaway), Dakota Fanning (Emily Callaway), Famke Janssen (Dr. Katherine Carson), Elisabeth Shue (Elizabeth Young), Amy Irving (Alison Callaway), Dylan Baker (Sheriff Hafferty). Directed by John Polson and produced by Barry Josephson. Screenplay by Ari Schlossberg.

A small girl is haunted by fears after her mother's suicide. Her father, a psychiatrist, feels powerless to console her, and thinks perhaps if they move out of the apartment where the death took place, that might help. Since John Polson's *Hide and Seek* is a thriller, he finds the ideal new home: a vast summer home, with lots of attics and basements and crannies and staircases, on a lakeside that must be jolly enough in the summertime, but is deserted now, in the wintertime. All except for some friendly but peculiar neighbors.

This is a setup for a typical horror film, but for the first hour, at least, *Hide and Seek* feels more like M. Night Shyamalan and less like formula. Robert De Niro and Dakota Fanning, as Dr. David Callaway, the father, and Emily, his preadolescent daughter, create characters that seem, within the extremes of their situation, convincing and sympathetic. De Niro's Dr. David Callaway is a patient and reasonable man, who treats his daughter with kindness, but there's something else going on . . .

Consider, for example, the night when Callaway brings home a neighbor woman, Elizabeth (Elisabeth Shue), for dinner. "Did Daddy tell you that my mommy died?" little Emily asks, volunteering: "She killed herself in our bathtub. Slit her wrists with a razor." Callaway gently tells his daughter he doesn't think their guest needs to hear that right now, at dinner, but there is a way Emily has of staring out of her big round eyes and seeming to look into darker spheres than the rest of us can see.

Then there is the matter of her imaginary friend, Charlie. Dr. Callaway knows kids have imaginary friends, and that troubled kids often invent confidants to share their fears. He consults a colleague (Famke Janssen), who specializes in children, meets Emily, and agrees. But then strange things begin to happen. Callaway is awakened in the middle of the night and finds a bloody message written on the bathroom walls. Something unpleasant happens to the family cat. Either Emily is acting out, or . . . well, perhaps Charlie is not imaginary at all.

This possibility is enhanced by the presence in the cast of Dylan Baker as the local sheriff, a nosy type who carries the keys to all the summer homes on a big ring on his belt. Baker is so reliable playing clean-cut but creepy types that once, when I saw him in a simply likable role, I was caught off guard. Here he hangs around way too much, and always seems about to ask a question and then deciding not to. There is also some oddness going on with the neighbors.

Up until about that point, the movie has played convincingly, within the terms of its premise. Dakota Fanning does an accomplished job of making us wonder what she knows and what she imagines. When she produces those scary drawings, for example, of people dying, are they prescient? Troubled? Or just a form of release?

To find out the answer to these and other more unexpected questions, you will have to see the movie. I found the third act to be a disappointment. There was a point in the movie when suddenly everything clicked, and the Law of Economy of Characters began to apply. That is the law that says no actor is in a movie unless his character is necessary. A corollary is that if a minor actor is set up as a suspect, he's a decoy. I began to suspect I knew the answer to Emily's nightmares and the nature of her imaginary friend, and I was right.

I would have been content, however, if the movie had found a way to make its solution more psychologically probable, or at least less contrived. In the best Shyamalan movies, everything fits, and you can go back and see them again and understand how all the parts worked. With *Hide and Seek*, directed by Polson from a screenplay by Ari Schlossberg, you don't get that satisfaction. It's not technically true to say the movie cheats, but let's say it abandons the truth and depth of its earlier scenes.

At Sundance, I saw Rebecca Miller's *The Ballad of Jack and Rose,* also a movie where the mother is killed. Also a movie where the father and daughter live together in isolation, on the far side of an island. Also a movie where the father brings home a woman for dinner, and the daughter resents her role in her father's life. But the Miller picture is interested in the dramatic developments in the situation—in character, and how it forms in one situation and tries to adapt to another.

Hide and Seek is not really interested in its situation, except as a way to get to the horror ending. I like horror films, but I don't like to feel jerked around by them. They're best when they play straight and don't spring arbitrary surprises. At the beginning of *Hide and Seek,* I thought I was going to be interested in the characters all the way to the end, but then the plot went on autopilot. In a movie like *The Ballad of*

Jack and Rose, the characters keep on living and learning and hurting and hungering, and there's no surprise at the end to let them off the hook.

High Tension ★

R, 91 m., 2005

Cecile De France (Marie), Maiwenn Le Besco (Alex), Philippe Nahon (The Killer), Franck Khalfoun (Jimmy), Andrei Finti (Alex's Father), Oana Pellea (Alex's Mother). Directed by Alexandre Aja and produced by Alexandre Arcady and Robert Benmussa. Screenplay by Aja and Gregory Levasseur.

The philosopher Thomas Hobbes tells us life can be "poor, nasty, brutish and short." So is this movie. Alexandre Aja's *High Tension* is a slasher film about a madman prowling a rural area of France, chopping, slicing, and crunching his way through, let's see, a body count of five or six people, including a small child that the film does not neglect to show crumpled and dead in a cornfield. That's what it's about, anyway, until we discover it actually consists of something else altogether, something I think is not possible, given our current understanding of the laws of physics.

The movie premiered at Toronto 2003 in a version that would clearly have received an NC-17 rating. It has been edited down to an R, perhaps the hardest R for violence the MPAA has ever awarded, and into the bargain Lions Gate has dubbed great parts of it into English. Not all: There are inexplicable sections where the characters swear in French, which is helpfully subtitled.

I had forgotten how much I hate dubbing, especially when it's done as badly as in *High Tension.* It's lip-flap on parade. The movie was originally shot in French, but for purposes of dubbing, one of the characters, Alex (Maiwenn Le Besco), has been given an American accent. As she and her friend Marie (Cecile De France) arrive at the country home of Alex's family, Alex warns her: "Their French is even worse than mine." Since the parents hardly speak except to scream bilingually, this is not a problem.

The story: Alex and Marie are driving out to a country weekend with Alex's parents. Alex seems normal, but Marie is one of those goofy sorts who wanders into a cornfield for no better reason than for Alex to follow her,

shouting "Marie! Marie!" while the wind sighs on the sound track—a track that beavers away with Ominous Noises throughout the movie; is there a technical term like Ominoise?

The girls are followed into the deep, dark woods by a large man in blood-soaked coveralls, who drives a battered old truck that must have been purchased used from a 1940s French crime movie. We know he's up to no good the first time we see him. We know this because he drops a woman's severed head out the window of his truck.

At the isolated country home, Marie gets the guest room in the attic, and goes out into the Ominoise night to have a smoke. There is a swing hanging from a tree limb, and she sways back and forth on it while she smokes, so that later we can get the standard thriller shot of the swing seat still swinging, but now suddenly empty. This is not because Marie has been shortened by the decapitator, but because she has gone back into the house. Soon it's lights out, although there is enough in the way of moonglow and night lights for us to see Marie masturbate, perhaps so that we can see if it makes her lose her mind or anything.

The killer (Philippe Nahon) breaks into the house, stomps around heavily, and slaughters everyone except Alex, whom he takes prisoner, and Marie, who hides under the bed—yes, *hides under the bed.* The killer lifts up the mattress to check, but looks under the wrong end. Uh-huh. Marie should then remain still as a church mouse until the killer leaves, but no, she follows him downstairs and eventually ends up locked in the back of the truck with the kidnapped and chained Alex.

From the point when Marie crawls out from under the bed and follows the killer downstairs, she persists in making one wrong decision after another and ignoring obvious opportunities to escape. Perhaps she feels her presence is needed for the movie to continue, a likely possibility as the list of living characters shrinks steadily. She does have wit enough to pick up a big kitchen knife, so that we can enjoy the slasher movie cliché where such knives make the noise of steel-against-steel all by themselves, just by existing, and without having to scrape against anything.

After the truck leaves the deserted house and stops at a gas station, Marie has another opportunity to get help, but blows it. Reader, take my advice and never hang up on a 911 operator just because you get mad at him because he's so stupid he wants to know where you're calling from, especially not if the slasher has picked up an ax.

The rest of the movie you will have to see for yourself—or not, which would be my recommendation. I am tempted at this point to issue a Spoiler Warning and engage in discussion of several crucial events in the movie that would seem to be physically, logically, and dramatically impossible, but clever viewers will be able to see for themselves that the movie's plot has a hole that is not only large enough to drive a truck through, but in fact does have a truck driven right through it.

Note: The film's British title is Switchblade Romance, *which, if you see the film, will seem curiouser and curiouser.*

Hijacking Catastrophe: 9/11, Fear and the Selling of American Empire ★ ★ ★
NO MPAA RATING, 68 m., 2004

Narrated by Julian Bond. With Daniel Ellsberg, Karen Kwiatkowski, Noam Chomsky, and Norman Mailer. A documentary directed and produced by Sut Jhally and Jeremy Earp.

I have here a commentary by John Eisenhower, son of the late president, who states in the *Union Leader* of Manchester, New Hampshire, that for the first time in fifty years he plans to vote for the Democratic candidate for president. "The fact is that today's 'Republican' Party is one with which I am totally unfamiliar," he writes, citing its $440 billion budget deficit and unilateral foreign policy. The current administration, he says, "has confused confident leadership with hubris and arrogance."

That is essentially the same argument made in *Hijacking Catastrophe: 9/11, Fear and the Selling of American Empire,* the most outspoken and yet in some ways the calmest of the new documentaries opposing the Bush presidency. It charges that America is in the hands of radicals at the right-wing extreme of the Republican Party. This view has some backing among traditional conservatives; none other than Patrick Buchanan has founded a magazine, the *American Conservative,* to argue against Bush and the war in Iraq.

For the neocons, the movie says, the invasion of Iraq has been a goal since the early 1990s, and deputy secretary of defense Paul Wolfowitz, called the "intellectual force" of the group, chillingly wrote in a 2000 report that it would be hard to sell a preemptive strike to the American people, unless a "catastrophic event—like a new Pearl Harbor" made it seem necessary. Immediately after 9/11, he and his associates argued for an attack on Iraq, making a connection between Saddam Hussein and Osama bin Laden that has now been proven false, and claiming Saddam had weapons of mass destruction, which we now know he did not.

Hijacking Catastrophe essentially consists of a parade of talking heads, all of them arguing that the Bush administration is more radical than most Americans realize. To be sure, the movie tells only one side. There are no defenders of the administration, and some of the speakers are well-known left-wing critics such as Noam Chomsky, Norman Mailer, and Daniel Ellsberg. Others are more centrist, including Lieutenant Colonel Karen Kwiatkowski (retired), an Air Force staff officer at the Pentagon, retired Army Special Forces master sergeant Stan Goff, weapons inspector Scott Ritter, and Nobel laureate Jody Williams.

What they do is look at the camera and talk. Although the film is only sixty-eight minutes long, it's so intense that it seems longer, and a point comes when I half-wished the filmmakers would relent and give us some of that goofy Michael Moore stuff. In urgent sound bites of mounting alarm, they charge that the neocon insurgents envision an "American colossus" that stands "astride the world," makes its own policies, and disdains cooperation with the family of nations. We went into Iraq without UN backing not because we had to, the movie argues, but because we wanted to; it was a good way to weaken the organization. By the same token, budget deficits are useful because they will bankrupt programs such as Social Security and Medicare that the neocons oppose but cannot destroy through conventional legislation.

Well, that's what the movie says, and a lot more. As your correspondent, I report it. And I will receive e-mails from readers who will protest this review and tell me a movie critic has no business getting involved in politics. But here is the movie, and here is what it says.

The most difficult aspect of *Hijacking Catastrophe* is to accept the argument that the neocons have wanted to invade Iraq for years, as part of a plan to conquer and occupy the Middle East, and that is why 9/11 inspired their curious decision to deflect American power from bin Laden to Saddam, an uninvolved bystander. Why does this make me think of Larry punching Curly, who retaliates by punching Moe? Fear of terrorists provided their cover, and Norman Solomon of the Institute for Public Accuracy says Roosevelt's statement "the only thing we have to fear is fear itself" has been rewritten by the neocons and their Orange Alerts into "the only thing we have to fear is not enough fear."

It is an ancient debating technique to identify your opponent's ideas with similar statements by evildoers. Nevertheless, this movie opens with a quote that seems eerie in its relevance:

The people can always be brought to the bidding of the leaders. That is easy. All you have to do is tell them they are being attacked, and denounce the peacemakers for lack of patriotism and exposing the country to danger. It works the same in any country.

Hermann Goering said that at the Nuremberg trials.

The Hills Have Eyes ★ ½
R, 107 m., 2006

Aaron Stanford (Doug Bukowski), Kathleen Quinlan (Ethel Carter), Vinessa Shaw (Lynn Bukowski), Emilie de Ravin (Brenda Carter), Dan Byrd (Bobby Carter), Tom Bower (Gas Station Attendant), Ted Levine (Bob Carter). Directed by Alexandre Aja and produced by Wes Craven, Marianne Maddalena, and Peter Locke. Screenplay by Aja, and Gregory Levasseur, based on the screenplay by Craven.

It always begins with the Wrong Gas Station. In real life, as I pointed out in my review of a previous Wrong Gas Station movie, most gas stations are clean, well-lighted places where you can buy not only gasoline but also groceries, clothes, electronic devices, Jeff Foxworthy CDs, and a full line of Harley merchandise. In horror movies, however, the only gas station in the world is located on a desolate road in a godforsaken backwater. It is staffed by a degenerate who shuffles out in his coveralls and runs through a disgusting repertory of scratchings, spittings, chewings, twitchings, and leerings, while thoughtfully shifting mucus up and down his throat.

The clean-cut heroes of the movie, be they a family on vacation, newlyweds, college students, or backpackers, all have one thing in common. They believe everything this man tells them, especially when he suggests they turn left on the unpaved road for a shortcut. Does it ever occur to them that in this desolate wasteland with only one main road, it *must* be the road to stay on if they ever again want to use their cell phones?

No. It does not. They take the fatal detour and find themselves the prey of demented mutant incestuous cannibalistic gnashing slobberers, who carry pickaxes the way other people carry umbrellas. They occupy junkyards, towns made entirely of wax, nuclear waste zones, and Motel Hell ("It takes all kinds of critters to make Farmer Vincent's fritters"). That is the destiny that befalls a vacationing family in *The Hills Have Eyes*, which is a very loose remake of the 1977 movie of the same name.

The Carter family is on vacation. Dad (Ted Levine) is a retired detective who plans to become a security guard. Mom is sane, lovable Kathleen Quinlan. A daughter and son-in-law (Vinessa Shaw and Aaron Stanford) have a newborn babe. There are also two other Carter children (Dan Byrd and Emilie de Ravin), and two dogs named Beauty and Beast. They have hitched up an Airstream and are on a jolly family vacation through the test zones where 331 atmospheric nuclear tests took place in the 1950s and 1960s.

After the Carters turn down the wrong road, they're fair game for the people who are the eyes of the hills. These are descendants of miners who refused to leave their homes when the government ordered them away from the testing grounds. They hid in mines, drank radioactive water, reproduced with their damaged DNA, and brought forth mutants who live by eating trapped tourists.

There is an old bomb crater filled with the abandoned cars and trucks of their countless victims. It is curiously touching, in the middle of this polluted wasteland, to see a car that was towing a boat that still has its outboard motor attached. No one has explained what the boat was seeking at that altitude.

The plot is easily guessed. Ominous events occur. The family makes the fatal mistake of splitting up; Dad walks back to the Wrong Gas Station, while the dogs bark like crazy and run away, and young Bobby chases them into the hills. Meanwhile, the mutants entertain themselves by passing in front of the camera so quickly you can't really see them, while we hear a loud sound, halfway between a *swatch* and a *swootch*, on the sound track. Just as a knife in a slasher movie can make a sharpening sound just because it exists, so do mutants make *swatches* and *swootches* when they run in front of cameras.

I received some appalled feedback when I praised Rob Zombie's *The Devil's Rejects* (2005), but I admired two things about it: 1) It desired to entertain and not merely to sicken, and 2) its depraved killers were individuals with personalities, histories, and motives. *The Hills Have Eyes* finds an intriguing setting in "typical" fake towns built by the government, populated by mannequins, and intended to be destroyed by nuclear blasts. But its mutants are simply engines of destruction. There is a misshapen creature who coordinates attacks with a walkie-talkie; I would have liked to know more about him, but no luck.

Nobody in this movie has ever seen a Dead Teenager Movie, so they don't know 1) you never go off alone, 2) you especially never go off alone at night, and 3) you never follow your dog when it races off barking insanely, because you have more sense than the dog. It is also possibly not a good idea to walk back to the Wrong Gas Station to get help from the degenerate who sent you on the detour in the first place.

It is not faulty logic that derails *The Hills Have Eyes*, however, but faulty drama. The movie is a one-trick pony. We have the eaters and the eatees, and they will follow their destinies until some kind of desperate denouement, possibly followed by a final shot showing that It's Not Really Over, and there will be a *The Hills Have Eyes II*. Of course, there was already a *The Hills Have Eyes Part II* (1985), but then again there was a *The Hills Have Eyes* (1977) and that didn't stop them. Maybe this will. Isn't it pretty to think so.

A History of Violence ★ ★ ★ ½
R, 96 m., 2005

Viggo Mortensen (Tom Stall), Maria Bello (Edie Stall), Ed Harris (Carl Fogarty), William Hurt (Richie Cusack), Ashton Holmes (Jack Stall), Stephen McHattie (Leland Jones), Greg Bryk (Billy Orser), Heidi Hayes (Sarah Stall). Directed by David Cronenberg and produced by Cronenberg, Chris Bender, and J. C. Spink. Screenplay by Josh Olson, based on a graphic novel by John Wagner and Vince Locke.

David Cronenberg says his title *A History of Violence* has three levels: It refers 1) to a suspect with a long history of violence, 2) to the historical use of violence as a means of settling disputes, and 3) to the innate violence of Darwinian evolution, in which better-adapted organisms replace those less able to cope. "I am a complete Darwinian," says Cronenberg, whose new film is in many ways about the survival of the fittest—at all costs.

The movie opens in a small Indiana town. Tom Stall (Viggo Mortensen) runs one of those friendly little diners that act as the village crossroads and clearinghouse. He's the kind of guy everybody likes, married to a lawyer named Edie (Maria Bello), father of the teenager Jack (Ashton Holmes) and young Sarah (Heidi Hayes). He has one of those middle American accents in which every word translates into "I'm just folks."

So persuasive are the Indiana scenes that, despite the movie's opening moments, we wonder if Cronenberg has abandoned his own history of violence and decided to make a small-town slice of life: a Capra picture, perhaps, with Viggo Mortensen as Jimmy Stewart. Then all hell breaks loose. Two tough guys enter the diner to try a stickup. They have guns, mean business, threaten the customers and a waitress. Moving so quickly he seems to have been practicing the scene as choreography, Tom Stall takes out the two guys and ends up on the local front pages as a hero.

He makes a shy hero. He doesn't want to give interviews or talk about what he has done, and there are strained moments in his household as his wife worries about a seismic shift in his mood, and his son can't understand an unstated change in their relationship. Read no further if you want to preserve the reasons for these changes.

Tom Stall, as it turns out, has a secret he has been guarding for twenty years. He is named not Tom Stall but Joey, is not from Indiana but from Philadelphia, has tried to start a new life in a small town and failed because of this unexpected publicity. Soon more strangers arrive in town: Carl Fogarty (Ed Harris) turns up with two hard men in his employ. Something really bad has happened to Carl earlier in life, and we don't want to know how his face got that way.

Tom Stall has transformed himself so completely into a small-town family man that maybe there were years when he believed the story himself. The arrival of Fogarty makes that an illusion impossible to sustain, and he must return to Philadelphia and to an extraordinary scene with a man named Richie Cusack (William Hurt), whose role in Tom's (or Joey's) life I will leave for you to discover. Let me say that Hurt has done a lot of good acting in a lot of intriguing roles, but during his brief screen time in *A History of Violence*, he sounds notes we have not heard before.

Another important element in the plot involves the Stall family, especially Edie, the wife, and Jack, the son. What do you do when you discover that your husband or father has concealed everything about his early life? Was he lying to you or protecting you? Did you love someone who did not really exist?

Cronenberg is a director with a wide range, usually played by the left hand. He has ventured into horror, the macabre, science fiction, satire, and the extremely peculiar. In his 2003 film *Spider*, he starred Ralph Fiennes as a mental patient in a halfway house whose reality balances between everyday details and haunting memories of his past. *Dead Ringers* (1988) has Jeremy Irons in a dual role as twins, one not so nice, the other not so nice either. *The Dead Zone* (1983) has Christopher Walken losing five years of his life and becoming a different kind of person. These shifts in personal reality seem fascinating to Cronenberg.

But what is Cronenberg saying about Tom, or Joey? Which life is the real one? The nature of Joey's early life was established by the world he was born into. His second life was created by conscious choice. Which is dominant, nature or nurture? Hyde or Jekyll? Are we kidding our-

selves when we think we can live peacefully? Is our peace purchased at the price of violence done elsewhere? In *A History of Violence*, it all comes down to this: If Tom Stall had truly been the cheerful small-town guy he pretended to be, he would have died in that diner. It was Joey who saved him. And here is the crucial point: Because of Joey, the son, Jack, makes discoveries about himself that he might not have ever needed (or wanted) to make.

A History of Violence seems deceptively straightforward, coming from a director with Cronenberg's quirky complexity. But think again. This is a movie not about plot, but about character. It is about how people turn out the way they do, and about whether the world sometimes functions like a fool's paradise. I never give a moment's thought about finding water to drink. In New Orleans after Hurricane Katrina, would I have been willing to steal from stores or fight other people for drinkable water? Yes, if it meant life for myself and my family. But I would have made a pitiful thief and fighter, and probably would have failed.

Since I am wandering, let me wander farther: At the Toronto Film Festival I saw a screening of *Nanook of the North*, the great documentary about Eskimos surviving in the hostile Arctic wilderness. They live because they hunt and kill. Of the three levels *A History of Violence* refers to, I think Cronenberg is most interested in the third, in the survival of the fittest. Not the good, the moral, the nice, but the fittest. The movie is based on a graphic novel by John Wagner and Vince Locke. It could also be illuminated by *The Selfish Gene* by Richard Dawkins. I think that's why Cronenberg gives his hero a son: to show that Jack inherited what he did not ever suspect his father possessed.

Hitch ★ ★ ½
PG-13, 120 m., 2005

Will Smith (Hitch), Kevin James (Albert), Eva Mendes (Sara), Amber Valletta (Allegra), Michael Rapaport (Ben), Adam Arkin (Max). Directed by Andy Tennant and produced by James Lassiter, Will Smith, and Teddy Zee. Screenplay by Kevin Bisch.

"Ninety percent of what you're saying isn't coming out of your mouth."

So says the Date Doctor. You communicate with your body language, your posture, your mood, your attitude about yourself. Nothing a guy can say will impress a woman nearly as much as the nonverbal messages she receives. So stand up straight, Fat Albert, and stop slumping around as if your tummy can be hidden in the shadows.

Hitch is a romantic comedy, timed for Valentine's Day, starring Will Smith as Alex "Hitch" Hitchens, professional dating consultant. In the cutthroat world of New York romance, where fates are decided in an instant, your average Lonely Guy needs skilled counseling. Hitch is your man. He understands women: how to get their attention, how to seem heroic in their eyes, what to tell them, and what definitely not to tell them.

Some of his strategies would be right at home in a silent comedy, such as an opening Meet Cute in which a babe's beloved pet dog is apparently saved from instant death by a guy who wants to get to know her. Others are more subtle, involving inside intelligence so that you seem able to read her mind. Then there are the grand dramatic gestures.

For Hitch's client Albert (Kevin James), the romantic quarry seems forever beyond his reach. He is in love with the rich, powerful, and beautiful Allegra (Amber Valletta), and surely she would not date a shy and pudgy accountant—would she? But at a board meeting he is outraged by investment advice she is being given, and in a Grand Dramatic, etc., he resigns. That gets her attention. She's touched that the guy would care so much.

Yes, but how can Albert follow up? He's one of those guys whose shirts seem to come back from the laundry with the mustard already on them. Hitch works desperately to smooth him out, clean him up, and give him some class. Meanwhile, his own romantic life is in a shambles. He's fallen in love with a really hot babe who is also smart and cynical. This is Sara (Eva Mendes), who writes for a gossip column not a million miles apart from Page Six. None of his advice seems to work for Hitch, maybe because in the game of romantic chess, Sara can see more moves ahead, maybe because—can this be possible?—he is losing his cool by trying too hard.

Hitch, you will have perceived, is not a great cinematic breakthrough. It depends for its ap-

peal on the performances, and gets a certain undeserved mileage because of the likability of Will Smith and Kevin James, who are both seen with sympathy. Allegra (Valletta) is a sweetheart, too, and not as unapproachable as she seems. But Sara is a real challenge, played by Eva Mendes as the kind of woman who seems more desirable the more she seems unattainable.

There is a purpose for a movie like *Hitch*, and that purpose is to supply a pleasant and undemanding romantic comedy that you can rent next Valentine's Day. It's not a first-run destination, especially with *Bride and Prejudice* and *The Wedding Date* playing in the same multiplex. It's not that I dislike it; it's that it just doesn't seem entirely necessary. The premise is intriguing, and for a time it seems that the Date Doctor may indeed know things about women that most men in the movies are not allowed to know, but the third act goes on autopilot just when the doctor should be in.

The Hitchhiker's Guide to the Galaxy ★ ★
PG, 110 m., 2005

Martin Freeman (Arthur Dent), Sam Rockwell (President Zaphod Beeblebrox), Mos Def (Ford Prefect), Zooey Deschanel (Trillian), Bill Nighy (Slartibartfast), Anna Chancellor (Questular Rontok), John Malkovich (Humma Kavula), Warwick Davis (Marvin the Paranoid Android), Alan Rickman (Marvin the Paranoid Android). Directed by Garth Jennings and produced by Gary Barber, Roger Birnbaum, Jonathan Glickman, Nick Goldsmith, and Jay Roach. Screenplay by Douglas Adams and Karey Kirkpatrick, based on the book by Adams.

It is possible that *The Hitchhiker's Guide to the Galaxy* should be reviewed by, and perhaps seen by, only people who are familiar with the original material to the point of obsession. My good friend Andy Ihnatko is such a person, and considered the late Douglas Adams to be one of only three or four people worthy to be mentioned in the same breath as P. G. Wodehouse. Adams may in fact have been the only worthy person.

Such a Hitchhiker Master would be able to review this movie in terms of its in-jokes, its references to various generations of the Guide universe, its earlier manifestations as books, radio shows, a TV series, and the center of a matrix of Websites. He would understand what the filmmakers have done with Adams's material, and how, and why, and whether the film is faithful to the spirit of the original.

I cannot address any of those issues, and I would rather plead ignorance than pretend to knowledge. If you're familiar with the Adams material, I suggest you stop reading right now before I disappoint or even anger you. All I can do is speak to others like myself, who will be arriving at the movie innocent of *Hitchhiker* knowledge. To such a person, two things are possible if you see the movie:

1. You will become intrigued by its whimsical and quirky sense of humor, understand that a familiarity with the books is necessary, read one or more of the *Hitchhiker* books, return to the movie, appreciate it more, and eventually be absorbed into the legion of Adams admirers.

2. You will find the movie tiresomely twee, and notice that it obviously thinks it is being funny at times when you do not have the slightest clue why that should be. You will sense a certain desperation as actors try to sustain a tone that belongs on the page and not on the screen. And you will hear dialogue that preserves the content of written humor at the cost of sounding as if the characters are holding a Douglas Adams reading.

I take the second choice. The movie does not inspire me to learn lots more about *The Hitchhiker's Guide to the Galaxy, The Ultimate Hitchhiker's Guide, The Salmon of Doubt,* and so on. Like *The Life Aquatic With Steve Zissou,* but with less visual charm, it is a conceit with little to be conceited about.

The story involves Arthur Dent (Martin Freeman), for whom one day there is bad news and good news. The bad news is that Earth is being destroyed to build an intergalactic freeway, which will run right through his house. The good news is that his best friend, Ford Prefect (Mos Def), is an alien temporarily visiting Earth to do research for a series of *Hitchhiker's Guides,* and can use his magic ring to beam both of them up to a vast spaceship operated by the Vogons, an alien race that looks like a cross between Jabba the Hutt and Harold Bloom. The Vogons are not a cruel race, apart from the fact that they insist on reading their poetry, which is so bad it has driven people to catatonia.

Once aboard this ship, Arthur and Ford are hitchhikers themselves, and quickly transfer to another ship named the *Heart of Gold,* commanded by the galaxy's president, Zaphod Beeblebrox (Sam Rockwell), who has a third arm that keeps emerging from his tunic like the concealed arm of a samurai warrior, with the proviso that a samurai conceals two arms at the most. Zaphod is two-faced in a most intriguing way. Also on the ship are Trillian (Zooey Deschanel), an earthling, and Marvin the Android (body by Warwick Davis, voice by Alan Rickman), who is a terminal kvetcher. There is also a role for John Malkovich, who has a human trunk and a lower body apparently made from spindly robotic cranes' legs; this makes him a wonder to behold, up to a point.

What these characters do is not as important as what they say, how they say it, and what it will mean to Douglas Adams fans. To me, it got old fairly quickly. The movie was more of a revue than a narrative, more about moments than an organizing purpose, and cute to the point that I yearned for some corrosive wit from its second cousin, the Monty Python universe. But of course I do not get the joke. I do not much want to get the joke, but maybe you will. It is not an evil movie. It wants only to be loved, but movies that want to be loved are like puppies in the pound: No matter how earnestly they wag their little tails, you can only adopt one at a time.

A Home at the End of the World ★ ★ ★ ½
R, 120 m., 2004

Colin Farrell (Bobby Morrow), Dallas Roberts (Jonathan Glover), Robin Wright Penn (Clare), Sissy Spacek (Alice Glover). Directed by Michael Mayer and produced by John Hart, Tom Hulce, Pamela Koffler, Hunt Lowry, Katie Roumel, Jeff Sharp, Christine Vachon, and John Wells. Screenplay by Michael Cunningham, based on his novel.

A Home at the End of the World tells the story of Bobby Morrow, who at seven sees his adored older brother walk into a glass door and die, who lost his mother even earlier, who finds his father dead in bed, who solemnly announces to his best friend, "I'm the last of my kind." Soon he is living with the friend's family, so comfortably that the mother eventually has to tell him, "You can't just live with us forever." By then he is twenty-four.

Bobby is played as an adult by Colin Farrell in a performance that comes as an astonishment. Farrell is a star who has appeared mostly in action pictures that reflect his bad-boy offscreen image. Here he plays a quiet, complex, unconventional character, a young man who has been deeply hurt, who fears abandonment, and whose guiding principle has become, "I just want everybody to be happy."

Bobby is sweet. Everybody likes him. But does anybody know him? He has such a need to please, to reassure, to comfort, to heal, that it is hard to say what might comfort and heal him. We attend to this character more than to most, because we like him but find him a mystery.

His best friend is Jonathan (played as an adult by Dallas Roberts), an outsider in high school until Bobby befriends him, gives him pot for the first time, and shares his dead brother's philosophy, which is basically that all is good, life is wonderful, so chill. Jonathan is clearly gay from an early age, and as the two boys share a bed, they eventually share a shy sexual experience. Jonathan moves to New York and Bobby eventually follows, joining a household that also includes Clare (Robin Wright Penn). She is older, experiments with bizarre hair-coloring strategies, embraces the unconventional, and eventually embraces Bobby. He confesses he is a virgin and may not be "adept"; she calls him "junior" and takes charge.

So is Bobby actually straight? "Bobby's not gay," Jonathan muses. "It's hard to say what Bobby is." Hard, because Bobby is much less interested in sex than in helping other people to feel better. That's why the filmmakers were correct in their well-publicized decision to leave out Farrell's scene of full frontal nudity; the movie is not about the size or function of Bobby's penis but about its friendliness. Consider his muted flirtation with Jonathan's mother, Alice (Sissy Spacek). He gives her pot, dances with her, turns her on to Laura Nyro, frees her to accept Jonathan's lifestyle, and to wonder what directions her own life might have taken, if she had not been so conventional, suburban, and married.

A Home at the End of the World, directed by Michael Mayer, is based on a novel and screenplay by Michael Cunningham, author of *The Hours*. Once again he is fascinated by very particular kinds of unconventional households, by nontraditional family groups that do not even fall into the usual nontraditional categories. One might think Bobby, Jonathan, and Clare were all gay, but no: Jonathan has an active homosexual life, but Clare is straight, and so concerned with remaining free that sex is approached warily. When she and Bobby have a daughter, their household makes a move toward a more conventional arrangement, and then backs off.

There is also the question of how Jonathan feels about their little family. He loves Bobby, and his many sexual partners are a way to escape that inescapable fact. Bobby loves him, but in the same way he loves everybody. Jonathan sometimes feels Bobby is elbowing him out of his own life: "You can be the son and I'll be the best friend." Clare studies Bobby and is baffled: "You can live in the suburbs, the East Village, the country—it just doesn't make any difference to you, does it?" By now they have moved to Woodstock, bought a little frame house, and opened a café in town.

The movie exists outside our expectations for such stories. Nothing about it is conventional. The three-member household is puzzling not only to us but to its members. We expect conflict, resolution, an ending happy or sad, but what we get is mostly life, muddling through. Some days are good and other days are bad. When Bobby makes the most important decision of the film, we know why he makes it, but Clare doesn't and it's hard to say about Jonathan. Bobby doesn't explain. He makes it because one of them needs him more than the other; there is really no thought of himself.

Plots in fiction are usually based on need, greed, fear, and guilt. Even love plays out in that context. All Bobby has is the need to please, in order to assure himself of a place where he belongs. A home. Colin Farrell is astonishing in the movie, not least because the character is such a departure from everything he has done before. Charlize Theron's leap of faith in *Monster* comes to mind, although Farrell's work here is less risky and lower-key. Rare, in a movie that sidesteps melodrama, for a character to fascinate us with his elusiveness.

"Is there anything you can't do?" one of them asks him.

"I couldn't be alone," he says.

Home on the Range ★ ★ ½
PG, 76 m., 2004

With the voices of: Roseanne Barr (Maggie), Judi Dench (Mrs. Caloway), Jennifer Tilly (Grace), Cuba Gooding Jr. (Buck), Randy Quaid (Alameda Slim), Richard Riehle (Sheriff Brown), Charles Dennis (Rico), Steve Buscemi (Wesley), Charles Haid (Lucky Jack), Estelle Harris (Audrey). Directed by Will Finn and John Sanford and produced by Alice Dewey Goldstone. Screenplay by Finn and Sanford.

Home on the Range, Disney's new animated feature, has the genial friendliness of a 1940s singing cowboy movie, and the plot could have been borrowed from Hopalong Cassidy or Roy Rogers, apart from the slight detail that they aren't cows. The new songs by Alan Menken ("The Little Mermaid," "Beauty and the Beast") are in the tradition of western swing; I can easily imagine Gene Autry performing any of them, including the yodeling number, and wasn't too surprised to find that the Sons of the Pioneers starred in a 1946 movie with the same name.

The pace is up-to-date, though. Gene Autry and Roy Rogers always had time to relax next to a campfire and sing a tune, but *Home on the Range* jumps with the energy of a cartoon short subject. The movie is said to be Disney's last release in the traditional 2-D animation style; its feature cartoons in the future will have the rounded 3-D look of *Finding Nemo.* Whether that is a loss or not depends on how you relate to animation; there are audiences even for those dreadful Saturday morning cartoon adventures that are so stingy on animation they're more like 1.5-D.

The story takes place on the Patch of Heaven ranch, which faces foreclosure because of the depredations of the vile cattle rustler Alameda Slim (voice by Randy Quaid). Pearl, the owner, could raise money by selling her cows—but they're family, you see, and so presumably they'll all be homeless soon. But then the cows get a bright idea: Why not track down Slim, collect the $750 reward, pay off the bank, and save the ranch?

Each of the cows has unique qualities to contribute to this effort. Mrs. Caloway (Judi Dench) is the voice of prudence. Grace (Jennifer Tilly) is the New Age cow, who makes observations like, "This is an organic problem and needs a holistic solution." Their catalyst is a newcomer to the farm, Maggie (Roseanne Barr), who quickly becomes the aggressive, in-your-face leader. Rounding out the team is Buck (Cuba Gooding Jr.), the stallion, who is a master of the martial arts.

The voices are all quickly recognizable, especially Barr's; the idea of using the voices of familiar stars instead of anonymous dubbing artists has added an intriguing dimension to recent animated features. Listen, for example, to Randy Quaid as the dastardly Slim. It's traditional in Disney animation to fill the edges of the screen with hyperactive little supporting characters, and we get Lucky Jack the jackrabbit (Charles Haid) and Audrey the chicken, who is chicken (Estelle Harris). There are also three very busy little pigs, and Steve Buscemi almost seems to be playing himself as a critter named Wesley.

Buck, by the way, has delusions of grandeur; he thinks maybe he can capture Slim and collect the reward, especially after he becomes the horse of the famed bounty hunter Rico (Charles Dennis), which leads to a fierce competition with the cows. The plot makes pit stops at all the obligatory Western sights: saloons, mine shafts, main streets, deserts with Monument Valley landscapes, and trains. All of these locations become the backdrops of chases in a movie that seldom stands still.

The songs are performed by k.d. lang, Bonnie Raitt, Tim McGraw, and the Bleu Sisters. None of the songs is likely to be requested by fans at future concerts. They sound generic and don't have the zest of Menken's earlier work.

A movie like this is fun for kids: bright, quick-paced, with broad, outrageous characters. But *Home on the Range* doesn't have the crossover quality of the great Disney films like *Beauty and the Beast* and *The Lion King.* And it doesn't have the freshness and originality of a more traditional movie like *Lilo & Stitch.* Its real future, I suspect, lies in home video. It's only seventy-six minutes long, but although kids will like it, their parents will be sneaking looks at their watches.

The Honeymooners ★ ★ ★
PG-13, 85 m., 2005

Cedric the Entertainer (Ralph Kramden), Mike Epps (Ed Norton), Gabrielle Union (Alice Kramden), Regina Hall (Trixie Norton), Eric Stoltz (William Davis), John Leguizamo (Dodge), Jon Polito (Kirby), Carol Woods (Alice's Mom), Anne Pitoniak (Miss Benvenuti). Directed by John Schultz and produced by Julie Durk, David T. Friendly, Eric Rhone, and Marc Turtletaub. Screenplay by Barry W. Blaustein, Danny Jacobson, Saladin K. Patterson, Don Rhymer, and David Sheffield.

The Honeymooners is a surprise and a delight, a movie that escapes the fate of weary TV retreads and creates characters that remember the originals, yes, but also stand on their own. Playing Ralph Kramden and Ed Norton, Cedric the Entertainer and Mike Epps don't even try to imitate Jackie Gleason and Art Carney; they borrow a few notes, just to show us they've seen the program, and build from there. And Gabrielle Union and Regina Hall, as Alice and Trixie, flower as the two long-suffering wives, who in this version get more story time and do not ever, even once, get offered a one-way ticket to the moon. Instead, Ralph even sweetly promises Alice he will "take her to the moon," although, to be sure, that's when he proposes marriage.

The externals of the movie resemble the broad outlines of the TV classic. The Kramdens live downstairs, the Nortons live upstairs, Ralph drives a bus, Ed is proud of his command of the sewer system's scenic routes. Ralph is a dreamer who falls for one get-rich-quick scheme after another, and the closet is filled with his failed dreams: the pet cactus, the Y2K survival kit. His wife, Alice, is the realist. All she wanted when she got married was to live in a home of their own. They're still renting.

Cedric the Entertainer is funny in the role, yes, but he's also sweet. He understands the underlying goodness and pathos of Ralph Kramden, who is all bluff. Mike Epps makes Norton into a sidekick like Sancho Panza, who realizes

his friend is nutty, but can't bear to see him lose his illusions.

The plot: Alice and Trixie, who work as waitresses at a diner, meet a sweet little old lady (Anne Pitoniak) who wants to sell her duplex at a reasonable price. They're up against a wily real estate king (Eric Stoltz) who wants to turn the whole block into condos, but if they can come up with a $20,000 down payment, the house is theirs. That means $10,000 from the Kramdens, who have $5,000 in the bank; Alice thinks maybe she can borrow the rest from her mother (Carol Woods), a fearsome force of nature who served in Vietnam, was a Golden Gloves champ, and despises her son-in-law (her advice to Ralph on eating his dinner: "When you get to the plate, stop").

There is a problem with Alice's financial plan. The problem is that Ralph has spent all the money on a series of failed dreams. Desperate to raise cash, Ralph and Ed try hip-hop dancing in the park, at which they are very bad, and begging as blind men, at which they are worse. Then they find a greyhound dog in a trash bin, and decide to race it at the dog track.

Enter John Leguizamo as Dodge, a "trainer" recommended by the track's shady owner (Jon Polito). Leguizamo is optimistic ("I started with nothing and still have most of it left") and fancies himself a Dog Whisperer, but Izzy the dog doesn't seem to understand the principle behind racing, which is that he has to leave the gate and run around the track. Ralph, however, believes in the "homeless Dumpster dog," and in a big scene describes him as "a survivor . . . like Seabiscuit, Rocky, and Destiny's Child."

All of this is handled by the director John Schultz *(Like Mike)* with an easygoing confidence in the material. There's nothing frantic about the performances, nothing forced about the plot; the emphasis is on Ralph's underlying motive, which is to prove to Alice that he is not invariably a failure and can buy her a house one way or another. That was the secret of Gleason's *Honeymooners*—Ralph lost his temper and ranted and raved, but he had a good heart, and Alice knew it.

The supporting performances bring the movie one comic boost after another. Leguizamo's con-man dog trainer is an inven-

311

tion in flim-flammery, Polito's track owner is an opportunist, Stoltz finds just the right slick charm as the real estate sharpie, and Carol Woods is the mother-in-law Ralph Kramden deserves for his sins. Regina Hall and Gabrielle Union spend a lot of their scenes with each other, while the boys are out getting in trouble. They provide the engine that drives the movie's emotions: They want that house, they have a deadline to meet, and Ralph grows increasingly desperate because he doesn't want to let Alice down yet once again.

I was afraid Cedric the Entertainer and Mike Epps would try to imitate Gleason and Carney. Not at all. What they do is work a subtle tribute to the earlier actors into new inventions of their own. Cedric has that way of moving his neck around inside his collar that reminds us of Gleason, and the slow burn, and the wistful enthusiasm as he outlines plans that even he knows are doomed. Epps has the hat always hanging on at an angle, the pride in the sewer system, the willingness to go along with his goofy pal. And the movie's story actually does work as a story and not simply as a wheezy Hollywood formula. Sometimes you walk into a movie with quiet dread, and walk out with quiet delight.

Hoot ★ ½
PG, 105 m., 2006

Logan Lerman (Roy Eberhardt), Luke Wilson (Officer Delinko), Brie Larson (Beatrice Leep), Cody Linley (Mullet Fingers), Eric Phillips (Dana Matherson), Dean Collins (Garrett), Tim Blake Nelson (Curly Branitt). Directed by Wil Shriner and produced by Frank Marshall and Jimmy Buffett. Screenplay by Shriner, based on the novel by Carl Hiaasen.

Hoot has its heart in the right place, but I have been unable to locate its brain. Here is a movie about three kids who begin by disliking or fearing one another and end up as urban guerrillas, sabotaging the construction of a pancake house that will destroy a nesting ground for burrowing owls. Yes, there are such birds, who sublet burrows originally dug by squirrels and prairie dogs and such, or occasionally dig their own dream burrows. They seem wide-eyed with astonishment at

their lifestyle, but actually that is just the way they look.

The hero of the movie is Roy Eberhardt (Logan Lerman), whom we meet on horseback in Montana, complaining that his family is moving again—this time to Florida. His dad has moved something like five times in eight years, which in the white-collar world means you are either incompetent or the CEO. In his new school, Roy is picked on by a bully and breaks the bully's nose, to create a subplot utterly unnecessary to the story.

His school career takes an upturn when he meets two extraordinary (not to mention unbelievable) students his own age. Beatrice the Bear (Brie Larson) is a soccer player with a fearsome reputation, which the movie halfheartedly establishes in a perfunctory manner before revealing her as a true-blue best pal who befriends Roy Eberhardt (he often is referred to by both names). Meanwhile, Roy Eberhardt is fascinated by a kid he sees running barefoot through the town. He tries to chase him, fails, finally catches up with him, is scared off by a sack of cottonmouth snakes, and eventually makes friends with him. This is Mullet Fingers (Cody Linley), a cross between Tarzan and Huckleberry Finn.

Mullet lives in hiding on a houseboat, doesn't go to school, and devotes his life to sabotaging the efforts by Curly (Tim Blake Nelson) to build the hated pancake house. He pulls up the surveying stakes, steals the seat from the bulldozer, and otherwise generates trouble for the local Keystone Kop, named Officer Delinko (Luke Wilson). Delinko is so incompetent that one night he stakes out the construction site and oversleeps because Mullet Fingers has painted all the windows of his prowler black.

The movie's climax involves one of those situations where everyone in the town arrives at the same time in the same place to hear incriminating evidence that forces the dastardly villains to abandon their plans. Oops, I gave away the ending, if you were expecting that the film would conclude with the death of the owls.

Hoot is based on a Newbery Honor novel by Carl Hiaasen, the Florida novelist. That gives it a provenance, but not a pedigree. (Having written the preceding sentence, I do not know what it means, but I like the way it reads.) I suspect the movie's target audience will think it plays suspiciously like an after-school special and lacks the punch and artistry of such superior family films as *Millions* and *Shiloh*. The villains are sitcom caricatures, the kids (especially Mullet Fingers) are likable but not remotely believable, and it is never quite explained why anyone would build a pancake house in a wilderness area that seems to be far from any major road.

Note: If you are a viewer of intelligence and curiosity and live in a city where human beings still program some of the theaters, there is a much better movie right now about guerrillas fighting to protect an endangered species. It is Mountain Patrol: Kekexili. *You have a choice: an inane dead zone of sitcom clichés, or a stunning adventure shot on location in the high deserts of Asia.*

Hostage ★ ★ ★
R, 113 m., 2005

Bruce Willis (Jeff Talley), Kevin Pollak (Mr. Smith), Jonathan Tucker (Dennis Kelly), Ben Foster (Mars), Jimmy Bennett (Tommy Smith), Michelle Horn (Jennifer Smith), Jimmy "Jax" Pinchak (Sean Mack), Marshall Allman (Kevin Kelly), Serena Scott Thomas (Jane Talley). Directed by Florent Emilio Siri and produced by Mark Gordon, Arnold Rifkin, and Bob Yari. Screenplay by Doug Richardson, based on a novel by Robert Crais.

The opening titles of *Hostage* are shot in saturated blacks and reds with a raw, graphic feel, and the movie's color photography tilts toward dark high-contrast. That matches the mood, which is hard-boiled and gloomy. Bruce Willis, who feels like a resident of action thrillers, not a visitor, dials down here into a man of fierce focus and private motives; for the second half of the movie, no one except for (some of) the bad guys knows what really motivates him.

There's also an interesting use of the movie's three original villains, who are joined later by evildoers from an entirely different sphere. As the film opens, three gormless teenagers in a pickup truck follow a rich girl being driven "in her daddy's Escalade" to a mountaintop mansion with fearsome security safeguards. Their motive: Steal the Cadillac. These characters are Mars (Ben Foster), a mean customer with a record, and two brothers: Dennis and Kevin

Kelly (Jonathan Tucker and Marshall Allman). Kevin is the kid brother along for the ride, appalled by the lawbreaking Mars leads his brother into.

Trapped inside the house when police respond to an alarm, they take hostages: Smith, the rich man (Kevin Pollak), his teenage daughter, Jennifer (Michelle Horn), and his young son, Tommy (Jimmy Bennett). Bruce Willis plays the police chief who leads the first response team, but after a bad hostage experience in Los Angeles, he has retired to Ventura County to avoid just such adventures, and hands over authority to the sheriff's department. Then, inexplicably, he returns and demands to take command again.

Moderate spoiler warning: What motivates him is that unknown kidnappers have captured Willis's own wife and child, and are holding them hostage. They want Willis to obtain a DVD in the Smith house, which (we gather) contains crucial information about illegal financial dealings. So we have a hostage crisis within a hostage crisis, and Willis is trying to free two sets of hostages, only one known to his fellow lawmen.

This is ingenious, and adds an intriguing complexity to what could have been a one-level story. Some other adornments, however, seem unlikely. Little Tommy is able to grab his sister's cell phone and move secretly throughout the house, using his secret knowledge of air ducts and obscure construction details. This development takes full advantage of the Air Duct Rule, which teaches us that all air ducts are large enough to crawl through, and lead directly to vantage points above crucial events in the action. Left unanswered is why the three hostage takers aren't concerned that the kid is missing for long periods of time.

Some elements exist entirely for the convenience of the plot. For example, the Kevin Pollack character functions long enough to establish his role and importance, then is conveniently unconscious when not needed, then is on the brink of death when Willis desperately wants to revive him, then miraculously recovers and is able to act with admirable timing at a crucial moment. I would love to examine his medical charts during these transitions.

But I am not much concerned about such

logical flaws, because the main line of the movie is emotional, driven by the Bruce Willis character, who is able to project more intensity with less overacting than most of his rivals. He brings credibility to movies that can use some, and that will be invaluable in *Die Hard 4*. The mechanics of the final showdown are unexpected and yet show an undeniable logic, and are sold by the acting skills of Willis and Pollak.

The movie was directed by Florent Emilio Siri, creator of two Tom Clancy–written video games, which may explain why some of my colleagues were chortling when the Willis character uses his knowledge of Captain Woobah and Planet Xenon (persons and places unknown to me) to reassure Little Tommy. I say, if you know it, flaunt it. If he had been quoting Nietzsche, now that would have been a red flag.

What Siri brings to the show is an intimate visual style that keeps us claustrophobically close to the action, an ability to make action sequences clear enough to follow, and a dark sensibility that leads to at least two deaths we do not really expect. In scenes where a hero must outgun four or five armed opponents, however, *Hostage* does use the reliable action movie technique of cutting from one target to the next, so that we never see what the others are doing while the first ones are being shot. Waiting for their close-ups, I suppose.

Hotel Rwanda ★ ★ ★ ★

PG-13, 110m., 2004

Don Cheadle (Paul Rusesabagina), Sophie Okonedo (Tatiana), Nick Nolte (Colonel Oliver), Joaquin Phoenix (Jack). Directed by Terry George and produced by Terry George and A. Kitman Ho. Screenplay by Keir Pearson and George.

You do not believe you can kill them all?
Why not? Why not? We are halfway there already.

In 1994 in Rwanda, a million members of the Tutsi tribe were killed by members of the Hutu tribe, in a massacre that took place while the world looked away. *Hotel Rwanda* is not the story of that massacre. It is the story of a hotel manager who saved the lives of 1,200 people by being, essentially, a very good hotel manager. The man is named Paul Rusesabagina, and

he is played by Don Cheadle as a man of quiet, steady competence in a time of chaos. This is not the kind of man the camera silhouettes against mountaintops, but the kind of man who knows how things work in the real world, and uses his skills of bribery, flattery, apology, and deception to save these lives who have come into his care.

I have known a few hotel managers fairly well, and I think if I were hiring diplomats they would make excellent candidates. They speak several languages. They are discreet. They know how to function appropriately in different cultures. They know when a bottle of Scotch will repay itself six times over. They know how to handle complaints. And they know everything that happens under their roof, from the millionaire in the penthouse to the bellboy who can get you a girl (the wise manager fires such bellboys, except perhaps for one who is prudent and trustworthy and a useful resource on certain occasions).

Paul is such a hotel manager. He is a Hutu, married to a Tutsi named Tatiana (Sophie Okonedo). He has been trained in Belgium and runs the four-star Hotel Des Milles Collines in the capital city of Kigali. He does his job very well. He understands that when a general's briefcase is taken for safekeeping, it contains bottles of good Scotch when it is returned. He understands that to get the imported beer he needs, a bribe must take place. He understands that his guests are accustomed to luxury, which must be supplied even here in a tiny central African nation wedged against Tanzania, Uganda, and the Congo. Do these understandings make him a bad man? Just the opposite. They make him an expert on situational ethics. The result of all the things he knows is that the hotel runs well and everyone is happy.

Then the genocide begins, suddenly, but after a long history. Rwanda's troubles began, as so many African troubles began, when European colonial powers established nations that ignored traditional tribal boundaries. Enemy tribes were forced into the same land. For years in Rwanda under the Belgians, the Tutsis ruled, and killed not a few Hutu. Now the Hutus are in control, and armed troops prowl the nation, killing Tutsis.

There is a United Nations "presence" in Rwanda, represented by Colonel Oliver (Nick

Nolte). He sees what is happening, informs his superiors, asks for help and intervention, and is ignored. Paul Rusesabagina informs corporate headquarters in Brussels of the growing tragedy, but the hotel in Kigali is not the chain's greatest concern. Finally it comes down to these two men acting as freelancers to save more than a thousand lives they have somehow become responsible for.

When *Hotel Rwanda* premiered at Toronto 2004, two or three reviews criticized the film for focusing on Rusesabagina and the colonel, and making little effort to "depict" the genocide as a whole. But director Terry George and writer Keir Pearson have made exactly the correct decision. A film cannot be about a million murders, but it can be about how a few people respond. Paul Rusesabagina, as it happens, is a real person, and Colonel Oliver is based on one, and *Hotel Rwanda* is about what they really did. The story took shape after Pearson visited Rwanda and heard of a group of people who were saved from massacre.

Don Cheadle's performance is always held resolutely at the human level. His character intuitively understands that only by continuing to act as a hotel manager can he achieve anything. His hotel is hardly functioning, the economy has broken down, the country is ruled by anarchy, but he puts on his suit and tie every morning and fakes business as usual—even on a day he is so frightened he cannot tie his tie.

He deals with a murderous Hutu general, for example, not as an enemy or an outlaw, but as a longtime client who knows that the value of a good cigar cannot be measured in cash. Paul has trained powerful people in Kigali to consider the Hotel Des Milles Collines an oasis of sophistication and decorum, and now he pretends that is still the case. It isn't, but it works as a strategy because it cues a different kind of behavior; a man who has yesterday directed a mass murder might today want to show that he knows how to behave appropriately in the hotel lobby.

Nolte's performance is also in a precise key. He came to Rwanda as a peace-keeper, and now there is no peace to keep. The nations are united in their indifference toward Rwanda. Nolte's bad-boy headlines distract from his acting gifts; here his character is steady, wise, cynical, and a master of the possible. He makes a considered

choice in ignoring his orders and doing what he can do, right now, right here, to save lives.

How the 1,200 people come to be "guests" in the hotel is a chance of war. Some turn left, some right, some live, some die. Paul is concerned above all with his own family. As a Hutu he is safe, but his wife is Tutsi, his children are at threat, and in any event he is far beyond thinking in tribal terms. He has spent years storing up goodwill, and now he calls in favors. He moves the bribery up another level. He hides people in his hotel. He lies. He knows how to use a little blackmail: Sooner or later, he tells a powerful general, the world will take a reckoning of what happened in Kigali, and if Paul is not alive to testify for him, who else will be believed?

This all succeeds as riveting drama. *Hotel Rwanda* is not about hotel management, but about heroism and survival. Rusesabagina rises to the challenge. The film works not because the screen is filled with meaningless special effects, formless action, and vast digital armies, but because Don Cheadle, Nick Nolte, and the filmmakers are interested in how two men choose to function in an impossible situation. Because we sympathize with these men, we are moved by the film. Deep movie emotions for me usually come not when the characters are sad, but when they are good. You will see what I mean.

Note: The character of Colonel Oliver is based on Lieutenant General Romeo Dallaire, a Canadian who was the UN force commander in Rwanda. His autobiography, Shake Hands with the Devil, *was published in October 2004.*

House Of D ★ ½
PG-13, 96 m., 2005

Anton Yelchin (Tommy), Tea Leoni (Mrs. Warshaw), David Duchovny (Tom Warshaw), Robin Williams (Pappass), Erykah Badu (Lady Bernadette), Magali Amadei (Coralie Warshaw), Harold Cartier (Odell Warshaw), Mark Margolis (Mr. Pappass), Zelda Williams (Melissa). Directed by David Duchovny and produced by Richard Barton Lewis, Jane Rosenthal, and Bob Yari. Screenplay by Duchovny.

Yes, I take notes during the movies. I can't always read them, but I persist in hoping that I can. During a movie like *House of D*, I jot down words I think might be useful in the review. Peering now at my three-by-five cards, I read *sappy, inane, cornball, shameless* and, my favorite, *doofusoid*. I sigh. The film has not even inspired interesting adjectives, except for the one I made up myself. I have been reading Dr. Johnson's invaluable *Dictionary of the English Language,* and propose for the next edition:

doofusoid, adj. Possessing the qualities of a doofus; sappy, inane, cornball, shameless. "The plot is composed of doofusoid elements."

You know a movie is not working for you when you sit in the dark inventing new words. *House of D* is the kind of movie that particularly makes me cringe, because it has such a shameless desire to please; like Uriah Heep, it bows and scrapes and wipes its sweaty palm on its trouser-leg, and also like Uriah Heep it privately thinks it is superior.

I make free with a reference to Uriah Heep because I assume if you got past Dr. Johnson and did not turn back, Uriah Heep will be like an old friend. You may be asking yourself, however, why I am engaging in wordplay, and the answer is: I am trying to entertain myself before I must get down to the dreary business of this review. Think of me as switching off my iPod just before going into traffic court.

So. *House of D.* Written and directed by David Duchovny, who I am quite sure created it with all of the sincerity at his command, and believed in it so earnestly that it did not occur to him that no one else would believe in it at all. It opens in Paris with an artist (Duchovny) who feels he must return to the Greenwich Village of his youth, there to revisit the scenes and people who were responsible, I guess, for him becoming an artist in Paris, so maybe a thank-you card would have done.

But, no, we return to Greenwich Village in 1973, soon concluding Duchovny would more wisely have returned to the Greenwich Village of 1873, in which the clichés of Victorian fiction, while just as agonizing, would at least not have been dated. We meet the hero's younger self, Tommy (Anton Yelchin). Tommy lives with his mother, Mrs. Warshaw (Tea Leoni), who sits at the kitchen table smoking and agonizing and smoking and agonizing. (Spoiler warning!) She seems deeply de-pressed, and although Tommy carefully counts the remaining pills in her medicine cabinet to be sure his mother is still alive, she nevertheless takes an overdose and, so help me, goes into what the doctor tells Tommy is a "persistent vegetative state." How could Duchovny have guessed when he was writing his movie that such a line, of all lines, would get a laugh?

Tommy's best friend is Pappass, played by Robin Williams. Pappass is retarded. He is retarded in 1973, that is; when Tommy returns many years later, Pappass is proud to report that he has been upgraded to "challenged." In either case, he is one of those characters whose shortcomings do not prevent him from being clever like a fox as he (oops!) blurts out the truth, underlines sentiments, says things that are more significant than he realizes, is insightful in the guise of innocence, and always appears exactly when and where the plot requires.

Tommy has another confidant, named Lady Bernadette (Erykah Badu), who is an inmate in the Women's House of Detention. She is on an upper floor with a high window in her cell, but by using a mirror she can see Tommy below, and they have many conversations, in which their speaking voices easily carry through the Village traffic noise and can be heard across, oh, fifty yards. Lady Bernadette is a repository of ancient female wisdom, and advises Tommy on his career path and the feelings of Pappass, who "can't go where you're going"—no, not even though he steals Tommy's bicycle.

The whole business of the bicycle being stolen and returned, and Pappass and Tommy trading responsibility for the theft, and the cross-examination by the headmaster of Tommy's private school (Frank Langella) is tendentious beyond all reason. (Tendentious, adj. Tending toward the dentious, as in having one's teeth drilled.) The bicycle is actually an innocent bystander, merely serving the purpose of creating an artificial crisis which can cause a misunderstanding, so that the crisis can be resolved and the misunderstanding healed. What a relief it is that Pappass and Tommy can hug at the end of the movie.

Damn! I didn't even get to the part about Tommy's girlfriend, and my case is being called.

House of Flying Daggers ★ ★ ★ ★
PG-13, 119 m., 2004

Zhang Ziyi (Mei), Takeshi Kaneshiro (Jin), Andy Lau (Leo), Song Dandan (Yee). Directed by Zhang Yimou and produced by William Kong and Yimou. Screenplay by Feng Li, Bin Wang, and Yimou.

Movie imagery, which has grown brutal and ugly in many of the new high-tech action pictures, may yet be redeemed by the elegance of martial arts pictures from the East. Zhang Yimou's *House of Flying Daggers*, like his *Hero* (2004) and Ang Lee's *Crouching Tiger, Hidden Dragon* (2000), combines excitement, romance, and astonishing physical beauty; to Pauline Kael's formula of "kiss kiss bang bang" we can now add "pretty pretty."

Forget about the plot, the characters, the intrigue, which are all splendid in *House of Flying Daggers*, and focus just on the visuals. There are interiors of ornate, elaborate richness, costumes of bizarre beauty, landscapes of mountain ranges and meadows, fields of snow, banks of autumn leaves, and a bamboo grove that functions like a kinetic art installation.

The action scenes set in these places are not broken down into jagged short cuts and incomprehensible foreground action. Zhang stands back and lets his camera regard the whole composition, wisely following Fred Astaire's belief that to appreciate choreography you must be able to see the entire body in motion. Tony Scott of the *New York Times* is on to something when he says the film's two most accomplished action scenes are likely to be "cherished like favorite numbers from *Singin' in the Rain* and *An American in Paris*." Try making that claim about anything in *The Matrix* or *Blade: Trinity*.

The scenes in question are the Echo Game and a battle in a tall bamboo grove. The Echo Game takes place inside the Peony Pavilion, a luxurious brothel that flourishes in the dying days of the Tang Dynasty, A.D. 859. An undercover policeman named Jin (Takeshi Kaneshiro) goes there on reports that the new dancer may be a member of the House of Flying Daggers, an underground resistance movement. The dancer is Mei (Zhang Ziyi, also in *Hero* and *Crouching Tiger*), and she is blind;

martial arts pictures have always had a special fondness for blind warriors, from the old *Zatoichi* series about a blind swordsman to Takeshi Kitano's *Zatoichi* remake (2004).

After Mei dances for Jin, his fellow cop Leo (Andy Lau) challenges her to the Echo Game, in which the floor is surrounded by drums on poles, and he throws a nut at one of the drums. She is to hit the same drum with the weighted end of her long sleeve. First one nut, then three, then countless nuts are thrown, as Mei whirls in midair to follow the sounds with beats of her own; like the house-building sequence in the Kitano picture, this becomes a ballet of movement and percussion.

Jin and Mei form an alliance to escape from the emperor's soldiers, Mei not suspecting (or does she?) that Jin is her undercover enemy. On their journey, supposedly to the secret headquarters of the House of Flying Daggers, they fall in love; but Jin sneaks off to confer with Leo, who is following them with a contingent of warriors, hoping to be led to the hideout. Which side is Jin betraying?

Still other warriors, apparently not aware of the undercover operation, attack the two lovers, and there are scenes of improbable delight, as when four arrows from one bow strike four targets simultaneously. Indeed most of the action in the movie is designed not to produce death, but the pleasure of elegant ingenuity. The impossible is cheerfully welcome here.

The fight in the bamboo grove inspires comparison with the treetop swordfight in *Crouching Tiger*, but is magnificent in its own way. Warriors attack from above, hurling sharpened bamboo shafts that surround the lovers, and then swoop down on tall, supple bamboo trees to attack at close range. The sounds of the whooshing bamboo spears and the click of dueling swords and sticks have a musical effect; if these scenes are not part of the sound track album, they should be.

The plot is almost secondary to the glorious action, until the last act, which reminded me a little of the love triangle in Hitchcock's *Notorious*. In that film, a spy sends the woman he loves into danger, assigning her to seduce an enemy of the state, which she does for patriotism and her love of her controller. Then the spy grows jealous, suspecting the woman really loves the man she was assigned to deceive. In *House of the Flying Daggers* the relationships contain additional levels of discovery and betrayal, so that the closing scenes in the snowfield are operatic in their romantic tragedy.

Zhang Yimou has made some of the most visually stunning films I've seen *(Raise the Red Lantern)* and others of dramatic everyday realism *(To Live)*. Here, and with *Hero,* he wins for mainland China a share of the martial arts glory long claimed by Hong Kong and its acolytes like Ang Lee and Quentin Tarantino. The film is so good to look at and listen to that, as with some operas, the story is almost beside the point, serving primarily to get us from one spectacular scene to another.

House of Wax ★ ★

R, 113 m., 2005

Elisha Cuthbert (Carly Jones), Chad Michael Murray (Nick Jones), Brian Van Holt (Bo), Paris Hilton (Paige Edwards), Jared Padalecki (Wade), Jon Abrahams (Dalton), Robert Ri'chard (Blake). Directed by Jaume Collet-Sera and produced by Susan Levin, Joel Silver, and Robert Zemeckis. Screenplay by Chad Hayes and Carey Hayes.

The Dead Teenager Movie has grown up. The characters in *House of Wax* are in their twenties and yet still repeat the fatal errors of all the *Friday the 13th* kids who checked into Camp Crystal Lake and didn't check out. ("Since all the other campers have been beheaded, eviscerated, or skewered, Marcie, obviously there's only one thing for us to do: Go skinny-dipping at midnight in the haunted lake.")

In *House of Wax,* two carloads of college students leave Gainesville for a big football game in Baton Rouge, and take an ominous detour along the way, leading them into what looks like the Texas Chainsaw Theme Park. "This town is not even on the GPS!" says one of the future Dead Post-Teenagers.

Some will complain that the movie begins slowly, despite a steamy sex scene involving Paris Hilton, and an ominous confrontation with a slack-jawed local man who drives a pickup truck, an innocent and utilitarian vehicle that in horror movies is invariably the choice of the depraved. I didn't mind the slow start, since it gave me time to contemplate the exemplary stupidity of these students, who surely represent the bottom of the academic barrel at the University of Florida.

Consider. They decide to camp overnight in a clearing in the dark, brooding woods. There is a terrible smell. The guy in the pickup truck drives up and shines his brights on them until Carly's ex-con brother, Nick (Chad Michael Murray), breaks one of the headlights. You do not get away with headlight-breaking in Chainsaw Country. The kids should flee immediately, but no: They settle down for the night.

In the morning, a fan belt is found to be mysteriously broken. An ominous sign: Fan belts do not often break in parked cars. Wade (Jared Padalecki) and girlfriend Carly (Elisha Cuthbert) unwisely take a ride into town for a replacement fan belt—from a guy they meet when they discover the source of the smell: a charnel pit of rotting road-kill. The guy is dumping a carcass into the pit at the time. Not the kind of person you want to ask for a lift. Is that a human hand sticking up from the middle of the pile? "This is weird," observes Paige. That night, when they are alone at the camp (not prudent), she treats her boyfriend, Blake (Robert Ri'chard), to a sexy dance that perhaps reminds him of a video he once saw on the Web.

The nearby town seems stuck in a time warp from the 1960s. The movie theater is playing *Whatever Happened to Baby Jane?* Yes, and for that matter, what happened to everybody else? No citizens prowl the streets, although some seem to be attending a funeral. Carly and Wade are attracted to a mysterious House of Wax that dominates the town, much as the Bates's home towered above *Psycho.* Wade scratches a wall of the house and says, "It *is* wax—literally!" This is either an omen, or the homeowners were victimized by siding salesmen. Had Wade and Carly only seen the 1953 Vincent Price thriller, they might have saved themselves, but no. They haven't even seen *Scream* and don't know they're in a horror movie.

The progress of the plot is predictable: One Post-Teenager after another becomes Dead, usually while making a stupid mistake like getting into a pickup or entering the House of

Wax ("Hello? Anyone home?"). Knowing that at least one and preferably two of the Post-Teenagers will survive for the sequel, along with possibly one of the Local Depraved, we keep count: We know Paris Hilton is likely to die, but are grateful that the producers first allow her to run in red underwear through an old shed filled with things you don't want to know about.

The early reviewers have been harsh with Miss Hilton ("so bad she steals the show," says the *Hollywood Reporter*), but actually she is no better or worse than the typical Dead Post-Teenager, and does exactly what she is required to do in a movie like this, with all the skill, admittedly finite, that is required. *House of Wax* is not a good movie, but it is an efficient one, and will deliver most of what anyone attending *House of Wax* could reasonably expect, assuming it would be unreasonable to expect very much.

Where the movie excels is in its special effects and set design. Graham "Grace" Walker masterminds a spectacular closing sequence in which the House of Wax literally melts down, and characters sink into stairs, fall through floors, and claw through walls. There is also an eerie sequence in which a living victim is sprayed with hot wax and ends up with a finish you'd have to pay an extra four bucks for at the car wash.

Howl's Moving Castle ★ ★ ½
PG, 120 m., 2005

With the voices of: Emily Mortimer (Young Sophie), Jean Simmons (Old Sophie), Christian Bale (Howl), Lauren Bacall (Witch of the Waste), Billy Crystal (Calcifer), Blythe Danner (Madame Suliman), Crispin Freeman (Prince Turnip), Josh Hutcherson (Markl). An animated film directed by Hayao Miyazaki and produced by Toshio Suzuki. Screenplay by Miyazaki, based on the novel by Diana Wynne Jones.

Almost the first sight we see in *Howl's Moving Castle* is the castle itself, which looks as if it were hammered together in shop class by wizards inspired by the lumbering, elephantine war machines in *The Empire Strikes Back*. The castle is an amazing visual invention, a vast collection of turrets and annexes, protuberances and afterthoughts, which makes its way across the landscape like a turtle in search of a rumble.

I settled back in my seat, confident that Japan's Hayao Miyazaki had once again created his particular kind of animated magic, and that the movie would deserve comparison with *Spirited Away, Princess Mononoke, My Neighbor Totoro, Kiki's Delivery Service,* and the other treasures of the most creative animator in the history of the art form.

But it was not to be. While the movie contains delights and inventions without pause and has undeniable charm, while it is always wonderful to watch, while it has the Miyazaki visual wonderment, it's a disappointment compared to his recent work. Adapted from a British novel by Diana Wynne Jones, it resides halfway between the Brothers Grimm and *The Wizard of Oz*, with shape-shifting that includes not merely beings but also objects and places.

Chief among the shape-shifters is the castle itself, which can swell with power and then shrivel in defeat. Inside the castle are spaces that can change on a whim, and a room with a door that opens to—well, wherever it needs to open. The castle roams the Waste Lands outside two warring kingdoms, which seem vaguely nineteenth-century European; it is controlled by Howl himself, a young wizard much in demand but bedeviled with personal issues.

The story opens with Sophie (voice by Emily Mortimer), a hat maker who sits patiently at her workbench while smoke-belching trains roar past her window. When she ventures out, she's attacked by obnoxious soldiers but saved by Howl (voice by Christian Bale), who is himself being chased by inky globs of shapeless hostility. This event calls Sophie's existence to the attention of Howl's enemy, the Witch of the Waste (Lauren Bacall), who fancies Howl for herself and in a fit of jealousy turns Sophie into a wrinkled old woman, bent double and voiced now by Jean Simmons. For most of the rest of the movie, the heroine will be this ancient crone; we can remind ourselves that young Sophie is trapped inside, but the shapeswitch slows things down, as if Grandmother were creeping through the woods to Red Riding Hood's house.

Sophie meets a scarecrow (Crispin Freeman) who bounces around on his single wooden leg and leads her to Howl's castle. Sophie names the scarecrow Turniphead, and we think perhaps a lion and a tin man will be turning up before long, but no. Nor is the castle run by a fraudulent wizard behind a curtain. Howl is the real thing, a shape-shifter who sometimes becomes a winged bird of prey. So is his key assistant, Calcifer (Billy Crystal), a fiery being whose job is to supply the castle's energy. Sophie also meets Markl (Josh Hutcherson), Howl's aide-de-camp, and sets about appointing herself the castle's housekeeper and maid of all work.

The plot deepens. Howl is summoned to serve both of the warring kingdoms, which presents him with a problem, complicated by the intervention of Madame Suliman, a sorceress voiced by Blythe Danner, who reminds us of Yubaba, the sorceress who ran the floating bathhouse in *Spirited Away*. These bloated old madame types seem to exert a fascination for Miyazaki scarcely less powerful than his fondness for young heroines. Howl cravenly sends old Sophie to represent him before King Sariman, and on her way there she gets into a race with the Witch of the Waste, who haunts the hinterlands where the castle roams. Sophie is obviously trapped in a web of schemes that's too old and too deep for her to penetrate, and there comes a moment when defeat seems certain and even Calcifer despairs.

All of this is presented, as only Miyazaki can, in animation of astonishing invention and detail. The castle itself threatens to upstage everything else that happens in the movie, and notice the way its protuberances move in time with its lumbering progress, not neglecting the sphincteresque gun turret at the rear. Sophie, old or young, never quite seems to understand and inhabit this world; unlike Kiki of the delivery service or Chihiro, the heroine of *Spirited Away*, she seems more witness than heroine. A parade of weird characters comes onstage to do their turns, but the underlying plot grows murky and, amazingly for a Miyazaki film, we grow impatient at spectacle without meaning.

I can't recommend the film, and yet I know if you admire Miyazaki as much I do you'll want to see it anyway. When his movies are working and on those rare occasions when they are not, Miyazaki nevertheless is a master who,

frame by frame, creates animated compositions of wonderment. Pete Doctor (writer of *Toy Story*) and John Lasseter (director of *Toy Story*), his great American supporters, have supervised the English dubbing; online anime sites say, however, that the Japanese voices are more in character (we'll be able to compare on the DVD). In the meantime, the big screen is the only way to appreciate the remarkable detail of the castle, which becomes one of the great unique places in the movies.

Hustle and Flow ★ ★ ★ ½
R, 114 m., 2005

Terrence Howard (Djay), Taryn Manning (Nola), Paula Jai Parker (Lexus), Anthony Anderson (Key), DJ Qualls (Shelby), Taraji P. Henson (Shug), Isaac Hayes (Arnel), Elise Neal (Yevette), Ludacris (Skinny Black). Directed by Craig Brewer and produced by John Singleton and Stephanie Allain. Screenplay by Brewer.

Sometimes you never really see an actor until the right roles bring him into focus. Terrence Howard has made twenty-two movies and a lot of TV (starting with the *Cosby Show*), but now, in *Crash* and *Hustle and Flow*, he creates such clearly seen characters in such different worlds that his range and depth become unmistakable.

In *Crash* he was the successful Hollywood television director, humiliated when his wife is assaulted by a cop. In *Hustle and Flow*, he plays a Memphis pimp and drug dealer who yearns to make something of himself—to become a rap artist. His quest for success is seen so clearly and with such sympathy by writer-director Craig Brewer that the movie transcends the crime genre and becomes powerful drama.

The movie's first achievement is to immerse us in the daily world of Djay, Howard's character. He is not a "pimp" and a "drug dealer," as those occupations have been simplified and dramatized in pop culture. He is a focused young man, intelligent, who in another world with other opportunities might have, who knows, gone to college and run for Congress. He can improvise at length on philosophical subjects, as he proves in an opening scene about—well, about no less than the nature of man.

He has a childhood friend named Skinny

Black (Ludacris), who has become a millionaire rap star. How close of a childhood friend is a good question; as nearly as I can tell, they went to different schools together. Skinny Black returns to the old neighborhood every Fourth of July for a sentimental reunion at the club where he got his start. The club owner (Isaac Hayes) is a friend of Djay's. The theory is, Djay will give his demo tape to Skinny Black, who will pull strings and make Djay a star.

But that's in the third act of the movie. The long second act, in some ways the heart of the film, involves Djay's attempts to meet his various business responsibilities while recording the demo. We get the ghetto version of renting the old barn and putting on a show. Djay picks up an ancient digital keyboard and enlists Key (Anthony Anderson), a family man and churchgoer, to work with him on the music. Key knows Shelby (DJ Qualls), a white kid with musical skills. They staple cardboard egg containers to the walls to soundproof a recording studio, enlist a hooker named Shug (Taraji P. Henson) to sing backup, and make the recording.

What Djay cannot be expected to understand is that Skinny Black gets countless demos pressed warmly into his hands every day. He does not have the power in the music industry that Djay imagines. Discovering a talented newcomer might be professional suicide. And beyond that is the whole worldview Skinny Black has bought into: his cars, his bodyguards, his image as a menacing rapper. Djay's first approach to him is miscalculated and all wrong. The way he uses his instincts to try again is smart, and brave.

But Hustle and Flow is not limited to Djay's rags-to-riches dream, because it is not a formula film. Much more interesting are his day-to-day relationships. Nola (Taryn Manning), the white woman who gets the benefit of his theory of human life, is his most profitable hooker, even though she tells Djay how much she hates getting into the cars of strange men. Shug, whom Djay gradually realizes he loves, is pregnant, probably not with Djay's child. Lexus (Paula Jai Parker) has an income as a stripper, which makes her more outspoken and independent.

Djay plays the pimp role and is effective enough, but his heart isn't in it. The dream of the demo record fills his mind—and obsesses Key and Shelby, to the dismay of Key's wife, who sees her churchgoing breadwinner spending his free time with a pimp ("What woman wouldn't be thrilled to have her man in a house full of whores?"). What happens is that Djay's horizon expands as his imagination is challenged. It isn't really the hope of stardom that keeps him going. It isn't the dubious connection with Skinny Black that inspires him. What we see in Hustle and Flow is rarely seen in the movies: the redemptive power of art. Djay is transformed when he finds something he loves doing and is getting better at. To create something out of your own mind and talent and see that it is good: That is a joy that makes the rest of his life seem shabby and transparent.

Terrence Howard modulates Djay with great love and consideration for the character. He never cheapens him, or condescends. He builds him inside out. He is a pimp and a dealer because he is smart and has ambition, and that is how, in his world, with his background, he can find success. The film accumulates many subtle moments to show how his feelings for Shug develop, how he begins by giving her the kind of "love" pimps use as a control mechanism, and slowly realizes that another kind of love is growing.

Shug is played by Taraji P. Henson as so wounded, so vulnerable, so loyal that we're astonished at the complex emotions developed by the story. Listen to her: "Letting me sing on the demo made me feel real. I know, moving up, you gonna get real good people, so I want you to know, it meant the world to me." What has transformed him has opened room for her transformation.

Hustle and Flow shows, among other things, what a shallow music-video approach many films take to the inner city, and then what complexities and gifts bloom there. Every good actor has a season when he comes into his own, and this is Howard's time.

I

I, Robot ★ ★
PG-13, 114 m., 2004

Will Smith (Del Spooner), Bridget Moynahan (Susan Calvin), Bruce Greenwood (Lance Robertson), James Cromwell (Dr. Alfred Lanning), Chi McBride (Lieutenant John Bergin), Alan Tudyk (Sonny). Directed by Alex Proyas and produced by John Davis, Topher Dow, and Laurence Mark. Screenplay by Jeff Vintar and Akiva Goldsman, based on the book by Isaac Asimov.

---

1. *A robot may not injure a human being or, through inaction, allow a human being to come to harm.*
2. *A robot must obey orders given it by human beings except where such orders would conflict with the First Law.*
3. *A robot must protect its own existence as long as such protection does not conflict with the First or Second Law.*
   —Isaac Asimov's *I, Robot*

I, Robot takes place in Chicago circa 2035, a city where spectacular new skyscrapers share the skyline with landmarks like the Sears (but not the Trump) Tower. The tallest of the buildings belongs to U.S. Robotics, and on the floor of its atrium lobby lies the dead body of its chief robot designer, apparently a suicide.

Detective Del Spooner is on the case. Will Smith plays Spooner, a Chicago Police Department detective, who doesn't think it's suicide. He has a deep-seated mistrust of robots, despite the famous Three Laws of Robotics, which declare above all that a robot must not harm a human being.

The dead man is Dr. Alfred Lanning (James Cromwell), who, we are told, wrote the Three Laws. Every schoolchild knows the laws were set down by the good doctor Isaac Asimov, after a conversation he had on December 23, 1940, with John W. Campbell, the legendary editor of *Astounding Science Fiction*. It is peculiar that no one in the film knows that, especially since the film is "based on the book by Isaac Asimov." Would it have killed the filmmakers to credit Asimov?

Asimov's robot stories were often based on

robots that got themselves hopelessly entangled in logical contradictions involving the laws. According to the invaluable *Wikipedia* encyclopedia on the Web, Harlan Ellison and Asimov collaborated in the 1970s on an *I, Robot* screenplay that, the good doctor said, would produce "the first really adult, complex, worthwhile science fiction movie ever made."

While that does not speak highly for *2001: A Space Odyssey* (1968), it is certain that the screenplay for this film, by Jeff Vintar and Akiva Goldsman, is not adult, complex, or worthwhile, although it is indeed science fiction. The director is Alex Proyas, whose great *Dark City* (1998) was also about a hero trying to make sense of the deceptive natures of the beings around him.

The movie makes Spooner into another one of those movie cops who insult the powerful, race recklessly around town, get their badges pulled by their captains, solve the crime, and survive incredible physical adventures. In many of these exploits he is accompanied by Dr. Susan Calvin (Bridget Moynahan), whose job at U.S. Robotics is "to make the robots seem more human."

At this she is not very successful. The movie's robots are curiously uninvolving as individuals, and when seen by the hundreds or thousands look like shiny chromium ants. True, a robot need not have much of a personality, but there is one robot, named Sonny and voiced by Alan Tudyk, who is more advanced than the standard robot, more "human," and capable of questions like "What am I?"—a question many movie characters might profitably ask themselves.

If Sonny doesn't have real feelings, he comes as close to them as any of the humans in the movie. Both Spooner and Calvin are kept in motion so relentlessly that their human sides get overlooked, except for a touching story Spooner tells about how a little girl dies because a robot was too logical. Sonny doesn't seem as "human" as, say, Andrew, the robot played by Robin Williams in *Bicentennial Man* (1999), based on a robot story by Asimov and Robert Silverberg. But his voice has a certain poignancy, and suggests some of the chilly chumminess of HAL 9000.

The plot I will not detail, except to note that

322

you already know from the ads that the robots are up to no good, and Spooner could write a lot of tickets for Three Laws violations. The plot is simple-minded and disappointing, and the chase and action scenes are pretty much routine for movies in the sci-fi CGI genre. The robots never seem to have the heft and weight of actual metallic machines, and make boring villains.

Dr. Susan Calvin is one of those handy movie characters who know all the secrets, can get through all the doors, and can solve all the problems. She helps Spooner move almost at will through the Robotics skyscraper, which seems curiously ill-guarded. When they team up against the eventual villain, it's an obvious ploy to create yet another space where characters can fall for hundreds of feet and somehow save themselves.

As for the robots, they function like the giant insects in *Starship Troopers,* as video game targets. You can't even be mad at them, since they're only programs. Although, come to think of it, you *can* be mad at programs; Microsoft Word has inspired me to rage far beyond anything these robots engender.

I Am David ★ ½

PG, 95 m., 2004

Ben Tibber (David), James Caviezel (Johannes), Joan Plowright (Sophie). Directed by Paul Feig and produced by Davina Belling, Lauren Levine, and Clive Parsons. Screenplay by Feig, based on a novel by Anne Holm.

I Am David tells the story of a twelve-year-old orphan boy who escapes from a Bulgarian forced labor camp and travels alone through Greece, Italy, and Switzerland to his eventual destiny in Denmark. He has awfully good luck: Along the way, he meets mostly nice people who do what they can to help him, and there's an enormous coincidence just when it's most needed. Benji encounters more hazards on his travels than this kid.

I know, I know, I'm supposed to get sentimental about this heartwarming tale. But I couldn't believe a moment of it, and never identified with little David, who is played by young Ben Tibber as if he was lectured to mind his manners. In an era with one effective child performance after another, here is a bad one.

The premise: In the cold war, enemies of the Bulgarian state are sent to forced labor camps, where they break up rocks into gravel under the merciless prodding of sadistic guards. I am sure the movie explains how David became an enemy of the state at his tender age, but the detail escaped me; maybe he inherited his status from his dead parents. Certainly he's lucky in his choice of friends, starting with Johannes (James Caviezel), a fellow inmate who gives him encouragement and dreams before—well, see for yourself.

A mysterious voice on the sound track advises David to escape. He is supplied with a bar of soap, half a loaf of bread, a compass, and an envelope not to be opened until he gets to Denmark, or finds Carmen Sandiego, whichever comes first. Sorry about that. The power is conveniently turned off for thirty seconds on the camp's electrified fences so that David can run across an open field and begin his long odyssey.

How, you may wonder, will the lad communicate in the many lands he must traverse? "You've picked up many languages from the others in the camp," the voice reminds him, and indeed David apparently speaks Bulgarian, Greek, Italian, and English, all with a wee perfect British accent. He lucks into rides on trucks, gets over the border to Greece through an unlikely series of events, stows away on a ship for Italy with astonishing ease, and fetches up in an Italian bakery where, please, sir, may I have a loaf? When the baker calls the cops, the kid is able to escape, although not with any bread.

Then something happens that would seem far-fetched even in a silent melodrama. He comes upon a burning cabin, hears screams, breaks in, and rescues a young girl who is tied to a chair. This girl, as it happens, is the victim of a prank by her younger siblings, who didn't mean to set the fire. The girl's rich parents embrace the lad and feed him, but ask too many questions, so he moves on to Switzerland and happens into friendship with a grandmotherly painter (Joan Plowright), who brings his story to a happy ending through a spectacularly unlikely coincidence.

As it turns out, the papers in his envelope could probably have been read by anyone in Greece or Italy and solved David's dilemma, and the advice to travel all the way to Denmark was not necessarily sound. But we forget that when we discover the secret of the mysterious voice that advised David—a secret I found distinctly underwhelming, although the movie makes much of it. The lesson, I guess, is that if you are a twelve-year-old orphan in a Bulgarian forced labor camp, you need not despair, because the world is filled with good luck and helpful people, and besides, you speak all those languages.

Note: In stark contrast to the fairy-tale events of I Am David, *the 2003 film* In This World, *by Michael Winterbottom, tells the story of a sixteen-year-old Afghan boy who journeys to London from a refugee camp in Pakistan. The film follows a real boy on a real journey, and includes scenes of documentary reality; it helps underline the unreal storytelling of* David.

Ice Age: The Meltdown ★ ★ ½
PG, 90 m., 2006

With the voices of: John Leguizamo (Sid), Denis Leary (Diego), Ray Romano (Manny), Queen Latifah (Ellie), Seann William Scott (Crash), Josh Peck (Eddie), Jay Leno (Fast Tony), Chris Wedge (Scrat), Will Arnett (Lone Gunslinger), Jason Fricchione (Grandpa Molehog). Directed by Carlos Saldanha and produced by Lori Forte. Screenplay by Peter Gaulke, Gerry Swallow, and Jim Hecht.

Only Scrat, the ferocious little saber-toothed squirrel, retains his magic from the original *Ice Age* (2002). Most of the other characters are back in *Ice Age: The Meltdown*, but their story is more of a slog than a sprint. Remarkable that they're still around, although tens of thousands of years must have passed since the previous film. But if I am going to require logical continuity in an animated comedy, I might as well admit that Daffy Duck is not real, and that I refuse to do.

As *Ice Age: The Meltdown* opens, it is Scrat who observes the first danger signal of global change. He's engaged as usual in a perilous chase after an acorn, which is all the more desirable because where is the oak from which it fell? The squirrel climbs a vertical ice wall with his claws, almost falls, is saved when his tongue freezes to the ice, and then has to pull himself up by his own tongue, paw over paw.

Don't you hate it when that happens? Then a jet of water springs from the ice face, and another, and another. The glacier is melting.

If kids have been indifferent to global warming up until now, this *Ice Age* sequel will change that forever. Giant chunks of icebergs and the polar ice cap fall off into the sea, the water levels rise, a temperate climate begins to emerge, and the animal family of the earlier film begins a long trek to save itself from drowning. There is said to be a hollow log at the end of the valley, in which they can float to safety.

The characters, as you will recall from the earlier film, have found a way to live together and not compete as species, although that leaves me a little vague about what the meat-eaters do at mealtimes. After Scrat (squeaks by Chris Wedge), we meet Manny the mammoth (voice by Ray Romano), who fears he is the last of his kind; Diego the tiger (Denis Leary); Sid the sloth (John Leguizamo); Fast Tony the turtle (Jay Leno); Lone Gunslinger the vulture (Will Arnett). And then, to the immeasurable delight of Manny, they encounter Ellie the female mammoth (Queen Latifah). Together, Manny and Ellie can save the mammoth race, if only Ellie can be convinced she is not a possum. Her delusion is encouraged by the possums Crash and Eddie (Seann William Scott and Josh Peck), who find having a mammoth as a sidekick is a great comfort.

Once the characters have been introduced and the ice shelf has started to melt, the movie essentially consists of a long trek, punctuated by adventures. Some of them are provided by the convenient thawing of two pre–ice age sea monsters, who are killing machines no doubt destined to evolve into sharks. There is also a perilous crossing of a melting ice bridge, which reminded me of the collapsing bridge in *The Lord of the Rings*.

The movie is nice to look at, the colors and details are elegant, the animals engaging, the action fast-moving, but I don't think older viewers will like it as much as the kids. The first *Ice Age* movie more or less exhausted these characters and their world, and the meltdown doesn't add much. Most of the conflict involves personalities: Can these species coexist? Well, of course they can, in a cartoon. And if global warming means simply that they don't have to freeze their butts off all the time and there are more acorns for Scrat, then what's the problem?

The Ice Harvest ★ ★ ★

R, 88 m., 2005

John Cusack (Charlie Arglist), Billy Bob Thornton (Vic), Connie Nielsen (Renata), Randy Quaid (Bill Guerrard), Oliver Platt (Pete Van Heuten), Mike Starr (Roy Gelles). Directed by Harold Ramis and produced by Albert Berger and Ron Yerxa. Screenplay by Richard Russo and Robert Benton, based on the novel by Scott Phillips.

It's a busy Christmas Eve for Charlie Arglist, who visits his former in-laws, steers his drunken buddy out of trouble, buys toys for his kids, waives the stage rental for a stripper at his topless club, and cheats, lies, steals, and kills. Perhaps of all actors only John Cusack could play Charlie and still look relatively innocent by Christmas Day. He does look tired, however.

Charlie is a mob lawyer in Wichita, Kansas. He is, in fact, the best mob lawyer in all of Kansas. We know this because his friend Pete (Oliver Platt) announces it loudly almost everywhere they go. "I wish you wouldn't do that," Charlie says, but Pete is beyond discretion. Pete is married to Charlie's former wife and has inherited Charlie's former in-laws, a circumstance that inspires in Charlie not jealousy but sympathy. They are fascinated that the woman they have both married is the only adult they know who still sleeps in flannel jammies with sewn-on booties.

Charlie's holiday has begun promisingly. He and his associate Vic (Billy Bob Thornton) have stolen $2.2 million belonging to Bill Guerrard (Randy Quaid), the local mob boss. They think they can get away with this. They certainly hope so, anyway, because Roy Gelles (Mike Starr), a hit man for Guerrard, has been asking around town for Charlie, probably not to deliver his Christmas bonus. As Charlie tells Vic: "I sue people for a living. You sell pornography. Roy Gelles hurts people." Charlie also runs a topless bar and is attracted to its manager, Renata (Connie Nielsen), who has suggested that Charlie's Christmas stocking will be filled with more than apples and acorns if certain conditions are met.

It is all very complicated. There is the matter of the photograph showing a local councilman in a compromising position with Renata. The question of whether good old Vic can be trusted. And the continuing problem of what to do with Pete, who is very drunk and threatens a dinner party with a turkey leg, which in his condition is a more dangerous weapon than a handgun.

The Ice Harvest follows these developments with the humor of an Elmore Leonard project and the interlocking violence of a *Blood Simple*. The movie, directed by Harold Ramis, finds a balance between the goofy and the gruesome, as in a rather brilliant scene in which a mobster who is locked inside a trunk is nevertheless optimistic enough to shout out muffled death threats. For some reason there is always humor in those crime scenarios where tough guys find it's easy to conceive diabolical acts, exhausting to perform them. It's one thing to lock a man in a trunk, another to get the trunk into the backseat of a Mercedes, still another to push it down a dock and into a lake. If the job ended with locking the trunk, you'd have more people in trunks.

The key to the movie's humor is Cusack's calm patience in the face of catastrophe. He has always been curiously angelic—the last altar boy you'd suspect of having stolen the collection plate. In *The Ice Harvest* he is essentially a kind man. Consider his concern for Pete, a friend who has gotten very drunk on Christmas Eve because, as he confesses, he's not man enough to fill his chair at the family dinner table. That Charlie takes time to bail his friend out of tight spots and give him good advice speaks well of a man so heavily scheduled with stealing and killing.

Vic, the Thornton character, is one of those Billy Bob specials whose smile is charming but not reassuring. Consider the moment after he and Charlie obtain the briefcase filled with the loot and Vic drops Charlie off at home and Charlie reaches for the case and Vic reaches for it first and they realize they have not discussed who will keep the case for the time being, and Vic asks if this is going to be a problem, and you know that if Charlie takes the case it is definitely going to be a problem.

Nielsen has a bruised charm as the sexy Renata. She's sexy, but weary of being sexy. It is such a responsibility. The movie has a quiet in-joke when Charlie asks her, "Where are you from, anyway?" He doesn't think she sounds like she's from around here. Of Nielsen's last sixteen movies, all but one was American, and she has a flawless American accent, but in fact she is Danish. She never does answer Charlie's question. The obvious answer is: "A long way from Kansas."

I liked the movie for the quirky way it pursues humor through the drifts of greed, lust, booze, betrayal, and spectacularly complicated ways to die. I liked it for Charlie's essential kindness, as when he pauses during a getaway to help a friend who has run out of gas. And for the scene-stealing pathos of Platt's drunk, who like many drunks in the legal profession achieves a rhetorical grandiosity during the final approach to oblivion. And I especially liked the way Roy, the man in the trunk, keeps on thinking positively, even after Vic shoots the trunk and says, "That must have been the head end."

Ice Princess ★ ★ ★
G, 92 m., 2005

Joan Cusack (Mrs. Carlyle), Kim Cattrall (Tina Harwood), Michelle Trachtenberg (Casey Carlyle), Hayden Panettiere (Gen Harwood), Kirsten Olson (Nikki), Jocelyn Lai (Tiffany), Juliana Cannarozzo (Zoe). Directed by Tim Fywell and produced by Bridget Johnson. Screenplay by Hadley Davis.

The computer doesn't make the jumps. You do.
—Casey to Gen

Yes, *Ice Princess* is a formula movie. Yes, it makes all the stops and hits all the beats and, yes, it ends exactly as we expect it will. It even has the inevitable scene where the gifted young heroine is in the middle of her performance and she looks up into the audience—and there she is! Her mother! Who disapproves of figure skating but came to the semifinals without telling her, and now nods and smiles like dozens of other parents in dozens of other movies, recognizing at last that their child has the real stuff.

Yes, yes, and yes. And yet the movie works. I started by clicking off the obligatory scenes, and then somehow the film started to get to me, and I was surprised how entertained I was. Like *Shall We Dance* or *Saturday Night*

Fever, it escapes its genre. That's partly because the screenplay avoids the usual rigid division of good and evil and gives us characters who actually change during the movie. Partly because the acting is so convincing. And partly because the actresses in the movie really can skate—or seem to. Well, no wonder, since two of them are figure skaters, but the surprise is that Michelle Trachtenberg seems able to skate too. That didn't look like a double on the ice, although *Variety,* the showbiz bible, reports, "Four different skaters sub for Trachtenberg in the more difficult performances."

Trachtenberg plays Casey Carlyle, a brilliant high school science student, who hopes to win a Harvard scholarship with a physics project. Her teacher advises her to find an original subject, and she gets a brainstorm: What if she films figure skaters, analyzes their movements on her computer, and comes up with a set of physics equations describing what they do and suggesting how they might improve?

Casey has always been a science nerd. She's pretty but doesn't know it, and so shy "I can't talk to anyone I haven't known since kindergarten." She goes to the ice rink in her Connecticut town run by Tina Harwood (Kim Cattrall), herself an Olympic figure skating contender until a disqualification at Saravejo. Now Tina coaches her daughter, Gen (Hayden Panettiere), toward championship status.

Casey's computer program works. She breaks down the moves, analyzes the physics, and advises Gen and other skaters on what they can change to improve their performance. Along the way, a funny thing happens; Casey has always enjoyed skating on the pond near her home, and now she grows fascinated by figure skating, and wants to start training.

This is horrifying news for her mom (Joan Cusack), a feminist and teacher who is pointing Casey toward Harvard and sniffs, "Figure skaters have no shelf life." Meanwhile, Gen confesses she envies Casey: "I hate to train all the time. I'd love to have a real life, like you." To her mom, Gen says, "I'm fed up with being a dunce in math class because I don't have time to do the homework."

The movie, written by Hadley Davis and directed by Tim Fywell, starts with a formula and then takes it to the next level. We have two obsessive stage mothers and two driven over-achievers, and the girls want to trade places, to the despair of their moms (no dads are in sight, except for a proud Korean-American father). This leads to more substance than we're expecting, and more acting, too, since the central characters don't follow the well-worn routines supplied by the GCFDDPO formula (Gifted Child Follows Dream Despite Parental Opposition). They strike out with opinions and surprises of their own.

I am informed that every actress in the movie does all of her own skating, but the movie's publicity is coy on the point, apart from pointing out that actresses Kirsten Olson (Nikki) and Juliana Cannarozzo (Zoe) are figure skaters making their first movie. All I know, as I said above, is that they look as if they do. What's important is not whether all the actors do their own skating, but that they play figure skaters so convincingly, and also bring a realistic dimension into their lives as high school students. Gen's first scene seems to set her up as the popular blond snob who's a fixture in all high school movies, but no: She makes a friend of Casey, and together the girls help each other figure out what they really want to do.

At one point, when a skater makes a really nice move on the ice, someone sniffs that it's because of Casey's computer. That's when she says the computer doesn't make the jumps. *Ice Princess* starts out with something like a computer formula too. But the formula doesn't make the moves. You can take it to another level, and that's what *Ice Princess* does. This movie is just about perfect for teenagers, and it's a surprise that even their parents are allowed to have minds of their own.

I Heart Huckabees ★ ★

R, 105 m., 2004

Jason Schwartzman (Albert Markovski), Dustin Hoffman (Bernard Jaffe), Isabelle Huppert (Caterine Vauban), Jude Law (Brad Stand), Lily Tomlin (Vivian Jaffe), Mark Wahlberg (Tommy Corn), Naomi Watts (Dawn Campbell). Directed by David O. Russell and produced by Russell, Gregory Goodman, and Scott Rudin. Screenplay by Russell and Jeff Baena.

I went to see *I Heart Huckabees* at the Toronto Film Festival. It was on the screen, and I was in my chair, and nothing was happening between us. There was clearly a movie being shown, but what was its purpose and why were the characters so inexplicable? To help myself focus, I found the pressure point that is said by the master Wudang Weng Shun Kuen to increase mental alertness. Then I dashed out for a cup of coffee. Then I fell into the yoga sutra of "yatha abhimata dhyanat va," literally clearing the mind by meditating on a single object until I become tranquil. I meditated on the theater exit door.

At festivals, the moment a movie is over everybody asks you what you thought about it. I said, "I didn't know what I thought." Then how did it make you feel? "It made me feel like seeing it again." You mean you liked it so much you want to see it twice? "No, I'm still working on seeing it the first time."

Now I have seen it twice. The movie is like an infernal machine that consumes all of the energy it generates, saving the last watt of power to turn itself off. It functions perfectly within its constraints, but it leaves the viewer out of the loop. This may be the first movie that can exist without an audience between the projector and the screen. It falls in its own forest, and hears itself. It's the kind of movie that would inspire a Charlie Kaufman screenplay about how it couldn't be made. The director and cowriter is David O. Russell, who made the brilliant *Three Kings* and the quirky *Flirting with Disaster,* and now . . . well, he has made this. God knows he's courageous.

I am about to commence a description. Not a plot description, as I am not sure it has a plot in a meaningful way, but an account of what transpires. Jason Schwartzman plays Albert, an environmentalist who wants to save nature, and begins by saving a large rock that is all that remains from a despoiled swamp (he reads a poem beginning, "You rock, Rock"). Albert makes a deal with Huckabees, a chain store, to underwrite his Open Space Coalition. Huckabees doesn't care about the environment, but cares deeply about seeming to care. Albert turns out to be a wild card for them, doing things like planting trees in the middle of parking lots to reclaim them for nature right then and there.

We meet Brad Stand (Jude Law), a Huckabees spokesman, and Dawn (Naomi Watts), a

Huckabees spokesperson. They are in what in their limited way they interpret as love. Brad's plan is to use Albert as a cover for a scheme to turn virgin marshland into a shopping mall. Albert meanwhile constantly crosses paths with a towering African exchange student, and knows this must Mean Something, so he hires two Existential Detectives to sort it out for him. These are Bernard and Vivian Jaffe (Dustin Hoffman and Lily Tomlin).

Their method is to follow a client everywhere, taking notes on all that he does. "Even into the bathroom?" Yes, even into the bathroom. Bernard and Vivian now begin to be seen in the backgrounds of many shots, or outside the windows, or behind the door, or under the furniture, taking notes. They need to see everything in his life because they believe that everything is connected, and so to know everything is to know all the connections. Perhaps they are followers of E. M. Forster, who wrote "Only connect!" in the novel *A Passage to India*, which was about a cave where, no matter what words you said, the echo always sounded like "boum." Curiously enough, a lot of Bernard and Vivian's dialogue has the same effect.

Brad, the double-crossing executive, decides to undercut Albert by hiring the detectives to also follow him and Dawn around. Albert meanwhile meets a fireman named Tommy (Mark Wahlberg). Tommy is so eco-conscious that he refuses to ride the fire truck to fires, pedaling alongside on his bike. (He usually gets there first.) Tommy for reasons unclear to me knows about another Existential Detective named Caterine Vauban (Isabelle Huppert), who is from France. She is an old enemy of the Jaffes, and no wonder: French existentialists define themselves by being old enemies. Caterine has a peculiar sex scene in a mud puddle.

Everybody talks a lot, the Jaffes in particular. They do a kind of double act, finishing or repeating each other's sentences. They seem to believe quantum physics is somehow involved in their theories, and talk about how two objects can be in different places at the same time—no, hold on, that's the easy part. They talk about how the *same* object can be in two places at once.

Their discussions about this quantum phenomenon reminded me wonderfully of the explanations of the same topic in *What the*

#$*! *Do We Know?* a "documentary" in which one of the "expert physicists" has been unmasked as a chiropractor, and the filmmakers are all followers of Ramtha, a 35,000-year-old spirit guide from Atlantis. Because nobody knows #$*! about quantum physics, this doc actually got respectful reviews from gullible critics like me, because it made about as much sense as most of what I've read on the subject.

Individual moments and lines and events in *I Heart Huckabees* are funny in and of themselves. Viewers may be mystified but will occasionally be amused. It took boundless optimism and energy for Russell to make the film, but it reminds me of the Buster Keaton short where he builds a boat but doesn't know how to get it out of the basement. The actors soldier away like the professionals they are, saying the words as if they mean something. Only Wahlberg is canny enough to play his role completely straight, as if he has no idea the movie might be funny. The others all seem to be trying to get in on the joke, which is a neat trick. I will award a shiny new dime to anyone who can figure out what the joke is.

I'll Sleep When I'm Dead ★ ★ ★ ½
R, 103 m., 2004

Malcolm McDowell (Boad), Jonathan Rhys-Meyers (Davey Graham), Clive Owen (Will Graham), Jamie Foreman (Mickser), Charlotte Rampling (Helen), Ken Stott (Turner). Directed by Mike Hodges and produced by Michael Corrente and Mike Kaplan. Screenplay by Trevor Preston.

Mike Hodges's gritty new *film noir, I'll Sleep When I'm Dead,* begins in enigma and snakes its way into stark clarity. At the beginning we don't even know who the characters are or why they matter to one another. For Hodges, this isn't a matter of keeping us in the dark, but follows simple logic: The characters know who they are and don't have to tell one another, and we are outsiders who will need to fit it together.

Some of the reviews have complained that *I'll Sleep When I'm Dead* is needlessly convoluted—that we're asked to spend too much time trying to identify the characters and become oriented within the plot. That assumes we want a simple story, simply told, and indeed many mainstream movies and TV shows treat audiences as simpletons. But there is a tangible pleasure in following enigmatic characters through the shadows of their lives; deprived for a time of a plot, given characters who are not clearly labeled and assigned moral categories, we're allowed to make judgments based on their manner and speech.

Hodges begins with parallel stories. In South London, an ingratiating charmer named Davey (Jonathan Rhys-Meyers) delivers drugs to parties, is popular on the circuit, picks up girls for a night, will steal anything not nailed down. Somewhere in a remote area, a man named Will (Clive Owen) lives alone in a van, is a manual laborer, finds a man who has been beaten, and helps him. In a third story, a car cruises through London with a hard man in the backseat, surrounded by hired muscle.

These stories will converge. Davey is dragged off the street and raped, he apparently kills himself, and when Will learns of this he returns to London. They are brothers. Whatever Will Graham did in the old days, whoever he was, there are a lot of people in South London who remember and fear him, even though he's been off the scene for years. In Clive Owen, Hodges has an actor who suggests the buried mystery and menace the role requires.

Hodges is a hard-boiled director who began with *Get Carter* (1971), with Michael Caine in one of his best performances, also as a gangster seeking vengeance for a dead brother. Hodges made a comeback in 1998 with *Croupier*, a sleeper hit starring Owen, who was not then widely known but was launched toward stardom by that film; you can currently see him in the title role of *King Arthur*, where he creates a harder, darker Arthur than the movies usually give us. In *I'll Sleep When I'm Dead*, he plays a familiar type, the retired killer forced to return to his old skills.

Will Graham still looms large in the memories of those he left behind when he chose to, or had to, disappear. He was a crime boss, we gather, and apparently he walked away from the life because he could no longer stomach it. Back on the scene but unrecognizable at first, because of his full beard and unshorn hair, he reconnects with his onetime lover Helen

(Charlotte Rampling) and his former lieutenant Mickser (Jamie Foreman), who was Davey's friend. Word travels through the underworld that Will is back in London, and all sorts of people stir uneasily at the news.

The movie's main line involves Will's methodical investigation as he traces a series of contacts and witnesses back to the name of the man who raped his brother. At the same time, Hodges and Owen, working with a screenplay by Trevor Preston, suggest other dimensions of Will Graham's life. There is, for example, the nature of his relationship with Helen, who is not a typical gangster's girl but an independent woman, wise and sad. That Will loved her—that he still has feelings for her—suggests he's a more complicated and thoughtful person than his fearsome reputation suggests. Indeed, his whole present life— his bare-bones lifestyle, his unkempt appearance—indicate a kind of self-chosen exile, as if he has not merely left the scene but is trying to purge himself of it.

More of the plot I must not reveal, although *film noir* exists more in detail, behavior, and mood than in what happens. But listen during a conversation Will has late in the film with a man named Boad, played by Malcolm McDowell in his most sneering and contemptuous mode, and you will sense all of the threads of the story coming together. "I wanted to show him what he was—nothing," says Boad. Then Will Graham shows Boad what he is, and gives him some time, not too much, to reflect upon it.

Imaginary Heroes ★ ★ ★
R, 112 m., 2005

Sigourney Weaver (Sandy Travis), Emile Hirsch (Tim Travis), Jeff Daniels (Ben Travis), Michelle Williams (Penny Travis), Kip Pardue (Matt Travis), Deirdre O'Connell (Marge Dwyer), Ryan Donowho (Kyle Dwyer), Suzanne Santo (Steph Connors). Directed by Dan Harris and produced by Ilana Diamant, Moshe Diamant, Frank Hubner, Art Linson, Gina Resnick, and Denise Shaw. Screenplay by Harris.

Imaginary Heroes gives us yet one more troubled suburban family, with suicide and drugs and a chill at the dinner table. But it gives us something else: a heroine with a buried but real sense of humor, and an ability to look at life from the outside instead of only through her own needs. That this person is the mother in the family, and that the father is cold and distant, goes without saying; fathers in the movies, as a group, supply only a few more heroes than Nazis. But the mother is worth having, and makes the movie work despite its overcrowded plot.

Her name is Sandy Travis, and she is played by Sigourney Weaver as someone whose teenage years were spent in the 1970s, which means that in a sense she will always be younger, or at least more unpredictable, than her children. When she makes it clear in early scenes how much she hates Marge, her neighbor, we feel a certain self-satire under the anger. When she talks to her son, Tim (Emile Hirsch), she's the kind of adult kids need to talk to when they can't communicate with their parents. Unusual to find that in a parent.

The film is narrated by Tim, who tells us about his older brother, Matt (Kip Pardue). Matt is the best swimmer anyone has ever seen. He holds all the records and is headed for the Olympics. Then, only a minute or two into the film, he shoots himself in the head. Tim knows something about Matt that few people were allowed to find out: Matt hated swimming. Mostly he hated it because of the way he was driven by his father, Ben (Jeff Daniels), a cold perfectionist who made Matt's life a daily final exam.

That's all prologue. *Imaginary Heroes* starts with the family trying to recover emotionally. Ben insists that a plate be served for Matt at every meal, on the table in front of his empty chair. "That creeps me out," says Penny (Michelle Williams), the older sister home from college. Sandy says: "I won't be making all this food for every meal. It's a waste." That's what she does, speaking her mind in front of the family, coming across as the one who may not be beloved but at least sees clearly.

Tim is going through unsettled times at school. He is smaller than Matt was, has no athletic gifts, looks young for his age, is assumed at the funeral to be headed for high school when in fact he is already a senior. He seems to have no communication with his father, who takes a leave of absence at work and drifts off into shapeless days of sad park benches.

But Sandy sees him and senses his needs, and talks with him. They have one extraordinary conversation on the front porch swing in which she observes that they may be the only mother and son in town who can talk openly about masturbation. She tells Tim: "You may never know how really good I am for you until I die. I never loved my parents until they died."

Tim, who looks uncannily like Leonardo DiCaprio's younger brother, is dating a girl at school named Steph. She thinks they may be ready for sex.

"Steph told me she loves me," he tells his mother.

"Well, do you love her?" she asks.

"I don't know."

"Then you don't."

The relationship between Sandy and her son is the heart of the movie, and works, and Sandy's character on her own is an unfolding fascination. Who else could get busted for pot quite the way she does? And who else would say to her would-be drug dealer, "Your parents should be ashamed of you." It was a wise decision for Dan Harris, the writer-director, to avoid getting bogged down in the legal aftermath of the arrest; the point, for the story the movie wants to tell, is that she felt an urgent need to get high, and behaved more like a kid than like a prudent adult.

Dan Harris is a kid himself, only twenty-two when he sent this screenplay to Bryan Singer, director of *X-Men* and (more to the point) *Apt Pupil* and *The Usual Suspects*. Singer liked it, hired Harris to work on the screenplay for *X-2*, and then the new *Superman* movie Singer is directing, and after that *Logan's Run*. Then Harris came back at twenty-four to direct his own screenplay.

I can see what Singer saw in it: a sensitivity to characters, an instinct for the revealing, unpredictable gesture, and good dialogue. I think I see a little too much more besides. The film might have been stronger as simply the story of the family trying to heal itself after its tragedy, with the focus on Sandy and Tim. But Harris feels a need to explain everything in terms of melodramatic revelations and surprise developments, right up until the closing scenes. The emotional power of the last act is weakened by the flood of new information. The key revelation right at the end explains a lot, yes, but it comes so late that all it can do is explain. If it had come earlier, it would have had to be dealt with, and those scenes might have been considerable.

I haven't gone into detail about Marge (Deirdre O'Connell), the neighbor, or her son, Kyle Dwyer (Ryan Donowho), who is Tim's best friend. Marge never really worked for me except as a plot convenience, and Tim's friendship with Kyle, while it produces some risky and effective scenes, is best left for you to discover. What remains when the movie is over is the memory of Sandy and Tim talking, and of a mother who loves her son, understands him, and understands herself in a wry but realistic way. The characters deserve a better movie, but they get a pretty good one.

Imagine Me & You ★ ★
R, 93 m., 2006

Piper Perabo (Rachel), Lena Headey (Luce), Matthew Goode (Heck), Celia Imrie (Tessa), Anthony Head (Ned), Darren Boyd (Coop), Sharon Horgan (Beth). Directed by Ol Parker and produced by Sophie Balhetchet, Andro Steinborn, and Barnaby Thompson. Screenplay by Parker.

Romeo: "I'm straight, and really attracted to you."
Juliet: "Good! I prefer men."

Ever notice how in heterosexual romances the characters rarely talk about how they're heterosexual? There have been a few homosexual romances in which the sexuality of the characters goes without saying, but *Imagine Me & You* is not one of them. Here's a movie that begins with a tired romantic formula and tries to redeem it with lesbianism. And not merely lesbianism, but responsible lesbianism, in which the more experienced of the two women does everything she can to preserve the marriage of the woman she loves.

She loves Rachel (Piper Perabo). She is Luce (Lena Headey), and she first sees Rachel on Rachel's wedding day. Their eyes meet, and the screenplay elaborates on that for ninety minutes. Both women know at that

moment, without a word being spoken, that they are destined for each other, but that doesn't prevent Rachel from going ahead with her marriage to Heck (Matthew Goode), although not without some alarming complications at the altar.

Much of the plot is devoted to explaining how Rachel and Luce (who runs a small but amazingly busy flower shop) can meet each other, go out on double dates with Heck and his pal Coop (Darren Boyd), and involve themselves in a romantic triangle; at one point Luce and Rachel are in the back room of the shop, snogging passionately among the petunias, when Heck walks in the front door. That generates one of those obligatory scenes in which the almost-discovered couple has to blush, breathe heavily, and make furtive adjustments to their clothes, while the unexpected visitor either notices nothing, or pretends to notice nothing. With Heck, there's a fine line between those two calibrations of noticing.

Luce does not want to break up Rachel's marriage. Unaware that as the more experienced lesbian she is required by tiresome clichés to be the predator, she nobly tries to suppress her feelings. But Rachel grows consumed by romantic obsession, and soon Heck senses that the honeymoon is over when technically it should still be humming right along.

The movie is set in London, which means that everyone can be more detached and civilized and unable to notice homosexuality than might be possible in, say, San Francisco. There are, however, no barriers between Rachel and Luce except for the fact of her marriage, which is easily disposed of once the plot gets down to work.

Most of the running time is devoted to sitcom devices involving family members, friends, double meanings, close escapes, and sincere heart-to-hearts, especially between Heck and Coop, who are awfully nice and terrifically sensitive. Rachel has a little sister named Beth (Sharon Horgan), who is so smart she says only things that are either accidentally or deliberately perceptive. And Rachel has parents (Celia Imrie and Anthony Head) who in the tradition of all British comedies are apparently insane right up to the point where they are required to demonstrate acceptance, insight, and unconditional love.

The sex in the movie is so mild that I assumed the R rating was generated primarily by the gay theme, until I learned the R is in fact because of too many f-words. That makes sense. If Rachel and Luce were of opposite genders, what they do together would be rated PG-13, and they'd have to hold on tight to keep from sliding into PG. There is a strange moment when Heck and Rachel decide to revive their marriage by making love outdoors on Hampstead Heath, and don't even get to the interruptus stage before two gay men emerge from the shrubbery and hold a conversation so innocuous they might have been taking a survey for the groundskeepers.

Perabo, as it happens, has made another movie about love between two women, the overlooked and underrated *Lost and Delirious* (2001), in which she costarred with Jessica Paré in a movie so infinitely superior (and sexier) that Perabo must have remembered it wistfully during the agonizingly belabored developments in this one.

I'm Not Scared ★ ★ ★ ½
R, 108 m., 2004

Guiseppe Cristiano (Michele), Aitana Sanchez-Gijon (Anna), Dino Abbrescia (Pino), Diego Abatantuono (Sergio), Giorgio Careccia (Felice), Mattia Di Pierro (Filippo). Directed by Gabriele Salvatores and produced by Marco Chimenz, Giovanni Stabilini, Maurizio Totti, and Riccardo Tozzi. Screenplay by Niccolo Ammaniti (based on his novel) and Francesca Marciano.

Michele is a ten-year-old boy whose summer is unfolding as one perfect day after another. He lives in a rural district in southern Italy, and spends his days exploring the countryside with his friends. One day they go poking about an old abandoned house, and later he returns alone to look for his sister's lost glasses. In the yard he finds a slab of sheet metal, and when he lifts it up he sees, at the bottom of a pit, a leg sticking out from under a blanket.

Michele (Guiseppe Cristiano) lets the covering slam down and races for home. He doesn't tell anyone what he has seen. Returning again, he discovers that the pit holds a small boy named Filippo (Mattia Di Pierro), who is

chained. On the television news Michele will learn that Filippo has been kidnapped.

I'm Not Scared tells its story mostly through Michele's eyes. He is just at that age when he has glimmers of understanding about adult life, but still lives within the strange logic of childhood. A year or two older, and he might have known to call the police. But no. Filippo becomes his secret, and he visits him frequently, bringing him bread to eat. It is almost as if he takes pride of possession.

We learn that Michele's father, Pino (Dino Abbrescia), is involved in the kidnapping, along with a friend named Sergio (Diego Abatantuono). Sergio has recently returned from Brazil, is clearly a criminal, is capable of violence. But Michele comes to understand this only gradually. His father is a figure of awe to him, a truck driver whose visits home are great occasions for Michele, his sister, and his mother, Anna (Aitana Sanchez-Gijon). The father is tall and strong and enveloped in a cloud of cigarette smoke, and his conversations with Sergio contain hints of menace.

This story unfolds surrounded by an almost improbable pastoral beauty. The children race their bicycles down country lanes, explore caves and ravines, roll down hillsides through boundless fields of golden wheat. Life at the farmhouse centers around dinners and much conversation, and later, when the children are asleep, the drinking and the talk continue. Michele pieces the clues together and understands that Filippo has been kidnapped by his father and Sergio, and when a police helicopter is seen in the neighborhood, he understands enough to realize that Filippo could be murdered—unless he saves him.

The film has been directed by Gabriele Salvatores, whose *Mediterraneo* won an Oscar for Best Foreign Film in 1992. The screenplay is by Niccolo Ammaniti and Francesca Marciano, based on Ammaniti's novel. The plot is essentially a thriller, but the film surrounds those elements with details of everyday life, with ambiguities and mysteries seen through a child's eyes, and a puzzle about the nature of the agreement between Pino and Sergio. Certainly the family is poor, and at one crucial moment, his mother asks Michele to promise, when he grows up, to "get away from here." The ransom money represents a hope for a new beginning.

Salvatores is not in a hurry to get to the climax. He allows summer days to follow one upon another, as Michele's secret grows in the boy's mind. There are details that enrich the portrait, as when he longs for a blue toy truck that belongs to a friend, and strikes a bargain to get it. We are acutely conscious of Filippo, chained in the hole, but for Michele, there are other things to think about, and the urgency of the situation only gradually grows upon him.

The film reminds us that, in childhood, days and weeks seemed to last forever. Summer was not a season but a lifetime. Parents represented a law that stood above our own best thinking, because they had demonstrated time and again that they knew best, that we were only children. The coming-of-age experience, which *I'm Not Scared* incorporates, involves that moment or season when we realize that we can see outside the box of childhood, that it is time to trust our own decisions.

Hollywood movies give us children who are miniature adults, secret agents like Cody Banks and the Spy Kids, who control technology and save the world. *I'm Not Scared* is a reminder of true childhood, of its fears and speculations, of the way a conversation can be overheard but not understood, of the way that the shape of the adult world forms slowly through the mist.

Incident at Loch Ness ★ ★ ★
PG-13, 94 m., 2004

Playing themselves, more or less: Werner Herzog, Zak Penn, Kitana Baker, Gabriel Beristain, Michael Karnow, Robert O'Meara, John Bailey, and David A. Davidson. Directed by Zak Penn and produced by Werner Herzog and Penn. Screenplay by Penn.

The story goes like this. Werner Herzog, the holy genius of the German New Wave, decides to make a documentary about the Loch Ness Monster. At the same time, a documentary is being made about Herzog by John Bailey, the famous cinematographer. Bailey and his crew follow Herzog and his crew to Loch Ness, where Herzog's producer turns out to be a jerk who hires his girlfriend as the "sonar expert" and expects everyone to wear official matching jumpsuits "so it will look like a real expedition." On the suits, he spells it "expediition."

Herzog realizes he is in the hands of a charlatan. The "sonar expert" (Kitana Baker) explains that her professional experience includes modeling for *Playboy* and appearing in the Miller Lite cat-fight commercials. The producer (Zak Penn) also springs a "cryptozoologist" on Herzog, and we learn that cryptozoology is "the study of undiscovered animals." The crypto guy produces a test tube containing a "mysterious" tentacle of which it can be said that it is definitely small. The sonar expert appears in an American flag bikini. Herzog is enraged that the producer has hired these people; the director should make such decisions.

They are all meanwhile on a boat named the *Discovery IV;* the producer liked the sound of that, despite the fact that there was no Discovery I, II, or III. The captain, a grizzled old sea dog (or loch dog) named David A. Davidson, mutters darkly about it being bad luck to change the name of a boat. A miniature fake Loch Ness monster is produced, and Herzog, asked to photograph it, says it is "stupid" and tells Bailey's doc camera: "I became aware that there was something seriously wrong." But then something attacks the boat, a crew member is eaten, the producer makes off in the only lifeboat, the sonar expert reveals, "I did study up a little," and tries to summon help on the radio, and Herzog dons a wet suit and announces plans to swim to shore for help.

This material falls somewhere between *This Is Spinal Tap* and *Burden of Dreams,* Les Blank's (real) documentary about the filming of Herzog's *Fitzcarraldo,* a movie shot deep in the Amazon jungles. There is even a moment when the producer pulls a gun on Herzog, echoing the story (inaccurate, Herzog says) that Herzog forced Klaus Kinski to act at gunpoint.

Is the film what it claims to be, or is it a contrivance from beginning to end? It must be said that Herzog himself is always completely convincing, and everything he says and does seems authentic. But was he really going to make a documentary? Or is that merely the pretext for this film? Or is this film what emerged from the collision of Herzog's failed film and Bailey's documentary? Is there a point at which reality becomes fiction and everybody redefines what they are really doing? It's intriguing to puzzle out such questions, while looking like a hawk for shots that betray themselves. There's one where two characters go upstairs to have a secret conference, and Bailey's camera sneaks up after them, and peeks through an open bedroom door and sees a crucial chart reflected in a mirror, and you know this shot didn't just happen; it was a setup.

On the other hand, an opening scene at Herzog's home in Los Angeles seems manifestly real, as Herzog and his wife, Lena, throw a dinner party for the crew of the film and some friends, including Jeff Goldblum and the magician Ricky Jay. It's at this party that the producer wants to discuss the "lighting package" that the cinematographer, Gabriel Beristain, will be using, and Herzog declares that a documentary needs no lights. Beristain is a real figure, who photographed *K2* and *S.W.A.T.*, and indeed everyone we see is who they say they are (in one way or another). Zak Penn, for example, is a writer of *Last Action Hero*.

Rather than say exactly what I think about the veracity of *Incident at Loch Ness,* let me tell you a story. A few years ago at the Telluride Film Festival, Herzog invited me to his hotel room to see videos of two of his new documentaries. One was about the Jesus figures of Russia, men who dress, act, and speak like Jesus and walk through the land being supported by their disciples. The other was about a town whose citizens believe that a city of angels exists on the bottom of a deep lake and can be seen through the ice at the beginning of winter. Wait too long, and the ice is too thick to see through. Crawl onto the ice too soon, and you fall in.

Herzog has made many great documentaries in his career, and I was enthralled by both of these. He's a master of the cinema, with an instinct for the bizarre and unexpected. After I saw the films, he said he only had one more thing to tell me: Both of the documentaries were complete fiction.

To what degree *Incident at Loch Ness* is truthful is something you will have to decide. Indeed, that's part of the fun, since some scenes are either clearly real, or exactly the same as if they were. Watching the movie is an entertaining exercise in forensic viewing, and the insidious thing is, even if it is a con, who is the conner and who is the connee?

Note: The Website www.truthaboutlochness.com supplies a lot of information, speculation, and gossip about the film, not all of it necessarily trustworthy.

An Inconvenient Truth ★ ★ ★ ★
PG, 100 m., 2006

Featuring Al Gore. A documentary directed by Davis Guggenheim and produced by Lawrence Bender, Scott Burns, and Laurie David.

I want to write this review so that every reader will begin it and finish it. I am a liberal, but I do not intend this as a review reflecting any kind of politics. It reflects the truth as I understand it, and it represents, I believe, agreement among the world's experts.

Global warming is real.

It is caused by human activity.

Mankind and governments must begin immediate action to halt and reverse it.

If we do nothing, in about ten years the planet may reach a "tipping point" and begin a slide toward destruction of our civilization and most of the other species on this planet.

After that point is reached, it would be too late for any action.

These facts are stated by Al Gore in the documentary *An Inconvenient Truth.* Forget that he ever ran for office. Consider him a concerned man speaking out on the approaching crisis. "There is no controversy about these facts," he says in the film. "Out of 925 recent articles in peer-review scientific journals about global warming, there was no disagreement. Zero."

He stands on a stage before a vast screen, in front of an audience. The documentary is based on a speech he has been developing for six years and is supported by dramatic visuals. He shows the famous photograph "Earthrise," taken from space by the first American astronauts. Then he shows a series of later space photographs, clearly indicating that glaciers and lakes are shrinking, snows are melting, shorelines are retreating.

He provides statistics: The ten warmest years in history were in the past fourteen years. Last year, South America experienced its first hurricane. Japan and the Pacific are setting new records for typhoons. Hurricane

Katrina passed over Florida, doubled back over the Gulf, picked up strength from unusually warm Gulf waters, and went from Category 1 to Category 5. There are changes in the gulf stream and the jet stream. Cores of polar ice show that carbon dioxide is much, much higher than it has been in a quarter of a million years.

It once was thought that such things went in cycles. Gore stands in front of a graph showing the ups and downs of carbon dioxide over the centuries. Yes, there is a cyclical pattern. Then, in recent years, the graph turns up and keeps going up, higher and higher, off the chart.

The primary manmade cause of global warming is the burning of fossil fuels. We are taking energy stored over hundreds of millions of years in the form of coal, gas, and oil and releasing it suddenly. This causes global warming, and there is a pass-along effect. Since glaciers and snow reflect sunlight but seawater absorbs it, the more the ice melts, the more of the sun's energy is retained by the sea.

Gore says that although there is "100 percent agreement" among scientists, a database search of newspaper and magazine articles shows that 57 percent question the fact of global warming, while 43 percent support it. These figures are the result, he says, of a disinformation campaign started in the 1990s by the energy industries to "reposition global warming as a debate." It is the same strategy used for years by the defenders of tobacco. My father was a Luckys smoker who died of lung cancer in 1960, and twenty years later it still was "debatable" that smoking and lung cancer were linked. Now we are talking about the death of the future, starting in the lives of those now living.

"The world won't 'end' overnight in ten years," Gore says. "But a point will have been passed, and there will be an irreversible slide into destruction."

In England, Sir James Lovelock, the scientist who proposed the Gaia hypothesis (that the planet functions like a living organism), has published a new book saying that in one hundred years mankind will be reduced to "a few breeding couples at the poles." Gore thinks "that's too pessimistic. We can turn this around just as we reversed the hole in the

ozone layer. But it takes action right now, and politicians in every nation must have the courage to do what is necessary. It is not a political issue. It is a moral issue."

When I said I was going to a press screening of An Inconvenient Truth, a friend said, "Al Gore talking about the environment! Bor . . . ing!" This is not a boring film. The director, Davis Guggenheim, uses words, images, and Gore's concise litany of facts to build a film that is fascinating and relentless. In thirty-nine years I have never written these words in a movie review, but here they are: You owe it to yourself to see this film. If you do not, and you have grandchildren, you should explain to them why you decided not to.

Am I acting as an advocate in this review? Yes, I am. I believe that to be "impartial" and "balanced" on global warming means one must take a position like Gore's. There is no other view that can be defended. Senator James Inhofe of Oklahoma, who chairs the Senate Environment Committee, has said, "Global warming is the greatest hoax ever perpetrated on the American people." I hope he takes his job seriously enough to see this film. I think he has a responsibility to do that.

What can we do? Switch to and encourage the development of alternative energy sources: solar, wind, tidal, and, yes, nuclear. Move quickly toward hybrid and electric cars. Pour money into public transit and subsidize the fares. Save energy in our houses. I did a funny thing when I came home after seeing An Inconvenient Truth. I went around the house turning off the lights. ☞

The Incredibles ★ ★ ★ ½
PG, 115 m., 2004

With the voices of: Craig T. Nelson (Bob Parr/Mr. Incredible), Holly Hunter (Helen Parr/Elastigirl), Samuel L. Jackson (Lucius Best/Frozone), Jason Lee (Buddy Pine/Syndrome), Sarah Vowell (Violet Parr), Elizabeth Pena (Mirage), Spencer Fox (Dashiell Parr), Eli Fucile (Jack Jack), Brad Bird (Edna "E" Mode). Directed by Brad Bird and produced by John Walker. Screenplay by Bird.

The Pixar Studio, which cannot seem to take a wrong step, steps right again with The Incred-

ibles, a superhero spoof that alternates breakneck action with satire of suburban sitcom life. After the *Toy Story* movies, *A Bug's Life, Monsters, Inc.,* and *Finding Nemo,* here's another example of Pixar's mastery of popular animation. If it's not quite as magical as *Nemo,* how many movies are? That may be because it's about human beings who have some connection, however tenuous, with reality; it loses the fantastical freedom of the fish fable.

The story follows the universal fondness for finding the chinks in superhero armor; if Superman hadn't had kryptonite, he would have been perfect and therefore boring, and all the superheroes since him have spent most of their time compensating for weaknesses. Think about it: Every story begins with a superhero who is invincible, but who soon faces total defeat.

Mr. Incredible, the hero of *The Incredibles,* is a superhero in the traditional 1950s mold, dashing about town fighting crime and saving the lives of endangered civilians. Alas, the populace is not unanimously grateful, and he's faced with so many lawsuits for unlawful rescue and inadvertent side effects that he's forced to retire. Under the government's Superhero Relocation Program, Mr. Incredible (voice by Craig T. Nelson) moves to the suburbs, joined by his wife, Elastigirl (Holly Hunter), and their children, Violet (Sarah Vowell), Dashiell (Spencer Fox), and little Jack Jack (Eli Fucile).

They are now officially the Parr family, Bob and Helen. Bob works at an insurance agency, where his muscle-bound supertorso barely squeezes into a cubicle. Helen raises the kids, and there's a lot of raising to do: The world is occasionally too much for the teenager Violet, whose superpowers allow her to turn invisible and create force fields out of (I think) impregnable bubbles. Dashiell, called "Dash," can run at the speed of light, but has to slow down considerably in school track meets (if they can't see you running around the track, they assume you never left the finish line, instead of that you're back to it already). Jack Jack's powers are still limited, not yet encompassing the uses of the potty.

Bob Parr hates the insurance business. Joining him in the suburb is another relocated superhero, Frozone (Samuel L. Jackson), who

can freeze stuff. Claiming they belong to a bowling league, they sneak out nights to remember the good old days and do a little low-profile superheroing. Then the old life beckons, in the form of a challenge from Mirage (Elizabeth Pena), who lures Mr. Incredible to a Pacific island where, overweight and slowed down, he battles a robot named Omnidroid 7.

This robot, we learn, is one of a race of fearsome new machines created by the evil mastermind Syndrome (Jason Lee), who once admired Mr. Incredible as a kid but became bitter when Incredible refused to let him become his boy wonder. He now wants to set up as a superpower by unleashing his robots on an unsuspecting world. That sets up the final climactic conclusion, which ranges from near-apocalyptic on the one hand to slapstick on the other (Elastigirl, whose body can stretch almost to infinity, gets trapped in two doors at once).

On the surface, *The Incredibles* is a goof on superhero comics. Underneath, it's a critique of modern American uniformity. Mr. Incredible is forced to retire not because of age or obsolescence, but because of trial lawyers seeking damages for his unsolicited good deeds; he's in the same position as the Boy Scout who helps the little old lady across the street when she doesn't want to go. What his society needs is not superdeeds but tort reform. "They keep finding new ways," he sighs, "to celebrate mediocrity."

Anyone who has seen a Bond movie will make the connection between Syndrome's island hideout and the headquarters of various Bond villains. *The Incredibles* also has a character inspired by Q, Bond's gadget-master. This is Edna Mode, known as "E" and voiced by Brad Bird, who also wrote and directed. She's a horn-rimmed little genius who delivers a hilarious lecture on the reasons why Mr. Incredible does not want a cape on his new uniform; capes can be as treacherous as Isadora Duncan's scarf, and if you don't know what happened to Isadora Duncan, Google the poor woman and shed a tear.

Brad Bird's previous film was *The Iron Giant* (1999), about a misunderstood robot from outer space and the little boy who becomes his friend. It had a charm and delicacy that was unique in the genre, and *The Incredibles,* too, has special qualities, especially in the subtle ways it observes its gifted characters trying to dumb down and join the crowd. Kids in the audience will likely miss that level, but will like the exuberance of characters like Dash. Grown-ups are likely to be surprised by how smart the movie is, and how sneakily perceptive.

Infernal Affairs ★ ★ ★
R, 100 m., 2004

Tony Leung (Chan Wing-yan), Andy Lau (Inspector Lau Kin-ming), Anthony Wong (Superintendant Wong), Eric Tsang (Hon Sam). Directed by Alan Mak and Andrew Lau and produced by Lau. Screenplay by Mak and Felix Chong.

Infernal Affairs is about a cop who is actually a gangster, and a gangster who is actually a cop. Early scenes show them being put into deep cover: A young gangster is assigned by a crime boss to enter the police academy, and a young academy graduate is spun off from the force and assigned to undercover work as a criminal. In each case, the strategy is to leave them in place for years, doing their jobs as well as possible, so they can rise in the ranks and become invaluable as moles.

This idea, made into the most successful Hong Kong production of recent years, is such a good one that a Hollywood remake is planned, perhaps by Martin Scorsese. What makes it so intriguing is that as the story grows more tangled, the lives of the two characters take on a hidden desperation. Both of them have spent so long pretending to be someone else that their performances have become the reality.

Andy Lau plays Lau, the young mobster who is assigned by his triad boss (Eric Tsang) to infiltrate the police force. He becomes a good cop, skilled at his job, smooth at departmental politics, cool as a cucumber.

Tony Leung, who won as best actor at Cannes for *In the Mood for Love,* plays Chan, the young police recruit who is assigned to infiltrate the mob. At first only two members of the force know his true identity, and eventually there is only one: Police Superintendent Wong (Anthony Wong), to whom he turns with increasing desperation. He is tired of being a

criminal, the work is depressing, he is the only person besides Wong who knows he's not a bad guy, and he wants to come in out of the cold.

These two characters come into full play ten years after the opening scenes, when both of them are brought in by their original employers, and both sides realize they have a traitor in their ranks. In a kind of symmetry that is unlikely and yet poetically appropriate, each one is assigned to find the mole—to find himself, that is.

There's another level of irony since Lau and Chan actually graduated in the same academy class, and knew each other if only by sight; Chan has no way of knowing Lau is a sleeper for the mob, but Lau knew at the time that Chan was a cop, and possibly knew he disappeared to go undercover. The two meet by chance years later in a stereo store, but don't recognize each other—a possibility easier for us to accept because they were played by other actors as younger men.

It's a long, tense buildup, with Lau prospering professionally while Chan begs with Wong to leave undercover work. Wong refuses; the department has invested years in putting him into place. Eventually, in a sustained virtuoso sequence, the two moles are in play at once, aware of each other's existence but not identity, and the plot ingeniously plays them against each other.

A lot of the action here has to do with cell phone strategy, brought to a level of complexity that would impress a logician. Each character is on the edge of discovering who the other is, and of being discovered himself, as a long-prepared police sting comes down on a long-planned criminal operation.

But this plot, clever and complex, is not the reason to see the movie. What makes it special is the inner turmoil caused by living a lie. If everyone you know and everything you do for ten years indicates you are one kind of person, and you know you are another, how do you live with that?

The movie pays off in a kind of emotional complexity rarely seen in crime movies. I cannot reveal what happens, but will urge you to consider the thoughts of two men who finally confront their own real identities—in the person of the other character. The crook has been the good cop. The cop has been the good crook. It's as if they have impersonated each other. All very lonely, ironic, and sad, and without satisfaction—especially if your superiors, the people you did it for, do not or cannot appreciate it. You might as well just forge ahead undercover for the rest of your life, a mole forever unawakened, and let the false life become the one you have lived.

In Good Company ★ ★ ★
PG-13, 131 m., 2005

Dennis Quaid (Dan Foreman), Topher Grace (Carter Duryea), Scarlett Johansson (Alex Foreman), Marg Helgenberger (Ann Foreman), David Paymer (Morty), Philip Baker Hall (Eugene Kalb). Directed by Paul Weitz and produced by Chris Weitz and Paul Weitz. Screenplay by Paul Weitz.

Corporations have replaced Nazis as the politically correct villains of the age—and just in time, because it was getting increasingly difficult to produce Nazis who survived into the twenty-first century (*Hellboy* had to use a portal in time). *The Manchurian Candidate* used a corporation instead of the Chinese Communists, and thrillers like *Resident Evil* give us corporations whose recklessness turn the population into zombies. *In Good Company* is a rare species: a feel-good movie about big business. It's about a corporate culture that tries to be evil and fails.

It doesn't start out that way. We meet Dan Foreman (Dennis Quaid), head of advertising sales at a sports magazine, who has the corner office and the big salary and is close to landing a big account from a dubious client (Philip Baker Hall). Then disaster strikes. The magazine is purchased by Teddy K (an unbilled Malcolm McDowell), a media conglomerator in the Murdoch mode, who takes sudden notice of a twenty-six-year-old hotshot named Carter Duryea (Topher Grace) and sends him in to replace Dan. Carter takes Dan's job and corner office, but instinctively keeps Dan as his "assistant," perhaps sensing that someone in the department will have to know more than Carter knows.

Dan accepts the demotion. He needs his job to keep up the mortgage payments and support his family. But Carter, known as a "ninja

assassin" for his firing practices, fires Morty (David Paymer), an old-timer at the magazine. As we learn more about Morty's home life, we realize this only confirms the suspicions of his wife, who thinks he's a loser.

Developments up to this point have followed the template of standard corporate ruthlessness, with lives made redundant by corporate theories that are essentially management versions of a pyramid scheme: Plundering victims and looting assets can be made to look, on the books, like growth.

Dan has a wife named Ann (Marg Helgenberger) and a pretty college-age daughter named Alex (Scarlett Johansson). He is concerned about Alex, especially after finding a pregnancy-testing kit in the garbage, but doesn't know how concerned he should be until he discovers that Carter, the rat, has not only demoted him but is dating his daughter.

In Good Company so far has been the usual corporate slasher movie, in which good people have bad things happen to them because of the evil and greedy system. Then it takes a curious turn, which I will suggest without describing, in which goodness prevails and unexpected humility surfaces. The movie was directed by Paul Weitz, who with his brother Chris made *American Pie* and the Hugh Grant charmer *About a Boy*, and with those upbeat works behind him I didn't expect *In Good Company* to attain the savagery of Neil LaBute's *In the Company of Men*, but I was surprised all the same when the sun came out.

Dennis Quaid has a comfort level in roles like this that makes him effortlessly convincing; as he tries to land the account from the big client, we see how Dan uses psychology and his own personality to sell the magazine. Young Carter is years away from that ease. Topher Grace plays him as a kid who doesn't know which Christmas present he wants to play with first; he has achieved success more quickly than the experience to deal with it. Like a pro sports rookie, he can think of no more imaginative way to celebrate his wealth than to buy a new Porsche; he finds that such joys do not last forever.

Scarlett Johansson continues to employ the gravitational pull of quiet fascination. As in *Lost in Translation* and *Girl with a Pearl Earring* (both much better films), she creates a zone of her own importance into which men are drawn not so much by lust as by the feeling that she knows something about life that they might be able to learn. That turns the Alex-Carter affair into something more interesting than the sub-*American Pie* adventure we might have expected.

David Paymer's character provides the movie with emotional ballast; he is not only out of work, but probably unemployable, at his age and salary level, and unsuited to survive at a lower level. His story is common enough. It is a corporate strategy to create narratives for employees to imagine, in which they begin as junior executives and ascend to the boardroom. Countless college graduates enter this dream world every year, without reflecting (a) that there are many fewer positions at the top than at the bottom, and (b) that therefore, if the corporations are still hiring at the bottom, it is because there are fatalities at the top. You can always get someone younger and cheaper to do the job of the older and more experienced.

There's one scene in the movie that works well even though it's less than convincing. The conglomerator Teddy K jets in for a meeting with the staff, at which he recites various corporate platitudes to an adoring audience (one of the keys to success in business is the ability to endure the gaseous inanities of Management-Speak as if they meant anything). Then Dan stands up and, with everything to lose, explains clearly and mercilessly just why Teddy K is full of it. Whenever anyone speaks the plain truth on such an occasion, there is a palpable shock; how can such enterprises survive realism? Consider the soldier who asked Donald Rumsfeld, please, sir, may we have some more armor?

I don't believe the real Dan would have made quite that speech, but then I don't believe the third act of *In Good Company*. I'd like to, but I just can't. I don't think corporate struggles turn out that way. Still, the movie is smart enough, the performances strong, and the subplots involving Johansson and Paymer have their moments. If nothing else, *In Good Company* shows that Paul Weitz has the stuff to tell a ruthless story—and he does, until he loses his nerve. Since most audiences no doubt will prefer his version to the one I imagine, who is to say he is wrong?

In Her Shoes ★ ★ ★ ½
PG-13, 129 m., 2005

Cameron Diaz (Maggie Feller), Toni Collette (Rose Feller), Shirley MacLaine (Ella Hirsch), Mark Feuerstein (Simon Stein), Francine Beers (Mrs. Lefkowitz), Ken Howard (Michael Feller), Candice Azzara (Sydelle), Norman Lloyd (The Professor). Directed by Curtis Hanson and produced by Ridley Scott, Carol Fenelon, Lisa Ellzey, and Hanson. Screenplay by Susannah Grant, based on the novel by Jennifer Weiner.

Curtis Hanson's *In Her Shoes* takes a good half-hour to make it clear it will not be a soppy chick flick, and for that matter, what is "chick flick" anyway but an insulting term for a movie that is about women instead of the usual testosterone carriers? The movie's setup would be right at home in a sitcom, but its next ninety-nine minutes do some rather unexpected things with characters who insist on breaking out of the stereotypes they started with. It's not every big-budget movie that gets its two biggest emotional payoffs with poems by Elizabeth Bishop and e. e. cummings.

Here are the opening stereotypes: Maggie Feller (Cameron Diaz) is a blonde bimbo who gets drunk at her high school reunion, has sex in the toilet, and passes out. Her sister, Rose (Toni Collette), is a plain-Jane Philadelphia lawyer who is fifteen pounds on the wrong side of her Weight Watchers target goal. Their mother is dead, and their father, Michael (Ken Howard), lives with his new wife, Sydelle (Candice Azzara). Maggie still lives at home because the rent is free, but Sydelle kicks her out because she wants her room for her own daughter, invariably described as "my Marsha."

Maggie moves in with Rose. Some measure of her desperation is suggested when Rose tells her she might consider going back to school. Maggie: "You know how well that worked out." Rose: "I meant the literacy place." Maggie indeed flunks an MTV audition when she can't read the words on the teleprompter.

Meanwhile, she trashes Rose's apartment while stealing her clothes, her money, and a potential boyfriend. Rose throws her out. Maggie is desperate when she finds birthday cards mailed to the girls by a grandmother whose existence was concealed from them. This is Ella (Shirley MacLaine), and in desperation Maggie travels to Ella's retirement home in Florida and throws herself on the mercy of a total stranger.

It's around here that the movie slips out of the cute stuff and develops a bite. Ella is the kind of no-nonsense older woman MacLaine has been playing ever since the wonderful *Madame Sousatzka* (1988). She's not a sentimental "oldster" but a tough cookie who observes Maggie stealing from her and asks her, "How much money were you hoping to get from me?" She makes Maggie a deal: She'll match, penny for penny, whatever Maggie can make while working at the retirement home's assisted living center. And as Maggie begins to bond with people such as Mrs. Lefkowitz (Francine Beers) and the Professor (Norman Lloyd), she discovers, slowly and uncertainly, that she can be competent and responsible and maybe even respectable.

The movie's key scenes take place with Maggie among the old people, and the screenplay by Susannah Grant (based on the novel by Jennifer Weiner) establishes them as characters who have lived their lives well by accumulating experience and instinctively knowing how to deal with the likes of Maggie.

The Professor, who taught college English, is especially important to Maggie. He wants her to read to him, gently helps her understand the technique and purpose of reading, and guides her through possible dyslexia. He needs a reader because he is blind, and that is important, too, because Maggie has maybe been thinking a lot about what Rose told her: "You're not going to look like this forever, you know." She knows the Professor doesn't like her for her looks. She reads him "One Art," a poem by Elizabeth Bishop that is about "the art of losing," and as a woman who has made a lifestyle out of misplacing people, possessions, and responsibilities, Maggie finds it strangely comforting and does some offscreen reading on her own, setting up a powerful appearance later in the film of the e. e. cummings poem that begins:

i carry your heart with me (i carry it in
my heart) i am never without it (anywhere
i go you go, my dear . . .

There are various male characters in the movie, attached to various possibilities of hearts being, or not being, carried in other hearts. But the movie is really about the transformation of the women, of all three women. That's what's surprising: This isn't simply about Maggie being worked on by Ella and Rose but about how her growth nudges both of the other women into new directions.

In Her Shoes starts out with the materials of an ordinary movie and becomes a rather special one. The emotional payoff at the end is earned, not because we see it coming as the inevitable outcome of the plot but because it arrives out of the blue and yet, once we think about it, makes perfect sense. It tells us something fundamental and important about a character, it allows her to share that something with those she loves, and it does it in a way we could not possibly anticipate. Like a good poem, it blindsides us with the turn it takes right at the end.

This movie by Curtis Hanson comes after *L.A. Confidential* (1997), *Wonder Boys* (2000), and Eminem's *8 Mile* (2002). Three completely different movies, you'd think, and yet all bound by a common thread: the transformative power of the written word. The first is about gossip journalism, the second about writers on a campus, the third about a hip-hop poet. Now a life is changed by reading.

In My Country ★ ★ ½
R, 100 m., 2005

Samuel L. Jackson (Langston Whitfield), Juliette Binoche (Anna Malan), Brendan Gleeson (de Jager), Menzi Ngubane (Dumi Mkhalipi), Sam Ngakane (Anderson), Aletta Bezuidenhout (Elsa), Lionel Newton (Edward Morgan), Langley Kirkwood (Boetie). Directed by John Boorman and produced by Robert Chartoff, Mike Medavoy, Kieran Corrigan, and Lynn Hendee. Screenplay by Ann Peacock, based on a book by Antjie Krog.

In the final decades of apartheid in South Africa, few observers thought power would change hands in the country without a bloody war. But white rule gave way peacefully to the Nelson Mandela government, and Mandela and F. W. de Klerk, the departing prime minister, shared the Nobel Peace Prize.

That miracle nevertheless left a nation scarred by decades of violence—not only of whites against blacks, although that predominated. The Truth and Reconciliation Commission, the inspiration of Mandela, Archbishop Desmond Tutu, and other leaders in the new society, found a way to deal with those wounds without resorting to the endless cycle of bloody revenge seen in Northern Ireland, Bosnia, and elsewhere. The commission made a simple offer: Appear before a public tribunal, confess exactly what you did, convince us you were acting under orders, make an apology we can believe, and we will move on from there.

John Boorman's In My Country is set at the time of the commission's hearings, and stars Samuel L. Jackson as Langston Whitfield, a Washington Post reporter covering the story, and Juliette Binoche as Anna Malan, a white Afrikaner, who is doing daily broadcasts for the South African Broadcasting Company. As the commission and its caravan of press and support staff travel rural areas, Whitfield and Malan find themselves in disagreement about the commission, but strongly attracted to each other.

I confess I walked into the film with strong feelings. I've spent a good deal of time in South Africa, including a year at the University of Cape Town. I had the opportunity to discuss the commission with Archbishop Tutu. I believe the transitional period in South Africa is a model for an enlightened and humane reconciliation with past evils. In My Country shows the process at work and argues in its favor, and I tended to approve of it just on that basis.

Yet there is something not quite right about the film itself. The affair between Whitfield and Malan seems arbitrary, more like two writers having sex on the campaign trail than like two people involved in a romance that would be important to them. Both are married, and neither wants to leave their marriage, although perhaps in the grip of infatuation they waver. Although apartheid imposed criminal penalties for interracial sex under its "Immorality Act," that does not necessarily mean that interracial sex has to be in the foreground of a movie about Truth and Reconciliation—particularly if it's

an affair involving a visiting foreigner. There seems something too calculated about the movie's pairing up of the political and the personal.

There is another unconvincing aspect: Whitfield, the Washington Post reporter, is not convinced that the commission hearings are useful or just. He thinks the wrongdoers are getting off too easy, and says so at press conferences, becoming an advocate and making no attempt to seem objective. It is up to Anna Malan (and the plot) to convince him otherwise. There is a certain poetic irony in an Afrikaner convincing an African-American that Mandela's new South Africa is on the right track, but isn't it more of a fictional device than a likely scenario?

A scene where Malan brings Whitfield home to her family farm seems contrived because we are not sure what Anna hopes to accomplish with it, and at the end of the scene, that is still unclear. True, during the visit we are able to see white unease about the transfer of power. ("They're not our police anymore. It's not our country anymore".) But the romance adds complications that are essentially a distraction from the main line of the story.

The movie, written by Ann Peacock, is based on a book by Antjie Krog, whose own radio and newspaper reports of the hearings inspired the character of Anna Malan. It has scenes of undeniable power. Many of them involve a character named de Jager (Brendan Gleeson), a South African cop with a zeal for torture and murder that went far beyond his job requirements. Whitfield's encounter with de Jager is tense and strongly played. There are also moments of real emotion during the testimony from a parade of whites (and one black) seeking forgiveness.

As it happens, I've seen another film on the same subject. That is Red Dust, a selection at Toronto 2004, starring Hilary Swank as a New York attorney who returns to her native South Africa to represent a political activist (Chiwetel Ejiofor) in the amnesty hearing for his torturer (Jamie Bartlett). Bartlett's character serves something of the same function as Gleeson's in the other film, but all of the characters and their stories are more complex and contradictory, reflecting their turbulent times.

Innocent Voices ★ ★ ★
R, 120 m., 2005

Leonor Varela (Kella), Carlos Padilla (Chava), Gustavo Munoz (Ancha), Jose Maria Yazpik (Uncle Beto), Ofelia Medina (Mama Toya), Daniel Gimenez Cacho (Priest), Jesus Ochoa (Bus Driver). Directed by Luis Mandoki and produced by Lawrence Bender, Mandoki, and Alejandro Soberon Kuri. Screenplay by Mandoki and Oscar Orlando Torres.

"When the war started, Dad left for the United States," the young narrator of *Innocent Voices* tells us. "Mom said now I was the man of the house." Chava is eleven years old, living in a barrio in El Salvador at the time of the civil war in the 1980s. Eleven is a dangerous age because when he turns twelve he will be drafted into the government army.

There have been several movies about civil wars in Latin America. In *Innocent Voices,* the government is being given American funds to fight the communist-led guerrillas. In Haskell Wexler's *Latino* (1985), the Contras are given American funds to fight the government. In Oliver Stone's *Salvador* (1986), a cynical journalist tries to cover both sides.

What sets *Innocent Voices* apart from these films is its resolute point of view through the eyes of Chava. He has no political opinions. His uncle is with the guerrillas, so he supports his uncle as he would a football team, and he fears the government because he does not want to be taken into the army. But he sees these choices as events in his own life and has no larger knowledge of their meaning.

In that way *Innocent Voices* resembles the best film about insurgencies in Latin America, which is *Men with Guns* (1997) by John Sayles, in which no country is named. It is, I wrote, "an allegory about all countries where men with guns control the daily lives of the people. Some of the men are with the government, some are guerrillas, some are thieves, some are armed to protect themselves, and to the ordinary people it hardly matters: The man with the gun does what he wants, and his reasons are irrelevant—unknown perhaps even to himself."

That is certainly the case in *Innocent Voices,* where politics seem meaningless at the local level, and it is simply a matter of armed men, some of them boys, who have machine guns and fire them recklessly, maybe because it is fun. Tactics and strategy seem lacking in this war; the armed teams on both sides travel the countryside, rarely encountering each other, intimidating the peasants, for whom the message from both camps is the same: Support us or we will kill you.

In this world, Chava (Carlos Padilla) lives a blessed life, as one of those streetwise kids like Pixote who knows everybody's business. His mother, Kella (Leonor Varela), scrambles to feed and protect her three children, and they retreat for a time to the more remote house of her mother, but Kella fears to move to a safer area because if her husband returns and they have moved, "he'll have no way to find us." Her mother sadly shakes her head: "Those who go north get swept away."

Chava makes a living, of sorts. He talks a bus driver into making him an unofficial conductor, shouting out the names of the stops. He goes to school, until the school is closed because of the war. He befriends Ancha (Gustavo Munoz), known as "fish brain" because he is retarded: "He is the only one not scared to have a birthday."

The most frightening scenes in the film are not necessarily the ones where men sweep the barrio with machine-gun fire and the residents cower behind their mattresses. They are the ones when the army comes to the school to take away the twelve-year-olds. On one of these sweeps, Chava improvises an inspired way for the boys to hide from the army; the secret is revealed in a single shot by director Luis Mandoki.

The frightening thing is that twelve-year-olds make good soldiers, up to a point. We see one kid transformed by a uniform and a weapon. He is too young to have a full appreciation of his own danger or the meaning of his actions, and it is great fun to have a real uniform and a real gun. That adults would use children in this way (and they do, all over the world) is a sin against the children and against the future.

The movie is effective without being overwhelming. It doesn't have the power of *City of God, Pixote, Salaam Bombay!* and other films about young boys living by their wits in the center of danger. Perhaps that is because Chava still has a safety net of sorts, in his home and his mother and in the help of the local priest (Daniel Gimenez Cacho), who takes a moral stand against violence but is given cruel thanks for his trouble. Chava is never entirely alone, and his personality assures that he knows many people and is liked by them. His story is not one of a child in the urban wilderness but of a child who was on a steady course through school and life when the war interrupted him.

There is a link between *Innocent Voices* and another recent film, *Lord of War*. In that one, Nicolas Cage plays an arms dealer who sells weapons to whoever has the money. His chief competitor will sell only to the side he believes to be right. The Cage character has no such reluctance, pointing out that guns and money attract each other, and he might as well profit as anyone else. That brings us full circle to *Men with Guns*. Wars had more meaning and were fought less lightly when men had to kill each other with their hands, at close quarters. Guns make it so easy, even a child can do it.

Inside Deep Throat ★ ★ ★
NC-17, 90 m., 2005

A documentary directed by Fenton Bailey and Randy Barbato and produced by Brian Grazer, Bailey, and Barbato. Screenplay by Bailey and Barbato.

In the beginning, Gerard Damiano was a hairdresser. Listening to his clients talk about sex, which in his salon was apparently all they talked about, he realized that pornography had cross-over appeal. All you had to do was advertise a movie in such a way that couples would come, instead of only the raincoat brigade. With a budget of $25,000 and an actress named Linda Lovelace, he made *Deep Throat* (1972), which inspired a national censorship battle, did indeed attract couples, and allegedly grossed $600 million, making it the most profitable movie of all time.

Deep Throat was made on the far fringes of the movie industry; Damiano later complained that most of the profits went to people he prudently refused to name as the mob. Since the mob owned most of the porn the-

aters in the prevideo days and inflated box office receipts as a way of laundering income from drugs and prostitution, it is likely, in fact, that *Deep Throat* did not really gross $600 million, although that might have been the box office tally.

Inside Deep Throat, a documentary that premiered at Sundance and is now going into national release, was made not on the fringes but by the very establishment itself. The studio is Universal, a producer is Brian Grazer *(A Beautiful Mind, How the Grinch Stole Christmas)* and the directors are Fenton Bailey and Randy Barbato *(Party Monster, The Eyes of Tammy Faye)*. The rating, of course, is NC-17. It is a commentary on the limitations of the rating system that Universal would release a documentary about an NC-17 film, but would be reluctant to make one.

The movie uses new and old interviews and newsreel footage to remember a time when porn was brand-new. In my 1973 review of *Deep Throat*, written three days after a police raid on the Chicago theater showing it, I wrote: "The movie became 'pornographic chic' in New York before it was busted. Mike Nichols told Truman Capote he shouldn't miss it, and then the word just sort of got around: This is the first stag film to see with a date."

A year or two earlier, porn audiences darted furtively into shabby little theaters on the wrong side of town; now they lined up for *Deep Throat* and talked cheerfully to news cameras about wanting to see it because, well, everybody else seemed to be going. The movie was not very good (even its director, Gerard Damiano, would tell you that), but it was explicit in a way that was acceptable to its audiences, and it leavened the sex with humor. Not very funny humor, to be sure, but it worked in the giddy, forbidden atmosphere of a mixed-gender porn theater.

The modern era of skin flicks began in 1960 with Russ Meyer's *The Immoral Mr. Teas,* which inspired Meyer and others to make a decade of films featuring nudity but no explicit sex. Then a Supreme Court ruling seemed to permit the hard-core stuff, and *Deep Throat* was the first film to take it to a mass audience. (Meyer himself never made hard-core, explaining (1) he didn't like to share his profits with the mob, and (2) he didn't

343

think what went on below the waist was nearly as visually interesting as the bosoms of his supervixens.) The movie was raided in city after city, it was prosecuted for obscenity, it was seized and banned, and the publicity only made it more popular. There were predictions that explicit sex would migrate into mainstream films, even rumors that Stanley Kubrick wanted to make a porn film.

But by 1974 the boomlet was pretty much over, and the genre had gone back into the hands of the raincoat rangers. When I interviewed Damiano that year, he said porn would soon be a thing of the past: "The only thing that's kept it going this long is the FBI and the Nixon administration. Without censorship to encourage people's curiosity, the whole thing would have been over six months ago." And that was pretty much the story until home video came onto the market, creating a new and much larger audience, but destroying what shreds of artistic ambition lurked in the styles of the film-based pornographers (see *Boogie Nights* for the story of that transition).

Inside Deep Throat has some headlines that go against popular wisdom:

—While everybody remembers that Linda Lovelace later said she had virtually been raped on screen, the movie suggests that her troubles were the doing of her sadistic lover at the time, not Damiano. By the time she was fifty, she was posing for *Leg Show* magazine and saying she thought she looked pretty good for her age.

—While everyone remembers the report of a presidential commission that found pornography to be harmful, not many people remember that was the *second* commission to report on the subject, not the first. The 1970 commission, headed by former Illinois Governor Otto Kerner, found that pornography was not particularly linked to antisocial behavior, and that indeed sex criminals as a group tended to have less exposure to pornography than nonsex criminals. This report, based on scientific research and findings, was deemed unacceptable by the Reagan White House, which created a 1986 commission headed by Attorney General Edwin Meese, which did no research, relied on anecdotal testimony from the witnesses it called, and found pornography harmful.

—Charles Keating Jr. and his Citizens for Decent Literature got a lot of publicity for leading the charge against *Deep Throat* and Larry Flynt. Keating got less publicity when he was charged with racketeering in the Lincoln Savings and Loan scandal, and eventually served four years in prison.

As for *Inside Deep Throat*, it remembers a time before pornography was boring, and a climate in which nonpornographic films might consider bolder sexual content. It has some colorful characters, including a retired Florida exhibitor whose wife provides a running commentary on everything he says. And it tells us where they are now: Damiano is comfortably retired, Linda Lovelace died in a traffic accident, and her costar, Harry Reems, is a recovering substance abuser who now works as a Realtor in Park City, Utah, home of the Sundance Film Festival.

Inside Man ★ ★ ½
R, 128 m., 2006

Denzel Washington (Detective Keith Frazier), Clive Owen (Dalton Russell), Jodie Foster (Madeline White), Willem Dafoe (Captain Darius), Chiwetel Ejiofor (Detective Bill Mitchell), Christopher Plummer (Arthur Case), Kim Director (Stevie). Directed by Spike Lee and produced by Brian Grazer. Screenplay by Russell Gewirtz.

Spike Lee's *Inside Man* has a detective tell a bank robber: "You saw *Dog Day Afternoon*. You're stalling." The problem is, we've seen *Dog Day Afternoon*, and Lee is stalling. Here is a thriller that's curiously reluctant to get to the payoff, and when it does, we see why: We can't accept the motive and method of the bank robbery, we can't believe in one character and can't understand another, and if a man was old enough in the early 1940s to play an important wartime role, how old would he be now? Ninety-five? He might still be chairman of the bank he founded, but would he look like Christopher Plummer?

To give the movie its due, many of these same questions occur to the hero, Det. Keith Frazier. Denzel Washington plays him as a cross between a street cop and one of those armchair sleuths who sees through a crime and patiently explains it to his inferiors. Frazier is early on the scene after four armed robbers invade a Wall Street bank, take hostages, and start issuing demands. As the crisis drags on, Frazier realizes the guys inside don't *want* their demands to be met; they're stalling. But why?

The robbers are led by Clive Owen, who spends most of the movie wearing a mask. Since we see him in the first shot of the film, talking about the crime in the past tense, we know he won't be killed. What we wonder is where he studied the craft of bank robbery. His gang walks in, bolts the door, has everyone lie flat on the floor, and does all the usual stuff such as leaping over teller partitions and intimidating weeping customers. They also throw around completely unnecessary smoke bombs, and the smoke drifts out to the street, alerting a beat cop that something is wrong. Did they *want* to be trapped inside the bank?

I'm not going to go into any detail about how the crisis plays out. And I'm going to conceal the purpose of the robbery. What I must point out is that Plummer, as the bank president, doesn't look to be in his nineties. Giving him a mustache, a walking stick, and some wrinkles doesn't do it. Yet we have to believe that in mid–World War II he was old enough to have risen high enough to do something important enough that after the bank is surrounded, he calls in a woman who seems to have mysterious links to powerful people.

This is Madeline White (Jodie Foster). She knows everybody. She can walk into the mayor's office without an appointment. The mayor orders the cops to "extend her every courtesy." Who or what is Madeline White? I've seen the movie, and I don't know. She is never convincingly explained, and what she does is not well-defined. She's one of those characters who is all buildup and no delivery.

I once knew a man named Jean-Jacques de Mesterton, whose biography described him as "a professional adventurer, political adviser, and international facilitator." You can Google him. I asked him what, exactly, he did. "If you have a problem," he said, "first, you call the police. Then you call the FBI. If you still have a problem, you call me." I guess Madeline White is supposed to be the Jean-Jacques of New York, but although she purses her lips, frowns, and won't take any nonsense, she's basically a red herring.

The whole plot smells fishy. It's not that the movie is hiding something but that when it's revealed, it's been left sitting too long at room temperature. *Inside Man* goes to much difficulty to arrive at too little. It starts with the taut action of a superior caper movie, but then it meanders; eventually the narration slows to the pace of a Garrison Keillor story on *A Prairie Home Companion,* which is nice if you are a prairie, but if not, not.

The screenplay by Russell Gewirtz needs a few more runs through rewrite. Because the film was directed by Spike Lee, it is not without interest; Lee finds so many interesting details that don't involve the plot that we're reluctant when he gets back to business. A cameo involving a little boy and his video game is a self-contained editorial. A Sikh is accused of being an Arab terrorist, and you want to say, "People! Listen up! Guy with a turban! Sikh! Not Arab!" There's a nutty sequence in which the hostage-takers use a foreign language that has to be translated by a bystander's ex-wife.

The performances, for that matter, are first rate; Washington is convincing even when he has little to be convincing about, and Foster is smart and tough as she decisively does more or less nothing. Well, to be fair, a little more more than less.

Intermission ★ ★ ★ ½
R, 105 m., 2004

Cillian Murphy (John), Kelly Macdonald (Deirdre), Colin Farrell (Lehiff), Colm Meaney (Detective Jerry Lynch), David Wilmot (Oscar), Brian F. O'Byrne (Mick), Shirley Henderson (Sally), Michael McElhatton (Sam), Deirdre O'Kane (Noeleen). Directed by John Crowley and produced by Neil Jordan, Alan Moloney, and Stephen Woolley. Screenplay by Mark O'Rowe.

Here is a movie where the characters discover that brown steak sauce tastes great in coffee, where a TV producer wants "more reality" after filming a rabbit race, where a cop's car is stolen while he's carrying out a drug bust, where . . . but *Intermission* goes on and on, in a tireless series of inventions, like a plot-generating machine in overdrive. That it succeeds is some kind of miracle; there's enough material here for three bad films, and somehow it becomes one good one.

The movie is a dark comedy—no, make that a dark, dark, *dark* comedy—set in Dublin and starring more or less everyone in town. That its cast includes Colin Farrell, now a big movie star, is less remarkable than the fact that the cast is so large and colorful that we sometimes lose track of him. Here is yet more evidence that *Pulp Fiction* was the most influential movie of recent years, as eccentric characters with distinctive verbal styles coil around a plot involving romance, betrayal, kidnapping, bank robbery, and a lot of brown sauce. Whether the sauce is Daddy's or HP, the two favorite brands in Ireland, is impossible to say, perhaps because both sauce manufacturers preferred to keep their labels out of this movie.

Like *Pulp Fiction*, the movie begins with sweet talk that suddenly turns violent, as Lehiff (Farrell) betrays a hard side. We meet his mates, including John (Cillian Murphy), who hates his job in a supermarket, and Oscar (David Wilmot), who despairs of finding a girlfriend and is advised to target older ladies who will be grateful for his attention. Meanwhile, John breaks up with his girlfriend, Deirdre (Kelly Macdonald), who begins dating a married bank manager, Sam (Michael McElhatton), while Sam's abandoned wife, Noeleen (Deirdre O'Kane, not to be confused with the character Deirdre), goes to a lonely-hearts dance and meets, of course, Oscar.

But to summarize the plot is insanity. There are a dozen major characters whose lives intersect in romance, crime, and farce; the screenplay by Mark O'Rowe is so ingenious and energetic that we almost don't feel like we're being jerked around. The other character who must be introduced is Jerry Lynch (Colm Meaney), who has watched too many cop reality shows and thinks he should star in one himself. Oh, and I should mention Sally (Shirley Henderson), who after a tragic disappointment in love has become a recluse and doesn't seem to realize she has enough of a mustache to be referred to occasionally as Burt Reynolds. Her character brings a new dimension to the classic movie scene in which a plain girl is told she would be beautiful if she got rid of the glasses/braces/bangs, etc.

Director John Crowley, a first-timer with enormous promise, seems to know his way through this maze even if we don't, and eventually with a sigh and a smile we give up and let

him take us where he will. That will include a kidnapping that combines the motives of bank robbery and cuckold's revenge, and a bus crash caused by a particularly vile little boy in a red coat, who has no connection with the other characters except that he occasionally turns up and causes horrible things to happen to them.

The movie is astonishing in the way it shifts gears, again like Tarantino. There are scenes of sudden, brutal violence. Scenes of broad comedy (especially involving the detective's attempts to be *C.S.I.* when he was born to be *Starsky and Hutch*). Moments of raw truth, as when an older woman at a pickup bar tells a younger man exactly how she feels. Moments of poignancy, as when John tries to win back Deirdre by saying all the things he should have told her in the first place. And moments of exquisitely bad timing, as when the bank manager unzips his pants in the living room just as Deirdre's mother walks in.

It's interesting how the stars fit right into the ensemble. Not only Farrell but Colm Meaney have famous faces for American audiences, and devoted moviegoers will recognize Kelly Macdonald from *Trainspotting* and Shirley Henderson from the wonderful *Wilbur Wants to Kill Himself.* What all of these actors do is fit seamlessly into the large cast, returning in some cases to the accents and body language of their preacting days. *Intermission* is a virtuoso act from beginning to end, juggling violence and farce, coincidence and luck, characters with good hearts and others evil to the core. In a movie filled with incredulities, the only detail I was absolutely unable to accept is that brown sauce tastes good in coffee.

The Interpreter ★ ★ ★
PG-13, 128 m., 2005

Nicole Kidman (Silvia Broome), Sean Penn (Tobin Keller), Catherine Keener (Dot Woods), Jesper Christensen (Nils Lud), Yvan Attal (Philippe), Earl Cameron (Zuwanie). Directed by Sydney Pollack and produced by Tim Bevan, Eric Fellner, and Kevin Misher. Screenplay by Charles Randolph, Scott Frank, and Steven Zaillian.

Sydney Pollack's *The Interpreter* is a taut and intelligent thriller, centering on Nicole Kidman as an interpreter at the United Nations, and Sean Penn as a Secret Service agent. And, no, they don't have romantic chemistry: For once, the players in a dangerous game are too busy for sex—too busy staying alive and preventing murder. They do, however, develop an intriguing closeness, based on shared loss and a sympathy for the other person as a human being. There's a moment when she rests her head on his shoulder, and he puts a protective arm around her, and we admire the movie for being open to those feelings.

The story was filmed largely on location in and around the United Nations, including the General Assembly Room; it's the first film given permission to do that. I mention the location because it adds an unstated level of authenticity to everything that happens. There's a scene where a security detail sweeps the building, and it feels like a documentary. Like when Drew Barrymore runs onto the field at Fenway Park in *Fever Pitch,* the U.N. scenes provide what Werner Herzog calls "the voodoo of location"—the feeling of the real thing instead of the artifice of sets and special effects.

The movie has a realism of tone, too. This isn't a pumped-up techno-thriller, but a procedural, in which Secret Service agents Keller (Penn) and Woods (Catherine Keener) are assigned to the U.N. after an interpreter named Silvia Broome (Kidman) overhears a death threat. The threat is against an African dictator named Zuwanie (Earl Cameron), once respected, now accused of genocide. He announces that he will address the General Assembly to defend his policies. The head of the Secret Service (played by Pollack himself) says the last thing the United States needs, at this point in history, is the assassination of a foreign leader on American soil.

Zuwanie is clearly intended to represent Robert Mugabe of Zimbabwe, also once hailed as a liberator, now using starvation as a political tool. Silvia, we learn, grew up in Zuwanie's country, was a supporter of Zuwanie, saw her parents killed, became disillusioned. She speaks many languages, including Ku, the tongue of the (fictional) country of Matobo, and five years ago became a U.N. interpreter.

After she reports the death threat, she ex-

pects to be believed. But Keller draws an instant conclusion: "She's lying." A polygraph indicates "she's under stress, but not lying." Is she, or isn't she? We meet a gallery of suspects, including Zuwanie's white security chief and two of his political opponents. Keller looks into Silvia's background, convinced she has reasons for wanting Zuwanie dead, although she says she joined the U.N. because she supports peaceful change.

"Vengeance is a lazy form of grief," she tells the agent, who has some grief and vengeance issues of his own. She also tells him of a custom from Matobo: When a man kills a member of your family and is captured, he is tied up and thrown into the river, and it is up to your family to save him or let him drown. If he drowns, you will have vengeance, but you will grieve all of your days. If you save him, you will be released from your lament. This is not a practice I was familiar with, and seems even to have escaped the attention of the Discovery Channel; I'd like to see a family debating whether to save the killer or drown him. Maybe a family like the Sopranos.

What I admire most about the film is the way it enters the terms of this world—of international politics, security procedures, shifting motives—and observes the details of all-night stakeouts, shop talk, and interlocking motives and strategies. More than one person wants Zuwanie dead, and more than one person wants an assassination attempt, which is not precisely the same thing.

Nicole Kidman is a star who consistently finds dramatic challenges and takes chances. Consider her in *Birth, The Human Stain, Dogville, The Hours, The Others,* and *Moulin Rouge.* Here, with a vaguely South African accent and a little-girl fear peering out from behind her big-girl occupation, she sidesteps her glamour and is convincing as a person of strong convictions. Sean Penn matches her with a weary professionalism, a way of sitting there and just looking at her, as if she will finally break down and tell him what he thinks she knows. It's intriguing the way his character keeps several possibilities in his mind at once, instead of just signing on with the theory that has the most sympathy from the audience.

The final scene is perhaps not necessary; it

has "obligatory closure" written all over it. But at least we are spared romantic clichés, and I was reminded of Robert Forster and Pam Grier in Tarantino's *Jackie Brown*, playing two adults with so much emotional baggage that for them romance is like a custom in another country.

Note: I don't want to get Politically Correct; I know there are many white Africans, and I admire Kidman's performance. But I couldn't help wondering why her character had to be white. I imagined someone like Angela Bassett in the role, and wondered how that would have played. If you see the movie, run that through your mind.

Intimate Strangers ★ ★ ★ ½
R, 104 m., 2004

Sandrine Bonnaire (Anna Delambre), Fabrice Luchini (William Faber), Michel Duchaussoy (Docteur Monnier), Anne Brochet (Jeanne), Gilbert Melki (Marc), Laurent Gamelon (Luc), Helene Surgere (Madame Mulon), Urbain Cancelier (Chatel). Directed by Patrice Leconte and produced by Alain Sarde. Screenplay by Jerome Tonnerre.

Men in the films of Patrice Leconte sometimes find themselves in a kind of paralysis of admiration for women. Consider the hero of *The Hairdresser's Husband,* who as a child developed an erotic obsession involving female hairdressers and their rituals and powders, their scents and tools, and now operates a beauty shop simply so that he can gaze in admiration as his wife cuts hair. Or consider *Monsieur Hire,* about a mousy little man who becomes aware that he can see into a seductive woman's bedroom across the air shaft from his flat. When she makes it clear she knows he is watching her and doesn't mind, his distance from her is threatened and he is profoundly shaken.

Now here is William Faber (Fabrice Luchini), a quiet, precise, middle-aged man who still lives in the flat where he was raised, and carries on the accounting business his father established there. He hasn't gone far from home. Even his father's secretary, Madame Mulon, still works for him. He is a man for whom probity is a cardinal virtue, and revealing passion is unthinkable.

One day a nervous young woman named Anna Delambre (Sandrine Bonnaire) walks into his office, lights a cigarette, and begins to spill the beans. She is so nervous that the camera becomes uneasy, regarding her with jerky little noticing shots. She talks frankly of problems in her marriage. William remains almost motionless behind his desk, his face a study in astonishment and alarm. The few words that he speaks are noncommittal and open-ended.

She thinks he is a psychiatrist. He is not, but doesn't tell her that, and as she continues her visits he ignores the withering stares of Madame Mulon and sits sphinxlike behind his desk, hardly moving a muscle, listening to her story as it grows steadily more strange and, it must be said, more erotic—so much so you would almost think Anna was trying to arouse him.

You may think I have revealed a great secret by explaining the mistaken identity. If Leconte were a lesser filmmaker, that would be true. But Leconte and his writer, Jerome Tonnerre, present her error and his deception only to prepare their canvas. We find we cannot take anything at face value in this story, that the motives of this woman and her husband are so deeply masked that even at the end of the film we are still uncertain about exactly what to believe, and why.

What is real is William's fascination. He doesn't move a muscle, say an unnecessary word, reveal in any way how transfixed he is by Anna and her story. But certainly she knows. There's something deeply sexual in a woman's discovery that she has ultimate power over a man, and one possibility is that she continues her visits to the wrong office because they excite her. There is also the possibility that her original motive changes in response to new developments. There is the mystery of her relationship with her husband, whom she seems to have accidentally crippled with the car, so that he walks with a cane. And the matter of what her husband wants her to do. And the way in which this is made known to William.

Bubbling away beneath most of Leconte's films is a stream of wicked humor. He is incapable of a film that exists on one level, for one purpose. He is quite capable, as in *Intimate Strangers,* of telling a story that has completely different meanings for the major characters, so that although they occupy the same rooms and hear the same words, they don't perceive the same scenario. And then with what delight he surprises us—not with anything so vulgar as a twist, but with a revelation of character so sudden it's like a psychic blow.

His camera is a coconspirator in *Intimate Strangers.* We are invited to become voyeurs as we follow the progress of the perverse therapy sessions—sessions that may be doing Anna as much good as if William really were a psychiatrist, although what would be good for Anna becomes increasingly hard to say. William watches this woman as she does small but closely observed things, like tipping the ash of her cigarette into a wastepaper basket. No, that doesn't start a fire—not in a Leconte film—but functions simply to make her seem reckless.

Consider a high-angle shot late in the film, which establishes that Anna is wearing a dress displaying noticeable cleavage. Now watch as Leconte cuts to William, whose gaze begins to waver as he tries resolutely not to look, and then notice the reaction shot (now our point of view as well as William's), as the camera hovers almost unsteadily, begins to dip to regard her neckline, and then subtly refuses to. William has not looked, but Leconte has demonstrated that we wanted him to. No big point is made of this, but some members of the audience actually crane their necks, trying to get a better angle through the camera lens.

Leconte is not famous, but he is addictive. You could do worse than hole up for a weekend with half a dozen of his films, also including *Ridicule, The Girl on the Bridge, The Widow of Saint-Pierre,* and *The Man on the Train.* His characters are fascinated by other lives, and by missed opportunities in their own. They think they know their motives, and then life reveals their real motives to them. They are presented with feelings that may be shameful, but are undeniable, and are theirs. It is up to them to decide if they would become more miserable through the realization of their desires or through the tantalizing denial of them.

Into the Blue ★ ★ ★
PG-13, 110 m., 2005

Paul Walker (Jared), Jessica Alba (Sam), Scott Caan (Bryce), Ashley Scott (Amanda), Josh Brolin (Bates), James Frain (Reyes), Tyson Beckford (Primo), Dwayne Adway (Roy). Directed by John Stockwell and produced by David A. Zelon. Screenplay by Matt Johnson.

Into the Blue is, of all things, an adventure story. Not a high-powered thriller with goofy special effects, but a story about people and hazards and treasure and love, in which every single thing that everybody does is physically possible for people to really do (except that they can apparently hold their breath indefinitely). The movie is written, acted, and directed as a story, not as an exercise in mindless kinetic energy.

Paul Walker and Jessica Alba star as Jared and Sam, lovers who live on a leaky boat in the Bahamas and search for buried treasure. They haven't found much, but they have their love to keep them warm. Tied up at a nearby dock is the larger and more powerful boat of Bates (Josh Brolin), who has money and success and wants to hire Jared, but there's something creepy about him.

Jared's friend Bryce (Scott Caan) flies in from the mainland with a girlfriend named Amanda (Ashley Scott) he says he picked up the night before. They all go diving together and find two kinds of treasure in more or less the same place: one ancient, one right up-to-date. They could become very rich. But Bryce is greedy and wants to push them in a direction that Jared and Sam are ethically opposed to.

But my description sounds dry and abstract, and the movie is juicy with fun. I'm trying not to tell you too much about what happens, because one of the pleasures of *Into the Blue* is that it develops as a narrative, not as a series of action scenes, and the characters don't mindlessly hurry from one impossible stunt to another but weigh their options, advocate opposing strategies, and improvise when they get in danger.

A lot of the movie takes place underwater, and director John Stockwell and cinematographers Shane Hurlbut and Peter Zuccarini do a good job of keeping us oriented under the sea. We know more or less where everything is, and what it means, and how it can be involved in the story; when there's an underwater emergency that almost kills Bryce, it is handled as if the characters (or the writers) have some practical information about scuba diving. There is also the surprise of having something very bad happen to a character we had every reason to expect would be around until the end of the movie.

The opening scenes are deceptive. The Alba character seems to have wandered over from the *Sports Illustrated* Swimsuit Issue, or maybe she thinks she's in the video. Then the plot kicks in and she gets a lot to do while *still* looking fine in a swimsuit. She also looks surprisingly sweet, after the stripper she played in *Sin City*. Caan, like his old man, does a good job of playing a persuasive jerk, and Walker is intriguing in the way he has his standards but can be talked out of them. People actually change their minds during this movie; in most action films, they're issued with an identity in their first scene and are limited by that identity for the rest of the movie.

Into the Blue offers modest pleasures. It is not an essential film, but if you go to see it, it will not insult your intelligence, and there's genuine suspense toward the end. It is a well-made example in a genre that has been cheapened and made routine. There's evidence the filmmakers spent more time talking about the characters and story than about how special effects would allow them to cheat on the narrative logic. And at the end of the film, there are some small surprises about who has survived and who has not. Usually you can predict the final head count at the end of the first act.

The Island ★ ★ ★
PG-13, 127 m., 2005

Ewan McGregor (Lincoln Six Echo), Scarlett Johansson (Jordan Two Delta), Djimon Hounsou (Albert Laurent), Sean Bean (Merrick), Michael Clarke Duncan (Starkweather), Steve Buscemi (McCord). Directed by Michael Bay and produced by Bay, Ian Bryce, Laurie MacDonald, and Walter F. Parkes. Screenplay by Caspian Tredwell-Owen, Alex Kurtzman, and Roberto Orci.

The Island runs 127 minutes, but that's not long for a double feature. The first half of Michael Bay's new film is a spare, creepy science fiction parable, and then it shifts into a high-tech action picture. Both halves work.

Whether they work together is a good question. The more you like one, the less you may like the other. I liked them both, up to a point, but the movie seemed a little too much like surf 'n' turf.

The first half takes place in a sterile futuristic environment where the inhabitants wear identical uniforms (white for the citizens, black for their supervisors). Big-screen TVs broadcast slogans and instructions, and about twice a day everybody gathers before them for the lottery. This sealed world, its citizens believe, has been created to protect them from pollution that has poisoned the earth. There is, however, one remaining "pathogen-free zone," which looks a lot like a TV commercial for *The Beach*. Winners of the lottery get to go there.

Yeah, sure, we're thinking. But the citizens in the white suits don't think very deeply; "they're educated to the level of fifteen-year-olds," we're told. There was a time when that would have made them smarter than most of the people who ever lived, but in this future world, education has continued to degrade, and we see adults reading aloud from *Fun with Dick and Jane*, a book that on first reading I found redundant and lacking in irony.

The true nature of this sealed world is not terrifically hard to guess; even those who failed to see through *The Village* may decode its secret. But the inhabitants are childlike and blissful, all except for a few troublesome characters like Lincoln Six Echo (Ewan McGregor), who wants bacon for breakfast but is given oatmeal. This inspires him to develop what all closed systems fear, a curiosity. "Why is Tuesday night always tofu night?" he asks his supervisor. "What is tofu? Why can't I have bacon? Why is everything white?" Then one day he sees a flying bug where no bug should be, or fly.

Sidestepping some intervening spoilers, I can move on to the second half of the movie, in which Lincoln Six Echo and the equally naive Jordan Two Delta (Scarlett Johansson) escape from the sealed world and are chased by train, plane, automobile, helicopter, and hovercycle in a series of special effects sequences that develop a breathless urgency. How the heroes manage to discover the underlying truth about their world while moving at such a velocity suggests they are quicker studies than we thought.

The movie never satisfactorily comes full circle, and although the climax satisfies the requirements of the second half of the story, it leaves a few questions unanswered. We wonder, for example, why a manufacturing enterprise so mammoth could have been undertaken in secret. Were government funds involved? We don't need to know the answers to these questions, it's true, but they would have allowed Bay (*Armageddon*) to do what the best science fiction does, and use the future as a way to critique the present. Does stem cell research ring a bell?

The Island has certain special effects, not its largest or most sensational, that reminded me of the creativity in a film like Spielberg's *Minority Report*. For example, little ladybug-like robots that crawl up your face and into your eye sockets, and transmit information from your brain before working their way through your plumbing and being expelled like kidney stones. I hate it when that happens. And consider the effective way CGI is used to show the actors interacting with themselves.

McGregor and Johansson do a good job of playing characters raised to be docile, obedient, and not very bright. The way they have knowledge gradually thrust upon them is carefully modulated by Bay, so that we can see them losing their illusions almost in spite of themselves. Michael Clarke Duncan has only three or four scenes, but they're of central importance, and he brings true horror to them. Sean Bean has the Sean Bean role, as a smug corporate monster. And the beloved Steve Buscemi plays an important character who has brought all of his bad habits into the sterile future world.

Buscemi is an engineer, or maybe a janitor, and lives in what must be the boiler room. All closed systems, no matter how spotless and pristine, always have an area filled with rusty machinery, cigarette butts, oily rags, and a guy who reads dirty magazines and knows how everything really works. Even in *Downfall*, the harrowing drama about Hitler's last days, there was a boiler room in the bunker where Eva Braun and her buddies could sneak away for a smoke. The Buscemi character turns out to be surprisingly well-informed and helpful, but then again, if the plot had to depend on characters educated only to the level of fifteen-year-olds, we might still be in the theater.

Note (spoiler warning): It was a little eerie watching The Island *only a month after reading Kazuo Ishiguro's new novel,* Never Let Me Go. *Both deal with the same subject: raising human clones as a source for replacement parts. The creepy thing about the Ishiguro novel is that the characters understand and even accept their roles as "donors," while only gradually coming to understand their genetic origins. They aren't locked up but are free to move around; some of them drive cars. Why do they agree to the bargain society has made for them? The answer to that question, I think, suggests Ishiguro's message: The real world raises many of its citizens as spare parts; they are used as migratory workers, minimum-wage retail slaves, even suicide bombers. The Island doesn't go there, but, then, did you expect it would?*

Isn't This a Time! ★ ★ ★ ½
NO MPAA RATING, 90 m., 2006

A documentary directed by Jim Brown and produced by Brown, Michael Cohl, and William Eigen. With Pete Seeger, Ronnie Gilbert, Fred Hellerman, Erik Darling, Eric Weissberg, Leon Bibb, Theodore Bikel, Arlo Guthrie, and Peter, Paul, and Mary.

In September 2004 at the Toronto Film Festival, the Weavers sang together for possibly last time. The event had great meaning for those who knew the Weavers and remembered their songs; in progressive circles they supplied the sound track for a good part of the 1950s and 1960s—the Weavers, and those who followed in their footsteps, such as Arlo Guthrie, Peter, Paul, and Mary, and Leon Bibb. If feelings stir within you when you hear "Goodnight, Irene" and "Wimoweh" and "This Land Is Your Land" and "If I Had a Hammer" and "Midnight Special" and "Rock Island Line," then the Weavers are a part of you.

The Weavers were Pete Seeger, Ronnie Gilbert, Lee Hays, and Fred Hellerman. In 1982 they held what then was billed as their farewell concert, at Carnegie Hall, and it was documented in *The Weavers: Wasn't That a Time!* I thought it was one of the best and most moving musical documentaries ever made. More than twenty years later, in 2003, the Weavers gathered to sing in Carnegie one

351

more time, in honor of Harold Leventhal, who was celebrating fifty years as an impresario. It was Leventhal who booked them in the good years and the bad, after they fell victim to the McCarthy-era blacklist and were barred from the mainstream after spending the late 1940s at the top of the charts.

The gathering at Toronto marked the premiere of *Isn't This a Time!*, the doc about the 2003 concert. After it, the Weavers sang one last time. Jim Brown, who directed the 1982 doc, returned to film the 2003 concert. If the sequel is slightly less compelling than the 1982 film, that's because time has taken a toll; Lee Hays has died, Seeger, the grand old man of American folk music, was eighty-four in 2003, and Gilbert and Hellerman were almost eighty. They were joined by Erik Darling and Eric Weissberg, and it was an evening of tears and joy. No longer are the famous voices quite as they were, but the spirit is undimmed and the emotion is, if anything, more powerful.

The power of *Isn't This a Time!* comes partly from the songs themselves, including those listed above and many more, such as "On Top of Old Smoky" and "Kumbaya" and "When the Saints Go Marching In" and "Brother, Can You Spare a Dime?" and of course "So Long, It's Been Good to Know You." It comes from the contributions of Leon Bibb, Peter, Paul, and Mary, Theo Bikel, and Arlo Guthrie, who organized the concert. It comes too from history: It was Arlo's father, Woody Guthrie, who invented the kind of music that Seeger and the Weavers performed, and Seeger and Woody Guthrie sang in the original Almanac Singers, a group identified with the 1930s labor movement.

The Weavers of 2003 did not sing as well as they did in 1982, or 1952, but if anything they had more heart, because of more memories. Backstage before the 2004 Toronto reunion, Seeger expressed concerns about his voice, but that night he sang with a renewed strength, and in *Isn't This a Time!* the music is accompanied not merely by guitars and Seeger's recorder but also by conviction and a defiance of time. They were all older, but they were survivors, and they sang in tribute to Leventhal (who died in October 2005).

Leventhal, they said, was much more than an impresario; he was a man willing to risk his ca-

reer to stand up against the blacklist and the notion that artists should be prevented from working because of their political beliefs. As the film unfolds, the 2003 concert is intercut with older footage of the Weavers, with bits of their history, with memories of their lives and songs.

The night of the premiere in Toronto, I introduced the Weavers, having earlier amused Seeger backstage by reciting all of the Almanacs' "Talking Union," which he frankly doubted I really knew.

"There's a kind of eerie moment in the movie," I said to Seeger, "when Arlo Guthrie observes that he has now performed with you twice as long as his father did."

"Time," said Seeger. "Time, time. A beautiful mystery."

Hellerman smiled. "At least it keeps everything from happening at once," he said.

It's All Gone Pete Tong ★ ★ ★
R, 90 m., 2005

Paul Kaye (Frankie Wilde), Mike Wilmot (Max Haggar), Beatriz Batarda (Penelope), Kate Magowan (Sonja), Pete Tong (Himself). Directed by Michael Dowse and produced by Allan Niblo and James Richardson. Screenplay by Dowse.

Frankie Wilde is the king of the club scene in Ibiza, a Mediterranean island where jumbo jets ferry in party animals on package tours. He stands like a colossus above the dance floor, vibrating in sympathy with his audience. Lately he's even started to produce a few records. He has a big house, a beautiful wife, and a manager who worships him. What could go wrong?

Frankie goes deaf. Maybe it was the decibel level in his earphones, night after night. Maybe it's a side effect from his nonprescription drugs; given enough cocaine, he makes Al Pacino's Scarface look laid-back. Frankie (Paul Kaye) tries to fake it, but his sets become exercises in incompatible noise.

He and his manager, Max (Mike Wilmot), share a painful truth: "Generally, the field of music, other than the obvious example, has been dominated by people who can hear." (When I hear a line like that, I am divided between admiration for the writing, and concern for audience members who will be asking each other who the obvious example is.) Frankie goes berserk one night, and is carried out of his club and out of his world.

It's All Gone Pete Tong presents Frankie's story in mockumentary form. Like Werner Herzog and Zak Penn's *Incident at Loch Ness*, it goes to some effort to blur the line between fact and fiction. It insists Frankie Wilde was an actual disc jockey and interviews "real" witnesses to his rise and fall; there are fake Websites discussing his legend, but the movie is fiction. There really is a Pete Tong, however; he's a British disc jockey who is seen interviewing Frankie in a doc-within-the-mock.

The title is real, too. *It's All Gone Pete Tong* is Cockney rhyming slang for "It's all gone wrong," and that's what it's gone, all right, for Frankie Wilde. His wife and her son bail out, his manager despairs, and Frankie descends into a slough of despond, drink, and cocaine. Occasionally he is attacked by a large, hallucinatory stuffed bear, reminding me of the bats that attacked Hunter S. Thompson on the road to Vegas. There is a time when he has sticks of dynamite strapped like a crown to his head, but the movie was a little manic just at that moment and I am not completely sure if the dynamite was real or a fantasy. Real, I think.

The downward arc of the first two acts of the movie is made harrowing and yet perversely amusing by the performance of Paul Kaye, a British comedian who sees Frankie as a clown who overacts even in despair. Then comes salvation in the form of a speech therapist named Penelope (Beatriz Batarda), who begins by teaching Frankie to lip-read and ends by saving his life and restoring him to happiness. Much of the solution involves Frankie's discovery that he can feel the vibes of the music through the soles of his feet; the discovery comes because, as he claims at one point, he is "the Imelda Marcos of flip-flops."

The movie works because of its heedless comic intensity; Kaye and his writer-director, a first-timer named Michael Dowse, chronicle the rise and fall of Frankie Wilde as other directors have dealt with emperors and kings. Frankie may not be living the most significant life of our times, but tell that to Frankie. There is a kind of desperation in any club scene (as *24-Hour Party People* memorably demonstrated); it can be exhausting, having a good time, and the relentless pursuit of happiness becomes an effort to recapture remembered bliss from the past.

Note: For me, a bonus was the island of Ibiza itself. It became famous in America in the early 1970s as the home of an author named Clifford Irving, who forged the memoirs of Howard Hughes and almost got away with it. In his defense, let it be said that Irving probably did a better job on the book than Hughes would have, and that he gave to the world his mistress, Nina Van Pallandt, who starred in Robert Altman's The Long Goodbye *(1973) as a woman one would gladly forge for, and with.*

J

The Jacket ★ ★
R, 102 m., 2005

Adrien Brody (Jack Starks), Keira Knightley (Jackie), Kris Kristofferson (Dr. Becker), Jennifer Jason Leigh (Dr. Lorenson), Daniel Craig (Mackenzie), Kelly Lynch (Jean), Brad Renfro (Stranger). Directed by John Maybury and produced by George Clooney, Peter Guber, and Steven Soderbergh. Screenplay by Massy Tadjedin.

In Iraq in 1991, an American soldier momentarily trusts a small boy, who has a gun and shoots him in the head. "That was the first time I died," says Jack Starks, the soldier, played by Adrien Brody as if he's not quite sure he didn't. That's not a criticism, but a description: The metaphysical and real horrors undergone by Jack in this movie include dying, not dying, feeling like he's dead, wishing he were dead, and being locked alive for long periods in a morgue drawer. No way to treat a returning hero.

Adrien Brody is an ideal actor for such a role, since his face can reflect such dread and suffering. He also has a cocky, upbeat speed (see *Bread and Roses*), but since *The Pianist* directors have used him for mournfulness. He has a lot to mourn this time.

After being declared dead in Iraq, it's discovered he's alive after all, and Jack is returned to the States and treated for amnesia. Out on his own, he's hitching through Vermont when he comes upon a spaced-out mother (Kelly Lynch) and her worried young daughter; their car has broken down. After helping them, he gets a lift with a passing motorist, who soon enough kills a cop. Jack passes out and wakes up to find himself a convicted cop killer, sent to a mental asylum. If only he could find that woman and daughter, he could establish an alibi. But the woman was zoned out, and the daughter was only a child.

The asylum is not one of your modern and enlightened asylums. Edgar Allan Poe would raise his eyebrows. It's run by Dr. Becker (Kris Kristofferson), whose theories are a cover for his sadism, or maybe it's the other way around. He believes that locking cold, wet patients in morgue drawers for long hours will help them—I dunno, get in touch with their feelings, or remember why they're there. Who knows.

The movie now begins to play with time. In a gas station, Jack, forlorn and homeless, is befriended by a woman named Jackie (Keira Knightley, from *Bend It Like Beckham*). She takes him home, cares for him, and here's where we have to get crafty to preserve plot points. To make a long plot short, when he is in the morgue drawer, Jack's brain, traumatized by a head wound, amnesia, and shock treatments, is able to time travel. Or maybe Jack himself physically time travels; the people who meet him on his journeys certainly think he's really there.

It's up to Jackie to believe this story and act on it, so that Jack can use his knowledge of the future to make important decisions in the present. Or maybe it's in the future that he makes the decisions, and in the past that he carried them out. Take notes. Able to assist him, if she believes his story, is Dr. Lorenson (Jennifer Jason Leigh) and even the evil, retired Dr. Becker himself. Lorenson always looked askance at Becker's barbaric methods. Try it yourself sometime, looking askance. Can be fun.

Meanwhile, the movie, taking its cue from Jack's deep weariness and depression, trudges through its paces as if it were deep and meaningful, which I am afraid it is not. It involves two or three time-paradox tricks too many to take seriously as anything other than a plot crafted to jump through all the temporal hoops. I was reminded of *Jacob's Ladder* (1990), also about a traumatized vet who descends into the abyss between the real and the imagined. I admired it at the time, but have been meaning to view it again after Fr. Andrew Greeley told me he thinks it's one of the most spiritual films of our time.

The Jacket will probably not make Andy's list. It has some touching moments between Jack and Jackie, whose curious willingness to trust him is explained in reasonable terms. But Dr. Becker comes intact from an old Hammer horror film, and would be right at home in *Scream and Scream Again* (1969), which involves a character who keeps waking up to find his inventory of body parts is shrinking. Becker's torturous "treatments" of Jack are so bizarre that the gentler and more philosophical possibilities in the story go astray.

The director, John Maybury, made *Love Is the Devil* (1998), a film about the British artist Francis Bacon, whose portraits of his subjects often seemed to catch them in their post–*Scream and Scream Again* periods. It was a perceptive, good film. In *The Jacket* you can sense an impulse toward a better film, and Adrien Brody and Keira Knightley certainly take it seriously, but the time-travel whiplash effect sets in, and it becomes, as so many time-travel movies do, an exercise in early entrances, late exits, futile regrets. If there is anything worse than time creeping at its petty pace from day to day, it would be if time jumped around. Better to die at the end, don't you think, than randomly, from time to time?

Japanese Story ★ ★ ★ ½
R, 110 m., 2004

Toni Collette (Sandy Edwards), Gotaro Tsunashima (Tachibana Hiromitsu), Matthew Dyktynski (Bill Baird), Lynette Curran (Mum), Yumiko Tanaka (Yukiko Hiromitsu), Kate Atkinson (Jackie), John Howard (Richards), Bill Young (Jimmy Smithers). Directed by Sue Brooks and produced by Sue Maslin. Screenplay by Alison Tilson.

Toni Collette can have an angular presence on the screen; she can look hard and tough, and is well cast in *Japanese Story* as an unmarried geologist whose idea of dinner is a can of baked beans poured over two slices of toast. But then there comes another side that is tender and dreamy. Her body becomes sensuous instead of distant, and her eyes are seeing from a different part of her soul.

Both of those identities are used in Sue Brooks's *Japanese Story*, a film in which her character journeys into the Australian desert with a Japanese businessman she begins by hating, and then begins to . . . not love, but cherish. She plays Sandy, an expert on the mining of minerals. She's assigned to baby-sit Tachibana (Gotaro Tsunashima), who has flown in from Kyoto and whose father owns 9 percent of the company.

Sandy flies with him to a dorp town in the interior, rents a Jeep, and shows him the mine: a massive hole in the ground whose terraces remind him of a Mayan temple. Then he wants to drive on, further, into the vastness. She protests. There's only a one-track dirt road, and "People die in this desert. Frequently." Their Jeep gets mired in the fine powder of the red earth, they can't drive it out or dig it out, they spend a cold night around a campfire, and she is very, very angry, because Tachibana got them into this mess, and it looks as if they may die, and he refuses to use his cell phone because of shame: Having caused their trouble, he refuses to admit it to his colleagues.

This sounds like some sort of survival adventure, but even in the moments of despair in the desert, *Japanese Story* is about characters, not plot. The Japanese man is not fluent in English, but he knows a great many more words than he first reveals. He doesn't know she's a geologist, and treats her like his driver (he lets her wrestle his heavy suitcase into the Jeep). But during the long, cold night (at one point she shifts to put her back against his, for warmth), something rotates in his consciousness, and the next day there are scenes in which each looks at the other for a long time, thinking, sensing, beginning to like. That night in a motel, they make love; undressing, she puts on his pants before walking over to the bed.

And now you must put the review aside, if you plan to see the movie. There is something I want you to experience for yourself.

What future do they have? None, really, even before she sees the photograph of his wife and family in his billfold. They're strangers with a thousand words between them, in the middle of a limitless empty place. What they have is not merely sex, yet not love; it is more like a means of communication to show relief and acceptance. Then, in a moment of heedless fun, he has an absurd accident and dies. Snap, the movie breaks in two. She must wrestle his body into the Jeep, take it to a small town, find Smithers the undertaker ("We'll put it in the cold room so it doesn't go off"), and deal with the police, the report, her colleagues . . . and the widow, who is flying in from Japan.

It's here that the movie demonstrates what it's been trying to say all along. Alison Tilson's screenplay follows its logic into deep feelings. What does another person mean to us, really, if they are not available to share our lives, and we cannot really know them—but we cherish them for the transient joy they have shared with us? Who was he, really? She had to ask which was his first and which his family name. Did he ever know her surname? After surviving death in the desert, after saving each other's lives, after making love and looking at the belittling landscape and becoming a team of two in an ocean of emptiness, they have come to this: His corpse, its head lolling from side to side, as she cleans off the sand and mud with a cloth.

Japanese Story never steps wrong in its crucial closing passages, especially in the precise and exact way that Sandy and the widow have a limited but bottomless communication. The mundane details of the undertaker, the coroner, the police, and the funeral are like a series of events that are—wrong. Wrong, all wrong, because Tachibana should not be dead. There is no sense in it. He lost his life in a senseless instant, and brought a horrible finality to a relationship not real enough to support it; it should have ended with a kiss and some tears and a rueful smile at an airport. It imposed enormous significance on their time together, which did not deserve and cannot support such significance. What she feels at the end, I think, is not love for him or sorrow, but a great pity that his whole life should have been wiped away and lost for no reason at all, just like that, carelessly, thoughtlessly, in the middle of things.

The movie wants to record how such things happen, and how they present the survivor with an insoluble challenge: What does Sandy think, how does she behave, what should she feel, what should she do now? Patiently, observantly, it takes her through all of these questions and shows her clumsy, but honest attempt to answer them. And gradually the full arc of Toni Collette's performance reveals itself, and we see that the end was there even in the beginning. This is that rare sort of film that is not about what happens, but about what happens then.

Jarhead ★ ★ ★ ½
R, 122 m., 2005

Jake Gyllenhaal (Tony Swofford), Peter Sarsgaard (Allen Troy), Lucas Black (Chris Kruger), Chris Cooper (Lieutenant Colonel Kazinski), Jamie Foxx (Staff Sargeant Sykes). Directed by Sam Mendes and produced by Lucy Fisher and Douglas Wick. Screenplay by William Broyles Jr, based on the book by Anthony Swofford.

Jarhead is a war movie that rises above the war and tells a soldier's story. It tells it with the urgency and pointlessness that all men's stories have, because if something has happened to us, then it is important to us no matter how indifferent the world may be. "Four days, four hours, one minute. That was my war," the Marine sniper Tony Swofford tells us. "I never shot my rifle."

The movie is uncanny in its effect. It contains no heroism, little action, no easy laughs. It is about men who are exhausted, bored, lonely, trained to the point of obsession, and given no opportunity to use their training. The most dramatic scene in the movie comes when Swofford has an enemy officer in the crosshairs of his gun sight and is forbidden to fire because his shot may give advance warning of an air strike.

His spotter, Troy, goes berserk: "Let him take the shot!" Let him, that is, kill one enemy as his payback for the hell of basic training, the limbo of the desert, the sand and heat, the torture of months of waiting, the sight of a highway traffic jam made of burned vehicles and crisp charred corpses. Let him take the shot to erase for a second the cloud of oil droplets he lives in, the absence of the sun, the horizon lined with the plumes of burning oil wells. Let him take the goddamn shot.

The movie is based on the best-selling 2003 memoir *Jarhead,* by Tony Swofford, who served in the first Gulf War. It is unlike most war movies in that it focuses entirely on the personal experience of a young man caught up in the military process. At one point, Swofford (Jake Gyllenhaal) is being interviewed by a network newswoman who asks him why he serves. He has already given two or three routine answers. She persists, and finally he looks in the camera and says: "I'm twenty years old, and I was dumb enough to sign a contract."

His best friend is his spotter, Troy (Peter Sarsgaard). Their small unit of scout-snipers has been led through training by Staff Sargeant Sykes (Jamie Foxx), who knows why he serves: He loves his job. Others in the group include borderline psychos and screwups, but mostly just average young Americans who have decided the only thing worse than fighting a war is waiting to fight one—in the desert, when the temperature is 112 and it would be great for the TV cameras if they played a football game while wearing their anti-gas suits.

Jarhead is a story like Robert Graves's *Good-bye to All That*, in the way it sees the big picture entirely in terms of the small details. Sykes briefs them about Hussein's invasion of the Kuwait oil fields but says their immediate task is to guard the oil of "our friends, the Saudis." This they do by killing time. The narration includes one passage that sounds lifted straight from the book, in which Swofford lists the ways they get through the days: They train, they sleep, they watch TV and videos, they get in pointless fights, they read letters from home and write letters to home, and mostly they masturbate.

These are not the colorful dogfaces of World War II movies with their poker games, or the druggies in *Apocalypse Now*. They have no wisecracks, we see no drugs, they get drunk when they can, and there is a Wall of Shame plastered with the photos of the girls back home who have dumped them. They go on patrols in the desert, looking for nothing in the middle of nowhere, and their moment of greatest tension comes when they meet eight Arabs with five camels. They sense a trap. Their fingers are on their triggers. They are in formation for action. Swofford and one of the Arabs meet on neutral ground. He comes back with his report: "Somebody shot three of their camels."

In a war like this, the ground soldier has been made obsolete by air power. Territory that took three months to occupy in World War I and three weeks in Vietnam now takes ten minutes. Sykes warns them to expect seventy-thousand casualties in the first days of the war, but as we recall, the Iraqis caved in and the war was over. Now we are involved in a war that does require soldiers on the ground, against an enemy that no longer helpfully wears uniforms. Yet many of its frustrations are the same, and I am reminded of the documentary *Gunner Palace*, about an Army field artillery division that is headquartered in the ruins of a palace once occupied by Saddam's son Uday. They are brave, they are skilled, and death comes unexpectedly from invisible foes in the midst of routine.

Jarhead was directed by Sam Mendes (*American Beauty*), and it is the other side of the coin of David O. Russell's *Three Kings*, also about the Gulf War. If Russell had *Catch-22* as his guide, it is instructive that the book Swofford is reading is *The Stranger*, by Camus. The movie captures the tone of Camus' narrator, who knows what has happened, but not why, nor what it means to him, nor why it happens to him. Against this existential void the men of the sniper unit shore up friendships and rituals. Their sergeant is a hard-ass, not because he is pathological but because he wants to prepare them to save their lives. They are ready. They have been trained into a frenzy of readiness, and all they find on every side, beautifully visualized by the film, is a vastness—first sand, then sand covered with a black rain, then skies red with unchanging flames twenty-four hours a day.

It is not often that a movie catches exactly what it was like to be this person in this place at this time, but *Jarhead* does. They say a story can be defined by how its characters change. For the rest of his life, Swofford tells us, whether he holds it or not, his rifle will always be a part of his body. It wasn't like that when the story began.

Jersey Girl ★ ★ ★ ½
PG-13, 103 m., 2004

Ben Affleck (Ollie Trinke), Liv Tyler (Maya Harding), George Carlin (Bart Trinke), Raquel Castro (Gertie Trinke), Jason Biggs (Arthur Brickman), Jennifer Lopez (Gertrude). Directed by Kevin Smith and produced by Scott Mosier. Screenplay by Smith.

Jersey Girl is a romantic comedy written and

directed by a kinder, gentler Kevin Smith. It's the kind of movie Hugh Grant might make, except for the way Smith has with his dialogue, which is truer and more direct than we expect. There are a couple of scenes here where a video store clerk cuts directly to the bottom line, and it feels like all sorts of romantic rules and regulations are being rewritten.

The movie stars Ben Affleck as Ollie Trinke, a hotshot Manhattan publicist whose beloved wife, Gertrude (Jennifer Lopez), is great with child. I would hesitate to reveal that she dies in childbirth if I had not already read and heard this information, oh, like 500 times, so obsessed is the nation with Ben and J-Lo. Lopez is luminous in her few scenes, helping to explain why Ollie remains so true to her memory that he remains celibate for many years.

His career meanwhile goes to pieces. Under pressure to hold a job while raising a daughter, he loses it one day, fatally offending his employers by causing a scene at the opening of a Hard Rock Café; he fails to understand why he should take Will Smith seriously ("Yeah, like the Fresh Prince of Bel Air is ever gonna have a movie career"). By the time the story resumes, he has moved back to New Jersey and is living in the same house with his father, Bart (George Carlin), and his beloved daughter, Gertie (Raquel Castro), who is now about seven. He's not in public relations anymore; he works with his dad in the public works department.

Because Ben Affleck is a movie star and looks like one, you might expect him to start dating eventually, but no. You might expect that he could find another high-paying PR job, but no. He doesn't because *then there wouldn't be a movie.* When a movie isn't working, we get all logical about things like this, but when it works, we relax.

Several times a week, Ollie and Gertie go to the local video store, where she plunders the kiddie section while he makes a quick dash through the bamboo curtain to grab a porno. One night he's confronted by Maya (Liv Tyler), the clerk, who claims she's taking a survey about pornography usage and asks Ollie how many times a week he masturbates. She is seriously disturbed by his reply, alarmed to learn he has had no sex in seven years, and informs him, "We're gonna have some sex."

And it's in a scene like this that Kevin Smith shows why he's such a good comedy writer. There is a bedrock of truth in the scene, which is based on embarrassment and shyness and Maya's disconcerting ability to say exactly what she's thinking, and when Ollie tries to explain why he has remained celibate (except for his relationship with countless porno titles), she patiently explains about sex: "It's the same thing only you're saving the $2 rental fee."

Inarguable logic, but he demurs, finally breaking down and agreeing to a lunch date. And thus does love reenter Ollie's life. For Maya may be bold about sex, but she is serious about love, and soon Gertie is saying, "Hey, you're the lady from the video store" at a moment when it would be much, much better had she not walked into the room.

Liv Tyler is a very particular talent who has sometimes been misused by directors more in love with her beauty than with her appropriateness for their story. Here she is perfectly cast as the naive and sincere Maya, whose boldness is *not* a seduction technique but an act of generosity, almost of mercy. It takes a special tone for a woman to convince us she wants to sleep with a man out of the goodness of her heart, but Tyler finds it, and it brings a sweetness to the relationship.

Kevin Smith, I believe, has spent almost as much time in video stores as Quentin Tarantino, and his study of ancient clichés is put to good use in the closing act of his movie, which depends on not one but three off-the-shelf formulas: (1) the choice between the big city and staying with your family in a small town; (2) the parent who arrives at a school play just at the moment when the child onstage is in despair because that parent seems to be missing; and (3) the slow clap syndrome. Smith is a gifted writer and I believe he knew exactly what he was doing by assembling these old reliables. I'm not sure he couldn't have done better, but by then we like the characters so much that we give the school play a pass.

Besides—without the school play, we wouldn't get a chance to see the set constructed for little Gertie by two of the guys who work with Bart and Ollie in the public works department. Let it be said that the Lyric Opera's set for *Madame Butterfly* was only slightly more elaborate.

Jiminy Glick in La La Wood ★ ½
R, 90 m., 2005

Martin Short (Jiminy Glick/David Lynch), Jan Hooks (Dixie Glick), Elizabeth Perkins (Miranda Coolidge), Linda Cardellini (Natalie Coolidge), Janeane Garofalo (Dee Dee), Corey Pearson (Ben DiCarlo), Carlos Jacott (Barry King), John Michael Higgins (Andre Divine). Directed by Vadim Jean and produced by Bernie Brillstein, Paul Brooks, Peter Safran, and Martin Short. Screenplay by Martin Short, Paul Flaherty, and Michael Short.

The problem with Jiminy Glick is that he doesn't know who he is. Or, more precisely, Martin Short doesn't know who he is. Jiminy is allegedly a chubby TV news entertainment reporter from Butte, Montana, who alternates between fawning over celebrities, insulting them, and not quite knowing who they are. I can sympathize. When I ran into Jiminy at the Toronto Film Festival, I didn't know he was Martin Short; the makeup job was masterful, and I hadn't seen the character in his earlier TV manifestations. One of the side effects of seeing 500 movies a year is that you miss a lot of TV.

Martin Short himself is one of the funniest men alive, or can be, and has been. But Jiminy Glick needs definition if he's to work as a character. We have to sense a consistent comic personality, and we don't; Short changes gears and redefines the character whenever he needs a laugh. That means Jiminy is sometimes clueless, sometimes uses knowledgeable in-jokes, sometimes is a closeted gay, sometimes merely neuter, sometimes an inane talk show host, and at other times essentially just Martin Short having fun with his celebrity friends.

Jiminy Glick in La La Wood takes the character to the Toronto Film Festival, where he confronts celebrities in situations that are sometimes spontaneous, sometimes scripted. He stays in a hotel from hell with his wife, Dixie (Jan Hooks), and their twin sons, Matthew and Modine. He is obsessed with getting an interview with the reclusive Ben DiCarlo (Corey Pearson), director of *Growing Up Gandhi,* in which the young Mahatma is seen as a prizefighter. He is also entranced by the presence of the legendary star Miranda Coolidge (Elizabeth Perkins).

The movie combines two story lines: Jiminy interviewing celebs, and Jiminy trapped in a nightmarish murder scenario narrated by David Lynch (played by Short himself, uncannily well). Lynch lights his already-lit cigarette and intones ominous insights about the lonely highway of doom, and Miranda's blood-drenched handkerchief turns up in Jiminy's possession; perhaps he did not merely dream that he murdered her.

The murder plot is a nonstarter (not funny, not necessary), and although Short does a good David Lynch, he stops at imitation and doesn't go for satire. He's at his best in a couple of sit-down interviews with cooperative movie stars (Kurt Russell and Steve Martin), in what feel like improvised Q&A sessions; he asks Martin, for example, if it's true that the commies still run Hollywood, and Martin refuses to name names—except for Meg Ryan and Tom Hanks. There is also an intriguing discussion of Martin's theory of tabletops and testicles, which put me in mind of his famous magic trick where eggs and lighted cigarettes emerge from his fly.

A comedy could be made about inane celebrity interviewers, yes, but it would have to be more reality-oriented. When a real person like Joe Franklin exists, how can Jiminy Glick outflank him? A comedy could be made about the Toronto Film Festival, but it would need to know more about festivals; interviewers from Butte, Montana, do not ordinarily have their private festival publicity person to knock on the hotel room every morning with a list of the day's interviews, and Glick (or Short) misses a chance to skewer publicists, junkets, and the hissy fits of critics afraid they'll miss a big movie.

Some stand-alone moments are funny. Jiminy thinks Whoopi Goldberg is Oprah Winfrey ("Remember, my name is spelled O-p-e-r-a," she advises him). Rappers in a hotel corridor try to teach an African how to sound like an American hip-hopper, but try as he will, "Y'allknowhaimean" comes out as "Yao Ming." And Jiminy and Kurt Russell begin a discussion about Elvis Presley, whom Russell starred with as a child actor and later, as an adult, played in a movie. Where this discussion eventually leads is hard to believe, and impossible to describe. And when David

Lynch says, "My name is David Lynch. I'm a director," I like Jiminy's reply: "Well who isn't, dear?"

Johnson Family Vacation ★ ★
PG-13, 95 m., 2004

Cedric the Entertainer (Nate Johnson), Vanessa L. Williams (Dorothy Johnson), Bow Wow (DJ Johnson), Solange Knowles (Nikki Johnson), Shannon Elizabeth (Chrishelle), Gabby Soleil (Destiny), Steve Harvey (Max Johnson), Shari Headley (Jackie Johnson), Tanjareen Martin (Tangerine), Lorna Scott (Gladys), Aloma Wright (Glorietta). Directed by Christopher Erskin and produced by Cedric the Entertainer, Paul Hall, Wendy Park, and Eric Rhone. Screenplay by Todd R. Jones and Earl Richey Jones.

Cedric the Entertainer can be a break-out comic force if given the least opportunity, but *Johnson Family Vacation* tames him in a routine cross-country comedy that feels exactly like a series of adventures recycled out of every other cross-country comedy. There's even a semi that tries to run them off the road.

The movie begins in a California suburb, where the Johnson family is on thin ice. Nate (Cedric) lives in the family house with his son, DJ (Bow Wow), while his wife, Dorothy (Vanessa L. Williams), teenage daughter, Nikki (Solange Knowles), and preschooler Destiny (Gabby Soleil) have moved into a second house nearby. Dorothy agrees to go along on the trip in a last-gasp attempt to save the marriage. So off they go in Nate's new Lincoln Navigator, which has been pimped out by the overeager car dealer (hard to explain, however, the Burberry pattern on the head rests). It will be a running gag that Nate has to return the car unscratched in order to get a replacement, which of course means the car will be scratched, dented, crashed, and covered in concrete before the trip is over. To repair the car, Cedric turns up in a dual role as Uncle Earl, a wizard mechanic.

Many of their adventures along the way involve Nate's decision to pick up a sexy but obviously flaky hitchhiker named Chrishelle (Shannon Elizabeth), who for fairly obscure reasons sneaks a Gila monster into their hotel room, but this subplot just doesn't work; better to stick with family dynamics than have Nate pick up a hitchhiker his wife obviously wants nothing to do with. Dorothy's idea of revenge—luring her husband into a hot tub and stealing his clothes, so that he has to tip-toe through the "Four Seasonings" hotel in the nude—is meant to be funny, but is cringe-inducing. Nothing about Dorothy's character makes us believe she would do that.

The family reunion, when they finally arrive, is all too brief, considering its comic possibilities. We meet Nate's older brother and lifetime rival, Max (Steve Harvey), who always wins the reunion trophy, and his mother, Glorietta (Aloma Wright), whose comic possibilities aren't developed. The rest of the family consists mostly of extras, and the Johnsons seem to be on their way home again after only a few hours.

The success of a movie like this depends on comic invention. The general outline is already clear: During the trip, the Johnsons will endure many misadventures, but the broken marriage will be mended. Whether we laugh or not depends on what happens to them along the way. Cedric, whose character is channeling Chevy Chase from *National Lampoon's Summer Vacation,* is a gifted comedian who could have brought the movie to life, but the screenplay by Todd R. Jones and Earl Richey Jones is paint-by-numbers, and one-time music video director Christopher Erskin films in a style without zing.

There's one funny scene where Nate bans his son from playing rap music by "anyone who got shot"—like Tupac or Biggie. He throws those CDs out the window. Then the son goes to work on his dad's CD collection, also with singers who got shot, like Marvin Gaye. This is such a neat turnaround that you wonder why the movie doesn't have more inspirations like that. It deals with specifics, but the movie itself is genial and unfocused and tired.

Joyeux Noel ★ ★ ★
PG-13, 110 m., 2006

Diane Kruger (Anna Sorensen), Benno Furmann (Nikolaus Sprink), Guillaume Canet (Lieutenant Audebert), Dany Boon (Ponchel), Bernard Le Coq (General Audebert), Gary Lewis (Father Palmer), Daniel Bruhl (Horstmayer), Alex Ferns (Gordon), Steven Robertson

(Jonathan), Robin Laing (William). Directed by Christian Carion and produced by Christophe Rossignon. Screenplay by Carion.

On Christmas Eve 1914, a remarkable event took place in the trenches where the Germans faced the British and the French. There was a spontaneous cease-fire, as the troops on both sides laid down their weapons and observed the birth of the savior in whose name they were killing one another. The irony of this gesture is made clear in the opening scenes of *Joyeux Noel*, in which schoolchildren of the three nations sing with angelic fervor, each in their own language, about the necessity of wiping the enemy from the face of the earth.

The Christmas Eve truce actually happened, although not on quite the scale Christian Carion suggests in his film. He is accurate, however, in depicting the aftermath: Officers and troops were punished for fraternizing with the enemy in wartime. A priest who celebrated mass in No Man's Land is savagely criticized by his bishop, who believes the patriotic task of the clergy is to urge the troops into battle and reconcile them to death.

The trench warfare of World War I was a species of hell unlike the agonies of any other war, before or after. Enemies were dug in within earshot of each other, and troops were periodically ordered over the top so that most of them could be mowed down by machine-gun fire. They were being ordered to stand up, run forward, and be shot to death. And they did it. An additional novelty was the introduction of poison gas.

Artillery bombardments blew up the trenches so often that when they were dug out again, pieces of ordnance, bits of uniforms, shattered wooden supports, and human bones interlaced the new walls. A generation lost its leaders. European history might have been different if so many of the best and brightest had not been annihilated. Those who survived were the second team. *Goodbye to All That* by Robert Graves is the best book I have read about the experience.

Carion's film, a 2006 Oscar nominee, is a trilingual portrait of a short stretch of the front lines, a small enough microcosm of the war that we're able to follow most of the key players. We meet some of them as they volunteer for service. There is a German tenor named Sprink (Benno Furmann), who leaves the opera to serve in uniform. Two Scottish brothers sign up, Jonathan and William (Steven Robertson and Robin Laing), who agree, "At last, something's happening in our lives!" They are joined by their parish priest, Father Palmer (Gary Lewis), who follows them into uniform as a stretcher bearer. The French are led by Lieutenant Audebert (Guillaume Canet), whose father (Bernard Le Coq) is the general in charge of these lines. Audebert throws up before leading his men into battle, but that's to be expected.

On Christmas Eve, the Danish singer Anna Sorensen (Diane Kruger) is brought to a support area to sing for German officers and the crown prince, but she insists on being taken to the front lines. She says she wants to sing for the ordinary troops, but her real hope is to see Sprink, her lover. Reaching the lines, she is surprised to find that thousands of little Christmas trees have been supplied by Berlin and form a decoration on top of the German trenches.

The Scots and the French are equally surprised by the trees, and by the sound of singing as Sprink and Sorenson sing "Silent Night" and "Adeste Fidelis." Slowly, tentatively, soldiers begin to poke their heads up over the ramparts, and eventually they lay down their arms and join in the cratered No Man's Land to listen to the singing, and then to the bagpipes of the Scots, and then to celebrate Mass. The next morning, Christmas Day, there is even a soccer game. Precious bits of chocolate are shared. And they bury their dead, whose bodies have been rotting between the lines.

These men have much in common with one another. They come from the same kinds of homes, went to the same kinds of schools, and worship the same kinds of gods. They are required to fight, and most of them are required to die. In a remarkable moment of common interest, they share information about plans for artillery attacks, and all gather in one trench while the other is shelled, then switch trenches for the response. This is treason, I suppose.

Joyeux Noel has its share of bloodshed, especially in a deadly early charge, but the movie is about a respite from carnage, and it lacks the brutal details of films like *Paths of Glory, A Very Long Engagement*, and, from later wars, *Saving Private Ryan* and *Platoon*. Its sentimentality is muted by the thought that this moment of peace actually did take place, among men who were punished for it and who mostly died soon enough afterward. But on one Christmas they were able to express what has been called, perhaps too optimistically, the brotherhood of man.

Junebug ★ ★ ★ ★
R, 107 m., 2005

Alessandro Nivola (George), Amy Adams (Ashley), Embeth Davidtz (Madeleine), Scott Wilson (Eugene), Benjamin McKenzie (Johnny), Frank Hoyt Taylor (David Wark), Celia Weston (Peg). Directed by Phil Morrison and produced by Mike Ryan and Mindy Goldberg. Screenplay by Angus MacLachlan.

Junebug is a movie that understands, profoundly and with love and sadness, the world of small towns; it captures ways of talking and living I remember from my childhood with the complexity and precision of great fiction. It observes small details that are important *because* they are small. It has sympathy for every character in the story and avoids two temptations: It doesn't portray the small-town characters as provincial hicks, and it doesn't portray the city slickers as shallow materialists. Phil Morrison, who directed this movie, and Angus MacLachlan, who wrote it, understand how people everywhere have good intentions, and how life can assign them roles where they can't realize them.

Tone is everything in this movie; it's not so much what people say, as how they say it, and why. Consider this dialogue:

Peg: "You comin' to bed?"

Eugene: "Not now. I'm looking for something. My Phillips-head."

That much is exactly right. A certain kind of person (my father was one) finds a Phillips-head screwdriver easier to lose than almost everything else. So now wait until it's later at night, and observe Eugene in the kitchen. He looks in the refrigerator and then he says:

"Now where would I be if I was a screwdriver?"

If you get that right, you get everything else right, too. And here is other dialogue that rings with clarity and truth:

Ashley to Johnny: "God loves you just the way you are, but he loves you too much to let you stay that way."

Peg, under her breath at a baby shower, after her son's new wife from the city has given her other daughter-in-law a silver spoon: "That won't go in the dishwasher."

Who are these people? The story begins in Chicago, where an art dealer named Madeleine (Embeth Davidtz) is holding a benefit for Jesse Jackson Jr. At the event, she meets George (Alessandro Nivola), and they fall in love and get married. His family from North Carolina is invited but doesn't attend. Six months later, she learns of a folk artist named David Wark (Frank Hoyt Taylor), who lives near George's family in the Winston-Salem area. They decide to kill two birds with one stone: She'll sign up the artist and meet the family.

Here is the family she meets. Peg (Celia Weston) is the matriarch who criticizes everyone, second-guesses every decision, and is never wrong, according to her. Eugene (Scott Wilson) is her husband, who has withdrawn into a deep silence and a shadowy presence, and spends many hours in his basement wood-carving corner. Johnny (Benjamin McKenzie) is George's younger brother, newly married to his high school sweetheart, Ashley (Amy Adams). She is pregnant.

As George and Madeleine arrive, Ashley is about to give birth. Johnny is responding to this, as he does to everything, by withdrawing, not talking to anybody, working under his car in the garage. Ashley, on the other hand, is always chatty: She's a good soul, cheerful, optimistic, supportive. The four people in this household are so locked into their roles that the arrival of the Chicagoans is like a bomb dropping.

Madeleine, the outsider, smiles all the time. If she feels that this family is strange and disturbing, she doesn't say so. George behaves as he knows he should but remains enigmatic: We don't find out what he really thinks about his family until the movie's last line, if then.

The artist, David Wark, is a profound eccentric with an accent and values that seem to have been imported from the eighteenth century. His folk art incorporates imperfectly controlled images from a half-understood world. "I like all the dog heads and computers," Madeleine tells him, "and the scrotums." This is not intended as a funny line. Wark has just finished an allegorical painting about the freeing of the slaves. He explains that he can't paint a face unless it belongs to somebody he knows, and he doesn't know any black people, which is why all the slaves have white faces.

There is tension between George and Johnny, between Ashley and Johnny, between the world and Johnny. He spends long hours away from everyone, but watch him in the family room when a documentary about meerkats comes on TV. He knows his wife "loves meerkats." He races around desperately to find a blank video so he can tape the show. It would mean so much to him to give her this video. He fails. Ashley explains about the tab that keeps you from recording over something, but he responds with anger and, of course, takes it out on her.

Two events happen at once. Madeleine believes she can win David Wark away from a New York gallery, and Ashley goes into labor. George thinks Madeleine's place is with the family, at the hospital. She doesn't agree: "I'll be over as soon as I do this. You know how important this is to me."

Now here is the question: How important is Ashley and Johnny's baby to George? (Johnny, of course, is nowhere to be found, certainly not at the hospital.) If he were in Chicago, George certainly would not fly down to be at the hospital. But when he moves into his family's house, he follows its rules. This leads to a scene of incredible power between Ashley and her brother-in-law, in which we see that Ashley truly is good, and brave, and sweeter than peaches. Small wonder that Amy Adams won the Sundance acting award.

Junebug is a great film because it is a true film. It humbles other films that claim to be about family secrets and eccentricities. It understands that families are complicated and

their problems are not solved during a short visit, just in time for the film to end. Families and their problems go on and on, and they aren't solved; they're dealt with.

Consider a guarded moment between Madeleine and Eugene, her father-in-law. She observes cautiously of his wife, "She's a very strong personality." This is putting it mildly. Eugene replies quietly, "That's just her way. She hides herself. She's not like that inside." And then he adds two more words: "Like most." Thank God for actors like Wilson, who know how those two words must be said. They carry the whole burden of the movie.　☞

Just Friends ★

PG-13, 94 m., 2005

Ryan Reynolds (Chris Brander), Amy Smart (Jamie Palamino), Anna Faris (Samantha James), Chris Klein (Dusty), Christopher Marquette (Mike). Directed by Roger Kumble and produced by Chris Bender, William J. Johnson, Michael Ohoven, J. C. Spink, and William Vince. Screenplay by Adam "Tex" Davis.

The best scenes in *Just Friends* take place offscreen. If they were in the movie, they would involve the makeover of Chris, the hero. As the film opens he is a fat, unpopular nerd in high school. Flash forward ten years, and he is thin, fit, rich, handsome, and working in the music industry. Obviously, during the missing decade he hired Oprah's trainer and studied the self-help tapes sold by that guy on late-night TV—you know, the guy who will make you into a person willing to accept success. You have to *be willing*, that's the trick. The guy's methods are proven because he is a success himself, having been willing to make millions by selling his tapes.

But already we're off the subject of the film. This will be a hard subject to stay on. I am going to the kitchen right now to set the timer on the stove to go off every sixty seconds as a reminder to stay on the subject. Now I'm back from the kitchen. You know that late-night TV guy? Basically, he's offering an updated version of the old classified ad that said, "Send twenty-five cents to learn how to get hundreds of quarters through the mail." *Ding!*

In *Just Friends,* Ryan Reynolds plays Chris, who looks like he gets his fat suits from Jiminy Glick's tailor. He wants to hook up with a sexy babe named Jamie, played by Amy Smart. Jamie likes Chris a whole lot, but only as a friend. When a girl says she likes you as a friend, what she means is: "Rather than have sex with you, I would prefer to lose you as a friend."

Chris is crushed. In adventures that will no doubt be included in the deleted scenes on the DVD, he apparently moves to L.A., loses 150 pounds, becomes a hockey star, opens an account at SuperCuts, and turns into a babe magnet. His boss wants him to sign up an overnight pop superstar named Samantha, who is called Samantha because screenwriters love women named Samantha because when you call them "Sam" it sounds like you know them, when in fact their entire backstory may be limited to the fact that their nickname is "Sam." *Ding!*

Sam is supposed to make us think of Brittany or Britney or Britannia or whatever her name is. Now I remember: Her name is Paris Hilton. The other night at dinner I met a Motorola executive who told me Paris Hilton is their best customer for cell phones because she has gone through seventy of them. As Oscar Wilde once said, "To lose one cell phone may be regarded as a misfortune; to go through seventy looks like carelessness."

Sam is played by Anna Faris, who in *The Hot Chick* played the best friend of Rachel McAdams, whose character is magically transported into the body of Rob Schneider, causing the audience to urgently desire that he had been transported into her body instead, because then he would look like her. Actually, they do trade bodies, but the plot follows the Rob Schneider body, which is like taking the Gatorland exit on your way to Disney World. The assignment of Anna Faris is to relate to Rob Schneider's body as if it contained Rachel McAdams, a challenge I doubt even Dame Judi Dench would be equal to. *Ding!*

Sam and Chris are on a private jet to Paris Hilton when it makes an emergency landing in Chris's hometown in New Jersey, where he meets up with Jamie again on Christmas Eve. There is not a spark of chemistry between Chris and Jamie, although the plot clearly re-quires them to fall in love. There is so much chemistry involved with the Anna Faris character, however, that she can set off multiple chain reactions with herself, if you see what I mean. The problem with Chris is that although he's a cool dude in L.A., the moment he finds himself with Jamie again, he reverts to hapless dweebdom.

On the *Just Friends* message board at the Internet Movie Database, "ecbell-1" writes: "I live about a block away from where they filmed this movie." It was François Truffaut who said it was impossible to pay attention to a movie filmed in a house where you once lived because you would constantly be distracted by how it looked different and they had changed the wallpaper, etc. Did "ecbell-1" experience this phenomenon? "It was pretty cool," he writes, "because I watched some of it being filmed, and even got to meet some of the actors." Nothing about the Truffaut theory. The New Jersey house, by the way, is in "ecbell-1's" hometown of Regina, Saskatchewan. *Ding! Ding! Awopbopaloobop, Alopbamboom!*

Just Like Heaven ★ ★ ★
PG-13, 101 m., 2005

Mark Ruffalo (David Abbott), Reese Witherspoon (Elizabeth Masterson), Donal Logue (Jack Houriskey), Jon Heder (Darryl), Dina Spybey (Abby Brody), Ben Shenkman (Brett Rushton), Ivana Milicevic (Katrina), Rosalind Chao (Fran). Directed by Mark Waters and produced by Laurie MacDonald and Walter F. Parkes. Screenplay by Peter Tolan and Leslie Dixon, based on the novel *If Only It Were True* by Marc Levy.

In *Just Like Heaven,* a man falls in love with a woman only he can see. She's not a ghost, because she's not dead, but a spirit. Why is she visible only to him? Perhaps because he has moved into her apartment. In a movie like this there is no logical reason for such matters. They simply are, and you accept them.

The woman is Elizabeth, played by Reese Witherspoon. The man is David, played by Mark Ruffalo. These are two of the sweetest actors in the movies, and sweetness is what they give their characters in *Just Like Heaven.*

There is not a mean bone in their bodies, and not a dark moment in the movie, unless, of course, you take the plot seriously, in which case it is deeply tragic.

Elizabeth is a young doctor at a San Francisco hospital. She is still single in her late twenties, and pulls twenty-six-hour shifts in the emergency room. A friend despairs of her unmarried status and wants to fix her up. "I'm perfectly capable of meeting men on my own," she says. The friend: "I know you are. I just want you to meet one that's not bleeding."

David was a landscape gardener until two years ago, when his first wife, Laura, died suddenly. Now he drinks too much and pays a lot of attention to the sofa he is sitting on at the moment. He's astonished when Elizabeth suddenly appears in the apartment and orders him to stop making a mess of things.

Although a good long talk would clear up everything at any point during the movie, the talk is postponed because the movie must move toward happiness with agonizing reluctance. David, manifestly confronted with a supernatural presence, consults Darryl (Jon Heder), the clerk in a psychic bookstore. He brings in a priest for a painfully overacted exorcism. He employs Asian ghostbusters. Elizabeth taunts him about "Father Flanagan and the Joy Luck Club." But she lacks crucial knowledge about what has happened to her.

We meet her sister, her nieces, her coworkers, and the creepy doctor who took over her job when she became a spirit. Can Elizabeth and David, who are now in love, take steps to return her to a corporal existence that will make their relationship immeasurably more satisfactory? Can David's best buddy, Jack (Donal Logue), help him with a little body-snatching? Can one movie support these many coincidences and close calls and misunderstandings?

Yes. The movie works, and so we accept everything, even the preposterous scene where a man is unconscious on the floor and Elizabeth tells David the man's lung is leaking air into his chest cavity, or whatever, and he must open a hole with a paring knife and keep it open with the plastic pour spout of a vodka bottle. As the chest is vented and the victim breathes again, I was poignantly reminded of the heart valve that gave Ignatius Reilly so much concern in *A Confederacy of Dunces,* that funniest of all novels from sad New Orleans.

I also liked the dialogue, by Peter Tolan and Leslie Dixon, as when it turns out that Elizabeth's little niece can also see her: "My fate is in the hands of a four-year-old who has seven other imaginary friends." And when she finally persuaded David to take her case: "You have two realities to choose from. The first is that a woman has come into your life in a very unconventional way and she needs your assistance. The second is that you're a crazy person, talking to himself on a park bench."

The Idiot Plot is a term devised for bad movies where the problems could be cleared up with a few words, if everyone in the plot were not an idiot. When the movie is good, it is kept afloat by the very frustration that sinks an Idiot Plot. There is a contest between what we want and what the characters do, and we get involved in spite of ourselves. Elizabeth explains perfectly clearly how her sister Abby (Dina Spybey) could be made to believe he is in touch with her spirit: She could tell David family secrets only Elizabeth would know. Wonderful, brilliant, and yet instead they mope about on hilltops with bittersweet regret. This woman could have been saved with days to spare, and there they are with fifteen minutes on the clock.

Just My Luck ★ ★
PG-13, 108 m., 2006

Lindsay Lohan (Ashley Albright), Chris Pine (Jake Hardin), Faizon Love (Damon Phillips), Missi Pyle (Peggy Braden), Samaire Armstrong (Maggie), Bree Turner (Dana). Directed by Donald Petrie and produced by Arnon Milchan, Arnold Rifkin, and Petrie. Screenplay by I. Marlene King and Amy B. Harris.

Some movies make me feel like I'm someone else. Other movies make me wish I were. Watching *Just My Luck,* I wished I were a teenage girl, not for any perverse reason, but because then I might have enjoyed it a lot more. I don't think it's for grown-ups, and I don't much think it's for teenage boys. But a teenage girl (even better, a preteen) might enjoy a romantic fantasy in which the heroine is old enough to get a top job at a marketing firm and wear Sarah Jessica Parker's clothes, and innocent enough that she has an entire romance based entirely on kissing. It's not only the romance that's kiss-based; so is the plot.

Lindsay Lohan is the star, and I have liked her ever since *The Parent Trap* (1998) and I like her here, too, but like many another former child star, it's time for her to move on to more challenging roles. I am lucky enough to have seen her in Robert Altman's forthcoming *A Prairie Home Companion,* so I know what we have to look forward to. Just our luck that we'll have *Just My Luck* to look back on.

Lohan plays Ashley, a young Manhattan career woman with extraordinarily good luck. It stops raining when she steps outside. Paper money sticks to her shoes. She can always get a cab. One day Damon Phillips (Faizon Love), a powerful record mogul, turns up at her office while her boss, Peggy Braden (Missi Pyle), is stuck in the elevator. Ashley has taken notes at previous meetings, knows the pitch, and delivers it to keep the mogul from walking out. She wins the contract, gets a new title, a raise, and an office, and finds herself producing an extravagant masquerade ball as a promotion.

In a parallel story, we meet Jake (Chris Pine). His luck is always bad. It starts raining when he walks outside. He finds a $5 bill, but it's covered with dog poop. His pants split. He works as a janitor at a bar and bowling alley, where he also runs the sound board and manages a band of young Brits who apparently want to look and sound as much as possible like the Beatles, circa 1964. The movie uses a real band, McFly: "Unlike most boy bands today," the press notes inform us, "McFly write their own songs and play their own instru-

ments." The alternatives are too depressing to contemplate.

The entire plot hinges on a single kiss. At the masked ball, Ashley is kissed by Jake, and somehow her good luck leaps from her lips to his, and he is blessed while now it rains on her and she can't get a cab. Many other dire events occur before Ashley realizes what must have happened. Since the person who kissed her was one of the professional dancers at the party, Ashley tracks down all twenty of them and kisses them—but no luck, because Jake was only pretending to be one of the dancers, see, and was really a gate-crasher trying to get McFly's demo CD into the hands of Damon Phillips. If you're one of those people who think I have a great job, imagine me watching Ashley work her way down the kiss list.

Eventually everything is sorted out, not before many misunderstandings and a lot of complex luck-trading that involves spit-swapping. McFly sings several songs, one of them a production number looking like a road company version of *A Hard Day's Night,* and Ashley's friends (Bree Turner and Samaire Armstrong) take her in after her apartment floods and tirelessly support her, advise her, cheer her, and help dress her. When Sarah Jessica Parker's dry cleaning is mistakenly delivered to Ashley's apartment, that's good luck. What happens later is bad luck for Ashley, and especially for Sarah Jessica Parker.

Just My Luck is perfectly efficient in its own way, delivering exactly what anyone would expect in a Lindsay Lohan movie with this premise. I wish it delivered more. It's safe, competent, and bland. I had a fairly monotonous time. You may like it more. For your sake, I hope so.

K

Keane ★ ★ ★ ½
R, 100 m., 2005

Damian Lewis (William Keane), Abigail Breslin (Kira Bedik), Amy Ryan (Lynn Bedik), Liza Colon-Zayas (1st Ticket Agent), John Tormey (2nd Ticket Agent), Brenda Denmark (Commuter), Ed Wheeler (Bus Driver), Christopher Evan Welch (Motel Clerk). Directed by Lodge H. Kerrigan and produced by Andrew Fierberg and Steven Soderbergh. Screenplay by Kerrigan.

Lodge Kerrigan's *Keane* opens with a man ranging the Port Authority Bus Terminal, looking for his lost daughter. He has a newspaper clipping he shows to people, who hurry on, sensing madness. The girl has been missing for weeks or months. It's not clear. This search has been part of the daily life of the man, named William Keane, who then retreats into a rough street world: a bottle of beer at one gulp, vodka, cocaine, prostitutes, reckless sex.

Keane, like Peter Winter, the subject of Kerrigan's *Clean, Shaven* (1994), is a schizophrenic on a quest for his daughter. But Winter has a daughter. Did Keane have a daughter, did she disappear, did she even exist? There is an enormous difference between the two films, generated by the urgency of Keane's desire to function in the world. He reminds himself he must look presentable to go on his search. He buys clothes for the missing girl. His episodes of abandon and confusion alternate with moments when he is quiet and tries to calm himself and focus.

Keane is played by Damian Lewis, a British actor recently seen in *An Unfinished Life* as the abusive boyfriend of Jennifer Lopez. Here he inhabits an edge of madness that Kerrigan understands with a fierce sympathy. There is no reason for us to believe that Keane (or his daughter) would be better off if he found her. The camera regards him mercilessly, and his performance involves us because he portrays not hopeless madness but his drive to escape his demons.

In a cheap flophouse, he meets Lynn (Amy Ryan) and her seven-year-old daughter, Kira (Abigail Breslin). They're down and out. Her husband has abandoned them, maybe to seek work, maybe to escape. Keane receives disability checks and gives Lynn money, which she needs badly enough to accept, especially since he is in a sweet, calm phase and doesn't want anything for it, or at least not anything she might not be willing to provide.

Lynn can't pick up Kira after school. Will Keane meet her, bring her home, and keep an eye on her from 4 to 7? He will. He does. They go to McDonald's. They go ice skating. This Keane might have made a good father. Which Keane is it? The mother goes seeking her husband and entrusts Kira to Keane overnight. What will happen? The suspense grows not out of the child's danger, if she is in any, but out of Keane's fears about himself. He has been going through a calm period. He is terrified of the responsibility he has suddenly been given. Does he confuse Kira with his lost daughter?

Kerrigan's films create worlds of personal obsession. After *Clean, Shaven*, he made *Claire Dolan* (1998), the story of an Irish prostitute (Katrin Cartlidge, 1961–2002, her early death from a sudden infection a sad loss after great performances). She works in Manhattan, wants to leave the life, must escape a dangerous pimp. In all three films, characters on the margins seek children they think will bring them happiness.

Some movies shed light on others. Regarding *Keane,* I think of *Flightplan,* the Jodie Foster thriller that opened a week earlier. Both films are excellent in their own way, seeking their own intentions, aimed at different audiences. Both begin with a lost daughter. The characters played by Foster and Lewis realize that if they are perceived as mad, all hope is lost for their search. Both try to function in a way that will allow them to continue.

There are some critics who will honor *Keane* and scorn *Flightplan,* and others who will praise *Flightplan* and never see, or even hear of, *Keane.* One is a commercial thriller, the other made by a transgressive independent. They both appeal to the same feelings in the audience. The parent has lost a daughter. The world presents a danger to the parent's search. *Keane* adds the grave complication of Kira.

367

The suspense in both films comes from our desire to see the parents survive and prevail.

The complete filmgoer is open to the movie on the screen and asks it to work in its own ways for its own purposes. He does not fault one for not being the other but is grateful for both if they are successful. Anyone seeking an understanding of the ways movies work might want to see both of these films and think about the ways they are different, and the ways they are not.

Keeping Up with the Steins ★ ★ ★
PG-13, 99 m., 2006

Jeremy Piven (Adam Fiedler), Larry Miller (Arnie Stein), Jami Gertz (Joanne Fiedler), Daryl Hannah (Sandy Sacred Feather), Garry Marshall (Irwin Fiedler), Daryl Sabara (Benjamin Fiedler), Doris Roberts (Rose Fiedler), Cheryl Hines (Casey Nudelman), Carter Jenkins (Zachary Stein). Directed by Scott Marshall and produced by A. D. Oppenheim, David Scharf, and Mark Zakarin. Screenplay by Zakarin.

I never tire of quoting Godard, who said, "The way to criticize a movie is to make another movie." Now comes more proof. A few weeks after *When Do We Eat?* a dreary comedy about a dysfunctional Jewish family at Passover, here is *Keeping Up with the Steins*, a fresh and lovable comedy about a dysfunctional Jewish family planning their son's bar mitzvah.

The family is headed by Adam Fiedler (Jeremy Piven), a Hollywood agent who is envious when his archrival, Arnie Stein (Larry Miller), throws a bar mitzvah for his own thirteen-year-old that includes an ocean cruise, a giant model of the Titanic, and a trained porpoise wearing a yarmulke. "I'm king of the world," the younger Stein cries, his arms outstretched as the *Titanic* sails into a ballroom and Adam Fiedler grows morose.

Adam consults with his wife, Joanne (Jami Gertz), about a bar mitzvah to shame the Steins. It may involve booking Dodger Stadium and having his son, Benjamin (Daryl Sabara of *Spy Kids*), arrive from the sky. Money is no object. Hiring a singer? How about Neil Diamond?

The problem with this grandiose scheme is that young Benjamin has no heart for it. Be-cause he narrates the movie, we learn from his point of view that he feels embarrassed by all the attention, overwhelmed by the scope of the ceremony, and terrified by his inability to master Hebrew in time to read it aloud during the religious prelude to the conspicuous consumption. He is also sad that his grandfather Irwin (Garry Marshall) has not been invited; Irwin and Adam have not been on speaking terms for years.

Benjamin appeals to his mother to downsize the bar mitzvah plans and secretly invites Grandfather Irwin to the ceremony. We discover that Irwin now enjoys a delightful new lifestyle on an Indian reservation with his young girlfriend, Sacred Feather (Daryl Hannah). When Irwin and Sacred Feather arrive at the Fiedlers' for dinner, Sacred Feather turns out to have dietary restrictions that make Jewish customs seem positively permissive. Marshall and Hannah have small roles, but they're perfectly realized.

Another key character is Benjamin's grandmother and Irwin's first wife, Rose (Doris Roberts). How will the once-married couple get along, and will Sacred Feather get caught in the middle? The movie could handle these questions with overacting, screaming matches, and overwrought drama, as *When Do We Eat?* does, but no. The screenplay by Mark Zakarin (a writer for *The L Word* on TV) uses its share of exaggeration and hyperbole, but the characters behave according to their natures and needs, as we all do.

The movie was directed by Scott Marshall, son of Garry, nephew of Penny, and, therefore, born with comic timing in his genes. His plot is not astonishingly original; it bears some similarity to the competition over holiday decorations in the awful *Christmas with the Kranks* (2004) and cheerfully goes for one-liners and sight gags. But it is always about something, and if a bar mitzvah marks a boy's entry into manhood, Benjamin's shows him becoming his own man.

I was grateful to Piven and Gertz for making the parents into people who act more like parents than like movie characters. To be sure, any Hollywood agent has a tendency toward the grandiose and the cocky, but Joanne is a steadying influence on Adam, who after all loves his son more than he loves outspending his rival.

At one point in the film, Adam looks at home movies of his own bar mitzvah, a humble backyard affair. His wife has never seen them before. They are a reminder of the underlying purpose of the ceremony, which is not to outspend the neighbors but to wish a young man godspeed in his life. Because the movie never really forgets this, *Keeping Up with the Steins* never loses its footing.

Kicking and Screaming ★ ★ ★
PG, 95 m., 2005

Will Ferrell (Phil Weston), Robert Duvall (Buck Weston), Kate Walsh (Barbara Weston), Mike Ditka (Himself), Dylan McLaughlin (Sam Weston), Josh Hutcherson (Bucky Weston), Musette Vander (Janice Weston), Elliott Cho (Byong Sun). Directed by Jesse Dylan and produced by Jimmy Miller. Screenplay by Leo Benvenuti and Steve Rudnick.

The problem with team sports involving kids is that the coaches are parents. The parents become too competitive and demanding, and put an unwholesome emphasis on winning. One simple reform would enormously improve childhood sports: The coaches should be kids, too. Parents could be around in supervisory roles, sort of like the major league commissioner, but kids should run their own teams. Sure, they'd make mistakes and the level of play would suffer and, in fact, the whole activity would look a lot more like a Game and less like a Sporting Event. Kids become so co-opted by the adult obsession with winning that they can't just mess around and have fun.

This insight came to me midway through *Kicking and Screaming*, which illustrates my theory by giving us a father-and-son coaching team who will haunt the nightmares of their players for decades to come. The movie is actually sweet and pretty funny, so don't get scared away: It's just that when a kid hears an adult say, "I eat quitters for breakfast and I spit out their bones," that kid is not going to rest easier tonight.

Will Ferrell stars as Phil Weston, an adult who still feels like a kid when his dad, Buck (Robert Duvall), is around. Buck is a version of Bull Meechum, the character Duvall played in *The Great Santini* (1979), where he was try-

ing to run his family like a Marine unit. Buck coaches in the local kids' soccer league, and as the movie opens, he trades his grandson—*his own grandson*—because the kid is no good. That makes Phil mad: He was always told he was a loser, and now his own kid is getting the same treatment from Buck.

So Phil decides to become a coach himself. But he's just as obsessed with winning as his dad. He makes three key recruits. Two of them are the kids of the local Italian butcher; they're great players. The third is Mike Ditka, as himself; he's Buck's neighbor, the two men hate each other, and Ditka agrees to become Phil's assistant coach.

Phil's basic coaching strategy is simple: Get the ball to the Italians. The movie could have taken better advantage of Ditka by really focusing on his personality, but that would have shouldered aside the father-son rivalry, and so I guess they have it about right, with Ditka supplying advice and one-liners from the sidelines. He makes one crucial contribution to the plot: He introduces Phil to coffee. Phil has never been a coffee drinker, but from the first sip he finds it addictive, and then maddening. "What is that fascinating aroma?" he asks, before going on a caffeine binge that actually leads to him being barred for life from a coffee shop.

With Ferrell in the movie, we might expect a raucous comedy like *Old School*, or maybe *Dodgeball*, a movie I have to keep reminding myself Ferrell was not in. But no, *Kicking and Screaming* is more like *The Bad News Bears* or *The Mighty Ducks*, with the underdogs coming from the bottom of the league standings to eventually—but I dare not reveal the ending, even though it will be obvious to every sentient being in the theater.

Will Ferrell is now a major movie star. I learn of his status from the industry analyst David Poland, who has crunched the numbers and come up with the "real" list of box-office heavyweights. He says the top ten stars in terms of actual ticket sales are, in order: Will Smith, Tom Cruise, Adam Sandler, Jim Carrey, Russell Crowe, Tom Hanks, Eddie Murphy, Ben Stiller, Will Ferrell, and Denzel Washington. The highest-ranking woman on the list is Reese Witherspoon, at No. 12.

The list is fascinating because it sets Ferrell apart from several other recent *Saturday*

Night Live alums cycling through hapless comedies; he has broken loose from the *SNL* curse that, for example, haunts Martin Short in *Jiminy Glick*. Ferrell plays actual characters, as he did in *Elf*, rather than recycled *SNL* skit creatures. In *Kicking and Screaming*, he understands that the role requires a certain vulnerability and poignancy, and although he goes berserk with all the coffee, it is kept within character. His soccer coach has an emotional arc and is not simply a cartoon. Duvall, of course, is superb. No one has a meaner laugh. He even begins to smile and you wish you were armed. He goes head-to-head with Ditka and you wait for them to spit out the bones.

The movie is pure formula from beginning to end, and it doesn't pay as much attention to the individual kids as it might have—especially to Byong Sun (Elliott Cho), the smallest member of the team, who seems to have something really going on down there among the knees of his opponents. There is also the usual thankless role of the hero's wife, played here by Kate Walsh; her job is to talk sense to Phil, which is never much fun. Buck's wife is a sexy bombshell played by Musette Vander, but she turns out to be sensible and sane, which is a disappointment. Still, *Kicking and Screaming* is an entertaining family movie, and may serve a useful purpose if it inspires kids to overthrow their coaches and take over their own sports.

The Kid and I ★ ★ ★
PG-13, 93 m., 2005

Tom Arnold (Bill Williams), Eric Gores (Aaron Roman), Richard Edson (Guy Prince), Joe Mantegna (Davis Roman), Henry Winkler (Johnny Bernstein), Shannon Elizabeth (Shelby Roman), Linda Hamilton (Susan Mandeville), Arielle Kebbel (Arielle). Directed by Penelope Spheeris and produced by Tom Arnold, Spheeris, and Brad Wyman. Screenplay by Arnold.

There is something I don't know about *The Kid and I*. Although I could easily find it out, I have decided to write the review without knowing it. The movie is about a kid with cerebral palsy, whose favorite movie is *True Lies* with Arnold Schwarzenegger, and whose dream is to star in an action movie of his own.

He wants to jump out of airplanes, beat up bad people, and kiss a girl, and because his father is a millionaire, he gets his chance.

Here is what I don't know: Is Eric Gores, who plays the kid, really disabled, or is he an actor? I ask because the answer involves how we respond to the difference between documentary and fiction. The performance by Gores is so convincing that if he's an actor, it's an impressive achievement. If he's not an actor, then it's impressive in a different way, because he overcomes disabilities to create a character we believe and care about.

Ten seconds on the Internet, and I would know. But the answer would skew my review. If Gores is an actor, we are looking at fiction. If he is disabled, then we are looking at a documentary in which a professional cast and crew interact with him. Or are we? Should it matter? That's where it gets tricky. Isn't a disabled actor as capable of playing a role in a movie as anyone else? Didn't the Italian neorealists teach us that everyone has one role he can play perfectly, and that role is himself?

I think the most honest strategy, having put my cards on the table, is to review the film on its own terms. *The Kid and I*, written by Tom Arnold and directed by Penelope Spheeris, doesn't sentimentalize the material, that's for sure. It begins as a dark comedy, with Bill Williams (Arnold) playing a has-been onetime movie star who is out of work and out of hope. He prepares a press release on his suicide and various other suicide notes, then leaves his house to give away his clothes to a bum named Guy (Richard Edson). The bum follows him home and sabotages the suicide plans. Now Bill is still alive and has no money *and* no clothes, and the trade papers are reporting his death. This could be the setup for a Preston Sturges story.

A millionaire named David Roman (Joe Mantegna) contacts him. He wants to hire Bill to write and act in an action movie like *True Lies*, which would star Roman's son Aaron. The real Tom Arnold did star in the original *True Lies*, and in this and many other details, the movie incorporates facts and names from real life. Bill is incredulous. When he meets Aaron, he is not instantly won over by the kid's courage, charm, personality, etc., and states flatly that the film cannot be done. But Aaron has a way of ignoring or deflecting negativity. He just keeps right on making his plans: "In the movie," he explains, "I want a girlfriend. I want to kiss a girl." He even specifies the girl he wants to kiss: Arielle Kebbel, who he has studied in the pages of *Maxim*.

The rich David Roman has a new spouse named Shelby (Shannon Elizabeth), who may quality as a "trophy wife" but is not a bad person, and helps convince Bill to take on the project. The details of the movie they make I will leave for you to discover. "We can get Penelope Spheeris to direct," Bill says at one point, adding that she won't cost a lot of money.

Spheeris plays herself in the film, is seen on camera, and her approach to both the outer and inner films is the same: She depends on realism, up to a certain point, and then it becomes "a movie." We see how stunts are handled, how effects are obtained, how shots are cheated to make it appear that the star does things he is not really doing. We see, in fact, more or less what might really happen if a disabled kid with a rich dad made this movie. Or if an actor played a disabled kid, etc.

And the result is—well, what is it? Heartwarming? In a technical sense, yes, but the movie doesn't pander and there aren't a lot of violins playing (or any, as I recall). The overall tone reflects the sardonic comedy Arnold might really make, right down to his suggestion that the kid's girlfriend could be Rosie O'Donnell. I wonder why he didn't suggest Roseanne Barr.

One tricky scene is handled especially well. That's the one they leave until the last day of the shooting, the hot-tub scene involving Kebbel. When Kebbel turns up on the set, she turns out to be not an alarmingly erotic menace from *Maxim* but a sweet girl who treats Aaron well, doesn't condescend to the situation, and is, let it be said, a charming hot-tub companion.

In this and other dicey moments, the movie finds a way to avoid being creepy on the one hand and corny on the other: It works by being forthright and businesslike about the movie-within-the-movie. And this is accurate: Movies cost a lot of money and involve skilled and impatient professionals; just because the kid's dad is rich changes nothing. Executive producers are always rich. That's how they get to be executive producers.

The Kid and I is not a great film, but you know what? It achieves what it sets out to achieve, and it isn't boring, and it kept me intrigued and involved. As an actor, Gores creates an engaging and convincing character that I liked and cared about—and believed.

I make it a practice to avoid watching trailers and reading Internet speculation on forthcoming movies, and in this case I'm relieved that I knew nothing about the movie going in. When you come out, check the Internet, which is what I'm about to do, and then ask yourself if your thinking about the movie is affected, knowing what you know now. The answer to that question cuts to the heart of the mystery about how we relate to movies.

Kids in America ★ ★ ★
PG-13, 91 m., 2005

Gregory Smith (Holden Donovan), Stephanie Sherrin (Charlotte Pratt), Nicole Richie (Kelly Stepford), Malik Yoba (Will Drucker), Julie Bowen (Principal Weller), Caitlin Wachs (Katie Carmichael), Emy Coligado (Emily Chua), Crystal Celeste Grant (Walanda Jenkins), Chris Morris (Chuck McGinn), Alex Anfanger (Lawrence Reitzer), Adam Arkin (Ed Mumsford), George Wendt (Coach Thompson), Andrew Shaifer (Chip Stratton), Rosanna Arquette (Abby Pratt), Elizabeth Perkins (Sondra Carmichael). Directed by Josh Stolberg and produced by Andrew Shaifer. Screenplay by Shaifer and Stolberg.

Once in a blue moon, a movie escapes the shackles of its genre and does what it really wants to do. *Kids in America* is a movie like that. It breaks out of Hollywood jail. You know all those "brainless high school comedies"? Here's what one would look like if it had brains. It's a movie for every kid who was different, every kid with a political thought, every kid who ever got suspended for exercising the freedom of speech, every kid who had an article censored in the school paper, or did something shocking in a talent show, or actually believed what the idealistic teachers told him.

Yes, all of that, but I'm making it sound too serious. This is also a comedy that bites, and a romance during which a boy and a girl fall in love while they are engaged in an experiment to reproduce movie kisses. They start with the greatest movie kiss of all time, which he thinks is the one between John Cusack and Ione Skye in *Say Anything*, the kiss in the rain that lasts about three seconds and you almost miss it. When Holden (Gregory Smith of *Everwood*) describes it to Charlotte (Stephanie Sherrin), she simply says "show me" and walks out into the rain. They eventually get around to the longest kiss in movie history, which I always thought was the one between Cary Grant and Ingrid Bergman in *Notorious*, but no, it was between Jane Wyman and Regis Toomey in *You're in the Army Now*, and it clocked in at 185 seconds. Of course, only a kid who works in a video store would know that.

There is nobody stupid in this movie. Not even Kelly (Nicole Richie of *The Simple Life*), the head of the cheerleader squad. Not even Principal Weller (Julie Bowen), who enforces medieval policies but is scary, she's so articulate. Not even the football coach (George Wendt). Not even the drama coach (Andrew Shaifer), who once staged a reading of Oliver Stone's *Platoon* with all the expletives removed, and what's more, he has Harvey Fierstein's autograph. The stupid people are all offscreen, like the anatomy teacher described by Holden: "He lives with his mom and has never seen a naked body, including his own."

The characters talk about real things in real words. Amazing. Consider the girl who runs the school's Celibacy Club but gets suspended for wearing a "Safe Sex or No Sex" button and sticking condoms to her blouse. The school policy is: no sex. But what about girls who do have sex, she wants to know, and get pregnant or have abortions? Principal Weller's policy is celibacy or else. Consider the crisis involving the school's Minority Club, which has "traditionally" been for African-Americans only. "You can kiss my Chinese ass," says an Asian student. Another kid wants in because he's fat. And what about Lawrence (Alex Anfanger)? The head of the club concedes: "You're so gay, Cher dresses like you."

The school reaches the crisis point during the annual Holiday Hoopla talent show, when Holden does a reading from Shakespeare. He gets as far as "to be or not to be" and decides "I choose not to be," attacking school policies and ending up with a real showstopper.

Principal Weller tries to contain the uprising; she's running for superintendent of schools and is worried about her image. But the students outmaneuver her and her flunkies, leading up to a hijacked pep rally where Holden commandeers the audiovisual hookup and shows a montage of heterosexual kissing in the corridors, leading up to a protest about the expulsion of the gay student. This leads to a development that will certainly add to the list of famous movie kisses.

Kids in America was directed by Josh Stolberg; he and Shaifer coproduced and wrote the screenplay. They say it was inspired by actual news stories, including one about a girl thrown out of school after her journal was seized and read without her permission. Another girl got expelled for wearing a "Barbie is a lesbian" T-shirt. The movie is properly angry at the repression and discrimination that masquerades as school policy, but the surprising thing is how funny and entertaining they make it. High school students are so consistently depicted as substance-abusing, sex-crazed airheads, you'd think Hollywood is trying to teach them they're as dumb as the movies about them. *Kids in America* is a call to the barricades, and a lot of fun.

Kill Bill: Vol. 2 ★ ★ ★ ★
R, 137 m., 2004

Uma Thurman (The Bride), David Carradine (Bill), Daryl Hannah (Elle Driver), Michael Madsen (Budd), Gordon Liu (Pei Mei). Directed by Quentin Tarantino and produced by Lawrence Bender and Tarantino. Screenplay by Tarantino and Uma Thurman.

Quentin Tarantino's *Kill Bill: Vol. 2* is an exuberant celebration of moviemaking, coasting with heedless joy from one audacious chapter to another, working as irony, working as satire, working as drama, working as pure action. I liked it even more than *Kill Bill* (2003). It's not a sequel but a continuation and completion, filmed at the same time; now that we know the whole story, the first part takes on another dimension. *Vol. 2* stands on its own, although it has deeper resonance if you've seen *Kill Bill*.

The movie is a distillation of the countless grind house kung-fu movies Tarantino has absorbed, and which he loves beyond all reason. Web sites have already enumerated his inspirations—how a sunset came from this movie, and a sword from that. He isn't copying, but transcending; there's a kind of urgency in the film, as if he's turning up the heat under his memories.

The movie opens with a long close-up of the Bride (Uma Thurman) behind the wheel of a car, explaining her mission, which is to kill Bill. There is a lot of explaining in the film; Tarantino writes dialogue with quirky details that suggest the obsessions of his people. That's one of the ways he gives his movies a mythical quality; the characters don't talk in mundane, everyday dialogue, but in a kind of elevated geekspeak that lovingly burnishes the details of their legends, methods, beliefs, and arcane lore.

Flashbacks remind us that the pregnant Bride and her entire wedding party were targeted by the Deadly Viper Assassination Squad in a massacre at the Two Pines Wedding Chapel. Bill was responsible—Bill, whom she confronts on the porch of the chapel for a conversation that suggests the depth and weirdness of their association. He's played by David Carradine in a performance that somehow, improbably, suggests that Bill and the Bride had a real relationship despite the preposterous details surrounding it. (Bill is deeply offended that she plans to marry a used record store owner and lead a normal life.)

The Bride, of course, improbably survived the massacre, awakened after a long coma, and in the first film set to avenge herself against the Deadly Vipers and Bill. That involved extended action sequences as she battled Vernita Green (Vivica A. Fox) and O-Ren Ishii (Lucy Liu), not to mention O-Ren's teenage bodyguard Go Go Yubari (Chiaki Kuriyama) and the martial arts team known as the Crazy 88.

Much of her success came because she was able to persuade the legendary sword maker Hattori Hanzo (Sonny Chiba) to come out of retirement and make her a weapon. He presented it without modesty: "This my finest sword. If in your journey you should encounter God, God will be cut."

In *Vol. 2*, she meets another Asian legend, the warrior master Pei Mei, played by Gordon Liu. Pei Mei, who lives on the top of a high, lonely hill reached by climbing many stairs, was Bill's master, and in a flashback, Bill delivers his protégé for training. Pei Mei is a harsh and uncompromising teacher, and the Bride sheds blood during their unrelenting sessions.

Pei Mei, whose hair and beard are long and white and flowing, like a character from the pages of a comic book, is another example of Tarantino's method, which is to create lovingly structured episodes that play on their own while contributing to the legend. Like a distillation of all wise, ancient, and deadly martial arts masters in countless earlier movies, Pei Mei waits patiently for eons on his hilltop until he is needed for a movie.

The training with Pei Mei, we learn, prepared the Bride to begin her career with Bill ("jetting around the world making vast sums of money and killing for hire"), and is inserted in this movie at a time and place that makes it function like a classic cliff-hanger. In setting up this scene, Tarantino once again pauses for colorful dialogue; the Bride is informed by Bill that Pei Mei hates women, whites, and Americans, and much of his legend is described. Such speeches function in Tarantino not as long-winded detours, but as a way of setting up characters and situations with dimensions it would be difficult to establish dramatically.

In the action that takes place "now," the Bride has to fight her way past formidable opponents, including Elle Driver (Daryl Hannah), the one-eyed master of martial arts, and Budd (Michael Madsen), Bill's beer-swilling brother, who works as a bouncer in a strip joint and lives in a mobile home surrounded by desolation. Neither one is a pushover for the Bride—Elle because of her skills (also learned from Pei Mei), Budd because of his canny instincts.

The showdown with Budd involves a sequence where it seems the Bride must surely die after being buried alive. (That she does not is a given, considering the movie is not over and Bill is not dead, but she sure looks doomed.) Tarantino, who began the film in black and white before switching to color, plays with formats here, too; to suggest the claustrophobia of being buried, he shows the Bride inside her wooden casket, and as clods of earth rain down on the lid, he switches from wide-screen to the classic 4x3-screen ratio.

The fight with Elle Driver is a virtuoso celebration of fight choreography; although we are aware that all is not as it seems in movie action sequences, Thurman and Hannah must have trained long and hard to even seem to do what they do. Their battle takes place inside Bill's trailer home, which is pretty much demolished in the process, and provides a contrast to the elegant nightclub setting of the fight with O-Ren Ishii; it ends in a squishy way that would be unsettling in another kind of movie, but here all the action is so ironically heightened that we may cringe and laugh at the same time.

These sequences involve their own Tarantinian dialogue of explanation and scene-setting. Budd has an extended monologue in which he offers the Bride the choice of Mace or a flashlight, and the details of his speech allow us to visualize horrors worse than any we could possibly see. Later, Elle Driver produces a black mamba, and in a sublime touch reads from a Web page that describes the snake's deadly powers.

Of the original *Kill Bill*, I wrote: "The movie is all storytelling and no story. The motivations have no psychological depth or resonance, but are simply plot markers. The characters consist of their characteristics." True, but one of the achievements of *Vol. 2* is that the story is filled in, the characters are developed, and they do begin to resonate, especially during the extraordinary final meeting between the Bride and Bill—which consists not of nonstop action but of more hypnotic dialogue, and ends in an event that is like a quiet, deadly punch line.

Put the two parts together, and Tarantino has made a masterful saga that celebrates the martial arts genre while kidding it, loving it, and transcending it. I confess I feared that *Vol. 2* would be like those sequels that lack the intensity of the original. But this is all one film, and now that we see it whole, it's greater than its two parts; Tarantino remains the most brilliantly oddball filmmaker of his generation, and this is one of the best films of the year.

The King ★ ★ ★ ½
R, 105 m., 2006

Gael Garcia Bernal (Elvis Valderez), William Hurt (David Sandow), Pell James (Malerie Sandow), Paul Dano (Paul Sandow), Laura Harring (Twyla Sandow). Directed by James Marsh and produced by Milo Addica and James Wilson. Screenplay by Addica and Marsh.

He is straight out of the Navy. He travels to Corpus Christi, Texas, takes a motel room, and attends church. After the service, he asks the pastor for a hug. The pastor hugs him and says, "I don't believe I know you." The young man says his name is Elvis: "My mother told me about you. Her name was Yolanda. She told me your name." This is not the sort of thing an evangelical minister wants to hear when his wife's name is not Yolanda.

Going to church was not quite the first thing Elvis (Gael Garcia Bernal) did in Corpus Christi. First he met the preacher's sixteen-year-old daughter, Malerie (Pell James). Now he moves on both fronts, seducing the daughter while playing a devout churchgoer for the father. Minister David Sandow is played by William Hurt as a man who once was a sinner but, as he tells Elvis, "That was before I became a Christian. Before I met my wife."

William Hurt can be so subterranean, we don't know where he's tunneling. Here he seems to be one thing while becoming its opposite. The last thing he wants in his life is a child from an early affair. On the other hand, Elvis makes a good impression. The pastor's son, Paul (Paul Dano), sings with his band at church services and at school is the leader of a campaign to introduce intelligent design into the curriculum. But we sense, and maybe the pastor does, that the energy Paul is channeling into Christian activism could turn against the church in a flash. Paul and his band perform a song one Sunday that enrages the pastor. Not long after, the son goes missing. The pastor, his family, and the congregation pray for his safe return, but the Lord is not in a position to answer their prayers.

At some point during this setup, we realize *The King* will *not* be a movie about the hypocrisy of the pastor. Pastor David is about as good a man as is possible under the circumstances, although there is room for improvement. And Elvis is not a blameless victim.

I have slipped over crucial sections of the movie because things occur that should come as a complete surprise to you. One thing that will not astonish anyone is Elvis's ability to sneak into Malerie's bedroom almost at will. We know from *Down in the Valley* and countless other movies that the bedrooms of teenage girls are sadly lacking in security and that their parents sleep the sleep of the dead. Malerie falls in love with Elvis, but his feelings for her are a good question: He knows, and she doesn't, that they have the same father.

The King descends so deeply and steadily into evil that it generates a dread fascination. After Paul disappears, the preacher reaches out to Elvis, acknowledging him in front of the congregation, treating him as a son, inviting him into his house. Because at any moment we possess more information than anyone except Elvis (and more insight into Elvis than he ever will have about himself), we see mistakes being made for perfectly reasonable motives. The preacher's decision comes under the heading of forgiveness and charity, but no good can come of it.

What has Elvis been planning in the years since David and Yolanda sinned? Certainly some of his actions in the movie are unpremeditated, but the way he responds to them shows a frightening degree of calculation. That Garcia Bernal's character looks open-faced and trustworthy is a great advantage; that he is utterly amoral helps him, too, because he can look straight in your eye and lie pleasingly and with conviction.

The movie was directed by James Marsh, a British documentarian, from a screenplay by Milo Addica (*Monster's Ball*). It's the kind of work where characters develop on their own, without consulting the book of clichés. We have so many preconceived notions about the types in this movie (hellfire preacher, sexpot daughter, dutiful son, black sheep) that it's surprising to see them behaving as individuals; they make decisions based on what they know and when they know it, and that's always too little and too late. The character who sees clearly, or intuits accurately, is the preacher's wife, Twyla (Laura Harring). At the service when David welcomes Elvis to the church, she walks out the door and straight down the middle of the street. But even that isn't the close of anything.

What the movie leaves us with are theological questions. Are the sins of the father visited on the son? Are we justified in protecting ourselves when fate threatens us? Are some people just plain bad? Should you think twice before doing the right thing? Are you sure you know

what it is? Underneath all these is a fundamental question: Why does God allow bad things to happen to good people? I was startled the other day when the pope visited Auschwitz and asked God the same question. The party line, in the pope's church and in Pastor David's, is that the Lord works in mysterious ways, his wonders to unfold. Some wonders we can do without.

King Arthur ★ ★ ★
PG-13, 130 m., 2004

Clive Owen (Arthur), Keira Knightley (Guinevere), Stellan Skarsgard (Cerdic), Stephen Dillane (Merlin), Ray Winstone (Bors), Hugh Dancy (Galahad), Til Schweiger (Cynric), Ioan Gruffudd (Lancelot), Joel Edgerton (Gawain). Directed by Antoine Fuqua and produced by Jerry Bruckheimer. Screenplay by David Franzoni.

For centuries, countless tales have been told of the legend of King Arthur. But the only story you've never heard . . . is the true story that inspired the legend.

—trailer for *King Arthur*

Uh, huh. And in the true story, Arthur traveled to Rome, became a Christian and a soldier, and was assigned to lead a group of yurt-dwelling warriors from Sarmatia on a fifteen-year tour of duty in England, where Guinevere is a fierce woman warrior of the Woads. His knights team up with the Woads to battle the Saxons. In this version, Guinevere and Lancelot are not lovers, although they exchange significant glances; Arthur is Guinevere's lover. So much for all those legends we learned from Thomas Malory's immortal *Le Morte d'Arthur* (1470), and the less immortal *Knights of the Round Table* (1953).

This new *King Arthur* tells a story with uncanny parallels to current events in Iraq. The imperialists from Rome enter England intent on overthrowing the tyrannical Saxons, and find allies in the brave Woads. "You—all of you—were free from your first breath!" Arthur informs his charges and future subjects, anticipating by a millennium or so the notion that all men are born free and overlooking the detail that his knights have been pressed into involuntary servitude.

The movie is darker and the weather chillier than in the usual Arthurian movie. There is a round table, but the knights scarcely find time to sit down at it. Guinevere is not a damsel in potential distress, but seems to have been cloned from Brigitte Nielsen in *Red Sonja*. And everybody speaks idiomatic English—even the knights, who as natives of Sarmatia might be expected to converse in an early version of Uzbek, and the Woads, whose accents get a free pass because not even the Oxford English Dictionary has heard of a Woad. To the line "Last night was a mistake" in *Troy*, we can now add, in our anthology of unlikely statements in history, Arthur's line to Guinevere as his seven warriors prepare to do battle on a frozen lake with hundreds if not thousands of Saxons: "There are a lot of lonely men over there."

Despite these objections, *King Arthur* is not a bad movie, although it could have been better. It isn't flat-out silly like *Troy*, its actors look at home as their characters, and director Antoine Fuqua curtails the use of CGI in the battle scenes, which involve mostly real people. There is a sense of place here, and although the costumes bespeak a thriving trade in tailoring somewhere beyond the mead, the film's locations look rough, ready, and green, (it was filmed in Ireland).

Clive Owen, who has been on the edge of stardom for a decade, makes an Arthur who seems more like a drill instructor, less like a fairy-tale prince, than most of the Arthurs we've seen. Lean, dark, and angular, he takes the character to the edge of antihero status. Keira Knightley, who was the best friend in *Bend It Like Beckham*, here looks simultaneously sexy and muddy, which is a necessity in this movie, and fits right into the current appetite for women action heroes who are essentially honorary men, all except for the squishy parts. The cast is filled with dependable actors with great faces, such as Ray Winstone as a tough-as-nails knight who inexplicably but perhaps appropriately anticipates the Cockney accent, and Stephen Dillane as Merlin, leader of the Woads and more of a psychic and sorcerer than a magician who does David Copperfield material.

The plot involves Rome's desire to defend its English colony against the invading Saxons, and its decision to back the local Woads in their long struggle against the barbarians. But Rome, declining and falling right on schedule, is losing its territorial ambitions and beginning to withdraw from the far corners of its empire. That leaves Arthur risking his neck without much support from the folks at home, and perhaps he will cast his lot with England. In the traditional legends he became king at fifteen, and went on to conquer Scotland, Ireland, Iceland—and Orkney, which was flattered to find itself in such company.

The movie ends with a pitched battle that's heavy on swords and maces and stabbings and skewerings, and in which countless enemies fall while nobody we know ever dies except for those whose deaths are prefigured by prescient dialogue or the requirements of fate. I have at this point seen about enough swashbuckling, I think, although producer Jerry Bruckheimer hasn't, since this project follows right on the heels of his *Pirates of the Caribbean*. I would have liked to see deeper characterizations and more complex dialogue, as in movies like *Braveheart* or *Rob Roy*, but today's multiplex audience, once it has digested a word like *Sarmatia*, feels its day's work is done.

That the movie works is because of the considerable production qualities and the charisma of the actors, who bring more interest to the characters than they deserve. There is a kind of direct, unadorned conviction to the acting of Clive Owen and the others; raised on Shakespeare, trained for swordfights, with an idea of Arthurian legend in their heads since childhood, they don't seem out of time and place like the cast of *Troy*. They get on with it.

Kingdom of Heaven ★ ★ ★ ½
R, 145 m., 2005

Orlando Bloom (Balian of Ibelin), Eva Green (Sibylla), Liam Neeson (Godfrey of Ibelin), David Thewlis (Hospitaler), Marton Csokas (Guy de Lusignan), Brendan Gleeson (Reynald), Jeremy Irons (Tiberias), Ghassan Massoud (Saladin), Edward Norton (King Baldwin). Directed by Ridley Scott and produced by Scott. Screenplay by William Monahan.

The first thing to be said for Ridley Scott's *Kingdom of Heaven* is that Scott knows how to direct a historical epic. I might have been kinder to his *Gladiator* had I known that *Troy* and *Alexander* were in my future, but *Kingdom of Heaven* is better than *Gladiator*—deeper, more thoughtful, more about human motivation, and less about action.

The second thing is that Scott is a brave man to release a movie at this time about the wars between Christians and Muslims for control of Jerusalem. Few people will be capable of looking at *Kingdom of Heaven* objectively. I have been invited by both Muslims and Christians to view the movie with them so they can point out its shortcomings. When you've made both sides angry, you may have done something right.

The Muslim scholar Hamid Dabashi, however, after being asked to consult on the movie, writes in the new issue of *Sight & Sound:* "It was neither pro- nor anti-Islamic, neither pro- nor anti-Christian.· It was, in fact, not even about the Crusades. And yet I consider the film to be a profound act of faith." It is an act of faith, he thinks, because for its hero, Balian (Orlando Bloom), who is a nonbeliever, "All religious affiliations fade in the light of his melancholic quest to find a noble purpose in life."

That's an insight that helps me understand my own initial question about the film, which was: Why don't they talk more about religion? Weren't the Crusades seen by Christians as a holy war to gain control of Jerusalem from the Muslims? I wondered if perhaps Scott was evading the issue. But not really: He shows characters more concerned with personal power and advancement than with theological issues.

Balian, a village blacksmith in France, discovers he is the illegitimate son of Sir Godfrey (Liam Neeson). Godfrey is a knight returning from the Middle East, who paints Jerusalem not in terms of a holy war but in terms of its opportunities for an ambitious young man; it has a healthy economy at a time when medieval Europe is stagnant. "A man who in France has not a house is in the Holy Land the master of a city," Godfrey promises. "There at the end of the world you are not what you were born, but what you have it in yourself to be." He makes Jerusalem sound like a medieval Atlanta, a city too busy to hate.

For the 100 years leading up to the action, both Christians and Muslims were content to see each other worship in the Holy City. It was only when Christian zealots determined to

control the Holy Land more rigidly that things went wrong. The movie takes place circa 1184, as the city is ruled by the young King Baldwin (Edward Norton), who has leprosy and conceals his disfigured face behind a silver mask. Balian takes control of the city after the death of its young king. Then the Knights Templar, well known from *The Da Vinci Code,* wage war on the Muslims. Saladin (Ghassan Massoud) leads a Muslim army against them, and Balian eventually surrenders the city to him. Much bloodshed and battle are avoided.

What Scott seems to be suggesting, I think, is that most Christians and Muslims might be able to coexist peacefully if it were not for the extremists on both sides. This may explain why the movie has displeased the very sorts of Muslims and Christians who will take moderation as an affront. Most ordinary moviegoers, I suspect, will not care much about the movie's reasonable politics, and will be absorbed in those staples of all historical epics, battle and romance.

The romance here is between Balian and Sibylla (Eva Green), sister of King Baldwin. You might wonder how a blacksmith could woo a princess, but reflect that Sir Godfrey was correct, and there are indeed opportunities for an ambitious young man in Jerusalem, especially after his newly discovered father makes him a knight, and Tiberias (Jeremy Irons) enlists him as an aide to Baldwin.

One spectacular battle scene involves the attack of Saladin's forces on Christian-controlled Jerusalem, and it's one of those spectacular set-pieces with giant balls of flame that hurtle through the air and land close, but not too close, to the key characters. There is a certain scale that's inevitable in films of this sort, and Scott does it better than anybody.

Even so, I enjoyed the dialogue and plot more than the action. I've seen one or two vast desert cities too many. Nor do thousands of charging horses look brand-new to me, and the hand-to-hand combat looks uncannily like all other hand-to-hand combat. Godfrey gives Balian a lesson in swordsmanship (chop from above), but apparently the important thing to remember is that if you're an anonymous enemy, you die, and if you're a hero, you live unless a glorious death is required. You'd think people would be killed almost by accident in the middle of a thousand sword-swinging madmen, but every encounter is broken down into a confrontation between a victor and a vanquished. It's well done, but it's been done.

What's more interesting is Ridley Scott's visual style, assisted by John Mathieson's cinematography and the production design of Arthur Max. A vast set of ancient Jerusalem was constructed to provide realistic foregrounds and locations, which were then enhanced by CGI backgrounds, additional horses and troops, and so on. There is also exhilarating footage as young Balian makes his way to Jerusalem, using the twelfth-century equivalent of a GPS: "Go to where they speak Italian, and then keep going."

The movie is above all about the personal codes of its heroes, both Christian and Muslim. They are men of honor: Gentlemen, we would say, if they were only a little gentle. They've seen enough bloodshed and lost enough comrades to look with a jaundiced eye at the zealots who urge them into battle. There is a scene where Baldwin and Saladin meet on a vast plain between their massed troops, and agree, man-to-man, to end the battle right then and there. Later, one of Balian's prebattle speeches to his troops sounds strangely regretful: "We fight over an offense we did not give, against those who were not alive to be offended." Time for a Truth and Reconciliation Commission?

King Kong ★ ★ ★ ★
PG-13, 187 m., 2005

Naomi Watts (Ann Darrow), Jack Black (Carl Denham), Adrien Brody (Jack Driscoll), Andy Serkis (Kong/Lumpy), Thomas Kretschmann (Captain Englehorn), Colin Hanks (Preston), Kyle Chandler (Bruce Baxter). Directed by Peter Jackson and produced by Jan Blenkin, Carolynne Cunningham, Fran Walsh, and Jackson. Screenplay by Walsh, Philippa Boyens, and Jackson, based on a story by Merian C. Cooper and Edgar Wallace.

It was beauty killed the beast.

There are astonishments to behold in Peter Jackson's new *King Kong*, but one sequence, relatively subdued, holds the key to the movie's success. Kong has captured Ann Darrow and carried her to his perch high on the mountain. He puts her down, not roughly, and then begins to roar, bare his teeth, and pound his chest. Ann, an unemployed vaudeville acrobat, somehow instinctively knows that the gorilla is not threatening her but trying to impress her by behaving as an alpha male—the king of the jungle. She doesn't know how Queen Kong would respond, but she does what she can: She goes into her stage routine, doing backflips, dancing like Chaplin, juggling three stones.

Her instincts and empathy serve her well. Kong's eyes widen in curiosity, wonder, and finally what may pass for delight. From then on, he thinks of himself as the girl's possessor and protector. She is like a tiny, beautiful toy that he has been given for his very own, and before long they are regarding the sunset together, both of them silenced by its majesty.

The scene is crucial because it removes the element of creepiness in the gorilla/girl relationship in the two earlier Kongs (1933 and 1976), creating a wordless bond that allows her to trust him. When Jack Driscoll climbs the mountain to rescue her, he finds her comfortably nestled in Kong's big palm. Ann and Kong in this movie will be threatened by dinosaurs, man-eating worms, giant bats, loathsome insects, spiders, machine guns, and the Army Air Corps, and could fall to their death into chasms on Skull Island or from the Empire State Building. But Ann will be as safe as Kong can make her, and he will protect her even from her own species.

The movie more or less faithfully follows the outlines of the original film, but this fundamental adjustment in the relationship between the beauty and the beast gives it heart, a quality the earlier film was lacking. Yes, Kong in 1933 cares for his captive, but she doesn't care so much for him. Kong was always misunderstood, but in the 2005 film there is someone who knows it. As Kong ascends the skyscraper, Ann screams not because of the gorilla but because of the attacks on the gorilla by a society that assumes he must be destroyed. The movie makes the same kind of shift involving a giant gorilla that Spielberg's *Close Encounters of the Third Kind* did when he replaced 1950s attacks on alien visitors with a very 1970s attempt to communicate with them (by 2005, Spielberg was back to attacking them in *War of the Worlds*).

King Kong is a magnificent entertainment. It is like the flowering of all the possibilities in the original classic film. Computers are used not merely to create special effects but to create style and beauty, to find a look for the film that fits its story. And the characters are not cardboard heroes or villains seen in stark outline but quirky individuals with personalities.

Consider the difference between Robert Armstrong (1933) and Jack Black (2005) as Carl Denham, the movie director who lands an unsuspecting crew on Skull Island. A Hollywood stereotype based on C. B. DeMille has been replaced by one who reminds us more of Orson Welles. And in the starring role of Ann Darrow, Naomi Watts expresses a range of emotion that Fay Wray, bless her heart, was never allowed in 1933. Never have damsels been in more distress, but Fay Wray mostly had to scream, while Watts looks into the gorilla's eyes and sees something beautiful there.

There was a stir when Jackson informed the home office that his movie would run 187 minutes. The executives had something around 140 minutes in mind, so they could turn over the audience more quickly (despite the greedy twenty minutes of paid commercials audiences now have inflicted upon them). After they saw the movie, their objections were stilled. Yes, the movie is a tad too long, and we could do without a few of the monsters and overturned elevated trains. But it is so well done that we are complaining, really, only about too much of a good thing. This is one of the great modern epics.

Jackson, fresh from his *Lord of the Rings* trilogy, wisely doesn't show the gorilla or the other creatures until more than an hour into the movie. In this he follows Spielberg, who fought off producers who wanted the shark in *Jaws* to appear virtually in the opening titles. There is an hour of anticipation, of low, ominous music, of subtle rumblings, of uneasy squints into the fog and mutinous rumblings from the crew, before the tramp steamer arrives at Skull Island—or, more accurately, is thrown against its jagged rocks in the first of many scary action sequences.

During that time we see Depression-era bread lines and soup kitchens, and meet the unemployed heroes of the film: Ann Darrow (Watts), whose vaudeville theater has closed, and who is faced with debasing herself in burlesque; Carl Denham (Black), whose work for a new movie is so unconvincing the backers want to sell it off as background footage; and Jack Driscoll (Adrien Brody), a playwright whose dreams lie off-Broadway and who thrusts fifteen pages of a first-draft screenplay at Denham and tries to disappear.

They all find themselves aboard the tramp steamer of Captain Englehorn (Thomas Kretschmann), who is persuaded to cast off just as Denham's creditors arrive on the docks in police cars. They set course for the South Seas, where Denham believes an uncharted island may hold the secret of a box-office blockbuster. On board, Ann and Jack grow close, but not *too* close, because the movie's real love story is between the girl and the gorilla.

Once they reach Skull Island, the second act of the movie is mostly a series of hair-curling special effects, as overgrown prehistoric creatures endlessly pursue the humans, occasionally killing or eating a supporting character. The bridges and logs over chasms, so important in 1933, are even better used here, especially when an assortment of humans and creatures falls in stages from a great height, resuming their deadly struggle whenever they can grab a convenient vine, rock, or tree. Two story lines are intercut: Ann and the ape, and everybody else and the other creatures.

The third act returns to Manhattan, which looks uncannily evocative and atmospheric. It isn't precisely realistic, but more of a dreamed city in which key elements swim in and out of view. There's a poetic scene where Kong and the girl find a frozen pond in Central Park, and the gorilla is lost in delight as it slides on the ice. It's in scenes like this that Andy Serkis is most useful as the actor who doesn't so much play Kong as embody him for the f/x team. He adds the body language. Some of the Manhattan effects are not completely convincing (and earlier, on Skull Island, it's strange how the fleeing humans seem to run beneath the pounding feet of the T-rexes without quite occupying the same space). But special effects do not need to be convincing if they are effective, and Jackson trades a little realism for a lot of impact and momentum. The final ascent of the Empire State Building is magnificent, and for once the gorilla seems the same size in every shot.

Although Watts makes a splendid heroine, there have been complaints that Black and Brody are not precisely hero material. Nor should they be, in my opinion. They are a director and a writer. They do not require big muscles and square jaws. What they require are strong personalities that can be transformed under stress. Denham the director clings desperately to his camera no matter what happens to him, and Driscoll the writer beats a strategic retreat before essentially rewriting his personal role in his own mind. Bruce Baxter (Kyle Chandler) is an actor who plays the movie's hero and now has to decide if he can play his role for real. And Preston (Colin Hanks) is a production assistant who, as is often the case, would be a hero if anybody would give him a chance.

The result is a surprisingly involving and rather beautiful movie—one that will appeal strongly to the primary action audience and cross over to people who have no plans to see *King Kong* but will change their minds the more they hear. I think the film even has a message, and it isn't that beauty killed the beast. It's that we feel threatened by beauty, especially when it overwhelms us, and we pay a terrible price when we try to deny its essential nature and turn it into a product, or a target. This is one of the year's best films.

Ebert's Great Movie review of the 1933 King Kong *is online at rogerebert.com.* ☞

King of the Corner ★ ★ ★ ½

R, 93 m., 2005

Peter Riegert (Leo Spivak), Eli Wallach (Sol Spivak), Isabella Rossellini (Rachel Spivak), Eric Bogosian (Rabbi Evelyn Fink), Beverly D'Angelo (Betsy Ingraham), Jake Hoffman (Ed Shifman), Rita Moreno (Inez), Harris Yulin (Pete Hargrove), Ashley Johnson (Elena Spivak). Directed by Peter Riegert and produced by Lemore Syvan. Screenplay by Riegert and Gerald Shapiro.

Leo Spivak is trapped in the Bermuda Triangle of middle age: He hates his job, his father is dying, his teenage daughter is rebelling.

He'd rather be the father, the child, or the boss—anything but Leo, the man in the middle, well paid and with a corner office, but devoting his days to market research. When he subjects instant stew to a blind taste-testing and the consumers say it tastes like dog food, they know how he feels most of the time.

King of the Corner is Peter Riegert's movie. He directed it, he cowrote it, and he stars as Leo. It's a well-chosen project for one of his particular talents, which is to play intelligent, sardonic losers. One of Leo's problems is that he knows his goals are worthless: If his market-research firm makes its money testing lousy products on dim-witted consumers, why would he even want to be the vice president?

One reason might be that Ed Shifman also wants the job. Ed (Jake Hoffman) is Leo's young protégé, or "management trainee," and scores points by stealing Leo's ideas and taking them directly to the boss (Harris Yulin). Ed will work for half the money, and won't be borderline depressive all the time. Together, they test products such as the Flaxman Voice-Altering Telephone, which answers the phones of timid widows with sturdy male voices, including Gregory Peck's.

At home, Leo is worried about his daughter, Elena (Ashley Johnson), who is staying out too late with an elusive lout named Todd who would rather honk for her than come to the door. He's worried, but not as worried as his despairing wife, Rachel (Isabella Rossellini), who seems borderline hysterical. Leo tries one of those excruciating conversations where he simultaneously advises Elena against sex and in favor of precautions. "Dad," she whines, "we're not doing anything." Uh-huh.

Every other weekend Leo flies out to Arizona, where his father, Sol (Eli Wallach), is in a retirement home. Sol was a salesman like Leo, always on the road, dragging his samples around like Willy Loman. When his wife died he moved to Arizona, found a girlfriend (Rita Moreno), and did a lot of fox-trotting before age caught up with him. Now he wants to die: "Why is it so hard for me to die? Other people do it every day." Leo has had an uneasy relationship with his father, but Leo, we begin to understand, is a good man who desperately wants to be seen as a good man: by his wife, his daughter, his father, even by Ed.

King of the Corner is not plot-driven. It's like life: just one damn thing after another. It's based on a collection of short stories named Bad Jews and Other Stories by Gerald Shapiro, who cowrote the screenplay with Riegert. Leo and his father were both bad Jews in the sense that they were not believers, although to a certain degree they were observant, if only because of family tradition. What it means to be a good Jew, or a good son or a good man, is discovered by Leo only after his father dies.

The whole movie has been leading up to this moment, and I don't want to describe it in detail because it needs to happen to you, to unfold as the logical answer to the question of why the movie exists and where it thinks it is going. I will say a brief word about a freelance rabbi named Evelyn Fink (Eric Bogosian), who begins every conversation by specifying there be no jokes about his names.

Other rabbis from his class have nice jobs with good congregations, but Rabbi Fink is still picking up a living from funeral homes that need a rabbi in a hurry. He begins to question Leo about his father at the funeral home, but when sobbing from the next room becomes a nuisance, he suggests they go somewhere else to talk. Where they go tells you a lot about the freelance rabbi.

Bogosian's role is brief, but perfectly realized. His eulogy at the funeral does what no eulogy should dare; it tells the truth. And then Leo discovers what he thinks about his father, his life, and himself. It is a scene that brings the whole movie into a poignant focus. In the "kaddish," the prayer for the dead, he becomes a good Jew at last.

A movie like this depends on the close observation of behavior. It is not so much about what the characters do as who they are, who they fear they are, and who they want to be. Leo, as played by Riegert, has reached an accommodation with life by keeping a certain dry distance from it. That's why a midmovie meeting seems so odd. He accidentally runs into the girl he lusted after in high school (Beverly D'Angelo), and that sets into motion a peculiar chain of events.

I am not sure I believe them, especially when he visits her home and meets her husband, but observe Riegert's body language. There are times, here and in his boss's office,

when he does things that are completely inexplicable. He falls to his knees, or invites a fight, or behaves with sudden recklessness. Why does he do these things? Is he crazy? No, not at all; he is reminding himself he is alive by stepping right outside the ordained limits of his life. At times like these he reminds me of the line in the Stevie Smith poem about the swimmer who is "not waving, but drowning."

Kings and Queen ★ ★ ★
NO MPAA RATING, 150 m., 2005

Emmanuelle Devos (Nora Cotterelle), Mathieu Amalric (Ismael Vuillard), Maurice Garrel (Louis Jenssens), Catherine Deneuve (Mme. Vasset), Magalie Woch (Arielle), Elsa Wolliaston (Dr. Devereux), Nathalie Boutefeu (Chloe Jenssens), Jean-Paul Roussillon (Abel Vuillard). Directed by Arnaud Desplechin and produced by Pascal Caucheteux. Screenplay by Roger Bohbot and Desplechin.

When you ask someone for the truth about themselves, you may get the truth, or part of the truth, or none of the truth, but you will certainly get what they would like you to think is the truth. This is a useful principle to keep in mind during Kings and Queen, a film that unfolds like a court case in which all of the testimony sounds like the simple truth, and none of it agrees.

We begin with a character named Nora (Emmanuelle Devos), smart, chic, an art gallery owner who buys a rare illustrated edition of Leda and the Swan as a present for her father, a famous author. We learn she has been divorced twice, will soon marry a very rich man, and has an eleven-year-old son named Elias. She visits her father, Louis (Maurice Garrel), who is in great pain; it is revealed he's dying of stomach cancer. What does he think about his daughter, and she of him? We think we know.

We meet another character, a violinist named Ismael (Mathieu Amalric). He was Nora's most recent lover. He is functional enough in a strange way, but behaves so unwisely that he finds himself in a mental institution. We sit in on his consultations with the hospital administrator (Catherine Deneuve), who is onscreen just about long enough for him to tell her, "You're very beautiful," and for her to reply, "I've been told." There is also his French-African psychiatrist (Elsa Wolliaston). Neither is much charmed by his theory that women lack souls. Ismael makes a friend at the hospital, a young woman named Arielle (Magalie Woch), who is so fond of attempting suicide that it would be a shame if she should succeed and thus bring her pastime to an end.

Nora has seemed like a decent enough woman, but what kind of a mother would not want to raise her own child? The boy's father is out of the picture (in more ways than one), and she strikes on the notion that Ismael, the former lover, is just the person to adopt Elias. Ismael loves the little boy, who loves him, and if this were a different sort of a movie such an arrangement might work.

Kings and Queen is, however, a *very* different sort of movie, in which it will not work for reasons that are explained by Ismael in a way both insightful and peculiar. Nora's father meanwhile leaves a journal entry that completely redefines everything we thought we knew about their relationship, and Ismael has an encounter with the leader of the string quartet where he thinks he is a valued member, but is mistaken. Sometimes you don't really want to know what people really think about you.

I have revealed nothing crucial, except that there are crucial revelations. The point of the movie is to call into question our personal versions of our own lives, and the emphasis on *Leda and the Swan* may be a nudge to suggest we construct myths to give a shape and meaning to lives we have lived with untidy carelessness.

The movie, directed by Arnaud Desplechin and written by him with Roger Bohbot, begins as such a straightforward portrait of ordinary life that it's unsettling to find layer after layer of reality peeled away. It opens with what seems like a conventional array of emotions, and then shows that they're like the bandages on Arielle's wrists, concealing deep desperation. The feelings of the dying father are particularly painful because of the way he has chosen to reveal them.

By the end of the film, we're a little stunned; everything seemed to be going so nicely, to be sure with the ordinary setbacks and tragedies

of life, but nothing approaching mythic, tragic, chaotic, emotional decay. You think you know someone, you think they know themselves, and suddenly you're both dealing with a complete stranger. Meanwhile, "Moon River" is playing on the sound track, but is far from a comfort.

Kinky Boots ★ ★ ★
PG-13, 94 m., 2006

Joel Edgerton (Charlie Price), Chiwetel Ejiofor (Lola/Simon), Sarah-Jane Potts (Lauren), Nick Frost (Don), Ewan Hooper (George), Linda Basset (Melanie), Jemima Rooper (Nicola). Directed by Julian Jarrold and produced by Nicholas Barton, Suzanne Mackie, and Pater Ettedgui. Screenplay by Geoff Deane and Tim Firth.

One of the gifts of movies is the way they introduce us to new actors, turning them this way and that in the light of the screen, allowing us to see the fullness of their gifts. Consider Chiwetel Ejiofor, whose first leading role was in *Dirty Pretty Things* (2002), as a Nigerian doctor reduced in London to working in a mortuary. Then came a romantic role in *Love Actually* (2003), a South African activist in *Red Dust* (2004), a space opera villain in *Serenity* (2005), and a New York detective in Spike Lee's *Inside Man* (2006). Along the way he has worked for Steven Spielberg, Woody Allen, and John Singleton (as a vicious mobster in *Four Brothers* in 2005) and has done Shakespeare and *The Canterbury Tales* for TV. Born in London in 1974, he works easily with British, American, and Nigerian accents.

Now he plays a drag queen in *Kinky Boots*. It is a performance all the more striking because he doesn't play any kind of drag queen I've ever seen in the movies. He plays the role not as a man pretending to be a woman, and not as a woman trapped in a man's body, and not as a parody of a woman, and not as a gay man, but as a *drag queen*, period: Lola, a tall, athletic performer in thigh-high red boots who rules the stage of a drag club as if she were born there, and who is a pretty good singer, too. In preparing for the role, Ejiofor must have decided not to simper, not to preen, not to mince, but to belt out songs with great good humor that dares the audience to take exception. If "simper," "preen," and "mince" are stereotypical words, well, then most drag queens, including Lola's backup dancers, are stereotypical performers. Not Lola.

With *Kinky Boots* we find ourselves watching another one of those British comedies in which unconventional sex is surrounded by a conventional story. The film's other hero is Charlie Price (Joel Edgerton), whose father dies and leaves him a Northampton shoe factory that is nearly bankrupt because men aren't buying traditional dress shoes. Through a coincidence we must accept, Charlie meets Lola, who complains that women's shoes don't stand up to the weight of a full-sized man in drag. Charlie thinks maybe his factory could supply a proper pair of boots with stiletto heels for Lola, and he lovingly crafts the boots himself, only to hear Lola respond: "Please, God, tell me I have not inspired something burgundy." What does he prefer? "Red! Red!"

Lola comes to Northampton to design a line of footwear, receiving a chilly reception from some of the union men in the factory, especially the gay-hating Don (Nick Frost). Don is the reigning arm-wrestling champion in a local pub, and of course it is only a matter of time until Don and Lola are elbow to elbow in a showdown. Meanwhile, Charlie's snotty fiancée, Nicola (Jemima Rooper), is a real estate agent hoping to recycle his factory into condos, while the plucky shoe worker Lauren (Sarah-Jane Potts) believes in Charlie, Lola, and the factory.

Drag queens are more mainstream in British entertainment than they are in America, even if we exclude Dame Edna Everage, who seems to be in drag not as a man, not as a woman, but as a self-contained gender. The movie is in the naughty-but-nice British tradition in which characters walk on the wild side but never seem to do anything else there. If Lola, whose birth name is Simon, has sex of any kind in *Kinky Boots*, it is offscreen. I was reminded of the wholesome kinkiness of *Personal Services* (1987), Terry Jones's comedy about Cynthia Payne, the "luncheon voucher madam" who treated retired gents to naughty noontime lingerie shows, heavy on whips, boots, and corsets. Some of them paid with the luncheon vouchers they received as old-age pensioners. A recent example of this innocent genre is *Mrs. Henderson Presents,* in which Dame Judi Dench runs the most wholesome strip club in Soho.

Kinky Boots has few surprises, unless you seriously expect the factory to go bankrupt. The climax comes at the annual shoe show in Milan, where last-minute developments unfold right on schedule; having provided us with Lola, the movie is conventional in all other departments. But Ejiofor's performance as Lola shows an actor doing what not every actor can do: taking a character bundled with stereotypes, clearing them out of the way, and finding a direct line to who the character really is. Just in the way she walks in those kinky red boots, Lola makes an argument that no words could possibly improve upon.

Note: It's pronounced Chew-i-tell Edge-o-for. Kinky Boots is based on a true story. Check it out at www.divine.co.uk.

Kinsey ★ ★ ★ ★
R, 118 m., 2004

Liam Neeson (Alfred Kinsey), Laura Linney (Clara McMillen), Chris O'Donnell (Wardell Pomeroy), Peter Sarsgaard (Clyde Martin), Timothy Hutton (Paul Gebhard), John Lithgow (Alfred Sequine Kinsey), Tim Curry (Thurman Rice), Oliver Platt (Herman Wells), Dylan Baker (Alan Gregg). Directed by Bill Condon and produced by Gail Mutrux. Screenplay by Condon.

Everybody's sin is nobody's sin. And everybody's crime is no crime at all.

Talk like that made people really mad at Dr. Alfred C. Kinsey. When his first study of human sexual behavior was published in 1947, it was more or less universally agreed that masturbation would make you go blind or insane, that homosexuality was an extremely rare deviation, that most sex was within marriage, and most married couples limited themselves to the missionary position.

Kinsey interviewed thousands of Americans over a period of years, and concluded: Just about everybody masturbates, 37 percent of men have had at least one homosexual experience, there is a lot of premarital and extramarital sex, and the techniques of many couples venture well beyond the traditional male-superior position.

It is ironic that Kinsey's critics insist to this day that he brought about this behavior by his report, when in fact all he did was discover that the behavior was already a reality. There's controversy about his sample, his methods, and his statistics, but ongoing studies have confirmed his basic findings. The decriminalization of homosexuality was a direct result of Kinsey's work, although there are still nine states where oral sex is against the law, even within a heterosexual marriage.

Kinsey, a fascinating biography of the Indiana University professor, centers on a Liam Neeson performance that makes one thing clear: Kinsey was an impossible man. He studied human behavior but knew almost nothing about human nature, and was often not aware that he was hurting feelings, offending people, making enemies, or behaving strangely. He had tunnel vision, and it led him heedlessly toward his research goals without prudent regard for his image, his family and associates, and even the sources of his funding.

Neeson plays Kinsey as a man goaded by inner drives. He began his scientific career by collecting and studying 1 million gall wasps, and when he switched to human sexuality he seemed to regard people with much the same objectivity that he brought to insects. Maybe that made him a good interviewer; he was so manifestly lacking in prurient interest that his subjects must have felt they were talking to a confessor imported from another planet. Only occasionally is he personally involved, as when he interviews his strict and difficult father (John Lithgow) about his sex life, and gains a new understanding of the man and his unhappiness.

The movie shows Kinsey arriving at sex research more or less by accident, after a young couple come to him for advice. Kinsey and his wife, Clara McMillen (Laura Linney), were both virgins on their wedding night (he was twenty-six, she twenty-three) and awkwardly unsure about what to do, but they worked things out, as couples had to do in those days. Current sexual thinking was summarized in a book named *Ideal Marriage: Its Physiology and Technique,* by Theodoor Hendrik van de Velde, a volume whose title I did not need to double-check because I remember so vividly finding it hidden in the basement rafters of my childhood home. Van de Velde was so cautious in his advice that many of those using the book must have succeeded in reproducing only by skipping a few pages.

One of the movie's best scenes shows Kinsey giving the introductory lecture for a new class on human sexuality, and making bold assertions about sexual behavior that were shocking in 1947. His book became a bestseller, Kinsey was for a decade one of the most famous men in the world, and he became the target of congressional witch-hunters who were convinced his theories were somehow linked with the Communist conspiracy. That patriotic middle Americans had contributed to Kinsey's statistics did not seem to impress them, as they pressured the Rockefeller Foundation to withdraw its funding. One of the quiet amusements in the film is the way the foundation's Herman Wells (Oliver Platt) wearily tries to prevent Kinsey from becoming his own worst enemy through tactless and provocative statements.

The movie has been written and directed by Bill Condon, who shows us a Kinsey who is a better scientist than a social animal. Kinsey objectified sex to such an extent that he actually encouraged his staff to have sex with one another and record their findings; this is not, as anyone could have advised him, an ideal way to run a harmonious office. Kinsey didn't believe in secrets, and he brings his wife to tears by fearlessly and tactlessly telling her all of his. Laura Linney's performance as Clara McMillen is a model of warmth and understanding in the face of daily impossibilities; she loved Kinsey and understood him, acted as a buffer for him, and has an explosively funny line: "I think I might like that."

Kinsey evolved from lecturing to hectoring as he grew older, insisting on his theories in statements of unwavering certainty. His behavior may have been influenced by unwise use of barbiturates, at a time when their danger was not fully understood; he slept little, drove himself too hard, alienated colleagues. And having found that people are rarely exclusively homosexual or heterosexual but exist somewhere between zero and six on the straight-to-gay scale, he found himself settling somewhere around three or four. Condon, who is homosexual, regards Kinsey's bisexuality with the kind of objectivity that Kinsey would have approved; the film, like Kinsey, is more interested in what people do than why.

The strength of *Kinsey* is finally in the clarity it brings to its title character. It is fascinating to meet a complete original, a person of intelligence and extremes. I was reminded of Russell Crowe's work in *A Beautiful Mind* (2001), also the story of a man whose brilliance was contained within narrow channels. *Kinsey* also captures its times, and a political and moral climate of fear and repression; it is instructive to remember that as recently as 1959, the University of Illinois fired a professor for daring to suggest, in a letter to the student paper, that students consider sleeping with each other before deciding to get married. Now universities routinely dispense advice on safe sex and contraception. Of course there is opposition, now as then, but the difference is that Kinsey redefined what has to be considered normal sexual behavior.

Kiss Kiss, Bang Bang ★ ★ ½
R, 103 m., 2005

Robert Downey Jr. (Harry Lockhart), Val Kilmer (Gay Perry), Michelle Monaghan (Harmony Faith Lane), Corbin Bernsen (Harlan Dexter). Directed by Shane Black and produced by Joel Silver. Screenplay by Black.

"All you need to make a movie is a girl and a gun," as I so tirelessly quote Jean-Luc Godard. Pauline Kael refined that insight after seeing a movie poster in Italy that translated as "Kiss Kiss Bang Bang." These four words, she wrote, "are perhaps the briefest statement imaginable of the basic appeal of the movies. The appeal is what attracts us and ultimately makes us despair when we begin to understand how seldom movies are more than this."

Shane Black has dealt with lots of girls and guns in his screenplays, including the *Lethal Weapon* pictures, *The Long Kiss Goodnight*, and *Last Action Hero*. Now comes his directorial debut, *Kiss Kiss, Bang Bang*, to which he adds a comma and a lot more. After Tony Scott's *Domino*, which has a narrator who says, "I'll never tell you what it all meant," here's another narrator who chats with the audience. His parting words: "Don't worry. I saw *Lord of the Rings*; I'm not gonna have the movie end twenty times."

Both of these movies may be action retreads of Charlie Kaufman's screenplay for *Adaptation*, in which the process of writing the screenplay becomes part of the story. *Domino* makes next to no sense but is shot in a style that makes sense irrelevant. *Kiss Kiss, Bang Bang* is slowed down and straightened out just enough so that we can see it makes no sense. Does that matter? Two answers: 1) No, when what is happening on the screen works as itself, without regard for the plot, and 2) Yes, when we can see that the movie is plainly spinning its wheels.

The movie is narrated by Harry Lockhart (Robert Downey Jr.), a would-be actor from New York who moves to Los Angeles and finds himself taking private-eye lessons from Gay Perry (Val Kilmer), a gay detective. We could play a version of the Kevin Bacon game with this movie, because Downey also starred in the movie version of *The Singing Detective* (2003), also about a detective who narrates his own story.

Kiss Kiss, Bang Bang is made for a fairly specific audience; it helps if you are familiar with the private-eye genre in general and the works of Raymond Chandler in particular (the movie has five chapter headings, all taken from Chandler's titles). But do the titles come from Harry Lockhart, or do they exist outside his mind and suggest that Black's screenplay has another level of comment on top? That would be roughly like the subtitles in *Domino*, which have a different point of view than the narration.

But now the review is spinning its wheels. *Kiss Kiss, Bang Bang* contains a lot of comedy and invention but doesn't much benefit from its clever style. The characters and plot are so promising that maybe Black should have backed off and told the story deadpan, instead of mugging so shamelessly for laughs. It could still be a comedy, but it wouldn't always be digging its elbow into our ribs. I kept wanting to add my own subtitles: "I get it! I get it!"

The film begins with Harry's stage debut as a child magician who saws a girl in half as she screams, "I'm going to be an actress!" Flash forward to years later in Los Angeles, where he meets Gay Perry (get it?), who agrees to tutor him in private-eyeing and sends him to a Hollywood party where he meets that very same girl, Harmony Faith Lane (Michelle Monaghan). Maybe it's inevitable she turns up here; Harry's narration observes of the women in Los Angeles: "It's like someone took America by the East Coast and shook it, and all the normal girls managed to hang on."

Then ensue events so complex that Harry loses a finger not once but twice, which is bad, because fingers have fingerprints, although the danger of being fingerprinted is greatly reduced by the manner of his losing the finger for the second time. This is in the process of investigating a series of murders, which he does primarily to impress Harmony Faith Lane.

The movie might reward deep textual study; consider that in the chapter named after Chandler's *The Lady in the Lake*, a gun is thrown into the lake, giving us the girl-and-the-gun formula in a form so subtle that right now you are wondering why I don't simply cave in and tell you if the movie is any good or not.

Well, yes and no. See above. I've seen the movie twice, foolishly thinking I might understand it better the second time. Understanding it is not the point. The dialogue exists not to explain anything or advance the story. It exists entirely in order to be dialogue. When the characters speak, it is an example of their verbal style, which is half film noir and half smart-ass. The dialogue, and just about everything else in the movie, is there for its own sake. Like a smorgasbord, it makes no attempt at coherence. Put a little of everything on your plate and you'll be stuffed by the end, but what did you eat?

I dunno. I liked Downey's pose that he was writing the movie as he was living it, and Kilmer's gay detective, who functions as a parody of gay parodies. But did I need to see it twice? Not really. Do you need to see it once? Not exactly.

Kontroll ★ ★ ★ ½
R, 105 m., 2005

Sandor Csanyi (Bulcsu), Zoltan Mucsi (Professor), Csaba Pindroch (Muki), Sandor Badar (Lecso), Zsolt Nagy (Tibi), Bence Matyassy (Bootsie), Gyozo Szabo (Shadow), Eszter Balla (Szofi). Directed by Nimrod Antal and produced by Tamas Hutlassa. Screenplay by Jim Adler and Antal.

On the London underground you sometimes realize the train has roared through an abandoned station, past a ghost platform illuminated only from the train windows; you get a murky glimpse of advertising posters from decades ago. In *Kontroll*, which takes place entirely within the Budapest subway system, such a subterranean world has a permanent population.

The trains are run on an honor system, and inspectors with red-and-black armbands prowl the underground, asking riders to show their tickets. The passengers descend from the sunshine to be accosted by kontrollers who are slovenly, unkempt, sallow-faced, with a certain madness in their eyes. Many riders consider the trains to be free and treat the inspectors like vagrants asking for a handout.

It is strange to work entirely under the ground in noisy, hostile, rat-infested caverns, and even stranger for those like the kontroller Bulcsu (Sandor Csanyi), who never ever returns to the surface. Once he was an architect who dreamed of buildings that would reach to the sky, but now he has retreated to a waking grave, sleeps on benches, eats the indescribable food vended in the system, and heads a crew of three other inspectors as haunted as he is.

Theirs is a miserable job, made more unbearable by the periodic visits of their boss, who descends from light and comfort to urge greater vigilance. The kontrollers don't really care if people are riding free; what they care about is meeting a daily quota of deadbeats in a duel of wills. They risk their lives, they engage in reckless chases and fights, not because they care about the fares, but because it is the price they pay to continue their melancholy existence.

There is a killer in the system, a hooded figure who emerges from the shadows to push passengers in front of trains. He seems to know the underground as well as the kontrollers, and, like the Phantom of the Opera, to occupy his own hidden world. The security cameras see only his hood. Bulcsu and his crew are faced with daily train delays because of jumpers, and while they can't blame those who were pushed, they wonder why suicides don't have the decency to kill themselves with less inconvenience to others.

Kontroll is the first feature by Nimrod Antal, born of Hungarian parents, raised in Los Angeles, returning to Budapest for this haunting film shot during the five hours every night when the subway shuts down. His film opens with a statement read by a self-conscious spokesman for the subway system, explaining that Antal was granted permission to film with some reluctance, and with the hope that audiences will realize the film is only symbolic. Is this spokesman real or fictional? Certainly the symbolism is more Kafkaesque than political, as the kontrollers apply logic (you must have a ticket) to an illogical situation (riders know they will rarely be asked to show one). We feel we've entered one of those postnuclear science-fiction societies where the surface has become uninhabitable, and a few survivors cling to subterranean life.

Bulcsu's colleagues include a new recruit named Tibi (Zsolt Nagy), who is trying to learn a job he has not yet realized is his doom. There is the Professor (Zoltan Mucsi), who seems to consider kontrolling a holy vocation, and Muki (Csaba Pindroch), who is a narcoleptic, a dangerous condition when you work next to subway tracks.

One day a bear wanders into the system. This is a young woman named Szofi (Eszter Balla), who always wears a bear suit, perhaps because she is employed as a bear, or more likely because it is her fashion choice. She keeps an eye out for her father, an alcoholic train driver who possibly thinks he sees bears and is occasionally comforted to find out he is correct. Bulcsu begins to have feelings for the bear.

In a world denied respect by society, the inhabitants seek it from each other. Bulcsu's crew stages competitions with other crews, most dangerously at the end of the day, when they challenge each other to foot races down the tracks between stations, just before the last train of the day. The point is not so much to win as to survive. That is also perhaps the point of the film.

Kontroll is the first work by a director who is clearly gifted, and who has found a way to make a full-bore action movie on a limited budget; there are no special effects in the movie, all of the trains are real, and I gather that at one point when we see Bulcsu barely crawling onto a platform ahead of a moving train, he is really doing exactly that.

Nimrod Antal has a feeling for action, but what distinguishes *Kontroll* is his control of characters and mood. He could have given us a standard group of misfits, but his characters are all peculiar in inward, secretive ways, suggesting needs they would rather not reveal. His visuals create a haunted house where the lights are off in most of the rooms, and there may indeed be a monster in the closet.

Kung Fu Hustle ★ ★ ★
R, 99 m., 2005

Stephen Chow (Sing), Yuen Wah (Landlord), Yuen Qiu (Landlady), Leung Siu Lung (The Beast), Huang Sheng Yi (Fong), Chan Kwok Kwan (Brother Sum), Lam Tze Chung (Sing's Sidekick), Dong Zhi Hua (Doughnut), Chiu Chi Ling (Tailor). Directed by Stephen Chow and produced by Chow, Po Chu Chui, and Jeffrey Lau. Screenplay by Tsang Kan Cheong, Chow, Lola Huo, and Chan Man Keung.

There is an opinion in some quarters that martial arts movies are violent. Many are, to be sure, but the best ones have the same relationship to violence that Astaire and Rogers have to romance: Nobody believes they take it seriously, but it gives them an excuse for some wonderful choreography.

Lurking beneath the surface of most good martial arts movies is a comedy. Sometimes it bubbles up to the top, as in Stephen Chow's *Kung Fu Hustle*. The joke is based not so much on humor as on delight: The characters have overcome the laws of gravity and physics. To be able to leap into the air, spin in a circle, and kick six, seven, eight, nine enemies before landing in a graceful crouch is enormously gratifying.

Realists grumble that such things are impossible. Well, of course they are. The thing about Astaire and Rogers is that they were really doing it, in long unbroken takes, and we could see that they were. Stephen Chow uses concealed wires, special effects, trick camera angles, trampolines, and anything else he can think of. We know it, and he knows we know it. But the trickery doesn't diminish his skill, because despite all the wires and effects in the world, a martial arts actor must be a superb athlete. Hang your average movie star on the end of a wire and he'll look like he's just been reeled in by the Pequod.

Kung Fu Hustle is Chow's seventh film as a director and sixty-first job as an actor, counting TV. He is forty-two years old, and has been busy. His only other film seen by me is *Shaolin Soccer* (2002), the top-grossing action comedy in Hong Kong history. Purchased by Miramax, it was held off the market for two years, cut by thirty minutes, and undubbed: Yes, Harvey Weinstein replaced the English sound track with subtitles. The movie opened a year ago, inspiring a review in which I gave my most rational defense of the relativity theory of star ratings.

Now comes *Kung Fu Hustle*. This is the kind of movie where you laugh occasionally and have a silly grin most of the rest of the time. It must have taken Chow a superhuman effort to avoid singing a subtitled version of *Let Me Entertain You*—or, no, I've got a better example—of *Make 'em Laugh*, the Donald O'Connor number in *Singin' in the Rain*. In that one, O'Connor crashed into boards and bricks, wrestled with a dummy, ran up one wall and through another one, and sang the whole time. Stephen Chow doesn't sing, but he's channeling the same spirit.

The movie is centered in a Shanghai slum named Pig Sty Alley. It's ruled by a dumpy landlady (Yuen Qiu) who marches around in slippers and has one of those cartoon cigarettes that always stays in her mouth no matter what happens. Shanghai is terrorized by the Axe Gang, which mostly leaves Pig Sty Alley alone because the pickings are too slim. But when counterfeit gang members are confronted by neighborhood kung fu fighters, the real gang moves in to take revenge. The Axe

Gang doesn't exactly blend in: They all wear black suits and top hats, and carry axes. That'll make you stand out. I am reminded of Jack Lemmon's story about the time he saw Klaus Kinski buying a hatchet at Ace Hardware.

The war between the Pig Stygians and the Axe Gang is an excuse for a series of sequences in which the stylized violence reaches a kind of ecstasy. Of course nothing we see is possible, but the movie doesn't even pretend it's possible: Maybe everyone is having matching hallucinations. One of the jokes is that completely unlikely characters, including the landlady and local middle-aged tradesmen, turn out to be better warriors than the professionals.

Chow not only stars and directs, but cowrote and coproduced. We get the sense that his comedies are generated in the Buster Keaton spirit, with gags being worked out on the spot and everybody in orbit around the star, who is physically skilled, courageous, and funny. Chow plays Sing, also the name of his character in *Shaolin Soccer* and at least six other movies. This time he's an imposter, pretending to be an Axe Gang member in order to run a shakedown racket in Pig Sty Alley. Imagine how inconvenient it is when the real Axe Gang shows up and he's in trouble with everyone. By the end of the movie, he's going one-on-one with The Beast (Leung Siu Lung), in a kung fu extravaganza. The joke is that most of what Sing knows about kung fu he learned by reading a useless booklet sold to him by a con man when he was a child.

It's possible you don't like martial arts movies, whether funny or not. Then why have you read this far? Or, you prefer the elegant and poetic epics like *Crouching Tiger, Hidden Dragon* or *House of Flying Daggers*. Those are not qualities you will find in *Kung Fu Hustle*. When I saw it at Sundance, I wrote that it was "like Jackie Chan and Buster Keaton meet Quentin Tarantino and Bugs Bunny." You see how worked up you can get, watching a movie like this.

L

Ladder 49 ★ ★ ★ ½
PG-13, 120 m., 2004

Joaquin Phoenix (Jack Morrison), John Travolta (Mike Kennedy), Morris Chestnut (Tommy Drake), Jacinda Barrett (Linda Morrison), Robert Patrick (Lenny Richter), Jay Hernandez (Keith Perez), Kevin Daniels (Don Miller), Kevin Chapman (Frank McKinny), Balthazar Getty (Ray Gauquin). Directed by Jay Russell and produced by Casey Silver. Screenplay by Lewis Colick.

The best compliment I can pay *Ladder 49* is to say that it left me feeling thoughtful and sad. I was surprised it had such an effect. I walked in expecting an action picture with heroic firemen charging into burning buildings for last-minute rescues. *Ladder 49* has the heroes and the fires and the rescues, but it's not really about them. It's about character, and about the kind of man who risks his life for a living. And it's about work, about what kind of a job it is to be a fireman.

The movie stars Joaquin Phoenix as Jack Morrison, a fireman assigned to search and rescue. John Travolta plays Kennedy, his chief. The other guys at the firehouse include Tommy (Morris Chestnut), Don (Kevin Daniels), Lenny (Robert Patrick), and Frank (Kevin Chapman).

We see them in action before we really meet them. A warehouse is on fire, and people are trapped on the twelfth floor. There's grain dust in the building that could explode at any moment. Jack and his team charge into the building, and Jack finds a survivor on the twelfth floor—which is too high for the cherry pickers or ladders to reach. "Stick with me. I'll take care of you," he tells the guy, and lowers him out a window on a rope until firemen below can grab him, calm his panic, and return him safe to earth.

The grain dust blows. Jack falls through a hole in the center of the building and lands a few floors below, stunned, half-buried by debris. Eventually he regains consciousness and is able to radio Travolta, who coordinates the rescue effort. It is clear that there's a limited window of opportunity to save Jack before the building kills him.

The movie flashes back to Jack's first day as a rookie in the fire department, and we understand what the structure will be: His present danger will be intercut with the story of his life as a fireman. So far, everything in *Ladder 49* has been basic and predictable, by the numbers, although the special effects and stunt work inside the burning building were convincing. But as the movie explores Jack's life, it shows an attention and sensitivity that elevates the flashbacks from the usual biographical stops along the way.

Yes, he's the victim of practical jokes. Yes, he does a lot of after-hours drinking with his firehouse buddies, chugging beer competitively. Yes, he and a buddy pick up two girls in the supermarket, and the one named Linda (Jacinda Barrett) becomes his wife. And they have kids. And some of his friends have bad things happen to them during fires. And he volunteers for search and rescue. And Linda worries about him, and dreads the day a red fire chief's car may pull up in front of her house to deliver a man with dreadful news.

As I list these scenes, you may think you can guess what they contain and how they play, but you would be wrong. The director, Jay Russell, working from Lewis Colick's screenplay, brings a particular humanity to the scenes; I am reminded of how his movie *My Dog Skip* transcended the basic elements of a boy and his dog. The marriage of Jack and Linda is not a movie marriage, but a convincing one with troubles and problems and love that endures. Linda is not one more of those tiresome wives in action movies, who appear only to complain that the hero should spend more time with his family. She is Jack's partner in their family, and a source of his pride and courage at work. And Jack's relationship with Chief Kennedy (Travolta) is complex, too, because Kennedy worries about him, and is not at all sure he should allow him to volunteer for search and rescue.

After Jack has lost one friend and another has been badly burned, Kennedy offers him a transfer to a safe job downtown. Jack stays where he is, not because he is a fearless hero, but because it is his job, and he is faithful to it. There is the sense that the men of Ladder 49 go into danger and take risks largely out of loyalty to their comrades. Soldiers in battle, it is said, fight not so much for the flag or for a cause as for their buddies, to not let them down. Russell allows small details to accumulate into the subtle but crucial fact that the camaraderie of the firehouse is what motivates these men above all.

The effort to rescue Jack is desperate but skilled. Diagrams are used to figure out where he must be inside the building. He gives them clues based on what he can see. Kennedy asks if he can get to a brick wall, knock a hole in it, and crawl through it to a room they think they can reach. He thinks he can.

The movie is not about a dying man whose life passes before his eyes, but about a man who saved a life and put himself in danger, and how he got to that place in his life, and what his life and family mean to him. Because it is attentive to these human elements, *Ladder 49* draws from the action scenes instead of depending on them. Phoenix, Travolta, Jacinda Barrett, and the others are given characters with dimension, so that what happens depends on their decisions, not on the plot.

As I said, I was surprisingly affected by the film. After I left the screening, I walked a while by the river, and sat and thought, and was happy not to have anything that had to be done right away.

Ladies in Lavender ★ ★
PG-13, 103 m., 2005

Judi Dench (Ursula Widdington), Maggie Smith (Janet Widdington), Daniel Bruhl (Andrea Marowski), Miriam Margolyes (Dorcas), Natascha McElhone (Olga Danilof), David Warner (Dr. Francis Mead). Directed by Charles Dance and produced by Nicolas Brown, Elizabeth Karlsen, and Nik Powell. Screenplay by Dance.

Ladies in Lavender assembles those two great dames, Judi Dench and Maggie Smith, and sends them off to play sisters sharing a cozy little cottage on the Cornwall coast. That is an inspiration. What they do there is a disappointment. Their days are spent gardening and having tea, their evenings with knitting and the wireless, until one dark and stormy night a strange young man is washed up on their shore.

This is Andrea Marowski (Daniel Bruhl). He is handsome, sweet, and speaks hardly a word of English. But Janet Widdington (Maggie Smith) discovers he has some German, and unearths her ancient textbook. Soon she and her sister, Ursula (Dench), discover that Andrea is Polish, a violinist, and a gifted one at that. What they do not discover is how he happened to be in the sea on that stormy night, which is the very thing we want to know. There is no word of a shipwreck. Perhaps he is a magical creature, left over from *The Tempest*.

The sisters have lived in calm and contentment for many years. Janet is a widow; Ursula has never married, and probably never had sex, although from the way she regards Andrea she may be thinking it's never too late to start. Ursula becomes possessive of the handsome young man; Janet observes this, doesn't like it, and mostly but not entirely keeps her thoughts to herself.

Andrea is visited by good Dr. Mead (David Warner), who advises bed rest, although perhaps not as much as Andrea chooses to enjoy; it is pleasant, watching the sun stream in through the window and being served tea by the sisters' crusty maid, Dorcas (Miriam Margolyes), who was born to play Doll Tearsheet. Eventually, however, Andrea ventures outside and catches the eye of Olga Danilof (Natascha McElhone), a landscape painter; she is not a very good painter, but she is a beautiful young woman, speaks German, and is soon spending time with Andrea while Ursula goes into a quiet and tactful form of anguish. Of course, coincidentally, Olga happens to possess the key to Andrea's fate as a violinist.

There is a moment's suspense when Dr. Mead, who also fancies Olga, ventures the suggestion that Olga and Andrea, chattering away in German, might be spies observing coastal activities; in which case, apparently, he thinks an appropriate punishment would be for Andrea to go to prison and Olga to fall in love with the doctor. It is 1936, and Europe seems on the brink of war, although for the Widdington sisters that's not much of a concern. The local police chief drops by for a chat, is satisfied, and leaves. He is so polite that if they had been spies, I wonder if he would have wanted to spoil such a nice day by mentioning it.

Ladies in Lavender, directed by the actor Charles Dance, is perfectly sweet and civilized, and ends with one of those dependable scenes where—gasp!—look who's in the audience at the concert! It's a pleasure to watch Smith and

Dench together; their acting is so natural it could be breathing. But Daniel Bruhl is tiresome as Andrea; he has no dark side, no anger, no fierceness, and although we eventually discover why he left Poland, we do not know if it was from passion or convenience. He is an ideal dinner guest; the kind of person you are happy enough to have at the table, but could not endure on a three-day train journey.

I am reminded of Lindsay Anderson's *The Whales of August* (1987), also about two elderly sisters in a house on a coast. That one starred Bette Davis and Lillian Gish, who engaged in subtle verbal gamesmanship, both as characters and as actors. It is probably true that we should not attend a movie about old ladies in a big old house expecting much in the way of great drama (although *Whatever Happened to Baby Jane?* has its moments), but *The Whales of August* had a fire that the relaxed *Ladies in Lavender* is entirely lacking.

In the category of movies about older women risking a last chance on love, you could hardly improve on *A Month by the Lake* (1995), with Vanessa Redgrave falling for, and being dropped by, Edward Fox. We want her to win her man, and the problem with *Ladies in Lavender* is that although Ursula can kid herself, we can't.

The Ladykillers ★ ★ ½
R, 104 m., 2004

Tom Hanks (Professor G. H. Dorr), Marlon Wayans (Gawain MacSam), J. K. Simmons (Garth Pancake), Tzi Ma (The General), Ryan Hurst (Lump Hudson), Irma P. Hall (Marva Munson). Directed by Joel Coen and Ethan Coen and produced by Ethan Coen, Joel Coen, Tom Jacobson, Barry Sonnenfeld, and Barry Josephson. Screenplay by Joel Coen and Ethan Coen, based on *The Ladykillers*, written by William Rose.

The genius of Alec Guinness was in his anonymity. He could play a character so ingratiating that he ingratiated himself right into invisibility, and that was the secret of his work in *The Ladykillers*, a droll 1955 British comedy that also starred Peter Sellers and Herbert Lom. Now comes a Coen brothers remake with Tom Hanks in the Guinness role, and although Hanks would be the right actor to play a low-key deceiver, the Coens have made his character so bizarre that we get distracted just by looking at him.

Hanks plays Goldthwait Higginson Dorr, who claims to be a professor of Latin and Greek, who dresses like Colonel Sanders, and who seems to be channeling Tennessee Williams, Edgar Allen Poe, and Vincent Price. As in the original, he rents a room from a sweet little old lady, and plans to use her home as a base for a criminal scheme. In this case, he and four associates will tunnel from her root cellar into the cash room of a nearby casino named the Bandit Queen. The professor explains to the little old lady that the five of them are a classical music ensemble who need a quiet place to practice; they play music on a boom box to cover the sounds of their tunneling.

The other crooks represent the extremes of available casting choices; all of them, like the professor, are over the top in a way rarely seen outside Looney Tunes. Gawain MacSam (Marlon Wayans) is a trash-talking hip-hop janitor at the casino; Garth Pancake (J. K. Simmons) is a mustachioed explosives expert who asphyxiates a dog in an unfortunate gas mask experiment; the General (Tzi Ma) is a chain-smoker who once apparently specialized in tunnels for the Viet Cong; and Lump (Ryan Hurst) is a dimwitted muscle man who will do the hard labor.

The little old lady is named Marva Munson, and she is played by Irma P. Hall in the one completely successful comic performance in the movie. Yes, she's a caricature, too: a churchgoing widow who doesn't allow smoking in the house, has regular conversations with the portrait of her dead husband, and is not shy about complaining to the sheriff. But her character is exaggerated from a recognizable human base, while the others are comic-strip oddities.

Even Marva is sometimes betrayed by the Coens, who give her speeches that betray themselves as too clever by half (protesting a neighbor's loud "hippity-hop" music, she complains that the songs use the n-word "2,000 years after Jesus! Thirty years after Martin Luther King! In the Age of Montel!" If she'd said "Oprah," it might have been her talking, but when she says "Montel" you can feel the Coens' elbow digging in your side. There's also a subplot involving Mrs. Munson's generous donations to Bob Jones University; she is apparently unaware of its antediluvian attitudes about race. There are too many moments where dialogue seems so un-matched to the characters that they seem to be victims of a drive-by ventriloquist.

Now let me say that although the movie never jells, its oddness keeps it from being boring. Tom Hanks provides such an eccentric performance that it's fun just to watch him behaving—to listen to speeches that coil through endless, florid ornamentation. That the purpose of a criminal in such a situation would be to become invisible—as Guinness, despite the bad teeth, tried to do in the 1955 film—escapes the Coens. But I am importing unwanted logic into a narrative that manifestly is uninterested in such fineries of specification, as the professor might declare. There are some big laughs in the movie, some of them involving body disposal and another one as Garth Pancake demonstrates the safe handling of explosives. When Mrs. Munson invites the church ladies over for tea and invites the nice gentlemen in the basement to play something, Hanks offers a poem by Poe as a consolation prize, and rises to a peak of mannered sublimity. As the church ladies gaze in speechless astonishment at his performance, I was reminded of a day in the 1960s I was in a working-class pub in a poor neighborhood of Sligo, in the west of Ireland. The TV set over the bar was tuned to *The Galloping Gourmet*. The regulars stared at him speechlessly, until finally one said: "Will you *look* at that fellow!" That's how they feel about Professor G. H. Dorr.

There's a lot of high-spirited gospel music in the movie, which brings the plot to a halt for a concert in Mrs. Munson's church. It's wonderful as music, but not really connected to the movie, unlike the music in the Coens' *O Brother, Where Art Thou?* For that matter, the four- and twelve-letter dialogue of the Wayans character fits awkwardly into a story where no one else talks that way; his potty mouth also wins the film an otherwise completely unnecessary R rating.

What the movie finally lacks, I think, is modesty. The original *Ladykillers* was one of a group of small, inspired comedies made at the low-rent Ealing Studios near London, where Alec Guinness was the resident genius; his other titles from the period include *Kind Hearts and Coronets* (1949), *The Lavender Hill Mob* (1950), and *The Man in the White Suit* (1951). These were self-effacing films; much of their humor grew out of the contrast between nefarious schemes and low-key, almost apologetic behavior.

The Coens' *Ladykillers*, on the other hand, is always wildly signaling for us to notice it. Not content to be funny, it wants to be *funny!* Have you ever noticed that the more a comedian wears funny hats, the less funny he is? The old and new *Ladykillers* play like a contest between Buster Keaton and Soupy Sales.

The Lake House ★ ★ ★ ½
PG, 105 m., 2006

Keanu Reeves (Alex Wyler), Sandra Bullock (Kate Forster), Christopher Plummer (Simon Wyler), Ebon Moss-Bachrach (Henry Wyler), Dylan Walsh (Morgan), Shohreh Aghdashloo (Anna). Directed by Alejandro Agresti and produced by Doug Davison and Roy Lee. Screenplay by David Auburn.

The Lake House tells the story of a romance that spans years but involves only a few kisses. It succeeds despite being based on two paradoxes: time travel, and the ability of two people to have conversations that are, under the terms established by the film, impossible. Neither of these problems bothered me in the slightest. Take time travel: I used to get distracted by its logical flaws and contradictory time lines. Now, in my wisdom, I have decided to simply accept it as a premise, no questions asked. A time-travel story works on emotional, not temporal, logic.

In *The Lake House*, it works like this: A woman (Sandra Bullock) lives in a glass house built on stilts over a lake north of Chicago. She is moving out and leaves a note for the next tenant (Keanu Reeves). He reads the note and sends a strange response to the address she supplies: He thinks she has the wrong house because, "No one has lived in this house for years." She writes back to disagree. It develops that he thinks it is 2004 and she thinks it is 2006, and perhaps she moved in after he left, instead of moving out before he arrived, although that wouldn't fit with—but never mind.

This correspondence continues. They both leave their letters in the mailbox beside the sidewalk that leads to the bridge that leads to the glass house. The mailbox eventually gets into the act by raising and lowering its own little red flag. The two people come to love each other, and this process involves the movie's second impossibility. We hear them having voice-over conversations that are ostensibly based on the words in their letters, but unless these letters are one sentence long and are exchanged instantaneously (which would mean crossing time travel with chat rooms), they could not possibly be conversational.

Never mind. They also have the same dog. Never mind, I tell you, never mind! I think, actually, that I have the answer to how the same dog could belong to two people separated by two years, but if I told you, I would have to shoot the dog. The key element in *The Lake House* that gives it more than a rueful sense of loss is that although Alex's letters originate in 2004 and Kate's in 2006, *he is, after all, still alive in 2006*, and what is more, *she, after all, was alive in 2004*. Is there a way for them to send letters across the gap that will allow them to meet where she was in 2004, or where he will be in 2006, or vice versa? There is, although it involves many paradoxes, including the one that in 2004 all of this is ahead of both of them, and in 2006 Alex knows everything but Kate either knows nothing or knows it too late to act on it. None of this prevents her letter of romantic anguish: *That was you that I met!*

Enough of the plot and its paradoxes. What I respond to in the movie, directed by Alejandro Agresti and written by the Pulitzer and Tony winner David Auburn (*Proof*), is its fundamental romantic impulse. It makes us hope these two people somehow will meet. All during the movie, we're trying to do the math: It should be possible, given enough ingenuity, for them to eventually spend 2007 together, especially since he theoretically can keep the letters he received from her in 2004 and ask her out on a date and show them to her, although by then she'd know she wrote them—or would she? They do arrange one date, which involves them in some kind of time-loop misunderstanding, I think. She later understands what happened, but I don't think I do. I mean, I understand the *event* she refers to, but not whether it is a necessary event or can be prevented.

A great deal depends on the personalities involved. Bullock is an enormously likable actor in the right role, and so is Reeves, although here they're both required to be marginally depressed because of events in their current (but not simultaneous) lives. Many of his problems circle

around his father, Simon Wyler (Christopher Plummer), a famous Chicago architect. The old man is an egocentric genius who designed the lake house, which his son dislikes because, like Louis himself, it lives in isolation; there aren't even any stairs to get down to the water.

Alex is an architect himself, currently debasing himself with suburban condos, and Kate is a doctor whose confidante is an older mentor at the hospital (Shoreh Aghdashloo). Alex has a confidant too, his brother Henry (Ebon Moss-Bachrach). A plot like this makes confidants more or less obligatory, since the protagonists have so little opportunity to confide in each other, except for their mysterious ability to transform written correspondence into a conversation. Now about that dog: Dogs live outside of time, don't you think?

La Mujer de mi Hermano ("My Brother's Wife") ★
R, 89 m., 2006

Barbara Mori (Zoe Edwards), Christian Meier (Ignacio Edwards), Manolo Cardona (Gonzalo Edwards), Gabriela Espino (Laura), Angelica Aragon (Cristina), Beto Cuevas (Padre Santiago), Bruno Bichir (Boris). Directed by Ricardo de Montreuil and produced by Stan Jakubowicz. Screenplay by Jaime Bayly.

I do not, alas, remember every detail of those steamy Isabel Sarli melodramas from Argentina that used to play on Times Square and provide such a diversion from the New York Film Festival. Having now seen the new Argentinean-Mexican-Peruvian-American film *La Mujer de mi Hermano* (*My Brother's Wife*), I suspect I know the reason: There were no details.

Sarli, a former Miss Argentina, was married to her director, Armando Bo, who cast her in films never to be forgotten, such as *Thunder Among the Leaves, Positions of Love, The Hot Days, Naked Temptation, Tropical Ecstasy, Fuego,* and *Fever*. In these films the plot was entirely disposable, except as a device to propel Sarli on an insatiable quest not so much for sex as for admiration. She clearly thought she was the sexiest woman alive, and that itself made her erotic, even in a scene where she attempted suicide by jumping off some rocks and into a pride of sea lions.

I have not thought about Isabel Sarli in years,

not since reviewing Theo Angelopoulos's *Ulysses' Gaze* in 1997. It starred Harvey Keitel as a movie director who returns to his roots in Greece and makes love to lots of women. I quote from my review: "I was reminded of Armando Bo's anguished 1960s Argentinean soft-core sex films, which starred his wife, Isabel Sarli, whose agony was terrible to behold and could only be slaked in the arms of a man. (Keitel) and the women make love in this movie as if trying to apply unguent inside each other's clothes."

The Sarli role in *La Mujer de mi Hermano* is filled (and that is the word) by Barbara Mori, a TV Azteca and Telemundo star who provides persuasive reasons why there are ever so many more plunging necklines on the Spanish-language channels than on their chaste Anglo equivalents. If Oprah were on Telemundo, Tom Cruise would have stayed on the couch.

The movie's title translates as *My Brother's Wife*, although it would be more accurate to call it *My Husband's Brother*, since it is told entirely from the point of view of Zoe (Mori). She has been married for ten years to Ignacio (Christian Meier), who is a "businessman." In these movies, "businessman" translates as "doesn't satisfy his wife." Zoe complains to a friend that Ignacio likes to have sex only on Saturdays. We find this hard to believe until a scene where a symbolic unguent application is interrupted by Ignacio: "Remember that today's not Saturday." When she cannot believe her ears (or any other organ), he whines, "Honey, that's the way I am."

What a contrast with his brother Gonzalo (Manolo Cardona), an artist with the kind of 5 o'clock shadow where the whiskers seem forced out through his skin by testosterone. Zoe attends one of Gonzalo's gallery openings and purchases a painting, which Ignacio throws into the pool of his multimillion-dollar house, an example of modern domestic architecture that looks as if Frank Lloyd Wright's Fallingwater had conceived a child with Donald Trump.

Ignacio begins to suspect something, although not nearly enough and none too quickly, as Zoe and Gonzalo star in *Never on Saturday*. The two brothers, they love each other, and yet dark secrets from their past beg to be revealed. Indeed, by this point secrets from anybody's past would be welcome. The movie is astonishingly simpleminded, depicting characters who obediently perform their assigned roles as adulterers,

cuckolds, etc. At least with Isabel Sarli you had the impression she was not only having a good time while she made her movies, but enjoyed hours and hours just looking at them.

Lana's Rain ★ ★ ★
R, 107 m., 2004

Oksana Orlenko (Lana), Nickolai Stoilov (Darko Lucev), Luoyong Wang (Julian), Stephanie Childers (Katrina), Stacey Slowid (Vermonica), David Darlow (General Donoffrio). Directed by Michael S. Ojeda and produced by Joel Goodman. Screenplay by Ojeda.

Lana's Rain tells the dark, hard-edged story of a brother and sister who escape from the war-torn Balkans, conceal themselves in a shipping container to travel to America, and try to survive on Chicago streets that have never seemed meaner. The picture is even bleaker than that: The brother is a war criminal who forces his sister into prostitution, and by the end of the film he's a low-life Scarface, with a stable of hookers, a big cigar, and a bottle and gun under his coat.

The story is seen through the eyes of the sister, Lana (Oksana Orlenko), who grew up apart from her brother and meets him again after many years on the eve of his escape from the Balkans. In a grisly prelude, the brother is having facial reconstruction to disguise himself, and is interrupted in the middle of the surgery; he wears an eye patch through the movie, while his enemies and Interpol search for him.

Lana speaks no English, is naive, is dominated by her brother, and despises the life of prostitution. She is savagely beaten by one client. Darko (Nickolai Stoilov), her brother, keeps all her earnings, scornfully tossing her $10 for "spending money." She speaks so little English that she tries to learn the language from a Dr. Seuss book she finds in a Dumpster. Her only friend is an Asian-American sculptor named Julian (Luoyong Wang), who befriends her, likes her, offers her shelter, but cannot get her away from the insidious domination of her brother.

The film, written and directed by Michael S. Ojeda, shows a sure sense of *noir* style and a toughness that lasts right up to the very final scene, which feels contrived and tacked-on. It lives through the performance of Oksana Orlenko, who won the best actress award at Milan.

On the basis of his work as the brother, Nickolai Stoilov has a future as a Bond villain. They are both never less than convincing, and Ojeda makes no effort to glamorize their lifestyle; even after Darko is running three or four call girls (advertising "Eastern European Beauties"), he lives in a shabby trailer in a neighborhood that looks more like Siberia than Chicago.

The movie has a lot of plot, including a revenge twist so ingenious I will not even hint of it. It also has too many endings; there is a time when it seems that Darko must certainly be dead, but with the resilience of a zombie he reappears. In a late confrontation where they are both drenched with gasoline, Lana's decision is drawn out for too long, and then the situation is settled with a shameless *deus ex machina*. And as for the nice Asian man, is it really that nice of him to make love to her in the night and reveal in the morning that he is committed to another woman? Well, given her need and desperation, maybe he did the right thing, but the subplot disappears just when we think it might amount to something interesting.

So *Lana's Rain* is not a perfect picture, but it has the flaws of ambition, not compromise. It doesn't soften the character of the brother, who is unremittingly evil from beginning to end, and it doesn't sentimentalize the sister's ordeal. Her stamina and endurance, during a harsh Chicago winter, give some hint of the harsh world she was raised in, and her struggle is all the more moving because it comes from courage, not cleverness. Even as I noted a glitch here and there in the plot, I was aware that the movie itself, and especially the character of Lana, had enlisted my sympathy.

La Petite Lili ★ ★ ★
NO MPAA RATING, 104 m., 2004

Nicole Garcia (Mado Marceaux), Bernard Giraudeau (Brice), Jean-Pierre Marielle (Simon Marceaux), Ludivine Sagnier (Lili), Robinson Stevenin (Julien Marceaux), Julie Départdieu (Jeanne-Marie), Yves Jacques (Serge), Anne Le Ny (Leone), Marc Betton (Guy). Directed by Claude Miller and produced by Annie Miller. Screenplay by Claude Miller and Julien Boivent, based on Anton Chekhov's *The Seagull*.

There is nothing the equal of a summer cottage to assemble all the characters needed for a drama, and nobody else. There are spare bedrooms and secluded groves for adultery, and long tables on the shady lawn for boozy lunches at which truth is told. European films get enormous mileage out of the device; Hollywood is more likely to send the parents off with their kids to Wally World or the Johnson family reunion, which is why this adaptation of Chekhov's *The Seagull* would play strangely in a station wagon.

The play, you will recall, if you received a liberal education and didn't major in ways to make money, involves a family gathering that includes an aging diva, a famous writer, the diva's idealistic son, and a young actress. The son falls in love with the actress, who knows which side of her bread she wants buttered and goes after the writer, who is the lover of the diva. Minor characters have minor dalliances, and the point of the play is to show how all of these passions are transmuted into art.

Claude Miller, a French director of dry humor and great skill, has taken the Chekhov outline and updated it to present-day France, substituting the cinema for literature. His film stars the elegant Nicole Garcia as Mado Marceaux, a movie star acutely aware of her age and determined to retain possession of her lover, the successful director Brice (Bernard Giraudeau). Her son, Julien (Robinson Stevenin), is one of those intolerable young men who guards the candle of integrity on the birthday cake of materialism. As the movie opens, Julien and Lili (Ludivine Sagnier), an ambitious young actress, are found making love, but Julien is like the young filmmaker in *Last Tango in Paris*, and sees his life as a movie and his lover as a character in need of direction.

Filling out the cast are old Uncle Simon (Jean-Pierre Marielle), who likes to nap in the sun and pose as a cynic, the handyman Guy (Marc Betton), his wife, Leone (Anne Le Ny), and their daughter, Jeanne-Marie (Julie Départdieu), who is genuinely in love with Julien and believes he is a genius.

Whether he is or not becomes clear one day when Julien announces the world premiere of his new experimental film. All of the guests troop out to the barn for a viewing, especially the famous director Brice; Julien despises him, his work, and everything he stands for, but desires his praise and support. The film, which stars Lili, is awful. Everybody knows it, but finds

395

ways to praise it (Gene Siskel's response in such a situation: "Thank you for making a film"). Lili doesn't find her future in Julien's avant-garde, and goes after Brice: "I could make you happy again." This is true only if it would give him joy to make her a star. Mado is crushed to lose to her younger rival. Jeanne-Marie stands by alertly to pick up Julien's pieces.

Flash forward five years and Julien is making a film on a set built to look like the location of their summer of passion. Some of the actors are playing themselves; others have been cast by famous look-alikes (the beloved Michel Piccoli among them). It is ironic that art has been transmuted into life, but more ironic that Julien has been transmuted into Brice, and now works on a sound stage with a full crew and a big budget. "Why did you make your movie for $24,000?" I heard an indie filmmaker asked at Sundance. "So I will never have to again."

The third act departs from Chekhov and is original with Miller; it not only makes a nicely ironic point, but, because he takes his time with it, allows for a meditation on the distance between art and life. We see that even the actors playing "themselves" are not playing the selves we have seen, but new selves invented by Julien. The character who best understands this, and actually forgives it, is the older director Brice.

And did Brice find happiness with young Lili? Almost on the very day he became her lover, he knew he would "fall into a well of loneliness." It has been said that the reason we establish relationships is to assure ourselves of a witness to our lives. Happy relationships have two witnesses, but Brice's has only one.

Last Days ★ ★ ★ ★
R, 97 m., 2005

Michael Pitt (Blake), Lukas Haas (Luke), Asia Argento (Asia), Scott Patrick Green (Scott), Nicole Vicius (Nicole), Ricky Jay (Detective), Thadeus A. Thomas (Salesman). Directed by Gus Van Sant and produced by Van Sant and Dany Wolf. Screenplay by Van Sant.

Gus Van Sant has made three movies in which the camera follows young men as they wander toward their deaths. All three films resolutely refuse to find a message in the deaths. No famous death can take place in our society with-out being endlessly analyzed by experts, who find trends, insights, motives, and morals with alarming facility. It's brave of Van Sant to allow his characters to simply wander off, in John Webster's words, "to study a long silence."

In *Gerry* (2002), death is accidental, caused by carelessness. Two friends fecklessly wander into a desert, get lost, and don't get found. In *Elephant* (2003), death is preceded by murder and is deliberate but pointless. Two friends carry out a plan to kill students and teachers at their high school, and then they too are shot. Now in *Last Days,* death is a condition that overtakes a character as he mumbles and stumbles into the final stage of drug addiction.

These deaths are not heroic or meaningful, and although they may be tragic, they lack the stature of classical tragedy. They are stupid and careless, and in *Elephant* they are monstrous, because innocent lives are also taken. If Van Sant is saying anything (I am not sure he is), it's that society has created young men who do not live as if they value life.

Last Days is dedicated to the suicide of Kurt Cobain, who led the band Nirvana, influential in the creation of grunge rock. Grunge as a style is a deliberate way of presenting the self as disposable. In a disclaimer that distances itself from Cobain with cruel precision, the movie says its characters are "in part, fictional."

The movie concerns a singer named Blake (Michael Pitt), who wanders about a big stone house in a wet, gloomy forest area. The first scenes show him throwing up, stumbling down a hillside to a stream, bathing himself, drying his clothes at a campfire, and, in the middle of the night, singing "Home on the Range." The movie seems unwilling to look at his face very clearly; it is concealed by lanky hair and a hooded coat, and the camera prefers long shots to close-ups. We notice that he is wearing the sort of wrist tag you get in a hospital. Blake walks aimlessly through the house, prepares meals (Cocoa Puffs, macaroni and cheese), and listens without comment as people talk to him in person and on the phone.

They're worried about him. Kim Gordon of Sonic Youth plays a woman who asks him, "Do you talk to your daughter? Do you say I'm sorry that I'm a rock and roll cliché?" No answer. "I have a car waiting, and I want you to come with me." No answer. A detective (Ricky Jay) turns up, cannot find Blake (who hides in the woods), and relates an anecdote about a magician who could catch a bullet in his teeth (most of the time). A musician turns up and wants Blake's help with a song he is writing about a girl he left behind in Japan. A (real) Yellow Pages salesman (Thadeus A. Thomas) turns up and tries to sell Blake an ad. Harmony Korine turns up (all the characters have the same names as the actors) and talks about playing Dungeons & Dragons with Jerry Garcia.

None of this interests Blake. One night he wanders into a nearby town, into a bar, and out of the bar again. No doubt some of the people in the bar know he is a famous rock star, but his detachment is so complete it forms a wall around him; you look at him, and you know nothing is happening there.

There is a moment at the house when some friends are about to leave, and one man pauses and looks for a long time as Blake, seen indistinctly through the windows of a potting shed, moves aimlessly. That is where his body will be found in the morning. In a curious coda to such a minimalist film, Van Sant shows Blake's ghostly image leaving his body and ascending, not by floating up to heaven, but by climbing—using the frames of a window as a ladder.

Last Days is a definitive record of death by gradual drug exhaustion. After the chills and thrills of *Sid & Nancy* and *The Doors*, here is a movie that sees how addicts usually die, not with a bang but with a whimper. If the dead had it to do again, they might wish that, this time, they'd at least be conscious enough to realize what was happening.

Last Holiday ★ ★ ★
PG-13, 112 m., 2006

Queen Latifah (Georgia Byrd), LL Cool J (Sean Matthews), Timothy Hutton (Matthew Kragen), Gerard Depardieu (Chef Didier), Alicia Witt (Ms. Burns), Giancarlo Esposito (Senator Dillings), Michael Nouri (Representative Stewart). Directed by Wayne Wang and produced by Laurence Mark and Jack Rapke. Screenplay by Jeffrey Price, Peter S. Seaman, and J. B. Priestly.

Last Holiday is a movie that takes advantage of the great good nature and warmth of Queen Latifah, and uses it to transform a creaky old formula into a comedy that is just plain lovable. To describe the plot is to miss the point, because this plot could have been made into countless movies not as funny and charming as this one.

Latifah plays a salesclerk named Georgia Byrd who works in a big chain store in antediluvian New Orleans, giving cooking demonstrations. At home alone in the evenings, she prepares elaborate gourmet dishes, watching TV cooking shows and training herself to be a great chef. Then, more often than not, she eats a lonely Lean Cuisine, because she's on a diet.

The need for dieting comes to a sudden halt when she receives bad news: She has three or four weeks to live. Her HMO won't cover the expensive treatment, which might not work anyway, and so Georgia throws caution to the wind, cashes in her 401(k), and buys a ticket to Karlovy Vary in the Czech Republic. That's where her hero, Chef Didier (Gerard Depardieu), rules the kitchen, and she decides to go out in style, eating everything on the menu and treating herself to all the services of the spa and the ski slopes.

Karlovy Vary is a jewel box of a spa town ninety minutes outside of Prague. Its hotels are high and wide but not deep because steep mountain walls rise close behind them. A stream runs down the center of the town, and at the top of the little valley is the Grandhotel Pupp, where Georgia checks in. My wife and I were in Karlovy Vary four years ago for a film festival, and, like Georgia, we did a double take when we discovered that the correct pronunciation of the hotel rhymes with "poop." Yes, but it is a magnificent edifice, and soon Georgia is walking eagerly into the dining room to order—well, everything on the menu.

Visiting this hotel is another party, consisting of a retail tycoon named Matthew Kragen (Timothy Hutton), who owns the chain of giant stores, including the one Georgia resigned from in New Orleans. At his table are his mistress (Alicia Witt), a senator (Giancarlo Esposito), and a congressman (Michael Nouri). They are startled when Chef Didier pays more attention to the woman dining by herself than to their self-important table. They don't know that Georgia has already invaded the chef's kitchen and impressed him with her cooking skills—both disciplined and improvised.

Who is this woman? Kragen's table becomes consumed with curiosity, especially since Georgia Byrd is obviously very wealthy. There's a montage that reminds us of *Pretty Woman*, as she raids a high-fashion dress shop (while "If I Were a Rich Girl" plays on the sound track) and subjects herself to being beaten with birch leaves at the spa ("I Feel Pretty"). A spa in Karlovy Vary is not quite as spartan as one in America and does not count so many calories; after your treatments, you are free to recover with roast duck and dumplings, followed by apple strudel.

By making no claims, putting on no airs, telling no lies, and acting as if she has nothing to lose, Georgia transforms the hotel. The important guests are in awe of her. The staff is in love with her. The chef adores her. And there is even romance in the air because of her unmistakable chemistry with Sean Matthews (LL Cool J), a New Orleans coworker who is shy but—I will not reveal more.

All of these things may be true and yet not inspire you to see this movie. I am the first to admit that the plot is not blindingly original, although transporting the action to Karlovy Vary at least adds an intriguing location. The movie is a remake of a 1950 film that starred Alec Guinness in the Queen Latifah role, and the story was not precisely original even then.

All depends on the Queen, who has been known to go over the top on occasion but in this film finds all the right notes and dances to them delightfully. It is good to attend to important cinema like *Syriana* and *Munich*, but on occasion we must be open to movies that have more modest ambitions: They want only to amuse us, warm us, and make us feel good. *Last Holiday* plays like a hug.

When a movie can do that, a strange transformation takes place. Scenes that in a lesser movie would be contrived and cornball are, in a better movie, redeemed by the characters. There is a moment here when Georgia and another hotel guest find themselves on a ledge on the roof of the Hotel Pupp. A crowd gathers below. Such a scene could be creaky and artificial. Not here. It works.

And what, you ask, about the Idiot Plot? The whole story depends on a series of elaborate misunderstandings. One word would set everybody straight. Yes, true, and yet the movie

smiles and winks at its own contrivances, and we enjoy them. The point of this story is not to discover the truth about Queen Latifah's past life, but to enjoy the unfolding of her future life (if, of course, she has one).

The movie was directed by Wayne Wang, whose *Joy Luck Club* and *Maid in Manhattan* showed a sure feel for romantic comedy with a human dimension. The key thing he does with Queen Latifah is to accept her. She is not elbowed into an unlikely comic posture or remade into a cliché but accepted for who she is. Or perhaps not for who she really is (for which of us knows the mystery of another?) but for whom she can play so comfortably and warmly on the screen. One of the movie's best scenes comes when she gives advice to the tycoon's mistress—who is conventionally sexy but senses that Georgia is sexy in a transcendent way because of who she is. The mistress is sexy to look at. Georgia is sexy when you *see* her. The men at the other table can't take their eyes off her.

The Last Shot ★ ★ ★
R, 93 m., 2004

Matthew Broderick (Steven Schats), Alec Baldwin (Joe Devine), Toni Collette (Emily French), Calista Flockhart (Valerie Weston), Ray Liotta (Jack Devine), Tim Blake Nelson (Marshal Paris), James Rebhorn (Abe White), Tony Shalhoub (Tommy Sanz), Buck Henry (Lonnie Bosco). Directed by Jeff Nathanson and produced by Larry Brezner and David Hoberman. Screenplay by Nathanson, based on an article by Steve Fishman.

Like *Danny Deckchair*, *The Last Shot* is based on a real story that provides the inspiration for otherwise unbelievable events. Yes, the FBI really did once produce a phony movie as a sting operation. And yes, the filmmakers had no idea their producer was an undercover agent. Directors get screwed all the time by phony money men, but this was one time they couldn't go to the FBI.

The movie stars Matthew Broderick and Alec Baldwin as two men who desperately want to escape dead-end jobs. Broderick plays Steven Schats, an usher at Graumann's Chinese Theater, who, like almost everyone with even the most tenuous connection to the movie industry, has a screenplay he'd like to make into a movie. Baldwin plays Joe Devine, an FBI agent trapped in a low-level job in Rhode Island and hungry to move up. When he learns that mob-connected firms are muscling in on show-biz jobs in Providence, he has a brainstorm: He will set a trap by producing a movie that will tempt mobsters into incriminating themselves.

But first he needs a screenplay, probably from a would-be filmmaker so naive he could be deceived by Joe Devine's lack of credentials and, for that matter, his blissful ignorance of the movie business. Steven Schats is his pigeon. With the innocent enthusiasm that Broderick specializes in, the usher pitches a screenplay set in Arizona, about a tragic heroine who staggers out of the desert and into a series of murky flashbacks.

Devine green-lights *Arizona,* but has one stipulation: The movie has to be shot in Providence. Schats is thunderstruck: How can he shoot a location Western in Rhode Island? Devine says it's necessary for "production reasons," and talks about backdrops, special effects, and fake cacti. Schats needs a Hopi Indian cave for a sacred ceremony. Devine suggests a storage locker.

The Last Shot is not a well-oiled enterprise but more of a series of laughs separated by waits for more laughs. It has a kind of earnest, eager quality, and it's so screwy you feel affection for it; it creates completely gratuitous characters like the production executive played by an unbilled Joan Cusack, who barks into her intercom, "Bring me my back brace and my banjo!" There is no reason for the Cusack character except that she is relentlessly hilarious.

The screenplay, by the director Jeff Nathanson, has a nice line on funny free-standing dialogue. My favorite is probably, "Your dog is dead. She killed herself." I also like Tony Shaloub, as a gangster, saying: "I see you noticed my face. My wife set me on fire. Six months later, our marriage fell apart." And Devine boasting to Schats, "My wife did the hair on *Jaws.*" She must have been very young at the time, but never mind. I also liked the moment when Schatz talks about "the business" and Devine thinks he means prostitution. A mistake anyone could make.

Toni Collette is funny as a ditzy would-be sex bomb who desperately needs the lead and desperately plays it, staggering out of the Rhode Island "desert" in full overacting mode. Calista Flockheart plays Valerie, Steven's flywheel girlfriend, who takes acting so seriously that she stabs herself in the leg to generate a Method "sense memory" of anguish. Familiar actors like Tim Blake Nelson, Buck Henry, and Ray Liotta work their supporting roles for everything they can get out of them.

I had the sense that one more trip through the word processor might have done the screenplay some good, but at the same time I enjoyed *The Last Shot* almost unreasonably, considering its rough edges. If a comedy makes you laugh you can forgive its imperfections. What is seductive about this one is the way Joe Devine begins to think of himself as a real movie producer, and gets caught up in the struggle to bring *Arizona* to the screen. What the movie gets right is the way even the most hopeless production can engender love and loyalty from its cast and crew, who talk themselves into believing it could be great. Nobody ever sets out to make a bad movie, and that's the lesson Joe Devine learns in spite of himself.

Latter Days ★ ★ ½
NO MPAA RATING, 108 m., 2004

Steve Sandvoss (Davis), Wes Ramsey (Christian), Rebekah Jordan (Julie), Amber Benson (Traci), Khary Payton (Andrew), Jacqueline Bisset (Lila), Joseph Gordon-Levitt (Ryder), Rob McElhenney (Harmon). Directed by C. Jay Cox and produced by Kirkland Tibbels and Jennifer Schafer. Screenplay by Cox.

A movie should present its characters with a problem and then watch them solve it, not without difficulty. So says an old and reliable screenplay formula. Countless movies have been made about a boy and a girl who have a problem (they haven't slept with each other) and after difficulties (family, war, economic, health, rival lover, stupid misunderstanding) they solve it, by sleeping with each other. Now we have a movie about two homosexuals that follows the same reliable convention.

Although much will be made of the fact that one of the characters in *Latter Days* is a Mormon missionary and the other is a gay poster boy, those are simply titillating details. Consider the subgenre of pornography in which nuns get involved in sex. We know they're not really nuns, but the costuming is supposed to add a little spice. By the same token, Davis (Steve Sandvoss) is a Mormon only because that makes his journey from hetero- to homosexual more fraught and daring. He could have been a Presbyterian or an atheist vegan and the underlying story would have been the same: A character who considers himself straight is seduced by an attractive gay man, and discovers he has been homosexual all along.

Since it is obvious to us from the opening shots that these two characters are destined for each other, the plot functions primarily to add melodrama to the inevitable. And there's change in both men. Christian (Wes Ramsey), who at the beginning is a shameless slut, bets a friend $50 he can seduce his new neighbor, but by the end of the film he truly loves him, and has been so transformed by this experience that he volunteers for an AIDS charity and in general is transformed into a nice guy. It's as if the Mormon missionary achieved his goal and converted him, in slightly different terms than he expected.

The $50 bet is a cliché as old as the movies, and of course it always results in the bettor *really* falling in love, while the quarry finds out about the bet and is crushed. One of the sly pleasures of *Latter Days* is the sight of this gay-themed movie recycling so many conventions from straight romantic cinema, as if it's time to catch up.

The film is made with a certain conviction, and the actors deliver more than their roles require; there are times when they seem about to veer off into true and accurate drama (as when Christian encounters a bitter dying man), but by the end, when Davis is back in Pocatello, Idaho, and his homophobic mother (Mary Kay Place) is sending him for shock treatment, we realize the movie could have been (a) a gay love story, or (b) an attack on the Mormon church, but is an awkward fit by trying to be (c) both at the same time.

I also question the character of one of Davis's fellow missionaries, who is outspokenly antigay in a particularly ugly way. Is this character modeled on life, or he is a version of the mustache-twirling villain? And then there's Christian's best friend, Julie (Rebekah Jordan), who of course is a hip and sympathetic African-American woman. You get to the point where you realize everyone in this movie has been ordered off the shelf from the Stock Characters Store, and none of them wandered in from real life.

Is there a way in which the movie works? Yes, it works by delivering on its formula. We sense immediately that Davis and Christian are destined to be lovers, and so we watch patiently as the screenplay fabricates obstacles to their destiny. We identify to some degree with them because—well, because we always tend to identify with likable characters in love stories. Maybe the fact that they're gay will help some homophobic audience members to understand homosexuality a little better, although whether they will attend the movie in the first place is a good question.

What I'm waiting for is a movie in which the characters are gay and that's a given, and they get on with a story involving their lives. Or maybe for a satire in which two heterosexuals move in next to each other and battle their inner natures until finally love tears down the barriers and they kiss, even though one is a boy and the other a girl. That would obviously be silly, and the day will come when a movie like this seems silly, too.

Laws of Attraction ★ ★
PG-13, 90 m., 2004

Pierce Brosnan (Daniel Rafferty), Julianne Moore (Audrey Woods), Parker Posey (Serena), Michael Sheen (Thorne Jamison), Nora Dunn (Judge Abramovitz), Frances Fisher (Sara Miller). Directed by Peter Howitt and produced by Julie Durk, David T. Friendly, Beau St. Clair, and Marc Turtletaub. Screenplay by Aline Brosh McKenna and Robert Harling.

Opposites attract, it's true, but the problem with the two divorce lawyers in *Laws of Attraction* is that they're not opposites. They're perfectly well suited to each other, recognize that almost immediately, and tumble into bed at least half an hour, maybe an hour, before that's permitted by the movie's formula. Then they annoy us by trying to deny the attraction while the plot spins its wheels, pretending to be about something.

The two attractive people are Daniel Rafferty (Pierce Brosnan) and Audrey Woods (Julianne

Moore). Neither one has ever lost a case. Both are, somewhat oddly, still single despite being awesomely attractive. Maybe it's because of all the divorces they see. Audrey blames it on being the plain daughter of a raving beauty (Frances Fisher), but, I don't know about you, I can't picture Julianne Moore as plain. As for Pierce Brosnan, anyone who thinks he needs to be replaced as James Bond is starkers.

As we all know, the formula for this kind of movie requires the two protagonists to hate each other at first sight. Only gradually do they discover they're in love. I recommend *Two Weeks Notice* (2002), with Sandra Bullock and Hugh Grant, as a superior example of the formula. But in *Laws of Attraction*, Brosnan is always more or less in love with Moore, usually more, and so the movie has to resort to wheezy devices to be about anything at all.

It gives him offices, for example, above a grocery in Chinatown. Why? Because Chinatown is a colorful location, although an undefeated divorce lawyer could afford uptown rents. I am reminded of *What a Girl Wants* (2003), in which Amanda Bynes and her mother, Kelly Preston, live in an apartment in Chinatown, again without a single Chinese person saying one word in the movie, simply because you get the colorful location for free.

One colorful location is not enough. Brosnan and Moore find themselves on opposite sides of a divorce case involving a rock star (Michael Sheen) and a dress designer (Parker Posey), who both want possession of a castle in Ireland, which of course requires Brosnan and Moore to jet to Ireland, visit the castle, attend a local fete, participate in Irish jigs, get drunk, and get married. Come to think of it, they were drunk when they went to bed for the first time too. Maybe Brosnan was drunk when he rented the apartment in Chinatown.

Now these two actors are perfectly lovable people, and so we are happy for them, and enjoy watching them and listening to them, but this is a movie, not an audition, and they really deserved more from the director, Peter Howitt, and cowriters Aline Brosh McKenna and Robert Harling, who between them come up with less than one serviceable screenplay.

One of the consequences of a reedy story like this is that you start looking in the corners. I remember that during *What Women Want*

(2000), a much better movie starring Mel Gibson, I was gobsmacked by the office for his ad agency, which was the neatest office I had ever seen in a movie. In *Laws of Attraction*, I liked Brosnan's apartment, which is not in Chinatown and so we don't need to know where it is. It looks like a showroom for the Arts and Crafts Movement, with dark wood everywhere. It was a little shadowy, to be sure, but I wonder if even things like the sink and the sofa were made out of wood. Possibly even the sheets. This apartment looks so odd that one of the movie's most implausible moments comes when Moore sees it and says nothing about it. Oh, she was drunk.

Layer Cake ★ ★ ★ ½
R, 105 m., 2005

Daniel Craig (XXXX), Colm Meaney (Gene), Sienna Miller (Tammy), Michael Gambon (Eddie Temple), Kenneth Cranham (Jimmy Price), George Harris (Morty), Jamie Foreman (Duke). Directed by Matthew Vaughn and produced by Adam Bohling, David Reid, and Vaughn. Screenplay by J. J. Connolly, based on his novel.

Like Scorsese's *Casino* and *GoodFellas*, the British crime movie *Layer Cake* opens with a narration describing a criminal world made in heaven. Also like *Casino* and *GoodFellas*, it is about an inexorable decline toward the torments of hell. The voice explaining everything to us belongs to Daniel Craig, who plays the competent and conservative middleman in a well-run London cocaine operation. Nobody ever calls him by name during the movie, and in the closing credits he's referred to as "XXXX," which may be one-upmanship on "XXX," or probably not.

Craig's credo, spelled out as if he's lecturing at a management seminar, involves knowing your suppliers, knowing your customers, paying your bills, and never getting too greedy. His front is real estate. His exit plan is retirement in the near future. All of that changes when he is summoned to a private club for a luncheon meeting with his immediate superior, Jimmy Price (Kenneth Cranham), a hard man with cold eyes and a menacing Cockney charm. Jimmy wants him to sort out an Ecstasy deal that went bad, and as a sort of twofer, also find the missing daughter of *his* boss, Eddie Temple

(Michael Gambon), the kind of man whose soul has warts on its scars.

XXXX does not much like either assignment. They involve cleaning up the kinds of messes he has scrupulously avoided in his own dealings. What's the use of playing it safe if you work for people who want you to take their chances for them? The Ecstasy deal is especially dicey: One of Jimmy's cronies named Duke (Jamie Foreman) stole Ecstasy pills allegedly worth a million pounds. The Serbs he stole them from want them back. Jimmy's ideal scenario, never stated in so many words, would involve XXXX grabbing the pills for Jimmy while Duke is thrown to the Serbs.

XXXX has some hard men who work for him and might be able to get this job done. More complicated is the matter of the girl, especially when another girl named Tammy (Sienna Miller) enters the picture. There are key supporting roles for such actors as the indispensable Colm Meaney, who looks as if he should be found guilty and sent down for life just for the way he has of listening to you.

The movie was directed by Matthew Vaughn, who produced *Lock, Stock and Two Smoking Barrels* and *Snatch,* and this one works better than those films because it doesn't try so hard to be clever and tries harder to be menacing. It's difficult to take danger seriously when it's packaged in fancy camera work, although Guy Ritchie's *Lock, Stock* did have a carefree visual genius. *Layer Cake* is more in the Scorsese vein, in which a smart and ambitious young man has it all figured out, and then gradually loses control to old-fashioned hoods who don't have the patience for prudence when it's easier to just eliminate anyone who gets in their way. The problem is that every dead enemy tends to leave a more dangerous living enemy standing next in line.

There is a kind of scene that both American and British crime movies do very well, in which low-lifes enjoy high life. They've had success in their business of crime, but their preparation for life has not equipped them with interesting ways to stay amused. They almost always lack imagination about what constitutes fun, and dutifully spend their money on cars, cigars, women, champagne, and memberships in private clubs, none of which finally seem to be worth the trouble. We are reminded of the last days of Scarface, a young man who desperately

needed something constructive to do with his spare time.

XXXX's dilemma is that he has the resources to enjoy himself, but works for people who speak a different language. He is really in the wrong line of work. He could steal more money with the kinds of high finance that distinguished Enron, and run a smaller risk of finding his head in a bucket of ice and his body elsewhere. As his life begins to heat up and events unfold more quickly than he can follow them, we're reminded of Ray Liotta in *GoodFellas,* whose life spun out of control.

Daniel Craig was said to be the front-runner for the next James Bond, until it began to be said that Pierce Brosnan might return for a farewell lap. My own money is on Clive Owen, but who would wish James Bond on anyone? Craig is fascinating here as a criminal who is very smart, and finds that is not an advantage because while you might be able to figure out what another smart person is about to do, dumbos like the men he works for are likely to do anything.

The Legend of Zorro ★ ½
PG, 129 m., 2005

Antonio Banderas (Zorro), Catherine Zeta-Jones (Elena), Adrian Alonso (Joaquin), Rufus Sewell (Armand), Rick Chinlund (McGivens), Raul Mendez (Ferroq). Directed by Martin Campbell and produced by Laurie MacDonald, Walter F. Parkes, and Lloyd Phillips. Screenplay by Alex Kurtzman and Roberto Orci.

The Legend of Zorro commits a lot of movie sins, but one is mortal: It turns the magnificent Elena into a nag. You will recall *The Mask of Zorro* (1998), which first united Antonio Banderas and Catherine Zeta-Jones as Zorro and Elena, in a resurrection of the character first played by Douglas Fairbanks Sr. and subsequently by Tyrone Power, John Carroll, Guy Williams and—here's a team for you—George Hamilton and Anthony Hopkins.

Hopkins played the elder Zorro in the 1998 film, and Banderas played a street urchin who grew up to be a bandit but was taken under old Zorro's wing and taught the tricks of the trade, such as swordsmanship, horsemanship, and charm. That was a grand movie, filled with swashes and buckles. Banderas and Zeta-Jones rose to the occasion with performances of joy and unbounded energy, and it was probably the best Zorro movie ever made, although having not seen them all I can only speculate.

Now come Banderas and Zeta-Jones again, with the same director, Martin Campbell, and of all the possible ideas about how to handle the Elena character, this movie has assembled the worst ones. The sublime adventuress has turned into the kind of wife who wants her husband to quit Zorroing because "you do not know your own son," and besides, Zorro comes home late, she never knows where he is, etc. We are inflicted with such dialogue as:

"People still need Zorro!"

"No—you still need Zorro!"

"You're overreacting!"

Saints preserve us from Mr. and Mrs. Zorro as the Bickersons. And what are we to make of their son, Joaquin (a good little actor named Adrian Alonso)? He dresses like Little Lord Fauntleroy but has developed, apparently by osmosis, all of the skills of his father, such as shadowing bad guys, eavesdropping on plots, improvising in emergencies, and exposing a dastardly scheme to overthrow the government.

He's a bright kid, but not bright enough to recognize that Zorro is his own father. To be sure, Zorro wears a mask, but let me pose a hypothetical exercise for my readers. Imagine your own father. That's it. Now place him in a typical setting: pushing back from the dinner table, cutting off some jerk in an intersection, or scratching his dandruff. Now imagine your dad wearing black leather pants, a black linen shirt, a black cloak, a flat black hat, and a black mask that covers his eyes. Got that? Now imagine him pushing back from the table. Still your dad, right? You can almost hear your mom: "Now don't you go getting any ideas about that whip."

To be sure, Zorro's work keeps him away from home a lot, which is one of the things Elena is complaining about. Maybe the son has never seen his father. In that case, Elena has a point. Meanwhile, the villains have a plot to use a superweapon in order to bring about the collapse of the union and protect us from "inferior races," by which they mean Zorro and all of his kind. Strange, how movie characters who hate "inferior races" somehow themselves never look like breeding stock. If they reproduced,

they would found a line of dog whisperers and undersecretaries of defense.

The circumstances under which Zorro and the villain fight a duel with polo mallets is unprecedented in the annals of chivalry, but never mind: What's with this secret society named the Knights of Aragon, who have secretly controlled the world for centuries? When you belong to an ancient order that runs the world and you're reduced to dueling with polo mallets, it's like you're running the Scientology office in Thule.

There is a neat scene here where Zorro and his horse race a train, and then the horse leaps from a trestle and lands on top of the train. That Zorro thinks a horse would do this shows that Zorro does not know as much about horses as he should. For that matter, the horse itself is surprisingly uninformed. It must have had the mumps the week the other horses studied about never jumping blind from a high place onto something that, assuming it is there, will be going 40 mph.

I am searching for the correct word to describe the scene where Zorro is served with divorce papers. Ah, I've found it! Shame I can't use it. Four letters. This is a family newspaper. Starts with "s." Then Zorro has to attend a fancy dress ball where Elena turns up as the escort of Armand (Rufus Sewell), a wealthy French vineyard owner. This is like Supergirl dating Jughead. For maximum poignancy, we need a scene where little Joaquin approaches Armand and says, "Father?"

Lemony Snicket's A Series of Unfortunate Events ★ ★ ½
PG, 97 m., 2004

Jim Carrey (Count Olaf), Jude Law (Lemony Snicket), Emily Browning (Violet Baudelaire), Liam Aiken (Klaus Baudelaire), Kara and Shelby Hoffman (Sunny), Timothy Spall (Mr. Poe), Catherine O'Hara (Justice Strauss), Billy Connolly (Uncle Monty), Meryl Streep (Aunt Josephine). Directed by Brad Silberling and produced by Laurie MacDonald and Walter F. Parkes. Screenplay by Robert Gordon, based on the books by Daniel Handler.

The first time I picked up a Lemony Snicket adventure in a bookstore, I was intrigued by the message on the back cover: "I'm sorry to say that the book you are holding in your hands is extremely unpleasant . . ." It goes on to warn that "the three youngsters encounter a greedy and repulsive villain, itchy clothing, a disastrous fire, a plot to steal their fortune, and cold porridge for breakfast" and suggests "putting this book down at once."

As a marketing ploy, this is brilliant. It was all I could do to prevent myself from buying the book. And the film *Lemony Snicket's A Series of Unfortunate Events* opens on the same note, with Lemony Snicket himself (Jude Law) bent double over an old typewriter and typing out the dire story of the three Baudelaire children who suddenly and decisively become orphans. The family banker, Mr. Poe (Timothy Spall), breaks the news that a fire has destroyed their mansion and killed their parents.

The children seem to take this news rather well. I would say they take it too well, except that demonstrations of grief are not helpful in macabre comedies, where there is so much to grieve about that there would be no end to it. Perhaps tragedy is in the family tree; I assume they are descended from the French poet Charles Baudelaire, whose poems about sex and death "became a byword for unwholesomeness," according to Wikipedia.com. The only thing standing in the way of this theory is that Charles left no descendants.

The Baudelaire children are Violet (Emily Browning), Klaus (Liam Aiken), and the infant Sunny (Kara and Shelby Hoffman), who possesses only two teeth but such a firm bite that she can hang in midair from the edge of a table for minutes on end, an occupation she finds amusing. Violet is beautiful, Klaus is intense, and they are immediately beset with life-threatening difficulties.

Mr. Poe takes them to live with their "closest relative," a fourth cousin three times removed, or perhaps it's the other way around. This is Count Olaf (Jim Carrey), who lives in a Gothic mansion so creepy his interior decorator must have been Nosferatu. The count wants to kill the children and inherit the family fortune, and is not very subtle in his methods, parking his ancient Imperial on the train tracks with the children locked inside. As there are eleven novels so far in the series, they necessarily escape.

It's odd how the movie's gloom and doom are amusing at first, and then dampen down

the humor. Although many Unfortunate Events do indeed occur in *Lemony Snicket*, they cannot be called exciting because everyone is rather depressed by them. There is no one in the movie to provide a reasonable reaction to anything; the adults are all demented, evil, or, in the case of Mr. Poe, stunningly lacking in perception, and the kids are plucky enough, but rather dazed by their misfortunes.

Jim Carrey is over the top as Count Olaf, but I suppose a character named Count Olaf is over the top by definition. The next relative to harbor the children is nice Uncle Monty (Billy Connolly), a herpetologist who shares his mansion with countless snakes, vipers, and other reptiles, and announces an immediate departure for Peru. Before the expedition can get under way, Count Olaf turns up again, this time in disguise as an Italian; although he prides himself on his acting and makeup skills, the kids take one look at him and announce that he is obviously Count Olaf. Uncle Monty, alas, is slow to take heed.

The children eventually arrive at yet another potential foster home, this one the residence of Aunt Josephine (Meryl Streep), whose Victorian mansion teeters on spindly supports that allow it to extend far above a rocky coast and stormy sea. Strange that her house is so precarious, since Josephine is literally afraid of everything, a condition I believe is called phobiaphobia.

The movie looks wonderful. Director Brad Silberling *(Moonlight Mile, City of Angels)* has assembled production designer Rick Heinrichs *(Sleepy Hollow)* and art directors John Dexter *(Planet of the Apes)* and Martin Whist, who have created wondrous and creepy spaces. The cinematography by Emmanuel Lubezki finds foreboding even in sunlight.

But there is a problem, and the problem is, everything seems to be an act. Nothing really seems to be at stake. The villains are teeth-gnashing hams, the hazards are more picturesque than frightening, and the children are unnaturally collected and capable. There is some kind of family secret, involving spyglasses, which will be resolved no doubt in later films; it's brought onstage and then not really dealt with.

I liked the film, but I'll tell you what. I think this one is a tune-up for the series, a trial run in which they figure out what works and what needs to be tweaked. The original *Spider-Man* was a disappointment, but the same team came back and made *Spider-Man 2* the best superhero movie ever made. The Lemony Snicket series has enormous potential, and I expect the next film will look just as good, and have the same wonderful kids, and be scarier and tell more of a real story, and discover that while gloom is an atmosphere, depression is a condition.

L'Enfant ★ ★ ★ ★
R, 100 m., 2006

Jeremie Renier (Bruno), Deborah Francois (Sonia), Jeremie Segard (Steve), Fabrizio Rongione (Young Thug), Olivier Gourmet (Plainclothes Officer), Stephane Bissot (Receiver), Mireille Bailly (Bruno's Mother). Directed by Jean-Pierre and Luc Dardenne and produced by Jean-Pierre and Luc Dardenne and Denis Freyd. Screenplay by Jean-Pierre and Luc Dardenne.

We talk about the "point of view" of a film. *L'Enfant* sees with the eye of God. The film has granted free will to its central character, Bruno, and now it watches, intense but detached, to see how he will use it. Bruno is so amoral he doesn't register the meaning of his actions. At first his behavior is evil. He attempts repairs. Whether he is redeemed is a good question. At the end he is weeping, but he cannot weep forever, and he has a limited idea of how to survive and make a living.

But let me just bluntly tell you what happens in the film, while observing that *L'Enfant,* more than almost any film I can think of, is not about plot development but about putting one foot in front of the other. We meet Sonia and Bruno. She has just borne his child. The baby in her arms, she finds Bruno begging from cars at a traffic light, while serving as a lookout for a burglary in progress. She shows him their child. He is as interested as if she had shown him her new phone card.

Sonia (Deborah Francois) looks in her late teens. Bruno (Jeremie Renier) looks older, yet in no way seems an adult, and indeed his criminal pals are all kids of around fourteen. He lives entirely in the moment. While Sonia was in the hospital, he sublet her apartment. When he divides loot from a robbery, he spends his share immediately. He buys a used perambulator be-cause Sonia wants one. He rents an expensive convertible because he wants one. There will always be more money. Working? Working is for losers.

In a cafe, he meets a woman he does business with. He mentions the baby. She tells him, "People pay to adopt." Promising Sonia to watch the baby for an afternoon, he arranges to sell the child. Bruno lives in a grim world of unfriendly streets; he and Sonia have spent nights huddled on a river bank. But no place in the movie is bleaker than the empty building where the sale of the child takes place. He never sees the buyers. They never see him. The child is left in a room, is taken, the money left behind. He returns to Sonia and proudly shows her the money ("This is ours!"). When she despairingly asks about the baby, he says, "We can have another one." She faints dead away and is taken to the hospital. This is a surprise to him.

L'Enfant, which won the Golden Palm at Cannes 2005, is the new film by the Dardenne brothers, Jean-Pierre and Luc, whose *The Son* (2002) made such an impact, audiences were moved in a deep, rare way. The Dardennes do not make morality tales. Their character Bruno is not aware that what he does is good or bad. He is unformed. There is a scene where he and Sonia tussle playfully in a car and then romp outside in a park like a couple of kids. Does he love her? Love is outside his emotional range. He takes money, spends it, doesn't even cultivate the persona of a hustler. He is that most terrifying kind of human being, the one who doesn't feel ordinary emotions or even understand that other people do.

The Dardennes achieve their effects through an intense visual focus. They follow their characters as if their camera can look nowhere else. In *L'Enfant,* their gaze is upon Bruno. They deliberately do not establish the newborn child as a character. Unlike the (equally powerful) *Tsotsi,* their film doesn't show Bruno caring for the child. The child is simply something he carries, like loot or a video game. The movie also avoids the opportunity to develop Sonia, except as her behavior responds to Bruno's. When she lets out a cry of grief and faints, this is not so much what she does as what Bruno sees her do.

Observe particularly the camera strategy in the last half of the film. Often when a handheld camera follows a character, it feels subjective; we are invited to identify, as if the camera is a point of view we share with the character. In the passages after Sonia faints in *L'Enfant*, the camera focuses so intensely on Bruno that everything else seems peripheral vision. But it doesn't "identify" with him, and it doesn't represent his point of view. It watches to see what he will do.

There is a theological belief that God gives us free will and waits to see how we will use it. If he were to interfere, it would not be free will at all. If we choose well, we will spend eternity in the sight of God; if badly, banished from his presence. If God were to issue instructions, what would be the point of his creation? If we are not free to choose evil, where is the virtue in choosing good?

It's with that in mind that the visual strategy of the Dardennes reflects the eye of God. Having made a universe that has set this creature Bruno into motion, God (and we) look to see what he will do. Bruno has little intellectual capital and a limited imagination. He has been so damaged that he lacks ordinary feelings; when he visits his mother to arrange for an alibi, we get some insights into his childhood. After Sonia faints, he sets about trying to get the baby back. Does he do this because he knows that selling the baby was wrong? Or because Sonia is a companion and convenience for him, and he must try to restore her to working order?

The greatness of the Dardennes is that they allow us to realize that these are questions, and leave us free to try to answer them. What happens at the end of the film perhaps suggests grief and a desire to repent. I hope it does. But *L'Enfant* is not so simple as to believe that for Bruno there can be a happy ending. Here is a film where God does not intervene, and the directors do not mistake themselves for God. It makes the solutions at the ends of other pictures seem like child's play.

The Libertine ★ ★ ★
R, 114 m., 2006

Johnny Depp (Rochester), Samantha Morton (Elizabeth Barry), John Malkovich (King Charles II), Rosamund Pike (Elizabeth Malet), Tom Hollander (Sir George Etherege), Johnny Vegas (Charles Sackville). Directed by Laurence Dunmore and produced by Lianne Halfon, John Malkovich, and Russell Smith. Screenplay by Stephen Jeffreys.

"You will not like me," the Earl of Rochester assures us, staring fiercely out of darkness. "You will not like me now, and you will like me a good deal less as we go on." These are the opening words of Stephen Jeffreys's play *The Libertine*, where in Scene 2 we find Rochester in conversation with the actress Elizabeth Barry: "In my experience, those who do not like you fall into two categories: the stupid, and the envious. The stupid will like you in five years' time, the envious never."

So there's our choice: stupid, or envious. I think I would choose stupid. To be envious of John Wilmot, the second earl of Rochester (1647–1680), would be difficult; he died at thirty-three of venereal diseases that ate away his nose, so that he attended Parliament wearing a silver replacement. One of those who did like Rochester was his king, Charles II, restored to the throne after the death of Cromwell. One of Charles's first acts was to allow women back on the English stage, which is why Elizabeth Barry can be an actress in the first place, although one gathers that if her role had been played by a boy, the second earl might have been no less interested.

The Libertine, a film by Laurence Dunmore, is based on Jeffreys's play, which opened in 1994 at the Royal Court in London and was brought to Chicago's Steppenwolf Theater with John Malkovich as Rochester. Here Malkovich plays Charles, and Johnny Depp plays Rochester as the kind of decaying rogue and licentious voluptuary who reaches such an alarming state that it is not a matter of liking or disliking him, but hoping not to catch something from him. Depp has an affection for outrageous roles, and Rochester is not as far removed as you might imagine from Jack Sparrow, the hero of *The Pirates of the Caribbean*, especially in personal hygiene and dental care. Rochester was in youth a hero of British naval engagements, a gifted and mercurial man whose father had helped protect young Charles during his exile. Now Charles has returned and is amused by Rochester's audacity and impudence: The earl composes poetry of startling obscenity, writes reckless satires, is not afraid to lampoon the king to his face. Sometimes Charles banishes Rochester to the country, but then he relents and invites him back to London, because for all his sins the earl is one of the smartest and most entertaining men of his time: good value for the money. All Charles asks is that Rochester keep the lid on, cool it a little. Alas, discretion does not come easily to Rochester.

The film doesn't follow the earl's rise and fall so much as his fall and fall. As a sex addict, he equals Casanova in willingness: "Now, ladies, an announcement," Depp's character says in his opening monologue. "I am up for it. All the time." He is up for gentlemen as well, although the movie is not as interested in that side of his activities. We see him offering Elizabeth Barry (Samantha Morton) lessons on acting, then falling in love with her; she is the smartest woman he has ever met, although that must be tempered with the observation that a smart woman would stay away from him. He welcomes his good wife, Elizabeth Malet (Rosamund Pike), when she comes up from the country, yet does not curtail his visits to the fleshpots and bordellos. She has a touching scene observing that when he returns after an evening with the harlots, she might not mind so much if he were happy—but no, he is sad, and will complain to her, and wish that he had been with her. These sentiments are not as consoling as he imagines.

Rochester crawls in and out of countless embraces, engages in an orgy of remarkable ingenuity, and writes, produces, and performs in a play that Charles commissions for the entertainment of the French king. This play is so outrageous that the Kings Are Not Amused, as we say in capital letters. The movie is pretty much downhill after that, but of course it is. There is no way the story can end happily, as Rochester descends into wine, women, and the pox. There comes a time when a comely wench no longer makes his eye sparkle, and the second earl is no longer up for it all the time. Watching the earl conquer one erotic target after another, I was reminded of a lecture I once attended by the authors of The 60-Minute Orgasm. An attentive older woman in the front row asked, "Do you have anything at around five minutes?"

I admire Depp's performance, which plays fair with his opening comment and contains nothing that would inspire us to like him. I was

engaged by the patience of Charles II, played by Malkovich as a man smart enough to prefer amusement to flattery; when he cautions Rochester to dial down, it isn't that he's personally offended but that it's a bad idea for the king to be seen giving license to offense. Morton's character bewitches Rochester by out-thinking him, which he finds more intriguing than any sexual favor. And Pike, as Rochester's wife, is touching as a woman who will put up with almost anything but not, finally, with everything.

Libertines are not built for third acts. No self-respecting libertine lives that long. Depp finds sadness in the earl's descent, and a desire to be loved even as he makes himself unlovable. What a brave actor Depp is, to take on a role like this. Still, at the screenplay stage, The Libertine might have seemed a safer bet than The Pirates of the Caribbean, a movie studio executives reportedly thought was unreleasable. In both cases, Depp accepts the character and all of its baggage, and works without a net. He is capable of subtle nuances, but the pirate and the earl are not, and Depp gamely follows them into wretched excess. You will not like the second earl of Rochester. But you will not be able to take your eyes from him. Having made his bed, he does not hesitate to sleep in it.

The Life Aquatic with Steve Zissou ★ ★ ½
R, 118 m., 2004

Bill Murray (Steve Zissou), Owen Wilson (Ned Plimpton), Cate Blanchett (Jane Winslett-Richardson), Anjelica Huston (Eleanor Zissou), Willem Dafoe (Klaus Daimler), Jeff Goldblum (Alistair Hennessey), Michael Gambon (Oseary Drakoulias), Noah Taylor (Vladimir Wolodarsky), Bud Cort (Bill Ubell). Directed by Wes Anderson and produced by Anderson, Barry Mendel, and Scott Rudin. Screenplay by Anderson and Noah Baumbach.

My rational mind informs me that this movie doesn't work. Yet I hear a subversive whisper: Since it does so many other things, does it have to work too? Can't it just *exist?* "Terminal whimsy," I called it on the TV show. Yes, but isn't that better than halfhearted whimsy, or no whimsy at all? Wes Anderson's *The Life Aquatic with Steve Zissou* is the *damnedest* film. I can't recommend it, but I would not for one second discourage you from seeing it.

To begin with, it has a passage of eerie beauty, in which the oceanographer Steve Zissou (Bill Murray) and his shipmates glide in a submarine past an undersea panorama of wondrous and delightful creatures. They are seeking the dreaded jaguar shark that ate Steve's beloved partner, and when they find it, well, they fall silent and just regard it, because it's kind of beautiful. This could have been a scene from *20,000 Leagues Under the Sea* if Captain Nemo had been a pothead.

Zissou is, we learn, the auteur of a series of increasingly uneventful undersea documentaries, in which the momentum is sliding down a graph that will intersect in the foreseeable future with a dead standstill. *The Life Aquatic* opens with the premiere of his latest work, which ends with the audience gazing up at the screen as if it is more interesting now that it is blank. Zissou himself seems to be in the later stages of entropy, and may become one of those Oliver Sacks people who just sit there on the stairs for decades, looking at you. His crew would seem slack-witted to SpongeBob.

On board the good ship Belafonte, Zissou has assembled his ex-wife, Eleanor (Anjelica Huston), her ex-husband, Alistair (Jeff Goldblum), the salty dog Klaus Daimler (Willem Dafoe), the plummy producer Oseary Drakoulias (Michael Gambon), and the financial guy Bill (Bud Cort, so that's what happened to him). Along the way they collect Ned Plimpton (Owen Wilson), who thinks he may be Steve's son, although my theory is he's just another one of George Plimpton's unfinished projects. Their mission is to find the deadly shark, exact revenge, and film the adventure. Covering the expedition is Jane Winslett-Richardson (Cate Blanchett), whose surname suggests she is the result of an affair involving the matriarchs of two great acting families and a designated male, perhaps Ned's birth father.

These characters involve themselves in great plot complications, which are facilitated by the design of the boat, which looks like a rust bucket on the outside but conceals innumerable luxuries, including a spa. There is also a "scientific laboratory" with equipment that looks as if it might have been bought at auction from a bankrupt high school in 1955. Anderson has built a wonderful set with a cutaway front wall so that we can look into all the rooms of the boat at once; it's the same idea Jerry Lewis used in *The Ladies' Man.*

Events on the boat are modulated at a volume somewhere between a sigh and a ghostly exhalation. Steve Zissou is very tired. I suggest for his epitaph: "Life for him was but a dreary play; he came, saw, dislik'd, and passed away." Ned makes an effort to get to know his father, a task made difficult because Steve may not be his father and is not knowable. Jane, Ned, and Steve form a romantic triangle, or perhaps it is just a triangle. A folksinger performs the works of David Bowie in Portuguese, and the ship is boarded by Filipino pirates.

So you see, it's that kind of movie. The colors are like the pastels produced by colored pencils, and kind of beautiful, like the shark. The action goes through the motions of slapstick at the velocity of dirge. Steve Zissou seems melancholy, as if simultaneously depressed that life is passing him by, and that it is taking so long to do it. Anjelica Huston seems privately amused, which is so much more intriguing than seeming publicly amused. Cate Blanchett proves she can do anything, even things she should not do. I forgot to mention that Steve's friend is played by Seymour Cassel, who I think I remember told me one night in Dan Tana's that he had always wanted to be eaten by a shark in a movie.

Lipstick & Dynamite, Piss & Vinegar: The First Ladies of Wrestling ★ ★ ½
NO MPAA RATING, 83 m., 2005

Featuring Ella Waldek, Gladys "Killem" Gillem, Ida May Martinez, Johnnie "The Great" Mae Young, Lillian "The Fabulous Moolah" Ellison, Penny Banner, and Diamond Lil. A documentary directed by Ruth Leitman and produced by Anne Hubbell, James Jernigan, Leitman, and Debbie Nightingale.

Lipstick & Dynamite, Piss & Vinegar: The First Ladies of Wrestling tells us just enough about the early days of professional women wrestlers to suggest there must be a great deal more to tell. The documentary visits elderly women who, then and now, can best be described as tough broads, and listens as they describe the early days of women's wrestling. What they say is not as revealing as how they say it; as they talk we envision not a colorful chapter in showbiz history, but a hard-scrabble world in which they were mistreated, swindled, lied to, injured, sometimes raped or beaten—and tried, it must be said, to give as good as they got.

The documentary, by Ruth Leitman, does an extraordinary job of assembling the survivors from the early days of a disreputable sport, beginning with Gladys "Killem" Gillem, whose sideshow act began as a change of pace from the strippers. Footage from the late 1930s and 1940s includes a sideshow barker describing the unimaginable erotic pleasures to be found inside the All-Girl Revue. I remember such sideshows at the Champaign County Fair, where you worked your way past the Octopus and the Tilt-a-Whirl to the girlie tent, always at the bottom of the midway, where dancers in ratty spangled gowns paraded before we horny teenagers, and then the barker said, "All right, girls, back inside the tent!" We followed them in, slamming down the exact change; if a murder had taken place during the show, there would have been no witnesses, because there was absolutely no eye contact between the sinners.

But I digress. The appeal of women's wrestling, then and, I suspect, even now, had a lot to do with the possibility of a Janet Jackson moment. But the sideshow wrestlers gave way to a sport that toured the same venues as men's professional wrestling; sometimes the women were the curtain-raisers, although, as they tell it, the men were terrified that the women would become a bigger draw. We meet such legends of the sport as The Fabulous Moolah (Lillian Ellison), who was the biggest star of the sport and had the most longevity, surviving even into the heyday of the WWF and finding a new generation of fans.

Moolah, now in her eighties, still works as a wrestling promoter. We get a glimpse of her home life; she lives with The Great Mae Young and Diamond Lil, a dwarf wrestler, in a household that would give pause to John Waters. Although Moolah and Young are apparently a couple, the role of Diamond Lil becomes harder to define the more Moolah praises her skills as an invaluable maid of all work. Among the film's other unforgettable characters are Penny Banner, "the blond bombshell," and Ella

Waldek, who sounds as if she has chain-smoked Camels from birth and later went into the detective business.

Men seem to have come into the lives of these women primarily as exploiters, rapists, and occasional transient husbands. The promoter Billy Wolfe, a key figure in the early days, is remembered without affection for taking half of what he said were their earnings, and sleeping with as many of them as he could. When the women describe their sexual experiences, their voices reflect more hardened realism than indignation. They were often abandoned when young, made their way on their own, paid their dues.

Magicians have a credo: "The trick is told when the trick is sold." They don't give away their secrets for free. Neither, I suspect, do women wrestlers. Glimpsed on every face in this movie, echoing in every voice, are hints of the things they've seen and the stories they could tell if they didn't have a lifelong aversion to leveling with the rubes. What we get is essentially the press-book version of their careers, which is harrowing enough; Ruth Leitman is said to be working on a fictional screenplay based on her material, and I have a suspicion it may be blood-curdling. At the end of the film, at the Gulf Coast Wrestlers' Reunion, there is not a lot of sentiment, and no visible tears. One woman after another seems to have attended in order to say, "I'm still here," as if being alive after what they've been through is a form of defiance.

Little Black Book ★ ★ ★
PG-13, 95 m., 2004

Brittany Murphy (Stacy Holt), Kathy Bates (Kippie Kann), Holly Hunter (Barb), Ron Livingston (Derek), Josie Maran (Lulu Fritz), Julianne Nicholson (Joyce), Rashida Jones (Dr. Rachel Keyes), Stephen Tobolowsky (Carl). Directed by Nick Hurran and produced by Elaine Goldsmith-Thomas, Deborah Schindler, William Sherak, and Jason Shuman. Screenplay by Melissa Carter and Elisa Bell.

Well, in the first place, I think Brittany Murphy is a great deal more talented than some people do. I wouldn't compare her with Marilyn Monroe, who is incomparable, but she has a similar ability to draw our eyes to her segment of the screen, even when the action is ostensibly elsewhere. She does this not with sex appeal but with life force. See her in such completely various roles as Eminem's tough girlfriend in *8 Mile* and a rich girl's nanny in the underrated *Uptown Girls*; she has the quality of seeming immediately there on the screen, open to possibility, unrehearsed, unstudied, natural, appealing. She hasn't had the roles yet to prove it, but she is a born movie star.

In *Little Black Book,* Murphy has the necessary qualities to function as a sort of decoy. She lures us into the picture on false pretenses; she's cute and chirpy in the early scenes, we assume this is going to be a routine career-girl comedy, and we're surprised when it moves deeper into its subject until finally it's a satirical comedy about television that invades some of the same territory as *Network* or *Broadcast News.*

Murphy plays Stacy Holt, who worships above all living beings Diane Sawyer, and dreams not of becoming Diane Sawyer, but simply of becoming her assistant, to serve this great woman with the devotion she deserves. Stacy begins a little more humbly, in cable TV, and works her way up to the Kippie Kann show, a daytime talk show whose hostess, played by Kathy Bates, is a wannabe Jerry Springer/Jenny Jones. Stacy's mentor on the show is a producer named Barb (Holly Hunter), who could be a more experienced, more cynical version of the TV news producer Hunter played in *Broadcast News.*

Kippie Kann is on the brink of being canceled. Her ratings are tanking, and the show is shamelessly seeking sensationalism. Young Stacy suggests a show on "little black books"— in particular, the Palm Pilot, Treo, or Blackberry of the person you're dating, which may contain evidence that you're being cheated on. She is meanwhile dating the hunky Derek (Ron Livingston), a hockey scout who's maybe ten years older and has dated a lot of women.

Stacy meets some of them: a supermodel named Lulu Fritz (Josie Maran), a chef named Joyce (Julianne Nicholson), a gynecologist named Dr. Rachel Keyes (Rashida Jones). Abusing her position on the Kippie Kann show, Stacy calls them in for interviews. They think they're possible guests; she thinks they're possible rivals.

Where the movie goes with this is fairly hard to anticipate, although by the end we have been given a convincing demonstration of the amorality of a television show in search of better ratings. The long closing sequence is virtuoso, redefining what went before and requiring Murphy to become a more complex character than she gave any hint of in the opening scenes.

The movie, directed by Nick Hurran and written by Melissa Carter and Elisa Bell, is every bit as cynical as *Network,* but at the same time engenders a sweet onscreen romance, although not between the people we anticipate. Certain tricky scenes work well because of the presence of Julianne Nicholson, an actress of fresh charm and uninflected honesty who glowed in a movie named *Tully* that you should rent immediately. There is nothing false about her, which is very important.

As for Brittany Murphy, for me it goes back to the 2003 Independent Spirit Awards, held the day before the Oscars in a big tent on the beach at Santa Monica, California. Murphy was assigned to present one of the awards. Her task was to read the names of the five nominees, open an envelope, and reveal the name of the winner.

This she turned into an opportunity for screwball improvisational comedy, by pretending she could not follow this sequence, not even after the audience shouted instructions and the stage manager came out to whisper in her ear not once but twice. There were those in the audience who were dumbfounded by her stupidity. I was dumbfounded by her brilliance. I had a front-row seat, and was convinced her timing was too good, her double-takes too perfect, her pauses too wicked, to even possibly be authentic. She was taking a routine task and turning it into the opportunity to steal a scene and leave everybody in the tent chattering about her performance. You can't screw up that entertainingly by accident. You have to know exactly what you're doing.

Loggerheads ★ ★ ★
NO MPAA RATING, 93 m., 2005

Tess Harper (Elizabeth), Bonnie Hunt (Grace), Michael Kelly (George), Michael Learned (Sheridan), Kip Pardue (Mark), Ann Owens Pierce (Ruth), Chris Sarandon (Robert), Valerie Watkins (Lola), Robin Weigert (Rachel).

Directed by Tim Kirkman and produced by Gill Holland. Screenplay by Kirkman.

All of the characters in Tim Kirkman's *Loggerheads* are good people, by their own lights. The lights of some people allow them to be content, while the lights of others fill them with sadness and regret. Sometimes you can move from one group to another. Not always.

The story involves the years 1990 and 1991 and three areas of North Carolina: Asheville, Eden, and Kure Beach. The characters are dealing in one way or another with homosexuality and adoption. One of the characters provides a connecting link involving the others. That makes it sound like things are all figured out, but *Loggerheads* is not a movie where the emotions are tidy and the messages are clear. It is about people trying to deal with the situations they have landed in.

We meet a woman named Grace (Bonnie Hunt) who works behind a rental-car counter and has moved back to Asheville to live with her mother, Sheridan (Michael Learned). In Eden, we meet a pastor named Robert (Chris Sarandon) and his wife, Elizabeth (Tess Harper). On Kure Beach, George (Michael Kelly) runs a shabby motel, and Mark (Kip Pardue) sleeps on the beach and observes the nocturnal behavior of loggerhead turtles. Loggerheads always return to the place where they were born, and that is something not everyone in the movie finds it easy to do.

I want to go slow in describing the plot because its developments unfold according to the needs of the characters. The movie is not about springing surprises on us but about showing these people in a process of discovery. The performances are not pitched toward melodrama; the actors all find the right notes and rhythms for scenes in which life goes on and everything need not be solved in three lines of dialogue.

George and Mark, for example, sense easily that they are both gay but become more friends than lovers. The pastor and his wife had a son they have not seen since he was seventeen, and they observe that among their friends and neighbors, "nobody ever asks about him." Grace gave up a child for adoption when she was seventeen and now wants to find that child, but in North Carolina an "anonymous" adoption cannot be undone.

These characters are not extreme examples of their type. The pastor is not a religious extremist but has ordinary conservative values. Here's how that works: When a new family moves in across the street, Robert suggests to Elizabeth that she ask them to come to church on Sunday. Then she informs him, "There is no woman in that house," and she thinks they're a gay couple. "Should I invite them to church?" she asks. Her husband says, "Let's just wait and see if they come on their own."

Elizabeth is much distracted by her longtime neighbor Ruth (Ann Pierce), who has placed an anatomically complete reproduction of Michelangelo's *David* on her front lawn. "If it were the *Venus de Milo*," Ruth says, "you wouldn't hear a peep out of anybody." Elizabeth suggests she put the statue in the backyard, so the neighbors won't have to look at it. "That's your solution to everything," Ruth says. "Move it to the backyard."

On Kure Beach, George gives Mark a room to stay in, and Mark thinks this may involve a "barter arrangement," but no, George is just doing him a favor. Unlike many gay men in movies, these two characters are not as concerned with sex as with their life choices; in different ways, both choose to live on the beach and are content to be far from the action. They talk about matters of life and death, George often seated comfortably, Mark usually standing or pacing, smoking.

In Asheville, Grace and Sheridan have issues going back to the day the mother insisted that her pregnant daughter give the baby up for adoption. "I was just trying to do what was best for everyone involved," she says in her defense. "I know you were," says Grace, and she does, however much she wanted to keep the baby and however empty the rest of her life has become.

Events now happen to these people that I will not describe. They bring some happiness, some sadness, some closure. It is Elizabeth, the pastor's wife, who moves most decisively to put her life in line with her feelings. Curiously, we are by no means sure that her husband, Robert, will not someday follow her in that direction.

These people are not robots programmed by the requirements of the plot. They want to be happy, and they want to feel they are doing the right thing. One of the characters, in my opinion, does the wrong thing but thinks it's the right thing. Sad, but there you are. *Loggerheads* offers these hopes: that our understanding of happiness can encompass more possibilities as we grow older, and that to find that happiness, we will have to do what we decide is the right thing, and not what someone else has decided for us.

London ★
R, 92 m., 2006

Chris Evans (Syd), Jessica Biel (London), Jason Statham (Bateman), Joy Bryant (Mallory), Kelli Garner (Maya), Isla Fisher (Becca). Directed by Hunter Richards and produced by Paul Davis-Miller, Ash R. Shah, and Bonnie Timmermann. Screenplay by Richards.

At one point in *London*, a Japanese experiment is described. Scientists place containers of white rice in two rooms. One container is praised. Nice rice. Beautiful rice. The other container is insulted. Ugly rice. Bad rice. At the end of a month, the rice in the first container is fresh and fragrant. The rice in the other room is decayed and moldy. If there is any validity to this experiment, I expect *London* to start decaying any day now. Bad movie. Ugly movie.

Another experiment is described. Baby bunnies. They are removed from their mother. Every time one is killed, the mother's vital signs show a sudden spike. *London* was given birth by the writer and director Hunter Richards, and if there is anything to the bunny theory, he's going to get jumpy when the reviews of his movie appear. There may be perspiration and trembling. Maybe anxiety attacks.

The rice and bunny experiments are two of many topics discussed by Syd (Chris Evans) and Bateman (Jason Statham) as they pace the floor of an upstairs bathroom at a Manhattan party, inhaling untold amounts of cocaine. Syd also guzzles tequila from a bottle. He met Bateman in a bar and insisted the older man, a Brit, accompany him to the party. He needed someone along for moral support because it was a going-away party for his girlfriend, London (Jessica Biel), and Syd wasn't invited. After I got to know Syd, I was not surprised that he wasn't invited, and I was not surprised that she was going away.

Let's track back a little. When first we see Syd, he has just treated himself to cocaine and the remains of a beer, and passed out in his apartment. The phone rings, he learns about the party, uses the f-word for the first of, oh, several hundred times, and smashes up the place, including a big aquarium. Curious that when the aquarium shatters, there are no shots of desperate fish gasping on the floor. Maybe Nemo has already led them to freedom.

At the party, Syd and Bateman get relentlessly stoned while discussing the kinds of tiresome subjects that seem important in the middle of the night in a bar when two drunks are analyzing the meaning of it all. Bartenders have been known to drink in order to endure these conversations. They usually consist of the two drunks exchanging monologues. During the parts when sober people would be listening, drunks are waiting until they get to talk again. Syd and Bateman are powerless over dialogue and their scenarios have become unmanageable.

There are personal confessions. Syd relates his unhappy romance with London, and we get flashbacks of them fighting, loving, talking, weeping, and running through all the other exercises in Acting 101. Bateman was married once, but it didn't work out. What a surprise. Now he pays good money to have S&M mistresses humiliate him. He describes their procedures in clinical detail, and we get flashbacks of those, too. Ugly. Bad. Syd is amazed that Bateman pays two-hundred dollars to be treated in such a way, although I am not sure if he is amazed that it is so much, or so little.

Occasionally one of the women from downstairs drifts into the bathroom. We meet Mallory (Joy Bryant) and Maya (Kelli Garner). Beautiful. Nice. They could do better. One of them says she heard Syd tried to commit suicide. That's a lie, says Syd, explaining a misunderstanding that occurred involving the drugs his dog takes for epilepsy. There is also a great deal of talk about God and faith, and whether Syd or Bateman feels the most pain. This discussion is theoretical, since neither one is feeling anything. "With all the drugs on the market, you'd think they'd have a pill to take the edge off of leaving a chick," Syd observes. Of course, he didn't leave her; she left him. But the treatment would probably be the same.

Evans and Statham have verbal facility and energy, which enables them to propel this dreck from one end of ninety-two minutes to the other, and the women in the movie are all perfectly adequate at playing bimbo cokeheads. I have seen all of these actors on better days in better movies, and I may have a novena said for them.

Two things mystify me. 1) How can you use that much cocaine and drink that much booze and remain standing and keep speaking, especially in the case of Syd, who was already stoned when he started? 2) Where is the camera? At least half of the movie is shot in the bathroom, which has a mirror along one wall. The mirror should be reflecting a camera, but I didn't see one. Well, of course, it's the job of the professionals to keep the camera hidden, and maybe cinematographer Jo Willems was trying to hide it in another movie.

Lonesome Jim ★ ★ ★
R, 91 m., 2006

Casey Affleck (Jim), Liv Tyler (Anika), Mary Kay Place (Sally), Seymour Cassel (Don), Kevin Corrigan (Tim), Jack Rovello (Ben), Mark Boone Junior (Evil), Rachel Strouse (Rachel), Sarah Strouse (Sarah). Directed by Steve Buscemi and produced by Jake Abraham, Buscemi, Galt Niederhoffer, Celine Rattray, and Gary Winick. Screenplay by James C. Strouse.

God loves you just the way you are, but he loves you too much to let you just stay that way.
—Ashley to her husband in *Junebug*

There was a time when young men in fiction went to big cities, seeking victory. Now they return to small towns, escaping defeat. *Lonesome Jim* follows, for example, *Winter Passing, Elizabethtown,* and *Garden State.* These movies tell us the big city will crush you but your hometown is a center of depression, weirdness, and parents near to madness. It's risky even when you only visit, as in *Junebug.*

These movies are not bad; they range from good to great. But they dramatize a disintegration of native American optimism. You can't make it there, and you can't make it anywhere. Consider Lonesome Jim. He went to New York City to be a great writer, although his choice of role models sends up an ominous signal; the photos on the wall of his childhood bedroom,

he explains, show victims of alcohol, drugs, or suicide, sometimes all three. He ought to have an alternative wall for modern writers who are successful and yet sane, such as Don DeLillo, Paul Theroux, Dave Eggers, Rohinton Mistry, and Eudora Welty.

But never mind. Jim returns home to Indiana, portrayed here as a sinkhole of failed dreams and nutty losers. This is unfair to Indiana; look what a cherished home the state made for the hero of *A History of Violence.* Perhaps Jim would find any state depressing, particularly in a film directed by Steve Buscemi, who is one of the best actors alive and a director of movies such as *Trees Lounge* and this one, in which the heroes are sad sacks. The sad sack Buscemi plays in *Trees Lounge* at least is fueled by resentment and anger and flashes of romantic optimism; Lonesome Jim is mired in the slough of despond. Played by Casey Affleck, he's in the same hole as his brother Tim (Kevin Corrigan), who never left home. One brother tells the other: "You're divorced, with a s— job in a lumberyard, and live with mom and dad. I'm a f—up, but you're a damn tragedy." Apart from the divorce, this could be either brother describing the other.

Jim moves in with Tim and their mom and dad (Mary Kay Place and Seymour Cassel). Dad is sour and jaundiced. Mom is implacably cheerful, which may be worse. She runs the lumber and ladder works, which her brother, called Evil (Mark Boone Junior), uses as a depot for drug deals. Tim and Jim discuss suicide. Tim runs his car into a tree, and although he survives, Jim has to take over his duties as the coach of a girls' basketball team that has not scored a single point in fourteen games. Not even Gene Hackman, in *Hoosiers,* could coach this team to victory. Luckily, Jim's brother's nurse is the sympathetic single mother Anika (Liv Tyler). It happens that Anika and Jim already know each other from a night of sudden sex.

In sad-sack movies there is often a helpful woman around to help the despairing heroes. In *Garden State* it was Natalie Portman, in *Elizabethtown,* Kirsten Dunst. Both were salvation angels, but Tyler has a gentle approach to this kind of role that is perfect for the tone of *Lonesome Jim.* Watch her eyes when he tells her, "There are so many fun and cheery people in the world. Don't you think you'd be better off with one of them?" She's a born nurse. Affleck finds a nice gradation in the way he allows his need for her to struggle with his fear for her.

Meanwhile, things go from worse to much worse for the family. Evil's schemes manage to get his sister arrested as a drug dealer, but look how optimistic she is when Jim visits her in prison. She enjoys talking to the other inmates, she says; arguably they're more entertaining than her family. God help her, the character played by Mary Kay Place could be Ashley from *Junebug*, grown up and with a family of her own.

The hero Buscemi played in *Trees Lounge* had even more desperate problems than Jim, but he at least dredged from his alcoholism the desire to survive. Lonesome Jim seems to embrace defeat. Having mastered the part about great writers being depressed and suicidal, he seems ready to retire without bothering to do the actual writing.

The movie is based on a screenplay by the Indiana writer James C. (Jim) Strouse. He has written a forlorn and poetic story, and Buscemi has made it into a movie about taking a deep breath and deciding to stop being a mope. The question is, can Jim accept the love of a woman like Anika? Can he allow himself to be happy? It's a close call for Jim, but it's his choice to make. You can actually be ecstatic living right there in Indiana. I know lots of people who are.

The Longest Yard ★ ★ ★
PG-13, 113 m., 2005

Adam Sandler (Paul "Wrecking" Crewe), Chris Rock (Caretaker), Burt Reynolds (Coach Nate Scarborough), James Cromwell (Warden Hazen), Walter Williamson (Errol Dandridge), Michael Irvin (Deacon Moss), Nelly (Earl Megget), Edward Bunker (Skitchy Rivers). Directed by Peter Segal and produced by Jack Giarraputo. Screenplay by Sheldon Turner, based on the story by Albert S. Ruddy and the screenplay by Tracy Keenan Wynn.

Before I left for the Cannes Film Festival, I saw *The Longest Yard,* and I did an advance taping of an episode of *Ebert & Roeper* on which I gave a muted thumbs-up to Roeper's scornful thumbs-down. I kinda liked it, in its goofy way. There was a dogged ridiculousness to the film

that amused me, especially in the way Adam Sandler was cast as a star quarterback. Once you accept Sandler as a quarterback, you've opened up the backfield to the entire membership of the Screen Actors Guild.

Now I have seen twenty-five films at Cannes, most of them attempts at greatness, and I sit here staring at the computer screen and realizing with dread that the time has come for me to write a review justifying that vertical thumb, which is already on video and will go out to millions of TV viewers seeking guidance in their moviegoing.

I do not say that I was wrong about the film. I said what I sincerely believed at the time. I believed it as one might believe in a good cu p of coffee; welcome while you are drinking it, even completely absorbing, but not much discussed three weeks later. Indeed, after my immersion in the films of Cannes, I can hardly bring myself to return to *The Longest Yard* at all, since it represents such a limited idea of what a movie can be and what movies are for.

Yet there are those whose entire lives as moviegoers are spent within the reassuring confines of such entertainments. In many cities and some states, there are few ways for them to get their eyes on movies that can feed their souls. They will have to be content with a movie in which Adam Sandler plays an alcoholic has-been football hero who gets drunk, drives dangerously, is thrown into jail, and becomes the pawn in a football game pitting a team of fellow prisoners against a team made up of prison guards. As I sit here, so help me God, I can't remember who got the idea for this game or why. I could look it up, but it's fascinating to watch myself trying to reconstruct a movie that was not intended to be remembered as long as it takes to get to the parking lot. This is how you learn. Through experience.

I recall that for some reason the big game is broadcast live on a sports network, maybe because the Sandler character was once a football hero and went down in flames over the drunk-driving scandal, and so there is a possibility of good ratings. His mentor is a former prisoner, played by Burt Reynolds, who starred in Robert Aldrich's original *The Longest Yard* (1974) and whose character this time is described in my notes as the Heisman Trophy winner of 1955.

Assuming my notes are correct, he was about twenty-one when he won the trophy and now Reynolds is about seventy-one, although now that I have done the math I don't know where to go with it. Certainly he is older than Sandler and younger than God.

James Cromwell plays the warden. I have met him on industry occasions. He is a militant Screen Actors Guild spokesman and a fiercely intelligent man who takes roles like this for the same reason I review them, because we are professionals and this is what we do. He would rather be in better movies and I would rather review them, but we have both seen a lot worse than this. There is a sense in which attacking this movie is like kicking a dog for not being better at calculus.

You think you know where I am headed. I am going to admit that I was wrong. I am going to withdraw that upturned thumb even as its ghostly video image beams out across the nation. I will compare it to the shimmering authority of a hologram of Obi-Wan Kenobi, expressing wisdom that was true enough when the hologram was recorded, but may not be helpful by the time it is seen.

But no, I am not going to do that at all. When the show was recorded I said what I believed, and for my sins I am appending three stars to the top of this review. I often practice a generic approach to film criticism, in which the starting point for a review is the question of what a movie sets out to achieve. The Longest Yard more or less achieves what most of the people attending it will expect. Most of its audiences will be satisfied enough when they leave the theater, although few will feel compelled to rent it on video to share with their friends. So, yes, it's a fair example of what it is.

I would, however, be filled with remorse if I did not urge you to consider the underlying melancholy of this review and seek out a movie you could have an interesting conversation about. After twelve days at Cannes, I was reminded that movies can enrich our lives, instead of just helping us get through them.

It may be that your local multiplex is not showing any films that have, or will, or would qualify for Cannes. There is a studied unwillingness among the major distributors to rise very frequently above the lowest common denominator, except during Oscar season. But there are actually some very worthy films in national release. If Kontroll is playing in your town, for example, that would be an idea. Or Brothers, or Dominion: Prequel to the Exorcist, or Layer Cake, or Unleashed. These are not great films, you understand, but they exist in a world that knows what greatness is, and they urge themselves toward it. If you can get to Crash, that is the movie you must see, and you should immediately drop any thought of seeing anything else instead.

Note: I attended a press conference of the Cannes jury. Its president, Emir Kusturica, said at one point that Cannes "kills uniformity." Its films are made one at a time. "To be global," he said, "to make a film that plays everywhere, you have to be slightly stupid." How do you like that; the bastard went and spoiled The Longest Yard for me.

Look at Me ★ ★ ★ ½
PG-13, 100 m., 2005

Marilou Berry (Lolita Cassard), Jean-Pierre Bacri (Etienne Cassard), Agnes Jaoui (Sylvia Miller), Laurent Grevill (Pierre Miller), Virginie Desarnauts (Karine Cassard), Keine Bouhiza (Sebastien), Gregoire Oestermann (Vincent), Serge Riaboukine (Felix), Michele Moretti (Edith). Directed by Agnes Jaoui and produced by Jean-Philippe Andraca and Christian Berard. Screenplay by Jean-Pierre Bacri and Jaoui.

Here is a difference, small but not insignificant, between Hollywood and French films. Consider the inevitable scene where the child is performing onstage, and the theater door opens, and there is the parent who has denied the child's talent, but now nods and smiles and sees that the child is truly gifted after all.

Now turn to Look at Me, the unforgiving new French film about a chubby classical singer and her egotistical father. She rehearses stubbornly and has a beautiful voice. He is a famous writer and a snob, absorbed in the appreciation of himself. She gives a recital in an old church in the country, and the audience admires her singing. Does the father arrive late, his eyes filled with tears as he acknowledges her gifts? No, the father arrives on time, but sneaks out to smoke and make cell calls.

People can be cruel out of ignorance or carelessness, but it takes a knack to be cruel as a strategy. Etienne Cassard (Jean-Pierre Bacri), the father, is a man full of himself. He has written great books, or at least people assure him they are great, and he is a publisher. People are wary of him and suck up to him.

Etienne has a gift for ignoring his twenty-year-old daughter, Lolita (Marilou Berry), perhaps because he doesn't think it helps his image to have her plumpness in view. He has a sleek, younger trophy wife named Karine (Virginie Desarnauts), who he is happy to display, but he ignores her, puts her down, ridicules her, gently corrects her, doesn't listen to her.

Given this situation, you'd think you could anticipate the drift of the film, but no: It doesn't pity its characters just because they are badly treated. Lolita, for example, is suspicious and defensive. She has felt unpopular for so long that she's developed a paranoia that prevents her from trusting others. No, not even Sebastien (Keine Bouhiza), the boy who cares for her, attends to her, would like her if she were not so sure no one could possibly like her.

There is also the matter of Lolita's music teacher, Sylvia, played by Agnes Jaoui, who cowrote the movie with Bacri and directs it. Sylvia's teaching helps support her husband, Pierre (Laurent Grevill), a novelist who is stuck in obscurity. Does Sylvia's attitude toward Lolita change when she learns that the girl's father is a famous writer and publisher? A man who could help her Pierre? Lolita thinks it does, and is probably right. So Lolita uses her father as leverage with her teacher, and soon Etienne has seen to the publication of Pierre's book.

Now watch closely. Pierre's book is an enormous success. This (a) reflects well upon Etienne because he discovered Pierre and sponsored him, but (b) underlines the inconvenience that Etienne himself has published nothing much in recent years. Pierre meanwhile follows Etienne like a fawning dog, ignoring his wife because he's blinded by the famous people at Etienne's parties. Lolita observes all of this and detests it, and carefully nurtures her misery.

There are scenes in this movie of social cruelty beyond all compare. Etienne is capable of making his daughter think he is calling her attractive, and then correcting her: He was talking to the woman next to her. Whoever he's talking to on his cell phone is always more important than whoever he's talking to in person. At dinner, when the attention strays from him for long, Etienne's eyes narrow and his conversational knives are thrown.

This performance comes from an actor who was so vulnerable in the previous movie he made with Jaoui. That was *The Taste of Others* (2000), where he plays an unremarkable man who falls in love with an amateur actress and her circle in a local theater company. In that movie, he was essentially playing the Pierre character—the adoring dog. He goes from meekness to arrogance so convincingly he even seems to have a different face in the two films. Marilou Berry's performance is remarkable, too, in the defiant way she faces the world, and in the way she uses a miraculous voice that is not miracle enough for her.

The most sympathetic character is the one who would be the heavy in the Hollywood version: Karine, the young stepmother. She reaches out to Lolita even after being rejected. She wants to be the girl's friend. She puts up with the boorish behavior of her husband, and she tries to repair the wounds he causes to their friends. In some sense, the overbearing father and the resentful daughter have created each other; the stepmother is the innocent bystander. The thing about a movie like this is, the characters may be French, but they're more like people I know than they could ever be in the Hollywood remake.

Look Both Ways ★ ★ ★ ½
PG-13, 100 m., 2006

William McInnes (Nick), Justine Clarke (Meryl), Anthony Hayes (Andy), Lisa Flanagan (Anna), Andrew S. Gilbert (Phil), Daniella Farinacci (Julia), Sacha Horler (Linda), Maggie Dence (Joan), Edwin Hodgeman (Jim), Andreas Sobik (Train Driver). Directed by Sarah Watt and produced by Bridget Ikin. Screenplay by Watt.

Death is for the living, and not for the dead so much.
　　　　　　　—Errol Morris's *Gates of Heaven*

It doesn't really matter if you look both ways. The piano may be falling from the sky. If we gave much thought to the possibility that we could die at any moment, we could hardly endure life. Sarah Watt's *Look Both Ways* tells the stories of several people who come close to death and deal with that experience. What choice do they have? The movie is not cheerful, nor is it morbid; it leaves us not encouraged but resolute.

Watt weaves together their stories, like *Crash* or perhaps even more like *Magnolia*. In Adelaide, Australia, a man is struck and killed by a train, and that event attracts a photographer named Nick (William McInnes), a reporter named Andy (Anthony Hayes), their editor Phil (Andrew S. Gilbert), and the victim's wife, Julia (Daniella Farinacci). Andy has a theory that many "accidents" are in fact suicides, and his examination of the death scene inspires an article speculating that the victim deliberately stepped in front of the train. Andy even stands on the tracks himself, as an experiment.

Nick takes a photograph of the wife, Julia, in anguish as she learns of her husband's death. Phil the editor runs the photo across half the front page, and Andy's speculations inside. These are not the acts of an editor much concerned with the feelings of the widow.

All the men have things on their minds. Nick has just learned that testicular cancer has spread throughout his body. Andy has learned that his girlfriend, Anna (Lisa Flanagan), is pregnant.

And then there is Meryl (Justine Clarke), a witness to the man's death. She is a painter of seascapes for sympathy cards, and she meets the photographer Nick on the scene. Their first meeting is casual, the next less so, and then to their surprise they are making love. The next day, Nick says he "isn't ready" for a relationship. "I meet you on the first day, we sleep together on the second, and on the third you're not ready," Meryl says. "That's a pretty tight schedule." They fight, they separate, and then they meet again and he tells her the truth.

With Andy and Anna, the pregnancy is a surprise. They hadn't seen each other in a month. "I've been incredibly busy," he says. Uh-huh. He doesn't want a kid. She points out that she didn't intend to get pregnant, and for that matter, "You were there, too." Will she get an abortion? On the other hand, will she stop smoking?

As the film considers these questions, the live action is interrupted from time to time by Meryl's violent fantasies in which a train roars off a bridge and crushes her, a monster attacks

from the woods, and so on. To these animated visuals, which are abrupt and violent, the movie adds montages from the pasts of the characters, especially Nick; when he learns of his cancer, his life flashes before his eyes, somewhat prematurely.

This kind of description, of course, could apply to a bad movie as well as a good one. What distinguishes Sarah Watt's writing and direction is that she doesn't allow her characters to stand for anything other than themselves. They are confused, uncertain, imperfect, yearning, lonely, scared. They bumble in the direction of survival. And the movie enriches their lives with memories; Nick, for example, recalls his own father's death, which he sees much differently after he learns of his cancer. He is also very mildly impatient by the way people react to his news. When he uses the word "cancer," two of them say exactly the same thing: "*Cancer* cancer?" Is there any other kind?

It's pretty brutal, the way the newspaper treats the dead man's widow to all that coverage the next morning. But she receives a heartwarming visit from the engineer of the train. It's harsh the way a pregnancy forces Andy and Anna to decide what, exactly, is the reality of their relationship. There is cosmic irony involved in Nick and Meryl falling in love just when they have absolutely no future. After they kiss and make up, notice especially a montage of images used by Sarah Watt. In that montage are love and death and the whole damn thing.

I watched the movie in a kind of fascination. It is poetic and unforgiving, romantic and stark. Death is the subject we edge around. If it is on the sidewalk, we step into the street. If it is on the telephone, we hang up. We don't open its letters. To know that we will die is such a final and unanswerable rebuke. And yet without death we'd all be bored out of our minds, if indeed we had even developed minds in the first place. Sometimes I think the whole process of evolution leads up to our ability to comprehend the words: *Gather ye rosebuds while ye may.*

Looking for Comedy in the Muslim World ★ ★ ★
PG-13, 98 m., 2006

Albert Brooks (Albert Brooks), John Carroll Lynch (Stewart), Sheetal Sheth (Maya), Jon

417

Tenney (Mark), Fred Dalton Thompson (Committee Chair). Directed by Albert Brooks and produced by Steve Bing, Herb Nanas, and Tabrez Noorani. Screenplay by Brooks.

Q: *Why is there no Halloween in India?*
A: *They took away the Gandhi.*

Ho, ho. Of course, if there is no Halloween in India, then they wouldn't know they didn't have one, so the joke would not be funny. In a country that does have Halloween, such as the United States, anyone young enough to find the joke funny (under eight, say) wouldn't know who Gandhi was.

So you see we're in a minefield here. Who knows what makes people laugh? In an opening scene of *Looking for Comedy in the Muslim World*, Albert Brooks is summoned to a secret State Department meeting. It's chaired by Fred Dalton Thompson, who was an actor before he was a senator, and now plays one in the movies. The president is concerned about reaching the world's Muslims, Thompson explains. He's tried wars and spying, the usual stuff, and now he thinks he might try humor. Brooks's assignment: Spend a month in India and Pakistan and write a five-hundred–page report on what makes Muslims laugh.

That's the premise for a movie that might inspire a sequel titled *Searching for Comedy in the Albert Brooks World*. I mean that as a compliment. Brooks's movie has a lot of humor in it, but it's buried, oblique, throwaway, inside, apologetic, coded, and underplayed. Midway through the movie he does a free stand-up comedy show in New Delhi, and nobody laughs at anything. Rodney Dangerfield attacked sullen audiences aggressively: "Folks! Folks! There's a guy up here onstage, telling jokes!" Brooks is incapable of bluntness. He sidles up to his material and slinks away from it.

I recall that Brooks did once perform the material from his New Delhi concert on TV (references are made to the *Tonight* show and Ed Sullivan). It was funny then: the "improv" set where he changes all of the audience suggestions, and the skit about the incompetent ventriloquist. But everything he does bombs in Delhi. It would also bomb in America, because he performs as if it's not funny.

His concert is an experiment: see what the audience does and doesn't laugh at, and put it in his report. Of course, he has no idea how many people in the audience are Muslims; India has lots of them, but a lot more Hindus. And when he tries to go to Pakistan, it involves an illegal border crossing and a stand-up session before a bunch of would-be stand-up comics sitting around a campfire.

Brooks is aided in his survey by a local woman, Maya (Sheetal Sheth), who types 125 words a minute, is terrifically encouraging, and has a jealous Iranian boyfriend. He has a couple of minders from the State Department, the *Fine Woodworking* subscriber Stuart (John Carroll Lynch) and his partner, Mark (Jon Tenney), always carrying on a simultaneous conversation on a cell phone. They try the man-on-the-street approach, asking people what makes them laugh with about as much success as Jay Leno has asking people how many states there are.

The laughs tend to be hidden in the crevices. Brooks walks by offices every day, for example, filled with people who are answering the phone for big American corporations. There are two bigger laughs in the movie, one involving his dressing room for the stand-up show, the other involving his meeting with executives of the Al-jazeera network. And some medium laughs. And a lot of chuckles. And a stubborn unwillingness to force the laughs. Brooks has a persona that apologizes for everything, including being a persona. No matter how much you laugh, you get the feeling he wanted you to laugh less.

Because I have seen all of Brooks's movies, liked most of them, and loved some, I was in training for *Looking for Comedy in the Muslim World*. Veteran Brooks watchers will be able to hear the secret melodies and appreciate the way he throws away even the throwaways. It's also interesting how he *doesn't* take cheap shots at India or Pakistan. When a Muslim woman asks him, "Are you a Jew?" he's set up for a slam dunk, but he walks away from it. He acts not like a comic wiseguy but like a clueless citizen sent on a baffling State Department mission. Well, that's what he's playing.

I liked the movie. I smiled a lot. It maintained its tone in the face of bountiful temptations to get easy laughs. It never identifies a Muslim (or Hindu) sense of humor, but then again, Brooks never does anything funny, so maybe that's why.

Of course they have a sense of humor in India, because the best-selling English-language novelist in the country is P G. Wodehouse. If you don't know who Wodehouse was, that's all right; you didn't know who Gandhi was, either. If you know who Gandhi was but still don't get the Halloween joke, that may have been because you were pronouncing "Gandhi" correctly.

Lord of War ★ ★ ★ ½
R, 122 m., 2005

Nicolas Cage (Yuri Orlov), Ethan Hawke (Jack Valentine), Jared Leto (Vitaly Orlov), Bridget Moynahan (Ava Fontaine), Ian Holm (Simeon Weisz), Sammi Rotibi (Baptiste Junior), Eamonn Walker (Baptiste Senior). Directed by Andrew Niccol and produced by Niccol, Philippe Rousselet, and Norman Golightly. Screenplay by Niccol.

Yuri Orlov argues that his products kill fewer people than tobacco and alcohol. He has a point, but it's more fun and takes longer to die that way. There are few pleasures to be had from an AK-47 bullet to the brain, and no time to enjoy them. Yuri is an international arms dealer who has "done business with every army but the Salvation Army." He cheerfully tours the world's flashpoints, a war-to-war salesman in a dark suit and tie.

Lord of War is a bleak comedy, funny in a *Catch-22* sort of way, and at the same time an angry outcry against the gun traffic that turns twelve-year-olds into killers and cheapens human life to the point where might makes not only right but everything else as well. Yuri is played by Nicolas Cage in another of those performances you cannot easily imagine anyone else doing; he plays an immigrant from Ukraine who has the cocky self-assurance, the snaky surface charm, the breezy intellectual justification for the most indefensible acts. He will sell to anyone, anytime, he tells us during his narration, which confides the secrets of his trade: He never sold to Osama bin Laden because, "He was always bouncing checks."

Yuri's world is a small one. He has few competitors and a short but frequently updated list of clients. The world's leading arms dealer when Yuri goes into business is Simeon Weisz (Ian Holm), who prefers not to do business with people he thinks are evil, although his definition of evil is extremely flexible. Yuri asks Simeon to let him team up, an offer Simeon rejects; he'll eventually lose a lot of business by that decision.

The clients come from all over. There is a moment in the film when Yuri gets some bad news: Peace talks have started in a particularly promising market. He shifts his focus to the Bosnian arena. When they say they're having a war, "they keep their word."

He also finds two good customers in Africa: the Liberian dictator Baptiste Senior (Eamonn Walker) and his son, Baptiste Junior (Sammi Rotibi). Senior is capable of shooting people dead without notice just in a fit of pique. During a meeting with Yuri, he kills an inattentive aide and seems ready to shoot Yuri next, but Yuri grabs the gun back and says, "Now you'll *have* to buy it because it's a used gun." It's the kind of joke that appeals to Senior. Yuri's life and even his fortune are saved.

Yuri lives in Manhattan luxury with the former model Ava Fontaine (Bridget Moynahan), who believes him, or pretends to believe him, when he says he's in the international shipping business. That business takes a turn for the better with the collapse of the Soviet Union and the sudden appearance on the black market of enormous caches of weapons. Luckily, Yuri is related to a now-retired general in Ukraine, and they do business.

The movie, written and directed by Andrew Niccol (*The Truman Show, Gattaca*), has some of the same stylistic aggressiveness as David O. Russell's *Three Kings*. Consider a brilliant early montage that takes a bullet's-eye view as it moves from ore to the assembly line to finishing, packaging, distribution, sale, and eventual use; the montage ends with the bullet passing through the brain of a young man. It makes the point that at every step along the way, arms manufacturers are producing death as their end product.

That doesn't much bother Yuri, who believes that wars will be fought regardless of whether he sells arms. In that he is correct. There is the disagreement, however, of a stubborn Interpol agent named Valentine (Ethan Hawke), who thinks he could save some lives by putting Yuri out of business. Some of their encounters resemble the "Spy vs. Spy" feature in *Mad* maga-

419

zine, as when Valentine chases a ship filled with arms, and Yuri is able to repaint its name and disguise it before the law gets close enough.

Helping Yuri at first, and then a distinct problem for him, is his younger brother Vitaly (Jared Leto). When they're desperately disguising the ship and need a Dutch flag they do not have, it is Vitaly's lateral thinking that suggests a French flag flown sideways looks like a Dutch flag.

After movies like *Hotel Rwanda, Before the Rain*, and *Welcome to Saravejo*, the cold cynicism of *Lord of War* plays like a deadly footnote. People are killed because guns are available; wars lower the average age of soldiers until in some places they are fought by children with no idea of their original cause. It's hypnotic, like the gaze of a poisonous snake, how Yuri stares into the face of this horror and counts his profits. Will fate and justice eventually catch up with him? Maybe, unless money is the answer. In Yuri's experience, it usually is.

Lords of Dogtown ★ ★
PG-13, 107 m., 2005

Emile Hirsch (Jay Adams), Victor Rasuk (Tony Alva), John Robinson (Stacy Peralta), Michael Angarano (Sid), Nikki Reed (Kathy Alva), Heath Ledger (Skip Engblom), Rebecca De Mornay (Philaine), Johnny Knoxville (Topper Burks). Directed by Catherine Hardwicke and produced by John Linson. Screenplay by Stacy Peralta.

In the summer of 1975, modern skateboarding was invented in the Santa Monica and Venice Beach areas of California. The young members of the Zephyr Team, sponsored by a permanently stoned surfboard store owner, revolutionized the sport, performing acrobatics and crazy stunts on skateboards that had until then been seen as fancy scooters. They became famous, they made a lot of money, they grew up, and one of them, Stacy Peralta, made a 2002 documentary about them named *Dogtown and Z-Boys*.

It was a good documentary. As I wrote at the time: "It answers a question I have long been curious about: How and why was the first skateboarder inspired to go aerial, to break contact with any surface and do acrobatics in midair?

Consider that the pioneer was doing this for the very first time over a vertical drop of perhaps fifteen feet to a concrete surface. It's not the sort of thing you try out of idle curiosity."

Now we have *Lords of Dogtown*, a fiction film based on the very same material, and indeed, written by Peralta. Not only is there no need for this movie, but its weaknesses underline the strength of the doc. How and why Peralta found so much old footage of skateboarding in 1975 is a mystery, but he was able to give us a good sense of those kids at that time. Although Catherine Hardwicke, the director of *Lords of Dogtown*, has a good feeling for the period and does what she can with her actors, we've seen the originals, and these aren't the originals. Nobody in the fiction film pulls off stunts as spectacular as we see for real in the documentary.

The story line remains the same. The kids live in what was then one of the remaining beachfront slums, down the coast from the expensive Malibu area. The beach was ruled by surfers, but in the afternoon, when the waves died down, some of the surfers, or their younger brothers, fooled around on skateboards. One day, Skip Engblom, the shop owner, comes up with a key breakthrough, polyurethane wheels: "They grip." With the additional traction, the Z-Boys try skating the sides of the big open drainage canal that runs through the area. Then comes a brainstorm: Because of a drought, the area's swimming pools were drained. They started "borrowing" pools when the owners weren't home, to skate the curved sides.

Emile Hirsch stars as Jay Adams, Victor Rasuk is Tony Alva, and John Robinson, with long blond hair that gets him photographed a lot in the emerging skateboarding magazines, plays Stacy Peralta. They all seem like pale imitations of the originals, as indeed they must be. Heath Ledger plays Skip, their mentor, who sponsors the Zephyr Team, gives them their first priceless T-shirts, and eventually, stoned and drunk, ends up making surfboards in somebody else's back room. But he was the catalyst.

In the documentary, there was a Z-Girl along with the Z-Boys, but here all we get is Nikki Reed as Kathy, Tony's sister. We also meet Rebecca De Mornay, as Jay's mother, who, like all mothers in southern California films, looks like she oughta be in pictures.

Both the surfing and skateboarding sequences are fun to watch, within reason, but after seeing *Dogtown and Z-Boys* and the haunting surfing documentary *Riding Giants* (2004), we know the real thing is more awesome. The best surfing scenes take place when surfers ride waves dangerously close to the Pacific Island Pier and the rocks at its base; the pier mysteriously burns down that summer. "They wanted it gone," Skip mourns.

Skateboarding is a sport combining grace, courage, and skill, and here we see it being born. What we do not quite understand is how long one can be a skateboarder before you feel like you've been there and done that. Stacy Peralta obviously feels great nostalgia for that period in his life, which was the foundation for fame and fortune, but at this point it is time for him to either (a) move on to films about something else, or (b) deal with the dark aftermath of those golden days.

There were a lot of drugs around; although we see Skip here as a survivor, he's more of a victim. And like the earlier movie, this one doesn't really deal with injuries or accidents. In a sport where you can free fall to concrete, were there deaths? Was anyone paralyzed? There's a touching scene here where the kids take a friend in a wheelchair into one of the empty swimming pools and let him ride the sides a little, but he's in the chair because of cancer, not skateboarding.

The Lost City ★ ★ ★
R, 143 m., 2006

Andy Garcia (Fico Fellove), Bill Murray (The Writer), Ines Sastre (Aurora Fellove), Lorena Feijoo (Leonela), Tomas Milian (Don Federico Fellove), Elizabeth Pena (Miliciana Munoz), Dustin Hoffman (Meyer Lansky), Millie Perkins (Dona Cecilia Fellove), Enrique Murciano (Ricardo Fellove), Nestor Carbonell (Luis Fellove), Richard Bradford (Don Donoso Fellove). Directed by Andy Garcia and produced by Frank Mancuso Jr. and Garcia. Screenplay by Guillermo Cabrera Infante.

Andy Garcia's *The Lost City* feels like the distillation of countless conversations and family legends, rehearsed from time immemorial by Cubans who fled their homeland and sought to re-create it in their memories. In every family such stories, repeated endlessly, can become tedious, but there is another sense in which they are a treasured ritual. There was a Cuba, remembered firsthand only by those who are growing older now, that was a beloved place and stopped existing when Castro came to power in 1959.

Garcia's family lived in that older Cuba, and so did Guillermo Cabera Infante, the Cuban writer and film critic who wrote this screenplay. (The project, long discussed, was not easy for Garcia to finance; Infante died in February 2005.) Infante and Garcia do not deceive themselves that the old Cuba was a paradise: It is seen as corrupt, controlled in key areas by the Mafia, and built on a class system in which many were poor so that a few could be rich. The problem is that Castro did not cure the ills so much as distribute them more evenly, so that more could be miserable. Garcia and Infante are against the old and the new, against both the rotten Batista regime and the disappointment of Castro and Che Guevara. There is a moment in the film when a senator agrees that Batista must be overthrown but argues wistfully that it must be done "constitutionally." Fat chance.

Garcia stars in the film as Fico Fellove, a suave operator who owns and runs a Havana nightclub named El Tropico. Showgirls perform a Vegas-style revue, the customers are elegant and intriguing, and at the door their big, sleek American cars glisten in the neon lights. Fico wants this life to continue forever, and like Rick in *Casablanca*, he is not particularly political. At a time when Batista's grip seems to be weakening, when reports from the mountains magnify Castro's popularity, he receives a visitor: the gangster Meyer Lansky (Dustin Hoffman), who wants to become Fico's partner in turning El Tropico into a casino. It is the kind of offer Fico can refuse, although that might not be prudent.

Fico's brothers have a different orientation in the dying days of the old regime. Luis (Nestor Carbonell) embraces the revolutionary cause, and Ricardo (Enrique Murciano) journeys into the mountains to fight with the rebels. The rest of the family deplores their decisions; Fico comforts Aurora (Ines Sastre), Luis's wife, who complains that her husband is away so much he must be cheating. He is not cheating but rebelling, but never mind: Fico ends by falling in love with her himself.

Commenting on all of these events is an enigmatic character named The Writer, played by Bill Murray as a jester who speaks in jokes that contain the truth. His running commentary on Meyer Lansky is bold to the point of recklessness. It is never quite explained who The Writer is, although some articles on the film claim he represents the screenwriter, Infante.

If so, he gives Infante an opening into the story that he can use to speak directly, if obliquely, of the absurdity of the times. Indeed, Infante himself played such a role under both Batista and Castro, saying what he believed in such a way that no one could be quite certain he had gone too far. Batista nevertheless jailed him, and Castro uneasily made him a cultural attaché in Belgium, not then a key posting. A lifelong communist, Infante felt Castro betrayed the party's principles, and he eventually chose exile. His *Twentieth Century Job*, a collection of his movie reviews, has some of the same wry, dubious philosophy expressed by The Writer in the film.

I enjoyed Murray and his scenes, but the character doesn't fit with the rest of the film. Fico Fellove is not a particularly witty or sunny character and does not suffer fools gladly. Why does he make an exception for The Writer? There are scenes where we almost wonder if The Writer is intended to be physically present at all; for all that Fico takes notice of him, perhaps he is a ghost visible only to us.

The main line of *The Lost City* involves the fall of Batista, Castro's entry into Havana, the divisions that open up in the family, and the quick disillusionment with the new regime, which is as arbitrary as the old, and more dogmatic. A musicians' union dispute at the nightclub symbolizes the way power is misused by those who have only just possessed it. Fico's loss is magnified by the heartbreak of the old musician who choreographed the shows and danced as a counterpoint to the girls; he has lost his whole world.

The movie evokes that long-ago world carefully and with a certain poetry; it was shot in the Dominican Republic. There is a lot of music, much of it from the period and performed by the same musicians or their successors. The costumes and the interiors set off the way the

characters carry themselves, with grace and confidence.

At 143 minutes, the movie is too long, but it has a lot to cover and a lot to say, and I imagine Garcia has a reason why every scene is necessary. There is romance and some action, but it is not a romance or an adventure film; it is a personal version of what happened in Cuba and what it felt like at the time. Communicating that effectively, it lacks a larger view; newsreel footage covers historical events that another film might have tried to stage, and the implication is that for characters like Fico, the revolution took place more in the news than in his own life, and he was not quite prepared for such an upheaval. At the end he and a great many others leave Cuba for Miami or New York, where, for Fico, Meyer Lansky awaits.

The Lost Skeleton of Cadavra ★ ½
PG, 90 m., 2004

Larry Blamire (Dr. Paul Armstrong), Fay Masterson (Betty Armstrong), Jennifer Blaire (Animala), Brian Howe (Dr. Roger Fleming), Susan McConnell (Lattis), Andrew Parks (Krobar), Dan Conroy (Ranger Brad), Robert Deveau (The Farmer). Directed by Larry Blamire and produced by F. Miguel Valenti. Screenplay by Blamire.

"It is a curious attribute of camp that it can only be found, not made." So observes Dave Kehr, in his *New York Times* review of *The Lost Skeleton of Cadavra*. I did not read the rest of the review, because (1) I had to write my own, and (2), well, his first sentence says it all, doesn't it? True camp sincerely wants to be itself. In this category I include the works of Ed Wood and the infinitely more talented Russ Meyer. False camp keeps digging you in the ribs with a bony elbow. In this category falls *The Lost Skeleton of Cadavra*. Movies like the *Austin Powers* series are in a different category altogether, using the framework of satire for the purpose of comedy.

The Lost Skeleton of Cadavra, which is a loving tribute to the worst science fiction movies ever made, is about a three-way struggle for possession of the rare element atmosphereum. The contestants include an American scientist and his wife, a married (I think) couple from outer space, and a mad scientist and his sidekick, which is, of course, the lost skeleton of Cadavra. There is also a creature that seems to have been created by an explosion at a sofa factory, and a sexy girl named Animala, whose role is to appear in the movie and be a sexy girl. More about her later.

The photography, the dialogue, the acting, the script, the special effects, and especially the props (such as a space ship that looks like it would get a D in shop class) are all deliberately bad in the way that such films were bad when they were *really* being made. The locations remind me of the old *Captain Video* TV series, in which the same fake rocks were always being moved around to indicate we were in a new place on the alien planet. The writer and director, Larry Blamire, who also plays the saner of the scientists, has the look so well mastered that if the movie had only been made in total ignorance fifty years ago, it might be recalled today as a classic. A minor, perhaps even minuscule, classic.

A funny thing happened while I was watching it. I began to flash back to *Trog* (1970). This is an example of camp that was made, not found. That it was directed by the great cinematographer Freddie Francis I have absolutely no explanation for. That it starred Joan Crawford, in almost her final movie role, I think I understand. Even though she was already enshrined as a Hollywood goddess, she was totally unable to stop accepting roles, and took this one against all reason.

The plot of *Trog*, which I will abbreviate, involves a hairy monster. When it goes on a killing spree and is captured, Joan Crawford, an anthropologist, realizes it is a priceless scientific find: the Missing Link between ape and man. Then Trog kidnaps a small girl and crawls into a cave, and reader, although many years have passed since I saw the movie, I have never forgotten the sight of Joan Crawford in her designer pants suit and all the makeup crawling on her hands and knees into the cave and calling out, "Trog! Trog!" As if Trog knew the abbreviation of its scientific name.

But never mind; you see the point. *Trog* is perfect camp because Freddie Francis and Joan Crawford would never have allied themselves with a movie that was deliberately bad. (I am not so sure about Joe Cornelius, who played Trog.) It is bad all on its own. *The Lost Skeleton*

of *Cadavra* has been made by people who are trying to be bad, which by definition reveals that they are playing beneath their ability. Poor Ed Wood, on the other hand, always and sincerely made the very best film he possibly could. How rare is a director like Russ Meyer, whose work satirizes material that doesn't even exist except in his satire of it, and who is also very funny; no coincidence that the *Austin Powers* movies are always careful to quote him.

But what have I neglected to tell you about *The Lost Skeleton of Cadavra*? Reading my notes, I find that "there is enough atmosphereum in one teaspoon to go to the moon and back six times," which is not quite the statement it seems to be. Oh, and the sexy girl named Animala is described as: "part human, part four different forest animals, and she can dance! Oh, how she can dance! Like I've never seen a woman dance before!" A possible mate for Trog?

A Lot Like Love ★

PG-13, 95 m., 2005

Ashton Kutcher (Oliver), Amanda Peet (Emily), Kathryn Hahn (Michelle), Kal Penn (Jeeter), Ali Larter (Gina), Taryn Manning (Ellen), Gabriel Mann (Peter), Jeremy Sisto (Ben). Directed by Nigel Cole and produced by Armyan Bernstein and Kevin J. Messick. Screenplay by Colin Patrick Lynch.

A Lot Like Love is a romance between two of the dimmer bulbs of their generation. Judging by their dialogue, Oliver and Emily have never read a book or a newspaper, seen a movie, watched TV, had an idea, carried on an interesting conversation, or ever thought much about anything. The movie thinks they are cute and funny, which is embarrassing, like your uncle who won't stop with the golf jokes. This is not the fault of the stars, Ashton Kutcher and Amanda Peet, who are actors forced to walk around in Stupid Suits.

When I was at Boulder for a conference at the University of Colorado, I found myself walking across campus with a kid who confessed he was studying philosophy.

"What do you plan to do with it?" I asked.

He said he wasn't sure. All of his friends were on career tracks, but "I dunno. I just find this stuff interesting."

Yes! I said. Yes! Don't treat education as if it's only a trade school. Take some electives just because they're interesting. You have long years to get through, and you must guard against the possibility of becoming a bore to yourself.

A Lot Like Love, written by Colin Patrick Lynch and directed by Nigel Cole, is about two people who have arrived at adulthood unequipped for the struggle. The lives of Oliver and Emily are Idiot Plots, in which every misunderstanding could be solved by a single word they are vigilant never to utter. They Meet Cute, over and over again. They keep finding themselves alone because their lovers keep walking out on them. Well, no wonder. "I'm going," one of her lovers says, and goes. Any more of an explanation and she might have had to take notes.

He has an Internet start-up selling diapers over the Web. She's dumped by a rock musician in the opening scene, where she seems to be a tough Goth chick, but that's just the costume. Later Ollie gives her a camera and she becomes a photographer, and even has a gallery exhibit of her works, which look like photos taken on vacation with cell phone cameras and e-mailed to you by the children of friends.

The movie is ninety-five minutes long, and neither character says a single memorable thing. You've heard of being too clever by half? Ollie and Emily are not clever enough by three-quarters. During a dinner date they start spitting water at each other. Then she crawls under the table, not for what you're thinking, but so they can trade sides and spit in the opposite direction. Then it seems like she's choking on her food, but he refuses to give her the Heimlich maneuver, and even tells the waitress not to bother. So take a guess: Is she really choking, or not? If she's playing a trick, she's a doofus, and if she isn't, he's a doofus. They shouldn't be allowed to leave the house without a parent or adult guardian.

They continue to Meet Cute over many long years, which are spelled out in titles: "Three Years Later," "Six Months Later," and so on. I was reminded of the little blue thermometers telling you the software will finish downloading in nineteen hours. Their first Meet Cute is a doozy: On a flight to New York, she enlists him in the Mile-High Club before they even know each other's names. But that's Strike One against him, she says, because she had to make the first move. Yeah, like a guy on an airplane should push into the rest room for sex with a woman he doesn't know. That's how you get to wear the little plastic cuffs.

Later they Meet Cute again, walk into a bar, drink four shots of Jack Daniels in one minute, and order a pitcher of beer. No, they're not alcoholics. This is just Movie Behavior; for example, at first she smokes and then she stops and then she starts again. That supplies her with a Personality Characteristic. Still later, they sing together, surprisingly badly. The movie is filled with a lot of other pop music. These songs tend toward plaintive dirges complaining, "My life can be described by this stupid song." At one point he flies to New York to pitch his dot-com diapers to some venture capitalists, and is so inarticulate and clueless he could be a character in this movie. To call the movie dead in the water is an insult to water.

Love Me If You Dare ★ ★
R, 99 m., 2004

Guillaume Canet (Julien), Marion Cotillard (Sophie), Thibault Verhaeghe (Julien at Eight), Josephine Lebas-Joly (Sophie at Eight), Gerard Watkins (Julien's Father), Emmanuelle Gronvold (Julien's Mother), Laetizia Venezia (Christelle). Directed by Yann Samuell and produced by Christophe Rossignon. Screenplay by Jacky Cukier and Samuell.

Do I dislike this film, or only its characters? There can be good films about bad people. Remember Travis Bickle. For that matter, do I dislike it because the characters are bad, or simply because they make me feel uneasy? Perhaps they're simply insane, and trapped in their mutual obsession. Perhaps because the film makes me feel so crawly, it is actually good. Yet still I cannot like it.

Love Me If You Dare tells the story of Julien and Sophie, who meet in grade school and make a pact that binds them together for a lifetime. Their treaty revolves around a little tin box, a toy painted to look like a merry-go-round. When one hands the other the box, along with it comes a dare. The other *must* do what they've been dared to do. This begins as a childhood game and continues into adulthood, where it gathers dangerous and dark undertones.

The movie will appeal to lovers of *Amelie,* according to the ads. Not if they loved *Amelie* for its good cheer. This is *Amelie* through the looking-glass. Yes, it has some of the same visual invention and delight, and director Yann Samuell's camera swoops and circles and flies through windows and into dreams. Yes, there's a bright color palate. Yes, the movie riffs through techniques, including animated sequences. Yes, Marion Cotillard has sweetness and appeal as Sophie, and yes, she and Julien (Guillaume Canet) seem destined to spend their lives together. But like this?

When they meet, they're eight years old and Sophie is being picked on at school because she's a foreigner. Julien defends her. They become friends for life. Even their first childish dares are risky, as when Sophie dares Julien to release the parking brake on the school bus; as it rolls downhill, do they get a fix of excitement that hooks them for life? Before long Julien is in the principal's office, peeing his pants—not because he's scared, but because Sophie dared him to.

The dares get riskier and more embarrassing as they grow older. Julien dares Sophie to take an oral exam at university while wearing her panties and bra outside her clothes. Sophie dares Julien to say "no" at the altar on his wedding day. Of course he won't be marrying her; that would be too easy, because she'd be in on the joke.

For that matter, what *is* their relationship? Are they in love, or simply trapped in a hypnotic mutual fascination? There's a flashforward in the movie from a scene where Sophie sleeps over at Julien's house when they're eight, to the two of them as adults, still in the same position in bed. But have they had sex in the meantime? Does it matter? Their bond is deeper than sex and love; it's the bond of shared madness.

At one point in the movie, they dare each other to stay completely out of contact for ten years. Will they get their pact out of their system? Not at all. Every moment of those ten years, they're acutely aware of the passage of time and the fulfillment of their dare, and when they meet again at the end it's to escalate the dare to a new and disturbing level.

The movie's first shot tells us something we don't understand at the time. The last scene explains it, and is profoundly creepy. There is, I suppose, a tradition of lovers' pacts, but are they lovers, and what are they proving with the way they end their own pact? I know these are questions not intended for answers. I realize that the movie establishes a premise and follows it relentlessly. I understand that the playful camera strategies are supposed to take the edge off, and that scenes are played like comedy so that we won't grow completely depressed by the strange fate of Sophie and Julien.

But at the end, I didn't like them. In fact, reader, I loathed them. Did I loathe them as people, or as characters? Are their characters intended as real people, or as a fictional device? I'm not sure. What I do know is that the movie is strangely frustrating, because Julien and Sophie choose misery and obsession as a lifestyle, and push far beyond reason. Perhaps I should applaud the movie for its conviction? Perhaps the snakier it made me feel, the better it was? Perhaps, but I can't say so if I don't think so. I can say this: If despite everything my description has intrigued you, go ahead and take a chance. You won't be bored, he said with a little smile.

Love Object ★ ★
R, 88 m., 2004

Desmond Harrington (Kenneth), Melissa Sagemiller (Lisa), Rip Torn (Novak), Brad Henke (Dotson), Udo Kier (Radley), John Cassini (Jason), Lyle Kanouse (Stan). Directed by Robert Parigi and produced by Kathleen Haase and Lawrence Levy. Screenplay by Parigi.

Robert Parigi's *Love Object* tells the story of a painfully shy writer of software manuals, a man inhibited to the point of paralysis, who discovers a Web site that sells realistic, life-size love dolls. Kenneth (Desmond Harrington) is already a user of porn, frequenting a cryptlike adult shop that looks like the horror chamber at Madame Tussaud's and seems to have the Elephant Man behind the cash register. Now he maxes out his line of credit to order Nikki, a custom-crafted mannequin made to his specifications: hair color, eyes, etc.

While this drama is unfolding in his private life, Kenneth is under pressure from his boss. That would be Mr. Novak (Rip Torn), who seems to have modeled his performance on Samuel Ramey as Mephistopheles. Gravel-voiced and goateed, he alternates threat and praise as he assigns Kenneth to produce a three-volume instruction manual in a month. To assist him, Novak supplies a temp who can do the typing. This is Lisa (Melissa Sagemiller), an attractive young blond.

Kenneth doesn't want help. He prefers to work alone. But then an eerie thing occurs; Lisa, as it happens, looks a little like the love doll, Nikki. Kenneth starts buying things for the doll: dresses, wigs, lipstick, fingernail polish. He rigs up a harness so he can dance with the doll. And meantime, Lisa makes no secret of her attraction to him, which is odd, since Kenneth is so odd he might as well have "Weirdo Freak" tattooed on his forehead.

The establishing scenes of *Love Object* are voyeuristic in a creepy way; there's a strange fascination in stories about sexual fetishes, and as Kenneth works to make Nikki look more like Lisa, and then to make Lisa look more like Nikki, the music by Nicholas Pike subtly reminds us of the *Vertigo* theme. The *Vertigo* connection seems deliberate: There's even a scene in a dress store, where Kenneth takes Lisa to buy the same dress he earlier bought for Nikki, and the sales clerk looks at him in that same complicit way the clerk regarded James Stewart in the Hitchcock film. Kenneth wants Lisa and Nikki to look alike, just as Stewart coached Kim Novak to resemble the woman of his dreams.

Both times there was a trap for the man: In Hitchcock, because Novak secretly really was the woman Stewart was obsessed by, and in Parigi, because Kenneth begins to confuse the woman and the doll. We can't be sure exactly what defines the level of his madness, but certainly he believes Nikki has the upper hand—she orders him around, calls him at work, handcuffs him in his sleep, and so on. Sooner or later Lisa is going to find out about this, and then . . .

Well, up to that point Parigi had me fairly well involved. I was reminded of Michael Powell's *Peeping Tom* (1960), about a voyeuristic photographer who kills with his camera, and *Kissed* (1996), the Canadian film about a woman's strangely sympathetic necrophilia. It wasn't as good as those films, but it had the same attention to the sad, inward obsession of the character. If Parigi had continued in the way he began, he might have produced a successful film.

But he lacks confidence in Kenneth and his inward life, and so the movie reaches with increasing desperation toward humor and grisly sadism, and the mood is broken. There is a workable subplot involving Kenneth's strange building manager (Udo Keir), who listens in amazement through the walls, but another neighbor, a Los Angeles detective named Dotson (Brad Henke), is a goofball who does everything wrong that he possibly can, just to wring cheap laughs out of a situation that by then is desperately unfunny.

And the film's violent conclusion is too gruesome to be earned by what has gone before. Instead of somehow finding a psychological climax for his hero's dilemma, as Hitchcock and Powell did, Parigi goes for horror film developments that he pushes far beyond any possible interest we have in seeing them. The movie turns cruel and ugly, and hasn't paid the dues to earn its last scenes. Parigi had me there for a while, but when he lost me, it was big time.

A Love Song for Bobby Long ★ ★ ★
R, 119 m., 2005

John Travolta (Bobby Long), Scarlett Johansson (Pursy Will), Gabriel Macht (Lawson Pines), Deborah Kara Unger (Georgianna), Dane Rhodes (Cecil), David Jensen (Junior), Clayne Crawford (Lee), Sonny Shroyer (Earl). Directed by Shainee Gabel and produced by Gabel, David Lancaster, R. Paul Miller, and Bob Yari. Screenplay by Gabel, based on the novel *Off Magazine Street* by Ronald Everett Capps.

There is a lazy, seductive appeal to the lives of the two boozers in *A Love Song for Bobby Long*. The notion of moving to New Orleans and drinking yourself to death is the sort of escape plan only an alcoholic could come up with, involving the principle of surrender to the enemy. If you are a writer and a failed English professor like Bobby Long, you can even wrap yourself in the legend of other literary drunks. It's all wonderfully romantic, especially in the movies, where a little groaning in the morning replaces nausea, headaches, killer hangovers, and panic attacks. A realistic portrait of suicidal drinking would contain more terror and confusion, but never mind. *Leaving Las Vegas* did that, and this is a different movie.

Bobby Long is played by John Travolta like a living demonstration of one of those artist's conceptions of what Elvis would look like at seventy. White-haired, unshaven, probably smelly, he lives on Magazine Street in the Quarter with a former student named Lawson Pines (Gabriel Macht), who thinks he is a genius. Years ago, Bobby was a legend on campus, Lawson's charismatic mentor. Then something happened, which we are pretty sure we will find out about, and here he is without wife or family, living on the sofa surrounded by piles of books.

He and Lawson spend a lot of time quoting literature to each other. Ben Franklin, Charles Dickens, the usual twentieth century gods. This is entertaining all by itself, apart from the good it does for the characters. It reminded me of Alan Bennett's play, *The History Boys*, in which memorizing literary quotations is recommended as a means of fertilizing the mind. Bobby and Lawson are well fertilized, but too disorganized to plant anything; an unfinished novel and a would-be memoir languish in the shadows. In *Sideways*, when Miles (Paul Giamatti) says he can't commit suicide because he has a responsibility to his unpublished novel, his buddy Jack (Thomas Haden Church) helpfully points out that the New Orleans legend John Kennedy Toole killed himself before *A Confederacy of Dunces* was published. So there is a precedent.

Bobby and Lawson seem prepared to keep on drinking and quoting and smoking forever, when a sudden change occurs in their lives. Their housemate, a jazz singer named Lorraine, has died. Now her daughter, Pursy (Scarlett Johansson), materializes, too late for the funeral. Pursy is a discontented and suspicious eighteen-year-old, who will soon prove to be the most mature member of the household. The boys tell Pursy her mother left her a third of the house, which is sort of true; actually, her mother left Pursy all of the house, but information like that could only confuse Pursy about the right of Bobby and Lawson to continue living there forever.

Pursy moves in, creating a form of family in which she is both the child and the adult, and Bobby and Lawson drift in between. At one point Lawson's halfway girlfriend Georgianna (Deborah Kara Unger) asks, "They know you're not going to school?" Pursy: "Yeah, it ranks right up there with being out of vodka and cigarettes."

The revelations in *A Love Song for Bobby Long* are not too hard to spot coming. There are only a few fictional developments that seem possible, and it turns out that they are. The movie is not about plot anyway, but about characters and a way of living. Pursy acts as a catalyst to create moments of truth and revelation, and those in turn help Bobby find a limited kind of peace with his past, and Lawson to find a tentative hope in his own possible future.

What can be said is that the three actors inhabit this material with ease and gratitude: It is good to act on a simmer sometimes, instead of at a fast boil. It's unusual to find an American movie that takes its time. It's remarkable to listen to dialogue that assumes the audience is well read. It is refreshing to hear literate conversation.

These are modest pleasures, but real enough. The movie tries for tragedy and reaches only pathos, but then Bobby lost his chance to be a tragic hero by living this long in the first place. Travolta has an innate likability quotient that works with characters like this; you can sense why a student would follow him to New Orleans and join him in foggy melancholy. There doesn't have to be a scene explaining that. You can also sense how Pursy would change things, just by acting as a witness. Alcoholics get uncomfortable when they're surrounded by people with insights. They like to control the times and conditions of their performances, and don't want an audience to wander backstage. Just by seeing them, Pursy forces them to see themselves. Once they do that, something has to give.

Lucky Number Slevin ★ ★
R, 109 m., 2006

Josh Hartnett (Slevin), Morgan Freeman (The Boss), Ben Kingsley (The Rabbi), Lucy Liu (Lindsey), Stanley Tucci (Brikowski), Bruce Willis (Mr. Goodkat). Directed by Paul McGuigan and produced by Christopher Eberts, Andreas Grosch, Kia Jam, Robert Kravis, Tyler Mitchell,

Anthony Rhulen, and Chris Roberts. Screenplay by Jason Smilovic.

Lucky Number Slevin is too clever by half. It's the worst kind of con: It tells us it's a con, so we don't even have the consolation of being led down the garden path. The rug of reality is jerked out from under us in the opening scenes, and before long the floor is being dismantled. Crouched in the dark, I am resentful. Since the plot is irrelevant and the dialogue too mannered to be taken seriously, all I'm left with are the performances and the production design.

The performances, to be sure, are juicy. A team of A-list actors do their specialty numbers, and it's fun to see pros at work. The movie begins with a man in a wheelchair (Bruce Willis) telling an inexplicable story to a stranger in an airport lounge—an empty lounge, which immediately labels the scene as dubious at best, fantasy at worst. The story involves a fixed horse race, and there is mention of the Kansas City Shuffle. It is not clear exactly what the Kansas City Shuffle is, but Willis observes that you can't have one without a body. This is not what you want to hear from a stranger in an empty airport lobby.

Cut to Josh Hartnett, playing Slevin, arriving at the New York apartment of his friend Nick and being mistaken for Nick by hired goons working for The Boss (Morgan Freeman). The Boss, played by Freeman with his usual suave charm, tells Slevin (or Nick) he owes a lot of money but the debt can be forgotten if he will kill the son of The Boss's rival crime kingpin, The Rabbi (Ben Kingsley). In no time at all, Slevin/Nick is hauled by an alternative set of goons before The Rabbi, who makes him an alternative offer he can't refuse.

The Rabbi and The Boss occupy Manhattan penthouses that face each other, and at times they stalk their terraces, fiercely glaring across the street. I was reminded of *The Singing Kid* (1936), in which Al Jolson and Cab Calloway occupy facing penthouses and perform a duet from their balconies. Even in a crime movie as peculiar as *Lucky Number Slevin,* a duet between Freeman and Kingsley would be too much to hope for.

Willis meanwhile resurfaces as Mr. Goodkat, a gun for hire who, as nearly as we can tell, is not currently hired. There's also the cop Brikowski (Stanley Tucci), who seems about to do something at any moment. Much more intriguing is Lindsey (Lucy Liu), who introduces herself to Slevin as his friend Nick's neighbor and moves into his life. She works in the coroner's office, which may mean she will be seeing a lot more of Slevin.

Mannered put-ons like this raise the hairs on the back of my neck. They think they're more clever than I am, and they may be right, but that doesn't make me like them. One of the redeeming graces of *Brick,* which opened the same weekend, is that although it stars modern teenagers who talk and act as if they're in a 1940s film noir, it plays it straight: As far as the movie is concerned, they really do talk and act that way, and the plot is treated as sincerely as if Bogart were starring in it.

Lucky Number Slevin, on the other hand, goes to some pains to make it clear it is only an exercise in style. Here we are, looking at a crime mystery involving warring hoodlums and beautiful neighbors and a confused guy from out of town and a gunman and a cop, and the movie knows we're deluded and they're all just conceits. It's smarter than we are. Well, it must be, because it got us to watch it.

Do I rule out all trickery in movies? Of course not. I was happy to be fooled by *The Sixth Sense,* but that's because I *was* fooled. I had problems with *The Usual Suspects,* but at least I didn't see the last scene coming. When a movie makes it clear that its characters are going through a charade for the amusement of the director (and when the characters themselves make it clear they all but know they are actors in a movie), I get restless: They're having such a good time with each other, why do they need me? Then when there's a level of trickery even beyond the apparent foolery—reader, I feel like they're yanking my chain.

M

The Machinist ★ ★ ★
R, 102 m., 2004

Christian Bale (Trevor Reznik), Jennifer Jason Leigh (Stevie), Aitana Sanchez-Gijon (Marie), John Sharian (Ivan), Michael Ironside (Miller). Directed by Brad Anderson and produced by Julio Fernandez. Screenplay by Scott Kosar.

"If you were any thinner," Stevie tells him, "you wouldn't exist." Trevor Reznik weighs 121 pounds and you wince when you look at him. He is a lonely man, disliked at work, up all night, returning needfully to two women who are kind to him: Stevie, a hooker, and Marie, the waitress at the all-night diner out at the airport. "I haven't slept in a year," he tells Marie.

Christian Bale lost more than sixty pounds to play this role, a fact I share not because you need to know how much weight he lost, but because you need to know that is indeed Christian Bale. He is so gaunt, his face so hollow, he looks nothing like the actor we're familiar with. There are moments when his appearance even distracts from his performance, because we worry about him. Certainly we believe that the character, Trevor, is at the end of his rope, and I was reminded of Anthony Perkins's work in Orson Welles's *The Trial,* another film about a man who finds himself trapped in the vise of the world's madness.

Trevor works as a machinist. There's a guy like him in every union shop, a guy who knows all the rules and works according to them and is a pain in the ass about them. His coworkers think he is strange; maybe he frightens them a little. His boss asks for a urine sample. One day he gets distracted and as a result one of his coworkers loses a hand. The victim, Miller (Michael Ironside), almost seems less upset about the accident than Trevor is. But then Trevor has no reserve, no padding; his nerve endings seem exposed to pain and disappointment.

Stevie (Jennifer Jason Leigh) is a consolation. They have sex, yes, but that's the least of it. She sees his need. Trevor is reading Dostoyevsky's *The Idiot* and perhaps there is a parallel between Stevie and Nastassia, Dostoyevsky's heroine, who is drawn to a self-destructive and dangerous man. Leigh has played a lot of prostitutes in her career, but each one is different because she defines them by how they are needed as well as by what they need.

Marie (Aitana Sanchez-Gijon) is the other side of the coin, a cheerful presence in the middle of the night. "You're lonely," she tells Trevor. "When you work graveyard shift as long as I have, you get to know the type." She wonders why he comes all the way out to the airport just for a cup of coffee and a slice of pie. She wouldn't mind dating him.

Then there is the matter of Ivan (John Sharian), the distracting and disturbing coworker who perhaps contributed to the accident. He lost some fingers in a drill press once, and the docs replaced them with his toes. "I can't shuffle cards like I used to," he says. Nor, apparently, can he punch in on the time clock: The guys at the shop claim he doesn't exist. Is Trevor imagining him? And what is the meaning of the Post-it notes that look like an incomplete version of a Hangman puzzle?

The Machinist has an ending that provides a satisfactory, or at least a believable, explanation for its mysteries and contradictions. But the movie is not about the plot, and while the conclusion explains Trevor's anguish, it doesn't account for it. The director Brad Anderson, working from a screenplay by Scott Kosar, wants to convey a state of mind, and he and Bale do that with disturbing effectiveness. The photography by Xavi Gimenez and Charlie Jiminez is cold slates, blues and grays, the palate of despair. We see Trevor's world so clearly through his eyes that only gradually does it occur to us that every life is seen through a filter.

We get up in the morning in possession of certain assumptions through which all of our experiences must filter. We cannot be rid of those assumptions, although an evolved person can at least try to take them into account. Most people never question their assumptions, and so reality exists for them as they think it does, whether it does or not. Some assumptions are necessary to make life bearable, such as the assumption that we will not die in the next ten minutes. Others may lead us, as they lead Trevor, into a bleak solitude. Near the end of the movie, we understand him when he simply says, "I just want to sleep."

Madagascar ★ ★ ½
PG, 80 m., 2005

With the voices of: Ben Stiller (Alex the Lion), Chris Rock (Marty the Zebra), David Schwimmer (Melman the Giraffe), Jada Pinkett Smith (Gloria the Hippo), Sacha Baron Cohen (Julian), Cedric the Entertainer (Maurice). Directed by Eric Darnell and Tom McGrath and produced by Teresa Cheng and Mireille Soria. Screenplay by Mark Burton and Billy Frolick.

One of the fundamental philosophical questions of our time is why Goofy is a person and Pluto is a dog. From their earliest days when Mickey Mouse was still in black and white, cartoons have created a divide between animals who are animals and animals who are human—or, if not human in the sense that Paris Hilton is human, then at least human in the sense that they speak, sing, have personalities, and are voiced by actors like Ben Stiller, Chris Rock, David Schwimmer, and Jada Pinkett Smith.

Now comes *Madagascar,* an inessential but passably amusing animated comedy that has something very tricky going on. What happens if the human side of a cartoon animal is only, as they say, a veneer of civilization? Consider Alex the Lion. In the Central Park Zoo, he's a star, singing "New York, New York" and looking forward to school field trips because he likes to show off for his audiences.

Alex (voice by Ben Stiller) lives the good life in the zoo, dining on prime steaks every day provided by his keepers. His friends include Marty the Zebra (Chris Rock), Melman the Giraffe (David Schwimmer) and Gloria the Hippo (Jada Pinkett Smith). If Alex likes it in the zoo, Marty has wanderlust. He wants to break out and live free. One night he escapes from the zoo, and his three friends catch up with him just as he's about to board a train for Connecticut, acting on bad advice from the giraffe, who has informed him that is where "the wild" can be found.

The animals are captured, crated up, and shipped off aboard a cargo ship to a wild animal refuge in Africa. On the way, a mutiny by rebellious penguins leads to them being swept off the deck and washed ashore in Madagascar. They're back in the wild, all right, but without survival training. The local population, pri-

marily a colony of lemurs, is ruled by King Julian (Sacha Baron Cohen) and his right-paw man Maurice (Cedric the Entertainer).

Some of the locals think maybe the New Yorkers are obnoxious tourists, even though Alex stages his zoo act, much in the same sense captured prisoners of war entertain the commandant. Then the intriguing problem of the human/animal divide comes into play. Alex misses his daily stacks of sirloin and porterhouse. He is a meat-eater. He eats steak. "Which is you," Marty the Zebra is warned. At one point, driven wild by hunger, Alex even tries to take a bite out of Marty's butt.

This is the kind of chaos that always lingers under the surface of animal cartoons. How would Goofy feel if Pluto wanted to marry one of his daughters? There is a moment at which *Madagascar* seems poised on the brink of anarchy, as the law of the wild breaks down the detente of the zoo, and the animals revert to their underlying natures. Now that could have been interesting, although one imagines children being led weeping from the theater while Alex basks on a zebra-skin rug, employing a toothpick.

The movie is much too safe to follow its paradoxes to their logical conclusions, and that's probably just as well. The problem, though, is that once it gets the characters to the wild it doesn't figure out what to do with them there, and the plot seems to stall. *Madagascar* is funny, especially at the beginning, and good-looking in a retro cartoon way, but in a world where the stakes have been raised by *Finding Nemo, Shrek,* and *The Incredibles,* it's a throwback to a more conventional kind of animated entertainment. It'll be fun for the smaller kids, but there's not much crossover appeal for their parents. ☞

Madison ★ ★ ★
PG, 94 m., 2005

James Caviezel (Jim McCormick), Jake Lloyd (Mike McCormick), Mary McCormack (Bonnie McCormick), Bruce Dern (Harry Volpi), Brent Briscoe (Tony Steinhart), Paul Dooley (Mayor Vaughn). Directed by William Bindley and produced by William Bindley and Martin Wiley. Screenplay by William Bindley and Scott Bindley.

What is it about Indiana that inspires movies

about small-town dreamers who come from behind to win? William Bindley's *Madison,* the story of a town that races its own hydroplane on the Ohio River, joins *Breaking Away* (a bicycle race), *Hoosiers* (high school basketball), and *Rudy* (local boy is too small to play football for Notre Dame, but that doesn't stop him). All four stories are inspired by fact; maybe that has something to do with it. A story about Bobby Knight would of course have to be based on fiction.

As *Madison* opens in 1971, times are hard for the town, which was once the busiest port above New Orleans and one of the richest cities in the state. Factories are closing, people are moving to big cities to find work, and although Madison is the only town to enter its own boat in the Gold Cup, things look grim for this year's race.

The boat is *Miss Madison,* an unlimited hydroplane (I think that means anything goes with engines and speed). The Gold Cup has been held since 1950; local businessman Jim McCormick (James Caviezel) used to pilot his boat, but retired after an injury ten years earlier. Now he is suddenly needed again, by the town and the boat, and comes out of retirement to the pride of his son, Mike (Jake Lloyd), and the concern of his wife, Bonnie (Mary McCormack), who like so many movie wives frets that her spouse is either (a) going to get killed, or (b) not be home for dinner.

Miss Madison's engine has exploded during a time trial and the boat itself is seriously damaged. It looks as if the town will not have an entry in the very year it hosts the famous annual race, but then Mike and his crew go to work. They need a new engine and can't afford one, so under cover of darkness they slip off to a nearby town and steal the engine from an airplane displayed in the courthouse square. Without being a mechanic, I am fairly sure such an engine, if it were indeed still in the plane, would be filled with dead leaves and hornets' nests and would need more than a trip through Jiffy-Lube, but never mind: It purrs right along on race day.

For the town, meanwhile, the race is heavensent. It provides a boost for civic morale, keeps a few more citizens from moving away, attracts tourist dollars and television publicity, and gives everyone a chance to sit on the river banks in their lawn chairs with their picnic baskets. Much of this is made possible by Mayor Don Vaughn (Paul Dooley, who played the father in

Breaking Away). He shifts some city funds, probably illegally, to find the money to back *Miss Madison.*

As sporting events go, hydroplane racing is pretty straightforward. The powerful boats race around a river course, making lots of waves and noise. Some of the boats have commercial sponsors, and one of the unique elements in *Madison* is negative product placement. One of the boats has "Budweiser" written all over it, and much is made about the rich and high-powered brewery team, but they're the bad guys and we want to see Bud lose to *Miss Madison.*

The cast is stalwart. Jim Caviezel, who made this movie in his pre-*Passion* days, is a salt-of-the-earth small-town dad who shares a secret with his son: a hidden cave that's "one of the special things about where we live." Mary McCormack, as wife and mother, is stuck with the obligatory speech, "You have a choice to make—me or the boat." But after she pays her dues with that tired line, she perks up and brings some sunshine into the movie. There is also sadness, which I will not reveal, except to say that driving one of these boats might be a good way to compete for the Darwin Award.

Who else? Oh: Bruce Dern. He's the expert mechanic who can turn around a stolen antique airplane engine in twenty-four hours. I saw him not long ago while revisiting *After Dark, My Sweet* (1993) and was happy to see him again. He has a way of chewing his dialogue as if he wants to savor it first before sharing it with us.

The Man ★ ½
PG-13, 79 m., 2005

Samuel L. Jackson (Agent Derrick Vann), Eugene Levy (Andy Fidler), Miguel Ferrer (Agent Peters), Luke Goss (Joey Trent), Anthony Mackie (Booty), Susie Essman (Lieutenant Rita Carbone), Horatio Sanz (Diaz). Directed by Les Mayfield and produced by Robert N. Fried. Screenplay by Jim Piddock, Margaret Oberman, and Stephen Carpenter.

The Man is another one of those movies, like *Lethal Weapon 2,* where the outsider finds himself in the dangerous world of cops and robbers. The cop this time is Derrick Vann, a hard-boiled Detroit ATF agent played by Samuel L. Jackson, and the outsider is Andy Fidler (Eugene Levy), a dental supplies salesman from Wisconsin. Fidler loves his product so much he chats up strangers about the glories of flossing.

The plot: Agent Vann's partner, who is on the take, has died in connection with a heist of guns from the ATF lock-room. A crook named Booty (Anthony Mackie) may be the key to the killing. Vann, an honest agent, mistakes Fidler for an underworld contact working with Booty. When he finds out how very wrong he is, he still needs Fidler to pretend to be a black market arms dealer if the sting is going to work.

Whether the sting and the movie work are two different questions. Jackson and Levy are in full sail as their most familiar character types: Jackson hard as nails, Levy oblivious to the world outside his own blissfully limited existence. They could play these characters in their sleep. Their differences provide the setup for the whole movie: these two guys linked together in an unlikely partnership during which their personalities (and Fidler's problems with intestinal gas) will make it difficult for them to share the front seat of Vann's customized Caddy.

The Man is very minor. The running time of seventy-nine minutes indicates a) thin material, and b) mercy toward the audience by not stretching it any further than what is already the breaking point. You know a movie like this is stalling for time when it supplies Agent Vann with a family so that his wife can call him in the middle of the action: "Your daughter wants to know if you'll be at her recital tonight." Yes, it's the ancient and sometimes reliable Dad Too Busy for Child's Big Moment formula. Does Vann wrap up the case in time to walk into the room just as the recital is beginning? Do he and his daughter exchange a quiet little nod to show family does, after all, come first? I would not dream of giving away such a plot detail.

Levy has funny moments as the fussy dental supplies fetishist but never goes into full obnoxious mode as Joe Pesci did in Lethal Weapon 2. He plays the character like a conventioneer trying to be nice to an alarming taxi driver. Jackson plays the cop like a man who has found a bug in the front seat of his car. What's interesting, however, is that they don't get locked into a lot of black-white shtick; their differences are defined through occupation, not race, except for the odd ethnic in-joke involving hot sauce.

The inescapable fact about The Man is that this movie is completely unnecessary. Nobody needed to make it, nobody needs to see it, Jackson and Levy are too successful to waste time with it. It plays less like a film than like a deal.

At Telluride I was talking to James Mangold, the director of Walk the Line and other ambitious pictures, and he said an interesting thing: Hollywood executives are reluctant to greenlight a project that depends on the filmmakers being able to pull it off. They want familiar formulas in safe packages. An original movie idea involves faith that the script will work, the director knows what he's doing, and the actors are right for the story. Too risky. Better to make a movie where when you hear the pitch you can already envision the TV commercial, because the movie will essentially be the long form of the thirty-second spot.

Go online, look at the trailer for The Man, and you will know everything you could possibly need to know about this movie except how it would feel if the trailer were eighty minutes long.

The Manchurian Candidate ★ ★ ★
R, 130 m., 2004

Denzel Washington (Ben Marco), Meryl Streep (Eleanor Shaw), Liev Schreiber (Raymond Shaw), Jon Voight (Senator Thomas Jordan), Kimberly Elise (Rosie), Jeffrey Wright (Al Melvin), Ted Levine (Colonel Howard), Bruno Ganz (Richard Delp), Simon McBurney (Dr. Atticus Noyle), Vera Farmiga (Jocelyn Jordan), Robyn Hitchcock (Laurent Toker). Directed by Jonathan Demme and produced by Scott Rudin, Tina Sinatra, Ilona Herzberg, and Demme. Screenplay by Daniel Pyne and Dean Georgaris.

Corporations, not commies, are the sinister force behind Jonathan Demme's The Manchurian Candidate, in which poor Raymond Shaw is told by a liberal senator: "You are about to become the first privately owned and operated vice president of the United States." There's a level of cynicism here that is scarier than the Red Chinese villains in John Frankenheimer's 1962 classic. It's a stretch to imagine a Communist takeover of America, but the idea that corporations may be subverting the democratic process is plausible in the age of Enron.

Demme is not shy about suggesting parallels with current politics, and he borrows a neat bit of indirection from Frankenheimer: In the 1962 version, Communists posed as anti-Communists to drum up hysteria that could be used to subvert American freedoms. In the new version, right-wingers pose as liberals to win office while neutering the left. Meryl Streep plays Senator Eleanor Shaw, who has sold her soul to the Manchurian Global corporation. A stage mother from hell, she pushes her son, Raymond (Liev Schreiber), into the vice presidency; a timely assassination will make him president. Raymond has a chip implanted in his skull that will allow Manchurian to control him.

This plan is on track and will succeed unless two men can make sense of their nightmares. Ben Marco (Denzel Washington) and Al Melvin (Jeffrey Wright) both fought in the Kuwait War as members of a patrol that was saved by the heroism of Sergeant Shaw—whose Medal of Honor launched his political career. But did Shaw really save them? Marco and Melvin have fragmented nightmares of an alternate reality. Marco notes that all the patrol members use identical words to describe their experience. "I remember that it happened," Shaw confesses to Marco, "but I don't remember it happening."

Audiences of the earlier film will know that during the patrol's missing days, as Marco eventually concludes, "Somebody got into our minds with chain saws." The brainwashing is front-loaded in Demme's version; it's revealed fairly early, perhaps because he and his writers concluded there was no use being coy about a secret that most of the audience already knows. Instead, Demme wisely conceals other secrets, leading to a wickedly different ending just when you think you know everything that will happen.

Washington plays Marco as a man with the public face of a decorated officer and the private tortures of a haunted man. After he discovers a chip under the skin of his shoulder, he desperately tries to get to Shaw to talk about their experience. At one point Marco actually leaps upon the vice presidential candidate, rips off his shirt, and tries to bite a chip out from under his skin. The Secret Service comes to the rescue, but Shaw declines to press charges, leaving us to wonder how the news organizations cover the remarkable spectacle of a decorated veteran biting a heroic candidate. Somehow, it should be a bigger story.

Schreiber, as Shaw, has the role played by Laurence Harvey in the original, and Washington follows Frank Sinatra. Meryl Streep has the assignment of playing the alarming and incestuous Mrs. Shaw, a role for which Angela Lansbury won an Oscar nomination, while essentially stealing the movie. Streep wisely goes for oblique humor rather than straight-ahead villainy, making the character different and yet just as loathsome. Gossips have whispered for months that her performance is modeled on Senator Hillary Clinton, but I dunno; Streep has mentioned Peggy Noonan, Condi Rice, and Dick Cheney.

Making parallels like that is risky. Demme's movie has all sorts of characters on the screen who tempt us to name their real-life counterparts, but he doesn't do simplistic one-to-one parallels; instead, he allows sly contemporary references to enter the film through many characters, as when one candidate calls for "compassionate vigilance." Another bold line, by Mrs. Shaw: "The assassin always dies, baby. It's necessary for the national healing."

Frank Rich writes in the *New York Times* that the movie is "more partisan" than *Fahrenheit 9/11*, but that requires a simpler and more translatable plot than the one I saw. Demme sticks his knife in everywhere, suggesting that the whole system and both parties have been compromised by the power of corporations. (For truly uninhibited parallelism in interpreting the movie, read Paul Krugman's *NYT* column "The Arabian Candidate.")

Every time I watch the original *Manchurian Candidate*, I'm teased by the possibility that there may be another, deeper, level of conspiracy, one we're intended to sense without quite understanding. It involves the character of the woman named Rose or Rosie, whom Marco meets on a train; she was played in 1962 by Janet Leigh and this time by Kimberly Elise. These characters materialize out of nowhere, fall instantly in love with Marco, and say inexplicable things. To accept them as simply a romantic opportunity is too easy; why would a woman fall for a complete stranger who (in the Sinatra version) is shaking so badly he can't light his cigarette and (in the Washington version) biting vice-presidential candidates? She's up to something.

To compare Demme's version with Frankenheimer's is sort of irrelevant. That was then and this is now. Frank Sinatra and Denzel Washington are both complete and self-contained and cannot be meaningfully compared. What we can say is that Demme has taken a story we thought we knew and, while making its outlines mostly recognizable, rotated it into another dimension of conspiracy. Are corporations really a threat to America's security? The rotten ones are. When you consider that the phony California electric crisis, with its great cost in lives and fortune, was an act of corporate terrorism, he has a point.

Manderlay ★ ★ ★
NO MPAA RATING, 139 m., 2006

Bryce Dallas Howard (Grace), Isaach De Bankole (Timothy), Danny Glover (Wilhelm), Willem Dafoe (Grace's Father), Lauren Bacall (Mam), Zeljko Ivanek (Gambler). Directed by Lars von Trier and produced by Vibeke Windelov. Screenplay by von Trier.

Alabama, 1933. A caravan of black limousines carries gangsters from a gold mining town in Colorado to a rural Alabama area where slavery still survives as an institution. Alabama looks uncannily like Colorado, as it must: The story that began in Lars von Trier's *Dogville* (2004) continues here, with the same visual strategy of placing all the action on a sound stage, with chalk lines indicating the outlines of locations. A few rudimentary props flesh out the action, including doors, windows, and machine guns.

The movie is the second in a trilogy by von Trier, who has never visited the United States but has set several movies here, all of them generated by his ideas about American greed, racism, and the misuse of power. To say his America is not recognizable to any American is beside the point; neither is the America in most Hollywood entertainments. Presenting imaginary worlds as if they were real is how movies work.

Von Trier's purpose is fiercely polemical. The Danish iconoclast holds strong ideas about our society and expresses them in satiric allegories of such audacity that we cast loose from realism and simply float with his conceits. The crucial difference between *Manderlay* and the almost unbearable *Dogville* is not that his politics have changed but that his sense of mercy for the audience has been awakened. The movie is thirty-eight minutes shorter than *Dogville* (although none too fleeting at 139 minutes), and the story is more clearly and strongly told.

He begins with a plantation in Alabama where slavery has never been abolished: Mam (Lauren Bacall) rules with an iron hand, assisted by her foreman, Wilhelm (Danny Glover), a slave who believes his people are not ready for the responsibilities of freedom. Driving up to the gates of the imaginary plantation, Grace (Bryce Dallas Howard) and her gangster father (Willem Dafoe) are surprised to find slavery still flourishing. Grace declares this cannot be, that the plantation must be informed of such historical events as the Civil War and the Emancipation Proclamation.

Grace's father has crimes to commit and wants to keep moving: "This is a local matter," he tells his daughter, echoing the argument used for generations. She thinks not and persuades him to leave behind a lawyer and four thugs with machine guns. Using brute force if necessary, she will impose democracy on this backwater. Von Trier's parallels with Iraq are not impossible to find; this Alabama is no more fictional than the pre-war Iraq depicted by the neocon advocates of war.

Mam dies soon after Grace frees the slaves, and Grace herself steps into the power vacuum, establishing a benevolent transitional authority. She will teach the slaves to vote, and then hold elections. Soon, but not yet, they will govern themselves. Doubts are expressed by the slave Wilhelm, who cites the insights in a book hidden under Mam's mattress—a volume categorizing the various kinds of slaves and their abilities. The slaves, he says, have grown accustomed to the plantation routine; dinner under Mam was always at seven, but what time will it be if the matter is open for discussion? And who will plant the crops and plan the harvest? Jobs don't get done by themselves.

Grace has her gangsters wear blackface and serve dinner to the slaves, who find the exercise offensive. She orders crops planted and rejoices at the harvest, although gamblers arrive to cheat the slaves, and company stores recycle the wages right back into the pockets of those who pay them. Again, there are contemporary parallels: One of the purposes of every colonial exercise is to open up markets for the occupying power.

I wouldn't go so far as to claim *Manderlay*

is fun to watch. Von Trier, who can make compulsively watchable films *(Breaking the Waves)*, has found a style that will alienate most audiences. Maybe it's necessary. On his bargain budgets, he certainly couldn't afford to shoot on a real plantation, with period detail. His actors work for peanuts (and even so, Nicole Kidman and James Caan bailed out after *Dogville*). The stark artificiality of his sets makes it clear he's dealing with parable and excuses his story from any requirement of reality. The real action generated by his story begins after the film ends. If audiences still exist for movies like this and debate them afterward—if, that is, not every single moviegoer in America is lost to mindless narcissistic self-indulgence—the arguments afterward will be the real show. Many moviegoers are likely to like the film less than the discussions it drags them into.

The film has a closing montage of photographs showing the history of African-Americans in America, from slavery through decades of poverty and discrimination to the civil rights movement, both its victories and defeats. Von Trier no doubt intends this montage to be an indictment of America, but I view it more positively: From a legacy of evil, our democracy has stumbled uncertainly in a moral direction and within our lifetimes has significantly reduced racism.

No doubt if everyone in America had always been Danish, we could have avoided some of our sins, but there you have it.

Note: Just in time to be tacked on to the end of this review, von Trier has issued a statement of revitality to Variety. *Ray Pride of* Movie City News *quotes him in part: ". . . I intend to reschedule my professional activities in order to rediscover my original enthusiasm for film. Over the last few years I have felt increasingly burdened by barren habits and expectations (my own and other people's) and I feel the urge to tidy up. In regards to product development this will mean more time on freer terms; i.e., projects will be allowed to undergo true development and not merely be required to meet preconceived demands. This is partly to liberate me from routine, and in particular from scriptural structures inherited from film to film. . . ."*

The most delightful element of this statement is his assumption that his films are "required to meet preconceived demands."

Man on Fire ★ ★ ½
R, 146 m., 2004

Denzel Washington (Creasy), Dakota Fanning (Pita), Marc Anthony (Samuel), Radha Mitchell (Lisa), Christopher Walken (Rayburn), Giancarlo Giannini (Manzano), Rachel Ticotin (Mariana), Jesus Ochoa (Fuentes), Mickey Rourke (Jordan). Directed by Tony Scott and produced by Lucas Foster, Arnon Milchan, and Scott. Screenplay by Brian Helgeland, based on a novel by A. J. Quinnell.

Tony Scott's *Man on Fire* employs superb craftsmanship and a powerful Denzel Washington performance in an attempt to elevate genre material above its natural level, but it fails. The underlying story isn't worth the effort. At first we're seduced by the jagged photography and editing, which reminds us a little of *City of God* and *21 Grams*. We're absorbed by Washington's character, an alcoholic with a past he cannot forgive himself for. And we believe the relationship he slowly develops with the young Mexico City girl he's hired to protect. But then the strong opening levels out into a long series of action scenes, and the double-reverse ending works more like a gimmick than a resolution.

The screenplay is by Brian Helgeland, whose work on *Mystic River* dealt with revenge in deep, painful, personal terms. But this time, action formulas take over. The hero outshoots and outsmarts half the bad guys in Mexico City. He seems to be homeless, yet has frequent changes of wardrobe and weaponry, even producing a shoulder-mounted missile launcher when necessary. And as he plows his way through the labyrinth of those responsible for kidnapping the girl, the body count becomes a little ridiculous, and Washington's character, who seemed very human, begins uncomfortably to resemble an invulnerable superhero. Sure, he gets shot now and again, but can you walk around Mexico City as an accused cop-killer and outgun professional killers indefinitely? When it seems that everyone who could possibly be killed is dead and the movie must surely be over, there's another whole chapter. We count those still alive, and ask ourselves if the Law of Economy of Characters applies: That's the one that says a movie contains no unnecessary characters, and so the otherwise unexplained presence of a star in a seemingly insignificant role will be richly explained by the end.

All of this is true, and yet the movie has real qualities. Denzel Washington creates a believable, sympathetic character here—a character complex enough to deserve more than fancy action scenes. Even the last scene involving his character is a disappointment; there's a moment when one thing and one thing only should happen to him, and it doesn't, and the movie lets him, and us, down gently.

Washington plays Creasy, whose résumé includes antiterrorism. He's fallen on hard times, drinks too much, and travels to Mexico for a reunion with his old military buddy Rayburn (Christopher Walken). "Do you think God will forgive us for what we've done?" Creasy asks Rayburn. "No," says Rayburn. "Me either," says Creasy.

Rayburn has a job for him: acting as a bodyguard for Mexico City industrialist Samuel Ramos (Marc Anthony), his American wife, Lisa (Radha Mitchell), and their daughter, Pita (Dakota Fanning). At the job interview, Creasy is frank about himself: "I drink." Ramos is able to live with this information, but advises Creasy to tell nobody, especially Mrs. Ramos. As we think back over the film, this conversation will take on added importance.

Creasy keeps his distance on the job. Pita wants to be his friend; he explains he was hired as a bodyguard, not a friend. But eventually he bottoms out in his despair, begins to love the little girl, and becomes her swimming coach, Marine-style. These scenes have a real resonance. After she is kidnapped, the movie goes through the standard routine (police called in, telephones tapped, ransom drop arranged), but with additional local color, since off-duty Mexico City police were apparently involved in the snatch, and Creasy feels surrounded by vipers. Rayburn may be the only person he can trust.

At the Ramos home, Samuel negotiates with the kidnappers, gets advice from his family lawyer (Mickey Rourke), and consults with the head of the Anti-Kidnap Squad, who is a busy man if the movie is correct in its claim that someone is kidnapped in Mexico every ninety minutes. Creasy, meanwhile, depends on a plucky journalist named Mariana (Rachel Ticotin), and she depends on an ex-Interpol expert named Manzano (Giancarlo Giannini). As the net and the cast widen, we begin to wonder if anyone in Mexico City is not involved in the kidnapping in one way or another, or related to someone who was.

Man on Fire has a production too ambitious for the foundation supplied by the screenplay. It plays as if Scott knows the plot is threadbare and wants to patch it with an excess of style. He might have gotten away with that in a movie of more modest length, but *Man on Fire* clocks in at close to two and a half hours, and needs more depth to justify the length.

Too bad, because the performances deserve more. Denzel Washington projects the bleak despair he's revealed before, and his character arc involves us. Christopher Walken supplies another of his patented little speeches: "Creasy's art is death. He's about to paint his masterpiece." Dakota Fanning *(Uptown Girls)* is a pro at only ten years old, and creates a heart-winning character. Ticotin and Giannini supply what is needed, when it's needed. There are scenes that work with real conviction. The movie has the skill and the texture to approach greatness, but Scott and Helgeland are content with putting a high gloss on formula action.

The Manson Family ★ ★ ★
NO MPAA RATING, 95, m., 2004

Marcelo Games (Charlie), Marc Pitman (Tex), Leslie Orr (Patty), Maureen Allisse (Sadie), Amy Yates (Leslie), Jim Van Bebber (Bobbi). Directed by Jim Van Bebber and produced by Carl Daft, David Gregory, and Mike King. Screenplay by Van Bebber.

The Manson Family has scenes so foul and heartless they can hardly be believed. Killers stab victims again and again and again, relentlessly, with glee. A throat is cut on camera. A dog is sacrificed. Victims plead piteously for their lives.

The action is recorded in low-tech film and video footage, some of it scratched and faded to look archival. There are passages as amateurish as a home movie. Actors snarl at the camera as if they're doing screen tests for snuff films. Some images (like an opening shot of blood dripping onto white flowers) are groaningly ham-handed. Although Charles Manson is extolled in the film by members of his "family" as a messiah and seer, he says nothing of value and has the charisma of a wino after a night in a Dumpster.

All of this will lead you to conclude that *The Manson Family* is a wretched film, but I am not sure I would agree with you. It filled me with disgust and dismay, but I believe it was intended to, and in that sense was a success. It has an undeniable power and effect, but be sure you understand what you are getting yourself into. This is not a "horror" film or an "underground" film, but an act of transgression so extreme and uncompromised, and yet so amateurish and sloppy, that it exists in a category of one film, this film.

I'm tempted to say you should see it just because you will never see a film like this again, but then I wonder: What need is there to see a film like this at all? Its insight into the Manson Family is that they were usually drugged, had absorbed the half-assed hippie philosophy of the time, and fell into the hands of a persuasive, gravely damaged man who convinced them to gladly murder for him.

I do accept that those who did the actual killing were acting under the influence of Manson. What I cannot find in this film is the slightest clue as to how Manson obtained or exercised such power. He seems like the kind of deranged and smelly lunatic any reasonable person would get away from quickly and permanently. That such figures as Dennis Wilson of the Beach Boys even briefly gave him friendship and shelter makes a persuasive argument against drug abuse.

The Manson Family has been around in several unfinished forms for many years. Its director, Jim Van Bebber, began shooting it in 1988, ran out of funds on various occasions, showed rough cuts at underground venues, and finally found completion money to make this theatrical version. If there is not perfect continuity because the actors grew older during the shooting, you'll never notice it because the filming technique uses such fragmentation, jagged editing, and chronological anarchy that we're rarely sure anyway what shot belongs before or after another shot.

What we absorb from the experience, as if wringing it free from the miasma of its making, is that Manson gathered followers with the lure of drugs and sex orgies, that they lured others, that they found an old and confused man and turned his farm into a commune.

Charlie was addled by dreams that he would become a rock 'n' roll god and found portents, patterns, and messages in rock songs and, for all I know, in his tea leaves. In a way that is far from clear, his disappointment at his lack of progress led to Helter-Skelter, an operation during which innocent people, including the pregnant Sharon Tate, were murdered. His theory was that the Black Panthers would be framed and a race war would result in—what? Charlie taking over? This makes no sense, but did you expect it to?

What Van Bebber does accomplish is to make a film true to its subject. It doesn't bring reason, understanding, analysis, or empathy to Manson; it wants only to evoke him. It is not pro-Manson, simply convinced of the power he had over those people at that time. In a paradoxical way, it exhibits sympathy for his victims by showing their deaths in such horrifying detail. In its technical roughness, its raw blatant crudeness, it finds a style suitable to the material; to the degree that it was more smooth and technically accomplished, to that degree it would distance itself from its subject and purpose.

We come to the question of a star rating. Convention requires me to assign stars to every film. Do I give *The Manson Family* four stars because it does what it does so successfully and uncompromisingly, or do I give it zero stars, for the same reason? I will settle on three, because it is remarkable enough I do not want to dismiss it. That doesn't mean I think you should see it.

March of the Penguins ★ ★ ★ ½
G, 80 m., 2005

Morgan Freeman (Narrator). A documentary directed by Luc Jacquet and produced by Yves Darondeau, Christophe Lioud, and Emmanuel Priou. Screenplay by Jordan Roberts.

After a long summer of feasting, their bodies stately and plump, the emperor penguins of Antarctica begin to feel, toward autumn, a need to march inland to the breeding grounds "where each and every one of them was born." They are all of a mind about this and walk in single file, thousands of them, in a column miles long. They all know where they are going, even those making the march for the first time, and when they get there these countless creatures, who all look more or less the same to us, begin to look more or less desirable to one another. Carefully, they choose their mates.

This is not a casual commitment. After the female delivers one large egg, the male gathers it into a fold of his abdomen, plants his feet to protect it from the ice below, and then stands there all winter with no food or water, in howling gales, at temperatures far below zero, in total darkness, huddled together with the other fathers for warmth. The females meanwhile march all the way back to the sea, now even more distant, to forage for food. When the females return to the mass of countless males, they find their mates without error and recognize the cries of chicks they have never seen. As they nurse the chicks, the males crawl back to the sea for food.

March of the Penguins is simply, and astonishingly, the story of this annual cycle. It was filmed under unimaginable conditions by the French director Luc Jacquet and his team, including cinematographers Laurent Chalet and Jerome Maison. There is not much to choose from in setting up their shots: On the coldest, driest, and (in winter) darkest continent on earth, there is snow, and there is ice, and there are penguins. There is also an ethereal beauty.

Although the compulsion to reproduce is central to all forms of life, the penguins could be forgiven if they'd said the hell with it and evolved in the direction of being able to swim to Patagonia. The film's narrator, Morgan Freeman, tells us that Antarctica was once a warm land with rich forests that teemed with creatures. But as the climate grew colder over long centuries, one life form after another bailed out, until the penguins were left in a land that, as far as they can see, is inhabited pretty much by other penguins, and edged by seas filled with delicious fish. Even their predators, such as the leopard seal, give them a pass during the dark, long, cold winter.

"This is a love story," Freeman's narration assures us, reminding me for some reason of Tina Turner singing "What's Love Got to Do with It?" I think it is more accurately described as the story of an evolutionary success. The penguins instinctively know, because they have been hardwired by evolutionary trial and error, that it is necessary to march so far inland

because in spring the ice shelf will start to melt toward them, and they need to stand where the ice will remain thick enough to support them. As a species, they learned this because the penguins who paused too soon on their treks had eggs that fell into the sea. Those who walked farther produced another generation, and eventually every penguin was descended from a long line of ancestors who were willing to walk the extra mile.

Why do penguins behave in this manner? Because it works for them, and their environment gives them little alternative. They are Darwinism embodied. But their life history is so strange that until this century it was not even guessed at. The first Antarctic explorers found penguins aplenty but had little idea where they came from, where they went to, and indeed whether they were birds or mammals.

The answers to those questions were discovered by a man named Apsley Cherry-Garrard, as described in one of the most remarkable books ever written, *The Worst Journey in the World* (1922). He was writing not about the journey of the penguins but about his own trek with two others through the bitter night to their mating grounds. Members of Robert F. Scott's 1910–1912 expedition to the South Pole, they set out in the autumn to follow the march of the penguins, and walked through hell until they found them, watched them, and returned with one of their eggs. Cherry-Garrard retired to England, where he lived until 1959; his friends felt the dreadful march, and the earlier experience of finding the frozen bodies of Scott and two others, contributed to his depression for the rest of his life.

For Jacquet and his crew, the experience was more bearable. They had transport, warmth, food, and communication with the greater world. Still, it could not have been pleasant, sticking it out and making this documentary, when others were filming a month spent eating at McDonald's. The narration is a little fanciful for my taste, and some of the shots seem funny to us, but not to the penguins. When they fall over, they do it with a remarkable lack of style. And for all the walking they do, they're ungainly waddlers. Yet they are perfect in their way, with sleek coats, grace in the water and heroic determination. It's poignant to watch the chicks in their youth, fed by their parents, playing with their chums, the sun climbing higher every day, little suspecting what they're in for.

Maria Full of Grace ★ ★ ★ ½
R, 101 m., 2004

Catalina Sandino Moreno (Maria), Yenny Paola Vega (Blanca), Giulied Lopez (Lucy), Jhon Alex Toro (Franklin), Patricia Rae (Carla), Orlando Tobon (Don Fernando). Directed by Joshua Marston and produced by Paul S. Mezey. Screenplay by Marston.

Long-stemmed roses must come from somewhere, but I never gave the matter much thought until I saw *Maria Full of Grace*, which opens with Maria working an assembly line in Colombia, preparing the roses for shipment overseas. I guess I thought the florist picked them early every morning, while mockingbirds trilled. Maria is young and pretty and filled with fire, and when she finds she's pregnant she isn't much impressed by the attitude of Juan, her loser boyfriend. She dumps her job and gets a ride to Bogotá with a man who tells her she could make some nice money as a mule—a courier flying to New York with dozens of little Baggies of cocaine in her stomach.

Maria (Catalina Sandino Moreno) is being exploited by the drug business, but she sees it as an opportunity. Her best friend, Blanca (Yenny Paola Vega), comes along, and they get tips from Lucy (Giulied Lopez), who has been a mule before—it's a way to visit her sister in New York.

At Kennedy Airport, the customs officials weren't born yesterday and consider the girls obvious suspects, but Maria can't be X-rayed because she's pregnant. The girls slip through and make contact with two witless drug workers whose job is to guard them while the drug packets emerge. But Lucy is feeling ill. A packet has broken in her stomach, and soon she's dead of an overdose. Her body is crudely disposed of by the two workers; her death is nothing more than a cost of doing business.

Maria is a victim of economic pressures, but she doesn't think like a victim. She has spunk and intelligence and can think on her feet. The movie wisely avoids the usual clichés about the drug cartel and instead shows us a fairly shabby importing operation,

run by people more slack-jawed than evil. Here is a drug movie with no machine guns and no chases. It focuses on its human story, and in Catalina Sandino Moreno finds a bright-eyed, charismatic actress who engages our sympathy.

The story of the making of the movie is remarkable. It was filmed on an indie budget by Joshua Marston, a first-time American director in his thirties, who found Moreno at an audition, cast mostly unknowns, and used real people in some roles—notably Orlando Tobon, who in life as in the film operates out of a Queens storefront, acting as middleman and counselor to Colombian immigrants in need.

The movie has the freshness and urgency of life actually happening. There's little feeling that a plot is grinding away; instead, Maria takes this world as she finds it and uses common sense to try to survive. She makes one crucial decision that a lesser movie would have overlooked; she goes to find the sister that Lucy came to visit.

I learn from Ella Taylor's article in the *LA Weekly* that one of Marston's favorite directors is Ken Loach, the British poet of working people. Like Loach, Marston has made a film that understands and accepts poverty without feeling the need to romanticize or exaggerate it. Also like Loach, he shows us how evil things happen because of economic systems, not because villains gnash their teeth and hog the screen. Hollywood simplifies the world for moviegoers by pretending evil is generated by individuals, not institutions; kill the bad guy, and the problem is solved.

Maria Full of Grace is an extraordinary experience for many reasons, including, oddly, its willingness to be ordinary. We see everyday life here, plausible motives, convincing decisions, and characters who live at ground level. The movie's suspense is heightened by being generated entirely at the speed of life, by emerging out of what we feel probably would really happen. Consider the way the two drug middlemen are seen as depraved and cruel, but also as completely banal, as bored by their job as Maria was with the roses. Most drug movies are about glamorous stars surrounded by special effects. Meanwhile, in a world almost below the radar, the Marias and Lucys hopefully board their flights with stomachs full of death.

Marilyn Hotchkiss' Ballroom Dancing and Charm School ★ ★

PG-13, 103 m., 2006

Robert Carlyle (Frank Keane), Marisa Tomei (Meredith Morrison), Mary Steenburgen (Marienne Hotchkiss), Sean Astin (Joe Buco), Donnie Wahlberg (Randall Ipswitch), Danny DeVito (Booth), John Goodman (Steve Mills), David Paymer (Rafael Horowitz), Camryn Manheim (Lisa Gobar), Adam Arkin (Gabe DiFranco), Sonia Braga (Tina). Directed by Randall Miller and produced by Eileen Craft, Miller, Morris Ruskin, and Jody Savin. Screenplay by Miller and Savin.

When he was twelve years old, Steve promised Lisa that they would meet again on the fifth day of the fifth month of the fifth year of the new millennium, at a reunion of their class at Marilyn Hotchkiss' Ballroom Dancing and Charm School. Now Steve is forty-eight, it is May 5, 2005, and he's piloting his station wagon down a lonely highway to make that rendezvous. If you're still reading, I'm as surprised as I am that I'm still writing.

Think about this. You liked a schoolmate when you were twelve and for almost forty years have focused on this reunion. Are you crazy? When I was twelve, I did not even take ballroom dancing classes, for which I thank the nuns of St. Mary's Grade School. It was all we could do to practice for the rhythm band. A rhythm band, as you rich kids may not know, is a band consisting entirely of cheap rhythm instruments. Sister Marie Donald would put a record on the Victrola and we would accompany it by ringing our triangles, rubbing our ratchet sticks together and pounding on tambourines. If a kid was left over, he would bang a desk lid up and down. The school had a piano, but it was in the auditorium.

Anyway, while racing to his rendezvous with Lisa, Steve (John Goodman) is in a car crash. The crash is witnessed by Frank (Robert Carlyle), who is driving a bakery truck. Frank calls 911, encourages Steve to hang in there, and accompanies him in the ambulance to the hospital. Steve keeps blubbering about Lisa: "I made this appointment almost forty years ago! I promised Lisa I'd be there!"

"Keep him talking!" a paramedic advises

Frank. This is not a problem. Steve talks on and off during the entire movie, telling the story of his relationship with Lisa and the dynamics of their class at the Marilyn Hotchkiss school. Occasionally his heartbeat falters, and we hear the ominously level tone of a heart monitor flatlining. But then Frank asks him another question, and thank God! The monitor starts beeping again, as Steve shares another memory from his past. He talks so much, the HMO must be shipping him to a hospital in another state.

Frank himself is grieving; his wife has committed suicide, for unexplained reasons. He promises Steve he will go to the Marilyn Hotchkiss reunion and look for Lisa, and this he does. He is painfully shy as he asks one woman after another if she is Lisa, but Lisa does not seem to have taken the appointment as seriously as Steve. Meanwhile, Frank has a run-in with Randall Ipswitch (Donnie Wahlberg), who warns him to keep his hands off his half-sister Meredith Morrison (Marisa Tomei). Randall is so angry, he even gives Frank's bakery truck four flat tires.

Was there ever a place in this or any reasonably adjacent universe where *Marilyn Hotchkiss' Ballroom Dancing and Charm School* could be considered a plausible story? I doubt it. It matches nothing in my experience. I have written before about the Thelma Leah Rose Ballroom Dancing Academy, which was above the Princess Theater on Main Street in Urbana, Illinois, and where I learned the fox-trot, the waltz, the mambo, the canasta, the pinochle, and many other dances—all of them, my wife confides, very badly.

We were younger than today's twelve-year-olds have ever been. I can assure you that the little Steves and Lisas in our class did not make appointments for forty years hence. We looked at each other with fear and loathing. The only reason I took the dance class in the first place was that I was in training for the St. Mary's Seventh- and Eighth-Grade Prom, at the Urbana-Lincoln Hotel. Sister Nathan and Sister Rosanne laid down the ground rules: They wanted to see daylight between the dancers. As far as I was concerned, they could have seen Indiana.

The adults at the Hotchkiss reunion are played by an assortment of splendid actors. Mary Steenburgen is the heir to the Hotchkiss legacy, and the students include Sean Astin,

David Paymer, Adam Arkin, and Sonia Braga. Tomei is adorable as the bighearted Meredith, who despite her attack-dog half-brother sees that Frank has a wounded heart, and she attempts to mend it. I hope she gets the flour out of her hair. All I can say about Lisa is, when we finally meet her, she's smoking. As a far better critic than I once wrote, there wasn't a wet eye in the house.

Masculine, Feminine ★ ★ ★
NO MPAA RATING, 103 m., 2005

Jean-Pierre Leaud (Paul), Chantal Goya (Madeleine), Marlene Jobert (Elisabeth), Michel Debord (Robert), Catherine-Isabelle Duport (Catherine-Isabelle). Directed by Jean-Luc Godard and produced by Anatole Dauman. Screenplay by Godard, based on *La Femme de Paul* and *Le Signe* by Guy de Maupassant.

We went seeking greatness in movies, and were most often disappointed. We waited for a movie like the one we wanted to make, and secretly wanted to live.

That's the line I remember best from Godard's *Masculine, Feminine,* and not the more famous "We are the children of Marx and Coca-Cola." When we found a movie like the one we secretly wanted to live, we did not even seek greatness; greatness could take care of itself. The joke at the center of *Masculine, Feminine* (1966) is that its young French characters were fascinated by America, and its young American audiences were fascinated by them. When the movie came out, we all focused on "Marx and Coca-Cola," but now I see that the operative word is "children."

I was barely older than the characters when I wrote my review of the film. I affected a certain detachment ("the French New Wave is coming full circle and recording what has happened to those influenced by it"). I didn't own up to what I really liked about the movie: the way its young hero moves casually through a world of cafés and bistros and the bedrooms of beautiful young girls, including a pop star who is maddeningly indifferent to him.

I wanted to be Paul, the character played by Jean-Pierre Leaud, or at least be Leaud, and appear in movies by Truffaut and Godard, or at least live in Paris and walk down the same streets. All of the rest—the radical politics, the sex talk, the antiwar graffiti Paul sprayed on the car of the American ambassador—was simply his performance art. By acting in that way, he could meet girls like the pop singer Madeleine (Chantal Goya) and her sexy roommates. If you didn't have the money to live in the world of a girl like that, it was a useful strategy to convince her of the purity of your poverty.

I call them "girls" deliberately, and Leaud's character is a boy. Pauline Kael, who loved the film, was even more heartless in her description, calling them "this new breed between teenagers and people." She is alert to the way they boldly discuss birth control, but don't in fact have the pill or know much about sex. Yes, the French are said to be great sophisticates, but the birth control method promised to Madeleine by Paul is one with many a slip 'twixt the method and the control.

The movie has been restored in a new 35mm print. You can appreciate Godard's vigorous early visual style; long before the Dogma movement, he shoots with natural sound and light, he inserts his characters into real times and places, and he practices his own form of withdrawal by separating the movie into fifteen chapters, each one with a title. There is an extended sequence where Leaud's character "interviews" a beauty contest winner, and the entire conversation is completely understood by both of them to be a pick-up attempt.

In a buried sense, everything Leaud does in the film is single-mindedly designed to get him into bed with girls who are not very interested (or interesting). He says he is a Communist. He supports the workers. He paints slogans. He makes radical political comments. He is at the barricades in the sense that barricades are found in the streets, and when he hangs out in cafés the streets are right outside. In the movie's first shot, we see him trying to flip a cigarette into his mouth in one smooth movement, Belmondo-style, as in Godard's first film, *Breathless.* He never gets it right. From the way he smokes we suspect that smoking is not the point: Smoking like Belmondo is the point.

The movie was inspired by two short stories by Guy de Maupassant. I have just read one of them, *The Signal,* which is about a married woman who observes a prostitute attracting

441

men with the most subtle of signs. The woman is fascinated, practices in the mirror, discovers she is better than the prostitute at attracting men, and then finds one at her door and doesn't know what to do about him. If you search for this story in *Masculine, Feminine,* you will not find it, despite some talk of prostitution. Then you realize that the signal has been changed but the device is still there: Leaud's character went to the movies, saw Belmondo attracting women, and is trying to master the same art. Like the heroine of de Maupassant's story, he seems caught off guard when he makes a catch.

The actress Chantal Goya was interviewed about her experience on the movie. She remembers the first day: "Jean-Pierre Leaud, whom I didn't know from Adam, or Eve, came over to me and, looking me straight in the eye, asked me point blank, 'Will you marry me?' I told him, 'We'll see later. I'm in a hurry. Bye.' I went home at noon." I'll have to see the film again to be sure, but I have the strangest feeling that moment is in the movie. The appeal of *Masculine, Feminine* may be that it's not a movie like the one they wanted to make and secretly wanted to live, but the movie they did make, and were living.

The Matador ★ ★ ★ ½
R, 96 m., 2006

Pierce Brosnan (Julian Noble), Greg Kinnear (Danny Wright), Hope Davis (Bean), Philip Baker Hall (Mr. Randy), Adam Scott (Phil Garrison), Dylan Baker (Lovell). Directed by Richard Shepard and produced by Pierce Brosnan, Bryan Furst, Sean Furst, and Beau St. Clair. Screenplay by Shepard.

I walked into *The Matador* expecting one film, and saw another. On paper, this sounds like a formula thriller, and the casting seems to confirm that: Pierce Brosnan as a hit man, and Greg Kinnear as a businessman who meets him in a hotel bar. But Brosnan redefines "hit man" in the best performance of his career ("I facilitate fatalities"), and Kinnear plays with, and against, his image as a regular kinda guy. By the time Hope Davis, Kinnear's wife, meets this killer her husband has told her so much about, she has her first question ready: "Did you bring your gun?"

The movie has a plot in which I suppose it matters who gets whacked, and why, but it's essentially a character study, in which Brosnan, Kinnear, and Davis are invited to riff on the kinds of characters they often play—maybe even get even with them. Every actor who has ever played James Bond spends years reading about how his latest role helps him to "shed the Bond image," but Brosnan appears in *Matador* with his character of Julian Noble so firmly in place that no shedding, molting, or other divestment is necessary.

Julian and Danny Wright (Kinnear) meet in the middle of the night in the hypermodern bar of a Mexico City hotel so sterile it makes the facilities in *Lost in Translation* look funky. During a moment of alcoholic truth, Mr. Wright shares with Mr. Noble the story of the death of his infant son. Julian counters with a dirty joke. Danny is insulted and walks out. But the next day they begin again after Danny demands, and receives, an apology.

Julian Noble's awkward joke is a defining moment in the movie, establishing him as a man cut off from all others, a man who confesses, "I don't live anywhere," a man wandering lost through booze and hookers, a man afraid of losing the skills that make him a useful hit man. He has lost the ability to carry on an appropriate conversation, and when Danny Wright is willing to listen to him, simply listen, he becomes grateful and they become friends.

If Julian needs a confidant, Danny needs a distraction from financial desperation. He has lost not only his child but also his job, and he is in Mexico City trying to cobble together some kind of improbable business deal. Julian offers to take him to a bullfight, and in a wonderfully written scene the conversation turns to the mechanics of hired killing. Julian picks out a man from the crowd, a man obviously with bodyguards, and walks Danny through a dress rehearsal of how he would kill the guy and get away safely.

Months pass. Back in Denver, we meet Carolyn (Hope Davis), Danny's wife. She is known as Bean. Yes, Bean. Bean and Danny are still in love; there's a sweet scene where she remembers how in high school he told her how pretty she was. The doorbell rings and it's Julian, desperate, falling to pieces, telling Danny something that we suspect may be true: "You are my only friend in the world."

Julian moves in, fascinating Bean, Danny, and their young son. Ironically, Julian is equally fascinated by Bean and Danny's love for each other: He's made his way through life, he says, "running from any emotion."

Other characters become involved. There is talk of Julian's panic attacks and a meltdown in the Philippines. His employer, Mr. Randy (Philip Baker Hall), has lost patience; he's like an investor who loved a stock but knows it's time to dump it. Julian's life may be in danger. At a crucial moment he walks through a hotel lobby carrying a gun and wearing only boots and Speedos, and although there is a reason for this, the real reason is to show Julian reduced to despair and public humiliation and meeting it with jaunty indifference.

Brosnan is so intriguing to watch in the movie. Unshaven, trembling, hungover, fearful, charming, confiding, paranoid, trusting, he clings to Danny and Bean like a lost child at the zoo. Where did he get those shirts he wears? They look like they were bought six at a time out of the back of a van at a truck stop. The richness of his comic performance depends on the way he savors and treasures this character; at no point does Brosnan apologize for Julian, or stand outside of him, or seem to invite our laughter. He is like the charming stranger you meet in a bar, who you know could become your best friend if he were not so obviously a time bomb.

Against Brosnan, Kinnear and Davis are perfect foils, enjoying his character as much as he does. The three actors do something that is essential to this kind of comedy: They refuse to be in on the joke. It's not funny for them. They never wink. The movie's writer-director, Richard Shepard, balances the macabre and the sentimental, and he understands that although his film contains questions like, "Don't successful people always live with blood on their hands?" its real subject is friendship.

Match Point ★ ★ ★ ★
R, 124 m., 2006

Jonathan Rhys-Meyers (Chris Wilton), Scarlett Johansson (Nola Rice), Emily Mortimer (Chloe Hewett Wilton), Matthew Goode (Tom Hewett), Brian Cox (Alec Hewett), Penelope Wilton (Eleanor Hewett). Directed by Woody Allen and produced by Letty Aronson, Lucy Darwin, Stephen Tenenbaum, and Gareth Wiley. Screenplay by Allen.

One reason for the fascination of Woody Allen's *Match Point* is that each and every character is rotten. This is a thriller not about good vs. evil but about various species of evil engaged in a struggle for survival of the fittest—or, as the movie makes clear, the luckiest. "I'd rather be lucky than good," Chris, the tennis pro from Ireland, tells us as the movie opens, and we see a tennis ball striking the net; it is pure luck which side it falls on. Chris's own good fortune depends on just such a lucky toss of a coin.

The movie, Allen's best since *Crimes and Misdemeanors* (1989), involves a rich British family and two outsiders who hope to enter it by using their sex appeal. They are the two sexiest people in the movie—their bad luck, since they are more attracted to each other than to their targets in the family. Still, as someone once said (Robert Heinlein, if you must know), money is a powerful aphrodisiac. He added, however, "Flowers work almost as well." Not in this movie, they don't.

The movie stars Jonathan Rhys-Meyers as Chris, a poor boy from Ireland who was on the tennis tour and now works in London as a club pro. He meets rich young Tom (Matthew Goode), who takes a lesson, likes him, and invites him to attend the opera with his family. During the opera, Tom's sister Chloe (Emily Mortimer) looks at Chris once with interest and the second time with desire. Chris does not need to have anything explained to him.

Tom's own girlfriend is Nola (Scarlett Johansson), an American who hopes to become an actress or Tom's wife, not in that order. Tom and Chloe are the children of Alec and Eleanor Hewett (Brian Cox and Penelope Wilton), who have serious money, as symbolized by the country house where the crowd assembles for the weekend. It's big enough to welcome two Merchant-Ivory productions at the same time.

Chloe likes Chris. She wants Chris. Her parents want Chloe to have what she wants. Alec offers Chris a job in "one of my companies"—always a nice touch, that. Tom likes Nola, but to what degree, and do his parents approve? All is decided in the fullness of time, and now I am going to become maddeningly vague in order not to spoil the movie's twists and turns, which are ingenious and difficult to anticipate.

Let us talk instead in terms of the underlying philosophical issues. To what degree are we prepared to set aside our moral qualms in order to indulge in greed and selfishness? I have just finished rereading *The Wings of the Dove* by Henry James, in which a young man struggles heroically with just such a question. He is in love with a young woman he cannot afford to marry, and a rich young heiress is under the impression he is in love with her. The heiress is dying. Everyone advises him he would do her a great favor by marrying her; then after her death, inheriting her wealth, he could afford to marry the woman he loves. But isn't this unethical? No one has such moral qualms in Allen's film, not even sweet Chloe, who essentially has her daddy buy Chris for her. The key question facing the major players is: Greed or lust? How tiresome to have to choose.

Without saying why, let me say that fear also enters into the equation. In a moral universe, it would be joined by guilt, but not here. The fear is that in trying to satisfy both greed and lust, a character may have to lose both, which would be a great inconvenience. At one point this character sees a ghost, but this is not Hamlet's father, crying for revenge; this ghost drops by to discuss loopholes in a "perfect crime."

When *Match Point* premiered at Cannes 2005, the critics agreed it was "not a typical Woody Allen film." This assumes there is such a thing. Allen has worked in a broad range of genres and struck a lot of different notes, although often he uses a Woody Figure (preferably played by himself) as the hero. *Match Point* contains no one anything like Woody Allen, is his first film set in London, is constructed with a devious clockwork plot that would distinguish a film noir, and causes us to identify with some bad people. In an early scene, a character is reading *Crime and Punishment*, and during the movie, as during the novel, we are inside the character's thoughts.

The movie is more about plot and moral vacancy than about characters, and so Allen uses typecasting to quickly establish the characters and set them to their tasks of seduction, deception, lying, and worse. Rhys-Meyers has a face that can express crafty desire, which is not pure lust but more like lust transformed by quick strategic calculations. Goode, as his rich friend, is clueless almost as an occupation. Mortimer plays a character incapable of questioning her own happiness, no matter how miserable it should make her. Johansson's visiting American has been around the block a few times, but like all those poor American girls in Henry James, she is helpless when the Brits go to work on her. She has some good dialogue in the process.

"Men think I may be something special," she tells Chris.

"Are you?"

"No one's ever asked for their money back."

Match Point, which deserves to be ranked with Allen's *Annie Hall, Hannah and Her Sisters, Manhattan, Everyone Says I Love You,* and *Crimes and Misdemeanors*, has a terrible fascination that lasts all the way through. We can see a little way ahead, we can anticipate some of the mistakes and hazards, but the movie is too clever for us, too cynical. We expect the kinds of compromises and patented endings that most thrillers provide, and this one goes right to the wall. There are cops hanging around trying to figure out what, if anything, anyone in the movie might have been up to, but they're too smart and logical to figure this one out. Bad luck.

Mayor of the Sunset Strip ★ ★ ★
R, 94 m., 2004

As themselves: Rodney Bingenheimer, David Bowie, Deborah Harry, Courtney Love, Cher, Nancy Sinatra, Mick Jagger. A documentary directed by George Hickenlooper and produced by Chris Carter, Greg Little, and Tommy Perna. Screenplay by Hickenlooper.

Mayor of the Sunset Strip tells the story of Rodney Bingenheimer, a man who loved music and musicians so much that he willed himself from obscurity into a position of power as the most influential hit-maker on the most important rock radio station in Los Angeles, and then faded from view as his moment passed. Now he is like a ghost, haunting the scenes of his former triumphs, clinging to a last gig from midnight to 3 A.M. every Sunday night on the station he once ruled. "They're afraid to fire him," another employee speculates, "because he's the soul of KROQ."

The Rodney Bingenheimer of today seems

always to be smiling through a deep sadness. He is a small man who still has the youthful cuteness that must have won him friends in his early days. His hair is still combed in the same tousled, mid-1970s, rock star style, and his T-shirts are the real thing, not retro. He lives now in an inexpensive apartment jammed with records, tapes, discs, and countless autographed photos of his friends the stars. And, yes, they are still his friends; they have not forgotten him, and David Bowie, Cher, Deborah Harry, Courtney Love, Nancy Sinatra, and Mick Jagger all appear in this film and seem genuinely fond of Rodney.

Well they might. He introduced some of them—Bowie in particular—to American radio. He was known for finding new music and playing it first: the Ramones, the Sex Pistols, the Clash, Nirvana. Stations all over the country stole their playlists from Rodney. "Sonny and Cher were kinda like my mom and my dad," he says wistfully at one point. He ran a little club for a while, featuring British glam rock, and the stars remember with a grin that it was so small the "VIP Area" consisted simply of a velvet rope separating a few chairs from the dance floor.

The story of how Bingenheimer entered into this world is apparently true, unlikely as it sounds. As a kid, he was obsessed with stars, devoured the fan magazines, collected autographs. One day when he was a teenager, his mother dropped him off in front of Connie Stevens's house and told him he was on his own. He didn't see his mother for another five or six years. Connie wasn't home.

He migrated to Sunset Strip, but instead of dying there or disappearing into drugs or crime, he simply ingratiated himself. People liked him. He hustled himself into a job as a gofer for Davy Jones of the Monkees (they looked a little alike), and then became a backstage caterer; a survivor of a Doors tour remembers a Toronto concert where Rodney had enormous platters of fresh shrimp backstage. But the Beatles were backstage visitors, and Rodney gave them the shrimp, so there were only a few left for the Doors, who had paid for them. Challenged by the Doors, Rodney shrugged and said, "Well, they're the Beatles."

Wherever Bingenheimer went in the music and club scene, his face was his passport.

Robert Plant says, "Rodney got more girls than I did." We hear a little of his radio show from the old days, and what comes across is not a vibrating personality or a great radio voice—it's kind of tentative, really—but an almost painful sincerity. He loves the music he plays, and he introduces it to you like a lover he thinks is right for you.

The road downhill was gradual, apparently. We get glimpses of Rodney today, repairing his mom's old Nova with a pair of pliers, shuffling forlornly through souvenirs of his glory days. He seems very even, calm, sad but resigned, except for one moment the documentary camera is not supposed to witness, when he finds that another deejay, a person he sponsored and gave breaks to, is starting a show of new music—stealing Rodney's gig. He explodes in anger. We're glad he does. He has a lot to feel angry about.

The film was directed by George Hickenlooper, who made the classic doc *Hearts of Darkness* (1991) about the nightmare of Francis Ford Coppola's *Apocalypse Now,* and the wonderful fiction film *The Man from Elysian Fields* (2001). Why did he make this film (apart from the possibility that someone named Hickenlooper might feel an affinity for someone named Bingenheimer)? Hickenlooper has been around fame from an early age. He was twenty-six when he released the doc about the Coppola meltdown. He cast Mick Jagger and James Coburn in *Elysian Fields.* He was aware of Rodney Bingenheimer when the name opened doors. His film evokes what the Japanese call "mono no aware," which refers to the impermanence of life and the bittersweet transience of things. There is a little Rodney Bingenheimer in everyone, but you know what? Most people aren't as lucky as Rodney.

Mean Creek ★ ★ ★
R, 89 m., 2004

Rory Culkin (Sam), Ryan Kelley (Clyde), Scott Mechlowicz (Marty), Trevor Morgan (Rocky), Josh Peck (George), Carly Schroeder (Millie). Directed by Jacob Aaron Estes and produced by Susan Johnson, Rick Rosenthal, and Hagai Shaham. Screenplay by Estes.

Mean Creek opens with a schoolyard bully picking on a smaller kid, develops into a story of revenge, and then deepens into the surprisingly complex story of young teenagers trying to do the right thing. It could have been simple-minded and predictable, but it becomes a rare film about moral choices, about the difficulty of standing up against pressure from your crowd.

Sam (Rory Culkin) is small for his age, bright, articulate. He has become the favorite target of George (Josh Peck), a chubby, spoiled kid whose aggression, we eventually learn, masks a deep loneliness. Certainly George is obnoxious on the surface; I was reminded of specific bullies who operated in the schools of my youth, bullies who never seem to attend our class reunions, although if they did I would cross the room to avoid them. Childhood wounds are not forgiven.

Sam gets pounded by George in a schoolyard fight one day, and that angers his older brother, Rocky (Trevor Morgan). Rocky is a teenager whose triumphs are behind him: He got points for smoking and drinking before anyone else did, was probably sexually active at an early age, was macho and good-looking, was popular within a narrow range, and is now facing his working years without the skills or education to prevail. He's a type familiar from Richard Linklater's *Dazed and Confused,* the recent high school graduate still hanging out with younger kids because those his own age have moved on.

Sam runs with a crowd of close friends, including Marty (Scott Mechlowicz), Clyde (Ryan Kelley), and Millie (Carly Schroeder), who will become his girlfriend when they figure out their half-formed feelings. Marty has problems including a father's suicide and an older brother who picks on him, and of course, the bully George knows how to push his buttons.

George is smart and observant, able to hurt with his words as well as his fists, and it's only in a scene where he's alone at home that we see how desperately he depends on his video toys and the neat stuff in his room as compensation for a deep loneliness. His problem is his big mouth, his habit of using words to wound even when they put him in danger. His out-of-control rant at a crucial moment is a very bad idea.

The other kids hang out as a crowd, and, pushed by Rocky and Marty, decide to pull a practical joke on George. "We need to hurt him without really hurting him," Sam says. They devise a fake birthday party as a way of luring George along on a boat trip, and it is during that trip that their practical joke begins to seem like a bad idea.

Jacob Aaron Estes, who wrote and directed *Mean Creek,* shows in this first film a depth of empathy for his characters, and for the ways the strong-willed ones control the others. It's extraordinary, the small words and events he uses to demonstrate the discovery by the more sensitive kids—Sam and especially Millie—that George isn't a monster after all. They begin to feel sorry for him, and talk quietly among themselves about calling off the practical joke. But Rocky and Marty, who personally have nothing against George, want to go ahead; they're using a crude interpretation of justice to mask their own needs.

The final act of the film is extraordinary. How unusual it is to see kids this age in the movies seriously debating moral rights and wrongs and considering the consequences of their actions. *Mean Creek* makes us realize how many films, not just those about teenagers but particularly the one-dimensional revenge-driven adult dramas, think the defeat of the villain solves everything. Such films have a simplistic, playground morality: The bully is bad, we will destroy him, and our problems will be over. They don't pause to consider the effects of revenge—not on the bully, but on themselves.

Mean Creek joins a small group of films, including *The River's Edge* and *Bully,* that deal accurately and painfully with the consequences of peer-driven behavior. Kids who would not possibly act by themselves form groups that cannot stop themselves. This movie would be an invaluable tool for moral education in schools, for discussions of situational ethics and refusing to go along with the crowd.

But the MPAA in its wisdom has recommended it not be seen by those who would find it most useful and challenging; it has the R rating. At Cannes, where the movie was selected for the Director's Fortnight, Jacob Aaron Estes ruefully said the rating was "because of a scene where the f-word is used about 1,000 times." Let it be said that the f-word has been heard and undoubtedly used by everyone the MPAA is shielding from it, and that the dialogue in that scene and throughout *Mean Creek* is accurate in the way it hears these kids talking.

It is especially accurate, in fact, in showing how the f-word lends power to half-formed and wrong ideas, coloring them with a dangerous aura. Kids who are familiar with the f-word but uncertain about the f-act are likely to feel challenged and insecure when they hear it, suspecting that those who use it must have access to hidden knowledge. All forbidden words work that way, which is how rap music gets some of its power; people who obsessively use that kind of language are covering up for their inability to articulate or even know what they really mean. The kids in *Mean Creek* learn such lessons in a hard and painful way, and will be forever touched by them.

Me and You and Everyone We Know ★ ★ ★ ★

R, 95 m., 2005

John Hawkes (Richard), Miranda July (Christine), Miles Thompson (Peter), Brandon Ratcliff (Robby), Carlie Westerman (Sylvie), Hector Elias (Michael), Brad Henke (Andrew), Natasha Slayton (Heather), Najarra Townsend (Rebecca), Tracy Wright (Nancy). Directed by Miranda July and produced by Gina Kwon. Screenplay by July.

Miranda July's *Me and You and Everyone We Know* is a film that with quiet confidence creates a fragile magic. It's a comedy about falling in love when, for you, love requires someone who speaks your rare emotional language. Yours is a language of whimsy and daring, of playful mind games and bold challenges. Hardly anybody speaks that language, the movie suggests—only me and you and everyone we know, because otherwise we wouldn't bother knowing them.

As a description of a movie, I suppose that sounds maddening. An example. A young woman walks into a department store, and in the shoe department she sees a young man who fascinates her. His hand is bandaged. She approaches him and essentially offers the gift of herself. He is not interested; he's going through a divorce and is afraid of losing his children. She asks him how he hurt his hand. "I was trying to save my life," he says. We've already seen how it happened: He covered his hand with lighter fluid and set it on fire to delight his two sons. He didn't think lighter fluid really burns you when you do that. He was wrong. He was thinking of rubbing alcohol.

Now imagine these two characters, named Christine (Miranda July) and Richard (John Hawkes), as they walk down the street. She suggests that the block they are walking down is their lives. And so now they are halfway down the street and halfway through their lives, and before long they will be at the end. It is impossible to suggest how poetic this scene is; when it's over, you think, that was a perfect scene, and no other scene can ever be like it.

Richard and Christine are at the center of the film, but through Richard's sons we meet other characters. His seven-year-old is named Robby, and is played by Brandon Ratcliff, who read my review from Sundance and wrote me a polite and helpful letter in which he assured me he's as smart as an eleven-year-old. In the movie, he visits an online sex chat room even though he knows nothing about sex. He knows enough about computers to sound like he does, however, by cutting and pasting words, and using open-ended questions. Asked what turns him on, he writes "poop," not because it does, but possibly because it is the only word he can spell that he thinks has something to do with the subject.

His fourteen-year-old brother, Peter (Miles Thompson), is being persecuted by two girls in his class named Heather (Natasha Slayton) and Rebecca (Najarra Townsend). They are intensely interested in oral sex, but unsure about its theory and technique. They decide to practice on Peter. I know this sounds perverse and explicit, and yet the fact is, these scenes play with an innocence and tact that is beyond all explaining. They are about what an embarrassment and curiosity sex is when you're old enough to know it exists but too young to know how it's done and what it's for. They are much intrigued by a neighbor who is a dirty old man in theory but not in practice.

Other characters have other plans for perfect lifetimes. Young Peter, once he shakes off the relentless Heather and Rebecca, is fascinated by Sylvie (Carlie Westerman), a ten-year-old neighbor who does comparison shopping to get the best price on kitchen appliances. Peter catches her ironing some towels. They are going straight into her hope chest, she explains. She is preparing her own dowry. Her future husband, when she grows up and finds him, had better be ready to be good and married.

There is also an art curator (Tracy Wright) who has a strange way of evaluating art, as if she's afraid it may violate rules she's afraid she doesn't know. She has a sexual hunger that proves particularly hard to deal with. She is, however, able to project her longings into the uncomprehending world; the strategy she uses, and the result it brings, is a scene of such inevitability and perfection that we laugh at least partly out of admiration.

Miranda July is a performance artist; this is her first feature film (it won the Special Jury Prize at Sundance, and at Cannes won the Camera d'Or as best first film, and the Critics' Week grand prize). Performance art sometimes deals with the peculiarities of how we express ourselves, with how odd and wonderful it is to be alive. So does this film. As Richard slowly emerges from sadness and understands that Christine values him, and he must value her, for reasons only the two of them will ever understand, the movie holds its breath, waiting to see if their delicate connection will hold.

Me and You and Everyone We Know is a balancing act, as July ventures into areas that are risky and transgressive, but uses a freshness that disarms them, a directness that accepts human nature and likes to watch it at work. The MPAA gave it an R rating "for disturbing sexual content involving children," but the one thing it isn't is disturbing. When the movie was over at Sundance, I let out my breath and looked across the aisle at another critic. I wanted to see if she felt how I did. "What did you think?" she said. "I think it's the best film at the festival," I said. "Me too," she said.

Mean Girls ★ ★ ★
PG-13, 93 m., 2004

Lindsay Lohan (Cady Heron), Rachel McAdams (Regina George), Lizzy Caplan (Janis), Daniel Franzese (Damian), Jonathan Bennett (Aaron), Lacey Chabert (Gretchen), Tina Fey (Ms. Norbury),Tim Meadows (Mr. Duvall), Amanda Seyfried (Karen). Directed by Mark S. Waters and produced by Lorne Michaels. Screenplay by

Tina Fey, based on the book *Queen Bees and Wannabes* by Rosalind Wiseman.

In a wasteland of dumb movies about teenagers, *Mean Girls* is a smart and funny one. It even contains some wisdom, although I hesitate to mention that, lest I scare off its target audience. The TV ads, which show Lindsay Lohan landing ass over teakettle in a garbage can, are probably right on the money; since that scene is nothing at all like the rest of the movie, was it filmed specifically to use in the commercials?

Lindsay Lohan stars as Cady Heron, a high school junior who was home-schooled in Africa while her parents worked there as anthropologists. She is therefore the smartest girl in school when her dad is hired by Northwestern and she enrolls in Evanston Township High School—which, like all American high schools in the movies, is physically located in Toronto. What she's not smart about are the ways cliques work in high school, and how you're categorized and stereotyped by who you hang with and how you dress.

Cady makes two friends right away: Janis (Lizzy Caplan), a semi-Goth whose own anthropology includes an analysis of who sits where in the cafeteria, and why; and Damian (Daniel Franzese), Janis's best friend, described as "too gay to function." They clue her in: The three most popular girls in the junior class are the Plastics, so-called because they bear an uncanny resemblance to Barbie. They're led by Regina George (Rachel McAdams), a skilled manipulator whose mother's boob job has defined her values in life. Her sidekicks are Gretchen (Lacey Chabert) and Karen (Amanda Seyfried).

Janis and Damian warn Cady against the girls from hell. But when Regina invites Cady to join their table, Janis urges her to: She can be a spy and get inside information for their campaign to destroy Regina. And she can recommend an obscure brand of Swedish "diet bar" actually used by athletes to gain weight, so that slim Regina with her flawless complexion can find out how it feels to be chubby and spotty.

Mean Girls dissects high school society with a lot of observant detail that seems surprisingly well informed. The screenplay by *Saturday Night Live*'s Tina Fey is both a comic and a sociological achievement, and no wonder; it's inspired not by a novel but by a nonfiction book by Rosalind Wiseman. Its full title more or less summarizes the movie: *Queen Bees and Wannabes: Helping Your Daughter Survive Cliques, Gossip, Boyfriends, and Other Realities of Adolescence.* The mothers in the movie are not much help, however, and Fey's screenplay wisely uses comedy as a learning tool.

Fey also plays a math teacher named Ms. Norbury, who is more plausible and likable than most high school teachers in the movies, and also kind of lovable, especially in the vicinity of the school principal, Mr. Duvall (Tim Meadows, a former *SNL* star). Although many of producer Lorne Michaels's movies with *SNL* cast members have been broad, dumb, and obvious, this one has a light and infectious touch, and it's a revelation to see how Meadows gets real laughs not with big gestures but with small ones: Notice particularly his body language and tone of voice during the new prom queen's speech.

The movie was directed by Mark S. Waters, who also made *Freaky Friday* (2003), a superior remake, and emerged from Sundance 1997 with *The House of Yes,* an uneven but intriguing dark comedy with Parker Posey convinced she was Jackie Onassis. Here he avoids amazing numbers of clichés that most teenage comedies cannot do without. When Cady throws a party while her parents are out of town, for example, a lot of uninvited guests do crash, yes, but amazingly they do *not* trash the house. Although Principal Duvall lectures the student body about a pushing-and-shoving spree, he does *not* cancel the prom ("We've already hired the deejay"). When Cady gets a crush on Aaron (Jonathan Bennett), who sits in front of her in math class, she deals with it in a reasonable way that does *not* involve heartbreak. When there are misunderstandings, they're understandable, and *not* awkward contrivances manufactured for the convenience of the plot.

In the middle of all this, Lindsay Lohan, who was seventeen when the movie was filmed, provides a center by being centered. She has a quiet self-confidence that prevents her from getting shrill and hyper like so many teenage stars; we believe her when she says that because of her years in Africa, "I had never lived in a world where adults didn't trust me." She never allows the character to tilt into caricature, and for that

matter, even the Plastics seem real, within their definitions of themselves, and not like the witch-harridans of some teenage movies.

Will teenage audiences walk out of *Mean Girls* determined to break with the culture of cliques, gossip, and rules for popularity? Not a chance. That's built into high school, I think. But they may find it interesting that the geeks are more fun than the queen bees, that teachers have feelings, and that you'll be happier as yourself than as anybody else. I guess the message is, you have to live every day as if you might suddenly be hit by a school bus.

Meet the Fockers ★ ★
PG-13, 116 m., 2004

Robert De Niro (Jack Byrnes), Ben Stiller (Greg Focker), Dustin Hoffman (Bernie Focker), Barbara Streisand (Roz Focker), Blythe Danner (Dina Byrnes), Teri Polo (Pam Byrnes), Owen Wilson (Kevin Rawley), Spencer and Bradley Pickren (Little Jack), Alanna Ubach (Isabel). Directed by Jay Roach and produced by Jane Rosenthal, Robert De Niro, and Roach. Screenplay by Jim Herzfeld and John Hamburg.

As a categorical rule, I avoid statements beginning, "If you loved/liked (name of movie), you'll love/like (name of another movie)." So let me put it this way. If you went to *Meet the Parents* (2000), you will probably find yourself going to *Meet the Fockers,* because having met one set of crazy parents, you are curious about the other set. Also, you may be the kind of person who finds it entertaining to mention that you are on your way to meet the Fockers. When the MPAA objected to the title, by the way, the filmmakers produced several real people who said they were Fockers, and proud of it.

The movie opens with Greg Focker (Ben Stiller) and Pam Byrnes (Teri Polo) still in the embrace of their interminable courtship. In the original film, Pam took Greg home to meet her parents, Jack and Dina (Robert De Niro and Blythe Danner), and you will recall that Greg was a threat to Jack's beloved cat, human ashes made an inappropriate appearance, a septic tank overflowed, and Jack the ex-CIA man gave Greg a lie-detector test.

Now it is time to drive down to Focker Isle

in Florida, where live Father and Mom Focker (Dustin Hoffman and Barbra Streisand). Roz is a successful sex therapist, author of books such as *Meet Your Orgasm!* Bernie was a lawyer until he took paternity leave to raise Greg and never went back to work. The Fockers only had the one child, Jack Byrnes discovers. And with a memory so long that I hope audiences can also recall the funniest moment in the first movie, he accuses Greg: "I thought you had a sister. You said you milked your sister's cat."

Hoffman and Streisand are such positive thinkers, so quick to hug and approve and embrace (and meet their orgasms) that it's amazing they produced such an uptight child as Greg. The household is so open-minded, there's a breeze. Consider, for example, Roz Focker's collection of erotic wood carvings of small ethnic people sporting enormous phalli. Jack scowls at such displays, and doesn't want to take his shirt off when Roz offers him a massage. The massage scene, sad to say, doesn't really pay off. Its only point is that Roz works him over so thoroughly that he's stiff and sore afterward. There must have been some comic way, I think, for Jack to meet his orgasm, or at least give it a friendly wave.

There is a tradition at dinners in these families that something unappetizing makes its appearance at the table, but Greg's childhood souvenir is so *very* unappetizing that, I dunno, I cringed instead of laughing. To the cat of the first movie we now add the Fockers' sex-mad dog, which, like a curious number of dogs, has a pants-leg fetish, proving Darwin was right because dogs have existed so much longer than pants. The cat is not only toilet-trained but knows how to flush, leading to another septic joke. And Jack calls on his old CIA buddies to investigate suspicions he has involving his future son-in-law and the family's former maid, the buxom Isabel (Alanna Ubach).

The movie is pleasant enough, but never quite reaches critical mass as a comedy. The director, Jay Roach, who made *Meet the Parents* and the Austin Powers movies, has some funny stuff, including Father Focker's proud display of all of his son's trophies ("I didn't know they made ninth-place ribbons," Jack muses). There's some wordplay involving the Byrnes family Circle of Trust and who is in it, who is outside it, and whose circle it is. Streisand and Hoffman

create characters who are, under the circumstances, not only likable but actually sort of believable. And yet, even if you loved *Meet the Parents*, you will only sorta, kinda like *Meet the Fockers*.

Note: There's a cute baby in the movie, Jack Jr., played by twins Spencer and Bradley Pickren. The kid is too young to talk, but Jack Sr. has already started him on sign language. I learn that the Pickren twins actually can sign, and that long before they can speak, babies can learn and use signs.

Melinda and Melinda ★ ★ ★ ½
PG-13, 99 m., 2005

Radha Mitchell (Melinda), Chloe Sevigny (Laurel), Jonny Lee Miller (Lee), Will Ferrell (Hobie), Amanda Peet (Susan), Chiwetel Ejiofor (Ellis), Wallace Shawn (Sy), Larry Pine (Max). Directed by Woody Allen and produced by Letty Aronson. Screenplay by Allen.

Woody Allen's *Melinda and Melinda* begins with friends having dinner in a Chinese restaurant. One of the friends is played by Wallace Shawn, who (Allen's audiences will know) has had a famous restaurant meal or two. Shawn is a playwright, debating another playwright (Larry Pine) about whether the world is essentially tragic or comic. They devise two versions of a story, which changes in detail and tone according to whether it is comedy or tragedy, and the film cuts between those possibilities.

The exercise involves two couples, both disrupted by the unexpected entrance of a character named Melinda (played by Radha Mitchell). For Susan the independent filmmaker (Amanda Peet) and her husband, Hobie (Will Ferrell), an out-of-work actor, she is the downstairs neighbor. For the rich woman Laurel (Chloe Sevigny) and her husband, Lee (Jonny Lee Miller), an alcoholic actor, she is Laurel's old college friend.

In both cases, Melinda is the catalyst for adultery, which does not play out the same way in the two stories. Indeed, almost all the characters except Melinda are different in the two stories because you would cast a comedy differently than a tragedy. Unexpected characters like Ellis Moonsong (Chiwetel Ejiofor), a composer, turn up to supply the third point in two romantic triangles at once.

From time to time, Allen reminds us that all of these characters are being imagined by people at dinner, and all of their feelings are being created out of thin air. The film's last shot, a bold masterstroke, leaves this perfectly clear, and strands us looking at the closing credits, which as always are played over some good traditional jazz. Why won't Woody choose one of these stories or the other? Why won't he either cheer or sadden us? When he abandoned comedy for neo-Bergman exercises like *Interiors*, at least they were Bergmanesque all the way through, with no excursions into romantic comedy. Why can't he make up his mind?

But you see, he has. Allen has made up his mind to pull the rug out from under us as we stand at the cocktail party of life, chattering about how we got there, when we plan to leave, and how we'll get back home. He has shown that the rug, the party, and all of the guests are shadows flickering on the walls. *Melinda and Melinda* is a movie about the symbiosis of the filmmaker and the audience, who are required to conspire in the creation of an imaginary world. He shows us how he does it and how we do it. In its complexity and wit, this is one of his best films.

That creates a particular challenge for the actors, who are expected to act as if they are in either a comedy or a tragedy and do not know about the other half of the movie. Radha Mitchell, who is the crossover character, rises to the challenge and is impudent in the comedy and touching in the tragedy; she must have had to compartmentalize her emotions, but then that's what actors do.

The two stories are a little sketchy because neither one is required to have a beginning, middle, and end—to deliver in traditional terms. They're works in progress. That may sound frustrating, but it's sort of exciting, as if Allen is allowing us to read his early drafts. Perhaps in Woody Allen's mind a dinner party is held nightly at which his optimistic and pessimistic selves argue about his next project. *Melinda and Melinda* may be a dramatization of his creative process.

Before the movie opened, A. O. Scott wrote a provocative article in the *New York Times*, concluding: "Instead of making the movies we expect him to, (Allen) stubbornly makes the movies he wants to make, gathering his A-list casts for minor exercises in whimsy and bile that tend not to be appreciated when they arrive in theaters. How could they be? Mr. Allen will never again be his younger self, and his audience, as long as we refuse to acknowledge that fact, will never grow up, guaranteeing our further disappointment. Maybe what we have on our hands is a dead shark."

That's a reference to *Annie Hall*, which won the Oscar and was the high point of America's relationship with Woody Allen ("A relationship is like a shark. It has to constantly move forward or it dies"). With Scott's words I have some sympathy. Woody Allen made members of my generation laugh when we were young, and now he doesn't make us feel young anymore. Scott argues that by refusing to repeat himself, Allen has left himself open to the charge of repeating himself: There he goes again, doing something different. I cannot escape the suspicion that if Woody had never made a previous film, if each new one was Woody's Sundance debut, it would get a better reception. His reputation is not a dead shark but an albatross, which, with admirable economy, Allen has arranged for the critics to carry around their own necks.

Melinda fails the standards of most audiences because it doesn't deliver a direct emotional charge. It doesn't leave us happy or sad for the characters, or even knowing which characters we were supposed to care about. That, however, is not Allen's failure, but his purpose. More than any other film that comes to mind, *Melinda and Melinda* says, clearly and without compromise, that movies are only movies. They're made up of thin air, the characters are not real, they could turn out however the director wants them to. We get all worked up about what Frankie does in *Million Dollar Baby*, and would get just as worked up if he did the opposite, both times talking about Frankie as if he were real and had actually done something. At the end of *Melinda and Melinda*, we realize that neither Melinda nor Melinda is real, but Woody Allen certainly is.

Memoirs of a Geisha ★ ★ ½
PG-13, 137 m., 2005

Ziyi Zhang (Sayuri), Ken Watanabe (The Chairman), Michelle Yeoh (Mameha), Gong Li

(Hatsumomo), Koji Yakusho (Nobu), Youki Kudoh (Pumpkin), Kaori Momoi (Mother), Suzuka Ohgo (Chiyo). Directed by Rob Marshall and produced by Douglas Wick, Lucy Fisher, and Steven Spielberg. Screenplay by Robin Swicord and Doug Wright, based on the book by Arthur Golden.

I suspect that the more you know about Japan and movies, the less you will enjoy *Memoirs of a Geisha*. Much of what I know about Japan I have learned from Japanese movies, and on that basis I know this is not a movie about actual geishas but depends on the romanticism of female subjection. The heroines here look so very beautiful and their world is so visually enchanting as they live trapped in sexual slavery.

I know, a geisha is not technically a prostitute. Here is a useful rule: Anyone who is "not technically a prostitute" is a prostitute. As dear old Henry Togna, proprietor of the Eyrie Mansion in London, used to cackle while describing to me his friend the Duchess of Duke Street, "Sex for cash, m'dear. That's my definition."

Is the transaction elevated if there is very little sex, a lot of cash, and the prostitute gets hardly any of either? Hard to say. Certainly the traditions of the geisha house are culturally fascinating in their own right. But if this movie had been set in the West, it would be perceived as about children sold into prostitution, and that is not nearly as wonderful as "being raised as a geisha."

Still, I object to the movie not on sociological grounds but because I suspect a real geisha house floated on currents deeper and more subtle than the broad melodrama on display here. I could list some Japanese films illustrating this, but the last thing the audience for *Memoirs of a Geisha* wants to see is a more truthful film with less gorgeous women and shabbier production values.

This is one of the best-looking movies in some time, deserving comparison with *Raise the Red Lantern* (in more ways than one). On the level of voluptuous visual beauty, it works if you simply regard it. The women are beauties, their world swims in silks and tapestries, smoke and mirrors, and the mysteries of hair when it is up vs. hair when it is down.

I am not disturbed in the least that the three leading Japanese characters in the film are played by women of Chinese descent. This casting has been attacked as ethnically incorrect, but consider that the film was made by a Japanese-owned company; the intent was not to discriminate against Japanese, but in favor of the box office. The movie was cast partly on the basis of star power: Ziyi Zhang, Gong Li, and Michelle Yeoh are not only great beauties and gifted actresses but box-office dynamite. Even in Japan, Zhang and Li outgross any Japanese actress.

They do wonders with their characters, who are trapped in a formula fiction but suggest possibilities they cannot explore. There isn't the faintest suggestion of free will, but then free will has never played much of a role in the world of a geisha. That's made clear at the outset, circa 1929, when a widowed fisherman sells his daughters on the human market in Kyoto. The older girl, although hardly old enough for sex, is sold directly into prostitution, while the nine-year-old Chiyo (Suzuka Ohgo) is sold to a geisha house where she will be an unpaid servant until it is determined if she is elegant enough for the house's clientele.

The house is run by Mother (Kaori Momoi), and its ruling geisha is Hatsumomo (Li). Chiyo quickly becomes best friends with Pumpkin (Youki Kudoh), a girl about her age, and they are raised by the house under a strict discipline that trains them for a lifetime of flattering wealthy men. They learn that love has no role in this world (although Hatsumomo sets a bad example). Geisha lore hints that they do fall in love with clients, but the operative word is "client" and the love is not free. Nobody wants it to be— not the geisha, who is earning her living, or the client, who is using money to control a woman while maintaining his independence and, for that matter, to observe a distinction between his geisha and his wife.

The key male in the story is the Chairman (Ken Watanabe), who first encounters Chiyo when she is a child and suggests her to Mother. As Chiyo and her beauty grow, it becomes clear she may represent a threat to the dominance of Hatsumomo. The story resumes when she is in her mid-teens and is purchased from Mother by Mameha (Yeoh), Hatsumomo's rival, whose master plan is to use her control of the younger girl to win control of Mother's house away from Hatsumomo, who expects to inherit the reins.

Hatsumomo in response acquires Pumpkin as her own proxy in the battle. It is amazing that a client stepping through their doors is not killed in the crossfire.

Chiyo is renamed Sayuri and is now played by Zhang. The movie, almost like a tourist, prowls the geisha quarter of Kyoto, visits a sumo wrestling match and attends a dance performance where Sayuri stars. Then World War II intervenes (that is the best word for its role in the film), and in peacetime the Chairman now desperately needs Sayuri, who has always loved and still does love him, perhaps because he steered her as a child into the best geisha house. It suits him for Sayuri to become the friend of his colleague Nobu (Koji Yakusho), and there is great intrigue surrounding the auctioning of Sayuri's virginity. This takes place, if my math is sound, at her fairly advanced age of about twenty-six, which reminds me that Oscar Levant claimed: "I've been in Hollywood so long, I knew Doris Day before she was a virgin."

I realize that my doubts and footnotes are completely irrelevant to the primary audience for this movie, which wants to see beauty, sex, tradition, and exoticism all choreographed into a dance of strategy and desire. *Memoirs of a Geisha* (directed by Rob Marshall of *Chicago*) supplies what is required elegantly and with skill. The actresses create geishas as they imagine them to have been, which is probably wiser than showing them as they were. There is a sense in which I enjoyed every frame of this movie, and another sense in which my enjoyment made me uneasy. I felt some of the same feelings during *Pretty Baby*, the 1978 film in which Brooke Shields, playing a girl of twelve, has her virginity auctioned away in New Orleans. The difference is that *Pretty Baby* doesn't evoke nostalgia or regret the passing of the world it depicts. ☞

The Memory of a Killer ★ ★ ★ ½
R, 120 m., 2005

Koen De Bouw (Eric Vincke), Jan Decleir (Angelo Ledda), Werner De Smedt (Freddy Verstuyft), Hilde De Baerdemaeker (Linda De Leenheer), Jo De Meyere (Baron De Haeck), Geert Van Rampelberg (Tom Coemans). Directed by Erik Van Looy and produced by Hilde De Laere and Erwin Provoost. Screenplay by Carl Joos and Van Looy, based on a novel by Jef Geeraerts.

The Memory of a Killer contains the elements of a typical police procedural, transcended and brought to a sad perfection by the performance of a veteran Belgian actor named Jan Decleir. In his appearance Decleir reminds me of Anthony Quinn, and in his behavior of Jean Gabin—the Gabin of the late gangster films, playing men who are weary of crime and yet live by an underworld code.

Decleir plays Angelo Ledda, a professional hit man. He is assigned to go to Antwerp in Belgium and kill a man. He protests that he is too old—he's retired. "Men like us never retire," his boss says. Angelo tells the waitress to bring fries with his steak, and she reminds him that he's already ordered them. Here is the first hint: He is in the early stages of Alzheimer's. In Belgium, he visits his senile older brother in an institution. An orderly describes the onset of his brother's symptoms. "I know how it begins," Angelo says firmly.

He is a contract killer who knows he is losing his mind. Like the hero of *Memento*, he writes notes to himself on his arm. But *The Memory of a Killer* is not another version of *Memento;* it is a full-bore traditional "policier," beginning with a plainclothes cop busting a man who is selling his eleven-year-old daughter, and continuing with a series of killings, as powerful men try to conceal their connection to child prostitution. The first man Angelo kills is a prosecutor who will not drop the investigation. His second assignment . . .

I'll leave that for you to discover. It is an assignment he will not accept. "No one will," he tells the man who wants him to do the job. Angelo is a killer, but he is also a man unwilling to cross a certain line. In her review of this movie, Manohla Dargis has a lovely observation: "Here is a thriller that asks, Are men essentially good or do they just sometimes forget to be bad?" Angelo is forgetting to be anything.

The police/criminal side of the plot could be from a novel by Ed McBain or Nicholas Freeling; the psychological side could be from Georges Simenon. The movie is based on the novel *The Alzheimer Case* by the Belgian writer Jef Geeraerts, which unthreads a plot involving buried perversion and aristocratic hauteur, contrasting it with the declining years of this hardworking professional man, the contract killer.

Koen De Bouw plays Eric Vincke, the fortyish cop assigned to the original child prostitution case; he follows the thread as it leads to powerful people and stays on the case in defiance of his superiors. Along the way, he comes to realize that Angelo Ledda is on both sides of the moral equation: as a murderer to begin with, and then as a man working against the same perverts Vincke is after. His first challenge is to figure out who Ledda really is; the old man may be declining, but he is experienced and canny, and he uses a masterstroke to throw the police off his scent.

There are crime stories, and then there are stories about people involved in crime. *The Memory of a Killer* is in the second category. It follows a rich European fictional tradition, which in addition to the authors I've mentioned also includes Michael Dibdin, Henning Mankell, and Maj Sjowall and Per Wahloo. In their work, crime is used as a quick entry into the secrets of the heart, and guilt is not assigned so easily. When Gabin plays a crook in a movie like *Touchez pas au Grisbi*, he somehow becomes the hero.

As the plot of *The Memory of a Killer* leads into a labyrinth of decadence and obscurity, one murder connects to another, and desperate men take risky measures. Old Angelo is the wild card, sought by both sides, working in the shadows, hiding out in places remembered from his childhood in Antwerp. He knows his way around. He realizes that, one way or another, he is on his last job. And that makes him doubly dangerous, because he has nothing to lose but his life, which is slipping away anyway.

Watch Decleir's performance. He never goes for the easy effect, never pushes too hard, is a rock-solid occupant of his character. Everything he has to say about Angelo is embodied, not expressed. By the end we care so much for him that the real suspense involves not the solution of the crimes but simply his well-being. Talks are already under way for a Hollywood remake of *The Memory of a Killer*, and the names of many actors have been proposed; the *Hollywood Reporter* lists DeNiro, Caan, Hopper, Hopkins. But this performance will not be easily equaled. Gene Hackman, maybe. Morgan Freeman. Robert Mitchum, if he were alive. Decleir is the real thing.

The Merchant of Venice ★ ★ ★ ½
R, 138 m., 2005

Al Pacino (Shylock), Jeremy Irons (Antonio), Joseph Fiennes (Bassanio), Lynn Collins (Portia), Zuleikha Robinson (Jessica), Kris Marshall (Gratiano), Charlie Cox (Lorenzo). Directed by Michael Radford and produced by Cary Brokaw, Michael Cowan, Barry Navidi, and Jason Piette. Screenplay by Radford, based on the play by William Shakespeare.

Thinking to read *The Merchant of Venice* one more time, I took down the volume of Shakespeare's tragedies, only to be reminded that this dark and troubling play is classified with his comedies. Its two natures come from different spheres; sunny scenes of romance alternate with sadness, desperation, and guile. When Jessica, Shylock's daughter, steals his fortune and leaves his home to marry Lorenzo, it's as if she's escaping from one half of the play to the other.

Michael Radford's new production is, incredibly, the first theatrical film of the play in the sound era. There were several silent versions, and it has been done for television, but among the most important titles in Shakespeare's canon this is the play that has been sidestepped by not only Hollywood but every film industry in the world. The reason is plain to see: Shylock, the moneylender who demands repayment with a pound of flesh, is an anti-Semitic caricature; filmmakers turn away and chose more palatable plays.

Yet Shylock is an intense, passionate character in a great play, and Radford's film does him justice. Although Shylock embodies anti-Semitic stereotypes widely held in Shakespeare's time, he is not a one-dimensional creature like Marlowe's *The Jew of Malta*, but embodies, like all of Shakespeare's great creations, a humanity that transcends the sport of his making. Radford's Shylock, played with a rasping intensity by Al Pacino, is not softened or apologized for—that would deny the reality of the play—but he is *seen* as a man not without his reasons.

The film opens by visualizing an event referred to only in dialogue in the original: We see the merchant Antonio (Jeremy Irons) spit at Shylock on the Rialto bridge, as part of a demonstration against the Jews who are both needed and hated in Venice—needed, because without moneylenders the city's economy cannot function, and hated, because Christians must therefore do business with the same people they have long executed a blood libel against.

That Antonio spits at Shylock, asks him for a loan of 3,000 ducats, and boldly tells him he would spit at him again is, in modern terms, asking for it. That Shylock loans him the money against the guarantee of a pound of flesh is not simply a cruelty, but has a certain reason; Shakespeare's dialogue makes it clear that Shylock proudly declines to accept any monetary interest from Antonio and has every reason to think Antonio can repay the loan, which means that Shylock will have borrowed the money at cost to himself and loaned it to Antonio for free.

That Antonio comes within a whisper of losing his flesh and his life is, after all, the result of a bargain he quickly agreed to, because he also thought he would escape without paying interest. Shakespeare's great courtroom scene, in which the Doge must decide between the claims of Shylock and the life of Antonio, is undercut by the farce of the cross-dressing Portia's last-second appeal; on the merits of the case, Shylock should win.

But I have written as if you know who Shylock and Antonio and Portia are, and you may not; *The Merchant of Venice* is studiously avoided in those courses that seek to introduce Shakespeare to students, who can tell you all about Romeo and Juliet. One of the strengths of the film is its clarity. A written prologue informs us of the conditions of Jewish life in Venice in 1586; Jews were forced to live in a confined area that gave the word "ghetto" to the world, were forbidden to move through the city after dark (although they seem to do a lot of that in the film), and were tolerated because Christians were forbidden to lend money at interest, and somebody had to.

The plot is driven from the comic side by the desire of Bassanio (Joseph Fiennes) to wed the fair Portia (Lynn Collins). She has been left by her father's will in the position of a game show prize; her suitors are shown chests of gold, silver, and lead, and made to choose one; inside the lucky chest is the token of their prize. Elementary gamesmanship cries out "Lead! Choose the lead!" but

one royal hopeful after another goes for the glitter, and the impoverished Bassanio still has a chance.

He will need money to finance his courtship, and turns to his friend Antonio. The play famously opens with Antonio's melancholy ("I know not why I am so sad"), but the casting of Jeremy Irons makes that opening speech unnecessary; he is an actor to whom sadness comes without effort, and a dark gloom envelops him throughout the play. The reason for this is implied by Shakespeare and made clear by Radford: Antonio is in love with Bassanio, and in effect is being asked for a loan to finance his own romantic disappointment. Whether he and Bassanio were actually lovers is a good question. How genuinely Bassanio can love Portia the lottery prize is another. That these two questions exist in the same place is a demonstration of the way in which Shakespeare boldly juxtaposes inner torment and screwball comedy.

Shylock is a cruel caricature, but isn't he also one of the first Jews allowed to speak for himself in gentile European literature, to argue his case, to reveal his humanity? It's possible that Shakespeare never actually met a Jew (to be a Catholic was a hanging offense in his England), but then he never visited Venice, either—or France, Denmark, or the seacoast of Bohemia. His Shylock begins as a lift from literary sources, like so many of his characters, and is transformed by his genius into a man of feelings and deep wounds. There is a kind of mad incongruity in the play's intersecting stories, one ending in sunshine, marriage, and happiness, the other in Shylock's loss of everything—daughter, fortune, home, and respect. And Shylock's great speech, beginning "Hath not a Jew eyes?" is a cry against anti-Semitism that rings down through the centuries. It is wrong to say that *The Merchant of Venice* is not "really" anti-Semitic—of course it is—but its venom is undercut by Shakespeare's inability to objectify any of his important characters. He always sees the man inside.

Pacino is a fascinating actor. As he has grown older he has grown more fierce. He is charged sometimes with overacting, but never with bad acting; he follows the emotions of his characters fearlessly, not protecting himself, and here he lays bare Shylock's lacerated soul. He has a way of attacking and caressing Shakespeare's language at the same time. He loves it. It allows him reach and depth. His performance here is incandescent.

Of the others, Irons finds the perfect note for the treacherous role of Antonio; making his love for Bassanio obvious is the way to make his behavior explicable, and so Antonio for once is poignant, instead of merely a mope. The young people, Bassanio and Portia, resolutely inhabit their comedy, unaware of the suffering their romance is causing for others. Only Jessica (Zuleikha Robinson) still seems inexplicable; how can she do what she does to her father, Shylock, with such vacuous contentment?

The film is wonderful to look at, saturated in Renaissance colors and shadows, filmed in Venice, which is the only location that is also a set. It has greatness in moments, and is denied greatness overall only because it is such a peculiar construction; watching it is like channel-surfing between a teen romance and a dark abysm of loss and grief. Shylock and Antonio, if they were not made strangers by hatred, would make good companions for long, sad conversations punctuated by wounded silences.

Metallica: Some Kind of Monster ★ ★ ★
NO MPAA RATING, 120 m., 2004

A documentary directed and produced by Joe Berlinger and Bruce Sinofsky.

Metallica: Some Kind of Monster doesn't require you to know anything about the band Metallica or heavy metal music, but it supplies a lot of information about various kinds of monsters. Some of them have been around since childhood, some live in the bottle, and others are generated by the act of making millions as a rock god. When the film opens, the band has been around some twenty years and its surviving members, now middle-aged, are exhausted, neurotic, and on each other's nerves. Their bass player, Jason Newsted, has quit the band, citing "the physical damage I've done to myself playing the music live."

In 2001, Metallica goes into an improvised studio in San Francisco's Presidio to create a

new album from scratch. They're starting with "no riffs, no songs, no titles, nothing." For reasons that must have seemed excellent at the time, they invite two documentary filmmakers to film them in this process. Joe Berlinger and Bruce Sinofsky have made some of the best docs of recent years, including *Paradise Lost: The Child Murders at Robin Hood Hills* (1996), which follows the trial and conviction of three heavy metal fans who almost certainly had nothing to do with the grisly murders they're charged with (in a 2000 sequel, *Paradise Lost 2: Revelations*, the likely murderer does all he can to draw suspicion to himself).

Sinofsky and Berlinger possibly thought this assignment would be more routine, even music-driven. In fact, there is little music in *Metallica* and a great deal of talking, as the three band members (lead singer James Hetfield, drummer Lars Ulrich, and guitarist Kirk Hammett) recruit their producer, Bob Rock, to play bass. There is another recruit: a therapist named Phil Towle. The relationship between Hetfield and Ulrich has become poisonous, and Towle's assignment is to bring peace and healing—or at least the ability to function.

The band members exhibit a certain courage in allowing their sessions to be filmed warts and all, as tempers flare, hurtful words are exchanged, and Towle's skills as a therapist make us wonder if his scenes were deleted from *This Is Spinal Tap*. That he is being paid $40,000 a month makes him feel like keeping his job, until finally Hetfield and Ulrich find they agree on something at last, getting rid of him.

The progress of the album is interrupted when Hetfield unexpectedly signs into rehab. For weeks and months the others have no idea how long he'll be gone; he returns in a year, sober and solemnly following instructions from the rehab center. He can work only four hours a day, for example. This drives Ulrich up the wall: How can you make an album without sleepless nights? He charges Hetfield with being "self-regarding," which was probably more true before he went into rehab; now, in his free time, we see him attending his daughter's ballet class and otherwise trying to learn how to be a husband and father.

There are hints in the film that a little rehab

would not be amiss for Ulrich. He gets a visit from his long-haired hippie Danish father, who still treats him like a kid taking music lessons, and at one point suggests deleting a song from the album because "It just doesn't sound right." Hammett meanwhile keeps a low profile, like the child in a dysfunctional marriage who has learned how to stay below the radar.

The band eventually finishes the album *(St. Anger)*. The movie opens with the press junket promoting it, at which they repeat conventional sound bites that the movie shows bear little correspondence with reality. If *Metallica: Some Kind of Monster* has a message, it's that it's great being a rock god up to a point, but most rock gods play the role long after it's much fun. Some people sing and tour forever (Willie Nelson, the Stones, McCartney). What Dr. Phil should probably advise Metallica is to call it a day. Why work with people you can't stand, doing work you're sick of, and that may be killing you? Lots of people have jobs like that, but Metallica has a choice.

Million Dollar Baby ★ ★ ★ ★
PG-13, 132 m., 2004

Clint Eastwood (Frankie Dunn), Hilary Swank (Maggie Fitzgerald), Morgan Freeman (Scrap), Jay Baruchel (Danger), Mike Colter (Big Willie Little), Lucia Rijker (Billie [The Blue Bear]), Brian F. O'Byrne (Father Horvak), Margo Martindale (Earline Firzgerald). Directed by Clint Eastwood and produced by Tom Rosenberg, Paul Haggis, Albert S. Ruddy, and Eastwood. Screenplay by Haggis, based on stories from *Rope Burns*, by F. X. Toole.

Clint Eastwood's *Million Dollar Baby* is a masterpiece, pure and simple, deep and true. It tells the story of an aging fight trainer and a hillbilly girl who thinks she can be a boxer. It is narrated by a former boxer who is the trainer's best friend. But it's not a boxing movie. It is a movie about a boxer. What else it is, all it is, how deep it goes, what emotional power it contains, I cannot suggest in this review, because I will not spoil the experience of following this story into the deepest secrets of life and death. This is the best film of the year.

Eastwood plays the trainer, Frankie, who runs a seedy gym in Los Angeles and reads poetry on the side. Hilary Swank plays Maggie, from southwest Missouri, who has been waitressing since she was thirteen and sees boxing as the one way she can escape waitressing for the rest of her life. Otherwise, she says, "I might as well go back home and buy a used trailer, and get a deep fryer and some Oreos." Morgan Freeman is Scrap, whom Frankie managed into a title bout. Now he lives in a room at the gym and is Frankie's partner in conversations that have coiled down through the decades. When Frankie refuses to train a "girly," it's Scrap who convinces him to give Maggie a chance: "She grew up knowing one thing. She was trash."

These three characters are seen with a clarity and truth that is rare in the movies. Eastwood, who doesn't carry a spare ounce on his lean body, doesn't have any padding in his movie, either: Even as the film approaches the deep emotion of its final scenes, he doesn't go for easy sentiment, but regards these people, level-eyed, as they do what they have to do.

Some directors lose focus as they grow older. Others gain it, learning how to tell a story that contains everything it needs and absolutely nothing else. *Million Dollar Baby* is Eastwood's twenty-fifth film as a director, and his best. Yes, *Mystic River* is a great film, but this one finds the simplicity and directness of classical storytelling; it is the kind of movie where you sit very quietly in the theater and are drawn deeply into lives that you care very much about.

Morgan Freeman is the narrator, just as he was in *The Shawshank Redemption*, which this film resembles in the way the Freeman character describes a man who became his lifelong study. The voice is flat and factual: You never hear Scrap going for an effect or putting a spin on his words. He just wants to tell us what happened. He talks about how the girl walked into the gym, how she wouldn't leave, how Frankie finally agreed to train her, and what happened then. But Scrap is not merely an observer; the film gives him a life of his own when the others are offscreen. It is about all three of these people.

Hilary Swank is astonishing as Maggie. Every note is true. She reduces Maggie to a fierce intensity. Consider the scene where she and Scrap sit at a lunch counter, and Scrap tells the story of how he lost the sight in one eye, how Frankie blames himself for not throwing in the towel. It is an important scene for Freeman, but what I want you to observe is how Hilary Swank has Maggie do absolutely nothing but listen. No "reactions," no little nods, no body language except perfect stillness, deep attention, and an unwavering gaze.

There's another scene, at night driving in a car, after Frankie and Maggie have visited Maggie's family. The visit didn't go well. Maggie's mother is played by Margo Martindale as an ignorant and selfish monster. "I got nobody but you, Frankie," Maggie says. This is true, but do not make the mistake of thinking there is a romance between them. It's different and deeper than that. She tells Frankie a story involving her father, whom she loved, and an old dog she loved too.

Look at the way the cinematographer, Tom Stern, uses the light in this scene. Instead of using the usual "dashboard lights" that mysteriously seem to illuminate the whole front seat, watch how he has their faces slide in and out of shadow, how sometimes we can't see them at all, only hear them. Watch how the rhythm of this lighting matches the tone and pacing of the words, as if the visuals are caressing the conversation.

It is a dark picture overall. A lot of shadows, many scenes at night, characters who seem to be receding into their private fates. It is also a "boxing movie" in the sense that it follows Maggie's career, and there are several fight scenes. She wins right from the beginning, but that's not the point; *Million Dollar Baby* is about a woman who is determined to make something of herself, and a man who doesn't want to do anything for this woman, and will finally do everything.

The screenplay is by Paul Haggis, who has worked mostly on TV but with this work will earn an Oscar nomination. Other nominations, and possibly Oscars, will go to Swank, Eastwood, Freeman, the picture, and many of the technicians—and possibly the original score composed by Eastwood, which always does what it required and never distracts. *[Indeed, the film won four Oscars.]*

Haggis adapted the story from *Rope Burns: Stories from the Corner,* a 2000 book by Jerry Boyd, a seventy-year-old fight manager who wrote it as "F. X. Toole." The dialogue is poetic but never fancy. "How much she weigh?" Mag-

gie asks Frankie about the daughter he hasn't seen in years. "Trouble in my family comes by the pound." And when Frankie sees Scrap's feet on the desk: "Where are your shoes?" Scrap: "I'm airing out my feet." The foot conversation continues for almost a minute, showing the film's freedom from plot-driven dialogue, its patience in evoking character.

Eastwood is attentive to supporting characters, who make the surrounding world seem more real. The most unexpected is a Catholic priest who is seen, simply, as a good man; the movies all seem to put a negative spin on the clergy these days. Frankie goes to Mass every morning and says his prayers every night, and Father Horvak (Brian F. O'Byrne) observes that anyone who attends daily Mass for twenty-three years tends to be carrying a lot of guilt. Frankie turns to him for advice at a crucial point, and the priest doesn't respond with church orthodoxy but with a wise insight: "If you do this thing, you'll be lost, somewhere so deep you will never find yourself." Listen, too, when Haggis has Maggie use the word "frozen," which is what an uneducated backroads girl might say, but is also the single perfect word that expresses what a thousand could not.

Movies are so often made of effects and sensation these days. This one is made out of three people and how their actions grow out of who they are and why. Nothing else. But isn't that everything?

Millions ★ ★ ★ ★
PG, 97 m., 2005

James Nesbitt (Ronnie Cunningham), Daisy Donovan (Dorothy), Lewis McGibbon (Anthony Cunningham), Alex Etel (Damian Cunningham), Christopher Fulford (The Man). Directed by Danny Boyle and produced by Graham Broadbent, Andrew Hauptman, and Damian Jones. Screenplay by Frank Cottrell Boyce.

"It isn't the money's fault it got stolen."

That is the reasoning of Anthony Cunningham, who at nine is more of a realist than his seven-year-old brother, Damian. Therefore, it isn't their fault that a bag containing 265,000 British pounds bounced off a train and into Damian's playhouse and is currently stuffed under their bed.

Danny Boyle's *Millions*, a family film of limitless imagination and surprising joy, follows the two brothers as they deal with their windfall. They begin by giving some of it away, taking homeless men to Pizza Hut. Damian wants to continue their charity work, but Anthony leans toward investing in property. They have a deadline: In one week the U.K. will say goodbye to the pound and switch over to the euro; maybe, thinks Anthony, currency speculation would be the way to go.

Here is a film that exists in that enchanted realm where everything goes right—not for the characters, for the filmmakers. They take an enormous risk with a film of sophistication and whimsy, about children, money, criminals, and saints. Damian collects the saints—"like baseball cards," says Richard Roeper. He knows all their statistics. He can see them clear as day, and have conversations with them. His favorite is St. Francis of Assisi, but he knows them all: When a group of Africans materializes wearing halos, Damian is ecstatic: "The Ugandan martyrs of 1881!"

The boys' mother has died, and Damian asks his saints if they have encountered a Saint Maureen. No luck, but then heaven is limitless. Their dad, Ronnie (James Nesbitt), has recently moved them into a newly built suburb outside Liverpool, where the kids at school are hostile at first. Anthony finds it cost-efficient to bribe them with money and neat stuff. Damian, under advice from St. Francis, wants to continue giving money to the poor. Anthony warns him urgently that throwing around too much money will draw attention to them, but Damian drops 10,000 pounds into a charity collection basket. When the boys find out the money was stolen, Damian thinks maybe they should give it back, which is when Anthony comes up with the excellent reasoning I began with.

Perhaps by focusing on the money and the saints I have missed the real story of *Millions*, which involves the lives of the boys, their father, and the woman (Daisy Donovan) who works at the charity that finds the fortune in its basket. The boys are dealing with the death of their mother, and the money is a distraction. Their father is even lonelier; maybe too lonely to ever marry again, maybe too distracted to protect his boys against the bad guy (Christopher Fulford), who dreamed up the perfect train robbery and is now skulking about the neighborhood looking for his missing bag of loot.

By now you may have glanced back to the top of the review to see if I really said *Millions* was directed by Danny Boyle, who made *Shallow Grave*, *Trainspotting*, and the zombie movie *28 Days Later*. Yes, *the* Danny Boyle. And the original screenplay and novel are by Frank Cottrell Boyce, who wrote *Hilary and Jackie* and *24 Hour Party People*. What are these two doing making a sunny film about kids?

I don't require an answer for that, because their delight in the film is so manifest. But they are serious filmmakers who do not know how to talk down to an audience, and although *Millions* uses special effects and materializing saints, it's a film about real ideas, real issues, and real kids. It's not sanitized, brainless eye candy. Like all great family films, it plays equally well for adults—maybe better, since we know how unusual it is.

One of its secrets is casting. In Alex Etel and Lewis McGibbon the film has found two of the most appealing child actors I've ever seen. Alex is like the young Macaulay Culkin *(Home Alone)* except that he has no idea he is cute, and like the young Haley Joel Osment *(The Sixth Sense)* in that he finds it perfectly reasonable to speak with dead people. There is no overt cuteness, no affected lovability, not a false note in their performances, and the movie allows them to be very smart, as in Anthony's theory about turning the pounds into dollars and buying back into euros after the new currency falls from its opening-day bounce.

Of course, that involves the difficulty of two boys ages seven and nine trying to convert 265,000 pounds into anything. They can't just walk into a bank with a note from their dad. The movie handles this and other problems with droll ingenuity, while also portraying a new suburban community in the making. An opening shot by Boyle, maybe a sly dig at Lars von Trier's *Dogville*, shows the boys visiting the site of their new neighborhood when it consists only of chalk outlines on the ground. After the new homeowners move in, a helpful policeman cheerfully advises a community meeting that they should expect to be burgled, and he tells them which forms to ask for at the police station.

Boyce, a screenwriter who often works with Michael Winterbottom, is so unpredictable and original in his work that he could be called the British Charlie Kaufman, if they were not both completely distinctive. He got the inspiration for *Millions,* he says, from an interview in which Martin Scorsese said he was reading the lives of the saints.

The idea of characters getting a sudden cash windfall is not new, indeed has been a movie staple for a century. What's original about the movie is the way it uses the money as a device for the young brothers to find out more about how the world really works, and what is really important to them. The closing sequence is a bit of a stretcher, I will be the first to admit, but why not go for broke? One of the tests of sainthood is the performance of a miracle, and since Damian is clearly on the road to sainthood, that is permitted him. For that matter, Boyce and Boyle have performed a miracle with their movie. This is one of the best films of the year.

Mindhunters ★ ★ ½
R, 106 m., 2005

Val Kilmer (Jake Harris), Christian Slater (J. D. Reston), LL Cool J (Gabe Jensen), Jonny Lee Miller (Lucas Harper), Kathryn Morris (Sara Moore), Clifton Collins Jr. (Vince Sherman), Will Kemp (Rafe Perry), Patricia Velasquez (Nicole Willis), Eion Bailey (Bobby Whitman). Directed by Renny Harlin and produced by Cary Brokaw, Akiva Goldsman, Robert F. Newmyer, Jeffrey Silver, and Rebecca Spikings. Screenplay by Wayne Kramer and Kevin Brodbin.

One of Those Among Us Is a Killer, and We Cannot Leave This (a) Isolated Country Estate, (b) Besieged Police Station, (c) Antarctic Research Outpost, (d) Haunted House, (e) Space Station, (f) Rogue Planet, or (g) Summer Camp Until We Find Out Who It Is—or Until We All Die. It is a most ancient and dependable formula, invariably surprising us with the identity of the killer, because the evidence is carefully rigged to point first to one suspect and then another, until they persuasively clear their names by getting murdered.

In *Mindhunters,* a thriller directed by Renny Harlin, the suspects and/or victims are assembled on an isolated island that has been rigged up by the FBI as a training facility. It looks like a real town, but is equipped with video cam-

eras and hidden technology so supervisors can see how well trainees handle real-life problems, not that getting your head shattered into supercooled fragments is a challenge they'll be facing every day on the job.

The formula was used early and well by Agatha Christie, whose influence on *Mindhunters* has been cited by such authorities as the *Hollywood Reporter* and *Film Threat.* In the London play *The Mousetrap,* which is now in the second century of its run, she assembled a group of characters in a snowbound country house; one of them died, and the others tried to solve the murder during long conversations in the sitting room involving much malt whiskey, considerable tobacco, unwise "looks around the house," and the revelation that some of the people are not really strangers to one another. It was possibly this play that gave us the phrase, "Where were you when the lights went out?"

To the Agatha Christie formula, *Mindhunters* adds another literary inspiration: George Orwell's *Decline of the English Murder,* a brilliant essay in which he celebrated the golden age of British poisoning and other ingenious methods of disposal. The victims were usually married to their killer, who tended to be a meek accountant who had fallen into a trap set by a floozy: "In the last analysis," Orwell writes, "he (commits) murder because this seems to him less disgraceful, and less damaging to his career, than being detected in adultery."

But by 1946, when Orwell was writing, British standards had fallen off fearfully, and in the famous case of the Cleft Chin Murder, "The background was not domesticity, but the anonymous life of the dance-halls and the false values of the American film." So there we go again, vulgar Americans with our wicked influence on the Brits, who in murder as elsewhere maintained elegant traditions until we spoiled the game by just having people kill each other.

Orwell might have been cheered by *Mindhunters,* although Christie would have wanted a more ingenious solution. They both might have thought that the killer in the movie goes to a dubious deal of difficulty to create elaborate murder situations that depend on perfect timing, skillful mechanics, a deep knowledge of the characters, and a single-minded focus on providing the movie with Gotcha! scenes. Does the killer in any one of these movies ever have a moment of weariness and depression? ("What the hell, instead of rigging the liquid nitrogen and rewiring the town, I think I'll just shoot somebody.")

Not in *Mindhunters*. The people who arrive on the island are there for an exercise in the profiling of a mass killer. Can they construct a psychological profile to narrow the search to the likely suspects? Val Kilmer plays their instructor, as the kind of expert you suspect has studied *The Dummy's Guide to Profiling*. The others include LL Cool J as Gabe Jensen, a Philadelphia cop who is along as an observer; the brainy Sara Moore (Kathryn Morris); the sexy Nicole Willis (Patricia Velasquez); Vince Sherman (Clifton Collins Jr.), who uses a wheelchair; J. D. Reston (Christian Slater), a cocky showboat, and so on.

They all have a single character trait, announced with such frequency that apparently, when they packed for the island, they were allowed to bring along only one. There is the character who likes to smoke. The character who will not go anywhere without a gun. Perhaps not amazingly, each victim dies because of the weakness revealed by his trait. The ingenuity of their deaths is impressive. Murder traps are rigged all over the island; you may think they are unbelievably complicated, but I say they're nothing a rogue agent couldn't accomplish if he were assisted by an army of key grips, carpenters, best boys, electricians, set designers, art directors, special effects wizards, makeup experts, and half a dozen honey wagons.

Is the film worth seeing? Well, yes and no. Yes, because it is exactly what it is, and no, for the same reason. What always amuses me in Closed World Murders is how the survivors keep right on talking, scheming, suspecting, and accusing: They persist while bodies are piling up like cordwood. At some point, even if you were FBI material, wouldn't you run around screaming and looking for a boat so you could row the hell off that island?

The mystery, when it is solved, is both arbitrary and explained at great length. The killer gives a speech justifying his actions, which is scant comfort for those already dead. As a courtesy, why not post a notice at the beginning: "The author of a series of murders that will begin this evening would like his victims to know in advance that he has good reasons, which follow." Of course, expert profilers might

be able to read the note and figure out his identity, although not, I suspect, in this case.

I will leave you with only one clue. In *House of Wax*, the movie theater is playing *Whatever Happened to Baby Jane?* In this movie, the theater marquee advertises *The Third Man*. No, the male characters are not numbered in order, so you can't figure it out that way, nor is the killer necessarily a woman. So think real hard. What else do you know about *The Third Man*? If you have never seen *The Third Man*, I urge you to rent it immediately, as a preparation (or substitute) for *Mindhunters*.

Miracle ★ ★ ★
PG, 135 m., 2004

Kurt Russell (Herb Brooks), Patricia Clarkson (Patti Brooks), Noah Emmerich (Craig Patrick), Michael Mantenuto (Jack O'Callahan), Eddie Cahill (Jim Craig), Patrick O'Brien Dempsey (Mike Eruzione), Nathan West (Rob McClanahan). Directed by Gavin O'Connor and produced by Mark Ciardi and Gordon Gray. Screenplay by Eric Guggenheim.

Miracle is a sports movie that's more about the coach than about the team, and that's a miracle too. At a time when movies are shamelessly aimed at the young male demographic, here's a film with a whole team of hockey players in their teens and early twenties, and the screenplay hardly bothers to tell one from another. Instead, the focus is on Herb Brooks (Kurt Russell), a veteran hockey coach from Minnesota who is assigned the thankless task of assembling a team to represent America in the 1980 Winter Olympics. The United States hasn't won since 1960, and the professionals on the Soviet team—not to mention the Swedes, the Finns, and the Canadians—rule the sport.

This is a Kurt Russell you might not recognize. He's beefed up into a jowly, steady middle-aged man who still wears his square high school haircut. Patricia Clarkson, playing his wife, has the thankless role of playing yet another movie spouse whose only function in life is to complain that his job is taking too much time away from his family. This role, complete with the obligatory shots of the wife appearing in his study door as the husband burns the midnight oil, is so standard, so ritualistic, so boring, that I propose all future movies about workaholics just make them bachelors, to spare us the dead air. At the very least, she could occasionally ask her husband if he thinks he looks good in those plaid sport coats and slacks.

Herb Brooks was a real man (he died just after the film was finished), and the movie presents him in all his complexity. It's fascinated by the quirks of his personality and style; we can see he's a good coach, but, like his players, we're not always sure if we like him. That's what's good about the film: the way it frankly focuses on what a coach does, and how, and why. Brooks knows hockey and disappointment: He was cut from the 1960 American hockey team only a week before the first game, and so in this film, when he has to cut one more player at the last moment, we know how he feels—and he knows how the player feels.

Brooks's strategy is to weave an air of mystery about himself. He assigns his assistant coach, Craig Patrick (Noah Emmerich), to become a friend to the players—because Brooks deliberately does not become a friend, stays aloof, wants to be a little feared and a little resented. At one point, after chewing out his team in the locker room, he stalks out and, passing Patrick, says in a quiet aside, "That oughta wake 'em up."

After Brooks is selected for the job, his first task is to select his team. He immediately breaks with tradition. Amateur sports are overrun with adults who are essentially groupies, loving to get close to a team, treasuring their blazers with the badges on the breast pockets. These guys think they will join Brooks in choosing the American finalists after a week of tryouts, but Brooks announces his final cut on the first day of practice; he already knows who he wants, and doesn't require any advice. He's looking for kids who are hungry and passionate and *need* to win.

Most of the time, the team is seen as a unit. We begin to recognize their faces, but not much is done to develop them as individuals. The exception is the goaltender, Jim Craig (Eddie Cahill). He refuses to take a psychological exam that Brooks hands out, and Brooks tells him that, by not taking it, "you just took it." Later,

when Craig seems to falter, he benches him, and says, "I'm looking for the guy who refused to take the test."

We know all the clichés of the modern sports movie, but *Miracle* sidesteps a lot of them. Eric Guggenheim's screenplay, directed by Gavin O'Connor, is not about how some of the players have little quirks that they cure, or about their girl, or about villains that have to be overcome. It's about practicing hard and winning games. It doesn't even bother to demonize the opponents. When the team finally faces the Soviets, they're depicted as—well, simply as the other team. Their coach has a dark, forbidding manner and doesn't smile much, but he's not a Machiavellian schemer, and the Soviets don't play any dirtier than most teams do in hockey.

Oddly enough, the movie this one reminds me of is Robert Altman's *The Company*, about the Joffrey Ballet. Altman was fascinated by the leadership style of the company's artistic director, and how he deliberately uses strategy and underlings to create an aura of mysterious authority. And he dealt dispassionately with injuries, which are a fact of life and end a career in a second. *Miracle* has a similar orientation.

In keeping with its analytical style, the movie doesn't use a lot of trick photography in the hockey games. Unlike the fancy shots in a movie like *The Mighty Ducks*, this one films the hockey matches more or less the way they might look in a good documentary, or a superior TV broadcast. We're in the middle of the confusion on the ice, feeling the energy rather than focusing on plot points.

That leaves Kurt Russell and his character Herb Brooks as the center and reason for the film. Although playing a hockey coach might seem like a slap shot for an actor, Russell does real acting here. He has thought about Brooks and internalized him; the real Brooks was available as a consultant to the film. And Russell and O'Connor create a study of a personality, of a man who is leading young men through a process that led him to disappointment twenty years earlier. He has ideas about hockey and ideas about coaching, and like the Zen master Phil Jackson, begins with philosophy, not strategy. The film doesn't even end with the outcome of the Big Game. It ends by focusing on the coach, after it is all over.

MirrorMask ★ ★
PG, 101 m., 2005

Stephanie Leonidas (Helena), Gina McKee (Joanne), Jason Barry (Valentine), Rob Brydon (Helena's Father), Dora Bryan (Nan), Robert Llewellyn (Gryphon), Andy Hamilton (Small Hairy), Nik Robson (Pingo). Directed by Dave McKean and produced by Simon Moorhead. Screenplay by Neil Gaiman and McKean.

MirrorMask must have been a labor of love to make. Watching it is also a labor of love. The movie is a triumph of visual invention, but it gets mired in its artistry and finally becomes just a whole lot of great stuff to look at while the plot puts the heroine through a few basic moves over and over again.

The story involves Helena (Stephanie Leonidas), who is fed up with working for the Campbell Family Circus. "It's your father's dream," says her mother, Joanne (Gina McKee). Yes, but it's not Helena's dream, and she resents her parents for denying her an ordinary girlhood. "I hope you die," she tells her mom, which is an unwise move for any character who even vaguely suspects she might be in a fantasy movie. Her mom promptly collapses and is hospitalized with an unspecified but alarming illness.

Helena's fantasy life is lived through drawings of an imaginary city that looks as if Ralph Steadman were the mayor. Through a process best described by that reliable shortcut "magical," she enters this world, a fantastical universe where fish swim through the air and the people from her real world appear transformed by bizarre masks and costumes. It is a world of light and dark; the Queen of Light (also played by Gina McKee) is in a trancelike state, and apparently it's up to Helena to venture into the Dark Lands and return with the means to restore goodness and awaken the queen.

The movie's fantasy world has an eerie beauty. This beauty enchanted me for several minutes, and then it began to wear on me, and finally it was a visual slog. Sorry. The story resembles what happens in Bernard Rose's *Paperhouse* (1988), in which a girl draws a house in another world, falls ill, enters that world, and finds herself responsible for saving the lonely little boy who lives in the house. In Rose's film, the images are stark and clear, with the directness of a child's drawings. In *MirrorMask*, with artist Dave McKean as director and production designer, the images are fuzzy and foggy, and Helena encounters one weird scenario after another in a world where the nonsense logic seems cloned from Wonderland.

Helena's more hazardous adventures occur after she crosses over to the dark side and is mistaken for her mirror image, a dark and sinister girl who apparently embodies all the sinister aspects of her subconscious. The Queen of Shadows (McKee again) mistakes good Helena for bad Helena, placing good Helena in some danger but also giving her access to information that may save the day—always assuming that real Helena (who seems to have a separate existence) doesn't bring everything to a sudden end by ripping her drawings from the walls.

Jason Barry has an important role as Valentine, a juggler who becomes Helena's counselor in this alternative universe, and there are countless very strange creatures, some of them with shoes for heads, others weirder than that, who seem to be by Hieronymus Bosch on an acid trip. One by one, frame by frame, these inventions are remarkable; stills from the film will give you an idea of the imagination that went into it.

But there's no narrative engine to pull us past the visual scenery. Landscapes recede vaguely into dissolving grotesqueries as Helena wanders endlessly past one damn thing after another, and since everything that happens in this world is absolutely arbitrary, there's no way to judge whether any action is helpful. It's a world where no matter what Helena does, an unanticipated development will undo her effort and require her to do something else. Watching *MirrorMask*, I suspected the filmmakers began with a lot of ideas about how the movie should look, but without a clue about pacing, plotting, or destination.

Miss Congeniality 2: Armed and Fabulous ★ ½
PG-13, 115 m., 2005

Sandra Bullock (Gracie Hart), Regina King (Sam Fuller), William Shatner (Stan Fields), Heather Burns (Cheryl), Ernie Hudson (McDonald), Diedrich Bader (Joel), Enrique Murciano (Jeff Foreman), Treat Williams (Collins). Directed by

John Pasquin and produced by Sandra Bullock and Marc Lawrence. Screenplay by Lawrence.

Having made the unnecessary *Miss Congeniality,* Sandra Bullock now returns with the doubly unnecessary *Miss Congeniality 2: Armed and Fabulous.* Perhaps it is not entirely unnecessary in the eyes of the producers, since the first film had a worldwide gross of $212 million, not counting home video, but it's unnecessary in the sense that there is no good reason to go and actually see it.

That despite the presence of Sandra Bullock, who remains a most agreeable actress and brings what charm she can to a character who never seems plausible enough to be funny. Does a character in a comedy need to be plausible? I think it helps. It is not enough for a character to "act funny." A lot of humor comes from tension between who the character is and what the character does, or is made to do. Since Miss Congeniality is never other than a ditz, that she acts like one is not hilarious.

You will recall that Gracie Hart (Bullock) is an FBI agent who in the first film impersonated a beauty pageant contestant in order to infiltrate—but enough about that plot, since all you need to know is that the publicity from the pageant has made her so famous that *MC2* opens with a bank robber recognizing her and aborting an FBI sting. Gracie is obviously too famous to function as an ordinary agent, so the FBI director makes her a public relations creature—the new "face of the bureau."

Since the Michael Caine character in the first film successfully groomed her into a beauty pageant finalist, you'd think Gracie had learned something about seemly behavior, but no, she's still a klutz. The bureau supplies her with Joel (Diedrich Bader), a Queer Guy for the Straight Agent, who gives her tips on deportment (no snorting as a form of laughter), manners (chew with your mouth closed), and fashion (dress like a Barbie doll). She is also assigned a new partner: Sam Fuller (Regina King), a tough agent with anger management issues, who likes to throw people around and is allegedly Gracie's bodyguard, assuming she doesn't kill her.

As Gracie is rolled out as the FBI's new face, there's a funny TV chat scene with Regis Philbin (Regis: "You don't look like J. Edgar Hoover." Gracie: "Really? Because this is his dress"). Then comes an emergency: Miss United States (Heather Burns), Gracie's buddy from the beauty pageant, is kidnapped in Las Vegas, along with the pageant manager (William Shatner).

Gracie and Sam fly to Vegas and humiliate the bureau by tackling the real Dolly Parton under the impression she is an imposter. Then they find themselves doing Tina Turner impersonations in a drag club. They also reenact the usual clichés of two partners who hate each other until they learn to love each other. And they impersonate Nancy Drew in their investigation, which leads to the thrilling rescue of Miss United States from the least likely place in the world where any kidnapper would think of hiding her.

Now a word about the name of Regina King's character, Sam Fuller. This is, of course, the same name as the famous movie director Sam Fuller *(The Big Red One, Shock Corridor, The Naked Kiss).* Fuller (1912–1997) was an icon among other directors, who gave him countless cameo roles in their movies just because his presence was like a blessing; he appeared in films by Amos Gitai, Aki Kaurismaki, his brother Mika Kaurismaki, Larry Cohen, Claude Chabrol, Steven Spielberg, Alexandre Rockwell (twice), Wim Wenders (three times), and Jean-Luc Godard, the first to use him, in *Pierrot le Fou,* where he stood against a wall, puffed a cigar, and told the camera, "film is like a battleground."

It may seem that I have strayed from the topic, but be honest: You are happier to learn these factoids about Sam Fuller than to find out which Las Vegas landmark the kidnappers use to imprison Miss United States and William Shatner. The only hint I will provide is that they almost drown, and Sandra Bullock almost drowns, too, as she did most famously in *Speed 2,* a movie about a runaway ocean liner. I traditionally end my reviews of the *Miss Congeniality* movies by noting that I was the only critic in the world who liked *Speed 2,* and I see no reason to abandon that tradition, especially since if there is a *Miss Congeniality 3* and it doesn't have Sam Fuller in it, I may be at a loss for words.

Mission: Impossible III ★ ★ ½

PG-13, 126 m., 2006

Tom Cruise (Ethan Hunt), Philip Seymour Hoffman (Owen Davian), Ving Rhames (Luther

Stickell), Billy Crudup (John Musgrave), Michelle Monaghan (Julia), Jonathan Rhys Meyers (Declan), Keri Russell (Lindsey), Maggie Q (Zhen), Laurence Fishburne (Theodore Brassel). Directed by J. J. Abrams and produced by Tom Cruise and Paula Wagner. Screenplay by Alex Kurtzman, Roberto Orci, and Abrams, based on the TV series created by Bruce Geller.

Ethan Hunt is in some respects the least inquisitive man in action movie history. In *Mission: Impossible* (1996), he risked his life to (I quote from my original review) "prevent the theft of a computer file containing the code names and real identities of all of America's double agents." But Ethan (Tom Cruise) must prevent this theft *after* it happens because first he must "photograph the enemy in the act of stealing the information and then follow him until he passes it along." The plot also involves crucial uses for latex masks and helicopters, one of which flies through the Chunnel from England to France, which is difficult considering helicopter blades are wider than the Chunnel.

In *Mission: Impossible 2* (2000), Ethan has to stop a villain with a deadly virus: Twenty-four hours after exposure, you die. The heroine (Thandie Newton) does, however, survive at the end of the movie, leaving her available for the sequel, although by *Mission: Impossible III*, Ethan Hunt is engaged to a sweet nurse named Julia (Michelle Monaghan), who thinks he is a highway traffic control engineer. Helicopters are again involved, and Ethan falls for the old latex mask trick again and even uses a latex mask himself, so that others can be fooled and he doesn't have to feel so bad. In a nice visual pun, the helicopters encounter giant energy-generating windmills in deserts near Berlin that uncannily resemble deserts near Palm Springs. It's kind of neat when one propeller slices off another, wouldn't you agree? Observing the curious landscape outside Berlin, I was reminded that Citizen Kane built his Xanadu "on the desert coasts of Florida."

Ethan Hunt's assignment in *M:I3* is to battle the villain Owen Davian (Philip Seymour Hoffman) for control of the Rabbit's Foot. In Ethan's final words in the movie, after countless people have been blown up, shot, crushed, and otherwise inconvenienced, he asks his boss, Brassel (Laurence Fishburne), "What is the Rabbit's Foot?" Ethan should know by now it is a MacGuffin, just like the virus and the computer file.

Why does Ethan risk his life and the lives of those he loves to pursue objectives he does not understand? The answer, of course, is that the real objective of all the *M:I* movies is to provide a clothesline for sensational action scenes. Nothing else matters, and explanatory dialogue would only slow things down. This formula worked satisfactorily in *M:I*, directed by Brian De Palma, and *M:I2*, directed by John Woo, and I suppose it works up to a point in *M:I3*, directed by J. J. Abrams, if what you want is nonstop high-tech action. Even the deadlines are speeded up this time; instead of a twenty-four-hour virus, we have an explosive capsule that detonates five minutes after it zips up your nose.

The action takes us to Berlin, the Vatican City, Shanghai, and the Chesapeake Bay Bridge, although there seems to be no real reason to visit any of those cities except to stage CGI stunts involving their landmarks. I did smile at a scene where Ethan parachutes from a building and ends up hanging upside down in his harness in front of a speeding truck. I liked a moment when he jabs a needle of adrenaline into a woman's heart to bring her out of her drugged stupor; Quentin Tarantino should send him a bill. And there is the intriguing speech by an agency techie about the Anti-God Compound, a deadly by-product of technological over-achievement, which might simply destroy everything. If there is an *M:I4*, I recommend the Anti-God Compound as the MacGuffin.

I didn't expect a coherent story from *Mission: Impossible III*, and so I was sort of surprised that the plot hangs together more than in the other two films. I was puzzled, however, by the nature of Ethan's relationship with Julia, his sweet fiancée. If he belongs to a secret organization that controls his life and can order him around, doesn't she deserve to know that? Or, if not, is it right for him to marry her? And when she meets his coworkers from the office, do they all talk like he does, about how if you hit the brakes, it can cause a chain reaction, slowing down traffic for hundreds of miles?

Such questions are beside the point. Either you want to see mindless action and CGI sequences executed with breakneck speed and technical precision, or you do not. I am getting to the point where I don't much care. There is a theory that action is exciting and dialogue is boring. My theory is that variety is exciting and sameness is boring. Modern high-tech action sequences are just the same damn thing over and over again: high-speed chases, desperate gun battles, all possible modes of transportation, falls from high places, deadly deadlines, exotic locations, and characters who hardly ever say anything interesting. I saw *M:I* and *M:I2* and gave them three-star ratings because they delivered precisely what they promised. But now I've been there, done that, and my hope for *M:I4*, if there is one, is that it self-destructs while mishandling the Anti-God Compound.

Mondovino ★ ★ ★
PG-13, 135 m., 2005

Featuring Michael Broadbent, Hubert de Montille, Aime Guibert, Jonathan Nossiter, Robert Parker, Michel Rolland, and Neal Rosenthal. A documentary directed by Jonathan Nossiter and produced by Emmanuel Giraud and Nossiter. Screenplay by Nossiter.

Mondovino applies to the world of wine the same dreary verdict that has already been returned about the worlds of movies, books, fashion, politics, and indeed modern life: Individuality is being crushed, marketing is the new imperialism, people will like what they are told to like, and sales are the only measurement of good. Briefly (although his movie is not brief), the wine lover Jonathan Nossiter argues that modern tastes in wine are being policed by an unholy alliance involving the most powerful wine producer, the most ubiquitous wine adviser, and the most influential wine critic. Together, they are enforcing a bland, mass-produced taste on a world of wine drinkers who fancy themselves connoisseurs, but basically like what they are told to like.

This does not surprise me, since I have long suspected that "oenophile" is a polite word for a trainee alcoholic who has money and knows how to pronounce the names of several wines that have worked for him in the past. I thought *Sideways* was particularly observant as it watched Miles, the oenophile played by Paul Giamatti, advance during the course of a day from elaborate sniffing, chewing, and tasting

rituals to pouring the bucket of slops over his head. I treasure the Mike Royko column in which he advised the insecure on how to deal with a snotty sommelier: He will present you with the cork. Salt it lightly and eat it. This will clear your palate.

There are people who know good wine from bad, and some of them are in this movie, although you will have to take their word for it, all the time remembering that every wine drinker thinks he knows good wine from bad, even at the level where Paisano is judged superior to Mogen David, as indeed some believe. *Mondovino* says distinctive wines are being punished because they do not taste familiar; the unique local taste of great wines is being leveled by "microoxygenization," a mysterious process that is recommended by the wine consultant Michel Rolland, which produces wines that are approved by the wine critic Robert Parker, and therefore becomes the standard for mass producers like Robert Mondavi. As Mondavi and other giants march through Europe buying up ancient vineyards, Rolland and Parker are right behind him to standardize the product.

Rolland is described in the movie as "always laughing; you have to like him." Indeed, the man seems bubbling over with private humor as he speeds in his chauffeured car from one vineyard to another, dispensing valued advice one step ahead of the serious, even self-effacing Parker, whose opinion can make or break a vineyard. That Parker is so powerful is proof that countless wine drinkers do not have taste of their own, because by definition there can be no such thing as a wine that everyone values equally; a great wine should be a wine that you think is great, and if you think it's great because Parker does, then you don't know what you like and simply require a prelubrication benediction.

This much I know from common sense. How many of the rest of Nossiter's charges are true, I cannot know, but he is persuasive. He is fluent in the language of every country he visits, talks with the powerful vintners and the little local growers, visits veteran retailers, and consults with a wine expert from Christie's who wonders "to what extent individuality has flown out the window," and concludes it has taken wing to a very great extent indeed.

Much is made of "terroir," a French word meaning "soil" but also meaning a region, a specific place, a magical quality that a particular area imparts to the grapes it produces. Every great wine should be specifically from its own time and place, in theory, but in practice that would mean that some wines were great and most wines were not, and that's no way to run a global industry. The new goal, Nossiter believes, is to produce pretty good wine and train consumers to consider it great because they're told it is and can find the real thing only with some difficulty. Nossiter thinks some French vineyards are holding out, but that the Italians have more or less caved in to Mondavism.

He makes this argument in a film that is too long and needlessly mannered. There is no particular reason for a restless hand-held camera in a documentary about wine. If we are watching a documentary about cock-fighting or the flight of the bumble bee, we can see the logic of a jumpy camera, but vineyards don't move around much and are easy to keep in frame. I am more permissive about Nossiter's other camera strategy, which is to interrupt a shot whenever a dog comes into view, in order to focus on the dog. This I understand. Whenever a dog appears at a social occasion, I immediately interrupt my conversation to greet the dog, and often find myself turning back to its owner with regret.

Despite its visual restlessness and its dogs, *Mondovino* is a fascinating film, not because Nossiter turns red-faced with indignation, but because he allows his argument to make itself. There comes a point when we learn all we are likely to learn about modern wine, and the movie continues cheerfully for another 30 or 40 minutes, just because Nossiter is having so much fun. Although modern wines may have lost their magic, traveling from one vineyard to another has not, and just when we think Nossiter is about to wrap it up, off he goes to Argentina. It was certainly only by an effort of will that he prevented himself from visiting our excellent Michigan vineyards. They have some magnificent dogs.

Monsieur Ibrahim ★ ★ ★
R, 95 m., 2004

Omar Sharif (Monsieur Ibrahim), Pierre Boulanger (Momo), Gilbert Melki (Momo's Father), Isabelle Renauld (Momo's Mother), Lola Naynmark (Myriam), Anne Suarez (Sylvie), Mata Gabin (Fatou), Celine Samie (Eva), Isabelle Adjani (Brigitte Bardot). Directed by François Dupeyron and produced by Michele Petin and Laurent Petin, based on the book and play by Eric-Emmanuel Schmitt.

On the rue Bleue in a working-class Jewish neighborhood in Paris, people know each other and each other's business, and live and let live. That includes the streetwalkers who are a source of fascination to young Momo, who studies them from the window of his flat before preparing supper for his father. Momo's mother is dead, an older brother has left the scene, and his father is distant and cold with the young teenager. But his life is not lonely; there is Monsieur Ibrahim, who runs the shop across the street. And there is Sylvie, who provides Momo with his sexual initiation after the lad breaks open his piggy bank.

Although Brigitte Bardot (played by Isabelle Adjani) pays a visit to the street one day to shoot a scene in a movie, there was another movie character I almost expected to see wandering past: Antoine Doinel, the hero of *The 400 Blows* and four other films by François Truffaut. Not only are both films set within about five years of each other (circa 1958 and 1963), but they share a similar theme: the lonely, smart kid who is left alone by distant parents and seeks inspiration in the streets.

Antoine found it at the movies and in the words of his hero, Balzac. Momo (Pierre Boulanger), whose life is sunnier and his luck better, finds it from Monsieur Ibrahim (Omar Sharif). Although Ibrahim is Turkish, his store is known in Parisian argot as "the Arab's store," because only Arabs will keep their stores open at night and on weekends. Ibrahim establishes himself like a wise old sage behind his counter, knows everyone who comes in, and everything they do, so of course he knows that Momo is a shoplifter. This he does not mind so much: "Better you should steal here, than somewhere you could get into real trouble."

The old man sees that the young one needs a friend and guidance, and he provides both, often quoting from his beloved Koran. He knows things about Momo's family that Momo does not know, and is discreet about Momo's friendship with the hookers. What Ibrahim dreams about is to return someday to the villages and mountains of his native land, to the bazaars and dervishes and the familiar smells of the food he grew up with. What Momo desires is a break with a home life that is barren and crushes his spirit.

The movie was directed by François Dupeyron, based on a book and play by Eric-Emmanuel Schmitt. Its best scenes come as the characters are established and get to know one another. Omar Sharif at seventy-one still has the fire in his eyes that we remember from *Lawrence of Arabia*, and is still a handsome presence, but he settles comfortably into Monsieur Ibrahim's shabby life, and doesn't bore us with his philosophy. And young Boulanger, like Jean-Pierre Leaud all those years ago, has a quick, open face that lets us read his heart.

The last third of the film is more like a fantasy. Momo and Ibrahim both want to escape. Ibrahim buys a fancy red sports car (like the one Bardot was driving), and they drive off to Turkey. What happens there, you will have to discover on your own, but while *The 400 Blows* ended on a note of bleak realism, *Monsieur Ibrahim* settles for melodrama and sentiment. Well, why not? Momo is not as star-crossed as Antoine Doniel, and Ibrahim achieves a destiny he accepts.

But isn't it sort of sad that a movie has to be set forty years ago for us to accept an elderly storekeeper buying a sports car and driving away with a teenager, without ever for an instant suspecting the purity of his motives? The innocence that Antoine and Momo lose in their stories is nothing compared to the world teenagers live in today.

Monster ★ ★ ★ ★
R, 109 m., 2004

Charlize Theron (Aileen Wuornos), Christina Ricci (Selby Wall), Bruce Dern (Thomas), Scott Wilson (Horton Rohrback), Lee Tergesen (Vincent Corey), Pruitt Taylor Vince (Gene), Annie Corley (Donna Tentler), Marco St. John (Evan). Directed by Patty Jenkins and produced by Mark Damon, Donald Kushner, Clark Peterson, Charlize Theron, and Brad Wyman. Screenplay by Jenkins.

What Charlize Theron achieves in Patty Jenkins's *Monster* isn't a performance but an embodiment. With courage, art, and charity, she empathizes with Aileen Wuornos, a damaged woman who committed seven murders. She does not excuse the murders. She simply asks that we witness the woman's final desperate attempt to be a better person than her fate intended.

Wuornos received a lot of publicity during her arrest, trial, conviction, and 2002 execution for the Florida murders of seven men who picked her up as a prostitute (although one wanted to help her, not use her). The headlines, true as always to our compulsion to treat everything as a sporting event or an entry for the *Guinness Book,* called her "America's first female serial killer." Her image on the news and in documentaries presented a large, beaten-down woman who did seem to be monstrous. Evidence against her was given by Selby Wall (Christina Ricci), an eighteen-year-old who became the older woman's naive lesbian lover and inspired Aileen's dream of earning enough money to set them up in a "normal" lifestyle. Robbing her clients led to murder, and each new murder seemed necessary to cover the tracks leading from the previous one.

I confess that I walked into the screening not knowing who the star was, and that I did not recognize Charlize Theron until I read her name in the closing credits. Not many others will have that surprise; she won the Academy Award for Best Actress. I didn't recognize her— but more to the point, I hardly tried, because the performance is so focused and intense that it becomes a fact of life. Observe the way Theron controls her eyes in the film; there is not a flicker of inattention, as she urgently communicates what she is feeling and thinking. There's the uncanny sensation that Theron has forgotten the camera and the script and is directly channeling her ideas about Aileen Wuornos. She has made herself the instrument of this character.

I have already learned more than I wanted to about the techniques of disguise used by makeup artist Toni G. to transform an attractive twenty-eight-year-old into an ungainly street prostitute, snapping her cigarette butt into the shadows before stepping forward to talk with a faceless man who has found her in the shadows of a barren Florida highway.

Watching the film, I had no sense of makeup technique; I was simply watching one of the most real people I had ever seen on the screen. Jenkins, the writer-director, has made the best film of the year. Movies like this are perfect when they get made, before they're ground down by analysis. There is a certain tone in the voices of some critics that I detest—that superior way of explaining technique in order to destroy it. They imply that because they can explain how Theron did it, she didn't do it. But she does it.

The movie opens with Wuornos informing God that she is down to her last $5, and that if God doesn't guide her to spend it wisely she will end her life. She walks into what happens to be a lesbian bar and meets the eighteen-year-old Selby, who has been sent to live with Florida relatives and be "cured" of lesbianism. Aileen is adamant that she's had no lesbian experience, and indeed her sordid life as a bottom-rung sex worker has left her with no taste for sex at all. Selby's own sexuality functions essentially as a way to shock her parents and gratify her need to be desired. There is a stunning scene when the two women connect with raw sexual energy, but soon enough sex is unimportant compared to daydreaming, watching television, and enacting their private soap opera in cheap roadside motels.

Aileen is the protector and provider, proudly bringing home the bacon—and the keys to cars that Selby doesn't ask too many questions about. Does she know that Aileen has started to murder her clients? She does and doesn't. Aileen's murder spree becomes big news long before Selby focuses on it. The crimes themselves are triggered by Aileen's loathing for prostitution—by a lifetime's hatred for the way men have treated her since she was a child. She has only one male friend, a shattered Vietnam veteran and fellow drunk (Bruce Dern). Although she kills for the first time in self-defense, she is also lashing out against her past. Her experience of love with Selby brings revulsion uncoiling from her memories; men treat her in a cruel way and pay for their sins and those of all who went before them. The most heartbreaking scene is the death of a good man (Scott Wilson) who actually wants to help her, but has arrived so late in her life that the only way he can help is to be eliminated as a witness.

Aileen's body language is frightening and fascinating. She doesn't know how to occupy her body. Watch Theron as she goes through a repertory of little arm straightenings and body adjustments and head tosses and hair touchings, as she nervously tries to shake out her nervousness and look at ease. Observe her smoking technique; she handles her cigarettes with the self-conscious bravado of a thirteen-year-old trying to impress a kid. And note that there is only one moment in the movie where she seems relaxed and at peace with herself; you will know the scene, and it will explain itself. This is one of the greatest performances in the history of the cinema.

Christina Ricci finds the correct note for Selby Wall—so correct some critics have mistaken it for bad acting, when in fact it is sublime acting in its portrayal of a bad actor. She plays Selby as clueless, dim, in over her head, picking up cues from moment to moment, cobbling her behavior out of notions borrowed from bad movies, old songs, and barroom romances. Selby must have walked into a gay bar for the first time only a few weeks ago, and studied desperately to figure out how to present herself. Selby and Aileen are often trying to improvise the next line they think the other wants to hear.

We are told to hate the sin but not the sinner, and as I watched *Monster* I began to see it as an exercise in the theological virtue of charity. It refuses to objectify Wuornos and her crimes and refuses to exploit her story in the cynical manner of true crime sensationalism—insisting instead on seeing her as one of God's creatures worthy of our attention. She has been so cruelly twisted by life that she seems incapable of goodness, and yet when she feels love for the first time she is inspired to try to be a better person.

She is unequipped for this struggle, and lacks the gifts of intelligence and common sense. She is devoid of conventional moral standards. She is impulsive, reckless, angry, and violent, and she devastates her victims, their families, and herself. There are no excuses for what she does, but there are reasons, and the purpose of the movie is to make them visible. If life had given her anything at all to work with, we would feel no sympathy. But life has beaten her beyond redemption.

Monster-in-Law ★

PG-13, 100 m., 2005

Jennifer Lopez (Charlie Cantilini), Jane Fonda (Viola Fields), Michael Vartan (Kevin Fields), Wanda Sykes (Ruby), Adam Scott (Remy), Annie Parisse (Morgan), Monet Mazur (Fiona), Will Arnett (Kit). Directed by Robert Luketic and produced by Paula Weinstein, Chris Bender, and J. C. Spink. Screenplay by Anya Kochoff and Richard La Gravenese.

Faithful readers will know I'm an admirer of Jennifer Lopez, and older readers will recall my admiration for Jane Fonda, whom I first met on the set of *Barbarella* (1968), so it has been all uphill ever since. Watching *Monster-in-Law*, I tried to transfer into Fan Mode, enjoying their presence while ignoring the movie. I did not succeed. My reveries were interrupted by bulletins from my conscious mind, which hated the movie.

I hated it above all because it wasted an opportunity. You do not keep Jane Fonda offscreen for fifteen years only to bring her back as a specimen of rabid Momism. You write a role for her. It makes sense. It fits her. You like her in it. It gives her a relationship with Jennifer Lopez that could plausibly exist in our time and space. It gives her a son who has not wandered over after the *E.R.* auditions. And it doesn't supply a supporting character who undercuts every scene she's in by being more on-topic than any of the leads.

No, you don't get rid of the supporting character, whose name is Ruby and who is played by Wanda Sykes. What you do is lift the whole plot up on rollers, and use heavy equipment to relocate it in Ruby's universe, which is a lot more promising than the rabbit hole this movie falls into. *Monster-in-Law* fails the Gene Siskel Test: "Is this film more interesting than a documentary of the same actors having lunch?"

The movie opens by establishing Charlotte "Charlie" Cantilini (Lopez) as an awfully nice person. She walks dogs, she works as a temp, she likes to cook, she's friendly and loyal, she roughs it on Venice Beach in an apartment that can't cost more than $2,950 a month, she has a gay neighbor who's her best bud. I enjoyed these scenes, right up until the Meet Cute with Young Dr. Kevin Fields (Michael Vartan), a surgeon who falls in love with her. She can't believe a guy like that would really like a girl like her, which is unlikely, since anyone who looks like Jennifer Lopez and walks dogs on the boardwalk has already been hit on by every dot.com entrepreneur and boy band dropout in Santa Monica, and Donald Trump and Charlie Sheen.

Dr. Kevin's mother, Viola, played by Fonda, is not so much a clone of Barbara Walters as a rubbing. You get the outlines, but there's a lot of missing detail. In a flashback, we see that she was a famous television personality, fired under circumstances no one associated with this movie could possibly have thought were realistic—and then allowed to telecast one more program, when in fact security guards would be helping her carry cardboard boxes out to her car. Her last show goes badly when she attempts to kill her guest.

When we meet her, she's "fresh off the funny farm," guzzling booze, taking pills, and getting wake-up calls from Ruby, who is played by Sykes as if she thinks the movie needs an adult chaperone. Viola is seen as a possessive, egotistical, imperious monster who is, and I quote, "on the verge of a psychotic break." The far verge, I would say. When she learns that Dr. Kevin is engaged to marry Charlie, she begins a campaign to sabotage their romance, moaning, "My son the brilliant surgeon is going to marry a temp."

The movie's most peculiar scenes involve Charlie being steadfastly and heroically nice while Viola hurls rudeness and abuse at her. There is a sequence where Viola throws a "reception" for her prospective daughter-in-law and invites the most famous people in the world, so the little temp will be humiliated; Charlie is so serene in her self-confidence that even though she's dressed more for volleyball than diplomacy, she keeps her composure.

All during her monster act, we don't for a second believe Fonda's character because if she really were such a monster, she would fire Ruby, who insults her with a zeal approaching joy. Anyone who keeps Ruby on the payroll has her feet on the ground. Another problem is that Dr. Kevin is a world-class wimp, who actually proposes marriage to Charlie while his mother is standing right there. No doubt Dr. Phil will provide counsel in their wedding bed.

Eventually we realize that Fonda's character

consists entirely of a scene waiting to happen: The scene where her heart melts, she realizes Charlie is terrific and she accepts her. Everything else Viola does is an exercise in postponing that moment. The longer we wait, the more we wonder why (a) Charlie doesn't belt her, and (b) Charlie doesn't jump Dr. Kevin—actually, I meant to write "dump," but either will do. By the time the happy ending arrives, it's too late, because by then we don't want Charlie to marry Dr. Kevin. We want her to go back to walking the dogs. She was happier, we were happier, the dogs were happier.

Monty Python's Life of Brian ★ ★ ★
R, 94 m., 2004

Multiple roles by Monty Python's Flying Circus: Graham Chapman, John Cleese, Terry Gilliam, Eric Idle, Terry Jones, and Michael Palin. Directed by Terry Jones and produced by John Goldstone. Screenplay by the Monty Python Troupe.

Monty Python's Life of Brian has been re-released, I suspect, because of the enormous box office of *The Passion of the Christ.* This is a classic bait-and-switch, because Brian, of course, is not Christ, but was born in the next stable. In cinema as in life, poor Brian never did the big numbers. When the film was released in 1979 it was attacked as blasphemous by many religious groups. Consulting my original review, I find I quoted Stanley Kauffmann in the *New Republic,* who speculated that Jesus might have enjoyed it; he had a sense of humor, proven by his occasional puns. That opens up another line of controversy: Are puns funny? Certainly *Monty Python's Life of Brian* is funny, in that peculiar British way where jokes are told sideways, with the obvious point and then the delayed zinger.

The tragedy of Brian (Graham Chapman) is that he has everything it takes be a success, except divinity. Not that he has any desire to found a religion. He attracts followers who convince themselves he is the savior, is the object of cult veneration, and unsuccessfully tries to convince his (small) multitudes that he is not who they think he is. No, that's the other guy. His followers seize upon the smallest hints and misunderstood fragments of his speech to create an orthodoxy they claim to have received from him.

We see the real Jesus twice, once in the next manger (unlike Brian, he has a halo) and again when he delivers the Sermon on the Mount. Most biblical movies show the sermon from a point of view close to Jesus, or looking over his shoulder. *Life of Brian* has the cheap seats, way in the back at the bottom of the mount, where it's hard to hear: "What did he say? Blessed are the cheesemakers?"

Unlike Brian, Monty Python's Flying Circus gang had a distinguished family line. It was in direct descent from the *The Goon Show* on BBC radio (Spike Milligan, Peter Sellers) and the satirical revue *Beyond the Fringe* (Peter Cook, Dudley Moore, Jonathan Miller, Alan Bennett), which was inspired by Second City. Cook and Moore also had a TV show named "Not Only . . . But Also," which along with Second City more or less invented *Saturday Night Live.* Then came the Pythons, who adapted best to movies *(Monty Python and the Holy Grail, Monty Python's The Meaning of Life).*

The success of *Life of Brian* is based first of all on Brian's desperation at being a redeemer without portfolio. He's like one of those guys you meet in a bar who explains how he would have been Elvis if Elvis hadn't been so much better at it. Brian is, in fact, not a religious leader at all but the member of an underground political organization seeking to overthrow Pontius Pilate and kick the Romans out of the Holy Land. There are uncomfortable parallels with the real-life situation in the Middle East, and a jab at the second-class status of women in the scene where men stone a blasphemer. The joke is that the "men" are women pretending to be men, because as women they never get to have fun attending stonings and suchlike. Monty Python rotates the joke into another dimension, since all of the women in the movie are men in drag (some of them risking discovery, you would think, by wearing beards).

The movie benefits by looking vaguely historically accurate (it used the sets built by Lord Lew Grade for Franco Zeffirelli's *Jesus of Nazareth*). It incorporates familiar figures such as Pontius Pilate (Michael Palin), but observes that he speaks with a lisp (his centurions helplessly crack up behind his back). At crucial moments it breaks into song, and

471

there is a particular irony, considering how it is used in the movie, that "The Bright Side of Life" has taken on a long life in exactly the opposite context.

If the film has a message, and it may, it's that much of what passes in religion for truth is the result of centuries of opinion and speculation. Its version of the Brian legend is like a comic parallel to the theories of Christian history in *The Da Vinci Code*—itself a ripe target for Pythonizing. The difficulty with a literal interpretation of the Bible is that it is a translation of a translation of a translation of documents that were chosen by the early church from among a much larger cache of potential manuscripts. "You've all got to think for yourselves!" Brian exhorts his followers, who obediently repeat after him: "We've all got to think for ourselves!"

Moolaade ★ ★ ★ ★
NO MPAA RATING, 124 m., 2004

Fatoumata Coulibaly (Colle Ardo Gallo Sy), Maimouna Helene Diarra (Hadjatou), Salimata Traore (Amasatou), Dominique T. Zeida (Mercenaire), Mah Compaore (Doyenne des Exciseuses), Aminata Dao (Alima Ba). Directed and produced by Ousmane Sembene. Screenplay by Sembene.

Sometimes I seek the right words and I despair. What can I write that will inspire you to see *Moolaade*? This was, for me, the best film at Cannes 2004, a story vibrating with urgency and life. It makes a powerful statement and at the same time contains humor, charm, and astonishing visual beauty.

But even my words of praise may be the wrong ones, sending the message that this is an important film, and therefore hard work. Moviegoers who will cheerfully line up for trash are cautious, even wary, about attending a film they fear might be great. And if I told you the subject of the film is female circumcision—would I lose you? And if I placed the story in an African village, have you already decided to see *National Treasure* instead?

All I can tell you is, *Moolaade* is a film that will stay in my memory and inform my ideas long after other films have vaporized. It takes place in a village in Senegal, where ancient customs exist side-by-side with battery-powered

radios, cars, and trucks, and a young man returning from Paris. Traditional family compounds surround a mosque; they are made in ancient patterns from sun-baked mud and have the architectural beauty of everything that is made on the spot by the people who will use it, using the materials at hand. The colors of this world are the colors of sand, earth, sky, and trees, setting off the joyous colors of the costumes.

It is the time for several of the young women in the village to be "purified." This involves removing parts of their genitals so they will have no feeling during sex. The practice is common throughout Africa to this day, especially in Muslim areas, although Islam in fact condemns it. Many girls die after the operation, and during the course of this movie two will throw themselves down a well. But men, who in their wisdom assume control over women's bodies, insist on purification. And because men will marry no woman who has not been cut, the older women insist on it too; they have daughters who must find husbands.

Colle (Fatoumata Coulibaly), the second of four wives of a powerful man, has refused to let her daughter be cut. Now six girls flee from a purification ritual, and four of them seek refuge with her. Colle agrees to help them, and invokes "moolaade," a word meaning "protection." She ties a strand of bright yarn across the entrance to her compound, and it is understood by everyone that as long as the girls stay inside the compound, they are safe, and no one can step inside to capture them.

These details are established not in the mood of a dreary ethnographic docudrama, but with great energy and life. The writer and director is Ousmane Sembene, sometimes called the father of African cinema, who at eighty-one can look back on a life during which he has made nine other films, founded a newspaper, written a novel, and become, in the opinion of his distributor, the art film pioneer Dan Talbot, the greatest living director. Sembene's stories are not the tales of isolated characters; they always exist within a society that observes and comments, and sometimes gets involved. Indeed, his first film, *Black Girl* (1966), is the tragedy of a young African woman who is taken away from this familiarity and made to feel a stranger in Paris.

The village in *Moolaade* has an interesting division of powers. All authority allegedly resides with the council of men, but all decisions seem to be made by the women, who in their own way make up their minds and achieve what they desire. Men insist on purification, but it is really women who enforce it—not just the fearsome women who actually conduct the ceremony, but ordinary women who have undergone it and see no reason why their daughters should be spared.

Colle has seen many girls sicken and die, and does not want to risk her daughter. She knows, as indeed most of those in the village know, that purification is dangerous and unnecessary and has been condemned even by their own government. But if a man will not marry an unpurified daughter, what is a mother to do? This is particularly relevant for Colle, whose own daughter, Amasatou (Salimata Traore), is engaged to be married to a young man who will someday rule their tribe, and who is a successful businessman in Paris. Yes, he is modern, is educated, is cosmopolitan, but in returning to his village for a bride, of course he desires one who has been cut.

Local characters stand out in high relief. There is Mercenaire (Dominique T. Zeida), a peddler whose van arrives at the village from time to time with pots, pans, potions, and dry goods, and who brings news from the wider world. There's spontaneous fun in the way the women bargain and flirt with him. And there is the *doyenne des exciseuses* (Mah Compaore), whose livelihood depends on her purification rituals, and who rules a fierce band of assistants who could play the witches in *Macbeth*.

Much of the humor in the film comes from the ineffectual debates of the council of men, who deplore Colle's action but have been checkmated by the invocation of moolaade. One ancient tradition is thwarted by another. Colle's husband, who has been away, returns to the village and insists that she hand over the girls, but she flatly refuses, and in a scene of drama and rich humor, the husband's first wife backs up the second wife's position and supports her.

All of this nonsense is caused by too much outside influence, the men decide. All of the radios in the village are collected and thrown onto a big pile near the mosque—where, in an image that lingers through the last scenes of the film, some of them continue to play, so that the heap seems filled with disembodied voices. Colle stands strong. Then the young man from Paris arrives, and the whole village holds its breath, poised between the past and the future.

The Mother ★ ★ ★ ½
R, 112 m., 2004

Anne Reid (May), Peter Vaughan (Toots), Cathryn Bradshaw (Paula), Steven Mackintosh (Bobby), Daniel Craig (Darren), Oliver Ford Davies (Bruce), Anna Wilson-Jones (Helen). Directed by Roger Michell and produced by Kevin Loader. Screenplay by Hanif Kureishi.

The Mother peers so fearlessly into the dark needs of human nature that you almost wish it would look away. It's very disturbing. It begins as one of those conventional family dramas with a little love, a little sadness, and a few easy truths, but it's anything but conventional. By the end we've seen lives that aren't working and probably can't be fixed, and we've seen sex used so many different ways it seems more a weapon than a comfort.

The film opens in the reassuring environs of British domesticity. A long-married couple travel into London to visit their children. May (Anne Reid) still has her health and the remains of her beauty, but Toots (Peter Vaughan) seems always out of breath. They arrive at the expensive new home of their son, Bobby (Steven Mackintosh), go for dinner at the flat of their daughter, Paula (Cathryn Bradshaw), and then Toots dies of a heart attack.

It's clear that Bobby and Paula do not much love their mother, although Paula goes through the motions; Bobby is always darting away for urgent conversations on his cell phone. May understands this, and yet when she returns home she finds she simply cannot stay there: "I'll be like all the other old girls around here, and then I'll go into a home. I'd rather kill myself." She returns to London, is greeted coolly by Bobby and his wife, but finds a role with Paula, who needs a baby-sitter.

At Bobby's expensive house, work is under way: His best friend, Darren (Daniel Craig), is building a new solarium. One night May hears Paula having sex in her living room, peers into the room, and discovers that Darren is Paula's lover. This discovery causes something to shift within May, who becomes friendly with Darren, brings him breakfast and lunch on a tray, and asks him, "Would you come to the spare room with me?"

She is in her sixties; he is in his thirties (and married, with an autistic child). She is a sweet-faced matron; he is bearded and muscular. I was reminded of Fassbinder's *Ali: Fear Eats the Soul* (1974), with its tall Moroccan immigrant and its doughy German widow, and indeed Anne Reid looks a little like Brigitte Mira, Fassbinder's star. But Fassbinder's couple had nothing in common but need; May and Darren find that they talk easily, laugh at the same things, are comfortable together. We follow them to lunch along the Thames and to the churchyard where Hogarth is buried; they are probably the only two people in the story who know who Hogarth was.

We think we know where the film stands: It will be about love transcending age. Not at all. That reassuring subject would leave Paula out of the picture, and she desperately pursues Darren and expects him to leave his wife. As sex gives May an inner glow and inspires her to improve her hair and wardrobe, desperation eats away at Paula until she looks almost as old as her mother, and more haggard and needy. She drinks, which doesn't help. After she and her brother guess the truth about May and Darren, Paula pushes to the center of the story with cold, unforgiving fury.

The Mother was written by Hanif Kureishi, whose screenplays include *My Beautiful Laundrette* and *My Son the Fanatic*. It has been directed by Roger Michell, who, hard to believe, is also the director of the comedy *Notting Hill.* Kureishi is relentless in peeling away the defenses of his characters, exposing their naked needs and fears. Familiar with the conventions of fiction, we expect to like someone in this movie. In the middle stretch we like May and Darren, even while we're aware of something not right in their relationship (it isn't the age gap, it's something trickier). But by the end there is nobody to like; we're faced with the possibility that to truly know someone is to wish you knew them less.

There is courage everywhere you look in *The Mother*. In Anne Reid, who follows May with unflinching honesty into the truth of her life. In Cathryn Bradshaw, whose Paula has never felt loved or valued by anyone. In Daniel Craig, who seems to understand why Darren wants to have sex with May, and helps us understand it, and then, when we think we do, shows us we don't. By the end, *The Mother* has told us all we need to know about the characters, except how to feel about them. It shows how people play a role and grow comfortable with it, and how that role is confused with the real person inside. And then it shows the person inside, frightened and pitiful and fighting for survival. I have a lot of questions about what happens in this movie. I am intended to.

The Motorcycle Diaries ★ ★ ½
R, 128 m., 2004

Gael Garcia Bernal (Ernesto "Che" Guevara), Rodrigo de la Serna (Alberto Granados), Mia Maestro (Chichina Ferreyra), Mercedes Moran (Celia de la Serna), Jorge Chiarella (Dr. Bresciani). Directed by Walter Salles and produced by Michael Nozik, Edgard Tenenbaum, and Karen Tenkhoff. Screenplay by Jose Rivera, based on books by Che Guevara and Alberto Granado.

The Motorcycle Diaries tells the story of an 8,000-mile trip by motorcycle, raft, truck, and foot from Argentina to Peru, undertaken in 1952 by Ernesto Guevara de la Serna and his friend Alberto Granados. If Ernesto had not later become "Che" Guevara and inspired countless T-shirts, there would be no reason to tell this story, which is interesting in the manner of a travelogue but simplistic as a study of Che's political conversion. It belongs to the dead-end literary genre in which youthful adventures are described, and then ". . . that young man grew up to be (Benjamin Franklin, Einstein, Rod Stewart, etc.)."

Che Guevera makes a convenient folk hero for those who have not looked very closely into his actual philosophy, which was repressive and authoritarian. He said he loved the people but he did not love their freedom of speech, their freedom to dissent, or their civil liberties. Cuba has turned out more or less as he would have wanted it to.

But all of that is far in the future as Ernesto

(Gael Garcia Bernal) and Alberto (Rodrigo de la Serna) mount their battered old 1939 motorcycle and roar off for a trip around a continent they'll be seeing for the first time. Guevara is a medical student with one year still to go, and Alberto is a biochemist. Neither has ever been out of Argentina. From the alarming number of times their motorcycle turns over, skids out from under them, careens into a ditch, or (in one case) broadsides a cow, it would appear neither has ever been on a motorcycle, either.

First stop, the farm of Ernesto's girlfriend, whose rich father disapproves of him. Chichina (Mia Maestro) herself loves him, up to a point: "Do you expect me to wait for you? Don't take forever." Shy around girls and not much of a dancer, Ernesto is unable to say whether he does or not.

The film, directed by Walter Salles (*Central Station*), follows them past transcendent scenery; we see forests, plains, high chaparral, deserts, lakes, rivers, mountains, spectacular vistas. And along the way the two travelers depend on the kindness of strangers; they're basically broke, and while Ernesto believes in being honest with people, Alberto gets better results by conning them.

They do meet some good new friends. A doctor in Lima, for example, who gets them an invitation to stay at a leper colony. The staff at the colony, and the lepers. A farmer and his wife, whom they meet on the road, and who were forced off their land by evil capitalists. Day laborers and their sadistic foreman. A garage owner's lonely wife. To get to the leper colony, they take a steamer down a vast lake. Guevara stands in the stern and looks down at a shabby smaller boat that the steamer is towing: This is the boat carrying the poor people, who have no decks, deck chairs, dining rooms, orchestras, and staterooms, but must hang their hammocks where they can.

By the end of the journey, Ernesto has undergone a conversion. "I think of things in different ways," he tells his friend. "Something has changed in me." The final titles say he would go on to join Castro in the Cuban Revolution, and then fight for his cause in the Congo and Bolivia, where he died. His legend lives on, celebrated largely, I am afraid, by people on the left who have sentimentalized him without looking too closely at his beliefs and methods. He is an awfully nice man in the movie, especially as played by the sweet and engaging Gael Garcia Bernal (from *Y Tu Mama Tambien*). Pity how he turned out.

The movie is receiving devoutly favorable reviews. They are mostly a matter of Political Correctness, I think; it is uncool to be against Che Guevara. But seen simply as a film, *The Motorcycle Diaries* is attenuated and tedious. We understand that Ernesto and Alberto are friends, but that's about all we find out about them; they develop none of the complexities of other on-the-road couples, like Thelma and Louise, Bonnie and Clyde, or Huck and Jim. There isn't much chemistry. For two radical intellectuals with exciting futures ahead of them, they have limited conversational ability, and everything they say is generated by the plot, the conventions of the situation, or standard pieties and impieties. Nothing is startling or poetic.

Part of the problem may be that the movie takes place before Ernesto became Che and Alberto became a doctor who opened a medical school and clinic in Cuba (where he still lives). They are still two young students, middle-class, even naive, and although their journey changes them, it ends before the changes take hold.

Salles uses an interesting device to suggest how their experiences might have been burned into their consciousness so that lessons could be learned. He has poor workers, farmers, miners, peasants, beggars pose for the camera, not in still photos, but standing as still as they can, and he uses black-and-white for these tableaux, so that we understand they represent memory. It's an effective technique, and we are meant to draw the conclusion that the adult Che would help these people, although it is a good possibility he did more harm to them.

As a child I faithfully read all of the titles in a book series named *Childhoods of Famous Americans*. George Washington chopped down a cherry tree, Benjamin Franklin got a job at a print shop, Luther Burbank looked at a potato and got thoughtful. The books always ended without really dealing with the adults those children became. But, yes, in retrospect, we can see how crucial the cherry tree, print shop, potato, and Che's motorcycle were, because Those Young Men Grew Up, etc. It's a convenient formula, because it saves you the trouble of dealing with who they became.

Note: To be fair, I must report that a Spanish-speaking friend tells me the spoken dialogue is much richer than the subtitles indicate.

Mountain Patrol: Kekexili ★ ★ ★ ½
No MPAA rating, 90 m., 2006

Duobuji (Ri Tai), Lei Zhang (Ga Yu), Liang Qi (Liu Dong), Xueying Zhao (Leng Xue). Directed by Chuan Lu and produced by Wan Zhongjun. Screenplay by Chuan Lu.

You are away from home for two or three years at a stretch. You belong to a band of armed men who patrol the desolate Kekexili region of Tibet in mud-covered jeeps and military vehicles. Your existence is sanctioned by the government, but you are not "officially employed." You have not been paid in a year. Your leader observes, "We are short of men, short of money, short of guns." You are four miles above sea level, the air is thin, the sun pitiless, you cannot see a living thing on the horizon, and there are others out there, better equipped, ready to kill you.

This is the life of the characters in *Mountain Patrol: Kekexili*, and what is their mission? To save the endangered Tibetan antelope, whose pelts were so prized by silly women that their population was reduced in the 1990s from millions to thousands. Why do you dedicate your life and endure this misery for such a cause? The movie contains no idealistic speeches, and the patrol members are not tree-huggers.

A journalist from Beijing (Lei Zhang) ventures to this far country to spend some time living with the mountain patrol. He meets their legendary leader, Ri Tai (Duobuji). They roar off into the desolation, a band of hardened men, hunting their dinner, roasting it over fires, cutting it with knives that are also weapons. Ri Tai is a man of few words, a man consumed by his mission, and he and his men remind me of the desperadoes in Cormac McCarthy's *Blood Meridian*. They are hunting poachers instead of Native Americans, but their focus is as intense. They consider themselves the hand of justice.

What is remarkable is that this film is based on a true story and filmed on the actual locations. These are hard, violent men, risking their lives to save an animal species. In appearance and behavior, they could be commandos, insurgents, terrorists. The poachers are no less des-

perate, and the film opens with the murder of a patrolman. In a strange way, the patrol and the poachers feel a bond; they are the only humans on this high plateau, both drawn there by a fascination for the antelope, and they share an existence no one else knows.

It is conventional to speak of the beauty of a vast, unspoiled wilderness, but the Kekexili is not where you would choose to live for three years. It is very dry. Color has been bleached from the land, which is sand and ochre and stark shadows. The desert offers no relief, and the mountains offer ambush. There is a particularly horrifying scene where a man steps into dry quicksand. He struggles, and then he simply stops moving and becomes utterly passive as inch by inch he sinks to his death, and then there is nothing to show he was there.

The journalist makes some discoveries. Ri Tai, the patrol leader, tells him that when they capture antelope pelts from the poachers, they sometimes sell them, because it is the only way to finance their operation. He explains that technically they lack the power to arrest the poachers, although in this country where anyone can disappear without a question, the measures they take are not closely scrutinized. When after long intervals they return to their wives and families, the women seem to accept their mission, although some wives, even in Tibet, might reasonably ask why their husband must leave his family unprovided for while roaming around in search of poachers.

Mountain Patrol is a Chinese film, which raises questions that are hard to answer. Is it designed to paint a positive picture of China's occupation of Tibet? Or can it be read as a parable: Protecting the antelope from poachers is the same as protecting Tibet from Chinese poaching? Because there are no ideological speeches, because the motives of the patrolmen are expressed in actions instead of words, we cannot be sure.

One of the American distributors of the film is National Geographic, and in its landscapes and ethnographic insights this looks at times like a documentary. But it plays like a Western involving foes who are equally hard and unsparing. The movie leaves us with the encouraging news that the Chinese government has taken over patrol duties, that the poaching has been reduced, and that the antelope herds are starting to grow again, that rich women no longer have the nerve or the heart to wear shawls made of shahtoosh, the wonderful fabric made from the pelts of four murdered Tibetan antelope. We are also left with wonder about what drew these desperate men to this desolate place for their thankless struggle.

Mr. and Mrs. Smith ★ ★ ★
PG-13, 119 m., 2005

Brad Pitt (John Smith), Angelina Jolie (Jane Smith), Adam Brody (Benjamin), Kerry Washington (Jasmine), Vince Vaughn (Eddie). Directed by Doug Liman and produced by Lucas Foster, Akiva Goldsman, Eric McLeod, Arnon Milchan, and Partrick Wachsberger. Screeplay by Simon Kinberg.

There is a kind of movie that consists of watching two people together on the screen. The plot is immaterial. What matters is the "chemistry," a term that once referred to a science, but now refers to the heat we sense, or think we sense, between two movie stars. Brad Pitt and Angelina Jolie have it, or I think they have it, in *Mr. and Mrs. Smith,* and because they do, the movie works. If they did not, there'd be nothing to work with.

The screenplay is a device to revive their marriage by placing them in mortal danger, while at the same time providing an excuse for elaborate gunfights and chase scenes. I learn from *Variety* that it was written by Simon Kinberg as his master's thesis at Columbia. If he had been studying chemistry instead of the cinema, he might have blown up the lab, but it wouldn't have been boring.

Pitt and Jolie play John and Jane Smith, almost certainly not their real names, who met in Bogota "five or six" years ago, got married, and settled down to a comfortable suburban lifestyle while not revealing to each other that they are both skilled assassins. John keeps his guns and money in a pit beneath the tool shed. Jane keeps her knives and other weapons in trays that slide out from under the oven.

As the movie opens, they're in marriage counseling; the spark has gone out of their relationship. On a typical day, they set off separately to their jobs: He to kill three or four guys, she to pose as a dominatrix while snapping a guy's neck. Can you imagine Rock Hudson and Doris Day in this story? Gable and Lombard and Hepburn and Tracy have also been invoked, but given the violence in their lives, the casting I recommend is The Rock and Vin Diesel. In the opening scene, they could fight over who has to play Mrs. Smith.

Sorry. Lost my train of thought. Anyway, John and Jane individually receive instructions to travel to a remote desert location in the Southwest and take out a mysterious target. They travel there separately, only to discover that their targets are themselves. It's one of those situations where they could tell each other, but then they'd have to kill each other. "If you two stay together, you're dead," says Eddie (Vince Vaughn), another tough guy, who lives at home with his mother because it's convenient and she cooks good and on and on.

The question becomes: Do John and Jane kill each other like the professionals they are, or do they team up to save their lives? The solution to this dilemma requires them to have a fight that reminded me of the showdown between Uma Thurman and Daryl Hannah in *Kill Bill 2.* After physical violence that should theoretically have broken every bone in both their beautiful bodies, they get so excited that, yes, they have sex, which in their case seems to involve both the martial and marital arts.

There is a chase scene. The movie was directed by Doug Liman *(The Bourne Identity),* who is good at chase scenes, and here he gets a laugh by having Jolie drive a van while being pursued by three muscle cars. Liman is able to find a lot of possibilities in the fact that it's one of those vans with two sliding doors in the rear.

The movie pauses from time to time for more sessions with the marriage counselor, during which it appears that professional killing is good for their relationship. After we get our money's worth of action, their problems are resolved, more or less. Although many lives have been lost, the marriage is saved.

None of this matters at all. What makes the movie work is that Pitt and Jolie have fun together on the screen, and they're able to find a rhythm that allows them to be understated and amused even during the most alarming developments. There are many ways that John and

477

Jane Smith could have been played awkwardly, or out of sync, but the actors understand the material and hold themselves at just the right distance from it; we understand this is not really an action picture, but a movie star romance in which the action picture serves as a location.

I've noticed a new trend in the questions I'm asked by strangers. For years it was, "Seen any good movies lately?" Now I am asked for my insights into Brad and Angelina, Tom and Katie, and other couples created by celebrity gossip. I reply that I know nothing about their private lives except what I read in the supermarket tabloids, which also know nothing about their private lives. I can see this comes as a disappointment. So I think I'll start speculating about threesomes enlisting The Rock, Vin Diesel, and Vince Vaughn, selected at random. This may be an idea for the sequel.

Mrs. Henderson Presents ★ ★ ★
R, 103 m., 2006

Judi Dench (Laura Henderson), Bob Hoskins (Vivian Van Damm), Kelly Reilly (Maureen), Christopher Guest (Lord Cromer), Will Young (Bertie), Thelma Barlow (Lady Conway). Directed by Stephen Frears and produced by Laurie Borg and Norma Heyman. Screenplay by Martin Sherman.

All the way across the Atlantic, on a flight that took twenty-four hours and involved refueling in Newfoundland and Iceland, I studied Arthur Frommer's *Europe on $5 a Day*. You will guess from the title this was some time ago. Following Frommer's instructions, I took the tube to Russell Square, checked into a hotel that would give me bed and breakfast for $2.50, took the tube to Westminster, and gazed upon Big Ben.

Then the throbbing magnetic pull of Soho attracted me, as it has so many young men, and soon I stood regarding the facade of the Windmill Theater. WE NEVER CLOSE, said the neon sign. That meant they were open and that I would soon be over my daily budget.

Yes, it was just like you see it in this movie, but a little shabbier. There were comics and song-and-dance acts, and above all there were dancing girls, and then the lighting shifted and you could see nude models, posed without moving, in "artistic tableaux." I gazed in bliss and won-

der. The lighting shifted again, and they disappeared, because how long, really, could a girl be expected to pose like that on a clamshell? All very well for Venus, but hard work six times a day for a variety artiste.

The Windmill Theater introduced nudity to the British stage through the brilliant expedient of convincing the Lord Chamberlain (who censored the shows) that a nude, *if she did not move*, was not "theater" but "art" and fell under the same exemption that permitted nudes in the National Gallery. Oh, how I agreed. Faithful readers will have followed the controversy over whether video games can be an art form. If I argue that they cannot, how then can I claim that a nude model at the Windmill could be art? Anyone who can ask such a question has been spending too much time in the basement with a joystick.

I visited the Windmill in the summer of 1961. Within a few years the barriers fell. Strip clubs opened all over Soho and the Windmill was yesterday's news, one of the casualties of the sexual revolution. Philip Larkin, who would have become poet laureate had he not declined the honor, did what a poet laureate is supposed to do and wrote a poem to mark the changing climate:

Sexual intercourse began
In nineteen sixty-three
(which was rather late for me)
Between the end of the Chatterley ban
And the Beatles' first LP.

Mrs. Henderson Presents is a fond showbiz tale directed by Stephen Frears, who is one year older than I am and, therefore, would also remember the Windmill as it used to be. That he attended it in his youth I have not the slightest doubt. So would have the Beatles, and Denis Thatcher and Stephen Hawking.

The film tells the story of the theater's founding by Laura Henderson (Judi Dench), whose husband left her a widow in the 1930s. She came home from India with some money and nothing to do. "I'm bored with widowhood," she told a friend. "I have to smile at people. In India there was always someone to look down on." One day she saw the abandoned theater on Great Windmill Street and decided to buy the old barn and put on a show.

As her impresario she hired Vivian Van

Damm (Bob Hoskins). They presented a variety programme. Her inspiration was a "nonstop revue" all day and evening. The theater was a hit until it was widely copied and began to lose money, and then she had an inspiration. "Let's have naked girls—don't you think?" she asked Vivian.

Their decision to include nudity saved the theater, and when war came Mrs. Henderson refused to close her doors, because a) the theater was below street level and, therefore, somewhat safe, and b) it was important for troop morale. When her son died in the first war, she told people, she found a French postcard among his possessions, and thought it likely he had never seen a real nude woman. She was determined to spare the new generation of British heroes this depressing fate.

"We never closed" became the war cry of the Windmill. All during the blitz, theaters, restaurants, and pubs closed, but never the Windmill. Frears, working from a screenplay by Martin Sherman, tells this story through the relationship of Mrs. Henderson and Van Damm, both high-spirited and stubborn. Van Damm may have been running a nude show, but his discipline was strict and his standards high—higher, I suspect, in this movie than in life. Although they became fast friends, the owner and her manager maintained a British reserve, and it is some years before Mrs. Henderson learns there was a Mrs. Van Damm.

Other key roles in the story are played by Maureen (Kelly Reilly), a Windmill girl whom Mrs. Henderson approves of for her "British nipples," and Lord Cromer (Christopher Guest), the Lord Chamberlain, who one suspects approves of them, too. Mrs. Henderson has a droll luncheon audience with Cromer where they debate exactly what she proposes to reveal in her revue. "Will you show the foliage?" he asks. "Try the brie," she suggests. He tries the cheese, finds it agreeable, and returns to "the somewhat sordid topic of the pudendum." Why are men always so concerned, Mrs. Henderson wonders, about "the Midlands"? She promises that her lighting will be subtle, but by the time I attended the Windmill the illumination of geography encompassed the Lake District all the way to Land's End.

Dench and Hoskins bring ineffable personal styles to roles that could have been potted show-

biz. One touch is just right: Van Damm is always natty in dress and grooming. Impresarios in that era glowed with prosperity, no matter how shaky their finances. Mrs. Henderson is in the tradition of British ladies whose age, bearing, and accent set the stage for the occasional shocking word; watch the Lord Chamberlain as she suggests a synonym for pudendum.

Mrs. Henderson Presents is not great cinema, and neither was the Windmill great theater, but they both put on a good show. As I recall those days, the nudes fade and what I am nostalgic for are the desperately jolly song-and-dance numbers and the earnest young magicians pulling pigeons from their pants. A few years ago my wife and I were among sixteen people in a tiny theater on Jermyn Street for a one-man show named "Is It Magic, or Is It Manilow?" It was neither. But it would have worked at the Windmill, if enriched by the occasional artistic tableau.

Mrs. Palfrey at the Claremont ★ ★ ★
No MPAA RATING, 108 m., 2006

Joan Plowright (Mrs. Palfrey), Rupert Friend (Ludovic Meyer), Zoe Tapper (Gwendolyn), Anna Massey (Mrs. Arbuthnot), Robert Lang (Mr. Osborne), Marcia Warren (Mrs. Post), Georgina Hale (Mrs. Burton), Millicent Martin (Mrs. De Salis). Directed by Dan Ireland and produced by Lee Caplin, Carl Colpaert, and Zachary Matz. Screenplay by Ruth Sacks, based on the novel by Elizabeth Taylor.

You may think there is no hotel in London like the Claremont, where Mrs. Palfrey becomes a lodger. No hotel where respectable gentlefolk can live by the month and have their breakfasts and dinners served to them in a dining room where good manners prevail. No hotel where the bellman is an aged ruin who nevertheless barks commands at the desk clerk. No hotel where the elevator is a brass cage that rises and falls majestically and discharges its passengers from behind ornate sliding doors.

But here and there such relics survive. A very few of my readers will have stayed at the Eyrie Mansion on Jermyn Street when it was run by Henry and Doddy Togna, and they will nod in recognition, although the Mansion, to be sure, had no dining room. They will remember Bob the hall porter, who drove Henry crazy by getting drunk every eighth day ("If Bob got drunk every seventh day, on a regular schedule like, we could plan for it").

Mrs. Palfrey (Joan Plowright) books into the Claremont almost blindly. She is in flight from life with her grown daughter in Scotland and wants to be independent. She is a stoic. Shown her room (twin beds of different heights, a desk, a mirror, a straight chair, and an arm chair), she says, "Oh, dear!" Learning from the aged ruin that the bathroom is down the hall and the early bird gets the hot water, she cannot even manage an "Oh, dear!"

In the dining room, she meets the regulars, particularly the brisk Mrs. Arbuthnot (Anna Massey), who tells the others to shut up when they require such coaching. There is also dear Mr. Osborne (Robert Lang), who asks her to a "do" at the Masons' Hall. Mrs. Palfrey hopes to spend time with her grandson Desmond, who works in the city, but he is an ingrate who never returns her calls. Then one day, while returning from the branch library with a copy of *Lady Chatterley's Lover* for Mrs. Arbuthnot, she stumbles on the sidewalk and is rescued by a nice young man named Ludovic (Rupert Friend). He invites her into the borrowed basement flat where he lives, serves her tea, rubs disinfectant on her bruise, and explains he is a writer who supports himself as a street musician.

Ludovic is too good to be true, really. Too kind, too gentle, too patient with a lady sixty years his senior. But *Mrs. Palfrey at the Claremont* is the kind of movie where nice people turn up, and soon Ludovic is doing Mrs. Palfrey a favor. She is embarrassed that everyone in the dining room wonders why her grandson has never appeared at dinner, so she asks Ludovic to pretend to be Desmond, and he agrees.

Just as teenagers enjoy escapist movies, so do the elderly. They simply prefer a gentler pace. What is touching about *Mrs. Palfrey* is that she is allowed to be elderly and not turned into a hip-hop granny. This movie is based on a novel by Elizabeth Taylor (the novelist, not the actress) and a screenplay by Ruth Sacks, herself in her eighties. Incredibly, it represents the biggest screen role that the great Joan Plowright (herself seventy-seven) has ever had, and it's little surprise she has won the AARP award as actress of the year.

Among the regulars in the Claremont dining room, there is that minute scrutiny inmates of such establishments always carry out because of boredom, jealousy, or simple curiosity. All I really miss are complaints about the food. I recall my aunt Mary O'Neill sadly surveying her dinner at a retirement home and complaining: "How am I expected to eat this, Rog? Sliced chicken, mashed potatoes, and cauliflower. It's all white, honey! It needs carrots."

Mrs. Palfrey at the Claremont has a parabola that is not startling. Mrs. Palfrey will undergo some disappointments and surprises, and Ludovic will learn a life lesson or two, and we accept all that because it comes with the territory. The movie is a delight, in ways both expected and rare. The scenes between Plowright and Lang, as the old gentleman, are classic—both the Masonic "do" and his proposal of marriage, which is argued on admirably practical grounds but inspires more than one "Oh, dear!"

Mr. 3000 ★ ★ ★
PG-13, 104 m., 2004

Bernie Mac (Stan Ross), Angela Bassett (Mo Simmons), Brian J. White (T-Rex Pennebaker), Michael Rispoli (Boca), Chris Noth (General Manager Shembri), Paul Sorvino (Coach Gus Panas). Directed by Charles Stone III and produced by Gary Barber, Roger Birnbaum, and Maggie Wilde. Screenplay by Eric Champnella, Keith Mitchell, and Howard Gould.

Baseball heroes are not necessarily the nicest guys on earth, but do moviegoers want to know that? Two movies about flawed legends, Ty Cobb and Babe Ruth, bombed at the box office. Now here is *Mr. 3000*, starring Bernie Mac as a player so disliked that even the team's mascot disses him. This time, however, the movie is a comedy, not a dirge, and Bernie Mac gives a funny and kind of touching performance as a man who attains greatness once and then has to do it again.

Mac plays Stan Ross, a legend in more ways than one with the Milwaukee Brewers, where he retired after getting 3,000 hits. In fact, he retired immediately after hit No. 3,000, leaving his team in the middle of the season to devote himself to his car dealership and TV commercials. Even his best friend doesn't sound sincere when he speaks on Stan Ross Day. Maybe there's still some bad feeling because Stan climbed into the stands to get the ball he hit for No. 3,000, and grabbed it out of the hands of a little kid.

Time passes. Stan basks in the afterglow of his 3,000 hits. He is considered for the Baseball Hall of Fame, and then a statistician discovers a crucial error: Because of a discontinued game, some of his hits were counted twice, and he in fact only has 2,997 hits. Too bad he didn't finish out that season.

That's all setup. The fun is in the payoff, as Stan comes out of retirement at forty-seven to try to get three more hits. He's past his prime and even past his decline, but his comeback makes a good story and ticket sales zoom. But the kids on the team hardly know who he is, and his attitude wears badly when he's batting 0 for 27. You may be in trouble if you're starring every night in Jay Leno monologues.

The thing about Stan, though, is that he knows baseball. He thinks his team is loafing, and he's right. He calls them a Little League team. He notices things, like an opposing pitcher's "tell" before he throws a curve. He starts passing out advice and criticism in the dugout. There's room for that, because the team's manager (Paul Sorvino) sits with sphinxlike detachment at the end of the bench, never uttering a single word.

The Bernie Ross story is a big one for ESPN, which assigns ace reporter Mo Simmons (Angela Bassett). She's an old girlfriend of Stan's, maybe the only woman he ever loved, although love for Stan does not come easily. She puts the pieces in place for what becomes the redemption of Mr. 3000, as he struggles to attain his crucial hits, but somehow at the same time becomes a nicer and even a wiser guy.

Bernie Mac is a meat-and-potatoes kind of actor, at least in the roles he's given to play. In his characters, what you see is what you get: a no-BS straight talker with unlimited self-confidence. He's a good choice to play Stan Ross because we believe him when he says what he thinks, and we especially believe him when he says what he shouldn't be thinking. Stan's romantic relationship with Mo Simmons is obviously based on a lot of history, and Angela Bassett plays what could have been a routine role with a convincing emotional

spirit; she'll cover the story, but Mr. 3000 has not earned an entry in her record book.

Almost all sports movies end with the big play, the big point, the big pass, the big putt, whatever. I guess they have to. There's not much point in showing the *next* play, point, etc. And, of course, the big moment has to come in the last moment of the last game of the season, after countless setbacks, in a sudden death situation. *Mr. 3000* follows this formula up to a point, and then, to my surprise, it finds a variation. Don't assume I'm hinting that Stan Ross doesn't get hit No. 3000, or, for that matter, that he does. It's more a case of allowing the implacable logic of baseball strategy to take over.

The Mudge Boy ★ ★ ★
R, 94 m., 2004

Emile Hirsch (Duncan Mudge), Tom Guiry (Perry Foley), Richard Jenkins (Edgar Mudge), Pablo Schreiber (Brent), Zachary Knighton (Travis), Ryan Donowho (Scotty), Meredith Handerhan (Tonya), Beckie King (April). Directed by Michael Burke and produced by Beth Alexander, Alison Benson, and Randy Ostrow. Screenplay by Burke.

The Mudge Boy tells the story of a strange and quiet mama's boy whose mother dies in the film's first scene, leaving him defenseless in the hard world of men—men like his stern and distant father, and the beer-swilling local kids who haunt the back roads in their red pickup truck. They're in basic training for a lifetime of alcoholism and wife-beating.

Duncan Mudge (Emile Hirsch) doesn't fit into this rural world. He is so direct we think at first he might be retarded; but no, he's simply clueless about how to relate to the louts who circle him. The great love of his life is a chicken, named Chicken, who follows him around and rides in the basket of his bicycle. Chicken is called "she" by just about everybody, but looks like a rooster to me; this may be a reference to the sexual uncertainty that uncoils during the film.

Duncan, who is fifteen or sixteen, has no friends as the story opens, but makes one: Perry (Tom Guiry), a neighbor, who is friendlier to him than the other local boys. One day at the swimming hole Duncan reaches out to feel the muscles in Perry's arm, and Perry recoils as if stung. But the touch sets something into motion between them. We think at first it may be Duncan's discovery that he is gay, but we're getting ahead of the plot, and Duncan may not be gay at all. Perry, the macho tough kid with the swagger, is another story.

Watching the movie, I wondered if *The Mudge Boy* is supposed to take place in the real world, and decided it is not quite. Duncan and his father, Edgar (Richard Jenkins), live not in a farmhouse but in a Farmhouse, an archetypal place filled not with furniture but with props—a dresser, a chair, a couch, a kitchen table. The district seems less like working farmland than like offstage in a psychological problem play. The local boys arrive in their pickup like messengers of fate, and Duncan passively allows himself to be swept up in their ignorance. He buys his way in by paying for their beer; when they come by looking for him, Edgar stares at them long and hard, suspecting their motives.

Edgar is not a cruel father. He is simply unable to talk with his son, except for a few rigid rules no doubt handed down by his own father. After he catches Duncan in an embarrassing situation, his response is to make him dig a hole, wide and deep, to learn what work is like. "You can't even get into trouble like a normal boy," he complains.

Some scenes work with cruel precision. Others seem uncertain—like the scene in church, with Duncan singing "The Old Rugged Cross" way off-key. The movie doesn't seem to know the point of this scene. Certainly it understands Perry, the neighbor boy, whose behavior toward Duncan is directly related to the fact that his father beats him. Duncan has at least been freed by his upbringing to be the person that he is; Perry is trapped in a maze of macho acting-out and baffled by his own behavior.

The film was written and directed by Michael Burke, who seems to be tapping deep, fearful feelings. The movie wants to be dark and truthful, but the spell is sometimes broken by scenes that edge too close to silly, such as the chicken cemetery, and others that seem just plain weird: Did you know you can "becalm" a chicken by putting its head in your mouth? Dr. Johnson said it was a brave man who ate the

first oyster, but that was nothing compared to the discovery of chicken becalming.

At the end there is a scene of sudden emotional truth that explains nothing but feels like it does. Duncan will go out into life and probably find a way, in a big city, to be himself. We should seek Perry's future adventures on the shelves of true crime books. *The Mudge Boy* is odd and intense, very well acted, and impossible to dismiss. I think the key is to understand that Duncan is not the one with the problems, but the kind of person who, by being completely and mysteriously on his own wavelength, causes the uncertain people around him to insist loudly and with growing unease on how certain they are of themselves.

Munich ★ ★ ★ ★
R, 164 m., 2005

Eric Bana (Avner), Daniel Craig (Steve), Geoffrey Rush (Ephraim), Mathieu Kassovitz (Robert), Ciaran Hinds (Carl), Hanns Zischler (Hans), Michael Lonsdale (Papa), Mathieu Amalric (Louis), Lynn Cohen (Golda Meir). Directed by Steven Spielberg and produced by Barry Mendel, Kathleen Kennedy, Spielberg, and Colin Wilson. Screenplay by Tony Kushner, based on the book *Vengeance* by George Jonas.

Steven Spielberg's *Munich* is an act of courage and conscience. The director of *Schindler's List*, the founder of the Shoah Foundation, the most successful and visible Jew in the world of film, has placed himself between Israel and the Palestinians, looked at decades of terrorism and reprisal, and had one of his characters conclude, "There is no peace at the end of this." Spielberg's film has been called an attack on the Palestinians and he has been rebuked as "no friend of Israel." By not taking sides, he has taken both sides.

The film has deep love for Israel and contains a heartfelt moment when a mother reminds her son why the state had to be founded: "We had to take it because no one would ever give it to us. Whatever it took, whatever it takes, we have a place on Earth at last." With this statement, I believe, Spielberg agrees to the bottom of his soul. Yet his film questions Israel's policy of swift and full retribution for every attack.

Munich opens with a heart-stopping reenactment of the kidnapping and deaths of Israeli athletes at the 1972 Munich Olympics. It then shows Prime Minister Golda Meir (Lynn Cohen) with her cabinet, stating firmly, "Forget peace for now." It shows the formation of a secret Israeli revenge squad to kill those responsible. It concludes that although nine of the eleven eventually were eliminated, they were replaced and replaced again by men even more dangerous, while the terrorists responded with even more deaths. What was accomplished?

The movie is based upon a book by George Jonas, a 1956 Hungarian freedom fighter, now a conservative Toronto political writer, who has been an acquaintance for twenty-five years. I thought to ask him what he thought of Spielberg's view of his material, but I didn't. I wanted to review the movie as an interested but not expert outsider, sharing (with most of the film's audience) not a great deal more knowledge than the film supplies. Those who know more, who know everything, are often the wrong ones to consult about a film based on fact. The task of the director is to transmute fact into emotions and beliefs—and beliefs, we need to be reminded, are beliefs precisely because they are not facts.

Munich takes the form of a thriller matched with a procedural. Eric Bana stars as Avner, a former bodyguard to Meir, who is made leader of the secret revenge squadron. He and his men are paid off the books, have no official existence, and are handled by a go-between named Ephraim (Geoffrey Rush). Why it is necessary to deny their existence is not quite explained by the film, since they are clearly carrying out Israeli policy and Israel wants that known; they even use bombs instead of bullets to generate more dramatic publicity.

Avner is assigned only four teammates: Robert (Mathieu Kassovitz), a toymaker, expert at disarming bombs, now asked to build them; Carl (Ciaran Hinds), who removes the evidence after every action; Steve (Daniel Craig), the trigger man; and Hans (Hanns Zischler), who can forge letters and documents. They travel with assumed names and false passports, and discover the whereabouts of many of their targets by paying bounties to a shadowy Frenchman named Louis (Mathieu Amalric).

Eventually Avner meets Louis' "Papa" (Michael Lonsdale), who has been selling information for years. Papa fought in the French Resistance and is now disillusioned: "We paid this price so Nazi scum could be replaced by Gaullist scum. We don't deal with governments." The family, he believes, is the only unit worth fighting for. His speech is moving, but does he really believe Avner and his money do not come from a government?

The film's most exciting moments are in the details of assassination. Plastic bombs are planted, booby traps are baited, there is a moment of Hitchcockian suspense when the team waits for a little girl to leave for school before calling her father's telephone; they have failed to see her reenter the house and are astonished when she answers the phone. As the team tries to prevent the explosion, we reflect how it is always more thrilling in a movie, when someone needs to run desperately, for it to be an awkward older man.

The teammates move among world capitals. One night, in a comic screwup with deadly possibilities, Avner's men and a PLO team are booked into the same "safe house." As the operation proceeds, it takes a psychic toll on Avner, who moves his family to Brooklyn, who grows paranoid, who questions the ethical basis of the operation he heads: "Jews don't do wrong because our enemies do wrong," he argues, and "if these people committed crimes we should have arrested them." To which he is told, "Every civilization finds it necessary to negotiate compromises with its own values."

The same debate is going on right now in America. If it is true that civilizations must sometimes compromise their values, the questions remain: What is the cost, and what is the benefit? Spielberg clearly asks if Israel has risked more than it has gained. The stalemate in the Middle East will continue indefinitely, his film argues, unless brave men on both sides decide to break with the pattern of the past. Certainly in Israel itself it is significant that old enemies Ariel Sharon, from the right, and Shimon Peres, from the left, are now astonishingly both in the same new party and seeking a new path to peace. For the Palestinians, it may be crucial that the PLO's corrupt Arafat no longer has a personal stake in the status quo and a new generation of leaders has moved into place.

Spielberg's film is well-timed in view of these unexpected political developments, which he could not have foreseen (Sharon left his Likud Party on November 21, 2005, and Peres left his Labour Party a week later). Far from being "no friend of Israel," he may be an invaluable friend, and for that very reason a friend of the Palestinians as well. Spielberg is using the effective form of a thriller to argue that loops of mutual reprisal have led to endless violence in the Middle East, Ireland, India and Pakistan, the former Yugoslavia, the former Soviet Union, Africa, and on and on. Miraculous that the pariah nation of South Africa was the one place where irreconcilable enemies found a way to peacefully share the same land together.

At crucial times in a nation's history, its best friends may be its critics. Spielberg did not have to make *Munich,* but he needed to. With this film he has dramatically opened a wider dialogue, helping to make the inarguable into the debatable. As a thriller, *Munich* is efficient, absorbing, effective. As an ethical argument, it is haunting. And its questions are not only for Israel but for any nation that believes it must compromise its values to defend them.   ☞

Murderball ★ ★ ★ ★

R, 85 m., 2005

Featuring Mark Zupan, Joe Soares, Keith Cavill, Andy Cohn, Scott Hogsett, and Bob Lujano. A documentary directed by Henry Alex Rubin and Dana Adam Shapiro and produced by Jeffrey Mandel and Shapiro.

"How do you eat your pizza with your elbows?"

It's a natural question for a little boy to ask a quadruple amputee, and Bob Lujano is happy to answer it. He and the other stars of the documentary *Murderball* wish more people would ask more questions, instead of becoming inhibited around people in wheelchairs. After this movie, maybe they will. You don't have to feel shy around quadriplegics who play wheelchair rugby.

This is one of those rare docs, like *Hoop Dreams,* where life provides a better ending than the filmmakers could have hoped for. Also like *Hoop Dreams,* it's not really a sports film; it's a film that uses sport as a way to see into lives, hopes, and fears. These tough all-Americans compete in international championships. Once they were shattered young men waking up in hospital beds and being told they would never walk again.

Consider Mark Zupan, probably the best player in the sport today. He was paralyzed when he was eighteen. He fell asleep in the bed of a pickup driven by his friend Christopher Igoe, who drove away not realizing Mark was aboard. The truck crashed, and Mark was thrown into a canal and wasn't found for thirteen hours. It took them a long time, but he and Igoe are friendly again.

During a discussion after a festival screening of the movie, he was asked, "If you could, would you turn back the clock on that day?" You could have heard a pin drop as he answered: "No, I don't think so. My injury has led me to opportunities and experiences and friendships I would never have had before. And it has taught me about myself." He paused. "In some ways, it's the best thing that ever happened to me."

This is hard to believe, but from him, I believe it. The movie follows Zupan and his teammates on Team USA during a couple of seasons where the off-court drama is fraught with tension. We meet Joe Soares, an all-American for many years, who with advancing age is dropped from the American team, is angry, and gets revenge by joining the Canadians. Under Soares, Canada beats the United States for the first time in twelve years. There is no love between Soares and Zupan ("If he were on fire, I wouldn't piss on him to put it out").

Wheelchair rugby is a full-contact sport. Chairs are reinforced to take the hammering. One strategy is to knock over your opponent's chair and land him on the floor; that's not a foul, although the referees helpfully put the players back on their wheels. Has anybody been injured *again* while playing the game? So far, no.

Many people think quadriplegics have no control over their four limbs, like Christopher Reeve, but most of them retain some degree of movement. Their level of disability is rated on a scale from 0.5 to 3.5, and a team can have a total of 8 points on the court at once. This leads to an ironic paradox: The athletes spend their lives overcoming and diminishing their disabilities, then hope for higher handicaps.

Although the sports scenes are filled with passion and harrowing wheelchair duels, the heart of the movie is off the court. We follow a young man named Keith Cavill, who has been wounded in a motocross accident and is painfully undergoing the slow process of rehabilitation. Encouragement from wheelchair athletes is crucial to his state of mind. Later, Team USA visits Walter Reed Army Medical Center, where newly arrived casualties from Iraq are facing the new reality of their lives. War injuries such as his are becoming more common; explosions cause more casualties than gunfire in Iraq, and *Harper's* magazine reports that improved body armor has created a large number of wounded soldiers whose body trunks are unblemished but whose arms and legs are devastated.

If Zupan is the hero of the movie, Soares is its enigma. He had a tough childhood. After losing the use of his legs from polio, he dragged himself around for years before his poor Portuguese-American family provided him with a chair. He fought for respect in school, fought for an education, was a fierce competitor on the court, and seems ferocious as he leads Team Canada against his former teammates.

At home, he wants his son Robert to be a jock like Dad. But Robert prefers to play the viola and observes wistfully that one of the household tasks he doesn't like involves "dusting Dad's trophy wall." Then an unexpected development (miraculously caught on camera) causes Soares to take a deep breath and re-evaluate his life and his relationship with his son. Rehabilitation is not limited to the body.

As the players talk frankly about their lives, we learn everything we always wanted to know about quadriplegic sex but were afraid to ask. One player says the chair works like a babe magnet: Women are dying to ask him if he can perform sexually. The answer, according to a documentary quoted in the film, is often "yes," and little animated figures show us some of the moves. We also learn that people in chairs have long since gotten over any self-consciousness in talking about their situation, and they hate it when people avoid looking at them or interacting with them. "I'm a guy in a chair," Zupan says. "I'm just like you, except I'm sitting down."

Murderball, directed by Henry Alex Rubin and Dana Adam Shapiro, produced by Jeffrey Mandel and Shapiro, and photographed by Rubin, works like many great documentaries to transcend its subject and consider the human condition. We may not be in chairs and may not be athletes, but we all have disabilities, sometimes of the spirit. To consider the bleak months and sleepless nights when these men first confronted the reality of their injuries, and now to see them in the full force of athletic exuberance, is to learn something valuable about the human will. Remember Bob Lujano, whom the kid asked about eating pizza? He has a motto: "No arms, no legs, no problem." ☞

Must Love Dogs ★ ★
PG-13, 98 m., 2005

Diane Lane (Sarah), John Cusack (Jake), Elizabeth Perkins (Carol), Christopher Plummer (Bill), Dermot Mulroney (Bob), Stockard Channing (Dolly), Ali Hillis (Christine), Brad William Henke (Leo). Directed by Gary David Goldberg and produced by Goldberg, Jennifer Todd, and Suzanne Todd. Screenplay by Goldberg, based on the novel by Claire Cook.

Must Love Dogs is like a puppy with big brown eyes and a wagging tail who weeps with eagerness to lick your hand, but you take a look around the pound and decide to adopt the sad-eyed beagle who looks as if she has seen a thing or two. In dogs, as in love stories, it is better to choose wisdom over infatuation.

The movie stars two of the most likable actors in the movies, Diane Lane and John Cusack. There is a sense in which you can simply sit there in the theater and regard them with satisfaction.

Cusack in particular has a gift of intelligent speech that no doubt inspires discerning women to let him know, one way or another, that he can have his way with them if he will just keep talking. Here he plays a man named Jake who builds racing boats by hand, out of wood. "They may not win," he observes, "but they lose beautifully." His divorce recently became final.

Diane Lane is a fortyish kindergarten teacher named Sarah who is also divorced; her family despairs because it seems she will never remarry. She belongs to one of those families that functions like the supporting cast of *Cheers,* offering one-liner insights and unwanted advice. Her sister Carol (Elizabeth Perkins) posts a phony singles ad about her on the Internet. This leads to an obligatory scene in which she has one date apiece with a series of spectacularly unlikely candidates, including one who bursts into tears almost continuously.

Fate and a helpful prod from the plot eventually bring Sarah and Jake together, although it is not love at first sight, or if it is, they deny it to themselves. Meanwhile, there is another man in the picture; Dermot Mulroney plays the separated father of the cutest of her little preschool toddlers and seems like a plenty nice guy. What she should know, as the screenplay certainly does, is that "separated" is not the same thing as "divorced." A wise woman of my acquaintance advises her single female friends, "Married men are for married women"—a rule that is more complex than at first it seems.

It is a pleasure to regard Cusack and Lane, or Jake and Sarah, as they Meet Cute and go through the usual romantic calisthenics of the love story. They must each doubt their own feelings, and each doubt the other's feelings, and miss a connection through a misunderstanding, and become convinced the other person is dating someone else, and clear all of the other hurdles placed with clockwork precision before the inevitable finish line. The movie is pleasant, sedate, subdued, and sweet, but there is not a moment of suspense in it.

It is melancholy to reflect that Cusack played a teenager in his first romantic comedies, the masterpieces *The Sure Thing* (1985) and *Say Anything* (1989), and now he plays an adult in a screenplay not anywhere near as risky, truthful, or moving. Consider the depth and truth of the girl's father in that film, played by John Mahoney, and then consider Diane Lane's father in this movie, played by Christopher Plummer.

Plummer is a great actor; he played the best Iago I have ever seen on the stage. But here his character is created from off-the-shelf sitcom templates. He was allegedly happily married for forty-five years, but after his wife dies he plunges into the Internet dating game so avidly that one of his blind dates turns out to be—his own daughter. He offers kindly wisdom, twinkling eyes, a wee hint of a brogue, and the audacity to keep two or three middle-aged ladies on the string at the same time, just so they won't grow overconfident.

Stockard Channing, who plays one of them, handles his heartlessness with such wisdom that

I'd like to see her in a whole film about a woman in such a predicament.

Lane and Cusack, meanwhile, take one step forward (they both say *Dr. Zhivago* is their favorite movie!) and two steps back (she sleeps with Mulroney but hates herself in the morning). Given the fact that his occupation is building boats by hand, what do you think the odds are that she will sooner or later commandeer a racing crew to help her pursue her dream? All too good?

The movie toys with heartbreak because it knows, and we know, no hearts will be broken. If one should get dropped by accident, well, the Cusack character thinks that when your heart breaks, "it grows back bigger." So maybe it's a good thing for it to be broken? Or what? These actors with their gifts deserve characters that the movie takes more seriously and puts at more risk. The Channing character is like a visitor from a parallel universe in which such movies are made.

My Architect: A Son's Journey ★ ★ ★ ½
NO MPAA RATING, 116 m., 2004

A documentary directed by Nathaniel Kahn and produced by Susan Rose Behr and Kahn. Screenplay by Kahn.

What a sad film this, and how filled with the mystery of human life. When Nathaniel Kahn read the obituary of his father, the great American architect Louis I. Kahn, he expected, somehow, to see his own name listed among the survivors. But in death as in life his father kept his secrets. Louis Kahn had an "official" family including his wife, Esther, and daughter Sue Ann. He had two other secret families: With fellow architect Anne Tyng he had a daughter, Alexandra, and with his colleague Harriet Pattison he had Nathaniel.

That Kahn was a great architect is clear from the loving photography of his work by his son. His masterpiece, the capitol of Bangladesh in Dhaka, is a building that invites the spirit to soar. His other works included the Kimball Art Museum in Fort Worth, the Yale Art Gallery, the Salk Institute in California, and, most surprising, a "music boat" he designed almost like a vessel from a cartoon. The boat sails into a harbor, folds up into a proscenium stage, and presents a concert for the listeners on shore.

Against these achievements the movie sets a lifetime of struggle, secrecy, stubbornness, deception, and frequent failure. He was "short, scarred, and ugly, and had a funny voice," a colleague states flatly. His face badly burned by a fire when he was an infant, Louis moved with his family from Estonia to Philadelphia when he was six. Called "Scarface" in school, he buried himself in his studies, won a college scholarship, had grand ideas about architecture, but was supported for twenty years by his first wife and didn't open his own office until he was almost fifty.

He would die at seventy-three, and only in the last ten years of his life did he achieve the stature for which he is remembered. But what a death. Returning from Bangladesh—a hard journey for a man his age—he collapsed and died in a rest room of Penn Station, and his body went unclaimed for two days because he had scratched out his address on his passport, and the police did not recognize his name. To this day, Nathaniel's mother remains convinced he blotted out the address because he planned to make good on a promise to come and live with them. Nathaniel is not so sure.

The movie begins as the story of a son searching for his father, and ends as the story of the father searching for himself. Kahn would visit Nathaniel and Harriet unexpectedly, always leaving before morning. He told the boy stories about his life, drew him a book of funny boats (at the time he was designing the music ship), but "left no physical evidence he had ever been in our home—not even a bow tie hanging in the closet."

Nathaniel interviews both his mother and Anne; Esther, who died in 1996, is seen in an old video. He talks to many of his father's colleagues, from contemporaries like Philip Johnson and I. M. Pei to Frank Gehry, who once worked in Kahn's shop. Their memories mix affection and respect with exasperation. He was a difficult man. When his plan to redesign downtown Philadelphia was rejected, there was a hint that anti-Semitism might have been involved, but when Nathaniel tracks down Ed Bacon, the czar in charge of the project, he gets a sharp verdict: "Totally irresponsible. Totally impractical." Kahn wanted Philadelphians to

park their cars in a ring around the city and walk to work, a utopian idea not likely to win tax dollars.

There are moments of sudden poignance. A colleague remembers that Kahn always spent Christmas with them, and Nathaniel repeats "Christmas?" and we realize he never spent a Christmas with his father. And Robert Boudreau, the man who commissioned the music ship, realizes he is talking to Louis's son, and tears well in his eyes. "I saw you when you were six years old," he says. "At the wake." Kahn's wife had sent orders for Anne and Harriet to stay away from the funeral, but they came anyway, and were ignored.

A portrait emerges of Louis I. Kahn as a man constantly in motion, an elusive target who lived more at his office than in any home, who worked his employees beyond the endurance of some of them, who would appear for two or three days and then fly off in search of a commission or to supervise a job. It was his great disappointment that his plans for a synagogue in Jerusalem were never taken up; ironic, that his greatest work was built by a Muslim country.

When he died, Nathaniel says, his father was $500,000 in debt. He narrates a catalog of projects that were canceled or never commissioned. At the end of the film, meeting with his two half-sisters, he wonders if they are a family, and they decide they are because they choose to be—not because of who their father was. That was the only choice Louis left them.

My Sister Maria ★ ★ ★ ½
NO MPAA RATING, 90 m., 2004

With Maria and Maximilian Schell and members of their family. A documentary directed by Maximilian Schell and produced by Dieter Pochlatko. Screenplay by Schell and Gero von Boehm.

My Sister Maria is brave, heartless, and exceedingly strange, a quasi-documentary in which the actor Maximilian Schell mercilessly violates the privacy of his older sister, Maria. It is filmed mostly on the Schells' family farm in Austria, where Maria, a famous star from the 1940s through the 1960s, lives in decline and seclusion. Like a modern Norma Desmond from *Sunset Boulevard,* she is surrounded by television sets, all playing videos of her old movies. "It all comes back, and I'm inside the scene," she says. "I was happy then."

She is not senile, precisely, or at least Maximilian refuses her the escape of that diagnosis. She has simply arrived at a decision: Having given her life to entertaining others, she has arrived at a time when the others must care for her. A psychiatrist explains to Max that his sister's mental "center for discipline" has been destroyed—something that sounds more like a punishment in a horror film than an actual condition.

For Maximilian, his sister's condition is explicable, and her recovery clear: She has given up and wants to spend all day in bed, and if she will only get up and walk, each day a little farther, her heart will pump blood to her brain and she will—what? Recover? That this regimen is forced upon Maria in the middle of an Alpine winter leads to scenes bordering on black comedy, as the pathetic old woman is sent out into the snow to laboriously walk a slippery path. More than once, she slips and falls. That a body double is obviously being used relieves us of concern that she will break a hip, but provides us with unsettling questions about the movie: How much of it is real, and how much devised, staged, or contrived? Once after the double falls, there is a close-up of Maria's face on the ground. Is she willingly acting here? Was the scene contrived? You rarely know exactly what the screenplay means with a documentary, and certainly not this time.

The film opens with paparazzi forcing themselves into Maria's home to grab photos of the old woman, which appear the next day in a paper. What are we to make of this? Did Maximilian use secret cameras to record this transgression? Unlikely, since we see the paparazzi approaching the wrong house, talking with a housekeeper and moving on to the right house; and then we see them inside. So the paparazzi were actors, apparently, directed by Maximilian for the film. And when Maria is shown the newspaper, her dialogue is right on target: "I used to be on Page One. Now I'm on Page Three." We can accept that the film restaged a paparazzi invasion that may really have happened, but how much indignation can we feel when Maximilian himself shows his sister at length, her beauty ravaged by time?

There is another strangeness in the scenes when Maximilian, his Russian-born wife, Natasha, and their children talk with Maria. To me, at least, Maria seems of essentially sound mind. Max asks her about their family, about her husbands, about her career, about romance, and her answers are lucid, concise, and sometimes even witty. What we want to hear, and never do, is how she feels about this use of herself, her history, and her present life.

Max must love his sister, and yet he resents her, too, especially in the way she has spent herself into bankruptcy. He asks on the sound track why others should be asked to sacrifice their financial status to support her. Max is finally forced to auction his art, and there are scenes perhaps a little boastful, where we're shown what famous artists he has collected ("This is Rothko's last painting"), and what enormous bids they inspire.

The film is intercut with scenes from Maria's long career. She was a star in Europe and Hollywood, was the first actress on the cover of *Time*, acted opposite everyone from Gary Cooper and Yul Brynner to Oskar Werner, had a radiant smile and a quick, healthful beauty, and then, gradually, faded away into age, as we all must.

I agree that a documentary that simply reviewed her career would be routine and pointless. I know Maximilian is a filmmaker obsessed with the subject of the loss of fame and beauty, because he demonstrated that so memorably in his 1984 documentary about Marlene Dietrich. But Dietrich resolutely (perhaps wisely) refused to appear on screen. Was Maria given a choice? Because we don't know if she's as sane as she seems or as crazy as the movie claims, we can't decide. If she is indeed demented, then the movie is not fair to her, and might even be interpreted as a form of revenge for the demands she has made on Maximilian's time, patience, and financial resources.

There is, however, another possibility: That the film, in some bold and original way, is a conscious collaboration between brother and sister to devise a work about the loss of fame and youth—a work that is all the more powerful because it seems to be factual, and seems to violate Maria's right to privacy. That this film may be substantially fictional, devised in its "documentary" form as an artistic tactic, is a fascinating possibility.

I was always, in any event, fascinated by the experience of watching it, and of trying to decide exactly what I was watching. If we accept the film on its own terms, then it takes, I think, immoral liberties with a woman powerless to protect herself. Yet Maria Schell in this film does not seem unaware, and retains enough authority that those around her do her bidding (even bringing her another TV set on a sled, through a blizzard). So I am unsure what to think.

Whatever the underlying reality, the film is now a fact, and if damage has been done, it is too late to undo it. To watch *My Sister Maria* requires us to decide what we think a film is, what we think a documentary should do, how far we think art justifies its cost in human feelings. Those who think *Fahrenheit 9/11* blurs the line between fact and interpretation have no idea how mysterious and challenging that line can become. The fundamental drama of *My Sister Maria* takes place within our own minds, as we struggle with the enigma of viewing it.

Mysterious Skin ★ ★ ★ ½
NO MPAA RATING, 99 m., 2005

Joseph Gordon-Levitt (Neil McCormick), Brady Corbet (Brian Lackey), Michelle Trachtenberg (Wendy Peterson), Jeffrey Licon (Eric Peterson), Bill Sage (Coach Heider), Mary Lynn Rajskub (Avalyn Friesen), Elisabeth Shue (Ellen McCormick), George Webster (Young Brian), Chase Ellison (Young Neil). Directed by Gregg Araki and produced by Araki, Jeffrey Levy-Hinte, and Mary Jane Skalski. Screenplay by Araki, based on a novel by Scott Heim.

"The summer I was eight years old," a character says at the beginning of *Mysterious Skin*, "five hours disappeared from my life." He remembers being at a Little League game, and then the next thing he remembers is being found hiding in his basement at home, with blood from a nosebleed all over his shirt. What happened during those five hours? And why does he continue to have blackouts, nosebleeds, and nightmares for the next ten years?

This character's name is Brian, and he is played as a child by George Webster, wearing glasses too large for his face. As a teenager, played by Brady Corbet, he has grown into

the glasses, but remains a shy and inward boy. He sees a TV show about a girl named Avalyn in a nearby Kansas town who believes she was abducted by aliens. He meets her, solemnly regards the scar on her leg where a "tracking device" was implanted, and when he talks about his nosebleeds she nods knowingly: "The old nose trick, so the scar can't be seen."

Although Brian's narration opens *Mysterious Skin*, he isn't the film's central character. That would be Neil, played by Chase Ellison as an eight-year-old and by Joseph Gordon-Levitt as a young man. He remembers Little League very well. He idolized his coach (Bill Sage), went home with him, was seduced with video games and sexually molested. The molestation continued that whole summer, as Neil identified with the coach as a father figure, valued his importance in the coach's life, and developed a compulsion to please older men. That leads him in adolescence to become a prostitute, not so much for the money as because he has been programmed that way.

Mysterious Skin, written and directed by Gregg Araki and based on a novel by Scott Heim, is at once the most harrowing and, strangely, the most touching film I have seen about child abuse. It is unflinching in its tough realism; although there is no graphic sex on the screen, what is suggested, and the violence sometimes surrounding it, is painful and unsentimental. There is little sense that Neil enjoys sex, or that he is "gay" in the way, for example, that his friend Eric is—Eric, who likes flamboyant hairstyles and black lipstick but never seems to have sex. Then there's Neil's soul mate, Wendy (Michelle Trachtenberg). "If I hadn't been queer, we would have gotten married and had kids and all of that," Neil tells us. She accepts Neil's nature, warns him of its risks, and at one point objectively observes, "Where normal people have a heart, Neil McCormick has a bottomless black hole."

The film's scenes set in childhood are filled with the kinds of mysteries childhood contains, including Neil's feelings about the endless string of boyfriends brought home by his mother (Elisabeth Shue), and Brian's conviction that a UFO hovered one night over his house. In their later teen years, the two boys

489

have no contact. Neil turns tricks at the public park, while Brian hangs out at the library and keeps a notebook of his nightmares about aliens. His friendship with Avalyn (Mary Lynn Rajskub) is based on memories of balloon-headed aliens performing weird sex probes, until Avalyn tries a weird probe of her own, which Brian is completely unable to deal with.

Neil's experiences are sad and harsh, and sometimes comic, as when he has sex while stoned, and simultaneously provides the public address commentary on a local baseball game. He follows Wendy to New York, and in the early 1990s learns some things about AIDS that cause him to leave hustling for a while and test opportunities in the fast food industry. His encounter with a dying AIDS victim is sad and tender ("This is going to be the safest encounter you've ever had. If you could just rub my back. I really need to be touched"). And then there is a brutal encounter that sends him fleeing home to Kansas on Christmas Eve, and to a crucial encounter with Brian, who thinks maybe since they were on the same Little League team, Neil might remember something helpful. He does.

Mysterious Skin begins in the confusion of childhood experiences too big to be processed, and then watches with care and attention as its characters grow in the direction that childhood pointed them. It is not a message picture, doesn't push its agenda, is about discovery, not accusation. Above all it shows how young people interpret experiences in the terms they have available to them, so that for Neil the memory of the coach remains a treasured one, until he digs more deeply into what really happened, and for Brian the possibility of alien abduction seems so obvious as to be beyond debate. The film begins with their separate myths about what happened to them when they were eight, and then leads them to a moment when their realities join. How that happens, and what is revealed, is astonishing in its truthfulness.

There is accomplished acting in this film, and there needs to be. This is not an easy story. Joseph Gordon-Levitt evokes a kind of detached realism that holds him apart from the sordid details of his life, while Brady Corbet's character seems frozen in uncertain childhood,

afraid to grow up. Both are lucky to have friends of tact and kindness: Michelle Trachtenberg's Wendy knows there is something deeply wounded about Neil, but accepts it and worries about him. And Jeffrey Licon, as Eric, becomes Brian's closest friend without ever seeming to require a sexual component; he watches, he is curious about human nature, he cares.

Mysterious Skin is a complex and challenging emotional experience. It's not simplistic. It hates child abuse, but it doesn't stop with hate; it follows the lives of its characters as they grow through the aftermath. The movie clearly believes Neil was born gay; his encounter with the coach didn't "make" him gay, but was a powerful influence that aimed his sexuality in a dangerous direction. Brian on the other hand was unable to process what happened to him, has internalized great doubts and terrors, and may grow up neither gay nor straight, but forever peering out of those great big glasses at a world he will never quite bring into focus.

My Summer of Love ★ ★ ★
R, 85 m., 2005

Natalie Press (Mona), Emily Blunt (Tamsin), Paddy Considine (Phil), Dean Andrews (Ricky), Paul Antony-Barger (Tamsin's Father), Lynette Edwards (Tamsin's Mother), Kathryn Sumner (Sadie). Directed by Pawel Pawlikovsky and produced by Chris Collins and Tanya Seghatchian. Screenplay by Pawlikovksy and Michael Wynne, based on the novel by Helen Cross.

Her brother has gone bonkers. He's pouring all the booze down the drain and announcing he's turning the pub into a worship center for Jesus people. Mona and Phil inherited the pub from their parents, and live upstairs; Phil (Paddy Considine) has come to Jesus belatedly, after a spell in prison. Mona (Natalie Press) gets on her moped, which has no engine but nevertheless functions as a symbol of escape, and wheels it into the country outside their small Yorkshire town. That's the day she meets Tamsin.

The title of *My Summer of Love* gives away two games at once: that she will fall in love, and that autumn will come. Mona is a tousled blonde, sixteen years old, dressed in whatever came to hand when she got up in the morning, bored by her town, her brother, and her life. Her boyfriend has just broken up with her in a particularly brutal way. Tamsin (Emily Blunt) is a rich girl, about the same age, sleek and brunette, on horseback the first time Mona sees her. She's spending the summer at her family's country house. "You're invited," she tells Mona. "I'm always here."

Tamsin's mother is absent. Her father is present but seems absent. The first time Mona visits, Tamsin shows her the room of her dead sister: "It's been kept as a shrine." The sister died, Tamsin says, of anorexia. The country girl and the city girl become friends almost by default; there seems to be no one else in the town they would want to talk to—certainly not the members of Phil's worship group.

That their summer leads to love is not quite the same thing as that it leads to a lesbian relationship. It's more like a teenage crush, composed in equal parts of hormones and boredom. But Tamsin and Mona promise to love each other forever, and as they swim in forest pools and ride around the countryside, they form their own secret society.

Phil, in the meantime, is engaged in the construction of a giant cross, made of iron and wood, which he wants to place on the top of a hill overlooking the town. Mona passes through the pub on her way upstairs, avoiding the prayer groups; left unexplained is how the brother and sister are supporting themselves. For Phil, religion seems less a matter of spiritual conviction than emotional hunger; he has been bad, now is good, and requires forgiveness and affirmation. Nothing wrong with that, unless he begins to impose his new lifestyle on Mona.

The movie is sweet and languid when the girls are together, edgier when Mona is around Phil. The question of Tamsin's father is complicated by the presence of his "personal assistant." The big summer house is empty and lonely, lacking a mother and haunted by the ghost of the dead sister. Pawel Pawlikovsky, the director and cowriter (with Michael Wynne), wisely allows the time to seem to flow, instead of pushing it. That's why, when Phil visits Tamsin's house looking for Mona, how Tamsin behaves and what happens is such a cruel surprise. She is, we realize, a convincing actress. When more revelations come in a closing scene, they are not exactly a surprise, not exactly a tragedy, not exactly very nice. We begin to sense the buried irony in the title.

Emily Blunt is well cast as Tamsin, a rich girl, product of the best schools, who cultivates decadence as her way of standing apart from what's expected of her. Natalie Press as Mona, on the other hand, is straight from the shoulder: She's without illusions about life, has given up on her brother, looks forward to marriage and family as a dreary prospect. Without quite saying so, she knows she'll never find a husband in her Yorkshire valley who is up to her speed. Will she, after this summer, identify as a lesbian? Doubtful. The summer stands by itself.

I'm not sure if the movie has a point. I'm not sure it needs one. I learn from *Variety* that the screenplay is inspired by a novel by Helen Cross that also involves a miner's strike and some murders. All of that is missing here, and what's left is a lazy summer of sweaty, uncertain romance; this isn't a coming-of-age movie so much as a movie about being of an age. At the end, when Tamsin tries to explain herself to Mona, we understand how completely different these two teenage girls are; how one deals in irony and deception, and with the other, what you see is what you get, whether you want it or not.

N

Nacho Libre ★ ½
PG, 91 m., 2006

Jack Black (Ignacio/Nacho), Hector Jimenez (Esqueleto), Richard Montoya (Guillermo), Ana de la Reguera (Sister Encarnacion). Directed by Jared Hess and produced by Jack Black, David Klawans, Julia Pistor, and Mike White. Screenplay by Jared Hess, Jerusha Hess, and White.

Jack Black is not very funny in *Nacho Libre*, and that requires some meditation. Jack Black is essentially, intrinsically, and instinctively a funny actor. He has that Christopher Walken thing going where you smile when he appears in a movie. It takes some doing to make a Jack Black comedy that doesn't work. But *Nacho Libre* does it.

The premise of the movie is just fine in theory and must have sounded great at the pitch meeting: Black plays Brother Ignacio, a monk who lives in a backwater of Mexico, cooks slop for orphans, and lusts after the beautiful Sister Encarnacion (Ana de la Reguera). Because he wants to be famous and make money and buy better food to cook for the orphans, he begins a secret career as a masked wrestler.

The sport he attempts to infiltrate actually exists in Mexico and the American Southwest. It is called *lucha libre*, and I learn from Wikipedia that it's freestyle wrestling with more freedom and less strategy than the American variety. A lucha libre wrestler is known as a *luchador*. The sport is depicted with affection in the movie. If the luchadors (especially the giant Ramses, with his golden mask) seem a little ridiculous, well, all professional wrestlers seem a little ridiculous, don't they? What can you say about a sport whose heroes include Haystacks Calhoun?

The problem with *Nacho Libre* is not its content but its style. It is curiously disjointed. Episodes meander on and off the screen without much conviction. While in training, Brother Ignacio climbs a rocky cliff to eat the yolk of an eagle's egg, and what's the payoff? He eats it and dives back into the water. Jokes do not build to climaxes, confrontations are misplaced, the professional wrestling itself is not especially well-staged, and Black's tag-team partner, Esqueleto (Hector Jimenez), is not well-defined; it's funny that he answers all of Ignacio's theories by saying he "believes in science," but what's the punch line? He tags along all too literally because the writers haven't carved out a role for him to play.

As for Sister Encarnacion, she is neither sexy enough nor pious enough to be funny as one or the other. She seems like an innocent not sure what she thinks about Brother Ignacio or anybody else. Nor is Brother Ignacio especially lecherous; his seduction technique is to ask her to "join me in my quarters for some toast." Again, funny, but freestanding and leading nowhere.

One of the writers on the film is Mike White (*Chuck & Buck, The School of Rock, The Good Girl, Orange County*), who usually can do no wrong. The director is Jared Hess, whose *Napoleon Dynamite* (2004) is much beloved by many moviegoers. I have been assured so often that I missed the boat on *Napoleon* that I plan to go back and have another look at it; but now here is *Nacho Libre*, which has the same incomplete and fitful comic timing I thought I found in the earlier film.

I suppose there will be those who find *Nacho Libre* offensive in one way or another, but with comedy, a little political incorrectness comes with the territory. Yes, Mexico in the movie seems to be a country where English is the language and Spanish is a hobby. Yes, Brother Ignacio is mugged by a wild child for a bag of nacho chips. And yes, Brother Ignacio's cooking is so bad that this may be the first orphanage in the history of fiction where an urchin approaches the cook and asks, "Please, sir, may I have less food?" (This doesn't actually happen in the movie, but it should have.)

I dunno. I sat there and watched scenes flex their muscles and run off in the direction of comedy and trip over something. I saw the great Jack Black occasionally at wit's end. I saw wrestling matches that were neither painful nor funny, and not well enough choreographed to make much sense. The film begins with a certain air of dejection, as if it already suspects what we're about to find out.

Nanny McPhee ★ ★ ★
PG, 97 m., 2006

Emma Thompson (Nanny McPhee), Colin Firth

(Cedric Brown), Angela Lansbury (Great Aunt Adelaide), Kelly Macdonald (Evangeline), Celia Imrie (Selma Quickly), Imelda Staunton (Mrs. Blatherwick), Thomas Sangster (Simon Brown). Directed by Kirk Jones and produced by Tim Bevan, Lindsay Doran, Eric Fellner, and Debra Hayward. Screenplay by Emma Thompson, based on the Nurse Matilda books by Christianna Brand.

There is a darkness in a lot of British children's fiction, from Roald Dahl to Harry Potter, and it provides both scariness and relief: The happy endings are arrived at via many close calls. Consider *Nanny McPhee*, named for a governess who seems closer to Mrs. Doubtfire than Mary Poppins. Garbed in a black dress that looks stuffed with flour sacks, she has warts on her face, fire in her eyes, and a walking stick that sends off sparks when she slams it on the cobblestones, which is a lot.

Nanny McPhee (Emma Thompson) is the eighteenth governess employed in the Brown household after the death of his wife left Cedric Brown (Colin Firth) to raise seven children on his own. These children, who seem to have been born within about eight years of each other, are a lawless tribe dedicated to driving away nannies, and we see several of them fleeing the house, one of them screaming, "They've eaten the baby!"

Cedric starts getting mysterious messages: "The person you need is Nanny McPhee." They are followed by Nanny herself, a formidable and foreboding presence who seems to command magical powers and quickly whips the children into shape. She has a set of rules for them to learn and a frown that terrifies them, and soon all is peaceful (or perhaps apprehensive), even at bedtime in the dormitory room the kids all share.

The Browns inhabit a big old country house with countless architectural grotesqueries and lots of gardens and staircases; only in fiction could this be the residence of a man facing financial ruin. Cedric Brown is the local funeral director, in debt and counting on an inheritance from his rich Great Aunt Adelaide (Angela Lansbury), who has made one stipulation: He must marry within thirty days.

There is an obvious candidate for his heart: Evangeline (Kelly Macdonald), the scullery maid, who is beloved by the children and by Cedric, although he's such a doofus he doesn't

realize it. Instead, Cedric seems doomed to marry Mrs. Quickly (Celia Imrie), who is well named, since like Shakespeare's Mistress Quickly she seems to be one step removed from a tart, possibly in the wrong direction.

As plans for the marriage advance, Nanny McPhee admirably improves the behavior of the Brown children, and here's a funny thing: Every time she succeeds in getting one of her rules enforced, a wart disappears from her face. She also seems to be slimming. By the end of the movie she will look like the Emma Thompson we know and love, and not a moment too soon.

Will Cedric marry Mrs. Quickly? Or will he realize Evangeline is his true love? Will the children turn into model kids? Will it snow in August? All of these questions are answered in due time, in a movie that embraces eccentricity as a social value.

Watching the movie, I reflected that the difference between American and British children in the movies is that the American kids tend to run their families, and the British kids (Harry Potter excepted) tend to require, and deserve, many hard lessons in life. It is also refreshing that British kids do not succeed because they find out they are good at sports (Quidditch excepted). In American movies the kids end in triumph, pumping their fists into the air and chanting "yes!" In British movies, they end as well-behaved miniature adults who have come to see the truth of all the wisdom bestowed upon them.

All of this is connected somehow with the decision that Cedric Brown makes to admit Nanny McPhee into his house in the first place. If a formidable and terrifying female, dressed in black and banging a lethal walking stick, should arrive at an American door all covered with warts, the residents would push the panic button on their security systems. Only in this world (based on the Nurse Matilda books by Christianna Brand) would such a creature be welcomed.

Will kids like the movie? I suspect they will. Kids like to see other kids learning the rules even if they don't much want to learn them themselves. Here is the Brown family, teetering on the brink of poverty and yet living in a house rich American kids could only envy. Lots of staircases, lots of hiding places, lots of gardens, and even a big old kitchen ruled by a red-faced cook, Mrs. Blatherwick (Imelda Staunton), who throws things at them but always seems to have a few chickens in a pot in case anyone should want sandwiches.

Napoleon Dynamite ★ ½
PG, 86 m., 2004

Jon Heder (Napoleon Dynamite), Jon Gries (Uncle Rico), Aaron Ruell (Kip Dynamite), Efren Ramirez (Pedro), Tina Majorino (Deb), Diedrich Bader (Rex), Haylie Duff (Summer). Directed by Jared Hess and produced by Jeremy Coon, Sean Covel, and Chris Wyatt. Screenplay by Jared Hess and Jerusha Hess.

There is a kind of studied stupidity that sometimes passes as humor, and Jared Hess's *Napoleon Dynamite* pushes it as far as it can go. Its hero is the kind of nerd other nerds avoid, and the movie is about his steady progress toward complete social unacceptability. Even his victory toward the end, if it is a victory, comes at the cost of clowning before his fellow students.

We can laugh at comedies like this for two reasons: because we feel superior to the characters, or because we pity or like them. I do not much like laughing down at people, which is why the comedies of Adam Sandler make me squirmy (most people, I know, laugh because they like him). In the case of Napoleon Dynamite (Jon Heder), I certainly don't like him, but then, the movie makes no attempt to make him likable. Truth is, it doesn't even try to be a comedy. It tells his story and we are supposed to laugh because we find humor the movie pretends it doesn't know about.

Napoleon is tall, ungainly, depressed, and happy to be left alone. He has red hair that must take hours in front of the mirror to look so bad. He wants us to know he is lonely by choice. He lives outside of town with his brother, Kip (Aaron Ruell), whose waking life is spent online in chat rooms, and with his grandmother, who is laid up fairly early in a dune buggy accident.

It could be funny to have a granny on a dune buggy; I smile at least at the title of the Troma film *Rabid Grannies*. But in this film the accident is essentially an aside, an excuse to explain the arrival on the farm of Napoleon's Uncle Rico (Jon Gries), a man for whom time has stood still ever since the 1982 high school sports season, when things, he still believes, should

have turned out differently. Rico is a door-to-door salesman for an herbal breast enlargement potion, a product that exists only for the purpose of demonstrating Rico's cluelessness. In an age when even the Fuller Brush Man would be greeted with a shotgun (does anyone even remember him?), Rico's product exists in the twilight zone.

Life at high school is daily misery for Napoleon, who is picked on cruelly and routinely. He finally makes a single friend, Pedro (Efren Ramirez), the school's only Latino, and manages his campaign for class president. He has a crush on a girl named Deb (Tina Majorino), but his strategy is so inept that it has the indirect result of Deb going to the prom with Pedro. His entire prom experience consists of cutting in.

Watching *Napoleon Dynamite*, I was reminded of *Welcome to the Dollhouse*, Todd Solondz's brilliant 1996 film, starring Heather Matarazzo as an unpopular high school girl. But that film was informed by anger and passion, and the character fought back. Napoleon seems to passively invite ridicule, and his attempts to succeed have a studied indifference, as if he is mocking his own efforts. I'm told the movie was greeted at Sundance with lots of laughter, but then, Sundance audiences are concerned to be cool, and to sit through this film in depressed silence would not be cool, however urgently it might be appropriate.

National Treasure ★ ★
PG, 100 m., 2004

Nicolas Cage (Benjamin Franklin Gates), Harvey Keitel (Agent Sadusky), Jon Voight (Patrick Henry Gates), Diane Kruger (Dr. Abigail Chase), Sean Bean (Ian Howe), Justin Bartha (Riley Poole), Christopher Plummer (John Adams Gates). Directed by Jon Turteltaub and produced by Jerry Bruckheimer and Turteltaub. Screenplay by Jim Kouf, Cormac Wibberley, and Marianne Wibberley.

Here is a movie about a fabled ancient treasure from the Middle East, protected through the ages by the Knights Templar and the Masons, and hidden for centuries until a modern investigator follows a series of baffling clues that lead him first to a priceless work in a national gallery, and then to a hiding place beneath an ancient church.

If you are one of the millions, like me, who plowed through *The Da Vinci Code*, you can be forgiven for thinking they've made it into a movie. And in a way, they have, but the movie is titled *National Treasure*. This new Jerry Bruckheimer production is so similar in so many ways to the plot of the Dan Brown best-seller that either (a) the filmmakers are the only citizens of the entertainment industry who have never heard of *The Da Vinci Code*, no, not even while countless people on the set must have been reading the book, or (b) they have ripped it off. My attorneys advise me that (a) is the prudent answer.

That I have read the book is not a cause for celebration. It is inelegant, pedestrian writing in service of a plot that sets up cliff-hangers like clockwork, resolves them with improbable escapes, and leads us breathlessly to a disappointing anticlimax. I should read a potboiler like *The Da Vinci Code* every once in a while, just to remind myself that life is too short to read books like *The Da Vinci Code*.

The Da Vinci movie will be directed by Ron Howard, who should study this one for clues about what to avoid. The central weakness of the story is the absurdity of the clues, which are so difficult that no sane forefather could have conceivably believed that anyone could actually follow them. That the movie's hero, named Benjamin Franklin Gates and played by Nicolas Cage, is able to intuitively sense the occult meanings of ancient riddles and puzzles is less a tribute to his intelligence than to the screenplay supplying him with half a dozen bonus A-ha! Moments. An A-Ha! Moment, you will recall, is that moment at which a movie character suddenly understands something which, if he did not understand it, would bring the entire enterprise to a halt.

Benjamin Franklin Gates is named, of course, after the famous software millionaire. His family of historians has been scorned for generations because of its belief that a vast treasure was brought back from the Crusades by the Knights Templar and has been hidden by the Masons—in this case, Masons who were the Founding Fathers of America. Benjamin's father, Patrick Henry Gates (played by Jon Voight and named after O. Henry), scoffs at the family legend, but his grandfather, John Adams Gates

(played by Christopher Plummer and named after the inventor of the toilet), gives Benjamin a clue handed down through the generations from Charles Carroll, the last surviving signer of the Declaration of Independence.

This clue, which involves the word "Charlotte," seems baffling until Benjamin has an A-Ha! and leads an expedition north of the Arctic Circle in search of a nineteenth-century sailing ship that, he calculates, must have frozen in the ice and then been shifted miles inland by the gradual movement of the floes. To say the expedition finds the ship without much trouble is putting it mildly; Benjamin digs about a foot down into the permafrost, and then bends over and wipes clean a brass nameplate that helpfully says "Charlotte."

Clues on the ship lead him to believe the map to the treasure may be written in invisible ink on the back of the Declaration of Independence—a safe place for it, because such a document would be guarded down through the ages. Of course, there is the problem of convincing the National Archives to allow you to remove the Declaration from its vacuum-sealed vault and molest it with lemon juice and a hair dryer. Luckily the national archivist, Dr. Abigail Chase (Diane Kruger), named after her scenes in the movie, is convinced by Benjamin, and together they team up to steal the Declaration before the villain (Sean Bean) can steal it first.

After many chases and close calls and quick thinking and fast footwork and hanging from swinging doors and leaping chasms, etc., the heroes find themselves in a collapsing mine shaft beneath a church tomb—a shaft that must have been created secretly, although it seems roughly the size of Boston's Big Dig. Whether they're on a wild goose chase or find the fortune of the ages, I will leave for you to discover. I understand why it is necessary in *The Da Vinci Code* to conceal information associated with the Holy Grail, but I am less convinced in *National Treasure* that the treasure had to be hidden because it was so vast that if all that wealth came suddenly into the world it would, I dunno, capsize the economy or cause the brains of accountants to explode.

Nicolas Cage, one of my favorite actors, is ideal for this caper because he has the ability to seem uncontrollably enthusiastic about almost anything. Harvey Keitel, who plays FBI agent Sadusky, falls back on his ability to seem grim about almost anything. Jon Voight calls on his skill at seeming sincere at the drop of a pin. Diane Kruger has a foreign accent even though she is the national archivist, so that our eyes can mist at the thought that in the land of opportunity, even a person with a foreign accent can become the national archivist. *National Treasure* is so silly that the Monty Python version could use the same screenplay, line for line.

Never Die Alone ★ ★ ★ ½
R, 90 m., 2004

DMX (King David), David Arquette (Paul), Michael Ealy (Mike), Clifton Powell (Moon), Reagan Gomez-Preston (Juanita), Aisha Tyler (Nancy), Jennifer Sky (Janet), Keesha Sharp (Edna). Directed by Ernest Dickerson and produced by Earl Simmons and Alessandro Camon. Screenplay by James Gibson, based on a novel by Donald Goines.

Ernest Dickerson's *Never Die Alone* is a doom-laden morality tale centered on a character who not only refers to *Scarface*'s Tony Montana but is more evil, more vicious, more self-pitying, and more cold-blooded. This is a man named King David, played by DMX as a midlevel drug dealer whose favorite trick is to hook a girl on cocaine and then switch her to heroin without telling her, so that she'll be completely dependent on him. If that is vile, he has a little "test" for them that is monstrous.

The movie begins with King David dead and in his coffin. I am not giving anything away; it's the first shot. Dead he may be, but he narrates the story of his own life from beyond the grave, like Tupac Shakur in *Tupac: Resurrection*. He has kept a diary on cassette tapes, and they come into the possession of an earnest white writer named Paul (David Arquette). Paul has a poster of Hemingway on the wall of his shabby rented room, and engages in the risky business of hanging out around tough types in Harlem drug bars. He's doing research, he thinks, or looking for trouble, we think.

The movie's plot is not nearly as linear and simple as I've made it sound so far. It loops back and forth through ten years of time, in flashbacks and memories, and there are several other major players. As it opens, King David has returned from Los Angeles to New York in order to "make amends" by repaying a debt to a higher-level drug kingpin named Moon (Clifton Powell), and Moon has sent his relatively untested lieutenant Mike (Michael Ealy) and another man to collect the cash payment. When that turns violent against Moon's specific instructions, it sets in motion a chain of events with beginnings that coil back through time, including the connection King David does not know he has with Mike.

Never Die Alone, written by James Gibson and based on a novel by the legendary ex-con writer Donald Goines, is not a routine story of drugs and violence, but an ambitious, introspective movie in which a heartless man tells his story without apology. The evil that he did lives after him, but there is no good to inter with his bones. What he cannot quite figure out at the end is how this white kid came into his life, and is driving him to the hospital, and seems to know his story.

There's action in the movie, but brief and brutal; this is not an action picture but a drama that deserves comparison with *Scarface* and *New Jack City*. The many characters are all drawn with care and dimension, especially the three women who have the misfortune to enter David's life; they're played by Reagan Gomez-Preston, Jennifer Sky, and Keesha Sharp. Each is onscreen relatively briefly; each makes a strong impression.

DMX is hard and cold as King David, and never more frightening than when he seems so charming to the women he encounters. It's a fearless performance, made more effective because we begin the movie by sort of liking him—so that we're being set up just like his victims. Michael Ealy, as Mike, has the difficult assignment of going through most of the movie being motivated by events we don't yet know about, so that we have to change our idea of him as the story develops. David Arquette is more the pawn of the plot than its mover, and his character functions mostly as a witness and facilitator; that's scary, because most of the time he has no idea how much danger he's in. After he inherits King David's Stutz pimpmobile, he essentially turns himself into a shooting gallery target.

The director Dickerson, who began as Spike Lee's NYU classmate and cinematographer, has done strong work before, starting with his debut film *Juice* (1992) and including the overlooked *Our America* (2002), based on the true story of two Chicago ghetto teenagers who were given a tape recorder by NPR and made an award-winning documentary. *Never Die Alone* is his best work, with the complexity of serious fiction and the nerve to start dark and stay dark, to follow the logic of its story right down to its inevitable end.

The New World ★ ★ ★ ★
PG-13, 130 m., 2006

Colin Farrell (Captain John Smith), Q'Orianka Kilcher (Pocahontas), Christopher Plummer (Captain Newport), Christian Bale (John Rolfe), August Schellenberg (Powhatan), Wes Studi (Opechancanough), David Thewlis (Captain Wingfield). Directed by Terrence Malick and produced by Sarah Green. Screenplay by Malick.

Terrence Malick's *The New World* strips away all the fancy and lore from the story of Pocahontas and her tribe and the English settlers at Jamestown, and imagines how new and strange these people must have seemed to one another. If the Indians stared in disbelief at the English ships, the English were no less awed by the somber beauty of the new land and its people. They called the Indians "the naturals," little understanding how well the term applied.

Malick strives throughout his film to imagine how the two civilizations met and began to speak when they were utterly unknown to each other. We know with four centuries of hindsight all the sad aftermath, but it is crucial to *The New World* that it does not know what history holds. These people regard one another in complete novelty, and at times with a certain humility imposed by nature. The Indians live because they submit to the realities of their land, and the English nearly die because they are ignorant and arrogant.

Like his films *Days of Heaven* and *The Thin Red Line*, Malick's *The New World* places nature in the foreground, instead of using it as a picturesque backdrop as other stories might. He uses voice-over narration by the principal characters to tell the story from their individual points of view. We hear Capt. John Smith describe Pocahontas: "She exceeded the others not only in beauty and proportion, but in wit and

spirit, too." And later the settler John Rolfe recalls his first meeting: "When first I saw her, she was regarded as someone broken, lost."

The New World is Pocahontas's story, although the movie deliberately never calls her by any name. She is the bridge between the two peoples. Played by a fourteen-year-old actress named Q'Orianka Kilcher as a tall, grave, inquisitive young woman, she does not "fall in love" with John Smith, as the children's books tell it, but saves his life—throwing herself on his body when he is about to be killed on the order of the chief, her father—for far more complex reasons. The movie implies, rather than says, that she is driven by curiosity about these strange visitors, and empathy with their plight as strangers, and with admiration for Smith's reckless and intrepid courage. If love later plays a role, it is not modern romantic love so much as a pure, instinctive version.

And what of Smith (Colin Farrell)? To see him is to know he knows the fleshpots of London and has been raised without regard for women. He is a troublemaker, under sentence of death by the expedition leader, Captain Newport (Christopher Plummer), for mutinous grumblings. Yet when he first sees Pocahontas, she teaches him new feelings by her dignity and strangeness. There is a scene where Pocahontas and Smith teach each other simple words in their own languages, words for sky, eyes, and lips, and the scene could seem contrived, but it doesn't because they play it with such a tender feeling of discovery.

Smith is not fair with Pocahontas. Perhaps you know the story, but if you don't, I'll let the movie fill in the details. She later encounters the settler John Rolfe (Christian Bale) and from him finds loyalty and honesty. Her father, the old chief Powhatan (August Schellenberg), would have her killed for her transgressions, but "I cannot give you up to die. I am too old for it." Abandoned by her tribe, she is forced to live with the English. Rolfe returns with her to England, where she meets the king and is a London sensation, although that story, too, is well-known.

There is a meeting that she has in England, however, that Malick handles with almost trembling tact, in which she deals with a truth hidden from her, and addresses it with unwavering honesty. What Malick focuses on is her feelings as a person who might as well have been transported to another planet. Wearing strange clothes, speaking a strange language, she can depend only on those few she trusts, and on her idea of herself.

There are two new worlds in this film, the one the English discover, and the one Pocahontas discovers. Both discoveries center on the word "new," and what distinguishes Malick's film is how firmly he refuses to know more than he should in Virginia in 1607 or London a few years later. The events in his film, including the tragic battles between the Indians and the settlers, seem to be happening for the first time. No one here has read a history book from the future.

There are the familiar stories of the Indians helping the English survive the first winter, of how they teach the lore of planting corn and laying up stores for the winter. We are surprised to see how makeshift and vulnerable the English forts are, how evolved the Indian culture is, how these two civilizations could have built something new together—but could not, because what both societies knew at that time did not permit it. Pocahontas could have brought them together. In a small way, she did. She was given the gift of sensing the whole picture, and that is what Malick founds his film on, not tawdry stories of love and adventure. He is a visionary, and this story requires one.

Note: This review is based on a viewing of the re-edited version of The New World, *which runs about 130 minutes; I also saw the original 150-minute version and noticed no startling changes.*

New York Minute ★ ½
PG, 91 m., 2004

Mary-Kate Olsen (Roxy Ryan), Ashley Olsen (Jane Ryan), Eugene Levy (Lomax), Andy Richter (Bennie Bang), Jared Padalecki (Trey), Riley Smith (Jim Wessler), Andrea Martin (Senator). Directed by Dennie Gordon and produced by Denise Di Novi, Mary-Kate Olsen, Ashley Olsen, and Robert Thorne. Screenplay by Emily Fox, Adam Cooper, and Bill Collage.

They say baseball is popular because everyone thinks they can play it. Similar reasoning may explain the popularity of the Olsen twins: Teenage girls love them because they believe they could *be* them. What, after all, do Mary-

Kate and Ashley do in *New York Minute* that could not be done by any reasonably presentable female adolescent? Their careers are founded not on what they do, but on the vicarious identification of their fans, who enjoy seeing two girls making millions for doing what just about anybody could do.

The movie offers the spectacle of two cheerful and attractive seventeen-year-olds who have the maturity of silly thirteen-year-olds and romp through a day's adventures in Manhattan, a city that in this movie is populated entirely by hyperactive character actors. Nothing that happens to them has any relationship with anything else that happens to them, except for the unifying principle that it all happens to *them*. That explains how they happen to be (1) chased by a recreational vehicle through heavy traffic, (2) wading through the sewers of New York, (3) getting a beauty makeover in a Harlem salon, (4) in possession of a kidnapped dog, (5) pursued by music pirates, (6) in danger in Chinatown, and (7) . . . oh, never mind.

Given the inescapable fact that they are twins, the movie of course gives them completely opposite looks and personalities, and then leads us inexorably to the moment when one will have to impersonate the other. Mary-Kate Olsen plays Roxy Ryan, the sloppy girl who skips school and dreams of getting her demo tape backstage at a "punk rock" video shoot. Ashley Olsen plays Jane Ryan, a Goody Two-shoes who will win a four-year scholarship to Oxford University if she gives the winning speech in a competition at Columbia. Perhaps in England she will discover that the university is in the town of Oxford, and so can correct friends who plan to visit her in London. (I am sure the screenwriters knew the university was in Oxford, but were concerned that audience members might confuse "going to" Oxford and "being in" Oxford, and played it safe, since London is the only city in England many members of the audience will have heard of, if indeed they have.)

But I'm being mean, and this movie is harmless, and as eager as a homeless puppy to make friends. In fact, it has a puppy. It also has a truant officer, played by Eugene Levy in a performance that will be valuable to film historians, since it demonstrates what Eugene Levy's irreducible essence is when he plays a character who is given absolutely nothing funny to say or do. His performance suggests that he stayed at home and phoned in his mannerisms. More inexplicable is Andy Richter's work as a limousine driver with sinister connections to music piracy rackets. He is given an accent, from where I could not guess, although I could guess why: At a story conference, the filmmakers looked in despair at his pointless character and said, "What the hell, maybe we should give him an accent."

Because the movie all takes place during one day and Roxy is being chased by a truant officer, it compares itself to *Ferris Bueller's Day Off*. It might as reasonably compare itself to *The Third Man* because they wade through sewers. *New York Minute* is a textbook example of a film created as a "vehicle," but without any ideas about where the vehicle should go. The Olsen twins are not children any longer, yet not quite poised to become adults, and so they're given the props and costumes of seventeen-year-olds, but carefully shielded from the reality. That any seventeen-year-old girl in America could take seriously the rock band that Roxy worships is beyond contemplation. It doesn't even look like a band to itself.

The events involving the big speaking competition are so labored that occasionally the twins seem to be looking back over their shoulders for the plot to catch up. Of course, there is a moment when all the characters and plot strands meet on the stage of the speech contest, with the other competitors looking on in bafflement, and of course (spoiler warning, ho, ho), Jane wins the scholarship. In fact (major spoiler warning), she does so without giving the speech, because the man who donates the scholarship reads her notes, which were dropped on the stage, and *knows* it would have been the winning speech had she only been able to deliver it. Unlikely as it seems that Jane could win in such a way, this scenario certainly sidesteps the difficulty of having her deliver a speech that would sound as if she could win.

Night Watch ★ ★
R, 114 m., 2006

Konstantin Khabensky (Anton Gorodetsky), Vladimir Menshov (Boris Geser), Valery Zolotukhin (Kostya's father), Mariya Poroshina (Svetlana), Galina Tyunina (Olga), Viktor Verzhbitsky (Zavulon), Dmitry Martynov

(Yegor). Directed by Timur Bekmambetov and produced by Konstantin Ernst and Anatoli Maksimov. Screenplay by Bekmambetov and Sergei Lukyanenko.

I confess to a flagging interest in the struggle between the forces of Light and Darkness. It's like Super Sunday in a sport I do not follow, like tetherball. We're told the future of the world hangs in the balance, and then everything comes down to a handful of hungover and desperate characters surrounded by dubious special effects. I want to hear Gabriel blow that horn.

Movies about apocalyptic showdowns always begin with an origin story; the rules for the struggle were established long ago, but now a recent crisis has altered the balance. That's the case with Timur Bekmambetov's *Night Watch*, the first in a fantasy trilogy from Russia. We learn that in the year 1342, the Warriors of Light and the Warriors of Darkness met in battle on a bridge, and so bloody was their carnage that it appeared both teams of Others (so called, I think, because they are not Sames) would lose all of their warriors, which might have been a good thing for Earth in the long run. But it was not to be; Geser and Zavulon, the leaders of Light and Darkness, establish a truce, which holds until Moscow 1992, when a new Other is born whose existence may reopen the ancient struggle.

We learn that during all the centuries in between, the truce was enforced; the Warriors of Light ran a Night Watch, and the Warriors of Darkness ran a Day Watch, to keep tabs on each other. Sometimes, when they were shorthanded, they hired a freelancer from the other side, which is like trusting mercenaries because now they're working for you. But now a young boy has been born who senses the Call and is drawn toward vampires—but hold on, how did they get in here? It appears that Others and Vampires are either interchangeable or operate in sync with each other, and the vampire hero Anton (Konstantin Khabensky), working for Light, attempts to rescue young Yegor (Dmitry Martynov) from the vampires of Darkness. Whichever team gets Yegor holds the edge. This is like Quidditch in hell.

You will sense that my understanding of the plot is not crystal clear. Do not depend upon me for a rational synopsis. In the meantime, a vortex is heading for Moscow, as symbolized by

499

ground-level shots of special-effects birds whirling about the roof of a tall building. Severe turbulence seizes an airplane, and the power plant in Moscow blows up, throwing everything into darkness. Then Anton is savagely attacked and brought into the office of the president of the light company, who sweeps everything off his desk and turns it into an operating theater to save him by plunging his fist into the chest of the victim, just like those magic healers we used to hear about in the Philippines. The Others are hardy; one warrior removes his own spine and uses it as a bludgeon. I wondered how he remained standing and had movement in his limbs, but it didn't seem to bother him.

Let us return to the endangered airplane. The passengers scream; the plane plunges wildly through the air and at one point is actually seen so close to the ground that it passes power cables. Then it's left to bounce about forgotten by the plot, until a perfunctory shot shows it aloft again and cruising smoothly. That's after the lights go back on in Moscow, which is odd, since how can the power plant function after it has exploded into smithereens? The movie is so plot-heavy it scurries between developments like a puppy surrounded by pigeons. I cringe in anticipation of the e-mails explaining all of this to me; those who understand the plot of *Night Watch* should forget about the movies and get right to work on string theory.

One interesting quality of the film is its use of characters who seem as if they might actually live in Moscow. They have a careworn look. Most Light vs. Darkness movies involve elaborate wardrobes, as if, between Apocalypsi, the warriors refit at a custom leather shop. But the Others look scruffy, drink vodka and blood more or less interchangeably, and speed around the city not in a customized Vampiremobile but in a truck of the sort used to transport refrigerated meat. While indoors, they spend a lot of time in rooms that remind me of Oscar Wilde's dying words: "Either this wallpaper goes, or I do."

The subtitles for the movie rise to the occasion, literally. They do not simply materialize at the bottom of the screen but rather unspool dynamically, dance across the picture, evaporate, explode, quiver, and seem possessed. Not since a modern benshi version of the Mexican silent classic *The Grey Automobile* (1919) have I seen such subtitles. Benshis, of course, were the Japanese performers who stood next to the screen during silent films and explained the plot to the audience. If ever a benshi were needed in a modern movie, *Night Watch* is that film.

Nine Lives ★ ★ ★ ½
R, 115 m., 2005

Kathy Baker (Camille), Amy Brenneman (Lorna), Elpidia Carrillo (Sandra), Glenn Close (Maggie), Stephen Dillane (Martin), Dakota Fanning (Maria), William Fichtner (Andrew), Lisa Gay Hamilton (Holly), Holly Hunter (Sonia), Jason Isaacs (Damian), Joe Mantegna (Richard), Ian McShane (Larry), Molly Parker (Lisa), Mary Kay Place (Alma), Sydney Tamiia Poitier (Vanessa), Aidan Quinn (Henry), Miguel Sandoval (Ron), Amanda Seyfried (Samantha), Sissy Spacek (Ruth), Robin Wright Penn (Diana). Directed by Rodrigo Garcia and produced by Julie Lynn. Screenplay by Garcia.

They meet by accident in the supermarket. It's been—how many years? They were in love once. They were a couple. They were "Damian and Diana" to everyone who knew them. Now they're both married to others. She's pregnant. They smile and exchange meaningless commonplaces. They separate. Each of their carts is filled with items for the use of a person the other will never meet.

In another aisle, they meet again. Not by accident. There is more to be said, but not very much that can be safely said without an enormous upheaval in their lives. It is clear to us, perhaps to them, that they never should have broken up. No matter what has happened, no matter whom they married, he says, "we're Damian and Diana." That will never change.

Thank God *Nine Lives* is an episodic film, so everything they have to say or do has to be contained in about twelve minutes. To know why they broke up or to see them get back together would involve us in a full-length love story of the sort we are familiar with.

It might be a good one. But here, in this meeting that is seen in one unbroken shot in a supermarket, we see the crucial heart of their relationship. It is based on the truth that their lives have moved on. Perhaps they should have stayed together. But they didn't. It's not important to know whether they start seeing each other again. But it is important for them to know that they want to, because to live without that knowledge is to dishonor their real feelings. This little story, starring Robin Wright Penn and Jason Isaacs, is told in *Nine Lives*, a collection of nine vignettes written and directed by Rodrigo Garcia. Each one contains a moment of truth, each one is about the same length, each one is told in a single shot, although the camera work isn't showy.

Sometimes the episodes seem obvious at first. Kathy Baker plays a woman who will undergo breast surgery in a few hours. In her hospital bed, she is frightened and angry; she's short-tempered with the nurses and hard on her husband (Joe Mantegna). A nurse adds a sedative to her IV drip, and she grows calmer and then—well, happy. She sees the good in things. The sedative has done its work.

But the episode is about so much more than that. It is about the indignity of surgeons inserting knives into your unconscious body, and about the fear of loss, and the impersonality of hospitals but the humanity of nurses, and the patience and love of her husband. Was she acting bitchy? When you're about to get a breast removed, you're not going for a good grade in deportment. Sometimes we behave badly for the best reasons in the world, and this movie knows that.

Other scenes. There is a prisoner (Elpidia Carrillo) who gets crazy because this is visitors' day and her daughter is on the other side of the glass, and the telephone doesn't work. An angry daughter (Lisa Gay Hamilton) who returns after a long absence to the home where she was raised and abused; this woman, so wounded, so borderline, is the same woman who, we discover in the hospital scene, is the nurse who is gentle and cares. Sissy Spacek plays a despairing mother in a dysfunctional household in one segment, and turns up in another prepared, perhaps, to have a forbidden night in a motel with Aidan Quinn. Glenn Close and Dakota Fanning visit a cemetery together in the last story, where the final shot will blindside you.

There is notoriously not a market for short films. You can't book them or advertise them, it's impossible to try to review them (and besides, where can the readers see them?). But short films are a form with purpose, just as short stories are. Some stories need only introduce us to a character or two and spend enough time with them for us to discover something about their natures, and perhaps our natures. The greatest short-story writers, such as William Trevor and Alice Munro, can awe us; their stories are short but not small.

Here Garcia does the same thing. The son of the novelist Gabriel Garcia Marquez, he has the same love for his characters, and although his stories are all (except for one) realistic, he shares his father's appreciation for the ways lives interweave and we touch each other even if we are strangers. A movie like this, with the appearance of new characters and situations, focuses us; we watch more intently, because it is important what happens. These characters aren't going to get bailed out with 110 minutes of plot. Their lives have reached a turning point here and now, and what they do must be done here and now, or forever go unknown.

9 Songs ★ ★
NO MPAA RATING, 71 m., 2005

Kieran O'Brien (Matt), Margo Stilley (Lisa). Directed by Michael Winterbottom and produced by Andrew Eaton and Winterbottom. Screenplay by Winterbottom.

Show rock concert, show sex, show icy wastes of Antarctica. Repeat eight times. That's essentially the structure of Michael Winterbottom's *9 Songs*, a movie that marks an important director's attempt to deal with explicit sex. As an idea, the film is fascinating, but as an experience it grows tedious; the concerts lack close-ups, the sex lacks context, and Antarctica could use a few penguins.

To begin with the sex: The story involves a British scientist named Matt (Kieran O'Brien) and an American named Lisa (Margo Stilley) who is visiting London for obscure reasons; she mentions jobs and studying. They meet at a rock concert in Brixton, go back to his place, and have sex. It is real sex. Real, in the sense that the actors are actually doing what they seem to be doing, and real, in the sense that instead of the counterfeit moaning and panting of pornography, there is the silence of concentration and the occasional music of delight.

All together, they go to nine concerts and hear nine songs, but this is not a concert film and the performers mostly are seen in long shot, over the heads of the crowd, which is indeed the way most of us see rock concerts. That works for realism, but it does the musicians no favors.

The nine sex scenes are filmed with the detachment of someone who has no preconceived notion of what the characters will be doing, or why. They lack the choreography of pornography, and they act as a silent rebuke to the hardcore image of sex. Winterbottom seems deliberately reluctant to turn up the visual heat; he accepts shadows and obscurities and creates a certain confusion (in the words of the limerick) about who is doing what and with which and to whom. The occasional shots of genital areas are not underlined but simply occur in the normal course of events.

There is also some dialogue. No attempt is made to see Matt and Lisa as characters in a conventional plot. They talk as two people might talk, who have fallen into an absorbing sexual relationship but are not necessarily planning a lifetime together. Matt likes her more than she likes him. There's a revelation late in the film, concerning the flat where she lives, that is kind of a stunner. What Winterbottom is charting is the progress of sex in the absence of fascination; if two people are not excited by who they are outside of sex, there's a law of diminishing returns in bed. Yes, they try to inspire themselves with blindfolds and bondage, but the more you're playing games, the less you're playing with each other. Their first few sexual encounters have the intricacy and mystery of great tabletop magic; by the end, they're making elephants disappear but they know it's just a trick.

The Antarctic footage is mostly of limitless icy wastes. Matt's narration observes that a subzero research station causes simultaneous claustrophobia and agoraphobia—"like a couple in bed." Yes. They're afraid to be trapped, and afraid to leave. There is some truth here.

The sex scenes betray the phoniness of commercial pornography; when the Adult Film Awards give a prize for best acting, they're ridiculed, but after seeing this film you'll have to admit the hard-core performers are acting, all right; *9 Songs* observes the way real people play and touch and try things out, and make little comments and have surprised reactions.

That said, *9 Songs* is more interesting to write about than to see. Its minimalism is admirable as an experiment but monotonous as an experience. To the degree that O'Brien and Stilley exchange dialogue on-screen and inhabit characters, they suggest that a full-blown movie about these characters might be intriguing. What Winterbottom does in part I'd like to see him do in whole: show a relationship in which two reasonably intelligent and sensitive adults pick each other up for sex, enjoy it, repeat it, and then have to decide if they want to take the relationship to the next level.

In many movies, the first sexual encounter is earthshaking, and then the lucky couple is magically in love forever—or at least until the story declares otherwise. In real life, sex is easy but love is hard. Sex is possible with someone you don't know. Love is not. In a way, *9 Songs* is about the gradual realization by Lisa and, more reluctantly, by Matt, that there is not going to be any love and that the sex is, therefore, going to become kind of sad.

Nobody Knows ★ ★ ★ ½
PG-13, 141 m., 2005

Yuya Yagira (Akira), Ayu Kitaura (Kyoko), Hiei Kimura (Shigeru), Momoko Shimizu (Yuki), Hanae Kan (Saki), You (Keiko). Directed and produced by Hirokazu Kore-eda. Screenplay by Kore-eda.

As *Nobody Knows* opens, we watch a mother and two kids moving into a new apartment. They wrestle some heavy suitcases up the stairs. When the movers have left, they open the suitcases and release two younger children, who are a secret from the landlord. "Remember the new rules," the mother says. "No going outside. Not even on the veranda—except for Kyoko, to do the laundry."

Kyoko is the second oldest, about ten. The oldest, a boy named Akira, is about twelve. He regards his mother with guarded eyes. So do we. There is something too happy about her, as she acts like one of the kids. It is not the forced happiness of a person trying to keep up a brave front, or the artificial happiness of someone who is high, but the crazy happiness of a person who is using laughter to mask the reality of her behavior. It fools the little kids, Shigeru and Yuki, who are perhaps seven and four.

The mother, named Keiko, played by a pop star named You, leaves Akira some money and goes away. She returns very late at night, still cheerful, as if it is the most natural thing in the world to leave her children alone, let them prepare their own dinners, and save some for her. "She stinks of booze," Akira says quietly to Kyoko.

Keiko confides in Akira that she has met a new guy, who seems "sincere" and might marry her. "Again?" he says. He is very quiet around her. She goes away again, for a much longer time, until the money she left runs out, and then she returns with gifts, including a backpack for Kyoko—ironic, since Kyoko is forbidden to leave the building. Keiko gives Akira more money, leaves again, and days and weeks pass; when Kyoko asks if she will return, Akira says she will not.

This story, written and filmed by Hirokazu Kore-eda, is based on a true story from Tokyo, where four children were abandoned by their mother and lived in an apartment for months, unmissed and undetected. He tells the story not as a melodrama about kids in danger, but as a record of long, lonely days, of the younger children playing their games and watching TV, of Akira going out into the city to buy food and find money. He gets some from a man in a pachinko parlor, who tells him not to ask again: "You know, Yuki isn't my kid." All four of the children have different fathers. Now they have no mother, but they have each other. Akira could contact the authorities, but "that happened before," he tells a friend, "and it was a real mess."

Akira is played by Yuya Yagira, who filmed the role over eighteen months, during which he grew a little and his voice broke. It is not just a cute kid performance, but real acting, because Kore-eda doesn't give him dialogue and actions to make his thoughts clear, but prefers to observe him observing, coping, and deciding. Yagira won the best actor award at Cannes.

What is most poignant is the sight of these kids wasting their lives. Kyoko asks her mother if she can go to school, but her mother laughs and says she will be happier at home. Akira was in school at one point, and studies his books at night, until finally his only subject is arithmetic—figuring how much longer their

money will last. There's a wistful shot of him looking at kids in a schoolyard, and one idyllic moment when he is asked to join a baseball game, and given a shirt and cap to wear.

He meets a girl his age named Saki (Hanae Kan), who prefers the streets to her home. They are too young for sex, but too old to be children. She picks up a guy, goes into a bar with him, comes out, and gives Akira some money. He tries to push it away, but she says, "All I did was sing karaoke with him." This time.

Kore-eda is the most gifted of the young Japanese directors. His *Maborosi* (1995), about a widow who remarries and takes her child to live in a small village, and *After Life* (1998), about a waiting room in heaven, are masterful. Here he is more matter-of-fact, more realistic, in suggesting the slow progress of time, the cold winter followed by the hot summer days, the desperation growing behind Akira's cautious expression. The fact that he doesn't crank up the energy with manufactured emergencies makes the impending danger more dramatic: This cannot go on, and it is going to end badly.

But don't the adults in the building, or anywhere else, know what is happening in the apartment? Hard to say. The landlady comes at one point to collect the rent, but then seems to let the subject drop. The gas, lights, and water are turned off, but that doesn't ring an alarm bell. Yuki's possible father knows Keiko has been away, but doesn't follow up to see if she's returned; perhaps he'd rather not know.

There are moments in Yuya Yagira's performance that will break your heart. One comes when he takes a few precious coins to a pay telephone to call a number where he might find his mother, or news of her. He's put on hold, and drops in one coin after another until they are all gone and he is disconnected, and bends his head forward against the telephone.

Kore-eda creates a sense of intimacy within the apartment. He shoots close to the kids (there's no room to get farther away), and underlines their claustrophobic imprisonment. They like each other, they have some toys, they get more or less enough to eat, usually less. One day Akira even takes their shoes out of a closet and lets them put them on, and takes them outside for a walk in the great, free, wide-open world that is so indifferent to them.

No Direction Home:
Bob Dylan ★ ★ ★ ★
NO MPAA RATING, 225 m., 2005

Featuring Bob Dylan, Joan Baez, Liam Clancy, Peter Yarrow, Dave Van Ronk, Allen Ginsberg, Maria Muldaur, and others. Directed by Martin Scorsese and produced by Margaret Bodde, Susan Lacy, Jeff Rosen, Scorsese, Nigel Sinclair, and Anthony Wall.

It has taken me all this time to accept Bob Dylan as the extraordinary artist he clearly is, but because of a new documentary by Martin Scorsese, I can finally see him freed from my disenchantment. I am Dylan's age, and his albums were the sound track of my college years. I never got involved in the war his fans fought over his acoustic and electric styles: I liked them all, every one.

Then in 1968 I saw *Don't Look Back*, D. A. Pennebaker's documentary about Dylan's 1965 tour of Great Britain. In my review I called the movie "a fascinating exercise in self-revelation" and added, "The portrait that emerges is not a pretty one." Dylan is seen not as a "lone, ethical figure standing up against the phonies," I wrote, but is "immature, petty, vindictive, lacking a sense of humor, overly impressed with his own importance, and not very bright."

I felt betrayed. In the film, he mercilessly puts down a student journalist and is rude to journalists, hotel managers, fans. Although Joan Baez was the first to call him on her stage when he was unknown, after she joins the tour, he does not ask her to sing with him. Eventually she bails out and goes home.

The film fixed my ideas about Dylan for years. Now Scorsese's *No Direction Home: Bob Dylan*, a 225-minute documentary that played in two parts on PBS, creates a portrait that is deep, sympathetic, perceptive, and yet finally leaves Dylan shrouded in mystery, which is where he properly lives.

The movie uses revealing interviews made recently by Dylan, but its subject matter is essentially the years between 1960, when he first came into view, and 1966, when after the British tour and a motorcycle accident he didn't tour for eight years. He was born in 1941, and the career that made him an icon essentially happened between his twentieth and twenty-fifth years. He

was a very young man from a little Minnesota town who had the mantle of a generation placed, against his will, upon his shoulders. He wasn't there at Woodstock; Arlo Guthrie was.

Early footage of his childhood is typical of many Midwestern childhoods: the small town of Hibbing, Minnesota, the homecoming parade, bands playing at dances, the kid listening to the radio and records. The early sounds he loved ran all the way from Hank Williams and Webb Pierce to Muddy Waters, the Carter Family, and even Bobby Vee, a rock star so minor that young Robert Zimmerman for a time claimed to be Bobby Vee.

He hitched a ride to New York (or maybe he didn't hitch; his early biography is filled with romantic claims, such as that he grew up in Gallup, New Mexico). In Greenwich Village he found the folk scene, and it found him. He sang songs by Woody Guthrie, Pete Seeger, others, then was writing his own. He caught the eye of Baez, and she mentored and promoted him. Within a year he was—Dylan.

The movie has a wealth of interviews with people who knew him at the time: Baez, Pete Seeger, Mike Seeger, Liam Clancy, Dave Von Ronk, Maria Muldaur, Peter Yarrow, and promoters such as Harold Leventhal. There is significantly no mention of Ramblin' Jack Elliott. The 2000 documentary *The Ballad of Ramblin' Jack* says it was Elliott who introduced Dylan to Woody Guthrie, suggested the harmonica holder around his neck, and essentially defined his stage persona; "There wouldn't be no Bob Dylan without Ramblin' Jack," says Arlo Guthrie, who also is not in the Scorsese film.

Dylan's new friends in music all admired the art but were ambivalent about the artist. Van Ronk smiles now about the way Dylan "borrowed" his "House in New Orleans." The Beat generation, especially Jack Kerouac's *On the Road*, influenced Dylan, and there are many observations by the Beat poet Allen Ginsberg, who says he came back from India, heard a Dylan album, and wept, because he knew the torch had been passed to a new generation.

It is Ginsberg who says the single most perceptive thing in the film: For him, Dylan stood atop a column of air. His songs and his ideas rose up from within him and emerged uncluttered and pure, as if his mind, soul, body, and talent all were one.

Dylan was embraced by the left-wing musical community of the day. His "Blowin' in the Wind" became an anthem of the civil rights movement. His "Only a Pawn in Their Game" saw the killer of Medgar Evers as an insignificant cog in the machine of racism. Baez, Pete Seeger, the Staple Singers, Odetta, and Peter, Paul, and Mary—all sang his songs and considered him a fellow warrior.

But he would not be pushed or enlisted, and the crucial passages in this film show him drawing away from any attempt to define him. At the moment when he was being called the voice of his generation, he drew away from "movement" songs. A song like "Mr. Tambourine Man" was a slap in the face to his admirers, because it moved outside ideology.

Baez, interviewed before a fireplace in the kitchen of her home, still with the same beautiful face and voice, is the one who felt most betrayed: Dylan broke her heart. His change is charted through the Newport Folk Festival: early triumph, the summit in 1964 when Johnny Cash gave him his guitar, the beginning of the end with the electric set in 1965. He was backed by Mike Bloomfield and the Butterfield Blues Band in a folk-rock-blues hybrid that his fans hated. When he took the new sound on tour, audiences wanted the "protest songs" and shouted "Judas!" and "What happened to Woody Guthrie?" when he came onstage. Night after night, he opened with an acoustic set that was applauded and then came back with the Butterfield Blues Band and was booed.

"Dylan made it pretty clear he didn't want to do all that other stuff," Baez says, talking of political songs, "but I did." It was the beginning of the Vietnam era, and Dylan had withdrawn. When he didn't ask Baez onstage to sing with him on the British tour, she says quietly, "It hurt."

But what was happening inside Dylan? Was he the jerk portrayed in *Don't Look Back*? Scorsese looks more deeply. He shows countless news conferences where Dylan is assigned leadership of his generation and assaulted with inane questions about his role, message, and philosophy. A photographer asks him, "Suck your glasses" for a picture. He is asked how many protest singers he thinks there are: "There are 136."

At the 1965 Newport festival, Pete Seeger recalls: "The band was so loud, you couldn't understand one word. I kept shouting, 'Get that distortion out!' If I had an ax I'd chop the mike cable right now!" For Seeger, it was always about the words and the message. For Dylan, it was about the words, and then it became about the words and the music, and it was never particularly about the message.

Were drugs involved in these years? The movie makes not the slightest mention of them, except obliquely in a scene where Dylan and Cash do a private duet of "I'm So Lonesome I Could Cry," and it's clear they're both stoned. There is sad footage near the end of the British tour, when Dylan says he is so exhausted, "I shouldn't be singing tonight."

The archival footage comes from many sources, including documentaries by Pennebaker and Murray Lerner *(Festival)*. Many of the interviews were conducted by Michael Borofsky, and Jeff Rosen was a key contributor. But Scorsese provides the master vision, and his factual footage unfolds with the narrative power of fiction.

What it comes down to, I think, is that Robert Zimmerman from Hibbing, Minnesota, who mentions his father only because he bought the house where Bobby found a guitar, and mentions no other member of his family at all, who felt he was from nowhere, became the focus for a time of fundamental change in music and politics. His songs led that change but they transcended it. His audience was uneasy with transcendence. It kept trying to draw him back down into categories. He sang and sang, and finally, still a very young man, found himself a hero who was booed. "Isn't it something, how they still buy up all the tickets?" he asks, about a sold-out audience that hated his new music.

What I feel for Dylan now and did not feel before is empathy. His music stands and it will survive. Because it embodied our feelings, we wanted him to embody them, too. He had his own feelings. He did not want to embody. We found it hard to forgive him for that. He had the choice of caving in or dropping out. The blues band music, however good it really was, functioned also to announce the end of his days as a standard-bearer. Then after his motorcycle crash in 1966, he stopped touring for eight years and went away into a personal space where he remains.

Watching him singing in *No Direction Home,*

we see no glimpse of humor, no attempt to entertain. He uses a flat, merciless delivery, more relentless cadence than melody, almost preaching. But sometimes at the press conferences we see moments of a shy, funny, playful kid inside. And just once, in his recent interviews, seen in profile against a background of black, we see the ghost of a smile.

Noel ★ ★

PG, 96 m., 2004

Penelope Cruz (Nina), Susan Sarandon (Rose), Paul Walker (Mike), Alan Arkin (Artie), Robin Williams (Charlie), Marcus Thomas (Jules), Chazz Palminteri (Arizona), Erika Rosenbaum (Merry). Directed by Chazz Palminteri and produced by Al Corley, Eugene Musso, Bart Rosenblatt, and Howard Rosenman. Screenplay by David Hubbard.

Noel tells the usual story of sad strangers who seek happiness on Christmas Eve, with the variation that most of the characters are stark staring mad. Christmas is a holiday fraught with hazards anyway, and these people are clearly not up to it. Thanksgiving is the most angst-free holiday, with no presents to buy, no cards to send, and mountains of turkey. But the genre of Thanksgiving movies is dominated by miserable, destructive family reunions; only the wonderful *What's Cooking?* gives the holiday a break.

If Thanksgiving in the movies is about lethal families, Christmas movies tend to be about loners who most keenly feel their aloneness as they engage in that quintessential activity of the Lonely Person, watching a Yule log on TV. The thing is, we're obsessed with the conviction that we're *supposed* to feel happy at Christmastime.

In Chazz Palminteri's film, the most miserable character is probably Rose (Susan Sarandon), a divorced, middle-aged book editor whose mother has disappeared into Alzheimer's. At one point she stands on the banks of a river, looking longingly at the icy water, but she's talked back from the edge by Charlie (Robin Williams), whom she met in her mother's nursing home, where he was sitting in the corner in the dark in a room with an unmoving body on the bed—a body that Rose, in her desperation, one night told, "I love you!"

Well, she needs somebody to love. "You need sex. Good sex," advises her secretary, who seems to speak from experience. Rose gets fixed up with the office stud, but at the point of decision she finds that it's all just too sad and sordid. Meanwhile, we meet Nina (Penelope Cruz), who is engaged to a cop named Mike (Paul Walker), who is consumed by such anger and jealousy that she threatens to postpone their wedding.

Mike has his own problems: Artie (Alan Arkin), a waiter in a restaurant, follows him around with lovesick eyes, not because he is gay, but because it only took him one look at Mike to realize he is the reincarnation of his dead wife. He could see it in the eyes. Even people who believe in reincarnation would probably not want to meet Artie.

Oh, and then there's the sad case of Jules (Marcus Thomas), who has had only one happy Christmas in his entire life, and that was when he was in a hospital emergency room and they had a Christmas party. Early in the film, he wanders into his local ER and asks what time the party starts, but is informed, alas, that he will require an emergency. This leads to easily the movie's most peculiar scene, in which Jules approaches a sinister man who seems to live on the stage of an abandoned theater, and says to him: "Glenn said that you break hands."

All of these plot developments are further complicated by the movie's intersecting plotlines and time lines; this is one of those stories where the characters always seem to be crossing paths. Some of the characters, like Susan Sarandon's Rose, are convincing and poignant; others, like Arkin's lovesick waiter, are creepy, and the guy who gets his hand broken should have tried the party at the Salvation Army, where they have great hot chocolate and sometimes you get a slice of pumpkin pie.

Only a cynic could dislike this movie, which may be why I disliked it. I can be sentimental under the right circumstances, but the movie is such a calculating tearjerker that it played like a challenge to me. There's a point at which the plot crosses an invisible line, becoming so preposterous that it's no longer moving and is just plain weird. If it's this much trouble to be happy on Christmas, then maybe Rose should consider doing what Susan Sontag does every year, which is to fly to Venice all by herself, walk around alone in the fog and the mist, cross lonely bridges over dark canals, and let the chill seep into her bones, and then curl up in bed in an empty hotel with a good book. It's kind of a judo technique: You use loneliness as a weapon against itself.

North Country ★ ★ ★ ★
R, 123 m., 2005

Charlize Theron (Josey Aimes), Frances McDormand (Glory), Sean Bean (Kyle), Richard Jenkins (Hank Aimes), Jeremy Renner (Bobby Sharp), Michelle Monaghan (Sherry), Woody Harrelson (Bill White) Sissy Spacek (Alice Aimes). Directed by Niki Caro and produced by Nick Wechsler. Screenplay by Michael Seitzman, based on the book *Class Action* by Clara Bingham and Laura Leedy Gansler.

After Josey Aimes takes her kids and walks out on the boyfriend who beats her, she doesn't find a lot of sympathy back at home. "He caught you with another man? That's why he laid hands on you?" asks her father. "You can actually ask me that question?" she says. He can. In that place, at that time, whatever happened was the woman's fault. Josey has returned to her hometown in northern Minnesota, where her father works in the strip mines of the Mesabi Iron Range.

She gets a job as a hairdresser. It doesn't pay much. She can make six times more as a miner. She applies for a job and gets one, even though her new boss is not happy: "It involves lifting, driving, and all sorts of other things a woman shouldn't be doing, if you ask me. But the Supreme Court doesn't agree." Out of every thirty miners, twenty-nine are men. Josey, who is good-looking and has an attitude, becomes a target for lust and hate, which here amount to the same thing.

North Country, which tells her story, is inspired by the life of a real person, Lois Jenson, who filed the first class-action lawsuit for sexual harassment in American history. That the suit was settled as recently as 1991 came as a surprise to me; I would have guessed the 1970s, but no, that's when the original court decision came down. Like the court's decisions on civil rights, it didn't change everything overnight.

The filmmakers say Josey Aimes is a character inspired by Jenson's lawsuit but otherwise is fictional; the real Jenson is not an Erin Brock-

ovich–style firebrand and keeps a low profile. What Charlize Theron does with the character is bring compelling human detail. We believe she looks this way, sounds this way, thinks this way. After *Monster*, here is another extraordinary role from an actress who has the beauty of a fashion model but has found resources within herself for these powerful roles about unglamorous women in the world of men.

The difference is that her Aileen Wuornos, in *Monster*, was a murderer, no matter what society first did to her. All Josey Aimes wants is a house of her own, good meals and clothes for her kids, and enough money to buy her son hockey skates once in a while. Reasonable enough, it would seem, but even her father, Hank (Richard Jenkins), is opposed to women working in the mines, because it's not "women's work," and because she is taking the job away from a man "who needs it to support his family." Josey replies, "So do I." But even the women in the community believe there's something wrong if she can't find a man to take care of her.

North Country is the first movie by Niki Caro since the wonderful *Whale Rider*. That was the film about a twelve-year-old Maori girl in New Zealand who is next in an ancestral line to be chief of her people but is kept from the position because she is female. Now here is another woman told what she can't do because she is a woman. *Whale Rider* won an Oscar nomination for young Keisha Castle-Hughes, who lost to Charlize Theron. Now Theron and Caro have gone to the Academy Awards again.

Caro sees the story in terms of two worlds. The first is the world of the women in the community, exemplified by a miner named Glory (Frances McDormand), who is the only female on the union negotiating committee, and has a no-nonsense, folksy approach that disarms the men. She finds a way to get what she wants without confrontation. The other women miners are hardworking survivors who put up with obscenity and worse, and keep their heads down because they need their jobs more than they need to make a point. Josey has two problems: She is picked on more than the others, and one of her persecutors is a supervisor named Bobby Sharp (Jeremy Renner), who shares a secret with her that goes back to high school and has left him filled with guilt and hostility.

In the male world, picking on women is all in

a day's work. It's what a man does. A woman operates a piece of heavy machinery unaware that a sign painted on the cab advertises sex for sale. The women find obscenities written in excrement on the walls of their locker room. When McDormand convinces the union to ask for portable toilets for the women, "who can't hold it as long as you fellas," one of the first women to use one has it toppled over while she's inside.

There is also all sorts of touching and fondling, but if a woman is going to insist on having breasts, how can a guy be blamed for copping a feel? After Bobby Sharp assaults Josey, his wife screams at her in public: "Stay away from Bobby Sharp!" It is assumed and widely reported that Josey is a tramp, and she is advised to "spend less time stirring up your female coworkers and less time in the beds of your male coworkers."

She appeals to a local lawyer (Woody Harrelson), who takes the case partly because it will establish new law. It does. The courtroom protocol in the closing scenes is not exactly conventional, but this isn't a documentary about legal procedure; it's a drama about a woman's struggle in a community where even the good people are afraid to support her. The court scenes work magnificently on that level.

North Country is one of those movies that stir you up and make you mad because it dramatizes practices you've heard about but never really visualized. We remember that McDormand played a female police officer in this same area in *Fargo*, and we value that memory because it provides a foundation for Josey Aimes. McDormand's role in this movie is different and much sadder but brings the same pluck and common sense to the screen. Put these two women together (as actors and characters) and they can accomplish just about anything. Watching them do it is a great movie experience.

The Notebook ★ ★ ★ ½
PG-13, 120 m., 2004

Rachel McAdams (Young Allie Nelson), Ryan Gosling (Young Noah Calhoun), Gena Rowlands (Allie Nelson), James Garner (Noah Calhoun), Joan Allen (Allie's Mother), Heather Wahlquist (Sara Tuffington), Nancy De Mayo (Mary Allen Calhoun), Sylvia Jefferies (Rosemary). Directed by Nick Cassavetes and produced by Lynn Harris and Mark Johnson. Screenplay by Jeremy Leven and Jan Sardi, based on the novel by Nicholas Sparks.

The Notebook cuts between the same couple at two seasons in their lives. We see them in the urgency of young romance, and then we see them as old people, she disappearing into the shadows of Alzheimer's, he steadfast in his love. It is his custom every day to read to her from a notebook that tells the story of how they met and fell in love and faced obstacles to their happiness. Sometimes, he says, if only for a few minutes, the clouds part and she is able to remember who he is and who the story is about.

We all wish Alzheimer's could permit such moments. For a time, in the earlier stages of the disease, it does. But when the curtain comes down, there is never another act and the play is over. *The Notebook* is a sentimental fantasy, but such fantasies are not harmful; we tell ourselves stories every day, to make life more bearable. The reason we cried during *Terms of Endearment* was not because the young mother was dying, but because she was given the opportunity for a dignified and lucid parting with her children. In life it is more likely to be pain, drugs, regret, and despair.

The lovers are named Allie Nelson and Noah Calhoun, known as Duke. As old people they're played by Gena Rowlands and James Garner; as young people, by Rachel McAdams and Ryan Gosling. The performances are suited to the material, respecting the passion at the beginning and the sentiment at the end, but not pushing too hard; there is even a time when young Noah tells Allie, "I don't see how it's gonna work," and means it, and a time when Allie gets engaged to another man.

She's a rich kid, summering at the family's mansion in North Carolina. He's a local kid who works at the sawmill but is smart and poetic. Her parents are snobs. His father (Sam Shepard) is centered and supportive. Noah loves her the moment he sees her, and actually hangs by his hands from a bar on a Ferris wheel until she agrees to go out with him. Her parents are direct: "He's trash. He's not for you." One day her mother (Joan Allen) shows her a local working man who looks hard-used by life, and tells Allie that twenty-five years ago she was in love with him. Allie thinks her parents do not love one another, but her mother insists they do; still, Joan Allen is such a precise actress that she is able to introduce the quietest note of regret into the scene.

The movie is based on a novel by Nicholas Sparks, whose books inspired *Message in a Bottle* (1999), unloved by me, and *A Walk to Remember* (2002), which was so sweet and positive it persuaded me (as did Mandy Moore as its star). Now here is a story that could have been a tearjerker, but—no, wait, it *is* a tearjerker, it's just that it's a good one. The director is Nick Cassavetes, son of Gena Rowlands and John Cassavetes, and perhaps his instinctive feeling for his mother helped him find the way past soap opera in the direction of truth.

Ryan Gosling has already been identified as one of the best actors of his generation, although usually in more hard-edged material. Rachel McAdams, who just a few months ago was the bitchy high school queen in *Mean Girls*, here shows such beauty and clarity that we realize once again how actors are blessed by good material. As for Gena Rowlands and James Garner: They are completely at ease in their roles, never striving for effect, never wanting us to be sure we get the message. Garner is an actor so confident and sure that he makes the difficult look easy, and loses credit for his skill. Consider how simply and sincerely he tells their children: "Look, guys, that's my sweetheart in there." Rowlands, best known for high-strung, even manic characters, especially in films by Cassavetes, here finds a quiet vulnerability that is luminous.

The photography by Robert Fraisse is striking in its rich, saturated effects, from sea birds at sunset to a dilapidated mansion by candlelight to the texture of southern summer streets. It makes the story seem more idealized; certainly the retirement home at the end seems more of heaven than of earth. And the old mansion is underlined, too, first in its decay and then in its rebirth; Young Noah is convinced that if he makes good on his promise to rebuild it for Allie, she will come to live in it with him, and paint in the studio he has made for her. ("Noah had gone a little mad," the notebook says.) That she is engaged to marry another shakes him but doesn't discourage him.

We have recently read much about Alzheimer's because of the death of Ronald Reagan.

His daughter Patti Davis reported that just before he died, the former president opened his eyes and gazed steadily into those of Nancy, and there was no doubt that he recognized her. Well, it's nice to think so. Nice to believe the window can open once more before closing forever.

The Notorious Bettie Page ★ ★ ★ ½
R, 100 m., 2006

Gretchen Mol (Bettie Page), Chris Bauer (Irving Klaw), Jared Harris (John Willie), Sarah Paulson (Bunny Yeager), Cara Seymour (Maxie), David Strathairn (Estes Kefauver), Lili Taylor (Paula Klaw), Jonathan M. Woodward (Marvin). Directed by Mary Harron and produced by Christine Vachon, Pamela Koffler, and Katie Roumel. Screenplay by Harron and Guinevere Turner.

In the 1950s a pretty girl from Nashville named Bettie Page became the most famous model of her time—in certain circles. Marilyn Monroe followed a nude calendar photo into Hollywood stardom, but Bettie Page's fame was within the specialist market of pinups and bondage photography. She was tied, trussed, handcuffed, chained, and restrained while wearing high heels, nylons, garter belts, corsets, and pointy brassieres, or nothing much at all, and yet her posing was so unaffected and her attitude so cheerful that she was like sunshine in the dark world of porn.

These things I know in a secondhand way because Page has been a cult figure for years, the subject of quasi-scholarly books and grainy videos. My friend Russ Meyer described her once as "the nicest girl you'd ever want to meet." Now she is the subject of a curiously moving biopic, *The Notorious Bettie Page*, which is not very sexy or scandalous, nor is Bettie Page (Gretchen Mol) very notorious. "Celebrated" might have been a better word.

You might expect such a film would aim for scandal. Not at all. Nor is it an attack on censorship or prudery; it doesn't defend Bettie and the pornographers she worked with, but presents them as mundane laborers in the world of sex, finding a market and supplying it. Most of Bettie's bondage photos were taken by Irving Klaw (Chris Bauer), an unremarkable New Yorker who worked with his sister, Paula (Lili Taylor).

509

"Boots and shoes, shoes and boots," Paula muses to Bettie. "They can't get enough of them. Why? I guess it takes all kinds to make a world."

Klaw became one of the targets of 1955 Senate hearings into pornography, and Klaw retired from the business. Bettie moved south to Miami and worked with cheesecake photographer Bunny Yeager. Then she drifted out of modeling as casually as she drifted in, becoming a born-again Christian but never apologizing for her work, because if God created the female form, why would he be offended by its display?

I have here a three-DVD set called *The Bettie Page Collection*, in which Bettie says the bondage work was pleasant because "we were always tied up by Paula, who was gentle and didn't make the knots too tight." Except for that time she was suspended from two trees. Bunny Yeager recalls that her most popular photos featured Bettie with two cheetahs, and we see both women posing with the animals, Bettie wearing a cheetah bikini. Yeager then provides a tour of her one hundred most famous models, remembering something about every single woman, including one who sewed her own posing costumes.

I looked through Bettie Page's photos and films hoping to find the same kinds of clues that must have inspired Mary Harron, who directed *The Notorious Bettie Page*, and Guinevere Turner, who wrote it with her. What I see is a pretty young woman with a spontaneous smile, who seems completely at home in whatever degree of nudity or distress. As Yeager famously said, "When she's nude, she doesn't seem naked." The material doesn't even come close to later notions of hard core, and if there were men anywhere, I missed them on fast-forward. The bondage and spanking sessions are between playful women, in short loops with titles involving sorority initiations and bad girls. Sometimes you can clearly see that the spanking is pretend, with no actual contact.

So that is the real Bettie Page. Who is this woman created by Mol, Harron, and Turner? It was Harron who starred Taylor in *I Shot Andy Warhol* (1996), another film about the underside of fame. Here she sees Bettie Page as a young woman not so much naive as simply incapable of depravity; she glides through the porno scene as a grateful visitor having a good time. The film suggests that after being abused as a child and gang-raped as a teenager, Bettie found a friendly refuge in the smut mills of the Klaws; on her first visit to Irving's studio she's immediately offered a sandwich.

The tone of the movie is subdued and reflective. It does not defend pornography but regards it (in its 1950s incarnation) with quiet nostalgia for a more innocent time. There is a kind of sadness in the movie as we reflect that most of these women and the men they inflamed are now dead; their lust is like an old forgotten song. Bettie Page is still alive in her eighties and corresponds with some of her faithful fans, also in their eighties.

In the Senate hearings held by Senator Estes Kefauver (David Strathairn), a father testifies that his son died while attempting something he may have learned from one of Klaw's films. In the movies, the witnesses at such hearings are routinely mocked as puritanical hypocrites, but Harron's film feels sympathy for the father, and so do we. We also feel, on the other hand, that Irving and Paula Klaw were not so very evil, and the clients of their "photography studio" (usually professional men) are so awed by the opportunity to photograph naked women that they treat the models as goddesses.

Mol is finally the key to the mysterious appeal of the film, to its sweetness and sadness. She plays a woman who for whatever reason does not consider her body an occasion for sin but a reason for celebration. In a haunting scene in an acting class (taught by Austin Pendleton), she is assigned to "do nothing" on the stage and responds by absentmindedly beginning to remove her clothes. The way I read the scene, she was undressing *in order* to do nothing, because for Bettie Page, to be dressed was to be doing something.

November ★ ★ ★
R, 73 m., 2005

Courteney Cox (Sophie), James Le Gros (Hugh), Michael Ealy (Jesse), Nora Dunn (Dr. Fayn), Anne Archer (Sophie's Mother), Nick Offerman (Officer Roberts). Directed by Greg Harrison and produced by Jake Abraham, Danielle Renfrew, and Gary Winick. Screenplay by Benjamin Brand.

November opens in a perfectly conventional way, as the story of an ordinary evening that goes wrong. Sophie and Hugh (Courteney Cox and James Le Gros) are driving home when she gets a snack attack and pulls the car to the curb by an all-night convenience store. He goes in to buy her something. A young man enters to rob the store. He starts shooting. Hugh is killed.

The film has developed this episode as if it will be about its aftermath. We anticipate a story in which Sophie deals with the death of someone she loves, and indeed the movie continues in that vein, as she visits a psychiatrist (Nora Dunn), complains of headaches, confesses to being unfaithful to Hugh, and in general seems to be gearing up for some heavy-duty soul-searching.

But then a strange thing happens. A lot of strange things happen. To tell you all of them would be unfair to the film, but I can tell you the first, I think. Sophie is a photographer. She met Hugh by taking his portrait. She teaches a photography class. Students present slide shows of their work for discussion and criticism. Sophie is clicking her way through one student's work when the last photo is revealed as . . .

She looks at the screen, stunned. The photo shows the convenience store on the night of the death. There's her car, parked at the curb. An indistinct figure inside may be Hugh. Who took this picture? How did it end up in the carousel of the slide projector? What does it mean?

The police send around a cop named Roberts (Nick Offerman), who is not particularly helpful. Although Sophie has been routinely questioned in connection with the death, there is no suspicion that she was involved with it. Was the taker of the photograph involved? How could the photograph have been taken by someone who then crossed the street, committed the crime, and was not seen by Sophie? Or was the photo taken as a coincidence?

Sophie tells the cop how to do his job. He should go to the photo store that developed the slide and get a list of everyone who was a customer the day the slide was developed. Officer Roberts follows her advice. Funny thing: It turns out it's Sophie's photo, paid for with her credit card.

And now I will say no more about the plot, except to observe that the movie cycles two more times through the events of that night, providing us with additional but not necessarily helpful versions of what happened.

As audience members, we can choose two responses: 1) intrigue with the method of the film, as it explores the nature of parallel realities, or 2) impatience with the film because it seems to be toying with us. I found myself poised between the two responses, experiencing a conflict that I rather enjoyed. It's intriguing when a film is about tension, and its method is about tension, and the two seem to be pulling against each other.

Cox, well-known from TV, rarely gets an opportunity to revise her famous image, but here she is serious, inward, coiled. She carries the film; the other characters circulate through her consciousness as possibilities and hypotheses. The opening scenes are dark, with blue-green lighting, and then later the film seems to break into red and black; I was reminded of the mother of this technique, the moment in Ingmar Bergman's *Persona* when the film breaks and must repair itself.

The one thing the film does not provide is an explanation. At seventy-three minutes, it barely has time to pose its questions, let alone answer them. But answers would be beside the point. When reality seems to splinter, there is only one answer, and it is: "Reality has seemed to splinter." Any other explanation, for example a speech by the psychiatrist or the cop explaining exactly what has really happened, would be contrivance. Better to allow *November* to descend into confusion and despair.

Ah, but the final segment of the film is subtitled "Acceptance," and we are reminded that acceptance is the fifth of Elisabeth Kübler-Ross's five stages of dying. The others are denial, anger, bargaining, and depression. It is useful to note that Kübler-Ross does not define "acceptance" as a "happy" stage. It is simply an end of resistance to death.

A movie that explained Hugh's murder, or whatever really happened in the convenience store, would be ending at the "bargaining" stage. It would not deny death. It would be beyond anger. It would have decided that to understand what happened would be the "answer." Most movies are satisfied to arrive at that point. Most audiences think that's what movies should aim for. But *November* does not bargain and does not explain. Take note of what happens at the end, consider that the final section is titled "Acceptance," and you may have the key to the mystery.

O

Oasis ★ ★ ★
NO MPAA RATING, 133 m., 2004

Sol Kyung-gu (Hong Jong-du), Moon So-ri (Han Gong-ju), Ahn Nae-sang (Hong Jong-il), Ryoo Seung-wan (Hong Jong-sae), Chu Kwi-jung (Jong-sae's Wife), Son Byung-ho (Han Sang-shik), Yun Ga-hyun (Sang-shik's Wife). Directed by Lee Chang-dong and produced by Cho Min-cheul, Jeon Jay, and Myeong Gye-nam. Screenplay by Chang-dong.

Oasis is a love story involving two young people abandoned by families unwilling to give them the love and attention they require. We in the audience may be equally unwilling to give them love and attention, and that's why the film works so powerfully. Its heroine is a woman rendered almost powerless by cerebral palsy. Its hero is a man so obnoxious and clueless that while he's in prison his family moves and leaves no forwarding address. They meet when he rapes her.

The new South Korean cinema is transgressive and disturbing, open to forms of behavior that are almost never seen in the films of the West. It can be about urgent, undisciplined, perverse needs; it can have the graphic detail of pornography yet show no hint of an erotic purpose; it can accept extreme characters and make no attempt to soften them or make them likable. There's something stunning and even inspiring in its indifference to popular taste. *Oasis* depends on scenes that could not be contemplated within the Western commercial cinema; it is unconventional to the point of aggression.

The movie opens with Hong Jong-du (Sol Kyung-gu), newly released from prison, seeking out his younger brother. He needs help because, in his passive-aggressive way, he has ordered food in a restaurant without being able to afford it (no, they don't want to accept his shoes as payment).

Jong-du is one of those people the rest of us instinctively avoid. He looks at people strangely, asks inappropriate questions, assumes an unwanted intimacy, violates their space, doesn't know the rules of social interaction, and in general inspires his targets to make a perfunctory and inane response and get away as quickly as possible. He may be retarded, but the movie

doesn't make that judgment; perhaps he is intelligent enough, but socially dysfunctional.

Jong-du has just served time for a hit-and-run episode. He has no money and no job prospects, and his family would be happy to never see him again. One day he buys a fruit basket and goes to visit the family of the man he killed with his drunk driving. It is impossible to say why he thinks this gesture would be appropriate, and his manner is so odd that the dead man's son and his wife are understandably enraged.

But it is through this visit that Jong-du learns of the existence of the dead man's daughter, Han Gong-ju (Moon So-ri). Severely disabled, she remains in what was the family apartment; her brother and sister-in-law have moved out and have as little to do with her as possible. We gather she is cared for by a combination of sketchy social services and the kindness of neighbors.

Jong-du returns to the apartment when Gong-ju is alone, rapes her, and leaves. He is amazed when, a few days later, he receives a message from her. He goes to see her, and they begin a romance that seems to meet their particular needs. For Jong-du, who senses other people trying to shrink from him, Gong-ju has the admirable quality of not being able to avoid him—or even, without immeasurable effort, arguing with him. For Gong-ju, her new friend is a prize who provides sex, companionship, and a way to get out of the house. Their needs and motives come together, for example, when Jong-du takes his new friend to dinner with his family; we (and they) are completely unable to read his motive. Is he being kind to her, standing up for what he believes in, or merely hoping to piss them off?

There are fantasy scenes when Gong-ju seems miraculously restored, and can move with grace and speak with eloquence. I am not sure if these moments are poetic, or somehow cruel. I am reminded of a better film involving a similar character: Rolf de Heer's *Dance Me to My Song* (1998), which starred and was written by the late Heather Rose, herself a victim of cerebral palsy. For her there was no possibility of fantasy scenes in which she danced about the screen, and her limitations became the movie's greatest strength.

Still, *Oasis* is a brave film in the way it shows two people who find any relationship almost impossible, and yet find a way to make theirs work. The problems with the film come because it overstays its welcome. There's a scene in which Gong-ju's family misinterprets something they witness, and their reaction leads to dire consequences that could surely have been avoided by a simple explanation. This is an Idiot Plot situation, in which the plot continues only because everyone acts stupidly. The closing scenes dissipate what has been accomplished, and seem not only unnecessary but harmful.

In the matter of romance between the disabled and the able-bodied, sentiment is usually the great weakness. A magnificent film like *Dance Me to My Song* was denied an American release because *The Theory of Flight* (1998, with Kenneth Branagh and Helena Bonham Carter) offered a more commercial, palatable treatment of a similar subject. Heather Rose's film was frank and graphic. *Oasis* falls somewhere in between, with the twist that the able-bodied character is more incapable of dealing with everyday life than the CP victim.

Ocean's Twelve ★ ★ ★
PG-13, 125 m., 2004

George Clooney (Danny Ocean), Brad Pitt (Rusty Ryan), Matt Damon (Linus Caldwell), Catherine Zeta-Jones (Isabel Lahiri), Andy Garcia (Terry Benedict), Don Cheadle (Basher Tarr), Bernie Mac (Frank Catton), Julia Roberts (Tess Ocean), Elliott Gould (Reuben Tishkoff), Vincent Cassel (Francois Toulour). Directed by Steven Soderbergh and produced by Jerry Weintraub. Screenplay by George Nolfi.

Just as most caper movies end with the thieves comfortably basking in retirement, so most sequels to caper movies begin with the thieves forced to go back to work and pull one more job. *Ocean's Twelve* does not disappoint. Tess Ocean (Julia Roberts) is chatting on the phone with her husband, Danny (George Clooney), when she looks out the window and says, "Oh, no." Terry Benedict (Andy Garcia) is ringing the door bell.

You will recall that in *Ocean's Eleven* Benedict was the owner of the Bellagio, a casino in Las Vegas from which the eleven stole—well, let's see, with interest, it works out to about $19 million

apiece. Benedict is accompanied on his visit by evil-looking twins and has an off-putting practice of poking people with a putter, the better to suggest dire consequences if his money is not returned. Yes, the insurance company has already paid off, but he envisions double indemnity.

With some movies, you begin to notice implausibilities. With others, you begin to admire them. For example, since Terry Benedict eventually pays a personal call on each and every one of the original eleven, why don't Danny and Tess simply telephone the other nine and warn them Benedict is coming? The reason you don't want to ask that question is because it would prevent the movie from introducing all the crooks and showing us what they're doing now.

One of the problems with a movie like this is directing traffic: How do you establish eleven characters (not counting Benedict, police inspector Catherine Zeta-Jones, rival thief Vincent Cassel, etc.) and keep them alive? You have a roll call every once in a while, is what you do, or you have them thrown in jail so the camera can pan across their faces and remind us who they are. Occasionally you have a scene for no other reason than to get an actor's face on the screen for five seconds, so he will not be misplaced. Elliott Gould puffs on his cigar three different times for this very reason.

The movie takes inventory of its characters with the same droll wit it does everything else. The *original* original *Ocean's Eleven*, made in 1960 by the Rat Pack, was a send-up of 1950s caper movies (it was inspired by Jean-Pierre Melville's French classic *Bob le Flambeur*). The *new* original *Ocean's Eleven* (2001) was a successful attempt by Soderbergh to doodle with the formula, much as a pianist might pick out a tune just well enough to show he could play it if he wanted to. Now, with *Ocean's Twelve*, Soderberg and his scenarist, George Nolfi, are doing a jazz riff. This isn't a caper movie at all; it's an improvisation on caper themes. If at times it seems like a caper, well, as the fellow said when he got up from the piano, it might not be Beethoven, but it has a lot of the same notes.

What Soderbergh is working with here is the charm of his actors, particularly Clooney, Roberts, Brad Pitt, and Zeta-Jones, who have the key roles, and the puppy-dog earnestness of Matt Damon, who wakes up Pitt on a transatlantic flight to tell him he thinks he's ready to play "a more central role." Damon's character is named Linus, a good choice of role model, since he is sincere and intense, and everyone else in the movie seems inspired by Snoopy.

When one character is excoriated as agoraphobic (what a wonderful phrase that is, "excoriated as agoraphobic"; don't you think it's almost musical?), Linus earnestly argues, "I don't think we have to be the kind of organization that labels people." There is a scene of mad invention in which Clooney and Pitt take him along for a meeting with Robbie Coltrane, an underworld contact, and their entire conversation is nonsense—an exchange of elegantly meaningless paradoxes. Linus doesn't understand a word, which is reasonable, but what he doesn't realize is that they don't either.

Their scheme has to do with stealing enough stuff to pay Benedict the $19 million apiece that they owe him. They doubt they can raise this much money in the three weeks until their deadline, especially since it appears that another thief, the Night Fox, is in business against them, and is either more skilled than they are or a supernatural being. As they contemplate the security surrounding one of their targets, Pitt flatly states: "In the physical universe we live in, it cannot be done." But the Night Fox can do it.

Occasionally their plans take the long way around. Consider a man in Amsterdam who has sealed himself and his treasures inside a house guarded with multiple alarm systems, and never leaves home. Surveillance indicates there is a control pad on an inner wall that might be manipulated to bypass the alarms. How to reach it? Their plan involves getting *underneath* the house, which is beside a canal and rests on underwater pylons, and using hydraulic lifts to raise the house one inch, so that a difficult shot with an arrow becomes possible. Uh-huh. With overhead like that, when do they reach their break-even point?

Rather than describe some of their other targets, such as a priceless jeweled egg, I will observe that all of the targets are MacGuffins, that it matters not what they go after but how they do it, and what they say in the process. The movie is all about behavior, dialogue, star power, and wiseass in-jokes. I really sort of liked it.

Example of the cleverness: There are two cameos in the movie that, for once, contribute

something more than allowing us to say, "Hey! There's (name of star)!" The genius is that one of the stars is really there, and the other star is not really there, although she is there in the person of the character who seems to be her. This will all become clear when you see the movie. What I liked is that the one cameo role is used to expose the other cameo role. When you get to the point of interlocking cameos, you have ascended to a level of invention that is its own reward.

Off the Map ★ ★ ★ ½
PG-13, 108 m., 2005

Joan Allen (Arlene Groden), Valentina de Angelis (Bo Groden), Sam Elliott (Charley Groden), J. K. Simmons (George), Jim True-Frost (William Gibbs), Amy Brenneman (Adult Bo). Directed by Campbell Scott and produced by Scott and George Van Buskirk. Screenplay by Joan Ackermann.

Somewhere in the back of nowhere, in an adobe house with no lights or running water, a family lives in what could be called freedom or could be called poverty. We're not sure if they got there because they were 1960s hippies making a lifestyle experiment, or were simply deposited there by indifference to conventional life. They grow vegetables and plunder the city dump and get $320 a month in veteran's benefits, but they are not in need and are apparently content with their lot.

Now there is a problem. "That was the summer of my father's depression," the narrator tells us. She is Bo Groden, played in the movie by Valentina de Angelis at about age twelve, and heard on the sound track as an adult (Amy Brenneman). "I'm a damn crying machine," says her dad, Charley (Sam Elliott). He sits at the kitchen table, staring at nothing, and his wife and daughter have learned to live their lives around him.

His wife is Arlene, played by Joan Allen in a performance of astonishing complexity. Here is a woman whose life includes acceptance of what she cannot change, sufficiency within her own skin, and such simple pleasures as gardening in the nude. She is a good wife and a good mother, but not obviously; it takes us the whole movie to fully appreciate how profoundly she observes her husband and daughter, and provides what they need in ways that are below their radar.

Charley has a friend named George (J. K. Simmons), who sort of idolizes him. Sometimes they fish, sometimes they talk. Arlene wants George to impersonate Charley, visit a psychiatrist, and get some antidepressants. George would rather fish. One day a stranger arrives at their home, which is far from any road. He carries a briefcase, says he is from the IRS, and is there to audit them, since the Groden family has reported an annual income of less than $5,000 for several years.

This man is William Gibbs (Jim True-Frost). He is stung by a bee, takes to the sofa, confesses his dissatisfaction with tax-collecting and, what with one thing and another, never leaves. Eventually he lives in an old school bus on the property. He falls in love with Arlene, in a nondemonstrative way, and is good company for Charley. "Ever been depressed?" Charley asks him. "I've never not been," William says.

These characters in this setting could become caricatures or grotesques. But the director, Campbell Scott, and the writer, Joan Ackermann, refuse to underline them or draw arrows pointing to their absurdities. They accept them. Their movie is freed from a story that must hurry things along; life unfolds from day to day. Will Charley recover from his depression? Will William leave? Will Bo, who is being home-schooled, get to go to a real school? The movie suggests no urgency to get these questions answered.

Instead, in a stealthy and touching way, it shows how people can work on one another. Charley may be depressed because of a chemical imbalance, or he may be stuck because his life offers him no opening for heroism. Arlene keeps herself entertained by surprising herself with her oddities; she handles financial emergencies by observing with detachment that sooner or later they will probably have to deal with them. Bo keeps busy writing letters to food corporations, complaining about insect parts found in their products, and composing personal questions for the "Ask Beth" newspaper column. William Gibbs starts to paint, and completes a watercolor, three feet high by forty-one long, showing the earth meeting the sky.

It is not clear if William has joined them to heal, to escape, or to die. But his presence in the family, which is accepted without comment, budges the emotional ground under Charley just enough so that he slides toward the edge of his depression. Perhaps it is William's undemonstrative love for Arlene, never acted on, that reawakens Charley's desire for this magnificent beast, his wife.

Campbell Scott is an actor, and as a director he is able to trust his actors entirely. If they are doing their jobs, we will watch, no matter if the story centers on a man sitting at a table and everyone else essentially waiting for him to get up. The life force bubbling inside young Bo, suggested by Valentina de Angelis in a performance of unstudied grace, lets us know things will change, if only because she continues to push at life. *Off the Map* is visually beautiful, as a portrait of lives in the middle of emptiness, but it's not about the New Mexico scenery. It's about feelings that shift among people who are good enough, curious enough, or just maybe tired enough to let that happen.

Variety, the show-biz bible, always assesses a movie's commercial prospects in its reviews. Its chief critic, the dependable Todd McCarthy, loves this film, but does his duty to the biz by noting: "Pic's unmelodramatic nature and unmomentous subject matter will make this a tough sell even on the review-driven specialized circuit." True, and by now you have sensed whether you would like it or not. If you think you would not, be patient, for sooner or later you will find yourself compelled to get up from the table.

Oldboy ★ ★ ★ ★
R, 120 m., 2005

Min-sik Choi (Dae-su Oh), Ji-tae Yoo (Woo-jin Lee), Hye-jung Gang (Mido). Directed by Chan-wook Park and produced by Dong-joo Kim. Screenplay by Jo-yun Hwang, Joon-hyung Lim, and Park.

A man gets violently drunk and is chained to the wall in a police station. His friend comes and bails him out. While the friend is making a telephone call, the man disappears from an empty city street in the middle of the night. The man regains consciousness in what looks like a shabby hotel room. A bed, a desk, a TV, a bathroom cubicle. There is a steel door with a slot near the floor for his food tray. Occasionally a little tune plays, the room fills with gas, and when he regains consciousness the room has been cleaned, his clothes have been changed, and he has received a haircut.

This routine continues for fifteen years. He is never told who has imprisoned him, or why. He watches TV until it becomes his world. He fills one journal after another with his writings. He pounds the wall until his fists grow bloody, and then hardened. He screams. He learns from TV that his blood and fingerprints were found at the scene of his wife's murder. That his daughter has been adopted in Sweden. That if he were to escape, he would be a wanted man.

Oldboy, by the Korean director Chan-wook Park, watches him objectively, asking no sympathy, standing outside his plight. When, later, he does talk with the man who has imprisoned him, the man says: "I'm sort of a scholar, and what I study is you."

In its sexuality and violence, this is the kind of movie that can no longer easily be made in the United States; the standards of a puritanical minority, imposed on broadcasting and threatened even for cable, make studios unwilling to produce films that might face uncertain distribution. But content does not make a movie good or bad—it is merely what it is about. *Oldboy* is a powerful film not because of what it depicts, but because of the depths of the human heart it strips bare.

The man, named Dae-su Oh (Min-sik Choi), is a wretch when we first meet him, a drunk who has missed his little daughter's birthday and now sits forlornly in the police station, ridiculously wearing the angel's wings he bought her as a present. He is not a bad man, but alcohol has rendered him useless.

When he suddenly finds himself freed from his bizarre captivity fifteen years later, he is a different person, focused on revenge, ridiculously responsive to kindness. Wandering into a restaurant, he meets a young woman who, he knows from the TV, is Korea's "Chef of the Year." This is Mido (Hye-jung Gang). Sensing that he has suffered, feeling an instinctive sympathy, she takes him home with her, hears his story, cares for him, comes to love him. Meanwhile he sets out on a methodical search to find the secret of his captivity. He was fed pot stickers day after day, until their taste was burned into his memory, and he travels the city's restaurants

until he finds the one that supplied his meals. That is the key to tracking down his captors.

It is also, really, the beginning of the movie, the point at which it stops being a mystery and becomes a tragedy in the classical sense. I will not reveal the several secrets that lie ahead for Dae-su, except to say that they come not as shabby plot devices, but as one turn after another of the screws of mental and physical anguish and poetic justice. I can mention a virtuoso sequence in which Dae-su fights with several of his former jailers, his rage so great that he is scarcely slowed by the knife sticking in his back. This is a man consumed by the need for revenge, who eventually discovers he was imprisoned by another man whose need was no less consuming, and infinitely more diabolical.

I am not an expert on the Korean cinema, which is considered in critical circles as one of the most creative in the world (*Oldboy* won the Grand Jury Prize at Cannes 2004). I can say that of the Korean films I've seen, only one *(The YMCA Baseball Team)* did not contain extraordinary sadomasochism. *Oldboy* contains a tooth-pulling scene that makes Laurence Olivier's Nazi dentist in *Marathon Man* look like a healer. And there is a scene during which an octopus is definitely harmed during the making of the movie.

These scenes do not play for shock value, but are part of the whole. Dae-su has been locked up for fifteen years without once seeing another living person. For him the close presence of anyone is like a blow to all of his senses. When he says in a restaurant, "I want to eat something that is alive," we understand (a) that living seafood is indeed consumed as a delicacy in Asia, and (b) he wants to eat the life, not the food, because he has been buried in death for fifteen years.

Why would Mido, young, pretty, and talented, take this wretched man into her life? Perhaps because he is so manifestly helpless. Perhaps because she believes his story, and even the reason why he cannot reclaim his real name or identity. Perhaps because in fifteen years he has been transformed into a man she senses is strong and good, when he was once weak and despicable. From his point of view, love is joined with salvation, acceptance, forgiveness, and the possibility of redemption.

All of this is in place during the several scenes of revelation that follow, providing a context and giving them a deeper meaning. Yes, the ending is improbable in its complexity, but it is not impossible, and it is not unmotivated. *Oldboy* ventures to emotional extremes, but not without reason. We are so accustomed to "thrillers" that exist only as machines for creating diversion that it's a shock to find a movie in which the action, however violent, makes a statement and has a purpose.

Oliver Twist ★ ★ ★ ½
PG-13, 130 m., 2005

Ben Kingsley (Fagin), Barney Clark (Oliver Twist), Jamie Foreman (Bill Sykes), Harry Eden (Artful Dodger), Leanne Rowe (Nancy), Edward Hardwicke (Mr. Brownlow), Mark Strong (Toby Crackit), Liz Smith (Old Woman). Directed by Roman Polanski and produced by Robert Benmussa, Polanski, and Alain Sarde. Screenplay by Ronald Harwood, based on the novel by Charles Dickens.

Roman Polanski's *Oliver Twist* and his previous film, *The Pianist*, seem to be completely unlike, but I believe they have a deep emotional connection. *Oliver Twist* tells the story of an orphan in a dangerous city, whose survival sometimes depends upon those very people who would use him badly. *The Pianist* is about a Jew who hides himself in Warsaw during the Holocaust and at a crucial moment is spared by a German soldier. Both Oliver and the pianist do benefit from the kindness of strangers, but the intervention of their captors is crucial.

Oliver is about ten when he is taken into the world of Fagin and his young pickpockets, and Polanski was ten in 1943, when his parents were removed by the Nazis from the Krakow Ghetto and he was left on his own, moving from one temporary haven to another in the city and the countryside. In the black market economy of wartime Poland, he would have met or seen people like Fagin, Bill Sykes, Nancy, and the Artful Dodger, resorting to thievery and prostitution to survive. In that sense, *Oliver Twist* more directly reflects his own experience than *The Pianist*.

Now rotate the story another turn, and we find that Charles Dickens himself spent a similar childhood. With his father in debtor's prison, he was sent at twelve to work in a bootblacking factory not unlike the workhouse where Oliver briefly lands; he asks in his memoirs "how I could have been so easily cast away at such an age." That Oliver, Dickens, and Polanski all survived to find prosperity and success could not erase the early pain, and in *Oliver Twist* Polanski approaches the material not as another one of those EngLit adaptations but with a painful and particular focus.

The story, like many of Dickens's stories, centers on a young person who is thrown into a stormy sea of vividly seen adult characters and who is often entirely in the dark about his own history and prospects. David Copperfield asks at the beginning of his story "whether I shall turn out to be the hero of my own life, or whether that station will be held by anybody else." He is writing, of course, after its events have all taken place, and he still does not know the answer.

Because the adult characters possess the power and make the decisions, it's particularly interesting to see what Polanski does with the key character in *Oliver Twist*, who is Fagin (Ben Kingsley), the grotesque old man who rules a household of pickpockets. Fagin is a Jew in the Dickens novel, an anti-Semitic caricature (although to be sure the Christians in the novel are also named by religion and are seen for the most part as hypocrites, sadists, and fools). Polanski's version never identifies Fagin as Jewish and does not depict him as the usual evil exploiter of young boys. Exploiter, yes, but evil, no: It is likely, as Fagin observes, that he has saved his charges from far worse fates awaiting them in the cruel streets of London and taught them the skills and cunning to survive.

That is why the next-to-final scene of the movie is so intriguing. Oliver has been rescued by his benefactor, the kind bookseller Mr. Brownlow (Edward Hardwicke), and has become a young gentleman. Fagin has been condemned to death. Oliver asks to see Fagin, and Brownlow takes him to the old man's cell, where they find a pathetic, self-pitying ruin. In the novel, Oliver asks Fagin to pray with him and says, "Oh! God forgive this wretched man!" In the movie, he says that, and something more: "You were kind to me."

For so Fagin was, after his fashion. It was Bill Sykes, the cruelest of all Dickens's villains, who meant him harm. In a movie that is generally faithful to Dickens, despite some smoothing out of the labyrinthine plot, Polanski's key change is to observe that Fagin does not simply exploit the boys; the old man and his pickpockets are struggling together to survive, according to the hard law that society has taught Fagin and he is teaching the boys. Fagin in his way is kinder than the workhouses and the courts of respectable society. The line "You were kind to me" is not a sentimental addition intended to soften the ending, but proceeds, I believe, directly from Polanski's heart and is a clue to why he wanted to make the movie. He must have met a Fagin or two, who were not good people yet not as bad as they might have been.

In Dickens there is always the contrast between horror and comedy; his biographer Peter Ackroyd observes that the novelist sometimes referred to his plots as "streaked bacon," made of fat, meat, and gristle. There is the sunny benevolence of Mr. Brownlow, who trusts the accused pickpocket with money and books. The pure goodness of the old country woman (Liz Smith), who pities and dotes on the child. The heroism of Nancy (Leanne Rowe), who risks her own life to save Oliver's. And even the mixed feelings of the Dodger (Harry Eden), who betrays Nancy to Bill and then has second thoughts and regrets.

True evil in the film is seen in Bill Sykes, who comes to such a ghoulish and appropriate end, and in the society that surrounds and permits all of the characters. Dickens grew up in a world of workhouses for children, child prostitution, "charity" institutions run with cruelty and greed, schools that taught nothing and were run for profit, and people who preyed on children, starved and mistreated them, and praised themselves for their benevolence. Those who haven't read Dickens since school, or never, may confuse him with the kindly storyteller of popular image; his works are filled with such fury that he must create a Mr. Brownlow from time to time simply to return calm to the story.

Polanski's film is visually exact and detailed without being too picturesque. This is not Ye Olde London, but Ye Harrowing London, teeming with life and dispute. The performances are more vivid and edgy than we might suspect; Kingsley's Fagin is infinitely more complex than in the usual versions. Jamie Foreman's Bill Sykes has a piggish, merciless self-regard. Rowe, as Nancy, becomes not a device of the plot but a resourceful young woman whose devotion to Bill is outlasted by her essential goodness. And Barney Clark, who was eleven when the film was made, is the right Oliver, a child more acted against than acting. *Oliver Twist* was Dickens's first proper novel, after the episodic *Pickwick Papers*. In it he found his voice by listening to the memories of the child he had been. Polanski, I think, is listening to such memories as well.

The Omen ★ ★ ★
R, 110 m., 2006

Julia Stiles (Katherine Thorn), Liev Schreiber (Robert Thorn), Mia Farrow (Mrs. Baylock), David Thewlis (Jennings), Pete Postlethwaite (Father Brennan), Michael Gambon (Bugenhagen), Seamus Davey-Fitzpatrick (Damien). Directed by John Moore and produced by Moore and Glenn Williamson. Screenplay by David Seltzer.

The Omen is a faithful remake of the 1976 film, and that's a relief; it depends on characters and situations and doesn't go berserk with visuals. In an age of effects run wild, what would a "contemporary" remake look like? No doubt lightning would zap from little Damien's ears, and his mother would not merely topple from a balcony but spin down to the bowels of the earth.

The story outline is as before: Worried astrotheologians in Vatican City ponder the meaning of comets in the heavens and upheavals on Earth, and an American diplomat and his wife have a baby boy in a Rome hospital. The husband is told the child has died, and he is urged by a sinister doctor to substitute a baby born the same day to an unwed mother. He agrees, keeps this a secret from his wife, and together they raise Damien, of whom it can be said that if he were made of snips and snails and puppy-dog tails, it would be an improvement.

The parents are Robert and Katherine Thorn (Liev Schreiber and Julia Stiles). After his boss's tragic death, the way becomes clear for Robert to become the American ambassador to Great Britain. Since he is the president's godson, it is all too clear that Damien's path ahead is preordained: He could become president and hasten Armageddon. I suppose there also will be remakes of *Damien: Omen II* (1978) and *Omen III:*

The Final Conflict (1981), although after *The Final Conflict, Omen IV: The Awakening* (1991) did not seem urgently required.

The most shocking scene in the 1976 movie was set at Damien's garden party, when his nanny cried out to him from the roof of the ambassador's mansion, jumped off with a rope around her neck, and hanged herself. When the replacement nanny turns up, a chuckle runs through the audience: She is Mrs. Baylock, played by Mia Farrow, who as Rosemary also had a baby not destined to become a Gerber model.

Enough of the plot. Let us consider instead the genre of theological sensationalism. I've observed before that when it comes to dealing with demons and suchlike, Roman Catholics have the market cornered. Preachers of other faiths can foam and foment all they want about Satanic cults, but when it comes to knowing the ground rules and reading ominous signs, what you want at the bedside is a priest who knows his way around an exorcism.

The Omen begins in the Vatican observatory, where the heavens are seen to fulfill prophecy by placing a star above Rome on the night of Damien's birth, just as there was a star above Bethlehem when Jesus was born. That the Antichrist gets his own star makes you wonder who's running the heavens, but never mind. The pope is informed, and his advisers add up the signs: The Jews have returned to the land of Zion, there are tumults of the earth and sea, and in a parallel I think needs a lot of looking into, the common market is an ominous portent. The film opens with a montage of such preapocalyptic events as the collapsing World Trade Center, Hurricane Katrina, and the 2004 tsunami; perhaps the haste with which *The Omen* incorporates real-life tragedy into a horror movie is also a sign that the end is near.

Father Brennan (Pete Postlethwaite) is the point man for the Catholics, breathlessly bursting into Robert's office to warn him, "The child must die!" What child? "Your son, Mr. Thorn! The son of the devil!" Father Brennan must have skipped class at the seminary during the sessions on pastoral counseling techniques. He does not make an impressive appearance, looking less like a messenger of truth and more like he has a problem with the sacramental wine.

Other events conspire to convince Robert that Damien is a peculiar child, something his wife has suspected from the first, and especially after the kid uses his scooter to knock her off a balcony and smiles as she falls to the marble floor far below. There is also the matter of the paparazzo (David Thewlis) whose photographs turn up so many hidden images we could possibly reconstruct *Blow-Up* from them.

The two men visit a remote monastery that can be reached only by rowboat (here, with the lonely lake covered in mist, we are getting some visual effects, but lovely ones). There they meet an old priest so close to death that the Grim Reaper would be livelier, and the trail leads on to a demonologist (Michael Gambon, in full wretched decadence mode). Before long they're opening graves and making you wonder what the standards are for coroners in the area.

All of this is done with mood and style by director John Moore (*Behind Enemy Lines*), who knows that the story itself is engrossing enough that we don't need X-Men stuff in the visuals. Schreiber is, I think, a good choice for Ambassador Thorn; he is readier to fear the worst than Gregory Peck, who played the role in 1976. Farrow is never creepier than when she's at her most sweetly reassuring. Stiles has a difficult role; how can a mother want her own child dead, even if he is the Antichrist? I guess that's a question that answers itself.

The British character actors (Thewlis, Gambon, Postlethwaite) bring so much creepy atmosphere onto the screen that they could have walked right over from the matinee performance of *Nosferatu*. It was George Orwell who said, "At fifty, everyone has the face he deserves." We can only marvel at what they must have done to deserve theirs. ☞

On a Clear Day ★ ★
PG-13, 99 m., 2006

Peter Mullan (Frank Redmond), Brenda Blethyn (Joan Redmond), Jamie Sives (Rob), Billy Boyd (Danny Campbell), Sean McGinley (Eddie Fraser), Ron Cook (Norman), Jodhi May (Angela), Benedict Wong (Chan). Directed by Gaby Dellal and produced by Sarah Curtis and Dorothy Berwin. Screenplay by Alex Rose.

Do you know who Peter Mullan is? A lot of people don't, but since 1990 he has moved quietly but firmly into the first rank of British film actors. A Scot, he had small roles in pictures such as *Riff-Raff, Shallow Grave, Braveheart,* and *Trainspotting,* and then in 1998 he starred in Ken Loach's *My Name Is Joe,* playing a recovering alcoholic just at that stage when he begins to believe that he might be able to trust himself. The performance came out of nowhere to win the Best Actor award at Cannes.

Since then, one powerful performance after another. In Mike Figgis's *Miss Julie* (1999), he was the servant who has an affair with a countess in a film based on the Strindberg play. In Michael Winterbottom's *The Claim,* a Thomas Hardy story moved to the Sierra Nevada, he runs a frontier town with an iron hand. He directed *The Magdalene Sisters* (2002), an angry exposé of the practice in Ireland of condemning sexually curious girls to a lifetime of unpaid servitude in church laundries. In *Young Adam* (2003), he was the barge captain whose wife is stolen away by a young man they hire as crew.

I mention these titles to call attention to an extraordinary talent, and as a way of backing into my review of *On a Clear Day,* which is a conventional film for an unconventional actor. When you start out working with Ken Loach, Danny Boyle, and Michael Winterbottom, it shows recognition of sorts, I suppose, but not necessarily progress to qualify as the lead in a Baked Potato People movie (see note). Mullan is at about the same stage in his career as Al Pacino was when he made *Bobby Deerfield.* Actors sometimes make the mistake of thinking that because they can play anyone, they should.

Mullan plays Frank Redmond, who has just been laid off his job after half a lifetime spent working as a shipbuilder in Glasgow. He is a man with inner torments (he blames himself for the drowning of a small son), and with time on his hands he sinks into depression and is hospitalized with a panic attack. Not to fear: The movie offers those varieties of depression and panic that function not as real problems but as plot conveniences, setting the other characters astir.

His wife, Joan (Brenda Blethyn), decides the time has come at last to take the test and become a bus driver. His other buddies turn into natural-born male bonders and turn up as a kind of chorus, led in wisdom by Chan (Benedict Wong), owner of the local takeaway shop, who advises them, "A gem cannot be polished without friction, or a man perfected without trials." Or

maybe that's just in one of his fortune cookies. No matter; Frank's crisis has served to budge them all out of their ruts, and his friends listen to Chan's proverb, confess they didn't know he spoke English, and enlist him on the buddy team.

Frank starts to swim. One day, impulsively, he swims the Clyde. Eventually a plan takes shape: He will swim the English Channel. This will budge him out of depression, and he can prove to himself that he is still to be reckoned with, despite his unemployment. Joan meanwhile is afraid to tell him of her bus-driving plans.

The movie leads up, as it must, to his Channel swim. Whether Frank succeeds I will leave for you to discover. It's a safe bet this is not the kind of movie where he is going to drown. But nothing in *On a Clear Day* is especially compelling. The movie doesn't dig deep enough. And after the Channel attempt—what then? Attempt to better his record? Get a job at the takeaway? Joan, the wife, seems altogether more sensible and goal-oriented, and although we are happy for Frank as he attempts to realize his dream, we are not so happy that we make offerings to the gods of cinema for allowing us to see this movie. I would, however, be prepared to sacrifice this movie as an offering toward Peter Mullan's future career.

Note: Baked Potato People movies are named in honor of my friend Billy "Silver Dollar" Baxter, who liked to announce: "I've been tubbed, I've been rubbed, I've been scrubbed. I'm huggable, lovable, and eatable." He said he found those words on a little paper flag stuck into a baked potato.

Ong-Bak: The Thai Warrior ★ ★ ★
R, 107 m., 2005

Tony Jaa (Ting), Petchthai Wongkamlao (George), Pumwaree Yodkamol (Muay Lek), Rungrawee Borrijindakul (Ngek), Chetwut Wacharakun (Peng), Sukhaaw Phongwilai (Khom Tuan). Directed by Prachya Pinkaew and produced by Pinkaew and Sukanya Vongsthapat. Screenplay by Suphachai Sithiamphan.

"No stunt doubles.
"No computer graphics.
"No strings attached."
These nine words represent the most aston-

ishing element of *Ong-Bak: The Thai Warrior*, the first Thai film to break through in the martial arts market. Having seen documentaries showing how stunt men are "flown" from wires that are eliminated in postproduction, having seen entire action sequences made on computers, I sat through the movie impressed at how real the action sequences seemed. Then I went to the Web site and discovered that they *were* real.

Yes, they do a lot with camera angles and editing tricks. With the right lens and angle and slow-motion you can make it look like an actor is defying gravity, when in fact he is simply making a big jump from a trampoline. But some of the shots cannot easily be faked.

In *Red Trousers* (2004), a documentary about Hong Kong stuntmen, we find that they perform a lot of falls simply by—falling. *Ong-Bak* opens with a tree-climbing contest in which the competitors try to capture a red flag at the top of a tree, while kicking and shoving their opponents off the limbs. Say all you want about wide-angle lenses that exaggerate distance, but we see the tree in an undistorted shot that establishes its height, and these guys are falling a long way and they are landing hard.

The movie stars Tony Jaa, a young actor who is already an accomplished stuntman and expert in Muay Thai boxing, a sentence I have typed just as if I had the slightest idea what Muay Thai boxing is. Thank you, Web site. Jaa, who plays the hero, Ting, is an acrobat and stuntman in the league of Jackie Chan or Buster Keaton, and there's an early chase through city streets where he does things just for the hell of it, like jumping through a large coil of barbed wire, jumping over two intersecting bicycles, and sliding under a moving truck.

This chase, and the tree-climbing scene, set the pace for the movie. It is 107 minutes long, and approximately seven minutes are devoted to the plot, which involves the theft of an ancient Buddhist statue from the hero's village. He has been trained by Buddhist monks and will not fight for reasons of vengeance, money, or personal gain, but he agrees to go to Bangkok and retrieve the sacred statue, and for a monk with a vow of pacifism he certainly relaxes his rule against fighting. One bloody sequence has him taking on three opponents in an illegal boxing club where enormous sums are wagered by Khom Tuan (Sukhaaw Phongwilai), the local crime lord.

I arrived at the movie prepared to take notes on my beloved Levenger Pocket Briefcase, which I lost at Sundance and then miraculously had restored to me. But I found when the movie was over that I had written down its title, and nothing else. That's because there's really nothing to be done with this movie except watch it. My notes, had I taken them, would have read something like this:

"Falls from tall tree.

"Chase through streets.

"Runs on tops of heads of people.

"Runs across the tops of market stalls, cars, and buses.

"Barbed wire!

"Fruit Cart Scene!!! Persimmons everywhere!

"Illegal boxing club. Breakaway chairs and tables pounded over heads.

"Chase scene with three-wheeled scooter-taxis, dozens of them.

"Ting catches fire, attacks opponents with blazing legs."

And so on, and on. The movie is based on the assumption, common to almost all martial arts movies, that the world of the hero has been choreographed and cast to supply him with one prop, location, and set of opponents after another. Ting needs a couple dozen three-wheelers for a chase scene? They materialize, and all other forms of transportation disappear. He fights twenty opponents at once? Good, but no one is ever able to whack him from behind; they obediently attack him one at a time, and are smashed into defeat.

The plot includes a pretty girl (Pumwaree Yodkamol), who I think is the girlfriend of George (Petchthai Wongkamlao), a friend of Ting's from the village who has become corrupted by Bangkok and betrays him. I was paying pretty close attention, I think, but I can't remember for sure if Ting and the girl ever get anything going, maybe because any romance at all would drag the action to a halt for gooey dialogue. I think they look at each other like they'll get together after the movie.

Did I enjoy *Ong-Bak*? As brainless but skillful action choreography, yes. And I would have enjoyed it even more if I'd known going in that the stunts were being performed in the old-fashioned, precomputer way. *Ong-Bak* even uses that old Bruce Lee strategy of repeating shots of each stunt from two or three angles, which wreaks havoc with the theory that time flows ceaselessly from the past into the future, but sure does give us a good look when he clears the barbed wire.

Open Water ★ ★ ★ ½
R, 79 m., 2004

Blanchard Ryan (Susan), Daniel Travis (Daniel), Saul Stein (Seth), Estelle Lau (Estelle), Michael E. Willimson (Davis), Jon Charles (Junior), Christina Zenarro (Linda). Directed by Chris Kentis and produced by Laura Lau. Screenplay by Kentis.

Rarely, but sometimes, a movie can have an actual physical effect on you. It gets under your defenses and sidesteps the "it's only a movie" reflex and creates a visceral feeling that might as well be real. *Open Water* had that effect on me. So did *Touching the Void,* the mountain-climbing movie. After both movies were over, I felt the need to go outside and walk in the sunshine and try to cheer myself up.

That's not to say *Open Water* is a thriller that churned my emotions. It's a quiet film, really, in which less and less happens as a large, implacable reality begins to form. The ending is so low-key we almost miss it. It tells the story of a couple who go scuba diving and surface to discover that a curious thing has happened: The boat has left without them. The horizon is empty in all directions. They feel very alone.

Touching the Void affected me because I'm not fond of heights and cannot imagine hanging from a mountainside. *Open Water* reached me in a different way. I'm not afraid of water and don't spend much time thinking about sharks, but the prospect of being lost, of being forgotten about, awakens emotions from deep in childhood. To be left behind stirs such anger and hopelessness.

When night follows day, when thirst becomes unbearable, when jellyfish sting, when sharks make themselves known, when the boat *still* does not come back for them, their situation becomes a vast, dark, cosmic joke. It is one thing to be in danger of losing your life. It is another thing to have hours and hours to think about it, and to discuss how casually the Caribbean vacation was settled on, instead of a ski holiday. The angriest line in the whole movie may be: "We

paid to do this." They went to a good deal of trouble and expense in order to be abandoned at sea.

The movie stars Blanchard Ryan and Daniel Travis as Susan and Daniel. They come from a world of SUVs and cell phones and busy work schedules, and now their lives have been reduced to the fact that they are floating in the ocean. With their scuba outfits, they can float for a long time. Much longer, indeed, than will be of any interest to them.

The sea is calm. The water is cold but not cold enough to kill them. The opening scenes explain, with implacable logic, the series of events that leads to two scuba divers being counted twice, so that the boat returns to port with eighteen divers, although it left with twenty. If this seems like inexcusable carelessness, well, we can kind of understand how it happened. And the movie is based on a true story of two divers left behind.

The movie, written, directed, and edited by Chris Kentis, tells its story with a direct simplicity that is more harrowing than any fancy stuff could possibly be. The movie was filmed with digital video cameras, but of course it was; what would a 35mm camera be doing out there? And they are out there; the actors were in deep water, I learn, with real sharks.

For most of an hour we are essentially watching Susan and Daniel float, and talk, and think. Their dialogue is believable: no poetry, no philosophy, no histrionics, just the way people talk when they know each other well and are trying to kid themselves that things are not as bad as they seem. How could they be *forgotten*? How could the crew not notice their gear on board, or their missing air tanks? Surely the boat will return. Certainly there will be a search.

They try to remember information from the Discovery Channel. Daniel knows it is fatal to drink seawater. (You can drink urine, but that's tricky when you're floating in a scuba suit.) Those are certainly shark fins cutting the surface of the sea. Most sharks won't bother you, but the word "most" is not anywhere near inclusive enough to reassure them. There is even a period when Susan discusses whether this might have all been Daniel's fault: He spent too much time on the bottom looking at that damned eel.

"Fault" is as meaningless as any other concept. Nothing they think or believe has any relevance to the reality they are in. Their opinions are not solicited. Their past is irrelevant. Their success, dreams, fears, loves, plans, and friends are all separated from them now by this new thing that has become their lives. To be still alive, but removed from everything they know about how and why to live, is peculiar: Their senses continue to record their existence, but nothing they can do has the slightest utility.

So you see I was not afraid as I watched the movie. I was not afraid of sharks, or drowning, or dehydration. I didn't feel any of the *Jaws* emotions. But when it began to grow dark, when a thunderstorm growled on the far horizon, a great emptiness settled down upon me. The movie is about what a slender thread supports our conviction that our lives have importance and make sense. We need that conviction in order to live at all, and when it is irreversibly taken away from us, what a terrible fate to be left alive to know it.

Osama ★ ★ ★ ½
PG-13, 82 m., 2004

Marina Golbahari (Osama), Arif Herati (Espandi), Zubaida Sahar (Mother), Khwaja Nader (Mullah), Hamida Refah (Grandmother). Directed by Siddiq Barmak and produced by Barmak, Julia Fraser, Julie LeBrocquy, and Makoto Ueda. Screenplay by Barmak.

The movies are a little more than a century old. Imagine if we could see films from previous centuries—records of slavery, the Great Fire of London, the Black Plague. *Osama* is like a film from some long-ago age. Although it takes place in Afghanistan, it documents practices so cruel that it is hard to believe such ideas have currency in the modern world. What it shows is that, under the iron hand of the Taliban, the excuse of "respect" for women is used to condemn them to a lifetime of inhuman physical and psychic torture. No society that loves and respects women could treat them in this way.

The heroine of the film, Osama (Marina Golbahari), is a preadolescent in a household without a man. Under the rules of the Taliban, women are not to leave the house without a male escort or take jobs, so Osama, her mother, and grandmother are condemned to cower in-

side and starve, unless friends or relatives bring food. They do not. Finally the grandmother suggests that Osama cut her hair and venture out to find work, pretending to be a boy.

This story is told against a larger context of institutional sadism against women. An opening scene shows women in blue burkhas holding a demonstration—they want the right to take jobs—and being attacked by soldiers who begin with water cannons and eventually start shooting at them. Obviously, Osama is risking her life to venture out into this world, and soon she's in trouble: She is snatched away from her job and sent to a school to indoctrinate young men in the ways of the Taliban.

Then it is only a matter of time until her real sex is discovered. The punishment handed down by a judge is revealing: This child becomes one of the many wives of a dirty old man, a mullah who keeps his young women as prisoners. At that, Osama gets off lightly; another woman in the film is buried up to her neck and stoned for . . . well, for behaving like a normal person in a civilized society.

The movie touches some of the same notes as *Baran* (2001), an Iranian movie about an unspoken love affair between a young Iranian worker and an Afghan immigrant who is a girl disguised as a boy. The film is not as tragic as *Osama*, in part because Iran is a country where enlightened and humanistic attitudes are fighting it out side-by-side with the old, hard ways. But in both cases Western audiences realize that to be a woman in such a society is to risk becoming a form of slave.

What is remarkable is the bravery with which filmmakers are telling this story in film after film. Consider Tahmineh Milani's *Two Women* (1999), which briefly landed her in jail under threat of death. Or Jafar Panahi's harrowing *The Circle* (2000), showing women without men trying to survive in present-day Tehran, where they cannot legally work or pause anywhere or be anywhere except inside and out of sight. The real weapons of mass destruction are . . . men.

Who will go to see *Osama*? I don't know. There is after all that new Adam Sandler movie, and it's a charmer. And *The Lost Skeleton of Cadavra* is opening, for fans of campy trash. I'm not putting them down. People work hard for their money, and if they want to be entertained, that's their right. But brave, dissenting Islamic filmmakers are risking their lives to tell the story of the persecution of women, and it is a story worth knowing, and mourning. In this country Janet Jackson bares a breast and causes a silly scandal. The Taliban would have stoned her to death. If you put these things into context, the Jackson case begins to look like an affirmation of Western civilization.

Oscar Nominated Shorts 2005
★ ★ ★ ★
NO MPAA RATING, 120 m., 2005

The 2005 short subject Oscar nominees. Animated: *Birthday Boy*, directed by Sejong Park; *Ryan*, directed by Chris Landreth; and *Gopher Broke* directed by Jeff Fowler. Live action: *Two Cars, One Night*, directed by Taika Waititi and Ainsley Gardiner; *7:35 in the Morning*, directed by Nacho Vigalondo; *Wasp*, directed by Andrea Arnold; and *Little Terrorist*, directed by Ashvin Kumar.

Seven of 2005's Oscar-nominated short subjects and the 2004 Oscar-winning student animated film have been gathered into a two-hour package going into release around the country. Every year readers ask me where and how they can see the shorts nominated for Oscars, and every year until now I've had to reply that, well, they can't. The distribution of short subjects is a notoriously difficult challenge, but a package like this, timed for release at Oscar time, is the perfect solution.

Only one of the animated films and none of the live-action shorts are by American directors. The finalists come from Australia, Canada, New Zealand, Spain, India, and Britain. (The student Oscar winner saves the day; it's from filmmakers at the New York University film school.)

Also a trend: One of the animated nominees and three of the four live-action films are about children who are neglected or in danger.

And the nominees are:

Live Action Short Subjects
—*Wasp*, from the United Kingdom, directed by Andrea Arnold, is a heartbreaking and angering twenty-three-minute drama about a single mother and her four children, one a baby. She fears having the children taken away from her, and with good reason: During a long day

and night, she chats up a former boyfriend, claims she is only baby-sitting the children, takes them home, and finds only white sugar from a bag to feed them. Then she brings them along to the pub where she's meeting the boyfriend, parking them outside and rushing out to give them potato chips and a Coke, "to share around." Hour follows hour as she plays pool and is sweet-talked by her date, while the kids wait outside, sad and hungry. The film is notable above all for not underlining its points, but simply making them: This woman should not be a mother, and these children should not have these lives. The movie won the 2005 Oscar.

—*7:35 in the Morning*, from Spain, directed by Nacho Vigalondo, is an odd and haunting eight-minute film that begins with a woman entering a café and sitting down with coffee and a pastry. She notices two musicians standing by the back wall. "What's with that?" she asks the owner, who does not answer. The customers all seem stiff, frightened, uncertain. A man appears and begins to sing a song about the woman, her coffee and pastry, and his thoughts about her. The customers and employees have already been rehearsed, and sing parts of the song from lyrics cupped in their hands. Then there is a scene where, frightened and awkward, they dance. The reason for their behavior eventually becomes clear, and terrifying.

—*Little Terrorist*, from India, directed by Ashvin Kumar, takes place along the border between India and Pakistan. A young boy crawls beneath a barbed-wire fence and enters a minefield in order to retrieve a cricket ball. Guards, who cannot see how young he is, fire warning shots and he runs in fear—to the other side of the field. Now he is in another country. A village schoolmaster and his wife give him shelter and a quick alibi during a house-to-house search, but now he must get back home. In fifteen minutes, the film builds genuine and poignant drama.

—*Two Cars, One Night*, from New Zealand, directed by Taika Waititi and Ainsley Gardiner, begins with two cars parked in the lot of a hotel with a bar and restaurant. There are two boys, one nine, one younger, in one car, and a twelve-year-old girl in the other. The adults who brought them are in the bar for the evening. The kids make faces and then they make friends, sharing without even mentioning it the loneliness of sitting in the cars at night and waiting for who knows how long.

Animated Short Subjects

—*Ryan*, from Canada, the 2005 Oscar winner by Chris Landreth, is an animated fourteen-minute documentary that cuts deeply into the truth of a human life. The subject is Ryan Larkin, who circa 1970 made animated films considered among the best and most influential in Canadian history, and then went astray into drug addiction and alcoholism. The film takes place largely in a vast room filled with long, empty tables, where Landreth talks with Larkin about his life; there are cutaways to important figures from his past.

The animation technique is dramatic, striking, and wholly original. Apparently beginning with live-action footage, Landreth converts the figures into grotesque cutaways of skull and sinew, eyes and hair, partial faces surrounded by emptiness or marred by bright visual scars representing angst. The effect is hard to describe, impossible to forget; the animation takes the documentary content to another emotional level.

—*Birthday Boy*, from Australia, by Sejong Park, is set in Korea in 1951 and shows a young boy all alone in a deserted wartime village. He plays, he wanders, he talks to himself, he sees tanks passing on rail cars, he sees planes flying overhead, he misses his mother. Like *Grave of the Fireflies*, it shows war providing a landscape in which childhood is exposed and vulnerable.

—*Gopher Broke*, from the USA, directed by Jeff Fowler, is in the tradition of Hollywood animated cartoons; it follows a gopher who digs a hole in a dirt road so that produce trucks will bounce fruit and vegetables into the road. All fine, except for the squirrels, crows, and other varmints who are faster than the gopher. Then there is a problem with a cow.

—*Rex Steele: Nazi Smasher*, is the bonus film, winner of the 2004 student animation Oscar. Directed by Alexander Woo, it's Indiana Jones crossed with Sky Captain, as a superhero enters a Nazi citadel atop a South American volcano and faces dire peril. High-spirited and kinetic.

Not included in the program, presumably because their makers chose not to participate, are the animated shorts *Guard Dog*, by Bill Plympton, and *Lorenzo*, by Mike Gabriel and

Baker Bloodworth of Disney, and the live-action short *Everything in This Country Must*, by Gary McKendry.

Oscar Nominated Shorts 2006

Every year readers ask where they can see the Oscar nominees in the short film categories. This year, there was an answer. The complete programs ran in Chicago, New York, Los Angeles, San Francisco, Detroit, Berkeley, Atlanta, Seattle, and Denver. I saw them all; here are capsule reviews:

Animated Shorts

—*The Moon and the Son: An Imagined Conversation*, from the USA, directed by John Canemaker and Peggy Stern. Re-creation of a painful relationship between a son and his angry father, who does prison time for arson. Photographs dissolve into animation that uses bold symbols and childlike drawings to create powerful emotions. The father and son (voiced by Eli Wallach and John Turturro) have an afterlife conversation where much is explained, nothing is resolved, and the pain continues: "I'm damned sure it's not the film you hoped for," the son says, "but it's the conversation we could never have."

—*9*, from the USA, directed by Shane Acker. In a futuristic world of ominous machinery and scraps of technology, humanoid creatures with camera lenses for eyes defend themselves against a fearsome mechanical ant. The sound track by David Steinwedel creates an atmosphere of creeping, crashing menace. The warfare is elaborated as a game of hide-and-seek, beautifully animated and intriguingly unwholesome.

—*Badgered*, from Great Britain, directed by Sharon Colman, is a fable involving a badger, two crows, and an underground missile silo. The badger's problems begin when he tries to silence the crows, scratches through the floor of his den, and lands on the control panel of the missile launcher.

—*One Man Band*, from the USA, directed by Andrew Jimenez and Mark Andrews, is from Pixar. In a town square in Europe, two one-man bands compete for the golden coin of a hard-to-please little girl. They one-up each other with virtuosity and amazing musical tricks, but it's a buyer's market. (This film played commercially before Pixar's *Cars*.)

—*The Mysterious Geographic Explorations of Jasper Morello,* from Australia, directed by Anthony Lucas. A short that plays like an epic collaboration between H. G. Wells and Tim Burton. An extraordinary airship voyage in the steam age, through storms and shipwreck to an uncharted land where strange blood-eating creatures seem to offer the cure for a plague. The animation style is haunting and evocative, and the narration establishes the mood of eerie unknown.

Documentary Shorts
—*The Death of Kevin Carter: Casualty of the Bang Bang Club,* directed by Dan Krauss. The Bang Bang Club comprised the white South African photographers who covered the violence of apartheid. Kevin Carter won the 1994 Pulitzer Prize for a famous picture of a starving girl in the Sudan being tracked by a vulture. He was criticized for not helping the girl. Carter increased his drug use, lost eighteen crucial rolls of film, sank into depression, and killed himself. A friend regrets that he didn't live to see the new South Africa; his daughter wonders if he died at the right time; the subtext is that drug addiction was the real problem.

—*God Sleeps in Rwanda,* by Kimberlee Acquaro and Stacy Sherman. The 1994 massacre of a million Tutsi by the Hutu tribe left the country 70 percent female. We follow the lives of five women in the next decade. They tell of being raped and tortured; some become pregnant, many die of AIDS (drugs for the disease cost as much as a typical salary). A former Hutu government minister is charged, and the trial is the first to define rape as a war crime. One survivor studies law, another works as a tailor; the female majority is both a burden and an opportunity, as the nightmare of genocide still haunts the land.

—*The Mushroom Club,* directed by Steven Okazaki. In Hiroshima sixty years after the bomb, some remember, some forget. Vandals set fire to paper cranes children have left at the war memorial. Loud-speaker trucks prowl the streets, chanting militaristic slogans. Jet Skis and rock music mar the quiet of the Peace Park. We meet bomb survivor Keiji Nakazawa, whose anime film *Barefoot Gen* remembers the attack. And an old woman who was fifteen when the bomb fell and needed twenty-seven operations to repair her face and her fused fingers. Another old woman combs the river banks for bits of fused steel and glass. And we meet a woman whose parents were told it was their fault, and not the radiation, that caused their child to be born disabled. An annual ceremony remembers the tragedy, but many young people seem to have forgotten.

—*A Note of Triumph: The Golden Age of Norman Corwin,* by Corinne Marrinan and Eric Simonson. Corwin, who still teaches at USC, was the producer of *On a Note of Triumph,* a historic 1945 radio broadcast on V-E Day. He appears along with others who remember the broadcast: Walter Cronkite, Robert Altman, Norman Lear, Studs Terkel. The night of the broadcast, "there was hope for the world," Terkel says. "I can still recite most of it," Altman says. Corwin was a poet who used radio as his medium. He recalls early days as a newspaperman, and how he created experimental radio simply because he didn't know what couldn't be done. The film stands as a rebuke to modern formula broadcasting.

Live-action Shorts
—*Our Time Is Up,* from the USA, by Rob Pearlstein and Pia Clemente. Kevin Pollack stars as a cold, detached psychiatrist who listens impassively as his clients complain of obsessive fondling, fear of the dark, fear of germs, bad relationships, and fear of turtles. Developments in his life inspire him to begin telling them the truth. They improve and are grateful. A simplistic fable, competently made but hardly of Oscar caliber.

—*The Last Farm,* from Iceland, directed by Runar Runarsson and Thor S. Sigurjonsson. Spare, deeply moving: An old farmer and his wife are scheduled to enter a retirement home. It is their last few days on the farm. Using his skill as a farmer and ingenuity in his use of materials, he carries out one final task. The bleak photography complements the impassive performance by Jon Sigurbjornsson as the farmer.

—*Cashback,* from Great Britain, directed by Sean Ellis and Lene Bausager. Sean Bigerstaff plays an art student who works overnight at a supermarket. Time passes exceedingly slowly, and his boss is an oaf. Fellow employees hold scooter races and play dodgeball with milk cartons. He imagines he can freeze time, move unobserved among the staff and customers, and undress the women to sketch them for his art classes. Workday comedy edges into imagination and eroticism.

—*The Runaway (Ausreisser)*, from Germany, directed by Ulrike Grote. Walter (Peter Jordan) is an architect confronted by a small boy (Maximilian Werner) who wants to be taken to school. He has no idea who the boy is, but the boy follows him and calls him "Father," and it develops that he may be Walter's child by a former girlfriend. Walter tries to shake the kid but can't. Where is the boy's mother? Takes an unexpected turn that may please some but left me underwhelmed.

—*Six Shooter*, from Ireland, directed by Martin Mcdonagh. Brendan Gleeson is touching as a man whose wife dies in a hospital. On the train ride home across Ireland, he sits across from an obnoxious young man of heartless cruelty who learns that the couple across the aisle have lost their baby. The kid is loud, obscene, and cruel; how long can the others put up with him? The film ends in macabre developments, but what is remembered is Gleeson's quiet suffering and the boy's extraordinary inhumanity.

Overlord ★ ★ ★ ★
No MPAA RATING, 88 m., 1975 (rereleased 2006)

Brian Stirner (Tom), Davyd Harries (Jack), Nicholas Ball (Arthur), Julie Neesam (The Girl), Sam Sewell (Trained Soldier), John Franklyn-Robbins (Dad), Stella Tanner (Mum). Directed by Stuart Cooper and produced by James Quinn. Screenplay by Christopher Hudson and Cooper.

I wrote from the 2004 Telluride Film Festival:

"The most remarkable discovery at this year's Telluride is *Overlord*, an elegiac 1975 film that follows the journey of one young British soldier to the beaches of Normandy. The film, directed by Stuart Cooper, won the Silver Bear at Berlin—but sank quickly from view after a limited release and was all but forgotten until this Telluride revival.

"Unlike *Saving Private Ryan* and other dramatizations based on D-day, *Overlord* is an intimate film, one that focuses closely on Tom Beddoes (Brian Stirner), who enters the British army, goes through basic training, and is one of the first ashore on D-day. Beddoes is not a macho hero but a quiet, nice boy, who worries about his cocker spaniel and takes along *David Copperfield* when he goes off to war.

"The movie tells his story through a remarkable combination of new and archival footage. It was produced by the Imperial War Museum in London, where Cooper spent three years looking at documentary and newsreel footage from World War II. About 27 percent of the film is archival, and awesomely real—for example, a scene where soldiers and their landing boat are thrown against rocks by furious waves.

"There are sights I had never seen before, including monstrous mechanical wheels that propel themselves across the beach to explode land mines and flatten barbed wire. One of these machines is driven by a ring of rockets around its rim, and as it rolls forward, belching fire and smoke, it looks like a creature of hell.

Overlord, whose title comes from the code word for one of the invasion plans, uses archival footage to show the devastation of bombing raids, from above and below. Cooper's cinematographer, the Kubrick favorite John Alcott, used lenses and film stock that matched the texture of this footage, so the black-and-white film seems all of a piece. Tom's story is not extraordinary; he says goodbye to his parents, survives some hazing during basic training, makes a few close friends, and becomes convinced he will die in the landing. This prospect does not terrify him, and he writes a letter to his parents, consoling them in advance.

"He meets a local girl (Julie Neesam) at a dance, in a club filled with soldiers on leave. All of the clichés of such scenes are abandoned. She is a nice girl, he is a nice boy, they are kind to each other, tender and polite, and agree to meet again on Monday. But on Monday he is part of the early stages of the invasion, which seems, he writes his parents, like an entity that is growing to unimaginable proportions while he becomes a smaller and smaller speck of it. He has a fantasy in which he meets the girl again; to describe it would reveal too much about this film, which is a rare rediscovery."

I reprint this earlier report because I'm writing this from Cannes and was not able to see the film again before deadline. *Overlord* remains firmly and clearly in my memory as a different kind of war film, one that sees through the eyes of one soldier and follows his story not through exciting adventures but through the routine steps designed to deliver an efficient and useful warrior to a place where he is needed.

The poignancy in the film comes because he knows, and his parents know, and the girl he meets knows, that his future is on hold. He may return home, he may have a future with the girl, and then again, maybe not, and this is the reality they all acknowledge in one sense or another.

The movie has been restored in a new 35mm print and combines its newsreel and fictional footage so effectively that it has a greater impact than all fiction, or all documentary, could have achieved. I still remember the rocket-driven mechanical wheel I wrote about from Telluride. I do not recall ever having seen such a machine depicted in a movie; that it is real is awesome. ☞

Overnight ★ ★ ★

R, 82 m., 2004

Featuring Troy Duffy, Willem Dafoe, Billy Connolly, and Jeffrey Baxter. A documentary directed by Tony Montana and Mark Brian Smith and produced by Montana.

Overnight tells a riches-to-rags story, like Project Greenlight played in reverse. Greenlight, you will recall, is the Miramax contest to choose and produce one screenplay every year by a hopeful first-time filmmaker. In *Overnight,* the director starts out with a contract and money from Miramax, and works his way back to no contract, no film, and no money. Call it Project Red Light.

The documentary tells the Hollywood story of a nine-day wonder named Troy Duffy. He was a bartender at a sports bar named J. Sloan's on Melrose, and had written a screenplay named *The Boondock Saints.* He, his brothers, and some friends had a rock band. In Los Angeles, every bartender under the age of seventy has a screenplay and is in a rock band, and they all want Harvey Weinstein of Miramax to read their script. After all, Harvey made Matt Damon and Ben Affleck stars by producing their screenplay of *Good Will Hunting.*

Troy Duffy hits the trifecta. Not only does Harvey buy his screenplay, but he signs Duffy to direct it, *and* the band gets a recording contract, *and* he agrees to buy the bar; they'll own it together. To celebrate his good fortune, Duffy asked two friends, Tony Montana and Mark Brian Smith, to make a documentary of his rise. It turned out to be about his fall.

I'd give anything to see footage of the early

meetings between Weinstein and Duffy. What magic did the bartender have to so bedazzle Harvey? By the opening scenes of *Overnight,* Duffy has sold a $300,000 script, has been given a $15 million budget, has signed with the William Morris Agency, and brags, "I get drunk at night, wake up the next morning hungover, go into those meetings in my overalls, and they're all wearing suits." Being Hollywood agents, they are probably also more familiar with the danger signals of alcoholism than Duffy is.

One of the subtexts of the movie involves how people look at Troy Duffy. He is very full of himself. At one point he actually says that Harvey Weinstein would like to be him. He keeps all of the money, tells the guys in the band they will get paid later, later tells them they don't deserve a dime, and still later tells them, "You do deserve it, but you're not gonna get it."

He is deeply satisfied with himself: "We got a deep cesspool of creativity here," he says, and boasts, "This is the first time in history they've signed a band sight unseen." Also, he might have reflected, sound unheard. As he's acting out his ego trip, the camera shows the others in the room looking at him with what can only be described as extremely fed-up expressions. His family, we sense during one scene, has been listening to this blowhard for a lifetime, and although they are happy to share his success, they're sort of waiting to see how he screws up.

So are we. The movie is pieced together out of uneven footage, and the idea of a documentary seems to have occurred in the midst of filming; at one point, a Morris agent walks into the room, looks at the lens, and says, "Oh, you got a better camera!" There are unfortunately no scenes between Duffy and Weinstein; the initial infatuation happens before the film starts, and then Weinstein pulls out of the deal by putting *The Boondock Saints* into dreaded "turnaround." The recording contract is also canceled.

Eventually a Hollywood producer named Elie Samada, who has been behind some good films but is a controversial character, picks up *The Boondock Saints* for much less than the Miramax price, and Duffy is elated again. Having dissed Keanu Reeves, Ethan Hawke, and Jon Bon Jovi ("I didn't even know he was an actor"), he hires the excellent Willem Dafoe; we see one scene being filmed, in which characters a lot like

Duffy and his friends get drunk and go berserk. The finished movie is taken to the Cannes marketplace, where not one single offer is made to purchase it. *Saints* eventually plays for one week in five theaters. The sound track album sells less than 600 copies. Then a car jumps the curb and hits Duffy, who "flees his apartment and arms himself."

Ah, but there's a happy ending! *The Boondock Saints* becomes a cult favorite on DVD, and Duffy is currently directing *Boondock II: All Saint's Day*. Unfortunately, the Morris agency neglected to secure for him any portion of the DVD profits.

Over the Hedge ★ ★ ★
PG, 87 m., 2006

Voices of: Bruce Willis (RJ the Raccoon), Garry Shandling (Verne the Turtle), William Shatner (Ozzie the Possum), Steve Carell (Hammy the Squirrel), Wanda Sykes (Stella the Skunk), Nick Nolte (Vincent the Bear), Thomas Haden Church (Dwayne the Verminator), Allison Janney (Gladys), Avril Lavigne (Heather the Possum), Eugene Levy (Lou the Porcupine), Catherine O'Hara (Penny the Porcupine). Directed by Tim Johnson and Karey Kirkpatrick and produced by Bonnie Arnold. Screenplay by Len Blum, Lorne Cameron, David Hoselton, and Kirkpatrick.

Over the Hedge is one of the few comic strips in which you will find debates about the Theory of Relativity, population control, and global warming. None of those issues are much discussed in the new animated feature inspired by the strip, but there is a great deal about suburban sprawl, junk food, and the popularity of the SUV. ("How many people does it hold?" "Usually one.")

The movie opens with the coming of spring and the emergence from hibernation of many forest animals, including some that do not actually hibernate, but never mind. Vincent the bear (voice by Nick Nolte) awakens to find that his entire stash of stolen food has been—stolen! He apprehends the master thief RJ the raccoon (Bruce Willis) and gives him a deadline to return the food or else. RJ cleverly mobilizes the entire population of the forest to help him in this task (during which he does not quite explain the bear and the deadline). And together they confront an amazing development: During the winter, half of their forest has been replaced by a suburb, and they are separated from it by a gigantic hedge.

That's the setup for a feature cartoon that is not at the level of *Finding Nemo* or *Shrek*, but is a lot of fun, awfully nice to look at, and filled with energy and smiles. It's not a movie adults would probably want to attend on their own, but those taking the kids are likely to be amused, and the kids, I think, will like it just fine.

Once again we get an animal population where all the species work together instead of eating each other, and there is even the possibility of interspecies sex, when a human's housecat falls in love with Stella the skunk (Wanda Sykes). There is also the usual speciesism: Mammals and reptiles are first-class citizens, but when a dragonfly gets fried by an insect zapper, not a tear is shed.

These animals once ate leaves and roots and things, but all that has changed since Hammy the golfing squirrel (Steve Carell) discovered nacho chips. The animals find these so delicious they are the forest equivalent of manna, and RJ is happy to lead them to the promised land of nachos and other junk food in the garbage cans and kitchens of humans.

Like all humans who like to live with a view of beautiful forests, the humans in *Over the Hedge* are offended that they are occupied by animals. Gladys (Allison Janney), the head of the homeowners' association, is personally affronted that RJ and his cronies might violate her garbage can, and she brings in Dwayne (Thomas Haden Church), a pest control expert known ominously as the Verminator.

"I want them exterminated as inhumanely as possible," she tells him. She's all heart.

The encroachment of the animals and the efforts of the Verminator don't approach the wit and genius of a similar situation in the Oscar-winning *Wallace & Gromit: The Curse of the Were-Rabbit* (2005), but, then, how could they? This movie is pitched at a different level. But the action scenes are fun, the characters are well-drawn and -voiced, and I thought the film's visual look was sort of lovely. If the animals lack the lofty thinking of their originals on the comics page, they are nevertheless a notch or two above the IQ levels of many an animated creature. They have to be. It's a hard life for a forager these days, when you're caught between an angry bear on one side of the hedge and a street hockey game on the other.

529

P

The Pacifer ★ ★
PG, 90 m., 2005

Vin Diesel (Shane Wolfe), Lauren Graham (Claire Fletcher), Faith Ford (Julie Plummer), Carol Kane (Helga), Brad Garrett (Vice Principal Murney), Brittany Snow (Zoe Plummer), Max Thieriot (Seth Plummer), Morgan York (Lulu Plummer). Directed by Adam Shankman and produced by Gary Barber, Roger Birnbaum, and Jonathan Glickman. Screenplay by Thomas Lennon and Ben Garant.

In *The Pacifer*, Vin Diesel follows in the footsteps of those Arnold Schwarzenegger comedies where the muscular hero becomes a girly-man. Diesel doesn't go to the lengths of Schwarzenegger in *Junior*, where Arnold was actually pregnant, but he does become a baby-sitter, going where no Navy SEAL has gone before.

Diesel plays Shane Wolfe, hard-edged commando ("We are SEALs—and this is what we do"). In the pretitle sequence, he and three other scuba-diving SEALs shoot down a helicopter, wipe out four gunmen on jet skis, bomb a boat, and rescue Plummer, an American scientist kidnapped by Serbians. They want "Ghost," the scientist's foolproof encryption key. That the scientist uses the names of his children as the password for his locked briefcase suggests that the Serbians could have saved themselves a lot of trouble by just finding the geek who hacked Paris Hilton's cell phone and aiming him at Plummer's hard drive.

Anyway. One thing leads to another, and soon Wolfe has a new assignment, which is to baby-sit and protect Plummer's five children while his wife and a navy intelligence officer go to Geneva to open his safety deposit box. They're supposed to be gone only a couple of days, but one week follows another as they unsuccessfully try to, yes, guess the password.

From time to time the movie cuts to a Swiss bank, where two executives wait patiently while the wife and the navy guy try one word after another. That two Swiss bank officials are willing to sit in a room day after day and listen to people guessing a password is yet one more example of why the Swiss banking system has such an exemplary reputation.

That leaves Wolfe in charge of an unhappy teenage boy, a boyfriend-crazy teenage girl, and three noisy moppets. Because he is not good at names, he tags them the Red Team, and calls them "Red One," "Red Two," and so on. They do not much take to this, and make his life a living hell.

This premise is promising, but somehow the movie never really takes off. We know that Diesel will begin as gravel-voiced and growly, and that he'll soften up and get to love the kids. We know that in two weeks all of the kids' personal problems will be solved, their behavior will improve, and they'll start cleaning up around the house. We're not much surprised when the Plummer nanny, a curious creature created by Carol Kane with an impenetrable accent, stalks out. Using the Law of Economy of Characters, we know that any neighbors who seem unnecessary yet are given dialogue will be more than merely neighbors.

There's one subplot that seems to offer more opportunities for comedy than it does. Seth (Max Thieriot), the older Plummer boy, wants to be an actor, despite the kidding he gets at high school. He's appearing in a production of *The Sound of Music*, where, unfortunately, he keeps dropping members of the Trapp family. The play's director, who seems to have been imported from *Waiting for Guffman*, walks off the job, and Shane Wolfe takes over the direction. Uh-huh. And he has a tender heart-to-heart with the kid about following his dream and being an actor if that's what will make him happy.

Meanwhile, Wolfe is also supposed to be guarding the kids against, I dunno, more Serbian kidnappers, maybe, although North Koreans also come into the mix. He has an uncanny ability to follow events on supermarket security monitors, which are not usually positioned where customers can see them, and so protects the Plummer girls when their firefly Girls cookie stand is attacked by rival scouts. He is also challenged to a wrestling match with a coach who is more than strange (Brad Garrett), and deals with an anal-retentive school principal by showing that Navy SEALs have better split-second timing than clock-watching bureaucrats.

All very nice, sometimes we smile, but nothing compelling. The director is Adam

Shankman, whose previous film, *Bringing Down the House,* starred Queen Latifah as a convict who moves in on Steve Martin's middle-class life. Shankman begins with situations that should work, but he doesn't quite boost them over the top into laugh-out-loud. Maybe he's counting too much on the funny casting. Casting is funny only when the cast is given something funny to do, a truth that should be engraved above the portals of every film school.

Palindromes ★ ★ ★ ½
NO MPAA RATING, 100 m., 2005

Ellen Barkin (Joyce Victor), Stephen Adly Guirgis (Joe/Earl/Bob), Jennifer Jason Leigh (Aviva), Emani Sledge (Aviva), Will Denton (Aviva), Hannah Freiman (Aviva), Shayna Levine (Aviva), Valerie Shusterov (Aviva), Sharon Wilkins (Aviva), Rachel Corr (Aviva/Henrietta), Richard Masur (Steve Victor), Debra Monk (Mama Sunshine), Matthew Faber (Mark Wiener), Robert Agri/John Gemberling (Judah), Stephen Singer (Dr. Fleischer), Alexander Brickel (Peter Paul), Walter Bobbie (Bo Sunshine), Richard Riehle (Dr. Dan). Directed by Todd Solondz and produced by Mike S. Ryan and Derrick Tseng. Screenplay by Solondz.

Todd Solondz's *Palindromes* is a brave and challenging film for which there may not be much of an audience. That is not a fault of the film, which does not want to be liked and only casually hopes to be understood. What it wants is to provoke. You do not emerge untouched from a Solondz film. You may hate it, but you have seen it, and in a strange way it has seen you.

Palindromes contains characters in favor of abortion and characters opposed to it, and finds fault with all of them. The film has no heroes without flaws and no villains without virtues, and that is true no matter who you think the heroes and villains are. To ambiguity it adds perplexity by providing us with a central character named Aviva, a girl of about thirteen played by eight different actresses, two of them adults, one a boy, one a six-year-old girl. She is not always called Aviva.

The point, I think, is to begin with the fact of a girl becoming pregnant at a too-early age and then show us how that situation might play out in different kinds of families with different kinds of girls.

The method by which Aviva becomes pregnant is illegal in all cases, since she is underage, but there is a vast difference between a scenario in which Aviva persuades a reluctant young son of a family friend to experiment with sex, and another where she runs away from home and meets a truck driver.

Perhaps Solondz is suggesting that our response to Aviva's pregnancy depends on the circumstances. He doesn't take an obvious position on anything in the movie, but simply presents it and leaves us to sort it out. We probably can't. *Palindromes* is like life: We know what we consider to be good and bad, but we can't always be sure how to apply our beliefs in the messy real world.

Consider an early scene in the film where one of the Avivas gets pregnant and wants to have the child. Her mother (Ellen Barkin) argues that this will destroy her life; an abortion will allow her to continue her education and grow up to be a normal adolescent, rather than being a mother at thirteen. The mother goes on to make a long list of possible birth defects that might occur in an underage pregnancy.

Later in the film, we meet the "Sunshine Family," a household full of adopted children with birth defects: one with Down's syndrome, one born without arms, and so on. It occurs to us that these are the hypothetical children Barkin did not want her daughter to bear. The children are happy and seem pleased to be alive. Yes, but does Solondz consider the adoptive parents of the Sunshine Family to be good and moral people? Not precisely, not after we find Father Sunshine conspiring to bring about a murder.

The plot circles relentlessly, setting up moral situations and then pulling the moral ground out from under them. The movie is almost reckless in the way it refuses to provide us with a place to stand. It is all made of paradoxes. Pregnancy is pregnancy, rape is rape, abortion is abortion, murder is murder, and yet in the world of *Palindromes* the facts and categories shift under the pressure of human motives—some good, some bad, some misguided, some well-intentioned but disastrous.

We look for a clue in the movie's title. A "palindrome" is a word which is spelled the same way forward and backward: Aviva, for example, or madam or racecar. Is Solondz saying that it doesn't matter which side of the issue we enter from, it's all the same and we'll wind up where we started?

While following the news during the Terri Schiavo case, I was struck by how absolutely sure of their opinions everyone was, on both sides. Could the reporters have found a few people willing to say that after giving the matter a lot of thought, they'd decided it was a tragedy no matter which way you looked at it? Solondz is perhaps arguing for moral relativism, for the idea that what is good in a situation is defined by the situation itself, not by absolute abstractions imposed from outside.

Todd Solondz has made a career out of challenging us to figure out what side of any issue he's on. You can't walk out of one of his movies *(Welcome to the Dollhouse, Happiness, Storytelling)* and make a list of the characters you like and the ones you don't. There's something to be said for and against everybody. Most movies, like most people, are so certain, and we like movies we can agree with. He makes movies where, like a member of the debate team, you sometimes feel as if you're defending a position just because that's the side you were assigned.

If the movie is a moral labyrinth, it is paradoxically straightforward and powerful in the moment; each individual story has an authenticity and impact of its own. Consider the pathos brought to Aviva by the actress Sharon Wilkins, who is a plus-size adult black woman playing a little girl, and who creates perhaps the most convincing little girl of them all. Or Jennifer Jason Leigh, three times as old as Aviva but barely seeming her age. These individual segments are so effective that at the end of each one we know how we feel, and why. It's just that the next segment invalidates our conclusions.

I look at a movie like this, and I consider what courage it took to make it. Solondz from the beginning has made a career out of refusing to cater to broad, safe tastes. He shows us transgressive or evil characters, invites us to identify with their pathos, then shows us that despite our sympathy, they're rotten anyway. You walk out of one of his films feeling like you've just failed a class in ethics, and wondering if in this baffling world anyone ever passes.

Paper Clips ★ ★ ★
G, 82 m., 2005

Linda Hooper (Herself), Sandra Roberts (Herself), Dagmar Schroeder-Hildebrand (Herself), Peter Schroeder (Himself), David Smith (Himself). A documentary directed by Elliot Berlin and Joe Fab and produced by Fab, Robert M. Johnson, and Ari Daniel Pinchot. Screenplay by Fab.

In 1998, three middle-school teachers in Whitwell, Tennessee (population 1,500), came up with a project for the eighth-grade class: Learn about intolerance by studying the Holocaust. The students read *The Diary of Anne Frank* and did Internet research, discovering that during World War II, the Norwegians wore paper clips in their lapels as a silent gesture of solidarity and sympathy with Hitler's victims.

A student, no one seems to remember which one, said it was impossible to imagine 6 million of anything, let alone Jews who died in the Holocaust. That led somehow to the notion of gathering 6 million paper clips in one place at one time, as a tribute to the victims. The project started slowly, with a clip here and a clip there, and 50,000 from one donor, and then *The Washington Post* and Tom Brokaw got on the story and by the time Whitwell's third group of eighth-graders were running the project, they had 29 million paper clips.

That could be a story like the one about the kid who was dying and wanted to collect business cards, and got millions and millions as his desperate parents announced he had recovered and no longer wanted more cards. But the Whitwell story goes to another level, a touching one, as the students make new friends through their project. Two of them are Peter and Dagmar Schroeder, White House correspondents from Germany, who visit the town and write about it. Many more were Holocaust survivors, who as a group visited Whitwell for a potluck dinner at the Methodist church, classes at the school, and a community reception.

And then there was the train car. The Schroeders found one of the actual rail cars used to transport Jews to the death camps, and arranged for it to be shipped to Whitwell. Local carpenters repaired the leaky roof and rotting floor, and the car was placed outside the high school as a Holocaust memorial. Inside were 11 million paper clips, representing 6 million Jews and 5 million gypsies, homosexuals, Jehovah's Witnesses, and others who were murdered by the Nazis. Also a suitcase that German children had filled with notes to Anne Frank.

Paper Clips, which tells this story, is not a sophisticated or very challenging film, nor should it be. It is straightforward, heartfelt, and genuine. It plays more like a local news report, and we get the sense that the documentary, like the paper clip project, grows directly out of the good intentions of the people involved. Whitwell at the time had no Jews, five African-Americans, and one Hispanic, we learn; there weren't even any Catholics. By the time the project was completed, the horizons of the population had widened considerably.

David Smith, one of the teachers involved, says he knows he is stereotyped as a southerner, and admits that he stereotypes northerners. In changing their perceptions about minorities, the students of Whitwell also changed perceptions others may have held about them. That America has been divided by pundits into blue states and red states does not mean there are not good-hearted people living everywhere; in a time of divisiveness, there is something innocently naive about the paper clip project, which transforms a silly mountain of paper clips into a small town's touching gesture.

Paradise Now ★ ★ ★
PG-13, 90 m., 2005

Kais Nashef (Said), Ali Suliman (Khaled), Lubna Azabal (Suha), Amer Hlehel (Jamal), Hiam Abbass (Said's Mother), Ashraf Barhom (Abu-Karem), Mohammad Bustami (Abu-Salim). Directed by Hany Abu-Assad and produced by Bero Beyer. Screenplay by Abu-Assad, Beyer, and Pierre Hodgson.

What I am waiting for is a movie about a suicide bomber who is an atheist, who expects oblivion after his death and pulls the trigger after having reasoned that the deaths of his victims will advance a cause so important that he, and they, must die. When religion enters into the picture, it clouds the meaning of the act: How selfless is your sacrifice if you believe you will be instantly rewarded for eternity?

"What happens afterward?" asks one of the two suicide bombers in *Paradise Now.*
"Two angels will pick you up."
"Are you sure?"
"Absolutely."

The movie involves two days in the lives of Said (Kais Nashef) and Khaled (Ali Suliman), two Palestinians, garage mechanics, best friends, who are recruited to cross into Israel and blow themselves up. They are not shown as fanatics. They prepare for their task as one would prepare for any difficult assignment. The organization that supports them provides training, encouragement, praise, shaves and haircuts, suits and ties, a ceremonial dinner, and a chance to make videos that will be shown on television.

On his video, Said articulates the Palestinian position, expressing anger that the Israelis have stolen the status of victims he believes belongs by right to his own people. Does this speech make the film propaganda, or does it function simply as a record of what such a man would say on such an occasion? I'm not sure it matters. If we are interested in a film that takes us into the lives of suicide bombers, we must be prepared to regard what we find there. Certainly what Said says will not come as a surprise to any Israeli. It's simply that they disagree.

We may disagree, too, and yet watch the film with a fearsome fascination. The director and cowriter, Hany Abu-Assad, uses the interesting device of undercutting the heroism of his martyrs with everyday details. During one taping of a farewell message, the camera malfunctions. During another, one of the bombers interrupts his political sermon with a personal shopping reminder for his mother. When the leader of the terrorist group personally visits the two men, he seems less like a charismatic leader than a bureaucrat a little bored by this obligatory task.

Then there is the matter of the woman Suha (Lubna Azabal); she and Said are beginning to love each other. A Palestinian born in France and raised in Morocco, she has great status in the Palestinian community because she is the daughter of Abu Assam, a revered leader. But she is not an advocate of suicide bombs. Influenced no doubt by the skepticism of the West, she questions terrorist acts on both theological and practical grounds: Islam forbids suicide, and she wonders if one qualifies as a martyr if one has martyred oneself. She believes the effect of the bombings is to create innocent victims and inspire retaliation in a never-ending cycle of violence.

The director Abu-Assad is himself a Palestinian, born in Israel; his crew included Palestinians, Israelis, and Westerners, and during the filming was reportedly threatened by both sides in the conflict. It hardly matters, in a way, which side his protagonists are on; the film is dangerous because of its objectivity, its dispassionate attention to the actual practical process by which volunteers are trained and prepared for the act of destruction.

Paradise Now, like another 2005 film, *The War Within,* and the 1999 Indian film *The Terrorist,* humanizes suicide bombers. But in my mind, at least, that creates not sympathy but pity; what a waste, to spend your life and all your future on behalf of those who send you but do not go themselves. These movies by necessity tell us versions of the same story: A true believer prepares for death, and we watch to see if death will come.

That is why I await the movie about the atheist who blows himself up. He will need to convince himself objectively of the wisdom of his decision. When religion is involved, it sidesteps the issue, since religion provides an absolute rationale. The problem is that all religions provide this service—yours, mine, theirs. When higher powers are invoked to justify death on both sides of a dispute, does heaven send four angels?

The Passenger ★ ★ ★ ½
PG-13, 119 m., 1975 (rereleased 2005)

Jack Nicholson (David Locke), Maria Schneider (Girl), Jenny Runacre (Rachel Locke), Ian Hendry (Martin Knight), Steven Berkoff (Stephen), Ambroise Bia (Achebe), Jose Maria Caffarel (Hotel Keeper), James Campbell (Witch Doctor). Directed by Michelangelo Antonioni, and produced by Carlo Ponti. Screenplay by Peter Wollen, Antonioni, and Mark Peploe.

There is an emptiness in the films of Michelangelo Antonioni that the director seems to love more than the people who intrude upon it. His films are never crowded. Even *Blow-Up,* set in London, and *La Notte,* in Milan, seem barely inhabited; he is drawn to spaces empty of people, save a few characters who wander irresolutely through in search of—well, of nothing. They want not to find but to seek.

The Passenger (1975) begins with a man in a North African village surrounded by desert. He hires a boy to lead him out into the wilderness, and then a man appears to lead him farther still and abandon him. Emptiness surrounds him. The man returns to the town alone. He is David Locke (Jack Nicholson), a journalist who was seeking an interview with guerrillas rumored to be somewhere in the desert hills.

His hotel lacks the usual comings and goings. There is a clerk, and one other resident, a man named Robertson (Charles Mulvehill). They have had a conversation about nothing much. Locke enters Robertson's room and finds him dead. Without premeditation, he exchanges identities with the corpse. He swaps their passports, switches their clothes, tells the clerk there of the dead man, and in London it is thought that David Locke is dead. His wife (Jenny Runacre) and associate (Ian Hendry) begin to edit the footage he took in the desert.

They are looking in the footage for David Locke himself, just as the photographer in *Blow-Up* seeks a corpse he thinks he sees on the grass of a park. The more intensely these characters look, the less they see. The new Robertson meanwhile decides to meet certain appointments that the old Robertson had made; this takes him to Munich and a meeting with representatives of the guerrillas. He finds he is a gun dealer.

Locke (we will call him that) meets a young woman (Maria Schneider), whose name is never given; in the credits she is the Girl. She joins him on his travels. He has no plans—neither his own nor Robertson's. "What are you running away from?" she asks him as they drive in a big American convertible. "Turn your back to the front seat." She does, sees the road receding behind her, and laughs.

He is not running away, or toward. He is simply in motion. Many of the shots suggest people with time on their hands in empty cities. The girl wants to invest his movements with importance, wants him to be someone and want something. He has revealed his secret, and at one point she says: "But Robertson made these appointments. He believes in something. That's what you wanted, isn't it?" In other words, he became Robertson because he had no plans or desires and Robertson did?

Not really. Locke does desire not to be found by his wife or associate, and the one moment of urgency in the film comes as he is almost recognized, and flees with the girl. There is a brief scene indicating that they have made love, but the movie is not about love or sex. He wants to leave the girl behind because she will get into trouble—his trouble, or Robertson's. She follows.

All leads up to a final shot of great beauty and complexity, in which he falls back exhausted on a hotel bed. The camera moves with infinite slowness toward a window with iron bars, and then somehow through the window into the piazza outside. A car appears and disappears. Another car appears. It contains people looking for him. The girl appears in the square, walking at a distance, observing, not implicated. The camera, still in the same unbroken shot, reenters the hotel and the room.

I have limited myself to describing the action because the film resolutely exists through its action, to which it declines to give meaning. At the outset Locke wanted to interview the rebels and Robertson wanted to sell them guns. By taking Robertson's place, Locke has abandoned his own plan without taking up Robertson's. Nicholson plays him as a man with no purpose; the appearance of the girl provides him with a companion and a witness, but not with a plan or a future.

What of the girl? Schneider gives a performance of breathtaking spontaneity. She is without calculation, manner, or affect. She reacts cleanly and without complication to events, she is concerned about the man and loyal to him, she understands nothing, and at the end she understands less. She is the only witness to his adventure. Without her, it would scarcely have happened. What did it mean? This is not a question to ask in a film by Antonioni. In *L'Avventura*, a character disappears on an island and never appears again. Her friends search for her and then abandon the search, which for a time gave them purpose. In *Blow-Up* a photographer shoots an event in a park and in studying his photographs thinks he may have photographed a murder. But there is no body, and the photographs yield less the more he studies them. In *The Passenger*, one man becomes another and then both evaporate. The girl is left in the empty piazza.

I did not admire the film in 1975. In a negative review, I observed that Antonioni had changed its title from *The Reporter* to *The Passenger*, ap-parently deciding it was about the girl, not Locke. Maybe it is simply about passengers who travel in someone else's life: Locke in Robertson's, the girl in Locke's. I admire the movie more thirty years later. I am more in sympathy with it.

When a film so resolutely refuses to deliver on the level of plot, what we are left with is tone. *The Passenger* is about being in a place where nobody knows you or wants to know you, and you are struck by your insignificance. There was a world where it was important that Robertson was Robertson and Locke was Locke. In the desert among strangers, it is not even important that Robertson be Robertson and Locke be Locke. The little white car that crisscrosses the square in the final shot belongs to a driving school. To its driver, it is important to pass the course and get a driver's license. Robertson and Locke disappear, and this is first gear, this is second, here is the clutch, here is the brake.

The Passion of the Christ ★ ★ ★ ★
R, 126 m., 2004

James Caviezel (Jesus, the Christ), Maia Morgenstern (Mary), Monica Bellucci (Mary Magdalene), Mattia Sbragia (Caiphas), Hristo Shopov (Pontius Pilate), Claudia Gerini (Pilate's Wife), Luca Lionello (Judas). Directed by Mel Gibson and produced by Bruce Davey, Gibson, and Stephen McEveety. Screenplay by Gibson and Benedict Fitzgerald.

If ever there was a film with the correct title, that film is Mel Gibson's *The Passion of the Christ*. Although the word *passion* has become mixed up with romance, its Latin origins refer to suffering and pain; later Christian theology broadened that to include Christ's love for mankind, which made him willing to suffer and die for us. The movie is 126 minutes long, and I would guess that at least 100 of those minutes, maybe more, are concerned specifically and graphically with the details of the torture and death of Jesus. This is the most violent film I have ever seen.

I prefer to evaluate a film on the basis of what it intends to do, not on what I think it should have done. It is clear that Mel Gibson wanted to make graphic and inescapable the price that Jesus paid (as Christians believe) when he died for our sins. Anyone raised as a Catholic will be familiar with the stops along the way; the screenplay is inspired not so much by the Gospels as by the fourteen Stations of the Cross. As an altar boy, serving during the Stations on Friday nights in Lent, I was encouraged to meditate on Christ's suffering, and I remember the chants as the priest led the way from one station to another:

At the Cross, her station keeping . . .
Stood the mournful Mother weeping . . .
Close to Jesus to the last.

For us altar boys, this was not necessarily a deep spiritual experience. Christ suffered, Christ died, Christ rose again, we were redeemed, and let's hope we can get home in time to watch the Illinois basketball game on TV. What Gibson has provided for me, for the first time in my life, is a visceral idea of what the Passion consisted of. That his film is superficial in terms of the surrounding message—that we get only a few passing references to the teachings of Jesus—is, I suppose, not the point. This is not a sermon or a homily, but a visualization of the central event in the Christian religion. Take it or leave it.

David Anson, a critic I respect, finds in *Newsweek* that Gibson has gone too far. ". . . (T)he relentless gore is self-defeating," he writes. "Instead of being moved by Christ's suffering, or awed by his sacrifice, I felt abused by a filmmaker intent on punishing an audience, for who knows what sins." This is a completely valid response to the film, and I quote Anson because I suspect he speaks for many audience members, who will enter the theater in a devout or spiritual mood and emerge deeply disturbed. You must be prepared for whippings, flayings, beatings, the crunch of bones, the agony of screams, the cruelty of the sadistic centurions, the rivulets of blood that crisscross every inch of Jesus' body. Some will leave before the end.

This is not a Passion like any other ever filmed. Perhaps that is the best reason for it. I grew up on those pious Hollywood biblical epics of the 1950s, which looked like holy cards brought to life. I remember my grin when *Time* magazine noted that Jeffrey Hunter, starring as Christ in *King of Kings* (1961), had shaved his armpits. (Not Hunter's fault; the film's crucifixion scene had to be reshot because preview audiences objected to Jesus' hairy chest.) If it does nothing else, Gibson's film will break the tradition of turning Jesus and his disciples into

neat, clean, well-barbered middle-class businessmen. They were poor men in a poor land. I debated Scorsese's *The Last Temptation of Christ* with Michael Medved before an audience from a Christian college, and was told by an audience member that the characters were filthy and needed haircuts.

The Middle East in biblical times was a Jewish community occupied against its will by the Roman Empire, and the message of Jesus was equally threatening to both sides—to the Romans, because he was a revolutionary, and to the establishment of Jewish priests because he preached a new covenant and threatened the status quo. In the movie's scenes showing Jesus being condemned to death, the two main players are Pontius Pilate, the Roman governor, and Caiphas, the Jewish high priest. Both men want to keep the lid on, and while neither is especially eager to see Jesus crucified, they live in a harsh time when such a man is dangerous.

Pilate is seen going through his well-known doubts before finally washing his hands of the matter and turning Jesus over to the priests, but Caiphas, who also had doubts, is not seen as sympathetically. The critic Steven D. Greydanus, in a useful analysis of the film, writes: "The film omits the canonical line from John's gospel in which Caiphas argues that it is better for one man to die for the people that the nation be saved. Had Gibson retained this line, perhaps giving Caiphas a measure of the inner conflict he gave to Pilate, it could have underscored the similarities between Caiphas and Pilate and helped defuse the issue of anti-Semitism."

This scene and others might justifiably be cited by anyone concerned that the movie contains anti-Semitism. My own feeling is that Gibson's film is not anti-Semitic, but reflects a range of behavior on the part of its Jewish characters, on balance favorably. The Jews who seem to desire Jesus' death are in the priesthood, and have political as well as theological reasons for acting; like today's Catholic bishops who were slow to condemn abusive priests, Protestant TV preachers who confuse religion with politics, or Muslim clerics who are silent on terrorism, they have an investment in their positions and authority. The other Jews seen in the film are viewed positively; Simon helps Jesus to carry the cross, Veronica brings a cloth to wipe his face, Jews in the crowd cry out against his torture.

A reasonable person, I believe, will reflect that in this story set in a Jewish land, there are many characters with many motives, some good, some not, each one representing himself, none representing his religion. The story involves a Jew who tried no less than to replace the established religion and set himself up as the Messiah. He was understandably greeted with a jaundiced eye by the Jewish establishment while at the same time finding his support, his disciples, and the founders of his church entirely among his fellow Jews. The libel that the Jews "killed Christ" involves a willful misreading of testament and teaching: Jesus was made man and came to Earth *in order* to suffer and die in reparation for our sins. No race, no religion, no man, no priest, no governor, no executioner killed Jesus; he died by God's will to fulfill his purpose, and with our sins we *all* killed him. That some Christian churches have historically been guilty of the sin of anti-Semitism is undeniable, but in committing it they violated their own beliefs.

This discussion will seem beside the point for readers who want to know about the movie, not the theology. But *The Passion of the Christ*, more than any other film I can recall, depends upon theological considerations. Gibson has not made a movie that anyone would call "commercial," and if it grosses millions, that will not be because anyone was entertained. It is a personal message movie of the most radical kind, attempting to re-create events of personal urgency to Gibson. The filmmaker has put his artistry and fortune at the service of his conviction and belief, and that doesn't happen often.

Is the film "good" or "great"? I imagine each person's reaction (visceral, theological, artistic) will differ. I was moved by the depth of feeling, by the skill of the actors and technicians, by their desire to see this project through, no matter what. To discuss individual performances, such as James Caviezel's heroic depiction of the ordeal, is almost beside the point. This isn't a movie about performances, although it has powerful ones; or about technique, although it is awesome; or about cinematography (although Caleb Deschanel paints with an artist's eye); or music (although John Debney supports the content without distracting from it). It is a film about an idea. An idea that it is necessary to fully comprehend the Passion if Christianity is

to make any sense. Gibson has communicated his idea with a single-minded urgency. Many will disagree. Some will agree, but be horrified by the graphic treatment. I myself am no longer religious in the sense that a long-ago altar boy thought he should be; but I can respond to the power of belief whether I agree or not, and when I find it in a film I must respect it.

Note: I said the film is the most violent I have ever seen. It will probably be the most violent you have ever seen. This is not a criticism but an observation; the film is unsuitable for younger viewers, but works powerfully for those who can endure it. The MPAA's "R" rating is definitive proof that the organization either will never give the NC-17 rating for violence alone, or was intimidated by the subject matter. If it had been anyone other than Jesus up on that cross, I have a feeling that NC-17 would have been automatic.

Peaceful Warrior ★ ★ ½
PG-13, 121 m., 2006

Nick Nolte (Socrates), Scott Mechlowicz (Dan Millman), Amy Smart (Joy), Ashton Holmes (Tommy Warner), Paul Wesley (Trevor Scott), Agnes Bruckner (Susie), Tim DeKay (Coach Garrick). Directed by Victor Salva and produced by Mark Amin, Cami Winikoff, Robin Schorr, and David Welch. Screenplay by Kevin Bernhardt, based on the book *Way of the Peaceful Warrior* by Dan Millman.

If *Peaceful Warrior* were not based on a true story, I might have an easier time believing it. It's the kind of parable that is perfectly acceptable as the saga of Mr. Miyagi, but when the movie opens with the words "inspired by true events," I get edgy. I keep wondering what "inspired" means. Did Dan Millman, the author of the book that inspired the movie, really meet a man who could levitate?

What I do believe is that Nick Nolte can play a man who can levitate. Nolte sounds a note of weary clarity in the film; when he utters self-help clichés ("Stop gathering information from outside yourself and start gathering information from inside"), he underplays it so well and looks so serious that we think maybe he knows this firsthand.

Nolte plays the only attendant at an all-night

Texaco station that looks so old-fashioned it could be the Fatal Gas Station in a horror movie: you know, where the sinister old scarecrow in overalls tells the kids to turn left and go down the old dirt road into the swamp. This station, however, seems well-lighted and orderly, and Nolte's character is always busy under the hood of a car. "This is a service station," he says at one point. "We offer service. There's no higher purpose."

He has such conversations with Dan Millman (Scott Mechlowicz), a character based on the author of the 1980 self-help best seller that has inspired the movie. Dan is a gymnast on the Berkeley team, a hotshot who's always trying out risky stuff in the gym. After a nasty fall his coach tells him, "Nobody on this planet can do what you're trying to do."

Dan is out jogging the first night he meets the Nolte character, whom he eventually thinks of as Socrates. As he's leaving, he turns back and finds that Socrates is now standing on the roof of the station, fifteen feet or more above the ground. How did he do that? Later, Dan also wants to know how Socrates appears in his bedroom during sex, and on top of a beam in the gymnasium. Quizzed on such puzzles, Socrates has helpful answers such as pointing to his forehead while saying, "Take out the trash, Dan."

Dan's motorcycle hits a car and he breaks his femur in seventeen places. This is inspired by the real Dan's accident in which he broke his leg in twenty-one places. Told he will never compete in gymnastics again, he contemplates suicide but eventually finds himself back at the service station, where Socrates shares such wisdom as, "The journey is what brings us happiness, not the destination." I was happy to hear this, because it explains what Godard meant when he said, "The cinema is not the station; the cinema is the train."

The story arc of *Peaceful Warrior* is so familiar that in addition to being inspired by fact, it is inspired by at least two-thirds of all the sports movies ever made. To quote myself (this situation has come up before): I can't give away the ending because it gives itself away. Oddly enough, it's not the plausible stuff like the gymnastics that fascinates me in the story, but the mystery of Socrates. Does Socrates even exist? Is his gas station really there? If Dan bought himself a Baby Ruth from the candy machine, could he eat it? Of course these questions betray me as hopelessly focused on realism.

Sometimes in an imperfect movie there is consolation simply in regarding the actors. You possibly have the impression that Nolte has been in a lot of commercial hits and is, or was until recently, an action star. But run his name through IMDb.com and you'll discover that he is, and essentially always has been, an art film actor. Yes, he had some big hits, but *48 Hours* was a breakthrough at the time, and when he does a superhero epic, it's the inventive *Hulk* by Ang Lee.

Nolte has been through some hard times and posed for at least one mug shot that went around the world. He has picked himself up and patched himself back together, and is convincing as a wise survivor. A movie based on his life might have the same parabola as Millman's, if you substituted drinking for gymnastics. There is a sense in which the role of Socrates speaks to him more loudly than to Dan, and that sense makes the performance sort of fascinating.

All the rest is formula: the coach, the team, the training, the accident, the comeback. The fact that doubles and visual effects are used for some of the gymnastics stunts is obvious but not objectionable, because of course they are. But it's funny, isn't it, how the most amazing stunt in the movie is performed off-screen. How *did* he get up there?

The Perfect Man ★
PG, 96 m., 2005

Hilary Duff (Holly Hamilton), Heather Locklear (Jean Hamilton), Chris Noth (Ben Cooper), Mike O'Malley (Lenny Horton), Ben Feldman (Adam Forrest), Aria Wallace (Zoe Hamilton), Vanessa Lengies (Amy). Directed by Mark Rosman and produced by Susan Duff, Marc E. Platt, and Dawn Wolfrom. Screenplay by Gina Wendkos.

Is there no one to step forward and simply say that Heather Locklear's character in *The Perfect Man* is mad? I will volunteer. Locklear plays Jean Hamilton, a woman whose obsessive search for the "perfect man" inspires sudden and impulsive moves from one end of the country to another, always with her teenage daughter, Holly (Hilary Duff), and Holly's seven-year-old sister, Zoe (Aria Wallace). Apparently, there can only be one Perfect Man candidate per state.

As the movie opens, Holly is preparing to attend a prom in Wichita when her mother announces, "It's moving time!" Her latest boyfriend has broken up with her, so they all have to pile into the car and head for New York, where Mom providentially has a job lined up at a bakery—a job that pays well enough for them to move into an apartment that would rent for, oh, $4,000 a month.

Holly keeps an online blog named GirlOn-TheMove.com, where she chronicles her mom's craziness for all the world. "Post me on Match.com," her mom tells Holly after they arrive in New York, but Holly thinks maybe it might be fun to see if her mom just—you know, *meets* someone. Jean's way of meeting someone is certainly direct: She attends a PTA meeting at Holly's new school, and suggests special PTA meetings for single parents and teachers. In desperation, Holly creates an imaginary online friend for her mom, who says all the things a woman wants to hear.

How does Holly know this is true? Because she's made a new friend at school (she's always making new friends, because she's always moving to new schools). This friend, named Amy (Vanessa Lengies) has an Uncle Ben (Chris Noth) who runs a bistro and is a bottomless well of information about what women want to hear, and what a Perfect Man consists of. Holly names the imaginary friend Ben, sends her mom Uncle Ben's photo, and recycles what he tells her into the e-mail. Example of his wisdom: "When a woman gets an orchid, she feels like she's floating on a cloud of infinite possibility." If I met a woman who felt like she was floating on a cloud of infinite possibility after receiving an orchid, I would be afraid to give her anything else until she'd had a good physical.

The Perfect Man takes its idiotic plot and uses it as the excuse for scenes of awesome stupidity. For example, when Jean walks into Uncle Ben's restaurant and there is a danger they might meet, Holly sets off the sprinkler system. And when Holly thinks Ben is marrying another woman, she interrupts the wedding—while even we know, because of the tortured camera angles that strive not to reveal this, that Ben is only the best man.

Meanwhile, Jean has another prospect, a baker named Lenny (Mike O'Malley), who is a real nice guy but kind of homely, and invites her to a concert by a Styx tribute band. This involves driving to the concert in Lenny's pride and joy, a

1980 Pontiac Trans-Am two-door hardtop; Jean has to take off her shoes before entering the sacred precincts of this car. My personal opinion is that Lenny would be less boring after six months than the cloud of infinite possibilities guy.

The Perfect Man crawls hand over bloody hand up the stony face of this plot, while we in the audience do not laugh because it is not nice to laugh at those less fortunate than ourselves, and the people in this movie are less fortunate than the people in just about any other movie I can think of, simply because they are in it.

The Perfect Score ★ ★
PG-13, 93 m., 2004

Scarlett Johansson (Francesca), Erika Christensen (Anna), Chris Evans (Kyle), Darius Miles (Desmond), Leonardo Nam (Roy), Bryan Greenberg (Matty), Fulvio Cecere (Francesca's Father), Kyle Labine (Dave), Bill Mackenzie (Bernie). Directed by Brian Robbins and produced by Roger Birnbaum, Jonathan Glickman, Robbins, and Michael Tollin. Screenplay by Mark Schwahn, Marc Hyman, and Jon Zack.

The dialogue in *The Perfect Score* mentions *The Breakfast Club*, which is nice (how come the characters in movies never seem to know there are movies—except the ones they attend but never watch?). And there are similarities between the two films, not least in the way that Scarlett Johansson, with her red lips and brunette haircut, resembles Molly Ringwald. There is also a certain seriousness linking the two films, although this one tilts toward a caper comedy.

The film takes place in Princeton, New Jersey, which in addition to being Albert Einstein's place of last employment is also home to the Princeton Testing Center, home of the SAT exam. The SATs, we learn, were once known as the Scholastic Aptitude Test, but since this name presumably reeked of common sense, it was dropped, and now "SAT" simply stands for—SAT. "Ess Ay Tee," the Website explains, making it easy for us.

We meet Kyle (Chris Evans), who for as long as he can remember has wanted to be an architect. That for him translates into being admitted to Cornell, but for Cornell, alas, he will need to score a 1,430 on his SAT, and his first score is

539

down close to triple digits. He can take the test again, but he doubts he can improve his score.

"Kyle," says one of his buddies, "this is your dream, man. If they want to put a number on that, then the hell with them." Yeah. So Kyle and his posse decide to break into the Princeton Testing Center, steal the answers to the test, and realize their dream. And that they set out to do, in a film that sketches various motives for a half-dozen characters. You may be able to find parallels between these characters and those in *The Breakfast Club*. On the other hand, you may decide life is too short.

I wasn't thinking about *The Breakfast Club* anyway, while I watched the film. I was thinking about *Better Luck Tomorrow*, the 2002 film by Justin Lin about a group of Asian-American high school students in Orange County, who started by selling exam answers and ended up involved in drugs and murder, all without getting caught. In the original ending of the film when it played at Sundance, the central character considers turning himself in to the police, but "I couldn't let one mistake get in the way of everything I'd worked for. I know the difference between right and wrong, but I guess in the end I really wanted to go to a good college."

Lin reshot some of the film, including that ending, but I've always thought it was a good one. It shows an ability to separate achievement from morality, and places so much value on success that it finally justifies any action. Lin's young heroes, I wrote in my article about the best films of the year, have positioned themselves to take over from the fallen leaders of Enron.

I thought about the film because *The Perfect Score* considers similar material without the bite and anger and savage determination. It's too palatable. It maintains a tone of light seriousness, and it depends on the caper for too much of its entertainment value. *Better Luck Tomorrow* also has a plot that involves crime, but the difference is, *The Perfect Score* is about the intended crime and depends on it, while in *Better Luck Tomorrow* we see a process by which the behavior of the characters leads them where they never thought to go.

There is a kind of franchising of movies going on right now, in which the big studio product is like fast food: bad for you, but available on every corner. Good and challenging movies are limited to release in big cities and in a handful of independently booked cinemas. Whole states and sections of the country never see the best new films on big screens, and they're not always easy to find on video.

And that's a shame. What does it say when a dozen of the titles nominated for major Academy Awards this year did not play in a majority of the markets? Have I drifted from the movie under review? I'm not drifting, I'm swimming.

The Phantom of the Opera ★ ★ ★
PG-13, 143 m., 2004

Gerard Butler (The Phantom), Emmy Rossum (Christine), Patrick Wilson (Raoul), Miranda Richardson (Madame Giry), Minnie Driver (Carlotta), Ciaran Hinds (Firmin), Simon Callow (Andre), Victor McGuire (Piangi). Directed by Joel Schumacher and produced by Andrew Lloyd Webber. Screenplay by Webber, based on the novel by Gaston Leroux.

The question at this point is whether *The Phantom of the Opera* is even intended to be frightening. It has become such a product of modern popular art that its original inspiration, "the loathsome gargoyle who lives in hell but dreams of heaven," has come dangerously close to becoming an institution, like Dracula, who was also scary a long, long time ago.

Lon Chaney's Phantom in the 1925 production had a hideously damaged face, his mouth a lipless rictus, his eyes off-center in gouged-out sockets. When Christine tore off his mask, she was horrified, and so was the audience. In the Andrew Lloyd Webber version, now filmed by Joel Schumacher, the mask is more like a fashion accessory, and the Phantom's "good" profile is so chiseled and handsome that the effect is not an object of horror but a kinky babe magnet.

There was something unwholesome and pathetic about the 1925 Phantom, who scuttled like a rat in the undercellars of the Paris Opera and nourished a hopeless love for Christine. The modern Phantom is more like a perverse Batman with a really neat cave. The character of Raoul, Christine's nominal lover, has always been a fatuous twerp, but at least in the 1925 version Christine is attracted to the Phantom only until she removes his mask. In this version, any red-blooded woman would choose the Phantom over Raoul, even knowing what she knows now.

But what I am essentially disliking is not the film but the underlying material. I do not think Andrew Lloyd Webber wrote a very good musical. The story is thin beer for the time it takes to tell it, and the music is maddeningly repetitious. When the chandelier comes crashing down, it's not a shock, it's a historical reenactment. You do remember the tunes as you leave the theater, but you don't walk out humming them; you wonder if you'll be able to get them out of your mind. Every time I see Webber's *Phantom*, the bit about the "darkness of the music of the night" bounces between my ears, as if, like Howard Hughes, I am condemned to repeat the words until I go mad. (I have the same difficulty with "Waltzing Matilda.") Lyrics such as

Let your mind start a journey through a strange new world,
leave all thoughts of the world you knew before,
let your soul take you where you long to be,
only then can you belong to me.

wouldn't get past Simon Cowell, let alone Rodgers and Hammerstein.

Yet Joel Schumacher has bravely taken aboard this dreck and made of it a movie I am pleased to have seen. To have seen, that is, as opposed to have heard. I concede that Emmy Rossum, who is only eighteen and sings her own songs and carries the show, is a phenomenal talent, and I wish her all the best—starting with better material. What an Eliza Dolittle she might make. But the songs are dirges or showlounge retreads, the dialogue laboriously makes its archaic points, and meanwhile the movie looks simply sensational. Schumacher knows more about making a movie than the material deserves, and he simply goes off on his own, bringing greatness to his department and leaving the material to fend for itself.

I attended a rehearsal of the Lyric Opera's new production of *A Wedding* and talked with its cowriter and director, Robert Altman. "I don't know $#!+ about the music," he told me. "I don't even know if they're singing on key. That's not my job. I focus on how it moves, how it looks, and how it plays." One wonders if Schumacher felt the same way—not that it would be polite to ask him.

He has a sure sense for the macabre, going back to his 1987 teenage vampire movie *The Lost Boys* and certainly including his *Flatliners*

(1990), about the medical students who induce technical death and then resuscitate themselves to report on what death was like—whether they saw the white tunnel, and so on. His *Batman Forever* was the best of the Batman movies, not least because of its sets, and here, working with production designer Anthony Pratt *(Excalibur)*, art director John Fenner *(Raiders of the Lost Ark)*, set decorator Celia Bobak (Branagh's *Henry V* and *Hamlet*), and costume designer Alexandra Byrne *(Elizabeth)*, he creates a film so visually resonant you want to float in it.

I love the look of the film. I admire the cellars and dungeons and the Styx-like sewer with its funereal gondola, and the sensational Masked Ball, and I was impressed by the rooftop scenes, with Paris as a backdrop in the snow. The scarlet of the Phantom's cape acts like a bloodstain against the monochrome cityscape and Christina's pale skin, and she rises to an occasion her rival lovers have not earned. She responds to more genuine tragedy than the film provides for her, she has feelings her character must generate from within, she is so emotionally tortured and romantically torn that both Raoul and the Phantom should ask themselves if there is another man.

I know there are fans of the Phantom. For a decade in London, you couldn't go past Her Majesty's Theater without seeing them with their backpacks, camped out against the north wall, waiting all night in hopes of a standby ticket. People have seen it ten, twenty, a hundred times—have never done anything else in their lives but see it. They will embrace the movie, and I congratulate them, because they have waited too long to be disappointed.

Some still feel Michael Crawford should have been given the role he made famous on stage; certainly Gerald Butler's work doesn't argue against their belief. But Butler is younger and more conventionally handsome than Crawford, in a *GQ* kind of way, and Lloyd Webber's production has long since forgotten that the Phantom is supposed to be ugly and aging and, given the conditions in those cellars, probably congested, arthritic, and neurasthenic.

This has been, I realize, a nutty review. I am recommending a movie I do not seem to like very much. But part of the pleasure of moviegoing is pure spectacle—of just sitting there and looking at great stuff and knowing it looks terrific. There wasn't much Joel Schumacher could have done with the story or the music he was handed, but in the areas over which he held sway, he has triumphed. This is such a fabulous production that by recasting two of the three leads and adding some better songs it could have been, well, great.

The Pink Panther ★ ½
PG, 92 m., 2006

Steve Martin (Inspector Jacques Clouseau), Kevin Kline (Chief Inspector Dreyfus), Beyonce Knowles (Xania), Jean Reno (Gendarme Ponton), Emily Mortimer (Nicole), Henry Czerny (Yuri), Kristin Chenoweth (Cherie). Directed by Shawn Levy and produced by Robert Simonds. Screenplay by Len Blum and Steve Martin.

What is the moviegoer with a good memory to do when confronted with *The Pink Panther*, directed by Shawn Levy and starring Steve Martin? Is it possible to forget Blake Edwards and Peter Sellers? It is not. Their best Pink Panther movies did wonderfully what could not be done so well by anyone else, and not even, at the end, by them. (There was the sad *Trail of the Pink Panther* in 1982, cobbled together from outtakes after Sellers died in 1980.) Inspector Clouseau has been played by other actors before Martin (Alan Arkin and Roger Moore), but what's the point? The character isn't bigger than the actor, as Batman and maybe James Bond are. The character is the actor, and I would rather not see Steve Martin, who is himself inimitable, imitating Sellers.

Clouseau is wrong, and so is Kevin Kline as Inspector Dreyfus, the role Herbert Lom made into a smoldering slow burn. Kline and Martin both wear the costumes and try the bad French accents, but it's like the high school production of something you saw at Steppenwolf, with the most gifted students in drama class playing the John Malkovich and Joan Allen roles. Within thirty seconds of Kline's appearing on the screen, I was remembering the Kevin Kline Rule from my "Little Movie Glossary," which observes that whenever Kline wears a mustache in a movie, he also has a foreign accent. Please do not write in with exceptions.

The movie credits Edwards as one of the sources of the story, which is fair enough, since the movie's ambition is to be precisely in the tra-

dition of the Pink Panther movies. It's a prequel, taking place before *The Pink Panther* (1963) and showing Clouseau plucked from obscurity for his first big case. The French soccer coach has been murdered on the field in view of countless cheering fans, and the Pink Panther diamond has been stolen at the same time. The pressure is on Dreyfus to solve the case. His inspiration: Find the most incompetent inspector in France, announce his appointment, and use him as a decoy while the real investigation secretly goes on.

Clouseau, of course, qualifies as spectacularly incompetent, and his first meeting with Dreyfus begins unpromisingly when he succeeds in piercing the chief inspector's flesh with the pin on his badge. Clouseau is assigned Ponton (Jean Reno), an experienced gendarme, as his minder. Reno survives the movie by dialing down.

Clouseau, as before, has the ability to begin with a small mistake and build it into a catastrophe. Consider a scene where he drops a Viagra pill, and in trying to retrieve it, short-circuits the electricity in a hotel, sets it on fire, and falls through a floor. The mounting scale of each disaster is like a slapstick version of the death scenes in *Final Destination 3*, where a perfectly ordinary day in the stock room can end with a death by nail gun.

The Panther movies always featured beautiful women or, in the case of Capucine, a woman rumored to have been born a man, although I'll bet John Wayne hadn't heard that when they costarred in *North to Alaska*. The beauties this time are Beyonce Knowles, Emily Mortimer, and Kristin Chenoweth, and their task is essentially to regard Clouseau as if they have never seen such a phenomenon before in their lives.

Ponton, in the meantime, is subjected to the same kinds of attacks that Sellers used to unleash on Cato (Burt Kwouk), but I dunno: Even in purely physical scenes, something is missing. I think maybe the problem is that Steve Martin is sane and cannot lose himself entirely to idiocy. Sellers, who liked to say he had no personality, threw himself into a role as if desperate to grab all the behavior he could and run away with it and hide it under the bed.

There are moments that are funny in a mechanical way, as when Clouseau causes a giant globe to roll out of an office and into the street, and it turns up much later to crash into a bicycle racer. But at every moment in the movie, I was aware that Sellers was Clouseau, and Martin was not. I hadn't realized how thoroughly Sellers and Edwards had colonized my memory. Despite Sean Connery, I was able to accept the other James Bonds, just as I understand that different actors might play Hamlet. But there is only one Clouseau, and zat ees zat.

Polar Express ★ ★ ★ ★
G, 100 m., 2004

Body movement performers: Tom Hanks (Hero Boy/Father/Conductor/Hobo/Scrooge/Santa), Michael Jeter (Smokey/Steamer), Nona Gaye (Hero Girl), Peter Scolari (Lonely Boy), Eddie Deezen (Know-It-All), Charles Fleischer (Elf General), Steven Tyler (Elf Lieutenant/Elf Singer), Leslie Zemeckis (Sister Sarah/Mother). Voice performers if different than above: Daryl Sabara (Hero Boy), Andre Sogliuzzo (Smokey/Steamer), Jimmy Bennett (Lonely Boy), Isabella Peregrina (Sister Sarah). Directed by Robert Zemeckis and produced by Gary Goetzman, Steve Starkey, William Teitler, and Zemeckis. Screenplay by Zemeckis and William Broyles Jr., based on the book by Chris Van Allsburg.

The Polar Express has the quality of a lot of lasting children's entertainment: It's a little creepy. Not creepy in an unpleasant way, but in that sneaky, teasing way that lets you know eerie things could happen. There's a deeper, shivery tone, instead of the mindless jolliness of the usual Christmas movie. This one creates a world of its own, like *The Wizard of Oz* or *Willy Wonka*, in which the wise child does not feel too complacent.

Those who know the Chris Van Allsburg book will feel right at home from the opening moments, which quote from the story: *On Christmas Eve, many years ago, I lay quietly in my bed*... The young hero, who is never given a name, is listening for the sound of sleigh bells ringing. He is at just the age when the existence of Santa Claus is up for discussion.

The look of the film is extraordinary, a cross between live action and Van Allsburg's artwork. Robert Zemeckis, the same director whose *Who Framed Roger Rabbit* juxtaposed live action with animation, this time merges them, using a process called "performance capture," in which human actors perform the movements that are translated into lifelike animation. The characters in *Polar Express* don't look real, but they don't look unreal, either; they have a kind of simplified and underlined reality that makes them visually magnetic. Many of the body and voice performances are by Tom Hanks, who is the executive producer and worked with Zemeckis on *Forrest Gump* (1994) — another film that combined levels of reality and special effects.

The story: As Hero Boy lies awake in bed, there is a rumble in the street and a passenger train lumbers into view. The boy runs outside in his bathrobe and slippers, and the conductor advises him to get onboard. Having refused to visit a department store Santa, having let his little sister put out Santa's milk and cookies, Hero Boy is growing alarmingly agnostic on the Santa question, and the *Polar Express* apparently shuttles such kids to the North Pole, where seeing is believing.

Already on board is Hero Girl, a solemn and gentle African-American, who becomes the boy's friend, and also befriends Lonely Boy, who lives on the wrong side of the tracks and always seems sad. Another character, Know-It-All, is one of those kids who can't supply an answer without sounding obnoxious about it. These four are the main characters, in addition to the conductor, a hobo who lives on top of the train, Santa, and countless elves.

There's an interesting disconnect between the movie's action and its story. The action is typical thrill-ride stuff, with the *Polar Express* careening down a "179-degree grade" and racing through tunnels with a half-inch of clearance, while Hero Boy and the Hobo ski the top of the train to find safety before the tunnel. At the North Pole, there's another dizzying ride when the kids spin down a corkscrewing toy chute.

Those scenes are skillful, but expected. Not expected is a dazzling level of creativity in certain other scenes. Hero Girl's lost ticket, for example, flutters through the air with as much freedom as the famous floating feather at the start of *Forrest Gump*. When hot chocolate is served on the train, dancing waiters materialize with an acrobatic song-and-dance. And the North Pole looks like a turn-of-the-century German factory town, filled with elves who not only look mass-produced but may have been, since they mostly have exactly the same features (this is not a cost-cutting device, but an artistic decision).

Santa, in this version, is a good and decent man, matter-of-fact and serious: a professional man, doing his job. The elves are like the crowd at a political rally. A sequence involving a bag full of toys is seen from a high angle that dramatizes Santa's operation, but doesn't romanticize it; this is not Jolly St. Nick, but Claus Inc. There is indeed something a little scary about all those elves with their intense, angular faces and their mob mentality.

That's the magic of *The Polar Express:* It doesn't let us off the hook with the usual reassuring Santa and Christmas clichés. When a helicopter lifts the bag of toys over the town square, of course it knocks a star off the top of the Christmas tree, and of course an elf is almost skewered far below. When Santa's helpers hitch up the reindeer, they look not like tame cartoon characters, but like skittish purebreds. And as for Lonely Boy, although he does make the trip and get his present, and is fiercely protective of it, at the end of the movie we suspect his troubles are not over, and that loneliness may be his condition.

There are so many jobs and so many credits on this movie that I don't know who to praise, but there are sequences here that are really very special. Some are quiet little moments, like a reflection in a hubcap. Some are visual masterstrokes, like a POV that looks straight up through a printed page, with the letters floating between us and the reader. Some are story concepts, like the train car filled with old and dead toys being taken back to the Pole for recycling. Some are elements of mystery, like the character of the hobo, who is helpful and even saves Hero Boy's life but is in a world of his own up there on top of the train and doesn't become anybody's buddy (when he disappears, his hand always lingers a little longer than his body).

The Polar Express is a movie for more than one season; it will become a perennial, shared by the generations. It has a haunting magical quality because it has imagined its world freshly and played true to it, sidestepping all the tiresome Christmas clichés that children have inflicted on them this time of year. The conductor tells Hero Boy he thinks he really should get on the train, and I have the same advice for you.

Note: I've seen the movie twice, once in the IMAX 3-D process that will be available in *larger markets. New oversized 3-D glasses, big enough to fit over your own glasses, light enough so you can forget them, made this the best 3-D viewing experience I've ever had. If there's a choice, try the IMAX version. Or go twice. This is a movie that doesn't wear out.*

Poseidon ★ ★
PG-13, 99 m., 2006

Kurt Russell (Robert Ramsey), Josh Lucas (Dylan Johns), Richard Dreyfuss (Richard Nelson), Jacinda Barrett (Maggie James), Emmy Rossum (Jennifer Ramsey), Mike Vogel (Christian), Mia Maestro (Elena), Jimmy Bennett (Conor James), Andre Braugher (Captain Bradford), Freddy Rodriguez (Valentin), Kevin Dillon (Lucky Larry), Stacy Ferguson (Gloria). Directed by Wolfgang Petersen and produced by Petersen, Duncan Henderson, Mike Fleiss, and Akiva Goldsman. Screenplay by Mark Protosevich, based on the novel by Paul Gallico.

An odd and unexpected word kept nudging its way into my mind as I sat watching *Poseidon.* That word was "perfunctory." I hoped that other words would replace it. I knew I was not enjoying the movie, but I hoped it would improve or, lacking that, discover an interesting way to fail. But no. It was perfunctory, by which I mean, according to the dictionary that came with my computer: cursory, desultory, hurried, rapid, fleeting, token, casual, superficial, careless, halfhearted, sketchy, mechanical, automatic, routine, and offhand.

Yes. And if you want to see the opposite of those qualities, consider some of the other films by the director Wolfgang Petersen, most notably *Das Boot* (1981), but also *In the Line of Fire* (1993) and *The Perfect Storm* (2000). It may have been the latter movie that won him the assignment to remake *The Poseidon Adventure* (1972). In *The Perfect Storm,* he shows a fishing boat trying to climb an overwhelming wall of water, and failing. It is one of the best adventure movies of recent years, with vivid characters, convincing special effects, and a tangible feel for the relentless sea.

Having made such considerable movies, Petersen does not seem to have been inspired by the opportunity to remake a movie that was not all that good to begin with. Everyone in his audience already knows the story, and much of the suspense depends on who gets the Shelley Winters role and has to hold his or her breath for a long time under water. *Poseidon* follows, as it must, the formula for a disaster movie, which involves 1) a container holding a lot of characters; 2) cameos to establish them in broad, simplistic strokes; 3) a catastrophe; 4) the struggle of the survivors; and 5) the loss of at least one character we hate and one character we like, and the survival of the others, while thousands of extras die unmourned. It might be interesting to add 6) deadly snakes on the loose, but they've all been signed up for the forthcoming *Snakes on a Plane.*

The container can be an ocean liner, an airplane, a skyscraper, a Super Bowl stadium, whatever. Doesn't matter. This time it is an ocean liner, overturned by a "rogue wave" that leaves it floating upside down. The ship's captain (Andre Braugher) assures the passengers, who were just celebrating New Year's Eve, that they will be safe in the giant ballroom. A few daring souls think otherwise. They decide to save themselves by, essentially, escaping up the down staircase.

These characters include the heroic Dylan Johns (Josh Lucas), the equally heroic Robert Ramsey (Kurt Russell), his daughter Jennifer (Emmy Rossum), the obnoxious Lucky Larry (Kevin Dillon), the suicidal Richard Nelson (Richard Dreyfuss), the mother (Jacinda Barrett) and her son, Conor (Jimmy Bennett), and a stowaway (Mia Maestro). All of their human stories will play out against the drama of the endangered ship. As they say.

What do I mean by "perfunctory"? I mean that Petersen's heart isn't in it. He is too wise a director to think this is first-rate material, and too good a director to turn it into enjoyable trash. We realize with a sinking heart that we will have to experience various stock situations, including 1) a perilous traverse over a dizzying drop; 2) escape from seemingly locked rooms; 3) repeated threats of drowning and electrocution; 4) crucial decisions in which the right button will save them and the wrong one will doom them; and 5) ingenious reasoning by people who know nothing about ships but are expert at finding the charts, maps, and diagrams they can instantly decode. ("This is the ballast tank!" "The bulkheads are activated by water pressure!" "This is the way out!")

During all this time, exterior CGI shots will show the ship being rocked by enormous explosions, although curiously the lights come on from time to time when they are convenient, and the characters have all the flashlights they need to allow us to see the action. The characters will also all find time to sort out all the romantic complications, family differences, personal hangups, and character flaws that have been carefully introduced for this purpose.

There is nothing wrong with the performances. All of the actors are professionals, although none have as much fun as Shelley Winters, who is the actor everyone remembers from the 1972 movie. They are wet a lot, desperate a lot, endangered a lot, and surrounded by a lot of special effects. Then some of them survive and others die. You don't know a thing at the end of the movie you didn't know at the beginning. In the proper hands, this could have been a sequel to *Airplane!* named *Ocean Liner!* in which once the characters battle their way to the top (i.e., bottom) of the overturned ship, a second wave flips it again, and they have to retrace their steps.

Postmen in the Mountains ★ ★ ★
NO MPAA RATING, 90 m., 2004

Teng Rujun (Father), Liu Ye (Son), Gong Yehong (Grandmother), Chen Hao (Dong Girl). Directed by Huo Jianqi and produced by Kang Jianmin and Han Sanping. Screenplay by Si Wu, based on a short story by Peng Jianming.

The father prepares the postbag the night before, arranging the mail in the order it will be needed, and wrapping everything carefully against the possibility of bad weather. This will be the last time he packs the bag, and the first time the route will be carried by his son—who is inheriting his job.

The next morning unfolds awkwardly. The boy's mother is worried: Will he find the way? Will he be safe? The father (Teng Rujun) is unhappy to end the job that has defined his life. But his son (Liu Ye) will be accompanied by the family dog, who has always walked along with the father and knows the path. It is a long route, 112 kilometers through a mountainous rural region of China, and the trip will take three days. The son shoulders the bag and sets off, and then there is a problem: The dog will not come along. It looks uncertainly at the father. It runs between them. It is not right that the son and the bag are leaving, and the father is staying behind. This is the excuse the father is looking for to walk the route one last time and show his son the way. The two men and the dog set off together in Huo Jianqi's *Postmen in the Mountains*, a film so simple and straightforward that its buried emotions catch us a little by surprise.

The trek represents the longest time father and son have ever spent together; the boy was raised by his mother while his father was away, first for long periods, then for three days at a time. They've never even had much of a talk. Now the son observes that his father, who seemed so distant, has many friendships and relationships along the way—that he plays an important role as a conduit to the outside world, a bringer of good news and bad, a traveler in gossip, a counselor, adviser, and friend.

The villages and isolated dwellings are located in a region that must have been chosen for its astonishing beauty. Here are no factories, freeways, or fast food to mar the view, and the architecture has the beauty that often results when poverty and necessity dictate the function, and centuries evolve the form. The dog seems proud to show these things to his new young master.

There are several vignettes, as the postman brings personal news between villages, and in one case continues a long-running deception he has practiced on a blind woman. Her son in the city sends money, but does not write; the postman invents a letter to go with every delivery, "reading" to her out of his imagination. Now that will become part of the son's job.

They receive food and shelter along the way. One night they build a campfire under the stars. They don't share deep, philosophical truths, but simple facts about the job, which gradually become the father's explanation to his son about the life he has led, about his satisfactions and regrets. It is too bad he was never at home very much—but now his son will find out for himself that carrying the mail is an important job and must be taken seriously.

And that's about it. The movie consists of the journey, the conversations, the scenery, the little human stories. No big drama. No emergencies. Just carrying the mail, which over the years has supplied the threads to bind together all of these lives. When the son sets out alone on his next journey, the dog cheerfully goes along.

A Prairie Home Companion ★ ★ ★ ★
PG-13, 105 m., 2006

Woody Harrelson (Dusty), Tommy Lee Jones (Axeman), Garrison Keillor (G.K.), Kevin Kline (Guy Noir), Lindsay Lohan (Lola Johnson), Virginia Madsen (Dangerous Woman), John C. Reilly (Lefty), Maya Rudolph (Molly), Meryl Streep (Yolanda Johnson), Lily Tomlin (Rhonda Johnson), L. Q. Jones (Chuck Akers), Tim Russell (Stage Manager), Sue Scott (Makeup Lady), Tom Keith (Effects Man). Directed by Robert Altman and produced by Altman, Wren Arthur, Joshua Astrachan, Tony Judge, and David Levy. Screenplay by Garrison Keillor.

What a lovely film this is, so gentle and whimsical, so simple and profound. Robert Altman's *A Prairie Home Companion* is faithful to the spirit of the radio program, a spirit both robust and fragile, and yet achieves something more than simply reproducing a performance of the show. It is nothing less than an elegy, a memorial to memories of times gone by, to dreams that died but left the dreamers dreaming, to appreciating what you've had instead of insisting on more.

This elegiac strain is explained by the premise that we are watching the last performance of the weekly show. After a final singing of *Red River Valley* (the saddest of all songs), the paradise of the Fitzgerald Theater will be torn down so they can put up a parking lot. After thirty years, the show will be no more.

The show is hosted by a man referred to as G.K., and played by Garrison Keillor as a version of himself, which is about right, because he always seems to be a version of himself. Keillor, whose verbal and storytelling genius has spun a whole world out of thin air, always seems a step removed from what he does, as if bemused to find himself doing it. Here his character refuses to get all sentimental about the last program and has a dialogue with Lola (Lindsay Lohan), a young poet who likes suicide as a subject. It seems to her G.K. should offer up a eulogy; there is sufficient cause, not only because of the death of the program but also because a veteran of the show actually dies during the broadcast.

"I'm of an age when if I started to do eulogies, I'd be doing nothing else," he says.

"You don't want to be remembered?"

"I don't want them to be *told* to remember me."

So the last show is treated like any other. In the dressing room, incredibly cluttered with bric-a-brac and old photos, we meet Lola's mother and her aunt, Yolanda and Rhonda Johnson (Meryl Streep and Lily Tomlin). They are the two survivors from a four-sister singing act: "The Carter Family was like us, only famous." Their onstage duets are hilarious, depending on a timing that rises above the brilliant to the transcendent; they were doing this double act on the Academy Award telecast in March 2006.

We also meet Chuck Akers (L. Q. Jones), an old-time C&W singer, and Dusty and Lefty (Woody Harrelson and John C. Reilly), two cowboy singers who threaten to make the last program endless as they improvise one corny joke after another. We also meet the people who make the show work: the stage manager, Molly (Maya Rudolph), and, borrowed from the show itself, the makeup lady (Sue Scott), Al the backstage guy (Tim Russell), the sound effects man (Tom Keith), the bandleader (Rich Dworsky), and the P.H.C. house band. Molly is surely so pregnant she should stay calm, but she is driven to distraction by G.K.'s habit of never planning anything and moseying up to the microphone at the last conceivable moment.

Adding another level is the materialization in the real world of Guy Noir, Private Eye (Kevin Kline). Listeners of the program will know that Keillor and his stock company perform adventures from the life of Noir as a salute to old-time radio drama. In Altman's movie, Noir is a real person, a broken-down gumshoe who handles security for the show (he lights his cigarettes with wooden kitchen matches, just like Philip Marlowe in Altman's *The Long Goodbye*). Guy is visited by a character described as the Dangerous Woman (Virginia Madsen), who may perhaps be an angelic one.

The final visitor to the Fitzgerald Theater is Axeman (Tommy Lee Jones), who represents the investors who have bought the lovely theater and will tear it down. He doesn't recognize the bust of a man in the theater's private box, but we do: It is F. Scott Fitzgerald, that native son of St. Paul in whose honor the theater is named. A little later, Ed Lachman's camera helps Altman

observe that Fitzgerald and Guy Noir have profiles so similar as to make no difference.

Like the show that inspired it, *A Prairie Home Companion* is not about anything in particular. Perhaps it is about everything in general: about remembering, and treasuring the past, and loving performers not because they are new but because they have lasted. About smiling and being amused, but not laughing out loud, because in Minnesota loud laughter is seen as a vice practiced on the coasts. About how all things pass away, but if you live your life well, everything was fun while it lasted. There is so much of the ghost of Scott Fitzgerald hovering in the shadows of this movie that at the end I quoted to myself the closing words of *The Great Gatsby*. I'm sure you remember them, so let's say them together: "And so we beat on, boats against the current, borne back ceaselessly into the past."

Pretty Persuasion ★ ★

NO MPAA RATING, 104 m., 2005

Evan Rachel Wood (Kimberly Joyce), Ron Livingston (Percy Anderson), James Woods (Hank Joyce), Jane Krakowski (Emily Klein), Elisabeth Harnois (Brittany Wells), Selma Blair (Grace Anderson), Adi Schnall (Randa Azzouni), Stark Sands (Troy), Danny Comden (Roger Nicholl), Jaime King (Kathy Joyce). Directed by Marcos Siega and produced by Todd Dagres, Carl Levin, and Matt Weaver. Screenplay by Skander Halim.

Pretty Persuasion is the kind of teenage movie where James Woods can play the heroine's dad and not be the worst person in the story. He comes close, but then everyone comes close, except for the innocent bystanders. The movie stars Evan Rachel Wood, who is amazingly good playing a spiteful, cruel high school student. There are so many movies where the heroine is persecuted by the popular bombshell and her posse that it's almost a genre, but never has the bombshell been this evil.

Wood plays Kimberly Joyce, the product of a Bel Air home where malice is served at every meal. Her millionaire father, Hank (James Woods), is aggressively hateful, a fast-talker who mows down the opposition in every conversation and amuses himself by telling racist jokes to his daughter and her new stepmother, Kathy (Jaime King). What Kimberly learns at home, she improves on at school. Her sidekicks are Brittany (Elisabeth Harnois) and Randa (Adi Schnall), an Arab girl who gets to listen to Kim's ranking of the races (Arabs come last, but Kim is gentle when she tells Randa). What Randa thinks is hard to say, since she rarely speaks, is intimidated and dominated by Kimberly, and has been chosen as a mascot, not a friend.

Kimberly dislikes her English teacher, Percy Anderson (Ron Livingston), partly because of his classroom matter, partly because she dislikes all teachers, and partly because she suspects (correctly) that he harbors lustful thoughts for them. The thoughts don't bother Kimberly, a sexual predator, but they give her an idea: Why don't the three girls accuse Mr. Anderson of sexually molesting them? It could be good publicity for the acting career Kimberly dreams about. The two friends go along, carefully schooled by Kimberly.

The movie, directed by Marcos Siega and written by Skander Halim, exists uneasily somewhere between comedy and satire. When Mr. Anderson gives his wife (Selma Blair) a skirt like the students wear and asks her to read an essay while he "grades" her, it might be funny if the movie itself were not so much more lethal.

What the movie gets right is that sexual molestation, especially against attractive, articulate students in rich neighborhoods, is a publicity magnet. The story attracts predatory TV reporter Emily Klein (Jane Krakowski), who turns it into a running commentary on the virus of social depravity, without realizing she's a carrier. Mr. Anderson loses his job, the case is taken to trial, and the rest you will learn.

I admired the willingness of the screenplay to venture into deep waters; the movie's rating is still pending as I write, possibly because the MPAA thinks it is an R and the distributors would like a PG-13 audience, many of whom would find it shocking and disturbing. Like *Lolita*, this is a movie about young girls, but not for them. It makes some hard-edged observations about the current popularity, if that is the word, of suits charging sexual harassment (I refer not to the crime itself, which is evil, but to the way it is sometimes exploited to destroy innocent reputations). It is also dead right about the way some TV news outlets cover such "news" stories with a fervor entirely lacking as

they regard more important topics. Coverage of molestation easily shades into voyeurism.

I also admire Wood, who in a few movies has emerged as a young actress who can bring an eerie conviction even to tricky and complex scenes. In *Thirteen* (2003), she played a good girl who makes the mistake of friendship with a girl her age who introduces her to drugs, sex, and lying. Here she essentially takes the other role and is just as convincing: She finds a coldness and heartlessness in Kimberly that moves beyond the high-school hellion category and into malevolence.

So the movie is daring and well acted. Yet it isn't very satisfying because the serious content keeps breaking through the soggy plot intended to contain it. The material in *Pretty Persuasion* needed to be handled as heavy drama or played completely for comedy, and by trying to have it both ways, the movie has it neither way. The audience gets emotional whiplash, its laughter interrupted by scenes where lives are destroyed.

I am also uneasy about the racism in the dialogue. I understand its purpose, I guess: to expose the way it works as a sickness, passed from generation to generation. But is the movie using its pose of exposing racism as a cover to slip in offensive jokes about Jews and Arabs that are, strictly speaking, not necessary to tell this story? It would have been interesting to see the movie with its opening night audience and see if anyone laughed at those jokes. I have a feeling they might have, and for them, the point of the movie will be lost. It is, I admit, rather easily lost.

Pride & Prejudice ★ ★ ★ ★
PG, 127 m., 2005

Keira Knightley (Elizabeth Bennet), Matthew Macfadyen (Darcy), Brenda Blethyn (Mrs. Bennet), Donald Sutherland (Mr. Bennet), Simon Woods (Charles Bingley), Rupert Friend (Lieutenant Wickham), Tom Hollander (William Collins), Rosamund Pike (Jane Bennet), Jena Malone (Lydia Bennet), Judi Dench (Lady Catherine), Carey Mulligan (Kitty Bennet), Talulah Riley (Mary Bennet). Directed by Joe Wright and produced by Tim Bevan, Eric Fellner, and Paul Webster. Screenplay by Deborah Moggach, based on the novel by Jane Austen.

It is a truth universally acknowledged, that a

single man in possession of a good fortune, must be in want of a wife.

Everybody knows the first sentence of Jane Austen's *Pride and Prejudice*. But the chapter ends with a truth equally acknowledged about Mrs. Bennet, who has five daughters in want of husbands: "The business of her life was to get her daughters married." Romance seems so urgent and delightful in Austen because marriage is a business, and her characters cannot help treating it as a pleasure. *Pride and Prejudice* is the best of her novels because its romance involves two people who were born to be in love, and who care not about business, pleasure, or each other. It is frustrating enough when one person refuses to fall in love, but when both refuse, we cannot rest until they kiss.

Of course all depends on who the people are. When Dorothea marries the Reverend Casaubon in Eliot's *Middlemarch*, it is a tragedy. She marries out of consideration and respect, which is all wrong; she should have married for money, always remembering that where money is, love often follows, since there is so much time for it. The crucial information about Mr. Bingley, the new neighbor of the Bennet family, is that he "has" an income of four or five thousand pounds a year. One never earns an income in these stories, one has it, and Mrs. Bennet (Brenda Blethyn) has her sights on it.

Her candidate for Mr. Bingley's hand is her eldest daughter, Jane; it is orderly to marry the girls off in sequence, avoiding the impression that an older one has been passed over. There is a dance, to which Bingley brings his friend Darcy. Jane and Bingley immediately fall in love, to get them out of the way of Darcy and Elizabeth, who is the second Bennet daughter. These two immediately dislike each other. Darcy is overheard telling his friend Bingley that Elizabeth is "tolerable, but not handsome enough to tempt *me*." The person who overhears him is Elizabeth, who decides she will "loathe him for all eternity." She is advised within the family circle to count her blessings: "If he liked you, you'd have to talk to him."

These are the opening moves in Joe Wright's new film *Pride & Prejudice*, one of the most delightful and heartwarming adaptations made from Austen or anybody else. Much of the delight and most of the heart comes from Keira Knightley, who plays Elizabeth as a girl glowing in the first light of perfection. She is beautiful, she has opinions, she is kind but can be unforgiving. "They are all silly and ignorant like other girls," says her father in the novel, "but Lizzie has something more of quickness than her sisters."

Knightley's performance is so light and yet fierce that she makes the story almost realistic; this is not a well-mannered *Masterpiece Theatre* but a film where strong-willed young people enter life with their minds at war with their hearts. The movie is more robust than most period romances. It is set earlier than most versions of the story, in the late 1700s, when Austen wrote the first draft; that was a period more down to earth than 1813, when she revised and published it. The young ladies don't look quite so much like illustrations for *Vanity Fair*, and there is mud around their hems when they come back from a walk. It is a time of rural realities: When Mrs. Bennet sends a daughter to visit Netherfield Park, the country residence of Mr. Bingley, she sends her on horseback, knowing it will rain and she will have to spend the night.

The plot by this point has grown complicated. It is a truth universally acknowledged by novelists that before two people can fall in love with each other, they must first seem determined to make the wrong marriage with someone else. It goes without saying that Lizzie fell in love with young Darcy (Matthew Macfadyen) the moment she saw him, but her pride has been wounded. She tells Jane: "I might more easily forgive his vanity had he not wounded mine."

The stakes grow higher. She is told by the dashing officer Wickham (Rupert Friend) that Darcy, his childhood friend, cheated him of a living that he deserved. And she believes that Darcy is responsible for having spirited Bingley off to London to keep him out of the hands of her sister Jane. Lizzie even begins to think she may be in love with Wickham. Certainly she is not in love with the Reverend Collins (Tom Hollander), who has a handsome living and would be Mrs. Bennet's choice for a match. When Collins proposes, the mother is in ecstasy, but Lizzie declines and is supported by her father (Donald Sutherland), a man whose love for his girls outweighs his wife's financial planning.

All of these characters meet and circle one another at a ball in the village Assembly Hall, and the camera circles them. The sequence involves one unbroken shot and has the same elegance as Visconti's long single take as he follows the count through the ballrooms in *The Leopard*. We see the characters interacting, we see Lizzie avoiding Collins and enticing Darcy, we understand the politics of these romances, and we are swept up in the intoxication of the dance. In a later scene, as Lizzie and Darcy dance together, everyone else somehow vanishes (in their eyes, certainly) and they are left alone within the love they feel.

But a lot must happen before the happy ending, and I particularly admired a scene in the rain where Darcy and Lizzie have an angry argument. This argument serves two purposes: It clears up misunderstandings, and it allows both characters to see each other as the true and brave people they really are. It is not enough for them to love each other; they must also love the goodness in each other, and that is where the story's true emotion lies.

The movie is well cast from top to bottom; like many British films, it benefits from the genius of its supporting players. Judi Dench brings merciless truth-telling to her role as a society arbiter; Sutherland is deeply amusing as a man who lives surrounded by women and considers it a blessing and a fate; and as his wife, Blethyn finds a balance between her character's mercenary and loving sides. She may seem unforgivably obsessed with money, but better be obsessed with money now than with poverty hereafter.

When Lizzie and Darcy finally accept each other in *Pride & Prejudice*, I felt an almost unreasonable happiness. Why was that? I am impervious to romance in most films, seeing it as a manifestation of box office requirements. Here it is different, because Darcy and Elizabeth are good and decent people who would rather do the right thing than convenience themselves. Anyone who will sacrifice their own happiness for higher considerations deserves to be happy. When they realize that about each other their hearts leap and, reader, so did mine. ☞

Prime ★ ★ ★
PG-13, 105 m., 2005

Meryl Streep (Lisa Metzger), Uma Thurman (Rafi Gardet), Bryan Greenberg (David Bloomberg), Jon Abrahams (Morris), Madhur Jaffrey (Rita). Directed by Ben Younger and produced by Jennifer Todd and Suzanne Todd. Screenplay by Younger.

Flawed is a word movie critics use more often than jewelers. They have looked into the heart of a sparkling gem and found an imperfection. Every movie should be perfect, and on such grounds, *Prime* is flawed. Its flaw is that it employs an Idiot Plot in a story that is too serious to support it. I can forgive and even embrace an Idiot Plot in its proper place (consider Astaire and Rogers in *Top Hat*). But when the characters have depth and their decisions have consequences, I grow restless when their misunderstandings could be ended by words that the screenplay refuses to allow them to utter.

Prime is such a movie, yet I must recommend it because in its comedy of errors are actors who bring truth at least to their dialogue. Meryl Streep and Uma Thurman have line readings that work as delicate and precise adjustments of dangerous situations. They're dealing with issues that are real enough, even if they've been brought about by contrivance. And Streep has that ability to cut through the solemnity of a scene with a zinger that reveals how all human effort is, after all, comic at some level: How amusing, to think we can control fate!

The movie crosses two dependable story structures: 1) the romance between lovers widely separated in age, and 2) a mistaken identity that leads to complications. The trouble begins when Rafi Gardet (Uma Thurman) and David Bloomberg (Bryan Greenberg) fall in love. They know there is an age difference, but because they both lie a little, they don't realize how big it is: Rafi is thirty-seven and David is twenty-three.

Rafi discusses her concerns with her psychiatrist, Lisa Metzger (Streep), who argues tolerantly that if the relationship is otherwise sound and healthy, then age alone is not a reason to terminate it. In this matter Lisa is counseled by her own psychiatrist, Rita (Madhur Jaffrey). Now comes a spoiler warning for anyone who has not seen a commercial or trailer for the movie, where Universal eagerly reveals the plot secret. It is: David is Lisa's son. Since they have different last names and his age has been lied about, she has no reason to guess this. On one hand you have a hypothetical case of a man about twenty-seven dating a woman about thirty-four, and on the other you have the real case of a Jewish son of twenty-three dating a thirty-seven-year-old divorced Gentile. This disconnect creates some interesting moments for the Streep character, who is not narrow-minded but whose feelings as a mother are not hypothetical, while her opinions as an analyst certainly are.

Prime gets too much mileage by persisting in the device of the mistaken identity. But it does lead to interesting moments. After Lisa discovers to her horror that the man in Rafi's life is her son, she flees to her own psychiatrist for advice and is told she has a responsibility to her client. In my opinion, that responsibility is to declare a conflict of interest, but then I'm not a shrink and besides, then we wouldn't have a movie. So Lisa continues the sessions, and perhaps only Streep could produce such gradations of facial expressions as her client describes her son's lovemaking, his opinion of his mother, and admirable details of his physique.

As the movie develops, we're asked to take sides: Should this romance continue? I am in favor of love but do not believe it conquers all. Rafi's clock is ticking. David has no eagerness to be a father. Rafi is a babe who looks much younger than her years, but the day will come when someone assumes she is David's mother, and they had better be prepared for that day. There is also the religious difference, but here Lisa the psychiatrist strikes a reasonable note that I will leave for her to explain.

The movie works through the performances. The director, Ben Younger *(Boiler Room)*, does some nice things with scenes such as the family dinner where everyone makes nice and ignores the elephant in the room. There are some one-liners that zing not only with humor but also truth. On the whole I was satisfied. The Idiot Plot was necessary up to a point. I thought that point was too long delayed. It is also a problem that this is a comedy about matters that are not, in most people's lives, very funny. There is a final shot in which Rafi and David regard each other with affection and nostalgia, and I wondered if the characters were expressing something else, as well: the wish that they could meet in another movie and start over.

Primer ★ ★ ★ ½
PG-13, 78 m., 2004

Shane Carruth (Aaron), David Sullivan (Abe), Casey Gooden (Robert), Anand Upadhyaya (Phillip), Carrie Crawford (Kara). Directed and produced by Shane Carruth. Screenplay by Carruth.

Shane Carruth's *Primer* opens with four tech-heads addressing envelopes to possible investors; they seek venture capital for a machine they're building in the garage. They're not entirely sure what the machine does, although it certainly does something. Their dialogue is halfway between shop talk and one of those articles in *Wired* magazine that you never finish. We don't understand most of what they're saying, and neither, perhaps, do they, but we get the drift. Challenging us to listen closely, to half-understand what they half-understand, is one of the ways the film sucks us in.

They steal a catalytic converter for its platinum, and plunder a refrigerator for its xenon. Their budget is so small, they could cash the checks on the bus. Aaron and Abe, agreeing that whatever they've invented, they're the ones who invented it, subtly eliminate the other two from the enterprise. They then regard something that looks like an insulated shipping container with wires and dials and coils and stuff. This is odd: It secretes protein. More protein than it has time to secrete. Measuring the protein's rate of growth, they determine that one minute in the garage is equal to 1,347 minutes in the machine.

Is time in the machine different from time outside the machine? Apparently. But that would make it some kind of time machine, wouldn't it? Hard to believe. Aaron (Shane Carruth) and Abe (David Sullivan) ponder the machine and look at their results, and Aaron concludes it is "the most important thing any living being has ever witnessed." But what is it?

There's a fascination in the way they talk with each other, quickly, softly, excitedly. It's better, actually, that we don't understand everything they say, because that makes us feel more like eavesdroppers and less like the passive audience for predigested dialogue. We can see where they're heading, especially after . . . well, I don't want to give away some of the plot, and I may not understand the rest, but it would appear that they can travel through time. They learn this by seeing their doubles before they have even tried time travel—proof that later they will travel back to now. Meanwhile (is that the word?) a larger model of the machine is/was assembled in a storage locker by them/their doubles.

Should they personally experiment with time travel? Yes, manifestly, because they already have. "I can think of no way in which this thing would be considered even remotely close to safe," one of them says. But they try it out, journeying into the recent past and buying some mutual funds they know will rise in value.

It seems to work. The side effect, however, is that occasionally there are two of them: the Abe or Aaron who originally lived through the time, and the one who has gone back to the time and is living through it simultaneously. One is a double. Which one? There is a shot where they watch "themselves" from a distance, and we assume those they're watching are themselves living in ordinary time, and they are themselves having traveled back to observe them. But which Abe or Aaron is the real one? If they met, how would they speak? If two sets of the same atoms exist in the same universe at the same time, where did the additional atoms come from? It can make you hungry, thinking about questions like that. "I haven't eaten since later this afternoon," one complains.

Primer is a puzzle film that will leave you wondering about paradoxes, loopholes, loose ends, events without explanation, chronologies that don't seem to fit. Abe and Aaron wonder, too, and what seems at first like a perfectly straightforward method for using the machine turns out to be alarmingly complicated; various generations of themselves and their actions prove impossible to keep straight. Carruth handles the problems in an admirably understated way; when one of the characters begins to bleed a little from an ear, what does that mean? Will he be injured in a past he has not yet visited? In that case, is he the double? What happened to the being who arrived at this moment the old-fashioned way, before having traveled back?

The movie delights me with its cocky confidence that the audience can keep up. *Primer* is a film for nerds, geeks, brainiacs, academic decathlon winners, programmers, philosophers, and the kinds of people who have made it this far into the review. It will surely be hated by those who "go to the movies to be entertained," and embraced and debated by others, who will find it entertains the parts the

others do not reach. It is maddening, fascinating, and completely successful.

Note: Carruth wrote, directed, and edited the movie, composed the score, and starred in it. The budget was reportedly around $7,000, but that was enough: The movie never looks cheap, because every shot looks as it must look. In a New York Times *interview, Carruth said he filmed largely in his own garage, and at times he was no more sure what he was creating than his characters were.* Primer *won the award for best drama at Sundance 2004.*

The Prince & Me ★ ★ ½
PG, 111 m., 2004

Julia Stiles (Paige Morgan), Luke Mably (Prince Edvard), Ben Miller (Soren), James Fox (King Haraald), Miranda Richardson (Queen Rosalind), Eliza Bennett (Princess Anabella), Alberta Watson (Amy Morgan), John Bourgeouis (Ben Morgan). Directed by Martha Coolidge and produced by Mark Amin. Screenplay by Jack Amiel, Michael Begler, and Katherine Fugate.

The Prince & Me recycles a story so old that it must satisfy some basic yearning in the human psyche—or at least that portion of the psyche installed in teenage girls. It is, as you have probably guessed, about a romance between a prince and a commoner—in this case, between the future king of Denmark and a Wisconsin farm girl. He enrolls in a Wisconsin university, they fall into hate and then into love, but when she follows him back to Denmark she has to ask herself if she really wants to be the future queen.

If the story felt more than usually familiar, maybe it's because I saw *Win a Date with Tad Hamilton!* In that version, a small-town girl won a date with a big Hollywood star, flew to Los Angeles, and in her simplicity and sincerity inspired the star to fall in love. But was she really cut out to be a movie star's wife? In both cases, the movies start by establishing the men as targets of paparazzi because of their steamy romantic lives; in both cases, the men are won over by the freshness of a woman unlike any they have ever dated.

The Prince & Me is an efficient, sweet, sometimes charming PG-rated version of the story, ideal for girls of a certain age but perhaps not for everybody else. It stars Julia Stiles as Paige Morgan, a serious, focused student of bio-chemistry, who was raised on an organic dairy farm and is famous as "the last unengaged girl in town." Stiles is gifted at conveying intelligence, which is a mixed blessing here; any smarter, and she'd realize she was in a movie.

Luke Mably plays Prince Edvard of Denmark, a.k.a. "Eddie," who flies to Wisconsin to escape the paparazzi and also because he saw a video in which Wisconsin college girls flash their boobs for the camera, and he assumes this is typical behavior in Wisconsin. This is such a stupid motivation for the prince's trip that it throws the character a little out of balance; it takes him several scenes in Wisconsin to reestablish himself as a person of normal intelligence.

Eddie arrives incognito with his valet Soren (Ben Miller) in tow, but because his parents have cut off his allowance he's short on funds and has to take a job in the campus cafeteria where Paige works. They clash almost at once, and find a temporary truce when she can help him with chemistry and he can help her with Shakespeare (he knows a lot about princes of Denmark). This stretch of the film is fun because it's based on tension; not so much fun is the formulaic part where she discovers his true identity, is angry at the deception, he returns to his father's sickbed, she follows him to Denmark, he proposes marriage, and so forth.

The movie does struggle to make something interesting of the royal family. The king (Edward Fox) and queen (Miranda Richardson) are played by fine actors who bring dimension and conviction to their roles; they are not simply marching through clichés. The queen's initial disapproval of Paige and her gradual acceptance are well handled. But the plot jerks Paige and Eddie back and forth romantically so many times we lose patience with it; we know, because the story is so familiar, that she must accept his proposal, then have second thoughts, then . . . well, you know.

As pure escapism, there are some sublime moments. I like the one where the queen takes Paige into the royal vault to show her the crown jewels, and ask her to pick out something to wear to the coronation ball. As Paige's eyes sweep the glittering shelves, there is a certain intake of breath among some of the women in the audience, and I was reminded of a similar moment in *The Greek Tycoon* when Aristotle Onassis outlines their marriage contract to Jackie Kennedy, and adds, "plus a million dollars a month walking-around money."

So there's good stuff here, and the stars are likable, but the director, Martha Coolidge, throws so many logical roadblocks in our path that we keep getting distracted from the story. When Paige arrives unannounced in Denmark and stands in the crowd at a royal parade, Eddie sees her and sweeps her up on his horse as the Danes shout, "Paige! It's Paige!" That's because they know her from photos the paparazzi took in Wisconsin. Okay, but how about later, when Eddie is giving his first speech as king, and Paige walks through the middle of the crowd and *no one* notices her, just because at that point the plot doesn't want them to? Despite the fact that she's now infinitely more famous in Denmark as the girl who accepted Eddie's proposal and then rejected it?

Quibble, quibble. The movie's target audience won't care. Others will. *The Prince & Me* has the materials to be a heartwarming mass-market love story, but it doesn't assemble them convincingly. *Win a Date with Tad Hamilton!* is less obviously blessed, but works better. Strange,

The Princess Diaries 2: Royal Engagement ★ ½
G, 120 m., 2004

Julie Andrews (Clarisse Renaldi), Anne Hathaway (Mia Thermopolis), Hector Elizondo (Joe), Heather Matarazzo (Lilly Moscovitz), Chris Pine (Sir Nicholas). Kathleen Marshall (Charlotte), John Rhys-Davies (Viscount Mabrey), Callum Blue (Andrew Jacoby). Directed by Garry Marshall and produced by Debra Martin Chase, Whitney Houston, and Mario Iscovich. Screenplay by Shonda Rhimes.

The Princess Diaries 2: Royal Engagement offers the prudent critic with a choice. He can say what he really thinks about the movie, or he can play it safe by writing that it's sure to be loved by lots of young girls. But I avoid saying that anything is sure to be loved by anybody.

In this case, I am not a young girl, nor have I ever been, and so how would I know if one would like it? Of course, that's exactly the objection I get in e-mails from young readers, who complain that no one like me can possibly like a movie like this. They are correct. I have spent a long time, starting at birth and continuing until this very moment, evolving into the kind of person who could not possibly like a movie like this, and I like to think the effort was not in vain.

So to girls who think they might like this movie, I say: Enjoy! Movies are for fun, among other things, and if you love *The Princess Diaries 2*, then I am happy for you, because I value the movies too much to want anyone to have a bad time at one.

But to Garry Marshall, the often-talented director of the original *Princess Diaries* as well as this sequel, I say: Did you deliberately assemble this movie from off-the-shelf parts, or did it just happen that way? The film is like an homage to the clichés and obligatory stereotypes of its genre. For someone like Marshall, it must have been like playing the scales.

The beautiful Anne Hathaway, still only twenty-two, stars as Princess Mia. You will remember that she was a typical American teenager whose mother raised her in a converted San Francisco firehouse, where she could slide down the pole every morning. Then a visit from Queen Clarisse of Genovia (Julie Andrews) revealed that she was, in fact, the queen's granddaughter and next in line to the throne.

In *Part 2*, she is the beloved Princess Mia of Genovia, a kingdom the size of a movie set, which is apparently located somewhere in Europe and populated by citizens who speak American English, except for a few snaky types with British accents. This kingdom has two peculiarities: (1) The shops and homes all seem to be three-quarter-scale models of the sorts of structures an American Girl doll would occupy; and (2) a great many of the extras get a few extra frames, in order to look uncannily as if they might be personal friends of the director. So many prosperous men in their sixties, so well barbered, groomed, and dressed, so southern California in their very bearing, are unlikely to be visiting Genovia for any other reason, since the kingdom doesn't seem to have a golf course.

There's no need for me to spoil the plot; as I was saying about *The Village*, it spoils itself. If I were to describe the characters, you could instantly tell me what happens in the movie. Let's try that, as an experiment.

There is Princess Mia, who is given a deadline of one month to either marry or forfeit her rights to the throne. The evil Viscount Mabrey (John Rhys-Davies) wants to disqualify her because his nephew, Sir Nicholas (Chris Pine), is next in line to the throne. Desperate for a husband, and learning that Queen Clarisse was perfectly happy in an arranged marriage, Mia decides to marry for the love of her country.

A suitable bachelor is discovered: nice Andrew Jacoby, duke of Kensington (Callum Blue). Mia accepts his proposal, despite, as she writes in her diary on the Web site, "He's everything a girl should want in a husband-to-be. It's . . . just that . . . something . . . you know." Meanwhile, of course, she hates the handsome young Sir Nicholas, who hangs around a lot and annoys her. Dear Diary: "Just look at him . . . all sneaky and smug and . . . and . . . cute."

Okay now, given those clues, see if you can figure out who she ends up with. And for that matter, consider Joseph (Hector Elizondo), the chief of palace security. He has been in love with the widow Clarisse for years, and she knows it, and is pleased. That provides us with a romance without closure that has persisted ever since the first movie, and if there is anything nature abhors more than a vacuum, it is a loving couple kept asunder when they should be sundering.

Director Marshall puts his cast and plot through their paces with the speed and deliberation of Minnesota Fats clearing the table. He even provides a fountain for two characters to stand beside, so they can illustrate Gene Siskel's maxim that nobody in a comedy ever comes within ten yards of water without falling in.

Yes, it's nice to see Julie Andrews looking great and performing a song, although the line "Give the queen a shout-out, and she'll sing" is one I doubt will ever be heard in Buckingham Palace. It is also rather original that at her slumber party, Mia and her friends don't get wasted at a private club, but engage in the jolly indoor sport of mattress surfing.

The Prize Winner of Defiance, Ohio ★ ★ ★ ½
PG-13, 99 m., 2005

Julianne Moore (Evelyn Ryan), Woody Harrelson (Kelly Ryan), Laura Dern (Dortha Schaefer), Trevor Morgan (Bruce Ryan at 16), Ellary Porterfield (Tuff Ryan at 13–18), Simon

Reynolds (Ray the Milkman), Frank Chiesurin (Freddy Canon). Directed by Jane Anderson and produced by Jack Rapke, Steve Starkey, and Robert Zemeckis. Screenplay by Anderson, based on the book by Terry Ryan.

The Prize Winner of Defiance, Ohio, said to tell a true story, subtitles itself: "How my mother raised ten kids on twenty-five words or less." And she does; in an era when companies gave valuable prizes for jingles and slogans, Evelyn Ryan is the best "contester" in America. She wins cash prizes, a deep freezer, trips, cars, and lots and lots of the sponsors' products. When her entry is chosen over 250,000 others in a big Dr Pepper contest, she proudly tells a daughter: "And it wasn't even my best one!"

Evelyn, played by Julianne Moore, is like the small-town cousin of Cathy, the Connecticut housewife she played in *Far From Heaven* (2002). Cathy was trapped in a sterile marriage and a world where men made all the decisions and women were locked in supporting roles. Judging by the body count around her dinner table in Ohio, Evelyn Ryan's marriage is not sterile, but it is a trap.

Her husband, Kelly (Woody Harrelson), puts back a six-pack and a pint of whiskey every night, drinking up his paycheck. He's a nice guy when he's sober but undergoes such terrifying personality changes that the family is afraid to enter the kitchen when he's listening to a baseball game. He never actually beats Evelyn, although she is sometimes injured as a side effect of his rages and suffers emotional anguish when he pounds on the brand-new freezer with a frying pan. When the cops are called, they stand around with him in the kitchen, discussing those Red Sox.

Evelyn handles her domestic situation with an eerie detachment and a relentless cheerfulness. She smiles, she looks on the bright side, she charms, she showers her children with attention and praise, and she lives tensely through her husband's rages. She doesn't scream at him but makes quiet comments about his drinking, and sad little asides he doesn't always understand. "You know what your problem is?" he says at one point. "You're too damn happy." A little later in the film, she tells him: "I don't need you to make me happy. I just need you to leave me alone when I am."

The power in the film comes from the dis-connect between the anger and emotional violence in the marriage, and the way Evelyn keeps her dignity, protects her children, fights to put food on the table, and deals with a husband she always calls "Father." She is "Mother," of course. She has never been outside of Ohio, never had a spare dollar in the bank, never been able to express her creativity except through the contests. Moore plays this woman as a victim whose defenses are dignity and optimism. It's a performance of a performance, actually: Evelyn Ryan plays a role that conceals the despair in her heart.

The word "alcoholic" is never used in the household, although Kelly Ryan is a classic alcoholic. When the parish priest comes to offer advice, it is to advise Evelyn to submit and pray and support her husband; when he leaves, one of the kids observes that the priest's breath "smells just like Dad's."

There is a running battle with the milkman over the weekly bill. They are hours from being homeless when a contest prize allows them to put a down payment on a house. Homework goes on around the dining room table while Kelly, in the kitchen, swings between bitterness and tears; he feels shame because his wife supports the family with her contests, and it comes out either weepy or angry. Of course, if he would stop drinking and go to AA, he could hold up his end of the marriage, but that does not occur to him as a possibility.

"So far, three of my chicks have found their nests, and I am so very proud of them," Evelyn tells us in narration at one point. "That's where my prayers went. That's where they all went." It's the repetition, the use of the word "all," that carries the message. She did not pray for herself, or for her husband. She does have one ambition: to travel to Goshen, Indiana, for a meeting of a "Contester Club" convened by a fellow contestant (Laura Dern) who is a pen pal.

The movie is based on a memoir by Terry ("Tuff") Ryan, one of two children who became authors. The other kids all turned out well, too. The film ends with one of those moments that blindsides you with an unexpected surge of emotion. But for the most part *Prize Winner*, written and directed by Jane Anderson, avoids obvious sentiment and predictable emotion, and shows this woman somehow holding it together year after year, entering goofy contests that for her family mean life and death.

This is Anderson's feature film debut as a director, after work on television. As a writer, she was responsible for *The Positively True Adventures of the Alleged Texas Cheerleader-Murdering Mom* (1993), starring Holly Hunter in one of the lost treasures among recent films. She is fascinated by mothers driven to extremes by the problem of having all of the responsibility and none of the power.

The Producers ★ ★ ★
PG-13, 120 m., 2005

Nathan Lane (Max Bialystock), Matthew Broderick (Leo Bloom), Uma Thurman (Ulla), Will Ferrell (Franz Liebkind), Roger Bart (Carmen Ghia), Gary Beach (Roger De Bris), Jon Lovitz (Mr. Marks). Directed by Susan Stroman and produced by Mel Brooks and Jonathan Sanger. Screenplay by Brooks and Thomas Meehan.

I know the 1968 movie *The Producers* virtually by heart, and it's one of the funniest movies I've ever seen. That makes it tricky for me to review this 2005 musical version—both because it's different and because so often it is the same. There are stretches in Susan Stroman's opening scenes that follow Mel Brooks's 1968 version so closely it's as if Gus Van Sant, having finished his shot-by-shot remake of *Psycho*, advanced directly to this assignment.

The new movie is a success, that I know. How much of a success, I cannot be sure. Someone who has seen the original once or twice, or never, would be a better judge. It is unfair to observe of Nathan Lane and Matthew Broderick that they are not Zero Mostel and Gene Wilder, but there you have it: They're not.

There is poetic justice here. When Broderick and Lane left the Broadway and London productions and were replaced by other actors, their replacements were sniffed at in some quarters as "the road company." Now comes the movie, and in following Mostel and Wilder, *they* become the road company. Each and every actor in the 1968 movie, including Kenneth Mars, Christopher Hewett, Andreas Voutsinas, Lee Meredith, Dick Shawn, William Hickey, and Renée Taylor, was so perfectly cast that a kind of inevitability befell them.

Now I look at Uma Thurman as the sexpot Ulla and Will Ferrell as the Nazi playwright Franz, and I think they're really good, they bring both new and old things to their roles, but—well, it's just not fair to them for me to remember the older movie, but I cannot help myself. When they sing and dance, I like them the most, because they're not reminding me of anything from 1968. When Thurman refers to herself in the third person as "Ulla" and describes the high standards of her low conduct, she achieves a kind of joy of performance that deserves to be seen without Meredith standing just offstage tapping her toe.

The story itself is a great construction. Brooks wrote an original screenplay whose characters are driven by greed, need, neurosis, cheerfully shameful sexual behavior, and a deep cynicism about show business. It is a tribute to his work that it could be transferred virtually intact to the musical stage thirty-five years later and effortlessly become a historic hit.

The new songs written by Brooks embodied the original film's spirit, and Stroman added a few inspired touches, such as little old ladies choreographed with their walkers; they were transgressive in the same outrageous Brooks tradition. The only flaw was one of excess; in a scene set in prison toward the end, he has Lane recap virtually the entire movie as a one-man repertory troupe, and if it goes on too long, well of course it does. Moderation is not a quality possessed by anyone associated with a movie that advises us, "If you've got it, baby—flaunt it!"

It is a tribute to this film that it worked for me despite my personal history. It was fun, it was funny, it was alive, although the color palette seemed to have darker colors and I remember the original as a movie made from golds and yellows and browns. There is a moment when Max Bialystock, the con-man producer, promises wealth and triumph to Leo Bloom, the nervous accountant who has cooked up their crooked financing, and a fountain erupts on cue behind him. In 1968 it was the fountain at Lincoln Center; now it's one in Central Park. I am absolutely incapable of judging the impact of this scene because I was startled and delighted in 1968, but watching this film I could hardly focus on the dialogue, I was so intent on waiting for the eruption.

So I had better end these meditations with a simple observation: If I had fun, most other viewers are likely to have more fun, because they won't have my baggage. I've painted myself into a corner. I cannot do better than to end with my favorite Mel Brooks story. Mel and I were in an elevator in New York at the time of the original film, and a lady got on, looked at him, and said, "Sir, I have seen your film and it is vulgar!" Brooks replied: "Madame, my film rises below vulgarity."

The Promise ★ ½

PG-13, 103 m., 2006

Cecilia Cheung (Princess Qingcheng), Dong-Kun Jang (Kunlun), Hiroyuki Sanada (General Guangming), Nicolas Tse (Wuhuan), Liu Ye (Snow Wolf), Hong Chen (Manshen). Directed by Chen Kaige and produced by Chen Hong, Han Sanping, and Ernst "Etchie" Stroh. Screenplay by Chen Kaige and Zhang Tan.

The Promise is pretty much a mess of a movie; the acting is overwrought, the plot is too tangled to play like anything *but* a plot, and although I know you can create terrific special effects at home in the basement on your computer, the CGI work in this movie looks like it was done with a dial-up connection. What a disappointment from Chen Kaige, who has made great movies (*Farewell, My Concubine*) and no doubt will make them again.

The plot involves a touch of the crucial romantic misunderstanding in *Vertigo*. Princess Qingcheng (Cecilia Cheung) thinks she is in love with the great General Guangming (Hiroyuki Sanada), who has saved her life after she offended the king (Cheng Qian). But actually she is in love with the slave Kunlan (Dong-Kun Jang), who is impersonating the general. Kunlan has been assigned to protect the king from an outlander assassin named Wuhuan (Nicolas Tse) and another assassin named Snow Wolf (Liu Ye). This is all going to be on the final.

Qingcheng's love for the general (or Kunlan) is doomed whether or not she discovers that the former slave is impersonating his master. That is because in the early scenes of the movie, we saw Qingcheng as a child, being told by the Goddess Manshen (Chen Hong) that although she will have beauty and power and be a princess, she will lose every man she ever loves. This has possibilities. Since she loves Kunlan (thinking he is the general), what would happen if Kunlan were lost as per the prophecy, and she

ended up with the real general? Would she then think she loved him and live happily ever after, not realizing he is not really the man she loves? Would her mistake grant him immunity? At some point I wanted James Stewart to appear and herd everybody up into a bell tower.

One of Kunlan's gifts is the ability to run really, really fast. I'm thinking of the Flash here. The problem with attaining that velocity is that Kunlan obviously must abandon the world of gravity and physical reality, and become a computer-generated graphic, and you know, it's a funny thing, CGI running may be faster than real running, but it never seems like anybody is really working at it. We're watching an effect instead of an achievement.

The CGI work in the movie is cheesy. One problem with CGI is that it inspires greed in directors. Chen Kaige reportedly had 1,000 real extras for one of his battle scenes, and considering that Orson Welles put on a great battle in *Falstaff* with close-ups of about nine actors, that should have been plenty. But no. He uses CGI to multiply those soldiers until they take on all the reality of the hordes of *Troy*, who were so numerous that in one shot it was obvious they would all fit inside their city only by standing on each other's shoulders. Enough is enough.

Another difficulty is that the story is never organized clearly enough to generate much concern in our minds. The characters are not people but collections of attributes, and isn't it generally true that the more sensational an action scene, the less we care about the people in it? It's as if the scene signals us that it's about itself, and the characters are spectators just as we are.

I spent a fair amount of time puzzling over my notes and rummaging on the Web for hints about the details of the plot, and in the process discovered a new Movie Law. You are familiar with the Law of Symbolism: If you have to ask what something symbolized, it didn't. Now here is the Law of Plots: If you can't describe it with clarity, there wasn't one. I know someone will throw up *Syriana* as an objection, but there is a difference between a plot that is about confusion and a plot that is merely confused.

Proof ★ ★ ★ ★

PG-13, 99 m., 2005

Gwyneth Paltrow (Catherine), Anthony

Hopkins (Robert), Hope Davis (Claire), Jake Gyllenhaal (Hal). Directed by John Madden and produced by John Hart, Robert Kessel, Alison Owen, and Jeff Sharp. Screenplay by David Auburn and Rebecca Miller, based on the play by David Auburn.

John Madden's *Proof* is an extraordinary thriller about matters of scholarship and the heart, about the true authorship of a mathematical proof and the passions that coil around it. It is a rare movie that gets the tone of a university campus exactly right and at the same time communicates so easily that you don't need to know the slightest thing about math to understand it. Take it from me.

The film centers on two remarkable performances, by Gwyneth Paltrow and Hope Davis, as Catherine and Claire, the daughters of a mathematician so brilliant that his work transformed the field and has not yet been surpassed. But his work was done years ago, and at the age of twenty-six or twenty-seven he began to "get sick," as the family puts it. This man, named Robert and played by Anthony Hopkins, still has occasional moments of lucidity, but he lives mostly in delusion, filling up one notebook after another with meaningless scribbles. Yet he remains on the University of Chicago faculty, where he has already made a lifetime's contribution; his presence and rare remissions are inspiring. Recently he had a year when he was "better."

Catherine was a brilliant math student, too—at Northwestern, because she wanted to be free of her father. But she returned home to care for him when he got worse, and her life has been defined by her father and the family home. Hal (Jake Gyllenhaal), her father's student and assistant, is hopelessly in love with her; she shies away from intimacy and suspects his motives. Most of the movie takes place after the father's death (flashbacks show him in life and imagination), and Hal is going through the notebooks. "Hoping to find something of my dad's you could publish?" Catherine asks him in a moment of anger.

Claire, the older sister, flies in from New York and makes immediate plans to sell the family home to the university: "They've been after it for years." Catherine is outraged, but the movie subtly shows how Claire, not the brilliant sister, is the dominant one. There is the sinister possibility that she thinks (in all sincerity) that

Catherine may have inherited the family illness and should not be allowed to stay alone in Chicago. Claire expresses love and support for her sister in terms that are frightening.

There is a locked drawer in Robert's desk. Catherine gives Hal the key. It contains what may be a revolutionary advance on Robert's earlier work; a new mathematical proof of incalculable importance. Did Robert somehow write this in a fleeting moment of clarity? The authorship of the proof brings into play all of the human dynamics that have been established among Catherine and Claire and Hal, and indeed among all of them and the ghostly presence of the father.

Proof, based on the award-winning Broadway and London play by David Auburn, contains one scene after another that is pitch-perfect in its command of how academics talk and live. Having once spent a year as a University of Chicago doctoral candidate, I felt as if I were back on campus. There is a memorial service at which the speaker (Gary Houston) sounds precisely as such speakers sound; his subject is simultaneously the dead mathematician and his sense of his own importance. There is a faculty party at which all of the right notes are sounded. And when Catherine and Hal speak, they talk as friends, lovers, and fellow mathematicians; they communicate in several languages while speaking only one.

What makes the movie deep and urgent is that Catherine is motivated by conflicting desires. She wants to be a great mathematician but does not want to hurt or shame her father. She wants to be a loyal daughter and yet stand alone as herself. She half-believes her older sister's persuasive smothering. She half-believes Hal loves her only for herself. At the bottom, she only half-believes in herself. That's why the Paltrow performance is so fascinating: It's essentially about a woman whose destiny is in her own hands, but she can't make them close on it.

It would be natural to compare *Proof* with *A Beautiful Mind* (2001), another movie about a brilliant and mad mathematician. But they are miles apart. *A Beautiful Mind* tries to enter the world of the madman. *Proof* locates itself in the mind of the madman's daughter, who loves him and sorrows for him, who has lived in his shadow so long she fears the light and the things that go with it.

Note: It doesn't make the movie any better or worse, but it's unique in that all of the locations match. There are no impossible journeys or nonexistent freeway exits. The trip from Hyde Park to Evanston reflects the way you really do get there. So real do the locations feel that it's a shock to find that most of the interiors were filmed in England; they match the Chicago locations seamlessly.

The Proposition ★ ★ ★ ★
R, 104 m., 2006

Guy Pearce (Charlie Burns), Ray Winstone (Captain Stanley), Danny Huston (Arthur Burns), John Hurt (Jellon Lamb), David Wenham (Eden Fletcher), Emily Watson (Martha Stanley), David Gulpilil (Jacko), Richard Wilson (Mike Burns), Tommy Lewis (Two Bob). Directed by John Hillcoat and produced by Chris Brown, Chiara Menage, Cat Villiers, and Jackie O'Sullivan. Screenplay by Nick Cave.

The Proposition plays like a Western moved from Colorado to hell. The characters are familiar: the desperado brothers, the zealous lawman, his civilized wife, the corrupt mayor, the old coots, the resentful natives. But the setting is the outback of Australia as I have never seen it before. These spaces don't seem wide open because an oppressive sky glares down at the sullen earth; this world is sun-baked, hostile, and unforgiving, and it breeds heartless men.

Have you read *Blood Meridian*, the novel by Cormac McCarthy? This movie comes close to realizing the vision of that dread and despairing story. The critic Harold Bloom believes no other living American novelist has written a book as strong. He compares it with Faulkner and Melville but confesses his first two attempts to read it failed, "because I flinched from the overwhelming carnage."

That book features a character known as the Judge, a tall, bald, remorseless bounty hunter who essentially wants to kill anyone he can, until he dies. His dialogue is peculiar, the speech of an educated man. *The Proposition* has such a character in an outlaw named Arthur Burns, who is much given to poetic quotations. He is played by Danny Huston in a performance of remarkable focus and savagery. Against him is Captain Stanley (Ray Winstone), who is not

precisely a sheriff since this land is not precisely a place where the law exists. He is more of an Ahab, obsessed with tracking down Arthur Burns and his brothers Charlie (Guy Pearce) and Mike (Richard Wilson). They are not merely outlaws, desperadoes, and villains but are dedicated to evil for its own sake, and the film opens with a photograph labeled "Scene of the Hopkins Outrage." The Burns boys murdered the Hopkins family, pregnant wife and all, perhaps more for entertainment than gain.

Ray Winstone, who often plays villains, is one of the best actors now at work in movies (see him in *Sexy Beast, Ripley's Game, Last Orders*). Here he plays a man who would be fearsome enough in an ordinary land but pales before the malevolence of the Burns brothers. He lives with Martha (Emily Watson), his fragrant wife from England, who fences off a portion of wilderness, calls it their lawn, plants rosebushes there, serves him his breakfast egg, and behaves, as colonial women did in Victorian times, as if still at "home."

"I will civilize this land," Captain Stanley says. In the 1880s, it is an achievement as likely as Ahab capturing the whale. He is able to capture Charlie and Mike Burns: Mike, a youth like the Kid in *Blood Meridian*, still half-formed but schooled only in desperation, and Charlie, an inward, brooding, damaged man whose feelings are as instinctive as a kicked dog. The captain is not happy with his prisoners because he lacks the real prize. He makes a proposition to Charlie. If Charlie tracks and kills his brother Arthur, the captain will spare both Charlie and Mike.

Charlie sets off on this mission. He feels no particular filial love for Arthur; they are bonded mostly by mutual hatred of others. The captain himself ventures out on the trail, finding such settlers as have chosen to live in exile and punishment. The most colorful—no, "colorful" is not a word for this movie—the most gnarled and cured by the sun is Jellon Lamb, played by John Hurt as if he is made of jerky.

Why do you want to see this movie? Perhaps you don't. Perhaps, like Bloom, it will take you more than one try to face the carnage. But the director, John Hillcoat, working from a screenplay by Nick Cave (the sometime punk rocker and actor in *Johnny Suede*), has made a movie you cannot turn away from; it is so pitiless and uncompromising, so filled with pathos and disregarded innocence, that it is a record of those things we pray to be delivered from. The actors invest their characters with human details all the scarier because they scarcely seem human themselves. In what place within Arthur Burns does poetry reside? What does he feel as he quotes it? What does Martha, the Emily Watson character, really think as she uncrates a Christmas tree she has had shipped in from another lifetime? If Captain Stanley is as tender toward her as he seems, why has he brought her to live in these badlands?

What of the land itself? There is a sense of palpable fear of the outback in many Australian films, from *Walkabout* to *Japanese Story*, not neglecting the tamer landscapes in *Picnic at Hanging Rock*. There is the sense that spaces there are too empty to admit human content. There are times in *The Proposition* when you think the characters might abandon their human concerns and simply flee from the land itself.

And what of the Aborigines, who inhabit this landscape more or less invisibly and have their own treaty with it? The Stanleys have a house servant named Two Bob, played by Tommy Lewis, who sizes up the situation and walks away one day, carefully removing his shoes, which remain in the garden.

P.S. ★ ★ ★
R, 97 m., 2004

Laura Linney (Louise Harrington), Topher Grace (F. Scott Feinstadt), Gabriel Byrne (Peter Harrington), Paul Rudd (Sammy), Marcia Gay Harden (Missy Goldberg), Lois Smith (Louise's Mother), Jennifer Carta (Sarah), Ross A. McIntyre (Jimmy). Directed by Dylan Kidd and produced by Anne Chaisson, John Hart, Robert Kessel, and Jeff Sharp. Screenplay by Kidd, based on the novel by Helen Schulman.

P.S. is the second movie in 2004 to use reincarnation as the excuse for transgressive sex. The earlier film was *Birth*, in which a woman in her mid-thirties becomes convinced that her dead husband has been reincarnated as a ten-year-old boy. Now comes *P.S.*, in which a woman in her late thirties is struck by the uncanny resemblance, in name and appearance, between a twenty-year-old student and the boy she loved when she was that age. The age gap makes both

relationships problematic; *P.S.* involves sex, while *Birth* prudently sidesteps it.

Both films are fascinating because they require us to see the younger character through two sets of eyes—our own, which witness an attractive woman drawn to a younger male, and the women's, which see a lost love in a new container. *Birth* considers the possibility that actual reincarnation is involved, while *P.S.* is willing to consider the possibility of an amazing coincidence. In *Birth*, it is the little boy who insists he is the dead husband, and tries to prove it; in *P.S.*, the woman is struck by the uncanny similarity between a student and the young man she once loved, and tries to prove it—to him, and to a friend her own age who once loved him too. That both her dead boyfriend and the young student are named F. Scott Feinstadt seems too good to be true. Even, indeed, if only one were named F. Scott Feinstadt, it would be a reach.

Watching these movies, we are fascinated by the disconnect between romance and reality. If the ten-year-old boy in *Birth* really is the dead husband, what then? The older woman (Nicole Kidman) actually suggests at one point that they wait until he comes of age, and then, well, what? It might have been wiser for her to say: "It's been ten years since you died. Life goes on. You should grow up and find a girl your age. Look at it this way: You're the first person in history who gets his wish to be ten again, knowing what you know now."

As for *P.S.* and the new F. Scott (Topher Grace), there's little doubt in the mind of Louise Harrington (Laura Linney) about what she should do, which is to take him home in the middle of the afternoon so they can have safe sex immediately. That she is a Columbia University admissions officer and he is a student applying for admission creates an ethical conflict, but should ethics stand in the way of earthshaking metaphysical lust? We would all agree that ethics certainly should not, although of course if a thirty-nine-year-old male admissions officer were to sleep with a twenty-year-old female applicant, castration would be too good for the fiend.

These logical considerations are not much discussed in *P.S.*, although one of the best things about *Birth* is that the woman's family think she's crazy and her mother threatens to call the cops. In *P.S.*, reincarnation is not insisted on, and while Louise sleeps with F. Scott because she wants to relive her treasured memories of first love, F. Scott sleeps with Louise because he can. Both genders are programmed by eons of Darwinian genetic strategy, and so we believe them, and because Linney and Grace are sexy and play well together, the age gap is not a barrier so much as additional seasoning.

In *Birth*, it must be admitted, the ten-year-old doesn't bring much to the party. He stands there like a little scold, insisting on his identity and completely failing to see the humor in his predicament. F. Scott, on the other hand, is a wiseass who treats Louise with an informality bordering on rudeness; she likes this, because it reminds her of the other F. Scott, and because it means she is being treated more like an equal than like an older authority figure. Louise has been saving up for a long time for the opportunity to get medieval on some guy. Like the fortyish Kim Basinger character in *Door in the Floor*, who has a wild fling with a sixteen-year-old boy (who resembles her dead son, of course), she brings great appetites to the task.

Louise comes supplied with an ex-husband, a brother, and a best friend who complicate matters. The ex-husband, inevitably named Peter (Gabriel Byrne), has decided he is a sex addict, and is twelve-stepping his way to restraint at just that moment when Louise casts it to the winds. Her brother Sammy (Paul Rudd) is a recovering addict with a fund of handy mantras. Her friend Missy Goldberg (Marcia Gay Harden) flies in from the coast to get a good look at F. Scott, and invites him to her hotel suite to get a better look. There is some question whether it was Louise or Missy who loved the original F. Scott first, or last, or best.

The plot mechanisms of these movies are at the service of justifying scenes that would otherwise be impossible, improbable, or criminal. The achievement of *Birth* is to take an entirely unacceptable situation (older woman, child) and make it dramatically possible by inhabiting the young body, so it would seem, with an older man. *P.S.* uses the stunning power of the boy's uncanny resemblance to the lost love, and *Door in the Floor* uses the grief of the mourning mother, who is reminded of her dead son by this teenage boy, although that doesn't exactly explain why she sleeps with him.

Watching these movies negotiate the hazards of their plots is part of the fun. Watching good actresses at the top of their form is another. Because these are not European films like Louis Malle's *Murmur of the Heart* or Agnes Varda's *Kung Fu Master*, they depend on plot more than emotion to motivate their forbidden behavior, but they seem to be taking chances even when they aren't really, and besides, stories like this are gold mines of terrific reaction shots.

The Punisher ★ ★
R, 124 m., 2004

Thomas Jane (Frank Castle [Punisher]), John Travolta (Howard Saint), Will Patton (Quentin Glass), Laura Harring (Livia Saint), Rebecca Romijn-Stamos (Joan), Samantha Mathis (Maria Castle), John Pinette (Mr. Bumpo), Ben Foster (Spacker Dave), Marcus Johns (Will Castle), Roy Scheider (Mr. Castle). Directed by Jonathan Hensleigh and produced by Avi Arad and Gale Anne Hurd. Screenplay by Michael France and Hensleigh, based on the comic book by Gerry Conway, Garth Ennis, Johnny Romita, and Michael Tolkin.

The Punisher is a long, dark slog through grim revenge. Unlike most movies based on comic book heroes, it doesn't contain the glimmer of a smile, and its hero is a depressed alcoholic—as well he might be, since his entire family, including wife, child, father, and even distant cousins have been massacred before his eyes. As he seeks vengeance, he makes the Charles Bronson character in *Death Wish* look relatively cheerful and well adjusted.

I wonder if the filmmakers understand quite how downbeat and dark their movie is? It opens with an FBI sting that leads to the death of a mobster's son. The operation, we learn, was the last assignment before retirement for agent Frank Castle (Thomas Jane). The criminal, a wealthy, high-profile money launderer named Mr. Saint (John Travolta), orders Castle's death, and then his wife, Livia (Laura Harring), adds, "His family. His whole family."

This sets up a sequence from which the movie hardly recovers. Castle has a romantic walk on the beach with his wife, Maria (Samantha Mathis), a hug with his child, and sentimental moments as his father (Roy Scheider) speaks at a family reunion. Then Saint's gun-

561

men mow down the entire family in a series of gruesome vignettes, not neglecting to linger on the death of wife and child after their pitiful attempt to flee.

Castle kills a few of the attackers, but is cornered on a pier, shot repeatedly, doused with gasoline, blown up, and lands in the water. This establishes a pattern for the movie: No one is killed only once. (Later in the film, a target is shot, chained to the back of a car and dragged into a car lot where all of the cars explode.) Miraculously, Castle survives and is nursed back to health by one of those useful clichés, the black loner who lives by himself on an island and possesses the wisdom of the ages.

The rest of the movie involves his recovery, his preparations, and his methodical revenge against Mr. Saint and all of his people. Several colorful supporting characters are introduced, especially the three oddballs who live in the shabby rooming house Castle occupies. They are Joan (Rebecca Romijn-Stamos), a sexy but frightened woman with an abusive boyfriend; Mr. Bumpo (John Pinette), a tubby sissy, and Spacker Dave (Ben Foster), who is pierced in ways you don't even want to think about. We have all been indoctrinated in the notion that "we are family!" and these three attempt to include Castle in their circle despite his need to isolate, drink, kill, and brood. There is something a little odd when he's invited over for ice cream and cake.

The movie is relentless in its violence. There is a scene where Spacker Dave is tortured by having his piercings removed with pliers; the scene breaks the fabric of the film and moves into a different and macabre arena. *The Punisher* opened on the same weekend as another movie about a gruesome massacre and an elaborate revenge, *Kill Bill: Vol. 2*, but they are as different as night and day; *Kill Bill* vibrates with humor, irony, over-the-top exaggeration, and the joy of filmmaking. *The Punisher* is so grim and cheerless you wonder if even its hero gets any satisfaction from his accomplishments.

That said, I have to note that the film, directed by Jonathan Hensleigh, is consistently well acted, and has some scenes of real power. That the Punisher is a drear and charmless character does not mean that Thomas Jane doesn't play him well: He goes all the way with the film's dark vision, and is effective in the ac-

tion scenes. John Travolta, as Mr. Saint, finds a truth you would not think was available in melodrama of this sort; his grief over his son and possessive jealousy over his wife are compelling.

The film doesn't simply set up Saint as a bad guy and a target, but devotes attention to the character, and develops an intriguing relationship between Saint and his right-hand man Quentin Glass (the always effective Will Patton). The Punisher is able to use Saint's jealousy to drive a wedge between the two men, but here's the strange thing: What happens between Saint and Glass is convincing, but what the Punisher does to sabotage their relationship is baffling and ludicrous, involving false fire hydrants and the improbable detail that Saint would allow his wife to go to the movies alone after he knows the Punisher is alive and at war.

Right down the line, the performances are strong. Even the three misfits in the run-down rooming house are given the dimension and screen time to become interesting. The screenplay, by Michael France and Jonathan Hensleigh, based on the Marvel comic, doesn't simply foreground the Punisher and make everyone else into one-dimensional cartoons. There's so much that's well done here that you sense a good movie slipping away. That movie would either be lighter than this one or commit to its seriousness, like *Scarface*. This one loses control of its mood and doesn't know what level of credibility it exists on. At the end, we feel battered down and depressed, emotions we probably don't seek from comic book heroes.

Pure ★ ★ ★
NO MPAA RATING, 96 m., 2005

Molly Parker (Mel), Harry Eden (Paul), Vinnie Hunter (Lee), David Wenham (Lenny), Keira Knightley (Louise), Geraldine McEwan (Nanna), Marsha Thomason (Vicki), Gary Lewis (Detective French). Directed by Gillies MacKinnon and produced by Howard Burch. Screenplay by Alison Hume.

If acting is so hard, why are so many children so good at it? Perhaps they're still in direct touch with emotions that adults have to reach through their art. Consider Harry Eden, who plays ten-year-old boy Paul in *Pure*. In the movie's first scene, he is making breakfast in bed for his mother, Mel (Molly Parker). This involves preparing a hit of heroin. "I told you never to touch my medicine," she says when she sees what he has done. And then: "Are you sure you made it up properly?"

Paul is sure. He has seen his mother do it countless times. He still barely believes the story that the drug is "medicine," and during the movie he will learn the truths that are right there to be seen all around him: His mother is a junkie, her boyfriend, Lenny (David Wenham), is a dealer, her best friend, Vicki (Marsha Thomason), claims she's not an addict because she only smokes crack instead of shooting up. The film's story centers on Paul, and Eden plays him as a good-hearted, frighteningly sincere kid who desperately tries to deal with a situation beyond his understanding. Where the performance comes from, I can't say, but there it is: strong, sure, touching.

Paul and his younger brother, Lee, live with his mother in a London welfare estate. His dad is dead of a heart attack; drugs may have had something to do with that, but we don't know. Lenny was his dad's best friend and is now his mother's lover and supplier. He's a hard man, but not as hard as some drug dealers we've seen; he likes Mel, and he thinks that supplying her addiction is a form of helping her.

Addiction wears down ordinary standards of human conduct until people behave in ways they would have considered unthinkable. Consider Vicki, a hooker whose small child, Rose, is sometimes watched by Mel. Mel is on the bus with the baby, and a man who says he is a doctor tells her the child has an infection and needs immediate attention. What Mel does then makes sense only if you understand that heroin has to come first before anything else in her life can proceed.

Paul is always on the move, running or riding his bicycle, acting as a parent for Lee and in a way for his mother. He makes friends where he finds them. The waitress Louise (Keira Knightley), for example, is nice to him and he confides in her. Like everyone in his world, she's into drugs. Eventually he asks her if he can try some: "I want to know how Mom feels." Her first response: "You can wait until you're eleven."

Always lurking about is a police detective (Gary Lewis) who knows that Lenny is an important supplier in the neighborhood but can't prove it. As the plot plays out, young Paul finds himself involved in the game between Lenny and the detective, in ways he does not understand or even guess.

One scene in the movie is painful almost beyond describing. Mel determines to get off drugs, cold turkey. She will lock herself in her room and Paul is not to listen to her, no matter what she says, until she is clean. To assist in this process, her resourceful son nails her bedroom door shut. This leads to a confrontation between mother and son that no child should ever have to endure, although I have a sad feeling that many do.

Parker is an extraordinary actress of the ordinary. In the strange and daring *Kissed* (1996), she played a necrophiliac employee of a funeral home whose feelings about the dead were not only perverse but, in an inexplicable way, tender and sorrowful as well. Not many actresses could have made the role acceptable, let alone believable, but Parker did. She did it by calmly accepting the reality of her character and never stepping outside it. Here she plays a drug addict whose treatment of her children is cruel and uncaring, and yet she is the best mother it is possible for her to be. She doesn't make Mel into a grotesque caricature; Mel is even more disturbing, really, because she tries to behave better than the drugs will allow her to.

One of the movie's intriguing qualities is that its horrors take place within a world that is not as cruel and painful as we know it could be. Mel's association with Lenny makes the getting of drugs safer and more manageable, and in a way she can kid herself that she leads a normal enough life except for this one area she imagines to be private. Paul has somehow been raised well enough to be capable and self-confident; we sense he will not be destroyed by his childhood. Lenny, like the hero of the recent *Layer Cake*, believes drug dealing can be run like a reasonable business, without unnecessary risk or violence. They are all living in foolishness and self-deception, but there are days that must seem almost normal and happy. After the medicine.

R

Racing Stripes ★ ★
PG, 101 m., 2005

Bruce Greenwood (Nolan Walsh), Hayden Panettiere (Channing Walsh), M. Emmet Walsh (Woodzie), Wendie Malick (Clara Dalrymple). And the voices of: Frankie Muniz (Stripes), Mandy Moore (Sandy), Michael Clarke Duncan (Clydesdale), Jeff Foxworthy (Reggie), Joshua Jackson (Trenton's Pride), Joe Pantoliano (Goose), Michael Rosenbaum (Ruffshodd), Steve Harvey (Buzz), David Spade (Scuzz), Snoop Dogg (Lightning), Fred Dalton Thompson (Sir Trenton), Dustin Hoffman (Tucker), Whoopi Goldberg (Franny). Directed by Frederik Du Chau and produced by Broderick Johnson, Andrew A. Kosove, Edward McDonnell, and Lloyd Phillips. Screenplay by David Schmidt.

Racing Stripes is a compromise between *National Velvet* and *Babe*, leading to the inescapable question: Why not see them instead of this? It tells the story of the young girl who has faith in a disregarded animal and rides it to victory in a derby, and it has the barnyard full of cute talking animals. There are kids who will like it, but then there are kids who are so happy to be at the movies that they like everything. Adults are going to find it a little heavy on barnyard humor.

The story: On a night journey, a circus truck breaks down, and when the caravan resumes its journey, a basket has been forgotten by the side of the road. It contains a baby zebra. Horse trainer Nolan Walsh (Bruce Greenwood) and his daughter, Channing (Hayden Panettiere), find the orphan. Nolan wants to trace its owners, but Channing, of course, falls in love with it and wants it for a pet. It wouldn't seem that hard to find the owners of a baby zebra in Kentucky, but Nolan agrees, and the baby is named Stripes.

The Walsh farm occupies high ground above a race track, which absorbs much of the attention of the farm's animals. Walsh himself was a trainer, we learn, until he fell into depression after his wife died in a riding accident. He has forbidden Channing to follow her lifelong dream of being a jockey, but are

we all agreed it's only a matter of time until she rides Stripes to victory in the local derby?

The animals in the movie are all real animals, except for the animated flies (voices by Steve Harvey and David Spade). Computer effects are used, however, to synch their mouths with the dialogue—an effect that's a little creepy. Cartoon animals have a full range of facial expressions, but when real animals are given CGI lip movements there often seems to be a disconnect between the lips and the face.

The Walsh farm is that anachronism in these days of agribusiness, a diversified barnyard filled with examples of every farm animal that might show promise as a character. They're voiced by actors who are quickly identifiable (Dustin Hoffman as a short-tempered Shetland, Joe Pantoliano as a goose who seems to be hiding out from the mob, Whoopi Goldberg as a goat, and Mandy Moore as a mare who falls in love with Stripes, although the movie wisely avoids the question of what would happen should they decide to begin a family). Stripes is voiced by Frankie Muniz of *Agent Cody Banks* and the wonderful *My Dog Skip* (an infinitely better movie about a friendship between a kid and his pet).

The racetrack is run by a Cruella DeVille type named Clara Dalrymple (Wendie Malick), reminding us of how reliable Dalrymple is as a movie name for upper-crust snobs. Her own horse, Trenton's Pride (voiced by Joshua Jackson), is favored to win the derby, and she doesn't see any point in letting a zebra enter the race. In a way, she has logic on her side. It's a horse race. There aren't any gazelles or ostriches, either.

I will get the usual feedback from readers who took their children to see *Racing Stripes* and report that the whole family loved the movie. For them, I am happy. It is a desperate thing to be at a movie with children who are having a bad time. But when you think of the *Babe* pictures, and indeed, even an animated cartoon like *Home on the Range*, you realize *Stripes* is on autopilot with all of the usual elements: a heroine missing one parent, an animal missing both, an underdog (or underzebra), cute animals, the big race. This is the kind of movie you might grab at the video store, but it's not worth the trip to the theater.

Raise Your Voice ★
PG, 103 m., 2004

Hilary Duff (Terri Fletcher), Rita Wilson (Frances Fletcher), David Keith (Simon Fletcher), Jason Ritter (Paul Fletcher), Oliver James (Jay), Rebecca De Mornay (Aunt Nina), John Corbett (Mr. Torvald), Lauren C. Mayhew (Robin), Dana Davis (Denise). Directed by Sean McNamara and produced by David Brookwell, A. J. Dix, McNamara, Anthony Rhulen, Sara Risher, and William Shively. Screenplay by Sam Schreiber.

Hilary Duff has a great smile, and she proves it by smiling pretty much all the way through *Raise Your Voice*, except when there's a death in the family, or her roommate Denise says something mean to her, or she sees her kind-of boyfriend Jay kissing Robin after he said he'd broken up with her, or when her dad says she can't go to music camp. The rest of the time she smiles and smiles, and I love gazing upon her smile, although a still photo would achieve the same effect and be a time-saver.

She smiles in *Raise Your Voice*, a carefully constructed movie that doesn't make her a contemporary teenager so much as surround her with them. She plays Terri Fletcher, a young music student, who after a personal tragedy wants to begin again by attending a three-week camp for gifted young musicians in Los Angeles. Her dad (David Keith) is against it: Terrible things can happen to a young woman in Los Angeles. Her mother (Rita Wilson) conspires with her artistic Aunt Nina (Rebecca De Mornay) to sneak her off to the camp while Dad thinks she's visiting Nina in Palm Desert. Aunt Nina is one of those artists who does alarming things up on stepladders with an acetylene torch.

All the kids are snobs at the camp, primarily so they can soften later. (If they soften right away, there goes the plot.) Terri's new roommate is Denise (Dana Davis), who plans to work hard for a scholarship, and resents Terri as a distraction. Sizing up Terri's wardrobe and her smile, Denise tells her: "You're like some kind of retro Brady Buncher." I hate it when a movie contains its own review. For that matter, earlier in the movie her brother tells her she's a "Stepford daughter," but he encourages her to go to the camp, direly predict-

ing: "If you don't, you're going to end up doing *Cats* at the Y when you're forty."

Terri meets a nice kid named Jay (Oliver James), who has a British accent and is very encouraging and warm, and brings her out of herself and encourages her to sing with joy, and writes a song with her and says he doesn't date the bitchy Robin (Lauren C. Mayhew) anymore because she was "last summer." There is also an inspiring music teacher (John Corbett), who wants to find the best in her, and doesn't have to look very deep.

All of this plays out against the backdrop of Terri's deception of her dad, who is convinced she's in Palm Desert because Terri and Aunt Nina phone him on a conference call. Dad only wants the best for her, of course, but when he finds out about the deception, he declares, "I want her home, right now!"

Does that mean (a) she comes home, right now, or (b) her mom and Aunt Nina work on Dad, and, wouldn't you know, the auditorium door opens and Dad walks in just in time for his daughter to see him from the stage halfway through her big solo. The answer of course is (b), right down to the obligatory moment when the disapproving parent in the audience nods at the gifted child onstage and does the heartfelt little nod that means, "You were right, honey." But her dad was right about one thing. Something terrible did happen to her in Los Angeles. She made this movie.

Raising Helen ★ ★
PG-13, 119 m., 2004

Kate Hudson (Helen Harris), John Corbett (Pastor Dan), Joan Cusack (Jenny), Hector Elizondo (Mickey Massey), Helen Mirren (Dominique), Hayden Panettiere (Audrey), Spencer Breslin (Henry), Abigail Breslin (Sarah), Sakina Jaffrey (Nilma Prasad), Felicity Huffman (Lindsay). Directed by Garry Marshall and produced by Ashok Amritraj and David Hoberman. Screenplay by Jack Amiel and Michael Begler.

Raising Helen is a perfectly pleasant comedy in which nice people do good things despite challenges that are difficult but not excessive. As a pilot for a TV sitcom it would probably be picked up, but it's not compelling enough to involve a trip to the movies. From beginning to end, we've been there, seen that.

Kate Hudson, who stars, seems to be following in the footsteps of her mother, Goldie Hawn; both have genuine talent, but choose too often to bury themselves in commercial formulas. Hudson plays Helen Harris, a high-powered Manhattan career woman who works as the personal assistant to the head (Helen Mirren) of a famous modeling agency. She works hard, is on call 24-7, and even when she parties she's talent-scouting. She has a sister named Jenny (Joan Cusack) who lives in the suburbs and raises her children as a disciplined time-and-motion study. Jenny's house, Helen observes, looks like a showroom at Pottery Barn.

Tragedy strikes. Their sister Lindsay (Felicity Huffman) and her husband are killed in an accident, and in her will Lindsay leaves custody of her small son and daughter not to Jenny the perfect homemaker, but to Helen the fast-track girl. How can this be? Helen and Jenny are both appalled, but Helen takes on the task of raising little Henry and Sarah, played by real-life siblings Spencer and Abigail Breslin.

If Helen has any notions that she can be a mom and keep her agency job, she's disabused by Mirren, who expects total dedication. Soon Helen has lost her job, moved her little family to a lower-middle-class neighborhood in Queens, and enrolled the kids in a nearby Lutheran school run by Pastor Dan (John Corbett), who is single and therefore preordained to fall in love with Helen, although not before many plot-laden details have been worked through. She gets a job in a car dealership run by the unfailingly dynamic Hector Elizondo.

The movie, directed by Garry Marshall (*Pretty Woman*), is not unaware of the lifestyle differences between single Manhattan career women and receptionists in Queens. Not even after Helen unloads an eyesore green Lincoln and is promoted to sales does she have the money, or the skills, to make things work—even though she learns fast. But she's let off fairly easily. The movie exists in the kind of economy where one working-class paycheck can just about support a family, and where city kids go to the wholesome parochial school down the street. Times are harder now, but the movie doesn't know it—can't afford to, if its sunny disposition is to prevail.

Most of Helen's lessons in survival come not from her sister, a forbiddingly humorless caricature, but from her across-the-hall Indian neighbor Nilma Prasad (Sakina Jaffrey), who, just like all neighbors in sitcoms, is willing to drop her own life at a moment's notice to play a supporting role in the heroine's; she channels Ethel Mertz.

The romance between Helen and Pastor Dan progresses with agonizing slowness, complicated by Helen's belief that Lutheran ministers cannot marry (her attempts to fake Lutheranism to get her kids into the school are amusing, but could have been subtler). Finally, Pastor Dan breaks the ice: "I'm a sexy man of God, and I know it." Then there are the scenes where the kids resent this man who seems about to replace their father, and the obligatory group visit to the zoo, scored with the obligatory use of Simon and Garfunkel's "At the Zoo."

Garry Marshall is a smart director with more of a comic edge than this movie allows him. I wonder if at any point he considered darkening the material even a little, and making Hudson's character a shade more desperate and less Lucy-like. There's nothing at risk in *Raising Helen*. We're not even surprised the kids go to Helen and not her sister, because the sister is written in a way that makes her impossible as a parental candidate.

Pastor Dan is the conveniently available, nearby eligible male, but somehow we doubt there are many ordained Lutheran bachelors in Queens; why not rotate the plot toward more complexity? Surely that nice Mrs. Prasad across the hall has a brother who is a widower with two children of his own? To obtain comedy, you don't give Helen problems and then supply a man who solves them; you supply a man who brings in additional problems. I can imagine this premise being passed through the imagination of a director like Gurinder Chadha (*Bend It Like Beckham, What's Cooking?*) and emerging fresh and exciting. *Raising Helen* is tame and timid from beginning to end, and relentlessly conventional. Because Helen takes no real risks, because she lives surrounded by the safeguards of formula fiction, the movie is fated from its first shot to be obedient to convention.

Rana's Wedding ★ ★ ★
NO MPAA RATING, 90 m., 2004

Clara Khoury (Rana), Khalifa Natour (Khalil), Ismael Dabbag (Ramzy), Walid Abed Elsalam (Marriage Official), Zuher Fahoum (Father), Bushra Karaman (Grandmother). Directed by Hany Abu-Assad and produced by Bero Beyer and George Ibrahim. Screenplay by Ihab Lamey and Liana Badr.

Rana's father is going to the airport at 4 P.M., and she can either get married or leave the country with him. He supplies her with a list of eligible bachelors who have asked for her hand in marriage. But she is in love with Khalil. Can she find him, ask him to marry her, find a registrar, get her hair done, gather the relatives, and get married—all before 4 o'clock?

This could be the description of a Hollywood romantic comedy. And indeed it is a romantic comedy of sorts, as romance and comedy survive in the midst of the conflict between Palestinians and Israelis. The movie takes place on both sides of the armed border separating Jerusalem and the Palestinian settlement of Ramallah, and although the comedy occupies the foreground, the background is dominated by checkpoints and armed soldiers, street funerals and little boys throwing rocks, bulldozers tearing down buildings and a general state of siege.

Rana (Clara Khoury) is a Palestinian who is seventeen; her lover, Khalil (Khalifa Natour), a theater director, seems to be around forty. Although her father has grave doubts about their marriage, they cite Islamic law that allows them to wed if they inform the father in the presence of a registrar. Her problem is to find her lover, find the registrar, find her father, and get them all together in the same place at the same time. This involves several trips back and forth through armed roadblocks that quietly make the point that Palestinians spend all day every day facing hostility and suspicion.

What's interesting is that the movie, made by the Netherlands-based Palestinian filmmaker Hany Abu-Assad, makes little overt point of its political content; the politics are the air that the characters breathe, but the story is about their short-term romantic goals. And those are made more complicated because Rana is not a simple woman. She changes her mind, she gets jealous, she risks missing the deadline in order to get her hair done, she sometimes seems older, sometimes like a child.

The premise is a little hard to accept: Has her father actually sent her a note on the morning when he is to leave the country, setting the 4 P.M. deadline? She seems very independent; is there any way she can stay behind? Could she have considered marriage days or weeks earlier, or has all of this come about at the last moment? And what, exactly, is her father's reasoning? Although we see him briefly, we have no real ideas about who he is and how he thinks.

It is also rather startling that Khalil is prepared to get married at a moment's notice. Rana finally tracks him down on the stage of a theater in the Palestinian sector, where he's asleep with some of his cast; the roadblocks make that easier than going home. She awakens him with the news that they are to get married this very day, and he takes it fairly well, I'd say. Enlisting a friend with a yellow VW beetle, he sets off with Rana on a mission to find the registrar (who is not at home, of course) and meet the deadline.

We have to accept this unlikely plot, I suppose, because there it is—a device to add suspense. More suspense comes because Rana sometimes seems in no hurry. But the strength of the movie comes in its observation of details, as when Rana sees small boys throwing rocks at a barricade, and Israeli soldiers firing back; this scene, and other border scenes, look like real life captured by the film, although I have no way of knowing if that's true. There's also a scene where Rana and Khalil stop for a quiet talk, and notice a security camera pointed at them, and when Rana forgets the plastic carryall with her possessions in it, and runs back to find she's too late: the police, thinking it might contain a bomb, have just blown it up with a remote-controlled cannon.

There are, of course, two sides to such an experience; if Palestinians use hidden explosives and suicide bombers, then the Israelis of course must try to prevent them. But the movie doesn't preach; it simply observes. This is how daily life is. The movie is passable as a story but fascinating as a document. It gives a more complete visual picture of the borders, the Palestinian settlements, and the streets of Jerusalem than we ever see on the news, and we understand that the Palestinians are not all suicide bombers living in tents, as the news sometimes seems to imply, but in many cases middle-class people like Rana and her circle, sharing the same abilities and aspirations as their neighbors. I think the point is to show how their conditions of life are like a water torture, breaking them down a drop at a time, reminding them that having lived in this place for a long time, they are nevertheless homeless.

Ray ★ ★ ★ ★
PG-13, 152 m., 2004

Jamie Foxx (Ray Charles), Kerry Washington (Della Bea Robinson), Clifton Powell (Jeff Brown), Harry Lennix (Joe Adams), Terrence Dashon Howard (Gossie McKee), Larenz Tate (Quincy Jones), Richard Schiff (Jerry Wexler), Aunjanue Ellis (Mary Ann Fisher), Bokeem Woodbine (Fathead Newman), Sharon Warren (Aretha Robinson), Curtis Armstrong (Ahmet Ertegun), Regina King (Margie Hendricks), Warwick Davis (Oberon). Directed by Taylor Hackford and produced by Howard Baldwin, Stuart Benjamin, and Hackford. Screenplay by James L. White.

Ray Charles became blind at age seven, two years after witnessing the drowning death of his little brother. In a memory that haunted his life, he stood nailed to the spot while the little boy drowned absurdly in a bath basin. Why didn't Ray act to save him? For the same reason all five-year-olds do dumb and strange things: Because they are newly in possession of the skills of life, and can be paralyzed by emotional overload. No one seeing the scene in *Ray*, Taylor Hackford's considerable new musical biography, would think to blame the boy, but he never forgives himself.

If he had already been blind, he could not have blamed himself for the death, and would not have carried the lifelong guilt that, the movie argues, contributed to his drug addiction. Would he also then have not been driven to become the consummate artist that he was? Who can say? For that matter, what role did blindness play in his genius? Did it make him so alive to sound that he became a better musician? Certainly he was so attuned to the world around him that he never used a cane

or a dog; for Charles, blindness was more of an attribute than a handicap.

Jamie Foxx suggests the complexities of Ray Charles in a great, exuberant performance. He doesn't do the singing—that's all Ray Charles on the sound track—but what would be the point? Ray Charles was deeply involved in the project for years, until his death in June 2004, and the film had access to his recordings, so of course it should use them, because nobody else could sing like Ray Charles.

What Foxx gets just right is the physical Ray Charles, and what an extrovert he was. Not for Ray the hesitant blind man of cliché, feeling his way, afraid of the wrong step. In the movie and in life, he was adamantly present in body as well as spirit, filling a room, physically dominant, interlaced with other people. Yes, he was eccentric in his mannerisms, especially at the keyboard; I can imagine a performance in which Ray Charles would come across like a manic clown. But Foxx correctly interprets his body language as a kind of choreography, in which he was conducting his music with himself, instead of with a baton. Foxx so accurately reflects my own images and memories of Charles that I abandoned thoughts of how much "like" Charles he was, and just accepted him as Charles, and got on with the story.

The movie places Charles at the center of key movements in postwar music. After an early career in which he seemed to aspire to sound like Nat "King" Cole, he loosened up, found himself, and discovered a fusion between the gospel music of his childhood and the rhythm and blues of his teen years and his first professional gigs. The result was, essentially, the invention of soul music, in early songs like "I Got a Woman."

The movie shows him finding that sound in Seattle, his improbable destination after he leaves his native Georgia. Before and later, it returns for key scenes involving his mother, Aretha (Sharon Warren), who taught him not to be intimidated by his blindness, to dream big, to demand the best for himself. She had no education and little money, but insisted on the school for the blind, which set him on his way. He heads for Seattle after hearing about the club scene, but why there and not in New York, Kansas City, Chicago, or New Orleans? Certainly his meeting with the Seattle teenager Quincy Jones was one of the crucial events in his life (as was his friendship with the dwarf emcee Oberon, played by Warwick Davis, who turns him on to pot).

The movie follows Charles from his birth in 1930 until 1966, when he finally defeats his heroin addiction and his story grows happier but also perhaps less dramatic. By then he had helped invent soul, had moved into the mainstream with full orchestration, had moved out of the mainstream into the heresy of country music (then anathema to a black musician), and had, in 1961, by refusing to play a segregated concert in Georgia, driven a nail in the corpse of Jim Crow in the entertainment industry.

In an industry that exploits many performers, he took canny charge of his career, cold-bloodedly leaving his longtime supporters at Atlantic Records to sign with ABC Paramount and gain control of his catalog. (It's worth noting that the white Atlantic owners Ahmet Ertegun and Jerry Wexler are portrayed positively, in a genre that usually shows music execs as bloodsuckers.) Charles also fathered more children than the movie can tell you about, with more women than the movie has time for, and yet found the lifelong love and support of his wife, Della Bea Robinson (Kerry Washington).

The film is two and a half hours long—not too long for the richness of this story—but to cover the years between 1966 and his death in 2004 would have required more haste and superficial summary than Hackford and his writer, James L. White, are willing to settle for. When we leave him, Ray is safely on course for his glory years, although there is a brief scene set in 1979 where he receives an official apology from his home state of Georgia over the concert incident, and "Georgia on My Mind" is named as the state song.

Charles's addictions were to drugs and women. He beat only drugs, but *Ray* is perceptive and not unsympathetic in dealing with his roving ways. Of the women we meet, the most important is his wife, Della Bea, played by Washington as a paragon of insight, acceptance, and with a certain resignation; when one of his lovers dies, she asks him, "What about her baby?" "You knew?" says Charles. She knew everything.

His two key affairs are with Mary Ann Fisher (Aunjanue Ellis), a blues singer, and

Margie Hendricks (Regina King), a member of his backup group, the Raelettes. Who knows what the reality was, but in the film we get the sense that Charles was honest, after his fashion, about his womanizing, and his women understood him, forgave him, accepted him, and were essential to him. Not that he was easy to get along with during the heroin years, and not that they were saints, but that, all in all, whatever it was, it worked. "On the road," says Margie, in a line that says more than it seems to, "I'm Mrs. Ray Charles."

The movie would be worth seeing simply for the sound of the music and the sight of Jamie Foxx performing it. That it looks deeper and gives us a sense of the man himself is what makes it special. Yes, there are moments when an incident in Ray's life instantly inspires a song (I doubt "What'd I Say?" translated quite so instantly from life to music). But Taylor Hackford brings quick sympathy to Charles as a performer and a man, and we remember that he directed *Hail! Hail! Rock 'n' Roll*, a great documentary about Chuck Berry, a performer whose onstage and offstage moves more than braced Hackford for this film. Ray Charles was quite a man; this movie not only knows it, but understands it.

The Real Dirt on Farmer John ★ ★ ★ ½
NO MPAA RATING, 83 m., 2006

With John Peterson, Anna Peterson, John Edwards, Isa Jacoby, Rosemary Palmer, Jesus Briano, Robert Clothier, Lesley Freeman. A documentary directed by Taggart Siegel and produced by Siegel and Teri Lang. Screenplay by John Peterson.

The filming of *The Real Dirt on Farmer John* essentially began on that day in the 1950s when John Peterson's mother, Anna, brought home a super-8 movie camera. A farmer's wife and schoolteacher from Caledonia, Illinois, she filmed her family working in the fields, her children playing in the yard, the raising of a barn, the changing of the seasons, and the harvest dinners supplied to neighbors who came to help with the threshing.

Her husband died at about the time her son John started to attend nearby Beloit College. By then it was the 1960s, and John and his friends took over the filmmaking; he was a farmer who was also a hippie, and his friends descended on the farm to create their art and, as was said in those days, do their thing. Peterson had his hands full running the farm, a dairy and hog operation, and eventually too many bank loans came due and he had to sell most of it.

That led to a long depression, to trips to Mexico to find himself, and finally, by a meandering route that the movie traces with great love for the meanders, to the present day, when Peterson's farm has been reborn as Angelic Organics, is co-owned with several hundred Chicago and northern Illinois investors, and raises so many organic vegetables, he says, "that I don't know the names of some of them."

The film has been directed and photographed by Taggart Siegel, who has been filming Peterson and his farm for more than twenty years. This is a loving, moving, inspiring, quirky documentary that was made while the lives it records were being lived. We get a sure sense for the gradual death of the American family farm, the auctions of land and farm equipment, the encroachment of suburban housing, and then an almost miraculous rebirth through the introduction of organic gardening. Fruits and vegetables in America have lost half their nutritive value in the past century, and those pretty hothouse tomatoes contain a fraction of the nutrients and phytochemicals in an organic tomato, but visionaries such as Peterson are finding a way back to the land.

Let it be observed, however, that Peterson is a strange man and celebrates his own oddities. He wrote and reads the narration, which is that of a man who has one foot in the counterculture and the other in rich organic soil. He likes to dress strangely, in Dr. Seuss hats or bumblebee costumes. He is taken to dancing wildly in the fields. He is told his speech and body language make him appear to be homosexual, but there is persuasive evidence of heterosexuality in the series of girlfriends who keep him in "relationships" through the decades.

The heroine of the film is his mother, a highspirited eighty-three-year-old when we meet her, who persuades John not to quit the farm because how could she live without her roadside produce stand? A freethinker who likes Jim Morrison although he didn't "dress nice," she is an articulate life force. Through her we glimpse

John's father, his uncles and aunts, and the neighbors of a vanished farm culture.

The miracle of Angelic Organics begins the day in the 1990s some Chicago investors in Community Supported Agriculture buy one of his organic onions, call him up, and offer to go into business with him. Today the Peterson farm is co-owned and -operated with his CSA partners, delivers fresh produce to hundreds of customers every week, has expanded, is working in a way Peterson's father could never have imagined. Oh, and John has finally put to rest those rumors about devil worship, orgies, and drug abuse, which were never true, but if a man is going to wear a Dr. Seuss hat and have hippies living in his barn, he's got to expect that people will talk.

Rebound ★ ★
PG, 103 m., 2005

Martin Lawrence (Roy McCormick), Wendy Raquel Robinson (Jeanie Ellis), Breckin Meyer (Tim Fink), Horatio Sanz (Mr. Newirth), Megan Mullally (Principal Walsh), Oren Williams (Keith Ellis), Tara Correa (Big Mac), Steven C. Parker (Wes), Steven Anthony Lawrence (Ralph), Gus Hoffman (Goggles). Directed by Steve Carr and produced by Robert Simonds. Screenplay by Jon Lucas and Scott Moore.

Rebound leads us patiently once more through the well-charted formulas of sports movies. We have the team of losers lacking all self-confidence, combined with the hotshot coach who has problems with anger management. Will the team pull itself together and become champions? Will the coach humble himself and take these underdogs seriously? Will he even rehabilitate himself and get his old job back? Can we be made to care?

Movies like this are easy to watch at one level. They usually contain cute kids who are surprisingly effective actors. And they give the grown-up actors opportunities for broad emotion. In *Rebound*, the coach with the temper problem is played by Martin Lawrence, and he looks like a kinder, gentler, happier, and rounder Martin Lawrence than we're accustomed to. He also talks nicer. Lawrence's dialogue may be reduced by 25 percent by the elimination of some of his favorite words, but the PG rating is justified, and the movie is family-friendly.

His character, Roy McCormick, is a big-time college coach who gets into a lot of trouble when he throws a basketball at the opposing team, the Vultures, killing the mascot's pet bird. He's in trouble anyway; he misses the first half of one game because he's doing a photo shoot for *Details* magazine. His endorsement deals seem to cover almost everything offered at retail.

The league threatens him with banishment for life. His agent, Tim Fink (Breckin Meyer), thinks he might be able to rehabilitate himself by doing some pro bono work, and he finds Roy a job coaching a hopeless middle school team. It's at the very school that Roy himself once attended ("I grew up in the mean streets of the suburbs").

If you thought the Vultures was a strange nickname for a team, consider that Roy's team is the Smelters. The team he inherits is so inept, its passing drills look like dodgeball. Tom Arnold, of the *Best Damn Sports Show Period*, finds a second career simply reporting on how bad the Smelters are.

Of the kids on the team, the most endearing, because he's the most like me, is Goggles (Gus Hoffman), who can barely see the ball, let alone pass it. Ralph (Steven Anthony Lawrence) is well named, since he barfs every time he gets nervous. There's a tough girl named Big Mac (Tara Correa), who looks and plays tough but has a sweet spot for the tall, shy Wes (Steven C. Parker). Coach gives him some snarling lessons. And the team starts to come together when Keith Ellis (Oren Williams) joins it. He looks uncannily like a young Dee Brown.

All of this is fun enough in a sweet but predictable way. It bears no resemblance to basketball as it is played and coached in the real world, and it is doubtful if even a school with a teacher played by Horatio Sanz would entrust its thirteen-year-olds with a mad-dog version of Bobby Knight. No matter. We wait complacently until the last second of the last minute of the final game of the season, confident that no matter how grim the situation looks, the underdog tradition of sports movies will be upheld. I can't recommend the movie, except to younger viewers, but I don't dislike it. It's *Coach Carter* lite, and it does what it does.

The Reckoning ★ ★ ★
R, 112 m., 2004

Willem Dafoe (Martin), Paul Bettany (Nicholas), Gina McKee (Sarah), Brian Cox (Tobias), Ewen Bremner (Damian), Vincent Cassel (Lord de Guise), Simon McBurney (Stephen), Elvira Minguez (Martha). Directed by Paul McGuigan and produced by Caroline Wood. Screenplay by Mark Mills, based on the novel *Morality Play* by Barry Unsworth.

In England circa 1380, a troupe of traveling actors makes its way across the medieval landscape, where to go twenty miles from home was to enter a world of strangers. In London at about the same time, Geoffrey Chaucer was writing about another group on the road—pilgrims on their way to Canterbury. His Knight, learning from the journey, declared:

This world is but a thoroughfare full of woe,
And we be pilgrims, passing to and fro.
Death is an end to every worldly sore.

The actors arrive at much the same conclusion in *The Reckoning*, when they arrive at a village where a murder trial is under way. A mute woman (Elvira Minguez) has been charged with the death of a local boy, and been sentenced to death as a witch. The actors by their nature are more worldly and sophisticated than the village folk, and after questioning the woman through sign language, they begin to doubt her guilt.

It is at first no affair of theirs, however, and they unload their props and costumes from a lumbering covered wagon and stage the wheezer they've been touring with: a morality tale about Adam and Eve. That this is probably the first play ever seen by the locals does not give it the virtue of novelty; it is ever so much more entertaining to hang witches than to attend allegory. In desperation, the players decide to devise a play based on the murder case, and the more they discover, the more they doubt the woman's guilt. The village in fact is a hotbed of sin and suspicion, and only a conspiracy of fear has kept the lid on. The actors are stirring the pot.

Ah, but there's a twist. One of the troupe, Nicholas (Paul Bettany, the surgeon in *Master and Commander*), is not an actor at all, but a

571

priest who was discovered at the wrong kind of devotions with a wife from his congregation— not the Wife of Bath, alas, or he might have gotten away with it. Fleeing for his life, he is taken on by the troupe, whose leader, Martin (Willem Dafoe), agrees to shelter him. Martin's sister Sarah (Gina McKee) is intrigued by Nicholas's aura of sensual guilt, but the veteran actor Tobias (Brian Cox) thinks they have enough mouths to feed without a freeloader. These tensions all play a role when the troupe begins to suspect a village scandal, and Lord Robert de Guise (Vincent Cassel) orders them to leave.

The Reckoning has been directed, perhaps incredibly, by Paul McGuigan, the Scots filmmaker whose previous work (*Gangster No. 1*) did not seem to point him in this direction. And yet the previous movie shows the same taste for dissecting the evil beneath the skin. Basing his film on the novel *Morality Play* by Barry Unsworth and a screenplay by Mark Mills, McGuigan shows a world in which characters project a rigid self-confidence which, when cracked, reveals venom.

The medieval world of the film has been convincingly re-created (it was photographed in Spain), and the ambience and plot suggest connections with three other medieval mystery films: *The Name of the Rose*, about a murder at a monastery, *The Return of Martin Guerre*, about a man who may be Martin or may have murdered him, and Bergman's *The Virgin Spring*, about a girl murdered by itinerant farmworkers. In those years, superstition and ignorance were the key elements in any criminal investigation.

The Reckoning has just a little too much of the whodunit and the thriller and not enough of the temper of its clash between cultures, but it works, maybe because the simplicity of the underlying plot is masked by the oddness of the characters. Willem Dafoe is invaluable in an enterprise like this, always seeming to speak from hard experience, giving mercy because he has needed it. Bettany plays the priest as a man left rudderless by his loss of status, and Cox plays the kind of malcontent who, on a modern movie location, would be angry about the quality of the catering. Given the vast scale of a quasi-medieval epic like *The Lord of the Rings*, it is refreshing to enter the rude poverty of the real Middle Ages, where both the peasant and

his lord lived with death and disease all around, and trusted sorcery and superstition to see them through.

Red Eye ★ ★ ★
PG-13, 85 m., 2005

Rachel McAdams (Lisa Reisert), Cillian Murphy (Jackson Rippner), Brian Cox (Joe Reisert), Jayma Mays (Cynthia), Jack Scalia (Charles Keefe). Directed by Wes Craven and produced by Chris Bender and Marianne Maddalena. Screenplay by Carl Ellsworth.

Wes Craven's *Red Eye* is a movie that wants to be a good thriller and moves competently, even relentlessly, toward that goal. It's helped enormously by Rachel McAdams, whose performance is convincing because she keeps it at ground level; thrillers are invitations to overact, but she remains plausible even when the action ratchets up around her. When she's stalking a terrorist with a hockey stick, she seems like a real woman stalking a real terrorist with a real hockey stick. It's not as easy as it sounds.

The terrorist is played by Cillian Murphy, who was the Scarecrow in *Batman Begins* and here plays a young man who seems pleasant and attractive to the heroine, until she asks him what his business is. All the warmth goes out of his eyes as he says, "As fate would have it, my business is all about you."

They meet in the Dallas–Fort Worth airport. She's Lisa, a hotel desk manager, on her way home to Miami. He's the cute guy who helps her put down a jerk, buys her a drink, and ends up with the seat next to hers on the overnight flight.

Murphy is handsome, but, like James Spader, the good looks come with a warning: There are ominous undertones here. Speaking softly, he explains that her father is being held hostage, that her help will be needed in a plot to blow up the deputy secretary of homeland security, and that her job is to call the hotel and have the security guy put him in a suite where he can be more easily assassinated. The encouraging angle is that the deputy secretary is taken that seriously.

What makes this goal worthy of a thriller is that the terrorist plan is of course nine times more complicated than it needs to be and is constructed entirely out of things that could go wrong. It's remarkable that terrorists like these still possess feet they have not shot off.

About the plot I will say no more, except in a general way: The scenes on board the airplane are about as convincing and plausible as they can be, given the situation. And the scenes, after the plane lands bring a cool excellence to the standard scenario in which the killer and the victim stalk each other.

Maybe what I like best about the movie is its reticence. After a summer of crashes, bangs, endless chase scenes and special effects that belittle the actors standing in front of them, what a pleasure to see characters in a thriller doing what people like themselves possibly could do. There are no supernatural or superhuman feats in the film, unless you count the piddling detail that a character isn't slowed down by an unexpected tracheotomy. The movie, bless its heart, even tries to make *this* development plausible by providing a doctor who eyeballs the victim and says (I quote from memory), "It's not too bad—only the larynx."

The rise of McAdams has been spectacular, if only because it has been so steep; in 2002, she had eighth billing in *The Hot Chick*. The only thing better would have been ninth billing. But then in 2004 she starred in *Mean Girls*, as the bitchiest girl in Lindsay Lohan's high school. It was a surprisingly good movie. And then came a straight romantic lead in *The Notebook* and a comic romantic lead in *Wedding Crashers*, where Owen Wilson fell in love with her and caught a heartwarming case of sincerity. Now this.

The previous three movies positioned McAdams as a rising star. *Red Eye* will be more important because casting directors, who know what to look for, will see that she brings more presence and credibility to her role than is really expected; she acts without betraying the slightest awareness that she's inside a genre. I wonder if that has anything to do with the fact that she's Canadian and thus culturally trained to avoid calling unnecessary attention to herself. Too many young Hollywood actors, especially in thrillers, think it's all about them. Her performance qualifies her for heavy-duty roles. Murphy is already established and does not need discovering, but here he shows an ability to modulate his character

instead of gnashing the scenery. They're very effective together.

Craven, the director, has been making thrillers for a long time and knows how to do it. From *The Last House on the Left* (1972) through *Swamp Thing* (1982), *The Serpent and the Rainbow* (1988), *Wes Craven's New Nightmare* (1994), and the *Scream* movies, he has put stories and characters ahead of "gotcha!" moments. Watching *Red Eye* function so smoothly, doing exactly what it was intended to do, I was reminded of Howard Hawks's definition of a good movie: "Three great scenes. No bad scenes." Craven scores two and one. Not bad.

Red Trousers: The Life of the Hong Kong Stuntmen ★ ★
R, 93 m., 2004

Robin Shou (Himself), Beatrice Chia (Silver), Keith Cooke (Kermuran), Hakim Alston (Eyemarder), Ridley Tsui (Himself), Craig Reid (Jia Fei). A documentary directed and produced by Robin Shou. Screenplay by Shou.

There's no room for the concept of workman's compensation in the world of the Hong Kong stuntman. Although certain stunts involve an 80 percent chance of a trip to the hospital, that's all in a day's work, and the stuntman who complains risks losing face with his employers—and his fellow stuntmen.

So we learn in *Red Trousers: The Life of the Hong Kong Stuntmen*, a rambling and frustrating documentary that nevertheless contains a lot of information about the men and women who make the Hong Kong action film possible. Not for them the air bags and safety precautions of Hollywood stuntmen. Quite often, we're stunned to learn, their stunts are done exactly as they seem: A fall from a third-floor window, for example, involves a stuntman falling from a third-floor window.

There is a sequence in the film where a stuntman is asked to fall off a railing, slide down a slanting surface to a roof, and bounce off the roof to the floor below. It is rehearsed with pads on the floor. When the shot is ready, the director tells his stuntman, "No pads. Concrete floor." And when the stuntman lands on the concrete incorrectly the first time, he insists on doing the stunt again: "I came off the roof at the wrong angle. This time I will get it right."

Are stuntmen ever killed? No doubt they are, but you will not hear about it in this doc, directed by the onetime stuntman and current actor and director Robin Shou *(Mortal Kombat)*. We do learn of a stuntman who was gravely injured when his wire snapped and he fell from a great height to land on jagged rocks. We see the shot as the wire snaps, and then the cameras keep rolling, Jackie Chan–style, as the crew race over to the man, who is screaming in pain. There's a call for pads to put him on, and then he's carried off on the shoulders of five or six crew members. We realized with astonishment that there is no medical team standing by, no ambulance, no provision at all should the stunt go wrong.

Later, visiting the injured stuntman in his village, we learn that he needed many operations over a period of two years on a shattered leg, but thank goodness his facial cuts didn't leave scars. He was paid $25 a day for two days of work, he observes. What about compensation? No mention. Good thing they have socialized medicine.

Wires are, of course, often used in stunts, to make the characters appear to defy gravity, but it would be wrong to assume they make stunts any easier. We see stunts where the wires are used to slam a stuntman against a wall, or spin him into a fall. The wires do not break the impact or slow the fall.

We hear a lot about how carefully Hollywood stuntmen prepare their "gags," but consider a scene in this movie where a stuntman jumps off a highway overpass, lands on top of a moving truck, and then rolls off the truck onto the top of a van before falling to the highway. How was the stunt done? Just as it looks. "My call was for 5:30 and the stunt was finished by 5:45," the stuntman reports cheerfully. Good thing the truck and the van were in the right places, or he might have been run over, or have fallen from the overpass to the pavement.

There are a lot of interviews with stuntmen in the movie, who repeat over and over how they love their work, how excited they are to be in the movies, how of course they're frightened but it's a matter of pride to do a stunt once you have agreed to it—if word gets around that they've balked, the jobs might dry up. They take pride in

the fact that Hong Kong stuntmen are allowed to make physical contact with the stars, while in Hollywood, the stars must never be touched.

All of this has a fascination, and yet *Red Trousers* is a jumbled and unsatisfying documentary. It jumps from one subject to another, it provides little historical context, it shows a lot of stunts being prepared and executed but refuses to ask the obvious questions in our minds: Are there no laws to protect injured stuntmen? Are they forced to sign releases? How many are killed or crippled? Why not use more safety measures?

Instead, Shou devotes way too much screen time to scenes from *Lost Time* (2001), a short action film he directed. Yes, we see stunts in preparation and then see them used in the movie, but sometimes he just lets the movie run, as if we want to see it. He explains that the term "red trousers" originated with the uniforms of students at the Beijing Opera School, which produced many of the early stuntmen, and shows us students of the opera school today; they begin as children, their lives controlled from morning to night, just as depicted in Kaige Chen's great Chinese film *Farewell, My Concubine* (1993). He interviews some of the students, who are still children, and as they affirm their ambitions and vow their dedication, we glimpse a little of where the stuntman code comes from. But if the wire breaks some day, they may, during the fall, find themselves asking basic questions about their working conditions.

Reel Paradise ★ ★ ★

R, 110 m., 2005

Featuring John Pierson, Janet Pierson, Georgia Pierson, Wyatt Pierson. A documentary directed by Steve James and produced by Scott Mosier and James.

I know a couple named Jon and Jennifer Vickers, who moved to Three Oaks, Michigan, (population 1,829), and bought the local movie theater. It's thirty miles from the closest multiplex. They show first-run art films and after eight years are a solid success. "The audience isn't just the Chicago weekend people," my friend Mary Jo Broderick tells me. She goes every week. "I see the same people I see in the supermarket in February." The Vickerses' theater doesn't show only

March of the Penguins but also Herzog, Wong Kar Wai, Bergman, Jarmusch. Every summer they have a silent-film festival.

Steve James's new documentary, *Reel Paradise*, is about a couple with similar idealism, who also move to a small town and buy the movie theater. Their theater is the 180 Meridian, on Taveuni, one of the Fiji Islands. They aren't trying to bring art cinema to Fiji. They're trying to bring the movies, period. The audience favorite is *Jackass*, a film so popular it is banned by the local authorities.

The man behind this idea is John Pierson, a producer's rep well-known in indie film circles and crucial to the early success of such directors as Spike Lee (he invested in *She's Gotta Have It*) and Michael Moore *(Roger and Me)*. I've run into him over the years at festivals such as Sundance. He tired of the indie circuit routine and convinced his wife, Janet, and their children, Georgia, sixteen, and Wyatt, thirteen, to join him for a year running a movie theater in Fiji. They do not entirely share his enthusiasm.

Steve James, who made *Hoop Dreams*, arrives in time to chronicle the final month of this experiment. What Pierson proved for sure is that if you show movies for free, you will get an audience. He also proved that a certain kind of great film, such as Buster Keaton's *Steamboat Bill Jr.*, will draw a crowd. It's always claimed that silent comedy is universal in its appeal; here's your proof.

Pierson wanted to show all kinds of movies. He has a hit with *The Hot Chick*. He doesn't do so well with more ambitious films. By the time James arrives with his camera, Pierson has contracted dengue fever and his son, Wyatt, has taken over the day-to-day operations at the 180 Meridian. He may be the son of a legendary art film supporter, but Wyatt keeps his eye firmly on the box office: "If you show *Apocalypse Now* twice," he tells his dad, "I guarantee no one will come the second night." If a fortune is to be made by the Pierson family in the movie business, it may be made by Wyatt.

Fiji seems like a paradise from a distance, but when you live there it turns into a real place with real problems. There is the heat, the humidity, the lack of a power grid (the theater has its own generator). The projectionist tends to get drunk. There is the reality that Georgia is a teenager and interested in boys

and, like all teenagers, wants to stay out past her curfew.

There are also two burglaries of the Piersons' home. Suspicion for this crime falls upon people the Piersons like and trust. Considering that the island has only one road, it should not be hard to find their computer, but it is. I am reminded of my visit to Bora Bora when *Hurricane* was being shot there. The movie publicist's Jeep was stolen. The sheriff advised him to stand outside and wait until it came around; the island had one road, which circled the island.

The priests at the Catholic mission disapprove of many of Pierson's movies (especially *Jackass*) and think that by showing them for free, he is undercutting the work ethic. The local teenagers hang out together and sometimes seem up to no good, but that is the nature of teenagers, and the dangers on Taveuni are mild compared to those in New York.

When the experiment ends and the Piersons return to America, the theater closes again. It is hard to say what they accomplished. It's nice to think that if you show people movies, especially good movies, that will somehow change or improve their lives. But movies out of context are a curiosity and may play in unexpected ways. The politically correct might question a Three Stooges movie involving a South Seas cannibal's boiling pot, but the audience explodes with such uncontrolled laughter that you can forget about hearing the dialogue.

The Piersons went, they showed movies, they returned. Taveuni is more or less the same. But by living and coping together for a year, the family is probably stronger and richer: Years from now, Georgia and Wyatt are going to be telling people about how their crazy parents opened a movie theater in Fiji, and in their voices you will hear that although they had their doubts at the time, they now think they were lucky to have such parents. Sometimes it's not whether you succeed, but whether you try.

Rent ★ ★ ½

PG-13, 128 m., 2005

Rosario Dawson (Mimi Marquez), Taye Diggs (Benjamin Coffin), Wilson Jermaine Heredia (Angel Schunard), Jesse L. Martin (Tom Collins),

Idina Menzel (Maureen Johnson), Adam Pascal (Roger Davis), Anthony Rapp (Mark Cohen), Tracie Thoms (Joanne Jefferson). Directed by Chris Columbus and produced by Jane Rosenthal, Robert De Niro, Columbus, Michael Barnathan, and Mark Radcliffe. Screenplay by Columbus and Stephen Chbosky, based on the musical drama *Rent* by Jonathan Larson.

Rent is a stage musical that wants to be a movie musical. Many stage musicals, from *Oklahoma!* to *West Side Story,* feel right at home on the screen. *Rent* on film is missing a crucial element of its life-support system: a live audience. The stage production surrounded the audience with the characters and the production. It lacked the song *We Are Family,* but that was the subtext. On film, *Rent* is the sound of one hand clapping.

It is not a bad film. It may be about as good a film as the material can inspire. The performances have a presence and poignancy that can feel surprisingly real, given the contrivances of the story. The film uses many of the same actors who starred in the original 1996 New York production, and the newcomers, Rosario Dawson and Tracie Thoms, earn their roles. But if you stand back from the importance of *Rent* as a cultural artifact and a statement about AIDS, does it stand on its own as a musical?

I don't think so. The song lyrics by Jonathan Larson have an ungainly quality, perhaps deliberate; the words often seem at right angles to the music. I do not demand that lyrics scan, rhyme, and make sense, but I do think they should flow with, or even against, the music; here the words and the music sometimes play as if two radios have been left on at the same time ("My T-cells are low" doesn't strike me as an especially singable line). The music serves the choreography, the words serve the story, but they don't serve each other.

The film left me in a curious state: I felt more respect than affection. From some of the more compelling characters, including Mimi (Dawson) and Angel (Wilson Jermaine Heredia), there are three-dimensional portraits that are convincing on any level. But the roommates in that artist's loft seem just as much of a casting call as they do in Puccini's *La Boheme,* the opera that inspired *Rent.*

They're so busy being bohemian and defying authority that they never find time to be themselves.

I no more believe Mark (Anthony Rapp) is a documentary filmmaker and Roger (Adam Pascal) is a musician than I believed Marcello and Rodolfo were an artist and a playwright in the Puccini version. There is not a person reading this review who couldn't make a better film than Mark, who doesn't even know that the handle of his hand-cranked 8 mm camera should not be revolving as he films, and whose footage looks like jerky home movies. To be given $3,000 to supply his sub-Warhol indulgences to TV is about as likely as Ozzy Osbourne getting his own reality show, ho, ho.

When the roommates feed a fire with their screenplays and compositions because it is cold in their unheated loft, I know they are only following Puccini, but I didn't believe it in *La Boheme* and I believe it less now. No matter; the job of the roommates in both versions is to be good friends of Mimi, but careless, so that they misplace her and she risks dying alone in the cold before being hurried onstage for her death scene.

The characters who did convince me have lives apart from the opera (or soap opera) elements in the story. Mimi is played by Dawson as a stripper who shoots drugs and has AIDS because of a tainted needle. She tries to clean up but falls back into drugs and they kill her. Angel (Heredia) is a transvestite who finds Tom Collins (Jesse L. Martin) mugged in an alley and tenderly cares for him as they fall in love. Angel's life force inspires a particularly moving tribute late in the film—one of those scenes that affect us like the real thing might.

There is a romantic triangle involving Mark, whose girlfriend, Maureen (Idina Menzel), dumps him for a girlfriend of her own, Joanne (Thoms). I believed the character of Joanne, but neither Maureen nor Roger. He doesn't seem much depressed by being dumped, and she's so superficial that she flirts with the cute female bartender at her partnering ceremony with Joanne. That Joanne sincerely cares for her and is really hurt I did believe. When she's accused of flirting by Joanne, Maureen sings the showstopper "Take Me for What I Am." I wanted Joanne to reply in her own song:

"Okay, You're a Promiscuous Slut, So Take Me for What I Am, Your New Former Partner." Roger and Mark had a third roommate, Benjamin (Taye Diggs), before he married, moved out, and became their landlord. Benjamin is a character conceived entirely for the convenience of the plot. When needed, he threatens eviction, sics the cops on their rent strike, is partly responsible for the riot after Maureen's performance, does evict them, padlocks the door, confiscates their possessions, and then relents and lets them move back in. All of this is done while he has two poker-faced middle-aged white men (PFMAWM), one of them his father-in-law, hanging around in the background saying nothing and apparently thinking nothing. Their job is to supply poker-faced reaction shots during same-sex dancing. Two guys dance together, PFMAWM see them. Two dolls dance together, PFMAWM see them. What are they thinking? For all I know, they're envious. Why Benjamin would take them to the same club where rent strikers cavort on tabletops is arbitrary if not capricious.

The story is set in 1989, a time when AIDS provided the same kind of death sentence that tuberculosis provided in nineteenth-century novels and operas. Through the story characters remind each other, "take your AZT," but some of them do not, apparently so they can exhibit, I dunno, a death wish, self-hatred, denial, or a desire to supply the playwright with tragedy. This is much the function provided by Puccini's original Mimi, who coughs in Act Three so that she can die in Act Four. More convincing is the treatment of Mimi's drug addiction in the modern version; Dawson plays Mimi as hooked and hopeless, and we believe her.

I think there is an audience for the movie version of Rent, and that would be fans of the stage version. If you came to know and love the material in its original form, this will be a way to see the characters and actors again, and you will bring those memories with you to the movie, as sort of a commentary track. Those who haven't seen Rent on the stage will sense they're missing something, and they are.

Note: I gave the movie a marginal thumbs up on Ebert & Roeper because I felt people might want to see it based on what was good in it, but I am fine-tuning that to a 2.5-star rating because, on the whole, I don't think the movie re-ally works on its own, without reference to the theatrical version.

Resident Evil: Apocalypse ½ ★
R, 93 m., 2004

Milla Jovovich (Alice), Sienna Guillory (Jill Valentine), Oded Fehr (Carlos Olivera), Thomas Kretschmann (Major Cain), Jared Harris (Dr. Charles Ashford), Sandrine Holt (Terri Morales). Directed by Alexander Witt and produced by Paul W. S. Anderson, Jeremy Bolt, and Don Carmody. Screenplay by Anderson.

I'm trying to remember what the city was called in the original Resident Evil (2002). I don't think it was called anything, but in Resident Evil: Apocalypse, it's called Raccoon City, just like in the original video game. Call it what you will, it has the Toronto skyline. Toronto played Chicago in Chicago and now it plays Raccoon City. Some you win, some you lose.

The movie is an utterly meaningless waste of time. There was no reason to produce it except to make money, and there is no reason to see it except to spend money. It is a dead zone, a film without interest, wit, imagination, or even entertaining violence and special effects.

The original film involved the Umbrella Corp. and its underground research laboratory called The Hive. The experimental T-virus escaped, and to contain it, The Hive was flooded and locked. But its occupants survived as zombies and lurched about infecting others with their bites. Zombies can appear in interesting movies, as George Romero proved in Dawn of the Dead and Danny Boyle in 28 Days Later. But zombies themselves are not interesting because all they do is stagger and moan. As I observed in my review of the first film, "they walk with the lurching shuffle of a drunk trying to skate through urped Slushies to the men's room."

Now time has passed and the Umbrella Corp. has decided to reopen The Hive. Well, wouldn't you know that the T-virus escapes again, and creates even more zombies? Most of the population of Raccoon City is infected, but can be easily contained because there is only one bridge out of town. The story involves three sexy women (Milla Jovovich, Sienna

Guillory, and Sandrine Holt), the first a former Umbrella Corp. scientist, the second a renegade cop, the third a TV reporter. Picking up some guys along the way, they battle the zombies and try to rescue a little girl so her dad can pull some strings and get them out of the quarantined city before it is nuked.

We pause here for logistical discussions. In a scene where several characters are fighting zombies inside a church, the renegade scientist comes to the rescue by crashing her motorcycle through a stained-glass window and landing in the middle of the fight. This inspires the question: How did she know what was on the other side of the window? Was she crashing through the stained glass on spec?

My next logistical puzzlement involves killing the zombies. They die when you shoot them. Fine, except Umbrella Corp. has developed some mutants who wear bulletproof armor. Zillions of rounds of ammo bounce off this armor, but here's a funny thing: The mutants do not wear helmets, so we can see their ugly faces. So why not just shoot them in the head? Am I missing something here?

What I was missing were more of the mutants from the first picture, where they were little monsters with nine-foot tongues. They have a walk-on (or maybe a lick-on) in the sequel, but it's no big deal. *Resident Evil: Apocalypse* could have used them, but then this is a movie that could have used anything. The violence is all video-game target practice, the zombies are a bore, we never understand how Umbrella hopes to make money with a virus that kills everyone, and the characters are spectacularly shallow. Parents: If you encounter teenagers who say they liked this movie, do not let them date your children.

The Return ★ ★ ★

NO MPAA RATING, 106 m., 2004

Vladimir Garin (Andrey), Ivan Dobronravov (Ivan), Konstantin Lavronenko (Father), Natalia Vdovina (Mother). Directed by Andrey Zvyagintsev and produced by Dmitry Lesnevsky. Screenplay by Vladimir Moiseenko and Alexander Novototsky.

Here is the latest and most disturbing of three films about children and their ominous fathers.

Bill Paxton's *Frailty* was about two brothers who are fearful about their father's conviction that an angel of God has assigned him to kill the Satan-possessed among us. *I'm Not Scared,* by Gabriele Salvatores of Italy, was about a small boy who stumbles upon a chained kidnap victim and gradually realizes his father is the kidnapper. Now we have *The Return,* from Russia, which is all the more frightening because two young brothers never do fully understand their father's alarming behavior. It is a Kafkaesque story, in which ominous things follow each other with a certain internal logic, but make no sense at all.

As the movie opens, Andrey (Vladimir Garin) and his younger brother Ivan (Ivan Dobronravov) return home one day to hear their mother whisper, "Quiet! Dad's sleeping." This is a father they have not seen for years, if ever, and the movie gives us no explanation for his absence. Almost immediately he proposes a fishing trip, and the boys are less than overjoyed at this prospect of leaving home with a man who is essentially a stranger.

The father (Konstantin Lavronenko) drives them to a lakeside. He attempts to impose stern discipline in the car, but this seems less the result of cruelty than because of his awkwardness around young boys. Indeed, the movie's refusal to declare the father a villain adds to the ambiguity; eventually he creates a disturbing situation, but does he act by design, compulsion, or impulse? And what are his motives?

Whatever they are, it's clear that catching fish is not one of them. There is an ominous scene under a lowering sky and scattered rain, as he and the boys row a small boat to an island far away in the middle of the lake. On the island, the boys explore, and there is a tower that tests their fear of heights. They spy on their father, and see him retrieve a small buried trunk. What's in it? We think perhaps he is a paroled convict, returning for his loot. Or a man who has learned of buried treasure. Or . . .

Doesn't matter. The box, which has caused so much trouble, is lost to history by the end of the film, along with the reason why the father thought he needed to bring his two sons along. Was he acting from some kind of stunted impulse to make up time with his boys? Was he subjecting them to an experience he had undergone? Are they safe with him?

The Return, directed by Andrey Zvyagintsev

and cowritten by Vladimir Moiseenko and Alexander Novototsky, does not conceal information from the audience, which would be a technique of manipulation—but from the young boys, which is a technique of drama. The movie is not about the father's purpose but the boys' confusion and alarm. Like the other two films I mentioned, it eventually arrives at the point where the boys must decide whether or not to act, and here the interior dynamic of their own relationship is more important than how they feel about their father.

Zvyagintsev films on chilly, overcast days, on an island that in this season is not a vacation spot. His cinematographer, Mikhail Kritchman, denatures the color film stock to deny us cheer. We do not like this island, or trust this father, or like the looks of the boat—which for a long time is left untethered on the beach, so that there's a constant underthought that it might float away. What finally happens is not anything we could have anticipated, except to observe that something like that seemed to be hanging in the damp, cold air.

Note: An additional sadness creeps into the film if we know that Vladimir Garin, the older of the two boys, drowned not long after the film was completed, in a situation not unlike one in the film.

Rick ★ ★ ★
R, 100 m., 2004

Bill Pullman (Rick), Aaron Sanford (Duke), Agnes Bruckner (Eve), Dylan Baker (Buck), Sandra Oh (Michelle). Directed by Curtiss Clayton and produced by Ruth Charny, Jim Czarnecki, and Sofia Sondervan. Screenplay by Daniel Handler.

Rick is a vicious SOB and a bully. He ridicules those weaker than he is, and rolls on the floor to please his boss. In other words, he's in middle management. Bill Pullman brings the character to full bloom in *Rick,* a movie that paints a corporate world of lust, hypocrisy, racism, and cruelty. No mention is made of the product or service produced by the corporation where Rick works, perhaps because the product is beside the point: This corporate culture works to produce itself.

The movie goes beyond dark comedy into dank comedy. Rick and his boss, Duke (Aaron Sanford), are creatures without redeeming merit, and Rick's old buddy Buck (Dylan Baker) is a killer for hire. His daughter is a regular in an X-rated chat room. Perhaps it is not astonishing that the screenplay is by Daniel Handler, who writes the Lemony Snicket books, the first of which warns its young readers: "These books are among the most miserable in the world."

With Lemony Snicket he's kidding, I think. With *Rick,* we have misanthropy run riot. I don't know if it works, but it's not boring, and there is a kind of terrible thrill in seeing an essentially nice guy like Bill Pullman play a character who is hateful beyond all measure. The story line is lifted from Verdi's *Rigoletto,* but if you could not sit down right now and compose 200 words summarizing the plot of that opera, it matters little; the movie has a life of its own.

The tone is set in a remarkable early scene in which Rick (Pullman) bounds into the office of Duke, who is half his age, and debases himself in a paroxysm of male bonding behavior. They curse, they drink, they smoke cigars, they pound each other to show what great guys they are, and Rick at one point actually crawls on the floor and seems likely to hump Duke's leg. They go out for a drink in a curious club supplied with video monitors so the customers can spy on each other, and then Duke excuses himself to go back to the office, where he can't wait to log on as BIGBOSS in that X-rated Web chat room.

Earlier in the film, a young woman named Michelle (Sandra Oh) came to Rick's office to be interviewed for a job. He made her go out, come in, go out, and wait and then come in again, and then systematically and cruelly humiliated and insulted her, deliberately confusing her Asian origins. In the club, wouldn't you know she's his waitress. Rick starts in on her again. She takes a little more than she should, and then, in a magnificent scene, she retaliates: "You're an evil person and you can't get away with it. I curse you. Your evil will come right back at you." This curse resonates through the film, reaching that deep part of Rick's ego where even he is disgusted by himself.

Rick has a daughter named Eve (Agnes Bruckner, so good as the student who deals with a molesting teacher in *Blue Car*). She's a regular in the chat room, logging on as VIXXXEN, and she and BIGBOSS have worked up to the point where a meeting might be in order. Meanwhile, Duke sees Rick with the pretty Eve on his arm, and concludes that Eve is Rick's wife, not his daughter. As his wife, she's fair game, Duke concludes; but then, as his daughter she probably would be too.

Enter Buck the alleged college chum. "I've started my own company," Buck tells Rick, and hands him his card:

Buck—My Own Company

What Buck does is eliminate your competitors at work, clearing the way for your own advancement. He does this by killing them, which he justifies as the price of getting ahead in business. In *Rigoletto* as in Shakespeare, much depends on improbably mistaken identities, and so we're not in much suspense about whether the wrong person will get killed, or be seduced, or whatever.

There is no one in this movie to like. It has a heroine, the young woman Michelle, but she's around only long enough to stand up for herself, put a curse on Rick, and get the hell out of there. The remaining characters are hateful, except for Eve the daughter, who is blameless apart from her practice of inflaming the fantasies of anonymous men with her chat room scenarios.

Movies like this are kind of a test for a viewer. If you require that you "like" a movie, then *Rick* is not for you, because there is nothing likable about it. It's rotten to the core and right down to the end. But if you find that such extremes can be fascinating, then the movie may cheer you, not because it is happy, but because it goes for broke.

Note: The director is Curtiss Clayton, who has edited many of Gus Van Sant's movies. He was scheduled to be the editor of Vincent Gallo's The Brown Bunny, *but walked off the job on the first day of postproduction when* Rick *was green-lighted. I don't know what passed between them, but Gallo told me he "freaked out" when Clayton bailed; is it possible that Gallo's propensity for putting hexes on people was the inspiration for Michelle's great scene?*

Riding Giants ★ ★ ★ ½
PG-13, 105 m., 2004

A documentary directed by Stacy Peralta and produced by Peralta, Agi Orsi, and Jane Kachmer. Screenplay by Peralta and Sam George.

For fifteen years, Jeff Clark surfed alone. He paddled through forty-five minutes of wave and chop to reach Maverick's, "a veritable graveyard of jagged rocks" in the Pacific off San Francisco. There he found the most challenging surfing he had ever seen or heard about. For all those years other surfers didn't join him; the area was too remote, and they were focused on southern California and Hawaii.

Well, you wonder, how dangerous could the "graveyard" be if Clark survived it solo for fifteen years? Then word of Maverick's gets around, and legendary surfers from Hawaii's North Shore come to visit. One of the sport's champions, Mark Foo, is killed after wiping out on a medium wave. One theory is that the tether to his board got caught on rocks and he drowned. Another surfer thinks he felt or sensed somebody under the water who shouldn't have been there. Exactly one year later, during a memorial to Foo, another surfer is drowned.

The documentary *Riding Giants* shows surfers gathered to discuss and mourn the lost men. It does not show Jeff Clark during those previous fifteen years because, of course, he was alone. And what a species of aloneness it was, to plunge into the cold ocean and swim out forty-five minutes for a few seconds of exhilaration at the risk of your life. Clark and his kind live at the intersection of courage, madness, skill, and obsession.

Consider Laird Hamilton, the current golden boy of the sport, who has cashed in with endorsement contracts, modeling assignments, and magazine covers. But no, I am not comparing him unfavorably to Clark, because Hamilton is also a superb athlete and a driven man. Hanging around as a kid with Hawaii's big wave riders of the 1960s, he introduced his divorced mom to one of them, who became his stepfather and tutor; Laird grew up to become surfing's first superstar.

What Hamilton has done is go farther from

land than any rider had thought to go, seeking "remote offshore reefs capable of producing unimaginable waves." At first this involved paddling two hours and then waiting up to two hours for a wave. Then Hamilton invents "towing surfing," in which a jet ski tows him out to the far reefs and slings him onto waves moving so fast it is impossible to access them any other way.

The jet ski driver's other job is to pick up Hamilton again after the ride, or be prepared to rescue him. The thriller *Open Water* shows a couple lost at sea after being left behind on a scuba-diving tour. For Hamilton, being lost at sea is a possibility several times a day. *Riding Giants* was directed by Stacy Peralta, whose *Dogtown and Z-Boys* (2002) documented the invention and culture of southern California skateboarding. In both films his archival work is the key; he seems to have access to limitless historical footage, sometimes in home movie form; we see Hamilton at the dawn of towing surfing, when at first it was scorned and then embraced by the sport's champions.

In August 2000, Hamilton goes to Tahiti in search of a legendary wave so big it is "a freak of hydroponics." He finds it and rides it, and we see him precariously balanced on its terrifying immensity in what the movie calls "the most significant ride in surfing history." Other surfers, providing voice-over commentary, say the wave's characteristics were so different from ordinary waves that Hamilton had to improvise new techniques, some of them violating years of surfing theory and instinct, right there on the wave.

What a long time it seems since that summer of 1967, when I sat in a Chicago beer garden with the suntanned and cheerful Bruce Brown. He'd just made a documentary named *Endless Summer*, and was touring the country with it, at the moment when surfing was exploding (there were 5,000 surfers in 1959, 2 million today). For Brown, surfing was a lark. With a $50,000 budget, he followed two surfers on an odyssey that led to Senegal, Ghana, South Africa, Australia, New Zealand, Tahiti, and Hawaii. They were searching for the "perfect wave" and found it off Durban, South Africa: "A four-foot curl that gave rides of fifteen minutes and came in so steadily it looked like it was made by a machine."

A four-foot curl? Hamilton and his contemporaries challenge waves of sixty or seventy feet. *Endless Summer* charts a world of beaches and babes, brews and Beach Boys songs, and surfers who live to "get stoked." In *Riding Giants* the sport is more like an endless winter—solitary and dangerous. Even as Brown was making *Endless Summer*, modern surfing was being invented by pioneers like Greg Noll of Hawaii, who ventured fifteen miles up the coast from Honolulu to Waimea Bay. It was thought to be unsurfable; a surfer asks himself, "Can the human body survive the wipeout?" It could. The discovery of the North Shore of Oahu, the movie says, "was surfing's equivalent of Columbus discovering the New World."

More vintage footage. The "storm of the century" descends upon Hawaii, and Noll, known as "The Bull," determines to surf it. His chances of surviving are rated at 50/50 by the movie, at zero by any reasonable person watching it. He survived. It was "the biggest wave ever ridden"—until, perhaps, a monster that Hamilton found off Tahiti, too big to be measured.

After Bruce Brown finds his Perfect Wave in *Endless Summer*, he marvels: "The odds against a wave like this are twenty million–to-one!" The odds that Laird Hamilton could get stoked on a four-foot curl are higher than that. Before seeing *Riding Giants*, my ideas about surfing were formed by the Gidget movies, *Endless Summer*, the Beach Boys, Elvis, and lots of TV commercials. "Surfin' Safari" was actually running through my head on the way into the screening.

Riding Giants is about altogether another reality. The overarching fact about these surfers is the degree of their obsession. They live to ride, and grow depressed when there are no waves. They haunt the edge of the sea like the mariners Melville describes on the first pages of *Moby-Dick*. They seek the rush of those moments when they balance on top of a wave's fury and feel themselves in precarious harmony with the ungovernable force of the ocean. They are cold and tired, battered by waves, thrown against rocks, visited by sharks, held under so long they believe they are drowning—and over and over, year after year, they go back into the sea to do it again.

The Ringer ★ ★ ★
PG-13, 94 m., 2005

Johnny Knoxville (Steve Barker), Brian Cox (Gary Barker), Katherine Heigl (Lynn Sheridan), Jed Rees (Glen), Bill Chott (Thomas), Edward Barbanell (Billy), Leonard Earl Howze (Mark), Geoffrey Arend (Winston), John Taylor (Rudy), Luis Avalos (Stavi), Leonard Flowers (Jimmy). Directed by Barry W. Blaustein and produced by Peter Farrelly, Bobby Farrelly, John L. Jacobs, and Bradley Thomas. Screenplay by Ricky Blitt.

The Ringer is a comedy about a man who poses as mentally disabled in order to fraudulently enter the Special Olympics. Yes, it's connected to the Farrelly brothers, specialists in bad taste, the same Bobby and Peter who showed the guy's artificial thumb rolling down the alley stuck in his bowling ball; indeed, the same Peter and Bobby who in *There's Something About Mary* gave us the hair gel that could have taken cell cloning research in a new direction. They are the producers of *The Ringer*, which means they came up with the money, and my guess is a lot more than that.

So the movie is in horrible taste and politically incorrect and an affront to all that is decent, right? After all, it stars Johnny Knoxville, whose *Jackass* TV show is probably the Farrellys' idea of *Masterpiece Theater*. But not so fast, Ex-Lax. The movie surprised me. It treats its disabled characters with affection and respect, it has a plot that uses the Special Olympics instead of misusing them, and it's actually kind of sweet, apart from a few Farrellian touches, such as the ex-janitor who gets his fingers chopped off in the lawn mower.

What happens is that the hero, Steve Barker (Knoxville), listens to one self-help tape too many: "Hey, you! Yes, you! I'm talking to you—the loser who bought this tape!" The tape works him into a lather and he demands a promotion. "Sure," says the boss. "You can start now. Fire the janitor."

But, jeez, Stavi the janitor (Luis Avalos) is a nice guy, and a widower with five kids to feed. So Steve fires him and then hires him to mow the lawn at his condo and gives him a raise out of his own salary, and then "Stavi Lose Fingers." Stavi, who always refers to himself in the third person, seems to speak in capitalized words, as in "Stavi's Kids Will Starve," or "HMO Says Stavi Has No Finger-Sewing Insurance."

Steve has an uncle, Gary (Brian Cox), who is wanted by the mob regarding a past-due loan and who knows how he and Steve can raise the money they need. Steve will pose as a Special Olympian, run rings around the other athletes, and Uncle Gary will bet a lot of money on him. Steve is a lot of things, but he is not a Special Actor. He poses as mentally challenged, calls himself Jeffy, forgets his last name and his Uncle Gary suggests Dahmer. The real Special Olympians are not fooled by him for one second: "You talk different," they tell him.

The competition includes Jimmy (Leonard Flowers), the Special Superstar, who arrives in a stretch limo with his agents and trainers, and has a lot of endorsement contracts. Also some regular Special Guys who, once they've blown Jeffy's cover, think it's cool that anyone would be stupid enough to try a stunt like that. And there's a beautiful volunteer named Lynn (Katherine Heigl), whom Steve falls in love with—as Jeffy, leading to complications.

The plot takes care of itself on the level of a competent sitcom. This is not a great movie, but I kinda liked its spirit. It might have been better if the Farrellys had directed instead of Barry W. Blaustein. Some of the Special characters are disabled, some are not, but all are seen as engaging and valuable people.

Although the Farrellys have made a career out of comedies in bad taste, I happen to know they have a sincere interest in mentally challenged people because they have a good friend named Rocket who knows *everything* about the movies. When we were trying out cohosts on the TV show, they called me and pitched Rocket for the job. "For cohost?" I asked. "Or your job," they said. I was tempted but afraid the audition might come across the wrong way.

The Ringer could have been a better movie, but that would have depended more on the screenplay than the cast, which is effective and generates real affection. Knoxville is on target as nothing Special, and Cox demonstrates why he is not only in every movie made, but deserves to be.

Note: Is the movie appropriate for developmentally disabled young people? There is a sincere note on the Internet Movie Database from the mother of a disabled child and Special Olympics participant. I pass along her opinion without comment. She writes:

While you may find the story uplifting, it may elude your students' understanding. It may be painful for them to see the type of teasing and disrespect they experience. Don't assume they will get the same thing out of the movie that you do. You may do a lot more harm than good. . . .

I did not allow my son to see Forrest Gump *or* I Am Sam *specifically because he will view these types of films from an entirely different perspective. Because the film is about the disabled, the journey itself is far too personal for many developmentally disabled people to endure and perhaps difficult for them to understand the good intentions.*

The Ring Two ★ ★ ½
PG-13, 111 m., 2005

Naomi Watts (Rachel Keller), David Dorfman (Aidan Keller), Simon Baker (Max Rourke), Sissy Spacek (Evelyn), Elizabeth Perkins (Dr. Emma Temple), Gary Cole (Martin Savide). Directed by Hideo Nakata and produced by Laurie MacDonald, Walter F. Parkes, and Mark Sourian. Screenplay by Ehren Kruger, based on the novel *Ringu* by Koji Suzuki.

I am not sure I entirely understand the deer. In *The Ring Two,* Rachel and her young son, Aidan, visit a farmer's market. Aidan wanders off and observes some deer that emerge from a nearby forest and stare at him. He stares back. Later, as mother and son are driving down a little-traveled road, a deer appears in front of their car. "Keep moving," Aidan says urgently, but his mother hesitates, and soon the car is under attack by a dozen stags, their antlers crashing through the windows. She speeds away and hits another stag, doing considerable damage to the car's front end.

This is in a movie that also involves a mysterious video that brings death to whoever watches it, unless they pass it on to someone else within a week. The video is connected to the death of a young girl named Samara who had a cruel childhood. Samara's ghost is trying to possess Aidan's body. Because she died at the bottom of a well, much water is produced wherever her ghost manifests itself.

Usually the water is on the floor, but sometimes it flows up to the ceiling.

Rachel visits the old farm where the girl was mistreated and died. In the basement, she finds antlers. A whole lot of antlers. So maybe the deer sense Samara's ghost's presence in Aidan and are attacking the car in revenge? But Samara was presumably not the deer hunter, being far too occupied as a cruelly mistreated little girl at the time. So is it that the deer are psychic, but not very bright?

One does not know but, oddly, one does not care. The charm of *The Ring Two,* while limited, is real enough; it is based on the film's ability to make absolutely no sense, while nevertheless generating a convincing feeling of tension a good deal of the time. It is like an exercise in cinema mechanics: Images, music, photography, and mood conspire to create a sense of danger, even though at any given moment we cannot possibly explain the rules under which that danger might manifest itself.

We do get some information. Samara, for example, can hear everything Rachel (Naomi Watts) and Aidan (David Dorfman) say to each other, except when Aidan is asleep. So Rachel talks to him a lot while he's asleep, with dubious utility. They also appear in each other's dreams, where they either (a) find a loophole by talking to each other while they're asleep, or (b) are only dreaming.

Meanwhile, the video gimmick, which supported *The Ring* (2002), is retired and the action centers on Samara's assaults on Aidan's body and Rachel's attempts to defend him. At one point this involves almost drowning him in a bathtub, which is the second time (after *Constantine*) that being almost drowned in a bathtub is employed as a weapon against supernatural forces.

The movie has been directed by Hideo Nakata, who directed the two famous Japanese horror films *Ringu* (1998) and *Ringu 2* (1999), although *The Ring Two* is not a remake of *Ringu 2.* It is a new departure, as Rachel, a newspaper reporter, leaves Seattle and gets a job on the paper in the pretty but rainy coastal town of Astoria, Oregon. Here perhaps the tape and its associated menace will not follow them.

Naomi Watts and David Dorfman are always convincing, sometimes very effective, in their roles; in the scene where she's going down into the basement, we keep repeating, "It's only a basement," but I was surprised that the ancient cinematic techniques still worked for me. In all such scenes it is essential for the camera to back into the basement while focused on the heroine, so that we cannot see what she sees, and therefore, through curious movie logic, neither can she.

The scenes involving Aidan's health are also well handled, as his body temperature goes up and down like an applause meter, reflecting the current state of Samara's success in taking over his body. If he becomes entirely a ghost, does he go down to room temperature? Elizabeth Perkins plays a psychiatrist who thinks Aidan may have been abused, and there is a creepy cameo by Sissy Spacek, wearing scary old lady makeup, as Samara's birth mother. Aidan always calls his mother "Rachel," by the way, and when he starts calling her "Mommy" this is not a good sign.

When I say the film defies explanation, that doesn't mean it discourages it. Websites exist for no other reason than to do the work of the screenwriters by figuring out what it all means. At the end, for example, when Rachel rolls the heavy stone across the top of the well, does that mean Samara is out of business? Rachel seems to think so, but wasn't the stone *always* on top of the well?

Rize ★ ★ ★
PG-13, 85 m., 2005

Featuring Tommy the Clown, Lil Tommy, Larry, Swoop, El Nino, Dragon, Lil C, Tight Eyez, Baby Tight Eyez, Daisy, Big X, Miss Prissy, La Nina, and Quinesha. A documentary directed by David LaChapelle and produced by Marc Hawker, Ellen Jacobson-Clarke, and LaChapelle. Screenplay by LaChapelle.

The footage in this movie has not been speeded up in any way.

We need to be told that, right at the beginning of *Rize*, because krumping, the dance style shown in the movie, looks like life in fast-forward. You haven't heard of krumping? Neither had I. And I didn't know that dressing up like a clown has become an alternative to join-

ing a street gang in the South Central and Watts areas of Los Angeles. When this movie was made, there were more than 50 clown groups; now there are said to be more than 100.

Rize is the rare documentary that plays as breaking news. Krumping and clowning have become so big in L.A. that the fifth annual krumping competition, known as Battle Zone, was held in the Great Western Forum. Yet until this movie was made by *Vanity Fair* photographer David LaChapelle, it was a phenomenon that existed below the radar of the media. It's an alternative to the hip-hop style that is growing a little old; because recording labels and cable TV have so much invested in hip-hop, however, they have been slow to embrace it. Or maybe they just couldn't believe their eyes.

The clowns in these groups are real clowns. Bozo should get royalties. They have rainbow wigs and putty noses and weirdly made-up faces and wildly colored costumes, and they would have floppy shoes except then they couldn't dance. The dance they do, krumping, sometimes looks like a fistfight in fast motion, sometimes borrows moves from strippers, sometimes looks like speeded-up martial arts, sometimes is beyond description.

Borrowing a page from poetry jams, krumpers face off one-on-one and try to out-krump one another, and the final showdown in Battle Zone V is between the two main factions of the movement, the krumps and the clowns. (Just to spell out the difference: While clowns krump, not all krumps are clowns. Krumping was invented by Lil C, Tight Eyez, and Dragon after they left Tommy to start their own school. So now you know.)

This world is the invention, we learn, of Tommy the Clown (Tom Johnson), who as a young man was into drugs and gangs. "Living like that," he says, "you either wind up shot dead or in jail. I was lucky. I wound up in jail." When he was released and unsure what direction his life would take, he was asked to play a clown at a friend's birthday party. He liked the way people responded to him as a clown; they regarded him as if he had dropped out of ordinary categories and lived in a separate world.

Tommy the Clown became "a ghetto celebrity," he tells us, and we see footage of Tommy making unannounced appearances at shopping malls, movie theater lines, and street corners. He takes his first disciple, Lil Tommy ("When my mom was in jail, he took me in"), and soon he's running a clown academy. A key moment comes when the clowns evoke a new kind of dancing; a clown named Larry is a key innovator. Soon there are groups of krump-dancing clowns all over the streets of neighborhoods that were once afire (the film opens with footage from the Watts and Rodney King rioting).

In these neighborhoods to wear the wrong gang colors in the wrong place at the wrong time is to risk being shot dead. But a clown wears every possible color at once, and in a way becomes disqualified. "The gangs sort of leave us alone," one of the clowns says, and there is a sense that joining a clown group may be a way to survive outside the gang culture. It is also a very weird lifestyle.

We see clowns devising elaborate facial makeup, owing more to Batman villains than to Bozo. We witness artistic rivalries between various styles of clowning and dancing. And there are suggestions that not everyone loves clowns; while Tommy is running the face-off at the Forum, his home is trashed. Late in the film, one of the most lovable characters is shot dead by drive-by killers, firing at random. Guns don't kill people; people with guns kill people.

Still, *Rize* on the whole brings good news, of a radical social innovation that simultaneously sidesteps street gangs and bypasses hip-hop. Krumping should turn up any day now on BET and MTV, if it hasn't already; whether the dancers will be dressed as clowns is less likely. There is something a little eerie about clowns, and to see dozens of them at once perhaps inspires even gang members to go elsewhere.

The most remarkable thing about *Rize* is that it is real. I remember hearing vaguely at Sundance about an earlier short subject that LaChapelle made about this phenomenon; was it on the level or a mockumentary? If *Rize* were a fake doc, it would look about the same as it does now, and would be easier to absorb, since the idea of gangs of clowns sounds like a put-on. But it isn't.

Robots ★ ★ ★ ½
PG, 91 m., 2005

With the voices of: Ewan McGregor (Rodney Copperbottom), Halle Berry (Cappy), Greg Kinnear (Phineas T. Ratchet), Mel Brooks (Big Weld), Amanda Bynes (Piper Pinwheeler), Drew Carey (Crank Casey), Jim Broadbent (Madame Gasket), Jennifer Coolidge (Aunt Fanny), Robin Williams (Fender), Stanley Tucci (Herb Copperbottom). Directed by Chris Wedge and Carlos Saldanha and produced by Jerry Davis, John C. Donkin, and William Joyce. Screenplay by David Lindsay-Abaire, Lowell Ganz, and Babaloo Mandel.

The thing that struck me first of all about *Robots* was its pictorial beauty. I doubt that was the intention of the animators, who've made a slapstick comedy set in a futurist city that seems fresh off the cover of a 1942 issue of *Thrilling Wonder Stories*. Towers and skyways and strange architectural constructions look like an Erector set's erotic dreams, and the ideal skyscraper is a space needle ringed by metallic doughnuts.

This world is inhabited by robots who are human in every respect except that they are not human in any respect, if you follow me. They even have babies. As the movie opens, Herb Copperbottom and his wife are unwrapping their new little boy, who has arrived in a shipping crate, some assembly required. This being a PG-rated movie aimed at the whole family, the robots even have the ability to fart, which is a crucial entertainment requirement of younger children.

But look at the design and artistic execution. Each robot is a unique creation, made of nuts and bolts, but also expressing an individual personality, and moving in a way that seems physical and mechanical at the same time. And consider the color palate, which seems to have been borrowed from Fiestaware, which was inspired by the cheap table settings that used to be given away as prizes at Saturday matinees and is now collected by those who inexplicably find it beautiful, such as myself. Even the shapes of some of the robots resemble the plump art deco lines of a Fiestaware teapot or water pitcher.

Like *Finding Nemo*, this is a movie that is a joy to behold entirely apart from what it is about. It looks happy, and more to the point, it looks harmonious. One of the reasons this entirely impossible world works is because it looks like it belongs together, as if it evolved organically.

Of course, organics are the last concern of young Rodney Copperbottom (voice by Ewan McGregor), who is born in Rivet City but dreams of a journey to Robot City, where he hopes that a mysterious tycoon named Big Weld will be amazed by his inventions. Rodney's father (Stanley Tucci) is a dishwasher (the appliance is built right into his midsection), and Rodney has invented a tiny helicopter robot that can whiz around the kitchen, stacking plates and silverware. What is served on the plates I will leave to your imagination.

Encouraged by his father to follow his dream, Rodney takes the train to Robot City. This train apparently uses the same technology as the *Polar Express;* it's pulled by a traditional steam locomotive, which casually takes off and chugs through the air. In Robot City, almost the first robotperson Rodney meets is Fender (Robin Williams), a tourist tout who snaps pictures, sells postcards, and introduces Rodney to the city's public transportation system.

Their trip across town is when we realize how joyously the filmmakers have imagined this world. Chris Wedge and Carlos Saldanha, who worked together on *Ice Age* (2002), create a Rube Goldberg series of ramps, pulleys, catapults, spring-loaded propulsion devices, spiraling chutes, and dizzying mechanical slingshots that hurtle Fender and poor Rodney on a stomach-churning ride, or would if they had stomachs.

Robots has a plot that centers on the availability of spare parts, and uses a lot of them itself, borrowed from other movies. There's a little of *The Wizard of Oz* in the character of Big Weld (Mel Brooks), who does a TV program extolling the virtues and perfection of his vast corporation, but does not seem findable when Rodney visits Big Weld headquarters. Nor are Big Weld's executives interested in Rodney's inventions.

The company is being run day-to-day by Phineas T. Ratchet (Greg Kinnear), who is uninterested in improving the product because a perfect product would be bad for sales. "Upgrades! That's how we make the dough!" he explains, sounding like a consumer electronics executive.

Phineas is dominated by his mother, Madame Gasket, played by Jim Broadbent.

Yes, Jim Broadbent, but reflect that in a robot society the genders are elements of design, not function. If you have a screwdriver and swappable attachments, you can come out of the closet as whatever you feel like. Madame Gasket's master plan is to create a shortage of spare parts, so that robots will have to be replaced, instead of being indefinitely repaired like a 1959 Chevy in Havana.

Rodney now meets a sexpot, or would that be an oilpot, named Cappy (Halle Berry), who serves as his guide to some of the secrets of Robot City. She looks great, but of course in a robot society everybody has had some work done. She becomes his sidekick in an invasion of Big Weld headquarters, which leads to a confrontation with the Weld himself.

I have observed before that giant corporations have replaced Nazis as dependable movie villains. Phineas T. Ratchett, who plans an inside takeover of Big Weld's empire, is obviously a student of the theories of conspicuous consumption and planned obsolescence. Such truths of human marketing would presumably have no place in the logical world of robots, but perhaps somewhere in the dim prehistory of Robot City there were human programmers, who added a few lines of code to make the robots endearingly greedy, selfish, and wasteful.

Darwinian processes seem irrelevant in robot society since, as nearly as I can tell, every robot is a unique example of intelligent design, including Aunt Fanny (Jennifer Coolidge), whose enormous derriere would no doubt confer an evolutionary advantage not immediately apparent, if robots reproduced according to the laws of DNA instead of the whims of manufacturers and repairmen. Imagine going to the garage after a breakdown and asking, "How long will it be before I can get myself back?"

Rock School ★ ★ ★
R, 93 m. 2005

With Paul Green, C. J. Tywoniak, Will O'Connor, Madi Diaz Svalgard, Tucker Collins, Asa Collins, Napoleon Murphy Brock, Eric Svalgard, Andrea Collins, Chris Lampson, Monique Del Rosario, Brandon King, Lisa Rubens, Lisa Green, and Jimmy Carl Black. A documentary directed by

Don Argott and produced by Argott and Sheena M. Joyce.

Paul Green is a great teacher. We have this on the authority of Paul Green. He wanted to be a great rock musician, and when that didn't pan out, he picked something he could be great at, and now, he admits, he is great at it. He is the founder and apparently the entire faculty at the Paul Green School of Rock, a Philadelphia after-school program that takes kids ages nine to seventeen and trains them to be rock musicians. Maybe he would like to start even sooner; at one point he asks his infant son, "Can you say 'Jethro Tull'?"

The school is crammed into a narrow brick building where every classroom seems jammed with kids who do not measure up to Green's standards. He warns them, berates them, shouts at them, waves his arms, issues dire predictions, and somehow gets them to play music. Some of them are pretty good. There is a guitar player named C. J. Tywoniak, who stands about five feet tall and can play better than most of the guitarists you see on *Saturday Night Live*. And a singer named Madi Diaz Svalgard, who comes out of a Quaker background and knows people involved in a group named Quaker Gangsta.

"The whole thing in education now is that you don't compare children," Green says. "Well, I do." It's difficult to figure out what the kids are thinking as they stare at him during his tirades, but he has a certain level of self-mockery that takes the edge off. Green is not an angry jerk so much as a guy playing an angry jerk because he loves rock music and wants these kids to play it well. He is not Mr. Nice Guy, like the Jack Black character in *School of Rock*.

But what does he mean by rock music? "I wanted life as a rock star in 1972," he said. "I'd never want to be a rock star now." His god is Frank Zappa, and he leads the kids through difficult Zappa songs like *Inca Roads,* preparing them for the annual Zappanale Festival in Germany. "We gotta be the best band there," he says, and during his preshow pep talks he sounds uncannily like a coach in a high school sports movie. In Germany they get a chance to play with two Zappa veterans, Napoleon Murphy Brock and Jimmy Carl Black, and Murphy

Brock gets down on his knees and bows to young C. J., and is about half-serious.

One of the most intriguing students in the school is Will O'Connor, who provides a description of his rocky beginnings: His was a difficult birth, his head was too large, he had to wear a neck brace for three years, he was misdiagnosed as mentally challenged, he was suicidal, etc., and then he discovered the School of Rock, and while he has not emerged as much of a musician, he no longer thinks of suicide and can even kid about it. Paul Green establishes the school's "Will O'Connor Award for Student Most Likely to Kill Himself," which sounds one way when it's an in-joke in the school corridors and another way when it's quoted in the *Philadelphia Inquirer*. One thing becomes clear when O'Connor is on the screen: Far from being "slow," he talks like the smartest person in the movie. The School of Rock is made for difficult cases like his.

There are scenes showing Lisa, Paul's wife, and his home life, which looks conventional. There are interviews with a few parents, who seem pleased with what their children are learning at school. One even styles her kid's hair in a spiky punk style, but draws the line at stenciling pentagrams on his face. Scenes of nine-year-olds rehearsing to sing in a menacing fashion are illuminating, revealing the nine-year-olds inside many rock singers.

Green uses the f-word incessantly, along with all the other words he can think of, and anyone in the conventional educational system would be horrified, I suspect, by moments in this film. What is important is that he doesn't talk down to the students, and he is deadly serious about wanting them to work hard, practice more, and become good musicians. He rants and raves, but at least he doesn't condescend. "By the time I'm thirty," his student Will O'Connor says, evaluating his musical progress, "I think I could be decent. If I live that long."

All very well, but how good a teacher is Paul Green, really? There are no scenes in the movie showing him actually teaching his students to play a guitar. Not a single musical note is discussed. No voice lessons. There are times when the point of the school doesn't seem to be making students into rock stars, but rewriting Green's own lost childhood. There are other times when the students regard him blankly, waiting for his wacky behavior to be over so that they can get back to playing. We see no friendships between the students. Not much school spirit; they're playing for Green's glory, not their own. Green's approach certainly opens up opportunities for his students, and is a refreshing change from the lockstep public school approach, which punishes individualism. But sooner or later, a kid like C. J. Tywoniak is going to have to move on—to Julliard, maybe.

Roll Bounce ★ ★ ★
PG-13, 107 m., 2005

Bow Wow (Xavier ["X"]), Chi McBride (Curtis Smith), Mike Epps (Byron), Wesley Jonathan (Sweetness), Kellita Smith (Vivian), Meagan Good (Naomi), Khleo Thomas (Mixed Mike), Nick Cannon (Bernard), Rick Gonzalez (Naps), Jurnee Smollett (Tori). Directed by Malcolm D. Lee and produced by Robert Teitel and George Tillman Jr. Screenplay by Norman Vance Jr.

Film by film, the makers of *Roll Bounce* have been creating a new world in American movies. This is a world in which black people live in well-kept homes, have jobs, don't do drugs, don't have guns, aren't in gangs, don't call anybody "bitch," and do not use a famous twelve-letter word. It is sad that I need to write such a paragraph, but relevant: The dominant image of African-Americans in the movies is of the lawless, the violent, and the drugged. This image does not represent the majority of black people, but it works as subtle propaganda in the minds of audiences of all races.

Now consider some titles. The producers of *Roll Bounce*, Robert Teitel and George Tillman Jr., also made *Soul Food, Men of Honor* (with Cuba Gooding Jr. as the first black Navy diver), *Barbershop* and its spin-offs, and *Beauty Shop*. Some of the movies are better than others, but all of them have good hearts. They reflect a reality that is missing in the Friday night multiplex specials.

Roll Bounce, a nostalgic memory of disco roller dancing in the late 1970s, has warm starring performances from Bow Wow (formerly "L'il") and Chi McBride, who are funny, lov-

able, and sometimes touching. In their different ways, they're mourning the death of a mother and wife; Xavier (Bow Wow) hangs out with four friends at a Chicago South Side roller rink, and Curtis (McBride) obsesses on repairing his dead wife's car. It is his secret that after ten years as an engineer, he lost his job when his company closed and is out of work.

Xavier feels his dad is distant. He is right; the father is distracted by his grief and worries. At the Palisades Gardens, "X" and his friends practice synchronized skating routines, but then the rink closes: "There goes our summer." Not quite. On the North Side there's the Sweetwater rink, an establishment so grand that special effects are used to create its facade. Sweetwater is ruled by a showboat dancer named Sweetness (Wesley Jonathan), who has a court of three male backup skaters and three sexy girls who hold his cape and his hat and look at him yearningly.

X is reluctant to go to Sweetwater until he sees Sweetness in action and his competitive spirit is aroused. He and his buddies decide to enter the big $500 skate-off at the end of the summer. Joining them as a mascot is the new girl next door, Tori (Jurnee Smollett), who has braces on her teeth that the boys kid her about—but then the screenplay by Norman Vance Jr. is filled with sharp-edged dialogue in which ritualistic insults are exchanged in language that is colorful precisely because it is not made out of tired vulgarities. Tori's mom, Vivian (Kellita Smith), also lives next door, which eventually becomes of interest to Curtis.

At the rink, X and his friends encounter Naomi (Meagan Good), whom Xavier once almost dated, apparently, before he dropped out because of the loss of his mother and of his self-confidence. She's gotten a lot prettier in the year since he saw her, but she's still nice— too nice to be impressed by Sweetness, for example. It is astonishing Naomi and Tori do not become rivals; instead, Tori encourages X to ask Naomi out, because she thinks they'd be good together. A move like that away from the predictable story line allows all sorts of truth into a situation that would otherwise be on autopilot.

There are two climaxes in the movie: the skate-off, and the inevitable moment of truth between Xavier and his dad. Both are handled well: the skate-off like a reprise of *Saturday Night Fever*, the father-son conversation filled with earnest sentiment. McBride and Bow Wow, who between them have specialized in comedies and music videos, find serious emotion well within their reach. In the skate-off, Sweetness and his gang are so talented that it's unlikely Bow Wow's crowd would be in contention, but there you go.

Roll Bounce is not a great film, but it does a good job of doing exactly what it intends: showing a summer in the lives of ordinary teenagers and their parents, and remembering the roller disco craze that preceded hip-hop. It's based on fact. Chicago black kids in the 1970s really did move between a neighborhood rink and a ritzier North Side rink, and it was kind of a territorial thing. The movie gets something else right (and wrong). Xavier has a paper route, which is right, but he throws the wrong paper.

Rory O'Shea Was Here ★ ★ ★
R, 104 m., 2005

James McAvoy (Rory O'Shea), Steven Robertson (Michael Connolly), Romola Garai (Siobhan), Gerard McSorley (Fergus Connolly), Tom Hickey (Con O'Shea), Brenda Fricker (Eileen). Directed by Damien O'Donnell and produced by James Flynn and Juanita Wilson. Screenplay by Jeffrey Caine.

Don't you want to get drunk, get arrested, get laid?
—Rory to Michael

When Rory O'Shea arrives at the Carrigmore Home for the Disabled, Michael Connolly's life is on hold. Michael's cerebral palsy makes his speech difficult to decipher, except by Rory, who understands every word. Rory himself is exuberantly verbal, but muscular dystrophy has left him with control over two fingers of one hand, and that's it.

Are you still even reading this review? "Marketing challenges don't come much tougher," says *Variety*, the showbiz bible. So I should shift gears and say that *Rory O'Shea Was Here* is funny and moving, and more entertaining than some of the movies you are

considering—more than *Son of the Mask* or *Constantine*, that's for sure.

In fact, trying to keep you from tuning out because of the subject matter, I've just gone back and added the quote at the top of this review. That's said by Rory to Michael in his attempt to blast him out of his silent corner at the care home, and get him out in the world—where, Rory is convinced, they both belong.

Rory wears his hair in a weird arrangement of spikes. I didn't notice his shoes, but they were probably Doc Martens. Yes, muscular dystrophy has thrown him a curve, but he's still at the plate and swinging. In no time at all he has Michael following him into a pub, where he tries to pick up girls and at one point seems prepared to start a fight, which with anybody else would be a bad sign but for Rory may actually represent growth.

Rory wants to get out of the institutional world and into independent living. A well-meaning board of supervisors doesn't think he's ready for that yet, not with his disabilities combined with his recklessness. Michael is perfectly prepared to spend forever in the home, until Rory blasts him loose and uses him as his ticket to freedom. He convinces Michael to apply for independent living, and after Michael's application is approved by the board, Rory adds sweetly that of course Michael will need an interpreter.

They'll also need a care giver, and they interview the usual assortment of hopeless cases. There should be a *Little Glossary* entry about the obligatory scene where a job interview or an audition inevitably involves several weirdly unacceptable candidates, before the perfect choice steps forth.

In this case, they meet Siobhan (Romola Garai) in a supermarket, and convince her that life with them will have to be more exciting than stacking toilet tissues. It is more or less inevitable that they'll both get a crush on Siobhan, made more poignant because Rory will have to interpret whatever Michael wants to say to her. How this works out is not predictable, and is the occasion for some of the film's best written and acted scenes.

James McAvoy plays Rory as a would-be Dublin punk turned into the R. P. McMurphy of the care home. It's a performance combining joy and determination as if they feed off each other. Steven Robertson has more limited opportunities with his character, but let it be said that by the end of the film we can sort of understand what Michael is saying, and we always know what he means. Sometimes, on the other hand, amusingly, a word or two of Rory's Dublin accent slips past undetected.

Both actors are able-bodied in real life. I could not watch the movie without being powerfully reminded of an Australian film that never got theatrical distribution in the United States, Rolf de Heer's *Dance Me to My Song*. It was the first film in my first Overlooked Film Festival, and on stage we greeted Heather Rose, who, like Rory, could control only a finger or two. Yet she wrote the film and starred in it, as a woman with two goals in life, which Rory would have approved of: (1) get revenge on the minder who is mistreating her and stealing from her, and (2) meet a bloke and get laid. Heather Rose was a great and funny woman, who died last year. After the Q&A session, she typed out on her voice synthesizer, in the true Aussie spirit, "Now let's all go out and get pissed."

You can rent *Dance Me to My Song,* and you may want to, after seeing *Rory O'Shea Was Here.* There has been much talk involving the messages about disability sent by two major recent movies. Here is a movie that sends the message that if you want to be a punk and you're in a wheelchair, you can be a punk in a wheelchair. If you're in a chair and want to play rugby, you can, as a documentary named *Murderball* makes perfectly clear. Some are more disabled than others; Rory will not be able to play wheelchair rugby, but he'd make a hell of a coach.

Rumor Has It ★ ★ ★
PG-13, 96 m., 2005

Jennifer Aniston (Sarah Huttinger), Kevin Costner (Beau Burroughs), Shirley MacLaine (Katharine Richelieu), Mark Ruffalo (Jeff Daly), Mena Suvari (Annie Huttinger), Richard Jenkins (Earl Huttinger). Directed by Rob Reiner and produced by Ben Cosgrove and Paul Weinstein. Screenplay by Ted Griffin.

Now here is a curious thing. When I see Jennifer Aniston playing any halfway ordinary character, I have the same reaction: Hey, a friend of mine has somehow gotten into the same movie with all of those stars. I've never actually met Aniston, although once at Sundance I saw paparazzi fight to photograph her with Brad Pitt, in response to a tragic shortage of pictures showing them together. Most of these photos later appeared on the covers of gossip mags with the couple torn in two by a jagged line and Angelina Jolie leering over the bar code, but none of that has anything to do with how I feel when I see Aniston in a movie. It's the damnedest thing. I don't ever want to meet her because then I might lose her as a friend.

In *Rumor Has It,* she plays a character named Sarah Huttinger, who unless she is vigilant may become the *third* woman in her family to sleep with Benjamin Braddock—you remember, the Dustin Hoffman character in *The Graduate.* This, of course, is all based on rumor. In Pasadena, the movie explains, everyone knew the real Charlie Webb, who wrote the novel *The Graduate,* and rumor has it that he based his book on real people who really lived in Pasadena. There really was a bride who ran away with this guy three days before her wedding, and the guy had earlier slept with her mother, who was the original Mrs. Robinson, and so on.

Now another generation has passed. Sarah's mother was the original Elaine Robinson, and a guy named Beau Burroughs (Kevin Costner) was the original Benjamin Braddock, and the original Mrs. Robinson was, therefore, of course, Sarah's grandmother. Can you believe Shirley MacLaine as the original Mrs. Robinson? I can, with no trouble at all.

I could also have believed Anne Bancroft. Sigh. The movie was directed by Rob Reiner, a friend of Anne Bancroft and Mel Brooks since he was a child, and at first I wondered if perhaps the role was intended for her before she become ill. But no: In the film's logic, the characters have *seen* the 1967 movie with Bancroft and Hoffman, and discuss it. It wouldn't make sense for the "real" Mrs. Robinson to be played by the same actress who played the fictional character.

The plot, written by Ted Griffin, sounds like a gimmick. That's because it is a gimmick. But it's a good gimmick. And *Rumor Has It* works for good reasons, including sound construction and the presence of Costner, who is posted sturdily at the balance point between Mrs. Robinson and her granddaughter. We can see him with either one. In fact, at times we seem about to.

As the film opens, Sarah (Aniston) is engaged to marry Jeff (Mark Ruffalo), but they are keeping their engagement a secret until after the wedding of Sarah's sister Annie (Mena Suvari). In "reality," we learn, the original Elaine dumped Benjamin, came back to Pasadena, married Earl (Richard Jenkins), had Sarah and Annie, and then died, which is a neat touch because it sidesteps the Idiot Plot (if their mom is dead, she can't tell them what really happened).

Jeff hears the rumors in Pasadena, does the math, and suggests to Sarah that it's possible she was conceived during the three days her mother ran away with Beau. Obsessed with learning the truth, she tracks down Beau, who is a San Francisco dot-com millionaire, and finds herself attracted to him as a possible dad—and more than a dad, if you see what I mean. Beau is a very attractive guy, but if he's her real father, then that would mean, like, yeechh! Try it out loud.

It's for the movie to reveal who does (or doesn't) do what, and with which, and to whom. I will observe that Costner has quietly been reminding us in recent roles (Open Range, The Upside of Anger) that when he doesn't play characters who stride astraddle the apocalypse, he is a natural actor with enormous appeal. Ruffalo has a good line in heartfelt sincerity, Richard Jenkins can turn on a dime as good pop/bad pop, and MacLaine plays Mrs. Robinson by just acting naturally.

This is not a great movie, but it's very watchable and has some good laughs. The casting of Aniston is crucial because she's the heroine of this story, and the way it's put together there's danger of her becoming the shuttlecock. Aniston has the presence to pull it off. She has to maybe scuttle her sister's wedding and her own, maybe abandon the guy who loves her, maybe break her official father's heart, maybe (yeechh!) sleep with her (maybe) real dad, yet always retain our sympathy. Well of course she does. She's one of my closest friends.

Running Scared ★ ★ ★
R, 122 m., 2006

Paul Walker (Joey Gazelle), Cameron Bright (Oleg Yugorsky), Vera Farmiga (Teresa Gazelle), Chazz Palminteri (Detective Rydell), Johnny Messner (Tommy "Tombs" Perello), Michael Cudlitz (Sal "Gummy Bear" Franzone), Alex Neuberger (Nicky Gazelle), Ivana Milicevic (Mila Yugorsky), Karel Roden (Anzor Yugorsky), Idalis DeLeon (Divina). Directed by Wayne Kramer and produced by Sammy Lee, Michael A. Pierce, and Brett Ratner. Screenplay by Kramer.

Speaking of movies that go over the top, Running Scared goes so far over the top it circumnavigates the top and doubles back on itself; it's the Möbius strip of over-the-topness. I am in awe. It throws in everything but the kitchen sink. Then it throws in the kitchen sink, too, and the combo washer-dryer in the laundry room, while the hero and his wife are having sex on top of it.

I never tire of quoting the French director Truffaut, who said that he was interested only in movies that were about the agony of making cinema or the ecstasy of making cinema. Running Scared eliminates the middle man. It's not even about making cinema. It's just about the agony and the ecstasy.

The movie stars Paul Walker. You won't catch him acting in Running Scared. The movie never slows down enough. He simply behaves, at an alarming velocity. After an opening flash-forward that features a car crash, the movie flashes back to a drug deal that goes bad. All the crooked cops and drug dealers in the room are killed, except for Joey Gazelle (Walker) and a guy who tells him to take all of the guns and lose them. Actually, maybe some other guys survived, too. This is the kind of movie where the next scene starts before the body count.

Gazelle hides the guns in his basement. His son Nicky (Alex Neuberger) is best friends with Oleg (Cameron Bright), the Russian kid who lives next door. Oleg's father, Anzor (Karel Roden), grew up in Russia watching John Wayne's The Cowboys over and over again, maybe a thousand times. But Anzor had only a ten-minute version of the film. So profoundly did it affect him that he had an image of the Duke tattooed on his back. When he came to America and saw the whole movie, he found out Wayne gets shot. This was so traumatic that he turned bitter, beat his wife, and terrorized his son, who steals a gun from the Gazelles' basement and shoots his father, wounding him right about where the sheriff's badge would be.

This is very bad because that is the same gun that killed a cop in the shootout. So Joey Gazelle has to race all over town trying to find the gun and collect the slugs that came out of it (this process involves both impersonating a doctor and chewing gum, although not at the same time). Meanwhile, Oleg runs away, so Joey and Nicky have to find him to get the gun back.

You understand I am giving only the bare bones of the plot. I barely have time to explain why Oleg, who has asthma, is befriended by a hooker (Idalis DeLeon) who gets him a fresh inhaler at gunpoint. And how Oleg is kidnapped by perverts who are so evil they have a body bag in their closet, and how Nicky's mother, Teresa (Vera Farmiga), comes to the rescue, extremely decisively.

Meanwhile, Joey is attacked with an acetylene torch by a mechanic who mistakenly sets himself on fire; Joey delays extinguishing him while screaming, "Where is my gun?" Oh, and there's the scene in the hockey rink where a crime boss has his hockey stars slam pucks at the hero's teeth. Just in case that scene might somehow lack interest, it is shot in black light, so everything glows like a purple necktie at a stag party. Yes, there is extreme material here. The opening sex scene is startling in its exploration of the Midlands. It is certainly a big surprise how the John Wayne tattoo gets shot. The perverts are so creepy they belong in a Satanic sitcom. All of this is done using strong characterizations, crisp action, and clear dialogue; this isn't one of those berserk action movies that look like the script was thrown into a fan and the shreds were filmed at random.

Wayne Kramer, the filmmaker, writes and directs with heedless bliss. He's best known for *The Cooler* (2003), that splendid Las Vegas movie about how a casino hired William H. Macy to stand next to lucky gamblers so their luck would turn bad. Kramer is such an overachiever that he actually succeeded in getting

The Cooler an NC-17 rating for a sex scene starring, yes, William H. Macy. Some would say it starred Maria Bello, but that would be missing the point. The scene had to be trimmed for an R rating, leading to a bitter complaint from the fifty-two-year-old Macy: "I have been working out for thirty years, staying in shape in the dream that someday I would get to play a sex scene. Finally I get one, and they cut it." The Macy specialty they cut out of *The Cooler* ends up in this movie on top of the washerdryer, in a thrilling combination of sex and the spin cycle.

One of the pleasures of the movie is how supporting characters are given big scenes all for themselves. John Noble has a Tarantinian soliloquy on his childhood obsession with the Duke. Vera Farmiga decisively escapes the cliché of the Thriller Hero's Wife, becomes the Hero's Thrilling Wife, and makes the neatest kills of the movie. Cameron Bright, who played the child containing the reincarnated husband of Nicole Kidman in *Birth*, seems to be a child containing the reincarnated Philip Seymour Hoffman in this one. Chazz Palminteri is such an evil cop that the planes of his face seem to have shifted into a sinister new configuration; I saw him in January at Sundance, where he was pleasant and smiling, and here he looks like a Batman villain who tried to shave with Roto-Rooter.

If you stand way back from *Running Scared*, the plot has certain flaws. For example, close attention to the ending will reveal that Joey Gazelle spent the whole movie risking his life and the lives of his son, his wife, and the neighbor kid in a desperate quest for a gun that *he didn't really need to find*. Don't be depressed if you miss this detail; Joey Gazelle misses it, too. Doesn't matter. The gun is only the MacGuffin. If you don't know what a MacGuffin is, the good news is, you don't need to know.

RV ★ ★
PG, 98 m., 2006

Robin Williams (Bob Munro), Cheryl Hines (Jamie Munro), Jeff Daniels (Travis Gornicke), Kristen Chenoweth (Mary Jo Gornicke), Joanna "JoJo" Levesque (Cassie Munro), Josh Hutcherson (Carl Munro), Hunter

Parrish (Earl Gornicke), Chloe Sonnenfeld (Moon Gornicke), Will Arnett (Todd Mallory). Directed by Barry Sonnenfeld and produced by Bobby Cohen, Lucy Fisher, and Douglas Wick. Screenplay by Geoff Rodkey.

The problem with traveling in a recreational vehicle, Jamie Munro tells her husband, is that you have to spend the night in an RV park with other RV people. "Remember," she tells him, "we're not friendly." The members of the Munro family are not even very friendly with one another. As Bob Munro tells his wife, "We watch TV in four separate rooms and IM each other when it's time to eat dinner." Yet here they are in a gigantic rented RV, traveling cross-country to Colorado and calling it a vacation.

It's almost a genre, the cross-country family vacation movie. In fact, it is a genre. Yellowstone is almost always involved, or at least mentioned. There is trouble with unfriendly animals, reckless driving, and sewage disposal. The genre usually stars Chevy Chase, but this time it's Robin Williams as Pop Munro, Cheryl Hines as his wife, and Joanna "JoJo" Levesque and Josh Hutcherson as their kids, Cassie and Carl. The boy is young enough to still be nice, but Cassie has arrived at that age when parents were put on this earth merely as an inconvenience for her.

Bob had originally thought to take the family to Hawaii, but then his obnoxious boss, Todd (Will Arnett), ordered him to make a presentation in Boulder, Colorado. Afraid to confess the business purpose of his trip, Bob simply rents the giant RV and announces that they'll go camping instead. "But we aren't a camping family," Jamie says. That becomes clear the moment Bob has to perform that least pleasant of RV tasks, emptying the sewage. In real life, this job can theoretically be performed with a minimum of difficulty, but in the movies it always results in the hero being covered by a disgusting substance that oddly never seems to involve toilet paper.

On their first night away, the Munros meet the friendly Gornicke family—Travis and Mary Jo (Jeff Daniels and Kristen Chenoweth) and their kids, Earl, Moon, and Billy (Hunter Par-

rish, Chloe Sonnenfeld, and Alex Ferris). The Gornickes are mighty friendly. They do country songs as a family. She sells franchise goods from the mobile home. They are masters of sewage, RV lore, route directions, and poking their noses into the business of the Munros, who, as we recall, are not friendly people.

The movie settles down into a rhythm of the road, with the Munros getting into trouble and the Gornickes getting them out of it. There are troublesome raccoons, that emergency brake that doesn't work, and a scene high up on Diablo Pass where Bob gets the RV balanced on a peak and tries to rock it back and forth to get it down onto the road; I was reminded of the tilting cabin in Chaplin's *The Gold Rush*, as I imagine the filmmakers were, too.

All of this is pleasant enough, after a fashion, but it never reaches critical mass. There is nothing I much disliked, but little to really recommend. At least the movie was not nonstop slapstick, and there were a few moments of relative gravity, in which Williams demonstrated once again that he's more effective on the screen when he's serious than when he's trying to be funny.

What else did I like? The good feeling within the Gornicke family. The reptilian loathsomeness of Bob's boss, Todd. Some of the negotiations involving the merger of Bob's giant corporation with a sweet little Boulder beverage company run by the Ben & Jerry of the Rockies. What I didn't much enjoy were extended sequences in which Bob had to run, drive, or pedal desperately. They were intended as comedy but amounted only to behavior.

Now I am going to tell you a strange thing. At one point in the movie, an older man appears on the screen and serves them plates of food. They don't want meat. "It's okay," he says, "it's not meat. It's just organs." The strange thing is: We have never seen this man before, and we never see him again, and no one on screen seems to notice him. Who is he? If there is one thing you should know before driving cross-country in an RV, it is: Never eat organ meats supplied by a man you have never seen before, just because he happens to turn up with a lot of organs.

S

The Saddest Music in the World
★ ★ ★ ½
NO MPAA RATING, 99 m., 2004

Mark McKinney (Chester Kent), Isabella Rossellini (Lady Port-Huntly), Maria de Medeiros (Narcissa), David Fox (Fyodor), Ross McMillan (Roderick/Gavrillo). Directed by Guy Maddin and produced by Niv Fichman, Daniel Iron, and Jody Shapiro. Screenplay by Maddin and George Toles, based on an original screenplay by Kazuo Ishiguro.

So many movies travel the same weary roads. So few imagine entirely original worlds. Guy Maddin's *The Saddest Music in the World* exists in a time and place we have never seen before, although it claims to be set in Winnipeg in 1933. The city, we learn, has been chosen by the *London Times*, for the fourth year in a row, as "the world capital of sorrow." Here Lady Port-Huntly (Isabella Rossellini) has summoned entries for a contest which will award $25,000 "in depression-era dollars" to the performer of the saddest music.

This plot suggests, no doubt, some kind of camp musical, a sub–Monty Python comedy. What Maddin makes of it is a comedy, yes, but also an eerie fantasy that suggests a silent film like *Metropolis* crossed with a musical starring Nelson Eddy and Jeannette McDonald, and then left to marinate for long forgotten years in an enchanted vault. The Canadian filmmaker has devised a style that evokes old films from an alternate time line; *The Saddest Music* is not silent and not entirely in black and white, but it looks like a long-lost classic from decades ago, grainy and sometimes faded; he shoots on 8mm film and video, and blows it up to look like a memory from cinema's distant past.

The effect is strange and delightful; somehow the style lends quasi-credibility to a story that is entirely preposterous. Because we have to focus a little more intently, we're drawn into the film, surrounded by it. There is the sensation of a new world being created around us. The screenplay is by the novelist Kazuo Ishiguro, who wrote the very different *Remains of the Day*. Here he creates, for Maddin's visual style, a fable that's *Canadian Idol* crossed with troubled dreams.

Lady Port-Huntly owns a brewery, and hopes the contest will promote sales of her beer. Played by Rossellini in a blond wig that seems borrowed from a Viennese fairy tale, she is a woman who has lost her legs and propels herself on a little wheeled cart until being supplied with fine new glass legs, filled with her own beer.

To her contest come competitors like the American Chester Kent (Mark McKinney of *The Kids in the Hall*), looking uncannily like a snake-oil salesman, and his lover, Narcissa (Maria de Medeiros), who consults fortune-tellers on the advice of a telepathic tapeworm in her bowels. If you remember de Medeiros and her lovable little accent from *Pulp Fiction* (she was the lover of Bruce Willis's boxer), you will be able to imagine how enchantingly she sings "The Song Is You."

Kent's brother Roderick (Ross McMillan) is the contestant from Serbia. Their father, Fyodor (David Fox), enters for Canada, singing the dirge "Red Maple Leaves." One night while drunk, he caused a car crash and attempted to save his lover by amputating her crushed leg—but, alas, cut off the wrong leg, and is finally seen surrounded by legs. And that lover, dear reader, was Lady Port-Huntly.

Competitors are matched off two by two. "Red Maple Leaves" goes up against a pygmy funeral dirge. Bagpipers from Scotland compete, as does a hockey team that tries to lift the gloom by singing "I Hear Music." The winner of each round gets to slide down a chute into a vat filled with beer. As Lady Port-Huntly chooses the winners, an unruly audience cheers. Suspense is heightened with the arrival of a cellist whose identity is concealed by a long black veil.

You have never seen a film like this before, unless you have seen other films by Guy Maddin, such as *Dracula: Pages from a Virgin's Diary* (2002), or *Archangel* (1990). Although his *Tales from the Gimli Hospital* was made in 1988, his films lived on the fringes, and I first became aware of him only in 2000, when he was one of the filmmakers commissioned to make a short for the Toronto Film Festival. His *The Heart of the World*, now available on DVD with *Archangel* and *Twilight of the Ice Nymphs* (1997), was a triumph, selected by some critics as the best film in the festival. It, too, seemed to be preserved from some alternate universe of old films.

The more films you have seen, the more you may love *The Saddest Music in the World*. It plays like satirical nostalgia for a past that never existed. The actors bring that kind of earnestness to it that seems peculiar to supercharged melodrama. You can never catch them grinning, although great is the joy of Lady Port-Huntly when she poses with her sexy new beer-filled glass legs. Nor can you catch Maddin condescending to his characters; he takes them as seriously as he possibly can, considering that they occupy a mad, strange, gloomy, absurd comedy. To see this film, to enter the world of Guy Maddin, is to understand how a film can be created entirely by its style, and how its style can create a world that never existed before, and lure us, at first bemused and then astonished, into it.

Sahara ★ ★ ★
PG-13, 127 m., 2005

Matthew McConaughey (Dirk Pitt), Steve Zahn (Al Giordino), Penelope Cruz (Eva Rojas), Lambert Wilson (Massarde), Glynn Turman (Dr. Hopper), Delroy Lindo (Carl), William H. Macy (Admiral Sandecker), Rainn Wilson (Rudi), Lennie James (General Kazim). Directed by Breck Eisner and produced by Stephanie Austin, Howard Baldwin, Karen Elise Baldwin, and Mace Neufeld. Screenplay by Thomas Dean Donnelly, Joshua Oppenheimer, John C. Richards, and James V. Hart, based on the novel by Clive Cussler.

Clive Cussler, who wrote the novel that inspired *Sahara*, is said to have rejected untold drafts of the screenplay, and sued Paramount over this one. One wonders not so much what Cussler would have left out as what else could have gone in. *Sahara* obviously contains everything that could possibly be included in such a screenplay, and more. It's like a fire sale at the action movie discount outlet.

Do not assume I mean to be negative. I treasure the movie's preposterous plot. It's so completely over the top, it can see reality only in its rearview mirror. What can you say about a

movie based on the premise that a Confederate ironclad ship from the Civil War is buried beneath the sands of the Sahara, having ventured there 150 years ago when the region was, obviously, damper than it is now?

Matthew McConaughey plays Dirk Pitt, the movie's hero, who is searching for the legendary ship. Dirk Pitt. Dirk Pitt. Or Pitt, Dirk. Makes Brad Pitt sound like William Pitt. Dirk has a thing about long-lost ships; readers may recall that he was also the hero of *Raise the Titanic* (1980), a movie so expensive that its producer, Lord Lew Grade, observed, "It would have been cheaper to lower the ocean."

Dirk has a sidekick named Al Giordino, played by Steve Zahn in the time-honored Movie Sidekick mode. Was it Walter Huston who explained that movie heroes need sidekicks "because somebody has to do the dance." You know, the dance where the sidekick throws his hat down on the ground and stomps on it in joy or anger? You can't have your hero losing his cool like that.

The two men arrive in Africa to find that a dangerous plague is spreading. The plague is being battled by the beautiful Eva Rojas (Penelope Cruz), and it turns out that Dirk and Eva share mutual interests, since if the plague spreads down rivers and "interacts with salt water," there is a danger that "all ocean life will be destroyed." Actually, I am not sure why that is only a mutual interest; it's more of a universal interest, you would think, although General Kazim (Lennie James), the African dictator, and an evil French zillionaire (Lambert Wilson) don't seem much disturbed. That's because they're getting rich in a way I will not reveal, although there is something grimly amusing about converting pollutants into other pollutants.

The movie, directed by Breck Eisner, son of Michael, is essentially a laundry line for absurd but entertaining action sequences. Dirk, Eva, and Al have an amazing series of close calls in the desert, while Admiral Sandecker (ret.) (William H. Macy) keeps in touch with them by radio and remains steadfast in his course, whatever it is. There are chases involving planes, trains, automobiles, helicopters, dune buggies, wind-propelled airplane carcasses, and camels. The heroes somewhat improbably conceal themselves inside a tank car on a train going toward a secret desert plant (improbably, since the car going in that direction should have been full), and then find themselves one of those James Bondian vantage points inside the plant, from where they can observe uniformed clones carrying out obscure tasks.

There is a race against time before everything explodes, of course, and some bizarre science involving directing the sun's rays, and then what do you suppose turns up? If you slapped yourself up alongside the head and shouted out, "The long-lost Civil War ironclad?" you could not be more correct. Gee, I wonder if its cannons will still fire after this length of time?

I enjoyed this movie on its own dumb level, which must mean (I am forced to conclude) in my own dumb way. I perceive that I have supplied mostly a description of what happens in the film, filtered through my own skewed amusement. Does that make this a real review?

Funny you should ask. As it happens, I happened to be glancing at Gore Vidal's article about the critic Edmund Wilson in a 1993 issue of the *New York Review of Books*. There Vidal writes: "Great critics do not explicate a text; they describe it and then report on what they have described, if the description itself is not the criticism." In this case, I think the description itself is the criticism. Yes, I'm almost sure of it.

Saints and Soldiers ★ ★ ★
PG-13, 90 m., 2004

Corbin Allred (Nathan "Deacon" Greer), Lawrence Bagby (Shirl Kendrick), Kirby Heyborne (Oberon Winley), Peter Asle Holden (Gordon Gunderson), Alexander Niver (Steven Gould), Lincoln Hoppe (Heinrich), Ruby Chase O'Neil (Sophie), Melinda Renee (Catherine), Ethan Vincent (Rudy). Directed by Ryan Little and produced by Adam Abel and Little. Screenplay by Geoffrey Panos and Matt Whitaker.

Just as it stands, *Saints and Soldiers* could have been made in 1948. That is not a bad thing. It has the strengths and the clean lines of a traditional war movie, without high-tech special effects to pump up the noise level. I saw it when the new restoration of Sam Fuller's *The Big Red One* (1980), made by a director who was an infantryman throughout World War II, and was struck by how the two films had similar tone: The No.

1 job of a foot soldier is to keep from getting killed. Doing his duty is a close second.

The film is inspired by actual events. We're told of a massacre of American soldiers at Malmedy, in Belgium, six months after the Normandy invasion; Nazis opened fire on U.S. prisoners and most were killed, but four were able to lose themselves in the surrounding forest. The movie is about their attempt to walk back to the American lines through snow and bitter cold; along the way, they're joined by a British paratrooper who has intelligence about a major Nazi offensive, and they decide they have to get that to the Allies in time to do some good.

These five soldiers are ordinary people; well, the Americans are, although the Brit seems odd to them, and they don't always appreciate his sense of humor. They are tired and hungry all the time, and guard cigarettes like a precious hoard. Unlike the characters in modern war movies, they don't use four-letter words, and we don't miss them. I don't know if that's accurate or not. Certainly in the 1940s that language was much rarer that it is now, but Norman Mailer uses the f-word all through *The Naked and the Dead*, spelling it "fugg" to get it past the censors.

The movie's hero is quiet and troubled rather than gung-ho. That would be Corporal Nathan Greer (Corbin Allred), nicknamed "Deacon" because he treasures his Bible and was once a missionary in Berlin. That's where he learned the German that saves them. We assume he's a Mormon, but aren't actually told so. His little group is led by Sergeant Gordon Gunderson (Peter Holden), who shields him from criticism after he freezes at a crucial moment; he's the best sharpshooter in the group, but can he actually kill someone? Steven Gould (Alexander Niver), the medic, is the obligatory soldier from Brooklyn who is required in all World War II movies, and Shirl Kendrick (Lawrence Bagby) is the equally obligatory farm boy from the South. The British pilot, Oberon Winley (Kirby Heyborne), may have seen one David Niven movie too many.

The story follows them as they trek through the forest and try to stay alive. There are some close calls as German troops comb the area, but also a friendly Belgian housewife (who will remind film lovers of the farm wife in *Grand Illusion*), and maybe a little too coincidentally, a German soldier who was friendly with Deacon during his missionary days in Berlin.

The director, Ryan Little, used the mountains of Utah for Belgium, and a firm hand to insist on character and story in a movie that doesn't have a lot of money for extras and effects; many of the Germans are played by military hobbyists who stage battle reenactments, and they also lent Little some of their equipment. *Saints and Soldiers* isn't a great film, but what it does, it does well.

Saraband ★ ★ ★ ★
R, 107 m., 2005

Liv Ullmann (Marianne), Erland Josephson (Johan), Borje Ahlstedt (Henrik), Julia Dufvenius (Karin), Gunnel Fred (Martha). Directed by Ingmar Bergman and produced by Pia Ehrnvall. Screenplay by Bergman.

Ingmar Bergman is balancing his accounts and closing out his books. The great director is eighty-seven years old and announced in 1982 that *Fanny and Alexander* would be his last film. So it was, but he continued to work on the stage and for television, and then he wrote the screenplay for Liv Ullmann's film *Faithless* (2000). Now comes his absolutely last work, *Saraband*, powerfully, painfully honest.

Although you can see the film as it stands, it will have more resonance if you remember Bergman's *Scenes from a Marriage* (1973). That film starred Ullmann and Erland Josephson as Marianne and Johan, a couple married twenty years earlier and divorced ten years earlier, who meet again in the middle of the night in a cabin in the middle of the woods. Their marriage has failed, their relationship has faded, and yet on this night it is more real than anything else. I wrote in 1973: "They are in middle age now but in the night still fond and frightened lovers holding on for reassurance."

Now there is no more reassurance to be had. They must be in their eighties now; in real life, Josephson is eighty-two and Ullmann sixty-six. Because Bergman's films can be seen again and again, and because he believes the human face is the most important subject of the cinema, we are as familiar with these two faces as any we have ever seen. I saw Ullmann for the first time in Bergman's *Persona* (1966), which I reviewed seven months after I became a film critic. Now here she is again. When I interviewed her about

Faithless at Cannes five years ago, I noted to myself that she had not, like so many actresses, had plastic surgery. She wore her age as proof of having lived, as we all must. Now I see *Saraband* and the movie is possible because she did not allow a surgeon to give her a face yearning for its younger form.

As the film opens, she is looking through some old photographs. Marianne and Johan had two daughters together, who are now middle-aged. She never sees them; one lives in Australia, and the other has gone mad. She tells us she has not seen Johan for all of those years but now thinks she will go to visit him. We follow her and find that Johan is now living in misery left over from an earlier marriage. He is rich, lives in the country, owns a nearby cottage that is occupied by his sixty-one-year-old son, Henrik (Borje Ahlstedt), and Henrik's nineteen-year-old daughter, Karin (Julia Dufvenius). Anna—Henrik's wife, Karin's mother—has been dead for two years. She is missed because she was needed, as cartilage if nothing else, to keep her husband and daughter from wearing each other down.

They are not Marianne's problem. But she visits them and witnesses appalling unhappiness. Johan is scornful of his son, who has value in his eyes only as the parent of Karin. Henrik is bitter that his father has money but doles it out reluctantly, to keep his son in constant need and supplication. Karin, who plays the cello, feels trapped because she wants to develop her career in the city and her father possessively hangs onto her (they sleep, Marianne discovers, in the same bed).

The movie is not about the resolution of this plot. It is about the way people persist in creating misery by placing the demands of their egos above the need for happiness—their own happiness and that of those around them. In some sense, Johan and Henrik live in these adjacent houses, in the middle of nowhere, simply so that they can hate each other. If they parted, each would lose a reason for living. Karin is the victim of their pathology.

Oh, but Bergman is sad, as he lives decade after decade on his island of Faro and writes these stories and assembles his old crew, or their children and successors, to film them. His *Faithless* showed an old filmmaker (working in Bergman's office, living in Bergman's house on Bergman's island). He hires an actress to help him think through a story he wants to write.

The actress, who is imaginary, is in fact playing a woman he once loved; their love caused pain to her husband, her child, and even to the director. Now in his old age he is working through it, perhaps trying to make amends. We know from Bergman's autobiography that the story is loosely based on fact. We know, too, that Ullmann, who is directing it, was also Bergman's lover and had his daughter.

If *Faithless* was an attempt to face personal guilt, *Saraband* is a meditation on the pathology of selfish relationships. It is filled with failed parents: All three adults lack love in their bonds with their children. It is filled with unsettled scores: Now that Henrik is sixty-one, what does it matter that he has never become as successful as his father? The game is over. It is time to enjoy the success of his daughter—a success he will not permit because he fears losing her. When Marianne, a witness to this triangle of resentment, returns to her own life, she returns to even less—to nothing, to photographs.

The overwhelming fact about this movie is its awareness of time. Thirty-two years have passed since *Scenes from a Marriage*. The years have passed for Bergman, for Ullmann, for Josephson, and for us. Whatever else he is telling us in *Saraband*, Bergman is telling us that life will end on the terms by which we have lived it. If we are bitter now, we will not be victorious later; we will still be bitter. Here is a movie about people who have lived so long, hell has not been able to wait for them.

Sarah Silverman: Jesus Is Magic ★ ½
NO MPAA RATING, 70 m., 2005

Sarah Silverman (Herself), La'vin Kiyano (Tough Guy), Laura Silverman (Herself), Bob Odenkirk (Himself), Brian Posehn (Himself), Brody Stevens (Agent). Directed by Liam Lynch and produced by Heidi Herzon, Randy Sosin, and Mark Williams. Screenplay by Sarah Silverman.

Sarah Silverman: Jesus is Magic is a movie that filled me with an urgent desire to see Sarah Silverman in a different movie. I liked everything about it except the writing, the direction, the editing, and the lack of a parent or adult guardian. There should have been somebody to stand up sadly after the first screening and say: "Sarah, honey, this isn't the movie you want

people to see. Your material needs a lot of work; the musical scenes are deadly, except for the first one. And it looks like it was edited by someone fooling around with iMovie on a borrowed Macintosh."

Apparently the only person capable of telling Sarah Silverman such things is Sarah Silverman, and she obviously did not. Maybe the scene of her kissing herself in the mirror provides a clue. The result is a film that is going to make it hard to get people to come to the second Sarah Silverman film. Too bad, because Silverman is smart and funny, and she blindsides you with unexpected U-turns. She could be the instrument for abrasive and transgressive humor that would slice through the comedy club crap. But here, she isn't.

You have seen her before. She started on *Saturday Night Live* and has been in fifteen movies and a lot of TV shows. She's tall, brunette, and good-looking, and she says shocking things with the precise enunciation and poise of a girl who was brought up knowing how to make a good impression. The disconnect between what she says and how she says it is part of the effect. If she were crass and vulgar, her material would be insupportable: If you're going to use cancer, AIDS, and 9/11 as punch lines, you'd better know how to get the permission of the audience. She does it by seeming to be too well-bred to realize what she's saying. She's always correcting herself. When she uses the word *retards* she immediately registers that it's non-PC and elaborates: "When I say 'retards,' I mean they can do anything."

So that's one of her lines. It would be a cheap shot for me to quote a dozen more and do her act here in the review. Better to stand back and see why she's funny but the movie doesn't work. The first problem is with timing. None of her riffs go on long enough to build. She gets a laugh, and then another one, maybe a third, and then she starts in a different direction. We want her to keep on, piling one offense on top of another. We want to see her on a roll.

That's in the concert documentary parts of the movie. She stands on a stage and does the material and there are cuts to the audience, but curiously not much of a connection; it doesn't seem to be *this* audience at *this* performance, but a generic audience. Then she cuts away from the doc stuff to little sketches. The first one, in which her sister (Laura Silverman) and her friend (Brian Posehn) brag about their recent accomplishments, is funny because she perfectly plays someone who has never accomplished anything and never will, and lies about it. Then we see her in a car, singing a song about getting a job and doing a show, and then she does a show. Fair enough.

But what's with the scene where she entertains the old folks at her grandma's rest home by singing a song telling them they will all die soon? She is rescued by the apparent oblivion of the old folks, who seem so disconnected she could be working in blue screen. Then there's the scene where she angrily shakes the corpse of her grandmother in its casket. Here is a bulletin from the real world: Something like that is not intrinsically funny. Yes, you can probably find a way to set it up and write it to make it funny, but to simply do it, just plain do it, is pathetic. The audience, which has been laughing, grows watchful and sad.

To discuss the film's editing rhythm is to suggest it has one. There are artless and abrupt cuts between different kinds of material. She's on the stage, and then she's at the nursing home. There is a way to make that transition, but it doesn't involve a cut that feels like she was interrupted in the middle of something. And the ending comes abruptly, without any kind of acceleration and triumph in the material. Her act feels cut off at the knees. The running time, seventy minutes including end credits, is interesting, since if you subtract the offstage scenes that means we see less of her than a live audience would.

Now if Silverman had been ungifted or her material had lacked all humor, I would maybe not have bothered with a review. Why kick a movie when it's down? But she has a real talent, and she is sometimes very funny in a way that is particularly her own. Now she needs to work with a writer (not to provide the material but to shape and pace it), and a director who can build a scene, and an editor who can get her out of it, and a producer who can provide wise counsel. On the basis of this movie, it will be her first exposure as a filmmaker to anyone like that.

Saved! ★ ★ ★ ½
PG-13, 92 m., 2004

Jena Malone (Mary), Mandy Moore (Hilary Faye), Macaulay Culkin (Roland), Patrick Fugit (Patrick), Martin Donovan (Pastor Skip), Mary-Louise Parker (Lillian), Eva Amurri (Cassandra), Chad Faust (Dean). Directed by Brian Dannelly and produced by Michael Stipe, Sandy Stern, Michael Ohoven, and William Vince. Screenplay by Dannelly and Michael Urban.

Saved! is a satire aimed at narrow-minded Christians, using as its weapon the values of a more tolerant brand of Christianity. It is also a high school comedy, starring names from the top shelf of teenage movie stars: Mandy Moore *(The Princess Diaries)*, Jena Malone *(Donnie Darko)*, Patrick Fugit *(Almost Famous)*, and Macaulay Culkin, who is twenty-three but looks younger than anyone else in the cast. That Hollywood would dare to make a comedy poking fun at the excesses of Jesus people is, I think, an encouraging sign; we have not been entirely intimidated by the religious right.

The film follows the traditional pattern of many other teenage comedies. There's a clique ruled by the snobbiest and most popular girl in school, and an opposition made up of outcasts, nonconformists, and rebels. We saw this formula in *Mean Girls*. What's different this time is that the teen queen, Hilary Faye, is the loudest Jesus praiser at American Eagle Christian High School, and is played by Mandy Moore, having a little fun with her own good-girl image.

Her opposition is a checklist of kids who do not meet with Hilary Faye's approval. That would include Dean (Chad Faust), who thinks he may be gay; Cassandra (Eva Amurri), the only Jew in school and an outspoken rebel, and Roland (Culkin), Hilary Faye's brother, who is in a wheelchair but rejects all forms of sympathy and horrifies his sister by becoming Cassandra's boyfriend. There's also Patrick (Fugit), member of a Christian skateboarding team and the son of Pastor Skip (Martin Donovan), the school's principal. Patrick is thoughtful and introspective, and isn't sure he agrees with his father's complacent morality.

The heroine is Mary (Jena Malone), whose mother, Lillian (Mary-Louise Parker), has recently been named the town's No. 1 Christian Interior Decorator. Mary's boyfriend is Dean (Chad Faust, an interesting name in this context). One day they're playing a game that involves shouting out secrets to each other while

599

underwater in the swimming pool, and Dean bubbles: "I think I'm gay!" Mary is shocked, bangs her head, thinks she sees Jesus (he's actually the pool maintenance guy), and realizes it is her mission to save Dean. That would involve having sex with him, she reasons, since only such a drastic act could bring him over to the hetero side. She believes that under the circumstances, Jesus will restore her virginity.

Jesus does not, alas, intervene, and Mary soon finds herself staring at the implacable blue line on her home pregnancy kit. Afraid to tell her mother, she visits Planned Parenthood, and is spotted by Cassandra and Roland.

> *Cassandra:* There's only one reason Christian girls come downtown to the Planned Parenthood!
> *Roland:* She's planting a pipe bomb?

You see what I mean. The first half of this movie is astonishing in the sharp-edged way it satirizes the knee-jerk values of Hilary Faye and her born-again friends. Another target is widower Pastor Skip, who is attracted to Mary's widowed mother, Lillian; she likes him, too, but they flirt in such a cautious way we wonder if they even realize what they're doing. A big complication: Skip is married, and his estranged wife is doing missionary work in Africa, making his feelings a torment.

At the time Mary sacrifices her virginity to conquer Dean's homosexuality, she's a member of Hilary Faye's singing trio, the Christian Jewels, and a high-ranking celebrity among the school's Jesus boosters. But the worldly Cassandra spots her pregnancy before anyone else does, and soon the unwed mother-to-be is hanging out with the gay, the Jew, and the kid in the wheelchair. They're like a hall of fame of outsiders.

Dean's sexuality is discovered by his parents, and he's shipped off to Mercy House, which specializes in drug detox and "degayification." Once again the screenplay, by director Brian Dannelly and Michael Urban, is pointed: "Mercy House doesn't really exist for the people that go there, but for the people who send them," says Patrick, who is having his own rebellion against Pastor Skip, and casts his lot with the rebels.

Now if the film were all pitched on this one note, it would be tiresome and unfair. But having surprised us with its outspoken first act, it gets religion of its own sort in the second and third acts, arguing not against fundamentalism but against intolerance; it argues that Jesus would have embraced the cast-outs and the misfits, and might have leaned toward situational ethics instead of rigid morality. Doesn't Mary, after all, think she's doing the right thing when she sleeps with Dean? (What Dean thinks remains an enigma.)

Saved! is an important film as well as an entertaining one. At a time when the FCC is enforcing a censorious morality on a nation where 8.5 million listeners a day are manifestly not offended by Howard Stern, here is a movie with a political message: Jesus counseled more acceptance and tolerance than some of his followers think. By the end of the movie, mainstream Christian values have not been overthrown, but demonstrated and embraced. Those who think Christianity is just a matter of enforcing their rule book have been, well, enlightened. And that all of this takes place in a sassy and smart teenage comedy is, well, a miracle. Oh, and *mirabile dictu,* some of the actors are allowed to have pimples.

Saving Shiloh ★ ★ ★ ½
PG, 90 m., 2006

Scott Wilson (Judd Travers), Jason Dolley (Marty Preston), Gerald McRaney (Ray Preston), Ann Dowd (Louise Preston), Kyle Chavarria (Dara Lynn Preston), Taylor Momsen (Samantha Wallace), Liberty Smith (Becky Preston). Directed by Sandy Tung and produced by Carl Borack and Dale Rosenbloom. Screenplay by Rosenbloom, based on the novel by Phyllis Reynolds Naylor.

Saving Shiloh is the third and final *Shiloh* film, and fully as worthy as the others. It's a family film that deals with real problems and teaches real values, and yet is exciting and entertaining. We come to really care about the young boy Marty, his family and friends, and the ominous presence of their neighbor Judd. Marty, now played by Jason Dolley, has grown up during the series and does some wise thinking in this film.

All three films are based on much-loved novels by Phyllis Reynolds Naylor, and the tension in all three centers on the neighbor, Judd (Scott

Wilson), who has a drinking problem, gets in fights, wrecks his car, and as before seems to have no occupation except for shooting squirrels in the trees around his cabin. Wilson plays the character full-bore, not as a villain in a family film, but as a complex and wounded person, earnestly trying to change.

Marty believes in him. His father, Ray (Gerald McRaney), has known Judd most of his life and disliked him until recently. His change of heart came in the first film, after Marty rescued the abused dog Shiloh from Judd, made him his own, and in the process broke into Judd's isolation for the first time. By this third film, Marty has won Judd's confidence to such a degree that the man shares a painful memory of his own father: "Sometimes he beat me when he was sad. Sometimes he beat me when he was happy. Sometimes he was just happy to beat me."

Judd becomes the suspect when a local man disappears after the two men get in a bar fight. Judd is suspected again in a series of thefts. Marty believes in him, and his dad backs him up: Judd is a troubled man, but not a thief and certainly not a killer. Local gossip is quick to blame Judd for everything that goes wrong, but Marty's teacher focuses on the principle that a man is innocent until proven guilty, and Marty puts that into practice. Judd still keeps his dogs chained, but Marty learns from the local vet that chained dogs are unhappy and mean and tells Judd he and his dad will help fence in his yard. In this and other ways, Marty stands true.

All of this may sound too much like an After School Special, so I should add that Marty, his best friend, Samantha (Taylor Momsen), and his sisters, Dara Lynn (Kyle Chavarria) and Becky (Liberty Smith), live ordinary kid lives, have ordinary kid days, fool around, and bring us lots of smiles. His dad and mom (Ann Dowd) are loving and supportive, and that's rare when so many movie parents are wrongheaded or missing.

It's commendable, too, that in this film, growing old and dying are treated respectfully; there's a visit to the grave of Samantha's grandfather Doc Wallace, and a visit to the nursing home where Marty's grandmother is slipping into Alzheimer's. Saving Shiloh doesn't overplay its lessons on life, but it contains them, and they give it values many family movies simply ignore. Carl Borack produced and Dale Rosenbloom directed the first film; they co-produced Shiloh 2: Shiloh Season (1999) and Saving Shiloh, both directed by Sandy Tung.

As for melodrama, there is some business involving the thieves that is fairly exciting but also fairly unbelievable. And a climactic scene where Dara Lynn slips off a bridge into the river, and Marty and Shiloh dive in to save her. The film nicely modulates the danger, making it scary but not traumatizing. Everyone involved with this film obviously had respect for the family audiences they are aiming at, and it's surprising how moving the film is, and how wise, while still just seeming to be about a boy and his dog, his family, and the mean man next door who isn't so mean if you get to know him.

Saw ★ ★
R, 100 m., 2004

Leigh Whannell (Adam), Cary Elwes (Dr. Lawrence Gordon), Danny Glover (Detective David Tapp), Ken Leung (Detective Steven Sing), Dina Meyer (Kerry), Mike Butters (Paul), Paul Gutrecht (Mark), Michael Emerson (Zep Hindle), Benito Martinez (Brett). Directed by James Wan and produced by Mark Burg, Gregg Hoffman, and Oren Koules. Screenplay by Leigh Whannell.

Saw is an efficiently made thriller, cheerfully gruesome, and finally not quite worth the ordeal it puts us through. It's a fictional machine to pair sadistic horrors with merciless choices, and so the question becomes: Do we care enough about the characters to share what they have to endure? I didn't.

Two films, Touching the Void and Open Water, involved characters who experienced almost unimaginable ordeals of pain and despair, and I was with them every step of the way—not least because I understood how they found themselves in their terrifying situations, and how they hoped to escape.

Saw, by contrast, depends on an improbably devious and ingenious villain who creates complications for the convenience of the screenplay. Named "The Jigsaw Killer," he joins that sturdy band of movie serial killers with time on their hands to devise elegant puzzles for their victims and the police. Sometimes that works, as in The Silence of the Lambs, and sometimes we simply feel toyed with. That said, Saw is well made and acted, and does what it does about as well as it could be expected to. Horror fans may forgive its contrivances.

The movie opens in a locked public toilet. A clock on the wall says it is 2 o'clock. Two men are chained by leg irons to opposite walls. In the center of the floor is a corpse in a pool of blood. Near the corpse are a revolver, a tape recorder, and a saw. The men are Adam (played by Leigh Whannell, who wrote the screenplay) and Dr. Lawrence Gordon (Cary Elwes). The corpse remains a mystery for a long time, but the tape recording is helpful: It informs both men that Dr. Gordon has to kill Adam by 6 o'clock, or his wife and daughter will be murdered.

A parallel story involves the efforts of two detectives to track down the Jigsaw Killer, who has posed such deadly ultimatums to earlier victims. (One involves a machine bolted to the victim's head, with a mechanism inserted into the mouth that is timed to rip the jaws apart after the deadline. I hate it when that happens.) The detectives are David Tapp (Danny Glover) and Steven Sing (Ken Leung), and they're racing, as you might expect, against time.

Who is the Jigsaw Killer, and why has he gone to such diabolical lengths to devise such cruel predicaments? Well might you ask. The answer, of course, is that he is a plot device lowered into the movie with a toolbox filled with horrors, dangers, and unspeakable choices. He exists not because he has his reasons or motivations (although some are assigned to him, sort of as a courtesy, at the end). He exists because he tirelessly goes to great trouble and expense to fabricate a situation that the movie can exploit for 100 minutes. And he is almost certainly not who he seems to be, because of the screenwriting workshop principle that a false crisis and a false dawn must come before the real crisis and the real dawn.

Elwes and Whannell, chained by their ankles in the locked room, not only have to act their socks off but perhaps even their feet. Actors like roles like this, I suppose, because they can vibrate at peak intensity for minutes on end, screaming and weeping and issuing threats and pleas, and pretty much running through the gamut of emotions by knocking over all of the hurdles. You hope at the end of the movie they have a hot shower, a change of clothes, and a chicken dinner waiting for them.

As for the (possible) Jigsaw Killer, he of course is glimpsed imperfectly in some kind of a techno-torture lair, doing obscure things to control or observe the events he has so painstakingly fabricated. We see another version of the killer, also annoying: Jigsaw (or someone) disguises himself as a grotesque clownlike doll on a tricycle. Uh-huh. Whenever a movie shows me obscure, partial, oblique, fragmented shots of a murderous mastermind, or gives him a mask, I ask myself—why? Since the camera is right there in the lair, why not just show us his face? The answer, of course, is that he is deliberately obscured because he's being saved up for the big revelatory climax at the end.

A movie that conceals the identity of a killer is of a lower order, in general, than one that actually deals with him as a character. To get to know someone is infinitely more pleasing than to meet some guy behind a hockey mask, or in a puppet suit, or whatever. There is always the moment when the killer is unmasked and spews out his bitterness and hate and vindictive triumph over his would-be victims. I find it a wonder this obligatory scene has survived so long, since it is so unsatisfying. How about just once, at the crucial moment, the killer gets squished under a ton of canned soup and we never do find out who he was?

Schultze Gets the Blues ★ ★ ★ ½
PG, 114 m., 2005

Horst Krause (Schultze), Harald Warmbrunn (Jurgen), Karl Fred Muller (Manfred), Ursula Schucht (Jurgen's Wife), Hannelore Schubert (Manfred's Wife), Wolfgang Boos (Gatekeeper), Leo Fischer (Head of Music Club), Loni Frank (Schultze's Mother). Directed by Michael Schorr and produced by Jens Korner. Screenplay by Schorr.

Do they have salt mines in Germany? Or is Schultze's job simply a symbol of a lifetime of thankless toil? Day after day he ventures down into the salt mine until, with a shock, he and three friends are forced to retire. There is a little party at the beer hall, his coworkers singing a lugubrious song of farewell, and Schultze is a retired man. Not married, he passes his days in the sad enjoyment of unwanted freedom. Sometimes he contemplates his retirement present, a lamp made from large block of crystallized salt with a bulb inside. If it ever falls into other hands, will its new owners think to lick it?

Schultze (Horst Krause) is a bulky, stolid, unlovely man who wipes the dust from his garden gnomes, spends as much time as possible napping on his sofa, visits his mother in a nursing home, plays the accordion at a polka club, and plays chess at a club where the level of play is not too high; one should not reach retirement age as a chess player still arguing over applications of the "touch-move" rule. He gets around town on his bicycle, dealing with the delays caused by a rail crossing guard who is distracted by the study of alchemy.

One night Schultze's world changes forever. On the radio he hears zydeco music from Louisiana. I was reminded of *Genghis Blues,* the 1999 film where a blind musician in San Francisco, Paul Pena, hears Tuva throat-singing over the radio, teaches it to himself, and travels to the Republic of Tuva for the annual competition. Schultze becomes a man possessed. He takes up his accordion, begins to pump through a tired song he has played a thousand times, and then gradually increases the tempo and turns up the heat until he is playing, well, zydeco polka.

That is not an impossible musical genre. David Golia, a friend of mine from San Francisco, leads a polka band that explores what he sees as the underlying connection between polka, rock, and Mexican and Brazilian music. It's not all about beer barrels.

Schultze now becomes a man obsessed. His lonely life is filled with fantasies of far-off bayous. He gets a cookbook and prepares jambalaya on his kitchen stove. His polka club listens to his zydeco arrangements and votes to send him to a German music festival in the town's sister city in Texas—not so much to honor him, we suspect, as to get him out of town.

Schultze is not much of a traveler, and speaks perhaps a dozen words of English. Unlike the travelers in many movies, he doesn't magically learn many more. The Texas festival does not nurture his inner man, and he does what any sensible person in Schultze's position would do, which is to purchase a boat and set off across the Gulf and into the waterways of Louisiana.

What may not be clear in my description is that *Schultze Gets the Blues* is not entirely, or even mostly, a comedy, even though it has pas-

sages of droll, deadpan humor. It is essentially the record of a man who sets himself into motion and is amazed by the results. I was reminded of Aki Kaurismaki's *The Man without a Past* (2002), the story of a man whose amnesia frees him to begin an altogether different life. The film has also been compared with *About Schmidt* (2002), although Schmidt was a madcap compared to Schultze.

Schultze is not an object of fun, but a focus of loneliness and need, a man who discovers too late that he made no plans for his free time and is deeply bored by his life. His American journey is not travel but exploration—not of a new land, but of his own possibilities. He suddenly realizes that he, Schultze, can move from one continent to another, can medicate his blues with Louisiana hot sauce, and play music that sends his accordion on crazy trills of joy.

He does not, during his journey, meet a soul mate, fall in love, become discovered on *American Idol,* or do anything else than live his new life. He meets people easily because he is so manifestly friendly and harmless, but finds it hard to form relationships because of his handful of words. No matter. We suspect it was the same for him even in Germany, and now he wanders where every single thing he sees is new to his eyes.

The writer and director, Michael Schorr, is making his first film, but has the confidence and simplicity of someone who has been making films forever. Unlike many first-timers, he isn't trying to see how much of his genius one film can contain. He begins, I think, not with burning ambition, but with a simple love and concern for Schultze. He creates the character, watches him asleep on the sofa, and then follows a few steps behind as Schultze backs away from the dead-end of retirement. He begins his journey with a single step, as we know all journeys must begin, and arrives at last on a boat in the Gulf of Mexico, where not all journeys end, and where Schultze must be as surprised as his director to find himself.

Scooby-Doo 2: Monsters Unleashed ★ ★
PG, 93 m., 2004

Freddie Prinze Jr. (Fred), Sarah Michelle Gellar (Daphne), Matthew Lillard (Shaggy), Linda Cardellini (Velma), Seth Green (Patrick), Peter

Boyle (Old Man Wickles), Tim Blake Nelson (Jacobo), Alicia Silverstone (Heather). Directed by Raja Gosnell and produced by Charles Roven and Richard Suckle. Screenplay by James Gunn.

The Internet was invented so that you can find someone else's review of Scooby-Doo. *Start surfing.*

Those were the closing words of my 2002 review of the original *Scooby-Doo*, a review that began with refreshing honesty: "I am not the person to review this movie." I was, I reported, "unable to generate the slightest interest in the plot, and I laughed not a single time, although I smiled more than once at the animated Scooby-Doo himself, an island of amusement in a wasteland of fecklessness."

Whoa, but I was in a bad mood that day. I gave the movie a one-star rating. Now I am faced with *Scooby-Doo 2*. There is a subtitle: *Monsters Unleashed*. As the story commences, our heroes in Mystery Inc. are attending the opening night of a museum exhibiting souvenirs from all of the cases they have solved. The event turns into a disaster when one of the monster costumes turns out to be inhabited and terrorizes the charity crowd.

Now I don't want you to think I walked into 2 with a chip on my shoulder because of the 2002 film. I had completely forgotten the earlier film, and so was able to approach the sequel with a clean slate. I viewed it as the second movie on a day that began with a screening of *Taking Lives*, with Angelina Jolie absorbing vibes from the graves of serial killer victims. The third movie was Bresson's 1966 masterpiece *Au Hasard Balthazar*, which could have been called *The Passion of the Donkey*. So you see, we have to shift gears quickly on the film crit beat.

What I felt as I watched *Scooby-Doo* was not the intense dislike I had for the first film, but a kind of benign indifference. There was a lot of eye candy on the screen, the colors were bright, the action was relentless, Matthew Lillard really is a very gifted actor, and the animated Scooby-Doo is so jolly I even liked him in the first movie. This film is no doubt ideally constructed for its target audience of ten-year-olds and those who keenly miss being ten-year-olds.

Once again, to quote myself, I am not the person to review this movie, because the values

I bring to it are irrelevant to those who will want to see it. This is a silly machine to whirl goofy antics before the eyes of easily distracted audiences, and it is made with undeniable skill. Watching it is a little like watching synchronized swimming: One is amazed at the technique and discipline lavished on an enterprise that exists only to be itself.

But a little more about the movie. The original cast is back, led by Lillard as Scooby-Doo's friend Shaggy, and containing Freddie Prinze Jr., Sarah Michelle Gellar, and Linda Cardellini. Alicia Silverstone plays a trash-TV reporter who is determined to debunk the myth of Mystery Inc. The always reliable Peter Boyle is mean Old Man Wickles, who, if he is not involved in skullduggery, is in the movie under false pretenses. Seth Green is funny as the museum curator. And there are a lot of cartoon monsters.

Is this better or worse than the original? I have no idea. I'll give it two stars because I didn't feel anything like the dislike I reported after the first film, but no more than two, because while the film is clever it's not really trying all that hard. I think the future of the republic may depend on young audiences seeing more movies like *Whale Rider* and fewer movies like *Scooby-Doo 2*, but then that's just me.

The Seagull's Laughter ★ ★ ★ ½
NO MPAA RATING, 102 m., 2004

Margrét Vilhjálmsdóttir (Freya), Ugla Egilsdóttir (Agga), Heino Ferch (Björn Theódór), Hilmir Snær Guðnason (Magnús), Kristbjörg Kjeld (Grandma), Edda Bjorg Eyjólfsdóttir (Dodo), Guðlaug Ólafsdóttir (Ninna), Eyvindur Erlendsson (Granddad). Directed by Ágúst Guðmundsson and produced by Kristin Atladóttir. Screenplay by Guðmundsson, based on the novel by Kristin Marja Baldursdóttir.

The most beautiful woman in the Icelandic village of Hafnarfjordur ran off to New York with an American serviceman, or so it is said, and now returns to her hometown without her husband but with seven trunks of sexy dresses. Is she a widow, as she claims, or did she never marry the serviceman, or did he come to a bad end? Freya is the kind of woman who inspires such speculation, especially in the inflamed imagination of her eleven-year-old cousin Agga, who adores and hates her, sometimes at the same time. *The Seagull's Laughter,* an uncommonly engaging comedy with ripe, tragic undertones, begins with the fact that everybody in town lives in everybody else's pockets. There are few secrets. Certainly Freya (Margret Vilhjálmsdóttir) is a sex bomb in search of a husband, and there are only two eligible men in the village: an engineer who lives with his mother and is engaged to the mayor's daughter, and a young policeman. The engineer has the better job and house, and so the mayor's daughter must go.

All of this is seen through the eyes of Agga, played by Ugla Egilsdóttir with such spirit and deviousness that when I was on the jury at the Karlovy Vary festival in 2002, we gave her the best actress award. She is on the trembling edge of adolescence, and her ambiguous feelings about sexuality cause her to worship the older woman while at the same time trying to frame her with arson, murder, and other crimes, during regular visits to the young cop. He dismisses her breathless eyewitness reports as the fantasies of an overwrought would-be Nancy Drew, but the movie suggests some of her reports—especially involving the mysterious fire that kills the wife-beating husband of Freya's best friend—may contain bits of truth.

Freya has essentially returned from America with no prospects at all. She takes a job in the chemist's shop, and finds popularity with the local drunks by selling them rubbing alcohol. She has moved into her grandfather's house, displacing the resentful Agga from her bed, and joins a matriarchy. The grandfather is almost always away at sea, and his house is ruled by his wife, Agga's grandmother, who also provides a home for her daughters, Dodo and Ninna, and her pipe-smoking sister-in-law, Kidda. Death is a fact in this home; Kidda's husband has died, and so have young Agga's parents. (When the police arrive at the door and ask to speak with her mother, she calmly tells them, "That will be difficult. She's dead.") The women are supportive of Freya and delighted by all of her dresses; they hold a spontaneous dress-up parade, and end by admiringly measuring her waist, bustline, and long hair.

Freya captures the eye of the engineer, Bjōrn Theódór (Heino Ferch), at a village dance, spirits him away, and doesn't return, Agga breathlessly tattles to the policeman, until 5 A.M. ("Five thirteen," he corrects her). Freya tells Agga how they spent the night, leaving out the detail of their lovemaking, but speaking of the softness of long summer nights, the look of the sea, and the stroll they took on the path through the . . . well, through the fish-drying racks.

The racks come up later, after winter sets in and Freya begins to take long, despairing walks in the snow. She hates Iceland, she cries out: the cold and the snow and the seagulls laughing at her, and the smell of fish. But home is where, when you have to go there, they have to take you in.

The understory involves Agga's gradual transition into womanhood. Watching Freya, sometimes spying on her, she gets insights into the adult world and translates them into bulletins for the young cop. She plays both sides of the street, at one point forging a letter to keep Freya and the engineer in contact. And she learns hard lessons when Freya's best friend is mistreated by her husband and threatens suicide, and Freya calms her in an extraordinary scene by getting on her hands and knees, letting down her long hair, creeping to the friend, and calming her with its smell. This seems to refer to a childhood memory, and has an unexpected emotional impact.

The movie balances between dark and light, between warmth and cold, like an Icelandic year. It's scored with Glenn Miller and other swing bands from the war era, and opens and closes with the 1950s hit "Sh-boom." The message I think is that tragedy is temporary and the dance of life goes on. Soon it will be Agga's turn to choose a partner.

The Sea Inside ★ ★ ★
PG-13, 125 m., 2004

Javier Bardem (Ramon Sampedro), Belen Rueda (Julia), Lola Duenas (Rosa), Clara Segura (Gene), Mabel Rivera (Manuela), Celso Bugallo (Jose), Tamar Novas (Javi), Joan Dalmau (Joaquin), Francesc Garrido (Marc). Directed and produced by Alejandro Amenabar. Screenplay by Amenabar and Mateo Gil.

When you can't escape and you depend on others, you learn to cry by smiling.

So says Ramon Sampedro, who has been in

the same bed in the same room for twenty-six years, not counting trips to the hospital. He was paralyzed from the neck down in a diving accident as a young man. He has his music, his radio and television, his visitors, his window view. He can control a computer, and write using a pen he holds in his mouth. He is cared for by his family, who love him and welcome the money they get from the government for his support. As *The Sea Inside* opens, Ramon demands the right to die.

"A life in this condition has no dignity," he says. He is tired of his bed, his limitations, and his life. He argues his point with great conviction, aided above all by his smile. Ramon is played by Javier Bardem, that Spanish actor of charm and gentle masculine force, and the smile lights up his face in a way that isn't forced or false, but sunny and with love. People truly care for him—his brother and sister-in-law, his nephew, the lawyer from a right-to-die organization, and Rosa, the woman from town who works as a disc jockey and peddles her bike out one day to meet him. Those who love me, he lets them all know, will help me to die.

The Sea Inside is based on the true story of a quadriplegic from Galicia, Spain, who in 1998 did succeed in dying, after planning his death in such an ingenious way that even if all the details were discovered no one could be legally charged with the crime. What we see in *The Sea Inside* is fiction, based on the final months. His lawyer, Julia (Belen Rueda), is herself suffering from a degenerative disease, and he feels that will make her more sympathetic to his cause. They fall in love with each other. The local woman Rosa certainly loves him. His family loves him and doesn't complain about the burden; his brother, in fact, is adamantly opposed to euthanasia. Ramon waits in his bed, smiles, is charming, and figures out how this thing can be made to happen.

Bardem and Alejandro Amenabar, the film's director, are adamant that they do not believe everyone in Ramon's position should die. This is simply the story of one man. Yes, and on those terms I accept it, and was moved by the humanity and logic of the character. But it happens I know a few things about paraplegia, which I hope you will allow me to share.

At the University of Illinois, my alma mater, there are more students in wheelchairs than at any other university in the country (the campus is completely lacking in hills, a great convenience), and they were in all my classes; when I was editor of the student paper, our photo editor was in a chair. The most outspoken student radical on campus could walk only with an exoskeleton of braces and crutches—it would have been easier in a chair, but not for him. Among other paraplegics I have known, a lifelong friend recently retired as a sportscaster, a young woman was largely responsible for getting the Americans with Disabilities Act passed, and I once joined a dozen wheelchair athletes on a teaching tour of southern Africa. A high school classmate was paralyzed in his senior year; a few years ago I got news of his romance and marriage. Some of these people have had children, and have raised them competently, lovingly, and well. I remember the remarkable Heather Rose, whose condition limited her to the use of one finger, which she used to tap on a voice synthesizer. She wrote and starred in *Dance Me to My Song*, and flew from Australia to attend my first Overlooked Film Festival. Only recently I got an e-mail from a fellow film critic I have been in communication with for years; discussing this movie, he revealed to me that he is a quadriplegic.

These people are all functioning usefully, and it is clear they have happy and productive days, no doubt interrupted sometimes by pain, doubt, and despair. To be sure, most of them are not quads. But whatever their reality, they deal with it. Ramon, on the other hand, refuses to be fitted with a breath-controlled wheelchair because he finds it a parody of the freedom he once had.

What would I do in the same situation as the man in Spain? I am reminded of something written by another Spaniard, the director Luis Buñuel. What made him angriest about dying, he said, was that he would be unable to read tomorrow's newspaper. I believe I would want to live as long as I could, assuming I had my sanity and some way to communicate. If I were trapped inside my mind, like the hero of Dalton Trumbo's *Johnny Got His Gun*, that would be another matter—although consider the life of Helen Keller.

In *The Sea Inside*, Ramon Sampedro has considered all these notions, and is not persuaded. He does not care to live any longer. Julia, the woman from the right-to-die agency, supports him, and so do "backers" from around the country. Rosa, the local girl, desperately wants him to live. A quadriplegic priest visits to talk Ramon out of his decision, and there is a macabre scene in which messages are carried up and down stairs between the two men. Julia's own health becomes an issue.

What finally happens to Ramon Sampedro I will not say. The movie invites us to decide if we are pleased or not. I agree with Ramon that, in the last analysis, the decision should be his to make: To be or not to be. But if a man is of sound mind and not in pain, how in the world can he decide he no longer wants to read tomorrow's newspaper?

Secret Things ★ ★ ★
NO MPAA RATING, 115 m., 2004

Coralie Revel (Natalie), Sabrina Seyvecou (Sandrine), Roger Mirmont (Delacroix), Fabrice Deville (Christophe), Blandine Bury (Charlotte), Olivier Soler (Cadene), Viviane Theophildes (Mme. Mercier). Directed by Jean-Claude Brisseau and produced by Brisseau and Jean-Francois Geneix. Screenplay by Brisseau.

Secret Things is a rare item these days: an erotic film made well enough to keep us interested. It's about beautiful people, has a lot of nudity, and the sex is as explicit as possible this side of porno. If you enjoyed *Emmanuelle*, you will think this is better. And, like Bertolucci's more considerable film *The Dreamers*, it will remind you of the days when movies dealt as cheerfully with sex as they do today with action. Of course, it is French.

What is amazing is how seriously the French take it. I learn from *Film Journal International* that *Secret Things* was named Film of the Year by *Cahiers du Cinema*, the magazine that brought Godard, Truffaut, Chabrol, and Rohmer into the world, and became the bible of the auteur theory. But then *Cahiers* has long been famous for jolting us out of our complacency by advocating the outrageous.

The movie is an erotic thriller that opens with a woman alone on a sofa, doing what such women do on such sofas in such movies. The camera slowly draws back to reveal the location: a strip club. We hear the voice of the narrator, Sandrine (Sabrina Seyvecou), who is a bartender in the club and new to this world; she needed the job. When she seems reluctant to

have sex with the customers, the performer, named Natalie (Coralie Revel), tells her that is her right, and they are both fired.

Sandrine cannot go to her flat because she is behind on the rent. Natalie invites her to spend the night with her. You see how these situations develop in erotic fiction. They have a tête-à-tête, and vice versa. We hear frank, revealing, and well-written dialogue about their sexual feelings. Natalie is a realist about sex, she says. When it comes to pleasure, she is more interested in herself than in her partners, who are nonparticipants in the erotic theater of her mind. What turns her on is being watched by strangers, and although Sandrine is shocked at first, in no time at all they are doing things in a Metro station that would get you arrested if you were not in a movie.

"Let's climb the social ladder," Natalie suggests to Sandrine. They target a small but wealthy company whose cofounder is about to die. His son, a notorious rake and pervert, will inherit. Sandrine gets a job as a secretary and is provocative in just such a way as to attract the attention of the other cofounder, Delacroix (Roger Mirmont). Soon she is his private secretary, and almost immediately his lover; her boldness in seducing him shows a nerve that is almost more interesting than her technique. She has him so completely in her power, she feels sorry for the poor guy.

Sandrine arranges for Natalie to be hired by the company, and soon they have both fallen into the orbit of Christophe (Fabrice Deville), the son and heir. This is a disturbed man. As a child, he watched his mother die and sat for days beside her body. As an adult, he has been such a cruel lover that not one but two women committed suicide by setting themselves afire in front of him. He has a sister, Charlotte (Blandine Bury), and feels about her as such men do in such movies.

If the film is erotic on the surface, its undercurrent is as hard and cynical as *In the Company of Men*. The difference is that, this time, women are planning the cruel jokes and deceptions—or they would like to think they are. The writer and director, Jean-Claude Brisseau, devises an ingenious plot that involves corporate intrigue and blackmail, double-crossing and sabotage, and sex as the key element in the control of the country.

And all the time, Sandrine's narration adds

another element. She is detached, observant, and a little sad in her comments on the action; unlike an American narrator, who would try to be steamy, she talks to us like one adult to another, commenting on what she really felt, who she felt sorry for, what she regretted having to do, and who she trusted but shouldn't have. The ending, which resolves all the plotting and intrigue with clockwork precision, is ironic not like a Hitchcock film, but like a French homage to Hitchcock; Truffaut's *The Bride Wore Black*, perhaps.

The film is well made, well acted, cleverly written, photographed by Wilfrid Sempe as if he's a conspirer with the sexual schemers. There's an especially effective scene where Natalie stands behind an open door and drives poor Delacroix frantic as coworkers pass by right outside. The movie understands that even powerful men can be rendered all but helpless by women with sufficient nerve. *Secret Things* is not the film of the year, or even of the fortnight, but it is a splendid erotic film with a plot so cynical that we're always kept a little off balance.

Secret Window ★ ★ ★
PG-13, 106 m., 2004

Johnny Depp (Mort Rainey), John Turturro (John Shooter), Maria Bello (Amy Rainey), Timothy Hutton (Ted), Charles S. Dutton (Ken Karsch), Len Cariou (Sheriff). Directed by David Koepp and produced by Gavin Polone. Screenplay by Koepp, based on a Stephen King novella.

The first shot after the credits of *Secret Window* is an elaborate one. It begins with a view across a lake to a rustic cabin. Then the camera moves smoothly in to the shore and across the grounds and in through a window of the cabin, and it regards various rooms before closing in on a large mirror that reflects a man asleep on a couch.

The framing narrows until we no longer see the sides of the mirror, only the image. And then we realize we aren't looking at a reflection, but are in fact now in the real room. Not possible logically, but this through-the-looking-glass shot, along with a wide-brimmed black hat and some Pall Mall cigarettes, are the only slight ripples in the smooth surface of the movie's realism.

The movie stars Johnny Depp in another of those performances where he brings a musing eccentricity to an otherwise straightforward role. He plays Mort Rainey, a best-selling novelist of crime stories; like the hero of *Misery*, he reminds us that the original story is by Stephen King. The computer on his desk in the loft contains one paragraph of a new story, until he deletes it. He spends a lot of time sleeping, and has possibly been wearing the same ratty bathrobe for months. His hair seems to have been combed with an eggbeater, but of course with Johnny Depp you never know if that's the character or the actor.

A man appears at his door. He is tall and forbidding, speaks with a Mississippi accent, wears the wide-brimmed black hat, and says, "You stole my story." This is John Shooter (John Turturro), a writer who leaves behind a manuscript that is, indeed, almost word for word the same as Rainey's story *Secret Window*. The plot deals with a man who has been betrayed by his wife, murders her, and buries her in her beloved garden—where, after a time, she will be forgotten, "perhaps even by me." Rainey knows he did not steal the story, but Shooter is an angry and violent man who stalks the author and causes bad things to happen: a screwdriver through the heart of his beloved dog, for example. Shooter says he wrote his story in 1997, and Rainey has his comeback: He wrote his in 1994, and thinks he has an old issue of *Ellery Queen's Mystery Magazine* to prove it.

But that leads him back into the world of his estranged wife, Amy (Maria Bello), who is living with her new lover (Timothy Hutton). She has the big house in town, and that's why Rainey is living in sloth and despond in the lake cottage. To tell more would be wrong, except to note Rainey's decision to hire an ex-cop (Charles S. Dutton) as a bodyguard, and to complain to the local sheriff (Len Cariou), an arthritic whose hobby is knitting.

Rainey appears to be the classic Hitchcock hero, an innocent man wrongly accused. He has been cheated on by his wife, and now this nut from nowhere is threatening his life because of a story he did not steal. The situation is magnified nicely by the location at the isolated cottage, which leaves many opportunities for disturbing sounds, strange omens, broken lightbulbs, threatening letters, and Shooter himself, who appears at disconcerting moments and seems to be stalking Rainey wherever he goes.

All of this could add up to a straight-faced thriller about things that go boo in the night, but Johnny Depp and director David Koepp (who wrote *Panic Room* and directed *Stir of Echoes*) have too much style to let that happen. Like many men who have lived alone for a long time, Rainey carries on a running conversation with himself—dour, ironic, sometimes amused. He talks to the dog until the dog is killed. Aroused from a nap, he stumbles through a confused investigation, asks himself, "Now, where was I?" and returns to the same position on the couch.

Even his friends are entertaining. When he talks with the ex-cop, they use a chess clock, banging their button when the other guy starts talking. Maybe this has something to do with billing arrangements, or maybe they're just competitive. Probably the latter, since bodyguards are always on duty.

The story is more entertaining as it rolls along than it is when it gets to the finish line. But at least King uses his imagination right up to the end, and spares us the obligatory violent showdown that a lesser storyteller would have settled for. A lot of people were outraged that he was honored at the National Book Awards, as if a popular writer could not be taken seriously. But after finding that his book *On Writing* had more useful and observant things to say about the craft than any book since Strunk and White's *The Elements of Style,* I have gotten over my own snobbery.

King has, after all, been responsible for the movies *The Shawshank Redemption, The Green Mile, The Dead Zone, Misery, Apt Pupil, Christine, Hearts in Atlantis, Stand by Me,* and *Carrie. Secret Window* is somewhere in the middle of that range storywise, and toward the top in Depp's performance. And we must not be ungrateful for *Silver Bullet,* which I awarded three stars because it was "either the worst movie ever made from a Stephen King story, or the funniest," and you know what side of that I'm gonna come down on.

Seed of Chucky ★ ★

R, 86 m., 2004

Herself (Jennifer Tilly), Himself (Redman), Hannah Spearritt (Joan), John Waters (Pete Peters), Billy Boyd (Voice of Glen/Glenda Doll), Brad Dourif (Voice of Chucky Doll), Jennifer Tilly (Voice of Tiffany Doll). Directed by Don Mancini and produced by David Kirschner and Corey Sienega. Screenplay by Mancini.

Midway through *Seed of Chucky,* Jennifer Tilly complains: "I'm an Oscar nominee, and now I'm f---ing a puppet!" Yeah, and I'm a Pulitzer winner, and I was being f---ed by a puppet movie. Because Focus Features declined to preview its new movie for the press, and indeed went so far as to station a guard at the Thursday night sneak preview in case I could not contain my eagerness to attend, I went on Saturday morning. I'm not complaining. They had those poppable Snickers bits.

Seed of Chucky is actually two movies, one wretched, the other funny. The funny one involves the Jennifer Tilly scenes. She plays "herself" in the movie—a horror film star making *Chucky Goes Psycho* and little realizing that both the Chucky doll and its wife, the Jennifer doll, have been brought back to life by the Glen or Glenda doll, their child.

Tilly, who seems to supply most of her own dialogue and is certainly a good sport if she didn't, is portrayed as a has-been actress who hopes to make a comeback by starring as the Virgin Mary in a film being prepared by the rap artist Redman. After an audition, Redman tells her he's going with his first choice for the role, Julia Roberts. But he tells Tilly he loved that movie with her and the other girl. "'Bound'?" she says. "Yeah, everyone loves that one." He asks if, uh, she is still, uh, friends with the other girl. "Gina Gershon? Me and Gina are *very* close friends. Gee, maybe the three of us could hang out." Then she shamelessly suggests that Redman come over to her place so they can get better acquainted.

"You're prostituting yourself to play the Virgin Mary!" her best friend tells her. "You'll go to hell!"

"Hell," says Tilly, "would be ending up on *Celebrity Fear Factor* in a worm-eating contest with Anna Nicole Smith."

Tilly has lots of good one-liners ("They're executing Martha Stewart this morning") and argues convincingly that if she had played Erin Brockovich instead of Julia Roberts, she wouldn't have had to wear a push-up bra. She is completely unaware that Chucky and Tiffany have come to life, until she finds the prop man's head and thinks it's a prop until it starts to drip.

The Chucky side of the movie tells the story of how Chucky and Tiffany's child sees them on television, realizes he's not alone in the world, and escapes from a British ventriloquist to fly to L.A. and bring his parents back to life with an ancient incantation. They're delighted to find they have offspring, but get into a fight over whether the kid is a boy or a girl. Full frontal doll nudity solves nothing. Chuck likes Glen as a name; Tiffany likes Glenda. Ed Wood, director of *Glen or Glenda* (1953) would be proud (and another cult filmmaker, John Waters, turns up here long enough to have his face eaten away).

Chucky's master plan is to impregnate Jennifer Tilly so Glen/Glenda can have a brother/sister. This involves the first doll masturbation scene that, offhand, I can remember in the movies, as Chucky produces a sperm sample (as a visual aid, he rejects skin magazines and chooses *Fangoria*). A turkey baster makes its inevitable appearance.

If you're thinking of *Seed of Chucky* as a horror movie, you can forget about it. It's not scary. If you do not by now find Chucky and the other killer dolls tiresome, I do (this is their fifth movie). If you like the way Jennifer Tilly has fun with her image (and, in what can only be called selfless generosity, with Gina Gershon's image), *Seed of Chucky* is a movie to be seen on television. Free television.

Note: The print at the Webster Place theater in Chicago looked dim, murky, and washed-out. I complained to the management, suggesting that perhaps the projector bulb was set too low. There was no improvement. The movie's trailers on the Web have bright and vivid colors. The movie I saw was drab, as if filmed through a dirty window. So were the other trailers they showed.

Seeing Other People ★ ★ ½
R, 90 m., 2004

Jay Mohr (Ed), Julianne Nicholson (Alice), Lauren Graham (Claire), Bryan Cranston (Peter), Josh Charles (Lou), Andy Richter (Carl), Matthew Davis (Donald), Jill Ritchie (Sandy), Helen Slater (Penelope). Directed by Wallace Wolodarsky and produced by Gavin Polone. Screenplay by Maya Forbes and Wolodarsky.

Alice and Ed are happy. They've been happy for five years. They're engaged to be married. But then Alice begins to mope. She wonders if she's been unfairly shortchanged in the sexual experience sweepstakes, since before Ed she slept with only three guys, and two of them don't count, one because he was not a guy. So she makes a modest proposal: They should both fool around a little before they get married. That will jumpstart their own fairly tame sex life, and reconcile her to a lifetime of faithfulness.

Seeing Other People takes her suggestion and runs with it through several sexual encounters, arriving at the conclusion that the biggest danger of meaningless sex is that it can become meaningful. It isn't a successful movie, but is sometimes a very interesting one, and there is real charm and comic agility by the two leads, Julianne Nicholson and Jay Mohr. There is also finally a role for which Andy Richter seems ideally cast.

The movie has to overcome one problem: We like Ed and Alice. Their friends like them. They seem intended for each other. They aren't sitcom types, but solid, loyal, comfortable, smart people; Alice reminds me a little of Nicholson's great performance in *Tully* (2000) as a veterinarian who knows who she wants to marry and captures him with infinite subtlety and tenderness.

Here she suggests the rules. They will be completely honest with each other. They will be honest with their partners. They will somehow know when to stop. Alice takes the first leap: "I made out with someone," she tells Ed. "Made out?" "Yeah, like . . . made out." As she describes her experience, they grow excited, and have, they tell friends the next day, the best sex they've had—ever. It'll be downhill from there, as Alice meets a contractor named Donald (Matthew Davis) and Ed meets a waitress named Sandy (Jill Ritchie). Neither Sandy nor Donald see themselves as one-night stands, and are not content to play walk-through roles in the sexual adventures of an engaged couple.

Other characters include Alice's sister (Lauren Graham) and brother-in-law (Bryan Cranston), and Ed's two best friends, played by Josh Charles as a sexual cynic, and Andy Richter as a sincere, salt-of-the-earth guy who just absolutely knows no good can come of this experiment.

Seeing Other People is not so much about sex as about its consequences, and although we see

some heaving blankets, what the characters mostly bare are their souls. I liked it best in the tentative early stages, when Ed and Alice were unsure about their decision, not very brave about acting on it, and fascinated by talking about it. Then the movie starts working out various permutations of possible couples, and we get a traffic jam. I don't want to give away all the secrets, but Alice gets into bed with one person she should not, would not, and probably could not get into bed with—not if she's the person she seems to be.

There's a quiet joke in the fact that Alice wants to fool around and Ed is reluctant to go along. And there's a nice irony when Alice decides to call off the experiment just when Sandy has promised Ed a three-way with her college roommate. Ed perseveres, only to learn what many have discovered before him, that three-way sex tends to resemble a three-car race where one car is always in the pits.

This is not a boring movie, and the dialogue has a nice edge to it. It was written by a married couple, Maya Forbes and Wallace Wolodarsky, and directed by Wolodarsky; his credits include *The Simpsons* and hers include *The Larry Sanders Show*. I liked the way they had Alice and Ed actually discuss their experiment, instead of simply presenting it as a comic setup. But I don't know if the filmmakers ever decided how serious the movie should be, and so fairly harrowing moments of truth alternate with slapstick (man escapes through bedroom window as wife enters through door, etc.). And there are so many different pairings to keep track of that the movie loses focus and becomes a juggling act. Too bad, because in their best scenes together Nicholson and Mohr achieve a kind of intimacy and immediate truth that is hard to find, and a shame to waste.

The Sentinel ★ ★ ★
PG-13, 105 m., 2006

Michael Douglas (Pete Garrison), Kiefer Sutherland (David Breckinridge), Eva Longoria (Jill Marin), Kim Basinger (Sarah Ballentine), Martin Donovan (William Montrose), David Rasche (President Ballentine). Directed by Clark Johnson and produced by Michael Douglas, Marcy Drogin, and Arnon Milchan. Screenplay by George Nolfi, based on the novel by Gerald Petievich.

Michael Douglas is a skilled actor who often works within a narrow range, as he does in *The Sentinel*. Once again, he's a skilled professional who finds himself with problems on two fronts: the romantic and the criminal. Half of his movies, more or less, have involved that formula; the others show a wide variety, as in *Wonder Boys, Traffic, Falling Down,* and *The War of the Roses*. I might object when I see him wearing a suit and tie and juggling adultery and danger, but you know what? He's good at it.

In *The Sentinel*, he is a Secret Service agent named Pete Garrison, who in 1981 took a bullet during the assassination attempt on Ronald Reagan and is still guarding the president twenty-five years later. The movie doesn't identify President Ballentine (David Rasche) as belonging to either major party, although somehow his wife, Sarah (Kim Basinger), looks to me like a Democrat. She also looks like a dish and is having a passionate affair with, yes, Agent Garrison.

As the movie opens, another agent is shot dead after telling Garrison he wanted to talk to him. Did he know something about an assassination attempt? Garrison thinks so after meeting with a seedy informer who tells him there is a mole in the Secret Service—a turncoat agent on the White House detail who will set up the president for assassination. That this informer would know the secrets involved in this particular conspiracy seems unlikely, but then Clay Shaw never seemed like a likely suspect either, maybe because he wasn't one.

Without describing too many plot details, I can say that every agent assigned to the Office of the President is required to take a lie detector test and that only Garrison flunks. We know why: Asked if he has done anything to endanger the president, he naturally thinks of what he has done to endanger the president's marriage, and the needle redlines. That makes him a suspect and brings him into the crosshairs of David Breckinridge (Kiefer Sutherland), an ace investigator who used to be Garrison's best friend until, uh, Garrison apparently had an affair with *his* wife.

With the entire Secret Service looking for him, Garrison busts loose, goes underground, and uses all of his skills as an agent to stay free while trying to contact his informer and single-handedly stop the plot to kill the president. A deadline is approaching because Ballentine is scheduled to attend a summit in Toronto, where he might be a prime target. Since the presidential helicopter was shot down by a rocket while leaving Camp David a few days earlier (not with the president on board), and since the service knows it has a traitor, you might think the wise decision would be to skip Toronto and stay at home, maybe in a panic room. But no: Ballentine goes to Toronto, along with Garrison, Breckinridge, Sarah, the terrorists, and everybody else in the plot.

The Sentinel involves a scenario that is unlikely, I hope. But it's told efficiently and with lots of those little details that make movies like this seem more expert than they probably are. (Did you know that agents are trained to disengage the safety lock on their handguns as they draw them, instead of after, as cops do?) The Douglas character does a lot of quick thinking, and Sutherland is brisk, cold, and efficient as a super-sleuth. Eva Longoria plays Jill, his new assistant, whom he prefers to a veteran agent because she's still fresh and hasn't been worn down by the job. I was able to spot the mole almost the first time he (or she) appears on the screen by employing the Law of Economy of Characters, but his (or her) identity is essentially beside the point.

There comes a point in *The Sentinel*, as there did in Harrison Ford's *Firewall*, when you wonder how a guy in his early sixties can run indefinitely, survive all kinds of risky stunts, hold his own in a fight, and stay three steps ahead of the young guys in his strategy. You wonder, and then you stop wondering, because hey, it's a movie. As I so wisely wrote about the Ford movie, "Nobody can do anything they do in thrillers anyway, so why should there be an age limit on accomplishing the impossible?"

This is the second theatrical feature (after *S.W.A.T.*) directed by Clark Johnson, an actor who has also done a lot of work on television, mostly on shows that would be useful preparation, such as *Homicide, Law & Order, The West Wing,* and *The Shield.* Have I seen movies like *The Sentinel* before? Yes, and I hope to see them again. At a time when American audiences seem

grateful for the opportunity to drool at mindless horror trash, it is encouraging that well-crafted thrillers still are being made about characters who have dialogue, identities, motives, and clean shirts.

Separate Lies ★ ★ ★
R, 87 m., 2005

Emily Watson (Anne Manning), Tom Wilkinson (James Manning), Rupert Everett (William Bule), Hermione Norris (Priscilla), John Warnaby (Simon), Linda Bassett (Maggie), John Neville (Lord Rawston), David Harewood (Inspector Marshall). Directed by Julian Fellowes and produced by Steve Clark-Hall and Christian Colson. Screenplay by Fellowes, based on a novel by Nigel Balchin.

Is that what you say when a man dies? How inconvenient?

—*The Third Man*

Separate Lies opens with an event so sudden it is over before it can be registered; only later do we discover that a man was knocked from his bicycle by a speeding car, which didn't pause. The man was killed. It happened on a lane near the country home of a London lawyer, on the afternoon he and his wife invited some neighbors for drinks. The dead man was the husband of their housekeeper.

The movie is not so much about the solution to this crime as about the ethics involved in taking responsibility. If you can, should you get away with murder? What if you did not intend to kill—what if it was an accident? The man is dead. Should he be made to suffer? Many people have one answer to these questions when a stranger is involved, and another when it touches them personally. Not even a hanging judge wants to hang.

Separate Lies stars Tom Wilkinson as James Manning, the lawyer, and Emily Watson as Anne, his wife. Their marriage seems happy enough. He's one of those lawyers who specialize in making powerful clients more powerful. When it comes to matters of right and wrong, he likes to think of himself as inflexible. His wife is accommodating and dutiful and likes the life they lead, the house in London, the Buckinghamshire hideaway.

Serenity

In the village, a remembered face has reappeared. This is William Bule (Rupert Everett), son of a leading local family, recently returned from America, indolent and insinuating as he plays cricket on the village green. He catches Anne's eye, and it is because of him, really, that she tells her husband they should have neighbors over for drinks.

Everett plays Bule as a man detached and arrogant, dismissive of conventional values, attractive to women because he doesn't seem to care how they feel about him one way or the other. James Manning, on the other hand, is serious and responsible, and we catch glimpses of the idealistic undergraduate. Wilkinson, who often plays ordinary men, here emerges as a sleek London figure, no stranger to the shirtmakers of Jermyn Street; he has the impatience of a man who is always having to explain things to people who do not have his standards. Anne may be one of those people; perfect as she seems, she feels she never quite comes up to his mark.

Now there is the matter of the dead body in the grass beside the lane. There was a witness, as it happens: Maggie (Linda Bassett), whose husband was killed. She saw the car and might be able to identify it. Or perhaps not. Maggie knows William Bule, too; she worked for his family until she was dismissed. It was Anne who gave her a new start in the village. When the police constable comes around, he will want to talk to all of these people, not because they are suspects but because they might (as the British so carefully word it) be able to assist the police in their inquiries. Certainly Anne is not under suspicion: "One person not driving to a party," her husband observes, "is surely the hostess."

The unfolding of the plot I will leave for you to discover. The story, based on a 1950 novel by Nigel Balchin titled *A Way Through the Wood*, could as easily have been told by Agatha Christie, if the focus is on the whodunit aspects, or by Georges Simenon, if we know the whodunit but want to know how they feel about it, and how their feelings change as they discover more details. The movie's director, Julian Fellowes, takes the Simenon approach, although some of his moments of revelation could take place in an Agatha Christie drawing room where a word or two rotates a crime into a new dimension.

Fellowes, who has worked mostly as an actor, won an Academy Award with his screenplay for

Altman's *Gosford Park* (2001). There, as here, he is fascinated by the way class lingers on in Britain after its time has allegedly passed, how fierce loyalties and resentments are exchanged between upstairs and downstairs. The way he handles James and Anne is a case study in British manners: There is the sharp outburst, to be sure, and even the f-word, used for effect by a person who doesn't talk that way. But there's none of the screaming and weeping and acting-out of American domestic drama; James and Anne would rather be reasonable than be in love because there's less chance for embarrassment that way. At one point, when a possibility is suggested, James curtly replies: "I'm afraid that's a little too Jerry Springer for me."

Separate Lies reminded me of Woody Allen's *Crimes and Misdemeanors*. Its characters are above reproach—from themselves. Others deserve justice, but we deserve compassion and understanding. This is hypocrisy, but so what? Do unto others as you would not have them do unto you. *Separate Lies* is only seemingly about the portioning of blame. It is actually about the burden of guilt, which some can carry so easily, while for others it is intolerable.

Serenity ★ ★ ★
PG-13, 119 m., 2005

Nathan Fillion (Malcolm Reynolds), Gina Torres (Zoe Warren), Adam Baldwin (Jayne), Alan Tudyk (Wash Washburn), Jewel Staite (Kaylee), Morena Baccarin (Inara), Summer Glau (River Tam), Sean Maher (Simon), Ron Glass (Shepherd Book), Chiwetal Ejiofor (The Operative). Directed by Joss Whedon and produced by Barry Mendel. Screenplay by Whedon.

The thrill of a fistfight in a movie was altered for me forever the day I visited a set and watched the sound men beating the hell out of a Naugahyde sofa with Ping-Pong paddles. There was a moment in *Serenity* when I remembered that moment—no, not during a fistfight, but during a battle in interplanetary space. There are so many spacecraft, so large, so close together, it looks as if collision is a greater danger than enemy fire. Imagine spaceships in a demo derby.

As the battle continued and the heroes were hurled about inside their own spaceship, which

613

at times looked curiously like the interior of a loading dock, I made a note: "More banging than in your average space movie." Then something shifted inside my ears and I somehow knew I was hearing sound men, pounding the hell out of garbage can lids, sheets of steel, and big piles of pots and pans.

I say this not with disapproval, but with affection. *Serenity* is an old-fashioned space opera and differs from a horse opera mostly in that it involves space, not horses. It takes place in a solar system of a dozen terraformed planets and "hundreds of moons," and there is a war going on between the Alliance, which runs things and wants everybody to be happy, and a group of rebels who begin to make disturbing discoveries. As the film opens, a psychic named River Tam (Summer Glau) is rescued from Alliance mind-washers by her brother, Simon (Sean Maher), and then we learn that River was unwisely exhibited to a roomful of important Alliance parliamentarians. Because she can read minds, she knows their secrets.

River and Simon are soon enough allied with a team of freelance smugglers on a banged-up old ship named Serenity. Malcolm (Nathan Fillion) is the captain, and his crew includes the pilot, Wash (Alan Tudyk), his wife, Zoe (Gina Torres), the engineer, Kaylee (Jewel Staite), and the tough guy, Jayne (Adam Baldwin). On their trail is the most competent and feared of the Alliance's agents, the Operative (Chiwetal Ejiofor).

Science fiction fans will recognize the plot line and most of the characters from a short-lived Fox series named *Firefly*, which (I learn in a letter from Stephen McNeil of Sydney, Nova Scotia) was canceled in midseason, but not before the episodes were carelessly shown out of proper order. What a crock, especially considering that Joss Whedon, the TV series' author (and writer-director of *Serenity*), earlier created *Buffy, the Vampire Slayer*, and so deserved the benefit of the doubt.

Serenity is made of dubious but energetic special effects, breathless velocity, much imagination, some sly verbal wit, and a little political satire. Turns out the Alliance was simply trying to bring contentment to its crowded planetary system by distracting its inhabitants from their problems and making them feel like they had a life. River is in possession of a secret about this

process that the Alliance would do anything to suppress. Like *Brave New World* and *1984*, the movie plays like a critique of contemporary society, with the Alliance as Big Brother, enemy of discontent. But as River observes, "Some people don't like to be meddled with."

Some of the dialogue sounds futuristic, some sounds nineteenth century, and some sounds deliberately kooky. (Captain Mal: "Do you want to run this ship?" Discontented crew member: "Yes." Mal: "Well, you can't.") There are also unanticipated scenes of real impact, including a planet where—but see for yourself. I'm not sure the movie would have much appeal for non-sci-fi fans, but it has the rough edges and brawny energy of a good yarn, and it was made by and for people who can't get enough of this stuff. You know who you are. 🖝

Sex Is Comedy ★ ★ ½
NO MPAA RATING, 92 m., 2004

Anne Parillaud (Jeanne), Gregoire Colin (Actor), Roxane Mesquida (Actress), Ashley Wanninger (Leo), Dominique Colladant (Willy), Bart Binnema (Cinematographer), Yves Osmu (Sound Man). Directed by Catherine Breillat and produced by Jean-Francois Lepetit. Screenplay by Breillat.

Sex Is Comedy watches a French director as she attempts to film two sex scenes. She doesn't have an easy time of it. Her actor and actress hate each other, and she and the actor are having an affair. She begins with a summer beach scene that is being filmed on a cold day out of season. Her crew is bundled up warmly but her actors shiver in their swimsuits while she urges them to seem more sincere and passionate. Their hearts are clearly not in their work. When an actor's body is there but not his soul, she believes, "that is moral ugliness." Perhaps so, but as Woody Allen observed: "Sex without love is an empty experience, but, as empty experiences go, it's one of the best."

This is the new film by Catherine Breillat, the French woman who often takes sex—its mystery, its romance, its plumbing—as her subject. When her *Anatomy of Hell* opened, it showed a woman who pays a man to watch her, simply watch her, as she reveals her innermost physical and emotional secrets. Now here is another film about watching, this time curious about the director's personal and professional needs for sex, and how they differ.

The director, named Jeanne and played by Anne Parillaud *(La Femme Nikita)*, is pretty clearly supposed to be Breillat herself. The film within the film seems inspired by her *Fat Girl* (2002), a brave and shocking movie about two sisters, one fifteen and pretty, one twelve and pudgy, and the younger one's desire to follow her sister prematurely into the world of sexuality. The sex scenes in *Sex Is Comedy* are similar to scenes in *Fat Girl*, and indeed the actress is Roxane Mesquida, who played the older sister in that film.

Breillat is making a film, then, about herself making an earlier film. Like other films about filmmaking, ranging from Truffaut's *Day for Night* to Tim Burton's *Ed Wood*, it sees the director and the stars existing in a fever of their own, while the assistant director holds things together and the crew looks on dubiously. "It's always the same with her male leads," the sound man observes. "She picks them for their looks, then grows disillusioned."

Known as the Actor (Gregoire Colin) and the Actress (Mesquida), the two stars indeed seem to hate each other, although Jeanne suspects, probably correctly, that they're exaggerating their feelings as a way of dodging the scene. It is cold on the beach, soon it will rain, their lips are blue, it is a ridiculous situation, and the director seems to doubt her own wisdom. The second sex scene is at least in bed, but here, too, authentic feeling seems to be lacking, and finally the director climbs into bed with her leading man to rehearse, while the crew stands by—"for twenty-six minutes," observes the assistant director, whose job is to keep the production on schedule.

The bed scene is further complicated by the use of a large artificial phallus, which doubles (perhaps literally) for the Actor's own. The Actor walks around the set with the device bobbling out of his dressing gown, something Breillat thinks is funnier than it is; she should study the glow-in-the-dark condom scene from Blake Edwards's *Skin Deep* (1989).

The Actress is having difficulty "expressing herself" in the scene, which means that she doesn't seem to be faking an orgasm truthfully enough, and Jeanne shoots take after take as everyone's frustration grows. Finally there is a breakthrough, as the Actress experiences what may be hysteria but at least plays as sex, and Jeanne, obviously moved, hugs her afterward. It is not so much the Actress who must be aroused, apparently, as the director. This is a theory I heard more than once from Russ Meyer, with whom Breillat might have enjoyed shoptalk.

Sex Is Comedy is not really a comedy and not really about sex. It's about the way a director works with actors and uses them in a godlike way to create a new reality; first directors remake the world the way they see it, and then they guide us into seeing it that way too. It is often said that the movies allow us to empathize with the characters, but aren't we empathizing even more with the directors, since they're the ones who take over our eyes, ears, minds, and imaginations? A great director, by this definition, would be one who most successfully involves us in voyeurism.

Movie sex scenes are famously faked—except in porn and, on several occasions, in films by Breillat (who showed real sex in *Romance* and the *Anatomy of Hell*, where she used porn stars as actors or, sometimes, as body doubles). Her films are not pornography, however, because they do not share the purpose of pornography, which is to arouse. She is fascinated by our fascination with sex, and her movies demystify and deconstruct it. That is an interesting purpose, but *Sex Is Comedy* is not sure what it's really about, or how to get there; the director is seen as flighty and impulsive, the situations seem like setups, and we never know what the Actor and Actress are really thinking—or if thinking has anything to do with it.

The Shaggy Dog ★ ★
PG, 98 m., 2006

Tim Allen (Dave Douglas), Kristin Davis (Rebecca Douglas), Spencer Breslin (Josh Douglas), Zena Grey (Carly Douglas), Robert Downey Jr. (Dr. Kozak), Danny Glover (Ken Hollister), Jane Curtin (Judge Whittaker), Shawn Pyfrom (Trey). Directed by Brian Robbins and produced by Tim Allen and David Hoberman. Screenplay by Cormac Wibberley, Marianne Wibberley, Geoff Rodkey, Jack Amiel, and Michael Begler.

This is surely one of the fundamental laws of

fiction: When a man and a dog change bodies, it is funnier to see the man act like a dog than to see the dog act like a man. As Dr. Johnson observed so long ago, when a dog stands on its hind legs, "It is not done well, but you are surprised to find it done at all." A dog standing on its hind legs is considerably less convincing than a man on all fours, especially when he lifts his leg near a fire hydrant.

In *The Shaggy Dog*, Tim Allen plays an assistant DA prosecuting a case involving the use of laboratory animals. He is bitten by a three-hundred-year-old dog from Tibet that has been stolen from a monastery. The dog is destined to be used in the DNA research of a scummy longevity researcher in the form of Robert Downey Jr., who plays, as he does so well, a man whose agenda seems not merely buried but decomposing.

There is a special-effects shot of the dog's DNA racing into Allen's veins. The dog DNA looks like lots of little dogs. I suppose we should be relieved that the human DNA doesn't look like a lot of little Tim Allens, although the concept of dog DNA being taken for a walk by human DNA is intriguing.

Allen's rebellious daughter, Carly (Zena Grey), is filled with animal rights fervor after her social studies teacher is accused of setting a fire at a lab where animals were being mistreated. Dave is the prosecutor but finds his courtroom duties increasingly hard to perform as he transmutes into a dog. I think he is supposed to have become the clone of the dog from Tibet, although perhaps he has simply become a new but similar dog. He doesn't go through puppy stage, however, so perhaps he was simply occupied by the other dog, although then does that still leave the original dog behind? Are laws of the conservation of matter involved here? I have extraordinary difficulty in reasoning through the details of plots that are preposterous on principle.

Although he becomes a dog, Dave retains his own mind and tries to behave like a dad would. When Carly gets too friendly with her boyfriend, Trey (Shawn Pyfrom), he jumps on the bed between them. And on his wedding anniversary, as his wife waits forlornly at a table for two in a restaurant, he appears outside the window, wagging his tail, with a bouquet in his teeth. His family is extraordinarily obtuse, I must say, in not quickly realizing that

the shaggy dog is their father. How many clues do you need?

For that matter, is the shaggy dog occupied only by a human mind, or by a human mind and a canine mind fighting it out for space? If a human mind, why doesn't the dog need to learn from scratch how to bark, jump, scratch, and fetch? If a canine mind, why does it turn up for the wedding anniversary when so many attractive girl dogs are easily found? Certainly their sexual tastes must be at variance. These are silly questions but might have been promising avenues for the plot to explore.

It says something for Robert Downey Jr. that in a movie where a man becomes a dog, Downey creates the weirdest character. With tics and jerks and strange verbal sorties and a tuft of hair that seems electrified, he plays a scientist who is mad on his good days. To put this man on the witness stand is a foolhardy act by Allen and his boss (Danny Glover), but we are grateful to him, because Downey is entertaining. Maybe they have the wrong actor in the lead. Downey, playing the dog, would have run through a repertory of every canine shtick in *Best in Show*. Even in this movie, you should see him fetch.

At the end of the film, Allen (as the dog) is standing on his hind legs (not well, but one is surprised) and hugging his wife when suddenly he turns back into her husband, and what happens then? The hug continues because, yes, this is the happy ending! Ladies, if a dog turned into your husband while you were hugging it, would you scream? Dial 911? Tell him to roll over and play dead? There is an age above which this movie is unnecessary, and it may be in the low double digits. All through *The Shaggy Dog*, I kept remembering a classic headline in the *Onion:* "Millions of dog owners demand to know: Who's a good boy?" That headline doesn't have anything to do with this movie, but what does?

Shall We Dance? ★ ★ ★

PG-13, 106 m., 2004

Richard Gere (John Clark), Jennifer Lopez (Paulina), Susan Sarandon (Beverly), Stanley Tucci (Link), Bobby Cannavale (Chic), Lisa Ann Walter (Bobbie), Anita Gillette (Miss Mitzi), Omar Benson Miller (Vern). Directed by Peter

Chelsom and produced by Simon Fields. Screenplay by Masayuki Suo and Audrey Wells.

Richard Gere plays John Clark, not an unhappy man, in *Shall We Dance?* He loves his wife and daughter, he enjoys his job as a Chicago lawyer, and when his wife (Susan Sarandon) gets that funny look in her eye and asks him if everything is okay, he says sure, of course, everything is fine. But there is something missing.

One night as he is returning home on the L train, he notices a woman standing alone in the window of Miss Mitzi's Dance Studio. There is something intriguing about her solitude, her pensive attitude, and, let it be said, her figure. A few days later, he gets off the train, walks into the studio, and signs up for classes in ballroom dancing.

Is he interested in dancing? No. Is he interested in the woman, named Paulina and played by Jennifer Lopez? Yes. Is she interested in him? No: "I prefer not to socialize with students." What does he think of the others, including the giant-size Vern (Omar Benson Miller), the homophobic Chic (Bobby Cannavale), the would-be bombshell Bobbie (Lisa Ann Walter), the manic dynamo Link (Stanley Tucci), and of course dear Miss Mitzi (Anita Gillette)? Let us say these are not the kinds of people he usually associates with.

But Paulina exudes a true fascination, especially when she personally dances the rumba with him. In talking about dance, she allows herself a freedom and sensuality she denies herself in life. Listen to her: "The rumba is the vertical expression of a horizontal wish. You have to hold her like the skin on her thigh is your reason for living. Let her go like your heart's being ripped from your chest. Throw her back like you're going to have your way with her right here on the dance floor. And then finish, like she's ruined you for life."

And then ask her if it was as good for her as it was for you. *Shall We Dance?* is a reasonably close remake of *Dansu Wo Shimasho Ka,* a 1996 Japanese film that set box-office records at home and won audiences around the world. If you've seen it, you know precisely what happens in the Hollywood version, but the movie is a star vehicle; the plot isn't the point, Gere and Lopez are. When they dance together, it's a reminder that when dancing

became rare from the movies, so did a lot of grace and sexiness.

This is not a cutting-edge movie. The characters are broad, what happens is predictable, and of course everything ends up in a big ballroom dancing competition, and (are you ready for this?) at the crucial moment we get the obligatory scene where the loved one arrives in the audience, sees what is happening, and understands all. I'm averaging two versions of that scene a month; think of *Raise Your Voice.*

Conventional as it may be, *Shall We Dance?* offers genuine delights. The fact that Paulina is uninterested in romance with John comes as sort of a relief, freeing the story to be about something other than the inexorable collision of their genitals. It can be about how John feels about his life, about why it might be useful for a middle-aged lawyer to jump the rails and take up ballroom dance. And about the gallery of supporting characters, who get enough screen time to become engaging.

Stanley Tucci, for example, has fun with Link, who is John Clark's mild-mannered colleague in a Loop law firm. On the dance floor, wearing a flamboyant hairpiece, he becomes a wild man. His dream: "I want to dance before the world in my own name." He fears he would lose his job if he did that, but when John joins the class, he gains courage. He's one of the reasons John stays at Miss Mitzi's even after it becomes clear that Paulina is not available. "Ballroom is all or nothing," Link tells him.

There's one area where the American remake is less than convincing. In the Japanese version, we believe that a faithful wife might remain at home evening after evening while her salaryman husband returned long after work. That's part of the Japanese office culture. That an American wife would put up with it is more problematical. The Clark household, including their teenagers, is not very realistic, but then it exists only as the staging area for the last big scene. I enjoyed the Japanese version so much I invited it to my Overlooked Film Festival a few years ago; it's available on DVD, but this remake offers pleasures of its own.

Shaolin Soccer ★ ★ ★
PG-13, 87 m., 2004

Stephen Chow (Sing), Vicki Zhao (Mui), Man

Tat Ng (Golden Leg Fung), Patrick Tse (Hung), Yut Fei Wong (Iron Head). Directed by Stephen Chow and produced by Kwok-fai Yeung. Screenplay by Chow and Kan-Cheung Tsang.

Shaolin Soccer is like a poster boy for my theory of the star rating system. Every month or so, I get an anguished letter from a reader wanting to know how I could possibly have been so ignorant as to award three stars to, say, *Hidalgo* while dismissing, say, *Dogville* with two stars. This disparity between my approval of kitsch and my rejection of angst reveals me, of course, as a superficial moron who will do anything to suck up to my readers.

What these correspondents do not grasp is that to suck up to *my* demanding readers, I would do better to praise *Dogville*. It takes more nerve to praise pop entertainment; it's easy and safe to deliver pious praise of turgid deep thinking. It's true, I loved *Anaconda* and did not think *The United States of Leland* worked, but does that mean I drool at the keyboard and prefer man-eating snakes to suburban despair?

Not at all. What it means is that the star rating system is relative, not absolute. When you ask a friend if *Hellboy* is any good, you're not asking if it's any good compared to *Mystic River*, you're asking if it's any good compared to *The Punisher*. And my answer would be, on a scale of one to four, if *Superman* (1978) is four, then *Hellboy* is three and *The Punisher* is two. In the same way, if *American Beauty* gets four stars, then *Leland* clocks in at about two.

And that is why *Shaolin Soccer*, a goofy Hong Kong action comedy, gets three stars. It is piffle, yes, but superior piffle. If you are even considering going to see a movie where the players zoom fifty feet into the air and rotate freely in violation of everything Newton held sacred, then you do not want to know if I thought it was as good as *Lost in Translation*.

Shaolin Soccer has become a legend. It's the top-grossing action comedy in Hong Kong history, and was a big hit at Toronto 2002 (although, for some reason, I didn't see it; I must have been sidetracked by *Bowling for Columbine*). Miramax bought it, and shelved it for two years, apparently so Harvey Weinstein could cut it by thirty minutes, get rid of the English dubbing, restore the subtitles, and open it one week after his own *Kill Bill: Vol. 2*.

To put this movie up against Tarantino is like sending Simon Cowell against William H. Rehnquist, but Simon has his fans.

The movie has been directed and cowritten by Stephen Chow, who stars as Sing, a martial arts master turned street cleaner, who uses his skills in everyday life and is in love with Mui (Vicki Zhao), who sells buns from her little street stand and combs her hair forward to conceal a complexion that resembles pizza with sausage and mushrooms. It is a foregone conclusion that by the end of this film Mui will be a startling beauty. Less predictable is that Sing recruits seven soccer players from his former monastery to form a soccer team.

His inspiration to do this is Fung (Man Tat Ng), known as the Golden Leg because he was, years ago, a great soccer hero until his leg was broken by Hung (Patrick Tse). Hung now rules the soccer world as owner of Team Evil (yes, Team Evil), while Fung drags his leg like the Hunchback of Notre Dame. It is another foregone conclusion that Team Evil will meet the Shaolin soccer team formed by Fung and Sing in a thrilling match played before what looks like a vast crowd that has been borrowed from a computer game.

The game doesn't follow any known rules of soccer, except that there is a ball and a goal. As the players swoop high into the air and do acrobatics before kicking the ball, I was reminded more of Quidditch. There is also the matter of ball velocity. The players can kick the ball so hard that it actually catches fire as it rockets through the air, or digs a groove in the ground as it plows toward the goal.

Since the game is impossible and it is obvious Team Evil will lose, there's not much suspense, but there is a lot of loony comedy, a musical number, and the redemption of the Poor Spotted Little Bun Girl. As soccer comedies go, then, I say three stars. It's nowhere near as good as *Bend It Like Beckham* (2002), of course, but *Beckham* is in a different genre, the coming-of-age female-empowerment film. It's important to keep these things straight.

Shark Tale ★ ★
PG, 100 m., 2004

With the voices of: Will Smith (Oscar), Robert De Niro (Don Lino), Renee Zellweger (Angie),

Jack Black (Lenny), Angelina Jolie (Lola), Martin Scorsese (Sykes), Katie Couric (Katie Current), Doug E. Doug (Bernie), Ziggy Marley (Ernie), Michael Imperioli (Frankie). Directed by Bibo Bergeron, Vicky Jenson, and Rob Letterman and produced by Bill Damaschke, Janet Healy, and Allison Lyon Segan. Screenplay by Letterman, Damian Shannon, Mark Swift, and Michael J. Wilson.

Casablanca was only twenty-five years old when I started as a movie critic, but I thought of it as an old movie. *The Godfather,* which supplies most of the inspiration for *Shark Tale,* is thirty-two years old, and *Jaws,* its other inspiration, is twenty-nine years old. Time slips into the future, and movies still fresh in our hearts are considered by younger audiences to be ancient classics.

Since the target audience for *Shark Tale* is presumably kids and younger teenagers, how many of them have seen the R-rated *Godfather* and will get all the inside jokes? Not a few, I suppose, and some of its characters and dialogue have passed into common knowledge. But it's strange that a kid-oriented film would be based on a parody of a 1972 gangster movie for adults. Strange, too, that the movie's values also seem to come from *The Godfather,* a study in situational ethics that preferred good gangsters with old-fashioned values (the Corleone family) to bad gangsters who sold drugs. Sure, it would be better for your kids to grow up to be more like Don Vito than Scarface, but what a choice.

The movie is the latest production of DreamWorks Animation, codirected by Vicky Jenson *(Shrek),* Bibo Bergeron *(The Road to El Dorado),* and Rob Letterman. It takes place on an underwater reef where sharks are the local gangsters, and run things from their headquarters on the hulk of the *Titanic.* Coral formations, undersea debris, and vegetation combine to create an aquatic Times Square, and, as in *Shrek 2,* real retailers have their "'toon" equivalents.

The movie doesn't follow the plot of *The Godfather* so much as recycle its characters, and the *Jaws* inspiration gets an early smile when the famous theme music, scary for people, is as inspiring to sharks as the national anthem. The story's hero is Oscar (voice by Will Smith), who works down at the Whale Wash. It's a mob front, run by Sykes (voice by Martin Scorsese), a puffer fish who has extraordinary eyebrows, for

a fish. Oscar is deep in debt to Sykes, who assigns a couple of Rastafarian enforcers (Ziggy Marley and Doug E. Doug) to take Oscar on a trip and teach him a lesson he'll never forget.

The mob is ruled by Don Lino (voice by Robert De Niro, channeling Marlon Brando), who is a ruthless, but by his own standards, fair shark. His two sons are Frankie (Michael Imperioli), who has grown up to be a shark any dad can be proud of, and Lenny (Jack Black), who has disgraced the family by becoming a vegetarian. Lenny could found a reef chapter of PETA (Predators for the Ethical Treatment of Animals) on the basis of his activist intervention one night at dinner, when he sets a shrimp cocktail free.

Don Lino is fed up with Lenny, and orders Frankie to take the lad on a swimabout and teach him the life lessons of sharkhood. As luck would have it, they cross paths with Oscar and the enforcers, and when a falling ship's anchor kills Frankie, Oscar gets the credit. Since the reef lives in terror of the sharks, this makes him a local hero and creates romantic suspense: Will he remain faithful to his longtime girlfriend, Angie (Renée Zellweger), or be seduced by the charms of the local "finne fatale," Lola (Angelina Jolie)? Reporting on all of this is the local anchorwoman, Katie Current, voiced by Katie Couric.

The problem with this story is that the movie pays too much attention to it, as if we really cared. Most successful animation has a basic level that even small children can easily identify. Little Nemo wanted to escape from the fish tank and return to his father in the ocean. Every kid understood that. But how much will they care in *Shark Tale* that Oscar wants to clear his debt with the loan sharks and become rich and famous? Will they follow the romantic struggle involving the Zellweger and Jolie characters?

The movie lacks a port of entry for young viewers in a character they can identify with. All of the major characters are adults with adult problems like debt, romance, and running (or swimming) away from the mob. In dealing with their concerns, the characters do way too much talking, maybe because the filmmakers were so thrilled to have great voice-over talent.

In earlier days the voice-over dubbers for cartoons were anonymous, unless they were named Mel Blanc. Now they "star" in the movie, so that the posters for *Shark Tale* list De

Niro, Smith, Zellweger, and Jolie in big type at the top, as if we were really going to see them in the movie. To be sure, the fish look a little like their voice talents; I wonder if salaries go up when the voices for animation agree to have their faces and mannerisms borrowed.

There are a lot of funny moments in *Shark Tale*, free-standing gags, clever lines, neat twists, but the movie never comes together into a convincing enterprise. It's so in love with its origins in gangster movies, and has so much fun with the voices of its famous actors, that it never really defines and sells the characters in a way the audience cares about. There's a point when you wish the filmmakers would drop the in-jokes and the subtle Hollywood references and just get on with it. The movie is likely to appeal to movie buffs more than to typical family audiences.

Shaun of the Dead ★ ★ ★

R, 99 m., 2004

Simon Pegg (Shaun), Kate Ashfield (Liz), Nick Frost (Ed), Lucy Davis (Dianne), Dylan Moran (David), Bill Nighy (Phil), Penelope Wilton (Barbara). Directed by Edgar Wright and produced by Nira Park. Screenplay by Simon Pegg and Wright.

As movie characters, zombies are boring by definition: All they can do is shuffle, moan, catch up with much faster people, and chew on their arms. *Shaun of the Dead* shares my sentiments so exactly that during the opening scenes of the movie its hero walks among the undead and doesn't even notice them. He's too hungover and worried that his girlfriend will leave him.

The movie is a new British comedy about clueless layabouts whose lives center on the pub; for them, the zombies represent not a threat to civilization as we know it, but an interference with valuable drinking time. When it becomes clear that London is crawling (or shuffling) with zombies, best buddies Shaun (Simon Pegg) and Ed (Nick Frost) lead a small band of survivors to the obvious stronghold: the Winchester, their local.

The irony is that Shaun's girlfriend, Liz (Kate Ashfield), has been issuing ultimatums, asking Shaun to choose between her and the pub. She lives with Di (Lucy Davis) and David (Dylan

Moran), who think that in a showdown Shaun would choose the pub over his girl; when Shaun urges them to barricade themselves inside the Winchester, David is not encouraging: "Do you think his master plan is going to amount to anything more than sitting and eating peanuts in the dark?" This is not really fair, since Shaun is at least armed: He uses his cricket bat to wham zombies on the head. A cricket bat is to British movies as a baseball bat is to American movies: the weapon of choice for clueless heroes going downstairs to investigate a noise that was inevitably made by somebody packing a lot more than a bat.

Liz, Shaun, and Ed the best friend have a relationship not unlike the characters played by Jennifer Aniston, John C. Reilly, and Tim Blake Nelson in *The Good Girl* (2002). Liz is smart and ambitious and wants to get ahead in the world, but Shaun is happy with his entry-level job in retail and his leisure hours spent with Ed, watching the telly and drinking beer—at the pub, preferably, or at home in a pinch. When Liz complains that Ed is always around, Shaun says, "He doesn't have too many friends," which is often an argument for not becoming one.

Shaun of the Dead, written by Simon Pegg and Edgar Wright and directed by Wright, is a send-up of zombie movies, but in an unexpected way: Instead of focusing on the undead and trying to get the laughs there, it treats the living characters as sitcom regulars whose conflicts and arguments keep getting interrupted by annoying flesh-eaters. In the first two or three scenes, as he crawls out of bed and plods down the street wrapped in the misery of his hangover, Shaun doesn't even notice the zombies. Sure, they're on the TV news, but who watches the news? For Shaun and Ed, the news functions primarily as reassurance that the set will be operating when the football match begins.

The supporting characters include Shaun's stepfather, Phil (Bill Nighy), and mother, Barbara (Penelope Wilton). Nighy is that elongated character actor who looks as if he may have invaded Rhys Ifans's gene pool. He has a quality that generates instinctive sympathy, as in *Love Actually* (2002), where he played the broken-down rock star still hoping patiently in middle age for a comeback. Here there's something endearing about his response when he is bitten by a zombie. It has been clearly established that such bites always lead to death and then rebirth as a zombie.

Once bitten, your doom is sealed. But listen to Phil reassure them, "I ran it under the tap."

Shaun of the Dead has its pleasures, which are mild but real. I like the way the slacker characters maintain their slothful gormlessness in the face of urgent danger, and I like the way the British bourgeois values of Shaun's mum and dad assert themselves even in the face of catastrophe. There is also that stubborn British courage in times of trouble. "We never closed," bragged the big neon sign outside the Windmill strip club in Soho, which stayed open every night during the Blitz. In this movie, the Winchester pub exhibits the same spirit.

Good thing the movie is about more than zombies. I am by now more or less exhausted by the cinematic possibilities of killing them. I've seen thousands of zombies die, and they're awfully easy to kill, unless you get a critical mass that piles on all at once. George Romeo, who invented the modern genre with *Night of the Living Dead* and *Dawn of the Dead*, was essentially devising video-game targets before there were video games: They pop up, one after another, and you shoot them, or bang them on the head with a cricket bat. It's more fun sitting in the dark eating peanuts.

She Hate Me ★ ★ ★

R, 138 m., 2004

Anthony Mackie (Jack Armstrong), Kerry Washington (Fatima Goodrich), Ellen Barkin (Margo Chadwick), Monica Bellucci (Simona Bonasera), Jim Brown (Geronimo Armstrong), Chiwetel Ejiofor (Frank Wills), Brian Dennehy (Bill Church), Woody Harrelson (Leland Powell), John Turturro (Angelo Bonasera). Directed by Spike Lee and produced by Preston L. Holmes, Lee, and Fernando Sulichin. Screenplay by Michael Genet and Lee.

Spike Lee's *She Hate Me* will get some terrible reviews. Scorched-earth reviews. Its logic, style, presumption, and sexual politics will be ridiculed. The Tomatometer will be down around 20. Many of the things you read in those reviews may be true from a conventional point of view. Most of the critics will be on safe ground. I will seem to be wrong. Seeming to be wrong about this movie is one of the most interesting things I've done recently. I've learned from it.

After seeing the movie once, I would have complained that *She Hate Me* contains enough for five movies, but has no idea which of those movies it wants to be. Movie One: the story of a corporate whistle-blower (Anthony Mackie) and an indictment of the corporate culture. Movie Two: The hero inexplicably becomes a stud who is hired to impregnate lesbians at $10,000 a pop. Movie Three: He impregnates a Mafia daughter (Monica Bellucci), and John Turturro turns up as her father to do a Marlon Brando imitation. Movie Four: a free-standing sidebar about Frank Wills (Chiwetel Ejiofor), the Watergate security guard who brought down the Nixon administration, and reaped nothing but personal unhappiness. Movie Five: how a black man steps up to the plate and accepts responsibility for raising his kids, by bonding with his lesbian ex-girlfriend (Kerry Washington) and her lover, who have both borne one of his children.

What do these stories have to do with one another? How can we be expected to believe that not one but eighteen lesbians would pay a man to make them pregnant? And that he could perform with six women in the same night and bring every one of them to a loud and even thrashing climax? That his sperm count would go the distance? That seventeen of them would get pregnant after one encounter? That none of them would be alarmed at being sixth or eighteenth in a row of unprotected sex? And that when the movie shows its hero ready to "be there" for his children, it ignores the question of whether a lesbian couple would need or desire his presence, however noble his intentions?

Oh, I could go on and on. But read some of the other reviews for that. The standard review of this movie is unanswerable, unless you look beneath the surface.

I went to see the movie a second time, because my first response, while immediate and obvious, left me feeling unsatisfied. I knew I could plow into the movie and spare not a single frame, using implacable logic and withering sarcasm. But some seed of subversion in the film made that feel too easy. Whatever its faults, the movie had engaged and fascinated me in its various parts, even if it seemed to have no whole.

Spike Lee is a filmmaker on a short list with directors like Herzog, Sayles, Jarmusch, Altman, Paul Thomas Anderson, Todd Solondz, and the new kid, David Gordon Green. He dances to his own music. He no doubt knows all the objections that can be raised against his film. He knows that structurally it's all over the map. He knows the lesbian story line is logically and emotionally absurd. He knows Frank Wills came in from left field. He knows he begins with a conventional drama about rotten corporations, and then jumps ship. He knows all of that. He teaches film at Harvard, for chrissakes. *So why did he make this movie, this way?*

I could call him up and ask him, but maybe the point is to look at this film, ask myself that question, and avoid the easy answer, which is that he made a preposterous movie because he didn't know any better. He knows better. He could have delivered a safe, politically correct, well-made film without even breathing hard.

But this is the work of a man who wants to dare us to deal with it. Who is confronting generic expectations, conventional wisdom, and political correctness. Whose film may be an attack on the sins it seems to commit. Who is impatient with the tired, rote role of the heroic African-American corporate whistle-blower (he could phone that one in). Who confronts the pious liberal horror about such concepts as the inexhaustible black stud and lesbians who respond on cue to sex with a man—and instead of skewering them, which would be the easy thing to do, flaunts them.

His movie seems to celebrate those forbidden ideas. Why does he do this? Perhaps because to attack those concepts would be simplistic, platitudinous, and predictable. But to work without the safety net, to deliberately be offensive, to refuse to satisfy our generic expectations, to dangle the conventional formula in front of us and then yank it away, to explode the structure of the movie, to allow it to contain anger and sarcasm, impatience, and wild, imprudent excess, to find room for both unapologetic melodramatic romance *and* satire—well, that's audacious. To go where this film goes and still have the nerve to end the way he does (with a reconciliation worthy of soap opera, and the black hero making a noble speech at a congressional hearing) is a form of daring beyond all reason.

My guess is that Lee is attacking African-American male and gay/lesbian stereotypes not by conventionally preaching against them, but by boldly dramatizing them. The inspiration for *She Hate Me* may be his *Bamboozled* (2000), an attack on black stereotypes that was one of his least successful films. Having failed with a frontal assault, he returns to the battle using indirection. By getting mad at the movie, we arrive at the conclusions he intends. In a sense, he is sacrificing himself to get his message across.

Either that, or I have completely misread *She Hate Me*, but I couldn't write the obvious review. I couldn't convince myself I believed it. This film is alive and confrontational and aggressively in our face, and the man who made it has abandoned all caution even to the point of refusing to signal his intentions, to put in a wink to let us see he knows what he's doing.

It is exciting to watch this movie. It is never boring. Lee is like a juggler who starts out with balls and gradually adds baseball bats, top hats, and chainsaws. It's not an intellectual experience, but an emotional one. Spike Lee is like a jazz soloist who cuts loose, leaving behind the song and the group, walking offstage and out of the club, and keeps on improvising right down the street, looking for someone who can keep up with him. True, the movie is not altogether successful. It's so jagged, so passionate in its ambition, it raises more questions than it answers. But isn't that better than the way most films answer more questions than they raise? *She Hate Me* invites anger and analysis about the stereotypes it appears to celebrate; a film that attacked those stereotypes would inspire yawns. Think what you want on a "politically correct" level, but concede that *She Hate Me* is audacious and recklessly risky.

She's the Man ★ ★ ★
PG-13, 105 m., 2006

Amanda Bynes (Viola), Channing Tatum (Duke), Laura Ramsey (Olivia), Vinnie Jones (Coach Dinklage), Robert Hoffman (Justin), Alex Breckenridge (Monique), David Cross (Principal Gold), Julie Hagerty (Daphne), James Kirk (Sebastian). Directed by Andy Fickman and produced by Lauren Shuler Donner, Jack Leslie, and Ewan Leslie. Screenplay by Ewan Leslie, Jack Leslie, Karen McCullah Lutz, and Kirsten Smith, based on *Twelfth Night* by William Shakespeare.

I didn't for one second believe the plot of *She's the Man*, but I did believe for the entire movie that Amanda Bynes was lovable. She plays a girl who pretends to be a boy in order to play soccer. That this story is recycled from Shakespeare's *Twelfth Night* is something I report right here at the top so that we can work together to put it out of our minds.

Bynes plays Viola, the twin sister of Sebastian (James Kirk), who at the start of the movie conveniently sneaks away to London for two weeks without telling anybody. This is much easier on Viola than the Shakespeare version, in which she fears her brother has perished at sea. But I will not mention Shakespeare again. Viola is the star of the girls' soccer team at Cornwall Prep, a school that seems to have enough money to supply every girl with her own soccer team. She thinks she's good enough to play for the boys' team, but her hopes are scorned, so she takes advantage of Sebastian's absence to take his place at nearby Illyria Prep, named after the country in Shakespeare's play. There she tries out for the soccer team.

Can Bynes convincingly play a boy? Of course not. She plays a cute tomboy with short hair who keeps forgetting to talk low and then nervously clears her throat and talks like she's on the phone to the school office: "Viola is sick today, and this is her mother speaking." Can she play soccer and live with a male roommate and take showers and not be exposed as a girl? Of course not, but at least the movie doesn't make a big deal out of it; she has a few close calls, and thinks fast. When the coach (Vinnie Jones) announces a practice game between shirts and skins, she offers compelling reasons why she should be a shirt.

Viola/Sebastian's roommate at Illyria is Duke, no doubt inspired by Duke Orsino in Shakespeare. But enough about Shakespeare. Duke seems attracted to Olivia (Laura Ramsey), but Olivia is attracted to Sebastian/Viola, who gets a crush on Duke because he speaks with such sensitivity about women even when having a private conversation with her, or him. Duke is played by Channing Tatum, who sounds as if he should be the child of Carol Channing and Tatum O'Neal, which in this movie might be possible, although in real life he was born in Cullman, Alabama.

Tatum is twenty-five, a little old to play a high school kid, but Bynes at nineteen is convincing, and her poise, under the circumstances, is extraordinary. The movie develops interlocking romantic triangles and adds some funny supporting characters, including David Cross as the headmaster, whose exuberance is as boundless as his baldness. Her mother, played by Julie Hagerty, dreams of the day when her little girl will come out as a debutante; while being coached as a deb, Viola is advised to "chew like you have a secret." Does she ever.

Of Bynes let us say that she is sunny and plucky and somehow finds a way to play her impossible role without clearing her throat more than six or eight times. More important, we like her. She first won a following with her show on Nickelodeon, and was funny in *Big Fat Liar* (2002), but in this role, as Shakespeare might say, she achieves greatness, or maybe she has it thrust upon her. The movie is good-natured and silly, and at the end there is a big soccer game between Illyria and Cornwall during which both Viola and the real Sebastian are able to offer proof of their genders, although when the PG-13 rating cites "nudity," I am compelled to report that the movie includes none of the naughty bits. As a famous playwright once wrote in *Twelfth Night*, "Wherefore are those things hid?"

Shopgirl ★ ★ ★ ½
R, 116 m., 2005

Steve Martin (Ray Porter), Claire Danes (Mirabelle Butterfield), Jason Schwartzman (Jeremy), Bridgette Wilson-Sampras (Lisa Cramer), Sam Bottoms (Dan Butterfield), Frances Conroy (Catherine Butterfield), Rebecca Pidgeon (Christie Richards), Gina Doctor (Del Rey). Directed by Anand Tucker and produced by Ashok Amritraj, Jon J. Jashni, and Steve Martin. Screenplay by Martin, based on his novella.

One of the things you cannot do in this life is impose conditions on love. Another impossibility is to expect another's heart to accommodate your own desires and needs. You may think that cleverness, power, or money will work on your behalf, but eventually you will end up feeling the way you really feel, and so will the other person, and there is no argument more useless than the one that begins with the words, "But I thought we had an agreement."

Shopgirl is a tender and perceptive film that argues these truths. It is about an older man named Ray Porter, a millionaire, who sees a young woman named Mirabelle Butterfield standing behind the glove counter at Saks and desires her. He goes through the motions of buying some gloves. Perhaps the gray? "I prefer the black," she says, and so he buys the black, and that night on her doorstep she finds the gloves, neatly gift-wrapped and with a note inside: "Will you have dinner with me? Ray Porter."

Now compare the elegance of this approach with the other man who desires her company. This is Jeremy, who is about her age in years but about twelve in knowledge about the ways of women. You do not honk your horn on a first date and expect the woman to hurry out to your car. You do not pretend you want only to people-watch until she agrees to buy her own ticket to the movies. You do not attempt one of those dreadful snuffling blind approaches to a kiss, the kind where the girl doesn't know if you're trying to kiss her or maybe you just got something caught in your throat while staring at her breasts. I've been around a long time and, young men, if there is one thing I know, it is that the only way to kiss a girl for the first time is to look like you want to and intend to, and move in fast enough to seem eager but slow enough to give her a chance to say, "So anyway . . ." and look up as if she's trying to remember your name.

All of these things and more are known to Ray Porter (Steve Martin). Yes, he is thirty-five years older than Mirabelle (Claire Danes), but we're not talking marriage here; we're talking about a relationship based on shared assumptions and friendly sex, plus a lot of Ray Porter's money, which he is spending not to purchase Mirabelle but simply to provide himself with a woman who dresses, dines and travels up to his standards. Watch him get shifty when she suggests he stay at her place one night.

"I made myself perfectly clear," he assures his psychiatrist. He is not seeking marriage. He does not want a long-term commitment. Yes, he wants sex, but Mirabelle is not necessary to satisfy that desire, which is so easily solved by a single man of Ray's age and wealth. Mirabelle is necessary because she is young, smart, enter-

taining, unattached, and there. She is good company. She is a person of character.

Perhaps he shops for her at Saks because anyone working there will understand the finer things and spend a lot of time thinking about the customers who can so easily afford them. He makes the parameters of their relationship perfectly clear, as if he were a surveyor and she a vacant lot. When he says it gives him pleasure to be able to provide her with nice things, it is the truth: He has so much money that cost is irrelevant, and she looks so good wearing that dress, dining in that restaurant, sitting on that airplane.

Mirabelle understands all of these things and accepts them. That's the deal. The Saks job is a dead end, and she wants to work as an artist. She would be wary if Ray came after her with love and sincerity in his eyes. Is she technically a prostitute, since the money all flows in her direction while the sex flows both ways? Not at all. For Ray to spend money is exactly the same thing as for her to receive it. It is of no importance except that it makes their lives together possible.

Now about Jeremy. You know guys who are like him. When he accumulates enough empty pizza boxes, he stacks them up and has himself an end table. Doing the laundry involves sniffing for the most passable T-shirt. He is an artist, too. His art involves stenciling the boxes that amplifiers come in. As his muse, Mirabelle may inspire him to design a new typeface. Shortly after they meet, he conveniently leaves town on an extended road trip with a rock band, which is led by a musician who gets him started on self-help books. He needs a lot of all kinds of help.

No, the movie is not about how Mirabelle realizes that Ray is a phony and Jeremy, for all his faults, is lovable. Ray is not a phony. He really is exactly the man he seems to be, God help him. Jeremy is lovable like a puppy that you are delighted belongs to somebody else. What happens at the end is not tidy like in most romantic comedies, but bittersweet and objective. "I guess I have to choose whether to be miserable now, or miserable later," Mirabelle says. There is an argument to be made for both choices, but when all is said and done she will not be the most miserable person in the movie.

Should I write about the performances, the writing, and the direction? I already have. I just did. That's what you're reading. These are the thoughts they inspired. What thoughts they inspire in you may be entirely otherwise. You may think Ray is a rat, Mirabelle is a victim, and Jeremy cleans up well. If that's what you think, go back and read the first paragraph again, and save yourself some trouble.

Shrek 2 ★ ★ ★
PG, 105 m., 2004

With the voices of: Mike Myers (Shrek), Eddie Murphy (Donkey), Cameron Diaz (Princess Fiona), John Cleese (King Harold), Julie Andrews (Queen Lillian), Jennifer Saunders (Fairy Godmother), Antonio Banderas (Puss-in-Boots), Rupert Everett (Prince Charming), Larry King (The Ugly Stepsister). An animated film directed by Andrew Adamson, Kelly Asbury, and Conrad Vernon and produced by David Lipman, Aron Warner, and John H. Williams. Screenplay by J. David Stem, Joe Stillman, and David N. Weiss, based on the characters by William Steig.

Shrek 2 is bright, lively, and entertaining, but it's no *Shrek*. Maybe it's too much to expect lightning to strike twice. *Shrek* was so original in its animation and such an outpouring of creative imagination that it blindsided us; *Shrek 2* is wonderful in its own way, but more earthbound. It's more fun to see Shrek battle a dragon than to watch him meeting his new in-laws.

Shrek (voiced again by Mike Myers) actually seems teetering on the brink of middle-class respectability in the sequel. There's nothing like a good woman to tame an ogre. His outsider status as the loner in the swamp has changed dramatically through his romance with Princess Fiona (Cameron Diaz), although his table manners could stand improvement when he has dinner with her parents, King Harold (John Cleese) and Queen Lillian (Julie Andrews).

In the first film, as you may remember, Fiona's curse was that she had been taken captive by a dragon, but could be freed if the dragon was slain and she was kissed by the hero who did the deed. Ideally, that would be Prince Charming (Rupert Everett), but in *Shrek 2*, when he finally arrives in the neighborhood he discovers to his intense disappointment that the ogre has already dispatched the dragon and wed the princess—and that Shrek's kiss dramatically transformed Fiona. No longer petite, she is tall and broad and green, and an ogre.

A summons comes from the Kingdom of Far Far Away: Her parents want to meet her new husband. This involves a very long journey by Shrek, Fiona, and Donkey (Eddie Murphy), who insists on coming along. Donkey is the comic high point of the movie, with Murphy's nonstop riffs and inability to guess when he is not welcome. "The trick isn't that he talks," Shrek observed in the first movie. "The trick is to get him to shut up." The kingdom is indeed far, far away, which gives Donkey endless opportunities to ask, "Are we there yet?"

Their arrival at the castle of Fiona's parents provides big laughs; Harold and Lillian are shocked to find that their daughter has not only married an ogre, but also become one. A basket of doves is released to celebrate their arrival, and one of them is so astonished it flies bang into the castle wall, and drops dead at Harold's feet. Eventually the plot leads us into the environs of the Fairy Godmother (Jennifer Saunders), a sinister figure who operates a vast factory manufacturing potions and hexes. Is it possible that her Happily Ever After potion could transform ogres into humans? Not if she can help it; she wants to get rid of Shrek and marry Fiona to Prince Charming, according to her original plan.

The screenplay, by J. David Stem, Joe Stillman, and David N. Weiss, has the same fun *Shrek* did in playing against our expectations. Who would anticipate a fight between the ogre and his bride, with Shrek marching out of the house? What about the arrivals ceremony at the matrimonial ball, with all of the kingdom's celebrities walking down a red carpet while an unmistakable clone of Joan Rivers does the commentary? And there's real sweetness when Shrek and Fiona start smooching.

The movie has several songs, none of which I found very memorable, although of course I am the same person who said the Simon and Garfunkel songs in *The Graduate* were "instantly forgettable." The first song, "Accidentally in Love," explains how Shrek and Fiona fell for each other. It's cut like a music video, which is okay, but I think it comes too early in the film, before we really feel at home with the narrative.

A few minor characters from the first film, like the Gingerbread Man and the Three Blind Mice, return for the sequel, and there's a new major character: Puss-in-Boots, a cat who seems to have been raised on Charles Boyer movies, and is voiced by Antonio Banderas. Donkey and Puss build an enormous mutual resentment, because each one thinks he's the star.

Sequels have their work cut out for them. Some people think *Godfather, Part II* is better than *The Godfather*, but the first film loomed so tall in my mind that I gave "Part II" only three stars. In the same way, perhaps I would have liked *Shrek 2* more if the first film had never existed. But I'll never know. Still, *Shrek 2* is a jolly story, and Shrek himself seems durable enough to inspire *Shrek 3* with no trouble at all. Maybe it will be *Shrek Meets Cheaper by the Dozen*.

Sideways ★ ★ ★ ★
R, 124 m., 2004

Paul Giamatti (Miles Raymond), Thomas Haden Church (Jack Lopate), Virginia Madsen (Maya), Sandra Oh (Stephanie). Directed by Alexander Payne and produced by Michael London. Screenplay by Payne and Jim Taylor, based on the novel by Rex Pickett.

"There was a tasting last night," Miles Raymond explains, on one of those alcoholic mornings that begin in the afternoon and strain eagerly toward the first drink. That's why he's a little shaky. He's not an alcoholic, you understand; he's an oenophile, which means he can continue to pronounce French wines long after most people would be unconscious. We realize he doesn't set the bar too high when he praises one vintage as "quaffable." No wonder his unpublished novel is titled *The Day After Yesterday*; for anyone who drinks a lot, that's what today always feels like.

Miles is the hero of Alexander Payne's *Sideways*, which is as lovable a movie as *Fargo*, although in a completely different way. He's an English teacher in middle school whose marriage has failed, whose novel seems in the process of failing, whose mother apparently understands that when he visits her, it is because he

loves her, and also because he needs to steal some of her money. Miles is not perfect, but the way Paul Giamatti plays him, we forgive him his trespasses, because he trespasses most of all against himself.

Miles's friend Jack is getting married in a week. They would seem to have little in common. Jack is a big, blond, jovial man at the peak of fleshy middle-aged handsomeness, and Miles looks like—well, if you know who Harvey Pekar is, that's who Giamatti played in his previous movie. But Jack and Miles have been friends since they were college roommates, and their friendship endures because together they add up to a relatively complete person.

Miles, as the best man, wants to take Jack on a week-long bachelor party in the California wine country, which makes perfect sense, because whatever an alcoholic says he is planning, at the basic level he is planning his drinking. Jack's addiction is to women. "My best man gift to you," he tells Miles, "will be to get you laid." Miles is so manifestly not layable that for him this would be less like a gift than an exercise program.

Jack (Thomas Haden Church) is a not very successful actor; he tells people they may have heard his voice-over work in TV commercials, but it turns out he's the guy who rattles off the warnings about side effects and interest rates in the last five seconds. The two men set off for wine country, and what happens during the next seven days adds up to the best human comedy of the year—comedy, because it is funny, and human, because it is surprisingly moving.

Of course they meet two women. Maya (Virginia Madsen) is a waitress at a restaurant where Miles has often stopped in the past, to yearn but not touch. She's getting her graduate degree in horticulture, and is beautiful, in a kind way; you wonder why she would be attracted to Miles until you find out she was once married to a philosophy professor at Santa Barbara, which can send a woman down-market in search of relief. The next day they meet Stephanie (Sandra Oh), a pour girl at a winery tasting room, and when it appears that the two women know each other, Jack seals the deal with a double date, swearing Miles to silence about the approaching marriage.

Miles has much to be silent about. He has

been in various forms of depression for years, and no wonder, since alcohol is a depressant. He is still in love with his former wife, and mourns the bliss that could have been his, if he had not tasted his way out of the marriage. Although his days include learned discourses about vintages, they end with him drunk, and he has a way of telephoning the poor women late at night. "Did you drink and dial?" Jack asks him.

The movie was written by Payne and Jim Taylor, from the novel by Rex Pickett. One of its lovely qualities is that all four characters are necessary. The women are not plot conveniences, but elements in a complex romantic and even therapeutic process. Miles loves Maya and has for years, but cannot bring himself to make a move because romance requires precision and tact late at night, not Miles's peak time of day. Jack lusts after Stephanie, and casually, even cruelly, fakes love for her even as he cheats on his fiancée.

What happens between them all is the stuff of the movie, and must not be revealed here, except to observe that Giamatti and Madsen have a scene that involves some of the gentlest and most heartbreaking dialogue I've heard in a long time. They're talking about wine. He describes for her the qualities of the Pinot Noir grape that most attract him, and as he mentions its thin skin, its vulnerability, its dislike for being too hot or cold, too wet or dry, she realizes he is describing himself, and that is when she falls in love with him. Women can actually love us for ourselves, bless their hearts, even when we can't love ourselves. She waits until he is finished, and then responds with words so simple and true they will win her an Oscar nomination, if there is justice in the world. *[They did.]*

Terrible misunderstandings (and even worse understandings) take place, tragedy grows confused with slapstick, and why Miles finds himself creeping through the house of a fat waitress and her alarming husband would be completely implausible if we had not seen it coming every step of the way. Happiness is distributed where needed and withheld where deserved, and at the end of the movie we feel like seeing it again.

Alexander Payne has made four wonderful movies: *Citizen Ruth, Election,* the Jack Nicholson tragicomedy *About Schmidt,* and now this. He finds plots that service his characters, instead of limiting them. The characters are played not by the first actors you would think of casting, but by actors who will prevent you from ever being able to imagine anyone else in their roles.

Silent Hill ★ ½
R, 125 m., 2006

Radha Mitchell (Rose DaSilva), Sean Bean (Chris DaSilva), Laurie Holden (Cybil Bennett), Deborah Kara Unger (Dahlia Gillespie), Kim Coates (Officer Gucci), Tanya Allen (Anna), Alice Krige (Christabella), Jodell Ferland (Sharon DaSilva). Directed by Christophe Gans and produced by Don Carmody and Samuel Hadida. Screenplay by Roger Avary.

I had a nice conversation with seven or eight people coming down on the escalator after we all saw *Silent Hill.* They wanted me to explain it to them. I said I didn't have a clue. They said, "You're supposed to be a movie critic, aren't you?" I said, "Supposed to be. But we work mostly with movies." "Yeah," said the girl in the Harley T-shirt. "I guess this was like a video game that you, like, had to play in order to, like, understand the movie."

I guess. I was out in Boulder, Colorado, last week on a panel about video games and whether they can be art, and a lot of the students said they were really looking forward to *Silent Hill* because it's one of the best games, and they read on the Internet that the movie was supposed to live up to the game. That was all speculation, of course, because Sony Pictures declined to preview the film for anybody, perhaps because they were concerned it would not live up to the game, or because they were afraid it would. When I told one student that the movie was not being previewed, there was real pain on his face, as if he had personally been devalued.

Not only can I not describe the plot of this movie, but I have a feeling the last scene reverses half of what I thought I knew (or didn't know). What I can say is that it's an incredibly good-looking film. The director, Christophe Gans, uses graphics and special effects and computers and grainy, scratchy film stock and surrealistic images, and makes *Silent Hill* look more like an experimental art film than a horror film—except for the horror, of course. The visuals are terrific; credit also to cinematographer Dan Laustsen, production designer Carol Spier, and the art, set, and costume artists. But what are we to make of dialogue such as I will now describe?

A group of undead citizens of the ghost town of Silent Hill have gathered for some witch-burning. The town was abandoned thirty years ago because of the fumes from mine fires, which still smolder beneath the surface. Gray ash falls like rain. "Something terrible happened here," a character says perceptively. The townspeople pile wood on a bonfire in the center of an abandoned church and tie an alleged witch to a ladder, which is then lowered over the flames until the victim's skin gets extra crispy. Next up: little Sharon (Jodell Ferland), the daughter of the heroine, Rose (Radha Mitchell). She is tied to the ladder and prepared to be lowered and roasted, when her mother bursts into the church and cries out, and I quote, "It's okay, baby. Everything's gonna be okay!"

The people who live in Silent Hill are dead, I guess. Some of them glow like old embers on a fire, which is not a sign of life. They live in abandoned buildings and in the mines and in a Smoke and Flame Factory, which you will recall from my Little Movie Glossary is a factorylike location of uncertain purpose that generates a lot of smoke and flames. Also sharing their space are ratlike little CGI insects, who scurry around thinking they look a lot scarier than they do.

Rose has come here with her daughter, Sharon, because the girl has taken to sleepwalking at night and standing on the edge of high cliffs while saying Silent Hill in her sleep. Obviously the correct treatment is to take her to the abandoned town itself. Rose and Sharon race off in the night, pursued by Rose's husband (Sean Bean) and a motorcycle cop (Laurie Holden) who is dressed like a leather mistress. The usual zombielike little girl turns up in the headlights, there is a crash, and then everybody wanders through the town for two hours while the art direction looks great. I especially liked the snake-like wires at the end that held people suspended in midair. I also liked it when Johnny Cash sang "Ring of Fire" on the sound track, since if there was ever a movie in need of a song about a ring of fire, this is that film.

Now here's a funny thing. Although I did not understand the story, I would have appreciated a great deal less explanation. All through the movie, characters are pausing to offer arcane backstories and historical perspectives and metaphysical insights and occult orientations. They talk and talk, and somehow their words do not light up any synapses in my brain, if my brain has synapses and they're supposed to light up, and if it doesn't and they're not, then they still don't make any sense.

Perhaps those who have played the game will understand the movie and enjoy it. Speaking of synapses, another member of that panel discussion at Boulder was Dr. Leonard Shlain, chairman of laparoscopic surgery at California Pacific Medical Center and an author whose book *Art & Physics: Parallel Visions in Space, Time and Light* makes you think that if anyone could understand *Silent Hill*, he could.

Dr. Shlain made the most interesting comment on the panel. He said they took some four- and five-year-olds and gave them video games and asked them to figure out how to play them without instructions. Then they watched the children's brain activity with real-time monitors. "At first, when they were figuring out the games," he said, "the whole brain lit up. But by the time they knew how to play the games, the brain went dark, except for one little point." Walking out after *Silent Hill*, I thought of that lonely pilot light, and I understood why I failed to understand the movie. My damn brain lit up too much.

Silver City ★ ★ ★ ½
R, 129 m., 2004

Chris Cooper (Dickie Pilager), Danny Huston (Danny O'Brien), Maria Bello (Nora Allardyce). Thora Birch (Karen Cross), Richard Dreyfuss (Chuck Raven), Miguel Ferrer (Cliff Castleton), Daryl Hannah (Madeleine Pilager), Kris Kristofferson (Wes Benteen), Mary Kay Place (Grace Seymour), Michael Murphy (Senator Judd Pilager), Billy Zane (Chandler Tyson). Directed by John Sayles and produced by Maggie Renzi. Screenplay by Sayles.

John Sayles's *Silver City* can be read as social satire aimed at George W. Bush—certainly the film's hero mirrors the Bush quasi-speaking style—but it takes wider aim on the entire political landscape we inhabit. Liberals and conservatives, the alternative press and establishment dailies, environmentalists, and despoilers are all mixed up in a plot where it seems appropriate that the hero is a private detective. Even the good guys are compromised.

Sayles, like Robert Altman, is a master at the tricky art of assembling large casts and keeping all the characters alive. Here, as in his *City of Hope* (1991), he shows how lives can be unexpectedly connected, how hidden agendas can slip in under the radar, how information can travel and wound or kill.

The movie centers on the campaign of Dickie Pilager (Chris Cooper), who is running for governor of Colorado with the backing of his father (Michael Murphy), the state's senior senator. Dickie is the creature of industrial interests who want to roll back pollution controls and penalties, but as the movie opens he's dressed like an L.L. Bean model as he stands in front of a lake and repeats, or tries to repeat, platitudes about the environment. Cooper deliberately makes him sound as much like George II as possible.

The younger Pilager may be clueless, but he's not powerless. His campaign is being managed by a Karl Rove type named Chuck Raven (Richard Dreyfuss), who tells him what to say and how to say it. There's not always time to explain why to say it. Surrounding the campaign, at various degrees of separation, other characters develop interlocking subplots.

The most important involves the discovery of a dead body in a lake, and the attempts of private eye Danny O'Brien (Danny Huston) to investigate the case. O'Brien is in the tradition of Elliott Gould in Altman's *The Long Goodbye;* he's an untidy, shambling, seemingly distracted, superficially charming loser who often seems to be talking beside the point, instead of on it.

Maria Bello plays Nora Allardyce, a local journalist who used to be involved with Danny. She sniffs a connection between the body and politics. Once she was a fearless reporter for a fearless newspaper, but a conglomerate swallowed up the paper and taught it fear, and now she is an outsider. She's currently engaged to a lobbyist (Billy Zane), who knows where all the bodies are buried and swells with his pleasure in this knowledge. Other important characters include Kris Kristofferson as a millionaire mine owner and polluter, who is funding Pilager's campaign and is one of those gravel-voiced cynics who delight in shocking people with their disdain for conventional wisdom.

The best of the supporting characters is Madeleine Pilager, Dickie's renegade sister, played by Daryl Hannah with audacious boldness. She likes to shock, she likes to upset people, she detests Dickie, and she provides an unexpected connection between the private eye and the campaign manager. Those connections beneath the surface, between people whose lives in theory should not cross, is the organizing principle of Sayles's screenplay; one of the reasons his film is more sad than indignant is that it recognizes how people may be ideologically opposed and yet share unworthy common interests.

Sayles's wisdom of linking a murder mystery to a political satire seems questionable at first, until we see how Sayles uses it, and why. One of his strengths as a writer-director is his willingness to allow uncertainties into his plots. A Sayles movie is not a well-oiled machine rolling inexorably toward its conclusion, but a series of dashes in various directions, as if the plot is trying to find a way to escape a preordained conclusion. There's a dialogue scene near the end of *Silver City* that's a brilliant demonstration of the way he can deflate idealism with weary reality. Without revealing too much about it, I can say that it involves acknowledging that not all problems have a solution, not all wrongs are righted, and sometimes you find an answer and realize it doesn't really answer anything. To solve a small puzzle is not encouraging in a world created to generate larger puzzles.

It's a good question whether movies like this have any real political influence. Certainly Sayles is a lifelong liberal, and so is his cinematographer, the great Haskell Wexler. (So are Murphy and Dreyfuss, for that matter.) They create a character who is obviously intended to be George W. Bush. How do we know that? Because Dickie Pilager speaks in short, simplistic sound bites, uses platitudes to conceal his real objectives, and has verbal vertigo. Now, then: Am I attacking the president with that previous sentence, or only describing him? Perhaps to describe George W.'s speaking style in that way is not particularly damaging, because America is familiar with the way he talks, and about half of us are comfortable with it.

That's why *Silver City* may not change any votes. There is nothing in the movie's portrait of Pilager/Bush that has not already been absorbed and discounted by the electorate. Everybody knows that Bush expresses noble thoughts about the environment while his administration labors to license more pollution and less conservation. We know Bush's sponsors include the giant energy companies, and that Enron and Ken Lay were his major contributors before Lay's fall from grace. So when Dickie Pilager is revealed as the creature of antienvironment conglomerates, it comes as old news.

The movie's strength, then, is not in its outrage, but in its cynicism and resignation. There is something honest and a little brave about the way Sayles refuses to provide closure at the end of his movie. Virtue is not rewarded, crime is not punished, morality lies outside the rules of the game, and because the system is rotten no one who plays in it can be entirely untouched. Some characters are better than others, some are not positively bad, but their options are limited and their will is fading. Thackeray described *Vanity Fair* as "a novel without a hero." Sayles has made this film in the same spirit—so much so, that I'm reminded of the title of another Victorian novel, *The Way We Live Now*.

Since Otar Left ★ ★ ★
NO MPAA RATING, 102 m., 2004

Esther Gorintin (Eka [Grandmother]), Nino Khomassouridze (Marina [Daughter]), Dinara Droukarova (Ada [Granddaughter]), Temour Kalandadze (Tenguiz), Roussoudan Bolkvadze (Roussiko), Sacha Sarichvili (Alexo), Dputa Skhirtladze (Niko). Directed by Julie Bertuccelli and produced by Yael Fogiel. Screenplay by Bertuccelli, Bernard Renucci, and Roger Bohbot.

Since Otar Left tells a story of conventional melodrama and makes it extraordinary because of the acting. The characters are so deeply known, so intensely observed, so immediately alive to us, that the story primarily becomes the occasion for us to meet them. Nothing at the plot level engaged me much, not even the ending, which is supposed to be so touching. But I was touched deeply, again and again, simply by watching these people live their lives.

Three women live in a book-lined flat in Tbilisi, the capital of the one-time Soviet republic of Georgia. Eka is the grandmother, very old, very determined (she is played by Esther Gorintin, who was eighty-five when she began her acting career five years ago). Marina (Nino Khomassouridze) is her daughter, around fifty, a woman of quick peremptory dismissals and sudden rushes of feeling. Ada (Dinara Droukarova), late twenties, is Marina's daughter, a student of literature, bored with her life.

We gather that Eka was French, moved to Georgia with her Soviet husband, was a committed Communist. She still thinks Stalin was a great man. Marina says he was a murderer. Ada looks incredulous that they are still having this argument. The cramped quarters are made into an arena when Eka turns up her television, and both Marina and Ada crank up their CD players.

But look at the way these actresses move. Every step, every gesture, suggests long familiarity with these lives. A visit to the post office observes the body language of people long buried in their jobs. The way that Marina discards her fork as the three women have tea says everything about her impatience. The women use verbal and physical shorthand to illuminate what goes without saying. Eka is always certain of herself. Marina is never satisfied ("I wish I loved you," she says to her patient man friend). Ada is fed up and trapped.

The crowded flat is dominated by the person who isn't there—Otar, Eka's son, who has moved to Paris to look for work. He telephones, but the lines fail. He sends money, but the postal service is uncertain. Things worked better in Stalin's day, Eka is certain. When news comes that Otar has been killed in an accident, Marina decides they will not tell old Eka, to spare her. This leads to a deception, the details of which are familiar from similar films.

What is not familiar, what becomes increasingly fascinating, is the direct and relentless way Eka marches toward the truth. She determines to go to Paris to visit her son, takes along the other two, finds them missing from their hotel room, and mutters "Those two are leading me on."

What is clear is that this old woman has a life and will of her own. There is a wonderful scene while she is still at home in Georgia. She leaves the house alone, looks up some information in the library, buys two cigarettes, and smokes them while riding on a Ferris wheel. With a lesser actor or character, this would be a day out for a lovable granny. With Esther Gorintin playing Eka, it is the day of a woman who thinks she has it coming to her.

What happens, and how, need not concern us. What I remember is the way Julie Bertuccelli, the director and cowriter, sees right into the beings of her characters. Consider two scenes in which the old woman gets a foot massage. In one, her granddaughter absently massages her foot while reading aloud from Proust. In the other, her daughter, usually so wounded and stern, giggles helplessly while tickling her feet, and old Eka laughs and squirms like a child. After seeing this movie, you watch another one with less gifted actors, and the characters seem to have met each other for the first time on the set, earlier that day.

Sin City ★ ★ ★ ★
R, 126 m., 2005

Bruce Willis (Hartigan), Jessica Alba (Nancy), Rosario Dawson (Gail), Benicio Del Toro (Jackie Boy), Clive Owen (Dwight), Mickey Rourke (Marv), Brittany Murphy (Shellie), Nick Stahl (Yellow Bastard), Alexis Bledel (Becky), Devon Aoki (Miho), Jaime King (Goldie), Frank Miller (Priest), Powers Boothe (Senator Roark), Michael Clarke Duncan (Manute), Carla Gugino (Lucille). Directed by Robert Rodriguez, Frank Miller, and Quentin Tarantino and produced by Elizabeth Avellan, Miller, and Rodriguez. Screenplay by Rodriguez and Miller.

If *film noir* was not a genre but a hard man on mean streets with a lost lovely in his heart and a gat in his gut, his nightmares would look like *Sin City*. The new movie by Robert Rodriguez and Frank Miller plays like a convention at the movie museum in Quentin Tarantino's subconscious. A-list action stars rub shoulders with snaky villains and sexy wenches in a city where the streets are always wet, the cars are ragtops, and everybody smokes. It's a black-and-white world, except for blood that is red, eyes that are green, hair that is blond, and the Yellow Bastard.

This isn't an adaptation of a comic book; it's like a comic book brought to life and pumped with steroids. It contains characters who occupy stories, but to describe the characters and summarize the stories would be like replacing the weather with a weather map.

The movie is not about narrative but about style. It internalizes the harsh world of the Frank Miller *Sin City* comic books and processes it through computer effects, grotesque makeup, lurid costumes, and dialogue that chops at the language of *noir*. The actors are mined for the archetypes they contain; Bruce Willis, Mickey Rourke, Jessica Alba, Rosario Dawson, Benicio Del Toro, Clive Owen, and the others are rotated into a hyperdimension. We get not so much their presence as their essence; the movie is not about what the characters say or what they do, but about who they are in our wildest dreams.

On the movie's Website there's a slide show juxtaposing the original drawings of Frank Miller with the actors playing the characters, and then with the actors transported by effects into the visual world of graphic novels. Some of the stills from the film look so much like frames of the comic book as to make no difference. And there's a narration that plays like the captions at the top of the frame, setting the stage and expressing a stark, existential world view.

Rodriguez has been aiming toward *Sin City* for years. I remember him leaping out of his chair and bouncing around a hotel room, pantomiming himself filming *Spy Kids 2* with a digital camera and editing it on a computer. The future! he told me. This is the future! You don't wait six hours for a scene to be lighted. You want a light over here, you grab a light and put it over here. You want a nuclear submarine, you make one out of thin air and put your characters into it.

I held back, wondering if perhaps the spy kids would have been better served if the films had not been such a manic demonstration of his method. But never mind; the first two *Spy Kids* were exuberant fun (*Spy Kids 3-D* sucked, in great part because of the 3-D). Then came his *Once Upon a Time in Mexico* (2003), and I wrote it was "more interested in the moment, in great shots, in surprises and ironic reversals and close-ups of sweaty faces, than in a coherent story." Yes, but it worked.

And now Rodriguez has found narrative discipline in the last place you might expect, by choosing to follow the Miller comic books almost literally. A graphic artist has no time or room for drifting. Every frame contributes, and the story marches from page to page in vivid action snapshots. *Sin City* could easily have looked as good as it does and still been a mess, if it were not for the energy of Miller's storytelling, which is not the standard chronological account of events, but more like a tabloid murder illuminated by flashbulbs.

The movie is based on three of the *Sin City* stories, each more or less self-contained. That's wise, because at this velocity a two-hour, one-story narrative would begin to pant before it got to the finish line. One story involves Bruce Willis as a battered old cop at war with a pedophile (Nick Stahl). One has Mickey Rourke waking up next to a dead hooker (Jaime King). One has a good guy (Clive Owen) and a wacko cop (Benicio Del Toro) disturbing the delicate balance of power negotiated between the police and the leader of the city's hookers (Rosario Dawson), who despite her profession moonlights as Owen's lover. Underneath everything is a deeper layer of corruption, involving a senator (Powers Boothe), whose son is not only the pedophile but also the Yellow Bastard.

We know the Bastard is yellow because the movie paints him yellow, just as the comic book did; it was a masterstroke for Miller to find a compromise between the cost of full-color reproduction and the economy of two-color pages; red, green, and blue also make their way into the frames. Actually, I can't even assume Miller went the two-color route for purposes of economy, because it's an effective artistic decision.

There are other vivid characters in the movie, which does not have leads so much as actors who dominate the foreground and then move on. In a movie that uses nudity as if the 1970s had survived, Rosario Dawson's stripper is a fierce dominatrix, Carla Gugino shows more skin than she could in Maxim, and Devon Aoki employs a flying guillotine that was borrowed no doubt from a circa-1970 Hong Kong exploiter.

Rodriguez codirected, photographed, and edited the movie, collaborated on the music and screenplay, and is coproducer. Frank Miller and Quentin Tarantino are credited as codirectors, Miller because his comic books essentially act as storyboards, which Rodriguez follows with ferocity, Tarantino because he directed one brief scene on a day when Rodriquez was determined to wean him away from celluloid and lure him over to the dark side of digital. (It's the scene in the car with Clive Owen and Del Toro, who has a pistol stuck in his head.) Tarantino also contributed something to the culture of the film, which follows his influential *Pulp Fiction* in its recycling of pop archetypes and its circu-

lar story structure. The language of the film, both dialogue and narration, owes much to the hard-boiled pulp novelists of the 1950s.

Which brings us, finally, to the question of the movie's period. Skylines suggest the movie is set today. The cars range from the late 1930s to the 1950s. The costumes are from the trench coat and g-string era. I don't think *Sin City* really has a period, because it doesn't really tell a story set in time and space. It's a visualization of the pulp *noir* imagination, uncompromising and extreme. Yes, and brilliant.

Sir! No Sir! ★ ★ ★
NO MPAA RATING, 85 m., 2006

Narrated by Troy Garity and featuring Edward Asner, Jane Fonda, Donald Sutherland, Terry Whitmore, Donald Duncan, Howard Levy, Oliver Hirsch, Susan Schnall, Randy Rowland, Louis Font, Dave Cline, Bill Short, Dave Blalock, Greg Payton, Darnell Summers, Michael Wong, Terry Whitmore, Joe Bangert, Richard Boyle, Jerry Lembcke, Terry Iverson, Tom Bernard, and Keith Mather. A documentary written and directed by David Zeiger and produced by Evangeline Griego, Aaron Zarrow, and Zeiger.

Quick question: When Jane Fonda was on her "FTA" concert tour during the Vietnam era, who was in her audience? The quick answer from most people probably would be "antiwar hippies, left-wingers, and draft-dodgers." The correct answer would be: American troops on active duty, many of them in uniform.

Sir! No Sir! is a documentary about an almost-forgotten fact of the Vietnam era: Antiwar sentiment among U.S. troops grew into a problem for the Pentagon. The film claims bombing was used toward the end of the war because the military leadership wondered, frankly, if some of their ground troops would obey orders to attack. It's also said there were a few Air Force B-52 crews that refused to bomb North Vietnam. And in San Diego, sailors on an aircraft carrier tried to promote a local vote on whether their ship should be allowed to sail for Vietnam. One of the disenchanted veterans, although he is never mentioned in the film, was John Kerry, who first was decorated for valor and later became a leader of Vietnam Veterans Against the War and testified before Congress.

After the turning point of the Tet offensive in 1968, troop morale ebbed lower, the war seemed lost, and a protest movement encompassed active duty troops, coffeehouses near bases in America, underground GI newspapers, and a modern "underground railway" that helped soldiers desert and move to Canada. According to Pentagon figures, there were some 500,000 desertions during the Vietnam years.

The film has been written and directed by David Zeiger, who worked in an antiwar coffeehouse near Fort Hood, Texas. In a narration spoken by Troy Garity, the son of Fonda and Tom Hayden, his film says, "The memory has been changed." The GI antiwar movement has disappeared from common knowledge, and a famous factoid from the period claims returning wounded veterans were spit on by "hippies" as they landed at American airports. According to the film, that is an urban legend, publicized in the film *Rambo II: First Blood.*

When we reviewed *Sir! No Sir!* on *Ebert & Roeper,* we cited the film's questions about the spitting story. There is a book on the subject, *The Spitting Image* by Jerry Lembcke, whose research failed to find a single documented instance of such an event occurring in real life. I received many e-mails, however, from those who claimed knowledge of such incidents. The story persists, and true or false it is part of a general eagerness to blame our loss in Vietnam on domestic protesters while ignoring the substantial antiwar sentiment among troops in the field.

Parallels with the war in Iraq are obvious. One big difference is that the Vietnam-era forces largely were supplied by the draft, while our Iraq troops are either career soldiers or National Guard troops, some of them on their second or third tour of duty. The Vietnam-era draft not only generated antiwar sentiment among those of draft age but also supplied the army with soldiers who did not go very cheerfully into uniform. The willingness of today's National Guardsmen to continue in combat is courageous and admirable but cannot be expected to last indefinitely, and the political cost of returning to the draft system would be incalculable.

A group of recent documentaries has highlighted a conflict between information and "disinformation," that Orwellian term for attempts to rewrite history. The archetype of "Hanoi Jane" has been used to obscure the fact that Fonda appeared before about sixty thousand GIs who apparently agreed with her. The Swift Boat Veterans incredibly tried to deny John Kerry's patriotism. The global warming documentary *An Inconvenient Truth* is being attacked by a TV ad campaign, underwritten by energy companies, which extols the benefits of carbon dioxide.

No doubt *Sir! No Sir!* will inspire impassioned rebuttals. No doubt it is not an impartial film, not with Fonda's son as its narrator. What cannot be denied is the newsreel footage of uniformed troops in antiwar protests, of Fonda's uniformed audiences at "FTA" concerts, of headlines citing Pentagon concern about troop morale, the "fragging" of officers, the breakdown of discipline, and the unwillingness of increasing numbers of soldiers to fight a war they had started to believe was wrong.

The Sisterhood of the Traveling Pants ★ ★ ★

PG, 119 m., 2005

Amber Tamblyn (Tibby), Alexis Bledel (Lena), America Ferrera (Carmen), Blake Lively (Bridget), Jenna Boyd (Bailey), Bradley Whitford (Al), Nancy Travis (Lydia Rodman), Rachel Ticotin (Carmen's Mother). Directed by Ken Kwapis and produced by Debra Martin Chase, Denise Di Novi, Broderick Johnson, and Andrew A. Kosove. Screenplay by Delia Ephron and Elizabeth Chandler, based on the novel by Ann Brashares.

Four teenage girls in a clothing store, trying on things, kidding around, giggling. Girls of four different sizes and shapes. What makes them all want to try on the same pair of preowned jeans? And why are the jeans a perfect fit all four times? It's the summer before the girls begin their senior year in high school, and all four have big summer plans. Because the jeans magically fit them all, and perhaps because they all saw *Divine Secrets of the Ya-Ya Sisterhood,* they come up with a plan: Each girl will wear the jeans for a week and then FedEx them to the next on the list.

Along with the solemn vow to forward the jeans on schedule comes a list of rules that must not be violated, of which the most crucial is that the girls must never let anyone else remove the jeans from their bodies. There is, however, a loophole: They can take them off themselves. Here we have a premise that could easily inspire a teenage comedy of comprehensive badness, but *The Sisterhood of the Traveling Pants* is always sweet and sometimes surprisingly touching, as the jeans accompany each girl on a key step of her journey to adulthood.

The movie, like *Mystic Pizza* (1988), assembles a group of talented young actresses who have already done good work separately and now participate in a kind of showcase. America Ferrera (whose *Real Women Have Curves* remains one of the best recent coming-of-age films) plays Carmen, who lives with her Puerto Rican mother and is thrilled to be spending the summer with her absentee non–Puerto Rican father. Alexis Bledel, who struck entirely different notes in *Sin City,* is Lena, off to visit her grandparents and other relatives on a Greek island. Blake Lively plays Bridget, who attends a soccer camp in Mexico and falls in love with one of the hunky young counselors. And Amber Tamblyn (of *Joan of Arcadia*) is Tibby, the one with the sardonic angle on life, who wants to be a filmmaker and takes a low-paying job for the summer at a suburban megastore where she plans to shoot a video documentary about life and work.

The stories of the four girls comes, I learn, from a novel by Ann Brashares, who has written two more in the series. The usefulness of her four-story structure is that none of the stories overstays its welcome, and the four girls aren't trapped in the same dumb suburban teenage romantic plot. They live, and they learn.

Carmen has idealized her father, Al (Bradley Whitford), even though he dumped her mother (Rachel Ticotin) years earlier. She values her Puerto Rican roots and discovers, with a shock, that her dad is planning marriage with a WASP named Lydia (Nancy Travis), who comes equipped with children and a suburban home that her father seems to desire as much as his new bride. Is he ashamed of his golden-skinned daughter whose jeans show off a healthy and rounded but technically overweight body?

Tibby has perhaps been watching IFC too much, and possibly envisions herself at Sundance as she heads off to the Wal-Mart clone with her video camera. She gets a young assistant named Bailey (Jenna Boyd), who is a good soul, open and warmhearted, and with a secret that Tibby discovers one day when Bailey passes out right there on the floor of a store corridor. Tibby's tendency was to look at everything through a lens, objectively; Bailey removes the lens cap on her heart.

In Greece, Lena finds her family living a salt-of-the-earth existence in what are surely outtakes from a tourism commercial. If there really is an island this sun-drenched, with a village this filled with white stucco and deep shade, populated by people who are this jolly and loving and throw a feast on a moment's notice, then I don't know why I'm not there instead of here. Lena's Greek relatives are, however, extremely protective of her chastity, which may exist primarily in their dreams, and she gets a crush on a local teen god.

Meanwhile, in Mexico, Bridget and the counselor know they are violating unbreakable rules by even spending private time together, but Bridget sets her sights on the guy and stages a campaign of attraction and seduction that is more or less irresistible.

The role played by the jeans in all of these stories is, it must be said, more as a witness than as a participant, sometimes from a vantage point draped over a chair near to a bed. But no, the PG-rated movie isn't overloaded with sex, and its values are in the right place. The message for its primary audience of teenage girls is that to some degree they choose their own destinies and write their own stories, and while boys may be an unexplored country, they are not necessarily a hostile one. As for fathers who would like to become Anglo by marriage, and daughters who fiercely resent them, perhaps after all he is still her father and she is still his daughter, and there is hope.

Because the *Ya-Ya Sisterhood* was such a disappointment, I expected even less from what looked, going in, like a teenage retread. But in a world where one pair of jeans fits all, miracles can happen. This *Sisterhood* is real pleasure, a big-hearted movie where a group of gifted actresses find opportunities most younger movie stars can only dream about.

The Sisters ★ ★
R, 113 m., 2006

Maria Bello (Marcia Prior Glass), Mary Stuart Masterson (Olga Prior), Erika Christensen (Irene Prior), Eric McCormack (Gary Sokol), Chris O'Donnell (David Turzin), Tony Goldwyn (Vincent Antonelli), Steven Culp (Dr. Harry Glass), Alessandro Nivola (Andrew Prior), Elizabeth Banks (Nancy Pecket), Rip Torn (Dr. Chebrin). Directed by Arthur Allan Seidelman and produced by Judd Payne and Matthew Rhodes. Screenplay by Richard Alfieri, based on his play.

When a classic is transferred to the present time and place, does the material travel well? Can it be reasonably taken from its world and transplanted in ours? Sometimes the transfer works, as when Ian McKellen played Richard III in a fascist 1930s Britain, and Gus Van Sant transmuted *Henry IV* into *My Own Private Idaho.* Sometimes it does not, as in this attempt to take Chekhov's *Three Sisters* out of 1901 in Russia and place it in the faculty club of a modern American university.

It could be argued that Shakespeare's characters are more universal and Chekhov's more particular to time and place—which is a strength of both. Because they are interior, the problems of Hamlet can be set anywhere, as Ethan Hawke proved by asking "To be, or not to be?" in the "Action" aisle at Blockbuster. But with Chekhov's *Three Sisters,* we can more easily imagine characters trapped together in a remote country house than believe their timely entrances and exits in a clubroom on campus. Nor do modern families usually work out their problems in general debate, with friends and strangers joining in; the American practice in unhappy families is to choose alienation and limit contact to weddings, funerals, and tortured Thanksgivings.

Arthur Allan Seidelman's *The Sisters,* written by Richard Alfieri and based on his play, assumes that the three sisters and one brother of a dysfunctional family gather in the faculty club after the death of their patriarch. The occasion is the birthday of Irene (Erika Christensen), the middle sister, although this family doesn't seem practiced at birthday parties. The other sisters are the university chancellor Olga (Mary Stuart Masterson), who is the oldest; and Marcia, the youngest (Maria Bello), who is under the spell of the psychologist Harry (Steven Culp). Andrew (Alessandro Nivola) is their brother and brings along his girlfriend, Nancy (Elizabeth Banks). The others think Nancy isn't good enough for him, but if she's sane, she's good enough for this family.

Others who drop in include Irene's fiancé, David (Chris O'Donnell); the sharp-tongued Professor Sokol (Eric McCormack); and a married childhood friend named Vincent (Tony Goldwyn), who is trying to disengage as Marcia's lover. Vincent has known them since childhood and reminds them of events best left to the psychological compost heap. Observing all of this is the sardonic Dr. Chebrin (Rip Torn), who has nothing much to do with anyone and is on the scene because, damn it all, this *is* the faculty club, and he's a member. As an outsider with little stake in the outcome, he makes remarks that uncannily reflect some of our own feelings: "You're too young to be having such thoughts," he tells Irene. "They're all true, of course."

During the course of the birthday party, hurtful truths will be told, lesbianism will be revealed, a drug overdose will take place, a character will require medical attention, and as we watch the mayhem we understand why other faculty members do not seem to flock to the club.

In Laurence Olivier's *Three Sisters* (1970), made for the American Film Theater series, you could tell the players without the program, even though they did seem to bring an extraordinary burden of problems onstage with them. In this version, there are so many cross-purposes to keep straight that the entrance of a character is like a piece being added to the chessboard in the middle of a game. We had it all figured out and, good lord, now the rook is threatened!

Projects like this bring out the best in actors, who take salary cuts to work in Chekhov (even at one remove). What we can guess, watching the film, is that the same players would make a good job of *Three Sisters,* but are undermined by the faculty club, which works like a hotel lobby. There's no way to sustain dramatic momentum here. The doorway offers escapes and entrances as required, and the common room plays like a ring for a tag-team match; Chekhovian wrestlers keep climbing over the ropes and pounding on anyone still standing.

16 Blocks ★ ★ ★
PG-13, 105 m., 2006

Bruce Willis (Jack Mosley), Mos Def (Eddie Bunker), David Morse (Frank Nugent), Cylk Cozart (Jimmy Mulvey). Directed by Richard Donner and produced by Randall Emmett, Avi Lerner, Arnold Rifkin, John Thompson, Jim Van Wyck, and Bruce Willis. Screenplay by Richard Wenk.

Bruce Willis plays Jack Mosley, a tired drunk, in *16 Blocks*. He's a detective who doesn't have the energy to be a cop. As the film opens, he's surrounded by dead bodies and spilled cocaine and is told by an officer, "Sit on this until the uniforms get here." Jack rummages around in the apartment until he finds what he wants: a bottle. He pours himself a drink and sits down to wait for the uniforms. Then he goes back to headquarters, where the receptionist gives him a breath mint.

Jack's shift is over. The last thing he needs is another job. But his boss assigns him to transport a witness sixteen blocks to a grand jury hearing. The witness has to arrive in two hours, before the grand jury's term expires. Jack goes to get the guy, who is named Eddie Bunker and is played by Mos Def as a motormouth who talks all the time, and I mean *all* the time, in a litany of complaints about his treatment, his life, and his fate. Eddie has the kind of voice that makes fingernails on a blackboard sound like Kenny G.

The job looks like a piece of cake. Put a guy in a car and drive sixteen blocks. Jack can't make the sixteen blocks. He makes a pit stop at a liquor store. Coming out again, he sees the wrong kind of guy making the wrong kind of moves on the witness in the car, and he shoots the guy, which is admirable decision-making under the circumstances. He figures out someone wants the witness dead, so he takes him to a friendly saloon and calls his superior officer.

Not a wise decision. Frank Nugent (David Morse), his chief, is the lynchpin of a ring of corruption and drug dealing within the department. He is one of the people who want to prevent Eddie Bunker from testifying. Jack knows this. He's wise to the crooked cops because he's bought into the system. But there's something about Eddie Bunker, something about his innocence, something about his naive trust in Jack, something about the way he won't shut up that somehow gets to Jack. Just when Eddie is about to be killed in the bar, Jack shoots a cop and saves Eddie's life. Now they are both on the same side of the law.

That's the setup for *16 Blocks*, which is a chase picture conducted at a velocity that is just about right for a middle-aged alcoholic. Unlike *Running Scared*, which was pitched a few degrees above manic, *16 Blocks* is more of a character study, a two-hander about how Jack has been fed up with the department for a long time, and Eddie's sweet, goofy nature tilts the balance. Of course, it's a good question whether Eddie is *really* the nutty motormouth he seems to be, but that's not something Jack has the time to determine right now.

The movie has been directed by Richard Donner, a specialist in combining action, chase scenes and humor (see *Lethal Weapon*, etc.). Here he starts with three good performances: Willis, world-weary and yet with a spark of defiance; Mos Def, whose speaking role is more or less the same as the movie's running time; and David Morse, evil and bureaucratic in equal measure.

The chase scenes involve Chinatown (of course), traffic jams, and a standoff on a bus that may owe something to the 2002 Brazilian film *Bus 174*. None of this is particularly new, but all of it is done well, and Mos Def does the same thing here that Austin Pendleton did in *Dirty Work*: He comes in from left field with a character performance that's completely unexpected in an action movie. At first I found it irritating. Then I began to wonder if something was going on beneath the surface. Eventually I was able to pick up the buried message, which was frightened and sincere, and was hiding behind self-satire. I did not, however, necessarily buy the story about the bakery.

One key scene gave me problems. It involves an ambulance. Actually, it involves two ambulances, which was my problem. I think maybe one additional shot or one more line of dialogue might have oriented me, but there for a moment it seemed as if certain characters had dropped into another dimension. The plot device was explained to me by Dann Gire, president of the Chicago Film Critics Association, which is yet another reason his photograph should be displayed in every post office and schoolroom.

The bedrock of the plot is the dogged determination of the Bruce Willis character. Jack may be middle-aged, he may be tired, he may be balding, he may be a drunk, but if he's played by Bruce Willis, you don't want to bet against him. He gets that look in his eye that says, "It's going to be a pain in the ass for me to do this, but I couldn't live with myself if I didn't." I always believe that more easily than the look that merely says, "I will prevail because this is an action picture and I play the hero."

The Skeleton Key ★ ★ ½

PG, 104 m., 2005

Kate Hudson (Caroline), Gena Rowlands (Violet), John Hurt (Ben), Peter Sarsgaard (Luke), Joy Bryant (Jill), Ronald McCall (Papa Justify), Jeryl Prescott (Mama Cecile). Directed by Iain Softley and produced by Daniel Bobker, Softley, Michael Shamberg, and Stacey Sher. Screenplay by Ehren Kruger.

As I mentally review what happens in *The Skeleton Key*, I think there may be a couple of loopholes, but to describe them would betray too much of the plot, which depends on a series of escalating surprises. Besides, a movie that goes to this much trouble to work out its cosmology must have the answers. I must have missed something.

Doesn't matter. The film depends upon atmosphere, shock, and superstition; the logic of the plot is the last thing on our minds. It takes place in a creepy plantation house in a gloomy Louisiana backwater during a very, very rainy season. The district has something in common with every other horror movie set in the Deep South: a ramshackle backroads gas station operated by degenerates who frighten and repel their customers. In the real world, motorists get their gas at shiny twenty-four-hour travel plazas, many of them incorporating Taco Bells and sales on the latest cassettes by Jeff Foxworthy. Not in horror movies, where the Chainsaw Family lurks in the shadows behind the cash register and cackles unwholesomely about newcomers.

The visitor in this case is Caroline (Kate Hudson), a nurse who grows despondent when a beloved patient dies, and quits her hospital job to sign on as a private caregiver. Her first job pays $1,000 a week, which right there should send up a flare, especially since several earlier employees

have quit. She meets a lawyer named Luke (Peter Sarsgaard), and he sends her on to his client, an old lady named Violet (Gena Rowlands). She has lived in the decaying mansion since 1962, "when we came over from Savannah." Now her husband, Ben (John Hurt), has suffered a stroke and can't talk. But he sure can look like he really wants to tell Caroline something.

The big house has rooms Ben and Violet have never used. Caroline is given a skeleton key that opens all of them, except, wouldn't you know, a door in the attic. This door rattles loudly, as if someone is locked inside; the Self-Rattling Door is a variation on the Snicker-Snack Rule, which teaches us that in horror movies a knife will all by itself make a sound like it is being scraped on metal, even when it isn't. All movies with self-rattling doors and/or self-scraping knife sounds also contain Unexpected Foreground Surprises, when the heroine is terrified because a character (or a cat) suddenly leaps up out of nowhere.

The opening scenes of the movie promise a degree of intelligent menace that few movies could live up to, including this one. But it works while it's happening. Rowlands, looking far less elegant than when she played James Garner's fading Southern love in *The Notebook*, distrusts Caroline: "She wouldn't understand the house," she tells her lawyer. But then again, who would? And what's to understand?

Old Ben, meanwhile, grabs Caroline's wrist in a deathly grip and really, really has something on his mind. Although he uses a wheelchair, one evening during the nightly monsoon, she finds him missing from his room. He has crawled out of his window and onto the porch, and he falls to the ground, for reasons that seem clearer at the time than they do later. Caroline becomes convinced that Violet is a threat to Ben and tries to help him escape, ramming her VW into the big old iron gates, which are mysteriously locked.

Underlying all of these alarms is a local practice known as hoodoo, not to be confused with voodoo. Hoodoo, we learn, is American folk magic incorporating incantations, conjurations, herbal remedies, and suchlike; voodoo is a religion, Caroline is told, but "God don't have much to do with hoodoo." From Violet, she hears the story of Papa Justify (Ronald McCall) and his wife, Mama Cecile (Jeryl Prescott), who were servants at the plantation ninety years ago, and how their hoodoo practices got mixed up with the rich family that owned the house.

The Skeleton Key is one of those movies that explain too much while they are explaining too little, and it leaves us with a surprise at the end that makes more sense the less we think about it. But the movie's mastery of technique makes up for a lot. Hudson is convincing as the young nurse determined to help her patient, Rowlands is awesome in the Joan Crawford role, and Hurt, who says not a word, semaphores whole dictionaries with his eyes.

There's a kind of moviegoer who likes a movie like this no matter how it ends. It's about the journey, not the destination, even though the ending of The Skeleton Key really is a zinger. It's just that—well, what did a lot of the other stuff have to do with anything? How do all the omens and portents and unexplained happenings connect? And what's the deal with hoodoo? It doesn't work unless you really believe in it, we're told, but if you really do, it really does. Considering what happens when you do, I think it's better if you don't. Besides, I believe things either work or don't work regardless of whether you think they can. Especially things that God don't have much to do with.

Sketches of Frank Gehry ★ ★ ★
PG-13, 82 m., 2006

Featuring Frank O. Gehry, Sydney Pollack, Philip Johnson, Bob Geldof, Barry Diller, Michael Eisner, Dennis Hopper, Michael Ovitz, and Milton Wexler. A documentary directed by Sydney Pollack and produced by Ultan Guilfoyle.

From the room he occupied for years in the old Cliff Dwellers Club atop Orchestra Hall, Louis Sullivan could have looked out his window, with the aid of a time machine, seen Frank Gehry's Pritzker band shell in Chicago's Millennium Park. The man who wrote "form follows function" would have contemplated the work of a man who seems to believe that form is function.

Although the band shell functions as a stage for performances, most of its visitors probably regard it first of all as sculpture. By the same token, Gehry's most famous work, the Guggenheim Museum in Bilbao, Spain, has been accused of one-upping the art inside. Certainly

when I visited in 2001, the Giorgio Armani career retrospective on the third level was hard-pressed to hold its own against the building containing it.

"Logotecture," one of Gehry's critics calls the Chicago band shell. The charge is that Gehry, having designed some brilliant buildings, is now ripping himself off to provide one city after another with its very own Gehry. This is a cheap shot. Mies van der Rohe attempted as nearly as possible to do the same thing over and over again, only more elegantly. Is there an enormous difference between his residential high-rises at 860 and 880 Lake Shore Drive and his IBM Building? No, but it's not logotecture, and neither is Gehry. An architecture critic has the opportunity to travel widely and become jaded by many Gehry buildings. The average person regarding the band shell is looking at the only Gehry she will see in her lifetime.

Well, not quite the only: Gehry also designed the elegant bridge connecting Millennium Park with the gardens on the east side of Columbus Drive. One day as I was visiting the park, it occurred to me that if Anish Kapoor's vast Cloud Gate has been universally renamed the Bean, then obviously Gehry's bridge is the Snake. And what is the band shell? Stand at the south end of the lawn, notice the web of arches that enclose the space and carry the sound, and observe the shell crouching at the other end. The Spider, obviously.

These musings are inspired by Sketches of Frank Gehry, an engaging documentary made by Hollywood director Sydney Pollack (Out of Africa, Tootsie, The Way We Were). Pollack is not usually a documentarian, and Gehry had never been documented; they were friends, and Gehry suggested Pollack might want to "do something." The result is not a formal doc but an extended chat between two professionals who, as Pollack puts it, search for "a sliver of space in the commercial world where you can make a difference."

Gehry did not begin by designing sculptural buildings. He takes Pollack to look at Santa Monica Place, his conventional 1984 shopping center at the end of the Third Street Mall in Santa Monica. Does Gehry like it? No. We meet his psychiatrist, Milton Wexler, authorized by Gehry to speak about a period in the 1980s when the architect made a breakthrough into his modern work; this process apparently involved, or perhaps even required, divorcing his first wife. All we learn about her from the film is that she pushed for her husband to change his name from Goldberg to sidestep anti-Semitism. Since he then immediately told everyone "my real name is Goldberg," this was less than perfectly functional, but we understand the form.

Gehry's design process could be inspiring for a kindergarten student. First he doodles on sketch pads. A form emerges. He uses construction paper, scissors, and tape to make a three-dimensional model from it. He plays with the model. Eventually it looks about right. His assistants use computer modeling to work out the stresses and supports, and together with his team he works on the interior spaces. Gehry's buildings are so complex that he believes they would have been impossible before computers (which he does not know how to operate). Certainly the math would have been daunting. Computers assure him that his cardboard fancies are structurally sound.

In this connection I remember the first famous architect I met, Max Abramovitz. I was sent as a young reporter to interview him on the site of the University of Illinois Assembly Hall, the largest rim-supported building ever made. Seating 16,000 people in a circle, it had no interior supports and was held together by five hundred miles of steel cable wrapped around the rim where the top bowl rested on the bottom. "Will this be your greatest achievement?" I asked the man who designed the United Nations complex.

"If it doesn't fall down," he said.

Because Pollack has his own clout and is not merely a supplicant at Gehry's altar, he asks professional questions as his equal, sympathizes about big projects that seem to go wrong, and offers insights ("Talent is liquefied trouble"). Because he is Pollack, and because he has Gehry's blessing, he has access to the architect's famous clients, such as Michael Eisner, who commissioned the Walt Disney Concert Hall in Los Angeles, and Dennis Hopper, who lives in a Gehry home in Santa Monica. He talks to the (late) great architect Philip Johnson, old and secure enough to praise a competitor. There are also a few critics brought in to provide balance, although Pollack's opinion is clear: Gehry is a genius. Having gazed upon the Guggenheim

and the Disney and sat happily on the grass beneath the Spider's web, I think so, too. Gehry helped tempt modern architecture out of its well-behaved period.

Sky Captain and the World of Tomorrow ★ ★ ★ ★
PG, 107 m., 2004

Jude Law (Joe "Sky Captain" Sullivan), Gwyneth Paltrow (Polly Perkins), Angelina Jolie (Captain Franky Cook), Giovanni Ribisi (Dex Dearborn), Michael Gambon (Editor Morris Paley), Ling Bai (Mysterious Woman). Directed by Kerry Conran and produced by Jon Avnet, Sadie Frost, Jude Law, and Marsha Oglesby. Screenplay by Conran.

Sky Captain and the World of Tomorrow is even more fun than it sounds like. In its heedless energy and joy, it reminded me of how I felt the first time I saw *Raiders of the Lost Ark*. It's like a film that escaped from the imagination directly onto the screen, without having to pass through reality along the way.

Before I got into serious science fiction, I went through a period when my fantasies were fed by a now-forgotten series of books about Tom Corbett, Space Cadet. There was a gee-whiz vigor to those adventures, a naive faith in science and pluck, evoking a world in which evil existed primarily as an opportunity for Tom to have fun vanquishing it. *Sky Captain* has that kind of innocence.

Jude Law and Gwyneth Paltrow star, as Joe "Sky Captain" Sullivan, a free-lance buccaneer for truth and justice, and Polly Perkins, a scoop-crazy newspaperwoman who hitches a ride in his airplane. Manhattan has come under attack from giant mechanical men who lumber through the skies like flying wrestlers, and stomp down the city streets sending civilians scurrying. This is obviously a case for Sky Captain, who must be the richest man on Earth, judging by his secret hideaway and what seems to be his private air force and science lab.

The robots have been sent by the mysterious Dr. Totenkopf, a World War I–vintage German scientist who has nurtured his plans for world domination ever since. He has kidnapped many leading scientists, and now his metal men will enforce his rule, unless Joe and Polly can stop him.

639

Also on the side of the good guys are Franky (Angelina Jolie), a sexy pilot with her own agenda, and Dex Dearborn (Giovanni Ribisi), Sky Captain's head of research and development.

To summarize the plot would spoil the fun, and be pointless anyway, since the plot exists essentially to inspire silly grins. What needs to be described is the look and technique of the film. *Sky Captain* is filmed halfway between full color and sepiatone, so that it has the richness of color and yet the distance and nostalgic quality of an old photograph. Its production design and art direction remind me of covers for ancient pulp magazines like *Thrilling Wonder Stories*.

Much will be written about the technique, about how the first-time director, Kerry Conran, labored for years to bring forth on his Macintosh a six-minute film illustrating his vision for *Sky Captain*. This film caught the attention of the director Jon Avnet, who agreed to produce Conran's film and presented the idea to Paltrow and Law.

The actors did almost all of their scenes in front of a blue screen, which was then replaced with images generated on computers. The monsters, the city, and most of the sets and props never really existed except as digital files. This permitted a film of enormous scope to be made with a reasonable budget, but it also freed Conran and his collaborators to show whatever they wanted to, because one digital fantasy costs about as much as another.

The film is not good because it was filmed in this way, however; it's just plain good. The importance of the technique is that it allows the movie to show idealized versions of sci-fi fantasies that are impossible in the real world and often unconvincing as more conventional special effects. It removes the layers of impossibility between the inspiration and the audience.

Paltrow and Law do a good job of creating the kind of camaraderie that flourished between the genders in the 1930s and 1940s, in films like *The Lady Eve*, with Henry Fonda and Barbara Stanwyck, or *His Girl Friday*, with Cary Grant and Rosalind Russell. The women in this tradition are tomboys (Katharine Hepburn is the prototype), and although romance is not unknown to them, they're often running too fast to kiss anyone. We gather that Polly and Joe had a romance a few years ago that ended badly

(Franky may have had a role in that), but now their chemistry renews itself as they fly off to Nepal in search of Dr. Totenkopf's lair.

The evil doctor is played by Laurence Olivier, who died in 1989, and who is seen here through old shots recycled into a new character. A posthumous performance makes a certain sense, given the nature of Dr. Totenkopf. There's something ghoulish about using a dead actor's likeness without his knowledge, and in the past I've deplored such desecrations as the Fred Astaire dust-buster ads, but surely every actor on his deathbed, entering the great unknown, hopes he has not given his last performance.

Sky Captain will probably not inspire the universal affection of a film like *Indiana Jones*, in part because Steven Spielberg is a better director than Kerry Conran, in part because many of *Sky Captain*'s best qualities are more cinematic than dramatic; I responded to the texture and surfaces and very feel of the images, and felt some of the same quickening I remember from the cover of a new Tom Corbett book. If the Space Cadet ever graduated, he probably grew up to be Sky Captain.

Sleepover ★
PG, 90 m., 2004

Alexa Vega (Julie), Mika Boorem (Hannah), Scout Taylor-Compton (Farrah), Kallie Flynn Childress (Yancy), Sam Huntington (Ren), Jane Lynch (Gabby), Jeff Garlin (Jay), Sara Paxton (Staci). Directed by Joe Nussbaum and produced by Bob Cooper and Charles Weinstock. Screenplay by Elisa Bell.

I take it as a rule of nature that all American high schools are ruled by a pack of snobs, led by a supremely confident young woman who is blond, superficial, catty, and ripe for public humiliation. This character is followed everywhere by two friends who worship her, and are a little bit shorter. Those schools also contain a group of friends who are not popular and do not think of themselves as pretty, although they are smarter, funnier, and altogether more likable than the catty-pack.

In the classic form of this formula, the reigning blond dates a hunk whom the mousy outcast has a crush on, and everything gets cleared up at the prom when the hunk realizes the mouse is the real beauty, while the evil nature of the popular girl is exposed in a sensationally embarrassing way.

Sleepover, a lame and labored comedy, doesn't recycle this plot (the blond gets dumped by her boyfriend) but works more as a series of riffs on the underlying themes. It moves the age group down a few years, so that the girls are all just entering high school. And it lowers the stakes—instead of competing for the football captain, the rivals enter into a struggle over desirable seating in the school's outdoor lunchroom. Winners get the "popular" table, losers have to sit by the Dumpster. That a school would locate a lunch area next to the garbage doesn't say much for its hygiene standards, but never mind.

Julie is the girl we're supposed to like. She's played by Alexa Vega, from *Spy Kids.* Staci (Sara Paxton) is the girl we're supposed to hate. Julie's posse includes Hannah (Mika Boorem), a good friend who is moving to Canada for no better reason, as far as I can tell, than to provide an attribute for a character with no other talking points; and Farrah (the wonderfully named Scout Taylor-Compton), who functions basically as an element useful to the cinematographer in composing groups of characters.

Julie decides to have a sleepover, and at the last minute invites poor Yancy (the also wonderfully named Kallie Flynn Childress), who is plump and self-conscious about her weight. Julie's invitation is so condescending it's a form of insult, something that doesn't seem to occur to the grateful Yancy. Julie's mom, the wonderfully named Gabby (Jane Lynch), lays down rules for the sleepover, all of which will be violated by the end of the evening without anything being noticed by her dad, Jay (Jeff Garlin), reinforcing the rule that the parents in teenage comedies would remain oblivious if their children moved the Ringling Bros. and Barnum and Bailey Circus into their bedrooms.

Staci, the popular one, visits the slumber party to suggest a scavenger hunt, with the winner to get the desirable lunch table. So it's up to the girls to sneak out of the house and snatch all the trophies, including, of course, the boxer shorts of the high school hunk. There is a tradition in which movie teenagers almost always have bedrooms with windows opening onto roofs, porches, trellises, etc., which function perfectly as escape routes when necessary, but collapse instantly (a) when used by an unpopular character or (b) when the risk of discovery and betrayal needs to be fabricated.

What happens during the scavenger hunt I will leave to you to discover, if you are so unwise as to attend this movie instead of *Mean Girls.* One of the movie's strangest scenes has Julie, who is about fourteen, sneaking into a bar because the scavenger hunt requires her to get a photo of herself being treated to a drink by a grown-up. This scene is outrageous even if she orders a Shirley Temple, but is even weirder because the guy she chooses is a teacher from her junior high, who must live in a wonderland of his own since he obviously has no idea of the professional hazards involved in buying a drink in public for one of his barely pubescent students, and then posing for a photo so she will have proof.

I don't require all high school (or junior high) comedies to involve smart, imaginative, articulate future leaders. But I am grateful when the movie at least devises something interesting for them to do or expresses empathy with their real natures. The characters in *Sleepover* are shadows of shadows, diluted from countless better, even marginally better, movies. There was no reason to make this movie, and no reason to see it.

A Slipping-Down Life ★ ★ ★
R, 111 m., 2004

Lili Taylor (Evie Decker), Guy Pearce (Drumstrings Casey), John Hawkes (David Elliot), Sara Rue (Violet), Irma P. Hall (Clotelia), Tom Bower (Mr. Decker), Shawnee Smith (Faye-Jean), Veronica Cartwright (Mrs. Casey). Directed by Toni Kalem and produced by Richard Raddon. Screenplay by Kalem, based on the novel by Anne Tyler.

I first became aware of Lili Taylor in *Mystic Pizza* (1988), a star-making film that also introduced Julia Roberts. She plays the girl who walks away from the altar because her husband-to-be doesn't believe in sex before marriage and she doesn't think it's worth marrying him just to get him into bed. That kind of almost-logical circular reasoning is common in her characters; you can see it in other Taylor masterpieces, like *Dogfight* (1991), *Household*

Saints (1993), *Girls Town* (1996), her great work in *I Shot Andy Warhol* the same year, and in *Casa de los Babys* (2003).

I don't suppose Taylor was born to play Evie Decker, the heroine of *A Slipping-Down Life*, but I can't imagine any other actress getting away with this role. She has a kind of solemnity she can bring to goofy characters, elevating them to holy (and usually lovable) fools. Here she plays a young woman from a small town who is lonely and isolated and lives with her father, who loves her but spends his evenings talking to ham radio operators in Moscow. She needs for something to happen to her.

Something does. She hears a rock singer on the radio one night. His off-balance ad lib philosophizing turns off the disc jockey, but sends her out to a local bar to see him in person. He becomes to her a demigod, a source of light and wisdom, but she is too inept to attract his attention. So she goes into the rest room and uses a piece of a broken bottle to carve his name into her forehead.

His name is Drumstrings Casey. She just carves the "Casey." "Why didn't you use my first name?" he asks her. "I didn't have room on my forehead," she says. "They call me Drum," he says. "I wish I'd known that," she says. There is another problem: She carved the name backward, because that way it looked right in the mirror. But at least when she looks at herself in the mirror it looks okay to her.

Drumstrings is played by Guy Pearce, of *Memento* and *L.A. Confidential*. He fits easily into the role of a third-rate, small-town rock god. When his agent finds out what Evie did, he talks Drumstrings into coming to the hospital to get his picture taken with her, and the publicity leads to an offer to have her appear at his concerts, to drum up business. This works well enough that he gets a gig in a nearby town, and doesn't invite her along, which breaks her heart. But somehow without that crazy girl in the audience, Drumstrings has an off night, and realizes he needs her.

The movie, written by the director Toni Kalem and based on a novel by Anne Tyler, performs a delicate maneuver as it slips along. The film opens with Evie totally powerless and miserable, and with Drumstrings holding all the cards. But her self-mutilation empowers her, and it provides a way for her to hold Drum's at-tention long enough for him to begin to like her. What she doesn't understand at first is that he's holding cards as bad as her own.

The film is like a tightrope walk across possible disasters. It could so easily go wrong. The plot itself is not enough to save it; indeed, this plot in the wrong hands could be impossible. But Kalem, an actress herself, understands how mood and nuance shape film stories; it's not what it's about, but how it's about it. Lili Taylor never overplays, never asks us to believe anything that isn't right there for us to see and hear. She changes by almost invisible steps into a woman who knows what she wants in a man and in marriage, and is able to communicate that to Drumstrings in a way he can, eventually, imperfectly, understand.

The supporting performances are like sturdy supports when the movie needs them. Tom Bower plays Evie's father as a man who has receded into his own loneliness. Irma P. Hall plays their maid, who is the de facto head of the household. John Hawkes is Drumstring's manager, who understands managing and publicity only remotely, but with great enthusiasm. Drum's mother (Veronica Cartwright) does not consider it a plus that this woman has carved her son's name into her forehead. Backward.

The movie is not a great dramatic statement, but you know that from the modesty of the title. It is about movement in emotional waters that had long been still. Taylor makes it work because she quietly suggests that when Evie's life has stalled, something drastic was needed to shock her back into action, and the carving worked as well as anything. Besides, when she combs her bangs down, you can hardly see it.

Slither ★ ★
R, 95 m., 2006

Nathan Fillion (Sheriff Bill Pardy), Elizabeth Banks (Starla Grant), Gregg Henry (Jack MacReady), Michael Rooker (Grant Grant), Tania Saulnier (Kylie Strutemyer). Directed by James Gunn and produced by Paul Brooks and Eric Newman. Screenplay by Gunn.

Slither is the kind of horror movie where decent citizens are attacked by a nauseating slimy grub from outer space, and the characters watch

Troma movies on TV. If the name "Troma" means nothing to you, what are you doing reading a review of *Slither* in the first place? It takes place in a forlorn small town where the mayor screams four-letter words on Main Street. Where the traffic is so slow the cops use the radar gun to time whip-poor-wills. Where the kids in grade school all have acne. Where everybody gets drunk to celebrate the opening of deer-hunting season.

Near this town falls a meteorite that emits a nasty little creature that quickly burrows into the chest of Grant Grant, the richest guy in town. Grant is played by Michael Rooker, from *Henry: Portrait of a Serial Killer*. He is married to Starla (Elizabeth Banks), a poor girl who was trying to escape from poverty and an unhappy family. The funny thing is, she takes her marriage seriously. She takes it way too seriously, if you ask me, when she still talks sweet to Grant after he begins to resemble a rotting version of Jabba the Hutt.

It is difficult to give away too much of the plot; you already know from the ads that the slithering, crawling things leap down the throats of their victims, turning them into beings who still have their human memories but also develop an appetite for raw meat. From their chests spring suction tentacles to suck up your innards. How they reproduce is not a pretty sight.

The action centers around Sheriff Bill Pardy (Nathan Fillion), who runs a fairly incompetent department. He's still in love with Starla from junior high school. When it becomes clear that some kind of slug-tentacle-slime creature is killing the livestock, one of his deputies buys a dime-store octopus to help potential witnesses make an ID. If you see this creature, believe me, you won't need visual aids.

The sheriff, aided by his deputies, Starla and cute young Kylie Strutemyer (Tania Saulnier), confront the creature(s) during an extended action sequence in which the slugs ooze their way into bathtubs, under doorways, down throats, and so on. Once they've occupied a victim, their prey instantly loses speed and coordination and turns into a lurching example of the zombies so familiar from, well, from all those zombie movies.

So now you know the terrain. What's interesting is that this story sounds so worn-out and yet it works. There is some humor in the plot, effective action, and scenes that entertain us because of how stupidly the characters behave. Consider the possible reconciliation between Starla and her husband, who speaks in that gravelly, placating Michael Rooker voice but looks as if he was absentmindedly left overnight in a cement mixer. She should have suspected something when he padlocked the basement door and told her he was hiding a surprise for her birthday. Her birthday is two months off, and the surprise is getting riper by the hour.

There are better movies. But *Slither* has a competence to it, an ability to manipulate obligatory horror scenes in a way that works. Given my theory of the star rating system, which suggests movies should be rated by their genres, *Slither* gets two if *28 Days Later* gets three. On the other hand, in the genre of slick and classy big-star thrillers, if *Fatal Attraction* gets 2.5 stars, then *Basic Instinct 2* gets 1.5. On the third hand, a lot of people probably would enjoy *Basic Instinct 2* more than *Slither*. One of these days, I'm going to have to take that star rating system and feed it to a meat-eating slime-slug.

Something New ★ ★ ★ ½
PG-13, 100 m., 2006

Sanaa Lathan (Kenya), Simon Baker (Brian), Mike Epps (Walter), Donald Faison (Nelson), Blair Underwood (Mark), Wendy Raquel Robinson (Cheryl), Alfre Woodard (Joyce), Golden Brooks (Suzette), Taraji P. Henson (Nedra), Earl Billings (Edmond). Directed by Sanaa Hamri and produced by Stephanie Allain. Screenplay by Kriss Turner.

Something New opens with cotton-candy titles, arrives in time for Valentine's Day, and is billed as a romantic comedy. Okay, it *is* a romantic comedy, technically, but the romance and the comedy don't arrive easily, and along the way the movie truly is something new: a touching story about a black professional woman facing problems in the workplace and the marriage market. I found myself unexpectedly moved.

Sanaa Lathan stars as Kenya, a Los Angeles accountant who is a workaholic. She's pretty, but the movie doesn't rest on that; Lathan makes Kenya wary, protective, cautious. It's a performance that could have skated the surface but goes more deeply. She's fiercely driven, a child of ambitious parents, a graduate of top schools, a candidate to became a partner in her firm. She doesn't date. She doesn't do much of anything except work, although recently she bought a new house.

That's how she meets Brian Kelly (Simon Baker), who is single, attracted to her, and a landscape architect. And white. They're fixed up on a blind date, but she makes awkward apologies and leaves. She doesn't date white guys. She doesn't seem to date black guys either, but she would in theory, if the IBM (Ideal Black Man) came along. She does hire Brian to landscape her backyard and gradually finds herself drawn to him, against her will. The movie depends on a sudden rain shower, that old Victorian standby, to drive them into the shelter of a tree for an unexpected kiss.

So let's pause and deal with some things you're probably assuming. You probably think *Something New*, like the remake *Guess Who*, approaches interracial romance as a sitcom opportunity. You probably think the cards are stacked in favor of these two people falling in love. But it isn't that simple. The movie is, astonishingly, told from a point of view hardly ever visible in movies: African-American professionals. Kenya's father (Earl Billings) is head of his department at Cedars-Sinai. Her mother (Alfre Woodard) is a pillar of black society, and of course her daughter made her debut at a black-tie cotillion. Her brother is a lawyer for a movie studio. Her family and friends are not thrilled by the notion that she might date a white man.

Neither is Kenya. That is not a prejudice, she tells Brian, but a preference. The movie has frank dialogue about race—not platitudes about how we're all really the same, but realistic observations about race in modern America. There's talk of the "black tax" that requires someone like Kenya to work harder than her white colleagues to overcome doubts about her competence. At work, she advises an important client to stay away from a merger; this is not news the client wants to hear, and he is unhappy hearing it from a black woman who seems better informed than he is.

Kenya and Brian do eventually fall into the first stages of a romance. But they get side-tracked when he asks her to take out her weave and wear her "own hair." She's angry; she thinks this is none of his business (and indeed men of all races would be wise to avoid hair-care discussions with women of all races, because it's a touchier subject than a man can possibly realize). In social situations, Brian is aware of coolness from Kenya's brother and her friends, and at a comedy club the black comedienne makes comments about race that land around him like grenades.

They love each other, but are they ready to take on the responsibility of declaring their love and living with it? They have an argument in a grocery store that's real in a way love stories are rarely permitted to be. Kenya breaks up with him. An IBM comes into the picture, a wealthy black professional (Blair Underwood) who says and does all the right things.

How the movie finally ends will not be difficult to guess. It's how it gets there that's compelling. *Something New* doesn't settle for formulas or easy answers. Like its heroine, it knows good reasons for dating within one's race. It knows about social pressure, and how it works both ways. It's able to observe Kenya and Brian in a mostly black social situation, where Brian calls her, correctly, on making "black" comments as a way of holding her white date at arm's length. Interesting, how it gives a fair hearing to both characters.

But the movie knows that if two people truly connect, that is a rare and precious thing and must be respected. And it shows Kenya's family and friends observing the relationship carefully and observing that it seems to work for her, for this driven woman who seemed to be unmarriageable. They size up Brian and like what they see. "The boy's just white," her father tells her mother. "He's not a Martian."

By the end, *Something New* delivers all the usual pleasures of a love story, and something more. The movie respects its subject and characters, and is more complex about race than we could possibly expect. With this film and the completely different but also observant Queen Latifah comedy *Last Holiday*, black women are being paid a kind of attention they deserve but rarely get in the movies. Yes, and it's fun, too: You'll laugh and maybe you'll have a few tears, that kind of stuff.

Son of the Mask ★ ½
PG, 86 m., 2005

Jamie Kennedy (Tim Avery), Alan Cumming (Loki), Liam Falconer and Ryan Falconer (Alvey Avery), Bob Hoskins (Odin), Traylor Howard (Tonya Avery), Ben Stein (Dr. Arthur Neuman), Bear (Otis the Dog). Directed by Lawrence Guterman and produced by Erica Huggins and Scott Kroopf. Screenplay by Lance Khazei.

One of the foundations of comedy is a character who must do what he doesn't want to do because of the logic of the situation. As Auden pointed out about limericks, they're funny not because they end with a dirty word, but because they have no choice but to end with the dirty word—by that point, it's the only word that rhymes and makes sense. Lucille Ball made a career out of finding herself in embarrassing situations and doing the next logical thing, however ridiculous.

Which brings us to *Son of the Mask* and its violations of this theory. The movie's premise is that if you wear a magical ancient mask, it will cause you to behave in strange ways. Good enough, and in Jim Carrey's original *The Mask* (1994), the premise worked. Carrey's elastic face was stretched into a caricature, he gained incredible powers, he exhausted himself with manic energy. But there were rules. There was a baseline of sanity from which the mania proceeded. *Son of the Mask* lacks a baseline. It is all mania, all the time; the behavior in the movie is not inappropriate, shocking, out of character, impolite, or anything else except behavior.

Both *Mask* movies are inspired by the zany world of classic cartoons. The hero of *Son of the Mask*, Tim Avery (Jamie Kennedy), is no doubt named after Tex Avery, the legendary Warner Bros. animator, although it is *One Froggy Evening* (1955), by the equally legendary Chuck Jones, that plays a role in the film. Their films all obeyed the Laws of Cartoon Thermodynamics, as established by the distinguished theoreticians Trevor Paquette and Lieutenant Justin D. Baldwin. (Examples: Law III: "Any body passing through solid matter will leave a perforation conforming to its perimeter"; Law IX: "Everything falls faster than an anvil.")

These laws, while seemingly arbitrary, are consistent in all cartoons. We know that Wile E. Coyote can chase the Road Runner off a cliff and keep going until he looks down; only then will he fall. And that the Road Runner can pass through a tunnel entrance in a rock wall, but Wile E. Coyote will smash into the wall. We instinctively understand Law VIII ("Any violent rearrangement of feline matter is impermanent"). Even cartoons know that if you don't have rules, you're playing tennis without a net.

The premise in *Son of the Mask* is that an ancient mask, found in the earlier movie, has gone missing again. It washes up on the banks of a little stream, and is fetched by Otis the Dog (Bear), who brings it home to the Avery household, where we find Tim (Kennedy) and his wife, Tonya (Traylor Howard). Tim puts on the Mask, and is transformed into a whiz-kid at his advertising agency, able to create brilliant campaigns in a single bound. He also, perhaps unwisely, wears it to bed and engenders an infant son, Alvey, who is born with cartoonlike abilities and discovers them by watching the frog cartoon on TV.

Tim won an instant promotion to the big account, but without the Mask he is a disappointment. And the Mask cannot be found, because Otis has dragged it away and hidden it somewhere—although not before Otis snuffles at it until it attaches itself to his face, after which he is transformed into a cartoon dog and careens wildly around the yard and the sky, to his alarm.

A word about baby Alvey (played by the twins Liam and Ryan Falconer). I have never much liked movie babies who do not act like babies. I think they're scary. The first *Look Who's Talking* movie was cute, but the sequels were nasty, especially when the dog started talking. About *Baby's Day Out* (1994), in which Baby Bink set Joe Mantegna's crotch on fire, the less said the better.

I especially do not like Baby Alvey, who behaves not according to the rules for babies, but more like a shape-shifting creature in a Japanese anime. There may be a way this could be made funny, but *Son of the Mask* doesn't find it.

Meanwhile, powerful forces seek the Mask. The god Odin (Bob Hoskins) is furious with his son Loki (Alan Cumming) for having lost the Mask, and sends him down to Earth (or maybe these gods already live on Earth, I dunno) to get it back again. Loki, who is the god of mischief, has a spiky punk hairstyle that seems inspired by the jester's cap and bells, without the bells. He picks up the scent and causes no end of trouble for the Averys, although of course the dog isn't talking.

But my description makes the movie sound more sensible than it is. What we basically have here is a license for the filmmakers to do whatever they want to do with the special effects, while the plot, like Wile E. Coyote, keeps running into the wall.

Sophie Scholl: The Final Days ★ ★ ★
NO MPAA RATING, 117 m., 2006

Julia Jentsch (Sophie Scholl), Gerald Alexander Held (Robert Mohr), Fabian Hinrichs (Hans Scholl), Johanna Gastdorf (Else Gebel), Andre Hennicke (Dr. Roland Freisler). Directed by Marc Rothemund and produced by Christoph Müeller, and Sven Burgemeister. Screenplay by Fred Breinersdorfer.

At the heart of *Sophie Scholl: The Final Days* is a long interrogation conducted across a desk in a police headquarters. It is February 1943, in Munich. The questions are asked by Robert Mohr (Gerald Alexander Held), a provincial who has risen in rank under the Nazis and wears a little lapel pin proclaiming his patriotism. The answers come from Sophie Scholl (Julia Jentsch), a student of biology and philosophy. She is accused of helping distribute leaflets on her campus that attack Hitler and his war.

This is not a thriller but a police procedural, in which we have all the information we need, right from the outset. She is guilty. Sophie and her brother, Hans (Fabian Hinrichs), belong to the White Rose, an underground group that mimeographs statements critical of the regime and the continuation of a war that is already lost. In theory their leaflets were to be mailed. Hans gets the idea of distributing them on their campus. This is reckless and stupid, and exactly the sort of grand gesture beloved by idealistic kids. If the Scholls had been communists, party discipline would have mocked them. But they are Catholics carried away by conscience.

Even so, they might have gotten away with it. They put piles of leaflets outside classroom doors, and then Sophie, in a heedless moment, sends a stack of paper swirling down into a central hallway. It is the janitor who turns them in, in part because he is a Nazi toady, in part because they made extra work for him.

Sophie Scholl, an Oscar nominee for best foreign film, contains no artificial suspense or drama. Directed by Marc Rothemund and written by Fred Breinersdorfer, it is based on fact and uses the transcripts of Scholl's actual interrogation and trial, as kept by the Gestapo and liberated when East Germany fell. Most of the words in the questioning are literally what Scholl and Mohr said. He sits behind his desk, impassive and precise, asking her to explain her presence on the campus and her suitcase that is exactly large enough to hold the leaflets. Cool and calm, she answers every question precisely. She has an alibi that is almost good enough.

The effect of this scene is so powerful that I leaned forward like a jury member, wanting her to get away with it so I could find her innocent. But the law moves as the law always does, with no reference to higher justice; even in this Nazi procedure there are carbon copies and paper clips and rubber stamps and a need to see the law followed, as indeed it is. The law underpins evil, but it is observed. When Sophie is found guilty, it is legal enough.

The sentence against her is carried out with startling promptness; because of the movie's title, we are not surprised, but we are jolted. I was reminded of an exchange in *Thank You for Smoking* where the son of a tobacco lobbyist asks him, "Dad, why is the American government the best government?" And his father replies, "Because of our endless appeals system." It is a luxury to be able to joke about such things. One day Sophie Scholl thoughtlessly throws some leaflets off a balcony, and two days later she is dead. Notice how the final sounds of the movie play under a black screen. Does she hear them?

Are the policeman Robert Mohr and the judge Roland Freisler (Andre Hennicke) evil men? Yes, absolutely, but they are doing their duty. I learn from Anthony Lane in the *New Yorker* that Mohr's widow received a state pension after the war. The police and the court are shown to follow the law, and in the law resides either good or evil, depending on what the law says and how it is enforced. That is why it is crucial that a constitution guarantee rights and freedoms, and why it is dangerous for any government to ignore it. There should be no higher priority.

All of these thoughts are made particular in *Sophie Scholl: The Final Days*. Most of the dialogue involves specific questions of where Sophie was, and when, and why the evidence against her is so compelling. Perry Mason–type stuff. The policeman is so passive he is hardly there. Only the judge indulges in speechifying; those who know their actions are wrong are often the loudest to defend them, especially when they fear a higher moral judgment may come down on them. But the most powerful political statement in the film is one of the saddest. Sophie is allowed a few moments with her parents before being taken away forever. "You did the right thing," her father says of Sophie and her brother. "I'm proud of you both."

Sorry, Haters ★ ★ ★
NO MPAA RATING, 83 m., 2006

Robin Wright Penn (Phoebe), Abdellatif Kechiche (Ashade), Elodie Bouchez (Eloise), Aasif Mandvi (Hassan), Sandra Oh (Phyllis MacIntyre), Remy K. Selma (Imam). Directed by Jeff Stanzler and produced by Gary Winick, Karen Jaroneski, Jake Abraham, and Stanzler. Screenplay by Stanzler.

Sorry, Haters is a film that begins in intrigue, develops in fascination, and ends in a train wreck. It goes spectacularly wrong, and yet it contains such a gripping performance by Robin Wright Penn that it succeeds, in a way, despite itself. To see great work is a reason to see an imperfect movie, and to observe how the movie loses its way may be useful even if it's frustrating. My inclination was to give the film a negative star rating, but that would mean recommending you not see this performance by Penn, and that I am unwilling to do.

When I mention Penn, I must also mention Abdellatif Kechiche, who plays the movie's other leading role, and whose anguish is easy to identify with, even if we cannot believe where the plot takes him. He plays a New York cab driver, and she plays a woman who gets into his cab one night—a woman who has been drinking and clutches a child's toy. She has him drive out to New Jersey so they can park across the street and she can look at what was her husband, her child, and their house. Her ex-husband, she says, divorced her, married again, and got the house, custody, everything. Before they leave, she uses her keys to scratch the ex-husband's new car.

Everything about this woman, named Phoebe, feels real, including her mania bordering on madness. There is also the modulation of her gradually growing curiosity about the cab driver, named Ashade. We learn his story: He was a Ph.D. in chemistry in his native Syria. His brother has been a Canadian citizen for ten years and has a French-Canadian wife and a baby. The brother was stopped by U.S. officials on his way through LaGuardia and is now a prisoner at Guantanamo. Appeals have failed, even though the brother (according to Ashade) is completely innocent. Phoebe, an executive for a cable TV company, decides that she would like to help them.

That, in any event, is the surface of the story, the setup. There is a lot more, but as much as I deplore how the movie develops, I will not reveal its secrets, because if you are going to see it, you deserve to see it as I did—going in knowing nothing, and coming out knowing everything and feeling admiration for Penn and something between dissatisfaction and anger for the film. I learn that the producers tried to tell the director, Jeff Stanzler, that his third act didn't work, but he pressed on. And what's the use of making a low-budget film on digital video if you can't make precisely the film you want to make? That's what the low budget buys you: freedom.

With freedom comes responsibility, etc., but never mind. Just watch Penn. She has to move through wide emotional territory in this film, and she does. She has to make a speech explaining her emotions and motivations, and she does that, too. We do not believe it. We believe either that a) no one would feel as she feels, or b) if she does, she's too crazy to seem as sane as she does. But perhaps there are forms of self-delusion that can be masked by intelligent psychopaths, and perhaps that's the case here; she drives the taxi driver to an explosion of frustration and desperation.

Certainly Phoebe seems on the level, at least to begin with. She's smart, attractive, articulate, and kind of creepy as she insists on visiting the French-Canadian sister-in-law (Elodie Bouchez) and taking Ashade to her office at the cable company. Later, there is a dinner involving Phyllis MacIntyre (Sandra Oh), her boss at the company, and without going into details, I ask you to observe the dynamic at that restaurant table.

There is (I'm wording this carefully) a surprise that begins to emerge at about the halfway point, but I didn't have a problem with it. I could believe it and consider it consistent with what went before. What I could not accept, where I could not follow, was Phoebe's ultimate purpose and her reasons for it. Perhaps it would have helped if the speech where she explains herself had just been left out altogether. It reminds me too much of the Talking Killer Syndrome—like a T.K., she is compelled to explain and justify herself at a time when only action is called for. I am thinking of the speech involving the word "powerless." Perhaps if we had seen her behavior without explication or complaint, we could have simply followed her actions and then figured out her motivation for ourselves.

It must have taken courage for Penn to commit to *Sorry, Haters*. She must have doubted the ending. And yet like many great actresses, she was willing to give the director the benefit of the doubt, because an ending that raises no questions may also achieve nothing. *Sorry, Haters* is certainly not the kind of movie that should end happily with everything resolved. In its world, and our world, that doesn't happen, not in a case like this.

A Sound of Thunder ★ ★
PG-13, 102 m., 2005

Edward Burns (Travis Ryer), Catherine McCormack (Sonia Rand), Ben Kingsley (Charles Hatton), Jemima Rooper (Jenny Krase), David Oyelowo (Officer Payne). Directed by Peter Hyams and produced by Moshe Diamant, Howard Baldwin, and Karen Baldwin. Screenplay by Thomas Dean Donnelly, Joshua Oppenheimer, and Gregory Poirer, based on a short story by Ray Bradbury.

When I was the president of the Urbana High School Science Fiction Club, this would have been my favorite movie. But the movies have changed and so have I, and today there is something almost endearing about the clunky special effects and clumsy construction of *A Sound of Thunder*. The movie is made with a gee-whiz spirit, and although I cannot endorse it, I can appreciate it. There's a fundamental difference between movies that are bad because they're willfully stupid *(Deuce Bigalow, European Gigolo)* and movies that are bad because they want so much to be terrific that they explode under the strain.

A Sound of Thunder may not be a success, but it loves its audience and wants us to have a great time. The movie is inspired by a famous short story by Ray Bradbury, arguing that to travel back in time and change even one tiny element in the past could completely alter the future. In that it is firmly Darwinian, and indeed, if the common ancestor of all primates had died without reproducing, where would that leave us?

In the movie, a greedy entrepreneur (Ben Kingsley) charges millionaires a small fortune to travel back in time, kill a giant prehistoric reptile, and return with a video of themselves. In theory this will not change the present because a) frozen liquid nitrogen bullets are used, which will evaporate, making no difference, b) the targeted beast is selected because in another second it would have died anyway, and c) the travelers never leave anything behind.

Since the same scenario is played out time and again, it raises the question of why each hunting party doesn't run into the other ones. Subtle dialogue hints suggest that maybe even the "safe" visits are making small changes, but then something happens big time, and the "present" is socked with a series of "time waves," which look like optical tsunamis and leave a different world behind them.

The film's hero is Travis (Edward Burns), a scientist who hopes to recreate ancient DNA. He leads the time expeditions. The heroine is Sonia Rand (Catherine McCormack), who invented the computer that oversees the travel. The heart of the movie involves a series of desperate expeditions into the past to repair or prevent what went wrong, so that the familiar "present" will return. Meanwhile, in alternative realities, a futuristic Chicago becomes a tropical swamp inhabited by giant reptilian bats, sabertoothed eagles, and lots and lots of bugs.

Now about the special effects. The scenes where the giant brontosaurus attacks the travelers looks so precisely like actors standing in front of back projection that it scarcely improves on *King Kong*. In the first time-travel scene, as the travelers walk out of a wormhole and into a shimmering pathway, why do they all look in the same direction? Wouldn't some of them look the other way? Why does the thick rain forest not have any trees in front of a volcano, so we can see it clearly? How can a volcano be so far away that we can see all of it, and yet be so close that its lava arrives in seconds? How can the lava look like dirty shaving cream and not like molten rock? How come if the power is out all over the city, the time machine can work? How can . . .

But what the hell, once you realize the effects are not even going to try to be convincing, you start to enjoy them. Perfect special effects can have a cold detachment to them; lousy ones can be eerie, strange, or fun. The future Chicago in this film, which makes the city in *Batman Begins* look like a documentary, is fantastical and preposterous; seeing the futuristic skyscrapers, the roadways in the sky, the airships, and the cars that all move at exactly the same speed, I was reminded of the covers of old sci-fi pulp magazines. When Travis and Sonia are trapped in a flooded subway with giant eels and the tunnel is caving in, I found it wonderful that they eventually escape through the kind of manhole we see in *The Third Man*.

Some of the dialogue is worth repeating. When Sonia finds the computer incapacitated and says she needs another terminal, someone suggests, "How about Home Depot?" And consider this exchange:

"What's that?"

"The molecular structure of brontosaurus blood."

"No way! Cool!"

The movie was directed by Peter Hyams, who a lifetime ago was an anchor for Channel 2 News in Chicago. He has directed mostly science fiction, including *2010, Capricorn One, Outland, End of Days, Stay Tuned, Timecop,* and *The Relic* (1997), another movie in which creatures in flooded Chicago tunnels played an important role. *A Sound of Thunder* looks cobbled together from a half-baked screenplay and underdone special effects, but it's made with a certain heedless zeal that makes you smile if you're in tune with it.

Spanglish ★ ★ ★
PG-13, 128 m., 2004

Adam Sandler (John Clasky), Tea Leoni (Deborah Clasky), Paz Vega (Flor), Cloris Leachman (Evelyn), Shelbie Bruce (Cristina), Sarah Steele (Bernice Clasky). Directed by James L. Brooks and produced by Brooks, Julie Ansell, and Richard Sakai. Screenplay by Brooks.

James L. Brooks' *Spanglish* tells the story of a Mexican woman and her daughter who travel all the way to Los Angeles to bring sanity to a crazy Anglo family. When I mention that the father of the family is played by Adam Sandler and is not its craziest member, you will see she has her work cut out for her. And yet the movie is not quite the sitcom the setup seems to suggest; there are some character quirks that make it intriguing.

Consider Deborah Clasky, the mother of the Los Angeles family. She is played by Tea Leoni like an explosion at the multiple personalities factory. She is kind, enlightened, and politically correct. She is also hysterical, manic, and a drama queen whose daily life is besieged by one crisis after another. I am not sure this character has any connection to a possible human being, but as a phenomenon it's kind of amazing; Deborah doesn't just go over the top, she waves good-bye as she disappears into cuckooland. Somehow Leoni is able to play Deborah without frothing at the mouth, and indeed makes her kind of lovable.

One who loves her is her husband, John (Adam Sandler), although he treacherously observes, "I'm running out of excuses for the woman of the house." John is a chef—in fact, according to the *New York Times,* the finest chef in America. You would therefore expect him to be a perfectionist tyrant with anger management problems, but in fact he's basically just that sweet Sandler boy, and at one point he is asked, "Could you stop being so stark raving calm?"

Deborah's mother, Evelyn (Cloris Leachman), is a practicing alcoholic whose rehearsals start at noon. She's a former jazz singer, now relegated to resident Golden Girl, sending in zingers from the sidelines. Her drinking pays off in the last act, however, when she sobers up (no one notices) and gives her daughter urgent advice.

Into this household come Flor (Paz Vega) and her daughter, Cristina (Shelbie Bruce), who is about the same middle-school age as the Claskys' daughter, Bernice (Sarah Steele). Flor and Cristina have lived in the barrio for six years, and now venture into Anglo-land because Flor needs a better job. The story is narrated by the seventeen-year-old Cristina as an affectionate memory of her mother, who learned English the better to treat this needful family with enormous doses of common sense.

Now that we have all the characters on stage, what is their story about? Is it about Flor, whose daughter narrates the story, or about the Claskys' marriage, or about the way the two daughters, both smart, both sane, are the go-to members of their families? I'm not sure there's a clear story line; it's more as if all these people meet, mix, behave, and almost lose their happiness (if happiness it is) before all is restored and the movie can end.

Along the way there are some wonderful scenes. My favorite involves a sequence where Flor decides she must finally explain to the Claskys exactly what she thinks, and why. At this point she still speaks no English, and so Cristina acts as her interpreter. As mother and daughter, Paz Vega and Shelbie Bruce play the scene with virtuoso comic timing, the mother waving her arms and the girl waving her same arms exactly the same way a second later, as they stalk around the room, Cristina acting as translator, shadow, and mime.

There's also ironic dialogue in a sequence involving the *Times* review of John's restaurant, which to John is a catastrophe. Restaurants are ruined by four-star reviews, he explains: A line of @$$#o!>s immediately forms out in front. Please, lord, he prays, just give me three and a quarter stars. The restaurant isn't really crucial to the story, however; it's more like a way for John to get out of the house.

Oh, and Tea Leoni has the first onscreen orgasm that can seriously be compared with Meg Ryan's show-stopper in *When Harry Met Sally.* After Ryan's, you'll recall, another woman in the restaurant said, "I'll have what she's having." After Leoni's, you just want to dial 911.

When it comes to the experiences of a Latino maid in an Anglo household, nothing is likely to improve on the adventures of Zaide Silvia Gutierrez in *El Norte* (1983), where the space-age automatic washer-dryer proved so baffling that the young maid just spread the washing out on the lawn to dry in the sun. But *Spanglish* isn't really about being a maid; it's more about being a life force, as Paz Vega heals this family with a sunny disposition and an anchor of normality.

There are a couple of excursions toward adultery in the film, one offscreen, the other not quite realized, but they, too, exist not to cause trouble, but to provide trouble that can be cured. The movie is all about solutions, and the problems are more like test questions. At the end, I felt there hadn't been much at risk, but I got to see some worthy characters stumbling toward improvement.

Spartan ★ ★ ★ ★
R, 106 m., 2004

Val Kilmer (Robert Scott), Derek Luke (Curtis), William H. Macy (Stoddard), Ed O'Neill (Burch), Tia Texada (Jackie Black), Kristen Bell (Laura Newton). Directed by David Mamet and produced by Art Linson, David Bergstein, Elie Samaha, and Moshe Diamant. Screenplay by Mamet.

Spartan opens without any credits except its title, but I quickly knew it was written by David Mamet because nobody else hears and writes dialogue the way he does. That the film tells a labyrinthine story of betrayal and deception, a con within a con, also stakes out Mamet territory. But the scope of the picture is larger than Mamet's usual canvas: This is a thriller on a global scale, involving the Secret Service, the FBI, the CIA, the White House, a secret Special Ops unit, and Middle Eastern kidnappers. Such a scale could lend itself to one of those big, clunky action machines based on 700-page best-sellers that put salesmen to sleep on airplanes. But no. Not with Mamet, who treats his action plot as a framework for a sly, deceptive exercise in the gradual approximation of the truth.

Before I get to the plot, let me linger on the dialogue. Most thrillers have simpleminded characters who communicate to each other in primary plot points ("Cover me." "It goes off in ten minutes." "Who are you working for?") *Spartan* begins by assuming that all of its characters know who they are and what they're doing, and do not need to explain this to us in thriller-talk. They communicate in elliptical shorthand, in shoptalk, in tradecraft, in oblique references, in shared memories; we can't always believe what they say, and we don't always know that. We get involved in their characters and we even sense their rivalries while the outline of the plot is still murky. How murky we don't even dream.

Val Kilmer, in his best performance since *Tombstone*, plays a Special Ops officer named Scott, who as the movie opens is doing a field exercise with two trainees: Curtis (Derek Luke) and Jackie Black (Tia Texada). He's called off that assignment after the daughter of the president is kidnapped. The Secret Service was supposed to be guarding her, but . . . what went wrong is one of the movie's secrets. Ed O'Neill plays an agent in charge of the search for the daughter, William H. Macy is a political operative from the White House, and it turns out that the daughter, Laura Newton (Kristen Bell), was taken for reasons that are not obvious, by kidnappers you would not guess, who may or may not know she is the president's daughter. Kilmer's assignment: go anywhere and get her back by any means necessary. Curtis and Jackie want to get involved, too, but Kilmer doesn't want them, which may not be the final word on the subject.

And that is quite enough of the plot. It leaves me enjoying the way Mamet, from his earliest plays to his great films like *House of Games, Wag the Dog, Homicide,* and *The Spanish Prisoner,* works like a magician who uses words instead of cards. The patter is always fascinating, and at right angles to the action. He's like a magician who gets you all involved in his story about the king, the queen, and the jack, while the whole point is that there's a rabbit in your pocket. Some screenwriters study Robert McKee. Mamet studies magic and confidence games. In his plots, the left hand makes a distracting movement, but you're too smart for that, and you quick look over at the right hand to spot the trick, while meantime the left hand does the business while still seeming to flap around like a decoy.

The particular pleasure of *Spartan* is to watch the characters gradually define themselves and the plot gradually emerge like your face in a steamy mirror. You see the outlines, and then your nose, and then you see that somebody is standing behind you, and then you see it's you, so who is the guy in the mirror? Work with me here. I'm trying to describe how the movie operates without revealing what it does.

William H. Macy, who has been with Mamet since his earliest theater days, is an ideal choice for this kind of work. He always seems like the

ordinary guy who is hanging on for retirement. He's got that open, willing face, and the flat, helpful voice with sometimes the little complaint in it, and in *Spartan* he starts out with what looks like a walk-on role (we're thinking David found a part for his old pal) and ends up walking away with it. Val Kilmer, a versatile actor who can be good at almost anything (who else has played Batman and John Holmes?), here plays lean and hard, Sam Jackson style. His character is enormously resourceful with his craft, but becomes extremely puzzled about what he can do safely, and who he can trust. Derek Luke, a rising star with a quiet earnestness that is just right here, disappears for a long stretch and then finds out something remarkable, and Tia Texada, in the Rosario Dawson role, succeeds against all odds in actually playing a woman soldier instead of a sexy actress playing a woman soldier.

I like the safe rooms with the charts on the walls, and I like the casual way that spycraft is explained by being used, and the way Mamet keeps pulling the curtain aside to reveal a new stage with a new story. I suppose the last scene in the film will remind some of our friend the *deus ex machina,* but after reflection I have decided that, in that place, at that time, what happens is about as likely to happen as anything else, maybe likelier.

Spider-Man 2 ★ ★ ★ ★
PG-13, 125 m., 2004

Tobey Maguire (Peter Parker/Spider-Man), Kirsten Dunst (Mary Jane Watson), Alfred Molina (Dr. Otto Octavius/Doc Ock), James Franco (Harry Osborn), Rosemary Harris (Aunt May), J. K. Simmons (J. Jonah Jameson). Directed by Sam Raimi and produced by Avi Arad and Laura Ziskin. Screenplay by Alvin Sargent, Michael Chabon, Miles Millar, and Alfred Gough, based on the comic book by Stan Lee and Steve Ditko.

Now this is what a superhero movie should be. *Spider-Man 2* believes in its story in the same way serious comic readers believe, when the adventures on the page express their own dreams and wishes. It's not camp and it's not nostalgia, it's not wall-to-wall special effects and it's not pickled in angst. It's simply and poignantly a realization that being Spider-Man is a burden that Peter Parker is not entirely willing to bear. The movie demonstrates what's wrong with a lot of other superhero epics: They focus on the superpowers and short-change the humans behind them (has anyone ever been more boring than Clark Kent or Bruce Wayne?).

Spider-Man 2 is the best superhero movie since the modern genre was launched with *Superman* (1978). It succeeds by being true to the insight that allowed Marvel Comics to upturn decades of comic book tradition: Readers could identify more completely with heroes like themselves than with remote, godlike paragons. Peter Parker was an insecure high school student, in grade trouble, inarticulate in love, unready to assume the responsibilities that came with his unexpected superpowers. It wasn't that Spider-Man could swing from skyscrapers that won over his readers; it was that he fretted about personal problems in the thought balloons above his Spidey face mask.

Parker (Tobey Maguire) is in college now, studying physics at Columbia, more helplessly in love than ever with Mary Jane Watson (Kirsten Dunst). He's on the edge of a breakdown: He's lost his job as a pizza deliveryman, Aunt May faces foreclosure on her mortgage, he's missing classes, the colors run together when he washes his Spider-Man suit at the Laundromat, and after his web-spinning ability inexplicably seems to fade, he throws away his beloved uniform in despair. When a bum tries to sell the discarded Spidey suit to Jonah Jameson, editor of the *Daily Bugle,* Jameson offers him $50. The bum says he could do better on eBay. Has it come to this?

I was disappointed by the original *Spider-Man* (2002), and surprised to find this film working from the first frame. Sam Raimi, the director of both pictures, this time seems to know exactly what he should do, and never steps wrong in a film that effortlessly combines special effects and a human story, keeping its parallel plots alive and moving. One of the keys to the movie's success must be the contribution of novelist Michael Chabon to the screenplay; Chabon understands in his bones what comic books are, and why. His inspired 2000 novel, *The Amazing Adventures of Kavalier and Clay,* chronicles the birth of a 1940s comic book su-

perhero and the young men who created him; Chabon worked on the screen story that fed into Alvin Sargent's screenplay. *See entry in the Answer Man section.*

The seasons in a superhero's life are charted by the villains he faces (it is the same with James Bond). *Spider-Man 2* gives Spider-Man an enemy with a good nature that is overcome by evil. Peter Parker admires the famous Dr. Otto Octavius (Alfred Molina), whose laboratory on the banks of the East River houses an experiment that will either prove that fusion can work as a cheap source of energy, or vaporize Manhattan. To handle the dangerous materials of his experiments, Octavius devises four powerful tentacles that are fused to his spine and have cyber-intelligence of their own; a chip at the top of his spine prevents them from overriding his orders, but when the chip is destroyed the gentle scientist is transformed into Doc Ock, a fearsome fusion of man and machine, who can climb skyscraper walls by driving his tentacles through concrete and bricks. We hear him coming, hammering his way toward us like the drums of hell.

Peter Parker meanwhile has vowed that he cannot allow himself to love Mary Jane because her life would be in danger from Spider-Man's enemies. She has finally given up on Peter, who is always standing her up; she announces her engagement to no less than an astronaut. Peter has heart-to-hearts with her and with Aunt May (Rosemary Harris), who is given full screen time and not reduced to an obligatory cameo. And he has to deal with his friend Harry Osborn (James Franco), who likes Peter but hates Spider-Man, blaming him for the death of his father (a.k.a. the Green Goblin, although much is unknown to the son).

There are special effects, and then there are special effects. In the first movie I thought Spider-Man seemed to move with all the realism of a character in a cartoon. This time, as he swings from one skyscraper to another, he has more weight and dimension, and Raimi is able to seamlessly match the CGI and the human actors. The f/x triumph in the film is the work on Doc Ock's four robotic tentacles, which move with an uncanny life, reacting and responding, doing double-takes, becoming characters of their own.

Watching Raimi and his writers cut between the story threads, I savored classical workmanship: The film gives full weight to all of its elements, keeps them alive, is constructed with such skill that we care all the way through; in a lesser movie from this genre, we usually perk up for the action scenes but wade grimly through the dialogue. Here both stay alive, and the dialogue is more about emotion, love, and values, less about long-winded explanations of the inexplicable (it's kind of neat that Spider-Man never does find out why his web-throwing ability sometimes fails him).

Tobey Maguire almost didn't sign for the sequel, complaining of back pain; Jake Gyllenhaal, another gifted actor, was reportedly in the wings. But if Maguire hadn't returned (along with Spidey's throwaway line about his aching back), we would never have known how good he could be in this role. Kirsten Dunst is valuable, too, bringing depth and heart to a girlfriend role that in lesser movies would be conventional. When she kisses her astronaut boyfriend upside-down, it's one of those perfect moments that rewards fans of the whole saga; we don't need to be told she's remembering her only kiss from Spider-Man.

There are moviegoers who make it a point of missing superhero movies, and I can't blame them, although I confess to a weakness for the genre. I liked both of *The Crow* movies, and *Daredevil*, *The Hulk*, and *X2*, but not enough to recommend them to friends who don't like or understand comic books. *Spider-Man 2* is in another category: It's a real movie, full-blooded and smart, with qualities even for those who have no idea who Stan Lee is. It's a superhero movie for people who don't go to superhero movies, and for those who do, it's the one they've been yearning for.

The Spongebob Squarepants Movie ★ ★ ★
PG, 90 m., 2004

With the voices of: Tom Kenny (SpongeBob SquarePants), Bill Fagerbakke (Patrick Star), Mr. Lawrence (Plankton), Clancy Brown (Eugene H. Krabs), Jeffrey Tambor (King Neptune), Alec Baldwin (Dennis), Rodger Bumpass (Squidward Tentacles). Directed by Sherm Cohen and Stephen Hillenburg and produced by Derek Drymon, Albie Hecht, Hillenburg, Julia Pistor, and Gina Shay. Screenplay by Hillenburg, Drymon, Tim Hill, Kent Osborne, Aaron Springer, and Paul Tibbett.

Q: *Why does a lobster make the ideal pet?*
A: *It doesn't bark, and it knows the secrets of the deep.*

I've been telling that joke for years, to people who regard me in silence and mystification. If it made you smile even a little, you are a candidate for *The SpongeBob SquarePants Movie*. This is the "Good Burger" of animation, plopping us down inside a fast-food war being fought by sponges, starfish, crabs, tiny plankton, and mighty King Neptune.

SpongeBob (voice by Tom Kenny) has a ready-made legion of fans, who follow his adventures every Saturday morning on Nickelodeon. I even know parents who like the show, which is fast-paced and goofy and involves SpongeBob's determination to amount to something in this world. In the movie, he dreams of becoming manager of Krusty Krab II, the new outlet being opened by Eugene H. Krabs (Clancy Brown), the most successful businesscrab in the ocean-floor community of Bikini Bottom. SpongeBob may only be a kid, but he's smart and learns fast, and reminded me of Ed, the hero of the live-action Nickelodeon series *Good Burger* ("Welcome to Good Burger, home of the Good Burger! Can I take your order *please?*").

SpongeBob, like all sponges I suppose, has a thing about cleanliness, and to watch him take a shower is inspiring. First he eats a cake of soap. Then he plunges a hose into the top of his head and fills up with water, exuding soap bubbles from every pore, or would that be orifice, or crevice? Then he pulls on his SquarePants and hurries off for what he expects to be a richly deserved promotion.

Alas, the job goes to Squidward Tentacles (Rodger Bumpass), who has no rapport with the customers but does have seniority. A kid can't handle the responsibility, Eugene Krabs tells SpongeBob. This is a bitter verdict, but meanwhile, intrigue is brewing in Bikini Bottom. Plankton, who runs the spectacularly unsuccessful rival food stand named Chum Bucket, plans to steal Eugene's famous recipe for

653

Krabby Patties. As part of this plot, Plankton (Mr. Lawrence) has King Neptune's crown stolen and frames Eugene Krabs with the crime, so it's up to SpongeBob and his starfish friend Patrick (Bill Fagerbakke) to venture to the forbidden no-go zone of Shell City (which is no doubt near Shell Beach, and you remember Shell Beach). There they hope to recapture the crown, restore it to King Neptune (Jeffrey Tambor), save Mr. Krabs from execution, and get SpongeBob the promotion.

All of this happens in jolly animation with bright colors and is ever so much more entertaining than you are probably imagining. No doubt right now you're asking yourself why you have read this far in the review, given your near-certainty that you will not be going anywhere near a SpongeBob SquarePants movie, unless you are the parent or adult guardian of a SpongeBob SquarePants fan, in which case your fate is sealed. Assuming that few members of SpongeBob's primary audience are reading this (or can read), all I can tell you is, the movie is likely to be more fun than you expect.

The opening, for example, is inexplicable, unexpected, and very funny, as a boatload of pirates crowd into the front of a movie theater to see SpongeBob. These are real flesh-and-blood pirates, not animated ones, and part of the scene's charm comes because it is completely gratuitous. So, for that matter, is the appearance of another flesh-and-blood actor in the movie, David Hasselhoff, who gives SpongeBob and Patrick a high-speed lift back to Bikini Bottom and then propels them to the deeps by placing them between his pectoral muscles and flexing and popping. This is not quite as disgusting as it sounds, but it comes close.

I confess I'm not exactly sure if the residents of Bikini Bottom are cannibals; what, exactly, is in Eugene H. Krabs's Krabby Patties if not . . . krabs? Does the Chum Bucket sell chum? No doubt faithful viewers of the show will know. I am reminded of the scene in *Shark Tale* when Lenny, the vegetarian shark, becomes an activist and frees a shrimp cocktail.

One of the stranger scenes in *SBSP* comes when SpongeBob and Patrick get wasted at Goofy Goober's nightclub, where ice cream performs the same function as booze. This leads to the ice-cream version of a pie fight, and terrible

hangovers the next morning; no wonder, as anyone who has ever used a sponge on ice cream can testify.

The Squid and the Whale ★ ★ ★ ½

R, 88 m., 2005

Jeff Daniels (Bernard Berkman), Laura Linney (Joan Berkman), Jesse Eisenberg (Walt Berkman), Owen Kline (Frank Berkman), Halley Feiffer (Sophie), William Baldwin (Ivan), Anna Paquin (Lili). Directed by Noah Baumbach and produced by Wes Anderson, Charlie Corwin, Clara Markowicz, and Peter Newman. Screenplay by Baumbach.

I don't know what I'm supposed to feel during *The Squid and the Whale*. Sympathy, I suppose, for two bright boys whose parents are getting a messy divorce. Both parents are writers and use words as weapons; the boys choose sides and join the war. In theory, I observe their errors and sadness and think, there but for the grace of God go I. In practice, I feel envy.

I would have loved to have two writers as parents, grow up in a bohemian family in Brooklyn, and hear dinner-table conversation about Dickens. These kids have it great. Their traumas will inspire them someday. Hell, the movie was written and directed by Noah Baumbach, whose parents were writers (the novelist Jonathan Baumbach, the film critic Georgia Brown), and look how he turned out. By the time he was twenty-six, he had already directed *Kicking and Screaming* (1995), about sardonic and literate college graduates whose only ambition was to remain on campus. I felt the same way. Left to my own devices, I would still be a student of English literature, entering my forty-fourth year as an undergraduate.

In the movie, the parents, Bernard and Joan Berkman, are played by Jeff Daniels and Laura Linney, and if that's who it takes to play your parents, what are you complaining about? The movie centers on their troubled sons. Joan has been having an affair for four years, their father is moving out, and in theory their divorcing parents will share custody (there is even a plan for time shares of the cat). In practice, Walt (Jesse Eisenberg), who is sixteen, moves in with his father, and Frank (Owen Kline), who is about ten, stays in the family home with his mother.

Both kids have issues with their parents' sexuality. Walt thinks his mother is a "whore" for bringing one of her lovers into their home, but then his father begins an affair with one of his students, and what does that make him? Walt falls into true adolescent love but is compelled to deny it to himself because his father urges him to play the field, and he values his father's opinions more than is wise. "You have too many freckles," he tells Sophie (Halley Feiffer), the girl he likes. I guess he thinks that shows he has high standards. He's so dumb he doesn't know how wonderful too many freckles are.

Frank, his younger brother, has meanwhile discovered masturbation and taken to distributing his semen here and there around his school—on library books, for example. This is an alarming breach of school decorum and leads to a parent-teacher-student conference, during which I kept hoping someone would quote Rodney Dangerfield: "When I was a kid we were so poor, if I hadn't been a boy I wouldn't have had anything to play with."

Bernard, the father, published a good novel some years earlier and is now in a protracted drought season. It doesn't help when his wife sells a story to the *New Yorker*. He is played by Daniels as a man with wise-guy literary opinions that his son remembers and repeats; Bernard says *A Tale of Two Cities* is "minor Dickens," which is correct, and arms Walt with useful terms such as "Kafkaesque." Walt informs Sophie a book is Kafkaesque, and Sophie says, "It's written by Franz Kafka. It has to be." Point, match, and game. Walt's performance in the school talent show is a great success. Everyone is impressed by his songwriting ability except for a fellow student familiar with the lyrics of Pink Floyd. Life lesson: Okay to steal from your father to impress people, not okay to steal from Pink Floyd.

The Squid and the Whale is essentially about how we grow up by absorbing what is useful in our parents and forgiving what is not. Joan may cheat on her husband, but he deserves to be cheated on, and she demonstrates a faith in romance that is, after all, a lesson in optimism. Bernard may be a gold mine of shorthand literary opinions, but in his case he has actually read the books, and sooner or later his son Walt will probably feel compelled to read minor Dickens for himself—and major Dickens,

which is so good all you can do is just helplessly stare at the book and turn the pages.

These kids will be okay. Someday Bernard and Joan will be old and will delight in their grandchildren, who will no doubt be miserable about the flaws and transgressions of Walt and Frank, and then create great achievements and angry children of their own. All I know is, it is better to be the whale than the squid. Whales inspire major novels.

Note: Since writing this, I have reread A Tale of Two Cities, and I no longer agree it is minor Dickens. ☞

Stage Beauty ★ ★ ★
R, 110 m., 2004

Billy Crudup (Ned Kynaston), Claire Danes (Maria), Rupert Everett (King Charles II), Tom Wilkinson (Thomas Betterton), Ben Chaplin (Duke of Buckingham), Hugh Bonneville (Samuel Pepys), Richard Griffiths (Sir Charles Sedley), Edward Fox (Sir Edward Hyde), Zoe Tapper (Nell Gwynn). Directed by Richard Eyre and produced by Robert De Niro, Hardy Justice, and Jane Rosenthal. Screenplay by Jeffrey Hatcher, based on his play *Compleat Female Stage Beauty*.

Stage Beauty opens in a London weary of Puritan dreariness. The monarchy has been restored, and Charles II is a fun-loving king whose mistress, Nell Gwynn, whispers mischief in his ear. They take a lively interest in the theater. Women are not allowed to perform on the stage, so all the women's roles are played by men—chief among them Ned Kynaston (Billy Crudup), whom Samuel Pepys described in his diary as the most beautiful woman on the London stage.

Ned is most comfortable playing a woman both onstage and off. But is he gay? The question doesn't precisely occur in that form, since in those days gender lines were not rigidly enforced, and heterosexuals sometimes indulged their genitals in a U-turn. Certainly Ned has inspired the love of Maria (Claire Danes), his dresser, who envies his art while she lusts for his body. We see her backstage during one of Ned's rehearsals, mouthing every line and mimicking every gesture; she could play Desdemona herself, and indeed she does one night, in an illicit secret theater, even borrowing Ned's costumes.

Word of her performance reaches the throne, and Charles (Rupert Everett) is intrigued; a courtier tells him the French have long allowed women on the stage. His adviser Sir Edward Hyde (Edward Fox) observes, "Whenever one is about to do something truly horrible, we always say the French have been doing it for years." But Charles, nudged by Nell, decrees that henceforth women shall be played by women. This puts Ned Kynaston out of work, and turns Maria into an overnight star. "A woman playing a woman?" Ned sniffs. "What's the trick of that?"

The film, written by Jeffrey Hatcher and based on his play *Compleat Female Stage Beauty*, is really about two things at once: the craft of acting and the bafflement of love. It must be said that Ned is not a very convincing woman onstage (although he is pretty enough); he plays a woman as a man would play a woman, lacking the natural ease of a woman born to the role. Curiously, when Maria takes over his roles, she also copies his gestures, playing a woman as a woman might play a man playing a woman. Only gradually does she relax into herself. "I've always hated your Desdemona," she confesses to Ned. "You never fight; you only die."

Like *Shakespeare in Love*, which is set half a century earlier and also centers on men playing women (and on a woman playing a man, and a woman playing a man playing a woman), *Stage Beauty* explores the boundaries between reality and performance. The difference is the Gwyneth Paltrow character in *Shakespeare* knows she is a woman in real life, while Ned Kynaston (based on a real actor) knows he is a woman on the stage but is not so sure about life.

It is a cruel blow when he finds fame and employment taken from him in an instant and awarded to Maria. Yet Maria still has feelings for Ned, and rescues him from a bawdy music hall to spirit him off to the country—where their lovemaking has the urgency of a first driving lesson. Like the couple in the limerick, they:

Argue all night
As to who has the right
To do what, and with which, and to whom.

Claire Danes is as fresh as running water in this role, exhibiting the clarity and directness that has become her strength; her characters tend to know who they are and why. That makes her a good contrast to Crudup, playing a character who is adrift between jobs and genders. Life for him is confusing, as men like the duke of Buckingham (Ben Chaplin) court him as a woman, forgiving him the inconvenience that he is not one, while saucy women delight in rummaging through his netherlands on a treasure hunt.

The movie lacks the effortless charm of *Shakespeare in Love,* and its canvas is somewhat less alive with background characters and details. But it has a poignancy that *Shakespeare* lacks, because it is about a real dilemma and two people who are trying to solve it; must Ned and Maria betray their real natures in order to find love, or accept them?

The London of the time is fragrantly evoked, as horses attend to their needs regardless of whose carriage they are drawing, and bathing seems a novelty. I wonder if the court of Charles II was quite as Monty Pythonesque as the movie has it, and if Nell Gwynn was quite such a bold wench, but the details involving life in the theater feel real, especially in scenes about the fragility of an actor's ego. Poor Ned. "She's a star," the theater owner Thomas Betterton (Tom Wilkinson) tells Ned about Maria. "She did what she did first; you did what you did last."

Note: Our best record of this period, of course, is Pepys's diary (if you do not have six months to read it all, try the audiobook abridgement by Kenneth Branagh, or look at the daily entries at www.pepysdiary.com). Pepys was a high official in the navy, with access to the court, and is the source for some of what we know about Ned Kynaston. We often see him at the edge of the screen, busily scribbling (in fact, he wrote at home in code). "Mr. Pepys," he is asked at one point, "who do you write down all those little notes for?"

Stander ★ ★ ½
R, 111 m., 2004

Thomas Jane (Andre Stander), Dexter Fletcher (Lee McCall), David Patrick O'Hara (Allan Heyl), Deborah Kara Unger (Bekkie Stander), Ashley Taylor (Deventer). Directed by Bronwen Hughes and produced by Martin Katz, Chris Roland, and Julia Verdin. Screenplay by Bima Stagg.

Stander begins with white South African police firing on black demonstrators during an infamous massacre at Soweto. Andre Stander, a police captain, has ordered his men to stand fast, but after a sniper in a helicopter starts firing, the tragedy begins. Stander kills a man and fires three more times. He is appalled by what he has done. When some of his men ask, "Think we'll get paid double-time on this?" he attacks them.

Stander, played by Thomas Jane, is in conflict with himself and his society. He hates his job, which he does so well he is about to be promoted. "A white man could get away with anything while the police are out watching the blacks," he observes. To prove it, he holds up a bank. He gets away with it.

The real Andre Stander was eventually to rob twenty-seven banks on his way to becoming a South African folk legend. He was bold to the point of recklessness, at one point returning as a police officer to the bank he had just robbed. He asks a teller for a description. "He looked just like you," the teller says. The cops get a good laugh out of that. On another occasion, he robs the bank next door to the special task force set up to catch him. On a third, when a bank manager brags he missed his other safe, he goes back to empty it.

He gathers a gang of two partners, whom he met in prison after being convicted of some of his earlier robberies. After their escape, they roam South Africa robbing banks almost on impulse. Yes, they use disguises, but disguises that look like disguises—and besides, everybody knows anyway that it's the Stander gang. Various girlfriends cause conflicts and problems, and Stander has a problematic relationship with his furious wife, Bekkie (Deborah Unger).

In court, the real Stander made the statement, "I'm tried for robbing banks—but I have killed unarmed people." So were his robberies a protest against apartheid and the cruel laws of white South Africa? In this movie, not precisely. He steals from the rich and gives to himself. The robberies seem to continue because the first one fed some kind of a need. It was self-destructive and thrilling at the same time; there may be a key in the opening scene, where he is drunk and driving recklessly, and is stopped by cops who apologize when they realize who he is. Does he need to flaunt his lawlessness as a way of dealing

with his conflicts as a police officer? It's not so much that he wants to get caught, as that he wants a cop to get caught.

Stander, directed by Bronwen Hughes and written by Bima Stagg, is as conflicted as its hero. Does it see Stander as an antihero or a case study? There's a long middle passage devoted mostly to bank robberies that seems almost perfunctory. We miss the timing, irony, and drama of the robberies in *Bonnie and Clyde,* where comedy was punctuated by violence, but don't get that tension here. The style is more deadpan, as if to demystify Stander: He was famous as a turncoat cop who performed dozens of daring daylight robberies, but he was not a criminal mastermind, and at times seemed almost childish.

The movie has few intimate insights into Andre Stander; it knows him as the reader of a newspaper might know him. It uses apartheid as a backdrop, but an uninformed moviegoer would not learn much about the South Africa of those days from this movie. The ending, which takes place in Fort Lauderdale during spring break, is ironic, yes, but all too conveniently existential; in a way it lets Stander off the hook.

There is one extraordinary scene. In his personal version of the Truth and Reconciliation process, Stander walks boldly into Soweto to visit the family of the man he killed. His audacity protects him, up to a point: A white man walking alone down those angry streets must have a good reason to think he can get away with it. When he finds the family, he identifies himself as the policeman who killed their son, and says he has come to apologize. Then he is beaten almost to death by young men from the crowd that has gathered. Well, of course he is, as he must have known he would be.

This scene involves elements that, properly presented and understood, might have provided insights into Stander and his culture, but it is played as a stand-alone event, an enigmatic choice by Stander that doesn't seem to connect with what comes later. We are not sure if his motive is to rid himself of guilt, to seek forgiveness, or simply to invite death in a form of suicide.

Stander's long run of brazen bank robberies would have made him a legend in any nation, but in South Africa there was the additional crucial factor that he was not only white, but had been a respected police official. His court statement, contrasting robbery with the killing of unarmed civilians, must have had wide circulation. What did black South Africans think of him? The movie gives us no real idea. The blacks provide backdrop and context, their deaths motivate the plot, but none of them emerge as individuals and their opinion of Stander is not solicited.

Starsky & Hutch ★ ★ ★
PG-13, 97 m., 2004

Ben Stiller (Dave Starsky), Owen Wilson (Ken Hutchinson), Snoop Dogg (Huggy Bear), Vince Vaughn (Reese Feldman), Juliette Lewis (Kitty), Fred Williamson (Captain Doby). Directed by Todd Phillips and produced by William Blinn, Stuart Cornfeld, Akiva Goldsman, Tony Ludwig, and Alan Riche. Screenplay by John O'Brien, Phillips, Scot Armstrong, and Stevie Long.

As Hollywood works its way through retreads of TV series from the 1960s and 1970s, I find I can approach each project with a certain purity, since I never saw any of the original shows. Never saw a single *Starsky and Hutch*. Not one episode of *I Spy*. No *Mod Squad*. No *Charlie's Angels*. What was I doing instead, apart from seeing thousands of movies? Avoiding episodic television like a communicable disease, and improving myself with the great literature of the ages. Plus partying.

So here is *Starsky & Hutch*, adding the ampersand for a generation too impatient for "and." It's a surprisingly funny movie, the best of the 1970s recycling jobs, with one laugh ("Are you okay, little pony?") almost as funny as the moment in *Dumb and Dumber* when the kid figured out his parakeet's head was Scotch-taped on.

Ben Stiller and Owen Wilson star, in their sixth movie together. They use the same comic contrasts that worked for Hope and Crosby and Martin and Lewis: one is hyper and the other is sleepy-eyed and cool. In a genial spoof of the cop buddy genre, they're both misfits on the Bay City police force. Starsky (Stiller) is the kind of cop who would ask another cop if he had a license for his firearm. Hutch (Wilson) has done nothing useful at all for months, aside from enriching himself illegally by stealing from

dead bodies. Their captain (Fred Williamson) thinks they deserve each other, and makes them partners in a scene where Hutch immediately insults Starsky's perm.

The bad guy is Reese Feldman (Vince Vaughn), coils of cigarette smoke constantly rising in front of his face. He's a big-time cocaine dealer who has invented, or discovered, a form of cocaine that has no taste or smell and can fool police dogs. He's also a vicious boss who kills an underling in the opening scene and pushes him off his yacht. Discovery of the floater gives Starsky and Hutch their first big case, although they almost blow it, since Hutch's first suggestion is to push it back out to sea and hope it floats to the next precinct.

Although the plot survives sporadically, the movie is mostly about the rapport between Stiller and Wilson, who carry on a running disagreement about style while agreeing on most other issues, such as the importance of partying with sexy cheerleaders as part of their investigation. Carmen Electra and Amy Smart are the cheerleaders, improbably attracted to the guys, and there's a very funny scene where Wilson croons a minor David Soul hit from the 1970s while a psychedelically fueled cartoon bird chirps on his shoulder.

The movie doesn't make the mistake of relying entirely on its stars. Apart from Vaughn and the cheerleaders, the supporting cast benefits mightily from Juliette Lewis, as Vaughn's mistress, and Snoop Dogg as Huggy Bear, a combo pimp/superfly/police informer whose outfits are like retro cubed. Will Ferrell turns up in a weird cameo as a jailhouse source whose sexual curiosity falls far outside anything either Starsky and Hutch had ever imagined ("arch your back and look back at me over your shoulder, like a dragon").

Another character is Starsky's beloved bright-red, supercharged Ford Gran Torino, which he drives like a madman while obsessing about the smallest scratch. The closing stunt involves something we've been waiting to happen in car stunt scenes for a very long time.

The film's director is Todd Phillips, of *Road Trip* and *Old School*. I was not a big fan of either movie, but they both contained real laughs, and now in *Starsky & Hutch* he reaches critical mass. Will the movie inspire me to watch reruns of the original series? No. I want to quit while I'm ahead.

Star Wars: Episode III — Revenge of the Sith ★ ★ ★ ½
PG-13, 140 m., 2005

Ewan McGregor (Obi-Wan Kenobi), Hayden Christensen (Anakin Skywalker), Natalie Portman (Padme Amidala), Ian McDiarmid (Chancellor Palpatine), Samuel L. Jackson (Mace Windu), Jimmy Smits (Senator Bail Organa), Christopher Lee (Count Dooku), Frank Oz (voice) (Yoda), Anthony Daniels (C-3PO), Kenny Baker (R2-D2). Directed by George Lucas and produced by Rick McCallum. Screenplay by Lucas.

George Lucas comes full circle in more ways than one in *Star Wars: Episode III—Revenge of the Sith,* which is the sixth and allegedly, but not necessarily, the last of the *Star Wars* movies. After *Episode II* got so bogged down in politics that it played like the Republic covered by C-Span, *Episode III* is a return to the classic space opera style that launched the series. Because the story leads up to where the original *Star Wars* began, we get to use the immemorial movie phrase, "This is where we came in."

That Anakin Skywalker abandoned the Jedi and went over to the dark side is known to all students of *Star Wars.* That his twins, Luke Skywalker and Princess Leia, would redeem the family name is also known. What we discover in *Episode III* is how and why Anakin lost his way—how a pleasant and brave young man was transformed into a dark, cloaked figure with a fearsome black metal face. As Yoda sadly puts it in his inimitable word-order: "The boy who dreamed, gone he is, consumed by Darth Vader." Unexplained is how several inches grew he in the process.

As *Episode III* opens, Anakin Skywalker (Hayden Christensen) and his friend Obi-Wan Kenobi (Ewan McGregor) are piloting fighter crafts, staging a daring two-man raid to rescue Chancellor Palpatine (Ian McDiarmid). He has been captured by the rebel General Grievous (whose voice, by Matthew Woods, sounds curiously wheezy considering the general seems to use replacement parts). In the spirit of all the *Star Wars* movies, this rescue sequence flies in

the face of logic, since the two pilots are able to board Grievous's command ship and proceed without much trouble to the ship's observation tower, where the chancellor is being held. There is a close call in an elevator shaft, but where are the guards and the security systems? And why, for that matter, does a deep space cruiser need an observation tower when every porthole opens onto the universe? But never mind.

Back within the sphere of the Jedi Council, Anakin finds that despite his heroism he will not yet be named a Jedi Master. The council distrusts Palpatine and wants Anakin to spy on him; Palpatine wants Anakin to spy on the council. Who to choose? McDiarmid has the most complex role in the movie as he plays on Anakin's wounded ego. Anakin is tempted to go over to what is not yet clearly the dark side; in a movie not distinguished for its dialogue, Palpatine is insidiously snaky in his persuasiveness.

The way Anakin approaches his choice, however, has a certain poignancy. Anakin has a rendezvous with Padme (Natalie Portman); they were secretly married in the previous film, and now she reveals she is pregnant. His reaction is that of a nice kid in a teenage comedy, trying to seem pleased while wondering how this will affect the other neat stuff he gets to do. To say that George Lucas cannot write a love scene is an understatement; greeting cards have expressed more passion.

The dialogue throughout the movie is once again its weakest point: The characters talk in what sounds like Basic English, without color, wit, or verbal delight, as if they were channeling Berlitz. The exceptions are Palpatine and, of course, Yoda, whose speech (voiced by Frank Oz) reminds me of Wolcott Gibbs's famous line about the early style of *Time* magazine: "Backward ran sentences until reeled the mind."

In many cases the actors are being filmed in front of blue screens, with effects to be added later, and sometimes their readings are so flat they don't seem to believe they're really in the middle of amazing events. How can you stand in front of exploding star fleets and sound as if you're talking on a cell phone at Starbucks? "He's worried about you," Anakin is told at one point. "You've been under a lot of stress." Sometimes the emphasis in sentences is misplaced. During the elevator adventure in the opening rescue, we hear, "Did I miss *something?*" when it should be, "Did I *miss* something?"

The dialogue is not the point, however; Lucas's characters engage in sturdy oratorical pronunciamentos and then leap into adventure. *Episode III* has more action per square minute, I'd guess, than any of the previous five movies, and it is spectacular. The special effects are more sophisticated than in the earlier movies, of course, but not necessarily more effective. The dogfight between fighters in the original *Star Wars* and the dogfight that opens this one differ in their complexity (many more ships this time, more planes of action, complex background) but not in their excitement. And although Lucas has his characters attend a futuristic opera that looks like a cross between Cirque du Soleil and an ultrasound scan of an unborn baby, if you regard the opera hall simply as a place, it's not as engaging as the saloon on Tatooine in the first movie.

The lesson, I think, is that special effects should be judged not by their complexity but by the degree that they stimulate the imagination, and *Episode III* is distinguished not by how well the effects are done, but by how amazingly they are imagined. A climactic duel on a blazing volcanic planet is as impressive, in its line, as anything in *The Lord of the Rings*. And Yoda, who began life as a Muppet but is now completely animated (like about 70 percent of the rest of what we see), was to begin with and still is the most lifelike of the *Star Wars* characters.

A word, however, about the duels fought with lightsabers. When they flashed into life with a mighty whizzing "thunk" in the first "Star Wars" and whooshed through their deadly parabolas, that was exciting. But the thrill is gone. The duelists are so well matched that saber fights go on forever before anyone is wounded, and I am still not sure how the sabers seem able to shield their bearers from incoming ammo. When it comes to great movie swordfights, Liam Neeson and Tim Roth took home the gold medal in *Rob Roy* (1995), and the lightsaber battles in *Episode III* are more like isometrics.

These are all, however, more observations than criticisms. George Lucas has achieved what few artists do, and created and populated a world of his own. His *Star Wars* movies are among the most influential, both technically and commercially, ever made. And they are fun. If he got bogged down in solemnity and theory

in *Episode II: Attack of the Clones*, the Force is in a jollier mood this time, and *Revenge of the Sith* is a great entertainment.

Note: I said this is not necessarily the last of the Star Wars movies. Although Lucas has absolutely said he is finished with the series, it is inconceivable to me that 20th Century-Fox will willingly abandon the franchise, especially as Lucas has hinted that parts VII, VIII, and IX exist at least in his mind. There will be enormous pressure for them to be made, if not by him, then by his deputies.

The Statement ★ ★
R, 120 m., 2004

Michael Caine (Pierre Brossard), Tilda Swinton (Anne-Marie Livi), Jeremy Northam (Colonel Roux), Charlotte Rampling (Nicole), Noam Jenkins (Michael Levy), Matt Craven (David Manenbaum), Alan Bates (Armand Bertier). Directed by Norman Jewison and produced by Jewison and Robert Lantos. Screenplay by Ronald Harwood, based on a novel by Brian Moore.

Michael Caine is such a lovely actor. In a movie like *The Statement*, where he is more or less adrift among competing themes, it's a pleasure to watch him craft a character we can care about even when the story keeps throwing him curves. He has such patience with a moment, such an ability to express weariness or fear without seeming to try. Here he plays a weak man baffled by life and by his own motives, and he arouses so much sympathy that even though he's supposed to be the villain, the movie ends up with substitute villains who are shadowy and ill-explained.

Caine plays Pierre Brossard, a Frenchman who was involved in the execution of Jews during World War II. Wanted as a war criminal, he has been living in hiding ever since, in a series of Roman Catholic monasteries and other safe houses. It's explained that he is a member of an ultrasecret Catholic society that protects its own, and that presents one of the movie's many hurdles: Although the story is based on fact, the movie never convinced me of its truth.

The screenplay, by Ronald Harwood (*The Pianist*), based on a novel by Brian Moore, is inspired by the real-life Paul Touvier, who executed Jewish hostages and then was protected for many years by an informal network of right-wing Catholics. Would a series of abbots and cardinals place the church at risk for this insignificant man for years after the war has ended? Yes, apparently, some did; but a movie must seem to be based on its own facts, not those in research consulted by the screenwriters. The situation on screen is not made to seem real.

Caine himself is virtually made to play two different characters. Early in the film we see him cool and merciless as he perceives that he is being followed, and calmly kills the man who wants to kill him. Later, we see him weak, pathetic, and confused. Perhaps he contains both men, but the movie seems to write the character first one way and then the other, showing not contrasts but simply contradictions.

Scene after scene works on its own terms. The director, Norman Jewison, has skill and conscience and obviously feels for the material, even if he hasn't found the way to tell it. There is a confrontation, for example, between Brossard and his estranged wife (Charlotte Rampling), which for edge and emotional danger could come from Le Carré or Graham Greene, but in *The Statement* it works on its own terms but doesn't fit into the whole, giving us one more facet of a personality that doesn't seem to fit together in any sensible way.

Presumably the moral thrust of the movie is against elements within the Church that supported anti-Semitism and continued to protect war criminals after the war. That there were such elements, and that the real Touvier was such a criminal, is beyond doubt. But then why does the movie supply a murky third element—a conspiracy to murder Brossard and pin the death on Zionists? The film fails to explain who these conspirators are, or to make clear exactly what they hope to achieve. We are not even quite sure which side they are on: Do they want to attack anti-Semites, or protect the Church, or support Israel, or what? I don't require that a movie have a message, but in a message movie it is helpful to know what the message is.

Stateside ★ ★
R, 96 m., 2004

Rachel Leigh Cook (Dori Lawrence), Jonathan Tucker (Mark Deloach), Agnes Bruckner (Sue Dubois), Joe Mantegna (Mr. Deloach), Carrie Fisher (Mrs. Dubois), Diane Venora (Mrs. Hengen), Ed Begley Jr. (Father Concoff), Val Kilmer (SDI Skeer). Directed by Reverge Anselmo and produced by Robert Greenhut and Bonnie Wells-Hlinomaz.

Stateside tells the story of a rich kid who joins the marines to stay out of jail, and then finds himself in love with a famous actress and rock singer who is being treated for schizophrenia. Stated as plainly as that, the plot could have been imported from a soap opera, but the writer-director, Reverge Anselmo, assures us it is "based on a true story." Perhaps. Certainly he rotates it away from sensationalism, making it the story of an irresponsible kid who is transformed by boot camp and then becomes obsessed with what he sees as his duty to the actress.

The kid is named Mark (Jonathan Tucker). He goes to an upscale Catholic high school, drinks too much one night, and is driving a car that broadsides the car of the headmaster, Father Concoff (Ed Begley Jr.). The priest is paralyzed from the waist down, but doesn't sue (he explains why, but so enigmatically it doesn't work). Mark's millionaire father (Joe Mantegna) pulls strings to have the charges dropped in exchange for Mark enlisting in the marines.

Mark goes to Parris Island for basic training, under the command of a drill instructor named Skeer (Val Kilmer). Skeer doesn't like the rich kid and makes it hard on him; the kid puts his head down and charges through, emerging at the end of the ordeal as what Skeer, if not all of the rest of us, would consider a success.

Home on leave before more training, he visits his girlfriend. That would be Sue (Agnes Bruckner), who lost her front teeth in the crash, but lost her freedom after her mother (Carrie Fisher) found some sexually explicit letters she wrote. The letters are obviously evidence of madness, so she's institutionalized, in the Connecticut version of *The Magdalene Sisters*. When Mark visits her, he meets her roommate, Dori (Rachel Leigh Cook), and they fall in love.

All of this sounds simpler than the movie makes it. The opening scenes are disjointed and confusing, and it doesn't help that the characters sometimes seem to be speaking in poetic code. We meet Dori early in the film, before Mark does, when she has a breakdown onstage and walks away from her band. But the movie doesn't make it clear who she is or what has happened, and we piece it together only later.

Famous as she is, she is also troubled, and Mark's steadfast loyalty and level gaze win her heart. She wouldn't ordinarily date a man from boot camp, even a rich one, but Mark's letters tell her he will stand by her, and she believes him. So do we, after he manages to balance the marines with trips home, springing her at various times from mental institutions and hospitals. These moments of freedom are heady for her, and she enjoys getting out from under her medication too. But her therapist (Diane Venora) solemnly explains to Mark that he is bad for Dori, that she needs her medication, that she can be a danger to herself. One conversation between them is especially well handled.

The point of the movie, I think, is that the marines make Mark into a man, but he takes his newfound self-confidence and discipline and uses it to commit to a lost cause. He doggedly persists in his devotion to Dori because he loves her, yes, but also because her helplessness makes him feel needed, and her illness is a test of his resolve.

Perhaps the movie is based on more of the true story than was absolutely necessary. Toward the end of the film, Mark is part of the marine landing in Lebanon, and returns home gravely wounded. This happens too late in the film for the consequences to be explored, especially in terms of his relationship with Dori. *Stateside* might have been wiser to bring the Mark-Dori story to some kind of a bittersweet conclusion without opening a new chapter that it doesn't ever really close.

The performances are strong, although undermined a little by Anselmo's peculiar style of dialogue, which sometimes sounds more like experimental poetry or song lyrics than like speech. It is also hard to know how to read Dori; we believe the therapist who says she is very ill, but her illness is one of those movie conveniences in which she is somehow usually able to do or say what the screenplay requires. There's also the enigma of Mark's father, played by Mantegna as a remote, angry man who carts an oxygen bottle around with him. We sense there's more Anselmo wants to say about the character than he has time for. *Stateside* plays like urgent ideas for a movie that Anselmo needed to make, but they're still in note form.

Stay ★ ★ ★ ½
R, 99 m., 2005

Ewan McGregor (Sam Foster), Naomi Watts (Lila Culpepper), Ryan Gosling (Henry Letham), Kate Burton (Mrs. Letham), Elizabeth Reaser (Athena), Bob Hoskins (Dr. Leon Patterson), Janeane Garofalo (Dr. Beth Levy), B. D. Wong (Dr. Ren). Directed by Marc Forster and produced by Arnon Milchan, Eric Kopeloff, and Tom Lassally. Screenplay by David Benioff.

The visual strategy in Marc Forster's *Stay* is so subtle you might miss it, but it provides a clue to the movie's secret. I will describe the strategy but not the secret. It involves transitions from one shot to the next, some subtle, some bold, all of them so agile we're not always sure what we've seen.

On a camera move, for example, an element in one shot becomes the whole of the next shot, but it's not a close-up; it's a new location. Or, as two men walk together, they pass behind pillars and it is possible, although not certain, that while out of sight they do a left-right flip. There is the matter of repeating almost unnoticed elements: Three out-of-focus spheres in the foreground, not lighted so you'd much notice them, turn up in the next shot, also out of focus, also not much noticed. And there are costume details: choices of shoes and socks, the length and style of pants.

The strategy is not underlined. The movie is facile and quick in its editing, and I'm sure another viewing would reveal transitions I missed. Accustomed to fancy footwork in modern movies, we may think Forster, his cinematographer, Roberto Schaefer, and his editor, Matt Chesse, are simply showing off: There are lots of visual flourishes without meaning in movies, and you can see dozens, maybe hundreds, in Tony Scott's *Domino*. True, they are a style and set a pace. But in *Stay*, the visuals are crucial to the movie's point of view and ultimately to its meaning.

Audiences are not always alert to styles, or they may notice them passively, not asking what function they serve. It is possible to watch an Ozu film and not register that he never moves his camera. During a Fred Astaire dance number, you may not notice that he is always shown full frame and in long takes. What Forster is doing in *Stay*, I think, is suggesting we watch the movie on two levels, although the deeper level can be glimpsed only at a tangent, passingly.

There is so much happening on the surface and in the story that we may get entirely involved up there, and Forster, in a departure from his films *Monster's Ball* and *Finding Neverland*, would be pleased if we did. The other level is beavering away in the shadows. Occasionally he'll spring a visual surprise that has a logical explanation; his hero walks through a door, for example, and seems to be undersea, and then we realize he has simply walked into a room where one wall is a very large aquarium.

But who is in this movie and what is it about? No spoilers follow. The film stars Ryan Gosling as Henry, an art student at university, who is in crisis. Asked to put out his cigarette on the subway, he stubs it out on his arm. He is seeing a university psychiatrist, but when he turns up for his appointment, a strange man is in her office. This is Sam (Ewan McGregor), who explains that he is filling in for a few weeks. Henry is angered by the substitution, walks out, returns on another day, and announces that at midnight Saturday he will kill himself.

We see more of Sam's life than Henry's. He plays chess with a blind man (Bob Hoskins). He consults a colleague (B. D. Wong). He visits Henry's usual psychiatrist (Janeane Garofalo), who is sitting at home with the lights out, depressed. He moves within the geometric architecture of the university campus, which seems to repeat itself, and there is repeating, too, in a curious scene where the corridors and stairways are suddenly populated by twins and triplets.

Sam lives with Lila (Naomi Watts), an artist who was his patient. She's suicidal, too. At various points people make little mistakes. She calls him "Henry" instead of "Sam." Understandable; they were just discussing Henry. Henry thinks the blind chess player is his father, but Henry is clearly going mad. Henry had been dating an actress named Athena (Elizabeth Reaser); Sam visits a rehearsal where she is playing Hamlet. A female Hamlet? No: "I'm just running the lines. I play Ophelia." He follows her down a spiral staircase and trips and falls and loses her. Interesting what happens next.

When the movie is over and we know all that is to be known, it deserves some thought. The ending is an explanation, but not a solution. For a solution we have to think back through the whole film, and now the visual style becomes a guide. It is an illustration of the way the materials of life can be shaped for the purposes of the moment.

The surface story of the film then becomes more interesting than before because we know more about it. Its shape and content mean something. It is the record of how we deal with the fundamental events of life by casting them into terms we can understand: terms like what we did, and what they did, and what we did then, all arranged so they seem to add up and lead somewhere. Maybe they don't. But the mind is a machine for making them seem to. Otherwise, all would be event without form and, therefore, without meaning. How desperately we need for there to be form, and meaning.

Stealth ★ ½
PG-13, 121 m., 2005

Josh Lucas (Lieutenant Ben Gannon), Jessica Biel (Lieutenant Kara Wade), Jamie Foxx (Lieutenant Henry Purcell), Sam Shepard (Captain George Cummings), Joe Morton (Captain Dick Marshfield), Richard Roxburgh (Keith Orbit). Directed by Rob Cohen and produced by Laura Ziskin, Mike Medavoy, and Neal H. Moritz. Screenplay by W. D. Richter.

Stealth is an offense against taste, intelligence, and the noise pollution code—a dumbed-down *Top Gun* crossed with the HAL 9000 plot from *2001*. It might be of interest to you if you want to see lots of jet airplanes going real fast and making a lot of noise, and if you don't care that the story doesn't merely defy logic, but also strips logic bare, cremates it, and scatters its ashes. Here is a movie with the nerve to discuss a computer brain "like a quantum sponge" while violating Newton's laws of motion.

The plot: Navy fliers have been chosen to pilot a new generation of stealth fighter-bombers. They are Lt. Ben Gannon (Josh Lucas), Lt. Kara Wade (Jessica Biel), and Lt. Henry Purcell (Jamie Foxx, who in his speech on Oscar night should have thanked God this movie wasn't released while the voters were marking their ballots).

They're all aboard the aircraft carrier Abraham Lincoln in the Philippine Sea, under the command of Capt. George Cummings (Sam Shepard, who played the test pilot Chuck Yeager in *The Right Stuff*). In a movie like this, you're asking for trouble if you remind people of *2001*, *Top Gun*, and *The Right Stuff*.

The pilots believe that three is a lucky number, because it is a prime number. One helpfully explains to the others what a prime number is; I guess they didn't get to primes at Annapolis. In a movie that uses unexplained phrases such as "quantum sponge," why not just let the characters say "prime number" and not explain it? Many audience members will assume "prime number" is another one of those pseudoscientific terms they're always thinking up for movies like this.

Captain Cummings has bad news: They're being joined by a "fourth wingman." This is a UCAV (Unmanned Combat Aerial Vehicle) controlled by a computer. The pilots are unhappy, but not so unhappy that Gannon and Wade do not feel a powerful sexual attraction, although pilots are not supposed to fraternize. At one point Gannon visits Wade's cabin, where she has laundry hanging on the line, and is nearly struck by a wet brassiere. "Pardon my C-cup," she says, a line I doubt any human female would use in such a situation.

Suddenly the pilots have to scramble for an emergency: "Three terrorist cells are about to meet in twenty-four minutes in Rangoon," Captain George tells them. Remarkable, that this information is so precise and yet so tardy. The pilots find they not only have time to take off from the aircraft carrier and fly to Burma, but also to discuss their strategy via radio once they get there. The meeting is in a building that is still under construction. Computer simulations show that if it falls over, it will kill a lot of people on the ground. Amazing what computers can do these days. However, if the building is struck from directly above, it may fall down in its own footprint.

Alas, the rocket bombs carried by the planes do not achieve the necessary penetration velocity. Lieutenant Gannon decides that if he goes into a vertical dive, he can increase the velocity.

The bomb is released, he pulls out of the dive low enough for everyone in Rangoon to get a good look at his plane, and the building collapses. It looks so much like the falling towers of the World Trade Center that I felt violated by the image.

Whoops! Another emergency. Lightning strikes the UCAV, which goes nuts and starts to download songs from the Internet. "How many?" "All of them." The computer also starts to think for itself and to make decisions that contradict orders. Meanwhile, the three human pilots, having participated in a mission that destroyed a skyscraper in Burma, may be on a worldwide most-wanted list, but they're immediately sent to Thailand for R&R. This gives Gannon a chance to photograph Wade in a bikini under a waterfall, while Purcell picks up a beautiful Thai girl. Soon all four of them are having lunch, and the three pilots are discussing military secrets in front of the Thai girl, who "doesn't speak English." Beautiful Thai girls who allow themselves to be picked up by U.S. pilots almost always speak English, but never mind. It's not that Purcell is too stupid to know that trusting her is dangerous; it's that the movie is too stupid.

How stupid? Nothing happens. The girl *can't* speak English.

Next mission: A nuclear crisis in Tajikistan! A warlord has nuclear bombs. The team flies off to the "former Soviet republic," where a nuclear cloud threatens 500,000 people, and Lieutenant Wade helpfully radios that they're going to need medical attention.

Various unexpected developments lead to a situation in which Lieutenant Wade's plane crashes in North Korea while Lieutenant Gannon is diverted to Alaska (they get such great fuel mileage on these babies, they must be hybrid vehicles). Then Gannon and the UCAV fly an unauthorized mission to rescue Wade, a mission that will succeed if the North Koreans have neglected to plant land mines in the part of the DMZ that Wade must cross.

Now about Newton's laws of motion. Let me try this out on you. A plane is about to explode. The pilot ejects. The plane explodes, and flaming debris falls out of the sky and threatens to hit the pilot and the parachute. If the plane is going at Mach 1, 2, or 3, wouldn't the debris be falling miles away from the pilot's descent path?

I'm glad you asked. The parachute sucks up that flaming debris like a quantum sponge. ☞

Steamboy ★ ★
PG-13, 106-126 m., 2005

With the voices of: Anna Paquin (Ray Steam), Alfred Molina (Eddie Steam), Patrick Stewart (Lloyd Steam). Directed by Katsuhiro Otomo and produced by Shinji Komori and Hideyuki Tomioka. Screenplay by Sadayuki Murai and Katsuhiro Otomo.

Steamboy is a noisy, eventful, and unsuccessful venture into Victorian-era science fiction, animated by a modern Japanese master. It's like H. G. Wells and Jules Verne meet *Akira*. The story follows three generations of a British family involved in a technological breakthrough involving steam, which the movie considers the nineteenth-century equivalent of nuclear power. There may be possibilities here, but they're lost in the extraordinary boredom of a long third act devoted almost entirely to loud, pointless, and repetitive action.

The movie opens in 1866 with the collection of water from an ice cave; its extraordinary purity is necessary for experiments by the Steam family, which is perfecting the storage of power through steam under high pressures. Young Ray Steam (voice by Anna Paquin) is the boy hero, whose father, Eddie (Alfred Molina), and grandfather, Lloyd Steam (Patrick Stewart), are rivals in the development of the technology. One day Ray gets a package in the mail from his grandfather, its delivery followed immediately by ominous men dressed in alarming dark Victorian fashions that proclaim, "I am a sinister villain."

The box contains a steam ball, which we learn contains steam under extraordinary pressure. The ball, invented by Lloyd, is either a revolutionary power source or an infernal device that could explode at any moment, take your choice. Ray tries to escape on a peculiar invention that seems to combine the most uncomfortable experiences of riding a unicycle and being trapped in a washing machine, but is captured and taken to the headquarters of the O'Hara Foundation, which wants to control the invention and use it to power new machines of war. It goes without saying, or does it, that the O'Hara family daughter is named Scarlett.

The movie is the result of ten years of labor by Katsuhiro Otomo, whose *Akira* (1988) was the first example of Japanese anime to break through to world theatrical markets. That one created a futuristic Tokyo where a military dictatorship cannot control rampaging motorcycle gangs. The animation was state of the art, the vision was bleak, the tone was a radical departure for American audiences raised to equate animation with cute animals and fairy tales.

Otomo also wrote *Rojin Z* (1991), about a computerized machine that contains elderly patients within an exoskeleton/bed that transports, diagnoses, treats, massages, and entertains its occupants; once installed in the new Z-100 model, owners are expected never to leave, whether or not they want to.

The movie has intriguing ideas about human lives ruled by machines, which is why the technology in *Steamboy* seems promising. Otomo has reportedly been working on the film for ten years, drawing countless animation cels by hand and also using computer resources; why, with all the effort he put into the film's construction, did he neglect to go anywhere interesting with the plot?

We have hope at first, just because Otomo creates Manchester and London at the dawn of the industrial era, when steam power offered limitless possibilities and the internal combustion engine was still impractical. His machines and the interior of the O'Hara Foundation look like the ancestors of pulp sci-fi magazine covers, but without the bright colors. For reasons that don't pay off, Otomo's visuals tend toward the pale and drab. Maybe he's going for period atmosphere. I wondered at first if the movie was being projected on video, but no, Otomo wants it to look washed-out.

His plot holds promise: The evil O'Hara Foundation wants to hijack the Great Exhibition, for which Prince Albert built the Crystal Palace to showcase Britain's leadership of the industrial revolution. But the Great Exhibition was held in 1851, and if the movie is set in 1866, is the chronology off? There may have been an explanation that eluded me, this not being a question that riveted my attention at the time.

The O'Hara people want to jettison the notion of progress for peace, and use the exhibition to promote its expensive new engines of war, hoping every country will buy some, go to war, and need to buy more. At this point, when the movie could potentially get its teeth into something, Otomo goes nuts with brainless action sequences in which one retro-futuristic device after another does battle, explodes, dives, surfaces, floats, opens fire, flies, attacks, defends, and so on.

Some of his ideas are promising, including a zeppelin fitted with iron claws that can lift a speeding train car from the tracks. A fearsome strategy indeed, although it would be awkward for the dirigible if the train ever went through a tunnel or under a bridge, or raced past big hard buildings close to the tracks. Other ideas are just collisions of hardware, punctuated by frantic expostulations.

It is a theory of mine that action does not equal interest. Objects endlessly in motion are as repetitive as objects forever at rest. Context is everything. Why are they moving, who wants them to move, what is at risk, what will be gained? By the end of *Steamboy* I was convinced the answers to all of these questions were: Otomo has abandoned the story and, in despair, is filling the screen with wonderfully executed but pointless and repetitive kinetic energy. Action doodles.

Note: The movie is available in a 106-minute English-dubbed version and a 126-minute Japanese version with English subtitles.

The Stepford Wives ★ ★ ★
PG-13, 93 m., 2004

Nicole Kidman (Joanna Eberhart), Matthew Broderick (Walter Kresby), Bette Midler (Bobbie Markowitz), Jon Lovitz (Dave Markowitz), Roger Bart (Roger Bannister), David Marshall Grant (Jerry Harmon), Faith Hill (Sarah Sunderson), Glenn Close (Claire Wellington), Christopher Walken (Mike Wellington). Directed by Frank Oz and produced by Donald De Line, Gabriel Grunfeld, Scott Rudin, and Edgar J. Scherick. Screenplay by Paul Rudnick, based on the book by Ira Levin.

The Stepford Wives depends for some of its effect on a plot secret that you already know, if you've been paying attention at any time since the original film version was released in 1975. If you don't know it, stay away from the trailer,

which gives it away. It's an enticing premise, an opening for wicked feminist satire, but the 1975 movie tilted toward horror instead of comedy. Now here's a version that tilts the other way, and I like it a little better.

The experience is like a new production of a well-known play. The original suspense has evaporated, and you focus on the adaptation and acting. Here you can also focus on the new screenplay by Paul Rudnick, which is rich with zingers. Rudnick, having committed one of the worst screenplays of modern times (*Isn't She Great*, the Jacqueline Susann story), redeems himself with barbed one-liners; when one of the community planners says he used to work for AOL, Joanna asks, "Is that why the women are so slow?"

Nicole Kidman stars, as Joanna Eberhart, a high-powered TV executive who is fired after the victim of one of her reality shows goes on a shooting rampage. Her husband, Walter (Matthew Broderick), resigns from the same network, where he worked under her, and moves with his wife and two children to the gated community of Stepford, Connecticut.

It's weird there. The women all seem to be sexy clones of Betty Crocker. Glenn Close is Claire Wellington, the real-estate agent, greeter, and community cheerleader, and she gives Joanna the creeps (she's "flight attendant friendly"). Nobody in Stepford seems to work; they're so rich they don't need to, and the men hang out at the Men's Association while the women attend Claire's exercise sessions. In Stepford, the women dress up and wear heels even for aerobics (no sweaty gym shorts), and Claire leads them in pantomimes of domestic chores ("Let's all be washing machines!").

Walter loves it in Stepford. Joanna hates it. She bonds with Bobbie Markowitz (Bette Midler), author of a best-selling memoir about her mother, *I Love You, But Please Die.* Her house is a pigpen. Every other house in Stepford is spotlessly clean, even though there seem to be no domestic servants; the wives cheerfully do the housework themselves. They also improve themselves by attending Claire's book club. A nice example of Rudnick's wit: When Joanna shares that she has finished volume two of Robert Caro's biography of Lyndon Johnson, Claire takes a beat, smiles bravely, and suggests they read *Christmas Keepsakes* and discuss celebrating Jesus' birthday with yarn.

Christopher Walken is Claire's husband and seems to be running Stepford; it's the kind of creepy role that has Walken written all over it, and he stars in a Stepford promotional film that showcases another one of his unctuous explanations of the bizarre. A new touch this time: Stepford has a gay couple, and Roger (Roger Bart), the "wife," is flamboyant to begin with, until overnight, strangely, he becomes a serious-minded congressional candidate.

What's going on here? You probably know, but I can't tell you. When Ira Levin's original novel was published in 1972, feminism was newer, and his premise satirized the male desire for tame, sexy wives who did what they were told and never complained. Rudnick and director Frank Oz don't do anything radical with the original premise (although they add some post-1972 touches like the Stepford-style ATM machine), but they choose comedy over horror, and it's a wise decision. Kidman plays a character not a million miles away from her husband-killer in *To Die For*, even though this time she's the victim. Bette Midler is defiantly subversive as the town misfit. And Walken is . . . Walken.

The movie is surprisingly short, at 93 minutes including end titles (the 1975 film was 115 minutes long). Maybe it needs to be short. The secret is obvious fairly early (a woman goes berserk and when Walter says she was probably just sick, Joanna says, "Walter, she was sparking!"). It could probably work as a springboard for heavy-duty social satire, but that's not what audiences expect from this material, and Rudnick pushes about as far as he can without tearing the envelope. Some movies are based on short stories, some on novels. *The Stepford Wives* is little more than an anecdote, and like all good storytellers, Oz and Rudnick don't meander on their way to the punch line.

Stick It ★ ★
PG-13, 105 m., 2006

Jeff Bridges (Burt Vickerman), Missy Peregrym (Haley Graham), Vanessa Lengies (Joanne), Tarah Paige (Tricia Skilken), Nikki SooHoo (Wei Wei), Maddy Curley (Mina), Kellan Lutz (Frank), John Patrick Amedori (Poot). Directed by Jessica Bendinger and produced by Gail Lyon. Screenplay by Bendinger.

Stick It uses the story of a gymnast's comeback attempt as a backdrop for overwrought visual effects, music videos, sitcom dialogue, and general pandering. The movie seems to fear that if it pauses long enough to actually be about gymnastics, the audience will grow restless. It often abandons realism, unless it is possible, which I doubt, that you can do a head-spin on a balance beam.

The movie stars Missy Peregrym as Haley, a once-promising gymnast who disqualified herself by walking away from Team USA during an important final match. She had her reasons for bailing out, but for now she's in disgrace. She spends her time back home in Plano, Texas, hanging out with teenage boys and doing insane stunts with bicycles and skateboards that involve rooftops and empty swimming pools. The cops give chase, and we get the obligatory scene where the mystery character takes off her helmet and lets down her hair, and—gasp!—it's a girl!

Haley did thousands of dollars in damage after crashing her bike through a window and is ordered by the judge to attend, on probation, the Vickerman Gymnastics Academy in Houston. This is a legendary establishment, rumored to be producing "more injuries than champions." Vickerman, played by Jeff Bridges, is a sharp-talking iconoclast with an offhand manner, but then everyone in this movie speaks in a strange, stylized, enigmatic way, and their dialogue sounds like—dialogue.

The story will be familiar to anyone who has ever seen a movie about a troubled athlete and a brilliant coach. It will also be familiar to anyone who has not. We have scenes in which the other students resent Haley for walking off Team USA, scenes where Haley rebels against Vickerman's discipline, scenes of injury and disappointment, moments of heartfelt revelation, some jealousy among the gymnasts, and finally a comeback in which, we sense, Haley probably will not walk off the floor.

All of this is well enough made, although it appears to my untrained eye that some of the better gymnastics stunts are done with CGI effects. Jessica Bendinger, the writer and director, wrote the better *Bring It On* (2000), about competing cheerleading squads.

667

Here she shows visual mastery but not visual judgment: She can do a lot of stuff that the movie doesn't really require, and it acts like a stylistic barrier between the audience and the emotions. With its stark red and white sets, Vickerman's looks more like a backdrop for an ad than like a working gymnasium. And the characters are rarely so spontaneous they can't find an epigrammatic way of expressing themselves. (By "epigrammatic," I mean smart-ass.)

I liked Peregrym as Haley, in part because she doesn't fit the stereotype of women gymnasts as short and underfed. I shared her anger at birdbrained judges who discount a difficult trick because a bra strap is showing. Bridges does what he can with the Vickerman role but is too good an actor to fit into such a shallow character. All through the movie, I kept thinking of Robert Towne's *Personal Best* (1982), with Mariel Hemingway as an athlete and Scott Glenn as her coach. That film has such honesty and integrity that *Stick It* seems childish by comparison. ☞

The Story of the Weeping Camel ★ ★ ★
PG, 90 m., 2004

Janchiv Ayurzana (Janchiv [Great Grandfather]), Chimed Ohin (Chimed [Great Grandmother]), Amgaabazar Gonson (Amgaa [Grandfather]), Zeveljamz Nyam (Zevel [Grandmother]), Ikhbayar Amgaabazar (Ikchee [Father]), Odgerel Ayusch (Odgoo [Mother]), Enkhbulgan Ikhbayar (Dude [Older Brother]), Uuganbaatar Ikhbayar (Ugna [Younger Brother]), Guntbaatar Ikhbayar (Guntee [Baby Brother]), Ingen Temee (Mother Camel), Botok (Baby Camel). Directed by Byambasuren Davaa and Luigi Falorni and produced by Tobias Siebert. Screenplay by Davaa and Falorni.

On the edges of the Gobi Desert live to this day nomadic herders who travel with their animals and exist within an ancient economy that requires no money. *The Story of the Weeping Camel*, which despite its title is a joyous movie, tells the story of one of those families, and of their camel, which gives birth to a rare white calf and refuses to nurse it. It is a terrible thing to hear the cry of a baby camel rejected by its mother.

The movie has been made in the same way that Robert Flaherty made such documentaries as *Nanook of the North, Man of Aran,* and *Louisiana Story.* It uses real people in real places, and essentially has them play themselves in a story inspired by their lives. That makes it a "narrative documentary," according to the filmmakers. A great many documentaries are closer to this model than their makers will admit; even *cinema verité* must pick and choose from the available footage and reflect a point of view.

We meet four generations of the same family. Do not think of them as primitive; it takes great wisdom to survive in their manner. I learn from the press materials that the older brother, Dude (Enkhbulgan Ikhbayar), went away to boarding school but then returned to his family because he enjoyed the way of life. Certainly these people live close to the land and to their animals, and their yurts are masterpieces of construction—sturdy, portable homes that can be carried on the back of a camel, but are sturdy enough to withstand winter storms.

It is spring when the movie begins, and a mother camel (Ingen Temee) has just given painful birth to her white calf (Botok). It is only reasonable to supply the names of these animals, since they are so much a part of their nomad families. Does the mother refuse her milk because the calf looks strange to her, or because of her birth agony? No matter; unless the calf is fed, it will die, and the family needs it.

When bottle-feeding fails, Dude and his younger brother Ugna (Uuganbaatar Ikhbayar) travel by camel some fifty kilometers to the nearest town to bring back a musician who will play a traditional song to the camel and perhaps persuade it to relent. While in the village, they watch television and brush against other artifacts of modern life with curiosity, but without need.

The musician accompanies them to the village. He plays the traditional song. Legend has it that if a camel finally agrees to nurse her young, this will cause her to weep. There are also a few damp eyes among members of the family. All of this is told in a narrative that is not a cute true-life animal tale, but an observant and respectful record of the daily rhythms and patterns of these lives. We sense the dynamics among the generations, how age is valued and youth is cherished, how the lives of these people make sense to them in a way that ours never will, because they know why they do what they do, and what will come of it. The causes and effects of their survival are visible, and they are responsible.

The filmmakers are Byambasuren Davaa and Luigi Falorni. They cowrote and directed; he photographed. They met at the Munich Film School, where she told him that her grandparents had been herders. Their film was shot on location in about a month, and has an authenticity in its very bones. In a commercial movie, sentiment would rule, and we would feel sorry for the cute baby camel. Well, yes, we feel sorry for the calf in *The Story of the Weeping Camel*, but we also understand that the camel represents wealth and survival for its owners, and in what they do, they're thinking, as they should, more about themselves than about the camel.

I believe this film would be fascinating for smart children, maybe the same ones who liked *Whale Rider*, because so much of it is told through the eyes of the younger brother. Although the desert society is alien to everything we know, in another way it is instantly understandable, because we know about parents and grandparents, about working to put food on the table, about the need of babies to nurse. Here is a film that is about life itself, and about those few humans who still engage it at first hand.

Note: Two other splendid documentaries cover similar ground. Taiga *(1995), the remarkable eight-hour documentary by Ulrike Ottinger, lives and travels with nomads for a year, and witnesses their private lives and religious ceremonies.* Genghis Blues *is the wonderful 1999 documentary about a blind San Francisco blues singer who hears Tuvan throat singing on the radio, teaches himself that difficult art, and journeys to Tuva, which is between Mongolia and Siberia, to enter a throat-singing contest.*

Strayed ★ ★ ★

NO MPAA RATING, 95 m., 2004

Emmanuelle Béart (Odile), Gaspard Ulliel (Yvan), Grégoire Leprince-Ringuet (Philippe), Clémence Meyer (Cathy), Jean Fornerod (Georges), Samuel Labarthe (Robert). Directed by André Téchiné and produced by Jean-Pierre Ramsay-Levi. Screenplay by Gilles Taurand and Téchiné, based on the novel *The Boy with Gray Eyes* by Gilles Perrault.

Who is this Yvan, this boy with the shaved head who has crawled out of the mud to lead them to safety? And why should she trust him? Odile (Emmanuelle Béart) is a bourgeois Parisian woman with two children and no way to protect them, and Yvan (Gaspard Ulliel) has a toughness that is reassuring and at the same time menacing. She really has no choice but to follow him into the forest, after Nazi planes have strafed and bombed the column of refugees streaming south from Paris.

It is 1940, and all of the certainties of Odile's life have evaporated. She is a pretty widow in her late thirties, a teacher, who fled Paris and joined the flight from the Germans with her thirteen-year-old son, Philippe, and her daughter, Cathy, who is seven. Her children trust her, but she doesn't trust herself, because her experience and values are irrelevant in this sudden war. "It's every man for himself," someone shouts on the road, not originally but cogently, as bullets kill some and spare others.

Yvan is tough and sure of himself, and her instincts as a teacher tell her he is dangerous. The teenager Philippe is frightened but more realistic; he believes they need this strange young man. Yvan has a sweet side, and seems to want to help them; there is perhaps even the suggestion that he needs this family to replace one he lost, and he needs this chance to be helpful and competent. Or perhaps the fact that Philippe secretly bribed him with his father's watch convinced him to stay; we never know for sure what he's thinking.

Strayed begins and ends with facts of war, but it is really a film about the nature of male and female, about middle-class values and those who cannot afford them, about how helpless we can be when the net of society is broken. The French director André Téchiné, no sentimentalist, creates a separate world for his four characters, and the war goes on elsewhere.

Separated from the other refugees, they walk through a forest of such beauty that war seems impossible, and they sleep under the stars. The next day, they come upon a country home, comfortable, isolated, and tempting. The owners have fled. Yvan believes they should break in and stay there for a while; the roads are mobbed, there is no sure safety in the south, and no one will look for them here. Odile argues that the house is private property. Her bourgeois instincts are so strong that she would sleep with her children in the woods, or try to rejoin the exodus, rather than break in. For Yvan, there is no choice: They must survive.

We realize that the war is very new to her, that she clings to the certainties of her ordered life and must learn that the rules have changed. They break in, of course. There is a wine cellar, many bedrooms, some food. Yvan hunts for game. Odile establishes a domestic routine. They could almost be on holiday, the children vibrating with the sense of adventure, Odile putting good French food on the table, and Yvan . . . Yvan . . . enjoying it too, but on guard, and always aware of their danger. Their danger and, we sense, his own.

When you put a beautiful woman and a forceful young man in an isolated situation where they must live closely together, sexual tension coils under the surface. At first it is not obvious, because Odile's bourgeois certainties make it impossible that she could sleep with a rough working-class stranger twenty years younger. And there are the children, although Philippe admires Yvan: Here is an older brother, or perhaps a father figure, who can protect them when his own father has failed.

There are certain mysteries, which I will not reveal, involving secrets Odile keeps from Yvan and those he keeps from her, and certain questions about how long they should stay in the house—questions that seem to depend, in Yvan's mind, on more than the simple matter of survival. There are things Philippe observes and keeps to himself. And always there is the knowledge between Odile and Yvan that they could sleep together, that the nature of their relationship is shifting, that the war has changed the rules and that Yvan has become necessary to her family.

We sense the story will not end here, and we know this temporary family cannot live in this house forever, with time suspended. We are not sure how near a town might be, and Odile wonders why the telephone doesn't work. Someone will find them, and what will happen then? Those questions occur to us as they occur to the characters, adding an urgency, an unreality,

as the days pass comfortably. Téchiné, a master of buried power struggles, increases the level of uncertainty and apprehension until we know something must happen, and then something does, and the essential natures of Yvan and Odile, and their way their society formed them, becomes clear.

Subject Two ★ ★
No MPAA rating, 93 m., 2006

Christian Oliver (Adam), Dean Stapleton (Vick), Courtney Mace (Kate), Jurgen Jones (Hunter), Thomas Buesch (The Professor). Directed by Philip Chidel and produced by Chidel, Christian Oliver, and Dean Stapleton. Screenplay by Chidel.

Having flunked his final exam on medical ethics, a student named Adam gets an e-mail asking him to venture to a remote, snowbound cabin where, his correspondent promises, he will share in revolutionary advances in medical science. Adam (Christian Oliver) takes the bait, is met by a young woman, driven to a remote mountain road, handed cross-country skis, and told he can find the doctor's cabin by following the red ribbons on the trees. After a long, cold journey, he finds the cabin, occupied by young Dr. Vick (Dean Stapleton).

Adam discovers (although not before being choked to death, left outside to freeze, and then brought back to life) that Dr. Vick has invented a serum that offers immortality. Death has no dominion in the mountain cabin, where Adam will be killed several more times (shot, hit by a snowmobile, etc.) and brought back to life several more times. These transitions are necessary because when Vick gets things wrong, it's necessary to kill Adam and leave him dead while making improvements.

I was reminded of *Scream and Scream Again*, in which every time the victim woke up, another body part was missing. In *Subject Two*, it doesn't much matter. There's not even anything special about the brain, apparently, and you don't need it to think. But Adam complains bitterly to Vick that he cannot feel: He lacks both physical and emotional sensations, he says, but since he feels so much anger about that, he must not be quite correct. Still, there's one consolation: He doesn't have those migraines anymore.

Subject Two is a horror film crossed with a workshop on the theory and practice of an earlier doctor, Frankenstein. When you bring the dead to life, what do you have then? Something that is alive? Something that is dead but can walk and talk and think? Would you want to be immortal if you had to keep being killed all the time? Is life worth living for the undead?

These questions play out in a movie that for most of its length involves just the two actors. One problem, for me, is that Vick doesn't seem particularly demented, and Adam doesn't seem particularly disturbed. The usual ramping up of emotions in a horror film doesn't take place; too much of the film consists of the characters using normal speaking voices, however distraught. One promising development, however, is that a man who was apparently Subject One is buried up to his neck out in the yard and apparently is dead. Seeing him planted with tubes going into him, I was reminded for the second time in a month of *Motel Hell,* the movie where Farmer Vincent planted the residents of his motel and used them as a cash crop.

Subject Two, written and directed by Philip Chidel and produced by him along with his two stars, is a good-looking movie, well-acted, but the material seems curiously inert. Even with some surprises at the end, we're left with too little desperation and too much conversation. There are big ideas nibbling around the edges of the screenplay, but the movie seems underwhelmed by its own startling material. There is, however, an idea here that's intriguing: If you had immortality, would you be begging someone to kill you? Can life be too much of a good thing?

Superman Returns ★ ★
PG-13, 140 m., 2006

Brandon Routh (Superman/Clark Kent), Kate Bosworth (Lois Lane), James Marsden (Richard White), Frank Langella (Perry White), Eva Marie Saint (Martha Kent), Parker Posey (Kitty Kowalski), Sam Huntington (Jimmy Olsen), Kevin Spacey (Lex Luthor). Directed by Bryan Singer and produced by Jon Peters and Singer. Screenplay by Michael Dougherty and Dan Harris.

It's no fun being Superman. Your life is a lie, there's nobody you can confide in, you're in love but can't express it, and you're on call twenty-four hours a day. But it can be fun being in a Superman movie. The original *Superman* (1978) was an exuberance of action and humor because Christopher Reeve could play the character straight and let us know he was kidding.

Superman II (1980) was just about as good, but *Superman III* (1983) and *Superman IV* (1987) were disappointments, and then the series disappeared for nineteen years. Now the Man of Steel is back in Bryan Singer's *Superman Returns,* which, like its hero, spends a lot of time dead in the water.

This is a glum, lackluster movie in which even the big effects sequences seem dutiful instead of exhilarating. The newsroom of the *Daily Planet,* filled with eccentricity and life in the earlier movies, now seems populated by corporate drones. Jimmy Olsen, the copy boy, such a brash kid, seems tamed and clueless. Lois Lane (Kate Bosworth) has lost her dash and pizzazz, and her fiancé, Richard White (James Marsden), regards her like a deer caught in the headlights. Even the editor, Perry White (Frank Langella), comes across less like a curmudgeon, more like an efficient manager.

One problem is with the casting. Brandon Routh lacks charisma as Superman, and I suppose as Clark Kent he isn't supposed to have any. Routh may have been cast because he looks a little like Reeve, but there are times when he looks more like an action figure; were effects used to make him seem built from synthetics? We remember the chemistry between Christopher Reeve and Margot Kidder (Lois Lane) in the original Superman movie, and then observe how their counterparts are tongue-tied in this one. If they had a real romance (and they did), has it left them with nothing more than wistful looks and awkward small talk?

It's strange how little dialogue the title character has in the movie. Clark Kent is monosyllabic, and Superman is microsyllabic. We learn Superman was away for five years on a mission to the remains of his home planet, Krypton, and in the meantime Lois got herself a boyfriend and a little son, played by Tristan Lake Leabu, who mostly stares at people like a beta version of Damien, the kid from *The Omen.* Now Superman and (coincidentally) Clark have returned, Clark gets his old job, and Lex Luthor

671

(Kevin Spacey) is out of prison and plotting to rule the earth.

Lex's plan: use crystals from Krypton to raise up a new continent in the mid-Atlantic and flood most of the surface of the populated world. Then he'll own all the real estate. Location, location, location. Alas, the craggy landscape he produces couldn't be loved by a mountain goat and won't be habitable for a million years, but never mind. Spacey plays Luthor as sour and sadistic; he has no fun with the role, nor do we.

As for Superman, he's a one-trick pony. To paraphrase Archimedes: Give me a lever and a place to stand, and I will move the universe. Superman doesn't need the lever or the place to stand, but as he positions himself in midair, straining to lift an airplane or a vast chunk of rock, we reflect that these activities aren't nearly as cinematic as what Batman and Spider-Man get up to. Watching Superman straining to hold a giant airliner, I'm wondering: Why does he strain? Does he have his limits? Would that new Airbus be too much for him? What about if he could stand somewhere?

Superman is vulnerable to one, and only one, substance: Kryptonite. He knows this. We know this. Lex Luthor knows this. Yet he has been disabled by Kryptonite in every one of the movies. Does he think Lex Luthor would pull another stunt without a supply on hand? Why doesn't he take the most elementary precautions? How can a middle-aged bald man stab the Man of Steel with Kryptonite?

Now about Lois's kid. We know who his father is, and Lois knows, and I guess the kid knows, although he calls Richard his daddy. But why is nothing done with this character? He sends a piano flying across a room, but otherwise he just stares with big, solemn eyes, like one of those self-sufficient little brats you can't get to talk. It would have been fun to give Superman a bright, sassy child, like one of the Spy Kids, and make him a part of the plot.

There is, I suppose, a certain bottom line of competence in *Superman Returns,* and superhero fans will want to see the movie just for its effects, its plot outrages, and its moments of humor. But when the hero, his alter ego, his girlfriend, and the villain all seem to lack any joy in being themselves, why should we feel joy at watching them?

Super Size Me ★ ★ ★
NO MPAA RATING, 96 m., 2004

A documentary directed by Morgan Spurlock and produced by Spurlock. With Dr. Daryl Isaacs, Ronald McDonald, and Dr. Lisa Ganjhu.

Of course it is possible to eat responsibly at McDonald's, as spokesmen for the chain never tire of reminding us. Fast food is simply one element of a balanced nutritional plan. Of course, it's the *unbalanced element* unless you order the fish filet sandwich with no mayonnaise and one of those little salads with the lo-cal dressing; then you'll be fine, except for the refined white flour in the bun and the high intake of sodium. Eating responsibly at McDonald's is like going to a strip club for the iced tea.

I say this having eaten irresponsibly at McDonald's since I was in grade school, and one of the very first McDonald's outlets in the nation opened in Urbana, Illinois. Hamburgers were fifteen cents; fries were a dime. Make it two burgers and we considered that a meal. Today it is possible to ingest thousands of calories at McDonald's and zoom dangerously over your daily recommended limits of fat, sugar, and salt. I know because Morgan Spurlock proves it in *Super Size Me.*

This is the documentary that caused a sensation at Sundance 2004 and allegedly inspired McDonald's to discontinue its "supersize" promotions as a preemptive measure. In it, Spurlock vows to eat three meals a day at McDonald's for one month. He is examined by three doctors at the beginning of the month and found to be in good health. They check him again regularly during the filming, as his weight balloons thirty pounds, his blood pressure skyrockets, his cholesterol goes up sixty-five points, he has symptoms of toxic shock to his liver, his skin begins to look unhealthy, his energy drops, he has chest pains, and his girlfriend complains about their sex life. At one point his doctors advise him to abandon McDonald's before he does permanent damage. The doctors say they have seen similar side effects from binge drinkers, but never dreamed you could get that way just by eating fast food.

It's amazing, what you find on the menu at McDonald's. Let's say you start the day with a sausage and egg McMuffin. You'll get ten grams of saturated fat—50 percent of your daily recommendation, not to mention 39 percent of your daily sodium intake. Add a Big Mac and medium fries for lunch, and you're up to 123 percent of your daily saturated fat recommendation and 96 percent of your sodium. For dinner, choose a quarter-pounder with cheese, add another medium order of fries, and you're at 206 percent of daily saturated fat and 160 percent of sodium. At some point add a strawberry shake to take you to 247 percent of saturated fat and 166 percent of sodium. And remember that most nutritionists recommend less fat and salt than the government guidelines.

There is a revisionist interpretation of the film, in which Spurlock is identified as a self-promoter who, on behalf of his film, ate more than any reasonable person could consume in a month at McDonald's. That is both true and not true. He does have a policy that whenever he's asked if he wants to "supersize it," he must reply "yes." But what he orders for any given meal is not uncommon, and we have all known (or been) customers who ordered the same items. That anyone would do it three times a day is unlikely. Occasionally you might want to go upscale at someplace like Outback, where the Bloomin' Onion Rings all by themselves provide more than a day's worth of fat and sodium, and 1,600 calories. Of course, they're supposed to be shared. For best results, share them with everyone else in the restaurant.

We bear responsibility for our own actions, so . . . is it possible to go to McDonald's and order a healthy meal? A Chicago nutritionist told a *Sun-Times* reporter that of course Spurlock put on weight, because he was eating 5,000 calories a day. She suggested a McDonald's three-meal menu that would not be fattening, but as I studied it, I wondered: How many customers consider a small hamburger, small fries and a diet Coke as their dinner? When was the last time you even *ordered* a small hamburger (that's not a quarter-pounder) at McDonald's? Don't all raise your hands at once.

Oh, I agree with the nutritionist that her recommended three meals would not add weight; her daily caloric intake totaled 1,460 calories, which is a little low for a child under four, according to the USDA. But even her menu would include fifty-four grams of fat (fifteen saturated), or about one-third of calories (for best heart health, fat should be down around 20 percent). And her diet included an astonishing 3,385 megagrams of sodium (daily recommendation: 1,600 megagrams to 2,400 megagrams). My conclusion: Even the nutritionist's bare-bones 1,460-calorie McDonald's menu is dangerous to your health.

I approached *Super Size Me* in a very particular frame of mind because in December 2002, after years of fooling around, I began seriously following the Pritikin program of nutrition and exercise, and I have lost about eighty-six pounds. Full disclosure: Fifteen of those pounds were probably lost as a side effect of surgery and radiation; the others can be accounted for by Pritikin menus and exercise (the 10,000 Step-a-Day Program plus weights two or three times a week). So of course that makes me a true believer.

You didn't ask, but what I truly believe is that unless you can find an eating program you can stay on for the rest of your life, dieting is a waste of time. The pounds come back. Instead of extreme high-protein or low-carb diets with all their health risks, why not exercise more, avoid refined foods, and eat a balanced diet of fruits and veggies, whole grains, fish, and a little meat, beans, soy products, low-fat dairy, low fat, low salt? Of course, I agree with McDonald's that a visit to Mickey D's can be part of a responsible nutritional approach. That's why I've dined there twice in the last seventeen months.

Suspect Zero ★ ★
R, 99 m., 2004

Aaron Eckhart (Thomas Mackelway), Carrie-Anne Moss (Fran Kulok), Ben Kingsley (Benjamin O'Ryan). Directed by E. Elias Merhige and produced by Gaye Hirsch and Paula Wagner. Screenplay by Zak Penn and Billy Ray.

We should be grateful, I suppose, when the serial killers in movies pause in their carnage long enough to concoct elaborate webs of clues, hints, and tantalizing challenges for their pursuers. Lives may be saved because of the time it takes them to plant enigmatic clues, send cryptic faxes, and pose for extreme close-ups in which they look like some guy in a photo booth trying to look tortured.

The serial killer or killers in *Suspect Zero* have obviously spent a lot of time watching old thrillers. They have learned in particular that it is important to zero in on one particular lawman, show that they're familiar with his secrets, and then challenge him to stop them before they kill or fax again.

In *Suspect Zero*, the fated target is FBI agent Thomas Mackelway (Aaron Eckhart), who got in some kind of trouble in Texas and has been demoted to New Mexico. He chews handfuls of aspirin to ease his pain, as Travis Bickle did in *Taxi Driver*; this is a behavior limited almost entirely to the movies, where the characters are too masochistic to wash them down with water.

Never mind. Mackelway investigates a murder involving a man whose car is found precisely on the state line between Arizona and New Mexico. "The killer must have used a global positioning system," Mackelway deduces. Why? To take the crime out of the jurisdiction of state authorities and make it the business of the FBI. And not just the FBI, but Mackelway personally, as a series of taunting faxes makes clear.

The faxes come from someone with inside knowledge about a serial killer. The problem with this killer is that he has no modus operandi, no pattern, no telltale habits, and strikes entirely at random, which makes him difficult to find. Does the writer of the faxes know the killer, or is he the killer? Or is there a third, more occult, explanation? As we ponder these possibilities, what looks like the world's longest and blackest semitrailer truck cruises inappropriately down city streets near playgrounds, and we wonder: Assuming the truck is not in the movie by accident, could it be connected to the killings, and, if so, wouldn't the presence of such a gargantuan truck be the very M.O. the killer allegedly lacks?

Mackelway has been joined in New Mexico by agent Fran Kulok (Carrie-Anne Moss). They share some unsuccessful romantic history. He has issues. Maybe they both do. But they have to work together, and so inevitably they will come to a new knowledge of each other in order to provide the fax writer with additional insights, and the ending with additional chills.

Ben Kingsley meanwhile looks like he should be chewing aspirin too. He plays a man named Benjamin O'Ryan who is often seen in such extreme close-ups that if pores could talk, the movie would be over. Is he the killer? The Law of Economy of Characters would seem to suggest that he must be, since the movie contains no other eligible candidate. But perhaps there is another, more bizarre and involved explanation, and the killer is either hidden in plain view among the major characters or is never seen at all until the climax. I am not spoiling any secrets, but simply applying logic to a plot that offers zero sum as well as zero suspects.

The director, E. Elias Merhige, made the splendid *Shadow of the Vampire* (2001), a macabre thriller about the filming of F. W. Murnau's silent classic *Nosferatu* (1922). Murnau, played by John Malkovich, has a dreadful secret he was keeping from his cast: Max Schreck (Willem Dafoe), who is playing the vampire, is so good in the role because he is in fact a vampire, and has been promised the blood of the leading lady, which even in an industry famous for its catering is one star perk too many. (Midway through production, Schreck dines on the cinematographer and when Murnau is furious at him, wonders to himself if they really need the writer.)

Merhige is a gifted director with a good visual sense and a way of creating tension where it should not exist. But *Suspect Zero* is too devised and elaborate to really engage us. There's a point at which its enigmatic flashes of incomprehensible action grow annoying, and a point at which we realize that there's no use paying close attention, because we won't be able to figure out the film's secrets until they're explained to us. All of the clues and faxes and close-ups and flashbacks are revealed as devices that are in the movie not because they add up to anything, but because they surround a fairly simple story with gratuitous stylistic mystery.

One final thought. Imagine the underlying material rewritten so that it was all seen and told from the point of view of the Ben Kingsley character. Wouldn't it be more interesting that way? His dilemma is much more dramatic than the elaborate charade concocted for the FBI. In a movie where one character knows everything and the others know nothing, it seems unkind to stick the audience with the dummies.

Syriana ★ ★ ★ ★
R, 126 m., 2005

George Clooney (Robert Barnes), Matt Damon (Bryan Woodman), Jeffrey Wright (Bennett Holiday), Chris Cooper (Jimmy Pope), William Hurt (Stan Goff), Mazhar Munir (Wasim), Tim Blake Nelson (Danny Dalton), Amanda Peet (Julie Woodman), Christopher Plummer (Dean Whiting), Alexander Siddig (Prince Nasir), Akbar Kurtha (Prince Meshal). Directed by Stephen Gaghan and produced by Jennifer Fox, Georgia Kacandes, and Michael Nozik. Screenplay by Gaghan, based on the book by Robert Baer.

Syriana is an endlessly fascinating movie about oil and money, America and China, traders and spies, the Persian Gulf states and Texas, reform and revenge, bribery and betrayal. Its interlocking stories come down to one thing: There is less oil than the world requires, and that will make some people rich and others dead. The movie seems to take sides, but take a step back and look again. It finds all of the players in the oil game corrupt and compromised, and even provides a brilliant speech in defense of corruption by a Texas oil man (Tim Blake Nelson). This isn't about Left and Right but about Have and Have Not.

The movie begins with one of the Gulf states signing a deal to supply its oil to China. This comes as a strategic defeat for Connex, a Texas-based oil company. At the same time, an obscure oil company named Killen signs a deal to drill for oil in Kazakhstan. Connex announces a merger with Killen, to get its hands on the oil, but the merger inspires a Justice Department investigation, and . . .

Let's stop right there. The movie's plot is so complex we're not really supposed to follow it; we're supposed to be surrounded by it. Since none of the characters understands the whole picture, why should we? If the movie shook out into good guys and bad guys, we'd be the good guys, of course. Or if it was a critique of American policy, we might be the bad guys. But what if everybody is a bad guy because good guys don't even suit up to play this game? What if a CIA agent brings about two assassinations and tries to prevent another one, and is never sure precisely whose policies he is really carrying out?

What if . . . well, here's a possibility the movie doesn't make explicit, but let me try it out on you. There is a moment when a veteran Washington oil analyst points out that while Kazakhstan has a lot of oil, none of it is where Killen has drilling rights. Yet Killen is undoubtedly shipping oil. Is it possible the Chinese are buying oil in the Gulf, shipping it to Kazakhstan, and selling it to the United States through Killen?

I bring up that possibility because I want to suggest the movie's amoral complexity without spoiling its surprises. *Syriana* is a movie that suggests Congress can hold endless hearings about oil company profits and never discover the answer to anything, because the real story is so labyrinthine that no one—not oil company executives, not Arab princes, not CIA spies, not traders in Geneva—understands the whole picture.

The movie has a lot of important roles and uses recognizable actors to help us keep everything straight. Even then, the studio e-mailed critics a helpful guide to the characters. I didn't look at it. Didn't want to. I liked the way I experienced the film: I couldn't explain the story, but I never felt lost in it. I understood who, what, when, where, and why, but not how they connected. That was how I wanted to relate to it. It created sympathy for individual characters in their specific situations without dictating what I was supposed to think about the big picture.

Some of the characters I cared about included Robert Barnes (George Clooney), a veteran CIA field agent; Bryan Woodman (Matt Damon), a trader based in Geneva; Jimmy Pope (Chris Cooper), who runs Killen; Dean Whiting (Christopher Plummer), a well-connected Washington lawyer whose firm is hired to handle the political implications of the merger; Bennett Holiday (Jeffrey Wright), assigned by Whiting to do "due diligence" on the deal, by which is meant that diligence that supports the merger; Prince Nasir (Alexander Siddig), who sold the rights to the Chinese; his younger brother Prince Meshal (Akbar Kurtha), who is backed by those who do not want Nasir to inherit the throne; and the mysterious Stan, played by William Hurt as someone who is keeping a secret from the rest of the movie.

675

Already I regret listing all of these names. You now have little tic-tac-toe designs on your eyeballs. *Syriana* is exciting, fascinating, absorbing, diabolical, and really quite brilliant, but I'm afraid it inspires reviews that are not helpful. The more you describe it, the more you miss the point. It is not a linear progression from problem to solution. It is all problem. The audience enjoys the process, not the progress. We're like athletes who get so wrapped up in the game we forget about the score.

A recent blog item coined a term like "hyperlink movie" to describe plots like this. (I would quote the exact term, but irony of ironies, I've lost the link.) The term describes movies in which the characters inhabit separate stories, but we gradually discover how those in one story are connected to those in another. *Syriana* was written and directed by Stephen Gaghan, who won an Oscar for his screenplay for *Traffic*, another hyperlink movie. A lot of Altman films, such as *Nashville* and *Short Cuts* use the technique. Also, recently, *Crash* and *Nine Lives*.

In a hyperlink movie, the motives of one character may have to be reinterpreted after we meet another one. Consider the Damon character. His family is invited to a party at the luxurious Spanish villa of the Gulf oil sheik whose sons are Nasir and Meshal. At the party, Damon's son dies by accident. The sheik awards Damon's firm a $100 million contract. "How much for my other son?" he asks. This is a brutal line of dialogue and creates a moment trembling with tension. Later, Damon's wife (Amanda Peet) accuses him of trading on the life of his son. Well, he did take the deal. Should he have turned it down because his son died in an accident? What are Damon's real motives, anyway?

I think *Syriana* is a great film. I am unable to make my reasons clear without resorting to meaningless generalizations. Individual scenes have fierce focus and power, but the film's overall drift stands apart from them. It seems to imply that these sorts of scenes occur, and always have and always will. The movie explains the politics of oil by telling us to stop seeking an explanation. Just look at the behavior. In the short run, you can see who wants oil and how they're trying to get it. In the long run, we're out of oil. ☞

The Syrian Bride ★ ★ ★
No MPAA rating, 94 m., 2006

Hiam Abbass (Amal), Makram Khoury (Hammed), Clara Khoury (Mona). Directed by Eran Riklis and produced by Bettina Brokemper, Antoine de Clermont-Tonnerre, Michael Eckelt, and Riklis. Screenplay by Suha Arraf and Riklis.

The Syrian Bride takes place at such a remote corner of the Golan Heights that when an Israeli official refers to it as a "military outpost," a Syrian scoffs at its ramshackle guardhouse and token military contingent. This obscure border crossing is crucial, however, to the future of Mona (Clara Khoury), who hopes to cross from Israel into Syria and be married. Her problem is that Syria considers her to already be in Syria, and Israel considers her to be in Israel. How can she cross from a place one side says does not exist to a place the other side says does not exist?

If *The Syrian Bride* seems vaguely familiar, it is because the same actress, Clara Khoury, starred in the 2004 film *Rana's Wedding*, playing a bride whose wedding is endangered by red tape at the checkpoint between Jerusalem and the Palestinian settlement of Ramallah. Only in the Middle East does a romantic comedy star specialize in border crossings. Odd, too, that in both cases romance has little to do with it; in *The Syrian Bride*, Mona is entering an arranged marriage with a Syrian soap opera star she's never met.

There is a note of gloom in the opening scenes of *The Syrian Bride*, because after Mona crosses into Syria she can never return to Israel and "will never see her family again." True, she will never see them again by crossing into Israel, but there are such things as airplane flights from both Syria and Israel to perfectly pleasant destinations that will welcome them both, and since the soap opera star presumably can afford the tickets, I was not in tears.

What is real is that these personal lives have become unmanageable because of the political positions of the two nations. Mona gets her passport stamped by the Israelis and then crosses to the Syrian checkpoint, which refuses to accept the passport because it has an Israeli stamp even though, the Syrian says, she has not come from Israel at all, but from Syria. Can she get the stamp whited out? No, because the Israelis require it for her to leave the country.

Meanwhile, the soap opera star's intended bride and his relatives wait in the burning sun on one side of the border, and her father and her family wait on the other. Their situation is more complex because her father has just been released by Israel as a political prisoner, and the terms of his parole forbid him to be this close to the border. Theoretically, he could be put back in jail, but an Israeli police official's shrug is the sort of gesture that makes life possible at all in such a situation.

Like many recent films from this part of the world, including *Rana's Wedding* and the 2006 Oscar nominee *Paradise Now, The Syrian Bride* was made by both Israelis and Arabs. *Rana's* director was a Palestinian based in the Netherlands; the director of *Syrian* is Eran Riklis, an Israeli. The crews are drawn from all the populations involved. What is interesting is that *Rana*, by a Palestinian, and *Syrian*, by an Israeli, seem to share exactly the same ideology: We live side by side, we are separated by a history of enmity, we are only people, we deserve to live our lives. Such films, which are said to be popular in Middle Eastern theaters, may assist in the gradual relaxation of tensions, although optimism regarding the Middle East often seems difficult. When *Paradise Now* was nominated for the Oscar, I received indignant e-mails from both sides, charging that the film favored the other side.

As for *The Syrian Bride*, it is difficult to get worked up about a bride and groom who have never met each other. If their marriage does not take place, their hearts will not be broken. That leaves us free to observe the world in which the film takes place, near a remote Druze desert settlement. Not precisely a flash point. It is possible that on some days, the guards on either side have only each other as company.

The real interest in the film enters by the side door, through supporting characters. Mona's family has gathered from far and wide for the ceremony. Her father is just out of jail, one of her brothers is a businessman in Europe, another has moved to Russia with his Russian bride. Most intriguing is Amal (Hiam Abbass), Mona's older sister, who is married, a feminist, has been accepted by the Israeli university at Haifa, and plans to attend despite the objections of her husband. Amal stands between the modern and the traditional, not so much a negotiator as a translator. What gives her intrinsic importance is Hiam Abbass's striking physical presence; if you remember Irene Papas in *Zorba the Greek* (or anything else), you'll get the idea.

Movies like *The Syrian Bride* are not overtly political but nibble around the edges, engaging our tendency to take a big political position and then undermine it with humanitarian exceptions. I am reminded of an appearance by Louis Farrakhan on the Larry King show. King asked him if he was still adamantly opposed to interracial marriages. Farrakhan said he certainly was, and then he shrugged and almost smiled: "But the young people, what can you tell them?"

T

The Take ★ ★ ★
NO MPAA RATING, 87 m., 2005

A documentary directed by Avi Lewis and produced by Lewis and Naomi Klein. Screenplay by Klein.

As one documentary after another attacks the International Monetary Fund and its pillaging of the Third World, I wish I knew the first thing about global economics. If these films are as correct as they are persuasive, international monetary policy is essentially a scheme to bankrupt smaller nations and cast their populations into poverty, while multinational corporations loot their assets and whisk the money away to safe havens and the pockets of rich corporations and their friends. But that cannot be, can it? Surely the IMF's disastrous record is the result of bad luck, not legalized theft?

I am still haunted by *Life and Debt* (2001), a documentary explaining how tax-free zones were established on, but not of, Jamaican soil. Behind their barbed-wire fences, Jamaican law did not apply, workers could not organize or strike, there were no benefits, wages were minimal, and factories exported cheap goods without any benefit to the Jamaican economy other than subsistence wages.

Meanwhile, Jamaican agriculture was destroyed by IMF requirements that Jamaica import surplus U.S. agricultural products, which were subsidized by U.S. price supports and dumped in Jamaica for less than local (or American) farmers could produce them for. That destroyed the local dairy, onion, and potato industries. Jamaican bananas, which suffered from the inconvenience of not being grown by Chiquita, were barred from all markets except England. Didn't seem cricket, especially since Jamaican onions were so tasty.

Now here is *The Take,* a Canadian documentary by Avi Lewis and Naomi Klein, shot in Argentina, where a prosperous middle-class economy was destroyed during ten years of IMF policies, as enforced by President Carlos Menem (1989–1999). Factories were closed, their assets were liquidated, and money fled the country, sometimes literally by the truckload. After most of it was gone, Menem closed the banks, causing panic. Today more than half of all Argentineans live in poverty, unemployment is epidemic, and the crime rate is scary.

In the face of this disaster, workers at several closed factories attempted to occupy the factories, reopen them, and operate them. Their argument: The factories were subsidized in the first place by public money, so if the owners didn't want to operate them, the workers deserved a chance. The owners saw this differently, calling the occupations theft. Committees of workers monitored the factories to prevent owners from selling off machinery and other assets in defiance of the courts. And many of the factories not only reopened, but were able to turn a profit while producing comparable or superior goods at lower prices.

A success story? Yes, according to the Movement of Recovered Companies. No, according to the owners and the courts. But after Menem wins his way into a run-off election he suddenly drops out of the race, a moderate candidate becomes president, the courts decide in favor of the occupying workers, and the movement gains legitimacy. The film focuses on an auto parts plant and ceramics and garment factories that are running efficiently under worker management.

Is this sort of thing a threat to capitalism, or a revival of it? The factories are doing what they did before—manufacturing goods and employing workers—but they are doing it for the benefit of workers and consumers, instead of as an exercise to send profits flowing to top management. This is classic capitalism, as opposed to the management pocket-lining system, which is essentially loot for the bosses and bread and beans for everybody else. Sounds refreshing to anyone who has followed the recent tales of corporate greed in North America. Is it legal? Well, if the factories are closed, haven't the owners abandoned their moral right to them? Especially if the factories were built with public subsidies in the first place?

I wearily anticipate countless e-mails advising me I am a hopelessly idealistic dreamer, and explaining how when the rich get richer, everybody benefits. I will forward the most inspiring of these messages to minimum-wage workers at Wal-Mart, so they will understand why labor

678

unions would be bad for them, while working unpaid overtime is good for the economy. All I know is that the ladies at the garment factory are turning out good-looking clothes, demand is up for Zanon ceramics, and the auto parts factory is working with a worker-controlled tractor factory to make some good-looking machines. I think we can all agree that's better than just sitting around.

Take My Eyes ★ ★ ★ ½
No MPAA rating, 109 m., 2006

Laia Marull (Pilar), Luis Tosar (Antonio), Candela Pena (Ana), Rosa Maria Sarda (Aurora), Kiti Manver (Rosa), Sergi Calleja (Therapist). Directed by Iciar Bollain and produced by Santiago Garcia de Leaniz. Screenplay by Bollain and Alicia Luna.

I knew a woman who stayed for years with a man who abused her. He couldn't help himself. Neither could she. I think she was addicted to the excitement. She was the center of his world, the focus of his obsessions, the star of his disease. Some of the reviews of Iciar Bollain's *Take My Eyes* can't understand why Pilar returns to Antonio after his violent explosions. That's the point of the movie: Logic becomes irrelevant when she's caught in the drama. Just as he goes to therapy groups to learn how to guard against his anger, she flees to her sister to hear what a bastard Antonio is. Then some dread tidal force draws them together again.

The movie is not neutral. Pilar (Laia Marull) has a problem, but Antonio (Luis Tosar) has a much graver one. He is a sick man whose insecurity and self-hatred boils up into violent outbursts against his wife. Even kicking a soccer ball around with his son, he finds himself kicking it too hard, thinking about his wife and taking it out on the kid. It is clear that Pilar should leave him and never return.

What makes the movie fascinating is that it doesn't settle for a soap opera resolution to this story, with Pilar as the victim, Antonio as the villain, and evil vanquished. It digs deeper and more painfully. The film opens with Pilar desperately waking her young son, grabbing a few clothes, and fleeing in the night to the home of her sister Ana (Candela Pena). In a sane world, this would be the end of the story, with Pilar

getting a protection order and Antonio forever out of the picture.

But he pleads to return. He promises to change. He goes into counseling and therapy. He talks sweet. Her deep feelings for the man begin to stir. We saw this process in *What's Love Got to Do With It* (1993), with Tina Turner finally breaking free from Ike. In *Take My Eyes*, which is about middle-class people in Toledo, Spain, the story is less sensational but trickier, because Antonio is a complex man. As we follow his attempts to reform, as we see that he's really serious about controlling his anger, we begin to feel sympathy for him. We even pity him a little as we see how, step by step, his defenses fall, his lessons are forgotten, and rage once again controls him.

Pilar has not asserted herself much in the marriage, but now in a period of independence she gets a job as a volunteer in an art museum, and quickly reveals an aptitude for talking about art. Soon she is a tourist lecturer; Antonio haunts the shadows of the museum, and as his wife describes the passions in paintings, he imagines she is focusing on men in her audience, sending them signals. She isn't, but never mind: The point is that anything Pilar does in the outside world, any skill she demonstrates or independence she shows, is a challenge to him. He cannot bear the possibility that she could live without him, could exist as herself and not as his possession.

The movie doesn't go in for elaborate set pieces of beatings and bloodshed. He is violent toward her, yes, but what's terrifying is not the brutality of his behavior but how it is sudden, uncontrollable, and overwhelming. There is a time, after she has returned to him once again, where his anger grows and grows until finally he strips her down to a brassiere and shoves her out onto the balcony, to be seen by the neighbors, since after all that's what she wants, isn't it? To parade before strange men?

Marull is powerful as Pilar, a woman who slowly, through hard lessons, is learning that she must leave this man and never see him again and not miss him or weaken to his appeals or cave in to her own ambiguity about his behavior. She may think (and some viewers of the film might think) that she is simply a victim, but when she returns to him, she gives away that game. She knows it's insane and does it anyway.

679

As Antonio, Tosar gives a performance comparable to Laurence Fishburne's in *What's Love Got to Do With It* or Temuera Morrison's in *Once Were Warriors* (1994). He makes his anger absolutely convincing, and that is necessary or this is merely a story. The difference is that Marull's Pilar is less confident, more implicated, than the strong women played by Angela Bassett and Rena Owen in the other two films. That creates a complex response for us. We sympathize at times with both characters, but curiously enough we are more willing to understand why Antonio explodes than why Pilar returns to him. Surely she knows she's making a mistake. Yes, she does. They both know they're spiraling toward danger. If only knowledge had more to do with how they feel and why they act.

Take the Lead ★ ★ ★
PG-13, 108 m., 2006

Antonio Banderas (Pierre Dulaine), Rob Brown (Rock), Yaya DaCosta (LaRhette), Alfre Woodard (Augustine James), John Ortiz (Mr. Temple), Laura Benanti (Tina), Dante Basco (Ramos), Jenna Dewan (Sasha), Marcus T. Paulk (Eddie). Directed by Liz Friedlander and produced by Diane Nabatoff and Christopher Godsick. Screenplay by Dianne Houston.

Take the Lead begins with rudeness, ends with good manners, and argues that poor inner-city schools can be redeemed by ballroom dancing. The only thing wrong with this vision, I suspect, is that it works for the ballroom dancers but not for the gang-bangers, who continue on their chosen careers. There is a more pessimistic view of urban high schools in another movie that opened the same day as *American Gun*, and I fear it's closer to the truth. But *Take the Lead* is said to be based on a true story, it tells a heartening fable, and Antonio Banderas is uncommonly charming as a dance teacher who walks into a high school and announces that he will improve it by his very example.

Public manners have degenerated in recent decades. It is now routine to hear obscenities shouted in public, and by all sorts of people, not just in traffic but even in Starbucks. I am as fond of colorful language as anyone, but I try not to inflict it upon strangers. I suspect that many people sense they should have better manners

and need only a nudge. In high school I was addressed for the first time in my life as "Mister Ebert" by Stanley Hynes, an English teacher, and his formality transformed his classroom into a place where a certain courtliness prevailed.

In *Take the Lead*, Banderas plays Pierre Dulaine, a Manhattan ballroom dancing instructor who rides the streets, impeccably dressed, on his bicycle. One day he witnesses a student named Rock (Rob Brown) attacking a teacher's car with a golf club. Rock has his reasons, but never mind; instead of calling the cops, Dulaine walks into the school the next day and announces to the principal (Alfre Woodard) that he wants to teach ballroom dancing to the detention class.

She is a take-charge realist who walks the hallways ordering students to take off their hats, pull up their pants, and remove their hands from the netherlands of others, and her impulse is to laugh at Pierre, or throw him out. But he prevails and walks into the detention hall, where the students regard him as a visitor from the moon. They resist him, but he fascinates them, especially when he brings in one of his sexiest ballroom colleagues to show them what is surely true, that the tango is more manly, more feminine, more sexy, and more plain damn hot than any other form of motion requiring clothes.

Having seen the charming documentary *Mad Hot Ballroom* (2005), about New York grade school kids learning to dance, which is based on the same real-life story of Dulaine, I anticipated the general direction of *Take the Lead*. It is not a particularly original movie, and it lacks the impact of such earlier classroom parables as *Stand and Deliver, Lean on Me, Mr. Holland's Opus*, and the similar *Music of the Heart* (1999). The vulgar, rebellious, resentful, potentially criminal students are transformed by dancing as surely as music transforms the hero of *Hustle & Flow*. And of course the film ends in a ballroom dancing competition, with full-court choreography that in real life takes weeks of rehearsal but in the movies springs spontaneously from the souls of the dancers.

The film is more fable than record, and more wishful thinking than a plan of action. Yet the end credits leave me no doubt that the real Pierre Dulaine's programs have spread to many other schools and that thousands of students are now learning the tango, the fox-trot, and other dances that are taught with so much less effect in another movie that opened the same day, *Marilyn Hotchkiss' Ballroom Dancing and Charm School*. Strange, how movies can open simultaneously and cast light on each other.

Still, I felt the Woodard character had something to be said for her dubious realism (the high school principal played by Forest Whitaker in *American Gun* certainly would agree with her) and that the ascendancy of Pierre Dulaine was a little too smooth. I began to suspect that he drew a good hand in that detention class, which is made of basically good and misunderstood kids. One really hard case might have capsized the ship.

That said, Banderas is reason enough to see the movie. There are some people who by their personal style can make us want to be better. "Whenever you're in doubt in a social situation," the director Gregory Nava once assured me, "just ask yourself, what would Fred Astaire do?" Pierre Dulaine must ask himself this question several times a day. He dresses well, carries himself with grace and self-respect, treats everyone politely, and all but shames them into returning his courtesy. By being so resplendent in his bearing and effect, he generates envy: The kids follow him not because they want to improve and reform but because they would like to be that cool.

Taking Lives ★ ★ ★
R, 103 m., 2004

Angelina Jolie (Illeana Scott), Ethan Hawke (James Costa), Kiefer Sutherland (Martin Asher), Olivier Martinez (Paquette), Tcheky Karyo (Leclair), Gena Rowlands (Mrs. Asher). Directed by D. J. Caruso and produced by Mark Canton and Bernie Goldmann. Screenplay by Jon Bokenkamp, based on the novel by Michael Pye.

Taking Lives is another one of those serial killer thrillers where the madman is not content with murder but must also devise an ingenious and diabolical pattern so that it can be intuited by an investigator who visits the crime scene and picks up his vibes. The vibe jockey this time is FBI agent Illeana Scott (Angelina Jolie), and the first time the other cops see her, she's on her back in the open grave of one of the victims, feeling the pain or sensing the hate or just possibly freaking out the cops so they won't take her for granted.

Although she's American, she's in Canada because her special skills have been called in by the Montreal police. Before you find it odd that the Canadian cops lack a single law enforcement person with her expertise, reflect on this: They don't even know they're not in Montreal. At almost the very moment we hear "Montreal" on the sound track, there is a beautiful shot of the Chateau Frontenac in Quebec City. This is a little like Chicago cops not noticing they are standing beneath Mount Rushmore.

But I quibble. *Taking Lives* is actually an effective thriller, on its modest but stylish level. Agent Scott quickly figures out that there's a pattern behind the killings—each victim is a few years older than the previous one, and the killer steals his identity, so he must be a person so unhappy to be himself that he has to step into a series of other lives. A moment's reflection might have informed him that his victims, were they not dead, would be keeping up with him chronologically, but maybe, you know what, he's insane.

There's a big break in the case when an artist and gallery owner named James Costa (Ethan Hawke) surprises the killer at work, and is able to supply a high-quality sketch of a suspect. Another development: Mrs. Asher (Gena Rowlands), mother of one of the supposed victims, says the dead body is not her son. Then, not long after, she sees her son quite alive on a ferry. "He's a dangerous man," she tells the cops. He was one of twins, but let's not go there.

The cops include Olivier Martinez and Tcheky Karyo, one of whom resents Scott, while the other respects her. Her methods include devising elaborate time lines of the victims and their photographs, but her greatest gift is to notice little clues. When she spots a draft beneath a bookcase, for example, Nancy Drew is the only other sleuth who would have guessed that behind the case is a hidden door to a secret room.

The movie gets a lot more complicated than I have indicated, and I will not even refer to the last act except to observe that it recycles a detail from *Fatal Attraction* in an ingenious and merciful way. The ending is, in fact, preposterous, depending as thrillers so often do on elaborate plans that depend on the killer hitting all his marks and the cops picking up on all his cues.

For that matter (I will speak cautiously), why is there a person under that bed? To kill Scott, I suppose, but when they struggle, why oh why does she not recognize him? To sacrifice this scene would have meant losing the clue of the draft under the bookcase, but with a little more imagination the hidden room could have been played for creepy chills and occult clues, and we could have lost the big *Carrie* moment. Another excellent question: How can a driver crash a speeding car and be sure who will live and who will die?

This keeps reading like a negative review. I've got to get a grip on myself. See, I *like* movies that make me ask goofy questions like this, as long as they absorb and entertain me, and have actors who can go the distance. Angelina Jolie, like Daryl Hannah, is one of those beauties you somehow never see playing a domesticated housewife. She's more of a freestanding object of wonder, a force of intrigue. Ethan Hawke has the ability to be in a thriller and yet actually seem like a real gallery owner; the art on the walls during his gallery opening looks like a group show from Mrs. Gradgrind's third-grade class, but that's contemporary art for you. And all I can say about Kiefer Sutherland, apart from praise for his good work in the past, is that he seems to have graduated from prime suspect to the parallel category of obvious suspect.

The movie was directed by D. J. Caruso, whose *The Salton Sea* (2002) included the most unforgettably weird villain in recent memory; you remember Vincent D'Onofrio's Pooh-Bear and his little plastic nose. In *Taking Lives*, he understands that a certain genre of thriller depends more upon style and tone than upon plot; it doesn't matter if you believe it walking out, as long as you were intrigued while it was happening.

The Talent Given Us ★ ★ ★ ½
NO MPAA RATING, 97 m., 2005

Judy Wagner (Judy), Allen Wagner (Allen), Emily Wagner (Emily), Maggie Wagner (Maggie), Andrew Wagner (Andrew), Judy Dixon (Bumby), Billy Wirth (Billy). Directed by Andrew Wagner and produced by Wagner, Tom Hines, and Chelsea Gilmore. Screenplay by Wagner.

In some families, certain topics are never discussed. In Andrew Wagner's family, every possible topic is discussed endlessly. It's remarkable that they have the courage (or recklessness) to speak so frankly to each other, and astonishing that they do it in front of a camera. Wagner's *The Talent Given Us* is a brave, funny, affecting film that follows his parents and two sisters as they drive from New York to Los Angeles, picking up a family friend in Iowa. The film rides along with them, stops for meals, eavesdrops in motels, sees the sights.

This is a "fiction film using the materials of documentary," Wagner told me when I met him at Sundance 2005. "My parents, sisters, and friends play my parents, sisters, and friends." They do a convincing job of it; the film feels like cinema verité, even though Andrew is behind the camera while they are allegedly driving to California to visit him. By pretending he's not there, they're acting. Many other details must be fictional.

Consider the family friend nicknamed Bumby (Judy Dixon). In the film we learn she's a publicist who has just been fired from *Field of Dreams 2*. The Internet Movie Database makes no mention of such a film. It must have been invented as an excuse to introduce another character halfway across the country.

Andrew's parents, Judy and Allen, have been married for forty-six years and are still warmly considering divorce. Are we watching them or "characters"? The biographical details match: he was a Wall Street stock specialist and tax consultant; she was a dancer, writer, and technical editor. Both are semi-retired. They wonder if they have been failures as parents, but any family that can make this film has been a success. Maybe their carping at one another is a way of expressing affection.

The cross-country trip happens with all the premeditation of a John Cassavetes plot. Allen, Judy, and their daughter Maggie go to the airport to pick up their daughter Emily, who has flown in from L.A. Both girls are actresses. Leaving the airport, Judy decides on impulse they must all drive as a family *back* to Los Angeles to visit Andrew. Emily reasonably says this is insane, but later she's the one who insists on continuing the trip.

They talk a lot. Allen has apparently had a stroke, which affects his speech, although we understand every word. He keeps a straw in his mouth for reasons never explained; maybe it helps him talk. He's on drugs that have sent his sex life to hell, a fact Judy is unhappy about; her frankness in a motel scene is startling. Emily uses a few drugs, too. She develops alarming symptoms while they're conveniently visiting the Menninger Clinic, and she tells the doctor she has prescriptions for Prozac, Wellbutrin, Synthroid, Xanax, Ativan. "Any unusual stress in your life right now?" the doctor asks. "I'm driving across the country with my parents," Emily explains.

The Wagners fight about driving skills, the route they should take, where they should stop for meals, what they should eat, and about the years when the children were small. "I'm not in therapy because you were a good mother," Emily tells Judy. Because her mother wouldn't pick her up after school, "I became a compulsive masturbator." Now she compensates with plastic surgery and liposuction. Oh, and sadomasochism. At one point, Emily corners both of her parents and quizzes them about their affairs.

Old Allen, meanwhile, has his eye on Bumby, the curvy family friend, and there is a scene between them where he clearly doesn't think his libido has gone completely to hell. Since Bumby seems to be a character introduced into the film, and Allen is contemplating adultery while being photographed by his son, this scene is probably fictional, wouldn't you say? With the Wagners, you never know. It leads, in any event, to midnight motel room confessions between Allen and Judy that are touching: They have lived together for so long that they no longer have a marriage, they have a condition of life, and sometimes they speculate about other lives they might have lived.

The Wagners look at houses they used to live in. They see the sights. They make hypothetical plans for the future. They meet Andrew, who finally appears in front of the camera, briefly. They meet Andrew's friend, the actor Billy Wirth. Allen and Billy have a heart-to-heart. Ever notice how your friends sometimes like your parents more than you do? That's because they didn't experience them as parents.

All of this somehow adds up, as I wrote from Sundance, to a movie that is "seemingly honest." It's the "seemingly" that fascinates me. Is this a documentary based on truth that has been given shape, like *Nanook of the North,* or a documentary that's fiction in the form of truth,

like *Best in Show?* Hard to be sure. I do believe we are really looking at the members of Andrew Wagner's family, and *The Talent Given Us* is a documentary in this sense: It is a record of these people doing these things. Whether they "really" did them is beside the point. They did them for the film, so if they hadn't done them before, they've done them now. ☞

Tarnation ★ ★ ★ ★
NO MPAA RATING, 88 m., 2004

With Jonathan Caouette, Renee LeBlanc, Adolph and Rosemary Davis, and David Sanin Paz. A documentary directed by Jonathan Caouette and produced by Caouette and Stephen Miller. Screenplay by Caouette.

The child is father of the man.
—Wordsworth

Renee LeBlanc was a beautiful little girl; she was a professional model before she was twelve. Then Renee was injured in a fall from the family garage, and descended into depression. Her parents agreed to shock therapy; in two years she had more than 200 treatments, which her son blames for her mental illness, and for the pain that coiled through his family.

Tarnation is the record of that pain, and a journal about the way her son, Jonathan Caouette, dealt with it—first as a kid, now as the director of this film, made in his early thirties. It is a remarkable film, immediate, urgent, angry, poetic, and stubbornly hopeful. It has been constructed from the materials of a lifetime: old home movies, answering-machine tapes, letters and telegrams, photographs, clippings, new video footage, recent interviews, and printed titles that summarize and explain Jonathan's life. "These fragments I shored against my ruins," T. S. Eliot wrote in *The Waste Land,* and Caouette does the same thing.

His film tells the story of a boy growing up gay in Houston and trying to deal with a schizophrenic mother. He had a horrible childhood. By the time he was six, his father had left the scene, he had been abused in foster homes, and he traveled with his mother to Chicago, where he witnessed her being raped. Eventually they both lived in Houston with her parents, Adolph and Rosemary Davis, who had problems of their own.

Caouette dealt with these experiences by stepping outside himself and playing roles. He got a video camera, and began to dress up and film himself playing characters whose problems were not unlike his own. In a sense, that's when he began making *Tarnation*; we see him at eleven, dressed as a woman, performing an extraordinary monologue of madness and obsession.

He was lucky to survive adolescence. Drugs came into his life, he tried suicide, he fled from home. His homosexuality seems to have been a help, not a hindrance; new gay friends provided a community that accepted this troubled teenager. He was diagnosed with "depersonalization disorder," characterized by a tendency to see himself from the outside, like another person. This may have been more of a strategy than a disorder, giving him a way to objectify his experiences and shape them into a story that made sense. In *Tarnation* he refers to himself in the third person. The many printed titles that summarize the story are also a distancing device; if he had spoken the narration, it would have felt first-person and personal, but the written titles stand back from his life and observe it.

The *Up* series of documentaries began with several children at the age of seven. It revisits them every seven years (most recently, in *42 Up*). The series makes it clear that the child is indeed the father of the man; every one of its subjects is already, at seven, a version of the adult he or she would become. *Tarnation* is like Caouette's version of that process, in which the young boy, play-acting, dressing up, dramatizing the trauma in his life, is able to deal with it. Eventually, in New York, he finds a stable relationship with David Sanin Paz, and they provide a home for Renee, whose troubles are still not over.

The method of the film is crucial to its success. *Tarnation* is famous for having been made for $218 on a Macintosh, and edited with the free iMovie software that came with the computer. Of course, hundreds of thousands were later spent to clear music rights, improve the sound track, and make a theatrical print (which was invited to play at Cannes). Caouette's use of iMovie is virtuoso, with overlapping wipes, dissolves, saturation, split screens, multiple panes, graphics, and complex montages. There is a danger with such programs that filmmakers will use every bell and whistle just because it is available, but *Tarnation* uses its jagged style without abusing it.

Caouette's technique would be irrelevant if his film did not deliver so directly on an emotional level. We get an immediate, visceral sense of the unhappiness of Renee and young Jonathan. We see the beautiful young girl fade into a tortured adult. We see Jonathan not only raising himself, but essentially inventing himself. I asked him once if he had decided he didn't like the character life had assigned for him to play, and simply created a different character, and became that character. "I think that's about what happened," he said.

Looking at *Tarnation*, I wonder if the movie represents a new kind of documentary that is coming into being. Although home movies have been used in docs for decades, they were almost always, by definition, brief and inane. The advent of the video camera has meant that lives are recorded in greater length and depth than ever before; a film like *Capturing the Friedmans* (2003), with its harrowing portrait of sexual abuse and its behind-the-scenes footage of a family discussing its legal options, would have been impossible before the introduction of consumer video cameras. Jonathan Caouette not only experienced his life, but recorded his experience, and his footage of himself as a child says what he needs to say more eloquently than any actor could portray it or any writer could describe it.

The film leaves some mysteries. Caouette visits his grandfather and asks hard questions, but gets elusive answers; we sense that the truth is lost in the murkiness of memory and denial. The 200 shock treatments destroyed his mother's personality, Caouette believes, and they could have destroyed him by proxy, but in *Tarnation* we see him survive. His is a life in which style literally prevailed over substance; he defeated the realities that would have destroyed him by becoming someone they could not destroy.

Taxi ★

PG-13, 97 m., 2004

Queen Latifah (Belle), Jimmy Fallon (Washburn), Henry Simmons (Jesse), Jennifer Esposito (Lieutenant Marta Robbins), Gisele

Bundchen (Vanessa), Ann-Margret (Washburn's Mom). Directed by Tim Story and produced by Luc Besson. Screenplay by Ben Garant, Thomas Lennon, and Jim Kouf.

The taming of Queen Latifah continues in the dismal *Taxi*, as Queen, a force of nature in the right roles, is condemned to occupy a lame-brained action comedy. In a film that is wall-to-wall with idiocy, the most tiresome delusion is that car chases are funny. Movie audiences are bored to the point of sullen exhaustion by car chases, especially those without motivation, and most especially those obviously created with a computer.

As the movie opens, Latifah plays a bicycle messenger who races through Macy's, rattles down the steps of the subway, zips through a train to the opposite platform, goes up a ramp, bounces off the back of a moving truck, lands on the sidewalk, jumps off a bridge onto the top of another truck, and so on. This is, of course, not possible to do, and the sequence ends with that ancient cliché in which the rider whips off a helmet and—why, it's Queen Latifah!

It's her last day on the job. She has finally qualified for her taxi license, and before long we see the customized Yellow Cab she's been working on for three years. In addition to the titanium supercharger given by her fellow bike messengers as a farewell present (uh, huh), the car has more gimmicks than a James Bond special; a custom job like this couldn't be touched at under $500,000, which of course all bike messengers keep under the bed. Her dream, she says, is to be a NASCAR driver. In her Yellow Cab?

Then we meet a cop named Washburn (Jimmy Fallon), who is spectacularly incompetent, blows drug busts, causes traffic accidents, and has not his badge, but his driver's license confiscated by his chief, Lieutenant Marta Robbins (Jennifer Esposito), who used to be his squeeze, but no more. When he hears about a bank robbery, he commandeers Queen Latifah's cab, and soon she is racing at speeds well over 100 mph down Manhattan streets in pursuit of the robbers, who are, I kid you not, four supermodels who speak Portuguese. Luckily, Queen Latifah speaks Portuguese, too, because, I dunno, she used to be the delivery girl for a Portuguese take-out joint.

Oh, this is a bad movie. Why, oh why, was the lovely Ann-Margret taken out of retirement to play Fallon's mother, an alcoholic with a blender full of margaritas? Who among the writers (Ben Garant, Thomas Lennon, and Jim Kouf) thought it would be funny to give Latifah and the cop laughing gas, so they could talk funny? What's with Latifah's fiancé, Jesse (Henry Simmons), who looks like a *GQ* cover boy and spends long hours in fancy restaurants waiting for Queen Latifah, who is late because she is chasing robbers, etc.? Is there supposed to be subtle chemistry between Latifah and the cop? It's so subtle, we can't tell. (He's afraid to drive because he had a trauma during a driving lesson, so she coaches him to sing while he's driving, and he turns into a stunt driver and a pretty fair singer. Uh, huh.)

All these questions pale before the endless, tedious chase scenes, in which cars do things that cars cannot do, so that we lose all interest. If we were cartoons, our eyes would turn into X-marks. What is the *point* of showing a car doing 150 miles an hour through midtown Manhattan? Why is it funny that the cop causes a massive pile-up, with the cars in back leapfrogging onto the top of the pile? The stunt must have cost a couple of hundred thousand dollars; half a dozen indie films could have been made for that money. One of them could have starred Queen Latifah.

Latifah has been in movies since 1991, but first flowered in F. Gary Gray's *Set It Off* (1996), about four black working women who rob a bank. She was wonderful in *Living Out Loud* (1998), as a torch singer who has an unexpectedly touching conversation with a lovelorn elevator operator (Danny DeVito). She walked away with her scenes in *Chicago*.

Why was it thought, by Latifah or anyone, that she needed to make a movie as obviously without ambition, imagination, or purpose as *Taxi*? Doesn't she know that at this point in her career she should be looking for some lean and hungry Sundance type to put her in a zero-budget masterpiece that could win her the Oscar? True, it could turn out to be a flop. But better to flop while trying to do something good than flop in something that could not be good, was never going to be good, and only gets worse as it plows along.

685

Team America: World Police ★
R, 98 m., 2004

With the voices of Trey Parker, Matt Stone, Kristen Miller, Daran Norris, and Phil Hendrie. Directed by Trey Parker and produced by Scott Rudin, Matt Stone, Parker, and Pam Brady. Screenplay by Stone, Parker, and Brady.

What're you rebelling against, Johnny?
Whaddya got?
　　　　　　　　　　—The Wild One

If this dialogue is not inscribed over the doors of Trey Parker and Matt Stone, it should be. Their *Team America: World Police* is an equal opportunity offender, and waves of unease will flow over first one segment of their audience, and then another. Like a cocky teenager who's had a couple of drinks before the party, they don't have a plan for who they want to offend, only an intention to be as offensive as possible.

Their strategy extends even to their decision to use puppets for all of their characters, a choice that will not be universally applauded. Their characters, one-third life-size, are clearly artificial, and yet there's something going on around the mouths and lips that looks halfway real, as if they were inhabited by the big faces with moving mouths from Conan O'Brien. There are times when the characters risk falling into the Uncanny Valley, that rift used by robot designers to describe robots that alarm us by looking too humanoid.

The plot seems like a collision at the screenplay factory between several half-baked world-in-crisis movies. Team America, a group not unlike the Thunderbirds, bases its rockets, jets, and helicopters inside Mount Rushmore, which is hollow, and race off to battle terrorism wherever it is suspected. In the opening sequence, they swoop down on Paris and fire on caricatures of Middle East desperadoes, missing most of them but managing to destroy the Eiffel Tower, the Arch of Triumph, and the Louvre.

Regrouping, the team's leader, Spottswoode (voice by Daran Norris), recruits a Broadway actor named Gary to go undercover for them. When first seen, Gary (voice by Parker) is starring in the musical *Lease*, and singing "Everyone Has AIDS." Ho, ho. Spottswoode tells Gary:

"You're an actor with a double major in theater and world languages! Hell, you're the perfect weapon!" There's a big laugh when Gary is told that, if captured, he may want to kill himself, and is supplied with a suicide device I will not reveal.

Spottswoode's plan: Terrorists are known to be planning to meet at "a bar in Cairo." The Team America helicopter will land in Cairo, and four uniformed team members will escort Gary, his face crudely altered to look "Middle Eastern," to the bar, where he will go inside and ask whazzup. As a satire on our inability to infiltrate other cultures, this will do, I suppose. It leads to an ill-advised adventure where in the name of fighting terrorism, Team America destroys the pyramids and the Sphinx. But it turns out the real threat comes from North Korea and its leader, Kim Jong Il (voice also by Parker), who plans to unleash "9/11 times 2,356."

Opposing Team America is the Film Actors Guild, or F.A.G., ho, ho, with puppets representing Alec Baldwin, Tim Robbins, Matt Damon, Susan Sarandon, and Sean Penn (who has written an angry letter about the movie to Parker and Stone about their comments, in *Rolling Stone*, that there is "no shame in not voting"). No real point is made about the actors' activism; they exist in the movie essentially to be ridiculed for existing at all, I guess. Hans Blix, the UN chief weapons inspector, also turns up, and has a fruitless encounter with the North Korean dictator. Some of the scenes are set to music, including such tunes as "Pearl Harbor Sucked and I Miss You" and "America, F***, Yeah!"

If I were asked to extract a political position from the movie, I'd be baffled. It is neither for nor against the war on terrorism, just dedicated to ridiculing those who wage it and those who oppose it. The White House gets a free pass, since the movie seems to think Team America makes its own policies without political direction.

I wasn't offended by the movie's content so much as by its nihilism. At a time when the world is in crisis, the response of Parker, Stone, and company is to sneer at both sides—indeed, at anyone who takes the current world situation seriously. They may be right that some of us are puppets, but they're wrong that all of us are fools, and dead wrong that it doesn't matter.

Tell Them Who You Are ★ ★ ★ ½
R, 95 m., 2005

With Mark Wexler, Haskell Wexler, Peter Bart, Verna Bloom, Billy Crystal, Michael Douglas, Conrad L. Hall, Julia Roberts, Jane Fonda, Sidney Poitier, John Sayles, Albert Maysles, Tom Hayden, Studs Terkel, Norman Jewison, Dennis Hopper, Milos Forman, and Paul Newman. Directed and produced by Mark Wexler. Screenplay by Robert DeMaio and Wexler.

I have known Haskell Wexler for thirty-six years. When Haskell had a rough cut of *Medium Cool*, his docudrama shot at the 1968 Democratic Convention, he asked me to see it after Paramount got cold feet about distribution. Like many people since then, I thought it was a powerful and courageous film. Haskell and I became friends over the years. I remember swimming in Jamaica with Haskell and his wife, the actress Rita Taggart. I remember going through *Blaze* a frame at a time with Haskell at the Hawaii Film Festival, and taking apart *Casablanca* with him on Dusty Cohl's Floating Film Festival.

So he is a friend. He is also a great cinematographer. And he is an activist for progressive causes, a sometime director of features and documentaries, and the subject of a new documentary named *Tell Them Who You Are*. The documentary is by his son, Mark, who tells his father very clearly: "I'm not a fan. I'm a son." Mark made a previous doc, *Me and My Matchmaker*, which I found fascinating; he meets a matchmaker, thinks it would be interesting to watch her at work, asks her to find him a wife, and gets involved in a process neither he nor the matchmaker could possibly have anticipated.

Mark's new doc is frankly intended, we learn, as an attempt to get to know his father better. The child of Haskell's second marriage, he has an almost Oedipal rivalry that has, among other things, led him to politics that are the opposite of his father's. Haskell, now in his eighties, agreed to participate with misgivings, and is not very happy with the results.

Two of Haskell's longtime friends, the director John Sayles and producer Maggie Renzi, told me Mark has "issues" with his father and the film doesn't reflect Haskell's big-hearted kindness. Then again, they share Haskell's left-wing

beliefs. Mark, perhaps not coincidentally, does not. "Haskell gets up every morning and he rants against what's happening in the world," says Haskell's fellow documentarian Pam Yates, with admiration. In the film, he takes Mark along to a peace rally in San Francisco, where he seems to know everybody.

All fathers and sons have issues. If *Tell Them Who You Are* had been a sunny doc about how great the old man was, it wouldn't be worth seeing—and wouldn't be the kind of film Haskell himself makes. What Mark does, better perhaps than either he or his father realizes, is to capture some aspects of a lifelong rivalry that involves love but not much contentment.

Mark remembers his father advising him, "Tell them you're Haskell Wexler's son," which would have done him some good in Hollywood, but Mark has been trying for years to be defined as *not* simply Haskell's son, and this film about his father is paradoxically part of that struggle. This generational thing has been going on for a while with the Wexlers; as a young man, Haskell organized a strike against his own father's factory. And, although he came from a well-to-do family, we learn that Haskell volunteered for the Merchant Marines in World War II and survived a torpedoed ship. This is a man who has been there.

"I don't think there's a movie that I've been on that I wasn't sure I could direct it better," Haskell says in the film. We learn of a few films he was fired from when the directors felt he was making that all too clear; one of them was *One Flew Over the Cuckoo's Nest*, and we get the memories of director Milos Forman ("He was sharing his frustrations with the actors") and producer Michael Douglas ("He reminds me of my own father: critical and judging").

There were also films he walked away from on matters of principle. After one, he told me the director was lazy and didn't treat people with respect. Haskell isn't an obedient hired hand, but a strong-willed artist who gets the admiration of strong directors like John Sayles (*Limbo, The Secret of Roan Inish*), Norman Jewison (*In the Heat of the Night*), Mike Nichols (*Who's Afraid of Virginia Woolf*), and Hal Ashby (*Bound for Glory*). He won Oscars for his work on *Virginia Woolf* and *Bound for Glory*, and was nominated three other times.

On the other hand, Francis Ford Coppola replaced him on *The Conversation* (after Haskell had finished the legendary opening sequence). Haskell's version: He was working too quickly for Coppola, who wasn't prepared. Coppola's version: unstated. And Haskell believes he shot more than half of Terrence Malick's *Days of Heaven*, which Nestor Almendros won an Oscar for.

After the lights went up at the Toronto Film Festival premiere of the doc, there was Norman Jewison sitting across the aisle and observing, "He could be a son of a bitch." The way he said it, it sounded affectionate.

What Haskell is sure of is that he knows more about making documentaries than Mark does. He tells Mark he should have employed a sound man for some scenes shot at a party, and he turns out to be right. The two men get into a heated argument when Mark tries to set up a shot with his father standing in front of a sunset, and Haskell thinks his son is valuing form over content; forget the sunset, he says, because "I desperately want to say something." On the other hand, he criticizes Mark for having him "say everything" instead of using the technique of telling through showing.

Mark provides a good overview of his father's career: the Academy Awards, the great films, the legendary reputation. He talks to some who love him and some who don't. We learn of Haskell's business partnership and close friendship with Conrad L. Hall, another great cinematographer; Mark sometimes felt closer to Conrad than to his own father, and strangely enough, Conrad's son, also a great cinematographer, felt closer to Haskell.

Then there is the issue of Mark's mother, Marian, Wexler's wife for thirty years, now a victim of Alzheimer's. I've known Haskell only with his third wife, Rita, and I see a couple glowing with love. Mark resents his father for leaving his mother. But then we see probably the film's strongest scene, and it involves Haskell visiting Marian in a nursing home. Marian doesn't recognize him, but Haskell speaks softly to her: "We've got secrets, you, me. We've got secrets. We know things about each other that nobody else in the world knows." There are tears in his eyes.

Certainly only a family member could have had access to such a scene. Possibly Haskell did not expect it to be in the documentary. But it reflects well on him, and on Mark for including it. There is this: Haskell agreed to be in the film,

to some degree in order to help his son. And although Mark shows the tension between himself and his father, he also shows a willingness to look beyond the surface of his resentments. Jane Fonda says of them: "Intimacy was not their gift." They are still working at it. This is a film about a relationship in progress.

The Terminal ★ ★ ★ ½
PG-13, 121 m., 2004

Tom Hanks (Viktor Navorski), Catherine Zeta-Jones (Amelia Warren), Stanley Tucci (Frank Dixon), Chi McBride (Joe Mulroy), Diego Luna (Enrique Cruz), Barry Shabaka Henley (Ray Thurman), Kumar Pallana (Gupta Rajan), Zoe Saldana (Dolores Torres). Directed by Steven Spielberg and produced by Laurie MacDonald, Walter F. Parkes, and Spielberg. Screenplay by Sacha Gervasi and Jeff Nathanson.

Steven Spielberg and Tom Hanks have made, in *The Terminal*, a sweet and delicate comedy, a film to make you hold your breath, it is so precisely devised. It has big laughs, but it never seems to make an effort for them; it knows exactly, minutely, and in every detail who its hero is, and remains absolutely consistent to what he believes and how he behaves.

The hero is named Viktor Navorski. He has arrived in a vast American airport just as his nation, Krakozia, has fallen in a coup. Therefore his passport and visa are worthless, his country no longer exists, and he cannot go forward or go back. Dixon, the customs official, tells him he is free to remain in the International Arrivals Lounge, but forbidden to step foot on American soil.

This premise could have yielded a film of contrivance and labored invention. Spielberg, his actors, and writers (Sacha Gervasi and Jeff Nathanson) weave it into a human comedy that is gentle and true, that creates sympathy for all of its characters, that finds a tone that will carry them through, that made me unreasonably happy.

There is a humanity in its humor that reminds you of sequences in Chaplin or Keaton where comedy and sadness find a fragile balance. It has another inspiration, the work of the French actor-filmmaker Jacques Tati. Spielberg gives Hanks the time and space to develop elaborate situations like those Tati was always getting himself into, situations where the lives of those around him became baffling because of Tati's own profound simplicity.

In *The Terminal*, Viktor Navorski's unintended victim is Dixon, the customs and immigrations official, played by Stanley Tucci with an intriguing balance between rigidity and curiosity. He goes by the rules, but he has no great love of the rules. Sometimes the rules are cruel, but he takes no joy in the cruelty. As Navorski lingers day after day in the arrivals lounge, Dixon's impatience grows. "He's found out about the quarters," he says one day, staring grimly at a surveillance monitor. Navorski is returning luggage carts to the racks to collect the refund, and spending his profits on food.

Navorski is a man unlike any Dixon has ever encountered—a man who is exactly who he seems to be and claims to be. He has no guile, no hidden motives, no suspicion of others. He trusts. The immigration service, and indeed the American legal system, has no way of dealing with him because Viktor does not do, or fail to do, any of the things the system is set up to prevent him from doing, or not doing. He has slipped through a perfect logical loophole. *The Terminal* is like a sunny Kafka story, in which it is the citizen who persecutes the bureaucracy.

Dixon wants Navorski out of the terminal because, well, he can't live there forever, but he shows every indication of being prepared to. "Why doesn't he escape?" Dixon asks his underlings, as Navorski stands next to an open door that Dixon has deliberately left unguarded. Dixon's plan is to pass Navorski on to another jurisdiction: "You catch a small fish and unhook him very carefully. You place him back in the water, so that someone else can have the pleasure of catching him."

Dixon could arrest Navorski unfairly, but refuses to: "He has to break the law." Navorski, who speaks little English but is learning every day, refuses to break the law. He won't even lie when Dixon offers him political asylum. "Are you afraid of returning to your country?" "Not afraid," he says simply. "But aren't you afraid of *something?*" "I am afraid for . . . ghosts," says Navorski. The terminal is filled with other characters Navorski gets to know, such as Amelia the flight attendant (Catherine Zeta-Jones), who is having an affair with a married man and finds

she can open her heart to this strange, simple man. And Gupta the janitor (Kumar Pallana), who leaves the floor wet and watches as passengers ignore the little yellow warning pyramids and slip and fall. "This is the only fun I have," he says. And a food services employee (Diego Luna), who is in love with an INS official (Zoe Saldana) and uses Navorski as his go-between.

These friends and others have secret social lives in the terminal, feasting on airline food, playing poker. Navorski becomes their hero when he intervenes in a heart-rending case. A Russian man has medicine he needs to take to his dying father, but Dixon says it must stay in the United States. The man goes berserk, a hostage situation threatens, but Navorski defuses the situation and finds a solution that would have pleased Solomon.

Tom Hanks does something here that many actors have tried to do and failed. He plays his entire role with an accent of varying degrees of impenetrability, and it never seems like a comic turn or a gimmick, and he never seems to be doing it to get a laugh. He gets laughs, but his acting and the writing are so good they seem to evolve naturally. That is very hard to do. He did the same thing in *Forrest Gump,* and Navorski is another character that audiences will, yes, actually love. The screenplay also sidesteps various hazards that a lesser effort would have fallen to, such as a phony crisis or some kind of big action climax. *The Terminal* doesn't have a plot; it *tells a story.* We want to know what will happen next, and we care.

Most of this movie was shot on a set, a vast construction by production designer Alex McDowell. We're accustomed these days to whole cities and planets made of computerized effects. Here the terminal with all of its levels, with its escalators and retail shops and food courts and security lines and passenger gates actually exists. The camera of the great Janusz Kaminski can go anywhere it wants, can track and crane and pivot, and everything is real. Not one viewer in one hundred will guess this is not a real airline terminal.

Spielberg and Hanks like to work together *(Saving Private Ryan, Catch Me If You Can),* and here they trust each other with tricky material. It is crucial, perhaps, that they're so successful as to be unassailable, which allows them to relax and take their time on a production that

689

was burning dollars every second. Others might have heard the clock ticking and rushed or pushed, or turned up the heat by making the Dixon character into more of a villain and less of a character study. Their film has all the time in the world. Just like Viktor Navorski. He isn't going anywhere.

Thank You for Smoking ★ ★ ★ ½
R, 92 m., 2006

Aaron Eckhart (Nick Naylor), Maria Bello (Polly Bailey), Adam Brody (Jack), Sam Elliott (Lorne Lutch), Katie Holmes (Heather Holloway), Rob Lowe (Jeff Megall), William H. Macy (Senator Finistirre), Robert Duvall (The Captain), Cameron Bright (Joey Naylor), J.K. Simmons (B.R.), David Koechner (Bobby Jay Bliss). Directed by Jason Reitman and produced by David O. Sacks. Screenplay by Reitman, based on the novel by Christopher Buckley.

Here is a satire both savage and elegant, a dagger instead of a shotgun. *Thank You for Smoking* targets the pro-smoking lobby with a dark appreciation of human nature. It stars Aaron Eckhart as Nick Naylor, a spokesman for the Academy of Tobacco Studies. We meet him on the Joan Lunden show, sitting next to bald-headed little Robin, a fifteen-year-old boy who is dying of cancer "but has stopped smoking." Nick rises smoothly to the challenge: "It's in our best interests to keep Robin alive and smoking," he explains. "The antismoking people want Robin to die."

Nick Naylor is a pleasant, good-looking career lobbyist who is divorced, loves his son, Joey (Cameron Bright), and speaks to the kid's class on career day. "Please don't ruin my childhood," Joey pleads, but his dad cross-examines a little girl whose mother says cigarettes can kill you: "Is your mother a doctor?" Once a week he dines with the MOD Squad, whose other members are alcohol lobbyist Polly Bailey (Maria Bello) and firearms lobbyist Bobby Jay Bliss (David Koechner). They argue over which of their products kills the most people. The initials MOD stand for "Merchants of Death."

The movie was directed by Jason Reitman, now twenty-nine, who warmed up by making short subjects. What's remarkable in his first feature is his control of tone; instead of careen-

ing from one target to the next, he brings a certain detached logic to his method. Notice how Nick negotiates with a Hollywood superagent (Rob Lowe) on the challenge of getting movie stars to smoke on-screen once again. Right now, they agree, no one smokes in the movies except for villains and Europeans. The stars would have to smoke in historical pictures, since in a contemporary film other people would always be asking them why they smoke. Or—why not in the future, after cigarettes are safe? Smoking in a space station?

Jason Reitman grew up around movies; his father is Ivan Reitman (*Ghostbusters, Evolution*). But Jason has his own style, sneaky and subtle. Instead of populating his movie with people smoking and coughing and wheezing, he shows not a single person smoking, although the ancient Captain (Robert Duvall), czar of the tobacco industry, holds a cigar like a threat. Eckhart has a good line in plausible corporate villains (see his debut in *In the Company of Men*), and he is smiling, optimistic, and even trusting (as when he tells reporter Katie Holmes things he should know will not be off the record).

Naylor's opponent in the film is Senator Ortolan Finistirre (William H. Macy), a Vermont environmentalist whose office desk is covered with his collection of maple syrup bottles. The senator has introduced legislation requiring a skull and crossbones to be displayed on every cigarette pack, replacing the government health warning. The symbol is better than the words, he explains, because "they want those who do not speak English to die."

Reitman's screenplay is based on a novel by Christopher Buckley (son of William F.) and retains a literary flavor rare in a time when many movies are aimed at people who move their lips when they think. Consider this exchange between Nick and his young son, who wants help on a school assignment:

> *Joey:* "Dad, why is the American government the best government?"
> *Nick:* "Because of our endless appeals system."

Or this nostalgia by Duvall, as the Captain: "I was in Korea shooting Chinese in 1952. Now they're our best customers. Next time we won't have to shoot so many of them."

What I admired above all in *Thank You for*

Smoking was its style. I enjoyed the satire, I laughed a lot because it's a very funny movie, but laughs are common, and satire, as we all know, is what closes on *Saturday Night Live*. Style is something modern movies can't always find the time for. I am thinking for some reason of *The Thin Man* (1934), a movie that works in large part because of the way William Powell and Myrna Loy hold themselves, move, and speak; their attitude creates a space between the vulgarities of the plot and the elegance of their personalities, and in that space the humor resides. Their lives are their works of art. Nick Naylor is like them, not egotistical or conceited so much as an objective observer of his own excellence. It is the purpose of the movie to humble him, but he never grovels and even in a particularly nasty situation still depends on his ability to spin anything to his advantage. If you want to remake *The Thin Man*, I say Eckhart and Catherine Keener.

Should the movie be angrier? I lost both of my parents to cigarettes, but I doubt that more anger would improve it. Everyone knows cigarettes can kill you, but they remain on sale and raise billions of dollars in taxes. The target of the movie is not so much tobacco as lobbying in general, which along with advertising and spin control makes a great many evils palatable to the population. How can you tell when something is not good for you? Because of the efforts made to convince you it is harmless or beneficial. Consider the incredible, edible egg. "Drink responsibly." Prescription drug prices doubled "to fund research for better health."

At one point in the movie Nick pays a call on Lorne Lutch (Sam Elliott), a former Marlboro Man now dying of cancer and speaking out bitterly against cigarettes. Nick brings along a briefcase full of hundred-dollar bills. This is not a bribe, he explains. It is a gift. Of course, to accept such a gift and then continue to attack tobacco would be ungrateful. Lorne eyes the money and wonders if he could maybe take half of it and cut back on his attacks. Nick explains with genuine regret that it doesn't work that way. Once you're on board, you're along for the ride.

The Thing About My Folks ★ ★ ½
PG-13, 96 m., 2005

Peter Falk (Sam Kleinman), Paul Reiser (Ben Kleinman), Olympia Dukakis (Muriel Kleinman), Elizabeth Perkins (Rachel Kleinman), Ann Dowd (Linda), Claire Beckman (Hillary), Mimi Lieber (Bonnie). Directed by Raymond De Felitta and produced by Robert F. Newmyer, Paul Reiser, and Jeffrey Silver. Screenplay by Reiser.

One of the nice things about my job is that I get to enjoy the good parts in movies that aren't really necessary to see. *The Thing About My Folks* travels familiar movie territory: a grown son and his father get to know each other during a journey in, yes, a classic car. They do not discover much they couldn't have learned in screenwriting class, but we discover once again what a warm and engaging actor Peter Falk is. I can't recommend the movie, but I can be grateful that I saw it, for Falk.

He plays a crusty old guy named Sam Kleinman, who descends one day upon his son, Ben (Paul Reiser), with astonishing news: Muriel (Olympia Dukakis), his wife of countless years, has walked out on him. She left a note that essentially said: "I have to go. I have to be alone." Why? Why would she do anything? Why would Sam, who has been married to her for most of his life, expect her to do a crazy thing like that?

Ben is a successful professional, happily married to Rachel (Elizabeth Perkins). There has been talk of moving out of New York and buying a place in the country, and Ben takes Sam along to inspect a property. "This house was built by my grandfather after the Civil War," the owner tells them. Sam is unmoved and wants to know details about the septic tank drainage.

They have car trouble, and when they appeal to a mechanic, they find on his lot a beautifully restored 1940 Ford Deluxe coupe convertible. It reminds Sam of the first cars of his young manhood. They buy it right there on the spot, thereby following two rules of the Little Movie Glossary. One provides that characters drive classic cars whenever possible because modern cars are boring and all look alike; the other calls for ragtops because it makes it easier to see and light the characters. They begin an odyssey through the beautiful scenery and foliage of upstate New York.

The movie is sort of a sideways version of *Sideways*, even down to a scene where the two men join two women for dinner. The difference is, in *Sideways* the guys desperately want to impress the women, and in *The Thing About My Folks* they want to impress each other. The women excuse themselves to go to the powder room, and somehow we know they won't be coming back. Sam and Ben are so deep in conversation, it's awhile before they realize they've been dumped.

What do they talk about? The early days of Sam's marriage. The meaning of life. Why they never talked about important things. How Sam's job kept him away a lot of the time. All the usual stuff. They also do the usual things. They go on a fishing trip, although they are not fishermen, and play pool, and Sam turns out to know his way around the table.

What will be the result of this trip? Falk has a wonderful speech: "You'll be here when your old man finds himself. While we're at it, we can find you, too. We can find the whole goddamned family. We got a car."

Then a dramatic document emerges: A letter written by Muriel to Sam, two weeks before Ben was born, which has waited in its envelope ever since. What the letter says I will leave for you to discover, but it places the entire marriage in a different light and leads to some closing scenes in which Dukakis has little to do but does it wonderfully; I was reminded a little of her exasperated marriage in *Moonstruck*. Her great discovery about life ("things change, and you make adjustments") is not earthshaking, although it has the advantage of being true.

The movie was written by Reiser, who does an interesting thing with his performance: Instead of going through the usual anger and impatience of a son in this kind of story, he projects a certain protective concern; he humors his old man, sometimes feeds him straight lines, understands about his care and feeding. Old Sam, we feel, has gone at life full-bore for all these years without a lot of introspection, but he is not a monster, and his son feels love for him. Also incredulity.

The film was directed by Raymond De Felitta, whose *Two Family House* is an overlooked treasure. With this film he does what the screenplay requires, with admiration for the actors and sincere acceptance of the material. The problem is that the screenplay doesn't require enough. We have seen situations something like this so often that we need, I dunno, something either stranger or deeper. It would be nice if lifelong problems

and questions got solved during a week playing hooky in a 1940 Ford Deluxe coupe, but if it were that easy, you wouldn't need the car.

13 Going on 30 ★ ★
PG-13, 97 m., 2004

Jennifer Garner (Jenna Rink), Mark Ruffalo (Matt Flamhaff), Judy Greer (Lucy Wyman), Andy Serkis (Richard Kneeland), Kathy Baker (Beverly Rink), Phil Reeves (Wayne Rink), Christa B. Allen (Young Jenna Rink). Directed by Gary Winick and produced by Susan Arnold, Gina Matthews, and Donna Roth. Screenplay by Cathy Yuspa, Josh Goldsmith, and Niels Mueller.

Jennifer Garner is indeed a charmer, but she's the victim of a charmless treatment in *13 Going on 30*, another one of those body-switch movies (think *Big*, *Vice Versa*, *Freaky Friday*, etc.) in which a child magically occupies an adult body. The director, Gary Winick, came out of Sundance with *Tadpole* (2003), a movie in which a sixteen-year-old boy was seduced by a forty-year-old woman, and some of us wondered how well that plot would have worked with a sixteen-year-old girl and a forty-year-old man. Now Winick finds out, by supplying a thirteen-year-old girl with a thirty-year-old body and a boyfriend who's a professional hockey star. Their big makeout scene goes wrong when she thinks he's "gross," and we fade to black, mercifully, before we find out what happens then. Can you be guilty of statutory rape caused by magical body-switching?

The movie introduces us to Jenna Rink when she's a teenager (played by Christa B. Allen), who allows the most popular girls in school to push her around because she wants to be just like them. (There's a much superior version of this angle in *Mean Girls*.) She throws a party in her rec room and the girls play a nasty trick on her, which inspires her to be cruel to her only true friend, Matt, a chubby kid who lives next door and adores her.

Then she's sprinkled with magic dust (I think we have to let the movie get away with this), and discovers that she is thirty, lives in New York, is an editor of a magazine named *Poise*, and looks like Jennifer Garner. Her snotty high school classmate Lucy (Judy Greer) now works with her on the magazine, and they're friends, sort of, although the movie teaches us that career women will betray each other to get ahead.

In the best examples of this genre, there are funny scenes in which adult actors get to act as if they're inhabited by kids. Tom Hanks did this about as well as it can be done in *Big*, and I also liked Judge Reinhold in *Vice Versa*, and of course Jamie Lee Curtis in the 2003 version of *Freaky Friday*. Strangely, *13 Going on 30* doesn't linger on scenes like that, maybe because Jenna is established in a high-powered Manhattan world where she has to learn fast. The result is that most of the movie isn't really about a thirteen-year-old in an adult body, but about a power struggle at the magazine, and Jenna's attempts to renew her friendship with Matt (now played by Mark Ruffalo).

He's not cooperative. Apparently her missing seventeen years all actually occurred; it's just that she can't remember them. And after the disastrous party in the rec room, she never talked to Matt again, so why should he believe she's any different now? She's desperate, because she has no real friends, but Matt is engaged to be married, and what happens to the time line to solve that dilemma would make *Eternal Sunshine of the Spotless Mind* look as linear as a Doris Day romance.

Logical quibbles are, of course, irrelevant with a movie like this. You buy the magic because it comes with the territory. What I couldn't buy was the world of the magazine office, and the awkward scenes in which high-powered professionals don't seem to notice that they're dealing with a thirteen-year-old mind. Jenna's bright idea to redesign the magazine is so spectacularly bad that it's accepted, I suppose, only because the screenwriters stood over the actors with whips and drove them to it.

The writers, by the way, are Cathy Yuspa, Josh Goldsmith, and Niels Mueller. Yuspa and Goldsmith wrote the vastly superior office comedy *What Women Want* (2000), in which Mel Gibson was able to read the minds of the women in his office. This time there are no minds worth reading. Although we understand why Jenna is attracted to the adult Matt (who has undergone a transition from pudgy to handsome), the movie never really deals with (1) whether he fully comes to grips with the fact

that this is the *same* girl he knew at thirteen, and (2) how or why or whether or when a thirteen-year-old can successfully fall in love with a thirty-year-old man, with everything that would entail (in life, anyway, if not in this movie). There are so many emotional and sexual puzzles to tap-dance around, this should have been a musical.

39 Pounds of Love ★ ½
NO MPAA RATING, 70 m., 2005

A documentary directed by Dani Menkin and produced by Daniel J. Chalfen and Menkin. Screenplay by Ilan Heitner and Menkin.

When Ami Ankilewitz was born with spinal muscular atrophy, a doctor told his parents he might live for six years; we join him in Tel Aviv at his thirty-fourth birthday party. He is the thinnest human being I have ever seen. The skin on his arm is so tightly wrapped around the bone that only the center of a Harley-Davidson tattoo is visible. His life force is fierce and adamant.

"I just hope I live to fulfill all my dreams," Ami says. So do we all, and we don't want to die then, either. We want to sit around for years having fulfilled them. The documentary *39 Pounds of Love* informs us that Ami's dreams are three: to win the love of his caretaker, Christina, to visit America for a reunion with his brother, and to find that doctor and tell him he was wrong.

Christina is a pretty Romanian, about twenty-one years old, who lifts Ami out of his bath with frightening ease. "She is beautiful, young, alive," Ami says, using a Madonna-style microphone to amplify his fragile voice. "There is nothing in this world I want more than to be with her." Christina says she loves him, "but it is not the love of two lovers." Ami requires more love than that and sends her away: "I can't go on like this. Just tell her to go out of the house." She leaves.

Ami now plans his trip to America, against the urgent advice of his mother, Helene, who argues he is not strong enough to survive the trip. Ami insists on going and enlists his best friend and former caretaker, Asaf, to accompany him, along with Dani Menkin, the director of this film, and no doubt various crew members not seen.

They rent a van and return to his Texas birthplace for a reunion with the brother. In Santa Fe, he visits a church where miracles are said to take place, but none do, or seem about to, or seem to have occurred in the past. A motorcycle club gives him his chance to ride a Harley at last; he is placed in a sidecar, and there is a shot of the wind in his hair and a smile on his face. At the Grand Canyon, Ami passes out and is rushed away in an ambulance. Eventually he finds the elderly and perplexed Dr. Albert Cordova, who listens as Ami explains that he was the child who would die before he was six, that he is thirty-four and did not die, and that the doctor should not presume such confidence about the future. The doctor never says a word during this speech but then gets his own close-up in which he solemnly congratulates Ami on his longevity and wishes him good health.

These are the materials for a touching documentary, but that's what they feel like: the materials, so arranged as to suggest questions that undermine the effect of the film. We know that in most documentaries some casual re-arrangement of reality takes place, and events happen at least in part because the camera is there to witness them. But *39 Pounds of Love* feels uncomfortably stage-managed and raises fundamental questions that it simply ignores.

When Ami protests his love for Christina, and she replies, and he sends her away, there is the distinct sensation that all three events were pre-determined before they happened in front of the camera. "When was the first time you realized you were completely different?" he is asked, and replies, "When Christina walked out the door." Really? He realized it as late as the events in this film? There's an indefinable scent of reality *actually happening right now* in most documentaries. In this one, we feel that Ami knows Christina will leave before he says he loves her, and that she has already left before we see her leave.

Then the best friend and former caretaker arrives to support the trip to America. But is Asaf along merely as best friend, or has he been hired again as caretaker to make the film possible? It is suggested that the brother has been estranged from the family (there is another brother, never seen, and the Mexican mother's Israeli ex-husband, never dealt with). But when the brother emerges from his American house, it is for a joyous reunion. Was the estrangement settled offscreen? What was its cause? Had it never before occurred to anyone in Israel that Ami could

ride in a Harley sidecar? As for poor Dr. Cordova, he seems startled by his role, and there is some question in the film itself about whether this is one and the same man who made the dire prediction about Ami.

Those are questions involving what we see. More perplexing are questions about what we don't see. After Ami collapses and is taken away by ambulance, what happened then? How much time passed before the visit to Cordova? What risks were involved? Was the American visit cut short? The film itself is certainly cut short; it ends after seventy minutes, without any scenes of Ami returning home and without any feeling of closure; it simply stops and the credits begin, at a point when everything we know about story-telling suggests there should be scenes of closure.

How is Ami today? What are his thoughts about his journey? Isn't it ominous that there are no homecoming scenes? Were they not filmed, or were they not happy? "The trip is not going to end well," a friend predicts before it begins. Any experienced documentarian watching this film would be keeping a mental inventory of the missing scenes, realizing that without them, as the saying goes, "we don't have a movie."

None of this is intended to detract from the courage and will of Ami Ankilewitz. His life is extraordinary. But he has not been well-served by the documentarians. Having been assigned by fate to an undeveloped body, he is the victim for reasons unknown of an undeveloped film. That *39 Pounds of Love* was short-listed as an Oscar contender suggests that the short-listers were not knowledgeable about documentaries, or that they were honoring Ami and not his film. That this film but not Werner Herzog's *Grizzly Man* made the cut reflects bad judgment bordering on scandal.

This Girl's Life ★ ★ ★
R, 101 m., 2004

Juliette Marquis (Moon), James Woods (Pops), Kip Pardue (Kip), Tomas Arana (Aronson), Michael Rapaport (Terry), Rosario Dawson (Martine), Isaiah Washington (Shane), Ioan Gruffudd (Daniel), Cheyenne Silver (Cheyenne). Directed by Ash and produced by Ash, Chris Hanley, and David Hillary. Screenplay by Ash.

This Girl's Life is an imperfect movie with so

many moments of truth that you forgive its stumbles. You also note that it's probably of historical value, because it centers on the first performance of an actress who is going to be a big star. Juliette Marquis, Ukrainian-born, Chicago-raised, is a great beauty, yes, but beauty is not hard to find in the movies. What she has is courage and an uncanny screen presence. She spends a lot of the movie talking directly to the audience, and she looks at the camera clear-eyed and calmly confident, and we feel she is . . . *there*.

She plays a porn star named Moon, about twenty-three years old, who works for a Website that trains cameras on her house twenty-four hours a day. Whatever happens there, subscribers see. A lot happens (although she seems to be away from home for most of the movie). Moon went into porn with her eyes open, eagerly. She likes sex, and likes bold and risky situations, and she's articulate about her motives and feelings. There's a scene where she talks straight to the camera while . . . well, while otherwise engaged, and her focus never wavers.

She's a porn star, but *This Girl's Life* isn't a porn movie. We get a lot of R-rated nudity and dialogue, but the story isn't about sex; it's about the complications of Moon's life. She's worried about her father, Pops (James Woods), who has Parkinson's. She cares for him, races home when he needs her, worries about him. She is frightened by an AIDS scare in the industry. She is also conflicted about a guy, a blind date named Kip (Kip Pardue), who didn't know she is a porn star and doesn't know if he's all right with that.

The movie surrounds her with friends, including the real porn star Cheyenne Silver, playing herself. They get together for a birthday party for Pops, which I think he enjoys, although Woods is good at showing a man disappearing into the sadness of his disease. A few days later, one of her friends confides that her boyfriend has proposed. Before the friend says yes, she wants Moon to do her a favor: test him out. See if she can seduce him. If she can, the would-be bride will know he's not the faithful type.

All of this sounds like the material of a trashy sex comedy, but *This Girl's Life* plays it thoughtfully and doesn't avoid real issues. Intrigued by her power in the original situation, Moon takes out an ad for a "Sexual Investigation Agency." She'll test your husband or boyfriend for faithfulness. This turns out to be a very bad idea, as she finds out when a car dealer (Michael Rapaport) flunks the test, finds out his wife hired her, shows her his son's photo, and says if she tells the wife, he'll lose his family. Does she want to be responsible for that?

The cards are stacked in her favor in her "investigations," since Moon is sexy and subtle, and it would take a good and true man to resist her. She finds, indeed, that the more she exercises her sexual power, the less sure she is of herself; her early certainty shades into doubt and discontent. Should she renew her contract with Aronson (Tomas Arana), the porn king? He's played as a well-spoken, not uncharming businessman who is realistic about his business, not sleazy, and can be persuasive. But Moon's trip to an AIDS clinic is the sort of experience that makes you think.

This Girl's Life has a ragged construction and an ending that's patched together. I'm not sure I understood exactly why Moon's love for sex translated into employment in porn. And James Woods's performance, good as it is, is almost too strong for a supporting role in a movie that is, after all, not about him.

The film was made by a British writer-director named Ash, whose earlier films *Bang* (1995) and *Pups* (1999) showed real talent. The first starred Darling Narita as a woman who is abused by a cop, ties him up, steals his uniform and motorcycle, and learns a great deal about Los Angeles by impersonating a police officer. (Ash plugged her into real situations with people who didn't know they were in a movie.) *Pups* was about a couple of middle-school kids who find a gun and decide to stick up a bank. In those films and in *This Girl's Life,* Ash likes to place his characters in risky situations where a lot depends on their being able to act their way to safety.

Hollywood talks about good early roles as "calling cards." With this movie, Juliette Marquis proves she has the right stuff. She has completed two more films (one starring Steven Seagal, not necessarily a good sign), and after the casting directors see *This Girl's Life* I have a feeling she won't be looking for work.

The Three Burials of Melquiades Estrada ★ ★ ★ ★
R, 121 m., 2006

Tommy Lee Jones (Pete Perkins), Barry Pepper

(Mike Norton), Julio Cedillo (Melquiades Estrada), Dwight Yoakam (Sheriff Belmont), January Jones (Lou Ann Norton), Melissa Leo (Rachel). Directed by Tommy Lee Jones and produced by Michael Fitzgerald and Jones. Screenplay by Guillermo Arriaga.

The Three Burials of Melquiades Estrada tells the kind of story that John Huston or Sam Peckinpah might have wanted to film. It begins with a bedrock of loyalty and honor between men and mixes it with a little madness. In an era when hundreds of lives are casually destroyed in action movies, here is an entire film in which one life is honored, and one death is avenged.

The director and star is Tommy Lee Jones, and the story proceeds directly from fundamental impulses we sense in many of his screen appearances. Jones is most at home in characters who mean business and do not suffer fools gladly. Here he plays Pete Perkins, the hardworking operator of a small cattle operation who hires an illegal Mexican immigrant named Melquiades Estrada (Julio Cedillo) to work as a cowboy. When Melquiades is killed in a stupid shooting involving a rookie agent for the Border Patrol, Pete sees that the local sheriff (Dwight Yoakam) is going to ignore the case. So Pete takes justice into his own hands. And not simple justice, which might involve killing the agent, but poetic justice, which elevates the movie into the realm of parable.

All the action takes place in a small border town of appalling poverty of spirit. This is a hard land for men, and a heartbreaking one for women. We meet two in particular. Lou Ann Norton (January Jones) is the wife of Mike, the border patrolman. Rachel (Melissa Leo) is the waitress in the local restaurant, married to Bob the owner but available for afternoons in motel rooms, not because she is a prostitute but because she is friendly and bored.

The story is told in links between the present and the recent past; the writer, Guillermo Arriaga *(21 Grams)*, was honored at Cannes 2005 as best writer, and Jones was named best actor. We see that the Border Patrol agent, Mike Norton (Barry Pepper), is violent and cruel, perhaps as a way of masking his insecurity. He beats up a woman trying to enter the country and is told by his commander, "You were way overboard there, boy." He lives in a mobile home with Lou

Ann, who watches soap operas during sex and hangs out at the diner with Rachel because there is absolutely nothing else to do.

The lives of these characters, including Melquiades, are connected in ways that I will not reveal and that show how they all have two avenues of communication: the public and the personal. Some of the hidden connections produce ironies that only we understand, since the characters don't know as much about each other as we do.

The main line of the movie forms as Pete Perkins kidnaps Mike Norton, handcuffs him, and explains to him that Melquiades Estrada, the dead Mexican, was his friend. Melquiades often talked about his village in Mexico, Pete says, and about his wife and family. Now Mike is going to dig up Melquiades's body, and the two men are going to ride into Mexico, return the dead man to his village, and give him a proper burial.

This is a process involving a good deal of gruesome labor. I was reminded of the Peckinpah masterpiece *Bring Me the Head of Alfredo Garcia*, which is also about a journey through Mexico with a dead man—or more exactly, with his head, which suggests that the rest of the man is dead, too, and is quite enough to draw flies. Mike gags as he digs up the body, and Pete is practical about the problems they face: He fills the corpse with antifreeze.

The horseback journey of the two men is a learning experience, shall we say, for Mike the border patrolman. He begins with threats and defiance, tearfully tries to explain how the shooting of Melquiades was a stupid accident, is finally mired in sullen despair. Of their adventures along the way, two are remarkable. One involves an old blind man, living alone, who suspects his son in the city may have died. He welcomes them, offers them what he has, then makes a haunting request. The other comes when Mike is bitten by a snake, and his life is saved by a woman who has no reason to do so. This scene also has a poetic resolution.

The journey and its end will involve more discoveries and more surprises; it traverses the same kinds of doomed landscapes we picture when we read *Blood Meridian* by Cormac McCarthy. What gathers in this story of lonely men and deep impulses is a kind of grandeur; Jones plays Pete Perkins not as a hero but as a man who looks at what has happened to his friend and responds according to the opportunities at hand. He is a man who never puts two and two together without getting exactly four.

There is one word at the end of the film that carries a burden that a long speech could not have dealt with. It is a word that is also used near the beginning of the film. It contains whatever message Jones finds at the end of the journey. As for the rest, the journey of his body and the burials of Melquiades Estrada are an opportunity for all of the characters in the movie to discover who they are and what they are made of. By the end of the film no one is watching TV.   ☞

Three Days of Rain ★ ★ ½
NO MPAA RATING, 94 m., 2005

Don Meredith (John), Michael Santoro (Thunder), Joey Bilow (Denis), Peter Falk (Waldo), Merle Kennedy (Tess), Erick Avari (Alex), Blythe Danner (Beverly), Bill Stockton (Michael), Maggie Walker (Jen). Directed by Michael Meredith, and produced by Bill Stockton and Robert Casserly. Screenplay by Meredith, based on short stories by Anton Chekhov.

"You're not a kind person," a husband says to his wife of many years, after she won't give a doggie bag to a homeless man who asks for it. This is something he didn't realize and can't live with. There are other people, kind and unkind, in *Three Days of Rain*, and as a storm crouches over Cleveland we wonder if it makes much difference. It is not a kind world.

Consider John (Don Meredith), a taxi driver who has just learned that his son is dead. He runs a red light, is distracted, tells a customer of his loss. The passenger (Blythe Danner) is not sympathetic. "I'm *destined* to hear these things!" she cries out from the backseat. "I'm here to suffer pain. Let me out of this cab!"

There are another father and son in the movie. Waldo (Peter Falk) is a drunk whose charm is so meticulously practiced that we realize his personal style has entirely replaced his self-respect. He asks the bartender for another drink, is told he is out of money, agrees as if relieved to have resolved a great mystery, and then "wonders" if he could have just another "drop or two" to refresh his glass.

Waldo is forever asking his son (Bill Stockton) for an "advance" because his pension check is late, and then charmingly admitting that he has no pension and, therefore, no check. The son is patient with him—and kind, although the only kindness Waldo desires is money for more drinking. Since Waldo is so good at drinking, so courteous and elaborately courtly, would it be a kindness to impose sobriety and leave him with no lies with which to exercise his style?

Another story involves a retarded janitor (Joey Bilow) who is being edged out of his job to make room for a relative of his supervisor. The operation has to be done carefully, the boss observes, because "they don't want the National Association of Forrest Gumps getting on their ass." The janitor may be slow, but as it turns out, he is focused. Still another story involves a judge who with his wife has taken in a foster child. He knows, but his wife does not, that their babysitter (Merle Kennedy) is the baby's birth mother. Is it a kindness to let the mother see her child under those conditions? Is it kind for the judge to keep the secret from his wife?

Kindness and its opposite keep circling around the husband (Erick Avari) and his selfish wife (Maggie Walker). He can't get that homeless man out of his head; he goes back to the neighborhood, quizzes a newsstand guy, wants to do—what? Buy the homeless guy a meal? That would be kind, but what of the next meal?

The movie was written and directed by Michael Meredith (the actor playing the taxi driver is his father, the football star). He based it on six short stories by Anton Chekhov. In the genre of interlocking stories about lonely lives, *Three Days of Rain* is only a sketch compared to the power of Rodrigo Garcia's *Nine Lives*, which continues to grow in my memory. But there is a way in which movies like this create the stage on which we perform our own lives.

Say it is a cold December night and you live in Chicago. You go to Facets Multimedia, known as a home for those who love movies beyond all reason. You watch the movie, with its rain and unkindness and its lonely people, and you are not unhappy to have seen it. It was not made of ugliness and calculation, and it contained certain moments of human perception. Then you linger in the Facets video store and talk casually with someone else just coming out of the movie. You are both the kind of people who would go out into the cold to seek a movie you hope will be better than you expect.

One of you stays in the video store longer than the other, but you nod when you meet again on the Fullerton L platform. At least you are not the only person like yourself. When you get home, you look through Chekhov to see if you can find some of the stories that inspired the movie. It goes without saying that you have Chekhov on your shelf. Somewhere else in the city, the person you met is reading Chekhov, too.

Three . . . Extremes ★ ★ ★ ½
R, 126 m., 2005

"Dumplings"
With: Bai Ling, Miriam Yeung, Tony Ka-Fai Leung. Directed by Fruit Chan and produced by Peter Ho-Sun Chan. Screenplay by Lilian Lee.

"Cut"
With: Lee Byung-Hun, Lim Won-Hee, Gang Hye-Jung. Directed by Park Chan-Wook and produced by Ahn Soo-Hyun. Screenplay by Park.

"Box"
With: Kyoko Hasegawa, Atsuro Watabe. Directed by Takashi Miike and produced by Fumio Inoue, Naoki Sato, and Shun Shimizu. Screenplay by Haruko Fukushima, based on a story by Bun Saikou.

Three . . . Extremes collects directors from Hong Kong, Korea, and Japan to make horror films, each about forty minutes long. The device was common in Europe in the 1960s, where movies like *Boccaccio '70* set assorted directors loose on a vaguely related theme. Here the theme is horror, and by "horror" I don't mean the Hollywood routine of shock, blood, and special effects. These films are deeply, profoundly creepy.

The first one, "Dumplings," may be unwatchable for some people when they figure out what's actually going on. There could be walkouts. Some of those who wait until the end may wish they'd left with the others; the movie's closing image is depraved on a scale that might have shocked the surrealists. I say this not in opposition but simply as an observation.

All three short films are examples of the Extreme Asia movement, which began as a programming category at film festivals and seems to be expanding into a genre. The point is to push beyond the worn-out devices of traditional horror films, to essentially abandon the supernatural and move into horror that has its expression in the dreads and traumas of nightmare. *Three* (2002) was the first Extreme Asia trilogy, and now here are three more.

"Dumplings," directed by Hong Kong's Fruit Chan, takes the debate about stem cells and other recycling of human body material to its ultimate extremity. I don't think the film's science is sound (I sincerely hope not), but the motivation is unassailable: There are some people who will do anything to prolong their youth and beauty.

That's a classic theme in stories of horror and the supernatural, but consider the scenario here. A former TV star (Miriam Yeung) is still attractive but no longer acting. Her husband goes on long trips without her and doesn't even bother with alibis. She turns to a woman (Bai Ling) she has heard about—a perky, cheerful type who works out of a small apartment in a high-rise. This woman cooks and serves dumplings. "How old do I look to you?" she asks her client. The actress guesses—oh, about thirty. I would have said even younger. The cook says she's a lot older than that.

The secret is in her dumplings. The actress pays for an order, looks at them dubiously, eats them, comes back for more. She thinks she looks better. It's not a Dorian Gray situation but, yes, the dumplings do seem to have an effect. The actress wants more dramatic results, faster. That will not be so easy, the cook says, but she will try. What she does in assembling her ingredients is profoundly disturbing. In some cases it may not technically be illegal, on other occasions it is. Depends on the circumstances. I will not describe her secrets, but I will tell you that you may be profoundly disturbed, and that the movie's last scene, sick and evil as it is, doesn't flinch when it comes to confronting the story's ultimate implications.

The second film is "Cut," from Korea, by Park Chan-Wook, whose haunting *Oldboy* made a stir in 2003 with its story of a man kept captive for years for no reason he can imagine. In this story, a horror film director recovers from unconsciousness to find his wife, a pianist, suspended in midair above her piano by an arrangement of piano wires. A young child is bound and gagged on the sofa. The director is tied at the end of a tether allowing him to move only so far.

A laughing, angry man appears. His grudge against the director is interesting: He hates his victim because he is rich, handsome, successful—and a good man. The captor, on the other hand, is poor, ugly, a failure, and not a good man. He wants to force the director to commit evil so that he will realize he is not so good after all—that to be good sometimes means only to have escaped the need to be bad. What the director is asked to do, and whether he does it, and what happens then, you will see for yourself. "Cut" is an effective film but has a certain contrivance that's lacking in the implacable and selfish horror of "Dumplings."

The third film, "Box," is the most complex of all. Made by the Japanese director Takashi Miike, it involves small twin girls who work with their father in a magic act. Their trick is to fold themselves into impossibly small boxes. Their father throws darts at the boxes, which spring open to reveal that the girls have been replaced by flowers.

Backstage, we discover that the father favors one girl over the other, and there is a suggestion of incest. The neglected sister finds her twin rehearsing one day and slams the lid shut on her box. What happens next is horrible enough on the surface level, but there are other levels of possibility here. The story is a recurring nightmare of an adult novelist who may or may not have been one of the two young girls, and may or may not have performed just such an act. The last shot will give you a lot to think about.

What all three of these stories share is the quality found in Edgar Allan Poe, H. P. Lovecraft, and Stephen King: an attention to horror as it emerges from everyday life as transformed by fear, fantasy, and depravity. Here is not a joker in a Halloween mask, scaring screaming teenagers, but adults whose needs and weaknesses turn on them with savage, relentless logic. I imagine *Three . . . Extremes* will attract some customers who thought they wanted to see a horror movie but find they're getting more than they bargained for.

Three Times ★ ★ ★ ★
NO MPAA RATING, 130 m., 2006

Shu Qi (May/Ah Mei/Jing), Chang Chen (Chen/Mr. Chang/Zhen). Directed by Hou Hsiao-hsien and produced by Hua-fu Chang, Wen-Ying Huang, and Ching-Song Liao. Screenplay by Chu Tien-wen.

Three stories about a man and a woman, all three using the same actors. Three years: 1966, 1911, 2005. Three varieties of love: unfulfilled, mercenary, meaningless. All photographed with such visual beauty that watching the movie is like holding your breath so the butterfly won't stir.

The director is Hou Hsiao-hsien, from Taiwan, and this probably will be the first of his seventeen films you've seen. "The movie distribution system of North America is devoted to maintaining a wall between you and Hou Hsiao-hsien," I wrote after seeing this film at Cannes 2005. Here is a factoid from IMDb.com: "Of the ten films that Hou Hsiao-hsien directed between 1980 and 1989, seven received best film or best director awards from prestigious international film festivals. In a 1988 worldwide critics' poll, Hou was championed as one of the three directors most crucial to the future of cinema."

His subject in *Three Times* is our yearning to love and be loved, and the way the world casually dismisses it. His first story, "A Time for Love," set in 1966, involves Chen (Chang Chen), a soldier on his way to the army, who falls in love with the hostess of a pool hall (Shu Qi). The camera perfectly composes the room and the light pouring in from an open door, and the woman, named May, moves gracefully and without hurry to rack the balls, arrange the cues, serve the customers. Does she like Chen? I think she does. When he gets leave, he hurries back to the pool hall, but she is gone. On the sound track, Hou uses the 1959 recording by the Platters of *Smoke Gets in Your Eyes*. That is the song that tells us, "They said, some day you'll find, all who love are blind."

In the second story, "A Time for Freedom," set in 1911, the woman is named Ah Mei, and she is a prostitute in a brothel. The man, named Chang, often visits her, and between them a friendship and comfort grows. He is very filled

699

with his own importance and has plans to reform the world, although perhaps he might reflect that his reforms might start by freeing Ah Mei from the brothel. She begins to love him. He loves her, too, I think, but all who love are blind. She never lets him see how she feels. Only we see. The movie is shot like a silent film, although with a fluid moving camera the real films of 1911 certainly lacked. In some sort of accommodation with the rules, Ah Mei cannot be heard to speak in this story, but she can be heard to sing.

The third story, "A Time for Youth," takes place in the present, in modern Taipei. The characters are named Jing and Zhen. She is a pop singer. He works as a photographer. She has a female lover but neglects her while falling in love with the man. In each of the three films, the woman is a professional performer (hostess, prostitute, singer), and the man, in one way or another, is a client. Perhaps the message is that if people meet in a way involving money and their jobs, they are not free to see each other with the perfect clarity required by love. "When your heart's on fire, you must realize, smoke gets in your eyes."

There isn't any deep message in this film. Love never has any deep message. Meryl Streep once said that every good actor knows that the statement "I love you" is a question. We send our love out into the world hoping it will not be laughed at or destroyed. We trust the one we love to accept it. In these stories, acceptance doesn't come with the territory. The pool hall hostess meets a lot of pool players every day. Yes, Chen is nice enough, but when she gets a new job, she doesn't wait for him. The prostitute sees a lot of men. When she falls for Chang, he doesn't notice because he sees himself as her client. And the modern couple are so wrapped up in overlapping relationships and a running parallel life on cell phones that they can barely deal with each other at all.

More than three centuries ago, Andrew Marvell wrote a poem named *To His Coy Mistress*, in which he said they would be free to love, "Had we but world enough, and time." I think these three couples have world enough and time, but the woman in the first, the man in the second, and both in the third are not willing to accept happiness. They can't even see it's there for the having.

This observation is as shallow as a popular song. Maybe there isn't any deeper level. Most of the things we really believe about love are stated most simply and unforgettably in song lyrics. The lives in *Three Times* are not tragedies, unless the tragedy is that they never become the lives they could have been. Hou Hsiao-hsien shows us people who could make each other happy and be happy themselves, and he watches them miss their chance. "And yet today, my love has gone away. I am without my love."

Thumbsucker ★ ★ ★
R, 97 m., 2005

Lou Pucci (Justin Cobb), Tilda Swinton (Audrey Cobb), Vince Vaughn (Mr. Geary), Vincent D'Onofrio (Mike Cobb), Keanu Reeves (Dr. Perry Lyman), Benjamin Bratt (Matt Schraam), Kelli Garner (Rebecca). Directed by Mike Mills and produced by Anthony Bregman and Bob Stephenson. Screenplay by Mills, based on the novel by Walter Kirn.

Sometimes parents act like parents, and sometimes they want to be your best friends. The ideal parents would be both, since either role in isolation can lead to unhappy teenagers. Since teenagers are by their nature unhappy anyway, perhaps this paragraph can end now.

Thumbsucker is about a bright but obscurely discontented seventeen-year-old named Justin (Lou Pucci), who still sucks his thumb. His parents are Audrey and Mike (Tilda Swinton and Vincent D'Onofrio), who like to be called by their first names. Audrey is still channeling her teenager within and has a crush on a TV star named Matt (Benjamin Bratt). She sends in coupons from cereal boxes in hopes of winning a date with him. She may also be way too impressed by a celeb patient at the rehab center where she works. (Her family is intensely curious about her day job: "Who did you see? Matthew Perry? Whitney Houston? Robert Downey Jr.?")

Justin is embarrassed by his thumbsucking, especially when he gets a crush on a girl named Rebecca (Kelli Garner) who, like most girls nowadays, doesn't think it's cool for a thumb to get all the attention. Justin turns not to a shrink but to an orthodontist named Perry (Keanu Reeves). Perry tries hypnosis; when he asks

Justin to walk in an imaginary forest and conjure his "power animal," the best Justin can come up with is a fawn. After all these years it's amazing he doesn't need braces, but instead he gets Perry's mantras: "You don't need your thumb, and your thumb doesn't need you." Demonstrably not true.

The school principal prescribes Ritalin, perhaps in hopes that it will unharness Justin's inner power animal, or whatever. It does. Certain other pharmaceuticals occasionally make a contribution. Earlier in the movie Justin was dumbstruck when asked to rebut an argument in the speech class taught by Mr. Geary (Vince Vaughn), but he turns overnight into a confident, persuasive speaker who becomes the star of Geary's debate team. Geary coaches debate the way Mike Ditka coached football ("Be a stone-faced killer"). But even he grows uncomfortable with the inner animal Justin has unleashed, which turns out to be an egotistical monster.

I have focused on Justin, but really the movie is equally about the adult characters, who all seem to have lacked adequate parenting themselves. We talk about the tragedy of children giving birth to children; maybe that can happen at any age. Certainly Justin and Audrey look and behave a lot alike, and certainly Mike distances himself from his wife's obsessions with other men; perhaps having failed in an early dream of playing pro sports, he has felt inadequate ever since.

Then there is the matter of Rebecca, who is willing to go so far and no further with Justin. She has chosen him for sexual foreplay because "I need to educate myself," and Justin seems to have runway skills without all the dangers associated with a pilot's license.

The movie contains many of the usual ingredients of teenage suburban angst tragicomedies, but writer-director Mike Mills, who began with a novel by Walter Kirn, uses actors who can riff; Swinton and D'Onofrio are so peculiarly exact as their characters that we realize Audrey and Mike are supposed to be themselves in every scene and are never defined only as "Justin's parents." She wins the date, and she may be outta here. Or maybe not. In a lot of movies, you'd know one way or the other, but Audrey has free will and Swinton plays her as if neither one of them has looked ahead in the screenplay. Reeves, too, makes more of the orthodontist than what we'd expect. He comes up with a Val Kilmeresque detachment from the very qualities that made him famous, and when he apologizes for "hippie psychobabble," he doesn't even need to smile.

There is some symbology in the movie, involving a construction site and Rebecca's interest in ecology, but the movie is not really interested in saving the environment; it's interested in characters who say they are interested in the environment because, after all, who isn't, or shouldn't be? A subject like that functions as the foreground in suburban angst conversations: You talk about ecology because it shows you are good as a tree and, especially in Justin's case, high as the sky.

Thunderbirds ★ ½

PG, 94 m., 2004

Bill Paxton (Jeff Tracy), Anthony Edwards (Brains), Sophia Myles (Lady Penelope), Ben Kingsley (The Hood), Brady Corbet (Alan Tracy), Soren Fulton (Fermat), Vanessa Anne Hudgens (Tin-Tin), Ron Cook (Parker), Philip Winchester (Scott Tracy), Lex Shrapnel (John Tracy), Dominic Colenso (Virgil Tracy), Ben Torgersen (Gordon Tracy). Directed by Jonathan Frakes and produced by Tim Bevan, Eric Fellner, and Mark Huffam. Screenplay by William Osborne and Michael McCullers.

I run into Bill Paxton and Ben Kingsley occasionally, and have found them to be nice people. As actors they are in the first rank. It's easy to talk to them, and so the next time I run into one of them I think I'll just go ahead and ask what in the h-e-double-hockey-sticks they were *thinking* when they signed up for *Thunderbirds*. My bet is that Paxton will grin sheepishly and Kingsley will twinkle knowingly, and they'll both say the movie looked like fun, and gently steer the conversation toward other titles. *A Simple Plan,* say, or *House of Sand and Fog.*

This is a movie made for an audience that does not exist, at least in the land of North American multiplexes: fans of a British TV puppet show that ran from 1964 to 1966. "While its failure to secure a U.S. network sale caused the show to be canceled after thirty-two episodes," writes David Rooney in *Variety,* "the 'Supermarionation' series still endures in reruns and on DVD for funky sci-fi geeks and pop culture nostalgists." I quote Rooney because I had never heard of the series and, let's face it, never have you. Still, I doubt that "funky" describes the subset of geeks and nostalgists who like it. The word "kooky" comes to mind, as in "kooky yo-yos."

Thunderbirds is to *Spy Kids* as Austin Powers is to James Bond. It recycles the formula in a campy 1960s send-up that is supposed to be funny. But how many members of the preteen audience for this PG movie are knowledgeable about the 1960s Formica and polyester look? How many care? If the film resembles anything in their universe, it may be the Jetsons.

A solemn narrator sets the scene. The Thunderbirds, we learn, are in real life the Tracy family. Dad is Jeff Tracy (Paxton), a billionaire who has built his "secret" headquarters on a South Pacific island, where his secret is safe because no one would notice spaceships taking off. His kids are named after astronauts: Scott, John, Virgil, and Gordon, and the youngest, Alan (Brady Corbet), who is the hero and thinks he is old enough to be trusted with the keys to the family rocket. His best friend, Fermat (Soren Fulton), is named after the theorem, but I am not sure if their best friend, Tin-Tin (Vanessa Anne Hudgens), is named after the French comic book hero or after another Tin-Tin. It's a common name.

The plot: The Hood (Kingsley) is a villain who (recite in unison) seeks world domination. His plan is to rob the Bank of London. The Thunderbirds are distracted when a Hood scheme endangers their permanently orbiting space station (did I mention Dad was a billionaire?), and when Dad and the older kids rocket off to save it, the coast is clear—unless plucky young Alan, Fermat, and Tin-Tin can pilot another rocket vehicle to London in time to foil them. In this they are helped by Lady Penelope (Sophia Myles) and her chauffeur (Ron Cook).

As the Tracys rocket off to rescue the space station, I was reminded of the Bob and Ray radio serial where an astronaut, stranded in orbit, is reassured that "our scientists are working to get you down with a giant magnet." Meanwhile, his mother makes sandwiches, which are rocketed up to orbit. ("Nuts!" he says. "She forgot the mayonnaise!")

Among the big *Thunderbirds* f/x scenes are one where the kids use their rocket ship to rescue a monorail train that has fallen into the Thames. This and everything else the Thunderbirds do seems to be covered on TV, but try to control yourself from wondering where the TV cameras can possibly be, and how they got there.

Paxton was in *Spy Kids 2* and at least knows this territory. Let it be said that he and Kingsley protect themselves, Paxton by playing a true-blue 1960s hero who doesn't know his lines are funny, and Sir Ben by trying his best to play no one at all while willing himself invisible. A movie like this is harmless, I suppose, except for the celluloid that was killed in the process of its manufacture, but as an entertainment it will send the kids tip-toeing through the multiplex to sneak into *Spider-Man 2*.

Tim Burton's Corpse Bride ★ ★ ★
PG, 75 m., 2005

With the voices of: Johnny Depp (Victor Van Dort), Helena Bonham Carter (Emily the Corpse Bride), Emily Watson (Victoria Everglot), Tracey Ullman (Nell Van Dort), Paul Whitehouse (William Van Dort), Joanna Lumley (Maudeline Everglot), Albert Finney (Finis Everglot), Richard E. Grant (Barkis Bittern), Christopher Lee (Pastor Galswells). Directed by Tim Burton and Mike Johnson and produced by Allison Abbate and Burton. Screenplay by John August, Pamela Pettler, and Caroline Thompson.

Tim Burton's Corpse Bride is not the macabre horror story the title suggests, but a sweet and visually lovely tale of love lost. In an era when most animated films look relentlessly bright and colorful, *Corpse Bride* creates two palettes, and not the ones we expect.

The world of the living is a drab and overcast place with much of the color drained from it, and the remaining grays and purples and greens so muted they seem apologetic. The world of the dead, on the other hand, is where you'd want to spend your vacation. It's livelier, cheerier, and has brighter colors.

Also, as the hero discovers when he visits there, it *is* true that when your pets die they go to the same place you go: Victor Van Dort is greeted ecstatically by Scraps, the dog he had as a child. Scraps, to be sure, is all bones, but look at it this way: no more fleas. Or maybe skeletal fleas. I'm not sure about all the fine points.

Victor is voiced by Johnny Depp and reflects the current trend in animation by also looking like Johnny Depp. Once cartoons were voiced by anonymous drudges, but now big names do the work and lend their images to the characters. As the movie opens, a marriage is being arranged between Victor's parents and the Everglots. Nell and William Van Dort (Tracey Ullman and Paul Whitehouse) are rich fishmongers; as for Victoria Everglot (Emily Watson), her parents, Maudeline and Finnis (Joanna Lumley and Albert Finney), are poor aristocrats. A marriage would provide her family with money and his with class. Victor and Victoria have never met, except in the title of a Blake Edwards comedy, but when they're finally introduced, they're surprised to find that, despite everything, they love each other.

But is it meant to be? Victor is so shy he cannot blurt out the words of his marriage vow, and he flees to the overgrown graveyard outside the church to practice. Repeating the words to memorize them, he places the wedding ring on a twig that is not a twig but the desiccated finger of Emily (Helena Bonham Carter), whose arm is reaching up from the grave. This marriage, according to the rules of the netherworld, is a legitimate one, and soon Victor is at a wedding celebration where jolly skeletons sing and dance to a score by Danny Elfman, and the wedding cake is made of bones but looks yummy.

The movie's inspiration is to make Emily a figure of sympathy, not horror. She lost her own chance at happiness when she was murdered on the eve of her wedding and wants to be a good wife for Victor. She's rather sexy, in a spectral way, with those big eyes and plump lips, and only a few places where the skin has rotted away to reveal the bone beneath. Long dresses would be a good fashion choice.

A piano is shown at one point in the movie, and we get just a glimpse of its nameplate. It's a Harryhausen. That would be Burton's tribute to Ray Harryhausen, the man who brought stop-motion animation to the level of artistry *(Jason and the Argonauts, The Golden Voyage of Sinbad)*. These days most animated movies are computer-generated, creating effortlessly flowing images. But in the days when they had to be laboriously drawn one frame at a time, it was scarcely more trouble to do tabletop animation, building model figures and moving them a tiny bit between each frame.

Famous creatures like King Kong were partly made of stop-frame animation, shot in smaller scale and then combined with live action in an optical printer so that Kong seemed enormous. When you watch *King Kong*, you may notice that his fur seems to crawl or bristle slightly; you are looking at disturbances made by the fingers of the animators between each shot. My own feeling is that the artificiality of stop-motion animation adds a quality that standard animation lacks, an eerie, otherworldly, magical quality that's hard to pin down. Certainly the macabre world of *Corpse Bride* benefits from it, and somehow it is appropriate that a skeleton would move with a subtle jerkiness. The same odd visual quality added to the appeal of Burton's *The Nightmare Before Christmas*.

Meanwhile, aboveground, the blameless Victoria is about to be married off by her heartless parents to a Victorian villain with the Dickensian name Barkis Bittern (Richard E. Grant). She deserves better. It is, after all, not her fault that Victor contracted an unexpected marriage. Nor, really, is it Victor's. Nor, for that matter, the Corpse Bride's. Three young people are unhappy when two of them should be blissful; it's not fair, even if one of them is dead.

As he does in all of his pictures, Burton fills the frame with small grace touches and droll details. He seems to have a natural affinity for the Gothic, and his live-action *Legend of Sleepy Hollow* (also with Depp) remains one of the most visually beautiful films I've seen. He likes moonlight and drear places, trees forming ominous shapes in the gloom, eyes peering uneasily into the incredible, and love struggling to prevail in worlds of complex menace. All of that is a lot for an animated fantasy to convey, but *Corpse Bride* not only conveys it but also does it, yes, charmingly.

Note: The PG rating is about right, I think, although quite young or impressionable children may be scared by the skeletal characters. Everyone is relatively jolly, however, so maybe not. ☞

Tokyo Godfathers ★ ★ ★
PG-13, 90 m., 2004

With the voices of: Toru Emori (Gin), Yoshiaki Umegaki (Hana), and Aya Okamoto (Miyuki). Directed by Satoshi Kon and produced by Masao Maruyama. Screenplay by Kon and Keiko Nobumotu.

In Japan, animation is not seen as the exclusive realm of children's and family films, but is often used for adult, science fiction, and action stories, where it allows a kind of freedom impossible in real life. Some Hollywood films strain so desperately against the constraints of the possible that you wish they'd just caved in and gone with animation (*Torque* is an example).

Now here is *Tokyo Godfathers*, an animated film both harrowing and heartwarming, about a story that will never, ever, be remade by Disney. It's about three homeless people—an alcoholic, a drag queen, and a girl of about eleven—who find an abandoned baby in the trash on a cold Christmas Eve, and try for a few days to give it a home. The title makes a nod to John Ford's *3 Godfathers* (1948), where three desperados (led by John Wayne) rescue a baby from its dying mother on Christmas Eve and try to raise it, at one point substituting axle grease for baby oil.

The three urban drifters live in a Tokyo of ice and snow, where they have fashioned a temporary shelter of cardboard and plywood, and outfitted it with all the comforts of home, like a portable stove. Here they've formed a family of sorts, but each has a story to tell, and during the movie they all tell them.

Gin, the alcoholic, claims to have been a bicycle racer who abandoned his family after losing everything by gambling. Hana, the transvestite, has felt like an outsider since birth. Miyuki, the little girl, ran away from home after a fight with her father. The others tell her she should return, but she's afraid to. And then the cries of the infant alert them, and their rescue of the little girl is a catalyst that inspires each of them to find what's good and resilient within themselves.

The movie was cowritten and directed by Satoshi Kon, whose *Perfect Blue* and *Millennium Actress* have been among the best-received and most popular anime titles. Unlike Hayao Miyazaki (*Spirited Away, My Neighbor Totoro*), his style doesn't approach full-motion animation, but uses the simplified approach of a lot of anime, with simple backgrounds and characters who move and talk in a stylized way that doesn't approach realism. If you see this style for thirty seconds you're likely to think it's constrained, but in a feature film it grows on you and you accept it, and your imagination makes it expand into an acceptable version of the world.

The movie's story is melodrama crossed with pathos, sometimes startling hard-boiled action, and enormous coincidence. The streets of Tokyo seem empty and grim as the three godparents protect the child and eventually begin a search for its true parents. And the story involving those parents is more complicated than we imagine. There are scenes in an abandoned house, in an alley of homeless dwellings, in a drugstore, that seem forlorn and hopeless, and then other scenes of surprising warmth, leading up to a sensational ending and a quite remarkable development in which two lives are saved in a way possible only in animation.

Tokyo Godfathers is not appropriate for younger viewers, and I know there are older ones who don't fancy themselves sitting through feature-length adult animation from Japan. But there's a world there to be discovered. And sometimes, as with this film and the great *Grave of the Fireflies*, the themes are so harrowing that only animation makes them possible. I don't think I'd want to see a movie in which a real baby had the adventures this one has.

Torque ★ ★ ½
PG-13, 81 m., 2004

Martin Henderson (Cary Ford), Ice Cube (Trey Wallace), Monet Mazur (Shane), Jay Hernandez (Dalton), Christina Milian (Nina), Jaime Pressly (China), Matt Schulze (Henry). Directed by Joseph Kahn and produced by Brad Luff and Neal H. Moritz. Screenplay by Matt Johnson.

Long ago, at the dawn of motorcycle pictures, a critic who had been working for only four months encountered a film named *Hells Angels on Wheels* (1967). It was about a war between motorcycle gangs, and its cast included an actor named Jack Nicholson, whom the critic did not even name, although he found room to mention Adam Roarke, John Garwood, and Sabrina Scharf. The critic, observing that "sometimes good stuff creeps into exploitation pictures just because nobody cares enough to keep it out," made the following points:

— "The characters are authentically surly, irresponsible, mean, coarse, and human."

— Sabrina Scharf "makes you wonder how she keeps her makeup on while raising hell with the angels."

— The "accomplished camera work" includes "one shot where the camera moves in and out of focus through a field of green grass and then steals slowly across one of the big, brutal cycles. The contrast has an impact equal to David Lean's similar shots in *Doctor Zhivago* (remember the frosty window fading into the field of flowers?)."

— "The film is better than it might have been, and better than it had to be. Take it on its own terms and you might find it interesting."

Reader, that young critic was me. The film's director was Richard Rush, who went on to make *The Stunt Man*. The young cinematographer was "Leslie Kovacs," who, under his true Hungarian name of Laszló, went on to shoot *Five Easy Pieces* with Jack Nicholson, and fifty other films, including some of the best photographed of his time.

Today I went to see *Torque*, also a motorcycle picture. Whether it contains a future Nicholson is hard to say, because the dialogue is all plot-driven and as sparse as possible. But the characters are surly, irresponsible, mean, and coarse, if not human; the actresses keep their makeup on; and the look of the picture is certainly accomplished. I use the word "look" because the cinematographer has been joined by squadrons of special-effects and animation artists, platoons of stunt men, and covens of postproduction wizards.

I enjoyed the two pictures about the same. I'd rate them both two and a half stars, meaning this as faint praise, but praise nevertheless. As genre exercises they are skillful, quick, and entertaining. There is a difference, though. *Hells Angels on Wheels* was frankly intended as an exploitation picture by everyone involved, who all hoped to move up to the A-list and make better films (all except for the producer, Joe Solomon, whom we will get to in a mo-

ment). *Torque*, I fear, considers itself to be a real movie—top of the world, man! Although it's been kept on the shelf for nearly a year by Warner Bros., reportedly to avoid competing with *2 Fast 2 Furious* and *Biker Boyz*, that is a marketing judgment, not an aesthetic opinion. I suspect no one at Warners has an aesthetic opinion about *Torque*.

I spent some time with Joe Solomon once, to profile him for *Esquire*. I liked him immensely. He wasn't too big to involve himself personally in the smallest details of a production, as when he demonstrated how ice cubes could be used as a perkiness enhancer. He was never happier than when producing motorcycle pictures, and his credits included *Angels from Hell; Run, Angel, Run; Wild Wheels;* and *Nam's Angels*.

What has happened between 1967 and 2004 is that Hollywood genres have undergone a fundamental flip-flop. Low-budget pictures are now serious and ambitious and play at Sundance. Big-budget exploitation work, on which every possible technical refinement is lavished, are now flashy and dispensable and open in 3,000 multiplexes. Little did Joe Solomon suspect that he was making the major studio pictures of the future.

Now as for *Torque*. The director is Joseph Kahn, who started by directing music videos and moved to this project, I learn, after long months of frustration trying to get *Crow 4* off the ground. The first three minutes convince us we are looking at a commercial before the feature begins. Then we realize the whole movie will look like this. It's flashy, skillful work—as much CGI as real, but that's the name of the game.

The plot is about a biker (Martin Henderson) who has returned to Los Angeles from exile in Thailand. The leader of a rival gang (Ice Cube) thinks he killed his brother, and wants revenge. The two gangs clash in a series of elaborate stunt and effects sequences, including a duel between two sexy women. A Hummer is tossed into the air and spun like a top before crushing a sports car. One motorcycle chase takes place on top of a train, and then inside the train; we would care more if it were not on approximately the same level of reality as a *Road Runner* chase. One of the bikes is "built around a Rolls-Royce jet engine." It goes so fast it makes parking meters explode. The final fight sequence is so extravagantly choreographed that the props work together like a speeded-up version of a Buster Keaton sequence.

The film is better than it might have been, and better than it had to be. Take it on its own terms and you might find it interesting. Or did I say that already? One hopes that the filmmakers understand that *Torque* must be seen as the first step on their artistic journey, not its destination.

Touching the Void ★ ★ ★ ★
NO MPAA RATING, 106 m., 2004

Brendan Mackey (Simpson), Nicholas Aaron (Yates), Joe Simpson (Himself), Simon Yates (Himself). Directed by Kevin Macdonald and produced by John Smithson. Screenplay by Joe Simpson, based on his book.

For someone who fervently believes he will never climb a mountain, I spend an unreasonable amount of time thinking about mountain climbing. In my dreams my rope has come loose and I am falling, falling, and all the way down I am screaming: "Stupid! You're so stupid! You climbed all the way up there just so you could fall back down!"

Now there is a movie more frightening than my nightmares. *Touching the Void* is the most harrowing movie about mountain climbing I have seen, or can imagine. I've read reviews from critics who were only moderately stirred by the film (my friend Dave Kehr certainly kept his composure), and I must conclude that their dreams are not haunted as mine are.

I didn't take a single note during this film. I simply sat there before the screen, enthralled, fascinated, and terrified. Not for me the discussions about the utility of the "pseudo-documentary format," or questions about how the camera happened to be waiting at the bottom of the crevice when Simpson fell in. *Touching the Void* was, for me, more of a horror film than any actual horror film could ever be.

The movie is about Joe Simpson and Simon Yates, two Brits in their mid-twenties who determined to scale the forbidding west face of a mountain named Siula Grande, in the Peruvian Andes. They were fit and in good training, and bold enough to try the "one push" method of climbing, in which they carried all their gear

with them instead of establishing caches along the route. They limited their supplies to reduce weight, and planned to go up and down quickly.

It didn't work out that way. Snowstorms slowed and blinded them. The ascent was doable, but on the way down the storms disoriented them and the drifts concealed the hazard of hidden crevices and falls. Roped together, they worked with one man always anchored, and so Yates was able to hold the rope when Simpson had a sudden fall. But it was disastrous: He broke his leg, driving the calf bone up through the knee socket. Both of them knew that a broken leg on a two-man climb, with rescue impossible, was a death sentence, and indeed Simpson tells us he was rather surprised that Yates decided to stay with him and try to get him down.

We know that Simpson survived, because the movie shows the real-life Simpson and Yates, filmed against plain backgrounds, looking straight on into the camera, remembering their adventure in their own words. We also see the ordeal reenacted by two actors (Brendan Mackey as Simpson, Nicholas Aaron as Yates), and experienced climbers are used as stunt doubles. The movie was shot on location in Peru and also in the Alps, and the climbing sequences are always completely convincing; the use of actors in those scenes is not a distraction because their faces are so bearded, frostbitten, and snow-caked that we can hardly recognize them.

Yates and Simpson had a 300-foot rope. Yates's plan was to lower Simpson 300 feet and wait for a tug on the rope. That meant Simpson had dug in and anchored himself and it was safe for Yates to climb down and repeat the process. A good method in theory, but then, after dark, in a snowstorm, Yates lowered Simpson over a precipice and left him hanging in midair over a drop of unknowable distance. Since they were out of earshot in the blizzard all Yates could know was that the rope was tight and not moving, and his feet were slipping out of the holes he had dug to brace them. After an hour or so he realized they were at an impasse. Simpson was apparently hanging helplessly in midair, Yates was slipping, and unless he cut the rope they would both surely die. So he cut the rope.

Simpson says he would have done the same

thing under the circumstances, and we believe him. What we can hardly believe is what happens next, and what makes the film into an incredible story of human endurance.

If you plan to see the film—it will not disappoint you—you might want to save the rest of the review until later.

Simpson, incredibly, falls into a crevice but is slowed and saved by several snow bridges he crashes through before he lands on an ice ledge with a drop on either side. So there he is, in total darkness and bitter cold, his fuel gone so that he cannot melt snow, his lamp battery running low, and no food. He is hungry, dehydrated, and in cruel pain from the bones grinding together in his leg (two aspirins didn't help much).

It is clear Simpson cannot climb back up out of the crevice. So he eventually gambles everything on a strategy that seems madness itself, but was his only option other than waiting for death: He uses the rope to lower himself down into the unknown depths below. If the distance is more than 300 feet, well, then, he will literally be at the end of his rope.

But there is a floor far below, and in the morning he sees light and is able, incredibly, to crawl out to the mountainside. And that is only the beginning of his ordeal. He must somehow get down the mountain and cross a plain strewn with rocks and boulders; he cannot walk but must try to hop or crawl despite the pain in his leg. That he did it is manifest, since he survived to write a book and appear in the movie. How he did it provides an experience that at times had me closing my eyes against his agony.

This film is an unforgettable experience, directed by Kevin Macdonald (who made *One Day in September,* the Oscar-winner about the 1972 Olympiad) with a kind of brutal directness and simplicity that never tries to add suspense or drama (none is needed!), but simply tells the story, as we look on in disbelief. We learn at the end that after two years of surgeries Simpson's leg was repaired, and that (but you anticipated this, didn't you?) he went back to climbing again. Learning this, I was reminded of Boss Gettys's line about Citizen Kane: "He's going to need more than one lesson." I hope to God the rest of his speech does not apply to Simpson: ". . . and he's going to get more than one lesson."

Touch the Sound ★ ★ ★
NO MPAA RATING, 113 m., 2005

Featuring Evelyn Glennie and Fred Frith. A documentary directed by Thomas Riedelsheimer and produced by Stefan Tolz, Leslie Hills, and Trevor Davies.

Evelyn Glennie became aware as a child that she was losing her hearing. It was suggested she attend a school for the deaf. This did not appeal to her. "Hearing or not, she will do what she wants to do," her father declared. She has. Today she is a musician specializing in percussion, and she uses her body as a "resounding chamber" through which she experiences her work.

Touch the Sound is a documentary by Thomas Riedelsheimer that follows Glennie on a musical journey around the world. We visit the Aberdeenshire farm in Scotland where she was raised, and where her father's accordion was her first taste of music. She plays in the center of Grand Central Station, and with improvised devices in a pub, and by running her wet finger across a guitar case, and in the Cologne airport, and beside a rooftop pigeon coop, and with glasses and plates in a Japanese restaurant, and on an ocean shore, and on a marimba, and obtains the sound of space itself unfolding by hurling down from a high place long sheets of graph paper. Her preferred instrument is the snare drum.

"Hearing," she tells us, "is a form of touch." A music teacher in school suggested that while performing she stop using hearing aids and focus on the vibrations picked up by her body through the air and by her bare feet on the floor. "I could hear less through the ears but more through the body," she says. Her body grew more sensitive to the vibrations in the air.

She describes herself not as "deaf," which is an absolute term, but as "profoundly deaf," by which she means she does perceive a very low level of sound. She can lip-read. Her music takes on an eerie quality through the ways of its making; it must feel right to her, and when it does, it sounds slightly uncanny to us, as if appealing to senses we were not aware we possessed. We listen to this film more intensely than is usually the case.

In the closing passages of the film, Glennie

records music for a CD she is making with the musician Fred Frith. They occupy a huge abandoned factory, its empty space a sounding board. Frith plays a variety of conventional instruments, and she uses an astonishing variety of percussive ones. There is no doubt she touches the sound, because as they improvise together they develop a musical conversation.

The director, Riedelsheimer, earlier made *Rivers and Tides* (2001), about another artist from Scotland, Andy Goldsworthy, whose art involves materials found in nature. We watch as with infinite patience he builds a geometric structure of flat rocks, or assembles twigs, or directs ice as it thaws and then freezes again. Sometimes his projects collapse in mid-creation. Sometimes they exist in their final perfect form for minutes or hours. They are all doomed eventually to be swallowed up by the indifference of nature.

Glennie and Goldsworthy have in common a profound sensitivity to their environments. They look around wherever they find themselves and begin to discover ways to create the order of art out of the chaos of existence. Their art is intended to be evanescent. It can be recorded on CDs or film, but it exists most fully during its own creation. Both artists seem to live more fully because they are so completely in the moment. There is a kind of bliss about them.

Note: Touch the Sound *is not subtitled, and its words are therefore unavailable to the hearing-impaired. Riedelsheimer is said to oppose subtitles because they would affect his visual compositions. Presumably, he is as entitled to the same control over his art that his subjects exercise, but such directors as Ozu, Bergman, Scorsese, and Welles have lived with subtitles, and I imagine he could have, too.*

The music in the film might, in any case, be out of reach to most in a hearing-impaired audience, so perhaps the DVD will be a better way for them to access it. Volume can be manipulated, the actual speakers can be touched with hands and feet or sat upon, the bass can be boosted, and the experience might approximate what Glennie herself perceives. Almost all DVDs are subtitled even in the language of their making; if the DVD of Touch the Sound *lacks subtitles, then Riedelsheimer will have some explaining to do.* ☞

708

The Tracker ★ ★ ★ ½
NO MPAA RATING, 90 m., 2004

David Gulpilil (The Tracker), Gary Sweet (The Fanatic), Damon Gameau (The Follower), Grant Page (The Veteran), Noel Wilton (The Fugitive). Directed by Rolf de Heer and produced by Bridget Ikin, Julie Ryan, and de Heer. Screenplay by de Heer.

The Tracker is one of those rare films that deserve to be called haunting. It tells the sort of story we might find in an action Western, but transforms it into a fable or parable. Four men set out into the Australian wilderness to track down an accused killer, and during the course of their journey true justice cries out to be done. The men never use their names, but the credits identify them as The Fanatic, a merciless officer; The Follower, a greenhorn new to the territory; The Veteran, an older man of few words; and The Tracker, an Aboriginal who will lead them to their quarry, also an Aboriginal.

The live action is intercut with paintings of events in the story, and the sound track includes songs about what happens. We assume the story is based on fact that became legend, and that the songs commemorate it; several critics have said the paintings are "probably Aboriginal" and done at the time (1922). Not so. The story is an original by the director, Rolf de Heer; the paintings were done on location by Peter Coad; and the songs were written by the director and Graham Tardif. They have created their own legend from their own facts, but it feels no less real; it is a distillation from Australia's shameful history with the Aboriginals, and contains echoes of the hunt for escaped Aboriginal children in *Rabbit-Proof Fence*.

De Heer used a small crew and shot in the wilderness, camping out every night, and we see the film's events not as heightened action but as a long, slow trek across a vast landscape. It seems to be unpopulated, but no; on the first night, when the kid gets out his ukulele and starts to sing, the officer quiets him so they can hear anyone approaching. "You won't hear them," the older man says. "They're there," says the tracker.

They are there, everywhere, invisible, as spears materialize out of emptiness and pick off their horses and then one of the men. Once they come upon the camp of a small Aboriginal family group. These people are peaceful, the tracker tells the officer, but some of them are wearing discarded army uniforms, and so the officer kills them all. The greenhorn is shaken and distraught: "They were innocent." The tracker, who says what the officer likes to hear, tells him, "The only innocent black is a dead black."

This tracker is more complex than he seems. He plays a loyal army employee, but his eyes suggest other dimensions. And when one of the men is killed, how extraordinary that he recites a Catholic burial rite in Latin. He must have passed through a missionary school on his way to this day in the Outback, and is not the savage (however noble) imagined by the racist officer. At the same time, he knows his job, and when the greenhorn charges that he isn't really tracking but is only following his nose, the officer (who also knows his job) tells the tracker, "Show him," and he does—pointing out a small dislodged stone with the earth still damp where it has rested.

The tracker is played by David Gulpilil, whose career started in 1971 when he played the young Aboriginal boy who guides the lost white girl in *Walkabout*. He also played a tracker in *Rabbit-Proof Fence*. Here he has a disarming smile and an understated enthusiasm that seems genuine—to the officer, at least—while we sense a different agenda shifting beneath the surface. While it is clear that some kind of confrontation is coming, it would be unfair for me to suggest what happens.

The officer, played by Gary Sweet, is unbending and filled with certitude. There is not a doubt in his mind that he is justified in shooting innocent people, and he even claims to expect a medal. The greenhorn (Damon Gameau) is the moral weathervane; the mission at first seems justifiable, and then he wonders. The old-timer (Grant Page) is the taciturn type every society knows; he has accommodated himself to this way of doing business, but stands apart from it. Notice how while the massacre is under way, he sits on a log and smokes, and we guess something of his detachment from the way the smoke emerges as a very thin, steady stream.

The performances are all the more powerful for being in a minor key. De Heer seems determined to tell his story without calculated emotional boosts. "The brutal scenes," he told an Australian interviewer, "were basically shifted from the film itself to the paintings to make the viewer look at the death scenes and macabre scenes differently—to distance the audience." And when the officer is shouting at the family group, the volume of his dialogue is toned down and a song plays as counterpoint; here is a film about memory, sadness, tragedy, and distance, not a film that dramatizes what it laments. Truffaut said it was impossible to make an anti-war film because the action always argued for itself; de Heer may have found the answer.

Transamerica ★ ★ ★
R, 103 m., 2006

Felicity Huffman (Bree), Kevin Zegers (Toby), Graham Greene (Calvin), Fionnula Flanagan (Elizabeth), Burt Young (Murray), Elizabeth Pena (Margaret), Carrie Preston (Sydney). Directed by Duncan Tucker and produced by Rene Bastian, Sebastian Dungan, and Linda Moran. Screenplay by Tucker.

Transamerica stars Felicity Huffman as a man who feels compelled to become a woman. The surgery is only a week away when Sabrina (Bree, for short) learns that seventeen years ago she fathered a son. Margaret, her therapist, was under the impression that as a man named Stanley, her client was a virgin. "There *was* this one girl in college," Bree muses, "but the whole thing was so tragically lesbian I didn't think it counted." Well, it counts now: Margaret (Elizabeth Pena) insists that Bree must meet the son and come to terms with him before the final surgery.

Bree reluctantly leaves Los Angeles and travels to New York to meet young Toby (Kevin Zegers), a brooding street hustler who wants to improve himself by becoming a porn star. This career choice is distressing to Bree, a ladylike middle-class conservative. Unwilling to reveal her real identity, Bree poses as a Christian caseworker who specializes in converting sex workers to Jesus. Toby agrees to drive back to L.A. with Bree, mostly because he needs the ride.

By this point in the plot description, I have the attention of readers who fired off e-mails about *Brokeback Mountain*, informing me that homosexuality was "a sin promoted by the liberal left." I responded that most people are gay or straight before they can talk, let alone vote. In any event, surely my correspondents would approve of those who go to the length of gender reassignment surgery to be sure their genitals match their orientation.

My own impression is that most transgender people have little interest in homosexuality; if they did, they'd be "pre-op" forever. Bree seems to have had little sex of any kind, working two jobs as she does to save up for her operation. She's not a terrifically exciting person, dresses like Mary Worth, is terribly nice, and needs to get out more. In the early stages of their automobile journey to Los Angeles she spends a lot of time correcting Toby's grammar.

Toby: "I'd probably be, like, disemboweled by a ninja."
Bree: "You needn't say 'like.' Probably 'disemboweled by a ninja' is sufficient."

There is a quiet strain of humor throughout *Transamerica*, but this is not so much a comedy as an observation about human nature. I am grateful to Stephanie Zacharek of Salon.com for pointing out something I simply did not notice: The movie assumes a transsexual will be more welcome in a blue state than a red one, and that when a man is attracted to Bree, it is an American Indian named Calvin Two Goats (Graham Greene). "He's allowed to be open-minded," she writes, "because he's a Navajo—in other words, a spiritually open-minded outsider, as opposed to your typical Middle American." (It is significant that Bree works in L.A. as a waitress in a Mexican-American diner; Mexicans, like Indians, apparently have a genetic tendency to open-mindedness.)

Zacharek, who also makes points about lip-liner that fell outside my zone of awareness, is correct, and the movie has prejudices about Middle America. How could I have forgotten the documentary *Southern Comfort* (2001), about a group of post-op pipe-smoking, pickup-driving Georgia gun owners? And consider the transsexual support group Bree visits. The only thing that seemed likely to come out was Tupperware.

The movie works, and it does work, because Huffman brings great empathy and tact to her performance as Bree. This is not a person who wants to make a big point about anything. She (we might as well recognize Bree's nature with the pronoun) has spent a lifetime living in a body that does not fit, and just when deliverance seems at hand she is suddenly supplied with an ungrateful son. How ironic, as Wordsworth did not quite observe, that the mother is father to the child.

Bree's original strategy is to keep it a secret that she is a pre-op transsexual and Toby's biological father. Well, it's a lot to spring on a kid. The truth emerges gradually during the trip and would generate more drama if Toby weren't one of those teenagers who cultivates an infuriating detachment. Jeez, kid, you think Bree is a missionary and she turns out to be your father? What does it take to get a rise out of you?

There are, however, personal breakthroughs and discoveries during the journey, especially during a stopover in Phoenix, home to Bree's unpleasant sister (Carrie Preston) and vulgarian parents (Fionnula Flanagan and Burt Young—yes, Rocky's brother-in-law). Bree's mom answers for herself the enigma of pre- or post-op by grabbing Bree's netherlands. No doubt she courted her husband in the same way. Regarding the wide open spaces of his grandparents' minds, Toby perhaps begins to develop some identification with Bree. To escape this family, a child might be willing to change not merely gender but species.

That *Transamerica*, written and directed by Duncan Tucker, works as a film is because Bree is so persistently and patiently herself. If she had been wilder, stranger, more extroverted, the movie might fly off the rails. It is precisely because she is so conventionally sincere that the movie gathers power in deep places while maintaining a relative surface calm. How does she respond to the undeniable interest of Calvin Two Goats? Reader, she blushes.

This is all new for her, too. What Huffman brings to Bree is the newness of a Jane Austen heroine. She has been waiting a long time to be an ingenue, and what an irony that she must begin as a mother. But she is a good person to the bottom of her socks, and at the end of *Transamerica* you realize it was not about sex at all. It was about family values.

The Transporter 2 ★ ★ ★
PG-13, 88 m., 2005

Jason Statham (Frank Martin), Alessandro Gassman (Gianni), Amber Valletta (Audrey

Billings), Katie Nauta (Lola), Matthew Modine (Mr. Billings), Jason Flemyng (Dimitri), Keith David (Stappleton), Hunter Clary (Jack Billings). Directed by Louis Leterrier and produced by Luc Besson and Steven Chasman. Screenplay by Besson and Robert Mark Kamen.

Reviewing *The Transporter* in 2002, I expressed doubt that some of the action sequences were possible. *The Transporter 2* sidesteps my complaint by containing action scenes that are even ~~more~~ impossible. ~~For example: Seeing the reflec-~~ tion of a bomb in a pool of liquid under his car, and knowing that the bad guys will not explode it while they're standing right next to it, the hero races the car out of a garage and up an incline, spinning the car neatly through the air, so that it makes one complete rotation and the bomb is pulled off by a hook on a crane, exploding harmlessly as the car lands safely. Uh-huh.

I could observe that this is preposterous, but the fact is, I laughed aloud. Other stunts and computer-generated effects were equally impossible, as when Frank Martin (Jason Statham) flies a Jet Ski onto a highway and jumps from it into the back of a school bus. And when he uses a fire hose to immobilize a posse of killers. And when he escapes from a plane that has crashed into the ocean. And when he leads a police pursuit up the ramps of a parking garage and then crashes his car through a wall of the garage and it flies a couple hundred feet through the air to a safe landing.

Either *The Transporter 2* is wall-to-wall with absurd action, or it's not a sequel to *The Transporter*. And in fact the sequel is a better film than the original, as if writer-producer Luc Besson had a clearer idea of what he wanted to do (and didn't want to do); the direction is by Louis Leterrier, whose *Unleashed*, released only three months previously, had that savage chemistry between a gangster (Bob Hoskins) and a fighter (Jet Li) he had raised like a dog. That movie was also written and produced by Besson, who is the hardest-working man in show business. Look him up on IMDb.com if you want to feel tired just reading about his plans.

The Transporter 2 is better for a number of reasons, one of them that it has an ingenious plot that continues to reveal surprises and complications well into the third act; this is not simply a movie where the good guy chases the bad guys, but a movie where the story turns a lot trickier than we expected.

It begins with Frank Martin helping out a friend by filling in for a month as the driver and bodyguard for a cute kid named Jack (Hunter Clary), whose dad (Matthew Modine) heads the U.S. narcotics agency. The kid is kidnapped in a bizarre scheme involving a phony doctor, and then he's recovered too quickly and without the ransom money being picked up, and it turns out the kidnapping—well, you'll see for yourself. Let me just observe that the methods of the kidnappers involve scientific ingenuity raised to evil genius. Not recently have I seen a movie with a better reason why the worst bad guy cannot be allowed to sink to the ocean floor along with the crashed airplane.

But not another word about that. Statham is amusing as a man whose emotions are so well under control that he can barely be bothered to have any. He stars in several martial arts sequences in which he wipes out whole platoons of enemies. They're deployed by Gianni (Alessandro Gassman), a really big, really mean, really smart villain. Modine efficiently plays the role of the sniveling bureaucrat, Amber Valletta is effective as his long-suffering wife, and Kate Nauta plays Lola, a deadly vixen who considers herself dressed after she's troweled on her eye makeup; for Lola, it's run, mascara, run.

There's a development of some interest to students of product placement. The Transporter drives an Audi. The first shots of the titles play like a commercial for the car. It's quite a car, all right, taking full advantage of the all-wheel drive as it survives those incredible stunts. So sturdy is its construction that after it crashes through the concrete wall while jumping to the other building, there's not even a scratch on the shiny silver circles on the front of the car.

There is some history here. In the original film, Frank Martin drove a BMW. Now he drives an Audi. Apparently BMW did not sign on for the sequel. Strange: On the very same day I saw this movie, I saw another thriller, *Memory of a Killer*, in which the characters hate BMWs so much, they urinate into their keyholes. In between, I saw a movie about Truman Capote that mostly featured Chevrolets, which must come as a relief to the home office in Bavaria. It's bad enough when the Transporter switches brands, but when Capote drops you, you're over.

Tristan & Isolde ★ ★ ★

PG-13, 125 m., 2006

James Franco (Tristan), Sophia Myles (Isolde), Rufus Sewell (Lord Marke), David O'Hara (King Donnchadh), Henry Cavill (Melot), J. B. Blanc (Leon), Jamie King (Anwick). Directed by Kevin Reynolds and produced by Moshe Diamant, Lisa Ellzey, Giannina Facio, and Elie Samaha. Screenplay by Dean Georgaris.

Tristan & Isolde begins with bits of the same myth that has inspired works ranging from sword & sorcery movies *(Lovespell)* to operas by Wagner, and transforms them, rather surprisingly, into a lean and effective action romance. The movie is better than the commercials would lead you to believe—and better, perhaps, than the studio expected, which may be why it was on the shelf for more than a year. Distributors who are content with the mediocre grow alarmed, sometimes, by originality and artistry: Is this movie too good for the demographic we're targeting?

The movie dumps the magical love potion that is crucial in most versions of the story. This time, when Tristan and Isolde fall in love, it's because—well, it's because they fall in love. The story takes place in England and Ireland, circa the year 600. The Roman occupiers have withdrawn, leaving a disorganized band of English warlords feuding among themselves while King Donnchadh of the Celts (David O'Hara) rules England from Ireland.

We meet Lord Marke (Rufus Sewell), wisest of the English rulers, who seeks to unite England and repel the Irish. He adopts the young Tristan (James Franco), and raises him as his son. Tristan leads Marke's troops in setting a successful trap for Donnchadh's overconfident raiders but then is poisoned and falls into a coma resembling death. Good thing the early Brits don't believe in burial: They put Tristan's body on a boat and push it out to sea, and a few days later it washes ashore in Ireland and is found by the beautiful Isolde (Sophia Myles), daughter of Donnchadh. Tristan is alive!

All contrived, all melodramatic, yes, but seen in a rugged, muddy, damp, straightforward visual style by director Kevin Reynolds (*The Count of Monte Cristo, Waterworld*), his cinematographer, Artur Reinhart, and the produc-

tion designer, Mark Geraghty. The knights and ladies don't look like escapees from a Prince Valiant comic strip, but like physical, vulnerable survivors of the conflicts left behind by the Romans. The removal of magic from the story grounds it as a realistic power struggle, and although the device of mistaken identity is used to supply the heart of the plot, we can sort of see how things might have worked out that way.

I don't want to betray details that may come as a surprise. So let me comment on what happens without revealing what it is. Tristan and Isolde, who love each other even though they are the children of bitter enemies, are put into an impossible situation that no one really intended for them. The Irish and English lords don't even realize they know each other. Tristan is entered in a tournament and does not know what the prize is. Isolde thinks she knows what the outcome of the tournament means but is mistaken.

And then, in a decision that is brave of Tristan and Isolde and maybe even braver of the filmmakers, they try to accept the reality they're confronted with. When it is said that "this marriage will end one hundred years of bloodshed," they try to reflect, not without heartbreak, that the problems of two little people don't amount to a hill of beans in this crazy world.

I'm going to remain vague about what happens then, except to say that it all becomes a great deal more involving than you might expect from a movie with castles and swords and horses and secret passageways. There are some fairly delicate scenes involving the deepest feelings of Lord Marke, Tristan, and Isolde, and the actors don't ratchet up the emotions but try for plausibility. They are grown-ups who face an emotional crisis as we think perhaps they might have. The writing of the crucial closing scenes doesn't hurry for easy effects but pays attention to what is meant, and what is felt.

Myles plays Isolde as the daughter of a king, raised by the king's rules, true to her own emotions but true, too, to her duty. She doesn't mistake Isolde for the heroine of a teenage romance. James Franco (the *Spider-Man* movies, *The Great Raid, Annapolis*) is not a larger-than-life comic hero but a vulnerable warrior capable of doubts and schemes. Rufus Sewell (*Dark City*) plays Lord Marke as a statesman in a land of squabbling egos, who, when he discovers a surprising secret, is inspired not so much by jealousy as by the offense to his sense of the rightness of things.

One key to the quality of the movie may be the executive producers, Ridley (*Gladiator*) Scott and Tony (*Top Gun*) Scott. Ridley Scott wanted to direct this movie for fifteen years, and although *Gladiator* may have preempted it on his schedule, it's clear he was intrigued not only by the possibilities for action but also by the impossible personal dilemma that faces Tristan and Isolde. By removing elements of magic and operatic excess from the story, the brothers Scott focus on what is, underneath, a story as tragic (and less contrived) as the one cited in the ads, *Romeo and Juliet*.

Tristram Shandy: A Cock and Bull Story ★ ★ ★ ★
R, 91 m., 2006

Steve Coogan (Tristram Shandy/Walter/Steve), Rob Brydon (Toby Shandy/Rob), Raymond Waring (Corporal Trim), Dylan Moran (Dr. Slop/Dylan), Keeley Hawes (Elizabeth Shandy/Keeley), Gillian Anderson (Widow Wadman/Gillian), Shirley Henderson (Susannah/Shirley), Jeremy Northam (Mark), Naomie Harris (Jennie), Kelly Macdonald (Jenny). Directed by Michael Winterbottom and produced by Andrew Eaton. Screenplay by Frank Cottrell Boyce and Winterbottom, based on the novel *The Life and Opinions of Tristram Shandy, Gentleman* by Laurence Sterne.

I started reading Laurence Sterne's *The Life and Opinions of Tristram Shandy, Gentleman* in 1965, and I intend to finish it any day now. That is true, and also a joke (a small one) involving a novel about procrastination. *Tristram Shandy* begins with its hero about to be born and becomes so sidetracked by digressions that the story ends shortly after his birth. Perhaps Sterne considered writing a sequel describing the rest of Tristram's life but never got around to it (smaller joke).

Now comes *Tristram Shandy: A Cock and Bull Story*, the movie, which never gets around to filming the book. Since the book is probably unfilmable, this is just as well; what we get instead is a film about the making of a film based on a novel about the writing of a novel. As an idea for comedy, this is inspired, and Michael Winterbottom and his screenwriter, Frank Cottrell Boyce, show the filmmakers constantly distracted by themselves. "But enough about me," Darryl Zanuck once said. "What did *you* think of my movie?"

The film takes place on the set of a movie named *Tristram Shandy*. It involves actors named Steve Coogan, Rob Brydon, Gillian Anderson, and others, played by Steve Coogan, Rob Brydon, Gillian Anderson, and others. The opening scene takes place in a makeup room, where Coogan and Brydon discuss their billing and whether Brydon's teeth are too yellow. Coogan has the lead, playing both Tristram and his father, Walter. Brydon plays Tristram's uncle Toby, who devotes his life to constructing a large outdoor model of the battlefield where, as a young man, he suffered an obscure wound. The Widow Wadman (Anderson), who is considering marrying Toby, wants to know precisely how and, ahem, where he was wounded. "Just beyond the asparagus," Toby explains, pointing to his model landscape.

But I digress. Back to the dressing room. Coogan mentions that he has the lead in the movie. Yes, says Brydon, but Toby is "a featured co-lead." Coogan: "Well, we'll see after the edit." Both actors are competitive in that understated British way that involves put-downs hardly less obscure than Toby's wound. Coogan wants the wardrobe department to build up his shoes so that the "featured co-lead" will not be taller than the leading man. Brydon learns that Gillian Anderson has been hired to join the cast, and he is panic-stricken: He is afraid that in a love scene he might blush or be betrayed by stirrings beyond the asparagus.

There are elements of *This Is Spinal Tap* in the film, and a touch of Al Pacino's *Looking for Richard*, a semidocumentary about actors preparing to play *Richard III*. From *Spinal Tap* come the egos of the artists and the shabbiness of their art; from Pacino the film borrows the device of explaining the material to the viewers while it is being explained to the actors (only one person in *Tristram Shandy*, and possibly nobody in the audience, has read the book).

The art is endearingly shabby. There is a screening of some battle footage in which lackluster foot soldiers wander dispiritedly past the camera, looking like extras on their lunch break. And a scene in which a miniature unborn Tristram is seen inside a miniature womb; I was reminded of Stonehenge in *Spinal Tap*. The explanations of the material include witty dinnertime conversation by Stephen Fry, playing himself playing an actor playing a literary theorist. Coogan picks up enough to lecture an interviewer: "This is a postmodern novel before there was any modernism to be post about." Later it's claimed that *Tristram Shandy* was "No. 8 on the *Observer's* list of the greatest novels," which cheers everyone until they discover the list was chronological.

Now about that interviewer. He has information about a lap dancer that the actor met one recent drunken evening. It would be embarrassing to see the lap dancer on the front page of the tabloids, but the interviewer is willing to do a deal: He'll tidy the story in return for an exclusive about Coogan's relationship with his girlfriend, Jenny (Kelly Macdonald), who has just given birth to their baby. It would not be good for Jenny to read about the lap dancer.

Jenny, as it happens, has just arrived on the set, where Coogan has been having a flirtation with a production assistant named Jennie (Naomie Harris). Jennie is not merely sexy and efficient, but also is a film buff who offers analysis and theory to people who really want only a drink. She compares the ungainly battle scene to Bresson's work in *Lancelot du Lac,* and has a lot to say about Fassbinder, who Coogan vaguely suspects might have been a German director. Not surprisingly, Jennie is the only person on the set who has read the novel, and she tries to explain why the battle scene isn't exactly important.

Because their work is so varied, director Winterbottom and Boyce, his frequent writer, are only now coming into focus as perhaps the most creative team in British film. Their collaborations include films as different as *Butterfly Kiss, Welcome to Saravejo, The Claim, Code 46* and *24 Hour Party People.* That the same director and writer could make such different films is almost inexplicable, and consider, too, that Winterbottom directed *Wonderland* and Boyce wrote Danny Boyle's *Millions.*

Boyce told me *Tristram Shandy* might sound a little like Charlie Kaufman's screenplay for *Adaptation,* but he thinks it's closer to Truffaut's *Day for Night.* (Am I sounding a little like Jennie here?) It wonderfully evokes life on a movie set, which for a few weeks or months creates its own closed society. Wives and lovers visit the set but are subtly excluded from its "family," and even such a miraculous creature as a newborn baby is treated like a prop that is very nice, yes, but not needed for the scene. As the final credits roll, Coogan and Brydon are still engaged in their running duel of veiled insults. They are briefly diverted, however, by imitating Pacino as Shylock. Every actor knows what David Merrick meant when he said, "It is not enough for me to succeed; my enemies must fail." ☞

Troy ★ ★
R, 162 m., 2004

Brad Pitt (Achilles), Eric Bana (Hector), Orlando Bloom (Paris), Diane Kruger (Helen), Brian Cox (Agamemnon), Sean Bean (Odysseus), Brendan Gleeson (Menelaus), Peter O'Toole (Priam), Garrett Hedlund (Patroclus). Directed by Wolfgang Petersen and produced by Petersen, Diana Rathbun, and Colin Wilson. Screenplay by David Benioff, based on the poem "The Iliad" by Homer.

Troy is based on the poem by Homer, according to the credits. Homer's estate should sue. The movie sidesteps the existence of the Greek gods, turns its heroes into action movie clichés, and demonstrates that we're getting tired of computer-generated armies. Better a couple of hundred sweaty warriors than two masses of 50,000 men marching toward each other across a sea of special effects.

The movie recounts the legend of the Trojan War, as the fortress city is attacked by a Greek army led by Menelaus of Sparta and Agamemnon of Mycenae. The war has become necessary because of the lust of the young Trojan prince Paris (Orlando Bloom), who during a peace mission to Sparta seduces its queen, Helen (Diane Kruger). This understandably annoys her husband, Menelaus (Brendan Gleeson), not to mention Paris's brother Hector (Eric Bana), who points out, quite correctly, that when you visit a king on a peace mission it is counterproductive to leave with his wife.

What the movie doesn't explain is why

Helen would leave with Paris after an acquaintanceship of a few nights. Is it because her loins throb with passion for a hero? No, because she tells him: "I don't want a hero. I want a man I can grow old with." Not in Greek myth, you don't. If you believe Helen of Troy could actually tell Paris anything remotely like that, you will probably also agree that the second night he slipped into her boudoir, she told him, "Last night was a mistake."

The seduction of Helen is the curtain-raiser for the main story, which involves vast Greek armies laying siege to the impenetrable city. Chief among their leaders is Achilles, said to be the greatest warrior of all time, but played by Brad Pitt as if he doesn't believe it. If Achilles was anything, he was a man who believed his own press releases. Heroes are not introspective in Greek drama, they do not have second thoughts, and they are not conflicted.

Achilles is all of these things. He mopes on the flanks of the Greek army with his own independent band of fighters, carrying out a separate diplomatic policy, kind of like Ollie North. He thinks Agamemnon is a poor leader with bad strategy, and doesn't really get worked up until his beloved cousin Patroclus (Garrett Hedlund) is killed in battle. Patroclus, who looks a little like Achilles, wears his helmet and armor to fool the enemy, and until the helmet is removed everyone thinks Achilles has been slain. So dramatic is that development that the movie shows perhaps 100,000 men in hand-to-hand combat, and then completely forgets them in order to focus on the Patroclus battle scene, with everybody standing around like during a fight on the playground.

Brad Pitt is a good actor and a handsome man, and he worked out for six months to get buff for the role, but Achilles is not a character he inhabits comfortably. Say what you will about Charlton Heston and Victor Mature, but one good way to carry off a sword-and-sandal epic is to be filmed by a camera down around your knees, while you intone quasi-formal prose in a heroic baritone. Pitt is modern, nuanced, introspective; he brings complexity to a role where it is not required.

By treating Achilles and the other characters as if they were human, instead of the larger-than-life creations of Greek myth, director Wolfgang Petersen miscalculates. What happens in Greek myth cannot happen between psychologically plausible characters. That's the whole point of myth. Great films like Michael Cacoyannis's *Elektra,* about the murder of Agamemnon after the Trojan War, know that and use a stark dramatic approach that is deliberately stylized. Of course, *Elektra* wouldn't work for a multiplex audience, but then maybe it shouldn't.

The best scene in the movie has Peter O'-Toole creating an island of drama and emotion in the middle of all that plodding dialogue. He plays old King Priam of Troy, who at night ventures outside his walls and into the enemy camp, surprising Achilles in his tent. Achilles has defeated Priam's son Hector in hand-to-hand combat before the walls of Troy, and dragged his body back to camp behind his chariot. Now Priam asks that the body be returned for proper preparation and burial. This scene is given the time and attention it needs to build its mood, and we believe it when Achilles tells Priam, "You're a far better king than the one who leads this army." O'Toole's presence is a reminder of *Lawrence of Arabia,* which proved that patience with dialogue and character is more important than action in making war movies work.

As for the Greek cities themselves, a cliché from the old Hollywood epics has remained intact. This is the convention that whenever a battle of great drama takes place, all the important characters have box seats for it. When Achilles battles Hector before the walls of Troy, for example, Priam and his family have a sort of viewing stand right at the front of the palace, and we get the usual crowd reaction shots, some of them awkward close-ups of actresses told to look grieved.

In a way, *Troy* resembles *The Alamo.* Both are about fortresses under siege. Both are defeated because of faulty night watchmen. The Mexicans sneak up on the Alamo undetected, and absolutely nobody is awake to see the Greeks climbing out of the Trojan Horse. One difference between the two movies is that Billy Bob Thornton and the other *Alamo* actors are given evocative dialogue and deliver it well, while *Troy* provides dialogue that probably cannot be delivered well because it would sound even sillier that way.

Tsotsi ★ ★ ★ ★
R, 94 m., 2006

Presley Chweneyagae (Tsotsi), Terry Pheto (Miriam), Mothusi Magano (Boston), Israel Makoe (Tsotsi's father), Percy Matsemela (Sergeant Zuma), Jerry Mofokeng (Morris), Benny Moshe (Young Tsotsi), Nambitha Mpumlwana (Pumla Dube). Directed by Gavin Hood and produced by Peter Fudakowski. Screenplay by Hood, based on the novel by Athol Fugard.

How strange, a movie where a bad man becomes better, instead of the other way around. *Tsotsi*, a film of deep emotional power, considers a young killer whose cold eyes show no emotion, who kills unthinkingly, and who is transformed by the helplessness of a baby. He didn't mean to kidnap the baby, but now that he has it, it looks at him with trust and need, and he is powerless before eyes more demanding than his own.

The movie won the Oscar as best foreign film. It is set in Soweto, the township outside Johannesburg where neat little houses built by the new government are overwhelmed by square miles of shacks. There is poverty and despair here, but also hope and opportunity; from Soweto have come generations of politicians, entrepreneurs, artists, musicians, as if it were the Lower East Side of South Africa. Tsotsi (Presley Chweneyagae) is not destined to be one of those. We don't even learn his real name until later in the film; "tsotsi" means "thug," and that's what he is.

He leads a loose-knit gang that smashes and grabs, loots and shoots, sets out each morning to steal something. On a crowded train they stab a man, and he dies without anyone noticing; they hold his body up with their own, take his wallet, flee when the doors open. Another day's work. But when his friend Boston (Mothusi Magano) asks Tsotsi how he really feels, whether decency comes into it, he fights with him and walks off into the night, and we sense how alone he is. Later, in a flashback, we will understand the cruelty of the home and father he fled from.

He goes from here to there. He has a strange meeting with a man in a wheelchair and asks him why he bothers to go on living. The man tells him. Tsotsi finds himself in an upscale suburb. Such areas in Joburg are usually gated communities, each house surrounded by a security wall, every gate promising "armed response." An African professional woman gets out of her Mercedes to ring the buzzer on the gate so her husband can let her in. Tsotsi shoots her and steals her car. Some time passes before he realizes he has a passenger: a baby boy.

Tsotsi is a killer, but he cannot kill a baby. He takes it home with him, to a room built on top of somebody else's shack. It might be wise for him to leave the baby at a church or an orphanage, but that doesn't occur to him. He has the baby, so the baby is his. We can guess that he will not abandon the boy because he has been abandoned himself and projects upon the infant all of his own self-pity.

We realize the violence in the film has slowed. Tsotsi himself is slow to realize he has a new agenda. He uses newspapers as diapers, feeds the baby condensed milk, carries it around with him in a shopping bag. Finally, in desperation, at gunpoint, he forces a nursing mother (Terry Pheto) to feed the child. She lives in a nearby shack, a clean and cheerful one. As he watches her do what he demands, something shifts inside of him, and all of his hurt and grief are awakened.

Tsotsi doesn't become a nice man. He simply stops being active as an evil one and finds his time occupied with the child. Babies are singleminded. They want to be fed, they want to be changed, they want to be held, they want to be made much of, and they think it is their birthright. Who is Tsotsi to argue?

What a simple and yet profound story this is. It does not sentimentalize poverty or make Tsotsi more colorful or sympathetic than he should be; if he deserves praise, it is not for becoming a good man but for allowing himself to be distracted from the job of being a bad man. The nursing mother, named Miriam, is played by Terry Pheto as a quiet counterpoint to his rage. She lives in Soweto and has seen his kind before. She senses something in him, some pool of feeling he must ignore if he is to remain Tsotsi. She makes reasonable decisions. She acts not as a heroine but as a realist who wants to nudge Tsotsi in a direction that will protect her own family and this helpless baby, and then perhaps even Tsotsi himself. These two performances, by Chweneyagae and Pheto, are surrounded by temptations to overact or cave in to sentimentality; they step safely past them and play the characters as they might actually live their lives.

How the story develops is for you to discover. I was surprised to find that it leads toward hope instead of despair; why does fiction so often assume defeat is our destiny? The film avoids obligatory violence and actually deals with the characters as people. The story is based on a novel by the great South African writer Athol Fugard, directed and written by Gavin Hood. It won the Oscar one year after the South African film *Yesterday* was the first from that nation to be nominated. There are stories in the beloved country that have cried for a century to be told.

Turtles Can Fly ★ ★ ★ ★
NO MPAA RATING, 95 m., 2005

Soran Ebrahim (Satellite), Avaz Latif (Agrin), Hirsh Feyssal (Henkov). Directed by Bahman Ghobadi and produced by Ghobadi. Screenplay by Ghobadi.

I wish everyone who has an opinion on the war in Iraq could see *Turtles Can Fly*. That would mean everyone in the White House and in Congress, and the newspaper writers, and the TV pundits, and the radio talkers, and you—especially you, because you are reading this and they are not.

You assume the movie is a liberal attack on George W. Bush's policies. Not at all. The action takes place just before the American invasion begins, and the characters in it look forward to the invasion and the fall of Saddam Hussein. Nor does the movie later betray an opinion one way or the other about the war. It is about the actual lives of refugees, who lack the luxury of opinions because they are preoccupied with staying alive in a world that has no place for them.

The movie takes place in a Kurdish refugee camp somewhere on the border between Turkey and Iraq. That means, in theory, it takes place in "Kurdistan," a homeland that exists in the minds of the Kurds even though every other government in the area insists the Kurds are stateless. The characters in the movie are children and teenagers, all of them orphans; there

are adults in the camp, but the kids run their own lives—especially a bright wheeler-dealer named Satellite (Soran Ebrahim), who organizes work gangs of other children.

What is their work? They disarm land mines, so they can be resold to arms dealers in the nearby town. The land mines are called "American," but this is a reflection of their value and not a criticism of the United States; they were planted in the area by Saddam Hussein, in one of his skirmishes with Kurds and Turks. (Well, technically, they were supplied to Saddam by the United States.) Early in the film, we see a character named Henkov (Hirsh Feyssal), known to everyone as The Boy With No Arms, who gently disarms a mine by removing the firing pin with his lips.

Satellite pays special attention to a girl named Agrin (Avaz Latif), who is Henkov's sister. They have a little brother named Risa, who is carried about with his arms wrapped around the neck of his armless brother. We *think* he is their brother, that is, until we discover he is Agrin's child, born after she was raped by Iraqi soldiers while still almost a child herself. The armless boy loves Risa; his sister hates him, because of her memories.

Is this world beginning to take shape in your mind? The refugees live in tents and huts. They raise money by scavenging. Satellite is the most resourceful person in the camp, making announcements, calling meetings, assigning work, and traveling ceremonially on a bicycle festooned with ribbons and glittering medallions. He is always talking, shouting, hectoring, at the top of his voice: He is too busy to reflect on the misery of his life.

The village is desperate for information about the coming American invasion. There is a scene of human comedy in which every household has a member up on a hill with a makeshift TV antenna; those below shout instructions: "To the left! A little to the right!" But no signal is received. Satellite announces that he will go to town and barter for a satellite dish. There is a sensation when he returns with one. The elders gather as he tries to bring in a signal. The sexy music video channels are prohibited, but the elders wait patiently as Satellite cycles through the sin until he finds CNN, and they can listen for

English words they understand. They hate Saddam and eagerly await the Americans.

But what will the Americans do for them? The plight of the Kurdish people is that no one seems to want to do much for them. Even though a Kurd has recently been elected to high office in Iraq, we get the sense he was a compromise candidate—chosen precisely because his people are powerless. For years the Kurds have struggled against Turkey, Iraq, and other nations in the region, to define the borders of a homeland the other states refuse to acknowledge.

From time to time the aims of the Kurds come into step with the aims of others. When they were fighting Saddam, the first Bush administration supported them. When they were fighting our ally Turkey, we opposed them. The *New York Times Magazine* ran a cover story about Ibrahim Parlak, who for ten years peacefully ran a Kurdish restaurant in Harbert, Michigan, only to be arrested in 2004 by the federal government, which hoped to deport him for Kurdish nationalist activities that at one point we approved. Because I supported Ibrahim's case, I could read headlines on right-wing sites such as, "Roger Ebert Gives Thumbs Up to Terrorism."

I hope Debbie Schlussel, who wrote that column, sees *Turtles Can Fly*. The movie does not agree with her politics, or mine. It simply provides faces for people we think of as abstractions. It was written and directed by Bahman Ghobadi, whose *A Time for Drunken Horses* (2000) was also about Kurds struggling to survive between the lines. Satellite has no politics. Neither does The Boy With No Arms, or his sister, or her child born of rape; they have been trapped outside of history.

I was on a panel at the University of Colorado where an audience member criticized movies for reducing the enormity of the Holocaust to smaller stories. But there is no way to tell a story big enough to contain all of the victims of the Holocaust, or all of the lives affected for good and ill in the Middle East. Our minds cannot process that many stories. What we can understand is The Boy With No Arms, making a living by disarming land mines like the one that blew away his arms. And Satellite, who tells the man in the city he will trade him fifteen radios and some cash for a satellite dish. Where did Satellite get fifteen radios? Why? You need some radios?

Twelve and Holding ★ ★ ★ ½
R, 90 m., 2006

Conor Donovan (Jacob and Rudy Carges), Zoe Weizenbaum (Malee Chung), Jesse Camacho (Leonard Fisher), Linus Roache (Jim Carges), Annabella Sciorra (Carla Chung), Jeremy Renner (Gus Maitland), Marcia DeBonis (Grace Fisher), Tom McGowan (Patrick Fisher). Directed by Michael Cuesta and produced by Leslie Urdang, Jenny Schweitzer, and Brian Bell. Screenplay by Anthony Cipriano.

Michael Cuesta's *Twelve and Holding* weaves together the stories of three families and three children who take desperate measures to try to solve the problems in their lives. All three kids feel let down by their parents—who love them, but not usefully or with much insight. But this isn't one of those films where the kids are filled with wisdom and find wonderful solutions. What they find instead is danger.

The most harrowing story involves twins named Jacob and Rudy, both played by Conor Donovan. They get in a fight with some other kids, who threaten to destroy their tree house. So Rudy and his fat friend Leonard (Jesse Camacho) decide to spend the night in the tree house, and that leads to Rudy's accidental death and to the anguish of Jacob, who refused to come along. Jacob has another problem: a birthmark that covers half his face; sometimes he wears a hockey mask to cover it.

We learn more about Leonard, the fat kid. His family sits around the table gobbling their food, and when he's not eating, he's snacking. A coach gives him books of exercise and nutrition and encourages him to get in shape: "You can play center on my team when you get to high school." Leonard is puzzled. "Why are you doing this for me?" he asks. "Because," says the coach, "I've never met a child so out of shape in my life."

At first Leonard can barely run a block. But the accident that kills Rudy changes his life, too, and as he begins to lose weight, he presents a challenge to his fat mother, Grace (Marcia Debonis). This leads to his attempt to "help" her in a way so ill-advised and hazardous, and yet so ingenious, I will leave it for you to discover.

Quieter, but more heartrending, is the story of Malee (Zoe Weizenbaum), the possibly adopted Asian daughter of a psychiatrist (Annabella Sciorra). Eavesdropping on her mother's therapy sessions, she gets an obsession about a construction worker named Gus (Jeremy Renner). Because she has a lot of inside information about him, she's able to attract his attention and act on the big crush she has for him. But a twelve-year-old girl is clearly playing with fire when she talks about love with a grown man. Weizenbaum is remarkable in the transformations she brings to her character.

Jacob thinks he can make up for the death of his brother. Leonard thinks he can solve his family's obesity. Malee thinks she can find, in a way, a father figure to replace the father she feels abandoned her. The paths these kids take are all wrong, but Cuesta's direction and Anthony Cipriano's screenplay are gentle with them; the movie observes their mistakes and is horrified, but does not blame, and understands how emotions can lead to a failure of common sense. What scars these children may bear as adults we are left to imagine.

Cuesta also directed *L.I.E.* (2001), where the initials stood for, among other things, the Long Island Expressway and the lies of some teenage boys who lived near it. Brian Cox played a pedophile who preyed on them, in a movie of tangled emotional complexity. Here again Cuesta shows a perception for the way young people may observe an adult world, even be familiar with it, and yet completely fail to understand it. *Twelve and Holding* could have been a series of horror stories, but the filmmakers and their gifted young actors somehow negotiate the horrors and generate a deep sympathy.

The Twilight Samurai ★ ★ ★ ★
NO MPAA RATING, 129 m., 2004

Hiroyuki Sanada (Seibei Iguchi), Rie Miyazawa (Tomoe Iinuma), Nenji Kobayashi (Choubei Hisasaka), Min Tanaka (Zenemon Yogo), Ren Osugi (Toyotarou Kouda), Mitsuru Fukikoshi (Michinojo Iinuma), Miki Ito (Kayana Iguchi), Erina Hashiguchi (Ito Iguchi). Directed by Yoji Yamada and produced by Hiroshi Fukazawa, Shigehiro Nakagawa, and Ichiro Yamamoto.

Screenplay by Yamada Asama and Yoshitaka Asama, based on novels by Shuuhei Fujisawa.

One who is a samurai must before all things keep in mind, by day, and by night, the fact that he has to die. That is his chief business.
—Code of Bushido

The Twilight Samurai is set in Japan during the period of the Meiji Restoration, circa 1868—the same period as Kurosawa's great *Seven Samurai* and Edward Zwick's elegant *The Last Samurai*. The three films deal in different ways with a time when samurai still tried to live by the Code of Bushido, even as they faced poverty or unemployment in a changing society. *The Last Samurai* is about samurai opposing the emperor's moves to modernize Japan; ironically, we learn that the hero of *The Twilight Samurai* fought and died in that rebellion— after the story of this movie is over.

His name is Seibei (Hiroyuki Sanada), and he lives under the rule of his clan in northeast Japan, where he spends his days not in battle but as an accountant, keeping track of dried fish and other foods in storage. Seeing him bending wearily over a pile of papers, declining an invitation by his fellow workers to go out drinking, we're reminded of the hero of Kurosawa's film *Ikiru*. Seibei hurries home because he has a senile mother and two young daughters to support, and is in debt after the death of his wife.

His story is told by director Yoji Yamada in muted tones and colors, beautifully re-creating a feudal village that still retains its architecture, its customs, its ancient values, even as the economy is making its way of life obsolete. What kind of a samurai has to pawn his sword and make do with a bamboo replacement? The film is narrated by Seibei's oldest daughter (Erina Hashiguchi), who is young in the film but an old lady on the sound track, remembering her father with love.

After working all day in the office, Seibei hurries home to grow crops to feed his family and earn extra cash. His coworkers gossip that his kimono is torn, and that he smells. One day the lord of the clan comes to inspect the food stores, notices Seibei's aroma, and reprimands him. This brings such disgrace on the family that Seibei's stern uncle reminds him, "Only a generation ago, hara-kiri would have been called for." His uncle advises him to remarry to get another worker into the home to prepare meals and do laundry. It happens that his childhood sweetheart, Tomoe (Rie Miyazawa), has just divorced her wife-beating husband, and begins to help around the house. The girls love her, but Seibei is shy and tired and cannot imagine remarrying.

The clan comes to him with an assignment: He is to kill the unruly Yogo (Min Tanaka), a samurai who has been employed by the clan for only four years, after a long, destitute time of wandering the countryside. Yogo, considered crazy, has declined the clan's suggestion that he kill himself. That seems sane enough to me, but the clan must uphold its standards even as its time is passing, and so the reluctant Seibei is bribed and blackmailed into taking on the assignment.

The closing third of the film is magnificent in the way it gathers all we have learned about Seibei and uses it to bring depth to what could have been a routine action sequence, but is much more. We see Tomoe shyly preparing him for battle ("Allow me to comb your hair"), and after a crucial conversation, he leaves her and goes to Yogo's home, where the body of an earlier emissary lies in the courtyard, covered by a swarm of flies.

I will not, of course, tell you what happens inside the house, or what happens between Seibei and Tomoe. What I can refer to is the extraordinary conversation between Seibei and Yogo, while their swords remain undrawn. "I know, you're all keyed up," Yogo says. "But I'm going to run." He has no desire to fight. He recounts his weary history as a samurai in poverty, or in bondage to a clan: "I was an errand boy, too." At one extraordinary moment he takes the ashes of his dead daughter and crunches a piece of bone between his teeth. Yogo's motive for having this conversation may not be as clear as it seems; it is up to you to decide.

Director Yoji Yamada, now seventy-three, has made at least sixty-six films, according to IMDB.com. The Twilight Samurai, the first to be widely released in this country, was Japan's Oscar nominee this year. He has been nominated six times since he was sixty as Japan's best director, and won once. Yet no less than forty-eight of his films were B-pictures, involving the beloved character Tora-san, popular in Japan

from 1970 until the death in 1996 of Kiyoshi Atsumi, who played him. Tora-san is little known outside Japan, but for a class on Japanese cinema, I obtained one of his movies from Shochiku Studios and we watched it. Apparently they are all much the same: Tora-san, a meek, self-effacing comic figure (a little Chaplin, a little Jerry Lewis, a little Red Skelton), is a salesman who stumbles into a domestic crisis, makes it worse, and then makes it better.

One can only imagine what it would be like to direct that formula forty-eight times. Perhaps Yamada felt a little like Seibei, as he remained loyal to the studio and this character year after year. Perhaps when Seibei finds, at the end of *The Twilight Samurai*, that he may be poor and stuck in a rut but he still has greatness in him— well, perhaps that's how Yamada felt when he entered the home stretch. There is a kind of perfection in laboring humbly all your life only to show, as the end approaches, that you had greatness all along. I am half-convinced that as Seibei's daughter remembers her father's life, she is also describing Yamada's. I could probably find out if that is true, but I don't want to know. I like it better as a possibility.

Note: The Twilight Samurai *swept the 2003 Japanese Academy Awards, winning twelve categories, including best picture, director, screenplay, actor, actress, supporting actor, and cinematography.*

Twisted ★ ½
R, 96 m., 2004

Ashley Judd (Jessica Shepard), Samuel L. Jackson (John Mills), Andy Garcia (Mike Delmarco), David Strathairn (Dr. Melvin Frank), Russell Wong (Lieutenant Tong), Camryn Manheim (Lisa), Mark Pellegrino (Jimmy Schmidt). Directed by Philip Kaufman and produced by Barry Baeres, Linne Radmin, Arnold Kopelson, and Anne Kopelson. Screenplay by Sarah Thorp and Kaufman.

Phil Kaufman's *Twisted* walks like a thriller and talks like a thriller, but squawks like a turkey. And yet the elements are in place for a film that works—until things start becoming clear and mysteries start being solved and we start shaking our heads, if we are well mannered, or guffawing, if we are not.

Let me begin at the ending. The other day I employed the useful term *deus ex machina* in a review, and received several messages from readers who are not proficient in Latin. I have also received several messages from Latin scholars who helpfully translated obscure dialogue in *The Passion of the Christ* for me, and, as my Urbana High School Latin teacher Mrs. Link used to remind me, "*In medio tutissimus ibis.*"

But back to *deus ex machina*. This is a phrase you will want to study and master, not merely to amaze friends during long bus journeys but because it so perfectly describes what otherwise might take you thousands of words. Imagine a play on a stage. The hero is in a fix. The dragon is breathing fire, the hero's sword is broken, his leg is broken, his spirit is broken, and the playwright's imagination is broken. Suddenly there is the offstage noise of the grinding of gears, and invisible machinery lowers a god onto the stage, who slays the dragon, heals the hero, and fires the playwright. He is the "god from the machine."

Now travel with me to San Francisco. Ashley Judd plays Jessica Shepard, a new homicide detective who has a habit of picking up guys in bars and having rough sex with them. She drinks a lot. Maybe that goes without saying. Soon after getting her new job, she and her partner, Mike Delmarco (Andy Garcia), are assigned to a floater in the bay. She recognizes the dead man, who has been savagely beaten. It's someone she has slept with.

She reveals this information, but is kept on the case by the police commissioner (Samuel L. Jackson), who raised her as his own daughter after her own father went berserk and killed a slew of people, including her mother. The commissioner trusts her. Then another body turns up, also with the killer's brand (a cigarette burn). She slept with this guy, too. She's seeing the department shrink (David Strathairn), who understandably suggests she has to share this information with her partner. Then a third dead guy turns up. She slept with him, too. Wasn't it Oscar Wilde who said, "To kill one lover may be regarded as a misfortune. To kill three seems like carelessness"?

Detective Sheperd has a pattern. She goes home at night, drinks way too much red wine, and blacks out. The next day, her cell rings and

she's summoned to the next corpse. Wasn't it Ann Landers who said that killing people in a blackout was one of the twenty danger signals of alcoholism? To be sure, Delmarco helpfully suggests at one point that she should drink less. Maybe only enough to maim?

So anyway, on a dark and isolated pier in San Francisco, three of the characters come together. I won't reveal who they are, although if one of them isn't Ashley Judd it wouldn't be much of an ending. Certain death seems about to ensue, and then with an offstage grinding noise . . . but I don't want to give away the ending. Find out for yourself.

And ask yourself this question: Assuming the premise of the first amazing development, how did the San Francisco police department know exactly which dark and isolated pier these three people were on, and how did they arrive in sixty seconds (by car, truck, motorcycle, and helicopter), and how come the cops who arrived were precisely the same cops who have already been established as characters in the story? And isn't it convenient that, fast as they arrived, they considerately left time for the Talking Killer scene, in which all is explained when all the Killer has to do is blow everyone away and beat it?

The movie does at least draw a moral: *Nemo repente fuit turpissimus.*

Two Brothers ★ ★ ½
PG, 109 m., 2004

Guy Pearce (Aidan McRory), Jean-Claude Dreyfus (Eugene Normandin), Philippine Leroy-Beaulieu (Mathilde Normandin), Freddie Highmore (Raoul), Oanh Nguyen (His Excellency), Moussa Maaskri (Saladin), Vincent Scarito (Zerbino), Maï Anh Le (Naï-Rea). Directed by Jean-Jacques Annaud and produced by Annaud and Jake Eberts. Screenplay by Alain Godard and Annaud.

The brothers in *Two Brothers* are tiger cubs when we meet them, prowling the ruins of temples in the jungles of French Indochina, circa 1920. With their mother and father, Kumal and Sangha live an idyllic life, romping and wrestling and living on air, apparently, since no prey ever seems to be killed. The movie never really fesses up that tigers kill for their dinner; that would undercut its sentimentality. The result is a reassuring fairy tale that will fascinate children and has moments of natural beauty for their parents, but makes the tigers approximately as realistic as the animals in *The Lion King*.

The movie is astonishing in its photography of the two tigers, played by an assortment of trained beasts, augmented by CGI. It is less wondrous in its human story, involving such walking stereotypes as the great British hunter, the excitable French administrator, the misunderstood Indochinese prince, and the little French boy who makes friends with Sangha and sleeps with him when Sangha is at an age to be plenty old enough for his own bed, preferably behind bars.

Two Brothers was directed and cowritten by Jean-Jacques Annaud, whose international hit *The Bear* (1989) did not sentimentalize its bear cub but treated it with the respect due to an animal that earns its living under the law of the wild. In that one, the speech of the hunter (Jack Wallace) was presented not so much as language as simply the sounds that human animals make. In *Two Brothers*, the cubs may not understand English, but they get the drift. In both films, Annaud achieves almost miraculous moments, the result no doubt of a combination of training, patience, and special effects. We're usually convinced we are looking at real tiger cubs doing what they really want to do, even when it goes against their nature. Occasionally there will be a scene that stretches it, as when Kumal, who was trained in a circus to jump through a ring of fire, apparently uses telepathy to convince Sangha he can do it too.

The first half-hour or so involves only the cubs, and these scenes play like a scripted documentary. The beauty of the tigers and the exotic nature of the locations are so seductive we almost forget the movie has human stars and will therefore interrupt with a plot. But it does.

The villain, who becomes the hero, is Aidan McRory (Guy Pearce), introduced as an ivory hunter but then, after the bottom drops out of the ivory market, a tomb raider. When one of his assistants finds an ancient statue in the forest and regrets it's too heavy to bring back to Europe, McRory coldly tells him, "cut off its head." McRory is the one who kills the cubs' father and captures Kumal, selling him to a circus run by the harsh trainer Zerbino (Vincent Scarito).

Sangha is also captured, and adopted by young Raoul (Freddie Highmore), son of the French colonial administrator (Jean-Claude Dreyfus). He eventually ends up in the menagerie of a spoiled prince (Oanh Nguyen); Sangha is no longer safe as Raoul's playmate, the kid is told, "now that he has tasted blood." Apparently until that fatal taste, Sangha was a vegetarian. The prince decrees that the two tigers fight to the death in an amphitheater, but of course, being brothers, they ... well, do more or less exactly what we expect them to do.

The story is broad melodrama that treats Sangha and Kumal as if they were almost human in their motivations and emotions. Such comforting sentiment is a luxury wild animals cannot afford. Still, along with the beauty of the animals and the photography, there are moments of genuine tension, as when McRory faces the tigers up close. That McRory does not make his own contribution to their taste for blood is because of the tiger's uncanny ability to peer deeply into the eyes of the human actors and learn there what they must do for the benefit of the movie's plot.

There is a lot in *Two Brothers* I admire. Families will not go wrong in attending this film. Some kids will think it's one of the best movies they've seen. My objections are of a sort that won't occur, I realize, to many of the viewers. But I remember *The Bear* and its brave refusal to supply its bear cub with human emotions and motivations. W. G. Sebald writes that animals and humans view one another "through a breach of incomprehension." That is profoundly true, and helpful to keep in mind when making friends with the bears at Yellowstone, or reassuring tigers that we feel their pain.

Two for the Money ★ ★ ★ ½
R, 124 m., 2005

Al Pacino (Walter), Matthew McConaughey (Brandon), Rene Russo (Toni), Armand Assante (Novian), Jeremy Piven (Jerry). Directed by D.J. Caruso and produced by James G. Robinson, David C. Robinson, and Jay Cohen. Screenplay by Dan Gilroy.

In D. J. Caruso's *Two for the Money*, you can see Al Pacino doing something he's done a lot lately: having a terrific time being an actor. At sixty-five he's on a hot streak in one well-written role after another. In *Insomnia, People I Know, Angels in America,* and *The Merchant of Venice* he has given performances vibrating with tension and need, and now here he comes again. George C. Scott used to say when a good actor was in the right role, you could sense the joy of performance. Pacino has moments here when he doesn't quite click his heels.

Matthew McConaughey and Rene Russo are wonderful, too, in a movie with three well-written and fully functional roles, but their characters are by nature more contained than Pacino's. He plays Walter, who runs a sports betting hotline. McConaughey plays Brandon, the Vegas oddsmaker Walter imports to New York, renames, and turns into a star. Walter is a mesmerizer who assaults him with confidence and exuberance. Russo is Toni, Walter's wife, who loves him and despairs of him. He dazzles Brandon and he worries Toni, a recovering junkie. He's recovering from everything: "If it says 'anonymous' at the end, he goes," she tells Brandon.

The nature of Walter's operation is a little hard to grasp, maybe even to Walter. It appears that his offices and home are in the same building, all paneled Prairie-style in dark woods and window partitions. On the ground floor, he has guys manning hotlines where you pay twenty-five dollars and get the early line for your weekend bets. On the second floor, it's bigger business: For the best advice, gamblers are expected to pay a percentage of what they win from their bookies. That way Walter is technically not breaking the law: He's not taking bets; he's taking a percentage at arm's length.

Two for the Money is not about the mechanics of this business but about its emotions. Walter is a promoter who at one point admits his operation is made of smoke and mirrors. He imports Brandon after the kid startles Vegas with the accuracy of his predictions. He gives him a haircut, a wardrobe, a sports car, and a new name, and puts him on TV, and Brandon obliges one weekend by correctly calling twelve games out of twelve.

That's all the plot you need from me. The rest will be observation. Look at the monologue Pacino delivers at a Gamblers Anonymous meeting. It's got the passion, if not quite the language, of his soliloquies in *The Merchant of Venice.* He tells his fellow degenerate gamblers that their problem isn't gambling; it's themselves: "We're all lemons. We need to lose." When they lose everything—the job, the house, the family—they are most fully alive, he says. When they win, they keep gambling until they lose again.

Walter knows this so well he hasn't gambled in years. Brandon has never gambled. Toni has gambled: She gambled when she married Walter. They have a young daughter. The way Walter grabs for the nitroglycerin pills when his angina hits, he shouldn't be in a business that depends on point spreads. But Walter is an optimist: "It was only a small one," he says after one attack.

I won't tell you what happens involving these three people in this movie, but I want you to watch for the way all three change. The screenplay by Dan Gilroy isn't one of those deals where one guy acts out and everybody else watches him. It's about three people who are transformed in relation to one another, as a situation develops that is equally dangerous all the way around. It takes us awhile to understand what Brandon is doing, and then we realize that Walter *knows* what he's doing—and is seeing him and raising him. There are moments here, including one moment before a live TV broadcast, where Walter is pushing his whole stake into the pot, and the game isn't poker; it's life.

Is the movie a realistic portrait of these kinds of people in this kind of business? I'm not an expert, but I doubt it. What I don't understand is how Walter finds out how much his clients bet so he can collect his percentage. Bookies aren't real good at sharing information, especially for the benefit of an operation devoted to out-handicapping them. And besides, there are a lot of bookies. Why can't I get the tips from Walter's company, bet a grand with a bookie he knows about, and ten grand with some guy he doesn't know about?

This is a problem, but it is not a problem that bothers me. It's a classic MacGuffin. The point is that something happens on the second floor that means Walter and Brandon and the telephone guys make a pile of money when Brandon correctly predicts the weekend games, and they do it without placing bets or taking bets. That's what we need to know. Everything else is dialogue, direction, acting, and energy.

I've been watching Pacino a long time. I saw him at the beginning, in 1971, in *The Panic in Needle Park*. Already a great actor. His next movie was *The Godfather*. I could mention *Dog Day Afternoon, Glengarry Glen Ross, Scarface, Carlito's Way, Heat, Donnie Brasco*. I could keep going.

But good as he already was, I think something rotated inside and clicked as he was directing his documentary *Looking for Richard* (1996), which was about how Shakespeare should be acted, and how an actor should play Richard III. Here was an actor in his mid-fifties, asking undergraduate questions, reinventing how he approaches a role, asking what acting is. He chose Richard III, a character who looks in a mirror and asks himself how he should play himself. In his movies since then, Pacino seems to have found something in the mirror.

The Two of Us ★ ★ ★ ★
NO MPAA RATING, 83 m., 1967 (rereleased 2005)

Michel Simon (Pepe), Alain Cohen (Claude), Lucie Fabiole (Meme), Roger Carel (Victor), Charles Denner (Claude's Father), Paul Preboist (Maxime), Jacqueline Rouillard (Teacher). Directed by Claude Berri and produced by Paul Cadeac. Screenplay by Claude Berri, Gerard Brach, and Michel Rivelin.

"I was eight years old and already a Jew."

The famous opening line of Claude Berri's *The Two of Us* (1967) is spoken by an adult voice, the director's own. The film is loosely inspired by his own life. In 1944 in occupied Paris, his parents sent him away to live with Gentiles, who would claim him as one of their own and protect him from deportation and death. In Berri's version of the story, his parents are posing as Alsatians but fear the boy will reveal his true identity in a heedless moment. A friend who is Catholic suggests that young Claude be taught the Lord's Prayer, given a new last name, and sent to live with an old couple on a farm outside Grenoble.

That's the setup for a heartwarming movie that showcases one of the last performances of the great Michel Simon (1895–1975), who began his career by looking old and kept on looking older. He was only thirty-seven in Jean Renoir's *Boudu Saved from Drowning* (1932), and thirty-nine in Jean Vigo's *L'Atalante* (1934), but he looks sixtyish in both films, and by the time he made *The Two of Us*, he was seventy-two, a plump, tottering wreck of a man with a creased face and the subtlety of a bear.

Simon plays Pepe, the old farm owner whose life revolves around his dog, his wife, and his prejudices. He is an anti-Semite who believes World War II was started by an evil conspiracy involving Jews, Masons, communists, and the monster Winston Churchill. He listens to the nightly broadcasts of the BBC, only to rail against them. He has no idea that young Claude, who has come to live with them, is Jewish; he accepts the reasonable explanation that this Catholic child has been sent by his parents to be safe if Paris is bombed.

The small boy has been warned by his parents to be constantly on guard against discovery. For Claude that means keeping his circumcised "birdie" out of view, and there's a harrowing scene where Meme (Lucie Fabiole), the old lady, tries to plunge into the soapy bathwater for a good scrub. But the movie is not really about danger and concealment; it's about how love grows between the boy and the old man, and how the boy, who is "already a Jew," becomes a wiser one.

The heart of the film is in Simon's performance, though young Alain Cohen is convincing and lovable as Claude and would go on to play Berri's autobiographical hero in two more films (their relationship became a little like François Truffaut's with Jean-Pierre Leaud). Simon was a large, shambling fact of life, a man who always seemed too large for the space available. In *L'Atalante*, he is the hired hand on a barge occupied by newlyweds and constantly seems to be in their way. In *Boudu*, which is the story of a drunk "rescued" by a bourgeois couple, he occupies too much space in their lives. In *The Two of Us*, he threatens to overwhelm the little boy with his affection.

They become playmates. That is the only word for it, and it's miraculous how old Pepe chases the boy around the yard, joins in his imaginary games, gets on the swing, puts a knife between his teeth, and pretends to be a dirty Bolshevik about to kill and eat him. The boy squeals with delight and joins Pepe in spoiling the old man's beloved dog. He also has long talks with Pepe about life. One Sunday, after they all go to church and hear a sermon reminding the congregation that Christ was a Jew, he quizzes the old man:

"Was Jesus a Jew?"

"So they say."

"Then God is a Jew, too."

Pepe doesn't think so but is not sure why. The boy listens to Pepe's descriptions of Jews, but when Pepe says they have big noses, the boy points out that Pepe's nose is enormous. The scene where Simon examines himself in the mirror could have been played for laughs, or ironically, but he plays it as an exercise in mystified curiosity.

A good many of the old man's neighbors oppose the Petain government that rules occupied France on behalf of the Nazis, but Pepe keeps the marshal's portrait framed on the wall, and Meme dusts it every day. When D-Day arrives and it appears the tide of battle has turned, even sympathizers in the district studiously forget their sympathies for Petain, but not Pepe: "In my house, I decide who governs France."

The movie is not so much an argument against anti-Semitism as a demonstration that it feeds on ignorance. The old man has not given much thought to his prejudices, but caught them like a virus in his childhood and has carried them along uncritically into old age. He has no idea that the child he has come to love so much is a Jew. I suspect if he did know, he would make an exception for Claude while continuing to harbor his prejudices against theoretical Jews he has the advantage of knowing nothing about. He is not converted in his thinking by this movie, and one of its strengths is that it ends without him ever becoming enlightened.

Such a scene of discovery would be a sentimental irrelevance, because the movie is concerned not with what Pepe knows but with who Pepe is; the person who learns and grows is Claude. Berri was born in 1934 with the name Claude Beri Langmann, the same name little Claude has in the movie, and so it is fair to conclude that the movie is the result of what the little boy learned during his stay among the Gentiles. He learned that anti-Semitism is an evil, but he learned to forgive some of the Pepes of the world, for they know not what they do. For those who do know, forgiveness is another question, but that is another movie.

2046 ★ ★ ½
R, 129 m., 2005

Tony Leung (Chow Mo Wan), Gong Li (Su Li Zhen), Takuya Kimura (Tak), Faye Wong (Jing Wen Wang), Ziyi Zhang (Bai Ling), Carina Lau (Lulu/Mimi), Maggie Cheung (slz1960). Directed by Wong Kar-Wai and produced by Wong. Screenplay by Wong.

Jam yesterday and jam tomorrow, but never jam today.

—Alice in Wonderland

It is always too early or too late for love in a Wong Kar-Wai film, and his characters spend their days in yearnings and regrets. *In the Mood for Love* (2000) brought that erotic sadness to a kind of perfection in its story of a man and a woman who live in hotel rooms next to each other and want to become lovers, but never do because his wife and her husband are lovers, and "for us to do the same thing would mean we are no better than they are." Yes, but no worse, and perhaps happier. Isn't it strange that most of the truths about love are banal?

2046, Wong's new film, is an indirect, oblique continuation of the earlier one. It stars Tony Leung as Chow Mo Wan, also the name of his character in *In the Mood for Love*, and there is a brief role for Maggie Cheung, his co-star in that film; they are not necessarily playing the same characters. There was also a Room 2046 in the other film, so there are subterranean connections between the two, but they operate something like the express train to the year 2046 in this one: All memories are there in the future, we are told, but no one has ever returned.

No one, except for the narrator, who tells us about it. We gather that *2046* is the name of a science fiction novel being written by Chow. It is also the room next to his in the hotel where much of this movie takes place—a room lived in by a series of women he loves. Not coincidentally, 2046 is also the year set by China for the expiration of Hong Kong's quasi-independence from the mainland. Does that make the movie *2046* a parable about Hong Kong? You could find parallels, I'm sure, but that doesn't seem to be the point. Chow observes that if he hadn't seen the number 2046 on a room, he wouldn't have started his futuristic novel, and it is just barely possible that Wong is telling us this movie was inspired when he asked himself what happened in Room 2046 after *In the Mood for Love* was over. Or before it began. Whatever.

These speculations are probably of no help in understanding the movie, which exists primarily as a visual style imposed upon beautiful faces; Josef von Sternberg's obsession with Marlene Dietrich is mirrored here by Wong's fascination with the beauty of Ziyi Zhang, Gong Li, Faye Wong, Carina Lau, and Cheung, and in the careworn eyes and tired smile of Leung, his Bogart. Like von Sternberg, he films his actors mostly in close-up and medium shot, with baroque architectural details in the background, and cigarette smoke constantly coiling through the air. There are a lot of foreground screens (doorjambs, draperies, walls, furniture) to add texture and detail while concealing parts of those faces. The film is in lurid colors, a pulp counterpoint to the elegance of the action. Why Nat King Cole's version of "The Christmas Song" is heard two or three times is unclear; his songs were also heard in *In the Mood for Love*.

The story is either briefly summarized, or too complicated to be attempted. Briefly: Chow (Leung) leaves Singapore and Su Li Zhen (Li): "We have no prospects here, so I'll see how things are in Hong Kong." She does not follow. In Hong Kong, he moves into the hotel and meets a series of women: Lulu (Lau), a prostitute whose murder lingers as a troubling mystery throughout the film; Jing (Faye Wong), daughter of the hotel owner; and Bai Ling (Zhang), a prostitute who becomes Chow's confidante as they drown their sorrows, preferring drink to sex. All of these relationships are seen in carefully composed shots that seem to be remembering the characters more than seeing them. One spectacular shot shows Jing from above and behind, smoking a cigarette and listening to an opera. Its composition is really the subject of the shot.

An example of complications: Jing is in love with a Japanese man and earlier in the movie appears as an anime idol in the futuristic story within the story, where she has the same Japanese lover. The Japanese man is the film's original narrator, although later it appears the sci-fi story is being written by Chow, inspired by the present-day Jing and her lover. Whether and why this story is being written, and how the future world of 2046 shares a function with the present Room 2046, is an inviting mystery: Do we define the future as a place in our minds where things can happen later, or be shelved, or be hoped for, or be delayed?

Since it is by Wong Kar-Wai, *2046* is visually stunning. He uses three cinematographers but one style that tries to evoke mood more than meaning. The movie as a whole, unfortunately, never seems sure of itself. It's like a sketchbook. These are images, tones, dialogue, and characters that Wong is sure of, and he practices them, but he does not seem very sure why he is making the movie, or where it should end.

2046 arrived at the last minute at Cannes 2003, after missing its earlier screenings; the final reel reportedly arrived at the airport almost as the first was being shown. It was said to be unfinished, and indeed there were skeletal special effects that now appear in final form, but perhaps it was never really finished in his mind. Perhaps he would have appreciated the luxury that Woody Allen had with *Crimes and Misdemeanors;* he looked at the first cut of the film, threw out the first act, called the actors back, and reshot, focusing on what turned out to be the central story. Watching *2046,* I wonder what it could possibly mean to anyone not familiar with Wong's work and style. Unlike *In the Mood for Love*, it is not a self-contained film, although it's certainly a lovely meander.

U

Uncle Nino ★ ★
PG, 102 m., 2005

Joe Mantegna (Robert Micelli), Anne Archer (Marie Micelli), Pierrino Mascarino (Uncle Nino), Trevor Morgan (Bobby Micelli), Gina Mantegna (Gina Micelli). Directed by Robert Shallcross and produced by David James. Screenplay by Shallcross.

The loudest danger signal for Uncle Nino, after he arrives from Italy to visit his dead brother's family, is that the wine comes from a cardboard box with a spigot. There are other problems. The nephew and his wife are both working too hard, the kids are on the edge of rebellion, and the household has no dog. Obviously, a family in crisis; obviously, Uncle Nino is the solution. He will return them all to their old-world roots, and reawaken their sense of family.

And so he does, in *Uncle Nino*, a family movie that some will find wholesome and heartwarming and others will find cornball and tiresome. You know who you are. I know who I am. This is not my kind of movie, and I found myself feeling mighty restless by the end, or even halfway through, or even near the beginning, but objectively I know there are people who will embrace this movie, and my duty as a critic is to tell them about it.

The film goes into national release with an interesting marketing story behind it. Independently financed and made in Chicago, it was rejected by major distributors and festivals. It opened in one theater in Grand Rapids, Michigan, played fifty-five weeks, grossed $170,000, and has ecstatic user comments on the Internet Movie Database. It also has an IMDb "user rating" of 9.1, which is 0.1 higher than *The Godfather*. This rating is interesting because 79.4 percent of everyone voting for it gave it a perfect "10" rating, and because the breakdown of voters into males, females, age groups, U.S. and non–U.S. reveals that the approval rating in each and every group is uncannily close to 9 (every female under eighteen scored it 10, and the hardest to please were males thirty to thirty-four, at 7.4). Does this suggest to you that someone has been force-feeding the database?

Never mind. Let's regard the movie. It stars Joe Mantegna and Anne Archer as Robert and Marie Micelli, a Glenview, Illinois, couple who have moved into an expensive new home and are working hard to keep up. Their son, Bobby (Trevor Morgan), is a fourteen-year-old who belongs to a band that can't find a place to practice, and their twelve-year-old daughter, Gina (Gina Mantegna), spends a lot of time at her best friend's house because nobody is home at her house. She wants a dog, but Robert doesn't want the mess and bother.

Enter Uncle Nino (Pierrino Mascarino), one of those lovable movie ethnic types who speaks no English except for each and every word he requires in a specific situation. He is making a belated visit to America to visit the grave of his late brother. A quick study, he perceives that the Micelli family needs more quality time, more music, wine in bottles, and a dog. In attempting to remedy these needs, he blunders into various episodes of mistaken intentions, mistaken identities, and mistaken mistakes. He is simultaneously saintly and comic, and filled with a wisdom at which American suburbanites can only shake their heads with envy.

The film ends with the high school battle of the bands. Does Bobby's band get enough rehearsal time to qualify? What role do Uncle Nino and his violin play? Is there a scene in which the busy dad is able to tear himself away from the office in order to sit in the audience and make significant eye contact with his son, indicating that a lifelong bond has been forged, and that he'll be a better father in the future?

As it happens, Joe Mantegna has appeared in a much better movie about an older Italian man with deep innocence in his heart. That would be David Mamet's wonderful *Things Change* (1988), starring Don Ameche as an old shoeshine man who is mistaken as a Mafia don because of his way of looking mysterious and issuing truisms that sound like profundities. *Uncle Nino* made me wish I was seeing that movie again.

I am quite aware, however, that *Uncle Nino* will appeal to those who seek sunny, predictable, positive family entertainment and do not demand that it also be challenging or have any depth. The success in Grand Rapids was because of word-of-mouth, as people told each other about the film, and if it is allowed to find an audience in its national release, that will probably happen again. It's that kind of movie, for better or worse.

Undead ★ ½
R, 100 m., 2005

Felicity Mason (Rene), Mungo McKay (Marion), Rob Jenkins (Wayne), Lisa Cunningham (Sallyanne), Dirk Hunter (Harrison), Emma Randall (Molly), Noel Sheridan (Chip). Directed and produced by Michael Spierig and Peter Spierig. Screenplay by Spierig and Spierig.

Undead is the kind of movie that would be so bad it's good, except it's not bad enough to be good enough. It's, let's see, the sixth zombie movie I've seen in the past few years, after *28 Days Later, Resident Evil,* the remake of *Dawn of the Dead, Shaun of the Dead,* and *George Romero's Land of the Dead.* That is a lot of lurching and screaming and heads blown off.

Undead is the work of two brothers from Australia, Michael Spierig and Peter Spierig, who wrote, directed, edited, and produced it. They are of the kitchen-sink approach to film-making, in which zombies are not enough and we must also have aliens and inexplicable characters who seem to have wandered in from another movie without their name tags. It's comedy, horror, satire, and sci-fi, combined with that endearing Australian quality of finding their own country the nuttiest place on Earth. If the Australian cinema is accurate, once you leave the largest cities, the only people you meet are crazies, eccentrics, neurotics, parched wanderers in the outback, and the occasional disc jockey who is actually a fish.

This tradition continues in *Undead,* which even includes some zombie fish. It takes place in the hamlet of Berkeley, in Queensland, a fishing mecca that has just held a beauty pageant to crown Miss Catch of the Day. This is Rene (Felicity Mason), an adornment to any bait store. Excitement such as the crowning of Miss Catch of the Day is interrupted by a meteor shower; rocks from space rain down upon Berkeley, some of them opening up platter-sized holes in the chests of the citizens, who stagger about with daylight showing through them and have become zombies.

In the obligatory tradition of all zombie movies, a few healthy humans survive and try to fight off the zombies and preserve themselves. Rene is on her way out of town when the attack occurs; she has lost the mortgage on the family farm and is fleeing to the big city, or a larger hamlet, when she runs into a traffic jam. All attacks from outer space, natural or alien, immediately cause massive traffic pileups, of course, and the only functioning cars belong to the heroes.

In *War of the Worlds,* for example, Tom Cruise has the only car that works, after he and a friend peer under the hood and say, "It's the solenoid!" And so it is. This moment took me back to my youth, when cars could still be repaired without computers. They just had gas lines and spark plugs and things like that. I never understood anything about engines, but there were always kids in high school who would look under the hood and solemnly explain, "It's the solenoid." The solenoid, always the solenoid. You could impress girls with a line like that. "It's the solenoid." Works every time.

But I digress. Rene hits a traffic jam on the road out of town and meets a bush pilot named Wayne (Rob Jenkins) and his girlfriend, Sallyanne (Lisa Cunningham), who was runner-up to Miss Catch of the Day, which means, I guess, you throw her back in. Sallyanne is preggers, so she can do what all pregnant women in the movies and few pregnant women in life do, and hold her stomach with both hands most of the time. There is also a cop named Harrison (Dirk Hunter), who if you ask me should be named Dirk and played by Harrison Hunter, as Dirk is a better name than Harrison for a cop whose vocabulary consists of four-letter words and linking words.

They wander off the road and into the company of a local gun nut and survivalist named Marion (Mungo McKay), who if you ask me should be named Mungo and played by Marion McKay, as Mungo is a better name than Marion for a guy who has three shotguns yoked together so he can blast a zombie in two and leave its hips and legs lurching around with its bare spine sticking up in the air. For him, every shot is a trick shot; he'll throw two handguns into the air, kill a couple of zombies with a shotgun, and drop the shotgun in time to catch the handguns on the way down and kill some more.

Marion/Mungo hustles them all into his concrete-and-steel underground safe room, where their problems seem to be over until Marion announces, "There is no food or water." He didn't think of everything. Meanwhile, on the surface, the nature of the attack has changed, and some actual aliens appear. Who they are and what they want is a little unclear; I am not even absolutely certain if they were responsible for the meteorite attack that turned people into zombies, or have arrived shortly afterward by coincidence, making this the busiest day in local history, especially if you include the Miss Catch of the Day pageant.

There is a sense in which movies like *Undead* ask only to be accepted as silly fun, and I understand that sense and sympathize with it. But I don't think the Spierig brothers have adequately defined what they want to accomplish. They go for laughs with dialogue at times when verbal jokes are at right angles to simultaneous visual jokes. They give us gore that is intended as meaningless and funny, and then when the aliens arrive they seem to bring a new agenda. Eventually the story seems to move on beyond the central characters, who wander through new developments as if mutely wondering, hey, didn't this movie used to be about us?

Still, the horror genre continues to be an ideal calling card for young directors trying to launch their careers. Horror is the only non-porno genre where you don't need stars, because the genre is the star. *Undead* will launch the careers of the Spierigs, who are obviously talented and will be heard from again. Next time, with more resources, they won't have to repeat themselves. You see one set of hips and legs walking around with a spine sticking up out of them, you've seen them all.

Underclassman ★
PG-13, 95 m., 2005

Nick Cannon (Tracy Stokes), Roselyn Sanchez (Karen Lopez), Shawn Ashmore (Rob Donovan), Angelo Spizzirri (David Boscoe), Cheech Marin (Captain Delgado), Kelly Hu (Lisa Brooks). Directed by Marcos Siega and produced by Peter Abrams, Robert L. Levy, and Andrew Panay. Screenplay by Brent Goldberg and David Wagner.

Underclassman doesn't even try to be good. It knows that it doesn't have to be. It stars Nick Cannon, who has a popular MTV show, and it's a combo cop movie, romance, thriller, and high school comedy. That makes the TV ads a slam dunk; they'll generate a Pavlovian response in viewers conditioned to react to their sales triggers (smart-ass young cop, basketball, sexy babes, fast cars, mockery of adults).

Cannon plays Tracy Stokes, a bike cop who screws up in the title sequence and is called on the carpet by his captain (Cheech Marin), who keeps a straight face while uttering exhausted clichés ("You've got a long way to go before you're the detective your father was"). He gets a chance to redeem himself by working undercover at an exclusive L.A. prep school where a murder has been committed.

Turns out the murder is connected to a student car-theft ring, which is linked to drugs, which is an indictment of the rich students and their rich parents. It is a melancholy fact that a brilliant movie about high school criminals, Justin Lin's *Better Luck Tomorrow* (2002), got a fraction of the promotional support given to this lame formula film. If the teenagers going to *Underclassman* were to see *Better Luck Tomorrow,* they'd have something to think about and talk about and be interested in. *Underclassman* is a dead zone that will bore them silly while distracting them with the illusion that a lot of stuff is happening.

Why couldn't the movie at least have tried to do something unexpected, like making Tracy a good student? It's on autopilot: It makes him into a phenomenal basketball player (so good that most of his shots are special effects) and has him telling a classmate over dinner, "In my old neighborhood, crabs were not something you eat." Another food joke: A popular white student (Shawn Ashmore) mentions Benedict Arnold. "He makes good eggs," Tracy says. If he knows about eggs Benedict, he knows about crab cakes. But never mind. He also gets involved in a linguistic discussion of the difference between "up their asses" and "on their asses."

The movie is multi-ethnic, but guess which ethnic group supplies the stooges, villains, and fall guys. There's a cute Asian cop (Kelly Hu) who helps Tracy a lot, and a sexy Latino teacher (Roselyn Sanchez) he wants to date (he's dying to tell her he's not really a student). And the plot asks us to believe that behind the murder is a conspiracy involving the local white establishment. Uh-huh. The white establishment in a rich Los Angeles neighborhood has ways to make (or steal) lots more money in business, without having to get involved in street crime.

Did anyone at any time during the talks leading up to this film say, "Gee, guys, doesn't it seem like we've seen this a million times before?" Did anyone think to create an African-American character who was an individual and not a wiseass stand-up with street smarts? Was there ever an impulse to nudge the movie in the direction of originality and ambition? Or was everybody simply dazed by the fact that they were making a film and were, therefore, presumably filmmakers?

Underclassman will probably open well, make its money, drop off quickly, go to video in a few months, and be forgotten. The sad thing is that Cannon, who is only twenty-five, showed real promise in *Drumline*. If he thinks *Underclassman* represents the direction his career should be taking, he needs to find himself a mentor.

Undertow ★ ★ ★ ★
R, 107 m., 2004

Jamie Bell (Chris Munn), Devon Alan (Tim Munn), Josh Lucas (Deel Munn), Dermot Mulroney (John Munn), Kristen Stewart (Lila), Shiri Appleby (Violet). Directed by David Gordon Green and produced by Terrence Malick, Lisa Muskat, and Edward R. Pressman. Screenplay by Joe Conway and Green.

The two boys live in a rural area of Georgia with their father. The older, Chris, is quietly building a reputation as a troublemaker; the younger, Tim, is an odd kid who eats mud and paint and explains he is "organizing my books by the way they smell." Their father, John, mourns his dead wife and keeps his boys so isolated that on his birthday Chris complains, "We can't even have friends. What kind of a birthday party is it with just the three of us?"

A fourth arrives. This is Deel, John's brother, fresh out of prison and harboring resentment. "I knew your mom first—she was my girl," he tells Chris. Deel and John's father had a hoard of Mexican gold coins with a legend attached to them: They belonged to the ferryman on the river Styx. Deel believes he should have inher-

ited half of the coins, and believes John has them hidden somewhere around the place.

If this sounds as much like a Brothers Grimm tale as a plot, that is the intention of David Gordon Green, the gifted director of *Undertow*. Still only twenty-nine, he has made three films of considerable power, and has achieved what few directors ever do: After watching one of his films for a scene or two, you know who directed it. His style has been categorized as "southern Gothic," but that's too narrow. I sense a poetic merging of realism and surrealism; every detail is founded on fact and accurate observation, but the effect appeals to our instinct for the mythological. This fusion is apparent when his characters say something that (a) sounds exactly as if it's the sort of thing they would say, but (b) is like nothing anyone has ever said before. I'm thinking of lines like, "He thinks about infinity. The doctor says his brain's not ready for it." Or, "Can I carve my name in your face?"

Undertow, like Green's *George Washington* (2001) and *All the Real Girls* (2003), takes place in a South where the countryside coexists with a decaying industrial landscape. We see not the thriving parts of cities, but the desolate places they have forgotten. His central characters are usually adolescents, vibrating with sexual feelings but unsure how to express them, and with a core of decency they are not much aware of.

In writing *Undertow*, Green said at the Toronto Film Festival, he had in mind stories by the Grimms, Mark Twain, and Robert Louis Stevenson, and also Capote's *In Cold Blood*. He wears these sources lightly. While much is made about the family legends surrounding the gold coins, they inspire not superstition but greed and function in the story just as any treasure would. Although we see two generations in which there is a troubled brother and a strange brother, the parallels are not underlined.

Instead, we see largely through the eyes of Chris (Jamie Bell, from *Billy Elliot* and *Nicholas Nickleby*). He figures in the startling opening sequence, where he tries to get the attention of a girl he likes, is chased away, and lands on a board with a nail in it. The audience recoils in shock. But now watch how he *continues* to hobble along with the board still attached to his foot. This is technically funny, but in a very painful way, and who but Green would think of the moment when an arresting cop gives Chris his board back?

Chris is in rebellion against the isolated life created for them by their father (Dermot Mulroney). So is Tim (Devon Alan), but in an internal way, expressed by the peculiar things he eats and the chronic stomach pain that results. When their Uncle Deel (Josh Lucas) appears one day, he is at first a welcome change, with his laid-back permissiveness. John asks Deel to watch the kids during the day while he's at work, but Deel is not very good at this, and points his nephews toward more trouble than he saves them from.

The bad feeling over the gold coins comes to a head in an instant of violence, and the boys run away from home, entering a world that evokes *The Night of the Hunter* (1955). In both films, two siblings flee from a violent man through a haunted and dreamy southern landscape. The people they meet during their flight all look and sound real enough, but also have the qualities of strangers encountered in fantasies: the kindly black couple who lets them work for food, and the secret community of other kids, living in a junkyard. If these passages add up to a chase scene, Green directs not for thrills but for deeper, more ominous feelings, and the music by Philip Glass doesn't heighten, as it would during a conventional chase scene, but deepens, as if the chase is descending into ominous dreads.

Green has a visual style that is beautiful without being pretty. We never catch him photographing anything for its scenic or decorative effect. Instead, his landscapes have the kind of underlined ambiguity you'd find in the work of a serious painter; these are not trees and swamps and rivers, but Trees and Swamps and Rivers—it's here that the parallel with *The Night of the Hunter* is most visible.

Undertow is the closest Green has come to a conventional narrative, although at times you can sense him pulling away from narrative requirements to stay a little longer in a moment that fascinates him. He is not a director of plots so much as a director of tones, emotions, and moments of truth, and there's a sense of gathering fate even in the lighter scenes. His films remind me of *Days of Heaven*, by Terrence Malick (one of this film's producers), in the way they are told as memories, as if all of this happened and is over with and cannot be changed; you watch a Green film not to see what will happen, but to see what did happen.

Films like *Undertow* leave some audiences unsettled because they do not proceed predictably according to the rules. But they are immediately available to our emotions, and we fall into a kind of waking trance, as if being told a story at an age when we half-believed everything we heard. It takes us a while to get back to our baseline; Green takes us to that place where we keep feelings that we treasure, but are a little afraid of.

An Unfinished Life ★ ★ ★
PG-13, 107 m., 2005

Robert Redford (Einar Gilkyson), Morgan Freeman (Mitch Bradley), Jennifer Lopez (Jean Gilkyson), Becca Gardner (Griff Gilkyson), Josh Lucas (Crane Curtis), Damian Lewis (Gary Watson), Camryn Manheim (Nina), Bart (The Bear). Directed by Lasse Hallstrom and produced by Leslie Holleran, Alan Ladd Jr, and Kelliann Ladd. Screenplay by Mark Spragg and Virginia Korus Spragg.

The typical review of *An Unfinished Life* will mention that it was kept on the shelf at Miramax for two years and was released in 2005 as part of the farewell flood of leftover product produced by the Weinstein brothers. It will say that Robert Redford and Morgan Freeman are trying to be Clint Eastwood and Morgan Freeman. It will have no respect for Jennifer Lopez, because she is going through a period right now when nobody is satisfied with anything she does. These reviews will be more about showbiz than about the movie itself.

Sometimes you are either open to a movie, or closed. If you're convinced that *An Unfinished Life* is damaged goods, how can it begin its work on you? If you think Freeman is channeling the relationship he had with Eastwood in *Million Dollar Baby,* reflect that this movie was made a year earlier. And give Lopez your permission to be good again; she is the same actress now as when we thought her so new and fine.

The story takes place on a rundown ranch outside Ishawooa, Wyoming. It has seen better days. So has its owner, Einar Gilkyson (Redford), and his longtime ranch hand Mitch (Freeman), who lives in the little house behind

731

the bigger one. Mitch was mauled a year ago by a bear and is an invalid, given a daily needle of morphine by Einar. These men are essentially awaiting death together when they get visitors: Jean (Lopez) is the widow of Einar's son, who was killed in a car crash a dozen years ago. Griff (Becca Gardner) is Einar's granddaughter.

Einar thinks he hates Jean. He blames her for his son's death. She doesn't want to be at the ranch, but she has no choice; her latest boyfriend, Gary (Damian Lewis), beats her, and she has fled from him. It is a foregone conclusion, I suppose, that Einar will eventually unbend enough to love Griff, who after all is his son's child, and true also that Mitch is the ranch's reservoir of decency. The local sheriff (Josh Lucas) is not indifferent to the arrival in a small town of a good-looking woman.

It's not often noted, but Redford plays anger well. His face gets tight and he looks away. Freeman never seems to be playing anything; he sees what he sees. The four characters seem to be stuck, and then they're budged by the arrival of two predators: The bear comes back, and so does Gary, the boyfriend. The bear (played by Bart, who had the title role in *The Bear*) is more likable, because after all he behaves according to his nature. But he is captured and sold off to a shabby local zoo so that yokels can stare at him through the steel mesh of a cage.

Gary, on the other hand, is a psychopath whose gearbox includes a setting for charm. We can almost see what Jean almost saw in him. Now he lurks around town, intimidated even by the two old men on the ranch, one of them an invalid, because wife-beaters by their nature are cowards. Sooner or later the matter of Gary will have to be settled. Less clear is the fate of the bear.

The unfinished life in the title at first seems to refer to Einar's dead son. Then we realize the death has put Einar, Jean, Mitch, and Griff all on hold. Until they deal with it, they can't get on with things. How they deal with it is not original, but it is sincere, and the actors are convincing. I was not quite as ready for the solution involving the bear, not after seeing *Grizzly Man* and remembering Werner Herzog's scary narration: The "blank stare" of a bear, he says, reveals not wisdom but "only the half-bored interest in food." While it is reasonable for bears to want to be free, it may not be reasonable for humans to want to live close to free bears.

An Unfinished Life was directed by Lasse Hallstrom, who has made a better movie about a dysfunctional family *(What's Eating Gilbert Grape)* and a worse one *(The Cider House Rules)*. This one, based on an original screenplay by Mark Spragg and Virginia Korus Spragg, is modest and heartfelt, dealing directly with straightforward material. We don't expect any twists, and there aren't any, but as Jean tries to put her life back together, her healing makes it possible for the others to get on with things. That is enough.

United 93 ★ ★ ★ ★
R, 90 m., 2006

JJ Johnson (Captain Jason Dahl), Ben Sliney (Himself), Gregg Henry (Colonel Robert Marr), Christian Clemenson (Thomas Burnett), Becky London (Jean Headley Peterson), David Alan Basche (Todd Beamer), Trish Gates (Sandy Bradshaw), Cheyenne Jackson (Mark Bingham), Lewis Alsamari (Saeed Al Ghamdi), Chip Zien (Mark Rothenberg). Directed by Paul Greengrass and produced by Tim Bevan, Eric Fellner, and Lloyd Levin. Screenplay by Greengrass.

It is not too soon for *United 93*, because it is not a film that knows any time has passed since 9/11. The entire story, every detail, is told in the present tense. We know what they know when they know it, and nothing else. Nothing about al-Qaida, nothing about Osama bin Laden, nothing about Afghanistan or Iraq, only events as they unfold. This is a masterful and heartbreaking film, and it does honor to the memory of the victims.

The director, Paul Greengrass, makes a deliberate effort to stay away from recognizable actors, and there is no attempt to portray the passengers or terrorists as people with histories. In most movies about doomed voyages, we meet a few key characters we'll be following: the newlyweds, the granny, the businessman, the man with a secret. Here there's none of that. What we know about the passengers on United 93 is exactly what we would know if we had been on the plane and sitting across from them: nothing, except for a few details of personal appearance.

Scenes on board the plane alternate with scenes inside the National Air Traffic Control

Center, airport towers, regional air traffic stations, and a military command room. Here, too, there are no backstories, just technicians living in the moment. Many of them are played by the actual people involved; we sense that in their command of procedure and jargon. When the controllers in the LaGuardia tower see the second airplane crash into the World Trade Center, they recoil with shock and horror, and that moment in the film seems as real as it seemed to me on September 11, 2001.

The film begins on a black screen, and we hear one of the hijackers reading aloud from the Quran. There are scenes of the hijackers at prayer, and many occasions when they evoke God and dedicate themselves to him. These details may offend some viewers but are almost certainly accurate; the hijacking and destruction of the four planes was carried out as a divine mission. That the majority of Muslims disapprove of terrorism goes without saying; on 9/12, there was a candlelight vigil in Iran for the United States. That the terrorists found justification in religion also goes without saying. Most nations at most times go into battle evoking the protection of their gods.

But the film doesn't depict the terrorists as villains. It has no need to. Like everyone else in the movie, they are people of ordinary appearance, going about their business. *United 93* is incomparably more powerful because it depicts all of its characters as people trapped in an inexorable progress toward tragedy. The movie contains no politics. No theory. No personal chitchat. No patriotic speeches. We never see the big picture.

We watch United 93 as the passengers and crew board the plane and it prepares to depart. Four minutes later, the first plane went into the WTC. Living in the moment, we share the confusion of the air traffic controllers. At first it's reported that a "small plane" crashed into the tower. Then by a process of deduction, it's determined it must have been a missing American flight. The full scope of the plot only gradually becomes clear. One plane after another abandons its flight plan and goes silent. There are false alarms: For more than an hour, a Delta flight is thought to have been hijacked, although it was not. At the FAA national center, the man in charge, Ben Sliney (playing himself), begins to piece things together and orders

a complete shutdown of all American air traffic. Given what a momentous decision this was, costing the airlines a fortune and disrupting a nation's travel plans, we are grateful he had the nerve to make it.

As the outline of events comes into focus, there is an attempt to coordinate civilian and military authorities. It is doomed to fail. A liaison post is not staffed. Two jet fighters are sent up to intercept a hijacked plane, but they are not armed; there is discussion of having the fighters ram the jets as their pilots eject. A few other fighters are scrambled but inexplicably fly east, over the ocean. Military commanders try again and again, with increasing urgency, to get presidential authorization to use force against civilian aircraft. An unbearable period of time passes, with no response.

The movie simply includes this in the flow of events, without comment. Many people seeing the film will remember the scene in *Fahrenheit 9/11* in which George W. Bush sat immobile in a children's classroom for seven minutes after being informed of the attack on the WTC. What was he waiting for? Was he ever informed of the military request? The movie does not know, because the people on the screen do not have the opportunity of hindsight.

All of these larger matters are far off-screen. The third act of the film focuses on the desperation on board United 93, after the hijackers take control, slash flight attendants, kill the pilots, and seem to have a bomb. We are familiar with details of this flight, pieced together from many telephone calls from the plane and from the cockpit voice recorder. Greengrass is determined to be as accurate as possible. There is no false grandstanding, no phony arguments among the passengers, no individual heroes. The passengers are a terrified planeload of strangers. After they learn by phone about the WTC attacks, after an attendant says she saw the dead bodies of the two pilots, they decide they must take action. They storm the cockpit.

Even as these brave passengers charge up the aisle, we know nothing in particular about them—none of the details we later learned. We could be on the plane, terrified, watching them. The famous words "Let's roll" are heard but not underlined; these people are not speaking for history.

There has been much discussion of the

movie's trailer, and no wonder. It pieces together moments from *United 93* to make it seem more conventional, more like a thriller. Dialogue that seems absolutely realistic in context sounds, in the trailer, like sound bites and punch lines. To watch the trailer is to sense the movie that Greengrass did not make. To watch *United 93* is to be confronted with the grim, chaotic reality of that autumn day in 2001.

The movie is deeply disturbing, and some people may have to leave the theater. But it would have been much more disturbing if Greengrass had made it in a conventional way. He does not exploit, he draws no conclusions, he points no fingers, he avoids "human interest" and "personal dramas" and just simply watches. The movie's point of view reminds me of the angels in *Wings of Desire*. They see what people do and they are saddened, but they cannot intervene.

The United States of Leland ★ ★
R, 108 m., 2004

Don Cheadle (Pearl Madison), Ryan Gosling (Leland P. Fitzgerald), Chris Klein (Allen Harris), Jena Malone (Becky Pollard), Lena Olin (Marybeth Fitzgerald), Kevin Spacey (Albert T. Fitzgerald), Martin Donovan (Harry Pollard), Ann Magnuson (Karen Pollard), Michelle Williams (Julie Pollard), Kerry Washington (Ayesha). Directed by Matthew Ryan Hoge and produced by Bernie Morris, Jonah Smith, Kevin Spacey, and Palmer West. Screenplay by Hoge.

Early in *The United States of Leland*, a teenager named Leland stabs an autistic boy twenty times, is arrested for the murder, and explains why he committed it: "Because of the sadness." The movie will cycle through many characters and much fraught dialogue to explain this statement, but it never seems sure what it thinks about Leland's action. I believe it is as cruel and senseless as the killings in *Elephant*, but while that film was chillingly objective, this one seems to be on everybody's side. It's a moral muddle.

Leland P. Fitzgerald (Ryan Gosling) is the alienated child of a distant mother (Lena Olin) and an absent father who is a famous novelist (Kevin Spacey). Much is made of his father's decision to send his son on a trip every year—to

Paris, to Venice—but not to meet him there. Leland has recently broken up with Becky (Jena Malone), the drug-addicted sister of the murdered boy, but that doesn't seem to be the reason for his action.

We meet the victim's other sister, Julie (Michelle Williams), and her boyfriend, Allen (Chris Klein). They're also in a rocky time in their romance, but we can't be sure that's what prompts Allen to the action he takes in the film. The dead boy's parents are Harry and Karen Pollard (Martin Donovan and Ann Magnuson), and while they are bereft, they express themselves in ways borrowed from docudramas.

There are two perfectly crafted performances in the movie, by Spacey as Albert Fitzgerald, the novelist who flies in from Europe, and by Don Cheadle as Pearl Madison, a high school teacher in the juvenile detention facility where Leland is held. Pearl, who perhaps sees a book in the murder, encourages Leland to open up about his feelings, and much of the movie is narrated by Leland from writings in his journal.

Some of the scenes in the movie, written and directed by Matthew Ryan Hoge, are so perfectly conceived that they show up the rest. When the novelist and the teacher meet in a hotel bar, it's an opportunity for Spacey to exercise his gift for understated irony ("There are no private spaces in my son's heart reserved for me"), and for Cheadle to show a man conflicted between his real concern for Leland and his personal awe at meeting the great writer. Ryan Gosling, a gifted actor, does everything that can be done with Leland, but the character comes from a writer's conceits, not from life.

The movie circles through characters and subplots on its way to its final revelations, and some of the subplots are blatantly unnecessary. Why, for example, must Cheadle's character have an affair with a coworker (Kerry Washington) and then try to explain it to his apparently estranged girlfriend? What does this have to do with anything? Why, really, does Spacey's character fly in if he is only going to sit in a hotel bar and exude literate bitterness? Perhaps to show that his emotional distance from his son helped lead to the murder? But no, because Leland's problem is not alienation, but an excess of empathy.

Lost in all of this is the fate of the murdered boy. The character and his autism are used as plot points, and there is little concern about his fate except as it helps set the story into motion and provide the inspiration for Leland's action. Subplots involving his sisters, their problems, their romances, and their boyfriends are made more confusing because the movie makes it difficult for us to be sure who they are; for a long time we're not sure they're sisters. That's not subtle writing, but needless confusion.

The reason for Leland's action, when we understand it, has a clarity and simplicity that would be at home in a short story. The problem is that the movie follows such a tortured path in arriving at it that, at the end, his motive is not so much a moment of insight as a plot point. And there is another murder in the movie that had me leaving the theater completely uncertain about how I was intended to feel about it. Is it that the first murder, however tragically mistaken, was at least committed with loftier motives than the second? Or what?

Unknown White Male ★ ★ ★ ½
PG-13, 88 m., 2006

A documentary directed by Rupert Murray and produced by Beadie Finzi. Featuring Doug Bruce.

Amnesia has a dread fascination because it leaves its victims alive to experience the loss of self. Parents, lovers, photographs, and old letters testify to the existence of a person who lived in the body whose inhabitant now regards them without recognition.

In *Unknown White Male*, that person is named Doug Bruce, or so he is told. He was raised in Britain, immigrated to America, made money in the market, dropped out to study photography, had a girlfriend from Poland named Magda, and has a London pal named Rupert who is now making a documentary about him. All of this he is told, and it goes into his new collection of memories. Everything that happened to him before July 3, 2003, is gone. He is a victim of retrograde amnesia—rare, and total.

Because this documentary may be the inspiration for a fiction film, pause here for a story possibility. What if you awake from amnesia, and those around you, informing you of your earlier life, introducing themselves as parents, lovers, and friends, are lying to you? What if the person you have forgotten was someone other than the person they say you were? Would it make a difference? Does it matter? If a murderer experiences amnesia, would it be ethical to execute the body that formerly harbored his memories?

Such speculations are inspired by this intriguing and disturbing film. Questions have been raised about its truthfulness; is it a fraud? I have interviewed the filmmakers and am convinced of its truthfulness, but what difference does it make? As we watch the film, Bruce exists for us only in the sense that the film transfers him into our memories. Is that person any more or less real to us if the film is truthful or fraudulent?

Rupert Murray, who directed the film, has been asked why it does not contain more "proof" that it is truthful. He says it never occurred to him that anyone would doubt it, and he was more interested in the unfolding of Doug Bruce's new life. Maybe he took the correct path after all, bypassing proof to focus on the question he begins with: "How much is our identity determined by the experiences we have? And how much is already there? Pure us?"

These questions coil around the affable face of Bruce, who found himself on that July morning on a subway train in Coney Island with no idea of who he was or how he got there. A telephone number in his backpack provided a connection to a woman he had been dating, and she collected him from a hospital. There is footage taken less than a week later, as he talks about his complete loss of memory.

Murray hears what has happened to his old friend and starts making this film. Bruce is introduced to Magda, his former girlfriend. They lived together for eight years. She flies back from Poland and moves in (or does she, technically, move in with a person she has never known, and who never knew her?). Bruce travels to London and Spain, and meets his parents and old friends. He does not remember them. They say he is calmer, even nicer, than the old Doug. "Given a new lease on life," Murray tells us in his narration, "Doug seemed to be more

735

articulate than before, more serious, more focused, as if his senses had been sharpened by a rebooting of the system."

Gradually Bruce begins to collect a fresh set of memories. He continues his photography lessons, and his teacher says that "his work has gained enormous depth." He finds Narelle, a new girlfriend. "The longer that it goes on," he says about his current life, "the less I care if my memory comes back." Yes, because if it did, would it invalidate what he now considers to be his identity? Would there be two persons inside his memory, one nicer and more focused, the other burdened with the imperfections of his previous operating system?

The thing about a movie like *Unknown White Male* is that it starts you thinking in the most unsettling ways. Murray, who claims to have met Bruce in London when they were eighteen or nineteen, has been questioned because he knows so little about Doug. If his friend was a stockbroker, what brokerage did he work for? Murray has no idea. "Quite frankly," he told me when I raised this question, "I make films and went to art school. I didn't know or care what firm he worked for. I'd call him up in New York and we'd go out for a drink." Is this plausible? Of course it is. I have friends in London of whom I could say the same thing.

How much of what we know about each other is simply a shared set of words? How much of what we know about ourselves is hearsay? When our parents tell us about our second birthday party, we no more remember that party than Bruce remembers his thirtieth. Yet the party goes into our database. How much is "pure us"? What Doug Bruce seems to have lost is not only his memory but even the "pure us" part—he has a different personality now. Here's an irony: He found that he could still write his signature. But neither he nor anyone else could read it.

Unknown White Male is maddening at times because Murray doesn't ask questions we'd like to shout at the screen: "Magda, if it's not too personal ... is Doug the same in bed?" "Doctor, is there a way to tell for sure if someone is faking amnesia?" "Doug, do you resent these strangers who make emotional demands because they claim they were your parents?" "Mrs. Bruce, if your son cannot remember

you, does it still hurt your feelings if he doesn't call and visit?"

This is not the review I thought I would write. I thought I would describe what is in the film, what happens and is said. But if he meets one set of people who say they were his London friends and not another, what difference does it make? We've never seen them before and neither has he. The real subject of the film is Douglas Bruce sitting on two years of memories and told there is a 95 percent chance that another thirty years may return to him. A lot of people don't want to know when they're going to die. Maybe they wouldn't want to be reborn either.

Unleashed ★ ★ ★
R, 103 m., 2005

Jet Li (Danny), Morgan Freeman (Sam), Bob Hoskins (Bart), Kerry Condon (Victoria). Directed by Louis Leterrier and produced by Luc Besson, Steven Chaseman, and Jet Li. Screenplay by Besson.

The story is familiar. The dog has been raised from infancy as a killer, obedient to its master. When it wears its collar it is passive. When the collar is removed and an order is given, it turns into a savage murder machine. Then a confusing thing happens. The dog experiences kindness for the first time in its life. Does this mean its master is wrong and must be disobeyed?

Luc Besson has produced or written some of the most intriguing movies of the last twenty years (*La Femme Nikita, The Fifth Element, Kiss of the Dragon, Ong-Bak*). He takes this classic animal story and makes a simple but inspired change: He turns the dog into a human being. Jet Li stars in *Unleashed* as Danny, a lethal martial arts warrior who has been raised in captivity since childhood and is used by Bart, a Glasgow gangster, as a fearsome weapon. Danny lives in a cage under the floor of Bart's headquarters, travels quietly in the gangster's car, and, when his collar is removed, explodes into violent fury and leaves rooms filled with his victims.

This is a story that could have made a laughable movie. That it works is because of the performances of Jet Li and Bob Hoskins, who plays his master. "Danny the dog" is fearful of his owner, passive in captivity, and obedient in action, because he has been trained that way for his whole life. Bart the gangster is another one of those feral characters Hoskins specializes in, a man who bares his teeth and seems prepared to dine on the throats of his enemies. Hoskins, who can be the most genial of men, has a dimension of pitiless cruelty that he revealed in his first starring role, *The Long Good Friday* (1980).

But *Unleashed* would be too simple if it were only about Bart and Danny. Besson's screenplay now adds the character of Sam, a blind piano tuner played by Morgan Freeman. Sam lives in a gentle world of musicians and pianos and his beloved stepdaughter, Victoria (Kerry Condon). Danny falls into their lives by accident, after running away from Bart, as a dog is likely to do when it becomes fed up with its master.

In Danny's early memories, a piano figures somehow. A drawing of a piano triggers some of those old shadows, and when he hears piano music with Sam and Victoria, and when they give him his first simple music lessons, a great cloud lifts from his mind and he knows joy for the first time. He also begins to recall his mother, who was a pianist, and remembers fragments of the events that led to him becoming Danny the dog.

The film is ingenious in its construction. It has all the martial arts action any Jet Li fan could possibly desire, choreographed by Yeun Woo-ping, who is the Gerald Arpino of kung fu and creates improbable but delightful ballets of chops and socks, leaps and twists, and kicks and improvisations. Everything happens in a denatured sepia tone that is not black and white nor quite color, but a palate drained of cheer and pressing down like a foggy day.

Because Hoskins is so good at focusing the ferocity of Bart, he distracts us from the impossible elements in the trained-killer plot. Because Morgan Freeman brings an unforced plausibility to every character he plays, we simply accept the piano tuner instead of noticing how implausibly he enters the story. Freeman handles the role in the only way that will work, by playing a piano tuner as a piano tuner, instead of as a plot device in a martial arts movie. His stepdaughter, Victoria, is invaluable because, as Ann Coulter was ex-

plaining when she was so rudely shouted down the other day, women are a civilizing influence on men, who will get up to mischief in each other's company; Victoria's gentleness stirs Danny's humanity more than it inflames his lust.

So many action movies are made on autopilot that I am grateful when one works outside the box. Luc Besson, as producer and writer, almost always brings an unexpected human element to his action stories. *Unleashed* ends with a confrontation between Bart and Danny in which Bart reveals the truly twisted depth of his attachment to the "dog." They say dogs and their owners eventually start to resemble each other, but in this case an actual transference seems to be going on.

The Untold Story of Emmett Louis Till ★ ★ ★

NO MPAA RATING, 70 m., 2005

A documentary directed and produced by Keith Beauchamp. Screenplay by Beauchamp.

There is no statute of limitations on murder. Fifty years after the death of Emmett Till, the U.S. Justice Department reopened the case of the fourteen-year-old black boy from Chicago who went to visit his grandfather in Mississippi and was kidnapped, tortured, and killed because he whistled at a white woman.

The case electrified the nation in 1955, not least because Emmett's indomitable mother, Mamie, enlisted Chicago officials in her fight to gain possession of the boy's body, which authorities in Money, Mississippi, wanted to bury as quickly and quietly as possible. In a heartbreaking sequence in *The Untold Story of Emmett Louis Till*, she recalls saying: "I told the funeral director, 'If you can't open the box, I can. I want to see what's in that box.'"

What she found was the already decomposing body of her son, which had spent three days in a bayou of the Tallahatchie River, a heavy cotton gin fan tied to his neck with barbed wire. The mother is deliberate as she describes what she saw. She always thought her son's teeth were "the prettiest thing I ever saw." All but two were knocked out. One eyeball was hanging on his chin. An ear was missing. She saw daylight through the bullet hole in his head. His skull had been chopped almost in two, the face separated from the back of the head.

What Mamie Till did then made history. She insisted that the casket remain open at the Chicago funeral. Thousands filed past the remains. A photograph in Jet magazine made such an impression that, fifty years later, *60 Minutes* reporter Ed Bradley remembers seeing it; he discusses it on his program with Keith Beauchamp, director of this film, a much younger man who saw the photo and became obsessed with the case.

It was Beauchamp's nine years of investigation, summarized in the film, that was primarily responsible for Justice reopening the case. In the original trial, two white men, Roy Bryant and J. W. Milam, were charged with the crime. An all-white jury took only an hour to acquit them, later explaining they would have returned sooner, but took a "soda pop break" to make it look better. Only two months later, immune because of laws against double jeopardy, the two men sold their story to *Look* magazine for $4,000 and confessed to the crime.

Both are now dead. But Beauchamp's investigation indicates fourteen people were involved in one way or another in the murder, including five black employees of the white men, as well as the woman Till whistled at. Five of them are still alive.

The film inevitably invites comparison with *4 Little Girls* (1997), Spike Lee's powerful documentary about the 1963 Birmingham church bombing, which includes the long-delayed conviction of Robert ("Dynamite Bob") Chambliss, one of the bombers. Lee is the better filmmaker, with better source materials to work with, and his film is more passionate.

Beauchamp's film, on the other hand, has an earnest solemnity that is appropriate to the material. He has a lot of old black-and-white TV and newsreel footage, including shots of the accused men before, during, and after their trial. He interviews Emmett's young cousins who were in the house on the night the white men took him away. He recounts the courage of Emmett's uncle, who in the courtroom fearlessly pointed out the men who had taken Emmett, when such an act was a death sentence in Mississippi.

It is startling, the way the local sheriff casually tells TV reporters, "We didn't have any problems until our niggers went up north and talked to the NAACP and came back down here and caused trouble." And the way reporter Dan Wakefield recalls, "Everybody in the town knew they did it," even before they confessed in *Look* magazine. The defense attorneys informed the jury their forefathers would "roll over in their graves" if they voted to convict. But the case would not go away, and has not gone away. Mamie Till died in January 2003, just a little too soon to learn that the case was reopened.

Up and Down ★ ★ ★
R, 108 m., 2005

Petr Forman (Martin Horecky), Emilia Vasaryova (Vera), Jiri Machacek (Frantisek Fikes), Natasa Burger (Miluska), Jan Triska (Otakar), Ingrid Timkova (Hana), Kristyna Liska-Bokova (Lenka), Jaroslav Dusek (Colonel). Directed by Jan Hrebejk and produced by Milan Kuchynka and Ondrej Trojan. Screenplay by Hrebejk and Petr Jarchovsky.

In the middle of the night on a back road of the Czech Republic, two truck drivers unload a group of illegal immigrants from India. Then they drive away, unaware that they still have a passenger—a baby, left behind in the confusion. Should they try to return the infant to its mother? No, because they don't know how to find her without risking arrest. Should they dump the baby by the roadside? One thinks that would be a good idea, but the other doesn't, and they end up selling the baby to the owners of a shady pawnshop.

This opening sets up one of the story lines in *Up and Down*, a Czech film about working-class and middle-class characters, former and present wives, infant and grown children, current and retired soccer fans, professors and hooligans, criminals and the police. Director Jan Hrebejk and his cowriter, Petr Jarchovsky, are interested not so much in making a statement about their society as seeing it reflected in specific lives; in this, their film resembles the early work of the Czech director Milos Forman (*The Fireman's Ball*), whose son Petr plays one of the film's leads.

The first couple we meet after the pawnshop are the Fikeses, Miluska and Frantisek (Natasa Burger and Jiri Machacek). They're not very bright, but not bad people. He's a night watch-man, sensitive about his cleft palate, grateful to his wife for having dinner with him even though "I eat ugly." He's a member of a soccer team's fanatic group of supporters, who meet to watch the games on TV, get drunk, sing, chant slogans, and go through the emotional yo-yo of victory and defeat.

Miluska desperately wants a baby. She can't conceive. They can't adopt because Frantisek has a police record (he blames the soccer club for leading him into hooliganism). After almost stealing a baby in its carriage, she's afraid: "I'll do something and they'll arrest me." The baby at the pawn shop is a godsend. They buy it, bring it home, and love it. When Frantisek's booster club buddy makes racist remarks about the baby's dark skin, Frantisek boots him out, resigns from the club, and joins his wife in loving the baby.

Then we meet another family, the Horeckas. Martin (Petr Forman) has spent the last twenty years in Australia—a useful explanation for his English-accented Czech, no doubt. He returns home to visit his father, Otakar (Jan Triska), and mother, Vera (Emilia Vasaryova), who have divorced. He is also confronted with the fact that his former girlfriend, Hana (Ingrid Timkova), is now living with his father, and they have an eighteen-year-old daughter, Lenka (Kristana Bokova). No doubt the ro-mance between Otakar and Hana was one of the reasons Martin left for Australia.

Czech movies seem to have some of their finest moments around the dining table, and a Horecky family dinner is funny, sad, and har-rowing all at once. So is the uncertain relation-ship between Martin and his half-sister, Lenka. We learn that Vera is an alcoholic with the kinds of resentments, including racist ones, that drunks often use to deflect anger and at-tention away from themselves.

These two stories do not so much interact as reflect on each other with notions about fami-lies, parents, children, and class. For me, the most affecting character was Franta, the watchman, who is tattooed, muscular, and fe-rocious, yet so gentle with his wife and baby. He has been under the thumb of the "Colonel" (Jaroslav Dusek), a leader of the booster club, but for a brief moment breaks free into happi-ness and a content family life. The story of his history with the club is the story of the ups and downs of his life, and his final scene in the movie is heartbreaking in the way it shows the club becoming a substitute family.

There is, of course, the question of the baby's real parents. Can they go to the police without revealing their status as illegal immigrants? An-other of the movie's ups and downs is about the way we're simultaneously required to sympa-thize with the baby's birth mother while wit-nessing how the baby transforms the marriage of Miluska and Frantisek.

Jan Hrebejk was also the director of *Divided We Fall* (2000), a film about a couple in Prague whose Jewish employers are victims of the Nazis. When the son of the employers appears at their door, they give him shelter in a hidden space within their house. Meanwhile, a local Nazi makes it clear he is attracted to the wife of the couple providing the shelter. He also be-gins to suspect their secret. What should hap-pen next? Should the wife have sex with the Nazi to protect the man they are hiding?

Such moral puzzles are at the heart of Hre-bejk's work, and he has no easy answers. *Up and Down* also lacks any formulas or solutions, and is content to show us its complicated charac-ters, their tangled lives, and the way that our need to love and be loved can lead us in oppo-site directions.

The Upside of Anger ★ ★ ★ ★
R, 118 m., 2005

Joan Allen (Terry Wolfmeyer), Kevin Costner (Denny Davies), Erika Christensen, Andy Wolfmeyer), Evan Rachel Wood ("Popeye" Wolfmeyer), Keri Russell (Emily Wolfmeyer), Alicia Witt (Hadley Wolfmeyer), Mike Binder ("Shep" Goodman). Directed by Mike Binder and produced by Jack Binder, Alex Gartner, and Sammy Lee. Screenplay by Binder.

Joan Allen and Kevin Costner achieve some-thing in *The Upside of Anger* that may have been harder than costarring in *Macbeth*. They create two imperfect, alcoholic, resentful ordi-nary people, neighbors in the suburbs, with enough money to support themselves in the discontent to which they have become accus-tomed. I liked these characters precisely be-cause they were not designed to be likable—or, more precisely, because they were likable in spite of being exasperating, unorganized, self-destructive, and impervious to good advice. That would be true of most of my friends. They say the same about me.

Allen plays Terry Wolfmeyer, suburban wife and mother of four daughters ("One of them hates me and the other three are working on it"). Her husband has walked out of the marriage, and all signs point to his having fled the country to begin a new life in Sweden with his secretary. "He's a vile, selfish pig," Terry says, "but I'm not gonna trash him to you girls." The girls, of college and high school age, dress expensively, are well groomed, prepare the family meals, and run the household, while their mother emcees with a vodka and tonic; her material is smart and bitter, although she sees the humor in the situation, and in herself.

Costner plays her neighbor, Denny Davies, once a star pitcher for the Detroit Tigers, now a sports-talk host who is bored by sports and talk. He spends his leisure time at the lonely but lucrative task of autographing hundreds of baseballs to sell online and at fan conventions. When Terry's husband disappears, Denny materializes as a friend in need. In need of a drinking partner, mostly. Neither one is a sensational *Barfly/Lost Weekend* kind of alcoholic, but more like the curators of a constant state of swizzledom. They are always a little drunk. Sometimes a little less little, sometimes a little more little.

Allen and Costner are so good at making these characters recognizable that we may not realize how hard that is to do. For Allen, the role comes in a season of triumph; she is also wonderful in Campbell Scott's *Off the Map,* and wait until you see her in Sally Potter's *Yes.* Costner reminds us that he is best when he dials down; he is drawn to epic roles, but here he's as comforting as your boozy best pal.

In *The Upside of Anger,* written and directed by Mike Binder, they occupy a comedy buried in angst. The camaraderie between Terry and Denny is like the wounded affection of two people with hangovers and plenty of time to drink them away. The four daughters have sized up the situation and are getting on with their lives in their own ways, mostly competently. Hadley (Alicia Witt) is a cool, centered college student; Andy (Erika Christensen) re-

acts as second children often do, by deciding she will not be Hadley and indeed will accept an offer to be an intern on Denny's radio show—an offer extended enthusiastically by Shep (Binder), the fortyish producer, who is a shameless letch. Emily (Keri Russell) is at war with her mother; she wants to be a dancer, and her mother says there's no money or future in it. Popeye (Evan Rachel Wood) is the youngest, but maturing way too rapidly, like Wood's character in *13.*

Terry deals imperfectly with events in the lives of her daughters, such as Hadley's impending marriage and Andy becoming Shep's girlfriend. Although Terry is wealthy, stylish, and sexy—a thoroughbred temporarily out of training—she has a rebel streak maybe left over from her teens in the late 1970s. At a lunch party to meet Hadley's prospective in-laws, she tells Denny, "I was like a public service ad against drinking."

It is inevitable that Denny and Terry will become lovers. The girls like him. He is lonely, and Terry's house feels more like home than his own, where the living room is furnished primarily with boxes of baseballs. It is also true, given the current state of the drunk driving laws, that alcoholics are wise to choose lovers within walking distance. So the movie proceeds with wit, intelligence, and a certain horrifying fascination. Sometimes Terry picks up the phone to call the creep in Sweden, but decides not to give him the satisfaction.

And then comes an unexpected development. Because *The Upside of Anger* opened a week earlier in New York than in Chicago, I am aware of the despair about this development from A. O. Scott in the *New York Times* (the ending "is an utter catastrophe") and Joe Morgenstern in the *Wall Street Journal* (the ending is "a cheat").

They are mistaken. Life can contain catastrophe, and life can cheat. The ending is the making of the movie, its transcendence, its way of casting everything in a new and ironic light, causing us to reevaluate what went before, and to regard the future with horror and pity. Without the ending, *The Upside of Anger* is a wonderfully made comedy of domestic manners. With it, the movie becomes larger and deeper. When life plays a joke on you, it can have a really rotten sense of humor.

V

Valentin ★ ★ ★
PG-13, 86 m., 2004

Rodrigo Noya (Valentin), Julieta Cardinali (Leticia), Carmen Maura (His Grandmother), Alejandro Agresti (His Father), Mex Urtizberea (Rufo). Directed by Alejandro Agresti and produced by Laurens Geels, Thierry Forte, and Julio Fernandez. Screenplay by Agresti.

Valentin is a nine-year-old boy who is solemn and observant, and peers out at the world through enormous glasses that correct his wandering eye. He lives with his grandmother in Buenos Aires in the late 1960s. His mother is not on the scene. His father appears from time to time with a girlfriend, usually a new one. Valentin spends a lot of time "building stuff for astronauts" and observing the adults in his life with analytical zeal.

He narrates his own story, but here's an interesting touch: The voice belongs to the young actor (Rodrigo Noya), but the sensibility is that of an adult remembering his childhood. There is an interesting explanation. The movie was written and directed by Alejandro Agresti, who tells us it is his own life story. Interesting that he plays the father who causes this little boy so much grief.

Valentin's grandmother (Carmen Maura) is not a lovable movie granny. She does what is necessary for the boy, is miserly with her affections, is trying to stage-manage her son into a second marriage. One day his father comes home with a girlfriend Valentin likes. This is Leticia (Julieta Cardinali), and she likes Valentin too. They get along famously, until one day he makes the mistake of telling her disturbing things about his father. She makes the mistake of repeating them to his father. As a result, Leticia breaks up with his father, and his father is angry with Valentin.

The movie sets its story against an Argentina carefully remembered by Agresti. Buenos Aires looks and sounds cosmopolitan and embracing, and there is a leisurely feeling to the streets and cafés, especially one in which Valentin observes a man sitting and reading and smoking, day after day. This is Rufo (Mex Urtizberea), a musician, who gives Valentin some piano lessons and becomes his confidant. "Rufo gave me the feeling I was older and more useful," he explains.

Valentin feels that since the adult world handles its affairs badly, he must sometimes take things into his own hands. When he decides his grandmother is ill, he convinces a doctor to visit her. Later, he gives the doctor a painting as a present. Outside events penetrate unevenly into his mind; he is up-to-date on the astronauts, but not so sure what it means when Che Guevara is killed. In church, people walk out of a sermon about Che; at home, anti-Semitism is prevalent, even though Valentin's mother was Jewish (we begin to suspect why she may have left the family).

I am not always sure what I mean when I praise a child actor, especially one as young as Rodrigo Noya. Certainly, casting has a lot to do with his appeal; he looks the part and exudes a touching solemnity. But there is more. There's something about this kid, and the way he talks and listens and watches people, that is very convincing. Perhaps it helped that he was directed by a man who was once Valentin himself. The film is warm and intriguing, and he is the engine that pulls us through it. We care about what happens to him; high praise.

By the end of the film, Valentin feels, with some reason, that he has been set adrift by the adult world. But he is smart and resourceful, and he has a simple but effective working knowledge of human nature. What he does and how he does it, and who he does it for I will leave for you to discover, since the movie's closing scenes are filled with a sublime serendipity. Let me just say he earns his name.

Van Helsing ★ ★ ★
PG-13, 131 m., 2004

Hugh Jackman (Gabriel Van Helsing), Kate Beckinsale (Anna Valerious), Richard Roxburgh (Count Dracula), Shuler Hensley (Frankenstein's Monster), David Wenham (Carl), Will Kemp (Velkan Valerious), Kevin J. O'Connor (Igor), Samuel West (Dr. Frankenstein), Robbie Coltrane (Mr. Hyde). Directed by Stephen Sommers and produced by Bob Ducsay and Sommers. Screenplay by Sommers.

The zombies were having fun,
The party had just begun,
The guests included Wolf Man,
Dracula and his son.
    — "Monster Mash" by Bobby Pickett

Strange that a movie so eager to entertain would forget to play *Monster Mash* over the end credits. There have been countless movies uniting two monsters (*Frankenstein Meets the Wolf Man, King Kong vs. Godzilla,* etc.), but *Van Helsing* convenes Frankenstein, his Monster, Count Dracula, the Wolf Man, Igor, Van Helsing the vampire hunter, assorted other werewolves, werebats and vampires, and even Mr. Hyde, who as a bonus seems to think he is the Hunchback of Notre Dame.

The movie is like a greatest hits compilation; it's assembled like Frankenstein's Monster, from spare parts stitched together and brought to life with electricity, plus lots of computer-generated images. The plot depends on Dracula's desperate need to discover the secret of Frankenstein's Monster because he can use it to bring his countless offspring to life. Because Dracula (Richard Roxburgh) and his vampire brides are all dead, they cannot give birth, of course, to live children. That they give birth at all is somewhat remarkable, although perhaps the process is unorthodox, since his dead offspring hang from a subterranean ceiling wrapped in cocoons that made me think, for some reason, of bagworms, which I spent many a summer hand-picking off the evergreens under the enthusiastic direction of my father.

Van Helsing (Hugh Jackman, Wolverine in the X-Men movies) is sometimes portrayed as young, sometimes old in the Dracula movies. Here he's a professional monster-killer with a *Phantom of the Opera* hat, who picks up a dedicated friar named Carl (David Wenham) as his sidekick. His first assignment is to track down Mr. Hyde (Robbie Coltrane), who now lives in Notre Dame cathedral and ventures out for murder. That job doesn't end as planned, so Van Helsing moves on to the Vatican City to get new instructions and be supplied with high-tech weapons by the ecclesiastical equivalent of James Bond's Q.

Next stop: Transylvania, where the movie opened with a virtuoso black-and-white sequence showing a local mob waving pitchforks and torches and hounding Frankenstein's Monster into a windmill that is set ablaze. We know, having seen the old movies, that the Monster will survive, but the mob has worked itself into such a frenzy that when Van Helsing and Carl arrive in the village, they are almost forked and burnt just on general principles. What saves them is an attack by three flying vampiresses, who like to scoop up their victims and fly off to savor their blood; Van Helsing fights them using a device that fires arrows like a machine gun.

And that leads to his meeting the beautiful Anna Valerious (Kate Beckinsale), who with her brother, Velkan (Will Kemp), represents the last of nine generations of a family that will never find eternal rest until it vanquishes Dracula. (Conveniently, if you kill Dracula, all the vampires he created will also die.) Anna is at first suspicious of Van Helsing, but soon they are partners in vengeance, and the rest of the plot (there is a whole lot of it) I will leave you to discover for yourselves.

The director, Stephen Sommers, began his career sedately, directing a very nice *Adventures of Huckleberry Finn* (1993) and the entertaining *Jungle Book* (1994). Then Victor Frankenstein must have strapped him to the gurney and turned on the juice, because he made a U-turn into thrillers, with *Deep Rising* (1998), where a giant squid attacks a cruise ship, and *The Mummy* (1999) and *The Mummy Returns* (2001, introducing The Rock as the Scorpion King). Now comes *Van Helsing,* which employs the ultimate resources of CGI to create a world that is violent and hectic, bizarre and entertaining, and sometimes very beautiful.

CGI can get a little boring when it allows characters to fall hundreds of feet and somehow survive, or when they swoop at the ends of ropes as well as Spiderman, but without Spidey's superpowers. But it can also be used to create a visual feast, and here the cinematography by Allen Daviau (*E.T.*) and the production design by Allen Cameron join with Sommers's imagination for spectacular sights. The best is a masked ball in Budapest, which is part real (the musicians balancing on balls, the waiters circling on unicycles) and part fabricated in the computer. Whatever. It's a remarkable scene, and will reward study on the DVD. So will the extraordinary coach chase.

I also liked the movie's re-creation of Victor Frankenstein's laboratory, which has been a favorite of production designers, art directors, and set decorators since time immemorial (Mel Brooks's *Young Frankenstein* recycled the actual sets built for James Whale's *The Bride of Frankenstein*). Here Frankenstein lives in a towering Gothic castle just down the road from Dracula, and the mechanism lifts the Monster to unimaginable heights to expose him to lightning bolts. There are also plentiful crypts, stygian passages, etc., and a library in which a painting revolves, perhaps in tribute to Mel Brooks's revolving bookcase.

The screenplay by Sommers has humor, but restrains itself; the best touches are the quiet ones, as when the friar objects to accompanying Van Helsing ("But I'm not a field man") and when the Monster somewhat unexpectedly recites the 23rd Psalm. At the outset, we may fear Sommers is simply going for f/x overkill, but by the end he has somehow succeeded in assembling all his monsters and plot threads into a high-voltage climax. *Van Helsing* is silly, and spectacular, and fun.

Vanity Fair ★ ★ ★ ★
PG-13, 137 m., 2004

Reese Witherspoon (Becky Sharp), Eileen Atkins (Matilde Crawley), Jim Broadbent (Mr. Osborne), Gabriel Byrne (Marquess of Steyne), Romola Garai (Amelia Sedley), Bob Hoskins (Sir Pitt Crawley), Rhys Ifans (William Dobbin), Geraldine McEwan (Lady Southdown), James Purefoy (Rawdon Crawley), Jonathan Rhys-Meyers (George Osborne), Tony Maudsley (Joseph Sedley). Directed by Mira Nair and produced by Janette Day, Lydia Dean Pilcher, and Donna Gigliotti. Screenplay by Matthew Faulk, Julian Fellowes, and Mark Skeet, based on the novel by William Makepeace Thackeray.

"I had thought her a mere social climber. I see now she's a mountaineer."

So says one of her fascinated observers as Becky Sharp transforms herself from the impoverished orphan of an alcoholic painter into an adornment of the middle, if not the upper, reaches of the British aristocracy. *Vanity Fair* makes her a little more likable than she was in the 1828 novel—but then, I always liked Becky

anyway, because she so admirably tried to obey her cynical strategies and yet so helplessly allowed herself to be misled by her heart.

Reese Witherspoon reflects both of those qualities effortlessly in this new film by Mira Nair, and no wonder, for isn't there a little of Elle Woods, her character in *Legally Blonde*, at work here? Becky, to be sure, never goes through a phase when anyone thinks her stupid, but she does use her sexuality to advantage, plays men at their own game, and scores about as well as possible given the uneven nineteenth-century playing field.

When William Makepeace Thackeray wrote his funny and quietly savage novel, there were few career prospects for an educated young woman who did not fancy prostitution. She could become a governess, a teacher, a servant, a religious, or a wife. The only male profession open to her was writing, which she could practice without the permission or license of men; that accounts for such as Jane Austen, the Brontës, George Eliot, Mrs. Gaskell, and others who, as Virginia Woolf imagined them, wrote their masterpieces in a corner of the parlor while after-dinner chatter surrounded them.

Becky Sharp could probably have written a great novel, and certainly inspired one; Thackeray sees her dilemma and her behavior without sentiment, in a novel that must have surprised its first readers with its realism. We meet Becky just as she's leaving finishing school, where the French she learned from her Parisian mother won her a berth as a boarder and tutor. She made one good friend there: Amelia Sedley (Romola Garai), and now proposes to visit the Sedley family for a few days on her way to her first job, as a governess for the down-at-heels Sir Pitt Crawley (Bob Hoskins).

But working as a governess is not Becky's life goal. She wants to marry well, and since she has neither fortune nor title it would be best if her husband brought both of those attributes into the marriage. Does this make her an evil woman? Not at all; romantic love is a modern and untrustworthy motive for marriage, and in England and India (where both Thackeray and Mira Nair were born), marriage strategies have always involved family connections and financial possibilities.

Amelia likes Becky (she is the only one at school who did, Thackeray observes), and thinks it would be nice if Becky married her brother Joseph (Tony Maudsley). Amelia's own fiancé, Captain George Osborne (Jonathan Rhys-Meyers), discourages this plan, convincing the weak-willed Joseph that Becky is little better than a beggar with vague family irregularities, and would not adorn the Sedley household.

So Becky goes to Crawley Hall, where she mistakes the unshaven Sir Pitt for a servant. Servants, money, and provisions seem in short supply in the Crawley family, but Becky makes one important conquest; Sir Pitt's rich maiden sister, Matilde (played with magnificent, biting wit by Eileen Atkins), admires her pluck and becomes her friend and protector—up to a point. That point is reached when Becky secretly marries her nephew Rawdon Crawley (James Purefoy). As a second son, Rawdon will not inherit the title or house, and as a gambler can't live within his allowance, so this marriage gives Becky a liaison with a good family but not the benefits.

Some of the film's best moments come when characters administer verbal flayings to one another. Matilde is unforgiving when she is crossed. But the most astonishing dialogue comes from a character named Lord Steyne (Gabriel Byrne), whom Becky meets for the first time when she's a young girl in her father's studio. Steyne fancies a portrait of Becky's mother; her father prices it at three guineas, but Becky insists on ten, putting on a good show of sentimental attachment to her departed parent. Now, many years later, Steyne crosses Becky's path again. She reminds him of their first meeting. It occurs to him that having purchased a portrait of the parent, he might purchase the original of the daughter. This sets up a dinner-table scene in the Steyne household at which the lord verbally destroys every member of his family, not sparing the rich mulatto heiress from the Caribbean who married his son for his title even though "the whole world knows he's an idiot."

The peculiar quality of *Vanity Fair*, which sets it aside from the Austen adaptations like *Sense and Sensibility* and *Pride and Prejudice*, is that it's not about very nice people. That makes them much more interesting. There are some decent blokes in the story, but on the fringes: William Dobbin (Rhys Ifans), for example, who persists in loving Amelia even though she falls for George, a thoroughgoing bounder. Joseph is a good sort, too.

And for that matter, how evil is Lord Steyne, really? He and Becky meet again after her husband, Rawdon, has lost everything at the gambling tables and the bailiff is literally moving their furniture out of the house. Steyne pays off their debts. This would not have been considered by anybody as an act of selfless charity. Of course, he expects Becky to show her gratitude, although oddly enough she shows it more frankly in the 1848 novel than in the 2004 movie; its PG-13 rating no doubt inspired Nair and her writers to suggest to their tender young audiences that Becky can be friendly and grateful without, as the saying goes, Steyne having sex with that young woman. In the real world, the furniture would have been back on the sidewalk.

Is the India-born Mira Nair a strange choice to adapt what some think is the best English novel of the nineteenth century? Not at all. She has an instinctive feel for the comic possibilities of marital alliances, as she showed in her wonderful *Monsoon Wedding* (2001). And she brings to the movie an awareness of the role India played in the English imagination; in the nineteenth century, hardly a well-born family lacked relatives serving or living in India, and wasn't it Orwell who said the two nations deserved each other, because they shared the same love of eccentricity?

Vera Drake ★ ★ ★ ★

R, 125 m., 2004

Imelda Staunton (Vera Drake), Phil Davis (Stan Drake), Peter Wight (Inspector Webster), Adrian Scarborough (Frank), Heather Craney (Joyce), Daniel Mays (Sid Drake), Alex Kelly (Ethel Drake), Sally Hawkins (Susan), Eddie Marsan (Reg), Ruth Sheen (Lily). Directed by Mike Leigh and produced by Simon Channing Williams and Alain Sarde. Screenplay by Leigh.

Vera Drake is a melodious plum pudding of a woman who is always humming or singing to herself. She is happy because she is useful, and likes to be useful. She works as a cleaning woman in a rich family's house, where she burnishes the bronze as if it were her own, and then returns home to a crowded flat to cook, clean, and mend for her husband, son, and daughter, and cheer them up when they seem out of sorts. She makes daily calls on invalids to plump up their pillows and make them a nice cup of tea, and once or twice a week she performs an abortion.

London in the 1950s. Wartime rationing is still in effect. A pair of nylons is bartered for eight packs of Players. Vera (Imelda Staunton) buys sugar on the black market from Lily (Ruth Sheen), who also slips her the names and addresses of women in need of "help." Lily is as hard and cynical as Vera is kind and trusting. Vera would never think of accepting money for "helping out" young girls when "they got no one to turn to," but Lily charges two pounds and two shillings, which she doesn't tell Vera about.

In a film of pitch-perfect, seemingly effortless performances, Imelda Staunton is the key player, and her success at creating Vera Drake allows the story to fall into place and belong there. We must believe she's naive to be taken advantage of by Lily, but we do believe it. We must believe she has a simple, pragmatic morality to justify abortions, which were a crime in England until 1967, but we do believe it.

Some of the women who come to her have piteous stories; they were raped, they are still almost children, they will kill themselves if their parents find out, or in one case there are seven mouths to feed and the mother lacks the will to carry on. But Vera is not a social worker who provides counseling; she is simply being helpful by doing something she believes she can do safely. Her age-old method involves lye soap, disinfectant, and, of course, lots of hot water, and another abortionist describes her method as "safe as houses."

The movie has been written and directed by Mike Leigh, the most interesting director now at work in England, whose *Topsy-Turvy, High Hopes, All or Nothing*, and *Naked* join this film in being partly "devised" by the actors themselves. His method is to gather a cast for weeks or months of improvisation in which they create and explore their characters. I don't think the technique has ever worked better than here; the family life in those cramped little rooms is so palpably real that as the others wait around the dining table while Vera speaks to a policeman behind the kitchen door, I felt as if I were waiting there with them. It's not that we "identify" so much as that the film quietly and firmly includes us.

The movie is not about abortion so much as about families. The Drakes are close and loving. Vera's husband, Stan (Phil Davis), who works with his brother in an auto repair shop, considers his wife a treasure. Their son, Sid (Daniel Mays), works as a tailor, has a line of patter, is popular in pubs, but lives at home because of the postwar housing crisis. Their daughter, Ethel (Alex Kelly), is painfully shy, and there is a sweet, tactful subplot in which Vera invites a lonely, tongue-tied bachelor named Reg (Eddie Marsan) over for tea, and essentially arranges a marriage.

Vera Drake tells a parallel story about a rich girl named Susan (Sally Hawkins), the daughter of the family Vera cleans for. Susan is raped by her boyfriend, becomes pregnant, and goes to a psychiatrist who can refer her to a private clinic for a legal abortion. Like everyone in the movie, Susan is excruciatingly shy about discussing sex, and ignorant. "Did he force himself upon you?" the psychiatrist asks, and Susan is not sure how to answer. Leigh's point is that those with £100 could legally obtain an abortion in England in 1950, and those with £2 had to depend on Vera Drake, or on women not nearly as nice as Vera Drake.

Vera's world falls apart when the police become involved in an abortion that almost leads to death, and the tightly knit little family changes when the police knock on the door. Inspector Webster (Peter Wight) is a considerable man, large, imposing, and not without sympathy. He believes in the law and enforces the law, but he quickly understands that Vera was not working for profit, and is not ungentle with her. In a courtroom scene, on the other hand, it is clear that the law makes no room for nuance or circumstance.

Some of the film's best scenes involve the family sitting around the table, shell-shocked (after Vera whispers into her husband's ear, telling him what he had never suspected). There are moments when Leigh uses his technique of allowing a reticent character to stir into conviction. At Vera's final Christmas dinner, Reg, now engaged to Ethel, makes what for him is a long speech: "This is the best Christmas I've had in a long time. Thank you very much, Vera. Smashing!" He knows telling Vera she has prepared a perfect meal means more to her than any speech about rights and wrongs, although later he blurts out: "It's all right if you're rich, but if you can't feed 'em you can't love 'em."

Vera Drake is not so much pro- or antiabortion as it is opposed to laws that do little to eliminate abortion but much to make it dangerous for poor p5ople. No matter what the law says, then or now, in England or America, if you can afford a plane ticket and the medical bill you will always be able to obtain a competent abortion, so laws essentially make it illegal to be poor and seek an abortion.

Even in saying that, I am bringing more ideology into Vera Drake than it probably requires. The strength of Leigh's film is that it is not a message picture, but a deep and true portrait of these lives. Vera is kind and innocent, but Lily, who procures the abortions, is hard, dishonest, and heartless. The movie shows the law as unyielding, but puts a human face on the police. And the enduring strength of the film is the way it shows the Drake family rising to the occasion with loyalty and love.

A Very Long Engagement ★ ★ ★ ½
R, 134 m., 2004

Audrey Tautou (Mathilde), Gaspard Ulliel (Manech), Jean-Pierre Becker (Lieutenant Esperanza), Jodie Foster (Elodie Gordes), Albert Dupontel (Celestin Poux), Clovis Cornillac (Benoit Notre-Dame), Marion Cotillard (Tina Lombardi), Ticky Holgado (Germain Pire). Directed by Jean-Pierre Jeunet and produced by Francis Boespflug. Screenplay by Jeunet and Guillaume Laurant, based on the novel by Sebastien Japrisot.

In the horror of trench warfare during World War I, with French and Germans dug in across from each other during endless muddy, cold, wet, bloody months, not a few put their rifles into their mouths and sent themselves on permanent leave. Others, more optimistic, wounded themselves to get a pass to a field hospital, but if this treachery was suspected the sentence was death. A Very Long Engagement opens by introducing us to five French soldiers convicted of wounding themselves; one is innocent, but all are condemned, and it is a form

of cruelty, perhaps, that instead of being lined up and shot they are sent out into No-Man's-Land and certain death.

The movie is seen largely through the eyes of Mathilde (Audrey Tautou), an orphan with a polio limp, who senses in her soul that her man is not dead. He is Manech (Gaspard Ulliel), son of a lighthouse tender, a boy so open-faced and fresh he is known to all as Cornflower. After the war, Mathilde comes upon a letter that seems to hint that not all five died on the battlefield, and she begins the long task of tracking down eyewitnesses and survivors to find the Manech she is sure is still alive and needs her help.

This story is told in a film so visually delightful that only the horrors of war keep it from floating up on clouds of joy. Having not connected with his earlier films Delicatessen and The City of Lost Children, I was enchanted, as everyone was, by Jean-Pierre Jeunet's first film with Audrey Tautou, Amelie. Now he brings everything together—his joyously poetic style, the lovable Tautou, a good story worth the telling—into a film that is a series of pleasures stumbling over one another in their haste to delight us. I will have to go back again to those early films; maybe I am learning the language.

That is not too say A Very Long Engagement is mindless jollity. From Goodbye to All That by Robert Graves and from a hundred films like All Quiet on the Western Front, Paths of Glory, and King and Country, we have an idea of the trench warfare that makes World War I seem like the worst kind of hell politicians and generals ever devised for their men. To be assigned to the front was essentially a sentence of death, but not quick death, more often death after a long season of cold, hunger, illness, shell shock, and the sheer horror of what you had to look at and think about. Jeunet depicts this reality as well as I have ever seen it shown on the screen, beginning with his opening shot of a severed arm hanging, Christ-like, from a shattered cross.

Against these fragments he buttresses his fancies, his camera swooping like a glad bird over Paris and the countryside, his narrator telling us of Mathilde and her quest. These moments have some of the charm of the early scenes in Truffaut's Jules and Jim, before the same war destroyed their happiness. Mathilde enlists a dogged old bird of a private detective

(Ticky Holgado, who you may remember from the cover of Amelie's talking book). He plods about quizzing possible witnesses with the raised eyebrows of an Inspector Maigret, and gradually a scenario seems to form in which Manech is not necessarily dead.

As a counterpoint to Mathilde's hopeful search, Jeunet supplies another search among the same human remains, this one carried out by a prostitute named Tina (Marion Cotillard), who figures out who was responsible for the death of her lover. Her means of revenge are so unspeakably ingenious that Edgar Allan Poe would twitch in envy.

The barbarity of war and the implacable logic of revenge are softened by the voluptuous beauty of Jeunet's visuals and the magic of his storytelling. Here is a director who loves—adores!—telling stories, so that we sense his voluptuous pleasure in his own tales. He must work in a kind of holy trance, falling to his knees at night to give thanks that modern special effects have made his visions possible. Some directors abuse effects. He flies on their wings.

Whether Mathilde finds Manech is a question I should not answer, but reader, what do you think is the likelihood that an angel-faced girl with polio could spend an entire movie searching for her true love and not find him? Audiences would rip up their seats. The point is not whether she finds him, but how. Can Jeunet devise their reunion in a way that is not an anticlimax after such a glorious search? What can they do, Mathilde and Manech, and what can they say? Reader, the film's closing moments are so sad and happy that we know, yes, it has to end on just that perfect note, held and held and held.

V for Vendetta ★ ★ ★
R, 130 m., 2006

Natalie Portman (Evey Hammond), Hugo Weaving (V), Stephen Rea (Finch), Stephen Fry (Deitrich), John Hurt (Adam Sutler), Tim Pigott-Smith (Creedy), Rupert Graves (Dominic). Directed by James McTeigue and produced by Grant Hill, Joel Silver, Andy Wachowski, and Larry Wachowski. Screenplay by the Wachowski brothers.

It is the year 2020. A virus runs wild in the world, most Americans are dead, and Britain is ruled by a fascist dictator who promises security but not freedom. One man stands against him, the man named V, who moves through London like a wraith despite the desperate efforts of the police. He wears a mask showing the face of Guy Fawkes, who in 1605 tried to blow up the houses of Parliament. On November 4, the eve of Guy Fawkes Day, British schoolchildren for centuries have started bonfires to burn Fawkes in effigy. On this eve in 2020, V saves a young TV reporter named Evey from assault at the hands of the police, forces her to join him, and makes a busy night of it by blowing up the Old Bailey courtrooms.

V for Vendetta will follow his exploits for the next twelve months, until the night when he has vowed to strike a crushing blow against the dictatorship. We see a police state that holds its citizens in an iron grip and yet is humiliated by a single man who seems impervious. The state tries to suppress knowledge of his deeds—to spin a plausible explanation for the destruction of the Old Bailey, for example, but V commandeers the national television network to claim authorship of his deed.

This story was first told as a graphic novel written by Alan Moore and published in 1982 and 1983. Its hero plays altogether differently now, and yet, given the nature of the regime, is he a terrorist or a freedom fighter? Britain is ruled by a man named Sutler, who gives orders to his underlings from a wall-sized TV screen and seems the personification of Big Brother. And is: Sutler is played by John Hurt, who in fact played Winston Smith in *Nineteen Eighty-Four* (1984). V seems more like Jack the Ripper, given his ability to move boldly in and out of areas the police think they control. The similarity may have come easily to Moore, whose graphic novel *From Hell* was about the Ripper and inspired a good 2001 movie by the Hughes brothers.

V for Vendetta has been written and coproduced by the Wachowski brothers, Andy and Larry, whose *Matrix* was also about rebels holding out against a planetary system of control. This movie is more literary and less dominated by special effects (although there are plenty), and is filled with ideas that are all the more intriguing because we can't pin down the message. Is this movie a parable about 2006, a cautionary

747

tale, or pure fantasy? It can be read many ways, as I will no doubt learn in endless e-mails.

The character of V and his relationship with Evey (Natalie Portman) inescapably reminds us of the Phantom of the Opera. V and the Phantom are both masked, move through subterranean spaces, control others through the leverage of their imaginations, and have a score to settle. One difference, and it is an important one, is that V's facial disguise does not move (unlike, say, the faces of a *Batman* villain) but is a mask that always has the same smiling expression. Behind it is the actor Hugo Weaving, using his voice and body language to create a character, but I was reminded of my problem with Thomas the Tank Engine: If something talks, its lips should move.

Still, Portman's Evey has expressions enough for most purposes, as she morphs from a dutiful citizen to V's sympathizer, and the film is populated with a gallery of gifted character actors. In addition to Hurt as the sinister dictator, we see Stephen Rea and Rupert Graves as the police assigned to lead the search for V. Tim Pigott-Smith is an instrument of the dictator. These people exist in scenes designed to portray them as secure, until V sweeps in like a whirlwind, using martial arts, ingenious weapons, and the element of surprise. Why the mask does not limit his peripheral vision is a question I will leave for the experts. See the Answer Man entry for this movie.

There are ideas in this film. The most pointed is V's belief: "People should not be afraid of their governments. Governments should be afraid of their people." I am not sure V has it right; surely in the ideal state, governments and their people should exist happily together. Fear in either direction must lead to violence. But V has a totalitarian state to overthrow and only a year in which to do it, and we watch as he improvises a revolution. He gets little support, although Stephen Fry plays a dissident TV host who criticizes the government at his peril.

With most action thrillers based on graphic novels, we simply watch the sound and light show. *V for Vendetta*, directed by James McTeigue, almost always has something going on that is actually interesting, inviting us to decode the character and plot and apply the message where we will. There are times when you think the sound track should be supplying "An-

archy in the U.K." by the Sex Pistols. The movie ends with a violent act that left me, as a lover of London, intensely unhappy; surely V's enemy is human, not architectural.

The film has been disowned by Alan Moore, who also removed his name from the movie versions of his graphic novels *From Hell* and *The League of Extraordinary Gentlemen*, but then any sane person would have been unhappy with the Gentlemen. His complaint was not so much with the films as with the deal involving the use of his work. I have not read the original work, do not know what has been changed or gone missing, but found an audacious confusion of ideas in *V for Vendetta* and enjoyed their manic disorganization. To attempt a parable about terrorism and totalitarianism that would be relevant and readable might be impossible, could be dangerous, and would probably not be box office. ☞

The Village ★
PG-13, 130 m., 2004

Joaquin Phoenix (Lucius Hunt), Bryce Dallas Howard (Ivy Walker), Adrien Brody (Noah Percy), William Hurt (Edward Walker), Sigourney Weaver (Alice Hunt), Brendan Gleeson (August Nicholson). Directed by M. Night Shyamalan and produced by Sam Mercer, Scott Rudin, and Shyamalan. Screenplay by Shyamalan.

The Village is a colossal miscalculation, a movie based on a premise that cannot support it, a premise so transparent it would be laughable were the movie not so deadly solemn. It's a flimsy excuse for a plot, with characters who move below the one-dimensional and enter Flatland. M. Night Shyamalan, the writer-director, has been successful in evoking horror from minimalist stories, as in *Signs*, which if you think about it rationally is absurd—but you get too involved to think rationally. He is a considerable director who evokes stories out of moods, but this time, alas, he took the day off.

Critics were enjoined after the screening to avoid revealing the plot secrets. That is not because we would spoil the movie for you. It's because if you knew them you wouldn't want to go. The whole enterprise is a shaggy dog story, and in a way it is all secrets. I can hardly discuss it at all without being maddeningly vague.

Let us say that it takes place in an unspecified time and place, surrounded by a forest the characters never enter. The clothing of the characters and the absence of cars and telephones and suchlike suggests either the 1890s or an Amish community. Everyone speaks as if they had studied *Friendly Persuasion*. The chief civic virtues are probity and circumspection. Here is a village that desperately needs an East Village.

The story opens with a funeral attended by all the villagers, followed by a big outdoor meal at long tables groaning with corn on the cob and all the other fixin's. Everyone in the village does everything together, apparently, although it is never very clear what most of their jobs are. Some farming and baking goes on.

The movie is so somber, it's afraid to raise its voice in its own presence. That makes it dreary even during scenes of shameless melodrama. We meet the patriarch Edward Walker (William Hurt), who is so judicious in all things he sounds like a minister addressing the Rotary Club. His daughter Ivy (Bryce Dallas Howard) is blind but spunky. The stalwart young man, Lucius Hunt (Joaquin Phoenix), petitions the elders to let him take a look into the forest. His widowed mother, Alice (Sigourney Weaver), has feelings for Edward Walker. The village idiot (Adrien Brody), gambols about, and gamboling is not a word I use lightly. There is a good man and true (Brendan Gleeson). And a bridegroom who is afraid his shirt will get wrinkled.

Surrounding the village is the forest. In the forest live vile, hostile creatures who dress in red and have claws of twigs. They are known as Those We Do Not Speak Of (except when we want to end a designation with a preposition). We see Those We Do Not Speak Of only in brief glimpses, like the water-fixated aliens in *Signs*. They look better than the *Signs* aliens, who looked like large extras in long underwear, while Those We Do Not, etc., look like their costumes were designed at summer camp.

Watchtowers guard the periphery of the village, and flares burn through the night. But not to fear: Those We Do, etc., have arrived at a truce. They stay in the forest and the villagers stay in the village. Lucius wants to go into the forest, and petitions the elders, who frown at this desire. Ivy would like to marry Lucius, and

tells him so, but he is so reflective and funereal it will take him another movie to get worked up enough to deal with her. Still, they love each other. The village idiot also has a thing for Ivy, and sometimes they gambol together.

Something terrible happens to somebody. I dare not reveal what, and to which, and by whom. Edward Walker decides reluctantly to send someone to "the towns" to bring back medicine for whoever was injured. And off goes his daughter Ivy, a blind girl walking through the forest inhabited by Those Who, etc. She wears her yellow riding hood, and it takes us a superhuman effort to keep from thinking about Grandmother's House.

Solemn violin dirges permeate the sound track. It is autumn, overcast and chilly. Girls find a red flower and bury it. Everyone speaks in the passive voice. The vitality has been drained from the characters; these are the Stepford Pilgrims. The elders have meetings from which the young are excluded. Someone finds something under the floorboards. Wouldn't you just know it would be there, exactly where it was needed, in order for someone to do something he couldn't do without it.

Eventually the secret of Those, etc., is revealed. To call it an anticlimax would be an insult not only to climaxes but to prefixes. It's a crummy secret, about one step up the ladder of narrative originality from It Was All a Dream. It's so witless, in fact, that when we do discover the secret, we want to rewind the film so we don't know the secret anymore. And then keep on rewinding, and rewinding, until we're back at the beginning, and can get up from our seats and walk backward out of the theater and go down the up escalator and watch the money spring from the cash register into our pockets.

Virgin ★ ★ ★

NO MPAA RATING, 113 m., 2005

Robin Wright Penn (Mrs. Reynolds), Elisabeth Moss (Jessie Reynolds), Daphne Rubin-Vega (Frances), Socorro Santiago (Lorna), Peter Gerety (Mr. Reynolds), Stephanie Gatchet (Katie Reynolds), Charles Socarides (Shane). Directed by Deborah Kampmeier and produced by Raye Dowell and Sarah Schenck. Screenplay by Kampmeier.

Jessie Reynolds is not the kind of girl who gets nice things written under her picture in the high school yearbook. She's probably never going to graduate, for one thing. When we see her for the first time in *Virgin*, she's trying to talk a stranger into buying some booze for her, and when he does, he gets a kiss.

Jessie is not bad, precisely. It would be more fair to say she is lost, and a little dim. She clearly feels left behind, even left out, by her family. Her sister, Katie (Stephanie Gatchet), is pretty, popular, and a track star who dedicates her victories to Jesus. Her parents (Robin Wright Penn and Peter Gerety) are fundamentalists, strict and unforgiving. Jessie doesn't measure up and doesn't even seem to be trying.

There is, however, someone she would like to impress: Shane (Charles Socarides), a boy at school. She wanders off from a dance with him, is drunk, is given a date-rape pill, is raped, and wakes up with no memory of the event. When she discovers she is pregnant, there is only one possible explanation in her mind: There has been an immaculate conception, and she will give birth to the baby Jesus.

Jessie is played by Elisabeth Moss, from *West Wing*, as a girl both endearing and maddening. Her near-bliss seems a little heavily laid on, under the circumstances, but director Deborah Kampmeier has ways of suggesting it's the real thing. Whether or not there is a God has nothing to do with whether or not we believe he is speaking to us, and although in this case there's every reason to believe God has not impregnated Jessie, there's every reason for Jessie to think so. Among other things, it certainly trumps the religiosity of her parents and sister.

Fundamentalists almost always appear in American movies for the purpose of being closed-minded, rigid, and sanctimonious. Anyone with any religion at all, for that matter, tends to be suspect (the priest in *Million Dollar Baby* is the first good priest I can remember in a film in a long time). Movies can't seem to deal with faith as a positive element in an admirable life, and the only religions taken seriously by Hollywood are the kinds promoted in stores that also sell incense and Tarot decks. So it's refreshing to see the Robin Wright Penn character allowed to unbend in *Virgin*, to become less rigid and more of an empathetic

mother, who intuitively senses that although Jessie may be deluded, she is sincere.

There has, of course, been a great wrong committed here, but it would be cruel for Jessie to learn of that fact. How sad to believe you are bearing the Christ child and then be told, no, you got drunk and were raped. Better, perhaps, to let Jessie bear the child and find out gradually that, like all children, it displays divinity primarily in the eyes of its mother.

But Kampmeier is up to something a little more ambitious here. She uses visual strategies to suggest that Jessie, in the grip of her conviction, enters a state that is just as spiritual as if its cause were not so sad. The performance by Moss invests Jessie with a kind of zealous hope that is touching: Here is a slutty loser touched by the divine and transformed. What has happened to her is more real than the miracles hailed on Sundays by results-oriented preachers. The more you consider the theological undertones of *Virgin*, the more radical it becomes. Must you be the mother of God to experience the benefits of thinking that you are? Can those from a conventional religious background deal with your ecstasy?

There is a wonderful novel named *The Annunciation of Francesca Dunn* by Janis Hallowell, a friend of mine, that tells of a waitress in Boulder, Colorado, whom a homeless man becomes convinced is the Virgin Mary. The novel explores a little more poetically and explicitly than *Virgin* the experience of being blindsided by an unsolicited spiritual epiphany.

Both works are fascinating because in mainstream society, there are only two positions on such matters: either you believe, or you do not (and therefore, either you are saved, or you don't care). Is it not possible that faith is its own reward, apart from any need for it to be connected with reality? I am unreasonably stimulated by works that leave me theologically stranded like that. They're much more interesting than works that, one way or the other, think they know.

Theological footnote: Every once in a while my Catholic grade school education sounds a dogma alarm. Jessie is not a Catholic, which perhaps explains why she thinks the term "immaculate conception" refers to the birth of Jesus, when in fact it refers to the birth of Mary.

W

Wah-Wah ★ ★ ★
R, 97 m., 2006

Gabriel Byrne (Harry Compton), Miranda Richardson (Lauren Compton), Nicholas Hoult (Ralph Compton), Emily Watson (Ruby Compton), Julie Walters (Gwen Traherne), Celia Imrie (Lady Riva Hardwick), Julian Wadham (Charles Bingham), Fenella Woolgar (June Broughton). Directed by Richard E. Grant and produced by Jeff Abberley, Pierre Kubel, and Marie-Castille Mention-Schaar. Screenplay by Grant.

There is a scene early in *Wah-Wah* where the British family drives off in its car and the servants wave after them, smiling happily. The same image could serve at the end of the film, when the British turn Swaziland over to its citizens and leave forever. The only difference would be that in the final scene, the smiles would be sincere.

Wah-Wah takes place just at that moment in the early 1960s when Britain was granting independence to its colonies, one by one, a parade of royals commuting to one distant capital after another to watch the Union Jack being lowered. The movie is of that time, but not about it, and for that it has been criticized in some circles. I think its myopia is accurate.

The colonial Brits, and whites in general, lived within a closed system and were preoccupied with their own lives, ranks, salaries, security, and gossip, to the exclusion of the local population. "How dare you contradict me in front of a servant?" the hero's father asks in *Wah-Wah*. It has escaped his notice that his entire life, and every one of its secrets, is being lived in front of the servants.

The movie is autobiographical, based on the life of its writer-director, Richard E. Grant. We know him as an actor, notably in *Withnail & I* and *How to Get Ahead in Advertising*. He often plays sour and disaffected characters, and on the basis of his early life seen in this movie, no wonder. An early memory involves his mother, Lauren (Miranda Richardson), making love with a man not his father. His father, Harry (Gabriel Byrne), drinks, but then everybody drinks at that time, in that place. His mother leaves with an-

other man. His father's drinking escalates, without affecting his job as Swaziland's minister of education. Young Ralph goes off to boarding school, and when he returns there is a new stepmother, an American stewardess named Ruby (Emily Watson). His father is still drinking.

Life for the Brits revolves around the office, the club, sport, and sundowners (where the drinking begins promptly regardless of the position of the sun). The most excitement in years is when Princess Margaret is announced as the royal visitor who will attend the ceremonies marking the end of British rule. Although their own shining moment was all too brief, the locals decide to stage a performance of *Camelot* in her honor. Ralph (Nicholas Hoult) is involved, and this is essentially his entrance into acting.

Ralph is more of an observer than a participant in the life of his family; his father, nice enough when sober, develops alarming rages when drunk and then cannot remember, when sober again, how reasonable it is for his son to be frightened of him. The key performance in the movie is by Watson, as a good and sensible woman who married too quickly to know what she was getting herself into, and tries to help her husband and protect Ralph. She's the one who says the locals speak "snooty baby talk" that all sounds to her like "Wah-wah-wah-wah-wah." She gives her marriage a brave try, but eventually it's toodle-oo.

What the movie sees clearly is that Harry may have a high post in the colonial administration, but he survives only because of the self-protective colonial system. With independence, his incompetence will make it impossible for him to ever find such a good job again, even if he stops drinking. As a counterpoint to his defeat, we observe the tactics of Lady Riva Hardwick (Celia Imrie), the snotty baby-talking arbiter of British values in the colony, whose word is law in social matters, especially in her own mind. Notice her awkwardness as she adjusts, none too smoothly, to the fact that she will have to address black people in a modulated tone of voice and actually accept them, at least ostensibly, as her equals.

Wah-Wah has a sequence, based on old newsreels, in which the flag is lowered and the sun sets on another bit of the empire. Odd how many critics have felt the whole movie should be about this. I don't see why. The story is about people who lived closed lives, and a film about them would necessarily give independence only a supporting role.

I admired the movie and was happy to see it but can think of two other films about whites in Africa that do a better job of seeing their roles. *Nowhere in Africa* is about German Jewish refugees who become colonial farmers; their daughter makes African friends and comes to love the continent even as her father grows disillusioned. And *White Mischief* is the classic portrait of life in Kenya's "Happy Valley," where a messy case of adultery and murder interrupts the drinking. The old *Chicago Daily News* had a gossip columnist assigned to O'Hare Airport. Once when former Prime Minister Harold Macmillan was passing through, she asked him if the sun would ever set on the British Empire. His answer was a masterpiece of tact: "Not any more than it already has."

Waiting . . . ★ ½
R, 93 m., 2005

Ryan Reynolds (Monty), Anna Faris (Serena), Justin Long (Dean), Kaitlin Doubleday (Amy), Chi McBride (Bishop), Luis Guzman (Raddimus), David Koechner (Dan), Alanna Ubach (Naomi), Vanessa Lengies (Natasha), John Francis Daley (Mitch), Robert Patrick Benedict (Calvin). Directed by Rob McKittrick and produced by Adam Rosenfelt, Jeff Balis, Robert Green, Stavros Merjos, and Jay Rifkin. Screenplay by McKittrick.

Waiting . . . is melancholy for a comedy. It's about dead-end lives at an early age and the gallows humor that makes them bearable. It takes place over a day at a chain restaurant named Shenaniganz (think Chili's crossed with Bennigan's), where the lives of the waiters and cooks revolve around the Penis Game. The rules are simple: Flash a fellow worker with the family jewels, and you get to kick him in the butt and call him a fag. Ho, ho.

Not long ago the restaurant was in the doldrums, morale was low, customers were rare. "The penis-showing game became a catalyst for change and improvement," says a cook named Bishop (Chi McBride). I dunno; to me it seems more like a catalyst for desperate shock value

from a filmmaker who is trying to pump energy into a dead scenario.

I can imagine a good film based on the bored lives of retail workers whose sex lives afford them some relief. *The 40-Year-Old Virgin* is a splendid example, and given the slacker mentality of the waiters in *Waiting . . .* Kevin Smith's *Clerks* leaps to mind. Both of those films begin with fully seen characters who have personalities, possess problems, express themselves with distinctive styles.

The characters in *Waiting . . .* seem like types, not people. What they do and say isn't funny because someone real doesn't seem to be doing or saying it. Everything that the John Belushi character did in *Animal House* proceeded directly from the core of his innermost being: He crushed beer cans against his forehead because he was a person who needed to, and often did, and enjoyed it, and found that it worked for him. You never got the idea he did it because it might be funny in a movie.

The central character in *Waiting . . .* is Monty (Ryan Reynolds), a veteran waiter who justifies his existence in hell by appointing himself its tour guide. He shows the ropes to a new employee named Mitch (John Francis Daley), beginning with the Penis Game and moving on to details about the kitchen, the table rotation, and the cultivation of customers. He also places great importance on the nightly parties where the employees get hammered.

Other staff members include the perpetually snarling Naomi (Alanna Ubach), who could make more money as the dominatrix she was born to play; Dan (David Koechner), the manager who has risen to the precipice of his ability, replacing the Penis Game with the Peter Principle; Serena (Anna Faris), who is way too pretty to be working at Shenaniganz, and knows it; and Raddimus (Luis Guzman), the cook, who is a master at dropping food on the floor and seasoning it with snot, spit, and dandruff. The movie has a lesson for us, and it is: Do not get the food-handlers mad at you.

The hero of sorts is Dean (Justin Long), who is discouraged to learn that while he's been making his seventy dollars a day in tips, a high school classmate has become an electrical engineer. When the supercilious classmate leaves him a big tip, he feels worse than when a stiff leaves another waiter two dollars on a sixty-three dollar bill. The problem with the customers in both of those scenarios, and with the lady customer who is relentlessly bitchy, is that there's nothing funny about them. They're mean and cruel and do not elevate their hatefulness to the level of satire but sullenly remain eight-letter words (in the plural form) beginning with "a." Even the bitch's dinner companions are sick of her.

A subplot involves Natasha, the restaurant's sexy underage receptionist (Vanessa Lengies), who attracts both Monty and Dan the manager. I am trying to imagine how she could have been made funny, but no: The movie deals with her essentially as jailbait, something Monty is wise enough to just barely know and Dan reckless enough to overlook. I was also unable to see the joke involving Calvin (Robert Patrick Benedict), who a) can't urinate because he's uptight that some guy may be trying to steal a glimpse of his jewels, but b) is a champion at the Penis Game. There is a paradox here, but its solution doesn't seem promising.

What it comes down to is that Shenaniganz is a rotten place to work and a hazardous place to eat, and the people on both sides of the counter are miserable sods but at least the employees know they are. Watching the movie is like having one of these wretched jobs, with the difference that after work the employees can get wasted but we can only watch. It can actually be fun to work in a restaurant. Most of the wait-people I have known or encountered have been competent, smart, and if necessary amusing. All the restaurant's a stage, and they but players on it. Customers can be friendly and entertaining. Tips can be okay. Genitals can be employed at the activities for which they were designed. There must be humor here somewhere.

Walking Tall ★ ★
PG-13, 85 m., 2004

The Rock (Chris Vaughn), Neal McDonough (Jay Hamilton Jr.), Johnny Knoxville (Ray Templeton), John Beasley (Chris Vaughn Sr.), Barbara Tarbuck (Connie Vaughn), Kristen Wilson (Michelle), Khleo Thomas (Pete), Ashley Scott (Deni), Michael Bowen (Sheriff Watkins). Directed by Kevin Bray and produced by Ashok Amritraj, Jim Burke, Lucas Foster, and David Hoberman. Screenplay by David Klass, Channing Gibson, Brian Koppelman, and David Levien.

I didn't see the original *Walking Tall*. I was "out of town at the time," I explained in my review of *Walking Tall, Part 2*. Sounds reasonable. But I suspect the earlier film was tilted more toward populism and less toward superhero violence than the new *Walking Tall*, which is "dedicated to the memory of Buford Pusser," but turns the story into a cartoon of retribution and revenge.

The Rock stars as a war hero named Chris Vaughn who returns to his southern hometown and finds that the mill has closed, a casino has opened, and kids are addicted to drugs. His character is named Chris Vaughn and not Buford Pusser, possibly because The Rock, having gone to a great deal of trouble to adopt a name both simple and authoritative, could not envision himself being called "Buford" or "Sheriff Pusser" for any amount of money.

He finds that an old high school nemesis named Jay Hamilton Jr. (Neal McDonough) has closed the mill, opened the casino, and manufactures the drugs. We know Jay is the villain because he has that close-cropped, curly, peroxided hair that works like a name tag that says, "Hi! I'm the Villain!" Outraged by the corruption that has descended upon his town, The Rock picks up the famous Buford Pusser Model Oak Club, smashes up the casino, defends himself in court, and makes such an impassioned speech that he has soon been elected sheriff. I love those movie trials in which cases are settled not according to guilt and innocence and the law, but according to who is *really* right and *deserves* to go free.

Sheriff Vaughn hires an old high school pal named Ray Templeton to be his deputy. The role is played by Johnny Knoxville, famous for *Jackass*, who is, in fact, completely convincing and probably has a legitimate movie career ahead of him and doesn't have to stuff his underpants with dead chickens and hang upside down over alligator ponds anymore.

The scenes establishing all of these events are handled efficiently and have a certain interest, but then the movie, alas, goes on autopilot with a series of improbable fight scenes that are so heavy on stunts and special effects that we might as well be watching a cartoon. This is an action movie, pure and simple, and one can only wonder what the late Buford Pusser would have made of it. Maybe he would have advised Sheriff Vaughn that times have changed and he should forget the oak club and get himself an AK-47.

The Rock comes out of the movie more or less intact, careerwise. I've felt from the beginning that he had the makings of a movie star, and I still think so; he has a kind of inner quiet that allows him to inhabit preposterous scenes without being overwhelmed by them. His acting style is flat and uninflected, authoritative without pushing it; he's a little like John Wayne that way. Also like Wayne, he's a big, physically intimidating man who is able to suggest a certain gentleness; he's not inflamed, not looking for a fight, not shoving people around, but simply trying to right wrongs. I seriously doubt that he could play a convincing villain. Not even with a name tag.

Walk the Line ★ ★ ★ ½
PG-13, 135 m., 2005

Joaquin Phoenix (John R. Cash), Reese Witherspoon (June Carter), Ginnifer Goodwin (Vivian Cash), Robert Patrick (Ray Cash), Dallas Roberts (Sam Phillips), Dan John Miller (Luther Perkins), Larry Bagby (Marshall Grant), Shelby Lynne (Carrie Cash), Tyler Hilton (Elvis Presley), Waylon Malloy Payne (Jerry Lee Lewis), Shooter Jennings (Waylon Jennings). Directed by James Mangold and produced by James Keach and Cathy Konrad. Screenplay by Gill Dennis and Mangold, based on *Man in Black* by Johnny Cash and *Cash: The Autobiography* by Johnny Cash and Patrick Carr.

Johnny Cash sang like he meant business. He didn't get fancy and he didn't send his voice on missions it could not complete, but there was an urgency in his best songs that pounded them home. When he sang something, it stayed sung. James Mangold's *Walk the Line*, with its dead-on performances by Joaquin Phoenix and Reese Witherspoon, helps you understand that quality. Here was a man whose hard-drinking father blamed him for the death of his older brother, said God "took the wrong son," and looked at Johnny's big new house and all he could say was, "Jack Benny's is bigger." In the movie, you sense that the drive behind a Johnny Cash song was defiance. He was going to sing it no matter what anybody thought—especially his old man.

The movie shows John R. Cash inventing himself. He came from a hardworking Arkansas family and grew up listening to country music on the radio, especially the Carter Family. He wrote his first song while he was serving in the Air Force in Germany. When he came back to the states, he got married and got a regular job but dreamed about being a recording artist. When his first wife, Vivian, complained he was spending more time on music than on her, he referred to his "band" and she said, "Your band is two mechanics who can't even hardly play."

She was just about right. When they finally got the legendary Sam Phillips (Dallas Roberts) of Sun Records in Memphis to let them audition, they sounded like carbon copies of third-rate radio gospel singers. Sam should have shown them the door. Out of kindness, he asked John if he had anything of his own he wanted to play. Cash chose a song he wrote in Germany, "Folsom Prison Blues." One of the key passages in Phoenix's performance comes as Cash learns, while in the process of singing this song, how he should sound and who he should be. You can hear his musicians picking up the tempo to keep pace with him. He starts the song as a loser and ends as Johnny Cash.

Walk the Line follows the story arc of many other musical biopics, maybe because many careers are the same: hard times, obscurity, success, stardom, too much money, romantic adventures, drugs or booze, and then (if they survive) beating the addiction, finding love, and reaching a more lasting stardom. That more or less describes last year's *Ray*, but every time we see this formula the characters change and so does the music, and that makes it new.

What adds boundless energy to *Walk the Line* is the performance by Reese Witherspoon as June Carter Cash. We're told in the movie that June learned to be funny onstage because she didn't think she had a good voice; by the time John meets her she's been a pro since the age of four, and she effortlessly moves back and forth between her goofy onstage persona and her real personality, which is sane and thoughtful, despite her knack for hitching up with the wrong men. Johnny Cash, for that matter, seems like the wrong man, and she holds him at arm's length for years—first because he's a married man, and later because he has a problem with booze and pills.

The film's most harrowing scene shows Johnny onstage after an overdose, his face distorted by pain and anger, looking almost satanic before he collapses. What is most fearsome is not even his collapse, but the force of his will, which makes him try to perform when he is clearly unable to. You would not want to get in the way of that determination. When Cash is finally busted and spends some time in jail, his father is dependably laconic: "Now you won't have to work so hard to make people think you been to jail."

Although Cash's father (played with merciless aim by Robert Patrick) eventually does sober up, the family that saves him is June's. The Carter Family were country royalty ever since the days when their broadcasts came from a high-powered pirate station across the river from Del Rio, Texas. When they take a chance on Cash, they all take the chance; watch her parents as they greet Johnny's favorite pill-pusher.

It is by now well known that Phoenix and Witherspoon perform their own vocals in the movie. It was not well known when the movie previewed—at least not by me. Knowing Cash's albums more or less by heart, I closed my eyes to focus on the sound track and decided that, yes, that was the voice of Johnny Cash I was listening to. The closing credits make it clear it's Joaquin Phoenix doing the singing, and I was gob-smacked. Phoenix and Mangold can talk all they want about how it was as much a matter of getting in character, of delivering the songs, as it was a matter of voice technique, but whatever it was, it worked. Cash's voice was "steady like a train, sharp like a razor," said June.

The movie fudges some on the facts, but I was surprised to learn that Cash actually did propose marriage to Carter onstage during a concert; it feels like the sort of scene screenwriters invent, but no. Other scenes are compressed or fictionalized, as they must be, and I would have liked more screen time for the other outlaws, including Waylon and Willie. Elvis Presley and Jerry Lee Lewis make brief excursions through the plot, but essentially, this is the story of John and June and a lot of great music. And essentially, that's the story we want. ☞

Wallace & Gromit: The Curse of the Were-Rabbit ★ ★ ★ ½
G, 85 m., 2005

With the voices of: Peter Sallis (Wallace), Ralph Fiennes (Lord Quartermaine), Helena Bonham Carter (Lady Tottington), Peter Kay (PC Mackintosh), Liz Smith (Mrs. Mulch), Nicholas Smith (Reverend Clement Hedges). Directed by Nick Park and Steve Box and produced by Claire Jennings, Peter Lord, Park, Carla Shelley, and David Sproxton. Screenplay by Bob Baker, Box, Mark Burton, and Park.

Wallace and Gromit are arguably the two most delightful characters in the history of animation. Between the previous sentence and this one I paused thoughtfully and stared into space and thought of all of the other animated characters I have ever met, and I gave full points to Bugs Bunny and high marks to little Nemo and a fond nod to Goofy, and returned to the page convinced that, yes, Wallace and Gromit are in a category of their own. To know them is to enter a universe of boundless optimism, in which two creatures who are perfectly suited to each other venture out every morning to make the world into a safer place for the gentle, the good, and the funny.

Wallace is an inventor. Gromit is a dog, although the traditional human-dog relationship is reversed in that Gromit usually has to clean up Wallace's messes. No, not those kinds of messes. They're not that kind of movie. In three short subjects and now in their first feature, Wallace sails out bravely to do great but reckless deeds, and Gromit takes the role of adult guardian.

In *Wallace & Gromit: The Curse of the Were-Rabbit*, they face their greatest challenge. Lady Tottington is holding her family's 517th annual Giant Vegetable Fete, and all the gardeners for miles around are lovingly caressing their gigantic melons and zucchinis and carrots and such, and Wallace and Gromit are responsible for security, which means keeping rabbits out of the garden patches.

Their company is named Anti-Pesto. Their methods are humane. They do not shoot or poison the bunnies. Instead, Wallace has devised another of his ingenious inventions, the Bun-Vac, which sucks the rabbits out of their holes and into a giant holding tube, so that they can be housed in comfort at Anti-Pesto headquarters and feast on medium and small vegetables. Their tactics perfectly suit Lady Tottington's humane convictions.

They have a rival, the sniveling barbarian

Lord Victor Quartermaine, a gun nut with a toupee heaped on his head like a mess of the sort Gromit never has to clean up. Lord Victor dreams of marrying Lady Tottington and treating himself to the luxuries of her ancestral wealth, and that involves discrediting and sabotaging Anti-Pesto and all that it stands for. Thus is launched the affair of the Were-Rabbit, a gigantic beast (with a red polka-dot tie) that terrorizes the neighborhood and inspires the Reverend Hedges to cry out, "For our sins a hideous creature has been sent to punish us."

I dare not reveal various secrets involving the Were-Rabbit, so I will skip ahead, or sideways, to consider Wallace's new invention, the Mind-o-Matic, which is intended to brainwash rabbits and convince them they do not like vegetables. That this device malfunctions goes without saying, and that Gromit has to fly to the rescue is a given.

Wallace and Gromit are the inventions of a British animator named Nick Park, who codirects this time with Steve Box. In an era of high-tech CGI, Park uses the beloved traditional form of stop-action animation. He constructs his characters and sets out of Plasticine, a brand of modeling clay, and makes minute adjustments to them between every frame, giving the impression not only of movement but of exuberant life and color bursting from every frame. (As a nod to technology, just a little CGI is incorporated for certain scenes that would be hard to do in Plasticine, as when the vacuumed bunnies are in free fall.)

Remarkably, given the current realities of animation, *Wallace & Gromit: The Curse of the Were-Rabbit* was the second stop-motion animated film in two weeks, after *Tim Burton's Corpse Bride*. Both of these films are wonderful, but Wallace and Gromit have the additional quality of being lovable beyond all measure, inhabiting a world of British eccentricity that produces dialogue such as: "This is worse than 1972, when there were slugs the size of pigs."

Speaking of pigs, some of my favorite books are the Blandings Castle novels by P. G. Wodehouse, in which Lord Emsworth dotes on his beloved pig, Empress of Blandings. I have always assumed the Blandings stories to be unfilmable but now realize that Park is just the man for them, with Wallace as Lord Emsworth and Gromit as George Cyrill Wellbeloved, his Lord-

ship's expert pigman. True, Gromit does not speak, but Wellbeloved is a man of few words, and if Gromit can solve the mystery of the Were-Rabbit, he should be able to handle a pig. ☞

War of the Worlds ★ ★
PG-13, 118 m., 2005

Tom Cruise (Ray Ferrier), Dakota Fanning (Rachel), Miranda Otto (Mary Ann), Tim Robbins (Harlan Ogilvy), Justin Chatwin (Robbie). Directed by Steven Spielberg and produced by Kathleen Kennedy and Colin Wilson. Screenplay by Josh Friedman and David Koepp, based on the novel by H. G. Wells.

War of the Worlds is a big, clunky movie containing some sensational sights but lacking the zest and joyous energy we expect from Steven Spielberg. It proceeds with the lead-footed deliberation of its 1950s predecessors to give us an alien invasion that is malevolent, destructive, and, from the alien point of view, pointless. They've "been planning this for a million years" and have gone to a lot of trouble to invade Earth for no apparent reason and with a seriously flawed strategy. What happened to the sense of wonder Spielberg celebrated in *Close Encounters of the Third Kind,* and the dazzling imagination of *Minority Report?*

The movie adopts the prudent formula of viewing a catastrophe through the eyes of a few foreground characters. When you compare it with a movie like *The Day After Tomorrow,* which depicted the global consequences of cosmic events, it lacks dimension: Martians have journeyed millions of miles to attack a crane operator and his neighbors (and if they're not Martians, they journeyed a lot farther).

The hero, Ray Ferrier (Tom Cruise), does the sort of running and hiding and desperate defending of his children that goes with the territory, and at one point even dives into what looks like certain death to rescue his daughter. There's a survivalist named Ogilvy (Tim Robbins) who has quick insights into surviving: "The ones that didn't flatline are the ones who kept their eyes open." And there are the usual crowds of terrified citizens looking up at ominous threats looming above them. But despite the movie's $135 million budget, it seems curiously rudimentary in its action.

The problem may be with the alien invasion itself. It is not very interesting. We learn that countless years ago, invaders presumably but not necessarily from Mars buried huge machines all over Earth. Now they activate them with lightning bolts, each one containing an alien (in what form, it is hard to say). With the aliens at the controls, these machines crash up out of the earth, stand on three towering but spindly legs, and begin to zap the planet with death rays. Later, their tentacles suck our blood and fill steel baskets with our writhing bodies.

To what purpose? Why zap what you later want to harvest? Why harvest humans? And, for that matter, why balance these towering machines on ill-designed supports? If evolution has taught us anything, it is that limbs of living things, from men to dinosaurs to spiders to centipedes, tend to come in numbers divisible by two. Three legs are inherently not stable, as Ray demonstrates when he damages one leg of a giant tripod, and it falls helplessly to earth.

The tripods are indeed faithful to the original illustrations for H.G. Wells's novel *The War of the Worlds*, and to the machines described in the historic 1938 Orson Welles radio broadcast and the popular 1953 movie. But the book and radio program depended on our imaginations to make them believable, and the movie came at a time of lower expectations in special effects. You look at Spielberg's machines and you don't get much worked up, because you're seeing not alien menace but clumsy retro design. Perhaps it would have been a good idea to set the movie in 1898, at the time of Wells's novel, when the tripods represented a state-of-the-art alien invasion.

There are some wonderful f/x moments, but they mostly don't involve the pods. A scene where Ray wanders through the remains of an airplane crash is somber and impressive, and there is an unforgettable image of a train, every coach on fire, roaring through a station. Such scenes seem to come from a different kind of reality than the tripods.

Does it make the aliens scarier that their motives are never spelled out? I don't expect them to issue a press release announcing their plans for world domination, but I wish their presence reflected some kind of intelligent purpose. The alien ship in *Close Encounters* visited for no other reason, apparently, than to demonstrate that life existed elsewhere, could visit us, and was in-triguingly unlike us while still sharing such universal qualities as the perception of tone.

Those aliens wanted to say hello. The alien machines in *War of the Worlds* seem designed for heavy lifting in an industry that needs to modernize its equipment and techniques. (The actual living alien being we finally glimpse is an anticlimax, a batlike bug-eyed monster, confirming the wisdom of Kubrick and Clarke in deliberately showing no aliens in *2001*.)

The human characters are disappointingly one-dimensional. Tom Cruise's character is given a smidgeon of humanity (he's an immature, divorced hotshot who has custody of the kids for the weekend), and then he wanders out with his neighbors to witness strange portents in the sky, and the movie becomes a story about grabbing and running and ducking and hiding and trying to fight back. There are scenes in which poor Dakota Fanning, as his daughter, has to be lost or menaced, and then scenes in which she is found or saved, all with much desperate shouting. A scene where an alien tentacle explores a ruined basement where they're hiding is a mirror of a better scene in *Jurassic Park* where characters hide from a curious raptor.

The thing is, we never believe the tripods and their invasion are *practical*. How did these vast metal machines lie undetected for so long beneath the streets of a city honeycombed with subway tunnels, sewers, water and power lines, and foundations? And why didn't a civilization with the physical science to build and deploy the tripods a million years ago not do a little more research about conditions on the planet before sending its invasion force? It's a war of the worlds, all right—but at a molecular, not a planetary, level.

All of this is just a way of leading up to the gut reaction I had all through the film: I do not like the tripods. I do not like the way they look, the way they are employed, the way they attack, the way they are vulnerable, or the reasons they are here. A planet that harbors intelligent and subtle ideas for science fiction movies is invaded in this film by an ungainly Erector set. ☞

The Warrior ★ ★ ★
R, 86 m., 2005

Irfan Khan (Lafcadia), Puru Chibber (Katiba, his son), Damayanti Marfatia (Blind Woman), Noor

Mani (Thief), Anupam Shyam (Lord), Aino Annuddin (Pursuer), Firoz Khan (Biswas). Directed by Asif Kapadia and produced by Bertrand Faivre. Screenplay by Kapadia and Tim Miller.

The Warrior tells the story of a fierce warrior who changes the direction of his life after a mystical visionary moment.

Lafcadia is an enforcer in the employ of a cruel lord in the far northwest Indian state of Rajasthan. When a village cannot pay its taxes because of a bad harvest, the lord has their leader beheaded and orders the warrior: "Teach them a lesson."

Lafcadia and his men ride out to the village and rape, pillage, and burn—and then the warrior sees a young village girl wearing an amulet given to her earlier that day by Lafcadia's son; he understands that in killing any child he might as well be killing his own. He has an inexplicable image of a snowy mountain vista, and he vows: "I'll never lift a sword again." The lord is enraged: "No one leaves my service. Bring me his head by dawn."

And so now the hunter has become the hunted. And the man who is hunting him, an ambitious warrior who was eager to replace him, faces a death sentence of his own if he does not return with the warrior's head, or one that looks almost like it. This description makes *The Warrior* sound violent, I know, but almost all the violence takes place offscreen, and the action is located primarily in the warrior's mind.

To save his life, and because he is compelled to seek out the source of his snowy vision, he begins a long trek to the mountains of the north. He is accompanied by an orphaned thief (Noor Mani) whose family he may in fact have killed, and by a blind woman (Damayanti Marfatia) who is on a pilgrimage to a holy lake. "There's blood written on your face," she tells the warrior, and he tells the thief, "She's right about me."

The movie won the Alexander Korda Award for Best British Film at the BAFTA Awards and was named Best British Independent Film at the British Indies. Filmed on location near the Himalayas, it was written and directed by Asif Kapadia, a documentary maker for the BBC.

The film is interesting for what it does not show. Not only is violence offscreen, but so is a lot of motivation; it is only by following the action and then thinking back through the story that we can understand the warrior's thought process. And it is only because he eventually finds the source of his snowy vision that we understand the role it played early in the film. These are not flaws, just curiosities.

What is best in the film is its depiction of the warrior's epic journey, photographed with breathtaking beauty and simplicity by Roman Osin, who just finished filming the new British version of *Pride and Prejudice*. The lands through which the warrior travels are familiar to my imagination from novels like *The Far Pavilions*, and by not setting the film in a particular period, the story takes on a timelessness. It is about people stuck in an ancient culture of repression, greed, and revenge, and how some are able to escape it by a spiritual path. Parallels with the current eye-for-an-eye ideology of the Middle East are inescapable.

It may be that some American moviegoers will find the film's form unsatisfactory. We are accustomed to closure and completion. If a threat is established at the opening of a film, by the end we expect it to be enforced, or evaded. We do not expect it to be . . . outgrown. Our plots are circular; *The Warrior* is linear. There is a kind of strange freedom in the knowledge that a story has cut loose from its origins and is wandering through unknown lands.

Note: It is hilarious that this elegant and thoughtful film has an R rating "for some violence," while buildings are destroyed 9/11-style, thousands are killed, and a nuclear cloud poisons a city in the PG-13-rated Stealth.

Wassup Rockers ★ ★ ★ ½
R, 97 m., 2006

Jonathan Velasquez (Jonathan), Francisco Pedrasa (Kiko), Milton Velasquez (Milton/Spermball), Yunior Usualdo Panameno (Porky), Eddie Velasquez (Eddie), Luis Rojas-Salgado (Louie), Carlos Velasco (Carlos), Iris Zelaya (Iris), Ashley Maldonado (Rosalia), Laura Cellner (Jade), Jessica Steinbaum (Nikki). Directed by Larry Clark and produced by Clark, Kevin Turen, and Henry Winterstern. Screenplay by Clark.

You could think of Larry Clark's *Wassup Rockers* as *Ferris Velasquez's Day Off*. In Los Angeles a group of Latino friends, all about fourteen, spend a very long day traveling from South Central to Beverly Hills and back home again, and although they are lighthearted and looking for fun, they don't have Ferris Bueller's good luck. The movie evokes the sense of time unfolding thoughtlessly for kids who have no idea what could happen next.

Clark usually makes movies about teenagers and has a rapport with them that's privileged or creepy, depending on your point of view. His first film was the powerful *Kids* (1995), which launched the acting careers of four first-timers—Rosario Dawson, Chloe Sevigny, Leo Fitzpatrick, and Justin Pierce—and writer-director Harmony Korine. *Bully* (2001) saw how a group dynamic works to drive teenagers toward a murder none of them would have done alone. *Ken Park* (2002) was bold in its frankness about teenage sexuality; a success at Telluride, it was never released commercially in the United States, not because of its content but because, Clark says, a producer never cleared the music rights.

Now comes *Wassup Rockers,* containing one and probably two deaths, a lot of tension between Latinos and African-Americans, and run-ins with cops and homeowners. Perhaps because we hardly meet the first boy who dies, and the second is shot off-screen, the movie is not as fraught as it could have been, and indeed, is Clark's least harrowing work.

The heroes mostly are of Salvadorian descent, although they are routinely mistaken for Mexican-Americans. They come from a poor district; one kid's mother apparently is a lap dancer. But Clark's characters do not carry guns, steal, use drugs, or smoke (anything). At fourteen years old, you're thinking, let's hope not—but Clark's subject often is how children get into sex, drugs, and violence when they are way too young. These kids don't set out looking for trouble, although it finds them.

The movie opens with a monologue by Jonathan (Jonathan Velasquez), who tells us about his friends; he separates each statement with the phrase "and then . . . ." He's the one the others look up to. We meet Kiko (Francisco Pedrasa), Spermball (Milton Velasquez, who keeps asking everyone to call him Milton, not Spermball), Porky (Yunior Usualdo Panameno), and two girls: Iris (Iris Zelaya), Jonathan's girl-friend, and Rosalia (Ashley Maldonado), who wants to be everybody's girlfriend.

They have a band, which plays very loudly, and they hang around and tell stories on each other (one kid tried to commit suicide, not very seriously, by drowning himself in the sink). Kiko "borrows" a car, and they head in the direction of Beverly Hills High School but are stopped by cops on bikes. Since they have no license or ID, they abandon the car, but they've made it to Beverly Hills, and now they practice skateboard jumping on the steps of the high school. Having seen countless skateboarding scenes in the movies, I appreciated Clark's realism: They fall or crash, again and again and again, trying to get a trick right.

They meet two rich 90210 girls, Jade (Laura Cellner) and Nikki (Jessica Steinbaum), and one of them gives them her address: "Come over anytime." They do. Clark has a good feel for how there is no particular tension between these young teens of different race and class. They're curious and talk openly about their differences. But when the Latinos have to leave suddenly, they begin a tour of upper-class backyards in the hills above Sunset; in one, there's a party going on, and the host is a gay man who tells Jonathan, "You'd be a good model." In another, there's a gun owner who shoots one of them and arranges with the cops to "keep it quiet."

With police looking for them, they're taken in by a rich and drunken woman whose maid looks out for them while the drunk gives one a bath and obviously is interested in what could happen next, once he's cleaned up.

The long journey home is by bus, rapid transit, and foot, and they are tired and scared. The fate of their friend who was shot is left unclear, although he obviously was hit and perhaps was killed. The home streets of South Central are not welcoming to them, because the black kids are not friendly. But in the world of a Larry Clark film, they've gotten off relatively easy. Despite its horrors, this is his most easygoing movie, in large part because the young actors are at ease, like each other, and live with delight.

Clark was an honored photographer before getting into movies in his early fifties. The only subject he feels any passion for is, obviously, the private lives of teenagers. Does that make him a pervert? Look at it this way. Hollywood has a cottage industry in Dead Teenager Movies, all devising formulas in which the young characters die in sudden and colorful ways. Clark listens to them and takes them seriously. His films may be the only truthful ones about some aspects of American adolescence, however we might wish that were not so. *Wassup Rockers,* for better and worse, is about lives that might actually be lived.

Water ★ ★ ★
PG-13, 117 m., 2006

Sarala (Chuyia), Seema Biswas (Shakuntala), Lisa Ray (Kalyani), John Abraham (Narayan), Manorma (Madhumati), Raghuvir Yadav (Gulabi). Directed by Deepa Mehta and produced by David Hamilton. Screenplay by Mehta.

Her father asks Chuyia, "Do you remember getting married?" She does not. He tells her that her husband has died, and she is a widow. She is eight years old. Under traditional Hindu law, she will be a widow for the rest of her life. There are two alternatives: marry her husband's brother or throw herself on his funeral pyre.

Deepa Mehta's *Water* is set in 1938. Even then, laws existed in India that gave widows the freedom to marry, but as one character observes, "We do not always follow the law when it is inconvenient." Torn from her father's grasp, crying out for her mother, Chuyia (Sarala) disappears into an ashram controlled by the lifelong widows who live there. Her hair is cut off. She wears a white garment that marks her. The woman in charge is Madhumati (Manorma), fat, indolent, and domineering, who is frightening to the little girl.

Then she makes a friend. This is the beautiful Kalyani (Lisa Ray), who alone among the widows has been allowed to wear her hair long, but for a sad reason. Madhumati has an arrangement with the pimp Gulabi (Raghuvir Yadav) to supply Kalyani to wealthy clients as a source of income for the ashram. Kalyani has a puppy, which they hide and love together. Another friend in the ashram is Shakuntala (Seema Biswas), a wise, thoughtful woman who questions the foundations of the theory of widowhood. It is Narayan (John Abraham), a follower of Gandhi, who supplies the most pragmatic explanation for the ancient practice: "One less mouth to feed, four less saris, and a free corner in the house. Disguised as religion, it's just about money."

Water is the third film in a trilogy about India by Mehta, whose *Earth* (1998) dealt with the partition of India and Pakistan, and whose *Fire* (1996) dealt with lesbianism among traditional Indian women. She is not popular with Indian religious conservatives, and indeed after the sets for *Water* were destroyed and her life threatened, she had to move the entire production to Sri Lanka. That she is female and deals with political and religious controversy makes her a marked woman.

The best elements of *Water* involve the young girl and the experiences seen through her eyes. I would have been content if the entire film had been her story. But Chuyia meets Narayan, a tall, handsome, foreign-educated follower of Gandhi, and when she brings him together with Kalyani, they fall in love. This does not lead to life happily ever after, but it does set up an ending as melodramatic as it is (sort of) victorious. We're less interested in Kalyani's romantic prospects, however, than with Shakuntala's logical questioning of the underpinnings of her society. It is interesting that the same actress, Biswas, played the title role in the no less controversial *Bandit Queen* (1994).

The film is lovely in the way Satyajit Ray's films are lovely. It sees poverty and deprivation as a condition of life, not an exception to it, and finds beauty in the souls of its characters. Their misfortune does not make them unattractive. In many Indian films it is not startling to be poor, or to be in the thrall of 2,000-year-old customs; such matters are taken for granted, and the story goes on from there. I am reminded of Ray's *The Big City* (1963), in which the husband loses his work and his wife breaks with all tradition and good practice by leaving their home to take employment. The husband is deeply disturbed, but his wife finds that, after all, being a woman and having a job is no big deal.

The unspoken subtext of *Water* is that an ancient religious law has been put to the service of family economy, greed, and a general feeling that women can be thrown away. The widows in this film are treated as if they have no useful lives apart from their husbands. They are given life sentences. They are not so very different from the Irish girls who, having offended someone's ideas of proper behavior, were locked up in the church-run "Magdalene laundries" for the rest of their lives. That a film like *Water* still has the power to offend in the year 2006 inspires the question: Who is still offended, and why, and what have they to gain, and what do they fear? (The character name "Narayan" is a reminder of R. K. Narayan, the novelist whose works are delightful human comedies about life in India.)

The Weather Man ★ ★ ★ ½
R, 102 m., 2005

Nicolas Cage (David Spritz), Michael Caine (Robert), Hope Davis (Noreen), Michael Rispoli (Russ), Gil Bellows (Don), Nicholas Hoult (Mike), Gemmenne de la Pena (Shelly). Directed by Gore Verbinski and produced by Todd Black, Jason Blumenthal, and Steve Tisch. Screenplay by Steve Conrad.

We think of tragic heroes outlined against the horizon, tall and doomed, the victims of their vision and fate, who fall from a great height. *The Weather Man* is about a tragic hero whose fall is from a low height. David Spritz (Nicolas Cage) is a Chicago weatherman whose marriage has failed, whose children are troubled, whose father is disappointed, and whose self-esteem lies in ruins. "All of the people I could be," he tells us, "they got fewer and fewer until finally they got reduced to only one—and that's who I am. The weatherman."

There is nothing ignoble about being a weatherman, especially in Chicago, where we need them. David's fatal flaw (all tragic heroes have one) is that he does not value his own work. Perhaps his viewers sense that, which is why they throw fast food at him from passing cars. They sense that he has embraced victimhood and are tempted. To feel inadequate is Dave Spritz's life sentence. His father, Robert (Michael Caine), is a famous novelist who won the Pulitzer Prize and who has always been disappointed in his son—disappointed, we sense, at every stage of Dave's life, and by everything he has done.

In Robert's mind, it's not that Dave is a weatherman but that he is a bad one. He hasn't done the homework. He's not even a meteorologist. He gets the weather off the news service wires. "Do you know," his father asks him, "that the harder thing to do and the right thing to do are usually the same thing?" Dave has made life easy for himself, but Robert tells him, "Easy

doesn't enter into grown-up life." Dave's life does indeed seem easy. He does the weather for two hours a day with hardly any preparation and makes the occasional personal appearance; we see him in costume as Abraham Lincoln.

This is one of those Nicolas Cage performances where he seems consumed by worry, depression, and misdirected anger. He often parks his car in front of the house he once shared with his wife, Noreen (Hope Davis), his overweight daughter, Shelly (Gemmenne de la Pena), and his troubled son, Mike (Nicholas Hoult). Noreen is now engaged to Russ (Michael Rispoli), and one day Dave slaps Russ in the face with gloves. Now what in the hell kind of a thing is that to do? Something he saw in a movie? Even Dave's grand gestures are pathetic.

I find myself attracted to movies that are really about somebody. Dave Spritz, whatever his failings, is somebody, he is there, he suffers, he hopes. But he exists, as far as he can see, for no purpose. If his father were cruel in an overt way, that would allow him some focus, but Michael Caine's performance turns Robert into a man who wounds with a thousand little cuts, who is urbane and articulate, and whose words are a rebuke not so much because of what he says as by the tender regret with which he says them. That Robert is dying of lymphoma makes it all the more poignant: Dave's father will not only die but die disappointed, and along the way will attend a "living funeral" in honor of himself. Dave was probably fated to do something inappropriate at his father's funeral; how much more pathetic that he does it while his father is still alive to see him.

Dave's problem is that he is never able to find the right note, the appropriate gesture, the correct behavior, try as he does. Perhaps he tries too hard. Perhaps he is always trying, and people sense it. His wife is not an unreasonable woman and allows Dave access to the children. But she is amazed that, at this point, Dave seriously expects the two of them to remarry. The girl, meanwhile, puts on weight, and the boy's counselor wants the kid to take off his shirt for some photos.

Does all of this make for a good movie? I think so—absorbing, morbidly fascinating. One of the trade papers calls it "one of the biggest downers to emerge from a major studio in recent memory . . . an overbearingly glum look at a Chicago celebrity combing through the emotional wreckage of his life." But surely that is a description of the movie, not a criticism of it. Must movies not be depressing? Must major studios not release them if they are? Another trade paper faults the movie for being released by Paramount, when it "probably should have been made by Paramount Classics. For this is a Sundance film gussied up with studio production values and big stars."

I find this reasoning baffling. Are major stars not allowed to appear in offbeat character studies? Is it wrong for a "Sundance film" to have "studio production values"? What distinguishes Cage as an actor is his willingness to take chances. His previous film, *Lord of War,* was also about an off-the-map character. Should he stick with films like *National Treasure?* Before that he made *Matchstick Men* and *Adaptation,* both brilliant, but *Matchstick* was criticized because it was directed by a big name, Ridley Scott, while *Adaptation* was by the indie Spike Jonze. Both invaluable movies. *The Weather Man* seems to offend some critics because it doesn't know its place and wants to be good even though Paramount made it with a star.

The film was directed by Gore Verbinski, who previously made *Pirates of the Caribbean,* and now is making the *Pirates* sequel. How dare he take time off to make an art film? And yet this film has moments of uncommon observation and touching insight. Consider Dave's awkward attempt to bond with his daughter. Shelly unwisely says something about liking archery, and Dave buys her a lot of archery equipment and signs her up for lessons she hates. Has she no sympathy for her old man? Can't she shoot a few arrows? He's trying. The archery episode leads up to a moment of completely unanticipated suspense that concentrates all of Dave's passions and hurts into one moment and one choice.

Yes, *The Weather Man* is a downer, although the sun breaks through from time to time, and there are moments of comedy that are earned, not simply inserted. Do you never want to see a downer? Some time ago, tiring of people telling me, "Oh, I heard that movie was depressing," I started telling them: "Every bad movie is depressing. No good movie is depressing." Sometimes they get it. Sometimes they look at me as if I'm mad. I haven't had any fast food thrown at me yet.

Wedding Crashers ★ ★
R, 119 m., 2005

Owen Wilson (John Beckwith), Vince Vaughn (Jeremy Grey), Christopher Walken (William Cleary), Rachel McAdams (Claire Cleary), Jane Seymour (Kathleen Cleary), Isla Fisher (Gloria Cleary), Bradley Cooper (Sack Lodge), Keir O'Donnell (Todd Cleary), Ellen Albertini Dow (Grandma Cleary), Henry Gibson (Father O'Neil). Directed by David Dobkin and produced by Peter Abrams, Robert L. Levy, and Andrew Panay. Screenplay by Steve Faber and Bob Fisher.

Wedding Crashers is all runway and no takeoff. It assembles the elements for a laugh-out-loud comedy, but it can't make them fly. There are individual moments that are very funny. But it takes a merciless focus to make a good comedy, and the director, David Dobkin, has too much else on his mind. There are sequences involving Vince Vaughn and Owen Wilson where you sense that the actors should have just broken into the cockpit and taken over the controls. There are few lonelier sights than a good comedian being funny in a movie that doesn't know what funny is.

The concept is terrific. The ads will fill the theaters on opening weekend, but people will trail out thinking, gee, I dunno . . . why all the soppy sentiment and whose idea was the potty-mouthed grandmother? And don't they know that in a comedy the villain is supposed to be funny, and not a hateful, sadistic, egotistical monster who when he hits people he really wants to hurt them, and who kicks them when they're down?

Vaughn and Wilson play Jeremy and John, old buddies who crash weddings. They have it all figured out—how to pick up bridesmaids, available girls, unavailable girls, even the occasional straying wife. There's nothing like a wedding to get women feeling romantic. When they debate their seduction theories and go to work on their targets, they're very good, and we sit back expecting the movie to break loose, but the plot makes pointless detours.

Near the beginning, for example, there's a cute montage showing John and Jeremy at a lot of different weddings: Italian, Jewish, Irish, Indian. Different costumes, different food, different dances, great-looking babes. Okay, and then there's *another* montage showing the same stuff, or maybe it's more of the same montage. We feel like we're drifting too far from shore. We need some plot to hang on to.

Jeremy and John's greatest challenge: crashing the yacht club wedding of the daughter of Treasury Secretary Cleary (Christopher Walken). How can this go wrong? Walken can order pizza over the phone and we split a gut. But it goes wrong. Incredibly, the movie never fully exploits Walken's gift for weirdly inspired flights of logical lunacy.

Meanwhile, Jeremy scores down on the beach with the youngest Cleary daughter, Gloria (Isla Fisher), and John falls more seriously in love with the most beautiful Cleary daughter, Claire (Rachel McAdams). Gloria wants her daddy to invite the boys back to the family's shore place, and starts stomping her little feet and throwing a tantrum to get her way—but her tantrum, incredibly, is in long-shot, so we miss the interaction between Walken and his spoiled brat. The movie shows *that* the tantrum happens, as if it needs to explain why her daddy invites the boys to his house. It doesn't need to explain anything; it either has to make it funny, or not show it.

The Clearys are apparently studying to become Kennedys, and on their sprawling lawn Secretary Cleary suggests a game of touch football. That's when we become fully aware of Sack (Bradley Cooper), Claire's fiancé, who tackles with brutality and stares with cold little eyes out of a hard face. He has the charisma of a knife.

There are a lot of ways to make touch football funny, and *Wedding Crashers* misses all of them. Why keep the Walken character so disengaged from the action when it would be funnier for him to get tough than for the hateful Sack, who spreads a cloud of unease in every scene he occupies? I don't blame Cooper for this, by the way; he shows he's very effective. It's just that he should find a movie where he can pound on Vin Diesel.

Formal dining room scenes are often an opportunity for laughter. Remember in *The Party* when Peter Sellers was trying to cut his Cornish game hen, and it flew off his plate and onto the hat of the society lady? In this movie, the dippy daughter slips her hand under the table to rummage among Vaughn's netherlands, and the movie doesn't time the reaction shots and misses the golden opportunity to have someone else at the table realize what's going on—some-

one like Grandmother Cleary (Ellen Albertini Dow), for example. The actress seems well-chosen to utter sweet little hints of sexual encouragement, but the movie prefers to assign her clanking obscenities about Eleanor Roosevelt.

Toward the end, the movie goes gooey. Too many heartfelt speeches, and a scene at an altar that goes on and on and yet avoids exploiting the reactions of the congregation. Also toward the end, the movie brings in a surprise guest star like a pinch hitter who can clear the bases, but his specialty (picking up girls at funerals) is treated as if it's funny all by itself, and doesn't need to be *made* funny.

Also wandering through this stretch is a priest (the reliable Henry Gibson), who is dealt with mostly in bewildered reaction shots; his most crucial moment in the plot happens offscreen. Thinking of what he must have said offscreen makes me smile. And there is a hapless Cleary brother, Todd (Keir O'Donnell), a stoop-shouldered, spike-haired "artist" who hates his family; the movie keeps starting to do something with him and then misplacing him.

There were probably days on the set of *Wedding Crashers* when everyone thought they had a winner. Vaughn and Wilson do dialogue scenes together that achieve a poetry of comic timing and invention. McAdams is a honey, and Fisher has everything she needs to play a hilarious nymphomaniac except the dialogue and the opportunity.

But how do you misplace Walken in a movie like this? How do you end up with Will Ferrell looking like an afterthought? You know all those horror stories about a cigar-chomping producer who screens a movie and says they need to lose fifteen minutes and shoot a new ending? *Wedding Crashers* needed a producer like that.

The Wedding Date ★ ★ ½
PG-13, 90 m., 2005

Debra Messing (Kat Ellis), Dermot Mulroney (Nick Mercer), Amy Adams (Amy), Jack Davenport (Edward Fletcher-Wooten), Jeremy Sheffield (Jeffrey), Peter Egan (Victor Ellis), Holland Taylor (Bunny Ellis). Directed by Clare Kilner and produced by Jessica Bendinger, Paul Brooks, Michelle Chydzik, and Nathalie Marciano. Screenplay by Dana Fox.

The Wedding Date presents the curious case of two appealing performances surviving a bombardment of schlock. I have so many questions about the movie's premise that it seems, in memory, almost entirely composed of moments when I was shaking my head in disbelief. The character played by Dermot Mulroney is a romance novel fantasy, and yet that doesn't prevent him from also being subtle and intriguing. The character played by Debra Messing not only finds Mulroney through an article in the *Sunday New York Times Magazine,* but seems to have found herself there, too, in the spring fashion issue. But she is nevertheless lovable and touching.

The premise: Kat Ellis (Messing) is a British woman living in New York, who must fly back to London for her sister's wedding. The problem: The groom's best man, Jeff, is Kat's former fiancé, who dumped her. The solution: She hires a male escort named Nick (Mulroney) to go along with her and play the role of her fiancé, so that Jeff will be jealous and she won't look pathetic and single. Nick gets $6,000 plus his airfare on Virgin Upper Class, which is also what he offers: Sex would be extra.

The movie develops the usual assortment of impossible relatives and fun wedding activities; some scenes look like they're posed for snapshots in the *Tatler,* a British society magazine devoted to pretending to like twits. The story expertly compacts *Four Weddings and a Funeral, Pretty Woman,* and *My Best Friend's Wedding* into *One Wedding, an Ex-Best Friend, and a Pretty Man,* with Mulroney (who played the best friend in the original) as the escort with a heart of gold.

Yes, and yet the movie isn't giddy with silliness. There's a melancholy undertow. Mulroney seems to have taken a close look at his character and realized that the less Nick says, the better. His personal thoughts are a closely guarded secret, and he makes a point of separating his role as an escort from his feelings as a man. When there comes, as inevitably there must, a moment when his feelings win out, the movie signals this not with clunky dialogue but with the most romantic use of an anchovy I can recall.

Messing, from TV's *Will & Grace,* makes Kat a character who is dealing with two confusing situations at once. She doesn't know how she feels about hiring an escort, and she doesn't know how she feels about Jeff (Jeremy Sheffield). Does she want Jeff back, or does she just want to make him miserable? Subplots grind away to create last-minute problems for her sister, Amy (Amy Adams), and her fiancé, the forthrightly named Edward Fletcher-Wooten (Jack Davenport). Nick the escort is so handsome, so mysteriously knowledgeable, so at home in every situation, and so wise that Kat forgets everything a grown-up girl like her should know about prostitution, role-playing, and the dangers of STDs, and relates to him as if she were the heroine on the cover of a novel by Jennifer Blake.

"Every woman has the exact love life she wants," Nick believes, according to the *Times* magazine article. It is his job to figure out what that is, and create the illusion that he is supplying it. "It's not about the sex," he says, "it's about what people need." And what does Kat need? Nick says he heard something in her voice on the phone. "Desperation?" she asks. "I think it was hope," he says. Down, boy!

Part of the movie's appeal comes from the way the Nick character negotiates the absurdities of the plot as if he stands outside it. A lesser performance, or one not as skillfully written (by Dana Fox) would have pitched him headlong into the fray. By withdrawing, so to speak, he creates a great curiosity about himself, and the other characters see in him what they need to see. As for Messing, she has an appeal similar to Nia Vardalos's in *My Big Fat Greek Wedding.* We want her to be happy. Whether that happiness will come at the hands of Nick is an excellent question, made simpler by the certainty that Jeff would only make her miserable. The answer to this and other questions, every single one of them, is supplied by one of those romantic comedy endings where false crisis and false hope and real crisis and real hope alternate like a clockwork mechanism. Everyone appears and disappears exactly on cue, driving around in sports cars with the top down and running around in shoes meant only for walking down the aisle.

As for Nick, what makes him happy? Is it also true that every man has the exact love life he wants? Does he want his? When he watches *Five Easy Pieces* and Jack Nicholson says, "I faked a little Chopin, and you faked a big response," does he see himself as the pianist, or the piano?

We Don't Live Here Anymore ★ ★
R, 101 m., 2004

Mark Ruffalo (Jack Linden), Laura Dern (Terry Linden), Peter Krause (Hank Evans), Naomi Watts (Edith Evans), Sam Charles (Sean Linden), Haili Page (Natasha Linden), Jennifer Bishop (Sharon Evans). Directed by John Curran and produced by Jonas Goodman, Harvey Kahn, and Naomi Watts. Screenplay by Larry Gross, based on stories by Andre Dubus.

Jack and Edith, who are married to other people, are seized with the need to have sex right then and there, in the middle of the night, in Edith's living room. But what about her husband, Hank? If he wakes up, she says, "he'll go to the bathroom first; we'll hear him." That kind of domestic detail compounds the betrayal, taking advantage of her husband's humanity at just that moment when the last thing they should be doing is listening for poor Hank to flush the toilet.

We Don't Live Here Anymore is set in the shabby moral surroundings of two couples who know each other too well, and themselves not well enough. Jack Linden (Mark Ruffalo) and Hank Evans (Peter Krause) are professors on a small campus in Oregon; Jack is married to Terry (Laura Dern) and Hank to Edith (Naomi Watts). One night at a party Jack finds that the beer supply has run low and says he'll go get some more. Edith says she'll go along for the ride. Later that night Terry asks her husband if it isn't time for him to stop going off with Edith on their phony little missions and leaving her behind with Hank.

Jack plays innocent, but fairly early in the film it's clear that both couples (and eventually their children) have a pretty good idea of what's going on. *We Don't Live Here Anymore* isn't about shocking discoveries and revelations, but about four people who move with varying degrees of eagerness toward, and then away from, the kinds of sexual cheating they may have read about in the pages of John Cheever, Philip Roth, or John Updike—whose characters are too sophisticated to be surprised by adultery, but not very good at it.

The movie, directed by John Curran and written by Larry Gross, is based on two stories by Andre Dubus. As with *In the Bedroom* (2001), also based on the work of Dubus, it listens carefully to what couples say in the privacy of their own long knowledge of themselves. What we hear this time is that Jack thinks Terry drinks too much, and Terry agrees. But Jack isn't cheating with Edith because his wife is a drunk; he's cheating because he wants too, because he and Edith have fallen into a season of lust. Hank, meanwhile, is not particularly alarmed by his cheating wife, because he's a serial cheater himself. His philosophy, explained to Jack: Sure, you should love your wife and kids, but it's okay to fool around sometimes "just because it feels good."

For Jack and Edith, it feels really good that first time, on the blanket in the woods near the bike trail. It feels so good that Jack has flashbacks to it every time he's near the place where it happened—while taking his kids on a bike ride, for example. The movie presents those flashbacks with an odd undertone, as if they're bothering him. Is that because he regrets what he did, or regrets he isn't doing it again right now? Hard to say.

As for his wife, Terry, she tells Jack that she and Hank have had sex, and Jack's response is not the emotional reaction of a wounded man, but the intellectual combativeness of an English professor who wants details of their conversations because he thinks somehow he can win this battle on a logical level. Hank, for that matter, also seems to prefer the theory to the practice of sex, although he confesses to Jack that he cried after breaking up with his last mistress.

These people are such whiners. They mope and complain and recycle their petty little marital grudges, and we yearn for—well, not for more passion, which doesn't come with the territory in stories of academic adultery, but more edge, cruelty, psychological wounding, slashing sarcasm, sadistic button-pushing. Consider George and Martha, virtuosos of verbal spousal abuse in *Who's Afraid of Virginia Woolf?* Or Neil LaBute's coldly evil characters in *Your Friends and Neighbors* (1998). Or the sardonic battle of wits between David Strathairn and Saul Rubinek (and their wives, Bonnie Bedelia and Caroleen Feeney) in *Bad Manners* (1997).

Jack and Terry and Hank and Edith are halfhearted in their cheating. Yes, the sex is great between Jack and Edith when they're on the blanket in the woods, or downstairs listening for Hank to pee, but didn't Woody Allen observe that the worst sex he'd had wasn't that bad? That three children are involved, and all three sense what's happening, acts like an undertow, demonstrating to the adults that they don't really want to face the consequences of their actions.

What must be said is that the actors are better than the material. There are four specific people here, each one closely observed and carefully realized. Ruffalo's Jack, driven by his lust, finds his needs fascinating to himself; Naomi Watts's Edith finds them fascinating to her. Terry and Hank seem almost forced into their halfhearted affair, and Laura Dern and Peter Krause are precise in the way they show dutiful excitement in each other's presence, while Dern vibrates with anger and passion in her arguments with her husband.

The film's problem is that it's too desultory. Maybe the point of the Dubus stories was to show perfunctory transgressions between characters not sufficiently motivated to accept the consequences. They approach adultery the way they might approach a treadmill, jumping on, punching the speed and incline buttons, working up a sweat, coming back down to level, slowing to a walk, and then deciding the goddamn thing isn't worth the trouble.

Welcome to Mooseport ★ ★ ★
PG-13, 110 m., 2004

Gene Hackman (Monroe Cole), Ray Romano (Handy Harrison), Marcia Gay Harden (Grace Sutherland), Maura Tierney (Sally Mannis), Christine Baranski (Charlotte Cole), Fred Savage (Bullard), Rip Torn (Bert Langdon). Directed by Donald Petrie and produced by Marc Frydman, Basil Iwanyk, and Tom Schulman. Screenplay by Tom Schulman.

I knew a very good poker player who always lost money at bachelor parties. He'd turn a profit in Vegas, but down in the basement with the beer and the cigar smoke he invariably got cleaned out. The reason, he explained, was that the jerks he was playing against didn't know how to play poker. They bet on every hand. They raised when they should have folded. You

couldn't tell when they were bluffing because they knew so little they were always bluffing.

Gene Hackman plays a character like that in *Welcome to Mooseport.* The movie isn't about poker but the principle is the same. He is a former president of the United States who has moved to a colorful Maine hamlet and suddenly finds himself running for mayor. His problem is, he knows way too much about politics to run for mayor of Mooseport. And way too little about Mooseport.

Hackman is one of the most engaging actors on the face of the earth. He's especially good at bluster. "The Eagle has landed," he declares, arriving in town. His name is Monroe "The Eagle" Cole, and don't forget the nickname. His opponent in the race is Handy Harrison (Ray Romano), a plumber who owns the local hardware store. "Let me get this straight," says The Eagle. "I'm running for mayor against the man who is repairing my toilet?"

There are romantic complications. Handy has been dating local beauty Sally Mannis (Maura Tierney) for seven years, without ever having gotten up the nerve to pop the question. As the movie opens, his face lights up with joy as he races over to tell her he's come into some money, and so the time is finally right to . . . buy that pickup. When The Eagle asks her out to dinner, she accepts.

Of course, he has no idea Handy and Sally have been dating. For that matter, the only reason he's in Mooseport at all is that his bitchy ex-wife, Charlotte (Christine Baranski), got the big house in the divorce settlement. Now time hangs heavily on his hands, he's surrounded by a support staff with nothing to do, and a mayoral race has them all exercising their overtrained skills. The only sane voice in his entourage belongs to Grace Sutherland (Marcia Gay Harden), who may be hoping that someday The Eagle will land on her.

Rip Torn plays the Karl Rove role. What a pleasure Torn is. Like Christopher Walken and Steve Buscemi, he makes us smile just by appearing on the screen. His Machiavellian approach to Mooseport is all wrong, however, because the town is so guileless and goodhearted that schemes are invisible to them. We question that such a naive and innocent town could exist in America, and are almost relieved to find that the movie was shot in Canada. Has it seemed to you lately that Canada is the last remaining repository of the world Norman Rockwell used to paint?

There is a genre of movies about outsiders who arrive in small towns and are buffaloed by the guileless locals. Consider David Mamet's *State and Main* (2000) or *Win a Date with Tad Hamilton!*. There's always a romance with a local, always a visiting sophisticate who rediscovers traditional values, always a civic booster in a bow tie, always a microphone that deafens everyone with a shriek whenever it's turned on, always an embarrassing public display of dirty laundry, and almost always a Greek chorus of regulars at the local diner/tavern/launderette who pass judgment on events.

Whether the movie works or not depends on the charm of the actors. Gene Hackman could charm the chrome off a trailer hitch. Ray Romano is more of the earnest, aw-shucks, sincere, well-meaning kind of guy whose charm is inner and only peeks out occasionally. They work well together here, and Maura Tierney does a heroic job of playing a character who doesn't know how the story will end, when everybody else in the cast and in the audience has an excellent idea.

What the #$*! Do We Know? ★ ★ ½

NO MPAA RATING, 108 m., 2004

Marlee Matlin (Amanda), Elaine Hendrix (Jennifer), John Ross Bowie (Elliot). And appearances by David Albert, Joe Dispenza, Amit Goswami, John Hagelin, Stuart Hameroff, Dr. Miceal Ledwith, Daniel Monti, Andrew B. Newberg, Candace Pert, Ramtha, Jeffrey Satinover, William Tiller, and Fred Alan Wolf. Directed by Mark Vicente, Betsy Chasse, and William Arntz, and produced by Arntz and Chasse. Screenplay by Arntz, Chasse, and Mathew Hoffman.

Why does anything exist? How do I know it exists? What do I mean when I say "I"? It's convenient to pin everything on God, but if there is a God, he provided us with brains and curiosity and put us in what seems to be a physical universe, and so we cannot be blamed for trying to figure things out. Newton seemed to have it about right, but it's been downhill ever since.

And with the introduction of quantum physics, even unusually intelligent people like you and me have to admit we are baffled.

What the #$! Do We Know?* is a movie that attempts to explain quantum physics in terms anyone can understand. It succeeds, up to a point. I understood every single term. Only the explanation eluded me. Physicists, philosophers, astronomers, biologists, and neurologists describe their strange new world, in which matter (a) cannot be said to exist for sure, although (b) it can find itself in two places at the same time. Time need not flow in one direction, and our perception of reality may be a mental fabrication.

Among the experts on the screen, only one seemed to make perfect sense to me. This was a pretty, plumpish blond woman with clear blue eyes, who looked the camera straight in the eye, seemed wise and sane, and said that although the questions might be physical, the answers were likely to be metaphysical. Since we can't by definition understand life and the world, we might as well choose a useful way of pretending to.

Sounded good to me, especially compared to the cheerful evasions, paradoxes, and conundrums of the other experts. Only after the movie was over did I learn from my wife, who is informed on such matters, that the sane woman who made perfect sense was in fact Ramtha—or, more precisely, Ramtha as channeled by the psychic JZ Knight, who would seem to be quite distinctive enough without leaving the periods out of her name. And who is Ramtha? From Cathleen Falsani, the religion writer of the *Chicago Sun-Times*, I learn that Ramtha is a 35,000-year-old mystical sage from the lost continent of Atlantis. Well, weirder authorities have surfaced. Or maybe not.

What the Bleep Do We Know, as it is referred to for convenience, is not a conventional documentary about quantum physics. It's more like a collision in the editing room between talking heads, an impenetrable human parable and a hallucinogenic animated cartoon. The parts have so little connection and fit together so strangely that the movie seems to be channel surfing. This is not a bad thing, but wondrously curious. There are three directors, and I wonder if they made the movie like one of those party games where you write the first sentence of a story and pass it along, and someone else writes the second sentence and then folds the paper so the third person can't see the first sentence, and so on.

We meet many wise men and women from august institutions, who sit in front of bookshelves and landscapes and describe the paradoxes and inexplicabilities of quantum physics. They seem to agree that quantum physics accurately describes the universe, but they don't seem sure about the universe it describes. Perhaps the universe is going into and out of existence at every moment, or switching dimensions, or is a construct of our minds, or is mostly made of nothing. Perhaps we cannot observe it but only observe ourselves as we think we're observing it.

The experts do not know the answers to these questions, and admit it. They have quixotic little smiles as they explain why it is that there are no answers. What makes them experts? I guess it's because they have been able to formulate the questions, and intuit the ways in which they are prevented from being answered. Gene Siskel ended every interview by asking his subjects, "What do you know for sure?" These people know for sure that they can't know for sure. At some point in the movie I would have enjoyed, as a change of pace, a professor of French who explains he cannot speak the language, that perhaps nobody can, and cautions us that France may not exist.

Intercut with their intellectual flailing (which is charming, intelligent, articulate, and by definition baffled), we get the story of a young woman named Amanda (Marlee Matlin). She is a photographer who has many questions about her life. Many of these are the usual questions we all have, like what does my life mean, and why do I look like this in the mirror? She unhappily attends a wedding party at which people think they are dancing and having a good time, but may in fact be bouncing randomly through space and time without a clue. Well, most parties are like that, but what we don't suspect is that the subatomic particles in our bodies may be partying in exactly the same way.

To visualize this idea, the filmmakers use brightly colored animated blobs to represent emotions, tendencies, memes, engrams, delusions, behavior patterns, senses, and various forms of matter or energy, all wandering around the universe trying to get a drink or maybe meet someone. As we see how random

everything is, how much chance is involved, and what the odds are of anything happening or not happening, we ask ourselves, "What the #$*! Do We Know?" And we conclude that we don't know s#!t.

That's where Ramtha comes in. Cathleen Falsani, who must have been taking notes while I was staring gobsmacked at the screen, quotes the 35,000-year-old Atlantean: "That we simply are has allowed this reality we call real, from the power of intangibility, to pull, out of inertness, action . . . and mold it into a form we call matter." Like I said, Ramtha makes perfect sense. That I simply am a film critic has allowed this reality we call *What the #$*! Do We Know?*, however intangible, to be molded into a form I call a movie review. Isn't life great?

When Will I Be Loved ★ ★ ★ ★
R, 81 m., 2004

Neve Campbell (Vera), Fred Weller (Ford), Dominic Chianese (Count Tommaso), Karen Allen (Alexandra), Barry Primus (Victor), Mike Tyson (Himself). Directed by James Toback and produced by Ron Rotholz. Screenplay by Toback.

When Will I Be Loved is like a jazz solo that touches familiar themes on its way to a triumphant and unexpected conclusion. Neve Campbell plays the soloist, a rich girl who likes to walk on the wild side, is open to the opportunities of the moment, and improvises a devious and spontaneous revenge when her boyfriend betrays her. Here is a movie that doesn't start out to be about a con, but ends up that way.

Campbell's performance is carnal, verbally facile, physically uninhibited, and charged with intelligence. Not many actresses could have played this character, and fewer still could give us the sense she's making it up as she goes along. She plays Vera, daughter of wealth, girlfriend of a persuasive street hustler named Ford (Fred Weller). Ford is smart, quick, cynical, and believes in making his own opportunities. He's engaged in trying to scam Count Tommaso (Dominic Chianese), an Italian millionaire who turns out to be interested in only one thing Ford might have to offer: his girlfriend.

The count suggests an introduction. Ford

mentions money. Money is not a problem. The count is a man of the world, cultivated, with taste but without scruples. He would never make the mistake of implying that cash will be exchanged for sex. He uses the soothing language of money as a gift or tribute or simply a gesture, as if Vera deserves his money because she is so splendid a person.

Ford pitches the idea to Vera, after a scene in which they have enthusiastic sex; Vera has earlier had spontaneous sex with a girlfriend, and is a thoroughly sensual creature. We begin to understand why she is attracted to Ford, why she even likes him, why she's entertained by the audacity of his pitch to the world. But Ford is poor and needs money, and pushes too hard in the wrong way.

Vera agrees to meet with the count, as much for her own amusement as anything. She quickly ups the talking price from $100,000 to $1 million—both sums negligible to the count. She discovers that Ford, as the middle man, was going to cheat her on her share. She is dealing with a man who wants to sell her and another who wants to buy her, and neither one understands two things: (1) She is offended by being bought and sold, and (2) she doesn't need the money.

Toback began as a writer *(The Gambler)* before going on to write and direct such films as *Fingers* and *Black and White*, and to write *Bugsy* for Warren Beatty. In his work and in his life, he likes risk, likes gambling, likes women, and once tried to pick up so many in a short span of time that the late *Spy* magazine ran a four-page foldout chart of whom he hit on, what he told them, and how he scored. There's a little of Ford in his character, but also a little of Vera and the count, especially in his delight in verbal negotiation.

The centerpiece of the film is an extended scene between Vera and the count, as they discuss the amount of money and what it is being paid for. Vera is very specific about the money, and the count is politely vague about exactly what he expects for it, until Vera makes it clear that the count is likely to be pleased with the outcome. It is possible that Vera might have gone through with the deal, not for $1 million but for the danger, excitement, and audacity of negotiating for the $1 million and then delivering; the count is not young, but he is trim, elegant, sophisticated, and

probably good company—at dinner, you know, and the opera, and at what he means when he mentions dinner and the opera.

Now I can tell you no more of the plot, except to say that it involves Vera's evolving response to a situation that develops in ways no one could have foreseen. I've seen countless movies in which people were conned or double-crossed or trapped by a con within a con (*Criminal* is an example). They all have to clear one hurdle: How could the characters predict so accurately who would do what, right on schedule, to make the pieces fall into place?

What is fascinating and ingenious about *When Will I Be Loved* is that nothing need be anticipated, not even the possibility of a con. In scenes of flawless timing, logic, and execution, Vera improvises in a fluid situation and perhaps even surprises herself at where she ends up. The third act of this movie is spellbinding in the way Vera distributes justice and revenge, and adapts to the unexpected and creates, spontaneously and in the moment, a checkmate.

Toback's structure backs into his perfect ending. There's an early scene where he plays a professor who is interviewing Vera for a job as his assistant, and then the two of them begin to speak openly about what is "really" going on; that's the curtain-raiser for the later high-stakes negotiation. There is a scene with Mike Tyson (so effective in *Black and White*) that plays like comic relief, until you think about it in the context of the movie. There's the lesbian scene, which seems gratuitous at the time but later seems necessary to establish Vera's carnal curiosity and Ford's ignorance of her complexity.

And the verbal sparring between Vera and the count is an exercise in the precise and stylish use of language to communicate exact meanings while using inexact euphemisms. Dominic Chianese and Neve Campbell are like virtuoso soloists with conversation as their instrument; the way they test and challenge each other is underlined by their obvious joy in performance. Both characters seem pleased to find another person who can engage them on their level of emotional negotiation.

The song "When Will I Be Loved" is about someone who complains, "I've been cheated—been mistreated." In the movie, the cheater and the mistreater have no idea who they're dealing with.

Where the Truth Lies ★ ★ ★

NO MPAA RATING, 107 m., 2005

Kevin Bacon (Lanny Morris), Colin Firth (Vince Collins), Alison Lohman (Karen O'Connor), Rachel Blanchard (Maureen O'Flaherty), David Hayman (Rubin), Maury Chaykin (Sally SanMarco), Sonja Bennett (Bonnie). Directed by Atom Egoyan and produced by Robert Lantos. Screenplay by Egoyan, based on the novel by Rupert Holmes.

Where the Truth Lies is film noir right down to the plot we can barely track; we're reminded of William Faulkner asking Raymond Chandler who did it in *The Big Sleep* and Chandler saying he wasn't sure. Certainly somebody did it in *Where the Truth Lies,* or how would a dead waitress from Miami end up in a bathtub in Atlantic City? The waitress was last seen in the Miami suite of Lanny Morris and Vince Collins, two famous 1950s entertainers. Their alibi: They were on TV, doing their polio telethon, and then got directly on a plane and flew to New York with a lot of other people and had a police escort to their hotel, where the body was awaiting them.

Atom Egoyan, no stranger to labyrinthine plots, makes this one into a whodunit puzzle crossed with some faraway echoes of *Sunset Boulevard,* as an entertainer is confronted with events from the past that might best be left forgotten. The movie takes place in 1957 and 1972, and both of those years involve the crucial participation of beautiful young blondes who want to interview the two stars.

In 1957, Morris (Kevin Bacon) and Collins (Colin Firth) are at the height of their fame, doing a nightclub act not a million miles apart from Martin and Lewis. The secret of their around-the-clock energy is the use of pills, lots of pills, from their Dr. Feelgood, which give them more urgency than they need in the realm of sex. A college student named Maureen O'Flaherty (Rachel Blanchard) arrives at their suite with room service, and when they suggest another kind of service, she seems sort of willing. She wants to interview them for her school paper.

It is Maureen who is found dead in Atlantic City, leading to a mystery that is never solved and to the breakup of Morris and Collins. Flash forward to 1972, and another would-be re-

porter, Karen O'Connor (Alison Lohman). Still in her mid-twenties, she negotiates a million-dollar book contract for Collins, who needs the money, but tells him he will have to talk about the murder of Maureen O'Flaherty. What Collins doesn't know is that Karen earlier met Lanny Morris on an airplane, followed him to his hotel room, and was dumped the next morning. What a rotter. What neither man knows is that Karen first met them in 1957, when as a young polio victim she appeared on their telethon. Nor does she know that Morris's tears as he talked to her were inspired not by her plight but by his knowledge that a dead waitress was on the sofa in their hotel suite.

Who killed the waitress and why? It's a classic locked-room mystery; all the relevant doors were locked from the inside, and so either man could have done it. But what if neither did? One imagines Ellery Queen rubbing his hands and getting down to work.

The attempts of Karen O'Connor to get Collins to talk are complicated by his own secrecy, financial need, lust, and general depravity. From his hillside mansion in Los Angeles, he lives in lonely isolation, happy to come and go as he pleases. His former partner, Morris, maintains an office and is apparently more active in showbiz, and both of them have reasons to pressure and mislead the young woman.

Because I have seen *Where the Truth Lies* twice and enjoyed it more when I understood its secrets, I don't understand why several critics have found Alison Lohman wrong for the job of playing the reporter in 1972. Is she too young? If she was nine in 1957, she would be twenty-four in 1972. Would a publisher give her such responsibility? If she can really deliver Collins, maybe one would—and the money depends on delivering. Is it a coincidence that Miss O'Connor looks something like Miss O'Flaherty? No, not if what she represents for both men is an eerie shadow from the past.

The movie departs from film noir and enters the characteristic world of Egoyan in its depiction of sex. Both blondes, and a third one I will not describe, are involved in fairly specific sex scenes with one or both men, and the sad and desperate nature of this sex is a reminder of such Egoyan films as *Exotica.* The MPAA rated the film NC-17 and refused an appeal, so it's being released unrated, but the sex really isn't the point of the scenes in question; it's the application of power, and the way that showbiz success can give stars unsavory leverage with young women who are more impressed than they should be.

Bacon is on a roll right now after several good roles, and here he channels diabolical sleaze while mugging joylessly before the telethon cameras. His relationship with the Firth character involves love and hate and perhaps more furtive feelings. There is a stunning scene in a nightclub where a drunk insults Morris, and Collins invites him backstage for a terrifying demonstration of precisely how those happy pills do not make everyone equally happy.

Alison Lohman has the central role. I've known young reporters like her. Some of them may be reading this review. You know who you are. She is smart, sexy, hungering for a big story, burning with ambition, and (most dangerous of all) still harboring idealistic delusions. Would a young woman like this find herself suddenly inside two lives of secrecy and denial? Yes, more easily than Kitty Kelly would, because she doesn't seem to represent a threat. Her youth is crucial because in some way, the danger Maureen O'Flaherty walked into is still potentially there.

There's another way in which the movie works, and that's through the introduction of an unexpected character, Maureen's mother. Another director might handle the showbiz and the murder and intrigue with dispatch, but Egoyan thinks about the emotional cost to the characters, as he also did in *Felicia's Journey*. The mother and the young reporter have a meeting during which we discover the single good reason why the solution to the murder should not be revealed. It is a flawed reason because it depends on the wrong solution, but that isn't the point: It functions to end the film in poignancy rather than sensation.

White Chicks ★ ½
PG-13, 100 m., 2004

Marlon Wayans (Marcus Copeland), Shawn Wayans (Kevin Copeland), Anne Dudek (Tiffany Wilson), Maitland Ward (Brittany Wilson), Brittany Daniel (Megan Vandergeld), Jaime King (Heather Vandergeld), Rochelle Aytes (Denise), Lochlyn Munro (Agent Harper), Frankie Faison (FBI Chief), Terry Crews (Latrell). Directed by Keenen Ivory Wayans and produced by Keenen Ivory Wayans, Shawn Wayans, and Marlon Wayans. Screenplay by Keenen Ivory Wayans.

Various combinations of the Wayans family have produced a lot of cutting-edge comedy, but *White Chicks* uses the broad side of the knife. Here is a film so dreary and conventional that it took an act of the will to keep me in the theater. Who was it made for? Who will it play to? Is there really still a market for fart jokes?

Marlon and Shawn Wayans play Marcus and Kevin Copeland, brothers who are FBI agents. Fired after a sting goes wrong, they're given a second chance. Their assignment: Protect Tiffany and Brittany Wilson (Anne Dudek and Maitland Ward), high-society bimbos who seem to be the target of a kidnapping scheme. The girls get tiny cuts in a car crash and are too vain to attend a big society bash in the Hamptons. Marcus and Kevin have the answer: They'll disguise themselves as the Wilsons and attend the party in drag.

Uh-huh. They call in experts who supply them with latex face masks, which fool everybody in the Hamptons but looked to me uncannily like the big faces with the talking lips on Conan O'Brien. There is also the problem that they're about six inches taller than the Wilsons. I guess they're supposed to be, I dunno, Paris and Nicky Hilton, but at least the Hiltons look like clones of humans, not exhibits in a third-rate wax museum.

The gag is not so much that black men are playing white women as that men learn to understand women by stepping into their shoes and dishing with their girlfriends. Womanhood in this version involves not empowerment and liberation, but shopping, trading makeup and perfume tips, and checking out the cute guys at the party. "Tiffany" and "Brittany" pick up a posse of three friendly white girls, inherit the Wilsons' jealous enemies, and engage in the most unconvincing dance contest ever filmed, which they win with a break-dancing exhibition.

Meanwhile, a pro athlete named Latrell (Terry Crews) is the top bidder at a charity auction for Marcus, who represents his ideal: "A white chick with a black woman's ass!" This leads to all sorts of desperately unfunny situations in which Marcus tries to keep his secret while Latrell goes into heat. Also meanwhile, a labyrinthine plot unfolds about who is really behind the kidnapping, and why.

The fact that *White Chicks* actually devotes expository time to the kidnap plot shows how lame-brained it is, because no one in the audience can conceivably care in any way about its details. Audiences who see the TV commercials and attend *White Chicks* will want sharp, transgressive humor, which they will not find, instead of a wheezy story about off-the-shelf bad guys, which drags on and on in one complicated permutation after another.

Are there any insights about the races here? No. Are there any insights into the gender gap? No. As men or women, black or white, the Wayans brothers play exactly the same person: an interchangeable cog in a sitcom.

Because they look so odd in makeup, the effect is quease-inducing. They fall victims, indeed, to the Uncanny Valley Effect. This phenomenon, named in 1978 by the Japanese robot expert Masahiro Mori, refers to the ways in which humans relate emotionally with robots. Up to a certain point, he found, our feelings grow more positive the more the robots resemble humans. But beyond a certain stage of reality, it works the other way: The closer they get to humans, the more we notice the differences and are repelled by them. In the same way, the not-quite convincing faces of the two white chicks provide a distraction every moment they're on the screen. We're staring at them, not liking them, and paying no attention to the plot. Not that attention would help.

The White Countess ★ ★ ★
PG-13, 138 m., 2005

Ralph Fiennes (Todd Jackson), Natasha Richardson (Countess Sofia Belinsky), Vanessa Redgrave (Aunt Sara), Lynn Redgrave (Olga), Madeleine Daly (Katya Belinsky), Hiroyuki Sanada (Mr. Matsuda), Allan Corduner (Samuel). Directed by James Ivory and produced by Ismail Merchant. Screenplay by Kazuo Ishiguro.

The White Countess is a film about a man who dreams of owning the perfect little bar, a place of elegance that finds the delicate balance, as he thinks a woman should, "between the erotic and the tragic." Outside it is Shanghai in 1936, and the world is late for its appointment with war. Inside the bar—well, inside, Mr. Jackson muses, "With a good team of bouncers, you could conduct the place like an orchestra."

Mr. Jackson is a blind man who stands, or sometimes leans, at the center of the last of twenty-eight films to be made together in this life by the director James Ivory and the producer Ismail Merchant. There were two more in preproduction when Merchant died in May 2005. They have been operating their own perfect little bar since 1963. Outside it is Hollywood and the world is hurrying toward commerce and compromise. Inside their bar, cosmopolitan characters, elegant and tragic, have wandered out of the pages of good books; what many share is a personal style employed to conceal wounds, lusts, and disappointments.

Todd Jackson (Ralph Fiennes) is a classic Merchant-Ivory character. He is an exile. He hoped for great things as a young man and now, disillusioned, hopes for smaller victories. He placed great trust in romance, now sees it as a hazard. He has taste. He needs money. He is comfortable with disreputable behavior, as long as it is conducted by the rules. Inside his world, friendships are possible that are otherwise forbidden.

Consider his friend Mr. Matsuda (Hiroyuki Sanada). Everyone knows the Japanese are going to invade China and that Mr. Matsuda is their Shanghai advance man. Mr. Matsuda knows Mr. Jackson was once considered "the last hope of the League of Nations." Mr. Jackson knows that Mr. Matsuda "would like to visit the bar of his dreams."

What would this ideal bar be like? In another bar, which is not the right kind of bar, Mr. Jackson overhears a conversation involving the Countess Sofia Belinsky (Natasha Richardson), once Russian royalty, now supporting her exiled family by working as a taxi dancer. Everyone knows that to make ends meet, taxi dancers must sometimes "fall in love" with their clients. Sofia's Russian family lives on her earnings while insulting her as a whore. Sofia's little daughter Katya (Madeleine Daly) doesn't know what a whore is but defends her mother against her fierce grandmother and aunt (Vanessa and

Lynn Redgrave): "If Mama didn't go out to work, then you would have to." Quite so, and at wholesale.

One night Sofia sees a situation developing in the shabby little bar where Jackson drinks, and quietly speaks to the blind man. She warns him he is about to be mugged and advises him to behave as her client. That will get him home unharmed. She wants no payment for this favor. "You're perfect," Jackson tells her. "You're what I need." She will be the hostess in his perfect little bar, talk with the customers, dance with them, decidedly not sleep with them.

The bar, when he wins the money to open it, is called the White Countess, and yes, in its way it *is* perfect. The jazz is good, the clientele is select, and Jackson has the right bouncers. The rest of the movie will involve the approaching collision between this perfect little world and the cataclysm of war.

Merchant and Ivory have never been much concerned with conventional melodrama, excitement, and cheap thrills. Often working with the writer Ruth Prawer Jhabvala, they have adapted works by such as Henry James *(The Golden Bowl)*, E. M. Forster *(Howards End, A Room With a View)*, and Kazuo Ishiguro *(The Remains of the Day)*; Ishiguro wrote this original screenplay. They have catered to a literate minority. If you have read this far, they have catered to you. In the perfect bar, you are likely to meet someone with every taste—even good taste.

Fiennes and Richardson make this film work with the quiet strangeness of their performances; if they insist on their eccentricities, it's because they've paid them off and own them outright. Fiennes' Jackson seems a little shaky for a man long accustomed to being blind, but not if he is also long accustomed to being a little drunk. Richardson's Sofia seems a little too cultivated for a prostitute, and we are reminded of Marlene Dietrich's great line, said by a character who lived in the same time and place: "It took more than one man to change my name to Shanghai Lily." But Sofia was raised as a countess and can hardly shed her elegance when she abandons her morals. These two fallen and needy people are reminded by each other of better times.

What we do is sit and watch them try to live up to their standards in a world that simply doesn't care. I saw my first Merchant and Ivory film, *Shakespeare Wallah,* in 1965, so for forty years I have been watching them living up to their own standards when the world didn't care and, lately, even when it did. Sometimes they have made great films, sometimes flawed ones, even bad ones, but never shabby or unworthy ones. Here is one that is good to better, poignant, patient, moving. In the closing scenes the movie loses its way as Jackson, Sofia, and everybody else get caught up in the chaos of the Japanese invasion, and melodrama is forced upon these reclusive souls. But no matter. No perfect little place lasts forever. The more perfect it is, the more word gets around and the wrong people blunder in and start fights.

The White Diamond ★ ★ ★
NO MPAA RATING, 90 m., 2005

With Graham Dorrington, Mark Anthony Yhap, Werner Herzog, Anthony Melville, Michael Wilk, Jan-Peter Meewes, Jason Gibson, and Red Man (Mark Anthony's rooster). A documentary directed by Werner Herzog and produced by Annette Scheurich, Lucki Stipetic, and Herzog.

Werner Herzog's documentary *The White Diamond* is not about a diamond, but about an airship, one of the smallest ever built, designed to float above the canopy of equatorial rain forests. Every niche in the jungle is exploited by plants, animals, and insects that have evolved to make a living there, and biologists believe that undiscovered species might live their entire lives 80 or 120 feet from the ground.

Herzog introduces us to a London researcher named Graham Dorrington, who dreams of reaching out from his airship to study specimens on the ceiling of the jungle. Like many of Herzog's subjects, he is a dreamer who talks a little too fast and smiles when he doesn't seem to be happy: When a sudden storm threatens to tear his airship to pieces, he says he is philosophical, and we see that he isn't.

Dorrington's airship is shaped like an upside-down teardrop with a tail. It carries a two-man gondola and is powered and steered by small motors. It uses helium gas, which will not burn, unlike hydrogen gas, which caught fire inside the Hindenburg and brought an end to an era when the giant zeppelins served tourist routes between Europe, Brazil, India, and the United States. The zeppelins were cigar-shaped ships that were hard to turn, Dorrington says, unlike his ship, which can pivot in midair. That is the theory, anyway, as he explains his motors and his switches, and we hear Herzog's voice, always filled with apprehension, telling us, "He did not know then that this particular switch would cause a huge problem later."

Dorrington tested an earlier airship in 1993 in Sumatra, and that ended with catastrophe, Herzog tells us. Dorrington describes the death of his cinematographer, Dieter Plage, who fell from a gondola after it was broken on the high branches of a tree by a sudden wind. "It was an accident," Dorrington says, and all agree, but he blames himself every day. Now he is ready to try again.

His airship was built in a huge hangar outside London that once housed dirigibles. Strange, that it cannot be tested there but must be transported to South America and the rain forests of Guyana. Dorrington is a man after Herzog's heart—Herzog, the director who could have filmed *Aguirre, the Wrath of God*, and *Fitzcarraldo* a few miles from cities—but insisted on filming them hundreds of miles inside the rain forest. Herzog has made a specialty of finding obsessives and eccentrics who push themselves to extremes; see his doc *Grizzly Man* about Timothy Treadwell, who lived among the bears of Alaska until one killed him.

Now watch what happens during the first test flight. Herzog has an argument with Dorrington. The scientist wants to fly solo. Herzog calls it "stupid" that the first flight might take place without a camera on board. (It might, of course, be the only flight.) Herzog has brought along two cinematographers but insists he must personally take the camera up on the maiden voyage. "I cannot ask a cinematographer to get in an airship before I test it myself," he says. As Herzog buckles himself into the gondola, we reflect that if Dorrington's standards were those that Herzog insists on, *Dorrington* would not allow *Herzog* to get in the airship until he had tested it himself. It is sublimely Herzogian that this paradox is right there in full view.

There are some dicey moments as the ship goes backward when it should go forward, and Herzog observes a motor burning out and pieces of a propeller whizzing past his head. The

flight instructor who pilots the expedition's ultralight aircraft says Dorrington has not practiced "good airmanship." Dorrington moans that "seven different systems" failed. We wonder if the catastrophe in Sumatra will be repeated.

There is breathtaking footage of the ship's flights, as it skims the forest canopy and descends to dip a toe in the river. Mournful, vaguely ecclesiastical music accompanies these images. The vast Kaieteur Falls fascinates the party; its waters are golden-brown as they roar into a maelstrom, and countless swifts and other birds fly into a cave behind the curtain of water. Mark Anthony Yhap, a local man employed by the expedition, relates legends about the cave. The team doctor, Michael Wilk, has himself lowered on a rope with a video camera to look into the cave. It is typical of a Herzog project that the doctor would be "an experienced mountain climber." It is sublimely typical of Herzog that he does *not* show us the doctor's footage of the cave, after Yhap argues that its sacred secret must be preserved. What is in the cave? A lot of guano, is my guess.

There are times when this expedition causes us to speculate that the Monty Python troupe might have based its material on close observation of actual living Britons. Consider the "experiment" to determine if the downdraft of the waterfall is so strong it would threaten the airship. Dorrington and Herzog tie together four brightly colored birthday balloons and hang a glass of champagne from them as ballast. Sure enough, the balloons are sucked into the mist.

Yhap is one of the film's riches. Known as "Redbeard," he is a Rastafarian who gives the film its title, saying the airship looks like a "big white diamond floating around in the sunrise." Yhap is fond of his red rooster, a mighty bird that has five wives who present him with five eggs every morning. Toward the end of the film Yhap is given his own chance to ride in the airship and enjoys it immensely, but regrets that he could not take along his rooster.

Although *The White Diamond* is entire of itself, it earns its place among the other treasures and curiosities in Herzog's work. Here is one of the most inquisitive filmmakers alive, a man who will go to incredible lengths to film people living at the extremes. In *La Soufrière*, a 1977 documentary released on DVD in August 2005, he journeys to an island evacuated because of an impending volcanic eruption to ask the only man who stayed behind why he did not leave. What he is really asking, what he is always asking, is why he had to go there to ask the question.

The Whole Ten Yards ★
PG-13, 99 m., 2004

Bruce Willis (Jimmy "The Tulip" Tudeski), Matthew Perry (Nicholas "Oz" Oseransky), Amanda Peet (Jill St. Claire), Kevin Pollak (Lazlo Gogolak), Natasha Henstridge (Cynthia Oseransky). Directed by Howard Deutch and produced by Allan Kaufman, Arnold Rifkin, Elie Samaha, and David Willis. Screenplay by George Gallo.

A fog of gloom lowers over *The Whole Ten Yards*, as actors who know they're in a turkey try their best to prevail. We sense a certain desperation as dialogue mechanically grinds through unplayable scenes, and the characters arrive at moments that the movie thinks are funny but they suspect are not. This is one of those movies you look at quizzically: What did they think they were doing?

The movie is an unnecessary sequel to *The Whole Nine Yards* (2000), a movie in which many of the same actors sent completely different messages. "A subtle but unmistakable aura of jolliness sneaks from the screen," I wrote in my review of the earlier movie. "We suspect that the actors are barely suppressing giggles. This is the kind of standard material everyone could do in lockstep, but you sense inner smiles, and you suspect the actors are enjoying themselves."

The problem, I suspect, is that *The Whole Nine Yards* did everything that needed to be done with the characters, and did it well. Now the characters are back again, blinking in the footlights, embarrassed by their curtain call. The movie has the hollow, aimless aura of a beach resort in winter: The geography is the same, but the weather has turned ugly.

You will recall that the earlier film starred Bruce Willis as Jimmy "The Tulip" Tudeski, a professional hit man who has moved in next door to a Montreal dentist named Oz (Matthew Perry). The dentist's receptionist was Jill (Amanda Peet), a woman whose greatest ambition in life was to become a hit woman. Jimmy was in hiding from a Chicago gangster named Janni Gogolak (Kevin Pollak), who wanted him whacked.

In *The Whole Ten Yards*, Jimmy the Tulip and Jill are married and hiding out in Mexico, where Jill finds employment as a hit woman while Jimmy masquerades as a house-husband. That puts Willis in an apron and a head cloth during the early scenes, as if such a disguise would do anything other than call attention to him. Oz, meanwhile, has moved to Los Angeles and is married to Cynthia (Natasha Henstridge), who used to be married to the Tulip. (His first wife, played in the earlier movie by Rosanna Arquette with a hilarious French-Canadian accent, might have been useful here.)

Janni Gogolak was made dead by Oz and the Tulip in the first picture, but now his father, the crime boss Laszlo Gogolak, has been released from prison, and uses all of his power to find revenge against the two men; that fuels most of the plot, such as it is. Lazlo Gogolak is played by Kevin Pollak in one of the most singularly bad performances I have ever seen in a movie. It doesn't fail by omission, it fails by calling attention to its awfulness. His accent, his voice, his clothes, his clownish makeup, all conspire to create a character who brings the movie to a halt every time he appears on the screen. We stare in amazement, and I repeat: What did they think they were doing?

The movie's plot is without sense or purpose. It generates some action scenes that are supposed to be comic, but are not, for the inescapable reason that we have not the slightest interest in the characters and therefore even less interest in their actions. The movie is instructive in the way it demonstrates how a film can succeed or fail not only because of the mechanics of its screenplay, but because of the spirit of its making.

The Whole Nine Yards was not a particularly inspired project, but it was made with spirit and good cheer, and you felt the actors almost visibly expanding on the screen; Amanda Peet in particular seemed possessed. Here we see the actors all but contracting, as if to make themselves smaller targets for the camera. That there will never be a movie named *The Whole Eleven Yards* looks like a safe bet.

Why We Fight ★ ★
PG-13, 98 m., 2006

Featuring Dwight Eisenhower, Wilton Sekzer, Chalmers Johnson, William Solomon, Charles Lewis, Richard Perle, William Kristol, Lt. Col. Karen Kwiatkowski, Joseph Cirincione, Susan Eisenhower, John S. D. Eisenhower, Anh Duong, Gwynne Dyer, Sen. John McCain, Gore Vidal, Franklin Spinney. A documentary directed by Eugene Jarecki. Screenplay by Jarecki.

I agree with the politics of *Why We Fight*, and I concede it is a skillful assembly of its materials, but as a documentary it's less than compelling. Few people are likely to see this film unless they already agree with its conclusions, and few of those will learn anything new from it. All political documentaries face that dilemma to one degree or another; when one of its distributors said Michael Moore's *Fahrenheit 9/11* would defeat George W. Bush in 2004, he miscalculated, because there was little overlap between those planning to vote for Bush and those planning to see the movie.

The most effective recent political documentaries have focused on reporting rather than opinion. Movies such as *Enron: The Smartest Guys in the Room*, which blames the California energy crisis on deliberate Enron policy, or *Gunner Palace*, which recorded the day-to-day life of American troops in Iraq, added to our knowledge without lecturing us about what to think. The drama *Jarhead* was also effective, because it recorded the daily military routine in the first Gulf War without providing an artificial action structure. I got e-mails from people frustrated that the movie had no payoff—but the payoff for the first Gulf War was, of course, our intervention in Iraq.

Why We Fight compiles archival footage and intercuts it with recent interviews, many conducted for the film, but the movie tells us nothing we haven't heard before. It opens with Dwight Eisenhower warning, in the farewell address of his presidency, of a "vast military-industrial complex" that was placing the nation on a permanent war footing. His prophecy was correct. It is no longer even possible to arouse much indignation when the executives of war industries move freely between their board rooms and government offices. Yes, Vice President Dick Cheney headed a major war supplier and now, in office, backs policies that enrich that supplier; he might have made Ike indignant, but today conflicts of interest are forgiven as a convergence of interests.

Why We Fight is devoted to proving Eisenhower correct. It says, essentially, that we fight because we have constructed a military-industrial complex that needs business. Declaring war opens up markets; from a purely financial point of view, it's like signing free-trade agreements or negotiating tariffs. The documentary, directed by Eugene Jarecki, quotes sources from both sides—conservatives such as Richard Perle, liberals such as Gore Vidal, disillusioned military experts such as Lt. Col. Karen Kwiatkowski, and the descendants of Eisenhower. But after Ike makes his point in the opening minutes, the film itself essentially just elaborates on it.

There is one story thread that stands apart and is compelling. It involves a retired New York cop named Wilton Sekzer. His son died in the 9/11 attacks, and he successfully lobbied the government to put his son's name on one of the first bombs that was dropped in Iraq.

He wanted revenge, and to a degree he felt like he got it. That was before Bush observed (some felt rather belatedly) that Iraq and Saddam Hussein had no direct involvement in the 9/11 attacks. Now Sekzer is bitter: He feels that Bush lied to him and that his patriotism was manipulated and misused. The story of Sekzer is new and is suited to film. Much of the rest of *Why We Fight* says things that can be said as well or better in print, and have been. This doesn't need to be a film.

There are other disillusioned people in the documentary, in particular Kwiatkowski, who resigned from the Pentagon because she witnessed military officers being vetoed by outside consultants whose loyalty was to the defense contractors who employed them. One watches *Why We Fight*, and nods, and sighs, and leaves.

What it says should concern us, but apparently it does not. The film observes that some defense contracts are cleverly planned to spread the government wealth among as many states as possible; some weapons systems have suppliers in all fifty states, and woe to the elected official of either party who votes against them. Shouldn't it be obvious that a legislator who votes against government spending in his own district must have given the matter a lot of thought, and be courageous, and perhaps even correct? That's a useful thought. But it's not news, and when documentaries such as *Enron: The Smartest Guys in the Room* contain fresh and shocking information, a film such as *Why We Fight* is not very necessary.

Wicker Park ★ ★ ★
PG-13, 113 m., 2004

Josh Hartnett (Matthew), Rose Byrne (Alex), Diane Kruger (Lisa), Matthew Lillard (Luke), Jessica Pare (Rebecca). Directed by Paul McGuigan and produced by Andre Lamal, Gary Lucchesi, Tom Rosenberg, and Marcus Viscidi. Screenplay by Brandon Boyce and Gilles Mimouni.

Strangely enough, I saw *Wicker Park* on the same day I saw another film, *What the #$*! Do We Know?* The what-the-bleep film was about quantum physics, and included a dozen experts testifying that we don't know s#!t. I have never understood quantum physics, so it was a relief to discover that no one else does, either. That set my mind at ease regarding *Wicker Park*. By substituting "Wicker Park" for "quantum physics," I was able to experience the movie in the same way that I experience the universe, by treating it as if it exists even if it doesn't.

The plot, for example, hums along as if it's really there, like matter, when in fact it's mostly a vacuum, like the insides of atoms. The chronology isn't confusing because scientists believe it's only an illusion that time originates in the past and moves through the present on its way to the future. It might move in any direction, like it does in this movie.

I especially appreciated *What the #$*!*'s claim that we cannot see something we do not understand. When Columbus arrived in the New World, the movie says, the Indians standing on the beach could not see his ships, because they had no concept of ships. But a wise old shaman noticed that the waves were flowing differently, and by standing on the beach for a long time, he was finally able to see the ships, and point them out to his friends.

In exactly the same way, I could not see the plot of this movie, because I had no concept of what it was. But by looking and listening carefully, I was at last able to perceive that it was a love quadrangle taking place in three Chicago apartments, which, for convenience, I thought of as the *Nina*, the *Pinta*, and the *Santa Maria*.

Am I a slow study? I think I'm ahead of the curve. The reviewer for the BBC Web site reports that the movie takes place in New York. It is set in Chicago and was filmed in Chicago and Montreal. Quantum physics, of course, explains how the characters, like subatomic particles, can be in Chicago and Montreal at the same time.

Faithful readers will notice that I have said almost nothing about the movie. That is because the movie consists entirely of plot twists and turns that cannot even be described without being revealed. Let me say, as vaguely as possible, that it involves a romance between Matthew (Josh Hartnett) and Lisa (Diane Kruger) that is the Real Thing, but comes to a sudden end because of a tragic lack of communication and a mutual misunderstanding. Although the characters spend half the movie on the phone, neither one succeeds in making the single call that would clear everything up; it's one of those plots where incredible coincidences happen right on cue, but commonsense events are impossible.

Two years pass. Matthew is engaged to Rebecca (Jessica Pare). He is supposed to fly to China to seal a deal for her father's firm, but in a restaurant he thinks he sees Lisa. This leads him on a trail involving mysterious addresses, hotel room keys, and notes that are, or are not, received by those they are intended for. Since he originally met Lisa by following her like a stalker, and since he searches for her now by acting the same way, past and present mingle delightfully, and we're not always sure if he's following the Lisa he wants to meet or the Lisa he's lost.

Then there are Alex (Rose Byrne) and Luke (Matthew Lillard). They start dating each other. Luke is Matthew's best friend, but Alex doesn't know that. Alex becomes Lisa's friend, but Lisa doesn't know . . . oh, never mind. And I won't even mention the true object of Alex's erotomania.

The strange thing is, I liked all of this while it was happening. The movie is a remake of *L'Appartement*, a 1996 French film I did not see—which is just as well, because the American film *Criminal* is a remake of *Nine Queens,* a 2000 Argentinean film I did see, so that I knew everything that was going to happen. Even if I had seen *L'Appartement,* I might not have known everything that was going to happen in *Wicker Park,* however, because I don't think anyone does, including the director, Paul McGuigan, and the writers, Brandon Boyce and Gilles Mimouni.

Once we understand the principle (if not the details) of the plot, *Wicker Park* works because the actors invest their scenes with what is, under the circumstances, astonishing emotional realism. There's a scene between Josh Hartnett and Rose Byrne during which so much is said, and left unsaid, that we feel real sympathy for both characters. There's an emotional craziness to the way the Hartnett character misses his plane to China and starts skulking around Chicago/Montreal like a sleuth. There's an open innocence to the way Matthew Lillard's character fails to realize he is about to become an innocent bystander. And Diane Kruger, whose Lisa is subjected to logical whiplash by the plot, always seems to know when it is and how she should feel. Now that's acting.

Wilbur Wants to Kill Himself ★ ★ ★ ½
R, 111 m., 2004

Jamie Sives (Wilbur), Adrian Rawlins (Harbour), Shirley Henderson (Alice), Lisa McKinlay (Mary), Mads Mikkelsen (Horst), Julia Davis (Moira). Directed by Lone Scherfig and produced by Sisse Graum Olsen. Screenplay by Scherfig and Anders Thomas Jensen.

It strikes a note of optimism, I suppose, that *Wilbur Wants to Kill Himself* is not titled *Wilbur Kills Himself.* Wilbur certainly tries desperately enough, with pills, gas, hanging, and teetering on the edge of a great fall. But he never quite succeeds. He is saved more than once by his brother, Harbour, and on another occasion by Alice, who interrupts his hanging attempt. By this point we begin to suspect that *Wilbur Wants to Kill Himself* is not about suicide at all, that Wilbur is destined for better things, and that despite its title this is a warm human comedy.

The movie takes place in Glasgow, that chill city where many views are dominated by the Necropolis, the Gothic cemetery on a hillside

overlooking the town. Such a view must be a daily inspiration for Wilbur (Jamie Sives). He is, from time to time, a patient at a local psychiatric clinic, where the therapists seem to have limited their studies to viewings of *One Flew Over the Cuckoo's Nest.* His hopes depend on Harbour, who loves him, tries to save him from himself, and brings him home to live with him.

Harbour (Adrian Rawlins) runs the used book store left him by his father. It is a shabby but inviting place, its windows following the curve of the road, its stock in a jumble. There seems to be only one customer, a man who visits almost daily, demanding Kipling, and is invariably told that there must be some Kipling around here somewhere, but Harbour can't put his hands on it.

Another frequent visitor wants to sell, not buy. This is Alice, played by Shirley Henderson, that luminous actress from *Trainspotting, Bridget Jones's Diary, Topsy-Turvy,* and half a dozen others; do not be put off that she played Moaning Myrtle in *Harry Potter and the Chamber of Secrets.* She brings in books that were left behind by patients at the hospital where she works, but the books are really an excuse for seeing Harbour, with whom she feels a strange affinity; perhaps they met in earlier lives, since Rawlins played Harry Potter's father.

In no time at all Alice and Harbour have fallen in love. Alice and her daughter, Mary (Lisa McKinlay), bring order to the store, so that Kipling can easily be found, and then Alice and Harbour are married. That leads to rather cramped living conditions in the small flat above the store, where Wilbur is also established.

This doesn't add up to a lot of incident, but it occupies more than half the movie, because the director and cowriter, Lone Scherfig, loves human nature and would rather enjoy it than hurry it along with a plot. The pleasure of the movie is in spending time in the company of her characters, who are quirky and odd and very definite about themselves. There is also a certain amount of escapism involved, at least for somebody like me, who would rather run a used book store than do just about anything else except spend all my time in them.

Now then. The real heart of the movie involves events I do not want to even hint about. That's because they creep up on the characters so naturally, so gradually, that we should be as surprised as they are by how it all turns out. Let me say that the bleak comedy of Wilbur's early suicide attempts is replaced by the deepening of all of the characters, who are revealed as warm and kind and rather noble. The movie's ending is almost unreasonably happy, despite being technically sad, and the affection we feel for these characters is remarkable.

The filmmaker, Lone Scherfig, is a Danish woman whose first film, *Italian for Beginners*, was a Dogma comedy. That she was able to make a Dogma comedy tells you a great deal about her. Here she does away with the Dogma rules and makes a movie in the tradition of the Ealing comedies produced in England in the 1950s and early 1960s: modest slices of life about people who are very peculiar and yet lovable, and who do things we approve of in ways that appall us. The title may put you off, but don't let it. Here is a movie that appeals to the heart while not insulting the mind or forgetting how delightful its characters are.

The Wild ★ ★ ★
G, 94 m., 2006

With the voices of: Kiefer Sutherland (Samson [lion]), Greg Cipes (Ryan [lion cub]), James Belushi (Benny [squirrel]), Janeane Garofalo (Bridget [giraffe]), Richard Kind (Larry [snake]), William Shatner (Kazar [wildebeest]), Eddie Izzard (Nigel [koala]). Directed by Steve "Spaz" Williams and produced by Beau Flynn and Clint Goldman. Screenplay by Ed Decter, Mark Gibson, Philip Halprin, and John J. Strauss.

When *The Wild* and *Ice Age: The Meltdown* were over, they left me with a question: What did they eat? The animals were awfully chummy, considering that some of them have been known to dine on the others. *The Wild* answers my question, but not very accurately. Some animals, as we know, are carnivores. That would include lions. Others are omnivores. That would include humans. Still others are herbivores, or vegetarians. That would include the mighty wildebeest, also known as the gnu, although "the mighty gnu" lacks a certain je ne sais quoi. Wildebeests move around, we are told, in search of grasslands, not quarry.

Hold that thought. *The Wild* and another recent animated film, *Madagascar,* share the same premise, which is that animals escape from a zoo and find themselves back in the jungle again—Madagascar in the first film, Africa in this one. The premise this time is that little Ryan (voice by Greg Cipes), the lion cub, has wandered off and gotten into a shipping container that is being taken to Africa. His horrified father, Samson (Kiefer Sutherland), races off to save him and ends up chasing Ryan's ship all the way to Africa on a tugboat that gets very good mileage. Along for the ride are such zoo friends as Benny the squirrel (James Belushi), Bridget the giraffe (Janeane Garofalo), Nigel the koala (Eddie Izzard), and Larry the anaconda (Richard Kind).

Benny is in love with Bridget, not realizing he is a squirrel and she is not, which reminds me of the mammoth in *Ice Age: The Meltdown* who thinks she is a possum. The cast continues to grow. On the journey through New York they encounter a couple of alligators in the sewer system, and in Africa they meet other characters, including the undercover chameleons Cloak and Camo (Bob Joles and Chris Edgerly), a vulture (Greg Berg) who I think lacks a name, and then, the earth thundering, the dreaded Kazar (William Shatner), who is king of the wildebeests but can be king of the jungle only if he defeats a lion. That would be Samson, who has a secret in his past he hopes Kazar doesn't discover.

Now, then. Although Samson gets regular T-bones at the zoo, he no doubt would cheerfully eat many of these other animals. But what are we to make of a volcano scene with lots of flowing lava that helps set up a scenario in which it appears that Kazar plans to cook Samson? Is Kazar not a vegetarian, or did I miss something?

The movie has a lot more action than *Ice Age: The Meltdown,* which was essentially one long trek. There are savage beasts (wilde and other), exploding volcanoes, rivers of lava, and so on—some of it may be too intense for the youngest kids. This is the third animated feature in a row (after *Curious George* and *Ice Age: The Meltdown*) that aims at children and has no serious ambition to be all things to all people (i.e., their parents). But for kids, it's okay.

That leaves me with some observations about its technique. I doubt that many audience members will be disturbed by such matters, but

I thought the movie's lip-synching was too good. The mouths of the characters move so precisely in time with their words that the cartoon illusion is lost and we venture toward the Uncanny Valley—that shadowy area known to robot designers and animators in which artificial creatures so closely resemble humans that they make us feel kinda creepy. Lip-synching in animation usually ranges from bad to perfunctory to fairly good, and I think fairly good is as good as it should get. In *The Wild*, it felt somehow *wrong* that the dialogue was so perfectly in synch.

I also had some problems with the film's visual strategy. The director, Steve "Spaz" Williams, has a way of cutting to unexpected close-ups. That gives us a subtle feeling that the movie knows in advance what will happen next, when in theory it should seem to find out just when we do. I also think the framing of some of the characters is too close; they hog the foreground and obscure the background. And the fur, hair, and feathers on the creatures look so detailed, thanks to the wonders of CGI, that once again we're wandering toward the Uncanny Valley.

An animated film can approach reality, but it should never arrive there. It must always seem one magical arm's length away. The art is in the style, in the way reality is distorted or heightened. When Miyazaki gives us characters who shout so loudly we can see their tonsils, he knows what he's doing. None of these details will matter to the target audience for *The Wild*, of course, although maybe in some vague, unconscious way they will sense that the movie doesn't have that je ne sais quoi, a phrase I employ again to make you feel vindicated for looking it up in the first place. As French phrases go, it is one of the handiest, and especially useful when you don't know quite what to say.

The Wild Parrots of
Telegraph Hill ★ ★ ★
G, 83 m., 2005

A documentary about Mark Bittner, directed and produced by Judy Irving.

Mark Bittner is calm, intelligent, confiding, wise, and well spoken. You would be happy to count him as your friend. He has not worked in

thirty years, has lived on the street for fifteen of them, and in recent years has devoted his life to getting to know forty-five wild parrots who formed a flock in San Francisco. It takes a lot of time to get to know forty-five wild parrots as individuals, but as he points out, "I have all the time in the world."

The Wild Parrots of Telegraph Hill, a documentary about Bittner and his birds by Judy Irving, is not the film you think it is going to be. You walk in expecting some kind of North Beach weirdo and his wild-eyed parrot theories, and you walk out still feeling a little melancholy over the plight of Connor, the only blue-crowned conure in a flock of red-crowned conures.

Connor had a mate, Bittner tells us, but the mate died. Now Connor hangs around with the other parrots but seems lonely and depressed, a blue-crowned widower who can sometimes get nasty with the other birds, but comes to the defense of weak or sick birds when the flock picks on them. Picasso and Sophie, both red-crowned parrots, are a couple until Picasso disappears; Bittner begins to hope that maybe Connor and Sophie will start to date and produce some purple-headed babies.

Nobody knows how the parrots, all born in the wild and imported from South America, escaped captivity, found each other, and started their flock. Irving has several North Beach residents recite the usual urban legends (they were released by an eccentric old lady, a bird truck overturned, etc.). No matter. They live and thrive.

You would think it might get too cold in the winter for these tropical birds, but no: They can withstand cold fairly well, and the big problem for them is getting enough to eat. Indeed, flocks of wild parrots and parakeets exist in colder climates; the famous colony of parakeets in Chicago's Hyde Park was evicted from some of their nests in 2005, after fifteen or twenty years, because they were interfering with utility lines.

Oddly, some bird lovers seem to resent trespassers such as wild parrots on the grounds that they are outside their native range. That they are here through no fault of their own, that they survive and thrive and are intelligent and beautiful birds, is enough for Mark Bittner, and by the end of the film that's enough for us, too.

He gives us brief biographies of some of the

birds. Sometimes he takes them into his home when they're sick or injured, but after they recover they all want to return to the wild—except for Mingus, who keeps trying to get back into the house. Their biggest enemies are viruses and hawks. The flock always has a hawk lookout posted, and has devised other hawk-avoidance tactics, of which the most ingenious is to fly *behind* a hawk, which can only attack straight ahead and has a wider turning radius than parrots.

Bittner originally came to San Francisco, he tells us, seeking work as a singer. That didn't work out. He lived on the streets, did odd jobs, read a lot, met some of the original hippies (Ginsberg, Ferlinghetti, Gary Snyder). For the three years before the film begins, he has lived rent-free in a cottage below the house of a wealthy couple who live near the parrots on Telegraph Hill. Now he is about to be homeless again, while the cottage is renovated into an expensive rental property. The parrots are threatened with homelessness, too, and Bittner testifies on their behalf before the city council. San Francisco mayor Gavin Newsom vows nothing bad will happen to the parrots; would that we had such statesmen in Illinois.

As Bittner tends and feeds his flock, visitors to the wooded area on Telegraph Hill want to categorize him. Is he a scientist? Paid by the city? What's his story? His story is, he finds the parrots fascinating and lovable. He quotes Gary Snyder: "If you want to study nature, start right where you are." Can he live like this forever? He is about fifty, in good health, with a long red ponytail. He says he decided not to cut his hair until he gets a girlfriend. Whether either Connor the blue-crowned conure or Bittner the red-headed birdman find girlfriends, I will leave for you to discover.

Wimbledon ★ ★ ★
PG-13, 98 m., 2004

Kirsten Dunst (Lizzie Bradbury), Paul Bettany (Peter Colt), Sam Neill (Dennis Bradbury), Jon Favreau (Ron Roth), Austin Nichols (Jake Hammond), Bernard Hill (Edward Colt), Eleanor Bron (Augusta Colt). Directed by Richard Loncraine and produced by Eric Fellner, Liza Chasin, and Mary Richards. Screenplay by Adam Brooks, Jennifer Flackett, and Mark Levin.

Wimbledon is a well-behaved movie about nice people who have good things happen to them. That's kind of startling, in a world where movie characters, especially in sports movies, occupy the edge of human experience. What a surprise to hear conversation instead of dialogue, and to realize that the villain may actually be right some of the time.

The movie stars Paul Bettany and Kirsten Dunst as tennis pros—she a rising star, he a fading one. Lizzie Bradbury's greatness is ahead of her, but Peter Colt fears his is all behind. He was once ranked 11th in the world, is now down around 113 and falling. He gets a wild card berth at Wimbledon and vows that, win or lose, he'll retire from the pro circuit after this tournament.

The two players have parents representative of their respective civilizations. Lizzie's dad, Dennis (Sam Neill), is a hard-driving American control freak who has managed Lizzie's career since she was a child. Peter's parents (Bernard Hill and Eleanor Bron) are rich British eccentrics; his mother potters in the garden, and his father moves into the tree house after a fight with his wife. Stop to consider how few movie sports heroes even have parents (some do not even seem of woman born).

Lizzie and Peter have a Meet Cute early in the film, when he is mistakenly given the key to her suite at the Dorchester. She is nude in the shower, but handles the situation with such composure that we wonder if she arranged for him to get the key, especially after, with admirable frankness, she asks him, "Where do you come down on the whole fooling-around-before-a-match issue?"

She comes down in favor of it, and soon they're snuggling and holding hands. Her father, of course, believes sex before a match is a drain of precious bodily fluids, and warns Peter away. Peter tries to reassure him, but the father says, "This time it's different. She's falling for you."

And so she is, in a movie where the lovers keep late hours for finalists at Wimbledon. His nightly workouts seem to inspire Peter, who scores one upset after another over highly seeded players. But Lizzie's father is afraid she's tiring herself, tries to hide her, and even

781

tracks the lovers to Brighton in a scene embarrassingly captured on live television.

All of this is told in a movie more realistic about tennis than about love. The tennis scenes are well choreographed and acted (Bettany looks to me like a competent player). They make sense visually and dramatically, and they evoke the loneliness of a sport where everything depends on one person at one moment in time. Interior monologues allow us to hear Peter talking to himself, psyching himself out, quieting his fears. Is it ridiculous to believe he plays better because he's in love? Of course not.

But what kind of love is it? On Peter's part, it seems to be old-fashioned over-the-moon romance. But Lizzie is rather alarmingly direct in the way she originally recruits Peter, and later she seems too willing to give him up. Does she use lovers like a convenience? We've seen male characters like this in the movies, but a woman with such a casual attitude is unusual. For that matter, is she really casual? There's a stretch of the movie when we're not sure.

We're also not so sure we like Ron (Jon Favreau), Peter's once and future agent. He's a little too much of a caricature, and the movie uses his cell phone for easy laughs. Sam Neill, as Lizzie's father, could also be a caricature, but I liked the way the movie backed off toward the end, and showed a certain common sense beneath his decisions.

What I mostly liked was the warmth between the two leads. Lizzie and Peter like each other, and because they share the same profession they have more to talk about than their feelings. We get a sense for what it's like to be all alone on a court with everything depending on you and no possible excuses. This is not a great movie and you will be able to live quite happily without seeing it, but what it does, it does with a certain welcome warmth.

Win a Date with Tad Hamilton! ★ ★ ★
PG-13, 95 m., 2004

Kate Bosworth (Rosalee Futch), Topher Grace (Pete Monash), Josh Duhamel (Tad Hamilton), Gary Cole (Henry Futch), Ginnifer Goodwin (Cathy Feely), Nathan Lane (Richard Levy), Sean Hayes (Richard Levy). Directed by Robert Luketic and produced by Lucy Fisher and Douglas Wick. Screenplay by Victor Levin.

Here is a movie for people who haunt the aisles of the video stores searching for 1950s romances. I could have seen it at the Princess Theater in Urbana in 1959. Maybe I did. It's retro in every respect, a romantic comedy in a world so innocent that a lifetime is settled with a kiss. And because it embraces its innocence like a lucky charm, it works, for those willing to allow it. Others will respond with a horse laugh, and although I cannot quarrel with them, I do not share their sentiments.

Maybe it's something to do with Kate Bosworth's smile. She plays Rosalee Futch, a checkout clerk at the Piggly Wiggly in Fraser's Bottom, West Virginia. Her manager, whom she has known since they were children, is Pete Monash (Topher Grace). He loves her, but can't bring himself to tell her so. Then she wins a contest to have a date with Tad Hamilton (Josh Duhamel), a Hollywood star whose agent thinks his image could use a little touch-up after a supermarket tabloid photographs him speeding, drinking, letching, and littering all at the same time.

Well, of course Rosalee is ecstatic about the trip to L.A., the stretch limo, the suite at the W hotel, the expensive dinner date, and the moment when she teeters on the brink when Tad invites her to his home, and then says, gee . . . you know, it's late and I have to fly home tomorrow. That she is a virgin goes without saying. What she can't anticipate is that Tad will follow her back to Fraser's Bottom, because there was something in her innocence, her freshness, her honesty, that appealed to an empty place deep inside him.

Within days he has purchased a house in West Virginia, taken her to dinner several times at the local diner, and made friends with her father, Henry (Gary Cole), who starts surfing Variety.com and wearing a Project Greenlight T-shirt.

As it happens, I'm reading *Anna Karenina* right now, and for some foolish reason Rosalee started to remind me of Kitty, the ingenue in the novel. She and a good man named Levin have long been in love, but she's swept off her feet by the sudden admiration of a snake named Vronsky, and rejects Levin when in fact her fate is to be his wife, and Vronsky's love is a mirage. Just today I read the charming pages where Levin and Kitty, too shy to speak their hearts, play a word game in order to find out if they have survived Vronsky with their love still intact. I was startled by how happy it made me when they got their answers right.

Win a Date with Tad Hamilton! could have had a similar effect, since there is a real possibility that Rosalee will wed the slick Tad instead of the steady Pete. But it doesn't have that kind of impact because of a crucial misjudgment in the screenplay and casting.

To begin with, Josh Duhamel is more appealing than Topher Grace—maybe not in life, but certainly in this movie, where he seems sincere within the limits of his ability, while the store manager always seems to have a pebble in his shoe.

And then the movie devotes much more screen time to Rosalee and Tad than to Rosalee and Pete—so much more that even though we know the requirements of the formula, we expect it to be broken with a marriage to Tad. And yet—what is the function of Pete, within the closed economy of a screenplay, except to be the hometown boy she should marry?

You can guess for yourself (very easily) what decision she finally comes to, but let me observe that the courtship between Rosalee and Tad is charming, warm, cute, and applaudable, and that Pete spends a great deal of time grumping about in the store office and making plans to go off to Richmond and become a business major. In 1959, or any other year, a movie like this would have known enough to make Tad into more of a slickster. There is the strangest feeling at the end of the film that Rosalee might have made the wrong choice.

That imbalance at least has the benefit of giving a formula movie more suspense than it deserves. And I liked it, too, for the way it played Tad and Hollywood more or less straight, instead of diving into wretched excess. The dream date is handled with lots of little touches that will warm the innards of PG-13 females in the audience, and the movie wants to be gentle, not raucous in its comedy. Kate Bosworth holds it all together with a sweetness that is beyond calculation.

Note: That leaves just one other elbow stick- ing out of the sack. Tad's agent and manager, played by Nathan Lane and Sean Hayes and both named Richard Levy, are so over the top that they break the mood in their scenes. For Lane, *Win a Date* represents yet another peculiar career choice in the movies, a medium where he is successful mostly when heard but not seen, as voice-over talent. To be sure, this isn't the suicidal career move of his decision to play Jacqueline Susann's husband in *Isn't She Great*, but as roles go, it's thankless. Here's the highest-priced Broadway star of his generation, and what's he doing in this little role, anyway?

Winter Passing ★ ★ ★ ½
R, 98 m., 2006

Ed Harris (Don Holden), Zooey Deschanel (Reese Holden), Will Ferrell (Corbit), Amelia Warner (Shelly). Directed by Adam Rapp and produced by P. Jennifer Dana and David Koplan. Screenplay by Rapp.

Reese didn't attend her mother's funeral because "she treated me like a mild curiosity all my life," nor she was eager to see her father. Reese lives in New York, works at being an actress, sleeps around, is depressed. Her father, Don Holden, was a famous novelist, then a famous writing teacher, then a famous drunk, and is now a famous drunken recluse. The usual trajectory. Her mother was a writer, too. Did her parents write to each other? An editor offers her money for their correspondence, and Reese needs money. There's nothing to keep her in New York after the death of her cat.

Winter Passing is the story of how Reese (Zooey Deschanel) takes the bus to the Upper Peninsula of Michigan and finds her father (Ed Harris) living in a shack in the backyard. When she knocks on the front door of the big house, it is opened by Corbit (Will Ferrell), who says he wants to see some ID. Later he confides, "I know karate. I've amassed several belts." Corbit is the caretaker, or something. Also living in the house is Shelly (Amelia Warner), a British girl who cooks meals and was Don's writing student at Iowa.

What are the relationships among or between Don, Corbit, and Shelly? Don is mired in a profound alcoholic depression. Corbit and Shelly seem, like Bunuel's dinner guests in *The*

Exterminating Angel, to have entered the house only to find themselves unable to leave it. Shelly is maybe an enabler. Corbit is maybe an alien. Reese lives in the house for a few days and begins to understand its desperate chemistry. These people are hanging on by one another's fingernails.

Winter Passing is a sad story told in a cold season about lonely people. Written and directed by the playwright Adam Rapp, it could be inspired by any number of case histories; Frederick Exley (*A Fan's Notes*) comes to mind. There is something about a great author, even in the extremities of alcoholic self-destruction, that exerts a magnetic pull on those who respect his books. Don's house itself is filled with so many books that you wouldn't ask, "Have you really read all of these?" because you'd be afraid of the answer either way. Only one title is clearly visible among the thousands of volumes, but it's the right one: *The Thirsty Muse.*

Rapp's film skirts the edges of humor and love. Approached in a different way, this could be a comedy of eccentricity. Rapp sidesteps temptations for laughter, while nodding to them in passing. Consider the carefully modulated performance of Ferrell, an actor whose presence is an invitation to laughter. Here he finds a way to be peculiar without being silly; he has deep fears, enclosed in a deeper shyness. He can sing and play the guitar but has a phobia about doing both at once in public. That leads to open-mike evening at the local bar and a scene almost impossible to play, but Ferrell and Deschanel find a way. Notice his aborted project to build a sheltered walkway from the shack to the main house. He starts it on impulse, and the impulse fades. Nor does he know much about carpentry.

Ed Harris has played alcoholic artists before; his Oscar-nominated Jackson Pollock is a benchmark. Here he mixes alcoholism with madness. Why does he move his bed, table, and bureau into the yard and sleep under the sky in the deep of winter? The arrival of his daughter seems to awaken him, if only to alert him to let go. Shelly confides in Reese that the old man is still writing, but slowly: "As a teacher, he was always preaching compositional velocity. I've never seen anyone agonize over each sentence the way he does."

Slowly, the old writer surfaces from his slough of despond. His face appears from behind his beard. He talks to Reese, a little, enigmatically. He has been working on a novel. There may indeed be letters between her father and her mother, who could not live together and yet were bound in a terrible need. Watch Don drink and smoke not because he wants to or needs to, but because he has forgotten to stop. Observe the sweetness of the Ferrell character, terrified of being known. Warner, as the former student, is still learning because when you apprentice to a genius you don't bail out. Deschanel, in this film and the dismal *Failure to Launch,* shows the same ability to remain apart, to watch and listen, to move on her own terms. She can love her father or forgive her father, but it will be hard to do both.

This is the kind of movie some people think is too quiet, but it can be more exciting to listen than to hear. It will disappoint those looking for a Will Ferrell comedy. Disappoint, puzzle, maybe enrage. But some Ferrell fans will find a kind of film they may not have seen before. That's how you grow as a filmgoer; your favorite stars lead you by the hand into deep water.

Winter Solstice ★ ★ ★
R, 89 m., 2005

Anthony LaPaglia (Jim Winters), Allison Janney (Molly Ripken), Aaron Stanford (Gabe Winters), Mark Webber (Pete Winters), Ron Livingston (Mr. Bricker), Michelle Monaghan (Stacey), Brendan Sexton III (Robbie). Directed by Josh Sternfeld and produced by Doug Bernheim and John Limotte. Screenplay by Sternfeld.

Oh, what a sad movie this is: Sad not with the details of tragedy, but with the details of life that must go on after the tragedy. *Winter Solstice* is about a family living in emptiness that threatens to become hopelessness. Jim Winters, the father, is a landscape gardener. His boys Gabe and Peter are in high school. Five years ago, Pete was in the car with his mother when there was an accident and she was killed. The family has been broken ever since.

It's conventional in such stories to assign blame to the father, who is seen as distant or bitter. Not here. Jim (Anthony LaPaglia) is filled with desperation as he tries to reach out to his sons. But he doesn't have the tone or the gift, or perhaps they're at that maddening stage in adolescence when they just clam up, taking it out on everybody else that they're angry with themselves.

The movie is not plot-driven, for which we must be thankful, because to force their feelings into a plot would be a form of cruelty. The whole point is that these lives have no plot. The characters and their situation are on stage and waiting for something to happen, but Josh Sternfeld, the writer-director, isn't going to let them off that easily. If this movie ended in hugs it would be an abomination.

Gabe (Aaron Stanford) thinks he will leave town and move to Tampa. He has no firm plans for what he will do in Tampa and only vague reasons for choosing Tampa instead of any other place on the face of the Earth. "What about Stacey?" his father asks. Stacey (Michelle Monaghan) is Gabe's girlfriend, welcome in the house, well liked. "That's my problem and I'm dealing with it," Gabe says. He's dealing with it the way a lot of teenage boys deal with girls: He's dropping her, and letting her figure it out. Stacey isn't a weeper; she wisely doesn't answer his phone calls and leaves him without the opportunity for justification, blame, closure, or anything else except a feeling of being lonely on his own.

Pete (Mark Webber) is in trouble at school. His teacher, Mr. Bricker (Ron Livingston) knows he's smart and can do better and rather bravely tries to get around his defenses, but Pete is miserable and punishes himself. The worse he does, the worse he can feel, which is fine with him.

A woman named Molly (Allison Janney) moves in down the street. Jim helps her shift some boxes. She invites them to dinner. Jim has not looked at another woman in five years, and maybe isn't really looking at Molly when he accepts; maybe he just knows it's time to break the pattern. Gabe and Pete fail to turn up for the dinner, and Jim throws their mattresses out into the lawn and lets them sleep under the stars; this is perceived not as tough love but as anger, which is probably just as well, since these boys are well defended against love.

Josh Sternfeld, like his character Stacey, knows he will have more effect on us if he denies us closure. It would be simple to give this movie a happy ending, but why does the happiness have to come at the end of this particular winter? Maybe it will come five years down the road, with Gabe returning from Tampa with a wife and a kid, and Pete safely in college, and Jim and Molly living together. Or maybe it won't end that way.

The movie knows that life is sometimes very discouraging, and keeps on being discouraging, and sometimes you can't save everybody and have to try to save yourself. Who is to say that it's a bad idea for Gabe to move to Tampa? Sure, his father thinks it is, but is Gabe making any progress in New Jersey? Would it be an answer to marry Stacey? Marrying somebody to solve a problem is never the answer to the problem, just a way to share it. LaPaglia, who often stars in crime movies and comedies, has a sad, resigned tone that is just right for this movie, as it was for the overlooked *Lantana* (2001).

When *Winter Solstice* is over, we sit and look at the screen and wonder what will happen to them all. We don't expect dramatic developments; these lives don't seem on a course for tragedy or happiness, but for a gradual kind of acceptance. Maybe the movies do us no service by solving so many problems, in a world with so few solutions.

With All Deliberate Speed ★ ★ ★
NO MPAA RATING, 110 m., 2004

As themselves: Julian Bond, Rev. Joe DeLaine, Barbara Johns, Vernon Jordan, Thurgood Marshall Jr., E. Barrett Prettyman. Re-creating the words of historical figures: Alicia Keys, Mekhi Pfifer, Larenz Tate, Joe Morton, and Terry Kinney. Directed by Peter Gilbert and produced by Gilbert.

On May 17, 1954, the Supreme Court ruled unanimously that "separate but equal" could no longer be the rule of the land. Its decision in the case of *Brown vs. Board of Education* ended segregated schools and opened the door for a wide range of reforms guaranteeing equal rights not only to African-Americans but also, in the years to come, to women, the handicapped, and (more slowly) homosexuals. The decision was a heroic milestone in American history, but it was marred, this new documentary says, by four fateful words: "with all deliberate speed."

Those words were a loophole that allowed some southern communities to delay equal rights for years and even decades; the last county to integrate finally did so only in 1970. And there was the notorious case of Prince Edward County, Virginia, which closed its schools for five years rather than integrate them. Most people alive today were born after *Brown* and take its reforms for granted. But *With All Deliberate Speed*, the documentary by *Hoop Dreams* producer Peter Gilbert, doesn't end on May 17, 1954. It continues on to the present day, noting that many of America's grade and secondary schools are as segregated now as they were fifty years ago.

The most valuable task of the film is to recreate the historic legal struggles that led to *Brown*, and to remember heroes who have been almost forgotten by history. Chief among them is Charles Houston, who was the first African-American on the editorial board of the *Harvard Law Review*. As dean of the Howard University law school, he was the mentor for a generation of black legal scholars and activists who would transform their society. Although he died in 1950, before *Brown* became law, it was his protégé Thurgood Marshall who argued the case before the Supreme Court, and later became the first African-American on the court.

It was Houston, the film says, who shaped the legal groundwork for *Brown*, arguing in the 1930s and 1940s that "separate but equal" could not, by its very nature, be equal. He helped convince the NAACP to mount legal challenges against segregation, and Marshall led the organization's legal efforts from 1940 onward. The film talks with the descendants of Houston and Marshall, and with many of the law clerks, now elderly, who as young men served the justices who handed down the landmark decision.

It also recalls the crucial role of Chief Justice Earl Warren in guiding his fellow justices toward what he felt had to be a unanimous decision. The previous chief justice, Fred Vincent, had little enthusiasm for such a controversial ruling. When he died, President Dwight Eisenhower appointed the former California governor Warren as chief justice; Justice Felix Frankfurter famously told his clerk that the death of Vincent "showed there is a God." So hated was *Brown* in some right-wing circles that an Impeach Earl Warren campaign continued throughout his term.

The film also tracks down some of the children involved in the first crucial cases, such as Barbara Johns of Prince Edward County. And it brings belated recognition to another hero of the time, the Reverand Joe DeLaine of Summerton County, South Carolina, who led the legal struggle against a system that required many black students to walk seven miles each way to school. His church was burned, his home was fired on, he was forced to flee the South, and only in October 2000, twenty-six years after his death, were charges against him cleared by the state.

Gilbert, of course, has no audio or video footage of the arguments before the Supreme Court, but he uses an interesting technique: He employs actors to read from the words of Thurgood Marshall and his chief opponent, the patrician John W. Davis. And he does a good job of recapturing the 1954 impact of the decision—with which, he notes, Eisenhower at first privately disagreed, although Ike later came around, and sent federal troops to enforce integration in the late 1950s.

What is the legacy of *Brown*? It's here that Gilbert's film is most challenging. It observes that while many communities have truly integrated schools, patterns of residential segregation in many areas have resulted in schools where the students are almost entirely of one race. He talks with blacks and whites who are in a tiny minority in their schools, and listens to discussions of race by today's high school students. And in reunions held today, he gathers students, now grown, who were at the center of the original case, and hears their memories of what it was like then and what it is like now. America moves imperfectly toward the goal of equality, but because of *Brown*, it moves.

Wolf Creek no stars
NO MPAA RATING, 95 m., 2005

John Jarratt (Mick Taylor), Nathan Phillips (Ben Mitchell), Cassandra Magrath (Liz Hunter), Kestie Morassi (Kristy Earl). Directed by Greg McLean and produced by McLean and David Lightfoot. Screenplay by McLean.

I had a hard time watching *Wolf Creek*. It is a film with one clear purpose: to establish the commercial credentials of its director by showing his skill at depicting the brutal tracking, torture, and mutilation of screaming young women. When the killer severs the spine of one of his victims and calls her "a head on a stick," I wanted to walk out of the theater and keep on walking.

It has an eighty-two percent "fresh" reading over at the Tomatometer. "Bound to give even the most seasoned thrill seeker nightmares" *(Hollywood Reporter)*. "Will have Wes Craven bowing his head in shame" (Clint Morris). "Must be giving Australia's outback tourism industry a bad case of heartburn" (Laura Clifford). "A vicious torrent of bloodletting. What more can we want?" (Harvey Karten). One critic who didn't like it was Matthew Leyland of the BBC: "The film's preference for female suffering gives it a misogynist undertow that's even more unsettling than the gore."

A "misogynist" is someone who hates women. I'm explaining that because most people who hate women don't know the word. I went to the Rotten Tomatoes roundup of critics not for tips for my own review, but hoping that someone somewhere simply said, "Made me want to vomit and cry at the same time."

I like horror films. Horror movies, even extreme ones, function primarily by scaring us or intriguing us. Consider *Three . . . Extremes* recently. *Wolf Creek* is more like the guy at the carnival sideshow who bites off chicken heads. No fun for us, no fun for the guy, no fun for the chicken. In the case of this film, it's fun for the guy.

I know, I know, my job as a critic is to praise the director for showing low-budget filmmaking skills and creating a tense atmosphere and evoking emptiness and menace in the outback, blah, blah. But in telling a story like this, the better he is, the worse the experience. Perhaps his job as a director is to make a movie I can sit through without dismay. To laugh through the movie, as midnight audiences are sometimes invited to do, is to suggest you are dehumanized, unevolved, or a slackwit. To read blasé speculation about the movie's effect on tourism makes me want to scream like Jerry Lewis: "Wake up, lady!"

There is a line, and this movie crosses it. I don't know where the line is, but it's way north of *Wolf Creek*. There is a role for violence in film, but what the hell is the purpose of this sadistic celebration of pain and cruelty? The theaters are crowded right now with wonderful, thrilling, funny, warmhearted, dramatic, artistic, inspiring, entertaining movies. If anyone you know says this is the one they want to see, my advice is: Don't know that person no more. ☞

The Woodsman ★ ★ ★ ½
R, 87m., 2005

Kevin Bacon (Walter), Kyra Sedgwick (Vickie), Mos Def (Sergeant Lucas), Benjamin Bratt (Carlos), David Alan Grier (Bob), Eve (Mary-Kay), Kevin Rice (Candy), Michael Shannon (Rosen), Hannah Pilkes (Robin). Directed by Nicole Kassell and produced by Lee Daniels. Screenplay by Steven Fechter and Kassell.

For the first several scenes of *The Woodsman*, we know that Walter has recently been released from prison, but we don't know the nature of his crime. Seeing the film at Cannes, I walked in without advance knowledge and was grateful that I had an opportunity to see Kevin Bacon establish the character before that information was supplied. His crime has now been clearly named in virtually everything written about the film, and possibly changes the way it affects a viewer.

Walter is a pedophile. The film doesn't make him a case study or an object for our sympathy, but carefully and honestly observes his attempt to reenter society after twelve years behind bars. Maybe he will make it and maybe he will not. He has a deep compulsion that is probably innate, and a belief that his behavior is wrong. That belief will not necessarily keep him from repeating it. Most of us have sexual desires within the areas accepted by society, and so never reflect that we did not choose them, but simply grew up and found that they were there.

Bacon is a strong and subtle actor, something that is often said but insufficiently appreciated. Here he employs all of his art. He seems to have no theory about Walter and no emotional tilt toward his problems, and that is correct, because we do not act out of theories about ourselves, but out of our hopes and desires. Bacon plays the character day by day, hour by hour, detail by detail, simply showing us this man trying to deal with his daily life. Larger conclusions are left to the audience.

He gets an apartment across from a grade school playground. He did not choose the location; he found a landlord who would rent to an ex-con. He gets a job in a lumberyard. No one there knows about his crime, but a coworker named Mary-Kay (Eve) doesn't like him and senses something is wrong. Lucas, his parole officer (Mos Def), visits regularly and is hostile, convinced it is only a matter of time until Walter lapses.

There is a woman at work named Vickie (Kyra Sedgwick), who is tough-talking but has an instinctive sympathy for the newcomer. She's a fork-lift operator, a realist. They start to date. We know, but she doesn't, that this may be the first normal sexual relationship Walter has had. She is not only his girlfriend but, in a way, an unknowing sex therapist. He eventually feels he has to tell her about his past. How she deals with this, how she goes through a series of emotions, is handled in a way I felt was convincing.

Mary-Kay finds out the truth about Walter and posts a Web site at work. His privacy is gone. There are other developments. Watching the playground through his window, for example, he becomes aware of a pedophile who is obviously hoping to find prey there.

The film has a crucial scene involving Walter and a young girl named Robin (Hannah Pilkes). Without suggesting how the scene develops, I will say that it is so observant, so truthful, that in a sense the whole film revolves around it. There is nothing sensational in this film, nothing exploitative, nothing used for "entertainment value" unless we believe, as I do, that the close observation of the lives of other people can be—well, since entertaining is the wrong word, then helpful. It is easy to present a pedophile as a monster, less easy to suggest the emotional devastation that led into, and leads out of, his behavior. The real question in The Woodsman is whether Walter will be able to break the chain of transmission.

The movie is the first film by Nicole Kassell, a recent graduate of the NYU film school, who wrote the screenplay with Steven Fechter, based on his play. It is a remarkably confident work. It knows who Walter is, and to an extent why he is that way, and it knows that the film's real drama exists inside his mind and conscience. This is not a morality play but a study of character—of Walter's character, and of those who instinc-

tively detest him, and of a few, including Vickie and his brother-in-law Carlos (Benjamin Bratt), who are willing to withhold judgment long enough to see if he can find redemption.

The reason we cannot accept pedophilia as we accept many other sexual practices is that it requires an innocent partner whose life could be irreparably harmed. We do not have the right to do that. If there is no other way to achieve sexual satisfaction, that is a misfortune, but not an excuse. It is not the pedophile that is evil, but the pedophilia. That is true of all sins and crimes and those tempted to perform them: It is not that we are capable of transgression that condemns us, but that we are willing.

The Woodsman understands this at the very heart of its being, and that is why it succeeds as more than just the story of this character. It has relevance for members of the audience who would never in any way be even remotely capable of Walter's crime. We are quick to forgive our own trespasses, slower to forgive those of others. The challenge of a moral life is to do nothing that needs forgiveness. In that sense, we're all out on parole.

Wordplay ★ ★ ★
PG, 90 m., 2006

Featuring Will Shortz, Bill Clinton, Jon Stewart, Ken Burns, Mike Mussina, Bob Dole, and the Indigo Girls. A documentary directed by Patrick Creadon and produced by Christine O'Malley..

There are certain things in life you instinctively hold at arm's length, or they will move in with you and put their feet on the furniture. I've spent enough time working crossword puzzles to know I could become addicted. In the documentary Wordplay, we observe that to be a crossword champion you have to be incredibly intelligent, be capable of intuitive lateral thinking, know everything, and focus your knowledge into a narrow and ultimately meaningless pursuit. Yes, that makes you an obsessive eccentric, but they're really the only interesting people left, don't you sometimes think?

The movie centers around the twenty-eighth annual American Crossword Puzzle Tournament, hosted every year in Stamford, Connecticut, by Will Shortz, the editor of the New York Times crossword puzzles. It also visits fans of the *Times* puzzles (which run in countless other papers). These include Bill Clinton, Bob Dole, Jon Stewart, Ken Burns, Yankee pitcher Mike Mussina, and the Indigo Girls, although they missed my friend Dusty Cohl, who descends into a deep mental well once a day and does not emerge until the puzzle has been completed (I think "filled in" is not the approved terminology).

The film is made with a lot of style and visual ingenuity. Patrick Creadon, the director, uses graphics to show us crossword grids with the problem areas highlighted, and then we see the letters being written in. In one especially ingenious montage, he has all of his celebrities working on the same puzzle in interlocking shots. During the final championship round, with three contenders working on giant crosswords on a stage, he makes their progress easy to follow; I can imagine another film in which it would have been incomprehensible.

You have to be very well-informed to be a crossword puzzle champion. Scrabble and spelling bees require knowledge of a lot of words, but crosswords require unlimited facts, encyclopedic knowledge, and an ability to figure out the author's unstated assumptions about the nature of the clues. The puzzles can be tricky; both Dole and Clinton remember that on the day after their presidential campaign, one clue asked for the name of the winner. Diabolically, the correct seven-letter word could be either CLINTON or BOBDOLE.

All of these people think Merl Reagle is about the best crossword author now active. Mike Mussina, the pitcher, says solving a Reagle puzzle "is like pitching to Barry Bonds." Jon Stewart laments that the *Times* has banished certain words, including those involving bodily functions: "Words like 'urine' and 'enema,'" he says, "are terrific because they pack a lot of vowels in five letters." We meet some of the stars in the crossword world, including a former champ, Trip Payne, and twenty-year-old Tyler Hinman, who is the kid to watch. We also absorb the sense of a family reunion at the crossword tournament; the annual talent show is so democratic it includes baton twirling.

Will Shortz has been the god of this world since he founded the tournament, shortly after taking over as editor of the *Times* puzzles. How do you prepare for such a career? He went to In-diana University, which permits students to design their own majors, and got a degree in "enigmatology." He created the rules for the annual tournament.

The final championship round is incredibly intense. Not only do the finalists stand onstage in front of big boards everyone can see, but they wear headphones that pump music at them, so they can't hear clues or comments from the audience. There is a finalist this time who rips off his headphones, throws them to the ground, and uses a banished word involving a bodily function, and believe me, he has his reasons.

Word Wars ★ ★ ★
NO MPAA RATING, 80 m., 2004

A documentary directed by Eric Chaikin and Julian Petrillo and produced by Chaikin.

Spelling bees and Scrabble begin with the same skill: the ability to remember the correct spellings of a bewildering number of words, many of them obscure, illogical, and of slight everyday utility. Spelling bees end in sudden death, with one winner left standing. Professional Scrabble tournaments, to judge by the documentary *Word Wars*, are more like a living hell, a vortex into which its addicts disappear.

The movie uses the same structure as *Spellbound*, the charming doc about the national spelling bee. The difference is, Scrabble players are not charming. Both movies introduce us to leading contenders for the national championship, watch them train, worry, and obsess, and follow them to the national finals. For *Word Wars*, the end of the rainbow is in San Diego, which also spells "diagnose"; the movie has cute graphics rearranging one word into another, illustrating the Scrabble skill of looking at tiles that seem to spell nothing and willing then to spell *something, anything.*

We meet four players who are famous within the world of Scrabble, a world not of cute kids hoping for college scholarships but of desperate men and a few women with tunnel vision, who have chosen a sport as narrow and obsessive as championship poker, but without the big pots. The top prize in the tournament, if I recall correctly, is $25,000, and there are no cable stations paying to look over your shoulder while you play Scrabble with Ben Affleck.

Of finalists who are all unhappy in one way or another, the most miserable may be Joel Sherman, known in Scrabbleland as "G.I. Joel" because of his gastrointestinal tract, a battlefield of churning acids. He chugs drugstore remedies. Then there's Marlon Hill, an African-American who likes to come across as an angry militant, even if angry black militancy finds little opportunity to express itself in Scrabble. Oh, I forgot: Scrabble is an example of the way the world colonizes his mind by forcing him to use standard English since there is no Ebonics version of the game.

Matt Graham specializes in demanding goals with low chances of success: He wants to be not only a Scrabble champion but also a successful standup comic. If he played the lottery, he'd have a trifecta. He consumes mysterious pills that are allegedly not illegal. I believe him, but I also believe, based on their effect on him, that they should be.

Among the four contenders, the one who is relatively centered is Joe Edley, who has won the national championship three times, and thus would be a household name and the idol of millions if his sport were only professional tennis. Edley practices the entire New Age routine, with meditation, mantras, chants, Tai Chi, and various weird behaviors designed to intimidate his opponents by how much more together he is than they are. Ozzy Osborne is more together than they are.

We meet professional Scrabble hustlers in Washington Square Park, not far from the professional chess hustlers. The difference is, chess is an exercise in applied logic in which the better player always wins (if he loses, he is by definition not the better player). Poker is also a game where the better player usually wins, or has an edge, although something depends on the luck of the cards. Scrabble requires the most masochistic traits of both chess and poker. To some degree, you win because you know how to spell more words and are better at teasing them out from the alphabet soup on your rack. To some degree, you lose because you drew lousy tiles. There is a shot in *Word Wars* of the tiles a player draws at a crucial moment in a game, and the audience groans. They may be the worst tiles in history.

Word Wars is compellingly watchable because (a) we all know how to play Scrabble, (b)

the characters are such authentic oddballs, (c) their world seems more arcane and peculiar the longer we spend in it, and (d) there is suspense approaching desperation at the end; some of the players almost need to win in order to buy their next meal.

Scrabble is one way to kill time. I can think of better ways to pass obsessive, lonely, antisocial lives; a documentary named *Cinemania* is about people who literally attempt to spend every waking hour watching movies, seven days a week. At least they get to see the movies. After a Scrabble player has triumphantly played a word that contains Q without U, where does he go from there? How long can you treasure that memory?

The World ★ ★ ★
NO MPAA RATING, 139 m., 2005

Zhao Tao (Tao), Chen Taishen (Taisheng), Jing Jue (Wei), Jiang Zhongwei (Niu), Huang Yiqun (Qun), Wang Hongwei (Sanlai), Liang Jingdong (Liang), Ji Shuai (Erxiao), Xiang Wan (Youyou), Alla Chtcherbakova (Anna). Directed by Jia Zhangke and produced by Yoshida Takio, Ichiyama Shozo, and Ren Zhonglun. Screenplay by Zhangke.

There is something about a one-ring circus or a run-down theme park that appeals to me. There is a poignancy in the shabbiness of their glory. Once on the Lido in Venice, out of season, I was one of nine people in the audience as an old lady in spangles rode around the ring on a discouraged pony. I ate sugar-coated peanuts and wept inside, perhaps from joy.

The World takes place almost entirely within a theme park in Beijing. "America has lost her Twin Towers," a guide observes, "but we still have ours." Yes, and the Eiffel Tower, Piazza San Marco, St. Peter's Square, the Pyramids, the Taj Mahal, the Leaning Tower of Pisa, and Big Ben. All of these landmarks are about the height of the McDonald's arches; one is reminded of the miniature Stonehenge, descending from above in *This Is Spinal Tap*.

How do you visit these miniature tourist attractions? There is an exhausted two-car monorail that creeps along its elevated track. Or you can board a jet airplane that never leaves the ground, which lends a certain jollity to the instructions about how to use your seat belt and the oxygen masks.

An American documentarian like Errol Morris would visit this world and find easy humor in its stunted grandiosity. But *The World* has been made in China by Jia Zhangke, a director who has been in much trouble with the authorities—not because he embraces the West, but because he mocks modern China for trying to become Western in such haste. He doesn't yearn for the days of Chairman Mao, but he doesn't find the emerging China much of an improvement; the nation seems trapped between two sterilities.

His plot keeps most of the tourists at a distance. He is concerned with the people who work in this park, changing their costumes to become now an Italian dancer, now a camel driver. They live in shabby rooms hidden away behind the gaudy attractions and dream of someday visiting the countries whose citizens they impersonate. The dressmaker Qun (Huang Yiqun) is married to a husband she has not seen for years; he was part of a boatload of illegal immigrants to Europe, one of only six to survive. Now he is in Paris, and she hopes for a passport. But passports seem to lead to The World, not away.

Two Russian dancers arrive, and their passports are confiscated by a man who assures them "they will be safer with me."

Later we see Anna (Alla Chtcherbakova) in a club, where she appears to have become a prostitute, probably against her will. Meanwhile, Qun has a sort of affair with Taisheng (Chen Taishen), a security guard. Is she cheating on her husband in Paris, or does he even remember her? Both Taisheng and the dancer Tao (Zhao Tao) come from the same small town and remember it with nostalgia mixed with hopelessness; if The World offers them dubious futures, their childhoods seemed to offer none.

There is a sense that someone is getting rich somewhere in China, but not the owners and operators of The World. There is an irony that foreign tourists are visiting a theme park where poor Chinese wander dubiously among miniatures of a world they will never be able to visit. On New Year's Eve, the park originates a telecast that will be seen "by 1 billion viewers worldwide"—the same mythical billion who also don't really watch the Oscars.

The movie is long and slow. Either you will fall into its rhythm, or you will grow restless. At first I felt like someone who had spent a humid afternoon at The World and wanted to know, "Can I go home now?" Then I became invested in the backstage story, which emerges slowly and in uncertain pieces. There is integrity in a movie that refuses to pump up melodrama where none belongs. This is not a movie about an amusement park threatened by a bomb, or populated by colorful characters, or made into the object of satire. It is a movie about people doing boring and badly paid work day after day while being required to look happy.

In China, the grandparents of these characters no doubt worked in rice fields or garment sweatshops, or as street vendors. Now the young generation wears uniforms and costumes and occupies a replica of the modern world. Zhangke seems to think they are even unhappier than their ancestors were; is hard labor better than pointless labor? Consider the romance between Qun and Taisheng. Where will it lead? What plans can they make? And is China unique in offering this kind of employment as a dead end? Ask a clerk at Wal-Mart.

After the screening, I rode down on the elevator with the great film critic Jonathan Rosenberg. "I've seen it five times," he said. "It's one of my favorite films. I still don't understand the ending." Not only was I afraid to ask him what he didn't understand about the ending, but I also was afraid to ask him what he thought the ending was. In a sense, *The World* is about a story that never really begins.

The World's Fastest Indian ★ ★ ★
PG-13, 127 m., 2006

Anthony Hopkins (Burt Munro), Jessica Cauffiel (Wendy), Saginaw Grant (Jake), Diane Ladd (Ada), Christopher Lawford (Jim Moffet), Aaron Murphy (Sam), Paul Rodriguez (Fernando), Annie Whittle (Fran), Chris Williams (Tina). Directed by Roger Donaldson and produced by Donaldson and Gary Hannam. Screenplay by Donaldson.

The World's Fastest Indian is a movie about an old coot and his motorcycle, yes, but it is also about a kind of heroism that has gone out of style. Burt Munro is a codger in his sixties who lives in Invercargill, New Zealand, takes nitro pills for his heart condition, and has spent years tinkering with a 1920 Indian motorcycle. His neighbors wish he would take a break once in a while to mow the grass.

By 1967, Burt thinks the Indian may be about ready to travel to the Bonneville Salt Flats in Utah and take part in the annual Speed Week. This project involves fund-raising in Invercargill, and a long journey that takes him overland in America, where he meets, among others, an accommodating widow who takes him to visit her husband's grave. In Bonneville, where millionaire drivers are sponsored by big corporations, no one has ever seen anyone like Burt or anything like his ancient machine.

He should have registered weeks ago, but the officials lack the heart to turn him away. They are amazed when they inspect his machine. No braking chute? No brakes? "Where's your fire suit?" Can that be a cork on his gas tank? There is no tread on his tires. Is that mechanical part a—kitchen hinge? Why do they allow this man to risk his life in defiance of every safety standard at Bonneville? I think it is because Burt loves his motorcycle and cannot believe she would harm him; the steadfastness of his trust seduces them. When Burt discusses his motorcycle, which he rhymes with Popsicle, he gets into theories he must have pondered long into the night in his garage in New Zealand: "The center of pressure is behind the center of gravity," he explains, as if that explained anything. Or maybe it does. With Burt you can never be sure.

This is one of Anthony Hopkins's most endearing, least showy performances. The man who created Hannibal Lecter and Richard Nixon is concerned here with the precise behavior of a quiet, introverted man who is simultaneously obsessed and a little muddled. It's as if his fellow racing drivers have been visited by a traveler from the dawn of their sport, when guys tinkered with their machines in the tool shed and roared up and down country roads. Burt Munro is a man for whom the world seems brand new: He is amazed to enter a restaurant and see, for the first time in his life, a menu with photographs. Bonneville involves not racing but time trials. Burt has customized his Indian into a low, streamlined machine that he rides while flat on his stomach. He has a pair of goggles and a battered helmet that looks like Lindy once wore it, and he roars off into the desert sun like a crazy kid.

Burt Munro was a real man, and the film is based on fact. Roger Donaldson, the movie's writer and director, grew up in New Zealand, where Munro was a folk hero. Donaldson wrote the first draft of this script in 1979, after a 1971 documentary, and then life took him to Hollywood and to big-budget thrillers such as *No Way Out*, and now at last he has returned to tell the story of a hero of his youth.

It is also the story of certain New Zealand characteristics, among which is self-effacing modesty. Burt Munro would think it unseemly to call attention to himself, although he is happy for his Indian to get attention. (Before one race, he pops a nitro pill into the gas tank and as he swallows the second, he explains, "One for myself and one for the old girl.") In an era of showboat sports superstars, how strange to see old Burt challenge one of the most durable records in racing and then actually be embarrassed by the attention.

Read no further if you do not want to know how Burt does at Bonneville, although perhaps you have already guessed that *The World's Fastest Indian* is not about the second-fastest Indian. Yes, in 1967 Burt coaxed the Indian to 201.85 mph, even as a muffler was burning the flesh on his leg. That set a record in the category of "streamlined motorcycles under 1,000 cc." It is a record, the film assures us, that stands to this day. Burt returned nine times to Bonneville, becoming a hero, although deflecting attention with his diffidence, his shyness, his way of talking about the Indian instead of about himself. We are reminded that when Lindbergh flew the *Spirit of St. Louis* across the Atlantic, he titled his autobiography *We*—so that it included his airplane. That's how Burt feels about the old girl.

X

X-Men: The Last Stand ★ ★ ★
PG-13, 104 m., 2006

Patrick Stewart (Charles Xavier), Hugh Jackman (Logan/Wolverine), Ian McKellen (Eric Lensherr/ Magneto), Halle Berry (Ororo Munroe/Storm), Famke Janssen (Dr. Jean Grey/Phoenix), Anna Paquin (Marie/Rogue), Kelsey Grammer (Dr. Hank McCoy/Beast), Rebecca Romijn (Raven Darkholme/ Mystique), Ben Foster (Angel), Michael Murphy (Warren Worthington II), Vinnie Jones (Cain Marko/Juggernaut), Eric Dane (Multiple Man), Cameron Bright (Leech), Shohreh Aghdashloo (Dr. Kavita Rao). Directed by Brett Ratner and produced by Avi Arad, Lauren Shuler Donner, and Ralph Winter. Screenplay by Zak Penn and Simon Kinberg.

The government has a Department of Mutant Affairs in *X-Men: The Last Stand*, and it is headed by the mutant Dr. Hank McCoy (Kelsey Grammer), also known as Beast. The Mutant Community seems on its way into the mainstream, the goal long envisioned by Professor Charles Xavier (Patrick Stewart), head of the school where young X-Men learn to develop and control their powers. The school purrs along proudly with Wolverine (Hugh Jackman) as a role model, but then a kid named Leech surfaces, and all bets are off.

His body produces an antibody to mutation; inject it into X-Men, and their mutant powers disappear. They become regular folks with the same limited powers the rest of us use to scrape by. Leech is played by Cameron Bright, whom you may remember from *Birth*, the movie where he was a child whose body was occupied by the mind of Nicole Kidman's late husband. Bright has large dark eyes and ominously sober features that make you think he might grow up to become chairman of the Federal Reserve, or a serial killer.

He's invaluable to the billionaire Warren Worthington II (Michael Murphy), who lives in shame because his son Warren III (Ben Foster), also known as Angel, has a sixteen-foot wingspan. A flashback shows young Angel in a room full of blood and feathers, having tried to cut the wings from his back. This self-hate is nurtured by Worthington, whose shame about his son translates into hatred of mutants in general. He buys Alcatraz, imprisons Leech, begins to manufacture the antibody and campaigns for a "cure" for mutants.

But what if mutants don't want to be "cured"? What if they're happy the way they are, and cherish their differences? Xavier has always tried to encourage that kind of thinking, but Magneto (Ian McKellen), his archenemy in X-Man land, takes a more direct approach. He wages war against Worthington and all those who would foist a "cure" on the mutants. Although Magneto has always been the villain of the series, this time he makes a good point.

So strong is Leech's anti-mutant power that a mutant need only stand near him to lose his or her abilities; maybe the antibody works through pheromones. Meanwhile, Mutant Cure Clinics spring up around the country, and are picketed by pro-mutant militants. Extremists arm themselves with guns that can fire the antibody and go out to shoot themselves some mutants. Beast, as the administration's cabinet minister in charge of mutant affairs, is caught in the middle.

There are so many parallels here with current political and social issues that to list them is to define the next presidential campaign. Just writing the previous paragraph, I thought of abortion, gun control, stem cell research, the "gay gene," and the Minutemen. "Curing" mutants is obviously a form of genetic engineering, and it stirs thoughts of "cures" for many other conditions that humans are born with, which could be loosely defined as anything that prevents you from being just like George or Georgette Clooney. The fact is, most people grow accustomed to the hand they've been dealt, and they rather resent the opportunity to become "normal." (Normal in this context is whatever makes you more like them and less like yourself.)

X-Men: The Last Stand raises all of these questions in embryo form but doesn't engage them in much detail, because it is often distracted by the need to be an action movie. Consider, for example, the lengths Magneto goes to in order to neutralize young Leech. The kid is being held on Alcatraz? Very well then, Magneto will stand on the Golden Gate Bridge and use his powers of industrial-strength levitation to rip loose a whole span of the bridge and rotate it so that it joins Alcatraz with the mainland, and his forces can march on Worthington's fortress. Countless innocent citizens die during this operation, falling from the bridge or otherwise terminating their commute. It seems to me that Magneto in this case is, well, a terrorist. So fanatic is his devotion to mutation that he will destroy the bridge in the service of his belief. Charles Xavier, on the other hand, is like (how does it go?) the vast majority of mutants who are peaceful and responsible citizens.

One of the distractions in all the X-Men movies is that the X-Men are always getting involved in local incidents that have little to do with the big picture. They demonstrate their powers during disagreements and courtships, neighborhood emergencies, psychological problems, or while showing off. After three movies you'd think they would have learned to coordinate their efforts so that Storm (Halle Berry), for example, is not suddenly needed to brew up a last-minute storm and save the neighborhood/city/state/world.

My guess is, there are just plain too many mutants, and their powers are so various and ill-matched that it's hard to keep them all in the same canvas. The addition of Beast, Angel, and Leech, not to mention Multiple Man, Juggernaut, and the revived Dr. Jean Grey (reborn as Dark Phoenix), causes a Mutant Jam, because there are too many X-Men with too many powers for a 104-minute movie. There are times when the director, Brett Ratner, seems to be scurrying from one plotline to another like that guy who had to keep all of his plates spinning on top of their poles. All the same, I enjoyed *X-Men: The Last Stand*. I liked the action, I liked the absurdity, I liked the incongruous use and misuse of mutant powers, and I especially liked the way it introduces all of those political issues and lets them fight it out with the special effects. Magneto would say this is a test of survival of the fittest. Xavier would hope they could learn to live together.

XXX: State of the Union ★ ★ ½
PG-13, 94 m., 2005

Ice Cube (Darius Stone), Willem Dafoe (George Deckert), Samuel L. Jackson (Agent Augustus Gibbons), Peter Strauss (President), Xzibit (Zeke), Robert Alonzo (Guard), Rich Bryant (Man in Trench Coat), Steve Carson (Prisoner). Directed by Lee Tamahori and produced by Gillian Libbert, Neal H. Moritz, and Arne Schmidt. Screenplay by Rich Wilkes and Simon Kinberg.

XXX: State of the Union is theater of the absurd, masquerading as an action thriller. Consider. The president of the United States is giving his State of the Union message, unaware that outside the U.S. Capitol building, storm troopers in black body armor, with little red pin-points for eyes, are attempting to break in and assassinate him, as well as the vice president and everyone else in the chain of command, until they get to the secretary of defense, who has hired them for his attempted coup.

Opposing them—well, we have an ex-con named Darius (Ice Cube), who has recruited a gang of black street warriors from an up-market chop shop and outfitted them with supercharged dragsters and heavy-duty weapons. These men have been put into play by a national security agent named Gibbons (Samuel L. Jackson), who is temporarily a prisoner of the secretary of defense (Willem Dafoe), although he will be freed in time to participate in a high-speed chase after the president (Peter Strauss) is spirited out of the Capitol on a secret bullet train.

In the climax of the movie, Darius (now known as XXX) will pursue the bullet train in his 220 mph car, shredding its tires so that it can run on the rails, and so that Darius can leap from his car onto the back of the train, enter it, grab the president, and attempt to swing him to safety via a helicopter before . . . well, before other stuff happens.

How strange to see this movie on the very day when a bullet train in Japan jumped the rails and crashed into a building. And in the very week when Amtrak appealed once again for rescue from its permanent fiscal crisis, caused in part by the lack of adequate rails for bullet trains. As the president's escape train was rocketing along, did he reflect that the tracks were only safe up to about 60 mph? Should have signed that transportation bill! Or was he too busy wondering why he was being rescued from his own secretary of defense by a black dude?

I showed Mario Van Peebles's *Baadasssss* at my Overlooked Film Festival. It is a movie about the making of a 1970 movie by his father, Melvin, about a black man who defies society and yet does not die at the end of the movie. It suggests that there may be corrupt police officers. This movie was very controversial thirty-five years ago. Now we have a movie in which the entire defense establishment is corrupt, and the president is rescued by a posse of baadassssses, who capture a tank and use it to blast their way into the Capitol, at which point I assume but cannot be sure that the media finally notice that all hell is breaking loose.

I am not sure because *XXX: State of the Union* has such a breakneck pace that it doesn't pause for the customary news updates in which the State of the Union Address is interrupted with the information that a war is raging on Capitol Hill. No, there's not even a crawl across the bottom of the screen: *Snows blanket New England . . . Armored vehicles attacking U.S. Capitol . . . Illinois 98, Michigan 91* . . . Just wondering: Are there any kind of security arrangements around the Capitol Building? You know, TV cameras or security guards who might notice when heavily armed bands of warriors dressed like Darth Vader are using rocket launchers?

The premise of the movie is apparently that within the nation's security apparatus there is a deeper, more lethal level of countersecurity agents whose job it is to defeat the regular security guys should they turn traitor. This force is always led by a superwarrior code-named XXX, and now that the original XXX (Vin Diesel) has been killed, Sam Jackson springs Ice Cube from prison to take over the assignment. (Diesel does not appear in the sequel after a salary dispute, which may explain why a Diesel lookalike plays a cameo role as a dead businessman.)

You are eager to know if any of the characters resemble current or former presidents or vice presidents or defense secretaries of the United States. No, they do not. They barely resemble fictional presidents, and so on. The president in the movie believes we must make our enemies our allies. The secretary of defense disagrees, which is why he wants to assassinate the president and half his administration. No political parties are named. There is a moment when the president says something in his speech and everybody on the Republican side of the chamber stands up to applaud, and I thought, a-ha, he's a Republican!—until I saw that all the Democrats stood up, too, and I realized they were all probably applauding praise for themselves.

Did I enjoy this movie? Only in a dumb, mindless way. It has whatever made the original *XXX* entertaining, but a little less of it. Does it make the slightest sense? Of course not. Its significance has nothing to do with current politics and politicians, the threat of terrorism, and the efficiency of bullet trains. It has everything to do with a seismic shift in popular culture.

Once all action heroes were white. Then they got a black chief of police, who had a big scene where he fired them. Then they got a black partner. Then they were black and had a white partner. Now they are the heroes and don't even need a white guy around, although there is one nerdy white guy in *XXX* who steps in when the plot requires the ineffectual delivery of a wimpy speech. So drastically have things changed that when Ice Cube offers to grab the president and jump off a train and grab a helicopter, all the president can do is look grateful.

Oh, and later, in his new State of the Union speech, our nation's leader quotes Tupac, although he doesn't know he does. Well, you can't expect him to know everything.

Y

Yes ★ ★ ★ ★
R, 99 m., 2005

Joan Allen (She), Simon Abkarian (He), Sam Neill (Anthony), Shirley Henderson (Cleaner), Sheila Hancock (Aunt), Samantha Bond (Kate), Stephanie Leonidas (Grace), Gary Lewis (Billy). Directed by Sally Potter and produced by Christopher Sheppard and Andrew Fierberg. Screenplay by Potter.

Sally Potter's *Yes* is a movie unlike any other I have seen or heard. Some critics have treated it as ill-behaved, as if its originality is offensive. Potter's sin has been to make a movie that is artistically mannered and overtly political; how dare she write her dialogue in poetry, provide a dying communist aunt, and end the film in Cuba? And what to make of the housecleaner who sardonically comments on the human debris shed by her rich employers? The flakes of skin, the nail clippings, the wisps of dead hair, the invisible millions of parasites?

I celebrate these transgressions. *Yes* is alive and daring, not a rehearsal of safe material and styles. Potter easily could have made a well-mannered love story with passion and pain at appropriate intervals; or perhaps, for Potter, that would not have been so easy, since all of her films strain impatiently at the barriers of convention. She sees no point in making movies that have been made before. See, for example, *Orlando,* in which Tilda Swinton plays a character who lives for centuries and trades genders.

Yes is a movie about love, sex, class, and religion, involving an elegant Irish-American woman (Joan Allen) and a Lebanese waiter and kitchen worker (Simon Abkarian). They are known only as She and He. She is a scientist, married lovelessly to a rich British politician (Sam Neill). He was a surgeon in Beirut, until he saved a man's life only to see him immediately shot dead. Refusing to heal only those with the correct politics, he fled Lebanon and now uses his knives to chop parsley instead of repairing human hearts.

They meet at a formal dinner. They do it with their eyes. He smiles, she smiles. Neither turns away. An invitation has been offered and accepted. Their sex is eager and makes them laugh.

They are not young; they are grateful because of long experience with what can go wrong.

There is a scene in the movie of delightful eroticism. It involves goings-on under the table in a restaurant. The camera regards not the details of this audacity, but the eyes and faces of the lovers. They take their time getting to where they are almost afraid to go. They look at each other, enjoying their secret, he looking for a reaction, she wary of revealing one. Her release is a barely subdued shudder of muffled ecstasy. This is what sex is about: two people knowing each other and using their knowledge. Compared to it, the sex scenes in most movies are calisthenics.

She was born in Belfast, raised in America, is Christian, probably Catholic. He is Arabic and Muslim. Both come from lands where people kill each other in the name of God. They are above all that. Or perhaps not. They have an economic imbalance: "You buy me with a credit card in a restaurant," he says in a moment of anger. And: "Even to pronounce my name is an impossibility." With his fellow kitchen workers he debates the way Western women display their bodies, the way their husbands allow them to be looked at by other men. He is worldly, understands the West, and yet his inherited beliefs about women are deeply ingrained, and available when he needs a vocabulary to express his resentment.

She, on the other hand, displays her body with a languorous, healthy pride to him, and to us as we watch the movie. There is no explicit nudity. There is a scene where she goes swimming with her goddaughter, and we see that she is athletic, subtly muscled, with the neck and head of a goddess. To recline at the edge of the pool in casual physical perfection is as natural to She as it is disturbing to He. Their passion cools long enough for them to realize that they cannot live together successfully in either of their cultures.

Now about the dialogue. It is written in iambic pentameter, the rhythm scheme of Shakespeare. It is a style poised between poetry and speech; "to be or not to be, that is the question," and another question is, does that sound to you like poetry or prose? To me, it sounds like prose that has been given the elegance and discipline of formal structure. The characters never sound as if they're reciting poetry, and the rhymes, far from sounding forced, sometimes can hardly be heard at all. What the dialogue brings to the film is a certain unstated gravity; it elevates what is being said into a realm of grace and care.

There is her dying aunt, an unrepentant Marxist who provides us her testament in an interior monologue while she is in a coma. This monologue, and others in the film, are heard while the visuals employ subtle, transient freeze-frames. The aunt concedes that communism has failed, but "what came in its place? A world of greed. A life spent longing for things you don't need." The same point is made by She's house-cleaner (Shirley Henderson) and other maids and lavatory attendants seen more briefly. They clean up after us. We move through life shedding a cloud of organic dust, while minute specks of life make their living by nibbling at us. These mites and viruses in their turn cast off their own debris, while elsewhere galaxies are dying; the universe lives by making a mess of itself.

Can She and He live together? Is there a way for their histories and cultures to coexist as comfortably as their genitals? The dying aunt makes She promise to visit Cuba. "I want my death to wake you up and clean you out," she says. You and I know that Cuba has not worked, and I think the aunt knows it, too. But at least in Cuba the dead roots of her hopes might someday rise up and bear fruit. And Cuba has the advantage of being equally alien to both of them. Neither is an outsider when both are.

Potter has said, "I think 'yes' is the most beautiful and necessary word in the English language"—a statement less banal the more you consider it. Doesn't it seem to you sometimes as if we are fighting our way through a thicket of no? When He and She first meet, their eyes say yes to sex. By the end of the film, they are preparing to say yes to the bold overthrow of their lives up until then, and yes to the beginning of something hopeful and unknown.

The Yes Men ★ ★ ★
R, 80 m., 2004

A documentary directed by Dan Ollman, Sarah Price, and Chris Smith and produced by Price and Smith.

From an economic point of view, the Civil War was the least profitable of all our wars, because the destruction of lives and property involved Americans on both sides. In our other wars, most of the lives and property belonged to foreigners. The war was fought to abolish slavery, but slavery would soon have faded away on its own because it made no economic sense. Think how much it costs to support a slave.

The involuntary servitude of imported labor, which is what slavery amounts to, has been replaced in our times by the much more efficient system of exporting jobs to countries that are poor to begin with, and thus have lower maintenance costs for labor. This "remote labor" is the natural alternative to slavery, and, as a bonus, there is no reason for the worker not to be free. Thus he is responsible for his own housing, feeding, and medical care—which can be at a cost level much lower than a slave owner could safely provide.

The new "remote labor system," enforced by the World Trade Organization through its system of loans and regulations for poor countries, is much more efficient for First World capitalism. It exports manufacturing and assembly jobs to Third World countries where athletic shoes, clothing, home appliances, tools, computers, and toys are assembled by labor forces paid only pennies an hour. The use of child labor further reduces the cost, and by removing the children from school, diminishes the threat of educated opposition to the system.

On the statements above we can all agree, right? Or was there a point at which you realized I was making an outrageous and immoral argument, and you were offended? I ask because when a fake "spokesman" for the World Trade Organization made the same argument before a WTO trade forum in Finland, the audience listened politely, applauded, and had no questions.

The Yes Men is a disturbing documentary in which a couple of tricksters named Mike Bonanno and Andy Bichlbaum create a fictional WTO spokesman named Hank Hardy Unruh, and a fake WTO Web site where he can be contacted. Real-world groups contact Hank Hardy, and he flies out to their meetings to deliver a speech at which he summarizes the anti-WTO argument in terms the audience, incredibly, absorbs and passively accepts. Apparently (a) no one is really listening, (b) no one is thinking, or (c) the immorality of the WTO's exploitation of cheap foreign labor becomes invisible when it is described in purely economic terms. Answer: All three, which is why the United States and the other nations controlling the WTO can live with the inhuman cost of its policies, and why so many people simply don't understand what the demonstrators at world trade forums are so mad about.

What is incredible in the film is the lengths to which a trade audience can be pushed without realizing it is the butt of a joke. At the meeting in Finland, which is about "Textiles of the Future," Hank Hardy Unruh concludes his speech, has an assistant rip off his "business suit," and reveals beneath it a gold lamé body suit. It has an inflatable appendage that pops up to allow him to view a computer screen at eye level. This appendage looks uncannily like a large phallus. Do the audience members laugh uproariously or walk out in anger? No, *they just sit there.* They have lost all ability to apply reality to the ideological construction they inhabit.

The film shows another fake lecture, before a group of New York students. At this one, McDonald's hamburgers are passed out, and the students chow down as the fake speaker laments the fact that the human body is inefficient in processing food. In fact, 90 percent of all the calories we eat are eliminated by the body. The challenge, they're told, "is to recycle postconsumer waste into fast food. A single hamburger can be eaten ten times!"

The students, thank God, don't just sit there. They are outraged—which means, however, that they took the speech seriously. "Do you think you guys are lacking kind of, like, a human element?" one student asks. And a cynic shouts: "How much did McDonald's pay you guys to come here today?"

Yeah, like McDonald's is really going to recycle excrement into Cheese McCraps. I watched the movie in astonishment and dismay. Have we lost all balance, all critical ability, all the instincts that should warn an intelligent person that a joke is being played? Is satire possible in a world where nobody gets it? Have modern forms of corporatespeak so depersonalized language that no one expects it to mean anything?

No one with a feeling for literature and poetry can read the typical best-selling business or self-help book with a straight face, because their six rules or nine plans or twelve formulas are so manifestly idiotic, and couched in prose of such insulting simplicity. If I were a boss, I would fire any employee reading such a book, on the grounds that he was not smart enough to be working for me. If I were the employee of a company that hired one of those motivational gurus, I would quit on the grounds that management had been taken over by pod people.

But I am a film critic, and must report that *The Yes Men* is amazing in what it shows, but underwhelming in what it does with it. The film seems a little hasty and disorganized, as if available footage is being stretched further than it wants to go. The filmmakers are Dan Ollman, Sarah Price, and Chris Smith; Price and Smith made *American Movie* (2000), without a doubt the funniest documentary I have ever seen, and one of the best.

This time, they have such colorful characters and such an alarming story to tell that the film works in spite of its imperfections. Yes, we'd like to know more about the infrastructure that supports the Yes Men, and have more objective information about the WTO. Or maybe the blank looks on the faces of the audience regarding the inflatable phallic "Employee Visualization Appendage" tells us everything we need to know.

Young Adam ★ ★ ★ ½
NC-17, 93 m., 2004

Ewan McGregor (Joe Taylor), Tilda Swinton (Ella Gault), Peter Mullan (Les Gault), Emily Mortimer (Cathie Dimly). Directed by David Mackenzie and produced by Jeremy Thomas. Screenplay by Mackenzie, based on a novel by Alexander Trocchi.

Two men and a woman on a barge. No one who has seen Jean Vigo's famous film *L'Atalante* (1932) can watch *Young Adam* without feeling its resonance. There cannot be peace unless the woman or one of the men leaves. In the Vigo film, newlyweds make the barge their occupation and home, and the bride feels pushed aside by the crusty old deckhand (the immortal Michel Simon). In *Young Adam,* the chemistry is more lethal. The barge is owned by Ella Gault

(Tilda Swinton), who has a loveless marriage with her husband, Les (Peter Mullan). Les has hired the young and cocky Joe Taylor (Ewan McGregor), who fancies himself a writer.

It is a foregone conclusion that Joe will eventually have sex with Ella, as the barge *Atlantic Eve* trades on the dank canals between Glasgow and Edinburgh, circa 1960. But that's really not the movie's subject, even though it provides rich opportunities for Peter Mullan, that intense and inward Scotsman, to underplay his rage and suppress his feelings. (At one point, as Joe and Ella linger in bed, they hear Les's boots on the deck overhead and decide, "He's letting us know he's back.") No, the *Atlantic Eve* is not the setting for adultery so much as for guilt and long silences.

As the film opens, Joe sees the body of a young woman floating in the canal, dressed only in lingerie. He uses a hook to pull it closer, and Les helps him haul her on board. The police are summoned. It is a drowning, perhaps a suicide. No foul play, apparently.

But Joe knows more about the body than he reveals—more, much more, than anybody would ever be able to discover, and he reads the papers with interest as it is learned the woman was pregnant, and that her boyfriend, a plumber, has been charged with the murder.

Joe is a hard case. Opaque. Not tender, not good with the small talk. Around women he has a certain intensity that informs them he plans to have sex with them and it is up to them to agree, or go away. He is not a rapist, but he has only one purpose in his mind, and some women find that intensity of focus to be exciting. It's as if, at the same time, he cares nothing for them and can think only of them. No amount of sweet talk would conquer them, but his eyes penetrate to their souls and rummage around.

As the murder case goes to trial, Joe finds himself attending the court sessions. He becomes fascinated by the defendant. Flashbacks fill in chapters of Joe's earlier life, episodes known only to him, including a moment when he could have acted, and did not act, and does not even begin to understand why he didn't. He is not a murderer, but a man unwilling to intervene, a man so detached, so cold, so willing to sacrifice others to his own convenience, that perhaps in his mind it occurs to him that he

would feel better about the young woman's death if he had actually, actively, killed her. Then at least he would know what he had done, and would not find such emptiness when he looks inside himself. This is an almost Dostoyevskian study of a man brooding upon evil until it paralyzes him.

Although Britain and Ireland now enjoy growing prosperity, any working class person thirty or older was raised in a different, harder society. That's why actors like Ewan McGregor and Colin Farrell, not to mention Tim Roth and Gary Oldman, can slip so easily into these hard-edged, dirty-handed roles. With American actors you have the feeling they bought work clothes at Sears and roughed them up; with these guys, you figure they got their old gear out of their dad's closet, or borrowed their brother's. Peter Mullan, who is older, is a sublime actor, too much overlooked, who can play a working man with a direct honesty that doesn't involve a single extra note. Look at his movie *My Name Is Joe*, where he plays a recovering alcoholic who tries to help a friend and to risk a romance. As for Tilda Swinton, here is directness so forceful you want to look away; she doesn't cave in to Joe because of his look, but because he can match hers.

A movie like *Young Adam* is above all about the ground-level lives of its characters. The death of the girl and the plot surrounding it is handled not as a crime or a mystery, but as an event that jars characters out of their fixed orbits. When you have a policy of behavior, a pose toward the world, that has hardened like concrete into who you are, it takes more than guilt to break you loose. It takes the sudden realization that the person you created continues to function, but you are now standing outside of him. He carries on regardless, and you are stranded, alone and frightened.

Yours, Mine & Ours ★ ½
PG, 90 m., 2005

Dennis Quaid (Frank Beardsley), Rene Russo (Helen North), Rip Torn (The Commandant), Linda Hunt (Mrs. Munion), Jerry O'Connell (Max), David Koechner (Darrell). Directed by Raja Gosnell and produced by Robert Simonds and Michael Nathanson. Screenplay by Ron Burch and David Kidd, based on the 1968 screenplay by Melville Shavelson and Mort Lachman and the book by Helen Eileen Beardsley.

Yours, Mine & Ours has one thing to be thankful for: Frank and Helen realize immediately that they're still in love, all these years after they were the prom king and queen in high school. They see each other, they dance, they talk while dancing, they kiss while talking, and in the next scene they're engaged to be married. That saves us the Idiot Plot device in which they're destined for each other but are kept apart by a series of misunderstandings. In this version, they're brought together by a series of misunderstandings, mostly on the part of the filmmakers, who thought they could remake the 1968 Henry Fonda/Lucille Ball film without its sweetness and charm.

The story: He is a Coast Guard admiral with eight children. She is a fashion designer with ten children. They were in love in high school and darn!—they shoulda gotten married then, if for no other reason than that they'd probably not have eighteen kids, although you never know, and some of hers are adopted. With a little willpower they could be merely starring in a sequel to the remake of *Cheaper by the Dozen.* Too late: *Cheaper by the Dozen 2* opened December 21.

Frank likes everything shipshape. Helen is comfortable with a certain messiness. His kids line up for roll call and mess duty. Her kids are free spirits with a touch of hippie. Her family has a pig for a pet. I think his family has two dogs. That's how many I counted, about forty-five minutes into the movie, although as nearly as I can recall nobody ever claims them. Of course, I may have missed something. I wish I had missed more.

Dennis Quaid can be the most effortlessly charming of actors, but give him a break: It helps when he has effortlessly charming material. Here he has a formula to race through at breakneck speed, as if the director, Raja Gosnell, is checking off obligatory scenes and wants to get home in time for the lottery drawing. Rene Russo can play a convincing and attractive mother of ten, but that's not what this material needs. It needs a ditzy madcap, to contrast with the disciplined Coast Guard man. The earlier casting of Lucille Ball gives you an idea of what the role required, and Russo is simply too reasonable to provide it. If ever there was a role calling out "Goldie! Goldie!" this is the one.

No matter; we never get a sense of a real relationship between Frank and Helen. Their marriage seems like an extended Meet Cute. Gosnell and his writers, Ron Burch and David Kidd, crack the whip while making the characters jump through the obligatory hoops of the plot. We know, because we have seen one or two movies before this one, that it is necessary a) for the two tribes of kids to become instant enemies, b) for food fights to erupt on a moment's notice, c) for there to be a Preliminary Crisis that threatens the marriage, and a Preliminary Solution, followed by d) a Real Crisis and a Real Solution, and happily ever after, etc., with a farewell sight gag or two involving the pig. There is even a truce among the children, who oppose the marriage and have a plan: "We gotta stop fighting and get them to start."

There's not a moment in this story arc that is not predictable. Consider the outing on the sailboat. The *moment* Admiral Frank warns everybody that the boom can swing around and knock you overboard, I would have given 19-to-1 odds that the person knocked overboard would be—but you already know.

Now about those opening logos before the movie started. This one sets some kind of a record. In no particular order, I counted Columbia Pictures, Nickelodeon Movies, Paramount Pictures, and Metro-Goldwyn-Mayer. Why did no studio in Hollywood want to back a single one of last year's best picture nominees, and every studio in town wanted to get involved with this one? To be sure, Fox, Disney, and Warner Bros. got left out. Too slow off the mark?

Z

Zathura ★ ★ ★
PG, 113 m., 2005

Josh Hutcherson (Walter), Jonah Bobo (Danny), Tim Robbins (Dad), Dax Shepard (Astronaut), Kristen Stewart (Lisa), Frank Oz (Voice of Robot). Directed by Jon Favreau and produced by Michael De Luca, Scott Kroopf, and William Teitler. Screenplay by David Koepp and John Kamps, based on the book by Chris Van Allsburg.

Zathura's opening credits are close-ups of an old science-fiction board game, a game that should have existed in real life and specifically in my childhood but that was created for this movie. In these days of high-tech video games, it's remarkable that kids once got incredibly thrilled while pushing little metal racing cars around a cardboard track: The toy car was *yours,* and you invested it with importance and enhanced it with fantasy and pitied it because it was small, like you were.

Such games were weapons against the ennui of endless Saturdays. In *Zathura,* time hangs heavily on the hands of Walter and Danny Budwing, two brothers, one ten, one six, whose father has left them alone in the house for a few hours. Not quite alone: Their teenage sister, Lisa, is allegedly babysitting, from her vantage point under the covers of her bed with her iPod. Walter and Danny fight, as brothers do; Danny hides in the dumbwaiter (a device that will come as news to many of the kids watching this movie), and Walter lowers him into the basement, which for every six-year-old is a place filled with ominous noises and alarming unseen menaces.

There Danny (Jonah Bobo) discovers the *Zathura* board game and tries to get Walter (Josh Hutcherson) to play it with him. Walter would rather watch sports on TV. Danny plays by himself. The game is an ingenious metal contraption; you wind it up and push a button and your little car moves around a track and the game emits a card for you to read. Danny has Walter help him read it: METEOR SHOWER. TAKE EVASIVE ACTION. Just about then, the meteors start showering, sizzling through the living room ceiling and drilling through the floor, pulverizing coffee tables and floor lamps.

The game is a portal to an alternative universe of startling adventures; the movie wisely attempts no rational explanation. It resembles the game in *Jumanji* (1995), which ported its players into a world of fearsome beasts and harrowing dangers, and indeed is based on a book by the same author, Chris Van Allsburg, who also wrote the book that inspired *The Polar Express* (2004). The differences between the three movies are fundamental: *Polar Express* is a visionary fable, *Jumanji* is an uneasy thrill ride whose young heroes endure dangers too real to be funny, and *Zathura* is the only board game in history that lives up to the picture on its box.

A key to the film's charm comes during that meteor shower: The living room is pulverized, but Danny and Walter are untouched. They run around as if evading meteors, but actually the meteors evade them. Incredible things will happen while they play Zathura, but they will survive. That helps explain why they can still breathe when they open the front door and discover that their house is now in orbit around Saturn.

Zathura is the third film directed by Jon Favreau, an actor who, like Ron Howard, possibly was born to be a director. His first film was *Made* (2001), his second was *Elf* (2003), and his next will be inspired by Edgar Rice Burroughs's *John Carter of Mars,* a series I have always assumed was unfilmable, but on the basis of these three films, maybe not. Favreau brings a muscular solidity to his special effects; they look not like abstract digital perfection but as if hammered together from plywood, aluminum, and concept cars. By that I don't mean they look cheap; I mean they have the kind of earnest sincerity you can find on the covers of *Thrilling Wonder Stories.* Since you may not know of this publication, I urge you to Google *Thrilling Wonder Stories* magazine and click on "images." You'll find the same kind of breathless pulp absurdity that *Zathura* brings to a boil.

The brothers take turns. The game is inexhaustible. Another card reads, SHIPMATE ENTERS CRYONIC SLEEP CHAMBER. This means that their sister, Lisa, who likes to sleep past noon, has been frozen into immobility in the upstairs bathroom. Other cards produce a) a fearsome but badly coordinated robot, whose designers spent more time on its evil glowing red eyes than on its memory chips, b) giant alien lizards who are directly from the pulp sci-fi tradition of bug-eyed monsters, c) assault fire from spaceships that look like junkyard porpoises, and d) a descent into a black hole. As the two kids hang on for dear life and lizards get sucked into the black hole, I was reminded of the kind of hubris celebrated by such *Thrilling Wonder Stories* titles as "Two Against Neptune."

What makes this fun is that Danny and Walter obviously are not going to get hurt. Alien fire blasts away whole chunks of their house, but never the chunks they're in, and the giant lizards seem more preoccupied with overacting than with eating little boys. The young actors, Hutcherson and Bobo, bring an unaffected enthusiasm to their roles, fighting with each other like brothers even when threatened with broasting by a solar furnace. Their father, I should have mentioned, is played by Tim Robbins, although his role consists primarily of being absent. Kristen Stewart makes the most of the sister Lisa's noncryonic scenes. And then there is the character of the Astronaut (Dax Shepard), who materializes at a crucial point and helps shield the kids from intergalactic hazards. Lisa's crush on the Astronaut becomes cringy after all is known.

Zathura lacks the undercurrents of archetypal menace and genuine emotion that informed *The Polar Express,* a true classic that was rereleased in 2005. But it works gloriously as space opera. We're going through a period right now in which every video game is being turned into a movie, resulting in cheerless exercises such as *Doom,* which mindlessly consists of aliens popping up and getting creamed. *Zathura* is based on a different kind of game, in which the heroes are not simply shooting at targets but are actually surrounded by real events that they need to figure out. They are active heroes, not passive marksmen. Nobody even gets killed in *Zathura* . . . well, depending on what happens to the lizards on the other side of the black hole.

Zatoichi ★ ★ ★ ½
R, 116 m., 2004

Beat Takeshi (Zatoichi), Michiyo Ookusu (Aunt O-Ume), Gadarukanaru Taka (Shinkichi), Daigoro Tachibana (Geisha O-Sei), Yuuko Daike (Geisha O-Kinu), Tadanobu Asano (Gennosuke Hattori), Yui Natsukawa (O-Shino), Ittoku Kishibe (Ginzo). Directed by Takeshi Kitano and produced by Tsunehisa Saito. Screenplay by Kitano, based on novels by Kan Shimozawa.

Zatoichi embodies the kinds of contradictory elements that make Takeshi Kitano Japan's most intriguing contemporary actor-director. He plays, as usual, a man with an impassive face, few words, and sudden bursts of action that end in a few seconds. He is vastly amused at private jokes. He has a code, but enforces it according to his own rules. And then there is the style of the movie, and what can only be called its musical numbers.

Kitano, who acts under the name Beat Takeshi, has played mostly modern tough guys, but here he ventures back to the nineteenth century to step into the shoes of Zatoichi, a blind swordsman who was the hero in one of the two most popular movie series in Japanese history. Zatoichi, always played by Shintaro Katsu, appeared in twenty-six Zatoichi films before his death in 1997. (Tora-san, a sort of Japanese Jerry Lewis, was played by Kiyoshi Atsumi in no less than forty-eight films between 1969 and 1995.)

Kitano playing Zatoichi is a little like Clint Eastwood playing Hopalong Cassidy; the star brings along a powerful persona that redefines the pop superficiality of his character. He poses as a humble, wandering, blind masseur whose hearing and instinct are so razor-sharp that he knows better what is going on around him than those who are limited to sight. He walks with a slight stoop, sometimes smiles or laughs to himself, carries his head cocked to one side, never seems tense or coiled, and then in an instant his cane-sword has found its target.

In its broadest outlines, *Zatoichi* is a revenge drama. The blind swordsman encounters on his travels two sisters (one actually a transvestite) who work as geishas at a wayside rest station. They were orphaned when their parents were killed by the merciless Ginzo gang, which shakes down small merchants. Zatoichi learns about their story, and although he never declares his intention to do anything, eventually the gang's retainers begin to die while trying to kill him. Finally all comes down to a duel between Zatoichi and the crime boss's high-priced bodyguard Hattori (Tadanobu Asano), a warrior of fierce talents.

This plot, however conventional it may sound, plays quite differently in Kitano's hands because of his acute and distinctive style of pace and timing. Not for him the ten-minute Hong Kong–style martial arts extravaganzas. In one scene set in a stony wasteland, Zatoichi is attacked by eight enemies, kills them one after another with almost blinding speed, and leaves the gray stones splashed with red blood, in what is, apart from anything else, a rather effective abstract color pattern.

Zatoichi is hardly on screen every moment, or even in every scene. The movie devotes full time to the Ginzo boss (Ittoko Kishibe) and his auditions for a bodyguard, and establishes Aunt O-Ume (Michiyo Ookusu), who befriends the two geishas, O-Kinu (Yuuko Daike) and O-Sei (the transvestite Daigoro Tachibana). We get a sense of village life, of gossip and speculation, of keen interest in this curious blind masseur.

And then there is the matter of the music of syncopation. Kitano often combines violence with artistic excursions of the most unexpected sorts, and here he weaves a thread of percussive rhythm through the film. In an early scene, we see four men with hoes, breaking up the earth in a field, and their tools strike the ground in a rhythm that the sound track subtly syncopates with music. Later, there is a duet for music and raindrops. Still later, the men with hoes are stomping in their field, again in rhythm. There is a scene of house-building where the hammers of all the workmen are timed to create a suite for iron against wood. And the final curtain call, worthy of *42nd Street*, begins with a boldly choreographed stomp dance—and then all of the actors come on from the wings and join in the dance, including actors who played some of the characters at younger ages.

This element of the film is almost unreasonably delightful, because it's completely irrelevant and uncalled-for; Kitano allows fanciful playfulness into what might have been a formula action picture. Remarkably, some of the people I saw the movie with (at two different viewings) came out complaining, as if there were a rigid template for action movies and Kitano had broken the rules. I was surprised and grateful.

Takeshi Kitano, born in 1947, has directed eleven films, written thirteen, and acted in thirty-two (there are some overlaps). An expert entry in the online encyclopedia Wikipedia says he has also published more than fifty books of poetry, film criticism, and fiction, and is also a game show host (one of his shows, retitled *MXC*, plays on Spike TV). He also hosts a weekly talk show of Japanese-speaking foreigners, who comment on Japan from their foreign perspectives.

Like many artists of long experience and consistent success, he gives himself permission to work outside the box. *Zatoichi* is not a continuation of the original series (itself available on DVD), but a transformation. It's the kind of film I more and more find myself seeking out, a film that seems alive in the sense that it appears to have free will; if, in the middle of a revenge tragedy, it feels like adding a suite for hoes and percussion, it does. Kitano is deadpan most of the time on the screen, but I have a feeling he smiles a lot in the editing room.

Zhou Yu's Train ★ ★
NO MPAA RATING, 97 m., 2004

Gong Li (Zhou Yu/Xiu), Tony Leung Ka Fai (Chen Qing), Honglei Sun (Zhang Qiang). Directed by Sun Zhou and produced by Huang Jianxin, Zhou, and Bill Kong. Screenplay by Zhou, Bei Cun, and Zhang Mei.

Zhou Yu's Train tells a pointlessly convoluted version of a love story that would really be very simple, if anyone in the movie possessed common sense. We know love is blind, but need it be obtuse? The three lovers in Sun Zhou's film, controversial in China for sex scenes that are more fond than fervent, make life miserable for themselves and, to a lesser degree, for us.

Our misery is leavened by the visual qualities of the film, which like most recent work from China is spectacularly good to look at. There's also the central presence of the Chinese superstar Gong Li, who plays a dual role so confusingly written that it might as well be one person, but plays it well.

Her character is a painter of porcelain pottery named Zhou Yu, who is secretive, with an active romantic imagination. A teacher and poet named Chen Qing (Tony Leung Ka Fai) falls in love with her, and gives her a poem comparing her to a mystical lake named Xan Hu. That this poem to her also appears in the district newspaper makes a deep impression, and soon she is taking a long train ride twice a week from her city to his.

The movie backs into this straightforward narrative by beginning in the middle of one of the journeys, as a veterinarian named Zhang Qiang (Honglei Sun) flirts with her and asks to buy the painted porcelain vase she is taking as a present to Chen Qing. Zhang is so insistent that she finally ends the conversation with a bold dramatic gesture. She dislikes Zhang as much as she loves Chen Qing—she thinks.

But Chen Qing is a case rewarding further study. He seems to be a squatter in a kind of forgotten library, where his simple bachelor existence suits him well. He is happy enough to make love two afternoons a week, but a little frightened of Zhou Yu's fervor. Mention is made of a teaching position he could take in Tibet.

It occurs to us, long before it occurs to Zhou Yu, that the vet would make a better partner than the poet. This would be even more obvious if the film weren't needlessly fragmented, so that we jump around in time and have to piece together the actual chronology of her relationships with the two men.

The vet at one point actually follows her on one of her train journeys, discovering a secret about Chen Qing that is well known to Zhou Yu but will not be mentioned here.

In my notes, I wrote: "Who is the short-haired girl? Looks like Gong Li." Reader, it was Gong Li, in the dual role, playing a character named Xiu. She is apparently a former lover of Chen Qing's who is now a narrator telling us about his affair with Zhou. All very well, except by casting the same actress the movie led me to assume I was seeing Zhou herself at two stages of her life, or at least at two stages of her hairstyling history. Xiu works mostly as an unnecessary diversion.

The qualities of the movie come during small, well-observed moments. Zhou covering her lover's face with hungry kisses. The train conductor reminding the vet, "That's the same girl who fainted one day, and you refused to treat her." The vet pointing out he has been trained to work with animals. Above all, the loneliness of the long-distance journeys, which seem to take on an existence of their own, as if Zhou prefers faithfully traveling to and from her lover to actually being with him, or apart from him.

The film is impeccably photographed, and the characters become convincing as themselves, if not always in their relationships. The story, once the complex telling is unraveled, invests these people with more romantic significance than they deserve. And if it is true, as I suspect, that Zhou Yu's train journeys have an importance for her apart from their alleged purpose—if, to put it simply, she just plain likes to take the train—the movie could have been a little more amused, and amusing, about that. Does she get frequent traveler miles?

The Best Films of 2005

December 18, 2005—How in the world can anyone think it was a bad year for the movies when so many were wonderful, a few were great, a handful were inspiring, and there were scenes so risky you feared the tightrope might break? If none of the year's ten best had been made, I could name another ten and no one would wonder at the choices. There were a lot of movies to admire in 2005.

The year's ten best films:

1. *Crash*

Much of the world's misery is caused by conflicts of race and religion; Paul Haggis's film, written with Robert Moresco, uses interlocking stories to show we are in the same boat, that prejudice flows freely from one ethnic group to another. His stories are a series of contradictions in which the same people can be sinned against or sinning. There once was a simple morality formula in America in which white society was racist and blacks were victims, but that model is long obsolete. Now many more players have entered the game: Latinos, Asians, Muslims, and those defined by sexual orientation, income, education, or appearance.

America is a nation of minority groups, and we get along with each other better than many societies that criticize us; France recently has been reminded of that. We are all immigrants here. What is wonderful about *Crash* is that it tells not simpleminded parables but textured human stories based on paradoxes. Not many films have the possibility of making their viewers better people; anyone seeing it is likely to leave with a little more sympathy for people not like themselves. The film opened quietly in May 2005 and increased its audience week by week, as people told each other they must see it.

2. *Syriana*

Stephen Gaghan's film doesn't reveal the plot but surrounds us with it. Interlocking stories again: There is less oil than the world requires, and that will make some rich and others dead, unless we all die first. The movie has been called "liberal," but it is apolitical, suggesting that all of the players in the oil game are corrupt and compromised and, in some bleak sense, must be to defend their interests—and ours.

The story involves oil, money, and politics in America, the Middle East, and China. The CIA is on both sides of one situation, China may be snatching oil away from us in order to sell it back, and no one in this movie understands the big picture because there isn't one, just a series of tactical skirmishes. *Syriana* argues that in the short run, every society must struggle for oil, and in the long run it will be gone.

3. *Munich*

Steven Spielberg's film may be the bravest of the year, and it plays like a flowing together of the currents in *Crash* and *Syriana,* showing an ethnic and religious conflict that floats atop a fundamental struggle over land and oil. Working from a screenplay by Tony Kushner, Spielberg begins with the massacre of Israeli athletes at the Munich Olympiad of 1972 and follows a secret assassination team as it attempts to track down the eleven primary killers. Nine eventually die, but not before the Israeli (Eric Bana) who leads the team loses his moral certainty and nearly his sanity, and not before the film sees revenge as a process that may have harmed Israel more than its targets.

The film is not critical of Israel, as some believe, but a more general mourning for the loss of idealism in a region marching steadily toward terrorism and anarchy. In defending itself, can Israel afford to compromise its standards—or afford not to? Spielberg doesn't have the answer. He has the courage to suggest that some of Israel's post-Munich policies have not made it a better or safer place.

4. Junebug

At last, a movie about ordinary people. Or put it this way: Phil Morrison's *Junebug* was the best non-geopolitical film of the year. In simply human terms, there was no other film like it. It understands, profoundly and with love and sadness, the world of small towns; it captures ways of talking and living I remember from my childhood and has the complexity and precision of great fiction.

The story, written by Angus MacLachlan, involves Alessandro Nivola and Embeth Davidtz as Chicagoans who return to North Carolina to visit his family: his mother (Celia Weston), mercilessly critical of everyone; his father (Scott Wilson), who has withdrawn into his wood carving; his brother (Benjamin McKenzie), who loves his wife but has been brought to a halt by his demons and shyness; and the pregnant wife (Amy Adams), who is a good soul. *Junebug* is a great film because it is a true film. It understands that families are complicated and their problems are not solved during a short visit, just in time for the happy ending. Families and their problems go on and on, and they aren't solved; they're dealt with. There is one heartbreaking moment of truth after another, and humor and love as well.

5. Brokeback Mountain

Two cowboys in Wyoming discover, to their surprise, they love each other. They have no way to deal with that fact. Directed by Ang Lee, based on a short story by E. Annie Proulx and a screenplay by Larry McMurtry and Diana Ossana. In the summer of 1963, Ennis (Heath Ledger) and Jack (Jake Gyllenhaal) find themselves one night on a distant mountainside suddenly having sex. "You know I ain't queer," Ennis tells Jack after their first night together. "Me neither," says Jake. But their love lasts a lifetime and gives them no consolation, because they cannot accept its nature and because they fear, not incorrectly, that in that time and place they could be murdered if it were discovered. Oh, what a sad and lonely story this is, containing what truth and sorrow.

6. Me and You and Everyone We Know

The previous films have waded fearlessly into troubled waters. Miranda July's walks on them. It's a comedy about falling in love with someone who speaks your rare emotional language of playfulness and daring, of playful mind games and bold challenges. July writes, directs, and stars. In her first film, she trusts a delicate sense of humor that negotiates situations that would be shocking if they weren't so darn nice. Can you imagine a scene involving teenage sexual experimentation that is sweet and innocent and not shocking at all, because it's not about sex but about what funny and lovable creatures we humans can be? And when have you seen a woman seduce a man not with sex but with unbridled and passionate whimsy?

7. Nine Lives

Rodrigo Garcia's film started as a 3.5-star movie and worked its way onto this list because I found myself admiring it more and more. It involves nine stories told in a total of nine shots. It is not a stunt. Most audiences will probably never notice that each scene is told in one shot, although they will sense the tangible passage of real time. The best story involves Robin Wright Penn and Jason Isaacs as two former lovers, now married, who meet by chance in a supermarket and during a casual conversation realize that although their lives are content, they made the mistakes of their lifetimes by not marrying each other. Stating this so boldly, I miss the subtle sympathy that Garcia has for all of his characters, who are permitted those tender moments of truth by which we learn what a tease life is—so slow to teach us how to live it, so quick to end.

8. King Kong

A stupendous cliff-hanger, a glorious adventure, a shameless celebration of every single resource of the blockbuster, told in a film of visual beauty and surprising emotional impact. Of course this will be the most popular film of the year, and nothing wrong with that: If movies like *King Kong* didn't delight us with the magic of the cinema, we'd never start going in the first place.

Peter Jackson's triumph is not a remake of the 1933 classic so much as a celebration of its greatness and a flowering of its possibilities. Its most particular contribution is in the area of the heart: It transforms the somewhat creepy relationship of the gorilla and the girl into a celebration of empathy, in which a vaudeville acrobat (Naomi Watts) intuitively understands that when Kong roars he isn't threatening her but stating his territorial dominance; she responds with acrobatics that delight him, not least because Kong is a gorilla few have ever tried to delight. From their relationship flows the emotional center of the film, which spectacular special effects surround and enhance but could not replace.

9. *Yes*

An elegant Irish-American woman, living with a rich and distant British politician, makes eye contact with a waiter. Neither turns away. Their sex is eager and makes them laugh. They are not young; they are grateful because of long experience with what can go wrong. He was a surgeon in Lebanon. Sally Potter tells their story in iambic pentameter, the rhythm scheme of Shakespeare. The dialogue style elevates what is being said into a realm of grace and care.

Joan Allen stars, and has ever a movie loved a woman more? To recline at the edge of the pool in casual physical perfection is natural to her, disturbing to him. They realize they cannot live together successfully in either of their cultures. A third place is required. Their story is told in counterpoint with the bold asides of a cleaner (Shirley Henderson), who notes that for all their passion they shed the same strands of hair and flakes of skin and tiny germs as the rest of us, and must be cleaned up after. Bold, erotic, political, and like no other film I have ever seen.

10. *Millions*

The best family film of the year is by the unlikely team of director Danny Boyle (*Trainspotting*) and writer Frank Cottrell Boyce (*Hilary and Jackie, 24 Hour Party People*). Nine-year-old Anthony Cunningham and his seven-year-old brother, Damian (Lewis McGibbon and Alex Etel), find a bag containing loot that bounced off a train and is currently stuffed under their bed. With limitless imagination and joy, the film follows the brothers as they deal with their windfall. They begin by taking homeless men to Pizza Hut. Damian wants to continue their charity work, but Anthony leans toward investing in property.

Oh, and Damian gets advice from saints—real ones. St. Francis of Assisi, his favorite, provides advice that Anthony is sure will get them into trouble. Despite how it sounds, this isn't a "cute little film." The director makes hard-boiled movies, the writer has worked at the cutting edge, and this is what a family film would look like if it were made with the intelligence of adults.

The Jury Prize

I have created as usual the Special Jury Prize and, taking my lead from the Academy Awards, spun out such categories as feature documentary and animated films. I've also listed five prime candidates for my Overlooked Film Festival.

At film festivals, the "jury prize" is how some jury members urgently signal that *this* is the film they like better than the eventual winner. It's not second place but somebody's idea of first place. This year there has been an eleven-way tie, listed alphabetically:

Best of Youth by Marco Tullio Giordana, the story of two Italian brothers and their lives from 1963 to 2000, as they intersect with politics and history: the hippie period, the disastrous flood in Florence, the Red Brigades, kidnappings, hard times and layoffs, and finally a certain peace.

Broken Flowers by Jim Jarmusch. Another inward, intriguing performance from Bill Murray, as a millionaire who lives in isolation and loneliness until he learns he might once have fathered a child, and visits the possible mothers (Sharon Stone, Frances Conroy, Jessica Lange, Tilda Swinton, and Julie Delpy).

Cinderella Man by Ron Howard. Russell Crowe gives another strong performance in the comeback story of boxer Jim Braddock, who was washed up after an injury but fought back from poverty to win the heavyweight title from the dreaded Max Baer. Crowe's accomplishment is to play Braddock as a good man, even-tempered, loyal to his family above all.

Downfall by Oliver Hirschbiegel. We do not recognize Bruno Ganz, hunched over, shrunken, his left hand fluttering behind his back like a trapped bird. This is Adolf Hitler in his final days in the bunker beneath Berlin, where after his war was lost he waged it in fantasy. Pounding on maps, screaming ultimatums, he moved troops that no longer existed and issued orders to commanders who were dead. A chilling portrait of evil and madness.

Duane Hopwood by Matt Mulhern. A career-transforming performance by David Schwimmer, as an Atlantic City pit boss who loves his wife and children and is losing everything because of alcoholism. Not the sensational drunk scenes of melodrama, but the daily punishment of the disease: Sometimes he drinks way too much. Sometimes he drinks too much. Sometimes he drinks almost too much. Sometimes he doesn't drink enough. Those are the only four "sometimes" for an alcoholic.

Good Night, and Good Luck by George Clooney. David Strathairn stars as Edward R. Murrow, who with his CBS News colleagues helped to bring about the downfall of the demagogue Senator Joseph McCarthy. McCarthy (shown in archival footage) is a liar and a bully, surrounded by yes-men, recklessly calling his opponents traitors; he destroys others and then is destroyed by the truth.

Match Point by Woody Allen. A return to greatness for Allen, not with a "Woody Allen picture" but with a thriller based on stomach-churning guilt. Jonathan Rhys-Meyers is a poor, ambitious tennis pro who marries well (to rich girl Emily Mortimer) while dallying with Scarlett Johansson, the former fiancée of his brother-in-law. Can he solve his problems with a perfect murder?

North Country by Niki Caro. Another powerful performance by Charlize Theron, as a working mother who becomes a miner on the Minnesota iron range and becomes the target of her male fellow union members. Based on the true story of the woman who inspired the first class-action lawsuit on sexual harassment. With great supporting work by Frances McDormand.

The New World by Terrence Malick. A visionary story of Pocahontas (Q'Orianka Kilcher) that places her, John Smith (Colin Farrell), and John Rolfe (Christian Bale) in an unspoiled sylvan forest where the Indians live in harmony with the land and the English blunder in with guns and ignorance. Poca-

hontas falls in love with Smith, and her transformation leads to an unimaginable personal journey.

The Three Burials of Melquiades Estrada, directed by and starring Tommy Lee Jones (best actor, Cannes 2005). He plays a ranch hand whose Mexican friend is killed by a border patrolman (Barry Pepper). He forces the younger man to join him on a long journey with the body to the friend's birthplace, in a film that could have been directed by John Huston and starred Humphrey Bogart.

Pride & Prejudice by Joe Wright. Keira Knightley is the first among equals in a gifted cast that captures all the charm and romance of the Jane Austen novel. Set a little earlier and closer to the land than most Austen adaptations, so that the urgency of a fortunate marriage is underlined, and the characters seem less precious. Gloriously romantic.

Special Jury Awards

Film festivals also hand out special awards for excellence, and so do I, because, in the words of Mickey Spillane, "I, the Jury." Alphabetically:

Batman Begins, the best and darkest of the *Batman* pictures. *Bee Season*, with its wondrous performance by Flora Cross as a young woman with mystical gifts. *Caché*, the French thriller about a family that knows it is being watched—but not why, or by whom, or how. *Capote*, with Philip Seymour Hoffman's Oscar-bound performance as Truman Capote. *Fear and Trembling*, with Sylvie Testud, who takes a job in Japan and finds herself a definitive outsider. *Firecracker*, Steve Balderson's brilliant indie about a murder in small-town Kansas. *Harry Potter and the Goblet of Fire*, with Harry surviving not only Lord Voldemort but the prom. *Head-On*, a harrowing portrait of Turkish "guest workers" in Germany and their desperation on the margins. David Cronenberg's *A History of Violence*, with Viggo Mortensen as a small-town diner owner who is pulled back roughly into his past.

Hustle & Flow, with Terrence Howard's great performance as a pimp who transforms himself through art. *Last Days*, Gus Van Sant's uncompromising look at the decline and death of a character based on Kurt Cobain. *Lord of War*, vibrating with the energy of Nicolas Cage's performance as a freelance arms dealer. *The Merchant of Venice,* another reminder of Al Pacino's passion and fierce focus. *Mysterious Skin,* about growing up gay in Kansas and thinking maybe aliens were involved. *Oldboy,* from Korea, about a man who is kept prisoner for fifteen years for reasons he cannot imagine.

Palindromes, Todd Solondz's challenging use of eight actors in an examination of the moral complexities of abortion. *Proof,* with Gwyneth Paltrow as the daughter of a great mathematician (Anthony Hopkins) who loses his mind but leaves behind historic work—or is it his? *Saraband,* Ingmar Bergman's return in his eighties to the same characters and actors (Liv Ullmann and Erland Josephson) from his *Scenes From a Marriage* (1973). *Schultze Gets the Blues,* starring Horst Krause as a simple German accordion player who wins a contest and finds himself in New Orleans playing zydeco polka.

Shopgirl, the bittersweet relationship between a millionaire (Steve Martin) and a clerk (Claire Danes) who are divided not so much by age or money as by courage. *Sin City,* the visual extravaganza adapted from Frank Miller's dark graphic novels. Noah Baumbach's *The Squid and the Whale* involves two divorcing writers (Jeff Daniels and Laura Linney), two sons with divided loyalties and all the mysteries of parents and children. *The Ballad of Jack and Rose,* Rebecca Miller's film about an aging hippie (Daniel Day-Lewis) and his daughter (Camilla Belle), living in isolation on an island. *The Constant Gardener,* with Ralph Fiennes and Rachel Weisz stumbling across reckless programs to test drugs in Africa. *The Memory of a Killer,* with Jan Decleir as an aging Italian hit man, undertaking a last assignment although senility is approaching. *The Upside of Anger,* with housewife Joan Allen and retired baseball pitcher Kevin Costner building a relationship on booze and the wrong assumptions. *The World,* Zhang Ke Jia's revealing look at the culture of the workers in a Beijing theme park. *Turtles Can Fly,* about children living amid the wreckage of war on the Iraqi-Turkish border. And *Walk the Line,* for its astonishing performances by Joaquin Phoenix and Reese Witherspoon.

Best Documentaries

Grizzly Man, Werner Herzog's portrait of a man who loves bears unwisely and too well. *Aliens of the Deep,* James Cameron's visual astonishment from the ocean floor. *Enron: The Smartest Guys in the Room,* mercilessly explaining how Enron fabricated the California energy crisis. *Gunner Palace,* about the daily lives of American soldiers in Iraq. *March of the Penguins,* about the responsibilities of parenthood. *Murderball,* about the sport of full-contact quadriplegic wheelchair rugby (yes). *No Direction Home: Bob Dylan,* Martin Scorsese's look at the singer's odyssey. *Tell Them Who You Are,* Mark Wexler's portrait of his complex and gifted father, cinematographer Haskell Wexler. *Touch the Sound,* about the deaf percussionist Evelyn Glennie. *The Wild Parrots of Telegraph Hill,* about Mark Bittner, who knows San Francisco's wild parrots by name.

Best Animated Films

Wallace & Gromit: The Curse of the Were-Rabbit, one of the most delightful films ever made. *Tim Burton's Corpse Bride,* surprisingly cheerful under the circumstances. *Robots,* with its jolly little children of Rube Goldberg in a future that looks like Fiestaware.

Overlooked

Off the Map, Campbell Scott's film with Joan Allen living in the New Mexico desert with her depressed husband (Sam Elliott) and imaginative daughter (Valentina de Angelis). Gore Verbinski's *The Weather Man,* and Nicolas Cage, brilliant again, as a man without a clue for his own happiness. *Keane,* Lodge Kerrigan's portrait of a schizophrenic (Damian Lewis) trying to hold himself together. *Duma,* Carroll Ballard's magnificent story of a boy and his cheetah. *The Woodsman,* Nicole Kassell's film starring Kevin Bacon as a recovering pedophile.

Interviews

Nicolas Cage

October 25, 2005—Ten things I learned while talking with Nicolas Cage:

1. His new movie, *The Weather Man*, is about a Chicago weatherman whose life is coming apart at the seams. His ex-wife (Hope Davis) despairs for him, his children are troubled, his father (Michael Caine) deplores him, and his fans throw food at him.

"Not too many weathermen get pelted with food, but if it were ever going to happen, it would probably happen in a place like Chicago. The Chicago weatherman is an entirely different weatherman than one anywhere else in our country. I'm from Los Angeles, and we don't have to rely on our weathermen as much as the Chicagoan does. If they get it wrong, you have to reschedule the bar mitzvah, so it's a pretty intense job."

2. Tom Skilling, the meteorologist from WGN-TV, was the technical adviser on the picture.

"He coached me. He has a warm persona and I wanted that to come across with my character, Dave Spritz. There's something about when these guys smile on camera, you just feel you're gonna get through it no matter how cold it gets. Gore Verbinski, the director, used Skilling's forecasts, and he told me he would call Skilling and yell at him because he was giving him weather reports that were not always accurate."

3. "This is a coming-of-middle-age story about a guy who is dealing with the fact that basically he's failed at everything, including success. I saw it as a reflection of the broken families that we have today in our country. I am certainly no stranger to the divorce club (after divorces from wives Patricia Arquette and Lisa Marie Presley), and when I decided to make *The Weather Man* I was processing those feelings. I wanted to make something productive and positive with them as opposed to just letting them succumb to the wildfire of the negative emotions. I was able to channel all those feelings into Dave Spritz, who's a character who's trying to put his family back together."

4. No matter how successful Dave Spritz is as a weatherman, he will always be in the shadow of his father (Michael Caine), a Pulitzer Prize–winning novelist. Nicolas Cage, born Nicolas Coppola, was born into some shadows, too: His father, August, is a professor of literature, and his uncle is the filmmaker Francis Ford Coppola.

"They are formidable people. I would go into a casting office, it would be clear that I was gonna talk about *The Godfather* and *Apocalypse Now,* and by the time they got around to the actual audition, I'd forgotten my lines. I needed to change my name just to liberate myself and find out I could do it without walking into a Hollywood casting office with the name Coppola."

5. In the movie, the Caine character finds his son a lasting disappointment.

"He's not exactly cruel, although he does inflict horrible wounds in his kindly advice that just makes you want to kill yourself. In between setups Caine would refer to my character as a loser, and I knew right then what the dynamic of the father-son relationship would be like."

6. They shot in Chicago in the winter, using artificial snow when the real stuff wasn't on the ground.

"I actually got to the movie later than intended, because I was shooting another picture. When I arrived we had a month of snow, and then we started building artificial snow. To be honest, I was relieved by that, because it's impossible to act when you're freezing. You can't relax when you're shaking and shivering. I learned that on *Moonstruck,* back in Brooklyn."

7. Cage won his Oscar for *Leaving Las Vegas* (1995), where he gave an unforgettable performance as an alcoholic who goes to Vegas to drink himself to death and finds a hooker (Elisabeth Shue) who pities him and eases his journey toward oblivion.

"It was so amazing how that worked out. We shot it so quickly, in just over three weeks, it just flowed out of everybody. Mike Figgis (the director) is like music, he is music, he had music playing on the set. Elisabeth Shue was very relaxed, there was nothing painful at all about the experience, and it just was one of those magical moments when all the elements came together perfectly. The irony was, when I made the movie, everyone said it was career death. I told them I'm never going to win an Academy Award anyway, so let me do this and just let me express myself the way I want to."

8. *The Weather Man* is a big studio production with a big budget and a big star, but it's written and played like an art picture. Is that a contradiction?

"It's very risky for an actor who's a bankable star to make pictures like *The Weather Man* or *Lord of War* (also released in 2005), because they inevitably promote them like big studio releases. And they're not big studio movies; they're more edgy, thought-provoking, independent-spirited films. What happens is, it goes into the computer and everyone says they can't open the movie because they thought it was X when it actually was Y. I want to make all kinds of movies. I do want to make big movies that are a lot of fun to go to, but I also want to make movies that are going to stimulate some thought and maybe raise some awareness. And so please don't think you're gonna go on a roller coaster ride with those movies."

9. Cage and his wife, Alice Kim, have a new son, born October 3, 2005.

"His name is Kal-El. Alice and I wanted a name that was exotic and American and stood for something good, because our son is exotic and he's American and we think he's good. And Kal-El was Superman's name when he was born. I just liked the sound of it."

10. His work in Ridley Scott's *Matchstick Men* (2003) was brilliant, I thought, but the movie got mixed to negative reviews.

"I'm at the point now where I know I'm doing something right when a movie gets mixed reviews, because then I'm not in the box. I don't want to make it too easy for people, and I don't want to make it too easy for myself. I want to try something unusual. I feel good about the bad reviews because I feel like I've affected them on some level. They may not know what I was trying to do, but they felt something.

"I met David Bowie once years ago, and I said, 'David, how do you do it? How do you keep reinventing yourself?' He said, 'I never got comfortable with anything I was doing.'"

Flora Cross

Toronto, Canada, November 6, 2005—Flora Cross is a beautiful young girl and a wise old soul. She has a gravity about her. By that I mean not that she is sad but that she weighs matters, considers what they are, and says what she thinks. That is a rare quality in anyone. Flora Cross is twelve.

She is essentially the star of *Bee Season,* which opened November 11 and is an extraordinary and haunted film. She's billed below Richard Gere and Juliette Binoche, who play her parents, but the film centers on her character and she carries its weight on her shoulders. It requires a solemnity in the young character, who takes it seriously and knows that her decisions matter.

I interviewed Flora at the Toronto Film Festival, where she arrived at the Four Seasons coffee shop with her father, Joe Cross, his fiancée, Vianna Bargas, and the movie's publicist. I asked for a table for five. "No," said her father. "I think Flora would rather talk to you by herself. We'll come back later."

Unusual. Young actors routinely arrive with support staffs, although to be sure, Dakota Fanning also abandoned her mother and her publicist and talked on her own. But Fanning is a Hollywood veteran. This is Flora Cross's first movie. She's a sixth-grader from Argentina. But there is never any doubt she's her own woman.

In the movie, she plays Eliza, whose father barely seems to notice her until she starts winning spelling bees. Richard Gere is the father, a Berkeley professor of religious studies, specializing in the Kabbalah and Jewish mysticism. His home life centers around a compulsive need to cook food and serve it to his family. Juliette Binoche, as her mother, lives a secret life of her own, which includes entering strange houses for personal reasons. Eliza's older brother, Aaron (Max Minghella), neatly trumps his father by joining Hare Krishna.

The girl's secret is that while her father theorizes about the Kabbalah, for Eliza it is a reality.

The Kabbalah treats words as if they are the objects from which the world is created. They have their own reality, and for Eliza they float in front of her eyes and she can spell them even if she has never seen them. Believe me when I say I have not revealed too much: This is not a movie about using mysticism to win spelling bees. It is a movie about a brave girl in a wounded family.

"I got the script in Argentina," Flora told me. "I read it with my dad, and I really wanted to make it."

Argentina, I said.

"That's where we live right now. I was born in Paris. I've lived all around. My first language is French. Second is English. I speak Spanish also. My father was a journalist and still is. He writes about boxing and horses. He has worked in Panama, Israel . . . he was doing his job in Jerusalem and it was supposed to be dangerous to be in the old city with the Arabs. I'm a Jew, but nobody said anything about my Jewish star, which I wore around my neck. One of the reasons I didn't like *Million Dollar Baby* is that I used to go and watch my father at work, and from what I know about boxing, it wasn't very accurate."

I really liked it, I said.

"Depends on how important you think the boxing is."

So you read the script, and then you auditioned . . .

"It originally wasn't going to be Juliette Binoche as the mother," she said. "It was going to be somebody else. Then Juliette got the role. The daughter was going to be Dakota Fanning. But when they cast Juliette, they were thinking, I looked like I could be Juliette's daughter. So I got the role."

You do look a lot like her, I said.

"My mom left me when I was six years old," Flora said. "I've only seen her once since."

She left?

"Just . . . she left. I don't know why."

And now you live with your father and his fiancée?

"I don't know why they say that. They're really not fiancées. Just girlfriend and boyfriend. I go to a French school; I've never gone to an American school in my life. I've also done a lot of homeschooling."

Did you want to be an actress?

"An actress, or a vet. Now I think I just want to be an actress. This movie was very difficult. There were scenes I didn't like, where I had to tremble. I had never acted before, although my brothers were actors. Or are. Not very famous. My brother Harley Cross, he made *The Believers* and *The Fly 2*. Remember that little boy? That's him. He's in *Kinsey* for just a couple of minutes. Now he makes mints. Hint Mints. You can get them at Barnes & Noble. They come in little curved tins, like this."

She made a little curved tin with her hand.

"My other brother is Eli Marienthal. He was in *American Pie*."

Did you see *Spellbound*, that documentary about spelling bees?

"I saw it. My brother rented it. I visit New York every Christmas to see my big brother and his family. I have a friend who won a spelling bee. She told me it was incredible pressure. What's strange is, I know how to spell in French. Before this movie, I could hardly spell in English."

Before she made *Bee Season*, she said, she rented the DVD of *The Deep End*, the 2001 film by the same directors, Scott McGehee and David Siegel.

"I listened to their commentary track—very informative about their methods as filmmakers. I have always loved films—more old films than new ones. Chaplin is my hero. I have lots of his stuff in my room. Jason Lee, who is directing the next movie I'm making, lives right next door to where Chaplin worked. Bette Davis is my favorite actress. *All About Eve*, that's a great movie. I like the French. *The 400 Blows* and *Jules and Jim*. Juliette worked with Kieslowski, and we talked a lot about his films."

Not every twelve-year-old knows about Charlie Chaplin, Bette Davis, Francois Truffaut, and Krzysztof Kieslowski, I said.

"I wonder why not. I really love Juliette. She's a great actress and a wonderful personality. *The English Patient* is a classic movie. We spoke French with each other. Or English. Sometimes we didn't know what we were speaking. When I was in the movie I really felt like I was her daughter, since I don't have a mother. Richard Gere, he's funny in real life. In the beginning, he ignores his daughter. He doesn't know she's alive until she starts winning. Then he sees her. She knows winning isn't everything. Most of all, for her mother, she wants her family to be all together again. That's very touching, when her mother comes and says, 'That's my daughter.'"

John Dahl

August 7, 2005—"The raid was so successful," John Dahl was saying, "that at the movie's first test screenings, audiences wouldn't believe it. We had to add titles at the end telling them it was a true story."

The titles come at the end of Dahl's new film *The Great Raid,* and they summarize the results of a 1945 rescue mission when 120 Army Rangers and 250 Philippine guerrillas staged a surprise attack on the Japanese POW camp at Cabanatuan. The prisoners, 511 of them, were freed. The dead: twenty-one Filipinos, two Americans (one of them a freed prisoner), about 250 Japanese in the camp, and 650 at a nearby bridge.

The movie's ads call it "the most daring rescue mission of our time." The challenge: move the Rangers and their guerrilla partners through Japanese-controlled territory, creep across an open field by daylight, make the final approach at night, and stake everything on the element of surprise.

There was another, more famous rescue raid in the Philippines at about the same time (2,146 prisoners were freed from a Japanese POW camp at Los Banos), but the Cabanatuan raid, smaller and more desperate, is ideal for a war movie: We understand the strategy, we follow the progress of the raid, we can keep track of individual leaders.

The movie, which opened August 12 on about eight hundred screens, is a stark contrast to the silliness of the new high-tech action movie *Stealth,* in which three Navy pilots and four airplanes mop up enemies in Tajikistan and Burma, and rescue a downed pilot in North Korea. If only it were that simple. Dahl has made a well-crafted, classic war movie, in which special effects are minimal and the focus is on soldiers and strategy.

The movie stars Benjamin Bratt as Col. Henry Mucci, who leads a Ranger battalion he calls "the best-trained soldiers in the Army." Well-trained, yes, but inexperienced; for many, the raid is their first action. James Franco (from *Spider-Man*) is Capt. Bob Prince, his point man, and Cesar Montano plays Capt. Juan Pajota, a Filipino hero who

leads the guerrillas. These three characters are from real life, and so is Margaret Utinsky (Connie Nielsen), an American nurse who stays in Manila during the war and is a resistance leader. But the role of Major Gibson (Joseph Fiennes), leader of the POWs, seems to be a fictional composite. Utinsky and Gibson are depicted as being in love, but since they barely meet during the movie, the romance doesn't sidetrack the action as it did in the ludicrous *Pearl Harbor.*

For director Dahl, *The Great Raid* represents a U-turn from the kinds of movies he had been making. Carefully and clearly told, old-fashioned in the best sense of the word, the movie is a contrast to four earlier Dahl movies I admired enormously: *Red Rock West, The Last Seduction, Rounders,* and *Joy Ride.* The first two were modern, twisted noirs, *Rounders* was a thriller about poker and other matters, and *Joy Ride* was an extended combination of horror and a chase.

Dahl is still a little puzzled about why Miramax approached him to make the war movie. But he understands the timing. He showed *Joy Ride* at the Toronto Film Festival two days before 9/11. He flew to Los Angeles on 9/10. The terrorist attack perhaps made a film about traditional American military heroism more attractive than it might have seemed a few days earlier.

The screenplay, by Carlo Bernard and Doug Miro, is based on the books *The Great Raid on Cabanatuan* by William B. Breuer and *Ghost Soldiers* by Hampton Sides. "At the time, Universal had optioned *Ghost Soldiers,*" Dahl said, "so it was a question of who would make their film first. Harvey Weinstein got the rights away from Universal, and we were a go."

In earlier drafts of the story, Dahl said during a Chicago visit, a fictional raid was staged by twelve American heroes. In another version, the Filipino hero Cesar Montano was replaced by a Caucasian, who would be easier to cast with a movie star. All of those drafts were dumped in favor of the more realistic approach.

"We thought it was important to show what a crucial role the Filipinos played," he said. "There were things we didn't have time for in the movie—for example, the total cooperation of the rural people, who rounded up all the dogs so they wouldn't bark and betray the silent troops. And the way hundreds of ox-carts were quietly readied to carry away the freed prisoners."

Dahl said there were a few facts he had to change. "A lot depends on the ditch where the raiders take cover before the attack. It was only thirty yards outside the prison fence, but that looked too close to audiences—because, of course, we had to add fictional searchlights in order to shoot at night. The real raid took place during a complete blackout. So we moved the ditch back to three hundred yards."

Another nod to storytelling techniques was the obligatory Chalk Talk Scene, done with a map drawn with a stick in the dust. Of course, the raiders would already be well-briefed, but such scenes are necessary so the audience can follow the action.

The movie represents, for Dahl, yet another chance of breaking through to wide audiences. I can't think of another director whose films have been more praised by critics while being less embraced by audiences. *Red Rock West* (1992) was a labyrinthine noir starring Nicolas Cage as a job-seeker who is mistaken for a hit man; a climactic scene in a cemetery is a classic combination of plotting, timing, and gallows humor. *The Last Seduction* (1994) starred Linda Fiorentino in an unforgettable performance as a femme fatale who deceives her husband, steals $1 million from a cocaine deal she talked him into, goes on the lam, and then seduces a small-town patsy into being her fall guy.

Rounders (1998) starred Matt Damon as a onetime cardsharp who returns to poker to pay the debts of an old friend (Ed Norton) whose life is threatened by a Russian mafioso (John Malkovich). *Joy Ride* (2001) is an extended chase thriller with Paul Walker, Steve Zahn, and Leelee Sobieski; they play a trick on a trucker named Rusty Nail, who makes them very sincerely regret it.

Red Rock West and *The Last Seduction* bombed at the box office, and the other two grossed less than $30 million. Perhaps there are reasons; *Red Rock West* was "funny but not a comedy, had action but was not an action picture," Dahl said, and the studio so lacked confidence in *The Last Seduction* that it was headed for video before a few good reviews won it a brief theatrical run.

These were all strong, exciting movies; Dahl

has directed movies that should have been big hits except that, well, they weren't. He is philosophical. He recalls his start in life:

"I was born in Billings, Montana (in 1956). My parents encouraged me to go to art school. I wasn't very good at fine art, so I switched to commercial art. I wasn't very good at that, either. I went into billboards. Nothing much happened. Animation. Same story.

"In 1982 I was accepted by the American Film Institute, in their second class. I got into directing. Francis Coppola liked my first film, *Kill Me Again*, and that's how I got his nephew, Nic Cage, to appear in my second film. And so on. The way I look at it, for a kid from Montana to even get to make movies is pretty good."

Perhaps *The Great Raid* will be his breakthrough. If word gets around that it is intelligent and gripping and not a dumb action picture, it may. If not, well, he's been able to show it to about seventy-five of the one hundred living survivors of Cabanatuan.

"They're all in their eighties now. They were told after the war that they wouldn't live past forty because of the POW experience. Actually, that low-fat, low-calorie, high-fiber diet and all the hard labor they did was good for them. Now, with this movie coming out, the local paper will call them one more time. People will be reminded of what an amazing thing they did."

Al Gore

When there is a new outrage, I have to download some of my existing outrages to a hard drive, to make room.

—Al Gore

Cannes, France, May 28, 2006—What he wants you to know is that he has not made a political film. Al Gore's *An Inconvenient Truth* tries to move outside politics and focus on the facts of global warming. Gore says those facts are established, the returns are in, there is almost unanimous scientific agreement about them, and we may have about ten years before the earth reaches a tipping point from which it cannot recover.

He has been traveling the world for six years making speeches in which this message has evolved. But all of those speeches put together have not had the impact of this new documentary, directed by Davis Guggenheim, which is horrifying and enthralling and has the potential, I believe, to actually change public policy and begin a process that could save the earth.

It is not only an important film, but a good one.

Guggenheim has found a way to make facts and statistics into drama and passion. He organizes Gore's arguments into visuals that overwhelm us. Gore begins with the famous photograph "Earthrise," which was the first photo taken of Earth from outer space. Then he shows later satellite photos. It is absolutely clear that the white areas are disappearing, that snow and ice are melting, that the shape of continents is changing. The polar areas and Greenland are shrinking, lakes have disappeared, the snows of Kilimanjaro have vanished, and the mountain reveals its naked summit to the sky for the first time in human history.

You owe it to yourself to see this film. If that sounds overdramatic, I understand. I could not have imagined writing that before seeing it myself. *An Inconvenient Truth* is not Al Gore's "opinion," or anyone's "political position," but a report on a process that the world's environmental scientists—almost literally every single one of them—are in agreement about.

Gore sits in a hotel room at the Cannes Film Festival and talks about these things. His film received a standing ovation here, but lots of films do. What's extraordinary is what an impact it has had. People are talking about it in that particular tone of voice that indicates they were moved beyond all their expectations. It opened May 24 in New York and Los Angeles, and on June 2 in Chicago and many other major cities. It then will roll out across the country, building (Gore hopes) on word of mouth—on people telling one another they must see it.

Gore makes no mention in the film of President George W. Bush or any of his policies. He deliberately avoids naming any names or pointing any fingers. "This is not a political movie," he says firmly. "Paramount did a lot of focus groups, and people said it was not like *Fahrenheit 9/11*. It played fair and supported what it said. It appealed equally to Republicans and Democrats, liberals and conservatives. You have to remember that the environment used to be a bipartisan issue in the United States. Religious leaders saw it as a matter of respecting God's creation."

In the film, Gore is shown as a man with a mission. Other retired politicians go into business or the media or teaching. Gore has devoted his life to the issue of global warming.

"The other day," he says, "I saw a TV ad which is being run to try to neutralize this film. It's sponsored by an industry front group underwritten largely by ExxonMobil. They have a line in the ad: *CO2. They call it pollution. We call it life.*

"Honest," he says. "This is a real ad. I know it sounds like a spoof from *Saturday Night Live*. It's funny, and we laugh, but the energy industry has paralyzed America for twenty years with disinformation like that. They're using exactly the same strategy the tobacco industry used. They're saying there is a 'controversy' and they refer to a 'debate,' when in fact the scientific consensus on global warming is definitive.

"We found an internal memo from an energy industry group from 1998, written by their disinformation specialists, saying their objective was: 'Reposition global warming as theory rather than fact.' That's the same language that tobacco used. The easiest defense is to simply deny reality and claim the truth is not the truth. Otherwise, they have to admit there is a moral imperative for change, and that would offend their big supporters in the oil and energy industries."

Gore says this, and behind him through the hotel window the sun shines down on Cannes and people make deals and go to movies and the world looks much as it always has. Then you go to his movie and discover that they drilled into the polar ice to extract an ice core that's a 650,000-year record of global climactic trends, and the current situation is going off the charts. There is no precedent. You learn that hurricanes in the Gulf of Mexico and typhoons in the Pacific Ocean have suddenly escalated in frequency and strength. That rainfall patterns are being disrupted. That arctic melting is having an effect on the Gulf Stream. That the ten hottest years in history have been in the last fourteen years. That the number of days the arctic tundra has been frozen enough to support trucks has gone down from 225 to 75.

"There is as strong a consensus on this issue as science has ever had," Gore says. "A survey of more than 928 scientific papers in respected journals shows 100 percent agreement. But a database search of newspapers and magazines shows 57 percent of the articles question global warming, and 43 percent accept it. That's disinformation at work.

"Even in the short run," he says, "we aren't heeding the warnings. Two or three days before Hurricane Katrina, the National Weather Service predicted a hurricane so severe it would create 'medieval conditions' in New Orleans. It issued clear warnings that the levees might be breached and the city flooded. Yet look what happened, and how slow the response was. Hurricane season starts again in a week."

"How do you feel about Bush's position on global warming?" I ask him, since his film never mentions the name and refers to him only indirectly, when Gore introduces himself: "I used to be the next president of the United States."

Gore shrugs. "There was a big new official study last month that said global warming is real and human activity is largely responsible. The White House, quote, 'accepted the study without endorsing its conclusions.' A White House spokesman said, 'This is only the first of twenty-one studies.' That sounds good until you realize it is also the latest of hundreds of studies."

He shrugs.

"The danger," he says, "is that people will go from denial to despair without stopping in between to ask themselves what action they can take."

In the movie, Gore suggests some actions, such as switching to higher-mileage and hybrid cars, developing and supporting clean energy sources, and even something as simple as turning off the lights.

"The leading scientists say we have about ten years. After that, we reach the tipping point, the point of no return. That doesn't mean the world ends, but it means that civilization as we know it gradually becomes impossible, more quickly than we can imagine.

"Is it too late? Look at the hole in the ozone layer. Everybody got together on that after the Montreal Accord, and the hole has grown a lot smaller and will have disappeared by the year 2050. So that worked. No, it's not too late. But it's too late to be sitting around."

This interview was on Sunday.

On Monday, an Associated Press story began:

Is President Bush likely to see Al Gore's documentary about global warming?

"Doubt it," Bush said coolly.

Philip Seymour Hoffman

October 16, 2005—"I don't think Capote knew exactly what he was setting himself up for," Philip Seymour Hoffman said. "He said later if he'd known what was going to happen he would have driven right through the town like a bat out of hell."

But he didn't. Truman Capote stayed in Holcomb, Kansas, and returned on and off over the next six years, writing *In Cold Blood*, a great book that after forty years is still read and valued but that destroyed its author. The book inspired a movie at the time, about the murder of the Clutter family, and now it has inspired another, about the triumph and self-destruction of Truman Capote.

Hoffman looks very much like himself and not particularly like Capote, but in Bennett Miller's *Capote* he has the inner music right, and he feels like Capote, like the small, precise gay man with the affectations and eccentricities who walked into the middle of America and brought back a portrait of ordinary people visited by tragedy. If there is such a thing as a lock on an Oscar nomination, Hoffman has one; in a year rich in performances, his is remarkable.

Hoffman will never be confused with a matinee idol, but by taking chances with good directors and unconventional projects he has become one of the most interesting actors of his generation: Consider such films as *Boogie Nights*, *The Big Lebowski*, *Happiness*, *Magnolia*, *Almost Famous*, *State and Main*, *Punch-Drunk Love*, *Flawless*, and *Owning Mahowny*. Consider the directors Paul Thomas Anderson, Todd Solondz, David Mamet, Cameron Crowe, Joel Schumacher, and the Coen brothers. This is a career.

Bennett Miller, who directed *Capote*, is not only Hoffman's director but also his old friend:

"I met Bennett and Danny Futterman, who wrote the screenplay, when we were all sixteen years old and in this summer theater program— and there we were on my porch in Manhattan when we're thirty-five, talking about making this film, and two years later we made it."

Hoffman and Miller were visiting Chicago to promote their film. I asked Miller how this actor he had known for twenty years became a character so completely unlike himself.

"One aspect is the mechanical aspect," Miller said, so softly he could have been talking to himself. The two men are opposites, Hoffman verbal and outgoing, Miller viewing the world with grave misgivings. "His performance begins with and depends on the voice. How Philip does Capote physically, that's something an actor does alone in a room with the door locked. He worked on it for five and a half months. We gave him audio- and video-tapes and it was a matter of methodical rehearsal. He's not a mimic by nature. But the deeper aspects of Capote are a little more mysterious, and how Phil managed to tune in to that frequency transcends the mechanical work he did."

Hoffman himself seems a little surprised by the uncanny way his performance resonates.

"An acting teacher of mine once said about Sissy Spacek in *Coal Miner's Daughter* that she was more Loretta Lynn than Loretta Lynn was. Spacek could capture a truth and essence that Loretta Lynn could never do because she *was* Loretta Lynn. Spacek could be objective, the way I can be objective about Capote and find the truth about what possibly made him tick.

"I wasn't concentrating on how to mimic him," he said. "I was concentrating on what put him into action. I got away from worrying about doing him exactly. I knew I had to get close to the voice and the mannerisms, but at the end of the day if I didn't understand what drove him, none of that stuff would have been any good."

He does understand. He portrays Capote as a man who finds himself the captive of an overwhelming opportunity. He goes to Kansas thinking he will write about how a small town deals with tragedy, and then he meets the two men arrested for the murders, Dick Hickock and Perry Smith, and he becomes their confidant. He sees the human beings inside the monsters. He falls in love with Smith. But he has a greater love for his book, which he correctly senses will be big and important. And in the end he betrays Smith. He pretends to work on their behalf for an appeal, but he needs for the men to die so that his book can end.

"It was an inevitable tragedy," Hoffman said. "He was unaware that it was happening until it was too late. He wanted to write this great book that would bring him more acclaim and love than ever before, but this other thing was just as powerful, this intimacy that was created, especially with Perry. He said later on he became closer with those two than he was with anyone else in his life.

"If you have that kind of intimacy alongside ambition, ultimately it's going to leave an incredibly tragic impression on his psyche and spirit. He paid a huge price to write one of the great books of the twentieth century. Capote didn't go to Kansas. Kansas reached out to New York and grabbed Capote. The minute he met Perry Smith it was inevitable that these two men were going to die, one literally and one figuratively, because the identification they shared was too deep. The minute he got Perry to open up about his own life, and he learned they were both orphans, they were both abandoned children, he sees his muse and that's the beginning of the end. Kansas sprung a trap on him."

Although Capote was an exotic original, Hoffman often plays characters who are so ordinary they seem to be making a point of it. I was remembering his work in *Owning Mahowny*, where he plays a Toronto bank officer who embezzles millions and loses it all in Atlantic City and Las Vegas, and seems to be in a trance when he's at the tables. At one point, he takes his girlfriend to Vegas and forgets she's there. Mahowny could get overlooked in a one-man lineup, and yet I will never forget the character. How does that happen?

"Acting is just hard for me," he said. "As I've gotten older I've gained a certain facility, but ultimately I know that if I don't feel for the material in a way that keeps me up at night, it's gonna be harder for me to act well. It might not ultimately be a great movie, but hopefully it will be a movie that somebody is gonna find interesting.

"It's not that I haven't made decisions based on money in my life. I definitely have and will again, but I try to keep those as far apart as possible. And even when I make those decisions, I still want to find something in the material that will get me active in finding out how I can act this thing well. Because if I'm left to my own devices, it's real empty in here."

He chooses directors, he said, because he likes their other work. "The way Bennett is and the way Cameron Crowe is and the Coen brothers, Paul Thomas Anderson—those are the guys you wanna work with. They're like children; they have the energy and excitement a child has, and that's necessary. Because if you've got somebody like me who's incredibly self-critical and can get down, you need an energy that is constantly reviving the atmosphere."

Hoffman says he's heard the talk about Oscars, and he doesn't beat around the bush: "I'm very excited people are talking like that. I usually hide my feelings about things like the Oscars. But I believe in the film. Hell or high water, here we are and people are actually going to see it, a lot more than we thought would, and they're responding the same way we felt about it. So I'm excited, and I hope the film is still in theaters six months from now, and the Oscar buzz is only gonna help. I don't want it to go away. I want it to be in the theaters in May."

Terrence Howard

August 10, 2005—Terrence Howard is having a good year. He has given two performances that are, by general agreement, of Oscar caliber. In *Crash,* which opened in May 2005, he plays a TV producer who finds himself in an impossible situation when his wife is assaulted by a white cop; he knows that if he protests, he'll be charged with resisting arrest, or worse. In *Hustle & Flow,* he plays a Memphis pimp named Djay who dreams of becoming a rap artist; as he works with new friends to make a demo record, the joy of creation changes the nature of his life. And in the film *Four Brothers,* he plays a cop, so this year he has been on both sides of the law and in the middle.

Howard is handsome in a Billy Dee Williams way, is soft-spoken and calm, and it's a surprise to see him as a street-smart pimp with a rough Memphis accent. That's what's known as acting. Sometimes it takes two or three performances to snap an actor into focus, so that you can see his gift and not simply his work. It happened last year to Jamie Foxx. This year, it's happening to Terrence Howard.

In a hotel suite in Chicago, we talked a long time. I found myself caught up in his energy; he wasn't "doing an interview" but was speaking directly from his heart. Here are some of the things I learned from him:

—"I've been at this for nineteen years. I'm one year from a pension. This year I got to work with Paul Haggis (*Crash*) and George Wolfe (*Lackawanna Blues,* for HBO) and Darnell Martin (*Their Eyes Were Watching God,* for ABC) and Craig Brewer (*Hustle & Flow*) and John Singleton (director of *Four Brothers,* producer and financer of *Hustle & Flow*), and I just finished a film with 50 Cent, directed by Jim Sheridan (*Get Rich or Die Tryin'*).

"I consider these directors to be my tutors. A director is your acting coach, fine-tuning you until you shine bright enough that everyone can see. Before, I was kept in the kitchen, but now I'm in the china cabinet a little bit. There's a lot I want to find inside myself, and directors find pieces of my personality scattered in these characters. Maybe when I'm seventy, I'll finally be who I wanted to be when I was a little kid."

—*Hustle & Flow* is an independent film that went against the formula. "We made it on a small budget, and we gathered twenty actors for way under scale. No one made more than $5,000 making the movie, but the actors brought their hearts into it. People want to see what's honest and real. The film industry needs this right now."

—He wanted to be an actor when he was five years old. "My great-grandmother Minnie Gentry was a stage actress. My grandmother was an actress. My mom auditioned in so many places it's like I'm living her dream. She had me at sixteen; she'd already had my older brother, she went on to have my two younger brothers, and then she finished high school, she went to college, she went to L.A. to try and be an actress, but as a single mom with four kids she couldn't go to the auditions. The spirit was strong in her and I was infected with it."

—"I've had sixty-year-old middle-class women coming to me after *Hustle & Flow* and saying they had no idea they had so much in common with a pimp. Everybody has lost a dream along the way, and seeing Djay try to find his is what people appreciate."

—He talked with 123 pimps during two years of research for the role. "None of them was the stereotypical pimp that's been portrayed. I didn't ask them what it took to be a pimp, but what they wanted to be when they were little kids. And, 'What circumstance pushed you into this life?' You could see them get silent; they'd hidden that vulnerable side, and when they'd start to speak you'd see a human being with nothing left to sell but his dignity and the humanity of the people who trusted him.

"I met this older woman whose son was a pimp, but still she had so much hope. She told me in every person there's a little piece of God. 'That's who you talk to,' she said, 'and my boy will be okay one day.' That was the moment I found Djay."

—In *Crash*, his character stands by impotently while a white cop essentially rapes his wife, and then he doesn't report it to Internal Affairs because he doesn't want to be perceived at work as a black man who is vulnerable, who despite his high salary and important job can be treated that way.

"What was so sad is that my character was taken from a real person that Paul Haggis knew. He told me he was walking down the hall of a studio and saw two white execs and a black junior exec, and one of the white guys told him a black joke, and he watched the black guy smile. You could see in his eyes it was tearing him to pieces, but he was more concerned with his job. Paul said he wondered how he found the strength and courage to come to work every day in those circumstances."

—A lot of people found it strange that Jim Sheridan, born in Ireland, was chosen to direct *Get Rich or Die Tryin'*, the semiautobiographical life story of the rap star 50 Cent. "But he dove right in," Howard said. "With Jim Sheridan, you're talking about a magician—a better actor than any actor on the planet and a better director, that's who Jim Sheridan is.

"Most directors give you a line reading, and you tell them thanks very much, I can handle this myself. When Jim does it, you ask him to do it again, because you want to do what he did. People were asking how this Irish guy was

going to write and direct this film about a drug dealer in the Bronx, and he told me he grew up poor in an urban area in Ireland, and the common factor is the struggle."

—*Crash* has been surprisingly successful at the box office, with its interleaved stories of racial tension between many groups in the Los Angeles melting pot. "Not once in that film did they use the words 'bigotry' or 'racism.' Haggis simply exposed the casual racism and allowed people to make their own judgment. He asked us as actors to dig inside ourselves and our own personal experiences. He was gonna try to weave them together into a tapestry of American society. I think Gandhi would stand behind that movie. I wish Martin Luther King was around to see it and say, 'Look how far we've come.'"

—John Singleton (*Boyz n the Hood*) put up his own money as the producer of *Hustle & Flow*, Howard said. "This film was turned down by every studio for two and a half years. They told him, if he would cast a rapper in place of me they'd give him $5 (million) or $10 million to make the movie. But John bet on a dead horse and reached inside his pocket and put $3 million on the line and made it."

—It was harder than you might think to play a rap artist in *Hustle & Flow*. Howard had taught himself guitar and piano, but rap was something else. "With guitar, I play country music. My grandfather was a truck driver, and during vacations we'd drive cross-country listening to country. I was sixteen years old, wearing cowboy boots, living in the middle of the projects in Cleveland. I asked Craig Brewer, why can't Djay play guitar? As an actor, I was trying to sneak my way out of it. And he said, 'Because Djay doesn't have that skill.'

"I still to this day don't think I pulled it off as a rapper. The movie works because people get caught up in Djay's passion. Now they're playing the videos on BET and MTV and trying to turn me into a rapper. No way. It was hard enough as it was."

—Terrence Howard is a chemical engineer. He studied chemical engineering in order to become an actor. It involved some fairly simple logic, which he smiled at while explaining:

"I was good at science. I was living in Cleveland in 1987 and had graduated high school and wanted to be an actor, but if I went to New

York and got a job, I wouldn't be free to go to auditions, and if I got a job as an actor, I'd get fired and lose my apartment. But I figured, if I'm in school I will always be free to go on auditions, and I'll have a place to live, because I'll be in the dorm."

Ang Lee and Heath Ledger

December 11, 2005—"I never was a citizen of any particular place," Ang Lee tells me. "My parents left China to go to Taiwan. We were outsiders there. We moved to the States. Outsiders. Back to China. Now we were outsiders there, too—outsiders from America."

He stirs his tea and inhales it. Doesn't drink it yet. Lee is such an outsider that both of his children were born in my hometown in Illinois. One year I was interviewing the arriving nominees at the Oscars and he told me proudly, "These are my two Urbana children!" People asked me, "What kind of children did he say they were? Did they have some kind of condition?"

"Everywhere can be home and everywhere is not really home, and you have to deal with loneliness and alienation," Lee tells me. "I'm old enough to realize that eventually you have to deal with loneliness anyway. I'm happily married, I love my children, but eventually you have to deal with yourself. I trust the elusive world created by movies more than anything else. I'm very happy when I'm making a movie. I live on the other side of the screen."

In that sentence, he explains why his movies are so different from one another. We look at their outer worlds. He lives inside them, where they are all the same world—his. He makes comedies like *Eat Drink Man Woman* and angst like *The Ice Storm* and science fiction like *Hulk* and martial arts fantasies like *Crouching Tiger, Hidden Dragon* and English lit adaptations like *Sense and Sensibility*, and now here is his *Brokeback Mountain*, about two young cowhands in Wyoming who discover they are gay and have absolutely no way of dealing with that fact.

The movie stars Heath Ledger and Jake Gyllenhaal, who take summer jobs in 1963 as sheepherders on a mountainside. For days and days they seem to be waiting for something, and then one night, suddenly, they make love. "That was a one-time thing," they

agree in the morning. But then it is night again, and their destinies are fixed. They are doomed to be in love for the rest of their lives, in a world that has given them no way to understand homosexuality and no one to discuss it with.

The movie is based on a short story by E. Annie Proulx. "I never asked her why she called it *Brokeback*," Lee says. "I was scared to ask her."

Later that same day, during the Toronto Film Festival, I spoke with Ledger, who sometimes seems as surprised to be an actor as his character is surprised to be a homosexual.

"He was fighting against his genetic structure," Ledger says of Ennis, his character. "He's fighting against every tradition and fear that has been passed down to him. I worked to try to physicalize his fear. His words have to battle their way out of his mouth."

Growing up in Australia, he says, he knew ranch hands and sheepherders. "They work daylight to nightfall on a horse, with gravity pulling down on their shoulders. At quitting time, when they dismount, they walk differently. Getting off a horse is like a sailor stepping ashore. Australian ranch hands speak with tense upper lips. I knew how to do that, had seen that, been around it. I figured that was to keep the flies out of their mouths."

Is that a smile?

Ledger won an Oscar nomination for this performance. "I never went to acting school," he says. "I never had a black, empty performing space and a pair of black pajamas to run around in and express myself. All of my mistakes are on film."

None of them are in *Brokeback Mountain*.

"Ennis hated himself for the form of love he felt for Jack," he says. "That's how I played his journey. What's so important about his relationship with his children is that's the one area in his life he felt confident about.

"It's a pattern of mine, no matter what the story is or the character, to find out whether I doubt myself. Doubt myself, or the character doubts himself, or both. Huge amounts of fear and doubt that I don't know how to do it. If I think far enough ahead, I wouldn't be brave enough to make a choice like this."

But he was.

"At one point I had to take a step back from a

career which was somewhat handed to me on a platter. Which I felt I didn't deserve. I had to walk away a little and make more interesting choices."

In the movie, the characters played by Gyllenhaal and Ledger both get married. Gyllenhaal is more willing to accept his hidden feelings. He thinks maybe one day they could run a ranch together. Ledger knows a couple of guys who got killed when they tried that.

"They don't really ever talk to each other," Lee tells me. "Not about that. This story is Larry McMurtry's *Lonesome Dove* in everything but its sexuality. I discussed this with McMurtry, who wrote the screenplay. *Lonesome Dove* was ripe for a homosexual love story. It took a foreigner like me or a woman like Annie to tip that over and spill it out and get rid of the metaphor and just see it. It's just there. I began to realize in that particular time, they have no understanding of their behavior. Nor do their wives. All they feel is a private, very romantic idea of falling in love, which they cannot discuss. We say we fall in love. It's like falling into a void. Are you afraid to take the fall? The most powerful thing in their lives is something that is missing.

"Heath Ledger, the movie rides on him. He's able to carry that mythical, elegiac Western thing. A macho environment in which he's scared and private. It happens after they climb higher to where the air is thinner and everything is unknown and a mystery. That's *Brokeback* to me."

Finally he sips his tea.

"I'm experienced enough to know," he says, "that the hardest thing to tell is an epic short story. Slices of life that add up to an epic feeling. You have to choose small details that feel like they add up to gaps of two or three years, between their meetings. It looks easy but it's not, especially since they never talk about it. One day I said to Annie, 'Your terse prose is very hard to bring to the screen.' You know what she said to me?"

What did she say to you?

"She said, 'That's your job.'"

Bai Ling

Honolulu, Hawaii, October 25, 2005—"I saw your new movie, and I thought it was really good," I told Bai Ling.

"You saw *Dumplings?*"

"I saw the 'Dumplings' episode in *Three . . . Extremes.*"

"You did not see whole film?"

"I saw all three episodes."

"But there is a whole feature film named *Dumplings*! I won the Golden Horse for it! That is Chinese Oscar! You only saw excerpt! Whole film has love-making scene so passionate, so powerful!"

Funny. I am already thinking so passionate, so powerful. Bai Ling was born in China and is now a famous star who appears mostly in American movies. She likes costumes for which nudity would not represent much of a compromise. Right now she is wearing an elegant Louis Vuitton gown that must have required half the spare change in Paris and hardly any of the fabric. We are standing in the Louis Vuitton store at the Ala Moana shopping mall in Honolulu, at a party for the Louis Vuitton Hawaii International Film Festival, which used to be called the Hawaii International Film Festival, so now you know why their party is at the Louis Vuitton store.

I have seen Bai Ling many times in the movies, often billed as Ling Bai. In China the practice is to put the family name first and the given name second. So properly she should be referred to as Ling Bai, right?

"Your theory is correct, but you have one thing wrong," I am told by Liwei Kiumra, the China expert of the Hawaii festival. "Ling is her first name."

Therefore, Bai Ling. Everyone who has it wrong has it right. I have never met her before. I'm sure I would have remembered if I had. She starts gabbing away like we're old friends and I want to catch up on what's been happening since our last sleepover.

"I am on reality TV! New VH-1 show! Named *But Can They Sing?* Celebrity super pop stars, can they sing? They give you four days to learn song. Models, actors, can you sing? I am on with Joey Pants, Larry Holmes, Morgan Fairchild, and Carmine Gotti. I tell them, have no trouble with Sinatra. 'The Way You Look Tonight,' no problem! You know what they want me to sing? 'Like a Virgin'! My God! Not my style! Show plays October 30 at 10 P.M." She makes sure I write that down. "Be sure to watch! You have to vote for me! Can vote by phone, Internet, every way."

Okay, so that's a plug. But she has already turned the plug into a parody of a plug, and now she hurtles ahead: "One day, I am begging them Sinatra, Sinatra, and they say can I sing old American song, 'McDonald Has Farm.' My God! I never heard of it. They teach me. I like the pig part. 'Oink oink here!'"

She laughs so cheerfully it is all I can do to watch the oinking and not what happens to her dress when she oinks.

Bai Ling has had an incredible life. I learn from IMDb.com that she was born in China in 1970 and at the age of fourteen enlisted in the Chinese People's Liberation Army and joined a troupe entertaining the soldiers in Tibet. Back in Beijing, she was active in theater, until she joined the antigovernment demonstrations at Tiananmen Square. That did nothing for her showbiz career. She immigrated to the United States two years later and has appeared mostly in American films. Her thirty credits include *The Crow, The Breed,* and *Sky Captain and the World of Tomorrow.* She was even the Chinese interpreter in Oliver Stone's *Nixon.* She had top billing recently in *The Beautiful Country* (opposite Nick Nolte), Spike Lee's *She Hate Me,* and Stuart Gordon's forthcoming *Edmond,* written by David Mamet, where she plays a temptress who misleads a fed-up husband played by William H. Macy.

After making *Red Corner* (1997), where she played Richard Gere's defense attorney in a movie critical of the Chinese legal system, she found trouble getting work in her homeland—although *Dumplings* and *Three . . . Extremes* were made in Hong Kong. *Three . . . Extremes* is a sampling of the Extreme Asia cinema; the term describes films that do not merely push outside the envelope but rip it to shreds and stomp on it.

There are two versions of the dumpling film because the director, Fruit Chan, made a ninety-one-minute version and then cut it down to forty minutes to be part of the Extreme Asia horror film trilogy also including Park Chan-Wook's "Cut," from Korea, and Takashi Miike's "Box," from Japan. *Three . . . Extremes* makes American slasher movies look like they're about can openers.

The character played by Bai Ling is a big departure from her usual glamorous and exotic roles. This time she plays a cook famous for her dumplings and always seems to have a little flour on her dress. Her dumplings are famous not because of how good they taste, but because rich, aging actresses believe the dumplings make them look younger. It's all in the recipe. What she puts into the dumplings I choose not to reveal at this point because you may be at breakfast, but let's say the story follows in the Extreme Asia tradition of transgressive and depraved behavior.

If you are thinking of waiting for the full-length version of *Dumplings,* I recommend seeing *Three . . . Extremes* first, both because all three films are so effective and because, frankly, you may not be able to take any more.

"Can I see the full-length version here at the festival?" I asked.

"Yes! Is playing here!"

"Great!" I said. "When?"

"Saturday at midnight," says Chuck Boller, the director of the festival.

"Midnight?" I say. "We just got off the plane from Chicago. I'll sleep right through the midnight screening. That's 5 A.M. in Chicago."

"Maybe take a nap between 7 and 10, be fresh," Bai Ling suggests.

"Why only at midnight?" I ask Boller.

"Well . . . you've seen the forty-minute version?"

I nod. We both nod.

"I make all dumplings myself!" Bai Ling told me. "All the time in that little kitchen. I was so pale, they asked me, what was my makeup? No makeup! Dying of heat! I am chopping away all the time, blood everywhere! Terrible smell. Much better in long version. There is a lovemaking scene in longer version that is amazing. Goes on forever. Wilder and wilder. Not, you know, too bad, just wild."

Her dumpling cook is a smiling and high-spirited creature who may live in a tenement but treats it like a palace. She is upbeat and supportive for her clients, who need a lot of support, but the film's horror involves what she does while she smiles.

"She's like a spirit, so bold, so innocent, so wise," Bai Ling tells me. "She is provocative, sexy, a free spirit. I think she is a Zen master. She is offering something to actress afraid of losing her looks. Myself, I will never have plastic surgery. When you do that, you start to lose yourself."

Bai Ling, now thirty-five, has not started to lose herself. In the movie, she asks her client, "How old do I look to you?" The actress guesses about thirty. As I wrote in my review, "I would have guessed even younger."

"For me, every day is a new day," Bai Ling tells me. "No thinking about growing old. We as individuals are perfect sculptures." Speak for yourself, Bai Ling.

Joaquin Phoenix and James Mangold

November 13, 2005—Johnny Cash had one requirement for the star of *Walk the Line*: "Whoever plays me, make sure they don't handle the guitar like it's a baby. Make them hold it like they own it!"

This was during a "real Southern breakfast" that John and his wife, June Carter Cash, cooked up for James Mangold and his wife, Cathy Konrad, who were going to direct and produce the movie.

"We went down to Hendersonville and checked into the hotel," Mangold remembered, "and John came and picked us up in the lobby. Not dressed in black. Just jeans and a checked shirt. At their house, John and June sang grace, holding hands. And John told us stories about his early days in the music business."

"I was sent by Sam Phillips of Sun Records with a record in an envelope, for a disc jockey to play," Cash told them. "The DJ dropped the record and it broke. I called up Sam and I was about in tears. 'John,' he said, 'I got a thousand more.' In those days there was no *Inside Edition*, so not every twenty-year-old knew how records were made."

This breakfast would have been around 1999. Mangold had been shopping the Johnny Cash biopic around Hollywood with no luck. Even after he had Joaquin Phoenix and Reese Witherspoon on board to play John and June, he was told the studios "don't want to make movies about people." William Goldman, the veteran screenwriter, had a gloomier analysis: "No one wants to make a movie that depends on you pulling it off."

They want, in other words, to make movies that don't need to be pulled off. Movies that are foolproof. Formula pictures, teenage action movies, video game adaptations, sequels. Last year every studio in Hollywood passed on *Ray*, the biopic about Ray Charles, and this year it can be said that they all passed on *Walk the Line* until Fox 2000 finally came through. What's ironic is that *Ray* won an Oscar for its star, Jamie Foxx, and Phoenix and Witherspoon are likely to be nominated for Oscars.

I talked to Mangold and Konrad at the Telluride Film Festival Labor Day 2005, and a week later I talked with Phoenix at the Toronto festival. The movie was well-received both places, and what amazed a lot of people was how well Phoenix and Witherspoon could sing—not "considering they aren't singers," but as if they actually were. When I saw the movie, I closed my eyes to focus on the sound track and convinced myself I was actually listening to Johnny Cash; the vocals were so convincing that when the credits rolled up and Phoenix was credited with doing all of his own singing, I was amazed, and so were a lot of other people.

"I didn't sing and I didn't have any experience," Phoenix told me. "Not even in the shower. I worked with a voice coach for an hour and a half a day. I had to go down an octave. T-Bone Burnett, our music consultant, helped me a lot. John had an amazing range. In *Walk the Line*, he changes keys with every verse. But it wasn't really so much how he sang as how he *acted* the songs.

"Then there was the challenge of showing him finding his voice. In biopics we always see the finished product, but not the development. But in his early albums, John sings very differently than later on. How does he find his voice, between his early twenties and his thirties? How did he discover his sound?"

Mangold said the most courageous thing about Phoenix's performance is, "He plays the growth. There is that early audition scene where he starts out lousy trying to sound like somebody on the radio, and by the end he is singing in his own voice."

That's the scene where, after weeks of trying, Cash gets an audition at Sun Records, where the legendary producer Sam Phillips launched Howlin' Wolf, Jerry Lee Lewis, and Elvis Presley. He listens to Cash listlessly grind through a spiritual, stops him, and asks him if he has anything of his own he can sing. Cash does. He wrote "Folsom Prison Blues" while he was serving in the Army in Germany. He sings it, and in that scene Phoenix shows Cash moving verse by verse toward his sound.

"Sam Phillips was like a great director," Phoenix said. "He helped develop the idea of the singer-songwriter. Country music took a hit with Elvis, and the country singers were wondering, what do we do? Sing like Elvis? John brought back the storyteller side of country, as opposed to the Nashville Sound. What you feel with John is empathy."

Mangold agrees. The director's earlier titles include the overlooked *Heavy* (1995), Sylvester Stallone in *Cop Land* (1997), Winona Ryder and Angelina Jolie in *Girl, Interrupted* (1999), and the weirdly wonderful time-travel romance *Kate & Leopold* (2001). *Walk the Line* is his first venture into a music-based film.

"Sam Phillips was kind of like Lee Strasberg at the Actors Studio," Mangold said. "He was doing the same kind of thing with Johnny Cash that Strasberg was doing with Brando, Newman, and Dean. He was asking them to call on real human experience more than a kind of glamour."

June Carter, he said, actually studied at the Actors Studio: "She grew up in a well-adjusted family, she was familiar with show business from the time she was born; the Carter Family was royalty in country music. She was acting more than people knew. There were two Junes. Onstage, she liked to joke and clown, because she wasn't as confident of her singing as she deserved to be. Offstage, she was a pro who knew how the business worked."

Mangold said Carter and Cash, who both died in 2003, were "excited" that Witherspoon and Phoenix were going to sing in their voices. Cash's only worry was about the guitar-handling. He had no objection to the frank way the movie handles his addiction to pills and his battle to get clean with June's help. That was all on the record and inspired one of the movie's best lines. After he's busted and spends some time behind bars, his father, whom John felt he could never please, said, "Well, at least now when you sing that 'Folsom Prison' song, you won't have to work so hard to make people think you been to jail."

Steven Spielberg

December 25, 2005—"I knew the minefield was there," says Steven Spielberg, describing the storm of controversy over his new film *Munich*. He has been attacked on three fronts: for being anti-Israeli, being anti-Palestinian, and being neither—which is, those critics say, the sin of "moral equivalency."

"I wasn't naive in accepting this challenge," he says about his film, which begins with the kidnapping and murder of eleven Israeli athletes at the 1972 Munich Olympiad and follows a secret Israeli team assigned by Prime Minister Golda Meir to hunt down those responsible and assassinate them.

"I knew I was going to be losing friends when I took on the subject," he told me during a telephone conversation at week's end. "I am also making new friends."

The film had already generated fiery discussion from those who've seen it in previews—or not seen it but objected to the very idea of it.

In his film, a character named Avner, played by Eric Bana, heads the assassination squad and begins to question the morality and utility of his actions. Others in the film articulate a defense of the strategy of revenge. Spielberg says that his film deliberately supplies no simple answers.

"It would make people more comfortable if I made a film that said all targeted assassination is bad, or good, but the movie doesn't take either of those positions. It refuses to. Many of those pundits on the left and right would love the film to land somewhere definite. It puts a real burden on the audience to figure out for themselves how they feel about these issues. There are no easy answers to the most complex story of the last fifty years."

Spielberg says he has been particularly struck by charges that his film makes him "no friend of Israel."

"I am as truly pro-Israeli as you can possibly imagine. From the day I became morally and politically conscious of the importance of the state of Israel and its necessity to exist, I have believed that not just Israel, but the rest of the world, needs Israel to exist.

"But there is a constituency that nothing you can say or do will ever satisfy. The prism through which they see things is so profound and deeply rooted and so much a part of their own belief system that if you challenge that, you challenge everything they believe in. They say the film is too critical of Israel. The film has been shown to Palestinians who think it is too pro-Israel and doesn't give them enough room to air their grievances.

"I guess what I'm trying to say is, if this movie bothers you, frightens you, upsets you, maybe it's not a good idea to ignore that. Maybe you need to think about why you're having that reaction."

Spielberg, who is the most popular filmmaker in modern history, has regularly chosen to make serious and thoughtful films, some of limited appeal, along with his box office blockbusters. It is striking that the director of *Jurassic Park* and the Indiana Jones movies is also the director of *Schindler's List, The Color Purple, Amistad,* and *Munich.*

"Some of my critics are asking how Spielberg, this Hollywood liberal who makes dinosaur movies, can say anything serious about this subject that baffles so many smart people. What they're basically saying is, 'You disagree with us in a big public way and we want you to shut up and we want this movie to go back in the can.' That's a nefarious attempt to make people plug up their ears. That's not Jewish, it's not democratic, and it's bad for everyone—especially in a democratic society."

Yet what *is* he saying that has people so disturbed? Careful attention to the film itself suggests that it's not so much what he says as that he dares to even open up the Middle East for discussion.

"My film refuses to be a pamphlet," Spielberg says. "My screenwriter, Tony Kushner, and I were hoping to make it a visceral, emotional, and intellectual experience, combined in such a way that it will help you get in touch with what you feel are the questions the film poses. The most important thing about peace in the Middle East is that people surrender their absolute certainty about what's going on."

He said he was taught by his parents, his rabbi, and his faith that discussion "is the highest good—it's Talmudic."

But what about the issue of "moral equivalence," the charge that he equates the Israeli and Palestinian causes, when the rightness of one (or the other) is seen as not debatable?

"Frankly, I think that's a stupid charge. The people who attack the movie based on 'moral equivalence' are some of the same people who say diplomacy itself is an exercise in moral equivalence and that war is the only answer. That the only way to fight terrorism is to dehumanize the terrorists by asking no questions about who they are and where they come from.

"What I believe is every act of terrorism requires a strong response, but we must also pay attention to the causes. That's why we have brains and the power to think passionately. Understanding does not require approval; understanding is not the same as inaction. Understanding is a very muscular act. If I'm endorsing understanding and being attacked for that, then I am almost flattered."

In his film, there is a scene where Ali, a member of the Black September group, which carried out the 1972 attacks, talks about his idea of a Palestinian homeland. Also a scene where Avner's mother, an original settler in Israel, defends their homeland. And a scene where an Israeli spymaster, played by Geoffrey Rush, provides a strong response to Avner's doubts.

"The whole Israeli-Palestinian idea of home suggests that there are two enormously powerful desires in competition," Spielberg says. "Two rights that are, in a sense, competing. You can't bring that to a simplicity. The film is asking you to surrender your simplicity on both sides and just look at it again. There was an article in *USA Today* by a Los Angeles rabbi, accusing me of 'blind pacifism.' That's interesting because there is not any kind of blind pacifism within me anywhere, or in *Munich.* I feel there was a justified need to respond to the terrorism in Munich, which is why I keep replaying images of the Munich massacre throughout the movie.

"In 1972, when Black September used the Olympics to announce themselves to the world, they broke all the rules and broke the boundaries of that conflict. Israel had to respond, or it would have been perceived as weak. I agree with Golda Meir's response. The thing you have to understand is, Munich is in Germany. And these were Jews dying all over again in Germany. For Israel it was a national

825

trauma. The Avner character, in the end, simply questions whether the response was right. Sometimes a response can provoke unintended consequences. The Rush character and Avner's mother reply. But people feel my voice is represented in Avner. The movie says I don't have an answer. I don't know anyone else who does. But I do know that the dialogue needs to be louder than the weapons."

Spielberg, a onetime boy wonder who directed his first commercial project at the age of twenty-two, is now fifty-nine.

"I guess as I grow older," he says, "I just feel more responsibility for telling the stories that have some kind of larger meaning. Most of my movies sum everything up. I try to make movies to give audiences the least amount of homework and the most amount of pleasure. The majority of my movies have done that. But as I get older I feel the burden of responsibility that comes along with such a powerful tool. I certainly have made movies by popular demand. There is a distinction between moviemaking and filmmaking. I want to do both."

He repeats that he was wounded by the charge that he is "no friend of Israel" because his film asks questions about Israeli policies.

"This film is no more anti-Israel than a similar film which offered criticism of America is anti-America. Criticism is a form of love. I love America, and I'm critical of this administration. I love Israel, and I ask questions. Those who ask no questions may not be a country's best friends."

Is the Middle East without a solution? I ask. Will there be an endless cycle of terror and reprisal? What about the startling fact that Israel's entrenched political enemies, Ariel Sharon from the right and Shimon Peres from the left, have resigned from their parties and joined in a new party that says it is seeking a path to peace?

"What I believe," Spielberg says, "is that there will be peace between Israelis and Palestinians in our lifetimes."

Spielberg Calls Back

The telephone rings, and it is Steven Spielberg once again. After the conversation reported in the article above, I sent him a defense of *Munich* written by Jim Emerson, editor of rogerebert.com (his article appears

on the Web site). It includes quotes from many Jews highly critical of Spielberg. I hear an urgency in Spielberg's voice.

"He brought together some sources and some criticisms I hadn't seen," Spielberg says, "and it made me want to be more specific about the responsibility of a Jewish artist.

"Everybody is sort of saying they wish I would be silent. What inspired me by what I read in Emerson's article is that silence is never good for anybody. When artists fall silent, it's scary. And when Jewish artists fall silent about Israel, it's maybe not so much because we think asking questions will do damage to Israel, but because we're intimidated by the shrillness and hysteria with which these questions are received sometimes.

"And I guess, because I'm a Jewish-American artist, that means that I'm not willing to shut up because somebody who claims to speak for the Jewish community tells me to. I guess I have a very deep faith in the intelligence and in the fairness and in the intellectual courage of the Jewish community, and I know that the questions I'm posing with *Munich* are also questions that many Jews here and in Europe and Israel are asking.

"I think that Jews have always understood that the combination of art and advocacy are not the work for the shy or the timid, and that's why Jews down through history have produced so many important advocates—because the Jewish community traditionally celebrates a variety of thought. I do not believe that *Munich* will polarize and was not intended to polarize that community which I love."

Charlize Theron

October 16, 2005—"She is a gazelle in a goddess suit."

We are discussing Charlize Theron, and that is how her director, Niki Caro, describes her. It is true enough, and yet consider the role for which Theron won an Oscar two years ago, and the new role for which she was nominated this year. In *Monster* (2003), she played a desperate hooker who worked freeway rest stops, was overweight, her face mottled, her teeth awry.

Now in *North Country,* she plays a female miner who inspired the first class-action suit against sexual harassment in American history. Astonishing that the suit was settled so recently, in 1991. As Josey Aimes, the miner, Theron looks good on Saturday nights when she goes to the local bar, but on the job at the mines she is covered with grime, deep in exhaustion, filled with despair as her male coworkers make her the target of relentless sexual outrage.

Because you are beautiful, I said when I interviewed Theron at the Toronto Film Festival, it is strange that in your two finest roles you work against the beauty or hide it.

"I find that a weird question," she said, "as if I'm expected to think a lot about how I look. I was raised in South Africa and didn't grow up in a way where much importance was placed on such things. I was raised on hard work and discipline. When I'm working in a movie, I'm almost fearless about how I look. I don't care, as long as I look right for the role."

In *North Country,* she plays the single mother of a teenage boy and younger girl who flees from an abusive boyfriend and moves back in with her parents on the Minnesota iron range. She gets a job as a hairdresser, then discovers she can make five times the money if she goes to work in the mines. Women have been hired as miners since 1971, but when she hires on in 1989, twenty-nine out of thirty mine workers are men, and women are resented because they are "taking a man's job." The man needs that job to feed his family, she's told. She needs the job to feed her family, she replies, but the answer is blunt: There must be something wrong with her if she can't find a man to take care of her.

"When I was growing up," Theron said, "my mother was the only woman in the road construction business, so I knew some of what goes on. When we were preparing for *North Country,* I met Lois Jenson, the woman the story was inspired by, the woman responsible for the class-action lawsuit. She wasn't the quintessential Norma Rae or Erin Brockovich character, the big personality who takes over a room. She was soft-spoken, she wasn't a ballbuster, but she found the strength to change history. For her, this wasn't just something that happened in the mines. She was haunted by it in every aspect of her life, because it was systematic degradation based on the fact that she happened to be a woman."

In the movie, Theron's character and other women are insulted physically and verbally, made the subjects of obscene graffiti, their locker rooms defaced with feces, and after they win the right to have portable toilets, to use one is to risk having it turned over while they're inside. Watching the movie, you're shocked at the viciousness of the male behavior but convinced it is portrayed accurately.

"The story is loosely based on real events," Theron said, "but my character is completely fictional. Lois, the woman who inspired the story, has seen the movie, and she's happy with it."

Her costar in the movie is Frances McDormand, who won an Oscar for *Fargo* (1996). In *North Country,* she plays a union representative who contracts Lou Gehrig's disease and has to fight physical deterioration as the case proceeds.

"McDormand is an incredible gift to the cinema," Theron said. "There's something so organic about her character, straight from the gut."

McDormand and the other actors in *Fargo* used the regional Minnesota accent to comic effect—you betcha they did.

"Preparing for these roles," Theron said, "we were concerned we were going to sound too broad, and maybe get laughs in the wrong way. We tried to fine-tune it a little, staying kind of neutral. Part of the transformation in any character is a new way of speaking. Also the physical look. Once again I worked with Toni G, who did my makeup for *Monster.*"

She said when she first saw the screenplay, "it was kind of black and white, and I like the gray zones. Five days after the Oscars, Niki Caro called and said she wanted to direct it. She'd just made *Whale Rider,* about another woman who was thought to be unsuited to man's work. She understood the gray zones, and she directed that way. Every sentence one of us started, the other one finished."

Mark Zupan

July 12, 2005—Mark Zupan went home to Austin, Texas, for fourteen hours on Saturday to attend a buddy's wedding. That was his third weekend at home since April. The star of the documentary *Murderball* has been caught in such a whirlwind of overnight stardom that the latest news—Eminem wants to play him in a fictional version of the story—is just one more news item.

Murderball, which looks poised to be the most successful documentary since *Fahrenheit 9/11,* is the story of athletes who play quadriplegic wheelchair rugby. It is a full-contact sport. One objective is to knock over the other guy's chair. It is also the story of overcoming obstacles, of fighting back.

"This film makes people say, hey, shit's gonna happen, so you gotta look beyond that and move on," Zupan said. "It bridges the gap between the disabled and the abled. For the disabled community, it's a change from the woe-is-me, I'm a poor gimp, feel bad for me because I'm in a chair, or happy for me because I brush my teeth."

It also answers questions people are too shy to ask.

"Audiences like the sex part," he said, "because they've always wondered how sex works if you're a quad. In general, the movie makes us seem approachable. Hey, we're just people. Talk to us. I had a guy tell me the other day he saw the movie, and afterwards he started talking to some guys in the theater who were in chairs, and before the movie he would have, like, sort of avoided them or felt sorry for them or something."

Zupan, who is in his early thirties, was paralyzed when he was eighteen. He fell asleep in the bed of a pickup truck after a party. Not knowing he was there, a friend drove away and got into an accident; Zupan was thrown from the truck and injured. The movie explains that most quadriplegics retain some movement of their limbs; not all are paralyzed from the neck down, like Christopher Reeve. To provide balanced competition, the sport assigns points to degrees of disability and limits the number of points a team can field at once.

The movie, directed by Henry Alex Rubin and Dana Adam Shapiro, has been a buzz magnet ever since it premiered at Sundance 2005. When I showed it in April at my Overlooked Film Festival at the University of Illinois at Urbana-Champaign, it was a huge audience favorite, winning a standing (and sitting) ovation. It makes stars of several of its subjects, including Zupan, a goateed and tattooed all-American who is an engineer in his day job, and the longtime all-American Joe Soares, who played on American wheelchair teams, winning one Olympic title after another, then left in a feud, signed with Canada, and led the Canadians to their first victory over the United States. Now back in his Florida home, Soares hopes to return as coach of the U.S. team and is signing an agent to help him deal with bookings as a motivational speaker.

Zupan was bemused that Eminem wants to play either him or Andy Cohn, another star of the film.

"He felt very strongly that he liked the film," Zupan said, "and there's been some talk in Hollywood about a fiction version, but if the doc does as well as we hope it does, it may be hard for a fiction film to follow it."

He said the film would be on 180 screens by the end of July, unusual for a documentary, and the word-of-mouth has caused week-to-week growth in box-office grosses.

"And, jeez, the Tomatometer at Rotten Tomatoes.com is 43 positive out of 43!" Zupan said. "That's a little unheard of. Sooner or later somebody has got to dislike it somewhere."

I asked Zupan what his life has been like since we talked in April.

"I've had the busiest month and a half I've ever experienced. We do *Regis* on Thursday (July 14), the *Today* show on Friday (July 15), Jay Leno on July 22, we did ESPN, there was a doc about the doc on HBO, and we even filmed a *Jackass* episode that will run at the end of the month. We did the wheelchair long jump and wheelchair jousting, with Johnny Knoxville and Steve-O. It had to be one of the most fun times I've ever had."

He's proudest, he said, of being featured in a print ad for the Reebok "I Am What I Am" campaign.

"They had the balls to say, yeah, we'll put a guy in a chair in a major print campaign."

What about wheelchair sports in general? Will they begin to get air time on cable sports networks?

"I don't know. The wheelchair rugby nationals are coming up in Austin in March or April. The way the movie is taking off, I think there might be some interest."

Essays

Duma at the Crossroads

August 10, 2005—Why penguins and not cheetahs?

Dan Fellman would like to know. Fellman, president of domestic distribution for Warner Bros., had two films about animals in release at the same time: *Duma,* about a boy and a cheetah who trek across the Kalahari desert, and *March of the Penguins,* about several thousand penguins who trek across the ice floes of Antarctica.

Both films have won rave reviews. *Duma* has a perfect 100 percent on the Tomatometer at RottenTomatoes.com; not a single critic dislikes it. *March of the Penguins* scored 94 percent on the Tomatometer; among major critics, only three were negative ("The Central Park Zoo is cheaper . . . and it has snow monkeys and beer," groused the *Village Voice*).

So howcum the penguins were the surprise box office hit of summer 2005, and *Duma* was fighting for its life? The movie was directed by Carroll Ballard, whose previous films involving animals have become classics: *The Black Stallion, Never Cry Wolf, Fly Away Home.* His new film, based on real life, tells the story of a twelve-year-old boy who raises a cheetah cub and then tries all by himself to return it to the wild.

That's a real cheetah (four, actually) in the same shots with young actor Alex Michaeletos. And those are real penguins, all right, standing for months without food or water at 60 below zero, incubating their precious eggs.

Duma is a well-crafted family movie in a marketplace dominated by overgrown video games. Warner opened the movie in the spring in test markets, using TV ads to pitch it to kids. "We struck out," says Fellman. But it got a positive review from Scott Foundas in *Variety.* I read his review, asked for a Chicago screening, and Richard Roeper and I decided to review it on *Ebert & Roeper.*

That inspired Warner to give it a chance in the Chicago market. It got E&R's two thumbs up, and praise from my *Sun-Times* review ("a grand tale of adventure"), Michael Wilming-ton of the *Chicago Tribune* ("sheer scenic magnificence and screen animal magnetism"), Dann Gire of the suburban *Daily Herald* ("keeps us in gut-tight suspense without scaring the bejabbers out of younger viewers"), and Stephanie Zacharek of Salon.com ("the greatest kids' movie of the year").

So how were the crowds?

"Disappointing," Fellman tells me. "We averaged around $5,000 per screen. However, with the positive response we got from audiences, and the press support and good word-of-mouth, we think we might see substantial improvement this week.

"What surprised us was that while the kid-oriented TV ads failed in the earlier markets, our print-based and review-driven approach in Chicago got a much larger nonfamily percentage—adults attending on their own. And the response from them was overwhelmingly positive. It's just that there weren't enough of them."

Marshall Field's vs. Macy's

September 21, 2005—I met J. C. Penney once. The old man visited the Penney's store on Main Street in Urbana, Illinois. He shook my hand, gave me a penny, and said if I took care of my pennies and nickels, my dimes and dollars would take care of themselves. At the end of a week, I had ten cents, which I used to see a movie at the Princess Theater. The movie was nine cents. The extra penny went for an all-day sucker.

Now I feel like the all-day sucker. Terry Lundgren, the three-headed chairman, president, and CEO of Federated Department Stores, came to town and informed Mayor Richard M. Daley that he is changing the name of Marshall Field's to Macy's. I thought the day would never come. I am looking at my Field's charge card, which I have cut up into tiny pieces. They look like little tears the color of money.

Initial reaction to the change was "mixed,"

say the Chicago news media, which have expressed an admirable degree of outrage despite licking their lips at all the new Macy's ads. Federated has surveys claiming a majority of Chicago shoppers support the change or are neutral. Federated should fire its marketing firm, because these results are a) unlikely, and b) useless, since nobody believes them anyway. If I had the job of the three-headed one, I would simply announce that Chicagoans supported the plan, and save the money I spent on the survey.

For that matter, if I were Lundgren, I would retain the name Marshall Field's simply because it would earn me goodwill and save me bad publicity. On CNN, business reporters based in New York and Atlanta were giving their own opinions that this decision was unwise, unexpected, and incredible. I think one used the word "crazy." In every corner of America that has lost a little of its soul to heartless corporate bean counters, the decision will have an echo.

Sure, sell Macy's merchandise in Marshall Field's. They have a lot of brand names already. Even call it "Macy's at Marshall Field's." But why slap the faces of Chicagoans who love the World's First and Greatest Department Store? There was never one day in the entire history of Macy's when anyone, in New York or anywhere else, thought it was the equal of Field's. What is Macy's? A Thanksgiving parade. Gobble, gobble.

The decision is a form of imperialism. The new corporate executives see their companies as empires and colonize new lands like the imperial powers of history. If Columbus could claim North America for Queen Isabella, if America could plant its flag on the moon, then why can't Terry Lundgren wade ashore in Chicago, plant his flag at Randolph and State, and tell the natives they only thought it belonged to them?

I hope we don't all catch chicken pox or the measles from him. That's what wiped out the Incas and Aztecs, you know. I hope Mayor Daley used Lifebuoy soap after shaking Lundgren's hand. My dad used to read the Lifebuoy label out loud: Protects against smallpox, scarlet fever, scarlatina, measles, whooping cough, typhoid, and typhus fever.

Lundgren threw Chicago two bones. He "may" return the manufacture of Frango Mints to the State Street kitchens. Great. I feel like the rat that spent three weeks crawling through a maze and all he found was a salted nut. And he "may" retain the actual brass Marshall Field's nameplate on the State Street store. He damn well should. I am calling on Alderman Burton F. Natarus, who mows the Loop like it's the front yard of his bungalow, to introduce legislation designating the brass nameplate as a landmark. If the measure does not pass the city council, then I am glad they gave me the key to the city. Next time I'll remember to lock up at night.

How I Gave Oprah Winfrey Her Start

November 16, 2005—Ever since Oprah Winfrey revealed on her twentieth anniversary program that I was the person who first suggested she go into syndication, I have been flooded with requests for interviews.

Yes, it is true, I persuaded Oprah to become the most successful and famous woman in the world. I was also the person who suggested that Jerry Springer not go into syndication, for which I have received too little credit.

All of these years I have maintained a discreet silence about my role as Oprah's adviser, but now that she has spilled the beans, the time is right to tell the whole story.

It began early one morning in Baltimore, where Gene Siskel and I were scheduled to appear on a morning talk show hosted by a newcomer named Oprah Winfrey. The other guests on the show included a vegetarian chef and four dwarfs dressed as chipmunks, who would sing "The Chipmunk Christmas Song" while dancing with hula hoops.

We were all standing in the wings. Siskel was staring straight ahead, in fierce concentration. "Whatever you do," he whispered, "don't look at the chipmunks. I know you too well. You'll start to laugh, and that will make me start to laugh, and we'll never be able to stop."

Following his example, I stared straight ahead in fierce concentration. I focused on the vegetarian chef. He was showing Oprah how to blend zucchini to make delicious zucchini bread for the holidays. He knocked over the blender, which sprayed pureed zucchini all over the interview couch. Then it was time for the commercial break.

Oprah did exactly what I would have done in the same situation, and turned over the cushions on the couch. She wiped off the back of the couch with the *Baltimore Sun*, and said, "Okay, boys, sit down and don't mention the zucchini." We sat down. During the interview I felt zucchini dripping into my shoes. The chipmunks were laughing so hard about the zucchini that they might not have been able to sing "The Chipmunk Christmas Song."

I realized during this show that Oprah Winfrey was a natural on television, although she could use a better booker. A few months later, the job of hosting *AM Chicago* opened up. I remember being the guest host one morning. My guest was Sophia Loren. She was promoting her new perfume. I'm not sure, but I think it was named "Sophia." I don't know much about perfume, but it was an opportunity to learn.

"What do you make the perfume from?" I asked Miss Loren.

"Make it?" she said. "What from?"

"Like flowers or stuff?"

"I don't make it myself, you know," she said. "I don't stir it up."

"No, but I just thought . . ."

"It doesn't matter what goes into it, as long as it smells so nice," she said.

I have found this a valuable rule over the years.

Oprah Winfrey was hired away from the Baltimore station to host *AM Chicago*. It was opposite the top-rated Phil Donahue. Within a few weeks, Phil Donahue was no longer top-rated. Oprah's show was expanded to an hour and became a smash hit.

At about this time, Oprah and I went out on a date. Well, actually two dates, but the one that made history began when we went to the movies. Afterward, we went to the Hamburger Hamlet for dinner, my treat.

"I don't know what to do," she told me. "The ABC stations want to syndicate my show. So does King World. The problem with syndication is that if your show isn't successful, you're off the air in three months. The ABC stations own themselves, so they can keep you on. Which way do you think I should go?"

I took a napkin and a ballpoint pen and made some simple calculations.

Line 1: How much I make in a year for doing a syndicated television show.

Line 2: Times 2, because Siskel makes the same.

Line 3: Times 2, because Oprah would be on for an hour, instead of half an hour.

Line 4: Times 5, because she would be on five days a week.

Line 5: Times 2, because her ratings would be at least twice as big as *Siskel & Ebert.*

I pushed the napkin across the table. Oprah studied it for ten seconds.

"Rog, I'm going with King World," she said.

With simple high school–level math, you can now figure out how much Oprah Winfrey makes in a year.

Step 1: Estimate how much I made in a year, twenty years ago.

Step 2: Carry out the other multiplications described above.

Step 3: Times 20.

Polar Express Rerelease

November 23, 2005—I've seen *The Polar Express* twice, once the regular way, once in 3 D at an IMAX theater. It returned in three dimensions to IMAX theaters in November 2005 and it was worth the special effort to seek it out. This was a wonderful moviegoing experience.

In general, I haven't been a fan of 3-D, with its murky images and pathetic little cardboard glasses. But IMAX does it right, and I was astonished by how effective *The Polar Express* was in 3-D on the big IMAX screen. The theater handed out new oversized 3-D glasses, big enough to fit over your own glasses, light enough so you can forget them, that made this the best 3-D viewing experience I had ever had.

As for the film, it's a movie in the process of becoming an enduring classic. It had the misfortune to open opposite *The Incredibles*, which was an enormous hit, but it didn't fold up and go away. Instead, week by week, it kept discovering new audiences, as word of mouth spread. Its 3-D screenings at IMAX theaters were almost always sold out.

Tom Hanks is everywhere in the movie. He voices five of the characters and provides the model for their body movements. Hanks and director Robert Zemeckis create something deeper and more mysterious, more filled with wonderment, than your usual slam-bang family entertainment. The film has the quality of a lot of lasting children's entertainment: It's a little creepy. Not creepy in an unpleasant way, but in that sneaky, teasing way that lets you know eerie things could happen. There's a deeper, shivery tone, instead of the mindless jolliness of the usual Christmas movie. This one creates a world of its own, like *The Wizard of Oz* or *Willy Wonka*, in which the wise child does not feel too complacent.

Those who know the Chris Van Allsburg book will feel right at home from the opening moments, which quote from the story: "On Christmas Eve, many years ago, I lay quietly in my bed. . . ." The young hero is listening for the sound of sleigh bells ringing. He is at just the age when the existence of Santa Claus is up for discussion.

The look of the film is extraordinary, a cross between live action and Van Allsburg's artwork. Zemeckis, the same director whose *Who Framed Roger Rabbit* juxtaposed live action with animation, this time merges them, using a process called "performance capture," in which human actors perform the movements, which are translated into lifelike animation. The characters in *Polar Express* don't look real, but they don't look unreal either; they have a kind of simplified and underlined reality that makes them visually magnetic.

The story follows Hero Boy as he awakens on Christmas Eve and finds himself aboard a train for the North Pole. On board are Hero Girl, Lonely Boy, Know It All, The Conductor, and the mysterious Hobo, who seems to live on top of the train. The North Pole is far from the jolly Santa's Workshop seen in routine kiddie pictures, and Hero Boy's experiences are more a coming of age than a cheerful adventure. The film resonates.

As I wrote in my original review, *The Polar Express* is a movie for more than one season; it will become a perennial, shared by the generations. It has a haunting, magical quality because it has imagined its world freshly and played true to it, sidestepping all the tiresome Christmas clichés that children have inflicted on them this time of year. The Conductor tells

Hero Boy he thinks he really should get on the train, and I have the same advice for you.

In Defense of *Crash*

January 3, 2006—Having selected *Crash* as the best film of 2005, I was startled to learn from Scott Foundas, a critic for *LA Weekly*, that it is the worst film of the year. In the annual Slate.com Movie Club, a roundtable also involving Slate's David Edelstein, the *Chicago Reader*'s Jonathan Rosenbaum, and A. O. Scott of the *New York Times*, he wrote:

"Not since *Spanglish*—which, alas, wasn't that long ago—has a movie been so chockablock with risible minority caricatures or done such a handy job of sanctioning the very stereotypes it ostensibly debunks. Welcome to the best movie of the year for people who like to say, 'A lot of my best friends are black.'"

That group must include (understandably, I suppose) the membership of the African-American Film Critics Association, who didn't get the wake-up call from Foundas in time to avoid voting *Crash* as their best film of the year. "The films selected for 2005 boldly reflect a bridge toward tolerance," said Gil Robertson IV, president of the association.

That's what I thought about *Crash*. I believe that occasionally a film comes along that can have an influence for the better, and maybe even change us a little.

Crash shows the interlinked lives of Los Angelinos who belong to many different ethnic groups, who all suffer from prejudice, and who all practice it. The movie, written and directed by Paul Haggis, doesn't assign simplistic "good" and "evil" labels but shows that the same person can be sometimes a victim, sometimes a victimizer. To say it "sanctions" their behavior is simply wrongheaded.

Crash is a film that, for much of its effect, depends on the clash of coincidental meetings. A white racist cop sexually assaults a black woman, then the next day saves her life. His white partner, a rookie, is appalled by his behavior but nevertheless later kills an innocent man because he leaps to a conclusion based on race. A black man is so indifferent to his girlfriend's Latino heritage that he can't be bothered to remember where she's from. After a carjacking, a liberal politician's wife insists all their locks be changed—and then wants them changed again, because she thinks the Mexican-American locksmith will send his "homies" over with the passkey. The same locksmith has trouble with an Iranian store owner who thinks the Mexican-American is black. But it drives the Iranian crazy that everyone thinks he is Arab, when they should know that Iranians are Persian. Buying a gun to protect himself, he gets into a shouting match with a gun dealer who has a lot of prejudices about, yes, Arabs.

And so on, around and around. The movie is constructed as a series of parables, in which the characters meet and meet again; the movie shows them both sinned against and sinning. The most poignant scene is probably the one in which a mother can see no evil in her son who is corrupt, and finds nothing but fault with her son who is a kind man and good to her. She thinks she knows them.

When *Crash* opened, I wrote: "Not many films have the possibility of making their audiences better people. I don't expect *Crash* to work any miracles, but I believe anyone seeing it is likely to be moved to have a little more sympathy for people not like themselves."

I believe that. The success of the film suggests it struck a lot of people the same way; opening in spring of 2005 as a low-profile release, it held its box office and slowly built through word of mouth. It opened in May 2005 with a $9 million weekend and by September had grossed $55 million. *Crash* and *March of the Penguins* were the two most successful "word of mouth" pictures of the year.

In my original review, I wrote: "If there is hope in the story, it comes because as the characters crash into one another, they learn things, mostly about themselves. Almost all of them are still alive at the end and are better people because of what has happened to them. Not happier, not calmer, not even wiser, but better."

How, then, can this be the worst movie of the year? It is not only Foundas who thinks so, but indeed even Jim Emerson, who edits rogerebert.com, and said it made him gasp and guffaw. But Emerson allows, "at least it has the up-front audacity to dare looking ridiculous by arguably reaching beyond its grasp." And here is Dave White of MSNBC: "Kids, racism is really, really, really bad and

wrong. Look, just watch this heavy, important movie about how everyone who lives in Los Angeles—all twelve of them—is super racist and awful. . . . it's really funny when Hollywood decides to tackle a serious moral issue and throw star-powered weight behind something that everyone but neo-Nazis agrees on already."

Foundas, in his Slate.com attack, says the movie is "one of those self-congratulatory liberal jerk-off movies that rolls around every once in a while to remind us of how white people suffer too, how nobody is without his prejudices, and how, when the going gets tough, even the white supremacist cop who gets his kicks from sexually harassing innocent black motorists is capable of rising to the occasion. How touching."

Of these three, Emerson is at least good-hearted, but Foundas and White seem actually angry at the film, even contemptuous. In a year that gave us *Chaos* and *Deuce Bigalow: European Gigolo,* this seems a strange choice of target.

White's comments indicate, I guess, that racism is dead in America, except for neo-Nazis, and that anyone making a movie about it is a fool. How glib, how smug, how insular. It is almost impossible these days to get financing and backing for any sort of serious film; White seems to think Hollywood makes them for fun.

Foundas is too cool for the room. He is so wise, knowing, and cynical that he can see through *Crash* and indulge in self-congratulatory superiority because he didn't fall for it. Referring to the wife who distrusts the locksmith, he writes: "When Sandra Bullock's pampered Brentwood housewife accuses a Mexican-American locksmith of copying her keys for illicit purposes, Haggis doesn't condemn her reprehensible behavior so much as he sympathizes with it."

This is a misreading of the film, but look at it more closely: Bullock is "pampered" and a "housewife," yet Haggis "sympathizes" with her behavior. Does he? No; I would say he *empathizes* with it, which is another thing altogether. She has just been carjacked at gunpoint and is hysterical. If Foundas were carjacked at gunpoint, would he rise to the occasion with measured detachment and sardonic wit? I wouldn't. Who will cast the first stone? And notice that the Mexican-American locksmith (Michael Pena) remains so invisible to Foundas that the actor is not named and Foundas has not noticed that the scene also empathizes with him.

Consider now Foundas describing the black TV director who stands by fearfully as a cop assaults his wife. Terrence Howard, Foundas says, plays the "creepy embodiment of emasculated African-American yuppiedom." Say what? As a black man in Los Angeles, Howard's character is fully aware that when two white cops stop you for the wrong reason and one starts feeling up your wife, it is prudent to reflect that both of the cops are armed and, if you resist, in court you will hear that you pulled a gun, were carrying cocaine, threatened them, and are lying about the sexual assault. Notice also, please, that the TV director's wife (Thandie Newton) makes the same charge of emasculated yuppiedom against her husband that Foundas does—and her husband answers it. Their argument may cut closer to some of the complex and paradoxical realities of race in America than any other scene this year.

It is useful to be aware of the ways in which real people see real films. I've had dozens of conversations about *Crash* with people who were touched by it. They said it might encourage them to look at strangers with a little more curiosity before making a snap judgment.

These real moviegoers are not constantly vigilant against the possibility of being manipulated by a film. They want to be manipulated; that's what they pay for, and that, in a fundamental way, is why movies exist. Usually the movies manipulate us in brainless ways, with bright lights and pretty pictures and loud sounds and special effects. But a great movie can work like philosophy, poetry, or a sermon.

It did not occur to many of its viewers that *Crash* was a "liberal" or for that matter a "conservative" film, as indeed it is neither: It is a series of *stories* in which people behave as they might and do and will, and we are invited to learn from the results. Not one in 10,000 audience members would agree with Foundas that *Crash* sympathizes with Bullock's character. They are not too cool, but at room temperature.

Now back to those awards from the African-American Film Critics Association. It named Howard as best actor for *Hustle & Flow*, and Felicity Huffman as best actress for *Transamerica*. Hold on! Huffman is white! How could she be the best-actress choice of the African-American critics? Because, Robertson says, they thought she gave the year's best performance. Is *Transamerica*'s story of a transsexual merely one more case of Hollywood (let's get this right) throwing its star-powered weight behind something that everyone but neo-Nazis agrees on already? Or could there possibly be a connection between such an award and the message of *Crash*? Now how about that?

Is *Unknown White Male* a Fake?

February 21, 2006—On July 3, 2003, a man named Doug Bruce found himself on a subway train in Coney Island with no idea of who he was or how he got there. After several days, authorities were able to establish that he was a New York stockbroker, in his early thirties, born in Britain. He was diagnosed with a rare case of retrograde amnesia.

Or maybe not. Maybe none of this is true.

Bruce is the subject of *Unknown White Male*, a documentary that played at Sundance 2005 and later went into release around the country. From the day it premiered, there has been speculation that it is actually a "mockumentary," an elaborate fraud. The charge is indignantly denied by the director, Rupert Murray, who says he'd known Bruce for years and became fascinated when he heard what had happened to his friend.

Bruce's hobby was photography, we learn, and he started keeping a video diary of his experiences that Murray was (conveniently) able to use in following his life after Coney Island. We see him being cared for by a former girlfriend, meeting family and old pals in London and Spain, and falling in love with a new girlfriend who says she's not concerned that he remembers nothing of his former life. Friends and family agree he's a nicer guy now than he used to be.

Articles in *Variety* on February 16, 2006, and in the London *Guardian* on February 20, 2006, reopen the controversy. *Variety* says Home Box Office considered buying the picture "but ultimately decided it was less than credible after some initial research." Michel Gondry, whose fiction film *Eternal Sunshine of the Spotless Mind* dealt with amnesia, told the *Guardian* he didn't think the story was authentic.

But Beadie Finzi, the film's coproducer, told the newspaper she was "outraged." The *Guardian* quotes her: "He had gone through so much, been brave enough to reveal and expose himself in this documentary. And then for people to dismiss it as a fake was appalling. I felt very protective and very angry."

All accounts point out that Bruce's form of amnesia is diagnosed by the reputable Daniel L. Schacter, chairman of psychology at Harvard. He is indeed seen on camera. But did he *diagnose* Bruce, or simply *describe* such a condition?

I saw the film not long ago and found it dramatic and convincing. Richard Roeper and I gave it two thumbs up on our TV show, Roeper saying he wondered about its credibility. The more I thought about *Unknown White Male,* the more I also began to find it faintly fishy. There is a moment when Bruce is back home in London, and as the car takes him past Buckingham Palace he says, "Who lives there?" Amnesia or not, isn't that a little too perfect? Who, looking at that vast building and knowing nothing about it, would think *anyone* lived there?

The film says that after the young man was found lost and confused, news accounts of his dilemma failed to identify him. Only a phone number in his knapsack, of the mother of a woman he had dated once or twice, led to his identification.

As a newspaperman, I wondered: How could a thirtysomething stockbroker live and work for several years in New York in both the financial and photography worlds, disappear, have his picture appear in the papers and on TV, and not be recognized by *someone*?

That led me to LexisNexis, a database search engine that prowls the complete texts of newspapers. I wanted to read the original news stories about Bruce's discovery in Coney Island and the search for his identity.

I couldn't find any. Searching both American and British papers for 2003, and then for the past five years, I found no news items at all

about Doug or Douglas Bruce, amnesiac, with or without the keywords Coney Island. Nor any stories about Coney Island and amnesia in 2003 without Bruce's name. Nothing at all. Separate searches of the *New York Times* and London *Telegraph* files also failed to turn up anything. All the stories on Google and Google News deal with the movie.

Either this case was not reported at the time, although the movie says it was, or I don't know how to use LexisNexis. The second theory is a good one. Still, I think it's fair to raise the question of the film's authenticity, since Josh Braun, a sales rep for the film at Sundance, told *Variety*: "The question mark of whether it's real or not could be a great way to direct people to see the movie. We believed it was 100 percent real. It seems too elaborate to keep the whole thing going. But even from the beginning, we said that an element of the marketing of the film is, 'Is this real or isn't it?'"

Documentary Is Not a Fake

February 22, 2006—I am persuaded that the documentary *Unknown White Male* is either a) factual and authentic, or b) the most convincing mockumentary ever made. In a recent story, I cited rumors and questions about the film. It tells the story of Doug Bruce, who on July 3, 2003, found himself on a subway train in Coney Island with no idea who he was or how he got there. He was subsequently diagnosed with retrograde amnesia, and the film charts his life as he deals with his condition.

The film is the remarkable story of a man trying to rebuild his sense of self. He remembers nothing about his earlier years as a stockbroker, a photographer, a son, a friend. The film's director, Rupert Murray, had known Bruce since they were both eighteen or nineteen, and began making the film when he learned of the amnesia.

The possibility that the film is a hoax has been raised in articles in *Variety, GQ,* the London *Guardian,* and the London *Daily Mail.* They point out that Murray coincidentally met with Bruce in New York three months before the amnesia incident, that he's vague on how he first met Bruce or where his friend worked or lived, that the Harvard expert cited in the film as an authority on amnesia never actually met Bruce. To these questions I added one of my own: Why did a LexisNexis search of the databases of all U.S. and U.K. newspapers reveal not a single story about this young man who was trying to find out who he was?

Excellent questions. I spoke with Murray and with the film's executive producer, Jess Search, and they provided answers.

Why no news items?

"Doug was taken to the hospital in Coney Island at 8 A.M. and by midnight had been collected at the hospital by his friend Nadine," said Search. In the film, Nadine is tracked down through the telephone number of her mother, found in Bruce's possession. "It never made the papers because there was no need to release a story and photo asking who he was. He'd been identified, so it remained a personal story."

Why was there convenient video material from very early in his experience?

The impression that there was a six-day search for his identity was perhaps given by the film's use of a video interview with Bruce six days after the event, Murray said, but the video was made in his home "by a couple of guys, friends of Nadine, that they met in a sushi bar. They thought his story was incredible and sat him down and did the interview. Doug told me about it when I started on the film."

Why is Murray vague about details of his friendship with Bruce, or details of his friend's life during the forgotten years?

"I can't actually remember the first time we met. We were eighteen or nineteen. It was in London. We had a large group of mutual friends. Most of those days for me are quite hazy. When you think about your friends, you may be surprised how few finite details you know. Why didn't I know the name of his stockbroking firm? Quite frankly, I made films and went to art school. I didn't know or care what firm he worked for. I'd call him up in New York and we'd go out for a drink."

What's the story with Daniel L. Schacter, chairman of psychology at Harvard?

"He is America's leading expert on amnesia," Search said. "His role in the film is to explain what it is. We used him as a reference point. He is not presented in the film as being Doug's doctor."

Why have so many viewers suspected the film was a hoax?

"It is possibly my fault as a filmmaker," said Murray. "I wasn't only a filmmaker; I was a friend. When I met him for the first time (after the incident), there was no doubt in my mind he was telling the truth. I didn't feel the need to wheel out doctor after doctor. I was more interested in the impact of the event on Doug and his family and friends."

Does the possibility of a hoax help promote the film?

"I would never compromise my reputation by being party to a hoax," says Search. "I worked five years as commissioning editor at Channel 4 in the U.K. I set up the British Documentary Film Foundation. I am the organizer of the new British documentary festival. I am 100 percent behind this film."

Murray adds: "The hoax issue clouds people's judgment. The film is so fascinating as a story of memory and identity that it would be a shame if it were discounted. The publicity may be great for the film, but it's not so great for Doug, after what he's been through."

But could it be the greatest mockumentary ever made?

"We've had that reaction many times over," Search said. "We're good, but not that good. If it's actually a piece of drama, it's unbelievably brilliant."

On Charles Dickens and *Crash*

February 16, 2006—I was reading Charles Dickens the other day and realized in a different way why *Crash* is such a good and useful film. Dickens is the best storyteller in the history of the novel, and although I've read him pretty much from end to end, I got into an argument about the character in *The Squid and the Whale* who tells his son that *A Tale of Two Cities* is "minor Dickens." I thought this opinion was correct, but I reread it for the first time since I was a child and found that it was not minor Dickens after all.

Dickens wrote melodramas and romances, comedies and tragedies, usually within the same story. He was a social reformer, filled with an anger that had its beginnings when his father was thrown into a debtor's prison and young Charles was yanked from a happy family into a precarious existence as a child laborer in a blacking factory. His targets were corrupt educators, exploiters of children and defenseless women, windbags, cheats, hypocrites, and toadies. He painted them with broad strokes and assigned them names to reflect their weaknesses: Mr. Gradgrind was a cruel schoolmaster, Scrooge the archetypal tightwad, the Cheeryble Brothers saw the good side of everything, Miss Havisham got a sham instead of a husband, and I don't know why Uriah Heep's name makes me think of bodily wastes, but it does.

These characters had flaws that defined their personalities. They occupied plots in which coincidence was the bedrock of the story. It was absolutely necessary that characters turn up precisely when the plot required them and that those with shady pasts turned out to be concealing the very secret that was needed in the present. *Masterpiece Theater* has serialized *Bleak House,* in which many scraps of paper are thrown out, but not the crucial one; in which a young woman's mother turns out to be the very person she is required to be; in which only those conversations are overheard that must be preserved; in which an orphan's protector fortuitously holds the key to her happiness.

Caricatures and coincidences are not weaknesses in Dickens, but his method. And *Crash,* which was my choice as the best film of 2005, uses exactly the same tools. The film's critics believe its characters are caricatures, and they say its Los Angeles seems to be populated by twenty people who are always crossing paths. Surely life is not a nonstop series of racist confrontations and coincidences?

Well, of course not. But the movie is not about life in general. It is about how racism wounds and stings, and makes its victims feel worthless and its perpetrators ugly and vicious. All true enough, but the brilliance of the movie's method is that victims and victimizers change places, and *Crash* demonstrates how in a complex multiracial society there is enough guilt to go around.

The story lines involving the two cops (Matt Dillon and Ryan Phillippe) and the upper-crust black couple (Terrence Howard and Thandie Newton) have inspired the most

discussion. On one day, Dillon stops Howard for DWB (driving while black) and commits a sexual assault against his wife, while the other two men stand by impotently—Howard aware that if he challenges the cop he could get arrested or killed, Phillippe a rookie who is intimidated by his brutal partner.

We follow the characters into their lives. Newton and Howard have a lacerating argument in which each says unforgivable things, and each blames the other for pain and ugliness that certainly was not either's fault. Dillon is seen in all the frustration of trying to care for his dying father in the face of heartless HMOs. Phillippe is seen as a decent cop trying to distance himself from Dillon's indecencies. And then, the next day . . .

Well, either you know what happens, or I should not tell you. The point is made that in different situations, the same people behave in different ways. One life is saved, another lost, not in the way we anticipate. The film does *not* forgive Dillon's character or excuse his crime; it simply shows that on both days he has done what it is in his nature to do. The film deals here and elsewhere in irony, in the bitter truth that human nature doesn't divide us into heroes and villains but gives us situations in which we behave badly, or well.

A lot of the film's scenes involve misunderstandings. Many of the racist assumptions are incorrectly aimed; a man of Iranian (i.e., Persian) descent is infuriated that anyone would think he is an Arab, but he leaps to immediate suspicions about the ethnic identity of the young man changing his lock. And then the locksmith . . .

I get in a lot of discussions with strangers about films. *Crash* is the one that keeps coming up. Those who dislike it assume it should be more "realistic," reflect "the Los Angeles I know," be less "manipulative," "not celebrate paranoia," not be so "facile." Those who admire it have a different tone in their voice. They say the movie made them think, made them look within themselves, made them realize that society has shuffled the packs of good and evil and made it more difficult for the good to always be Us and the evil to always be Them. The movie invited them to see that everyone has a story—a story that does not excuse or justify their actions but places them in a context.

People wrote me. I heard from a black woman who was surprised to find herself sympathizing with the Sandra Bullock character. Well, why shouldn't she? You don't have to be white to be paranoid after a carjacking (to think you do is racist). I heard from a Canadian with a North American Indian background ("First Nation," as they say in Canada). Because of his appearance, people can't immediately identify him by race, but sometimes they think they can, and he is treated in different ways by those who think he is Asian, Latino, Arabic, or African-Canadian; he learns firsthand about the subtleties of racial prejudice.

Crash is not a movie with answers, and maybe not even with questions. Maybe it is all made of observations. In a time when we are encouraged to draw sharp lines and leap to immediate conclusions, here is a movie that asks us to think twice, to look again, to look also within ourselves. "It made me think," a lot of people say.

Yes, you can dismiss it, deplore its contrivances, think that by exposing its methods you have invalidated the film. You can demolish Dickens in the same way. But social arguments are not won by drawing subtle logical distinctions. Dickens brought about actual changes in laws involving education, child labor, bankruptcy, insanity, and legalized theft from estates. He did it with caricature, coincidence, exaggeration, honesty, passion, and truth. *Crash* uses the same methods with the same hopes. It is not an unworthy undertaking.

Indie Spirits Awards

Santa Monica, California, March 6, 2006—On the eve of the Academy Awards, the Independent Spirits Awards sometimes provide advance clues to Oscar winners. But Saturday's indiefest under the big tent on the beach at Santa Monica spread the awards so evenly that omens were hard to spot. *Brokeback Mountain* and *Crash,* thought to be the Oscar front-runners, both won: *Brokeback* for best picture, *Crash* for best first film by a director.

Some wondered why such major Oscar contenders were even included in the indie field. Shouldn't the awards be focused more on outsider and overlooked films? "Welcome to the awards that spotlight struggling artists," said emcee Sarah Silverman, "like Ang Lee and George Clooney." Lee, who won as best director for *Brokeback,* remembered that he first attended the Indies with his little comedy *The Wedding Banquet* in 1994.

The best picture and directing awards for *Brokeback* didn't translate into acting prizes, however. Best actor, as expected, was Philip Seymour Hoffman, for *Capote,* who praised his fellow nominees and said on the day before the Oscars, "I've been given enough." Best actress was Felicity Huffman, who played a male-to-female transsexual in *Transamerica,* and got a big laugh remembering a day on location in the desert "when the driver got drunk and took the keys to Mexico, and the caterer quit and our producer had to go to Denny's, and a lamp exploded and blew glass all over the set, and I saw our key grip up on a fifteen-foot stepladder with a flashlight in his mouth, trying to rig another light, and saying, 'This ——ing story better win some ——ing prizes or we're all wasting our ——ing time.'"

The best supporting actress award went to Amy Adams, who won for playing the youthful earth mother who holds her improbable family together in *Junebug.* Best supporting actor was Matt Dillon, as a cop both corrupt and heroic in *Crash.*

Paradise Now, which has inspired opposition to its portrait of two Palestinian terror bombers, won as best foreign film; the voters apparently agreed with the nominating committee that the film's purpose was not to support bombers but to shed light on the world that produces them. The best documentary was *Enron: The Smartest Guys in the Room.*

For cinematography, Robert Elswit's black-and-white images in *Good Night, and Good Luck* won the Indie. Best screenplay went to Dan Futterman for *Capote,* and best first screenplay to Duncan Tucker of *Transamerica.* ("Isn't that a strange name for the man who wrote and directed *Transamerica*?" mused Silverman.

The John Cassavetes award for best feature under $500,000 went to the makers of *Conventioneers,* which plugged actors into the two 2004 political conventions. The $25,000 AMC/American Express Award to a visionary producer went to Caroline Baron, of *Capote* and *Monsoon Wedding*. The $25,000 IFC/ Acura Award for a director deserving wide recognition went to Ian Gamazon and Neill Dela Llana, directors of *Cavite*. And the $25,000 Truer Than Fiction award, to emerging documentary directors, went to Garrett Scott and Ian Olds for their Iraq documentary *Occupation: Dreamland*. A shaken Olds accepted the award: "Garrett Scott died of a heart attack four days ago, at thirty-seven. I wasn't going to come today, but I came for him."

Following hosts such as John Waters and Samuel L. Jackson, Silverman was hilarious as she negotiated a fine line between taste/no taste in her monologue about vaginal sprays. Director Kevin Smith broke through that line and did a couple of laps in his monologue, which recalled that he met his wife on a first date at the Indies nine years ago. Based on what he said next, he may be divorced by next year's ceremony.

Crash Takes Top Honor at Joyous Seventy-Eighth Oscar Ceremony

Los Angeles, California, March 6, 2006— *Crash*, a film about the complexities of racism in the American melting pot, was named the year's best picture at the 78th Academy Awards. It tells interlocking stories about many of America's ethnic groups, cops and criminals, the rich and the poor, the powerful and powerless, all involved in racism. The film's circular structure shows how a victim on one day could be a victimizer on another, and it doesn't let anyone off the hook.

In an evening when no single film dominated, four films took three Oscars apiece: *Crash, Brokeback Mountain, King Kong,* and *Memoirs of a Geisha.*

The win for *Crash* was a surprise to the Oscar audience (though I predicted it). *Brokeback Mountain* was thought to be the favorite going into the ceremony. It won other major awards, including one for its director, Ang Lee. The two films both won writing Oscars: *Crash* for original screenplay, *Brokeback Mountain* for adaptation.

Although actor Don Cheadle, one of the producers of *Crash*, was not among those onstage to collect the Oscar, the award was a personal victory because he was instrumental in assembling the large cast of stars who worked

for far less than their usual salaries in a labor of love.

The win also extended the winning streak of its writer-director Paul Haggis, who wrote the screenplay for last year's best film, *Million Dollar Baby*. His success comes after a long career as a writer for TV and films. When he won the Independent Spirit Award March 5 for best first film as a director, the fifty-two-year-old acknowledged "the other boys and girls" who were nominated for their first efforts.

In an evening that saw upsets and surprises, two of the victories were widely expected: Philip Seymour Hoffman, named best actor for *Capote*, and Reese Witherspoon, best actress for *Walk the Line*. Hoffman led up to the Oscars by winning every other acting award in sight, and when he won at the Independent Spirit Awards, he said, "I've been given enough." But the big prize was still ahead.

"I'm overwhelmed," he told the academy audience. Thanking his friends, he quoted Van Morrison's lyrics: "I love, I love, I love." He thanked his mother: "She brought up four kids alone. She took me to my first play, she stayed up with me and watched the NCAA Final Four—we're at the party, Ma!"

Hoffman's reputation has been made as a superb character actor, playing varieties of strange characters in films such as *Boogie Nights, Magnolia,* and *Happiness*. His starring role as author Truman Capote was all the more impressive because he didn't look much like the famous Capote and yet was able to occupy the character fully.

Witherspoon was a wildly popular winner for the audience at the Kodak Theatre. Her screen career began in 1991 with perhaps the sweetest first kiss in movie history, in *The Man in the Moon*. The twenty-nine-year-old has been a charmer ever since, in films such as *Election, Legally Blonde,* and *Vanity Fair,* but in *Walk the Line,* she found serious notes and a new dramatic range in her performance as country singer June Carter Cash.

"Oh, my goodness!" she said. "Never thought I'd be here in my entire life, growing up in Tennessee!" Her costar and conominee Joaquin Phoenix looked on proudly as she singled him out ("He put his heart and soul into this performance") and musician T-Bone

Burnett ("who helped me realize my lifelong dream of being a country and western singer!"). And she teared up as she acknowledged her family, saying she saw a lot of the qualities of her grandmother in the character of June Carter Cash. She quoted the legendary singer—"I'm just tryin' to matter"—and said that was her own goal in life.

It was an extraordinary Oscarcast for several reasons. Not just for the quality of the winners, not just for Jon Stewart's triumph as emcee, but for the legendary director Robert Altman's startling revelation that he had a heart transplant more than ten years ago. In an industry where rumors of bad health can end careers, it was a statement of unusual courage, typical of Altman.

The overall tone of the Oscarcast was— well, the word is joyous. Perhaps keyed by Stewart's own high spirits and the infectious grins inspired by George Clooney, Meryl Streep, Ben Stiller, Lily Tomlin, Three 6 Mafia, and Dolly Parton, the evening was warm and upbeat, and more relaxed than many Oscarcasts.

There were a lot of questions about the choice of Stewart as emcee, and he answered them all almost immediately, with an opening monologue that was on target, topical, and funny. After scenes of other hosts, from Billy Crystal to David Letterman, turning down the job, Stewart walked on the stage as if it was his second home. His biggest laugh, referring to the singer Björk and her famous dress designed like a swan: "Björk couldn't be here this year. She was trying on her Oscar dress, and Dick Cheney shot her." Another good line, about the film George Clooney directed, cowrote, and appeared in: "*Good Night, and Good Luck* was not just Mr. Murrow's sign-off, but how Mr. Clooney ends all of his dates."

Throughout the show, Stewart's one-liners and zingers were perfectly timed and almost always on target. After one of the packages of classic clips: "I can't wait for the tribute to Oscar's greatest montages!" After all of the speculation about the selection of Stewart as a host, his performance deserves perhaps the highest tribute: He was as relaxed, amusing, and at home as Johnny Carson. The assignment is his again in future years, and in one night he positioned himself as the likely heir of a major late-night network talk slot.

In the night's first big prize, Clooney won as best supporting actor for his CIA agent in *Syriana,* a film where none of the characters fully understood the situation, and his agent never knew what role he was really playing for the agency. His Oscar might also have been in recognition of his role in the best picture nominee *Good Night, and Good Luck,* the story of the battle between broadcaster Edward R. Murrow and Senator Joseph McCarthy. Clooney directed, cowrote, and costarred in that film. The Oscar came after a year in which both films solidified his reputation as a serious film artist.

"Unless we all played the same role, I don't know how you can compare these performances," he said of his other nominees, joking that the Oscar would forever change how he is referred to: Now he'll be an Oscar winner "in addition to being the sexiest man alive in 1997, and a former Batman."

As he gave praise to the academy for its attention to social issues over the years, Clooney was notable in his acceptance speech for avoiding all the usual boring lists of thankyous to agents, writers, coproducers, and so on. His speech was an Oscar rarity: actually interesting.

Rachel Weisz won for best supporting actress for *The Constant Gardener,* playing a woman who is murdered in Africa after learning of a conspiracy to test dangerous drugs on unsuspecting victims. The film, based on a novel by John Le Carre, drew admiring reviews, and Weisz's performance made a deep impression, even though it exists mostly in flashbacks as her husband (Ralph Fiennes) tries to solve the mystery of her death. The actress, seven months pregnant, was radiant in her acceptance speech, honoring Le Carre for "this unflinching, angry story."

Ang Lee was a popular winner as best director, for *Brokeback Mountain.* "I want to thank two people who don't even exist," he said, "except for the artistry of Annie Proulx, Diana Ossana, and Larry McMurtry. Their names are Ennis and Jack." Those characters, he said, taught us about "great love itself." "I made this film right after my father passed away, and more than any other, I made this film for him."

Paul Haggis, who shared his *Crash* award with Bobby Moresco, quoted Bertold Brecht: "Art is not a mirror to hold up to society, but a hammer with which to shape it." His film, he implied, was such a hammer. The third Oscar for *Crash* came for best editing, by Hughes Winborne, reflecting the complexity of its interlocking stories.

Brokeback Mountain, as expected, won for best adapted screenplay, by Larry McMurtry and Diana Ossana. McMurtry, the legendary author of novels set in the West (*The Last Picture Show*), strode down the red carpet wearing a tuxedo coat, blue jeans, and cowboy boots. Ossana thanked author E. Annie Proulx ("She's right over there") for trusting them with her story. McMurtry mostly thanked Ossana, and then the Texas used bookstore proprietor thanked "all the booksellers of the world—remember that *Brokeback Mountain* was a book before it was a movie."

After years of overwrought production numbers weighing down the performances of nominated songs, what an impact Dolly Parton made by simply walking onstage and singing her "Travelin' Thru." Kathleen "Bird" York brought a power to the performance of her song "In the Deep" from *Crash* with simple, heartfelt vocals, subtle backup singers, and a backdrop of flames that, oddly enough, was subtle, too: It was typical of a ceremony with more class and style than many another Oscarcast.

And consider the evident joy of the rap group Three 6 Mafia (Jordan "Juicy J" Houston, Paul "DJ Paul" Beauregard, and Darnell "Crunchy Black" Carlton), as they were joined by Taraji P. Henson, one of the stars of the film, performing "It's Hard Out Here for a Pimp" from *Hustle & Flow*. (Stewart's helpful definition of a pimp: "Sort of like an agent with a better hat.") The song's cowriter, Cedric "Frayser Boy" Coleman, told me on the red carpet he knew the nomination was for real "when they sent a limousine to pick me up at my mama's house."

They'll send him some more limousines. In another upset, the Oscar went to "It's Hard Out Here for a Pimp." In their exuberant acceptance speech, Three 6 Mafia thanked

everyone from George Clooney to Oscarcast director Gil Cates. "Now *that's* how to make an acceptance speech," Stewart said.

Meryl Streep and Lily Tomlin brought down the house while introducing legendary director Robert Altman with an inspired delivery in his trademark overlapping dialogue. But they didn't step on each other's lines when they read a list of his great credits. The director has been nominated five times (*MASH, Nashville, The Player, Short Cuts, Gosford Park*), but his first Oscar was an honorary one, for lifetime achievement.

He interrupted a tumultuous standing ovation by quipping, "I've got a lot to say and they've got a clock on me. I always thought this kind of award meant it was over. Then it dawned on me I was in rehearsals for a play in London that opened last night, and I just finished my new film, *Prairie Home Companion*. So it's not over. And no other film director," he said, "has gotten a better shake than I've had. I've never had to make a film I didn't want to make. And to me, I've just made one long film."

He said he couldn't thank all of his collaborators, "so I'm gonna thank a doctor who's taking care of me, Jodie Kaplan." Then the eighty-one-year-old Altman made a startling revelation: "I'm here, in a way, under false pretenses. I have to become straight with you. Ten, eleven years ago, I had a total heart transplant. I got the heart of a young woman who was in her late thirties, and so by that kind of calculation, you may be giving me this award too early. I think I've got about forty years left on it."

South Africa won its first Oscar, as *Tsotsi* was honored for best foreign film. "God bless Africa," said writer-director Gavin Hood, singling out his star, Presley Chweneyagae. The baby-faced actor plays a township thug who kills without emotion, until he accidentally comes into possession of a baby who changes his life. It was the second foreign film nomination in a row for South Africa, which placed *Yesterday* last year and is experiencing a filmmaking renaissance.

Best documentary, as expected, went to *March of the Penguins,* so successful, it actually outgrossed all of this year's best picture nominees. The filmmakers came onstage holding penguin plush toys and thanked the academy with whistles they claimed were penguin-speak.

The original scores of motion pictures are sometimes meant to be consciously listened to by the audience, sometimes intended as almost unheard background. The winner for best score was Gustavo Santaolalla, whose compositions for *Brokeback Mountain* were heard, and remembered, and contributed in an important way to the elegiac emotional tone of the film. He dedicated his award to his mother, his country Argentina, and Latinos everywhere.

Though *Memoirs of a Geisha* was shut out of the major categories, it drew honors for its superb technical credits. It was honored for its Japanese period costumes, designed by Colleen Atwood, who won in 2003 for *Chicago*. Backstage in the press room, she was asked about the film's controversial use of Chinese actresses to play Japanese roles. "Those choices were not up to me," she said, "but the film was about a story, not a race." The film also won best art direction and set decoration for John Myhre and Gretchen Rau. Myhre, who accepted on behalf of Rau, was asked backstage why she didn't attend. "She is having some serious health issues right now," Myhre said, "which I would prefer for her family to address."

Splotchy-faced Steve Carell and Will Ferrell introduced the Oscar for best makeup, which went to *The Chronicles of Narnia: The Lion, the Witch, and the Wardrobe*, a film that created fantastical creatures not only with animation but with live-action makeup and costuming.

Stewart's one-liner: "I'm disappointed that *Cinderella Man* didn't win. Imagine making Russell Crowe look like he got in a fight."

Ben Stiller got more laughs with a special-effects bit using a green suit that would have disappeared in front of a green screen that was, however, lacking. He announced the visual effects Oscar for *King Kong*, the first of three technical awards for the giant-ape epic, which also picked up Oscars for sound mixing and sound editing.

Winner for live-action short: *Six Shooter* by Martin McDonagh of Ireland, starring Brendan Gleeson as a man whose wife dies; on the train ride home across Ireland, he sits across from an obnoxious young man of heartless cruelty, who picks on a couple across the aisle who have lost their baby. How long can the others put up with him?

The Oscar winner for best animated short was another hand-drawn film, *The Moon and the Son: An Imagined Conversation* by John Canemaker and Peggy Stern. It had extraordinary weight for a short subject, as it re-created a painful relationship between a son and his angry father. The voices by Eli Wallach and John Turturro gave realism and depth to the images, which segued from photographs to drawings.

The Oscar for best documentary short went to *A Note of Triumph: The Golden Age of Norman Corwin* by Corinne Marrinan and Eric Simonson. Corwin, who still teaches at the University of Southern California, was the producer of "On a Note of Triumph," a historic 1945 radio broadcast on V-E Day. The film, which serves as a rebuke to modern formula broadcasting, assembled many who remember the broadcast, including Chicago's own legendary Studs Terkel, who says, "I can still recite most of it."

Crash and Its Critics

Los Angeles, California, March 6, 2006—One of the mysteries of the 2006 Oscar season is the virulence with which lovers of *Brokeback Mountain* savaged *Crash*. When the film about racism actually won the Oscar for best picture, there was no grace in their response. As someone who felt *Brokeback* was a great film but *Crash* a greater one, I would have been pleased if either had won.

But here is Ken Turan in the *Los Angeles Times*, writing on the morning after: "So for people who were discomfited by *Brokeback Mountain* but wanted to be able to look themselves in the mirror and feel like they were good, productive liberals, *Crash* provided the perfect safe harbor. They could vote for it in good conscience, vote for it and feel they had made a progressive move, vote for it and not feel that there was any stain on their liberal credentials for shunning what *Brokeback* had to offer. And that's exactly what they did."

And Nikki Finke, in the *LA Weekly*: "Way back on January 17th, I decided to nominate the Academy of Motion Picture Arts and Sciences for Best Bunch of Hypocrites. That's because I felt this year's dirty little Oscar secret was the anecdotal evidence pouring in to me about hetero members of the Academy of Motion Picture Arts and Sciences being unwilling to screen *Brokeback Mountain*. For a community that takes pride in progressive values, it seemed shameful to me that Hollywood's homophobia could be on a par with Pat Robertson's."

Yes, and more than one critic described *Crash* as "the worst film of the year," which is as extreme as saying John Kerry was a coward in Vietnam. It means you'll say anything to help your campaign.

What is intriguing about these writers is that they never mention the other three best picture nominees: *Capote; Good Night, and Good Luck*; and *Munich*. Their silence on these films reveals their agenda: They wanted *Brokeback Mountain* to win, saw *Crash* as the spoiler, and attacked *Crash*. If *Munich* had been the spoiler, they might have focused on it. When they said those who voted for *Crash* were homophobes who were using a liberal movie to mask their hatred of homosexuals, they might have said the same thing about *Munich*.

This seems simply wrong. Consider Finke's "anecdotal evidence" that puts Hollywood's homophobia on a par with Pat Robertson's. *Pat Robertson*? This is certainly the most extreme statement she could make on the subject, but can it be true? How many anecdotes add up to evidence? Did anyone actually tell her they didn't want to see the movie because it was about two gay men?

My impression, also based on anecdotal evidence, is that the usual number of academy voters saw the usual number of academy nominees and voted for the ones they admired the most. In a year without *Brokeback Mountain*, Finke, Turan, and many others might have admired *Crash*. It is not a "safe harbor," but a film that takes the discussion of racism in America in a direction it has not gone before in the movies, directing attention at those who congratulate themselves on not being racist, including liberals and/or minority group members. It is a movie of raw confrontation about the complexity of our motives, about how racism works not only top down but sideways, and how in different situations we are all capable of behaving shamefully.

Good Night, and Good Luck; Capote; and *Munich* were also risky pictures—none more so, from a personal point of view, than *Munich*, which afforded Steven Spielberg the unique experience of being denounced as anti-Semitic. *Good Night, and Good Luck* was surely a "safe harbor" for liberals, with its attack at a safe distance on McCarthyism—although it carried an inescapable reference to McCarthyism as practiced by the Bush administration in its equation of its critics with supporters of terrorism. *Capote* was a brilliant character study of a writer who was gay, and who used his sexuality, as we all use our sexuality, as a part of his personal armory in daily battle.

It is noticeable how many writers on "Hollywood's homophobia" were able to sidestep *Capote*, which was a hard subject to miss, being right there on the same list of best picture nominees. Were *Brokeback*'s supporters homophobic in championing the cowboys over what Jon Stewart called the "effete New York intellectual"?

Of course not. *Brokeback Mountain* simply was a better movie than *Capote*. And *Crash* was better than *Brokeback Mountain*, although they were both among the best films of the year. That is a matter of opinion. But I was not "discomfited" by *Brokeback Mountain*. Read my original review. I chose *Crash* as the best film of the year not because it promoted one agenda and not another, but because it was a better film.

The nature of the attacks on *Crash* by the supporters of *Brokeback Mountain* seem to proceed from the other position: *Brokeback* is better not only because of its artistry but because of its subject matter, and those who disagree hate homosexuals. Its supporters could vote for it in good conscience, vote for it and feel they had made a progressive move, vote for it and not feel that there was any stain on their liberal credentials for shunning what *Crash* had to offer.

In Memoriam

Richard Pryor

Richard Pryor, one of the best and most influential comedians of his time, died December 10, 2005, at sixty-five, of heart failure, in a suburban Los Angeles hospital, according to his wife, Jennifer, who told Reuters, "He was my treasure."

He was a national treasure. Born in a brothel, accused of obscenity in his early stand-up days, nearly burned to death in an accident while freebasing cocaine, he went on to star in movies both good and bad. But as a live performer he was brilliant and fearless and found truths his audiences instinctively identified with.

Although the obituaries will make much of his nearly fatal accident and his long battle with multiple sclerosis, the most significant entry may be this one: In 1998, he won the first Mark Twain Prize for humor from the John F. Kennedy Center for the Performing Arts. He said in his acceptance speech he had been able to use humor as Mark Twain did, "to lessen people's hatred."

When you look again at his three great performance films, you realize that was exactly what he did: It was when he was live in front of an audience that the full range of his gifts was seen most clearly. Drugs muddled some of the early stages of his career, and his disease finally silenced him, but in the early 1980s, after he was clean and sober and before he fell ill, there was a flowering of genius. In 2004, Comedy Central placed him first on its list of the greatest stand-up comedians of all time.

Pryor was born December 1, 1940, in Peoria, Illinois, in a brothel his grandmother owned. He recalled his early years in *Jo Jo Dancer, Your Life Is Calling* (1986), an autobiographical film he wrote, directed, and starred in. He said it was not entirely factual, but the broad outlines of his life are there, including the day in 1980 when he ran screaming into a Los Angeles street, his body in flames.

He began as a stand-up comic and made a handful of films before his breakthrough in *Lady Sings the Blues* (1972), as Piano Man, the confidant of Billie Holiday (Diana Ross). Other important roles included *Uptown Saturday Night* (1974), *The Bingo Long Traveling All-Stars and Motor Kings* (1976), *Blue Collar* (1978), *Stir Crazy* (1980), and *Brewster's Millions* (1985).

Although Whoopi Goldberg was the first black host of the Academy Awards (1994), Pryor was the Oscar cohost in 1977, following earlier black cohosts Sammy Davis Jr. and Diana Ross. By then he was a major Hollywood star, teamed by the Oscars with Warren Beatty, Ellen Burstyn, and Jane Fonda. Oscar invited him back in 1983.

He had about twenty-five starring roles, often opposite Gene Wilder, who would play the straight man when they did interviews together. This is from their visit to Chicago to promote their biggest hit, *Silver Streak* (1976):

Wilder: What are you doing next?

Pryor: It's a movie called *Which Way Is Up?* This Italian director, Lina Wertmuller . . ."

Wilder: No! Oh, my God! I'll kill myself!

Pryor: What you moaning about, man?

Wilder: You're going to work with Lina Wertmuller? She passed right by me and saw you and said, "I must have that young man"?

Pryor: You didn't let me finish. She made this movie called *The Seduction of Mimi,* and this will be a remake, set among the grape pickers of California.

Wilder: I would have killed myself out of envy.

Pryor: And then I'm in a remake of *Arsenic and Old Lace.*

Wilder: Oh, my God! My favorite play next to *Hamlet.* All-black cast, I suppose, nothing for me.

Pryor: And then I'm doing *Hamlet.*

In *Silver Streak,* they did their own stunts, including one where they hung out of a train at 50 mph, Pryor holding Wilder by the belt. "I'm thinking, one slip of my foot and goodbye, Gene!" Pryor said.

"What gave me a lot of confidence," Wilder said, "was that Richie promised me that if I went, he went, too. If I fell off the train and was killed, he would throw himself after me."

"Of course," said Pryor, "they had me wired to the train."

Some of his films after that were not as good, including the dreadful *Harlem Nights* (1989) with Eddie Murphy, and in the late 1980s there was a visible slowing down, the result of multiple sclerosis. Wilder told me that when they made *Another You* (1991), Pryor had a daily struggle on the set; his performance, although impaired, was a triumph over his disease.

There was no slowing down, however, in the three concert films that will preserve his work at its peak. In *Richard Pryor Live in Concert* (1979), *Richard Pryor Live on Sunset Strip* (1982), and *Richard Pryor Here and Now* (1983), he earned full comparison with Bill Cosby, the grandmaster of the autobiographical stand-up genre.

In the 1982 film, he dealt frankly with his cocaine addiction and his accident. The movie was filmed live over two nights. We sense at the beginning that he is shaky, but he gains confidence and builds into "the most talented one-man stage show in existence right now," I wrote in my review, effortlessly bringing to life a series of impressions ranging from Mafioso to water buffalo.

The racial content of his humor was observational, not confrontational. In the 1982 concert, he mimes an impression of two whites passing each other on the street in Africa. In *Silver Streak*, Pryor told me, there was concern about a scene where Wilder appears in blackface and fools a white man. Pryor suggested a simple change that turned a possibly embarrassing scene into one of the biggest laughs in the film:

"Instead of a white dude being fooled by the disguise, a black dude comes in and isn't fooled. Here's Gene snapping his fingers and holding his portable radio to his ear, and the black dude takes one look and says, 'I don't know what you think you're doing, man, but you got to get the beat.'"

In *Live on Sunset Strip,* Pryor does a brilliant extended sequence involving his addiction to cocaine. He depicts himself alone in his room with his cocaine pipe, which speaks to him in reassuring, seductive tones. Only gradually do we realize that the pipe is speaking in the voice of Richard Nixon.

It is unclear whether all of Pryor's drug use was behind him when he made *Sunset Strip.* But in *Richard Pryor Here and Now,* he firmly states he is clean and sober, seems more relaxed than we've ever seen him before, and is growing from a comedian into a wise social observer. He does impressions of characters of many races, the humor based on empathy, and has fun with himself as an African-American feeling like a foreigner in Africa. In Zimbabwe, he tells an African how surprised he is to be able to speak English everywhere.

"Everybody speaks English," the African tells him, "but what language do you speak at home?"

There is an extended sequence at the end of that film where he shows a street addict shooting heroin. It begins in comedy, ends in pain, moves from self-deception to honesty, and goes far beyond stand-up into what can be described only as inspired acting. That was the direction he was moving in, and we can only wonder what heights he would have achieved if MS had not taken its cruel toll.

Pryor had seven marriages to five wives, including twice to Jennifer Lee (in 1981 and 2001) and twice to Flynn Belaine (in 1986 and 1990). He had seven children—Renee, Richard Pryor Jr., Elizabeth Stordeur, Rain Kindlin (herself an actress), Kelsey Pryor, Steven Pryor, and Franklin Mason—and three grandchildren.

Film Festivals

Telluride Film Festival
Report No. 1:
Eclectic Mix of Old and New

Telluride, Colorado, September 2, 2005—When I first came to the Telluride Film Festival in 1980, screenings were held in Quonset huts and city parks, the Masons Hall, the old Nugget theater on Main Street, and in the faded glory of the tiny Sheridan Opera House, built when this was a boom town in mining days. The 2005 festival, which takes place Labor Day weekend, still uses the opera house and the Mason's Hall, but has added so many state-of-the-art theaters, some of them constructed inside the school gyms, that it feels like the most happening art-movie town in America.

The movies, however, have continued to be an eclectic mix of new and old, experimental and mainstream. Yes, this year we are able to see two of the most widely heralded new biopics: James Mangold's *Walk the Line,* with Joaquin Phoenix and Reese Witherspoon as Johnny Cash and June Carter Cash, and Bennett Miller's *Capote,* with Philip Seymour Hoffman playing Truman Capote at the time he wrote *In Cold Blood,* and Catherine Keener as his friend Harper (*To Kill a Mockingbird*) Lee. And there's the new David Mamet screenplay, *Edmond,* with two of his longtime collaborators: actor William H. Macy and director Stuart Gordon.

But we also can see a program of little movies made on Macintosh computers, led with the new film by performance artist Laurie Anderson. And three of the favorite films of guest programmer Don DeLillo, the novelist, who includes the neglected Spanish classic *Spirit of the Beehive.* And a newly restored print of *King Kong.*

The Telluride Tributes are known for their diversity, and who could be more diverse than this year's honorees: actor and legend Mickey Rooney, actress and legend Charlotte Rampling, and Belgian codirectors Jean-Pierre and Luc Dardenne, whose *The Son* is one of the best films of recent years and who are here with the new film *The Child.*

The festival takes over the resort town of Telluride, which had FOR SALE signs in a lot of windows on Main Street the first year I attended and now has empty lots selling for $1 million. It is not easy to get to, but thousands make the trek, usually by flying through Denver to Montrose and then driving for ninety minutes. There is a Telluride airport, but having observed the position of the runway here in the mountains, I, for one, prefer the drive. Local hotels and ski lodges double their prices for the festival, but moviegoers share lodgings and sleeping bags, and everyone seems reasonably cheerful because the films are so good and it's fun just to stand in line with people who are as interested in movies as you are.

A few of this year's American premieres are from Cannes 2005, including Michael Haneke's *Hidden,* now for some reason given the less-than-compelling title *Caché.* It's about a Paris TV presenter who begins to receive videos indicating his family is under surveillance. What seems to begin as a thriller develops into a harrowing excursion into family tragedy. Also from Cannes, *Three Times,* the wonderful new film by Hou Hsiao-hsien, which stars Shu Qi and Chang Chen in three stories in which they play lovers at different times in China in the past century: 1911, 1966, and the present day.

Among the films being seen here for the first time are Neil Jordan's *Breakfast on Pluto,* starring Cillian Murphy as a cross-dressing Irishman who tries his chances in London (Jordan's *The Crying Game* created a sensation with a transsexual character). There is Ang Lee's new *Brokeback Mountain,* with a screenplay by Larry McMurtry based on Annie Proulx's famous short story, and starring Heath Ledger and Jake Gyllenhaal. And Richard Gere in *Bee Season,* by David Siegel and Scott McGehee; Gere's character is married to Juliette Binoche, and they try to redeem their lives through their children.

Oh, and there are a lot more films: a silent classic with a piano in the pit, DeLillo's revival of Antonioni's *The Passenger*, with Jack Nicholson, films from Iran and Hungary and Singapore. On opening night, festival cofounder Bill Pence always cheerfully explains that the schedule has been carefully arranged so that no one can see everything, or even half of everything. Knowing that the Toronto festival begins the following Thursday, the veteran festivalgoer uses Telluride to see films that can be seen nowhere else—and might, for that matter, never be seen anywhere again.

Telluride Report No. 2: Oscar Contenders Get First Showing

September 3, 2005—Oscar season opens every September with the Telluride and Toronto film festivals, and again this year, biopics seem to be leading the field. Last year in September we got our first looks at *Ray, Hotel Rwanda*, and *Kinsey*, and so far this year the leading contenders are *Walk the Line* and *Capote*. If no two people could be more different than Ray Charles and Alfred Kinsey, no two other people could be less alike than Johnny Cash and Truman Capote.

Walk the Line stars Joaquin Phoenix and Reese Witherspoon as the man in black and his wife, June Carter Cash. A review can await the film's opening, but let me observe that at one point, during a musical number, I closed my eyes to focus entirely on the music. As someone who knows Cash's music virtually by heart, I was convinced the movie was dubbed: That was Johnny Cash's real voice, just as *Ray* used the original Ray Charles recordings.

At the end of the movie, watching the credits, I was thunderstruck to discover that Phoenix had performed all of Cash's vocals. It was more than just a good impersonation; he nailed them. Witherspoon does her own vocals, too, confirming (as Kevin Spacey did last year with *Beyond the Sea*) that gifted actors are sometimes also gifted singers; it's just that we don't know it. If this were an era of movie musicals, these would be singing as well as acting stars. And now that every pop singer since 1940 seems to have a biopic in the wings, that era may be returning indirectly.

In *Capote*, Philip Seymour Hoffman plays the twee New York writer who won notoriety with his reclining photo on the jacket of his first book, fame with his novel *Breakfast at Tiffany's*, and critical acclaim with his nonfiction best seller *In Cold Blood*. Capote claimed he had invented the "nonfiction novel" with his minutely observed story of the slaughtered Clutter family of Holcomb, Kansas, and their killers: Dick Hickock and Perry Smith.

At the time, rumors swirled that Capote did less than he could have to help the killers get an appeal, because until they were executed his book could not be finished. *Capote* also draws that conclusion, in a fascinating character study of a man who was relentlessly focused and ruthless, despite his image as a sissy. Catherine Keener costars as the novelist Harper Lee, his best friend, who goes along with him to Kansas to babysit and lend a steadying hand; during this period she published her *To Kill a Mockingbird*.

Whether Hoffman impersonates Capote as well as Phoenix duplicates Cash's voice is not really the question; Hoffman does create a Capote who is complex and real, in a film that is unforgiving about the way a journalist can focus on what he knows is the story of his lifetime.

Also premiering during the first two days of Telluride: Ang Lee's *Brokeback Mountain*, starring Jake Gyllenhaal and Heath Ledger as two cowboys in the 1960s who fall in love despite the danger that creates for them in the world they occupy. And Stuart Gordon's *Edmond*, starring William H. Macy in an adaptation of a David Mamet play never before filmed, because it is so raw and confrontational.

Brokeback Mountain is based on an Annie Proulx short story, adapted by Larry McMurtry and Diana Ossana. It's a reminder of the lifelong relationship between Call and Gus, the stars of McMurtry's *Lonesome Dove* trilogy, although they were straight (but not the marrying kind). A review awaits the film's opening, but I can point to the detail with which *Brokeback Mountain* portrays two homosexuals who in appearance and behavior fit the popular notion of stalwart heterosexuals. "This stays between us," they say after their first night together. But can it, even through marriage and children?

William H. Macy has worked in Mamet

847

material since their early days together on the Chicago stage. Mamet's verbal rhythms and ellipses come naturally to Macy: the indirect statements, the emphasis on precise detail, the obscenity, the tendency toward dogmatic truisms, the sudden anger. Here he plays an executive who is jolted by a fortune-teller, walks out on his wife, goes looking to buy sex, has trouble because he doesn't want to overpay or be cheated, and eventually finds himself—where you will find him when you see the movie.

Edmond contains a litany of four-, six-, and twelve-letter words, and a thesaurus of racist language. It is a bitter, misogynistic film, directed by Stuart Gordon in a world of neon-lit peep shows, alarming taverns, dangerous streets, and unhappy bedrooms. Where its hero finds himself at the end is an irony, especially given the opinions he has earlier expressed, and whether it provides closure or simply a conclusion is a good question.

Telluride has a way of springing surprise sneak previews; last year it was *Neverland*, and this year it's Martin Scorsese's Bob Dylan picture, *No Direction Home*. That's coming up, along with all sorts of other riches; you stagger from one end of the village to another, knowing you can't see everything, standing in line for one movie while being told you should be standing in line for another one.

Telluride Report No. 3: Mickey Rooney

September 3, 2005—It is the longest career in the history of show business. Mickey Rooney first appeared on stage when he was seventeen months old. He made his first movie in 1925, when he was five, and on Friday night, there he was on the stage of the Sheridan Opera House at the Telluride Film Festival, telling stories, doing imitations, singing the song he wrote when Judy Garland died, and then joining his wife in a duet of "Let's Call the Whole Thing Off."

Rooney received the Telluride Medal. After festival codirector Bill Pence hung it around his neck, I was supposed to join the Mick onstage for a Q&A, but that had to wait ten minutes as he stepped before the footlights, rhapsodized about the golden years of Hollywood, did impressions of Clark Gable and

Humphrey Bogart, and told some jokes. Standing in the wings, I realized: He's a little taller than you think.

Earlier, we'd seen an hour of clip highlights from his career: The early Mickey McGuire comedies, which he claimed gave Walt Disney the name for Mickey Mouse. Scenes from the Andy Hardy films he made at MGM ("Hey, gang! Let's rent the old barn and put on a show!"). Dramas such as *Requiem for a Heavyweight*. And a remarkable nine-minute scene with Judy Garland from *Babes on Broadway*, where he tells her about the magic of the theater and then they perform a song-and-dance routine that ends with Rooney doing "Yankee Doodle Dandy."

"I'll bet a lot of the audience thought you were imitating Jimmy Cagney when you did 'Yankee Doodle Dandy,'" I told him when the Q&A began at last. "But you made *Babes* a year *before* he made *Yankee Doodle Dandy*, so he was imitating you."

Not at all, Rooney said. Cagney was a great actor. So were they all, everyone he worked with. Asked who his favorite costar was, he began with Clark Gable and then simply said, "They all were." Who was the hardest to work with? "They were all great to work with. Some not so much as others."

Watching the session from a box by the side of the stage was Jan, Rooney's wife of thirty-one years. "Everybody knows I've been married all those times," he said, "but really I've been married only once." He praised Jan and God for his longevity and success: "But not any particular religion. Just faith. You gotta have faith."

Telluride makes a specialty out of surprising its audiences with unexpected treasures, and in connection with Rooney's tribute the festival showed *The Comedian*, a 1957 live-on-TV "Playhouse 90" drama written by Rod Serling and directed by John Frankenheimer (who called Rooney "the best actor I've ever worked with"). The film, recently released on DVD, is a revelation for anyone who identifies Rooney with Andy Hardy.

He plays a comic with a monstrous ego who is one of the biggest stars on TV, and one of the meanest. Mel Torme plays his brother, long the butt of the jokes in his monologues. The brother begs to be dropped from the act, but on the first show of the new season, the comic is in mid-monologue when the brother appears before the live cameras in tears and begs him to stop. Rooney plays a man for whom performing is more important than anything: He passes off his brother's tears as a joke and then, astonishingly, throws him over his shoulder and runs offstage with him.

All of this on live TV, with no breaks, no doubles, no stunts. Just lifting him up and running off with him. "It was working without a net," Rooney remembered. "Once the show started, you were live all the way. What went wrong, went wrong. Frankenheimer worked with six cameras, and he had his shots so carefully planned you never would have thought it was all happening in real time."

He shared memories of working with the two great child actresses of his early years, Judy Garland and Elizabeth Taylor. "Judy was a wonderful person," he said. "She worked hard. She got tired. Doesn't everybody have the right to get tired? She took pills, and they took hold of her. I took pills, too, but I was lucky and was abler to stop them."

When the news came of her death, he said, he wrote a song in her memory. I asked him to sing it, and he did, softly, movingly. I praised his acting, saying that early and late he seemed utterly unforced and natural—a modern unaffected actor before his time.

"Everybody is an actor," he said. "You're acting right now, playing an interviewer."

He's still active. He and Jan tour in a two-person show with musical backup. "She does a great Patsy Cline." I called her onstage, and she did some Patsy Cline, and then they did the duet: "You say tomato, I say tomahto." As an intro to the song, they argued about who was supposed to go first. "Were they acting, or really having a fight?" someone asked after the show. They were acting, but well enough that you had to wonder.

Telluride Report No. 4: Good Movie Season Opens

September 5, 2005—Like the rains after a dusty season, the movies of September wash and refresh. You walk out of a screening here and think you have surely seen an Oscar nominee. You leave a second and third, and think the same thing. The 2006 Academy

Awards could be populated from this festival, with Toronto still to begin on Thursday. And that doesn't even account for the riches of the foreign films, and the revived classics, and the program called "Made on a Mac," of films by such as Laurie Anderson.

Are they still making good movies? Yes, they are, but you have to find them. Millions of dollars will not be spent to shove them down your throat. Consider two movies I saw back-to-back on Sunday: Neil Jordan's *Breakfast on Pluto* and *Bee Season*, by Scott McGehee and David Siegel. Both are about characters who impose an alternative reality on the difficulties of their lives.

Breakfast on Pluto stars Cillian Murphy, that brave survivor of the post-apocalyptic *28 Days Later*, the Scarecrow from *Batman Begins*, as an entirely different species of character. He plays Patrick Brady, who prefers to be called Patricia Kitten Brady, and who from his earliest days has preferred to live as a girl. No, he is not a "man trapped in a woman's body," but a person who chooses to present himself as he does because that is his nature.

In the Catholic school of his small town in the west of Ireland, he is an exasperation and a scandal. A priest (Liam Neeson) walks out of the confessional and slams the door behind him when he sees through the grating the soft-spoken young man in lipstick and makeup. Kitten's life purpose is a quest for his mother, who he thinks may have gone to London. His father, who might be easier to find, he is not as interested in.

The movie follows his journey from Ireland to London and from early adolescence into his twenties, but is not founded on grim reality. So persistent is Kitten's fantasy that he sometimes imposes it on the rough world. Even two British interrogators, who pound on him for a week, convinced he planted an IRA bomb in a pub, end up being won over by him. He makes no attempt to defend or deny but acts in optimism that all will see him as he sees himself.

There are sequences that could come from Dickens, such as one where he becomes a magician's assistant and is sawn in half and made the target of a knife-throwing trick. He has an ambivalence toward sex: Kitten works for a time as a prostitute and even in a Soho peep show, but there is little nudity and no specific sex at all. What matters more is his inner journey, to find the Phantom Lady he believes gave him birth.

Bee Season is a film that astonishingly combines mysticism with spelling bees, and centers on an extraordinary performance by Flora Cross, as a girl of about eleven who goes to the finals of the National Spelling Bee. This movie is about spelling as much as *Breakfast on Pluto* is about employment in London. It explores a murky family dynamic.

Her father (Richard Gere) is a professor who teaches Jewish mysticism and the Kabbalah. He is forever preparing family meals, feeding his family as if it is a kind of passion. Her mother (Juliette Binoche) is a woman damaged early by the deaths of her parents, quiet, smiling too much, deferring to her husband, with a private life of astonishing complexity. Her brother (Max Minghella) is on a spiritual quest of his own—one that leads away from his father's beliefs.

The father teaches that if all the shards of word and light could be brought back together, we could look upon the face of God. During the course of the movie the girl advances in a spelling bee, and the way she spells the words has something to do with a literal application of her father's theories in a way he cannot imagine. He thinks he knows all about the Kabbalah, but in his own house live three people whose mystical lives are far beyond his theory.

Conversations with Other Women is another of the best films I have seen here. Directed by Hans Canosa, it stars Aaron Eckhart and Helena Bonham-Carter in an idea that seems like a stunt and then deepens into the sadness of unrealized love. The stunt is that the entire film has been made in split screen, so that we are always looking at two pictures. The left is usually occupied by Eckhart, the right by Bonham-Carter, although they are free to enter each other's frames and sometimes seem to be standing so close that the frame division is a formality; other characters sometimes enter either frame.

They meet at a wedding. She is a "substitute bridesmaid." They talk. They flirt. They spend the night together. The nature of their complete relationship I will leave for you to discover. The movie is really about the passage of time and the finality of decisions taken and not taken—about the loneliness of men, who seem condemned to regret what they have not had, and women, more content to accept what they have chosen. The two actors are talking for almost the entire movie, which depends on tone and pitch to sustain its deepening insights. The split screen comes to seem necessary.

There were many other films here, some of which I will be able to see at Toronto. And some films I remember from Cannes 2005, including Hou Hsiao-hsien's elegant masterpiece *Three Times,* from Taiwan, and Michael Haneke's *Caché,* from France, which played at Cannes under the better title *Hidden.* It is about a Paris TV presenter who receives videos indicating his family is under observation. Whom do they come from, and what do they mean?

Where do any of these films come from, and what do they mean? After a summer during which we knew precisely where most of the films came from and how little they meant, Good Movie Season begins at Telluride, and now the celebration moves on to Toronto.

Toronto Film Festival
Toronto Report No. 1: World's Most Important Film Festival

Toronto, Canada, September 7, 2005—Is the Toronto Film Festival the most important in the world, or does it only seem that way? In recent years I've described it as second only to Cannes. Now Toronto critic Liam Lacey says flatly, "Toronto now has the most important film festival in the world—the largest, the most influential, the most inclusive." Yes, you say, but he is a Canadian, so of course he thinks that. Lacey is ready for you: "One reason the Toronto festival has probably not received its full recognition is, frankly, because it takes place in Canada."

Frankly, only a Canadian would think that. Toronto is all he says it is, and that's that. Part of the festival's importance comes simply because of timing: Oscar season opens this weekend, and in the next ten days we likely will see most, maybe even all, of the major 2006 Academy Award winners.

Cannes, held in May, is well timed to launch

"summer pictures," which are precisely the kinds of movies that do not require festivals. The most important American festival, Sundance, serves an entirely different function, focusing on indie films.

Toronto programs indies and mainstream, experimental and blockbuster, long and short, new and old—it programs everything it can get its hands on that seems to be any good, and doesn't stop there.

There was a time, ten years ago, that Cannes was rumored to be considering a switch to the autumn. But the hard reality, even then, was that if the distributors of the major Oscar season pictures had to choose, they would choose Toronto. Cannes backed off from the confrontation. In the decade since, Toronto indeed has earned Lacey's praise as the most important, largest, most influential, most inclusive festival, and he could have added another crucial superlative: the cheapest.

Movies premiere in Toronto for the same reason so many are filmed here. The Canadian dollar is cheaper than the American dollar, although not as cheap as it once was, and prices by any standard are lower. To launch a film at Cannes can cost twice or three times as much as giving it a good push-off at Toronto. Just getting up in the morning, you can save 75 percent on your first cup of coffee, and a stalwart Canadian bran muffin will cost you half as much as a croissant.

There is another factor in Toronto's ascendancy. From the very first years, the festival has been aimed primarily at audiences of—well, moviegoers. To see a film at Cannes you allegedly must possess some sort of industry credential. Toronto is open to the public. Ordinary people with ordinary funds can gorge on movies; standing in line at passport control, I chatted with a woman who showed me her list of forty films. It's a rare Toronto screening of even the most obscure film that isn't sold out.

This year, the hot tickets include several movies already considered Oscar favorites. Philip Seymour Hoffman is said to have a lock on a nomination for his *Capote*, in which he makes the author simultaneously twee and hard-boiled. Joaquin Phoenix is tipped to fill the *Ray* slot with *Walk the Line*, his extraordinary performance as Johnny Cash, and Reese Witherspoon is no less favored as June Carter Cash. Ang Lee's *Brokeback Mountain* stars Heath Ledger and Jake Gyllenhaal as two cowboys who have a lifelong love affair and keep it a secret in a 1960s Wyoming that would murder them if it found out.

Slightly darker horses include Neil Jordan's *Breakfast on Pluto,* starring Cillian Murphy, the Scarecrow from *Batman Begins,* as an Irish transvestite whose only protection is his eccentric innocence; Cameron Crowe's autobiographical *Elizabethtown;* David Cronenberg's *A History of Violence,* with its Oscar-worthy Viggo Mortensen performance as an ordinary dad with a frightening past; Roman Polanski's *Oliver Twist,* with Ben Kingsley as Fagin; and Scott McGehee and David Siegel's remarkable *Bee Season,* which combines the Kabbalah and a spelling bee, and might get a nomination for a young woman named Flora Cross.

Charlize Theron gives another powerful and moving performance in Niki Caro's *North Country,* about a female mine worker who files the first class-action suit for sexual discrimination. Morgan Freeman and Kevin Spacey star in David J. Burke's *Edison,* a movie I know nothing about except that it's a film noir involving newspapers, and any movie with those actors, Piper Perabo and LL Cool J is not likely to be boring.

Atom Egoyan's *Where the Truth Lies* stars Kevin Bacon and Colin Firth in a murder mystery involving a showbiz team not a million miles away from Martin and Lewis. Gwyneth Paltrow reaches a career high in John Madden's *Proof,* also starring Anthony Hopkins, Hope Davis, and Jake Gyllenhaal in a thriller about higher mathematics.

I have already seen most of these movies. What lies ahead for me? Last year at this time *Ray, Kinsey, Yes, Palindromes, The Sea Inside, Undertow,* and *Hotel Rwanda* were only rumors to me. I write on Wednesday night, and will see three or four new movies tomorrow, and be astonished by completely unexpected treasures. I permit myself to be delighted until I reflect that in the real world, titles like this do not open every weekend, or play everywhere, or get much support, and there are perfectly nice people who are going to see *Deuce Bigalow: European Gigolo* under the impression that it is a movie.

Toronto Report No. 2:
Water Cheered as Festival Opener

September 9, 2005—It was seven years and many troubles in the making, but Deepa Mehta's *Water* was cheered here Thursday on opening night at the Toronto Film Festival. The heartrending story of an eight-year-old bride forced onto a lifetime of widowhood caused such controversy during its filming that Mehta, born in India, now a Canadian, had to move the production to Sri Lanka for her crew's safety.

The film stars the luminous young actress Sarala in a remarkable performance as a girl wed to an older man in childhood. When the man dies, she is taken by her father to live in a home of other widows of all ages. According to religious law quoted at the top of the film, "A woman who remains chaste when her husband has died goes to heaven." According to a follower of Gandhi in the film, locking widows away makes "one less mouth to feed, four less saris, and a free corner in the house. Disguised as religion, it's just about money."

In the widows' residence, filled with a Dickensian gallery of characters, the girl is protected by the beautiful Kalyani (Lisa Ray), who has been ordered into prostitution to help support the older widows. Kalyani attracts the son of a local Brahman, the follower of Gandhi, who rejects beliefs about widowhood and intends to marry her. The film plays out in heartbreaking anger and passion but is told with serenity and visual beauty; it reflects the way these characters in 1938 might have regarded the situation, not the way it would seem to modern eyes.

The premiere screening kicked off the largest film festival in the world, "with more corporate and government sponsors than any similar event," the audience was assured—and believed it, after forty-five minutes of speeches of thanks. Since the supporters have pledged some $132 million of the projected $192 million cost of the new Festival Centre, the gratitude was understandable and, after all, will not be repeated every night.

Toronto is wall-to-wall with movies. Some nine hundred critics and other professionals march in and out of a dozen preview screens at the Varsity Cinemas, where at 10 A.M. Thursday I saw a remarkable documentary about an African-American female basketball star in Seattle, at 2 p.m. the new Steve Martin–Claire Danes romantic tragicomedy, *Shopgirl*, and at 5 P.M. *L'Enfer*, with Emmanuelle Beart in a convoluted saga of family secrets. Then over to the vast Roy Thomson Hall for *Water*. It all starts again on Friday with Kevin Jordan's *Brooklyn Lobster* (he made *Goat on Fire and Smiling Fish*, which I liked even if you've never heard of it), and then *Tim Burton's Corpse Bride* and *Bubble*, Steven Soderbergh's new film. You see what I mean by variety.

That first film I saw was Ward Serrill's *The Heart of the Game*, a documentary that could flower into a sleeper hit. The movie tells the stories of Darnellia Russell, a high school basketball star in Seattle, and Bill Resler, a professor of tax law who becomes the coach of the women's basketball team at Roosevelt High School.

His Roughriders are drawn from a mostly white student body, but Darnellia's mother wants her to transfer because at Roosevelt she might get a better education and more of a shot at a college athletic scholarship. Darnellia starts slow, intimidated, she tells the coach, because she's never been around so many white people before. He's convinced she is not only a great player but also a bright student, and is proven right with a state championship in a year when she graduates with honors. Those triumphs do not come before a great many setbacks and hurdles, including two court challenges to a women's basketball governing body that wants to prevent Darnellia from playing in her final season.

The movie inevitably will be compared with *Hoop Dreams*, the great 1994 doc about two black inner-city basketball players recruited by a suburban powerhouse, but *The Heart of the Game* is more concerned with basketball and personalities, less interested in larger social issues. The strength of the film comes not so much from Darnellia Russell's undeniable skills on the court as by the way, supported by her family, she overcomes a series of challenges that would have derailed a less determined young woman.

Shopgirl, directed by Anand Tucker, is based on Steve Martin's novel about a serious young woman who clerks at Saks Fifth Avenue while aiming toward a career as an artist. Two men come into her life: the feckless Jeremy (Jason Schwartzman) and the smooth, assured millionaire Ray (Martin). Jeremy seems on track for forty-year-old geekhood. Ray gives Mirabelle (Claire Danes) gifts, attention, concern, and care—everything but love and marriage, which he is quite clear are not part of the package. He's too old for her, he tells his shrink; more likely, he's phobic about any form of commitment.

She understands that about him, likes him anyway, thinks he's a nice guy, and then the relationship develops in a way that leads, as it must, to heartbreak. The novel was uncommonly perceptive in showing how a limited man and an unlimited woman could follow the same path only up to a point; the film works with intelligence and sympathy, and is likely to inspire from its female viewers not sighs and tears but sad recognition and perception. Some men are not only undiscovered countries but undiscoverable ones.

I would like to tell you all about *L'Enfer,* but it has a fearsomely complicated plot, the time is now 2:46 A.M. and my coffee and bran muffin arrive at 8. The festival is so front-loaded that if you don't run as fast as you can through the weekend, you never catch up.

My own private festival got off to an interesting start on Thursday morning, when I went to the press office to pick up my credentials. The friendly volunteers gave me a shoulder bag filled with discs, press releases, schedules, timetables, and magazines. I swung it into the air to drape it around my neck and was struck sharply on the forehead by the corner of *Guess* magazine. "You're bleeding," my wife told me. All day long, people have been asking me, "What happened to your forehead?" Guess, I say.

Toronto Report No. 3: Movie City

September 13, 2005—It was like I had moved to a city where only movie people live. I wandered Toronto on Saturday, from screening to party, and on the busiest day of the thirtieth annual Toronto Film Festival there were more stars, as MGM liked to say, than in the heavens. Amazing: I ran into Deborah Kara Unger, Ed Harris, Kris Kristofferson, Steve Martin, Anthony Hopkins, Peter Saarsgard and Maggie Gyllenhaal without even trying, just because they were right there on the sidewalk, or in the hotel lobby.

The showbiz columnist George Christy held his twenty-first annual brunch, always at the Four Seasons, always with chicken pot pie on the menu, and I met and actually spoke with Philip Seymour Hoffman, who will be nominated for *Capote,* and Cuba Gooding, Jr. the conflicted hit man in *Shadowboxer.* And with the directors Norman Jewison (handing out samples of maple syrup from his farm), Lee Daniels (produced *Monster's Ball,* directed *Shadowboxer*), and Atom Egoyan (*Where the Truth Lies*), who was with his wife, actress Arsinee Khanjian; they met Paul Haggis (writer of *Million Dollar Baby* and director of *Crash*) and told him how extraordinary it was for a first-time director to make a film of the complexity of *Crash.* "Just the car crash scene," Egoyan said, "a lot of directors couldn't have done that without a few films under their belts."

Oh, and here was Jennifer Tilly, so funny she slipped into the dreadful horror film *Seed of Chucky* and created her own comedy right there under their noses ("I'm an Oscar nominee, and now I'm f---ing a puppet!"). She's at Toronto with Terry Gilliam's *Tideland,* which she says is wonderfully strange, and if it's strange to Jennifer Tilly, it's certainly going to be strange to me. And here were Cillian Murphy and director Neil Jordan, for the Toronto premiere of *Breakfast on Pluto,* a movie about an Irish boy who decides from an early age to present himself as a girl and imposes that vision on society by his very innocence. And Lisa Ray and Joseph Abraham, the costars of Deepa Mehta's opening-night film *Water,* about child widows in India.

That evening, after two screenings and an interview, I went to the dinner given by Sony Pictures Classics and saw Hoffman again and his director, Bennett Miller, and, good lord, here was Catherine Keener, costar of *Capote,* who plays Capote's best friend, author Harper Lee. Keener walks into every kind of movie and is simply splendid. Already this year: *The Ballad of Jack and Rose* and *The 40-Year-Old Virgin,* where her sweetness helps turn a sex comedy into a heart-warmer.

"Catherine Keener is an amazing woman," Michael Barker told me. He is copresident of

Sony Classics. "She's not contractually required to be here to promote the film, but we told her about it, and she's always there for you. And the thing is, she comes all by herself. Just gets on the plane. No publicist, no hairdresser, no retinue." And without a lot of time to pack, I observe, considering her Sonic Youth (I BELIEVE ANITA HILL) T-shirt.

At Barker's table were Henry S. Rosenthal and Jeff Feuerzeig, the kind of indies Toronto always has room for. They produced and directed *The Devil and Daniel Johnston*, a doc about a brilliant, reclusive, troubled singer-songwriter who makes his first public appearance in years. Turns out Rosenthal also produced Jon Jost's *All the Vermeers in New York* and Feuerzeig directed *Half Japanese*, a film about a garage band that aspires to stay in its garage. People like Rosenthal and Feuerzeig are like battlefield transfusions for the film industry, pumping in fresh blood from the front lines. Block that metaphor!

In the afternoon I had a talk with Bob Hoskins, Judi Dench's costar in *Mrs. Henderson Presents*. The movie tells the story of London's famed Windmill Theater, in the heart of Soho, which presented a nonstop revue featuring singers, dancers, jugglers, magicians, dancing girls, and (the crucial element) beautiful nude women, who were not allowed to move a single muscle while they were nude.

The movie involves the famous ruling by the Lord Chamberlain, who censored all British stage productions: If a nude woman onstage is moving, it is obscene. If she is perfectly still, it can be considered art, just like all those Botticellis in the National Gallery. This ruling is obscurely related, I feel, to Fanny Brice's opinion of the swimming-movie star Esther Williams: "Dry, she's not much. But wet, she's a star."

Hoskins has a lot of gears in his shift box. He can be the most savage and venomous of actors, or alternatively the sunniest and most reasonable. Earlier this year, in *Unleashed*, he played a gangster who kept a martial arts fighter (Jet Li) in a cage and treated him like his own attack dog. Now he plays a perfectly groomed and barbered West End impresario who despite the scandalous nature of his theater is always honest and kind, and takes the girls out to dinner once a week during rationing.

He and Dench have a rapport based on the eccentricity of her character and the perfect timing of them both. "Americans," she says. "Strange people. Good manners." When Hitler started bombing London, the Windmill alone among all theaters never closed. Dench's Mrs. Henderson confides that after her only son was killed in World War I, she found a French postcard in his room and realized he may never have seen a nude woman. That made her so sad, she says, that she determined to keep her theater open as a service to the boys going overseas, who if they were killed at least had the consolation of having gazed upon a Windmill girl.

My interview with Hoskins awaits the film's opening, because my space is limited and I want to move along to *The World's Fastest Indian*. The festival has seven days to go and who knows what wonders to unveil, but *Indian* is certainly going to be a contender for the People's Choice Award, voted on by the moviegoers themselves. Anthony Hopkins usually makes serious films, and the director, Roger Donaldson, often makes big-budget thrillers (*Species, The Recruit, White Sands, No Way Out*). This time they tell the true story of a sixty-eight-year-old New Zealander named Burt Munro, straight and true as a board, kind as a saint, innocent as a monk, who spends his entire life tinkering with an Indian motorcycle.

The cycle is rated to go 60 mph, maybe. He customizes it, streamlines it, lies almost prone atop it, and thinks it will go 200 mph. The first two-thirds of the movie involves his long and underfinanced journey from New Zealand to Speed Week on the Bonneville salt flats in Utah, where world speed records are broken. His goal: drive the Indian faster than an Indian has been driven before.

Whether he succeeds, I cannot reveal at this time. What's rich about the movie is that he meets a series of Americans as helpful as they are odd, including an Indian chief who gives him powdered dog bones for his prostate trouble (they work), a farm widow who helps him replace an axle and then says, "Burt, where you sleepin' tonight?" and a Nevada cop who clocks him at 140 on the Indian and observes that although Nevada has no speed limit, drivers are expected to drive sanely.

Good thing the cop doesn't know the Indian has no brakes.

Toronto Report No. 4: Six Stars

September 12, 2005—Charlize Theron heard about *North Country* the week she won the Oscar for *Monster*. She plays a female miner in Minnesota who in 1983 filed the nation's first class-action lawsuit against sexual harassment. Her director was Niki Caro, of *Whale Rider*.

"Josey Aimes isn't Norma Rae or Erin Brockovich. She's soft-spoken, kind of disappears in a room, not a ballbuster, but she found the strength to fight this for ten years. I grew up in South Africa, raised on hard work and discipline. My mother was in the road construction business. Here I was playing a character like I was raised to be. I look pretty grungy here and even more in *Monster*. I'm not real concerned with how I look. I like films with risk, films in the gray zone.

"Frances McDormand, my costar, is a gift to cinema. She's straight from the gut. We agreed we had to be careful with that Minnesota accent. She made it famous in *Fargo*, but we toned it down a little because there was a danger we might get a laugh when it wasn't supposed to be funny. We stayed kind of neutral."

* * *

Heath Ledger has starred in epics and thrillers and has his breakthrough role in Ang Lee's *Brokeback Mountain*, which just won the Golden Lion at Venice. He and Jake Gyllenhaal play Wyoming ranch hands, circa 1960, who surprise themselves by making love. They agree "this is nobody's business but ours." It is, for years, as they marry and start families, but their feelings do not change.

"He's fighting against his genetic structure, and the traditions and fears passed down to him. He's not comfortable expressing his love to Jack or to his wife; what's important is his love for his children. I worked to physicalize him. Words had to battle their way out of his mouth. He hated himself for the form of love he had for Jack.

"I never studied acting in Australia. I never had an empty stage and black pajamas to run around and express myself. All of my mistakes are on film. I learn by observing. Ranch hands

in Australia are like those in Nevada, gravity pulling down on their shoulders, squinting, walking different after a long time on a horse. They talk without moving their upper lips. I think it's to keep the flies out."

* * *

Darnellia Russell is a 5-6 basketball guard averaging 30 points per game in the Spokane junior college league. Ward Serrill's *The Heart of the Game* is about her high school career, when she won two court appeals in order to play; her coach, a bearded tax professor named Bill Resler, guided the team to the state championship her senior year.

"I started out with low grades, but I changed my attitude and graduated with honors, a 3.6. The girls on the team thought Bill was crazy; he was probably dropped as a baby. He told us we were moose, piranha, wolves, lions—one time we were a tropical storm.

"I played women's basketball hoping to get a four-year scholarship, but that hasn't happened. I scored 49 points in one game in the Spokane college tournament. There were some scouts in the crowd. Maybe it will still happen. In our state championship game, Bill wanted every girl to play, and he put in a freshman from the bench with eighty-one seconds to go and a one-point lead. She scored six points. That's Bill."

* * *

David Cronenberg is the Canadian master of horror, the macabre, and the merely strange. His titles include *The Dead Zone, Naked Lunch, Dead Ringers,* and *Spider*. In *A History of Violence,* Viggo Mortensen plays a small-business owner in Indiana, married for twenty years when his violent past catches up with him. It was a big success at Cannes.

"It's really two movies at once: the first time you see it, and the second time. Then you can see little tones, sounds that point ahead in the story. Viggo is a serious actor, and the things he does here are subtle; I wonder how many people notice how his accent shifts in the second half of the film.

"William Hurt, as his brother, has a small role but makes a big impression. He read the script and told me, 'I think I have some afterburners I haven't used yet.'

"People say most films are too long. I go the other way. I'm too brutal in the editing. With

Videodrome, I cut out too much, gave the studio seventy-two minutes that were totally incomprehensible. New Line asked how long this movie was: ninety-six minutes. Just long enough."

* * *

Gwyneth Paltrow starred in the stage version of *Proof,* the story of a brilliant mathematician's equally brilliant daughter. When her father (Anthony Hopkins) becomes mentally ill, she cares for him; after his death, her sister (Hope Davis) and her boyfriend (Jake Gyllenhaal) disagree about her future. Meanwhile, who wrote the earthshaking mathematical proof found in her father's locked drawer?

"I don't know a thing about math, but in this movie you don't need to; it's clear what the stakes are. After her father's death, she doesn't know how to redefine herself. It's devastating for her to even begin to claim ownership of that proof. She's fragile. You can see her sister's point: How can she let my character, who is maybe mentally ill, live alone in a filthy house that's a shrine to their father's madness?

"They were meticulous in matching the University of Chicago exteriors and the interiors, which were built on a London soundstage. When I saw the university, I was so reminded of Cambridge. I'm sure some people will see that magnificent chapel and think it has to be English; it can't be in Chicago."

* * *

Bob Hoskins costars with Judi Dench in *Mrs. Henderson Presents,* the story of the woman who owned London's naughty but heroic Windmill Theater, and the man who ran it for her. The theater presented variety shows with nude models in "artistic" poses; censorship laws said they could not move a muscle onstage while naked.

"When I was five, my mom and dad took me to the Windmill. It was a family show. After the war, you'd see Peter Sellers or Spike Mulligan onstage. I knew I was gonna see naked women, but it was treated so naturally I took it in stride.

"Judi Dench is completely fearless and will play anything. We were out to lunch to discuss the movie and I said, 'Judi, in this movie you get to dress up as a Chinese lady *and* a polar bear.' She was on board.

"Someone once said, 'Acting is something you should never get caught doing.' I don't know who said that. You can put it down to me if you like."

Toronto Report No. 5: Treasure Trove of Great Films

September 13, 2005—At the halfway point of the 2005 Toronto Film Festival, one thing is clear: This is the best autumn movie season in memory. One film after another has been astonishingly good. Critics gathered in the hallways after the Varsity press screenings, talking in hushed tones as if witnesses to a miracle.

These are movies for grown-ups. Intelligent, unusual, challenging, thoughtful. We plowed through a summer of the multiplex two-week wonders, some of them good at what they wanted to do, few of them wanting to do very much. At Telluride, James Mangold, director of *Walk the Line,* told me: "Nobody wants to make a picture that depends on someone being able to 'pull it off.'" Now here are all these movies that someone *did* pull off: films that aspire to be as good as they possibly can be.

It's a festival like this: Ang Lee shows *Brokeback Mountain* at Venice. It stars Heath Ledger and Jake Gyllenhaal as two macho ranch hands in Wyoming thirty-five years ago who have a love affair and no clue about how to deal with that fact. Lee flies to Toronto. He is told to get back on a plane two hours later to fly back to Venice and accept the Golden Lion Award. Then back to Toronto.

When I talk to him Monday, he is weary and happy: "I don't know where I am, but I never know where I am. I was born in China, then my parents moved to Taiwan, where we were outsiders, then to the States, then back to China, then back here. I trust the elusive world created by movies more than anything else. I live on the other side of the screen."

I think of *Bee Season* by Scott McGehee and David Siegel and I am astonished all over again by how a twelve-year-old girl named Flora Cross, who has never acted before, carries the weight of that movie on her shoulders and holds the screen with Richard Gere and Juliette Binoche and Max Minghella, and is so powerful it's scary. And I think, how did the directors know to take that risk? To trust their whole movie to a girl who had never acted, and who gave them something they could not have gotten any other way?

They took a chance. So did Liev Schreiber when he directed *Everything Is Illuminated,* starring Elijah Wood as a solemn young man who goes to Ukraine to thank the woman who saved his grandfather's life, and meets two half-crazy guides who specialize in "tours of dead Jews." There is the old grandfather (Boris Leskin) and his grandson (Eugene Hutz), an actor who sings with a gypsy punk band and is in his first movie. The film begins as a screwball comedy and finds a trajectory straight to the beating heart of truth, and how Schreiber controls that tonal shift in his directorial debut is hard to say, but he does.

I went to see the film a second time because I felt I had been paying the wrong kind of attention when I saw a screening a month ago, and I was right about being wrong. Yes, I gave it thumbs up on TV, but I wasn't focused on its greatness. I think it helps to see it twice, to understand the journey it takes.

Jason Reitman took a chance with *Thank You for Smoking,* his first film. His father is the famous director Ivan. Your dad can get you hired in the movie business, but you have to be a director all on your own. His movie stars Aaron Eckhart as a lobbyist for the tobacco industry, who defends a product he knows is deadly and at the same time tries to teach his young son what is important in life. There are broad satirical strokes and big laughs, but watch how its anger stays focused, and how its cynicism and idealism curiously sometimes seem to change places. It would have been easier to make this movie in a simple and obvious way, but Reitman, at twenty-six, is ambitious and wants to push harder and dig into tricky personal ethics.

Curtis Hanson's *In Her Shoes* stars Cameron Diaz, Toni Collette, and Shirley MacLaine (and some men) in the story of two daughters at lifelong war with each other, and a grandmother who has disappeared from their lives. I tell you the story, and you see how this could be a soppy weeper, but the movie is tough and perceptive. MacLaine plays the grandmother as if she doesn't know that after seventy you're supposed to be lovable, and thinks at any age you have to be smart and practical and do the

hard thing if the hard thing is right. The two sisters drive each other crazy and yet are joined in a hopeless love; hope enters by way of a blind professor who is the first person to really see Diaz, and not just her body.

I've already written about Philip Seymour Hoffman's Oscar lock with his performance in *Capote.* The problem is, there are way more than five obvious candidates in every category. To make a list is to leave out work as good as the work you mention. Joaquin Phoenix could be nominated for *Walk the Line,* and MacLaine for *Shoes,* Ledger for *Brokeback,* Charlize Theron for *North Country,* Cillian Murphy for *Breakfast on Pluto,* Gwyneth Paltrow for *Proof,* Claire Danes for *Shopgirl,* Catherine Keener for three pictures, and Judi Dench for *Mrs. Henderson Presents,* and think of all the earlier movies, such as *Lord of War, Junebug, Crash, Broken Flowers, Me and You and Everyone We Know, Millions,* and *Yes.*

And then there are the popular "audience pictures" here that are delightful, such as Anthony Hopkins in *The World's Fastest Indian,* and *Tim Burton's Corpse Bride,* and Dakota Fanning in *Dreamer,* the story of a girl's fierce trust in an injured horse, and Pierce Brosnan in *Matador,* and Aishwarya Rai in *Mistress of Spices,* which has all the depth of a romance novel but is essentially an entire film about her beauty, worth seeing for her beauty alone, and if you doubt me, go to see it and try to think about anything else.

I hate this list, because it leaves out as much as it puts in. And half the festival is still to come. People talk to me or write to me about how the movies aren't as good anymore and they can't find anything they want to see, and I'm going to have to find a way of telling them: You're not paying attention.

Toronto Report No. 6: Sound Bites from Toronto

September 15, 2005—Matthew Modine was attending the Toronto Film Festival launch party for the U.S. edition of Norman Jewison's autobiography, so the subject of his own memoirs came up.

"I don't know if that book will ever be written," he said. "But I am publishing *Full Metal Diary,* which is the diary I kept when I was making Stanley Kubrick's *Full Metal Jacket.* That was so long ago that when I read it, it's like the writings of a young actor who doesn't have a whole lot to do with me. An actor writing journal entries on the set every day, just excited to be working with this great director on this film."

Modine was at Toronto with two films: Udayan Prasad's sweet and good-hearted *Opa!* where he plays an archaeologist who falls in love with the high-spirited owner (Agni Scott) of a taverna on a Greek island—a beloved local institution that may be located directly above the ancient church holding St. John's Cup. Which is more important: the present or the past?

Modine's other film is much more controversial. Abel Ferrara's *Mary,* indirectly inspired by Mel Gibson's *Passion of the Christ,* stars Modine as the director of a film about Mary Magdalene (Juliette Binoche). He is cynical, she is spiritual, and a talk show host (Forest Whitaker) is the catalyst for their passionate disagreement over the film. *Mary* won the Jury Prize at Venice, which is essentially second place. Modine, who was there, said Ferrara grumbled, "I totally disapprove of awards for films. But if they give them, I want to win."

* * *

Michael Cuesta's *Twelve and Holding* is another of the treasures in this festival of one remarkable film after another. Set in a New York suburb, it involves twelve-year-olds in crisis who attempt to solve problems they do not understand.

Zoe Weizenbaum gives an astonishingly focused and intense performance as the daughter of a therapist (Annabella Sciorra) who provides her with psycho-babble but leaves her feeling abandoned by an absent father. She gets a crush on one of her mother's clients, a depressed construction worker (Jeremy Renner), and boldly goes about trying to attract him.

Meanwhile, a nighttime firebombing of a tree house leads to the accidental death of one twin and the anguish of his brother (both played by Conor Donovan). And a fat boy (Jesse Camacho) from a fat family begins to diet after asking a coach, "Why are you doing this for me?" "Because," says the coach, "I've never met a child so out of shape in my life."

All of these children love their parents, and all of them find dangerous ways of trying to express their love, in a film that negotiates carefully between drama and melodrama. The common thread is that the parents, who also love their children, are not expressing their love in a way that can help these kids at these moments in their lives.

* * *

Norman Jewison is the patron saint of Movieville. He has long since proven he is a great director of enormous reach, able to make both *Fiddler on the Roof* and *The Hurricane,* both *Moonstruck* and *In the Heat of the Night,* both *The Thomas Crown Affair* and *A Soldier's Story.* We know that. But there are other great directors of enormous reach.

What grants Jewison sainthood, I reflect as I attend the launch party for his autobiography, is how generous he is in helping newcomers and the movie industry in general. You sense his spirit in the title of his book, *This Terrible Business Has Been Good to Me.*

At the earliest Toronto festivals I attended, Jewison was the sponsor and backer of a young Canadian director named Atom Egoyan. He has advised and boosted countless others. In those years he held a picnic on his farm west of town for the visiting filmmakers, festival people, and critics. The first year, he recalls in his autobiography, there were 268 guests.

When the festival got too big for a picnic on his farm, he was ready for that, too: By then he had founded the Canadian Film Center, taking over an estate on the edge of Toronto and turning it into the northern version of the American Film Institute. He has also taken on the thankless task of directing Oscarcasts and, in general, somehow made good films while nevertheless being a good guy.

Oh, and he was the first director to wear a baseball cap, starting a global fashion trend all by himself. Hard to believe that such a trend actually had a beginning and didn't always exist, but someone had to be first, and it's hard to imagine Hitchcock in a baseball cap.

* * *

A festival like Toronto attracts hopeful filmmakers eager to pitch projects and find financing. Here, for example, are Alex Ferrari and Jorge Rodriguez, the director and producer of *Broken,* a nineteen-minute, $8,000 horror film containing, by their count, more than one hundred visual effects.

"We're here to talk about a development deal for a feature based on the short," Rodriguez tells me before the screening of *Twelve and Holding*. "Who you talking to?" I ask. "We'd better not say," Ferrari says.

He gives me a DVD of their short: "We've already sold one thousand copies online. It contains six commentary tracks and, like, three hours of information on how to shoot low-budget digital films and how to do the special effects. It's like a training course." They refer me to their Web site, www.whatisbroken.com, and back at the hotel I view the film and visit the site.

The film is effective and professional, and the ominous sound track works with the images to create the desired effect. Whether the plot quite rises above the level of "it was only a dream," I am not prepared to say. Whether the short someday will grow into a good film, we will know only if the development deal goes through.

But that's not really the point. The point is that gifted and ambitious young filmmakers can, with very little money, use the new digital technology to make a presentation that gets attention from industry pros. Kerry Conran's *Sky Captain and the World of Tomorrow* (2004) was floated the same way, with a homemade demo made on his Mac.

Whether this is better than the old-fashioned method of submitting a screenplay is a good question; *Broken* essentially is a demonstration of the mastery of horror imagery and techniques. A screenplay also has to have dimensional characters (one, two, or three dimensions, depending on its ambition) and a story. In an industry so impenetrable for newcomers, any way you break in is the right way. Then it depends on what you do. Looking forward to *Broken: The Feature*.

Toronto Report No. 7: The Festival Winds Down

September 16, 2005—I have a few more movies to see, and the awards are still to be announced, but Toronto 2005 is basically history, and now what remains is for its many wonderful films to find their audiences. There's general agreement that this will be an autumn to remember among those who care about good films.

The first movie I saw at this year's festival was *The Heart of the Game*, the documentary about young Seattle basketball star Darnellia Russell. It came here without distribution, Toronto audiences embraced it, and late in the festival it made history: It was the first acquisition by the "new" (i.e., post-Weinstein) Miramax.

There was also a stir when Jason Reitman's satiric comedy *Thank You for Smoking*, with Aaron Eckhart as a spokesman for the tobacco industry, sold for a reported Toronto record of $6.5 million, after one of those bidding disputes that used to be a specialty of Sundance.

For Atom Egoyan, the Canadian director of *Where the Truth Lies*, the news was bad and good. His film, which I thought was one of the best I saw at Cannes last May, played here while going through an appeal of its NC-17 rating by the MPAA. On Friday, Egoyan described the appeals process as a bad dream. The disputed scene involves three-way sex among the two members of a 1950s comedy team (Colin Firth and Kevin Bacon) and a young woman played by Alison Lohman, who later is found dead.

The scene cannot be cut without destroying the movie; it is crucial to the murder mystery in the plot and explains the breakup of the act. For that reason, Egoyan said, he did not make it sexually explicit, since he was under contract with producer Robert Lantos to deliver an R movie. The MPAA slapped on the NC-17, upheld its ruling on appeal, and under its own rules did not need to give reasons.

"Lantos is a stand-up guy and will release the film unrated," Egoyan said. "What disturbed and confused me was that in addition to the ten-member board, there were two other people in the room. I asked who they were. They were clergymen, one Catholic, one Episcopalian. I asked why they were there and didn't get an answer, but they were allowed to sit in on the secret deliberations of the rating board."

In the days of the Ontario Censor Board, now abolished, its guidelines were at least published and had the status of law. The baffling thing about the MPAA, Egoyan said, is that it does not specify what can and cannot be shown, and does not have to explain its decisions. His movie is not in any way a sex or exploitation film, he said, and I agree. "By giving it an NC-17, they are denying parents the privilege of deciding for themselves if their teenage children should be allowed to see it."

The last few days of Toronto are valuable to critics because most of the big-star must-see vehicles roared out of town after the weekend. You can make offbeat discoveries, and I made three:

—It will be fun to read the reviews of John Turturro's *Romance and Cigarettes* and watch the critics try to describe a film whose charm depends on how it can't be pinned down. It's a comedy suffused with melancholy, a musical in which the characters sing along with their favorite records, a slice of life crossed with magic realism, a story about everyday working people who have nothing everyday about them. Even its language ventures from vulgarity to high poetry.

James Gandolfini and Susan Sarandon star as a long-married Brooklyn couple with a family of wacky grown children. She finds evidence he's been fooling around and banishes him from her bed and her regard. He petitions for readmission. Kate Winslet plays the scarlet woman, part real, part dreams. Advice and dissent come from supporting characters played by Steve Buscemi, Christopher Walken, and Elaine Stritch, who steal not only every scene they're in but every word they use; occasionally even their body language in long shot steals a scene.

The musical numbers are gloriously messy with exuberance: Just like in real life, the characters have a jukebox in their heads playing their favorite songs, which sometimes burst out onto the sound track and cause whole neighborhoods to sing along, even the cops and garbage men. Toronto audiences love it. Its distribution rights went up for grabs after United Artists was absorbed by Sony, and now it has inspired, if not exactly a bidding war, certainly a border skirmish.

—Josh Gilbert's *a.k.a. Tommy Chong* is a documentary about the entrapment and prosecution of comedian Tommy Chong on charges of selling bong pipes through the mail. You do not have to approve of drugs to be offended by the way the Justice Department under John Ashcroft created a fictitious head shop in Pennsylvania for the specific purpose of ordering paraphernalia from the Chong family's Web-based retail store to nail him with that state's laws against such merchandise.

As the costar of druggie comedies of the 1970s, none of which I much liked, Chong was a symbol of an era hated by Washington's new Puritans. The movie argues that in federal courts the power is held not by judges but by prosecutors, who offer plea bargains to get what they want. They offered Chong a deal: Plead guilty and serve ten months, and we will not prosecute your wife and son. He pleaded. Of all the defendants of this particular government sting, Chong was the only one with no prior convictions who actually served time. Yes, Chong broke the law. But the paraphernalia law went unenforced and ignored for years until the Ashcroft minions dusted it off and aimed its cross-hairs straight at Tommy Chong.

—Annette Bening can play the sweetest, sunniest, most reasonable of women. There are times in *Mrs. Harris* when you would trust your children to the private school Jean Harris administers in Philadelphia. At other times she is shooting Dr. Herman Tarnower, the diet guru of Scarsdale, New York, in the notorious 1980 murder case. Did she mean to kill him, or did he die in a struggle over a gun while she was trying to kill herself? We will never know. What the movie argues, however, is that Tarnower was a right proper bastard, a monstrous egoist who treated Harris and his other mistresses with high-handed arrogance and low contempt.

Ben Kingsley plays the doctor as the kind of man who, awakened by a lover who has driven five hours in the rain to be with him, complains that she woke him up. A man who coldly promises to cut Jean Harris out of his life if she complains about his blatant affairs with other women. A man whose primary qualifications for writing the best-selling Scarsdale Diet book were his arrogance and his cook. Mrs. Harris, on the other hand, is a lonely and proper woman who, after years of his scorn, hath the fury of hell.

Toronto Report No. 8: Winners

September 18, 2005—Although the Toronto Film Festival lacks an official competition, lots of awards are handed out on closing day. As they were announced Saturday, I felt like I was standing on the pier waving sadly as the ship sailed. Although I saw forty-three of this year's films, either here or at Telluride, Cannes, or Sundance, I managed for the first time to get through the entire festival without having seen a single film that won a prize. This report therefore is based on descriptions in the official program.

The festival's most coveted honor, the People's Choice Award, is voted on by the moviegoers themselves, as they mark ballots on the way out of the theater. This year's winner was *Tsotsi*, by Gavin Hood, a South African/British coproduction. Inspired by a novel by Nobel winner Athol Fugard, it stars Presley Chweneyagae as a carjacker who steals a BMW and unexpectedly finds a baby in the backseat. Stirred by the infant's helplessness, he forces a young mother, at gunpoint, to care for the child.

The $30,000 Toronto City Award, given to the best Canadian feature, was won by *C.R.A.Z.Y.*, a film by Jean-Marc Vallee about a Montreal teenager who may be gay and is certainly a misfit in the middle of four rowdy brothers. It takes place in the 1970s, with a sound track inspired by his taste in music—the Stones, Pink Floyd, and of course, Patsy Cline.

The $15,000 Discovery Award, voted on by members of the international press who are covering the festival, went to *Look Both Ways*, by Sarah Watt of Australia. The characters all meet at the site of a train wreck, the lines of their tangled lives crossing in unexpected ways.

The City TV Award for best Canadian first feature was a tie between *Familia*, by Louise Archambault, and *The Life and Hard Times of Guy Terrifico*, directed by Michael Mabbott. The first film is about a mother addicted to gambling and a daughter who barely survives her first rave; they decide to drive (or escape) to California. The second is a mockumentary about a self-destructive singer-songwriter whose destruction outran his talent.

The Bravo!FACT Short Cuts Canada Award (yes, that's its official title) went to *Big Girl*, a fourteen-minute short by Renuka Jeyapalan about a daughter who disapproves of her mother's new boyfriend. Honorable mention

went to *There's a Flower in My Pedal*, directed by Andrea Dorfman, a four-minute short about a lost bicycle.

The FIPRESCI Award is given at most major festivals by members of the official international film critics' association. This year's Toronto winner was *Sa-Kwa*, by Kang Yi-Kwan of South Korea, a film about a woman who is jilted by the man she loves and unwisely, on the rebound, marries a man who is besotted with her.

The festival closed Saturday night, having in its thirtieth year established itself as the equal of Cannes in importance, and in terms of audiences and numbers of films shown, the largest festival in the world. Curiously, its influence is reduced because it does not have an official juried competition and, therefore, cannot give a film the kind of worldwide boost the Palme d'Or and other prizes provide at Cannes.

Hawaii Film Festival

Honolulu, Hawaii, October 27, 2005—I've been away from the Hawaii film festival for a few years, and things have changed. Two indications:

1. I went to see the Korean film *Bittersweet Life* and found the street in front of the theater blocked by screaming fans of the star Byung-hun Lee. By the time I'd fought my way to the door, an ambulance had arrived to cart away a fan who had fainted. In the old days no one screamed or fainted at Hawaii except at the movies.

2. On a more serious note, I was talking with Christa Marker, the German documentarian who is also an official of the Berlin festival, and she said: "This festival has arrived. It is now at the top level." Although that does not rank it with Cannes, Toronto, and Berlin, it means that the festival has passed a turning point.

I remember Sundance and Toronto in their earliest days, when everybody at the festival could fit into one hotel banquet room. Look at them now. Then I look at the enormous crowds at Hawaii, its two hundred films, its creative programming, and I think, yes, the dream that Jeannette Paulson had when she started the festival twenty-five years ago is becoming a reality.

861

It's officially called the Louis Vuitton Hawaii International Film Festival, and the sponsorship has made a difference, providing cachet and cash. Its director, Chuck Boller, has things humming along smoothly. The festival now occupies not only the beautifully restored Hawaii Theater, a movie palace from the 1920s, but also several big screens at the Regal cineplex at the Dole Cannery (which is not a cannery any longer; you don't sit on pineapple crates to watch the movies). I'm doing a shot-by-shot analysis of *Dark City* in the Doris Duke Theater of the Hawaii Academy of the Arts, and I remember when this two-hundred–seat theater was a main venue, not just for the sidebars.

Major directors are here; the most important is also the most symbolic. Zhang Yimou, one of the leading filmmakers of China, flew in for a "secret" screening of his new film *Riding Alone for Thousands of Miles*. Secret, because the Tokyo festival had the official world premiere four hours earlier. History: Paulson brought Yimou here circa 1980, and it was his first trip to a Western festival.

Another important director is Korea's Kim Ji-woon, whose *Bittersweet Life* provides the kind of hard-edged action that is making a name for Korea in new markets. Its star, Byung-hun Lee, no doubt will be ported into Hollywood movies before long, joining Chow Yun-Fat, Jackie Chan, and Jet Li; Asian stars have a special aura for young acting fans. I had also seen him in *Three . . . Extremes,* but I wasn't aware of his superstar status in certain circles.

"Tell me about him," I asked two ladies in front of me, after he was introduced and approximately five hundred teenage girls with digital cameras stormed the stage.

"Oh, he's the Korean Brad Pitt!" one said.

"He's bigger than that!" said the other one. "He's the American Brad Pitt!"

In the movie, Byung-hun Lee shot approximately everyone he met, although I will not give away the ending. The style was a mixture of film noir and Sundance chic.

Hawaii is still a launching pad for early films by younger directors, particularly Asian-Americans. I saw two I admired. Georgia Lee's *Red Doors* tells the story of a troubled Chinese-American family; the father has retired

into deep silence and eventually wanders away from the family on a personal spiritual quest. The mother presides over a twenty-nine-year-old professional (Jacqueline Kim), a young medical intern (Elaine Kao), and a teenager (Kathy Shao-Lin Lee) whose idea of letting a boy know she's interested in him is putting a bomb in his locker—a small bomb, to be sure. When the intern falls in love with an actress, the family life grows even more fraught, since there is some doubt that the mother can handle this information. The film handles this not as sitcom material but with a warm tenderness.

Telling the family about romance with an outsider is also the theme of Frank Lin's *American Fusion,* which stars Sylvia Chang as a divorced woman in her forties who falls in love with a Mexican-American dentist (Esai Morales). Question: Will her domineering, complaining mother allow her to live her own life? Chang plays a daughter who wants to be loving and dutiful but is thanked with guilt and criticism. Although the gloom lifts when the dentist supplies a timely blood transfusion, if Morales marries the woman he loves it will not be in hopes of spending more time with his mother-in-law.

The best movie I've seen here is a documentary named *Sisters in Law,* which follows several cases through the courts of Cameroon, West Africa. The judges, magistrates, and many of the lawyers are women, and they are dealing with women who have been beaten and mistreated. Muslim law suggests such matters be handled within the family, but the movie's women are strong and determined, and have the law of the land behind them. There is real drama here, but also enough humor to justify the description you often hear, that the movie is like a real-life version of *The No. 1 Ladies' Detective Agency* novels.

An American indie that got a lot of buzz is *I Am a Sex Addict* by Caveh Zahedi. The director uses some real people and some actors in a story he says is "entirely true," about how he destroyed his first two marriages and his peace of mind through an obsessive addiction to prostitutes. Life is strange: He hires an actress to play his first wife, then goes looking on the Web for a prostitute who looks like her, and finds an ad for the porn star Rebecca Lord, who under her real name is already playing the wife.

Zahedi seems less obsessed by prostitutes than he is obsessed by his obsession. He needs to talk about it, "share" with the women in his life, and now even make a film about it. I had the feeling that it was always about him; that he didn't need prostitutes so much as he needed to need them. Since he narrates the film in a style combining both the best and the worst of Woody Allen and Nick Broomfield, his saga is perversely interesting even when it may not be sending precisely the message he intends.

Later in the week, I'll be introducing my Critic's Choice program, Mark Dornford-May's *U-Carmen eKhayelithsha*, which is Bizet's opera filmed in Cape Town and sung in the Khosa language by Pauline Malefane and other South African singers of formidable ability. It was at Hawaii that I saw the extraordinary New Zealand version of Shakespeare's *The Merchant of Venice* performed entirely in the Maori language, so there is a tradition at work here. Besides, *Carmen* is always in a foreign language, as far as I'm concerned.

Sundance Film Festival
Sundance Report No. 1

Park City, Utah, January 19, 2006—The Sundance Film Festival officially started Thursday night with the premiere of *Friends with Money*, which stars Jennifer Aniston, who attracts so many photographers you would think she was a one-hour photo shop.

For the visiting movie critic, however, it started the night before. I drove up from Salt Lake City in a snowstorm, dragged my luggage through the snow across a parking lot to the wrong building, dragged it back to the car again, and dragged it through more snow to the right building. Those little wheelies are no damn good in the snow.

Then at midnight I set out to purchase the items necessary for life in a rented ski condo. They are:

1. Instant coffee
2. Whole-wheat bread
3. Peanut butter
4. Strawberry jam

I went to the 7-Eleven around the corner from my condo. I walked up and down the aisles, finding more than two hundred varieties of candy, an entire aisle of chips, vast coolers full of pop and beer, and a shelf of magazines, which all had Jennifer Aniston or supercharged trucks on their covers.

"Instant coffee?" I asked the guy behind the counter. He walked up and down the candy aisle and told me, "No instant coffee."

"Whole-wheat bread?"

He did not have to look.

"No bread."

"No whole wheat?"

"No bread."

"You don't sell any *bread* in this store?"

"We have doughnuts," he said helpfully.

This story is actually two parables.

Parable One. I do not attend Sundance expecting glamour. I will not eat a restaurant meal for the next seven days, will see vegetables only on the screen, will attend four movies on a slow day, will stand in the freezing dark for a shuttle bus to nowhere, and will make friends with the folks at the snack counters whose oatmeal cookies, microwave burritos, and bottled water sustain life.

Parable Two. For the average moviegoer, the local multiplex is like 7-Eleven—lots of candy and pop, but no coffee or bread. Sundance supplies the coffee and bread: movies to wake you up, and others to feed your soul. This is the festival that gives hope for the future, introduces new talents, celebrates the offbeat and the experimental, exists on the cutting edge. Sundance, in a sense, created a market for that kind of film; the big studios certainly weren't interested in them twenty years ago, but now they all have "classics divisions" devoted to marketing indie and foreign films.

It began with the Sundance story everybody tells, about how Steven Soderbergh's *sex, lies . . . and videotape* created a sensation at Sundance 1989, was picked up by Miramax, essentially put Miramax on the map, and created the situation at Sundance 1990 where every distributor in America was prowling the screenings looking for the next Soderbergh.

There have been a lot of next Soderberghs. There will be more this year. Soderbergh himself has gone on to big commercial hits, such as *Ocean's Eleven,* but he still has the Sundance spirit. On Friday, January 27, he opens *Bubble*, a great film shot with first-time actors on a tiny budget. In a distribution strategy that has exhibitors angry, it will play on cable the same day it opens in theaters and will come out on DVD four days later. This experiment with simultaneous release may be the salvation of little indie films, which have trouble making themselves seen behind the walls of $30 million ad campaigns.

Now take Jennifer Aniston. Yes, she is a big star. Big because, to paraphrase Stuart Smalley, doggone it, people like her. She makes commercial movies, such as *Rumor Has It* (2005), about what would happen if *The Graduate* were a real story and she might be about to sleep with the "real" Benjamin, who also slept with her mother and grandmother. A nice movie.

But Aniston, like Soderbergh, is also interested in independent films. Her *Friends with Money* is the new film by Nicole Holofcener, the director of the wonderful *Lovely & Amazing* (2001), which might have been the best film you didn't see that year. I showed it at my Overlooked Film Festival, which tells you something right there.

Sometimes actors are like brand names; you see a few of them together in the same movie, and you sense it might be good. *Friends with Money* also stars Frances McDormand, Joan Cusack, and Catherine Keener. If that doesn't make your heart leap up, you've been missing some good movies.

As I write this, I haven't seen *Friends with Money* or anything else here, except for a few I saw earlier, such as Wim Wenders's *Don't Come Knocking*, which was at Cannes. There are premieres by Nick Cassavetes, Terry Zwigoff, Jonathan Demme, Michel Gondry. Yes, I'm eager to see them. But I have never heard of the directors in the official competition, and that's where the new Soderbergh or Holofcener will be found.

We all plunge in. At 2:30 Friday afternoon I will be seeing *Somebodies*, a film written and directed by a college student from Georgia named Hadjii. I know the producer, Nate Kohn, who was Hadjii's film professor at the University of Georgia. He read the script and liked it so much he found the backing to make it. Its budget was—don't even ask. In a way,

the film comes from nowhere. Now it is one of sixteen titles in the official dramatic competition. Next year, Jennifer Aniston may be working with Hadjii. Now that's what I'm talking about.

Sundance Report No. 2: *Somebodies* Makes a Splash

January 21, 2006—John Cooper, who has been programming films at Sundance for almost twenty years, had a particular tone in his voice as he introduced *Somebodies* Friday afternoon. This wasn't a routine introduction. "Certain moments at Sundance we remember," he said, "because they were the beginning of something great."

You would expect that *Somebodies* then would unreel as a profound social statement or bold visual breakthrough. But no. This new film by a director from Georgia named Hadjii is great in a different way, for how it breaks through the conventions that wall in films about African-Americans. It is not uplifting or angry or about drugs or crime or sports or music or sex. It is about ordinary young people who are very, very funny because they don't seem to know they're in a movie, and aren't performing for any imagined audience, black or white. Their purpose is to celebrate themselves.

"Black films are under so much pressure to provide 'role models,'" Hadjii said in a Q&A after the screening. "These characters are not good or bad. They're going through a transitional period." They're living, in other words.

Hadjii stars, as Scottie, a college student who drinks too much and sleeps through church services and meets a girl (Kaira Whitehead) who likes him but isn't going to sleep with him until he has his "paperwork." At a clinic where she takes him to get tested for AIDS, she suggests the "player's special," a package price for tests for all the popular STDs.

Scottie's friends, concerned about his drinking, decide to stage an intervention. But he's late getting home, and they start to drink and play cards, and when he arrives they decide to put off the intervention while they go out and get something to eat. There are several church services in the movie, one featuring a black preacher whose holy rants are punctuated by the sober, factual footnotes and responses of the deacon who stands beside him. Their rhythm in these sermons achieves a kind of comic verbal ecstasy. No less funny is the all-white Campus Christian Coalition meeting Scottie attends. These scenes don't make fun of church or religion; they are funny, but fond.

So is the whole movie. It's more a matter of tone than plot, of letting characters (including uncles, aunts, friends, visitors) run loose in verbal riffs of astonishing invention and remarkable sexual speculation. If along the way Scottie is somewhat redeemed, that happens in the margins; the movie is not about the salvation of Scottie, but about the process by which he gradually moves in a better direction.

Like all really good films, *Somebodies* defies description because it's not about plot; it's about how it celebrates its characters. It started life as a screenplay when Hadjii was a student at the University of Georgia; his professor, Nate Kohn, and Nate's wife, Pamela Kohn, admired it and decided to produce it. Local money supplied the small indie budget. What you feel, watching the film, is that moments of truth are being set free; that unlike many films about African-Americans, this one isn't made with the slightest concern for the "impression" it might make; it is being generated by the joy of the characters.

Somebodies was the third of four films I saw at Sundance on Friday—all comedies. The funniest laugh-out-loud audience pleaser was *Little Miss Sunshine,* a first film by Jonathan Dayton and Valerie Faris, written by Michael Arndt, which begins with a family that seems destined to explode. The father (Greg Kinnear) is obsessed with positive thinking and hopes to get rich with a self-improvement scheme. His wife (Toni Collette) is a center of sanity. Her brother (Steve Carell) has come to live with them after attempting suicide. Her son (Paul Dano) is training for the Air Force and living under a vow of silence. Her daughter (Abigail Breslin) is a finalist in the Little Miss Sunshine contest. And her father-in-law (Alan Arkin) has been thrown out of the retirement home for loudly and obscenely advocating 1960s values while sniffing heroin.

The plot, never mind why, lands them all in an ancient VW bus that has to be pushed to 20 mph before it will turn over. The whole family, never mind why, has to pile in the bus and drive to the Little Miss Sunshine contest in Redondo Beach. This contest, with its little girls made up to look like hookers, is blown to pieces by the astonishing performance of the little girl, who thanks her grandfather for "teaching me the moves."

As we moviegoers huddled afterward in the cold, waiting for the shuttle bus, a buyer told her friend, "That movie is going to sell for a *lot* of money."

Nicole Holofcener's *Friends with Money* is about four friends, three rich, one (Jennifer Aniston) working as a maid. The others are Frances McDormand, Catherine Keener, and Joan Cusack, and all of their marriages are going through varieties of crises, in a series of scenes built on satirical psychological excavations. I didn't like it as much as *Lovely & Amazing,* but, then, how could I? It has the moves and the moments, but not as much heart.

Kinky Boots, by Julian Jarrold, is like a throwback to the British comedies of the 1950s, although in 1957 it might not have starred the strapping actor Chiwetel Ejiofor as a drag queen. Joel Edgerton, who looks uncannily like a young Albert Finney, plays the heir to a failing shoe factory in Nottingham. He meets the drag queen by accident and has a brainstorm: The factory can be saved by converting from men's dress shoes to men's kinky boots, built to hold the greater weight of a male drag queen during the wear and tear of a drag show. Well, why not? The movie is conventional, even old-fashioned, in its structure, but Ejiofor, as "Lola," transforms the material with what can be described only as a muscular performance. It was somehow inevitable that *Kinky Boots* was "based on a true story."

Sundance Report No. 3: Tunney Stars in *Open Window*

January 22, 2006—Robin Tunney sits in the corner of an empty coffeehouse and smiles about the fact that her TV series, *Prison Break,* has made her recognizable everywhere she goes. "It's not something I pursued, doing TV. I've been broke in my career, and that's okay. I love doing indie films."

I love seeing her in them, too. You may not

have heard of *Niagara, Niagara* (best actress at Venice, 1997) and *Cherish* and *The Secret Lives of Dentists* (both 2002), but they were very good—especially *Cherish*, with Tunney under house arrest and wearing an ankle bracelet that will sound an alarm if she leaves her apartment—which she must do for reasons of diabolical precision.

Now here she is at Sundance in Mia Goldman's *Open Window,* her most serious drama and most challenging role. She plays a photographer happily engaged to Joel Edgerton, when a stranger breaks into her studio and rapes her. She is not quick to recover. She refuses to press charges, won't talk about what happened, retreats into depression and withdrawal. The movie is about the slow healing of her relationship.

"Revenge is silly except in Elizabethan drama," she says. "To confront the rapist doesn't heal anything. I like the way the movie allows her to be silent, to do nothing, to not really react for a long time."

Tunney says she was surprised by how difficult the rape scene was: "I'm not an emotional person. I don't cry, I'm pretty composed, but I just broke down and started crying and couldn't stop, and finally had to go to a hospital for a sedative. It was embarrassing. But at least we got through it. Mia Goldman, the director, was the velvet knife: She got exactly what she wanted, but she asked for it in the best way."

Tunney grew up in Chicago, graduated from the Chicago Academy of the Arts, is happy to be back home for *Prison Break,* which shoots around Chicago through March. She thinks a lot, she says, about how she'll handle the next twenty years of her career:

"Acting is so youth-driven, especially for women, who start doing crazy things to their faces. No woman enjoys getting older. In fact, a lot of old actors don't seem very happy. I worked once with G. D. Spradlin, though, who was almost eighty, and he told me an old actor is like an old hooker: You don't like to do it anymore, but you're flattered when you're asked."

* * *

It's astonishing, the range of films you see here in a day. *Open Window* was quiet and intense, and paid great attention to the emotional weather of the characters. In the morning I saw Julia Kwan's luminous *Eve and the Fire Horse,* the only feature here from Canada, which tells the story of two young Chinese-Canadian sisters growing up in a family obsessed with good luck. One becomes a Christian, one becomes a Buddhist, and the scene everybody will remember is Jesus and Buddha dancing together in the Eng family living room, although I forgot to take notes on who was leading.

The film is about religion without being a religious film. It's about how children ask each other profound questions and supply answers that are admirably practical. This is not a children's film, but a film about children, which allows them their own space and time, and the freedom to think for themselves without being driven ahead by the plot. I was reminded of *Millions,* another film in which siblings confront the supernatural and don't blink.

* * *

The big evening hit at the Eccles was Patrick Stettner's *The Night Listener,* an eerie, Hitchcockian thriller starring Robin Williams as a gay late-night disc jockey whose publisher friend (Joe Morton) asks him to read a manuscript about a young boy (Rory Culkin) tortured by his parents and now dying of AIDS under the care of a foster mother in Wisconsin (Toni Collette).

The Williams character is depressed by the breakup of a long-term love affair and gets involved by telephone in the boy's life-and-death story. But the more he finds out, the more questions are raised, until the movie takes turns that no one in the audience can anticipate. The screenplay is by Armistead Maupin and Terry Anderson, based on Maupin's novel, and is scary, fascinating, and elusive. Williams pursues versions of reality in a series of events that grow nightmarish. This is a movie that ends more than once, in more than one way.

* * *

You see some unexpected moviegoers at Sundance. In the audience at *The Night Listener* was Rep. Rahm Emanuel (D-Ill.), the Democratic strategist: "We have four couples who come to the opening weekend of Sundance every year." Did he say anything else? Only, "We'll have another war right before the next election." He seemed prepared to elaborate, but the lights were going down and the ushers told us to take our seats.

* * *

In yesterday's report, I quoted a woman overheard at the shuttle bus stop predicting that the Sundance comedy hit *Little Miss Sunshine* would "sell for a *lot* of money." Today I add a conversation overheard at a screening: "I hear two numbers—$8 million and $10 million." Either one would be a Sundance record.

Sundance Report No. 4: Interview with Julia Kwan

January 22, 2006—Julia Kwan, the director of one of the most beloved films at Sundance this year, didn't touch a film camera until she was twenty-three. She was studying to be a legal assistant. Her dad worked in a restaurant. Her mom worked in the garment industry.

"I've yet to meet a relative who makes a living as an artist," she said. When she told her mom she was studying writing at Ryerson University in Toronto, her sister told her, "Mom thinks you're studying calligraphy."

After more study at Norman Jewison's Center for Advanced Film Study, where she made a short subject that played Sundance, she is back this year with *Eve and the Fire Horse*. It is the heartwarming story of two little sisters growing up near Vancouver and trying to combine Buddhism and Catholicism with Chinese beliefs about fate and luck. It is not a children's movie. It is a movie about children.

"I've had this idea for a long time," Kwan told me Sunday afternoon. We were in the corner of a hotel suite with the sign GERMAN AND CANADIAN CINEMA on the door. It's cheaper to double up.

"My grandmother died, and my father told me she was reincarnated as a goldfish. I thought that was beautiful. Then, when I was eight years old, I was told in Christian school that my grandmother was in hell because she was a Buddhist."

The Catholics told you that?

"Just Christians, but I made them Catholic in the movie because it's more cinematic. What I wanted to show was how the minds of children work. They're told the story of Moses closing the waters of the Red Sea over the Egyptians, and they want to know, why did all the horses have to drown? Kids see such matters as either right or wrong. What did the horses do to make God drown them?"

Kwan's movie opened nationwide January 17 in Canada. It doesn't have a U.S. distributor yet. "It's a specialized sell," she said. "That's what they say."

These could be any kids, I said, but then I realized the distribution problem isn't that the kids are Chinese; the problem is that the film is intelligent, delicate, and touching, and distributors look for films that are hard, cynical, and uncouth.

"The success of the movie *Hostel* broke my heart," Kwan said.

Yeah, I said, make a horror movie that's more gruesome than the last one, and that's what will sell.

"At least Cronenberg's *A History of Violence* was about the *consequences* of violence," Kwan said.

Where did you find those two little girls? I asked. Phoebe Jojo Kut and Hollie Lo play Eve (born in the year of the fire horse) and her slightly older sister, Karena.

"They came in as friends of other girls who were auditioning. We needed Chinese-Canadians who spoke English but could at least understand Cantonese, so when their parents were talking they'd look like they understood. Phoebe's second audition, she did the scene where she tells her mother she saw her grandmother's ghost, and she had everybody in the room in tears."

Are your parents proud that you're at Sundance?

"I don't think they know where Utah is. The film was screened in Vancouver, and a friend who was sitting behind my father said he cried. I have only seen him cry twice in my life. So I know he liked it. We don't really talk much about things like this. Some Chinese magazine interviewed my mother, and she talked proudly about how I had a job at a bank that paid $10 an hour."

Your adult lead is a big star, I said—Vivian Wu.

"A wonderful actress. She was so big I didn't even know if she would read my script, but she said right away she wanted to do it. She is so good. Here at Sundance some interviewers have actually asked her if *Eve and the Fire Horse* will be her American breakthrough. Here is a woman who starred in *The Pillow Book* and *The Joy Luck Club* and *Heaven and Earth* and a lot of other big movies. I thought that was kind of insulting."

If they're that dumb and yet they think *Eve* could be a breakthrough, I thought, at least that means the film made an impression. Although I wouldn't recommend it to the audience for the horror movie of the week. You don't want to overload those brain cells. Could cause a thought or something.

Sundance Report No. 5: Ashley Judd's Quiet Side

January 24, 2006—Most of Ashley Judd's biggest hits have been thrillers, but most of her very best work has been in closeup character studies. That was true of her first film, *Ruby in Paradise,* and it's true again of *Come Early Morning,* the story of a small-town woman whose pattern is to get drunk, sleep with a guy she picks up in a bar, and make a quick getaway the next morning.

But her character is not quite that simple. She also holds down an important desk job in a construction company, goes to church with her dad in hopes of getting closer to him, and is a good friend—or girlfriend, because no guy gets very close, until she meets a nice man, played by Jeffrey Donovan.

In a more conventional movie, she would learn to love him and leave all her issues behind. "But I didn't want this movie to be about how all her problems are solved when she meets the right guy," Joey Lauren Adams told the audience at the Sundance premiere. Adams, an actress who works too rarely (she was wonderful in Kevin Smith's *Chasing Amy*), makes her directing debut with *Come Early Morning,* and it has the assurance of a thoughtful filmmaker who knows her characters and how to tell their stories with no wrong steps or awkward moments.

We watch Lucy, the Judd character, and we sense how deep her problems are, and there is an answer somewhere in the shyness of her father, who sits alone and drinks and smokes and once played guitar good enough to go head-to-head with Chet Atkins but never had the nerve to do it again.

* * *

The South African film renaissance continues with one of the most extraordinary and powerful films at Sundance, *Son of Man.* This is the story of Jesus, told in episodes from the New Testament but set in present-day Africa. This is a Jesus (Andile Kosi) who says the same sorts of things he says in the Bible, is not "updated" except in some of his terms of reference, and yet sends an unmistakable message: If Jesus were alive today, he would be singled out as a dangerous political leader, just as he was the first time around.

The movie has relatively little spoken dialogue, but a great deal of music, that joyous full-throated South African music that combines great technical skill with great heart. Some of the best moments belong to a chorus, singing the praises of the lord. Others belong to an actress named Pauline Malefane, who plays Mary and sings in celebration after being told she will be the mother of Jesus.

She's told by an angel; the angels in the movie are small African boys with a few feathers attached here and there, looking on with concern. Jesus's disciples include a few women along with the men this time, and they follow him through the townships of Cape Town as he preaches nonviolence. Television news tells of occupying forces and uprisings, the modern version of the Roman concern with the Jews. Judas spies on Jesus with a video camera. The secret of the movie is that it doesn't strain to draw parallels with current world events— because it doesn't have to.

The movie was directed by Mark Dornford-May, but it is an improvisational collaboration of the Dimpho Di Kopane theater company, which also created Dornford-May's great *U-Carmen* (2005), a version of Bizet's opera sung entirely in Khosa. That, too, starred Malefane, a trained opera singer.

* * *

Haskell Wexler and his wife, Rita Taggart, held a little dinner on Monday night after the Sundance premiere of *Who Needs Sleep?,* the new doc by Wexler and Lisa Leeman. But I had to get up early Tuesday to see the 8:30 A.M. screening of, yes, *Who Needs Sleep?* Here is a movie that could supply Sundance with its official motto.

"I started working on this film when I was

seventy-five," says Wexler, the Oscar-winning cinematographer, who is now eighty. He started it soon after a camera operator named Brent Hershman fell asleep at the wheel and was killed after finishing a nineteen-hour day on the set.

Wexler argues that long hours are running out of control in Hollywood. He's involved in a group called 12 On and 12 Off, which tries to limit shifts to twelve hours. A more typical work schedule for cast and crew members is fourteen, sixteen, even eighteen hours. Such hours are unheard of on movie sets elsewhere in the world.

Wexler visits sleep experts who say Americans exist with a "sleep debt," take pride on going without sleep, and are doing damage to their health, their thinking, and their safety. He visits union officials who were early to sign on to shorter hours after Hershman's death but now, curiously, claim they're powerless. No one seems to have the will to act.

Overtime is a way to hide budget moneys, one insider tells Wexler. "The studio doesn't notice overtime, but they notice extra days." Spouses complain they never see each other. One production worker has never had dinner with his family. Toward the end of shooting, another film worker was killed, asleep at the wheel.

Wexler has been a political activist since day one. Here, because he's dealing with a glamorous industry, he runs into opposition from people who argue that if you want to make movies, you gotta be willing to pay the price. Yes, some actors make $20 million paychecks, but the average actor makes around $40,000, and because they are often out of work, the average crew member is also around that level. Many of them need longer hours to qualify for health insurance. And their unions seem co-opted by the industry.

* * *

It's official: Rights to *Little Miss Sunshine,* the hit comedy from Sundance, have been purchased by Fox Searchlight for $10.5 million, a festival record. Meanwhile, *Son of Man* and *Eve and the Fire Horse* (which I wrote about yesterday) are still seeking distribution deals. Terrific comedies are a lot of fun and an easy sell. Quieter, more human films, those made at the edge of imagination and artistry, are another matter.

Sundance Report No. 6

January 24, 2006—I have seen one of the wisest films I can remember about love and human intimacy. It is a film of integrity and truth, acted fearlessly, written and directed with quiet, implacable skill. I will not forget it. Now here is a dilemma: The film is so truthful and observant, so subtle and knowing about human nature, that it may be too much for most audiences. Moviegoers demand a little something in the way of formula, if only for reassurance, or as a road sign.

The movie is *Flannel Pajamas,* directed by Jeff Lipsky. It is his second feature in ten years, after *Childhood's End* (1997, no relation to the Arthur C. Clarke novel). That one I never saw. But I see Lipsky a lot because he is a tireless distributor of independent films, a regular at all the festivals. He started at New Yorker Films and founded both October Films and Lot 47. He knows the cinema.

Now he is back with this difficult, relentless, sad, and true film about two people who meet on a blind date, fall deeply in love, get married, and see the marriage gradually fall apart. It is clear to us whose fault the failure really is, but not clear to either of the characters. It may be that childhood events made a marriage impossible. We see a lot of their family members, who give us a good idea of what they were up against.

The film stars Julianne Nicholson and Justin Kirk as New Yorkers who meet on a blind date arranged by their therapist. They fall in love during their first conversation, are married, are happy at first, and then become unhappy. But their unhappiness is not the stuff of melodrama; it's an accumulation of small moments that build a deep divide between them. Lipsky demands of his actors no less than Bergman required in *Scenes from a Marriage* or *The Passion of Anna,* and although the acting here is not showy, it is quietly, powerfully good.

I've noticed Nicholson a lot in good movies; rent *Tully* for a heartwarming American family drama. She played Jenny on *Ally McBeal.* She's thin, freckled, quiet, and warm, and pulls you in instead of going after you. Here she has a hard assignment: She must at all times seem reasonable, logical, and sane while in almost invisible ways sabotaging her marriage. Kirk's character desperately wants to please her but cannot and never understands that he can't, or why he can't.

The extended family scenes (especially a conversation between Kirk and Rebecca Schull, as his mother-in-law) are fraught with hidden messages. But most of the film takes place between two people who begin in happiness and are blindsided by their own hidden natures. The film is deep and demanding and not easy to experience, but it is formidable.

* * *

Faithful readers will recall The Kid. They will remember my reports about how hopeful filmmakers press copies of their DVDs upon me, hoping that I will ignore the official Sundance entries, repair to my room, and watch their work on video. Regretfully but firmly I must decline these gifts, because I have not come all this way to miss official screenings in order to look at the latest product of the DVD-R drive on somebody's computer.

But it was a different matter with The Kid. He accosted me on opening night in 1999 in the theater lobby. His film, named *Bobby Loves Mangos*, was only twenty minutes long. It was brilliant, he assured me. "Someday I'll be a great director, and I will remind you of this moment," he told me. I wished him well but did not allow him to press the video into my hands.

The next day I was standing in the coffee bar of the Yarrow Hotel, and a voice in my ear confided that The Kid's film would begin in ten seconds on the giant-screen TV over the bar. It was The Kid.

"What'd you do? Bribe the manager?" I asked.

"Kind of," he said.

"But I have to go to a press screening in ten minutes," I said.

"I'll have them hold it for you," he assured me. "I work here."

"Hold it?" I said. "They're not gonna keep three dozen people waiting so that . . ."

"Don't miss the opening scene," he said.

I watched the film. Sitting next to me was Paul LeMat, star of *American Graffiti* and many other movies. He watched it too. "This is pretty good," I said. He agreed. It was.

I wrote about The Kid, whose name was Stuart Acher. He got an agent. He started making commercials and music videos. He wrote some TV shows. There was a bittersweet triumph when his commercial "Super Absorbent," starring the Gap girl Shalom Harlow, was on Fox's "best commercials you'll never see." But there was no feature film. It is not that easy to get a feature film off the ground, no matter how well your short subject plays in the Yarrow coffee bar.

Now it is Sundance 2006. I am on the shuttle bus to the Eccles Center. A voice in my ear says, "I'm still here." It was The Kid. He had good news for me.

"I'm directing my first feature film this summer! This is Kimberley Boyd. She is my producer."

I can't wait to see Acher's film. I hope it plays Sundance. If it doesn't, I have a feeling I will see it anyway, maybe in the Yarrow coffee bar. Will Acher be a great director someday? I think it is a promising sign that he made a commercial too good to be aired.

Sundance Report No. 7

January 26, 2006—Since 1968, the MPAA Code and Ratings Administration has been an anonymous group enforcing secret guidelines on almost all movies seeking release in America. The difference between its R and NC-17 ratings can mean life or death for a movie. A rating can be appealed—to another anonymous group, also with guidelines that are never made clear. The board's founder and great defender, Jack Valenti, explained for years that the movie raters were "ordinary parents" with young children, trying to advise other parents on how appropriate movies might be for younger viewers.

That mysterious cloak of secrecy was ripped asunder (to use Valenti's beloved hyperbole) here at Sundance Wednesday night, with the premiere of Kirby Dick's new documentary, *This Film Is Not Yet Rated*, a devastating attack on the MPAA's ratings and how they are administered. Yes, it's one-sided, especially in the way Dick sidesteps a good point that Valenti makes: The national ratings system headed off the threat of countless local censor boards. But the system penalizes many nonpornographic but adult-themed movies and is administrated inconsistently behind a bewildering smoke screen.

In the film, Dick hires a doughty private

eye, a middle-aged woman with a van, a pair of binoculars, and a niece to write down license plates, and they successfully discover the names of all the movie raters; interestingly, only a few have young children, many have children in their twenties and thirties, and one has no children at all.

They get a couple of former raters to talk and even interview Richard D. Heffner, a former head of the board. The bottom line is not much of a surprise: The board is much more lenient toward violence than toward sex, won't suggest helpful edits to indie filmmakers but supplies suggestions to studio films, and has an interesting voting system: If there's a tie vote of the eight-member board, the chair casts the deciding vote, which means he gets to vote twice.

Dept. of Rich Irony: The *Los Angeles Times* reports that the MPAA obtained a copy of Dick's film and made DVD copies of it for internal scrutiny. That, of course, would be precisely the kind of bootleg piracy the MPAA is waging war against.

* * *

One of the strongest and most touching films in the competition is *Quinceañera* by Wash Westmoreland and Richard Glatzer. It tells the story of a fifteen-year-old Mexican-American girl in the Echo Park district of Los Angeles. Like the wonderful 2002 film *Real Women Have Curves,* it's about a generation gap between parents and children, about the challenge of being in love and remaining a virgin, and about an extended circle of family and friends. There is rich human comedy here, and sadness, and a portrait so textured that we get very involved.

Emily Rios stars as Magdalena, whose fifteenth birthday milestone is approaching and who knows her father isn't rich but hopes she can have a Hummer stretch limo like her best friend for her own *quinceañera* (a traditional celebration of a Latina's fifteenth birthday). Then she becomes pregnant while technically still a virgin ("My sperm sure can swim," her boyfriend observes ruefully). Her father banishes her from the family home, and she finds refuge with her great-uncle, played by Chalo Gonzalez with such warmth and wisdom that this is surely one of the best performances of the year. The story also involves

her cousin (Jesse Garcia), who gets involved with the yuppie gays who are their landlords. Life lessons are learned in a film that is serious, joyful, and filled with heart.

* * *

Tilda Swinton and Amber Tamblyn share scenes of painful personal revelation in Hilary Brougher's *Stephanie Daley,* which is also about a pregnant teenager. Tamblyn's character, whose pregnancy is a secret, partly even from herself, gives birth in a restroom, and, when the baby is found dead and discarded, is charged with a crime.

Swinton plays the psychologist assigned by the prosecution to interview the girl. This process is fraught with emotion because the older woman recently went through a stillbirth and now is pregnant again. As the two women talk, flashbacks show the complexities of their experiences with pregnancy.

The film avoids the conventional moves of a Q&A investigation to show both women somehow sharing their emotions. "There's a kind of a conspiracy among women to conceal how painful and difficult pregnancy can be," Swinton, the mother of two, said after the screening. The film avoids a simple criminal solution to the death of the teenager's baby and involves instead the deepest feelings both women have about the lives within them.

* * *

The Darwin Awards began as a Web site, became a book, and have now become a movie. The awards were inspired by the theory that some people die in such idiotic ways that their passing may be a benefit to the gene pool. Finn Taylor's comedy stars Winona Ryder as an insurance investigator who is told by a neurotic former police detective (Joseph Fiennes) that his brilliance at creating victim profiles can help the insurance company single out likely candidates for stupid accidental deaths.

The film intercuts their investigations with scenes based on famous Darwin Award winners; the funniest and most gruesome involves a couple of stoners who try to sneak into a Metallica concert and end up in a catastrophe so unlikely that a kind of insane logic informs it. The movie doesn't have much of a through-line, and the investigators mostly exist as segues between horrible accidental deaths, but there is a certain gruesome fascination to the episodes.

Sundance Report No. 8

January 26, 2006—As Sundance 2006 approaches its end, and we stagger from one screening to another fueled almost entirely by blueberry muffins and microwave burritos, it is time to reflect that most moviegoers will have little chance of seeing many of the Sundance films. The system is set up that way. Numskull action pictures are pounded into the desires of teenage boys by multimillion-dollar ad campaigns, and it takes the special moviegoer to seek and find the treasures. A moviegoer exactly like you, for why else would you be reading about this festival of directors who hope to make wonderful films even if the system is indifferent?

I'm writing this in the press room at Sundance, because it has free Wi-Fi access, free coffee, and (instead of burritos) ham sandwiches and chili. A gourmet paradise. Because I am at a table near the door, people stop to talk to me, and as I meet them I am reminded of the idealism that fuels Sundance. No, the festival has not "gone Hollywood" and is not too "commercialized," although these people dearly wish Hollywood would notice them and pay cash for the movies they made by mortgaging their lives.

Here are some people I have met:

—Mike Wilson, a member of the Tohono O'odham Nation, is featured in *Crossing Arizona,* a documentary about Native American people who give aid to Mexicans trying to enter the United States through the Sonora Desert, a journey that can take four days. "Hundreds of these people die," he tells me. "We give them water. That has nothing to do with the law. People do not deserve to die." Because Indian lands are exempt from federal laws, what he does is in a legal shadowland, but "it is a moral issue, not a legal issue," he tells me. He hopes I can see the film.

—Susan Norget is the publicist for *Madeinusa,* a title that is one word made of three. It's a Peruvian film about a village where every year, from the hour of Christ's crucifixion until the hour of his resurrection, "sin does not exist" because God is dead. She tells me the director, Claudia Llosa, cast all local actors and gets a feeling of immediacy that is uncanny. She hopes I can see the film.

—John Jota Leanos and Sean Levon Nash give me tickets to the Animation Spotlight program Saturday. They worked on *Los ABCs,* a Chicano animated film "which catalogues the real-life testimonies of skeletons who have returned to tell their stories of life and death." It is, according to the postcard they hand me, a "mariachi sing-along," and its "silences will be broken with much operatic wagon-burning." They hope I can see the film.

—Mia Goldman is the director of *Open Window,* starring Robin Tunney as a woman who is raped and is slow to recover; she retreats deeply into herself, where her husband cannot find her. Her film, at least, I have seen, and admired. She tells me Tunney was sad that the work schedule for her *Prison Break* TV series shortened her Sundance stay. Goldman does not say, but I intuit, that although only a fraction of the *Prison Break* audience will ever see *Open Window,* it is for roles like this that actresses like Tunney dream, because they can reach the far edges of their talent.

—I run into Steven Wallace, a publicist for *Eve and the Fire Horse,* a magical first film from Canada by Julia Kwan. I loved its story of two young Chinese-Canadian girls who bring about a charming and formidably logical fusion of Buddhism and Catholicism in their lives. "It doesn't have U.S. distribution yet," he says, "but it opens this weekend in Canada, and the Sundance reception has generated a lot of interest."

—A little earlier, in the breakfast room at the Yarrow, I met Jim Bennett, who is a vice president of Netflix; Bronagh Hanley, its director of public relations; and Stan Lanning, whose card says he is an "employee." That means he is either very low down or, more likely, very high up in the Netflix hierarchy. They talk about the retailing theory of the "long tail," which teaches that although immediate business can be raked in by current best sellers, the real money is made by churning the backlist. Netflix's system of "cinematches" tries to pair customers with movies they might like but have not heard of. Sundance films are tailor-made for matching; the depth of their selection provides hope for films that must live and die outside the mainstream hype.

Now, as I meet Mike Wilson, as I hear about

Claudia Llosa and the hours without sin, as I am intrigued by the mariachi sing-along and operatic wagon-burning, as I remember Tunney's great performance, as I think of the two little girls picturing Jesus and Buddha dancing together, I consider that although the best place to see a good movie is in a theater, the worst thing is not to see it at all. No video store can carry every film, but companies like Netflix can try to, and although the retail terminology about "churning the long tail" may not be precisely poetic, at least these films have a chance of being seen.

Note: For that matter, you can watch Los ABCs *and a lot of other shorts for free on the Sundance Web site, at http://festival.sundance. org/2006/watch/index.aspx.*

Sundance Report No. 9

January 29, 2006—Closing pages from a festival diary:

If many of the best films at Sundance find it hard to attract a teenage audience, *Alpha Dog*, the festival's big closing film, may explain why. Nick Cassavetes's harrowing true-life drama, based on a notorious Los Angeles kidnapping, portrays affluent kids and their parents who live in a wasteland of ignorance, moral bankruptcy, and general cluelessness. It is impossible to imagine any character in this movie attending a movie, reading a book, or having a thought not focused on self-gratification.

Half an hour into the film, two audience members walked out loudly, as the film wallowed in a lifestyle of drug abuse, alcoholism, careless sex, and nonstop f-wordery. Good thing they didn't stay to watch scenes of cruelty and violence, and a murder as stupid as it is heartless. One reaction might be to recoil from the film. My reaction was to admire Cassavetes and his cast for so mercilessly portraying a worthless segment of society.

The cast is a roll call of A- and B-plus younger actors, including Emile Hirsch, Justin Timberlake, Anton Yelchin, Shawn Hatosy, Lukas Haas, and Dominique Swain. Ben Foster is especially scary as a stoned speed-freak martial artist with eyes that seem to spin in his head. The film's message appears to be: These people and their world are the spawn of hell.

* * *

But at Sundance you switch gears quickly.

On the last day or two you hurry between screenings, trying to catch films everybody tells you not to miss. One I especially admired was *Crossing Arizona*, the story of how changes in the U.S. border patrol strategy have funneled illegal immigration toward the Sonoma Desert. More than one thousand Mexicans have died of thirst in recent years, and we meet Native Americans who distribute bottles of water along immigration pathways. They also advise the immigrants to turn themselves in to the Border Patrol to save their lives.

The movie observes that illegal immigrant farm workers are crucial to the Arizona economy, and an American farmer says that without them the state's agriculture would fail. We meet right-wing Minute Men who appoint themselves as unofficial border guards, fanned on by TV commentators such as Bill O'Reilly, who says the North Koreans line their border with Red Army troops and says he agrees with that approach. Meanwhile, Border Patrol agents consider the Minute Men dangerous bozos, and an Indian pastor finds that someone has slashed open the plastic bottles of water he leaves in the desert.

* * *

The movie title *Madeinusa* is intended to be pronounced "Madanusa," and it's the name of the heroine of Claudia Llosa's magical film from Peru. She's a young girl who lives with her sister under the sway of a tyrannical father. In her village, it is believed that between 3 P.M. on Good Friday, when Christ died, and dawn on Easter, when he arose from the dead, it is impossible to commit a sin—because God is dead. The villagers take full advantage of this in alarming ceremonies involving their virgins.

A traveler from Lima is marooned in the village over the weekend, falls in love with Madeinusa, and becomes a victim of local customs. The film is enriched with countless eerie details, including an old man who stations himself in the square, squints at the sun to tell the time, and flips over cardboard numbers to act as a living digital clock.

* * *

Has there ever been a gloomier-looking movie than *A Little Trip to Heaven*? Here is a gothic noir that is set in America but was filmed in Iceland, where director Baltasar

873

Kormakur finds a landscape and a shambling farmhouse so cold, dark, and forbidding it becomes like another character.

Forest Whitaker is lovably engaging as an insurance investigator who suspects that the crispy body in a burned-out car may not belong to a client with a $1 million insurance policy. Jeremy Renner plays a scary creep who specializes in fake accidents, and Julia Stiles is the woman horrified by his schemes but trapped in them because of her love for her child. Whitaker gives his investigator an absentminded insecurity that makes us like him, and fear for him.

* * *

Wristcutters: A Love Story is the kind of macabre fantasy that may find an audience just because its premise is so audacious. Patrick Fugit stars as a pleasant young man who commits suicide for reasons never explained. He awakens on the other side to discover that life goes on as before except everything is a little more run-down and depressing. He falls in love with Shannon Sossamon, who believes she got a raw deal because she didn't kill herself but died of an accidental overdose. She appeals to a guy who seems to be in charge, who is played by Tom Waits, which tells you something right there.

Sundance Report No. 10

January 29, 2006—On the last day of Sundance 2006, I went to see one final film, named *Man Push Cart*. It was playing at 8:30 A.M. in the Prospector Square Theater, which is a large room filled with fairly comfortable folding chairs. The movie tells the story of a young man who was once a rock star in his native Pakistan but now operates a stainless steel push cart on the streets of Manhattan, vending coffee, tea, muffins, and bagels ("You want cream cheese?").

The room was filled. In front of me were a woman from Ogden and her brother from Philadelphia. They said they attend Sundance to see films that are really about something. After *Man Push Cart* was over, they said they loved it. So did I. But I loved it not only for itself but because of the conditions of its making.

At the end of ten days and hundreds of films and hype about movie stars and swag

bags and midnight parties, this is what Sundance is really about: this man pushing this cart.

The movie was written and directed by Ramin Bahrani, an American born in Iran. It stars Ahmad Razvi, an American born in Pakistan. It was shot in less than three weeks, on a small budget, with Bahrani grabbing a lot of his shots by filming from across the street.

There's a scene where the hero, also named Ahmad, offers to sell some bootleg videos to a couple of guys loading merchandise. He says they're $8 each, two for $15. "I can get them for four bucks in Brooklyn," says one of the guys. This guy did not know he was in a film; Bahrani got him to sign a release so he could keep the scene. As for (the real) Ahmad, when he was not acting he was working on locations and continuity. Everybody on the film worked on everything.

Ahmad is a sad man whose wife has died and whose in-laws will not let him see his son. His career as a singing star is long forgotten. He gets up at 3 every morning, stocks his cart, and pulls it through the streets. He makes friends with a Spanish woman who is filling in for a relative at a nearby magazine stand. She likes him. But can he see a future for himself?

Bahrani said one of the inspirations for his film was *The Myth of Sisyphus* by Albert Camus. That's the story of a man who spends his life rolling a heavy rock up a hill, only to see it roll back down again. The life of Ahmad resembles the plight of Sisyphus. At the end of the film, we see him helping a friend pull a cart through the streets. *Two Men Push Cart*, I guess. Is this progress? Is it reason for hope?

It's almost impossible to convey the particular tone and effect of *Man Push Cart*. It is an experience, not a synopsis. My purpose is to show that with very little money but a lot of effort, a director can push a movie all the way uphill to Sundance. This man may have been born in Iran and his star may be from Pakistan, but they are Americans, their film is mostly in English, it is entered in the "Spectrum" section, and people from Ogden and Philadelphia come to see it because they hunger for such films. The whole experience contains the Sundance idea: Anyone can make a movie, and if it is good enough, Sundance can help it find an audience.

Man Push Cart didn't win any prizes later that night at the award ceremony. But the winning films were also uphill battles. *Quinceanera*, the winner as best dramatic film, takes us into the life of a fifteen-year-old Latina in Los Angeles who faces a crisis and finds hope from her elderly great-uncle and her gay cousin. The film was made by a Brit named Wash Westmoreland and a New Yorker named Richard Glatzer, "and we are both gay," Westmoreland said, perhaps to underline how their film enters lives completely unlike their own and views them with empathy.

I wish *Man Push Cart* could be seen by the Minute Men, the self-anointed patriots shown in the Sundance documentary *Crossing Arizona*. They man the Mexican border with night-vision binoculars and hope to repel illegal immigrants without whom Arizona's agricultural economy would collapse. I wonder if the Minute Men see themselves as the children of immigrants. Can they see Ahmad as an American?

The best Sundance documentary this year was *God Grew Tired of Us* by Christopher Quinn, who told the stories of some 27,000 starving Sudanese boys who trekked through a desert to survive while the world ignored them. When the screening was over, a member of the audience wrote a check for $25,000 for Sudanese relief. Certainly Quinn did not go to the Sudan hoping for fame or fortune; he saw a story that he felt he had to tell.

Julia Kwan felt the same way. She is a young woman from Vancouver who made *Eve and the Fire Horse*, about two young Chinese-Canadian sisters who take religion very seriously. They ask questions a theologian would find tricky, such as, "When the Egyptians were drowned in the Red Sea, why did God drown their horses, too?" One sister becomes a Catholic, the other a Buddhist. Their stories are based on Kwan's childhood memories. Her film won a special jury prize in the world cinema section. Although it is visually beautiful and moves with poetic grace, it was as hard to make as the others. It must have looked impossible at one point.

Most of the movies that open every week are calculated financial investments made by people who expect to see a profit. Many of the smaller Sundance films are made by people who never expect to be able to pay them off. They make them because they are filled with a vision or a message and want to share their experience. To see them is to participate in their lives. It is hard for a man to push a cart. It is easier when there are two men. Maybe Sundance is like the other guy, helping to push the cart.

Overlooked Film Festival
Marni Nixon Headlines Eighth Annual Overlooked Film Festival

Chicago, March 20, 2006—An Oscar nominee, an offscreen singing star, a *really* bad Santa, and a Carmen from Cape Town will be among the selections at my Eighth Annual Overlooked Film Festival. Playing April 26–30 at the University of Illinois at Urbana-Champaign, the fest honors overlooked films, formats, and genres. Their makers join me onstage for discussions after the screenings.

Opening night will feature a famous movie with a star who was required by Hollywood to remain anonymous. We'll have a rare 70mm screening of a restored print of *My Fair Lady*, with a personal appearance by Marni Nixon, who dubbed the singing voice of Audrey Hepburn in the movie. As Hollywood's most gifted unseen musical star, she also sang for Natalie Wood in *West Side Story* and Deborah Kerr in *The King and I*.

Amy Adams, an Academy Award nominee this year for *Junebug*, will appear after a screening of her film, along with its writer-director, Phil Morrison. Of all the performances I saw last year, hers was the most heart-warming.

A two-time Oscar nominee, John Malkovich of Chicago's Steppenwolf Theater, has tentatively agreed to join us to discuss his 2002 film *Ripley's Game*. Directed by Liliana Cavani, it is the best of all the films inspired by Patricia Highsmith's amoral villain but was never released theatrically in the United States. Russell Smith, the executive producer and a longtime Steppenwolf associate, also will be onstage.

Terry Zwigoff, director of *Bad Santa*, will be at the festival with his personal print of what he calls *Really, Really Bad Santa*. The original *Bad Santa* (2003) starred Billy Bob Thornton as an alcoholic department store Santa who used his job as a cover for robberies. It was rated R on general release, and then additional material was added for an "unrated" DVD. Zwigoff says the print he's bringing includes material not even on the DVD.

We always salute a musical film on the closing Sunday of the festival, and this year my choice is *U-Carmen e-Khayelitsha* (2005), a version of Bizet's opera *Carmen* filmed in Cape Town and sung entirely in Khosa. The South African diva Pauline Malefane and the film's director, Mark Dornford-May, will appear in person.

Lodge Kerrigan is a legendary independent director whose films, including *Clean, Shaven* and *Keane* (2005), explore lives on the margin. He will appear with his film *Claire Dolan* (1998), starring Katrin Cartlidge, a brilliant actress who died too young at forty-one in 2002.

Nate Kohn, director of the Overlooked Festival and professor of cinema at the University of Georgia, is not often seen on the stage of the Virginia Theater. But he can't escape the spotlight this year. I've invited *Somebodies*, the official Sundance entry he coproduced with his wife, Pam. Also in person: the film's gifted young writer-director, Hadjii, and one of its stars, Kaira Whitehead. The film is a human comedy about an African-American college student in Georgia and his friends and relatives.

One goal of the festival is to spotlight new indie films still seeking distribution. This year we'll show *Man Push Cart*, a 2006 Sundance entry about the life of a former Pakistani rock star who now operates a Manhattan bagel and coffee wagon. The writer-director, Ramin Bahrani, and its star, Ahmad Razvi, will be onstage in person.

One of the best indie films I saw last year was *Duane Hopwood*, with its brilliant, career-best performance by David Schwimmer as an alcoholic who works the overnight shift at a casino in Atlantic City. Despite its power it received only a small theatrical release; its writer-director, Matt Mulhern, will be onstage.

David Mamet is not only one of the world's leading playwrights but also a film director of great distinction. His *Spartan* (2004), about the kidnapping of a daughter of the president, got a four-star review from me but grossed only about $2 million at the box office. In a precedent-breaker, it will be followed onstage by Michael Barker, cohead of Sony Classic Pictures, which did *not* release the film; he is simply a great admirer of the Warner Bros. release. One of the stars may also be present.

Millions (2005), a family film from the U.K. that was on my ten best list, will be our Saturday morning family matinee. Directed by Danny Boyle (*28 Days Later*) and written by Frank Cottrell Boyce (*Hilary and Jackie, Tristram Shandy*), it's about two brothers who find loot from a robbery; one of them takes advice from his favorite saints about how to dispose of it.

My personal highlight at each year's festival is the silent film, accompanied by the Alloy Orchestra of Cambridge, Massachusetts, world leaders in performing musical scores. They'll be in the pit of the Virginia accompanying a restored print of *The Eagle* (1925), starring Rudolph Valentino.

Cannes Film Festival

Cannes Report No. 1:
Da Vinci at Cannes

Cannes, France, May 18, 2006—On second thought, maybe it was not such a great idea to hold the world premiere of *The Da Vinci Code* at the Cannes Film Festival. The critical reception here was negative, but what would you expect? As someone who enjoyed the film (good, not great, better than the book), I am possibly typical of many of the people who will pay to see it. But when you open at Cannes, those are not the people in your audience.

You must understand that Cannes always opens with a French film. Always. Well, almost always. It always opens with a movie that has big stars, that's for sure. Every network in Europe covers the opening night, as celebrities march up the red-carpeted staircase and fashion commentators give a gown-by-gown description of the action. So Cannes got its stars: Tom Hanks, yes, and Sir Ian McKellen, and two of the biggest stars in France, Jean Reno and Audrey Tautou of *Amelie*. It got a film that opens and closes at the Louvre, has a chase scene in Paris, includes a villa in the French countryside, and has a lot of subtitled French. But it did not get a French film, and that caused some resentment.

Then there was the circus atmosphere. Sony Pictures actually chartered a train to bring press here from London, as the stars wandered the aisles giving interviews. The kinds of journalists who take such train rides are, in the language of Cannes, not critics but chroniclers. In other words, celebrity and gossip writers. As for the critics, who saw the film here on Tuesday, they are very serious, never more serious than on opening night, when they suspect they are witnessing the death of the cinema. They have suspected this every year since 1946, I believe it was.

There is also the delight of a scandal: Big film comes to Cannes, opening-day Tomatometer stands at 20 percent, Drudge runs headline that *Da Vinci* was greeted with jeers, etc. David Germain of the Associated Press looked on the bright side: "There were fewer departures than many Cannes movies provoke among harsh critics." And he found a critic who liked it: ". . . for two hours it was good entertainment. As a Hollywood movie, it's a very nice picture." This critic was Igor Soukmanov of Unistar Radio in Belarus.

I suppose it takes a certain perversity to say, hey, it's not that bad; it's more or less precisely what you would imagine a movie made from *The Da Vinci Code* would be like. Having actually read the Dan Brown novel, however, I imagine the movie was harder to appreciate for those who hadn't slogged through his theological treasure hunt, and I doubt it is the sort of novel favored by opening-night critics at Cannes.

So maybe Sony should have just opened the movie in the usual way and not spent millions setting itself up for crucifixion at Cannes. Speaking of those millions, we never did make it to the opening-night party, which began at midnight and was held in a pyramid that was said to be somewhere out at the end of the harbor. When you fly all night to France, you do not seek out midnight parties involving two thousand strangers jammed into a pyramid. Instead of a VIP area, do they use the pharaoh's burial chamber?

My wife, Chaz, and I did, however, attend the official opening dinner in the Palais du Festival after the screening. We sat at a table with a woman who said her name was Monica and that she spoke English, but did not say anything more than that. Also at the table was our good friend Baz Bamigboye of the *Daily*

Mail, a London paper that is like if the *New York Post* died and went to heaven. Baz on opening night: "It's a movie about whether the greatest story ever told is true or not, and it's not the greatest movie ever screened, is it?"

True enough. We ran into Sir Ian McKellen, who seemed, after years of toiling at greatness in Shakespeare, to be enjoying his current superstar status as a Hollywood villain. This week, *The Da Vinci Code*. Next week, Magneto in *X-Men: The Last Stand.*

"I'm the sort who pays his way into the Universal Studio tour because I love the movies so much," he said. "Just think, I get paid to be in a movie with Tom Hanks!" This struck me as such an improbably nice statement that it might possibly be true. He was hanging out with Tim Roth and Alfred Molina, two other great actors with jolly Hollywood credits (you will recall Molina as Doc Ock in *Spider-Man 2*).

Ron Howard and his producer, Brian Grazer, passed by on their way to the pyramid. Howard seemed reasonably cheerful, perhaps because he suspects *The Da Vinci Code* will gross a fortune despite its Cannes reception. They left through a nearby door.

"I wonder if that's how you get to the pyramid?" Chaz said.

I asked a waiter, "Is that the way to the pyramid?"

"The pyramid, monsieur?" he said. "That is the way you get to the kitchen."

We sat back down at our table with Monica and Baz. There was a little printed menu at every place. I asked Chaz if she wanted to stay for dessert.

"What are they having?" she asked. "I don't have my reading glasses, and I can't see the menu."

"Luckily, I do, and I can," I said.

"But it is in French, and you won't know what it says."

"I read a lot of French," I said. "You're forgetting the summer I spent reading the Tin Tin comics with the French dictionary."

"All you learned from that," she said, "was how to say, 'Not by foot, I hope!'"

"A useful phrase," I said.

"Can you understand what it says we're having for dessert?" she said.

"Of course I can," I said. "It says, 'Surprise.'"

Cannes Report No. 2: Blood and Guts

May 19, 2006—In one of the bravest acts of courage I have performed in the exercise of my duties at the Cannes festival, I went out to dinner Thursday night. The company was exhilarating and the food was superb, but let me tell you about two movies I saw before dinner. Both were official selections. *Fast Food Nation* is about how meat arrives in franchise burgers, and what might be in it besides meat. *Taxidermia* is about a man who invents a machine that eviscerates and stuffs its occupant, stitches up the incisions, and chops off his head and one arm.

During these films I saw great big gobs of greasy, grimy guts: livers, spleens, intestines, hearts, lungs, and a young woman taught how to "pull out the kidneys." I saw hooves, ears, and snouts sliced off, skin stripped from carcasses, rivers of blood, intestines poured into pots. That was in a meat processing factory in *Fast Food Nation*. In *Taxidermia*, a pig is reduced to its elements, and what goes on sexually does not bear mentioning.

Taxidermia is by Gyorgy Palfi, the Hungarian director of *Hukkle* (2003), a sort of wonderful movie almost entirely without human sounds except for hiccups. I am sure *Taxidermia* is an important film and certainly a brave one, but I doubt if I know anyone who would thank me for recommending it.

Fast Food Nation was written by Eric Schlosser, author of the best seller of the same name, and directed by Richard Linklater, the brilliant Austin-based director of *Waking Life, Slacker, School of Rock, SubUrbia, Tape,* and *Dazed and Confused*. It is not a documentary, but a fact-based dramatization using parallel stories. One involves Greg Kinnear as a fast-food marketing executive on a fact-finding mission; his boss asks him to investigate reports that fecal matter is being found in the chain's hamburgers. The other is about undocumented Mexicans supplied as low-salaried employees in a vast food processing plant where not all the legs sliced off belong to cows.

The movie is not sensational, unless we consider factual footage of cattle being slaughtered on an assembly line to be sensational, and why should we? That's how most of America's meat gets to most of America's meat-eaters. The film has no special statement to make on "guest workers" in terms of the current national debate: It simply observes how they are imported (at their own cost) and supplied as cheap labor to a meat factory where Americans are not keen to work.

The film produces a great sadness and a greater queasiness. It is not about heroes, but about ordinary working people. There is a conversation between the Kinnear character and a key supplier of meat (Bruce Willis) that in its quiet, factual ruthlessness is probably just about how such people discuss such matters. The Willis character argues that there has always been a lot of stuff in meat besides meat, and if the burgers are grilled at a high temperature, what's the difference?

College students who work part time in a fast food outlet begin to hate their jobs and learn that the meat plant's holding lots for cattle produce more urine and feces than all of the people in Denver, none of it treated, all of it seeping into groundwater. They take direct action against the company; the result is not high drama but a sad joke—on the cattle, I think.

You can't make an omelet without breaking eggs, or a burger without slaughtering cows, which reminds me of the chicken who suggested ham 'n' eggs to the pig, who replied: "For you it's a donation, but for me it's a commitment." I am also reminded of Roy Rogers having Trigger stuffed and joking, "When I die, I want to be stuffed and mounted on Trigger," and Dale Evans saying, "Now, Roy, don't you be gettin' any ideas about me."

I want to write a lot more about *Fast Food Nation*—and *Taxidermia*, for that matter. I've gone through periods of being a vegetarian in my life, and I sense another one coming on. My interest in taxidermy remains minimal.

Cannes Report No. 3

May 22, 2006—One of the traditions at Cannes is the dramatic unveiling of advance footage from a blockbuster scheduled to open next Christmas. I avoid these opportunities. I prefer to see movies all at once. Therefore, I turned down an invitation to the preview party for *Dreamgirls*, the big musical that opens December 6, 2006.

"You're crazy," I was informed. "People are dying to get into that party."

I considered my latest report from the festival. It involved movies about cow manure in hamburger meat, and a taxidermist who invents a machine to kill and stuff himself. Perhaps, I thought, my readers would enjoy reading about something more cheerful, such as Beyoncé Knowles.

My wife, Chaz, and I arrived at the Hotel Martinez an hour late for the party, which would be starting before long. People were not dying to get into the party. They were killing to get into the party. The customary riot was under way. Jamie Foxx was entering the building, and gendarmes were holding back surging masses of paparazzi determined to repair the world's tragic shortage of photos of Jamie Foxx.

We fought through the crowd to the entrance point, where the barricades were manned by those fierce guards in tuxedos known at Cannes as the gorillas.

"*Non!*" explained a gorilla, as we indicated a desire to enter. "*Impossible!*"

"But we are invited!"

"*Enn-vee-tay!*" he said, pointing to the other end of the mob, a block down the street. Mark Twain once explained that all foreigners understand English if it is pronounced loudly and slowly enough, and so I said, "We . . . are . . . invited!"

"*Impossible!*" he explained in French. He jabbed his finger in a giant arc to indicate that we should overleap the mob. Luckily, in French I know how to say, "Not by foot, I hope!" When I told him that, the gorilla started talking into his cuff link.

I know when I am beaten. We plunged into the mob and emerged at a point where Richard and Mary Corliss, the film critic of *Time* and his wife, were shaking their heads and waving us off.

"We're at the wrong place," they told us. "We have to go up to the front of that mob."

A gorilla was fiercely watching for any excuse to apply a choke hold.

"We just came from there and they told us to come here," I said. Richard nodded curtly and translated this into English: "They just came from there and were told to come here!"

"Must go there!" said the gorilla.

"Not by foot, I hope!"

We hurled ourselves again into the mob and fought our way back up the street, where the original gorillas regarded us with total indifference as we walked directly into the hotel. The story has a happy ending. Inside the hotel, we were given badges that would admit us to the hotel.

As for the *Dreamgirls* preview, the theory is that after seeing twenty minutes from the movie I will write a story saying I can't wait until December 6 to see the rest of it. There is no sense in being coy. Those were twenty terrific minutes. They involved three unknown backup singers (Beyoncé Knowles, Anika Noni Rose, and Jennifer Hudson) rehearsing with a James Brown type played by Eddie Murphy. Then a musical montage. Then Jamie Foxx as a former car salesman who has transformed himself into a brilliant manager. "Didn't you sell me my Caddy?" asks Eddie Murphy. Then the famous scene where the sweet girl with the best voice (Hudson) is told she's being replaced as the lead by the Dreamgirl with more glamour (Knowles).

Bill Condon, director of the film (and an Oscar winner for *Chicago,* the famous musical filmed in Toronto), bounded onstage and introduced Knowles, Rose, Hudson, Foxx, and the choreographer, Fatima Robinson. Tumultuous cheering.

At the reception, Hudson, the *American Idol* loser from Chicago who is now the program's biggest winner, introduced her mother, Darnell, to Sir Ian McKellen, who starred in Bill Condon's 1998 movie, *Gods and Monsters.* McKellen confessed himself charmed by mother and daughter.

Also in the room was Chris Tucker, in an ice cream suit and shocking pink tie. "Do you have a film here?" I asked. "No," he said, "just hanging out." That possibly translates as, "No, but my people and Jackie Chan's people are meeting in hotel rooms to discuss *Rush Hour 3* and preselling it to most of the world."

And Lawrence Laws Watford and his wife, Angela Watford, were there. May 14 was their first wedding anniversary. He has a short film in the official competition, and she is the copy editor of *Star* magazine. "I never miss it," I said. They were such really nice people, I wanted to introduce them to McKellen, just to see three nice people at the same time. But by then, I myself was feeling so nice that I considered taking some cookies out to the gorillas. It is a lonely life they lead.

Cannes Report No. 4—
William Friedkin and *Bug*

May 22, 2006—William Friedkin's new horror film, *Bug*, begins as an ominous rumble of unease and builds to a shriek. The last twenty minutes are searingly intense: A paranoid personality finds its mate, and they race each other into madness. For Friedkin, director of *The Exorcist*, it's a work of headlong passion.

The film has caused a stir at Cannes, not least because its stars, Ashley Judd and Michael Shannon, achieve a kind of manic intensity that's frightening not just in itself but because you fear for the actors. The film is based on a play by Tracy Letts, an actor and playwright at Chicago's Steppenwolf Theater. It opened in London ten years ago and was playing in Chicago on 9/11. Friedkin saw it in 2004 in New York with his wife, Paramount studio chief Sherry Lansing. She said she thought it was fantastic. When he told her he wanted to make it into a movie, she told him he was crazy. Maybe it took craziness.

"I didn't want to take it to a big studio where there would be lots of young people eager to, quote, help out the director," Friedkin said here the day after the film played, joining Letts and Shannon over coffee. "A lot of big stars wanted to act in this piece and even tried to buy it, but I knew the film had to be true to the play, and Michael was inseparable from the role."

In the film we meet Agnes (Judd), a waitress in a honky-tonk bar, living in a shabby motel. Her violent ex-husband (Harry Connick Jr.), just out on parole, walks back into her life, still violent. At about the same time, her lesbian friend R.C. (Lynn Collins) drags in a stray with haunted eyes. This is the polite stranger named Peter (Shannon), who says he doesn't want sex or anything else, is attentive and courteous, and is invited by Agnes to spend the night even though he seems (to us) like the embodiment of menace.

The story involves this man's obsession with bugs that he believes infect his cells and may have been implanted by the government during his treatment for obscure causes after military service in the Gulf. We think he's

crazy. Agnes listens and nods, and doesn't want him to leave; she feels safer around him. He begins to seem more weird. This doesn't bother her. With mounting urgency, she begins to share his obsession about bugs, and together they escalate into a paranoid fantasy that ties together in perfect conspiracy all the suspicions they've ever had about anything. There is a scene we're not prepared for, in which they're peering into a cheap microscope and seeing whatever they think they see.

Peter is mad, and Agnes's personality seems to need him to express its own madness. Judd's final monologue is a sustained cry of nonstop breathless panic, twisted logic, and sudden frantic insight that is a kind of behavior very rarely risked in or out of the movies. It may not be Shakespeare, but it's not any easier.

"I wanted Ashley for her intelligence," Friedkin said. "The actors have to be able to understand this movie. It can't be explained to them. Her personal experience was a help: She grew up with her mother and sister, poor, living in trailers; she had some abusive relationships ... she had some things in common with Agnes. I didn't have to say a lot to her. We were on the same page."

I asked Shannon, a member of A Red Orchid Theatre in Chicago, about the challenge of delivering his own nonstop rapid-fire monologue of madness and not being able to come up for air until the end. He has a frightening speech that scares the audience but makes perfect sense to Agnes.

"You get nervous before those long takes," he said. "The scene I have outside the bathroom door, telling her my life story, I did it once and Billy said that was it. I said I wanted to do it again. He said, 'What are you trying to do, make Eastman Kodak rich?' He let me do it again. That time he said, 'You did it all with your eyes closed. Now try it with your eyes open.' The third take was like being shot out of a cannon. After it was over, it was all a blur. You have to trust the director."

Letts said the inspiration for the play came to him in Oklahoma, his home state. "The Oklahoma City bombing hit me hard," he said. "I was shocked that it was done by Americans. How far out of the matrix could you slip? The more I investigated paranoia, the more I saw how the connections feed on themselves and build out of control. What happens in this movie is that Agnes is leaping to catch up with Peter."

The film is lean, direct, unrelenting. A lot of it takes place in the motel room, which by the end has been turned into an eerie cave, a sort of psychic air raid shelter against government emissions or who knows what else? "They're watching us," Peter says.

Friedkin is often called a master of horror, but for him, most modern horror films are really just violent comedies.

"For me, *United 93* is a horror film," he said. "It puts you in a place where you don't want to go. The horror films that appeal to me are sort of reality: *Psycho, Diabolique, Rosemary's Baby.* That Austrian director, Michael Haneke, he's the real deal. His *Funny Games* is the scariest film I've ever seen."

"Me, too," said Letts.

The thing about *Bug* is that we're not scared for ourselves so much as for the characters in the movie. "At various times as I was reworking this play on the road," Letts said, "the conclusion involved various paranoid linkings of every conspiracy in history, from John Wilkes Booth to Lee Harvey Oswald to aliens kidnapping people for experiments. With a certain kind of paranoia, it all connects."

"I think that scaring people is what made me want to become a movie director," Friedkin said. "When I was six or seven, I was sitting on our front porch in Chicago telling two girls that a murderer was killing people on our block, and our houses were next on his list. They were spellbound. When I saw I could get to them, I just kept going."

Cannes Report No. 5

May 23, 2006—There are entries that have been liked and even loved, but the 2006 Cannes Film Festival reaches its halfway mark looking like a fairly lackluster year. Only Pedro Almodovar's *Volver*, a high-spirited memory inspired by his childhood in La Mancha, has been embraced by critics and audiences. *Volver* means "to return" and resembles in its exuberant nostalgia Fellini's *Amarcord* (*I Remember*).

Other warmly received films have included Ken Loach's *The Wind That Shakes the Barley*, a story of the Troubles in Ireland that centers on the ruthless finality with which the IRA enforced its codes; Nicole Garcia's *Charlie Says*, a French film in which a young boy is the witness and connection between several interlocking stories; and Andrea Arnold's *Red Road*, unseen by me, a British film about a woman whose job, watching public surveillance cameras, leads her to an unexpected discovery. Every year there is a film that everyone tells me I should not have missed, and in 2006 *Red Road* is apparently that film.

Outside the official competition, enormous enthusiasm has been generated by *An Inconvenient Truth*, the documentary with Al Gore citing alarming facts and terrifying trends about global warming. No, it doesn't sound thrilling. Take my word for it: It is.

The director, Davis Guggenheim, who has worked mostly in TV and is not particularly political, finds a way to present Gore, his information, and some sensational graphics on a 100-foot screen in a way that begins with a lecture and gives it the impact of a concert of ideas. I'll write more about *An Inconvenient Truth* later.

Another sensation here is *Shortbus*, the long-awaited, much-rumored explicit erotic film from John Cameron Mitchell (*Hedwig and the Angry Inch*). It's an official selection, playing out of competition. Yes, there's hardcore sex in this film (gay, straight, solo, amateur, professional, and all of the above). But you couldn't call it a hard-core film.

It just doesn't feel like one, and despite all the genitals on the screen it doesn't try to be one; it's not about sex but about sexuality, not about scoring but about living, and at its center is a remarkable performance by Sook-Yin Lee as Sofia, a sex therapist ("I prefer the term 'couples counselor'") whose search for her own first orgasm leads her into the gay, bi, trans, and S&M underworld of New York. It is a world that seems so gentle and friendly in this film that I overheard a strange comment afterward: "This is the first time New York has seemed Canadian."

Surveying the festival on its sixth day, Cannes veteran Michael Barker, copresident of Sony Pictures Classics, told me: "This is the first year I can remember when there seem to be more interesting films in the marketplace than in the competition."

Although he prudently didn't name names, one of those (according to me) is *Look Both Ways,* an Australian film. Sarah Watt's film involves interlocking stories about victims and survivors, locked together in guilt and hopeful romance.

The Wind That Shakes the Barley is set in Ireland in the early 1900s, during the Irish Republican Army's war against British occupation. Cillian Murphy stars as a young doctor who abandons his career to join the IRA, becomes involved in the merciless struggle with brutal British troops, and is forced into agonizing decisions and actions when the IRA enforces discipline by executing some of its members; friends are required to shoot friends. The film leads up to a historic truce negotiated by the IRA and the British, and its rejection by the IRA rank and file, who consider it a sellout. That turning point may have led to violence that continued until very recent years. For Ken Loach, who often deals with working-class people and political issues, this is an unblinking, involving, sad story of heroism that no one feels very good about. Murphy (*Breakfast on Pluto*) could be a candidate for a best actor award.

Nicole Garcia's French entry *Charlie Says* stars Jean-Pierre Bacri, an actor who usually embodies middle-aged machismo (as in *Look at Me*). Here he plays the lonely and clueless mayor of a small town on the French Atlantic coast. He's having an affair with a young local municipal worker; a onetime anthropologist (Benoit Magimel) has left that career to hide out as a local science teacher; his alienated Finnish wife (Minna Haapkyl) is having an affair; his famous mentor (Patrick Pineau) discovers him and challenges him to return to his former life; and there are subplots involving a tennis champion in crisis and an incompetent small-time thief. All of these stories are drawn together by young Charlie (Ferdinand Martin), who knows his father is having an affair with the wife of his teacher.

Interlocking plots have become increasingly popular in recent years; sometimes they're simply a tricky gimmick, but sometimes they work, and in *Charlie Says* the connections do pay off in insights about the characters.

The greatest disappointment so far this year is an easy choice: *Southland Tales,* the much-anticipated new film by Richard Kelly, whose *Donnie Darko* inspired a lot of enthusiasm. This one is a "fiasco," writes *Variety*'s Todd McCarthy, and he is not being unkind, only truthful.

Running an unendurable 161 minutes, it's an apocalyptic mess set in Los Angeles of the near future, where "neomarxists" and other neos, all of whom seem like retro retreads from the 1960s, stage an incomprehensible revolution. There's an all-star cast, headed by The Rock, Sarah Michelle Gellar, Mandy Moore, Wallace Shawn, Justin Timberlake, and Janeane Garofalo, who plays a uniformed general who stands inside a bookstore on Venice Beach and has inexplicable telephone conversations for obscure purposes with unestablished characters she never seems to meet.

Another disappointment, but on a higher level, is Nanni Moretti's official entry, *Il Caimano,* in which a onetime horror film director (Silvio Orlando) attempts a comeback with a first-time writer-director (Jasmine Trinca). He hasn't quite read or understood her screenplay, which is an unconcealed attack on the controversial Italian political figure and sometime government leader Silvio Berlusconi. The movie begins as a comedy about making movies, meanders, and ends uncertainly with scenes from the angry indictment they end up making.

Still ahead, I guess or hope, are most of the films that (in addition to *Volver* and *The Wind That Shakes the Barley*) will be among the winners on closing night.

Cannes Report No. 6

May 24, 2006—Like any good bookie, Derek Malcolm carries his odds in his head. He revises them after every screening of a film in the official competition. Wednesday morning, the odds got a little longer for Sofia Coppola's *Marie Antoinette,* which is tipped as a frontrunner for the Palme d'Or.

"Almodovar's chances up a little, Coppola down a little," Malcolm informed me. He is a British film critic, long with the *Guardian,* who early in life was a professional jockey. At Cannes he quotes the odds, you place your bet, he pays off at the end of the festival. This must be legal, since he makes no secret of it. Like all good bookies, he usually makes money no matter who wins.

"Pedro Almodovar is now the front-runner at 9–4," he told me. "Next best chance is *Babel*, by Alejandro Gonzalez Inarritu, at 7–2. *Marie Antoinette* is 5–1."

Almodovar's *Volver* has been a favorite since early in the festival, but *Marie Antoinette* was expected to roll into town and swamp the competition. After its first press screening, it is no longer a sure winner. There was some applause but more booing, and although a French film critic at the Coppola press conference blamed the booing on "petite bourgeoisie," other classes may also have been implicated.

"I wanted to see heads rolling," groused Baz Bamigboye, the famous *Daily Mail* columnist, and there seemed to be general disappointment that the film ends well before the king and queen are beheaded.

Marie Antoinette is an ambitious film, visually splendid, with some of the most elaborate costumes in movie history, and the real Versailles as a location. Kirsten Dunst's performance is perfectly suited to Coppola's view of the role: Marie Antoinette as an unschooled fourteen-year-old princess from Austria, wed to the future Louis XVI (Jason Schwartzman) and marooned in the sadistic rituals of the French court (she is dressed and undressed with a roomful of courtiers; in bed on their wedding night the newlyweds are blessed by an archbishop and given a pep talk by her father-in-law, Louis XV).

The movie shows husband and wife paralyzed on the brink of sex for months, maybe years, until Marie's brother (Danny Huston) visits Versailles and explains the conjugal mysteries to Marie's husband in terms of the young man's favorite hobby, locks and keys. Versailles is a court sealed against real life; Parisians starve and riot, while Marie shops, parties, gambles, and fools around with a Swedish count who is an expert locksmith.

All of these qualities in the film are real and tangible, and have a fascination. Yet I sensed a vague dissatisfaction not only at the lack of a guillotine but also at pacing that lingers over the early years of Marie's marriage and then hastens toward a conclusion it never quite

seems to reach. The film doesn't fail, but neither does it triumph.

* * *

Now what about *Babel*, at 7–2 the runner-up in the Cannes derby? This is another powerful group of interconnected stories by Inarritu, whose *Amores Perros* and *21 Grams* dealt with lives jolted by accident and joined by fate. In *Babel*, what the characters have is a problem in communication.

"Did you count the six languages in the film?" Cate Blanchett asked me at lunch. She plays an American tourist, married to Brad Pitt, who is shot and gravely wounded in Morocco. The bullet into their tourist bus is fired by a kid who is supposed to be protecting his goats from jackals; he shoots at the bus because he thinks the bullets won't reach that far. Other stories in *Babel* involve Mexicans, Americans, and a Japanese deaf-mute girl.

Six languages? Well, the languages of the Moroccans, the Mexicans, the Americans, the Japanese, and sign language. That's only five.

"The subtitles," Blanchett said. "In every scene, there is somebody who doesn't understand what somebody else is saying. That puts the audience in the position of knowing more than the characters, because we can read the subtitles and they can't."

For example, I said, when the doctor says you will bleed to death and the translator tells your husband you will be fine?

"Exactly. The tragedy is, in countries like Germany, the whole film will be dubbed into German, so they'll miss the additional dimension of the subtitles."

* * *

Gael Garcia Bernal, a rising star (*Amores Perros, Y Tu Mama Tambien, Motorcycle Diaries*) has personal experience with the situation of Mexicans who work in the United States.

"I have my visa renewed regularly," he said. "I've had what we call Little Room Moments. They call you aside: *Where do you come from?* I say, Mexico. *Where do you really come from?* Mexico? My mother? My address? *Are you here on business or pleasure?* How can anyone be anywhere for only business or only pleasure?"

Bernal said both countries share the responsibility for the problems over illegal entry into the United States. "America needs cheap labor or its food chain fails, and with undocumented workers, employers can pay low wages and not worry about insurance and health care. Yet the dollars these poor people send home are Mexico's second-largest source of income, after oil. So both countries profit from these 'invisible workers.' And when Mexicans wire their money home, the banks take a 20 percent commission."

American banks?

"Western Union, mostly."

* * *

Inarritu, the director, said he is making progress: "Six years ago, when I was here with *Amores Perros,* they wouldn't let it in the competition. Now at least the jury can see it."

He said his film *Babel* is about borders and barriers: The American tourist almost dies because American authorities assume she was shot by a terrorist; a Mexican nanny's American children almost die because her nephew recklessly flees a border check; and the Japanese girl desperately seeks sex as a way of breaking through her alienation.

"The one language everyone speaks," he said, "is touch. That is another language in the film. When the wife touches her husband's hand, when the Moroccan father lifts his child into his arms, when the Japanese girl is hugged by her father, then they understand. A doctor told me that when we touch one another, we cannot lie. If someone hugs you but they don't really like you, you can tell."

Maybe that was Marie Antoinette's problem.

Cannes Report No. 7

May 25, 2006—At last, on Day 9 of the Cannes Film Festival, an old-fashioned real movie, with a beginning, middle, and end, characters, a story, and a powerful message. But is Rachid Bouchareb's *Days of Glory (Indigenes),* a drama about French troops from the colonies of Northern Africa, too traditional to win the Palme d'Or?

The film begins as poor Algerians and Moroccans volunteer to join the Free French army and defend the "homeland" none of them have ever seen. It follows them through one battle after another, through the burning sands of Morocco and the freezing winters of northern Italy, to a lonely outpost in a French village where their heroism is dearly paid for.

All the time, they are promised they will be "remembered," but a French censor blocks all correspondence with the French girls they have met, a French Algerian officer argues their case but is essentially racist, and they are giving their lives for a "homeland" that wants them to return as quickly as possible to the Muslim nations of their birth. The human stories of the individual soldiers become enormously important to us.

After the screening, we journalists gathered as always in the area where our mailboxes hold daily piles of press releases. There was a kind of amazement in the air. We included Tony Scott of the *New York Times,* Lisa Schwarzbaum of *Entertainment Weekly,* Ken Turan of the *Los Angeles Times,* and Michel Ciment, the best-known French film critic. We were all smiling at having seen a "real movie"—remembering the pleasures of traditional craft and storytelling.

"It is the kind of movie the French have forgotten how to make," said Ciment. "We can make art films and silly sex comedies, but this is what I call a Saturday-night movie for real moviegoers. Not great art, but great moviemaking."

High praise, but higher still came from Turan: "I stayed right until the end." This statement has to be put in context. Turan's long-standing policy at all film festivals is to see the beginnings of as many films as possible, perhaps eight or ten a day.

"I want to get an overview of the whole festival," he explains. He'll see the complete film in Los Angeles when it opens. All the publicists know "it doesn't mean anything bad when Kenny leaves after thirty minutes."

"You are still here!" I said.

"I really got wrapped up in it," he said.

"I can see the ads now," I said. "Four stars— Ebert! 'I stayed right until the end!'—Turan."

* * *

As you're reading this, do you have the impression that Sofia Coppola's *Marie Antoinette* was booed here at Cannes? You can be excused for that impression, because the booing at the Wednesday morning press screening was widely reported, and I am one of those responsible, although I did not boo. Drudge headlined the boos and linked to a story in *Variety* saying they had "a Gallic accent," leading to my speculations about whether "boo" sounds different in French and English.

But now let's step back and be fair. Yes, there was booing. But I was present at the screening and would guess not more than five people, maybe ten, booed. Many others applauded. Booing is always shocking to North American critics; I am not sure I have heard booing more than once or twice in all my years at the Toronto, Sundance, Telluride, Chicago, Montreal, and New York festivals. In Europe, they boo all the time, sometimes because they think a film is bad, sometimes because it is (according to them) politically incorrect.

The reports of booing have disturbed Coppola, who on a few hours' notice unexpectedly withdrew as the guest of honor for festival president Gilles Jacob's formal dinner Thursday night at the Carlton Hotel.

"I don't know why *Variety* thought the French were booing," Pierre Rissient told me the next morning in the sunny breakfast room of the Hotel Splendid. Rissient is one of the best-connected people in the world of French cinema; he represents one degree of separation.

"The French critics saw the film in Paris before it played here. The reviews were mostly very good. It opened in Paris yesterday and is doing terrific business. The only thing we might question is the implication that Louis XVI was not the father of all of Marie Antoinette's children. DNA testing has shown all her descendants were Bourbons."

More evidence that the boos did not have a Gallic accent comes from Dave McCoy, who writes on MSN.com Movies:

"At one point, Marie, just awakened by a swarm of servants, stands naked and cold, while family members decide who gets the privilege of dressing her. Until this point, Marie has said little in the film. When finally clothed, she utters, 'This is ridiculous.' 'This is Versailles,' responds her servant.

"I laughed, as I had been doing for the past twenty minutes. I was laughing at the satire, at Coppola's brash approach and from the pure joy that a great film can trigger. That's when two French journalists to my right Frenched me. 'Those were the rules! They had rules!' one hissed, while the other sneered and added, 'Not funny! Not funny!' Of course, this

made me laugh harder. I briefly considered explaining the concept of satire to my hosts, but it was pointless."

So did those who booed perhaps have a Yankee accent? Or British, Italian, or Austrian? Who can say? The important point is that the film was not hated. The daily "critics' jury" of *Screen International,* a cross-section of nine international critics, gave it 2.44 points out of a possible 4; it's tied for fifth out of fourteen films. In *Le Film Francais,* the French trade paper, five of the fifteen critics gave it their highest rating—"worthy of the Palme d'Or." In another poll, Michel Ciment also rated it worthy of the Palme d'Or.

I've also noticed that opinions on the film seem to be growing more favorable as time passes. True, many viewers were disappointed that it doesn't end with Marie's beheading. On second thought, I realize Coppola was making a film about a performance: A fourteen-year-old girl from Vienna is brought to France to cement a diplomatic alliance and symbolize the bonds between the nations. Versailles is a stage upon which she plays a queen. She has her own theatrical ambitions, and her husband even builds her a theater where she can sing.

Then the revolutionary mob assails Versailles, and as she appears on a balcony, she majestically lowers her head, spreads her arms, and bows to them. Finally, a real curtain call. Perhaps a beheading would have been anticlimactic.

Cannes Report No. 8

May 26, 2006—It probably won't happen this way, but wouldn't everyone be pleased if Gerard Depardieu won the best actor award at Cannes this year? The festival's awards are given out Sunday night, and Depardieu received a tumultuous ovation Friday as the star of *Quand J'etais Chanteur,* or *The Singer.* Depardieu's character reminded many audience members of the actor himself: a beefy middle-aged artist still slugging away at a job he loves, smoking too much, adamantly on the wagon, given new hope by his feelings for a much younger woman (Cecile de France). "I've been written off a lot of times," he tells her, "but I always bounce back."

The film, directed by Xavier Giannoli, is

sentimental but not soppy, showing the singer as a specialist in romantic ballads at mixers for middle-aged single people "afraid of discos." Depardieu does all his own singing, most memorably "Save the Last Dance for Me" sung directly to de France as she dances with his rival. It's not a great movie, but it's such a quintessential Depardieu performance that—who knows—the jury might lean that way.

You hear a lot of predictions about this year's winners, many of them, like my mention of Depardieu, based more on hope than reality. The jury is headed by the Chinese director Wong Kar-Wai, himself a specialist in unrequited love, and its best-known members (to North Americans) are Samuel L. Jackson, Tim Roth, Helena Bonham Carter, and Ziyi Zhang.

Speculation is that the Palme d'Or for best film could go to Pedro Almodovar's *Volver*, with Penelope Cruz playing a character inspired by his mother; it played early in the festival and has been a favorite ever since. Or perhaps to Alejandro Gonzalez Inarritu's *Babel*, three interlocking stories of lives disrupted by borders. Or to Rachid Bouchareb's *Days of Glory*, about the North African French colonials who fought and died for the "homeland" in World War II and were ill-treated for their sacrifices.

Best actress could be Cruz, or Kirsten Dunst for Sofia Coppola's *Marie Antoinette*, or possibly Adriana Barraza, who plays a Mexican nanny in *Babel*. Best actor might go to one of the Algerian actors in *Days of Glory*, or Giacomo Rizzo, who plays a sour-tempered skinflint moneylender in Paolo Sorrentino's *The Family Friend*. Stock in Coppola's film has gone up since exaggerated early reports that it was booed at the festival, and it probably will win a major award—if not actress, then director, or perhaps a special prize for its decor and costumes.

A few films in the competition are still to play, notably *Pan's Labyrinth*, a Spanish film by the popular Guillermo del Toro, whose Hollywood work includes *Blade II* and *Hellboy*. It was del Toro, at an official festival dinner Thursday night, who defined the film festival awards as "like getting laid after a disco night—there's a flurry of passion, not always in the right order."

* * *

A Chicagoan, Jim Stern, is a prominent player at Cannes this year; his Endgame Entertainment is one of the investors in Todd Haynes's *I'm Not There*, a biopic about Bob Dylan that will film this summer. The film has received a lot of attention because of the actors who will portray Dylan in various incarnations. They include Heath Ledger, Richard Gere, Christian Bale, Ben Wishaw, and Cate Blanchett. Yes, Cate Blanchett.

Stern's participation got front-page notice in the British trade paper *Screen International*, which said his company is drawing on "an equity base of $100 million."

A former Chicagoan also got a lot of publicity at week's end: Hugh Hefner was here to celebrate his eightieth birthday on board a yacht in the harbor. He visited the American Pavilion to cut his birthday cake, accompanied by more girlfriends than any one man probably requires but a good many men probably envy.

* * *

No, the Cannes awards will not be seen on American TV this year. IFC, which carried them live, and Bravo, which repeated them in the evening, have dropped their coverage. That means you will not be able to hear my commentary with its spectacular mispronunciations, and the patient Annette Insdorf correcting me in six languages.

Cannes Report No. 9: Festival Winners

May 29, 2006—Ken Loach's *The Wind That Shakes the Barley* won the Palme d'Or in the Cannes Film Festival here Sunday, and that was a surprise and a delight in about equal measure. The film stars Cillian Murphy in the harrowing story of how the Irish Republican Army waged war against the British and enforced deadly discipline within its own ranks.

Secrecy surrounding the jury was tight, and pre-awards gossip entirely overlooked the Loach film, even though it got strongly positive reviews. When juror Samuel L. Jackson told one insider the jury "was going to kick some butt and surprise everybody," that seemed to mean the apparent front-runner, Pedro Almodovar's *Volver*, would be overlooked—but no one I talked to predicted the Loach victory.

The movie is a powerful drama in which

Murphy is a young medical student on his way to London in the early 1920s, when personal experience of British mistreatment of the Irish causes him to join the IRA instead. At one point, his commitment to the cause requires him to execute a friend.

Wong Kar-Wai, the Hong Kong director who was president of the jury, said after the awards that the decision was unanimous. Loach said in his acceptance speech that the film encouraged Britain to confront imperialism in its past, adding, "If we can tell the truth about the past, maybe we can tell the truth about the present." This marks the seventh Loach film in the official competition, but his first winner.

In a festival first, the jury honored ensembles with both of its acting awards. All the female stars of Almodovar's *Volver*, including Penelope Cruz and Carmen Maura, won as "best actresses," and the best actors were the stars of Rachid Bouchareb's *Days of Glory*, the story of Algerian and Moroccan troops who fought in the French army in World War II but were discriminated against at the time and later had their veterans' pensions taken away.

The Grand Prix, unofficially considered second prize, went to *Flanders*, by Bruno Dumont. The French film involves a young soldier who returns home much changed by the experience of combat.

Red Road, by British director Andrea Arnold, won the Special Jury Prize. It stars Kate Dickie as a woman who watches a public surveillance camera and one day sees an unexpected face.

Alejandro Gonzalez Inarritu's *Babel*, thought to be a front-runner for the Palme d'Or, won him the best director prize. The Mexican director of *Amores Perros* and *21 Grams* once again made a film of interlocking stories, this one involving barriers of borders and language in Morocco, the Mexican-U.S. border, and Japan. The film's best-known stars are Brad Pitt and Cate Blanchett.

Almodovar won the screenwriting award for the *Volver* screenplay, which he said was inspired by his mother and his friends, as he observed them while growing up in La Mancha. Cruz plays a character based on his mother, and Maura on his grandmother, who fakes her own death and then appears to people as a "ghost." The Camera d'Or prize, given to the best first film, went to *12:08 East of Bucharest*, a Romanian film by Corneliu Porumboiu.

The grand prize in the Critics' Week, given separately from the main event, went to *Poison Friends*, by Emmanuel Bourdieu of France. The FIPRESCI Award, voted on by members of the worldwide critics' organization, went to *Climates*, by the Turkish director Nuri Bilge Ceylan.

Jury members, in addition to Wong and Jackson, were Monica Bellucci, Helena Bonham Carter, Patrice Leconte, Lucrecia Martel, Tim Roth, Elia Suleiman, and Zhang Ziyi.

Cannes Report No. 10: Summing Up

May 29, 2006—All rumors about the prizes at Cannes are essentially worthless. Why don't I know this? I could make up my own and do just about as well. It is apparently true that Sam Jackson told somebody there were going to be "big surprises" when the awards were announced, and there were; never before has a jury honored the casts of two films with ensemble acting awards, and certainly no one predicted that Ken Loach's *The Wind That Shakes the Barley* would win the Palme d'Or. When it did, there was much agreement, and, yes, much surprise.

But the prognosticators were looking for bigger surprises than that. Sunday morning in the Hotel Splendid breakfast room, my favorite Cannes expert, Pierre Rissient, predicted that the big prize would shock everyone by going to *Colossal Youth*, by the Portuguese director Pedro Costa. Rissient is such a legend they are naming a theater after him at Telluride this year, but he was, to put it delicately, wrong.

Colossal Youth, unseen by me, tells the story of a Lisbon worker whose wife leaves him, and he moves from a slum to a housing complex. Why didn't I see it? Because Mary Corliss did. She is the wife of *Time* film critic Richard Corliss, who told me: "Mary walked out after an hour because the movie made her feel like rats were fighting in her skull."

Two other films mentioned as Palme candidates, Pedro Almodovar's *Volver* and Alejandro Gonzalez Inarritu's *Babel*, did win major prizes: *Volver*'s entire cast, led by Penelope

Cruz and Carmen Maura, was honored, and he won for screenplay. *Babel* won for best director.

But what about another much-touted film, Sofia Coppola's *Marie Antoinette*? No other film was so loved by the French critics, although of course they are not the jury. And as the festival came to its close, I found the film growing in my memory and appreciation. Others said the same: Once you get over the surprise that there's no beheading, you step back and realize what a stunning visual achievement it is, and how well Kirsten Dunst plays a fourteen-year-old girl who grows up into her fate and doom.

I thought the jury might give *Marie Antoinette* an award in part to correct the impression that the film was booed out of town. As I wrote earlier, the booing at the press screening (five or ten people, maybe) was blown up into a scandal. On balance, audiences here admired the film—some of them, a lot.

Another incorrect rumor, but one with a lot of passion behind it, was that Guillermo del Toro's *Pan's Labyrinth* might charge out of nowhere on the last day of screenings and grab the Palme d'Or. Not shown until Saturday (the last day for competition screenings), it would have been a worthy winner, a fairy tale for grown-ups that has surprising emotional power.

It takes place in 1944, as Franco's fascist regime holds control in Spain but the Nazis are facing the world-changing reality of the Normandy landings. In an isolated forest outpost, a band of fascist soldiers hunts down a band of rebels who are still holding out. The officer in command (Sergi Lopez) is a ruthless sadist. His new wife has a daughter named Ofelia (Ivana Baquero) from an earlier marriage, and this daughter is led by a fairy into a labyrinth where a fearsome faun tells her of her role in the Underworld Kingdom.

Del Toro (*Cronos, Blade II, Hellboy*) once again shows his mastery of serious fantasy as a genre, and despite fairies and fauns, this is a serious movie—also beautiful and exhilarating, with a payoff that combines emotion with magic and is astonishingly moving, considering it involves giant toads. The cinematographer Guillermo Navarro makes the movie's fantasy elements dark and painterly. That *Pan's Labyrinth* and *Marie Antoinette* didn't win some sort of prize is surprising.

The very last film I saw at Cannes was a three-hour restoration of Giovanni Pastrone's *Cabiria* (1914), an early silent epic, awesome in ambition. In a filmed introduction, Martin Scorsese says it was this film, a worldwide hit, that inspired great leaps forward by D. W. Griffith and C. B. DeMille, directors often given credit for Pastrone's innovations. He was perhaps the first to use a moving camera, his sets anticipated the colossal constructions in DeMille's epics, and in Maciste (Bartolomeo Pagano), the giant strongman, he created the first Italian movie star; Pagano changed his name to Maciste and starred as the North African Hercules in twenty-four more films.

One spectacular scene in the film shows a city's walls being scaled. Eight warriors bend over and balance their shields on their backs. Six more stand on the shields, bend over, and balance their own shields. Then four, then two, until finally the hero scales this pyramid of men and shields and reaches the top of the wall, in a splendid demonstration of how a film wins at Cannes.

Questions for the Movie Answer Man

Annapolis

Q. I noticed in your review of *Annapolis* some errors and maybe a misperception of what the Naval Academy is about. Tyrese Gibson plays *midshipman* Lieutenant Cole; he is not a "drill sergeant" and is not "on loan to the academy." Previously-enlisted Marines and sailors are a regular occurrence at USNA. I think, however, that your misperception of the Naval Academy illustrates what any other viewer would think and how the filmmakers didn't care about detail or a well-made story. Why make a movie about a unique institution like the United States Naval Academy if you can't do it right?

—Midshipman, name withheld
because of naval regulations

A. You had other interesting comments, which I am using in the Letters section of rogerebert.com. Regarding the rank of the Tyrese Gibson and Jordana Brewster characters, I did not understand they were both midshipmen and was not alone in my bewilderment. I find that the *New York Times* calls Gibson the "company commander" and Brewster the hero's "superior officer." The *Toronto Globe and Mail* calls her a "babelicious officer." The *Chicago Tribune* says Brewster is his "military superior" and Cole is a "company commander." Salon.com calls Gibson the "company commander." *Variety* has it about right, with ". . . his toughest instructor, Midshipman Lt. Cole," and says Brewster is "another superior among his overseers."

The Aristocrats

Q. There's a conspiracy theory on the Internet about *The Aristocrats,* claiming that "the world's dirtiest joke," which is the subject of the movie, is the creation of Penn Jillette, and the backstory was created to perpetrate a hoax on the movie audience. Do you think Penn is punking us?

—Victor Ireland, Redding, California

A. You sent me to slumbering.lungfish.com, where Lore Sjoberg offers two reasons for thinking the movie is a hoax: "First, Penn Jillette. If anyone was going to make up a dirty joke, then fool millions of people into thinking it's a super-secret comedian thing, it would be Jillette. Secondly, I can't find any evidence that the joke was posted to the Internet before 2001." But since authentic footage shows Gilbert Gottfried telling the joke at a Friar's roast in 2001, a hoax would have involved great foresight and patience, plus the total cooperation of all one hundred comedians in the film. And Gregory Kirschling describes it in *Entertainment Weekly* as "an ancient dirty joke out of vaudeville days." Isn't the *Aristocrats* joke really a version of a joke everybody knows, about the man who goes to be treated for a rash on his arm? "What do you do for a living?" the doctor asks him. "I work at the circus, giving enemas to the elephants," the guy says, adding disgusting details about how he administers the enemas. "Quit your job, and the rash will clear up," the doctor says. The guy says, "What! And leave show business?"

Q. In a recent column you printed a letter suggesting that *The Aristocrats* was a hoax by Penn Jillette, who made up the joke and claimed it was a tradition among comedians. I heard the story over 50 years ago. At that time the punch line was "The Sophisticates!"

—Richard Washburn, Cliffside Park, New Jersey

A. Case closed. In my review of the film, I said Buddy Hackett could have told the joke better than anyone else and wondered why he wasn't used. I received this reply from Jillette, who made the film with Paul Provenza: "I called Buddy and explained the project to him. He loved the idea and he got it. He told me a few versions of the joke and talked about how much it meant to him. Man, Buddy was perfect for our movie. I asked him and he said he'd love to but 'I'm old and sick.' It was as simple as that. He cheered us on, but he just wasn't up for being on camera. The 'old and sick' might have been a lie but, man, if you're willing to back up your lie by dying, well, I'm going to believe you. I called Rodney (Dangerfield) right after that and had just about the same phone call. They both should have been in the movie.

"Many people who aren't in the movie were very supportive. It was Johnny Carson's favorite joke, and he loved our idea but was no-kidding, no-Sinatra retired. We were setting up a time to go to Malibu and show it to him; the day after our first screening at Sundance, we got a phone call from Amazing Randi saying Johnny had died. So much for our comedy high.

"The project is not over. We used only comics that we knew personally for this go-around, but many more have loved the movie and want to be part of the project, so we will keep shooting people for posterity."

Art School Confidential

Q. In writing "O tempera! O mores!"—the headline for your online review of *Art School Confidential*—I assume you're quoting Cicero's "o tempora, o mores!" from the First Catalinarian Oration. It's spelled *tempora*, not *tempera*. I'm a Latin teacher in Cleveland.
—Nick Fletcher, Cleveland, Ohio

A. Yes, but artists use tempera paint, and the headline was a pun.

Asian Name Order

Q. In your interview with Bai Ling from the Hawaii festival, you wrote:

"I have seen Bai Ling many times in the movies, often billed as Ling Bai. In China the practice is to put the family name first and the given name second. So properly she should be referred to as Ling Bai, right?

"'Your theory is correct, but you have one thing wrong,' I am told by Liwei Kiumra, the China expert of the Hawaii festival. 'Ling is her first name.' Therefore, Bai Ling. Everyone who has it wrong has it right."

Congratulations, Roger! You could not have been any more confusing! What does "properly" mean in that context? Properly for the Asians or properly for us? And what does Mr. Kiumra mean when he says "first name"? Does he mean family name or given name? And while we're at it, is it Mr. Kiumra or Mr. Liwei?
—Alexandre Rowe, Montreal, Quebec

A. It's *Ms.* Liwei Kiumra, because that's what it says on her card. As for Bai Ling's name order,

of course by "first" she means "given." Whenever I review an Asian movie, this question arises in exchanges with the copy editors, because if you use the accepted Asian word order, Western readers get confused; should I write "Li Gong" when everybody in the West thinks of "Gong Li"? Consulting the reviews of *Raise the Red Lantern*, for example, I find that the *New York Times, Washington Post,* and *Variety* use "Gong Li," and director "Zhang Yimou," but the Internet Movie Database, which always follows local usage, has "Li Gong" and "Yimou Zhang."

Q. I think there's confusion in your column with regards to Gong Li's name. Her family name is Gong, her given name Li. The West knows her as "Gong Li," but this is in fact the correct Asian order. Same with "Zhang Yimou."
—Mengmeng Zhang, South Bend, Indiana

A. Copy editors, please note: Now I am wondering, is your given name Mengmeng and your family name Zhang? Which order should we use in the West?

Here is a useful answer from Jason Ishikawa of Honolulu: "I would recommend calling them by whatever name they are known as. Most Hollywood celebrities use fake names anyway, so I wouldn't consider it insulting either way. 'Gong Li' is Gong Li and 'Zhang Yimou' is Zhang Yimou, just as 'Kurosawa Akira' is Akira Kurosawa. However, 'Zhang Ziyi' is beyond me, because she has been billed both ways."

Ebert again. I applied the Google test and searched for her both ways. There are three million hits for "Ziyi Zhang" and 2.990 million hits for "Zhang Ziyi." Flip a coin.

Q. Replying to my Answer Man letter about Chinese name order, you asked about my own name. My family name is Zhang, given name Mengmeng. But I go by Mengmeng Zhang because I've been here for many years and that's how I think of myself in English. I'm not sure really how it should be done in the West. It's especially confusing in a case like Gong Li, because Li is a very common family name (the most common in China and, thus, the world at last count, I believe). A figure skater a few years ago was named Chen Lu, both of which are common Chinese family names, and I'm still not sure which is her actual family name. A slight correction again in regards to whether "Zhang Ziyi" or "Ziyi Zhang" is more popular: If you do the search on Google using quotes, so it searches only the exact phrase, "Zhang Ziyi" beats "Ziyi Zhang" 2.4 million to about 600,000.

—Mengmeng Zhang, South Bend, Indiana

A. Note to self and copy editors: It's "Zhang Ziyi" from now on. Except when the movie credits have it the other way, which is most of the time.

Ask the Dust and Nelson Algren

Q. In your review of Ask the Dust, you state, "I have been lucky enough to know a great writer in his shabby apartment, with his typewriter, his bottle, and his cigarettes, and I know he had a famous romance and that later he hated the woman, and having achieved all possible success was perhaps not as happy as when it was still before him."

I know to whom you refer. He is one of my literary heroes. I met him and you on a Saturday night in the early '70s. I was with my good friends Gary Houston and Hedda Lubin at the first Miomir's Serbian Club on Evergreen Street. I can still see the fake stalactites coming from the ceiling, backlighted with black light, and Miomir clapping his hands and dancing with the women to the music of the bald gypsy violinist. I knew that you and Gary worked at the Sun-Times together before he left for full-time acting. You came over to our table and asked Gary if we would like to join you and Nelson for dessert. After Gary assented I asked him, "Who's Nelson?" Gary replied, "Nelson Algren." My heart leaped. It is an evening I will never forget. We closed Miomir's, got a bottle of Bull's Blood, and went to Nelson's apartment down the street. The apartment was a wonderland of 1930s radicalism ephemera, mixed with autographed pictures and the usual bachelor apartment disarray.

I cried when sometime later I turned on the news and Nelson was being interviewed. He was selling all of his belongings to move to New Jersey to work on his Hurricane Carter book. I cried again when I heard of his lonely death.

—Martin Gaspar, Chicago, Illinois

A. The famous romance, as everyone knows, was with Simone de Beauvoir. Let us once again quote Algren's Law: "Never play poker with a man called Doc. Never eat at a place called Mom's. Never sleep with a woman whose troubles are worse than your own."

Audience Behavior

Q. I recently attended the screening of Citizen Kane at the free Chicago Outdoor Film Festival where you and Mr. Roeper gave a nice introduction. I am a film nut and have been accused of being a bit over-sensitive to crowd noise when I attend a screening at indoor movie theaters. At the outdoor festival, I adjusted my expectations, as a certain amount of noise and conversation is inevitable. One fellow, however, perhaps encouraged by his liquid dinner, insisted on shouting "Chicago!" every time a character in the film mentioned the broad-shouldered city. As if that was not enough, he gave a mighty yell of "Yeah! Slap that (expletive deleted)!" during one of the key scenes in the film—when Charles Foster Kane struck his second wife. I spoke up (rather rudely myself, I am afraid) by yelling, "Shut up!" While Mr. Chicago was more or less quiet after my outburst, I feel a bit conflicted. Is shushing a fellow moviegoer at an outdoor film festival a sign of hypersensitivity to sound?

—Jeff Waldhoff, Chicago, Illinois

A. I think you should have suggested what he could do with his sled.

Bart the Bear

Q. In your review of An Unfinished Life, you mention that the bear is played by Bart the Bear of The Bear (also of The Edge, Legends of the Fall, etc.). I'm also a fan of that Bart. But according to IMDb, the original Bart passed away in 2000. There's another Bart the Bear now.

Personally, I find this distasteful. By selecting an identical name so soon after the original Bart's passing, it's as if the new bear's handlers and agents are trying to dupe us and capitalize on the success of the beloved cinematic ursine. I imagine most people were not fooled by the appearance of Bruce Le and Bruce Lei after Bruce Lee's passing, but Bart's death wasn't widely publicized; most people could be fooled.

—Eric Petrisic, Orlando, Florida

A. Next you'll be telling me there was more than one Lassie. I'm pretty sure there was only one Trigger, however, because Roy Rogers had the horse stuffed, inspiring Dale Evans to say, "Now, Roy, don't you go getting any ideas about me."

Basic Instinct 2

Q. In your review of *Basic Instinct 2*, you struggle with whether to give it a favorable rating; you know it's not a good movie, but it's very watchable and you enjoyed viewing it. Doesn't that contradict a rule you usually apply? You have to be true to the moviegoing experience. If you got into the film, shouldn't you give it a positive review, even though you know it's flawed?

—Michael Hart, Staten Island, New York

A. I struggled with the conflict between my belief that it was a bad movie and my knowledge that it was not a boring one. I tried to reflect that in my review, as if signaling that you could like it even if you didn't admire it. Maybe it was a cop-out.

Q. Did you read that Paul Verhoeven, who made the original *Basic Instinct*, said that America has become antisexual? I agree with him, although I would say we have become not antisexual but antierotic. *Basic Instinct 2* and *Showgirls* are erotic films. Eroticism is about the feminine, whereas pornography is about the masculine. I live in Las Vegas, where sex-for-sale is male-dominated. It's one of the least "erotic" cities in the world, and the women who are the focus of sexual interest are in the service of the patriarchy. I write erotic fiction that has some elements of *Basic Instinct 2*—it can be hard and bitchy, but it's still definitely erotic. America doesn't seem to have a problem with the pornographic, but it frequently reviles the erotic. I wish critics would take note of this dichotomy and stand up for erotic movies.

—Martha Woodworth, Las Vegas, Nevada

A. Most sex in American movies indeed is seen from the male point of view, and *Basic Instinct 2* at least seems to be controlled by the female character. Did the movie fail at the box office because of its female eroticism? I doubt it: *BI2* was so quickly and definitively a commercial failure that potential moviegoers apparently had made up their minds they didn't want to see it whether it was good or bad or whatever anyone said about it.

Q. On reading your review of *Basic Instinct 2*, I was reminded of a *Siskel & Ebert* show years ago titled "Guilty Pleasures." One of the films reviewed positively was *Emmanuelle*. You knew what it was, and why you were watching it, and for what it was, it was well enough done; we've all seen much worse. I haven't yet seen *BI2* but I will go into it knowing that Sharon Stone at least will have enjoyed wringing what she can out of the character that gave her stardom.

—John Sukovich, Newberry, South Carolina

A. And that's not all she wrings.

Batman Begins

Q. I just saw *Batman Begins* and thought it was okay. There were children at the show, however, and I felt sorry for them because the movie contained nothing that might appeal to eight years and younger. Why have filmmakers decided to ignore young audiences? Aren't comic books at heart really meant for children? I'm not saying the movie should have catered to young minds exclusively, but I find it more than a little cruel that the film offers nothing to the age group that made Batman a success in the first place. What would the young Roger Ebert have thought of the movie? I think the eight-year-old me would have found it visually confusing and disturbing.

—Cameron Moneo, Saskatoon, Saskatchewan

A. Trying to appeal to every possible age group is one of Hollywood's fatal errors. Batman is the darkest of the superheroes, and the recent graphic novels about his life have been intended for teenagers and adults. One of the reasons the movie was so good was that it dealt with the darker side of the character's early life and wasn't dumbed down with too many special effects or the clowning of the villains. The young Roger Ebert, of course, would have agreed.

Bettie Page

Q. In your review of *The Notorious Bettie Page*, you state, "Bettie Page is still alive in her eighties, and corresponds with some of her faithful fans, also in their eighties." This gives the impression most of Bettie's fans are older. This is not the case. Bettie's fan base spans age, gender, sexual orientation, and a number of subcultures, ranging from rockabilly fans to fetishists. There are numerous books, comic books, T-shirts, trading cards, action figures, and just about any other kind of merchandise you can think of, and Grandpa isn't the only one buying this stuff.

—Bob Ignizio, Lakewood, Ohio

A. Bettie Page action figures! The mind boggles. Think of the possibilities for the video game.

Bewitched

Q. When you wrote a review of the movie *Bewitched*, you, sir, were a liar and a charlatan. You stated you never saw the program when it was on television because you were reviewing hundreds of films per year, which did not leave you much time to watch the tube. May I remind you that you did not write your first review until 1967 and by then *Bewitched* had been on for three years? Possibly you might like to rethink that line of reasoning and pursue another feeble excuse. All you had to do was look at one or two episodes and I suspect even you might be able to determine the present piece is nothing more than garbage that should not be considered in the same breath as the original series or movie.

—Gil Effertz, Frazier Park, California

A. My bad. I forgot when I started not watching it.

Beyond the Valley of the Dolls

Q. I read today that Fox is releasing a special edition of *Beyond the Valley of the Dolls*, featuring a commentary by you and some docs, etc. I'd read that *BVD* was due for a fully packed Criterion release at some point. Has the Criterion release been canceled and replaced by this new Fox special edition?

—Greg Vickers, Hamilton, Ontario

A. Yes, but through cooperation between the two companies, the commentary track I recorded for Criterion is the one used on the Fox disk. I've received a copy of the two-disc Fox special edition and (warning: conflict of interest!) was very impressed by it, especially by how many of the original cast members and other artists they got to collaborate on a series of docs on Disc 2. What comes across is nostalgia for the experience of making the movie, and

a genuine love for Russ Meyer. Several critics, from such publications as *Newsweek*, the *Village Voice*, and the *Onion*, also say the movie is actually very good, broke new ground, invented the MTV editing style, etc., and express a surprising amount of admiration for the songs and the performances of the Carrie Nations. There's also a sweet conversation between Cynthia Myers and Erica Gavin about their love scene.

Box Office Slump?

Q. About the record-breaking slump that movie ticket sales are experiencing:

1) Since a lot of the audience is being lost to DVDs, aren't the real losers in this the theaters and distributors? The studios still get their money, only a few months later.

2) And isn't another part of the problem that 2005 was a lackluster year for the movies? How many must-see movies were there? Do you think 2005 was a down year, both in terms of "event" films and quality small films?

—Tim Gregorek, Chicago, Illinois

A. There were some wonderful films in 2005, from *Batman Begins* to *Crash* to *Millions* to *Me and You and Everyone We Know* to *Yes* to *Murderball*. The most interesting thing about the "slump" is that there may not be one. David Poland of the Movie City News Web site has been calling the slump a nonstory all summer. He points out that the grosses for 2004 were skewed by the performance of Mel Gibson's *The Passion of the Christ*, one of the most successful movies ever made, which attracted enormous numbers of people who ordinarily do not go to the movies. Even so, 2005 may end up as the second- or third-highest-grossing year in movie history. "There is no real slump," Poland writes. "If you think you are analyzing a real trend, but it can be changed by the actions of a week or two or a movie or two, it is not really a trend, it is a blip."

Q. If 2005 was such a great year for movies, why were box office receipts down from 2004, even though admission prices are at an all-time high? Do you feel that there is such a growing disconnect between Hollywood and America that Hollywood had better wake up or face serious consequences?

—Cal Ford, Corsicana, Texas

893

A. No, I don't, because the "box office slump" is an urban myth that has been tiresomely created by news media recycling each other. By mid-December 2005, according to the *Hollywood Reporter*, receipts were down between 4 and 5 percent from 2004, a record year when the totals were boosted by *The Passion of the Christ*, which grossed $370 million. Many of those tickets were sold to people who rarely go to the movies. 2005 eventually will be the second- or third-best year in box office history. Industry analyst David Poland has been consistently right about this nonstory.

The Break-Up

Q. Re the Vince Vaughn character who refers to the "16th Chapel" in *The Break Up*: When I studied Italian in Rome, one of the funny things they told us was that the actual meaning of Sistine Chapel, or Cappella Sistina (which both sound so lovely), is actually Chapel No. 16, or the Sixteenth Chapel!
—Stan Blair, Miami, Florida

A. Unfortunately, what the movie needed was Love Potion No. 9.

Brit vs. Yank Fantasy

Q. In your review of *Chronicles of Narnia*, you write: "Remarkable, isn't it, that the Brits have produced Narnia, the Ring, Hogwarts, Gormenghast, James Bond, Alice, and Pooh, and what have we produced for them in return?" True, the Brits have given us many wonderful, fantastic worlds. But we are not as bereft as you make it seem. L. Frank Baum gave the world Oz and the wonders therein. Theodore Geisel gave us the wonderful world of Dr. Seuss. Not to mention Batman, Superman, Spider-Man, X-Men, etc. The world of fantasy extends to graphic novels, too. Most of the top writers of fantasy these days—David and Leigh Eddings, Terry Brooks, Mercedes Lackey—are American. You sell us short, sir. We hold our own.
—Dean Grant, Simpsonville, South Carolina

A. You neglect Tarzan, but be honest: Would you trade the movies inspired by my list for the movies inspired by yours?

Brokeback Mountain

Q. In your review of *Brokeback Mountain* you write, "In their own way, programs like

Jerry Springer provide a service by focusing on people, however pathetic, who are prepared to defend what they feel." Roger, really, now. Do you *really* think *anything* on *Jerry Springer* is real? *JS* is utterly useless. It's vapid. It's a waste of light and electricity. Gawd! Stop it!
—Kim Kersey

A. For the purposes of the point I was making, it makes no difference if the show is real, or whether I believe it, or whether it's vapid. In a sense, the lower he aims, the more he reaches the people who may be able to gain tolerance about the diversity in our society, if that doesn't sound too condescending, and it probably does.

Q. I was rooting for *Brokeback Mountain* to win the Best Picture Oscar. I thought it was a great film. I haven't seen *Crash*, but I'm curious now to see it and be able to make a comparison. I wish the academy voters had done the same. For the major categories, there is no requirement that academy voters have seen all nominees. Or that they've even seen any of the nominees. Or that the academy member is the person actually filling out the ballot. The process is a sham. If one of the Olympic ice-skating judges missed one of the performances but then was able to submit a score that helped determine who won the gold medal, people would be outraged. The academy should change its rules.
—Bob Bartosch, Somerville, Massachusetts

A. Although the academy requires members to see all five documentaries and all five foreign films before voting in those categories, there is no such requirement in any of the other categories. Perhaps it is time for new bylaws. It was widely reported that two academy members refused to see *Brokeback Mountain* because of its gay subject matter, and anecdotal evidence that others also refused. Of course, some members no doubt voted *for* the film because of its theme. Members are free to vote however they want, but I think it is reasonable to expect them to see the films first, and I am awaiting apologies from Tony Curtis and Ernest Borgnine, who shamelessly went public with their refusals.

Broken Flowers

Q. In his new movie *Broken Flowers*, Bill Murray wears a blue track suit with orange stripes. Since he was courtside to cheer Illinois during the NCAA tourney, is his wardrobe intended to represent the Illinois colors?

—Betsy Hendrick, Champaign, Illinois

A. Since they are the precise shades of orange and blue used by Illinois, it can't be a coincidence.

Bubble

Q. To call Bubble a masterpiece is like calling a hole in the ground the Grand Canyon. The acting (albeit by amateurs) was wooden and consisted mainly of mumbling, and the cinematography was second-rate, but worst of all was the story itself. Frankly, I didn't care who the killer was (even though it was obvious). Please reconsider how bad this movie was. Fortunately I watched it on HDNet, so I didn't have to shell out any dollars.

—Rick Young, Pittsford, New York

A. Except, of course, that you had to subscribe to HDNet through your cable service. Perhaps like a lot of quiet, introspective movies (*Lost in Translation, Last Days*) it plays better on a bigger screen that can envelop you. I stand by my review.

Caché

Q. *(Spoiler warning)* My wife and I attended a screening of *Caché*. Everyone in the theater was puzzled by the last scene. Does the last scene at the school reveal the identity of who had been doing the tapings? Someone in the audience said they thought they saw the two sons talking to each other as though this provided a possible answer.

—Al and Pat Ralston, Fullerton, California

A. *Caché* has struck a nerve and did surprisingly good business in the United States and Europe. I'm asked about it constantly, as if there is an answer. The last scene indeed does show the two sons talking, and there should be no way they know each other. But what does that explain? Does it account for the videos? Consider that the film's last shot is exactly in the style of the videos that were received. Is someone else behind the camera? The film offers no possible closure.

Q. No one in Peter Haneke's *Caché* made those videotapes. The culprit is us, the viewing

audience. There's even a scene early in the film where Georges tries to figure out where the camera could have been and can't figure out how he could have walked right past it without seeing it. That's because from his perspective, the camera wasn't "there" at all. I took the film as a commentary on how voyeuristic our society has become. Whenever the movie switches to the videotape point of view, we stare, waiting for what's going to happen. We become the voyeurs. I usually don't go off on crazy theories like this, but you can't take the movie literally. You mention that it doesn't make sense that the two boys would be talking in the last shot; why couldn't they know each other from school? They could even be unaware of who each other's father is.

—Kevin McMillen, Rochester, New York

A. *Caché* is the movie people will not stop devising theories about, and although I've discussed it several times in the Answer Man, the subject apparently is not closed.

At the Cannes Film Festival, I got into a discussion of *Caché* with the director William Friedkin. He told me: "I was talking to Barbet Schroeder, one of the producers on the film, and he said that after Haneke screened it, everybody told him he was crazy, because 99 percent of the audience would never see those two obscure kids in the upper left-hand corner of the final shot. So he re-edited it, put in a closer shot so you could see it was them, and put in the dialogue of what they were saying to each other. Then his psychiatrist in Vienna told him, 'No, no! Do it the way you wanted!' So he took all that stuff out again."

What were the kids saying? I asked.

"That," Friedkin said, "I don't know."

Cannes Tickets

Q. I am serving in the U.S. Army, deployed to Iraq. My R&R falls during the 2006 Cannes Film Festival, and as a movie lover I am excited about the possibility of joining in the excitement while practicing my French a little. Is there a way for a guy like me to not only view the open-air screenings but also the films in competition?

—1st Lt. William J. Sherman, Iraq

A. Yes, you can attend the free screenings on the beach every night. And if you get up early enough to stand in line, you may be lucky enough to get tickets to a few official screenings. But in general, you need a photo pass to get into anything. You can absorb a lot of the fun by just hanging around. Hotel reservations are scarce and expensive. Some people on a budget stay in Nice and take the train every morning.

Chaos

Q. I sincerely regret having given the makers of *Chaos* my money. This film is an excuse to graphically film two rapes and several murders under the guise of art, which brings up an interesting dilemma. I was one of those people who were upset with George Bush Sr.'s dismissal of *Trainspotting* as a worthless film when he hadn't seen the film. An aide to the then-president rationalized this with the reply, "You don't have to look in every single trash can to know there's garbage inside," or something along those lines.

At the time, I thought the comment was ignorant and pandering to the Right. I still think it is, as I found *Trainspotting* to be a powerful indictment not only of the drug culture but also of our consumer culture.

But *Chaos* raises the question: Although the comment was wrong in its original context and was said for political purposes in a struggling president's career—is there any merit to what that aide said? *Does* every trash can have to be peered into? I saw *Chaos* because I didn't want to be in what I thought was the intellectually indefensible position of dismissing or criticizing a film without having seen it. But now I've played into their hands and given these morons exactly what they want: attention and money just because they were willing to be more socially abhorrent than any filmmaker to date.
—Rob Olmstead, Chicago, Illinois

A. The critic peers into the trash can so that you don't have to, as long as you trust the critic to describe the trash accurately. What happens, though, is that even the most negative reviews probably sell some tickets. In theory, the service to readers outweighs the benefit to the film.

Charlie and the Chocolate Factory

Q. I keep hearing that Johnny Depp based his performance as Willy Wonka on Michael Jackson. I think everyone is looking through the wrong end of the telescope. It has seemed to

me for years that Michael Jackson at some point decided, perhaps unconsciously, to become Willy Wonka. It should be no surprise, then, if Depp evokes the character Jackson has become.
—Seth Derrick, Phoenix, Arizona

A. The strange thing about *Charlie and the Chocolate Factory* is the way Depp's performance seems to exist in a world of its own while the film succeeds despite him. Depp is so consistently good that this miscalculation may simply be an illustration of his willingness to take chances. It's not a bad performance, just somehow a wrong performance.

Q. The newly released home video of *Charlie and the Chocolate Factory* bears a PG rating for "quirky situations" (among other things). Once again I am baffled by the MPAA's logic. Having seen the movie, I do not deny that it contains situations that indeed are quirky; however, what degree of quirkiness is required to elevate a movie from the G-rated quirkiness of, say, *Wallace & Gromit* to the PG-rated quirkiness of *Charlie*?
—Maureen Stabile, Streamwood, Illinois

A. The MPAA Code and Ratings Administration never discusses its reasons for a rating. If you think you're confused, consider the reader in a previous Answer Man column who questioned the G rating for *Wallace & Gromit in the Curse of the Were-Rabbit* in view of its "sexual innuendo, curse words, and even some nudity." To be sure, Gromit displays full frontal nudity in every scene.

Chicken Little

Q. Not wishing to appear a sexist pig, I hesitate to approach this subject. However, in your review of *Chicken Little* you keep referring to the protagonist as "he." In my opinion Chicken Little was a "she." A male chicken is usually referred to as a rooster.
—Derek Verner, Tuckahoe, New York

A. Actually, the word "chicken" encompasses both genders of the domestic fowl. A hen is a female chicken and a rooster is a male chicken. This doesn't get me off the hook, however, since how did I know that Chicken Little was a male and not a female? Perhaps because he was supplied with a male voice by Zach Braff and referred to as "he" throughout the movie's publicity materials. Nevertheless, it is fairly clear that Chicken Little is *not* a rooster. Perhaps he is a capon, in which case more than the sky has fallen.

Another good question: Since Chicken Little has no ears, why don't his glasses slip off?

The Chronicles of Narnia

Q. You write that J. R. R. Tolkien and C. S. Lewis "hated each other's fantasy worlds." Although you are correct in saying Tolkien disliked elements of Lewis's *Chronicles of Narnia*, Lewis was most appreciative and enthusiastic of Tolkien's *Lord of the Rings*. He wrote several reviews and essays attesting to this fact, and current editions of Tolkien's work even boast the famous Lewis quote "Here are beauties which pierce like swords or burn like cold iron" as part of their back jacket copy.

—Frank Gruber, Paramus, New Jersey

A. Many other readers supplied similar information, including Kevin Bush of West Palm Beach, Florida, who wrote: "In fact, Lewis probably overpraised Tolkien. I remember one book review where he favorably compared *Lord of the Rings* to Ariosto's *Orlando Furioso*.

My correspondents were quite correct. Lewis did not hate *LOTR*, and I have corrected the online review. My information came from a British reference book named *The Reader's Companion to Twentieth Century Writers*, edited by Peter Parker. It reads bluntly: "Lewis and Tolkien, despite their friendship, despised each other's writings for children." In answer to your next question, yes, they considered *LOTR* and *Narnia* to be writings for children.

Cinderella Man

Q. I was fascinated by the portrayal of Max Baer in *Cinderella Man* as a bit of a bastard. Whenever I see an actual historical person portrayed negatively, two questions always pop into my head: 1) Is that an accurate portrayal? and 2) What do their families think about it? Now I'm wondering if there is counseling for descendants of people who come off badly in movies. I smell a potential industry.

—Myeck Waters, Cliffwood Beach, New Jersey

A. Relatives of Baer and boxing historians have complained that he was depicted unfairly

in *Cinderella Man*. Apparently he killed only one man in the ring, not two, and was considered to be a gentleman by the man who defeated him for the title, Joe Louis. My own feeling is that we go to print for facts and to movies for emotions. Even when movies are "based on" real stories, I assume they are essentially fictions.

Commercials and Moviegoing

Q. People seem to be blaming the movies for the 2005 slump in the box office. I feel it's the actual experience of going to the theater that makes people stay away. When I saw *War of the Worlds*, the projection was slightly off and fuzzy, and certain scenes weren't framed properly. That was nothing compared to the theatergoers who were talking and directing glib remarks to the screen. One answered his phone and started talking loudly. Going to the movies is my favorite thing in the world. But now incidents like that happen about four out of five times I go. Isn't there anything theater chains can do to promote quiet screenings and make going to the movies fun again?

—Mark Donahue, Philadelphia, Pennsylvania

A. I've received a lot of feedback just like yours. People are also angry at the commercials they're forced to sit through. I've heard from people who now mostly attend "art theaters," not because they dislike commercial films, but because they know the audience behavior will be more appropriate.

Q. I'm amazed at how the movie theater experience degrades every year, yet the movie industry has resisted all feedback from moviegoers on how to improve it, apparently preferring to sue large groups of them instead. After being expected to sit through extended commercials, dirty conditions, outrageous prices, poor projection on outdated equipment, appalling behavior from other theatergoers, and the annoyance of cell phones, I have decided to avoid theaters as much as possible. If you personally were in charge of remaking the theater experience to win back moviegoers, what changes would you make?

—Tom Woodward, Santa Monica, California

A. Here are a few suggestions:

1. Install equipment, which already exists, to block cell phone signals in movie theaters.

897

2. Sell tickets with bar codes on them, so that moviegoers can attend only the movie they paid for. This would reduce the comings and goings of patrons who believe one admission is their ticket to a double or triple feature, and kids who movie-hop with their friends from one theater to another. It also would help explain why ticket sales seem to be down even though theaters seem to be about as full as ever.

3. Eliminate commercials (see below).

4. Train projectionists to show films at the proper light and sound levels. Twenty years after I first wrote about this problem, many movie theaters continue the insane practice of dialing down the intensity of projector lamps under the mistaken belief that they can reduce their power bills and extend lamp life. As a result, many movies are projected so dimly that their impact is diminished. I've quoted Eastman Kodak experts who say the light level has no effect on bulb life.

5. Many adults avoid certain kinds of movies because they assume the theater will be filled with noisy teenagers. Let's say you're forty and you want to go see a Dead Teenager Movie like *Final Destination 3*. Would you think twice? Perhaps theater chains could create movie clubs for patrons above a certain age and advise them of screenings where reasonable audience behavior will actually be enforced by the presence of ushers. Even one usher should do it: It's the thought that counts.

In support of my fifth suggestion, here is a message from Keith Johnson of Olathe, Kansas: "When people write of bad movie experiences, I can relate. One helpful solution is to attend the matinees. If it is not a children's movie, the theater seems to have older, more mature audiences, and the behavior of the audience is much better."

Q. I took my family to see *Fun with Dick and Jane*. We arrived on time, stood in line twice, once to buy our tickets and then to buy popcorn and sodas. Once seated in the theater, we watched a local commercial slide show for about ten minutes. Then we watched about thirty minutes of nothing but television commercials, one after another, and then another twenty minutes of previews. Watching coming attractions of new movies is fine, but forty minutes of conventional commercials is intol-

erable. I am not surprised at all at the box office slump. It is induced by the theaters themselves.
—Dr. Alex Cullison, Fairfax, Virginia

A. People used to ask if I'd seen any good movies lately. Now the inevitable topic of conversation is how much they hate commercials in movie theaters. I emphasize the word *hate*. For some moviegoers, commercials are the straw that broke the camel's back. Unfortunately, theater chains continue to delude themselves on the subject. For example:

Charles S. Lewis III of Daly City, California, writes me: "*USA Today* is reporting that the nation's largest movie chains are telling audiences to expect even *more* on-screen advertisements than before! Is it just me, or do things like this make one think that the owners just *want* to drive audiences away? With so many complaints about audience drop-off, why would they want to encourage such a thing? Earlier this year, I wrote a letter to AMC complaining about all the commercials. They responded by saying that their research shows 'audiences actually enjoy the ads very much.'"

And Stephen Cummings of Coralville, Iowa, writes me: "According to the IMDb, Pam Blase, a spokeswoman for AMC Entertainment, states that only one movie patron per 600,000 guests complains about ads before movies and that most regard the ads as 'part of the theatergoing experience,' something to do rather than talk to the person they came with before the movie starts (talking to a friend when you could spend valuable time staring at ads is really bad in consumer culture)."

Ebert again. One patron per 600,000! I wish we had a video clip of Blase quoting that statistic without breaking into hysterical laughter. If the National Association of Theater Owners were to commission a survey designed to determine what their patrons honestly thought about commercials, they would, I suspect, receive a loud and clear message.

Q. I finally sat down to watch a video I purchased a few months ago. All I wanted to do was hit "play," sit back, and enjoy the film. Instead I got six commercials. Six commercials! There was Oprah's twentieth anniversary collection. (Yeah, I was so ticked off I made a list.) Bob Dylan's *No Direction Home*. *Rugrats*. *SpongeBob SquarePants*. *Lemony Snicket's A*

Series of Unfortunate Events. Everybody Hates Chris. I don't want Nike or Ford commercials when I go to the theater and I don't want Oprah or Bob or Chris on a video disc that isn't about them. The studio added that junk as if it was a bonus feature.

—Troylene Ladner, Jersey City, New Jersey

A. A special circle of hell should be reserved for video executives who place previews at the top of DVDs. You tell me that in this case, you could get rid of each preview by clicking "next," but it took six clicks to get to "play." In some cases the previews cannot be skipped but are unavoidable, like the FBI warning (which has wasted untold millions of man-hours and not prevented a single act of piracy). Here's a tip from Teresa Budasi of the *Sun-Times:* With some discs, hitting "menu" before you hit "play" will get you to the "play movie" prompt with no commercials.

A Confederacy of Dunces

Q. Are there future plans to produce *A Confederacy of Dunces?* This movie must be made!

—Ginger Williams, Knoxville, Tennessee

A. The movie of John Kennedy Toole's great comic novel, with David Gordon Green directing and a script by Scott Kramer and Steven Soderbergh, was put on hold in late 2004. Green told the Answer Man in May 2005: "Politics over the property rights—torn between Miramax, Paramount, and various camps of producers—put a weight on the project that wasn't creatively healthy to work within."

Green now tells me: "The rights to *A Confederacy of Dunces* have been cleared at Paramount. The project is in development once again. The adaptation from the last effort has been put aside for legal reasons and a new one is in the works. I'm editing a film I just shot and hoping to begin putting more energy toward the potential of what I believe a proper production of that book might be. We'll see."

Crash

Q. Re your defense of *Crash* and the theory of one of its critics that the movie "sympathizes" with Sandra Bullock's "reprehensible behavior": *Crash* is a film that was aimed at those of us who thought we were above bias and smart enough to recognize our own reflection when we see it. This movie "freaked me

out." Here I am a black woman in America. I am not supposed to be able to identify with the racist white cop (Matt Dillon)! Nor Bullock's racial slurs. Their prejudices were nurture, not nature. But I did! Why? Their experience transcended color and it broke it down to just plain human nature. Maybe it even made me a little less angry. It also made me reflect on my own behaviors and stereotyping, and I didn't like what I saw. A film that can make you connect to the human experience is a great film!

—Tracy Flood, Garland, Texas

A. That's the thing: The movie asks all of us to examine our own consciences. Here is another letter on that point, from Donnie Garrow of Ottawa, Ontario:

"Although I did not think *Crash* was the best movie of the year, I do hold it in high esteem. As a person who is constantly confused for a number of different backgrounds, I was engrossed by the movie's ability to show not only the apparent racism that of course still exists but also the subtlety with which people demonstrate their ignorance and fear of something they do not know. I see this every day, again and again. I can be confused for Middle Eastern, Southeast Asian, Italian, and of course the right one, which is First Nation person of Canada; it is amazing what I encounter. Even in Canada, where people like to think racism doesn't exist, it does, and in many of the forms seen in the movie. When watching this movie I did start to have an inner discussion about the subtle ways I myself put down people and that even as minute as I might think a statement is, it can be hurtful."

Critics at Work

Q. As the wife of *Salt Lake Tribune* critic and Sundance veteran Sean Means, I laughed and cringed at your references to your festival diet. Although we live in Salt Lake City, Sean lives in a Park City condo during the festival, and I worry about his health the entire time he's gone. Every year I send him up the mountain with as many bananas, granola bars, and multivitamins as he's willing to carry, and every year he winds up living off whatever cheese and crackers he can scavenge from hospitality suite tables. As unhealthy as this seems, I wonder sometimes if this fasting perhaps contributes to his appreciation of the festival, making the

899

whole experience a sort of vision quest in the snowy mountains.

—Leslie Means, Salt Lake City, Utah

A. There's a poignancy in the way we movie critics talk at Sundance about the days since our last balanced meal. A restaurant visit costs you one, maybe two movies. The jurors have it hard, too; at the awards I told actor Terrence Howard he was looking slim, and he said yes, he had lost weight for a role but had packed on five pounds at Sundance. It is a sad sight to see cinephiles in the lobby, munching oatmeal cookies against the clock.

Q. Did you happen to see the item about you in the April 2006 *Premiere* magazine? Sundance Film Festival people were polled for their good and bad memories.

—Kerry O'Connor, La Grange, Illinois

A. The item quotes Myles Rademan, director of public affairs for Park City: "One year we towed Clint Eastwood's car. He came in and said, 'I deserved to be towed. I'll pay the fine.' He sounded just like Dirty Harry. Roger Ebert was the worst when he got towed. He made a real scene about it, and we all gave him a thumbs down."

Rademan of course has had the Myles Rademan Spirit of Hospitality Award named after him, "presented to an individual who has contributed to the tourism business in the Park City area." Since I have been attending the festival since 1981, even before it was called Sundance, I have long dreamed of winning the Rademan Award, but now my hopes are dashed.

Yes, I recall that incident and wrote about it in 1997. I paid my fine and did not make a scene. I've been around too long to make scenes in police stations. I remember being treated pleasantly by the Park City police, who even gave me a lift to the distant lot where my car had been towed. The police sympathized with me about how the city had made a deal with freelance car towers who cruised the streets looking for cars to snatch. They were bounty hunters, paid by the car, in the Park City Spirit of Hospitality. Not only were the police nice, but also every single Park City citizen and Sundance volunteer I have ever met has been a warm and wonderful person; however, I have never met the director of public affairs.

The real headline, of course, is that a big star like Eastwood not only drove and parked his own car but also turned up in person to redeem it. Wouldn't you think he would have had a limo driver, and a publicist to pay the ticket? But it sounds like Rademan must have been an eyewitness at both of these incidents. At the very least, in the Myles Rademan Spirit of Hospitality, he should have torn up Eastwood's ticket. If Eastwood really sounded like Dirty Harry, I would have.

Q. A study by professors from Duke, Florida Atlantic, and Carnegie Mellon purports to examine "the meaning of silence" by film critics. Some do not review good films, some do not review bad films. You are listed among four critics giving "the most information" on bad films. What do you think of this study?

—Greg Nelson, Chicago, Illinois

A. The study has been greeted with howls of laughter and derision in the filmcrit community. It was made in ignorance of how critics actually work, and its findings are meaningless. It assumes that every critic has control over which films he or she reviews. But on a paper with several critics, the senior critic is likely to get the better films and the junior critic gets the leftovers. "Silence" simply means the other critic wrote the review. In my case, since I review everything I can (280 reviews in 2005) I presumably also should have been among the leaders writing about good films. My friend Mark Caro, another leading reviewer of bad films, demolishes the study in his blog, "Pop Machine," at chicagotribune.com.

Critic vs. Public

Q. I must take issue with your response to Jay Leno's question about whether Hollywood is out of step with the mainstream public. Your response was, "Maybe the moviegoing public is out of step with good movies." How incredibly insulting and arrogant!

Your comment illustrates an obvious belief on your part that the people involved with financing, writing, directing, and acting in films—most of whom live in the unnatural and aesthetic environments of Hollywood and other cloistered situations—know better than I and the rest of the public what *we* want and need in entertainment! Many of us are *tired* of the continual diet of political, environmental, and societal issues forced upon us by today's moviemakers. The overwhelming and continual box office success of the lighter fare versus the others proves my point.

—Donna Larson, Princeton, Minnesota

A. No, I think it proves *my* point. These 2006 films "won" their weekends or placed second: *Hostel, Underworld: Evolution, Big Mammas House 2, When a Stranger Calls, Madeas Family Reunion, The Hills Have Eyes, Ultraviolet,* and *Date Movie.* Only three of these, by the way, were "lighter fare," unless vivisection and evisceration make you smile. During the same weeks, these films were *not* embraced at the box office: *The Matador, Caché, The New World, Transamerica, The Three Burials of Melquiades Estrada, Tristram Shandy,* and *Tsotsi.* If I prefer the films on the second list, does that make me arrogant? Moviegoers "tired of the continual diet of political, environmental, and societal issues" are finding lots of films that entertain them, and those of us who prefer more challenging films have to look a little harder.

Here's some insight from Daniel R. Huron, of Texas City, Texas: "I was reading a review of *Syriana* from Reuters, but I stopped reading, not because I was offended by their opinion, but because the reviewer insisted on commenting on its box office potential. According to the reviewer, the film was unlikely to connect with the 'under-twenty-five, mainstream audience' because it is so 'dialogue heavy.' My feeling is, who cares? Shouldn't a reviewer critique the film for what it is and not for its potential to make money?"

Dark City

Q. I applaud your recent addition of Alex Proyas's *Dark City* to your Great Movies collection. I saw the film for the first time when I was fourteen and it changed my conception of what science fiction films could do. Yet my uncle, a true cinephile, assured me that it was a rehash of the superior *Blade Runner* and would be forgotten in ten years. It has been seven years since I had that conversation. Has the film left any lasting imprint on the cinema yet in your mind?

—Paul Babin, Yarmouthport, Massachusetts

A. After being missed by many moviegoers in its original release, it has become a best seller on DVD and developed a large and devoted following (see recent discussions at the blog Cinematical.com). Proyas is working on a new director's cut, to be released in 2006; I have expanded my commentary from the original DVD to reflect the changes. Tell your uncle the movie stands on its own and is not a rehash of anything—but that I feel I may have undervalued *Blade Runner. Dark City* helped me appreciate the values of the earlier film.

The Da Vinci Code

Q. Why did you refer to the novel *The Da Vinci Code* as a "preposterous" work of fiction yet fail to label the Bible as such? Do you honestly believe the Bible is a work of nonfiction? Aren't parts of the Bible "preposterous"? If your devotion to institutionalized religion colors your ability to write logically, perhaps you should recuse yourself from reviewing films that require an unbiased view.

—Fred Schultz, Dallas, Texas

A. The job of a critic is to express an opinion. If critics recused themselves from reviewing anything on which they held an opinion, there would be no criticism. The purpose of my review of *The Da Vinci Code* was not to review the Bible but to review the film adaptation of a novel.

Even doing that made some readers unhappy. Here is Lara Coates of Kennewick, Washington: "Maybe you should stick to reviewing the movie instead of reviewing and insulting people who might entertain the ideas that Dan Brown suggests. Although Brown's suggestions may be preposterous, as you suggest, there is no way for anyone to know exactly what happened during Jesus's time. I guarantee you that I am of 'sound mind' even though I question the validity of the Bible."

Ebert again. Some of the material on which Brown's book is based did not originate in the time of Jesus but is a French forgery from the 1950s. *60 Minutes* did a segment about that.

Q. One of the great ironies of Brown's book is that it assaults you with its greatest piece of idiocy before you've even picked it up. The man's name is Leonardo, please. "da Vinci" (note the lower-case *D*), is *not* his family name, it's his hometown. He was born in Vinci, Italy, in 1452, in a time before Europeans had started surnaming themselves. Brown's error is on par with writing a book on the life of Christ called *The Of Nazareth Code,* or assuming St. Joan was the daughter of Mr. and Mrs. *Of Arc.* It's amazing that anyone could take seriously the historical claims of a work whose title screams out, "penned by a historical ignoramus!"

—C. J. E. Culver

A. We have a policy at the Answer Man that all writers must provide the name of their hometown, but in your case, I'm making an exception.

Deleted Scenes

Q. I have a big complaint with the folks who release DVD versions of theatrical releases. I own *Titanic, Star Wars I–III,* and a lot of others. My question is: Why can't the directors put all the extended and deleted scenes within the context of the film itself? We are smart enough to sit through a longer version.

—Marianne Brzezinski, Oak Lawn, Illinois

A. Yes, but perhaps there was a reason those scenes were shortened or deleted? The "director's cuts" on DVDs reproduce the director's original vision, which in some cases (*Picnic at Hanging Rock*) may actually be shorter than the theatrical version. And when a director does incorporate longer or deleted scenes or makes other changes, I get complaints like this one from Robert Wiseman of Centennial, Colorado: "Do you have any idea if and when the original version of *Blade Runner* (i.e., the one that made the film a success, not the one that Ridley Scott's ego destroyed) will be available on DVD?"

Answer: An edition that includes three versions of the film, including the original version, was announced a year ago, but digitalbits.com reports rumors that the forthcoming special edition will feature, once again, only the director's cut. Versions of the original version, which opens with Harrison Ford's narration, are for sale on eBay, ranging from $1.99 to $30 (for the Criterion laser disc).

Deuce Bigalow: European Gigolo

Q. Did you really need to pick on Rob Schneider in your review of *Deuce Bigalow: European Gigolo*? RottenTomatoes.com shows that he scores a 10 out of 100 on the TomatoMe-

ter, which is even lower than Steven Seagal. Why not just say that the movie sucked, as opposed to saying *his* movie sucked?

—Willy Yu, Los Angeles, California

A. You say he's lower than Steven Seagal, yet you think I picked on him?

Q. Re *Deuce Bigelow*: You guys always seem puzzled how stuff like that gets made. Y'know . . . there's a huge audience for this crap in America. That's why it keeps getting made. And yes, I'll admit that even these crap movies can have their funny moments. I live in Indianapolis and I know there's a bunch of Deuce Bigalow fans in this town. They're beer-guzzlin', dope-smokin', truck-drivin', pit bull–ownin', head-shavin', ball cap–wearin', crime-committin', jackass psychopaths whose parents (if there were any) didn't want to bother with the job of teaching and controlling them. Garbage in, garbage out, so the parents are probably just like their offspring. The United States is rife with them. It's ugly and it's increasingly one of the causes for the ruination of a once civilized, safe nation.

—Tom McCullough, Indianapolis, Indiana

A. Indianapolis also harbors many heroic, civilized, and cultured citizens, as befits the home office of Steak 'n' Shake.

Q. Rob Schneider is one of the biggest actors in what I call the Stupid Movie Genre, which caters to the lowest of our culture. But what Tom McCullough from Indianapolis wrote in the Answer Man column really cheesed me off.

I don't live in Indianapolis. But I have enjoyed a stupid movie now and again. That includes the original *Deuce Bigalow,* as well as *Sorority Boys, Joe Dirt,* and *Josie and the Pussycats.* (It doesn't include *The Longest Yard,* a Stupid Movie that I hated and that you gave three stars.) I told my girlfriend early in our courtship when discussing my movie tastes, "On my DVD wall, I'm as proud to have *Pootie Tang* as *Citizen Kane.*" But I certainly wouldn't apply any of the adjectives to myself that Tom from Indiana does to the fans he knows. A person shouldn't try too hard to defend Stupid Movies, but I'll be darned if the people who like them shouldn't be defended from statements as ignorant as those of Mr. McCullough.

—Jason Millward, Northville, Michigan

A. I was with you right up until *Pootie Tang*. It's a difficult task, separating the good Stupid Movies from the bad ones, but if it saves you from seeing *Deuce Bigalow, European Gigolo*, it's worth it. The point is not to avoid all Stupid Movies but to avoid being a Stupid Moviegoer.

Devil's Rejects

Q. There exists an audience-fueled campaign to encourage the academy to recognize Bill Moseley's performance as Otis Driftwood in *The Devil's Rejects*. In addition to an online petition (www.petitiononline.com/otis78), fans are collecting signatures at theaters and rock concerts. Do you know of any previous instances when the public has taken an Oscar campaign into their own hands on behalf of an actor?

—Louise Fenton, New York, New York

A. The nearest thing I can think of is the campaign arguing that Michael Crawford should star in the film version of *Phantom of the Opera*. But surely the academy should begin by voting a posthumous Oscar to Groucho Marx's performance as Otis Driftwood in *A Night at the Opera*. My own feeling is that if Moseley has other plans for the night of March 5, 2006, he shouldn't rush out to change them.

Digital Matters

Q. What do you think of the new digital format agreed to by the studios? In the past, you have said digital projection was not as good as the current 35mm film format. Is the new format the same as the former digital format? Do you think the new format will help or hinder film piracy?

—Mike Coleman, Round Lake, Illinois

A. The digital projection system that was being touted four years ago, at a cost of $100,000 to $150,000 a machine, today would seem woefully substandard. Those promoting it claimed it was "as good as film." New digital projectors are much better, and the studios think they can save money on the cost of film prints by switching to digital. Still uncertain is: 1) Who will pay for the still-expensive projectors? 2) Will widespread digital distribution be an invitation to piracy? and 3) How will the public react to buying tickets to movies they essentially can see at home at about the same projection quality?

If the movie industry had true visionaries among its most powerful executives, Maxivision 48 would be given a try. It shows movies at forty-eight frames a second, uses only 50 percent more film than current technology, and because of a patented method for moving the film through the gate, eliminates scratching and jiggles; it would cost only $12,000 per screen to install the equipment. The picture is four times better than current film projection, and that would provide a powerful incentive for people to see movies in theaters. I've heard genuine enthusiasm from people who've seen movies such as *Batman Begins* and *Charlie and the Chocolate Factory* on IMAX screens, and I know that audiences do respond to picture quality. If one industry leader announced a movie in Maxivision, there would be a stampede to the format because digital would be upstaged instantly.

Domino

Q. Your review of *Domino* asks why they remove the man's arm for the combination tattooed on it, when it would be easier to just copy down the number. The movie makes it clear that the arm was removed by mistake because of a misunderstood cell phone call. Domino was told to remove the sleeve of the shirt to read the combo but the cell phones were breaking up, so there was the disastrous consequence. I'm surprised you missed this moment.

—Sandy Struth, Los Angeles, California

A. I'm not surprised. I enjoyed *Domino*'s hyperkinetic structure, but the movie is told so breathlessly and in such a fractured style that Tony Scott could have hidden *Doom* in there somewhere and I might have missed it.

Dreamer

Q. *Mariah's Storm* did not win the Breeders' Cup, as you say in your review of *Dreamer*, but actually finished ninth. Quite a difference.

—Joseph Smith, Forest Hills, New York

A. *Dreamer* is inspired by the true story of Mariah's Storm, one of the rare horses who were not put down after a broken bone. She was treated, recovered, and raced again. I consulted the great horse writer William Nack, author of the biography of Secretariat, for an expert answer. He replies:

"The letter is accurate but slightly misleading to the layperson who does not know the sport. Mariah's Storm finished ninth in the Breeders' Cup Distaff run at Belmont Park on October 28, 1995. There is a Breeders' Cup day every year in which all the best horses in the world gather at one U.S. track and run in a bunch of races to decide who is the best in various divisions: sprint, turf, mile, male two-year-old, female two-year-old, etc. Mariah's Storm competed in the $1 million BC Distaff, a race confined to female thoroughbreds age three and older. She was four that year. It's the championship event of the year for females older than two.

"In the lead-up to the Breeders' Cup, there are many events run around the country that have the tag 'Breeders' Cup' attached to them. These are races that are related to the main event but are not part of it. So Turfway Park in northern Kentucky ran the Turfway Breeders' Cup race for females that year and, yes, she won that and beat the champion Serena's Song. But then she finished ninth in the big one, at Belmont Park. Of course, then Mariah's Song went on to stud duty and became the mother of Giants Causeway, a wonderful racehorse who is proving himself to be a great stallion. So Mariah's Song's genetic influence has become powerful in the sport. She was a beautifully bred horse herself and a superior runner in her own right."

Ebert again. I have added the crucial word "Turfway" to my review.

The Dukes of Hazzard

Q. I was appalled at the pure venom in your review of The Dukes of Hazzard. As a movie critic, you have every right to blast a movie, but I am shocked at the personal character attack on Jessica Simpson. No, she may never win a Nobel Prize, but that is hardly a reason to so viciously attack her in print. Blast her performance, costumes, script, whatever, but I found it mean-spirited to be so cruel in regards to Simpson's personality and intelligence. Yes, she *should* watch the news more, but a movie review is hardly the place to point it out.

—Jenna Scott, Bowling Green, Kentucky

A. You're right. I was unkind, and it was uncalled-for. I was startled that Simpson didn't know who Lance Armstrong was, but then

again I'd never seen Dukes of Hazzard on TV. We live and learn. I made some reckless comments about her IQ and the school system of her birthplace, Abilene, Texas, and got a lot of messages like these:

• Her intelligence: "It might be you who is uninformed about middle America. I'm from North Carolina and my extended family wouldn't know who Lance Armstrong is, nor their friends, nor their friends. If you told them, they would respond, 'He pedals a bike up and down a mountain? Who cares? Now get back to work or I'll pedal *you* up a mountain.'" (Alan Grady, Raleigh, North Carolina)

• The Abilene school system: "As a graduate of the Abilene Independent School District, I was amused when I read your review of Dukes of Hazzard. Jessica Simpson grew up in the Dallas–Fort Worth area and not Abilene. While I am convinced that Simpson has several talents, I am not so sure that the Abilene Independent School District can take credit for her knowledge (or lack of it) about Lance Armstrong, buffalo wings, or any other of her trademark statements." (John Neese, Abilene, Texas)

• On never having seen Dukes of Hazzard: "This is why we, the liberal elite, get such a black eye. When you denigrate something that you admit you have never seen, I understand why the conservative right calls you, and by extension, the rest of us, elitist. The fact that you list never watching the TV show as a reason why you are 'so smart and cheerful' basically marks you as a fool. I happen to believe that there is something to be gained from many different forms of entertainment, even that which is 'popular.' I just wanted you to understand how insulted I felt by that particular review." (Ron Lindsey)

Okay, this is Ebert again. If we are, as you say, "we, the liberal elite," then why shouldn't conservatives call us elitist? Conservatives can be elitist, too. In fact, it is something we should all strive for, don't you think? Any reader of my reviews knows I love popular culture. I also love putting my tongue in my cheek, which is where it was parked when I wrote about being so smart and cheerful. Have we, the liberal elite, entirely lost our sense of humor?

Q. Recently you have come under fire from readers who don't get the humor in your

columns, as in your *Dukes of Hazzard* and *The Aristocrats* reviews. The print medium is the absolute hardest place to be witty. A little piece of me dies every time one of your witticisms is mistaken for a sincere attack.
—Andrew Zimmer, Los Angeles, California

A. I hope it is a very small piece. A depressing number of people seem to process everything literally. They are to wit as a blind man is to a forest, able to find every tree, but each one coming as a surprise.

Q. Regarding your comments on Jessica Simpson's early education, you should see Jay Leno's *Jaywalking* segment. A lot of young Californians apparently are getting the same quality of education as Simpson.
—John Marzan, Manila, Philippines

A. I suppose it's a whole lot better in your state.

Duma

Q. What will happen with the wonderful family film *Duma*? I know it was on a test run here, but I'm wondering, will it be released elsewhere?
—Katy Petersen, Chicago, Illinois

A. Keep your fingers crossed. It was held over for a fourth week in Chicago, although Dan Fellman, president of distribution for Warner Bros., says the last week's grosses were disappointing. All the same, he says the studio will release the film September 30 in forty Los Angeles theaters, "giving us a chance to market the film to a wide audience and use all we have learned from previous campaigns." *Duma* currently scores a perfect 100 on the Tomatometer.

Q. We have a cat who loves to watch TV (his faves are Teletubbies and anything with a live-action cat, big or small, in it). We had a screener of *Duma*, which I procured so I could watch it again before writing about it, so we put it on for him. He watched it for twenty minutes straight, without moving, except for going behind the TV cabinet for a moment to see if he could find a real cheetah. And I'm thinking, I could market this thing to cats, and Warner Bros. can't figure out how to market it to kids?
—Stephanie Zacharek, film critic, Salon.com

A. Yours is a brave cat. I certainly would not look behind the TV if I thought there might be a cheetah back there. You were one of the origi-

nal champions of *Duma*, a wonderful and overlooked family film that critics were able to help find a limited release in several major markets. In another strange marketing decision, Warner Bros. released it on DVD January 1, 2006, just a little too late to be a Christmas present.

The Dying Gaul

Q. I just saw *The Dying Gaul* and really liked it. I am a Buddhist, as is Robert, the character played by Peter Sarsgaard. Robert believes he may have encountered his dead lover in a chat room. You mentioned that you had two big problems with the film: "1) There is no reason to believe Robert particularly believes in the supernatural, and 2) Would it not occur to Robert that he had, after all, told Elaine about his favorite chat room?" Your second point is a good one. But as a Buddhist, I would differ a bit with your first point. Robert mentions that after his lover's death he was afraid to step on insects for fear that a bug might be his lover reincarnated. So the idea that perhaps his lover might speak to him through a chat room struck me less as a supernatural event than as a possible reincarnation manifestation.
—Dwight Okita, Chicago, Illinois

A. I wrote back to you: "Does the Buddhist theory of reincarnation include becoming reincarnated as the very same person, with the same memories, and the password to the correct chat room? In other words, was the lover reborn as the same person at the same age as when he died?"
You responded: "I'm not sure if most Buddhists believe one's memory is erased at the moment of reincarnation. I know that SGI Buddhists like me do believe that one is born back into the world with whatever wisdom one has achieved in previous lifetimes. So wherever you are on your progress toward enlightenment, you re-enter the world with that progress intact. Maybe passwords come with us, too! But in the end, one never really knows until one is there to experience it oneself."
Ebert again. To die, be reborn, and know that one is NightRider with the password "ledzeppelin" is too depressing to contemplate.

Eight Below

Q. In your review of *Eight Below*, you say the dogs should have been invisible, since there is total darkness during the Antarctic winter. You are correct. However, it's not dark so much as it is a murky twilight. The sun does rise but only to within a few degrees of the horizon—at least, if my recollection of sixth-grade earth science is correct.

—Jill C. McCoy, Chicago, Illinois

A. We should have heard only barking. The darkness is more total the closer you get to the pole, but in dead winter it is pretty much dark all over the continent. The man to ask is Mr. Matt, who spends the winter in Antarctica and answers kids' questions on globalclassroom.org. Here is an exchange he had:

"Dear Mr. Matt: Hi I heard that you're in total darkness. Do you have enough food? Do you have any games? I like your mustache. I am thirteen years old. How old are you? My favorite color is red. Your friend, Marquis

"Dear Marquis: Thank you for writing. We have been in total darkness, but the sun is showing signs of coming up. Today, the sky was a lighter shade of blue, and I could make out the mountains. Blue is my favorite color. We eat pretty good, considering all the food was brought here last summer. There are a few vegetables from the greenhouse. In April I turned fifty. Your friend, Mr. Matt."

The Exorcism of Emily Rose

Q. In your review of The Exorcism of Emily Rose, you wrote, "You didn't ask, but in my opinion, she had psychotic epileptic disorder, but it could have been successfully treated by the psychosomatic effect of exorcism if those drugs hadn't blocked the process." I have news for you, there is no such thing as a "psychotic epileptic disorder/seizure." The symptomatology of psychosis and epilepsy do not correlate. Next time, please base your opinion on something that the fields of psychiatry and psychology acknowledge.

—Jonathan Fink, psychologist, Hilton Head Island, South Carolina

A. Scott Derrickson, director of The Exorcism of Emily Rose, replies: "It's true that 'psychotic epileptic disorder' is not the name of any real medical condition—nor is the drug Gambutrol real, for that matter. The use of the actual names of recognized medical conditions and pharmaceuticals in movies typically must be changed for legal and copyright purposes.

"To further address your concerns, it should be noted that in the film, the name 'psychotic epileptic disorder' is meant to be taken as a dubious medical term—one that has been invented by the doctor on the witness stand. And the fact that the symptoms of psychosis and epilepsy do not correlate is pointed out by the defense, but that certainly doesn't negate the possibility that a person can have both conditions at once.

"This is all, however, beside the point, really. I can't speak for you, but it seemed quite obvious to me that your last paragraph was not intended as a literal evaluation of Emily Rose's condition or potential cure, but rather a symbolic acknowledgment that there are merits to both sides of the court case and that the truth probably lies somewhere in the murky overlap between them."

Ebert again: Derrickson may have been too quick to write off psychotic epileptic disorder, Barton Odom, philosophy professor at Tarleton State University, informs me: "According to epilepsy.com, there are several syndromes in which the symptomatologies of psychosis and epilepsy do indeed correlate. So your sentence was correct as written: There is such a thing as psychotic epileptic disorder (several, in fact)."

Q. I saw The Exorcism of Emily Rose, believing the ads: "based on a true story." However, at the end of the credits, it says in plain English: "The events in this film are fictitious." What?! It's not the first movie to pull this, either. Fargo is a big one that comes to mind. Why do movies need to disguise themselves as based on reality? Sure, it seems more scary that way, but why do the filmmakers lie to us?

—Steven O'Brien, Blauvelt, New York

A. Fargo's claim to be based on a true story was used by the Coen brothers, they explained, as a stylistic device. In the case of Emily Rose, the story is fiction but it is technically "based on a true story"—much changed in time, place, and details, to be sure. The movie moved the story to America, focused on one priest, and omitted most of the horrifying details of the real case, casting itself more as a sincere dispute between science and religion.

According to The Real Emily Rose at fotofetch.com, my source for all that follows, the film was inspired by a case in the 1970s that represents the last time the Catholic Church officially recognized a demonic possession. It involved a German girl named Anneliese Michel, who was treated for seizures and given drugs over a period of five years before the Church finally authorized an exorcism; its investigation indicated she was possessed by, among others, Lucifer, Judas, Nero, Cain, and Hitler. From September 1975 until July 1976 she underwent a series of exorcism rituals, while refusing all food and "her knees ruptured due to the 600 genuflections she performed obsessively during the exorcism." A forensic exam eventually found she died of starvation. Two priests and her parents were found guilty of manslaughter and sentenced to six months in jail and probation. The German bishops then asked Rome to abolish the exorcism ritual; a revised ritual was published by Rome in 1999 but has never been used.

Fantastic Four

Q. Let me start off by saying that Tim Story's *Fantastic Four* is a lackluster film, with very little going for it. In this sense, your appraisal is correct. To call the Fantastic Four "second-tier heroes," however, is not. The Four, one of Stan Lee and Jack Kirby's earlier creations, is also one of Marvel's longest-running comics. They have been rightly coined comics' "first family" and their own comic subtitles itself as "the world's greatest comic book." They are miles more popular than many other characters who have received the film treatment in recent years—for evidence of this, look at how this mediocre, critically panned film nearly doubled its initial box office projections.

How you could confuse the Human Torch with the Flash is baffling. One lights on fire and flies, the other runs really fast. At least mix him up with X2's Pyro, who could control flame (but not create it). And comparing Storm with the Invisible Woman—why, because they both have blond hair? I had thought you were beginning to catch on to the fact that powers and personality were intertwined—that comic-book films contain some depth of character. These are not films about flashy powers, they are stories about people. I will give you this much, however: The film's version of Dr. Doom (much changed for the worse from his comics incarnation) is derivative. Instead of a vengeful and scarred totalitarian dictator, the film offers up a

Trump-wannabe tycoon whose every "motive" scene to fuel his hatred for the Four is completely ripped from Willem Dafoe/Norman Osbourne's exposition in the original *Spider-Man*. I don't expect you to do all the homework in reviewing these films, with long and storied histories in other media. I do wish, however, that if you don't know what you're talking about, you wouldn't act as though you do.

—Justin Morissette, Vancouver, Washington

A. It is easy enough to label yourself "the world's greatest comic book," or "the world's greatest newspaper," for that matter. The trick is to get someone else to describe you that way. But you make a good point. Many, many, many Fantastic Four fans have written to me complaining that since the Four predated the appearance of X-Men, they hardly could be ripping them off. My defense is that I was thinking of the movies, not the original comic books, and so *Fantastic Four* seemed like an afterthought to *X-Men* and *The Incredibles*. What I learned while reading dozens of messages is that comics fans have made enormous psychic investments in their favorite characters and follow their origins, adventures, opponents, and character changes with an attention bordering on obsession. I saw a bad movie. Many of them saw a movie whose goodness or badness was secondary, since whatever happened on the screen was linked in their imaginations with an extensive prehistory.

First Descent

Q. Here is a quick answer to the question in your *First Descent* review, "How do snowboarders know where they're going?"

I asked the same question when my son Jeremy was riding as a professional in the BC back country, the U.S. Rockies, and the Andes and competing in World Cup competition. The answer is that they scout their drops beforehand. My son also told me about a couple of video shoots where he was guided over the lip of a cliff by a spotter in a helicopter who had a full view of the "drop."

—Bill Atkinson, Courtenay, British Columbia

A. This is good enough for your son, who is a professional at the World Cup level. But in my mind, when a "drop" is more than, oh, say, about fifty feet, I take away the quotes and italicize it.

Flightplan

Q. Have they started serving alcohol at press screenings in your neck of the woods? I ask because I'm a reviewer in Canada, and perhaps we could ask for the same courtesy here; it would help with movies like *Flightplan*. This is one of the most ridiculous movies I've seen this year. It doesn't even make sense *before* the drop into Steven Seagal territory in the last act. No one has seen the daughter, or anyone leading her away? As *MadTV*'s Marvin Tikvah would say: *Come on!* More important, how could anyone be sure that she would be on *that* plane at *that* time?

—Nicolas Lacroix, Quebec City, Quebec

A. I got a lot of complaints like yours, including a masterpiece of analysis by Andy Ihnatko of Boston, Massachusetts, that was so thorough I believe he even disproved the existence of the movie itself. The key passage in my review was: "After the movie is over and you are on your way home, some questions may occur to you. . . ." I now realize I should have written, "many fundamental, enormous, and unanswerable questions may occur to you." But let me explain the reasoning behind my review. I believe the movie worked while it was playing. It presented me with a baffling disappearance and then seemed to address it with logic. Then it turned into a film depending on the resourcefulness and imagination of the Jodie Foster character. Yes, I agree, after it's over you realize there is no way all of the necessary conditions could have been counted upon. But you don't know that at the time, and while watching a thriller, it's what you know at the time that's crucial. If you also want it all to be plausible in hindsight, you're probably disappointed when a magician doesn't saw a real person in half and leave the severed corpse on the stage.

Q. I just read Nicolas Lacroix's apoplectic response to the absurdity of *Flightplan* and to your review of it for failing to point out how illogical that movie was. Well, let me get apoplectic. I've heard many critiques like Lacroix's about the lack of logic or realism in various movies, and I'm tired of that kind of sniping. Every creative work has its own set of rules and expectations, and the work should be critiqued on those grounds; real-world logic hardly ever enters the picture. To criticize a movie because it's not logical is to criticize it for something it's not attempting to be.

—Juan Felipe Calle, Tamarac, Florida

A. Unless, to be fair, the lack of logic distracts us in the wrong way or at the wrong time. *Flightplan* becomes impossible only on reflection, after it's all over. Until then you don't know it's illogical because you don't know what's going to happen, unless you were unfortunate enough to read the Associated Press story about how flight attendants hate the movie; it gave away the ending in its first paragraph!

The 40-Year-Old Virgin

Q. I know you liked *The 40-Year-Old Virgin* more than your readers did. You also liked it more than I did. I do a review column for an ad people's newsletter, and my main problem with this movie was the casting of Steve Carell as Andy in the lead. I never believed him in that role. Everybody else was fine, especially Paul Rudd and Catherine Keener. But the role of Andy seemed made for either Adam Sandler or Ben Stiller, not Carell, which is ironic, since he cowrote the script. I wonder what you think about the job Carell did.

—Liz Craig, Roeland Park, Kansas

A. It is hardly true to say I liked the movie more than my readers did, since it is a phenomenal box office success, but I think Carell was perfect in the role. Sandler might have been too knowing and Stiller too macho; Carell projects an innocence that is crucial to the movie's success. I hope he will forgive me for saying so, but you can believe he is a virgin.

Q. While reading my local paper over the weekend, I saw an ad for *The 40-Year-Old Virgin* that called it "the best-reviewed movie of the year!" with a note stating this was from Rotten Tomatoes. So I went to rottentomatoes.com and looked up 2005 movies, and I found that *The 40-Year-Old Virgin* has a Tomatometer rating of 85 percent—very respectable, but hardly the best of 2005. In fact, Rotten Tomatoes rates it as No. 35 in its list of 2005 movies. Rated higher than *The 40-Year-Old Virgin* are such wide-release movies as *Murderball*, *March of the Penguins*, *Kung-Fu Hustle*, *Millions*, and *Broken Flowers*. Why (and how) can Universal Pictures get away with an ad that is blatantly lying?

—Doug Wicinski, Rockville, Maryland

A. A Universal spokesperson replies: "Every year, there are a number of films that make the unsubstantiated claim of being the 'best-reviewed film of the year,' but this is not the case with *The 40-Year-Old Virgin*. Upon the weekend of its release, the film received a 90 percent positive rating from Rotten Tomatoes, the online site that aggregates reviews from the widest collection of critics. With that rating, the film became the best-reviewed of eighty-two wide releases from major studios as of that date. On August 19, Rotten Tomatoes posted a news report on its site with the headline *The 40-Year-Old Virgin* is the best-reviewed film of the year.' While this ranking does not, as your reader notes, take into account specialty films, documentaries, and films that began in limited release, Universal Pictures cited the source as Rotten Tomatoes in all ads that touted the film as the 'best-reviewed film of the year,' should any consumer want to verify the legitimacy of that claim."

Q. I have read numerous reviews of *The 40-Year-Old Virgin*, but none of the reviewers, except you, could see the "Bollywood connection." Was the "Sunshine" song, which appears in the end, really done in Bollywood spirit? Were the filmmakers intentionally borrowing from Bollywood?

—Kapil Komireddi, London, England

A. Director and cowriter Judd Apatow replies: "I was inspired by Bollywood, but also the Blues Brothers and every other musical that can be stolen from." My own feeling is that the style of choreography is distinctively Bollywood.

Glory Road

Q. Re *Glory Road* and coach Don Haskins: Thought you would be interested to know that Haskins received roughly $375,000 for the movie. The players received about $7,500 apiece. When Haskins found out how little the players received, he insisted that his portion be divided evenly among all. Everyone then received roughly $37,000, including Haskins. What a man.

—Leta Mohrman, El Paso, Texas

A. His decency is clear in the movie. I also heard from Rob Reed of Bloomington, Indiana, whose father, Neil, was the assistant to Kentucky coach Adolph Rupp at the time of the famous 1966 NCAA championship game. Rupp (played by Jon Voight) comes over well in the film, his wife extends kindness to Mrs. Haskins, and the end titles observe that the next season, Rupp recruited the first black player in Kentucky's history. There was more to it than that, Reed writes me: Rupp and his father "were trying to integrate the team, much to the chagrin of segregationists of all types, including the board of trustees at the University (who eventually forced out Rupp on the pretense of his being at retirement age, despite his having the best win/loss record in college basketball history)." There were death threats, Rob Reed writes, and the FBI was called in; a TV news documentary about this period is at www.wkyt.com. Reed closes: "It's a wonderful thing to have pride in the raw, honest courage of one's father."

Good Night, and Good Luck

Q. In your review of *Good Night, and Good Luck*, the new George Clooney movie about Edward R. Murrow, you said about Senator Joseph McCarthy: "He destroys others with lies and then is himself destroyed by the truth." The only problem is that McCarthy wasn't lying. He might have gotten a few of the details wrong, but he was substantially correct. The Venona Project was a top-secret U.S. government effort to decode Soviet messages, which ran from 1943 until 1980. Untold thousands of diplomatic messages were decrypted, providing invaluable intelligence. Some of that intelligence proved that there were, indeed, spies embedded in the U.S. government in far greater numbers than the public suspected. Many of the people McCarthy singled out as being spies actually were working for Russia, traitors who were selling out their country to the most murderous regime the world has ever seen. The threat was very real, and Murrow did the free world no favors with helping to bring down McCarthy. The film has no mention of Venona, no mention of Soviet spies, who certainly did exist, no nuance, and no truth. Instead we're treated to a rehashing of the same old debunked story about how journalists managed to bring down a greater threat to freedom than Stalin. What is beyond my comprehension is how most of the people who know and care about the Red Scare of the 1950s are completely unaware of Venona. Many of the decoded documents have been available to the public for more than a decade.

—James R. Rummel, Columbus, Ohio

A. If McCarthy had that information, why didn't he cite it to save himself? Obviously, because it was not available until years after his death. Evidence at the Army-McCarthy hearings and elsewhere indicated that he fabricated most of his charges out of thin air. Do you have any sympathy for the majority of his targets, who were completely innocent? What about the blacklist that ended careers and destroyed lives because innocent people exercised their constitutional privileges? It is significant that government security officials in possession of facts about spies did not choose to share them with McCarthy, who was a loose cannon. Presumably the security experts were taking care of business while McCarthy was disgracing himself. Murrow is the public servant in this scenario.

Grizzly Man

Q. No movie stuck with me emotionally more than Werner Herzog's *Grizzly Man* did this year. Why did *Grizzly Man* not even qualify for the short list for Best Documentary?

—John Brightling, Listowel, Ontario

A. It was the best documentary of the year, after all, so maybe that counted against it.

Q. Wonderful to see that Werner Herzog's *Grizzly Man* was voted the best documentary of 2005 by the Los Angeles, New York, and San Francisco film critics, and shocking that it did not make the "final fifteen" cut at the academy for the Oscar!

—Tom Luddy, cofounder,
Telluride Film Festival, Berkeley, California

A. This follows in a shameful academy tradition. *Hoop Dreams* and *Crumb* also were not nominated.

Q. My roommates and I go to school in an area that doesn't get many independent films—let alone Werner Herzog documentaries—so we were excited that the Discovery Channel decided to air *Grizzly Man*. Unfortunately, the rhythm and beauty of Herzog's film

was destroyed by the Discovery Channel's decision to stretch the doc to three hours and add lots of commercials. With as little as five minutes between commercial interruptions, the film was rendered unwatchable. I understand that licensing can be expensive, but why would the Discovery Channel be so incredibly disrespectful to the film and its audience? And why would Herzog allow such a travesty?

—Clint Bland, College Station, Texas

A. Werner Herzog replies: "The answer to the interruptions by commercials lies completely within the rules of the market: Discovery financed a good part of the film, and they are a company that is out there to make money. However, Discovery added a full hour to the film (discussions, additional footage from Timothy Treadwell's treasure trove, and other statements) without delineating clearly where my film ends and where the additional materials start. Many viewers believed that the appendix belonged somehow to my film, as Discovery placed the end credits of my film at the very end of the three-hour special. I had no prior knowledge that this would happen. But we should not forget that Discovery supported my film and made it possible that we have it now.

"The only consolation I can offer is the DVD, and the knowledge in my guts that this film will pass the test of time, and that a TV airing like the one on Discovery belongs to the ephemeral and fleeting moments we have to endure. Sure, centuries from now our great-great-great-grandchildren will look back at us with amazement at how we could allow such a precious achievement of human culture as the telling of a story to be shattered into smithereens by commercials, the same amazement we feel today when we look at our ancestors for whom slavery, capital punishment, burning of witches, and the Inquisition were acceptable everyday events."

Harold Lloyd

Q. I was pleased and disappointed to read your assessment of silent-film comedian Harold Lloyd in your latest "Great Movies" installment; pleased by a piece on the neglected Lloyd and disappointed you didn't treat the great comic more favorably. It is tiresome to read another lament over Lloyd's inferiority to Chaplin and Keaton, especially when you admit that you had never seen a Lloyd film until *Safety Last*. You fault Lloyd for his "ordinariness" yet fail to note that Lloyd's naturalistic characterization was a big first for film comedy and paved the way for hundreds of romantic comedies to come. Or that Lloyd's feature films combined Chaplin's emotional resonance with Keaton's cinematic virtuosity. It was none other than Orson Welles who lobbied for Lloyd's genius years ago: "Harold Lloyd—he's surely the most underrated of them all. The intellectuals don't like the Harold Lloyd character—that middle-class, middle-American, all-American college boy. There's no obvious poetry to it, and they miss that incredible technical brilliance. . . . Someday he'll get his proper place—which is very high." I envy you. You have many Harold Lloyd films ahead of you, and Lloyd has many tricks up his sleeve to surprise you with, whether in the formal cinematic beauty of *The Kid Brother,* the uproarious surrealism of *Why Worry?* or the sheer crowd-pleasing fun of *The Freshman.* I urge you to watch these comedies with an open mind. Let Lloyd's brilliance come to you on his own terms.

—Yair Solan, Brooklyn, New York

A. So I will. The Lloyd films were very hard to see for many years and now are in national release in art and repertory theaters in preparation for DVD editions.

Hate Crime

Q. Read your review of *Hate Crime* and disagree when you say the movie presents a portrait of fundamentalists that does not reflect many of them. I live in Dallas and I know very few Southern Baptists who do not think gays are going straight to hell. Unfortunately, this includes some members of my family. I sadly do not think that the Pastor Boyd character was overplayed.

—Mike Schermer, Dallas, Texas

A. In my review I wrote in part: "Yes, there are plenty of fundamentalists who believe homosexuals are on the highway to hell. But there are other fundamentalists, a great many more, I believe, who are gentle and humane, positive and well-meaning, and although I may disagree with many of their beliefs, well, there are a lot of religious beliefs in the world and most people disagree with most of them."

I received dozens of letters telling me this statement was naive, and not a single letter in support of it. Here is Elaine Wood of Louisville, Kentucky: "Having been raised in that fundamentalist 'we're right and everyone else is wrong,' hate-mongering environment, I was subjected to ministers like the Pastor Boyd character repeatedly—until I refused to return to church when he tried to molest me as a teenager. This character is an accurate composite of many 'God-fearing' (as opposed to 'God-loving') tyrants. Are there less-lethal fundamentalists? Sure, but I've yet to encounter one who wasn't determined to 'fix' me, regardless of my spiritual beliefs, faith, and church membership. I saw the movie not as a statement about homosexuality (what other people do in the privacy of their homes is none of my business), but as a wake-up call for reducing judgment, bigotry, and intolerance."

Hitchcock

Q. I have a friend who buys DVDs just to have them. He was lured into buying a cheap movie for an even cheaper price. Until I looked at it closer, I refused to acknowledge it. But I realized it was *The Man Who Knew Too Much* and it was "directed by Alfred Hitchcock." The problem was that Peter Lorre starred in it. I watched it and it was trash. Did Hitchcock direct two versions of the film?

—Collin Welch, Madison, Indiana

A. Yes, and in the second one, Doris Day sings "Que Sera, Sera." If Lorre had sung it in the first version, now that would be a DVD worth owning.

An Inconvenient Truth

I've received so many messages about my review of Al Gore's *An Inconvenient Truth* that, frankly, I don't see how the Answer Man can process them. I could print a dozen or a hundred, but that would lead us into an endless loop.

Many letters are supportive. More letters are opposed to the movie and just about everything in it, and are written by people who have not seen the movie and will not see it for a variety of reasons, including the theory that it is "liberal propaganda." What I fail to understand is why global warming should be a liberal or conservative issue. It is either happening or it is not, and we can either take action to try to slow it or we cannot. That is why a great many conservatives have agreed with Gore on this.

When I am told "this is another one you're trying to blame on Bush and Halliburton," all I can say is, somebody is listening to way too much talk radio on which they are told global warming is being blamed on Bush and Halliburton. Actually, Gore blames neither and mentions neither. "It got worse on his watch as vice president." Yes, it did. "He flies around on a jet to warn against it." Yes, one of thousands of jet flights every day.

One person says that when Gore finds a "100 percent agreement" among scientists about global warming, that proves he is wrong, because 100 percent of scientists do not agree on anything. Then they quote scientists who disagree with Gore. What he said was, a random sampling of 935 recent articles *published in peer-review scientific journals* shows agreement with the basic findings reported in his film.

Many people inform me that they just read a story saying that the South Pole was tropical many eons ago. So it was, as reported in *March of the Penguins*. I don't know what they want me to do with this factoid—applaud our actions to bring that condition around again as quickly as possible?

I cannot get into a scientific discussion here. There will be no end to it. All I can say is, the Gore documentary made a deep impression on me. I urge you to see it. You will not be seeing a "campaign film," or "sour grapes," or "Gore still being bitter." George W. Bush has repeated for six years that global warming "requires more study." If Gore has spent six years studying it, aren't his findings worthy of attention? Yes, I'm "being political." But saying the issue "needs more study" is a political statement, when energy groups are among your major supporters and your family is in the oil business.

Junebug

Q. I would like to get your opinion of the artwork in *Junebug* that is a central plot point of the film. The local townspeople seem to have the upper hand on the art dealer. They realize that the "art" is nothing more than the racist and sexually explicit ravings of a disturbed man. Do you think the director is trying to show that the fatuous paintings are fooling the

pseudo-intellectual Embeth Davidtz character, or am I on my own here?

—Michael Hein, Cincinnati, Ohio

A. I do not believe the artist intends to be racist, although his limited intelligence and experience lead him to expressions that would be racist coming from a competent person. He is a disturbed man whose work falls within the definition of outsider art. He says, for example, that he cannot paint a face of someone he does not know, and since he knows only white people, the slaves in his paintings have white faces. This is not racism but naïveté shading into insanity.

Q. It's great to see *Junebug* on your Top 10 list. It easily makes my top five. This movie is heartbreaking and real and smart, smart, smart. I can't remember if it was you or Gene Siskel who said of *Mrs. Brown* that Judi Dench's performance was simply the best of the year, male, female, or otherwise. This year, that distinction goes to Amy Adams in *Junebug*. Her performance is the best acting in any film in any role this year. I loved her, I loved the movie.

—Paul Preston, Los Angeles, California

A. If Adams is not nominated for an Oscar, the academy voters have not done their homework.

P.S. On January 7, 2006, Adams was chosen as the year's best supporting actress by the National Society of Film Critics, in its annual awards.

P.P.S. On January 31, 2006, Adams was nominated for an Academy Award as best supporting actress.

King Kong

Q. We have just returned from *King Kong* bewildered, disappointed, and even angry that you gave it such a great review without mentioning its stunning racism. From the moment we saw the dark-skinned, aboriginal child, we knew it was going to be bad. It was worse than we expected. The African- and indigenous-influenced dance, drumming, and ritual, the elaborate face piercings, the bloodshot or rolling-back eyes, the striking ugliness (intended to imply inbreeding?), the skulls everywhere, and the sacrifice of the pure white-blond beauty by the nappy-haired old woman combine to produce an image that was so offensive it was nearly impossible for us to stay interested in the rest of the film.

—Maria Rosales and Tiffany Holland, Greensboro, North Carolina

A. I am not sure the islanders would agree with you that their face piercings, dancing, and "ugliness" are racist, or ugly. I agree that the stereotyping of the local population has been negative in the Kong pictures and wonder why Peter Jackson didn't simply show the island as having been abandoned by its human civilization after the erection of the wall failed to contain the creatures on the other side. How long could humans survive on Skull Island with all of those dinosaurs, snakes, giant insects, man-eating slugs, etc.?

Q. The character of the director character, Carl Denham, in *King Kong* wasn't based on DeMille so much as on Merian C. Cooper himself. Cooper, as you may know, had a very adventurous life, worthy of its own movie.

—Steven Doyle, Atlanta, Georgia

A. Here it gets complicated. Do you think Cooper based Denham, in his 1933 movie, on himself? I believe he was having a little fun with DeMille. You may be right that Jackson was thinking of Cooper. The Internet Movie Database says Cooper was "partially inspired by Douglas Burden, who brought the world's first captive Komodo dragons to the Bronx Zoo in 1926."

Lobsters as Pets

Q. In your review of *Aquamarine*, you say the mermaid reminds you of your friend McHugh explaining why lobsters make ideal pets: "They don't bark, and they know the secrets of the deep." Actually it was Gerard de Nerval who said that, shortly before hanging himself in 1855.

—David Gilmour, Toronto, Ontario

A. Of course it was. As Wikipedia writes about the French romantic poet: "Nerval had a pet lobster. He took it for walks in Paris on the end of a blue ribbon. He regarded lobsters as 'peaceful, serious creatures, who know the secrets of the sea, and don't bark.'" Apologies to my friend McHugh, who is never seen far from his well-thumbed volume of Nerval. His trans-

lation of Nerval, by the way, is funnier and more graceful than Wikipedia's.

Loose Change

Q. Mass media twist the arm of most Americans today because most know only what they see and hear on TV or radio. I do not rely on just mainstream media. I'd like you to review *Loose Change*. Considering you are a member of the mass media and since money is probably what motivates you in a day and age of greed and you are too busy of a man to reply to my one e-mail, please watch the online link I've provided if you have any real remorse for those lost due to what happened on 9/11.

—Kyle Kern, no hometown provided

A. Readers can find the film by Googling "*Loose Change* video" and clicking on the first link. I have received countless messages urging me to see this film, which essentially charges that 9/11 was a hoax generated by the Bush administration to justify the invasion of Iraq. It questions whether commercial aircraft actually crashed into the Twin Towers, says United 93 may have been shot down by a missile, doubts a plane crashed into the Pentagon, etc. Some of the film's historical information is correct, but its conspiracy theory regarding 9/11 seems cobbled together with a mixture of unsubstantiated speculation, paranoia, and pseudoscience.

Bredon Clay of DeKalb, Illinois, writes suggesting *Loose Change* believers read an article in the March 2005 *Popular Mechanics* that decisively demolishes the conspiracy theories (you can Google "*Popular Mechanics* 9/11" and click on the first link). On the same list are replies to the magazine's arguments. Another widespread conspiracy factoid is that United 93 landed safely at Hopkins Airport in Cleveland. If it did, how can we account for the fact that all of the relatives of those onboard believe it crashed? What happened to the survivors?

Lost in Translation

Q. My favorite scene in *The Island* is when Ewan McGregor congratulates Scarlett Johansson on being chosen to go to the island. He then leans over and whispers to her, "I'm sorry I didn't get to know you better." This is an obvious allusion to *Lost in Translation*, designed to inform us once and for all what Bill Murray whispered to her at the end of that movie.

—Abraham Leib, Bellevue, Washington

A. Yes, but how do you know that's what he said? When *Sight & Sound* magazine interviewed *Lost in Translation* director Sofia Coppola and asked her what Bob whispers to Charlotte at the end, she replied: "Someone asked Bill, and he said, 'It's between lovers.' I love that answer." She was asked if she had written lines for the scene, and said: "I wrote some stuff but I wasn't happy with it. There was dialogue but it was really sparse. Ultimately I liked it better that you don't hear it, that you can put in what you want them to say."

Q. Your reader Andrew Leib writes that in *The Island* Ewan McGregor whispers to Scarlett Johansson: "I'm sorry I didn't get to know you better." He believes this speech is "designed to inform us once and for all what Bill Murray whispered to her" at the end of *Lost in Translation*. I have a copy of the script dated September 2002, and it reads as follows:

BOB: Why are you crying?

CHARLOTTE: I'll miss you. (He kisses her, hugs her good-bye.)

BOB: I know, I'm going to miss you, too. (He holds her close.)

—Professor Nate Kohn,
University of Georgia, Athens, Georgia

A. So now we know what the Murray character would have said, if Murray and director Coppola hadn't decided it was better for the audience not to hear their final words. Leaving something out is often more effective than putting it in; in his *Grizzly Man,* Werner Herzog listens to the tape of Timothy Treadwell being killed by a bear but doesn't play it for us. In his *The White Diamond,* he shows a man lowered by rope to videotape a legendary cave behind a waterfall but doesn't show us the tape. In all three films, what isn't there is a challenge for our imaginations.

Madagascar

Q. The animated feature *Madagascar* has two illogical scenes where the male lion gets kicked from the front between his back legs and doubles over like a man kicked in the testicles. Problem: A male lion, like all cats, has his testi-

cles located on his back side and there is no way they could be kicked by standing in front of the lion who is "rampant" on his hind legs. I suspect that you noticed this error but were too politically correct, or lacked the *cajones,* to point this out in your review of the movie.

—Michael L. Stoianoff, Anchorage, Alaska

A. Just ignorance on my part, actually. This info could be a lifesaver.

Memoirs of a Geisha

Q. Re your review of *Memoirs of a Geisha:* As a half-Japanese woman, I have traveled to Japan every year to live with my mother's family for the summer. I have been raised with Japanese culture and traveled to Kyoto on several occasions. Every Japanese person knows that Kyoto is known for being very straight. Straight streets and lines, like a grid. This movie shows a Kyoto that is as accurate as shooting in Miami and calling it Chicago. The trees aren't quite right, the streets are winding and curved. My friend who is a quarter-Japanese and is boycotting the film likens the *Geisha* performances to an En Vogue video.

—Alisa Monnier, Chicago, Illinois

A. All true, as I remember from my visit to Kyoto, but what I found missing was emotional truth; if that had been there, the accuracy of the location would have been irrelevant.

MPAA Ratings

Q. Just read your Sundance piece on Kirby Dick's documentary about the MPAA ratings system, *This Film Is Not Yet Rated.* I want to note that our film *Gunner Palace* originally received R for language, which we successfully appealed to a PG-13. It is the most profane PG-13 movie ever—I stopped counting f-bombs after the first reel. Although I talk about our experiences with the MPAA in Kirby's film, I was unaware until a day ago that he doesn't point out that we in fact defeated the MPAA on its own terms. Although I don't agree with the current ratings system, I think you are right to point out that Valenti's system was born in response to regional ratings, which would be a *true* mess for indie pics such as *Gunner.* When we won our appeal, based on an argument to the appeals board, they did their job that day.

—Mike Tucker, director, *Gunner Palace*

A. The appeals board did its job in your case, but the problem, as Dick argues, is that it is inconsistent, anonymous, unaccountable, and, by refusing to reveal its standards, open to the charge that it rates films in an entirely subjective manner. Critics and audiences are entitled to be subjective, but presumably the MPAA should not be rating by the seat of its pants. If one film can get a PG-13 with countless f-words, why should, for example, the recent film *Imagine Me and You* get an R for, reportedly, one or two excess f-words?

Q. You were standing next to me at the premiere of *This Film Is Not Yet Rated* while taking the photo of Kirby Dick. I would like to make a statement. We never stalked any of the raters or anyone else associated with the MPAA, as some of the newspapers state. We went around them only long enough to obtain a photo, and we never followed any of the raters to a school. My job is not to hurt anyone, but only to find out the truth. As a licensed private investigator, it is my job to make sure I have all of the information accurate and to look at both sides, which I believe I did in this case. Unfortunately, not all of our work was told in the documentary, so I could see how you would see it as one-sided.

—Becky Altringer, Ariel Investigations, La Verne, California

A. You were the private eye hired by Kirby Dick to discover the identities of the MPAA's movie raters and appeals board members. This you did, discovering in the process that many of their children were in their twenties and thirties and that they were not the "ordinary parents" so often described by Jack Valenti. Other writers may have criticized your work on the case, but I did not. I did mention that the doc was one-sided, in part because the MPAA did not cooperate, in part because Dick sidesteps the fact that the ratings board does, at least, head off local censorship. On balance, I admire the film, although if someone were following me in a van and studying my license plates through binoculars, I might indeed feel stalked.

Munich

Q. I'd like your readers to know that most if not all reasonable American Jews have no problem whatsoever with *Munich*. In fact, quite the opposite is true. Last night, I went with my fa-

ther, an immigrant from Israel, to see the film. We both loved every minute of it and thought it portrayed Israeli/Palestinian relations in a positive and pretty realistic light. If Jewish-American critics of *Munich* would take a look at some of the best films coming out of Israel made by Israeli filmmakers for an Israeli audience (such as *Time of Favor*), they might notice the same kind of soul-searching done by Avner in *Munich*.

—Guy Handelman, Valley Village, California

A. I doubt that you are right when you say "most," and in fairness it is possible to be reasonable and still disapprove of the film. If *Munich* did not divide audience opinion, it would not be doing what Spielberg intended: to challenge his viewers to discuss issues that, in the minds of many, long have been settled one way or the other. Among dissent on the film, one of the sanest and most useful articles I've read was by Walter Reich, a former director of the U.S. Holocaust Museum, in the *Washington Post*.

Murderball

Q. I, like you, loved *Murderball*. It moved me almost to tears, yet we saw it in an almost-empty theater on opening day. Why do you think it hasn't caught on? I think the title is a problem, but I couldn't think of a better name for it.

—Bill Payne, Las Vegas, Nevada

A. Dana Adam Shapiro, *Murderball*'s codirector, tells me: "It is indeed odd, as I reckon we're one of the best-reviewed films of the year, if not the decade. The press has been so kind, and as mainstream as it gets. Maybe people just don't like wheelchairs. Maybe we alienated our base by trying to gloss it up and go mainstream: big theaters, no festival laurels, no 'documentary.' Maybe the title paired with Zupan's goateed mug scared off half the audience. For better or worse, people are hearing 'sports film.' Maybe the sportos don't want to see a wheelchair doc, and the doc-heads don't want to see a sports flick. Maybe everybody thinks it's one of those cue-the-violins 'inspirational' weepies. Who knows?"

Q. What's up with you not liking *Murderball*? You did not include it on your year-end top-ten list. What is up with that? Do you not know anything about good movies, or do you just hate cripples?

—Josh Radde, Algonquin, Illinois

915

A. *Murderball* was right there on my list of the year's top ten documentaries. Earlier in the year I gave it a four-star rating and invited it to my Overlooked Film Festival. For an example of a film I hate, you are going to have to look a little harder, maybe under the heading *Deuce Bigalow.*

My Fair Lady and the Beatles

Q. Re your Great Movie choice of *My Fair Lady:* The Beatles' film *A Hard Days Night* and the Cukor *My Fair Lady* were released in the same year, 1964. But I never noticed, until I read your comments, the revolutionary acts of Eliza against Higgins and the upper classes. I always thought that Eliza was a lazy protagonist pushed around by two men, but in fact she changed *their* lives. I used to feel that the revolutionary, black-and-white, low-budget, docu-style comedy about four rocker kids had nothing in common with the color, pageantry, scope, and studio-produced grandeur of a Cinderella tale. Now I see that John, Paul, George, Ringo, and Eliza have more in common than their lower-class British upbringing. The Beatles could be sticking it to the Higginses at Ascot and Eliza could be a rocker chick on *Ed Sullivan.*

—Nellie Kim, San Diego, California

A. And wouldn't that be lover-ly.

Old-timers

Q. In your article about Mickey Rooney, you say Rooney is the longest-working man in showbiz. Rooney is about eighty-five years old. George Burns was singing on the vaudeville stage at age seven, and he was still performing at age ninety-eight (screen credit for *Radioland Murders*) or later. So Rooney has to work for a few more years to catch up.

—Mike McGowan, Lombard, Illinois

A. In 1979, Burns told me: "I was acting when I was two. When I was seven, I was in the Pee Wee Quartet." Then he told me a story about another old-timer:

"There was a guy, a tramp comedian named Joe Jackson. He was famous for how he handled the curtain. He had these big, floppy shoes, and he'd stand onstage just where the curtain fell, so his toes would be sticking out under the curtain. So the audience knows he's still there. They go crazy, applauding. Meanwhile, Jackson slips out of the shoes. He waits

until the applause is dying down, and then he steps out from the side of the stage in his stocking feet. That brought the house down.

"One night, the curtain comes down. Jackson steps out of his shoes. Then he dies backstage. Drops dead. The audience knows the gag, see, and so they're cheering, applauding . . . the greatest ovation Joe Jackson ever got, and he didn't live to hear it.

"When I tell that story, people sometimes burst into tears. I hate to break the news to them that I made it up."

The Omen

Q. Re your mention of what little boys are made of in your review of *The Omen;* it's "snakes" (not "snips") "and snails and puppy dog tails."

—Rick Allen, Doylestown, Pennsylvania

A. Searching Google for "snips," etc., I got 28,900 hits, but with "snakes," etc., I got 119,000. You must be right. However, it's "snips" in a crucial line from *Rosemary's Baby.*

Oscar Footnotes

Q. There was confusion on Oscar nominations day about the producing roles of Don Cheadle (*Crash*) and George Clooney (*Good Night, and Good Luck*), and whether they were eligible to go onstage if their films won. Can you explain?

—Susan Lake, Urbana, Illinois

A. I was among the confused. Both men indeed were producers of the films involved. Cheadle did not go onstage when *Crash* won because the academy decided to end the cattle calls of countless producers and specified two of the film's other producers. This is unfortunate because a) Cheadle was instrumental in assembling the film's all-star cast at bargain-basement prices, and b) TV viewers would enjoy seeing an actor more than a Suit. As for Clooney, many reports said he got four nominations, but he took his producer's credit off *Good Night* and so disqualified himself for the fourth. Clooney told *Entertainment Weekly:* "Did I work as a producer on the film? Sure. But not anywhere near the extent that Grant [Heslov] did. Every day I'd come in and say, 'Okay, here's our fifteen problems with financing and our ten problems with archival footage,' and he dealt with them. And he deserves credit for that. Films are generally about people trying to grab credit where they don't deserve it. We had to [deal with] a lot of executive producers that I hadn't met before. Anyone who gives us $300,000 gets to put their name on the film."

Q. What was Tom Hanks so visibly irritated about as he came onstage at the Academy Awards?

—Brian McCarthy, Minneapolis, Minnesota

A. Many Oscarcast viewers thought they saw Hanks saying something angry to host Jon Stewart. Lip-readers who recorded it came up with highly colorful possibilities. But was he talking to Stewart? From the TV viewer's POV, Hanks seemed to be looking at Stewart. But he could also, in the same line of sight, have been looking at Bill Conti, the musical director, who was not visible in the TV shot. Defamer.com has produced a plausible theory. The site says Hanks thought he had a deal with Conti and the academy that they would not play the theme from *Forrest Gump* when he came onstage; he is tired of always being identified with it. But that was the music played, and that's why he was unhappy.

Q. With *Saraband* being Ingmar Bergman's very last film and taking his age and his amazing body of work into account, I feel it is time for the Academy of Motion Picture Arts and Sciences to reward Bergman with its lifetime achievement award. When I searched the Oscar database, I was surprised to discover that he has not yet received the award. Giving the award to a foreign film director is nothing new; in 1990, Akira Kurosawa received the lifetime award for his contributions to film.

—Nick Neely, Huntsville, Alabama

A. Absolutely. By general acclaim, Bergman is the greatest of living directors, and *Saraband* a magnificent farewell. Bergman won the Irving G. Thalberg Award in 1971, presented by the academy's Board of Governors to "creative producers whose bodies of work reflect a consistently high quality of motion picture production."

But it is not precisely a lifetime achievement award; that would be the academy's Honorary Award, which, according to the academy, "is not called a lifetime achievement award by the academy, but it is often given for a life's work in filmmaking—to Polish director Andrzej Wajda in 1999, for example, and to Elia Kazan the previous year."

Overlord

Q. In your review of the film *Overlord*, you mention a machine to clear mines on beaches that was powered by rockets on its wheels. The name of this machine was the Great Panjandrum, and one of the engineers involved in its development was Neville Shute, who later wrote the novel *On the Beach*. There is a film of a prototype Panjandrum in action with Shute operating the control cables. In the film the Great Panjandrum goes straight for about fifteen feet, then Shute engages a brake. The infernal engine makes a 540-degree turn and heads straight toward an audience of VIPs. Things get rather exciting at that point. There were no casualties, except to the egos of various admirals, generals, and bureaucrats.

—John Hobson, Bolingbrook, Illinois

A. At nevilshute.org there's a discussion of the Panjandrum, a photo of it upright, and another after it overturned.

Personal Matters

Q. Last week I went to see *Munich*, which was gripping but also nearly three hours long. About halfway through I felt the normal human need to visit a restroom. But I wasn't about to leave for a minute, afraid I'd miss the most important part. So I endured for an hour and a half rather than miss a minute of Spielberg's masterpiece. Maybe I have a small bladder, but I've never even been able to buy a soda while going to the theater, since an excruciating experience when I was twelve years old, bouncing up and down in agony during the last half of *Indiana Jones and the Last Crusade*. Why is it that theaters don't offer a few minutes in the middle the movie to make a quick run to the loo? I think they call it an intermission.

—Wade Mann, Orem, Utah

A. All movies in India have intermission, but then their Bollywood features are routinely more than three hours long. Hollywood had "roadshow" movies circa 1970, with intermissions built in, but now the idea is to show a movie as many times as possible during the day (and theaters lose up to an hour with commercials). My own strategy is to try to sit on the aisle so that I can slip in and out quickly. Your ability to "endure" for ninety minutes has my most sincere admiration.

Piracy

Q. My eighteen-year-old daughter and I went to the Loews-Cineplex Theater to see *Hustle & Flow*, starring Terrence Howard. I, along with other moviegoers, had a metal detector wand waved across my body by a security guard. Other security guards checked inside people's purses and backpacks. My daughter and I noticed that although there were other movies being shown at this same theater, such as *Herbie Fully Loaded*, *Madagascar*, and *Mr. and Mrs. Smith*, this procedure was not done for those movies. Why do you think this screening was done?
—Linda McEwen, Chicago, Illinois

A. It might appear that racial profiling was involved in selecting *Hustle & Flow*, but my guess is that, objectively, it was the most piratable movie at the theater. I have been wanded at press screenings, once had my turkey sandwich examined to see if it concealed a camera, and have noticed security people with night-vision goggles peering at me. Since on opening day you probably could have purchased a bootleg video of a *Hustle & Flow* screening, the studio's concern is real.

Poetry in the Cinema

Q. Okay, I've gone around my college asking my professors where I can locate poetry in film. I figured film is a language, and every language has a poetry. No one could tell me anything. No explanations, no examples. I think there are scenes of perfect poetry within a lot of narrative films. Can you think of any offhand?
—Adam Judd, Visalia, California

A. Two effective uses of verbal poetry in the movies: Victor Mature as Doc Holliday, in John Ford's *My Darling Clementine* (1946), reciting Hamlet's "To be, or not to be . . ." soliloquy in the saloon. And Cameron Diaz, in *In Her Shoes* (2005), reading poetry to a blind professor and later reciting some e. e. cummings at a crucial point.

But I suppose you mean the poetry of visuals or dialogue, rather than quoted poetry. The list could be endless, but some examples come to mind. Bonnie's farewell to her mother in *Bonnie and Clyde*. The death of the young cowboy on the suspension bridge in *McCabe and Mrs. Miller*. The corridor with candelabra held by living arms, in Cocteau's version of *Beauty and the Beast*. The night the children capture fireflies and use them to illuminate their cave in *Grave of the Fireflies*. The boy and the horse approaching each other from opposite sides of the screen in *The Black Stallion*. And Marge Gunderson (Frances McDormand) to Grimsrud (Peter Stormare), the killer in *Fargo*: "So that was Mrs. Lundegaard on the floor in there. And I guess that was your accomplice in the wood chipper. And those three people in Brainerd. And for what? For a little bit of money. There's more to life than a little money, you know. Don't you know that? And here ya are, and it's a beautiful day. Well, I just don't understand it."

Politics and Critics

Q. You believe that showing the bombing of a high-rise in *Stealth* was in bad taste because of 9/11. This is not the role of a movie critic. Movie critics fail when they are *not* open-minded and become melodramatic about what is right and wrong. For example, some might argue that George W. Bush should be imprisoned for crimes against humanity (innocent people killed in Iraq and lies about weapons). Would you be able to criticize a movie that deals with this issue? Probably not if you used your "bad taste" conservative scale to be a judge rather than a critic.
—Marlene DiFiori Locke, Maryland Heights, Maryland

A. First time in a while I've been called a conservative. I believe movies can deal with 9/11 or any other subject, but I reserve the right to have an opinion about how they do it. I felt there was something unworthy about a goofy special-effects thriller that showed the U.S. bombing a Rangoon high-rise from above so it would fall down in its own footprint. The shot of the falling building is uncanny in the way it resembles the falling Twin Towers. I don't think the movie has earned the right to use that imagery.

Q. I wonder if it was just a coincidence that you posted your Great Movie review of *Crimes and Misdemeanors* on September 11. I couldn't stop thinking that if the eyes of God are on us always (I grew up with that notion, and often it's not a very good feeling), what to think of those airplanes hitting the Twin Towers? Or what to think of natural disasters, such as Hurricane Katrina or the tsunami in Asia? Do you think the powers that be have the same "morals" as Martin Landau's character? Are we all poor romantic losers like Allen? I don't know. But the film sure is brilliant.

—Joao Solimeo, Vinhedo, Brazil

A. The timing was a coincidence, although the timing of my Great Movie review of *The Terrorist* was directly inspired by the bombings in London. I believe that events on Earth happen because they happen. If one believes, as many religions do, that God gave man free will, then surely he also set the universe free to realize itself.

Those who interpret natural disasters as messages from God almost always think God is sending a message that agrees with their own philosophy. God never seems to send messages that cause them to wonder if they are wrong. A rare exception was when the Dutch Reformed Church in South Africa, after upholding apartheid for years, decided it was immoral.

Q. I'm always amazed at the irrational nature of the debate on medical care. In your review of *The Death of Mr. Lazarescu,* you state, "At least in Romania he is not asked for his insurance company, and he has a theoretical right to free medical care." In the next sentence you quote a Romanian doctor who discusses the horrible condition of medical care in his country. Isn't it obvious that when something is "free" for everyone, it will be inadequate for everyone? Do people get left behind in a medical system that involves free enterprise? Of course they do. But when you have a system where personal responsibility plays no part, you certainly get the system you deserve. I for one am glad that I get asked for proof of insurance when I show up at a hospital. It annoys me that people who cannot do so get treated at my expense anyway.

—Jeff Grant, Centreville, Virginia

A. The hospitals are always looking for volunteers. Maybe you could help them turn away sick poor people.

Q. I am a student at the University of Northern Iowa, interested in becoming a film critic.

Today, I was discussing *Good Night, and Good Luck* with an acquaintance. I happen to be a somewhat politically conservative man and hated the film because I thought it was smugly left-wing and pompous in the extreme. My acquaintance, who reviewed films in high school, told me that his journalism teacher instructed him to look at a film for what it was and how good it was at reaching its potential. For example, if a film is intended to be a left-wing parable, then judge it purely on those merits, or if it is supposed to be a light romantic comedy, judge it based on that. I thought about this and am unable to agree. Although *Good Night, and Good Luck* certainly was well made, should I give it a good score despite the fact that I find its message and tone laughable and insulting? What would you say when asked how much a reviewer should inject their personal and political beliefs into a film?

—James Frazier, Cedar Falls, Iowa

A. An ideal review would provide a good idea of the film itself and include your own opinions. If you disagree with a film's message, then you can observe that it makes its point effectively but is unworthy for political reasons. See the struggle I had over this very dilemma in reviewing *The Birth of a Nation* in the Great Movies section on my Web site. Or note in *Silent Hill* that I praised the film as "incredibly good-looking," which is true, and should be reported even in a negative review.

Q. I enjoy reading your movie reviews. However, I have no desire to read your political opinions. You have expressed gratuitous political views in two recent reviews—*The Great Raid* and *The Constant Gardener*—and you need to stop. Stick to what you know. Keep your nose out of what you don't.

—Dick Brown, Matthews, North Carolina

A. Both movies were inescapably political, and to pretend they were not would have been dishonest. I have my views. You have yours. Please continue to express yours, which in fact you have done by urging me not to express mine.

Pride & Prejudice

Q. Why does Emma Thompson get thanks at the end of *Pride & Prejudice*?

—Cal Ford, Corsicana, Texas

A. She rewrote the script but would not take a screen credit.

Punctuation

Q. What's with the strange punctuation in movie titles these days? Especially titles with unnecessary use of ellipses. Last fall, *Waiting . . .* and now *Rumor Has It . . . .* Of course, the godfather of such titles is *When Harry Met Sally . . . .* This kind of punctuation abuse reminds me of my high school composition teacher, who used to ask, "Are you using those dots for decoration?"

—Laura Emerick, Chicago, Illinois

A. In my review I renamed *Rumor Has It . . .* as *Rumor Has It* because all titles ending in ". . ." annoy me. How do you say it? *Rumor Has It Dot Dot Dot? Rumor Has It Ellipsis?*

Russ Meyer

Q. I can only assume that your e-mail is clogged with reports that the recent Russ Meyer biography, *Big Bosoms and Square Jaws*, is being brought to the screen by Rob Cohen, the auteur of *The Skulls, The Fast and the Furious*, and *Stealth*. Two questions come to mind: 1) Who, dare I ask, do you see playing the ambitious young critic-turned-screenwriter? 2) Do you think they should just scuttle the whole damn thing if they can't get Rose McGowan to play Tura Satana?

—Peter Sobczynski, Chicago, Illinois

A. Cohen may be an excellent choice to make this biopic, since his films have the kind of high-energy audaciousness that Meyer loved. To answer your question 1), I'm thinking Jack Black or Philip Seymour Hoffman, and your question 2), there isn't a name actress in Hollywood today who could meet Russ Meyer's exacting standards. Another good question is, who should play Meyer? He was a tall, brawny combat veteran, a Signal Corps cameraman with a robust personality—not a dirty old man. James Garner at fifty would have been ideal.

Postscript, May 2006: The latest director connected with the project is Brett Ratner, of X-Men 3: The Last Stand.

Q. Any comment on the story that they're talking to Philip Seymour Hoffman about playing you in a proposed biopic about Russ Meyer?

—Bill Zwecker, Chicago, Illinois

A. Complete fiction. It happened this way. I was on the Howard Stern program with Jon Stewart, and we were talking about Hoffman's chances of winning the Oscar as best actor. I added: "They're making a movie about Russ Meyer, and I think he should play me." Just joking around, but a listener reported on Ain't It Cool News that Hoffman was actually being recruited for the role. That became an instant factoid.

Serenity

Q. You made the comment that one room on the spaceship in *Serenity* looked like a loading dock. Not the case here. *Serenity* was built as two huge sets—no preexisting sets were used. The reason that room looked like a loading dock was that, it *was* a loading dock. *Serenity* is a cargo ship and used to transport goods. She is nothing but a loading dock and warehouse with everything else built around them.

—Barbara Jungbauer, St. Paul, Minnesota

A. Then I was right!

Shelley Winters

Q. The death of Shelley Winters has me in mourning. I expected a tribute from you but didn't see one.

—Greg Nelson, Chicago, Illinois

A. I was on vacation with no phone and learned the news belatedly. Like you, I mourn the loss of a great life force of the cinema. The films and performances of Shelley Winters speak for themselves, but to meet her was to be in a presence of a whirlwind of great humor and fearless indiscretion. My favorite story: On an opening night of the Chicago Film Festival, Winters received the key to the city from our mayor, Richard M. Daley. Accepting it, she told him: "You look great. You haven't aged a day since I met you twenty years ago. Who does your work?" Did she know she was talking to Richard M., the son, and not Richard J., the father? With Shelley Winters, you never knew.

Slow Movies

Q. I am finding myself more and more attracted to "slow" movies. Slow. That's the word I want to use, and I'm not going to shy away from it. *Vera Drake, The Station Agent, Story of the Weeping Camel, Lost in Translation,* and most recently *Off the Map* are all slow, but I became completely enamored with the simple observation of character. I can tell I'm sold on one of these movies when I'm sad to see it end despite being steadily led to its resolution. *Schultze Gets the Blues,* which was a video pick on *Ebert & Roeper,* was "slow" from beginning to end, but had the director been more conventional with track shots and pans, I would have been bored. Instead, after sedately absorbing the final moments of the film, I found myself leaping off the couch at the end crying, "That's it?!" accidentally waking my roommate. I wanted more and completely loved the melancholy ending.

—Brandon Tomasello, Jacksonville, Florida

A. A slow movie that closely observes human beings and their relationships can be endlessly fascinating, while a thriller with nonstop wall-to-wall action can be boring, because it is all relentlessly pitched at the same tone.

Smorgasbord

Q. You say in your review of *Kiss Kiss, Bang Bang* that the dialogue is "there for its own sake. Like a smorgasbord, it makes no attempt at coherence. Put a little of everything on your plate and you'll be stuffed by the end, but what did you eat?" Oh dear, oh dear. How wrong! I trust your every word about film, but regarding Scandinavian smorgasbord you are out of your depth, like the blind discussing colors! If you are ever around Copenhagen I'll give you a crash course in the strict coherence and do's and don'ts about "smørrebrød"!

—Leif Barbré Knudsen,
Hveensvej, Vedbaek, Denmark

A. The word "smorgasbord" has a different meaning where I come from in downstate Illinois, where the salad bars include butterscotch pudding.

Snicker-snack Effect

Q. You mentioned in your *Resident Evil* review and again in reviewing *The Hills Have Eyes* that metal always makes a particular sound in horror movies. My favorite moment in *The Hills Have Eyes* is when the chain that slices the tires was pulled back and it growled. True inspiration.

—Phillip Kelly, Valley Village, California

A. Thank you for a previously unidentified variation on the Snicker-snack Effect, defined in Ebert's Little Movie Glossary: "In horror movies, whenever we see a knife with a big, shiny blade, we inevitably hear the scrape of metal against metal, even if it touches nothing."

Spitting on Vietnam Vets

Q. Re the comment made in the documentary *Sir, No Sir!* about soldiers being spit on as they returned from Vietnam through San Francisco: It is claimed this cannot be true because they did not go through San Francisco airport. They most certainly did. I came back from 'Nam in June 1968 and that was my first landing after leaving 'Nam. A great percentage flew into San Francisco airport.

—John Doto, Wakefield, Massachusetts

A. Your comment refers to the movie's claim that the "hippie chicks" who spit on "wounded veterans" were in fact an urban legend, because no wounded came through San Francisco airport and no documentary records exist of this ever having happened. After I wrote back, you clarified:

"All able-bodied returning from 'Nam were sent to San Francisco. Wounded went through Andrews Air Force, Walter Reed, or Bethesda Naval Hospital. All the military who went over with me came back at different times and flights through San Francisco. I did have someone ask me where I was coming from and when I said 'Nam they immediately asked to have their seat changed, which they did do as we did not have a full flight."

Ebert again. Since, as you say, you flew direct from Vietnam, why did the person in the next seat ask you where you were coming from? Wayne LeClear of Mentor, Ohio, writes: "There is a book titled *The Spitting Image* by Jerry Lembcke. He tries to debunk the whole idea of a vet being spit on. But no matter how hard he tries, it will probably not happen. This has become such an embedded belief in our culture that it will never be eliminated. I am a Vietnam vet (drafted, not enlisted). If you are around vets for very long, you will invariably find someone who 'knew someone whose cousin was friends with someone who was spit on. . . . ' Lembcke will never convince those people who want to hang on to this belief."

So I wrote Lembcke. He responded: "I've gotten challenged on this before and, like with the other facets of the spitting stories, I never say it didn't/couldn't have happened to someone, sometime. Travis AFB may have been fogged in and the plane diverted to SF but, in cases like that, how would the protesters have known ahead of time and rushed to the airport—none of it makes sense. I always ask for additional documentation and have never gotten it."

Q. I was bothered by your response to the reader who claimed he flew from Vietnam to San Francisco. He says he flew through SF and that while on the plane he was asked where he was coming from. When he said, Vietnam, the person asked for a different seat assignment. You, in a snide way, asked if he flew direct, why did the person need to ask? I don't think he ever said he flew direct to SF, or that he was speaking of the flight in from Vietnam. He very well could have meant his flight out of SF. It seemed biased on your part to immediately dismiss his claim.

—Dave Viola, San Francisco, California

A. The reader wrote: "I came back from 'Nam in June 1968 and that was my first landing after leaving 'Nam." That sounds to me like a nonstop flight. However, perhaps he was referring to his ongoing connection from San Francisco and did not make that clear, in which case you have a good point.

Troy Hinrichs of Riverside, California, writes me: "There were no direct flights from Vietnam to SF (or anywhere stateside). For one thing, it's too long, so the vet who lost his seatmate could have been coming from Tokyo, Manila, or any other spot in Southeast Asia, depending on where the rude seatmate boarded."

This is also quite true.

The Squid and the Whale

Q. I was put off by your opening sentence: "I don't know what I'm supposed to feel during *The Squid and the Whale*." Huh? Shouldn't you be asking what you are supposed to *think* during the film? I don't read your film reviews to better understand what makes Roger Ebert tick. To dis-

miss the point of view of this film because you, personally, wish you had had "cool" parents just like these kids is a dumbing-down of your role as a critic. What I wish you had reviewed was a film that thoughtfully explores the unintended consequences of divorce in a culture that collectively and individually tries to assuage its guilt about the effects, particularly on children. Divorce, like death, may be a part of life that we have no choice but to accept, but prevalence alone does not mitigate the effects of divorce on the children, who are the civilian casualties.

—Jane Levin Kroboth, Charlottesville, Virginia

A. You make a good point about the underlying subject of the film. But I think "feel" is the correct word. Movies are essentially a medium of emotion. Intellectual arguments are more suited to the written word; movies persuade us not by what they argue, but by how they make us feel. One purpose of a critic is to be open about exactly what he or she actually felt, instead of retreating into abstractions. When I saw *The Squid and the Whale*, I was not thinking about the unintended consequences of divorce, I was thinking that for all its faults the family functioned pretty well to produce useful and creative children, including the director of the film.

By the way, in that review I quote the father telling his son that *A Tale of Two Cities* is "minor Dickens," to which I add, "Which is correct." Lee Granas of St. Louis, Missouri, writes me: "Why is *A Tale of Two Cities* minor Dickens, and which books are major Dickens?" At the time I was reading some major Dickens, *Our Mutual Friend*, and was reminded I hadn't read *A Tale of Two Cities* in decades. So I just finished reading it again. It is not minor Dickens, but one of his most readable novels, with so many thriller elements it's amazing it hasn't been filmed since 1958.

Star Ratings

Q. It seems that in the past year most of your reviews end up awarding three or more stars. I had confidence in your three-star ratings until I realized that so many of them are mediocre films. For example, *Star Wars Episode III*, which is composed of bad acting and unimpressive dialogue. Please be more critical of average films.

—Bud Schauerte, Austin, Texas

A. I often hear I am "getting soft." A correspondent helpfully writes, "My friend says that since you had cancer, you give every movie three or four stars." A New York weekly critic says I "like everything," and he must be right, because I even liked the film he cited as an example of how much more discerning he is than critics like me.

I did some math and found that my average rating for a feature film in 2005 came to about 2.7 stars. On a bell curve the average should be 2.0, but consider that I reviewed 284 movies last year, and the extra titles were independent and foreign films that tended to skew higher. I am content with my 2.7 average. The problem is with the use of stars as a rating system. Star ratings go back to that simpler time when film critics stood on far hillsides and signaled to the grateful peasantry with torches and brightly colored flags. Indignant readers write me: "How could you give Film A three stars and Film B only two and a half stars? I will never read your reviews again." I reply: "A wise decision! My reviews are for those who are stronger in literature than math."

Q. Re your average 2005 review being 2.7 stars, when on a perfect curve it would have been 2.0: For what it's worth (maybe a half star?) there's likely a good reason your average movie rating isn't two stars. In the statistical world they call it a "survivor bias," which essentially means that you don't get the opportunity to review enough truly bad movies. Less-than-stellar movies generally are not shown for critics before the movie opens. If it follows that you don't write a review for those films, the average rating for "movies reviewed" will be higher than what it would be if you reviewed "every movie released." I have to tell you that one of my favorite moments on television was watching Rob Reiner read your zero-stars review of *North* before the Friars Club.

—John Fitch, Cary, Illinois

A. Yeah, I hated, hated, hated that movie. On the other hand, how to account for my three-star review of Reiner's *Rumor Has It*, the movie about the "real" sequel to *The Graduate*? Its average score at Metacritic.com was 36. I also took some heat for my three-star *Cheaper by the Dozen 2*. But I contend that if you read the reviews instead of merely counting stars, the

ratings make sense. Another way "survivor bias" works is that I am more likely to seek out and review an independent or foreign film than I am to try to catch up with *Aeon Flux* (unscreened for critics) in theaters.

Q. Having read your reviews of *Basic Instinct 2* and *Slither*, I must ask, why not just abandon your star rating system? This is not the first time you've dealt with your unhappiness about the stars. Since you provide full-length reviews, you have plenty of space to explain why the movie was good or not. Why torture yourself over whether *Basic Instinct 2* deserves one and a half or four stars? If it's a "good bad movie," just say that. If people are too lazy to read the review and must rely on the star rating alone, I say screw 'em!

—Colin Woodward, Richmond, Virginia

A. I think the *Sun-Times* would let me drop the stars if I asked to. But I've got thirty-nine years of star ratings in those thousands of past reviews on my Web site, and the ratings I gave those movies would hang around no matter what I did now. I was all set to drop the stars in the late 1960s, but Gene Siskel was named film critic of the *Chicago Tribune* and immediately insisted the *Trib* start using stars to compete. And that was that.

Stealth

Q. I just read your review of *Stealth*, where you wondered how a pilot could eject from a plane going Mach 1, 2, or whatever, but then have the plane explode and debris fall to Earth on top of him, not further ahead. You cite Newton's laws. Well, when an object in motion is ejected, that new object continues to move at the same speed and in the same direction as the original one until some outside force, such as friction from contact with air, slows it down. When the pilot ejects from the plane, he is still moving at the speed of the plane. Depending on when the plane exploded, it is possible that the debris might rain down on him.

—Peter Papachronopoulos,
Manchester, New Hampshire

A. I heard from many readers making the same argument, as well as producer Robert Swanson of Delta Max Productions, who himself has ejected from a jet fighter. Two things seem true: 1) If the pilot ejected at such a speed, the impact with the air would tear him to shreds. 2) If he survived, or if the plane was going slower, the air would slow him down a *lot* right away, not even accounting for his drag chute, so it is unreasonable to believe that a pilot descending by parachute still would be directly beneath the falling parts of a plane that does not explode for a few more seconds.

Stick It

Q. Your review of Jessica Bendinger's *Stick It* was informative and succinct, but you made a few errors. The character did her head spin on the balance beam. Also, in women's gymnastics, they use the uneven bars; the parallel bars are reserved for the men.

—Cindy Henry, Virginia Beach, Virginia

A. So now my question becomes, is it possible to do a head spin on a balance beam? Stefan Verstappen writes in *Black Belt* magazine for October 2002: "Dancers and figure skaters, when performing pirouettes, focus their eyes on a point in the horizon. As their body spins, the head and eyes remain focused on that spot until the neck will not twist any further, then the head turns around quickly ahead of the body and again focuses on that same spot. If you allowed the head to spin in tandem with the body, the overwhelming visual and vestibular sensations would cause immediate dizziness and disorientation."

Yet we do sometimes see break-dancers doing head spins, so perhaps they would be possible briefly on a balance beam, before the visual and vestibular sensations kicked in.

Stop-motion Animation

Q. I agree with you that stop-motion animation has a magical quality. I've always been an admirer of both *King Kong* and the battle of the skeletons in *Jason & the Argonauts*. Thank you for the Ray Harryhausen information; I didn't realize he was the genius behind *Jason* and *Sinbad*. Do you think that because we grew up with stop-motion animation, we think it has a magical quality, and our nostalgia is involved? On a less serious note, am I mistaken in thinking that Victor made the wrong choice of a bride in *Tim Burton's Corpse Bride*? Emily, voiced by Helena Bonham-Carter, had more spirit and was more attractive. Maybe it was her

alluring blue skin, or the exposed cheekbones, but I think Victor should have decided to go for the corpse. Plus, she gave him a fantastic present . . . his dog, Scraps.

—Jason Miller, Tucson, Arizona

A. What's more, Emily would never grow older. Stop-motion involves using actual physical models that are moved slightly between each frame of the film, giving the illusion of movement. Its modern incarnations include *Corpse Bride* and Nick Park's *Wallace & Gromit: The Curse of the Were-Rabbit*. For me, it is the very slight jerkiness of the motion that enhances their appeal, giving them a different kind of reality than the smooth movements within modern animation (whether drawn or produced by computer). It's not that I dislike state-of-the-art animation; it's that I like variety.

Superman

Q. Fans of Richard Donner's *Superman* film have launched a multiphase project to restore his *Superman II*, incorporating elements that Donner shot concurrently with the first film but were thrown out by the studio when he was replaced. Phase one was to locate copies of as many of Donner's original elements as possible. Most of these lost scenes were included in a special extended cut of *Superman II* that was aired on TV once, and only once, in 1984. But sure enough, there were plenty of fans out there who'd videotaped that broadcast and who'd held on to the tapes. The highest-quality elements from all of these tapes (that is, the one copy of a certain shot that didn't suffer from static or jitter or a promo for *Dukes of Hazzard*) were assembled into a restored "director's cut," which was released as a bootleg. In phase two, the phase one release was color-corrected and enhanced, resulting in much higher-quality video. And now the Superman fans have moved on to phase three: They're trying to upgrade all of the wonky seventies-era special effects with modern digital techniques. Phase three is still in progress. Naturally, releasing these cuts is entirely illegal. If you want a copy, you have to post a message on a certain message board at a certain time, and at some point to be determined later, a DVD magically appears in your mailbox. Download the cover art, print it, slide the disc and the art into a case, and presto. Partly, they're doing this just to put Donner's original vision out there, but I think the real goal is to convince the studio to go into its vaults, dig out the negatives, and do it for real. Talk about activism!

—Andy Ihnatko, Westwood, Massachusetts

A. The amazing thing is that Warner Bros. doesn't see the commercial potential in this lost film and simply release it on DVD, as they did with Paul Schrader's original version of the *Exorcist* prequel.

Sure to Be One of the ...

Q. I notice that the poster for *The Prize Winner of Defiance, Ohio,* includes the quote "Sure to be one of the best films of the year." Unfortunately, I saw the poster on the Web, and the type was too small for me to see which critic made this extraordinary statement. How can anyone know without seeing it that a film is "sure" to be good?

—Greg Nelson, Chicago, Illinois

A. I have also been squinting at the poster and can't read the name. Could this by any chance be a slogan entered in the family tradition by a member of the Ryan family of Defiance, Ohio?

Q. An Answer Man letter mentioned the poster for *The Prize Winner of Defiance, Ohio.* I have seen the poster, and the critic is Jeffrey Lyons of NBC-TV.

—Jerry A. Taylor, Tucson, Arizona

A. I hope he will not keep us waiting for his reviews of next year's best films.

Q. Earlier the Answer Man marveled at the prescience of critic Jeffrey Lyons. The AM wrote, "I hope he will not keep us waiting for his reviews of next year's best films." Your hope has come true. In an ad for *The Worlds Fastest Indian,* Lyons writes, "Anthony Hopkins gives one of his finest, most endearing performances in what is sure to be one of the year's best films."

—Greg Nelson, Chicago, Illinois

A. Because in this case he describes Hopkins's performance, we can assume Lyons has seen the film and is not, as appeared with the previous quote, to be acting as a psychic. What we are left with is the question, in what sense is it "sure to be" one of the year's best films? It is not now, but it will be in the future? It is sure to be on Lyons's list? It is sure to be nominated as such? Sure to be so acclaimed by others? Surely, having seen it, he has license as a critic to write simply "One of the year's best films," which still leaves wriggle room unless the word "ten" is inserted.

Syriana

Q. I read your review for *Syriana* and found that you did not mention one of the integral story threads in the film, about the Pakistani immigrant Wasim. Why? Other reviews made some reference to this story line, and the actors who played these Pakistani roles are even credited on the poster! It was an important part of the film. Was this intentional or a mistake?

—Shahab Yunus, Lahore, Pakistan

A. Neither one, but simply a case of too much plot to be summarized in one review. It was interesting that a somewhat similar story, told in the powerful *Paradise Now,* won the 2006 Golden Globe as best foreign film.

Q. I have read more than one review mentioning Tim Blake Nelson's "brilliant" speech in *Syriana* about corruption. It has been compared to Michael Douglas's speech in *Wall Street,* defending greed. I haven't seen the movie yet but I'd love to just be able to read the speech.

—Greg Nelson, Chicago, Illinois

A. The speech is the work of Stephen Gaghan, the Oscar-winning writer and director of the film. Nelson plays Danny Dalton, a Texas oilman who is speaking to Bennett Holiday (Jeffrey Wright), a lawyer investigating a merger of two oil companies. Gaghan supplies this transcript:

Danny: Some trust fund prosecutor, got off-message at Brown, thinks he's gonna run this up the flag pole, make a name for himself, maybe get elected some two-bit, no-name congressman from nowhere, with the result that Russia or China can suddenly start having, at our expense, all the advantages we enjoy here. No, I tell you. No, sir. (mimics prosecutor) "But, Danny, these are sovereign nations." Sovereign nations! What is a sovereign nation but a collective of greed run by one individual? "But, Danny, they're codified by the U.N. charter!" Legitimized gangsterism on a global basis that has no more validity than an agreement between the Crips and the Bloods! (beat) . . . Corruption charges. Corruption? Corruption ain't nothing more than government intrusion into market efficiencies in the form of regulation. That's Milton Friedman. He got a goddamn Nobel Prize. We have laws against it precisely so we can get away with it. Corruption is our protection. Corruption is what keeps us safe and warm. Corruption is why you and I are prancing around here instead of fighting each other for scraps of meat out in the streets. (beat) Corruption . . . is how we win.

The Talent Given Us

Q. The movie *The Talent Given Us* has a title that sounds like a quotation to me, but I can't find it in Bartlett's or anywhere else. Any clues?

—Greg Nelson, Chicago, Illinois

A. *The Talent Given Us*, directed by Andrew Wagner, is a fiction film in the form of a documentary, with Wagner's family playing themselves. I asked him if the title was a quotation. He responded: "It's from a line of dialogue in *Southern Man*, one of my own scripts that takes place in the South in the '50s, so it's possible it originates from the civil rights and period research I did. *Talent* had a different working title. Early into the editing I was on the lookout for a new title that better captured the themes and comedy of the film and I came across *The Talent Given Us* while doing a rewrite on *Southern Man*. It clicked for me. In my mind, 'talent' is a euphemism for the emotional patterns that are passed along in families."

Theater Mysteries

Q. News item: "An Associated Press–AOL poll last week found that 73 percent of adults prefer watching movies on DVD, videotape, or pay-per-view rather than going to the theater." As much is it pains me to agree, increasingly I find myself irritated by the theater experience. For example, I saw *Batman Begins* last week; the picture was dark and there was a row of drugged-out hippies laughing and talking during the whole movie. Do you think the AP-AOL poll is an accurate reflection of people's views or is the sample skewed? What impact do you think this will have on movies released theatrically? The box office returns *are* at their lowest point since 1985, after all.

—Matt Wolf, Burnsville, Minnesota

A. Movie exhibitors have reached a moment of truth. It is time to create and enforce a supe-rior viewing environment in theaters or accept the consequences. Ushers should have ejected the annoying patrons, but I am just as disturbed by your comment that the picture was dark. *Batman Begins* is a dark movie, set mostly at night, but if it is properly projected it is dark in a clear and atmospheric way. It is possible, however, that the theater you attended is one that practices the idiotic economy of turning down the power on the projector bulb for "savings"—on electricity, bulbs, who knows? The life span of a projector bulb is not shortened by using it at the correct setting.

Q. On a message board, someone reported that they went to see *Brokeback Mountain* and were issued tickets for *Eight Below*. There was discussion that some studios bump sales by issuing tickets to a different movie than the one you're attending. I've been issued tickets that were not for the film I was seeing. I thought it was just a mistake, but friends who went to see *The Iron Giant* said that none of their tickets were for *Iron Giant*. It smacks of something unfair. Might be worth checking your tickets from time to time.

—David Brewster, Burbank, California

A. I've heard this sort of thing attributed to cashier error. It also could be a device by the theaters to make more money. In the first few weeks of a run, the studios take up to 90 percent of the ticket price. As the run continues, the theater's share increases. So money could be made by substituting a ticket to an older movie. In this case, though, *Brokeback* is the older movie. A bar code system could ensure the correct movie was ticketed and prevent the Multiplex Shuffle.

Q. I remember watching movies as a kid. Looking up, you could see the light rays coming from the projection room, reflecting against the dust in the air. I never see that anymore. What happened?

—Wai Chu, New York City, New York

A. Moviegoers are no longer allowed to smoke in theaters.

The Three Burials of Melquiades Estrada

Q. *(Spoiler warning)* We saw *The Three Burials of Melquiades Estrada* yesterday. Loved it. Read your review of this film today. You say,

"There is one word at the end of the film that carries a burden that a long speech could not have dealt with. It is a word that is also used near the beginning of the film. It contains whatever message Jones finds at the end of the journey." What was this one word? My sidekick and I are baffled by this assertion.

—L. Singh, Chicago, Illinois

A. The word is "son."

3-D

Q. Re your unhappiness with *Sharkboy and Lavagirl in 3-D* in the inferior red/cyan anaglyph format: It was shown via digital light processing (DLP) in full-color polarized (clear glasses) 3-D at the film's premiere in Austin. Quite a different experience. *Sharkboy* is only the fourth major film to be released in anaglyph format, following *The Mask* (1961), *Freddys Dead: The Final Nightmare* (1991), and *Spy Kids 3-D* (2003). That's because Hollywood was smart enough to realize that looking through colored glasses is not an acceptable way to view a major film. The vast majority of 3-D movies, including all fifty-one that Hollywood churned out in 1952–55 and most since then, have been released in polarized clear-glasses form. I've seen nearly forty of the 1950s films in the original dual-projector polarized form in a controlled environment in recent years, and frankly, many of the films were breathtakingly good. Full color, full brightness, no headache, no distraction. IMAX 3-D can work, but often the films are shot in such a way that all the action takes place in front of your face, which causes eyestrain. *Polar Express* was great, but many of the others recently, such as *Wild Safari*, are intolerable. Bottom line: Red/blue isn't, and never has been, the standard. I suspect *Sharkboy* will be the last time Hollywood tries it. DLP via polarized glasses is the wave of the future.

—Steve Phillips, Las Vegas, Nevada

A. Digital light processing is state-of-the-art projection. What surprises me is that *Sharkboy* director Robert Rodriguez, who is a big-time gizmo freak and a pioneer of filming on digital, chose an inferior format for his movie. It would have been a perfectly entertaining movie for kids in 2-D, but the box office fell off quickly in 3-D because audiences hated watching it. The DVD should find a wider market.

Thumbs

Q. I got a nasty review (not from you) for my debut feature, the comedy *Four Dead Batteries*, which I wrote and directed. Those thumbs down haunt me now, as I prepare my sophomore effort. As a critic, do you take into consideration the damage a thorough drubbing might cause a beginning filmmaker?

—Hiram Martinez, Clifton, New Jersey

A. On the bright side, you didn't get any thumbs down, haunting or otherwise, because the thumbs are trademarked and were not employed on your film one way or the other. As for the drubbing, let's put it this way: If the review was useful to you, it did its job. Praise without merit is more harmful than unearned criticism. Developing that thought, I checked your movie's page on IMDb.com and found that your user rating is 8.8 out of 10, which seems fairly high, considering that the top-rated movies of all time, *The Godfather* and *Shawshank Redemption*, are rated 9 and *Casablanca* and *Star Wars* come in at only 8.7. An amazing 54 percent of all voters gave *Four Dead Batteries* a perfect 10, and only one of 26 voters rated it lower than 6. Can you think of any possible explanation for this extraordinary result?

Tim Burton's Corpse Bride

Q. Where was the spoiler warning in the Movie Answer Man question about *Corpse Bride*? I've really been looking forward to seeing the film (and I still am), but I wish you would've given readers a chance to avoid knowing Victor's choice in advance!

—Joe Madden, Urbana, Illinois

A. The name of the movie is, let's see here . . . yes, here it is: *Tim Burton's Corpse Bride*. The poster shows the movie's hero and the corpse dressed for a wedding and holding hands. Obviously different artwork should have been chosen and the movie's title should have been: *(Spoiler Warning) Tim Burton's Corpse Bride*.

Q. An oversight in your *Corpse Bride* review calls into question your competency as a critic. I speak of skeletal fleas. Fleas, like other insects, have exoskeletons; a skeletal flea would look just like a regular one, so there's no point in differentiating between the two.

—Ed Resnick, San Diego, California

A. It makes a great deal of difference to the flea.

Touch the Sound

Q. The documentary film *Touch the Sound*, which is about a deaf musician named Evelyn Glennie, will not be released theatrically with subtitles. Think about this for a second. Although many people might want to see this film, I would guess that the movie will be of particular interest to the hearing-impaired. They would require subtitles to appreciate the content in any meaningful way beyond visual imagery and perhaps lip-reading. But according to a representative of the distribution company, the director felt that "the visual aspect of the film is as important as the aural" and that "the subtitles would be hurtful" in the theatrical release. So this film is about deaf people but is not for deaf people. I believe that citing aesthetic reasons for not using subtitles is insensitive and against the very spirit behind this particular film.

—Heather Chan, Toronto, Ontario

A. I mentioned this peculiar decision in my review and queried the distributors, Shadow Distribution. Spokesman Ken Eisen replies:

Touch the Sound is being exhibited theatrically without subtitles, in its original English-language version. Although there are about 250 screens in U.S. theaters that have the capability of screening rear-projected closed-captioned versions of films, none of those screens show 'art' films, and so authorizing such a version would not be helpful. We are, instead, working with theaters in each city in which *Touch the Sound* plays to set up at least one special screening at which the film will be interpreted into sign language so that it is as accessible as possible to all audiences who wish to see it. Such a screening will happen in Chicago at the Music Box."

Ebert again. This answer sidesteps the possibility of actually subtitling all prints of film. The special screening with sign language is not much of a solution, since all the other screenings will be inaccessible, and watching signing during a movie is more difficult than reading subtitles, particularly given the lighting conditions. I believe the no-subtitle decision by director Thomas Riedelsheimer is wrong-headed.

Carla Leete, assistant to *Touch the Sound* star Evelyn Glennie, informs me: "We are currently in the process of creating a statement addressing the subtitle issue, which will eventually be found on Evelyn's site (www.evelyn.co.uk)."

Q. I was recently at the Santa Fe Film Festival, where I had the opportunity to see Thomas Riedelsheimer's amazing new documentary, *Touch the Sound*. Given that the subject of the film was the nature and spirit of sound and silence, I was traumatized to have the man sitting next to me fall asleep and snore through the entire film. It completely ruined my experience, but honestly, I didn't know what to do. I nudged him a few times to make him stop, which he did, but only temporarily. Bloody hell. Should I have awakened him, or asked him to leave?

—Sridhar Reddy, Chicago, Illinois

A. The Answer Man's expert on matters of etiquette is Dear Prudence of Slate.com, who responds:

"This is an unfair impediment to watching a movie, so if such an occurrence absolutely wrecks the movie for you, explain it to the box office and ask for a free return ticket. Your situation gives new meaning to the old exhortation 'Get a room.' Other strategies: 1) Try to move your seat. 2) If a new neighborhood in the theater is not possible, nudge the guy awake every time you hear the zzzs start. 3) Looking for the manager would take you from the movie, so go back to #2."

Tristram Shandy

Q. Has anyone you know ever finished reading *Tristram Shandy*? I have been a member of a book club dedicated to reading the book, and we've met every year for twenty-two years. None of us have finished it, although we do discuss how many pages we've read during the year. No one has missed at least one page per year!

—Vicki Halliday, Angus, Scotland

A. No one I know has finished the novel, and perhaps its author, Laurence Sterne, never finished it either, since it begins in the middle and claims to be getting around to its beginning and its end.

On the Internet Movie Database, we are told of the screenplay: "The credited writer, Martin Hardy, is actually a pseudonym for the writer

Frank Cottrell Boyce, who had his name taken off the film after a falling-out with longtime collaborator Michael Winterbottom." In the spirit of *Tristram Shandy,* this, too, is a fabrication. Boyce writes me, "Re Martin Hardy: So much of the script was improvised by Steve Coogan and Rob Brydon that it seemed like cheating and a bit churlish to take all the credit. Inventing a writer seemed the most shandean option. I recently won a British script award in which the other contender was Martin, and in my speech I called him a true genius and a great lover."

Q. You claim in discussing the movie *Tristram Shandy* that you have never met anyone who finished the novel. When I was an English major at Barnard College in the mid-1980s, I read it cover to cover. When I told my professor, she was surprised, claiming that although it was on the syllabus, she didn't expect anyone to read the thing in its entirety.

—Rachel Leventman Shwalb,
Brookline, Massachusetts

A. I now have heard from many readers who have indeed finished it, including:

• Clare Flanagan Ahearn, Rutherford, New Jersey: "As an English major at Emmanuel College, Boston, from 1966–70, I had to read *Tristram Shandy.* I did, because I was expected to. I recall little; like the pangs of childbirth, some things are too painful to remember. I was paying for college myself, and I wanted to get as much out of it as possible."

• Tracey S. Rosenberg, Edinburgh, Scotland: "I have read *Tristram Shandy.* I must admit, however, that I read it for the same reasons I read James Joyce's *Ulysses:* 1) I will be able to tell people that I have read it, and 2) having read it, I never have to read it again."

• David Van Court, Houston, Texas: "*Tristram Shandy* is not nearly as difficult as something like *Ulysses* and is a pure delight. I would put it on a list with *Tom Jones, David Copperfield, Lucky Jim,* and anything by Evelyn Waugh."

• John Marble, Los Alamos, New Mexico: "I've read *Tristram Shandy* three times. I think it inspired contemporary writers such as Vonnegut, Douglas Adams, and Philip Jose Farmer (writing as Kilgore Trout)."

Uncanny Valley

Q. I think you may be onto something with your critique of *The Wild,* when you say the animals fall into the Uncanny Valley of being too realistic. I think it may extend beyond the lip-synching. The day I saw the poster, I told one of my friends that it left me vaguely unsettled, because the animals looked simultaneously real and not real, which is, in essence, the basic idea behind the Uncanny Valley. The look of the creatures (especially the lion, for some reason) creeped me out. I will be interested to see if other critics and people I know have a similar reaction to the film.

—Matthew Lingo, Bakersfield, California

A. Most of my correspondents advised me to just shut up and review the movie, which I was under the impression I was doing with rare insight and breadth of knowledge, throwing in the Uncanny Valley theory as a bonus. I guess they don't want to read anything in a review they don't already know, but I am paid by the word and can't afford to write that concisely.

V for Vendetta

Q. In your review of *V for Vendetta* you write: "There are ideas in this film. The most pointed is V's belief, 'People should not be afraid of their governments. Governments should be afraid of their people.' I am not sure V has it right; surely in the ideal, state governments and their people should exist happily together. Fear in either direction must lead to violence."

I defer to Thomas Jefferson, who said, "When the people fear their government, there is tyranny; when the government fears the people, there is liberty."

—D. Saul Weiner, Buffalo Grove, Illinois

A. This reminds me of John F. Kennedy's statement at a White House dinner for Nobel Prize winners: "I think this is the most extraordinary collection of talent, of human knowledge, that has ever been gathered together at the White House, with the possible exception of when Thomas Jefferson dined alone."

Q. Re your statement about Hugo Weaving's character, V, in *V for Vendetta:* I see your point about the distraction when the lips of a character don't move when he talks. But I'm vividly reminded how effective both the characters

929

Darth Vader and C-3PO were in *Star Wars*. Anthony Daniels's performance as C-3PO stands out as an extraordinary use of vocal and body expression.

—Jason Burnett, Seoul, South Korea

A. C-3PO didn't bother me because I would expect a robot to have a mechanized voice, and it wouldn't make sense for his lips to move. Darth Vader, like V, has a good reason for covering his face, but in the beginning I somehow related to him as if there wasn't a human body under that cloak. In my review, I also asked why V's mask doesn't limit his peripheral vision. Corey Buran of Knoxville, Tennessee, informs me: "It's simple: He doesn't have eyes. Recall the scene at the prison camp, when the head doctor sees him emerge from the flames. 'He had no eyes, but he could see me. I could feel it.'"

Video Games

Q. If *Doom* were just another action thriller, then I would have to say you were too generous by giving it one star. Frankly, the movie deserves zero stars. But it is not just a movie. *Doom* was to games what *Rashomon* was to movies. It invented a way of showing something that had never been done before—what you call the "point-of-view shot looking forward over the barrel of a large weapon." *Doom* the movie is a tribute to this seminal event. This movie isn't about clever camera angles, witty dialogue, or subtle directorial touches. *Doom* has no pretensions, aspirations, or delusions about itself. You aren't supposed to wonder about the origins of mankind as you walk out of the theater. *Doom* the movie is *Doom* the game brought to the screen without messing around too much with the original. *Doom* works as a tribute because it fails so utterly as a movie. There is a reason so many video game–based movies suck: They are fundamentally different forms of representation. Thus, by being faithful to the game, the movie pisses off the critic and pleases the gamer.

—Vikram Keskar, Kirksville, Missouri

A. With friends like you, what does *Doom* need critics for? Surveys indeed show that more than half the movie's opening-weekend viewers had played the game. I suppose they got what they were expecting. I believe in the value-added concept of filmmaking, in which a movie supplies something a video game does not. As a moviegoing experience, this was not a good one. There are specialist sites on the Web devoted to video games, and they review movies in their terms. I review them in mine. As long as there is a great movie unseen or a great book unread, I will continue to be unable to find the time to play video games.

Q. I've been a gamer since I was very young, and I haven't been satisfied with most of the movies based on video games, with the exception of the first *Mortal Kombat* and *Final Fantasy: The Spirits Within*. These were successful as films because they didn't try to be tributes to the games, but films in their own right. I have not seen *Doom*, but don't plan to, nor do I think that it's fair to say that it pleases all gamers. Some of us appreciate film, too. That said, I was surprised at your denial of video games as a worthwhile use of your time. Are you implying that books and film are better media, or just better uses of your time? Films and books have their scabs, as do games, but there are beautiful examples of video games out there—see *Shadow of the Colossus, Rez*, or *PeaceMaker*.

—Josh Fishburn, Denver, Colorado

A. I believe books and films are better media, and better uses of my time. But how can I say that when I admit I am unfamiliar with video games? Because I recently have seen classic films by Fassbinder, Ozu, Herzog, Scorsese, and Kurosawa and recently have read novels by Dickens, Cormac, McCarthy, Bellow, Nabokov, and Hugo, and if there were video games in the same league, someone somewhere who was familiar with the best work in all three media would have made a convincing argument in their defense.

Q. I was saddened to read that you consider video games inherently inferior to film and literature, despite your admitted lack of familiarity with the great works of the medium. This strikes me as especially perplexing given how receptive you have been in the past to other oft-maligned media, such as comic books and animation. Was not film itself once a new field of art? Did it not also take decades for its academic respectability to be recognized? There already are countless serious studies on game theory and criticism available, including Mark S. Meadows's *Pause &*

Effect: The Art of Interactive Narrative, Nick Montfort's *Twisty Little Passages: An Approach to Interactive Fiction,* Noah Wardrip-Fruin and Pat Harrigan's *First Person: New Media as Story, Performance, and Game,* and Mark J. P. Wolf's *The Medium of the Video Game,* to name a few. I hold out hope that you will take the time to broaden your experience with games beyond the trashy, artless "adaptations" that pollute our movie theaters, and let you discover the true wonder of this emerging medium, just as you have so passionately helped me appreciate the greatness of many wonderful films.

—Andrew Davis, St. Cloud, Minnesota

A. Yours is the most civil of countless messages I have received after writing that I did indeed consider video games inherently inferior to film and literature. There is a structural reason for that: Video games by their nature require player choices, which is the opposite of the strategy of serious film and literature, which requires authorial control. I am prepared to believe that video games can be elegant, subtle, sophisticated, challenging, and visually wonderful. But I believe the nature of the medium prevents it from moving beyond craftsmanship to the stature of art. To my knowledge, no one in or out of the field has been able to cite a game worthy of comparison with the great dramatists, poets, filmmakers, novelists, and composers. That a game can aspire to artistic importance as a visual experience, I accept. But for most gamers, video games represent a loss of those precious hours we have available to make ourselves more cultured, civilized, and empathetic.

Q. Thank you for jump-starting a discussion about the relative artistic and critical merit of video games as compared to film and books. This can't help but have positive consequences for video games. I do take issue when you argue that video games never can have the merit of a great film or novel. You say, "Video games by their nature require player choices, which is the opposite of the strategy of serious film and literature, which requires authorial control."

Where you see a flaw, I see promise. It's not a bug that there is less authorial control, it's a feature. Arguing that games are inherently inferior because books and movies are better at telling stories and leading us through an author-driven experience is begging the question. It's like say-

ing that photography is better than painting because photos make more accurate visual records.

The invention of photography sparked a crisis in the world of painting: "Why should we paint if pictures can do it better?" But then painters figured out that there were lots of other things that they could do that cameras can't. Now we see an enormous explosion of creativity in the world of painting and another explosion in the world of photography.

We agree that games are inherently different from films and books. I believe they are at their worst when they try to mimic films and books and at their best when they exploit this difference to create experiences that films, books, and all the other art forms cannot. No one criticizes sculpture for failing to tell a story as well as a good movie.

Many people would agree with you that there aren't yet any games that rival the best films or books that you care to list. Game makers are just beginning to understand that games are not films/books with action sequences. I think you'll see that the more we work that out, the more we will find ways of creating meaningful artistic works that are unlike anything anyone's seen before.

—Tim Maly, designer, Capybara Games, Toronto, Ontario

A. If or when that happens, I hope I will approach it with an open mind. This debate has taken on a life of its own. In countless e-mails and on a dozen message boards, I've found that most of the professionals involved in video games are intelligent and thoughtful people like yourself. A large number of the video game players, alas, tell me "you suck" or inform me that I am too old. At sixty-three, I prefer such synonyms as "wise" and "experienced."

I received a message from retired Professor David Bordwell of the University of Wisconsin at Madison, who generally is thought of as the leading scholarly writer on film; the textbooks he has written by himself and with Kristin Thompson are used in a majority of the world's film classrooms. What he said was intriguing on a practical level:

"The last dissertation I'm directing is on video games as they compare to film. The guy is bright, so we let him do it. But he brought his games and game platform to my house to give me some experience on this medium. I lasted through fifteen minutes of *Simpsons Road Rage,* largely because my coordination is so poor. Even if I got good on the controls, what keeps me away is the level of commitment. The idea of spending hours at this boggles my mind.

"My student told me that the most sophisticated games require up to one hundred hours to master. In one hundred hours we can watch twenty-five Bollywood films or fifty-plus Hollywood/foreign features or eighty B-films or 750 Warner Bros. cartoons. Depending on how fast you read, in the same interval you can probably finish reading twenty to thirty books. Not to mention twenty-five to thirty-five operas or 100 to 120 symphonies. And that's just for one game! On the basis of my very limited experience, and given my tastes (a big part of the issue here), the problem with video games is that they're too much like life—too much commitment for thin and often frustrating results."

Q. I was surprised by *Silent Hill* director Christophe Gans's incendiary comments about you in *Electronic Gaming Monthly,* especially considering your positive review of his earlier work *Brotherhood of the Wolf.* Gans phrased his comments to indicate he wanted you to read them.

—David Seelig, Philadelphia, Pennsylvania

A. In the article, Gans praises video games as a form of art and says *The Legend of Zelda* was "a beautiful, poetic moment for me." Asked about my opinion that video games are not art, he said: "F*** him. I will say to this guy that he only has to read the critiques against cinema at the beginning of the twentieth century. It was seen as a degenerate version of live stage musicals. And this was a time when visionary directors like Griffith were working. That means that Ebert is wrong. It's simple. Most people who despise a new medium are simply afraid to die, so they express their arrogance and fear like this. He will realize that he is wrong on his deathbed. Human beings are stupid, and we often become a**holes when we get old. Each time a new medium appears, I feel that it's important to respect it, even if it appears primitive or naive at first, simply because some people are finding value in it. If you have one guy in the world who thinks that *Silent Hill* or *Zelda* is a beautiful, poetic work, then that game means something."

Ebert again. I am willing to agree that a video game could also be a serious work of art. It would become so by avoiding most of the things that make it a game, such as scoring, pointing and shooting, winning and losing, shallow characterizations, and action that is valued above motivation and ethical considerations. Oddly enough, when video games evolve far enough in that direction, they not only will be an art form, they will be the cinema.

A tip on the early cinema: No wonder it was seen as "a degenerate version of live stage musicals," since the talkies hadn't been invented yet, and there is nothing more degenerate than a musical without sound.

Your comments on age and the fear of death are thought-provoking. You know, Christophe, the older I get, the more prudent I become in how I spend my time. As David Bordwell has pointed out, it can take at least one hundred hours to complete a video game. Do you really feel you have mastered the mature arts to such an extent that you have that kind of time to burn on a medium you think is primitive and naive?

On my deathbed, I doubt that I will spend any time realizing that I was wrong about video games. Your theory reminds me of my friend Gene Siskel, who observed that nobody on his deathbed ever thinks, "I'm glad I always flew tourist."

Q. In your anecdote in the *Silent Hill* review about children's brain activity and video games, you cite Dr. Leonard Shlain describing the monitoring of brain activity by young children learning to play video games: "At first, when they were figuring out the games, the whole brain lit up. But by the time they knew how to play the games, the brain went dark, except for one little point."

As if this was a negative argument! I read and write plays and films all day long. I went to *Silent Hill* yesterday to give my brain a break, which is why most people play video games (or watch stupid movies). There is a place for entertainment that discourages thought—it gives us space to actually think.

—Tommy Smith, New York City, New York

A. That's exactly my problem. I watch stupid movies, and they make me actually think, and I write those reviews about brain waves. There also is a place for entertainment that encourages thought, I suppose, although then we also would actually be thinking. I am confused.

Walk the Line

Q. In your review of *Walk the Line*, you state: "The movie fudges some on the facts. Johnny didn't actually propose marriage to June onstage, but I'm glad he does in the movie." I just read Johnny Cash's autobiography *Man in Black* last week, and Cash himself tells the story of when he proposed to June Carter onstage in Toronto.

—Megan Breen, Chicago, Illinois

A. You are quite right. So was Johnny Cash, for that matter. The review has been corrected.

Wallace & Gromit: The Curse of the Were-Rabbit

Q. I was so excited to see that *Wallace & Gromit: The Curse of the Were-Rabbit* was rated G and that you gave it a good review, so I took my four-year-old to see it. I was blown away that a G movie would have so much sexual innuendo, curse words, and even some nudity. Did we see the same film? I am e-mailing everyone I know who has small children that this movie is clearly wrongly rated. Please be aware that you have a responsibility to acknowledge those facts when critiquing a film for the American public.

—Hope Otto, Houston, Texas

A. The most reliable and accurate source I know for parents who want detailed information on movies is screenit.com. In its discussion of *Wallace & Gromit* the site terms the nudity in the movie "moderate" and the profanity "minor." It summarizes: "Will kids want to see it? Yes, especially younger ones. Why the MPAA rated it G: For not containing material to warrant a higher rating."

War of the Worlds

Q. You may be on the wrong track with your objection to the three-legged aliens in *War of the Worlds*, when you write, "Three legs are inherently not stable." Amateur carpenters are advised to build three-legged stools rather than four-legged stools. Why? Because even if the seat is not level, all three legs will be in contact with the surface. The real problem with the machines in the movie is that they have a very high center of gravity, so high that any rapid lo-

comotion is likely to tip them over, especially when they stop or change direction.

—Mike Barnas, Chicago, Illinois

A. Seeking an expert opinion, I contacted Jessica Banks, a Ph.D. candidate at the MIT Computer Science and Artificial Intelligence Lab, whose thesis involves a robot with one point of contact. She consulted her colleague Dan Paluska, a Ph.D candidate at the MIT Media Lab, an expert on robot legged locomotion who was featured on the cover of *Wired* magazine.

They began by pointing out, "Your comment 'If evolution has taught us anything, it is that the limbs of living things, from men to dinosaurs to spiders to centipedes, tend to come in numbers divisible by four' is wrong and misleading. Numbers of limbs are divisible by two due to the principle of bilateral symmetry to which nature adheres."

I meant, of course, to write "two" instead of "four" but was attacked by a brain cloud. My online review has been corrected. Banks and Paluska continue with a fascinating discussion of the functions of three legs among both living and mechanical creatures, which I am printing in full on rogerebert.com. Here are some bullet points:

• A three-legged chair or table is very stable when it is still. However, the answer isn't so easy when one considers three-legged locomotion.... Things have a right and a left, a front and a back. This has to do with the fact that animals tend to travel in a certain direction, facing forward when doing so. Having an even number of legs allows animals to be balanced as they travel forward....

• There is a rhythm to walking and running that may be difficult to achieve with a three-legged machine. A kangaroo is the closest thing to a three-legged animal, because it uses its tail. However, its tail is not the same as its legs, and the tail does not touch the ground when the kangaroo is hopping....

• The argument that nature didn't 'come up' with such a creature doesn't hold much water. Nature didn't come up with the wheel for locomotion either.... We could, for instance, imagine a three-legged creature that stood still and upright for the vast majority of its life.... However, it would be hard to imagine such a robot being efficient at locomoting over any significant distances.

• The height of the tripods and the fact that

they are top-heavy makes it plausible that one would fall if one of its legs was damaged, especially if the alien was in motion at the time of injury. This doesn't really say that much, though; considering the fact that if you were to kick one of my legs while I was running or even give it a forceful unexpected blow when I was just loitering about, I would most likely fall to Earth as well. . . .

• So, who knows if it is *practical* or not for a robot to walk on three legs? . . . Ultimately, it would all depend on the system as a whole (speed, passive stability, simplicity, energy consumption, navigability, human-exterminating ability, etc.), the available technologies (sensors, computation, actuators, etc.), the environment in which the robot was supposed to perform, and, well, who was funding it. . . .

Q. I am disappointed that you have not actually read *The War of the Worlds* by H. G. Wells. If you had read it you'd know all the answers to the questions you posed. George H. W. Bush, Norman Schwarzkopf, George W. Bush, and Karl Rove did not invent the strategy of "shock and awe" to cow the enemy—Wells did, and they stole shamelessly from him without knowing this either. The aliens have a whole strategy of invasion, capitulation, domination, colonization, Martian-forming, and domestication of Earth. Humans are ancillary to their plans and quite inconsequential. Wells's book is quite remarkable. It's the first literary treatment of the hostile indifference of the universe, which points up our own relative insignificance, literally played out in the Martians' callous annihilation. You seem to have missed this.

—Kevin Mequet, San Jose, California

A. I did read the book, when I was ten. But if the explanations aren't in the movie, they aren't relevant, because the movie creates its own closed system.

Q. Are the couple standing on the mother's stoop in Boston at the end of *War of the Worlds*, Gene Barry and Ann Robinson, the leads from the 1953 version of the movie?

—Tony McFadden, Singapore

A. Yes.

Whit Stillman

Q. Is Whit Stillman still involved in making movies? All his films were excellent, even if they were not seen by a majority audience.

—Fred C. Mound, Los Angeles, California

A. Stillman is the director of such perceptive and witty slices of yuppie life as *Metropolitan*, *Barcelona*, and *The Last Days of Disco*, but his most recent film appeared in 1998. *Filmmaker* magazine reported in its winter 2006 issue: "'To justify the long silence, I've been working on a number of scripts that are in various stages,' Stillman says, adding that one of them is ready to go. But his writing process can't be hurried. *Metropolitan*, for example, took four years to write, on and off, in the wee hours of the night in a caffeinated haze. 'I don't think a script is very authentic until I've thought about it and gone over it a few times,' he adds. 'For me, time is the biggest luxury.'"

Wolf Creek

Q. Being a die-hard horror fanatic, I was surprised by your zero-star review of *Wolf Creek*. I'd read several positive reviews of the film, and I was hyped to see it. Now that I have, I think you were right about the misogynistic undertones in the film. The film did "cross a line." An example is the "head on a stick" scene versus the only male death scene in the flick. You can easily say which is more brutal and disturbing. The movie didn't act as though these women had names; it acted as though they were just numbers that would be mixed in and forgotten.

—Nate Frankel, Skokie, Illinois

A. I heard from a lot of readers who admired the film and apparently were able to disconnect from its heartless and extreme sadism. That is an ability I do not envy them.

X-Men: The Last Stand

Q. As *X-Men: The Last Stand* was wrapping up, I couldn't help asking, shouldn't Magneto have been in jail? I mean, here is someone who has killed hundreds or thousands of people and destroyed a national monument. Shouldn't there at least have been a trial?

—Jerry Roberts, Birmingham, Alabama

A. Yeah, it's gonna take a lot of work to get that Golden Gate Bridge back in place, now that Magneto has lost his powers.

Ebert's Little Movie Glossary

These are the year's new contributions to my glossary project. Hundreds of entries were collected in *Ebert's Bigger Little Movie Glossary*, published in 1999. Contributions are always welcome.

* * *

Building Code Violations. Whenever an object or person is thrown through a glass window in a movie, it invariably shatters into vicious shards. Even in the future, safety glass is not used. See *Minority Report.*

—Maryann Mynatt, Bolingbrook, Illinois

Clicker-Clack Effect. The firearm counterpart to the Snicker-Snack Effect. Whenever a character is holding a gun and waves it for emphasis, regardless of whether the character actually cocks the gun, or if the gun even has a hammer to cock, it makes a cocking noise.

—Matt Griffin

Corrected Bullet Velocity Rule. In the Bullet Velocity Rule, the equation should go as follows: HBS=RBS/IC, when Hollywood Bullet Speed equals Real Bullet Speed *divided by* (not "times") the importance of character, where the more important the character, the higher the number. That way, the more important the character, the *slower* the bullet will be, and the easier to jump out of the way. I know it's ridiculous for a grown man who is a director of a nonprofit and a teacher to spend time correcting this, but I love the Little Movie Glossary and want it to be perfect.

—Bob Diefendorf, Princeton, New Jersey

Dead for Sure, No Doubt About It. In a movie, the absolute proof of the death of a character is when blood drips slowly from the corner of the mouth. There are too many movies to document. An interesting variation was the dripping of liquid metal from the evil mutant's mouth in *X:2: X-Men United.* As a physician, I can tell you that blood coming from the mouth after a fight is either (1) a sign of a communication of the esophagus with a major blood vessel, which

would be fatal, or (2) a cut in the mouth, which would not be.

—Ken Rosenzweig, Englewood, New Jersey

Deadly Tweener Syndrome. The Tweener is, in horror movies, that creepy character introduced at the beginning of the movie who seemingly lives between two worlds: the "normal" world of the main characters and the dark, creepy world of the cannibalistic or sadistic family, clan, or tribe. The Tweener either warns the main characters to beware a certain road or area or directs them into the path of horror by offering a shortcut. Either way, the Tweener will later take part in the cruel maiming of the main characters. Often appearing as a gas station attendant, the Tweener can be seen in such movies as *The Devil's Rejects, The Texas Chainsaw Massacre,* and *The Hills Have Eyes* remake.

—Ben Schwenk, Cincinnati, Ohio

Don't Shoot the Piano Player. In movies, whenever a person asks a pianist whether he or she knows a tune, the answer is always a nod, followed immediately by the opening notes.

—Alberto Diamante, Toronto, Ontario

Don't Wait for Me. Whenever the hero in a movie says "If I'm not back in five/ten/fifteen minutes, get out of here/blow the whole thing up/call the cops," etc., he will be late. But his companions will ignore his instructions and wait until the hero (who is always wounded) returns. There is a 20 percent chance that they will go out to look for him and also get wounded.

—Roland Freist, Munich, Germany

Dorm Roomate Rule. When it's two to a room in a college dorm, it's highly likely that the protagonist's roommate will be a punk rocker/Goth and almost certain that the roomie will have sex with someone in their bed while the protagonist tries to do homework. See *The Butterfly Effect.*

—Matt Mintz, Murrieta, California

Either Enron or a Ghost. In potentially ominous

935

situations, when the skies are clouding over and something bad is about to happen, the electric lights will blink, stutter, and buzz, as if possessed by a ghostly outage.

—Roger Ebert

Every Minute, On the Minute. Whenever there is a close-up of a digital clock, the shot always shows it at the moment when the minute is changing.

—Brian Palatucci, Santa Monica, California

Explosion? Oh, *That* Explosion. To show he is grizzled or cynical, a character will walk toward the camera as an explosion happens in the background. He doesn't flinch while everyone in the background runs and screams. Examples include Robert Duvall in *Apocalypse Now,* Jake Gyllenhaal in *Jarhead,* and George Clooney in *Syriana.*

—James Flynn, Chicago, Illinois

Forehead Target Rule. When a character is shot in the head, the bullet will impact the victim precisely between the eyes, and a trickle of blood will indicate that it is, indeed, a bullet wound.

—Dat Pham, Ontario, California

Good Dog, Bad Dog. Every werewolf movie must have at least one scene in which a friendly dog (man's best friend) contrasts with the werewolf. The good dog may meet a grisly end at the hands of a werewolf (as with the doomed pooches in *Ginger Snaps* and its sequel), it may become greatly agitated by the person who will become a werewolf (the little terrier on the sidewalk in *An American Werewolf in London*), or it may just be there to remind us that dogs usually are our friends (the farmhouse border collie in *Dog Soldiers.*

—Peter Simpson, Ottawa, Ontario

Green Destiny Foreshadowing. This is any aspect of a film that foreshadows future films by the same director. In *Crouching Tiger, Hidden Dragon,* Ang Lee named the sword the *Green Destiny* and went on to make *Hulk.* Chris Nolan has a protagonist who has a Batman sticker on his front door. Nolan of course went on to direct *Batman Begins.* Willem Dafoe thinks he's Jesus Christ in *Platoon,* and he played Jesus in *The Last Temptation of Christ.*

—Jason Callen, Madison, Wisconsin

Human-Absorption Bus Rule. Whenever one character is looking at another from across the street, if a bus or truck passes between them, it will invariably make the other one disappear, possibly into another dimension.

—Alberto Diamante, Toronto, Ontario

The Loner's Vindication Rule. Whenever the fate of the world is on the line, governments turn to that lone scientist whose ideas and theories, once shunned as ludicrous, now become the last hope to save humanity.

—Eric Voisard, Toronto, Ontario

Picture Perfect Principle. When a character has a photograph of a location he is searching for, the camera will cut to a close-up of the photo being held in his hand. The photo will then drop away, revealing the location the character is looking for at exactly the same angle the photo was shot from. Corollary: If a person is in the photo but not in the scene, their absence is a plot point.

—Todd Doherty, Londonderry, New Hampshire

Prison Dossier Rule. In any prison movie, when the main character first arrives in prison, he will have a meeting at which the warden reads the prisoner's file aloud to him, including his name, his background, and the reason he has been sent to prison, in case the prisoner himself has forgotten any of these details. (See *Escape from Alcatraz, Escape from New York,* and *No Escape.*)

—Dan Wiencek, Riverside, California

Roadkill Syndrome. When unsuspecting victims are flattened by a speeding truck, the scene is always the same: Filmed from the side at a ninety-degree angle to the street, so the truck runs directly across the screen from one side to the other; the person just stands there and gets wiped out. Why didn't the victim see or hear the truck coming, and why didn't the driver see the victim? This is related to the Helicopter on Mute Syndrome, in which a helicopter suddenly appears in the scene, totally unseen and unheard until it is right on top of the hero.

—Joe Kappes, Plano, Texas

Rules for Movie Checkers. Movie checkers is a variation on the classic game of checkers, in which the pieces are placed irregularly on a checkerboard. The first player looks thoughtfully at the arrangement for several moments, and moves one checker. The second player then immediately jumps his checker over all of the opposing checkers, ending the game.

—Mike Gebert, Chicago, Illinois

The Tell-Tale Purse. When a female character has something of direct use to the plot in her purse (gun, real ID, pills), she will either put her purse down on the ground and leave it wide open so another character can look inside, or she'll drop it and the one thing she doesn't want anyone to see will spill out. Seen in numerous noir films, *Sneakers, Nightmare on Elm Street III,* etc.

—Patrick Keys, Houston, Texas

Time for Nemo's Close-up. No fish tank can be broken in any movie without a cutaway shot showing a fish flopping desperately on the ground.

—Grant Hawkins, Sydney, Australia

The Tom Hanks Shift. Phenomenon in which actors begin in comedies and progress to serious dramas. In modern times, the shift was pioneered by Tom Hanks (*Bachelor Party* to *Saving Private Ryan*) and followed by actors like Jim Carrey (*Ace Ventura* to *Eternal Sunshine of the Spotless Mind*), Robin Williams (*Popeye* to *One Hour Photo*), Jamie Foxx (*Booty Call* to *Ray*) and, recently, Will Ferrell (from *A Night at the Roxbury* to *Winter Passing*).

—Alberto Diamante, Toronto, Ontario

Two Guards, Two Dogs. Whenever a movie character tries to (a) escape from prison or (b) access an impregnable fortress, once he reaches its perimeter, two guards, each one leading one menacing dog, will walk past him side by side without noticing him.

—Gerardo Valero Perez Vargas, Mexico City, Mexico

Velocity Repudiation Rule. Movie characters in most genres can fall as far as one hundred feet before grabbing a loose pipe; their hands never lose their grip, and their arms are never ripped off by the sheer force.

—Robert Terry, Oxnard, California

Waterfall Immunity Rule. When a hero fleeing for his life jumps into a huge and menacing waterfall, the bad guys assume he's dead and walk away. But lo and behold, he survives! See *The Fugitive, Last of the Mohicans, Collateral Damage.*

—Jonathan Toren, New York City, New York

Index

A

Index